CW01545527

CIPA GUIDE TO THE
PATENTS ACTS

CIPA GUIDE TO THE PATENTS ACTS

SEVENTH EDITION

EDITOR
Paul G. Cole

CONSULTANT EDITOR
Stephen F. Jones

FOR
THE CHARTERED INSTITUTE OF PATENT ATTORNEYS

Founded 1882
Royal Charter 1891

SWEET & MAXWELL   THOMSON REUTERS

First Edition	1980
Second Edition	1984
Third Edition	1990
Fourth Edition	1995
Fifth Edition	2001
Sixth Edition	2009
Seventh Edition	2011

Published in 2011 by Sweet & Maxwell, 100 Avenue Road, London NW3 3PF
Part of Thomson Reuters (Professional) UK Limited
(Registered in England & Wales, Company No 1679046.
Registered Office and address for service:
Aldgate House, 33 Aldgate High Street, London EC3N 1DL)

Prelims, Tables and Index typeset by Interactive Sciences Ltd, Gloucester.
All other typesetting by Sweet & Maxwell electronic publishing system.
Printed and bound by
CPI Group (UK) Ltd, Croydon, CR0 4YY
For further information on our products and services, visit www.
sweetandmaxwell.co.uk

No natural forests were destroyed to make this product; only farmed
timber was used and re-planted.

A CIP catalogue record for this book is available from the British Library

ISBN 978 0 414 01863 1

Thomson Reuters and the Thomson Reuters logo are
trademarks of Thomson Reuters.
Sweet & Maxwell ® is a registered trademark of Thomson Reuters (Professional) UK
Limited.

Notice to Readers

This book has been prepared mainly for use by patent practitioners in the United
Kingdom. It is truly intended as a "guide" and is not a substitute for the exercise of
professional judgment.

CIPA GUIDE TO THE PATENTS ACTS

EDITOR

Paul G. Cole
Chartered Patent Attorney
Lucas & Co

CONSULTANT EDITOR
Stephen F. Jones
Solicitor-Advocate, Chartered Patent Attorney
Baker & McKenzie LLP

This edition of the "Black Book" has been produced by a team of contributors acknowledged below, in alphabetical order, who have generally contributed in respect of one or more individual sections. These include patent attorneys, solicitors, barristers and others. The Editor and Consultant Editor named above have also contributed in relation to certain sections.

Robert Ackroyd, WP Thompson & Co
James Anderson, Elkington and Fife LLP
Edward Barker, Baker & McKenzie LLP
Helen Brearley, Elkington and Fife LLP
Ruth Burstall, Baker & McKenzie LLP
Zoë Butler, Powell Gilbert LLP
Paul Casbon, Lucas & Co
Edward Cole, University of Durham
Trevor Cook, Bird & Bird LLP
Richard Davis, Hogarth Chambers
Alison Firth, University of Surrey
Gill Grassie, Maclay Murray & Spens LLP
Iona Harding, Baker & McKenzie LLP
Anna Hatt, Beck Greener
Jeremy Heald, 3 New Square

John Hull, Beck Greener
Richard Luetchford, Ministry of Defence
Jonathan Markham, Beck Greener
Joanna Martin, Baker & McKenzie LLP
Bhupendra Patel, Ministry of Defence
David Pearce, Potter Clarkson
Geoffrey Pritchard, 3 New Square
Michael Ralph, CIPA.
Vicki Salmon, IP Asset LLP
Kim Scallan, Baker & McKenzie LLP
Andrew Sheard, Andrew Sheard Patent Attorney
Susan Snedden, Maclay Murray & Spens LLP
Nick Wallin, Withers & Rogers LLP
Philip Walters, Celldex Therapeutics
Alan White, CIPA, Hon. Member
James Wilson, Baker & McKenzie LLP
Gordon Wright, Elkington and Fife LLP

In addition, the following post-graduate students from the University of Surrey assisted in writing and research for the Guide:

Margaret Cooper
Robert Grannells
Lana Haworth
Isabel Lu
Uzo Madu
Definite Moyo
Rochelle Sampy
James Whitney

FOREWORD

When Stephen Jones asked me to write a foreword for this edition, I thought "Blimey, haven't I just done it". Well it was not so long ago—the last edition was 2009. In the foreword to that I wrote in praise of the emergence of the patent agent/scholar. I withdraw none of that. The Black Book is the work of scholars —not scholars of an abstract, too theoretical-to-be-useful bent, but learned writers who seek to set out the law as it really is so that the reader knows where he or she stands. Some like Stephen have dual qualification as both patent agents and solicitors, but the bulk of the writing has been by "pure" patent agents.

None of that has changed so there is no point in repeating what I said then on that topic. This time I want to add something else—what about the patent agent/ cunning schemer? I illustrate what I mean by what happened about this very foreword. Stephen asked me to do it some time ago and I forgot and might not have got round to doing it. But then he told me that Paul Cole had asked Chief Judge Randall Rader of the Court of Appeal for the Federal Circuit to write an introduction from a US standpoint. Paul told Randy that I was writing the forward to induce him to write. Randy said he would be happy to be associated with anything in which I was involved and agreed. And because Randy had agreed, I got on with my bit. The cunning patent agent/scholars played one of us against the other. Well done! And more seriously I hope and expect that Randy will commend the work to US readers. I do, as well as to anyone else concerned with European patents. Note that I say "European Patents" rather than British Patents—for in essence, despite its title, that is what this book is about.

I have used the expression "patent agent/scholars" although I know that patent agents are now called "attorneys". I carry on saying patent agent. I know it sounds a bit old-fashioned, but I have a good reason to wonder whether the change to "attorney" was altogether a good idea. For "attorney" not only means something like legal agent, but it once, at least, had overtones. As, for instance when Dr Johnson said that "he did not seek to speak ill of any man behind his back, but he believed the gentleman was an attorney". And when Thomas Carlyle said "attorney cunning is a kind of thing that fancies itself to be talent".

Enough of that. Where are we now? Well the first thing to observe is how fast the new edition has come round. It will appear just two years after the previous edition. That is a reflection of how much is happening in the world of patents. The Enlarged Board continues to produce decisions of more or less opacity and the Black Book covers all this well.

More alarmingly, indeed most alarmingly, the Court of Justice of the European Union is beginning to assume patent jurisdiction. We now have two decisions based on the Biotech Directive. Looking back, I am far from convinced that any Directives touching patentability were within the EU's competence. Patents are governed by the EPC, a non-EU Treaty. What business is it of the EU by a Directive to attempt to override this Treaty? And both decisions are unsatisfactory. *Monsanto* (Case C-428/08) has the Court telling us that soya meal which contains bits of broken-up genes which could no longer work are not protected. I do not quarrel with that as an ultimate conclusion, but it was not arrived at, as it could have been, by claim construction (which is how Pumfrey J. did it in the corresponding English case). That would have been consistent with art.69 of the EPC. Instead we find the Court adding EU law to patent law—a dangerous precedent for the future because it is entirely foreseeable that there will be conflict between the EPC and EU law leading to fuzzy edges and uncertainty. Even more serious is *Brüstle v Greenpeace* (C-3410) where the Court set back European stem-cell research. It should have read the Directive down to its irreducible minimum. The result is not to stop the research, which is perfectly lawful, but to remove the patent incentive for it. Humanity is the loser. It is all tied up with "ethical", perhaps religious, considerations—as if an acorn were a tree.

It is decisions like these (and the chaotic tsunami of ECJ and CJEU trade mark cases) which have made it clear to all industry that the CJEU should not have competence in patents. The proposed Unitary Patent and European Patent Court —perhaps now rushing to a premature realisation—stand in danger of this threat as I write. I am alarmed more generally about the current proposals: they do not stand the acid test—are they better than what Europe has now? Forum shopping will remain high on the agenda of patentees. In particular the possibility of bifurcation with entrenched local divisions which may favour patentees of doubtful patents would tip the balance in favour of enforcing arguably invalid patents at least provisionally.

Another, much to be welcomed, development, are the changes to the Patents County Court. When Judge Fysh took it over it was more or less moribund. He breathed life into it but before long found himself shackled by Lord Woolf's one-size-fits all idea for civil procedure—that the rules should be the same everywhere. That made no sense for a court which was for small patent cases and which needed special rules to ensure swift and cheap resolution. Well that shackle has now gone—and the court has fit-for-purpose rules. It has also been fortunate that Colin Birss QC was willing to take on the job. I commend the court to patent agents—and I repeat the message I gave last time: one of the best ways to run a small patent case is by a patent agent working with a junior barrister.

Where will we be by the time of the next edition? I do not know. It is possible there will be a patent court for all of the EU or all of the EU except Spain and Italy. And there may be a "unitary patent".

On the other hand it may be that the current proposals will fail—if they proceed as they stand at present I frankly hope that they do. But if some key changes are made then it should all come to pass. If they do not, then next time it will happen. Whatever happens this time, the Black Book will set it all out clearly—or, given the problems of obscurity which increasingly affect all IP law, as clearly as possible.

I shall continue to keep the book within easy reach. So should anyone else concerned with European or British patents.

The Rt. Hon. Professor Sir Robin Jacob
Faculty of Laws,
UCL

October 2011

GUEST FOREWORD

The timing of this foreword is especially fitting because it follows shortly after the United States Congress passed the Leahy-Smith America Invents Act. The America Invents Act moves the United States closer to other patent systems, such as those in the United Kingdom and the rest of Europe. As the world's patent law systems converge legislatively, the national judiciaries are also recognizing the international import of their enforcement work. Just a month after the America Invents Act, the U.S. Court of Appeals for the Federal Circuit and the Tokyo Intellectual Property High Court met in a historic joint judicial conference— the first of a series of such conferences to promote international judicial cooperation.

Thus the significant work of making the law properly serve the international marketplace proceeds in both legislative and judicial arenas. Similar to the work done by the legislative branch with the America Invents Act, the judicial branch also has the capacity to learn from and incorporate the principles of judgments in other jurisdictions, either domestic or international. The global market means that decisions of the U.S. Court of Appeals for the Federal Circuit impact economic policy as well as commercial and trade relationships of the United States. These considerations are an undercurrent for the court's decisions and are useful to commercial actors, in the United States, United Kingdom and beyond, who engage in commercial transactions with the United States.

Thus convergence of process and substance amongst the international judiciaries has been a topic of discussion for years, as evidenced by the increase in international judicial exchanges, for example, conferences, committees, and forums. Further, at the 20th Anniversary Judicial Conference for the U.S. Court of Appeals for the Federal Circuit, then-Chief Justice William H. Rehnquist of the U.S. Supreme Court noted the following:

"But with the growth in global commerce and technology, the areas within the jurisdiction and expertise of the Federal Circuit have become more and more topical for international exchanges. As new judicial systems get past the initial efforts to put basic rules and systems in place, they become able to focus on areas such as patent and trade law."

For inventors and commercial actors, an international tapestry of laws that adhere to the same basic principles and outcomes promotes vital values of fairness and efficiency. These values include predictability, uniformity, lower costs to obtain and enforce patents rights, and reduction of forum shopping. If technology knows no geographical boundaries, then the law should not lag behind in providing a jurisprudence that does not tolerate wide variances from one part of the market to another. International corporations should not be required to make different products for each nation to accommodate different laws. The law must facilitate, rather than frustrate, an efficient global market.

Of course, a judge in the United States takes an oath to uphold the Constitution and laws of the United States. Thus the globalization of the market cannot alter that fundamental duty to uphold the law as written by the United States Congress. At the same time, that principle need not conflict with the exchange of information, views, and understandings amongst different enforcement bodies in the international legal world. Thus a judge in the United States can participate in a dialogue among international judiciaries and legal communities around the world with an eye to improving our own administration of justice by comparative learning.

The international marketplace already requires judges to learn and apply the law of other nations. For example, the U.S. Court of Appeals for the Federal Circuit may theoretically, under the principle of supplemental jurisdiction, be called upon to apply the law of a foreign country to resolve issues of infringement which arise under a "common nucleus of operative fact" with a United States case. In 2007, the U.S. Court of Appeals for the Federal Circuit rendered its decision in *Voda v Cordis*, which created a two-part test for determining whether a district court has supplemental jurisdiction over claims brought under a foreign patent. *Voda v Cordis* has similarities to and differences from the 2006 decision by the European Court of Justice in *Gesellschaft für Antriebstechnik mbH & Co. v Lamellen und Kupplungsbau Beteiligungs KG*. Therefore, judges must be prepared on occasion to apply the law of other nations.

As noted above, the United States has adopted in the America Invents Act many practices that have been in operation in Europe for years. For example, the new Act incorporates into United States practice many European-style post-grant opposition procedures. As these provisions encounter tests in the United States judiciary, the European experience may help ease the transition to new rules in the America Invents Act. Another example would be the similarities and differences between obviousness requirements of the United States and the United Kingdom by studying *Graham v John Deere Co.* by the United States Supreme Court in contrast to *Windsurfing International Inc. v Tabur Marine (GB) Ltd* by the United Kingdom Court of Appeal.

In sum, this new age of technology and global enterprise necessitates new learning in the practices of other nations. The legal scholarship found in this book has an important role to play in that new age. This study may well engender further development of legal scholarship and provide easy access to information about different patent systems to practitioners, commercial actors, and government officials around the world. These resources will then permit judges and other officials to seek the best practices among the international alternatives. This academic study will make it easier to assess the new judicial role in the international marketplace and to improve cooperation amongst international judiciaries and practitioners so that the legal landscape is compatible with the international marketplace.

The Honorable Randall R. Rader
Chief Judge, U.S. Court of Appeals for the Federal Circuit

November 2011

ACKNOWLEDGEMENTS

Earlier precursors of the CIPA Guide can be traced back to 1950 when with the encouragement of the late Gordon Edmunds the then the Chartered Institute of Patent Agents published *The Patents Act, 1949* which was intended to draw attention to the changes introduced by what was then a new statute. The second edition (1968) explained that: "The broad aim has been to provide a manual for reference, if not daily, at least whenever any doubt arises on the provisions of the Act or Rules and above all on the practice under them". The aim and format have continued unchanged to the present day.

The present Guide remains closely associated with the name of Dr Alan White, under whose leadership it evolved into one of the most comprehensive reference works in our field. Alan continues to be closely involved in its production, providing structured lists of cases which are invaluable for contributors, writing the Historical Background (Appendix A) together with the commentary on a number of sections of the Acts and reviewing several other contributions. His advice and practical help continues to underpin much of what we do.

This edition, like its predecessors, represents the cumulative endeavour of many contributors, past and present, and our team now totals 34. Originally the Guide was entirely the work of members of the Institute, but our team is now inclusive, with members of the Bar and solicitors long since having joined our ranks. It is encouraging to welcome two new contributors still in their 20s. If the Guide had to be started afresh, the average effort for a contributor would now approach that needed for an M. Phil. thesis. In some of the more active areas that level has indeed been approached for the present edition. Even where sections do not need to be rewritten completely they still have to be scrutinised afresh in order to take account of recent developments. As Sir Robin Jacob points out in his Foreword, our contributors can truly be described as both practitioners and scholars. They all give their services for no reward save that of knowing they have made a contribution. They therefore deserve the sincere thanks of the editors and publishers.

Particular thanks are due to Stephen Jones for his stalwart support as co-editor and contributor. The Foreword and Guest Foreword provided by Sir Robin Jacob and by Chief Judge Randall Rader from European and US perspectives respectively are much appreciated. A special debt of gratitude is owed to Tibor Gold who has proof-read almost all sections of the Guide; Gillian Herrod-Hempsall also helped with proof-reading, and several trainees from Baker & McKenzie helped with compilation of material and cross-reference checking. Caroline Bommer provided useful insight into recent Australian developments. The editors are grateful for the help and encouragement of Thien-Thu Luc and Lisa Mitchell of Sweet & Maxwell and for the support of the Chartered Institute of Patent Attorneys through its Textbooks and Publications Committee.

Paul Cole

November 2011

PREFACE

The Patents Act 1977 fundamentally changed the basis of the patent law of the United Kingdom and came into force on 1 June 1978. The first and second editions of this work were published in 1980 and 1984 under the title *C.I.P.A Guide to the Patents Act 1977*. For the third edition (1990), the title was changed to the current title, *C.I.P.A. Guide to the Patents Acts*, to reflect those provisions of the Copyright, Designs and Patents Act 1988 which made some changes to the 1977 Act, and this title is now even more appropriate having regard to the Patents Act 2004 which made further changes. In addition to this, the 1977 Act has been further amended by numerous statutory instruments, often giving effect to European directives, and also has to be interpreted in accordance with the relevant provisions of the European Patent Convention. The law of patents in the UK is therefore no longer contained in any single act and keeping up to date with all the various changes is a challenge.

Further, the rules made under the 1977 Act have also been in a state of regular revision, being completely re-issued in the Patents Rules 1995, and the fourth edition, published in that year, included treatment of those new Rules. The fifth edition, published in 2001, dealt with further significant changes made by three sets of Amendment Rules in 1999, which were followed by yet further changes in the Act and the Rules to meet the implementation of the European Biotechnology Directive. The sixth edition dealt with the implications of the Patents Act 2004 and EPC 2000 as well as incorporating the further completely revised form of the Rules in the Patents Rules 2007. Since then we have seen yet further changes introduced by the the Patents, Trade Marks and Designs (Address for Service) Rules 2009 and the Patents (Amendment) Rules 2011.

The Civil Procedure Rules were introduced in 1998 and at the time of writing are on their 57th update. Part 45 and Part 63 were amended by The Civil Procedure (Amendment No. 2 Rules) 2010 which inter alia introduced new procedures for the Patents County Court.

Nevertheless, the basic format of the book, known to practitioners as the "Black Book", remains essentially unchanged from the format first devised for the initial work in this series, The Patents Act 1949 (1950 and 1968), followed by a third edition of 1975, then entitled *Patent Law of the United Kingdom*, and used in the previous editions of the present work. The individual sections of the 1977 Act are reprinted followed by the relevant rules and any other relevant measures such as European regulations, directives etc; and then detailed commentaries on the law and practice under each section. This is followed by a similar treatment of sections of the 1988 Act relevant to patents and patent attorneys and the Patents County Court, and then by Appendices which deal with further relevant matters including an historical introduction, a reprint of the

European Biotechnology Directive and other relevant European legislation, the Civil Procedure Rules and practice directions applicable to litigation in the Patents Court and the Patents County Court, and the various rules and regulations relating to patent attorneys.

As well as a subject matter index, there are Tables of Cases (including decisions of the Boards of Appeal of the European Patent Office); and Tables of Statutes, Statutory Instruments, Rules of Court, International Conventions and Treaties and a list of abbreviations. Throughout the main text, there are frequent cross-references to provide an easy guide to the location of material. In the reprinting of statute sections and of the Patents Rules, deleted provisions are italicised within brackets and new wording is denoted by bold type.

As in the previous edition edition it has been decided not to reprint the forms specified under the Patents Rules because these are subject to change and are now readily available from the UK-IPO's own website. Nor, as in previous editions, have the Patents (Fees) Rules been reprinted, because this information would become misleading when the fees are increased. The reader has been referred to sources of information on the internet where such are readily available and will provide a better and more up to date source of material.

Decisions of the Appeal Boards of the European Patent Office are referred to whenever it is thought that these may be of assistance in interpreting UK national law. However, for detailed commentary on practice before the European Patent Office and under the European Patent Convention, see the *European Patents Handbook* (EPH), also prepared under the aegis of the Chartered Institute and published by Sweet & Maxwell. Likewise, for detailed commentary on the international phase of practice under the Patent Co-operation Treaty see The *PCT Handbook* prepared by Colin Jones for the Chartered Institute and also published by Sweet & Maxwell, although the commentaries under ss.89, 89A and 89B of the present work deal with practice in respect of PCT applications entering the United Kingdom national PCT phase.

When quoting decided cases it has been the formula in this book to give the reference for the case in the text, after the name of the case, to minimise the need to refer back to the Table of Cases and to continue the practice of previous editions, of eschewing the use of footnotes. For this edition, in the text normally only one reference is given, which should be the "best" reference available. For court cases, where there is an R.P.C. reference, that will generally be given as the "best" reference. If there is no R.P.C. reference, but there is an F.S.R., that reference will be given. Failing either of these, the "Neutral Citation" reference (EW number) will be given. Many decisions are now freely available on the website of The British and Irish Legal Information Institute (BAILII) and can be accessed there via the Neutral Citation number. For Patent Office decisions, the R.P.C. or F.S.R. number will be given if the case has been reported, but failing that a BL reference will be given. A feature of the book continues to be the many references to decisions not, or not as yet, published in the law reports, but available because of their deposit in the British Library. These decisions are referred to by this prefix BL. In the Table of Cases, all references which are likely to be useful to the reader will be given, thus R.P.C., F.S.R. and EW numbers will all be given where they are available. Other sources, such as I.P.D., the *Times* etc., or other reports such as the W.L.R. will be given where no R.P.C. or F.S.R. reference is available. The foregoing applies to patent and IP cases. For cases in other areas, such as competition law, reference to the appropriate specialist law report (if applicable) will be given instead of the R.P.C. reference.

The present edition could not have been produced without the diligent efforts of all those who have contributed to it, and the Chartered Institute expresses its grateful thanks to all of them. The Editors and all the contributors have given their services entirely voluntarily in order to provide for others the benefit of their expertise and experience. The Chartered Institute also thanks the editorial staff of its publishers, Sweet & Maxwell Ltd., for their co-operation and assistance and to Sir Robin Jacob and Chief Judge Randall Rader for writing a Foreword and a Guest Foreword to the Work.

The Chartered Institute would much appreciate any perceived or possible errors being reported to the Editors so that, if necessary, appropriate correction may be made in the next Cumulative Supplement and the value of the work to patent practitioners can be enhanced.

PUBLISHERS' NOTE

The material in this book has been collected up to the end of July 2011, with some material up to the beginning of November.

In order to keep the work up to date, Supplements will be issued approximately annually.

The names of customers who buy this book direct from Sweet & Maxwell will be recorded so that they can receive information about updating Supplements to it, unless customers ask not to be recorded. Those buying this book from a bookseller should either make sure that the bookseller makes arrangements to keep them updated or contact the publisher for this service.

Sweet & Maxwell
Cheriton House
PO Box 2000
Andover
SP10 9AH

Tel: 0845 600 9355 (calls charged at local rate)
Fax: +44 (0)20 7449 1144/1155
Email: sweetandmaxwell.customer.services@thomson.com

CONTENTS

TABLE OF CASES

References are to section (§) numbers.
An additional table of EPO Decisions arranged in numerical order follows this Table.
These decisions are also included in the Table below,
arranged under the proprietor's name.

TABLE OF EPO DECISIONS

(This Table is a list of decisions of the Appeal Boards of the European Patent Office and is arranged in numerical order. When the name of the patent proprietor is given, the decisions in this Table are also included within the alphabetical listing in the main Table of Cases. The references are to section (§) numbers. Decisions marked as "Unreported" are available on the "Espace-Legal" CD-Rom produced by the EPO and, for recent decisions also on the EPO website, see http://www.epo.org.

TABLE OF STATUTES

(References are to section (§) numbers.
***Bold** type indicates a reprinted section of statute.)*

TABLE OF STATUTORY INSTRUMENTS

(References are to section (§) numbers.
***Bold** type indicates a reprinted rule.)*

TABLE OF COURT RULES

(References are to section (§) numbers.
***Bold** type indicates a reprinted rule.)*

TABLE OF INTERNATIONAL CONVENTIONS, TREATIES AND RELATED RULES AND REGULATIONS

(References are to section (§) numbers.
***Bold** type indicates a reprinted article or rule.)*

TABLE OF EUROPEAN PATENT OFFICE GUIDELINES

(References are to section (§) numbers.)

TABLE OF ABBREVIATIONS

1949 Act	The Patents Act (c.87)
1986 Act	The Patents, Designs and Marks Act 1986 (c.39)
1977 Act	The Patents Act 1977 (c.37)
1968 Rules	Patents Rules 1968 (SI 1968/1389)
1978 Rules	Patents Rules 1978 (SI 1978/216)
1995 Rules	Patents Rules 1995 (SI 1995/2093)
2007 Rules	Patents Rules 2007 (SI 2007/3291)
A.C.	Appeal Cases
Act (the)	The Patents Act 1977 (c.37)
All E.R.	All England Law Reports
art.	Article (of a Convention or Treaty)
BL	British Library
BL C/#/#	Series of Court decision transcripts located in the Patents Section of the British Library
BL O/#/#	Series of UK-IPO decisions located in the Patents Section of the British Library
B.S.L.R.	BioScience Law Review
CA	Court of Appeal (for England and Wales)
CDPA 1988	Copyright, Designs and Patents Act 1988
CFI	European Court of First Instance
Ch.	Chapter
Ch.	Law Reports: Chancery Division
Ch. App.	Law Reports: Chancery Appeal Cases
CIPA	Journal of the Chartered Institute of Patent Attorneys
C.I.P.A.	Chartered Institute of Patent Attorneys
CJJA	Civil Jurisdiction and Judgments Act 1982 (c.27)
C.L.R.	Commonwealth Law Reports [Australia]
C.M.L.R.	Common Market Law Reports
Costs L.R.	Costs Law Reports
CPC	Community Patent Convention
CT	Community Treaty
DTI	Department of Trade and Industry
EAT	Employment Appeal Tribunal
EBA	EPO Enlarged Board of Appeals
ECJ	European Court of Justice
ECHR	European Court of Human Rights
E.C.R.	European Court Reports
E.C.L.R.	European Competition Law Review
EEC	European Economic Community
E.I.P.R.	European Intellectual Property Review
E.L.R.	European Law Review
E.N.P.R.	European National Patent Reports
EPB	European Patent Bulletin
EPC	European Patent Convention
EPC 2000	European Patent Convention 2000
EPH	European Patents Handbook

Epi	European Patent Institute (Institute of Professional Representative before the EPO)
epi-Information	Journal of the *epi*
EPO	European Patent Office
E.P.O.R.	European Patent Office Reports
EPSF	European Patents Sourcefinder
Formalities Manual	The Formalities Manual, published by the UK-IPO. See *http://www.ipo.gov.uk.*
F.S.R.	Fleet Street Reports
G.R.U.R.	Gewerblicher Rechtsschutz und Urheberrecht
Guidelines	Guidelines for Examination in the EPO
HL	House of Lords
I.C.R.	Industrial Cases Reports
I.I.C.	Intellectual Review of Industrial Property and Copyright
I.P.D.	Intellectual Property Decisions
I.P. & T.	Intellectual Property and Technology Cases
I.R.L.R.	Industrial Relations Law Reports
ITMA	Institute of Trade Mark Attorneys
K.B.	Law Reports: King's Bench Division
L.Q.R.	Law Quarterly Review
Litigation Manual	The Litigation Manual, published by the UK-IPO. See *http://www.ipo.gov.uk.*
MIP	Managing Intellectual Property
MOHP	The Manual of Hearing Practice, published by the UK-IPO. See *http://www.ipo.gov.uk.*
MOPP	The Manual of Patent Practice, published by the UK-IPO. See *http://www.ipo.gov.uk.*
N.S.W.L.R.	New South Wales Law Reports
N.Z.L.R.	New Zealand Law Reports
OJ EC	Official Journal of the European Community
OJ EPO	Official Journal of the European Patent Office
OHIM	The Office of Harmonization for the Internal Market
Opinions Manual	The Opinions Manual as published by the UK-IPO. See *http://www.ipo.gov.uk.*
Ord.	Order
Paris Convention	Intellectual Convention for the Protection of Industrial Property (1883)
PAT	Patents Appeal Tribunal (former)
Pat Ct	Patent Court
Patents Journal	Published by the UK-IPO, previously referred to as the Patents and Design Journal ("PDJ"), or the Official Journal (Patents) ("O.J.").
PC	Privy Council
PCC	Patents County Court
PCT	Patent Cooperation Treaty
PF No.	Patents Form No.# (under Patents Rules 1968)
PF #	Patents Form # (under Patents Rules 2000)
PLT	Patent Law Treaty
Protocol on Recognition	Protocol on Recognition, annexed to the EPC
Q.B.	Law Reports: Queen's Bench Division
r.#	Rule
rr.#	Rules
RPA	Register of Patent Agents

R.P.C.	Reports of Patents, Designs and Trade Mark Cases
RRO	The Regulatory Reform (Patents) Order 2004 (SI 2004/2357)
RSC	Rules of the Supreme Court (former)
Rules (the)	Patent Rules 2007 (SI 2007/3291)
s.#	Section
ss.#	Sections
SI	Statutory Instrument
SC	Session Cases (from the Court of Session in Scotland)
SCA	Supreme Court Act 1981 (c.54)
Sch.#	Schedule (to an Act or Rules)
S.L.T.	Scottish Law Times
SPC	Supplementary Protection Certificate for Medicinal (or Plant Protection) Products
TBA	EPO Technical Board of Appeals
TR	Treaty of Rome (now embodied in the European Community Treaty, CT)
Trans. Chart. Inst.	Transactions of the Chartered Institute of Patent Attorneys
TRIPS	Trade Related Aspects of Intellectual Property Rights, including Trade in Counterfeit Goods
UKAEA	United Kingdom Atomic Energy Authority
UK-IPO	United Kingdom Intellectual Property Office, also referred to as the "Patent Office"
U.S.	United States Supreme Court Reports
U.S.C.	United States Code of Law
U.S.P.Q.	United States Patents Quarterly
U.S.P.Q. (2d)	United States Patents Quarterly (2nd edition)
WIPO	World Intellectual Property Organization
W.L.R.	Weekly Law Reports
W.P.C.	Webster's Patent Cases
WTO	World Trade Organization

Patents Act 1977 (c.37)

This Act came into force on June 1, 1978. The 1977 Act has three parts: Pt I **0.01** (ss.1–76A) dealing with domestic law; Pt II (ss.77–95) dealing with the application of international conventions, particularly the European Patent Convention (the "EPC") and the Patent Cooperation Treaty ("the PCT"); and Pt III (ss.96–132) dealing with miscellaneous and general matters. Schedules 1–6 contain various transitional provisions and amend and repeal other statutes. The current Rules made under the 1977 Act are the Patents Rules 2007 (SI 2007/3291).

The 1977 Act has itself been amended in several respects by other statutes including the Patents Act 2004 (c.16) and has been supplemented by provisions contained in the Copyright, Designs and Patents Act 1988 (c.48) ("CDPA 1988"), the relevant parts of which are set out and discussed in §§274.00 et seq. Other matters of relevance to patent law and practice in the United Kingdom are dealt with in the Appendices.

The long title to the Act, its sections and Schedules

The Patents Act 1977 has the following long title and list of sections and Schedules: **0.02**

An Act to establish a new law of patents applicable to future patents and applications for patents; to amend the law of patents applicable to existing patents and applications for patents; to give effect to certain international conventions on patents; and for connected purposes.   [29th July 1977]

BE IT ENACTED by the Queen's most Excellent Majesty, by and with the advice and consent of the Lords Spiritual and Temporal, and Commons, in this present Parliament assembled, and by the authority of the same, as follows:

ARRANGEMENT OF SECTIONS
ARRANGEMENT OF SECTIONS

PART I [Sections 1–76A]

NEW DOMESTIC LAW

Licences of right and compulsory licences

Use of patented inventions for services of the Crown

Infringement

Revocation of patents

PART II [Sections 77–95]

PROVISIONS ABOUT INTERNATIONAL CONVENTIONS

PART III [Sections 96–132]

MISCELLANEOUS AND GENERAL

Legal proceedings

Offences

Patent agents

Immunity of department

Administrative provisions

Supplemental

Amendments to the Patents Act 1977

0.03 The 1977 Act has been amended in many respects. In the reprinted sections in this Work, where the amendments may have continuing significance, they are indicated by bold type signifying new wording and italic type within brackets signifying wording that has been deleted. Also, *Notes* indicate how these amendments were enacted and the date when each was made effective.

Effect of the Act

0.04 The Patents Act 1977 was intended to provide the United Kingdom with a new system of patent law as far as possible to be harmonised with the substantive law provisions of the EPC, and to deal with patents and applications processed via the EPO and the PCT as administered by the World Intellectual Property Organization ("WIPO").

Whichever route is chosen, any patent ultimately granted by, or for, the United Kingdom has the same effect, with an extent of protection governed by art.69 of the EPC and the Protocol thereto (each as amended by EPC 2000), for which see the commentary on s.125. Also, as was done in several other EPC Member States, the Act harmonised the law of infringement with that set out in the Community Patent Convention ("CPC"), although that Convention has never come into force.

Certain facets of United Kingdom patent law remain unique, e.g. particularly Crown user rights (for which see ss.55–59), and the provisions for post-grant amendment (for which see ss.27 and 75), although in the latter case any amendments made must conform to the substantive restrictions on either pre- or post-grant amendment set out in art.123 of the EPC (see s.76).

The Act provided various provisions of a transitional nature for dealing with or patents granted under the former Patents Act 1949. Such patents were termed "existing patents" but because all such patents have now expired, the effect of these transitional provisions is mentioned only in passing.

For a summary of the former statutes, and a historical introduction to the evolution of patent law of the United Kingdom from its founding statute of 1623, see Appendix A.

NEW DOMESTIC LAW

Patentability [Sections 1–6]

SECTION 1

Patentable inventions

1.—(1) A patent may be granted only for an invention in respect of which the **1.01**
following conditions are satisfied, that is to say—

(a) the invention is new;

(b) it involves an inventive step

(c) it is capable of industrial application;

(d) the grant of a patent for it is not excluded by subsections (2) and (3) **or
section 4A below**;

and references in this Act to a patentable invention shall be construed accordingly.

(2) It is hereby declared that the following (among other things) are not inventions for the purposes of this Act, that is to say, anything which consists of—

(a) a discovery, scientific theory or mathematical method;

(b) a literary, dramatic, musical or artistic work or any other aesthetic creation whatsoever;

(c) a scheme, rule or method for performing a mental act, playing a game or doing business, or a program for a computer;

(d) the presentation of information;

but the foregoing provision shall prevent anything from being treated as an invention for the purposes of this Act only to the extent that a patent or application for a patent relates to that thing as such.

(3) A patent shall not be granted [—*(a)*] for an invention the **commercial**
[*publication or*] exploitation of which would be **contrary to public policy or
morality** [*generally expected to encourage offensive or anti-social behaviour;
(b) for any variety of animal or plant or any essentially biological process for the
production of animals or plants, not being a micro-biological process or the
product of such a process*].

(4) For the purposes of subsection (3) above **exploitation** [*behaviour*] shall
not be regarded as **contrary to public policy or morality** [*offensive, immoral or
anti-social*] only because it is prohibited by any law in force in the United
Kingdom or any part of it.

(5) The Secretary of State may by order vary the provisions of subsection (2)
above for the purpose of maintaining them in conformity with developments in
science and technology; and no such order shall be made unless a draft of the order has been laid before, and approved by resolution of, each House of Parliament.

Notes

1. Subsection (1) was amended by the Patents Act 2004 (c.16) and Sch.2, para.2 with effect from December 13, 2007, SI 2007/3396.

9

2. To implement the European Biotechnology Directive 98/44/EC, subss.(3) and (4) were amended as shown by the Patents Regulations 2000 (SI 2000/2037). However, these changes have no effect on patents and applications filed before July 28, 2000 (SI 2000/2037 reg.9).

3. As regards "biotechnological inventions" a further set of things which are not patentable inventions was introduced by the Patents Regulations 2000, see new s.76A (for which see §76A.01) whose purpose is to introduce detailed provisions contained in Sch.A2 (see also §76A.01A). Again there is no effect on prior dated patent applications and patents.

4. For the replacement of former subs.3(b), see Sch.A2 para.3(f).

5. The amendments set out in Notes 2 and 3 above were applied to the Isle of Man from June 10, 2003 (SI 2003/1249).

"EPC 2000 Article 52—Patentable Inventions

1.02   **52**—(1) European patents shall be granted for any inventions, in all fields of technology, provided that they are new, involve an inventive step and are susceptible of industrial application.

(2) The following in particular shall not be regarded as inventions within the meaning of paragraph 1:
  (a) discoveries, scientific theories and mathematical methods;
  (b) aesthetic creations;
  (c) schemes, rules and methods for performing mental acts, playing games or doing business, and programs for computers;
  (d) presentations of information.

(3) Paragraph 2 shall exclude the patentability of the subject-matter or activities referred to therein only to the extent to which a European patent application or European patent relates to such subject-matter or activities as such."

TRIPS Article 27—Patentable Subject-Matter

1.03   **27**—(1) Subject to the provisions of paragraphs 2 and 3, patents shall be available for any inventions, whether products or processes, in all fields of technology, provided that they are new, involve an inventive step and are capable of industrial application [Note. For the purposes of this Article, the terms "inventive step" and "capable of industrial application" may be deemed by a member to be synonymous with the terms "non-obvious" and "useful" respectively]. Subject to paragraph 4 of Article 65 [Transitional arrangements], paragraph 8 of Article 70 [patent protection for pharmaceutical and agricultural chemical products] and paragraph 3 of this Article, patents shall be available and patent rights enjoyable without discrimination as to the place of invention, the field of technology and whether products are imported or locally produced.

(2) Members may exclude from patentability inventions, the prevention within their territory of the commercial exploitation of which is necessary to protect ordre public or morality, including to protect human, animal or plant life or health or to avoid serious prejudice to the environment, provided that such exclusion is not made merely because the exploitation is prohibited by their law.

(3) Members may also exclude from patentability: (a) diagnostic, therapeutic and surgical methods for the treatment of humans or animals; (b) plants and animals other than micro-organisms, and essentially biological processes for the production of plants or animals other than non-biological and microbiological processes. However, Members shall provide for the protection of plant varieties either by plants or by an effective sui generis system or by any combination thereof. The provisions of this subparagraph shall be reviewed four years after the date of entry into force of the WTO Agreement."

Note: The date for the review specified in art.27.3(b) was January 1, 1999, but no such review has yet taken place.

COMMENTARY ON SECTION 1

Scope of the section

Section 1 is the first of the group of ss.1–6 directed to considerations of patentability. It **1.04** provides a definition of patentability which replaced that which had been the basis of patent law in the United Kingdom for over 350 years, namely the wording of s.6 of the Statute of Monopolies (c.3).

The definition set out in s.1 requires a patentable invention to have: novelty (defined in s.2); inventive step (defined in s.3); capability of industrial application (defined in s.4); and not to be specifically excluded by the provisions of s.1(2) and (3). This definition of "patentable invention" displaced any residual element of common law in the application for and grant of a patent and its revocation: *Genentech's Patent* [1989] R.P.C. 147 CA. In some areas, however, e.g. novelty, inventive step and scope of claims, decisions of UK courts under the previous law continue to be relevant, whereas in other areas, e.g. industrial application and the exclusions of s.1(2) they are now no longer relevant.

To ensure conformity with the EPC, subss.(1)–(4) are declared by s.130(7) to have been so framed as to have, as nearly as practicable, the same effects as the corresponding provisions of the EPC, CPC and PCT (which by s.130(6) includes any other international agreement or convention replacing them and therefore covers EPC 2000).

The relevant article of the EPC is art.52 set out at §1.02, with which by s.130(7) the section should therefore be read in conformity. In a letter initiating Enlarged Board of Appeal G 3/08 *PRESIDENT'S REFERENCE/Patentability of programs for computers* (available on the EPO website) a concise history is given of the discussions which resulted in the present wording of art.52 of the EPC after amendment by EPC 2000. It is explained that it was decided to retain "programs for computers" in art.52(2)(c) but that the one amendment to art.52 that was adopted was the addition in para.1 of the statement that European patents should be granted "in all fields of technology". The President explained that:

"The intention of this amendment was to enshrine 'technology' in the basic provision of substantive patent law, as well as aligning the article with Article 27(1) TRIPS."

As previously explained, references to the EPC include references to EPC 2000 and the italicised words below are considered effectively to form part of UK law by virtue of s.130(7) even though the Act has not been explicitly amended. However, in *Symbian's Application* [2009] R.P.C. 1 Patten J. held that the addition of these words effected no change of the law.

As concerns provisions relating to varieties of plants and animals corresponding to the repealed provisions of s.1(3), see §1.21 below and the commentary on s.76A and Sch.A2.

Although not specifically provided for under the EPC, it appears clear that the extent of the patentability exclusions can move with the times, see, e.g. G3/08 at 7.3.3. Under the Patents Act, there is specific provision for potential movement. Subsection (5) gives the Secretary of State power, by positive resolution of each House of Parliament, to promulgate rules to vary the exception provisions of subs.(2) "for the purpose of maintaining these exceptions in conformity with developments in science and technology". No such order has yet been made.

As explained above, the section is (with effect from December 13, 2007 when EPC 2000 came into effect) intended to conform to art.27 of the TRIPS Agreement, see §1.03.

EPO decisions are only persuasive, not binding, authority (*Genentech's Patent*, above).

The extent to which the Court of Appeal could depart from one of its earlier decisions when considering decisions of the EPO Appeal Boards was considered in *Symbian's Application* [2009] R.P.C. 1. In principle, the Court of Appeal is bound by one of its previous decisions unless that previous decision is inconsistent with a subsequent decision of the House of Lords, now the SupremeCourt, (in which case, the previous decision cannot be followed), is inconsistent with an earlier Court of Appeal decision (in which case the court may choose which previous decision to follow), or can be shown to have been arrived at *per incuriam* (i.e. without reference to a relevant statutory provision or other authority), see *Young v Bristol Aeroplane Co Ltd* [1944] K.B. 718 However, in *Actavis UK Ltd v Merck & Co Inc* [2008] R.P.C. 26; [2008] EWCA Civ 444 the court held that it could depart from one of its previous decisions if satisfied that the EPO Boards of Appeal had formed a settled view which differed from that arrived at in the previous UK decision, but was not obliged to do so if it thought that the jurisprudence was plainly unsatisfactory; see also *Merrell Dow v Norton* [1996] R.P.C. 76 at 82, and *Conor v Angiotech* [2008] R.P.C. 28 where Lord Hoffmann emphasised the desirability of English courts adopting the same principles as that of the Boards of Appeal when assessing obviousness, see also *Human Genome Sciences v Eli Lilly* [2011] UKSC 51. It was not necessary for there to have been a decision of the Enlarged Board on the relevant issue and it sufficed if there had been a number of carefully considered decisions of the EPO Appeal Boards on that issue demonstrating a consistent approach and nothing to suggest that the reasoning of the Board was wrong.

The EPO Guidelines for Examination, although only advisory in nature, give a fully considered opinion on the interpretation of the EPC and its implementing regulations. However, the EPO itself recognises that these Guidelines are only "general instructions" intended to cover normal occurrences and has stated that there is a discretion for an EPO Examining Division to depart from general guidance in a particular case provided that the decision remains within the bounds defined by the EPC: T 162/82 *SIGMA/Classifying areas* OJ EPO 1987, 533; [1987] E.P.O.R. 375. The general and non-binding nature of the EPO Guidelines, particularly for the EPO Boards of Appeal, was also stressed in T 522/94 *TECHNO/Powered vehicle for operation of ladles* OJ EPO 1998, 421; [1999] E.P.O.R. 75.

It should be noted that the position in Europe differs from that in the USA where there is no equivalent of s.1(1)(c) and s.4 and the courts have positively held that types of patentable invention should be given wide scope; see *Aerotel* [2007] R.P.C. 7 citing *Diamond v Chakrabarty* (1980) 447 U.S. 303; *In re Apappat* (1994) 33 F.3d 1526, 31 U.S.P.Q.2d 1545; and *State Street Bank v Signature Financial Group* (1998) 149 F.3d 1368, 47 U.S.P.Q.2d 1596.

On June 28, 2010 the US Supreme Court handed down its opinion in *Bilski v Kappos* 08-0964 concerning the scope of 35 USC §101. It reaffirmed that the scope of the section was not unlimited, and in particular that it did not cover laws of nature, physical phenomena and abstract ideas. By a 5:4 majority it refused to hold that business methods in general were excluded. It further held that the "machine or transformation test was not the sole test for patent eligibility", although there was a consensus that it was useful and that few inventions which do not satisfy that test would be patent eligible. It was unanimous that the claimed invention which explained how commodities buyers and sellers in the energy market could protect, or hedge, against the risk of price changes was not patent eligible because it was a mere abstract idea.

History and development of the law of inherent patentability

1.05 Up to the granting of the Statute of Monopolies, the Crown would grant such monopolies on the basis of 'grace and favour'. The Statute (being probably one of the oldest forms of anti-trust legislation) limited the grant of such monopolies save for specific circumstances, one of which was letters patent for inventors. Section 6 of the statute provided as follows:

"shall not extend to any letters patents and grants of privilege for the term of fourteen years or under, hereafter to be made, of the sole working or making of any manner of new manufactures within this realm to the true and first inventor and inventors of such manufactures".

From the words "manner of new manufacture" grew up the various exempted areas of patentability. For example a discovery was not considered patentable as explained in *Reynolds v Herbert Smith & Co Ltd* (1903) R.P.C. 123:

"Discovery adds to the amount of human knowledge, but it does so only . . . by disclosing something. . . . Invention also adds to human knowledge, but not merely by disclosing something. Invention necessarily involves also the suggestion of an act to be done, and it must be an act which results in a new product, or a new result, or a new process, or a new combination for producing an old product or an old result."

The entry into force of the Patents Act 1977 harmonised the law of the United Kingdom with that of the European Patent Convention 1973. Thus when the European Patent Office opened its doors in the early 1980s, the requirements for patentability were to be the same regardless of the route by which grant of a patent was secured (i.e. via the EPO or the UK Intellectual Property Office).

Approach under the Patents Act 1977

The approach originates in the seminal case of T208/84 *VICOM/Computer-related* **1.06**
invention [1987] E.P.O.R. 74 and considers whether the invention exhibits technical contribution (sometimes technical effect). Initially there was little basis for the technical contribution criterion although it tended to be rationalised by the EPO on the basis of r.29 EPC 1973 that "the claims shall define the matter for which protection is sought in terms of the technical features of the invention". See *VICOM* §8.

VICOM itself concerned a method of digitally filtering a two-dimensional data array (representing a stored image). In reaching its conclusions, the Board stated as follows:

"12. The Board is of the opinion that a claim directed to a technical process which process is carried out under the control of a program (be this implemented in hardware or in software), cannot be regarded as relating to a computer program as such within the meaning of Article 52(3) EPC, as it is the application of the program for determining the sequence of steps in the process for which in effect protection is sought. Consequently, such a claim is allowable under Article 52(2)(c) and (3) EPC.

. . .

16. In arriving at this conclusion the Board has additionally considered that making a distinction between embodiments of the same invention carried out in hardware or in software is inappropriate as it can fairly be said that the choice between these two possibilities is not of an essential nature but is based on technical and economical considerations which bear no relationship to the inventive concept as such. Generally speaking, an invention which would be patentable in accordance with conventional patentability criteria should not be excluded from protection by the mere fact that for its implementation modern technical means in the form of a computer program are used. Decisive is what technical contribution the invention as defined in the claim when considered as a whole makes to the known art. Finally, it would seem illogical to grant protection for a technical process controlled by a suitably programmed computer but not for the computer itself when set up to execute the control."

Throughout the 1980s and 1990s, the question of inherent patentability had been considered by the English Court of Appeal on four occasions, namely in *Genentech's Patent* [1989] R.P.C. 147, *Merrill Lynch's Application* [1989] R.P.C. 561, *Gale's Application* [1991] R.P.C. 305 and *Fujitsu's Application* [1997] R.P.C. 608. Whilst there are various consistency issues between these decisions the touchstone of 'technical effect' was unanimously adopted.

The key point from *Merrill Lynch* can be summarised in the following passage from the judgment of Fox L.J. in the Court of Appeal who said at p.569 lines 2–10:

> "... it seems to me to be clear ... that it cannot be permissible to patent an item excluded by section 1(2) under the guise of an item which contains that item—that is to say, in the case of a computer program, the patenting of a conventional computer containing that program. Something further is necessary. The nature of that addition is, I think, to be found in the Vicom case where it is stated: 'Decisive is what technical contribution the invention makes to the known art.' There must, I think, be some technical advance on the prior art in the form of a new result (e.g., a substantial increase in processing speed, as in *Vicom*)."

On the facts the claim before the court was rejected but on the basis of its being a method of doing business rather than a program of computer. Moreover, the court remitted the matter back to the UK Intellectual Property Office for further prosecution and a claim was finally granted on the application.

The law in *Gale* was to the same effect. As in *Merrill Lynch*, the Court of Appeal held that, although a computer program was not patentable as such, that was not the end of the matter precisely because computer instructions might represent a technical process. In such a case the process was not barred from patentability by reason of the use of a computer as the medium by which it was carried out. *Gale* related to a method of calculating square roots which required reduced computational operation (mostly binary shifting which can be carried out speedily by a computer rather than more general multiplication and division which take computers longer). Per se it would seem to be no more than a mathematical method or algorithm. Moreover, it was held to be excluded from patentability since the numbers so processed had no physical significance.

Fujitsu summarised the position as follows at p.614 lines 40–46:

> ".....it is and always has been a principle of patent law that mere discoveries or ideas are not patentable, but those ideas and discoveries which have a technical aspect or make a technical contribution are. Thus the concept that what is needed to make an excluded thing patentable is a technical contribution is not surprising. That was the basis of the decision in *Vicom*. It has been accepted by this court and by the EPO and has been applied since 1987. It is a concept at the heart of patent law."

The question of patentability returned to the English Court of Appeal in 2006 in the context of a conjoined appeal in *Aerotel's Application* (a telecoms system alleged to be solely a 'program for a computer') and *Macrossan's Application* (company formation software alleged to be both a program for a computer and a method of doing business). At that time (i.e. pre-*Actavis*) the Court of Appeal was considered to be bound by its previous decisions and hence was obliged to follow *Merrill Lynch/Gale/Fujitsu*. In order to simplify the application of the approach, it adopted a distillation of the test suggested by the United Kingdom Intellectual Property Office (UK-IPO) which split it into four steps (now known as the *Aerotel* test) as follows:

(1) properly construe the claim;

(2) identify the actual contribution;

(3) ask whether it falls solely within the excluded subject-matter;

(4) check whether the actual or alleged contribution is actually technical in nature.

Justifying these steps and explaining how they were to be interpreted, the Court said the following:

> "42. No-one could quarrel with the first step—construction. You first have to decide what the monopoly is before going on the question of whether it is excluded. Any test must involve this first step.
>
> 43. The second step—identify the contribution—is said to be more problematical. How do you assess the contribution? Mr Birss submits the test is workable—it is an exercise in judgment probably involving the problem said to be solved, how the invention works, what its advantages are. What has the inventor really added to human knowledge perhaps best sums up the exercise. The formulation involves looking at substance not form—which is surely what the legislator intended.
>
> 44. Mr Birss added the words "or alleged contribution" in his formulation of the second step. That will do at the application stage—where the Office must generally perforce accept what the inventor says is his contribution. It cannot actually be conclusive, however. If an inventor claims a computer when programmed with his new program, it will not assist him if he alleges wrongly that he has invented the computer itself, even if he specifies all the detailed elements of a computer in his claim. In the end the test must be what contribution has actually been made, not what the inventor says he has made.
>
> 45. The third step—is the contribution solely of excluded matter?—is merely an expression of the "as such" qualification of Art.52(3). During the course of argument Mr Birss accepted a re-formulation of the third step: Ask whether the contribution thus identified consists of excluded subject matter as such? We think either formulation will do—they mean the same thing.
>
> 46. The fourth step—check whether the contribution is "technical"—may not be necessary because the third step should have covered that. It is a necessary check however if one is to follow Merrill Lynch as we must."

On the facts the Court of Appeal held that the *Aerotel* invention was clearly patentable (although this was later reversed by the trial judge once he had reached the view that the claims were not inventive (*Aerotel v Telco* [2008] EWHC 1180 (Pat)). By contrast, *Macrossan's* invention was held not to be inherently patentable as being both as a method of doing business and as a program for a computer. Mr Macrossan filed a petition for appeal to the House of Lords but permission to appeal was refused.

In *Aerotel* the Court of Appeal considered three approaches that had been put forward in previous cases.

The first or so-called "contribution" approach suggested at first instance in *Merrill Lynch's Application* [1988] R.P.C. 1 is to consider whether the inventive contribution resided only in excluded matter. However, when the case came before the Court of Appeal, it had already been rejected by that court in *Genentech's patent* [1989] R.P.C. 147 where it was observed that:

> "Such a conclusion, when applied to a discovery, would seem to mean that the application of the discovery is only patentable if the application is itself novel and not obvious, altogether apart from the novelty of the discovery. That would have a very drastic effect on the patenting of new drugs and medicinal or microbiological processes."

The Court of Appeal therefore rejected the "contribution" approach in favour of a second or so-called "technical effect" approach set out by the EPO in T 208/84 *VICOM/ Computer-related invention* [1987] E.P.O.R. 74:

> "Generally speaking, an invention which would be patentable in accordance with conventional patentability criteria should not be excluded from protection by the mere fact that, for its implementation, modern technical means in the form of a computer program are used. Decisive is what technical contribution the invention as defined in the claim when considered as a whole makes to the known art."

However, the Court of Appeal in *Merrill Lynch* adopted that "technical effect" approach subject to the rider that inventive excluded matter could not count as a technical contribution.

Three EPO decisions concerning technical effect are referred to in *Aerotel*. T 6/83 *IBM/ Data Processor Network* [1990] E.P.O.R. 91 which concerned improved communication facilities between programs and files held at different processors within the known network. T 115/85 *IBM/Text processing* [1990] E.P.O.R. 107 concerned a text processing program, and the Board formed the view that giving visual indications automatically about conditions prevailing in an apparatus or system, in this case input/output device of a text processor, was a technical problem whose solution included the use of a computer program and tables stored in a memory to build up phrases to be displayed. In T 26/86 *KOCH & STERZEL/X-ray apparatus* [1988] E.P.O.R. 72 the invention concerned X-ray apparatus for radiological imaging differing from the prior art in that it incorporated a new control program providing optimum exposure and overload protection for the X-ray tube. Technical character as a requirement of patentability is also a feature of two further significant EPO decisions: T 1173/97 *IBM/Computer program product* and T 935/97 *IBM/Computer program product II.*

The third approach, "any hardware", was adopted by the EPO in T 931/95 *PBS PARTNERSHIP/Controlling pension benefits system* OJ EPO 2001, 441; [2002] E.P.O.R. 522. The main request in that case was directed to a method of controlling a pension benefits program and was rejected on the ground that the subject-matter claimed was a business method as such. However, an auxiliary request directed to a suitably programmed computer or system of computers for carrying out the method could not simply be held to fall within EPC art.52(c) having regard to the wording of the Convention:

"In the Board's view a computer system suitably programmed for use in a particular field, even if that is the field of business and economy, has the character of a concrete apparatus in the sense of a physical entity, man-made for a utilitarian purpose and is thus an invention within the meaning of Article 52(1) EPC. This distinction with regard to patentability between a method for doing business and an apparatus suited to perform such a method is justified in the light of the wording of Article 52(2)(c) EPC, according to which "schemes, rules and methods" are non-patentable categories in the field of economy and business, but the category of "apparatus" in the sense of "physical entity" or "product" is not mentioned in Article 52(2) EPC."

The Board was not prepared to take into account a contribution which was essentially in the field of economics when assessing inventive step and the application was refused. For that reason the third approach was described in *Aerotel* [2007] R.P.C. 7 at [28] as: "The Lord giveth, the Lord taketh away" and as being in conflict with *Vicom*. However, it is apparent from [101] that the Court of Appeal equated the computer program objection with the business method objection and insufficiently appreciated that the EPO was endeavouring to achieve consistency with *Vicom* despite the difference in statutory language as between the business methods exclusion and the computer program exclusion.

The Court of Appeal correctly noted that subsequent EPO decisions negated the distinction between method and apparatus claims under EPC art.52: in T 258/03 *HITACHI/ Auction method* [2004] E.P.O.R. 55 another EPO Appeal Board differed from the *PBS PARTNERSHIP* decision and gave a broad interpretation to technical means which would avoid the exclusion of art.52(2)(c) of the EPC for both method and apparatus claims even where that means was as commonplace as pencil and paper, but held that merely changing the rules of an auction so that it could be carried out automatically was non-technical and did not contribute to inventive character. In T 424/03 *MICROSOFT/Data transfer with expanded clipboard formats* [2006] E.P.O.R. 39 it was held, contrary to the UK decision in *Gale*, that any concrete apparatus avoided EPC art.52(2) including a programmed computer and also including a data carrier such as a CD or floppy disk.

Subsequent to *Aerotel* there was a flurry of unsuccessful Patents Court appeals: *Capellini's/Bloomberg's Application* [2007] F.S.R. 26; *Oneida Indian Nation's Application* [2007] EWHC 954 (Pat); *Raytheon's Application* [2008] R.P.C. 3; *IGT's Applications*

[2007] EWHC 1341; *Autonomy Corp's Application* [2008] EWHC 146 (Pat); *IGT/Acres* [2008] EWHC 586 (Pat); and *Kapur's Application* [2008] EWHC 649 (Pat).

In addition to these appeals, inherent patentability became an issue in various infringement/validity cases leading to decisions that, since the patent was not inventive there can be no technical contribution and hence that the patent was also bad for lack of inherent patentability. See for instance *RIM v Visto* [2009] F.S.R. 10, [2008] EWHC 335 (Pat) and *Aerotel v Telco* [2008] EWHC 1180 (Pat) although note that Arnold J. declined to go down this route in *RIM v Motorola* [2010] EWHC 118 (Pat).

As regards the patentability of claims to computer programs on computer-readable media, the current position is that such claims are in principle allowable, see *Astron Clinica v Comptroller-General* [2008] R.P.C. 14; [2008] EWHC 85 Pat Ct.

The latest consideration by the Court of Appeal on of the state of the law was that in *Re Symbian's Application* [2009] R.P.C. 1. The specific facts of this case are considered in §1.10, below. The Court was urged to apply *Actavis* and to follow the law as applied in the EPO (for which see §1.07 below) However the court declined so to do or to give any real guidance as to the application of *Aerotel* other than to say:

"In deciding whether the application reveals a "technical" contribution, it seems to us that the most reliable guidance is to be found in the Board's analysis in Vicom and the two IBM Corp. decisions, and in what this court said in Merrill Lynch and Gale. Those cases involve a consistent analysis, which should therefore be followed unless there is a very strong reason not to do so.

. . .in this court at this stage, we should try to follow previous authority, we should seek to steer a relatively unadventurous and uncontroversial course, and we should be particularly concerned to minimise complexity and uncertainty. These aims are not necessarily mutually consistent, but, on this occasion, we believe they are achievable, namely by following the analysis adopted by the Board in Vicom and the two IBM Corp. cases [*T6/83 IBM/Data processor network* and *T115/85 IBM/computer related invention*], and of the Court of Appeal in Merrill Lynch and Gale." [59] & [51]

However, the Court was clear in upholding the potential patentability of software inventions stating:

"More positively, not only will a computer containing the instructions in question 'be a better computer', as in Gale, but, unlike in that case, it can also be said that the instructions 'solve a "technical" problem lying with the computer itself'. Indeed, the effect of the instant alleged invention is not merely within the computer programmed with the relevant instructions. The beneficial consequences of those instructions will feed into the cameras and other devices and products, which, as mentioned at [3] above, include such computer systems. Further, the fact that the improvement may be to software programmed into the computer rather than hardware forming part of the computer cannot make a difference—see Vicom; indeed the point was also made by Fox LJ in Merrill Lynch." [55]

Following *Symbian* the UK-IPO issued a yet further Practice Notice. This means that there are currently three such notices in force, dated November 2, 2006, February 7, 2008 and December 8, 2008.

There is some doubt as the extent to which tethering a product or process to industrial activity can confer patentability. Mere tethering would appear to promote form over function although following the dicta in *Halliburton v Smith* [2006] R.P.C. 2 the UK-IPO is inclined to insist upon it. For a rare example of a case in which tethering was not mandated and the patentability upheld see *NEC's Application* BL/202/08 which concerned a method for calculating the tilt angle of antennae. A claim which merely output the required tilt angle and which did not control means for positioning the antennae was upheld following the principles expounded in *Astron Clinica* [2008] R.P.C. 1. Similarly in *Halliburton Energy Services Inc* [2011] EWHC 2508 (Pat) it sufficed to specify "outputting to a resource the results of the method". Furthermore, in that decision the Patents Court reaffirmed that there had been a consistent line of jurisprudence in this area following *Vicom* (T6/83), including *Merrill Lynch* and *Gale* and that it should continue to be followed, see also *Symbian* at paras 48–51; see also §1.09.

Development of law in the EPO: The 'trio' of cases

1.07   A trio of cases in the EPO led away from the test of technical character, or at least applied it in a slightly different manner. This seminal trio now represents the law in Europe and little reference need be made to other cases. Indeed reference to other case law may serve only to confuse due to the profusion of cases in this area and the complexity of some of the subject-matter involved. Those cases are: T 931/95 *PBS PARTNERSHIP*, T 258/03 *HITACHI* and T 641/00 *COMVIK*, and their general approach has been approved by the Enlarged Board in G 3/08 *PRESIDENT'S REFERENCE/Program for Computers*.

PBS PARTNERSHIP decides that the contribution approach is no longer good law. Once one claims any concrete apparatus, there is more than a computer program as such. The same does not necessarily hold true for method claims. The (official) headnote in *PBS PARTNERSHIP* reads as follows:

> "1. Having technical character is an implicit requirement of the EPC to be met by an invention in order to be an invention within the meaning of Article 52(1)EPC. (following decisions T 1173/97 and T 935/97)
>
> 2. Methods only involving economic concepts and practices of doing business are not inventions within the meaning of Article 52(1) EPC. A feature of a method which concerns the use of technical means for a purely non-technical purpose and/or for processing purely non-technical information does not necessarily confer a technical character to such a method.
>
> 3. An apparatus constituting a physical entity or concrete product, suitable for performing or supporting an economic activity, is an invention within the meaning of Article 52(1) EPC.
>
> 4. There is no basis in the EPC for distinguishing between "new features" of an invention and features of that invention which are known from the prior art when examining whether the invention concerned may be considered to be an invention within the meaning of Article 52(1) EPC. Thus there is no basis in the EPC for applying this so-called contribution approach for this purpose. (following decisions T 1173/97 and T 935/97)."

Hence when considering an apparatus claim, the Board held that the "concrete nature" of such apparatus was sufficient to confer inherent patentability causing it to be an invention within the meaning of art.52(1) EPC. This Board (although not that of *HITACHI*—see below) held there to be a distinction with regard to patentability between a method and an apparatus for carrying out that method. The distinction was justified on the basis of art.52(2)(c) EPC which defines as non-patentable categories "schemes, rules and methods". Having set a low hurdle for inherent patentability, the Board re-iterated the requirement for technicality (which it would later require when considering inventive step). In so doing it made clear that the advance to be considered could not include advances in the field of business or economics. The skilled addressee for the purposes of inventive step was a software developer or application programmer. Moreover that person was assumed to have the "knowledge of the concept and structure of the improved pension benefits system and of the underlying schemes of information processing as set out in the . . . claims". This approach to the assessment of inventive step will be considered more fully in relation of *COMVIK* (see below and at §3.26).

HITACHI reconsiders the correctness or otherwise of the contribution approach and upholds the *PBS PARTNERSHIP* approach insofar as it says that the contribution approach is wrong. However it goes further in saying that a method of operating a concrete apparatus is sufficient to establish patentability. Part of the reason for this close re-analysis must been seen as the passing of the baton from the former chairman of Appeal Board 3.5.1 (the principal Board handling these types of appeals) Herr van der Berg to Dr Steinbrenner. In justifying its divergence on the question of methods it announced itself unconvinced by the reliance placed upon art.52(2)(c) EPC. In its view any implication of physical features was sufficient. The low level of the hurdle now considered to be imposed by art.52 was confirmed by the example given by the Board, the act of writing using pen and paper. However, again it was confirmed that technicality was of import in the assessment of inventive step, namely that to be patentable an invention must represent a non-obvious technical solution to a technical problem.

COMVIK follows *HITACHI* but develops it in a critical respect. For an invention to be patentable it must involve an inventive step and the assessment of that inventive step mandates technicality in that it requires a technical solution to a technical problem. As such, in formulating the objective technical problem to be solved it is permissible to include non-technical objects even if those objects are not known in the prior art since non-technical advances cannot contribute to inventive step. This test is well reflected in the headnote which reads as follows:

"An invention consisting of a mixture of technical and non- technical features and having technical character as a whole is to be assessed with respect to the requirement of inventive step by taking account of all those features which contribute to said technical character whereas features making no such contribution cannot support the presence of inventive step."

The Board went on to conclude that the formulation of the technical problem may legitimately include knowledge of the economic or business problem to be solved.

In T 154/04 *DUNS LICENSING ASSOCIATES/Estimating sales activity* [2007] E.P.O.R. 38 the Appeal Board considered inter alia the decision in *Aerotel*, reaffirmed absence of technical character as the common characteristic of excluded things and held that also to be true under EPC 2000, where the Basic Proposal (MR/2/00e, p.43, No.1) clearly confirmed its mandatory character:

"4. Nevertheless, the point must be made that patent protection is reserved for creations in the technical field. This is now clearly expressed in the new wording of Article 52(1) EPC. In order to be patentable, the subject-matter claimed must therefore have a 'technical character' or to be more precise—involve a 'technical teaching', ie an instruction addressed to a skilled person as to how to solve a particular technical problem using particular technical means. It is on this understanding of the term 'invention' that the patent granting practice of the EPO and the jurisprudence of the Boards of Appeal are based. The same considerations apply to the assessment of computer programs.

Thus, it will remain incumbent on Office practice and case-law to determine whether subject-matter claimed as an invention has a technical character and to further develop the concept of invention in an appropriate manner, in light of technical developments and the state of knowledge at the time."

The Board went on to hold that the presence of technical character was an absolute requirement that did not imply any new contribution to the prior art, was a distinct requirement and should not be mixed up with the requirements of novelty, inventive step and industrial applicability. In support of this position the Board relied on a number of earlier EPO decisions as well as Mustill L.J. in *Genentech's Patent* [1989] R.P.C. 147 at 262 and German Federal Court of Justice decision *X ZB 20/03—Elektronischer Zahlungsverkehr [Electronic banking] of 24 May* 2004 (see Reasons Nos II 3. b) (1) and II 4.). The inclusion in the claim of technical means (a method for estimating sales activity of products including the step of operating a processor) avoided the objection that it was excluded from patentability. The true objection was that the novel features did not contribute to the solution of a technical problem and therefore had to be ignored when assessing inventive step.

With few exceptions, this is the settled approach now adopted by the EPO. It is reflected in the EPO Guidelines for Examinations ("Guidelines") at C-IV 11.5.2 as follows:

"Features which cannot be seen to make any contribution, either independently or in combination with other features, to the technical character of an invention are not relevant for assessing inventive step (see T 641/00, OJ 7/2003, 352). Such a situation can occur for instance if a feature only contributes to the solution of a non-technical problem, for instance a problem in a field excluded from patentability (see T 931/95, OJ 10/2001, 441).

. . .

Where the claim refers to an aim to be achieved in a non-technical field, however, this aim may legitimately appear in the formulation of the problem as part of the framework of the technical problem to be solved, in particular as a constraint that has to be met (T 641/00, OJ 7/2003, 352 and T 172/03, not published in OJ)."

As to procedure, it was held in T 690/06 *AUKOL/Financial records* [2007] E.P.O.R. 39 that as long as no search has been performed an Examining Division should normally not refuse an application for lack of inventive step if the invention as claimed contains at least one technical feature which was not notorious, see also T 1515/07 *SAP/Cost estimate*. In T 1411/08 *IN_DEVELOPMENT/Pairing providers* with consumers the Board stated that the term 'notorious', meant: (i) prior art which was so well known that its existence at the date of priority could not be reasonably disputed, in contrast to the skilled person's common general knowledge, which could generally be reasonably questioned; and (ii) as implying that technical detail was not significant. The examination of a combination of features in relation to inventive step normally involved questions such as what advantages and disadvantages the combination was said to have, and in what technical areas it was used. That was the sort of information a search should uncover. On the other hand, a claim might be so drafted that such questions did not arise. It was prior art reflecting such generic features that the Board understood as 'notorious'. In the instant case, the Examining Division had not identified the prior art as 'notorious' or an indisputable part of the skilled person's common general knowledge. The Board concluded that the Examining Division could and should have ensured that a search was performed before refusing the application for lack of inventive step.

EPO Enlarged Appeal Board Decision in PRESIDENT'S REFERENCE

1.08   On October 22, 2008 a number of questions were referred to the Enlarged Board of Appeal under EPC art.112(1)(b) as G 3/08 *PRESIDENT'S REFERENCE*.

In its opinion, the first question was re-phrased by the Enlarged Board as follows:

"If a particular claim to a computer program *A program for a computer comprising instructions to carry out steps x, y, z*, is excluded from patentability by Article 52(2) EPC, are any of the following (or anything else) automatically excluded under the same article? *2. A computer system loaded with the program of claim 1. 3. A method of operating a computer comprising executing the program of claim 1. 4. A computer program product storing the program of claim 1.*"

According to T 1173/97 *IBM/Computer program* [2000] E.P.O.R. 219 some programs, claimed alone, were excluded from patentability and were also excluded when recorded on a computer-readable medium. A claim to a computer program was patentable only if the program produced a "further technical effect" when run. The further technical effect need not be new, and the "contribution approach" of earlier case law had been abandoned. T 1173/97 *IBM/Computer program* further held that determining the contribution that an invention achieved with respect to the prior art was more appropriate to examination of novelty and inventive step than to a decision concerning an exclusion under EPC art.54(2) and (3). A further approach characterised as "any hardware" had been put forward in T 258/03 *HITACHI/Auction method* [2004] E.P.O.R. 55 and T 424/03 *MICROSOFT/ Clipboard formats I* [2006] E.P.O.R. 39, and the consequences of abandoning the contribution approach had been explored in T 931/95 *PBS PARTNERSHIP/Controlling pension benefits systems* [2002] E.P.O.R. 52. The question whether a program itself caused a "further technical effect" when run was of importance for the question of inventive step taking into account that some of the claimed features when considered alone might be excluded, see T 154/04 *DUNS LICENSING ASSOCIATES/Estimating sales activity* [2007] E.P.O.R. 38.

The Enlarged Board held that there was a contradiction between T 1173/97 *IBM/ Computer program* and T 424/03 *MICROSOFT/Clipboard formats I* as to whether a computer program had technical character when recorded on a computer-readable medium, but the logic of T 424/03 *MICROSOFT/Clipboard formats I* was consistent and had not been challenged in any later decisions. A computer-readable data storage medium had the technical effects of being computer-readable and of being capable of storing data and was not excluded from patentability by EPC arts 54(2) and (3). On that basis it could not be excluded from patentability merely because it was "storing computer program X", any more than a cup which was a technical article could be excluded from patentability merely because it was decorated with picture X. There was no case law to support the view that a claim to "a computer-readable storage medium with program X written on it" should lose its technical character merely because it was too generic or functionally defined. The above arguments applied with equal force to claims which mentioned a computer. T 424/03 *MICROSOFT/Clipboard formats I* should be regarded as a legitimate development of the case law, and it was relevant that it introduced no change in the final outcome. The Enlarged Board summarised its conclusions as follows:

"10.13.1 In the section 3.1.IV, 'Consequences'(page 6), of the referral it is stated that, 'if one were to follow the reasoning of T 424/03, overcoming the exclusion of programs for computers would become a formality, merely requiring formulation of the claim as a computer implemented method or as a computer program product.' Indeed if the Boards continue to follow the precepts of T 1173/97 it follows that a claim to a computer implemented method or a computer program on a computer-readable storage medium will never fall within the exclusion of claimed subject-matter under Articles 52(2) and (3) EPC, just as a claim to a picture on a cup will also never fall under this exclusion. However, this does not mean that the list of subject-matters in Article 52(2) EPC (including in particular 'programs for computers') has no effect on such claims. An elaborate system for taking that effect into account in the assessment of whether there is an inventive step has been developed, as laid out in T 154/04, DUNS. While it is not the task of the Enlarged Board in this Opinion to judge whether this system is correct, since none of the questions put relate directly to its use, it is evident from its frequent use in decisions of the Boards of Appeal that the list of 'non-inventions' in Article 52(2) EPC can play a very important role in determining whether claimed subject-matter is inventive.

10.13.2 We note, in passing, that it is somewhat surprising that the referral does not address any of its questions to the validity of this way of judging an inventive step, an issue which is surely of general interest (and one which Lord Justice Jacob proposed should be put to the Enlarged Board—'How should those elements of a claim that relate to excluded subject-matter be treated when assessing whether an invention is novel and inventive under Articles 54 and 56?', *Aerotel/Macrossan* at 76, question (2)). The Board can only speculate that the President could not identify any divergence in the case-law on this issue, despite the fact that (at present) approximately seventy decisions issued by a total of fifteen different Boards (in the sense of organisational units) cite T 641/00, *COMVIK* (OJ EPO 2003, 352), and over forty decisions by eight Boards cite T 258/03, *HITACHI*, the decisions which essentially defined the approach. Nor is the Enlarged Board aware of any divergence in this case-law, suggesting that the Boards are in general quite comfortable with it. It would appear that the case-law, as summarised in T 154/04, has created a practicable system for delimiting the innovations for which a patent may be granted."

If an answer had to be given to the inadmissible first question, it therefore seems that the answer would have been negative, subject to the proviso that when considering the patentability of the subject-matter of claims 2, 3 and 4 the exclusions of EPC art.52 are relevant and non-technical features cannot be relied on in response to an objection of lack of novelty or of obviousness.

As to the second question ("Can a claim in the area of computer programs avoid exclusion under EPC art.52(2)(c) and (3) merely by explicitly mentioning the use of a computer or a computer-readable storage medium?"), it would appear that if the question had been found admissible, then an affirmative answer would have been given for the reasons expressed in relation to the first question. The Enlarged Board observed that, contrary to the arguments in the referral, computer program claims and computer-implemented method claims differed in scope. A computer program referred to a sequence of instructions specifying a method rather than to the method itself. In contrast, a computer-implemented method could not be divorced from the computer on which it was to be carried out. A method of operating a shoe polishing machine comprising placing a shoe in a position touching a surface rotatable in a direction clearly required the presence and involvement of the shoe polishing machine. There should not be confusion between a set of instructions for carrying out steps and the steps themselves. Furthermore, there was no conflict between T 1173/97 *IBM/Computer program* and T 38/86 *IBM/Text clarity processing* [1990] E.P.O.R. 606.

The third question was: Must a claimed feature cause a technical effect on a physical entity in the real world in order to contribute to the technical character of the claim? There were two problems with the question. Firstly, the question referred to individual features rather than to the claimed subject-matter as a whole. Although the *COMVIK/HITACHI* approach to deciding whether there was an inventive step could involve ignoring some features, it began with consideration of all the features together to determine whether the claimed subject-matter had technical character. Only once this determination had been made could the Board turn to the question of which claimed features contributed to that technical character and therefore should be taken into account for the assessment of whether there was an inventive step. It was well-established that features that taken in isolation belonged to matters excluded from patentability under EPC art.52(2) could nevertheless contribute to the technical character of the claimed invention, see T 208/84 *VICOM/Computer-related invention* [1987] E.P.O.R. 74. Secondly, neither T 163/85 *BBC/Colour television signal* [1990] E.P.O.R. 599 nor T 190/94 *MITSUBISHI* required a technical effect on a physical entity in the real world. They merely accepted this as something sufficient for avoiding exclusion from patentability. There was no divergence with T 125/01 *HENZE* and T 424/03 *MICROSOFT/Clipboard formats I* where the technical effects were essentially confined to the respective computer programs. Had an answer to this question been required, it is logical to conclude that the answer would have been negative.

The fourth question was whether the activity of programming a computer necessarily involved technical considerations, see e.g. T 1197/97 *SYSTRAN/Translating natural languages* [2005] E.P.O.R 13 and T 172/03 *RICOH/Order management*; see also T 833/91 *IBM/External interface simulation* [1998] E.P.O.R. 431; T 204/93 *AT&T/Computer system* [2001] E.P.O.R. 39; and T 769/92 *SOHEI/General purpose management system* [1996] E.P.O.R. 253 where programming was considered to be a mental act. There was no divergence between these positions. Designing a bicycle clearly involved technical considerations (it may also have involved non-technical, e.g. aesthetic, considerations) but it was a process which at least initially could take place in the designer's mind, i.e. be a mental act excluded from patentability. A computer algorithm could be regarded as a pure mathematical-logical exercise or it could be seen as a procedure for carrying making a machine carry out a task e.g. the application of the hypothetical Turing machine to the *Entscheidungsproblem* (David Hilbert, 1928). It was the intention of those who drafted the EPC that an abstract formulation of an algorithm should not be regarded as technical, and that a program should only be regarded as technical if when run it produced a "further technical effect", see T 1173/97 *IBM/Computer program product*.

Following this decision the UK-IPO declined to follow the approach by the EPO Boards embodied by *Pension Benefit* (T 931/95), *Hitachi* (T 2587/03) and *Microsoft/data transfer* (T 424/03), and their opinion is further set out in MOPP at 1.29.6 and 1.29.7. In *Halliburton Energy Services Inc.* [2011] EWHC 2508 (Pat) the Patents Court also declined to do so on the ground that the EPO's approach to patentability goes hand in hand with a special approach to inventive step. It was far from clear that the EPO's approach when applied as a whole and correctly was any more favourable to patentees than the UK approach. The difficulties perceived in the UK with the way the EPO now approached computer-implemented inventions were genuine jurisprudential concerns of respectful nature. As a matter of law computer-implemented inventions were just as patentable in the UK as in the EPO. The Patents Act is in accordance with the EPC in that both contain an exclusion for computer programs as such. That was a matter of legislation and it was not for any court to interpret that exclusion out of existence. Any change in the UK approach would now require a decision of the Court of Appeal: having regard to the finding in *Eli Lilly v Human Genome Sciences* [2011] UKSC 51 that the courts should normally follow the jurisprudence of the EPO, particularly where the Board has adopted a consistent approach in a number of decisions and having regard to strong policy reasons for seeking consistency of approach it is possible, but not certain, that future decisions will rule in favour of a change.

Standard of Proof

The relevant standard of proof was considered in *Blacklight Power Inc v Comptroller* **1.09** [2009] R.P.C. 6; [2008] EWHC 2763 Pat Ct. Any pure question of law should be decided during prosecution. On an issue of fact, it is not the law that any doubt, however small, should force the Comptroller to allow an application to proceed to grant. Rather he should examine the material before him and attempt to come to a conclusion on the balance of probabilities. If he considers that there is a substantial doubt about an issue of fact which could lead to patentability at that stage, he should consider whether there is a reasonable prospect that matters will turn out differently if the matter is fully investigated at a trial. If so he should allow the application to proceed.

Computer programs—further UK opinions

There is a widespread misconception both amongst those who devise computer **1.10** programs and those who advise them that there is a general prohibition on the patenting of inventions involving computer programs. Study of issued patents (whether granted under the 1977 Act or by the EPO), reveals that this is not the case.

The general approach taken to the consideration of patentability of computer software is that described at §,1.06 above. As previously stated, the leading cases on the patentability of software-related inventions in the UK are currently *Aerotel* and *Symbian*, and the judgments handed down in those cases discuss many significant earlier UK and EPO Appeal Board decisions. After *Aerotel* and before *Symbian* the approach adopted by the UK-IPO was to refuse an application for a computer program-related invention unless it related to a technical process outside the computer or a solution to a technical problem within the computer, and this approach opened a gap between the outcomes likely before the UK-IPO and the EPO. With the *Symbian* decision, the test applicable in the United Kingdom has been restored to "technical effect" and it is possible that outcomes before the two offices will become more similar.

This section looks at some of the more specific points relating to such inventions.

Gale's application [1991] R.P.C. 305 concerned a read-only memory chip programmed with an improved algorithm for calculating square roots and is notable as the basis of the approach adopted by the UK-IPO prior to *Symbian*. The Court of Appeal held that:

"That still leaves the difficulty that those instructions when written, and without more, are not patentable, because they constitute a computer program. Is there something more? In the end I have come to the conclusion that there is not. The attraction of Mr Gale's case lies in the simple approach that, as claimed, he has found an improved means of carrying out an everyday function of computers. To that extent, and in tha-trespect, his program makes a more efficient use of a computer's resources. A computer, including a pocket calculator with a square root function, will be a better computer when programmed with Mr Gale's instructions. So it may. But the instructions do not embody a technical process which exists outside the computer. Nor, as I understand the case as presented to us, do the instructions solve a 'technical' problem lying within the computer, as happened with patent applications such T 115/85 [1990] E.P.O.R. 107 and *IBM Corp./Data processor network* T 06/83, [1990] E.P.O.R. 91. I confess to having difficulty in identifying clearly the boundary line between what is and what is not a technical problem for this purpose. That, at least to some extent, may well be no more than a reflection of my lack of expertise in this technical field. But, as I understand it, in the present case Mr Gale has devised an improvement in programming. What his instructions do, but it is all they do, is to prescribe for the cpu in a conventional computer a different set of calculations from those normally prescribed when the user wants a square root. I do not think that makes a claim to those instructions other than a claim to the instructions as such. The instructions do not define a new way of operating the computer in a technical sense, to adopt the expression used in *IBM Corp./Document abstracting and receiving* T 22/85, [1990] E.P.O.R. 98, 105.

In short, therefore, the claim is in substance a claim to a computer program, being the particular instructions embodied in a conventional type of ROM circuitry, and those instructions do not represent a technical process outside the computer or a solution to a technical problem within the computer."

In *Fujitsu's Application* [1997] R.P.C. 608 the invention concerned a method and apparatus, for modelling a synthetic crystal structure. The Court of Appeal held that the result depended on the personal skill and assessment of the user, that having regard to the way that the image was produced there was no technical contribution, and further that even though the invention like *Vicom* related to image production, each case had to be decided on its own facts.

On the facts in *Aerotel* the Court of Appeal held that the claimed method and apparatus for making a telephone call was a new combination of apparatus. However, that case was an appeal after a successful application for summary judgment and this was uncontested because the parties had reached a settlement. Later the same patent came before the court at full trial in *Aerotel v Wavecrest* [2008] EWHC 1180 Pat Ct. Here, the different defendants brought evidence before the court and on this argued that the patent was no more than the implementation of an existing combination of hardware to perform a particular method of doing business between telephone company and customer, implemented by programming existing computers, the patentee's contribution to what was known being entirely in the fields excluded from patentability; and, based upon knowledge of the common general knowledge in the art at the priority date, that the invention as claimed also lacked inventive step. The Patents Court accepted this evidence and revoked the patent.

In *Symbian* (above) the application concerned the patentability of a method of accessing data in a dynamic link library device. The UK-IPO took the position that art.52(2)(c) of the EPC had the effect of excluding from patentability any program unless it had a novel effect outside the computer, whereas the applicants argued that it only excluded programs which did not provide a technical solution to a technical problem. A program which improved the performance of a computer would not be excluded any more than a program which improved the performance of any other machine. The Court of Appeal held that the important question was whether the claimed subject matter made a "technical" contribution to the state of the art. Despite an attack by the UK-IPO on the vagueness and arbitrariness of the term "technical", that question embodied the consistent jurisprudence of the EPO Appeal Boards (even though the precise meaning given to the term has not been consistent), and it has been applied by the UK Court of Appeal itself in *Merrill Lynch, Gale, Fujitsu* and *Aerotel*. The most reliable guidance as to the meaning of the term "technical" was to be found in *VICOM*; T 6/83 *IBM CORP/Data processor network*; T 115/85 *IBM/ Computer-related invention*; and in the UK decisions in *Merrill Lynch* and *Gale*. The fact that "the boundary line" between what is and what is not a technical contribution is imprecise might be attributable to three causes: (a) national tribunals and the Board may still be at an intermediate stage of working out and identifying the precise location of the line to be drawn; (b) the problem is inherent and never wholly satisfactorily soluble; and (c) competing views based on different philosophies (the "open source" movement represent one extreme, that of companies such as the present applicant, the other). The uncertainty was well demonstrated by the elusiveness of the meaning of "technical", the change of attitude manifested in the more recent decisions of the EPO Appeal Board, the contrasting outcomes in *Vicom* and *Fujitsu*, and indeed possible reconsideration of the correct view of computer program patents in the United States (see Professor John Duffy: *Death of Google's Patents*? Patently-O Patent Law Blog, July 21, 2008). However, bearing in mind the multifarious features of computer programs and the unpredictable developments which will no doubt occur in the IT field, the court believed that it would be dangerous to suggest that there was a clear rule available to determine whether or not a program was excluded by art.52(2)(c) of the EPC. Each case must be determined by reference to its particular facts and features, bearing in mind the guidance given in the decisions mentioned. Furthermore, a technical innovation, whether within (as in the last-mentioned cases) or outside the computer will normally suffice to ensure patentability (subject of course to the claimed invention not falling foul of the other exclusions in art.52(2) of the EPC).

In *AT&T Knowledge Ventures and CVON Innovations Ltd v Comptroller General of Patents Designs and Trade Marks* [2009] EWHC 343 Pat Ct, the court considered the tests set out in *Aerotel v Telco; Macrossan's Application* [2006] EWCA Civ 1371; [2007] R.P.C. 7 (*Aerotel*); and in *Symbian Ltd v Comptroller-General of Patents* [2008] EWCA Civ 1066; [2009] R.P.C. 1 (*Symbian*). Lewison J. stated that it was impossible to define the meaning of "technical effect" in the context of the *Aerotel* test, but at [45] that the following were useful signposts, whether:

(i) the claimed technical effect had a technical effect on a process which is carried on outside the computer;

(ii) the claimed technical effect operated at the level of the architecture of the computer; that is to say whether the effect was produced irrespective of the data being processed or the applications being run;

(iii) the claimed technical effect resulted in the computer being made to operate in a new way;

(iv) there was an increase in the speed or reliability of the computer; and

(v) the perceived problem was overcome by the claimed invention as opposed to merely being circumvented.

Additionally, the fact that there were several ways of putting a method of doing business into practical operation did not mean that the selection of one of them was relevantly technical. Each way of practical implementation might itself be a method of doing business, see para.[57].

AT&T's appeal concerned a content broker hosting service system. That was a system which acted as an intermediary between a user wishing to buy digital content (e.g. music) and digital content suppliers. The problem that the inventor identified was that digital content suppliers supply content without knowing the functionality of the device on which it is to be played. This may mean that the user devices cannot decode or display the digital content. For example, a user might have bought music that he could not play. The application solved the problem by the provision of a "device profile table" which indicated the capabilities of the various user devices that could be connected to the system, so that the system could select and supply content which was compatible.

CVON's application was for a messaging system, such as that used for transmitting text messages between mobile phones, which modified messages sent from one terminal to another dependent on the membership of sender or recipient of a group which might be anything from a supermarket loyalty scheme to a sports club or an online community such as Facebook. That was perceived to be slow, as the old way of modifying messages on the basis of group membership (where group membership records were held in a third-party database) was that the third party database periodically transferred data to the telecommunications network so as to update the latter's records of group membership. The claimed invention made the process more efficient by holding a database containing the group membership of its subscribers at the telecommunications network end.

Applying the above tests to the joined appeals before him, Lewison J. held that both applications related only to excluded subject-matter, as neither produced a relevant technical effect [46] and [57].

In *Gemstar v Virgin* [2009] EWHC 3068, the UK Patents Court considered the validity of a patent for an electronic programming guide and applied the technical contribution test stated in *Symbian Ltd* [2008] EWCA Civ 1066; [2009] R.P.C. 1; *Aerotel* [2007] R.P.C. 7, [2006] EWCA Civ 1371; *Macrossan* [2007] R.P.C. 7, and summarised in *AT&T Knowledge Ventures Ltd* [2009] F.S.R. 19, [2009] EWHC 343. In *Gemstar*, it was held that a different, or alternatively a better, user interface was not a technical effect. Many computers running a program were likely to have a display output, and if that were enough to be a technical effect, then every program in such a computer would be likely to fall outside the exclusion. That was unlikely to have been the intention of the Act, see paras [41]–[60].

In *Cranway v Playtech* [2010] F.S.R. 3, [2009] EWHC 1588 Pat Ct, the court considered the validity of a patent for an interactive, computer gaming system using general purpose computers, where the innovative aspects were claimed to concern auditing and security to ensure fairness for players and prevent players from defeating the outcome of a game. It was argued that if, ignoring the computer program, the invention were patentable, then the fact that a computer drives the invention does not deprive it of patentability. It was held that if that test were applied, there was nothing left of the invention. Its sole raison d'être was the computerisation of conventional gambling for real money. Accordingly, the patent described a computer program as such, see paras [132]–[143].

Computer programs—further EPO opinions

1.11   EPO decisions T 1173/97 *IBM/Computer program product* OJ EPO 1999, 609; [2000] E.P.O.R. 219; and T 935/97 *IBM/Computer program Product II* [1999] E.P.O.R. 301 stress that claims should be allowed provided that the subject-matter has technical character. Although it was stated that computer programs cannot be considered as having technical character merely because they operate computers, the required technical character could be found in the further effects (i.e. further to normal computer operations) deriving from the execution by the hardware of the instructions given by the program if the computer program is one of the necessary means of obtaining a particular technical effect. These two decisions approved two previous decisions (T 164/92 *BOSCH/Electronic computer components* OJ EPO 1995, 305; [1995] E.P.O.R. 585) where an improvement in computer re-set procedure was deemed sufficiently technical for patentability to be upheld; and T 71/91 *INTERNATIONAL BUSINESS MACHINES/Electronic document distribution network* which involved the reconstitution of a data stream passing between a plurality of workstations). However, the 1999 IBM decisions distinguished the earlier T 204/93 *AT&T/System for generating software source code components* [2001] E.P.O.R. 39 wherein it was stated that, for patentability, the computer must work in an essentially new way from a technical point of view.

In the past, the EPO also rejected some applications involving computer programs, sometimes under another of the excluded classes of invention. These included: T 22/85 *IBM/Document abstracting and retrieving* OJ EPO 1990, 12; [1990] E.P.O.R. 98 where it was held that operations of an automatic abstracting, storage and retrieval system amounted to mental acts excluded under EPC art.52(2)(c) and that patentable character could not be derived by defining the necessary steps in terms of functions to be realised with the aid of conventional computer hardware elements; T 52/85 *IBM/Semantically-related expressions* [1989] E.P.O.R. 454 where semantic relationships were not regarded as of technical character and the processing of the applicant's system involved only conventional computer techniques and programming; T 121/85 *IBM/Spelling checking*;

T 38/86 *IBM/Text processing OJ EPO* 1990, 384; [1990] E.P.O.R. 606; T 65/86 *IBM/Text processing* [1990] E.P.O.R. 181; and T 186/86 *IBM/Text editing* in each case where the invention concerned the editing and display of matter in a text processing system; and T 158/88 *SIEMENS/Character form* OJ EPO 1991, 566; [1992] E.P.O.R. 69 where the invention concerned the automatic selection of an orthographically correct form of a character depending upon its position in a word.

However, in T 110/90 *IBM/Transforming editable documents* OJ EPO 1993, 10 and 1994, 557; [1995] E.P.O.R. 185, the automatic translation of printer control codes was held to be of a technical character because the codes were not concerned with the linguistic meaning of the text and related to operations that in old mechanical typewriters had been performed by mechanical means; and, in T 1002/92 *PETTERSSON/Queuing system* OJ EPO 1995, 605; [1996] E.P.O.R. 1, claims were allowed to a system for determining a queue system for serving customers on the basis that such should be regarded as an apparatus and not a mere method of doing business. Also held patentable by the EPO was a method for interactive rotation of displayed graphic objects: T 59/93 *INTERNATIONAL Business Machines/Interactive rotation* and a computer system for plural types of independent management: T 769/92 *SOHEI/General-purpose management system* OJ EPO 1995, 525; [1996] E.P.O.R. 253.

In T 528/07 *ACCENTURE/Portal System* it was held that the *DUNS/COMVIK* approach of T 641/00 did not need modification having regard to the alignment of EPC art.52(1) with TRIPS art.27(1). TRIPS did not give a definition of the term "technology" but left it to the member states and their jurisdiction to define and apply this concept. TRIPS art.27(1) reflected on the one hand a minimum consensus and on the other hand the Member States' unreadiness uniformly to define the patentability requirements. The TRIPS Member States were free to adopt different standards for each patentability requirement, e.g. inventive step. The *COMVIK* approach was one facet of the standard applied by the EPO.

Conceptual processes and meta-methods ordinarily exhibit no technical characteristics and hence do not involve an inventive step, see T 354/07 *SIEMENS/Funktionspläne*.

In T 1656/06 *MICROSOFT/Digital Rights Management*, the Appeal Board restated the rule that claimed subject-matter specifying at least one feature not falling within the ambit of art.52(2) EPC was not excluded from patentability by the provisions of arts 52(2) and (3) EPC. All the claims under consideration were method claims which specified that the method was carried out by "computing devices". Claim 10 was a claim to a "computer-readable medium". Neither of those two features fell under the exclusions of art.52(2) EPC and hence the claimed subject-matter of the request was not excluded from patentability by the provisions of arts 52(2) and (3) EPC. In the circumstances, the Appeal Board held that the Examining Division had taken a position which was incompatible with the case law of the Boards of Appeal. However its decision had not been in contradiction to the Guidelines for Examination of the time and it is arguable that T 258/03, raised in argument, was not entirely established case law at the time of the refusal. Additionally, the Appeal Board re-stated that where one computer controlled another computer, that was a technical effect going beyond the effects observed when any computer program was run, and therefore all the claimed means involved in achieving that effect had to be taken into account when assessing the novelty and inventive step of the claimed invention. On the detailed facts, the Board considered that the combination of features claimed, inter alia the user's request to render some digital content triggering a communication with another system, the communication containing certain control data which was replaced by other control data and returned, could not be dismissed as common knowledge of such notoriety that it could not be challenged.

In T 1244/07 *AMAZON/1-Click*, the claimed invention relating to online shopping and sought to reduce the number of user interactions involved in selecting items and also to reduce the amount of sensitive information sent over the internet, which might be intercepted. The Appeal Board held that the way the claimed system operated related to forms of human behaviour and thinking that fell under mental acts, which were excluded from patentability. Additionally, apart from the question of whether omitting steps would be obvious in the light of the general desire to simplify computer interactions, the Board considered that such steps related to a method of doing business. Such steps could not contribute to inventive step.

—Scheme, rule or method for doing business—UK opinions

1.12 The legal position in UK and Europe concerning patents for business methods has been challenged by developments in the US and European practitioners should be aware of these developments.

In *State Street Bank & Trust v Signature Financial Group* 149 F.3d 1368 (Fed. Cir.1998) it was held that the "business methods" exception to patentability was no longer available absent some more well-defined statutory objection. The transformation of data representing discrete dollar amounts by a machine through a series of mathematical calculations into a final share price constituted a practical application of a mathematical algorithm, formula, or calculation, because it produced "a useful, concrete and tangible result"—a final share price momentarily fixed for recording and reporting purposes and accepted and relied upon by regulatory authorities and in subsequent trades. The effect of this decision has been to stimulate the filing of patent applications in the US for business method-related inventions, and a flood of counterpart applications in UK and Europe.

The US Supreme Court has now handed down its opinion in *Bilski v Kappos* (above at §1.04) that the concept of hedging as claimed was an unpatentable abstract idea like the algorithms in *Benson* and *Flook*. Furthermore, limiting an abstract idea to a particular field of use or adding token post-solution components did not make the concept patentable. The USPTO responded on July 27, 2010 by publishing draft interim guidelines. Factors that weigh in favour of patent-eligibility satisfy the criteria of the machine-or-transformation test or provide evidence that the abstract idea has been practically applied, and factors that weigh against patent-eligibility neither satisfy the criteria of the machine-or-transformation test nor provide evidence that the abstract idea has been practically applied. An explanatory memorandum further comments that since claims directed to abstract ideas were not patent-eligible prior to *Bilski*, subject-matter eligibility outcomes based on the *Interim Bilski Guidance* are not likely to change in most cases. The difference is that in some rare cases, factors beyond those relevant to machine-or-transformation may weigh for or against a finding that a claim is directed to an abstract idea.

A succession of applications originating in the financial community has been considered by the UK courts and the EPO. *Merrill Lynch's Application* [1989] R.P.C. 561 related to a computerised trading system that accommodated a random real-time order flow; after an unsuccessful appeal to the Court of Appeal, the case returned to the UK-IPO, the objections raised during examination were overcome and a patent was granted with revised claims as Patent No.GB-B-2180380. *Pintos Global Services' Application* BL O/171/01 was directed to an apparatus for controlling a pension benefit system and was rejected, following *Merrill Lynch*, because the fact that the claim was formally directed to "apparatus" was not conclusive: it essentially involved a method of doing business as such. In T 1284/04 *KING/Loan System* the application concerned an application claiming a method of and computer-based apparatus for creating financial instruments, administering an adjustable rate loan system, and the application was refused on the ground that inventive step could only result from features having a technical character, see also T 1161/04 *NASDAQ/Stock index*.

Many applications have related to features of gaming apparatus. See *CFPH LLC's Application* [2006] R.P.C. 5, which were refused and related to networked interactive wagering on the outcomes of events. *IGT's Applications* [2007] EWHC 1341 Ch concerned four applications which all related to systems for playing gambling games having a main game and a bonus game, the bonus game being of a different type to the main game and a player having to earn credits to get to the bonus game. The applications related to balancing payouts between individual machines in a linked system; to allowing a player to select between first and second bonus events shared between machines; to providing a bonus game involving challenges between players; and to enabling a player to enter or leave a game whilst a bonus game is continuing. All of the applications were held to relate to excluded matter and the appeals were dismissed. In *IGT/Acres Gaming Inc's Application* [2008] EWHC 568 Pat Ct the invention concerned apparatus for selecting an account for a player, comprising a card reader, designed to electronically read information off a pre-existing card issued by an entity other than a casino, a database of accounts, a network and a microprocessor programmed to access an account from the database over the network based on information read from the pre-existing card. The court held that it may or may not have been a clever business idea to piggy-back on pre-existing conventional cards, but what was defined was not a patentable invention. An application directed to an internet betting system was refused as relating to a method of doing business in *Sporting Exchange's Application* BL O/280/02. In *Oneida Indian Nation's Application* [2007] EWHC 954 Pat Ct the claimed subject-matter related to computerised apparatus for enabling players to play games from an off-site location with the new and inventive feature of iterative pre-generation and storage of results in response to a bet, with the associated advantages that: (a) the number of processing steps per bet was reduced; (b) the number of data transmission steps was reduced; (c) the system dispensed with the need to make an account check for every bet; and (d) as a result the system was more secure and robust. The court held, however, that these were advantages of a new way of doing business and devoid of relevant technical effect. European decisions where applications have been refused include T 1543/06 *GAMEACCOUNT/Game machine*; T 366/07 *IGT/Electronic multi-play poker* [2008] E.P.O.R. 18; and T 859/07 *DEQ SYSTEMS CIRP/Multi-player bet auxiliary game*.

An auction method was treated as a business method as such in T 258/03 *HITACHI/Auction method* where it was held that method steps consisting of modifications to a business scheme and aimed at circumventing a technical problem rather than solving it by technical means cannot contribute to the technical character of the subject-matter claimed.

As regards order processing and provision of discounts, decisions rejecting inventions under subs.(2)(c) are: *Dell USA's Application No.9919949.9* BL O/432/01, noted [2001] *CIPA* 576 in which a (very successful) web-based online user interface provided by Dell Corporation to enable users to custom configure a computer system for purchase was seen to be a computerised version of a salesman advising a client on the ordering of a suitable system and hence a "method of doing business" and unpatentable; and *Bilgrey Samson's Application* BL O/577/01 in which claims to the operation of a "fruit machine" type apparatus were held not to involve a technical contribution and to relate to a scheme, etc. for doing business. A further application by Dell was refused in *Dell USA's Application No.0005904.8* BL O/177/02 on the basis that the specification was silent with respect to the technical detail of the process, so that it offered no technical contribution to the art. This decision considered the UK, EPO and German case law in coming to this conclusion. An argument that the Dell website was able to offer a variety of choice amounting to 70 million options, more than a salesperson could handle, did not succeed because the specification imposed no limit on the complexity of the system; it could be set up to deal with fewer combinations. In any event, even with a large number of combinations, the computer was doing no more than its familiar function of performing a large number of iterations quickly. A divisional application out of the first application No.9919949.9 was considered in a further decision (*Dell USA's Application No.0127329.1* BL O/377/02) but rejected on the same basis, the hearing officer concluding that although the form and content of the claims had been changed, the substance of the invention claimed remained:

> "an interaction between a user and a computer, which … replicates what a customer may do in a store, by telephone or in writing".

In *e-Speed Inc* BL O/009/09, the application concerned a programme for the use of game controllers such as gamepads or joysticks for electronic trading, game controller signals being mapped to trading commands in the trading system. The specification explained that that enabled trading commands to be performed with greater speed and accuracy than with a keyboard or mouse. There was prior art in the electronic trading field disclosing the hand-held controller feature, and the hearing officer concluded that the subject-matter of claim 1 lacked inventive step, although the subject-matter of some dependent claims was allowable. What the invention had added to human knowledge as a matter of substance was an interface which allowed a trading command to be generated by making use of stored sets of game controller signals so that the command could be selected on the basis of both a particular user and a particular game controller, enabling a trading system to be controlled by two game controllers in a way that was not possible before However, the individual hardware items were conventional and any novelty in their overall arrangement was a consequence of using the interface of the invention rather than a contribution in its own right. As a matter of practical reality the contribution was a program which enabled trading commands to be generated more efficiently, but this advantage arose solely because there was a better program and not because there was any technical improvement in the operation of the hardware items making up the overall trading system. The hearing officer additionally stated that it was clear from *Symbian* (above) at para.[27] that the use of a program to implement a business method did not prevent the invention from being excluded on the latter ground. In the instant case, the application was for a method of doing business, see para.[41], and hence unpatentable.

—EPO decisions concerning business methods

1.13   A leading EPO decision is T 641/00 *COMVIK/Two identities* [2004] E.P.O.R. 10 in which the closest prior art against which the inventive character of the claimed subject-matter had to be judged was a paper describing the subscriber identity module for the European digital cellular system GSM. The differences between the subject-matter claimed and the prior art were that: (i) a subscriber identity module was allocated at least two identities; (ii) a user could select to which of the two or more identities a call was to be allocated, e.g. by reversing the attitude of a SIM card; and (iii) selective activated identities were used for distributing the costs amongst service and private calls or among different users. The Appeal Board held that these differences did not relate to the technical aspects of the network, but were a financial and administrative concept that did not require the exercise of technical skills and competence and did not involve the solution of a technical problem, the necessary commands already being available within the GSM system, and the discrimination required for cost distribution merely requiring minor modification of the network's home database. Accordingly the patent was revoked.

T 531/03 *CATALINA/Discount certificates* concerned a system for generating a printable cumulative discount certificate in a retail store solely in response to a customer's decision to purchase one or more pre-selected items. No support could be derived from non-technical features and it was held that an attempt to take into account the contribution of non-technical and technical aspects on an equal footing in the assessment of inventive step would not be in conformity with the EPC, since the presence of inventive step would in such an approach be attributed to features which are defined in the EPC as not being an invention. In T 154/04 *DUNS LICENSING ASSOCIATES/Estimating sales activity* [2007] E.P.O.R. 38 it was held that methods of business research are excluded "as such" from patentability under EPC art.52(2)(c) and (3) and that gathering and evaluating data as part of a business research method do not convey technical character to the business research method if such steps do not contribute to the technical solution of a technical problem. However, the German Federal Patent Court has accepted that a method of automatic sales control involving adjusting selling prices from sales prediction data is not merely an automatic method of putting a business method into effect and has technical character and so is not inherently unpatentable: *IBM/Automatic sales control* [Germany] [2000] E.I.P.R. 309.

In T 767/99 *PITNEY BOWES/System for processing mail*, apparatus for processing mail in accordance with departure data for a transportation system and shipping the mail to meet a just-in-time sequence was held not to be excluded, e.g. because of the use of a controlling computer and trays labelled with destination codes and departure times. In contrast, in T 388/04 *PITNEY BOWES/Undeliverable mail* [2007] E.P.O.R. 31 an application relating to a method of responding by a mailer to a notice from a postal service that a mail piece has not been delivered was refused, the Appeal Board holding that subject-matter remains excluded even where the use of unspecified technical means is implicit, and that activities may be excluded even where they have practical utility.

In T 1616/08 *AMAZON/Gift* order it was observed that the only relevant criterion for inventive step is the one stated in EPC art.56, namely whether the invention is obvious to a person skilled in the art. Since in accordance with established jurisprudence this "art" cannot be a field of business or administration, only elements of the solution falling within the competence of a technically skilled person (here: a programmer or computer scientist) can be taken into account.

The patent in T 588/05 *WEST DIRECT* [2010] E.P.O.R. 12 related to computer-assisted telemarketing. During a primary telemarketing transaction, a computer system attempted in real-time to suggest an "upsell", i.e. to offer the potential customer a secondary transaction opportunity in addition to, or in lieu of, the good or service for which the primary contact was made. The suggested secondary offer was supposed to present an optimum in terms of probability and profitability of commercial transactions. The thrust of the application was for using recent customer data (obtained from the current primary transaction) and archived customer data in order to tailor a secondary offer to the customer's presumed interests. It was held that the technical aspects specified or implied in the claim pertained to routine data communication and processing techniques and structures. Real-time access to databases while communicating with a person was a common technical means for efficient interaction in situations where more and more accuracy, complexity and data volume are desired and accepted based on the availability of increasing computing power. No specific technical problem was addressed by the application. Accordingly, the application disclosed no technical effect, see para.[5].

In T 511/06 *AMERICAN EXPRESS/Authenticating information*, analysis of characterising features allegedly contributing to inventive step was carried out feature-by-feature with some strictness. The differences between the claimed system for authenticating download of information and the prior art were (i) the specified external device was a third-party device which was remotely located from the information owner, the third-party device transferring blocks of information on behalf of the information owner, and (ii) the information device was configured to perform an acknowledgment process which sent the computed acknowledgment to the information owner for verification. The patentee submitted that the objective technical problem was providing means for the information owner to know whether the information, the download of which he had delegated, had really been downloaded to the customer. However, the Board did not agree with this formulation. In accordance with consistent case law, to arrive at the objective technical problem, it had first be established which technical effect the distinguishing features of the claim achieved. The technical problem was then formulated as the aim and task of modifying or adapting the closest prior art to provide the technical effects that the invention provided over the closest prior art. If a distinguishing feature did does not contribute to the solution of a technical problem, it could not support the presence of an inventive step. The effect of the first distinguishing feature was that the information owner could delegate the download of information to a third party, but this was not technical but merely concerned the distribution of tasks and related to a pure business model. The second distinguishing feature was that the delegating party (the information owner) could verify that the downloaded information had indeed been correctly received by the customer. Again this concerned administrative re-distribution of tasks and had no technical character. There were no technical advantages beyond those inherent in straightforward technical implementation, and the claimed subject-matter lacked inventive step since the only features which rendered the claimed subject-matter novel could not support inventive step.

In T 1108/06 *VISA INTERNATIONAL/Bill pay system*, the invention related to electronic bill payment systems which allowed a consumer to direct his bank to pay amounts owed to a biller. An important part of the invention was the generation of a unique number to increase the security of the transaction. In dismissing the appeal, the EPO held that it was the commercial method that underlay the invention and it could not, whether original or not, contribute to an inventive step, see para.[5].

In T 1029/06 *TOSHIBA/Environmental impact estimation* [2010] E.P.O.R. 13, the EPO considered a method to aid the planning, development, design and estimation of an environmentally conscious product by collecting information about how the product would be manufactured and used. The information, together with the costs of production, reuse and recycling, would be used to estimate the overall cost of the product. It was held that the application had no overall technical character, but was merely a mixture of subject-matter excluded as such under EPC art.52(2) and (3), specifically mathematical methods, methods for performing mental acts or doing business and presentations of information, see para.[11].

—Scheme, rule or method for performing a mental act

1.14   Subsection (2)(c), inter alia, prevents patents for inventions which consist of "a scheme, rule or method for performing a mental act".

At present, there appear to be conflicting decisions of the High Court on the extent of the exclusion. A number take the position that the prohibition denies protection for a function which in principle could be carried out in the human brain, even though the claimed subject-matter would not reflect a normal process of human reasoning. Others take the position that the exclusion is not so broad, see for instance *Aerotel* at [62] and [94] to [98] and *Halliburton Energy Services Inc.* [2011] EWHC 2508 (Pat).

In *Wang's Application* [1991] R.P.C. 463, the invention concerned an expert system which though seeking to produce results similar to those arrived at by a human expert, used procedures and steps that would not be replicated by such a person. The Patents Court held that:

> "a method of solving a problem, such as advising a person whether he has acted tortiously, can be set out on paper, or incorporated into a computer program. The purpose is the same, to enable advice to be given, which appears to me to be a mental act. Further, the result will be the advice which comes from performance of a mental act. The method may well be different when a computer is used, but to my mind it still remains a method for performing a mental act, whether or not the computer program adopts steps that would not ordinarily be used by the human mind."

The decision in *Wang* was followed in *Raytheon's application* [1993] R.P.C 427 which related to a method for automatically identifying objects such as ships from their silhouettes and was rejected by the Patent Office on the ground that the application related to no more than a method for performing a mental act using a computer and that decision was affirmed on appeal. In *Fujitsu's Application* [1996] R.P.C. 511, the Patents Court upheld the Comptroller's decision (see BL O/106/95) to refuse an application directed to methods for modelling a synthetic crystal structure by combining images of two such structures to display a third image representing a further crystal structure. The court held that the method claimed left it to the operator to select what data to work on, how to work on it and which, if any, results to use. Accordingly, what is produced was determined by the personal skill and assessment of the operator, and, as such, was held unpatentable because it consisted in substance of a scheme or method of performing a mental act. However, the court accepted that "prima facie, a novel technical development should be patentable". The Court of Appeal (see [1997] R.P.C. 608) dismissed a further appeal, regarding the invention as nothing more than a computer program, and stated that:

> "methods of performing a mental act, which means all methods of the type performed mentally, are unpatentable, unless some concept of technical contribution is present".

In *Halliburton v Smith* [2006] R.P.C. 2, Pumfrey J. held that claims to a method of designing a drill bit were methods of performing a mental act even though they could be carried out in a computer.

In *Westinghouse Electric's Application* BL O/105/95, the invention involved a computer programmed to classify data for the identification of targets and such identification was deemed to be a mental act, unpatentable as such; and, likewise, in *Cotterell's Application* BL O/53/97 for an application involving encoding of archaeological artefacts. In *Furuno Electric's Application* BL O/133/90, noted I.P.D. 14040, a claim to a method of detecting fish shoals by the use of radar was refused as a performance of a mental act contrary to subs.(2)(c). Nevertheless, a method of distinguishing genuine from counterfeit articles by marking them according to a secret algorithm has been found allowable in principle in *McNeight and Lawrence's Application* BL O/66/85, though the EPO later rejected a somewhat similar claim, see T 51/84 *STOCKBURGER/Coded distinctive mark* OJ EPO 1986, 226; [1986] E.P.O.R. 229 because the specification was not seen to identify a technical means for carrying out the claimed procedural steps.

In *Minnesota Mining's Application* BL O/259/00, the collection of data was seen as a rule, scheme or method for performing a mental act, it being possible to collect the same data using pen and paper; and, in *Fujitsu's Application* BL O/317/00, an application concerned with systems for handling conflicting demands for resources, such as reservations for meeting rooms, particularly involving "queuing" criteria, was denied patentability as directed to mental acts being "the mere automation of a manual method of prioritisation of human actions". In this *Fujitsu* case, the application was also seen as an unpatentable method of doing business.

International Business Machines' Applications BL O/390/01 and O/399/01 are further examples of applications being refused as directed to methods of performing mental acts. In *International Business Machines' Applications* BL O/390/01 (which was concerned with a method allowing a computer to identify the human language of a computerised document by breaking down words into all their constituent letter pairs, and comparing those with corresponding letter pairs of pre-selected words from the chosen languages under consideration) the agent for the applicant argued that there was a technical effect, being the electronic recognition of the language of the document, but had to concede that this argument was weakened by the fact that the documents being handled remained unchanged by the process. The Comptroller considered the operations performed by the computer to be "a purely intellectual exercise" and held that:

"no matter how broad an interpretation is put on the terms technical contribution, technical effect, or technical consideration, I cannot find such a contribution, effect or consideration in the invention of the present application."

A similar result was reached in BL O/399/01 in which the invention related to a method of translation. It was held irrelevant that the claims were directed to a translation "system", as (following *Merrill Lynch*):

"substance must prevail over form and it is therefore necessary to construe each claim carefully to determine whether it relates to an excluded matter in the guise of some other article".

McKirdy's Application BL O/278/98 concerned a "memory enzyme system" designed to facilitate recall from memory of characteristics of a literary work. The examiner rejected the application as being directed to a mental act, but the hearing officer favoured rejection under s.1(2)(d) as being directed to a presentation of information. However, although applications were refused in *Toyota Jidosha's Application* BL O/72/94 for an apparatus for controlling the ordering of parts for a vehicle assembly line, and in *Nissan's Application* BL O/90/94, in respect of the electronic evaluation of designs, in neither case would the application have been refused as no more than a mental act.

In *Halliburton Energy Services* BL O/080/11 the Hearing Officer held that he was bound by the decision of Pumfrey J. in *Halliburton v Smith* and therefore applied the broad interpretation of the exclusion, but as noted above this was reversed on appeal in

Halliburton Energy Services Inc. [2011] EWHC 2508 (Pat). The Patents Court held that the balance of authority in England was in favour of the narrow approach to the mental act exclusion. Furthermore, it favoured the narrow interpretation on its own merits. The wide construction was uncertain in scope and there was no good reason why the exclusion needed to be interpreted widely. On the other hand there was logic behind the narrow interpretation, preventing patents being granted which could be infringed by a purely mental process. Allowing for the possibility of patent infringement by thought alone was undesirable. The purpose of the exclusion was to make sure that patent claims could not be performed by purely mental means and that was all. The exclusion would not apply if there were appropriate non-mental limitations in the claim. A similar approach by the EPO could be discerned in T 1227/05 *INFINEON*.

As discussed above in §1.07, the EPO takes the position that a patentable invention must solve a technical problem by technical means, see T 258/03 *HITACHI/Auction method* and that if this is lacking, the claimed subject-matter is an abstract intellectual concept devoid of any technical implications. In T 914/02 *GENERAL ELECTRIC COMPANY/Nuclear core loading* [2006] E.P.O.R. 13 it was held that the involvement of technical considerations was not sufficient for a method which may exclusively be carried out mentally to have technical character, and that it was doubtful whether mere complexity could be used to disqualify an activity as a mental activity. However, by specifying "using a suitably programmed computer" the amended claim contained a definition of technical means to be used in the method which no longer related to a mental act as such and was therefore, not excluded from patentability. Cases that have been refused include T 22/85 *IBM/Document abstracting* (abstracting, storing and retrieving a document); T 121/85 *IBM/Spell checking*; T 38/86 *IBM/Text Processing* (automatically replacing difficult expressions in a text with expressions of improved understandability level); T 65/86 *IBM/Text Editing* (automatic detection and replacement of text homophones); and T 158/88 *SIEMENS/Character form* (automatically selecting the appropriate position-sensitive form of a character in a written oriental language). Contrast T 110/90 *IBM/ Transforming editable documents* (automatic translation of printer control codes held to be of a technical character), and also T 49/04 *WALKER/Text processor* [2007] E.P.O.R. 34 where the presentation of natural language text on a display in a manner which improved readability, enabling users to perform their task more efficiently related to how, i.e. by what physical arrangement of the text, cognitive content is conveyed to the reader and was thus considered as contributing a technical solution to a technical problem. A method for adaptable control of the accuracy of a value for rotation of an object by cursor input was allowed, see T 59/93 *INTERNATIONAL Business Machines/Interactive rotation*. Claims to a method of designing a computer chip have been refused, but allowed when amended to be directed to a method of manufacture of such a chip, the claim now being directed to a physical entity T 453/91 *INTERNATIONAL BUSINESS MACHINES/VLSI chip design*. However, it should be noted that this decision was no longer considered good law by the Board in T 1227/05 *INFINEON TECHNOLOGIES/Schaltkreisssimulation I*.

In T 756/06 *FUJITSU/Displaying a schedule*, the invention related to schedule display apparatus. The problem to be solved was how to make better use of a limited area on a display screen of a PC, electronic notebook or the like. The existing solutions all had disadvantages; displaying less information was not so useful to the user, using smaller fonts was harder to read and using a scroll bar required additional user input. The display of the invention solved this problem by allocating fewer lines to 'non-active' hours, e.g. those outside the working day. As a result, more detail about the activities in the 'active' hours could be displayed. The Board held that the layout of the schedule was for the user's mental use, i.e. according to the user's requirements and preferences, rather than for a technical purpose in a technical process. In particular, although the appellant mentioned the possibility of user input of the first time span, the Board considered that this only resulted in a subjective improvement of the appearance of the schedule and was not a part of any technical process, see para.[14].

A system used in designing a laminate part was considered in T 887/07 *McDONNELL DOUGLAS/Knowledge driven composite design optimisation* [2009] E.P.O.R. 47. The

Appeal Board held that the exclusion for mental acts did not extend to a system which represented technical means for implementing a design optimisation method.

In T 0784/06 *BECKMAN/Genotype determination*, the Appeal Board considered an application for a device for determining the genotype at a locus within genetic material obtained from a subject. The claim had several parts, some technical and some non-technical in nature. The Board confirmed the established rule that non-technical features, such as mental activities, were not to be ignored in assessing inventive step, insofar as they interacted with the technical subject-matter of the claim for solving a technical problem. The patentees argued that the claimed data treatment features were the key for determining the genotype of a biological sample whereas opponents argued that the steps were too general to provide a technical contribution. In the outcome the features were ignored and the patent was revoked, the information content in the specification relating to the relevant features being held to be sparse and insufficient.

In T 0311/08 *SAP/Reassigning data objects* the Board held that choosing a resource distribution algorithm to improve data distribution was a non-technical solution of a purely mathematical and theoretical nature, whereas the Appeal Board held that it was a concrete technical solution to the technical problem of smoothing the distribution of data, and the application was remitted for further prosecution.

—Presentation of information

Objections under this heading arise both in relation to conventional products and processes and in relation to computer-implemented inventions. **1.15**

EPO decisions of special significance are T 163/85 *BBC/Television signal* and T 1194/97 *PHILIPS/Data structure product* [2001] E.P.O.R. 25.

In the *BBC* case a signal of defined structure for a television picture was held to be patentable because it was a physical reality that could be detected by technical means. The claim read:

> "A colour television signal adapted to generate a picture with an aspect ratio of greater than 4:3, and in which the active-video portion of a line constitutes at least 85% and preferably 90% of the line period."

It should be noted that in the US the courts have reached the opposite conclusion, holding that a claim to a signal modified with an encoded "watermark" was not patentable since it did not fall into any of the statutory classes specified by 35 U.S.C. §101, see *In re Nuijten* 500 F. 3d 1346; Fed. Cir. 2007; and see the case comment by G. Kirsch and S. Anderson [2007] *CIPA* 614.

In *PHILIPS* (above), the question that had to be decided was whether a claim to a recording medium having stored information on it was precluded from protection. The Appeal Board followed the *BBC* decision and drew a distinction between information that can be protected and content which is excluded from protection and said:

> "... the deciding board considered it appropriate to distinguish between two kinds of information, when discussing its presentation. According to this distinction, a TV signal solely characterised by the information per se, e.g. moving pictures, modulated upon a standard TV signal, may fall under the exclusion of Article 52(2)(d) and (3) EPC but not a TV signal defined in terms which inherently comprise the technical features of the TV system in which it occurs. The present board regards a record carrier having data recorded thereon as being in this respect analogous to a modulated TV signal and considers it appropriate to distinguish in a corresponding way between data which encodes cognitive content, e.g. a picture, in a standard manner and functional data defined in terms which inherently comprise the technical features of the system (reader plus record carrier) in which the record carrier is operative. The significance of the distinction between functional data and cognitive information content in relation to technical effect and character may be illustrated by the fact that in the present context complete loss of

the cognitive content resulting in a humanly meaningless picture like 'snow' on a television screen has no effect on the technical working of the system, while loss of functional data will impair the technical operation and in the limit bring the system to a complete halt. In particular the board sees no reason to ascribe less technical character to a synchronisation signal recorded as digital data, e.g. a predetermined binary string, than to an analog synchronisation signal transmitted or recorded as a pulse having a distinctive shape."

The Board supported its position by reference to Claude E. Shannon and Warren Weaver, *The Mathematical Theory of Communication* (Illinois: University of Illinois Press, 1949):

"The word information, in this theory, is used in a special sense that must not be confused with its ordinary usage. In particular, information must not be confused with meaning. In fact, two messages, one of which is heavily loaded with meaning and the other of which is pure nonsense, can be exactly equivalent, from the present (information technology) viewpoint, as regards information. Information in communication theory relates not so much to what you do say, as to what you could say. That is, information is a measure of one's freedom of choice when one selects a message."

It also held that the definition that it had put forward was consistent with the legislative history of art.52(2)(d) and (3) of the EPC. The phrase "presentation of information" in art.52(2)(d) of the EPC had been adopted from r.39.1(v) of the PCT. The records of the PCT Washington Conference 1970, p.572 showed that the intention of the provision was to remove from what an International Searching Authority had to search, tables, forms, writing styles and the like. In the view of the Board this was subject-matter which merely conveyed cognitive or aesthetic content directly to a human.

In the UK under the 1949 Act, it has been held that, while a patent could not be "sustained on the basis of novelty in information, for example artistic or literary content alone", a novel method of presenting information, or novel article by which information can be presented, ought to be patentable under s.101 of the 1949 Act, see *Rhodes' Application* [1973] R.P.C. 243. Some other cases decided under the former law are mentioned in the *Manual of Patent Office Practice* (MOPP).

Applications which have been refused under the 1977 Act as being directed merely to the presentation of information include: *TDK Electronics' Application* BL O/97/83 for a magnetic tape cassette of conventional construction, but with one guide pole coloured to assist assembly; *Price's Application* BL O/105/84 for trading stamps which were regarded as unpatentable as either aesthetic creations or ways of presenting information; *Kettle's Application* BL O/41/86 for a vehicle licence plate with symbols denoting the month and year of first registration; *Turner's Application* BL O/14/88 for a chart identifying the growth stages for a particular plant, where the claimed method of use would only have been patentable if it had involved an inventive concept beyond the mere presentation of information; *Thompson's Application* BL O/50/89 for a drinking vessel characterised by displaying an informational message viewable through its base, claims only being allowed after addition of a structural feature which added novelty to the claim in addition to that novel informational feature; *Waring's Application* BL O/73/90, noted I.P.D. 13138 for a traffic violation ticket which was held unpatentable as being merely a presentation of information, the other characteristics of the ticket being known in a stationery pad intended for other purposes; *Crane Ltd's Application* BL O/41/92, noted I.P.D. 15156 for a juxtaposition of two graphs was held unpatentable as lacking an inventive step other than as regards the presentation of information; *Shahin's Application* BL O/149/95 directed to a gaming machine in which fruit pictures were replaced by advertisements; and *McKirdy's Application* (see §1.14 above) for a "memory enzyme system". In *Crawford's Application* [2006] R.P.C. 11; [2005] EWHC 2417 Pat Ct the invention related to a bus having a sign for displaying whether it was operating in a boarding mode where it would both pick up and drop off passengers and an exit mode where it would drop off passengers only. The only advance in the art was in the nature of the information to be displayed on the outside of the bus, which was not of a technical nature.

In *Raytheon Company's Application* [2008] R.P.C. 3; [2007] EWHC 1230 Pat Ct the invention related to a method for generating and displaying inventory data in which textual descriptions were replaced by visual representations permitting items to be identified more easily, the representations being synthesised in real time from individual images of the components of the facility which were stored in digital form in a database, so reducing the usage of memory and the load on the processor, and in which the system was navigable by a user starting with a high level interactive graphical representation and "drilling down" to the particular rack or component of interest by, for example, clicking a particular location on the screen. The court concluded that the contribution was no more than a reflection of how the programmer has chosen to create the desired representation. Just as in *Fujitsu* where the programmer had to devise a program to create a pictorial display which reproduced the effect of a model, so here the programmer had to devise a program to produce a visual representation of the rack and all it contained, and the fact he had done it by synthesising the representation from a number of smaller images was simply a matter of program design. The result was a computer of a known type operating according to a new program, albeit one which reduces the load on the processor and the contribution related to no more than the presentation of information and/or a computer program as such.

The extent of the exclusion was recently considered by the High Court in *Gemstar v Virgin Media* [2010] R.P.C. 10, see paras 52 to 60. The Court held that if the presentation of information had some technical features over and above the information and its delivery then it might be patentable. Hence the distinction was drawn between the content (and its mere delivery) and any additional technical aspects of its delivery. The decision was upheld on appeal: [2011] R.P.C. 25; [2011] EWCA Civ 302.

In *Trane International Inc's Application* BL O/429/10, the application concerned the selective presentation of alarm information. The UK-IPO held this to be patentable by reason of it being a presentation of information as such.

An application which has been refused by the EPO is T 119/88 *FUJI/Coloured disk jacket* OJ EPO 1990, 395; [1990] E.P.O.R. 615 which related to disk jackets coloured in a specific range of colours. However, the EPO has allowed claims to a method of selecting correct emergency patient treatment using a specially calibrated measuring tape as being more than a mere presentation of information T 77/92 *BROSELOW/Measuring tape* [1998] E.P.O.R. 266; and for the display of only valid commands in a computer "help" system as being of a technical character, the computer program constituting a technical means for carrying out the invention T 887/92 *IBM/On-line help facility*. T 790/92 *INTERNATIONAL BUSINESS MACHINES/Editing business charts* held that a discrepancy between normal and modified presentations of information failed to have the necessary "technical nature". However, in T 679/04 *MATSUSHITA/Transmission system* [2007] E.P.O.R. 18 a claim to a transmission system for television programmes was refused as originally worded characterised only by its information content, but the objection was overcome by addition of hardware features and the application was remitted for further examination. In T 362/90 *WABCO/Schaltanzeige für Gangschaltung* a device for displaying especially in a heavy goods vehicle both the gear in use and the best gear to be in was held to be patentable. A case which has been refused is T 603/89 *BEATTIE/Marker* OJ EPO 1992, 230; [1992] E.P.O.R. 221 for markers for facilitating the reading of music where the display of information had no effect on the physical properties or mechanical functioning of the known marker structure.

The invention in T 1505/05 *NORITSU KOKI/On line picture album* concerned a photo-processing system providing for dual-sided printing with a picture on the front surface of the resulting printed sheet and auxiliary information on the rear surface. The Board held that any concept of arranging pictures and text which did not solve a specific technical problem was a mere presentation of information. Such a concept did not provide a technical contribution over the prior art and thus could not form a valid basis for novelty and inventive step. The same situation existed with respect to the claims of the auxiliary requests, which characterised the invention by options to select the type of pictures and whether the text was printed on the front or back of the printing paper. These options were typical aspects of presentation of information and were also available to the user of prior art systems.

The invention in T 701/06 *CASIO/Determining group name* concerned the problem of organising digital photographs. When images taken at a number of holiday sightseeing locations were put in an album, they could be grouped by the date they were taken. A name corresponding to that date could be assigned to each group such that the group could be retrieved. However, it was difficult to associate the images in a group some time later from only the date they were taken. The invention assigned a meaningful name to the group. The name given to the group was the name of the nearest item in a map database to where the oldest (first) image in the group was taken, or the name of an area in the map database covering the places where all the images in the group were taken. It was held that the general idea of identifying images according to subjective criteria (time, location, event or combinations thereof) for easy retrieval was nontechnical. The appellant argued that the invention used both techniques in the same device in that it first looked for a name representative of the area and if one was not found it would give the group the name of the oldest image in the group. However, the appellant was unable to find support in the application for this sequence of operations and this was not reflected in the wording of the claim. Thus, the claim merely defined an apparatus that was capable of performing both alternatives. Since both alternatives were obvious and there was no surprising effect disclosed when combining these two alternatives in the same device, the Board considered that the claimed combination did not involve an inventive step, see para.[11].

In T 1143/06 *BRITISH TELECOMMUNICATIONS/Data selection system* [2010] E.P.O.R. 11 the invention concerned large computer databases in which it was extremely difficult to identify hidden patterns in the data. The invention allowed each data file to be represented visually as an element moving on a display. Patterns in the data were readily recognisable since each element moved in accordance with the relevance of sort statements to the data file they represented so that differences between respective data files could be observed on the display as relative movements between the respective elements, hidden patterns in the data being easily identified by observing groups of elements moving in a similar way. The Board considered that a direct technical effect was absent, the user's evaluation being a mental act. Only a speed feature had been added which amounted to presentation of information. The case law of the Boards of Appeal provided little support for the idea that screen representations inherently addressed technical problems, T 49/94 *HITACHI/Video Signal Recording* not being followed. Furthermore, as regards the way the trajectory over the screen was computed, it was not clear that this implementation was actually technical since the computed trajectory served to present information and the way of computing it was a mathematical method, similar to the graphical rendering of any mathematical function. However, this question did not need to be decided since the feature involved no inventive step.

In T 1244/07 *AMAZON/1-Click* the claim related to an online purchasing system having the feature that the step of displaying an indication that the order for the item that was requested in response to the single action could be cancelled within a predetermined time period. The Board agreed with the Examining Division that the feature might amount to nothing more than the screen displaying "you can cancel within 90 minutes". That feature amounted solely to the presentation of administrative information and did not provide a solution of any technical problem.

—Aesthetic creations: literary, dramatic, musical or artistic works

1.16   Section 1(2)(b) prohibits patents for inventions which consist of "a literary, dramatic, musical or artistic work or any other aesthetic creation whatsoever". This provision continues the prohibition on the patenting of the intellectual or visual content of a paper or card which relates to the fine, and not to the applied, arts. Under the former "manner of manufacture" test, that prohibition was extended to cover additional articles such as cinematograph films and gramophone records where the novelty lies only in the information to be conveyed to the brain see, e.g. *Virginia-Carolina's Application* [1958] R.P.C. 35; and claims to a squash ball characterised by its blue colour was allowed as having a technical, rather than mere, aesthetic effect, *ITS Rubber's Application* [1979] R.P.C. 318. An example under the present Act of rejection of claims directed solely to aesthetic factors is *Andrews and Hopkins' Application* BL O/65/92; and *Simon's Application* BL O/139/86 and C/6/87 is an example of refusal on the ground that the invention was only a scientific theory or literary work.

Claims to partitions for buildings intended "to provide a different appearance" in the finished building were refused in *Shanley's Application* BL O/422/02 although sub-claims introducing technical features were allowed to proceed, subject to amendment. An argument that the main claim should be allowed on the basis of T 931/95 *PBS PARTNERSHIP/ Controlling pension benefits system* was rejected.

The EPO Guidelines define an aesthetic creation with reference to an article (e.g. a painting or sculpture) having aspects which are other than technical and the appreciation of which is essentially subjective. The EPO Guidelines give the following examples:

- Tyre tread—mixture of aesthetic and technical features—patentable.

- Book claimed solely in terms of the aesthetic or artistic effect of its information content, of its layout or of its letter font—not patentable.

- Book defined by a technical feature of the binding or pasting of the back may be patentable, even though it has an aesthetic effect also, e.g. a literary, dramatic, musical or artistic work.

In T 244/00 *MATSUSHITA/Remote-control* [2005] E.P.O.R. 12 the invention concerned remote control apparatus for an audio-visual system in which diagonal cursor moves were permitted in order to facilitate the selection of menu items. The Appeal Board held that normally the arrangement of menu items on a screen was artistic rather than technical, and the same was true for the permitted directions of cursor movement, see also T 125/04 *COMPARATIVE VISUAL ASSESSMENTS/Assessment system* [2007] E.P.O.R. 33 where it was held that, in general, the task of designing diagrams is non-technical even if the diagrams arguably convey information in a way which a viewer may intuitively regard as particularly appealing, lucid or logical. These decisions may be contrasted with T 643/00 *CANON/Searching image data* [2007] E.P.O.R. 1 where it was held that an arrangement of menu items (or images) on a screen could be determined by technical considerations, e.g. searching and retrieving images stored in an image processing apparatus in a more efficient or faster manner. See also T 333/95 *IBM/Interactive animation* [2003] E.P.O.R. 43 where the objective problem was to design a display interface which allowed an operator interactively and in a simple way to define a sequence of operations to be performed on graphics objects, and the solution of making the graphics object the current cursor decreased the mental and physical effort of the operator, the used input means also functioning as "programming means".

The EPO has allowed claims to a building component having particular decorative features as technical features were seen in addition to the aesthetic features, see T 686/90 *HETTLING-DENKER/Lichtdurchlässiges Bauelement* [2004] E.P.O.R. 5, but it would, apparently, be reluctant to accept colour alone as a distinguishing technical feature, see T 119/88 *FUJI/Coloured disk jacket* where resistance to fingerprints was also seen as a mere aesthetic effect. A method of concealing surface inhomogeneities was also seen as confined to an aesthetic effect in T 962/91 *POLYGRAM/Plattenförmige Informationsträger*. In T 619/02 *QUEST INTERNATIONAL/Odour selection* [2006] E.P.O.R. 52 a method of odour selection using human test subjects was refused on the grounds that although the perceptual processes taking place in the mind of a test subject presented with odours in an odour selection test did not constitute mental acts within the meaning of art.52(2)(c) of the EPC, the distinguishing features of the invention over the closest state of the art did not perform any technical function or achieve any technical effect.

In T 50/07 *APPLE/Method of transition between window states* [2010] E.P.O.R. 20, the Board considered a method of transitioning a window on a computer screen between an open state and a minimised state. The objective problem to be solved was how to achieve the specific aesthetic effect, i.e. its technical implementation. The steps in the claim of defining the set of curves and displaying the window as successive positions within the curves while scaling it to fit within the curves imply some further unspecified data-processing as well as driving the computer screen. Hence, the technical implementation as claimed was merely limited to such implied data-processing and driving, which was considered to be a straightforward, if not the only, solution for obtaining this specified aesthetic effect on the computer screen, and would be obvious to a skilled person in the field of computer graphics and in particular of graphical user interfaces, see para.[3].

In T 1689/07 *PROCTOR & GAMBLE/Colour changing absorbent article* [2010] E.P.O.R. 19, the patent was for an absorbent article for feminine hygiene distinguished inter alia by the feature that it was provided with a colour change material. The Board held that the article as claimed was a technical product. The material changed colour in response to an external stimulus on the article, namely a change of temperature, an exertion of pressure and/or an exposure to light. Such a change of colour, which could also be described as a modification of the light absorption by the article, was a technical effect that could be measured by technical means, e.g. a colorimeter. It was common practice that inventions such as dyes or hair colouring compositions, although having only an aesthetic goal, were nevertheless patentable inventions in the sense of EPC art.52. The Board concluded that the claimed absorbent article was not an aesthetic creation per se in the sense of EPC art.52(2)(b) and (3).

Similarly in T 1793/09 *UNI-CHARM/Absorbent article*, the Board considered an application for an absorbent article comprising a liquid-permeable top and back layers around an absorbent body, heat-bonded together to form compressed and uncompressed portions. The claim differed from prior art by the arrangement of the compressed portions, which although having an aesthetic effect also changed the article's flexibility and absorbability and provided a solution to a technical problem.

—Discoveries

1.17 Section 1(2)(a) continues a long-standing prohibition on the patenting of subject-matter of an abstract character. In *Househill Coal and Iron v Neilson* (1843) 1 W.P.C. 673; 9 Cl & Fin 788; 8 E.R. 788, it was stated that an abstract philosophical principle could not be patented unless it were applied to a special purpose to achieve a practical result and benefit not previously attained. Thus Volta's discovery of the effect on a frog's leg of the current from an electric battery was not a patentable invention, see also *Jupe v Pratt* (1837) 1 W.P.C. 145. In *Reynolds v Herbert Smith* (1903) 20 R.P.C. 123 at 126 it was stated that discovery added to human knowledge only by disclosing something that had previously been unseen, whereas invention involved the suggestion of an act resulting in a new product or result, or a new process, or a new combination for producing an old product or result, see also, e.g. *British Thomson-Houston v Charlesworth Peebles (No.2)* (1925) 42 R.P.C. 180 at 209. However, in *Otto v Linford* (1882) 46 L.T. (NS) 35 CA, it was held that a new principle could provide good subject-matter for a patent even when embodied in a machine which was not in other respects sufficiently novel.

Under the present Act, in *Genentech's Patent* [1989] R.P.C. 147 CA, the question arose whether the first to determine the structure of the naturally occurring protein t-PA could obtain a monopoly for its synthesis by recombinant DNA technology. Purchas L.J. stated that the relevant legal question was whether the invention claimed was "a method embracing a new discovery" or was merely a claim in the form: "I claim this discovery harnessed to make useful artefacts". Genentech argued that, because it had discovered the formula of t-PA, any person who used some new expression vector, or some undiscovered method which used its structural data, would be using its invention. The Court of Appeal rejected this argument on the basis that claiming all possible future uses for the information amounted to claiming the discovery as such, see also *Kirin-Amgen Inc v Hoechst Marion*

Roussel Ltd [2005] R.P.C. 9 at 269 where the House of Lords held that a patent should not give a monopoly of the use of information as such. However, it is to be noted that an essentially similar claim was subsequently allowed by the EPO in a parallel case, see T 923/92 *GENENTECH/Human t-PA* [1996] E.P.O.R. 275; abridged OJ EPO 1996, 564.

In *Kirin-Amgen Inc v Roche Diagnostics GmbH* [2002] R.P.C. 1, the court held that although the essential feature of the patent was a discovery (of a certain DNA sequence) it was a discovery that made a technical contribution. Claim 1 was to an application of the discovery which was capable of industrial application.

As regards newly discovered properties of known materials, the EPO *Guideline* C–IV, 2.3.1 explains that:

"If a new property of a known material or article is found out, that is mere discovery and unpatentable because discovery as such has no technical effect and is therefore not an invention within the meaning of Art. 52(1). If, however, that property is put to practical use, then this constitutes an invention which may be patentable. For example, the discovery that a particular known material is able to withstand mechanical shock would not be patentable, but a railway sleeper made from that material could well be patentable."

In G 2/88 *MOBIL OIL III/Friction reducing additive* the Enlarged Board held that the fact that the idea or concept underlying the claimed subject-matter resides in a discovery does not necessarily mean that the claimed subject-matter is a discovery "as such". In relation to a claim whose wording defines a new use of a known compound, the proper interpretation of the claim will normally be that attaining a new technical effect which underlies the new use is a technical feature of the claimed invention. In T 279/93 *AMERICAN CYANAMID/Melamine derivatives* [1999] E.P.O.R. 88 it was held that noticing that an old product had less impurities and, as a consequence thereof, a lighter colour was a mere discovery. To convert that discovery into a patentable invention, and to show a new technical effect as required by G 2/88 *MOBIL OIL III/Friction reducing additive*, a use claim would have to exploit the discovery for some new technical purpose. However, the patent disclosed no such new purpose, but merely gave a skilled person reasons for preferring one known product over other known products for purposes that had already been suggested, which did not amount to a new industrial application, compare T 319/88 *BP Chemicals/Acetic acid* where the newly discovered property gave rise to a new use not correlated with the known use and independent of it and T 1642/06 *SPRUCE BARBARA ET AL/Sigma receptor* [2008] E.P.O.R. 12 where an undisclosed technical effect identified a new clinical situation. In T 1200/03 *THE CUPRON CORPORATION/Article of clothing* a prior document disclosed fabrics coated with copper oxides and the mere discovery that such fabrics had antimicrobial properties did not render them or the process for their production novel.

The status of naturally occurring materials is considered in the EPO *Guideline* C–IV, 2.3.1, the relevant portion of which reads:

"To find a previously unrecognised substance occurring in nature is also mere discovery and therefore unpatentable. However, if a substance found in nature can be shown to produce a technical effect, it may be patentable. An example of such a case is that of a substance occurring in nature which is found to have an antibiotic effect. In addition, if a microorganism is discovered to exist in nature and to produce an antibiotic, the microorganism itself may also be patentable as one aspect of the invention. Similarly, a gene which is discovered to exist in nature may be patentable if a technical effect is revealed, e.g. its use in making a certain polypeptide or in gene therapy."

An EPO Opposition Division has held that the isolation and characterisation of a DNA fragment encoding a human protein is not unpatentable as representing only a discovery when the claimed substance had not had a previously recognised existence, see *HOWARD*

FLOREY/Relaxin OJ EPO 1995, 388; [1995] E.P.O.R. 541 and this decision was upheld on appeal, see T 272/95 *HOWARD FLOREY INSTITUTE/Joint opposition* OJ EPO 1999, 589; [2000] E.P.O.R. 235. In T 338/00 *SALK INSTITUTE/Multimeric receptors* the EPO Appeal Board defined a mere discovery as the result of purely intellectual activity with no practical or technical character, and held that such a finding was not appropriate where there was a technical result, e.g. modulation of the expression of a gene/product of interest in a particular expression or system, screening of products with specific pharmacological activity.

The patent in *Tate & Lyle v Roquette Frères* [2010] F.S.R. 1 concerned a sugar substitute called maltitol. The patent concerned the crystallisation of maltitol, and in particular two different shapes of maltitol crystal. What it claimed, was that a by-product of the maltitol production process, called maltotriitol, could be used to modify or control the shape that the crystals took. It was settled law that an invention was a practical product or process, not information about the natural world. The patent was simply for a property of maltotriitol which the defendants discovered. That also explained why the patent had been anticipated by so much prior art. The patent explained why maltitol crystals took the habit that they did, but it did not add anything else to the sum of human knowledge. The claim was not saved from unpatentability simply by the addition of the phrase "the use of". What mattered was the substance of the claim rather than its form. It would have been possible to claim particular processes or products that took advantage of the discovery, for instance by claiming certain levels of concentration of maltotriitol within the syrup, or crystals produced with the aid of the discovery. Indeed that is what the defendants did, but all their claimed products and processes had been declared invalid or have been abandoned. In Molière's play *Le Bourgeois Gentilhomme*, Monsieur Jourdain asked something to be written in neither verse nor prose. A philosophy master said to him, "Sir, there is no other way to express oneself than with prose or verse". Jourdain replies, "By my faith! For more than forty years I have been speaking prose without knowing anything about it, and I am much obliged to you for having taught me that." That was the situation here: the industry had been using maltotriitol to control or determine crystal habit without knowing it. Consequently, what was left of the patent as granted was no more than a discovery as such, see paras [74]–[46].

—Scientific thoeories

1.18   Refusals of applications on this ground alone have been uncommon, possibly because applications in which such an objection arises are also uncommon. *Simon's Application* BL O/139/86 and C/6/87 is an example of refusal on the ground that the invention was only a scientific theory or literary work. An inventor in *Blacklight Power Inc v Comptroller* [2009] R.P.C. 6; [2008] EWHC 2763 Pat Ct claimed to have found a new hydrogen species called "the hydrino" which he alleged existed in a lower energy state than the lowest possible such state recognised by standard physical laws. He claimed the novel hydrogen species and a power-generating plasma reactor, but his patent applications were rejected as contrary to the laws of physics. On appeal, it was held that the hearing officer should have considered whether there was any reasonable prospect that on a fuller investigation evidence would emerge to support the truth of the applicant's theories. The application was remitted to him for examination of the voluminous evidence to see whether there was indeed a debatable question of fact on which there was a reasonable prospect of *Blacklight* succeeding. The court observed that the need to do so might have been avoided if the Comptroller had served a Respondent's Notice which can have the effect of discouraging appeals that have no real merit.

The application in *Robinson (Geoffrey)* BL O/336/08 claimed a more accurate way of determining the velocity of a remote object, based on a new relativistic effect which could account for anomalies in the Doppler data from the Pioneer 10 and 11 spacecraft. It was not the primary function of the Intellectual Property Office to validate new scientific theories. The examiner would consider the validity of a theory only to the extent necessary for him or her to be satisfied that the application complies with the requirements of the

Patents Act and Rules. Applying the test stated in *Blacklight Power*, the hearing officer, where he considers that there is a substantial doubt as to the validity of the theory, should consider whether, on a full investigation with the benefit of expert evidence, there is a reasonable prospect that the theory might in fact turn out to be valid. The application contravened a well-established scientific theory and could not therefore be put into practice. It follows that the invention was neither capable of industrial application as required by s.1(1)(c) nor sufficiently disclosed as required by s.14(3). Even if the application had not disclosed a new way of measuring velocity, it might conceivably have found a new way to derive the conventional relativistic Doppler equations. However, that would not be patentable, since s.1(2)(a) of the Act prevented the grant of a patent for a discovery, scientific theory or mathematical method as such, see paras [18]–[26].

For a decision of the EPO on this topic see T 1358/05 *ZAGYANSKY/New atomic scale physics* where it was observed that a Board of Appeal cannot be a discussion forum for new physical theories unless these are unambiguously proven, are of a technical nature and capable of industrial application.

—Mathematical methods

As regards computer-implemented inventions, decisions in UK and Europe to some **1.19** extent parallel those in the US. In *Gottschalk v Benson* 409 U.S. 36 (1972), an algorithm for converting binary coded decimal numbers into pure binary numbers was rejected by the Supreme Court on the ground that the applicant should not be permitted to pre-empt the algorithm itself which would be tantamount to allowing a patent on an abstract idea. In *Parker v Flook* 437 U.S. 584 (1978) the application concerned calculation of an alarm limit, the only novelty being in the algorithm used. The Supreme Court held that the claimed subject-matter was not patentable not because it contained a mathematical algorithm as one feature, but because once that algorithm was assumed to be within the prior art, the application, considered as a whole, contained no patentable invention. The court observed that even though a phenomenon of nature or mathematical formula may be well known, an inventive application of the principle could be patented. Conversely, the discovery of such a phenomenon could not support a patent unless there was some other inventive concept in its application. In contrast, in *Diamond v Diehr* 450 U.S. 175, applicants filed a patent application claiming invention for a process for moulding raw, uncured synthetic rubber into cured precision products. While it was possible, by using well-known time, temperature, and cure relationships, to calculate by means of the Arrhenius equation when to open the moulding press and remove the cured product, the industry had not been able to measure precisely the temperature inside the mould, thus making it difficult to make the necessary computations to determine the proper cure time. The applicants characterised their contribution to the art to reside in the process of constantly measuring the temperature inside the mould and feeding the temperature measurements into a computer that repeatedly recalculated the cure time by use of the Arrhenius equation and then signalled a device to open the press at the proper time. Decisive for patentability was the link between the moulding process, the computer-based calculation and the result of avoiding over-cure or under-cure of the product.

Under the 1949 Act, a claim to a ship's propeller in which the only novelty was in the method of calculating the blade thickness at different radial positions was refused in *Lips' Application* [1959] R.P.C. 35.

In *Gale's Application* (see §1.10 above) the claimed invention, though falling within the computer program exclusion was not a mathematical method as such. The Court of Appeal observed:

"In the present case Mr Gale claims to have discovered an algorithm. Clearly that, as such, is not patentable. It is an intellectual discovery which, for good measure, falls squarely within one of the items, mathematical method, listed in s.1(2). But the nature of this discovery is such that it has a practical application, in that it enables instruction to be written for conventional computers in a way which will, so it is claimed, expedite one of the calculations frequently made with the aid of a computer. In my view the application of Mr Gale's mathematical formulae for the purpose of writing computer instruction is sufficient to dispose of the contention that he is claiming a mathematical method as such."

The application in *Schlumberger Holdings* BL O/016/09 was for the provision of quality control indicators of improved reliability by processing sonic well-logging data to generate a slowness against frequency dispersion curve at each of a number of depths, and from that a projection log of curve data against depth. Although the invention was claimed as a method of performing a quality control analysis, the specification did not contemplate anything more than visual inspection of the data. Although the application could be implemented by a computer program, the contribution could not be said to relate solely to a computer program which was merely one way of implementing the invention. Applying the principles established by *WesternGeco* BL O/135/07 and *Institut du Français Petrol & Elf* BL O/201/03 which were disallowed as mathematical methods (although in the *WesternGeco* case a dependent claim specifying, the additional step of determining one or more parameters relating to physical properties of the earth's interior from the processed geophysical data and producing seismic images was potentially patentable), although the contribution increased the range of sonic emitters which could reliably be used, it did not produce any change in a physical entity, did not have any functional link to a physical system and did not have any internal technical feature and was therefore held to be a mathematical method. Unlike the claims in *VICOM*, *Elf* and *WesternGeco*, the claims did not set forth a precise series of mathematical steps, but that did not prevent the method from being mathematical, see paras [28]–[29]. The invention was concerned with the information content of an image rather than the physical properties of the image as in *VICOM*. See also *Marathon Oil Co* O/174/10 where an improvement in an existing model was not saved by the fact that real seismic data was used.

In T 208/84 *VICOM/Computer-related invention* the claim as initially presented more closely resembled the fact pattern in *Gottschalk v Benson* but after amendment more closely resembled that in *Diamond v Diehr* (both above). The invention related to an improved method for digitally filtering images by convolution which had the advantage that the volume of calculations required to be carried out was significantly reduced compared to the prior art. The key difference was that a conventional operator matrix was replaced by a "small generating kernel", e.g. of dimensions 3 elements by 3 elements which was scanned over the data matrix a plurality of times. The original claim was to "A method of digitally filtering data". This was held to be an abstract notion not distinguished from a mathematical method so long as it was not specified what physical entity was represented by the data and formed the subject of a technical process. The Board said:

"There can be little doubt that any processing operation on a mathematical signal can be described in mathematical terms. The characteristics of a filter, for example, can be expressed in terms of a mathematical formula. A basic difference between a mathematical method and a technical problem can be seen, however, in the fact that a mathematical method or mathematical algorithm is carried out on numbers (whatever those numbers may represent) and provides a result also in numerical form, the mathematical method or algorithm being only an abstract concept prescribing how to operate on the numbers. No direct technical result is produced by the method as such. In contrast thereto, if a mathematical method is used in a technical process, that process can be carried out on a physical entity (which may be a material object but equally an image stored as an electric signal) by some technical means implementing the method and provides as its result a certain change in that entity. A technical means might include a computer comprising suitable hardware or an appropriately programmed general purpose computer."

The claim that was held to be allowable in *VICOM* read: "A method of digitally processing images in the form of a two-dimensional data array". An important factor in the allowance of the above claim was that it was known in the prior art to process images by analog circuitry to improve their sharpness.

Similarly in T 471/05 *PHILIPS/Lens design* claims to a method for designing an optical system in which the rays satisfied a mathematical condition, and a method for making an optical system according to the design were refused as a mere conceptual teaching, but an auxiliary request which specified the use of an optical design program was held to define a physical, technical activity and to be allowable. Specifying codewords representing audio or image information in a method that reduces channel noise also avoided objection, see T 212/94 *AT&T/Channel noise*. In T 1227/05 *INFINEON TECHNOLOGIES/ Schaltkreisssimulation I* the claimed invention concerned a computer-implemented method for simulating the performance of a circuit subject to 1/f noise by feeding random numbers into a circuit model, see also T 421/06 *INFINEON/Schaltkreissimulation II*. The Board held that there was technical character because a computer was involved, and that computer simulation had technical character because it was a preparation for actual production. In T 27/97 *FRANCE TELECOM/Cryptographie à clés publiques* the claimed subject-matter concerned a method of encrypting or decrypting a message represented as a digital word using an RSA-type public-key algorithm. The Board held that the invention was clearly a method falling into the computer and telecommunications field and therefore not excluded under EPC art.52(2) and (3) even if based on an abstract algorithm or mathematical method. Similarly, in *IGT's Application* BL O/149/08 the invention related to gaming apparatus in which 2D image data was converted into 3D image data, but the applicant argued that the invention related to technical improvement of the 3D image by correction of image distortion, brightness distortion and colour aberration when displayed on a non-planar screen and a claim specifying these features was held not to be excluded under s.1(2).

Where a mathematical method is unpatentable per se, the EPO has allowed a claim directed to a method of controlling a physical process by such a method (T 953/94 *BRADFORD JOHN GEORGES/Functional analysis*).

—Scheme, rule or method for playing a game

The Comptroller had until recently considered the patentability of games in light of *Official Ruling 1926(A)* (1926) 43 R.P.C. (Appendix) i. Under this ruling, an apparatus for playing a game comprising one or more playing pieces and a board marked in a particular manner substantially as shown in drawings accompanying the specification, with the playing piece(s) being moved in accordance with specified rules, was considered to meet the requirements of an invention, subject to any other objections such as lack of novelty. The patentability of board games was discussed and analysed by *R.G.V. Doble* [1997] E.I.P.R. 587. Patents also continued to be granted for packs of cards when designed for the purpose of playing a game, in accordance with *Cobianchi's Application* (1953) 70 R.P.C. 199. However, in *Shopalotto.com Application* [2006] R.P.C. 7, Pumfrey J. said that the Official Ruling no longer provided a valid guide, and that as with other inventions a technical contribution was necessary, see Practice Notice "Patents Act 1977: Patentability of Games" [2006] R.P.C. 8.

1.20

T 928/03 *KONAMI/Video game* [2006] E.P.O.R. 53 related to a video game in which a guide mark (ball) was of enlarged size to avoid the risk of its being concealed behind a neighbouring playing character which was not excluded from patentability, although the shape of the guide mark was a merely aesthetic creation, see also T 1793/07 *KONAMI/ Video game device*.

IGT's Applications [2007] EWHC 1341 Ch concerned four applications relating to gaming apparatus of the sort where success in a main game lead to the chance to play a bonus game. In each case, the court held that the claims once construed related to known apparatus upon which a game was played. The contribution in each case therefore lay in the rules or methods used to play the game, and fell solely within the excluded category of "schemes, rules or methods of... playing a game...", see also T 1023/06 *IGT/Computer implemented game process* [2007] E.P.O.R. 36; T 1274/06 *IGT/Gaming device using programmable display switch*; T 1543/06 *GAMEACCOUNT/Game machine*; T 366/07 *IGT/Electronic multi-play poker*; T 859/07 *DEQ SYSTEMS CIRP/Multi-player bet auxiliary game*; and T 1793/07 *KONAMI/Video game device*. In contrast to these decisions, T 717/05 *LABTRONIX CONCEPT INC./Auxiliary game* related to gaming apparatus configured to operate principal and auxiliary games. The Appeal Board defined a problem in terms of maintaining the player's interest and accepted that displaying the outcomes of previous games informed a player about the internal state of the gaming apparatus and of the way it would behave under the occurrence of a further outcome and in this way was similar to any display of the internal state of an apparatus in a more classical field, such as displaying the temperature of an internal combustion machine or the pressure of an autoclave.

The invention in T 12/08 *NINTENDO/Game machine and storage medium* [2009] E.P.O.R. 31 concerned a games machine of the type wherein a player object was moved on a map and encountered game characters. Encounters were governed by chance, in that characters appeared according to an "appearance probability". To further increase this element of unpredictability of the game, and thereby hold a player's interest longer, the invention proposed to vary that appearance probability through time, and this was the distinguishing feature over Pokémon™ which was the closest prior art. The precise method by which the invention varied the appearance probability was indisputably novel. The games software produced the further technical effect of generating a random event, which was a technical feature not excluded from patentability; similarly interaction with a clock bestowed technical character and the problem of reducing predictability in a random event generator, itself of a technical character, "soundly resides in the technical domain.". Making chance encounters depend on time was not a "game rule" excluded from patentability since the invention concerned the manner in which the rule was realised and was not intended to be known or agreed to by a player. Accordingly the application met the requirements of the EPC. Similarly in T 1225/10 *NINTENDO/Game program* the Appeal Board considered a claim for a computer game in which a player character was to be moved on a display through a field of background objects, and in which collisions with certain ones elicited a game response that depended on collision direction. Collisions were detected from the overlap of character and objects, with the side of the object hit by the player character being determined from particular points on the player character that overlap with the object. It was the Board's view that the added feature of collision direction determination required an inventive insight on the part of the skilled person. Though collision detection per se was known, no prior art suggested detecting the collision direction using points on the player character. Accordingly, the claim involved an inventive step.

In T 2127/09 *BANDAI/Game* apparatus the application related to a computer game like "Tetris" and the EPO search division had carried out no search. On appeal the applicants added the feature of controlling a so-called "sequence bar" with a counter when a predetermined count was reached. The Board was unable to determine whether these amended features provide any further technical effects associated with the implementation of the modified "Tetris" game rules over and above those inherent in these rules themselves, and the application was remitted with an order to perform a search. Although this was not available as of right, in the exceptional circumstances of this application it was appropriate to make such an order since the Examining Division had taken the position that all the claimed features were notorious and did not contribute to inventive step and had at no time indicated an intention to perform a further search.

In T 1769/10 *IGT/Internet remote game server*, the Appeal Board considered a gaming system comprising a casino server communicating with a plurality of gaming devices allowing players to play wagering games. The objective technical problem to be solved was that of modifying the system of a prior reference so as to improve the player's access to games while maintaining confidentiality of the player's data in a database. The technical solution was to let the server for maintaining the player database communicate with a plurality of game outcome servers, with respective, different games. The server for maintaining the player database was physically separate and located remote from the game outcome servers. The game outcome servers were not allowed direct access to the player database, such that confidentiality of the player database is maintained. Player access is improved by letting the player navigate to each game outcome server through a game access interface offering game links to game outcome server-supported games at the game outcome servers through a game access interface supported by the player management server and displayable by the identified client device and without the player having to register or log-on into the game outcome servers. It was held that the claimed subject-matter was free from objection and grant of a patent was ordered. It was observed that there was no conflict in the Board's existing case law, and arguments that the case law was insufficiently developed were rejected, citing G 3/08 *PRESIDENT'S REFERENCE*, OJ EPO 2011, 10, reasons 10.13.2.

In T 1547/09 *M-COMM/System and method for playing a game* the claimed subject-matter concerned an SMS-based game that was based on skill rather than chance. The object was to guess a word corresponding to a game code which was a two- or more digit number in which each number identified a key of the mobile terminal, each key identifying any of three possible letters. A player's success depended on his skill in recognising possible letter combinations and his agility in forming a reply message. The claimed subject-matter was held to have technical character since the claims were directed to physical features of an entity, in this case a system with an interacting game unit and mobile terminals. However, it was not permissible to rely on excluded matter alone however original it might be and the question was how it was technically implemented and whether there were further technical effects over and above those inherent in the excluded subject-matter itself. It was a typical games insight that giving a player a better sense of achievement and more control could make the game more appealing, but such insight was not technical in nature and could not be relied on when formulating the objective technical problem. In accordance with T 336/07 *IGT/Electronic multi-play poker* [2008] E.P.O.R. 18 novelty could not reside in the game rules alone since these were merely an abstract mental construct. Implementation of the present rules was a matter of routine skill for a software engineer specialising in games systems, and there was no further effect inherent in the game concept itself, the new game merely adding to the variety of existing games. Accordingly the application was refused.

The UK MOPP as revised in July 2010 states at para.1.22.1:

"Thus a game implemented on a conventional computer system or network would be excluded as both a scheme, rule, or method for playing a game and a computer program as such."

It is therefore apparent that differences between the approach adopted in the United Kingdom and that adopted by the EPO are not confined to judicial reasoning but can in some cases lead to different outcomes since there are some computer games inventions for which the EPO may be willing to grant a patent where the UK-IPO will not.

—Contrary to public policy or morality

Following their amendment to comply with both art.27.2 of the TRIPS Agreement (see §1.03 above) and art.6 of the Biotechnology Directive (reprinted in §C06 and see also s.76A), subss.(3) and (4) now prohibit the grant of patents only where the exploitation (and not the mere publication) of the invention would be contrary to "public policy", a phrase which has to equate with the words "ordre public" used in the Directive and in art.53(a) of the EPC, or is contrary to "morality". While, formally, this change does not affect patents and applications filed before July 28, 2000, it can be argued that the provisions of the TRIPS Agreement have over-riding effect as regards such prior-dated applications and patents.

Article 27.2 of the TRIPS Agreement also permits exclusion from patentability of inventions for "the protection of human, animal or plant life or health or to avoid serious prejudice to the environment", but such exclusions do not appear in either the Act or in the

1.21

EPC, except that (under s.4(2)) inventions of a: "method of treatment of the human or animal body by surgery or therapy or of diagnosis practised on the human or animal body shall not be taken to be capable of industrial application" and, therefore, are unpatentable on this ground, as discussed in the commentary on s.4.

In addition, the Directive states (art.6(2)) that certain subject-matter is to be considered unpatentable as being deemed to be contrary to ordre public or morality, viz.:

(a) processes for cloning human beings;

(b) processes for modifying the germ line genetic identity of human beings;

(c) uses of human embryos for industrial or commercial purposes; and

(d) processes for modifying the genetic identity of animals which are likely to cause them suffering without any substantial medical benefit to man or animal, and also animals resulting from such processes.

These provisions are given effect by sub-paras (3)(b)–(e) of Sch.A2 (reprinted in §76A.01A), but only as regards patents and applications dated on or after July 28, 2000 (see note to §1.01).

Article 53(a) of the EPC is explained at EPO Guidelines C–IV, 4.1–4.3. The purpose of these exclusions is to render unpatentable inventions likely to induce riot or public disorder or to lead to other generally offensive behaviour. The meaning of "generally expected" is undefined, and it is not clear whether it means by a majority of the public or merely "widely". EPO *Guideline* C–IV, 4.1 states that a fair test is to consider whether it is probable that the general public would regard the invention as so abhorrent that the grant of patent rights would be inconceivable. Under the Act, the test under subs.(3) is, probably, whether exploitation of the invention would offend moral principles of right-thinking members of the public, such that it would be wrong for the law to protect it, following a similar principle on the registrability of designs (*Masterman's Design* [1991] R.P.C. 89) and the broadly similar sentiments ("not . . . in conformity with the conventionally-accepted standards of conduct pertaining to European culture") expressed in T 356/93. See also *Ghazilian's Trade Mark Application* [2002] R.P.C. 33 ("TINY PENIS"); *French Connection Ltd v Dennis Woodman* O/137/06; "FCUK" and *CDW Graphic Design Ltd v Manchester United Merchandising Ltd* (Trade Marks Registry, November 20, 2002, http://www.standupifyouhatemanu.com) in which it was held that normal and fair use would be liable to be "a badge of antagonism", even if that was not the applicant's intention. For an attempt to define Community standards of offensiveness, see the trade mark decision of the Grand Board of Appeal of OHIM, Case R 495/2005–G *Application of Kenneth (trading as SCREW YOU)* [2007] E.T.M.R. 7.

However, by subs.(4), an invention is not to be regarded as contrary to public policy (ordre public) or morality merely because it is prohibited by law in the United Kingdom. This provision is also included in art.53(a) of the EPC in accord with the final sentence of art.27.2 of the TRIPS Agreement and with the final clause of art.6(1) of the Directive. It thus appears that an invention should not be held unpatentable if only unobjectionable uses are mentioned in the specification. The MOPP §1.36 is unclear about the extent to which various outlawed weaponry which might have the potential to be exploited for a legitimate purpose would fall foul of subs.(3).

The Landmines Act 1998 (c.33) has the object (expressed in its long title) to "promote the control of anti-personnel landmines, and for connected purposes". Section 2(2) of that Act states that (subject to certain limited exceptions, not considered of relevance to the acquisition and maintenance of patents) "no person shall assist, encourage or induce any other person to engage in any conduct specified in subsection (1)" (which includes acts to develop or produce an anti-personnel mine (or a component of one); and, by s.3(2) this prohibition applies to assistance, encouragement and inducements in the United Kingdom or elsewhere, and applies irrespective of whether the conduct assisted, encouraged or induced takes place, or (if it takes place) will take place, in the United Kingdom or elsewhere. Section 4 provides some limited exceptions and in particular s.4(7) refers to the development of techniques of detection, clearance or destruction of mines.

Under these embracing provisions, the Comptroller views inventions relating to landmines as falling within s.1(3)(a) of the 1977 Act. Moreover, the Comptroller apparently takes the view that the terms of the Landmines Act require him not to publish (under the powers provided by ss.16(2) and 22(2)) any pending application relating to landmines, nor accept any international application relating thereto. He has also stated that any renewal fee tendered on any such patent will not knowingly be accepted by the UK-IPO and has suggested that patent attorneys will need to consider their personal position if asked to handle patent applications relating to landmines or parts thereof, see [1998] *CIPA* 600. These statements could be argued as, in part, exceeding the powers of the Comptroller, but in contesting the Comptroller's view, it could be considered that such contest may itself be a prohibited activity within the broad terms of s.2(2) of the Landmines Act.

In *HARVARD/Onco-mouse* OJ EPO 1992, 588; [1991] E.P.O.R. 525, the EPO Examining Division weighed claims for a mouse having a gene predisposing to tumour development against competing contentions as to the public interest; and then held that, in the circumstances of that case, the invention would lead to an overall reduction in the amount of animal suffering: accordingly, it was held that claims to oncogenic animals are not contrary to art.53(a) of the EPC, but warned that other cases under EPC art.53(a) could be viewed differently. However, the patent then granted was opposed by a large number of bodies concerned with animal welfare, and the patent was restricted to mice since this was the only species which had been commercialised and the only species for which the resulting medical benefits and animal suffering could be balanced one against another, see T 315/03 *HARVARD/Transgenic animals* [2005] E.P.O.R. 31. The same principle of weighing the benefit to mankind against the associated degree of animal suffering has since been built into the Biotechnology Directive, see art.6(2)(d).

T 356/93 *PLANT GENETIC SYSTEMS/Glutamine synthetase inhibitors* regarded inventions as unpatentable, as contrary to "ordre public", if their exploitation is likely to breach public peace or social order or seriously to prejudice the environment; and/or, as contrary to morality, if their exploitation would not be in conformity with the conventionally-accepted standards of conduct pertaining to European culture, although it is irrelevant whether the claimed invention concerns living matter. On this basis, claims to a means for rendering plants herbicide-resistant by genetic modification of their cells were held allowable under EPC art.53(a), although not under EPC art.53(b). The Board of Appeal in EPO decision T 315/03 confirmed the definition of "ordre public" and morality as set out in EPO decision T 356/93, adding that when assessing morality no one definition based on economic or religious principles represents an accepted standard of European culture. The use of opinion polls to assess majority opinion on morality was held to be of limited value. "Ordre public" was held to include the protection of public security and the physical integrity of individuals as part of society, which includes protecting the environment. The same principle of weighing the benefit to mankind against the associated degree of animal suffering has since been built into the Biotechnology Directive, see art.6(2)(d). However, the *PLANT GENETIC SYSTEMS* application, and the subsequent confirmatory decision by the same Board of Appeal in T 1054/96 *NOVARTIS/Transgenic plant* OJ EPO 1998, 511; [1999] E.P.O.R. 123, were later considered by the Enlarged Board of Appeal (G 1/98 OJ EPO 2000, 111; [2000] E.P.O.R. 303), which determined that a claim wherein specific plant varieties are not individually claimed is not excluded from patentability under EPC art.53(b) even though it may embrace plant varieties. On the other hand, the exception to patentability in art.53(b) applies to plant varieties irrespective of how they are produced, such that plant varieties containing genes introduced into an ancestral plant by recombinant gene technology are excluded from patentability.

In T 1213/05 *UNIVERSITY OF UTAH/Breast and ovarian cancer* regarding the human BRCA1 gene and its use to diagnose a predisposition to breast and ovarian cancer, the Board of Appeal held that the scope of the Biotechnology Directive does not include activities before or after the grant of a patent. In this case it was argued that the lack of proof that cell donors had given informed consent to the use of the cells to produce the claimed invention was against "ordre public" or morality. The Board disagreed. The EPC does not contain provisions that require submission of evidence regarding informed consent. It was also argued that socio-economic consequences of patenting the claimed invention should be considered under EPC art.53(a); however, the Board stated that EPC art.53(a) refers to "exploitation of the invention" rather than the "exploitation of the patent" and confirmed that the EPO had "not been vested with the task of taking account of economic effects of granting patents in specific areas and restricting the field of patentable subject-matter accordingly".

An EPO Opposition Division has also held that the isolation of mRNA encoding a human protein is not immoral, nor is the patenting of a DNA fragment encoding human proteins intrinsically unethical, see *HOWARD FLOREY/Relaxin* OJ EPO 1995, 388; [1995] E.P.O.R. 541. Here it was said that only in those cases where there appears to be an "overwhelming consensus" that the exploitation or publication of an invention would be immoral should its patentability be excluded under EPC art.53(a). The appeal on this case was eventually resolved, after some preliminary procedural questions were referred in G 3/99 to the Enlarged Board of Appeal, by the Technical Board in EPO decision T 272/95 of October 23, 2002 upholding the Opposition Division's decision essentially on the basis that then EPC rr.23(d) and 23(e) newly introduced by the Directive (now EPC rr.28 and 29) answered the appellants' arguments.

In T 866/01 *MICHIGAN STATE UNIVERSITY/Euthanasia Compositions*, an appeal that a patent for a chemical for use in euthanasia of lower mammals should be revoked under the "ordre public" provision was rejected. The Board held that patent protection should only be denied under EPC art.53(a) if the intended exploitation of the invention, i.e. the avowed use indicated in the patent (*"bestimmungsgemäßer Gebrauch"*), would infringe "ordre public" or morality; it is not enough to show that the invention can also be exploited in a proscribed way. The fact that the invention may be abused is not sufficient to deny patent protection if it can also be exploited in a way that would not be contrary to "ordre public" or morality.

The question of the patentability of human embryonic stem cells has now been considered by the Enlarged Board under case number G 2/06 *WARF/Stem cells* (Unreported); however, see the article by S. Mitchell and G. Schlich analysing the decision at [2008] *CIPA* 708. It was held that r.28(c) of the EPC, formerly EPC r.23(d) applied to all pending applications including those filed before the entry into force of the rule, that the rule forbade the patenting of claims directed to products that could as of the filing date be prepared exclusively by a method that involved the destruction of human embryos even if that method was not part of the claim, and that it was not relevant that after the filing date the same products could be obtained without having to destroy human embryos. No view was expressed as to the patentability in general of human stem cells or human stem cell cultures. In view of the result, it was not necessary to consider issues of ordre public or morality. See the commentary on s.76A for further discussion of the referral.

On March 10, 2011 in a referral from the German Federal Supreme Court to the CJEU in C-34/10 *Brüstle v Greenpeace*, Advocate-General Bot defined the task before the Court as defining what stage of the development of the human body should constitute an "embryo". There was a distinction between totipotent cells, which have the capacity to evolve into a complete human being, and pluripotent cells, which can develop into organs of the human body but cannot in themselves evolve separately into a complete human being. The former fell within the definition of "human embryo" and were thus excluded from patentability whereas the latter did not and could be the subject-matter of a patent. However, where the removal of the pluripotent cells would be to the detriment of the embryo, patenting would also be prohibited, e.g. at the blastocyst stage of development reached at about five days after fertilisation and which was from where Professor Brüstle took the pluripotent cells required for his invention. At the time of writing a decision of the court is awaited.

—Plant and animal varieties and biotechnological inventions

1.22   Schedule A2, para.3(f), in conformity with art.4(1) of the Biotechnology Directive, replaced former subs.(3)(b) as regards applications (and patents granted on such applications) dated on or after July 28, 2000. The exclusions relating to plant and animal varieties are therefore no longer to be found in s.1 and are discussed under s.76A in the context of the patentability of biotechnological inventions generally, where Sch.A2 is also reprinted and reference should be made to the commentary on that Schedule for any subject-matter likely to fall within the scope of its provisions.

In particular, Sch.A2 provides that an invention shall not be considered unpatentable solely on the ground that it concerns a product consisting of or containing biological material or a process by which biological material is processed, produced or used, and further provides that biological material may be patented if it previously occurred in nature and has been isolated from its natural environment or has been produced by a technical process. Supplementing the provisions of s.1(2) it provides another list of matters which are not considered patentable inventions, including the human body at various stages of its formation and development, the simple discovery of the sequence or partial sequence of a gene, processes for cloning human beings, processes for modifying the germ line genetic identity of human beings, uses of human embryos for industrial and commercial purposes, processes for modifying the genetic identity of animals which are likely to cause suffering without any substantial medical benefit, and plants and animal varieties. The patentability of microbiological and other technical processes and of the product of such processes is affirmed as also is the patentability of inventions concerning plants and animals whose technical feasibility is not confined to a particular plant or animal variety and elements isolated from the human body or otherwise produced by a technical process.

See the commentary on s.76A for a fuller discussion of patentability issues relating to plants and animals and biotechnological invention more generally.

SECTION 2

Novelty

2.—(1) An invention shall be taken to be new if it does not form part of the **2.01** state of the art.

(2) The state of the art in the case of an invention shall be taken to comprise all matter (whether a product, a process, information about either, or anything else) which has at any time before the priority date of that invention been made available to the public (whether in the United Kingdom or elsewhere) by written or oral description, by use or in any other way.

(3) The state of the art in the case of an invention to which an application for a patent or a patent relates shall be taken also to comprise matter contained in an application for another patent which was published on or after the priority date of that invention, if the following conditions are satisfied, that is to say—

(a) that matter was contained in the application for that other patent both as filed and as published; and

(b) the priority date of that matter is earlier than that of the invention.

(4) For the purposes of this section the disclosure of matter constituting an invention shall be disregarded in the case of a patent or an application for a patent if occurring later than the beginning of the period of six months immediately preceding the date of filing the application for the patent and either—

(a) the disclosure was due to, or made in consequence of, the matter having been obtained unlawfully or in breach of confidence by any person—

(i) from the inventor or from any other person to whom the matter was made available in confidence by the inventor or who obtained it from the inventor because he or the inventor believed that he was entitled to obtain it; or

(ii) from any other person to whom the matter was made available in confidence by any person mentioned in sub-paragraph (i) above or in this sub-paragraph or who obtained it from any person so mentioned because he or the person from whom he obtained it believed that he was entitled to obtain it;

(b) the disclosure was made in breach of confidence by any person who obtained the matter in confidence from the inventor or from any other person to whom it was made available, or who obtained it, from the inventor; or

(c) the disclosure was due to, or made in consequence of the inventor displaying the invention at an international exhibition and the applicant states, on filing the application, that the invention has been so displayed and also, within the prescribed period, files written evidence in support of the statement complying with any prescribed conditions.

(5) In this section references to the inventor include references to any proprietor of the invention for the time being.

(6) [*In the case of an invention consisting of a substance or composition for use in a method of treatment of the human or animal body by surgery or therapy or of diagnosis practised on the human or animal body, the fact that the substance or composition forms part of the state of the art shall not prevent the invention from being taken to be new if the use of the substance or composition in any such method does not form part of the state of the art.*]

Note. Subsection (6) was repealed by the Patents Act 2004 (c.16) Sch.3 para.1 (December 13, 2007 as SI 2007/3396). Now see s.4A.

RELEVANT RULE—RULE 5

Rule 5—International exhibitions

5.—(1) The statement mentioned in section 2(4)(c) that an invention has been displayed at an international exhibition must be in writing.

2.02

(2) The prescribed period for the purposes of section 2(4)(c) is four months beginning [with] immediately after the date of filing.

(3) But paragraphs (1) and (2) do not apply where rule 67(2) applies.

(4) The written evidence required by section 2(4)(c) must be in the form of—

(a) a certificate issued by the authority responsible for the international exhibition; and

(b) a statement, duly authenticated by that authority, identifying the invention as being the invention displayed at the exhibition.

(5) The certificate must include the opening date of the exhibition (or if later, the date on which the invention was first displayed).

(6) The comptroller may publish a statement in the journal that a particular exhibition falls within the definition of "international exhibition" in section 130(1) (interpretation).

Note. Amended by the Patents (Amendment) Rules 2011 (SI 2011/2052).

COMMENTARY ON SECTION 2

Scope of the section

Section 2 defines the concept of "novelty" introduced by s.1(1)(a), an absence of which is frequently referred to as "anticipation". Like s.1 it is declared by s.130(7) to have been framed to have, as nearly as practicable, the same effects as the corresponding provisions of the EPC, CPC and PCT.

2.03

Section 2(1) follows EPC art.54(1) verbatim. Subsection (2) follows EPC art.54(2) except that the word "everything" is replaced by "all matter (whether a product, a process, information about either, or anything else)", "date of filing" is replaced by "priority date" (see EPC art.89) and the words "made available to the public" are qualified by "whether in the United Kingdom or elsewhere". These verbal differences have not given rise to any difference in practice. Subsection (3) corresponds to EPC art.54(3) when read in association with EPC art.88(4). Subsections (4) and (5) correspond to EPC art.55(1)(a), the extended language being merely declaratory. These provisions were largely derived from arts 4 and 6 of the Strasbourg Convention (1963) Cmnd.8002. Provisions concerning methods of treatment and diagnosis formerly covered by the repealed s.2(6) are now covered by s.4A.

It should be noted that "published" in s.101(1) of the 1949 Act also defined "publication" as "making available to the public" and went on to explain that a document should be deemed to be published if it could be inspected as of right by members of the public whether on payment of a fee or otherwise. Decisions under the former law about what amounts to publication therefore continue to be relevant. The concept of something having been "made available to the public" is derived from *Humpherson v Syer* (1887) 4 R.P.C. 407, as elaborated by *Bristol-Myers' Application* [1969] R.P.C. 146, and reviewed and applied in *Catnic v Evans* [1983] F.S.R. 401: namely, that the state of the art includes anything which is in possession of any member of the public which he is free in law and equity to use as he pleases and so may disclose to others without any inhibiting fetter of confidence, whether express or implied. This concept is followed in EPO Guideline C–IV, 6.1. In *Genentech's Patent* [1989] R.P.C. 147 CA, it was stated that matter is not available to the public if it is merely known to one or two individual research workers pursuing their own experiments in private, the "public" being the community of research workers skilled in the art in general.

Novelty is defined by reference to the "state of the art" subs.(1) judged as of the day before the "priority date" if priority is available, for which see the commentary on s.5, or if there is no priority as of the day before the filing of the patent application. This "state of the art" is considered on a world-wide basis.

A valid claim must possess, inter alia, both novelty under s.2 and inventive step under s.3 as at the priority or filing date for the claimed subject-matter. The requirements for novelty and inventive step are distinct, and although the wording of a document covers subject-matter which it implicitly discloses, it does not cover subject-matter which it makes obvious, as to which see s.3. The boundary between implicitly disclosed subject-matter and subject-matter made obvious is fundamental, although sometimes difficult to define in particular cases.

Evaluation of novelty requires as a first step establishment of the state of the art, §§2.04–2.17. It then requires as a second step comparison of what is described and/or claimed in a patent specification with that which existed previously §§2.18–2.27. Under the Act, the same comparison has to be made at a variety of times and in a variety of contexts:

- *Priority*, s.5, the comparison being between the subject-matter expressly or implicitly disclosed in an earlier relevant application and that disclosed in the originally filed or amended version of the patent specification.

- *Entitlement to, and date of, priority* where there is more than one earlier relevant application, s.5(2), the comparison being between the subject-matter expressly or implicitly disclosed in the first relevant application and that expressly or implicitly disclosed in the subsequent application or applications.

- *Amendment* of a patent specification or filing of a divisional application under ss.15A(6), 18(3), 19(1), 27(1), 76, the comparison being between the subject-matter expressly or implicitly disclosed in the originally filed specification and that disclosed and/or claimed in the amended specification or the specification of the divisional application.

- *Novelty having regard to matter which had been disclosed to the public before the priority or application date of the patent or application*, the comparison being between the subject-matter claimed and the earlier disclosed matter.

- *Novelty having regard to the disclosure of an earlier unpublished patent application*, the comparison being between the subject-matter expressly or implicitly disclosed in the other patent application and that claimed in the later application.

It is implicit in the decision of the EPO Enlarged Appeal Board in G 3/93 *PRESIDENT'S REFERENCE/Priority Interval* OJ EPO 1995, 18; [1994] E.P.O.R. 97 that in each of the above cases the comparison should be objective and be based on what subject-matter a skilled person could derive directly and unambiguously, using the common general knowledge, from the earlier document, and that the suggestion that in some circumstances a lesser degree of correspondence would suffice should be rejected. That decision is qualified by a further Enlarged Appeal Board decision in G 1/03 *PPG/Disclaimer* that an unsupported disclaimer necessary to restore novelty or disclaim subject matter excluded for non-technical reasons is permitted, provided that it does no more than necessary to restore novelty and is not relevant to inventive step or sufficiency of disclosure.

The preliminary step of construing the extent of protection provided by claimed subject-matter (for which see the commentary on s.125) is crucial to the determination of novelty, as the same claim construction must be applied to anticipation as to infringement, see *Novamedix v NDM* BL C/78/97, noted I.P.D. 20108 CA and *Horne Engineering v Reliance Water Controls* [2000] F.S.R. 90. An example of the importance of claim construction to the outcome of a decision as to novelty is provided by *Glaverbel v British Coal* [1994] R.P.C. 443; and [1995] R.P.C. 255 CA where the Court of Appeal adopted a wider construction of the claims than had been adopted by the Patents Court and then found the claims to lack novelty. Construction of a prior art document is considered at §§2.17–2.18.

Novelty based "squeeze" arguments, i.e. that if a claim is narrow it is not infringed whereas if it is broader then it is invalid, (see the seminal speech of Lord Moulton in *Gillette v Anglo-American* (1913) 30 R.P.C. 465 at 480) may influence claim construction. For example, in *Lighting Electronics v Thorn Lighting* BL C/94/98, noted I.P.D. 22082, had the claim been found to have been infringed on the application of a wider construction than was adopted, then the court stated that it would have had difficulty in not finding it anticipated by that prior used device. Likewise, in T 370/90 *RICHARDSON/Nickel plating* [1999] E.P.O.R. 293, the claim was given a "sensible", rather than literal, construction and, on this basis, it was then upheld over the prior art.

Under art.3(2) of the European Biotechnology Directive (reprinted in §C03), which has been incorporated into the Act by Sch.A2 para.2 (reprinted in §76A.01A):

"Biological material which is isolated from its natural environment or produced by means of a technical process may be the subject of an invention even if it previously occurred in nature".

Article 5(2) thereof (reprinted in §C05 and incorporated into the Act as Sch.A2 para.5, reprinted in §76A.01A) states that:

"An element isolated from the human body or otherwise produced by means of a technical process, including the sequence or partial sequence of a gene, may constitute a patentable invention, even if the structure of that element is identical to that of a natural element".

However, these provisions can be seen as only confirming the previously held view that a natural product isolated from its natural environment, or one synthesised for the first time, should be regarded as a different product from that already existing in a natural environment. For example the EPO held that a DNA fragment encoding a human protein is not anticipated by its prior presence in the human body, it being said to be established practice to recognise novelty for a natural substance which has been isolated for the first time, see T 272/95 *HOWARD FLOREY/Relaxin* OJ EPO 1995, 388; [1995] E.P.O.R. 541. A similar conclusion as regards isolated DNA was reached by the US Court of Appeal for the Federal Circuit in *Association for Molecular Pathology v Myriad Genetics* (July 29, 2011), but further stages of appeal are possible.

The *Myriad* case is discussed in an article by Anthony Tridico and Nicole Parsons "The *Myriad* scare: isolated DNA molecules remain patent-eligible (for now!)", [2011] *CIPA*, p.598.

The state of the art (subss.(1)–(2))

—Documents in public places and/or that can be inspected as of right

Documents that were freely available for public inspection prior to the relevant date by distribution in a printed publication and/or presence in a library are the most convenient references both during examination of a patent application and during European opposition proceedings or UK revocation proceedings. Such publications include patent specifications, journal articles and much trade literature including instruction and repair manuals and brochures. Their dates of publication are usually simple to prove and issues of confidentiality do not arise. During prosecution of a patent application, cited matter within other categories is only rarely encountered. Documents made available to the public through the internet also fall into this category, but because the internet is being updated continuously more detailed investigation may be needed prove that publication took place on a particular date and to identify and prove the content that was published on that date.

2.04

A single document which has been made available to the public suffices for anticipation, see *Woven Plastic v British Ropes* [1970] F.S.R. 47 where a single Japanese utility model specification had been received in the former Patent Office Library only three days before the priority date. The EPO has held that if a document can be inspected by the public it is to be considered as part of the state of the art even if there is no evidence that the document was ever in fact inspected, see T 444/88 *JAPAN STYRENE PAPER/Foam particles* [1991] E.P.O.R. 94: here the pleaded art was an example added to the file of a Japanese patent application after this application had been published. On similar reasoning it was considered irrelevant that the cited subject-matter may have appeared only in a non-technical publication of limited circulation and may never have been seen by anyone skilled in the art, see T 165/96 *CAYLA/Délavage*, where an insert in a small-ads newspaper (circulation 24,000) distributed in the suburbs of Copenhagen was held to be citable.

Where a document is received by a library and placed in an archive or private room, in order to establish a date of publication it must have been indexed, otherwise the public would have no means of knowledge of its existence, see T 314/99 *EXXON MOBIL/Process and catalyst*, see also *Plimpton v Malcolmson* (1876) 3 Ch.D. 531 and *Plimpton v Spiller* (1877) 6 Ch.D. 412. However, in T 381/87 *RESEARCH ASSOCIATION/Publication* OJ EPO 1990, 213; [1989] E.P.O.R. 138 a copy of a journal was received by a library and, according to the evidence of the librarian, immediately placed on its open shelf and not in its archive. In these circumstances the Board held that the journal was published as of its date of receipt and that it was not necessary to show that it had been indexed.

Patent specifications carry a date of publication which is normally taken to be correct, although that presumption is rebuttable by convincing evidence that the specification did not in fact become available to the public on the date stated: see *Microsonics' Application* [1984] R.P.C. 29. In that case, a statement in the United States Patent Office Official Gazette that, though printing of certain patents had been delayed, the files thereof would be available from the official issue date was not overcome by affidavits merely reporting (hearsay) conversations with officials of the United States Patent Office which tended to contradict the official notice. In T 826/03 *SCHLUMBERGER/Electronic revenue meter* it was held that there was insufficient proof of the date of publication of a Canadian patent application since it was not clear beyond doubt that the indicated publication date was correct. In T 315/02 *JACQUET ORTHOPEDIE/Priority document* a patent specification not yet published in its country of origin was held to form part of the state of the art if it was accessible to the public as a priority document for a published European application. In T 877/98 *FUCHS UMWELTTECHNIK/Patent grant* the question was whether a German patent had become publicly available upon notification of the grant decision if the application had not been published previously. The Appeal Board took the view that the patent had not become available until publication of grant in the patent bulletin; only from that point on where the file was open for inspection. It thus endorsed the view of the German Federal Patents Court (decision of 23.12.1994, 4W (pat) 41/94, BlfPMZ 1995, 324).

In the case of other printed documents availability to the public at a sufficiently early date must be proved if not apparent. A date of publication which appears on, or in connection with, a particular document is evidence of the date on which its contents became available to the public. However, a date appearing on the face of a document may be proved not to be its publication date but only its intended date of dispatch to the public, see T 750/94 *AT&T/Proof of prior publication* OJ EPO 1998, 32; [1997] E.P.O.R. 509. In the case of a document in a library, more reliable evidence is provided by a dated receipt stamp as in T 729/91 *PANACHE PROMOTIONS/Wall-mounted hair dryer* [2000] E.P.O.R. 60. Such evidence was also accepted in T 287/86 *TOBIAS/Photoelectric densitometer* [1989] E.P.O.R. 214 in relation to a dated copyright notice appearing on a brochure, and in T 381/87 *RESEARCH ASSOCIATION/Publication*, where it was held that a scientific paper had been made available to the public on its stated date of publication, it being immaterial whether or not any member of the public actually then knew that the paper was available or actually asked to see it. Nevertheless, date of receipt evidence may be rebutted, e.g. as in T 1137/97 *ENI/Integral joint* where the received date was merely handwritten and evidence was adduced from three other libraries that they had received their copy of the journal after the relevant date. In T 308/87 *DU PONT/Yarn finish applicator* [1991] E.P.O.R. 464, a brochure was disregarded for lack of proof of its distribution date, whereas in T 804/05 *DAL GmbH/Sanitärinstallationen* a brochure dated 18 months before the priority date of an opposed patent was presumed to have been made available to the public. In T 861/04 *UNITED VIDEO PROPERTIES/Electronic television program guide* the date of the patent in issue was 1994 and the cited document was a manual for a colour television having the copyright notice "© 1993 by Sony Corporation Printed in UK." The Appeal Board held that a copyright notice could not be compared with a printing date because it had legal consequences and the stated facts should be presumed to be correct unless the contrary is proved. In the present case there was no evidence of an alternative date of publication, and it was highly unlikely that the relevant television models and the user manual would have been kept in stock for a whole year and not distributed. Accordingly the document was comprised in the prior art under EPC art.54(2).

In the case of a thesis submitted as part of a university degree, particular care may be needed if its precise date of publication is important. In *Codex v Racal-Milgo* BL C/135/81, noted I.P.D. 4100, publication of an abstract of a thesis was held (again under the former law) not to make the thesis itself available to the public in the absence of evidence that the offer of inspection of the thesis contained in the abstract was realistic. In *Vericore's Patent* BL O/125/02 evidence as to the likelihood that a thesis would have been put on the shelves of a library earlier than the catalogue date was not found sufficient to prove that the thesis had been made available to the public before the relevant date. However, evidence from the author of the thesis that he supplied copies to colleagues without confidentiality restriction before the relevant date was accepted. The Comptroller's decision was upheld on appeal to the court: [2003] EWHC 111 Pat Ct, noted I.P.D. 26026. In T 314/99 *EXXON MOBIL/Diplomarbeit*, it was undisputed that a diploma thesis arrived in the archive of the a library before the priority date of the patent in issue, but that did not mean it was as of that point in time catalogued or otherwise prepared for the public to acquire knowledge of it, and without such means of information the public would remain unaware of its existence, so that availability to the public had not been proved. In T 151/99 *KPN/Transmission of data cells* the Board held that it was highly plausible that a paper submitted to obtain an academic degree was not confidential, and this became a virtual certainty if the thesis was referred to in another document published before the priority date.

Publication can take place by display of a poster at a conference. In *Generics (UK) Ltd v Daiichi Pharmaceutical Co Ltd* [2009] R.P.C. 5; [2008] EWHC 2413 Pat Ct a poster was displayed at a meeting for a period of two hours in a public place where passers-by could see it, and the author was present and answered any questions posed to him, but the poster was not catalogued or indexed so as to be subsequently retrievable. Nevertheless, availability was sufficient to establish publication and it was irrelevant whether anybody actually had read the poster; see also *Lux v Pike* [1993] R.P.C. 107 at 133. Furthermore, information could not cease to be part of the state of the art once it had been made available. In opposition proceedings the EPO has held that the standard of proof in these circumstances is the same as for prior use, i.e. the onus of proof is on the opponent and the standard of proof is beyond reasonable doubt, especially where the supporting evidence lies within the power and knowledge of the opponent. For example, oral and written evidence from an author who prepared a poster as to the inclusion of particular content was not accepted in relation to events eight years previously since the relevant question was not whether she was honest but whether she might have made an honest mistake, see T 1210/05 *TAKEDA/2-2-(2-pyridylmethylsulfinyl)benzimidazole crystals*, see also as to proof of content T 759/03 *ST VINCENT'S INSTITUTE, et al/FIV* and as to evaluation of conflicting evidence and T 313/05 *APPLERA/Apparatus* for modifying a polymerase chain reaction.

In *HSBC France's Application* O/180/09 the standard of proof for publications on the internet was held to be balance of probabilities as in *Kavanagh Balloons v Cameron Balloons* [2004] R.P.C. 5 and not the higher standard called for by the EPO in T 1134/06 *KONAMI CORP/Game system*. Furthermore, only if there was substantial doubt should an applicant be given the benefit of that doubt. In the present case relevant websites were highly reputable with a long history of publishing both for IT consumers and for the IT industry, the dates they gave to articles were reliable and the contents of the articles were unlikely to be changed once published. Even under the EPO standard it would have been taken that there was proof "up to the hilt" and there was no need for additional supporting evidence, see also *Ranger Services Ltd's Application* O/362/09.

The EPO has now issued a notice concerning internet citations, see [2009] OJ EPO 456. In agreement with *HSBC France's Application* O/180/09, it now sets out that the appropriate standard of proof is balance of probabilities. It explains inter alia that establishing a publication date has two aspects. It must be assessed separately whether a given date is indicated correctly and whether the content in question was indeed made available to the public as of that date. Neither restricting access to a limited circle of people (e.g. by password protection), nor requiring payment for access (analogous to purchasing a book or subscribing to a journal) prevent a web page from forming part of the state of the art. It is sufficient if the web page is in principle available without any bar of confidentiality. If there is an explicit publication date which is generally considered reliable it will be accepted at face value and the onus will be on an applicant or patentee to prove otherwise. Online technical journals from scientific publishers will be considered as reliable as traditional paper journals, and this principle extends to other "print-equivalent" publications. Computer-generated time stamps (e.g. on blogs) will also normally be considered as reliable. Other evidence of availability may come from an internet archiving service, the most prominent being the internet archive accessible through the so-called "Wayback Machine" (*http://www.archive.org* [Accessed September 19, 2011]).

Operation of the EPO standard of proof "up to the hilt" is illustrated in T 1255/06 *EX-ERGEN CORP/Radiation detector* [2009] E.P.O.R. 23 where an opponent relied on a 20-year-old brochure and a simultaneous presentation at a conference. A witness was heard by the EPO but could not recall relevant detail, including the year in which the conference took place, whether or not the brochure accurately reflected what was displayed, which version of the brochure was distributed, whether there was feedback from customers and whether any sales had been made. Only the brochure survived and no other supporting documents, e.g. laboratory notebooks, manuals, invoices, etc. had been found. The opponent explained that it was not now possible to find such documents owing to the length of time that had elapsed. The supporting evidence was held to be insufficiently definite, and the fact that the alleged disclosure had happened long ago was no reason to relax the burden of proof. Neither the date of publication of the brochure nor the public prior disclosure of the invention had been proven to the required standard, so that these were not to be regarded as prior art.

A publication cannot be removed from the state of the art, even if it contains foolish-looking instructions, and the same applies to other publications irrespective of their geographical location or the alleged reputation of the periodical, see T 48/85 *NRDC/Eimeria necatrix* [1987] E.P.O.R. 138.

The EPO has held that a publication which is erroneous on its face, as in the case of an abstract inconsistent with the, inevitably cross-referenced, document which it purports to summarise, should be discounted, see T 77/87 *ICI/Erroneous abstract* OJ EPO 1990, 280; [1989] E.P.O.R. 246. Indeed, it is submitted that a document presented as an "abstract" should never be held to contain information broader than, and especially inconsistent with, the contents of the document which it purports to have abstracted, since the skilled reader would treat the original document as the true disclosure, of course assuming that this was itself published before the priority date in issue. In T 412/91 *KAWASAKI/Alloy steel powder* [1997] E.P.O.R. 538, in order to resolve doubt whether a disclosure was correct, reference was made to a corresponding patent from which it was deduced that the disclosure in the cited document was erroneous and could therefore be discounted. Where a document contains a mistake which the skilled reader would immediately perceive and correct, the corrected version contains the true disclosure, as in T 513/89 *SIEMENS/Contact medium* [1998] E.P.O.R. 63. However, the document can be discounted if the apparent defect cannot be corrected by the skilled reader, see T 591/90 *ALUMINIUM-WERKE/Deep-drawn aluminium container* [1998] E.P.O.R. 56. It appears to be a moot point whether a disclosure made in a work of fiction should be disregarded, presumably as one which the public would not accept as an actual disclosure.

Documents communicated in private correspondence and/or in private hands

2.05   Matter communicated by one person to another person may form part of the state of the art depending on the circumstances in which the communication was made. A single instance of supply of a single document to a single member of the public who is free in law and equity to use its information as he or she wishes is sufficient, see *Bristol-Myers Co's Application* [1969] R.P.C. 146. However, the matter will not form part of the state of the art if the supply was in circumstance where the recipient was under an obligation of confidence.

Matter is not available to the public if it is merely known to research workers pursuing their own experiments in private and keeping their knowledge to themselves, see *Genentech Inc's Patent* [1989] R.P.C. 147; *Catnic v Evans* [1983] F.S.R. 401; and *Dolland's Case* (1776) 1 W.P.C. 43. Drawings and notebooks, research reports and other documents generated by an individual or within an organisation but which have never been communicated to another, and in the case of an organisation have never been communicated outside that organisation, do not form part of the state of the art, this being referred to by the EPO as "in-house prior art", see T 405/86 *MOBIL OIL/film*.

United Kingdom courts require proof of publication on the normal standard of balance of probabilities, see *Kavanagh Balloons v Cameron Balloons* [2004] R.P.C. 5 at 97. The EPO more usually requires a more stringent standard of proof as is apparent, e.g. from

T 313/05 *APPLERA/Apparatus for modifying a polymerase chain reaction*, where extensive evidence from eminent scientists as to whether a report prior to the priority date had been made available at an internal workshop was evaluated, and the Board concluded that on the evidence it had not been established beyond reasonable doubt that the report had been made available at that workshop. As to the standard of proof, the Board concluded that a "beyond reasonable doubt" or "up to the hilt" standard was appropriate where the revocation of a granted European patent was at issue. To base a revocation decision on the mere balancing of probabilities of what might have occurred would be difficult to reconcile with the need for reliability in the decision-making procedures of the EPO, which is of utmost importance for users of the patent system as well as the general public.

As to onus of proof, in *Qualcomm Incorporated v Nokia Corp* [2008] EWHC 329 Pat Ct the court held that if what is proved is distribution through a channel which would normally be expected to make the document available to the public, then the burden will shift, at least temporarily. But if what is proved is distribution through an unconventional channel, particularly one where precautions to maintain confidentiality of some kind were taken, the burden will remain with the party seeking to establish that the document was made available to the public. It rejected an argument that where a document is effectively circulated to every person having an interest in it, it should be treated as made available to the public, even if individual recipients were supplied the document in confidence.

Oral description

In the case of an ephemeral disclosure such as a lecture, issues can arise concerning **2.06** standard of proof and concerning the content of the disclosure. It is also relevant whether the disclosure made the subject-matter available to the public or was made in circumstances where there was an obligation of confidence.

Often conference proceedings are followed by post-lecture publication, e.g. *Actavis v Janssen* [2008] F.S.R. 35, where publication was in a book, and the court held that since the book was intended to be a record of the proceedings it was improbable that information would have been incorporated into the material for publication in the book if it were not part of the original presentation. Similarly the EPO has held that although it is not to be presumed that an oral presentation of a scientific paper was identical with the text of that paper as subsequently published, on the balance of probabilities a salient feature of that paper can be expected to have been disclosed in that oral presentation: T 86/95 *ALCOA/Aluminium lithium alloys* [2000] E.P.O.R. 54. However, the situation may be different where the report was only published some years later, T 153/88 *STAHLWERKE PEINE-SALZGITTER/Hot strip* [1997] E.P.O.R. 371. In T 348/94 *SUMITOMO/Superconductive film* [2001] E.P.O.R. 20 at 161 it was held that there was no presumption that conference proceedings published 10 months afterwards were an accurate record of those proceedings. There was a burden of proof on the opponent to show this, in the absence of which alleged disclosures recorded in a document which had been published after the priority date did not form part of the state of the art.

No post-lecture publication was available for reference in T 1212/97 *GENENTECH/Immunoglobulin preparation*. Opponents averred that the claimed subject-matter had been disclosed at the lecture shortly before the relevant priority date. Declarations were filed from the lecturer identifying the slides that had been shown, from a technician who had prepared the slides and from the organiser of the meeting who was present at the lecture. The patentees filed a declaration from a member of the audience who did not recall any mention of the matters specifically relied on, and filed questionnaires from others present that they did not recall the lecture as disclosing anything not previously known. The Board wanted evidence from the audience, not from the lecturer. In the absence of evidence that any member of the audience actually did write down the relevant information or understand it, the Board was not prepared to make any presumption as to the information made publicly available. Similarly an oral disclosure to a circle of persons who are unable to understand its technical teaching, and are therefore unable to distribute the information further, may be insufficient to make it "available to the public" and hence not be novelty-destroying: T 877/90 *HOOPER TRADING/T-cell growth factor* [1993] E.P.O.R. 6.

Other cases where a prior oral disclosure was proved include: T 534/88 *IBM/Ion etching* [1991] E.P.O.R. 18 and T 739/92 *HERCULES/Thermosetting epoxy resin*, where an oral disclosure made at a conference open to specialists in the field who were free to disseminate information gained thereat, provided that they did not disclose the source of that information, was held to have been publicly disseminated. In contrast, in T 818/93 *PALMAZ/Expandible intraluminal vascular graft* discussions concerning the obtaining of equipment for research were implicitly confidential.

In T 379/92 *HERCULES/Thermosetting epoxy resin* an oral description represented by a manuscript of a lecture, in poster form, was held to belong to the state of the art since the conference at which the lecture was given was open to every specialist in the relevant field, there was no secrecy agreement and participants were not prohibited from disseminating oral information about the conference or from publishing information from it.

Again, the relevant standard of proof has been said by the UK courts to be the ordinary civil standard of what is more likely than not to have happened, see *Actavis v Janssen* [2008] EWHC 1422 at [137]; [2008] F.S.R. 35 Pat Ct, see also *Kavanagh Balloons v Cameron Balloons* [2004] R.P.C. 5 at 97. The EPO usually applies a "beyond any reasonable doubt" standard, see T 1212/97 *GENENTECH/Immunoglobulin preparations*. In order to establish the facts, it may make an order providing the attendance of particular witnesses at oral proceedings, see e.g. T 104/99 *WISCONSIN/Taking of evidence—witnesses*.

Prior public use

2.07   A single instance of use of an invention in public before the relevant date is an anticipation, see *Carpenter v Smith* 1 W.P.C. 530 in which a lock had been used on a gate adjoining a public road for sixteen years prior to the patent, *Taylor's Patent* in which a fire grate had been used in a private house where it was specially shown to visitors (see (1896) 13 R.P.C. 482), and more recently *Windsurfing v Tabur Marine* [1985] R.P.C. 59 in which use of a sailboard by a 12-year-old boy off the coast of Hayling Island put that sailboard in the public domain notwithstanding that it subsequently lay forgotten, but see *Boyce v Morris Motors* (1927) 44 R.P.C. 105 at 109 in which a thermometer fitted in cars driven on the public highway was held not to be public use if nobody had the opportunity of stopping the cars and asking to look at them. A single instance of supply of an invention to a single member of the public without inhibiting fetter is enough to make an invention available to the public, see *Fomento v Mentmore* [1956] R.P.C. 87. Where an article had been made and openly sold, that is not a secret or uninformative use, it being irrelevant whether the article had ever been tested to demonstrate the attributes claimed, see *Milliken Denmark v Walk Off Mats* [1996] F.S.R. 292. Examples of EPO decisions to the same effect are T 482/89 *TELEMECHANIQUE/Power supply unit* OJ EPO 1992, 646; T 953/90 *THOMSON-CSF/Tube électronique* [1998] E.P.O.R. 415; and T 1022/99 *VAN WONTERGHEM/Dispositif de transmission.*

In T 575/94 *GILL'S CABLES/Control cable assembly* [1997] E.P.O.R. 100, prior use of a cable control assembly was established on the testimony of recollection by employees of the opponent which was uncorroborated, but held to be substantiated by later documentation concerning further development. The assembly had been placed on about 100 cars sold to the public and had therefore been made available even though it was unlikely that any purchaser would have noticed their presence. Also, where an experiment had been carried out on a factory scale on the premises of another party and where there was neither a tacit nor express duty to maintain secrecy, the process of that experiment was found to have been made available to the public, see T 602/91 *BAYER/Plasterboard* [1996] E.P.O.R. 388. Similarly, there was prior public use of a process before the priority date in a factory which maintained an open policy towards visitors because it was believed that conventional products were being made in a conventional way and there was no need for confidentiality, see T 947/99 *UNILEVER/Confectionery.*

Sale of a product whose composition can be analysed makes that composition available to the public since it gives the means of knowledge to the purchaser, see *Miller's patent* (1919) 15 R.P.C. 205 at 211 and *Stahlwerk Becker Aktiengesellschaft's Patent* (1918) 36

R.P.C. 13 HL. In *Lux Traffic v Pike Signals* [1993] R.P.C. 107 at 134, it was stated that "what is made available to the public by a machine. is that which the skilled man would, if asked to describe its construction and operation, write down having carried out an appropriate test or examination. To invalidate the patent, the description that such a man would write down must be a clear and unambiguous description of the invention claimed." Here it was held that the system had been made available to contractors who were free in law and equity to examine it in operation and that, if a skilled person had taken the time to test it in operation, he would have obtained details of the invention as claimed. Likewise, in *BSH Industries' Patents* [1995] R.P.C. 183, novelty was held destroyed by prior use of a component which could have been reproduced by reverse engineering after examination.

In *PCME v Goyen Controls* [1999] F.S.R. 801 the court held that where the alleged prior use was a "black box" a notional skilled team evaluating what had been disclosed would include a skilled but uninventive forensic engineer, otherwise it would be possible to re-patent information which any competent forensic engineer could find out by obvious investigative techniques. The relevant questions were (1) what tests or analyses would it be obvious to carry out on the product, (2) what would be the result of those tests and (3) how would those results be interpreted by the person skilled in the art. What was made available to the public was the result of the obvious test procedures and their normal interpretation, and if the result was imprecise ("probably A but may be B") although it may not then be sufficient to support anticipation it was to be treated as published and might well render the claimed subject-matter obvious. On the evidence, obvious and simple testing techniques would have revealed that the prior device was a.c.-coupled and would have disclosed its frequency range. Even if a skilled worker was not certain that the prior device was a.c.-coupled it was obvious to try an a.c.-coupled amplifier if that was the most likely explanation of the behaviour of the prior device. In *Evans Medical's Patent* [1998] R.P.C. 517 (as discussed by I. Karet [1998] B.S.L.R. 28 and J. Marshall, [1998] E.I.P.R. 273) a vaccine had been made available to the public who would have been free to analyse it and thereby ascertain that it contained an antigen within the scope of the claims of the patent-in-suit, prior identification of that antigen not being a necessary element for a finding of lack of novelty. In *Cranway v Playtech* [2009] EWHC 1588 Pat Ct features of an online computer game that could have been ascertained by a software engineer at the client side using a debugger which was a standard tool were held to have been made available to the public.

A prototype had been shown by an inventor to a neighbour prior to the priority date of the patent in issue which was owned by a third party; see *Stockley v Husqvarna* O/402/09. The neighbour whose employment had familiarised him with patents asked whether the inventor should be showing him this invention as it might be considered prior art if a patent application had not been filed. The inventor told his neighbour that a patent application had been filed and there was nothing to worry about (the application was in fact subsequently withdrawn prior to publication). In the circumstances of the disclosure confidentiality was not an issue, the neighbour was free in law and equity to use the information disclosed to him and the prototype had indeed been made available to the public. A number of other allegations of prior disclosure had been relied on, but all of these were found to be under an obligation of confidentiality.

In *Folding Attic Stairs v The Loft Stairs Co* [2009] EWHC 1221 Pat Ct a prototype of a folding attic stairway had been shown to the Irish Minister for Trade and Tourism and to a newspaper photographer and a photograph had appeared in the *Irish Times*. No security precautions had been taken. However, it was held that the important feature of the invention could not be discerned from the photograph which was therefore not destructive of novelty. The case against the patent was also that the Minister and the photographer were free to examine the unit and to tell anybody about it, which was sufficient to have made the invention available to the public. The court held that it would be an unnecessary legal fiction to presume that information that could have been perceived by people who were on private premises was in fact perceived by them, and in the absence of evidence from the individuals concerned it was unlikely that they would have been able to describe the relevant features. Accordingly the objection of lack of novelty was not established. A similar point arose in *Loadhog v Polymer Logistics* O/195/10 where there was no evidence that the relevant member of the public had got down on his hands and knees to examine it, or that it had been turned upside down to reveal how its mechanism operated.

To the same effect, the EPO Enlarged Board of Appeal has held that where a product is available to the public and it could have been not only analysed but also reproduced by the skilled person without undue burden that product is part of the state of the art irrespective of whether or not particular reasons can be identified for analysing the composition: G 1/92 *Availability to the Public* OJ EPO 1993, 277; [1993] E.P.O.R. 241, overruling T 93/89 *HOECHST/Polyvinyl ester dispersion* OJ EPO 1992, 718; [1992] E.P.O.R. 155, see also T 952/92 *PACKARD/Prior use* OJ EPO 1995, 755; [1997] E.P.O.R. 457. Prior use was found where X-ray investigation could have been used to ascertain the internal structure of an electron tube without destroying it, see T 953/90 *THOMSON/Electron tube*. An invention embodied in a published computer program listing has been held to have been made available to the public where the listing contained expressions in plain text indicating its relevance to an electronics specialist who would have consulted a computer programmer to determine how the program operated, see T 164/92 *BOSCH/ Electronic computer components* OJ EPO 1995, 305; [1995] E.P.O.R. 585. However, it appears from T 461/88 *HEIDELBERGER/Microchip* OJ EPO 1993, 295; [1993] E.P.O.R. 529 that the EPO may be receptive to an argument that subject-matter, though ascertainable by reverse engineering, would have involved undue difficulty and expense, e.g. where the knowledge to be gained by the investigation would have been disproportionate to the time spent on the investigation and the economic loss by prolonged non-availability of a complex machine.

In *Pall Corp. v Commercial Hydraulics* [1990] F.S.R. 329 the supply prior to the priority date of test samples for customer evaluation had not made the invention "available to the public" because the nature of the samples had not then been disclosed and this was not apparently ascertainable by examination. In *Quantel v Spaceward Microsonics* [1990] R.P.C. 83 a demonstration at which no-one was allowed near the machine and no engineering description was given, did not provide an "enabling disclosure". In *PLG Research v Ardon* [1993] F.S.R. 197, a prior use was held not to have disclosed the nature of the starting material which was an essential element of claims having a process feature: the point was not discussed in the appeal decision: [1995] R.P.C. 287 CA. There is no prior use of an article where relevant constructional features are concealed and are not directly obvious to a skilled person who has an opportunity to see them, see T 1085/92 *ROBERT BOSCH/Electrical machine* [1996] E.P.O.R. 381, see also T 242/85 *CHEMIE LINZ/ Reinforced channels* [1988] E.P.O.R. 77 where anticipation by prior use was not established because this had not revealed to the public all of the features of the invention, but the claims were found to lack an inventive step over it.

In *Prout v British Gas* [1992] F.S.R. 478, an experimental field trial of the invention, necessarily conducted in public, was excused, but the reasoning used in this decision makes it of doubtful authority. Perhaps the decision could be supported on a similar basis to the decision in *Vax v Hoover* [1992] F.S.R. 307, where under the 1949 Act the mere act of a prior demonstration was held not to be a "use".

The question of claims to a process by which a product has been made raises further problems, since examination of a product will not always disclose how it had been made, see *PLG Research v Ardon* (above). Thus, even if product claims are invalidated by the prior use, claims directed to the process by which it is made may be upheld. This was the issue in *Gore v Kimal* [1988] R.P.C. 137, where it was held (under the former statute) that public distribution of a product in the course of trade before the priority date constituted a prior use of the process claimed, irrespective of whether it would have been possible to ascertain from the product what process had been used to make it and irrespective of whether the process took place in the United Kingdom or whether (as was the case) it took place abroad. It can be seen that, if the process claims had been upheld in these circumstances, importation of the resulting product would have been an infringement even though the same act had been done before the priority date. Thus, a "post-infringement" test was, in effect, here applied, though under the 1949 Act. However, it seems doubtful whether the same decision would be given under the present Act, because of the enablement require-ment for an effective prior use, see §2.09 below; but in *Pifco v Philips* [1998] EWHC Patents 276, noted I.P.D. 22026, a prior used article was held to anticipate a claim to a method of manufacture of that type of article because the claim embraced a method which would at least have been in the contemplation of the designer of that article, thereby mak-ing this an enabled prior use.

As regards clinical trials, it was held in *Merrell Dow v Norton* [1996] R.P.C. 76 HL that prior use was not established as regards participants in clinical trials who were given a drug for the sole purpose of swallowing it and were not at liberty to analyse the drug. Under the Patents Act 1949 such uninformative use would have invalidated the patent, but under the 1977 Act this was no longer the case and the decision in *Bristol-Myers Co (Johnson's) Application* [1975] R.P.C. 127 HL was no longer good law as discussed in more detail in §2.08. The same conclusion was reached in *Merz v Allergan* [2006] EWHC 2686 Pat Ct which was a further case involving clinical trial of a drug and by the EPO in T 494/96 *HOYA/Intraocular lens* [2002] E.P.O.R. 14 at 131 which concerned a clinical trial of artificial intra-ocular lenses that had been supplied by an opponent to a hospital for surgeons to use. The hospital paid for the lenses and billed the patients for them but the patients could not examine the lenses, there was no evidence that the surgeons had any clear knowledge of the composition of the lenses, and the question of a patient's ability to gain such information from the surgeon was "hypothetical". Prior use was established in T 0945/09 *GEISTLICH/Taurolidine in delivery systems*, the patient being aware of the identity of the drug being used, and the use having arisen from the instant necessity to help a patient in a desperate situation and not as part of a planned scientific experiment.

To prove a prior use in EPO opposition proceedings, the material provided must strictly identify the point or period of time for the alleged use; identify the object of the use suf-ficiently precisely for this to be equated with the object of the patent; and verify the cir-cumstances of the use to establish the manifest nature of the objects used, see T 538/89 *DEERE/Coupling rod* [1991] E.P.O.R. 445; T 232/89 *VEIDEKKE/Dam core machine* [1993] E.P.O.R. 37; T 600/90 *UNILEVER/Perborate* [1993] E.P.O.R. 28; T 328/87 *THOMSON-BRANDT/Admissibility* [1993] E.P.O.R. 191; T 194/86 *ALBANY/Shower fit-ting* [1994] E.P.O.R. 335; and T 326/93 T*HORN/Thermal limiting device* [1995] E.P.O.R. 297. In particular, the evidence may need to distinguish between personal and public knowledge of the witness, see T 448/90 *BRITISH GAS/Mains replacement method* [1994] E.P.O.R. 105.

A general statement of the standard of proof required by the EPO where prior use relied on is that of an opponent appears in T 738/04 MICROCHIP TECHNOLOGY/Circuit and its method of operation:

"It is the established practice of the boards of appeal to apply the criterion of 'absolute conviction' rather than the 'balance of probabilities' in cases of prior public use for which the evidence lies entirely within the sphere of the opponent. In decision T 472/92 (OJ 1998, 92, cf. headnote), the Board held that '. . . in those prior public use cases, where practically all the evidence in support of an alleged prior public use lies within the power and knowledge of the Opponent, the latter has to prove his case up to the hilt', which view was later reiterated in decision T 97/94 (OJ 1998, 467, point 5.1).

This implies not only that the reasoning referred to by the appellant should be complete and conclusive but also that all facts supporting that reasoning be fully substantiated by corresponding evidence. This requirement is the consequence of the principle accord-ing to which parties representing opposite interests should be given equally fair treat-ment and derives from the contentious character of the post grant opposition proceed-ings (cf. G 9/91, OJ 1992, 408, point 2). Usually the only possibility for a patentee who played no part in the alleged prior use is to take issue with the conclusive nature of the adduced evidence and consequently of the reasoning to which it gives rise; the unbal-anced factual situation resulting from the unilateral access of the opponent to the avail-able evidence is then compensated by the severe legal requirement developed by the case law that such prior use should be established beyond any reasonable doubt.

A more liberal approach, which would accept that facts could be established on the basis of the less demanding criterion of 'balance of probabilities' would, in unbalanced situations such as those referred to above, normally constitute a breach of said principle, since the patentee would be deprived of the opportunity to successfully challenge the opponent's reasoning, i.e. to question the conclusiveness of the adduced evidence."

In T 12/00 *PIRELLI/Hydrogen-absorbing composition* the appropriate standard of proof for prior use was balance of probabilities since neither of the parties was involved in the alleged prior use, see also T 1464/05 *PRYSMIAN/Hydrogen-absorbing composition* [2010] E.P.O.R. 1 which was a subsequent decision on the same opposition, the name of the patentee having changed during the course of the procedure.

In T 627/88 *ASAHI/Resin composition* [1991] E.P.O.R. 81, prior use was found where there was no reason to doubt the authenticity either of the evidence or the witness presenting it, see also T 124/88 *PEUGEOT/Electric motor* [1991] E.P.O.R. 255. However, in T 782/92 *TOKAI/Dual-type damper* [1996] E.P.O.R. 207, a delivery note evidencing delivery of a small quantity of articles was held to be insufficient evidence to establish that information had been made available to the public thereby; the small quantity of articles delivered was thought to be indicative of a supply in confidential circumstances. The decision was likewise in T 472/92 *SEKISUI/Shrinkable sheet* (above) where the Board was not satisfied that a supply by company A to company B, of which A was a joint owner, had taken place in non-confidential circumstances, see also: T 97/94 *CECA/Procedural timetable* OJ EPO 1998, 467; [1999] E.P.O.R. 65; T 848/94 *KANEGAFUCHI/Polyimide film* [1999] E.P.O.R. 270; and T 883/97 *CARROLL PRODUCTS/Display units* [1999] E.P.O.R. 248, in each of which prior use was held not to have been firmly proved, that is "up to the hilt". Prior use was also not found in T 245/88 *UNION CARBIDE/Atmospheric vaporizer* [1991] E.P.O.R. 373 where it was far from clear that the public had had sufficient access to the alleged prior-used apparatus to ascertain its nature.

Whether or not fabric that had been delivered was "available to the public" was in issue in T 681/01 *HUNTER DOUGLAS INDUSTRIES/Treated fabric*. Opponents filed evidence that material had been sent for delivery for resale and without any obligation of confidence and that so far as they knew the material had been received since no objection had been raised and the relevant invoices had been duly paid. As this had happened nine months before the priority date, it was held that there was sufficient evidence of actual delivery before the priority date and evidence as to the precise delivery date was not necessary and would have served no useful purpose: doubts raised by the patentees had no reasonable basis. Direct visual inspection of the fabric would have enabled a skilled person to determine that it possessed all of the physical features required by the claim under consideration. Accordingly the material had been made available to the public.

As regards pleadings in UK court proceedings, see CPR 63 PD 04 (reproduced in Appendix F). CPR 63 PD 4.4(1) applies to allegations of lack of novelty arising from prior written description and CPR 63 PD 4.4(2) provides for inspection of machinery or apparatus alleged to have been used before the priority date.

Prior non-public use

2.08   Under subs.(2), novelty is determined according to whether the invention has been made available to the public by written or oral description, by use or in any other way. Thus, unlike the position under the former statutes, prior secret use no longer anticipates, nor does a prior use which failed to provide a disclosure sufficient to enable the public to replicate the claimed invention, i.e. to make the invention "available to the public", see *Asahi's Application* [1991] R.P.C. 485 HL and *Merrell Dow v Norton* [1996] R.P.C. 76 HL. The EPO has also authoritatively stated that a hidden or secret use is not a ground of objection to the validity of a European patent because such use has not "been made available to the public", see G 2/88 *MOBIL III/Friction reducing additive* OJ EPO 1990, 93 and 469; [1990] E.P.O.R. 73; and G 6/88 *BAYER/Second non-medical indication* OJ EPO 1990, 114; [1990] E.P.O.R. 257.

Instead, the prior user acquires a prescriptive right to continue its former activity (see s.64 and the commentary thereon) leaving the patent enforceable against third parties, and perhaps even against the prior user in respect of a variant of its prior use because the s.64 right is quite limited, as explained by Isabel Davies and S. Cohen [1994] E.I.P.R. 239. The defence to infringement which it provides does not apply unless the prior act (or more probably an act which, before the priority date, a person had made "serious and effective preparations" to carry out) would, if carried out after the patent grant, have been an act of "infringement". Hence, the exceptions to infringement of "private and non-commercial use" s.60(5)(a) and of "experimental use relating to the subject-matter of the invention" (s.60(5)(b)) cause difficulties, as discussed in §64.03.

In *Bristol-Myers' (Johnson's) Application* [1975] R.P.C. 127 HL an alleged prior use was an uninformative use in which a batch of ampicillin trihydrate had been supplied to the public, albeit unknowingly and without intention and in circumstances where it would not have been detected by analysis, although there was an opportunity for the public to attempt such analysis. Under the former law this was held to amount to prior use. However in *Merrell Dow v Norton* [1996] R.P.C. 76 HL the *Bristol-Myers* case was held no longer to be good law because the invention must have been made available to the public, an invention being a piece of information. Use of a product makes an invention part of the state of the art only insofar as that use makes available the necessary information. In *PLG Research Ltd v Ardon International Ltd* [1993] F.S.R. 197, 225, Aldous J. had correctly stated that under the 1977 Act a patent may be granted for an invention covering a product that has been put on the market, provided the product does not provide an enabling disclosure of the invention claimed. In most cases, prior sale of the product would make available information as to its contents and its method of manufacture, but it was possible to imagine circumstances where that would not happen. In such cases a subsequent patent could be obtained and the only safeguard given to the public was s.64 of the Act. This was also the position set out in G 2/88 *MOBIL III/Friction reducing additive* [1990] E.P.O.R. 73 at 88 where the Enlarged Appeal Board explained that under the EPC, a hidden or secret use, because it has not been made available to the public, was not a ground of objection to the validity of a European patent. In this respect, the provisions of the EPC differed from the previous national laws of some contracting states, and even from the current national laws of some non-contracting states. The question of inherency did not arise as such under art.54 and any vested right derived from prior use of an invention was a matter for national law. In the *Merrell Dow* case the alleged prior use was in the course of clinical trials where the participants took terfenadine without being at liberty to discover its composition and produced within themselves a substance which had not then been readily capable of being identified but was now known to have been a subsequently claimed metabolite. Under the Patents Act 1949 such uninformative use would undoubtedly have invalidated the patent for the metabolite, but under the 1977 Act the claim for the metabolite could not be dismissed simply on the ground that making it was something that had been done before.

The corresponding *Merrell Dow* case in the United States (reported as *Merrell Dow v Baker Norton [USA]* [1998] F.S.R. 158, arrived at the same result as in Germany (*Terfenadin [Germany]* [1998] F.S.R. 145 where, in both cases, there was a decision of non-infringement by the terfenadine metabolite of a claim to a compound which was construed as limited to that compound when made synthetically. On this basis, the validity of the patent was not resolved in either case. For further information on the German case, see P. Tauchner, *Patent World*, No.111, April 1999, 19.

A prior use which is subject to an obligation of confidentiality does not make an invention available to the public. Whether or not a prior use which is not expressly in public is confidential depends on the relationship between the parties, as discussed below.

The requirement for a novelty-destroying disclosure to have an "enabling" character

The House of Lords in *Asahi's Application* [1991] R.P.C. 485 accepted the previously **2.09** expressed EPO view that a prior novelty-destroying disclosure must have an "enabling" character if the invention was thereby to have been "made available to the public", see T 206/83 *ICI/Pyridine herbicides* OJ EPO 1987, 5; [1986] E.P.O.R. 232 and T 81/87 *COLLABORATIVE/Preprorennin* OJ EPO 1990, 250; [1990] E.P.O.R. 361 and *Genentech's [Human Growth Hormone] Patent* [1989] R.P.C. 613. The requirement from *Asahi* that a novelty-destroying disclosure or use should have an enabling character was firmly endorsed in *Merrell Dow v Norton* [1996] R.P.C. 76 HL.

This means that a prior disclosure (whether this be written or oral, or a prior use, or a disclosure "in any other way") is only novelty-destroying if it conveys sufficient information for the invention to be reproduced from the total information content of that prior disclosure when this is received by the person skilled in the art and understood by him in the light of his common general knowledge at the time. In conformity with this principle, EPO Guideline C–IV, 9.5 states that a chemical compound whose name or formula is stated in a prior document is not to be considered as "known" from it unless the information provided enables that compound to be prepared and separated, or (in the case of a naturally-occurring compound) to be separated. It was this principle which was upheld in *Asahi*), thereby overruling *Gyógyszeripari's Application* [1958] R.P.C. 51, decided under the former law, which had held that a statement of prior existence of a chemical compound destroyed its novelty for subsequent claims, whether or not the skilled person would have then been able to make that compound.

T 977/93 *AMERICAN HOME PRODUCTS/Canine coronavirus* [2001] E.P.O.R. 36 at 274 confirms that the properties of a product are considered not to have been made available to the public if the skilled person has no means of establishing the composition or the internal structure of the product and was not able to reproduce it, in spite of the product being in the hands of the public before the priority date of the patent.

In *Mölnlycke v Brightwake* [2011] EWHC 376 Birss QCheld that in a normal case the court would proceed on the basis that the technical results set out in a document could be achieved as asserted. The case that a prior document is non-enabling must be more than a mere assertion and the pleadings should explain why the document is non-enabling. The pleaded assertions should be supported by evidence, and in some cases experimental evidence may be needed. In the present case the experiments intended to show non-enablement were rejected as contrived, only standard techniques were needed to practise the invention, the parameters to adjust would have been familiar to a skilled person and although it was a borderline case on balance the document relied on was an enabling disclosure.

In *SmithKline Beecham's [PMS] Patent* BL C/24/02; and [2003] R.P.C. 6 at 114 the court held that evidence of experiments to prove that a method described in the earlier application cited under s.2(3) gave the result alleged was admissible. The Court of Appeal agreed, holding that the word "content" in EPC art.54(3) referred to what was taught by the document. If the earlier application taught a process which inevitably produced the product claimed, that product was also taught, was part of the content of the application, and was therefore matter part of the state of the art by virtue of s.2(3). The quality of such matter must be the same whether the document was prior published or taken to be part of the state of the art under s.2(3). The judge was right to conclude that the tests in s.2(2) and (3) of the Act were the same. In reaching this conclusion the Court of Appeal considered EPO decisions including G 2/98 *Requirement for claiming priority of the "same invention"* OJ EPO 2001, 413; [2002] E.P.O.R. 17 at 167 in which it was held that for a valid priority claim the skilled person must be able to derive the subject-matter "directly and unambiguously" from the priority document. In this case it was assumed that the process in the prior application could be carried out and the application would provide proper support for a claim to the process. If so, the product produced by the process must be directly and unambiguously derived from the prior application. Evidence to enable the features of that product to be characterised would be admissible.

In the subsequent substantive revocation proceedings *SmithKline Beecham's [PMS] Patent (No.2)* [2003] R.P.C. 33 at 607, it was held at first instance that there had indeed been anticipation by the earlier application, but on appeal (see [2003] R.P.C. 43 at 769) it was held that because it was not possible to repeat the example of the prior art without modification there were no clear and unmistakable directions to make the claimed compound; therefore the claim could not be invalid for lack of novelty. On further appeal, the House of Lords sub nom. *SmithKline Beecham's PMS Patent* [2006] R.P.C. 10 at 323 emphasised that disclosure and enablement are distinct concepts, each of which has to be satisfied and each of which has its own rules. The role of the person skilled in the art is different in relation to disclosure and enablement. In the case of disclosure, when the matter relied upon as prior art consists of a written description, the skilled person is taken to be trying to understand what the author of the description meant and his common general knowledge forms the background to an exercise in construction. But once the meanings of the prior disclosure and the patent have been determined, the disclosure is either of an invention which, if performed, would infringe the patent, or it is not, and the person skilled in the art has no further part to play. However, for the purpose of enablement, the question is no longer what the skilled person would think the disclosure meant but whether he would be able to work the invention which the court has held it to disclose. In the present case the earlier application disclosed the existence of PMS crystals and claimed that they could be made. The attribution of a wrong IR spectrum was irrelevant to this finding. On enablement, the standards were those laid down, e.g. in *Mentor Corp v Hollister* [1993] R.P.C. 7. The finding at first instance that the skilled person would have tried some other solvent from the range mentioned in the application or forming part of his common general knowledge and would have been able to make PMS crystals within a reasonable time was a finding of fact with which an appellate court should be reluctant to interfere, and the Court of Appeal's rejection of the judge's findings were based on confusion between disclosure and enablement. In the case of a high-tech invention, in testing enablement it may be assumed that the skilled person will have to use his skill, and may have to learn by his mistakes (see Lord Reid's reference to "trial and error" in *Van der Lely v Bamfords* [1963] R.P.C. 61 HL at 71).

The corresponding European patent was considered in T 885/02 *SMITHKLINE BEECHAM/Paroxetine Methanesulfonate*. Here, the claim specified PMS in crystalline form having certain characteristic IR or XRD peaks, which were alleged to provide novelty over an earlier disclosure. However, the EPO was not satisfied that the peaks listed were the relevant peaks for distinguishing between polymorphs of the compound, and concluded that the claimed crystalline form was not distinguishable from that of the earlier disclosure. It also concluded that the earlier disclosure was enabling and the patent was revoked.

To deal with a contention that a prior publication should be discounted because of an allegedly non-enabling character, the Comptroller takes the view that any citation under s.2 should be regarded as an enabling one until the applicant satisfies him to the contrary, see *Toyama's Application* [1990] R.P.C. 555. This, of course, is a difficult task given the logical impossibility of proving a negative proposition, but the applicant must be prepared to put forward some positive evidence of the inability to reproduce the prior disclosure. In that case, the Patents Court granted extra time for the submission of experimental evidence of non-enablement on the appeal, but indicated that allowing new evidence on appeal would in future be a rare concession, see §18.15.

The doctrine of non-enablement has so far been applied mainly to overcome objections raised under s.2(3), or the corresponding EPC art.54(3). In such cases the issue of inventive step over the prior disclosure cannot arise, though the *Asahi* decision firmly takes the view that the same criteria apply in relation to lack of novelty arising under either s.2(2) or (3). Thus, both the *Asahi* and *Genentech* cases, as well as T 206/83 *ICI/Pyridine herbicides* and T 81/87 *COLLABORATIVE/Preprorennin* (above) were cases under s.2(3) or EPC art.54(3). In each it appears that, although the compound mentioned in the prior-dated application could have been made at the priority date of the invention in issue, the method of doing so was not described in it, nor could that compound be made on the basis of the common general knowledge of the skilled person at the time. Consequently, in each case, the compound mentioned in the prior-dated application did not destroy the novelty under the s.2(3) provision of a claim to it.

A prior use also has to be of an enabling nature. It is important to appreciate that, in view of this requirement, the *Asahi* and *Merrell Dow* decisions mean that those who work their invention in public, although in a manner which does not permit the public to reproduce the invention, are at risk of infringing a patent of later date which their prior use will fail to invalidate in view of its non-enabling character, unless that prior user can rely on rights granted by s.64 (for which see the commentary thereon), but this will only be so if that user had carried out his work within the United Kingdom, see Isabel Davies and S. Cohen [1994] E.I.P.R. 239 and §64.05. Other problems arising from an application of the "non-enablement" doctrine were illustrated by M. F. Vivian (1989) 20 I.I.C. 303.

A reference in a published scientific paper to a certain plasmid does not make it available to the public in an enabling manner, a presumed scientific custom of free exchange of such material not being sufficient to overcome a presumption of non-availability free of contractual obligations: T 576/91 *NORTH CAROLINA/Plasmid pTR2030* [1998] E.P.O.R. 382.

Confidentiality

2.10   Matter does not form part of the state of the art if the supply was in circumstance where the recipient was under an obligation of confidence, e.g. because the information was supplied for a limited purpose and the recipient was not entitled to use the information for other purposes, e.g. as was the case in *Saltman Engineering Co Ltd v Campbell Engineering Co Ltd* [1948] 65 R.P.C. 203 and *Suhner & Co AG v Transradio Ltd* [1967] R.P.C. 329 at 333, see also *Quantel v Spaceward Microsytems* [1990] R.P.C. 83. The Patents County Court has held that it is for the party alleging confidentiality to prove that the recipient was not free in law or equity to make use of the information. The obligation of confidence could best be tested by whether the recipient of information of commercial value was bound in conscience not to divulge it to anyone else, see *Kavanagh Balloons v Cameron Balloons* [2004] R.P.C. 5 at 97.

While disclosures truly made in confidential circumstances are not to be regarded as having been "made available to the public", the question is always one of fact or degree. Multiplication of copies, or the nature or position of the person or persons communicated to, may be relevant, see *Weir's Application* (1926) 43 R.P.C. 39. The EPO has ruled that there is no act of publication by the mere submission of a scientific paper for later publication even though the author had signed a release permitting publication: T 842/91 *BILFINGER/Sealing screen* [1999] E.P.O.R. 192; and, until actual publication, the contents of such a paper have been considered to be subject to an obligation of confidence extending also to a referee to whom the paper was submitted for vetting. A document which was marked "confidential" and "not to be disclosed to non-members", but which was sent to members of a trade association for them to use the information in it as they wished has been held to be published, see: *Dalrymple's Application* [1957] R.P.C. 449, and likewise with a document supplied to a salesman for him to distribute see: *Monsanto's (Brignac's) Application* [1971] R.P.C. 153. A document in the library of a learned society, and accessible only to its members, is published provided that there is no fetter on members using the information contained in that document. In *LG Electronics v Sony Europe Ltd & Ors* [2011] EWHC 2319 (Pat) the claimant contended that a "DVD Specification" marked "confidential" was such despite being distributed to a large number of persons, which the defendant sought to establish that all interested parties had the opportunity to gain knowledge of the contents of the document and that that is sufficient as a matter of law for the document to have been made available to the public; moreover, that fact amounted to the contents becoming common general knowledge. The judge refused to adjudicate on the point in an application for summary judgment, citing inter alia the conflicting decision of Floyd J. in *Qualcomm Inc. v Nokia Corp.* [2008] EWHC 3129 (Pat) and T/50/02 *Daikin Industries.* A "private" report which could be purchased by interested parties who had the opportunity of gaining knowledge of its contents for their own purposes was held to be published even if purchasers did not have the right to disseminate the report to third parties, see: T 50/02 *DAIKIN/Pentafluoroethane refrigerant.* The restriction on dissemination was merely to preserve the exclusivity and value of the report for its publisher, not to prevent use for their own purposes by purchasers of the information it contained. A draft standard sent to members of an international standards working party was not confidential and was available to the public since the task of the working party precluded any obligation of confidentiality, see T 202/97 *ERICH JÄGER/Electrical connector*. However, the EPO held that a report marked "confidential" and issued on loan terms to licensees had not been published, even though these licensees included the major manufacturers in the field, see: T 300/86 *RCA/TV receiver* [1994] E.P.O.R. 339.

In T 1619/06 *PLATTE/Spout inhibitors* [2009] E.P.O.R. 32 the parties had entered into a secrecy agreement providing that: "We will treat all information designated as Secret and Confidential in the manner prescribed." It was held that this provision excluded information exchanged between the parties and not marked to be secret and confidential with the effect that it did not need to be kept secret. The agreement left no room for an implicit secrecy obligation for any information not designated as being secret and confidential, and the situation differed from where no secrecy agreement had been entered into and the relationship between the parties exchanging information needed to be considered. The relevant documents did not have a secrecy designation and had therefore been made available to the public.

If the sender and receiver are, in effect, collaborators there is no publication, even if the document is not explicitly said to be confidential, see *Gallay's Application* [1959] R.P.C. 141, see also *Sommer Allibert v Flair Plastics* [1987] R.P.C. 599 where an inter-group communication not intended for, never communicated to and never reaching, a member of the public acting as such was held not to have been made available to the public; and *James Industries' Patent* [1987] R.P.C. 235, following *Gallay's Application* (above), where the sender and recipient of a letter were partners in a joint commercial venture leading to the inference of the existence of an obligation of confidence, despite the absence of an agreement between the parties. Similarly the EPO has held that a letter between contracting firms is implicitly confidential, see T 480/95 *FUSION SYSTEMS CORPORATION/Photoresists*, similarly in T 818/93 *PALMAZ/Expandible intraluminal vascular graft* where the relevant documents were communicated in attempts to obtain grants for research. The general nature of the relationship between the supplier and recipient of an article or of information as such is therefore relevant, see *Strix v Otter* [1995] R.P.C. 607 and T 830/90 *MACOR MARINE SYSTEMS/Secrecy agreement* OJ EPO 1994, 713; [1995] E.P.O.R. 21.

In T 1081/01 *NEW JAPAN CHEMICAL/Acetals* the Board held that if at the time of receipt of the information the recipient was in some special relationship to the donor of the information, then he could not be treated as a member of the public, and the information could not be regarded as published for the purpose of EPC art.54. Even if this special relationship later ceased, so that the recipient was now free to pass on the information, the mere cessation of this special relationship did not make the information available to anyone else. In *Zipher v Markem* [2009] F.S.R. 1; [2008] EWHC 1379 freedom of ex-employees to make use of an internal memorandum of their former employer was considered. It was held that the expression ''made available to the public'' involved more than a state of knowledge in one person's mind even if coupled with freedom to choose when to disclose it: it involved a handing over of (literally a transmission of) knowledge to the public. Although the court did not go so far as to say that the *Acetals* decision was wrong, it doubted its correctness on the basis that:

"The Board's reasoning raises the question of what would happen if a piece of information is disclosed by A to B with a restriction that it must be kept confidential for one hour. Is the legal consequence different from a disclosure without that restriction? One might think this was an odd result."

Subject-matter disclosed orally, e.g. at a lecture which was a private occasion, where an obligation of confidentiality might apply is not available to the public. The disclosure might, for example, be a private communication within a closed circle of persons bound by an obligation of confidentiality, as in T 838/97 *RESEARCH FOUNDATION/ Translational inhibition* where conferences open to up to 100 participants were subject to an explicit restriction that:

"information presented at the conferences is not to be used without the specific authorisation of the individual who makes the contribution, whether in formal presentation or in discussion".

In *Visx v Nidek* [1999] F.S.R. 405, there were allegations of oral disclosures from one scientist to another, but all but one allegation failed as an anticipation either because the court was not satisfied as to what had been actually said, the witnesses not being disinterested parties, or because the disclosures took place in confidential circumstances. The one disclosure upheld was made by a disinterested person giving evidence of his clear recollection and, combined with information published in an important paper in the art, was held to make the claimed subject-matter obvious.

Whether or not a prior use which is not expressly in public is confidential depends on the relationship between the parties, relevant authorities including *Pall v Commercial Hydraulics* [1990] F.S.R. 329; *Strix v Otter* [1995] R.P.C. 607; and *Kavanagh Balloons v Cameron Balloons* [2004] R.P.C. 5. In *Qual-Chem v Corus UK* [2008] EWPCC 1 relevant factors included (a) a long, ongoing, open and honest relationship between the parties, (b) a need for experimental tests to be conducted and the fact that this could only have been done at the defendant's premises, (c) the fact that the trials were devised and supervised by the patentees, (d) the origin of the trials from a practical need on the defendant's part, which need was not in the public domain and was commercially sensitive, and (e) a contention at one time by the defendant that it had a right to be nominated co-applicant for the patent. (The case was appealed but not on these points.)

The EPO has held that an express secrecy agreement is not needed since secrecy may result from the ethical conduct of employees of large corporations, see T 478/99 *INTERTECHNIQUE/Crew oxygen mask*. On the facts in that case the demonstration in question was for the purpose of technical evaluation, not making sales, the device was a prototype, and commercial launch took place three years after the demonstration. In T 782/92 *TOKAI/Dual-type damper* a delivery note evidencing delivery of a small quantity of articles was held to be insufficient evidence to establish that information had been made available to the public thereby; the small quantity of articles delivered was thought to be indicative of a supply in confidential circumstances. The decision was likewise in T 472/92 *SEKISUI/Shrinkable sheet* where the Board was not satisfied that a supply by company A to company B, of which A was a joint owner, had taken place in non-confidential circumstances. Clinical trials of a device whose status is investigational are implicitly confidential, see T 906/01 *DE PUY SPINE/Spinal column retaining apparatus*.

In *MMI v Cellxion* [2009] EWHC 418 the alleged prior use was the supply of a machine and its instruction manuals to the Australian government for evaluation. The defendants relied on T 1022/99 *VAN WONTERGHEM/Dispositif de transmission* where it was held that sale to a single purchaser with no obligation of secrecy towards the vendor was invalidating notwithstanding the fact that the object sold was destined to be incorporated into the purchaser's confidential prototype, and they further argued that in the present case any restrictions were self-imposed. It was held that normally if a piece of equipment was sold outright, there was no obligation of confidence. However, in the present case the relevant manuals were explicitly confidential, and it was held that it would be odd if a different regime applied to the machine itself so that the Australian government was not free to disclose information in the manuals, but could derive the same information from the machine and then disclose it. Therefore the totality of the circumstances implied an obligation of confidence. Furthermore there was no evidence about what a user of the machine could have inferred about its method of operation merely from possession and use. Consideration of additional material in the same case did not lead to any different conclusion, any supply of manuals or a disc being subject to confidentiality under general conditions of sale, see [2011] EWHC 426 (Pat).

Confidentiality in a second sale of a sample was not established in T1464/05 *PRYSMIAN/Hydrogen-absorbing composition* and it was held that the sale made the composition and its properties available to the public. The second sample, although larger than the first, was only sufficient for testing and insufficient for commercial production. However, there was no express secrecy agreement between the parties and no evidence of any special relationship other than that of vendor and purchaser such as a technical cooperation agreement or research and development program. The first small sample had been supplied free of charge, but a charge was made for the second larger sample, and the same product had been offered to three further companies. The sale was held to be a regular and unrestricted commercial transaction, and it was also held to be more likely than not that relevant information about the properties of the sample had been exchanged between the parties.

For a further decision where confidentiality in a sale of samples (throttle valves to a motor vehicle manufacturer) was not established see T 1511/06 *HITACHI/Air flow rate control apparatus*. The patentees argued that in the highly competitive automotive industry a parts manufacturer and a vehicle manufacturer were both interested in maintaining information confidential before production had started. However, in the present case the throttle valves were a generic product of the valve supplier which might be sold to other manufacturers, and although the vehicle manufacturer might have wanted the fact of sale kept secret to avoid leakage of information about its engines, this could not be equated with maintaining secret the constructional details of the throttle valve as such.

The onus of proof is discussed in T 818/93 *PALMAZ/Expandable intraluminal vascular graft*, where it was held that where there is convincing evidence that the circumstances of the relevant communication were confidential, the onus passes to the party endeavouring to prove the contrary.

The state of the art—subs.(3)

Treatment of earlier and later applications for the same subject-matter where the earlier application was still unpublished at the priority or filing date of the later application is governed by subs.3 which provides that the subject-matter is citable against the later application for lack of novelty but not for lack of inventive step. It corresponds to EPC art.54(3) and (4) and art.54(3) of EPC 2000. **2.11**

In *Yeda Research & Development Company v Rhône-Poulenc Rorer* [2007] UKHL 43 Lord Hoffmann pointed out that by s.3(3) the state of the art includes matter contained in a patent application with an earlier priority date. This rule of novelty is the only source, in English law, of the principle that if two people independently make the same invention, the "first to file" is the one entitled to a patent. In s.60(2) EPC the rule is stated expressly in those terms. But the way this principle operates is not by supposing some meta-patent for which the two inventors are in competition and which is awarded to the first to file. The inventor first to file is the one entitled to a patent, not to the patent. The second to file is not entitled to a patent because the invention he claims lacks novelty by virtue of s.2(3); *Synthon BV v Smithkline Beecham Plc* [2005] UKHL 59.

In order to be relevant the subject-matter must indeed to be entitled to an earlier date. It must have been present in the earlier application both as filed and as "published". That term as used in subs.(3) is defined in s.130(5) as meaning published (or deemed to be published) under s.16. A priority document as such is therefore not published in this sense, but merely laid open to public inspection; see *Smith's Patent* BL O/16/86. Further, if an application was filed with a description only but not claims which were added subsequently, then the description forms part of the state of the art under s.2(3) but the claims do not, nor does the abstract, see the *MOPP* at 2.31 and §§5.23 and 76.06.

If priority is claimed in the earlier application then that priority is not established until rr.6, 8 and 9 or the corresponding rules under the PCT or the EPC have been complied with, see the commentary on s.5 and particularly §§5.30-5.32. A claimed priority date that has been lost will be disregarded. Furthermore, if priority is formally available, then as a matter of substance the subject matter must be "supported by matter disclosed in the earlier relevant application, as to which see §5.23.

Only subject-matter published or deemed to be published under s.16 forms part of the state of the art under s.5(3) so that subject-matter in an earlier US application which was published by the USPTO but not elsewhere does not enter the state of the art. Applications which may be relied on under subs.(3) include:

(a) UK applications which have been published under s.16;

(b) International applications for patents designating the UK, published by WIPO under PCT art.21 which have entered the UK national phase (i.e. the relevant fee has been paid and if the application is in a foreign language an English translation has been filed at the UK-IPO, see ss.89(1), 89A(3)(a) and 89(b)(2));

(c) applications for European patents (UK) published by the EPO under EPC art.93; and

(d) International applications for European patents (UK) published by WIPO under PCT art.21 which have entered the European regional phase (i.e. the relevant fee has been paid and if the application is in a language other than English, French or German a translation into one of these languages has been filed at the European Patent Office, see s.79(1), (2)).

Subject-matter enters the state of the art under s.2(3) when an application containing it is published and in the case of an International application when that application has entered the national or regional phase. Once this has happened the subsequent fate of the application is irrelevant. For UK applications, it appears that withdrawal of the application in the period when it has become too late to prevent publication but before publication has actually taken place prevents the application from entering the state of the art, see *Woolard's Application* [2002] R.P.C. 39 at 767; [2002] I.P. & T. 897, over-ruling the decision in *Zbinden's Application* [2002] R.P.C. 13 at 310. The practice in the EPO for applications published prior to entry into force of EPC 2000 (December 13, 2007) was similar so that withdrawal of the entire application or withdrawal of the UK designation prevented the application from entering the state of the art. However, under EPC 2000 art.79(1) all EPC contracting states are automatically designated at the time of filing, and s.78(5A) provides that subsequent withdrawal of a UK designation does not affect the position under s.3, so that all European applications filed under EPC 2000 enter the state of the art under s.2(3) on publication

Subsection (3) specifies that the state of the art comprises the whole contents of (i.e. comprises all matter contained in) an earlier application published on or after the relevant priority date, provided that the matter concerned was contained in the earlier application both as filed and as published and provided it has an earlier priority date. The EPC achieves the same result by treating the priority date as if it were the filing date, see EPC art.89 and applying this date when the application is to be treated as part of the state of the art by virtue of EPC art.54(3).

In *Edwards Lifesciences v Cook Biotech* [2009] EWHC 1304 Pat Ct at [106]–[110] a claimed feature had been disclosed in generic terms but not specifically in an earlier application citable under s.2(3). Although the subsequently claimed embodiment was the most obvious embodiment, the prior disclosure covered other possible embodiments. It was held that the earlier disclosure was insufficient for anticipation. "Anticipation requires prior disclosure of subject matter which, when performed, must necessarily infringe the patent. The distinction between this and obviousness may seem artificial and, on occasion, difficult to draw. But it is a distinction the law demands and is the reason a generic disclosure will not normally take away the novelty of any specific example falling within that disclosure", citing the opinion of Lord Hoffmann in *Synthon v Smithkline Beecham* [2005] UKHL 59 at [23].

Although an application for a European patent (UK) or an international application (UK) having an earlier priority than the invention of an application or patent in suit is part of the state of the art for the purposes of the Act (for the consideration of novelty only), an opposition against a European patent in the EPO cannot be based on a prior national right, as distinct from a prior right arising from a European application, since the former is not part of the "state of the art" under EPC art.54(3), see T 550/88 *MOBIL/National prior right* OJ EPO 1992, 117; [1990] E.P.O.R. 391. Such an issue can be raised only in national revocation proceedings.

An objection under subs.(3) can be raised even after grant by the Comptroller, see s.73(1), as discussed in §73.05.

—Effect of secret applications under subsection (3)

If the publication of a patent application is prohibited under s.22, such an application **2.12** has no effect under subs.(3) unless and until it is eventually published. It will then have a "whole contents" effect as of its filing date and, if relevant, its priority date. However, if any matter is deleted under s.19, the deleted matter will not then have such an effect, and if the application as a whole is abandoned before publication it will have no "whole contents" effect. This leads to the following possibilities:

(i) a patent which is fully anticipated by a secret application may nevertheless remain valid in relation to that anticipation for the whole of its life if the secret application is never declassified and therefore is never published;

(ii) if the secret application is published, the later patent would be valid one day and invalid, with ab initio effect, the next day; or

(iii) the patent might be invalid retrospectively in the event that the publication of the secret application occurs after expiry.

—Excepted disclosures

Subsections (4) and (5) provide exemptions from the law of novelty in respect of matter **2.13** obtained unlawfully or disclosures made in breach of confidence or as regards disclosures made at certain international exhibitions.

—Scope of subsections (4) and (5)

Subsections (4) and (5) correspond to EPC art.55. Subsection (4)(a) and (b), corre- **2.14** sponding to EPC art.55(1)(a), relate to unauthorised disclosure by "obtaining" and/or breach of confidence from the inventor (or from the proprietor (subs.(5)). These provisions have a similarity to s.50(2) of the 1949 Act, and cases in which these have been discussed may therefore be relevant, see: *Tiefebrun's Application* [1979] F.S.R. 97; *Ethyl Corp's Patent* [1966] R.P.C. 205; and *Chemithon's Patent* [1966] R.P.C. 365. In the *Chemithon* case it seems to have been suggested that the court could in a suitable case restrain an applicant for revocation from relying on matters prejudicial to validity which had arisen as the result of a breach of confidence.

The provisions of subss.(4) and (5) should be relied upon only in those cases where no alternative exists, as the exceptions which they provide are limited in scope. In particular, the six-month grace period under subs.(4) is expressed to be reckoned back from the actual filing date of the application in suit and not from any claimed priority date, whether foreign or domestic. In G 03/98 *UNIVERSITY PATENTS/Six-month period* OJ EPO 2001, 62; [2001] E.P.O.R. 33 at 249, the EPO Enlarged Board of Appeal decided that the six months' grace period under EPC art.55(1) applies in respect of the date of filing of the application in the EPO, and not from the priority date, thereby over-ruling the first instance EPO decision in T 735/91 *PASSONI/Stand structure* [1992] E.P.O.R. 79.

Rule 111(5) (reprinted in §123.39) deals with the calculation of the grace period in cases which involve excluded days under s.120 or r.111(1); and r.111(6) (likewise reprinted) provides for an extension of the six months' period under subs.(4) upon a failure or undue delay in the postal services, as discussed in §§123.78 and 123.79.

—Disclosures in breach of confidence

Although subss.(4)(a) and (b) are supposed (by s.130(7)) to be in accord with EPC **2.15** art.55(1)(a), the latter refers to "an evident abuse" rather than to an unlawful act or a breach of confidence. Under the European wording, erroneous early publication of a foreign patent application by a government agency is not necessarily an "evident abuse": what is apparently important then is the state of mind of the abuser, see T 585/92 *UNILEVER/Deodorant detergent* OJ EPO 1996, 129; [1996] E.P.O.R. 579 where, under such test, the early erroneous publication of a Brazilian patent application was not excused. *Microsonics' Application* [1984] R.P.C. 29 indicates that a breach of confidence cannot be relied upon to exempt a prior disclosure under subs.(4) unless evidence is provided which establishes that, in all probability, a breach had occurred. In T 173/83 *TELECOMMUNICATIONS/Antioxidant* OJ EPO 1987, 465; [1988] E.P.O.R. 133 the EPO stated that there would be a disclosure in breach of confidence if a third party failed to honour a declaration of mutual trust linking him to the inventor, or if a third party acted in such a way as to cause harm to a person from whom he had received information which he was authorised to communicate to others, though in this case no breach of confidence was held to have occurred. A case where it has been held that prior disclosure was made by the applicants for the purpose of consultation and on the clear understanding that the recipient would treat the information as confidential is *Riekie and Simpfendorfer v McGrath* [Australia] (1987) 7 I.P.R. 120. M.G. Harman has raised some intriguing questions on the position when disclosure occurs in circumstances where any subsequent publication would be unlawful (1986–87) 16 *CIPA* 369.

In a decision concerning registered designs, the question whether a disclosure had taken place in circumstances of confidence (other than in terms of a contract) was held to depend on the subjective unspoken views of the parties, since an equitable obligation of confidence was involved and "equity looks at the conscience of the individual": *Carflow Products v Linwood Securities* [1996] F.S.R. 424.

In *Stanelco Fibre Optics v Bioprogress* [2005] R.P.C. 15 at 319 the court held that Bioprogress employees had conceived of an idea and were the inventors even though they were not responsible for actually putting the idea into practice and showing that it worked. Bioprogress disclosed the core inventive concept to Stanelco and there had been a misuse of that confidential information, to Bioprogress' detriment, when Stanelco used it as the basis for its own patent applications. An action for breach of confidence accordingly succeeded.

—Disclosures at international exhibitions

2.16   Subsection (4)(c) and r.5, for which see above, (made under s.130(2)) correspond to EPC art.55(1)(b) and (2) and concern disclosure at, or in consequence of, display by the inventor (or proprietor, subs.(5)) at an international exhibition. To take advantage of these provisions an applicant must so declare at the time of filing the application and provide an appropriate certificate within four months thereafter, see r.5(2) and §2.02.

The term "international exhibition" is defined in s.130(1) by reference to "the Convention on International Exhibitions". This term is also defined in s.130(1) as the Convention signed in Paris on November 22, 1928 (which was last revised on November 30, 1972), as amended or supplemented by any protocol to that convention which is for the time being in force. Only very large international exhibitions can qualify (*Patents Journal* February 23, 1977) and for further information on the requirements for such qualification, see A. C. Serjeant (1985–86) 15 *CIPA* 319 and §2.28.

Unless the Convention on International Exhibitions provides otherwise, the designation of an exhibition as an "international" one must, apparently, precede the opening of that exhibition if the protection of subs.(4)(c) is to be obtained for the reasons given (under the Registered Designs Act 1949 (c.88) s.6(2)) in *Mod-Tap v BI Communications* [1999] R.P.C. 33 3. The words "in consequence of" exclude reliance on the provision where publication occurs in a catalogue of the exhibition which becomes available to the public before the opening of the exhibition (*Steel's Application* [1958] R.P.C. 411).

The Patent Office does not appear to publish a list of International Exhibitions which it will recognise for the purposes of s.2(4)(c), but the EPO does publish notifications of recognition of such exhibitions under the corresponding EPC art.55(1)(b): see e.g. OJ EPO 1979, 159; OJ EPO 1981, 221; OJ EPO 1986, 43; OJ EPO 1987, 86; OJ EPO 1988, 159;

OJ EPO 1989, 156; OJ EPO 1990, 183; OJ EPO 1991, 240; OJ EPO 1992, 202; OJ EPO 1993, 266; OJ EPO 1994, 276; OJ EPO 1995, 270; OJ EPO 1996, 246; OJ EPO 1997, 190; and OJ EPO 1998, 230, see also the *European Patents Handbook* ("EPH") (London, Sweet & Maxwell) at s.58.9.1.

Comparison of earlier disclosed matter and subsequently claimed matter

—*The UK approach to construction of a prior art document*

While inventive step and sufficiency fall to be judged as at the priority date for an invention, novelty is a question of fact which falls strictly to be judged against the date when the alleged novelty-destroying document was published or the alleged prior use occurred. It is thus important that a prior art document is read as it would have been at the date when it was made available, and without regard to the patent in suit or any other subsequent information, see: *General Tire v Firestone* [1972] R.P.C. 457 at 484 CA; *Minnesota Mining v Bondina* [1973] R.P.C. 491; T 677/91 *ICI/Emulsion polymer* [1997] E.P.O.R. 480; and T 694/91 *TEKTRONIX/Schottky barrier diode* [1995] E.P.O.R. 384. It is, of course, possible that the person skilled in the art would, at a later date, read the prior art document in a different way from that at its date of publication, but that is then a question of obviousness. **2.17**

In *Schlumberger Holdings v Electromagnetic Geoservices* [2010] EWCA Civ 819 a reference was difficult to understand and the defendants submitted that it should be read as a two-part document, the first part being intelligible and anticipating the invention. They put to the patentee's witness a redacted document with the difficult passages omitted, but the witness refused to accept the notion of cutting out the relevant passages because he was of the view that they concerned essential aspects of the teaching and that it was not legitimate to cherry-pick the document. The court of appeal held that this approach was correct, and that the reference was a single disclosure which a notional skilled person should take as he found it.

In construing the prior art document as of its date of publication, ex post facto analysis of the content of that document is inadmissible, see *Glaverbel v British Coal* [1994] R.P.C. 443 at 505; and [1995] R.P.C. 255 CA. In *Hewlett Packard v Waters* [2002] EWCA Civ 612 the court accepted the correctness of a submission that it is its task to determine what the prior art: "clearly and distinctly taught the skilled person at the priority date, not what can be read out of [it] by the application of hermeneutical stress", which "admirable phrase" was said to concisely describe "the process of squeezing a document to extract every last drop of meaning". The decision on novelty was upheld on appeal, see [2002] EWCA Civ 612.

In *Merz v Allergan* [2006] EWHC 2686 Pat Ct, the invention concerned a Swiss-form claim to the use of the neurotoxic component of botulinum toxin for making a medicament for treating pain associated with muscle contracture. The patentees argued that the claim was limited to the use of the neurotoxic component alone, and stripped of associated proteins, otherwise it would read on what was expressly described in the specification as being old. However, the court pointed out that the invention as claimed was a novel use of the neurotoxic component for relieving pain, and what was acknowledged in the prior art was the use of the compounds for the relief of spasm, not pain. Accordingly, the force of the patentee's argument that the claim should be construed so as to avoid covering acknowledged prior art was much diminished. An earlier patent citable only under s.2(3) of the Act and disclosing a combination of at least two toxins fell within and therefore anticipated the subsequent claim.

Where a document cited as a prior publication is susceptible of two possible interpretations, the onus of proof is on an applicant for revocation to establish what is the correct disclosure, i.e. whether there truly is an anticipatory disclosure, see *James Industries' Patent* [1987] R.P.C. 235. Therefore, in ex parte proceedings, an applicant should be given the benefit of the doubt in such a circumstance.

A disclosure includes implicit features, see e.g. *Smoothysigns v Metro Products* BL C/57/95; [1995] E.I.P.R. D–289 in which it was contended, unsuccessfully, that the means of attachment specified should be construed as the sole such means. Likewise, in *Monsanto v Merck* [2000] R.P.C. 709 where a prior disclosure of a chemical formula which did not specify the position of a named substituent was held either to deprive of novelty, or render obvious (for which see §3.10), the compound with that substituent in the position which was the easiest of the class to prepare.

Evidence can be adduced to show what a document conveyed at its date of publication to a person skilled in the art. For example, in *Van der Lely v Bamfords* [1961] R.P.C. 296 CA and [1963] R.P.C. 61 HL it was held that a person skilled in the art could interpret a photograph and give evidence as to features that were not explicitly shown but which he could deduce and which were therefore implicitly disclosed to him. The interpretation of a technical drawing is (as with a photograph) a matter for expert evidence, see *BSH Industries' Patents* [1995] R.P.C. 183, to be decided on the balance of probabilities. Where a device illustrated in the prior art is reconstructed with a view to experiments being carried out to demonstrate that that device works in the same way as a later claimed device, it is important that such reconstruction be carried out on the same scale and without use of any later information, particularly that derived from the alleged infringement, see *Dyson v Hoover* [2001] R.P.C. 26 at 473. In *Inhale Therapeutics v Quadrant* [2002] R.P.C. 21 at 419, it was also held that, if a piece of prior art describes clearly a process or product, it is not enough for the patentee to hint that it might not work or have the properties asserted for it. If the assertion is that the prior art is in error in its description of what it has produced, it is for the party asserting the error to prove it. In relation to another piece of prior art the judge said:

"Just as it is no defence to infringement for the infringer to say he did not know that he had the features of the claim in his product, so it is no answer to an allegation of anticipation that no-one would have realised that the article or process described in, or obtained from, the prior art had the features of the claim".

Drawings in a patent specification should not be construed as scale drawings unless this is clearly indicated, see *Hadley Industries v Metal Sections* [1998] EWHC Patents 284, but scale could be inferred from an industry standard, see §14.23.

In *Gemstar TV-Guide v Virgin Media* [2011] EWCA Civ. 302, Jacob L.J. in rejecting a suggested meaning for a prior art document which he said made no technical sense added the following statement of general principle:

"One has to consider how they [i.e. cited items of prior art] would be understood on their date of publication ... by the notional person skilled in the art. There is no reason why such a person, just as in the case of a real person, *must* find a meaning. *In real life there are documents which have no clear meaning*, documents so obscure that one throws up one's hands saying 'I have no idea what this author was really trying to say.' The notional skilled reader can do likewise, and if he or she does, the document is not novelty-destroying. It is not 'clear and unambiguous,' per Jacob LJ in *Schlumberger Holdings Ltd v Electromagnetic Geoservices AS* [2010] EWCA Civ 819 at [163] – [165]."

—The EPO approach to construction when deciding on novelty

2.18   When deciding on the novelty of the subject-matter of a claim, its broadest technically meaningful interpretation should be taken into account; see T 79/96 *APV ANHYDRO/ Granulation by spray drying* and T 686/96 *CROSFIELD/Precipitated silicas*. The description cannot be construed to restrict the subject-matter of a claim which is in itself technically meaningful, see T 787/04 *DENTSPLY/Orthodontic appliances*.

Guideline C–IV, 9.1 points out that a mosaic must not be made of separate items of prior art. However, the disclosure of one document can be read together with that of another document if that the latter is sufficiently cross-referenced in it so as to form an integral part of its total disclosure, see T 153/85 *AMOCO/Alternative claims* [1988] E.P.O.R. 116, abridged OJ EPO 1988, 1.

The disclosure of a document has to be considered as a whole and not only on the basis of individual examples or embodiments. It is the overall disclosure that the skilled person can unambiguously take from a document which is decisive for establishing whether such disclosure is novelty destroying or not. That means that, when examining novelty, different passages of a single document may be combined provided that there are no reasons that would prevent a skilled person from making such a combination. In general the technical teaching of examples may be combined with that disclosed elsewhere in the same document, e.g. in the description of a patent document, provided that the example concerned is indeed representative for the general technical teaching disclosed in the respective document, see T 12/81 *BAYER/Diastereoisomers* at [7] and T 332/87 *SCOTT BADER/ Ceramic tile adhesives* [1991] E.P.O.R. 575. In the latter case the claimed subject-matter was distinguished from a composition exemplified in a prior art document by the presence of a filler that according to the description of the same prior art document could be added to all of the compositions exemplified and lack of novelty was established. For a contrary example where an argument based on cherry-picking only some examples then making a further selection from the general teaching of the document did not succeed see T 1630/07 *UNILEVER/fabric conditioner*. It is not legitimate to draw features pertaining to separate embodiments in order to create artificially a particular embodiment that would destroy novelty; see T 0305/87 *DIENER/Shear* and T 1722/06 *KSI/Communications localisation system*. Thus, a general statement contained in a prior art document cannot be combined with a specific statement which the skilled reader would not have read in combination with it, see T 291/85 *BAYER/Catalyst* OJ EPO 1988, 302; [1988] E.P.O.R. 371. Where the document contains a reasoned statement dissuading its reader from doing certain acts, novelty can reside as regards those acts but the claims must be limited thereto, see T 26/85 *TOSHIBA/Thickness of magnetic layers*. The EPO does not regard a document as disclosing claimed parameters unless it is shown that these are inevitably obtained by following its disclosure, see T 103/86 *DU PONT/Phenylenediamine* [1987] E.P.O.R. 265.

In assessing the contents of a prior document, the usual interpretation rules apply, i.e. taking the normal grammatical meaning and giving the words their usual meaning in the relevant art unless another meaning is clearly intended (EPO Guideline C–III, 4.2). In assessing novelty, a prior art document must be read as a whole in relation to the invention described and its technical teaching is to be considered in the light of its "total information content", whether explicitly or impliedly stated, see T 666/89 *UNILEVER/Washing composition* OJ EPO 1993, 495; [1992] E.P.O.R. 501. The achievement of a particular technical effect is neither a prerequisite for novelty nor can it confer novelty; its existence can merely serve to confirm a finding of novelty already achieved, a purposive selection being distinct from a mere arbitrary selection and permitting the inference that what is involved is a new invention and not a mere embodiment of an existing invention, see T 666/89 and T 198/84 *Hoechst/Thiochloroformates*.

EPO Guideline C-IV 9.1 proceeds to warn that the teaching of a document does not embrace well-known equivalents which are not disclosed in the document, that being a question of obviousness. Guideline C–IV, 9.5 then states that: "[A] generic prior disclosure does not usually take away the novelty of any specific example falling within the terms of that disclosure, but a specific prior disclosure does take away the novelty of a generic claim embracing that disclosure", aspects which are discussed below at 2.1*.

In the case of a published document, the lack of novelty may be apparent from what is explicitly stated in the document itself: alternatively, it may be implicit in that, in carrying out the teaching of the document, a skilled person would inevitably arrive at a result falling within the terms of the claim, see EPO Guideline C–V, 9.6. The interpretation of a claim for these purposes should be such as to disregard non-distinctive characteristics such as a statement of purpose (see EPO Guidelines C–III, 4.13 and C–IV, 9.7), but on this point see §2.15.

The limitations of what can be said to have been an implicit disclosure are apparent from T 1523/07 *NIPPON SHOKUBAI/Washing a device*. The patent in issue required rinsing subsequent to washing until the pH of the waste water was not more than 9. This feature had not explicitly been disclosed in a citation. However, opponents submitted evidence that it was implicit since even a trainee chemist would have realised that after an alkali wash, rinsing should be continued until the alkali had been removed. The Appeal Board held that implicit disclosure covered no more than the clear and unambiguous consequences of what had been disclosed: here rinsing with water did not inevitably mean that the specified pH in the waste water was obtained, this being the result of the amount of water used and the intensity of rinsing, as to which the citation was silent. Accordingly lack of novelty had not been established. Lack of novelty was also held not to have been established for similar reasons in T 221/05 *ALBEMARLE/Halogen exchange reactions*.

A prior art document must not be read with hindsight, i.e. with a knowledge of the invention, to deprive it of novelty; see T 125/89 S*COTT PAPER/Release coating* [1992] E.P.O.R. 41 and T 1967/08 *Medinol/Flexible expandible stent*. Also, a document published after the priority date cannot be used to interpret a prior-published summary of it, see T 507/89 *CELANESE/Polybutylene terephthalate* [1992] E.P.O.R. 229. However, post-priority documents can sometimes be used as evidence of the content of pre-priority disclosures, see T 316/86 *NILED/Electrical connecting apparatus* [1990] E.P.O.R. 217.

Subject-matter which is "reconditely submerged" in a cited prior document is not made available to the public, see T 666/89 *UNILEVER/Washing composition*; and a document makes its technical teaching available to the public only to the extent that the skilled person would seriously have contemplated applying that teaching in a particular area, see T 26/85 *TOSHIBA/Thickness of magnetic layers* OJ EPO 1990, 22; [1990] E.P.O.R. 267. In T 450/89 *ENTHONE/Electroless plating*, a cited document contained no more than an obscure and self-contradictory reference to a possibility of there being an outer coating of nickel and, no anticipation was found, because: "a conclusion of lack of novelty ought not to be reached unless the prior document contains a clear and unmistakable disclosure of the subject-matter of the subsequent invention".

Thus, where a disclosure in a prior art document could accidentally fall within the wording of a claim, a particularly careful comparison needs to be made between what can fairly be considered to fall within the wording of the claim and what is effectively shown in the document, see T 161/82 *AMP/Electrical contact* OJ EPO 1984, 551, where the novelty of the claimed invention was upheld over an alleged chance anticipation. However, where a prior art product could, and apparently often was, made in the configuration later claimed, a lack of novelty was established, see T 601/92 *SIEMENS/Radialventilator* although it is submitted that that decision ought to have been made as one of lack of inventive step, as in *Lubrizol v Esso* [1997] R.P.C. 195, abridged; and [1998] R.P.C. 727, not available in a case falling within EPC art.54(3) (corresponding to subs.(3).

Parts of a document may not be arbitrarily isolated to derive a technical teaching which is distinct from, or even in contradiction with, the integral teaching of, the whole document, see T 56/87 *SCANDITRONIX/Ion chamber* OJ EPO 1990, 188; [1990] E.P.O.R. 352: see also T 356/89 *FORD/Novelty* [1990] E.P.O.R. 370, where the drawings of the citation could not be taken in isolation. However, features in a prior art drawing are part of the state of the art when a person skilled in the art is able to derive a technical teaching from it, but dimensions obtained merely by measuring a diagrammatic representation in a prior patent specification do not form part of the art as no skilled person would rely upon dimensions so obtained, see T 204/83 *CHARBONNAGES/Venturi* OJ EPO 1985, 310; [1986] E.P.O.R. 1. Also, the EPO has accepted novelty for achieving success in a prior-disclosed uncompleted experiment, see T 694/92 *MYCOGEN/Modifying plant cells* OJ EPO 1997, 408; [1998] E.P.O.R. 114, although in the circumstances this result seems to have been a mere discovery (T.W. Roberts, [1998] E.I.P.R. N–18).

—The general test for anticipation

2.19   UK law does not permit a finding of anticipation based on a "mosaic" of prior disclosures, and the claimed subject-matter must be compared individually and in turn with each disclosure, see *Von Heyden v Neustadt* (1880) 50 L.J.Ch 126 at 128.

After it has been determined what matter is contained in the state of the art, the test for anticipation of claimed subject-matter by a disclosure of earlier date has been stated to be the same under the 1977 Act as under the former statutes, see *Helitune v Stewart Hughes* [1991] R.P.C. 78; [1991] F.S.R. 171 and *Merrell Dow v Norton* [1994] R.P.C. 1; and [1995] R.P.C. 233 CA. That test has been authoritatively stated by Sachs L.J. in *General Tire v Firestone* [1972] R.P.C. 457 at 485–486 in the following terms:

"When the prior inventor's publication and the patentee's claim have respectively been construed by the court in the light of all properly admissible evidence as to technical matters, the meaning of words and expressions used in the art and so forth, the question whether the patentee's claim is new for the purposes of section 32(1)(e) [1949 Act] falls to be decided as a question of fact. If the prior inventor's publication contains a clear description of, or clear instructions to do or make, something that would infringe the patentee's claim if carried out after the grant of the patentee's patent, the patentee's claim will have been shown to lack the necessary novelty, that is to say, it will have been anticipated. The prior inventor, however, and the patentee may have approached the same device from different starting points and may for this reason, or it may be for other reasons, have so described their devices that it cannot be immediately discerned from a reading of the language which they have respectively used that they have discovered in truth the same device; but if carrying out the directions contained in the prior inventor's publication will inevitably result in something being made or done which, if the patentee's patent were valid, would constitute an infringement of the patentee's claim, this circumstance demonstrates that the patentee's claim has in fact been anticipated.

If, on the other hand, the prior publication contains a direction which is capable of being carried out in a manner which would infringe the patentee's claim, but would be at least as likely to be carried out in a way which would not do so, the patentee's claim will not have been anticipated, although it may fail on the ground of obviousness. To anticipate the patentee's claim the prior publication must contain clear and unmistakeable directions to do what the patentee claims to have invented: *Flour Oxidizing Co Ltd v Carr & Co Ltd* (1908) 25 RPC 428 at p. 457, line 34, approved in *British Thomson-Houston Co Ltd v Metropolitan Vickers Electrical Co Ltd* (1928) 45 RPC 1 at p. 24, line 1. A signpost, however clear, upon the road to the patentee's invention will not suffice. The prior inventor must be clearly shown to have planted his flag at the precise destination before the patentee."

From the above statement, three attributes of an earlier disclosure that must be present for it to anticipate later-claimed subject-matter may be discerned. These are:

(a) Completeness, each and every feature of the claimed subject-matter being present in the earlier disclosure. The requirement of completeness is alluded to by the metaphor of planting a flag at the precise destination before the patentee (although sometimes the same metaphor is also used in relation to certainty), and by the suggested test that what infringes if subsequent to the relevant date anticipates if earlier than the relevant date.

(b) Certainty, there being no tolerance for doubt or ambiguity. The requirement of certainty is signalled by references to "clear instructions", "clear and unmistakeable directions to do what the patentee has invented" and "inevitable result".

(c) Substance, the earlier disclosure being in reality the same as the subsequently claimed matter, notwithstanding any differences of description or language that lack technical significance.

The infringement/anticipation test remains in the forefront of most decisions on anticipation. For example, in *Synthon BV v Smithkline Beecham Plc* Lord Hoffmann observed:

"Although it is sometimes said that there are two forms of anticipatory disclosure: a disclosure of the patented invention itself and a disclosure of an invention which, if performed, would necessarily infringe the patented invention (see, for example, Laddie J in *Inhale Therapeutic Systems Inc v Quadrant Healthcare Plc* [2002] RPC 21 at para 43) they are both aspects of a single principle, namely that anticipation requires prior disclosure of subject-matter which, when performed, must necessarily infringe the patented invention."

Insofar as it adds anything to the requirement for completeness, that addition is to be found in an implicit direction to interpret the language of the claim under consideration having regard to the principles of construction explained in the commentary on s.125, below or before the EPO.

As decided in *Asahi's Application* [1991] R.P.C. 485 HL, the test of novelty applicable for the purposes of subs.(3) is no different from that under subs.(2). Thus, anything disclosed in the relevant prior application must be taken into account under subs.(3), just as under subs.(2), see *Szucs' Application* BL O/34/89 and BL C/24/90, noted I.P.D. 13168. For this purpose the unpublished application will be deemed to have been published on the priority date of the later invention and its contents interpreted in the light of the common general knowledge in the art at that time, see *Genentech's [Human Growth Hormone] Patent* [1989] R.P.C. 613. However, the EPO has differently held that the date at which a prior-dated, but unpublished, application should be read is its own filing (or priority) date, so that it is only the common general knowledge then possessed by the skilled person which can be used to interpret it, see T 233/90 *KONICA/Magnetic recording medium*. In *Konica* the Board held in the case of a prior document under art.54(3) where there is a reference to a "usual manner" of preparing a product, it is permissible to use documents of reference such as handbooks, encyclopaedias or dictionaries in order to determine what the skilled person would have understood by such a reference on the effective date of the prior document.

The test for lack of novelty under subs.(3) (where an artificial line has to be drawn and obviousness cannot be considered) has been stated to be whether the specific embodiment described in the prior-dated priority document of an earlier application would fall within the claims in question, see *Beloit v Valmet* [1995] R.P.C. 705, where certain claims were held to lack novelty. A prior application falling to be considered under s.2(3) is novelty-destroying "if it explicitly teaches something within the claim or, as a practical matter, that is what the skilled man would see it as teaching him", see *Hoechst Celanese v BP Chemicals [Carbonylation]* [1998] F.S.R. 586, although here no anticipation was found because the teaching of the document was no more than "a cryptic signpost" to the claimed invention.

The test applied by the EPO is in essentials the same as that applied by the UK-IPO and courts. EPO Guideline C–IV, 9.2 states that: "A document takes away the novelty of any claimed subject-matter derivable directly and unambiguously from that document including any features implicit to a person skilled in the art in what is expressly mentioned in the document", a statement which has often been quoted in EPO decisions as the bedrock of the EPO criteria for assessment of lack of novelty, see e.g. T 450/89 *ENTHONE/ Electroless plating* [1994] E.P.O.R. 326.

EPO Guideline C–IV, 9.1 points out that a mosaic must not be made of separate items of prior art, unless, of course, the relevant documents are referenced to each other and would be read by the skilled person as one document. The above test is consistent with that set out in the EPO Guideline C–IV, 9.2, that a document anticipates any claimed subject-matter derivable directly and unambiguously from that document including any features that are implicit to a person skilled in the art from what has been expressly disclosed, but not including well-known equivalents which are a matter of obviousness. A convenient summary of the approach adopted by the EPO is contained in T 589/01 *PROCTOR & GAMBLE/Artificial tanning compositions* in the context of whether a feature could be inferred directly and unequivocally from an earlier disclosure as follows:

"According to the consistent case law of the boards of appeal, a document that is part of the state of the art under Article 54(2) or 54(3) EPC only constitutes anticipation if that document reveals all the features of the subject-matter claimed — not just the essential ones — directly and unmistakably. The disclosure also covers technical features which are not expressly mentioned in that document but which, for the person skilled in the art, are clearly and unambiguously implied by its content (see e.g. T 0059/87 published in OJ EPO, 1991, 561; T 0450/89 of 15 October 1991; T 0677/91 of 3 November 1991; T 0465/92 published in OJ EPO 1996, 32; T 0511/92 of 27 May 1993; and in general 'Case Law of the Boards of Appeal of the European Patent Office', 4th edition, 2001, I.C.2.)

As for the appellant's assertions concerning the implicit prior description of the claimed artificial tanning composition in the state of the art according to [a citation], it should be noted as a preliminary point that features which are not expressly mentioned in a prior-art document, such as in the present case both features (a) and (b), could only be considered as implicitly disclosed if they were directly and unequivocally derivable from that particular document. According to the consistent case law of the boards of appeal, when assessing novelty, the disclosure of a particular prior document must always be considered in isolation; in other words it is only the actual content of a document (as understood by a skilled man) which destroys novelty. It is not permissible to 'combine' separate items of prior art together (see e.g. T 0153/85, OJ EPO 1988, 1; and in general "Case Law of the Boards of Appeal of the European Patent Office", 4th edition, 2001, I.C.3). This general principle not only applies to explicit features but must apply with all the more justification if a feature is to be considered as implicit in what is explicitly disclosed in a particular single prior art document.

The disclosure of [the cited document] is determined by what knowledge and understanding can and may be expected of the average skilled reader in the technical field in question, when reading that disclosure in isolation (T 164/92, OJ EPO 1995, 305, corr. OJ EPO 1995, 387; T 0582/93 of 23 June 1994). The skilled person's function in the examination of novelty is limited to an individual comparison. He may only compare the filed invention with one citation at time. In addition, the skilled person may not automatically combine or link details from a citation. Considerations that go beyond this narrow examination of novelty are to be included in the examination of inventive step pursuant to Article 56 EPC (see e.g. T 0181/82, OJ EPO 1984, 401; T 0195/84, OJ EPO, 1986, 121; T 0572/88 of 27 February 1991)."

The EPO has held that, in order to mitigate the harshness of the "whole contents" approach and reduce the risk of "self-collision", a strict approach to lack of novelty arising from citations available only under EPC art.54(3) should be adopted and, therefore, a prior specification does not comprise other features which are "equivalent" to the features according to the claims, see T 167/84 *NISSAN/Fuel injector valve* OJ EPO 1987, 369; [1987] E.P.O.R. 344.

As regards features which are implicit within a written description, the Enlarged Appeal Board explained in G 2/88 *MOBIL/Friction reducing additive*:

"In each such case, however, a line must be drawn between what is in fact made available, and what remains hidden or otherwise has not been made available. In this connection the distinction should also be emphasised between lack of novelty and lack of inventive step: information equivalent to a claimed invention may be 'made available' (lack of novelty), or may not have been made available but obvious (novel, but lack of inventive step), or not made available and not obvious (novel and inventive). Thus, in particular, what is hidden may still be obvious."

A reference which is the closest prior art from the standpoint of novelty may also be the most promising starting point for an objection of lack of inventive step. It is, however, a matter of experience that this is often not the case, especially by the classic case of an "accidental anticipation" by a casual, though novelty-destroying, disclosure, see *Molins v Industrial Machinery* (1937) 54 R.P.C. 94 and (1938) 55 R.P.C. 31, see also §3.06.

It should be borne in mind that warnings against combining the disclosures of different documents apply only where the claimed features constitute a single invention and not one or more distinct inventions arbitrarily grouped together, see also §3.11. In *Dowling's Application* BL O/83/06, the claimed invention concerned a sofa-bed whose frame was entirely contained in a filling material and whose arms were movable to a second position where they rested on the floor and became legs. The Patent Office held that this was a mere juxtaposition of features without any difficulty in combining them, and therefore related to two separate inventions as set out in *SABAF v MFI and Meneghetti* [2005] R.P.C. 10 at 208; [2004] UKHL 45. Each feature should therefore be considered in turn applying the tests for patentability to them individually. That approach followed logically from *SABAF* and, in the present case, both inventions failed the test of novelty.

—Completeness as a necessary attribute of anticipation

2.20   Absence of a single feature is sufficient to avoid a finding of anticipation. For example, In *Flour Oxidizing v Carr* (1908) 25 R.P.C. 428 at 455, the patentability of a novel method of operating an old machine was upheld, it not being sufficient to prove that this machine could have been used in the new way, but rather it had to be shown that clear and unmistakable instructions had been provided to operate the machine in the manner claimed. In *Hickman v Andrews* [1983] R.P.C. 147, the prior art was held not to describe a "workbench" though all the other features of the claim were described in it. Also, in T 617/90 *AIR PRODUCTS/Cryogenic liquid dispenser* [1994] E.P.O.R. 396, a claim to an article "for" performing a type of operation was held to possess novelty over a similar article designed for a different operation, both operations being differentiated by those skilled in the art. However, a broader formulation of the test is to be found *Dow Chemical v Spence Bryson* [1984] R.P.C. 359 CA, where it was stated (at p.399) that:

> "a skilled technician, after considering [the cited document], would have been able to produce without anything more than ordinary workshop methods of trial and error a foam rubber which would have infringed claim 1 of the patent in suit."

The invention in *Tate & Lyle Technology Ltd v Manon Frères* [2009] EWHC 1312 Pat Ct was the use of maltotriol to modify or control the form of maltitol crystals. The teaching of the patent was that maltotriol was the sole determinant of crystal habit and it was held that the novelty of the patent should be determined on its own terms. In the prior art selecting the maltotriol content of the syrup used would have controlled crystal habit even if it was not known that it would have that effect. The patentees had explained why maltitol crystals had the habit which they did but had not added anything else to the stock of human knowledge. The prior art had been unknowingly using the invention just as in Molière's play *Le Bourgeois Gentilhomme* Monsieur Jourdain had for more than 40 years been speaking prose without knowing that fact. The claimed subject-matter was therefore not novel and claimed an unpatentable discovery, see also §1.10.

In *Cranway v Playtech* [2009] EWHC 1588 Pat Ct it was argued that if a known product had feature X and a skilled person examining it would assume that it had feature Y then because of the presence of feature X then both X and Y had been disclosed even though the product in reality did not have feature Y. This argument was rejected and it was held that if the product contained X but not Y, then Y had not been disclosed irrespective of how confidently a skilled person believed that it did.

A claim to substances used as alternatives was alleged in T 312/04 *PHILIPS/Reactive ion etching* to have been anticipated by a table in a prior document which when considered in isolation apparently disclosed the use of these substances as alternatives. However, elsewhere in the document the use of mixtures of them were disclosed. The Board emphasised that it was not legitimate to consider part of a document in isolation and that each part must be construed in the light of the document as a whole in order to derive its true meaning.

An isolated nucleic acid molecule having a polynucleotide sequence encoding for Neutrokine-α was claimed in T 18/09 *HUMAN GENOME SCIENCES/Neutrokine*. Opponents alleged that clones in the IMAGE consortium which were publicly available could have been analysed and the claimed sequence could have been found, so that the sequence was available to the public, citing G 1/92 *PRESIDENT'S REFERENCE/ Availability to the public* [1993] E.P.O.R. 241. However, the relevant clones had no assigned role and were only present in a collection of 540,000 such clones within the TNF super-family. Although they had been given identification numbers and could be ordered by anyone who wished, there was nothing which would have lead a skilled person in a straightforward manner to these identification numbers and the corresponding clones, and the situation therefore differed from that in G 1/92. There was no indexed information of the nature or properties of the clones which would have rendered them accessible to the public, and their mere existence in a large collection could not be seen as an implicit disclosure. This conclusion was in line with normal practice to consider the deposition of a strain of a plasmid as disclosing only the plasmid in toto but not specific recombinant sequences which are recognised later on, see T 301/87 *BIOGEN/Recombinant DNA* [1990] E.P.O.R. 190.

The novelty of one of the stereospecific forms of a chemical compound previously described as an equal mixture of such forms was upheld by the EPO in T 296/87 *HOECHST/Enantiomers* OJ EPO 1990, 195; [1990] E.P.O.R. 337 but it was held to lack an inventive step. In *Generics (UK) Ltd v Daiichi Pharmaceutical Co Ltd* [2009] R.P.C. 5; [2008] EWHC 2413 the UK High Court, differing from earlier decisions of the *Bundespatentgericht* held that a claim to an enantiomer was not anticipated by prior disclosure of the racemic mixture, and it was not obvious to resolve the mixture and produce the claimed compound because, on the evidence, resolution was not easy but required a research programme with a highly uncertain outcome, see also §3.12.

—Certainty as a necessary attribute of anticipation

Mere need to choose between alternatives does not amount to lack of certainty and is insufficient to avoid a finding of anticipation.   **2.21**

In *Novartis v Ivax* [2006] EWHC 2506 Pat Ct alleged anticipation was based on a single example in a prior patent, and other examples did not anticipate the claimed subject-matter. The patentees argued that this did not amount to directions that were clear or unmistakable. The court held that anticipation had been established and that there were clear and unmistakable directions to perform all the examples of the invention even though choice might be exercised between examples. The situation was not analogous to a single example containing one or more choices and in which the way choice was exercised affected whether the example fell within the claim. In the latter case the single example was incapable of supporting an allegation of anticipation by inevitable result. In *Ranbaxy and Arrow Generics v Warner-Lambert* [2005] F.S.R. 209 at 14, the court held that there was a clear case of anticipation in a document that gave clear and unmistakable directions to make three preferred enantiomers, one of which fell within the claim. It observed that to describe a thing as optional is to describe the thing, just as disclosure of something that is adjustable also discloses something that is not adjustable, see *Gillette v Anglo-American* (1913) 30 R.P.C. 465 and *Zipher v Markem* [2008] EWHC 1379 HC; [2009] F.S.R. 1. In *Dyson Technology v Samsung* [2009] EWHC 55 it was held that an option in a cited document that had been disclosed but was not preferred was relevant to novelty. Arguments that concerned the obviousness or otherwise of adopting the less preferred option did not alter the fact of its disclosure, see para.[135].

The information given by a direction not to do X because it will have adverse consequences is not equivalent to a direction to do X because it has beneficial consequences or because it does not have the supposed adverse consequences: *Union Carbide v BP Chemicals* [1998] R.P.C. 1. However, this situation is to be distinguished from one where there is no novelty in a composition as such but new information shows the prior disclosed composition to have an additional advantage, see *Bristol-Myers Squibb v Baker Norton* [1999] R.P.C. 253 and [2001] R.P.C. 1 at 1 CA.

Similarly the EPO has held in T 141/89 *SIBOLA/Packing machine* [1998] E.P.O.R. 425 that where a claim covers alternative constructions, the claim is invalid (unless and until amended) if any of those constructions is found to lack novelty. Furthermore if a prior document describes a process for the production of a class of compounds all of which can be prepared by a skilled person following its teaching, all the members of that class are thereby made available to the public and form part of the state of the art. A claim defining an overlapping class of compounds is anticipated, and in the absence of evidence of selection it is no answer that the working examples in the prior document do not produce compounds within the subsequently claimed class, see T 124/87 *DU PONT/Copolymer*.

The requirement of certainty or inevitability covers a situation where a method is described without it being explicitly stated what results from that method. In such a situation, the inevitable result of carrying out the described operation is considered to be an implicit feature of that description. This situation was first considered in *Fomento v Mentmore* [1956] R.P.C. 87 and was more fully considered in *Letraset v Rexel* [1974] R.P.C. 175 and [1976] R.P.C. 51 and in *Letraset v Dymo* [1976] R.P.C. 65, see also *Institut Français' Application* [1972] R.P.C. 364.

In *Evans Medical's Patent* [1998] R.P.C. 517 it was held that some prior documents disclosed processes which would inevitably lead to the production of a product falling within the scope of the claims: these claims were therefore invalid even though none of the prior disclosures explicitly identified the claimed product as one produced by those processes. However, in *Rocky Mountain Traders v Hewlett Packard* [2000] F.S.R. 411 HC; [2002] F.S.R. 1 at [1] a finding at first instance of lack of novelty was reversed on appeal because the directions in the prior art document could be carried out in a variety of ways and thus had not unambiguously described "planting the flag" in the same way as the claim required.

In *Lubrizol v Esso* [1997] R.P.C. 195; and [1998] R.P.C. 727 CA, it was not inevitable that carrying out a prior art process would have involved a starting material of the type required, but it was held that such a material would in all probability have been used. While novelty was upheld over this finding, the claim was held to lack inventive step, essentially on the application of the "right to work" principle. In *Inhale Therapeutics v Quadrant* [2002] R.P.C. 21 at 419 it was held that a disclosure which is capable of being carried out in a manner which does not fall within the claim does not anticipate, although it may be the basis of an obviousness attack. In *Koninklijke Philips v Princo Digital* [2003] EWHC 1598 Ch, the disclosures of the alleged anticipating documents were capable of different interpretations, so that the patent could not be invalid for lack of novelty (the relevant citations again being under s.2(3) only).

In *SmithKline Beecham's Patent (No.2)* [2003] R.P.C. 33 at 607, it was held (in revocation proceedings brought by Synthon against claims to paroxetine methanesulphonate (PMS) in crystalline form), that an earlier Synthon application (forming part of the state of the art under s.2(3) and therefore effective only against novelty) had disclosed a method of making crystalline PMS. Although there were found to be difficulties in reproducing the method of the earlier application, the judge found on the balance of probabilities that there was only one crystalline form of PMS and that this was what Synthon had made and described in their prior patent application. The decision was reversed on appeal (see [2003] R.P.C. 43 at 769), it being held that the example given in the *Synthon application* could not be made to work without modification and therefore there were no clear and unmistakable directions to make the claimed form of PMS. Accordingly, the prior disclosure did not make the PMS claimed in the patent available to the public A further appeal to the House of Lords sub nom. *SmithKline Beecham's PMS Patent* [2006] R.P.C. 10 at 323 was allowed, and the first instance decision restored. The example was held to be enabling, it being observed that there are two forms of anticipatory disclosure: a disclosure of the patented invention itself and a disclosure of an invention which, if performed, would necessarily infringe the patented invention. They were both aspects of a single principle, namely that anticipation required prior disclosure of subject-matter which, when performed, must necessarily infringe the patented invention.

In *SmithKline Beecham's [Paroxetine Anhydrate] Patent* [2002] EWHC 1373, the court stated the principle as being that:"if the prior disclosure does not contain a teaching which is of equal utility to the teaching of the patent, it may nevertheless anticipate if [in] carrying out its directions the skilled man carries out a process or makes a product falling within the claim." In this case the claims referred to the paroxetine anhydrate as free from bound propan-2-ol, which was the solvent used in its preparation. The prior art process used a different solvent in the process such that propan-2-ol could not be present in the end product. The patentee contended that the claim should be read as requiring the product to be free of any bound organic solvent used in its production, and not just free of propan-2-ol, in order to give fair protection to the patentee. The court found the claims invalid for lack of novelty and the Court of Appeal (see [2003] R.P.C. 49 at 855; [2004] I.P. & T. 846) agreed, holding that the suggestion that the word "propan-2-ol" should be read as "organic solvent" was a deviation from the ordinary rules of construction and would do violence to the language, which was a result to be avoided unless no other reasonable construction was possible. The judge had accordingly been entitled to reach the conclusion that the claims were invalid. His decision to uphold claims limited to crystallising the anhydrate in an organic solvent or mixture of solvents which form a solvate not removable by conventional drying techniques and displacing the solvated solvent or solvents using a displacing agent was also upheld.

This patent in amended form was later considered in another action *SmithKline Beecham v Apotex* [2005] F.S.R. 23 at 524 on appeal from a first instance decision (see [2004] F.S.R. 26 at 523). Whether or not the amended claims were anticipated depended on the interpretation of an example in an earlier patent which inter alia required paroxetine acetate to be dissolved in isopropanol (IPA) and then treated with concentrated hydrochloric acid and "more IPA". The parties differed as to whether this was a small amount of IPA or was enough to produce controlled crystallisation and whether the intermediate was anhydrate or solvent. The court held that what mattered, by analogy with the *Bolam* test for professional negligence, was not the answer that an expert would give as an individual, but what the notional skilled person would understand from the document. The court should distinguish its views on the experts as good witnesses from the more fundamental reasons for their opinions. In the present case the example was ambiguous and therefore could not anticipate the claimed subject-matter. Repetition of the example was criticised as contrived or "litigation chemistry".

Whether or not the inevitable result of carrying out what was disclosed in an example of an earlier patent would have resulted in the monohydrate of calcipotriol was a key issue in *Leo Pharma v Sandoz* [2009] EWHC 996 Pat Ct and [2009] EWCA Civ 1188. Repetition of what had been disclosed in that example was not persuasive since the starting material had not been prepared as disclosed in the earlier patent but was a bought-in material prepared by an undisclosed process and since a seed-free environment had not been used.

In *Halliburton v Smith International* [2006] R.P.C. 2 at 25, a claim to a drill bit having three rotary cones in which the axial force on each cone was required to be 31–35 per cent of the total axial force was held to be anticipated by two prior manufactured bits which were shown by computer simulation to be balanced as required by the claim. The court accepted arguments that it would have been possible to copy one of the prior manufactured bits and make another equally within the claim, and that patents are not available for discovering mere properties of old articles. It rejected the counter-argument that "dumb anticipation" was not enough and drew a distinction between products which could subsequently be reproduced so that their relevant properties could be ascertained and products where, e.g. in a chemical case, no analysis was possible and therefore there was no relevant information.

In the EPO it has also been held that there is a lack of novelty if the inevitable result of carrying out a described process is the product being claimed as an invention, see T 12/81 *BAYER/Diastereomers*, but this is not so if the prior document contains no clear and unmistakable directions and, in fact, a contrary teaching, see T 310/88 *TORAY INDUSTRIES/Photosensitive resin* [1991] E.P.O.R. 10.

The EPO has held that this test of inevitability needs to be satisfied "beyond all reasonable doubt", rather than on "the balance of probabilities": T 793/93 *ALLIED-SIGNAL/*

Polyolefin fiber [1996] E.P.O.R. 104. A finding of "inevitable result" will be made only if the prior disclosure has been experimentally repeated exactly as set out T 173/89 *ICI/ Gamma-sorbitol* [1991] E.P.O.R. 62; and T 207/94 *BIOGEN/Human beta–interferon* OJ EPO 1999, 273; [1999] E.P.O.R. 451, or so closely that there is no scope for serious challenge to the validity of the repetition, or it is shown convincingly that the deviation is not material to the end result: T 396/89 *UNION CARBIDE/High tear strength polymers* [1992] E.P.O.R. 312. A latex characterised by a low chloride ion content was the subject of T 142/06 *ASAHI/Polyvinylidine chloride latex*. A reworking of an example in a cited document had not demonstrated chloride content to the necessary standard of "beyond reasonable doubt". Furthermore, despite the general rule that disclosure of a compound made it available in all states of purity, in this case no need for purification to low chloride levels had been disclosed in the prior art and chloride level was important to the properties of films made from the latex. Accordingly the inventor had genuinely given the public something new, and the objection of lack of novelty failed.

If there is no evidence or reason for considering the explicit teaching of a prior art document as incomplete or wrong or giving rise to doubts about the results obtained, a party's allegation that a skilled person would have understood additional but undescribed features to be a necessary part of such prior art teaching cannot be accepted, see T 410/99 *MESTO/ Kraft pulp*. In T 824/05 *EASTMAN CHEMICAL/Polyesters* at 4.1.2 the claim referred to an inherent viscosity which was concentration-dependent but did not specify the concentration at which measurement was to be made. It was therefore incompletely defined and was therefore not a distinguishing feature of the invention.

—Substance as a necessary attribute of anticipation

2.22   The requirement of substance or actuality is further illustrated by *Merrell Dow v Norton* [1994] R.P.C. 1; [1995] R.P.C. 233 CA; and [1996] R.P.C. 77 HL. A prior written description of the administration to a patient of drug terfenadine was held to anticipate a claim to a metabolite on the patentee's admission that the metabolite was produced in vivo after that administration, such being the inevitable result of that administration. Here, the Court of Appeal stated:

> "a disclosure of a process makes available to the public, for the purpose of that process, everything which inevitably takes place as part of the process, whether appreciated or not".

The House of Lords endorsed the decision on essentially the same reasoning which it explained by reference to the history of the drug quinine:

> "The Amazonian Indians have known for centuries that cinchona bark can be used to treat malarial and other fevers. They used it in the form of powdered bark. In 1820, French scientists discovered that the active ingredient, an alkaloid called quinine, could be extracted and used more effectively in the form of sulphate of quinine. In 1944, the structure of the alkaloid molecule ($C_{20}H_{24}N_2O_2$) was discovered. This meant that the substance could be synthesised.
> Imagine a scientist telling an Amazonian Indian about the discoveries of 1820 and 1944. He says: 'We have found that the reason why the bark is good for fevers is that it contains an alkaloid with a rather complicated chemical structure which reacts with the red corpuscles in the bloodstream. It is called quinine'. The Indian replies: 'That is very interesting. In my tribe, we call it the magic spirit of the bark'. Does the Indian know about quinine? My Lords, under the description of a quality of the bark which makes it useful for treating fevers, he obviously does. I do not think it matters that he chooses to label it in animistic rather than chemical terms. He knows that the bark has a quality which makes it good for fever and that is one description of quinine."

On the facts under consideration, disclosure of the anti-histamine effect of terfenadine made available the effect of the metabolite as part of what occurs in the human body when terfenadine is ingested and the antihistamine effect is produced. Whether or not a person is working a product invention is an objective fact independent of what he knows or thinks about what he is doing. The position is different when the invention is a use for a product; in such a case, a person may only be working the invention when he is using it for the patented purpose. But the Amazonian Indian who treats himself with powdered bark for fever is using quinine, even if he thinks that the reason why the treatment is effective is that the tree is favoured by the gods. The teachings of his traditional medicine contain enough information to enable him to do exactly what a scientist in the forest would have done if he wanted to treat a fever but had no supplies of quinine sulphate. There is a distinction between anticipation by use and anticipation by written disclosure. In objection of anticipation by use the acts relied upon conveyed no information which would have enabled anyone to work the invention, i.e. to make the acid metabolite, whereas the objection of anticipation by disclosure relies upon the communication to the public of information which enables it to do an act having the inevitable consequence of making the acid metabolite and anticipation was established, see T 12/81 *BAYER/Diastereomers* [1979-85] E.P.O.R. Vol. B. 308, 312; T 303/86 *CPC/Flavour concentrates* [1989] 2 E.P.O.R. 95 and G 2/88 *MOBIL III/Friction reducing additive*.

The EPO also takes the view that mere difference in wording without any difference in substance is insufficient to establish novelty, see T 198/84 *Hoechst/Thiochloroformates*; see also T 455/98 *SPI/Crystalline sugar alcohols*, T 577/98 *US Surgical Corp/Medical Implants*, T 287/99 *GLAXO/Aerosol medicaments*, T 48/01 *Unilever/Reduced fat spread*, and T 1435/06 *DENFOTEX/Dental root canal filling*. For example in T 114/86 *ERIKSSON/Foam plastic filter* OJ EPO 1987, 485; [1988] E.P.O.R. 25 which related to the use of plastics foam the Board could discern no difference between the claimed perforated closed cells and interconnected cells constituting an open-cell structure as disclosed in an earlier document. The verbal distinction did not represent a real difference in structure and the patentee had made no attempt either to establish that there was such a difference or to identify what it was.

—Novelty of purpose

Although a new use of an old article is patentable, under traditional British patent juris- **2.23** prudence that new use has had to be claimed as a new method of using the old article because novelty has been held not to be conferred merely by specifying the purpose for which an old article is now intended. Thus, in *Adhesive Dry Mounting v Trapp* (1910) 27 R.P.C. 341, it was held that the scope of a claim to an article is not limited by a statement that the article is "for" use in a particular way, just as infringement of a claim to an article is not avoided by using that article for a purpose different from that envisaged by the patent.

It should be noted that although, under *Adhesive Dry Mounting v Trapp*, a claim stating that a product is "for [a particular use]" does not limit the article to that use, the stated purpose may import a dimensional limitation of the claim, thereby saving it from being anticipated by a prior disclosure of a similar article designed for a different purpose, it being so held in *Howley v Dronsfield* BL CC/40/95. This principle has also been upheld in *South Africa G.I. Marketing v Fraser-Johnston* [South Africa] noted [1996] E.I.P.R. D–75, see also EPO Guidelines C–III, 4.13–4.14. Likewise, article claims may be distinguished by a field of use definition, as in *Hickman v Andrews* [1983] R.P.C. 147 where a claim to a "workbench" was upheld over a description of a book press having the same general features.

The EPO Appeal Boards do not follow the *Adhesive Dry Mounting* approach either for inventions in the fields of human or veterinary medicine (see s.4A) or for other inventions. The Enlarged Board of Appeal has accepted that, in addition to inventions of a further medical indication, novelty can be conferred on a claim by including a statement of novel technical purpose. In T 59/87 *MOBIL II/Friction reducing additive* OJ EPO 1988, 347; [1989] E.P.O.R. 80; and G 2/88 *MOBIL III/Friction reducing* additive claims to the use of a substance as a friction-reducing additive in lubricants were allowed even though such use would have been inherent, but unappreciated, in the previously known use of the same substance in lubricants, in the same amounts, as a rust inhibitor. The Enlarged Board held that with respect to a claim to a new use of a known compound, such new use could reflect a newly discovered technical effect described in the patent. The attaining of such a technical effect should then be considered as a functional technical feature of the claim (e.g. the achievement in a particular context of that technical effect). If that technical feature had not been previously made available to the public, then the claimed invention was novel, even though such technical effect may have inherently taken place in the course of carrying out what was previously been made available to the public. Also, in T 231/85 *BASF/ Triazole derivatives* OJ EPO 1989, 74; [1989] E.P.O.R. 293 claims were allowed in principle to "Use of X for controlling and preventing fungus growth" when X was already known for use as a growth promoter, the fact that the new use may need no technical realisation over the previously known use being regarded as irrelevant, a decision specifically endorsed by the Enlarged Board in G 6/88 *BAYER/Second non-medical indication* which led to the allowance of claims to the use of known compounds "to regulate plant growth", see T 208/88 *BAYER/Growth regulation* OJ EPO 1992, 22; [1992] E.P.O.R. 74. In this last-cited decision it was stated that:

> "an effect not previously described, but actually occurring during the execution of a known teaching and intended as the basis of a use invention, becomes available to the public only when revealed so clearly during such execution as to disclose the invention's essential character, at least potentially, to an unlimited number of skilled persons".

These *Mobil* and *Bayer* decisions were discussed in papers by G. D. Paterson [1991] E.I.P.R. 16; A. W. White [1990] E.I.P.R. 315; and R. S. Crespi (1991) 2(1) I.P.B. 9 and 3(5) I.P.B. 17; and also in 1989–90 19 CIPA 111 and 171. The *Mobil* decision is not so easily distinguished from that in *Adhesive Dry Mounting*, but provides an illustration of the effect-based nature of examination in the EPO and the importance which the EPO Appeal Boards give to the discovery or achievement of a new technical effect, see also §3.31.

As a result of the *Mobil* and *Bayer* decisions, it may be that (at least in the EPO) objections of lack of novelty can be overcome in many cases if a different technical effect from that indicated by the prior art can be demonstrated, see T 20/88 *UNION CARBIDE/ Polymer-polyol compositions* [1990] E.P.O.R. 212; and T 361/88 *DU PONT/Hollow filaments* [1991] E.P.O.R. 1; and see also the continuation of these two decisions of the Enlarged Board of Appeal in T 59/87 *MOBIL IV/Friction reducing additive* OJ EPO 1991, 561; [1990] E.P.O.R. 514 and T 208/88 *BAYER/Growth regulation* (above). A similar case is T 290/86 *ICI/Cleaning plaque* OJ EPO 1992, 414; [1991] E.P.O.R. 157. Where it was not viable to define apparatus in a way other than by reference to its intended use, a claim has been allowed to a combination of the apparatus and its use unambiguously defined that apparatus over the prior art, see T 841/95 *JOHNSON & JOHNSON/Self-cleaning pipette tip*.

A hitherto unknown new purpose is an essential requirement for the *Mobil Oil* approach to be applicable. In T 892/94 *ROBERTET/Deodorant compositions* OJ EPO 2000, 1; [1999] E.P.O.R. 516 the Board held that a newly discovered technical effect does not confer novelty on a claim directed to the use of a known substance for a known non-medical purpose if the newly discovered technical effect already underlies the known use of the known substance, see also T 189/95 *L'OREAL/Composition amaigrissante* where the newly discovered effect merely explained the mechanism behind the known use. Discovery of a previously unknown technical effect does not confer novelty where the claimed process does not open the way to a new activity and occurs inherently when carrying out known processes, see T 1092/01 *INDUSTRIAL ORGANICA/Lutein*. There must be something more than a purely mental addition to the state of the art, see T 80/96 *LONZA/L–Carnitine* OJ EPO 2000, 50; [2000] E.P.O.R. 323 where the claim specified the use of a known substance together with an auxiliary substance and was seen to cover every conceivable use of the known preparation and therefore to lack novelty. The EPO has also held that anticipation is not avoided by adding a test procedure to be satisfied as a feature of the claim, unless there is evidence that prior art products would fail that test, see T 627/88 *ASAHI/Resin composition*. In T 706/95 *FUEL TECH/Reduction of nitrogen-based pollutants* it was held that the discovery that the same known means lead to an additional effect when they are used for the same known purpose (i.e. known use) of reducing the concentration of nitrogen oxides in the same effluent cannot confer novelty to this known use.

The Board held in T 1049/99 *L'OREAL/Composition cosmétique filtrante* that the *Mobil Oil* doctrine should not be extended to process claims because such claims cover the product of the process and claims should not be allowed whose effect was to cover an already known product, see also T 684/02 *E.I. DU PONT DE NEMOURS AND COMPANY/ Fluorocarbon resins*. A claim defining the physical step of applying a surface active agent to an absorbent material was held in T 304/08 *BASF/Method for reducing malodour* to be a process claim and not a use claim in the sense of decisions G 2/88 *Mobil Oil Corp v Chevron Research Co* [1990] E.P.O.R. 73 and G 6/88 *BAYER/Plant growth regulating agent* [1990] E.P.O.R. 257, which related exclusively to claims directed to the use of a substance for achieving an effect. Thus the purpose of the method in claim in issue, namely for reducing malodour, could not be regarded as a functional technical feature in the sense of the above decisions and did not render the method novel.

UK courts have criticised the *Mobil Oil* approach but have not gone so far as to say that it should not be followed. In *Merrell Dow v Norton* [1994] R.P.C. 1; [1995] R.P.C. 233 CA and [1996] R.P.C. 77 HL each of the courts who heard the case indicated that the *Mobil* decision would require careful consideration before it could be accepted into the patent law of the United Kingdom. The Court of Appeal indicated that this would be unlikely in circumstances where the *Gillette* defence was applicable, while the House of Lords merely stated that G 2/88 *MOBIL III/Friction reducing additive* (above) makes it difficult to apply the traditional United Kingdom doctrine of infringement under which infringement is absolute, i.e. independent of knowledge or intention to a patent for an old product used in an old way for a new purpose, but that this aspect did not arise in the case then before it. The relationship between the *Mobil* and *Merrell Dow* decisions was discussed by C.D. Floyd in the 1996 Herchel Smith Lecture [1996] E.I.P.R. 480 where G 2/88 *MOBIL III/ Friction reducing additive* was subjected to trenchant criticism. In *Bristol-Myers Squibb v Baker Norton* [1999] R.P.C. 253, not only was the *Mobil* decision again criticised, but it was pointed out that in later EPO decisions a distinction had been drawn between discovery of a new technical effect (as in *Mobil*) and a discovery of mere information concerning a previously known effect as in T 958/90 *DOW/Sequestering agent* [1994] E.P.O.R. 1 and T 279/93 *AMERICAN CYANAMID/Melamine derivatives* [1999] E.P.O.R. 88. The earlier T 290/86 *ICI/Cleaning plaque* (above) was then seen to be incompatible with these two later decisions. The Patents Court then indicated that further consideration of the *Mobil* decision by the EPO Enlarged Board would be desirable. In dismissing an appeal in the *Bristol–Myers Squibb case* [2001] R.P.C. 1 at [1] CA, the *Dow* and *American Cyanamid* cases were followed and the *Mobil* case was seen to be of a different kind dependent on a purposive claim construction.

A new surgical use cannot render novel the subject-matter of a claim relating to the use of the components of a known instrument system for its manufacture for that purpose, there being no new technical effect as in the case of a claim to the further medical indication of a known therapeutic substance; this anyway is distinguished by its destruction during its use as a medicament: T 227/91 *CODMAN/Second surgical use* OJ EPO 1994, 491; [1995] E.P.O.R. 82. A somewhat similar case is *Novamedix v NDM* [1997] EWCA Civ 1924 where the Court of Appeal (reversing the decision below, BL CC/60/95) found a lack of novelty in a claim to a medical appliance which specified the attainment by it of a particular effect. The prior art was held to have provided "clear and unmistakable directions to make an appliance of a particular construction" and this was sufficient as the invention was not claimed in terms of how the appliance would be fitted or used, this not being possible given that such use would be a method of therapy excluded from patentability by s.4(2). It was stated that: "The test for the purpose of novelty must be the same when deciding whether the device falls within the claim" and, as the patentee had proved (on the balance of probabilities) that its device did produce this effect when fitted in a particular way, the similarity of the prior art device indicated that it, likewise, would produce the stated effect when fitted in the same way, it being irrelevant whether that effect was described, or even intended, by the prior author. Thus, rather than overturning the *Mobil* and *Bayer* decisions, it may be that there will be an increasing tendency to distinguish these on the facts of the case in issue while continuing to avoid a decision on whether the *Adhesive Dry Mounting* decision remains part of at least United Kingdom patent law.

There has not yet been a decision where a UK court has held a use claim valid and infringed and formulated an order based on such a claim, and until this has happened the form of any such order and the practical effectiveness of use claims remains open to conjecture, notwithstanding the value placed by practitioners on the ability to obtain grant of such claims, although such a claim has been held to be valid and infringed in South Africa, see §4A.10.

Selection inventions

2.24   The UK approach is aligned with that adopted by the EPO following a decision of the Court of Appeal in *Dr Reddy's Laboratories v Eli Lilly* [2009] EWCA Civ 1362 and is now based on "individualised description", see also *Mölnlycke v Brightwake* [2011] EWHC 376 (Pat) at [235] although the degree of such alignment is still not fully established, see *Lundbeck v Norpharma* [2011] EWHC 907 (Pat) discussed below.

In the *Dr Reddy's* case, a generic disclosure in the prior art relied on covered some 1019 compounds and a preferred genus covered 86,000 compounds. The court rejected an argument that these prior disclosures amounted to the disclosure of individual members of each genus, referring to a quotation from G.K. Chesterton's *Father Brown* short story "*The Sign of the Broken sword*": "Where does a wise man hide a leaf? In a forest". The contention had no logical stopping place. Disclosure of a large number of compounds in a list should be treated in the same way as the disclosure of a Markush group: "To say a particular book is identified by saying 'the book is in the Bodleian' is no different from saying it is identified by providing access to the catalogue of the Bodleian." Furthermore a prior disclosure of "fixing means" was not a disclosure of a particular fixing means, e.g. welding or riveting even though you could list out a whole number of ways of fixing things together which would include these means. This conclusion was supported by an EPO Appeal Board decision in T 296/87 *Hoechst/Enantiomers* [1990] E.P.O.R. 337, by the earlier UK decisions in *Generics v H Lundbeck A/S* [2008] EWCA Civ 311; [2008] R.P.C. 19; *Synthon BV v SmithKline Beecham Plc (No.2)* [2006] R.P.C. 10 and by a decision of the *Oberlandesgericht* in Germany concerning the same patent; see also the decision of the Patents Court in *Laboratorios Almirall v Boehringer* [2009] EWHC 102 Pat Ct. The decision is reviewed by P.G. Cole, "Novelty and obviousness in an empirical research field" [2010] *CIPA* 105. The previous law, flowing from the decision in *IG Farbenindustrie's Patents* (1930) 47 R.P.C. 289 is explained in earlier editions of this work.

Earlier UK decisions raising genus/species issues include *Beecham Group's (Amoxycillin) Application* [1980] R.P.C. 261 CA and *Du Pont's (Witsiepe's) Application* [1981] F.S.R. 377 CA and [1982] F.S.R. 303 HL although each was decided under the former statute.

In *Beecham (Amoxycillin)*, a claim requiring a particular chemical compound to be comprised in "a pharmaceutical composition adapted for oral administration to human beings" was held not anticipated by a prior disclosure which hinted at both the epimeric compound in question and the possibility of formulation of the disclosed compounds for oral administration. The prior document did not contain clear and specific directions to make up the particular composition as claimed in the amended claim. A similar decision resulted in the corresponding case in New Zealand, see *Beecham Group's (Amoxycillin) Application [New Zealand]* [1982] F.S.R. 181.

In *Du Pont (Witsiepe's) Application*, a claim requiring the use of a C4 glycol was held not to be anticipated by a patent dated some 30 years previously that had specified in the same process the generic use of a C1-C10 glycol, and which had mentioned the C4 glycol, though not in any example but only in the context of prior art discussed in its preamble. Both the Court of Appeal and House of Lords applied the rule that the novelty of a claim is destroyed only by a clear disclosure and that a pointer is not sufficient. There was no clear instruction in the prior document to use the particular glycol in question and the fact that it was mentioned by name in a list therein was an irrelevance. It is apparent that prior disclosure of a genus will not anticipate a claim to a species within that genus if the species is new and exhibits a special advantage. The size of the group (or list) from which the selection was made was also considered to be irrelevant to the question of novelty. In addition, in *Witsiepe* both the Court of Appeal and the House of Lords emphasised the importance of a prior art chemical compound having previously been made and its properties ascertained before it could be regarded as "known" or "published", see also *Beecham v Bristol SA* [1978] R.P.C. 521 and also *Beecham Group's (Amoxycillin) Application (No.2)* [New Zealand] [1980] 1 N.Z.L.R. 192. The implication of these statements, that a chemical compound is not deprived of novelty unless the prior art document states that it has been made and reports some of its properties, has been considered by B.C. Reid [1982] E.I.P.R. 118.

It remains an open question whether and to what extent UK courts should follow somewhat more stringent EPO practice regarding the novelty of selection inventions (described below). In *Lundbeck v Norpharma* [2011] EWHC 907 (Pat) Floyd J. held that the law of novelty in relation to overlapping ranges is no different from novelty in other circumstances, and should not depend on whether a skilled person would "seriously contemplate" moving form a broad range to a narrow range because such dependence was inconsistent with the decision of the House of Lords in *Synthon* that a genus does not anticipate a species. A reference which was silent about concentration of a species did not implicitly refer to 1–99 per cent of that species and does not implicitly anticipate 20–33 per cent. In order to reach that conclusion, however, it was not necessary to reach a concluded view as to whether the "serious contemplation" test of T 666/89 *UNILEVER/Washing composition* (and other cases discussed below) was correct.

The EPO approach to selection inventions is set out in EPO Guideline C–IV, 9.8 which states that a generic disclosure does not usually take away the novelty of any specific example falling within the terms of that disclosure, but that a specific disclosure takes away the novelty of a generic claim embracing it. The EPO has upheld selection inventions in a number of cases, for example in: T 1/80 *BAYER/Carbonless Copying Paper* [1982] R.P.C. 321; OJ EPO 1981, 206; T 198/84 *HOECHST/Thiochloroformates* OJ EPO 1985, 209; T 433/86 *ICI/Modified Diisocyanates* [1988] E.P.O.R. 97; and T 7/86 *DRACO/Xanthines* OJ EPO 1988, 381; [1989] E.P.O.R. 65.

EPO Guideline C–IV, 9.8(1) explains that a selection from a single list of specifically disclosed elements does not confer novelty. Novelty can be found in selection from two lists of some length according to EPO Guideline C–IV, 9.8(1) which follows an approach explained in T 12/81 *BAYER/Diastereomers*. Here, it was stated that selection of the elements of a product from two lists of starting materials avoids anticipation, but where a starting material chosen from a list is combined with one of a number of listed processes, not only does the corresponding process lack novelty but, so also does the inevitably obtained end-product. The "selection from two lists" principle has been applied to find novelty in T 7/86 *DRACO/Xanthines* (above) and in T 61/85 *ICI/Polyester crystallisation* [1988] E.P.O.R. 20.

Much of the EPO jurisprudence in the area of selection has been developed in connection with attempts to patent a selection from a numerical range. In the *Thiochloroformates* decision (above), the principle was established that for a sub-range selected from a broader numerical range to be novel the selected sub-range must be narrow and sufficiently far removed from the known range as illustrated by examples in the prior disclosure. On this basis, a claim which met these criteria was allowed. The sub-range claimed was novel by virtue of an effect which was demonstrated to occur only within the sub-range and was not merely a newly discovered effect associated with the whole range. A favourable approach to the patentability of selection inventions within the EPO is discernible in T 279/89

TEXACO/Reaction injection moulded elastomer [1992] E.P.O.R. 294 where the Board held that novelty depended on whether a skilled person would "seriously contemplate" working within the narrower range selected from within the broader range disclosed in the prior art It further held that a selected sub-range from a broader range may be novel if it is: (a) narrow; (b) sufficiently removed from the specific description of the prior document; and (c) based on a purposive selection, i.e. not an arbitrary specimen of the prior description, see also T 366/90 *UNILEVER/Interesterification process* [1993] E.P.O.R. 383. Nevertheless, the technical teaching against which the "serious contemplation test" is to be applied must be the "total information content" of the prior art document, that is including information which is "hidden" or implicit in that document as well as that which is expressly stated by it, though not that which is "reconditely submerged" in it, see T 666/89 *UNILEVER/Washing composition.* Here it was also stressed that a technical effect is neither a prerequisite for novelty nor can it confer novelty: its existence can merely confirm a finding of novelty already achieved; see also T 230/07 *PAROC/Colloidal binder.* In T 247/91 *STAMICARBON/Cyclohexane oxidation* [1996] E.P.O.R. 120, a prior art document referred to a temperature range of 80–170°C and its teaching was held to extend to the whole of this range so that a claim limited to operation at 85–115°C was held to have been anticipated. T 17/85 *PLÜSS-STAUFER/Filler* OJ EPO 1986, 406; [1987] E.P.O.R. 66; T 124/87 *DU PONT/Copolymers* (above); and T 75/87 *INLAND STEEL/Tellurium-containing steel* [1994] E.P.O.R. 475 are other numerical range cases in which the criteria formulated in the *Thiochloroformates* case were held not to have been met, see also T 25/87 *UNION CARBIDE/Polyacrylate moulding composition* [1989] E.P.O.R. 381 where novelty was lacking because four ranges of numbers defined the claimed compositions and these ranges had been combined in the same way as the prior art. Lack of novelty was also found where the claims overlapped a prior art disclosure, as demonstrated by calculations showing that the skilled person has been informed that he could indeed apply the known technical teaching in the range later claimed, see T 560/90 *EUTECO/Ethyl t-butyl ether* [1996] E.P.O.R. 353.

Novelty was also found when the subject-matter claimed required combining various pieces of information contained in the cited document in a certain manner T 137/90 *SHELL/Amino-triazine* [1991] E.P.O.R. 381; and also in the case of a catalogue where it was doubted whether it was proper to regard this as a single document rather than as a selection of documents, see T 305/87 *GREHAL/Shear* OJ EPO 1991, 429; [1991] E.P.O.R. 389. For further cases where novelty was recognised on the basis of a "multiple selection", see T 427/86 *RHÔNE-POULENC/Ester production* [1999] E.P.O.R. 443 and T 653/93 *BP Oil/Process oils.*

In T 296/87 *HOECHST/Enantiomers* a claim to an enantiomeric compound was held to be novel, though not inventive, over the prior disclosure of that isomer as part of a racemic mixture. Novelty was also found in similar circumstances in T 1048/92 *PFIZER/Penem* [1995] E.P.O.R. 207; but in T 658/91 *SANOFI/Enantiomer* [1996] E.P.O.R. 24, the Pfizer case was noted as being apparently inconsistent with the *Hoechst* case. In T 1046/97 *ZENECA/Enantiomer* [2002] E.P.O.R. 30 at 325 it was held that it was not sufficient for lack of novelty that the claimed enantiomer belonged conceptually to the group of possible optically active forms mentioned in the prior art unless there was a pointer to the individual member of the group at stake. Although the skilled person would be expected to combine the disclosure of the specific example with the general teaching in the patent as to optically active forms, this could not be equated to the disclosure of a specific enantiomer.

In T 990/96 *NOVARTIS/Erythro-compounds* OJ EPO 1998, 489; [1998] E.P.O.R. 441, novelty was not recognised for a claim to an enantiomer defined by its purity, as the inherent disclosure of the prior art was that this compound could be prepared to any desired degree of purity. However, the rule indicated in T 990/96 *NOVARTIS/Erythro-compounds* is not absolute. T 803/01 *NOVARTIS/Purified polylactide composition* [2005] E.P.O.R. 26 at 220 shows that a product defined by a quantitative absence of certain impurities can be accepted provided that there is evidence that the product produced by the prior art process would have contained the now excluded impurities. Furthermore, a claim to a polymer having a specified degree of purity was held not to be anticipated by a prior disclosure that could not achieve the specified purity, see T 803/01 *NOVARTIS/Purified polylactide.*

The EPO view on the novelty of selection inventions was reviewed by R. Spannenberg (1997) 28 I.I.C. 808.

—Permissible amendments under subsection (3)

The same criteria of novelty are to be applied for selection inventions under s.2(3) as under s.2(2), see T 279/89 *TEXACO/Reaction injection moulded elastomer*. However, because inventive step considerations do not apply to disclosures effective only under s.2(3), somewhat different issues can arise in practice.

2.25

The practice of permitting unsupported disclaimers to restore novelty over an earlier reference published under EPC art.54(3) was approved by the EPO Enlarged Board of Appeal in G 1/03 *PPG/Disclaimer* which observed that agreement to adopt the "whole contents" approach would never have been reached without retaining the ability to distinguish from the earlier dated application by a disclaimer as had been permitted in particular in the UK. The disclaimer must, however, do no more than is necessary to restore novelty.

Accordingly there continues to be no reason why a s.2(3) objection should not be overcome by a claim of the "N–1" type, provided that what is left is described with sufficient particularity, see *Upjohn's Application* BL O/61/83. However, in *Fruehauf's Application* BL O/185/83, it was held that objection under subs.(3) could not be overcome by insertion of a disclaimer to "all matter disclosed" in the prior application, as the resulting scope of the claims would then be obscure, contrary to s.14(5).

—Product-by-process claims

The general rule both in the EPO and in the UK is that "product-by-process" claims should not be allowed because they are unnecessary having regard to s.64(2) EPC and s.60(1)(c) of the Act which extend the protection given to a process to cover products directly obtained by that process, see T 150/82 *IFF/Claim categories* OJ EPO 1984, 309, and *Kirin-Amgen v Hoechst Marion Roussel* [2005] R.P.C. 9 at 169 (HL).

2.26

In the latter case, the House of Lords held that the first requirement for such a claim is that the product must be new, and that a difference in the method of manufacture of a product that is otherwise identical to the prior art does not make it new, this being a proposition of law that a rule of practice within the IP Office could not overcome. In T 248/85 *BICC/Radiation processing* OJ EPO 1986, 261 a product-by-process claim was rejected on an admission that the product per se was indistinguishable from a product of the prior art. A process will not be new if the prior art discloses the same starting materials and reaction conditions, because, then, identical products must inevitably result, see T 303/86 *CPC/Flavour concentrates*.

The condition for product-by-process claims to be allowable was held by the EPO to be that the products themselves fulfil the requirements for patentability and there is no other information available in the application which could enable the applicant to define the product satisfactorily by reference to its composition, structure or some other testable parameter, see T 150/82 *IFF/Claim categories*. Such a claim was allowed in T 130/90 *UNIVERSITY OF TEXAS/Recombinant monoclonal antibody* [1996] E.P.O.R. 46, T 748/98 *BIOMIN/Pharmaceutical compositions based on egg shells* and T 59/97 *NIPPON PISTON RING/Member pressure fitted onto a shaft* where it was held that especially in the mechanical field, the method of manufacturing a product often leaves its mark on a finished product, e.g. a finished camshaft made by machining a one-piece cast blank or has been made by welding together separate parts.

If the product can be defined only by process, rather than structural, parameters, the onus is on the applicant to establish by evidence that modification of the stated process results in other products; e.g. by showing such other products to have different properties. Differences in properties which cannot be due to different structural parameters, such as merely the absence of malodorous monomer impurities, cannot be relied upon, see

T 205/83 *HOECHST/Vinyl ester/crotonic acid copolymers* OJ EPO 1985, 363; [1986] E.P.O.R. 57 where a claim to a copolymer defined solely by a "product-by-process" claim was disallowed. Likewise, in T 248/85 *BICC/Radiation Processing* OJ EPO 1986, 261; [1986] E.P.O.R. 311.

A catalyst specified in product-by-process terms using "obtainable by" language was considered in T 956/04 *JOHNSON MATTHEY/Cobalt on alumina catalysts*. However, the "obtainable by" features did not unambiguously define the claimed catalysts as inevitable products of the specified process because they did not specific starting materials and specific reaction conditions and did not give rise to any distinguishable product feature. According to T 552/91 *MERCK/Chroman derivatives* [1995] E.P.O.R. 455 "it is necessary to include in the claim the process parameters required for defining unambiguously the claimed substances as inevitable process products." Accordingly the "obtainable by" features were not clear and did not permit the conclusion that the claimed catalyst was novel.

See an article by G. Grant and D. Smyth, "Protection provided by product by process claims", [2010] EIPR 635.

PRACTICE UNDER SECTION 2

Avoiding self-collision with a related application

2.27 In order to prevent self-collision under subs.(3) with subject-matter contained in an earlier application of the same applicant, it may not be sufficient to delete the subject-matter in question from the earlier application before this is published under s.16 as that application will be published in the form as filed. As suggested in (1979–80) 9 *CIPA* 247, it would appear more prudent to file a divisional application on the earlier application before it is published under s.16. The divisional application can omit the offending subject-matter and the original application can be abandoned before publication.

Disclosures at international exhibitions

2.28 As with s.51 of the 1949 Act, the provisions of subs.(4)(c) concerning disclosure at an international exhibition before filing can be fatal to the validity of patents subsequently acquired, in some foreign countries, where a similar grace period based on art.11 of the Paris Convention is not afforded.

It would appear that an "international exhibition" is one registered with the International Exhibition Bureau. Lists of such exhibitions are published periodically in the OJ EPO, as noted above; and see §2.16 above.

The procedure when such exhibition has taken place is given in r.5 (reprinted above). At the time of filing the application for the patent, the Comptroller must be informed in writing that the invention has been displayed at the exhibition, r.5(1), and, within four months of the date of filing the application, there must be filed a certificate, issued by the authority responsible for the exhibition, stating that the invention was exhibited and the opening date of the exhibition and, if the invention was not disclosed on that date, the first date when it was disclosed; and the certificate must be accompanied by an authenticated identification of the invention r.5(4). No forms or fees are required for providing the information or to accompany the certificate and the period specified in r.5(2) is extensible under r.108(1) at the Comptroller's discretion.

SECTION 3

Inventive step

3.01 **3.** An invention shall be taken to involve an inventive step if it is not obvious to a person skilled in the art, having regard to any matter which forms part of the state of the art by virtue only of section 2(2) above (and disregarding section 2(3) above).

Note. Section 130(7) requires s.3 to be construed in conformity with the corresponding provision of the EPC. This is EPC art.56, reproduced in §3.02 below.

CORRESPONDING CONVENTION PROVISION

Article 56 EPC—Inventive step

56. An invention shall be considered as involving an inventive step if, having regard to the state of the art, it is not obvious to a person skilled in the art. If the state of the art also includes documents within the meaning of article 54, paragraph 3, these documents shall not be considered in deciding whether there has been an inventive step. **3.02**

COMMENTARY ON SECTION 3

Scope of the section

Section 1(1)(b) specifies that an invention patentable under the Act shall involve an "inventive step". Section 3 further requires that an invention shall be taken to involve an inventive step if it is not obvious to a person skilled in the art. It corresponds to art.5 of the Strasbourg Convention (1963) (Cmnd. 8002) and to EPC art.56 and is qualified by s.130(7) as being framed to have, as nearly as practicable, the same effect. This appears to require "inventive step" to be construed as "inventive activity" *Genentech's Patent* [1989] R.P.C. 147 CA. **3.03**

Regard has to be paid to the state of the art, as to the meaning of which see §§2.04–2.06. However, UK, European and International patent applications filed earlier than the priority date of the invention but published later are disregarded for evaluation of inventive step, see §2.24 and §3.24.

"Invention" comes from the Latin *invenire* meaning to find or to come upon. It calls for a positive attribute of an underlying discovery by the inventor.

Obviousness comes from the Latin *ob+via*, meaning by the wayside. It calls for the negative attribute of accessibility, i.e. that the skilled person would have come upon the claimed subject-matter sooner or later and without having to display ingenuity.

In the United Kingdom under the former statutes no practical distinction was made between the objections that claimed subject-matter was "obvious" and was "lacking in inventive step", see *Benmax v Austin* (1955) 72 R.P.C. 39 at 44–46 HL. It is arguable that there is no room for such a distinction under the present statute because of the requirement that an invention shall be taken to involve an inventive step if it is not obvious. Similarly the positive terms in which the section is written exclude other criteria, such as technical progress and inventive level as requirements of patentability. Nevertheless, inventive step is sometimes raised as a requirement in its own right. In *STEP v Emson* [1993] R.P.C. 513 at p.519 Hoffmann L.J. said that the question was whether the patent discloses something sufficiently inventive to deserve the grant of a monopoly. Jacob L.J. explained in *Actavis v Novartis* [2010] EWCA Civ 82 that although ''inventive step'' is defined as being one which is not obvious, the purpose of that definition must be remembered—to define what is inventive, see §3.26.

The Appeal Boards of the European Patent Office are "relevant convention courts" as defined by s.130(1). Under s.91(1)(c) judicial notice must be taken of their decisions or expressions of opinion on any question arising or in connection with the EPC, including opinions regarding inventive step. However, the relevant implementing regulations and rules have created a divergence in the way that the EPO on the one hand and the UK IP Office and courts on the other hand treat the issue of technical problem and its relationship to inventive step, see §3.28. As discussed in §3.04, UK courts do not consider themselves bound to follow problem/solution analysis (PSA) used by the EPO. They sometimes consider whether the outcome under PSA would be different from that given by the *Windsurfing/Pozzoli* approach normally used in the UK. Furthermore, the EPO may have considered issues which have not yet come before the UK courts or where the UK courts have decided to follow the EPO approach, e.g. concerning the criteria for selection patents, see §3.31, in which case the relevant decision(s) of the EPO Appeal Boards are routinely citable.

Historical development of the concept of obviousness—tests used by the UK and US within the common law and problem/solution analysis (PSA) used by the EPO

3.04   The UK approach to the evaluation of inventive step is the outcome of legal evolution that has continued in the common law tradition from the seventeenth century to the present day. The US approach also evolved within the common law tradition starting from UK approach as it stood at the end of the eighteenth century. Some US developments are mentioned to highlight similarities to and differences from the UK approach and also because of the practical importance of US law for those who draft specifications in the UK and require protection in the US. The EPO approach based on PSA, see below, was decided on by members of the Appeal Boards in discussions prior to the first decision that they handed down, T0001/80 *Carbonless copying paper/BAYER*, and is *sui generis*, although the influence of civil law tradition is significant.

Before the introduction of obviousness into UK and US law, the courts in both countries focused on inventiveness because that was the only requirement that could be gleaned from statute over and above bare novelty.

The Statute of Monopolies 1623 (21 Jac. 1, c3) provided for the grant of a patents for the sole working or making of any manner of new manufacture to the true and first inventor thereof. In the UK the courts held that a scintilla of invention was needed for patentability, see *Parkes v Cocker* (1929) 46 R.P.C. 241 at p.248. In the USA, the Supreme Court held that patentability called for more ingenuity than the work of a mechanic skilled in the art, see *Hotchkiss v Greenwood* 52 U.S. (11 How.) 248 (1850), and in 1941 went on to say that an invention should reveal the flash of creative genius, see *Cuno Engineering Corp. v Automatic Devices Corp.*, 314 U.S. 84, 91; 51 U.S.P.Q. 272, 275 (1941) per Douglas J.

The courts held that there could not be a patent for a well-known mechanical contrivance merely because it is applied in a manner or to a purpose which was analogous to the previous well-known use, see *Harwood v Gt. Northern Railway* 35 L.J.Q.B 27 and *Gadd & Mason v Mayor, etc. of Manchester* (1892) 9 R.P.C. 516. Issues of this kind frequently arose in the period following the industrial revolution and are discussed in many decisions of the UK and the US courts. They arise less commonly today. In relation to substances for the treatment of the human or animal body by surgery or therapy such an objection is now precluded by s.4A of the Act which gives effect to arts 54(4) and (5) EPC, see §§4A.01, and other new uses are protectable following the decision of the EPO Enlarged Appeal Board in G 2/88 *MOBIL OIL III/Friction reducing additive*.

Considerations of obviousness were introduced into UK patent law in the speeches of Lord Herschell in *American Braided Wire v Thompson & Co.* (1889) 6 R.P.C. 518 at p.528 and in *Vickers & Co. v Siddell* (1890) R.P.C. 292 at p.305. The need to treat anticipation and obviousness as distinct objections was explained by Lindley L.J. in *Gadd & Mason v Mayor etc. of Manchester* (above).

A question formulated by Sir Stafford Cripps was cited by the Master of the Rolls in *Sharp and Dohme Inc. v Boots Pure Drug Co.* (1928) 45 R.P.C. 153 at p.173:

"Was it for all practical purposes obvious to any skilled chemist in the state of chemical knowledge existing at the date of the patent, which consists of the chemical literature available . . . and his general chemical knowledge that he *could* manufacture *valuable* therapeutic agents by making the higher alkyl resorcinols?" (emphases added)

It was held that a skilled person could have made the higher alkyl resorcinols merely by following the teaching of the prior art and that he would have done so because it was predictable from the prior art that they would be valuable. It will be noted that the Cripps question like the subsequent *Windsurfing/Pozzoli test* §3.05 requires identification of the relevant skilled person §3.07–3.10, the common general knowledge to be attributed to that person §§3.11–3.17, the new human activity covered by the claim §3.18 and the result achieved by that new activity §3.29. In formulating that question it was taken as an established fact that the human activity lead to a valuable result (n-hexyl resorcinol being known as a valuable antiseptic at the time of trial), and the question then became firstly whether the road to the human activity was already open and secondly whether its value was recognisable in advance.

In the UK, it was as late as 1932 that the grounds upon which a patent could be revoked were codified and lack of novelty and obviousness became recognised by statute as distinct grounds of revocation, the latter being "that the invention is obvious and does not involve any inventive step having regard to what was known or used prior to the date of the patent" (Patents and Designs Act 1932, c.32, s.3, substituting a new s.25 into the Patents and Designs Act 1907, c.29). This definition remained substantially unchanged in the 1949 Act, save for reference to "priority date of a claim" instead of the "date of the patent". Similar codification did not take place in the USA until 1952 despite recognition of the objection of obviousness by the US courts since 1850 and in Australia also did not take place until 1952.

After 1932, the Cripps question in various forms continued to provide the framework for deciding obviousness for many years. In *Technograph v Mills and Rockley* [1969] R.P.C. 395 at 404 CA and [1972] R.P.C. 346 at 362 HL, the question was reformulated by replacing "could" with "would" or "should" and it was pointed out that inventive ingenuity can lie "in perceiving that the final result which it is the object of the invention to achieve was attainable from the particular starting point and in selection of the particular combination of steps which would lead to that result." In *Olin Mathieson v Biorex* ([1970] R.P.C. 157 at 187), there was a further reformulation of the question: "Would the notional research group at the relevant date, in the circumstances, ... directly be led as a matter of course to try [the invention claimed] in the expectation that it might well produce [a useful desired result]."

As explained above, a statutory obviousness test was introduced into US law in 1952 by 35 USC 103. For an explanation of the reasons for introduction of that test and the problems created by the previous inventiveness test see Giles S. Rich, *Laying the Ghost of the "Invention" Requirement*, AIPLA Quarterly Journal, Vol. 1, No. 1 pp.26–45 (1972). Judge Rich was a practising patent attorney, one of the two authors of the US patent statute, and a long-serving judge of the Court of Appeals for the Federal Circuit: he discusses 35 USC 103 not as a matter of legislative history but as one of its authors. He argues that "invention" was indefinite and subjective, had become the plaything of the judiciary and explains that non-obviousness had been intended to impose a more objective standard. How that test should be applied was explained by the US Supreme Court in *Graham v John Deere* 383 U.S. 1 (1966), in which Mr Justice Clark, delivering the opinion of the Court, said:

"While the ultimate question of patent validity is one of law, *Great A. & P. Tea Co. v. Supermarket Equipment Corp.* . . . 340 U. S. 155, the §103 condition, which is but one of three conditions, each of which must be satisfied, lends itself to several basic factual inquiries. Under §103, the scope and content of the prior art are to be determined; differences between the prior art and the claims at issue are to be ascertained; and the level of ordinary skill in the pertinent art resolved. Against this background, the obviousness or nonobviousness of the subject matter is determined. Such secondary considerations as commercial success, long felt but unsolved needs, failure of others, etc., might be utilized to give light to the circumstances surrounding the origin of the subject matter sought to be patented. As indicia of obviousness or nonobviousness, these inquiries may have relevancy.   .   .

This is not to say, however, that there will not be difficulties in applying the nonobviousness test. What is obvious is not a question upon which there is likely to be uniformity of thought in every given factual context. The difficulties, however, are comparable to those encountered daily by the courts in such frames of reference as negligence and scienter, and should be amenable to a case-by-case development."

The above formulation requires structured factual enquiries to be made, and thereafter leaves the issue to be decided according to the evidence and the arguments of the parties, with confirmation that circumstantial evidence may be relevant. No legal standard is imposed beyond that set out in the statute. The correctness of this analysis has not subsequently been questioned, and in *KSR v Teleflex* 550 U.S. 398 (2007) Mr Justice Kennedy, delivering the opinion of the US Supreme Court confirmed that "the factors continue to define the inquiry that controls" and that the appropriate approach was expansive, flexible and inconsistent with the application of any rigid rule that limits the scope of the inquiry.

The current test for inventive step used in the UK is derived from *Windsurfing v Tabur Marine* [1985] R.P.C. 59 CA and is in its essentials identical to that in *Graham v John Deere* insofar as it also calls for a structured enquiry followed by a decision according to the evidence adduced and arguments submitted by the parties, see §3.05.

The approach to inventive step adopted by the EPO has two principal characteristics. Firstly, it is an "effects-based" approach, so that whether or not a patent is granted ultimately depends on whether there is a new effect, a new function or result, flowing from the claimed features. Secondly, analysis for the presence or absence of inventive step is conducted within the so-called "technical problem" framework which is algorithmic and is applied universally and consistently by the EPO Appeal Boards, see §3.42.

It should not be assumed that the words "technical problem" have the same meaning when used by the EPO as they do when used by the United Kingdom IP Office or courts. It is submitted that much of the controversy which has continued in the UK for many years concerning the technical problem test arises through misunderstanding of the meaning given by the EPO to these words. In the UK they are generally understood to refer to a real-world problem whose existence is apparent from the cited literature or from the testimony of expert witnesses. In the EPO they are understood more usually to relate to an artificially constructed problem derived by considering the particular technical success achieved by the inventor(s) vis-à-vis the closest prior art.

Before decisions of the EPO Appeal Boards began to be handed down the approach that would be adopted by the EPO was uncertain: an article by J. Pagenberg, (1978) 9 IIC 1 and 121 describing and discussing the various sub-tests for presence, or absence, of inventive step which have been used particularly in the United States with the aim of improving the objectivity of the analysis is therefore of historical interest, as also is Hanns Ulrich, *Standards of Patentability for European Inventions*, IIC Studies Vol. 1, Max Plank, Munich, 1977 which extensively discussed the concept of technical advance then a feature of German law in comparison with developments in US law but did not advocate a technical problem test. The editors are not aware of any pre-1980 publication which predicted that the EPO would settle on the technical problem approach in the way that it did. For articles of a general nature, see: *"The inventive step: Its evolution in Canada, the United Kingdom and the United States"* by J. Bochnovic, IIC Studies, Vol. 5, Max Planck Institute, Munich, 1982; an article by Sir Douglas Falconer, (1989) 20 IIC 348 containing a pithy account of the manner in which objections of lack of subject-matter were dealt with respectively in grant, infringement and revocation proceedings under United Kingdom law and practice; and a paper by G.S.A. Szabo, "The Problem and Solution Approach in the European Patent Office" (1995) 26 IIC 457. A paper by P.G. Cole, "KSR and Standards of Inventive Step: A European View", 8 *J. Marshall Rev. Intell. Prop. Law* 14 (2008), available online, compares the test for obviousness applied by the US courts with that applied by the UK courts and by the EPO.

Serious consideration was given to the introduction in the UK of second-tier patents analogous to the *Gebrauchsmuster* system in Germany and corresponding systems, e.g. in China, Japan and Korea. The 2006 report of the *Gowers Review of Intellectual Property* did not recommend the establishment of such a system in the UK. However, the Australian government took a different view and in 2000 introduced so-called "innovation patents" having terms of eight years as compared to 20 years for standard patents. Innovative step is intended to be a less demanding requirement than inventive step, and appears to be an extended novelty test based on that set out in *Griffin v Isaacs* 12 A.L.J. 169 (1938). The statutory test is that an invention lacks an innovative step if when compared to the "prior art base" the invention varies in ways that make no substantial contribution to the working of the invention as judged by a person skilled in the art.

Innovative step was considered by the Full Court of the Federal Court of Australia in *Dura-Post v Delnorth* [2009] FCAFC 81. Delnorth had invented roadside posts of thin spring steel sheet which could flex through 90° when driven over by a vehicle wheel and could spring back without damage. The defendants Dura-Post contended that the invention was in the use of sheet spring steel for making roadside posts, and that the remaining differences specified in the claims were mere matters of common general knowledge. The primary judge had held at [2008] FCA 1225 at [52]–[54] that the phrase "no substantial contribution to the working of the invention" involved quite a different kind of judgment from that involved in determining whether there was an inventive step. Obviousness did not come into the issue. The idea behind it was that a claim which avoided a finding of lack of novelty because of an integer which made no substantial contribution to the working of the claimed invention should not receive protection but that, where the point of differentiation did contribute to the working of the invention, then it was entitled to protection, whether or not (even if), it was obvious. Indeed, the proper consideration of s.7(4) of the 2000 Act was liable to be impeded by traditional thinking about obviousness. The Full Court affirmed the unchallenged decision that the broader functional claims lacked innovative step over an earlier reference, but that claims specifying the use of a marker hole, a barb, a tapered end, longitudinally extending ribs and particular dimensions made a substantial contribution to the working of the invention as claimed and were valid.

Skeptics minded to doubt whether there is in reality a difference between innovative step and inventive step will observe that corresponding Delnorth applications matured into US Patent 7585127 and European Patent 1636427 so that the patents in issue satisfied both innovative step and inventive step requirements. Furthermore, the claims that were held valid were directed to generically similar features to those present in the granted US and European claims. The willingness of Australian courts to enforce patents that satisfy an innovative step requirement but clearly fail to satisfy an inventiveness requirement has not yet been tested. Nevertheless, the Australian Advisory Council on Intellectual Property in an "Issues Paper" dated August 2011has remarked that "an innovation patent is seen as being a very 'strong' patent that can be very difficult to revoke." It is arguable that the existence of an innovative step can act as strong indicator of inventive step. What may be of equal practical importance is that the enquiry as to innovative step involves a significantly narrower range of issues than the enquiry for inventive step, thus making enforcement a more realistic proposition for small and medium enterprises. Future developments will show whether the innovative step requirement provides a standard over and above novelty that is workable in the long term.

The test currently in use in the UK

Windsurfing/Pozzoli

The approach of UK courts has since 1985 been derived from *Windsurfing v Tabur Marine* [1985] R.P.C. 59 CA. The *Windsurfing* questions have been restated to provide a more logical presentation in *Pozzoli* [2007] EWCA Civ 588 CA. With slight re-ordering and more logical re-numbering we can re-define a sequence of questions as follows, inclusion of question (o) being a logical necessity since without it there is no antecedent basis for the reference to "the art":   **3.05**

[(o) identify the art or field of endeavour in which the invention arises;]

(i) identify the notional "person skilled in the art";

(ii) identify the relevant common general knowledge of that person;

(iii) identify the inventive concept of the claim in question or if that cannot readily be done, construe it (in *"Windsurfing"* originally stated as "identify the inventive concept embodied in the patent in suit");

(iv) identify what, if any, differences exist between the matter cited as forming part of the "state of the art" and the inventive concept of the claim or the claim as construed;

(v) viewed without any knowledge of the alleged invention as claimed, decide whether those differences constitute steps which would have been obvious to the person skilled in the art or whether they require any degree of invention.

Recent decisions show that *Windsurfing/Pozzoli* continues to provide the predominant questions that are asked and answered by the courts and UK IPO and it is submitted that they will continue for the foreseeable future to provide a structured approach which UK courts will follow. They are therefore used as the basis for discussion in the following sections.

Accordingly field of endeavour is considered at §3.06. The person or team skilled in the art is discussed at §§3.07–3.10. Common general knowledge is discussed at §§3.11–3.17. Identification of inventive concept and of differences between the invention and the prior art, including issues as to citable disclosures are discussed at §§3.18–3.25. Additional evidence and arguments relevant to question (v) is discussed at §§3.26–3.34. Further issues relating to evaluation, including the role of appellate courts, are considered at §§3.35–3.41. The EPO's problem/solution approach (PSA) which is sometimes used by UK courts as a cross-check on their evaluation is considered at §§3.42–3.51.

A slightly different way of evaluating invention was employed in *Mölnlycke v Brightwake* [2011] EWHC 376. Birss QCconsidered firstly whether the claimed product was obvious to conceive and secondly whether the skilled team could have made it without the exercise of invention. In the present case the invention was no more than the putting into effect the prior art proposals in an obvious way, the various choices being soundly based on the pleaded disclosure and the common general knowledge. In effect the choices operated in parallel and not as a series as in *Technograph*, where the series of steps needed to arrive at the invention required the cumulative application of hindsight.

Evidence and arguments covered by the structured enquiry

—The art or field of endeavour in which the invention arises—disclaimer practice

3.06 The first of the reformulated *Windsurfing/Pozzoli* question requires the person skilled in the art to be identified, after which the court or other tribunal has to identify the common general knowledge to be attributed to him. Obviously these questions cannot be answered without identifying the art or in the case of a complex invention the arts in question, as acknowledged by Jacob L.J. in *Schlumberger Holdings Ltd v Electromagnetic Geoservices AS* [2010] EWCA Civ 819, [2010] R.P.C. 33 at [65].

For a practitioner(s) prosecuting a patent application or litigating a granted patent, forming a view about the identity and scope of the art or field of endeavour in which the invention arises is an essential preliminary task. It is advisable to include in the claims features relating to or defining a field of endeavour, and both unduly wide and unduly restrictive definitions can create difficulty. For example, in *Windsurfing* (above) Oliver L.J. noted that although the patent covered the well-known Windsurfer sailing surfboard, the field of endeavour was defined to include ships in general and other types of vehicle e.g. land yachts. Prior art relating to ocean-going yachts was therefore legitimately citable. Because of the wide scope of the claimed subject-matter there was no basis for disputing the relevance of the evidence of a naval architect specialising in the design of such yachts rather than in the design of small sailing dinghies and surfboards in which the sole commercially significant embodiment had arisen.

A clear definition of the relevant art helps selection and assessment of the prior art. For example, in *Technograph v Mills & Rockley* [1972] R.P.C. 346 the field of endeavour was wiring for electrical circuits, and the technical problem was to replace the known method of point-to-point wiring. The solution was to form the conductors by printing a resist onto metal foil on a backing board and to etch away unwanted portions. The art cited also produced a pattern of conductors on a substrate by etching, although this method was not preferred. Its use was for producing a pattern of conductors for an electrostatic shield. It therefore lay outside the field of endeavour in which the inventors were working and was not relevant except with hindsight to the problem that they were endeavouring to solve. Not surprisingly, it did not provide a strong starting point for an obviousness attack, and the patent was held valid. Similarly in *Hickman v Andrews* [1983] R.P.C. 147 the invention as claimed was a workbench which was a field-defining limitation clearly differentiating the invention from the closest prior art which was an attachment for a workbench, and again the patent was held valid.

Limitation of a claim to distinguish prior art devices in which the problem solved by the subject-matter claimed does not arise can be an effective way of overcoming an obviousness objection. The classic UK decision on this point is *Molins v Industrial Machine Co. Ltd* (1938) 55 R.P.C. 31 CA. The claimed invention related to machines for forming cigarette rod and the problem was avoidance of irregularities in the rod. The inventive feature had been disclosed in an earlier specification, but that earlier disclosure related to a low-speed machine which did not produce rod suffering from the irregularities. Amendment of the claim to limit the claim to the high speed machines where the problem arose overcame objections as to both novelty and inventive step. The same fact pattern recurred in *Ferag v Muller Martini* [2007] EWCA Civ 15 where again a cited prior machine operated at low speed and did encounter the same problem as the invention which concerned high speed machines. For that reason it would have involved hindsight to start from the prior machine and make such variations as would bring it within the claim.

EPO and UK practice agree as regards the effects of disclaimers. For example, in T 59/87 *MOBIL I/Friction reducing additive* applicants as their main request claimed a lubricant composition containing an additive. The claim had been refused as lacking in novelty. An auxiliary request was directed to the use of the additive in a lubricant for reducing friction. The Appeal Board referred the issue of novelty to the Enlarged Board, but accepted that the narrowing amendment in the auxiliary request disposed of any objection as to lack of inventive step by more specifically defining the field of endeavour or technical problem with which the invention was concerned. Its reasoning therefore corresponds closely to that in *Molins*.

Amendment practice involving an unsupported disclaimer was considered in *Napp Pharmaceutical v Ratiopharm* [2009] R.P.C. 11, [2009] EWCA Civ 252. It was observed at [79]–[99] that what is important is the test laid down by the EPO Enlarged Appeal Board in G 1/03 *PPG/Disclaimer*, i.e. whether an introduced amendment is a mere disclaimer not contributing to the invention. If the added disclaimer renders the patent unobvious, it may be doing more than excluding protection for part of the subject-matter originally claimed and may be providing the patentee with an unwarranted advantage, see T 1139/00 *CORDIS/Balloons for medical device*. The disclaimer in one of the patents in issue was "other than an acrylic resin matrix selected so that the formulation provides pH independent dissolution characteristics." The case against the disclaimer was that it created two different classes of acrylic resin, one which was pH-independent and one which was not, and it would have been permissible to divide these two classes if they had been separately disclosed but not otherwise. At first instance it was held that the skilled person would not have derived any new technical teaching, but merely that such materials were not claimed. It was noteworthy that no expert had suggested that he would have learned anything new from the granted patent that he would not already have learned from the application as filed. Furthermore it was a fallacy that disclosure of subject-matter should be equated with scope of claim; see *A.C. Edwards v Acme Signs & Displays* [1992] R.P.C. 131 at p.143. The decision was affirmed on appeal. The latitude given by UK courts may be somewhat greater than that available in the EPO where a strict view that a disclaimer must do no more than what is necessary to restore novelty prevails, see e.g. G1/03 *PPG/Disclaimer*, G2/03 *GENETIC SYSTEMS/Disclaimer* and T 8/07 *IDEMITSU KOSAN/Disclaimer*.

The right to exclude by disclaimer an embodiment which was disclosed in positive terms in an application as filed was confirmed in T 1107/06 *ALLERGAN/Botulinum toxins*.

Disclaimer practice has been reviewed by A. Rudge, *The art of gracefully renouncing what's not yours—how the Boards of Appeal have applied G1/03 and G2/03 in practice*, EPI Information, 4/09, 134–140. A further review by A. Koch and G Weinzierl, *The concept of "unambiguous and direct disclosure"—future perspectives in view of T 1107/06 and 1443/05*, EPI Information 1/10, 15-17 warns of possibly conflicting standards as regards priority under a. 87 EPC and added subject matter under a.123(2) EPC and that an undisclosed disclaimer though allowable under a.123(2) EPC may result in denial of priority.

—The person skilled in the art

3.07 The teaching of the art is to be judged through the eyes of a person skilled in the art. The correct identification of the skilled person is therefore crucial to obviousness since everything (or in the alternative nothing) will be obvious to an incorrectly identified skilled person, *Actavis UK Ltd v Merck & Co. Inc.* [2007] EWHC 1311 (Pat). In revocation proceedings the parties normally provide expert evidence on this issue, see, e.g. *Handi-Craft Co. and others v B Free World Ltd and others* [2007] EWHC B10 (Pat).

An appropriate person must be directly involved in producing the product in question or in carrying out the process in question. In *Inhale Therapeutics v Quadrant* [2002] R.P.C. 419 it was held that where a claim covers a wide field, parts of it may be obvious to a notional skilled person in one area and other parts may be obvious to the notional skilled person in another area. This is not unfair to the patentee, but simply a reflection of the fact that the scope of protection is wide. Thus an argument that the claim fell to be construed by an expert in freeze drying, although the claims also covered other techniques such as spray drying (as used by the defendant), was held to be misconceived. Similarly in *European Central Bank v Document Security Systems Incorporated* [2007] EWHC 600 (Pat) the Court held that if the patentee has chosen to cast his monopoly so widely that it covers a number of different applications then its validity may be challenged in relation to each of them.

An appropriate person must be neither over- nor under-qualified. Lord Moulton said in *Gillette Safety Razor v American Trading* (1913) 30 R.P.C. 465 at 481 that a patent should not be tested by what it would convey or suggest to a mechanical genius but that it would be equally unjust to take it as though it were read only by mechanical idiots. In *Union Carbide v BP Chemicals* [1998] R.P.C. 1 and [1999] R.P.C. 409 CA, the Court of Appeal, in upholding a finding at first instance of inventive step, saw the defendant's evidence as based on an analysis by a distinguished expert in the field who could not be equated with the notional skilled man who would not have had the same level of expertise. The EPO takes a similar view; see T 39/93 *ALLIED COLLOIDS/Polymer powders* OJ EPO 1997, 134 at 7.8.4 where it was held that a person skilled in the art is an expert in the relevant field who is possessed of average knowledge and ability but is not an exceptional, outstanding or brilliant expert. That remains the case even if a number of scientists working in the field at the time were actually awarded the Nobel Prize; see T 60/89 *HARVARD/Fusion protein* OJ EPO 1992, 268, see also the *EPO Guidelines* at C IV 11.3.

The inventor himself may not be representative of a relevant skilled person, see *Wellcome Foundation v VR Laboratories [Australia]* [1982] R.P.C. 343 where there was a lengthy discussion concerning the state of mind of the inventor and the circumstances in which he came to make the alleged invention: the former is probably irrelevant, but the latter is not. The EPO takes a similar view; see T 39/93 *ALLIED COLLOIDS/Polymer powders* where it was held that the inventor is set apart from the average skilled person because he is possessed of inventive capability whereas the notional skilled person is not, and that the relevant person is a competent but uninventive person. Similarly in *Genentech's Patent* (above), it was argued that other workers in the art who had reached the same goal as the inventors possessed inventive capacity and should therefore not be equated with the persons skilled in the art, relying on *Valensi v British Radio* [1973] R.P.C. 337.

—Characteristics of a skilled person

Where the relevant skilled person is an individual, the characteristics of that individual **3.08** were explained by Laddie J. in *Pfizer's Patent* [2001] F.S.R. 20 in the following terms:

"The question of obviousness has to be assessed through the eyes of the skilled but non-inventive man in the art. This is not a real person. He is a legal creation. He is supposed to offer an objective test of whether a particular development can be protected by a patent. He is deemed to have looked at and read publicly available documents and to know of public uses in the prior art. He understands all languages and dialects. He never misses the obvious nor stumbles on the inventive. He has no private idiosyncratic preferences or dislikes. He never thinks laterally. He differs from all real people in one or more of these characteristics. A real worker in the field may never look at a piece of prior art—for example he may never look at the contents of a particular public library—or he may be put off because it is in a language he does not know. But the notional addressee is taken to have done so. This is a reflection of part of the policy underlying the law of obviousness. Anything which is obvious over what is available to the public cannot subsequently be the subject of valid patent protection even if, in practice, few would have bothered looking through the prior art or would have found the particular items relied upon. Patents are not granted for the discovery and wider dissemination of public material and what is obvious over it, but only for making new inventions. A worker who finds, is given or stumbles upon any piece of prior art must realise that that art and anything obvious over it cannot be monopolised by him and he is reassured that it cannot be monopolised by anyone else."

He has been described by Jacob L.J. in *Rockwater Ltd v Technip France SA (formerly Coflexip SA) and another* [2004] EWCA Civ 381 as a very boring person—a nerd and furthermore as very forgetful. Although he reads all the prior art, unless it forms part of his background technical knowledge, having read (or learnt about) one piece of prior art, he forgets it before reading the next unless the pieces of prior art can form an uninventive mosaic or there is a sufficient cross-reference, see the no-mosaic rule laid down by Lord Reid in *Technograph v Mills & Rockley* [1972] R.P.C. 346 at p.355, see also §3.23. Jacob L.J. went on to say that the attempt to approximate real people and in particular expert witnesses to the notional skilled man is not helpful because the role of an expert witness is to educate the court in the technology and not to provide an approximation to the skilled man.

The skilled person should be credited with sufficient time and the best available equipment to carry out the work and, where the art requires intellectual jumps and ingenuity of approach, that person must have a degree of inventiveness, but ability to perform known techniques is not a criterion *Genentech's Patent* [1989] R.P.C. 147.

In *Valensi v BRC* [1973] R.P.C. 337 at 377, Buckley L.J. said that the hypothetical addressee is not to be expected to exercise any invention nor any prolonged research enquiry or experiment. He must however be prepared to display a reasonable degree of skill and common knowledge of the art in making trials and to correct obvious errors if a means of correcting them can readily be found.

According to the *EPO Guidelines* C IV 11.3 a skilled person has the common general knowledge and a capacity for routine work and experimentation, as was explained in T 1030/06 *BROADCOM CORPORATION/Secure buffering*, particularly in relation to the ability to implement a feature disclosed in functional terms:

"The appellant argued generally that although the skilled person would be able to understand the invention, he would not be able to develop further or create ideas. The Board can only agree with this statement up to a point. The skilled person is a person of ordinary skill in the art which means not only having access to the state of the art and common general knowledge in the field, but also the capability to perform routine work and experimentation. Thus, the skilled person can be expected to seek out solutions and make choices to try to solve design problems that crop up. In the Board's view, this is particularly so where the problem is to come up with an implementation of an apparatus having certain required functions as in the present case. The implementation of the first part of the solution (here the provision of several processors) often leads to further design decisions that must be made (here the choice of encryption scheme and the identification of the source of data) in order to produce a working system. The skilled person cannot be expected to abandon the implementation half-way through in the form of a "black box" with undefined means for carrying out the required functions, but must attempt if possible to put such means into practice using knowledge available to him (see also T 623/97 of 11 April 2002, at point 4.4). These would literally be "further ideas" in the sense that they could be new in the given context, but they should be routine and thus not inventive."

Additionally, the EPO considers the skilled person to have notice of all the references found in the search report, which is not an assumption that would be made automatically by the UK IPO or a UK court.

—The skilled team

3.09   In appropriate cases the person skilled in the art may be a multi-disciplinary team, *General Tire v Firestone* [1972] R.P.C. 457 at 482–485, *American Cyanamid v Ethicon* [1979] R.P.C. 215 and *Genentech's Patent* [1989] R.P.C. 147 CA. Since patented inventions are commonly the work of teams of inventors, it is logical that in appropriate cases the state of the art should be judged for the purposes of inventive step through the eyes of such a team. For example, in *Chiron v Organon Teknika (No. 3)* [1994] F.S.R. 202, it was accepted that the notional skilled addressee would have the knowledge of a clinician, a virologist and a molecular biologist. In *Aloys Wobben v Vestas-Celtic Wind Technology Ltd* [2007] EWHC 2636 (Pat) the invention concerned wind turbine technology. The Patents Court held that the skilled addressee would be a multi-disciplinary team comprising a wind turbine design and development engineer (from a wind turbine design company); an electrical machines design and development engineer (from an electrical machines company); a power electronics and real time control design and development engineer (from a variable speed drives company); and a power systems operation and control engineer (from a distribution network or a transmissions systems operator).

In *Ivax v Akzo Nobel* [2006] EWHC 1089, BL C/61/06, noted IPD 29059, the court held, following an earlier decision in *Richardson-Vick's Patent* [1997] R.P.C. 888 (CA) that it is illegitimate to include in the team someone who was not directly involved in producing the product described in the specification or in carrying out the process of production. It had not been established on the evidence that knowledge of the regulatory requirements was part of the common general knowledge of the legitimate members of the team. Obstacles to regulatory approval of pharmaceutical products or to lawful sale were therefore not relevant to an obviousness attack. Similarly in *Generics (UK) Ltd and others v H. Lundbeck A/S* [2007] EWHC 1040 (Pat) which concerned the development of a new antidepressant drug the skilled addressee was held to be a team comprising medicinal chemists who were PhDs with two to three years' experience and were engaged in finding new drug candidates, an analytical chemist and a clinician, but not a process research chemist (for developing large-scale production methods) nor a pharmaceutical chemist (for development of formulations). In *Cranway v Playtech* [2009] EWHC 1588 (Pat) claims to a gaming system for playing an interactive casino game were not limited to gambling with real money and hence a casino operator was not part of the team, the skilled person being a computer software engineer who could actually implement the system called for by the patent. The purpose of trying to include a casino operator as part of the team from the standpoint of the patentee was to establish an alleged "mindset" hostile to or at least sceptical about online gambling at casino games for real money. But even if a casino operator had been included in the team, there would have been an internal debate about the technical feasibility of implementing the idea. It was not accepted that the casino operator would have been the dominant member of the team and that his views or prejudices would have prevailed. If the perceived difficulties were business difficulties, they were not relevant to the question of obviousness. If there were technical difficulties there was no reason why the casino operator would not have been convinced by the computer specialist that the solution was technically obvious.

In *Sandoz v Roche Diagnostics* [2004] EWHC 1313 (Ch), noted IPD 27076 which concerned the preservation of the protein human erythropoietin, the court held that a protein scientist would have the pivotal role and that a formulation scientist and a microbiologist who would be the other members of the team would play an essentially supplemental role.

In *Minnesota Mining v AT! Atlas* [2001] F.S.R. 514; [2001] IP&T 535, it was noted, as a matter of principle, that invention cannot lie in bringing into a notional team working on a particular problem a new notional member with different skills from those of the existing notional team.

The EPO also recognises teams of inventors, but identifies and focuses on the team member whose efforts are needed to solve the problem with which the invention is concerned. In T 32/81 *FIVES—CAIL BABCOCK/Cleaning apparatus for conveyor belt* OJ EPO 1982, 225 the invention related to cleaning apparatus for an endless conveyor belt, the problem was breakage of rod-shaped cleaning elements and the conveying equipment specialist was prompted by the nature of the problem to bring in a specialist in materials science whose skills permitted the problem to be solved. As a further example, in T 222/86 *GERBER/Laser engraving* the field was held to be an advanced technology involving a laser expert, an electronics expert and a chemist, with electronics expert being able so foresee the step necessary to solve the technical problem. In T 986/96 *M.A.I.L. CODE INC/Mail Processing System* the relevant team consisted of a first expert in the field of mail processing and a second expert in the field of weighing, but neither of them could solve the problem so that validity was affirmed. The approach adopted by the EPO is further illustrated in T 1160/07 *GILLETTE/Shaving razor handle*. In the development of plastic parts such as a shaving razor handle a product designer was active from the beginning of development but the issue of his knowledge of moulding methods could be left open since the invention concerned the manufacturing aspect and it was the knowledge of an expert in the technology of moulding small parts that was relevant.

—Different teams for different situations

A question that arises in relation to the composition of teams of skilled people is whether **3.10** the phrase "person skilled in the art" has the same meaning when considering the various concepts of novelty, obviousness and sufficiency.

In *Synthon BV v Smithkline Beecham Plc* [2005] UKHL 59 HL it was explained that the role of the skilled person differs as regards anticipation and insufficiency. For novelty the skilled person is interpreting what the prior description discloses, whereas for enablement the skilled person is ascertaining whether the invention held to have been disclosed can be reproduced. Whether or not the relevant teams differ as regards obviousness and insufficiency so that the notional skilled team should include a person skilled in a second discipline was again considered in *Schlumberger v Electromagnetic Geoservices* [2010] EWCA Civ 819. It was again held that there could be different teams for different purposes, and in particular for obviousness and sufficiency, provided that the invention was itself art-changing by putting together two disparate arts. Examples included *Dyson v Hoover* [2002] R.P.C. 465 where the real research team did not include an expert on cyclones because "no-one had the wit to bring one in" and doing that was the essence of the invention and T 422/93 *JALON/Luminescent security fibres* in which to perform the Jalon invention dyeing skills were needed but the person skilled in dyeing was rejected as being irrelevant when considering obviousness because the very invention consisted of bringing a dyer in—he was part of the solution. "The art" was not necessarily the same both before and after the invention had been made. It was not a matter of applying a different construction to the phrase "person skilled in the art" in the different sections of the Act but of applying the phrase to different situations. Where the issue was claim construction or sufficiency a post-patent situation was being considered where the person skilled in the art had the patent in hand to tell him how to perform the invention and what the monopoly claimed was. But *ex-hypothesi* the person skilled in the art did not have the patent when considering obviousness and "the art" could be different if the invention of the patent itself was art-changing. Such considerations could make all the difference when considering obviousness. If there were specialists in two different disciplines it could not just be assumed that each would know what was known to the other, proof was needed that this was indeed so. Was the marriage obvious to either notional partner? (Schlumberger) In that case if the specialist in the second field had been aware of the problem in the first field, the invention would have been obvious, but he was not. On the same reasoning Birss QC held that a team interested in developing wound dressings would not have included a silicone coating specialist if the prior art had not mentioned silicone coating, but that where the prior art did so, then a person or team in this art would have consulted a silicone specialist, see *Mölnlycke v Brightwake* [2011] EWHC 376.

—Common general knowledge in the art

3.11   The re-stated *Windsurfing* analysis requires consideration of the "common general knowledge" of the person skilled in the art. In *Beloit Technologies v Valmet Paper Machinery* [1997] R.P.C. 489 at 494–495 Aldous L.J. explained that:

> "It has never been easy to differentiate between common general knowledge and that which is known by some. It has become particularly difficult with the modern ability to circulate and retrieve information. Employees of some companies, with the use of libraries and patent departments, will become aware of information soon after it is published in a whole variety of documents; whereas others, without such advantages, may never do so until that information is accepted generally and put into practice. The notional skilled addressee is the ordinary man who may not have the advantages that some employees of large companies may have. The information in a patent specification is addressed to such a man and must contain sufficient details for him to understand and apply the invention. It will only lack an inventive step if it is obvious to such a man. It follows that evidence that a fact is known or even well-known to a witness does not establish that that fact forms part of the common general knowledge."

Such knowledge has been described by Aldous L.J. in *Dyson Appliances v Hoover Limited* [2001] EWCA Civ 1440 as distinct from that which is merely known and as being what is known by the ordinary addressee of the patent, e.g. generally known in the industry with which the invention is concerned. It was further explained in *Raychem's Patents* [1999] R.P.C. 497 CA as:

> ". . . the technical background of the notional person in the art against which the prior art must be considered. This is not limited to material which he has memorised and has in the front of his mind. It includes all that material in the field he is working in which he knows exists, which he would refer to as a matter of course if he cannot remember it and which he understands is generally regarded as sufficiently reliable to use as a foundation for further work and to help understand the pleaded prior art".

The importance of assessing common general knowledge was explained by Pumfrey J. in *Conor Medsystems Inc. v Angiotech Pharmaceuticals Inc. and Anor* [2006] EWHC 260 HC as follows:

"The most difficult part of any obviousness case is the attribution of the relevant skill and knowledge to the notional addressee of the patent. When the common general knowledge is identified, the height of the bar is set."

A further reason why the concept of common general knowledge is important under United Kingdom law is because, as explained by Jacob L.J. in *SmithKline Beecham Plc v Apotex Europe Ltd* [2004] EWCA Civ 1568, [2005] F.S.R. 23 at [96] the skilled person has his common general knowledge—the mental tools of his trade—but no more. The law of obviousness supposes that he can be given any individual piece of prior art and read it with that knowledge. What he cannot to do is to link one piece of art with another, unless so to do would be uninventive. A mosaic is permissible but it must be one which the skilled person can put together with no invention and in practice such situations are rare, see §3.23, see also the EPO approach at §3.47.

As explained by Aldous L.J. in *Dyson Appliances v Hoover Limited* [2001] EWCA Civ 1440, common general knowledge is a matter of evidence which must be given by a person in a position to know what was the common general knowledge in the industry, e.g. a member of a design department, and not e.g. given by an expert witness who had nothing to do with the industry at the relevant time. In *Tickner v Honda* [2002] EWHC 8 (Pat) there had been a meeting between experts for the parties to identify points of agreement and disagreement, and Jacob J. observed that it would be desirable in future cases if the experts could specifically address items of agreed common knowledge separately.

In *Maxluk Biotechnology Corp's Application* O/130/10 the Hearing Officer held, citing *Ratiopharm GmbH v Napp Pharmaceutical Holdings* [2009] R.P.C. 11 at 155–159, that when deciding what was common general knowledge it was not appropriate to just take those parts of a document that supported or rebutted the objection that was being made. To do so was hindsight selection. The notional skilled person came armed with all the common general knowledge, and could not pick and choose selectively with the benefit of hindsight. Some aspects of the common general knowledge might lead the skilled person from the prior art towards the inventive concept, but equally other aspects of common general knowledge might lead him away from the inventive concept. So the common general knowledge includes both of these apparently conflicting "pointers", see also *Nokia v Ipcom* [2011] EWHC 1470 (Pat) at [58].

The concept of common general knowledge is also important under the EPC and the approach to what is or is not to be considered part of such knowledge is similar to that which applies in the UK. The subject is reviewed in T 890/02 *Chimeric gene/BAYER* OJ EPO 2005. It is explained that assessment is made on the basis that firstly the skills of such a person include not only basic general knowledge of a particular technical field but also the ability to look up such knowledge in encyclopaedias and handbooks as well as, in exceptional cases, in a series of relevant studies or in a scientific publication or a patent specification, secondly the skilled person cannot be expected to carry out a comprehensive search of the literature covering virtually the whole state of the art because that would involve undue effort and thirdly the information found must be unambiguous and usable in a direct and straightforward manner without doubts or further research work. Databases such as the *EMBL Nucleotide sequence*, the *ENZYME database* or *SWISS PROT* were held to resemble an encyclopaedia rather than an abstracting service and to form part of the common general knowledge because they required no search strategy, retrieval of information required no undue effort and the retrieved information was unambiguous and straightforward.

—Mere paper proposals

In *British Acoustic Films Ltd v Nettlefold Productions* (1936) 53 R.P.C. 221 at p.250 **3.12** Luxmoore J. said that it was difficult to appreciate how the use of something which in fact has never been used in a particular art can ever be held to be common general knowledge in that art. This statement has been quoted with approval in *General Tire v Firestone* [1972] R.P.C. 457 and *Beloit v Valmet* [1977] EWCA Civ. 993.

In *Virgin Atlantic Airways v Premium Aircraft Interiors* [2009] EWHC 26 the idea of inwardly facing herringbone seating had been around for some time but had not become part of the common general knowledge as it had never been put into practice. On appeal, [2009] EWCA Civ 1062, Jacob L.J. observed at [27] that a well-known but unused idea may have less significance than one that was well in use, but neither side's case depended on this point because an inward facing herringbone had been referred to in cited prior art [116].

Prior art acknowledged in the specification

3.13   In *Storage Computer v Hitachi* [2003] EWCA Civ. 1155 the Court of Appeal upheld a decision at first instance that prior art acknowledged in the patent was part of the common general knowledge and could be used as the basis of a finding of obviousness, being at least an admission made against the patentee's interest. If the patentee had wished to contend that the statement in the patent did not provide an adequate statement of what was disclosed in the prior art, then it was for it to adduce the appropriate evidence, which it had not done.

In O/195/10 *Loadhog v Polymer Logistics* the introduction to the patent in issue stated that: "The prior art is replete with wheeled dollies and with pallets with retractable wheels". The patentees sought to resile from this statement, but it was held that their expert had not made a sufficiently clear rebuttal inter alia because he had not referred to the statement in the patent itself, and also because the rebuttal would have been expected to come from the patentee and not from another witness. However, the statement itself was not the same as saying that pallets with retractable wheels were part of the common general knowledge. For example, the prior art is replete with magnetic core memories, but that technology had been abandoned 30–40 years ago and such memories were not part of the common general knowledge today.

—Patent specifications and scientific papers

3.14   The Court of Appeal explained in *General Tire & Rubber Co. v Firestone Tyre & Rubber Co. Ltd* [1972] R.P.C. 457, at p.482, line 33 that individual patent specifications and their contents do not normally form part of the relevant common general knowledge, though there may be specifications which are so well known amongst those skilled in the art that they form part of such knowledge. Furthermore, there may occasionally be particular industries (such as that of colour photography) in which the evidence may show that all specifications form part of the relevant knowledge.

The circumstances in which scientific papers may become common general knowledge were explained by Luxmoore J. in *British Acoustic Films Ltd v Nettlefold Productions* (1936) 53 R.P.C. 221 at p.250 which was cited with approval by the Court of Appeal in *General Tire & Rubber Co. v Firestone Tyre & Rubber Co. Ltd* [1972] R.P.C. 457 at 482. This commonly cited passage is set out below with the modification introduced by Aldous L.J. in *Beloit Technologies Inc v Valmet Paper Machinery Inc* [1997] R.P.C. 489:

> "In my judgment it is not sufficient to prove common general knowledge that a particular disclosure is made in an article, or series of articles, in a scientific journal, no matter how wide the circulation of that journal may be, in the absence of any evidence that the disclosure is accepted generally by those who are engaged in the art to which the disclosure relates. A piece of particular knowledge as disclosed in a scientific paper does not become common general knowledge merely because it is widely read, and still less because it is widely circulated. Such a piece of knowledge only becomes general knowledge when it is generally known [and generally regarded as a good basis for further action] by the bulk of those who are engaged in the particular art; in other words, when it becomes part of their common stock of knowledge relating to the art . . ..".

The EPO regards isolated patents or scientific publications as common general knowledge only in special circumstances T 228/87 *BRIDGESTONE/Rubber composition* [1990]

E.P.O.R. 483. However, where the addressee of the patent was held to be a highly skilled physicist, a paper published in a prestigious scientific journal which such a person would read was held to have the status of "common general knowledge" T 378/93 *TOSHIBA/ Self-aligned FET*.

—Textbooks

In *HTC Corporation v Yozmot 33 Ltd* [2010] EWHC 786 (Pat) it was disputed whether **3.15** the use of electromagnetic loudspeakers in landline telephones as described in a "fairly elementary" textbook was common general knowledge in the cellular telephone art. Both parties were criticised for not dealing with the matter in cross-examination. The court held that although the onus of proof lay on HTC, the issue should not be resolved on onus unless it was impossible to come to conclusion one way or the other on the evidence: see *Stephens v Cannon* [2005] EWCA Civ 222. In the present case the relevant textbook itself was best evidence because the easiest way to prove that something is common general knowledge is to show that it is mentioned in an appropriate textbook, and the matter was held to be common general knowledge. In *Red Spider Technology v Omega Corporation* [2010] EWHC 59 (Pat) a feature was held to be common general knowledge on the basis of its prevalence and sufficiently clear appearance in catalogues which it would have been common practice for a designer to consult to keep abreast of products made by competitors.

The EPO regards information contained in textbooks or encyclopaedias (as distinct from patent specifications) as having the status of common general knowledge, T 671/94, *ICI/Solid emulsion* [1997] E.P.O.R. 155.

—Routine further investigations

In *Ivax v Akzo Nobel* [2006] EWHC 1089 Ch *noted* IPD 29059, the court held that it did **3.16** not matter if an average formulator was not aware of the drug in question since he would have acquired the relevant information either in the form of a pre-formulation brief which would tell him what drug he was required to formulate or in the course of pre-formulation literature searches which were part of the ordinary routine of a formulator. If that is what would happen in the real world as a matter of the routine of a skilled but unimaginative person, there was no reason why it should not happen in the world of patents. Although this information was not part of the common general knowledge, as that expression is usually understood, it was nevertheless to be treated in the same way as common general knowledge.

The above principles were further discussed in *Generics v Daiichi* [2009] R.P.C. 4, [2009] EWCA 646. There may be material which a skilled person is taken to know and which he will bring to bear on learning of a particular piece of prior art. There may be other material which he will not carry in his head but which he knows he can find if he needs to do so, but it does not follow that such material should be taken to be known to the skilled man if he has no particular reason for referring to it. The skilled person reads each specific piece of prior art with his common general knowledge and does not read it with another specific piece of prior art unless the first causes him to do so or both are part of the matter taken to be in his head. For example, if a skilled person knows that coefficient of expansion matters to the operation of a device, it is then legitimate to say that he knows that there are tables of coefficients of expansion and that he would consult them, but not if it was not apparent that coefficient of expansion mattered.

The relevant legal principles were reviewed by Arnold J. in *KCI Licensing v Smith & Nephew* [2011] F.S.R. 8, [2010] EWHC 1487 Pat at [105]–[112] and his conclusion was approved as an accurate statement of the law by Jacob L.J. [2010] EWCA Civ 1260 at [6]:

"[112] It follows that, even if information is neither disclosed by a specific item of prior art nor common general knowledge, it may nevertheless be taken into account as part of a case of obviousness if it is proved that the skilled person faced with the problem to which the patent is addressed would acquire that information as a matter of routine. For example, if the problem is how to formulate a particular pharmaceutical substance for administration to patients, then it may be shown that the skilled formulator would as a matter of routine start by ascertaining certain physical and chemical properties of that substance (e.g. its aqueous solubility) from the literature or by routine testing. If so, it is legitimate to take that information into account when assessing the obviousness of a particular formulation. But that is because it is obvious for the skilled person to obtain the information, not because it is common general knowledge."

—Prejudice (an aspect of common general knowledge)

3.17   It is necessary to take into account both the positive and the negative aspects of the common general knowledge held by a person skilled in the art, see O/332/10 *William Brownlie's Application*. Invention may lie in overcoming the preconceptions of the skilled person in a particular field of technology. As Jacob J put it in *Union Carbide v BP Chemicals* [1998] R.P.C. 1, 13: "Invention can lie in finding out that that which those in the art thought ought not be done, ought to be done. From the point of view of the purpose of patent law it would be odd if there were not patent incentive for those who investigate the prejudices of the prior art." Technical prejudice is also taken into consideration under the EPC, see e.g. T 341/94 *Oral Compositions/PROCTER III* where it was observed that a prejudice in any particular field relates to an opinion or preconceived idea widely or universally held by experts in that particular field. The existence of such prejudice is normally demonstrated by reference to the literature or to encyclopaedias published before the priority date and the prejudice must have existed at the priority date.

In *Glaxo Group Patent* [2004] R.P.C. 843, [43], it was held that a technical prejudice must be sufficiently widespread for it to be properly regarded as commonly shared, and if only some technically skilled people and not others were affected by the prejudice then that was not sufficient. In *Merz Pharma Gmbh & Co KGaA v Allergan* [2006] EWHC 2686 it was held that to be relevant a technical prejudice must be generally held by those skilled in the art. Similarly, in T 1212/01 *Pyrazolopyrimidinones for impotence treatment/ PFIZER* it was held that prejudice can only be established by proving that, in relation to the technical solution, a relatively widespread or universal error or misapprehension about the technical invention existed among skilled workers in the relevant field before the priority date of the patent in suit; a selection of the technical literature did not suffice. Laddie J. was also of the view that in the case of this particular patent there was no relevant prejudice, commenting that it was all too easy to raise a lurid fear and thereby obscure the issues, and the relevant risk was not that of killing anyone but that research would be unproductive, see *Lilly Icos v Pfizer* [2000] EWHC Pat 49, affirmed at [2002] EWCA Civ 1. In T 1671/06 *NOKIA/Reminders for a communications terminal* it was held that a nontechnical prejudice is not relevant to inventive step.

As explained in *Dyson v Hoover* [2002] R.P.C. 465, common general knowledge has both positive and negative aspects. In the relevant art there was seen to be a ''mindset'' against bag-less vacuum cleaners which "played a part in setting the notional addressee's mental horizon, making a true inventor of the individual who was able to lift his eyes above the horizon and see a bag-less machine." It was seen as "one of the ironies of the case" that the defendant, which had a pre-eminent reputation in domestic vacuum cleaners, had in fact rejected the invention when offered it, but then claimed that the judge was wrongly influenced by the existence of that mindset in coming to his decision that the invention was not obvious, see also the observations of Judge Rich at §3.39. The idea of mindset also played a part in the Court of Appeal's decision in *Panduit v Band-It* [2003] F.S.R. 127.

In *Schlumberger Holdings v Electromagnetic Geoservices* [2010] R.P.C. 33, [2010] EWCA Civ 819 Jacob L.J. held [42] that in considering the skills of the notional "person skilled in the art" the court should have regard to the reality of the position at the time and the combined skills and mindsets of real research teams in the art was what mattered when constructing the notional research team to whom the invention must be obvious. The patentees argued that exploration geophysicists had a mindset, thinking that CSEM was an academic technique of no practical use, just as in *Dyson v Hoover* vacuum cleaner engineers were "bag-ridden". However, it appears that this argument was not accepted [91]–[93], the court preferring to base its decision on the fact that the patent was for a useful technique which could have been developed long before, which those in the art had missed and which provided a new method for the direct and remote identification of hydrocarbon-filled layers in deep-water areas, permitting vast savings in the cost of drilling test wells into structures that did not contain measurable amounts of hydrocarbon [103].

An observation in *Pozzoli* at [28] that a patent for an old idea thought not to work and not explaining how or why, contrary to prejudice that the idea does indeed work, contributes nothing to human knowledge was reconsidered in *Dyson v Samsung* [2009] EWHC 55 [Pat] at [154]–[157]. Following the decision of the House of Lords in *Conor v Angiotech* it is now merely necessary for the patent to make it plausible that the invention would work or be practical contrary to the prejudice. Further, it is not necessary for the patent to expressly address the prejudice, but failure to mention any prejudice in the specification may be of evidential significance. Increase in pressure drop by addition of an additional cyclone to form a three-stage cyclone was not a reason for saying that such a cyclone would not work and was not worth bothering with, the possible need for a more powerful and hence expensive fan was a commercial and not a technical consideration and it would have been obvious to a skilled person that adding the third cyclone would have improved separation efficiency. For a further decision involving prejudice and plausibility see *FNM Corporation v Drammock International* [2009] EWHC 1294 (Pat) at [188].

In *Ancare's Patent [New Zealand]* [2003] R.P.C. 139 the Privy Council on appeal from the Court of Appeal of New Zealand held that the fact that scientific opinion thought that something was useless did not mean that practising it, or having the idea of making a preparation to do it, was an inventive step. Otherwise, anyone who adopted an obvious method for doing something which was widely practised but which the best scientific opinion thought was pointless could obtain a patent.

In *Vector Group v Glatt Air Techniques* [2006] EWHC 1638 (Pat) it was common ground that the behaviour of fluidized beds was not well understood and that although the science of fluidization had ceased to be a "black art", it was still reliant on trial and error. Partly for that reason the community of those involved in fluidization was conservative in outlook and this mindset meant that the skilled addressee was wary of modifying designs on paper in the prior art.

—Identifying the inventive concept

In *Van der Lely v Ruston's Engineering* [1985] R.P.C. 46 it was held that from the **3.18** standpoint of the patent office or a court the inventive concept will probably be the advance in the art which the patent itself asserts has been made. In *Unilever v Chefaro* [1994] R.P.C. 567 at p.580, Jacob J. observed:

> "The first stage of identification of the concept is likely to be a question of construction: what does the claim mean? It might be thought that there is no second stage - the concept is what the claim covers, and that is that. But that is too wooden and not what courts applying *Windsurfing* stage one have done. It is too wooden because if one merely construes the claim one does not distinguish between portions that matter and portions which, although limitations on the ambit of the claim, do not. One is trying to identify the essence of the claim in this exercise."

In *Conor Medisystems v Angiotech Pharmaceuticals* [2008] R.P.C. 28, [2008] UKHL 49 the House of Lords affirmed that the invention means prima facie that specified in the claim, and not some vague paraphrase based on the extent of the disclosure in the description.

In *Generics v Lundbeck* [2009] R.P.C. 13, [2009] UKHL 12 Lord Scott (with whom Lord Neuberger agreed) held that inventive concept was distinct from technical contribution to the art. Inventive concept is concerned with the identification of the core (or kernel, or essence) of the invention—the idea or principle, of more or less general application which entitles the inventor's achievement to be called inventive. The technical contribution of the invention to the art is concerned with the *evaluation* of its inventive concept—how far forward the state of the art has been carried. Lord Neuberger added that in the case of a product claim the inventive concept was primarily what was alleged to have been invented rather than how the invention had been made.

Thus in *Conor* the House of Lords affirmed that where a claim is to a new product the question is simply whether that product involves an inventive step. In the case in issue, there was nothing inventive about how to make the product, and the alleged inventiveness was in the claim that the product would have a particular property. It was sufficient that the specification contained enough information to make it plausible that the product would indeed have that property. There was no further requirement that the specification should demonstrate by experiment that the invention would work or should explain why it would work.

In *Lundbeck v Generics* [2008] R.P.C. 19, [2008] EWCA Civ 311 Lord Hoffmann (sitting in the Court of Appeal) cited with approval observations in EPO Case T 595/90 *Kawasaki Steel Corporation* [1994] OJ EPO 695 in which the Board held that a product which can be envisaged as such with all its characteristics determining its identity together with its properties in use, i.e. an otherwise obvious entity, could become nevertheless non-obvious and claimable as such if there was no known way or applicable (analogy) method in the art to make it and the claimed methods for its preparation were therefore the first to achieve this in an inventive manner. It was incorrect to read *Biogen v Medeva* [1977] R.P.C. 1 as casting any doubt upon the proposition that an inventor who finds a way to make a new product is entitled to make a product claim, even if its properties could have been fully specified in advance and the desirability of making it was obvious. The decision was affirmed by the House of Lords [2009] R.P.C. 13, [2009] UKHL 12, where Lord Neuberger said at [90]:

"In the light of this discussion, it appears clear to me that, unless precluded by the reasoning in *Biogen* [1997] RPC 1, on which Kitchin J primarily relied in his decision and on which Mr Thorley primarily relies in his argument, the product claim in the present case is valid. I appreciate that this means that, by finding one method of making a product, a person can obtain a monopoly for that product. However, that applies to any product claim. Further, where (as here) the product is a known desideratum, it can be said (as Lord Walker pointed out) that the invention is all the more creditable, as it is likely that there has been more competition than where the product has not been thought of. The role of fortuity in patent law cannot be doubted: it is inevitable, as in almost any area of life. Luck as well as skill often determines, for instance, who is first to file, whether a better product or process is soon discovered, or whether an invention turns out to be valuable. Further, while the law must be principled, it must also be clear and consistent."

The decision is criticised by Justine Pila, *Chemical Product Patents and Biogen Insufficiency before the House of Lords*, 920090 125 Law Quarterly Review 573-578, observing that the enantiomer in question, escitalopram, was an isolated chemical product, that this distinction was essential to the finding that the claimed subject-matter was not anticipated by the racemate, and that a claim to an isolated product was analogous to a claim to a recombinant product.

Especially in empirical research fields it may not be possible to rely on an unexpected effect not described or foreshadowed in the patent specification. The patentee cannot rely on a discovery that he had not made at the time that the patent was filed, but only some time later, see *Richardson-Vicks Inc.'s Patent* [1995] R.P.C. 568 and *Glaxo Group Ltd's Patent* [2004] EWHC 477 (Ch); [2004] R.P.C. 43 where the absence of supporting data in the specification was commented on. In *GE Healthcare v Perkin Elmer* [2006] EWHC 214 (Pat), the claims were very broad and were not limited to particular materials that were effective or to particular performance levels. After identifying a number of deficiencies in the teaching contained in the description, the court held that the inventive concept was a bare idea regardless of whether that idea yielded any improvement. The claimed subject-matter was then held to lack inventive step. In *Laboratorios Almirall v Boehringer Ingelheim* [2009] EWHC 102 (Pat) it was held that sufficient justification for the solution to a technical problem must be found in the application as filed and experiments performed thereafter cannot be relied on to make good an initial deficiency of disclosure, citing T 609/02 *SALK INSTITUTE/AP-1 complex*, T 1329/04 *JOHNS HOPKINS/Factor 9*, *Richardson-Vick's Patent* [1995] R.P.C. 568 at p.581 and *Glaxo Group's Patent* [2004] R.P.C. 843 at 852–853. In T 294/07 *PROTEXEON/Anaesthetic formulation* there was a reference to a higher than expected activity and examples where the claimed formulations had been administered to human patients, which was held to be sufficient to make it plausible that there was synergy between the components of the formulation, as established by post-published experimental data.

Where the claims are seen as prolix and opaque, the court should break free of the claim language used and concern itself with what the claims really meant, *Raychem's Patents* [1998] R.P.C. 31, disregarding meaningless and arbitrary parameters present in the claim wording. If an inventive concept cannot readily be identified, the claim should simply be construed. It was observed in *Actavis v Novartis* [2010] F.S.R. 18, [2010] EWCA Civ 82 (CA) at [19]–[20] that the "inventive concept" could be a distraction if there was an argument as to what it was, but could be helpful when the parties were agreed as to what it was. In the patent in issue although the claim had a numerical limitation defining what was meant by "sustained release", as a practical matter both sides proceeded on the basis that it was for a sustained release formulation.

—The collocation/combination test and its relevance to inventive concept

The restated *Windsurfing/Pozzoli* test implicitly assumes that the claimed subject-matter relates to a single inventive concept. However, a decision may have to be made whether the claimed features represent a combination or a mere collocation. Features form a combination when they all work together to produce a result, whereas they form a collocation when they can be divided into individual features or groups of features that work independently (see the "sausage machine" case, *Williams v Nye* (1890) 7 R.P.C. 62 CA, *British Celanese Ltd v Courtaulds Ltd* (1935) 52 R.P.C. 171, 193 HL, *International Paint's Application* [1982] R.P.C. 247 HC, see also the *EPO Guidelines for Examination* Ch.IV, para.11.7). An affirmative finding that a result flows from the claimed integers in combination can provide evidence in support of patentability §3.29. The present discussion is primarily concerned with implications where there is no such result. **3.19**

It was in the past unclear how the collocation/combination test fitted into the structured approach called for in *Windsurfing*, but it has become apparent since the judgment of the House of Lords in *Sabaf SpA v MFI Furniture Centres Ltd* [2004] UKHL 45 that the test is related to the third *Windsurfing/Pozzoli* question and is in truth related to the construction or interpretation of the claim see (see also the MOPP at 3.17). Lord Hoffmann observed:

"I quite agree that there is no law of collocation in the sense of a qualification of, or gloss upon, or exception to, the test for obviousness stated in section 3 of the Act. But before you can apply section 3 and ask whether the invention involves an inventive step, you first have to decide what the invention is. In particular, you have to decide whether you are dealing with one invention or two or more inventions. Two inventions do not become one invention because they are included in the same hardware. A compact motor car may contain many inventions, each operating independently of each other but all designed to contribute to the overall goal of having a compact car. That does not make the car a single invention.

Section 14(5)(d) of the Act provides (following article 82 of the EPC) that a claim shall 'relate to one invention or to a group of inventions which are so linked as to form a single inventive concept'. Although this is a procedural requirement with which an application must comply, it does suggest that the references in the Act to an 'invention' (as in section 3) are to the expression of a single inventive concept and not to a collocation of separate inventions.

The EPO Guidelines say that 'the invention claimed must normally be considered as a whole'. But equally, one must not try to consider as a whole what are in fact two separate inventions. What the Guidelines do is to state the principle upon which you decide whether you are dealing with a single invention or not. If the two integers interact upon each other, if there is synergy between them, they constitute a single invention having a combined effect and one applies section 3 to the idea of combining them. If each integer 'performs its own proper function independently of any of the others', then each is for the purposes of section 3 a separate invention and it has to be applied to each one separately."

In *Nokia v IPcom* [2009] EWHC 3482 at [108] which concerned cellular mobile phone technology the claim divided the invention into three separate compartments: initial, normal and lock-on synchronisation. This did not amount to a true combination: it was merely a juxtaposition of three methods which did not interact with one another, except to the extent that they were all required to be used in the same overarching method. It was legitimate to look at the separate parts and determine whether they were individually inventive.

In *Schlumberger v Elecgtromagnetic Geoservices* (above) in relation to one of the three patents in issue two elements of refraction seismics and CSEM were held not to achieve a new technical effect but only the aggregate of their individual effects, so that, following *Sabaf* (above) there was no invention in combining them. There was no appeal concerning the decision as to the invalidity of that patent, see [2010] R.P.C. 33, [2010] EWCA Civ 819.

In *Laboratorios Almirall v Boehringer Ingelheim* (above) it was held that if a synergistic effect was to be relied on, then it must be exhibited by everything within the claim and must be described in the specification. However, in the present case which related to combination therapy no effect was described in the specification that was not a natural prediction from the properties of the individual components.

The EPO prefers to consider collocation objections in terms of "partial problems" and a keyword search in the decisions database of the EPO Appeal Board revealed 75 instances where this concept had been referred to. The Appeal Board in T 966/05 *RAYTHEON/Man-portable modular system* agreed with the reasoning of the Examining Division that where distinguishing features (a) and (b) when taken in combination produced no extra technical effect they solved partial problems and could be assessed separately, and the same reasoning applies when they produce unrelated effects, see T 526/08 *MAASLAND/Contamination*. In T 175/94 *SILVANDERSSON/Insect trap* the Appeal Board rejected an argument that features of claim 1 of their main request supported one another on the ground that the effect alleged was based on a feature not specified in the main claim, but allowed an auxiliary request in which one of the features had been more specifically defined on the ground that the claimed features produced a combined effect that could neither be easily foreseen nor was suggested by the prior art. The above decisions express the established case law of the EPO Appeal Boards, see the Case Law of the Boards of Appeal of the European Patent Office, 6th edn 2010 at 8.2.1 and 8.2.2.

In T 1054/05 *NEC/Information Management* an applicant argued that the claimed new measures served the same purpose and that this was a combination effect not rendered obvious by the prior art. The Board's view was that this was not a synergistic effect. It is not enough that the features solve the same technical problem or that their effects are of the same kind and add up to an increased but otherwise unchanged effect. In the present case, sending messages in the form of minimum updates saved a certain amount of data per message, and sending the messages to fewer clients saved a certain number of messages. The data reduction achieved by the invention over the prior art was simply the sum of all the messages and message parts that did not have to be transmitted and there was no additional effect going beyond what could be expected. Hence the claimed subject-matter did not involve an inventive step, see also T 1303/06 *INTERNATIONAL BUSINESS MACHINES/Selectively viewing video information* where although claimed features aimed at the same general goal of improved information retrieval they addressed separate aspects and were not interrelated beyond their individual contributions so that the claimed subject-matter lacked inventive step.

In T 552/89 *TETRA PAK/Cold cathode replenishment*, objection was based on a primary reference disclosing electron beam apparatus, a first secondary reference disclosing a monitoring and control system and a second secondary reference disclosing a pair of rollers operated by a servo mechanism for advancing the cathode wire. The Appeal Board held that the invention was obvious over the three references and commented that:

"When the objective problem established having regard to the closest prior art as disclosed in a primary document is formed of individual problems then the skilled person can be expected to take account of solutions to the individual problems proposed in different secondary documents in the same or neighbouring technical fields. Thus the teaching of secondary documents may be combined with the disclosure of the closest prior art, if such secondary documents provide solutions to specific individual problems forming parts of the objective problem in progressing from the closest prior art, in particular when such individual solutions are merely aggregated together in the claimed invention."

The above decision was followed in T 302/02 *APPLERA/Amplification of nucleic acid sequences* where a primary reference disclosed an enzyme that survives undamaged in the heating part of a PCR heating/cooling cycle, a first secondary reference disclosed a microcomputer programmed to generate cyclical temperature profiles and a further secondary reference disclosed a block for heating and cooling medical samples using a Peltier element. The Appeal Board held that if a technical problem could only be solved by combining techniques from several fields, then it was a routine matter to do so and that in these circumstances the number of different pieces of prior art was likely to equal the number of technical fields to be combined.

It should be noted that, the courts and the EPO have at least until recently treated this type of analysis with caution and its use is infrequent. In *Koninkijke Philips v Princo Digital* [2003] EWHC 1598 (Ch) it was asserted that the skilled person would have taken a number of steps to proceed from another piece of prior art to reach the claimed invention, but it was held to be unfair to the inventor to dissect a combination into its component parts and then demonstrate that each of those parts is or may be obvious, this being an impermissible hindsight approach. The skilled team would not have made the invention without the insight of the invention. In *Triumph Actuation Systems LLC v Aeroquip-Vickers Ltd* [2007] EWHC 1367 a collocation objection was dismissed as involving unacceptable hindsight employed for improperly dissecting the invention into its component parts, together with a careful demonstration that each of the component parts was itself old or an obvious building-block to use. Similarly in *Abbott Laboratories v Evysio Medical Devices* [2008] R.P.C. 23, [2008] EWHC 800 (Ch) [182]–[185] an argument that various features of a claimed stent did not interact but merely served their ordinary function as they did in the prior art failed because on the evidence they interacted to produce a required balance of properties. It is not fair to break down an invention into two or more successive improvements of the closest prior art and to examine whether each improvement fulfills the requirement of unobviousness. That is particularly so when there is no suggestion in the closest prior art document, or in the teaching of the other relevant prior art, that a second improvement might be required or would be a necessary consequence of the first one, see T 26/98 *ALZA/Iontophoretic delivery device*.

—Citable disclosures and combinations of disclosures

3.20   The next step in the restated *Windsurfing/Pozzoli* test requires identification of differences between the prior art and the alleged invention, that is against the subject-matter protected by the claims. It is at this point that consideration has to be given to what disclosures or combinations of disclosures may validly be cited in support of an objection of lack of inventive step. As to whether alleged disclosures have indeed been made available to the public and are therefore citable, see §§2.04 to 2.06. As to the citability of prior co-pending patent applications, see §3.24.

Anything which has been made available to the public is citable including any earlier published document, any instances of prior use, any oral or written disclosure and anything which makes subject-matter available to the public in any other way, e.g. disclosure at an exhibition or conference. It was argued under the former Act that subject-matter ought to be citable only if it might be found by a diligent searcher so that fleeting and obscure disclosures should not count. That view was rejected in *Technograph v Mills and Rockley* [1972] R.P.C. 346 and in *Windsurfing* (above) and remains the position under the present Act and under the EPC. In *Procter & Gamble v Peaudouce* [1989] F.S.R. 180 CA, it was stated that the skilled, but unimaginative addressee, is to be assumed to have read carefully the literature, especially any relevant published patent specifications, and obviousness would then be assessed against the presumed knowledge of such a person.

Care should be taken in selecting the references to be relied on because a multiplicity of references weakens rather than strengthens the case on obviousness. In *Alan Nuttall Limited v Fri-Jado UK Ltd and Anor* [2008] EWHC 1311 the Court observed that if the alleged invention was obvious over one particular item of prior art, it does not make the case any better that there were other items that were not quite as good.

An allegation that a skilled person would not have taken forward the teaching of a reference so that the case was "anticipation or nothing" was rejected in *Wake Forest University v Smith & Nephew* [2009] F.S.R. 11, [2009] EWCA Civ 848 and doubt was expressed whether this could be a correct test for obviousness, although the point was not decided and instead it was held that the reasons for disregarding that reference did not stand up to examination. In *Red Spider Technology v Omega Completions Technology Ltd* [2010] EWHC 59 (Pat) disclosure in a US patent published in 1944 was not dismissed as irrelevant on account of its age. It was a detailed and apparently thought-through design to which a skilled addressee would have given attention irrespective of age. The assumption was not that a skilled person was sifting through many pieces of prior art with the risk that an old item might get overlooked, but instead that this particular item of prior art was put before him.

—Obviousness having regard to common general knowledge

3.21   Allegations of obviousness can be made based on common general knowledge alone. However, in such cases it is important to avoid hindsight, see *Coflexip v Stolt Connex Seaway CA* [2000] IP&T 1332 at [45] and *Abbott Laboratories v Evysio Medical Devices* [2008] EWHC 800 (Ch) at [180], *Ratiopharm v Napp* [2008] EWHC 3070 (Pat); [2009] R.P.C. 11 at [158] and *Nokia v Ipcom* [2011] EWHC 1470 at [58].

It should be noted that if the prior art in the specification is referred to as "conventional", then it is likely to be taken to be common general knowledge, see *NEC Corporation's Application* BL O/038/00.

—Obviousness having regard to a single reference and common general knowledge

3.22   The most common objections that come before the UK courts are based on a single reference in combination with the common general knowledge. Where several references are cited to the court, each reference is considered in turn together with the common general knowledge. References that do not form part of the common general knowledge are rarely considered in combination (a practice condemned under the former statutes as "mosaicing") because it has to be established that it would be obvious to combine them, and circumstances where such a finding is appropriate are rare, see §3.23. Thus, there is no point in preparing a "tick chart" to show that each feature of a claim is known from some document as inventive step has to be determined on the obviousness of the claimed combination, see *Hadley Industries v Metal Sections* [1990] EWHC 284 (Pat), noted IPD 22004. Section 7(3) of the Australian Patent Act 1990 now provides statutory basis in Australia for precisely the above approach and does not permit consideration of combinations of references neither of which form part of the common knowledge, see also the decision of the High Court of Australia in *Lockwood Security Products Pty Ltd v Doric Products Pty Ltd (No 2)* [2007] HCA 21. Investigation of inventive step by a court, however, is assisted by the evidence of technical experts, each of whom may be cross-examined by the opposing party and by disclosed documentary evidence, and with the assistance of such evidence an effective evaluation of inventive step is in practice possible without the court having to rely on combinations of published documents.

An argument of obviousness based on an old reference that had never been put into practice and was a mere paper proposal was considered untenable in *Grimme Landmaschinenfabrik GmbH & Co KG v Scott (t/a Scotts Potato Machinery)* [2011] F.S.R. 7, [2010] EWCA Civ 1110 at [59].

—Obviousness based on two or more references

The leading authority on obviousness objections based on combinations of references remains the observation of Lord Reid in *Technograph v Mills & Rockley* [1972] R.P.C. 346 at p.355: "When dealing with obviousness, unlike novelty, it is permissible to make a "mosaic" out of the relevant documents, but it must be a mosaic which can be put together by an unimaginative man with no inventive capacity.'' The UK courts have found few cases where it was appropriate to do so. For example, in *Inhale Therapeutic Systems Inc v Quadrant Healthcare Plc* (unrep.) Laddie J. held that a skilled person would not be expected to combine documents from remote fields so that a designer of an internal combustion engine would not be deemed to have read a document concerned with baking technology with the suspicion that it might be of assistance. Aldous L.J. citing *Inhale* with approval held in *Amersham Pharmacia Biotech v Amicon* [2001] EWCA Civ 1042 that an objection based on a first reference and on a second reference in a distant field was hopeless, the references being assembled with the aid of hindsight. In *Scinopharm Taiwan v Eli Lilly* [2009] EWHC 631 (Pat) it was held that whether it was obvious to read two documents together was a question to be considered in the light of the particular circumstances of each case. Relevant factors included whether one document referred to the other or whether one or both documents would be found in a literature search of the kind the skilled person would routinely have carried out before attempting to find a solution to the problem the patent addressed [84]. In *Schütz (UK) Ltd v Werit (UK) Ltd* [2010] EWHC 660 (Pat) it was held that there was no doubt that an obviousness attack could be maintained even if it required two documents to be read together e.g. the second document being found by a suitable search, but that the obviousness attack failed on the facts and again was driven by impermissible hindsight; see also *Gedeon Richter v Bayer Schering* [2011] EWHC 583 (Pat) where an allegation that the secondary references could have been found in a standard literature search, e.g. using PubMed, failed because there was little evidence that a skilled person would have taken the trouble to obtain copies of these references and reviewed their contents, the evidence being that the journals in which they were published were not part of the everyday reading of a relevant skilled person and that the titles were unpromising and not likely to stimulate his interest.

The UK Intellectual Property Office is not usually assisted by expert evidence during ex parte examination of a pending application, and even during revocation proceedings where expert evidence is normal, that evidence is by written witness statement and is only rarely tested by cross-examination. As a practical matter, obviousness examination can only be

3.23

carried out using documents in combination. The MOPP explains at paras 3.40–3.44 that there is no simple rule as to whether information from different documents, or from different parts of a single document, can properly be combined as a ''mosaic'' to provide a case that an invention is obvious. The Office adopts an intermediate position between the extremes that (a) no two documents can be combined unless at least one of them is well-known and (b) all information and documents can be combined provided that they are in the same technical field. However, if documents are to be combined, they should be ones that a skilled person would come across and consider together; see *Dow Chemical (Mildner's) Patent* [1973] R.P.C. 804. If the features disclosed in the documents are inherently incompatible or if one of them teaches away from the postulated mosaic, then that points towards inventive step. If the documents are from different technical fields the question is whether the problem would have prompted a search in those fields, e.g. to look for an adhesive having essential properties of moisture resistance and capacity to form a plastics-metal bond so as to fasten components of a known cable structure together.

In *Nampak Cartons v Rapid Action Packaging* O/342/09 a hearing officer observed that although it may be tempting to put together a combination of the cited prior art to show how the inventive concept may have been arrived at, this involved hindsight both in selecting the relevant disclosures and also in disregarding the irrelevant or unhelpful teaching in them, and there was no evidence that any of them had been put into use. In Opinion 34/09 claimed subject-matter was held to lack inventive step having regard to a primary reference and any one of three secondary references each disclosing the same further feature. The examiner observed that there was no simple rule as to whether different documents or different parts of the same document could be combined to create a "mosaic" to provide a case that an invention was obvious, but that following *Dow Chemical (Mildner's Patent)* (above) it was necessary to consider whether a seeker after information would come across the documents and consider them together. In the present case the primary reference and three of the four secondary references lay in the same field of endeavour as the invention and the fourth document lay in a closely related field. It was held that a skilled person would have recognised and easily appreciated the advantages of combining the teachings of the primary reference with any of the three secondary references in the same field and that it would be at least obvious to try so that obviousness over those combinations of references was established. However, the fourth reference was not in the same field of endeavour and no particular advantages were specified, so that there was nothing to motivate a combination of the primary and fourth references. In O/391/10 *Kezi Levin's application* the invention concerned preventing a sock from being pulled off an infant's foot using a tubular over-sock open at each end and formed with a hole located so that a heel of an infant's foot became positioned in the hole. A first reference showed a device for infants based on a pair of bands and a second reference showed a tubular over-sock as in the application but for use by adult walkers to prevent sock slippage when boots have been worn for a long time. The claimed subject-matter was held to lack inventive step having regard to the disclosures of the two references, which could legitimately be combined having regard to the small size of the art (there being few other solutions disclosed in the patent literature) and the solution in the second reference of the same general problem as in the application and in the first reference of keeping socks in place on feet.

Readers should be aware that reluctance to read references together is a peculiarity of UK law, and does not apply, or applies with significantly lesser force, in other jurisdictions. In EPO examination the citation of two or more references during examination of an application is commonplace, see §3.47. The citation of mere "mosaics" is discouraged, and examiners are required to show reasons before combining the disclosures of different documents, but such reasons can frequently be identified by an examiner as part of the examination process. There appears to be little complaint that the EPO practice in this regard creates injustice for applicants or patentees defending opposition proceedings. The USPTO also commonly cites two or three references together, giving reasons why (at least in the opinion of an examiner) it is right to do so, the US Supreme Court observing in *KSR v Teleflex* 550 US 398 (1987) that: "in many cases a person of ordinary skill will be able to fit the teachings of multiple patents together like pieces of a puzzle." An argument that is frequently used in the US against an objection of lack of inventive step over such a combination of references is that one or other of them teaches away from the invention.

US examination practice is reviewed in *Examination Guidelines for Determining Obviousness Under 35 U.S.C. 103 in View of the Supreme Court Decision in KSR International Co. v Teleflex Inc.*, Federal Register, Vol. 72, No. 195 page 57526 (2007) and *Examination Guidelines Update: Developments in the Obviousness Inquiry After KSR v Teleflex*, Federal Register, Vol. 75, No. 169, page 53643 (2010) which those prosecuting patent applications before the USPTO are advised to consult.

Limitations from section 2(3) prior art citable in support of obviousness objections

Where the state of the art includes a prior-dated application for a patent in the United **3.24** Kingdom having an earlier priority date, its contents have effect under s.2(3) as regards possible lack of novelty, but these contents are not permitted to have any effect in relation to the issue of inventive step. Thus the prior art disclosure anticipates both what is explicitly disclosed and what is implicitly disclosed but not what is rendered obvious, see, e.g. *Edwards Lifesciences v Cook Biotech* [2009] F.S.R. 27, [2009] EWHC 1304 Pat Ct at [106]–[110], discussed in §2.11.

—Identification of differences between prior art and the alleged invention

Application of a novelty test to the express or implicit disclosure of each cited reference **3.25** and the subject-matter of the claim or claims in issue usually enables the relevant differences to be identified with relatively little difficulty.

It should be noted that differences should be identified in relation to each individual item of prior art rather than cited or pleaded prior art as a group. Where claimed subject-matter is to a combination of features, it may be distinguished from individual prior disclosures by the presence of different features: a combination of features A, B and C may differ from prior art X by the inclusion of feature B and from prior art Y by feature C but this is not considered detrimental in itself or a source of inconsistency because the subject-matter claimed is the combination considered as a whole. For this reason UK law and practice has consistently declined to adopt the two-part structure preferred e.g. in German and EPO practice in which a claim is divided into classifying and characterising features. The function of claims was reviewed by Fletcher-Moulton L.J. in *British United Shoe Machinery Co. Ltd v A. Fussell & Sons Ltd* (1908) 25 R.P.C. 631 at p.651 where he concluded that:

> ". . . a man must distinguish what is old from what is new by his claim; but he has not got to distinguish what is old from what is new in his claim. If the combination which he has claimed, and for which he seeks a monopoly, is novel that is sufficient. There is no obligation to go further and state why it is novel or what in it is novel."

It is not apparent that the words "characterized in that" appearing in the claims of a European patent brought into effect in the United Kingdom have had any effect, affirmative or negative, on assessment of inventive step.

The fourth question—additional evidence and arguments commonly adduced

—Allegedly trivial differences, materials readily to hand

Inventive step cannot be based on trivial features, i.e. features which are neither **3.26** remarked on in the specification nor of significance to a person skilled in the art, see *LG Philips v Tatung* [2006] EWCA Civ 1774 at [41]. However, there may be a dispute whether a claimed feature is indeed a trivial variant, and many decisions support the proposition that a small difference from the prior art may nevertheless suffice for inventive step.

In *Gillette Safety Razor Co. v Anglo-American Trading Co.* (1916) 30 R.P.C. 465 HL Lord Moulton held that if what was alleged to infringe was not patentable over the pleaded prior art (see also §125.08) that was a defence to proceedings for infringement, and commented:

"In practical life it is often the only safeguard to the manufacturer. It is impossible for an ordinary member of the public to keep watch on all the numerous patents which are taken out and to ascertain the validity and scope of all their claims. But he is entitled to feel secure if he knows that what he is doing differs from that which has been done of old only in non-patentable variations, such as the substitution of mechanical equivalents or changes of material, shape or size."

Laddie J. in *Hoechst Celanese v B.P. Chemical (Iodide Removal)* [1997] F.S.R. 547 said that there had to be a motive for making such changes, but that if the changes were trivial, then a trivial motive would suffice:

"Before a step from the prior art can be held to be obvious there must be some reason why the man skilled in the art would wish to take it. If he has a problem and the step would occur to him as a solution to it, then he has a reason. But there is no requirement that it be demonstrated that the step would have been expected to produce significant commercial advantages. The problem might be very small. The courts will assume that he may just want an alternative way of achieving essentially the same result as in the prior art. Thus mere workshop modifications, none of which would be expected to produce significant technical or commercial benefits are still obvious. To adopt an example sometimes given by Jacob J., if it is known to make a 5 inch plate, it is obvious to make a $5^1/_4$ inch plate. Technicians and businessmen frequently want to make trivial variations in established or known products. Similarly if the prior art discloses two wooden parts held together by screws it would be obvious to glue them, even if so doing would not be expected to advance the industry. The notional addressee is likely to want to use materials readily at hand to make essentially the same thing as is disclosed in the prior art. That is sufficient motivation and the use of those materials is, accordingly, obvious."

In *Pharmacia v Merck* [2002] R.P.C. 775 CA at [124] Aldous L.J. held that the above statement of the law should not be followed generally and that there was no separate test of workshop variation:

"That statement of the law was, I expect, apt on the facts of that case, but should not be followed generally. A step from the prior art, albeit made without reason, can still be obvious. The judge categorises such a step as workshop modification and, in so doing, introduces a test not in the statute, namely whether the step from the prior art was a workshop modification. The statutory test is obviousness and any modification which is obvious will not be patentable, whereas one which is not obvious will be. The true test, as made clear in *Windsurfing*, is to ask whether the invention was obvious. Whether or not there is a reason for taking the step from the prior art may well be an important consideration, but that does not mean that it is an essential requirement of a conclusion of obviousness. In any case the judge in these proceedings did consider whether there was a reason for taking the step from the prior art and concluded that there was, namely a natural desire to investigate the analogs and the structural activity relationship of such compounds."

It has now been held to be settled law that the absence of a particular motive to take a particular step between the prior art and the invention is not fatal to an obviousness attack, see *Research In Motion UK Ltd v Visto Corp.* [2009] F.S.R. 10, [2008] EWHC 3325 (Pat) at [73] and *Datacard v Eagle Technologies* [2011] R.P.C. 17, [2011] EWHC 244 (Pat) at [94]. However, absence of motivation may lead to an objection being rejected, see O/361/10 *Honey Pot Trust* where a skilled person would have known that data partitioning systems could be incorporated into a prior verification system but absent the motivation to do so, i.e. that image data security needed to be improved or that data store partitioning was known to increase security, it was not apparent that a skilled person would have regarded the difference between the inventive concept and the prior art as obvious.

In *Actavis v Novartis* [2010] F.S.R. 18, [2010] EWCA Civ 82 Jacob L.J., returning to the 5¼ inch plate paradox and advanced the proposition that there is a category of arbitrary and non-technical features that should be disregarded when evaluating inventive step:

"Suppose the patent claim is for a plate of diameter 5¼ inches. And suppose no-one can find a plate of that particular diameter in the prior art. Then (a) it is novel and (b) it is non-obvious for there is no particular reason to choose that diameter. The conclusion, that the plate is patentable, is so absurd that it cannot be so.

What then is the answer to the paradox? It is this: the 5¼ inch limitation is purely arbitrary and non-technical. It solves no problem and advances the art not at all. It is not inventive. And although ''inventive step'' is defined as being one which is not obvious, one must always remember the purpose of that definition – to define what is inventive. That which is not inventive by any criteria is not made so by the definition. Trivial limitations, such as specifying the plate diameter, or painting a known machine blue for no technical reason are treated as obvious because they are not inventive."

It is apparent, therefore, that a feature may be disregarded if it is trivial or arbitrary, see *Phillips' (Bosgra's) Application* [1974] R.P.C 241, or has been introduced for no technical reason, that also being the basis of "parametritis" as discussed in *Raychem's Patents* [1998] R.P.C. 31 and *LG Philips v Tatung* [2006] EWCA Civ 1774—i.e. the introduction of an arbitrary or artificial stipulation to give a claim an apparent inventiveness or distinctiveness, when it has none.

At first instance in *Actavis* [2009] EWHC 41 (Ch) it was argued that making a sustained release formulation of a known drug was an inherently obvious step to take, like making a 5¼ inch plate, but Arnold J. commented that although this language might describe how the court had made its decision in particular situations, it was not of universal application and the correct test was that laid down in the statute, whether the invention was obvious to a skilled person [145]. There were factors, e.g. patient compliance and alleged technical difficulties in making such a formulation, such that detailed analysis was needed.

The EPO also takes the position that features that do not produce a technical effect cannot contribute to inventive step; see T 27/97 *FRANCE TELECOM/Crypthographie à clés publiques*, this position being confirmed, e.g. in T 619/02 *QUEST INTERNATIONAL/ Odour selection* where it was held that components resulting from a non-technical selection are arbitrary and hence irrelevant. Further examples where differences have been held by the EPO Appeal Boards to provide no technical effect and to be simple workshop variants of no technical significance are found in T 1026/97 *CASIO/Liquid Crystal display device* and T 452/91 *TOYO/Polyester fibres*. There are also numerous references in decisions of the EPO Appeal Boards to "routine measures" and "mere routine experimentation involving nothing more than general considerations and obvious choices", see T 542/02 *OWENS CORNING/Binders*, see also T 302/02 APPELERA/Automated amplification of nucleic acid sequences where a finding that the feature in question was a routine measure was supported by absence of information about it in the patent in issue. A selection (in this case of residues in an amino acid sequence) is arbitrary if it is a random choice amongst numerous equally good options, see T 1139/08 *CONSIGLIO NAZIONALE DELLE RICERCHE/Allergenic protein*. The EPO further applies the principle that features excluded by art.52 EPC as non-technical cannot be taken into account when assessing inventive step, see T 641/00 *COMVIK/Two identities* and T 258/03 *HITACHI/Auction Method*; see also G3/08 *PRESIDENT'S REFERENCE/Programs for computers* at 10.13.2 discussed at §1.04.

It cannot be too strongly emphasised, however, that blind concentration on the nature and magnitude of the differences from the prior art without consideration of any benefits that flow from such differences is at risk of misjudgement. Many warnings have been given, e.g. that of Jessel M.R. in *Hinks & Son v Safety Lighting Co.* (1876) 4 Ch. D. 607

that a small difference can produce a large result in which case it can fairly be the subject of a patent. The observation of Tomlin J. in *Samuel Parkes & Co v Crocker Bros.* (1929) 46 R.P.C. at p.248 is often cited, but a fuller than usual version is apt:

"Nobody however has told me, and I do not suppose anybody ever will tell me, what is the precise characteristic or quality the presence of which distinguishes invention from a workshop improvement. Day is day, and night is night, but who shall tell where day ends or night beings? The user of this particular clip has been large. Over 1¼ millions were sold up to the end of 1927. The Railway Companies have adopted it as standard, and to that extent it has beaten its competitors out of the field. The truth is that, when once it had been found, as I find here, that the problem had waited solution for many years, and that the device is in fact novel and superior to what had gone before, and has been widely used, and used in preference to alternative devices, it is, I think, practically impossible to say that there is not present that scintilla of invention necessary to support the Patent."

In *Oneac v Raychem* BL C/32/98, *noted* IPD 21085; [1998] EIPR N–188 , the step from the prior art was accepted as a small one which persons "could" have easily taken, but which the evidence was that in practice they would not take, and indeed had not taken. Here, Laddie J. said that "there can be invention in making a small modification to the prior art or realising that the solution had been at one's fingertips all along". The decision was not followed in *Cartonneries de Thulin S.A. v CTP White Knight Limited* BL/C85/98, noted IPD 22013 where Neuberger J. commented:

"This point is fine so far as it goes, and is undoubtedly a useful warning. Elegant simplicity can often be more inventive than confusing complexity, although it is easy to mistake the former for obviousness and the latter for inventiveness. However, it is equally true that one should not risk leaning over backwards to hold that a simple concept is inventive."

In *Mölnlycke v Procter & Gamble (No. 5)* (above), followed in *PLG Research v Ardon* [1995] R.P.C. 287 CA, the Court of Appeal observed that:

"The inventive step may not have been large and it is not surprising to us that more than one inventor may have broadly the same idea at around the same time. Where the subject-matter of a patent is an idea, the inventive step involves having an insight which, although simple, genuinely requires an act of insight rather than a mere development and application of existing ideas".

In *Haberman v Jackel International* ([1999] F.S.R. 683), the court stated that: "The simpler the solution, the easier it is to explain. The easier it is to explain, the more obvious it can appear. This is not always fair to inventors." The patent was upheld, see §3.33.

It is not persuasive to start with a modification, explain that it is simple and then explain its advantages since that involves impermissible hindsight, see *Nokia v IPcom* [2011] EWHC 1470 (Pat) at [74].

In *Sandoz v Roche Diagnostics* [2004] EWHC 1313 (Ch), noted IPD 27076, the invention concerned the preservation of human erythropoietin using a combination of preservatives. The defendants averred that these were part of a recognised group of about ten preservatives commonly in use in 1991 and that at the time the benefits of using the preservatives in combination to achieve synergy were well-known. However, the alleged synergy disclosed in the prior art related to anti-microbial properties and not to maintaining the integrity of a protein structure, relevant preservatives had been rejected for single use, and although combinations might have been interesting to investigate, they were not obvious or routine.

Furthermore, although a skilled person must be deemed to consider any piece of prior art properly and the public cannot be deprived of its right to do or make anything which is merely an obvious modification of what has been done or published before, the law does not deem the skilled person to assume that the prior art has any relevance to the problem he is addressing or require him to take it forward. Having considered it, he may conclude that it is simply not a worthwhile starting point and put it to one side, e.g. where the claimed starting point is merely one of tens of thousands of samples that would need to be worked through, analogously to isolating a bacterium from soil, see *Eli Lilly & Company v Human Genome Sciences* [2008] R.P.C. 29, [2008] EWHC 1903 (Pat).

—Obvious desiderata, automaticity

A claim is unduly wide if it covers all solutions to a known problem or no more than an **3.27** obvious desideratum. An example is *Raychem's Patents* [1998] R.P.C. 31, where many compositions having obviously desirable characteristics fell within the scope of the claims and, as such, they covered what was obvious. For one patent, the patentee "had done no more than seek to monopolise a group of compositions displaying obviously useful characteristics" in claims prolix and obscure in meaning (see §14.28). Similarly it has been held that a patentee cannot obtain a monopoly of all possible means of remedying a known defect, *Crabtree v Hoe* (1936) 53 R.P.C. 443.

A claim is also unduly wide if it covers all ways of automating a known operation; see *British United Shoe Machinery v Simon Collier* (1909) 26 R.P.C. 21 at p.49 where Parker J. said:

"... [T]he problem was simply how to do automatically what could already be done by the skill of the workman. On the other hand, the principle which the inventor applies for the solution of the problem is the capacity of a cam to vary the relative positions of two parts of a machine while the machine is running. Assuming this principle to be new, it might be possible for the inventor, having shown one method of applying it to the solution of the problem, to protect himself during the life of his Patent from any other method of applying it for the same purpose, but I do not think that the novelty of the principle applied would enable him to make a valid claim for all means of solving the problem whether the same or a different principle were applied to its solution."

A number of claims to software-based inventions have been drafted so broadly as to fall within this prohibition, which it is submitted is often the most straightforward objection in cases of this kind. Examples include the EPO decisions in T 121/85 *IBM/Spell checking*, T 38/86 *IBM/Text Processing* (automatically replacing difficult expressions in a text with expressions that are more intelligible), T 65/86 *IBM/Text Editing* (automatic detection and replacement of text hompohones) and T 158/88 *SIEMENS/ Character form* (automatically selecting the appropriate position-sensitive form of a character in a written oriental language).

—Technical problem—the UK approach

Inventions are often regarded as solutions of technical problems. If confirmation is **3.28** needed, see *Schlumberger Holdings Ltd v Electromagnetic Geoservices AS* [2010] R.P.C. 33, [2010] EWCA Civ 819 at [65] where Jacob L.J. said: "In the case of obviousness in view of the state of the art, a key question is generally 'what problem was the patentee trying to solve?'".

In *Haberman v Jackel International* [1999] F.S.R. 683 (HC) Laddie J. produced a checklist of factors which were helpful in determining whether or not commercial success was relevant insofar as it might throw light on the thought processes which pervaded the relevant industry, but which, as may be seen, focuses on the existence of a technical problem and the relevant surrounding circumstances:

(a) What was the problem which the patented development addressed? Although sometimes a development may be the obvious solution to another problem, that is not frequently the case.

(b) How long had that problem existed?

(c) How significant was the problem seen to be? A problem which was viewed in the trade as trivial might not have generated much in the way of efforts to find a solution. So an extended period during which no solution was proposed (or proposed as a commercial proposition) would throw little light on whether, technically, it was obvious. Such an extended period of inactivity may demonstrate no more than that those in the trade did not believe that finding a solution was commercially worth the effort. The fact, if it be one, that they had miscalculated the commercial benefits to be achieved by the solution says little about its technical obviousness and it is only the latter which counts. On the other hand, evidence which suggests that those in the art were aware of the problem and had been trying to find a solution will assist the patentee.

(d) How widely known was the problem and how many were likely to be seeking a solution? Where the problem was widely known to many in the relevant art, the greater the prospect of it being solved quickly.

(e) What prior art would have been likely to be known to all or most of those who would have been expected to be involved in finding a solution? A development may be obvious over a piece of esoteric prior art of which most in the trade would have been ignorant. If that is so, commercial success over other, less relevant, prior art will have much reduced significance.

(f) What other solutions were put forward in the period leading up to the publication of the patentee's development? This overlaps with other factors. For example it illustrates that others in the art were aware of the problem and were seeking a solution. But it also is of relevance in that it may indicate that the patentee's development was not what would have occurred to the relevant workers. This factor must be treated with care. As has been said on more than one occasion, there may be more than one obvious route round a technical problem. The existence of alternatives does not prevent each of them from being obvious. On the other hand where the patentee's development would have been expected to be at the forefront of solutions to be found yet it was not and other, more expensive or complex or less satisfactory, solutions were employed instead, then this may suggest that the ex post facto assessment that the solution was at the forefront of possibilities is wrong.

(g) To what extent were there factors which would have held back the exploitation of the solution even if it was technically obvious? For example it may be that the materials or equipment necessary to exploit the solution were only available belatedly or their cost was so high as to act as a commercial deterrent. On the other hand if the necessary materials and apparatus were readily available at reasonable cost, a lengthy period during which the solution was not proposed is a factor which is consistent with lack of obviousness.

(h) How well has the patentee's development been received? Once the product or process was put into commercial operation, to what extent was it a commercial success? In looking at this, it is legitimate to have regard not only to the success indicated by exploitation by the patentee and his licensees but also to the commercial success achieved by infringers. Furthermore the number of infringers may reflect on some of the other factors set out above. For example, if there are a large number of infringers it may be some indication of the number of members of the trade who were likely to be looking for alternative or improved products (see (iv) above).

(i) To what extent can it be shown that the whole or much of the commercial success is due to the technical merits of the development, i.e. because it solves the problem? Success which is largely attributable to other factors, such as the commercial power of the patentee or his licensee, extensive advertising focusing on features which have nothing to do with the development, branding or other technical features of the product or process, says nothing about the value of the invention.

It has been said that there is a temptation to turn the above list of factors into a checklist, which may not be helpful, see *Conor v Angiotech* [2006] EWHC 260 (Pat) HC. However, Jacob L.J. has referred to the "non-exhaustive" summary as "a masterpiece", see *Schlumberger Holdings v Electromagnetic Geoservices* [2010] R.P.C. 33, [2010] EWHC Civ 819 at [80]. Although the Laddie questions are not in common use as a checklist by the UK courts and the IPO, it is submitted that they provide a useful starting point for questioning expert witnesses in proceedings involving the issue of inventive step.

Laddie J. held in *Haberman* that there had been a long felt want, as demonstrated by the prior art and failure of others to reach the simple solution claimed, and that the commercialised product of the invention was "cheap, simple, effective and a remarkable commercial success". For other cases where a finding of long-felt want lead to failure of an objection as to lack of inventive step, see, e.g. *Parkes v Cocker* (1929) 46 R.P.C. 241 at 248 and *In re Kahn* 441 F.3d 997 (Fed. Cir. 2006).

Investigation of technical problem by the UK courts has a long history. For example, in *Gadd & Mason v Mayor, etc. of Manchester* (1892) 9 R.P.C. 516 Lindley L.J. held that a patent for the new use of a known contrivance without additional ingenuity in overcoming fresh difficulties could not be supported, whereas the patent was good if the new use involved practical difficulties that the patentee had been the first to see and overcome by his own ingenuity.

Hugh Fletcher-Moulton, *The Present Law and Practice relating to Patents for Inventions* (London: Butterworths, 1913) gave at p.24 the following insight into the inventive process which was cited with approval by the High Court of Australia in *Lockwood Security Products Pty Ltd v Doric Products Pty Ltd* (No 2) [2007] HCA 21:

"An invention may, and usually does, involve three processes. Firstly the definition of the problem to be solved or the difficulties to be overcome; secondly the choice of general principle to be applied in solving the problem or overcoming these difficulties; and thirdly the choice of the particular means used. Merit in any one of these three stages, or in the whole combined, may support the invention and it is therefore all important in considering subject matter to consider, at any rate in the first instance, the whole advance in knowledge due to the inventor, rather than to examine in detail the variations from former practice."

A similar explanation was given by Lord Hoffmann in *Biogen v Medeva* [1996] UKHL 18 which was cited with approval by the High Court of Australia in *Lockwood Security Products Pty Ltd v Doric Products Pty Ltd* (above):

"Whenever anything inventive is done for the first time it is the result of the addition of a new idea to the existing stock of knowledge. Sometimes, it is the idea of using established techniques to do something which no one had previously thought of doing. In that case, the inventive idea will be doing the new thing. Sometimes, it is finding a way of doing something which people had wanted to do but could not think how. The inventive idea would be the way of achieving the goal. In yet other cases, many people may have a general idea of how they might achieve a goal but not know how to solve a particular problem which stands in their way. If someone devises a way of solving the problem, his inventive step will be that solution, but not the goal itself or the general method of achieving it."

A difference of opinion has arisen between courts in Anglo-American based legal systems and the Appeal Boards of the EPO as to whether identifying a solved technical problem is a necessary condition for finding claimed subject-matter unobvious: the EPO takes an affirmative view whereas UK and US courts treat it as merely one of many factors to be taken into account in reaching a decision. However, there is a link between technical problem and new technical effect or result, discussed in §§3.29 and 3.42, these usually being opposite faces of the same coin. We can use the fact pattern in *Dolland's case* (1776) 1 W.P.C. 42 to provide an example. Replacement of the single component telescope objective lens of Lippershay (1608) and Galileo (1611) with a lens having crown and flint glass components can be regarded as the solution to the technical problem of poor focus in refracting telescopes. That problem had existed since 1611, had been alleviated but not overcome by the use of an objective of long focal length (Hevelius, 1673), had been the subject of a design-around by the Newtonian reflector (1668), but its solution had not been made public until the disclosure of the achromatic doublet (1758) for which Dolland was awarded the Copley medal of the Royal Society. The awkwardness of long-focus telescope designs used in the late seventeenth century shows that inability to achieve a sharp focus in a refracting telescope was a real-world problem only too well-known to those in the art of making telescopes, and that the achromatic doublet provides an outstanding example of a long-felt want. Equally the use of the crown and flint glass components can be regarded as providing a new technical effect permitting an image in a refracting telescope to be brought to a sharp focus for the first time. The above link provides the basis on which technical problem is defined under EPO practice, see §3.42.

—New or improved result flowing from a claimed combination of features; relationship to technical problem

3.29   The collocation/combination test has both positive and negative aspects, the former providing affirmative and persuasive evidence for inventive step. Decisions of courts in the USA and the United Kingdom and of EPO Appeal Boards agree on this point. It is a matter of experience that the ability to identify a new function or result flowing from a claimed combination of features is a strong indicator that the claim should be allowed during official examination and is also a good predictor of validity in subsequent EPO opposition or revocation proceedings. As will be apparent from the discussion which follows, that positive evidence can be rebutted by showing that the claimed subject-matter was obvious for a different purpose or that the new function or result was a mere bonus. For example if it is obvious to carry out a test it makes no difference that an unexpectedly good result has been found, T 296/87 *HOECHST/Enantiomers* or if the result flows from recommended practice prescribed in a handbook, T 423/09 *DE LAVAL/Milk sampling apparatus*.

Furthermore, if improved results are to be relevant, they must be obtainable over the full scope of the claim, see *Brugger v Medic-Aid* [1966] R.P.C. 635 at 656–657 and *Lundbeck v Norpharma* [2011] EWHC 907 (Pat). In the latter case the invention concerned a process for producing a substance in good yields and high purity under easily controllable conditions. However, there was no limitation in the claim about either yield or purity and the claim would have been infringed whenever the prescribed conditions were used to make the substance, even if the process was not taken to completion or low purity product was obtained. It was therefore not legitimate to use the results which the invention "allows" to formulate the question for the purposes of determining inventive step; further the relative terms "high yield and purity and easily controllable conditions" were nowhere defined. Obviousness could not be considered on the basis that the claimed process was better, or even as good as a cited prior art process; it was simply another set of process conditions for performing a known reaction which a skilled chemist would have arrived at without invention; see also §3.47.

The positive aspect of the test goes back to early days of patent law, and is a matter of wide agreement over a period of two centuries and in a many jurisdictions including the UK, the US, Germany and the EPO.

The first (1883) edition of *Terrell on Patents* quotes at p.32 Lord Ellenborough in *Huddard v Grimshaw* 1 Web. P.C. 85 (1803):

> "I suppose it will not now be disputed that a new combination of old materials, so as to produce a new effect, may be the subject of a patent."

George Ticknor Curtis was a US patent attorney practising in the early nineteenth century, at which time US jurisprudence concerning patentability was closely aligned with that of the UK. His clients included Samuel Morse, Charles Goodyear and Cyrus

McCormick. In his book *A Treatise on the Law of Patents for Useful Inventions* (Boston: Charles C Little and James Brown, 1849) (downloadable from the Antique Rare IP Library of IP Mall) he expressed the following conclusion:

"It is evident, therefore, that the whole of the act of invention, in the department of useful arts, embraces more than the new arrangement of particles of matter in new relations. The purpose of such new arrangements is to produce some new effect or result, by calling into activity some latent law, or force, or property, by means of which, in a new application, the new effect or result may be accomplished. In every form in which matter is used, in every production of the ingenuity of man, he relies on the laws of nature and the properties of matter, and seeks for new effects and results through their agency and aid."

German national courts have fundamentally the same viewpoint, as explained in the following passage from EPO Enlarged Appeal Board decisions G2/07 and G1/08 *Essentially Biological Processes*:

"Human intervention, to bring about a result by using the forces of nature, pertains to the core of what an invention is understood to be. Like national laws, the EPC does not define the term "invention" but the definition that was given many years ago in the "*Red Dove*" ("*Rote Taube*") decision of the German Federal Court of Justice ("Bundesgerichtshof"), BGH 27.3.1069, X ZB 15/67 set a standard which still holds good today and can be said to be in conformity with the concept of "invention" within the meaning of the EPC.
  In that decision, in the version of the translation into English published in 1 IIC (1970), 136, the German Federal Court of Justice defined the term "invention" as requiring a technical teaching. The term technical teaching was characterised as "a teaching to methodically utilize controllable natural forces to achieve a causal, perceivable result" (point 3 of the Reasons). . ."

The evidential nature of a new result was explained in the US Supreme Court in *Webster Loom Co. v Higgins* 105 U.S. 580, 1881 by Mr Justice Bradley:

"It may be laid down as a general rule, though perhaps not an invariable one that if a new combination and arrangement of known elements produce a new and beneficial result, never attained before, it is evidence of invention."

The importance of new result was again emphasised in *British Celanese Ltd v Courtaulds Ltd* (1935) 52 R.P.C. 171, 193 in the often overlooked second part of the observations of Lord Tomlin:

". . . where the old integers when placed together have some working inter-relation producing a new or improved result then there is patentable subject-matter in the idea of a working interrelation brought about by the collocation (*sic*) of the integers."

Examples of new function or result which have supported patentability in the United Kingdom in recent cases follow.
  In *Beecham Group's (Amoxycillin) Application* [1980] R.P.C. 261, the combination of properties exhibited by amoxycillin was significant: it exhibited high activity combined with high achieved blood level.
  In *Fichera v Flogates* [1984] R.P.C. 257 (CA), the invention concerned a ladle for molten steel having a bottom discharge outlet closed by a sliding gate valve, and the improvement involved the provision of a ring of refractory material in the bottom of the ladle, a bush with a vertical hole for tapping metal mounted in the ring, and a stationary refractory plate having an upper surface on which the bush rested and a lower surface

along which the valve slid. The bush was well known in a different form of bottom discharge outlet, and the defendants objected that the provision of this well-known bush in a known form of outlet was within the range of variants which a skilled person would make without invention. However, the effect of the change was to move the seat of erosion by the molten steel from the sliding parts of the valve to the top of the bush, where it is less damaging, and to enable the outlet to be used to pour many charges of molten steel instead of only one charge as in the prior art. Both the Patents Court and the Court of Appeal held on the basis of the evidence adduced that the patent was valid and warned against treating dismissively apparently small changes to seemingly simple structures.

In *Mölnlycke v Proctor & Gamble* [1994] R.P.C. 49 the invention concerned a disposable diaper which could be opened and re-fastened. Its novel feature was that a single plastics strip was provided extending across the diaper at one end for fastening of tape tabs from the other end, the surface texture of the plastics strip being such as to control adhesion and permit tab removal and re-fastening. The effect of this feature was to provide a landing surface with different characteristics from the back-sheet so that each could be independently optimised. Both the Patents Court and the Court of Appeal held that the added feature provided a novel solution to the problem of providing tapes that could be securely re-fastened without tearing the back-sheet and that the patent was valid. The Court of Appeal observed that:

"The inventive step may not have been large and it is not surprising to us that more than one inventor may have broadly the same idea at around the same time. Where the subject-matter of a patent is an idea, the inventive step involves having an insight which, although simple, genuinely requires an act of insight rather than a mere development and application of existing ideas".

In *Haberman v Jackel International* [1999] F.S.R. 683, the use in an infants' trainer cup of a self-closing slit valve solved the long-standing problem that such cups were prone to leak when upset.

In *Dyson Appliances v Hoover Ltd* [2002] R.P.C. 265 the use of an upstream low-efficiency cyclone in a vacuum cleaner enabled it to separate carpet fluff, thread, paper shreds, dog hairs and the like and avoid so-called "hang-up", i.e. material within the cyclone which kept spinning about without being deposited.

In *Vector Corporation v Glatt Techniques Ltd* [2006] EWHC 1638 (Pat) the invention concerned a fluidized bed processor having a spray nozzle for injecting coating material, wherein a gas stream was provided to shield the initial spray pattern to allow the droplet density to decrease before the sprayed particles contacted the fluidized bed, thereby permitting higher spray rates to be used with less agglomeration.

In *Schlumberger v Electromagnetic Geosciences* (above) it was a new geophysical technique based on the use at the sea bed of a wave refracted by a buried hydrocarbon layer which arrived faster than direct or reflected waves and at a relatively high signal level to detect the hydrocarbon layer, there being a large resistivity contrast between hydrocarbon-saturated reservoirs and surrounding sedimentary rocks saturated with aqueous saline fluids, and the signal being detectable even though the hydrocarbon layers were thin compared to their depth of burial.

In *Norbrook Laboratories' Patent* [2006] F.S.R. 302, it was observed that it is only where technical advantages are possessed by everything falling within the claim, or at least all sensible embodiments of what is claimed, that it is legitimate to bear in mind the technical advantages of the invention. A wide inventive concept which includes, but is not limited to, embodiments with technical merit may be more vulnerable to an attack on the ground of lack of inventive step than a narrow one which is limited and traps the advantageous features. However, occasional failure to achieve promised advantages can be excused so long as substantially all embodiments provide a solution to the problem to be solved, see T 1146/02 *SMITHKLINE BEECHAM/Vaccines containing a saponin and a sterol.*

Opioid analgesics are well known, as also are extended release formulations. The objection against the patent in *Napp Pharmaceutical v Ratiopharm* (above) was that it was obvious to make a sustained release formulation of oxycodone which was a known opioid analgesic. However, the evidence was that prior to the invention oxycodone had been known only as a co-drug for administration with aspirin or paracetamol to give additional analgesia and was not perceived as an alternative to morphine. In the claimed sustained release formulation oxycodone proved as potent against pain as morphine, and needed less dosage adjustment for individual patients than slow-release morphine because there was less patient-to-patient variation in response. At first instance, [2008] EWHC 3070, the judge had formed the provisional view that as a matter of common general knowledge it was uninventive to propose a controlled release formulation of a known drug, but had concluded on the evidence that as oxycodone had not been perceived as an alternative to morphine and clinicians had no practical experience of its use for that purpose the case on common general knowledge must fail. Affirming this decision, the Court of Appeal noted that the judge had rejected evidence that oxycodone would make a shortlist of known drugs as suitable alternatives for morphine, which it held was a crucial finding. Furthermore, development of prior art formulations would not be pursued without any apparent therapeutic reason. This was not a case like *Hallen v Brabantia* [1991] R.P.C. 195 where there was both a foreseeable advantage in a PTFE coating for all corkscrews and an unforeseeable advantage for corkscrews of the self-puller type and obviousness was established. In the present case it was not obvious that any advantage would be obtained. An unexpected advantage should only fail to defeat an obviousness attack where there had been a real motive to use the idea apart from that advantage because only then would the skilled man more or less inevitably encounter the unexpected advantage.

The High Court has observed in *Generics (UK) Ltd & Ors v H Lundbeck A/S* [2007] EWHC 1040 (Pat) that whether a surprising technical benefit provides an indication of inventive step depends upon all the circumstances. For example, if it is found that the claimed invention is obvious for one purpose then it is not saved because it is found to have added benefits, see *Hallen v Brabantia* [1991] R.P.C. 195 at 216. The EPO adopts a similar approach, see T 21/81 *Electromagnetically operated switch/ALLEN-BRADLEY*, OJ EPO 1983, 15 where it refers to it as a mere "bonus effect" §3.31. It also considers where there were alternatives available to the skilled person or the art was in a "one-way street" situation leading to predictable advantages which remain obvious in spite of the existence of some unexpected "bonus" effect, see T 0192/82 *BAYER/Polymer compositions*. However, there is no "one-way street" situation where there were even more promising candidates for trial to solve a particular problem, T 487/92 *PROCTER & GAMBLE/ Manual dishwashing* [1996] E.P.O.R. 637); here the problem was formulated as a real, rather than hypothetical one. There is also no "one-way street" situation where a number of other modifications to meet official requirements were possible, T 0766/91 *BOEING/ Decorative laminates* [1997] E.P.O.R. 247 and T 0848/94 *KANEGAFUCHI/Polyimide film* [1999] E.P.O.R. 270; or where the problem is a two-fold one and the documents do not contribute to the solution of this, see T 0155/88 *NGK INSULATORS/Zirconia ceramics* [1998] E.P.O.R 161. In T 294/07 *PROTEXEON/Anaesthetic formulation* the problem was recognised as being the provision of an improved formulation on the basis of post-published evidence, there was no mere bonus effect following inevitably from an obvious measure since prior to the invention a skilled person would have been deterred from incorporating one of the constituents because of reported side-effects. In *Abbott v Medinol* [2010] EWHC 2865 (Pat) the claimed improvement provided improved flexibility in a stent. Obviousness was not established because there was no pointer towards the invention in the cited art, and once the skilled team decided to modify the designs disclosed in that art they would have been faced with a multi-dimensional problem with a number of potential avenues to follow and a number of conflicting criteria to balance against each other. If the step had been an obvious one, it was difficult to see why it had not been thought of previously.

The credibility of an effect on which an applicant or patentee wishes to rely is diminished if that effect is not disclosed in the specification. For example, in *Datacard v*

Eagle Technologies [2011] R.P.C. 17, [2011] EWHC 244 (Pat) the invention concerned a print ribbon cartridge incorporating an RFID tag for identification of the type of ribbon, the tag having a body formed with an aperture configured to allow a spindle to pass through it and an antenna formed on the tag body. The patentees wished to amend their main claim by adding a feature from a dependent claim that the antenna was circular and surrounded the aperture. They put forward the advantage that with this arrangement the antenna was equidistant from the reader regardless of rotational position, so that the ribbon did not have to be advanced for identification purposes and ribbon wastage was avoided. However, although the specification had identified prior art it had not identified any problems in relation to that art and merely referred to a "continuing need for improvements". It had not identified advantages associated with a circular antenna, and the circular antenna had not been claimed in the application as originally filed. The claim as notionally amended were held not only to lack inventive step but also to give rise to an impermissible intermediate generalisation §76.06 inter alia because the application as filed had contained no suggestion that the feature was of inventive significance. In *Clay v Allcock* (1906) 23 R.P.C. 745 at 750 the Court set out the relevant principles as follows:

> "Counsel for the Plaintiff urged the well-known principle in Patent law that a man need not state the effect or the advantage of his invention, if he describes his invention so as to produce it. But that is not true where he has to rely on the presence or absence of such effect or advantage as a part of the necessary delimitation. The fact that it is a mere consequence cannot be pleaded by him as an excuse for not putting it in, if the leaving it out leaves his invention inadequately defined."

Although *Clay v Allcock* is authority for the proposition that effect or advantage need not be stated in the specification, and it has been mentioned in relevant textbooks, it appears not to have been cited since 1906 and it could be difficult now to persuade a court to follow it, possibly also having regard to the requirement in r.5.1(a)(iii) PCT to disclose the invention in such terms that the technical problem and its solution can be understood and any advantageous effects with respect to the background art are set out.

—Obvious to try?

3.30   In *Johns-Manville's Patent* [1967] R.P.C. 479 CA it was held that a particular flocculating agent, recently made available on a commercial scale, "was well worth trying out in a generally known process in order to see whether it would have beneficial results". However, in *Gedeon Richter v Bayer Schering* [2011] EWHC 583 (Pat) a preliminary distinction was made between experiments that a skilled person would carry out in any event as part of his routine work without necessarily having any expectation as to the outcome and additional experiments involving more of a value judgment.

An obviousness to try objection can arise from a published paper or even an oral disclosure as in T 455/91 *GENENTECH/Expression in yeast* OJ EPO 1995, 684; [1996] E.P.O.R. 85, where it was held that a skilled person working in one field (e.g. expression in yeast) would regard a means conveniently adopted in a neighbouring field (e.g. the bacterial art) as being readily usable also in that field, if this transfer of technical knowledge involved nothing out of the ordinary.

The second *Johns-Manville* requirement, of there being a reasonable expectation of a beneficial result, is an important qualification and both stages of the test must be satisfied. Essentially the same two-stage test is used by the EPO with essentially the same criteria for the second stage, as explained in T 296/93 *BIOGEN/HBV antigen production* OJ EPO 1995, 627:

> "The fact that other persons (or teams) were also working on the same project might suggest that is was 'obvious to try' or that it was 'an interesting area to explore', but it does not necessarily imply that there was 'a reasonable expectation of success'. A 'reasonable expectation of success', which should not be confused with the understandable

'hope to succeed', implies the ability of the skilled person to reasonably predict, on the basis of the existing knowledge before the starting of a research project, a successful conclusion to the said project within acceptable time limits. The more unexplored a technical field of research is, the more difficult is the making of predictions about its successful conclusion and, consequently, the lower the expectation of success."

The objection of "obvious to try" was explained in *Norbrook Laboratories' Patent* [2006] F.S.R. 3002 [18] in the following terms. An invention may simply consist in an idea which, once it has been conceived, is one which will obviously work. For those cases a party attacking the patent only needs to show that the idea was an obvious one. But there are other cases where the invention involves something more than the bare idea, because it is not immediately apparent that the idea could be made to work. In these cases the attacking party needs to show something more: that it was obvious to have the idea and to try it to see whether it would work. The combination of a long acting antimicrobial with an anti-inflammatory was held to be an idea that would have occurred to a skilled team without invention, but they would not have known that the long-acting effect of the antimicrobial would be preserved, and accordingly an objection of obviousness failed. Similarly in T 1599/06 *UNIVERSITY OF CALIFORNIA/Mycobacterium vaccinating agent* the Appeal Board explained that evaluation of reasonable expectation involved analysing the prior art to determine the degree of confidence that an envisaged result would be obtained. If confidence was too low, then a reasonable expectation turned into a mere hope to succeed, and a skilled person working on that basis followed a non-obvious course of action. In the case in issue a skilled person could not have made a rational reliable prediction of success and the claimed subject-matter was not obvious.

Relatively straightforward objections of the *Johns-Manville* type involve the testing of new products for logical uses and are likely to lead to a finding of obviousness. In *DuPont (Holland's) Application* [1971] R.P.C. 7 it was held to be obvious to try every new textile fibre for every reasonably possible use. The EPO agrees that it is obvious to test a recently marketed material to see if this would overcome deficiencies in the current use of similar materials for the same purpose T 306/93 *REVLON/Nail enamel*, unreported. Where modified egg yolk had been described as an alternative to egg yolk, it was obvious to use the modified, instead of the unmodified, material in a prior art process T 384/94, *UNILEVER/ Emulsions* [2000] E.P.O.R. 469.

In *Genentech's Patent* [1987] R.P.C. 553 and [1989] R.P.C. 147 CA, claims to a product ("t-PA") made by recombinant DNA technology were revoked by the Court of Appeal partly because the existence of t-PA in a natural environment together with its characterisation and utility was part of the prior art, and to attempt its preparation by such technology was an idea well worth trying out to see if it would have beneficial results. This was supported by the facts that others had been working in parallel, though slightly later, and that the research work, though difficult and time-consuming, required no more than pertinacity, sound technique and trial and error, and such could not be regarded as characteristic of a patentable invention. The *Genentech* claims were also invalidated as based solely on a discovery unpatentable as such, see §1.10, and an analogy was drawn with a claim covering all solutions to a problem, i.e. to a known desideratum, as for example in *British United Shoe Machinery v Collier (Simon)* (1909) 26 R.P.C. 21 and (1910) 27 R.P.C. 567. The *Genentech* case, its factual background and commercial and legal significance were analysed in papers by: P. G. Cole, *Patent World*, 13, January 1989, 31; J. P. Thurston, [1989] EIPR 66; and B. Sherman, (1990) 21 IIC 76 with some further information on the background of the case being given by I. Armitage, *Patent World*, 15, April 1989, 3. Subsequently, the EPO allowed a corresponding patent with differently worded, but still very broad, claims extending to "alleles and derivatives by way of amino acid deletion, substitution, insertion, addition or replacement" of the stated 527 amino acid sequence, provided that the product has the essential character of natural t-PA as being classified as a t-PA based on immunological properties, T 923/92 *GENENTECH/Human t-PA* [1996] E.P.O.R. 275; abridged OJ EPO 1996, 564; discussed [1996] CIPA 562.

In T 541/89 *BEECHAM-WÜLFING/PVD* [1992] E.P.O.R. 193, it was held obvious to subject each of 12 compounds indicated in a prior art document to comparative tests to ascertain the most effective of these for an obvious purpose. Similarly in *Pfizer v Apotex* 480 F.3d 1348 (Fed. Cir., 2007 it was held to be obvious to screen anions from a shortlist of seven to overcome problems of instability of a drug after it had been admitted that there was a reasonable expectation that one of them would solve the problem. In contrast, in T 922/94 *MITSUI/Photocurable resin composition* [2002] E.P.O.R. 208, inventive step was upheld where the problem was a general one and there was a wide field of variation open to the skilled person such that hindsight was needed to come to the conclusion that the patentee's solution was obvious.

In T 1212/01 *PFIZER/Pyrazolopyrimidones for the treatment of impotence* a primary reference disclosed a class of compounds which were inhibitors of an enzyme called cGMP PDE and that the compounds were useful inter alia as vasodilators. The objective problem was to provide a further medical indication for the compounds and a skilled person looking to solve the problem would have turned to a second document which was a review article suggesting that compounds that inhibited this enzyme would have a possible therapeutic utility for treatment of impotence. The combined disclosures of the two documents gave a skilled person an incentive to test the compounds for that purpose so that the invention would have been arrived at without the exercise of inventive skill. Cautious language ("possible therapeutic utilities could include") in the second document was not evidence of a speculative approach but was unsurprising because the document was not reporting actual new developments. A skilled person would not have dismissed these suggestions but instead would have taken them seriously, especially in the context of a review of most or all of the known prior art rather than an isolated suggestion of an individual researcher. That opinion was not displaced by arguments as to technical prejudice, peer recognition or commercial success. The same conclusion in relation to the same patent having regard to the same prior art was reached by the UK Court of Appeal in *Lilly Icos v Pfizer* [2002] EWCA Civ 1, affirming the view at first instance that the claimed invention was little more than a putting into practice of the recommendations and suggestions of a prior document which would have been appreciated by a skilled person as being sound and worth trying.

In *MMI Research v CellXion* [2009] EWHC 418 (Pat) the patent in issue related to a method for identifying a mobile phone user or for eavesdropping on outgoing calls. It was held in relation to an objection of obviousness over the common general knowledge that an important purpose of GSM was to make the system more secure, and that a skilled team could not be assumed to have appreciated that it was possible to break into it at all, still less proceed through a long sequence of steps without knowing that it was indeed possible. Listening methods that had worked with past analogue networks would not have worked for GSM, and there was no logical model to adapt for the purpose of tackling the new task, so that the objection failed.

If a particular route is an obvious one to take or try, it is not rendered any less obvious from a technical point of view merely because there are a number of other obvious routes as well: the order in which the skilled worker chooses to try these will depend on many factors, but there "is no rule of law or logic which says that only the option which is likely to be tried first or second is to be treated as obvious for the purposes of patent legislation" *Brugger v Medic-Aid* [1996] R.P.C. 635. In *Monsanto v Merck* [2000] R.P.C. 709 the claimed compounds were a structural variation of a compound previously indicated to have desired activity, although more difficult to make than the known compound. In view of the activity announced for the known compound, it was held obvious to make and test the claimed compounds because of their analogous structure. In *Intervet v Merial R's University of Belfast* [2010] EWHC 294 at [236] the mere fact that a proposed route was a research project in which experiments were required and that success was not guaranteed did not show that the invention was not obvious if the route was obvious to try, easy to try and worth trying and that the skilled team would have a reasonable expectation of success and would have been likely to succeed.

There are EPO decisions where a "try and see" situation was held not to equate with an absence of a reasonable expectation of success if, e.g. from the teaching of the prior art, a skilled person had already clearly envisaged a proposed solution and then determined by routine tests whether the proposed solution had the desired effect, see T 1599/06 *UNIVERSITY OF CALIFORNIA/Mycobacterium vaccinating agent*. In T 91/98 *WELLCOME/Antiviral nucleosides* in ascertaining whether a compound was active against retroviruses while remaining non-toxic the Board preferred a "try it and see" test to a "reasonable expectation of success" test which it commented had been developed to deal with the complexity inherent in some recombinant DNA techniques, see also T 111/00 *FARBER/Monokine*. In T 1391/05 *ACTELION PHARMACEUTICALS/Glucosylceramide inhibitors* first and second documents, which were cross-referenced, when read together disclosed that certain compounds might be useful for a new medical indication. A claim to the compounds for use in treating that indication was held to lack inventive step. If the first document presented the problem of finding a new indication for the compounds, the second cross-referenced document suggested the claimed solution. Whether or not a skilled person would have tried the compounds for treating the new indication depended on the difficulties that would have been encountered and by the urgency of the need to find a treatment for the new indication. Here the compounds were already available and the illness was severe and had no accepted treatment. The experimental data in the first document was only *in vitro*, but such data was accepted in the pharmaceutical field as prima facie evidence of clinical effect, and there was a reasonable expectation of success.

However, in *St. Gobain v Fusion Provida* [2005] EWCA Civ. 177, [2005] IP&T 880, at [35]), it was stated that the "obvious to try" doctrine needs to be applied with caution and that:

> "Mere possible inclusion of something within a research programme on the basis you will find out more and something might turn up is not enough. If it were otherwise there would be few inventions which were patentable. The only research which would be worthwhile (because of the prospect of protection) would be in areas totally devoid of prospect. The obvious to try test really only works where it is more-or-less self-evident that what is being tested ought to work."

Similarly in *Conor Medsystems v Angiotech* (above), Lord Walker doubted whether the standard set out in *Johns-Manville* of "sufficient to warrant actual trial" and also adopted by the EPO in some decisions was workable in fields such as pharmaceuticals and biotechnology where enormous resources are committed to research, the results are very great and competition is fierce. In these circumstances it might be held that it would be worthwhile for large players to examine all possible avenues to see if one gave the right result, so that a solution which was well down the list of alternatives, all of which were more or less worth trying, would fail for obviousness for the reasons set out in *Brugger* (above). Pumfrey J. had decided obviousness on whether it was obvious to test or screen taxol for use in a drug-eluting stent, and Lord Hoffmann held that this was an inappropriate test and whether it was obvious to try something without any expectation of success was an oxymoronic concept which had no precedent in the law of patents. In *American Cyanamid v Ethicon* [1979] R.P.C. 215 a material was "obvious to try" in the sense of being a suitable candidate for inclusion in a research programme, but the extent of the research programme was such that the invention was held not to be obvious.

Calcipotriol monohydrate has advantages over its un-hydrated form: superior stability and superior technical properties in the manufacture of crystal suspension formulations. In *Leo Pharma v Sandoz* [2009] EWCA Civ 1188 the case against the patent was that a skilled person would have conducted a full polymorph screen and would have detected the monohydrate. The purpose of a full screen was not to find a better crystalline form but simply to find out whether there were other such forms, and a negative outcome would have been as important as a positive outcome. However, the evidence was that real skilled teams did not work on this basis, full screening was not required by the regulators, crystallizing vitamin D analogues was very hard indeed and past experience had indicated that it was not worthwhile. The case against the patent was held to be much too speculative; the hydrate was simply not *ob via*.

In *Generics v Daiichi* (supra) the invention was concerned with an enantiomer of a known drug. The case against the patent was that enantiomers of a related compound had been made and tested, and that one of them had potent activity whereas the other was only weakly active. Guidance as to a possible stereospecific intermediate had been disclosed in a poster presentation using a specific and somewhat unusual resolving agent. It was contended that a skilled person would have been motivated to investigate whether a corresponding intermediate for the known drug could provide a route to the present enantiomer using the same resolving agent. However this contention was rejected. Use of an unusual resolving agent suggested difficulty and unpredictability, otherwise a standard resolving agent would have been used, and the absence of a track record for the resolving agent made it less apparent that it might be generally useful. It was relevant that the generally accepted method of resolution started from the final product, not from an intermediate. The judge had correctly found that the structure of the necessary intermediate was not part of the common general knowledge. Even if the unimaginative skilled person had found the necessary intermediate and had recognised its similarity in structure to the previously disclosed intermediate, "having the wit to draw conclusions from that" would have involved a level of invention. Furthermore, the synthetic reaction might or might not have worked and the skilled person had other things to try. In coming to the conclusion that the proposed route was not attractive enough, the judge had made no error of principle and had properly carried out the balancing task of forming an overall value judgment, which is so often the task of the first instance judge. As to reasonable expectation of success, the level of expectation needed depended on the facts of each case, see *Generics (UK) Ltd v H Lundbeck A/S* [2007] R.P.C. 32 at [72]. It was recognised that there may be a number of obvious routes, and that there is no rule of law that requires only that option that is likely to be tried first or second to be treated as obvious, see *Brugger v Medic-Aid* [1996] R.P.C. 635 at p.661 l. 6 and *Palmaz's Patents* [2000] R.P.C. 631. However, it held that this did not mean that a skilled person would pursue every avenue relentlessly when there were only the mildest of motives for doing so.

In *Teva UK Ltd v Merck* [2009] EWHC 2952 (Pat) the claimed invention concerned the use of two drugs as a synergistic co-formulation for the treatment of glaucoma. The Court observed that caution is needed when faced with an obviousness attack based on a suggestion that the skilled person would embark on a research program in the course of which he would discover that a product or compound was effective. This was particularly so where the technical effect was one which was newly discovered, or impossible or very hard to predict because the expectation of success might be zero or inadequate to drive the research forward. In the end it will all depend on weighing the various factors as they appear from the evidence in the case. That applied a fortiori in the case of a use claim traditionally drafted because the compound in question was itself old, and might even have been previously used for a medicinal purpose. However, on the particular facts of the case, given the published results with one of the drugs, the patient compliance benefits of a co-formulation and the expectation of success a skilled team would have arrived at the claimed subject-matter without invention. The decision was affirmed on appeal, [2011] EWCA Civ 382.

—Invention by way of selection from the prior art

3.31   A "selection invention" must first satisfy the criterion of novelty, for which see §2.18. Once novelty has been established, inventive step can be recognised if a surprising technical effect is demonstrated for the claimed product or process, so that an unpredictable solution is achieved to the known problem of improving already known products or processes T 1/80 *BAYER/Carbonless copying paper* [1982] R.P.C. 321; OJ EPO 1981, 206. The evidence of surprising effect must be unique to the selection, so that selection of a sub-range from a larger range requires a "purposive", rather than arbitrary, selection of that sub-range which must be novel per se T 198/84 *HOECHST/Thiochloroformates* OJ EPO 1985, 209.

In *Dr Reddy's Laboratories v Eli Lilly* (above at §2.24) it was held that pre-1977 decisions on selection patents such as *I.G. Farbenindustrie's Patents* (1930) 47 R.P.C. 289 at pp.322–3 and *Du Pont's Patent* [1982] F.S.R. 303 should now be regarded as part of legal history and not part of the living law. The better approach was to see what the EPO Appeal Boards did when a patented product or class of products fell within a greater class. The applicable law was now to be found in T 939/92 *AGREVO/Triazoles* and T 133/01 *WYETH/ Dopamine agonists* that a sub-class or individual member of a published class was taken to be obvious if it was a random selection but not if it provided a real technical advance, and sufficient justification were provided for the advance to be credible. For an example of a patent concerning a single compound selected from a small group see *Beecham Group's Amoxycillin Application* [1980] R.P.C. 261; see also *Du Pont's (Witsiepe's) Application* [1982] F.S.R. 303.

In *Generics v Daiichi* [2009] R.P.C. 4, [2009] EWCA Civ 646 the patent covered an enantiomer of a known drug. In rejecting an objection that the claimed enantiomer was obvious and affirming the decision at first instance [2008] EWHC 2413 (Pat), the court observed that the work disclosed in the patent had led to a better medicine which was not merely twice as active, which might have been expected, but was a lot more soluble and less toxic than was predictable. The enantiomer could be used in higher dosages than expected and "only a curmudgeon" would have said that there was no invention.

The use of a known material, on the basis of a known property of it, to obtain a known effect in a new combination is not normally considered inventive, but special cases are recognised where selection of the material brings an unexpected advantage, or overcomes a known prejudice, or unforeseen difficulties are encountered such as a need to alter another component of the combination, see T 130/89 *KÖMMERLING/Profile member* OJ EPO 1991, 514; [1992] E.P.O.R. 98 where the claims were disallowed because, although two disparate problems were solved, neither solution involved inventive ingenuity.

Also, the selection must not be of the most appropriate material for the required purpose, even if unexpected, advantageous results then arise, i.e. the selection itself must be an unobvious one T 21/81 *ALLEN-BRADLEY/Electromagnetically operated switch* OJ EPO 1983, 15; and there is no invention in the selection of one of several obvious possibilities T 162/89 *KONICA/Colour photographic material* [1992] E.P.O.R. 24). If the problem is only to find a further solution to those already known, because no unexpected effect has been demonstrated, small changes (such as reversal of the known arrangement) are unlikely to be held inventive, see T 170/87 *SULZER/Hot gas cooler* OJ EPO 1989, 441; [1990] E.P.O.R. 14.

—Contemporaneous peer activities and peer reaction

Peer recognition can provide evidence in support of invention. In *General Tire v Firestone* [1971] R.P.C. 173 and [1972] R.P.C. 457 CA a scientist working for the defendant had written a book on the art and described the invention as a breakthrough. In *Genentech's (Human Growth Hormone) Patent* [1989] R.P.C. 613, a textbook had described the inventors' experiment as a notable one. In each case an objection of obviousness did not succeed. In *Schlumberger Holdings v Electromagnetic Geoservices* ("EMGS") (above) documents from an academic researcher conveyed enthusiasm for a new and valuable idea and coming contemporaneously from a leader in the field of CSEM carried substantial weight in the decision to affirm validity. It was held that the contemporaneous real reactions of experts in the field were admissible evidence which would not have been tailored or selected for the trial, often many years later, involved no or little reconstruction and for that reason had always been treated as of real value in deciding a patent case. It was wrong to downgrade it. The absence of cross-examination was irrelevant because hindsight cross-examination years later could not have demonstrated that the expert did not mean what he wrote at the time. However, in T 521/90 *PROCTER & GAMBLE/Pouring and measuring package* [1993] E.P.O.R. 558 a patent was revoked in the face of articles in the technical press praising the invention because it was not clear that their writers had been aware of the teachings of the relevant art.

Patent applications for the same invention filed by third parties insofar as they demonstrate peer reaction can also provide evidence of invention. In *Mabuchi Motor's Patents* [1996] R.P.C. 387, a validity challenger had itself sought a patent for a feature of the

3.32

claimed invention, an act which was noted as suggesting though not proving that this was thought to be inventive, see also *Unilever v Chefaro* [1994] R.P.C. 567. In *Schlumberger Holdings v Electromagnetic Geoservices* (above), academics at the University of Southampton had applied for a patent on a technique which clearly covered the basic idea of the patent in issue, and Jacob L.J. held that this made no sense except in the context that people thought that there was something valuable, especially since there had been entitlement proceedings leading to a 6-day hearing with leading counsel on both sides (the IP Office decision following that hearing was O/204/05 *Statoil v University of Southampton* and the patent was assigned to EMGS). However, in *Amersham Pharmacia Biotech AB v Amicom Limited and others* [2001] EWCA Civ. 1042 Aldous L.J. held that the author of an earlier "Disclosure of Invention" which was not proceeded with had qualifications exceeding those of the notional skilled addressee and also that it was not possible to decide whether the decision not to patent was correct because the prior art taken into account in reaching that decision was not before the court. In *Minnesota Mining's Patent* [1999] F.S.R. 636, on the principle that secondary evidence must be kept firmly in its place, an application for discovery of a later, abandoned, patent application by the petitioner was refused as disproportionate.

Peer recognition may be apparent from the disclosed documents of a defendant or applicant for revocation. In *Mölnlycke v Procter & Gamble* [1994] R.P.C. 49 at p.113, documents disclosed by P & G showed that they had treated the plaintiff's invention as both novel and inventive, that they did not comment that it had been an obvious development from what had gone before, and that they considered it an idea worth copying, see also *Schlumberger v Electromagnetic Geoservices* (above) at [85].

A sceptical attitude to the invention when announced coupled with later success is discussed at §3.39 with reference to the comments of Judge Rich in his article entitled "Laying the Ghost of the 'Invention' Requirement" (above) and with reference to *Haberman v Jackel International* (above).

Evidence as to contemporaneous peer activity can provide an indication whether an objection of obviousness should succeed. The Court of Appeal has approved the statement that the best guide when considering obviousness is to ask the question: "What did people do?"—see *Fichera v Flogates* [1984] R.P.C. 257. Likewise in *Chiron v Organon Teknika (No. 3)* [1994] F.S.R. 202 it was noted that the attitudes and thinking of those in the art at the priority date can "best be ascertained by looking at what was happening and the attitudes of those concerned in the field in the 1980's", this evidence helping the court to decide "whether the opinions of witnesses are consistent with the facts or (as was held) are hindsight reconstructions of the type which are not persuasive".

Peer failure to solve the problem which was solved by the patentee provides evidence to rebut a suggestion of obviousness. In *Glaverbel v British Coal* [1994] R.P.C. 443 the defendant had itself failed to perform the process which it subsequently alleged unsuccessfully to have been obvious, and had later tried also unsuccessfully to work outside the scope of the patent. However, on appeal [1995] R.P.C. 255 a wider construction was given to the claim and it was then held, in the light of the later improved technology, obvious to use the only feature which could have added novelty to it.

In *Mölnlycke v Procter & Gamble (No. 5)* [1994] R.P.C. 49 CA several people had each had a similar idea by the date when the patented invention was made, but only the patentee had thought the idea worth developing. Furthermore, the patented system was seen to make use of an entirely different concept from that of the then common general knowledge in the art. Accordingly the Patents Court recognised the presence of an inventive step. The Court of Appeal affirmed the decision at first instance and placed emphasis on the attitude to the invention displayed in the defendant's contemporaneous internal memoranda which was considered preferable to the expert evidence which it felt was necessarily tainted by hindsight. However, as explained at §3.39, it warned against indiscriminate reliance on such secondary evidence, as the state of knowledge of skilled individuals, including the inventor, might not correspond to the statutory definition of the state of the art. In *Unilever v Chefaro* (above), the Court was influenced by the fact that the defendant's expert, faced with the same problem, had done something different from the solution covered by the patent.

In *Beloit v Valmet* [1995] R.P.C. 705 and [1997] R.P.C. 489, abridged, BL C/18/97, a number of independent persons had proposed the idea almost simultaneously. This was a different situation from that in *Mölnlycke*, leading to the inference that the simultaneous proposals were not "flashes of insight", but suggested a natural development in the art. In *Demel v Jefferson* [1999] F.S.R. 204, which concerned a prosthesis for overcoming lameness in cows, the expert for the party attacking validity admitted that he had not thought of taking the step from the prior art until aware of the patent and that this was not something he (and other veterinary surgeons also) would have been likely to think of: indeed, on cross-examination, he stated that he thought it "a very good invention". After this evidence, the patent was naturally upheld. However, unsuccessful attempts by others do not assist the patentee if the problems they faced cannot be solved by anything said in the specification: see *Johns-Manville's Patent* [1967] R.P.C. 479 and *Société Technique de Pulverisation STEP v Emson* [1993] R.P.C. 513 CA.

Contemporaneous peer activity, or the absence thereof, may be revealed by the disclosed documents of the parties. In *Schlumberger v Electromagnetic Geosciences* (above), the absence of relevant pre-patent documents of the applicant for revocation was telling: no-one at Schlumberger had, pre-patent, even contemplated the use of CSEM for detection of hydrocarbons, and their post-patent documents referred to CSEM as somewhat fringe geophysical methods of use only as regional exploration tools of low resolution and then only suitable for applications in certain more difficult geological provinces, whereas as now modified these methods had undergone a metamorphosis; see also the effect of the disclosed research documents of the parties in *Beecham Group's (Amoxycillin) Application* (above) at §3.39.

—Market reaction

A court views with suspicion arguments based on prior art that an invention was obvi- **3.33**
ous if, despite the prior art, the invention has been a commercial success; *Parkes v Cocker* (above).

The current UK approach is summarised by observations of Jacob L.J. *Schlumberger v Electromagnetic Geosciences* (above) at [79]. Commercial success of a patented product can point to inventiveness, particularly where the product meets a long-standing need. It is necessary to be able to strip out all other possible causes of that success, such as advertising, low production costs due to factors other than the invention, good design features and so on. But if that can be done (normally it works only in the case of simple inventions) and the result is a successful product, which, if anyone had thought of it earlier, would have met a large market earlier, there may well be an invention. *Haberman v Jackel* (above) was a particularly dramatic example where commercial success turned a case of apparent obviousness into one of non-obviousness, and Laddie J.'s "non-exhaustive summary" of the factors taken into account when considering commercial success (see §3.28), as previously noted, was acknowledged as a masterpiece. These observations repeat views previously expressed in *Angiotech v Conor Medsystems* [2007] EWCA Civ 5. In contrast to a simple invention, a taxol-eluting stent had not sprung on the market once the "invention" was made. On the contrary it was not until 10 years after the priority date that it came on the market at all. Work had to be done not only in establishing all the detail (appropriate polymer carrier, dose, safety and so on) but as to whether that which in principle ought to work, in fact did so. Commercial success had not shown to be the result of just an inventive idea. In the House of Lords in [2008] R.P.C. 28, [2008] UKHL 49, sub nom. *Conor Medsystems v Angiotech Pharmaceuticals Inc.* it was noted that the Angiotech stent had the largest market share amongst drug-eluting stents, but it is not apparent that this fact was more than incidental to the decision to allow the appeal and affirm the validity of the patent and no criticism was made of these observations of Jacob L.J.

Relevant success is not necessarily confined to national boundaries: in *Unilever v Gillette* [1989] R.P.C. 417 a pleading of foreign commercial success was allowed to remain as possibly, but not necessarily, relevant.

Licensing can form the basis of relevant success. However, at first instance in *SABAF v MFI and Meneghetti* BL C/37/01, noted IPD 24059 evidence of successful licensing did not help save the patent because the royalty rates charged were so low that it would have made little sense for anyone to refuse the offer of a licence and to have litigated instead. Commercial success was not in issue either before the Court of Appeal [2003] R.P.C. 264 [14] or before the House of Lords [2005] R.P.C. 209[10]. Similarly in *Aerotel v Wavecrest* [2009] EWCA Civ 408 which involved a method of making a telephone call using prepayment, allegations of commercial success were not persuasive and it was held that the circumstances were entirely different from those in *Haberman v Jackel* (above). A grateful market did not immediately fall upon this invention, saying "this is the answer to our problems." When the invention was made known absolutely nothing happened. The world beat a path to the door of Ralph Waldo Emerson's inventor of a better mousetrap, but the path to Aerotel's door remained untrodden. The patentees had made their income by licensing, litigation and the threat of litigation, and there was no evidence that any success was due to the merit of the invention.

In *Alan Nuttall v Fri-Jado UK Ltd and Anor* [2008] EWHC 1311 (Pat) evidence of commercial success and of copying by others was held to be legally irrelevant and unhelpful, and was not allowed to be adduced because it did not begin to establish what would need to be established, namely that as a fact, or proper inference in the circumstances, those skilled in this art had probably read the cited prior art yet had failed to come up with the invention. However, the patent was held valid on the basis of a brief and straightforward analysis of the relationship between the claimed invention and the prior art, which may have influenced the decision not to admit circumstantial evidence.

Where a party to proceedings before the Patents Court wishes to rely upon alleged commercial success to rebut a challenge of obviousness, it is required that full particulars of such success be given in a formal answer to the pleading containing the obviousness allegation, see CPR 63PD 0.4 at 4.6 (see Appendix F and discussed in §3.33). Thus, before pleading "commercial success", the implications for the disclosure stage of litigation should be considered, because putting commercial success in issue will require at least some disclosure of, probably sensitive, sales statistics as well requiring identification of the precise nature of the commercially successful product or process, and such may show that the success was due to an embodiment of a sub-claim rather than of the main claim, or be due to extraneous factors such as advertising. The extent of the disclosure that is not prima facie required to support such a pleading is particularised in CPR 63 PD 6.3. Even the UK IP Office may order disclosure of relevant documents related to exploitation of the invention by the proprietor, though this is likely to be more limited than would be ordered in proceedings before the court, see *John Guest's Patent* [1987] R.P.C. 259.

In general, like the UK courts, the EPO views evidence of commercial success with suspicion since that success may be due to factors other than the intrinsic inventiveness of the solution to the problem which the art had faced, see T 270/84 *ICI/Fusecord* [1987] E.P.O.R. 357 and T 490/89 *ENERGY CONVERSION/Silicon deposition* [1993] E.P.O.R. 46. However, it has accepted evidence of commercial success as indicating unobviousness where the adoption of the invention appears to have been uninfluenced by factors other than the merit of the invention e.g. where the invention was adopted in hospitals who could not easily be influenced by publicity or advertising, see T69/89 *SURGIKOS/Disinfection* [1990] E.P.O.R. 632. In T 626/96 *AVILON/Water tap commercial success* was recognised as this was seen as directly attributable to the new structure and had been achieved over a short period and also nearly 60 years had elapsed between publication of the closest prior art and the filing date of the patent; similarly T 915/00 *INTEGRAN TECHNOLOGIES/Nanocrystalline metals* where relevant circumstantial evidence included commercial implementation, licensing and recognition of the inventor's merits by the scientific community.

—Delay—"If obvious, why was it not done before?"

3.34   Unexplained delay points towards invention. In *Schlumberger Holdings v Electrogeomagnetic Geoservices* (above) it was observed by the Court of Appeal that if a useful development was, in hindsight, seemingly obvious for years and the apparently straightforward technical step from the prior art simply was not taken, then there was likely to have been an invention. In the present case the CSEM technique had been available for 20 years, the closest prior art had been available for nine years and various reasons why the invention had not been made earlier were put forward, none of which answered the question why the invention had not been made before, when the facts really called for a good explanation. "The simplest explanation—indeed the only one that fits the known facts—is that the inventors hit upon something which others had missed. Occam's razor points to invention." The invention had been "obvious" for too long for it really to have been obvious. A similar situation arose in *Fosroc International v W R Grace* [2010] EWHC 1702 (Pat) where the skilled person would have assumed that the commercialised compound was the best compound, that there was no expectation that superior or even equivalent compounds would be found amongst those already disclosed, and the failure of the art to come up with the invention was particularly telling. A six-year delay was held to be persuasive of inventive step in *Virgin Atlantic Airways v Premium Aircraft Interiors UK* [2010] R.P.C. 8, [2009] EWCA Civ 1062. Similarly a 10-year delay without any product emerging on the market was held to be conclusive against a finding of obviousness in a case based on the common general knowledge alone, the court observing that in such cases it is vital to look at what actually happened in the field and that although a person skilled in the art is a legal construct he or she is not supposed to be divorced from reality, see *Convatec v Smith & Nephew* [2011] EWHC 2039 (Pat).

However, the persuasive value of delay may be reduced or eliminated by the absence of real-world interest or of a long-felt want, see *Boehringer Mannheim v Genzyme* [1993] F.S.R. 716, *Brugger v Medic-Aid* [1996] R.P.C. 635 and *Optical Coating v Pilkington* [1995] R.P.C. 145.

The persuasive value of delay may also be reduced if, even though the problem had been long-standing, the means to solve it had only recently become available, see *Texas Iron Works' Patent* [2000] R.P.C. 207 CA. A warning given in *Angiotech's Patent* [2006] R.P.C. 665 [28] is that inventions may be obvious even though the art missed them; and that it is absurd to suggest that everything objectively obvious at the priority date should have been done or contemplated either then or at any time thereafter. Patents should not be granted for things that have been obvious for a long time.

Attitudes towards delay in the EPO are similar. Invention can be recognised if there is no adequate answer to the question: if obvious why was the solution not reached before? T 165/85 *BOEHRINGER MANNHEIM/Detection of redox reactions* [1987] E.P.O.R. 125. However, a long interval is only relevant if it can be shown that there had been an unsatisfied requirement during it T 324/94 *VDO ADOLF SCHINDLING/Illuminating device* [1997] E.P.O.R. 14.

The fourth question—evaluation of the evidence

—A decision according to the evidence

Obviousness is frequently referred to as a jury question; see, e.g. *Procter & Gamble v Peaudouce* [1989] F.S.R. 180 CA. The role of the Comptroller or of a court when deciding whether or not the claimed subject-matter is obvious is to give a true decision according to the evidence. The invention must be held either obvious or unobvious: there is no halfway house. **3.35**

In *Genentech's Patent* [1989] R.P.C. 147, it was stressed that obviousness is to be assessed by the judge in the light of the totality of the facts before him, the effect of which should first be analysed by him. However, this "jury question" is entirely a factual question, to be decided objectively without knowledge of the alleged infringement and it does not involve quantitative assessment of the size of the "step", that is this difference from the prior art. It has been said to be doubtful whether any particular verbal formula can be used in all cases, see *Johns-Manville's Patent* [1967] R.P.C. 479. A statement of Kitchin J. in *Generics v Lundbeck* [2007] R.P.C. 32 at [72] approved by Lord Hoffmann in *Conor v Angiotech* [2008] R.P.C 28 at [42] has been cited in many subsequent decisions:

"The question of obviousness must be considered on the facts of each case. The court must consider the weight to be attached to any particular factor in the light of all the relevant circumstances. These may include such matters as the motive to find a solution to the problem the patent addresses, the number and extent of the possible avenues of research, the effort involved in pursuing them and the expectation of success."

In *Windsurfing* the jury question was expressed in the neutral terms of the statute, which side-steps whether it should be formulated in terms of what a skilled person could do or what he would do. In *Pharmacia v Merck* [2002] R.P.C. 77 at [125] Aldous L.J. commented that prior to Oliver L.J.'s judgment in *Windsurfing*, many hours were spent arguing about the question to be considered, but this was no longer desirable and use of the structured approach in *Windsurfing* avoided such considerations. *Windsurfing* continues to provide the relevant test under the present Act and there has been no discontinuity in the British approach between the present Act and the former law. The decision in *Windsurfing* and the surrounding circumstances are discussed by P.G. Cole, "Fundamentals of Patent Drafting", *CIPA*, 2006 at pp.223–245.

—Precedent and fact issues

3.36   In *Hallen v Brabantia* [1989] R.P.C. 307 the Court of Appeal reviewed numerous cases on the issue of obviousness but found few of assistance and observed that "citing previous decisions on a question of fact is not a useful, nor is it a proper exercise". In *Angiotech Pharmaceuticals & Anor v Connor Medsystems Inc.* [2007] EWCA Civ 5 Jacob. L.J. said:

"I also take the view that one can over-elaborate a discussion of the concept of 'obviousness' so that it becomes metaphysical or endowed with unwritten and unwarranted doctrines, sub-doctrines or even sub-sub-doctrines. This can be coupled with a massive citation of authority . . . In the end the question is simply 'was the invention obvious?' This involves taking into account a number of factors, for instance the attributes and cgk [common general knowledge] of the skilled man, the difference between what is claimed and the prior art, whether there is a motive provided or hinted by the prior art and so on. Some factors are more important than others. Sometimes commercial success can demonstrate that an idea was a good one. In others 'obvious to try' may come into the assessment. But such a formula cannot itself necessarily provide the answer. Of particular importance is of course the nature of the invention itself."

A warning against relying on an earlier decision as to the relevant facts was given in *Actavis v Merck* [65]. The fact that a patent for sustained release formulation of oxycodone had been upheld in *Napp v Ratiopharm* [2009] EWCA Civ 252, [2009] R.P.C. 539 was not a reason for upholding a patent for a sustained release formulation of fluvastatin: the two cases were unalike, see also *Abbott Laboratories v Medinol* at [248] where an earlier cited decision was held to be of limited assistance since the obviousness attack in the earlier case was different as also was the evidence. In *Eli Lilly & Company v Human Genome sciences, Inc* [2010] R.P.C. 14, [2010] EWCA Civ 33 it was observed that the English courts had never given deference to the Technical Boards of Appeal in the case of the objection of obviousness, see also §1.04. That position was confirmed by the Supreme Court in *Eli Lilly v Human Genome Sciences* [2011] UKSC 51 at [85], [87] and [91] where it was explained that although the approach was binding, the reasoning or outcome might not be, e.g. where there was different evidence and arguments, where the same competing arguments and factual evidence were assessed differently or in a borderline case where they formed different judgments on the same view of the expert and factual evidence.

—Everything within the scope of the claim must be inventive

3.37   In *Pozzoli S.P.A v BDMO S.A.* [2006] EWHC 1398 (Pat), Lewison J. explained that if a claim covers anything that is obvious, it is invalid. It does not matter that the claim also covers things that are far from obvious. If the claim covers more than it should, the patentee's remedy is to amend it, see also *Novartis v Ivax* [2006] EWHC 2506 (Pat) and *Brugger v Medic-Aid* [1996] R.P.C. 635.

In *Norbrook Laboratories' Patent* ([2006] F.S.R. 302 [18]), it was observed that it is only where technical advantages are possessed by everything falling within the claim, or at least all sensible embodiments of what is claimed, that it is legitimate to bear them in mind. A wide inventive concept which includes, but is not limited to, embodiments with technical merit may be more vulnerable to an attack on the ground of lack of inventive step than a narrow one which is limited and traps the advantageous features. However, occasional failure to achieve promised advantages can be excused so long as substantially all embodiments provide a solution to the problem to be solved, see T 1146/02 *SMITHKLINE BEECHAM/Vaccines containing a saponin and a sterol* (unreported).

—Technical invention or a mere commercial idea?

The relevant question is whether something in the claim was technically obvious in the light of the disclosure relied upon, not whether it was commercially obvious: *Windsurfing v Tabur Marine* (supra), *Hallen v Brabantia* [1991] R.P.C. 195 at pp.211–212 CA; *Pharmacia v Merck* [2001] EWCA Civ 1610; [2001] R.P.C. 41 at [122]; *Asahi Medical v Macopharma* [2002] EWCA Civ 466 at [26]–[27] see also *Thermos v Isola* (1910) 27 R.P.C. 388 at pp.398–399. **3.38**

—Handling of evidence; direct and circumstantial evidence

There is a range of views as to the classification of evidence as to inventive step, being variously the results of technical analysis of an invention vis-à-vis the best starting point prior art, primary evidence of an appropriately qualified technical expert, and secondary evidence relating to the surrounding circumstances, e.g. commercial success. There is also a range of opinions about the probative value of evidence of each kind, and prevailing opinion or at least emphasis is liable to change depending on the nature of the cases that have recently come before the courts and the case which is currently under consideration. **3.39**

Forceful arguments for the position that obviousness should be decided on the basis of objective technical analysis, and that circumstantial evidence is of low probative value are found in an opinion of the EPO Appeal Board in T 24/81 *BASF/Metal refining* which outlines an approach which has consistently been adopted by the EPO:

"When assessing inventive step ... it is not a question of the subjective achievement of the inventor ... It is rather the objective achievement which has to be assessed. As in the case of novelty, inventive step is an objective concept. Objectivity in the assessment of inventive step is achieved by starting out from the objectively prevailing state of the art, in the light of which the problem is determined which the invention addresses and solves from an objective point of view ... and consideration is given to the question of the obviousness of the disclosed solution to this problem as seen by the man skilled in the art and having those capabilities which can be objectively expected of him ... The appellant sees the fact that the steel industry has passed by the method as applied for, despite the significant economic contribution it makes to solving the environmental problems in this field, as an indication of the presence of inventive step. The Board takes the view that, as against the assessment of inventive step from the objective point of view ... a mere investigation for indications of the presence of inventive step is no substitute for the technically skilled assessment of the invention vis-à-vis the state of the art, pursuant to Article 56 EPC."

The EPO approach was further explained in slightly more moderate terms in T 1212/01 *PFIZER/Pyrazolopyrimidones for the treatment of impotence*. Commercial success and similar arguments can only ever be secondary indicia of inventiveness, which are usually only important in cases where an objective evaluation of the prior art has not provided a clear answer. In such cases, secondary indicia may show that an inventive step is involved. Since in the present case the claimed subject-matter followed plainly and logically from the prior art, secondary indicia could not assist in the assessment of inventive step.

For an equally forceful contrary view, see the paper entitled "Laying the Ghost of the "Invention" Requirement" (above) in which Judge Rich pointed out that in a trial for murder evidence of a smoking gun or a bloody knife was compelling circumstantial evidence and argued that commercial success and similar circumstantial evidence should not be dismissed as "secondary" and relegated to situations of doubt but instead could have the highest probative value. For example, if a judge were presented with a defence of obviousness and the evidence showed that the defendant, long knowing about a problem in his product or his manufacturing process for which he had found no solution changed over to use his competitor's patented invention as soon as he heard of it, that evidence was not "secondary" and should not be ignored in considering his argument that it was an obvious invention.

From the mid–1990s onwards the UK courts, while admitting circumstantial evidence, have been sceptical about the weight that should be given to it, see for, e.g. *Glaverbel SA v British Coal* [1995] R.P.C. 155 CA:

"The primary evidence will be that of properly qualified expert witnesses who will say whether or not in their opinions the relevant step would have been obvious to a skilled man having regard to the state of the art. All other evidence is secondary to that primary evidence. . .

In the nature of things, the expert witnesses and the court are considering the question of obviousness in the light of hindsight. It is this which may make the court's task difficult. What with hindsight seems plain and obvious, often was not so seen at the time. It is for this reason that contemporary events can be of evidential assistance when testing the experts' primary evidence. For instance, many people may have been industriously searching for a solution to the problem for some years without hitting upon the allegedly obvious invention. When this type of evidence is adduced, the court can quickly find itself caught up in an investigation of what was or was not obvious to certain identified individuals at certain dates during the history of the development of the product or process involved. This gives rise to complications because the state of the knowledge of these individuals, though skilled, may not correspond to the statutory definition of the state of the art. A particular inventor may have been unaware of some aspect of the state of the art as defined in section 2(2), and may therefore have genuinely taken what was actually an inventive step, but nevertheless be unable to claim a patentable invention since the step was, in the terms of the statute, obvious. Further, this type of evidence invites the court to speculate whether particular individuals were of an inventive disposition, because the earlier making of the same invention by another or others does not necessarily mean that at the later date the invention was obvious. Yet again, evidence of the commercial success of the invention can lead into an investigation of the reasons for the success; there may be commercial reasons for this success unrelated to whether the invention was or was not obvious in the past.

Secondary evidence of this type has its place and the importance, or weight, to be attached to it will vary from case to case. However, such evidence must be kept firmly in its place. It must not be permitted, by reason of its volume and complexity, to obscure the fact that it is no more than an aid in assessing the primary evidence."

However, circumstantial evidence is sometimes influential or even decisive in UK proceedings. In *Beecham Group's (Amoxycillin) Application* [1980] R.P.C. 261, two of the judges in the Court of Appeal who had experience of patents had formed opposite views about the patentability of Amoxycillin and the third judge who admitted he did not have prior patent experience had to decide between them. He ruled between the opposing views on the basis of the internal research reports disclosed by the parties by way of discovery, which revealed that both Beecham and Bristol Myers had made Amoxycillin, but that only Beecham had recognised its outstanding properties. In *Haberman v Jackel*

International [1999] F.S.R. 683 a long-felt want combined with a history of industry rejection followed by commercial success and further followed by industry denial of inventiveness, conforming to the pattern outlined by Judge Rich (above), was a decisive factor in favour of validity.

In *Schlumberger Holdings v Electromagnetic Geoservices* [2010] R.P.C. 33, [2010] EWHC Civ 819 Jacob L.J. reaffirmed the important role of secondary evidence in relation to the question: why was it not done before? Secondary evidence and the history of the matter could point to inventiveness; see *Technograph Printed Circuits v Mills & Rockley* [1972] R.P.C. 346 at 353, *Haberman v Jackel* (above), *Chiron v Organon Teknika (No. 3)* [1994] F.S.R. 202 at 223, *Lucas v Gaedor* [1978] R.P.C. 297 at 358 and *Mölnlycke v Procter & Gamble* [1994] R.P.C. 49 at 113. In the present case the evidence of the defendant's expert was a mere assertion of opinion without supporting reasons, and his view should not be accepted in the face of compelling secondary evidence of inventiveness.

The significance of expert evidence, or lack of expert evidence, in relation to pleaded prior art was considered in *KCI Licensing v Smith & Nephew*. An objection in relation to a gel patent that a feature was obvious was held at first instance [2010] EWHC 1487 (Pat),to have failed for lack of evidence. On appeal [2011] F.S.R. 8, [2010] EWCA Civ 1260 the court resisted a temptation to find that the feature was so trivial as to be inherently obvious but nevertheless held that there was ample evidence to support the conclusion that it was indeed obvious to the relevant skilled team, that evidence all pointing in a single direction.

An appeal from the IP Office in an application for revocation where evidence had been adduced from experts acting for each side, and both experts had been subjected to cross-examination came before the Patents Court in *Nampak Cartons v Rapid Action Packaging* [2010] EWHC 1458 (Pat). It was held that a statement in the decision that the Hearing Officer had not found the expert evidence "directly" helpful should not be read that he had disregarded that evidence, or substituted his own judgment for that of the experts. At first instance O/342/99 the hearing officer had not been persuaded by a stage-wise cross-examination which was arrived at "starting from something known, and taking a series of apparently easy steps, see *British Westinghouse v Broulik* (1910) R.P.C. 209 at p.230 and *Technograph Printed Circuits v Mills & Rockley* [1972] R.P.C. 346 at p.362.

A long-standing principle of the assessment of inventive step before a British court has been that direct evidence may not be given on the very question that the court has to decide, so that it is impermissible for an expert witness to say that the invention would, or would not, have been obvious to him at the relevant date, see *British Celanese v Courtaulds* (1935) 52 R.P.C. 171 at 196 HL. Under this principle, the evidence should be directed to an explanation of the prior art and the surrounding circumstances, leaving the court to judge the vital question for itself, but the rival experts will no doubt, legitimately, try to influence the court by giving evidence of common practices and general knowledge in the art as at the priority date. In *Mölnlycke v Procter & Gamble (No. 5)* [1994] R.P.C. 49 at 113 CA and *Glaverbel v British Coal* [1995] R.P.C. 255 CA, it was suggested that this rule from this British Celanese decision had been altered by the Civil Evidence Act 1972 (c. 30) and that an expert ought to be able to give evidence on any matter on which he is qualified to give an opinion. However, this view does not appear to have been adopted and in *Beloit v Valmet* [1995] R.P.C. 705, it was stated in relation to the opinions of expert witnesses that it is the reasons which they give to support those expressed opinions that are more important than the opinions themselves.

Avoidance of hindsight

A classic warning against unintended but inevitable hindsight appears in a book by Diane Vaughan, *The Challenger Launch Decision* (University of Chicago Press, 1996) at 69–71. It is referred to inter alia by Roy Marsh, "The Continuing PSA debate" [2010] *CIPA* 59. Professor Vaughan explains that a problem that was ill-structured becomes well-structured after an event (in that instance a disaster, but equally the making of an invention), as people look back and reinterpret information ignored or minimised prior to the event that afterward takes on new significance. Information strung together in post-event accounts can present a coherent set of signals that was not characteristic of the situation as

3.40

it existed prior to the event. The result can be a systematic distortion of history that obscures the meaning of events and actions *as it existed and changed for the participants in the situation at the time the events and actions occurred.* (Professor Vaughan's emphasis) Making an invention is by definition an ill-structured problem whereas the task of examination of a patent application or deciding on an objection of lack of inventive step against a granted patent is a well-structured problem because the invention has become known. There is the same risk of deriving a coherent set of signals where none existed prior to the invention. Even the selection of a primary reference may be a product of hindsight and risks distorting history in the manner suggested by Professor Vaughan.

Care must therefore be taken not to construct an argument of obviousness based upon ex post facto analysis: hindsight is not to be confused with foresight. Such analysis "is unfair to inventors and not countenanced by English patent law", see *British Westinghouse v Braulik*, (1910) 27 R.P.C. 209 at 230, a statement said to be as true in 1975 as it was in 1910 *Hughes v Ingersoll* [1977] F.S.R. 406. Obviousness is to be considered without knowledge of the invention: otherwise that consideration amounts to impermissible ex post facto analysis *Shoketsu's Patent* [1992] F.S.R. 184. In *Coflexip v Stole Comex* BL C/32/00 CA Aldous L.J. said that there had been a classic instance of the kind of cross-examination rejected by Lord Diplock in *Technograph Printed Circuits Ltd v Mills & Rocky (Electronics) Ltd* [1972] R.P.C. 346 at p.362, and Chadwick L.J. added that obviousness has to be answered not by looking with the benefit of hindsight at what is known now and what was known at the priority date and asking whether the former flows naturally and obviously from the latter, but by hypothesising what would have been obvious at the priority date to a person skilled in the art to which the patent in suit relates, who is assumed to have access to what was known of the art immediately before the priority date. He also commented that adopting the structured approach in *Windsurfing* helped to avoid the error of hindsight.

In *Fichera v Flogates* [1984] R.P.C. 257, the invention was held to be unobvious, though it "was plainly obvious to anyone with the benefit of hindsight", because of the practical activities of experts in the field who had unsuccessfully been seeking to solve the same problems as the inventor. In *Intalite v Cellular Ceilings (No. 2)* [1987] R.P.C. 537, the claimed invention was, at first sight, one obvious to the skilled worker to try, but after hearing the evidence the Patents Court was satisfied that the objection of obviousness was unsustainable. It was observed that:

> "When skilled and inventive individuals, looking for improvements in the field, fail to arrive at the claimed construction it is impossible to suggest that it would have been obvious to the hypothetical skilled man."

A similar case is *Fairfax v Filhol* [1986] R.P.C. 499 CA where the claimed idea had not been arrived at by several others, including "the most prolific inventor in the field", see also *Windsurfing v Trilantic [Canada]* (1986) 8 CPR (3d) 241. In *Bonzel v Intervention (No. 3)* [1991] R.P.C. 553, it was held that the skilled man would not have seen the cited prior art to have been of relevance at the priority date, its relationship to the invention being seen only in hindsight by a person who then had knowledge of the invention.

In *Oneac v Raychem* BL C/32/98, noted IPD 21085; [1998] EIPR N–188, which concerned a telephone circuit, the court was not persuaded that the ordinary skilled worker would have realised that simple modifications from the prior art could be made until after the alleged invention had been made, the Court noting that "one has to look forward from the prior art, not backwards from the patentee's solution". The Court concluded:

> "This is one of those cases where, once an elegant and simple solution had been found to a problem, it is all too easy to think it obvious. Electrical components do not have minds of their own. They behave in predictable ways. It is possible to analyse why a circuit works when it has been designed. Once the solution has been found it is possible to re analyse the problem in a way which will lead to the solution. ... However, it can be misleading to analyse the problem with the patented solution in mind. A major part in making an invention may consist of analysing the problem and thinking of a new way

of avoiding it. Once this has been done, putting together the components to give effect to that new way may be easy."

Likewise, in *Cartonneries de Thulin* [2001] R.P.C. 264 CA, the alleged invention was seen as simple and elegant and the Patents Court recognised that, therefore, it was "particularly easy to fall into the trap of thinking it obvious with the benefit of wisdom of hindsight", that court also stating that "one should not be beguiled by the step-by-step analysis; in this case, as in many cases, it makes the alleged invention look more likely to be obvious than is justified"; this decision was upheld on appeal.

English Hop Products' Patent BL O/146/04 concerned a process for selective catalytic hydrogenation of unsaturated iso-α-acids of hops to partially hydrogenated products using super-critical carbon dioxide. The applicants for revocation relied on an earlier document disclosing a similar process that gave quantitative partial hydrogenation of isophorone, a simpler molecule, with no production of fully hydrogenated by-products and argued that it was obvious to try the same reaction conditions for iso-α-acids. However, it was concluded, following extensive evidence and cross-examination, that it was easy to see similarities between isophorone and iso-α-acids when that is what you wanted to find. Once you had seen the patent, it was easy to trawl through the many compounds listed in the reference relied on looking for those that had features in common with iso-α-acids. However, even if with hindsight one alighted on isophorone, the similarities were not that strong.

Novartis v Ivax [2006] EWHC 2506 (Pat), BL C/91/06 related to formulation of cyclos-porin as an oil-in-water microemulsion. Prior to the patent microemulsions had been described in a paper and had been taught to undergraduate students as a way of formulat-ing poorly soluble active ingredients but had not been used to formulate other drugs. Ac-cordingly microemulsions were not part of the common general knowledge. The problem was to improve on a known cyclosporin formulation to improve, e.g. stability or bioavailability. The defendants relied on a patent describing how to formulate microemul-sions and the common general knowledge. The Court held that this was a good example of an objection based on impermissible hindsight since a skilled person would not have said "this gives me what I want" unless he had already appreciated the merits of microemul-sion formulations. There could be technical merit in an obvious development from a non-obvious starting point, and if microemulsions were not part of the common general knowl-edge, their use was really research work.

In *Lundbeck v Generics* [2007] EWHC 1040 an argument that a reaction was obvious to try was rejected on the grounds that it was only with hindsight that it was possible to explain the outcome of the reaction which would otherwise have been unexpected and that the road towards achieving the overall goal of obtaining an enantiomer of a known drug was long and uncertain. This finding was upheld on appeal [2008] EWCA Civ 311.

In *SmithKline Beecham v Apotex* [2005] F.S.R. 524 [23], repetition of an example in a prior specification gave paroxetine hemihydrate rather than the promised anhydrate. It was argued that a skilled person would have realised that the problem was water, that the earlier steps of the example should be repeated under anhydrous conditions, and that then in order to remove bound isopropanol a water slurry step should be tried. The step had been disclosed in the example and a skilled person would go back to the recipe and see what it did. In rejecting this argument, the Court of Appeal accepted that for obviousness even a blind following of an apparently pointless or deleterious step might count, but in this case it had not been established that a skilled person trying to find out where the example had gone wrong would without imagination have put into water a product that had been kept dry up to the intermediate stage. See also: *Sandoz v Roche Diagnostics* BL C/89/04, noted [2004] *CIPA* 481; and *SmithKline Beecham v Apotex [Appeal]* [2004] EWCA (Civ) 1568, noted [2004] *CIPA*, 706 and IPD 28003.

It should, therefore, be borne in mind that, in choosing expert witnesses, the evidence of those with practical experience at the relevant time is likely to be preferred over that derived from reading publications and specialist papers. Such evidence in *Glaverbel v British Coal* [1994] R.P.C. 443 and [1995] R.P.C. 255 was discounted as being "affected by the wisdom of hindsight"; and, likewise, in *Assidoman Multipack v Mead Corp.* [1995] R.P.C. 321.

Defendants in *Ferag v Muller Martini* [2007] EWCA Civ 15 relied on certain models alleged to have been made in accordance with a prior disclosure, but these were criticised as "hindsight models".

—The UK approach to evaluation on appeal

3.41 At the appeal stage, deference should be given both to findings of primary fact by the Judge and to the evaluation of these facts by the judge, unless he had gone wrong in principle. In *Biogen v Medeva*, Lord Hofmann said at [54]:

> "The question of whether an invention was obvious has been called 'a kind of jury question' (see Jenkins L.J. in *Allmänna Svenska Elektriska A/B v. The Burntisland Shipbuilding Co. Ltd* (1952) 69 R.P.C. 63, 70) and should be treated with appropriate respect by an appellate court. It is true that in *Benmax v. Austin Motor Co. Ltd* [1955] A.C. 370 this House decided that, while the judge's findings of primary fact, particularly if founded upon an assessment of the credibility of witnesses, were virtually unassailable, an appellate court would be more ready to differ from the judge's evaluation of those facts by reference to some legal standard such as negligence or obviousness. In drawing this distinction, however, Viscount Simonds went on to observe, at p. 374, that it was "subject only to the weight which should, as a matter of course, be given to the opinion of the learned judge." The need for appellate caution in reversing the judge's evaluation of the facts is based upon much more solid grounds than professional courtesy. It is because specific findings of fact, even by the most meticulous judge, are inherently an incomplete statement of the impression which was made upon him by the primary evidence. His expressed findings are always surrounded by a penumbra of imprecision as to emphasis, relative weight, minor qualification and nuance (as Renan said, *la vérité est dans une nuance*), of which time and language do not permit exact expression, but which may play an important part in the judge's overall evaluation. It would in my view be wrong to treat *Benmax* as authorising or requiring an appellate court to undertake a *de novo* evaluation of the facts in all cases in which no question of the credibility of witnesses is involved. Where the application of a legal standard such as negligence or obviousness involves no question of principle but is simply a matter of degree, an appellate court should be very cautious in differing from the judge's evaluation."

In *Instance v Denny Bros.* [2002] R.P.C. 321 the Court of Appeal rejected an appeal against a finding of obviousness on the basis that an appeal court should only reverse a decision based on the facts and evidence if satisfied that the trial judge had made an error of principle. The error of principle that was alleged was that the judge had not, in his finding of obviousness, used the structured approach required by the *Windsurfing* judgment. The Court of Appeal held that this approach was not essential, provided the judge had asked the right questions, which he had done.

In *Saint-Gobain v Fusion Provida* [2005] EWCA Civ 177 it was held that the Court of Appeal should not apply the *Biogen* principle piecemeal. If an error of principle in an overall conclusion of obviousness is identified, then that conclusion as a whole is open for reconsideration. That approach was followed in *Wake Forest University v Smith & Nephew* [2009] F.S.R. 11, [2009] EWCA Civ 848. The Court held that if a judge had adopted the wrong approach to obviousness—for instance taking a mistaken view as what was disclosed by the prior art or what the difference between the prior art and the claim under attack was—then an appellate court would have to form its own evaluation on the basis of the facts as found by the judge or which appeared clearly from the documents or other evidence without having been expressly mentioned in the judgment. The judge had dealt only briefly with obviousness over a primary reference, expressing the view that the case was one of "anticipation or nothing" and that the skilled person would have no reason to have modified that reference. The defendants argued that the "anticipation or nothing" approach was wrong, modifications should not be limited to those to which the primary reference pointed clearly and the correct test was what was obvious to the skilled reader on the basis of that reference and his common general knowledge. The Court of Appeal held that evidence of what a skilled person would have done had been overlooked, findings that the primary reference taught away from the invention and would have been disregarded by a skilled person were incorrect, and that an error of principle had been made which might have been avoided if the *Pozzoli* structure had been followed and if there had been concentration on difference identification (the third step) so that the court would have put itself in the right position to make the decision as to obviousness (the fourth step). The evidence had not been properly evaluated and it was open to the Court of Appeal to reach its own conclusion applying the *Pozzoli* test.

In *Nampak Cartons v Rapid Action Packaging* [2010] EWHC 1548 (Pat) the Patents Court held, applying CPR 52.11 and CPR 63.16 that appeal from a decision of the Comptroller was limited to a review of the decision below, and that the court should not interfere unless persuaded that he had erred in principle or was clearly wrong. The degree of reluctance that should be exercised in relation to interfering with such a decision on an appeal were (a) the standing and specialist experience of the court or tribunal appealed and (b) whether the court or tribunal appealed from heard oral evidence, see the judgment of Robert Walker L.J. in *South Cone Inc v Bessant and others (trading as Reef)* [2002] EWCA Civ 763 at [26]–[28]. One ground of appeal was that the hearing officer failed to have regard to the expert evidence and has simply substituted his own view as to obviousness, but a statement by the Hearing Officer that he did not find the expert evidence "directly helpful" simply recorded the position that the experts employed by the parties took opposing stances, and other passages in the decision made it clear that he had relied extensively on the expert evidence. Nor had he reached a conclusion that was not open to him on the evidence. As regards alleged failure to apply the approach in *Pozzoli*, while the structured approach in that decision is of assistance to judges, not every slip in its application opened the decision to attack based on error of principle.

Problem/solution analysis at the EPO

—The EPO problem and solution approach to consideration of inventive step

As previously explained, the EPO's problem-solution analysis (PSA) applies a sequence **3.42** of questions in a consistent algorithmic manner to application and opposition cases where inventive step has to be determined. EPO Guideline C-IV, 11.5 sets out some of the questions in this sequence, but study of issues arising in EPO Appeal Board decisions permits a more complete sequence to be constructed:

  (i) What is the technical field, or the purpose and effect, of the invention §§3.43?

 (ii) What was the most promising starting point prior art ("closest prior art") §3.44?

(iii) Based on that prior art what is the technical problem that is solved by the claimed subject-matter §§3.45?

(iv) Does the claimed subject-matter indeed provide a solution for the technical problem?

 (v) Was the technical problem known or obvious §3.46? If not:

(vi) Does the claimed subject-matter provide no more than an obvious solution §3.47–3.49?

(vii) Especially in the chemical, biochemical and biotechnology arts:
    Was the claimed solution obvious to try §3.30? If so
    Was there a reasonable expectation of success §3.30?

(viii) Does the claimed subject-matter fall within exceptions for selection inventions §§2.24 and 3.31 and new uses, §2.23?

Many issues are common to PSA and *Windsurfing/Pozzoli*. These have, so far as possible, been discussed above, e.g. identity of the skilled person or team, common general knowledge, prejudice, collocations/combinations, obvious to try, selection, peer and market reaction and delay. The following sections consider those issues where the approach adopted by the EPO differs or where most or all the relevant case law is provided by decisions of the EPO Appeal Boards.

—Field of the invention

3.43   Definition and scope of the field of the invention, in combination with the definition of the technical problem which is attempted to be solved, determine the nature of the references that can be cited in support of an obviousness objection before the EPO. As regards definition of field there is broad agreement between the UK approach and that of the EPO and the relevant principles have been set out at §3.06.

Selection of the starting-point prior art

3.44   In PSA, a distinction is made between the primary reference and any secondary reference or references. It is necessary to identify the correct primary reference because the technical problem with which the invention is concerned is defined on the basis the disclosure of that reference and not on the basis of that of any secondary reference or on the basis what is disclosed in the set of references considered as a group.

The primary reference should be the most promising springboard towards the invention that was available to a skilled person on the day before the invention was made. It is not merely that reference that has the most technical features in common with the invention T 870/96 *PHILIPS/Optical illumination system*.

It is essential to PSA that the disclosure of the closest prior art should not be distorted or misrepresented based on hindsight knowledge of the invention so that it artificially meets specific features recited in the claim under consideration: this unfairly and tendentiously conceals the technical contribution of the invention and prejudices the subsequent objective determination of the technical problem, T 970/00 *MURATA/Acousto-optic deflector*.

A defective disclosure is not a promising starting point for assessing inventive step and should not be taken into account, especially where there is other prior art whose disclosure is not doubted and which is directed to the same purpose or effect as the patent in issue, T 211/01 *DOVER/Hydroxypolyalkylene amine*.

A generically different document does not qualify as a realistic starting point. For example in T 66/97 *SUMITOMO/Connecting optical fibres* the claimed invention concerned the connection of a pair of hermetic optical fibres. The Appeal Board selected an earlier reference disclosing fibres of this type in preference to another reference not disclosing such fibres and therefore not referring to the problems caused by the presence of hermetic layers, see also T 870/96 *PHILIPS/Optical illumination system*, T 1105/92 *Dürr/Rollenbahn*, T 464/98 *SCHWARTING/Festbettreaktor* and T 989/93 *FISHER SCIENTIFIC/Scintillation media*, Reasons [12]. In T 487/95 *SCHUBERTH/Schutzhelm* the defined use or field of endeavour of the invention was a military protective helmet, and it was held that a reference describing an earlier such helmet should be selected as the closest prior art in preference to references describing workers' safety helmets, although these might provide important secondary references providing a skilled person with indications and suggestions for solving the problem defined with reference to the primary reference. The same reasoning was applied in T 255/03 *ELECTROLUX ZANUSSI/ Washing machine* where the Board held that choice of a starting point machine with its respective benefits and drawbacks defines the framework of further development, and a change in type of machine during further development can only be the result of ex post facto analysis.

A document not mentioning a technical problem that is at least related to that derivable from the patent specification does not normally qualify as a description of the closest state of the art, regardless of the number of technical features it might have in common with the subject-matter of the invention, T 644/97 *BAYER/Crystallized aromatic polycarbonate*. The reason is that if the prior document was not closely related to the problem with which the invention was concerned, then the problem would have to be reformulated as: "The provision of a further [variant] with a different spectrum of utility". The solution of that problem could almost never be obvious because any attempt by a skilled person to establish a chain of considerations leading in an obvious way to the claimed subject-matter gets stuck at the start for want of an identifiable goal or object, see also T 835/00 *MITSUBISHI/Polypropylene resin expanded particles*, where it was observed that if the relevant problem is not derivable from the prior art, the measures necessary for its solution are a fortiorari not derivable.

Age of a disclosure is sometimes but not always relevant and the outcome may depend on the nature of the technical problem. In T 334/92 *EISAI/Benzodioxane derivatives* applicants had disclosed compounds suitable for the treatment of angina for which there was experimental evidence that they were more active and less toxic than the known compounds nitroglycerine and isosorbide dinitrate. A 20-year-old reference had been cited which disclosed structurally similar compounds but was silent about their activity. The Appeal Board held the cited document would not provide a realistic starting point for determining the technical problem of making improved compounds because it would be unrealistic to expect a skilled person to modify compounds within a class whose properties were unknown with a view to obtaining compounds of higher activity than those already in general use, and the application against which this reference was cited was granted. In contrast, T 964/92 *EISAI/Benzodioxane derivatives II* concerned a divisional application covering compounds for which there was no experimental data. The technical problem was therefore no more than finding alternatives to known compounds said to be suitable for the treatment of angina. The same document which had been ruled out for the parent application qualified as closest prior art for the divisional application because any document describing compounds said to be useful could qualify and the length of time for which the document had been published was now irrelevant.

In T 479/00 *VIGNALI/Colouring ceramics* the Appeal Board refused to treat a document as closest prior art because it was unrealistic to expect a skilled person to try to improve 65-year old technology that had never been put into practice. However, in T 153/97 *MINNESOTA MINING AND MANUFACTURING/Aerosol formulation* a 30-year-old document was considered not too old to take into account inter alia because new circumstances had arisen (concern about ozone depletion), see also T 69/94 *BEECHAM/Pharmaceutical composition* where a 20-year-old document was not considered too old and the claimed subject-matter was held to be obvious having regard to the disclosure of the disputed reference. An allegation that a five-year-old reference which had received no subsequent attention should be disregarded as closest prior art was rejected in T 1019/99 *AGFA-GEVAERT/Contrast enhancement* even in relation to the fast-moving field of image processing.

In T 79/96 *APV ANHYDRO/Granulation by spray drying* [2001] E.P.O.R. 309, the Appeal Board held that if there are several prior art documents disclosing subject-matter about equally close to that of the patent, the most recent should be regarded as the closest prior art since the person skilled in the art is expected to take into account the latest developments in the art.

In the case of a known chemical product, the closest prior art is that document which describes that product and an earlier process for its preparation, see T 339/03 *GENERAL ELECTRIC COMPANY/Tris(hydroxyphenyl)* compounds and earlier decisions cited therein. The same principle applies to other products, e.g. T 373/94 *MALLINCKRODT/Prefilled plastic syringe* where the invention claimed was a sterile plastic syringe and a reference describing an earlier plastic syringe was preferred to another reference relating to an earlier glass syringe. Where the invention concerns difficulties encountered in conventional processes for the manufacture of known chemical compounds, the documents to be considered when determining the closest prior art are those which describe those compounds and their manufacture. The reason is that only such documents allow a valid comparison of the technical effects and results of the respective processes, e.g. the yields achieved for the desired compounds according to the state of the art and according to the application in suit T 713/97 *NISSAN/N-alkylation* [1998] E.P.O.R. 456.

In T 18/09 *HUMAN GENOME SCIENCES/Neutrokine*, although every EST clone in a database was available to a skilled person, they were not equally valid starting points for assessing inventive step. An uncharacterised and un-annotated clone could not be singled out from all other clones present in the database without an objective reason for making such a selection. The sequence relied on by the opponents could not be regarded as the closest prior art without hindsight knowledge of the invention. Furthermore, automated pipeline screening would not have been undertaken out of idle curiosity given the size of the database and the effort required, and there was a difference between looking for members of a protein family having high sequence identity and those having only a low sequence identity. No particular group of EST sequences had been identified as a starting point for pipeline screening and an objection of lack of inventive step based on that approach was untenable. Hence the claimed subject-matter fulfilled the requirements of art.56 EPC. It should be noted that the patent in issue here was the same as in *Eli Lilly v Human Genome Sciences* see §§1.04, 3.36 and 4.03.

After choice of the closest prior art has been made, other prior art disclosures can be disregarded as starting points for assessment of inventive step because they are less relevant than the closest prior disclosure.

In T 570/91 *AE PLC/Pistons* the Board explained that although a skilled person is completely free to select a starting point, he is subsequently bound by that choice and went on to explain that:

> "If, for instance, for whatever reason it may be, a person skilled in the art prefers and decides to start from a specific compressor piston, he can further develop that piston but at the end of that development the normal result will still be a compressor piston and not an [internal combustion engine]. piston."

The EPO approach of identifying the starting-point prior art was discussed in *Actavis v Merck* [2010] EWCA Civ 82 at [27]–[29] and was held to be an immensely practical way of dealing with a very large number of pieces of prior art e.g. in opposition proceedings. If the best obviousness attack succeeded, it did not matter what other attacks there were which might also succeed, whereas if it failed other weaker attacks would also do so. There was no corresponding step in the *Pozzoli/Windsurfing* approach because practitioners had learned to confine themselves to their best cases, especially by the time of trial and English patent judges were simply not faced with profligate citations. If a party attempted to indulge in profligate citation it would be likely to find that when the case-management stage of the case was reached, it would be made to identify its best case, or few best cases. Moreover wasteful conduct, which would generally include profligate citation of prior art, was likely be met with adverse costs orders.

—Technical problem under the EPC

3.45   The EPO's problem/solution analysis (PSA) is derived from r.5(a)(iii) PCT which provides that the description of a patent specification shall:

> "disclose the invention, as claimed, in such terms that the technical problem (even if not expressly stated as such) and its solution can be understood, and state the advantageous effects, if any, of the invention with reference to the background art. . ."

Rule 42(1)(c) EPC [formerly r.27(1)(c) EPC] is identically worded. The EPO appeal boards regard the reference to technical problem contained in this rule as providing the fundamental basis for PSA. As explained in T 26/81 *ICI/Containers*:

"The provisions of Rule 27(1)(c) require that the description shall disclose how the invention can be understood as the solution to a technical problem. Indeed, the inventive step may be considered as a step from the technical problem to its solution. If, therefore, the requirements of the above rule are neither satisfied by the original description, nor, after request, by an amendment, it will emerge that an invention within the meaning of Article 52 does not exist. On the other hand, if the subject-matter of an independent claim, for which there is sufficient disclosure, is judged as being inventive in character, it must always be possible to derive a technical problem from the application."

As explained at §3.28 the link between problem and new result link underpins the EPO's PSA approach. In case T 939/92 *AGREVO/Triazole* which concerned a class of herbicides it was held that for patentability herbicidal activity had to be expected for all members of the class. The Appeal Board based its opinion on the principle that the extent of the patent monopoly should correspond to and be justified by the technical contribution to the art that was contained in the specification. The Boards of Appeal consistently decided the issue of obviousness on the basis of an objective assessment of the results achieved by the claimed subject-matter compared with the results achieved according to the state of the art. It was then assumed that the inventor did in fact seek to achieve these results and therefore these results were taken to be the basis for defining the problem. Mere structural ingenuity was not sufficient. If the result that the skilled person was seeking to achieve was simply obtaining further chemical compounds, then all known chemical compounds were equally suitable as starting points and all known methods of transformation could be used, so that the selection of particular compounds to be made was a mere arbitrary choice. For that reason:

". . .the selection of such compounds, in order to be patentable, must not be arbitrary but must be justified by a hitherto unknown technical effect which is caused by those structural features which distinguish the claimed compounds from the numerous other such compounds."

The above principles represent a settled approach to the evaluation of inventive step and have been written into the EPO Examination Guidelines, see CIV, 11.5.2. *Agrevo* was distinguished on the facts in T 294/07 *PROTEXEON/Anaesthetic formulation*: arguments were accepted that there was a class effect shared by all members of a group of compounds claimed by a generic formula, and there was no contrary evidence or arguments from the opponent.

Where detailed instructions for solving a particular problem are not to be found in the specification, the claim will probably lack an inventive step: otherwise, if inventive, the description will be insufficient, see T 292/87 *CONTROL SYSTEMS/Ticket-issuing machines* [1989] E.P.O.R. 333.

The objective problem must be formulated so as not to contain pointers to its solution, since including part of the solution must necessarily result in impermissible hindsight T 229/85 *SCHMID/Etching metal surfaces* OJ 6/1987, 237. In T 487/92 *PROCTER & GAMBLE/Manual dishwashing* [1996] E.P.O.R. 637 it was not accepted that the normal duties of the skilled man included trying to solve hypothetical technical problems, for example, to find further uses for certain compositions, this being a "retrospective approach" contrary to the "problem and solution approach" under which hindsight considerations should be avoided. The whole matter must be looked at in a practical, and not abstract, manner without hindsight, T 5/81 *SOLVAY/Production of hollow thermoplastic objects* OJ EPO 1982, 249. For example, if the technical problem is one which arises in large-scale production, it is incorrect to formulate the problem in terms of laboratory practice T 121/91 *GRACE/Nitro compounds* [1994] E.P.O.R. 114, see also T 619/88 *E. I. DU PONT/Suspension polymerization*. The problem must also be formulated from the state of the art as it exists, and not from what is obvious thereover, T 181/91 *NISSHIN/Steroid* [1994] E.P.O.R. 135. It should not be influenced by a definition of the skilled person set out in the specification if it turns out that the skilled person has been incorrectly identified, T 422/93 *JALON/Luminescent security fibres* OJ EPO 1997, 24; [1999] E.P.O.R. 486. In T 813/93 *NOBEL/Hexanitrostilbene* [1998] E.P.O.R. 151 the technical problem identified by the Examining Division was to provide an improved purification process that would yield a more satisfactory end product. The Appeal Board held that this definition was too vague to be resolved by specific technical means and therefore could not form a basis for evaluating inventive step. It therefore formulated a more specific problem of finding a simpler and faster process than that of the closest prior art.

It is established case lawof the Boards of Appeal that a definition of the problem should normally start from the problem that is described in the application or patent in issue. Only if that problem had not been solved or an incorrect state of the art had been used to define the problem can alternative problems be considered, see T 151/05 *TOYOTA JIDOSHA/ Producing a piston*, T 644/97 *ASAHI/Crystallised aromatic polycarbonate* and T 495/91 *TARKETT PEGULAN/Surface finish* [1995] E.P.O.R. 516.

Provision in the prior art of a solution to a problem does not preclude a patent for another method of solving the same problem, see T 92/92 *Valmet/Glide shoe* and T 495/91 *TARKETT PEGULAN/Surface finish* (supra). A lesser problem than that envisaged by the inventor can be accepted in an appropriate case T 132/84 *HÜLS/Tetramethylpiperidone* [1986] E.P.O.R. 303 and reformulation from the provision of improved variants to the provision of further alternatives, e.g. because of lack of convincing comparative data may not be fatal to grant of an application or maintenance of a patent where the evidence shows that the advantage claimed is not generally achieved or is based on an effect which is not provided over the full scope of the claim. The problem must be re-written in less ambitious terms T 742/89 *HÜLS/Polyurethanbesichichtubngen*. In chemical cases it is commonplace for the technical problem to be stated as the provision of further or additional compounds having a particular known function or effect, and classes of compound claimed in this way are commonly held to be inventive.

The extent to which reformulation of the problem is possible has to be assessed on the merits of each particular case. The problem need not be expressly described in the application as filed T 142/84 *BRITAX/Inventive step* OJ EPO 1987, 112; [1987] E.P.O.R. 148, and it is possible to reformulate the problem when more relevant prior art is brought to the attention of the applicant T 13/84 *SPERRY/Reformulation of the problem* OJ EPO 1986, 253; [1986] E.P.O.R. 289, e.g. when advantages can be demonstrated arising from small structural differences T 44/85 *SHELL/Curable binder preparation* [1986] E.P.O.R. 258. As a matter of principle any effect provided by the invention may be used as a basis for the reformulation of the technical problem, as long as said effect is derivable from the application as filed, see T 386/89 *GKN SANKEY/Wheels*. It is also possible to rely on new effects submitted by the applicant post-filing, provided that the skilled person would recognise these effects as implied by or related to the problem initially suggested, see the EPO Examination Guidelines at IV, 11.11 and T 184/82 *MOBIL/Thermoformed shaped articles* OJ 6/1984, 261. Later-discovered advantages can be used to establish patentability provided that these have a close technical relationship with the original problem set forth in the application T 440/91, *PHARLYSE/Mucolytic salts* [1999] E.P.O.R. 408.

In T 344/89 *GTE LABORATORIES/Coated composite* it was held that reformulation of the problem does not constitute added matter if the new problem is foreshadowed in the originally filed application; alternatively expressed if it can be deduced by a skilled person from the application as originally filed, see T 39/93 *ALLIED COLLOIDS/Polymer powders* [1997] E.P.O.R. 347.

The EPO approach of reformulating the technical problem was held by Jacob L.J. in *Actavis v Novartis* [2010] EWCA Civ 82 at [34] to be the weakest part of PSA because of its retrospective nature. In *Actavis* it was held that it would be wrong to reformulate the problem because no new prior art unknown to the patentee had turned up, and it would not be right to reformulate the problem as one of looking for better medical effects when that was not the problem as seen by the patentee or to reformulate the solution as having found such effects where the patentee had not promised any [65].

—The unobvious problem

The existence of so-called "problem inventions" was acknowledged in T 2/83 *RIDER/* **3.46**
Simethicone tablet OJ EPO 1984, 265 (cited at the time of writing in over 200 subsequent
decisions) in which it was explained that the discovery of a previously unrecognised
problem could give rise to patentable subject-matter even though the claimed solution was
retrospectively trivial and in itself obvious. The invention concerned tablets containing
simethicone which was a silicone oil together with an antacid. It was known that if the oil
came into contact with the antacid its activity would be inhibited. In commercial tablets
the oil was adsorbed onto a large excess of inert carrier which it was believed would stop
this from happening. The applicants had discovered that when such tablets were stored the
simethicone still lost its activity and recognised that the reason was that the simethicone
was migrating through the solid material of the tablet. The solution was therefore to
incorporate a barrier layer to stop oil migration. The Appeal Board held that in the previous state of knowledge a barrier layer would have been perceived as superfluous, wasteful
and devoid of any technical effect, whereas it had now been recognised that it produced a
substantial effect not predictable from the prior art. Accordingly a patent was granted.

The Simethicone fact pattern may be contrasted with that in T 109/82 *BOSCH/Hearing
aid* OJ EPO 1984, 473 where the deficiencies relied on could have been identified by a
skilled person so that identification of the problem did not amount to an inventive contribution; similarly T 195/84 *BOEING/High lift device* and T 280/96 *CORNILLEAU/Table
tennis table* [1998] E.P.O.R. 129. In T 188/95 *YAMANOUCHI/Tablets*, the drawback of
known tablets was their bitter aftertaste on oral administration. The Appeal Board held
that any person taking such a tablet would immediately recognise this drawback, and recognition of the problem could therefore not contribute to inventive step. Nor can recognition after the filing or priority date of a deficiency in a device or process forming part of
the prior art, especially where the invention is of the "problem" type, since the guiding
consideration in assessing inventive step is the knowledge of the skilled person before the
date of filing T 268/89 *LATZKE/Magnetic plaster*.

The Appeal Board explained in T 971/92 *AMOCO/Terephthalic acid* that the appreciation of conventional technical problems which form the basis of the normal activity of a
skilled person, e.g. removal of shortcomings, optimization of parameters and saving of
energy or time cannot involve an inventive step. If an applicant wishes to rely on the recognition of a technical problem whose solution is admittedly obvious, then the minimum
requirement is that the problem must be clearly and unambiguously disclosed in the application as filed.

The perception of a problem cannot contribute to the assessment of inventive step if
that problem is not of a technical nature T 579/88 *ESSWEIN/Automatic programmer*
[1991] E.P.O.R. 120 and T 1114/06 *HONEYWELL/Production of difluoromethane* where
cost-efficiency could not form part of the problem which should be of a technical nature
only so that economic considerations do not qualify.

Combining references—the EPC approach

As explained at §3.23, before the EPO objections of lack of inventive step are com- **3.47**
monly made on the basis of two or more documents or other disclosures. Two questions
arise when prior disclosures are sought to be combined: firstly, whether a skilled person
aware of the primary disclosure and seeking to solve the objective problem should be
taken to be aware of the secondary disclosure or disclosures, and if so, secondly, whether
there were good grounds for fitting the disclosures together.

As regards selection of secondary references from neighbouring fields, two cases are
referred to in the Case Law of the Boards of Appeal of the European Patent Office, 6th edn
pp.184–5 as "landmark decisions".

The first of these is T 176/84 *MÖBIUS/Pencil sharpener* OJ EPO, 1986, 50 where the
primary reference concerned a prior pencil sharpener and the question was whether that
disclosure should be considered in combination with another reference disclosing a securing mechanism for the slot of a savings box. It was held that a skilled person would, as
well as considering the state of the art in the specific technical field of the application, look
for suggestions in neighbouring fields and/or in a broader general technical field of which

the specific field was part, i.e. any field in which the same technical problem or one similar to it arose and of which the person skilled in the art should be expected to be aware. However, in this case the references were not combinable because the respective fields were too distant—storage of coins in a container as opposed to sharpening of pencils with provision for collection of shavings. The references were not part of the same broader field and it was held that the objection of obviousness did not succeed.

The second is T 0195/84 *BOEING/High lift device* OJ EPO 1986, 121 which concerned a mechanism for extending a high lift device such as an auxiliary aerofoil relative to a main aerofoil using a particular guide, carrier track and cable drive arrangement. The primary reference disclosed a similar mechanism which had the disadvantage of using long cable drives. The secondary reference was a 20-year-old reference disclosing individual cable drives as adopted in the invention, but was not specific as to field of use. The Board held that the state of the art when examining inventive step included a non-specific (general) field dealing with the solution of any general technical problem which the application sought to solve in its specific field. Solutions of general technical problems in such non-specific fields were to be considered part of the general knowledge which was to be attributed to a skilled person in a specific technical field. On the particular issues it was held that the cable drives of the secondary reference formed part of the general engineering knowledge of a person skilled in the art which was not restricted to a certain time or period of time and that having once recognised that long cables were the problem in the known high lift device, they could be replaced with drives known from the secondary reference without producing any unexpected effect whatsoever, and the application was refused. There was an alleged incompatibility of the references as regards, e.g. the use of straight or curved track but since the main claim was not restricted to a particular shape there was reason not to combine these teachings.

The skilled person is expected to consult textbooks outside his field if they describe a general theory or methodology T 426/88 *LUCAS/Combustion Engine* [1992] E.P.O.R. 458; and also literature in a non-parallel field to the invention where the same problem is well known to the public at large and there exists a relationship between the materials used in the two fields T 0560/89, *N.I. INDUSTRIES/Filler mass* OJ EPO 1992, 725; [1994] E.P.O.R. 120.

Opponents argued in T 28/87 *KERBER/Wire link bands* OJ EPO 1989, 383 that a reference in a remote field must be considered when examining for inventive step where the patentee himself discussed that reference in the application as filed and therefore was aware of it on the date of filing. The Appeal Board held that the association of ideas had not been disclosed until it was made by the patentee, it would be wrong to apply different standards depending on whether the remote reference was discussed in the specification or found only by an independent search, the patentee's association of ideas should not be held against him to his disadvantage, and that the reference was too remote to be taken into consideration.

Where the prior art contains well-founded reasoning for the existence of a particular mode of action and discloses that anything that has the mode of action will be suitable for the intended purpose (e.g. detergents), it would be obvious to a skilled person to search in related technical fields (biochemistry, medicine) for further things having that mode of action T 588/99 *PROCTOR & GAMBLE/Liquid detergents*.

If the claimed subject-matter merely concerns a number of aggregated individual or partial problems, then prior disclosures solving the individual problems may be combined without further purpose having to be demonstrated. In T 552/89 *TETRA PAK/Cold cathode replenishment*, objection was based on a primary reference disclosing electron beam apparatus, a first secondary reference disclosing a monitoring and control system and a second secondary reference disclosing a pair of rollers operated by a servo mechanism for advancing a cathode wire. The Appeal Board held that the invention was obvious over the three references and commented that:

"When the objective problem established having regard to the closest prior art as disclosed in a primary document is formed of individual problems then the skilled person can be expected to take account of solutions to the individual problems proposed in different secondary documents in the same or neighbouring technical fields. Thus the teaching of secondary documents may be combined with the disclosure of the closest prior art, if such secondary documents provide solutions to specific individual problems forming parts of the objective problem in progressing from the closest prior art, in particular when such individual solutions are merely aggregated together in the claimed invention."

If a technical problem is aggregated from individual problems in this way, then there is no point at which the number in the aggregation is sufficient for inventive step to be taken for granted, see T 0302/02 *APPLERA/Amplification of nucleic acid sequences* and T 1114/06 *HONEYWELL/Production of difluoromethane*.

It is also possible to combine disclosures with some freedom where the technical problem is to provide a mere alternative. In T 0631/06 *DU PONT DE NEMOURS/ Fungicidal mixtures* the invention concerned a two component fungicidal composition and the alleged problem was to find components that acted synergistically. However, the results in the specification indicated synergism for some experiments and not others, so the problem had not been solved over the whole claimed scope. Accordingly the problem was merely to provide an alternative composition, with the result that all the information contained in a cited document should be treated equally by the person skilled in the art, notwithstanding whether it was preferred or not, or whether the implementation of some of the said information presented some difficulties. The so-called "could-would" approach applied when the technical problem to be solved related to the provision of an improvement or in the suppression of disadvantages, not in the provision of an alternative. The claimed subject-matter was held to lack inventive step. In another synthetic fungicide case, T 0920/06 *SYNERGENTIA/Fungicidal compositions*, the specification contained no quantitative data, and test data provided during prosecution reported tests *in vitro* which were not a reliable guide to the effects of the composition *in vivo*. Therefore the technical problem was not that of finding an improved combination of compounds but merely that of providing an alternative combination of compounds. Starting from a first document which disclosed a first component a skilled person would have consulted a second document providing a list of 56 compounds as potential second components, one of which was as claimed. A skilled person would have considered each of the 56 listed compounds as an equally suitable solution to the problem, and therefore the selection of the particular second component specified was considered to be obvious. The same reasoning has also been applied by the UK Patents Court, see *Lundbeck v Norpharma* [2011] EWHC 907 (Pat).

Conversely, where the claimed features are functionally linked together to provide a combined result from which a technical problem can be reconstructed, then it can only convincingly be argued that disclosures will be combined in the expectation of a desired result. It is not permissible to mosaic various features, each from its particular context in a different document, so as to reconstruct with hindsight the combination claimed, see T 741/98 *NIPPON STEEL/Grain-oriented electrical steel sheet*, and an ex post facto mosaic of features taken arbitrarily from a group of prior disclosures is unallowable, see T 501/94 *DELPHI/Electrical double leaf spring contact*. Reason to adopt the features of the secondary reference or references must be demonstrated. The questions to be answered concerning inventive step are not only whether a skilled person, starting from the state of the art closest to the invention and examining the secondary disclosures in the light of his general common knowledge, would be provided with enough information that he could arrive at the solution claimed, but also whether, in the secondary disclosures, he would find hints or clues leading him to modify said closest state of the art in a way leading to the claimed invention in expectation of the improvement he was searching for. Moreover, it should be borne in mind that the technical disclosure in a prior art document should be considered in its entirety and that it is not justified arbitrarily to isolate parts of such document from their context in order to derive therefrom technical information which would differ from the integral teaching of the document, see T 414/98 *BOC/Treatment of poultry*. In T 564/89 *TORAY/Photosensitive polymer* it was explained that according to the established jurisprudence of the Boards of Appeal the decisive question is not whether a skilled person could have performed the subject of the patent in suit but rather whether he would have done so in the expectation of solving the underlying technical problem. It is often possible to show after an invention has been made that a skilled person could have been led to it by combining separate pieces of prior art, but such considerations must be disregarded as resulting from an ex post facto analysis.

It is inadmissible to combine unrelated, or conflicting, documents mosaically to deny inventive step T 2/81 *MOBAY/Methylenebis (phenyl isocyanate)* OJ EPO 1982, 394. The teachings of two documents ought rarely, if ever, to be combined, when it is apparent that their teachings are mutually conflicting. Before rejecting any patent as lacking in inventive step, all the documents in the case ought to be read carefully to ensure that the decision is not based on a selection involving too much hindsight. It is important not to overlook pointers in the direction opposite to the alleged invention, particularly if they are the kind of pointers would have been taken seriously by any skilled worker in the art who did not start from actual knowledge of the invention, see T 0176/89 *MITSUI/Ultra-high molecular weight polyethylene* [1996] E.P.O.R. 361. Nor should references be combined where the matter respectively described each suffers from the same shortcomings which had been overcome by the claimed invention T 0184/90 *GENERAL ELECTRIC/Polycarbonate composition* [1997] E.P.O.R. 341.

—The unobvious solution—advantages must be unpredictable

3.48   A mere arbitrary choice from amongst a host of possible solutions of a minimalist technical problem of finding further or alternative embodiments cannot involve an inventive step, T 939/92 *AGREVO/Triazoles*, and cannot give rise to a selection invention T 214/01 *EDICO/Teletext receiver*. If the claimed solution is obvious, it makes no difference that there are several other possible solutions T 0190/03 *Edico/Multiple subtitles*.

In contrast, a seemingly obvious solution to a known problem can be regarded as inventive if that solution provides an unexpected improved result or advantageous technical effect, see T 270/84 *ICI/Fusecord* [1987] E.P.O.R. 357. This, of course, is not the case if the technical effect asserted is one that could itself have been predicted, see T 271/84 *AIR PRODUCTS/Removal of hydrogen sulphide* OJ EPO 1987, 405; [1987] E.P.O.R. 23; and T 229/84 *ICI/Polyester polyols* [1988] E.P.O.R. 217. Where an unexpected advantage is relied upon for patentability, the features which give rise to that advantage must be specified in the claims T 215/85 *KERNFORSCHUNGSZENTRUM/Gas separation* [1999] E.P.O.R. 356.

The advantage can be a surprising effect of a generally known process coupled with some further development of that process T 361/88 *DU PONT/Hollow filaments* [1991] E.P.O.R. 1; and the technical effect can be the avoidance of a disadvantage, but that disadvantage must be one that would be expected otherwise to arise T 49/85 *AMERICAN CYANAMID/Melt spinning* [1989] E.P.O.R. 234. Also, the advantage demonstrated must be a genuine one. Thus, no invention is involved in merely worsening the prior art, as when applying techniques previously disclosed for comparative purposes T 155/85 *PHILLIPS PETROLEUM/Passivation of catalyst* [1988] E.P.O.R. 164; abridged OJ EPO 1988, 87.

The fact that a previously unappreciated technical effect is achieved does not necessarily mean that an inventive step has been made T 0329/89 *FUJITSU/Silicon oxynitride semiconductor* [1996] E.P.O.R. 224. Where the improvement provided by the invention was no more than the sum of unchanged known individual and non-interacting features, inventive step was not recognised T 141/87 *BOSCH/Diagnostic test system* [1996] E.P.O.R. 570.

A so-called "analogy process" becomes patentable if it leads to a novel and inventive result which is not derivable in an obvious manner from the state of the art T 119/82 *EXXON/Gelation* OJ EPO 1984, 217 and T 65/82 BAYER/Cyclopropane OJ EPO 1983, 327. The modifying feature, which provides the necessary novelty to the invention, must contribute causally to the improvement demonstrated: T 0192/82 *BAYER/Moulding composition* OJ EPO 1984, 415. Similarly a product whose characteristics can be envisaged in advance from the prior art may become non-obvious if there is no known way or applicable (analogy) method to make it known to the art and the disclosed method is the first to do so and is inventive T 0595/90 *KAWASAKI/Grain oriented silicon sheet* but in the patent in issue the relevant method was held not to be inventive. In T 0803/01 *NOVARTIS/Purified polylactide* the decisive question was whether polylactide having the claimed degree of purity was achievable at the priority date of the application or there was an obvious way leading to it. The answer was negative and a patent was granted with product claims defined by purity, see also §2.24.

—Advantages must be demonstrated

It may be necessary to rely on reports of experiments contained in the specification of a patent in support of an alleged technical result or advantage. **3.49**

Supporting experimental evidence may not be needed for grant of an application if there is no prima facie inference of obviousness T 390/88 *KONISHIROKU/Photographic film* [1990] E.P.O.R. 417, or where it was considered unlikely that the skilled person would anyway have consulted the prior art document in issue T 215/90 *AKZO/Rainwear* [1992] E.P.O.R. 1. The apparent futility of carrying out a claimed operation is itself an indication of non-obviousness T 1027/93 *L'AIR LIQUIDE/Gas separation* [1996] E.P.O.R. 188. If it appears plausible to a skilled person that it is plausible that a described method will solve the technical problem, the patent proprietor is not required to provide comparative examples or other evidence to demonstrate that this is indeed the case, see T 2151/08 *STORK/Slaughtered poultry*.

If a technical effect is relied upon to establish inventive step, sufficient evidence of this is required T 20/81 *SHELL/Aryloxybenzaldehydes* OJ EPO 1982, 217. Any required technical effect must be demonstrated, the EPO not considering mere allegations or assertions of such T 124/84 *UNIE VAN KUNSTMESTFABRIEKEN/Urea synthesis* [1986] E.P.O.R. 297 and T 94/84 *DUCO/Paint layers* OJ EPO 1986, 337; [1987] E.P.O.R. 37. Where experiments are carried out during opposition proceedings without agreement concerning the methodology, and in the absence of the other party(s), the results are to be considered cautiously though, where tests show contradictory results, the patentee should be given the benefit of the doubt T 547/88 *MOBIL/Metal-coated film* [1994] E.P.O.R. 349.

As previously explained, a technical effect can only be relied upon to demonstrate an inventive step if it manifests itself over the whole area of the claimed subject-matter; see T 939/92 *AGREVO/Triazoles* OJ EPO 1996, 309; [1996] E.P.O.R. 171, T 583/93 *HYMO CORP./Water-soluble polymer dispersion* OJ EPO 1996, 496; [1997] E.P.O.R. 129 and T 131/87 *OCCIDENTAL/Stabilised dielctric fluid* [1997] E.P.O.R. 293. The effect must be demonstrated with sufficiently comprehensive supporting evidence that it can reasonably be extrapolated over the whole scope of the claim, and a mere unsupported statement cannot suffice T 134/00 *Exxon/Additives and fuel compositions*. Where a claim is to a group of chemical compounds which can only be patented upon proof of a technical effect, and the specification does not contain sufficient information as to make it credible that an alleged technical effect is obtained for all the compounds claimed, objection arises for lack of invention under art.56 EPC rather than for lack of support under art.84 EPC; see T 939/92 *AGREVO/Triazoles* (above), see also §14.38, the Case Comment thereon by I. Karet [1996] EIPR 561 and T 626/90 *TERUMO/Production of peptides* [1996] E.P.O.R. 194.

If the alleged technical effect is an improvement rather than merely the provision of an alternative then that must also be proved for the whole scope of the claim, evaluation against the prior art differing depending on what has been proved and hence on which kind of technical problem applies. The technical effect demonstrated can be quite small if it has a worthwhile commercial significance T 38/84 *STAMICARBON/Oxidation of toluene* OJ EPO 1984, 368. While the required comparative tests must be carried out under all conditions likely to be encountered in practice, a technical effect is only required to be demonstrated in an overall manner T 57/84 *BAYER/Tolylfluanid* OJ EPO 1988, 53; [1987] E.P.O.R. 131 and need not show advantages as regards other properties of prior art compounds provided that the latter are maintained at a reasonable level so that the improvement is not completely off-set by disadvantages in other respects T 254/86 *SUMITOMO/Yellow dyes* OJ EPO 1989, 115; [1989] E.P.O.R. 257.

The improved effect must convincingly be shown to have its origin in the distinguishing feature of the invention, so that it may be necessary to modify the elements of comparison so that they differ only by the specific distinguishing characteristic T 197/86 *KODAK/ Photographic couplers* OJ EPO 1989, 371; [1989] E.P.O.R. 395. An example of the application of this principle is found in T 1114/06 *HONEYWELL/Production of difluoromethane* where the experimental evidence was subjected to searching scrutiny. The compared examples were found not to differ exclusively by the presence or absence of the relevant feature as required for a convincing comparison, and the benefits were alleged to be achieved on an industrial scale, whereas the claim covered production on any scale. As the advantages had not been demonstrated either convincingly or over the whole scope of the claim they could not be taken into account when formulating the problem, so that the objective problem was directed to providing an alternative process rather than an improved process. The claimed process was merely an aggregation of obvious steps, and since the problem concerned mere provision of an alternative there was no upper limit on the number of prior documents (in this case three) whose teachings could be combined to support an obviousness objection, see §3.47.

In a demonstration of advantage (or non-advantage by an opponent), care should be taken to carry out a strict comparison and, where materials used are identified by a trade mark, evidence should be provided of their identity with materials identified by a different trade mark T 343/90 *DSM RESINS/Polyester* [1996] E.P.O.R. 216. Comparative tests used to demonstrate an unexpected effect must also display the maximum possible adherence to the instructions, etc. used in the closest state of the art, and the unexpected effect has to be shown to be derived from the distinguishing feature of the invention over the closest state of the art T 317/95 *PROCTER & GAMBLE/Gastrointestinal composition* [1999] E.P.O.R. 528, see also T 92/86 *GRASS-AIR/Air-drying apparatus* [1999] E.P.O.R. 574 where no prejudice against the prior art had been shown, no advantages had been demonstrated and, anyway, the claim was not limited to the feature alleged to provide an inventive step. Objectivity and e.g. "blind" tests are particularly important for consumer products where what is being tested is an aesthetic quality such as "feel", see T 702/99 *SHISEIDO/ Cosmetic.*

Chemical compounds

—Structural obviousness

3.50   In the field of chemistry, the novelty of a compound is not enough for patentability. If the compound is a structure of a known type, inventive step will be recognised only if the new compound has a property not suggested by the prior art, see T 20/83 *CIBA-GEIGY/ Benzothiopyran derivatives* OJ EPO 1983, 419. This is because a structural difference has no value unless it gives rise to a valuable property or effect or an increase in an effect, see T 22/82 *BASF/Bis-epoxy ethers* OJ EPO 1982, 341. However, the position is different if the product compound is not structurally obvious over the prior art: then no improvement over the prior art need be demonstrated provided that a problem, redefined if appropriate, has been solved, see T 162/86 *HOECHST/Plasmid pSG2*, OJ EPO 1988, 452; [1989] E.P.O.R. 107.

If it can be assumed that compounds of similar chemical structure will have similar therapeutic activity, the EPO will not recognise an inventive step over a prior document, even if this is of some antiquity, which discloses such similar compounds unless it can be shown that the new compounds have an advantageous activity not possessed by the disclosed prior art compounds, see T 964/92 *EISAI/Benzodioxane derivatives* [1997] E.P.O.R. 201. However, mere apparent, but unestablished in the prior art, bioisosterism is not in itself sufficient to deny the presence of an inventive step: what is important is whether there is information on the impact of the isosteric replacement on pharmacological activity, T 643/96 *BEECHAM/Bioisosterism* [1998] E.P.O.R. 18. Thus invention can be recognised where the claimed compounds are structurally obvious over prior art compounds which have been described for a different therapeutic activity and it is not seen that these prior art compounds would have been considered to have the different activity found for the now claimed compounds, see T 116/90 *BEECHAM-WUELFING/Xanthine ketals* [1997] E.P.O.R. 307. Further cases in which mere structural similarity has been held insufficient to deny an inventive step are: T 309/91 *BEECHAM/Benzopyrans* [1998] E.P.O.R. 11 and T 852/91 *ICI AMERICAS/Leukotriene antagonist* [1998] E.P.O.R. 31.

If a product is unpatentable as such, there remains the possibility of seeking protection for a particular inventive method of making it, see T 84/82 *MACARTHYS/Chloral derivatives* OJ EPO 1983, 451. The converse also applies—although a chemical process may lack an inventive step, products made according to that process may nevertheless be unobvious, see T 189/88 *ASAHI/Polyethylene terephthalate fibres* [1990] E.P.O.R. 543. Indeed, an obvious product as such could become patentable if the skilled person could not see how to make it, T 595/90 *KAWASAKI/Grain-oriented silicon sheet* OJ EPO 1994, 695; [1995] E.P.O.R. 36, though it can be questioned whether the first to perform an obvious desideratum should be entitled to a monopoly which covers other routes to the same end.

—Patentability of chemical intermediates

The patentability of chemical intermediates is to be measured by the same yardstick as other chemical compounds and this requires a non-obvious (i.e. unexpected) enhancement of the art. This can be because the compound has been made in connection with an inventive preparation, or during an inventive further processing, or as part of an inventive complete process, see T 648/88 *BASF/Alpha-tocopherol* OJ EPO 1991, 292; [1991] E.P.O.R. 305. However, if the end product is neither novel nor inventive, a novel superior effect demonstrated for this cannot support patentability of an intermediate formed in the method used to make the final product, see T 18/88 *DOW/Pyrimidines* OJ EPO 1992, 107; [1992] E.P.O.R. 184.

3.51

To be patentable on the basis of the patentability of the final product, the intermediates must make a contribution to the structure of the final products, e.g. by displaying at least one of the features which differentiate the subsequent products from known compounds, T 372/86 *ICI/Diphenyl ethers* [1988] E.P.O.R. 93. However even then a chemical intermediate may be held obvious when judged in relation to the prior art, and here both "close to the intermediate" and "close to the product" art has to be considered T 65/82 *BAYER/Cyclopropane* OJ EPO 1983, 327.

An unexpected "process effect" will be recognised as conferring patentability on an intermediate compound T 22/82, BASF/Bis-epoxy ethers OJ EPO 1982, 341, e.g. where the further processing is itself an inventive concept T 163/84 BAYER/Acetophenone derivatives OJ EPO 1987, 301; [1987] E.P.O.R. 284.

Drafting of specification to assist argument of non-obviousness

The likelihood of an affirmative finding of inventiveness can be significantly increased by appropriate presentation of the case for patentability in the application as filed.

3.52

Rule 42(a) EPC requires the description to specify the technical field to which the invention relates. As explained in §§3.34 to 3.35 the definition of the art or field of endeavour contained in the application as filed and subsequently in the granted patent can significantly affect what prior art is validly citable both in the UK and before the EPO. Thoughtful definition of the technical field is therefore advisable.

Rule 42(b) requires the description to indicate the background art which so far as known to the applicant can be regarded as useful for understanding the invention and preferably to cite documents reflecting such art. Specifications in the electrical and mechanical arts usually have relatively short background sections, whereas those in the chemical and especially the biotechnology and medical arts are often more discursive. Because of so-called

"*Markman*" practice in the US, prior art discussions in specifications originating from that country have become more abbreviated, and US practitioners are cautious about citing particular documents, especially in the mechanical and electrical arts. However, citation of one or a few relevant documents in the field of endeavour of the invention (or even a chain of prior documents) and relevant to the technical problem assists drafting and assists understanding. However, it is extremely important that prior art discussion should reflect no more than what is actually contained in the prior art and should not acknowledge defects in the prior art and the causes of those defects as belonging to the prior art where in truth their identification is part of the inventive contribution. Confusion may be created by citation of multiple documents, especially where these include documents outside the field of endeavour, see T 0028/87 *KERBER/Wire link bands* OJ EPO 1989, 383. It is important not to acknowledge an association of ideas where that association does not occur in the prior art. Likewise, stating in the specification that a technique is "conventional" is likely to be taken as an acceptance that this technique was part of the common general knowledge of the addressee, as in *NEC Corp's Application* (BL O/38/00).

Rule 42(c) EPC requires the description to disclose the invention in such terms that the technical problem and its solution can be understood and to state any advantageous effects with reference to the background art. It is highly desirable that, if non-obviousness is to be successfully asserted on the basis of the attainment of a surprising technical effect, that effect should be mentioned in the specification, see *Petra Fischer's Application* [1997] R.P.C. 899 where this was not the case. In the case of a selection invention, it is essential for the new effect of the claimed selection to be specified in the specification. While a statement of new effect cannot be added to the specification after filing because such an amendment is precluded by s.76, such a statement may be submitted later for consideration by the examiner: such will then be placed in the open part of the file. The EPO adopts a similar position, see EPO Guidelines C–VI, 5.7a and 5.7b.

Submission of evidence of unobviousness

3.53   The submission of evidence, particularly of surprising technical effect or advantage, may often be useful in overcoming an objection of obviousness raised during the substantive examination under s.18. That evidence should be submitted to the Comptroller as it is unlikely to be permitted to be placed before the Patents Court for the first time on appeal, see *Wistar's Application* [1983] R.P.C. 255 and §18.14.

Pleading of commercial success

3.54   In proceedings before the Patents Court a defence of commercial success to an allegation of obviousness needs to be distinctly pleaded, see by CPR 63PD 0.4 at 4.6 (reprinted in Appendix F) and the discussion in §3.33. Such a pleading has the consequence of leading to distinct and detailed particularisation (see *Deks (John) v Aztec Washer* [1989] R.P.C. 413) and thus, potentially of considerably expanding the scope of disclosure. However, disclosure on this issue is now limited to a required disclosure of identification of the product or process involved and summaries of periods involved, revenue received therefrom and expenditure incurred in promotion, advertising or other financial support for that product or process, see CPR 63PD 06 at 6.1, but an application may be made to the court for additional disclosure if it can be demonstrated that what is required under this Practice Direction is insufficient in the circumstances of a particular dispute.

Pleading of multiple prior art

3.55   It is often counter-productive to plead a multiplicity of prior art as a large number of "near misses" is often indicative of unobviousness: the practice is also undesirable as a waste of the court's time, see *Hadley Industries v Metal Sections* BL C/68/98, *noted* IPD 22004.

SECTION 4

Industrial Application

4.—(1) **An** [*Subject to subsection (2) below, an*] invention shall be taken to be capable of industrial application if it can be made or used in any kind of industry, including agriculture.

(2) [*An invention of a method of treatment of the human or animal body by surgery or therapy or of diagnosis practised on the human or animal body shall not be taken to be capable of industrial application.*]

(3) [*Subsection (2) above shall not prevent a product consisting of a substance or composition being treated as capable of industrial application merely because it is invented for use in any such method.*]

Note. Subsections (2) and (3) and the words in subs.(1) were repealed by the Patents Act 2004 (c.16) Sch.3 para.1 (December 13, 2007 as SI 2007/3396).

4.01

COMMENTARY ON SECTION 4

Scope of the section

Section 4 further qualifies the requirement of s.1(1)(c) that an invention should be capable of industrial application, corresponds to art.57 of the EPC, and by s.130(7) must be considered so far as practical to have the same effect. The word "capable" corresponds to the wording of s.1(1)(c) whereas EPC art.57 adopts the word "susceptible".

4.02

Following the revisions to the EPC in 2000, the former subss.(2) and (3) have been replaced by s.4(a)(1) and (2) as discussed in the commentary on s.4A.

Inventions in the field of biotechnology are subject to s.76A which gives effect to European Biotechnology Directive 98/44/EC by introducing into that section the provisions of Sch.A2 to the Patent Regulations 2000 (SI 2000/2037) which is reprinted at §76A.01A. The Directive introduces a number of additional things which are not patentable inventions including aspects of the human body and processes for cloning human beings, modifying the germ line genetic identity of human beings, etc. The commentary on s.76A covers these provisions and their interpretation, and the Directive itself is reprinted in Appendix C.

Under former statutes, the corresponding requirement to be satisfied was whether the invention was directed to a "manner of manufacture" according to the principles set out in the Statute of Monopolies, for which see §A06. That phrase had the advantage that its application to particular technology could move with the times, as was said by the High Court of Australia in *NRDC's Application* [1961] R.P.C. 134. After that, barriers to patentability of biological and agricultural innovations became increasingly relaxed, save that methods of medical treatment carried out on the human body remained unpatentable, see particularly the decision to this effect by the Court of Appeal in New Zealand in *Wellcome Foundation's (Hitching's) Application* [New Zealand] [1983] F.S.R. 593, reversing [1980] R.P.C. 305.

It seems that the expression "capable of industrial application" derives from the Strasbourg Convention (1963) (Cmnd.8002) and that it was not intended to limit patentability but to extend it by reducing the limitations which then existed under the various European patent laws, e.g. in the United Kingdom "manner of manufacture". However, the meaning of "industrial application" has now gained increased importance because of the requirement (set out in Sch.A2 para.6) that, where a claim is directed to a sequence or partial sequence of a gene, its industrial application must be disclosed in the patent application as filed, see also §14.30.

Definition of "industrial application" (subs.(1))

As pointed out in §1.03, the Act does not define "invention" except that its extent is defined in s.125 as being that specified in the claims as interpreted by the description and

4.03

any drawings. To be patentable an invention has to be capable of industrial application, as defined in subs.(1), and must not fall into the excluded classes of subject-matter indicated in s.1(2)–(4) and s.4A(1) and (2). These are separate requirements, and inventions excluded by s.1(2)–(4) are not rendered patentable even if they are capable of industrial application, see T 116/85 *WELLCOME/Pigs I* OJ EPO 1989, 13; [1988] E.P.O.R. 1.

In the term "capable of industrial application", it is thought that "industrial" should be interpreted in a broad sense as involving some physical human activity of "technical character", i.e. an activity which belongs to the useful or practical arts, as distinct from the aesthetic or fine arts, see EPO Guideline C–IV, 5.1. The Guideline goes on to explain at C–IV, 5.4 that in most cases how the invention can be exploited in industry will be self-evident, so that no more explicit description on this point will be required; but that there may be a few instances, e.g. in relation to certain biotechnological inventions, i.e. sequences and partial sequences of genes, where the manner of industrial exploitation is not apparent and must therefore be explicitly indicated. Methods of testing would appear to be patentable if the test is applicable to the improvement or control of a product, apparatus or process which is itself capable of industrial application, see EPO Guideline C–IV, 5.2.

For example, in *Chiron v Murex* [1996] R.P.C. 535 CA, it was held that s.4 requires a claimed invention to be capable of being used in any kind of industry so that a claim covering subject-matter that had no connection with the invention made and that the patentee had not investigated was invalid for non-compliance with the section. The court stated that "industry" does not "exist to make or use that which is useless for any known purpose" and "intellectual property rights should be confined to that which has some useful purpose", although commercial profit is not necessarily involved. Moreover, although an invention must be capable of industrial application and the specification must indicate how (if it is not clear) it is to be so applied, the claims do not have to be restricted to industrial applications, see EPO Guideline C–IV, 5.3. Consequently, subs.(1) would seem to exclude from patentability few inventions which are not already excluded by s.1(2)–(4).

The leading UK authority on the interpretation of s.1(1)(c) and s.4 is now *Eli Lilly v Human Genome Sciences Inc* [2011] UKSC 51 which reversed the decisions of the Patents Court [2008] R.P.C. 29 and the Court of Appeal [2010] R.P.C. 14 discussed in earlier editions of this work. The case addressed industrial application in the context of a biotechnological invention in which a genetic sequence had been isolated encoding for a protein whose function in the body was incompletely understood, although the superfamily to which it belonged was known. The Supreme Court held that the principles adopted by the EPO Appeal Boards should be followed, their essence being summarised in the following points:

(i) The patent must disclose "a practical application" and "some profitable use" for the claimed substance, so that the ensuing monopoly "can be expected [to lead to] some . . . commercial benefit" (T 0870/04, para.4, T 0898/05, paras 2 and 4);

(ii) A "concrete benefit", namely the invention's "use . . . in industrial practice" must be "derivable directly from the description", coupled with common general knowledge (T 0898/05, para.6, T 0604/04, para.15);

(iii) A merely "speculative" use will not suffice, so "a vague and speculative indication of possible objectives that might or might not be achievable" will not do (T 0870/04, para.21 and T 0898/05, paras 6 and 21);

(iv) The patent and common general knowledge must enable the skilled person "to reproduce" or "exploit" the claimed invention without "undue burden", or having to carry out "a research programme" (T 0604/04, para.22, T 0898/05, para.6).

Where a patent discloses a new protein and its encoding gene:

(v) The patent, when taken with common general knowledge, must demonstrate "a real as opposed to a purely theoretical possibility of exploitation" (T 0604/04, para.15, T 0898/05, paras 6, 22 and 31);

(vi) Merely identifying the structure of a protein, without attributing to it a "clear role", or "suggest[ing]" any "practical use" for it, or suggesting "a vague and speculative indication of possible objectives that might be achieved", is not enough (T 0870/04, paras 6–7, 11, and 21; T 0898/05, paras 7, 10 and 31);

(vii) The absence of any experimental or wet lab evidence of activity of the claimed protein is not fatal (T 0898/05, paras 21 and 31, T 1452/06, para 5);

(viii) A "plausible" or "reasonably credible" claimed use, or an "educated guess", can suffice (T 1329/04, paras 6 and 11, T 0640/04, para.6, T 0898/05, paras 8, 21, 27 and 31, T 452/06, para.6, T 1165/06 para.25);

(ix) Such plausibility can be assisted by being confirmed by "later evidence", although later evidence on its own will not do (T 1329/04, para.12, T 0898/05, para.24, T 1452/06, para.6, T 1165/06, para.25);

(x) The requirements of a plausible and specific possibility of exploitation can be at the biochemical, the cellular or the biological level (T 0898/05, paras 29–30).

Where the protein is said to be a family or superfamily member:

(xi) If all known members have a "role in the proliferation, differentiation and/or activation of immune cells" or "function in controlling physiology, development and differentiation of mammalian cells", assigning a similar role to the protein may suffice (T 1329/04, para.13, T 0898/05, para.21, T 1165/06, paras 14 and 16, and T 0870/04, para.12);

(xii) So "the problem to be solved" in such a case can be "isolating a further member of the [family]" (T 1329/04, para.4, T 0604/04, para.22, T 1165/06, paras 14 and 16);

(xiii) If the disclosure is "important to the pharmaceutical industry", the disclosure of the sequences of the protein and its gene may suffice, even though its role has not "been clearly defined" (T 0604/04, para.18);

(xiv) The position may be different if there is evidence, either in the patent or elsewhere, which calls the claimed role or membership of the family into question (T 0898/05 para.24, T 1452/06, para.5);

(xv) The position may also be different if the known members have different activities, although they need not always be "precisely interchangeable in terms of their biological action", and it may be acceptable if "most" of them have a common role (T 0870/04, para.12, T 0604/04, para 16, T 0898/05, para.27).

In the present case the basis on which their decision was reached by the lower courts was not consistent with the approach of the EPO Appeal Board. The disclosure of the existence and structure of Neutrokine-α and its gene sequence, and its membership of the TNF ligand superfamily should have been sufficient, taking into account the common general knowledge, to satisfy the requirements of art.57 EPC. Where all known members of the superfamily also manifest to a significant degree common activities which are, of themselves, enough to bring the patent within the ambit of points (xi), (xii) and (xiii) it would be bizarre if the fact that they had additional, but differing, qualities, should preclude the grant of such a patent. The disclosure of a new member would not only be of greater potential value than if the additional qualities did not exist, but the reason for the grant of the patent is the perceived value of a new member because of the common features of all known members, a feature which is unaffected by the additional qualities. If the known activities of the TNF ligand superfamily were enough to justify patentability for the disclosure of a novel molecule (and its encoding gene) which was plausibly identified as a member of that family, the fact that further work was required to see whether the disclosure actually had therapeutic benefits does not, at least without more, undermine the validity of a patent. The dividing line between "plausibility" and "educated guess", as against speculation", just like the contrast between "a real as opposed to a purely theoretical possibility of exploitation", can be difficult to discern in terms of language and application, and is a point on which tribunals could often differ. However, as a result of the decisions discussed above, the Board's approach to patents such as that in this case was held to be tolerably clear.

The same issues were considered in corresponding opposition proceedings before the EPO, which were heard by the TBA under case T 18/09 *HUMAN GENOME SCIENCES/ Neutrokine*. The TBA accelerated proceedings in view of a request from the Court of Appeal and proceeded to find that the requirements of industrial applicability were met. The Board noted the close relationship between EPC art.57 (industrial applicability) and EPC art.83 (sufficiency) in that both provisions relate to the obligation on an applicant to give a sufficient description of the invention. They concluded that an objection of lack of industrial application requires the same standard of proof as an objection of insufficient disclosure, namely serious doubts substantiated by verifiable facts, which was not met in this case.

The later decision of the English Court of Appeal took the opportunity to contrast procedural differences between the Opposition Divisions and Technical Boards of Appeal of the EPO with the English courts and the opportunity for cooperation between the two. The Court of Appeal concluded that in this case the TBA and the English courts had applied the same principles of law, but their conclusions differed due to different assessments of the facts, including the reliance by the TBA on a last-minute affidavit which had not been tested by cross-examination. The Supreme Court disagreed, holding that in this case the reason for the contrasting outcomes was that the courts below had applied a stricter standard than the TBA's jurisprudence requires.

Apparently, an invention in the ordinary sense which meets all the criteria, except that it is not capable of industrial application—something associated with the person perhaps—is not patentable at all. It is not easy to think of such inventions, but the EPO has taken the view that, while it can be accepted that pregnancy is not a disease and therefore not automatically precluded from patentability by art.53(c) of the EPC, claims to contraceptive treatment should be denied patentability as applying only to private acts and therefore not an invention which is industrially applicable (T 74/93 *BRITISH TECHNOLOGY/ Contraceptive method* OJ EPO 1995, 712; [1995] E.P.O.R. 279). In T 1165/97 *ULTRAFEM/Feminine hygiene device* [2002] E.P.O.R. 35 the claimed method of using a vaginal discharge collector was held not to relate to a service satisfying only the strictly personal needs of the woman in question, as in T 74/93 *BRITISH TECHNOLOGY/ Contraceptive method*, above, as it was capable of being used by an enterprise of which the object is to assist women in collecting a sample of their vaginal discharge for subsequent examination or other purposes. It was said that:

"whether such enterprises actually exist is not relevant for the purposes of art.57 EPC; what counts is the possibility that such a service may be offered by an enterprise."

See also §4A.05 for whether such a method would be excluded in any event as a diagnostic method.

An idea for penal reform by the substitution of voluntary corporal punishment has been held to lack industrial applicability (as well as being a scheme for doing business) (*Melia's Application* BL O/153/92).

Inventions which have been excluded from patentability under subs.(1) include articles or processes alleged to operate in a manner clearly contrary to well-established physical laws. Thus, claims to an energy conservation device were rejected in *Paez's Application* BL O/176/83, and in *Yaou Song's Application* BL O/40/94, in each case because the operation of the invention was regarded as being contrary to well-established natural laws. In *Paez*, it was held that "made" in s.1(1)(c) embraces the operation of a device as well as its construction. The rejection in that case was also based on a failure to comply with s.14(3). Applications for apparatus of the perpetual motion type, or for machines held to be operating contrary to natural laws, were also rejected in: *Webb's Application* BL O/84/ 88, noted I.P.D. 1078; *Kershaw's Application* BL O/23/86; *Renaut's Application* BL O/25/86; *Wilkinson's Application* BL O/21/86; *Steney's Application* BL O/280/98; *Stott's Application* BL O/151–2/99; *Richardson's Application* BL O/368/00 and *Lister's Applications* BL O/100/11. For rejection of an application in which the claims "did not make technical sense" see *American Photo Booth's Patent* BL O/457/02. An application relating to a propulsion system alleged to work by the generation of magnetic energy through the transmission of microwaves through coils containing iron crystals and a honey-based substance was rejected, inter alia, on the ground that it would contravene the law of conservation of energy, and so was not capable of industrial application, see *Hickinbotham's Application* BL O/162/05. In *Ducketts' Application* BL O/228/05, an application relating to a propulsion unit including electric and hydraulic systems alleged to work by using an alternator to maintain a battery at full charge whilst providing further electricity for auxiliary power was held to contravene the law of conservation of energy since it appeared to create energy out of nothing and was refused as not having industrial application, see also §1.16.

Objections of insufficient description (under s.14(3)) or of claims not being supported by the description (under s.14(5)) can, at least sometimes, be used as alternative grounds for findings of unpatentability which might otherwise have been given as a failure to meet the criterion of s.4(1) see, e.g. T 5/86 *NEWMAN/Perpetual motion* [1988] E.P.O.R. 301 where a claim involving perpetual motion was refused for insufficiency of description.

SECTION 4A [ADDED]

Methods of treatment or diagnosis

4A.—(1) A patent shall not be granted for the invention of—   **4A.01**

  (a) a method of treatment of the human or animal body by surgery or therapy, or

  (b) a method of diagnosis practised on the human or animal body.

(2) Subsection (1) above does not apply to an invention consisting of a substance or composition for use in any such method.

(3) In the case of an invention consisting of a substance or composition for use in any such method, the fact that the substance or composition forms part of the state of the art shall not prevent the invention from being taken to be new if the use of the substance or composition in any such method does not form part of the state of the art.

(4) In the case of an invention consisting of a substance or composition for a specific use in any such method, the fact that the substance or composition forms part of the state of the art shall not prevent the invention from being taken to be new if that specific use does not form part of the state of the art.

Note. Section 4A was added by the Patents Act 2004 (c.16) s.1 (December 13, 2007) and the related (Commencement No.4 and Transitional Provisions Order) SI 2007/3396.

COMMENTARY ON SECTION 4A

Scope of the section

Section 4A corresponds to revised arts 53(c), 54(4) and (5) of the EPC 2000, which   **4A.02** relate to the exceptions to patentability and novelty, respectively. Subsections (l) and (2) replace former subss.(2) and (3). It is only the expression of the law, not the law itself, which changed when this statutory amendment took effect. Decisions relating to the interpretation of former subss.(2) and (3) are still applicable to the law under this section.

Subsection (3) replaces former s.2(6) to continue to permit inventions of the first medicinal utility of a known substance to be protected by a use-bound product claim, as discussed in §4A.08 below. Subs.(4) extends the same principle to an invention consisting of a new medicinal use for a substance already known to have a different medicinal use. With the coming into force of EPC 2000, it is no longer necessary to claim this type of invention by a "Swiss form" of claim expressed as "Use of X for the production of a medicament for use in the medical treatment of Y", and this form of claim will no longer be granted in the United Kingdom and in due course will no longer be allowed in the EPO, as set out in G 2/08 *ABBOTT RESPIRATORY/Dosage regime* [2010] E.P.O.R. 26 (see §4A.09 below). Instead, the simpler form "Substance X for use in the treatment of disease Y" will be allowable. Despite this new claim wording, it would appear that comments relating to decisions under former s.2(6) will apply to new s.4A(4). However, the relaxation of the law of lack of novelty under the provisions of subss.(3) and (4) continues to apply only where the actual use envisaged is one which cannot be patented as such under subs.(1).

In T 1319/04 *KOS LIFE SCIENCES, INC/Dosage Regimen* [2008] E.P.O.R. 27, the question of the applicability of the decisions under the provisions of former EPC arts 52(4) and 54(5) was referred to the Enlarged Board of Appeal, as G 2/08. In T 1319/04 *KOS LIFE SCIENCES, INC/Dosage Regimen*, the Board observed that it appeared from the *travaux préparatoires* for the Conference of the contracting states to revise the European Patent Convention which took place in Munich from November 20 to 29, 2000, that:

"as regards the second or further medical uses, the case law evolved by the EPO Enlarged Board of Appeal should be enshrined in the Convention" (point 139 conference proceedings).

Accordingly, the Board took the view that to understand art.54(5) of the EPC 2000, it was appropriate to refer to the case law as embodied in Enlarged Board of Appeal decision G 5/83 *EISAI/Second medical indication* OJ EPO 1985, 64; [1979–85] E.P.O.R. B241 issued on December 5, 1984 and the correspondingly worded decisions in other official languages in parallel cases (e.g. G 1/83 and G 6/83). However, for the sake of a consistent development of the case law, it referred three questions to the Enlarged Board:

1. Where it is already known to use a particular medicament to treat a particular illness, can this known medicament be patented under the provisions of arts 53(c) and 54(5) of the EPC 2000 for use in a different, new and inventive treatment by therapy of the same illness?

2. If the answer to question 1 is yes, is such patenting also possible where the only novel feature of the treatment is a new and inventive dosage regime?

3. Are any special considerations applicable when interpreting and applying arts 53(c) and 54(5) of the EPC 2000?

Following the referral in T 1319/04 *KOS LIFE SCIENCES, INC./Dosage Regimen* [2008] E.P.O.R. 27, the Enlarged Board in G 2/08 *ABBOTT RESPIRATORY/Dosage regime* [2010] E.P.O.R. 26 observed that no fundamental change was intended by the legislator in replacing art.54(5) EPC 1973 with art.54(4) EPC 2000 (relating to the first medical indication of a per se already known substance or composition). Further, the purpose of introducing art.54(5) EPC 2000 (relating to second and subsequent medical indications of substances or compositions already known as medicines) was to fill the lacuna in the former provisions which had been filled by the case law established by the Enlarged Board of Appeal with decision G 5/83 *EISAI/Second medical indication* OJ EPO 1985,64; [1979-85] E.P.O.R. B241 issued on December 5, 1984 and the correspondingly worded decisions in other official languages in parallel cases (e.g. G 1/83 and G 6/83).

Thus, the Board confirmed that the change in law was not intended to have any effect on the principles established by earlier case law, and so it would appear that comments relating to decisions under former s.2(6) will apply to the new s.4A(4).

However, Sterckx and Cockbain argue in their article "Purpose-limited pharmaceutical product claims under the revised EPC 2000" [2010] I.P.Q. 1, 88, that the change in the law relating to protection for second and subsequent medical indications under EPC 2000 does in fact result in a change in the scope of protection provided by such patents.

Unpatentability of medical and veterinary treatment (subss.(1) and (2))

Although a prohibition against patents for medical and veterinary treatment is permitted **4A.03** under the TRIPS Agreement, this increasingly appears as an anachronism; see the decisions permitting such claims in Australia under the former "manner of new manufacture" test, *Anaesthetic Supplies v Rescare* [Australia] (1994) 28 I.P.R. 383, discussed by D. Kell [1995] E.I.P.R. 202, and *Bristol-Myers Squibb v Faulding* [Australia] (1999–2000) 46 I.P.R. 553, in which the judgment of Finkelstein J. (at 586) reviewed the worldwide history of the allowability of this type of patent protection, particularly in the United States, and discussed the ethical questions involved. A similar position has been taken in New Zealand (*Pharmaceutical Management v Commissioner of Patents* [New Zealand] [2000] R.P.C. 857, for which see §4A.10. For further discussion on the patentability of methods of medical treatment and of second medical uses, see Audrey Horton, *Patent World*, 124 (August 2000), 9; and on *Bristol-Myers Squibb v Baker Norton* [1999] R.P.C. 253 and the Court of Appeal decision [2001] R.P.C. 1, see the paper by J. Williams [2000] B.S.L.R. 238. However, in *Actavis UK Ltd v Merck & Co Inc* [2008] R.P.C. 26; [2008] EWCA Civ 444, the Court of Appeal chose not to follow *Bristol-Myers Squibb v Baker Norton*, taking the view that the court is free but not bound to depart from the ratio decidendi of its own earlier decision if it is satisfied that the EPO Boards of Appeal have formed a settled view of European Patent law which is inconsistent with that earlier decision and stating that the court will follow such a settled view, referring in particular to T 1020/03 *GENENTECH/ Method of administration of IFG-I* [2006] E.P.O.R. 9 and subsequent decisions following it.

Subsection (1) corresponds to art.53(c) of the EPC and simply states that patents shall not be granted for methods for treatment of the human or animal body by surgery or therapy and diagnostic methods practised on the human or animal body, rather than saying that such methods shall be deemed not capable of industrial application as under the former s.4(2) and former art.54(2) of the EPC. This exclusion from patentability is permitted by the TRIPS Agreement (see art.27.3, reprinted in §1.03). Thus, claims to a method of medical or veterinary treatment as such are not allowed, see Decision G 5/83 *EISAI/ Second Medical Indication* adopted in the United Kingdom by *John Wyeth's and Schering's Applications* [1985] R.P.C. 545, though "use in treatment" claims are permitted in the German Federal Republic, see §4A.10 further below.

However, the prohibition of subs.(1) is alleviated by subs.(2) which is corresponds to the second clause of art.53(c) of the EPC which says that this provision shall not apply to products, in particular substances or compositions, for use in any of these methods. These provisions, taken together, allow (despite subs.(1)) protection by way of a "purpose-bound" product claim for an invention based on the first application of a known substance or composition in the methods of treatment by surgery or therapy, or diagnostic methods, when practised on the human or animal body. Subsection (3) corresponds to art.54(4) of the EPC and is considered in §4A.08 as a specific derogation from the requirement that claims should be directed solely to subject-matter which is "novel" in all its aspects. It is followed in §4A.09 by discussion of the eventual acceptance of patent protection for inventions of second or further medical indications, that is in respect of discoveries of new and inventive medicinal uses of substances already known to have some (other) pharmaceutical activity.

Thus, although claims for medical or veterinary treatment of the human or animal body are prohibited by subs.(1), useful (and broad) protection for such inventions may be obtainable by claims to chemical or biological substances or compositions which have useful activity in such methods, provided that these substances possess novelty per se under s.2. If this is not so, a purpose-bound substance claim may be possible under the exception to the law of novelty available under s.4A(3), provided that no medical or veterinary use for the substance or composition is already part of the state of the art, i.e. that the purpose for which the substance or composition is to be patented is not only a novel one, but is also the first such purpose to be suggested or used in the field of medical or veterinary treatment, as discussed in §4A.08. If such a claim is not possible, then a more limited purpose-bound claim directed to a specific novel use of that substance or composition in providing some novel and inventive treatment of the human or animal body may be possible under s.4A (4) by means of a claim either in the "Swiss form" or "for use" format, as discussed above and further in §4A.09.

There is no objection under s.4A(1)(a) or (b) to a claim directed to an apparatus for carrying out medical or surgical treatment, or for diagnosis, or to a claim to a device to be used in such procedures. However, s.4A(3) means that such claims must be construed as "apparatus claims" and not as "method claims", see *Visx v Nidek* [1999] F.S.R. 405. If the apparatus is not novel, then s.4(A)(2), (3) and (4) will not assist in obtaining claims to an "apparatus" as opposed to a "substance or composition"; see *National Research Development Corp's Application* BL O/117/85, noted I.P.D. 9047, referred to in §4A.08 below.

Normally, infringement actions are brought against manufacturers and vendors, not users, of a patented product. In the United States, where claims directed to medical treatment as such are permitted, the carrying out of the claimed treatment by a medical practitioner is a statutory exception to the acts otherwise regarded as patent infringing.

Decisions on the interpretation of subs.(1)(a) and (b) first involve the question whether the claim is directed to a method of treatment *"of the human or animal body"* or diagnosis "practised on the human or animal body". If this is not so, then the prohibition on patentability imposed by the subsection has no effect. Then, if the claim does involve a method in this sense, the further question arises whether that method involves "therapy" (discussed in §4A.05), or "surgery" (discussed in §4A.06), or "diagnosis" (discussed in §4A.07).

—The meaning of treatment of the human or animal body and diagnosis practised on the human or animal body

4A.04   So far as the exclusion from patentability of methods of treatment or diagnosis is concerned, only treatments of the human or animal body by surgery or therapy or diagnosis practised on the human or animal body are apparently excluded. Thus, a treatment or diagnostic method, to be excluded, must actually be carried out on the living animal or human body. Accordingly, the EPO Guidelines state that treatment of body tissues or fluids after removal from the body is not excluded insofar as these tissues or fluids are not returned to the same body (C–IV, 4.8.1). On this basis, claims directed to the cosmetic treatment of nails and hair (including methods of permanent waving) would appear to be patentable, as they were under the "manner of manufacture" test.

Nevertheless (as demonstrated in §4A.05 and §4A.06 respectively), the terms "surgery" and "therapy" have each been given broad interpretations so as to expand the scope of the exclusions created by subs.(1), despite the general rule of statutory construction that exclusions should be narrowly construed—a philosophy to which scant regard appears to have been paid in decisions under former s.4(2) and the corresponding former art.52(4) of the EPC.

Determination of whether a method is "a method for the treatment of the human body" cannot depend on the person carrying out the claimed method, see G 1/07 MEDIPHYSICS/Treatment by surgery [2010] E.P.O.R. 25 discussed further at §4A.06, although see also T 663/02 discussed also at §4A.06.

Patentability can, apparently, be recognised where no therapeutic or prophylactic effect could be seen: T 329/94 *BAXTER/Blood extraction method* OJ EPO 1998, 241; [1998] E.P.O.R. 363. In T 1165/97 *ULTRAFEM/Feminine hygiene device* [2002] E.P.O.R. 35 the claimed method of using a vaginal discharge collector was held not to relate to a method of treatment by surgery or therapy, because there was no curative or preventative treatment involved nor was any medical skill required for the use of the device. Nor was it deemed to be a method of diagnosis because the steps of providing and placing the collector and the use and disposal thereof as claimed did not involve all the steps involved in reaching a medical diagnosis. See also §4A.03. Similarly, in T 635/08 *DOW CORNING FRANCE S.A./Method for adhering substrates using adhesive devices containing silicone gels*, claims pertaining to a method of adhering a prosthesis to the skin of a human or animal body were not excluded from patentability under EPC art.53(c) because there was no specific therapeutic or surgical effect caused by said adhesion. Nevertheless, if the claims include a single technical operation performed on a human or animal body which defines a method for treatment of such a body by therapy or surgery, such is regarded as unpatentable, see T 82/93 *TELECTRONICS/Cardiac pacing* OJ EPO 1996, 274; [1996] E.P.O.R. 409 where the patent had been granted with claims to a method of operating a heart pacemaker during patient exercise, but, in an appeal against unsuccessful opposition proceedings, the claims were held to be contrary to former art.52(4) of the EPC (which now corresponds to EPC art.53(c)) because they involved, in part, treatment carried out on the human body. Attempts to amend the claims to direct these instead to "a pacer" were then rejected as extending the breadth of protection as granted contrary to art.123(3) of the EPC, see §76.22.

However, in some cases, claims have been allowed directed to an article for use in a medical treatment because these have been seen as not themselves directed to medical treatment as such, see: T 426/89 *SIEMENS/Pacemaker* OJ EPO 1992, 172; [1992] E.P.O.R. 149; and T 245/87 *SIEMENS/Flow measurement* OJ EPO 1989, 171; [1989] E.P.O.R. 241 in which a method of measuring the flow of liquid, particularly suitable for use in an implanted device for drug administration, was held to be patentable as it was a matter of apparatus design of no concern to the physician who used it and which left the physician completely free to exercise his skills.

In T 820/92 *GENERAL HOSPITAL/Contraceptive method* OJ EPO 1995, 113; [1995] E.P.O.R. 446 it was left undecided whether a method of contraception could be patentable under the EPC, but such claims were rejected as a method of therapy because the claimed method not only provided contraception but also a concurrent therapeutic treatment, this being sufficient for prohibition under the former EPC art.52(4) (which now corresponds to EPC art.53(c)): however, claims in the "Swiss form" were allowed. Then, in T 74/93 *BRITISH TECHNOLOGY/Contraceptive method* OJ EPO 1995, 712; [1995] E.P.O.R. 279 it was accepted that pregnancy is not a disease and therefore not automatically precluded from patentability by art.52(4) of the EPC, but the claimed method was denied patentability as not being industrially applicable for another reason, see §4.03.

The EPO has allowed claims limited to formulations adapted only for topical administration to the exclusion of oral and injectable administration after restrictively construing the prior art as relating only to injectable and oral compositions (T 289/84 *WELLCOME/3-Amino-pyrazoline derivatives* [1987] E.P.O.R. 58).

The EPO has previously allowed claims to cosmetic treatment, even where therapeutic activity is involved (e.g. T 36/83 *ROUSSEL-UCLAF/Thenoyl peroxide* OJ EPO 1986, 295; [1987] E.P.O.R. 1 and T 144/83 *DU PONT/Appetite suppressant* OJ EPO 1986, 30; [1987] E.P.O.R. 6). However, in later decisions a partial feature of medical or veterinary treatment has led to a finding of unpatentability. In T 438/91 *MEIJI/Feeds* [1999] E.P.O.R. 333, a dual purpose treatment was held to fall within the prohibition of art.52(4) of the EPC where the two effects (here the remedying of scours and obtaining a weight increase in the breeding of animals) are linked by the single action of feeding and it is the intention to obtain both effects. Likewise, in T 1077/93 *L'OREAL/Protection against UV radiation* [1997] E.P.O.R. 546, a cosmetic composition was found partly to produce its effect by an interactive mechanism with the epidermis and so was unpatentable as also having a therapeutic effect.

In *ICI's Application* BL O/73/82, a claim to a method of cleaning teeth for the removal of dental plaque from the teeth was rejected as a method of medical treatment; and, in T 116/85 *WELLCOME/Pigs I* OJ EPO 1989, 13; [1988] E.P.O.R. 1, claims were rejected to a method of controlling ectoparasites on pigs by localised application to the pig body surface of a known pesticidal composition as being a method of therapeutic treatment.

However, in T 584/88 *REICHART/Anti-snoring means* [1989] E.P.O.R. 449, a claim was allowed in the form: "Use of X to combat troublesome snoring", this type of snoring not being considered as medical treatment: claims in the "Swiss form" were also allowed as regards "the therapeutic treatment of snoring which might be harmful to health", see §4A.09.

T 35/99 *GEORGETOWN UNIVERSITY/Pericardial access* OJ EPO 2000, 447 held that:

"In contrast to procedures whose end result is the death of the living being 'under treatment', either deliberately or incidentally (*e.g.* the slaughter of animals or methods for measuring biological functions of an animal which comprise the sacrificing of the animal), those physical interventions on a human or animal body which, whatever their specific purpose, give priority to maintaining the life or health of the body on which they are performed, are 'in their nature' methods of treatment by surgery".

Also:

"the exclusion from patentability of such methods encompasses any surgical activity, irrespective of whether it is carried out alone or in combination with other medical or non-medical measures".

In *ICI's (Richardson's) Application* [1981] F.S.R. 609, a claim to:

"A method of producing an anti-oestrogenic effect in warm-blooded animals, including man, but excluding any method of treatment of the animal or human body by therapy, which comprises administering [the compound]"

was rejected as not relating to an invention within s.1(1)(c) because there was nothing left in the claim if effect were given to the exclusionary phrase. The specification described only the application of the compound for the treatment of breast cancer and infertility. The claim was also held to be indefinite and therefore objectionable under s.14(5).

In *Virulite Distribution Ltd's Application* BL O/058/10, a claim to a method of cosmetically treating an area of skin around the eye to reduce wrinkles that occur as a result of natural aging was held to be neither a method of treatment by surgery nor a method of treatment by therapy. The hearing officer applied a two-step test, derived from EPO case law, notably T 820/92 *GENERAL HOSPITAL/Contraceptive method* [1995] E.P.O.R. 446, to determine whether the method was a method of treatment by surgery and concluded that there was no "non-insignificant intentional physical intervention" and that the treatment was not "suitable, or potentially suitable, for maintaining or restoring the health, the physical integrity, or the physical well being of human beings or animals". The surgical exclusion would only apply in cases where both of these criteria were met. The method was not treatment by therapy since no medical conditions would benefit from the claimed method of wrinkle reduction.

—The meaning of "therapy"

4A.05   In *Unilever's (Davis's) Application* [1983] R.P.C. 219, the Patents Court held that "therapy", as used in former s.4(2), should be given its broader meaning of the medical treatment of disease rather than its narrower meaning of curative medical treatment because "surgery" is clearly not limited to curative surgery. On this basis, s.4(2) was held to prevent the patenting of prophylactic treatments such as immunisation or vaccination, these being treatments of disease even though effected on healthy persons or animals because they are directed to the prevention of disease. The EPO likewise gave a further broad meaning to the term "therapy" when, in T 19/86 *DUPHAR/Pigs II* OJ EPO 1989, 24; [1988] E.P.O.R. 10, it followed this *Unilever* decision in holding that "therapy" embraces both curative and prophylactic treatment.

The EPO also decided, in T 81/84 *RORER/Dysmenorrhoea* OJ EPO 1988, 202; [1988] E.P.O.R. 297, that the concept of "therapy" should not be construed narrowly and that it is undesirable to distinguish between basic and symptomatic therapy, i.e. between healing or cure and mere relief, so that the relief of pain, discomfort or incapacity should each be considered as therapy or therapeutic use and, therefore, unpatentable under former EPC art.52(4) (now EPC art.53(c)). Accordingly, claims to the relief of discomfort of a human female attributed to menstruation were rejected. The same principle can be seen in T 58/87,

SALMINEN/Pigs III [1989] E.P.O.R. 125 where a method of creating unpleasant conditions to prevent a sow lying upon and suffocating her litter was held patentable, this not being regarded as a "treatment". In this case, "therapy" was defined as:

"covering any non-surgical treatment which is designed to cure, alleviate, remove or lessen the symptoms of, or prevent or reduce the possibility of contracting any malfunction of the animal body."

Similarly, in *Ciba-Geigy's Application* BL O/30/85, noted I.P.D. 8083, the Comptroller rejected claims to a method of treating intestinal helminths, such as tapeworms, on the basis that to rid a patient's body of such parasites should be regarded as "therapy".

A method of purifying blood during renal dialysis was rejected in *Schultz's Application* BL O/174/86, noted I.P.D. 10003 as involving "therapy" because, like the administration of pain killers or insulin to diabetic persons, the method gives temporary alleviation of disease symptoms. This case also indicated that the phrase in subs.(2) "practised on the human or animal body" only qualifies the term "diagnosis" and not the terms "therapy" or "surgery", which therefore stand unqualified.

Also, claims to use of a known composition as an oral hygiene agent have been refused as being a therapeutic treatment of the human body (T 290/86 *ICI/Cleaning plaque* OJ EPO 1992, 414; [1991] E.P.O.R. 157). Likewise, general immunostimulation, or stimulation of the body's own defences, by the use of particular compounds in conjunction with specific prophylaxis against certain infections has been classed as therapeutic treatment, any increase in meat production of an animal as a result merely being a consequence of that (unpatentable) treatment (T 780/89 *BAYER/Immunostimulant* OJ EPO 1993, 440; [1993] E.P.O.R. 377).

Nevertheless, claims to a method of controlling bleeding in non-haemophilic mammals have also been allowed over prior art describing the same composition for controlling bleeding on haemophilic mammals (T 893/90 *QUEEN'S UNIVERSITY AT KINGSTON/ Controlling Bleeding* (Unreported)).

Whereas therapeutic treatment has the purpose of restoring a condition from a pathological state to its original condition, a non-therapeutic improvement of performance takes the normal state as its starting point (T 774/89 (Unreported)).

In *Commonwealth Scientific's Application* BL O/248/04, claims to a photodyanamic method of controlling wool growth were held not to be a method of therapy, the hearing officer deciding that for a treatment to constitute therapy, there must be a direct link between the treatment and disease state being cured, prevented or alleviated. In contrast to *Unilever Ltd (Davis's) Application*, above, the method did not result in any agent or effect that would in turn actively prevent the disease state.

In T 1230/05 *BIOENERGY/Increasing energy in vivo* the use of ribose for increasing skeletal muscle performance in normal healthy subjects was held not to be within EPC art.53(c). In T 1002/09 *NESTEC/High Fibre high calorie composition* novelty was in the proposed use for promoting gut health in an elderly patient. The claim was held to be a purpose-related product claim in analogy to EPC art.54(4) ("first medical use of a known compound"), alleviation of pain in the human body by regulating gut flora and improving intestinal transit being therapeutic measures and elderly patients being a distinct demographic group.

In T 170/07 *GAMBRO/Haemodialysis* the claimed subject-matter concerned extracorporeal haemodialysis of blood in which a parameter, e.g. sodium ion concentration in the dialysis liquid, was varied and calculations were made to determine the effectiveness of treatment. It had been shown in the prior art that patients undergoing dialysis could suffer from hypotension and that this could be overcome by increasing the concentration of sodium in the dialysate. The claimed method of parameter determination covered embodiments where there would be a beneficial effect on a patient exhibiting symptoms of hypotension, and the doses and times given by the applicant were of the same order as those necessary for treating hypotension. The Board held that the question was not whether or not the machine was intended to give a therapeutic dose of sodium, or whether the claim covered embodiments where there was no positive effect or even a negative effect, but simply whether the claim covered embodiments which would clearly produce a therapeutic effect. Claim 1 of the main request was not limited to any particular variation. Accordingly, the Board held that the step of varying the value of a characteristic inevitably resulted in a therapeutic step when the variation was of the size and type proposed by the prior art, a variation which fell within the scope of the claim. That was sufficient for the claimed method a method to fall within EPC art.53(c), and the claimed invention was not patentable.

—The meaning of "surgery"

4A.06   In *Occidental Petroleum's Application* BL O/35/84, noted I.P.D. 7070; (1985) 16 I.I.C. 216, it was concluded that, while "therapy" in former s.4(2) covers curative and prophylactic treatment, the term "surgery" is not limited to therapeutic surgery, but includes any method of surgical treatment which need not necessarily involve making an incision into body tissue. On this basis, claims to embryonic transplantation were rejected. A method of implanting an imaging marker in a human body has also been held unallowable as being both "surgical" and "treatment", each of these words being given a broad meaning (*Allen's Application* BL O/59/92, noted I.P.D. 16040). However, this principle does not extend to allow a "Swiss form" of claim for a new surgical use of a known surgical instrument (T 227/91 *CODMAN/Second surgical use* OJ EPO 1994, 491; [1995] E.P.O.R. 82).

The Enlarged Board's decision in G 1/07 *MEDI-PHYSICS/Treatment by surgery* sets out the current practice with regards to surgical methods. In the referring decision T 992/03 *MEDI-PHYSICS/Treatment by surgery* [2007] E.P.O.R. 32 the invention concerned magnetic resonance methods for imaging the pulmonary and/or cardiac vasculature and evaluating blood flow using dissolved polarised 129 Xe. The Appeal Board held that the claimed subject-matter did not fall within the diagnostic method exclusion because the claimed steps were confined to the examination phase and did not include steps considered constitutive for making a diagnosis. However, the claimed method covered administration of polarised xenon into the heart by injection, and the method was intended to be used inter alia for providing real-time feedback during surgery.

Existing case law of the Appeal Boards had held that introduction of a catheter into the pericardial space was an excluded method of surgical treatment (T 35/99 *GEORGETOWN UNIVERSITY/Pericardial access* [2001] E.P.O.R. 21; see also T 182/90 *SEE-SHELL/ Bloodflow* [1994] E.P.O.R. 320 as to methods of injection), but that applying radiation to the body for the purpose of cosmetic removal of hair was not excluded (T 383/03 *GENERAL HOSPITAL CORP/Hair removal method* [2005] E.P.O.R. 33). Issues arising in the appeal to the Enlarged Board included whether a physical intervention of the human or animal body was to be considered "surgical" even if there was no aim to maintain life and health, whether it was possible to exclude the administration step ("pre-delivered contrast agent") or whether the claim would be allowable if the administration step were defined at a higher level of abstraction ("administering a contrast agent").

The Enlarged Board reiterated that the meaning of "treatment by surgery" is not to be confined to surgical methods pursuing a therapeutic purpose and that the exclusion could not depend on the person carrying out the claimed method. However, whilst the Board limited its answer to the specific questions asked and declined to provide guidance on other kinds of methods which might potentially be considered to fall within the exclusion of "treatment by surgery", it did provide some guidance that the exclusion should perhaps be construed more narrowly in the future (see point 3.4.2 of the decision and T 663/02, below). Thus, the questions were answered by the Board as follows:

1. A claimed imaging method, in which, when carried out, maintaining the life and health of the subject is important and which comprises or encompasses an invasive step representing a substantial physical intervention on the body which requires

professional medical expertise to be carried out and which entails a substantial health risk even when carried out with the required professional care and expertise, is excluded from patentability as a method for treatment of the human or animal body by surgery pursuant to Article 53(c) EPC.

2a. A claim which comprises a step encompassing an embodiment which is a 'method for treatment of the human or animal body by surgery' within the meaning of Article 53(c) EPC cannot be left to encompass that embodiment.

2b. The exclusion from patentability under Article 53(c) EPC can be avoided by disclaiming the embodiment, it being understood that in order to be patentable the claim including the disclaimer must fulfil all the requirements of the EPC and, where applicable, the requirements for a disclaimer to be allowable as defined in decisions G 1/03 and G 2/03 of the Enlarged Board of Appeal.

3. Whether or not the wording of the claim can be amended so as to omit the surgical step without offending against the EPC must be assessed on the basis of the overall circumstances of the individual case under consideration.

4. A claimed imaging method is not to be considered as being a 'treatment of the human or animal body by surgery' within the meaning of Article 53(c) EPC merely because during a surgical intervention the data obtained by the use of the method immediately allow a surgeon to decide on the course of action to be taken during a surgical intervention.

With reference to the second question, the Board noted that terms such as "pre-delivered" and "pre-implanted" are not disclaimers and may be allowable in order to omit the surgical step without offending against the EPC. The relevant provisions of the EPC which must be considered for the allowability of the omission and the patentability of such a claim are EPC arts 56, 83 and 123.

In T 663/02 *METHOD FOR MAGNETIC IMAGING OF ARTERIES/PRINCE, MARTIN R.* the Technical Board of Appeal applied the reasoning of the Enlarged Boards in G 1/04 and G 1/07 to conclude that:

"I. *The fact that an intravenous injection of a magnetic resonance contrast agent can be delegated by a physician to a qualified paramedical professional indicates that such an injection may be considered as representing a minor routine intervention which does not imply a substantial health risk when carried out with the required care and skill. Such acts would be ruled out from the scope of the application of the exclusion clause pursuant to Article 53(c) EPC following the narrow understanding advocated by the EBA (G 0001/04 and 0001/07) (Reasons, 3.2.4).*

II. *A possible way of assessing health risks is to use a risk matrix permitting to combine the levels of likelihood and health impact of a complication of a medical act with regard to a large number of patients, so as to obtain statistical health risk scores which may be used to decide what action should be taken. Such a risk assessment supports the view that an intravenous injection of a magnetic resonance contrast agent represents a minor routine intervention involving no substantial health risks when carried out with the required care and skill (Reasons, 3.2.5).*"

Thus, the Board looked at criteria such as "substantial health risk" and "professional medical skills" in order to differentiate between excluded "substantial physical interventions on the body" and non-excluded subject-matter, despite an explicit statement from the Enlarged Board in G 1/07 that the exclusion cannot depend on the person carrying out the method.

In T 775/97 *EXPANDABLE GRAFTS/Surgical Device* [2002] E.P.O.R. 24 claims in the "Swiss-style" form were refused where directed to a method by which tubular members were assembled inside the body of a patient, such that the final construction of the product was only arrived at in the body following a surgical procedure. This was held to be a method of treatment by surgery and therefore unpatentable under former EPC art.52(4) (now EPC art.53(c)).

In T 556/07 *MELLES/Vital dyes for vitreo-retinal surgery* the claimed invention was:

"Use of at least one vital dye for the manufacture of a composition for staining a retinal membrane in an eye to visually distinguish the retinal membrane from the underlying retina in a method for performing retinal membrane removal."

The claim was held to be a use for the manufacture of a composition in Swiss-type format that was not in conflict with art.53(c) followed by a separate surgical method which was excluded, and accordingly the patent was revoked.

—The meaning of "diagnosis"

4A.07 Inventions involving diagnosis of a medical or veterinary condition which is carried out extra-corporeally do not involve a treatment carried out "on the human or animal body" and are, therefore, not excluded from patentability under subs.(1).

It is also significant that, unlike the more restrictive line taken over the meaning of the terms "therapeutic" and "surgical", it has been recognised by an EPO Board of Appeal (reversing the Examining Division) that former art.52(4) of the EPC (now EPC art.53(c)) should be construed narrowly "like all regulations governing exclusions", consequently placing a limited interpretation on what constitutes a diagnostic method excluded from art.53(c) of the EPC by holding patentable a non-invasive diagnostic method which did not provide results which enabled an immediate decision on medical treatment to be made (T 385/86 *BRUKER/Non-invasive measurement* OJ EPO 1988, 308; [1988] E.P.O.R. 357). Here it was considered important that the patent would not hamper a physician in the exercise of his healing skills. Thus, it appears that diagnostic methods are only excluded by art.53(c) of the EPC if the results therefrom can, as such, be utilised in making a diagnosis, see also T 83/87 *SIEMENS/Diagnostic method* [1988] E.P.O.R. 365.

T 964/99 *CYGNUS/Surgical Device* OJ EPO 2002, 4; [2002] E.P.O.R. 26 appeared to change that position in that it held that all methods practised on the human or animal body which relate to diagnosis or are of value for the purpose of diagnosis should be excluded from patentability. The controversy was referred to the Enlarged Board of Appeal, which opined as follows in EPO Opinion G 1/04 *Diagnostic methods* (in which reference to new EPC art.53(c) has been substituted for the former equivalent provision):

"1. In order that the subject-matter of a claim relating to a diagnostic method practised on the human or animal body falls under the prohibition of [EPC art.53(c)], the claim is to include the features relating to:

(i) the diagnosis for curative purposes *stricto sensu* representing the deductive medical or veterinary decision phase as a purely intellectual exercise,

(ii) the preceding steps which are constitutive for making that diagnosis, and

(iii) the specific interactions with the human or animal body which occur when carrying those out among these preceding steps which are of a technical nature.

2. Whether or not a method is a diagnostic method within the meaning of [EPC art.53(c)] may neither depend on the participation of a medical or veterinary practitioner, by being present or by bearing the responsibility, nor on the fact that all method steps can also, or only, be practised by medical or technical support staff, the patient himself or herself or an automated system. Moreover, no distinction is to be made in this context between essential method steps having diagnostic character and non-essential method steps lacking it.

3. In a diagnostic method under [EPC art.53(c)], the method steps of a technical nature belonging to the preceding steps which are constitutive for making the diagnosis for curative purposes *stricto sensu* must satisfy the criterion 'practised on the human or animal body'.

4. [EPC art.53(c)] does not require a specific type and intensity of interaction with the human or animal body; a preceding step of a technical nature thus satisfies the

criterion 'practised on the human or animal body' if its performance implies any interaction with the human or animal body, necessitating the presence of the latter."

In T 1255/06 *EXERGEN CORP/Radiation detector*, the relevant claim related to a method of determining ear temperature. The Board held that such a method was not a diagnostic method in the sense of EPC art.53(c) because it did not include features relating to "the diagnosis for curative purposes stricto sensu representing the deductive medical or veterinary decision phase as a purely intellectual exercise", as required by G 1/04 *CYGNUS/Diagnostic methods*. In contrast, the claimed method was a method of data acquisition, despite that such data acquisition could lead to the detection of a deviation from normal values, since it did not allow the attribution of a detected deviation to a particular clinical picture.

The Swiss Supreme Court has held, under a statutory provision analogous to subs.(1), that a particular procedure for monitoring, recording and transmitting electro-cardiographic data from a patient is unpatentable as a method of diagnosis because the procedure has no purpose other than for the diagnosis and for the conclusions to be drawn from it by the physician (*AEK v Federal Patent Office* [Switzerland] (1984) 15 I.I.C. 82).

—Patents for the first medical indication (subs.(3))

Subsections 4A(3) and (4) are concerned with the patentability of inventions consisting of a known substance or composition for use in a method of treatment or diagnosis and correspond to the new provisions of art.54(4) and (5) of the EPC which came into effect with the 2000 revision of the EPC.   **4A.08**

Subsection (3), which replaces former s.2(6), corresponds to, but is worded differently from, art.54(4) of the EPC; it is complementary to subss.(1) and (2) and allows a use-bound substance claim "if the use of the substance or composition in any such method does not form part of the state of the art".

The EPO has held that, provided the state of the art presents no restricting matter, the special form of claim permitted by former art.54(5) of the EPC (which corresponds the new EPC art.54(4) and to subs.(3)) can be expressed broadly, e.g. as "Derivatives of formula X for use as an active pharmaceutical substance" (T 128/82 *HOFFMANN-LA ROCHE/Pyrrolidine-derivatives* OJ EPO 1984, 164, and EPO Guideline C–IV, 4.8. Also, the EPO has held that the special form of claim permitted by former art.54(5) of the EPC may be directed to a "substance" or to a "composition" and, consequently, that this type of claim may be used when the "composition" consists of two components present "as a combined preparation for simultaneous, separate or sequential use in therapy", that is as a kit-of-parts, the word "composition" being interpreted as including a "combination" or "aggregate" (T 9/81 *ASTA/Cytostatic combination* OJ EPO 1983, 372). However, in *National Research Development Corp's Application* BL O/117/85, noted I.P.D. 9047, the Comptroller declined to permit a claim to a novel diagnostic use of a known diagnostic apparatus under former s.2(6) (now subs.(3)) holding this to be limited by its wording to "substances or compositions".

There is doubt as to when a use of a substance or composition in a method of treatment is to be taken to form part of the state of the art. It appears that the publication of laboratory tests results on animals might amount to such a disclosure when these tests establish a first medical or veterinary use. A mere paper allegation of a medical use (as contrasted with mere statements about pharmacological activity) in a patent specification relating to an invention which has nevertheless never been put into practice may amount to such a disclosure, and the substance or composition need not have actually been used for one of these purposes. However, according to the MOPP (para.4A.25), a prior disclosure of the possibility of use of a substance for a therapeutic, surgical or diagnostic purpose does not amount to disclosure of a "use" which would prevent a "purpose-bound" substance claim from being allowed under the subsection. The EPO disregards an alleged first indication if it is proved wrong or too general, for example a mere disclosure of the substance being "a medicament", see, for example, T 7/86 *DRACO/Xanthines* OJ EPO 1988, 381; [1989] E.P.O.R. 65 where an exemplified compound of a class, stated as such to have a diuretic action, was not regarded as itself having been disclosed thereby for use in a therapeutic method. See also §,4A.09 below.

Subsection (3) of itself provides no relaxation in the case of second or subsequent medical and veterinary applications of the substance or composition. Thus, in *Sopharma's Application* [1983] R.P.C. 195, and in *Bayer's (Meyer's) Application* [1984] R.P.C. 11, also reported as *Hydropyridine (UK)* OJ EPO 1984, 233, both approved by the Patents Court in *John Wyeth's and Schering's Applications* [1985] R.P.C. 545, former s.2(6) (now subs.(3)) was held to have the effect as if the end of it read:

> "…shall not prevent the invention from being taken to be new if the use of the substance or composition in any [method of treatment of the human or animal body by surgery, therapy or of diagnosis practised on the human or animal body] does not form part of the state of the art".

As explained in *John Wyeth's and Schering's Applications* (above), the position would have been different had the word "any" been omitted in subs.(6).

However, as discussed in §4A.09, second and subsequent medical and veterinary applications can now be protected by claims in the form "for use in the treatment of disease Y", or for earlier applications by means of the "Swiss form" of claim bearing in mind the decision in G 2/08 *ABBOTT RESPIRATORY/Dosage regime*. It should also be noted that subs.(3) applies only if the substance or composition in question lacks novelty per se. In view of the difficulty of establishing this under the tests applied in the *General Tire* case (discussed at §2.19); and, since bare novelty will often suffice because of an inventive step arising from the discovery of the previously unknown and unpredictable treatment provided by the new use for the previously known compound or substance, in many instances it may be possible to avoid questions of a second medical or veterinary use by appropriate drafting of claims to novel compositions as such, or as an allowable selection from a class of known compositions, for which see §2.24. The EPO has ruled that novelty is not imparted to a claim to a pharmaceutical composition merely by stating that this is a "contraceptive composition" (T 303/90 and T 401/90 (both Unreported)). A claim in the "Swiss form" (discussed in §2.17) would seem to be necessary in such cases.

A claim to a substance or composition for use in a method of treatment or diagnosis is to be construed as restricted to the substance or composition when presented or packaged for the special use (in contrast to the general position under EPO Guideline C–III, 4.13, for which see §2.23). Such claims will then be infringed under s.60(1) by the sale of packaged medicaments bearing or containing indications for the new medicinal use. As noted in *Actavis v Merck* [2008] R.P.C. 26, manufacturers, particularly for prescription medicines and probably many others, have to provide detailed instructions about the use(s) and dosage(s) of their product, generally in the form of a patient information leaflet, which is supplied with the product when sold. In practice, therefore, it is usually possible to establish that someone has used X in a medicament for treatment of Y. The patient information leaflet will have to say what diseases are to be treated with the product. If the compound or substance is sold without such indication, infringement may nevertheless arise under s.60(2), subject to s.60(3), see §§60.07–60.10.

—Patents for the protection of the second (or further) medical indications

4A.09   Section 4A(4) now specifically enables patent protection to be obtained for the second or further use of a substance or composition in a method or of treatment or diagnosis by a claim in the form "Substance X for use in the treatment of disease Y." The second or further use of a known substance or composition in a method of treatment or diagnosis is taken to be new if that "specific" use does not form part of the state of the art. Prior to the EPC 2000, a second or further medical indication was only patentable using the "Swiss form" claim, see §4A.10.

Following the decision of the Enlarged Board of Appeal in G 2/08 *ABBOTT RESPIRATORY/Dosage regime*, the "Swiss form" of claim will no longer be allowable. The subject-matter claimed in the referred case was in "Swiss-form" and related to nicotinic acid for the manufacture of a sustained release medicament for treatment of hyperlipidaemia once per day prior to sleep. The question before the Enlarged Board was whether such claims were patentable where the only novelty was in the dosage regime.

The Enlarged Board held that the provisions of EPC art.53(c) were clear and unambiguous, drawing a borderline between method claims directed to a therapeutic treatment which were forbidden in order to permit a physician to act unfettered and claims to products for use in such methods which were allowable if novel and inventive. EPC art.54(5) now expressly allowed further patent protection for second medical uses of substances or compositions and filled a lacuna which had previously been filled by the decision of the Enlarged Board in G 5/83 *EISAI/Second medical indication* [1979–85] E.P.O.R. B241. The new use need not be for the treatment of a further disease. It was well-established in case law under EPC 1973 that patents could be granted for (a) a new group of subjects (T 19/86 *DUPHAR/Pigs II* [1988] E.P.O.R. 10; T 893/90 *QUEEN'S UNIVERSITY KINGSTON/Controlling bleeding*; and T 233/96 *MEDCO RESEARCH/Adrenaline*, (b) a new routine or mode of administration (T 51/93 *SERONO/HCG*; T 138/95 *GENENTECH/Intrapulmonary delivery*, and (c) a different technical effect leading to a truly new application (T 290/86 *ICI/Cleaning plaque* [1991] E.P.O.R. 157; T 254/93 *ORTHO PHARMACEUTICAL/Prevention of skin atrophy* [1999] E.P.O.R. 1; and T 1020/03 *GENENTECH INC/Method of administration of IGF-I* [2006] E.P.O.R. 9). The Enlarged Board concluded that the legislators wished to maintain the status quo as regards the availability of protection for further therapeutic uses. There was no reason to apply a different treatment to a new dosage regime compared to any other specific new use provided that a new effect was achieved.

Owing to the praetorian approach in decision in G 5/83 *EISAI/Second medical indication*, and because the need for that approach had ended when the loophole in EPC 1973 had been closed, it was decided that Swiss-type claims should no longer be allowable. The Board set a time limit of three months after the publication of the decision in the Official Journal of the EPO in order that future applications comply with this provision by converting their claims to purpose-limited product claims of the form "Substance X for use in the treatment of disease Y", and for these applications the relevant date will be their filing date or, if priority has been claimed, their priority date. G 2/08 was published in the OJ EPO on 28 October 28, 2010. However, the decision in G 2/08 in relation to the allowability of the "Swiss form" of claim has no retroactive effect in the EPO and so claims of this form will continue to be allowable, alongside the simpler claim form, for applications having a filing (or priority) date of January 28, 2011 or earlier.

In contrast, the UK-IPO has issued a practice notice (dated May 26, 2010) indicating that the decision of the EBA in G 2/08 *ABBOTT RESPIRATORY/Dosage regime* will have an immediate effect in the United Kingdom for pre-grant applications in that all Swiss-type claims will be objected to as lacking clarity. Amendment of a patent application to replace a Swiss-type claim with the new form of second medical use claim will be allowed. For granted patents, there is no change in practice and a request to make a post-grant amendment to replace Swiss-type claims with the new form of second medical use claim is unlikely to succeed.

The Board in G 2/08 also confirmed that the Swiss form of claim and the direct form of claim are viewed as being the same scope and therefore no further protection is afforded by subs.(4) than was previously available. Accordingly, the case law concerning Swiss form claims (see §4A.10) is likely to apply equally to the simpler form of second medical use claims. However, Sterckx and Cockbain argue in their article "Purpose-limited pharmaceutical product claims under the revised EPC 2000" [2010] I.P.Q. 1, 88, that the change in the law relating to protection for second and subsequent medical indications under EPC 2000 does in fact result in a change in the scope of protection provided by such patents.

— "Swiss form" second medical use claims

4A.10   Following the decision of the Enlarged Board of Appeal in G 2/08 *ABBOTT RESPIRATORY/Dosage regime*, the "Swiss form" of claim will no longer be allowable (see §4A.09). The case law discussed in this section in relation to "Swiss form" claims is relevant to the simpler form of claim now allowed.

A claim of the form "Use of X in the treatment of disease Y" was upheld by the German Supreme Court on the basis that it was the industrially applicable aspects of such a claim that would be asserted and that the protection it gives goes beyond that of mere treatment (*Hydropyridine* [Germany] OJ EPO 1984, 26). However, the corresponding case in the EPO, together with seven similar cases, was referred to the EPO Enlarged Board of Appeal who held that a "use for medical treatment" form of claim could not, at least at that time, be permitted under the EPC (G 5/83 *EISAI/Second Medical Indication*). Previously, the same view had been expressed by the Comptroller in *Sopharma's Application* [1983] R.P.C. 185 and *Bayer's (Meyer's) Application* [1984] R.P.C. 11 also reported as *Hydropyridine (UK)* OJ EPO 1984, 233. Subsequently, the Patents Court, in *John Wyeth's and Schering's Applications* [1985] R.P.C. 545, also expressed its agreement with the Comptroller's view and expressed the opinion that the German Supreme Court's *Hydropyridine* decision appeared to be based on earlier German national case law.

However, the Enlarged Board in G 5/83 *EISAI/Second Medical Indication* stated that, having made a full study:

"no intention to exclude second (and further) medical indications from patent protection can be deduced from the terms of the EPC or its legislative history".

It then decided to permit claims directed to the use of a substance (or composition) for the manufacture of a medicament for a specified new and inventive therapeutic application. In doing so, the EPO Enlarged Board followed a precedent set by the Swiss Patent Office (*Second Medical Indication—Switzerland* OJ EPO 1984, 581) and indicated that a claim in the form: "Use of X for the manufacture of a medicament for treatment of Y" (now called the "Swiss form" of claim) should not be held to be deprived of novelty merely because some therapeutic use of the medicament was already known, stating that:

"It seems appropriate to take a special view of the concept of the 'state of the art' defined in EPC a. 54(2), though only in the case of inventions which fall within the terms of the first sentence of [former] EPC a. 52(4)" (now EPC art.53(c) and corresponding to s.4A(1))

These decisions were reviewed and discussed by I. B. de Minvielle-Devaux (1984–85) 14 *CIPA* 221; A. W. White [1985] E.I.P.R. 62; and R. Teschemacher (1988) 19 I.I.C. 18, and see particularly P. W. Grubb *Patents for Chemicals, Pharmaceuticals and Biotechnology* 5th edn (Oxford University Press, 2010) and "Examination Guidelines for Patent Applications relating to Medical Inventions in the UK Intellectual Property Office" available online from the Patent Office website at *http://www.ipo.gov.uk*.

In *John Wyeth's and Schering's Applications* (above), the Patents Court, sitting *en banc*, then specifically followed G 5/83 *EISAI/Second Medical Indication*. In doing so the court indicated that the Swiss form of claim would have lacked novelty under the 1949 Act having regard to the decision in *Adhesive Dry Mounting v Trapp* (1910) 27 R.P.C. 341 (for which see §2.23) and that, but for the EPO decision, the better view under the 1977 Act would be that the Swiss form of claim lacked novelty. However, taking judicial notice under s.91(1) of the EPO decision and acting in conformity with it, the court held that, in the special circumstances of an inventive discovery which would not otherwise be patentable because of s.4(2), a claim in this form would not lack novelty. G 5/83 *EISAI/Second Medical Indication* has been followed in Sweden *Hydropyridine* [Sweden] (1988) 19 I.I.C. 815) and in New Zealand (*Pharmaceutical Management v Commissioner of Patents* [New Zealand] [1999] R.P.C. 752 upheld on appeal (see (2000) 46 I.P.R. 655; [2000] 2 N.Z.L.R. 529; [2000] R.P.C. 857, noted [2000] E.I.P.R. N–34), discussed by C. Elliott and

Jane Calvert *Patent World* No.120, March 2000, 7 and by G. Arthur [2000] E.I.P.R. 380, but in the Netherlands the Patent Office held that such a claim in a Dutch national patent does not meet the requirements of novelty and inventiveness (*Second medical use/NL* OJ EPO 1988, 405). However, all these prior decisions are now superseded or confirmed by the EPC 2000 revisions which should put the patentability of medical use claims under the EPC beyond doubt.

The EPO Enlarged Board of Appeal subsequently expanded on the principle first expounded in G 5/83 *EISAI/Second Medical Indication* so that mere novelty of purpose was held to confer patentability on a claim whatever the field of the invention, see G 2/88 *MOBIL III/Friction reducing additive* OJ EPO 1990, 93 and 469; [1990] E.P.O.R. 73 discussed in §2.08 and §2.23 and at (1989–90) 19 *CIPA* 111 and 171. Thus, the Swiss form of claim for inventions of a further medical indication seems no longer to be a special case, and it would appear that, if G 2/88 *MOBIL III/Friction reducing additive* is accepted into the patent law of the United Kingdom, then, even outside the special situation of the further medical indication, s.2 should no longer operate, as did the law of novelty under the 1949 Act, to deny novelty to a claim where the sole statement of novelty is a mere indication of purpose for which the article or method is to be put. However, the English Courts have so far been able to avoid directly addressing this issue, see particularly *Merrell Dow v Norton* [1994] R.P.C. 1; [1995] R.P.C. 233 CA; and [1996] R.P.C. 77 HL where the House of Lords stated that G 2/88 *MOBIL III/Friction reducing additive* makes it difficult to apply "the traditional United Kingdom doctrine of infringement" under which infringement is absolute, i.e. independent of knowledge or intention, but that the case before it did not require further discussion of this aspect of that decision.

The EPO has tended, in applying G 5/83 *EISAI/Second Medical Indication* (above), to grant patents by adopting a very narrow view of lack of novelty of claims presented in the "Swiss form". Thus in T 289/84 *WELLCOME/3-Amino-pyrazoline derivatives*, the prior description of a pharmaceutical composition for systemic application was held not to anticipate a composition "adapted for only topical, to the exclusion of oral and injectable, administration". The EPO has also held the same treatment for the same ailment to be novel when applied to a new class of pigs (T 19/86 *DUPHAR/Pigs II*). Similarly, in T 584/88 *REICHART/Anti-snoring means*, a claim in the "Swiss form" was allowed covering the manufacture of an agent for the therapeutic treatment of snoring containing a substance defined (apparently very broadly) solely by its mode of action and with a disclaimer to substances acting according to the prior art, see also §4A.04. Claims in the Swiss form have also been allowed when the sole point of novelty was the mode of drug administration (T 51/93 (Unreported)) and also where novelty resided only in the frequency of drug administration (T 570/92 (Unreported)); and see the further discussion on *Bristol-Myers Squibb v Baker Norton* [1999] R.P.C. 253 and *Actavis v Merck* [2008] R.P.C. 26; [2008] EWCA Civ 444 below.

These decisions were confirmed by the Enlarged Board in G 2/08 where it was indicated that second medical use claims, which derive notional novelty from the intended therapeutic use, are not limited to new therapeutic indications (see also §4A.09). The Board confirmed the approach taken in decision T 1020/03 *GENENTECH INC/Method of administration* of IGF-1 OJ EPO 2007, 204, where the Board stated:

> ". . .there was a seamless fit, either a method of using a composition is not a treatment by therapy and therefore falls outside the provision of Article 52(4) EPC [1973] first sentence, and so is patentable subject to compliance with the other provisions of the EPC, or else a method is a treatment by therapy and therefore inside the provision of Article 52(4) EPC [1973] first sentence, and so not itself patentable, but use of a composition for making a medicament for use in such treatment by therapy is patentable for unspecified therapy as a first medical indication or for a specified therapy as a further medical indication, again subject to compliance with the other provisions of the EPC, particularly novelty and inventive step."

The Board in G 2/08 proceeded to answer the first 2 questions referred to them as follows:

"Question 1:
Where it is already known to use a medicament to treat an illness, Article 54(5) EPC does not exclude that this medicament be patented for use in a different treatment by therapy of the same illness.
Question 2:
Such patenting is also not excluded where a dosage regime is the only feature claimed which is not comprised in the state of the art."

This decision reviews many of the earlier EPO decisions relating to Swiss form claims. For example, T 1020/03 *GENENTECH/Method of administration of IFG-I* stated that a novel dosage regime can confer novelty to a Swiss form claim in a detailed decision which itself reviewed many of the earlier EPO decisions relating to Swiss form claims, identifying in particular decisions T 317/95 PROCTER & GAMBLE/Gastrointestinal compositions [1999] E.P.O.R. 528; T 56/97 *EURO-CELTIQUE/Thiazide diuretics*; T 584/97 *ELAN CORPORATION/Use of nicotine*; T 4/98 *SEQUUS/Liposome composition* [2002] E.P.O.R. 371; and T 485/99 *NOVARTIS/Method of improving the immune response* as conflicting with G 5/83 *EISAI/Second Medical Indication*. On the other hand, the Board apparently approved decisions T 51/93; T 19/86 D*UPHAR/Pigs II*; T 893/90; and T 290/86 *ICI/ Cleaning plaque* (see above) as well as T 836/01 *YEDA RESEARCH AND DEVELOP-MENT CO. LTD/Interferon-beta2*, concluding at [72] that:

"the Board interprets decision G 0005/83 as allowing Swiss form claims directed to the use of a composition for manufacture of a medicament for a specified new and inventive therapeutic application, where the novelty of the application might lie only in the dose to be used or the manner of application. This Board allowed such a claim, where only the manner of application was new, already eleven years ago in T 0051/93 of 8 June 1994. The discussion in decision G 0005/83 concerning further medical indications did indeed refer to use for treating a new illness. But the Board regards this significant only of the fact that most further medical use claims will refer to a new illness, as in that case novelty and inventive step are more likely to exist than in the case of a minor modification of the treatment known for an existing illness. The logic of decision G 0005/83 allowing claims to further medical uses of known compositions, seems equally applicable to any use of such known composition for a new and inventive treatment which cannot be claimed as such because of Article 54(4) EPC first sentence."

The Board also referred to the UK Court of Appeal decision in *Bristol-Myers Squibb v Baker Norton* (see below), noting that in spite of s.130, the wording of s.4(2) and (3), as they then were, had "substantially different wording" from the provisions of [former] art.52(4) of the EPC and commented that its interpretation of [former] art.52(4) of the EPC and of G 5/83 *EISAI/Second Medical Indication*, would have appeared to it much more problematic if [former] EPC art.52(4) had been worded, in all official languages, to correspond exactly to the wording of [former] s.4(2) and (3) of the UK Patents Act.

More recently, the Board in T 1127/05 *SCRIPPS RESEARCH INSTITUTE/Inhibition of angiogenesis*, considered the allowability of a claim to the use of specified αVβ3 antagonists for inhibiting αVβ3-angiogenesis. The specified compounds were known per se, as was their use in inhibiting (αVβ5-mediated) angiogenesis. Based on the evidence, the Board concluded that αVβ3- and αVβ5-mediated angiogenesis were associated with different diseases. Consequently the inhibition of αVβ3-mediated angiogenesis by the specified compounds is a novel "specific use" in the sense of art.54(5) EPC, as compared to their use in the inhibition of angiogenesis in general or the inhibition of αVβ5-mediated angiogenesis.

In T 1286/05 *R.P. SCHERER TECHNOLOGIES, INC./Use of a lipophilic surfactant*, the Board held that if a claim drawn up as a "Swiss-type" claim in fact relates to a further non-therapeutic use, then the feature defining the non-therapeutic use is of a merely illustrative character and, as a consequence, not suitable for establishing novelty. Thus, claims to "reducing the inhibitory effect of . . . [a] component on the in vivo lipolysis of . . . oil" and to "increasing the bioavailability of . . . [a] drug by substantially reducing the inhibitory effect of . . . [a] component on the *in vivo* lipolysis of . . . oil" were found to lack novelty.

In T 406/06 *NOVO NORDISK/Stimulation of beta cell proliferation*, the Board considered a "Swiss-type" claim in which the only novel feature was the mechanism of treatment of diabetes—by "stimulating beta-cell proliferation", it having been acknowledged that the prior art disclosed the specified compounds for treating diabetes. The Board held that the new effect could not reflect a new therapeutic use, and further that the new technical effect could not render the claim novel. However, in T 1642/06 *SPRUCE/Sigma Receptor*, the Board held that a novel effect could reflect a new therapeutic use where the effect identifies a new clinical situation (here targeting tumour vasculature rather than the cancer cells themselves).

The "Swiss form" of claim can also be directed to a "method" or "process" for making a medicament from X for treatment of disease Y (T 958/94 *THERAPEUTIQUES SUBSTITUTIVES/Anti-tumoral agent* OJ EPO 1997, 241; [1997] E.P.O.R. 417), but this decision was criticised by T. Beetz, *epi Information*, 4/1997 120; and, in T 655/92 *NYCOMED/Contrast agent for imaging*, it was stated that the "Swiss type" of claim is only permitted if the method of use of the substance or composition is one of those excluded from patentability under EPC art.52(4). A claim in the "Swiss form" is apparently acceptable even though no other medicinal use of the active compound or composition has been shown (T 143/94 *MAI/Trigonelline* OJ EPO 1996, 430; [1996] E.P.O.R. 613). However, subsequently, in T 1758/07 *HANKKIJA/Food additive*, it was held that if the claimed subject-matter relates to a first medical indication, G 1/83 *EISAI/Second medical indication* provides no legal basis to additionally claim the same subject-matter in terms of a second medical indication. Claims were allowed to a feed additive for the prevention of intestinal diseases and gastric disorders characterised by a particular preparative method, the feed additive belonging to the state of the art, but its use for a therapeutic treatment being novel, so that protection under EPC 1973 art.52(4) was available.

The scope and effect of this form of "purpose-bound process claim", or "utility-based use claim", is the subject of the papers by J. Utermann (1986) 17 I.I.C. 41; and B. Hansen (1988) 19 I.I.C. 272. Obviously, if mere novelty of purpose has to be recognised as an essential element of novelty in a claim, as in the "Swiss form" of claim, that claim should not be held to be infringed unless the alleged infringing act embraces, or is intended to embrace, that purpose, see §14.33 and §125.24. Indeed, in *Bristol-Myers Squibb v Baker Norton* [1999] R.P.C. 253, a plea was made for G 2/88 *MOBIL III/Friction reducing additive* to be re-visited in an infringement context, see §91.03, but on appeal (see [2001] R.P.C. 1 at 17), G 2/88 *MOBIL III/Friction reducing additive* was seen to differ from a "Swiss form" of claim and to be based on a particular purposive construction of claim.

In this *Bristol-Myers Squibb* case, the claim in issue was in the form:

"Use of taxol and sufficient medications to prevent severe anaphylactic reactions, for manufacturing a medicamentation for simultaneous, separate or sequential application for the administration of from 135 mg/m2 up to 175 mg/m2 taxol over a period of about 3 hours or less as a means of treating cancer and simultaneously reducing neutropenia."

The prior art was a lecture which had disclosed the ongoing clinical trial of using taxol (with pre-medication) by infusion for either 3 or 12 hours and at two different dose levels. Only interim results from these trials were then reported which indicated that there was efficacy at the lower dosage time and amount, but not that this resulted in reducing the known adverse side effect. Both the Patents Court and the Court of Appeal held that this claim was not a second medical treatment, but one tothe already disclosed treatment to which a new effect had been added, this being "a mere discovery about an old use". The court therefore found a lack of novelty in the claim, following the statement in T 958/90 *DOW/Sequestering agent* [1994] E.P.O.R. 1 that "A known effect cannot become novel for the sole reason that it is present to a hitherto unknown (greater) extent". The Court of

Appeal then went further and held the claim to be invalid also as claiming solely a method of medical treatment, see §4A.03. In this case, the Patents Court expressed the view that T 290/86 *ICI/Cleaning plaque*, was incompatible with this *Dow* decision. In this *Bristol-Myers Squibb* case, satisfaction was expressed by both courts that a similar conclusion had been reached to that found by the Dutch Court of Appeal in *Bristol-Myers Squibb v Yew Tree Pharmaceuticals* [Netherlands] [2000] E.N.P.R. 26. For case comment on the English decision, see Anna McKay, *Patent World*, No.107 (November 1998), 16; and for a general review of "Second Medical Use Claims", see B. Oosting *Patent World*, March 1999, 22.

However, as noted in §4A.03, in *Actavis UK Ltd v Merck & Co Inc* [2008] R.P.C. 26; [2008] EWCA Civ 444, the Court of Appeal chose not to follow *Bristol-Myers Squibb v Baker Norton*. The court also took the view that on the basis of G 5/93 alone Swiss form claims are allowable where the novelty is conferred by a new dosage form or other form of administration of a substance. The court reasoned that that it could depart from the precedent of *Bristol-Myers Squibb v Baker Norton* as that earlier decision was inconsistent with the "settled view" of EPO case lawas set out in T 1020/03 *GENENTECH/Method of administration of IFG-I* and subsequentlyT 36/04 *UNIVERISTY OF TEXAS/DNA damaging agents*; T 292/04 *EXOXEMIS/Haloperoxide*; T 380/05 *PRAECIS/GnRH Antagonists*; T 1074/06 *ARS/Infertility*; T 1399/04 *SCHERING/Combination therapy HCV*; and T 230/01 *SEPRACOR/Descarboxethoxyloratadine*. The court also drew attention to the decision of the German Supreme Court in *Carvedilol II* (2006) I.I.C. Vol.38, 479, which held a Swiss form claim whose novelty depended on a dosage regime to be novel and not a claim to a method of treatment.

In South Africa (*Elan Transdermal v Ciba-Geigy* [South Africa] [1994] B.R. 1), a claim in the Swiss form reading:

"Use of nicotine for the manufacture of a medicament for use in the one daily percutaneous administration of nicotine in a manner for the treatment of withdrawal symptoms associated with smoking cessation, and in which the nicotine is administered in an amount sufficient to maintain plasma levels of nicotine substantially equivalent to trough plasma levels resulting from intimate smoking."

was found valid and infringed.

In *Monsanto v Merck* [2000] R.P.C. 77 CA, a contention that a "Swiss form" of claim could be infringed when the specified compound was formed as an intermediate in the preparation of the active ingredient of the medicament supplied by the defendant was held not to be unarguable, but the argument failed at full trial (*Monsanto v Merck* [2000] R.P.C. 77). Likewise, in *American Home Products v Novartis* [2000] R.P.C. 547; and [2001] R.P.C. 159 CA, the Court of Appeal held that the claim (reprinted above) was not infringed by the use of a rapamycin derivative containing 8 per cent of unreacted rapamycin: such could not be regarded as use of rapamycin "as a medicament".

Advance Biofactures' Application BL O/303/04, illustrates some of the factors which might, exceptionally, lead to a new dosage form being considered both novel and inventive. The active agent was present at substantially higher concentration than the prior art, and it was impossible in practice to deliver the required dose with the prior art solutions. A Swiss-type claim was allowed covering use of a quantity of collegenase within a specified range in a pharmaceutically acceptable carrier and within a specified concentration range in the manufacture of a medicament for treating Peyronie's disease. The hearing officer took the view that the person skilled in the art would have considered this higher concentration to have unacceptable side effects, and the concentrated composition was successful in treating a group of patients who did not benefit from treatment with the prior art compositions.

—Patents for pharmaceutical packs

4A.11   An alternative approach to attempting to protect medical uses of known compounds has been to try to claim a pack comprising a pharmaceutical preparation associated with instructions for its (new and inventive) manner of use on the basis that this should be regarded as an appropriate claim directed to s.60(2), and not as merely a disguised claim to a method of treatment. However, the EPO made it clear that pharmaceutical use claims are regarded as claims to a method of therapeutic treatment and, therefore, are as such not allowable (EPO Guidelines C–III, 4.8 and C–IV, 4.8). Likewise, in *Bayer's (Meyer's) Application* [1984] R.P.C. 11 also reported as *Hydropyridine* [UK] OJ EPO 1984, 233, a claim to a package containing a known drug together with instructions for a new use were not allowed because the inventive step set out in the claim resided in the information given in the instructions, and this was the mere presentation of information and accordingly not an invention under s.1(2)(d). This followed unsuccessful attempts to obtain such type of claim under the former system of law, see: *Ciba-Geigy's (Dürr's) Applications* [1977] R.P.C. 83 CA; *Dow Corning's Applications* [1974] R.P.C. 235 Pat Ct; and *Wellcome Foundation's Australian Application* [1981] F.S.R. 72 HC of Australia.

However, a claim to a "pharmaceutical pack" has been accepted by the EPO in circumstances where one component has an interaction on the pharmaceutical effect of the other, even if the components are to be taken separately or sequentially rather than in combination (T 9/81 *ASTA/Cytostatic combination*). There is here an analogy with the claim allowed (under the 1949 Act) in *L'Oréal's Application* [1970] R.P.C. 565 to a two-pack product for permanent hair waving containing two known chemicals each to be used in a manner already known in themselves, in contrast to a card carrying two kinds of pill with printed instructions as to the order in which these should be taken, as in *Organon's Application* [1970] R.P.C. 574, where the two components were, in effect, held not to be interactive. For further discussion of the possibility of patenting a "pharmaceutical pack", see the note by I. B. de Minvielle-Devaux (1983–84) 13 *CIPA* 120.

See also parts of §2.24, Novelty of Purpose, as applied to medical, etc.

SECTION 5

Priority date

5.—(1) For the purposes of this Act the priority date of an invention to which an application for a patent relates and also of any matter (whether or not the same as the invention) contained in any such application is, except as provided by the following provisions of this Act, the date of filing the application.   **5.01**

(2) If in or in connection with an application for a patent (the application in suit) a declaration is made, whether by the applicant or any predecessor in title of his, complying with the relevant requirements of rules and specifying one or more earlier relevant applications for the purposes of this section made by the applicant or a predecessor in title of his and **the application in suit has a date of filing during the period allowed under subsection (2A) (a) or (b) below,** [*each having a date of filing during the period of twelve months immediately preceding the date of filing the application in suit*] then—

(a) if an invention to which the application in suit relates is supported by matter disclosed in the earlier relevant application or applications, the priority date of that invention shall instead of being the date of filing the application in suit be the date of filing the relevant application in which that matter was disclosed, or, if it was disclosed in more than one relevant application, the earliest of them;

(b) the priority date of any matter contained in the application in suit which was also disclosed in the earlier relevant application or applications shall be the date of filing the relevant application in which that matter was disclosed or, if it was disclosed in more than one relevant application, the earliest of them.

(2A) The periods are—

(a) the period of twelve months immediately following the date of filing of the earlier specified relevant application, or if there is more than one, of the earliest of them; and

(b) where the comptroller has given permission under subsection (2B) below for a late declaration to be made under subsection (2) above, the period commencing immediately after the end of the period allowed under paragraph (a) above and ending at the end of the prescribed period.

(2B) The applicant may make a request to the comptroller for permission to make a late declaration under subsection (2) above.

(2C) The comptroller shall grant a request made under subsection (2B) above if, and only if—

(a) the request complies with the relevant requirements of rules; and

(b) the comptroller is satisfied that the applicant's failure to file the application in suit within the period allowed under subsection (2A)(a) above was unintentional.

(3) Where an invention or other matter contained in the application in suit was also disclosed in two earlier relevant applications filed by the same applicant as in the case of the application in suit or a predecessor in title of his and the second of those relevant applications was specified in or in connection with the application in suit, the second of those relevant applications shall, so far as concerns that invention or matter, be disregarded unless—

(a) it was filed in or in respect of the same country as the first; and

(b) not later than the date of filing the second, the first (whether or not so specified) was unconditionally withdrawn, or was abandoned or refused, without—

(i) having been made available to the public (whether in the United Kingdom or elsewhere);

(ii) leaving any rights outstanding; and

(iii) having served to establish a priority date in relation to another application, wherever made.

(4) The foregoing provisions of this section shall apply for determining the priority date of an invention for which a patent has been granted as they apply for determining the priority date of an invention to which an application for that patent relates.

(5) In this section "relevant application" means any of the following applications which has a date of filing, namely—

(a) an application for a patent under this Act;

(b) an application in or for a convention country (specified under section 90 below) for protection in respect of an invention or an application which, in accordance with the law of a convention country or a treaty or international convention to which a convention country is a party, is equivalent to such an application.

(6) References in subsection (5) above to a convention country include

references to a country, other than the United Kingdom, which is a member of the World Trade Organisation.

Notes

1. Section 130(7) requires s.5 to be construed in conformity with the corresponding provisions of the EPC. These are arts 87–89 of the EPC, for which see §§5.02–5.04 below, arts 87 and 88 being set out in the forms as revised by EPC 2000. These revisions took effect on December 13, 2007, the date on which EPC 2000 entered into force.

2. Article 8 of the PCT and art.4 of the Paris Convention are also relevant. The appropriate parts of these are reprinted in §§5.05 and 5.06 below.

3. The amendment to subs.(2) and the insertion of new subss.(2A)–(2C) were made by the Regulatory Reform (Patents) Order 2004 (SI 2004/2357) ("RRO") (art.3) with effect from January 1, 2005. However, as explained in Note 1 to §5.01, the previous version of subs.(2) continues to apply to applications which were pending on that date.

4. Subsection (6) was added by SI 1999/1899 with effect from July 29, 1999 and applied to the Isle of Man by SI 2003/1249 with effect from June 10, 2003.

5. Subsections (1) and (3) of s.130 are also relevant. The term "priority date" is defined in s.130(1) as being the date determined as such under s.5. As regards s.130(3), see §§5.24 and 130.07.

RELEVANT CONVENTION PROVISIONS

EPC Article 87—Priority right

87.—(1) Any person who has duly filed, in or for   **5.02**
  (a) any State party to the Paris Convention for the Protection of Industrial Property or
  (b) any Member of the World Trade Organization,
an application for a patent, a utility model or a utility certificate, or his successor in title, shall enjoy, for the purpose of filing a European patent application in respect of the same invention, a right of priority during a period of 12 months from the date of filing of the first application.

(2) Every filing that is equivalent to a regular national filing under the national law of the State where it was made or under bilateral or multilateral agreements, including this Convention, shall be recognized as giving rise to a right of priority.

(3) A regular national filing shall mean any filing that is sufficient to establish the date on which the application was filed, whatever the outcome of the application may be.

(4) A subsequent application in respect of the same subject matter as a previous first application and filed in or for the same State shall be considered as the first application for the purposes of determining priority, provided that, at the date of filing the subsequent application, the previous application has been withdrawn, abandoned or refused, without being open to public inspection and without leaving any rights outstanding, and has not served as a basis for claiming a right of priority. The previous application may not thereafter serve as a basis for claiming a right of priority.

(5) If the first filing has been made with an industrial property authority which is not subject to the Paris Convention for the Protection of Industrial Property or the Agreement Establishing the World Trade Organization, paragraphs 1 to 4 shall apply if that authority, according to a communication issued by the President of the European Patent Office, recognizes that a first filing made with the European Patent Office gives rise to a right of priority under conditions and with effects equivalent to those laid down in the Paris Convention.

(As amended by the EPC 2000.)

Note. This Article is reprinted in the form into which it was amended by the revisions of the EPC in 2000. These revisions came into effect on December 13, 2007, being the date on which EPC 2000 entered into force. Revised art.87 applies to European patent applications filed on or after EPC 2000 entered into force (see Decision of the EPO Administrative Council of June 28, 2001).

EPC Article 88—Claiming priority

5.03   **88.**—(1) An applicant desiring to take advantage of the priority of a previous application shall file a declaration of priority and any other document required, in accordance with the Implementing Regulations.

(2) Multiple priorities may be claimed in respect of a European patent application, notwithstanding the fact that they originated in different countries. Where appropriate, multiple priorities may be claimed for any one claim. Where multiple priorities are claimed, time limits which run from the date of priority shall run from the earliest date of priority.

(3) If one or more priorities are claimed in respect of a European patent application, the right of priority shall cover only those elements of the European patent application which are included in the application or applications whose priority is claimed.

(4) If certain elements of the invention for which priority is claimed do not appear among the claims formulated in the previous application, priority may nonetheless be granted, provided that the documents of the previous application as a whole specifically disclose such elements.

(As amended by the EPC 2000.)

Note. This Article is reprinted in the form into which it was amended by the revisions of the EPC in 2000. These revisions came into effect on December 13, 2007, being the date on which EPC 2000 entered into force. Revised art.88 applies to European patents granted and European patent applications pending at the time EPC 2000 entered into force as well as European patent applications filed on or after EPC 2000 entered into force (see Decision of the EPO Administrative Council of June 28, 2001).

EPC Article 89—Effect of priority right

5.04   **89.** The right of priority shall have the effect that the date of priority shall count as the date of filing of the European patent application for the purposes of article 54, paragraphs 2 and 3, and article 60, paragraph 2.

PCT Article 8—Claiming priority

5.05   **8.**—(1) The international application may contain a declaration, as prescribed in the regulations, claiming the priority of one or more earlier applications filed in or for any country party to the Paris Convention for the Protection of Industrial Property.

(2)

    (a) Subject to the provisions of subparagraph (b), the conditions for, and the effect of, any priority claim declared under paragraph (1) shall be as provided in article 4 of the Stockholm Act of the Paris Convention for the Protection of Industrial Property.

    (b) The international application for which the priority of one or more earlier applications filed in or for a Contracting State is claimed may contain the designation of that state. Where, in the international application, the priority of one or more national applications filed in or for a designated state is claimed, or where the priority of an international application having designated only one state is claimed, the conditions for, and the effect of, the priority claim in that state shall be governed by the national law of that state.

PARIS CONVENTION (STOCKHOLM REVISION) ARTICLE 4

(as relevant to patents)   **5.06**

A. —

    (1) A person who has duly filed an application for a patent, or for the registration of a utility model, or of an industrial design, or of a trademark, in one of the countries of the Union, or his successors in title, shall enjoy, for the purpose of filing in the other countries, a right of priority during the periods hereinafter stated.

    (2) Every filing that is equivalent to a regular national filing under the domestic law of any country of the Union or under bilateral or multilateral treaties concluded between countries of the Union shall be recognised as giving rise to a right of priority.

    (3) By a regular national filing is meant any filing that is adequate to establish the date on which the application was filed in the country concerned, whatever may be the outcome of the application.

B. —Consequently, the subsequent filing in any of the other countries of the Union before the expiration of those periods shall not be invalidated through any acts accomplished in the interval, as, for instance, by another filing, by publication or exploitation of the invention, ..., and these acts cannot give rise to any right of third parties, or of any personal possession. Rights acquired by third parties before the date of the first application which serves as the basis for the right of priority are reserved under the domestic legislation of each country of the Union.

C. —

    (1) The above-mentioned periods of priority shall be twelve months for patents ... .

    (2) These periods shall start from the date of filing of the first application; the day of filing shall not be included in the period.

    (3) If the last day of the period is an official holiday, or a day when the office is not open for the filing of applications in the country where protection is claimed, the period shall be extended until the first following working day.

    (4) A subsequent application for the same subject as a previous first application within the meaning of paragraph (2) above and filed in the same country of the Union, shall be considered as the first application, of which the filing date shall be the starting point of the period of priority, provided that, at the time of filing the subsequent application, the previous application has been withdrawn, abandoned or refused, without being open to public inspection and without leaving any rights outstanding, and has not served as a basis for claiming a right of priority. The previous application may not thereafter serve as a basis for claiming a right of priority.

D. —

    (1) Any person desiring to take advantage of the priority of a previous filing shall be required to make a declaration indicating the date of such filing and the country in which it was made. Each country will determine the latest permissible date for making such declaration.

    (2) These particulars shall be mentioned in the publications issued by the competent authority, and in particular in the patents and the specifications relating thereto.

(3) The countries of the Union may require any person making a declaration of priority to produce a copy of the application (specification, drawings, etc.) previously filed. The copy, certified as correct by the authority which received the application, shall not require any authentication, and may in any case be filed, without fee, at any time within three months of the filing of the subsequent application. They may require it to be accompanied by a certificate from the same authority showing the date of filing, and by a translation.

(4) No other formalities may be required for the declaration of priority at the time of filing the application. Each of the countries of the Union shall decide what consequences shall follow the omission of the formalities prescribed by the present article, but such consequences shall in no case go beyond the loss of the right of priority.

(5) Subsequently, further proof may be required.

A person who avails himself of the priority of a previously filed application shall be required to specify the number of that application, which shall be published under the conditions provided for by paragraph (2) above.

E. —...

F. —No country of the Union may refuse a priority or a patent application on the ground that the applicant claims multiple priorities, even originating in different countries, or on the ground that an application claiming one or more priorities contains one or more elements that were not included in the original application or applications whose priority is claimed, provided that, in both cases, there is unity of invention within the meaning of the law of the country.

With respect to the elements not included in the original application or applications whose priority is claimed, the filing of the later application shall give rise to a right of priority under the usual conditions.

G. —

(1) If examination reveals that an application for a patent contains more than one invention, the applicant may divide the application into a certain number of divisional applications and preserve as the date of each the date of the initial application and the benefit of the right of priority, if any.

(2) The applicant may also, on his own initiative, divide a patent application and preserve as the date of each divisional application, the date of the initial application and the benefit of the right of priority, if any. Each country of the Union shall have the right to determine the conditions under which such division shall be authorised.

H. —Priority may not be refused on the ground that certain elements of the invention for which priority is claimed do not appear among the claims formulated in the application in the country of origin, provided that the application documents as a whole specifically disclose such elements.

I. —...

RELEVANT RULES—RULES 3 AND 6–9

Rule 3—The declared priority date

5.06A **3.**—(1) For the purposes of these Rules the "declared priority date" is the date of filing of the earliest relevant application specified in a declaration made for the purposes of section 5(2) in, or in connection with, an application in suit.

(2) For the purposes of these Rules there is "no declared priority date" if—

(a) no declaration has been made for the purposes of section 5(2); or

(b) every declaration made has been withdrawn or disregarded before the end of the relevant period.

(3) For the purposes of paragraph (2)(b) the relevant period ends—

(a) in the case of an application which falls to be treated as an application for a patent under the Act by virtue of a direction under section 81, when that direction is given;

(b) in the case of an international application for a patent (UK), when the national phase of the application begins; or

(c) in any other case, when preparations for the application's publication have been completed by the Patent Office.

(4) In this rule references to declarations made for the purposes of section 5(2) include declarations treated as made for those purposes.

Rule 6—Declaration of priority for the purposes of section 5(2) (priority date)

6.—(1) Subject to paragraph (2) and rule 7(9), a declaration for the purposes of **5.07** section 5(2) must be made at the time of filing the application for a patent.

(2) Subject to rule 7(9), a declaration for the purposes of section 5(2) may be made after the date of filing provided that—

(a) it is made on Patents Form 3;

(b) it is made before the end of the period of sixteen months beginning immediately following the date of filing of the earlier relevant application (or if there is more than one, the earliest of them) specified in that, or any earlier, declaration; and

(c) the condition in paragraph (3) is met.

(3) The condition is that—

(a) the applicant has not made a request under section 16(1) for publication of the application during the period prescribed for the purposes of that section; or

(b) any request made was withdrawn before preparations for the application's publication have been completed by the Patent Office.

(4) A declaration for the purposes of section 5(2) must specify—

(a) the date of filing of each earlier relevant application; and

(b) the country it was filed in or in respect of.

(5) In the case of a new application filed as mentioned in section 15(9), no declaration shall be made which has not also been made in, or in connection with, the earlier application.

Note. This rule came into force on December 17, 2007 (s.1 of the Patents Rules 2007, SI 2007/3291). Paragraph 5(3) of the transitional provisions in sch.5 to the Patents Rules 2007 provides that r.6(2) and (3) (declaration of priority made after date of filing) does not apply to applications made before January 1, 2005, being the commencement date of the amendments introduced to s.5 by the RRO.

Rule 7—Request to the comptroller for permission to make a late declaration under section 5(2B)

7.—(1) The period prescribed for the purposes of section 5(2A)(b) is two **5.08** months.

(2) Subject to paragraph (4), a request under section 5(2B) must be—

(a) made on Patents Form 3; and

(b) supported by evidence of why the application in suit was not filed before the end of the period allowed under section 5(2A)(a).

(3) Where that evidence does not accompany the request, the comptroller must specify a period within which the evidence must be filed.

(4) In relation to a new application, a request under section 5(2B) may be made in writing, instead of on Patents Form 3, and no evidence shall accompany it.

(5) Subject to paragraph (6) and rule 66(3), a request under section 5(2B) may only be made before the end of the period allowed under section 5(2A)(b).

(6) Where a new application is filed after the end of the period allowed under section 5(2A)(b), a request under section 5(2B) may be made on the initiation date.

(7) A request under section 5(2B) may only be made where—

    (a) the condition in paragraph (8) is met; or

    (b) the request is made in relation to an international application for a patent (UK).

(8) The condition is that—

    (a) the applicant has not made a request under section 16(1) for publication of the application during the period prescribed for the purposes of that section; or

    (b) any request made was withdrawn before preparations for the application's publication have been completed by the Patent Office.

(9) Where an applicant makes a request under section 5(2B), he must make the declaration for the purposes of section 5(2) at the same time as making that request.

Note. This rule came into force on December 17, 2007 (s.1 of the Patents Rules 2007, SI 2007/3291). Paragraph 5(3) of the transitional provisions in sch.5 to the Patents Rules 2007 provides that r.7 (permission to make late declaration under s.5(2B)) does not apply to applications made before January 1, 2005, being the commencement date of the amendments introduced to s.5 by the RRO.

Rule 8—Filing of priority documents to support a declaration under section 5(2)

5.09
    8.—(1) In respect of each priority application to which this paragraph applies the applicant must, before the end of the relevant period, furnish to the comptroller the application number of that application; otherwise the comptroller must disregard the declaration made for the purposes of section 5(2), in so far as it relates to the priority application.

(2) In respect of each priority application to which this paragraph applies the applicant must, before the end of the relevant period, furnish to the comptroller a copy of that application—

    (a) duly certified by the authority with which it was filed; or

    (b) otherwise verified to the satisfaction of the comptroller,

otherwise the comptroller must disregard the declaration made for the purposes of section 5(2), in so far as it relates to the priority application.

(3) Paragraph (1) applies to every priority application except where the application in suit is an international application for a patent (UK) and the application number of the priority application was indicated in compliance with the Patent Co-operation Treaty.

(4) Paragraph (2) applies to every priority application except where—

    (a) the application in suit is an international application for a patent (UK) and a certified copy of the priority application was filed in compliance with the Patent Co-operation Treaty; or

(b) the priority application or a copy of the priority application is available to the comptroller.

(5) For the purposes of this rule the relevant period is sixteen months beginning [with] immediately after the declared priority date, subject to rule 21.

Note. This rule came into force on December 17, 2007 (s.1 of the Patents Rules 2007, SI 2007/3291), while the amendment to r.8(5) came into force on October 1, 2011 as a result of The Patents (Amendment) Rules 2011 (SI 2011/2052).

Rule 9—Translation of priority documents

9.—(1) The comptroller may direct the applicant to comply with the require- **5.10**
ments of paragraph (4), if—

    (a) a copy of the priority application has been—
        (i) furnished in accordance with rule 8(2),
        (ii) filed in compliance with the European Patent Convention,
        (iii) filed in compliance with the Patent Co-operation Treaty, or
        (iv) made by the comptroller in accordance with rule 112(2);
    (b) that copy is in a language other than English or Welsh; and
    (c) the matters disclosed in the priority application are relevant to the determination of whether or not an invention, to which the application in suit relates, is new or involves an inventive step.

(2) In his direction under paragraph (1), the comptroller shall specify a period within which the applicant must comply with the requirements of paragraph (4).

(3) But the comptroller shall not specify a period that ends after the grant of the patent.

(4) Where the comptroller has given a direction under paragraph (1), the applicant must, before the end of the period specified by the comptroller, file—

    (a) an English translation of the priority application; or
    (b) a declaration that the application in suit is a complete translation into English of the priority application,

otherwise the comptroller must disregard the declaration made for the purposes of section 5(2), in so far as it relates to the priority application.

Note. This rule came into force on December 17, 2007 (s.1 of the Patents Rules 2007, SI 2007/3291).

COMMENTARY ON SECTION 5

Scope of the section

Sections 5 and 6 are concerned with priority, one of the fundamental concepts in patent **5.11**
law. Priority dates are provided for by s.5: the term "priority date" is defined in s.130(1) as "the date determined as such under section 5". While s.5 determines the priority date of an application, it says nothing about the effect of that date when determined. Section 6 provides that an application (and any patent granted from it) is not to be invalidated by "relevant intervening acts", see §§6.01–6.04.

Sections 5 and 6 are, primarily, intended to reflect the principles enshrined in art.4 of the Paris Convention (Stockholm revision), see §5.06, above. These sections (by virtue of s.130(7)) are also intended to conform with corresponding provisions of the EPC, CPC and PCT (in particular, s.5 broadly reflects arts 87, 88 and 89 of the EPC, see §§5.02–5.04, above), a subject which is discussed in §5.13.

Section 5 was amended by the RRO, which came into force on January 1, 2005, to incorporate the principles of art.13 of the Patent Law Treaty ("PLT"). The amended section applies to applications made on or after January 1, 2005; for earlier applications, the provisions of s.5 prior to this Order coming into force apply.

The right of priority is generally regarded as one of the cornerstones of the Paris Convention, originally signed in 1883. Its basic purpose is to safeguard, for a limited period, the interests of the patent applicant in his attempt to obtain international protection for his invention, thereby alleviating the negative consequences of the principle of territoriality in patent law. The bedrock of the Paris Convention is that an initial application in one contracting state can serve as a "priority document" for corresponding applications filed later in another contracting state, provided that the later filing is made within the period of 12 months from the date of filing of the initial application. In effect, the initial application is then treated as if it had been filed in the other State on the same date as the date of filing of the initial application. Consequently, patentability of the subject-matter of the later-filed application falls to be judged as to the "state of the art" as it existed at the date of filing of the priority document, rather than as at the actual date of filing the "application in suit". Also, where an application can have some prior art effect from its date of filing, although not then published, that prior art effect can then likewise be ante-dated to the date of filing of an initial application which has served as a priority document for the later application.

Of course, these principles are subject to various conditions, both formal and substantive, and it is these principles and conditions which form the subject of ss.5 and 6, and the accompanying rules (see rr.6 to 9, above) discussed in §§5.30–5.36. For the onus of establishing a priority date, see §5.14.

Under the Act, the prima facie priority date of an invention contained in an application ("the application in suit"), and also of any matter (whether or not the same as the invention) contained in such application, is the date of filing that application (subs.(1)). However, if a permitted priority date from an earlier "relevant application" is duly "declared" either at the time of filing the application in suit or within the time allowed by the relevant rules which is currently 16 months after the earliest priority date to be declared (as to which see below), an ante-dating effect occurs under subs.(2). The earlier application must be one which is not disregarded under subs.(3), see below.

For patentability of subject-matter claimed in the application in suit, priority is accorded from the earlier application if, and to the extent that, an invention to which the application in suit relates is "supported by matter disclosed" in the earlier relevant application (subs.(2)(a)), see §5.23. For assessing the prior art effect of the application in suit against claims in another application or patent, the application in suit is ante-dated to the filing date of the earlier application as regards matter "disclosed" therein (subs.(2)(b)), see §5.24.

The ability to claim priority is not open-ended. Under subs.(2) prior to amendment on January 1, 2005, priority could only be claimed from an earlier relevant application having a filing date during the period of 12 months immediately preceding the filing date of the application in suit. This requirement continues to apply to applications that were pending on January 1, 2005. However, under amended subs.(2) and new subs.(2A), for applications filed on or after January 1, 2005, the date of filing of the application in suit must be either: (1) during the period of 12 months following the date of the earlier (or earliest) relevant application (subs.(2A)(a)); or (2) 14 months following that date where the Comptroller has given permission for a late declaration to be made under s.5(2) (subs.(2A)(b) and r.7(1), previously r.6A(1) of the Patents Rules 1995, as amended). A request for permission to make a "late declaration" under subs.(2A)(b) must be sought by making a "request" to the Comptroller (subs.(2B)). Such request can only be granted if the Comptroller is satisfied that the failure to file the declaration within the normal 12-month period was "unintentional" and provided that the request has complied with the relevant requirements of the rules (subs.(2C) and r.7, previously r.6A of the Patents Rules 1995 as amended). The filing of a late declaration is discussed in more detail in §§5.18 and 5.30 below.

Subsection (3) deals with the position where an invention or other matter contained in the application in suit is disclosed in two earlier relevant applications by the same applicant (i.e. a first application and a second application), the second of which was specified in or in connection with the application in suit. This subsection provides that the second application be disregarded for the purposes of allocating a priority date to the common matter unless the second application was filed in or in respect of the same country as the first application and, not later than the filing date of the second application, the first application was withdrawn, abandoned or refused without having been made available to the public, without leaving any rights outstanding and without serving to establish priority for any other application. If both of these applications have been validly declared, then priority can only be claimed from the first application in relation to the subject-matter (i.e. the invention contained or the matter disclosed) in the application in suit that is common to the second application and the first application. However, in circumstances where the first application was not validly declared, then if one or more of the conditions of subs.(3) is not met, a priority date, other than the date of filing of the application in suit, cannot be accorded for such common subject-matter. This provision is thereby intended to prevent applicants from extending the priority period unless they first withdraw or abandon the earlier application in accordance with subs.(3). For further discussion of subs.(3), see §5.28.

Subsection (4) makes the provisions of the section equally applicable to applications and patents granted on them.

Subsection (5) defines the term "relevant application" by reference either to (a) an application filed under the Act, or (b) one filed in a "convention country" (as defined in s.90), including European and international patent applications; and sub.(6) further provides (for the reason explained in §90.02) an automatic designation as a "convention country" under the Act of each Member State of the World Trade Organization. These subsections are discussed further at §5.29, and a complete list of such "convention countries" is set out in §90.03. So long as it has a date of filing, the outcome of the earlier application is not relevant, subject of course to the implications of subs.(3). Thus an earlier application may serve to establish a priority date even if it is subsequently withdrawn or refused before or after a subsequent application is filed. However, if it is withdrawn prior to filing the subsequent application, it must be withdrawn explicitly reserving the right to claim priority therefrom if an applicant still wishes to use it as a priority application.

The declaration of priority (required under subs.(2)) is a prerequisite for the claiming of an ante-dating effect. However, independently of whether the other above-mentioned requirements are met so as validly to accord the requested priority date, the filing of the "declaration" determines the earliest date of publication under s.16. This is currently a date not earlier than 18 months after the earliest declared priority date, or (if no priority has been declared) 18 months after the filing date of that application, see §16.03.

It should be noted that the priority document does not form part of the application or patent granted from it (*Mitsui Engineering and Shipbuilding Co's Application* [1984] R.P.C. 471).

Differences between according priority under the 1977 and 1949 Acts

First, under the 1977 Act, priority is accorded to an invention claimed, or to matter disclosed, in a specification. Under s.5 of the 1949 Act, each claim had to have a single priority date (*Thornhill's Application* [1962] R.P.C. 199). Under the 1977 Act, a claim may now have multiple priority dates for the individual inventions or aspects of an invention, see §5.21.

5.12

Secondly, the test under s.5 of the 1949 Act for priority was whether the claim was "fairly based on the matter disclosed in the earlier application". Under s.5(2) of the 1977 Act, whether an invention claimed in the application in suit can be accorded a priority date from an earlier application depends on the test of whether the "invention to which the application in suit relates is supported by matter disclosed in the earlier relevant application" (subs.(2)(a)). However, when the priority date of the earlier application is important for determining whether it can have prior art effect against a later application under s.2(3), the test is whether "matter disclosed in the application in suit is also disclosed in the earlier relevant application" (subs.(2)(b)). The substantive test for priority under the 1977 Act is discussed in detail below at §§5.22–5.24.

Thirdly, priority can be claimed from an earlier, but different, application under the 1977 Act (subs.(5)(a)) or from an application filed in or for a "convention country" (subs.(5)(b)). Thus, the subject-matter of an earlier application under the Act can now be cognated with one filed in a convention country, even though under the Act the United Kingdom is not itself a "convention country"—as that term is defined in s.90, see subs.(6) and §90.02. This was not possible under the 1949 Act under which priority could either be claimed from one or more earlier "provisional specifications" (for which see §A10) *or* from one or more applications filed previously in one or more convention countries, the latter type of application being called "a convention application". There is now no distinction between claiming an external priority under subs.(5)(b) or an internal priority under subs.(5)(a), and multiple priorities can be claimed from either or both of these categories. Thus, subs.(5)(a) produces much the same effect as the former claiming of priority from a provisional specification under the 1949 Act when a "complete specification" was filed in respect of the same application for which a "provisional specification" had earlier been filed, but under the Act the later (cf. "complete") application has a fresh number.

Fourthly, if priority is incorrectly claimed, the effect is now merely a loss of priority (although the effect of a loss of priority may result in the patent being invalid due to intervening art), whereas up to the 1977 Act, the whole patent was lost upon a false priority date being claimed.

Fifthly, under the 1977 Act, priority is not lost for an invention if the invention of the later application is not the subject of the claims of the earlier application. In this regard, s.5 says that priority is accorded if the invention to which the later application relates is "supported by matter disclosed" in the earlier application (subs.(2)(a)). This provision must be construed more broadly than the test under the 1949 Act arising from *Stauffer's Application* [1977] R.P.C. 33 CA. Under that test, a "convention application" under s.1(2)(b) of the 1949 Act had to be in respect of an invention for which "protection had been sought".

Conformity of section 5 with the EPC

As discussed in §5.11 above, ss.5 and 6 are referred to in s.130(7) as having been intended to have the same effect as the corresponding provisions of the EPC, PCT and CPC. For the relevant sections of the EPC and PCT see §§5.02–5.05, above.

5.13   In terms of wording, the most noteworthy difference between s.5 and art.87 of the EPC is that, while s.5(2)(a) provides that priority is accorded to an invention "supported by matter disclosed", art.87(1) of the EPC requires that the earlier application was filed "in respect of the same invention". In *Unilin Beheer v Berry Floor* [2005] F.S.R. 6, the Court of Appeal made it clear that this difference in wording results in no difference in effect of the two provisions. In *Unilin*, Jacob L.J. focussed on the wording of art.87 of the EPC (as interpreted by G 2/98 *Requirement for claiming priority for the "same invention"* OJ EPO 2001, 413; [2002] E.P.O.R. 17, as well as arts 4A, B and F of the Paris Convention, rather than the way in which these principles had been incorporated into s.5 of the 1977 Act. His Lordship regarded art.87 as the key provision on priority, noting that s.5 was supposed to mean the same as art.87 (s.130(7)). He indicated that he preferred to work from the EPC itself, as does the EPO not only in its daily work but also in its jurisprudence, which UK Courts should endeavour to follow (again, s.130(7)). See also Jacob J.'s (as he then was) comments in *Beloit v Valmet* [1995] R.P.C. 705, the point not being pursued on appeal.

Jacob L.J. noted that, in relation to priority, the EPC is seeking to implement the Paris Convention (Stockholm revision), so it too is a relevant consideration, being the very foundation of the worldwide priority system (this appears also to be the view of the Enlarged Board of Appeal, see for example G 3/93 *Priority Interval* OJ EPO 1995, 18; [1994] E.P.O.R. 521 and G 2/98 *"Same invention"*). His Lordship endorsed the view previously expressed by the Court of Appeal in *Pharmacia v Merck* [2002] R.P.C. 41 that the leading authority in the UK on priority, *Biogen v Medeva* [1997] R.P.C. 1 HL, is consistent with the leading case in the EPO, G 2/98 *"Same invention"* (above), even though decided before it. Interestingly, the Technical Board of Appeal of the EPO came to a different conclusion to the House of Lords on the question of priority when considering the patent in issue in *Biogen* (T 296/93 *BIOGEN/Hepatitis B* [1995] E.P.O.R. 1), although this decision was also made before G 2/98 *"Same invention"*.

The substantive test for priority is considered in more detail below, see §§5.22 to 5.26.

The prima facie priority date (subs.(1)) and the onus of proof

Subsection (1) states that, unless subsequent provisions of the Act provide otherwise, **5.14** the priority date of an invention to which a patent application under the Act relates, or to any matter contained in it, is that of the filing date of the application, termed in s.5 "the application in suit". This is, therefore, the prima facie priority date. If any other (earlier) date for its subject-matter is to be established under subs.(2)(a), the onus for this should initially fall upon the applicant, but the evidential burden of showing that a prima facie disclosure in the priority document is insufficient (e.g. non-enabling—as to which see below) will rest with the person who challenges the prima facie priority date, see *Biogen v Medeva* [1995] R.P.C. 25 CA. Also, to establish this prima facie priority date, it is enough for the patentee to assert that the instructions in the priority document work to produce the results claimed for them and, if this assertion is challenged, the evidential burden then shifts to the challenger to satisfy the court that these instructions are not sufficient for this purpose (*Evans Medical's Patent* [1998] R.P.C. 517).

In *Medimmune Ltd v Novartis Pharmaceuticals UK Ltd & Another* [2011] EWHC 1669 (Pat), Arnold J. noted that the burden lies on the patentee to establish that the claims in issue are entitled to priority from the priority document, although it is usually convenient to proceed by considering the objections to the claim to priority advanced by the other party.

When defending an application against another application, which allegedly forms part of the state of the art under s.2(3) by virtue of an earlier priority accorded under s.5(2)(b), the task of verifying that the relevant matter in the other application is not entitled to an earlier priority date falls upon the applicant defending the application in suit.

The priority period and the necessity for a valid declaration (subss.(2) (both before and after amendment effective January 1, 2005), (2A), (2B) and (2C))

Subsection (2) was amended and new subss.(2A)–(2C) were introduced by the RRO **5.15** with effect from January 1, 2005. The primary aim of this statutory order was to introduce deregulation of the Act in certain respects to enable it to be administered in compliance with the Patent Law Treaty of the World Intellectual Property Organization ("the PLT"). One of the PLT-driven aspects to this deregulation was to allow the delayed making of priority claims.

The Patent Rules 1995 were also amended with effect from January 1, 2005 (SI 2004/2358), replacing r.6 and adding new rr.6A–6C, to reflect the amendments to s.5. Rule 6A of the 1995 Rules was then further amended by the Patents (Amendment) Rules 2007 on April 1, 2007 to comply with r.49 *ter* of the PCT (i.e. to allow r.6A to apply to late claiming of priority in relation to international applications). These rules were then replaced by rr.6–9 of the Patents Rules 2007 with effect from December 17, 2007; in overall effect, these new rules extensively reproduce rr.6, 6A–6C of the 1995 Rules as amended.

Under s.5(2) prior to amendment, the application in suit could not claim priority from an earlier application filed more than 12 months previously: this reflected the way in which the priority provisions of the Paris Convention have traditionally been interpreted (see art.4C at §5.06, above). Furthermore, the rules in force prior to January 1, 2005 required a claim to priority to be made on the date of filing of the application in suit. These requirements continue to apply to applications that were pending on January 1, 2005. Clearly, this priority regime made no allowance for so-called Acts of God or other incidents which would qualify for force majeure.

However, the PLT now requires contracting states to allow late priority claims in two instances which can be summarised as follows: (1) where the filing date of the application in suit is within 12 months of the filing date of the relevant application, a request to make a priority claim should be allowed after the time of filing the later application, often referred to as a late claim to priority; and (2) requests for late claims to priority must be allowed in respect of applications whose dates of filing are more than 12 months after the priority date to be claimed, providing that the later application is filed within a further period (to be set by the contracting state) consecutive to the expiry of the normal 12-month period and providing, at the option of the contracting state, that either due care was taken to file in time or the failure to file in time was unintentional. The latter is referred to in the Act as a "late declaration". This position is now reflected in the Act and the corresponding Rules as described below. In respect of applications filed on or after January 1, 2005, the following discussion focuses on the current rules in force, namely rr.6–9 of the 2007 Rules, highlighting any significant changes over rr.6, 6A–6C of the Patents Rules 1995 (as amended).

—Filing a declaration of priority pre-January 1, 2005

5.16   Rule 6 of the Patents Rules 1995 (prior to amendment on January 1, 2005) required that, to obtain a priority date earlier than the filing date of the application in suit, a priority declaration had to be made at the time of filing the application in suit, subject to an exception (under r.6(5) of the 1995 Rules prior to amendment) in the case of an international application for which the PCT Regulations permitted a priority declaration to be added, or corrected, within a limited period after the international filing date, see §89B.05.

The declaration of priority could be made only in respect of an application filed within the preceding 12 months (omitting excluded days, for which see §§120.04 and 120.05). This period was inextensible, other than under r.111 in the case of postal delays or disruption in the UK-IPO (for which see §§123.78 and 123.79). In the case of a divisional application (filed under s.15(4)), no priority could be claimed which had not been claimed in the parent application (final sentence to r.6(1), added in 1995 to remove any doubt on the point).

Although the declaration had to be made at the time of filing the application, it did not need to be made on PF 1 (as then was, r.6(1) of the 1995 Rules prior to amendment). The declaration had to include the date of filing of the earlier application and the country in or for which it was made. Within the time specified by r.6(2)–(5) (1995 Rules), there also had to be furnished to the UK-IPO details of the file number of the priority application and in most cases also a certified copy of it or equivalent conditions had to be complied with. If the priority application was not in English, a verified translation of it had to be timely supplied (r.6(6) of the 1995 Rules prior to amendment).

—Filing a declaration of priority claiming a priority date within the normal period post-January 1, 2005

5.17   The amendments made to s.5 maintain (under new s.5(2A)(a)) that priority may be declared provided the application in suit is filed within the period of 12 months immediately following the date of filing of the earlier specified relevant application, or, if there is more than one, of the earliest of them. This may conveniently be called "the normal period". New r.6(1) provides that normally a declaration of priority should be made at the time of filing the application.

However, where the application was filed within the normal 12-month period, it is possible to file a priority declaration after that date, provided that this is done by filing form PF 3 no later than 16 months after the earliest priority date to be declared and provided that, when PF 3 is filed, no application (unless by then this has been withdrawn) has been made for early publication of the application under s.16 (r.6(2) and (3)). This is referred to as a late claim to priority. This 16-month period (under r.6(2)(b)) is inextensible (2007 Rules, Sch.4 Pt 1, reprinted in §123.26). The possibility of making a late claim of priority mirrors a similar provision introduced into the EPC by the Implementing Regulations to EPC 2000 (r.52(2)).

For the formalities relating to making a declaration of priority under the rules, see §§5.30 to 5.36 below.

—Filing a late declaration of priority post-January 1, 2005

5.18   As compared to the situation under subs.(2A)(a) (discussed in §5.17 above), where a priority declaration may be filed late in respect of an application which was filed within the normal period of 12 months after the earliest priority date, subs.(2A)(b) can be used to permit a late filing of a priority declaration where the date of filing of the application in suit is more than 12 months after the earliest priority date to be declared. Rule 7 (reprinted above) is then applicable. Overall, the effect of these provisions is that exceptionally permission may be granted for a late declaration of priority to be made in which case the time period is 14 months from the filing of the earlier relevant application or, if there is more than one, the earliest of them.

Under subs.(2B), a request for permission to file a late declaration may be made to the Comptroller. Except in relation to a "new application" (see below), the request must be made on new form PF 3 (r.7(2)(a)), with its attendant fee, this being higher than that prescribed when PF 3 is filed under s.5(2A)(a), and must be filed within a period of two months after the end of the normal period (r.7(1) and 7(5)). The period specified in r.7(1) is the minimum provided by the PLT, and is inextensible (Rules, Sch.4, Pt 1, reprinted in §123.26). No such request can be accepted under s.5(2B) if the applicant has made a request for early publication of the application under s.16, unless this had been withdrawn before the preparations for such publication had been completed (rr.7(7)(a) and 7(8)).

Unless the request is in respect of a "new application" (see below), supporting evidence must be filed explaining why the application in suit was not filed before the end of the normal 12-month period allowed under subs.(2A)(a) (r.7(2)(b) and (4)). If such evidence is not filed with PF 3, the Patent Office must specify a period within which the evidence must be filed (r.7(3)), which will normally be two months (see *Formalities Manual*, ch.6, para.6.23). The required supporting evidence must establish, to the satisfaction of the Comptroller, that the omission to file the application within the normal period was "unintentional" (subs.(2C)(b)).

There is no definition in the Act or rules as to what is meant by "unintentional" in this context. Any indication that the applicant had had a change of mind, from an original intention not to file the application or to file it without a priority declaration, is, however, likely to be fatal to an application under subs.(2A)(b) and r.7. Case law, including case law under s.28, below, in which the word also appears, will elaborate the circumstances that can be regarded as "unintentional", but paramount will be a lack of evidence of any change of mind of the applicant. Often the failure to file timely the application in suit will have arisen from a clerical error and the intention to file the application should then be apparent from the records of the applicant or his agent.

To satisfy s.5(2C)(b), the applicant must have intended to file the very same UK application with the same application papers before the end of the normal 12-month period and not some other application, e.g. a PCT or EP application (*Sirna Therapeutics' Application* [2006] R.P.C. 351 at [12] (UK-IPO) and *Re Abaco Machines (Australasia) Pty Ltd's Application* [2007] Bus. L.R. 897 Ch.Div. Pat Ct; see also *Formalities Manual*, ch.6, para.6.25). Thus, in the *Sirna Therapeutics* and *Abaco Machines* cases, a request for a late declaration of priority was rejected where the applicant had unintentionally failed to file a PCT application (which would have designated the UK) and subsequently decided to file a UK national application instead with a request for a late declaration. In such circumstances, it was held that the non-existent PCT application could not be regarded as the "application in suit" within s.5(2C)(b); the "application in suit" could only be the UK national application and this application was filed intentionally, and not unintentionally, outside the normal 12-month period.

However, the *Formalities Manual* notes at para.6.26 that, if the applicant intended to file a PCT application claiming priority but failed to do so within the 12-month period, he may file his PCT application within 14 months and request that a late declaration be allowed under the PCT rules (late declarations to priority are permitted on international applications under PCT r.49 *ter*.2, see also paras 13.73 and 13.74 of the *Formalities Manual*). Alternatively, the applicant may wait until the international application enters the national phase and, provided the international application was filed within 14 months of the priority date, make the request using PF 3 within 1 month of entry (r.66(3); see paras 6.27, 13.73 and 13.74 of the *Formalities Manual*, see also r.7(5)).

There is here a parallel with new s.20A, under which an application which has been terminated for non-compliance with a time limit can be reinstated if the Comptroller can be satisfied that the non-compliance had been unintentional, see §20A.05; and also with the new condition for restoration of a lapsed patent, see §28.08. However, it has been held (the *Sirna Therapeutics* case, above) that the test applied under s.5(2C)(b) is different from the test of "continual underlying intention to proceed" applied under r.110(4) (as in *Heatex's Application* [1995] R.P.C. 546), which related to the Comptroller's discretion to extend certain time limits.

At the same time as filing PF 3, there must also be filed the declaration which it is desired to file if leave is granted (r.7(9)). The same formal requirements relating to the information and documents that must be provided with the declaration apply as to a declaration made under r.6, and these are discussed in §§5.30 to 5.36 below.

Where the request for permission relates to a "new application" (defined in r.2 as a new application filed under ss.8(3), 12(6) or 37(4) or as mentioned in s.15(9)), the request need only be made in writing, as opposed to form PF 3, and no evidence shall accompany it (r.7(4); see also para.6.28 of the *Formalities Manual* in respect of divisional applications). Under the 1995 Rules as amended, a request under s.5(2B) for a late declaration on a new application had to be made on the then PF 3 and accompanied by evidence, despite the fact that the same process had to be undertaken for the same late declaration on the earlier application. This was unduly burdensome in relation to new applications and so a more liberal regime was introduced under r.7 of the Patent Rules 2007 in relation to new applications. Where a new application is filed after the end of the two-month period allowed under s.5(2A)(b), a request under s.5(2B) may be made on the initiation date (r.7(6)).

—Person with right to make a declaration of priority

5.19   While the applicant for the application in suit must be, or derive title from, the applicant for the priority application (subs.(2)), there is no requirement under rr.6 to 9 to provide any proof of derivation of title to claim priority when the priority application is in another name. However, where there is no apparent connection between the applicant of the priority application and the applicant of the application in suit, the UK-IPO may request an explanation of the "new" applicant's right to claim priority and may call for evidence to substantiate any claim.

If there has been no assignment of at least the right to claim priority from the earlier application, it may be that any patent granted on the application in suit could be revoked under s.72(1)(b) because the patent was granted to a person not entitled to be granted the patent, for which see §72.13. Nevertheless, entitlement to apply and entitlement to claim priority are not necessarily the same so that a failure of entitlement to claim priority, but not to apply, may result only in a loss of priority by the false priority declaration merely being ignored. In *Beloit v Valmet* [1995] R.P.C. 705, the earlier patent-in-suit had claimed priority from a Japanese utility model application filed by a different entity. Although there was no formal assignment of priority right, it was held sufficient to claim priority on the basis of a pre-existing agreement allowing a licensee to apply for patents if the licensor decided not to do so itself. This decision was not challenged on the appeal: [1997] R.P.C. 489 CA. The entitlement to claim priority must exist at the date of making the declaration as otherwise that declaration would be a false one and presumably, therefore, void and of no effect, see *Edwards Lifesciences AG v Cook Biotech Inc.* [2009] F.S.R. 27.

See also discussion at §5.28 below of T 5/05 *DYSTAR TEXTILFARBEN/Mixtures of monoazodisperse dyes* (Unreported) and T 788/05 *TERUMO KABUSHIKI KAISHA/ Vascular Catheter* (Unreported).

—Effect of a "declared priority date"

5.20   The term "declared priority date" relates to the priority date referred to in the priority declaration. It is defined in r.3(1) (reprinted above) as the date of filing of the earliest relevant application specified in a declaration made for the purposes of s.5(2) in, or in connection with, an application in suit. According to the UK-IPO Concordance on the Patents Rules 2007 r.3 replaces the definition in r.2 of the Patents Rules 1995: in general, it is not intended to change the way the "declared priority date" is calculated for the purposes of the Rules, although it does address certain points raised in the 5th edition of the *CIPA Guide* at §5.07.

By virtue of r.3(4), references to declarations made for the purposes of s.5(2) include declarations treated as made for those purposes, thus covering declarations treated as declarations under s.5(2) by virtue of s.89B(1)(b) (an international application for a patent (UK)) and s.81(3)(c) (an application for a European patent (UK) converted into an application under the Act).

Rule 3(2) clarifies that there is "no declared priority date" (this term was used in the 1995 Rules, but not defined) if no declaration for the purposes of s.5(2) has been made or every declaration that has been made has been withdrawn or disregarded before the end of the "relevant period". The "relevant period" is defined in r.3(3) and varies according to the type of application. Where the declared priority date has arisen from an application for a European patent (UK) converted into an application under the Act by virtue of a direction under s.81(1), the relevant period ends when that direction is given (r.3(3)(a)). In the case of an international application for a patent (UK), the relevant period ends when the national phase of the application begins (r.3(3)(b)). Otherwise, the relevant periods ends when preparations for the application's publication have been completed by the Patent Office (r.3(3)(c)).

This means that, if priority is lost after completion of preparations for s.16 publication (for which see §16.06), the compliance period (defined in r.30(1), which replaces r.34 of the Patents Rules 1995, as the period prescribed for the purposes of ss.18(4) and 20(1)) is not affected, see §18.11. Therefore, if a copy of the priority document is required but not supplied within the prescribed period, the declared priority date under s.5(2) will be lost and time limits going forward will be affected accordingly. This is because the application in suit will necessarily not yet have been sent for publication. However, when the declaration is lost because of a failure to file a translation, this is likely to be after the s.16 publication date, and then there will be no change to the compliance period for the application.

It should be noted that the definition of "declared priority date" is of no relevance to the question of whether a priority declaration actually establishes that date as the priority date of an invention under s.5(2)(a) in relation to the state of the art, or establishes under s.5(2)(b) the prior art effect of the application claiming that invention against an invention of later priority. All that it does is to fix the date from which various time limits commence and potentially make possible that the date of the application in respect of which the declaration was made shall be regarded as the priority date in respect of the contents of that application. Thus, an application can have only one "declared priority date", whereas different priority dates may be assigned to various parts of the text and claims of the application; and, if an earlier application mentioned in a declaration of priority does not support any invention or disclose matter contained in the application in suit, that declaration may be nugatory but it is not objectionable. If no declaration of priority is filed, the various time limits run from the actual filing date of the application. In the absence of a priority declaration, the filing date becomes the priority date for the invention and subject-matter contained in the application.

According multiple priorities or a partial priority

Under s.5(2), an application may claim rights of priority based on more than one earlier **5.21** application. So, for example, if an application embraces more than one invention, each invention may have a different priority date. Provided they are all "relevant applications" (see §5.29), there is no requirement that they should have been filed under the same national law or international agreement.

Section 125(2) makes it clear that where more than one invention is specified in any claim, each invention may have a different priority date, see §125.27. Note that under s.14(5)(d) (discussed in §14.40), the separate inventions encompassed in an application should be so linked as to form a single inventive concept, although this is only an issue pre-grant, see s.26 (discussed in §26.02). Consequently, a single claim can embrace more than one invention each with a different priority date. A claim may, therefore, have multiple priorities (i.e. claim priority from more than one earlier application), or a partial priority (i.e. part of the claim has a priority date of an earlier application while the date of filing of the application applies to the remaining part). This is also the case under the EPC, see art.88(2) of the EPC, second sentence. On its face art.88(2) does not appear to require as a condition to a claim having multiple priorities that more than one invention is specified in the claim, but this would appear to follow from art.87(1) which refers to priority in the context of an invention.

In contrast with the practice under the 1949 Act (under which it was thought that a claim could have only a single priority date, see *Thornhill's Application* [1962] R.P.C. 199), it is no longer necessary to draft elaborate sets of claims to take into account multiple and partial priorities. As a result of s.125(2), where a claim contains a plurality of inventions, if one of those inventions is a patentable invention then the patent is partially valid (*Hallen v Brabantia (No.2)* [1990] F.S.R. 134). However, where an application clearly covers a number of inventions linked by a single inventive concept, it is still worth considering drafting claim sets such that, so far as possible, each claim has a single priority.

When assessing the extent to which multiple, or partial, priorities may be accorded to a claim, it is a question of construction whether that claim is directed to a single invention or a plurality of inventions. This is a question of substance not form, but whether a claim can have multiple priorities may depend in part on the way in which it is drafted.

So, for example, if a claim is drafted in such a way that it covers separately identifiable alternatives (such as in the case of a so-called "OR" claim, i.e. a claim to A or B, or a US Markush-type claim which defines a chemical compound by reference to a formula which may have specified alternative forms) then attributing a different priority to each alternative may not be problematic. For example, in *Hallen v Brabantia (No.2)* above, the court adopted an "alternatives" construction: the claim in issue (a subsidiary claim of the form "apparatus according to any preceding claim") was construed as being a number of discrete claims rather than a composite claim. In contrast, in the case of a claim that is truly generic (i.e. it specifies a unified class of species rather than clear alternatives) or encompasses a combination of features (such as in the case of a so-called "AND" claim, i.e. a claim to C+D), it is more difficult to see how multiple priorities could be conferred on such a claim. Indeed, in the latter case, it may not be possible to claim priority from an earlier application unless the claimed combination of features (e.g. C+D) is supported by matter disclosed in the earlier application (see §5.23). These principles were explored by the Enlarged Board of Appeal of the EPO in one of the leading EPO cases on priority, namely G 2/98 *"Same invention"*, see in particular paras 6.4 to 6.7, discussed further below. See also EPO Guideline C–V, 1.5 and T 665/00 *L'OREAL/Loose powder compositions*, noted [2006] *CIPA* 274.

It is important to remember when claiming multiple priority dates that, where there is more than one relevant application disclosing a particular invention encompassed in the application in suit, priority will be based on the earliest of these provided the invention is "supported by matter disclosed in the earlier relevant application" (subs.2(a)) and provided this earliest application was filed not more than 12 months before the filing date of the application in suit (subject to the ability to make a late declaration of priority, see §5.18). Otherwise, no priority is accorded to that invention unless the provisions of subs.(3) are met, for which see §5.28.

Although priority may be claimed from a number of earlier applications, an application may have only one "declared priority date", namely the date of filing of the earliest relevant application, see §5.20 for the effect of a "declared priority date".

The nature of the test for priority (subs.(2))

5.22   Determining a priority date arises in two contexts under s.5(2). First, for assessing the patentability of subject-matter claimed in an application, priority is accorded from an earlier application if, and to the extent that, an invention to which the application relates is "supported by matter disclosed" in the earlier application (subs.(2)(a)). Secondly, for assessing the prior art effect of an application against claims in another application or patent under s.2(3), the application in suit is ante-dated to the filing date of an earlier application as regards matter "disclosed" therein (subs.(2)(b)). The following two sections consider the tests applied by the UK courts in relation to each.

—Test of "supported by matter disclosed" (subs.(2)(a))

If a priority date earlier than the date of filing of the application is sought for an invention pursuant to s.5(2)(a), then the earlier priority will be obtained if the invention is "supported by matter disclosed in the earlier relevant application". The House of Lords decision in *Biogen v Medeva* [1997] R.P.C. 1, and in particular the speech of Lord Hoffmann, has long been cited as the leading UK authority on the extent to which priority can be claimed from an earlier application. Following the House of Lords decision in *Asahi Kasei Kogyo KK's Application* [1991] R.P.C. 485, Lord Hoffmann saw the test of "supported by matter disclosed" as being one for an enabling disclosure, the same test governing insufficiency (under ss.14(3) and 72(1)(c)) as well as permissible breadth of claim for grant (under s.14(5)): **5.23**

> "In *Asahi Kasei Kogyo KK's Application* [1991] RPC 485 this House decided that for matter to be capable of supporting an invention within the meaning of s 5(2)(a) it must contain an 'enabling disclosure', that is to say, it must disclose the invention in a way which will enable it to be performed by a person skilled in the art. This construction has not been challenged by the appellants before your Lordships' House. It is however important to notice the relationship between the requirement of 'support' in s 5(2)(a) and certain other provisions of the Act which share the concept of an enabling disclosure.
>
> The concept of an enabling disclosure is central to the law of patents. For present purposes, it touches the matters in issue at three different points. First, as we have seen, it forms part of the requirement of 'support' in s 5(2)(a). Secondly, it is one of the requirements of a valid application in s 14 and thirdly, it is essential to one of the grounds for the revocation of a patent in s 72. I shall start with s 14. Subsection (3) says:
>
> > 'The specification of an application shall disclose the invention is a way which is clear enough and complete enough for the invention to be performed by a person skilled in the art.'
>
> This is plainly a requirement of an 'enabling disclosure'. In addition, subsection (5)(c) says that the claim or claims shall be 'supported by the description'. It was by reference to subsection (3) that Lord Oliver of Aylmerton, who gave the leading speech in *Asahi*, reasoned at page 536 that a description would not 'support' the claims for the purpose of subsection (5)(c) unless it contained sufficient material to enable the specification to constitute the enabling disclosure which subsection (3) required: 'the Act can hardly have contemplated a complete application for a patent lacking some of the material necessary to sustain the claims made'. By parity of reasoning, he said that 'support' must have the same meaning in s 5(2)(a)."

Lord Hoffmann then noted that, while the need for an enabling disclosure to satisfy the requirements of support under s.5(2)(a), valid application under s.14 and sufficiency under s.72(1)(c) had been plain and undisputed since *Asahi*, what had been less clear was what the concept means. Commenting that part of the difficulty had been caused by a misinterpretation of what the Technical Board of Appeal of the EPO said in T 292/85 *GENENTECH I/Polypeptide expression* [1989] OJ EPO 275, he said that in fact the Board had been doing no more than applying a long-established principle of patent law in the UK that the specification must enable the invention to be performed to the full extent of the monopoly claimed. Thus, disclosure of a principle capable of general application may support claims in correspondingly general terms, such that the patentee need not show that he has proved the application of the principle in every individual instance. However, if the claims include a number of discrete methods or products, the patentee must enable the invention to be performed in respect of each of them. He went on:

"Thus if the patentee has hit upon a new product which has a beneficial effect but cannot demonstrate that there is a common principle by which that effect will be shared by other products of the same class, he will be entitled to a patent for that product but not for the class, even though some may subsequently turn out to have the same beneficial effect: see *May v Baker Ltd v Boots Pure Drug Co Ltd* (1950) 67 RPC 23, 50. On the other hand, if he has disclosed a beneficial property which is common to the class, he will be entitled to a patent for all products of that class (assuming them to be new) even though he has not himself made more than one or two of them."

Their Lordships held that the priority document did not support the invention claimed in the patent, which, in light of a subsequent publication before the application was filed, proved fatal to the validity of the patent. The claim in *Biogen* was to a recombinant DNA molecule characterised by the fact that it coded for Hepatitis B antigens. Priority was denied because the priority document disclosed that the recombinant DNA molecule had been derived in a particular way and yet the claim covered all ways of expressing the gene, ways which owed nothing to the teaching of the patent or any principle which it disclosed. In other words, the contribution of the inventor, as described in the priority document (and incidentally in the patent itself), did not justify a claim to a monopoly of any recombinant method of making the antigens and was therefore too broad for priority to be accorded.

In the context of sufficiency, this case had given rise to what was commonly referred to as "*Biogen* insufficiency"—see §72.14. As is described in more detail in there, the *Biogen* case had been considered as authority for the proposition that a patent claim may be insufficient if the breadth of the claim exceeds the technical contribution to the art embodied in the invention. However, in *H Lundbeck A/S v Generics (UK) Ltd* [2008] R.P.C. 19; [2008] EWCA Civ 311, (a case concerned with insufficiency rather than priority, again discussed in §72.14), Lord Hoffmann, sitting in the Court of Appeal, made it clear that the finding in *Biogen* was specific to its facts: as a matter of construction, the House of Lords had interpreted the claim as being to a class of products which satisfied specified conditions, one of which was that the molecule had been made by recombinant technology. The term "recombinant technology" includes a wide variety of possible processes, but the priority document in *Biogen* described only one method and disclosed no general principle. It was easy to contemplate other methods about which the priority document said nothing and which would owe nothing to the matter disclosed. Lord Hoffmann concluded, therefore, that the decision in *Biogen* is limited to the form of claim which their Lordships were there considering and could not be extended to, as in the *Lundbeck* case, an ordinary product claim in which the product is not defined by a class of processes of manufacture. In recent cases, the courts have tended to side-step the need explicitly to address *Biogen* and *Lundbeck* in the context of priority, referring instead to the decision of the EPO Enlarged Board of Appeal in G 2/98 *"Same invention"* [2002] E.P.O.R. 17 (discussed in more detail below in this section and at §5.25) and, for example, the *Unilin* and *Abbott Laboratories* cases (also discussed in this section below); see for example the decisions of Arnold J. in *Intervet UK Ltd v Merial* [2010] EWHC 294 (Pat) and *Medimmune Ltd vNovartis Pharmaceuticals UK Ltd & Another* [2011] EWHC 1669 (Pat).

In *Pharmacia v Merck* [2002] R.P.C. 41, the Court of Appeal held that *Biogen* was consistent with the then more recent decision of the EPO Enlarged Board of Appeal in G 2/98 *"Same invention"* (discussed in more detail below at §5.26), which had resolved a longstanding divergence of views in the EPO case law as to the meaning of "same invention" in art.87(1) (again, see §5.26 below). Aldous L.J. summed up the law as follows:

"What is required, as Lord Hoffmann pointed out in *Biogen*, is that the priority document must contain sufficient material for the priority document to constitute the enabling disclosure of [the claim concerned]".

The *Pharmacia* case concerned a claim to a class of chemical compounds defined by reference to a general formula and described in the specification as having a particular pharmaceutical activity. The key claim in issue specified that one of the substituents should have a particular invariant character whereas the priority document specified the presence of this substituent only as an optional possibility in the broadest class described, and in another, narrower general formula only in combination with different requirements for certain of the other substituents as compared to the granted claims. At first instance, in denying priority, the court stated that:

"a monopoly defined by one or other of these substitutions as an invariant feature across the whole width of the claim cannot be fairly based on a disclosure which does not hint at their materiality either textually or as a matter of necessary implication but only, at best, as a result of well-informed assessment of probabilities".

Moreover, the disclosure of the priority document did not support the basis for the claims, i.e. that they covered a class of compounds having a particular pharmaceutical activity, because the priority document contained no mention of that activity, particularly in view of the finding that some of the specified compounds had been shown to be inactive (first instance decision reported as *Monsanto Co v Merck & Co Inc* [2000] R.P.C. 709). The Court of Appeal upheld the finding of lack of priority noting that, while it is possible to claim in a patent a narrower range of compounds than that disclosed in the priority document, the mere fact that it is a narrower range does not mean that there is support for that range.

The Court of Appeal considered G 2/98 *"Same invention"* further in *Unilin Beheer NV v Berry Floor NV* [2005] F.S.R. 56. As discussed above at §5.13, Jacob L.J., who gave the leading judgment, regarded art.87 of the EPC (as interpreted by G 2/98 *"Same invention"*) as the key provision on priority, noting that s.5 was supposed to mean the same as art.87. His Lordship reiterated that the leading authority in the UK on priority, *Biogen*, is consistent with G 2/98 *"Same invention"*, even though decided before it. He quoted from G 2/98 *"Same invention"* as follows:

"The requirement for claiming priority of 'the same invention', referred to in Article 87(1) EPC, means that priority of a previous application in respect of a claim in a European patent application in accordance with Article 88 EPC is to be acknowledged only if the skilled person can derive the subject-matter of the claim directly and unambiguously, using common general knowledge, from the previous application as a whole."

Jacob L.J. explained that, following both *Biogen* and G 2/98 *"Same invention"*, the approach is not formulaic: priority is a question about technical disclosure, explicit or implicit. Is there enough in the priority document to give the skilled person essentially the same information as forms the subject of the claim and enables him to work the invention in accordance with that claim? His Lordship also held that the claims (if any—there is no rule that there should be) and consistory clauses of the priority document are just part of its disclosure: for the purposes of priority, one just looks at the disclosure as a whole (see also the House of Lords in the *Asahi* case). He noted that, if the rule were otherwise, one of the main functions of a priority document would be lost since inventors and their advisors would have to start worrying not only about the technical information disclosed but how it was to be claimed in the priority document. He noted that this was not the purpose of the priority system: the purpose at this point is to get the information justifying the later claim into a patent office of a Union country.

When asked to consider a disclosure in a priority document in the form of A+B+C, and whether such a disclosure supported a claim to only one of these features without the other two, Jacob L.J. held in *Unilin* that, whether there is also a disclosure of A or B or C independently depends on substance, not on a formula. Some inventions consist of a combination of features, in others features are independent one from the other. The ultimate question, his Lordship held, is simply whether the skilled person can derive the subject-matter of the claim from the priority document as a whole.

In *Abbott Laboratories Ltd v Evysio Medical Devices Plc* [2008] R.P.C. 23; [2008] EWHC 800, Kitchin J., citing G 2/98 *"Same invention"* and *Unilin*, noted that enablement is not the only requirement of a valid claim to priority. He reiterated that what is important is not the consistory clause or the claims of the priority document but whether the disclosure as a whole is enabling and effectively gives (directly and unambiguously) the skilled person what is in the claim whose priority is questioned. He noted that it is not sufficient that what is claimed in the later application may be an obvious development of what is disclosed in the priority document.

It would therefore appear to follow that priority cannot be accorded from a priority document which is wholly silent as to an essential feature of the eventually claimed subject-matter (*Balmoral Group v CRP Marine Ltd* [2000] F.S.R. 860 CA, which appears to be consistent with G 2/98 *"Same invention"*). Where a priority document does disclose certain features but does so without suggesting that they are essential, a claim omitting those features can properly claim priority (*Rocky Mountain Traders v Hewlett Packard* [2000] F.S.R. 411 (this point did not rise on appeal; again, it appears to be consistent with G 2/98 *"Same invention"*).

Further, since the priority document must be looked at as a whole, its general description is no less a part of the technical content than the examples (see *Evans Medical Ltd's Patent* [1998] R.P.C. 517). Laddie J. also noted in *Evans Medical* that the requirement of an enabling disclosure is a matter of substance not form: the reader would not necessarily be misled by incorrect nomenclature or other errors of description. However, the tests of enablement and obviousness differ. For a document to be enabling, it must lead the reader to the invention clearly. Although obvious errors might be corrected, this is not another version of the test for obviousness.

It is a matter of the national law of the country of the priority application whether an abstract provided with the priority application is considered as part of the application. Under s.14(2)(c), the abstract is part of a United Kingdom application, but this is not the case for patent applications filed in Germany as certified copies of applications therefrom make clear, and the EPO also does not consider the abstract to be part of an application, see §14.42.

What constitutes an "enabling disclosure" has now been further explained by the House of Lords in *Synthon BV v SmithKline Beecham* [2006] R.P.C. 10 at 323, a case concerning the test for lack of novelty, in which Lord Hoffmann stressed the importance of separating the concepts of disclosure and enablement, as discussed further in §2.09. It would appear to follow from Lord Hoffmann's comments in *Biogen* and *Synthon*, and those of their Lordships in *Asahi*, that the question of what will satisfy the test of enablement, i.e. the degree of effort required of the skilled person, is the same for priority under s.5(2)(a) and sufficiency under s.72(1)(c) (see authorities relied upon for assessing enablement at §§14.24–14.26, §§14.28–14.30 and §72.14).

—Test of "disclosed in the earlier relevant application" (subs.(2)(b))

5.24   Whereas subs.(2)(a) concerns the priority date of an invention to which an application relates, subs.(2)(b) concerns the priority date of "matter contained in the application in suit". Subsection (2)(b) provides that the priority date of any matter contained in the application in suit will be the date of filing of the earlier relevant application or applications if such matter "was also disclosed in the earlier relevant application or applications". In other words, the priority date of matter contained in an application is deemed to be the filing date of an earlier application if that matter was "disclosed in" that earlier application. Whereas subs.(2)(a) is ultimately concerned with the patentability of the claims in the application in suit, subs.(2)(b) is concerned with the prior art effect of the contents of an application in suit. This test of prior art effect can be applied to any matter in an application in suit whether it is claimed or not, and is available for use in a case of interlocking priorities to decide which claims, or parts of claims, have the earlier priority.

The distinction between the tests to be applied under subss.(2)(a) and (2)(b) was considered by the House of Lords in the *Asahi* case. Lord Oliver, who gave the leading judgment, noted that s.5 shows a distinction between the invention to which an application relates and "matter" contained in the application and contemplates that there may be different priority dates for the two. His Lordship found that a description in an earlier application which contains no enabling disclosure will not "support" the invention so as to enable it, as an invention, to claim priority from the date of that application under s.5(2)(a). However, he noted that the description will be entitled to a priority as "matter contained" in the application in suit under s.5(2)(b). He noted that s.130(3), which provides that matter shall be taken to have been disclosed in any relevant application within the meaning of s.5 if it was either claimed or disclosed in that application, simply directs attention to disclosure contained in the claims as well as in the body of the application in order to determine whether matter has been disclosed. Similarly, Lord Jauncey held that subs.(2)(b), unlike subs.(2)(a):

> "contemplates that the matter disclosed in the earlier relevant application will not be sufficient *per se* to support the invention in the patent in suit and may not within itself contain an enabling disclosure".

Thus, in the *Asahi* case, a formula for a chemical compound disclosed in an application cited as prior art was found to be entitled to an earlier priority date under s.5(2)(b) because the formula itself was identified in the priority document. The fact that the priority document did not disclose a method of manufacturing the compound (and the skilled person would not have known how to do so without specific teaching), and was therefore not enabling, was not found to prejudice the question of priority under s.5(2)(b). However, this lack of an enabling disclosure meant that the disclosure of the formula was not novelty-destroying under s.2(3) in relation to a claim to the compound with a later priority date (see §2.09).

According priority under the EPC

As noted above, the relevant sections of the EPC are arts 87 to 89 (see §§5.02–5.04, above), which provide a complete, self-contained code of rules of law (now together with the accompanying rules of the Implementing Regulations to the EPC 2000) on the subject of claiming priority for the purposes of filing a European patent application (see for example G 3/93 *"Priority interval"* and G 2/98 *"Same invention"*, above). Since the EPC constitutes, according to its preamble, a special agreement under the Paris Convention, it has been held by the EPO that arts 87–89 are clearly intended not to contravene the basic principles concerning priority laid down in the Paris Convention (again, see G 3/93 *"Priority interval"* and G 2/98 *"Same invention"*).

Article 87(1) of the EPC requires priority to be accorded from a relevant earlier application to the extent that the later application is "in respect of the same invention". Besides this basic rule for priority to be accorded to an earlier application, the "elements" of a claim must be included in the earlier application (EPC art.88(3)). If the elements do not appear in the claims of the earlier application, priority may nonetheless be accorded provided the documents of the earlier application as a whole specifically disclose such elements (EPC art.88(4)). These matters were primarily discussed in G 3/93 *"Priority interval"* in relation to matter disclosed after the date of the priority document depriving the later claim of novelty when priority from the priority document was not accorded in respect of this additional matter, as discussed more fully in §6.02.

Chapter V of the EPO Guidelines concerns priority, of which ss.2.1–2.4 deal in some detail with the test for priority under the EPC. The EPO Guidelines point out that an element may be a feature disclosed, or it may be the combination of certain features, but in this connection it is not permitted to make a mosaic of priority documents unless,

5.25

possibly, one refers to the other and explicitly states that features from the two documents can be combined in a particular manner (EPO Guideline C–V, 1.5). Also, a claim to a detailed embodiment of a certain feature is not supported by a general reference to that feature. Exact correspondence is not required: it suffices that on a reasonable assessment there is in substance a disclosure of all the important features of the claim (EPO Guideline C–V, 2.2). The EPO Guidelines also state that the basic test for entitlement to priority is "the same as the test for determining whether or not an amendment to an application satisfies the requirements of Art. 123(2)" so that:

> "the subject-matter of the claim must be directly and unambiguously derivable from the disclosure of the invention in the priority document, also taking into account any features implicit to a person skilled in the art in what is expressly mentioned in the document".

The EPO Guidelines specifically reference G 2/98 *"Same invention"* (discussed below).

—Test of "same invention" applied by the EPO (art.87(1))

5.26 Since the effect of s.130(7) is to require s.5 to be construed to have, as far as practicable, the same effect as the corresponding EPC provisions, EPO decisions on the interpretation of arts 87–89 of the EPC are highly relevant to the interpretation of s.5 (see §5.13 above).

The leading case on the substantive test for priority of inventions under art.87(1) is G 2/98 *"Same invention"*, referred to above. The significance of this case has now been recognised by the UK Court in a number of decisions and is generally the starting point for the court's analysis of the substantive test for priority under s.5(2)(a) (see §5.13 and §5.23 above).

G 2/98 *"Same invention"* was a decision of the EPO Enlarged Board of Appeal made following a request by the President of the EPO for clarification of the apparently inconsistent approaches which had been adopted by the EPO as to the meaning of "same invention" in art.87(1). The question referred to the Enlarged Board was as follows:

> "Does the requirement of the 'same invention' in Article 87(1) EPC mean that the extent of the right to priority derivable from a priority application for a later application is determined by, and at the same time limited to, what is at least implicitly disclosed in the priority application?"

This request had arisen because previous decisions of the Boards of Appeal diverged, falling broadly into one of two conflicting camps. Early decisions under the EPC adopted a strict approach to according priority, under which subject-matter had to have been at least implicitly disclosed in the priority application for priority to be accorded (the President of the EPO cited a number of decisions adopting this "traditional approach", such as T 184/84 *NGK INSULATORS/Ferrite crystal* [1986] E.P.O.R. 169 and T 85/87 *CSIRO/Arthropodicidal compounds* [1989] E.P.O.R. 24). According to this case law, the criterion of at least implicit disclosure used for the novelty test under art.54(2) and (3) of the EPC and the disclosure test under EPC art.123(2) were considered also to apply to the test for "same invention" under art.87(1). This so-called "traditional approach" was often referred to as the "novelty test" in order to distinguish it from the less strict approach which came to be adopted in the period 1990–95.

The more liberal approach followed the decision T 73/88 *HOWARD/Snackfood* OJ EPO 1992, 557; [1990] E.P.O.R. 112, where the EPO allowed a priority date of a claim to be maintained when the claim has been voluntarily amended by the inclusion of a feature disclosed in the application in suit that was not identifiable in, or unambiguously implicit from, the teachings of the priority document, provided that such feature was not an essential aspect of the invention in suit. In this case, it was indicated (contrary to views expressed previously) that the test for priority is different from that for added subject-matter wherein the inclusion of that feature would amount to a violation of the test for art.123(2) of the EPC. T 73/88 *Snackfoods* was subsequently approved and followed by others. For example, in T 16/87 *PROCATALYSE/Catalyst* OJ EPO 1992, 212; [1992] E.P.O.R. 305, it was held that the priority right is not lost when an arbitrary limitation is inserted to avoid prior art, provided that the alteration does not lead to the claiming of a new invention, and in T 582/91 *METAL-FREN/Friction pad assembly* [1995] E.P.O.R. 574, priority was upheld where a change had been made from the priority document which was not seen as changing the character and nature of the claimed invention. However, even after the T 73/88 *Snackfoods* decision was published, there were decisions from the Boards of Appeal that were more in line with the stricter regime of the traditional approach. For example, a rigid line in denying priority was taken in T 77/97 *RHÔNE-POULENC/ Taxoids* [1998] E.P.O.R. 256, where a claim in the priority document to a sub-group consisting of four compounds was held not to provide a concrete teaching for two of those compounds individually, these compounds only being part of the purely conceptual content of that claim which was insufficient for priority to be accorded to claims directed to these specific compounds.

In G 2/98 *"Same invention"*, the Board recognised the divergence in the case law. It found that a "narrow or strict" interpretation of the concept of "the same invention" was to be preferred over the "extensive or broad" interpretation of T 73/88 *Snackfoods*, and therefore answered the reference question in the affirmative, stating that:

"The requirement for claiming priority of 'the same invention', referred to in Article 87(1) EPC, means that priority of a previous application in respect of a claim in a European patent application in accordance with Article 88 EPC is to be acknowledged only if the skilled person can derive the subject-matter of the claim directly and unambiguously, using common general knowledge, from the previous application as a whole."

It held that such an approach, which equates "the same invention" to "the same subject-matter" in art.87(4), is solidly supported by the provisions of both the Paris Convention and the EPC, and is necessary to ensure a proper exercise of priority rights in full conformity with the principles of equal treatment of the applicant and third parties and legal certainty, and with the requirement of consistency with regard to the assessment of novelty and inventive step. This decision therefore discredits the T 73/88 *Snackfoods* approach whilst allowing room for implicit as well as explicit disclosures to be taken into account. It would appear to follow, therefore, that at least some of the case law applying the stricter, traditional approach is still relevant, see Ch.IV.B of the *Case Law of the Boards of Appeal of the European Patent Office* 5th edn (EPO, 2006).

—The question of exhaustion of priority rights

In T 15/01 *SDLO/Mystery swine disease* OJ EPO 2006, 153; [2005] E.P.O.R. 45 at 461, the EPO was asked to consider whether there existed under the EPC a "doctrine of exhaustion of priority rights", namely the legal proposition that a priority right which has been claimed in a patent application is thereafter exhausted and cannot be claimed any more in a later patent application for the same territory. In T 998/99 *L'OREAL/Skin equivalent* OJ EPO 2006, 229; [2005] E.P.O.R. 39 at 417, the Technical Board of Appeal had considered the doctrine applicable and had disallowed a claim to priority from a first filing for more than one application in the same state and in respect of the same invention. However, in T 15/01 *SDLO/Mystery swine*, the TBA disagreed with the earlier decision and rejected the doctrine. It acknowledged that the EPC is silent on this issue and that art.87(1) of the EPC is open to different interpretations. However, it was concluded that the priority system of the EPC allows patent applicants to claim and enjoy the same priority right in more than one European application. The TBA declined to make a reference, and it is understood that, as at the time of writing, the President of the EPO is not intending to refer the issue to the Enlarged Board of Appeal. The TBA took the same view in the later decision of T 5/05 *DYSTAR TEXTILFARBEN/Mixtures of monoazodisperse dyes*, again rejecting a doctrine of exhaustion of priority rights.

5.27

Regenerating the priority date (subs.(3))

5.28   If there is more than one "relevant application" (for the definition of which see §5.29) disclosing the same subject-matter filed in or in respect of the same country and by the same applicant as the application in suit, the later application(s) is/are ignored for the purposes of determining priority of the common subject-matter unless certain conditions are met as regards the earliest "relevant application". These are that the first application:

(i)   must have been unconditionally withdrawn, abandoned or refused;

(ii) must not have been made available anywhere to the public;

(iii) must not have left any outstanding rights; and

(iv) must not have served to establish a priority date for another application made anywhere,

these requirements having been met *not later than* the date of filing the second application.

In essence, subs.(3) is aimed at preventing applicants extending the normal 12-month priority period. However, applicants can "regenerate" their priority date by withdrawing or abandoning a first application before it is published and then filing a second application disclosing the same subject-matter as the first. Provided the conditions of subs.(3) are fulfilled, the priority date will be the date of filing of the second application. Such a strategy is not uncommon and affords an applicant further time in which, for example, to perfect the disclosure of his invention; of course, the applicant in so doing runs the risk of intervening art.

Subsection (3) derives from art.4C(4) of the Paris Convention (see §5.06, above) and is intended to correspond to art.87(4) of the EPC (see §5.02, above). However, the subsection is in the negative form so that in broad terms the second of two earlier relevant applications is to be disregarded unless filed in the same country as the first, and provided the first was unconditionally withdrawn, abandoned or refused for all purposes before filing the second. In contrast, the corresponding art.87(4) of the EPC and art.4C(4) of the Paris Convention are in the positive form, wherein the second application is considered to be the first when the previous application was filed in the same country and was earlier abandoned for all purposes. Thus, unlike subs.(3), EPC art.87(4) is not relevant to multiple earlier applications within the 12-month period. The intention of this provision was to enact art.4C(4) of the Paris Convention, which is concerned with the problem of alleviating the position of an applicant who is otherwise unable to replace an unsatisfactory first application without loss of priority (Bodenhausen: *Guide to the Paris Convention* (BIRPI, 1968) p.45).

However, subs.(3) also applies to multiple earlier applications whether filed within the normal 12-month period or not. Thus, if the first application was not abandoned for all purposes before filing the second application, whether or not it was specified for priority purposes in the substantive application, the second application is disregarded insofar as it concerns an invention or matter disclosed in the first application, with the result that the first application also does not give priority if dated more than 12 months (subject to the possibility of a late declaration) before the filing date of the application in suit (subs.(2)).

Under subs.(3), the second earlier application will be disregarded for priority purposes if the application in suit contains matter common to both earlier applications and the earlier applications were filed *by the same applicant* as the application in suit or by a *predecessor in title* of his. The predecessor in title referred to in subs.(3) must be a predecessor in title of the applicant in respect of the title to the right to make that application and thus the term "predecessor in title" does not include a predecessor of the applicant in respect of a different title, e.g. because this is derived from a different inventorship entity (*Genentech's [Human Growth Hormone] Patent* [1989] R.P.C. 613).

In T 5/05 *DYSTAR TEXTILFARBEN/Mixtures of monoazodisperse dyes*, it was held that a document may still be regarded as the first application within the meaning of art.87(4) even though this application, and the European patent in respect of which priority is claimed, share inventors in common with an earlier application (i.e. an application predating the claimed priority document). In this case, the applicant of the claimed priority document and the patent was different to the applicant of the earlier filing. Although sister companies under common control, the TBA held that this did not change the fact that the two applicants were independent legal persons: under EPC art.87 only an applicant for a patent or his successor in title can claim the priority right, art.87 does not refer to inventors. The inventor was not relevant. The TBA commented that, while the addition of an inventor in the later filing might be an indication of a change of subject-matter, it would be impractical to allocate subject-matter to each inventor. Thus, the contribution of an additional inventor could not be a criterion in determining the validity of a priority claim with respect to an alleged earlier first application.

In T 788/05 *TERUMO KABUSHIKI KAISHA/Vascular catheter*, it was decided that, where the original filing was made by two co-applicants, a subsequent application made in the name of only one of those co-applicants, without evidence that the other co-applicant had transferred his rights to that individual, was not entitled to the priority right as not being filed by the same ''person''. As a result, the first application was prior art against the second for novelty purposes under EPC art.54(3).

Note also that, if the conditions of subs.(3) are not met, the second earlier application is disregarded only so far as concerns the invention or matter disclosed in the first earlier application; the second application is not disregarded so far as concerns priority for matter which is not in common. But this causes problems when the second earlier application broadens a specific disclosure in the first application into a generic disclosure. Priority from the second application may then be lost because it cannot be regarded as a "*premier dépôt*" (first filing) for the specific matter also contained within the generic claim. To overcome this, it may be desirable to include a claim of the "N-1" type based solely on the second application.

If the first application was filed before the normal 12-month period, contains common subject-matter and was abandoned for all purposes before the second was filed, the second application is unaffected by it. However, if the first application was not abandoned for all purposes, the second application is not disregarded so far as concerns priority for the matter which is not in common but is otherwise disregarded. EPO Guideline C–V, 1.4 reaches the same conclusion. As noted above, the same effects arise under subs.(3), even when the first application was filed within the normal 12-month period. If, however, the first application was filed before the normal 12-month period and was published before the filing date of the application in suit, not only can it not provide a basis for priority, it also entered the state of the art as from its date of publication, both as regards novelty and inventive step. Even if the first application is not published, it may still be relevant for the purposes of novelty under s.2(3). This follows also from art.4 of the Paris Convention.

In T 449/04 *HITACHI METALS/Managing steel* (Unreported), it was held that an earlier application (from which priority had not been claimed) did not prevent a subsequent application from fulfilling the necessary "first application" condition for the relevant subject-matter claimed in a later European application (within the meaning of art.87(4)) where the subject-matter was presented in the earlier application merely as a non-inventive, comparative example. Applying G 2/98 *"Same invention"*, and noting that the concepts of "same subject-matter" and "same invention" of arts 87(4) and 87(a) of the EPC are to be interpreted narrowly and strictly, the TBA concluded that the subject-matter of the comparative example, which was "clearly and definitely excluded" from the scope of the invention of the earlier application, did not represent part of the invention taught by the earlier application.

If the failure to declare priority, or to sustain such a declaration, in respect of the first application results from an error or mistake, e.g. omission of the declaration of priority, or failure to supply details of its filing date or country of filing, or failure to supply any required certified copy or translation thereof, within the prescribed time limits, then priority is lost for all matter in the first application, see *Matsushita's Application* [1983] R.P.C. 105. This is consistent with subs.(2) requiring priority to be accorded only in respect of the earliest application when the matter in question was disclosed in more than one relevant earlier application. Article 87(1) of the EPC gives the same result when construed *a contrario* in the light of arts 4A(1) and 4C(2) of the Paris Convention (see Bodenhausen, above, p.36, §(3)). It confers priority only from the first application.

As noted above, an applicant is only able to regenerate a priority date if the first application is unconditionally withdrawn, abandoned or refused before the date of filing of the second application. In *Haberman v Comptroller-General* [2004] R.P.C. 21, Mr Peter Prescott QC, sitting as a deputy judge, commented that he considered this timing condition to be capricious: in his opinion, provided the first application was withdrawn/abandoned before it was published or before anything could come of it that would affect the rights of other persons, it should not matter that the second application may already have been filed. However, given the normal interpretation of subs.(3), it is important for any attorney considering regenerating a priority to ensure that the conditions of subs.(3) are fulfilled *before* the second application is filed. On the facts, he refused to make a declaration that the first application had been withdrawn in a timely manner, but commented that as the applicant was being professionally advised, if there was doubt it should be presumed that everything had been done correctly. Before the EPO, Mandy Haberman, the claimant in the *Haberman* case, was denied a priority claim because she was unable to establish for the purposes of art.87(4) of the EPC that an earlier application had been timely withdrawn before the filing of the relevant second application: T 1056/01 *HABERMAN/Drinking vessel* (Unreported), the EPO refusing to make the suggested presumption.

Particular care also needs to be taken when claiming priority from a United States "continuation-in-part ['c-i-p'] application". Priority is not claimable for features disclosed in such an application which were also present in the earlier United States application if the earlier application was filed more than 12 months before the application in suit, see *Whitin's Application* (1937) 54 R.P.C. 278, the principle of which continues to apply. However, under the 1949 Act, priority was accorded from a c-i-p application where the original United States application could be seen to be fatally defective as containing an insufficient disclosure (*Monsanto's Applications* [1964] R.P.C. 6), and this would still seem to be the position bearing in mind that for priority to be accorded the priority document must contain an enabling disclosure, see §5.23. In T 713/02 *AVECIA/ Phosporamidites* OJ EPO 4/2006, 267, an application was filed claiming priority from a US c-i-p application; thus, the claimed priority was inappropriate. Correction of priority (the original US application having been filed less than 12 months before the application in suit) was not sought until some years later and, because of the delay, was refused. As a consequence, the application failed for lack of novelty over a document published in the priority year. It is, therefore, important that attorneys asked to file, whether in the EPO or the UK, an application stated to have been based on a US c-i-p should routinely ask to examine the parent application to check whether the claims of the proposed application are only based on new matter set out in the c-i-p. A failure to do so could result in a loss of priority with potentially serious consequences.

"Relevant application" (subss.(5) and (6))

5.29   A "relevant application" (i.e. one from which priority may be claimed for an application under subs.(2), or for a patent under subs.(4)) is either one filed under the Act (subs.(5)(a)) or one filed in a "convention country" (subs.(5)(b)), for the definition of which see s.90 and §90.02, subs.(6) now automatically extending this definition to any Member State of the World Trade Organization, other than the United Kingdom. The "relevant application" must be an "application for protection in respect of an invention" or an application equivalent thereto under the law of, or applicable in, such convention country. Thus, priority cannot be claimed from an application filed in a country (other than the United Kingdom under subs.(5)(a)) which is not recognised as a "convention country", either under subs.(6) or by a designation under s.90. However, there are now few countries which fail to qualify for this status, see the list of "convention countries" set out in §90.03.

A "relevant application" can be an application which is equivalent to an application in a convention country as a result of local law or a treaty or international convention, see EPC art.66 and PCT art.11(4). Thus a European or an international patent application is to be treated as equivalent to an application in a convention country whether the United Kingdom is designated or not. The same result arises when the United Kingdom is designated, as a consequence of ss.78(1) and 89(1) whereby a European or international application is treated for the purposes of the Act as an application for a patent under the Act. Similar effects are envisaged in respect of EPC and PCT patent applications claiming priority from applications filed under an international convention (see EPC art.87(2) and PCT r.4.10(a)(iv)). These provisions follow from art.4A of the Paris Convention, Lisbon and Stockholm texts.

However, there is a danger that an originating European patent application might be held not to be capable of establishing a priority date in countries not a party to the EPC, particularly those countries which have not ratified the Stockholm text of the Paris Convention or whose ratification does not apply to arts 1 to 12 of it. The same is true of an originating PCT patent application.

Subsection (5)(b) needs further explanation. The "application in or for a convention country ... for protection in respect of an invention" should, under the law of that country, be a regular national filing adequate to establish the date on which it was filed in the country concerned, whatever may be the outcome of the application (Paris Convention art.4A, and see also EPC art.87(2) and (3)). In *Ishihara Sangyo v Dow Chemical* [1987] F.S.R. 137 CA, it was held that, under s.5 of the 1949 Act, an application duly filed in a convention country would give rise to a right of priority irrespective of its validity under its local law, unless the relevant priority application was not an application for a patent at all. Subsection (5) appears to be of like effect. Therefore, so long as it has a filing date, the outcome of the earlier application is not relevant, subject of course to the implications of subs.(3). Thus an earlier application may serve to establish a priority date even if it is subsequently withdrawn or refused before or after a subsequent application is filed. However, if it is withdrawn prior to filing the subsequent application, it must be withdrawn explicitly, reserving the right to claim priority from it, if an applicant still wishes to use it as a priority application.

The MOPP points out that the term "for protection in respect of an invention" is not defined in the Act. However, as s.5 is intended to have the same effect as art.87 of the EPC, art.87(1) could dictate what types of applications for protection of an invention are covered by subs.5. In this regard, art.87(1) (as amended by the EPC 2000) mentions a patent application and an application for a utility model or a utility certificate (prior to amendment by the EPC 2000, an application for an inventor's certificate was also referenced but this is now obsolete). Thus, the subject-matter of a German *"Gebrauchsmuster"* application, or a French *"Certificat d'Utilité"* may be considered relevant for the purposes of s.5(2). However, following *Agfa-Gevaert's Application* [1982] R.P.C. 441, priority for a patent application may not be claimed from a German design application (*"Geschmacksmuster"*) consisting only of drawings. The EPO decided likewise (J 15/80 *Arenhold/ Priority Right: earlier deposit of industrial design* OJ EPO 7/1981, 213). The same would also be true for an attempt to claim priority from a United Kingdom design application, not least because the United Kingdom is not a convention country within the meaning of s.90.

A United States "provisional application" is also accepted by the UK-IPO as a "relevant application" from which priority can be claimed, see the MOPP (para.5.30). There used to be doubt as to the validity of this practice: until recently such an application could never itself mature into a patent. However, it is understood that US law changed in 1999 such that a provisional application can now be converted into a full US patent application within one year of filing. The MOPP notes that the UK-IPO practice would have to be reviewed if doubt were cast upon it in any proceedings before the court or Comptroller.

The priority date cannot be earlier than the date on which the earlier relevant application was filed, even if the national law of the country in which the earlier application was filed allows it to be ante-dated. It is not possible, therefore, to claim priority from a date when the invention was exhibited before filing at an international exhibition (as permitted by s.2(4)(c)), see *Soudure Electrique's Application* (1939) 56 R.P.C. 218.

PRACTICE UNDER SECTION 5

The following sections focus on practice under rr.6 to 9 of the Patents Rules 2007 (reprinted at §§5.07 to 5.10), which came into force on December 17, 2007.

Filing of declaration of priority

5.30   Declarations of priority in connection with applications under the Act are now dealt with under rr.6 to 9 (for which see above). These rules are discussed in §§5.15–5.29 above and §§5.30–5.32.

In summary, the position for applications filed on or after January 1, 2005 is as follows:

(1) Where the application in suit is filed within the normal priority period (that is, within 12 months immediately following the date of filing of the earlier application (or earliest if there is more than one) (s.5(2A)(a)), a declaration should normally be made at the time of filing under r.6(1) and is usually (but not necessarily) on a completed form PF 1. Alternatively, if the declaration is not made at the date of filing, it may be made up to four months later (that is, within 16 months immediately following the date of filing of the earlier application (or earliest if there is more than one) (r.6(2)(b)) provided all the conditions of rr.6, 8 and 9 are met. Such a declaration must be made on PF 3 together with its attendant fee.

(2) In exceptional circumstances (essentially where the applicant "unintentionally" fails to file the application in suit within the normal 12-month priority period and provided the relevant rules are complied with, see s.5(2C) and r.7), permission may be granted under s.5(2B) for a late declaration of priority. Where permission is granted, the application in suit may be filed up to two months after the end of the normal 12-month priority period, i.e. 14 months from the filing of the earlier application (or earliest of them where there is more than one), (s.5(2A)(b) and r.7(1)). Unless the request relates to a "new application" (as defined in r.2(1) as being a new application filed under s s.8(3), s.12(6) or s.37(4) or as mentioned in s.15(9)), the request must be made on PF 3 (with its attendant fee) and supported by evidence of why the application in suit was not filed before the end of the normal 12-month period (r.7(2)). Where the evidence does not accompany the request, the Comptroller must specify a period in which the evidence must be filed (r.7(3)). In the case of new applications, the request may be made in writing, rather than on PF 3, and no evidence shall accompany it. The declaration which it is desired to file if permission is to be granted must be made at the same time as the request for permission (r.7(9)).

The time limits for making a late claim to priority under r.6(2)(b) and requesting permission to make a late declaration of priority under r.7(1) are inextensible (Rules, Sch.4 Pt 1, reprinted at §123.26). However, where the period for filing the application and/or declaration expires on a day which is specified by the Comptroller as an excluded day under s.120, or on a day which is certified under r.110(1) as one on which there was an interruption due to a general interruption or subsequent dislocation in postal services within the United Kingdom or an interruption in the normal operation of the Patent Office, then the period is extended to include the next following day which is not excluded or certified as interrupted (r.110(3)), reprinted in §123.28). The period may also be extended under r.111 in particular cases affected by a delay in, or failure of, a communication service, being a service by which documents may be sent or delivered such as post, electronic communications or courier, see §123.79.

A declaration made under the PCT in respect of an international application entering the national phase will be accepted and treated as a declaration under s.5(2) in accordance with s.89B(1)(b) (see §89B.05). Similarly, by s.78(3)(a), a declaration of priority made under EPC art.88(1) and EPC r.38 is treated as a declaration made under s.5(2) (see §78.03).

As regards the requirements to furnish the UK-IPO with the application number of and file a certified copy and translation of the priority application, the subject of the priority declaration, see §§5.31 and 5.32 below.

Filing of application number and copy of priority application

The furnishing to the UK-IPO of the application number of each priority application **5.31** and the filing of copies of each priority document is now covered by r.8 (reprinted above), the periods for each of these requirements remaining at 16 months from the declared priority date (r.8(5)) but extendible by a period of two months under r.108(2), subject to a further discretionary extension under r.108(3), reprinted at §123.25 and discussed in §§123.73 and 123.74. A failure to provide this information will result in the priority declaration being disregarded insofar as it relates to the priority application with respect to which there is non-compliance. In the case of a new application (i.e. one filed under ss.8(3), s.12(6),or s.37(4) or as mentioned in s.15(9) (divisional)), the period is two months beginning with the new application's initiation date, or the period specified in r.8(5) if it expires later (rr.8(5) and 21(1)(b)).

Except where the application in suit is an international application for a patent (UK) and the application number of the priority application was indicated in accordance with the PCT (r.8(3)), the file number of a priority application must be furnished to the UK-IPO within the 16-month period. It is recommended, however, that, if possible, this information be supplied when filing the declaration both as an aid to identification and to avoid overlooking this requirement at the possible later date. Where priority is claimed from a Japanese utility model application, care should be taken to include the preface "U" as part of its file number as otherwise the number may be taken to be that of a patent application having the same number, see *Patents Journal* April 9, 1997. The *Formalities Manual* at paras 6.37 to 6.40 sets out the correct numbers for Belgian, Hungarian and Irish priority documents.

Each priority application must be certified by the authority with which it was filed or otherwise verified to the satisfaction of the Comptroller, and a copy provided to the Comptroller. If more than one priority is claimed, then all the priority documents must be supplied within the 16-month period. There is an exception in the case of an international application for a patent (UK) where a copy of the priority application was filed in compliance with the PCT (r.8(4)). Further, there is also now an exception where a copy of the priority document is "available to the comptroller": this is to allow for the use of electronic libraries of priority applications.

Note that if a copy is not filed within the required 16-month period, then, subject to a request for an extension, the declared priority date will be lost before preparations for publication under s.16 have been completed. The period for placing the application in order for acceptance will then run from the actual filing date, with no earlier priority attached to the contents of the application (see §5.20).

For further discussion of the requirements for copies of priority documents for applications under the Act see §15.13 and (for divisional applications filed under s.15(9)) §15.23. Also see §§81.09, 89A.30 and 89A.31 for discussion of the filing of copies in relation to European patent applications (UK) converted into an application under the Act and international patent applications (UK). Note that rr.6B(3)(a) and 6B(4)(a) of the 1995 Rules (as amended), which expressly stated that rr.6B(1) and 6B(2) regarding supply of the application number and copy of the priority application did not apply where the application was one proceeding as a result of a direction under s.81, have been omitted from new r.7, as they are unnecessary by virtue of s.81(3)(c).

If a required copy is not filed, but this is not noticed by the UK-IPO and the application becomes published with a priority statement, the statement will be deleted under r.107 when the error is discovered (*Brossman's Application* [1983] R.P.C. 109), unless late filing under r.108(3) should be permitted.

Supply of translation of copy of priority application

Rule 9 (see above) absolves an applicant from automatically being required to file either **5.32** a translation of a priority document or a declaration that the application in suit is a complete translation of the priority application, as was the position prior to January 1, 2005. A translation (or declaration) is only required where the Comptroller has, in the exercise of his discretion, provided a direction for such supply, which he may only do where the priority application is not in English or Welsh and where it is considered that matters disclosed in the priority document are relevant to the determination of whether or not an invention, to which the application in suit relates, is new or involves an inventive step (r.9(1)(b) and (c)). The 2007 Rules have thus remedied the deficiency under r.6C(1)(c) of the Patent Rules 1995 (as amended), in which the assessment of novelty was not a relevant ground under which the Comptroller could require the filing of a translation.

Where such a direction is given, and the priority application is not in English or Welsh, a translation of it is required to be filed, or a declaration given that the application in suit is a complete translation of it into English (r.9(4)). This is to be done within the period of time specified by the Comptroller under r.9(2) (such period must not end after the grant of the patent (r.9(3)) and will normally be the same as the time given for replying to the examination report, *Formalities Manual*, para.6.54), failing which the declaration made under s.5(2) is to be disregarded as regards that priority application (r.9(4)). This period is extensible under s.117B and r.109. The translation does not need to be verified (unlike the position prior to January 1, 2005); if the examiner has doubts as to the accuracy of the translation, he may request evidence under r.115. What is meant by the words "complete translation" in relation to a declaration that the application in suit is a complete translation of the priority application was the subject of *Legal Advice No.19/99 from the EPO President* (EPO OJ 1999, 296–299) in relation to the corresponding provision of the EPC then in force (EPC r.38(4)).

The *Formalities Manual* specifies that where a translation was requested under the Patent Rules in force prior to January 1, 2005 (e.g. the examiner could require a verified translation rather than a declaration) then that request is still valid and the translation must be filed before the application is granted (see para.6.58 of the *Formalities Manual*).

If a required translation or declaration is not supplied in time, preparations for publication will have been completed and the time periods for the application will be unaffected, that is will remain as calculated from the originally declared priority date, even though no priority will now be accorded to the contents of the application (see §5.20).

Deleting or changing a priority claim by correction

5.33   As discussed in more detail in the commentary on s.117, it may be possible under s.117 to delete or correct a priority claim if the original inclusion or mistake in its details is due to a clerical error or mistake, see §117.07. The EPO has allowed a correction of this type, although only when requested in time for a warning to be published with the application, see §§117.08 and 117.11. The EPO has also allowed, under certain conditions, the addition of an omitted priority declaration, see J 3/82 *TAISHO/Correction-Priority* OJ EPO 1983, 171, although this should now be covered by the new provision introduced by the EPC 2000 allowing a late claim of priority. However, s.117 cannot be used to correct a mistake in the filing of a document, in contrast to a mistake in the document itself (*Klein Schanzlin's Application* [1985] R.P.C. 241). See T 713/02 *AVECIA/Phosporamidites* OJ EPO 4/2006, 267, referred to above in §5.28, where, because of delay, correction of a priority claim was refused.

Withdrawal of a priority claim by amendment

5.34   A declaration of priority may be withdrawn at any time before grant, and such a request should be made in writing (see *Formalities Manual*, para.6.59).

Applying for a certified copy

5.35   Where certified copies of a United Kingdom patent application are required to support claims to priority in foreign patent applications, application is made on PF 23, with the accompanying fee, as described in §32.38.

Inspection of a priority document

5.36   For several years, it was the practice of the UK-IPO to transfer from the public part of the application file to its secret part the copy of an earlier patent application from which priority had been claimed but had been withdrawn prior to publication. Third parties could not then determine whether that earlier application invalidated a subsequent priority claim, e.g. under subs.(3)(b). Now, the earlier application is maintained on the public file, see the correspondence on revoked Patent No. 2,128,706.

SECTION 6

Disclosure of matter, etc., between earlier and later applications

6.—(1) It is hereby declared for the avoidance of doubt that where an applica- **6.01**
tion (the application in suit) is made for a patent and a declaration is made in accordance with section 5(2) above in or in connection with that application specifying an earlier relevant application, the application in suit and any patent granted in pursuance of it shall not be invalidated by reason only of relevant intervening acts.

(2) In this section—

"relevant application" has the same meaning as in section 5 above; and

"relevant intervening acts" means acts done in relation to matter disclosed in an earlier relevant application between the dates of the earlier relevant application and the application in suit, as for example, filing another application for the invention for which the earlier relevant application was made, making information available to the public about that invention or that matter or working that invention, but disregarding any application, or the disclosure to the public of matter contained in any application, which is itself to be disregarded for the purposes of section 5(3) above.

Note. Section 130(7) requires s.6 to be construed in conformity with the corresponding provisions of the EPC and PCT, see Notes 1 and 2 to §5.01, and §5.13.

COMMENTARY ON SECTION 6

Scope of the section

Section 6 is a provision added to the Bill for the 1977 Act during the committee stage in **6.02**
the House of Commons on July 5, 1977, and was designed to re-enact the provision of s.52 of the 1949 Act, and arts 4A and 4B of the Paris Convention (reprinted at §5.06), in order to protect an applicant against invalidity of his claims due to an "intervening act" of disclosure or use of the invention during the "intervening period", namely the interval between the claimed date of the priority application and the filing date of the application in suit described in a priority application. However, by s.130(7), the section is to be construed in conformity with the EPC and the EPC contains no corresponding provision. Moreover, s.6 is stated to be only a declaratory provision "for the avoidance of doubt". As discussed in §6.04, the EPO Enlarged Board of Appeal has given a decision apparently contrary to the provisions of the section, even though that decision appears also to be contrary to the wording of the Paris Convention. Thus, unless that decision can be avoided or overruled, it seems doubtful whether the section actually has any real effect, although the relevant intervening act might provide a right of use under s.64 to avoid infringement of a patent based on an application filed by a third party at a later stage during the "intervening period".

Anyway, s.6 could only be operative when a declaration of priority has been made in accordance with s.5(2). It is not clear whether s.6 could apply when this declaration has been made, but is invalid or inoperative, because, for example, the requirements of r.8 have not been met as to the supply of a certified copy within the due time. The UK-IPO practice seems to be that priority is not then accorded (*Matsushita's Application* [1983] R.P.C. 105), but s.6 refers only to a priority having been "declared".

In any event, the word "between" in subs.(2) means that care should be taken when, for example, there are a number of earlier applications filed on the same day containing common subject-matter but each concentrating on a different aspect of an invention. If a subsequent application is filed for that common subject-matter claiming priority from one or more, but not all, of the earlier cases, subs.(2) might, anyway, have no effect because the other earlier applications were not filed between the date of filing of the earlier priority application and the subsequent application. In such a situation, it would be advisable to claim priority from all of the earlier applications.

Operation of section 6 in practice

6.03   In *Beloit v Valmet* [1995] R.P.C. 705, Jacob J. (as he then was) held that s.6 merely clarifies the consequences emerging from s.5(2)(a): it does not have any substantive effect, as indicated by the opening words "It is hereby declared for the avoidance of doubt". It was made clear that s.6 should be given a meaning consistent with the EPC, particularly because such meaning is required by s.130(7); and also because it would be absurd if a patent could be saved under the Act when it could previously have been revoked by the EPO under the terms of the EPC. Such uniformity could be achieved by holding the words in s.6, "declaration is made in accordance with section 5(2)", to mean a declaration made "in accordance with and having effect under section 5(2)" so that s.6 merely provides that it is a consequence of conferring priority that a subsequent filing, publication or exploitation of that for which priority is properly claimed cannot invalidate merely because this occurred before the actual filing date of the application. This view was held to be in conformity with art.4B of the Paris Convention, and the decision of G 3/93 *Priority interval* OJ EPO 1995, 18; [1994] E.P.O.R. 521, discussed in §6.04. This holding was not challenged on the appeal: [1997] R.P.C. 489 CA.

It therefore appears that section 6 has little effect in practice. Thus, if a development is made of an invention described in a priority application, a further priority application should be filed in respect of it and intervening publication by the inventor or his assignee should, if possible, be avoided since such is likely then to be effective prior art against any subject-matter later included in the application or in an application which claims priority from the earlier application, see also A. Maschio [1995] *CIPA* 269. The difficulties in drafting claims where there are multiple priorities and intervening publications were discussed by J.C.H. Ellis (1989–90) 19 *CIPA* 187, but it should be remembered that (unlike the position under the 1949 Act) a claim may now be in respect of a plurality of related inventions and priority dates are now accorded to an "invention", rather to a "claim", see §125.27.

In *Evans Medical's Patent* [1998] R.P.C. 517, it was contended that, if the priority document was non-enabling so that priority was lost, then an intervening publication of the work described in the priority document should likewise be held to be non-enabling. However, it was held that here the intervening publication gave more information than did the priority document and, although it described a procedure carried out on a different bacterium and so was not novelty-destroying, it would have been obvious to apply its teaching to the organism in issue: hence, the claims lacked an inventive step over the disclosure of the intervening publication, following loss of the declared priority date.

If the section does have any effect, then it may be noted that, in *International Paint's Application* [1982] R.P.C. 247, the word "described" in s.52 of the 1949 Act was held to have the same meaning as in s.5(2) so that it seems likely that the same test for the "matter disclosed in the earlier relevant application" applies under s.6 as it does under s.5, for which see §5.24. The corresponding s.52 of the 1949 Act was also discussed in *Ronson v Lewis* [1963] R.P.C. 103 and applied in *Letraset v Rexel* [1976] R.P.C. 51 CA.

Relevant EPO decisions

6.04   The EPC has no direct counterpart to the wording of s.6, though the provisions of EPC art.54 (novelty), EPC art.88(2) (multiple priority), EPC art.88(3) and (4) (substantive priority) and EPC art.89 (effect of priority) ought to be construed in such a way that art.4B of the Paris Convention (reprinted at §5.06) is satisfied, because the preamble of the EPC states that the EPC is a special agreement within the meaning of art.19 of the Paris

Convention. Although the EPO has held that it is not directly bound by the Paris Convention as the European Patent Organisation is not a party to it, see J 15/80 OJ EPO 1981, 213, it has said that the provisions of EPC arts 87–89 and EPC r.38, while forming a complete code of rules of law on the subject of priority rights, are nevertheless to be considered as based on the same principles as the priority provisions of the Paris Convention (T 301/87 *BIOGEN/Alpha-interferons* OJ EPO 1990, 335; [1990] E.P.O.R. 190).

This latter decision gave an interpretation to the EPC which seemed aligned with s.6, because it held that the contents of a prior application, published elsewhere, are not to be deemed to be part of the state of the art against matter contained in an application claiming priority from that application. However, the EPO Enlarged Board of Appeal subsequently specifically overruled that decision (G 3/93 *Priority interval* OJ EPO 1995, 18; [1994] E.P.O.R. 521) and held that:

> "a document published during the priority interval, the technical contents of which correspond to that of the priority document, constitutes prior art citable under EPC a. 54(2) against a European patent application claiming that priority, to the extent such priority is not validly claimed";

and that:

> "this also applies if a claim to priority is invalid due to the fact that the priority document and the subsequent European application do not concern the same invention because the European application claims subject-matter not disclosed in the priority document".

For a criticism of G 3/93 *Priority interval*, see G.W. Schlich [1995] E.I.P.R. 327.

It has been argued that this decision is contrary to the above-discussed terms of the Paris Convention (J. Boff, *epi-Information* 1995, 27 and L.J. Steenbeek, *epi-Information* 1999, 140), but so long as it stands then additional matter contained in a document published after the declared priority date will enter the state of the art and therefore can impugn the validity of a later-dated invention, see comment by R.S. Crespi (1990) 2(2) I.P.B. 24.

As discussed above, in *Beloit v Valmet* [1995] R.P.C. 705, the Patents Court followed G 3/93 *Priority interval*. However, on a literal interpretation of the EPC (read in conformity with art.4B of the Paris Convention) some doubt may continue to exist as to whether s.6 is in accord with it, in spite of s.130(7), because Bodenhausen (*Guide to the Paris Convention*, BIRPI 1968, 41–42) makes it clear that the protection provided by this Convention is in respect to "acts accomplished in the priority application" with respect to the invention, i.e. the one disclosed in the priority application and not one that is obvious with respect to it.

Also, particularly in a climate where the UK courts have stated that great significance should be attached to decisions of the EPO Boards of Appeal, particularly where the Boards have formed a settled view, see §91.03 and *Actavis UK Ltd v Merck & Co Inc* [2008] R.P.C. 26; [2008] EWCA Civ 444 CA, it seems that reliance should only be placed on s.6 as a last resort, and the old doctrine of "provisional protection" provided by s.52(1) of the 1949 Act is unlikely to be applicable for patents under the present Act, a matter which some regret, see J.C.H. Ellis, *epi-Information* 1994, 147.

Right to apply for and obtain a patent and be mentioned as inventor [Sections 7–13]

SECTION 7

Right to apply for and obtain a patent

7.—(1) Any person may make an application for a patent either alone or jointly with another. **7.01**

(2) A patent for an invention may be granted—

    (a) primarily to the inventor or joint inventors;

    (b) in preference to the foregoing, to any person or persons who, by virtue of any enactment or rule of law, or any foreign law or treaty or international convention, or by virtue of an enforceable term of any agreement entered into with the inventor before the making of the invention, was or were at the time of the making of the invention entitled to the whole of the property in it (other than equitable interests) in the United Kingdom;

    (c) in any event, to the successor or successors in title of any person or persons mentioned in paragraph (a) or (b) above or any person so mentioned and the successor or successors in title of another person so mentioned;

and to no other person.

(3) In this Act "inventor" in relation to an invention means the actual deviser of the invention and "joint inventor" shall be construed accordingly.

(4) Except so far as the contrary is established, a person who makes an application for a patent shall be taken to be the person who is entitled under subsection (2) above to be granted a patent and two or more persons who make such an application jointly shall be taken to be the persons so entitled.

Note. Although s.130(7) does not require s.7 to be construed in conformity with the EPC, art.60 of the EPC seems relevant, therefore see §7.02 below.

Relevent Convention Provision

EPC Article 60—Right to a European patent

7.02   **60.**—(1) The right to a European patent shall belong to the inventor or his successor in title. If the inventor is an employee the right to a European patent shall be determined in accordance with the law of the State in which the employee is mainly employed; if the State in which the employee is mainly employed cannot be determined, the law to be applied shall be that of the State in which the employer has the place of business to which the employee is attached.

(2) If two or more persons have made an invention independently of each other, the right to a European patent therefor shall belong to the person whose European patent application has the earliest date of filing, provided that this first application has been published.

(3) In proceedings before the European Patent Office, the applicant shall be deemed to be entitled to exercise the right to a European patent.

(As amended by the EPC 2000.)

Note. The amendments to art.60 of the EPC made by EPC 2000 apparently have little or no consequence.

Commentary on Section 7

Scope of the section

7.03   Section 7 deals with the right to apply for and obtain a patent. Sections 8–12 and s.37 deal with disputes regarding the entitlement or progress of UK and overseas patents and applications, with s.36 regulating the rights of co-owners. Section 13 deals with the right to be mentioned as inventor. Section 39 deals with the issue of entitlement as between an employer and employee.

Section 7 particularly concerns the identity of an applicant for a patent under the Act (subs.(1)) and of the person(s) entitled to be granted a patent (subs.(2)), including a European patent (UK) (s.77(1)(b)), with a presumption of entitlement set out in subs.(4).

The effect of the section is essentially different from that under the 1949 Act. This is a consequence of the change of the meaning of "inventor", now defined in subs.(3) and discussed in §7.10 and the automatic ownership by an employer of certain inventions made by his employees, see s.39 and §§39.07–39.12.

Who may apply for a patent (subs.(1))

Subsection (1) states that any person may make an application for a patent. There is no **7.04** requirement in subs.(1) for that person to be entitled to the grant of the patent at that stage. Under s.15(1)(b) the identity of the applicant for a patent must be made known. Where the applicant is not the sole inventor or the applicants are not the joint inventors, then, under s.13(2), a statement of the derivation of the right to grant must be filed in due time (see §13.09) or the application will be deemed to be withdrawn. Subsection (4) states that the applicant is presumed to be entitled to the grant, except where the contrary is shown. Therefore, the application may be made by a person not entitled to the grant in the expectation that the patent will be granted eventually to the rightful owner. Further, because of this presumption, if a third party seeks to challenge the entitlement, the onus of proof will be on the challenger (see §37.06).

Who is a person

Section 7 states that it is a "person" who may apply for and be granted a patent. In addi- **7.05** tion, s.30(1) provides that patents are "personal property".

In order to determine whether an entity is able to benefit from the protection of the Act, it is necessary to determine whether it is a "person" within the meaning of the Act, i.e. an entity capable under English (or Scots) law of becoming the owner of personal property in the form of a patent. Under the Interpretation Act 1978 (c.30), the term "person" includes "a body of persons corporate or unincorporate". Thus, a company may be a "person". In the case of partnerships, a limited liability partnership may be a "person", as it has legal personality separate from that of its members, but an unincorporated partnership under English law is not an entity distinct from its members, and in such case it is the partners themselves who are "persons". The general legal rule under English law as to ownership of personal property is, therefore, that an owner may be a single individual, several individuals (as co-owners) or a legal entity, such as a company, limited liability partnership or other form of corporation.

In order to benefit from the protection of the Act, an entity must be treatable as a "person". This means that a foreign entity will only be recognised as having legal personality, and therefore a capacity to sue or be sued, if such a body has been accorded legal personality under the law of a foreign state recognised by the United Kingdom, see *Westland Helicopters v Arab Organisation for Industrialisation* [1995] Q.B. 282. Although it may seem logical to conclude that, if an entity is a person for the purpose of legal proceedings, it should be able to own property under English law equally for the purposes of the Act, there is no case deciding this specific point.

To ensure that the patent can be properly granted, therefore, the applicant has the onus of describing its status properly, see *Schwarzkopf's Application* [1965] R.P.C. 387 which allowed an application to be made by a German "*Kommanditgesellschaft*". On similar principles, applications are allowed by a German or Austrian "*offene Handelsgesellschaft*", by a Swiss "*Société Commandite*" and by a "limited partnership" organised under the laws of certain of the United States of America. In *Discovision v Pioneer Electronics* BL C/55/98, noted I.P.D. 21103, the patentees were a general partnership under Californian law and as, under that law, the partnership could as such hold property in its own name a change in the partners was not a transaction, instrument or event to which s.68 (or s.33) applied. The *Formalities Manual* lists other US states where limited partnerships can hold property in their own right.

The Formalities Section at the UK-IPO holds an extensive, though non-exhaustive, list of foreign unincorporated bodies which are believed to be capable of holding property in their own name under the laws of their country of origin, the more common of which were listed in (1978–79) 8 *CIPA* 371. Others are listed in the MOPP, and include a Scottish partnership firm, although the partners' names must also be given. The UK-IPO's list of recognised overseas bodies can now be found on the UK-IPO website in Ch.7 of the MOPP and in s.2 of the *Formalities Manual*.

The *Formalities Manual* sets out what the Formalities Examiner should look for in the PF 1 and the steps to take if there is a problem. In particular, Annex 2E sets out a letter to be sent where the applicant is a trust in order to establish whether, like a National Health Service Hospital Trust, it is capable of holding property in its own right, or whether the names of up to four nominated trustees should be recorded on the register instead, there being an express prohibition against recording any notice of any trust on the register (see s.32(5)). Applications made on behalf of Government departments should proceed in the name of the "Secretary of State" or "Minister" responsible for the department and not in the name of the individual holding that office.

For a discussion on ownership of IP by children and the validity of the contracts into which they might enter for assignment or exploitation see Saunders and Robinson, "Can children own IP?" [2009] June *CIPA* 390–392.

Who may be granted a patent (subs.(2))

7.06　　Subsection (2) refers to the person(s) to whom the patent may be granted. In *Yeda v Rhône-Poulenc Rorer* [2008] R.P.C. 1; [2007] UKHL 43, Lord Hoffmann stated that subs.(2), with the definition of "inventor" in subs.(3), provided an exhaustive code for determining the entitlement to the grant of a patent. The wording at the end of that subsection "and to no other person" made that clear.

The subsections state that a patent may be granted: (a) "primarily" to the inventor(s); or (b) "in preference" to the inventor(s), to any person entitled to the whole of the property in the invention by virtue of law, convention or enforceable agreement made before the making of the invention. "Primarily" was taken by Lord Hoffmann in *Yeda v Rhône-Poulenc Rorer* as emphasising that the claim to the patent had to flow through the inventor. This reflects the traditional British view that the right to be granted a patent flows from the act of invention and not from the ownership of the invention. Such a view is consistent with art.60 of the EPC. Someone claiming through the inventor, must then base their claim either on subs.(2)(b) due to, e.g. a right of an employer under s.39 or on subs.(2)(c) by being the successor in title to the inventor or the person referred to in subs.(2)(b). So the first step in any dispute is to identify the inventor and then afterwards to decide if someone else is entitled to the patent under paras (b) or (c).

In *Markem v Zipher* [2005] R.P.C. 31, where a previous employer was contesting the ownership of an application filed by the inventors' new employer, the Court of Appeal held that reliance on paras (b) or (c) required the claimant in an entitlement dispute to show that there had been a breach of some rule of law which gave rise to the entitlement. However, whilst not doubting the outcome in *Markem v Zipher*, this as a broad point of principle was overturned by the House of Lords in *Yeda v Rhône Poulenc* (above), as in the latter case it was a question of identifying the inventor and so determining the entitlement, rather than knowing the inventor and then determining entitlement as between two companies.

The term "in preference" in para.(b) shows the point at which the primary assumption that the invention belongs to the inventor(s) is overridden when a legally enforceable right to the invention exists at the time when the invention is made, e.g. because the invention belongs to the inventor's employer by virtue of s.39(1). Paragraph (c) applies where the right to the patent arises after the making of the invention.

The entitlement qualification for grant of the patent is the legal title to the patent property, ignoring equitable interests. This, apparently, admits a grant to be held in trust for an equitable owner (on which see §30.04), and an equitable title can be registered, see §32.19.

The reference to "enactment or rule of law" in subs.(2)(b) will include the automatic right of an employer to ownership of the invention under the provisions of s.39(1), but preference over an inventor could also occur where, before the making of the invention, there is appointed: a trustee in bankruptcy for an insolvent inventor; a deputy appointed by the Court of Protection to control and manage a person's property under the Mental Capacity Act 2005 (c.9) s.16, s.18; the custodian of enemy property in times of war; and possibly also a guardian of a person under the age of 18, who has rights to inventions arising after the date of the appointment.

The "time of making the invention" is referred to in subs.(2)(b). In *Beecham v Bristol SA* [1978] R.P.C. 521, the time of making of an invention of selection was considered to be the date when the necessary advantage was appreciated, see also *El Du Pont's Patent* [1961] R.P.C. 336. *French v Mason* [1999] F.S.R. 597 confirms the "common sense" view that the question of ownership of an invention must first be considered as of the date on which the invention was made; and any question of equitable ownership, such as a constructive trust, must have arisen or subsisted at that time.

By subs.(2)(c), the rights of the successors in title will override those entitled under paras (a) and (b) (they are entitled "in any event"). Frequently such persons will be successors of such rights to the patent by virtue of an assignment made after the invention has been devised. Such an assignment of the right to apply for a patent would appear to be one covered by the common law (see further below). However, they also include, in respect of an existing invention, the personal representatives (i.e. executors or estate administrators) of a deceased inventor or the rightful applicant and the heirs following a distribution of his estate; or on appointment of: a trustee in bankruptcy for an insolvent inventor; a deputy appointed by the Court of Protection to control and manage a person's property under the Mental Capacity Act 2005 (c.9) s.16, s.18; the custodian of enemy property in times of war; and possibly also a guardian of a person under the age of 18.

Section 7(2)(b) specifically makes it possible to assign the right to file a patent application before an invention is made:

> "a patent for an invention may be granted. . . to any person. . . who,. . . by virtue of an enforceable term of any agreement entered into with the inventor before the making of the invention, was or were a the time of the making of the invention entitled to the whole of the property in it".

Consequently, s.7(2)(c) makes it possible to assign the right to file a patent application between the date on which the invention is made and the application is filed. Whilst at common law the assignment of a future chose in action is void, equity allowed a purported assignment for valuable consideration to be treated as a contract to assign in the future, when the chose came into being, although the legal title still needed to be perfected. (Note that under s.30, a patent is personal property, but without being a "thing in action".) However, in the light of the explicit statutory wording, this common law/equitable principle is not applicable to patentable inventions. The CDPA 1988 has a similar provision (s.91) to permit the assignment of future copyright. The only comparable provisions in relation to designs are where a UK registered or unregistered design is commissioned for money or money's worth, but this does not apply to Community design rights.

In *KCI Licensing Inc v Smith & Nephew Plc* [2010] F.S.R. 31, [2010] EWHC 1487 Pat Ct, the term in a confidentiality agreement by which the inventor assigned and agreed to assign to an employer "all right, title and interest to all confidential information, inventions and improvements conceived or developed by me, . . . during my employment . . . ." was enough to give the employer the rights to the PCT application, including the right to claim priority from the US priority application which had been filed in the name of the inventor. (See further the commentary under §5.19 above.)

The right to file the patent application and the right to claim priority are two separate rights. Whilst any person may file the patent application and the assignment only needs to be in place by the time of grant, this is not the position for a priority claim, where the right to make that claim must be in place from the outset, see *Edwards Lifesciences AG v Cook Biotech Inc* [2009] F.S.R. 28, [2009] EWHC 1304 Pat Ct. Although the patentee appealed, the first instance decision was upheld on other grounds and this point was not considered by the Court of Appeal, [2010] EWCA Civ 718 . See further the commentary under §5.19 above and also on *Lancaster University Business Enterprises Ltd and the University of Lancaster* BL O/040/09 at §37.10 below.

For further discussion on *Edwards v Cook* and *KCI v Smith & Nephew*, see Cordina and Stephen, "Can entitlement to priority be transferred, shared or divided?" [2010] July *CIPA* 408.

The issue of entitlement under s.7(2)(c) came before the Comptroller in *Raven v Williamson* BL O/259/10. The hearing officer looked first at the requirements of s.30(6) and agreed that there had been no written assignment of rights. However, he then went on to consider whether there was an oral agreement which was sufficient to give Williamson a beneficial interest in the case before the patent application was filed (Williamson having provided strategic advice, instructed the patent attorney with whom the inventors had liaised and paid the fees). He concluded that there was and that Williamson had the right to remain as a named applicant.

The hearing officer was not referred to *KCI v Smith & Nephew* (above), which was decided one month before *Raven*, although he did find support in the recent Court of Appeal decision regarding equitable and legal ownership of a registered design: see *Ifejika v Ifejika et al* [2010] EWCA Civ 563. The hearing officer's decision in *Raven* [2010] F.S.R. 29, is consistent with Arnold J.'s position in *KCI*. Although *KCI* largely dealt with written documents transferring the rights prior to the making of the invention, there is discussion as to the roles of equity and law and the extent to which formalities need to be complied with to transfer rights. In relation to the second applicant, the court held at para.[98]:

"Counsel for KCI accepted that he could not point to any written assignment, or even an oral agreement, but argued that the correct inference to be drawn from the circumstances surrounding the filing of the PCT Application was that KC Inc had agreed by conduct to transfer part of its interest in the invention to its subsidiary Mediscus. He submitted that this was sufficient to make Mediscus a successor in title for the purposes of claiming priority, and that no greater degree of formality was required. I accept that submission."

For a review of further case law and examples as to what will give rise a right to a patent in preference of that of the inventor under this subsection see §7.09, §37.05 and, for employees, see the commentary under s.39.

The MOPP indicates that only executors and administrators appointed in the UK of a deceased's estate fall within the meaning of "personal representatives". If no personal representative has been appointed for a deceased applicant by the date of grant nor the application assigned to a third party, the MOPP states that the patent is granted to the deceased applicant. The MOPP also indicates that applications should proceed in the name of the applicant even if he is of unsound mind and that applications by minors may proceed in their own names or that of a parent or guardian.

For procedure to change the applicant entity or entities, see §7.13.

Identifying inventors and applicants

7.07   Since a patent may be revoked under s.72(1)(b) on the ground that it was granted to a person who was not entitled to be granted that patent, presumably in accordance with s.7(2) (see §7.12) and since it may be a defence to an infringement action that the person suing is not the proprietor (*Cinpres v Melea* [2008] R.P.C. 17; [2008] EWCA Civ 9, it is obviously of importance that the facts concerning entitlement should be correctly established before grant.

Patent attorneys have a particular responsibility to identify, before filing an application, the inventor(s) from whom the entitlement to grant is to be derived, neither omitting a true deviser nor gratuitously naming any person who, in law, did not make a contribution to devising the inventive concept for which a patent is to be sought, see *Xaar's International Application* BL O/257/98, where it was stated that patent attorneys should take particular care to ensure that all employees and past employees who contributed to the actual devising of the claimed subject-matter should be named as inventors, and *BNOS Electronics' Patent* BL O/270/98, where naming the entire research team without apparent regard to consideration of actual inventorship was seen as a "simply too casual approach". Inventorship is a question of fact, rather than agreement between the parties as pointed out in *Meider v Whitfield* BL O/171/10.

However, an exhaustive review at this point in time is unlikely to be realistic and, indeed, may not be possible, not least because a full prior art review may not have been undertaken and, as Lord Hoffmann said in *Yeda v Rhône-Poulenc Rorer*:

> "the inventive concept is a relationship of discontinuity between the claimed invention and the prior art. Inventors themselves will often not know exactly where it lies".

Where an applicant decides to acknowledge another as an inventor in order to "get [alleged inventor] off his back", he may then store up an entitlement dispute, where the onus will now be on him to prove that the alleged inventor was not, in fact, an inventor (*Rose v Ability* BL O/247/11).

The inventor(s) has/have to be identified either on filing the application, see s.13 on PF 1 which asks questions about the identity of the inventors, or by the filing of a statement of inventorship on PF 7 within a defined period thereafter, see §§13.08, 13.09 and §13.15, although the, or each, inventor may waive his right to be named in the published application. The making of a change in the identified inventors is discussed in §§13.13 and §13.17.

The fact that an applicant has made an application for protection of the invention in a convention country does not in itself give any right under subs.(2), as it did under s.1(2) of the 1949 Act. Nevertheless, in order to obtain a priority date under s.5(2), the applicant in the United Kingdom must be the same as, or be able to show title from, the applicant of the relevant application referred to in s.5(5), see s.5(2) and (3). See also §7.06 re *KCI Licensing Inc v Smith & Nephew Plc* and *Edwards v Cook*.

Identifying the "invention"

Before identifying the "inventor", it is first necessary to establish the subject-matter of the alleged invention. **7.08**

Notwithstanding that, by s.125, the invention for which a patent has been granted is to be taken as that specified in the claims of the patent, the court will not just look at the form of the claims of a pending application to decide what the invention is and who is the deviser of that invention. Moreover, the issue of inventorship can arise even before an application has been filed, or where an application has been filed but no claims have yet been formulated. The Court of Appeal recognised in *Markem v Zipher* that patent attorneys often draft a first set of claims very broadly so as to get the most out of the search and claims will be amended prior to grant. The issue for the court will be to see what is "the heart" of the invention, even though there may be more than "one heart", and each claim may not need to be considered a separate "heart" on its own. Accordingly, the enquiry is one as to who contributed. But a distinction has to be drawn between contributing inventive information and contributing common general knowledge or non-patentable integers of the claim or even carrying out routine experiments to provide examples that the invention works as expected—see *IDA v University of Southampton* [2006] R.P.C. 21; [2006] EWCA Civ 145 CA, reported sub nom. *University of Southampton's Application* [2006] R.P.C. 21 at 567. Only after the inventor(s) for a particular invention have been identified can one determine what rights, if any, they (or another) have in it (*Yeda v Rhône-Poulenc Rorer*).

It is also worth considering the wording of s.43(3), which draws a distinction between the employee inventor and those who merely contribute advice or other assistance, but do not make the invention (see §43.04).

Issues of validity of claims will be relevant: especially where claim 1 is overly broad. Traditionally entitlement was determined according to the alleged inventor's perception of what he had discovered, rather than what might turn out in the light of the prior art actually to have been invented. In other words, validity considerations are not generally to be taken into account in assessing entitlement questions and "invention" in this context should not mean a "patentable invention", see *Norris's Patent* [1988] R.P.C. 159 and *Viziball's Application* [1988] R.P.C. 213. This may be due in part to the fact that s.74 does not allow invalidity to be put into issue in an inventorship or entitlement dispute and frequently references under s.8 become references under s.37. However, s.74 relates to a challenge to validity of a granted patent, and so has no application to a pending application, although, it can become relevant where the patent is granted before the entitlement proceedings are determined.

However, two recent important decisions have changed this practice.

In *Yeda v Rhône-Poulenc Rorer* [2008] R.P.C. 1; [2007] UKHL 43, Lord Hoffmann held that s.7(2) provided an exhaustive code to entitlement to the grant of a patent. Section 7(3) defined the inventor as "the actual deviser of the invention", and so it was necessary to distinguish between the person who had made the invention and the person who had made a non-inventive contribution.

"Deciding upon inventorship will therefore involve assessing the evidence adduced by the parties as to the nature of the inventive concept and who contributed to it. In some cases this may be quite complex because the inventive concept is a relationship of discontinuity between the claimed invention and the prior art. Inventors themselves will often not know exactly where it lies."

Also, in *Markem v Zipher* [2005] R.P.C. 31, the Court of Appeal felt that, as a matter of convenience, if a claim was clearly and unarguably invalid, then not only could the Comptroller take that into account when exercising his wide discretion, and deal accordingly with such claims, he ought to do so as there was no point in "handing rights in an invalid monopoly from one side to another" and "the sooner an obviously invalid monopoly is removed, the better from the public point of view". Where there was "self-evidently no bone", the "dogs [should] be prevented from fighting over it". So Jacob L.J. concluded:

"if an inherent part of a claim to entitlement is also an assertion of or acceptance of invalidity, the entitlement claim must fail."

The hearing officer proceeded to consider this aspect of *Markem* in *Statoil v University of Southampton* BL O/204/05 and found that the principle applied where either of the parties to the entitlement dispute raised the question of validity, and the defendant "should not be allowed to get away with pleading invalidity as an inherent part of his defence".

Thus, questions of patentability can now be raised pre-grant in entitlement proceedings and previous cases to the contrary will no longer be good law. However, care may be needed in applying this where the invention in question is patentable in an overseas jurisdiction but not patentable in the UK (e.g. because it relates to computer software or a method of doing business—as in *LIFFE v Pinkava* [2007] R.P.C. 30; [2007] EWCA Civ 217).

An example of how the hearing officer addresses the prior art can be found in *Welland Medical v Hadley* BL O/133/11. Here the prior art was used to assess the construction which should be put on claim 1, but without making any decisions on inventiveness. Thus the hearing officer was able to conclude that the claimant's contention as to the invention was too wide in the light of the prior art and that the defendant's narrower construction was to be preferred.

Disputed Entitlement

7.09   Sections 8 and 12 both require a determination of the ownership to "that invention" and s.37 requires determination of the ownership of "the patent". However, for all of these there will need to be an identification as to what the invention is, who made it, and how the applicant derives its title. In *Markem v Zipher* [2005] R.P.C. 31; [2005] EWCA Civ 267, the Court of Appeal reflected that, if two independent parties came up with the same invention, then the patent would go to the party who filed its application first. So it was not enough for A to be entitled to a patent itself. It had to show that, by some rule of law (that is more than just the provisions of s.7, but some breach of contract or breach of confidence), B was not entitled to the patent application that B had filed, or at least that A was entitled to a share of that application.

That general proposition was overturned by the House of Lords in *Yeda v Rhône-Poulenc Rorer* but resulted in three judgments. Lord Hoffmann held that s.7(2) provided a complete code to determining entitlement and one first had to start by identifying the inventor of the inventions set out in that patent or application. In determining the question as to who the inventor had been, Lord Hoffmann could see no reason to import questions of whether one of them had a personal cause of action against the other. Lord Hoffmann further held that the Court of Appeal was muddling up *entitlement* with *validity* and, in a system of first to file, the inventor who filed first was entitled to *a* patent, but not *the* patent and the second to file would suffer from lack of novelty under s.2(3). Lord Walker said that the Court of Appeal's proposition was likely to be relevant generally where s.39 was in play. Where there was more than one independent invention, in the hands of unconnected parties, then there was only an "inchoate property in the invention" until an application had been drafted and the subsequent application would have to contend with the earlier as prior art. (However, this case was brought under s.37 and so their Lordships might not have considered that applications under ss.8 and 12 can be brought even before the application has been filed, although the UK-IPO is likely to require a written description of the invention in question.) Lord Neuberger pointed to the wording of s.37(1) as showing that a person could not allege that they were the true proprietor of *the* patent in question if there no connection between that third party and the current proprietor or the chain of title. The wording in ss.8(1) and 12(1) is not quite so clear-cut, as at that stage there is no patent and, under s.8, the application may not even exist: the question that is referred is whether the claimant is entitled to a patent for *that* invention.

For examples of the application of s.7(2): in *Kokta's Patents* BL O/88/91, noted I.P.D. 15018, a general policy document issued by a University stating that patent rights in University inventions would pass to the appropriate professor was held sufficient to pass to the professor rights to inventions made by a co-inventor with him who at the time was a University employee and in *Walter's Applications* BL O/272/05, noted in [2006] *CIPA* 122, the claimants successfully relied upon an agreement which the parties had entered into, before setting up the claimant company, which provided for the company to own, under s.7(2)(b), the patent applications for the inventions created after the date of the agreement. However, an unenforceable assignment gives no rights under subs.(2)(b) or (c). Such an assignment is likely to be one made by an employee prior to the making of the invention and therefore unenforceable under s.42(2) (for which see §42.03) if the assignment diminishes the employee's rights. For further case law see generally at §37.04 and, for employees, see §§39.05–39.13.

Definition of "inventor" (subs.(3))

"Inventor" is defined in s.130(1) as having the meaning given to it by s.7 and is defined **7.10** in subs.(3) as the "actual deviser" of the invention. These words were used in s.16(2) of the 1949 Act where they were defined for the purposes of that section to exclude the first importer of an invention into the United Kingdom who was also regarded under former United Kingdom patent statutes as an inventor for the purposes of making an application. This distinction is irrelevant to the 1977 Act, and the first importer is no longer regarded as an inventor by virtue of the words "no other person" at the end of subs.(2). Thus, a person may no longer (as under previous statutes) file an application in his own name as a "communication" from abroad on the basis of being the first importer.

The statement in s.43(3) that, for the purposes of ss.39–42, a person who merely contributes advice or other assistance in the making of the invention by another person is not an inventor, is believed to be in harmony with case law that then existed on inventorship see, e.g. *Allen v Rawson* 135 E.R. 656; (1845) 1 C.B. 551; *Smith's Patent* (1905) 22 R.P.C. 57; and an article by R. P. Lloyd (1979–80) 9 *CIPA* 16.

In *Henry Bros v Ministry of Defence* [1997] R.P.C. 693; and [1999] R.P.C. 442 CA, the Court of Appeal assessed inventorship by asking who contributed to the underlying inventive concept, assuming such to exist, and on this basis held that the proprietor had no claim to entitlement as its employee had not even been a co-inventor. At first instance, stress had been laid on who had invented the claimed combination of elements, but the Court of Appeal saw the alleged invention in a different light, while reaching the same end result. In *Minnesota Mining's Patent* BL O/237/00 the "invention" was seen as not only the underlying idea, but also its means of realisation: on this basis those employees of another firm who had supplied the composition which brought the idea to fruition were entitled to be named as co-inventors and their employer consequently entitled to co-ownership, although not necessarily on the terms set out in s.36(3), see §37.07.

In *IDA v University of Southampton*, see §7.08 above, the Court of Appeal found that the invention had been made by an IDA employee before the University of Southampton was asked to assist in showing that it worked. The University employees had merely to find out "whether or not [the] idea worked" and "that was a matter of simple and routine experimentation—mere verification". They were not inventors; their "'contribution' amounted to no more than adding the common general knowledge in the art". See also *Stanelco Fibre Optics v Bioprogress (No.1) and (No.2)* [2005] R.P.C. 15 and 16; [2004] EWHC 2263 Pat Ct, Mr. C. Floyd QC, where, for some inventions, D (Bioprogress' employee) was found to have added common general knowledge to N's (Stanelco's employee) untested concept. For some claims there was co-inventorship and for some N was not an inventor. See also: *Clegg v Amcor Flexibles* BL O/206/05, noted [2005] *CIPA* 540, in which Dr Clegg was found not to have contributed to the research work which lay at the "heart of invention".

In *Welland Medical v Hadley* BL O/133/11, the hearing officer found that although there had been confidential discussions between the parties, they had come up with completely different solutions to the same problem. The defendant's patent application did not contain any disclosure of the claimant's solution and the defendant was the actual deviser and sole inventor of the content of his application.

Entitlement to grant (subs.(4))

7.11   Subsection (4) provides that, except insofar as the contrary is established, the applicant is entitled to grant of the patent. Thus, there is a rebuttable presumption that the person making the application under subs.(1) is entitled to the grant under subs.(2) and a referrer in an entitlement dispute has the onus of proving entitlement (*Viziball's Application* [1988] R.P.C. 213), and he will fail if there is an unresolvable conflict of evidence, see §37.06. However, there is an argument that, in an employer-employee entitlement dispute, s.39(2) (discussed in §§39.07–39.13) reverses the onus of proof, see §39.07. Note also the comments of Lord Hoffmann in *Yeda* (above), that the effect of this section is that "the person who seeks to be added as a joint inventor bears the burden of proving that he contributed to the inventive concept ... and a person who seeks to be substituted as sole inventor bears the additional burden of proving that the inventor named in the patent did not contribute to the inventive concept."

Section 7 provides for joint applicants and grantees. In the absence of an overriding agreement, the rights of co-owners inter se are governed by s.36, see the commentary under that section.

Entitlement can be challenged before grant under s.8(1) and after grant under s.37(1). Although lack of entitlement is a ground of revocation, this remedy is available only to the person who has been found to be properly entitled, see §7.12.

Under arts 60 and 61 of the EPC and the EPC Protocol on Recognition, entitlement is left as a matter for national law, see §§82.03–82.06. Entitlement to a European patent may be challenged before grant under s.12(1), subject to ss.82 and 83, see the commentaries on those sections. Entitlement to an international application and to a foreign patent application may also be challenged under s.12(1). It is not possible to challenge ownership of a foreign patent under the Act.

Revocation after grant to non-entitled person

7.12   By s.72(1)(b), it is a ground of revocation that the patent was granted to a person who was not entitled to be granted that patent, i.e. was not a person entitled under s.7(2) to be granted the patent. This corresponds to art.138(1)(e) of the EPC (reprinted in §72.02). Where a person entitled to be a co-owner was not named as one of the proprietors, there is doubt whether the patent ought to be revoked, but rather that an order should be made for that person to become a co-owner, see *Henry Bros v Ministry of Defence* [1999] R.P.C. 442 CA discussed in §72.13. At first instance in that case (see [1997] R.P.C. 693), it was decided that (by s.72(2)) the ground of revocation under s.72(1)(b) is available only to a person already found by the court under its general jurisdiction to grant a declaration, or the Comptroller under s.37, to be entitled to the patent, but the questions of entitlement and revocation may be considered sequentially in consolidated or linked proceedings, as also discussed in s.123 or §72.13, or, under the 2007 Rules, they can be raised in the same proceedings. Also, note the change to s.36(3)(a) with effect from January 1, 2005 by the 2004 Act, whereby a co-proprietor may no longer seek revocation of the patent without the consent of the other co-owner(s) (see §36.05).

Also, under s.72(2)(b) this ground of revocation is not available if the proceedings before the court or the Comptroller were commenced more than two years after the patent was granted, unless at the time of grant, or on transfer of the patent, the proprietor knew that the claim to entitlement was wrong. Indeed, s.37(5) and (8) respectively preclude the Comptroller and the court from making an order under s.37 unless this condition is found to have been met, see *Peart's Patents* BL O/209/87 where the Comptroller took the point on his own initiative. However, see also *Yeda v Rhône-Poulenc Rorer* (above), which stressed that it is the proceedings which need to have been begun, but where changing a reference from a claim to joint ownership to one of sole ownership occurred, that did not change the fundamental nature of the proceedings, namely "who is entitled?". The two-year time limit is reiterated in s.74(4). Given that it is no longer necessary to begin separate proceedings under the different provisions of the Act and the Comptroller has power to allow amendment of statements of case (r.82), it remains to be seen whether the late amendment to include a claim for revocation would be allowed in any particular case. The meaning of "knew" in this context is discussed in §37.11.

Other aspects of s.72(1)(b) and (2) are discussed in §72.13 and §74.05.

PRACTICE UNDER SECTION 7

Change of applicant

In summary, there are three routes available for addition or deletion of an applicant: **7.13**

(1) By applying, at any time either before or after grant, to make a correction to PF 1. This can be done in two ways: either

    (a) as a request for correction of an error in the register or document filed in connection therewith (by filing a written request under r.50 (request for correction of error) reprinted at §32.10 and discussed in §32.21); or

    (b) as a request for correction of error in a patent or application (by filing a written request under r.105 (correction of errors) reprinted in §117.02 and discussed in §117.12).

(2) By filing a written request under r.31 (amendment of application before grant), reprinted in §19.02 and discussed in §19.04.

(3) By filing PF 21 under r.47 (registration of transactions, instruments or events), reprinted at §32.07 and discussed in §§32.26–32.32.

SECTION 8

Determination before grant of questions about entitlement to patents, etc.

8.—(1) At any time before a patent has been granted for an invention (whether **8.01**
or not an application has been made for it)—

(a) any person may refer to the comptroller the question whether he is entitled to be granted (alone or with any other persons) a patent for that invention or has or would have any right in or under any patent so granted or any application for such a patent; or

(b) any of two or more co-proprietors of an application for a patent for that invention may so refer the question whether any right in or under the application should be transferred or granted to any other person;

and the comptroller shall determine the question and may make such order as he thinks fit to give effect to the determination.

(2) Where a person refers a question relating to an invention under subsection (1)(a) above to the comptroller after an application for a patent for the invention has been filed and before a patent is granted in pursuance of the application, then, unless the application is refused or withdrawn before the reference is disposed of by the comptroller, the comptroller may, without prejudice to the generality of subsection (1) above and subject to subsection (6) below—

(a) order that the application shall proceed in the name of that person, either solely or jointly with that of any other applicant, instead of in the name of the applicant

or any specified applicant;

(b) where the reference was made by two or more persons, order that the application shall proceed in all their names jointly;

(c) refuse to grant a patent in pursuance of the application or order the application to be amended so as to exclude any of the matter in respect of which the question was referred;

(d) make an order transferring or granting any licence or other right in or under the application and give directions to any person for carrying out the provisions of any such order.

(3) Where a question is referred to the comptroller under subsection (1)(a) above and—

(a) the comptroller orders an application for a patent for the invention to which the question relates to be so amended;

(b) any such application is refused under subsection 2(c) above before the comptroller has disposed of the reference (whether the reference was made before or after the publication of the application); or

(c) any such application is refused under any other provision of this Act or is withdrawn before the comptroller has disposed of the reference **(whether the application is refused or withdrawn before or after its publication)** [*, but after the publication of the application*];

the comptroller may order that any person by whom the reference was made may within the prescribed period make a new application for a patent for the whole or part of any matter comprised in the earlier application or, as the case may be, for all or any of the matter excluded from the earlier application, subject in either case to section 76 below, and in either case that, if such a new application is made, it shall be treated as having been filed on the date of filing the earlier application.

(4) Where a person refers a question under subsection (1)(b) above relating to

an application, any order under subsection (1) above may contain directions to any person for transferring or granting any right in or under the application.

(5) If any person to whom directions have been given under subsection (2)(d) or (4) above fails to do anything necessary for carrying out any such directions within 14 days after the date of the directions, the comptroller may, on application made to him by any person in whose favour or on whose reference the directions were given, authorise him to do that thing on behalf of the person to whom the directions were given.

(6) Where on a reference under this section it is alleged that, by virtue of any transaction, instrument or event relating to an invention or an application for a patent, any person other than the inventor or the applicant for the patent has become entitled to be granted (whether alone or with any other persons) a patent for the invention or has or would have any right in or under any patent so granted or any application for any such patent, an order shall not be made under subsection (2)(a), (b) or (d) above on the reference unless notice of the reference is given to the applicant and any such person, except any of them who is a party to the reference.

(7) If it appears to the comptroller on a reference of a question under this section that the question involves matters which would more properly be determined by the court, he may decline to deal with it and, without prejudice to the court's jurisdiction to determine any such question and make a declaration, or any declaratory jurisdiction of the court in Scotland, the court shall have jurisdiction to do so.

(8) No directions shall be given under this section so as to affect the mutual rights or obligations of trustees or of the personal representatives of deceased persons, or their rights or obligations as such.

Note. Subsection (3)(c) was amended by the Patents Act 2004 (c.16) s.6 with effect from January 1, 2005, except for any reference made before that date for which the previous form of the subsection continues to apply (SI 2004/3205, arts 2(b) and 9(2)).

RELEVANT RULE—RULE 20

Rule 20—New applications under sections 8(3), 12(6) and 37(4)

20.—(1) The period prescribed for filing a new application under section 8(3) **8.02** or section 12(6) is the relevant period.

(2) A new application for a patent may be filed under section 37(4) before the end of the relevant period.

(3) For the purposes of this rule the relevant period is—

(a) where the comptroller's decision to make an order under those provisions is not appealed, three months beginning [with] immediately after the date on which the order was made; or

(b) where that decision is appealed, three months beginning [with] immediately after the date on which the appeal was finally disposed of.

(4) But the comptroller may, if he thinks fit, shorten the relevant period after giving the parties such notice and subject to such conditions as the comptroller may direct.

Note. As amended by The Patents (Amendment) Rules 2011 (SI 2011/2052).

OTHER RELEVANT RULES—RULES 73–88

8.03   The rules reprinted at §§123.06–123.21 are those of Pt 7 of the Patents Rules 2007 and are general in nature to govern procedure in all proceedings to be heard before the Comptroller. These specifically include proceedings under s.8(1) and (5). These rules are discussed under the heading "Practice under Section 123", but are also mentioned, as appropriate, in the commentary and practice sections below.

Note. For "replacement" applications filed under s.8(3), rr.21, 28(4)–(7) and 30(3) and (4) (reprinted respectively at §§15.06, 18.02 and 18.04) are also relevant.

COMMENTARY ON SECTION 8

Scope of the section

8.04   Section 8 is part of a series of sections dealing with ownership and entitlement. Section 7 deals with the right to apply for and obtain a patent. Sections 8–12 and s.37 deal with disputes regarding the entitlement or progress of UK and overseas patents and applications, with s.36 regulating the rights of co-owners. Section 13 deals with the right to be mentioned as inventor. Section 39 deals with the issue of entitlement as between an employer and employee.

Section 8 provides a procedure by which any person claiming to have a right in an invention may apply to the Comptroller for him to resolve the matter and make an appropriate order. The nature of the claim will be based on the provisions of s.7(2). (See *Yeda v Rhône-Poulenc Rorer* [2008] R.P.C. 1; [2007] UKHL 43, where it was held that s.7(2) provides a complete code for entitlement, as discussed at §§7.06 and 37.04.) A claim under s.8 may be made at any time before grant of the patent, and even before any application for a patent is filed. A similar claim after grant may be made under s.37. Section 8 is not referred to in s.130(7) as having the same effect as a corresponding EPC article.

Under s.25(1), the date of grant is the date when the notice of grant is published. However, once a letter is issued under s.18(4) indicating that the patent application is due for grant, the application process comes to an end. The MOPP indicates (para 8.03.1) that entitlement applications under s.8 cannot be progressed during the hiatus thus created and any filed during the hiatus must wait until after publication of notice of grant and will then be treated as applications under s.37, (by virtue of s.9).

A reference under s.8 does not delay the publication or substantive prosecution of the patent application (*Brooks and Cope's Application* BL O/71/93) and there is no general power to stay the prosecution or grant of the application pending resolution of the entitlement dispute (see §8.07). (However, note, in contrast, the interim interdict granted by the Court of Session in *Quantum Glass v Spowart* [Scotland], [2000] ScotCS 299, noted [2001] *CIPA* 99, to prevent a patent applicant and inventor from further prosecuting an *international* application pending full trial of the issues of entitlement and breach of confidence, even though the effect of the interdict made it likely that the application could not proceed within the required time limits—see §12.03 and §37.07). If, as is often the case, grant of the patent occurs before the s.8 proceedings have been determined, s.9 causes the proceedings to be continued under s.37, for which see §9.02 and §37.04. Therefore, the commentary here deals mainly with cases that have actually been decided under s.8, or which have involved some point of interpretation thereof, and the commentary on s.37 deals generally with entitlement disputes whether commenced under s.8 or 37.

Entitlement disputes can also be dealt with under s.12 if they involve foreign, including international, patent applications and, in precedence to s.12, under s.82 if they involve certain applications for a European patent.

Entitlement disputes will rarely, if ever, begin without reliance also on s.7 and may frequently also have recourse to s.13. Indeed, the question of inventorship lies at the heart of any entitlement dispute because, under s.7, entitlement can only arise by a chain of rights which originate with those who have made an inventive contribution to the subject-matter of the alleged invention, and this may, therefore, involve a detailed analysis to identify the inventor: see the discussions in §§7.08–7.10 and §13.07. In making a determination as to ownership, it may also be necessary to consider issues of breach of contract or breach of confidence. The Comptroller does not have jurisdiction to adjudicate breach of confidence claims, but he does have jurisdiction to consider breach of confidence issues and other questions of general law such as breach of contract in the context of cases referred under this section and that may be important for the choice of jurisdiction in which to resolve any such dispute (see further at §8.05 below in relation to the *Henderson* point and under §37.08 in relation to the exercise of the Comptroller's power to decline jurisdiction).

Where the parties to an entitlement dispute involve an employer and an employee, the substantive law is contained in s.39, with ancillary provisions in ss.40–43; see the commentaries on these sections. In such cases, the decision on ultimate entitlement made under s.8, 12 or 37 may require an analysis of the facts by reference to the provisions of s.39.

Section 10 allows the Comptroller to decide between co-applicants as to how a patent application should be dealt with, and s.11 provides for directions consequent on a decision under s.8 (or s.10) to order transfer of a right arising under the application, although it is no longer necessary to start separate co-joint proceedings under either of those sections (cf. *West and Gibbon's Application* BL O/147/93, with subsequent proceedings noted I.P.D. 17100); and likewise (under s.13) if inventorship is also to be challenged (cf. *Mann and Northwood's Patent* BL O/109/94).

Section 8 deals with two disparate questions, each of which may be referred to the Comptroller by a person who used to be called the "referrer" but should now be referred to as the "claimant" (r.73(3)). These questions are: (a) whether any third party, usually of course the claimant, is entitled to be granted a patent or to have any rights in or under it (subss.(1)(a), (2), (3), (5) and (6)); and (b) whether a right in or under an application of co-proprietors who cannot agree should be transferred or granted to any other person (subs.(1)(b), (4) and (5)). The procedural rules are now set out in Pt 7 (reprinted under s.123) and are the same regardless of the type of claimant or the provision of the Act under which the reference is made. Each such reference is notified to the applicant for the patent and may be notified to others known, or presumed, to be interested, including for example any known licensee or the grantee of a security under the patent application (see §8.09). It may then be contested by a counter-statement lodged in accordance with Pt 7 of the Rules by a person who used to be called an "opponent" but is now called the "defendant" (r.73(3)), which term will include the existing applicant for the patent.

Question (a) is a straightforward claim to entitlement. Usually, the claim arises after an application for a patent has been filed and the claimant is a non-applicant; the topic is therefore more conveniently discussed in association with claims to entitlement made after grant and thus in the commentary on s.37. Question (b) concerns disputes between existing co-applicants and arises out of s.36(3) which governs co-ownership of applications as well as of patents by virtue of s.36(7)(a). In either situation, the claimant bears the onus of proof of his allegations—on the usual civil law test of the balance of probabilities—and will therefore fail if this onus is not discharged, see §37.06.

Under subs.(7), the Comptroller may decline to deal with any matter under the section and require any such dispute to be referred to the court for determination. This provision is analogous to that in s.37(8) and is therefore mentioned in §37.06 and discussed in §37.08.

Also, no direction may be given under s.8 which would affect the mutual rights or obligations of trustees or of the personal representatives of deceased persons, or their rights or obligations as such (subs.(8)).

Raising of questions of entitlement

A question of entitlement under s.8 may be referred to the Comptroller by any person **8.05** and thus by a co-applicant (under s.8(1)(b)), or (under s.8(1)(a)) by any other person who believes himself or herself to be entitled to a patent for the invention, see *Secretary of State for Defence's Application* BL O/135/89, noted I.P.D. 13063 and §8.09. The procedure is similar to that when a question of entitlement is raised before the Comptroller post-grant under s.37, as discussed in §37.13 and §37.14, but for the practice under s.8 see also §8.09.

In *Pelling and Campbell's Application* BL O/134/87, the question was raised whether the words "any other person" at the end of s.8(1)(b) have the narrow meaning of "any person other than a co-proprietor"; or the wider meaning of "any person other than the transferor or grantor", thereby allowing the "other person" to be a co-proprietor. No finding was made on the point as the dispute was resolved under s.10, see §10.04. The amendment made to s.37(1) by the CDPA 1988 now deals with the point for resolution of an objection post-grant, see §37.04. It is surprising that a corresponding amendment was not made likewise in ss.8(1) and 12(1) because ss.8(1), 12(1) and 37(1) each originally had closely similar wording. The wording of s.37(1) will ultimately be applied in many cases owing to the effect of s.9.

Under *Henderson v Henderson* (1843) 3 Hare 100, as reiterated by the House of Lords in *Johnson v Gore Wood* [2002] 2 A.C. 1:

"the parties [should] ... bring their whole case before the court so that all aspects of it may be finally decided ... once and for all".

Therefore, where a party sought to bring a new breach of confidence action, after the determination of an entitlement action in which no such allegations had been raised, and which was based on the same facts as the entitlement action, it was struck out as an abuse of process (*Markem v Zipher* [2005] R.P.C. 31; [2005] EWCA Civ 267). In the first action it had not been asserted that the employees had done anything wrong or unlawful. In response to points raised in the entitlement proceedings, the employees had started High Court declaratory proceedings to clear their names of wrongdoing, but these had been stayed in favour of following Markem's entitlement application.

However, an application made initially as a claim for joint ownership can subsequently be amended to be a claim to sole ownership. (See *Yeda v Rhône-Poulenc Rorer* [2008] R.P.C. 1; [2007] UKHL 43.) This is also consistent with *Ruttle Plant Hire v Secretary of State for the Environment* ([2007] EWHC 1773 (TCC)) where it was held that the rule in *Henderson* does not prevent late amendment of statements of case to add issues which might have been pleaded earlier. Also, where the intention is subsequently to pursue separate defendants who might have been involved in the initial case, but were not, see *Ashley Wilde Group v Kocak et al* (John Baldwin QC, March 17, 2010).

Nature of the invention to be considered under section 8

8.06   Because a reference under s.8 may be made even when no application for a patent has yet been filed, the form of any claims in such an application cannot determine the nature of the invention that has to be considered as to entitlement to its origin or ownership. The UK-IPO will review the full specification (or other description where there is no application) to determine what the invention is, then who devised it and finally who is entitled to it (see *Microscience Technologies v CRP Group* BL O/234/07—although note that this was decided before *Yeda*, see the discussion under §7.09 and *Welland Medical v Hadley* BL O/133/11).

An entitlement dispute may require inventorship to be assessed in relation to more than one inventive concept, where those concepts are contained in the same application, and in relation to the application as a whole and not just the wording of the claims. Entitlement to each of those may be different. See cases such as *Collag v Merck* [2003] F.S.R. 16 where a number of inventive concepts were contained in the application, and the court held that this had to be assessed from the application as a whole, not just the claims. Different inventive concepts may involve different contributions from the parties as in *BNOS Electronics' Patent* BL O/270/98, where inventorship was assessed not only in relation to the main concept alleged to be inventive (as assessed by the main claim originally filed), but also in respect of any other feature disclosed which might be considered as a subsidiary concept having an inventive character. For further discussion as to the assessment of the "invention" etc. see §§7.08–7.10.

Where the reference under s.8 is begun before the application has been published and the claimant does not have a copy, then the claimant will need to set out what he believes the patent application contains and the Comptroller will assess whether there is anything in common between those "ideas" and the inventions in the unpublished applications (*Toland & Coates Smith* BL O/79/08).

Relief under section 8

—General

Subsections (1) of each of ss.8 and 37 require the Comptroller to determine the question **8.07** referred to him and to make such order as he thinks fit to give effect to the determination. Therefore, his powers are not limited by the range of orders set out in subss.(2) and (3). In both *Szucs' Application* BL O/4/86 and *University College London's Application* BL O/381/02, declarations were made respectively that: (1) certain matter in the abandoned application was the referrer's property; and (2) the applicant was the inventor and entitled to the invention. Where the invention was the subject of a corresponding international application, a declaration will also made under s.12 (see §12.04).

Types of order available under s.8 are set out in subs.(2) and include orders that the application should proceed only in certain specified names (subs.(2)(a)(b)); the application be refused or that it be amended to exclude non-entitled subject-matter (subs.(2)(c)); or that a licence should be granted or transferred to specified persons (subss.(2)(d) and (4)). In view of the similarity of these provisions with the types of order which may be made under s.37, the various categories of relief available in the various types of entitlement disputes are primarily discussed in the commentary on s.37.

The Comptroller has no power to declare an application void ab initio in order that a later-filed application can validly stand in its place. In contrast to the provisions of the EPC, which allow the EPO to suspend applications pending the resolution of entitlement disputes, the Comptroller appears to have no power to stay proceedings, or to require an applicant to maintain the application in contention pending determination of entitlement proceedings under s.8. In fact, the MOPP indicates that the application should continue to be progressed and the officer managing the entitlement dispute should regularly check to see whether grant has occurred and the s.8 proceedings treated pursuant to s.9 as proceedings under s.37. However, where the entitlement proceedings are transferred to the court, the Comptroller may well accede to requests by the parties for extensions of time to respond to official actions pending resolution of the dispute by the court, although the parties will need to watch the deadlines for putting the case in order for allowance (r.30). Further, if the entitlement application succeeds but the original application no longer subsists, the Comptroller does have power (under subs.(3)) to permit the filing of a new application (herein called a "replacement application") claiming the filing date from the earlier application, as discussed in §8.08 (although, for entitlement disputes begun prior to January 1, 2005, only if the wrongly filed application has been published). Accordingly, although the UK-IPO did change its practice so that steps could not be taken which would jeopardise the position of a claimant/referrer, this is no longer required and had been deleted from the MOPP. Where joint proprietorship has been established, but the two applicants have fallen out, an order has been made for the additional applicant to be sent copies of all the papers and an indication given that any further dispute could be resolved upon an application made under s.10 (*Rutherford's Application* BL O/61/99). See also the comments at §§8.04, 12.03 and §37.07, regarding the interim interdict granted by the Court of Session in *Quantum Glass v Spowart* [Scotland], [2000] ScotCS 299, noted [2001] *CIPA* 99, in relation to an *international* application.

Should the Comptroller order a transfer or assignment of any right in the application to any other person (subs.(4)), or decide that there should be a variation in entitlement, he may need to consider whether the rights of the apparently entitled parties are subordinated to one or more employers under the provisions of s.39(1). Thus, in *Inrad's Application* BL O/164/88, where the parties to an entitlement dispute under s.8 were agreed that one of the four named inventors was not an inventor, the Comptroller ordered PF 7 to be endorsed with his decision; a correction slip to be issued for the specification; and publication of the order in the *Patents Journal*. The proceedings were then adjourned for the remaining inventors to put forward proposals on proprietorship. Meanwhile (and in contrast to the decisions referred to above) the applicant was not permitted to amend or abandon the application.

—Filing of new application (subs.(3))

8.08   If the original application is withdrawn, refused or amended by exclusion of the matter in dispute, ss.8(3), 12(6) and 37(4) allow the person who referred the question to file a new application (a "replacement application") for the relevant matter. Where the entitlement reference under this section was made before January 1, 2005, the original application had to have been published before the Comptroller could allow a replacement application to be filed. However, the revision of subs.(3)(c), noted in §8.01 above, allows a replacement application, which is permitted to be filed under subs.(3), to be back-dated to the date of filing of the original application, irrespective of whether the original application had been published before it was withdrawn. A corresponding amendment has been made to s.12, see §12.01.

Where the claimant could not take advantage of subs.(3), the entitled person might still have been able to file his own new application and, if necessary, seek to overcome any publication of the invention under s.2(4). However, the change to this section should now allow the entitled person to backdate their application to the date of filing of the original application, even if it was not published, claiming any priority claimed in the original application and so deal with prior disclosure that way. This means that, where the original application was never published, but its contents had been disclosed after its filing, the novelty of the replacement application is no longer impugned. However, that may not assist where the earlier application did not originally claim priority from another relevant earlier application (r.6(1)) (although see further below), unless the provisions of s.2(4) are applicable to the replacement application.

The claimant must identify the subject-matter over which he claims ownership, and for which he can put forward a case for patentability (*Stevens' Application* BL O/63/93). He cannot merely assert that there is subject-matter in the earlier application which he devised without setting out the particulars.

In *Amateur Athletic Association's Applications* [1989] R.P.C. 717, specifically with reference to s.8 proceedings, it was indicated that, by analogy with reviving an apparently abandoned application by extension of time under the rule which is now r.108(1), it might be possible to allow an application to proceed in the name of the claimant notwithstanding that it had previously been treated as withdrawn (this would now be subject to the provisions of Sch.4 (to the Rules) and the other provisions of r.108, for which see §123.25). Furthermore, in *Shape and Potemkin's Applications* BL O/140/92, the register was rectified as to ownership of an abandoned application in order that a successful claimant/ referrer could claim priority from it in a replacement application which he was permitted to file under s.8(3). However, this type of relief is possible only where the priority application was filed as one under the Act (when s.8(3) or 37(4) may apply), or as a European or international application (when s.12(6) may apply). See *Dodge's European Application* BL O/20/90, noted I.P.D. 13136, discussed in §12.05 where (not without misgivings as to the effect of the decision on third parties) a replacement application was allowed to be filed over five years after the lapse of the wrongfully filed case, see further §12.05.

Subsequently, in *Stafford Rubber Company's Application* BL O/255/02 the claimant was allowed to file a new application under s.8(3) taking the date of the defendant's earlier application, but the order was made subject to third party terms analogous to those employed in s.28A for revocation actions, because of the perceived risk that a third party may have begun working the invention in reliance on the lapsing of the earlier application, at least in respect of matter common to the two applications. It was accepted as likely that such terms would be academic, but in the event that they were invoked, the hearing officer thought that the claimant might have a case for damages against the defendant.

This was followed in *Mastermover's Application* BL O/269/05, noted [2005] *CIPA* 668, where the claimant was allowed to file a new application under s.8(3), subject to third party terms. The claimant argued strongly that it was blameless, but then so too would be a third party who relied on the notice of abandonment of the earlier application filed by the claimant's ex-employees. However, where the third party obtained information or assistance from the ex-employees or where the acts would have infringed various registered and unregistered design rights, then such acts were not to be exempted.

A replacement application is possible where the original applicant had abandoned its application (*Earl Engineering's Application* BL O/18/91; and it need not be identical with the original application, see *Acoustech's Application* BL O/95/94) where the replacement application had to omit one paragraph which the claimant/referrer agreed described a feature which was not his invention and which anyway he asserted was unpatentable.

If the original application is allowed to lapse before determination of proceedings commenced under s.8, a replacement application can nevertheless be permitted (*Jessamine Holdings' Application* BL O/138/85). Also, where a non-entitled application has been abandoned but had served as a priority document for a second application, a claimant/ referrer has been allowed to file two replacement applications, with the second claiming priority from the first (*Amateur Athletic Association's Applications*, referred to above) it being here recognised that, while there is no specific power to allow a replacement application to claim priority, such has long been the settled practice with divisional applications with which there is an analogy. Moreover, only in this way could the claimant/ referrer here be given any effective relief because the first non-entitled application had been filed one day before his own application and such was therefore prior art against him under s.2(3). Similar relief was granted in *Coin Controls' Application* BL O/95/89, noted I.P.D. 13034, though in each case with the new applications being limited to that part of the two earlier non-entitled applications which it was held the referrer had invented. Here, the fact that the claimant/referrer had abandoned his own, later, applications did not affect the right to file replacement applications.

In contrast, there is no power to permit a replacement application under s.8(3) to deem a further priority claim. This has the result that, if the earlier applicant had prior-published the invention, a replacement application under s.8(3) will not result in a valid patent, see *Georgia Pacific's Application* [1984] R.P.C. 467.

If entitlement proceedings take place prior to filing the international application, then the claimant may not be looking to file a "replacement application". In these circumstances, any international application must be filed before the expiry of the earliest priority period as it may not be possible to seek reinstatement of a priority claim which had been missed. See *John Terence Crilly's Application* (BL O/182/10) where entitlement proceedings had only been determined after the 12–month period had expired, the patent attorney had not diarised the priority date of the earliest case as it was in the name on the non-entitled party and being prosecuted by that party's attorney and, until conclusion of the entitlement proceedings, they had not been clear as to the contents of the earliest application and hence any need to claim priority from it.

A replacement application can be filed even if the original application has been withdrawn or deemed to be withdrawn (*Vet Health's Patent* BL O/49/90, noted I.P.D. 13165), but, if the original application had been refused as a result of a prior art objection, a similar objection would no doubt be raised against the replacement application. However, no estoppel would have been created in view of the different applicant entities.

In *Young and Chatwin's Application* BL O/174/01 the Comptroller had in an earlier decision (see BL O/70/01) determined that the claimant was entitled to part of the subject-matter included in the patent application in dispute. He accordingly made an order allowing the claimant to make a new application under s.8(3) limited to that subject-matter only. Even though this was an unusual order, the hearing officer commented that orders under s.8(3) are uncommon, and when they have been made, they have usually been in respect of the whole contents of the patent application in question.

No new matter can be included in a "replacement application" (s.76(1)), and if any such matter is added to the original application, the replacement application should not be allowed to proceed until amended, see §76.02 and §76.03.

Any replacement application has to be put in condition for grant, i.e. comply with the Act and Rules within the later of 18 months of its actual date of filing; or four years and six months from the earliest declared priority date or, if none, the filing date of the original application (r.30(3)) or, if the first official letter is sent out in the last three months of that period, then three months from the date of the official letter (r.30(4)). Although there is no specific restriction against filing an application under s.8(3), 12(6) or 37(4) with wider claims based on the same text, it seems unlikely that this would be permitted, see §76.07 and, in *X Ltd's Application* [1982] F.S.R. 143, a replacement application with broader claims was not accepted under the 1949 Act, see also §37.09. However, there is no prohibition against broadening claims before grant, provided that there is no added matter.

The applicant of the original application and its licensees, even if acting in good faith, had no rights under a "replacement application" where the reference was filed before January 1, 2005. However, s.11 was amended by the 2004 Act so that certain rights may be given in respect of both the original application and any replacement application when this proceeds after having been transferred to a new applicant. See further under §11.05.

PRACTICE UNDER SECTION 8

Raising of questions under subsection (1)

8.09   Rules 73–88 of the Rules (reprinted at §§123.06–123.21) are applicable to proceedings under s.8(1)(a) or 12(1)(a) initiated by a non-applicant and to proceedings under s.8(1)(b) or 12(1)(b) initiated by a co-applicant. The procedure for non-applicants and co-applicants used to be separate but similar and were regulated by rr.7 and 8 respectively of the 1995 Rules. Now there is only one set of rules to apply to all inter partes proceedings in the Patent Office and it is no longer necessary to start separate proceedings under each relevant section. Instead one set of proceedings can cover applications under, e.g. s.13 and s.8 or under s.8 and s.10. See the commentary under s.123 for a detailed discussion of these provisions.

PF 2 is initially filed in duplicate by the claimant (as defined in r.73(3)) accompanied by a statement of grounds also in duplicate (r.76(1)). The statement of grounds must include a concise statement of all facts and grounds relied upon and specify the remedy sought (r.76(4)). The Comptroller sends a copy of PF 2 and the statement to the persons specified in rr.77(1) and (2), i.e. he *must* send a copy to the patent applicant(s) and he *may* send a copy to an one else who appears to him to be likely to have an interest in the proceedings. As s.8(6) precludes orders from being made under s.8(2)(a), (b) and (d) unless notice of the reference has been communicated to affected parties, presumably all those mentioned in the relevant transaction, instrument or event will also be sent the PF 2 and statement of grounds, notwithstanding the provisions of r.77.

The Litigation Manual, Ch.7 deals with applications under ss.8, 10, 12 and 37. Paragraph 7.21 lists the types of persons to whom notices will be sent. This includes proprietors not a party to the reference, anyone mentioned in the reference as having a right under the patent or so identified on the register, any person who has applied to register a transaction, instrument or event, anyone named as inventor or believed to be an inventor any other person who is likely to have an interest in the case.

The Comptroller will set a period within which counter-statements may be filed (r.77(5)). However, the Comptroller is not required to send papers for a reference under s.8(1) or 12(1) to any person who has already indicated in writing that he supports the reference, or to the claimant himself (r.77(3)). Where a potential party has given consent to an application, then this is best communicated to the Comptroller, by sending him the actual signed notice of consent. See *Farmer v Yardley* BL O/52/08, for a request for an extension of time for filing a counter-statement.

Any defendant (as defined in r.73(3)) must file his counter-statement in duplicate (r.77(6)). The Comptroller is only obliged to forward a copy to the clamant (r.80(1)), but in practice is likely to send a copy to other parties to the proceedings. This is unlikely to include any party which has consented or is deemed to have consented to the claimant's case and that includes a party notified under r.77(1) or (2) but who failed to file their own counter-statement (r.77(9)).

For the procedure which follows, including for the Preliminary Opinions, directions, evidence and hearings, see the commentary on s.123.

Note that sequential exchange of evidence was ordered in *Orbita 2 Ltd v Urs Vikor Giger* BL O/033/10, in a reference under s.12, where the defendant had applied to strike out the entire reference as the claimant had not identified the inventive concept and so "disclosed no reasonable grounds for bringing the claim". Relying on *Yeda*, the hearing officer felt that the questions of "inventive concept" and "actual deviser" could only be determined in the light of the evidence and the burden was on the claimant to prove its case. Ordering sequential evidence would assist the defendant in knowing the case he was expected to meet.

Where the Preliminary Opinion indicates that there is no case to answer, the Comptroller may use it under his case management powers as a basis, after giving the parties the opportunity to be heard, for striking out part of the claim and giving summary judgment on other parts—see *Meider v Whitfield* BL O/171/10.

If the applicant does not contest the reference, then previously the matter was decided on the basis that the assertions made by the referrer should be accepted if, prima facie, they were credible, see *Kitelane's Application* BL O/15/94 and *Coventry University's Application* BL O/223/00. Now r.77(9) specifies that if a person does not file a counter-statement (in this case the original patent applicant(s)) then he is treated as supporting the claimant's case and r.78(3) specifies that allegations in the statement of grounds which are not dealt with in the counter-statement will be taken to be admitted.

Previously a referrer (now claimant) was not permitted to allege a new case at the stage of evidence-in-reply, for example that the invention had in fact been made some years earlier by another, when by due diligence that point could have been raised earlier (*Manthorpe's Application* BL O/1/91): and, the possibility remained of a new reference being made to raise that further new allegation. Now the Comptroller manages the case subject to the "overriding objective" set out in r.74 (which includes the saving of expense) and has the power to allow amendment of a statement of case under r.82. (See further under s.123.)

If confidential material is to be filed with the UK-IPO in relation to a reference under s.8, then the Comptroller has power to keep that information confidential (r.53, reprinted at §118.04). However, the party wishing such material to be kept confidential must explain what element of that material is confidential and why, and cannot use obligations of confidentiality to prevent another party from filing that material with the UK-IPO for determination of an entitlement dispute (see *Microscience Technologies v CRP Group* BL O/16/07 and BL O/234/07).

Security for costs is now required only from a claimant who neither resides nor works within the European Community or, more precisely, not resident in a "Brussels" or "Lugano" contracting state or a "Regulation State", these terms being defined by s.1(3) of the Civil Jurisdiction and Judgments Act 1982, as amended (see r.85 reprinted at §123.18 and §107.05 generally as to security).

As noted in §8.04, s.9 has the effect that most cases commenced under s.8 come to be decided under s.37. For practice under s.37, see §§37.12–37.14. A parallel plea for revocation under s.72 may then also be appropriate. For the procedure where the Comptroller decides to refer the matter to the court, see §37.14.

Orders made under sections 8 or 12

The Comptroller will allow the parties to be heard, but where the patent applicant does **8.10** not oppose an entitlement reference (together with request under s.13 for change of inventorship), the Comptroller has ordered a change of applicant and of inventor without a hearing (*Powell's Application* BL O/154/92). However, the Comptroller is not required to decide a case adversely to the referrer if he withdraws his reference (*Lupa's Application* BL O/59/90, noted I.P.D. 13167).

An order made under s.8 or 12 that an application is to proceed in the name of someone else who was not the original applicant, the effect of that order and the procedure to be followed, particularly as regards subsequent proceedings, are governed by s.11 and discussed in §11.05 (and see §11.06 for a discussion as to who will be notified and when). A person making a request under s.11(3), (3A) or 12(5) must apply within the period specified in r.90(2) (reprinted at §11.02). The time period is now two months from the making of the order, whether the claimant will be the, or any of the, original applicants or an existing licensee.

If there is non-compliance with an order under s.8(2)(d) or (4), or s.37(2)(c), an application for an order for substituted authority to act is made to the Comptroller. Section 8(5) is not mentioned in Sch.3. Accordingly, the MOPP states that this means that the application can be made to the Office in writing without the need to file form PF 2. However, the application should still set out all the facts upon which the claimant relies and the nature of the authorisation sought. The Office will then send a copy to the person who has failed to comply with the previous directions and make such further directions for the proceedings as he sees fit. If satisfied, the Comptroller will grant the authorisation.

Filing of new application under section 8(3), 12(6) or 37(4)

8.11   The procedure for filing a new application under s.8(3), 12(6) or 37(4) is discussed in §15.18, this being generally similar to that for filing a divisional application under s.15(4), for which see §§15.16–15.25 and §§15.32–15.35. However, PF 1 must be filed and the filing fee paid not later than three months after the date of expiry of the term for appeal from the order under s.8(3), 12(6) or 37(4), or after disposal of such appeal (see r.20, above). This period is extensible at the Comptroller's discretion (r.108(1)) and may also be shortened by him (r.20(4)). The requirements of r.21(1) and (2) and of r.28(4) to (6) (reprinted respectively in §15.06 and §18.02) must be complied with, and the application must be placed in order for grant in accordance with the provisions of r.30(3) or (4) (reprinted in §18.04) (i.e. within 18 months from its actual date of filing, unless the four years and six month period from the priority date (or, if none, the filing date) expires later, unless the first substantive examination report is sent within the last three months of such period, in which case it can be extended to three months after the report is sent). The period under r.21 (insofar as applied to r.6(5)) is inextensible (Pt 1, Sch.4 and r.108(1)), but the other periods under r.21 and the periods under rr.28(5) and 30 may each be extended as of right by two months under r.108(2) by filing PF 52, and further on application under r.108(3), on PF 52 with supporting evidence, in the discretion of the Comptroller, see the commentary on s.123. See also §§12.05, 12.06 and §37.13 for the analogous practice for replacement applications permitted under ss.12(6) and 37(4).

SECTION 9

Determination after grant of questions referred before grant

9.01   **9.** If a question with respect to a patent or application is referred by any person to the comptroller under section 8 above, whether before or after the making of an application for the patent, and is not determined before the time when the application is first in order for a grant of a patent in pursuance of the application, that fact shall not prevent the grant of a patent, but on its grant that person shall be treated as having referred to the comptroller under section 37 below any question mentioned in that section which the comptroller thinks appropriate.

COMMENTARY ON SECTION 9

9.02   Section 9 sets out the procedure to be followed in those cases where a reference is made to the Comptroller under s.8 before a patent is granted and the matter is not resolved by the time that the patent is granted. The grant of a patent is not stayed, but thereafter the matter is to be treated as a reference under s.37. This has the effect that the majority of applications under s.8 are eventually resolved in proceedings continued under s.37, see the commentaries on those sections and particularly §37.04. However, the operation of s.9 to continue (under s.37) entitlement proceedings commenced under s.8 is not obligatory; and in *Goddin and Rennie's Application* [1996] R.P.C. 141, the Comptroller exercised his power under s.10 to delay the grant of a patent until entitlement proceedings under s.8 were concluded, see §10.04.

Grant under s.25(1) occurs when notice of grant is published in the journal. However, once a letter under s.18(4) has issued indicating that the patent application is in order for grant, the application process ends. There will thus be a hiatus between these dates where entitlement proceedings under s.8 end, but cannot yet be started under s.37. Entitlement proceedings begun after the s.18(4) letter but prior to the publication of grant should be brought under s.8, but will then not progress until after grant and progress under s.37. (See MOPP para.8.03.1.)

The procedure is different in the case of a challenge to entitlement to an application for a European patent (including one designating the United Kingdom). Subject to the jurisdiction requirement of s.82 being met (for which see the commentary on s.82), such a challenge takes place by a reference under s.12, rather than under s.8, and then the examination proceedings in the EPO can be suspended (after publication of the application) under EPC r.14 until a decision has been given under s.12. However, if the s.12 proceedings become protracted, the EPO may set a date to resume the examination and even process the application to grant. Presumably, thereafter, declaratory relief would still be available. If the European application has been allowed to lapse, e.g. by failure to pay a renewal fee, a replacement application is possible according to G 3/92 *LATCHWAYS/ Unlawful applicant* OJ EPO 1994, 633; [1995] E.P.O.R. 141. See the discussion of this decision in §12.05.

PRACTICE UNDER SECTION 9

When proceedings under s.8 have been initiated and the patent proceeds to grant, the parties can expect to be informed by the UK-IPO that the proceedings will henceforth be continued under s.37, although such continuance is not obligatory, see *Goddin and Rennie's Application* [1996] R.P.C. 141, referred to above, and §10.04.   **9.03**

The letter from the UK-IPO will inform the parties that the case will continue under s.37 and this may affect the relief available. However, the MOPP does not indicate that any response or amendment of the statements of case will be required. Silence from the parties will be treated by the UK-IPO as consent that the question of relief be deferred to the substantive hearing of the application.

SECTION 10

Handling of application by joint applicants

10. If any dispute arises between joint applicants for a patent whether or in what manner the application should be proceeded with, the comptroller may, on a request made by any of the parties, give such directions as he thinks fit for enabling the application to proceed in the name of one or more of the parties alone or for regulating the manner in which it shall be proceeded with, or for both those purposes, according as the case may require.   **10.01**

RELEVANT RULES—RULES 73–88

The above are reprinted at §§123.06–123.21 and are general in nature to govern procedure in all proceedings to be heard before the Comptroller. These specifically include proceedings under s.10. These rules are discussed in the commentary under s.123, but are also mentioned, as appropriate, in the commentary and practice sections below.   **10.02**

COMMENTARY ON SECTION 10

Scope of the section

Section 10 relates to the resolution of disputes between joint applicants as to their rights   **10.03** inter se, perhaps as a parallel proceeding to an entitlement application made under s.8(1)(b), but s.10 applies only to matters concerned with the continued prosecution of the application. Disputes concerning entitlement to the whole of, or a share in, patent rights involving a non-applicant or non-patentee are to be resolved under one of the "entitlement sections" 8, 12, 37 or 82, see §8.04 and, mainly, §37.05; and inventorship disputes are to be settled by proceedings under s.13. Thus one or more of these other sections may be required to be listed on the application form, but these can now proceed in a single set of proceedings.

Any proceedings under s.10 must be terminated within the time limit set for compliance with the Act and Rules by r.30 under ss.18(4) and 20(1) for which see §18.11. Although analogous proceedings after grant are possible under s.37, proceedings under s.10 do not automatically continue under s.37 (contrast s.9 which specifically so provides in the case of entitlement disputes initiated under s.8, see §9.02).

By virtue of s.12(4), s.10 applies to disputes between joint applicants in respect of foreign, European or international applications except that the Comptroller has no power to "regulate the manner in which an application is to proceed" (i.e. in relation to the prosecution of such applications, as opposed to the proceedings for determination of the dispute). Although a court could be asked to make orders binding upon the parties to a s.10 dispute, the court would probably not do so unless it had jurisdiction over the person(s) involved. Once an international application has entered the UK phase (for which see §89.10 and §89A.12), then (by virtue of ss.89(1) and 89A(3)) s.10 fully operates upon it in the same way as it does on an application filed under the Act.

Section 11 deals with the effects of directions given under s.10 in relation to licences or other rights in or under the application-in-suit.

Application of section 10 in practice

10.04   In *Pelling and Campbell's Applications* BL O/134/87, it was observed that, under s.10:

"the correct approach is for the Comptroller to seek to implement the overall purpose of the Act in the most equitable manner that he can".

It was also here stated that the Comptroller will not make a pronouncement upon any alleged contract between applicants unless required to do so as part of his statutory duties. In this case, one co-applicant, C, refused to bear any costs of the application. It was held that, if he wished to be treated as a full co-applicant, he should bear a fair share of the costs involved in obtaining the patent protection under which he sought to shelter and, if he was not prepared to pay his fair share, he had no good cause to complain if his rights as co-applicant were restricted. It was held that within three months, C should assign his interest to the other co-applicant P and that P should then grant to C a free, non-assignable, non-revocable licence in similar terms to that produced under s.36, but excluding any right for C to grant sub-licences, and that P should agree to assign the application and any patent granted thereon to C in the event that P should relinquish his interest in it.

In *Change Controls' Application* BL O/34/91, noted I.P.D. 14139, C and E were joint applicants. E became uncontactable after instructing different agents. C obtained an order that the application should proceed solely in its name, but with an undertaking that, upon request from E, C should grant E a free, personal, non-assignable licence under the patent, which C was not required to keep in force.

In *Melco Products Application* BL O/49/91, a verbal agreement was found for collaboration in the filing, but with no concluded agreement on future exploitation. Because it was not considered appropriate for the application to proceed in only one of the joint applicants' names, nor for exploitation to be governed by s.36, the matter was adjourned to give the parties a chance to reach an exploitation agreement. Subsequently (see BL O/14/92, noted I.P.D. 15139), when one co-owner had gone into liquidation, it was held that the patent should be granted to the other co-owner with the insolvent co-owner having a right to a non-exclusive licence with the royalty to be settled by the Comptroller in default of agreement.

In *Brooks and Cope's Application* BL O/71/93, each of the joint applicants claimed (under s.8) sole entitlement to the application, but the Comptroller decided (under s.10) that substantive examination should continue pending resolution of the entitlement dispute with the examination report being sent to both the agents representing the respective applicants. Subsequently (see BL O/145/93), it was held that C had been the sole inventor but that there had been an initial agreement that the patent rights should be held jointly on a promise by B to arrange finance for exploitation. That had not happened and, accordingly, it was held that B should not benefit and that the application form, the published specifications and the register should each be amended to show C as sole proprietor.

In *West and Gibbon's Application* BL O/147/93, the Comptroller declined to adjudicate on inventorship in the absence of any application under s.13. There had been litigation between the parties resulting in an order made by consent, the effect of which was in dispute. The Comptroller held that, since this referred to "giving all rights" and "without let or hindrance", that order should be regarded as an assignment in favour of G, and not merely the grant of a licence to work the invention. However, on appeal (noted I.P.D. 17100), it was held that the previous order did not have this effect and therefore that the application should proceed in the original joint names, but with prosecution responsibility vested in only one of them. (Since the coming into force of the Patents Rules 2007, it is only necessary to make a single application, although all relevant sections should be mentioned on the PF 2.)

The operation of s.9 to continue (under s.37) entitlement proceedings commenced under s.8 is not obligatory. In *Goddin and Rennie's Application* [1996] R.P.C. 141, the Comptroller exercised his power under s.10 to delay the grant of a patent until entitlement proceedings under s.8 were concluded, see §9.02.

PRACTICE UNDER SECTION 10

The practice under s.10 (and also under s.12(4)) is governed by rr. 73–88 of the Rules (discussed and reprinted at §§123.06–123.21). PF 2 is filed in duplicate with a duplicate statement of grounds (r.76). A copy of PF 2 and the statement is then sent by the Comptroller to each other joint applicant inviting him to oppose within a term set by the Comptroller (r.77). Any opponent must file a counterstatement in duplicate within the specified period and the Comptroller sends a copy thereof to each other joint applicant, specifying a time for filing any evidence in support, for which see the commentary under s.123.

10.05

SECTION 11

Effect of transfer of application under section 8 or 10

11.—(1) Where an order is made or directions are given under section 8 or 10 above that an application for a patent shall proceed in the name of one or some of the original applicants (whether or not it is also to proceed in the name of some other person), any licences or other rights in or under the application shall, subject to the provisions of the order and any directions under either of those sections, continue in force and be treated as granted by the persons in whose name the application is to proceed.

11.01

(2)   Where an order is made or directions are given under section 8 above that an application for a patent shall proceed in the name of one or more persons none of whom was an original applicant (on the ground that the original applicant or applicants was or were not entitled to be granted the patent), any licences or other rights in or under the application shall, subject to the provisions of the order and any directions under that section and subject to subsection (3) below, lapse on the registration of that person or those persons as the applicant or applicants or, where the application has not been published, on the making of the order.

(3) If before registration of a reference under section 8 above resulting in the making of any order mentioned in subsection (2) above—

    (a) the original applicant or any of the applicants, acting in good faith, worked the invention in question in the United Kingdom or made effective and serious preparations to do so; or

    (b) a licensee of the applicant, acting in good faith, worked the invention in the United Kingdom or made effective and serious preparations to do so;

that or those original applicant or applicants or the licensee shall, on making a request within the prescribed period to the person in whose name the application is to proceed, be entitled to be granted a licence (but not an exclusive licence) to continue working or, as the case may be, to work the invention.

(3A) If, before registration of a reference under section 8 above resulting in the making of an order under subsection (3) of that section, the condition in subsection (3)(a) or (b) above is met, the original applicant or any of the applicants or the licensee shall, on making a request within the prescribed period to the new applicant, be entitled to be granted a licence (but not an exclusive licence) to continue working or, as the case may be, to work the invention so far as it is the subject of the new application.

(4) **A licence under subsection (3) or (3A) above** [*Any such licence*] shall be granted for a reasonable period and on reasonable terms.

(5) Where an order is made as mentioned in subsection (2) **or (3A)** above, the person in whose name the application is to proceed **or, as the case may be, who makes the new application** or any person claiming that he is entitled to be granted any such licence may refer to the comptroller the question whether the latter is so entitled and whether any such period is or terms are reasonable, and the comptroller shall determine the question and may, if he considers it appropriate, order the grant of such a licence.

Note. The marked amendments to s.11 were made by the Patents Act 2004 (c.16) s.6, with effect from January 1, 2005, except in relation to any reference made before that date (SI 2004/3205, arts 2(b) and 9(2)).

RELEVANT RULE—RULE 90

Rule 90—Licences following entitlement proceedings

11.02   **90.**—(1) The period prescribed for the purposes of section 11(3) and (3A) shall be two months beginning with—

    (a) where section 11 is applied by section 12(5), the date on which the order under section 12(1) was made; and

    (b) in any other case, the date on which the order under section 8 was made.

(2) The period prescribed for the purposes of section 38(3) shall be two months beginning with the date on which the order mentioned in section 38(2) was made.

OTHER RELEVANT RULES—RULES 73–88

11.03   The above rules are reprinted at §§123.06–123.21 and are general in nature to govern procedure in all proceedings to be heard before the Comptroller. These specifically include proceedings under s.11(5). These rules are discussed in the commentary under s.123, but are also mentioned, as appropriate, in the commentary and practice sections below.

COMMENTARY ON SECTION 11

Scope of the section

As a result of the operation of s.8 or s.10 or (by virtue of s.12(4) and (5)) of s.12(1), the **11.04** patent application may be transferred to different applicants while the application under s.8 or s.10 is still pending. If, at the time of the transfer, there still exists a licence or mortgage granted by the original applicant, then s.11 sets out the rights of the licensee or mortgagee in such circumstances. The effect depends on whether the new applicant(s) include(s) at least one of the original applicants. The provisions of s.11 are similar to those of s.38 for orders made after grant on the resolution of a dispute on entitlement under s.37 and the same rules apply to applications under s.38.

Effect of transfer of application under section 8 or 10

If the Comptroller has ordered under s.8 or s.10 that there shall be a change of applicant, **11.05** and if any of the original applicants remains as such, any licence or other right continues in force, subject to the provision of the order and any directions of the Comptroller (subs.(1)). Alternatively, if the application has been ordered to proceed in the name of a person or persons none of whom was an original applicant, as a result of a determination that none of the original applicants was entitled to be granted a patent, any licence or other right under the application lapses (subs.(2)). This lapse takes effect from the date of registration of the new applicant(s), or from the date of the order if the application has not by then been published, unless the order or directions given under the section should provide otherwise.

However, in the circumstances of subs.(2), an original applicant or his licensee who, acting in good faith, had worked the invention in the United Kingdom or made serious and effective preparations to do so before the entitlement proceedings commenced is entitled to be granted a non-exclusive licence (see s.130(7) for definition of "exclusive licence" and hence "exclusive and non-exclusive licensees") to continue that working, or to work the invention, each for a *reasonable* period and on *reasonable* terms (subss.(3) and (4)). Subsections (3) and (4) are also applied to foreign, European and international applications for a patent by virtue of s.12(5).

The amendments made to s.11 by the Patents Act 2004, particularly the insertion of new subs.(3A), provide that, where a replacement application is permitted to be filed, the original applicant and any existing licensees can acquire a non-exclusive licence under the replacement application and under the provisions of subss.(3) and (4), but only provided that such a person had already begun to work the invention in good faith. The provisions of s.38 already referred to the filing of a new application but clarifying amendments were also made to this section by the Patents Act 2004, see §38.01 and §38.04. The amendments of s.11 only took effect in relation to references made under s.8 or 12 after January 1, 2005.

The terms "good faith" and "serious and effective preparations" also appear in s.28A(4) and s.64(1) and are discussed particularly in §28A.06 and §64.06. The term "non-exclusive licence" is defined in s.130(1) by reference to "exclusive licence". It would seem appropriate to construe "reasonable", both in relation to duration and to the terms of the ordered licence, as connoting an objective test as between willing, but arm's length, parties in the light of usages of the relevant industrial sector.

Result of making order falling within subsection (2)

Under the 1995 Rules, the Comptroller was obliged to notify all original applicants and **11.06** their licensees of whom he was aware that he had made an order falling within subs.(2) and inform them of the deadline for requesting a licence from the new patent applicant. There is no longer a rule to this effect. Rule 80(6) requires the Comptroller to notify all "parties" of his decision and the reason for making the decision, but there is room for doubt as to whether all relevant persons will be "parties". The Comptroller must notify the patent applicant of the entitlement proceedings under s.8 and/or s.12 when they start (r.77(1)). When the entitlement proceedings start, he *may* notify any person who appears to him to be likely to have an interest in the case (r.77(2)) (emphasis added). Further, where s.8(6) applies, the Comptroller is obliged to notify relevant persons (see §8.09). Although this may not impose a duty on the Comptroller to notify a mortgagee, presumably all interested parties will be aware of the entitlement proceedings. Further, the MOPP states at para.123.05.5:

"generally the Comptroller will notify any person named in the register of patents or in the statement of grounds and any other person who appears likely to a case-by-case basis to have an interest".

However, under r.77(3) the Comptroller is not obliged to notify anyone who has consented in writing to the claimant's case of the start of proceedings and a person who does not file a counter-statement is then treated as supporting the claimant's case, so such persons might not be "parties". However, paras 8.03 and 11.05 of the MOPP state that "the Office notifies all original applicants and their licensees of whom it is aware of the making of the order".

The term for making an application to the new patent applicant for a licence to continue working, whether under subss.(3) or (3A), is two months from the date of the order itself (see r.90). (Existing licensees had longer under the 1995 Rules—but now there is only one period for all potential new licensees.) The periods under r.90 are extensible at the Comptroller's discretion under r.108(1), see also the discussion at §8.11.

Any dispute following the making of an order to which s.11(2) applies may be referred to the Comptroller (subs.(5)) by either the new patent applicant or the person seeking the licence, the procedure being prescribed by Pt 7 (reprinted under s.123). No time limit is specified for the making of a reference under s.11(2).

Any licence granted under the section has effect as if it were a deed executed by the proprietor and other necessary party (s.108, discussed in §108.02).

PRACTICE UNDER SECTION 11

11.07   The first step for anyone seeking a licence under this section is to apply to the new applicant for such a licence, whether under subss.(3) or (3A). It is only when a person entitled to make such an application does so within the prescribed period that they become entitled to be granted a non-exclusive licence (although the Comptroller can be asked to extend this retrospectively).

A dispute to be referred to the Comptroller under s.11(5) is commenced by filing PF 2 in duplicate with a statement of grounds, also in duplicate. This must set out not only the question referred and the facts relied on, but also the period and/or terms of the licence which the applicant is prepared to accept or grant (r.76(4)). The Comptroller must send a copy of the PF 2 and statement to each other patent applicant. He will also presumably notify any other prospective licensee or other interested party of whom he is aware (from either an entry on the register or from the papers in the file), however, r.76(2) uses the phrase "may", not "must", so the Comptroller retains a discretion here. However, where the application is made by the new applicant and not by the person seeking a licence, that person will have to be notified. The Comptroller will also specify a period for filing any counterstatement. If the draft licence is not accepted and opposition is lodged, a counter-statement must be filed in duplicate within the period specified and the Comptroller sends a copy of this to the claimant under r.80(1). Thereafter, the Comptroller may make such case management orders as are appropriate. See the commentary under s.123 for more detail.

SECTION 12

Determination of questions about entitlement to foreign and convention patents, etc.

12.01   12.—(1) At any time before a patent is granted for an invention in pursuance of an application made under the law of any country other than the United Kingdom or under any treaty or international convention (whether or not that application has been made)—

(a) any person may refer to the comptroller the question whether he is entitled to be granted (alone or with any other persons) any such patent for that invention or has or would have any right in or under any such patent or an application for such a patent; or

(b) any of two or more co-proprietors of an application for such a patent for that invention may so refer the question whether any right in or under the application should be transferred or granted to any other person;

and the comptroller shall determine the question so far as he is able to and may make such order as he thinks fit to give effect to the determination.

(2) If it appears to the comptroller on a reference of a question under this section that the question involves matters which would more properly be determined by the court, he may decline to deal with it and, without prejudice to the court's jurisdiction to determine any such question and make a declaration, or any declaratory jurisdiction of the court in Scotland, the court shall have jurisdiction to do so.

(3) Subsection (1) above, in its application to a European patent and an application for any such patent, shall have effect subject to section 82 below.

(4) Section 10 above, except so much of it as enables the comptroller to regulate the manner in which an application is to proceed, shall apply to disputes between joint applicants for any such patent as is mentioned in subsection (1) above as it applies to joint applicants for a patent under this Act.

(5) Section 11 above shall apply in relation to—

(a) any orders made under subsection (1) above and any directions given under section 10 above by virtue of subsection (4) above; and

(b) any orders made and directions given by the relevant convention court with respect to a question corresponding to any question which may be determined under subsection (1) above;

as it applies to orders made and directions given apart from this section under section 8 or 10 above.

(6) In the following cases, that is to say—

(a) where an application for a European patent (UK) is refused or withdrawn, or the designation of the United Kingdom in the application is withdrawn **whether before or** after publication of the application but before a question relating to the right to the patent has been referred to the comptroller under subsection (1) above or before proceedings relating to that right have begun before the relevant convention court;

(b) where an application has been made for a European patent (UK) and on a reference under subsection (1) above or any such proceedings as are mentioned in paragraph (a) above the comptroller, the court or the relevant convention court determines by a final decision (whether before or after publication of the application) that a person other than the applicant has the right to the patent, but that person requests the European Patent Office that the application for the patent should be refused; or

(c) where an international application for a patent (UK) is withdrawn, or the designation of the United Kingdom in the application is withdrawn, whether before or after the making of any reference under subsection (1) above [*but after*] **or the** publication of the application;

the comptroller may order that any person (other than the applicant) appearing to him to be entitled to be granted a patent under this Act may within the prescribed period make an application for such a patent for the whole or part of any matter comprised in the earlier application (subject, however, to section 76 below) and that if the application for a patent under this Act is filed, it shall be treated as having been filed on the date of filing the earlier application.

(7) In this section—

(a) references to a patent and an application for a patent include respectively references to protection in respect of an invention and an application which, in accordance with the law of any country other than the United Kingdom or any treaty or international convention, is equivalent to an application for a patent or for such protection; and

(b) a decision shall be taken to be final for the purposes of this section when the time for appealing from it has expired without an appeal being brought or, where an appeal is brought, when it is finally disposed of.

Note. The marked amendments to s.12 were made by the Patents Act 2004 (c.16) Sch.2(5), with effect from January 1, 2005, except in relation to any reference made before that date (SI 2004/3205, arts 2(f)(k) and 9(2)).

<h2 style="text-align:center">RELEVANT RULES—RULES 73–88</h2>

12.02   The above rules are reprinted at §§123.06–123.21 and are general in nature to govern procedure in all proceedings to be heard before the Comptroller. These specifically include proceedings under s.12(1) and (4). These rules are discussed under the heading "Practice under Section 123", but are also mentioned, as appropriate, in the commentary and practice sections below. Rule 20 (reprinted in §8.02) is also relevant to the filing of a new application under s.12(6).

Note. For "replacement" applications filed under s.12(6), rr.21, 28(4)–(7) and r.30(3) and (4) (reprinted respectively at §§15.06, 18.02 and 18.04) are also relevant.

<h2 style="text-align:center">COMMENTARY ON SECTION 12</h2>

Scope of the section

12.03   Section 12 is part of a series of sections dealing with ownership and entitlement. Section 7 deals with the right to apply for and obtain a patent. Sections 8–12 and 37 deal with disputes regarding the entitlement or progress of UK and overseas patents and applications, with s.36 regulating the rights of co-owners. Section 13 deals with the right to be mentioned as inventor. Section 39 deals with the issue of entitlement as between an employer and employee. Where the dispute involves the ownership of a European application, then s.82 is also relevant.

Section 12 extends the provisions of s.8 from the resolution by the Comptroller of entitlement disputes relating to existing, or prospective, applications under the Act to existing, or prospective, applications filed under a foreign national law or a treaty or international convention, including applications claiming priority under the Paris Convention, and applications under the EPC and/or PCT. For this purpose, when s.12 applies, there is an extended meaning to be given to the terms "patent" and "application for patent" (subs.(7)(a)), though arguably not so extended as under s.43(4) by virtue of the absence of the word "other" before "protection". Thus, the extension under subs.(7)(a) is likely, in practice, to be confined to supplementary protection certificates, utility models and inventor's certificates. However, semiconductor topography rights and copyrights cannot be ruled out with any certainty. Subsection (1) is analogous to s.8(1) and thus provides for an entitlement dispute to be raised: (a) by a non-applicant party; and (b) by a co-applicant.

A question of inventorship can also be raised in s.12 proceedings because there is no other provision which would enable this to be done as a necessary preliminary to settlement of a question of entitlement under the section (*Staeng's Patent* [1996] R.P.C. 183), whereas under s.8, inventorship can only be disputed by reference to (but no longer needing a separate application under) s.13. As inventorship may give rise to rights under a foreign patent, a claim to co-inventorship of an international application may be made under s.12, as in *Xaar's International Application* BL O/257/98 and *SCS Consultancy Services' Application* BL O/174/00 and may lead to a declaration or a finding of fact as to co-inventorship. However, the absence of proceedings under s.13 was not fatal to the grant of relief under s.12 in *Ladney and Hendry's International Application* [1998] R.P.C. 319; and BL O/84/96 and now it would probably not be fatal if s.13 was not mentioned on the PF 2. In *RS Brookhouse Engineering v Pro-Tek Engineering* BL O/218/07, the Comptroller granted a certificate under s.13(3) as to which inventors should and should not be designated in the UK part of the European application, but could not grant such a declaration for the whole of the new application. But an order for ownership of the new application to be filed with the EPO could be made following the settlement agreement entered in parallel court proceedings.

Since subs.(1) expressly applies to entitlement disputes before any application has been filed, the word "invention" in s.12 has to be given the broad meaning referred to in §8.06, see *Rawlplug's European Application* BL O/145/88. However, unless "protection" for inventions is interpreted broadly enough to bring in design and/or copyright types of protection, there must presumably be some application in existence somewhere to bring s.12 into play, since otherwise the reference to "treaty or international convention" makes little sense. In practice, proceedings under s.12 are often combined with proceedings commenced under s.8 in respect of a parent or parallel application filed under the Act; and, where proceedings were brought under s.8 in respect of an application which had been abandoned, but which had served as a priority date for an international application, the Comptroller suggested that proceedings under s.12 might be appropriate and these then led to a declaration of entitlement for all pending applications claiming this priority (*Carbury Herne's Application* BL O/182/00 and O/269/00).

There can be an issue where the continued prosecution or abandonment of overseas applications may prejudice the rights of the person challenging entitlement. In *Quantum Glass v Spowart* [Scotland], [2000] ScotSC 299, noted [2001] *CIPA* 99, the Court of Session granted an interim interdict to prevent a patent applicant and inventor from further prosecuting an international application pending full trial of the issues of entitlement and breach of confidence, even though the effect of the interdicts made it likely that the application could not proceed within the required time limits—see §§8.04, 8.07 and §37.07. However, the 1977 Act does not confer any such jurisdiction on the Comptroller. Indeed, s.12(4), expressly does not extend the Comptroller's power to regulate the manner of prosecution of an application under the 1977 Act, as conferred by s.10 where there is a dispute between co-applicants, to overseas, European or international applications. Also, see §12.05 regarding filing replacement applications.

With regard to co-ownership and co-applicants, as with s.8(1) (for which see §8.05), it is surprising that s.12(1) was not likewise amended to maintain its wording in conformity with that of the corresponding amendment of s.37(1).

The language of subs.(1) excludes consideration by the Comptroller of a reference where at the date of its submission the (or all) foreign patent(s) had already been granted, see *Magill's Application* BL O/256/00. However, the Comptroller retains jurisdiction over other foreign patent applications in the same family. However, given that the Comptroller's enquiry is focussed on the ownership of "that invention", any decision might well be of assistance in any foreign tribunal which is then called to rule upon the ownership of the granted patent.

While s.11 concerns licences or mortgages following a reference under s.8 or 10 in respect of a United Kingdom application, s.12 deals with similar circumstances arising in connection with an application filed or to be filed in a country other than the United Kingdom, and s.11 is made to apply to such cases by subs.(5). However, the Comptroller cannot make orders binding under foreign law, and his powers under the section may often be limited to making a declaration as to ownership, leaving such to be implemented at the discretion of a foreign tribunal, as in *Marchbank's Applications* BL O/12/96. Alternatively, the Comptroller may choose to make no order in respect of applications for which no evidence of the local law of inventorship, and particularly ownership, especially in relation to employee inventors has been provided see, e.g. *Norris's Patent* [1988] R.P.C. 159, where an order for joint entitlement was made under ss.8 and 37; and *Xaar's International Application* (above). However, the decision might be accepted by a foreign court or patent office at least as a declaration of rights as seen under English law. As an order of the Comptroller under the section should operate in personam, if such an order is made in respect of a person normally resident in the United Kingdom, courts of the United Kingdom ought then to enforce it.

In the case of an international application, any order made as to entitlement under s.12 may need to be implemented before each national office for which protection is sought as the International Bureau has quite limited powers to record changes of ownership or of entitlement, unless perhaps sought by the current applicant, see the *Patent Cooperation Treaty Handbook* ("PCTH") (London: Sweet & Maxwell). Thus, when an order is sought under s.12, this should likewise be in terms of an order to operate in personam against the existing applicant requiring him to take steps to record the rightful entitlement as found by the Comptroller.

The power of the Comptroller to make "such order as he thinks fit to give effect to the determination" (at the end of subs.(1)), is very wide, but not so wide as to enable the Comptroller to make a costs order under this section. Costs are dealt with under s.107 (see *IDA v Southampton* BL O/46/07), but can include some of the costs of "vesting" the application in the name of the correct proprietor (*EI Du Pont de Nemours & Co (Rebouillat's) Applications* [1996] R.P.C. 740).

Subsection (2) is analogous with ss.8(7) and 37(8) in giving power to the Comptroller to decline to deal with any question raised under the section and for this therefore to be raised before a permitted "court" as defined in s.130(1) and as discussed in §37.08. Disputes between joint applicants under subs.(1)(b) are dealt with as under s.10 (subs.(4)). As noted above, subs.(5) imports the effects of s.11 and applies these also to any orders made by "the relevant convention court", as defined in s.130(1) and discussed in §103.02. Subsection (6) (discussed particularly in §12.05) provides that a new application may be allowed to be filed analogously with s.8(3), for which see §8.08 and §8.11. Otherwise, the commentaries on ss.8, 10, 11 and 37 are generally relevant for application mutatis mutandis. A person making a reference under s.12 who is not resident in the European Union, or more precisely, does not qualify by virtue of s.1(3) of the Civil Jurisdiction and Judgments Act 1982 as amended, may be required to give security for costs, see §107.05 and r.85 (reprinted at §123.18).

However, the jurisdiction with regard to applications for European patents (UK) is subject to s.82 (subs.(3)), as discussed in §§82.03–82.06. Whether the Comptroller has jurisdiction over these applications under this section is decided by him as a preliminary point, even if the reference is not contested by the proprietor, see *Bundy's European Application* BL O/113/88 and *CSIRO's Application* BL O/74/98. In the *CSIRO* case jurisdiction was accepted over two European applications because the only parties involved were Australian and United Kingdom entities. Once granted, a European patent (UK) is treated as a patent granted under the Act and, consequently, s.37 will then apply to questions of entitlement which are raised.

As under ss.8 and 37, entitlement proceedings may take place in Scotland and may be referred to courts other than the Patents Court, see §37.08.

Application of section 12 in practice

12.04   In *University College London's Application* BL O/381/02—see §8.07—although the

UK application had been withdrawn before publication, a declaration was made under s.12 so that it could be used by the applicant in support of any request to the International Bureau or to national or regional authorities in connection with the corresponding international application or any national or regional applications deriving from it.

In *Kitelane's Application* BL O/101/96, the Comptroller accepted that a previous determination of entitlement under s.8 should have res judicata effect under s.12 and, accordingly, subsequently granted a declaration under that section in respect of an international application.

In contrast, in *Statoil v University of Southampton* BL O/268/05, noted [2005] *CIPA* 735, consideration was given to the foreign applications following the earlier decision BL O/204/05, noted [2005] *CIPA* 538, on entitlement to the UK patent under s.37. There was no suggestion that the inventive concept in the foreign applications differed from that in the UK patent. The decision on UK entitlement already being in the claimant's favour, the Office was only interested in any quirks of local law that would affect inventorship or ownership. The University had the onus of proving that different considerations applied in other jurisdictions. It had already been given the opportunity to investigate the position and had not discharged that onus. Although noting that the US approach was to look at entitlement on a claim by claim basis, rather than the current approach in the UK mandated by *Markem v Zipher* [2005] R.P.C. 31 at 761; [2006] I.P. & T. 102—see §7.08—the hearing officer thought that the same result would be achieved in this case. The evidence also suggested that the other countries identified applied the same principles as the UK. So there was no need to stay the order to assign the foreign applications to Statoil.

In *Rawlplug's European Application* BL O/145/88, it was held that part of the invention claimed had been obtained from the referrer and that the subject-matter of the application should be divided. This was achieved by an order to delete specified subject-matter from the application, the Comptroller noting that the referrer should then be able (under EPC art.61 and (what is now) r.16 of the EPC) to file its own application for the subject-matter, but limited to the matter arising from itself and excluding subject-matter arising from the original applicant. In this division of subject-matter it was stressed that no prior art had been taken into account. Such was a matter for the substantive examination of the applications; see also *AEA Technology's Reference* BL O/36/99 for a similar case.

The ECJ has held (*Duijnstee v Göderbauer (288/82)* [1983] E.C.R. 3663; [1985] F.S.R. 221) that art.16(4) of Sch.1 to the Civil Jurisdiction and Judgments Act 1982 (c.27), which repeats the same article in the Brussels Convention providing for exclusive jurisdiction in proceedings concerned with registration or validity of patents, etc. has no applicability to questions of entitlement. Thus, now, within the European Economic Area, only a single court should have jurisdiction in relation to an employer-employee dispute over ownership of corresponding patents in various countries in accordance with the provision of that Article of the Brussels Convention (in force in the United Kingdom since January 1, 1987). The Brussels Convention has now been replaced by the EC Regulation 44/2001, the Jurisdiction Regulation (also known as the Brussels Regulation), for most contracting states and art.16(4) of the Convention is equivalent to art.22(4) of the Regulation.

For proceedings which initially involved an application under s.12 in relation to an international and a European application, see *Kakkar v Szelke* [1989] 1 F.S.R. 225; [1989] E.P.O.R. 184 CA. Here, s.82(3) required that the proceedings under s.12 had to be struck out as regards a European application once this had become assigned to a Swedish company; and it was held on appeal that this was so, even as regards a claim for a declaration that the applicant would hold the patents on a constructive trust for the referrers, see §82.05 and §82.06. The fact that the application also involved an international application does not appear to have been separately argued. In contrast to *Kakkar v Szelke*, the Office did have jurisdiction over a California-based company where the applicant was resident in the UK—see *Actineon's Applications* BL O/309/05, noted [2005] *CIPA* 799. There was both an EPC and a PCT application and so s.82 was considered as well. The hearing officer noted that s.12 "is very wide in ambit." It "places no restriction at all on the place of business, or residence or indeed any other factor associated with" the defendant.

In *Cannings' US Application* [1992] R.P.C. 459, a former employee-inventor had refused to execute an assignment of a United States application in favour of his employer but had not contested the s.12 proceedings. On the uncontested facts the employer was held to be entitled to the benefit of the application and the inventor was ordered to execute an assignment. The Comptroller held that he had power to authorise another to execute the assignment if the inventor failed to obey this order, by analogy with s.8(5), although s.12 gave him no express power to do so. Subsequently, he exercised this power after efforts to have the inventor sign had failed and after an assurance that an assignment executed by another under his authorisation would be recorded in the United States Patent and Trademark Office, see also *Edenlist's Patent* BL O/121/97; O/141/97 and O/1/98 for a similar case. Also, in *British Telecommunications' Applications* BL O/402/01, the inventor had left the applicant (BT) after the priority application had been filed and could not be traced. An application for an international application designating the USA and Canada had been rejected by the UK-IPO (acting as receiving office) because the power of attorney for the United States application had not been signed by the inventor. The Comptroller was satisfied that BT was entitled to the invention under s.39 for the purposes of the United States and Canadian applications and therefore BT's head of IP was authorised to sign the power of attorney and to execute assignments of the inventor's rights to BT.

In *Xaar's International Application* BL O/257/98, the referrer successfully claimed co-inventorship. As under the law of the United States a patent application must be initially filed by the inventor(s), an order was made that the applicant seek to correct inventorship (and consequently the initial applicant entities) in that country. However, the referrer/co-inventor was also ordered to execute an assignment of rights to *Xaar* who had been her employer at the time the invention was devised. Armed with the decision, the referrer could now seek to correct inventorship in the Euro-PCT application under EPC art.61 and (what is now) r.19 of the EPC. No order was made in respect of the international application in other countries because of the absence of evidence as to the provisions for correcting inventorship therein.

In *James Campbell v University of Aberdeen* BL O/274/08, the pursuer failed to show that an exchange student who was both working for him and at the University had been the "deviser" of the invention, rather than a different University employee. However, the Comptroller heard the case in Scotland and there was a considerable amount of documents put in by the unrepresented pursuer. If the University had not declined to mediate the dispute, then it might have obtained an off-scale award of costs with respect to the unnecessary paperwork.

In *Raven v Williamson* BL O/259/10, the Comptroller ordered that, even though he had no power under s.12 to regulate the manner in which the application would proceed, the order of the applicants for the European application should be changed so that one of the other applicants might be deemed to be the common representative, in order to try to reinstate the European application (the parties having fallen out and the European application having been deemed withdrawn).

New application under subsection (6)

12.05 The amendments in subs.(6) echo those made to s.8(3)(c), for the effect of which see §8.08.

Where the Comptroller decides under subs.(1) that a person, other than the applicant, is entitled to a patent, that person may file a new application under the Act which is treated as if it had been filed on the date of filing of an earlier application for a European patent (UK) or an international application (UK) that has been withdrawn, or refused, or in which the designation of the United Kingdom has been withdrawn after publication of the application (subs.(6)(a)). In the case of an application for a European patent (UK), the withdrawal must have occurred before the initiation of entitlement proceedings, or after a final determination (as defined in subs.(7)(b)) of entitlement has been made by the Comptroller, court or relevant convention court (as defined in s.130(1)) and the person entitled has requested the EPO to refuse the application for a European patent or withdraw the designation of the United Kingdom (subs.(6)(b)). Note that, after the initiation of entitlement proceedings and notification to the EPO, an application for a European patent, or the designation of a country therein, cannot be withdrawn until the entitlement proceedings are concluded (EPC r.15); and that a stay of the examination proceedings in the EPO can be requested until the question of entitlement has been settled in national proceedings, although publication of that application proceeds normally (EPC r.14). See §9.02 and §12.06 for further discussion on the imposing and lifting of a stay at the EPO.

A new application may likewise be filed if an international application designating the United Kingdom without a request for a European patent is withdrawn, or the designation of the United Kingdom is withdrawn and the international application has been published (subs.(6)(c)). In the case of subs.(6)(b), a new application can be filed whether or not the withdrawn application has been published.

The new application need not be one under the Act. It can be an application for a European patent (UK) filed under EPC art.61(1)(b). Thus, in *Dodge's European Application* BL O/20/90, noted I.P.D. 13136, the Comptroller allowed a new European application to be filed even though five years had elapsed since the filing of the non-entitled application. Although there is no provision for protection for those who might have started to work the invention in reliance on the initial application having been abandoned, the Comptroller left it to the courts to devise relief in any such circumstances. (Cf. *Stafford Rubber Company's Application* BL O/255/02 where the Comptroller imposed third party terms analogous to those employed in s.28A—see §8.08.) Subsequently, in G 3/92 *LATCHWAYS/Unlawful applicant* OJ EPO 1994, 633; [1995] E.P.O.R. 141, the facts of which are described in J 1/91 *LATCHWAYS/Entitlement to patent* OJ EPO 1993, 281, the EPO Enlarged Board of Appeal accepted (by a majority decision) that it is not a precondition for a replacement application to be accepted under the EPC that the earlier original usurping application should be still pending when the new application is filed. Although the previous edition of this Work noted that this decision was controversial, the practice seems to be followed. Thus in *RS Brookhouse Engineering v Pro-Tek Engineering* BL O/218/07 the EPO Legal Division had written to advise that a new application could be filed for the same invention, even though the original one had ceased over three years previously, provided that there was a final decision for the UK-IPO that the new applicant was entitled to the grant of the European patent on the original application.

In *Bradford Hospital's Application* BL O/85/01, the filing of a replacement application under subs.(6) was allowed, in accordance with G 3/92 *LATCHWAYS/Unlawful applicant*, (above), following a decision as to entitlement on European and international applications which had been allowed to lapse by the original applicant. See §39.08 regarding entitlement by the employee in this case.

Where a competent national court has adjudged by a final decision (in the *Dodge* case, the unappealed decision of the Comptroller) that a person other than the applicant is entitled to the grant of a European patent, EPC art.61(1) requires that person to exercise his remedies, including the filing of a new European application in respect of the same invention under EPC art.61(1)(b), within three months of the date when the national court decision became final, though this is subject to the proviso that the disentitled European patent has not by then been granted (EPC r.16). This should not have happened if the permitted stay of the examination of the European application had been sought and obtained under EPC r.14 and not subsequently lifted.

Whether the filing, if permitted, of a new international application under s.12(6)(c) is effective will depend upon the national laws of the countries to be designated in that international application. In *Solargen's Applications* BL O/147/98, the Comptroller doubted whether, in the circumstances, any such applications would have validity under national laws having regard to the prior filing of a Russian application, but gave the successful referrer an opportunity to request relief under this provision, preferably after taking professional advice.

A problem also arises (as it did in the *Dodge* case, above) if the non-entitled application has invalidating prior art effect because it claimed priority from an earlier application, even though that priority application had been withdrawn. Under s.78(5) and (5A) (as amended on December 13, 2007 to bring it into line with EPC 2000), this invalidates a replacement European application (UK) permitted to be filed under s.12(6). Under art.79 of the EPC 2000 every European patent application will, upon filing, be deemed to be an application for protection in all the then contracting states. However, for further discussion on the historical position of when and how published EP applications designating the UK were prior art under s.2(3) but not necessarily prior art under the EPC, see §78.03. When such a situation occurred under s.8, the problem was solved by permitting a second new application to be filed replicating the priority document, see *Amateur Athletic Association's Applications* [1989] R.P.C. 717 discussed in §8.08, but, even if such filing were permitted under s.12(6), it is problematical whether this would be accepted in a foreign country or by the EPO as giving rise to a valid priority claim.

PRACTICE UNDER SECTION 12

12.06   Practice under s.12 follows that for corresponding applications under ss.8, 10 and 11, see §§8.09–8.11, §10.05 and §11.07. In all such cases, proceedings under s.12, of whatever variety, are now commenced on PF 2. The Comptroller can make no order under s.8 or s.37 relating to foreign applications or patents. Such requires a separate reliance on s.12. The practice under the 1995 Rules was that the Comptroller would not permit amendment of an existing reference (under ss.8 or 37) if that would delay the conclusion of that reference (*Vet Health's Patent* BL O/49/90, noted I.P.D. 13165). However, now references under these different sections are brought in the same proceedings and the Comptroller has power to allow amendment of statements of case under r.82(1). This will be exercised in accordance with the overriding objective (r.74), which includes dealing with the matter in a proportionate way and the saving of expense. For further discussion see the commentary on s.123.

While proceedings under s.12 are pending on an application for a European patent, the EPO is required, upon application, to stay its examination of the application (EPC r.14). However, the EPO may withdraw such stay if the s.12 proceedings become too prolonged, see T 146/82 *TAG/Suspension of proceedings* OJ EPO 1985, 267; [1979–85] E.P.O.R. B618.

A new application permitted to be filed under s.12(6) cannot contain new matter (s.76(1)) and should be filed within three months from the date when the entitlement was finally disposed of on appeal, or from the last day for lodging an appeal if there was no appeal (r.20, reprinted at §8.02). The commentaries on the corresponding s.8(3) or 37(4) (for which see §8.08 and §37.09 respectively) apply likewise to a new application under s.12(6) with the requirement that the application has to be placed in order within the period specified in r.30(3) or (4) (reprinted in §18.04), and other requirements also satisfied, all as specified in §8.11. The practice on the filing of any such new application is discussed in §8.11 and §37.13 and the other paragraphs referred to in those sections.

SECTION 13

Mention of inventor

13.01   **13.**—(1) The inventor or joint inventors of an invention shall have a right to be mentioned as such in any patent granted for the invention and shall also have a right to be so mentioned if possible in any published application for a patent for the invention and, if not so mentioned, a right to be so mentioned in accordance with rules in a prescribed document.

(2) Unless he has already given the Patent Office the information hereinafter mentioned, an applicant for a patent shall within the prescribed period file with the Patent Office a statement—

(a) identifying the person or persons whom he believes to be the inventor or inventors; and

(b) where the applicant is not the sole inventor or the applicants are not the joint inventors, indicating the derivation of his or their right to be granted the patent;

and, if he fails to do so, the application shall be taken to be withdrawn.

(3) Where a person has been mentioned as sole or joint inventor in pursuance of this section, any other person who alleges that the former ought not to have been so mentioned may at any time apply to the comptroller for a certificate to that effect, and the comptroller may issue such a certificate; and if he does so, he shall accordingly rectify any undistributed copies of the patent and of any documents prescribed for the purposes of subsection (1) above.

Note. Although s.130(7) does not require s.13 to be construed in conformity with the EPC, arts 62 and 81 of the EPC seem relevant. See below for these Articles.

RELEVANT CONVENTION PROVISIONS

EPC Article 62—Right of the inventor to be mentioned

62. The inventor shall have the right, *vis-a-vis* the applicant for or proprietor of a European patent, to be mentioned as such before the European Patent Office.　　**13.02**

EPC Article 81—Designation of the inventor

81. The European patent application shall designate the inventor. If the applicant is not the inventor or is not the sole inventor, the designation shall contain a statement indicating the origin of the right to the European patent.　　**13.03**

RELEVANT RULES—RULES 10 AND 11

Rule 10—Mention of inventor

10.—(1) An inventor or joint inventor of an invention, if not mentioned in any published application for a patent, or in any patent granted, for the invention, must be mentioned in an addendum or an erratum to the application or patent.　　**13.04**

(2) A person who alleges that any person ought to have been mentioned as the inventor or joint inventor of an invention may apply to the comptroller for that person to be so mentioned—

　(a) in any patent granted for the invention; and

　(b) if possible in any published application for a patent for the invention,

and, if not so mentioned, in the manner prescribed by paragraph (1).

(3) Subject to rules 21, 58(4), 59(3) and 68(2), the period prescribed for the purposes of section 13(2) is sixteen months beginning [with] immediately after

—

　(a) where there is no declared priority date, the date of filing of the application; or

　(b) where there is a declared priority date, that date.

(4) A statement filed under section 13(2) must be made on Patents Form 7.

Rule 11—Waiving the right to be mentioned

11.—(1) The inventor may, before preparations for the application's publica-　　**13.05**

tion have been completed by the Patent Office, apply to the comptroller in writing to waive his right—

    (a) to have his name and address mentioned as those of the inventor; or

    (b) to have his address mentioned as that of the inventor.

  (2) An application by an inventor under paragraph (1)(a) must—

    (a) include his reasons for making the application; and

    (b) be accepted by the comptroller where the comptroller is satisfied by those reasons.

  (3) An application by an inventor under paragraph (1)(b) must be accepted by the comptroller.

  (4) Where the comptroller has accepted an inventor's application to make a waiver under this rule, the inventor may apply to the comptroller to end that waiver.

  (5) The comptroller may, if he thinks fit, accept an application to end a waiver, and his acceptance may be made subject to such conditions as he may direct.

  (6) An application under paragraph (1)(a) or (b) or under paragraph (4) may also be made by a person who is not the inventor, but who has been identified as such for the purposes of section 13(2).

  (7) Where a person makes an application in reliance on paragraph (6), the reference in this rule to an application to waive his right to have his name and address (or his address) mentioned shall be construed as a reference to an application not to have his name and address (or his address) mentioned; and paragraphs (4) and (5) shall be construed accordingly.

Note. Rule 10 was amended as from October 1, 2011 by The Patents (Amendment) Rules 2011 (SI 2011/2052).

OTHER RELEVANT RULES—RULES 73–88

13.06   The rules reprinted at §§123.06–123.21 are those of Pt 7 of the Patents Rules 2007 and are general in nature to govern procedure in all proceedings to be heard before the Comptroller. These specifically include proceedings under r.10(2) and s.13(3). These rules are discussed under the heading "Practice under Section 123", but are also mentioned, as appropriate, in the commentary and practice sections below.

COMMENTARY ON SECTION 13

Scope of the section

13.07   Section 13 concerns the right of an inventor to be named as such in the patent and further provides that the inventor shall have the right to be mentioned "if possible" in a published application or in a prescribed document. The power to make rules in respect of the inventor's right to be mentioned or to waive such rights is set out in r.123(2)(i) (reprinted in §123.01). Rule 44(1)(b) (reprinted in §32.04 and discussed in §32.17) provides for entry of identified inventor's name and address in the register. However, r.11 (see §13.05), allows the inventor to apply to the Comptroller to waive this right, either in respect of his name and address or just in respect of his address (see §13.12 below for discussion).

Inventorship alone, without "entitlement" (for which see §7.06), for inventors who are not also employees, gives no right to an invention, other than the right to be named as inventor under the section. Employee-inventors who are not entitled to the rights in their inventions have other rights in the circumstances set out in ss.40–43, see the commentaries on these sections. Entitlement to patent rights needs to be derived in some way from an inventor, see s.7(2), discussed in §7.06.

The definition of "inventor" is discussed in §7.10 in the light of cases mainly decided under the common law. Cases involving the application of s.39 (ownership of inventions made by employee-inventors) are also relevant, see §§39.07–39.12.

The meaning of "invention" in s.13 is open to some doubt. On the one hand, the courts have tended to shy away from discussions of validity in dealing with inventorship questions. However, on the other, it is necessary to identify the inventive concept in issue, and then to identify the person or persons who had come up with it (*University of Southampton's Applications* [2005] R.P.C. 11; [2004] EWHC 2107 Pat Ct). A person is not an inventor merely because he has contributed to the work embodied in a patent claim. The contribution must be to the inventive concept. However, it may sometimes be necessary to assess this question. In *Yeda v Rhône-Poulenc Rorer* [2008] R.P.C. 1; [2007] UKHL 43, Lord Hoffmann pointed out:

"In some cases this may be quite complex because the inventive concept is a relationship of discontinuity between the claimed invention and the prior art. Inventors themselves will often not know exactly where it lies."

Care should be taken to include all such persons as co-inventors while not naming as an inventor anyone who did not make such a contribution, see *Xaar's International Application* BL O/257/98; *BNOS Electronics' Patent* BL O/270/98 and §7.07. Accordingly, where one inventor is wholly responsible for the full disclosure, no difficulty is likely to arise. Where two or more inventors are concerned, the practice of looking only at the claims and identifying inventors by reference to individual claims appears to have been doubted. One must look for "the heart" of the invention. Although "there may be more than one 'heart', each claim is not to be considered as a separate 'heart' if its own". (*University of Southampton's Applications* [2005] R.P.C. 11; [2004] EWHC 2107 Pat Ct.)

If the claims include an "omnibus" claim of the usual form, it is still possible that the application for mention as a co-inventor may relate to subject-matter described in the application, even though not otherwise specifically claimed.

Declaration of inventorship (PF 7)

13.08

Where the inventor is the applicant, or all the inventors are co-applicants, with no other person involved as an inventor, then all the relevant information will be included in the application form (PF 1). Section 7 of the form contains two questions "Are all the applicants named above also inventors?" and "If yes, are there any other inventors?" If the answers are "Yes" and "No" respectively, then no further form is required.

However, where there is an inventor who is not an applicant, or an applicant who is not an inventor, a separate declaration of inventorship must normally be filed on PF 7, see r.10(4), unless the Office has already been informed of the inventorship details. This might be due to compliance with the EPC for an application converted (under s.81(3)(c)) or compliance with the PCT for an international application entering the UK national phase (under s.89B(1)(c)).

In the case of a divisional application, a PF 7 will be required; care should be taken in such cases because it is by no means automatically true that the invention as defined by the claims of the divisional application was made by the same inventors (where there are two or more) as those who made the invention defined by the claims of the parent application.

PF 7 must state how the applicant derives the right to be granted the patent (subs.(2)(b)), for example by assignment or operation of law, as discussed in §13.15. As s.7(4) presumes that the applicant is the person entitled, unless this is successfully challenged, the Office do not require any statement as to how the rights are derived to be substantiated.

Time for filing PF 7

13.09   Under r.10(3) PF 7 must normally be filed within 16 months of the "declared priority date" (as defined in r.3, reprinted at §5.06A), or (where priority has not been claimed) within 16 months of the filing date of the application. It is thus possible to file an application to serve as a priority document without, at that stage, naming any inventor. Absence of the naming of inventors initially can cause problems in entitlement disputes and the Comptroller has indicated that a failure to investigate inventorship is too casual an approach and that patent attorneys should take particular care to ensure that all inventors, and only those persons, are named, see §7.07 with reference to *Xaar's International Application* BL O/257/98; and *BNOS Electronics' Patent* BL O/270/98.

The timing of filing PF 7 in the case of a divisional application under s.15(4), or of a new or "replacement" application under ss.8(3), 12(6) or 37(4) is dealt with in r.22, reprinted at and discussed in §15.07).

The 16-month period for complying with r.10(3), or with r.21(1), by the filing of PF 7 may be extended as of right by two months by filing PF 52 (r.108(2)) and for a further period of up to two months on application under r.108(3) at the discretion of the Comptroller (which is exercised under r.108(5)), for which see §123.25. A request for an extension for the further period requires supporting evidence. There is a fee for filing the PF 52. For the time limits for filing PF 7 in the cases of a European application converted under s.81 and of an international application, see §13.10.

The request for a two-month extension of time under r.108(2) may be made up to two months after the relevant period of time has expired (r.108(2)(c)) and extensions of time under r.108(3) may also be made after the relevant period of time of time has expired (r.108(6)). So this can extend the time beyond the date for publication of the application.

Where the extension request involves the exercise of the Comptroller's discretion, then it will generally be necessary to show that the failure to meet the time period was unintentional. However, the MOPP indicates that there may be circumstances where discretion will be favourably exercised, even though this requirement has not been met (see the MOPP at para.123.37).

The MOPP indicates that, even now, the provisions of s.117 (correction) cannot be invoked to overcome the mandatory requirements of s.13(2) (i.e. the requirement to identify the inventors and the derivation of title) because of *Payne's Application* [1985] R.P.C. 193.

A failure to file PF 7 is not a "formal requirement" within the terms of r.25 (reprinted at §15A.04). Thus, the Office has no obligation to draw attention to its absence and accordingly invite observations or amendment under s.15A(6). However, the *Formalities Manual* states that, if the PF 7 is required and missing, the outstanding procedural matter should be communicated to the applicant, if necessary by telephoning the agent.

Note that under s13(2), the failure to file a statement indicating the identities of those believed to be inventors and the derivation of title within the prescribed period means that the application is deemed to be withdrawn.

Inventor designation in international and European applications (UK)

13.10   The procedure prescribed by r.10 for designating inventorship is generally similar to that for a European application under EPC r.19. Thus, under s.81(3)(c), it is sufficient for r.19 of the EPC to have been complied with in the EPO when a European application (UK) is converted into an application under the Act under s.81(2)(b), see also r.10(3). However, if a European application (UK) is deemed to have been withdrawn because it has not been received in due time by the EPO, and r.19 of the EPC has not been complied with, PF 7 will be required when the application is converted under s.81. In these circumstances, PF 7 should be filed within a period of two months of the request for conversion being made to the Comptroller where the applicant makes the conversion request under s.81(2)(b)(i), or within four months where the request for conversion is made by a patent office of another EPC contracting state under s.81(2)(b)(ii), see rr.58(4) and 59(3) (reprinted in §81.02 and §81.03 and discussed in §81.08). These periods are each extensible under r.108(2) and (3) in the same way as indicated in §13.09.

For an international application (UK), if the inventorship was correctly stated in the request form, no declaration of inventorship is required under the Act (s.89B(1)(c), r.10(4)). In these circumstances (and only in these circumstances) the applicant is not required by subs.(2)(b) to state how he derives his right to be granted the patent, but a question of entitlement can of course still be raised at any time under s.12(1)(a) (during the international phase–by virtue of s.89B(4)), but subject to s.82 in the case of a Euro-PCT application, or under s.8(1)(a) or s.37(1)(a) as appropriate. If the inventors have not been named in the international application, PF 7 should be filed when the filing fee is paid for entering the United Kingdom phase (preferably by the filing of PF NP.1), see r.68 (reprinted in §89A.04) as discussed in §89A.32. These periods are each extensible under r.108(2) and (3) in the same way as indicated in §13.09.

Sufficient copies of PF 7

The Rules no longer require an applicant to file more than one copy of the PF 7. The Office will make such copies as are required to send a copy to each non-applicant inventor. However, where there are more than three inventors, then the back of a further copy of the form will need to be used for the other inventors and attached to the first one. **13.11**

Waiver by Inventor of right to be mentioned

Rule 11 (see §13.05), allows the inventor to apply to the Comptroller to waive the right, either to have his name and address or just his address mentioned. Rule 11(7) makes it clear that this really means that he is applying not to have his name and address or just his address published. The application must be made in writing and must be made before preparations for the publication have been completed by the Office. **13.12**

If the application is just to in respect of the address, then the Comptroller must accept it (r.11(3)). However, where it is to withhold both the name and address from publication, then the applicant must set out the reasons for making the application and the Comptroller need only accept it where he is satisfied by those reasons (r.11(2)).

The procedure under r.11 also applies to someone who has been identified under s.13(2) as an inventor, but is not an inventor (r.11(6)).

An inventor can change his mind about the waiver and subsequently apply for the waiver to be ended, i.e. for his name and/or address to be published. The Comptroller has discretion as to whether or not to accept this subsequent application and to impose conditions for any acceptance (r.11(4) and (5)).

Where an application for waiver is accepted, then r.26(2) requires the Comptroller to ensure that that persons name and address is not published as an inventor with the publication of the application (see §123.49), r.44(2) (reprinted in §32.04) gives the Comptroller the power (but not the obligation) to omit the inventor's details from the register and r.51(3)(e) requires that no document disclosing that name and address may be inspected, unless the Comptroller directs to the contrary. These details might need to be disclosed if there is an entitlement or inventorship dispute.

Amendment of inventorship entities

The Act provides means in subs.(1) for adding the name of an inventor and in subs.(3) for deleting the name of an inventor, although applications to add inventors should be made under r.10(2) and not subs.(1). For comments on the procedure see §13.17 below. The procedure in both instances is governed by the rules in Pt 7 (reprinted and discussed in under s.123, by virtue of r.73(1)(a) and Sch.3 Pt 1). Any person may apply to add a name of an inventor who ought to have been mentioned as inventor, but has been omitted. (Under the previous rules, this had to be the inventor himself, but now this application can be made by the applicant or proprietor of the patent.) Any person may apply for the deletion of the name of an inventor. **13.13**

The direct result of an application under r.10(2) or subs.(3) is the issue of an addendum or erratum to the patent or published application showing the corrected inventorship and (where appropriate) a certificate that a person formerly named as inventor should not have been so named (subs.(3)). It is not, apparently, possible to correct an inventorship designation of an application which did not proceed to publication, but the Comptroller may make a "finding of fact" which may facilitate the correction of inventorship in a European, international or foreign application, see *Carbury Herne's Application* BL O/182/00.

As an alternative to application under s.13 and Pt 7, other procedures are available for "correction" of inventorship entities. If the statutory period for filing PF 7 has not expired, correction of the inventorship of an application may be made simply by filing a substitute PF 7. If, as a result of amendment of the patent application, a named inventor should no longer be included in the stated inventorship entities, the MOPP indicates that application under subs.(3) is not the appropriate starting point. Instead, the relevant facts should be set out in a letter and that all those interested (including the applicant and named inventors) indicate their consent. The Office will write to any party whose consent has not already been given. If the Office is satisfied, then the relevant inventor will cease to be named on the grant of that application. Where the matter cannot be resolved by agreement, then an application under subs.(3) may become necessary.

However, the *Formalities Manual* states that a request to delete the names of one or more inventors from a parent application, when filing a divisional application under s.15(9), should be made on PF 2 with supporting grounds, but that this is not required when this follows amendment of the claims of the parent application. This seems a little confused and further clarification may be required.

Otherwise, correction may be effected under s.117 and r.105 (correction of errors) for which see §117.01 and §117.02. Where the correction is to a name or address, then PF 20 should be filed (r.49; see §32.09). However, amendment under s.19 does not seem possible, since PF 7 is not part of an "application", see s.14(2).

In the case of a European patent (UK), an application may be made to amend the stated inventorship entities as from publication of the mention of grant in the EPB (*Kinetron's Patent* BL O/110/95). Prior thereto, inventorship details may be corrected by application to the EPO under EPC r.21 and, by proceeding under s.13(3), it is possible to obtain, prior to grant of a European patent (UK), a certificate from the Comptroller as to inventorship. Presumably, this could then be applied to correct inventorship once the European patent (UK) has been granted.

Reasons for proceedings under section 13

13.14   Proceedings under s.13 are not directly concerned with entitlement to the patent (for which, see the commentaries on ss.8 and 37), although question under these different sections may be raised in parallel. Under the previous rules, applications either to add or remove an inventor were dealt with in the same way.

Whereas previously it was necessary to issue concurrent applications, now PF 2 can be used to initiate proceedings under more than one section of the Act and/or the Rules, provided that they relate to the same cause of action.

"Although there is no express requirement in s.40 for a claimant to have been identified as inventor in the patent, r.10(1) requires that all inventors must be mentioned. It would thus seem necessary for a claimant who is not so mentioned to make an application under r.10(2) to be added as an inventor. A claimant who has identified himself to the IPO as an inventor but has successfully applied under r.11 to waive his right to have his name mentioned could, presumably, pursue an application for compensation without the need for remedial action under r.10(2)."

Even in the absence of a question of entitlement, however, the possibility of compensation under s.40 gives employees a material reason to seek under s.13 a correct designation of inventorship. There is no time limit for making an application under r.10(2); and, if an omitted inventor can establish his claim, even many years after grant, he would appear to have an absolute right to be named as such and then to claim compensation under s.40. This means that full records of inventorship should be maintained throughout the life of the patent and, indeed, for one year thereafter in view of r.91 (reprinted in §40.02), see §39.18. Section 40 does not contain an express requirement for the employee claiming under that section to have first been identified as an inventor. However, r.10(1) does require that all inventors are identified either initially or in an addendum or erratum. Therefore, it appears necessary for an employee not already identified as an inventor to make an application under r.10(2) to be named as inventor either before or at the same time as the application under s.40, not least as any such claim for compensation from an unnamed inventor is a challenge to the correctness of the PF7 and, potentially, the standing of the other inventors. Indeed the IPO consider this necessary—see the *Litigation Manual* at Ch.10, para.10.02. The Act and Rules do not explain the position of an employee-inventor who has successfully applied for his name to be withheld from publication. However, this is only the waiver of the right to be named, and not a waiver of other rights: so presumably such a person is still able to claim under s.40, without needing first to end the waiver. However, it may well be a corollary, of any application for compensation, that the inventor's name will be published as part of any decision.

When initially filed claims are restricted during examination and an initially named co-inventor of the original claimed subject-matter is not an inventor for the invention of the restricted claims, then the applicant may wish to correct the inventorship, if only to avoid that person subsequently claiming compensation under s.40. See §13.13 above for the way to proceed.

PRACTICE UNDER SECTION 13

Filing of declaration of inventorship on PF 7

Naming the inventor is effected by filing PF 7, which must normally be done within 16 **13.15** months of the declared priority date or (where priority has not been claimed) the filing date of the application. It is not necessary to give the nationality of an inventor, but the surname or family name of the or each inventor should be underlined in black print or ink, see Note on p.2 of PF 7. If this underlining is omitted, the Office will probably only require this to be rectified where there is doubt is seen as to which name given should be regarded as the surname/family name, this name being used for indexing purposes.

PF 7 may be signed by an agent and no signature by the inventor is required. The Comptroller will, unless there is a foreign priority claim, send one copy of the form to each inventor who is not an applicant (see the *Formalities Manual*), but the rule which previously required this, and for the Form to be filed in multiple copies, has been deleted.

The correctness of the information, e.g. as to the name and address of the, or each, inventor in the "boxes" printed on the reverse of PF 7 is important, because the Comptroller uses these "boxes" directly as address labels and will send a query to the agent if the postal services return a PF 7 which apparently bears an incorrect or out-of-date address. If the postal authorities return a PF 7 to the Office because the letter was undeliverable, the Office will contact the Agent or applicant (by telephone where possible) to seek a corrected address. It is understood that this situation does not hold up publication under s.16, and that if a correct address is not forthcoming, the Office does not persist.

It is also understood that no objection is raised if the address of the inventor is given as that of his employer. However, this practice is not as important as it was, as, if the inventor wishes to keep his domestic address out of the public domain he can now make an application under r.11, before the Office has completed preparation for publication. When such a request is made, then not only will those details not appear on the published application (r.26(2)), but they will also be kept off the Register (r.44(2)) and any document which sets out that address cannot be inspected (r.51(3)(e)). (See §13.12 above, §13.16 below and the MOPP at para.13.03.)

PF 7 must indicate the derivation of the applicant's right to be granted the patent. The Office does not require a full substantiation of the applicant's rights to the patent, but will require that "sufficient" information is given to identify the facts. Generally the Office looks for wording to show direct assignment (or a full chain of assignments) from the inventors named on the PF 7 to the applicant, an indication that there is a contract of employment *and* s.39 applies or that there has been an inheriting of rights from the inventor or original applicant (or that this is the personal representative). The date of any such document or event is not required. The bald statement "by assignment" or an incomplete chain of title is not be accepted (e.g. where the derivation is stated to be by virtue of an assignment from A to B, but the applicant is C). Statements such as "by operation of law" or "by virtue of section 7(2)" are regarded as too vague, although in the case of the latter it would be sufficient to indicate whether the right to apply arises under s.7(2)(b) or s.7(2)(c). Thus, in *Nippon Piston's Applications* [1987] R.P.C. 120, two applications were refused for failure to comply with s.13(2)(b) because adequate identification of the applicant's right to apply had not been provided. However, in that case it was accepted that the requirement to identify the inventor(s) under s.13(2)(a) had been met by supplying a certified copy of the priority document which did name the inventor. Naturally, the applicant must always be in a position to substantiate his right to a patent, and the statement on PF 7, should this ever be disputed.

When naming an inventor it is worth ensuring that the inventor is aware that his or her details will be made available on public registers and to check whether they wish to use the employer's address instead. See Burt, "Designation of inventor: what contact address should be used?" [2009] Sep. *CIPA* 610–611, for a discussion on the outcome of requests to the EPO to remove such data from the PATSTAT database.

Meider v Whitfield BL O/171/10 is a reminder that inventorship is a question of fact, rather than agreement between the parties.

Application under rule 11

13.16 It is for the inventor to make the application under r.11. There is no form, but as the request must be made in writing, it seems that a letter would be sufficient. Where the request is only to withhold the address, then no reasons are required and this request has to be complied with. If more than one inventor is named on the PF 7, the Office will place the original form in the closed part of the file and make up a new one, with that address removed, to be placed in the open part of the file. Correspondence from that inventor which sets out his address will be placed in the closed part of the file.

If the inventor also wishes to withhold his name, then he will have to file supporting reasons. The Comptroller will only accede to this request if satisfied by those reasons. The *Formalities Manual* states that each case will be judged on its merit. Factors to be balanced are the concerns of the inventors in certain fields versus the removal of a useful patent searching and evaluation tool. Where the request is granted, a footnote will appear on both the A and B publications indicating that at least one inventor has waived the right to be mentioned. In addition to keeping the name off the Register, it will also be withheld from the certificate of grant. The details of other inventors who have not made such a request will be published and again documents which identify the inventor who has sought anonymity will be kept in the closed part of the file and copies without that information will, where relevant, be made and placed in the open part for inspection.

The inventor can change his mind and request publication. The Office does not have to republish the application.

Amendment of named inventors(s)

13.17 Where the alternative and less formal ways of changing the named inventors (discussed at §13.13 above) are not available, the procedure to add an inventor under r.10(2) (rather than under subs.(1)) and to delete an inventor under subs.(3) is governed by Pt 7 of the Rules (see under s.123) and is made on PF 2. The PF 2 has to be filed in duplicate, together with a statement in duplicate setting out fully the facts relied upon (r.76(1)). Only one application is needed where there are proceedings under s.13 and proceedings under, e.g. s.8 or s.37 on an issue of entitlement, provided that they relate to the same cause of action. Only one fee is required (see note (e) on PF 2).

Although PF 2 will allow proceedings under both subs.(3) and s.12, there are questions as to whether that would be the most effective way to correct inventorship in international or foreign applications and so the rules relating to the international or foreign application would need to be considered. However, proceedings under s.13, applicable only to the international application (UK), may well be appropriate.

When PF 2 is filed, the Comptroller sends a copy of it and the supporting statement to all the inventors identified to date and to the proprietor (other than to the s.13 applicant himself and any other person who has already consented in writing to the application) as well as to any other person whose interests the Comptroller considers may be affected by the application (presumably including anyone who has filed a request to be notified of a relevant event (the so-called, PF 49, caveat) for this purpose under r.54(1) and (7) (r.77(1) and (2)). Oppositions/counterstatements can be filed in duplicate under r.77(6) within the period specified r.77(5). For further details of what the statements must contain and the procedures see the commentary on Pt 7 of the Rules under s.123.

The onus of proof is on the applicant who seeks deletion of an inventorship entity, see *Bond Knittings Systems' Patent* BL O/125/87 and C/35/88;and *Mawzones' Patent* BL O/17/95, noted I.P.D. 18026, in each of which the application failed on its facts, and *Rose v Ability* BL O/247/11, which succeeded. In *Rose v Ability*, the applicant had decided to acknowledge Rose as an inventor in order to "get Mr Rose off his back", but this had proved a mistake as Mr Rose then launched entitlement proceedings.

If, in an application for change of inventorship, the named inventors are notified of the proceedings and do not oppose, the Comptroller will allow the application and order the issue of an addendum or erratum to the specification (*Ferguson Ltd's Patent* BL O/85/91). However, the procedure is simplified even further if written consents to the application from all persons which the application seeks to add or remove as named inventors and from all the other named inventors are filed with the application.

There is no provision to transfer entitlement proceedings under s.13 to the court. Accordingly, in *Stanelco Fibre Optics' Applications and Patents* BL O/381/03, noted [2004] *CIPA* 35, with the consent of the parties, the Office stayed the s.13 proceedings pending the outcome of the related court case.

Applications [Sections 14–16]

SECTION 14

Making of application

14.—(1) Every application for a patent—   **14.01**

    (a) shall be made in the prescribed form and shall be filed at the Patent Office in the prescribed manner; and

    (b) [*rendered ineffective*]

(1A) Where an application for a patent is made, the fee prescribed for the purposes of this subsection ("the application fee") shall be paid not later than the end of the period prescribed for the purposes of section 15(10)(c) below.

(2) Every application for a patent shall contain—

    (a) a request for the grant of a patent;

    (b) a specification containing a description of the invention, a claim or claims and any drawing referred to in the description or any claim; and

    (c) an abstract;

but the foregoing provision shall not prevent an application being initiated by documents complying with section 15(1) below.

(3) The specification of an application shall disclose the invention in a manner which is clear enough and complete enough for the invention to be performed by a person skilled in the art.

(4) [*repealed*]

(5) The claim or claims shall—

(a) define the matter for which the applicant seeks protection;

(b) be clear and concise;

(c) be supported by the description; and

(d) relate to one invention or to a group of inventions which are so linked as to form a single inventive concept.

(6) Without prejudice to the generality of subsection (5)(d) above, rules may provide for treating two or more inventions as being so linked as to form a single inventive concept for the purposes of this Act.

(7) The purpose of the abstract is to give technical information and on publication it shall not form part of the state of the art by virtue of section 2(3) above, and the comptroller may determine whether the abstract adequately fulfils its purpose and, if it does not, may reframe it so that it does.

(8) [*repealed*]

(9) An application for a patent may be withdrawn at any time before the patent is granted and any withdrawal of such an application may not be revoked.

(10) Subsection (9) above does not affect the power of the comptroller under section 117(1) below to correct an error or mistake in a withdrawal of an application for a patent.

Notes

1. Subsections (1A) and (10) were added by Regulatory Reform (Patents) Order 2004 (SI 2004/2357) ("RRO") art.4 with effect from January 1, 2005 when subs.(1)(b) was also made ineffective, although without effect for applications which were pending on that day.

2. Subsections (4) and (8) were repealed by the CDPA 1988 (c.48) Sch.8, but with eventual replacement by new s.125A (SI 1990/2168) with effect from January 7, 1991, see §125A.01.

Relevant Rules—Rules 12–14, Schedule 2, and Rules 15–16

Rule 12—Applications for the grant of patents under sections 14 and 15

14.02   **12.**—(1) A request for the grant of a patent must be made on Patents Form 1.

(2) Where the documents filed at the Patent Office to initiate an application for a patent do not include the applicant's name and address, the comptroller shall notify the applicant that his name and address are required.

(3) Where the applicant has been so notified, he must, before the end of the period of two months beginning [with] immediately after the date of the notification, file his name and address; otherwise the comptroller may refuse his application.

(4) The specification mentioned in section 14(2)(b) must be preceded by the title of the invention and must be set out in the following order—

(a) description;

(b) the claim or claims; and

(c) any drawing referred to in the description or any claim.

(5) But paragraph (4) does not apply where an application is delivered in electronic form or using electronic communications.

(6) The title of the invention must be short and indicate the matter to which the invention relates.

(7) Where the specification includes drawings, the description must include a list of drawings briefly describing each of them.

(8) Where—

(a) the documents filed at the Patent Office to initiate an application for a patent include something which is or appears to be a description of the invention in a language other than English or Welsh; and

(b) the applicant has not filed a translation into English or Welsh of that thing, the comptroller shall notify the applicant that a translation is required.

(9) Where the applicant has been so notified, he must, before the end of the period of two months beginning with the date of the notification, file a translation; otherwise the comptroller may refuse his application.

Note. Rule 12(3) was amended as from October 1, 2011 by The Patents (Amendment) Rules 2011 (SI 2011/2052).

Rule 13—Biological material and sequence listings

13.—(1) The provisions of Schedule 1 prescribe the circumstances in which the specification of an application for a patent, or of a patent, for an invention which involves the use of or concerns biological material is to be treated as disclosing the invention in a manner which is clear enough and complete enough for the invention to be performed by a person skilled in the art.   **14.03**

(2) Where the specification of an application for a patent discloses a sequence, it must include a sequence listing.

(3) Where an applicant has not provided a sequence listing on filing the application, the comptroller may specify a period within which the applicant must provide the sequence listing; and if it is not provided within this period, the comptroller may refuse the application.

(4) Where a sequence listing is provided after the date of filing the application, the listing must be accompanied by a declaration that it does not contain matter extending beyond the sequence disclosed in the application.

(5) The sequence listing must comply with any requirements and standards adopted under the Patent Co-operation Treaty for the presentation of sequence listings in patent applications.

(6) A sequence listing shall, if it is reasonably possible, be delivered to the comptroller in electronic form or using electronic communications, even where the application for the patent is not delivered in electronic form or using electronic communications.

(7) A sequence listing may be set out either in the description or at the end of the application, but if set out at the end of the application rule 12(4) shall not apply.

Note. Schedule 1 is reprinted at §§125A.03–125A.10.

Rule 14—Size and presentation of application

14.—(1) The contents of all documents (including annotations to drawings) contained in an application for a patent must be in English or Welsh.   **14.04**

(2) The requirements for the documents contained in an application for a patent (other than drawings) are set out in Parts 1 and 2 of Schedule 2.

(3) The requirements for a drawing contained in an application are set out in Parts 1 and 3 of that Schedule.

(4) All documents contained in an application (including drawings) must comply with the requirements set out in Part 4 of that Schedule.

(5) Paragraphs (2) and (3) do not apply to an application, or a sequence listing contained in an application, which is delivered in electronic form or using electronic communications.

Rule 14

SCHEDULE 2

Formal and other Requirements

PART 1

REQUIREMENTS: ALL DOCUMENTS

14.05

1. A4 matt white paper must be used.

2. A document in paper form must be free from tears, folds or similar damage and its contents must be suitable for reproduction.

3. Frames (lines surrounding matter) must not be used.

PART 2

REQUIREMENTS: DOCUMENTS (OTHER THAN DRAWINGS)

4. The pages of the description and claims must be numbered consecutively in a single series.

5. But where a sequence listing is set out at the end of the application, it must be numbered consecutively in a separate series.

6. Page numbers must be located at the top or bottom of the page (but not in the margin) in the centre.

7. The minimum margins in any document must be 20mm.

8. Each of the following—
   (a) the request for the grant of a patent;
   (b) the description;
   (c) the claims;
   (d) the abstract,
must begin on a new sheet of paper.

9. The abstract, description and claims must use at least 1.5 line spacing, except where they form part of a translation or a sequence listing.

10. The capital letters in any typeface or font used must be more than 2mm high.

PART 3

REQUIREMENTS: DRAWINGS

11. There must be a margin around any drawing which must be at least—
   (a) at the top and left side, 20mm;
   (b) at the right side, 15mm; and
   (c) at the bottom, 10mm.

12. All drawings must be numbered consecutively in a single series.

13. The drawings must begin on a new sheet of paper.

14. The pages containing the drawings must be numbered consecutively in a single series.

15. Drawings must comprise black lines and must not be shaded.

16. Drawings may include cross-hatching to illustrate the cross-sections of a thing.

17. Any scale or other reference for making measurement must be represented diagrammatically.

18. Any drawing must be produced in such manner that it would still be clear if it were reduced by linear reduction to two thirds of its original size.

19. A drawing must not be included in the description, the claims, the abstract or the request for the grant of a patent.

20. The capital letters in any typeface or font used in any drawing must be more than 3mm high.

PART 4

OTHER REQUIREMENTS

21. References must only be included in the drawing where they are mentioned in either the description or the claims.

22. Tables of information may only be included in the claims if the comptroller agrees.

23. The terminology and any references used must be consistent throughout the application for a patent.

24. Where units of measurement used in the application are not standard international units of measurement, the equivalent standard international units of measurement must be provided, and where no international standard exists, units must be used which are generally accepted in the field.

25. Only technical terms, signs and symbols which are generally accepted in the field may be used.

DIRECTIONS UNDER SECTION 124A OF THE PATENTS ACT 1977

Filing Patent Applications by Electronic Means

(*Note.* These Directions were amended by a Direction effective from 31 March 2008. **14.06** They are reproduced here in their amended form as of that date.)

Introduction

1. The comptroller has given the following Directions under section 124A of the Patents Act 1977 (''the Act'') to direct the form and manner in which patent applications and certain other documents may be delivered to him in electronic form or using electronic communications.

2. These Directions and any others made under s.124A set out the extent to which such documents may be delivered to the comptroller in electronic form or using electronic communications.

3. These Directions come into force on 17 December 2007.

4. The Directions given on 16 March 2007 are revoked.

Interpretation

5. In these Directions:

"appropriate hardware" means either:

(a) a smart card reader and a smart card supplied by the Office; or

(b) a smart card reader and smart card supplied by any other person and which are acceptable to the Office;

"appropriate software" means version 3.20 or above of the UK epoline® software;

"description of the invention" means the description required under section 14(2)(b) of the Act

"digital media" means

(i) a compact optical disk containing electronic data conforming to ISO 9660;

(ii) a digital versatile disk (DVD) containing electronic data conforming to ISO 9660 or ISO 13346; or

(iii) a 3.5" floppy disk;

"electronic application" means:

(a) an application for a patent under the Act; or

(b) in relation to an international application for a patent (UK), a request to enter the national phase processed using the appropriate software and appropriate hardware or delivered via the web interface;

"the Office" means the Patent Office or, where appropriate, the comptroller;

"online", in relation to a document being delivered, refers to a document that has been transmitted from one device to another by means of an electronic communications network (within the meaning of section 32 of the Communications Act 2003);

"original format", in relation to a document, means a document in the file format in which it was originally created before it was converted into a PDF file;

"priority application" has the meaning given by rule 2(1) of the Rules;

"smart-card application" means an electronic application processed using the appropriate software and appropriate hardware;

"the Rules" means the Patents Rules 2007;

"user" means a person using the appropriate software and appropriate hardware, or the web interface, to deliver an electronic application;

"web application" means an electronic application delivered via the web interface;

"web interface" means the Office's dedicated web page for filing patent applications.

6. In these Directions, "Patents Form" shall be construed as a reference to a document containing the information required by the relevant Patents Form as set out in directions under section 123(2A) of the Act.

7. In these Directions, "delivered" and related expressions, means delivered to the Office and for the purposes of the Act and the Rules a document shall be treated as filed at the time it was delivered.

Delivery of smart–card applications

8. A smart-card application may be delivered either online or on digital media, except that no smart–card application may be submitted by a person who has not registered with the Office.

9. A smart-card application may only be sent from a computer that uses a version of Microsoft Windows® supported by the Office.

Online filing

10. An electronic application can be sent online at any time, except between 01:00 and 02:30 hours UK time.

11. A user may only deliver a web application if he also submits his email address.

12. A user may only deliver a smart–card application online if he has

(a) an account with the Office;

(b) registered with the Office; and

(c) registered for PKI certification.

13. A smart-card application delivered online shall be submitted using the appropriate software.

14. A smart-card application shall be sent online to the electronic address (URL address) provided to the user for that purpose by the Office.

Filing a smart-card document using digital media

15. A smart-card application delivered on digital media must be accompanied by a paper document identifying:

(a) that the digital media contains an application for a patent;

(b) the person applying for a patent or contain information sufficient to enable that person to be contacted by the Office;

(c) a list of the Patents Forms and documents making up the application (or which can be delivered at the same time as the application (as listed in paragraph 21, 22 or 23)) which are stored on the digital media.

Formal requirements

16. Where an electronic application includes a description of the invention, rule 12(4) of the Rules shall apply to the extent that the description shall be preceded by the title of the invention.

17. The following provisions of the Rules shall apply to electronic applications and shall be formal requirements: Schedule 2 Part 1 paragraph 3, Schedule 2 Part 2 paragraphs 4–7, 9 and 10 and Schedule 2 Part 3 paragraphs 11, 12 and 14–20.

Illegible or incomplete documents and infected files

18. Where part or all of a document delivered under these Directions is illegible or incomplete, the whole document shall be treated as not complying with these Directions.

19. Where a document delivered under these Directions is reported as having a virus (or other malicious software) by the Office's virus checking software, the document shall be treated as not complying with these Directions.

20. Where a document is treated as not complying with these Directions under paragraph 18 or 19, provided the user can be identified, he shall be notified of this fact by the Office.

Other documents

21. In relation to an application for a patent under the Act, the following documents may be delivered at the same time as the electronic application:

- Patents Form 3

- Patents Form 7

- Patents Form 9A

- Patents Form 10

- Patents Form 23

- a copy of a priority application where that application was filed with the United States Patent and Trademark Office

- translations of priority applications

- evidence to support a request for a late declaration of priority made on Patents Form 3

- covering letter

and if it is a smart-card application the following document may also be delivered, using the appropriate software, at the same time as the application:

- Patents Form 8A

22. In relation to a request for an application for an international patent (UK) to enter the national phase, the following documents may be delivered at the same time as a smart–card application:

- Patents Form 3

- Patents Form 7

- Patents Form 9A

- Patents Form 10

- Patents Form 52

- translation of the international application

- translation of information relating to the deposit of a micro–organism
- translation of amendment under the Patent Cooperation Treaty
- translations of priority applications
- copy of the application under the Patent Cooperation Treaty
- copy of amendment under the Patent Cooperation Treaty
- evidence to support a request for a late declaration of priority made on Patents Form 3
- evidence to support a request for a further extension made on Patents Form 52
- covering letter

23. In relation to a request for an application for an international patent (UK) to enter the national phase, the following documents may be delivered via the web interface at the same time as a web application:

- Patents Form 3
- Patents Form 7
- Patents Form 9A
- Patents Form 10
- Patents Form 52
- translation of the international application
- translation of information relating to the deposit of a micro-organism
- translation of amendment under the Patent Cooperation Treaty
- translations of priority applications
- copy of the application under the Patent Cooperation Treaty
- copy of amendment under the Patent Cooperation Treaty
- evidence to support a request for a late declaration of priority made on Patents Form 3
- evidence to support a request for a further extension made on Patents Form 52
- covering letter

Delivery of documents in their original format

24. The user may deliver documents related to a smart-card document in their original format. These documents shall be submitted using the appropriate software at the same time as the smart-card application.

25. The documents mentioned in paragraph 24 shall not be part of the application. They shall only be used in the subsequent processing of the smart–card application for verification of its contents at the time it was delivered.

Signatures

26. Where a document requiring a signature is delivered online or on digital media, it shall only be treated as signed where the signature takes the form of a facsimile signature, a text string signature or an enhanced electronic signature.

27. In paragraph 26:

"facsimile signature" means a TIFF or JPEG image of the signatory's signature;

"text string signature" means a string of characters, preceded and followed by a forward slash (/), selected by the signatory to provide evidence of his identity and of his intent to sign the document in question;

"enhanced electronic signature" means a signature created using an electronic PKI-based certificate recognised by the Office.

Acknowledgement and time of delivery

28. Where an electronic document has been delivered online an acknowledgement ("the receipt") will be issued to the user electronically.

29. Where no receipt is issued in accordance with paragraph 28, the electronic application will be treated as not complying with these Directions.

30. The receipt will specify:

(a) the date and time of delivery at the Office;

(b) the application number allocated to the electronic application; and

(c) a list of the Patents Forms and documents delivered at the same time as the electronic application.

31. The receipt for an electronic application delivered on digital media will include the information referred to in paragraph 30, but will be sent to the user by post.

Payment of fees

32. Where a Patents Form or other document is required by the Patents (Fees) Rules 2007 to be accompanied by a fee, that Patents Form or document shall be treated as not complying with these Directions until the fee has been paid.

33. Where such a form is filed with a web application, the fee shall be paid via the web interface at the time of making the application.

34. Fees payable with a web application may be paid using a deposit account held with the Office or by credit–card or debit–card.

35. Fees may be paid on a smart–card application from a deposit account held with the Office or by a credit–card or debit–card registered with the Office for that purpose.

Note. For filing documents relating to pending patent applications, see further Directions under s.124A entitled "Filing documents relating to pending patent applications by electronic means" which can be downloaded from the UK-IPO website. The terms of these further Directions closely follow those reproduced above. Both Directions are accompanied by brief guidance and notes downloadable from the UK-IPO website.

Rule 15—The abstract

15.—(1) The abstract must start with a title for the invention.   **14.07**

(2) The abstract must contain a concise summary of the matter contained in the specification.

(3) That summary must include—

(a) an indication of the technical field to which the invention belongs;

(b) a technical explanation of the invention;

(c) the principal use of the invention.

(4) Where the specification contains more than one drawing, the abstract must include an indication of the drawing which should accompany the abstract when it is published.

(5) Where it appears to the comptroller that a drawing included in the specification better characterises the invention he shall publish it with the abstract.

(6) Where a feature of the invention included in the abstract is illustrated in a drawing, the feature must be followed by the reference for that feature used in that drawing.

(7) The abstract must not contain any statement on the merits or value of the invention or its speculative application.

Rule 16—Single inventive concept

14.08 16.—(1) For the purposes of the Act, two or more inventions shall be treated as being so linked as to form a single inventive concept where there exists between those inventions a technical relationship which involves one or more of the same or corresponding special technical features.

(2) In paragraph (1) "special technical features" means those technical features which define a contribution which each of the claimed inventions, considered as a whole, makes over the prior art.

Commentary on Section 14

Scope of the section

14.09 Section 14 prescribes the manner of making a patent application, lays down requirements as to the form and contents of a patent application, and provides for withdrawal of a patent application. (The minimum requirements to establish a filing date are prescribed by s.15(1) discussed below.) The practice under the section is comprehensively described in the MOPP, and in any case of doubt, it would be wise to consult the latest version of this on the website: *http://www.ipo.gov.uk.*

In s.14: subs.(1) provides for the form of a patent application and the manner in which it may be filed; subs.(1A) provides for an application fee; subs.(2) prescribes the contents required for a patent application, these matters being discussed in §§14.10–14.23 below. Otherwise, subs.(3) specifies the sufficiency requirements for a specification; subs.(5) specifies the requirements for the claims; subs.(6) provides for unity of invention; subs.(7) refers to the required abstract; and subss.(9) and (10) refer to withdrawal of an application. Repealed subs.(1)(b) provided for a "filing fee". Repealed subss.(4) and (8) stipulated special requirements for the sufficiency of a specification in the case of inventions involving the use of micro-organisms, but this subject is now dealt with in s.125A and in rules made thereunder (amended to extend the term "micro-organism" to "biological material"), see the commentary on s.125A, below.

Section 130(7) states that subss.(3) (sufficiently clear and complete disclosure of invention), (5) (requirements to be met by the claims), and (6) (unity of invention) are intended to have the same effect as the corresponding provision of the EPC (i.e. EPC arts 83, 84 and 82 respectively) and of the PCT (i.e. PCT arts 5, 6 and PCT r.13.1, which have corresponding effect). These EPC articles are in the following terms:

"EPC Article 82—Disclosure of the invention

The European patent application shall relate to one invention only or to a group of inventions so linked as to form a general inventive concept."

"EPC Article 83—Disclosure of the invention

The European patent application shall disclose the invention in a manner sufficiently clear and complete for it to be carried out by a person skilled in the art."

"EPC Article 84—The claims

The claims shall define the matter for which protection is sought. They shall be clear and concise and be supported by the description."

Section 14 is also in conformity with the obligatory part of art.29(1) of the TRIPS Agreement, which reads:

"TRIPS ARTICLE 29—Conditions on Patent Applicants

1. Members shall require that an applicant for a patent shall disclose the invention in a manner sufficiently clear and complete for the invention to be carried out by a person skilled in the art."

Subsection (3) corresponds to the provisions of EPC art.83 and of TRIPS art.29. In accordance with art.138(1) of the EPC a national court can revoke a European patent granted for its country for breach of art.83 of the EPC and this is applied under UK law by the terms of s.72(1)(c), as discussed particularly in §72.14. However, the grounds set out in art.138(1) of the EPC constitute the **only** grounds upon which a European patent can be revoked nationally. Consequently, while subs.(5) corresponds to EPC art.84, a finding of breach thereunder does not enable a national court to revoke a granted patent because such breach is not within the ambit of art.138(1) of the EPC, as was made clear when, in *Genentech's Patent* [1989] R.P.C. 147, the Court of Appeal reversed much (but not all) of the decision below, seeing that the first instance decision had improperly relied upon the terms of subs.(5), see §14.39, below. Thus, non-compliance with subs.(5) can only be dealt with in pre-grant proceedings. This is becoming increasingly important and, consequently, there is a tendency to try to raise grounds akin to breach of subs.(5) under the ambit of subs.(3). The effect of subs.(3), and its limitations, for dealing with alleged invalidity of a granted patent is discussed in §§14.24–14.30 below, while the effect of subs.(5), necessarily only effective in pre-grant proceedings, is discussed in §§14.31–14.39.

Entitlement to obtain a patent is discussed at §§7.06–7.11. Time limits for filing documents are discussed at §§15.10–15.13, and extensions of time limits under r.108 are discussed in §§15.14 and 123.25–123.27.

Filing of application (subss.(1) and (2))

An application must be made in the prescribed form and filed in the prescribed manner (subs.(1)(a) introducing r.12, reprinted at §14.02). The application may be filed electronically under directions made under s.124A, for which see §14.06 above.   **14.10**

Subsection (1A) replaces the former filing fee with a requirement to pay an "application fee" (referred to in an addition made to s.130(1), as noted in §130.01), which is the fee to cover the "preliminary examination" under s.15A.

The payment of the application fee is discussed in §14.18, below.

Subsection (2) specifies that an application for a patent shall contain: (a) a request for the grant of a patent; (b) a specification containing a description, the claim or claims, and any drawings; and (c) an abstract. Rule 12(1) requires that the request for the grant of a patent be made on PF 1, as discussed further in §14.45. Rule 12(4) requires that the specification be preceded by the title of the invention (which formally therefore is not part of the specification and which, by r.12(6), must be short and indicate the matter to which the invention relates) and include in the following order: the description; the claim or claims; and any drawings. According to r.12(5), the requirements of r.12(4) do not have to be met when an application is delivered in electronic form or using electronic communication, under the directions indicated in §14.06 above and as discussed further in the commentary on s.124A.

According to r.12(7), the description must include a list of the drawings briefly describing each of them. The claims may be filed later (s.15(10)(a); and r.22(5)(a), reprinted in §15A.07), as discussed in §15A.15.

Rules 12(2) and (3) provide that, where the documents initially filed omit the name and address of the applicant, the Comptroller is required to notify the applicant of the deficiency and, if this is not rectified within two months of that notification, the application may be refused. This period may be extended (under r.108(1) by discretion), but this must be requested within this two-month period (r.108(5)), and the extension may not exceed two months (r.108(7) and Rules, Sch.4 Pt 3), see §123.25 and §123.26).

Rules 12(8) and (9) provide that where a document initially filed is or appears to be a description and is not in English or Welsh and no English or Welsh translation has been filed, the Comptroller is required to notify the applicant of the deficiency and require a translation to be filed within two months of the notification. If a translation is not filed by this date, the application may be refused. This period may be extended under r.108(1) by discretion, but this must be requested within this two-month period (r.108(7)) and the extension may not exceed two months (r.108(5) and Rules, Sch.4 Pt 3, see §§123.25 and 123.26).

The filing of an application may be made by hand or post, either at or to the UK-IPO at its main address in Newport, South Wales NP10 8QQ, or by hand at its London Office at 21 Bloomsbury Street, London, WC1B 3HF, see §123.88, and any filing by post will be deemed to have been received on its date of receipt or, if received on an excluded day, will be treated as having been received on the next non-excluded day, see §119.03. Alternatively, filing may be by fax transmission to 01633 817 777, as discussed in §119.05. When an application is received on a day when the UK-IPO is not open for business in respect of filing an application of the type in question, (for which see §120.02 and §120.03), that is, on a "*dies non*", the filing date accorded will be the next day of business for that class of business at the UK-IPO, but any time period expiring on a *dies non* is automatically extended to the next business day as discussed in §§120.04–120.05. Directions under s.124A (reprinted at §14.06) enable an application to be filed in electronic form or by way of an electronic communication.

The Request (subs.(2)(a))

—General

14.11   The request on PF 1 calls for the following information to be provided:

(1) an optional reference;

(2) the name and address of the or each applicant;

(3) the title of the invention;

(4) the name of an appointed agent (if any) and an address for service (which may be in the UK, another European Economic Area state or the Channel Islands, see §32.15);

(5) any declaration of priority, as discussed in §14.15;

(6) details of any earlier application whose filing date is claimed under ss.8(3), 12(6), 15(9) or 37(4);

(7) a statement relating to inventorship (for which see §13.17);

(8) an indication of whether the application fee is being paid with the form;

(9) a summary of the pages of the specification being filed or a reference to a previous application that is to be relied upon in place of the filing of a description with the application; and

(10) a listing of other documents being filed if any.

PF 1 requires signature by the or each applicant or by their appointed agent (who need not be a registered patent attorney see §274.03).

A statement of inventorship may be included on the PF 1 if the applicant(s) and the inventor(s) are identical. Otherwise, a separate statement of inventorship on PF 7 must be filed (for which see §§13.08–13.11).

Rule 101 (reprinted at §274.02 and discussed at §§274.04–274.09) does not require the filing of a written authorisation when any action is taken for the first time by an agent acting on behalf of the applicant(s). Naming the appointed agent on the form commencing that action is sufficient, and the address of the agent is then taken as the address for service, as required to be supplied by r.103 (reprinted at §32.02 and discussed in §32.15). Personal signature on PF 1 by the applicant or authorised agent is not required, in contrast to practice before the EPO, see §274.10.

The filing of the request for grant on PF 1 is designated a formal requirement by r.25 unless the application is filed in electronic form or using electronic communications. If PF 1 is not used for a paper filing, time for compliance with r.12(1) must be given under s.15A(6) and r.25(1)(a) during preliminary examination (assuming that the application fee has been paid), see §15A.06.

—Applicant's or Agent's Reference

Although there is no obligation to provide a reference on the PF 1, it is in the applicant's **14.12** or agent's interest to do so since, until an application number has been accorded by the UK-IPO, there is no other reliable way of identifying a particular application. It may also be useful should any confusion arise over the application numbers accorded to several cases that are filed at the same time. If provided, the UK-IPO will use the applicant's or agent's reference in correspondence related to the application.

—Applicant's Name and Address

The full name and address, including the postcode, should be given for the or each **14.13** applicant. All surnames (family names) should be underlined for natural persons. For natural persons, the name given should normally be the person's true name (and not a pseudonym or nickname for example). For corporate applicants or other legal persons, the full legal name should be given. Whilst the PF 1 no longer asks for the country or state of incorporation for corporate applicants, the MOPP and the relevant "Factsheet" from the UK-IPO for filling in the PF 1 refer to giving the country of incorporation and, where appropriate (e.g. for US or Canadian corporate applicants), the state or province of incorporation of the applicant. If an application is made on behalf of a Government Department, the applicant should be stated to be the Secretary of State or Minister responsible for the department, and not the individual holding such office. Applications from police forces should be made by the relevant Police Authority.

—Title of the invention

The title of the invention (discussed more fully in §14.46) must be short and indicate **14.14** the subject of the invention (see r.12(6), above). The title should, however, not be too informative since it is published in the *Patents Journal* shortly after filing and from that date could in itself become prior art against a later application. Nevertheless, failure to comply with r.12(6), for example by the use of a wholly uninformative title such as "Electrical circuit" or "Chemical compound" could ultimately result in refusal of the application for failure to comply with s.14(1)(a), should the applicant fail to supply a better title when called upon to do so by the UK-IPO. It should be noted that compliance with r.12(6) itself is not regarded as a "formal requirement" under r.25 for which time for compliance must be given under s.15A(6), see §15A.06. The MOPP indicates that in the absence of a title on PF 1, the applicant should be required to give one or to confirm that the title on the specification is to be used on the PF 1. In any event, presumably amendment to comply with r.12(6) is permissible under s.18(3) or 19(1). The UK-IPO has indicated that the title should not contain a fancy or trade name, a personal name, the word "patent", nor the abbreviation "etc." Official guidance as to titles for inventions in patent documents can be found in WIPO Standard ST.15 (available on the WIPO website *http://www.wipo.org*). The title will, if necessary, be abbreviated by the UK-IPO to 158 characters or less as that is the maximum length of a title permitted in the OPTICS computerised register operated by the UK-IPO.

—Claiming of priority

14.15   When priority is being claimed under s.5(2) from an earlier "relevant application" (i.e. from a UK patent application or an application in or for a "convention country"), the declaration of priority should normally be made at the time of filing the application (r.6(1), reprinted in §5.07). Provision is made for inclusion of this declaration in the PF 1. The date of filing of the relevant application or of the earliest relevant application identified in such declaration is the "declared priority date" for the purposes of the rules, provided that such priority date has not been lost, abandoned or withdrawn before the completion of preparations for publication of the application under s.16 (r.2, reprinted at §123.04). It is now possible to make a late priority claim and/or to add a priority claim and even to file a priority-claiming application after the usual 12-month period under ss.5(2A) to (2C), as discussed further in the commentary on s.5 at §5.18.

—Claiming an earlier application date

14.16   If the application is a divisional application and so claims an earlier application date under the provisions of s.15(9), then the number and filing date of the earlier application must be given on PF 1. If the application claims an earlier application date under the provisions of ss.8(3), 12(6) or 37(4) (order of the Comptroller following a dispute about entitlement), then the number and filing date of the earlier application or patent should be given on PF 1.

—Statement relating to inventorship

14.17   A section is provided on PF 1 for giving an indication as to inventorship. This conveniently allows a statement of inventorship to be included on the PF 1 although only if the applicant(s) and the inventor(s) are identical. Otherwise, a separate statement of inventorship on PF 7 must be filed (for which see §§13.08–13.13).

—Application fee

14.18   A section is provided on PF 1 for giving an indication as to whether the application fee is being paid with the PF 1. The application fee required by subs.(1A) is to be paid within the "relevant period" as prescribed for s.15(10)(c) by r.22(2) in conjunction with r.22(7) (reprinted respectively in §15.01 and §15.07). This period is 12 months from the date of filing the application where there is no declared priority date. Where there is a declared priority date, this period is the later of 12 months starting from that date or two months from the date of filing the application. The application fee may be paid in conjunction with the filing of PF 1 or with the filing of PF 9A together with the required search fee. If the application fee is not paid with either of these forms, the non-statutory form AF 1 may conveniently be used when paying this fee.

—Documents making up or accompanying the application

14.19   A section is provided on PF 1 for entering the number of pages of any continuation pages of the PF 1, the description, the claims, the abstract and the drawings accompanying the PF 1. Where the application is not accompanied by a description, and instead a reference to an earlier application under s.15(1)(c)(ii) is relied upon for qualifying for a date of filing, the application number, country of filing and date of filing of that earlier application should be entered in this section of the PF 1. Such a reference must be substantiated by the filing of a certified copy of the earlier application within the time specified by r.22(3), which is four months from the date of filing, and a description must be filed within the time specified by r.22(1), which is the same period as for the claims and abstract and is 12 months from the date of filing the application where there is no declared priority date or, where there is a declared priority date, the later of 12 months starting from that declared priority date or two months from the date of filing the application. A separate section is provided on the PF 1 for indicating other documents being filed with the PF 1, including in particular any priority documents, statement of inventorship (PF 7), request for search (PF 9A) and request for substantive examination (PF 10), as well as any other documents.

Where the application is online, either by web application or smart card application, the documents making up the application must be pdf documents. The number of pages in each document is calculated automatically. However, where a single specification document is provided, it is required to provide details of which pages make up the description, claims, abstract and drawings.

Documents and language

As discussed more fully in §§14.47–14.50, by r.14(2), (3) and (4) the documents mak‑ **14.20** ing up the patent application must be in the format prescribed by Sch.2 to the Rules (see Sch.2, above), with exceptions for applications filed electronically under directions made under s.124A, see §14.06 above and as discussed in the commentary on s.124A.

Whilst it appears not to be prescribed by the Rules, the UK-IPO still apparently prefers that all documents other than forms be typed or printed on one side only. Only a single copy of the specification and abstract (and any replacement thereof) need be filed.

Rule 14(1) requires all wording (including that contained in drawings) in any document contained in a patent application to be in English or Welsh. By s.14(2), an application for a patent contains: (a) a request for the grant of a patent; (b) a specification containing a de‑ scription, the claim or claims, and any drawings; and (c) an abstract, and it is therefore these documents that must be in English or Welsh. This requirement is in general not satis‑ fied by the subsequent filing of replacement documents in English or Welsh because, save for the documents specified in r.113(2) (which include in particular a description of the invention), documents not in English or Welsh are acceptable only if "accompanied by" a translation into English (r.113(1), reprinted in §123.30).

As noted in §14.10 above and discussed further in §15.10, r.12(8) and (9) provide that where a document initially filed is or appears to be a description and is not in English or Welsh and no English or Welsh translation has been filed, the Comptroller is required to notify the applicant of the deficiency and require a translation to be filed within two months of the notification. If a translation is not filed by this date, the application may be refused. This period may be extended under r.108(1) by discretion, but this must be requested within this two-month period (r.108(5)) and the extension may not exceed two months (r.108(7) and Rules Sch.4 Pt 3), see §123.71). For a case of an attempt at filing a descrip‑ tion in a foreign language with a subsequently filed English language translation under the old law, see *Rohde and Schwarz's Application* [1980] R.P.C. 155, the facts of which were more fully described (1979–80) 9 *CIPA* 268). Following *A's Application* [1974] R.P.C. 663, it was noted by the hearing officer in that case that the words "accompanied by" define an infinitely short period, which can apparently be extended by discretion under r.108(1), see §123.71. On the facts of that case, discretion was not exercised in favour of the applicant.

In addition, again as discussed further in §15.08, in accordance with s.15(1)(c)(ii) the description can be substituted at the time of filing with a reference to an earlier application. In that case, by s.15(10)(b)(i) and r.22(1) and (7), an English or Welsh description must be filed by 12 months beginning with the date of filing, where there is no declared priority date. Where there is a declared priority date, the English or Welsh description must be filed by the latest of 12 months from the claimed priority date and two months from the ap‑ plication date and, by s.15(10)(b)(ii) and r.22(3), a copy of the earlier relevant application must be filed within 4 months from the application date. By r.17(2)(a), the copy of the priority application must be a certified copy or "otherwise verified to the satisfaction of the Comptroller". Where the priority application is not in English or Welsh, r.17(2)(b) requires that the (certified) copy of the priority application be filed together with a translation into English of the priority application or a declaration that the description filed under s.15(10)(b)(i) is a complete and accurate translation into English of the description of the priority application. This latter reference in r.17(2)(b) to the description filed under s.15(10)(b)(i) being a complete and accurate translation into *English* suggests that, to be able to rely on this provision, the late-filed description can only be in English and not in Welsh. Rule 17(3) provides that, where a copy of the earlier relevant application is available to the Comptroller, it shall be treated for the purposes of subs.(10)(b)(ii) as having been filed as required.

The Specification (subs.(2)(b))

—General

14.21   The "Code of Practice for Patent Applicants and Agents", which is available on the UK-IPO website at *http://www.ipo.gov.uk*, should be consulted for general information about the content of the specification, see also §14.42 below. For further discussion on the contents of a description, see the book *Fundamentals of Patent Drafting* by P.G. Cole (The Chartered Institute of Patent Attorneys, 2006).

The specification must be preceded by the title of the invention, which is therefore not formally part of the specification, and must be set out in the order of the description of the invention, the claim or claims, and any drawings to which the description or any claim refers (r.12(4)). Subsection (2)(b) contrasts with EPC art.78(1) and PCT art.3(2) which do not refer to a specification as such. The physical requirements for the application, including the specification, are discussed in §§14.47–14.50.

For the effect of a missing part of the description or drawings, see r.18 (reprinted at §15.03) and the discussion in §15.13 in relation to s.15(2) and (3A).

An application need not contain claims in the specification at its date of filing (s.15(10)(a) and r.22, reprinted at §15.07). However, failure initially to file claims, or at least a statement of invention in the description, may create uncertainty over the priority date of an invention which is subsequently claimed because of potential difficulties in determining the scope of the invention that was described in the first application, though some assistance may be provided by art.4H of the Paris Convention. In any event, any subsequently filed claims will need to be supported by the specification as filed in order to avoid contravening s.76(1). This is also discussed at §15.40.

A priority document is not part of the specification and, therefore, its contents do not form part of the contents of the application as originally filed for the purpose of support for a divisional application, or for amendment without contravening s.76(1) or (2), but the priority document may, nevertheless, have evidentiary value, see T 260/85 *AMP/Coaxial connector* OJ EPO 1989, 105; [1989] E.P.O.R. 403. The priority application can also act as a basis for including missing parts in the application whilst maintaining the original date of filing (see §15.13).

The specification must disclose the invention in a manner which is clear enough and complete enough for the invention to be performed by a person skilled in the art (subs.(3)), as discussed further in §§14.24–14.30. Where a claim is directed to a sequence or partial sequence of a gene, the industrial application of this has to be disclosed in the specification in order to comply with art.5(3) of the European Biotechnology Directive (reprinted in §C05) and incorporated into the Act by Sch.A2 para.6 (reprinted in §76A.01A).

By "invention" for the purposes of s.14(2)(b) and (3) is meant that which is specified in any claim (s.125(1), which is itself to be interpreted in accordance with the Protocol on the Interpretation of EPC art.69 (s.125(3)). Accordingly, it is useful to refer to the EPO Guidelines for guidance as to what matter ought to be included in the description. Since the claims themselves form part of the specification, the content of the claims as well as that of any drawings (but not the abstract) can apparently be taken into account when determining whether the requirement of subs.(3) has been met, see also *Procter & Gamble's Application* [1982] R.P.C. 473.

A defect in the specification under subs.(3) can normally not be cured by amendment as this would result in subject-matter being added to the specification, contrary to s.76 (for which see §76.06). However, such a defect can be overcome by amending the claims so that the description of invention that remains claimed does satisfy the requirements of the subsection.

—The description

The purpose of the description is twofold: firstly, to disclose the invention clearly **14.22** enough and completely enough for it to be performed (subs.(3)); and secondly to provide support for the claims (subs.(5)). The Act itself imposes no further requirements on the content of the description (other than the requirement that the industrial application of a claimed sequence or partial sequence of a gene must be described, see §14.21), and the Rules merely impose the further requirement that the description shall include a list briefly describing the drawings, if any (see r.12(7), above).

The description must be preceded by the title (see r.12(4), above). This should be the same as the title given on PF 1 (for which see §14.14), though the title appearing in the abstract (see r.15(1), above) may be different. The title published in the *Patents Journal* under s.118(3)(b) and r.55 is that of the abstract, see §14.42.

It is usual (though not essential, unlike practice before the EPO, see r.27 of the EPC, or under the PCT, see PCT r.5.1, and see further below) for the description to begin with a summary or brief statement of the relevant state of the art, with specific references to relevant documents, such as prior patent specifications, where appropriate. If any prior United Kingdom application (or European or international application designating the UK) referred to was published after the declared priority date of the application in suit so that such publication forms part of the state of the art under s.2(3) and is to be disregarded when considering whether the invention involves an inventive step, it is recommended that the description should draw attention to this fact, or at least to the date of publication of the prior specification (EPO Guideline C–II, 4.3). Following any discussion of the prior art, there may then appear an indication of its disadvantages or shortcomings which are allegedly overcome or avoided by the invention as claimed in the broadest claim or claims. The specification should avoid disparaging statements, but if they are included they may be omitted by the Comptroller from the specification as published under s.16, see s.16(2) and §16.03.

Although not always required by the Comptroller, it is recommended that a "statement of invention" or "consistory clause" be included in the description in exact agreement with the or each independent claim. It is doubtful whether such a statement of invention helps to provide support for the claim, but it may be necessary or helpful in order to provide some link or intermediate generalisation between the statement of invention and the particular embodiment or embodiments of the invention subsequently described, unless such link is self-evident. Otherwise the requirements of subs.(5), discussed in §14.39, may not be met. The UK-IPO (like the EPO) does not object to the inclusion in the description of a reference to one or more of the claims in order to avoid repetition, though by convention this is perhaps rarely done in practice.

Where the description contains a statement of invention, the statement should be consistent with the definition of the invention as contained in the claims. Consequently, where it becomes necessary to amend a claim, the corresponding statement of invention should normally be correspondingly amended.

The MOPP reminds the reader that:

"Since disclosure of the invention is the consideration in return for which the applicant is granted a monopoly, the highest degree of good faith is called for, and the disclosure should be clear, precise, honest and open. A designedly ambiguous description or one that is wanting in distinctness, either by negligence or unskilfulness, will invalidate a patent (*British Ore Concentration Syndicate Ltd v Minerals Separation Ltd*, (1910) 27 RPC 47; *Cincinnati Grinders (Inc) v BSA Tools Ltd*, (1931) 48 RPC 33)."

If material is included for comparative purposes, or to illustrate the prior art, the nature of this material should be made clear. Also, the MOPP indicates (with reference to decisions made under former statutes) that the specification should not contain "superfluous or irrelevant matter" (citing *Francis' Application* (1910) 27 R.P.C. 86) and that curtailment of an inordinately long specification may be requested (citing *LD Corp's Application* (1949) 66 R.P.C. 4), although it is stated that this will be done only "in the most extreme cases".

Thus, the description should be clear and straightforward with avoidance of unnecessary technical jargon. Terms that are well known in the art in question may be used and indeed it will often be desirable or necessary to use such terms (see Sch.2 para.25, see §14.05). Little known or specially formulated terms may also be used provided that they are adequately defined (see the MOPP).

Sch.2 para.24 (reprinted above) requires that units of measurements shall be expressed, at least in the alternative, in "standard international units of measurement". This may normally be taken to mean metric units. The MOPP refers to the EC Units of Measurement Directive (Council Directive 80/181/EEC, as amended by Council Directive 89/617/EEC and Directive 1999/103/EC of the European Parliament and of the Council of 24 January 2000) and indicates that no objection should be raised against the use of non-SI metric units. The MOPP indicates that temperatures should normally be given in degrees Celsius, except that the Kelvin scale may be used as customary for cryogenic temperatures and colour temperatures. Units said to be recognised in international practice and complying with the relevant EPC Rule are set out in the EPO Guidelines as an Annex to C–II.

As regards cross-references to patent applications that are unpublished at the priority date or filing date, see §14.27.

Trade marks should preferably not be used in the description but, if used, must bear an initial capital and be properly acknowledged as a trade mark, whether or not registered. For acknowledgment of a registered trade mark, see §19.09. If a trade mark is registered, the validity of the registration is irrelevant, even if the mark has fallen into general usage in the art. If a trade mark is not registered, it is considered good practice to indicate the name of the owner. As a trade mark can rarely be an unambiguous statement of the nature of a commercial product, it is generally an unacceptable term for use in a claim, see further §14.37.

As discussed more fully in §14.35, there is no objection to the inclusion in the specification of an "omnibus" claim directed to the particular embodiment(s) "substantially as described and shown (or illustrated) in the accompanying drawings" or by reference to examples (e.g. in chemical cases) or to tables, though the EPO does not allow such claims. The Comptroller will require a statement of invention when there is an independent omnibus claim and the description of those embodiments itself includes generalisations and the omnibus claim is not of a narrow form (e.g. the omnibus claim does not refer to the drawings).

The significance of the wording of the description was emphasised in the decision in *Kirin-Amgen v Hoechst Marion Roussel* [2005] R.P.C. 9 at 169 HL. Referring to the famous dictum of Lord Diplock in *Catnic v Hill and Smith* [1982] R.P.C. 183 at 243, s.125, art.69 of the EPC and the Protocol on the Interpretation of Article 69, Lord Hoffmann stressed that the claims of a patent have to be construed in accordance with what the person skilled in the art would have understood the patentee to be using the language of the claims to mean, the person skilled in the art construing the claims purposively in the context of the description and drawings. Thus, the extent of protection provided by a claim cannot extend to the exclusion of a feature that the description has indicated (explicitly or implicitly) as one essential to the performance of the invention.

Injudicious statements made by a patent draftsman, particularly as regards claims made speculatively on the basis of analogy with the prior art, can lead to decisions of insufficiency or obviousness, as for example in *Hoffmann-La Roche's Application* O/192/04.

For a European application, the contents of a specification are more closely controlled by r.42 of the EPC. This rule can be paraphrased as requiring the description to: (a) specify the technical field to which the invention relates; (b) indicate the background art known to the applicant and regarded as useful for understanding the invention; (c) disclose the invention, as claimed, in such terms that the technical problem and its solution can be understood and advantageous effects over the prior art should be stated; (d) contain a brief description of the drawings; (e) describe in detail at least one way of carrying out the invention; and (f) explain explicitly the way in which the invention is capable of industrial exploitation if this is not already obvious. These elements of the description should preferably also be stated in above-stated order. As regards the element (b), T 450/97 *PROCTER & GAMBLE/Shampoo composition* OJ EPO 1999, 67 states it is also necessary to include in the description (if necessary by amendment) a reference to the document that represents the "closest state of the art", against which inventive step is generally to be assessed before the EPO (see §3.44) as this is regarded by the EPO (although not by the United Kingdom courts) as being "essential for understanding the invention". Rule 5 of the PCT is in essentially the same terms (though it refers to description setting forth "at least the best mode contemplated by the applicant for carrying out the invention claimed"; however, failure to describe the best mode shall have no effect in any State that does not require the best mode to be described).

—The drawings

Schedule 2 Pt 3 to the Rules, (see §14.05, above) sets out the requirements to be met by any drawings forming part of the application, the details of these requirements being discussed in §14.49. While drawings will almost always be useful in mechanical and electrical cases, there was once perceived to be a slight risk that a copyright or design right recorded in a drawing contained in a patent application may thereby be lost. The latest view is that this is not so and that the different forms of intellectual property are independent of each other, see §60.31. If possible, it is nevertheless prudent for drawings in patent specifications to be diagrammatic in nature, rather than full working or engineering drawings which might disclose know-how additional to the information otherwise contained in the application which, in itself, is already sufficient to enable the skilled person to make the invention as claimed. It should also be realised that sometimes the dimensions of the article are derivable from the drawings, for example because of some industry standard, as in *Catnic v Hill and Smith* [1982] R.P.C. 183 HL; see *Gardex v Sorota* [1986] R.P.C. 623. **14.23**

No mention as such is made of the purpose of any drawings forming part of the specification, except that, in conjunction with the description, they shall be used to interpret the claims (s.125(1), discussed in §125.12); and, presumably, may contribute to the fulfilment of the requirements of subss.(3) and (5)(c). The Comptroller cannot require drawings to be furnished.

Where drawings are contained in an electronic filing, only some of the rules for presentation of drawings have to be complied with, see para.17 of the Directions for Filing Patent Applications by Electronic Means, reproduced in §14.06 above.

Sufficiency of description (subs.(3))

—Requirements for sufficiency

Subsection (3) imposes requirements of clarity and completeness which if not complied with are grounds for refusal of an application and for revocation of a granted patent, s.72(1)(c). Lack of completeness is traditionally referred to as invalidity for "insufficiency". However, in contrast to the former patent statutes, subs.(3) does not actually require a specification to be "sufficient", but rather the subsection is in terms of the adequacy of disclosure to enable the invention as claimed to be performed. Such is often called an "enabling disclosure", see *Asahi's Application* [1991] R.P.C. 485 HL and *Biogen v Medeva* [1997] R.P.C. 1 HL. **14.24**

In *Kirin-Amgen v Roche Diagnostics* [2002] R.P.C. 1, the court at first instance drew a distinction between two kinds of insufficiency: "classic insufficiency" was said to occur where the teaching of the patent does not support that which it specifically purports to deliver; and "Biogen insufficiency", based on the House of Lords decision in *Biogen*, above, that was said to occur where the claim is cast more widely than the teaching of the patent enables. On appeal (*Kirin-Amgen v Transkaryotic Therapies* [2003] R.P.C. 31) it was held by the Court of Appeal that it was incorrect to say that there were two types of insufficiency: s.72(1)(c) provides just one ground of invalidity. However, the names for the variants have continued in use see, e.g. *Laboratorios Almirall v Boehringer International* [2009] EWHC 102 at [255] Pat Ct. Biogen insufficiency is further discussed at §14.25.

The difference in the effects of subss.(3) and (5), is that the latter cannot be used in post-grant proceedings, as explained in §14.09 above. While both subsections are grounds of objection available pre-grant, it should be realised that objections under sub.(3) often require to be established on the basis of factual evidence or expert testimony which, in reality, can only be put forward by a third party because an examiner will often not have available to him the facts upon which a successful attack could be substantiated that the specification is deficient under the requirements of this subsection. However, as explained below, there are some types of cases, although rare, where the specification can be seen to be so implausible that objection under the subsection could be raised without the need to rely upon technical expertise or evidence.

In *Genentech's Patent* [1989] R.P.C. 147 CA, sufficiency of the description was treated as referrable to the claims, so that some claims would be invalid for insufficient description and others not. Also, in *Chiron v Organon Teknika (No.3)* [1994] F.S.R. 202, upheld on appeal sub nom. *Chiron v Murex* [1996] R.P.C. 535 CA, some claims were held invalid for insufficiency, but broader claims were upheld despite the fact that the subject-matter of the invalid claims could not, in practice, be worked without infringement of the valid broader claims, see §14.25. Statutory basis for this approach can perhaps be found in the definition of an invention implied by s.125(1), see §125.04.

In general, it will often be difficult to overcome an objection of an insufficient specification without adding subject-matter contrary to s.76, except by restricting the scope of the claims to an extent that the specification becomes sufficient with regard to the more limited scope of protection then claimed (see, for example, *Genentech's Patent* (above). However, it is possible that an objection under subs.(3) arising from lack of clarity, rather than incompleteness of description, could be overcome by amendment without contravening s.76.

Subsection (3) does not require that the specification must disclose the best method of performing the invention known to the applicant. However, disclosure of the "best mode" remains a most important requirement for patents in the United States, and care therefore needs to be taken if the specification is also to be used for an application in that country. (The America Invents Act of 2011 also requires an inventor to "set forth" the best mode for accomplishing the invention, but failure of disclose of a best mode cannot be used as a basis for invalidating an issued patent)

The specification consists of the description, the claims and any drawings: s.14(2)(b). As the claims must be supported by the description, as required by s.14(5)(c), in practice the requirement is that the description and any drawings must disclose the invention in a manner which is clear enough and complete enough for the invention to be performed by a person skilled in the art.

As explained by Lord Hoffmann in *Kirin-Amgen v Hoechst Marion Roussel* [2005] R.P.C. 9; [2004] UKHL 46, whether or not a specification is sufficient is highly sensitive to the nature of the invention. The first step is to identify the invention and decide what it claims to enable the skilled person to do. Then one can ask whether the specification enables him or her to do it.

Insufficiency often involves a deficiency of information e.g. about essential starting materials and process conditions. In *Badische Anilin und Soda Fabrik v La Société Chimique des Usines du Rhône and Wilson* (1898) 15 R.P.C. 359 the invention concerned the production of a particular dye in an autoclave. At trial it emerged that the process failed unless the autoclave was made of iron, as was often the case, but that enamelled autoclaves were also in common use. The patent was held invalid for insufficiency because the description did not contain an instruction which turned out to be essential for the performance of the invention.

In *DSM's Patent* [2001] R.P.C. 675, claims extending to hybridised DNA sequences were, if construed literally, held invalid as covering unworkable embodiments, and, if (as the patent proprietor contended) construed to include an implied functional limitation, there was no supporting teaching as to the conditions to be applied (other than trial and error) to achieve that result; the claims were invalid for insufficiency in either situation, see also §76A.18.

The threshold explained by Aldous J. and approved by the Court of Appeal in *Mentor Corporation v Hollister* [1993] R.P.C. 7 at 13 is the ability to construct a workable prototype as opposed to a commercial embodiment. There may be no insufficiency where a promised result can generally be obtained by a skilled person working with his presumed skills to produce the promised result to some degree even if that is not sufficient to produce a commercially viable product, see *American Cyanamid v Ethicon* [1979] R.P.C. 215 at 265. The position may, however, be different if the claimed invention is a "selection" made from the prior art on the basis of a surprising beneficial effect obtained with the selected subject-matter, as then there is an insufficiency if that effect cannot be obtained throughout the range of claimed subject-matter, on which see §14.25 below. The requirements were further explained in *Mentor* above as follows:

"The section requires the skilled man to be able to perform the invention, but does not lay down the limits as to the time and energy that the skilled man must spend seeking to perform the invention before it is insufficient. Clearly there must be a limit. The subsection, by using the words, clearly enough and completely enough, contemplates that patent specifications need not set out every detail necessary for performance, but can leave the skilled man to use his skill to perform the invention. In so doing he must seek success. He should not be required to carry out any prolonged research, enquiry or experiment. He may need to carry out the ordinary methods of trial and error, which involve no inventive step and generally are necessary in applying the particular discovery to produce a practical result. In each case it is a question of fact, depending on the nature of the invention, as to whether the steps needed to perform the invention are ordinary steps of trial and error which a skilled man would realise would be necessary and normal in order to produce a practical result."

A clear exposition of the criteria for assessing so-called "classical insufficiency" appears in paras 361–437 of the judgment of Floyd J. in *Zipher v Markem* [2009] F.S.R. 1 in relation to an invention in the electro-mechanical arts, a drive mechanism for a ribbon or tape for a thermal transfer printer. The essential points there in issue were summarised in a note on the decision at [2008] *CIPA* 395. The judgment explained:

"The test which I need to apply to all this evidence is whether the patent imposes an undue burden on the skilled reader to arrive at a workable prototype of the invention".

The court held that the novel and ingenious feature was the use of current to monitor and control tension, that the skilled person would not readily see in the case of a stepper motor how to measure the relevant current, and that what had to be decided was whether the teaching of the patent as to how to obtain tension or work-related current made something possible for a person seeking success which would have been considered thought-challenging or impractical before. The court held that the description was inadequate and that:

"Simply to direct a reader to sample, filter and average a noisy waveform a few times per cycle does not approach an adequate teaching. The skilled reader is left with very much the same puzzle as he would have had if the idea had crossed his mind independently. This is not a matter of allowing for reasonable trial and error. I think it would take something approaching invention—certainly a research project—to fill the gaps left by the patent's teaching".

A number of further defects were held to be present, e.g. an erroneous equation which would give rise to errors in tension control and unmatched temperature variations between the motors. The overall conclusion of the court was that the patent presented the skilled reader with such a combination of defects that it did not serve as a clear or complete description of how to perform the invention.

A similar factual situation was found in *Halliburton v Smith International (North Sea) Ltd* [2006] R.P.C. 2, where the invention related to drill bits having three roller-cones for drilling into rock, the claimed method involved equalising the volume of rock cut by each cone, and the objections were that a skilled person could not have set up a geometrical model of the bit, could not have calculated the cutting forces on the teeth of the cones and could not have calculated the cone/bit speed ratio. In relation to mathematically modelling the action of the teeth, for example, the court held that:

"There was no convincing demonstration of any common general knowledge in relation to modelling the force on a tooth…It is not up to the modeller to decide what is the exact nature of the elemental analysis he is performing. It is his job to follow the directions in the specification to construct the model, using such description as there is of the model. If no model is fully described, the specification is insufficient unless the deficiency can be made good from the common general knowledge. In this case, it was not."

On appeal to the Court of Appeal, [2007] R.P.C. 17; [2006] EWCA Civ 171, the issue of undue effort was raised, e.g. a concept that would take 20 years of routine work to implement. It was held that if what is "taught" involved too much to be reasonable allowing for all the circumstances including the nature of the art, then the patent could not be regarded as an "enabling disclosure." The setting of a gigantic project, even if merely routine, would not do. There was no analogy with genetic engineering and pharmaceutical inventions because in those fields the work that went into bringing them to market related to testing efficacy and safety—not in actually making the invented product. Furthermore, there was an interrelationship between obviousness and insufficiency. As a matter of first impression it might be supposed that an idea that required masses of work to implement would be more readily rejected by, or less likely to occur to, a notional unimaginative skilled person or team. This produced an apparent paradox that the less sufficient the description, the less an idea was likely to be obvious. The answer to the paradox was that if the notional skilled person/team was one that was prepared to contemplate an immense amount of work, that attribute must also be considered part of the person/team's consideration of what was obvious. On the facts, the decision of the Patents Court was affirmed.

Insufficiency can also arise where a feature is specified for which there is no workable criterion or test, e.g. if tests are specified about which there is no general agreement or consistency in application, see *Minnesota Mining & Manufacturing Co's (Suspension Aerosol Formulation) Patent* [1999] R.P.C. 135. In *Kirin-Amgen* (above) an independent product claim specified a polypeptide characterised by being an expression product (rEPO) of a DNA sequence having a higher molecular weight by SDS-PAGE from (sic) erythropoietin isolated from urinary sources (uEPO). The claim was based on the assumption that all uEPOs had effectively the same molecular weight irrespective of source and method of isolation, whereas this had been shown not to be correct. The House of Lords held that the deficiency did not merely create a fuzzy boundary between what would work and what would not but made it impossible to work the invention at all until it was ascertained what ingredient was needed. Considerations of "seeking success" were irrelevant because the concepts of ''success'' or ''failure'' were irrelevant to the choice of uEPO, which had nothing to do with making the invention work but was simply a criterion against which to test whether rEPO fell within the claims. All the skilled man could do was to guess which uEPO the patentee had in mind and if the specification did not tell him, then it was insufficient.

In *Baxter Healthcare Corp v Abbott Laboratories* [2007] EWHC 348 Pat Ct an active ingredient was combined with an inhibitor in an amount sufficient to prevent degradation of the active ingredient. The specification did not provide any workable criterion for determining what the amount was, and the relevant claim was construed so as to be coextensive with a dependent claim in order to avoid insufficiency, the court observing that if that construction was wrong then the relevant claims were hopelessly insufficient, see also *Mayne Pharma v Debiopharm* [2006] F.S.R. 37 discussed at §14.34. For further cases concerning inadequately defined tests decided under the 1949 Act, see §14.29.

As to errors, in *No-Fume Ltd v Frank Pitchford & Co Ltd* (1935) 52 R.P.C. 231 it was stated that:

"The test to be applied for the purpose of ascertaining whether a man skilled in the art can readily correct the mistakes or readily supply the omissions, has been stated to be this: Can he rectify the mistakes and supply the omissions with[out] the exercise of any inventive faculty? If he can, then the description of the specification is sufficient. If he cannot, the patent will be void for insufficiency."

The above test was further explained by Buckley L.J. in *Valensi v British Radio Corp* [1973] R.P.C. 337 in relation to a mistake in the specification:

"Further, we are of the opinion that it is not only inventive steps that cannot be required of the addressee. While the addressee must be taken as a person with a will to make the instructions work, he is not to be called upon to make a prolonged study of matters which present some initial difficulty: and, in particular, if there are actual errors in the specification—if the apparatus really will not work without departing from what is described—then, unless both the existence of the error and the way to correct it can quickly be discovered by an addressee of the degree of skill and knowledge which we envisage, the description is insufficient."

Further as to errors, see the discussion of the decision of the House of Lords in *SmithKline Beecham's PMS Patent* [2006] R.P.C. 323 discussed at §2.09. In *Evans Medical's Patent* [1998] R.P.C. 517, the patent claimed an antigen P. In the priority document it had been indicated that the invention was based on the discovery that a known enzyme (AC) had antigenic activity. However, the antigenic material was in fact P and not AC, which was then found not to be an antigen. Nevertheless, the patent continued to indicate that, in the isolation process from a bacterium culture, the desired fraction could be tracked by monitoring AC activity. On this basis the specification was held to be insufficient, see also I. Karet [1998] B.S.L.R. 28 and J. Marshall [1998] E.I.P.R. 273.

In *Eli Lilly & Company v Human Genome Sciences Inc* [2008] R.P.C. 29, [2008] EWHC 1903 at 241 Pat Ct it was explained that the *Valensi* reasoning is equally apt to cover an omission. In relation to claims to pharmaceutical and diagnostic compositions insufficiency was found because it would have required a research programme and been far from routine for the skilled person to produce a candidate pharmaceutical or diagnostic composition comprising an antibody to the disclosed protein, i.e. the pharmaceutical or diagnostic equivalent of a workable prototype, on the basis of the information contained in the patent and the common general knowledge. The patentees should not have broad protection over an unexplored technical field without providing an adequate compensating benefit to the public.

The decision in *Eli Lilly v Human Genome Sciences* was affirmed by the Court of Appeal, see [2010] R.P.C. 14, [2010] EWCA Civ 33. The patent had previously been found to be sufficient by the EPO Appeal Board, see T 18/09 *HUMAN GENOME SCIENCES/ Neutrokine* [2010] *CIPA* 116, but the Court of Appeal emphasised that it was at liberty to differ from the Appeal Board on the facts, and even if plausibility had been established that was not enough to prove an immediate and concrete benefit, see para.[146], nor would a skilled person approach the patent with an ability to distinguish the kernel from the rest, see para.[148]. The Court of Appeal decision is now reversed, see [2011] UKSC 51. The Supreme Court held that the arguments of industrial applicability and sufficiency went hand-in-hand, especially since the claim was simply to the encoding gene of Neutrokine-α without any express reference in the claim to the polypeptide having certain activities.

In *Zipher* (above) the court considered the position in which a skilled team would be able to make something falling within the claim, but which was not as good as the patent promised. Insufficiency would not be established, although in relation to the separate objection of lack of inventive step it would show that the technical advance represented by the claim was less than contended for by the description. In chemical and pharmaceutical cases, failure to achieve a promised activity is usually fatal to validity see, e.g. *Pharmacia v Merck* [2002] R.P.C. 41 at 775.

The Comptroller takes the view that a specification that describes a device that functions contrary to an established natural law (e.g. where the alleged invention is a perpetual motion machine) cannot satisfy subs.(3) unless it is established either that that law is wrong or that it does not apply to the device in issue, *Paez's Application* O/176/83, and, most recently, *Blacklight Power Inc v Comptroller* [2009] R.P.C. 6. In *Lister's Applications* BL O/100/11, three separate applications were found to be lacking in sufficiency of disclosure because they could not be performed by a skilled person. All three applications related to an arrangement of magnets such that magnetic repulsion produced perpetual motion. However, if a claim is directed to the structure of the device, without reference to its function, it could perhaps be argued (relying on s.125(1)) that the specification sufficiently describes the invention if it enables the reader to construct a device falling within the claim, even if that device is useless, though the EPO Guideline at C-II, 4.9 states that, in order to meet the requirement for sufficiency:

"It is necessary that the invention is described not only in terms of its structure but also in terms of its function, unless the functions of the various parts are immediately apparent".

See also *Eastman Kodak Co v American Photo Booths Inc* O/457/02, in which the hearing officer held that the invention could not function as described and claimed, and so lacked both industrial applicability and sufficiency of disclosure contrary to s.4(1) and s.14(3) respectively.

Classical insufficiency can arise in relation to generic claims in empirical research fields, where some species within the genus provide the benefit on which patentability is based whereas others do not. An early statement of the relevant principles was made by the US Supreme Court in *Consolidated Electric Light Co v McKeesport Light Co* 159 U.S. 465 (1895). The invention was an incandescent conductor for an electric lamp of carbonised fibrous or textile material and of an arch or horseshoe shape. Evidence was adduced that Edison and his assistants had tested 6000 vegetable products, of which only a very few could be made into incandescent filaments, and that wood, for example, was unsuitable. The court held that if the patentee had discovered a quality common to a genus of materials that distinguished them from other materials and adapted them particularly to the purpose, then the claim might not be too broad, but that in the case before it the facts were otherwise. The same distinction between an entirely empirical field where each species is a separate invention and a field that is at least semi-empirical so that effectiveness can be predicted on the basis of a law or principle found by the inventor was made by the House of Lords in *May & Baker v Boots* (1950) 67 R.P.C. 23 at 50 and was reaffirmed in *Biogen v Medeva* [1997] R.P.C. 1 at 49 in terms of "a beneficial property which is common to the class".

In *Olin Mathieson v Biorex* [1970] R.P.C. 157 a claim was affirmed where a particular new substituent had been introduced at one position into a genus of pharmaceutical compounds of known type for which structure-activity relationships in the other relevant positions in molecules of that genus had already been investigated. The defendants argued that the claim was over-broad and covered inactive compounds, but there was no experimental evidence to support that proposition. In *Chiron v Murex* the invention related to polypeptides for use in a test kit for the hepatitis C (HPC) virus, and the Court of Appeal held that this was a single invention properly defined by the common denominator of the existence of an antigenic determinant of HPC virus, notwithstanding that the resultant polypeptides would have divergent characteristics in other respects. The invention of one of the polypeptides was the invention of all of them because that which was common to all was of the essence of the discovery and that which distinguished one from the other was irrelevant to that discovery. In contrast, in *American Home Products v Novartis* [2001] R.P.C 8 at 159 the patentees had discovered the immunosuppressant properties of a macrolide antibiotic called rapamycin, but structure/activity relationships for derivatives had not been established and the Court of Appeal held (reversing a decision of the Patents Court that the patentees had made available to the art the opening through which a new class of immunosuppressants could be found) that a generic claim covering all derivatives that were effective would not relate to a class with a unifying characteristic and hence would be insufficient, and would stifle further research. In *Monsanto v Merck* [2000] R.P.C. 77 experimental evidence was adduced that compounds falling within the claimed genus did not have the postulated activity, the Patents Court held that the patentee had given no information such as a structure/activity relationship, which enabled the reader to draw any conclusions as to the properties of any particular compound without further experiment, so that insufficiency had been established. All he had done was to describe the scope of the claim with spurious precision. The decision was affirmed by the Court of Appeal sub nom. *Pharmacia v Merck*, above.

It is not possible to provide an enabling disclosure by a cross-reference to an application that was unpublished, at least at the filing date, or by side reference to a publication which the addressee would not have been motivated to read by the rest of the description. See *Halliburton v Smith International* [2006] R.P.C. 2 where it was also said that in general cross-referencing for the purpose of supplementing the disclosure was highly undesirable. This was referred to by the hearing officer in *Blacklight Power's Applications* (O/076/08) where it was seriously doubted:

"whether the court would consider it acceptable to rely on passages plucked from within the 1000-plus pages of a document which is itself but one of some 40 or so cross-referenced documents in a patent specification to support an amendment."

(Although the point was made in regard to whether a claim was supported by the specification to avoid unpatentability as something excluded under s.1(2) rather than whether the specification was sufficient.) See also the discussion on this point in §14.27.

CoreValve v Edwards Lifesciences [2010] F.S.R. 34, [2009] EWHC 6 Pat Ct concerned a cardiac valve prosthesis. It was held that the description of the physical device was sufficient, and the issue then arose whether it was necessary for the patent to describe how the device was to be used clinically. The court held that it was doubtful whether any patent could be sufficient in that respect because it would be akin to learning to fly a helicopter by reading the manual, and there was no substitute for hands-on experience. It went on to observe:

"I have referred to aircraft. The real merit of the Wright Brothers was perhaps not so much that they invented a device that was capable of controlled heavier-than-air powered flight, but that they realised that it would be a strong idea to teach themselves to fly before actually flying. And so they proceeded in small, cautious steps, starting with gliders. Their first flight in their powered machine covered a distance that was less than the length of the aisle in a modern Boeing 747. It took several years before any realistic distances were achieved. But nobody says that the Wright patent should have been held invalid for lack of enablement.

I stress those points because, in my judgement, *CoreValve's* case confuses the sufficiency of the instructions for making a device falling within the claims of the patent and the sufficiency of instructions for telling the reader how to use it.

There was much evidence about the difficulties of implanting the device in the iliac artery without needing a general anaesthetic. But the patent was not required to teach the reader how to do this. In my judgment it was enough that the skilled device manufacturer could, by reasonable trial and error, construct a device that could be inserted via the femoral route. I do not believe the patent had to go on and describe all possible operational alternatives."

Ratiopharm v Alza [2009] EWHC 213 Pat Ct concerned a skin patch containing "an amount of [X] sufficient to induce and maintain analgesia in a human for at least three days". Defendants averred that this was an unclear criterion because there was a five-fold variation in skin permeability between individuals, patients had different drug clearance rates, and their response to pain was highly subjective. It was therefore impossible to determine conclusively whether any particular patch contained the required amount of X. In rejecting this argument, the court held that it was enough if the patches gave rise to analgesia in some patients for three days, and it was not necessary that it would do so for all patients because the range of variability meant that no patch would ever satisfy the requirement. A skilled person could determine whether the requirement was satisfied by tests in vitro and in vivo using information in the specification, so that there was no undue burden in determining whether a particular patch fell within the claimed scope.

HTC Corp v Yozmot 33 [2010] EWHC 786 Pat Ct concerned the provision of ringtones for cellular telephones, and it was established that although the invention could be used for simple musical ringtones and audio files, its use with complex audio files such as mp3 files would have been "a considerable technical challenge". The court held that this was not a reason to find the patent insufficient since the specification did not promise that the invention could be carried out using complex audio files, and it was not necessary for the specification to teach the skilled reader how to implement the claimed method with regard to all possible subject-matter that might be the subject of that method.

In *Schlumberger v Electromagnetic Geosciences* [2010] R.P.C. 33, [2010] EWCA Civ 819 it was held that there could be different teams of skilled people for different purposes and in particular for obviousness and sufficiency, see §3.07.

In *Novartis AG v Johnson & Johnson Medical Ltd* [2010] EWCA Civ 1039 the invention related to hydrogel contact lenses intended for extended wear and which were based on a polymeric material formed from oxygen-permeable material and ionically permeable material, the lens allowing oxygen permeation in an amount sufficient to maintain corneal health and ion or water permeation in an amount sufficient to enable the lens to move on the eye "such that corneal health is not substantially harmed and wearer comfort is acceptable during a period of extended continuous contact with ocular tissues and ocular fluids". The polymers were defined in very wide terms and selection parameters in terms of oxygen diffusion rate and ion diffusion rate were "woolly". Ophthalmic compatibility was a requirement demanding testing on real people and was uncertain since it was not clear what should happen where a minority of patients showed adverse reactions. The court concluded that although the claim defined a number of features, hardly any of them had any significance. It was to a lens derived from two vast classes of polymerisable materials, one having a high oxygen diffusion rate and the other having a high ion or water diffusion rate and in substance the claim amounted to this: "if you try any pair of polymers, to see if they work (perhaps only after surface treatment) and find anything that does, we claim it." Furthermore the patent gave the reader no help in finding a combination of polymers that worked. Although it would normally be understood by a skilled person that the specific embodiments in the invention worked, there was nothing in the data that showed that any of the 33 examples in the specification actually did so and instead the data showed that nine examples did not work. None of the patentee's disclosed documents showed that the invention did work. The patent had been held sufficient in parallel proceedings before the EPO (see T 246/04 which was apparently a decision reached without any expert testimony) and in Holland, Germany and France, and in this regard Jacob L.J. observed:

"As regards the Dutch proceedings, the District Court of the Hague said this: 'Novartis has rightly pointed out that the patent specification contains many examples of lenses that have the required ophthalmic compatibility and which the person skilled in the art can easily reproduce.'

If that accurately records what was submitted, then Novartis are saying different things in this court to what they were saying to the Dutch Court. I hope that is not so. Whether or not there was this inconsistency the Dutch Court clearly thought the examples 'worked'. That lay at the heart of its decision to reject the sufficiency attack. What the Court would have said if it had known what has emerged in these proceedings—that even Novartis has no idea whether the 'examples' or any of them, 'work'— one can only guess ...

I would add one other thing about these parallel decisions. None of them recognise just how devoid of meaningful limitations claim 1 is. Quite why is perhaps explicable on the basis that the courts concerned assumed that the examples worked and did not have the benefit of the intensive probing of the facts and expert evidence afforded by cross-examination which is provided by English procedure. Sometimes that procedure is wasteful, but not in this case."

At first instance it had been held that the patent did not disclose any unifying characteristic or principle of general application which would have enabled the skilled person to predict which silicone hydrogel formulations were likely to be useful for producing an ophthalmically compatible lens suitable for extended wear, and that it would have required a research programme to do so. In conclusion:

"The upshot of all this is that the Judge was entirely right to decide that the Patent was insufficient. It is no more than a 'if you can find it, we claim it' patent. Its avaricious ambit coupled with its failure to provide any help makes it nothing but a hazard to those conducting research into extended wear contact lenses. It should be revoked in its entirety."

Special provisions apply for sufficiency of a specification involving an invention which requires for its performance the use of a micro-organism, see s.125A and the commentary thereon at §125.01.

—Relationship between extent of sufficiency and scope of the claims

For several years, the EPO took the view that, if any embodiment of the claimed invention was sufficiently described for the skilled person to reproduce it, not only was an enabling disclosure for that embodiment provided but also the patent as a whole was regarded as complying with the requirements of EPC art.83 (and correspondingly of s.14(3)), see particularly: T 292/85 *GENENTECH/Polypeptide expression-I* OJ EPO 1989, 275; [1989] E.P.O.R. 1; T 226/85 *UNILEVER/Stable bleaches* OJ EPO 1988, 336; [1989] E.P.O.R. 18; and T 301/87 *BIOGEN/Alpha-interferons* OJ EPO 1990, 335; [1990] E.P.O.R. 190. A further similar decision was given in T 740/90 *LESAFFRE/Yeast* [1993] E.P.O.R. 459 as well as, apparently, in the similar case under the 1949 Act (*Lesaffre's Patent* [1994] R.P.C. 521). This view was followed in Morritt J. in *Mölnlycke v Procter & Gamble (No.5)* [1994] R.P.C. 49

A significant break with the above approach was represented by T 409/91 *EXXON/Fuels oils* OJ EPO 1994, 653; [1994] E.P.O.R. 149 which concerned diesel oils having wax crystals of a certain size, the claim being of a functional nature. It was held that the specification provided no guidance on how to choose the so-called "suitable additive" in order to obtain the required effect with a reasonable expectation of success; and the applicant's submission, that sufficiency should be acknowledged simply because one way of performing the invention was disclosed was expressly rejected. The Board stated that there would only be sufficiency within the meaning of art.83 of the EPC if the specification

14.25

allowed a person skilled in the art to perform the invention across the whole range that was claimed. This situation was distinguished from a case where a class of chemical compounds was claimed and only one method of preparing them was necessary to enable a skilled person to prepare all compounds of the claimed class. The disclosure would not be sufficient if it disclosed only a method of obtaining some members of the claimed class: T 206/83 *ICI/Pyridine herbicides* OJ EPO 1987, 5; [1986] E.P.O.R. 232 was cited as being consistent with this approach.

T 435/91 *UNILEVER/Detergents* OJ EPO 1995, 188 is to similar effect as this *EXXON* decision and, since these decisions, their stronger line has been followed in the rejection of broad claims under EPC art.83 (and also under art.84 in pre-grant proceedings), see particularly T 694/92 *MYCOGEN/Modifying plant cells* OJ EPO 1997, 408; [1998] E.P.O.R. 114 and in the revised form of EPO Guidelines C–II, 4.1 and 4.9. The *MYCO-GEN* decision stressed that, where the gist of the claimed invention is the achievement of a given technical effect by known techniques in different areas of application and serious doubts exist as to whether this effect can readily be obtained for the whole range of applications claimed, ample technical details and more than one example may be necessary to support claims of a broad scope. Insufficiency was also found in: T 612/92 (Unreported), where the general process claimed required some adaptation for each species, the specification being silent on the means for this and the adaptation would require an undue burden of experimentation; and, also in T 440/92 *SUMITOMO/Oxygen-enriched gas* [1998] E.P.O.R. 240, where inventive step had been upheld on the basis of improved results but it was not seen that the same process conditions and results could be obtained across the range of the claim. See also T 322/93 (Unreported) where sufficiency over the full range of the claim has to be determined on a case-by-case basis and even 25 examples may not be sufficient where the claims are broad. A further case following T 612/92 and 694/92 *MYCOGEN/Modifying plant cells* is T 187/93 *GENENTECH/Vaccines* [2002] E.P.O.R. 21, which held the technical effect relied on to demonstrate that the claimed subject-matter involved an inventive step could not be achieved by the skilled person without undue burden within the whole range of application claimed, so that claims of broad scope were not allowable under arts 83 and 84.

The definitive view of the inter-relationship between sufficiency and scope of claim under United Kingdom law was set out by Lord Hoffmann in the further appeal in *Biogen v Medeva* [1997] R.P.C. 1 HL which upheld the decision of the Court of Appeal on insufficiency but on different reasoning. Lord Hoffmann saw the crucial issue as being the requirement for an enabling disclosure on each of the following issues: for priority (under s.5(2)(a)); for sufficiency of description (under ss.14(3) and 72(1)(c)); and for supporting description at the application stage (under s.14(5)). As explained in §5.23, it was stated by Lord Hoffmann that "the specification must enable the invention to be performed to the full extent of the monopoly claimed", and a distinction was seen between an invention that "discloses a principle capable of general application", for which the claims may be in correspondingly general terms, and claims directed to a number of discrete methods or products, for each of which an enabling disclosure is required. T 292/85 *GENENTECH/ Polypeptide expression-I* (noted above) was then seen to be an example of the former, whereas T 409/91 *EXXON/Fuel oils* (noted above) was seen as an example of the latter, as also was the position in the *Biogen* decision itself. In this respect Lord Hoffmann differed from T 296/93 *BIOGEN/Hepatitis B* [1995] E.P.O.R. 1, where the validity of the same patent had been upheld in the EPO. These points were discussed by A.W. White [1997] *CIPA* 1020 and by I. Karet and Isabel Britton [1997] B.S.L.R. 1. It is also noted here that subsequently, in *Kirin-Amgen v Roche Diagnostics* [2002] R.P.C. 1 discussed further below, Lord Hoffmann explained that when he referred in *Biogen* to a "principle capable of general application", this "applies to any element of the claim, however humble, which is stated in general terms", and that such a claim is "sufficiently enabled if one can reasonably expect the invention to work with anything which falls within the general term." and gave as a simple example the requirement of "connecting means" in a hypothetical claim. But now see Lord Hoffmann's further explanation of *Biogen* in *H. Lundbeck A/S v Generics* [2008] R.P.C. 19, discussed below, in which Lord Hoffmann stated that so-called "Biogen sufficiency" is applicable to product-by-process claims, and not ordinary product claims.

In *Minnesota Mining's (Suspension Aerosol Formulation) Patent* [1999] R.P.C. 135, the view of Lord Hoffmann in *Biogen* was paraphrased as meaning that:

"a patent will be insufficient if it covers matters which owe nothing to the disclosure or if the teaching is inadequate to produce all the promised results".

The court noted that the second formulation has an interesting overtone of the old requirement for utility. The Minnesota Mining patent was held insufficient when its claims were construed to give effect to functional phrases, see §14.34.

In *Pharmacia v Merck* [2002] R.P.C. 41 the Court of Appeal, following the House of Lords decision in *Biogen*, held that the specification must enable the invention to be performed to the full extent of the monopoly claimed. If the invention is a selection of certain compounds having a particular characteristic, the specification must contain sufficient information on how to make the compounds having that characteristic and the compounds of the claim must all have that characteristic. If certain subclasses of the claimed class did not have the characteristic asserted, the extent of the monopoly exceeded the technical contribution. This would not necessarily be rebutted if one compound in a subclass showed some activity. The evidence must be considered as a whole, and any evidence of activity weighed against the rest of the evidence.

In *H. Lundbeck A/S v Generics* [2008] R.P.C. 19; [2008] EWCA Civ 311 the Court of Appeal said that at first instance the Patents Court, in following the approach set out in *Biogen*, Lundbeck had only "contributed to the art" a new method of resolving a racemate into its individual enantiomers and were therefore only entitled to claims to that method, and were not entitled to claims to the particular enantiomer that they had identified as having a particular therapeutic effect. In the Court of Appeal, Lord Hoffmann, who had "stepped down" from the House of Lords to hear this appeal, explained that in *Biogen*, the relevant claim was to "A recombinant DNA molecule" having a specified function. Lord Hoffmann stated that a claim to the DNA molecule per se was not possible in *Biogen* because the molecule per se already existed (in the human body, for example) and, furthermore, already existed in purified form (because it had already been obtained in pure form by a purification process, though that yielded small quantities, hence the desire to synthesise it) so a claim to the "pure" or "purified" DNA molecule was also not possible in that case. Thus, Lord Hoffmann explained that in *Biogen*, it was only permissible to claim the newly invented way of synthesising the molecule, and it was not permissible to claim the molecule per se (because that would lack novelty) nor for any method claim to go beyond the newly invented way of synthesising the molecule because other methods were not "described clearly enough and completely enough to be carried out by the person skilled in the art". The present case was different because the product per se (the enantiomer identified as having a particular therapeutic effect) was regarded as new, Lord Hoffmann, quoting T 296/87 *Hoechst/Enantiomers* OJ 1990, 19 at [6.2]; T 1048/92 *Pfizer/Penem* [1995] E.P.O.R. 207; and T 1046/97 *Optically active triazole derivatives and compositions* [2002] E.P.O.R. 325, point 2.1.2.2 said:

"It is settled jurisprudence in the European Patent Office that disclosure of a racemate does not in itself amount to disclosure of each of its enantiomers".

Having identified the useful function of that enantiomer, Lundbeck were entitled to a claim to the enantiomer per se: the product (that enantiomer) is new in law and Lundbeck described how to make it, and therefore had described the invention "clearly enough and completely enough to be carried out by the person skilled in the art". Lord Hoffmann said that it did not matter that Lundbeck would thereby cover all methods of making the product: that was always the case with inventions involving new and inventive products because the "invention" was the product itself. This was echoed by Jacob L.J. who said:

"I turn to sufficiency. There is a very short answer to this point. The claim is to the (+) enantiomer. That is novel and non-obvious. If one asks the straightforward question 'Does the patent enable the skilled man to make it?' the answer is an equally straightforward: 'Yes.' So, in the language of EPC Art 83, the patent discloses 'the invention in a manner sufficiently clear and complete for it to be carried out.'".

The House of Lords affirmed the decision of the Court of Appeal in *Generics v H. Lundbeck A/S* [2009] R.P.C. 13, [2009] UKHL 12, on the ground that the reasoning in *Biogen* [1997] R.P.C. 1 is not relevant to the validity of a simple product claim as opposed to a process or product-by-process claim. A review of *Generics v Lundbeck* is provided in "Product per se claim survives Biogen attack" [2009] *CIPA* 250 and Kitchin J. discussed the impact of this decision in "How much for how little?" [2009] *CIPA* 522.

In *Zipher v Markem* [2009] F.S.R. 1, Floyd J. saw the essential difference between these *Biogen* and *Lundbeck* cases to be that *Biogen* involved claims to a group of compounds, whereas in *Lundbeck* the claim covered only a single compound, itself novel and inventive.

In *MedImmune v Novartis* [2011] EWHC 1669 Pat Ct, the patent contained broad method claims. Arnold J. considered the case to be closer to *Biogen v Medeva* and *Kirin-Amgen v Hoechst* than *Generics v Lundbeck*. Arnold J. took the view that the invention could be characterised as a principle of general application and in this case, implementation did not involve undue burden on the part of the skilled team to undertake the method. Therefore, he found the patent sufficient.

It should also be noted that there is a relationship between sufficiency of description and inventive step. For example, in *Raychem's Patents* [1999] R.P.C. 497 CA, an unsuccessful attempt was made to uphold claims, admitted to cover obvious subject-matter, on the basis that the prior art failed to teach how to make the claimed compositions, with insufficiency not having been pleaded. Only some of the 77 examples contained in the specification taught the making of these compositions with no indication that this was so: thus, the reader was "necessarily forced back to the general teaching of the specification" admitted to lack invention.

The EPO has also noted (T 187/93 *GENENTECH/Vaccines*) that arguments to support sufficiency can be counter-productive as regards inventive step. However, there can be rare cases where objections of obviousness and insufficiency are not inconsistent. Thus, in *Horne Engineering v Reliance Water Controls* [2000] F.S.R. 90, the specification was held not to have provided the reader with sufficient directions:

"always to remain within the claim; he understands that the length of the baffle is crucial, as to which the specification is silent".

Thus, "in so far as the invention is not obvious, the specification gives insufficient instructions for putting it into effect".

Moreover, a contention of non-literal infringement can sometimes be met by the argument that, if the extent of the patent is such as to cover the alleged infringement, then the patent fails for insufficiency. This will particularly be so where the defendant's apparatus works in a different way, as in *Visx v Nidek* [1999] F.S.R. 405 where had the claims been infringed (which was not so), there would have been a finding of insufficiency.

As with infringement, claims must be construed purposively rather than literally (see §125.10) so that insufficiency will not be found upon an over-literal interpretation of a term used in the claim, see *Hadley Industries v Metal Sections* BL C/68/98, noted I.P.D. 22004 and also *Kirin-Amgen v Roche Diagnostics* (above).

—Date at which sufficiency of the specification is required

14.26   In *Biogen v Medeva* [1995] R.P.C. 25, the Court of Appeal held that under the present Act, since further subject-matter cannot be added to an application after filing without invalidating (under s.72(1)(d)) any patent granted thereon, it would be illogical to hold that a specification, which is insufficient at its date of filing, could be rendered sufficient by subsequent publication of the additional subject-matter thereby making this known by the publication date of the application, reversing the decision on this point at first instance (co-reported with it). This decision was upheld on further appeal [1997] R.P.C. 1 HL where it was further stated that, citing *Asahi's Application* [1991] R.P.C. 485 CA, if the proprietor needs to rely upon a declared priority date, the description of the priority application needs to contain an enabling disclosure if the filing date of this is properly to accord priority to an invention claimed in the later application, see §5.23.

The Rules (Sch.1, reprinted at §125A.03) and the corresponding r.31 of the EPC both indicate that, for a description of a micro-organism (that is not itself publicly available) to be sufficient under s.125A, a deposit thereof must have been made by the date of filing. Thus, each of these assumes that the specification must be sufficient as of its date of filing, but again it would seem that a priority date may be lost if the priority document fails to contain a sufficient enabling disclosure (which can be achieved in this respect in such a case by filing a deposit no later than the claimed priority date).

In *Cellartis AB's Application* BL O/050/11, the deposit was not filed prior to the priority date. Therefore, the claim to the cell line in the priority application was found to be insufficiently supported, and therefore the claim was not entitled to priority. An intervening publication rendered the claim not novel.

References to other applications and documents

An application may contain a reference to another document, which may be another patent application or other document or another source (e.g. a Web page), in which information may be found. As noted in the EPO Guideline C–II, 4.19, such references relate either to the "background" or prior art or to part of the disclosure of the invention. Where the reference relates to the background art, it may have been in the application as filed or added at a later date (the latter usually being required in the EPO when the document represents relevant prior art). Where the reference relates to part of the disclosure of the invention, normally the reference can legitimately only have been present in the application as filed because to add such a reference later will almost certainly add subject-matter to the application or patent specification, contrary to s.76(2) and s.76(3) respectively. The MOPP indicates that the allowability of a reference to another document need only be considered by the examiner if the further information to be found in the other document is essential for there to be a clear and complete disclosure of the invention.

14.27

Where the reference relates to part of the disclosure of the invention and is to be relied on when determining whether the invention has been disclosed completely and clearly enough to meet the requirements of s.14(3), great care must be taken to ensure that it is a proper and sufficient reference. As mentioned in the judgment in *Halliburton v Smith International* [2006] R.P.C. 2, "Patent specifications should be complete in themselves . . ." and "In general, cross-referencing for the purpose of supplementing the disclosure is highly undesirable . . .". Thus, it seems that the safest option is to include the relevant material in the specification of the application as filed. Where it is not possible or perhaps impractical to do so, perhaps because of the length of the document or relevant material to which the reference is being made, the following points should be noted, including particularly the difference between current UK law and the current practice of the EPO in relation to European patent applications.

The current UK law is as follows. As noted in §14.26 above, it was held in *Biogen v Medeva* [1997] R.P.C. 1 HL that the date for assessing sufficiency is the filing date of the application. Citing this decision, it was held in the *Halliburton* decision (above) that a document referred to in a specification must have been published by the date of filing of the application in order for that reference to be effective. As further noted in §14.26, it was also held in *Biogen v Medeva* that, following *Asahi's Application* [1991] R.P.C. 485 CA, if a declared priority date is to be relied on, the description of the priority application needs to contain an enabling disclosure. Presumably, therefore, a document referred to in the priority application must have been published at the priority date if that reference is to be effective in contributing to the priority application containing an enabling disclosure.

The MOPP indicates that references in applications under the Act to documents containing essential information and published later than the filing date or not at all should be deleted as irrelevant by the applicant. The MOPP further indicates that supplementing or replacing such a reference by an indication of the contents of the documents (beyond what is already explicitly contained in the application as filed) is not allowed. Otherwise, provided that the publication requirements set out above are met, the examiner should permit the applicant to replace the reference with the matter referred to, though apparently the applicant is not required to do so unless the referenced document is in a language other than English, see further below.

References in the form of patent application numbers should be objected to under s.14(3), and replaced with the relevant publication numbers by the applicant, provided again that the referenced application was published at the time of filing the application in suit.

As set out in the EPO Guideline C–II, 4.19, the current practice of the EPO is somewhat different in respect of both the requirements as to the publication date of the referenced document and the permissibility of the reference remaining in the specification. The former point is discussed in an annex to the *Halliburton* decision (above). In particular, if the referenced document was not available to the public on the date of filing of the application, it can only be considered if: (i) a copy of the document was available to the EPO on or before the date of filing of the application; and (ii) the document was made available to the public no later than on the date of publication of the application (under EPC art.93). The EPO Guidelines indicate that the latter requirement can be met by, for example, the document being present in the application dossier and therefore made public (under EPC art.128(4)) at the time that the application is published (under EPC art.93). This is said to be following T 737/90 (Unreported) (where a cross-reference to an application filed on the same day was only identifiable because only one other application had been filed by the applicant on that day).

Moreover, in the EPO, references to other documents relating to part of the disclosure of the invention are not normally permitted to remain in the specification. As further discussed in the EPO Guideline C–II, 4.19, where the reference document relates directly to the disclosure of the invention (e.g. details of one of the components of a claimed apparatus), then the examiner should first consider whether knowing what is in the reference document is in fact essential for carrying out the invention. If not essential, the usual expression "which is hereby incorporated by reference" or similar should be deleted from the description. If matter in the document referred to is essential to satisfy the requirements for a complete and clear disclosure of the invention, the applicant should be required to delete the above-mentioned expression and expressly incorporate the matter into the description. This is on the basis that a patent specification should be self-contained, i.e. capable of being understood without reference to any other document, at least in respect of the essential features of the invention.

In addition to the need for the referenced document to meet the publication/availability requirements discussed above, the reference to the document must in itself be a sufficient reference. The reference should be explicit in directing the skilled person to a specific document, or to a specific part or parts of a long document, for the purpose of supplementing the disclosure in the specification as filed so as to obtain a complete and clear disclosure of how to perform the claimed invention. Thus, two references in the specifications of the two patents concerned were held in the *Halliburton* decision (above) to be deficient in the circumstances in any event. A reference to and discussion of one document was held to be merely a discussion of a prior art document and the problems associated with that prior art proposal. A reference to a commonly owned US provisional application and a US final patent application claiming priority from the US provisional application, which were said in the specification as filed to be "incorporated by reference", was also held to be inadequate to allow reliance on the disclosure in the referenced US final and provisional patent applications for the purpose of supplementing the disclosure of the patent in question. This was principally on the basis that the reference did not direct the skilled person to those documents for the purpose of supplementing the disclosure of the patent. Moreover, on the specific facts of that case, the referenced documents were not available at the filing date of the patent in suit (following the UK approach discussed above) nor at the publication date of the application for the patent in suit (following the more generous EPO approach discussed above). In particular, and given that at that time the US Patent and Trademark Office did not publish pending US patent applications, the first publication of the referenced US final and provisional patent applications was effectively when a US patent was granted, which was some time after the publication date of the application for the patent in suit. The fact that a PCT application claiming priority from the referenced US provisional application was published on the same day as the application for the patent in suit was deemed irrelevant as the reference was not to the PCT application.

The *Halliburton* decision (above) was also referred to by the hearing officer in *Blacklight Power's Applications* O/076/08, for which see §14.24 above, and in view of it, the validity of the previous practice adopted by some of including the specification of another unpublished patent application (whether one under the Act or otherwise) or a copy of some other unpublished document as an "appendix" in order to assist in meeting the requirements for sufficiency is doubtful, and the only safe option in respect of unpublished material is to include the relevant material in the specification of the application as filed.

The MOPP indicates that if an application contains an applicant's or agent's identifying reference to another application filed on the same day or earlier under the Act, the search examiner should supplement it by the application number, even if it is necessary to telephone the applicant or agent to ascertain the number. All other references are published as filed.

—Addressee as a person skilled in the art

14.28

The specification must be construed as it would be understood by a person skilled in the art. Accordingly, in an action or counterclaim for revocation on this ground, such a person should give evidence of the alleged insufficiency (*Fichera v Flogates* [1983] F.S.R. 198; and [1984] R.P.C. 257 CA). Although the phrase "person skilled in the art" was not used in previous Acts, the "addressee of the specification" has been so described in numerous decisions following *Edison and Swan v Holland* (1889) 6 R.P.C. 243 CA, see particularly: *Valensi v British Radio* [1973] R.P.C. 337 at 375 and 380; *Dual Manufacturing's Patent* [1977] R.P.C. 189 at 194; *Fuji Photo's (Kiritani's) Application* [1978] R.P.C. 413; *American Cyanamid v Ethicon* [1979] R.P.C. 215 at 261; and *Standard Brands' Patent (No.2)* [1981] R.P.C. 499 at 531. Thus, it seems that "persons skilled in the art" are:

"persons having a reasonably competent knowledge of what was known before on the subject to which his [the proprietor's] patent relates, and having reasonably competent skill in doing what was then known".

The specification may be addressed to several persons skilled in respective arts (*Edison v Holland* above; and *Osram v Pope* (1917) 34 R.P.C. 369. Indeed, as discussed in §3.20, nowadays the person skilled in the art is increasingly seen as a multi-disciplinary team of persons, especially in complex cases, such as in the field of biotechnology, see: *American Cyanamid v Ethicon* [1979] R.P.C. 215 at 245; *Chiron v Organon Teknika (No.3)* [1994] F.S.R. 202; T 60/89 *HARVARD/Fusion protein* OJ EPO 1992, 2668; [1992] E.P.O.R. 320; and EPO Guideline C–IV, 11.3.

In drafting a patent specification it is essential to presume that its intended addressee (i.e. the person or team skilled in the art) is of no more than average knowledge and competence, see *Dual Manufacturing's Patent* (above) and *Blendax-Werke's Application* [1980] R.P.C. 491. Most pungently and succinctly, Jacob L.J. called that person a "nerd" and the team "an assembly of nerds" in *Rockwater Ltd v Technip France SA (formerly Coflexip SA)* [2004] R.P.C. 46. Also, that person or team must not be required to exercise any invention in carrying out the instructions given in the specification (*Valensi v British Radio* [1973] R.P.C. 337 at 377). However, it is permissible to have to perform *non-inventive* experiments in order to discover how to obtain the desired result, and it is also permissible to have to exercise individual judgment about the degree of adjustment of a feature (*Fichera v Flogates* above). Nevertheless, it has been questioned whether the phrase "person skilled in the art" necessarily has the same meaning when applied to the consideration of obviousness, see *Genentech's Patent* [1989] R.P.C. 147 CA and §3.07. In any event, what the proprietor meant by the words he has used in his specification is irrelevant (*Osram v Pope* (1917) 34 R.P.C. 369 at 391); and see the reference to *Kirin-Amgen v Hoechst Marion Roussel* in §14.22 above.

A skilled person is expected to make use of common general knowledge (T 51/87 *MERCK/Starting compounds* OJ EPO 1991, 177; [1991] E.P.O.R. 329 and *Halliburton v Smith International* [2006] R.P.C. 2. However, he cannot be presumed to have special knowledge, see *Hsiung's Patent* [1992] R.P.C. 497 CA where the specification was held not to have given the skilled reader enough information to manufacture the patented product without undue experiment. Accordingly, a specification is not insufficient if the skilled addressee can carry out its concepts without difficulty and without using ingenuity (*Helitune v Stewart Hughes*), or through using his skill to perform the invention while seeking success, see *Mentor v Hollister* [1991] F.S.R. 557; and [1993] R.P.C. 7 CA where the patent was upheld on the basis that only routine trial and error experiments were needed to perform the invention. In each of the *Hsiung*, *Mentor* and *Helitune* cases, the test used in *Valensi v British Radio* (above), i.e. that the relevant person or team must not be required to exercise any invention in carrying out the instructions given in the specification, was applied. Thus, this test should be regarded as that currently controlling the meaning of the term "sufficiency" under ss.14(3) and 72(1)(c)). In *Helitune v Stewart Hughes* [1991] R.P.C. 78; [1991] F.S.R. 171, the addressee would have appreciated that the specification contained an error and would notionally and, automatically, have corrected this to render the specification sufficient.

According to EPO Guideline C–IV, 11.3, the skilled reader may be presumed to have *access* to everything in the state of the art. However, this does not mean that the skilled reader has *knowledge* of everything in the state of the art. Thus, in considering sufficiency of a specification, recourse may legitimately be had to the common general knowledge of the skilled addressee of the specification, which knowledge can be taken as impliedly included within the text, but not to the specialised knowledge of that person (or team). Therefore, in drafting a specification, specific references should be given to published documents of whose existence the average person skilled in the art cannot be presumed to be aware, the contents of which are deemed to be included in the specification; if specific prior art is to be relied upon to provide necessary details for working of the invention, reference thereto should be included in the application as filed (T 165/88 *IBM/Insufficient disclosure* [1989] E.P.O.R. 157).

Nevertheless, care should be taken on relying for sufficiency on the common general knowledge of the skilled person as being impliedly included within the information possessed by the applicant because, if the missing feature of the claim is the only feature that can provide inventive step to the claim, the patent must either be invalid for insufficiency or for lack of an inventive step, see *Discovision v Pioneer Electronics* BL C/55/98, noted I.P.D. 21103. Also, in *Kirin-Amgen v Roche Diagnostics* [2002] R.P.C. 1, it was held that the court should be careful before it ascribed to the skilled addressee information outside his common general knowledge as this would be "entering into a field of uncertainty". However, it might not be impossible for the skilled man to consult someone else when trying to implement the teaching of the patent. The court should not adopt a rigid approach. If a document was referred to on one point it did not necessarily follow that the addressee should be taken to be aware of information contained in it relating to another point which may have been relevant to the teaching of the patent. This would depend on the facts.

Subsequently, Lord Hoffmann also indicated that the requirement for enablement of disclosure does not require the reader to follow the explicit description precisely. The addressee is entitled to use his common general knowledge to add to the explicit or implicit disclosure to obtain (if he can) the promised result, provided that in doing so no step is taken which was itself of an inventive character, see *Synthon v SmithKline Beecham* [2006] R.P.C. 10 at 323 HL where this view was applied to the sufficiency of a prior art disclosure.

It is submitted that this principle applies likewise to questions of sufficiency of the description in a patent.

In *Mayne Pharma v Teva* [2005] EWHC 2141 Pat Ct, noted I.P.D. 28004 it was held that, although the description specified the use of a defined pH value for a non-aqueous reaction medium with no indication of how this should be measured, it was held that, in the absence of any other disclosure, the skilled addressee would use a conventional pH meter without any calibration and rely upon the value thus obtained, whether this was right or wrong in the circumstances of a non-aqueous medium. The specification was therefore not insufficient on this point.

—Comparison with requirement of sufficiency under the 1949 Act

For a discussion on this topic, and in particular on the former objections of "inutility" **14.29** and "false suggestion" which have no counterparts under this Act, reference may be made to earlier editions of this work.

—EPO decisions on insufficiency

The former view of the EPO was that a specification was sufficient if it described a **14.30** single method of practising the invention in an enabling manner, but the position has changed and this is now only so if the invention is one directed to a novel principle: otherwise, the wording of the application/patent must enable the claimed invention to be performed over the full range of the claim, as discussed more fully in §14.25. Other EPO decisions arising under EPC art.83 (corresponding to subs.(3)) are now discussed.

Insufficiency has been found by the EPO when it was shown that specific directions in the description failed to provide the promised result (T 60/89 *HARVARD/Fusion proteins*); and when excessive experimentation was required in order to obtain the promised result (T 79/88 *JSR/Impact resistant resin composition* [1992] E.P.O.R. 387); and also when a ratio was specified in the claim lacking sufficient disclosure of how that ratio could be measured (T 654/90 *UNION CARBIDE/Coatings* [1994] E.P.O.R. 483). Although each example in the patent need not be exactly repeatable, the claimed process must reliably lead to the desired product (T 281/86 *UNILEVER/Preprothaumatin* OJ EPO 1989, 202; [1989] E.P.O.R. 313).

On the burden of proof required of an opponent to establish an objection of insufficiency under EPC art.100(c) the EPO has held that a mere statement that one of the patent examples has been repeated "exactly as described", but without obtaining the stated result, is inadequate to establish insufficiency in those proceedings (T 182/89 *SUMITOMO/Extent of opposition* OJ EPO 1991, 391; [1990] E.P.O.R. 438); and, if the described example is on an industrial scale, the repetition must be carried out on a similar scale (T 740/90 *LESAFFRE/Yeast*).

The EPO has held that an application is not insufficient merely because a feature essential for the operation of an invention is not explicitly disclosed (T 22/83 *FUJITSU/Surface acoustic wave device* [1988] E.P.O.R. 234). Nevertheless, the reader must not add to the explicit and implicit teaching of the patent anything of an inventive character (T 32/84 *COMMISSARIAT/Redefining an invention,* OJ EPO 1986, 9; [1986] E.P.O.R. 94); and any required processing conditions must be apparent to such a reader (T 219/85 *HAKOUNE/Inadequate description*).

Sufficiency can be demonstrated by adding to the content of the specification the common general knowledge of the person skilled in the relevant art, see T 124/85 *ASTEN/Papermaking fabric* [1995] E.P.O.R. 464). However, in doing so, an argument of inventive step may be compromised, see T 412/93 *KIRIN-AMGEN/Erythropoietin* [1995] E.P.O.R. 629 where evidence of alleged obviousness, showing that the invention could easily be performed, was seen to be contrary to an allegation of insufficiency, for comment on which see [1996] *CIPA* 26. While common general knowledge is normally demonstrated by reference to textbooks and basic handbooks (T 206/83 *ICI/Pyridine herbicides*), in an appropriate case it can consist of a recently published patent application (T 51/87 *MERCK/Starting compounds*).

Sufficiency can also be based on the contents of a document cross-referenced in the original disclosure (T 449/90 *CEDARS-SINAI/Treatment of plasma* [1993] E.P.O.R. 54). Here the reference had been deleted during examination, but its reinstatement was permitted to provide sufficiency. In T 787/89 *BRITISH PETROLEUM/Diamond identification* [1991] E.P.O.R. 178, the EPO refused an application because the applicant did not respond to the invitation to provide a pre-published document indicating how a particular claimed feature could in practice be attained.

In T 923/92 *GENENTECH/Human t-PA* [1996] E.P.O.R. 275; abridged OJ EPO 1996, 564, there was a finding of insufficiency where the examples and information provided were inadequate to allow the skilled person using common general knowledge to perform the invention (defined in terms of products having certain functions) without undue burden in the whole area claimed, but the objection was overcome by limiting the features expressed within the claim wording, even though the allowed claims continued to have a very broad literal scope. Where a claim specifies a feature to have a particular value and there is no way by which the skilled person could measure that value, an objection of insufficiency arises, see T 626/91 (Unreported); and, likewise, where the value of a specified parameter cannot be meaningfully measured (T 780/95 [2001] E.P.O.R. 449), see also T 954/05 (Unreported). However, no insufficiency was found where methods for the measurement of the specified parameter were known, even though these did not give identical results (T 492/92 (Unreported)).

Insufficiency has been found on the basis of documents, published after the priority date, from the inventors which indicated that they themselves had been unable to carry out the invention according to their own written disclosure, see: T 418/89 *ORTHO/Monoclonal antibody* OJ EPO 1993, 20; [1993] E.P.O.R. 338; T 495/89 *ORTHO/Monoclonal antibody* [1992] E.P.O.R. 48; and T 498/94 (Unreported).

The EPO is prepared to allow an open-ended claim in certain circumstances, see T 487/89 *ASAHI/Polyamide fibre* [1992] E.P.O.R. 32. It has also held that a chemical specification need not contain an illustrative example if performance of the invention would require routine experimental investigations only (T 407/87 *TOSHIBA/Semiconductor device* [1989] E.P.O.R. 470; and T 561/96 (Unreported)), see further §14.37.

The EPO has used the objection of insufficiency to reject an application of the perpetual motion type on the basis that "the person of average skill in the art would not be able to fill in the missing details from his own knowledge or following reasonable trial and error (T 5/86 *NEWMAN/Perpetual motion* [1988] E.P.O.R. 301. Other instances of findings of insufficiency when the description and claims were seen to be contrary to the laws of thermodynamics are T 442/97 *COSBY/Fluid circuit* [1998] E.P.O.R. 212 and T 451/89 *BOLESTA/Power generator* [1998] E.P.O.R. 333.

In T 727/95 *WEYERSHAEUSER/Cellulose* [2001] E.P.O.R. 35 it was held that there was an undue burden on a person skilled in the art in respect of the isolation of relevant micro-organisms because the reproducibility of the exercise depended on chance. Reliance on chance was unsatisfactory unless there was evidence that the probability of the chance events occurring was sufficiently high to guarantee success.

In T 604/04 *GENENTECH/Human PF4A receptors* (Unreported), claims to the therapeutic use of specified monoclonal antibodies (Mabs) were refused for insufficiency of description because, although it was accepted that such antibodies are capable of industrial applicability, it could not be deduced from the description that they had any specific therapeutic activity.

In T 491/08 *Government USA/Improved immunogenicity* (Unreported), it was held that the patent application itself did not provide any information that the generically described compounds according to claim 1, when administered to a human by whatever inoculation protocol, would have a direct effect on a metabolic mechanism specifically involved in HIV-1 infection i.e. the medical indication claimed. As a result, there was only a weak presumption of sufficiency, and therefore less substantial arguments and evidence were required to overcome the presumption.

It is no objection to the sufficiency of the description of the invention for the skilled person to be obliged to carry out tedious experimentation to execute it where this is nothing out of the ordinary in the relevant field and would involve only routine trials (T 391/91 *UNIVERSITY OF CALIFORNIA/Ice nucleating* [2002] E.P.O.R. 8).

In T 608/07 *INEOS/Polymerisation process* [2009] *CIPA* 483, it was held that, for insufficiency arising out of ambiguity, it was not enough to show that an ambiguity exists, for example at the edge of the claims. Instead, it will normally be necessary to show that the ambiguity deprived the person skilled in the art of the promise of the invention, see T 256/07 *SCA HYGIENE/Absorbing product* and *Zipher v Markem* [2009] F.S.R. 1, [2008] EWHC 1379 which was cited with approval.

The above decisions may be contrasted with T 815/07 *PROCTOR & GAMBLE/Absorbent articles* in which it was held that where a claimed article is defined by reference to a parameter to be measured by a specified method, and that method for any particular article produces values which sometimes fall within the claimed range and sometimes fall significantly outside it, a skilled person has no means of knowing whether the article in question will solve the problem or not. It placed upon him an undue, if not insuperable burden when trying to reproduce the invention, such an objection being established on the facts before the Board so that the specification was insufficient.

Similarly in T 560/09 *ADVANCE HOLDINGS/Semi-synthetic platelet*, the invention concerned a platelet gel required to be "not capable of forming a clot in less than 15 minutes". There was no standard method of determining this feature, and results would vary depending on the skill of the experimentalist and the conditions used, so that the public was left in doubt as to which materials were covered by the claim and which were not, and the objection of insufficiency was held to be established.

A claim to the use of certain compounds for treatment of vascular disorders, the compounds being defined in functional terms in respect of their ability to stimulate a certain enzyme was held to be objectionable as a "reach-through" claim directed to future inventions based on the invention actually being disclosed, and hence to be objectionable under EPC art.83, see T 1063/06 *BAYER SCHERING/Reach through claim* [2010] E.P.O.R. 17.

In T 952/06 *THE REGENTS OF THE UNIVERSITY OF CALIFORNIA/Compounds for the treatment of sexual dysfunction* the applicants' main request related to compounds defined by a Markush formula for use in the treatment of sexual dysfunction, and containing a functional definition concerning the ability of the compounds to up-modulate certain receptors to natural ligand binding. Although 25 specific compounds had been exemplified, the Board held that there was not fair support for all the structural variations claimed since the specification was silent as to their origin (known or unknown compounds) and specific preparation and a full research programme would be required to fill the gap. In relation to a first auxiliary request with a more restricted genus of compounds, it was not plausible in the context of the description that there was a causal link between the generally defined medical indication (sexual dysfunction) and the compounds in the purpose-related product claim. A second auxiliary request limited to a more restricted subclass of compounds and restricted to medical indications for which animal tests provided valid evidence was held to meet the requirements of sufficiency and was remitted for further prosecution. A similar situation arose in T 290/05 *IDEA/Associates of macromolecules* where there were 158 examples, but little variation in their composition, and a requirement for a skilled person to select from three very large pools of compounds whose definition was vague and then ascertain whether a functional requirement was met required considerable effort on the part of a skilled person and imposed an undue burden, see also T 352/07 *CHUGAI SEIYAKU/IL-6 antagonist* where the Appeal Board held that the applicants' teaching exhaustively defined a problem, but not its solution.

In T 63/06 *HITATCHI/Fuel injection and ignition*, it was held that in opposition proceedings the burden of proof generally lies upon an opponent to establish insufficiency of disclosure. When the patent does not give any information of how a feature of the invention can be put into practice, only a weak presumption exists that the invention is sufficiently disclosed, and the opponent can then discharge his burden by plausibly arguing that common general knowledge would not enable the skilled person to put this feature into practice. The patent proprietor then has the burden of proof for contrary assertion that common general knowledge would indeed enable the skilled person to carry out the invention.

In T1138/09 *CONSIGLIO NAZIONALE DELLE RICERCHE/Variants of allergic protein*, the claims contained a broad structural definition and only a narrow range of examples were present in the description. The Appeal Board stressed that a broad definition is not prima facie a reason to assume that all members of the group do not share the same properties. Secondly, the number of examples required to make it credible is dependent on the particular circumstances in each case.

The claims (subs.(5))

—Purpose and requirements of claims

14.31   The claims define the matter for which the applicant seeks protection (subs.(5)(a)). The extent of protection is determined by the claims, as interpreted by the description and drawings (s.125(1), which is to be interpreted in accordance with the Protocol to EPC art.69, s.125(3) and *Kirin-Amgen v Hoechst Marion Roussel* [2005] R.P.C. 9 at 169 HL) as discussed in more detail in §125.05. Subsection (5) also requires that the claims: (b) be clear and concise (discussed in §14.36); (c) be supported by the description (discussed in §14.37 and §14.38); and (d) conform to the requirement for unity of invention (discussed in §14.40). However, non-compliance with any of these provisions (b)–(d) gives rise to objections that can only be raised pre-grant, because (unlike the position with subs.(3)) non-compliance with them is not a ground of revocation, see §14.09 above. For further discussion on this aspect, see also §14.36 below.

The Rules are silent as to any required form of the claims, so that the so-called two-part or "characterising" form of claims (as is normally required by the EPO under EPC r.29(1)) and the presence of reference numerals in claims (as also is normally required by the EPO) is neither required nor forbidden. "Omnibus" claims, that is, claims which are in terms of the invention substantially as described in the description, the drawings and/or the examples in a chemical case, are permitted. Omnibus claims are discussed further in §14.35, but it is here noted that, under most circumstances, omnibus claims are forbidden by r.29(6) of the EPC and r.6.2(a) of the PCT, except possibly if such were "absolutely necessary" to obtain protection (T 150/82 *IFF/Claim categories* OJ EPO 1984, 309).

However, objection will normally be taken if a claim is divided into separate phrases by one or more full stops: it is then considered to be ambiguous in scope, see *Leonard's Application* [1966] R.P.C. 269 which the MOPP indicates remains the current practice.

As explained in §14.21, a "Code of Practice for Patent Applicants and Agents" is made available on the UK-IPO website *http://www.ipo.gov.uk/codeofpractice.pdf*. This summarises some of the sections from the MOPP. It states that claims as filed should be structured to have:

(a) one independent claim defining all the technical features essential to the invention or inventive concept. This should include the core integers as well as sufficient details of interrelationship, operation or utility to establish that the invention achieves the intended objectives; and

(b) dependent claims incorporating all the features of the independent claim and characterised by additional non-essential features.

(c) Further independent claims are only justified where the inventive concept covers more than one category, e.g. apparatus, use, process, product; complementary versions within one category, e.g. plug and socket, transmitter and receiver, which work only together, or distinct medical uses of a substance or composition.

Therefore claims as filed should not, where it might have been avoided, contain:

(d) Multiple unrelated inventions that would clearly give rise to a plurality objection.

(e) Multiple independent claims in any one category, even if only one inventive concept is present.

(f) Claims of a total number or complexity not justified by the nature of the invention.

(g) Claims which are in principle unsearchable by reason of the number of alternatives embraced, or the choice of characterising parameters or desiderata.

(h) Dependent claims that are not fully limited by the terms of the preceding independent claim, e.g. dependent claims which omit, modify or substitute a feature of an independent claim.

Further, the claims as filed should not, where it might have been avoided, define an invention that is clearly excluded from being patentable under the Act.

—Categories of claims

Claims can generally be divided into two broad categories: (1) claims to things, such as **14.32** a device or apparatus, or substances (products); and (2) claims to actions, which are processes, methods and uses. A single application can, and indeed in most cases should, contain more than one type of claim in order for adequate protection to be obtained, though see the discussion on unity of invention at §14.40.

An apparatus generally comprises a number of integers cooperating to produce a result. The apparatus may be claimed by specifying the integers, and normally the claim will be unclear unless the interrelationships between the integers are also given. A product claim is a claim to an article or substance and the invention in such a case may be defined by reference to features of the product, that is by reference to its structure or composition, or by reference to its use or, in some circumstances, by reference to features of its manufacture (for which, see the discussion of "product-by-process" claims and the *Kirin-Amgen v Roche Diagnostics* case (above), each discussed below. Where the apparatus or product is of a known type, it is generally not necessary to specify all the integers (EPO Guideline C–III, 4.5). In such a case, the apparatus or product may sometimes be claimed by specifying features of its operation. Where the invention resides in a new or modified integer (or integers) in a generally known type of apparatus or product, the claim may refer to the known type and then specify the new or modified integers.

A process may be directed to a single process step or to a series of such steps, not necessarily a process of manufacture, but the process must have industrial applicability (s.1(1)(c)).

Sometimes there is an overlap between these two types of claims, resulting in a hybrid product/process claim. For example, an apparatus claim may include limitations relating to its mode (or method) of operation. Also, a process claim may be limited to the use of a particular apparatus or may consist in the use of a particular article or substance.

Special problems may arise in claiming computer-related inventions, which may be refused under s.1(2)(c), and/or as not industrially applicable under s.1(1)(c) and (4), see the commentary above on s.1

In United Kingdom practice, it is not usual for claims to contain reference numerals for fear that their presence may have some limiting effect on the claim. However, in *Virgin Atlantic Airways Ltd v Premium Aircraft Interiors UK Ltd* [2010] R.P.C. 23, [2009] EWCA Civ 1062, it was held that the EPO approach to reference numerals applies in the United Kingdom.

"In particular we do not think that numerals should influence the construction of the claim at all—they do not illustrate whether the inventor intended a wide or narrow meaning. The patentee is told by the rule that if he puts numerals into his claim they will not be used to limit it. If the court subsequently pays attention to the numbers to limit the claim that is simply not fair. And patentees would wisely refrain from inserting numbers in case they were used against them. That is not to say that numbers are pointless. They help a real reader orient himself at the stage when he is trying to get the general notion of what the patent is about. He can see where in the specific embodiment a particular claim element is, but no more. Once one comes to construe the claim, it must be construed as if the numbers were not part of it. To give an analogy, the numbers help you get the map the right way up, they do not help you to read it to find out exactly where you are."

It should be noted that for very many years, product-by-process claims (i.e. claims to a product, which may not be new itself, defined by reference to a new process by which it is made) were permitted in the United Kingdom. However, following the House of Lords decision *Kirin-Amgen Inc v Hoechst Marion Roussel Ltd* [2005] R.P.C. 9, 169), Lord Hoffmann reassessed this aspect of UK patent law and commented that it was important that the United Kingdom should apply the same law as the EPO and the other Member States when deciding what counts as new for the purposes of the EPC. He held that, since art.64(2) of the EPC and s.60(1)(c), extend the protection afforded by a process claim to a product directly made by that process, it makes it "unnecessary to claim the product defined by reference to the process". This overturns many years of practice in the UK and means that "product-by-process claims" will not be valid, and should not in future be accepted by the UK-IPO, except in the circumstances permitted under the EPO Guidelines, i.e. where the product cannot satisfactorily be defined by other parameters. In that case, however, the claim will be interpreted as covering the product however made, and hence will be anticipated if the product has been disclosed in the prior art, but made by a different process. For a discussion on, and examples of, claims in the form "Product X *obtainable by process Y*", see the article by R. K. Percy (1991–92) 21 *CIPA* 218.

—Effect of claim containing a statement of purpose

14.33   When the claim states that apparatus, a product or a method, is "for a" purpose, the traditional British view has been that the claim is considered to be limited as to dimensions or as to type so as to be suitable for the stated purpose (and possibly for other purposes as well), but not limited to apparatus, etc. specifically limited or intended to be useful in, or as used in, such purpose, see: *Adhesive Dry Mounting v Trapp* (1910) 27 R.P.C. 341, where the rule was first enunciated though on the facts it may have arisen because otherwise two claims would have had identical effect; and *Raleigh v Miller* (1948) 65 R.P.C. 141 HL: EPO Guideline C–III, 4.13 is in similar terms. Thus, in *Du Pont's (Buege's) Application* [1984] R.P.C. 17, a claim to a known resin limited by the phrase "for use in" was rejected, in accordance with the *Adhesive Dry Mounting* and *Raleigh v Miller* decisions (above) as not clearly defining the invention as required by s.14(5)(a) and (b), because the phrase was seen as a mere statement of intent.

However, exceptions to this rule occur when claiming an invention of a first, or further, medical indication for a known pharmaceutical product by a claim in the form of "X for use in treatment of disease Y" (as permitted by s.4A and discussed in §§2.23 and 4A.09). The "Swiss form" of claiming further medical indications is no longer permissible following the EPO Enlarged Board decision G 2/08. A practice note of May 26, 2010 issued by the UK-IPO confirms that it will follow this practice for all pending applications, although an application for post-grant amendment of granted claims is unlikely to be successful, potentially because the allowed form of claim may be broader in scope than the "Swiss form" of claim.

Moreover, at least in the EPO, a claim to the use of a known compound for a particular purpose, which is based on a technical effect which is described in the specification, is interpreted as including that technical effect as a functional technical feature, at least as regards its patentability over the prior art, see G 2/88 *MOBIL III/Friction reducing additive* OJ EPO 1989, 93; [1990] E.P.O.R. 73 and G 6/88 *BAYER/Second non-medical indication* OJ EPO 1990, 114; [1990] E.P.O.R. 257, as discussed in §2.23.

In *Schwihag Gesellschaft's Patent* O/29/04 the Comptroller construed the opening claim words "A sleeper for a railway track" as applicable only (in the context of the description) when the sleeper was assembled into railway track. On this basis, the claim had a restricted meaning and was not invalidated by a reference which did not disclose the presence of shock absorbing elements as specified in the claim wording.

—Claims of a functional nature

A claim may be a "functional" claim in the sense that it defines the invention or a **14.34** feature of the invention by reference to the *function* of the feature rather than more explicitly by reference to the *structure* or other precise nature of the feature. Examples might be where a claim to a mechanical invention refers to "fastening means" rather than to a "nail" or a "rivet", or where a claim to a chemical invention refers to "a fat-dissolving substance" rather than to one or other particular fat-dissolving substances. A claim may also, in appropriate circumstances, claim an invention or a feature of the invention by reference to a result to be achieved, as in the classic case of *No Fume v Pitchford* (1935) 52 R.P.C. 231. Often the *No Fume* functional type of claim defines some or all of the features of the claim by use of the phrase "the arrangement being such that ...". When claiming by reference to a result to be achieved, the claim must recite those features that must be chosen to enable the result to be achieved, and the person skilled in the art must know from the description or common general knowledge how to conduct tests, which must be routine and not themselves involve invention, in order to find out how to achieve the result and to know that the result has been achieved, see *Hughes v Ingersoll* [1977] F.S.R. 406. Otherwise, the requirements for sufficiency of the functional type of claim are no different from those for other claims (*IBM's Application* [1970] R.P.C. 533), see also *Nestlé's Application* [1970] R.P.C. 84.

Where these principles are not followed, a finding of insufficiency should result. Thus, in *Birtcher Medical Systems' Patent* O/70/96, the claim specified a device for creating an "improved" effect, but the patent did not indicate what degree of improvement was required or how this could be determined. This led the Comptroller to disregard the word "improved" and, as a result, the patent was held to lack novelty and inventive step. Also, in *Minnesota Mining's (Suspension Aerosol Formulation) Patent* [1999] R.P.C. 135, it was held that, if functional wording in the claim were given any effect, then the patent was invalid for insufficiency because the specification "simply provides no teaching relating to the criteria according to which the skilled man is to be taken to be using the invention", the assessment of the attainment of the stated characteristics here being essentially subjective and based on experience, with skilled persons possibly reaching different conclusions.

The EPO has adopted a similar approach, see: EPO Guidelines C–III, 4.10, 4.22 and 6.5 and T 14/83 *SUMITOMO/Vinylchloride resins* OJ EPO 1984, 105; T 48/85 *NRDC/Eimeria necatrix* [1987] E.P.O.R. 138; T 68/85 *CIBA-GEIGY/Synergistic herbicides* OJ EPO 1987, 228; [1987] E.P.O.R. 302; T 139/85 *EFAMOL/Pharmaceutical compositions* [1987] E.P.O.R. 229; and T 226/85 *UNILEVER/Stable bleaches*, and a paper by P. Ford (1985) 16 I.I.C. 325 and 358. Indeed, the EPO has stated that functional phrasing is proper where features cannot be defined more precisely without restricting the scope of the invention (T 292/85 *GENENTECH/Polypeptide expression-I*); and, in T 430/92 *SUMITOMO/Growth of tulips* [1999] E.P.O.R. 341 a claim was allowed in which the characterising feature was expressed in entirely functional terms as its distinction from the prior art, according to which the specified effect was not obtained, and where an objection was dismissed that this form of claim was an attempt to claim all solutions to the problem. Similarly, the EPO accepts that an invention may be functionally defined by an unambiguous mathematical formula if a skilled person can determine therefrom whether the claim is infringed (T 126/89 *FILTRATION/Fluid filter cleaning system* [1990] E.P.O.R. 292). Indeed, a claim can be characterised by functional features if, from an objective viewpoint, the features of the invention cannot otherwise be defined more precisely without restricting the scope of the invention, but the features must provide instructions sufficiently clear to the expert to reduce them to practice without undue burden, if necessary with reasonable experiments (T 204/90 *LINDHOLM/Breathing apparatus* [1992] E.P.O.R. 282).

A claim will be rejected by the EPO under EPC art.84 if it does not specify *all* features that are necessary for solving the technical problem with which that application is concerned (T 283/84 *ROHM/Ultra-violet emitters* [1988] E.P.O.R. 16). Also, a finding of insufficiency will result where the specification discloses only isolated examples and without sufficient technical teaching which, taken together with common general knowledge in the art, is sufficient to enable the skilled person to achieve the envisaged result without undue difficulty within the whole ambit of the claim containing the functional definition (T 435/91 *UNILEVER/Detergents* and T 694/92 *MYCOGEN/Modifying plant cells*), discussed in §14.25. Insufficiency was also found in T 225/93 and T 805/93 (each Unreported) where no specific method was specified for measuring a required parameter and different methods gave inconsistent results.

An example of a functional claim being upheld on the basis of performance by one of its embodiments, despite evidence that performance failed with other constructions, is T 524/98 *IMPERIAL TOBACCO/Smoking article* [2000] E.P.O.R. 412.

However, in *Mayne Pharma v Debiopharm* [2006] F.S.R. 37 at 656, where the patent was based on an improved storage stability of a pharmaceutical product by the presence of a "an effective stabilising amount of a material", it was held that "it must be possible to devise a test which can answer the question 'Have I used such an amount or not?'", but here a prior art document showed that such better stability had already been achieved. Thus, the claims were regarded as "hopelessly insufficient" because the answer to this question was "You don't have to add any at all." See also *SmithKline Beecham v Apotex [Appeal]* [2005] F.S.R. 23.

Care should be taken when drafting functional claims for use in the US because features claimed in the "means-plus-function" or step-plus-function can be and typically are construed to be of narrow scope that is closely tied to the specific embodiments or examples described in the specification, see 35 U.S.C. 112(b).

—Claims of the "omnibus" type

14.35   "Omnibus" claims referring to the drawings or in a chemical case the examples are not forbidden by the Act or the Rules, although this is out of step with the Resolution on the Adjustment of National Patent Law contained in the CPC and the provisions of r.43(6) of the EPC. Such claims will probably be upheld in the United Kingdom, in accordance with numerous decisions under former patent statutes. Claims of the omnibus type were the only ones held valid and infringed in: *Raleigh v Miller* (1948) 65 R.P.C. 141 HL; *Surface Silos v Beal* [1959] R.P.C. 331; and [1960] R.P.C. 154; and *Rotocrop v Genbourne* [1982] F.S.R. 241. See also *Deere v McGregor* [1965] R.P.C. 461 and the article by P.W. Grubb (1974–75) 4 *CIPA* 3. It is generally considered that the scope of such claims is narrow, although as indicated above, they may be construed so as to omit or broaden a feature in the main independent claims. There is no apparent disadvantage resulting from their inclusion. Therefore, it is normally prudent to include a specific claim of this kind limited to any of the particular embodiments or examples given to illustrate the invention more generally described. However, such claims should be carefully drafted to avoid ambiguity, see the criticism in *Daikin Kogyo's (Shingu's) Application* [1974] R.P.C. 559 CA.

In *Philips Electronics' Patent* [1987] R.P.C. 244, amendment of a European patent (UK) was permitted by adding an omnibus claim thereto, though this was carefully worded so as not to extend beyond the scope of the remainder of the claims.

—EPC requirements as to claims

14.36   By contrast with the position stated under United Kingdom law in §14.31, the PCT and EPC each require that "whenever appropriate" each independent claim (but not dependent claims) to be divided into a preamble, setting forth the claimed features that are shown in combination in the most relevant single item of prior art, and a second, "characterising" portion setting forth the novel claimed features, divided by "characterised in that" or "characterised by" or similar (EPC r.43(1); PCT r.6.3(b)).

The EPO also normally requires reference numerals in the claims, particularly when they are required for an understanding of the claims (EPC r.43(7)). Rule 43(7) of the EPC indicates that the presence of reference numerals in a claim of a European patent does not limit the scope of the claim, there is no corresponding provision in the Act. This is confirmed in *Virgin Atlantic Airways Ltd v Premium Aircraft Interiors UK Ltd* [2010] R.P.C. 23, [2009] EWCA Civ 1062, discussed in §14.32.

Product-by-process claims are allowable by the EPO only if the product cannot be satisfactorily defined by reference to its composition, structure or some other testable parameter (T 150/82 *IFF/Claim categories*), and the novelty of a product-by-process claim can only depend on a process feature if this necessarily provides the product with a characteristic which is inevitably achieved by the skilled person (T 412/93 *KIRIN-AMGEN/Erythropoietin*). The same principle has been applied to "device-by-process" claims (T 227/91 *CODMAN/Second surgical use* OJ EPO 1994, 491; [1995] E.P.O.R. 82). Also, in the EPO, a product-by-process claim is allowable only if the product is novel per se (T 434/87 *FABRE/Toothbrush fibres* [1990] E.P.O.R. 141), that is if the product is distinguishable per se from products of the prior art (T 248/85 *BICC/Radiation processing* OJ EPO 1986, 261; [1986] E.P.O.R. 311), for example because it is the process by which the product is prepared that renders that product novel, as in T 130/90 *UNIVERSITY OF TEXAS/Recombinant monoclonal antibody* [1996] E.P.O.R. 46. Here a distinction was also drawn between the words "produced by" and "obtainable by". See also T 73/92 *BALFOUR/Feedstuff* [2004] E.P.O.R. 73. In T 124/93 *AMOCO/Olefin catalyst* [1996] E.P.O.R. 624, it was stated that:

"according to established case law of the EPO Boards of Appeal, product-by-process claims give protection for the products as such, independent from the process by which they were made".

Similarly, in T 20/94 *ENICHEM/Amorphous TPM* [2003] E.P.O.R. 56, the EPO applied its previous decisions on the interpretation of product by-process claims in holding that an amendment of a process claim to claim a product "directly obtained" by the process extended the scope of protection because the product by process claim was a claim to the product itself. Further EPO decisions on product-by-process claims include: T 219/83 *BASF/Zeolites*; T 93/83 *MONTEDISON/Ethylene polymers* [1987] E.P.O.R. 144; and T 205/83 *HOECHST/Vinyl ester/crotonic acid copolymers* OJ EPO 1985, 363; [1986] E.P.O.R. 57, also discussed in §2.26.

The EPO has permitted a product-by-process form of claim as a way of correcting a claim to a chemical product which had been originally defined by an erroneous structure, though only in circumstances where it is possible to define all the measures (e.g. starting materials, reaction conditions, purification) required to obtain such product, it not being possible to insert the correct chemical structure since that would involve inadmissible addition of subject-matter (T 552/91 *MERCK/Chroman derivatives* OJ EPO 1995, 100; [1995] E.P.O.R. 455).

As discussed further in §14.32, the House of Lords in *Kirin-Amgen v Transkaryotic Therapies* [2005] R.P.C. 9 at 169 HL determined that the EPO practice should now be followed, meaning that product-by-process claims will no longer be generally allowable or upheld in the UK.

—Claims to be clear and concise (subs.(5)(b))

The MOPP states that: **14.37**

"The requirement that the claims shall be clear applies to individual claims and also to the claims as a whole, and is of the utmost importance in view of the function of the claims in defining the monopoly sought."

The EPO Guideline C–III, 4.1 are in practically identical terms. Similarly, the MOPP states that:

"The requirement that the claims shall be concise refers to the claims in their entirety as well as to the individual claims"

and the EPO Guideline C III, 5 are all but identical. An objection under subs.(5)(b) can only be raised pre-grant, see §14.39.

A relative or imprecise term in a claim is not objectionable if its meaning is clear to the skilled addressee. Thus, under previous statutes, in *British Thomson-Houston v Corona* (1922) 39 R.P.C. 49 HL, claims referring to a "filament of large diameter" were upheld; as likewise, in *Cleveland Graphite v Glacier Metal* (1950) 67 R.P.C. 149 HL, where claims referred to a "thin and flexible bearing liner". In *General Tire v Firestone* [1971] R.P.C. 173, the main claim also contained a number of relative and imprecise terms. This first instance judgment (at 229 and 230) is valuable in its exposition of the propriety (in a suitable case) of the use of such terms under English law. That judgment was upheld on appeal: [1972] R.P.C. 457. In *Bugges v Herbon* [1972] R.P.C. 197, the phrase "quick-breaking or unstable emulsion" was also held to be perfectly clear to the addressee of the specification.

In *Chevron Research's Patent* [1975] F.S.R. 1, the court remarked that "specifications are intended primarily to give practical information" and "should be drafted in such a way that a man skilled in the field in question should be able to understand the meaning of the words used" In *Mobil Oil's Application* [1970] F.S.R. 265, it was held that, although there may be cases, as in *Du Pont's Application* (1952) 69 R.P.C. 246, in which a chemical specification is insufficient without an example. There are many chemical cases which can be sufficiently described without examples.

A claim may still be upheld as to its clarity even though something clearer and shorter might have been drafted: the test of clarity is whether the skilled person would have difficulty in understanding the language used (*Strix v Otter* [1995] R.P.C. 607). However, where a claim contains a term that is so vague and ambiguous as to be incapable of any reasonable meaning, an argument may succeed that such a claim can never be infringed (*Milliken Denmark v Walk Off Mats* [1996] F.S.R. 292) though the point did not succeed in that case. In *Scanvaegt v Pelcombe* BL C/5/97, it was observed that, where there is a lack of clarity in a claim, there is no reasonable degree of certainty for third parties (as required by s.125(3) in compliance with art.69 of the EPC and its Protocol, reprinted in §§125.01–125.03) because the extent of protection cannot be properly discerned and accordingly the patent is then invalid as *ex hypothesi* the invention as disclosed cannot be performed. On appeal in that case (see [1998] F.S.R. 786), the obiter statement in the *Milliken* case was accepted, also obiter, with the remark that: "If you cannot define the invention claimed, you cannot conclude that it is being used."

In T 454/89 *ICI/Optical sensing apparatus* [1995] E.P.O.R. 600, it was stated that EPC art.69 (and its Protocol) only applies to the question of extent of protection and not to clarity of the claims under EPC art.84. This was echoed in T 1129/97 *GALDERMA/ Benzimidazole derivatives* OJ EPO 2001, 273, [2001] E.P.O.R. 478, where the applicant was required to amend the claims to include the definition of "lower alkyl" from the description. Explicit disclosure of the meaning of the term in the description and not in the claims was not sufficient. Although art.69(1) of the EPC stated that the description was to be used to interpret the claims, that article was said to be only concerned with determining the extent of protection (e.g. when that had to be determined for the benefit of third parties), and not with defining the matter for which protection was sought by means of a claim, as required by art.84. However, this view, which seems to be widely held at the EPO, must be questionable because "the extent of protection" (EPC art.69(1)) and "the matter for which protection is sought" (EPC art.84) would appear to mean precisely the same thing in this context. In any event, if a claim is not "clear", how can the extent of protection which it provides be determined? But the EPO has held that art.69(1) of the EPC may have a role in deciding whether a claim may be amended without breach of art.123 of the EPC (T 808/05 (Unreported)).

In *Raychem's Patents* [1998] R.P.C. 31 the claims were seen to have been drafted in terms of functional parameters in a way calculated, in the legal sense, to make them difficult to understand, with simple concepts dressed up in an elaborate clothing of quasi-science and complicated terminology. The court construed these prolix and opaque claims free of the language used and concerned itself with what they really meant. It held that the claims were invalid as directed to obvious desiderata, see §3.27. The court commented that patents are not given for skill in inventing technically meaningless parameters. An appeal was unsuccessful: BL C/88/98, noted I.P.D. 22032.

The EPO requires a claim to be clear in itself, when read in the light of the common general knowledge of the skilled person, without the use of further knowledge given in the description (T 454/89 *ICI/Optical sensing apparatus* above). The EPO also appears to regard the requirement of art.84 of the EPC for clarity of claim to be satisfied if the claim contains all the features that are required for performance of the invention, even if these are defined in functional terms, provided that the claim is distinguished from the prior art (T 1055/92 *AMPEX CORP./Clarity* OJ EPO 1995, 214; [1995] E.P.O.R. 469). Nevertheless, the fact that a claim to a process does not explicitly specify certain steps does not mean that these steps are implicitly excluded if that would mean that some of the protected embodiments could not then be reproduced (T 7/88 *DU PONT/Flange formation process* [1990] E.P.O.R. 149).

The mere breadth of a claim does not in itself diminish its clarity provided that it is unambiguous to the skilled person (T 238/88 *KODAK/Crown ether* OJ EPO 1992, 709; [1993] E.P.O.R. 100); and the EPO has allowed a claim to a chemical-type product which was defined by physical parameters (T 94/82 *ICI/Gear crimped yarn* OJ EPO 1984, 75), though it was important that the parameters chosen were readily capable of being determined by analysis or measurement. Also, where it was not viable to define apparatus in a way other than by reference to its intended use, a claim to a combination of the apparatus and its use which unambiguously defined that apparatus over the prior art was held to have sufficient clarity and be allowable under EPC art.84 (T 841/95 (Unreported)).

Of course, the scope of a claim should be determinable and the use of vague and ill-defined terms in a claim may cause invalidity. Thus a qualitative term may, but need not always, require reference to a test by which the value of that qualitative term is to be determined (T 860/93 *AQUALON/Protective coating composition* OJ EPO 1995, 47; [1995] E.P.O.R. 391). This decision is to be contrasted with T 124/85 *ASTEN/Papermaking fabric* where the absence of explicit reference to the intended text was excused because the skilled person would appreciate the test to be used from his general knowledge, but T 337/95 *NIHON NOHYAKU/Lower alkyl* OJ EPO 1996, 628; [1997] E.P.O.R. 333 held that, as the term "lower alkyl" does not have an unambiguous meaning, a claim containing this term could not be allowed for the sake of legal certainty, as required by art.84 of the EPC. Also, the phrase "artificial diamond or zircon" has been held to lack clarity because it indicated that zircon is not an artificial diamond (T 787/89 *BRITISH PETROLEUM/ Diamond identification*).

The existence of a grey area, where measurement error may make it difficult to determine whether a particular product falls within a claim or not, does not justify an objection under EPC art.84, nor necessarily does the use of a relative term in claim wording (T 412/93 *KIRIN-AMGEN/Erythropoietin*), for comment on which see [1996] *CIPA* 26; see also the follow-up decision (T 636/97 *KIRIN-AMGEN/Erythropoietin II* [2000] E.P.O.R. 135). However, if functional language is not used and a claim feature is of unclear limiting effect, pre-grant objection under EPC art.84 has been taken, see T 349/97 *PHILIPS/Picture signal* [1999] E.P.O.R. 52 and T 216/97 *XEROX/High addressability image generator* [1999] E.P.O.R. 111.

In T 1055/92 *AMPEX CORP./Clarity* (above) it was stressed that the requirements for clarity are to be distinguished from those of sufficiency under EPC art.83, but the EPO has held that an objection of lack of clarity (ambiguity) can be raised as one of insufficiency under EPC art.83 (T 684/89 *CYBEREXACT/Printer ribbon errors* [1993] E.P.O.R. 173). Although (as discussed in §14.39) an objection of non-compliance with s.14(5)(b) (or with EPC art.84) is not available after grant, the question of clarity can have consequences for reproducibility under subs.(3) (corresponding to EPC art.83). As to the permissible breadth of claim having regard to subs.(3) (and EPC art.83), see §§14.25 and 14.37.

The EPO has stated that the word "comprising" is inherently ambiguous as meaning either "including" or "consisting of" or "composed of", but the phrase "consisting essentially of" was accepted as meaning that unspecified components could be present if the characteristics of the claimed composition were thereby not materially affected (T 472/88 *GENERAL ELECTRIC/Thermoplastic resin* [1991] E.P.O.R. 486; T 340/89 *GENERAL FOODS/caffeine* [1992] E.P.O.R. 199; see also T 522/91 and T 759/91 (each Unreported). In T 589/89 *NATIONAL RESEARCH/Polyurethane compositions* [1994] E.P.O.R. 17, the word "comprising" was held to have left over the possibility of the presence of further reactive ingredients and, on that basis, the claim lacked novelty. However, where the word "consisting" is used, the proportions of the specified ingredients must total 100 per cent (T 711/90 (Unreported)). Also, the EPO Guideline C–III, 4.21 currently says:

"in drafting patent claims legal certainty normally requires the word 'comprising' to be interpreted by the broader meaning 'include', 'contain' or 'comprehend'."

The EPO has refused to allow the word "approximately" to appear in a claim as being inherently vague but it did allow the word to remain in the specification on the applicant's representation that the word merely implied a possible lack of perfection (T 194/89 *IBM/Brushless DC motor* [1991] E.P.O.R. 411). The EPO Guidelines say at C–III, 4.7 that whenever the word "about" or "approximately" is used in a claim, "the examiner should use his judgement as to whether the meaning is sufficiently clear in context".

A claim which incorporates reference to an unpublished document should be objectionable as lacking clarity, but there is no objection as such to a disclaimer within a claim provided that the claim as a whole is clear and concise (T 4/80 *BAYER/Polyether polyols* OJ EPO 1982, 149). Nevertheless, if a claim contains an exclusionary clause which is indefinite, the claim itself fails to meet the requirements of subs.(5), as also it does if its operative part is unsupported by the body of the specification (*ICI's (Richardson's) Application* [1981] F.S.R. 609).

Special considerations apply to inventions relating to alloys, the present practice continuing to be that established by the decision in *Mond Nickel's Application* (1948) 65 R.P.C. 123. Following this decision, it became usual for claims to an alloy to specify the range of the respective proportions of each of its essential ingredients, followed by a reference to incidental constituents and impurities whose ranges do not normally need to be specified, see the paper by C.H. Greenstreet (Trans. Chart. Inst. LXXVII (1958–59) C119 and LXXVIII (1959–60) B57). In this vein, the EPO has held that a claim to a mixture is not clear if the proportions stipulated for its constituents cannot add up to the requisite total (100 per cent in the case of percentages) for each composition claimed (T 2/80 *BAYER/Polyamide moulding compositions* OJ EPO 1981, 431).

In *Fruehauf's Application* BL O/185/83, a mere disclaimer to "all matter disclosed in" a prior concurrent application to overcome an objection under s.2(3) was refused as leaving the scope of the claims unclear contrary to s.14(5); and in *Toyama's Application* BL O/125/88 an attempt to overcome an objection under s.2(3) by a disclaimer to matter validly claimed in the cited application and having an earlier priority date was also rejected as leaving the claims unclear. Likewise, the EPO has refused to allow a claim containing an internal disclaimer to materials "as disclosed in" an earlier application because that disclaimer would not be unequivocal (T 11/89 *GÖDECKE/Naphthyridinone derivatives* [1991] E.P.O.R. 336). Claim wording which defines elements in terms of trade marks or other trade names lacks clarity and is therefore not normally accepted by the UK-IPO or the EPO (see for example T 762/90 *VON BLÜCHER/Surface filter* [1993] E.P.O.R. 296).

The MOPP and the EPO Guidelines both say that trade marks may only be used exceptionally in a claim if their use is unavoidable and they are generally recognised as having a precise meaning or do not introduce ambiguity. In T 480/98 *CIUFFO GATTO/Trade mark* [2000] E.P.O.R. 494, it was held that, where a trade mark is used as a definition of an element in a claim, it is inherently lacking in clarity and an attempt to replace the mark by a description of the product as it was sold under that mark at the priority date was rejected as impermissibly adding subject-matter.

In *L. B. (Plastics)' Application* BL O/90/86, the application contained a claim to "any novel subject matter" contained in the application. It was argued that this prevented an objection under s.76 of broadening the protection claimed, but it was held that the claim failed in this purpose and that a reader was free with impunity to disregard such a claim.

In *Bilgrey Samson's Application* BL O/577/01 claims to the operation of a "fruit machine" type apparatus were held to lack clarity because a claim limited to tax thresholds prevailing at a given time may result in apparatus not originally an infringement becoming so upon a change in the law, and because reference to a "dark and uninviting corner" of an amusement arcade was too subjective to provide a sufficiently clear description of the invention.

As to conciseness of claiming, in T 246/91 *OXY/Gel-forming compositions* [1995] E.P.O.R. 526 it was stated (in referring an application back for further examination) that "157 claims imposed a severe and totally undue burden on the public"; and, in *Contravision's Patent* BL O/79/00, noted I.P.D. 23048, amendment was disallowed partly on the ground that the proposed amendment would have increase the total number of claims from 65 to 239 with 68 independent claims which would have imposed an intolerable burden on the public. The UK-IPO is likely to raise objections that the claims lack clarity and/or conciseness if a large number of independent claims is present.

—Claims to be supported by description (subs.(5)(c))

Subsection (5)(c), which corresponds to art.84 of the EPC, requires that the claims be supported by the description. An objection under subs.(5)(c) can only be raised pre-grant, see §14.38. Cases decided under former statutes, which related to a "lack of fair basis", have to be applied with caution, see *Schering Biotech Corp's Application* [1993] R.P.C. 249 and, whilst the classic precedents under the 1949 Act on the content of the claims are still relevant, they are no longer binding. Such precedents include *Esau's Application* (1932) 49 R.P.C. 85, following which objection is raised against a claim that is speculative in that it embraces fields not yet explored by the applicant. In *Glatt's Application* [1983] R.P.C. 122, it was observed that, in rejecting a divisional application for failure to comply with s.14(5)(c), it is not permissible to select certain features at will from the initial disclosure and otherwise rely on vague and inexplicit passages taken out of context, and that third parties should not have to face monopolies which were neither clearly sought nor founded by the inventor at the date of filing, but which were conceived later and claimed *post hoc*. In dismissing an appeal, the Patents Court held that the literal wording of the proposed claim covered something that was never within the contemplation of the inventor.

14.38

The definitive view of the effect of subs.(5)(c) was set out by Lord Hoffmann in *Biogen v Medeva* [1997] R.P.C. 1 HL. Here, the requirement for a sufficiently supporting description under s.14(5)(c) was seen as an aspect of the overall need for an enabling disclosure, the substantive effect of this requirement being given effect by s.72(1)(c) (for which see §72.14). This was seen as a requirement of substance rather than form and, although the purposes for which the question is asked (under ss.14(5)(c) and 72(1)(c) respectively) are different, the underlying concept is the same, as it is also with the concept of according a priority date because the phrase "supported by matter disclosed" is also used in s.5(2) to establish whether priority from an earlier application can be accorded, as discussed in §§5.21 and 5.22. Accordingly, Lord Hoffmann saw "no gap or illogicality in the scheme of the Act".

In *Biogen*, Lord Hoffmann indicated that broad claims are justifiable when the inventive discloses a principle capable of general application, but the vital question is:

"not whether the claimed invention could deliver the goods, but whether the claims cover other ways in which they might be delivered: ways which owe nothing to the teaching of the patent or any principle which it disclosed."

See also §14.25 above. On the facts of the *Biogen* case itself, Lord Hoffmann said:

"I accept the judge's findings that the method was shown to be capable of making both antigens and I am willing to accept that it would work in any otherwise suitable host cell. Does this contribution justify a claim to a monopoly of any recombinant method of making the antigens? In my view it does not".

Lord Hoffmann also stated that when dramatically new things are done for the first time, the technical contribution deserves to be recognised, but:

"care is needed not to stifle further research and healthy competition by allowing the first person who has found a way of achieving an obviously desirable goal to monopolise every other method of doing so."

On the facts of the case, the *Biogen* patent was then found invalid for insufficiency due to its breadth of claim although, because the priority date was denied, it had already been conceded that an intervening publication resulted in a lack of inventive step. These views were discussed by A.W. White [1996] *CIPA* 1020 and subsequently by: I Karet [1997] E.I.P.R. 21; Diana Sternfeld *MIP* February 1997, 32; and J.M. Marshall *Patent World*, March 1997, 34. The patent was subsequently amended, as noted [1997] *CIPA* 738.

The *Biogen* decision was followed in *American Home Products v Novartis* [2000] R.P.C. 547; and [2001] R.P.C. 8 CA where, initially, the Patents Court found infringement by derivatives of the claimed rapamycin on the basis of the Protocol to EPC art.69 and also held that the claimed invention (as construed to cover the derivatives) was sufficiently disclosed, pointing out that there is no requirement that every embodiment of the protected invention should have been demonstrated to provide the promised effect: in this case, it was stated that the discovery of the new immunosuppressant effect of rapamycin "made available to the art the opening through which a new class of immunosuppressives could be found." However, the Court of Appeal disagreed. A submission that:

"the inventor had disclosed in the specification a beneficial property of a class of products, namely that rapamycin and derivatives with rapamycin-effect had immunosuppressant qualities"

was not accepted and, on the contrary, it was held that there had only been a sufficient disclosure in respect of rapamycin and not of any of its derivatives. Thus, had the claim been construed to cover the derivatives (which the Court of Appeal held it should not be, disagreeing with the Patents Court on this point), it would have been invalid for insufficiency: no guidance had been given as to which derivatives of rapamycin would exhibit the immuno-suppressive effect of the claimed use of rapamycin and, as admitted, not all such derivatives would have this property, and thus there would be an undue burden on the skilled person to find out which of such derivatives would and which would not exhibit this effect.

In the *Schering Biotech* case (above), the Patents Court upheld an objection from the Comptroller (see BL O/77/88) that, while claims to the preparation of a plasmid containing a specified cDNA insert were allowable, extension of these claims to cover use also of a nucleotide "capable of hybridisation with such insert" should not be permitted as not being supported by the description, particularly because it was admitted that such hybridised product would not necessarily produce the same result as a plasmid with the specified insert. It was stated by the Patents Court that "the word support requires the description to be the base which can fairly entitle the patentee to a monopoly of the width claimed" and that a mere mention in the specification of the features of the claims is not sufficient support for them.

This theme was followed in *Monsanto v Merck* [2000] R.P.C. 709 where the court was satisfied that many of a very large class of chemical compounds covered by the claim did not possess the qualities promised by the specification leading to its invalidity for insufficiency. Here the court stated:

"If compounds having the features of the claim may or may not possess the qualities which the patent says unify the class, it cannot be said that the claim reflects a true class at all. It is just a generalised description of a large number of chemical compounds. Such a claim is not analogous to a claim to a new principle, since the patentee has given no information, such as a structure/activity relationship, which enables the reader of the specification to draw any conclusions as to the properties of any particular compound without further experiment. All he has done is to describe the scope of the claim with spurious precision."

This was upheld on appeal, reported as *Pharmacia v Merck* [2002] R.P.C. 41.

In contrast to these decisions under the Act, at one time the EPO took the view that objection does not arise under EPC art.84 merely because a claim is "unreasonably broad" and that "support by the description" merely requires that technical features stated in the description to be essential to the invention should appear as features of the claims. The decision in T 939/92 *AGREVO/Triazoles* OJ EPO 1996, 309; [1996] E.P.O.R. 171 signalled a change in attitude against the former ready allowance by the EPO of broad claims by stating that, in respect of an alleged technical effect that is not part of the definition of the claimed invention, where the specification does not contain sufficient information in order to make it credible that the alleged technical effect is obtained, then objection of lack of inventive step can arise, at least where this technical effect is the sole reason for the alleged inventiveness of the compounds. In that case a reference in the claim to a "substituted phenyl group" was construed as meaning substituted by anything and inventive step was denied in the absence of credible evidence that any such substituent would provide the promised herbicidal activity of the class of compounds claimed.

Also, claims that extend to a group of inter-related products have been regarded under EPC art.84 as not being sufficiently enabled across the total breadth of the claim and therefore in the circumstances not allowable, see: T 409/91 *EXXON/Fuel oils*; T 435/91 *UNILEVER/Detergents*; and T 694/92 *MYCOGEN/Modifying plant cells*, each as discussed in §14.25.

The EPO has also held, though before these decisions, that the absence of an upper limit to a feature claimed by reference to a minimum value is not necessarily objectionable, at least where it would be obvious to the skilled person that there is an inherent upper limit and it would be unjustified to limit the feature to the highest value disclosed in the specific examples (T 297/90 *DU PONT/Nonwoven sheet* [1993] E.P.O.R. 389). Also, an essential feature for performing the invention need not be present in the main claim if the claimed sub-combination can be seen as an intermediary building block for providing the inventive full combination, the position being likened to the patenting of a chemical intermediate having no utility except as such (T 888/90 *BAXTER/Sub combination* OJ EPO 1994, 162; [1994] E.P.O.R. 98). Where there was an inconsistency between the wording of a claim and that of the examples of the invention in the description, it was held that the requirements of art.84 of the EPC had not been met (T 150/85 (Unreported)). It is not clear whether these decisions would today be followed in view of the recent trend against the allowance of broad claims.

Following *Hoerrmann's Application* [1996] R.P.C. 341 and *McManus' Application* [1994] F.S.R. 558, the Comptroller stated that a "Swiss form" claim based on a further medical use for a known therapeutic compound requires to be supported by at least some:

"part of the description which is dedicated to showing how the applicant arrived at the knowledge that a pharmaceutical compound or composition, known to be effective in the treatment of one kind of condition, is also effective in the treatment of another", although the tests carried out to provide this support "can be of a rudimentary nature", see *Prendergast's Applications* [2000] R.P.C. 446; *Consultants Supplies' Application* [1996] R.P.C. 348; *Hoffmann-La Roche's Application* BL O/192/04, noted [2004] *CIPA* 479; and *Commonwealth Scientific's Application* BL O/248/04, noted [2004] *CIPA* 521. As discussed in §14.33 above, the "Swiss form" of claim is no longer allowed. However, the subsequent medical indication claims will probably require the same support. In similar vein, in *Protoned's Application* [1983] F.S.R. 110, leave was refused (pre-grant) to change claim wording from "mechanical compression spring" to "mechanical spring" inter alia because the specification would not support a claim broadened in this way. For further cases on the impermissibility of claims in divisional, or other back-dated, applications because of matter having been added thereto over the parent application as filed, see §§76.13–76.16.

A claim which, in effect, claims all solutions to the problem which faced the inventor is objectionable unless the invention lies in the identification of that problem, see: *British United Shoe Machinery v Simon Collier* (1909) 26 R.P.C. 21 at 48–51; *NV de Bataafsche Petroleum's Applications* (1940) 57 R.P.C. 65; and *Kahn (David) v Conway Stewart* [1974] R.P.C. 279 at 319–320. Perhaps *H. Lundbeck v Generics* [2008] EWCA Civ 311; [2008] R.P.C. 19 (discussed in §14.25 above) was such a case. Here the claim was limited to a single new chemical compound, the production of which was held to have been inventive, and a claim to that compound per se was not seen to be objectionable, Lord Hoffmann saying:

> "Parliament has chosen to allow product claims and the jurisprudence of the EPO, which we have always regarded as carrying great weight, shows that such claims can be made in the latter case as well. It is too late to have regrets about the breadth of the monopoly which such claims confer."

To this Jacob L.J. added:

> "The fact that compound claims may give a patentee 'more than he deserves' has not in practice proved to be much of a problem. Their certainty and pragmatic value has proved itself over the years. What matters for present purposes is that the concept 'that the patentee should not have more than he deserves' does not form part of the statutory test for sufficiency."

Thus, this decision may come to be seen as a limited one based on the product claim not extending beyond the single chemical compound which the inventor had invented, his invention having been enabled by the special process which he had inventively devised for this purpose, as to which see *Zipher v Markem* [2008] EWHC 1379 Pat Ct; [2009] F.S.R. 1 also discussed in §14.25.

The abstract is part of the application, but not part of the specification generally and the description in particular. Therefore, it cannot in itself provide support for the claims under subs.(5)(c). In *Abbott Laboratories Ltd v Medinol Ltd* [2010] EWHC 2865 Pat Ct, it was held that s.14(7) should be interpreted in the same manner as EPC art.85, and therefore the abstract was ignored when considering the disclosure of the application.See also the discussion in §14.41.

—Raising, post-grant, objections of lack of supporting description or lack of clarity or conciseness of claims

14.39   Objections of lack of clarity or conciseness of the claims under s.14(5)(b) or lack of support in the description for the claims under s.14(5)(c) can be raised only during substantive examination of the application and, after grant, claims may not be held invalid on these grounds because these grounds are not among those listed in s.72(1), as was authoritatively held in *Genentech's Patent* [1989] R.P.C. 147 CA, reversing the Patents Court, [1987] R.P.C. 553, and reiterated in *Strix v Otter* [1995] R.P.C. 607. The position is the same under the EPC. Thus, art.84 of the EPC (which corresponds to s.14(5)) is separate from the question of sufficiency under EPC art.83 (which corresponds to s.14(3)). Consequently, objection under EPC art.84 as such cannot be raised in opposition proceedings before the EPO, see: T 48/85 *NRDC/Eimeria necatrix*; and T 23/86 *NAIMER/ Computer-controlled switch* OJ EPO 1987, 316; [1987] E.P.O.R. 383. Likewise, the Comptroller has no power to consider an objection under s.14(5)(c) during revocation proceedings before him (*Smith's Patent* BL O/16/86).

In the *Genentech* case (above), the Court of Appeal observed that, since objection under s.14(5) is not available after grant, the UK-IPO ought to have clearly in mind during examination the undesirability of allowing claims the object of which was to cover a wide and unexplored field, or where there was no disclosure in the specification coterminous with the monopoly indicated in the claims. However, this does not seem to happen in practice and it is, apparently, the policy of the EPO and its Boards of Appeal to adopt, in ex parte pre-grant procedures, a liberal view concerning the application of art.84 of the EPC, see: T 610/90 *AMERICAN COLLOID/Clay layer* [1993] E.P.O.R. 1. Indeed, the EPO further stated that determination of the extent of protection is not a matter for the EPO, statements made by opponents and proprietors merely being noted (T 175/84 *KABELMETAL/Combination claim* OJ EPO 1989, 71; [1989] E.P.O.R. 181). This attitude is surprising and has led to claims of very broad scope in the field of genetic engineering being upheld, see T. Roberts [1994] E.I.P.R. 371; M. Brandi-Dohrn (1994) 25 I.I.C. 648; and J. Wibblemann [1997] E.I.P.R. 515.

In the *Genentech* decision (above), it was observed that objection under s.14(5) could possibly arise if an attempt is made to amend a granted patent, on which see §27.12. However, that seems not so likely in practice, see *Chiron v Organon Teknika (No.5)* [1994] F.S.R. 258. In opposition proceedings before it, the EPO will consider objections under EPC art.84, although such is not a permissible ground of opposition under EPC art.100, only when amendments are proposed in EPO opposition proceedings (T 434/87 *FABRE/Toothbrush fibres*), and then only if the objection arises out of the amendments proposed to be made (T 301/87 *BIOGEN/Alpha-interferons*), see also T 923/92 *GENENTECH/Human t-PA*, although here a very broad claim was eventually allowed, see §3.30.

Accordingly, for some time a problem existed of finding a way in which claims that contravene the provisions of s.14(5) can be attacked post-grant. In *Chiron v Organon Teknika (No.3)* [1994] F.S.R. 202, an attempt was made to do this by arguing, not that the claims were too broad, but that the description was not sufficient to enable the invention claimed to be made, but the court held that objections of alleged insufficiency could not be used as a substitute for an objection that the claims are not supported by the description—a plea which "unfortunately is not available under section 72"—and that the broad claims were not invalid for insufficiency because at least one embodiment of these could be made, see §14.25. In this case, an attempt was made to challenge support for the broad claims when a narrower claim fell to be deleted, but such challenge was not permitted because it is "not relevant or right to consider matters which have no nexus with the amendment nor with the cause for the amendment" (*Chiron v Organon Teknika (No.5)*, above), see §§27.12 and 75.06. This decision was unsuccessfully appealed, see the consolidated report (*Chiron v Murex* [1996] R.P.C. 535).

The grant of claims of very broad scope, particularly by the EPO and in the field of biotechnology, was criticised at a broadly-based seminar in London where a call was made for amendment of the EPC to make art.84 of the EPC a ground of invalidity post-grant, see [1995] *CIPA* 262 and *epi-Information* 2/1995, 44. However, there was no enthusiasm elsewhere in continental Europe for any change to the EPC on this point, art.84 of the EPC being strangely seen only as a question of formal support for claim wording, e.g. by including in the description statements of invention with parallel wording, see *epi-Information* 2/1995, 46 and [1996] *CIPA* 650 and 655. Thus, there remains the illogicality of having s.14(5) (and EPC art.84) available only as an objection to patentability pre-grant with the EPO Opposition Divisions and national courts seemingly impotent to deal with an objection of non-compliance with these provisions post-grant, unless it is possible to formulate an objection under some other provision, i.e. under the Act under one of the heads of permissible revocation set out in s.72(1) or by refusing a requested amendment under the terms of s.76.

However, since these decisions, there has been a marked change of emphasis in EPO decisions concerning claims of broad scope and it now appears that the allowability of a broad claim can be a question of lack of inventive step (under EPC art.56), or of an insufficiency of description (under EPC art.83), as discussed in §§14.25 and 14.38. Also, at least in the United Kingdom, over-broad claims may some times be challenged, post-grant, as an insufficiency of description under s.72(1)(c), see the discussion in §14.37 above of *Biogen v Medeva* [1997] R.P.C. 1 HL and *H. Lundbeck A.S. v Generics* [2008] R.P.C. 19.

Unity of invention (subss.(5)(d) and (6))

14.40   The claims of an application must relate to a single invention or to a group of inventions which are linked by a single inventive concept (subs.(5)(d)). Subsection (6) provides for rules to govern what may be termed "a single inventive concept", though without prejudice to the generality of subs.(5)(d). Accordingly, r.16 (reprinted at §14.08 above) sets out that two or more inventions may be claimed in a single application (either in the same or in different claims) when there exists among such inventions a "technical relationship" which involves one or more of the same or corresponding "special technical features", a term that means "those features which define a contribution which each of the claimed inventions, considered as a whole, makes over the prior art". This form of r.16 was adopted in 1992 in conformity with similarly revised forms of r.13 of the PCT and r.44 of the EPC (r.33 when it was adopted in 1991).

What constitutes a single invention is a question of fact, not law, and is commonly decided by the Comptroller on the basis of practical considerations, including the size of the field of search and whether a single search is sufficient. In a little-developed field the Comptroller may exercise discretion to allow claims which in a true sense may be said to be for different inventions, see *Celanese's Application* (1952) 69 R.P.C. 227, confirmed as applying to the present Act in *Nissan Chemical's Application* BL O/142/83. The MOPP also indicates that any doubt as to whether unity of invention exists should be resolved in the applicant's favour.

The MOPP indicates that one criterion, which "would be suitable for some sets of claims", would be to determine whether the common subject-matter of the claims is novel and involves an inventive step. Mere novelty of the common subject-matter is unlikely in itself to avoid objection, particularly having regard to the current form of r.16. Other examples where unity of invention exists include: (a) in addition to an independent claim for a product, an independent claim for a process specially adapted for the manufacture of the product, and an independent claim for use of the product; (b) in addition to an independent claim for a process, an independent claim for an apparatus or means specifically designed for carrying out the process; and (c) in addition to an independent claim for a product, an independent claim for a process specially adapted for the manufacture of the product and an independent claim for an apparatus or means specifically designed for carrying out the process. In addition, claims to separate articles which are inter-related, for example, by being characterised in that they are to be used together, may be regarded as linked to form a single inventive concept. Such cases include inventions relating to plugs and sockets, transmitters and receivers, (computer) clients and servers, etc.

A lack of unity of invention is typically identified by an examiner when conducting the search (see §§17.01 and 17.05, below). Only the first-claimed invention in an application will be searched although an opportunity to pay additional search fees will be given.

Article 82 of the EPC (see §14.09 above) relates to unity of invention and EPC r.44 and r.22 are in similar terms. Unity of invention is considered in EPO Guideline C–III, 7. One approach adopted by the EPO is to consider whether the claimed invention(s) in question are directed to solutions of the same technical problem, see W 7/86 *MUCKTER/Lithium salts* OJ EPO 1987, 67; [1987] E.P.O.R. 176 and W 9/86 *NRDC/Thromboxane antagonists* OJ EPO 1987, 459; [1988] E.P.O.R. 34 where more restrictive objections made by another PCT international searching authority appear to have been criticised. W decisions of the EPO are decision on cases where additional search fees have been paid under protest as permitted by PCT r.40.2(c). Two different ways of solving the same problem can be regarded as involving a single inventive concept (W 11/89 *X/Fibre fleece* [1993] E.P.O.R. 514). Similar to statements in the MOPP, the EPO Guidelines indicate that an objection of lack of unity of invention should neither be raised nor persisted in on the basis of a narrow, literal or academic approach. It should be borne in mind, however, that r.43 of the EPC currently restricts the number of independent claims to a single independent claim in any category except for certain, specified, cases. Thus, in the EPO, whilst plural independent claims may have unity of invention, objection may nevertheless be raised simply to the presence of more than one independent claim in any category. Similarly, UK examiners will object to the presence of a large number of independent claims in any category, typically for lack of clarity and/or conciseness under s.14(5)(b) as noted in §14.37.

Unity of invention is according to the EPO present in a claim defining a number of alternatives where the alternatives are of a "similar nature". In the case of alternative chemical compounds (in so-called "Markush claims", named after the inventor Eugene Markush), this requirement may be met if these alternatives share a common property or activity and either a significant structural element is shared by all the alternatives, or all the alternatives belong to a class for which there is an expectation in the art that its members will behave in the same way in the context of the invention (W 3/94 *HOECHST/Ketonoxim-O-ether* OJ EPO 1995, 775). Where there is no novel common structural element, unity of invention may still be present where the compounds share a common property or activity and there is a common part of the chemical structure which distinguishes the claimed compounds from known compounds having the same property or activity, see: W 1/94 (Unreported); W 6/95 (Unreported); and W 4/96 *UNILEVER/Teeth whitening* OJ EPO 1997, 552; [1997] E.P.O.R. 502 although, if the alternatives belong to a class of compounds members of which have already been shown in the prior art to behave in the manner disclosed in the application, then there may be a lack of unity (W 4/96 *UNILEVER/Teeth whitening*, above).

The "single general concept" required by the EPO for unity of invention to be present must have an "inventive character", that is there must be an inventive common feature in those parts of the independent claims differing from the closest prior art, otherwise unity of invention will be denied (W 6/90 *DRAENERT/Single general concept* OJ EPO 1991, 438, [1991] E.P.O.R. 516; and W 32/92 *WISAP/Cervical punch* OJ EPO 1994, 239).

It is also sufficient that different groups of chemical intermediates, which are intended to be inter-reacted to form the desired final products, contribute an essential structural element to the final products so that they are technically inter-connected with those final products (T 470/91 *ICI/Unity* OJ EPO 1993, 680; [1994] E.P.O.R. 231). Accordingly, in the EPO, claims to a chemical intermediate may be included in a single application together with claims to a final product and with claims to a process for making this final product using such an intermediate so long as the intermediates are oriented towards the final product and there is a sufficiently close technical interrelation between the two (T 57/82 *BAYER/Copolycarbonates* OJ EPO 1982, 306; T 110/82 *BAYER/Benzyl esters* OJ EPO 1983, 274). Where this is the case, the claims to the intermediates can be of narrower scope (T 35/87 *BASF/Hydroxy-pyrazoles* OJ EPO 1988, 134; [1988] E.P.O.R. 260). Claims directed to products and to processes for their preparation do not lack unity merely because the claimed process can be used for making other compounds; a process can usually be considered specially adapted for manufacture of a product if the process is new and suited to making the product and, if so, it is irrelevant whether other products can be obtained using the process (W 11/99 *N.N./Percarbonate* OJ EPO 2000, 186; [2000] E.P.O.R. 515).

As r.16 conforms with the current form of r.44 of the EPC, UK-IPO examiners ought to be inclined to follow EPO decisions concerning unity of invention.

The citation of further prior art during examination may create a non-unity situation, see W 6/97 (Unreported) where it was stressed that unity can only be assessed once the underlying problem which the invention seeks to solve has been properly defined. Non-unity of remaining claims may arise during prosecution as a result of rejection of a broader claim. Filing of a divisional application would normally be appropriate in such a case (provided that, in the EPO, the subject-matter for that divisional application had not been abandoned during prosecution of the European patent application (see T 178/84 *IBM/Lack of unity* [1989] E.P.O.R. 364, abridged OJ EPO 1989, 157; and W 8/87 *ELECTRO-CATHETER/Protest* [1989] E.P.O.R. 390, *abridged* OJ EPO 1989, 123).

Where the UK-IPO is of the opinion that there is lack of unity of invention, it is the first invention encountered in the claims that forms the basis of the official search, see §17.05.

Section 26 expressly provides that objection cannot be raised that the claims of a granted patent lack unity of invention, see §26.02. In any case, such objection would apparently fall outside the scope of s.72(1)(c) assuming that this is limited in effect to a failure of the specification to comply with s.14(3).

Biological material

14.41   The special requirements for sufficiency of a specification for an invention which requires for its performance the use of a "micro-organism" (originally contained in subss.(4) and (8)) were removed from s.14 into a new s.125A, which has now been extended to relate to "biological material", as discussed in the commentary on that section.

Abstract (subss.(2)(c) and (7) and r.15)

14.42   According to subs.(7), the purpose of the abstract required by subs.(2)(c) is to give technical information. If it is determined that the abstract as filed does not adequately fulfil this purpose, subs.(7) provides the examiner with the power (as to which see §130.04) to revise the submitted abstract (including its title) before it is published and without appeal being possible by the applicant (s.97(1)), who indeed is not necessarily even informed of this revision. Whilst no longer a requirement of the rules as such, the MOPP and Code of Practice for Patent Applicants and Agents (both available at *http://www.ipo.gov.uk*) still indicate that the abstract should be drafted so that it constitutes an efficient instrument for the purposes of searching and disclosure in the particular technical field, in particular by making it possible to assess whether there is a need to consult the specification itself.

Rule 15 (reprinted at §14.07 above) sets out more explicitly the requirements for the abstract. The abstract must start with a title for the invention (which need not be the same as the title that precedes the specification, though typically it will be, see §14.22) and must contain a concise summary of the matter contained in the specification, including an indication of the technical field to which the invention belongs, a technical explanation of the invention, and the principal use of the invention. Rule 15(4) requires that the abstract include an indication of the drawing which should accompany the abstract when it is published (if there is more than one drawing in the specification), but under r.15(5) the Comptroller can choose another figure if thought more suitable. For features in the abstract that are shown in any of the drawings, reference characters must be included in the abstract following the relevant features, see r.15(6). The rules no longer require that the abstract should normally have a maximum of 150 words, apparently because this was never a strict requirement, though an overly long abstract is likely to be amended under the general power given to the Comptroller under s.14(7) to amend abstracts. Conveniently, the abstract may be headed "Abstract for identification purposes".

In accordance with subs.(7), on publication the abstract does not form part of the state of the art against a later co-pending application under s.2(3), though it will be effective under s.2(2) as from the date of publication of the application under s.16. Although the abstract, reframed by the Comptroller if he wishes (subs.(7)), is published under s.16, because it forms part of the application (s.14(2)(c)), the abstract is not included in the granted patent which is published under s.24(3) because this refers to the specification which does not include the abstract (s.14(2)(b)). The abstract does not assist in defining the extent of the invention, see s.125(1).

As noted in §14.38, the abstract is part of the application, but not part of the specification generally and the description in particular and, therefore, it cannot in itself provide support for the claims under subs.(5)(c). In the EPO where it has been decided that, in accordance with art.85 of the EPC ("[t]he abstract shall serve the purpose of technical information only; it may not be taken into account for any other purpose. . ."), the abstract has only a documentation purpose and therefore that it cannot be used for the purposes of overcoming an objection under EPC art.123(2) (T 246/86 *BULL/Identification system* OJ EPO 1989, 199; [1989] E.P.O.R. 344). In *Abbott Laboratories Ltd v Medinol Ltd* [2010] EWHC 2865 Pat Ct, it was held that s.14(7) should be interpreted in the same manner as EPC art.85, and therefore the abstract was ignored when considering the disclosure of the application.

Whilst the Comptroller has the power to rewrite an abstract that has been filed but is deemed not to meet the requirements of r.15, the MOPP indicates that in the case that the abstract as filed is wholly inadequate (the example of the abstract being little more than a title being given in the MOPP), then objection should be raised that no abstract has been filed and the applicant requested to remedy this. Because it is a requirement that an abstract be filed (s.15(5)), a failure to file within the prescribed period, including any permitted extended period (for which see §15.10), anything which could not be regarded as an abstract will result in the application being deemed withdrawn.

Withdrawal (subs.(9))

An applicant may withdraw a patent application at any time before grant (subs.(9)), the **14.43** procedure for which is discussed in §14.51. The date of grant for this purpose is the date of the letter to the applicant informing him of the grant of a patent under s.18(4), see §24.05 and therefore the withdrawal must be made before this letter is issued. Where there are co-applicants, an effective act of withdrawal requires the consent or agreement of each applicant. Withdrawal has effect from the date of its receipt at the UK-IPO, rather than the date on which the UK-IPO takes action upon it for example, *Siemens Medical System's Patent* O/63/00.

If an application is to be withdrawn in order to avoid it becoming published under s.16, the notice of withdrawal must reach the UK-IPO before the preparations for this publication have been completed, see, §14.51 and §16.10 also. Where an application is withdrawn after either PF 9 or PF 10 has been filed, but not acted upon, it is possible that the UK-IPO in its discretion may refund the fee paid thereon, though the applicant has no formal entitlement to such a refund. It is possible for a withdrawn application to serve as a priority application for another application, see §5.28. If a written request for withdrawal is received in the Office before the issue of the grant letter but not in time to prevent issue of the letter, then the grant may be rescinded.

There is no possibility of reviving or securing restoration of a withdrawn application (s.14(9)) unless the withdrawal was made in error. In particular, s.14(10) was added, s.117 was amended and s.117(A) was added, all with effect from January 1, 2005, to allow an application to be resuscitated when the withdrawal was made in error or by mistake and to set out the effect of such resuscitation, see §§117.01, 117.03 117A.01 and 117A.02.

In *General Motors' (Longhouse's) Application* [1981] R.P.C. 41, an attempt at restoration, on the ground that a letter of withdrawal had been signed by someone other than the authorised agent, failed on a finding that the signatory had acted under an implied authority, see also *Moskovsky Nauchno-Issledovatelsky's Application* O/5/88. Nevertheless, it was observed, obiter, by the Comptroller in *Tokan Kogyo's Application* [1985] R.P.C. 244 that, if an application has wrongly been treated by the UK-IPO as having been withdrawn, the withdrawal might, and indeed should, be cancelled. This has in fact been done in a few instances, see §123.62.

If an application is withdrawn after its publication, and if a dispute about entitlement to the grant of a patent on the application has been referred to the Comptroller under s.8(1), the Comptroller still has the power under s.8(3)(c) to allow a new application to be filed. This procedure contrasts with that under the EPC in which r.15 of the EPC forbids withdrawal of an application for a European patent whilst proceedings concerning the entitlement to the grant are pending.

Practice under Section 14

Scope of discussion on practice under section 14

14.44   As stated in §14.09, the MOPP is available on the UK-IPO website: *http://www.ipo.gov.uk.*

It contains detailed and updated information on the way in which UK-IPO operates under s.14. However, for convenience, §§14.45–14.50 below summarise the operation of practice under s.14. Filing of an application may also be made by electronic means under the terms of directions made under s.124A, for which see §14.06 above. When these directions are used, care should be taken to see that they are strictly followed, see the commentary on s.124A. The Patents Forms are downloadable from the UK-IPO website.

Also, the manner in which the documents can be filed at the UK-IPO (including the facilities for fax filing) is discussed in §123.88. For the hours of operation of the Office, see §120.04. For the filing of documents outside these hours, see §120.05. For the payment of fees, see §123.64. Matters which can be dealt with after the initial filing are discussed in the commentary on s.15, see particularly §15.12 (times for filing claims and abstract and for paying search fee), as also are the filing and content of divisional applications (see §§15.18–15.24 and 15.38 and 15.42). Any priority claim should normally be made at the time of filing the application, though it is now possible to make a late priority claim and/or to add a priority claim and even to file a priority-claiming application after the usual 12-month period under ss.5(2A) to (2C), as discussed further in §14.15 and the commentary on s.5 at §5.18.

Filing of an application

14.45   The request form PF 1 should be personally signed by each of the applicants, or by an agent acting on their behalf, see §14.11.

In completing the necessary forms for filing, each applicant should be identified by a full and proper name and a permanent address given. In the case of an individual applicant, the surname and forename(s) are to be given separately on the request (PF 1), with the surname underlined. On the Statement of Inventorship (PF 7) the surname or family name of the or each inventor should likewise be underlined. It is not required to state the nationality of an individual applicant or inventor. When the applicant is a legal entity, the proper full legal name should be given. When the applicant is a corporate body, the country and, if relevant, the state of incorporation must be stated below the company name. Note that, e.g. for a United States or Australian corporation, the state of incorporation may be different from that given in its address. Where the applicant has a trading name different from its proper legal name, this trading name should not be given. Applications filed on behalf of a government department are filed in the name of the Secretary of State or the appropriate Minister, each stated as such. Where there are multiple applicants and/or inventors, the required information should be continued on separate sheets as necessary and this fact recorded in the relevant spaces provided on PF 1. The designation "Republic of China" should not be used in an address given for an applicant or inventor resident in Taiwan.

Space is provided on PF 1 for insertion of the applicant's ADP number where known. It is highly desirable that an identifying reference be used on at least PF 1, particularly when similar applications are filed at the same time. The MOPP indicates that this reference or other identification may be lightly written in pencil on the back of any drawings, but neither the applicant's nor the agent's name nor the title of the invention should appear on the face of the drawings.

For applications filed on or after January 1, 2005, in accordance with r.9(1)(c) and r.9(4), an English translation (which no longer normally needs to be a verified translation) of a priority application that is not in English or Welsh, or a declaration that the application in suit is a "complete translation" into English of the priority application, will only be required:

"where the matters disclosed in the priority application are relevant to the determination of whether or not an invention, to which the application in suit relates, is new or involves an inventive step".

Where an examiner considers that such a translation or declaration is necessary, a direction will be issued to the applicant and a period for complying with the direction will be specified. See §5.32.

When an application is filed, the UK-IPO issues a filing receipt identifying the application by a number which is a seven digit figure wherein the first two digits indicate the year and the other five digits the sequential number for applications filed in that year. A check digit is also added after a decimal point. This is determined according to the same algorithm used by the EPO. As explained in the *Patents Journal* November 23, 1988, this involves: multiplying each digit from right to left alternatively by 2, 1, 2, 1 etc.; adding the separate resulting digits together; dividing by 10; and subtracting the remainder from 10 to give the check digit. For example, if the base number is 8807000, the digits are respectively multiplied by 2, 1, 2, 1, 2, 1, 2 to give 16, 8, 0, 7, 0, 0, 0, the sum of which is 22 which, after division by 10, leaves a remainder of 2 and consequently a check digit of 8.

The agent or applicant should check this filing receipt for accuracy and particularly check if all papers intended to be filed with PF 1 were duly filed, and should see that appropriate diary entries have been made for the dates by which other matters have to be dealt with. One difficulty here is monitoring the date for the filing of PF 10, which is required six months after the publication of the application under s.16(1). However, since this publication should take place on or shortly after 18 months from the earliest declared priority date (as defined in r.3, reprinted at §5.06A), a preliminary diary entry can be made based on this 18-month date.

The title

A title must be stated on the request (PF 1), in the specification and also in the abstract. **14.46** At the time of filing, these three titles ought to be identical, but there is no official requirement that this be so and the title may eventually change, for example when the specification is amended during substantive examination. After filing, each may become amended, the examiner having power to amend the title in the abstract as he thinks appropriate (s.14(7), discussed in §14.42). The requirements for the title of the specification are set out in r.12(6) and discussed in §14.14. The title stated on PF 1 is of practical importance, because it is this title that identifies the newly filed application in the *Patents Journal* and the indexes in the British Library. Thus, this should be worded with care if it is not desired to disclose details of the invention prior to publication of the application under s.16. The use of a wholly uninformative title may jeopardise the application, see §14.14. However, it should always be possible to devise a title that is reasonable enough to satisfy the UK-IPO and yet does not disclose information which it is desired should not be published before the rest of the specification.

Formal and Other Requirements

—All Documents

The documents making up the patent application must be in the format prescribed by **14.47** Sch.2 to the Rules (see Sch.2, above), with exceptions for applications filed electronically as discussed further above. The requirements are similar to, though more relaxed than, previous versions of the Rules.

For all documents, Sch.2 Pt 1 requires that all paper must be matt white and of A4 size, must be free from tears and folds and the contents suitable for reproduction, and frames (i.e. lines surrounding any matter) must not be used. Only a single copy of the specification and abstract (and any replacement thereof) need be filed, the previous requirement for duplicate copies having been dropped for all patent applications irrespective of filing date.

The MOPP indicates that "the overriding consideration is that the specification shall be capable of being directly reproduced". As such, all documents shall be reasonably free from deletions and other alterations, overwritings and interlineations and in any event shall be legible. Each application is examined shortly after filing for compliance with Sch.2, and if necessary an official letter is issued setting out what is required and by when. However, textual corrections, additions or deletions are permitted in manuscript provided that these are of a de minimis nature and the manner of their execution does not spoil the appearance of the finished document; for example: deletions should be made by erasure or by visible obliteration in black ink with a straight edge being used for striking out, other than for single letters.

Rule 14(1) (see §14.04 above) requires all wording (including that contained in drawings) in any document contained in a patent application to be in English or Welsh (such documents being the request for grant of a patent; the specification containing the description, the claim or claims, and any drawings; and the abstract). Notwithstanding the requirement to file an application in English or Welsh, an application can qualify for a date of filing if the description (or what appears to be the description) is in a foreign language, providing that the indication that a patent is sought and the identity of the applicant (or the means of contacting him) are in English or Welsh. Where a date of filing is accorded to an application comprising a description in a foreign language, the applicant must be notified of the failure to comply with r.14(1). The Comptroller may refuse the application if the applicant fails to file a description in English or Welsh within two months of such a notification (extendable at the discretion of the Comptroller under r.108(1) together with r.108(5)–(7)). See further §14.20.

If any of these requirements are not met at the time of filing, the terms of r.25(1) make them "formal requirements", and an opportunity of amendment to comply with these requirements must be given, see §15A.06.

—Documents Other Than Drawings

14.48   Schedule 2 Pt 2 to the Rules (reprinted above) sets out specific requirements for all documents other than the drawings (for which, see §14.49). The pages of the description and claims must be numbered consecutively in a single series, though where a sequence listing is set out at the end of the application, it must be numbered consecutively in a separate series. Page numbers must be located at the top or bottom of the page (but not in the margin) in the centre. The minimum margins in any document must be 20mm. The description, claims and abstract must use at least 1.5 line spacing, except where they form part of a translation or a sequence listing. The capital letters in any typeface or font used must be more than 2mm high. The Request for Grant (PF 1), the description, the claims and abstract (and the drawings) must each begin on a new sheet of paper.

It is not necessary to number every fifth line in the description, claims or abstract, as it was prior to March 1987, but line numbering can be helpful and is recommended as it assists in subsequent proceedings. The margins should contain no markings whatsoever and thus page and line numbers, agent's or applicant's references, etc. should not appear within the required margins.

No drawings can be present in the request for grant, the description, claims or abstract (Sch.2 para.19). The claims may contain tables of information only if the Comptroller agrees (Sch.2 para.22).

Pages of new or amended claims for publication under s.16 (for which see §16.01) must be self-explanatory and not rely on instructions in a covering letter, and should preferably be headed "Amendments to the claims". Such pages are checked for formal requirements prior to s.16 publication, but their contents are not otherwise examined until the substantive examination under s.18: *Patents Journal* March 30, 1988.

Conveniently, the first page of the description and claims and the abstract page should be headed "Description", "Claims" and "Abstract" respectively for ease of identification. The EPO has ruled that the claims are not definitively identified by the heading used to introduce them but by their inherent nature, see J 5/87 *PHILLIPS/Number of claims incurring fees* OJ EPO 1987, 295; [1987] E.P.O.R. 316. Somewhat to the contrary, the EPO has also held that individual statements of desired protection will rank as "claims" only if presented as such (J 5/88 *NEORX/Claims fees* OJ EPO 1990, 445; [1991] E.P.O.R. 76) and a specification has been allowed to proceed with a set of "clauses" preceding the claims and setting out preferred features of the invention, the EPO taking the view that such "clauses" could not be regarded as claims per se (T 490/90 *ARI/Clauses* [1998] E.P.O.R. 44).

The listing in specifications of sequences of nucleotides or amino acids to indicate a DNA or protein structure is now, effectively, the subject of special stringent presentation requirements, for which see §76A.19.

—Drawings

Schedule 2 Pt 3 to the Rules (reprinted above) sets out specific requirements for **14.49** drawings. The main criterion is that any drawing must be produced in such a manner that it would still be clear if it were reduced in size by linear reduction to two thirds of its original size (Sch.2 para.18). Thus, drawings must use black lines and must not be shaded (Sch.2 para.15). Colouring should not be used. Cross-hatching should be used to indicate cross-sections (Sch.2 para.16). Capital letters of text in a drawing must be more than 3mm high (Sch.2 para.20).

The margin requirements for the drawings of an application are different from those for other documents. For drawings, the top and left side margins are required to be at least 20mm, the right side margin at least 15mm and the bottom margin at least 10mm (Sch.2 para.11). By convention, these margins are those when the sheet of the drawings is viewed in "portrait", i.e. with the short edges of the sheet at the top and bottom and the long edges of the sheet to the left and right, irrespective of the orientation on the page of the figures themselves. If a figure is placed sideways on the sheet, it is suggested that the top of the figure be to the left of the sheet for consistency with r.46(2)(h) of the EPC and r.11.13(j) of the PCT and by convention.

The drawings themselves, i.e. the individual figures, must be numbered consecutively in a single series (Sch.2 para.12), and are typically numbered in Arabic numerals, i.e. Fig.1, Fig.2, etc. The drawings must begin on a new sheet of paper (Sch.2 para.13) and the pages of the drawings must be numbered consecutively in a single series (Sch.2 para.14), and are thus to be numbered separately from the other pages of the specification. By convention, the pages of the drawings are numbered with the sheet number and the total number of sheets separated by a stroke or slash (e.g. 1/5, 2/5, etc.), typically top centre on the sheet when viewed in portrait. All reference signs in drawings must have a counterpart in the description or claims (Sch.2 para.21).

Given that the drawings may be reproduced in a different size from that originally filed, no scale should be specified in words and no dimensions should be given in the drawings, see the MOPP. Any scale or other reference for making measurement must be represented diagrammatically (Sch.2 para.17).

Whilst no longer a requirement of the Rules, the following are still required under the corresponding provisions of the EPC and PCT (EPC r.46 and PCT r.11.13 respectively) and referred to in the MOPP and may be considered good practice. All numbers, letters and reference signs should be presented in a simple and clear manner, without brackets, circles or inverted commas. The Latin alphabet and, where customary, the Greek alphabet should be used for the lettering of drawings. The drawings should not use extensive textual matter, though a few short keywords, such as "water", "steam", "open", "closed", "section on AB", etc. may be included. (Somewhat ironically, it is not unusual for examiners in the US Patent and Trademark Office to require that *more* text be added to drawings in a US patent application.) The term "drawings" here includes flow sheets and diagrams.

—Other Requirements

Schedule 2 Pt 4 to the Rules (reprinted above) sets out other requirements for **14.50** documents. As noted in §14.49, reference signs in drawings must have a counterpart in the description or claims (Sch.2 para.21). As noted in §14.48, the claims may contain tables of information only if the Comptroller agrees (Sch.2 para.22). The terminology and any references used must be consistent throughout the application (Sch.2 para.23). Only technical terms, signs and symbols which are generally accepted in the field may be used (Sch.2 para.25).

As noted in §14.22, Sch.2 para.24 requires that units of measurements shall be expressed, at least in the alternative, in "standard international units of measurement". This may normally be taken to mean metric units. The MOPP refers to the EC Units of Measurement Directive (Council Directive 80/181/EEC, as amended by Council Directive 89/617/EEC and Directive 1999/103/EC of the European Parliament and of the Council of 24 January 2000) and indicates that no objection should be raised against the use of non-SI metric units. The MOPP indicates that temperatures should normally be given in degrees Celsius, except that the Kelvin scale may be used as customary for cryogenic temperatures and colour temperatures. Units said to be recognised in international practice and complying with the relevant EPC Rule are set out in the EPO Guidelines as an Annex to C–II.

Voluntary withdrawal

14.51   As noted above, withdrawal has effect from the date of receipt at the UK-IPO, rather than the date on which withdrawal takes action upon it (*Siemens Medical System's Patent* O/63/00). To avoid publication of the application, the withdrawal must have effect before the preparations for publication have been completed, see §16.10.

Withdrawal may be by letter, sent by post or fax in the usual way. Alternatively, (and the IPO website notice recommends this) in accordance with directions given under s.124A, withdrawal may be effected by e-mail to *withdraw@ipo.gov.uk*. E-mail withdrawal requests should be titled (i.e. the subject line should be) "Withdrawal of patent application number GBYYXXXXX.X" and include in the main body of the message a clear statement of withdrawal and an indication that the sender is authorised to make the withdrawal. This e-mail address should not be used for other proceedings under the Act or any other correspondence relating to business carried out by the UK-IPO. The e-mail should not include any attachment and should be in plain text (RFC822-compliant). The UK-IPO notice indicates that messages in MS-TNEF/RTF or HTML formats and messages that are encrypted or digitally signed will not be accepted. An email reply will be sent and it should not be assumed that the withdrawal has had effect until this is received. (Indeed, the MOPP indicates that the request cannot be treated as being delivered unless this acknowledgement has been sent.) This e-mail reply will be followed by written confirmation from the UK-IPO. The email will be given the time and date when it enters the UK-IPO internal e-mail system which may be later than the time of actual receipt. To ensure withdrawal before publication of an application, such an email must be received not later than 23:59 on the day before preparations for publication are deemed to be complete (see §16.10 also); otherwise, publication will occur.

If it is desired to withdraw an application in time to prevent publication under s.16, the request must reach the Office by 23:59 on the day before preparations for publication ("PPC date") are complete. Such requests should be marked "URGENT—PUBLICATION IMMINENT". If requested, the Office will supply the PPC date.

In view of the provisions of subs.(9) (discussed in §14.43) that any voluntary withdrawal of an application may not be revoked (unless the withdrawal was made in error), only a clear and unqualified statement of withdrawal is regarded by the UK-IPO as effective in this respect. Statements which fall short of this (e.g. that it is not intended to seek substantive examination, or that it is not intended to respond to an examination report) have no effect, and an application in such as case is treated as withdrawn or refused only when and if this becomes appropriate in due course. If it appears that withdrawal is being sought in order to avoid publication and the statement is not unequivocal, or the applicant or agent purports to effect a conditional withdrawal, the MOPP indicates that the UK-IPO will request the filing of an unqualified statement of withdrawal, failing which the application will not be treated as withdrawn.

Thus, if an application complies with the requirements of the Act and Rules, then, in the absence of an unequivocal and unconditional written statement of withdrawal, it will proceed to publication and in due course to grant.

The EPO also requires that the request for withdrawal is unambiguous For example, see J 11/80 OJ EPO 1981, 141. Likewise, in J 11/87 *DORIS/Abandonment* OJ EPO 1988, 367; [1989] E.P.O.R. 54, and in J 7/87 *SCHWARZ ITALIA/Abandonment* OJ EPO 1988, 422; [1989] E.P.O.R. 91, statements that "the Applicant has decided to abandon" the application were held to be equivocal because it was not clear whether this was a statement of present action or of future intent. However, in J 6/86 *RIKER/Withdrawal* OJ EPO 1988, 124; [1988] E.P.O.R. 277, the statement that the "Applicant wishes to abandon the application" was held to be unambiguous in the absence of any circumstances suggesting that the statement be qualified; and, in J 15/86 *AUSONIA/Withdrawal of application* OJ EPO 1988, 417; [1989] E.P.O.R. 152, a statement of withdrawal, which contained a request for confirmation, and an enquiry on possible reimbursement of fees, was held to be a firm one. The EPO has allowed retraction of a withdrawal made erroneously by an agent as a correction under EPC r.88, though only because publication of the withdrawal in the OJ EPO had not then been made (J 10/87 *INLAND STEEL/Retraction of withdrawal* [1989] E.P.O.R. 437, abridged OJ EPO 1989, 323), but because s.14(9) is in different terms to art.79(3) of the EPC and r.88 of the EPC, this decision does not apply under the 1977 Act (*Spectra-Tech's Application*, [1999] R.P.C. 187).

However, unlike the UK-IPO approach, it is possible to make a conditional withdrawal of a European patent application. Suitable examples include making the withdrawal conditional on the application not being published or on the refund of some or all of the substantive examination fee.

SECTION 15

Date of filing application

15.—(1) Subject to the following provisions of this Act, the date of filing an application for a patent shall be taken to be the earliest date on which documents filed at the Patent Office to initiate the application satisfy the following conditions—

    (a) the documents indicate that a patent is sought;

    (b) the documents identify the person applying for a patent or contain information sufficient to enable that person to be contacted by the Patent Office; and

    (c) the documents contain either—

        (i) something which is or appears to be a description of the invention for which a patent is sought; or

        (ii) a reference, complying with the relevant requirements of rules, to an earlier relevant application made by the applicant or a predecessor in title of his.

(2) It is immaterial for the purposes of subsection (1)(c)(i) above—

    (a) whether the thing is in, or is accompanied by a translation into, a language accepted by the Patent Office in accordance with rules;

    (b) whether the thing otherwise complies with the other provisions of this Act and with any relevant rules.

(3) Where documents filed at the Patent Office to initiate an application for a patent satisfy one or more of the conditions specified in subsection (1) above, but do not satisfy all those conditions, the comptroller shall as soon as practicable after the filing of those documents notify the applicant of what else must be filed in order for the application to have a date of filing.

15.01

(4) Where documents filed at the Patent Office to initiate an application for a patent satisfy all the conditions specified in subsection (1) above, the comptroller shall as soon as practicable after the filing of the last of those documents notify the applicant of—

    (a) the date of filing the application, and

    (b) the requirements that must be complied with, and the periods within which they are required by this Act or rules to be complied with, if the application is not to be treated as having been withdrawn.

(5) Subsection (6) below applies where—

    (a) an application has a date of filing by virtue of subsection (1) above;

    (b) within the prescribed period the applicant files at the Patent Office

        (i) a drawing, or

        (ii) part of the description of the invention for which a patent is sought, and

    (c) that drawing or that part of the description was missing from the application at the date of filing.

(6) Unless the applicant withdraws the drawing or the part of the description filed under subsection (5)(b) above ("the missing part") before the end of the prescribed period—

    (a) the missing part shall be treated as included in the application; and

    (b) the date of filing the application shall be the date on which the missing part is filed at the Patent Office.

(7) Subsection (6)(b) above does not apply if—

    (a) on or before the date which is the date of filing the application by virtue of subsection (1) above a declaration is made under section 5(2) above in or in connection with the application;

    (b) the applicant makes a request for subsection (6)(b) above not to apply; and

    (c) the request complies with the relevant requirements of rules and is made within the prescribed period.

(8) Subsections (6) and (7) above do not affect the power of the comptroller under section 117(1) below to correct an error or mistake.

(9) Where, after an application for a patent has been filed and before the patent is granted—

    (a) a new application is filed by the original applicant or his successor in title in accordance with rules in respect of any part of the matter contained in the earlier application, and

    (b) the conditions mentioned in subsection (1) above are satisfied in relation to the new application (without the new application contravening section 76 below),

the new application shall be treated as having, as its date of filing, the date of filing the earlier application.

(10) Where an application has a date of filing by virtue of this section, the application shall be treated as having been withdrawn if any of the following applies—

    (a) the applicant fails to file at the Patent Office, before the end of the prescribed period, one or more claims and the abstract;

(b) where a reference to an earlier relevant application has been filed as mentioned in subsection (1)(c)(ii) above—

(i) the applicant fails to file at the Patent Office, before the end of the prescribed period, a description of the invention for which a patent is sought,

(ii) the applicant fails to file at the Patent Office, before the end of the prescribed period, a copy of the application referred to, complying with the relevant requirements of rules;

(c) the applicant fails to pay the application fee before the end of the prescribed period;

(d) the applicant fails, before the end of the prescribed period, to make a request for a search under section 17 below and pay the search fee.

(11) In this section "relevant application" has the meaning given by section 5(5) above.

Notes

1. Section 15 was replaced by the form set out above by the Regulatory Reform (Patents) Order (SI 2004/2357) ("RRO") with effect from January 1, 2005. The former wording of the section has no current relevance except (under arts 20–22 of that Order) the previous version of s.15 (as well as the provisions of ss.5, 14(1)(b), 17, 18, 72, 76, 78 and 130(1)) continued to apply to: applications which were pending before that date, i.e. with a filing date on or before December 31, 2004, see the Rules Sch.6 para.5. As these transitioned provisions seem now to have no further effect, except perhaps for applications placed under a secrecy order made under s.22, they are merely here noted without further explanation.

2. The relevant rules under s.15 are r.12 (reprinted in §14.02 and discussed in §14.10) and rr.17–22 (see below). Rule 108 (Extension of time limits), reprinted in §123.25, and discussed in §123.69–123.75, is also relevant as mentioned in the commentary below.

Rule 17—References under section 15(1)(c)(ii)

17.—(1) A reference made under section 15(1)(c)(ii) must include—   **15.02**

(a) the date of filing of the earlier relevant application;

(b) its application number; and

(c) the country it was filed in or in respect of.

(2) Subject to paragraph (3), the copy of the application provided under section 15(10)(b)(ii) must—

(a) be duly certified by the authority with which it was filed or otherwise verified to the satisfaction of the comptroller; and

(b) where it is in a language other than English or Welsh, be accompanied by—

(i) a translation into English of that application; or

(ii) a declaration that the description filed under sub-paragraph (i) of section 15(10)(b) is a complete and accurate translation into English of the description contained in the application provided under sub paragraph (ii) of that provision.

(3) Where the application or a copy of the application is available to the comptroller it shall, for the purposes of section 15(10)(b)(ii), be treated as having been filed in accordance with rules.

Rule 18—Missing Parts

15.03   **18.**—(1) The period prescribed for the purposes of section 15(5)(b) and (6) is the period beginning [with] immediately after the date of filing of the application for a patent and ending with the date of the preliminary examination.

(2) But where the applicant is notified under section 15A(9) that a drawing or part of the description of the invention has been found to be missing, the period prescribed for the purposes of section 15(5)(b) and (6) shall be the period of two months starting on the date of the notification.

(3) An applicant may only withdraw a missing part by giving written notice to the comptroller.

(4) A request made under section 15(7)(b) must—

    (a) be made in writing;

    (b) include sufficient information to identify where in the priority application the contents of the document filed under section 15(5)(b) were included; and

    (c) be made before the end of the period prescribed for the purpose of section 15(5)(b).

(5) Any request under section 15(7)(b) shall be considered never to have been made where—

    (a) the priority application does not contain every missing part filed under section 15(5); or

    (b) the applicant fails, before the end of the relevant period to furnish to the comptroller copies of all earlier relevant applications—

        (i) duly certified by the authority with which they were filed, or

        (ii) otherwise verified to the satisfaction of the comptroller

(6) But paragraph (5)(b) does not apply in respect of an earlier relevant application where that application or a copy of the application is available to the comptroller.

(7) For the purposes of paragraph 5(b) the relevant period is—

    (a) sixteen months beginning [with] immediately after the declared priority date; or

    (b) if it expires earlier, the period of four months beginning with the date the request was made under section 15(7)(b).

Note. The amendments are made as a consequence of The Patents (Amendment) Rules 2011 (SI 2011/2052) that came into force on October 1, 2011.

Rule 19—New applications filed as mentioned in section 15(9)

15.04   **19.**—(1) A new application for a patent may be filed as mentioned in section 15(9)—

    (a) before the end of the relevant period; or

(b) if earlier, before the earlier application is terminated or withdrawn.

(2) Such an application must include a statement that it is filed as mentioned in section 15(9).

(3) For the purposes of this rule the relevant period is—

(a) where an applicant is notified under section 18(4) that his earlier application complies with the requirements of the Act and these Rules, two months beginning [with] immediately after the date of that notification; or

(b) in any other case, the period ending three months before the compliance date of the earlier application.

Note. The amendments are made as a consequence of The Patents (Amendment) Rules 2011 (SI 2011/2052) that came into force on October 1, 2011.

Rule 20—New applications under sections 8(3), 12(6) and 37(4)

20.—(1) The period prescribed for filing a new application under section 8(3) or section 12(6) is the relevant period.   **15.05**

(2) A new application for a patent may be filed under section 37(4) before the end of the relevant period.

(3) For the purposes of this rule the relevant period is—

(a) where the comptroller's decision to make an order under those provisions is not appealed, three months beginning [with] immediately after the date on which the order was made; or

(b) where that decision is appealed, three months beginning [with] immediately after the date on which the appeal was finally disposed of.

(4) But the comptroller may, if he thinks fit, shorten the relevant period after giving the parties such notice and subject to such conditions as the comptroller may direct.

Note. The amendments are made as a consequence of The Patents (Amendment) Rules 2011 (SI 2011/2052) that came into force on October 1, 2011.

Rule 21—Extensions for new applications

21.—(1) Where a new application is filed—   **15.06**

(a) the period prescribed for the purposes of section 13(2) is—

(i) two months beginning [with] immediately after its initiation date, or

(ii) if it expires later, the period prescribed by rule 10(3); and

(b) the relevant period for the purposes of rule 8 is—

(i) two months beginning [with] immediately after its initiation date, or

(ii) if it expires later, the period specified in rule 8(5),

and the reference in rule 10(3) to the date of filing of the application is a reference to the date of filing of the earlier application.

(2) But where the new application is filed less than six months before the compliance date—

(a) the period prescribed for the purposes of section 13(2) is the period ending with its initiation date; and

(b) the relevant period for the purposes of rule 8 is the period ending with its initiation date.

(3) The second requirement in Schedule 1 must be complied with—

(a) on the initiation date; or

(b) if it expires later, before the end of the relevant period specified in paragraph 3(3) of that Schedule.

Note. The amendments are made as a consequence of The Patents (Amendment) Rules 2011 (SI 2011/2052) that came into force on October 1, 2011.

Rule 22—Periods prescribed for the purposes of sections 15(10) and 17(1)

15.07   **22.**—(1) The period prescribed for the purposes of section 15(10)(a) and (b)(i) is the relevant period.

(2) Subject to rules 58(4), 59(3) and 68(3), the period prescribed for the purposes of section 15(10)(c) and (d) and section 17(1) is the relevant period.

(3) The period prescribed for the purpose of section 15(10)(b)(ii) is four months beginning [with] immediately after the date of filing of the application.

(4) But paragraphs (1) to (3) do not apply to a new application.

(5) In relation to a new application—

(a) the period prescribed for the purposes of section 15(10)(a), (b)(i), (c) and (d) and section 17(1) is—

(i) two months beginning [with] immediately after the initiation date, or

(ii) if it expires later, the relevant period; and

(b) the period prescribed for the purposes of section 15(10)(b)(ii) is—

(i) two months beginning [with] immediately after its initiation date, or

(ii) if it expires later, the period of four months beginning [with] immediately after the date of filing of the earlier application,

and the reference in paragraph (7) to the date of filing of the application is a reference to the date of filing of the earlier application.

(6) But where the new application is filed less than six months before the compliance date, the period prescribed for the purposes of section 15(10)(a) to (d) and section 17(1) is the period ending with its initiation date.

(7) For the purposes of this rule the relevant period is—

(a) where there is no declared priority date, twelve months beginning [with] immediately after the date of filing of the application; or

(b) where there is a declared priority date—

(i) twelve months beginning [with] immediately after the declared priority date, or

(ii) if it expires later, the period of two months beginning [with] immediately after the date of filing of the application.

Note. The amendments are made as a consequence of The Patents (Amendment) Rules 2011 (SI 2011/2052) that came into force on October 1, 2011.

COMMENTARY ON SECTION 15

Scope of the section

Section 15 relates to the date of filing of a patent application (s.14 deals more generally **15.08** with the making of a patent application). The current form of s.15 was introduced with effect from January 1, 2005, for compliance with the Patent Law Treaty.

Subsections (1)–(4) deal with the conditions necessary to have a date of filing assigned to an application. Two possibilities are available:

(a) filing documents including at least a description of the invention for which a patent is sought; or

(b) filing by reference to an earlier relevant application made by the applicant or its predecessor in title for which see §15.12. By subs.(11) such an application may be an application under the Act, or an International or European application designating the UK, or an application filed in a convention country, for which see §5.29.

Subsections (5)–(8) allow for the possible correction of the originally filed documents if these are missing a drawing or part of the description of the invention. This discussed in §15.13.

Subsection (9) provides for the filing of a "new application", being either: (a) a divisional application in which subject-matter has been divided out of an earlier-filed application (the parent application); or (b) a replacement application, filed under any of ss.8(3), 12(6) or 37(4) following a decision that an earlier filed application has been made by an applicant who did not have entitlement to file it. In either case, the new application, if validly made, is to be treated as having the date of filing of the earlier application. These matters are discussed in §§15.18, 15.34 and 15.38–15.42, below.

Subsection (10) deals with the actions needed to prevent the application "from being treated as withdrawn", and is discussed in §§15.14–15.15 below. The relevant time periods, and the possibilities for extension, are discussed in §§15.15–15.17, below.

A useful summary and information as to the approach of the UK-IPO to actions required under s.15 can be found in the MOPP.

The procedures for filing applications under the EPC or PCT are generally not now dealt with in the present work.

Definition of the "date of filing"

The term "date of filing" is defined in s.130(1) in relation to an application under the **15.09** Act with reference to s.15. It was held by the Patents Court in *Antiphon's Application* [1984] R.P.C. 1 (in response to an argument that s.15 did not apply to a so-called "formal" application meeting the requirements of s.14) that this definition applies to any application for a patent under the Act, however initiated.

Under s.15(1), the "date of filing of an application for a patent" is the earliest date on which documents filed at the UK-IPO satisfy the three minimal conditions set out in §15.10.

The terms of subs.(1) are further subject to the provisions for service to, and the hours of business of, the UK-IPO, as discussed in the commentaries on ss.119 and 120.

Under certain circumstances the "date of filing" will be different from the date at which documents initiating the application are lodged at the UK-IPO. The term "initiation date" is defined in r.2 (reprinted in §123.04) as the date on which a new application is initiated by documents mentioned in s.15(1) being filed at the UK-IPO. This term is particularly useful in relation to applications of the second and third types discussed below.

First, if the documents initially lodged at the UK-IPO do not meet the requirements of s.15(1) the date of filing will be when the remaining required documents are provided. This is made clear in s.15(1).

Secondly, where the application is a "new application under s.15(9), that is, a divisional application or a replacement application under any of ss.8(3), 12(6) and 37(4), it will take the date of filing of the earlier (parent) application, see the final clause of s.15(9).

Thirdly, where missing drawings or description are provided late, the application may be redated so that its date of filing is the date on which the missing description or drawings is provided. This is discussed under §15.13 below.

The date of filing of an application meant for a European Patent (UK) is defined in s.78(1), subject to s.78(3)(c) and discussed in §78.04; and the date of filing of a converted European application is defined in s.81(3)(a), discussed in §81.07. The date of filing of an international application (UK) is normally defined by s.89B(1)(a) as the date of filing to be applied under the Act (see §89B.04); but if an international date of filing is refused and the international application is nevertheless allowed to enter the United Kingdom national phase, then s.89(5) applies, see §89.30.

It should also be noted that, in the case of any other application, i.e. an application other than one for a United Kingdom patent, or a European patent (UK), or an international application (UK), the date of filing is defined by s.130(1) to be the date which, under the laws of the country where the application was made or in accordance with a treaty or convention to which that country is a party, is to be treated as the date of filing that application or is equivalent to the date of filing an application in that country (whatever the outcome of that application). This wording is not unlike that used in art.4A of the Paris Convention (Stockholm Text). This definition includes the date of filing of applications under the EPC and PCT when the countries designated do not include the United Kingdom.

Documents necessary to establish a date of filing

15.10   To establish a date of filing the supplied document(s) must satisfy the UK-IPO of three minimal conditions:

- that a patent is sought;

- that the person applying for the patent is sufficiently identified for contact to be made by the UK-IPO; and

- that the submitted document either (i) contains something which is or appears to be a description of the invention for which a patent is sought; or (ii) contains a reference (complying with the rules) to an earlier relevant application made by the applicant or its predecessor in title.

No form or fee is required for an application to be given a date of filing.

The submission(s) must be made in documentary form, so that any statement made only verbally has no effect.

The MOPP and the *Formalities Manual* contain useful discussions of the minimum documents necessary to establish a date of filing. In particular, the MOPP states that the indication that a patent is sought may be informal but must be in English or Welsh. It also indicates that a telephone number or e-mail address rather than a postal address is sufficient contact information for an applicant, but that contact information is needed for each applicant. It indicates that the name of a firm as applicant is sufficient for a date of filing to be given. However, under r.12(2) and (3), the applicant's name and address must be provided within two months of notification that they are required, or the application may be refused (see §14.10).

No formal specification is needed to be given a date of filing. There are two options for the description of the invention. First, under subs.(1)(c)(i), a description of the invention may be filed. This must contain at least a small amount of technical information. The description need not necessarily be in English or Welsh. However, under r.12(8) and (9), an English or Welsh translation of the description must be provided within two months of notification that it is required, or the application may be refused (see §14.10 and also r.14(1)).

Second, under subs.(1)(c)(ii), a reference may be made to an earlier relevant application, see §15.12.

Where the provisions of subs.(1)(c)(ii) are relied on, the reference to the earlier relevant application must include (under r.17(1)):

- the date of filing of the earlier relevant application;

- its application number; and

- the country it was filed in or in respect of.

When the documents submitted do not satisfy all the conditions for a date of filing to be accorded, the Comptroller shall, as soon as practicable, notify the applicant of what else still needs to be submitted in order for the application to be given a date of filing (subs.(3)).

When these minimal conditions have been met to the satisfaction of the Comptroller, he notifies the applicant of the date of filing which he has assigned (subs.(4)(a)) and this date then becomes the official date of filing.

Applications filed initially under the EPC or PCT

15.11

The conversion of European patent applications to UK patent applications is dealt with under s.81. The treatment of international applications as United Kingdom patent applications is discussed under ss.89, 89A and 89B. The prosecution of international applications for patents (UK) before the UK Patent Office is also discussed under s.89A, see the commentaries on these respective sections.

Filing by reference to an earlier relevant application (subs.(1)(c)(ii))

15.12

As explained under §15.10, subs.(1)(c)(ii) provides for filing by reference to an earlier relevant application as an alternative to providing a description of the invention by the date of filing.

Under subs.(11), and the terms of s.5(5), the relevant application can be an international application for a patent UK being entered into the UK national phase (under s.89A(3), and discussed in §§89A.08 and 89A.35). The earlier relevant application will typically be an application from which priority is claimed, but need not be.

There appear to be no limits as to the permissible period between the dates of filing of the earlier relevant application and the later application which refers to it. In particular, there is no requirement that the later application be filed within the 12–month period for claiming priority from the earlier relevant application. However, if published, the earlier relevant application will of course constitute prior art against the later application.

A description must be filed subsequently (s.15(10)(b)(i)), and must not add subject-matter to the content of the earlier relevant application (s.76(1A)). It is not necessary for the description to be identically worded to the description of the earlier relevant application. For the relevant time period, see §15.15.

Section 15(10)(b)(ii) and r.17(2) require a copy of the earlier relevant application to be filed which:

- must be duly certified or verified; and

- if not in English or Welsh, must be accompanied by a translation into English or a declaration that the description of the earlier relevant application. This is also discussed in §14.20, which notes the reference in r.17(2)(b) to English but not Welsh.

Rule 17(3) provides that, where a copy of the earlier relevant application is available to the Comptroller, it shall be treated for the purposes of subs.(10)(b)(ii) as having been filed as required.

The requirement for a certified copy of the earlier relevant application is a separate requirement from the requirement to provide a description, and the MOPP makes clear that the certified copy of the earlier application cannot serve as the description for the application itself. However, the *Formalities Manual* indicates that a single certified copy may serve as priority document and as copy of the earlier relevant application. For the relevant time period, see §15.15.

For the situation where a divisional application is filed by reference to an earlier relevant application, see §§15.33 and 15.39.

Missing parts of documents (subss.(5)–(8) and r.18)

15.13   Subs.(5) deals with "missing parts" of the description or drawings that should have been, but apparently were not, included in the description provided, and which are supplied later. Rule 18 (see §15.03 above) deals with this situation.

The MOPP indicates that to be treated as missing the parts must not be present at all on filing. It is not possible, for example, to replace a drawing which was already present under these provisions.

Missing parts may be identified either by the UK-IPO or by the applicant. The MOPP indicates that the UK-IPO Documents Reception will check for missing parts, although it is not required to do so. Where the UK-IPO identifies missing parts, it will notify the applicant. The notification may be either part of a formal preliminary examination report (s.15A(4)) or a separate notification (s.15A(9)(b)). It may be included in the notification of a date of filing and outstanding requirements (under subs.(4)(a) and (b)).

The MOPP indicates that parts will only be considered as missing when this is evidently the case. That may be for example because: there is an inconsistency between the pages listed in the request and those of the specification; there is a problem with the specification itself e.g. it refers to a drawing which is not present or it does not follow from page to page.

The applicant can choose not to supply the missing part, but this may cause difficulties, for example with sufficiency under s.14 or basis for amendment under s.76.

Once a missing part has been supplied, the applicant can proceed in various ways:

- the applicant can have the application redated to the date on which the missing part was supplied (subs.(6));

- the applicant can withdraw the missing part and retain the original date of filing, but without the missing part being included in the application (subs.(6)); or

- the applicant can supply the missing part and rely on the priority document as a basis for including it in the application while retaining the original date of filing (subs.(7)).

The applicant often seeks to withdraw the missing part to avoid re-dating of the application. The missing part must be withdrawn in writing (subs.(3)). If the missing part is not withdrawn, the new date of filing is likely to cause any claimed priority date to be lost because the new date of filing will in most cases be outside the generally inextensible 12-month priority period specified in s.5(2) and (2A). The possibility of using subss.5(2B) and (2C) is unlikely to be possible or effective in these circumstances. However, it might be possible to have the application redated without losing the priority claim where the missing parts were filed within a day or so after the original filing so that the new date of filing was still within the priority period, or where the priority-claiming application was filed early in the priority period. Loss of the original date of filing (and possibly the priority claim) may cause claims to become invalid for lack of novelty or inventive step over prior art made available to the public before that new date of filing. The applicant must decide whether to accept redating, balancing the risk of further prior art being found against the risk of the specification being insufficient or without adequate basis for amendment if the missing parts are not reinstated.

Redating of a divisional application, if permitted, does not affect its date of filing as this is based on the parent application. However, the initiation date is redated. This may mean that the divisional application is considered to have been initiated outside the r.19 period, in which case it will not be validly filed unless a discretionary extension of time can be obtained (see the *Formalities Manual*).

Where it is possible to rely on the priority application under subs.(7), this is likely to be a better option than the alternatives under subs.(6). To rely on the priority application, a request must be made under subs.(7)(b) to avoid redating under subs.(6)(b). The terms for compliance with subs.(7)(b) are set out in r.18(4)–(7). The request must:

- be made in writing (r.18(4)(a));

- include sufficient information to identify where in the priority document the missing parts were included (r.18(4)(b)); and

- be filed before the end of the prescribed period (see below).

The priority application must contain every missing part (r.18(5)(a)). The usual period for supplying the priority documents (unless available to the Comptroller under r.112) of 16 months from the declared priority date (under r.8) is limited to four months from the date of the request to rely on the priority document if this expires earlier (r.18(5)(b), (6) and (7)).

Any supply or withdrawal of missing parts or request to rely on a priority document must be made by the end of the prescribed period under r.18(1) and (2). Under r.18(1), the prescribed period is from the date of filing up to the end of the preliminary examination under s.15A. However, where notification of missing parts is given under s.15A(9), the period is limited to two months beginning with the date of the notification (r.18(2)). For the possibility of extensions of the periods relating to missing parts, see §15.17.

It should be noted that (under subs.(8)) subss.(6) and (7) discussed above do not affect the power of the Comptroller under s.117(1) to correct an error or mistake. This is discussed in the commentary on that section. The MOPP indicates that a request for correction can be made with a request under s.15(5)–(7) in the alternative as a fallback position. Requests to introduce missing drawings by way of correction were considered in *Antiphon's Application* [1984] R.P.C. 1 and *Alps Electric Co.'s Application* BL O/12/90. In the latter case it was argued unsuccessfully that the term "drawing" referred to a sheet, so that a missing figure in a sheet of drawings constituted an error and not a missing drawing.

Where the application with missing parts was an initial filing, a further option is to file a subsequent interim application including the missing parts. At the end of the priority period, applications claiming priority from both these applications can be filed. The second application may itself claim priority from the application including the missing parts if desired (although this will prevent it from being abandoned and refiled under s.5(3)).

An application with withdrawn missing parts will be printed with a notice to that effect. The missing parts will not be published but are available via file inspection.

Time limits after application has been given date of filing

—General

On notifying the applicant of the date of filing, the Comptroller is also required to notify the applicant of the requirements which remain to be complied with, and the relevant time limits, if the application is not to be treated as having been withdrawn (subs.(4)(b) and (10)). **15.14**

When the Office is satisfied that these further conditions have been met, the application is referred to an examiner for a preliminary examination under s.15A.

Rule 22 sets out the principal time limits which must be met for an application which has been given a formal date of filing to be treated and maintained as an admissible application. These time limits may run from the date of filing, the initiation date or the declared priority date, which will normally have been declared in the initiating documents. The time limits are primarily discussed in §15.15 below, §15.17 dealing with the availability of extensions of time.

When the application is a new application (as defined and discussed in §15.08 above, i.e. a divisional or replacement application), there are different time limits which are discussed in §§15.24 onwards below.

§15.16 also mentions some other relevant rules which impose time limits which are required to be met generally under either of ss.15 and 15A and to which subs.(10) does not explicitly apply. These rules also lead to the application being treated as having been withdrawn or being refused if not complied with. Again, §15.17 deals with the availability of extensions of time.

Time limits set by subsection (10) and rule 22

15.15   Listed below are the time limits for specified actions set out in s.15(10) which are required to be carried out within specified time periods ending between the assigned date of filing and the end of the preliminary examination under s.15A. Extensions of the time limits that may be available are explained in §15.17 below.

Special rules apply in the case of a new application (i.e. a divisional or replacement application), to which r.22(4)–(6) particularly apply. These special rules, and the time limits for complying with them, are discussed below under §15.24.

The mandatory actions specified in s.15(10) are divided into five categories as set out in paras (a), (b)(i), (b)(ii), (c) and (d) of s.15(10). The five categories are:

(a) filing of one or more claims and the abstract (as required by rr.12 and 14 (reprinted at §14.02 and §14.04));

(b)(i) where the application was filed by reference to an earlier application, filing of a description of the invention (as also required by r.12 and as discussed in §15.10 above);

(ii) filing a copy of the earlier application and translation if necessary (r.17(2));

(c) paying the application fee, as required by s.14(1A) (reprinted in §14.01 and discussed in §14.18); and

(d) requesting a search and paying the fee for this by the filing of PF 9A (as required under s.17(1) and r.27 (reprinted respectively in §§17.01 and 17.02) and discussed in §17.09.

Rule 22 (reprinted above) specifies the relevant period within which these actions must be performed, failing which the application is to be deemed withdrawn. For all but category (b)(ii), the relevant period period is defined in r.22(7) as follows. Where there is no priority date, the period is 12 months from the date of filing the application. Where there is a declared priority date, the period is 12 months from the priority date, or two months from the date of filing of the application if that expires later. For category (b)(ii), the relevant period is defined in r.22(3) as four months beginning with the date of filing of the application.

If an application is treated as withdrawn under the effect of s.15(10), reinstatement of the withdrawn application under s.20A may be possible.

—Time limits set by other rules for application prosecution

15.16   Below, there is a list of other rules in Pts 1 and 2 of the Patents Rules 2007, as amended by The Patents (Amendment) Rules 2011 (SI 2011/2052), as from October 1, 2011, (Introduction and Applications for patents) which impose time limits for the filing of certain forms and other documents before the UK-IPO during the prosecution of a patent application under the Act. Again, extensions of the time limits that may be available are explained in §15.17 below.

Rules that relate solely to a new application (i.e. a divisional or replacement application) are not included in the present list, but such rules are discussed in §§15.24–15.33. Those paragraphs also discuss the present rules as they apply (usually with some modification) to new applications.

Some of the rules noted in the lists apply with modifications to converted European applications (s.81) or international applications (ss.89, 89A or 89B). These modifications are not mentioned in these lists, but for their effect see the commentaries below on these sections.

In addition to r.22 discussed in §15.15, the following rules specify various time limits within which a specified procedure must be carried out. Possible extension of these limits, and those arising under r.22, are discussed in §15.17.

These rules are:

Rule 5:	(International exhibitions), stating that the prescribed period for providing a statement as mentioned in s.2(4)(b) is normally four months from immediately after the date of filing (r.5(2)).
Rule 6:	(Declaration of priority for the purposes of s.5(2), priority date), stating that the normal position is that such a declaration must "be made at the time of filing the application" (r.6(1)), but such can be made thereafter provided that it is made before the end of the period of 16 months immediately following the date of filing the earlier relevant application, although not if a request for publication under s.16(1) had already been made unless any request for such publication had been withdrawn (r.6(2)(b) and (3)).
Rule 7:	(Request to the Comptroller for permission to make a late priority declaration under s.5(2B)), stating that a request under s.5(2B) is to be made within two months from the end of the 12-month period allowed under s.5(2A)(a) (r.7(1)), or after that, on the initiation date of the application (r.7(5), and (6)).
Rule 8:	(Filing of priority documents to support a declaration under s.5(2)), stating that the relevant period for furnishing the number of the priority application (r.8(1), and also for the filing of a copy of this is 16 months beginning with the declared priority date (r.8(2)).
Rule 9:	(Translation of priority documents), stating that the time limit for the filing of an English translation of the priority application and a declaration that the application in suit is a complete translation into English of the priority application (r.9(4)) is to be set by the Comptroller (but not extending beyond the grant of the patent, r.9(3)).
Rule 10:	(Mention of the inventor), stating that the normal period for filing a statement (under s.13(2) and made on PF 7, to mention the name of the or each inventor) is 16 months beginning (a) where there is no declared priority date on the date of filing of the application, or (b) that date of filing where there is a declared priority date (r.10(3)). Rule 21 applies likewise as regards a "new application" (i.e. a divisional or replacement application). The effects of these two rules are fully discussed in the commentary on s.13 above, and see §15.24 below as regards r.21.
Rule 11:	(Waiving the right to be mentioned), stating that any waiving by an inventor of his right to be named must be made before preparations for publication of the application have been completed by the UK-IPO (r.11(1)).
Rule 12:	(Applications for the grant of patents under ss.14 and 15), referring to some additional time limits other than those mentioned above in relation to r.22, these being: where there has been a notification of the absence of the applicant's name and address (r.12(3)) and/or where a translation is required (r.12(8)), under which the time limit is two months after such notification (r.12(9)).

Rule 13:	(Biological material and sequence listings), referring to the provisions of Sch.1 to the Rules (which is discussed in the commentary on s.125A) as to the furnishing of information indicated as applicable under this rule title. Generally, the Comptroller may specify a time limit for compliance with the requirements specified in this rule and its Schedule where these have not been met at the time of filing, but the Schedule states two particular time limits which have importance in relation to the availability of possible extensions thereof, as indicated in §15.17 below (Sch.1 paras 3(2) and 8(5)).
Rule 18:	(Missing parts), discussed in §15.13 above.
Rules 19–21	these rules relate only to new applications (i.e. divisional or replacement applications) and are discussed in §15.19 and 15.24–15.33 below.
Rule 22:	discussed immediately above this list of other rules.
Rule 24:	(Correcting priority declaration for the purposes of s.5(2)), stating that, where an incorrect priority date has been noted in a preliminary examination report and this notified to the applicant, a corrected priority date is to be provided within two months of that notification.
Rule 27:	(Search under s.17), discussed under s.17 below.
Rule 28:	(Request for substantive examination under s.18), discussed under s.18 below.
Rule 30:	(Period for putting application in order), specifying a compliance period within which an application must be placed in compliance with the Act and Rules. This period is four years and six months beginning with the earliest priority date or the date of filing but with a minimum period of 12 months from the date when the first substantive examination report is sent. A minimum period of three months from any third party observations also applies. This period is explained further and discussed in §15.19 and §15.25 below in relation to its effect upon new applications (i.e. divisional or replacement applications) (r.30(2) and (4)).
Rule 32:	(Reinstatement of applications under s.20A), stating that a request for reinstatement of an application which has been deemed to have been withdrawn must be made within two months from the date when the cause of removal was removed (r.32(2)(a)), or if this period expires earlier, then within 12 months from the date on which the application was terminated (r.32(2)(b)). This is discussed in the commentary on s.20A.

Extension of time for compliance with subsection (10) and time limits set by other rules for prosecution of an application

15.17   The extension of time limits in all proceedings in the UK-IPO is governed by r.108 and Sch.4 to the Rules (reprinted respectively at §§123.25 and 123.26) and which are discussed generally (including details of the relevant forms and fees) in §§123.69–123.75).

Sch.4 does not apply to extensions which can be obtained under r.108(1) under general discretion and without fee and where an extension may be granted if the Comptroller "thinks fit", i.e. an extension can here be granted by the exercise of the Comptroller's discretion, which may be exercised without further limit of time (as discussed in §123.69). Of the rules listed in §15.16, rr.5, 9, 11, 18(2), 20, 24, and 27 are not mentioned in Sch.4.

Part 1 of Sch.4 lists rules specifying periods that are inextensible. Of the rules listed in §15.16, the inextensible rules are rr.6(2)(b) and 7(1) (each discussed in the commentary on s.5); r.32(1) (discussed in the commentary on s.20A); and para.8(5) of Sch.1 under r.13 (discussed in the commentary on s.125A).

Part 2 of Sch.4 lists rules specifying periods for which a first extension as of right of up to two months is obtainable under r.108(2), with further discretionary extension also being possible. Included in Pt 2, but not in Pt 3 (see below), are r.8(1) and (2) (filing of information and priority documents) and r.18(1) (missing parts).

Part 3 of Sch.4 lists rules for which each extension (or further extension) is limited to a period of two months only (under r.108(5)), and for which the extension (or further extension) must be requested within that two-month period (under r.108(7)). Pt 3 rules may also appear in Pt 2, or may appear in Pt 3 only.

Part 3 of Sch.4 is particularly important because it specifies several of the rules discussed or listed in §15.16, i.e. rr.10(3); 12(3) and (9); 19; 21(1)(a) and 21(2)(a); 22; 28; and 30.

In particular, Pt 3 extends to all parts of r.22 (discussed in detail in §15.15). However, only paras (1), (2) and (5) of r.22 are specified in Pt 2 of Sch.4. The effect of this is that an extension of time as of right of two months is available for the time limits specified in paras (1), (2) and (5) of r.22 for filing claims and abstract; for filing a description of an application filed by reference to an earlier application; for paying the application fee; for requesting a search and paying the search fee), but further extensions are subject to the restrictions indicated above for the Pt 3 rules. No extension of time as of right is available for the time limit specified in para.(3) of r.22 (for filing a copy of an earlier relevant application), but extensions may be available subject to the restrictions indicated above for the Pt 3 rules.

Rule 18(1) and r.18(2) each specify periods for dealing with missing parts. Rule 18(1), setting a period ending with the date of preliminary examination, appears in Pt 2 (but not Pt 3) of Sch.4 and the period can thus be extended at least by two months as of right. However, r.18(2), setting a period of two months from notification, does not appear in Sch.4. Thus, any extension of this period is discretionary under r.108(1).

It will be seen (from §15.24 and §15.33 below) that analogous rules exist which are applicable to new applications (i.e. divisional or replacement applications; sometimes under rules mentioned above, but with special provisions for new applications) and that these are also usually rules listed in Pt 3 of Sch.4.

Divisional and replacements applications (subs.(9))

—Definitions of "new application", "divisional application" and "replacement application"

15.18 The term "new application" is defined in r.2 (reprinted in §123.04) as meaning either: (i) an "application filed under section 8(3), 12(6) or 37(4)" (i.e. one which is called herein a "replacement application"); or (ii) one as "mentioned in section 15(9)" (i.e. one which is commonlycalled a "divisional application").

Divisional applications take the date of filing of an earlier "parent application" and contain matter divided out from it. Divisional applications are typically filed to obtain protection for subject-matter which has been deleted from the parent application following an objection of lack of unity of invention under s.14(5)(d) (see §14.40). Divisional applications are discussed in detail below.

Replacement applications are filed following a decision that an earlier-filed application was filed by an applicant who did not have entitlement to do so. Replacement applications also take the date of filing of the earlier-filed application. They are much less commonly filed than divisional applications. Replacement applications are discussed in §15.34 below.

—Divisional applications under EPC and PCT

15.19 EPC divisional procedure is different from that under the Act and was changed with effect from 2010. This procedure is not dealt with here. In *Nokia v IPCom* [2011] EWCA Civ 6 Jacob L.J. commented that the previous EPO "uncontrolled" divisional procedure did not serve the public interest.

The PCT does not provide for the filing of divisional applications on international applications, although art.17(3) of the PCT and r.40 of the PCT provide for additional searches and PCT art.34(3) and PCT r.68 provide for the examination of claims directed to several inventions. §89B.18 discusses divisional applications from international applications (UK).

—Time for filing divisional application

15.20 A divisional application can be initiated by compliance with the requirements of subs.(1) (as described in §15.10 above), with the facility for filing the other required documents at a later date.

Where the parent application is an international application (UK), a divisional application of it filed after the application has entered the UK national phase will be an application under the Act governed by r.66 (beginning of national phase) and r.68 (altered prescribed periods). These matters are discussed in the commentaries on ss.89A and 89B.

The time within which a divisional application may be filed is governed by r.19 (see §15.04 above).

Rule 19(1)(a) requires a divisional application to be filed "before the end of the relevant period" but r.19(1)(b) prohibits the filing of a divisional application after the earlier application has been terminated or withdrawn which includes the position where a patent has already been granted on the application because this then no longer exists.

The relevant period is defined in r.19(3)(b) as normally expiring three months before the "compliance date", which is the date on which an application fails if not then in condition for acceptance as required by ss.18(4) and 20(1), this period being defined in r.30 (reprinted in §18.04 and discussed in §18.11) and often described as the "rule 30 period". This is the period permitted by that rule for placing the application in compliance with the Act and Rules, including any extension of it under r.108. The compliance date is four-and-a-half-years from the earliest declared priority date if any, or otherwise from the date of filing, but with the proviso of a minimum period of 12 months after the date of the first substantive examination report issued under s.18, and three months from the filing of third party observations (see r.30(2)(b) and (4) discussed in §18.11).

However, where the first examination report is made under s.18(4), i.e. stating that the application is already in compliance with the Act and Rules, the time period for filing divisional applications is defined as two months from the date of such report (r.19(3)(a)).

Thus (provided that the parent application has not been refused or withdrawn), there will always be available for the filing of a divisional application a minimum period of two months from the first examination report; and, in most circumstances, an applicant should be able to file a divisional application up to three months before the end of the r.30 period, provided that before then the fate of the earlier application has not been determined, for example by issue of a letter under s.18(4) which operates as the administrative date of grant (on which see *ITT's Application*, [1984] R.P.C. 23 and §18.10).

It is advisable to indicate any intention to file a divisional application when responding to an examination report. In *Luk Lamellan's Application* [1997] R.P.C. 104, it was indicated that, where an applicant has indicated an intention to file a divisional application and the application is otherwise in order for grant, it is the practice of the UK-IPO to postpone grant for one month pending clarification of that indicated intention (see also MOPP 15.46).

—Late filing of divisional applications

15.21 Rule 108(1) confers no discretionary power which would allow the requirements of the Act with regard to filing of divisional applications to be varied, see *Ogawa Chemical's Application* [1986] R.P.C. 63. However, extensions of the time periods set out in rr.19 and 30 are possible.

The r.19 period is extendable by a discretionary extension under r.108(1). The r.30 period is a Sch.4, Pt 2 rule, extendable as of right by two months with a further discretionary extension of time possible. Note that extension under rr.19 and 30 is restricted because they are Pt 3 rules (as discussed in §15.17). The *Formalities Manual* indicates that a situation may arise where a discretionary extension under r.19 for late filing of a divisional application is refused, but the compliance period of the parent application can be extended as of right and the divisional application can then be re-filed.

It was held in *Ian A. Ferguson's Application* BL O/272/09 that the same criteria should apply to discretionary extensions of time to file a divisional application under r.108(3) (further extension to r.30 compliance period) or r.108(1) (extension of r.19 period).

Late filing of a divisional application under this discretionary power is only appropriate "where the circumstances are exceptional and there has been proper diligence by the applicant", see *Asahi's Application* (BL O/98/89, noted I.P.D. 12113), where the case failed for both of these reasons; and *Kiwi Coders' Application* [1986] R.P.C. 106. This was not the case where there had been no prior indication of a desire to file a divisional application and where the divisional application was filed shortly after the parent application had been put in order, following an extension of the r.30 period (*Motorola's Application* BL O/118/98).

In *Fieldturf's Application* BL O/371/04, it was explained that a discretionary extension to allow a divisional application to be filed within the limit of three months before expiry of the r.30 period as set out in r.19(3)(b) should only be exercised in "circumstances which are exceptional" and where the applicant "has been properly diligent". This was not here considered to be the case. Although the agent had clearly warned the UK-IPO of an intention to file a divisional application nothing had then been done and no evidence had been submitted to explain the delay.

Discretion will not be exercised outside the periods permitted by r.19 if the effect would be to circumvent a refusal to grant an extension of time for response to a substantive examination report under s.18(3), see *Goodhart's Application* BL O/242/97 and §18.16. *Central Research Laboratories' Application* BL O/419/00 is another example of discretion being refused to permit late filing of a divisional application: here, there were indications of a change of mind and insufficient diligence in the period before the application was filed. In *Anderson's Application* BL O/297/02, the applicant filed a divisional application out of time but an extension of time was refused because the applicant had not been sufficiently diligent in prosecuting his application. An argument under the Human Rights Act 1998 (c.42) failed.

In *Ian A. Ferguson's Application* (above), however, the compliance period of the application in issue was further extended under r.108(3) by two months to allow a divisional application to be filed. The applicant had intended to file a divisional application but had been prevented by financial difficulties and the circumstances were exceptional. It was held that it was not necessary for the failure to file the divisional application in time to have been unintentional.

It may be possible to invoke r.107 to enable a divisional application to be filed where the applicant, having indicated an intention to file a divisional application, can demonstrate that he has been misled by a statement or action of the UK-IPO. On appeal in *Howmet Research Corp's Application* [2006] R.P.C. 27 at 657, an application to rescind grant of the parent application was allowed so that a divisional application could be filed. In *Weatherford/Lamb Inc.'s Application* O/028/09, following *Howmet Research Corp's Application*, rescission of grant of a patent was permitted with the compliance date of the re-created patent application set at six months from the date of rescission. In a response letter, *Weatherford* had stated that they intended to file a divisional application, but the UK-IPO had not sent them the usual (though non-statutory) notice that the application was likely to be re-examined and if in order granted, and the application was forwarded for grant. A two-year delay in detecting the error was not a reason for refusal of discretion. It was held that third party terms should be imposed in respect of the invention protected by any divisional application

However, a request for rescission of grant was refused in *Irwin Industrial Tool Co's Application* O/247/09, where the applicant had not indicated an intention to file a divisional application. The applicants had filed revised claims overcoming a lack of unity objection, and the case was forwarded for grant before the two-month extended period for response to objection had expired. The applicants argued that the request for an extension foreshadowed the filing of a divisional application, or that if there was any doubt about their intentions that doubt should have been resolved before grant. It was held that deletion of independent claims was something different from foreshadowing a divisional application, and it was not correct that the UK-IPO should clarify any doubt of any kind about the applicant's intentions.

—Divisional applications of divisional applications

15.22   There is no prohibition against the filing of a divisional application on an application that already has divisional status. However, the practice of filing a series of "cascading divisionals" is inhibited in the UK because of the overall time limit for acceptance being calculated for each divisional from the declared priority date, see r.30(2)(a)(ii).

—Content of divisional applications

15.23   A divisional application usually contains claims of a different type and/or scope from those in the parent application (although this is not necessarily the case at the time of filing). "Double patenting" provisions prevent a divisional application from being granted with claims granted in the parent application.

The claim to divisional status must be made at the time of filing. The applicant must (under r.19(2)) include a statement that the application is a divisional application and should identify (e.g. in Pt 6 of PF 1) the parent application by date of filing and number. Thus, a non-divisional application cannot be converted to a divisional application after filing (*P's Application* [1983] R.P.C. 269). However, a divisional application can be converted into a non-divisional application after filing.

Any priority claim for a divisional application must normally be made at the time of filing, but the rules for making a late priority claim for a new application are less onerous than for a normal application (r.7(4), see §5.18).

There is no obligation for a cross-reference to the parent application to be included in the specification of a divisional application, although the fact that the application has this status will be apparent from the front page of the published application, and likewise with the front page of an ensuing patent. Nevertheless, it is good practice for the appropriate part of the text in the description of one application to refer to the number of the other application and state that it claims the matter concerned.

Under s.76, (for which see §76.01), a divisional application containing new matter is allowed to be filed initially, but will not proceed unless and until it is amended (by an application under s.19) so as to exclude the additional matter, as discussed further in §15.40. While there is no objection as such that the claims of a divisional application are broader than those of the parent, for the reasons explained in §76.08, it will of course not be possible to obtain valid claims in a divisional application which are broader in scope than those that could have been obtained on the basis of the disclosure in the parent application, see also §76.06. Consolidated EPO Decisions G 1/05 *ASTROPOWER/Divisional* and G 1/06 *SEIKO/Sequences of divisionals* (above) held that:

> "it is a necessary and sufficient condition for a divisional application that anything disclosed in the divisional application be directly and unambiguously derivable from what is disclosed in each of the preceding applications as filed."

The practice of filing divisional applications in exactly the same form as the initial form of the parent application and seeking to make amendments later is not necessary, but it may be desirable to avoid objection under s.76, see §15.40, and to provide basis for further divisional applications. However, the MOPP comments that "this practice is discouraged". It may be preferable at least to change the claim order to ensure that the claims of interest are searched.

If a divisional application contains new matter by error or mistake, correction may also be possible under s.117 and reference could be made to the parent application for evidence that nothing other than the offered correction was intended. For further details, see §117.05.

It is possible to relinquish divisional status to retain additional matter in the new application over that in the parent application.

For missing parts in divisional applications, see §15.13.

Time limits on divisional and replacement applications

—The applicable rules

As discussed in §15.12 above, the provisions applicable to the time limits for filing documents as required by ss.15(10) and 17(1) are set out in r.22 (reprinted above). In relation to normal applications, the procedure has been explained in §15.15. For such normal applications only paras (1)–(3) and (7) of r.22 apply, it being stated in para.(4) that these paragraphs do not apply to a new application (i.e. a divisional or replacement application). **15.24**

For new applications it is paras (5) and (6) of r.22 which stipulate the different time limits for meeting the requirements of s.15(10) and s.17(1). Rule 21 stipulates the time limits under s.13(2) (statement of inventorship), r.8 (priority document) and Sch.1 (sequence listing). Other rules (e.g. r.28) apply with modifications to new applications. The time limits are summarised in this section and discussed in more detail in §§15.25–15.33 below.

These matters apply likewise to the filing of a divisional or replacement application based on an international application for a patent UK after it has entered the UK national phase, for which see ss.89A and 89B.

A useful table setting out time limits applying to divisional applications and possible extensions thereof is provided in the *Formalities Manual*.

For normal applications, all but one of the time limits under r.22(1)–(3) are expressed in terms of the relevant period, which is explained in §15.15 above. However, for new applications this definition of relevant period is only used (as explained below) as an exception to the general rule which is defined instead by reference to the initiation date (i.e. the date of filing papers at the UK-IPO to initiate an application, see §15.09).

This different treatment arises because divisional or replacement applications need to be processed more quickly in view of the shorter time available for the applicant and the UK-IPO to meet the compliance requirements of r.30 discussed in §15.25. Also, in the case of both divisional and replacement applications, the applicant will typically already have to hand copies of the required documents or at least the information necessary to complete the appropriate forms (although this may not always be the case: for example, some of the information needed to complete PF 7 may be missing for a divisional application from an international patent application (UK)). Moreover, r.22(3) refers to "the date of filing" which is inappropriate with respect to a new application which takes the date of filing of the earlier application. Therefore, different language is needed.

Paragraphs (5) and (6) of r.22 state that all the actions required under s.15(10) (that is: filing the claims and abstract; filing a description for an application filed by reference to an earlier relevant application; filing a certified copy of an earlier relevant application; paying the application fee; requesting search and paying the search fee) should be taken within the period of only two months beginning with the initiation date (r.25(5)(a)(i)/(b)(i)) or within the period for the earlier application if that should be longer (r.22(5)(a)(ii)/(b)(ii)).

However, if the new application is filed less than six months before the compliance date, the period for meeting all five requirements of s.15(10) is the initiation date.

The periods set out in r.21 are similar.

Extensions of time for periods under r.21 and r.22 are complicated, with r.21 being included fully in Pt 2 and partially in Pt 3 of Sch.4 of the rules, and r.22 being included partially in Pt 2 and fully in Pt 3 of Sch.4. The effect of this is that extensions of time as of right (under r.108(2)) are available for some periods under these rules but not others, and that some extensions (e.g. for filing PF 7 on a divisional application) are subject to restrictions under r.108(5) and (7).

It is therefore good practice to file all the necessary documents and forms (PF 1, PF 7 and PF 9A) on a new application at the initiation date, as well as filing the claims and abstract and paying the application fee.

In exercising an extension discretion on a divisional application, the Comptroller may feel that insufficient time will remain for the search and substantive examination to be done properly within the compliance period, even if it should be extended (see §15.25).

—Compliance period

15.25   The compliance period under r.30 on the divisional application is that for the parent application at the initiation date of the divisional application, see §18.11. Thus, if the compliance period on the parent application has already been extended, this extended period will be the unextended compliance period on the divisional application. However, the MOPP indicates that extension of the compliance period on the parent application after the initiation date of the divisional application will not affect the compliance period of the divisional application, with a separate request for extension being needed.

The compliance period for a replacement application is a minimum of 18 months from its initiation date (r.30(3)(a)), see §18.11.

It should be appreciated that any extension sought for a period under r.21 or r.22 does not of itself extend the r.30 period for the new application, for which a separate extension application is needed, although this may be made on the same form under r.108(4). The r.30 period is listed under Pts 2 and 3 of Sch.4 to the rules so that extension is available as of right but subject to restrictions.

—Application fee

15.26   Section 15(10)(c) requires an application fee to be paid before the end of the prescribed period.

For new applications, the deadline is two months beginning with the initiation date, or within the period for the parent application if that is longer (r.22(5)(a)). This period is listed under Pts 2 and 3 of Sch.4 to the Rules so that an extension as of right is available but subject to restrictions.

However, where the new application is filed less than six months before the r.30 compliance date, the prescribed period is the period ending on the initiation date (r.22(6)). This period is listed under Pt 3 but not Pt 2 of Sch.4 to the Rules so that extension is discretionary and subject to restrictions.

—Payment of search fee by filing PF 9A

15.27   Sections 17(1)(c) and 15(10)(d) require PF 9A to be used to request the required search and for the search fee to be paid, before the end of the prescribed period. For normal applications (under r.22(2)), this period is defined in r.22(7), as a 12-month period, from the date of filing or priority date, with a two-month period from the date of filing as a minimum.

For new applications, the deadline is two months beginning with the initiation date, or within the period for the parent application if that is longer (r.22(5)(a)). This period is listed under Pts 2 and 3 of Sch.4 to the Rules so that an extension as of right is available but subject to restrictions.

However, where the new application is filed less than six months before the r.30 compliance date, the prescribed period is the period ending on the initiation date (r.22(6)). This period is listed under Pt 3 but not Pt 2 of Sch.4 to the Rules so that extension is discretionary and subject to restrictions.

For possible remission of the search fee on a new application, see §§17.06 and 123.65.

—Filing of claims and the abstract

The need for the filing of one or more claims and the abstract for a new application is **15.28** also governed by s.15(10), see para.(10)(1)(a) and r.22. The deadlines are the same as those for filing of the search request §15.27.

Thus, the claims and abstract are due within two months of the initiation date, or within the period for the parent application if that is longer (r.22(5)(a)). This period is listed under Pts 2 and 3 of Sch.4 to the Rules so that an extension as of right is available but subject to restrictions.

However, where the new application is filed less than six months before the r.30 compliance date, the prescribed period is the period ending on the initiation date (r.22(6)). This period is listed under Pt 3 but not Pt 2 of Sch.4 to the Rules so that extension is discretionary and subject to restrictions.

—Payment of examination fee by filing PF 10

Section 18(1) requires that a request be made for a substantive examination by filing PF **15.29** 10 and paying the required fee within a prescribed period, see §18.06. The relevant rule is r.28 (reprinted at §18.02). For normal applications this period ends six months after the application is published (under r.28(2) as discussed under §18.06).

For new applications, the deadline (under r.28(4), (5) and (7)) is two months beginning with the initiation date, or within two years from the priority date or date of filing (where there is no priority claim) if that is longer. Note that, exceptionally, this second deadline is not the same as the deadline for the parent application. This period is listed under Pts 2 and 3 of Sch.4 to the Rules so that an extension as of right is available but subject to restrictions.

However, where the new application is filed less than six months before the r.30 compliance date, the prescribed period is the period on the initiation date (r.28(6)). This period is listed, under Pt 3 but not Pt 2 of Sch.4 of the rules so that extension is discretionary and subject to restrictions.

The filing of PF 10, should, in practice, always be done as a routine matter when the steps are taken to file a new application.

—Filing of inventorship statement on PF 7

Section 13(2) requires information to be provided which identifies the person(s) **15.30** believed to be the inventor(s). Rule 10 stipulates that this is to be done by the filing of PF 7 and (for a normal application) within the period of 16 months after the priority date or date of filing. These requirements have been discussed in the above commentary on s.13. However, for a new application, r.10 is replaced by r.21 (reprinted above).

Under r.21(1), the prescribed period under s.13(2) is two months beginning with the initiation date (r.21(1)(a)(i)), or the period for the parent application if that is longer (r.21(1)(a)(ii)), and last part of r.21(1)). This period is listed under Pts 2 and 3 of Sch.4 to the Rules so that an extension as of right is available but subject to restrictions.

However, where the new application is filed less than six months before the r.30 compliance date, the prescribed period is the period ending on the initiation date, (r.21(2)(a)). In this case, unlike the cases listed in §§15.27–15.28, this period is listed in Pts 2 and 3 of Sch.4 to the Rules, so that an extension as of right is available but subject to restrictions.

—Priority claims and filing of priority document

If the parent application claims priority, it will usually be necessary to claim the same **15.31** priority for a divisional or replacement application based on it, since otherwise the parent application is likely to become effective prior art against the claims in the divisional application under s.2(3). However, it is of course possible that the subject-matter claimed in the divisional application is not entitled to the priority claim. This should not cause difficulty, as the effective date of the subject-matter in the parent application, will be similarly affected.

It is not possible to claim any priority which was not claimed for the parent application, see r.6(5).

When priority is claimed, the requirements for the furnishing of the application number of it (r.8(1)) and, if required, a copy of it (priority document) (r.8(2)) are set out in r.8(3)–(5). A priority document will not normally be required for a divisional or replacement application because it will normally already be available to the Comptroller (r.8(4)).

These actions for a normal application, are required (by r.8(5)) to be met within 16 months of the declared priority date (as discussed in §5.31 above). However, for a new application, r.8(5) states that these periods are subject to the provisions of r.21 (see r.21 at §15.06 above) and r.21(1)(b) states that for new applications the relevant period (under r.8(1) and (2)) is the period of two months beginning with the initiation date, or the period on the parent application if longer. This period is listed under Pt 2 but not Pt 3 of Sch.4 so that an initial extension of time of two months is available as of right and further extensions can be obtained on payment of further fees and at the discretion of the Comptroller.

However, where the new application is filed less than six months before the end of r.30 compliance date, the relevant periods for meeting the required provision of information and copies of the priority documents (under r.8(1) and (2)) each expire on the "initiation date". Again, exceptionally, this period is listed under Pt 2 but not Pt 3 of Sch.4 so that an initial extension of time of two months is available as of right and further extensions can be obtained on payment of further fees and at the discretion of the Comptroller

—Providing details of biological material

15.32   Schedule 1 to the Rules (reprinted in §125A.03) deals with deposits of samples of biological material. For further discussion of the deposit requirements of this Sch.1, see the commentary on s.125A. For a normal application, action to meet the requirements of para.3(2) of this Schedule is needed by 16 months after the priority date, or date of filing if there is no priority date. When a divisional application is filed later than this, the requirements will normally have to be complied with by the initiation date of the divisional application (r.21(3)(a)). This paragraph is listed in Pt 2 but not Pt 3 of Sch.4 to the Rules (reprinted at §123.26), so that an initial extension of two months is obtainable as of right and further extensions can be obtained on payment of further fees and at the discretion of the Comptroller.

—Filing of documents on application filed by reference to earlier relevant application

15.33   For a divisional application filed by reference to an earlier relevant application (see §15.12), the description must be filed within two months of the initiation date, or within the period for the parent application if that is longer (s.15(10)(b)(i) and r.22(5)(a)). A certified copy of the earlier application must be filed within two months of the initiation date, or within four months of filing the parent application (again, this is the period for the parent application) if that is longer (s.15(10)(b)(ii) and r.22(5)(b)). These periods are listed under Pts 2 and 3 of Sch.4 to the Rules so that an extension as of right is available but subject to restrictions.

However, where the new application is filed less than six months before the r.30 compliance date, the prescribed period in each case is the period ending on the initiation date (r.22(6)). This period is listed under Pt 3 but not Pt 2 of Sch.4 to the Rules so that extension is discretionary and subject to restrictions.

Replacement applications under sections 8(3), 12(6) and 37(4)

New applications under s.8(3) (determination before grant of entitlement to patents, etc.), s.12(6) (determination of questions of entitlement to foreign and convention patents, etc.) and s.37(4) (determination of right to patent after grant), are conveniently called "replacement applications" because they take the place of a previously filed application made by a non-entitled person, and these applications are particularly discussed in the commentaries on those sections and, in relation to "Practice", in §8.11.

15.34

Rule 20 (reprinted above) sets out the period within which such a replacement application may be filed. This is necessarily different from the period prescribed for filing a divisional application under s.15(9), which is defined in r.19 (and discussed in §§15.19 and 15.21). However, replacement and divisional applications are collectively termed "new applications" and the periods of time applicable to both types of such applications are then dealt with in commonly expressed rules that have been discussed in §§15.24–15.33. This discussion is mainly concentrated on divisional applications because these are much more numerous than replacement applications. There is generally no need to discuss replacement applications separately other than as regards the time permitted to file such applications and the r.30 compliance period.

Replacement applications must be filed within three months from the date when the Comptroller or court makes an order which is not appealed; or, if appealed, from the date when that appeal is finally disposed of (r.20(3)). The Comptroller may, after giving notice to the parties, shorten this period and make it subject to conditions (r.20(4)).

Where the application which gave rise to the decision that a replacement application could be filed was an international application (UK), such replacement application will be an application under the Act.

The compliance period for a replacement application is a minimum of 18 months from its initiation date (r.30(3) (a)), see §15.25.

The EPC provides for replacement applications under art.61. There is no provision in the PCT allowing for the filing of a replacement application in the international phase.

PRACTICE UNDER SECTION 15

Filing of initial application

The term "initial application" is used here to refer to an application which does not include a priority claim. Such an application may serve as a priority application for other applications in due course.

15.35

As described in §15.10, an application can be initiated merely by fulfilling the minimal requirements set out in subs.(1). If these are not met, a date of filing is not accorded until the deficiencies have been rectified. However, many of the formal requirements to establish an application can be dealt with at a later date, see §15.15.

Applicants wishing to file an initial application in the United Kingdom in order to secure a priority date may file a specification without claims or abstract. This can be done at no cost as there is no filing fee (the application fee can be paid later, see §15.15). Thus, the UK-IPO has advantages over many other Patent Offices for filing an initial application. However, the description of this initial application must disclose the invention in a manner which will enable the invention to be performed by a person skilled in the art and will support the ultimate claims, and also to provide an adequate basis for the establishment of a priority date for a later application in other countries. Thus, a statement of invention should be included at the very least. As to the effectiveness of a priority claim, see G 2/98 *"Same Invention"* and the strict novelty test that is applied (discussed in §5.23). An initial filing is unlikely to provide priority, in the United Kingdom at least, for any generalisation not expressly included in the specification.

At any time within 12 months following the date of filing, the applicant may add claims to the initial application, or he may file another application in the United Kingdom claiming priority from the earlier application or he may file an application for a European patent or an international application designating, inter alia, the United Kingdom and claiming priority from the earlier United Kingdom application.

If a new United Kingdom, European or international application is filed, additional matter can be included and multiple priorities can be claimed. It is possible to claim priorities from an earlier United Kingdom application and an earlier foreign application jointly.

The documents of an initial application can be informal, and formal replacements are not needed if the initial application serves solely as a priority basis. However, care should be taken that the documents are clear enough to enable legible certified copies to be obtained.

If the initial application is intended to serve as a basis for claiming priority only, it may be convenient not to include an abstract. This will mean that the application is treated as withdrawn following failure to file the abstract, see §15.14.

The 12-month period for filing the claims and the abstract and for paying the search fee specified in r.22(1) can be extended under r.108(2) and/or (7) (see §15.17). For discretionary extension of the priority period under s.5(2A) and (2B), see §§5.17–5.18.

For withdrawal of an initial application before publication, see §16.10. If the application has served its sole intended purpose of establishing priority, the UK-IPO prefers its specific withdrawal once the second application claiming priority has been filed, in order to avoid duplicate publication (although if the application does not contain an abstract it will normally be treated as withdrawn before this stage).

There is however no obligation to withdraw an earlier United Kingdom application that has served to establish a priority date for a later United Kingdom application, an application for a European patent (UK) or an international application for a patent (UK). For example, if the earlier application discloses several inventions, the application can be pursued for protection of one of those inventions and the later United Kingdom application or the European or international application can be pursued, possibly with additional subject-matter, in respect of another of those inventions.

Moreover, applicants may wish to pursue the UK priority application and application for a European patent (UK) or international application for a patent (UK) to take advantage of an early grant date on the former, which can then be replaced by the latter to give an extended term (see below). Advantage can also be taken of any differences in scope between the two patents.

Section 18(5) gives the Comptroller power to prevent two patents from being granted in the United Kingdom to the same person for the same invention and a United Kingdom patent will normally be revoked on the Comptroller's own initiative under s.73(2) (subject to s.73(3) and (4)) if a European patent (UK) is granted to the same patentee for the same invention, see §73.06.

Since the term of a patent is calculated from the date of filing (s.25(1)), the filing of a second application claiming priority from a first application results in a later expiry of the patent and a later date for the payment of the first renewal fee. However, the period prescribed by s.16 for publication is calculated from the declared priority date (defined in r.3, reprinted at §5.06A), and publication is therefore not delayed by filing a second application claiming priority from the first. The compliance period prescribed by r.30 (reprinted at §18.04) for complying with the requirements of the Act and Rules is also calculated from the declared priority date and is therefore not affected by filing a second application claiming priority from the first.

Filing of Application

15.36 It is good practice to file an application with a completed application form PF 1. An application other than an initial filing should also be filed with PF 7 and PF 9A.

The application will normally include a description, claims, drawings if appropriate and an abstract (although see §15.35 on filing an application without abstract), all in the English language. For formal requirements, see §14.46.

It is good practice to pay the application fee on filing, by enclosing it with PF 1. The application fee can otherwise be paid on PF 9A, or by using the non-statutory form AF 1.

For the procedure for filing documents after normal hours of opening of the UK-IPO, see §120.04.

For the progression of the application to preliminary examination, search and substantive examination, see s.15A, 17 and 18 respectively.

Disclosure at international exhibition prior to filing

A patent application may be protected against the prior art effect of a disclosure of the **15.37** invention at an international exhibition (i.e. one certified as such and usually notified as such in the *Patents Journal*, see r.5(6)). This requires the application to be accompanied by a statement under s.2(4)(c) that the invention was displayed at such an exhibition. The application must be filed within six months of the exhibition. It is not sufficient for the application to have a priority date within six months of the exhibition. The position under art.55 of the EPC is similar, see G 3/98 *UNIVERSITY PATENTS/Six month period* OJ EPO 2001, 62; [2001] E.P.O.R.33.

Divisional applications

—Deadline for filing

Where a divisional application is filed at a time when it appears that the parent applica- **15.38** tion could proceed to administrative grant, an accompanying letter should be filed marked "URGENT" in order that the parent application should not proceed to grant before the divisional application is accorded a date of filing, see the *Patents Journal* October 9, 1991. Note that the UK-IPO does not provide an advance notification of grant as the EPO does.

However, applicants may not foreshadow such filing as a way of postponing grant which should be automatic once the conditions for grant have been met, see §18.10.

—Documents required for filing

The filing of a divisional application requires compliance with the general provisions **15.39** for filing a normal application, but the time periods within which the various actions must each be completed are different as explained in §§15.24–15.33. In particular, PF 1 must be filed with box 6 completed providing the number of the earlier UK application (i.e. parent application) from which the contents of the divisional application are being divided. Each priority document must be identified by its application number, this being particularly important when more than one priority was claimed for the parent application. See also §14.16 for information on filling in PF1 for a divisional application.

These requirements are complicated and it is safest for the filing of any divisional application to be accompanied by the claims and abstract and PF 1, PF 9A and PF 10, payment of the search and examination fees and the filing of a PF 7 (if the inventor(s) is/are not the applicant(s)). Reference to r.112 may also be desirable to show that copies of the priority documents (and any translation of them) should not need to be provided because the Comptroller will have copies of them in the file of the parent application and can make certified copies of them under r.112(2). When, as is usual for a divisional application PF 9A and PF 10 are filed together, the search and examination will normally be carried out together.

It is not clear whether a divisional application can be filed by reference to a parent application as the earlier relevant application under s.15(1)(c)(ii).

Remission of the search fee (under r.106(2)(b), reprinted at §123.23, and discussed in §123.65 and §17.09) may be possible when no additional search is needed for the divisional application, see MOPP 15.47–49. A request for fee remission must be made in writing, and it is suggested that this be done when filing the divisional application. However, the MOPP indicates that any such refund may sometimes not be made until the divisional application is ready for grant.

If the request for a divisional application (PF 1) names an agent different from that on the original PF 1, it would seem prudent, in view of the terms of r.101 (reprinted in §274.02), also to file PF 51.

A divisional application is given an application number based on its initiation date.

—Content of divisional application

15.40   As discussed in §15.23, it is useful to file the divisional application with a description identical to that originally filed in the parent application and to include the original claims of the parent application, in order to ensure that all the description contained in the parent application is available to support claims in the divisional application (and any later generation divisional applications), and then to make appropriate amendment subsequently. If the claims of the parent application are initially included in the divisional application, the claims desired for grant in the divisional application should be placed first to ensure that the search report is directed to the invention of the divisional application since, where there is non-unity of the invention, these claims are those searched initially, see §17.05. Doing this may have increased importance in view of subss.17(8) and 18(1A) (supplemental search fees), discussed in §17.05 and §18.09 respectively. Before grant, it will be necessary to excise the claims which are to be granted on the parent application, since the two applications cannot claim the same invention, see s.18(5) and §18.12. Here "the same invention" seems to mean that the claims of the two applications must not overlap with each other, as discussed in §73.06, in the context of a UK patent and a European Patent (UK) directed to the same invention.

An objection that the divisional application contains additional matter can be raised as a preliminary point. It will then be necessary to satisfy the requirements of s.76(1) before the then-deferred substantive examination is carried out. Alternatively, the search may be carried out first and an objection under s.76 then be raised. Otherwise, the first examination report under s.18 should, inter alia, confirm the divisional status of the application. Any view expressed in the first examination report must, however, be regarded as provisional, it being possible for an examiner to raise an objection (under s.18(3)) on the basis of additional matter at any time before grant. What constitutes added matter is discussed in §76.06 and §§76.13–76.16. Where an objection is raised, amendment to remove the additional matter should be possible under s.18(3).

The Comptroller appears to take into account the public interest in deciding whether the claims of a divisional application find adequate support in the accompanying description, see *Glatt's Application* [1983] R.P.C. 122.

In view of the provisions of s.72(1)(d), if the applicant becomes aware of any new matter in a divisional application or a patent granted thereon, voluntary application to amend the specification to delete the offending matter should be made under s.19(1), 27(1) or 75 as appropriate.

—Prosecution of divisional application

15.41   When prosecuting a divisional application, particularly in the last six months of the compliance period permitted under r.30 for placing the application in order for acceptance, it is prudent to endorse correspondence prominently with the words "DIVISIONAL: URGENT". This is in order that the examiner be alerted that the expiry of the acceptance period will occur before the date which the application number would suggest. Note that (under r.30(3)(b), and (4), reprinted in §18.04) for a divisional application (including a second or later generation divisional application, i.e. one where the parent application is itself a divisional application), then the compliance period for the divisional application will be the same as that applicable to the parent application.

It is understood that entries are made in the register for the parent application when a divisional application therefrom has been filed. It is further understood that a divisional application will not be found to be formally in order for acceptance until the parent application is likewise in order and vice versa. Thus, the parent and all divisional applications therefrom are likely to proceed to grant on or about the same date.

—Applicant for divisional application

The applicant(s) must normally be the same as in the parent application.   **15.42**

Section 15(9) requires that a divisional application be filed by the original applicant of the parent application or his successor in title (at the time of filing the divisional application), such as an assignee or a personal representative of a deceased applicant. A parent application, may be filed in joint names; because it contain separate inventions to which different applicants are separately entitled. In this situation, a divisional application may be filed in the name of the applicant entitled to the invention covered. This applicant may request that his name be removed from the applicants in the parent application on filing PF 11 (under s.19) requesting the change together with evidence showing that he has no interest in, or right to, the invention of the parent application.

Where the relationship between the applicants in the parent and divisional applications is not self-evident and no explanation is submitted with the application, the UK-IPO will query the relationship and the application will not be permitted to proceed as a divisional if it is found that there has not been compliance with the requirements of s.15(9).

SECTION 15A [ADDED]

Preliminary examination

15A.—(1) The comptroller shall refer an application for a patent to an   **15A.01**
examiner for a preliminary examination if—

(a) **the application has a date of filing;**

(b) **the application has not been withdrawn or treated as withdrawn; and**

(c) **the application fee has been paid.**

(2) **On a preliminary examination of an application the examiner shall—**

(a) **determine whether the application complies with those requirements of this Act and the rules which are designated by the rules as formal requirements for the purposes of this Act; and**

(b) **determine whether any requirements under section 13(2) or 15(10) above remain to be complied with.**

(3) **The examiner shall report to the comptroller his determinations under subsection (2) above.**

(4) **If on the preliminary examination of an application it is found that—**

(a) **any drawing referred to in the application, or**

(b) **part of the description of the invention for which the patent is sought,**

is missing from the application, then the examiner shall include this finding in his report under subsection (3) above.

(5) **Subsections (6) to (8) below apply if a report is made to the comptroller under subsection (3) above that not all the formal requirements have been complied with.**

(6) **The comptroller shall specify a period during which the applicant shall have the opportunity—**

(a) **to make observations on the report, and**

(b) **to amend the application so as to comply with those requirements (subject to section 76 below).**

(7) **The comptroller may refuse the application if the applicant fails to amend the application as mentioned in subsection (6)(b) above before the end of the period specified by the comptroller under that subsection.**

(8) Subsection (7) above does not apply if—

(a) the applicant makes observations as mentioned in subsection (6)(a) above before the end of the period specified by the comptroller under that subsection, and

(b) as a result of the observations, the comptroller is satisfied that the formal requirements have been complied with.

(9) If a report is made to the comptroller under subsection (3) above—

(a) that any requirement of section 13(2) or 15(10) above has not been complied with; or

(b) that a drawing or part of the description of the invention has been found to be missing.

then the Comptroller will notify the applicant accordingly.

Note. Section 15A was introduced by the Regulatory Reform (Patents) Order 2004 (SI 2004/2357) ("RRO") to have effect from January 1, 2005, but without effect on applications which were then "pending", for which see Note 1 to §15.01.

Relevant Rules—Rules 23–25

Preliminary examination

Rule 23—Preliminary examination under section 15A

15A.02
23.—(1) In the preliminary examination under section 15A of an application the examiner shall determine whether the application complies with the requirements of rules 6 to 9.

(2) The examiner must report to the comptroller his determinations under paragraph (1), and the comptroller must notify the applicant accordingly.

Rule 24—Correcting a declaration made for the purposes of section 5(2)

15A.03
24.—(1) Where, on the preliminary examination under section 15A of an application, the examiner finds that a declaration made for the purposes of section 5(2) specifies a date of filing for an earlier relevant application—

(a) more than twelve months before the date of filing of the application in suit; or

(b) where the comptroller has given permission for a late declaration to be made under section 5(2), more than fourteen months before the date of filing of the application in suit,

he must report this finding to the comptroller, and the comptroller must notify the applicant accordingly.

(2) Where the comptroller has notified the applicant under paragraph (1), the applicant must, before the end of the period of two months beginning [with] immediately after the date of that notification, provide the comptroller with a corrected date; otherwise the comptroller must disregard the declaration in so far as it relates to the earlier relevant application.

(3) In paragraph (2) "corrected date" means a date that would not have been reported by the examiner under paragraph (1).

Note. The amendments are made as a consequence of The Patents (Amendment) Rules 2011 (SI 2011/2052) that came into force on October 1, 2011.

Rule 25—Formal requirements

25.—(1) Subject to paragraphs (2) and (3), the requirements of the following **15A.04**
provisions of these Rules are formal requirements—

    (a) rule 12(1) (application for a patent on Patents Form 1);

    (b) rule 14(1) (application in English or Welsh);

    (c) rule 14(2) and (3) (form of documents and drawings).

(2) Where an application is delivered in electronic form or using electronic
communications, only the requirements of rule 14(1) are formal requirements.

(3) Where an international application for a patent (UK) was filed in accordance with the provisions of the Patent Co-operation Treaty, the requirements
mentioned in paragraph (1) shall be treated as complied with to the extent that the
application complies with any corresponding provision of that Treaty.

COMMENTARY ON SECTION 15A

Scope of the section

Section 15A provides for a "preliminary examination" of an application by an examiner **15A.05**
before it proceeds to a search under s.17.

Subsection (1) deals with the conditions which must be met for preliminary examination to take place.

Subsections (2) and (4) set out the matters which are checked during preliminary
examination.

Subsections (3) and (5)–(9) provide for a preliminary examination report which is notified to the applicant, and sets out the applicant's possibilities for response.

Further information on the ways in which the UK-IPO operates under s.15A can be
found in the MOPP.

Preliminary examination

By subs.(1), an application only proceeds to preliminary examination if: **15A.06**

— it has a date of filing (see §15.10);

— it has not been withdrawn or treated as withdrawn (see §15.15); and

— the application fee has been paid (see §15.15).

The preliminary examination starts as soon as possible after payment of the application
fee.

If an application has been treated as withdrawn before preliminary examination, it may
be possible to apply for reinstatement under s.20A, for which see the commentary on that
section.

The examiner will check various matters during preliminary examination, some of
which are set out in the section and some in the rules. These matters are listed below.

Under subs.(2)(a), the examiner is required to determine: whether the application
complies with the "formal requirements" designated as such by r.25 (reprinted above).
That is:

— PF 1 has been filed fully completed including an address for service (under r.12(1),
   reprinted in §14.02 and discussed in §14.10;

— all documents have been supplied in English or Welsh (under r.14(1) (reprinted in
   §14.04 and discussed in §14.20; and

— the requirements for the presentation of the documents and drawings are met (as set out in Pts 1–3 of Sch.2 to the Rules, under r.14(2) and (3), reprinted in §14.05 and discussed in §§14.21–14.30). Under r.25(2), this does not apply to documents that have been filed by electronic means under directions under s.124A for which see §14.06. These requirements are automatically treated as complied with in the case of an international application for a patent (UK) which complies with any corresponding provision under the PCT (r.25(3)).

Under subs.(2)(b); the examiner is also required to check whether the requirements of ss.13(2) and 15(10) have been met, that is:

— whether PF 7 has been filed to identify the designated inventor(s) unless the sole applicant(s) is named on PF 1 under r.10, reprinted at §13.05 and discussed in §§13.09–13.10; also discussed in §15.16); and

— whether the applicant has failed to take any of the steps needed to keep an application having a date of filing from being withdrawn. These are discussed in §15.15 for normal applications, and in §15.24 for divisional and replacement applications (for which the required time periods are different and generally reduced). Limited extensions of the prescribed periods under s.15(10) are available as discussed in §15.17.

Under subs.(4), the examiner will check whether any part of the description or drawings appear to be missing (see §15.13).

Under r.23, the examiner will check whether the requirements of rr.6–9 (relating to priority and discussed under s.5) have been met.

Under r.24, the examiner will check whether the application was filed within 12 months of the first claimed priority date.

Under r.13(2)–(7), the examiner will check for a sequence listing where the application concerns biological material and includes one or more sequences.

Preliminary examination report

15A.07 Preliminary examination leads (under subs.(3)) to a report by the examiner made to the Comptroller setting out his determinations under subs.(2).

Where the examiner's report to the Comptroller identifies formal requirements that have not been complied with, the Comptroller is required (under subs.(6)) to specify a period during which the applicant has the opportunity to contest the report by making observations and/or by amending the application.

The Comptroller is also required (under subs.(9)) to notify the applicant of any requirements under ss.13(2) and 15(10) which have not been complied with and/or any missing parts.

In addition, the preliminary examination report will indicate whether the application complies with the requirements of rr.6–9 relating to priority (r.23(2)). If the application appears to have been filed too late for the priority claim to be valid, the examiner will indicate this (r.24(1)) and advise the applicant of possibility of a late declaration of priority under s.5(2B). If the priority date needs to be corrected, this must be done within two months of notification (under r.24(2)), or the priority claim will be disregarded.

If no sequence listing has been provided, the preliminary examination report will set a period of two months to provide the sequence listing (r.13(3)). The application may be refused if this is not done.

The period for response to formal requirement objections raised in the preliminary examination report is set by the UK-IPO (subss.(5) and (6)). The MOPP indicates that the usual period is 15 months from the priority date (or date of filing where there is no priority claim), or two months from notification where that period has expired or nearly expired. However, the preliminary examination report may also list outstanding requirements for which a different deadline applies, for example filing of PF 7 (see §15.16), filing of a priority document, or dealing with a missing part (see §15.13).

The MOPP indicates that a two-month extension of time for responding to a preliminary examination report will be allowed on receiving a request for extension in writing before the end of the extended period, and that a further discretionary extension may be possible.

If satisfactory amendments are not made within the specified period, or the observations are not accepted, the application may be refused (subss.(7) and (8)). The MOPP indicates that an opportunity to submit observations or request a hearing will be given first.

Reinstatement of an application refused for failure to respond adequately to the preliminary examination report may be possible under s.20A, although only if the Comptroller can be satisfied that the failure to comply was "unintentional", for which see the commentary on s.20A.

Where no deficiencies are found during preliminary examination, no preliminary examination report is normally sent to the applicant. However, the *Formalities Manual* indicates that a "no objection" letter will be sent to private applicants.

SECTION 16

Publication of application

16.—(1) Subject to section 22 below **and to any prescribed restrictions,** where an application has a date of filing, then, as soon as possible after the end of the prescribed period, the comptroller shall, unless the application is withdrawn or refused before preparations for its publication have been completed by the Patent Office, publish it as filed (including not only the original claims but also any amendments of those claims and new claims subsisting immediately before the completion of those preparations) and he may, if so requested by the applicant, publish it as aforesaid during that period, and in either event shall advertise the fact and date of its publication in the journal.

16.01

(2) The comptroller may omit from the specification of a published application for a patent any matter—

(a) which in his opinion disparages any person in a way likely to damage him, or

(b) the publication or exploitation of which would in his opinion be generally expected to encourage offensive, immoral or anti-social behaviour.

Note. The additional words in the first line of the section were inserted by SI 2005/2471, with effect from October 1, 2005. Rule 11 (reprinted in §6.02) provides such a restriction.

RELEVANT RULE—RULE 26

Rule 26—Publication of application

26.—(1) The period prescribed for the purposes of section 16(1) is eighteen months beginning [with] immediately after—

16.02

(a) where there is no declared priority date, the date of filing of the application; or

(b) where there is a declared priority date, that date.

(2) Where a person's application under rule 11(1)(a) or (b) has been accepted by the comptroller, the comptroller must ensure that the application for the patent as published does not mention that person's name and address as those of the person believed to be the inventor (or, as the case may be, that person's address as that of the person so believed).

Note. The amendments are made as a consequence of The Patents (Amendment) Rules 2011 (SI 2011/2052) that came into force on October 1, 2011.

COMMENTARY ON SECTION 16

Scope of the section

16.03 Section 16 deals with the publication of a pending application (patents are also published following grant under s.24). This is referred to as "early publication" by the UK-IPO. Subsection (1) provides for automatic publication of a pending application as soon as possible after a prescribed period, unless a secrecy order is in force under s.22 the application has been withdrawn or refused before the UK-IPO's preparations for publication have been completed. Subsection (1) also provides for possible earlier publication if the applicant so requests and requires the Comptroller to advertise the publication (and its date) in the *Patents Journal*. By r.26, the prescribed period is 18 months from the declared priority date or, where there is no declared priority date, from the date of filing.

The reference to "prescribed restrictions" in subs.(1) provides the basis for r.11 (reprinted in §13.06) under which an inventor may apply either to waive his right to have his name and address, or just his address mentioned as that of and/or the inventor in the publication under s.16 (see r.26 above). An inventor may find it desirable to make such a waiver in a situation where activists may seek to harass him because of his involvement in the research leading to the invention. This information will then also be withheld from file inspection under r.51(3)(e) (reprinted at §118.02). This topic is discussed in §13.12.

Subsection (2) allows the Comptroller to omit from the publication any material that he considers disparaging or encouraging offensive, immoral or anti-social behaviour see §16.05.

References throughout the Act to an application for a patent being published are defined (by s.130(5)) as references to the application being published under s.16.

Although s.16 is not one of the sections specified in s.130(7) as being intended to have the same effect as the corresponding provisions of the EPC or the PCT, there are similar provisions in art.93 of the EPC and rr.48, 67, 68 and 69(1) of the EPC and in PCT arts 21 and 29 and PCT rr.9.1 and 48. Thus, applications for a European patent and international applications are each published, also about 18 months after their first claimed priority date. Publication of pending applications 18 months after the earliest claimed priority date is a common pattern of international patent practice. By s.78(3)(d), an application for a European patent (UK) published under EPC art.93 is deemed to be published under s.16, see §78.04. Likewise, by s.89B(2), an international application for a patent (UK) published under PCT art.21 is deemed to be published under s.16, but only if the international application has subsequently entered the UK phase, and subject to the provisions of s.89B(3), see §89B.10.

Under s.118(3)(b), the bibliographic information defined in r.55 (reprinted at §118.06) may be published before the publication date of the application. In fact it is published in the *Patents Journal* about five weeks after the date of filing.

Publication usually takes place every Wednesday.

"Contents of published application"

16.04 The contents of the application to be published are defined by s.14(2). Publication under s.16 gives rise to the "A-specification", that is the printed specification having a new "Publication Number" with the suffix "A", see §16.13. The published A-specification includes:

— a front page

— the specification (description, claims and drawings if present), and

— the search report.

The front page of the A-specification published under s.16 contains the bibliographic information defined in r.55 (reprinted at §118.06), that is: the date of filing and filing number; the name of the applicant; the date of filing, the filing number and country of any earlier application in respect of which a declaration of priority has been filed; and the title. The various items of bibliographic data are linked to the numbers of the INID standard code of WIPO, as explained in §123.84.

In addition, the front page contains: the address of the applicant; the name of the inventor (unless his right to be mentioned has been waived); the name and address of the appointed agent, if any; a list of the documents cited in the search report under s.17(5); the international classification; the abstract (which may have been amended by the UK-IPO); and possibly one or more drawings.

A divisional application will be identified as such.

If a statement that the invention was exhibited at an international exhibition has been filed, this information also appears on the front page of the printed specification.

Footnotes indicate if the claims and/or drawings were filed after the date of filing, or when originally filed informal drawings have been subsequently replaced, but no indication is given whether any matter has been divided out into a separate application.

Any amendments to PF 1 will be reflected in the published A-specification, together with an explanatory notice.

The specification is published in the form in which it was originally filed (see subs.(1)). The MOPP indicates that the "as filed" state of an application refers to the papers present at the UK-IPO at the close of business on the date of filing.

The specification is no longer typeset, but is published by reproduction of the pages filed. Where, as previously, a specification was published in typeset form, it should be remembered that this could contain printing errors and that the authentic text is not the printed form but that held on the UK-IPO file.

The published specification also includes any original or amended claims filed after the date of filing but before completion of the preparations for publication together with a notice that these were filed after the date of filing. The MOPP indicates that amended claims may be omitted if they do not appear on self-explanatory fresh pages, which should preferably be headed to indicate that they present amended claims. Amendments to the description and drawings are not included in the published specification. The form of the claims on publication are complete is important in determining the rights arising on publication in accordance with s.69(2) and (3) (infringement of rights conferred by publication of application), see §69.06.

Corrections to obvious clerical errors should be included in the published specification, provided that these have been made in timely fashion under s.117.

If replacement pages are filed to comply with formal requirements (for example, formal drawings), these replacement pages will be published, together with a notice that the replacement pages were filed after the date of filing.

If the application was originally filed in a foreign language, the translated specification will be published, together with a notice that the application was originally filed in a foreign language.

If a divisional application is filed including additional subject-matter which must be excluded before it can proceed (s.76), the application will still be published as filed i.e. including the additional subject-matter.

As the search under s.17(5) is carried out before the application is published under s.16(1), a list of the documents cited in the search report is included on the front sheet of the published specification. The A-specification also includes a copy of the examiner's search report which (as with EPO and PCT search reports) indicates the apparent relevance of each cited document, for which see §17.08.

The UK-IPO endeavours to issue the search report within 15 months of the declared priority date, or within three months of the date of filing if there is no declared priority date, provided that PF 9A and the claims have already been filed. If, for any reason, the issue of the search report is delayed, publication under s.16 is also delayed. This contrasts with the provisions of art.93 of the EPC under which the search report and the definitive abstract are published either as an annex to the description and claims and any drawings, or separately later if they are not ready by the time the technical preparations for publication have been completed. Rule 48.2(g) of the PCT has a similar provision to art.93 of the EPC.

The MOPP contains further information on the practice of the UK-IPO in relation to variations in the contents of the application as published under s.16, e.g. where documents have not become available in time, including missing parts of documents or drawings, or have been presented in an unclear or illegible form or where some wording has been deleted (under s.16(2)) because of apparent disparaging or offensive wording. In such cases the front page of the "A-specification" will contain information on what has not been included in the printed version, including notes on new claims and other matter that had been submitted after the date of filing. However, such non-included information will normally be available upon a file inspection. Where later printer's errors are discovered in the A-specification, an erratum notice can be issued which will then become part of the published application when accessed on the UK-IPO website or when further copies are purchased.

Material omitted from published application

16.05   Material may be omitted from publication because it is objectionable or because it is very detailed.

Subsection (2) provides that the comptroller may omit certain matter from the published specification, i.e. matter which disparages any person in a way likely to damage him, or the publication or exploitation of which would be generally expected to encourage offensive, immoral or anti-social behaviour. Apparently, under this provision and having regard to the Landmines Act 1998 (c.33) s.2(2), the Comptroller will refuse to publish any specification which relates to anti-personnel landmines, see §1.21.

The applicant is informed that matter has been expunged under this provision and has the opportunity of contesting the decision, although there is no appeal from a final decision of the Comptroller on this point (s.97(1)(b)). Note that the Comptroller considers that he has the power under s.16(2) to refuse to publish the application in its entirety should he consider this appropriate in all the circumstances.

Where this provision is used, the printed specification contains a statement at the place of deletion that "certain matter has here been suppressed from publication under section 16(2)", and this matter is also removed from the file copy of the specification.

Certain very detailed information may be removed from the text for publication purposes because of its specific nature. This provision is used, for example, in the case of complicated computer programs or long sequence listings, details of which are indicated to be available for inspection in the file.

Accelerated publication

16.06   Section 16(1) provides that publication may take place within the 18-month period after the priority date or date of filing on request by the applicant.

Such a request should be made in writing and marked "REQUEST FOR ACCELER-ATED PUBLICATION", see [2000] *CIPA* 107. No reason need be given.

Accelerated publication may be desirable if there is a potential infringer, so that rights arising on publication in accordance with s.69(2) and (3) come into effect as soon as possible. Accelerated publication may also be desirable so that the patent application is full prior art for novelty and inventive step purposes against third party patent applications from as early a date as possible.

For accelerated publication to take place, the claims and abstract must have been filed, the search must have taken place (see s.17) and the formal requirements must have been met (see ss.14 and 15A).

Accelerated publication allows the application to be moved to the start of the five week publication cycle. The publication cycle cannot itself be accelerated.

Any request for early publication must be withdrawn before a priority claim can be corrected under r.6.

Delayed publication

An application on which, for security reasons, directions prohibiting publication have **16.07** been imposed under s.22(2) will not be published unless and until such directions have been revoked under s.22(5)(e), see §22.11.

If priority has been claimed, but a copy of each required priority document has not been filed, publication will be delayed until it is decided whether priority has been lost because of the failure to file the priority document.

If this is so, then the application is re-dated with publication delayed until 18 months after the new priority date or date of filing as appropriate.

Effects of publication under section 16

The publication of the application is advertised in the *Patents Journal* (subs.(1)). **16.08**

Normally, printed copies of the A-specification are made available on the advertised publication day but, if not, publication is still deemed to have taken place on that day. The A-specifications are available on various websites, including the ESP@CENET® database (which can be accessed via the UK-IPO website).

The date of advertised publication is important as it defines the start of the term of six months prescribed by r.28(2) (reprinted in §18.02) for requesting substantive examination under s.18. This period is unusual in not being determined with reference to the date of filing or declared priority date, and special care in its monitoring is therefore needed, see §18.06. For further details of the availability of published specifications, see §123.83.

Upon publication of the application, an entry is created in the register of patents (see §16.09).

Under s.118(1), after publication of an application, all documents relating to it subject to certain exclusions, are available or open to inspection, as discussed in §118.10. Online inspection is now available via the IPSUM database on the UK-IPO website. Note that under s.118(4), any person threatened with a future infringement action on an application can have sight of the file before publication, see §118.12.

Creation of entry in the register

Upon publication of the application, an entry is created in the register of patents (as **16.09** maintained under s.32, see §32.01). By r.44(1) (reprinted in §32.04), this entry is of each of:

(a) the name of the applicant(s);

(b) the name and address of the person identified as the inventor;

(c) the address of the applicant and his address for service;

(d) the title of the invention;

(e) the date of filing of the application for a patent;

(f) the application number;

(g) where a declaration has been made for the purposes of s.5(2)—

   (i) the date of filing of each earlier relevant specified in the declaration,

   (ii) its application number, and

   (iii) the country it was filed in or in respect of; and

(h) the date of the application's publication.

For subsequent entries in the register, see r.44(3) and (4) (reprinted in §32.04) and §24.10 and §32.17. Since computerisation of the register in late 1989, the filing of a divisional application has been recorded in the register entry for the parent application/ patent. Under r.44(2), the applicant may request that the name and address of the inventor(s) be omitted from the register and file inspection.

Once the application has been published, the file of the application is open to public file inspection.

Date when preparations for publications are complete

16.10   A warning that automatic publication of the application will take place unless the application is withdrawn, or is deemed to be withdrawn, before preparations for its publication are complete is given on the reverse of the filing receipt issued by the UK-IPO.

The applicant may wish to take action before preparations for publication are complete, in particular to withdraw the application to prevent publication, or to file amended claims which will determine the scope of provisional protection.

Unless a request for accelerated publication has been made, the search report is issued with a covering letter indicating the estimated date when preparations for publication will be complete. The MOPP states that this estimated date will normally be the later of 16 months and three weeks, after the earliest priority date (or the date of filing if no priority is claimed) or four weeks after issue of the search report. A letter of intended publication will be sent to the applicant giving three days' notice of the date on which preparations for publication will be complete.

The date when preparations for publication of the specification have been completed by the UK-IPO (according to s.16(1)) has to be determined objectively on a case-by-case basis, this probably being the date when the specification has been allocated to one of the printing contractors and these are ready to be sent to, or collected by, him from the UK-IPO (the MOPP indicates that following computerisation the nearest equivalent point in the procedure applies). Accordingly, up to that date, the applicant is entitled to withdraw or amend the application, but thereafter the Comptroller has no discretion. In *Peabody International's Application* [1986] R.P.C. 521, that date had already been reached, and indeed the printer had already collected the papers: withdrawal of the application was therefore not permitted.

Rule 3(3)(c) (reprinted at §5.06A) indicates that there is no "declared priority date" if every priority declaration has been withdrawn or disregarded by the time when preparations for publication are complete.

Practice under Section 16

Filing of further applications before publication

16.11   On publication the contents of a patent application become public, i.e. citable for novelty and inventive step purposes, see ss.2 and 3 and in particular s.2(3). Therefore, consideration should be given to filing further patent applications for developments of an invention before publication of the original application.

Examination and search [Sections 17–21]

SECTION 17

Search

17.01   **17.—(1) The comptroller shall refer an application for a patent to an examiner for a search if, and only if—**

    (a) the comptroller has referred the application to an examiner for a preliminary examination under section l5A(1) above;

    (b) the application has not been withdrawn or treated as withdrawn;

    (c) before the end of the prescribed period—

       (i) **the applicant makes a request to the Patent Office in the prescribed form for a search; and**

       (ii) **the fee prescribed for the search ("the search fee") is paid;**

    (d) **the application includes—**

       (i) **a description of the invention for which a patent is sought; and**

       (ii) **one or more claims; and**

    (e) **the description and each of the claims comply with the requirements of rules as to language.**

(2) [*repealed*]

(3) [*repealed*]

(4) Subject to subsections (5) and (6) below, on a search requested under this section, the examiner shall make such investigation as in his opinion is reasonably practicable and necessary for him to identify the documents which he thinks will be needed to decide, on a substantive examination under section 18 below, whether the invention for which a patent is sought is new and involves an inventive step.

(5) On any such search the examiner shall determine whether or not the search would serve any useful purpose on the application as for the time being constituted and—

    (a) if he determines that it would serve such a purpose in relation to the whole or part of the application, he shall proceed to conduct the search so far as it would serve such a purpose and shall report on the results of the search to the comptroller; and

    (b) if he determines that the search would not serve such a purpose in relation to the whole or part of the application, he shall report accordingly to the comptroller;

and in either event the applicant shall be informed of the examiner's report.

(6) If it appears to the examiner, either before or on conducting a search under this section, that an application relates to two or more inventions, but that they are not so linked as to form a single inventive concept, he shall initially only conduct a search in relation to the first invention specified in the claims of the application, but may proceed to conduct a search in relation to another invention so specified if the applicant pays the search fee in respect of the application so far as it relates to that other invention.

(7) After a search has been requested under this section for an application the comptroller may at any time refer the application to an examiner for a supplementary search, and **subsections (4) and (5)** [*subsection (4)*] above shall apply in relation to a supplementary search as **they apply** [*it applies*] in relation to any other search under this section.

(8) **A reference for a supplementary search in consequence of—**

    (a) **an amendment of the application made by the applicant under section 18(3) or 19(1) below, or**

    (b) **a correction of the application, or of a document filed in connection with the application under section 117 below,**

shall be made only on payment of the prescribed fee, unless the comptroller directs otherwise.

Notes

1. The section title was amended and subs.(1) replaced by Regulatory Reform (Patents) Order 2004 (SI 2004/2357) ("RRO") with effect from January 1, 2005 except for applications then pending. This rendered subss.(2) and (3) ineffective for applications filed from that date, see Note 2 to §15.01.

2. Subsection (7) was amended and new subs.(8) added by Sch.5 para.3 to the CDPA 1988, with effect from January 7, 1991 (SI 1990/2168).

RELEVANT RULE—RULE 27

Rule 27—Search under section 17

17.02 **27.**—(1) A request under section 17(1)(c)(i) for a search must be made on Patents Form 9A.

(2) The comptroller may, if he thinks fit, send to the applicant a copy of any document (or any part of it) referred to in the examiner's report made under section 17.

(3) Where an examiner conducts a search in relation to the first only of two or more inventions, in accordance with section 17(6), he must report this fact to the comptroller, and the comptroller must notify the applicant accordingly.

(4) The applicant must pay any search fee in relation to those inventions (other than the first) on or before the relevant date.

(5) The relevant date is the first day of the three month period ending with the compliance date of the application.

(6) The fee for a supplementary search under section 17(8), or a search under section 17(6), must be accompanied by Patents Form 9A.

COMMENTARY ON SECTION 17

Scope of the section

17.03 The substantive examination of patent applications is effected in three distinct stages: (1) a preliminary examination under s.15A (as discussed above in the commentary on it) to establish whether the application is in an appropriate form for it to proceed; (2) a search (under s.17) to search for and provide material upon which it may be appropriate for the patentability of the submitted claims to be assessed (as discussed in this commentary); and (3) a substantive patentability examination under s.18 based on the provisions of the Act and Rules, with particular reference to the material revealed by the search under s.17 (as discussed below). These sections are not included in s.130(7) and so are not specified as having been intended to have the same meanings as the corresponding sections of the EPC and the PCT, but similar provisions exist under the EPC and PCT articles and regulations. Section 17 (as in force from January 1, 2005) deals only with the search, as distinct from the "preliminary examination".

Rule 27 (reprinted above) is the operative rule for making the necessary request for a search. This has to be done on PF 9A. Old form PF 9 is generally redundant as it only applies to applications which were pending on January 1, 2005.

The search (subss. (4) and (5))

17.04 The search will not be commenced before the requirements of subs.(1) have been met and, therefore, not until the deficiencies in the preliminary examination report have been rectified.

By subs.(4) the purpose of the search is to identify documents which the examiner thinks will be needed to enable a decision to be made as to whether the invention is new in accordance with s.2 and whether it involves an inventive step in accordance with s.3. The search scope and strategy is discussed in the "Matter to be searched for" section of the MOPP, currently in paras 17.36–17.43. Where the application claims priority from an earlier application, any search report issued thereon will normally be examined by the search examiner. Also, the MOPP indicates that the search examiner should pay particular attention to prior art referred to in the application's description of the invention sought to be patented. Additionally, the MOPP suggests that if the search examiner is of the opinion that the claims as they stand do not clearly define the invention, then the search should primarily be directed to what the search examiner perceives to have been invented. This may arise in situations where, for example, due to an inappropriate choice of wording the claims in fact define something different from what has been described or unwittingly embrace matter which is well known.

The examiner may issue a preliminary report where it is thought that this may lead to amendments being proposed which would simplify the completion of a full report.

However, while a search of the prior art is the primary purpose of the search, the search examiner may also point to any concern that he may have from his study of the supplied description of the invention as to whether this is objectionable on grounds other than those under s.2 or s.3. Thus, he may raise other objections to the allowability of the application on other grounds, such as, e.g. inherent unpatentability under s.1(2); whether the description of the invention contained in the application is sufficient to enable the invention to be practised (s.14(3)): whether the application has claims defining the invention which are supported by the description (s.14(5)); and whether the description contains subject-matter additional to that in the description of the invention as present in the application at its date of filing (s.76(2)). However, the MOPP indicates that such points should only be raised in the search report if they appear to be clear and substantial, and should otherwise be left to be raised in the substantive examination report under s.18(3).

The aim of the UK-IPO is that the search report should be issued within four months of PF 9A being filed so that, it can be included in the printed "A–specification". However, this aim is not always achieved across all technologies, especially electronics and biotechnology. If, for any reason, the issue of the search report is delayed, publication under s.16 is also delayed (see §16.04). Also, early receipt of the search report may assist the applicant as regards filing corresponding applications abroad, or through the EPO, or of possible filing of an additional application for further subject-matter claiming priority from the present application provided that sufficient time exists for this to be done within the period of 12 months (or potentially longer, see s.5(2A) and s.5(2B)) from the date of filing of the searched application; and also consideration of the possible desirability of seeking some amendment of the text and claims before the substantive examination under s.18 takes place, and having regard also to the benefit such amendment may bring under s.69, see the commentary there.

A copy of the search report is sent to the applicant, usually together with a copy of any document (or part thereof) referred to in the report (as provided for in r.27(2)), but it may be too difficult to do this at the same time, as explained in the MOPP (currently in para.17.104.1). No charge is made for this supply. Applicants are also able to order, at the time of filing the or each PF 9A, as many extra sets of cited documents as required (see the *Patents Journal* March 30, 1994). The Office makes a non-statutory charge in order to cover the cost of this service. No refund is made in the event of there being no citations. This non-statutory charge is additional to the search fee and should be shown immediately after the search fee on the Fee Sheet accompanying PF 9A. The supply of these copies of cited references does not involve any infringement of copyright, see ss.45 and 178 of the 1988 Act.

It is possible to combine the search and substantive examination (under ss.17 and 18 respectively). This happens automatically if PF 10 (for substantive examination) is filed at the same time as PF 9A (for the search), unless the application is an international application which has entered the national phase after communication to the Patent Office of the international search report, or if a specific written request to the contrary is made at the time the two forms are filed together; substantive examination then being delayed until after publication of the application under s.16. A combined examination can also be requested when filing PF 10 after PF 9A, but this request, which must be in writing, will not be entertained if the search has already been commenced. The effect of such combined examination is discussed in §18.13.

A request for an accelerated search can be made, as a distinct procedure separate from requesting combined search and examination. The request for this should be made clearly and unambiguously and be accompanied by a reasoned statement of the reason for the request, and a statement made whether accelerated publication is also being requested, see the *Patents Journal* August 2, 2000 and [2000] *CIPA* 107. For further information on accelerated search procedure see the MOPP (para.17.05).

By subs.(5), the search is conducted only insofar as it will serve a useful purpose. Accordingly, the search examiner confines the search to material which is relevant to novelty and inventive step in relation to the invention as presented at the time of the search. Consequently, the search report (in contrast to search reports from the EPO) tends to cite documents of background interest only if these are considered relevant to an argument of lack of inventive step (see [1994] *CIPA* 122), but see §17.08 as regards a change in practice since 1994.

If the search examiner decides that a search would serve no useful purpose, for example where the examiner sees that the alleged invention is not patentable as seemingly clearly falling within the class of inventions which s.1(2) regards as unpatentable as such, then the applicant is notified under subs.(5)(b) by a letter containing the examiner's report to this effect, and the applicant may amend his application after receipt of such report under the terms of s.19 or request a hearing on this objection, as discussed in the commentary on s.1 above. If the application is, however, abandoned, the MOPP indicates that no refund of the search fee will be made. Where no search is carried out because it is seen that the application appears to be unpatentable as relating only to subject-matter excluded from patentability under s.1(2), the Comptroller is entitled to proceed directly to a rejection under s.18(3), even if no examination fee has been paid.

When amendments are made to the claims which will enable the examiner to conduct the search, the search will be carried out before publication under s.16 if the amendments are received in time. Otherwise the search is deferred until after publication.

When it appears that an application has been filed without professional assistance, the practice of the UK-IPO is to issue its examination report in a different style, and perhaps even to supply the applicant with some of the UK-IPO literature on the filing and prosecution of a patent application. For an explanation of the steps taken by the Office when an application is filed apparently without professional assistance, see *Hulmes' Application* BL O/176/86. In that case, the application was rejected for insufficient disclosure as originally filed; no search could be performed and the search fee was certified for refund, see also *Poon's Application* BL O/51/89 for a similar case where the applicant representing himself insisted on a hearing.

With regard to applications from private applicants for which a search fee has been paid, the MOPP indicates that such applications should be sent to the Private Applicant Unit (PAU) for consideration before preliminary examination and search. PAU examiners should consider whether the application is insufficient under s.14(3), or clearly unpatentable under s.1(1)(c) or (d). They should also consider whether the application appears to clearly lack novelty, and if so may carry out a rudimentary search to identify documents illustrating this. If the PAU examiner considers that the application has no patentable content, then the applicant should be sent a letter informing him of the shortcomings and giving him the option to withdraw the application with a refund of the search fee.

Much more information on how the UK-IPO handles unusual situations and how it deals with applications apparently made without professional assistance can be found in Ch.17 of the MOPP. For the possibility of remission of the search fee, see §17.06 below.

Search against further inventions and supplementary search (subss.(6)–(8))

17.05   If the examiner conducting the search considers that the claims are directed to two or more inventions not so linked as to form a single inventive concept, he is required (by subs.(6)) to restrict the search to the first-claimed invention. Rule 27(3) requires that the examiner must notify the applicant of the fact that he has done so. A supplementary search can then be carried out on the claims identified as relating to a different inventive entity, but this requires the filing of a further PF 9A and payment of a further search fee which can perhaps later be remitted, see §17.06. This further PF 9A must identify the claims to be searched; and must be filed not later than three months before the end of the compliance period under r.30 (as discussed in §18.11). Extension of this period is implicitly available if the r.30 period is extended (as of right under r.108(2) or in the exercise of the Comptroller's discretion under r.108(3)—this is restricted by r.30 being specified in Pts 2 and 3 of Sch.4 to the Rules.

When only a partial search is carried out in the first instance, and the non-searched claims are retained in the application, an objection of plurality of invention (contrary to s.14(5)(d) and (6)) can be expected during the substantive examination, as discussed in §18.14. On the concept of unity of invention, see §14.40.

When a broad claim has been drawn with a view to obtaining a broad search, there is the risk that the search examiner will not proceed further once he has found some prior art anticipating the broad claim so that the applicant remains in the dark as to whether subject-matter in some of the sub-claims may or may not be patentable. With a view to avoiding a requirement for a subsequent supplementary search, PF 9A can be accompanied by a letter indicating which of the sub-claims are regarded as significant. If these are few in number, the examiner may then extend the primary search to these claims also, although he is under no obligation so to do.

A supplementary search may be carried out at any time, see subs.(7), and copies of documents (or any parts thereof) which are referred to in that supplementary search report are provided as for a primary search.

Subsection (7) also enables an update of the primary search to be carried out as part of the s.18 examination procedure so as to extend it to include recently published UK, European and international applications and to extend the field of search in the event that the examiner finds the search report to be inadequate for the making of a decision under s.18(4) as to patentability of the invention. Such updating of the original search is distinct from an additional search under subs.(6) and the MOPP (paras 17.115–17.118) explains this. Thus, the provisions of subs.(6) do not apply to a supplementary search carried out under subs.(7) as an "additional search".

Subsection (8) allows the Comptroller to require a fee for a supplementary search if the need for such a search arises from an amendment under s.18(3) or 19(1) or from a correction under s.117. The situation arises typically when an amendment to remove a lack of unity leaves the application containing claims to an unsearched invention. The UK-IPO can use this power to avoid examining an invention for which a search fee has not been paid under subss.(1), (6) or (8). In this respect, UK practice differs from that of the EPO, where r.137 provides that amended claims may not relate to unsearched subject-matter and the EPO Guidelines C–III, 7.12 require the applicant to be informed that he can pursue the unsearched subject-matter only in a divisional application.

Under s.18(1A), if a fee is required under s.17(8), substantive examination will not proceed until the fee is paid or the application is amended to render the supplementary search unnecessary. If neither the fee is paid nor the application amended, the Comptroller will be entitled to refuse the application, see §18.06. Presumably, there will first be an opportunity to contend that a supplementary search is unnecessary even without amending the application.

Refund of the search fee

17.06

Provision for refund of the search fee in certain specified circumstances is provided for by r.106 (reprinted at §123.23 and discussed at §123.65). A refund may also arise (under r.107) where the Comptroller is satisfied that there had been an irregularity of procedure, see §17.09.

If it is successfully argued during substantive examination under s.18 that the inventions of claims against which separate search reports have been drawn up under subs.(6) or (8) do involve the same invention for which a search report was drawn up under subs.(6) on the parent application, the search fee paid on the divisional application may, and is likely to, be refunded (r.106(2)(b)). Also this may be applicable to an international application (UK) which has entered the UK national phase, and the Comptroller already has available to him a copy of the International Search Report (r.106(2)(a)), see also §89A.37.

If an application is irrevocably withdrawn after the search fee has been paid, but before the search has been issued, the search fee may be refunded, though this is a matter of discretion (*Spectra Tech's Application* BL O/171/98). There is apparently no rule which authorises the Comptroller to refund all or part of the search fee paid on an application claiming priority from an earlier United Kingdom application on which a search report for the same invention has already issued, and the MOPP states (para.17.48) that this should not be done.

The MOPP indicates that, if the examiner's opinion is that the application has no patentable content, a letter suggesting action before search (ABS) (or, if appropriate, action before combined search and examination (ABCSE) may be issued. This letter states the examiner's view that there is no likelihood of a patent being granted, and sets out the reasons why the examiner considers that the invention is not patentable. The letter specifies a period for response (usually one month, but can be longer if appropriate) in which the applicant may withdraw the application with a refund of the search fee.

Furnishing of translations of cited documents

17.07 A search report may refer to documents in a foreign language and copies of such will, if possible, normally be sent with the search report. The search report may also, helpfully, list any corresponding English-language documents, see the MOPP. Where in the subsequent substantive patentability examination an objection is made to a foreign language document in a s.18(3) report and the applicant wishes to refer in detail to such a document, he will be filing a copy of the cited document; an English translation of this may then be required (under r.113(1) and (4)), see §123.81.

PRACTICE UNDER SECTION 17

The extent of the search

17.08 No limit is placed by subs.(4) on the field and extent of the search. In practice, the area of search will include: United Kingdom patents published since about 1925 and applications published under the present Act; published European patent applications; international applications published up to the date of the search; and United States patents published since at least 1974. The MOPP (at the "Matter to be searched for" and "Performing the search"sections) discusses the extent of the search and the strategy used in it. Search reports issued on apparently corresponding applications elsewhere and available to the UK-IPO, perhaps confidentially via a private website or by publicly accessible databases such as the PAIR database operated by the US Patent and Trademark Office may also be studied by the search examiner.

The eventual search report sent to the applicant indicates the field of the search which was carried out and the claims to which the search was applied (see the MOPP section "The Search Report"). The relevant documents founding the search are then cited, in standard abbreviated form, in the search report sent to the applicant, as explained in the MOPP.

As with the EPO search, the references cited in the search report are categorised as to their perceived relevance. Category X denotes a document considered relevant when taken alone. Category Y denotes a document considered relevant only when taken in combination with some other document and so is not considered as a novelty-destroying disclosure, though seen to be relevant to an objection of obviousness, as of course can a category X document be also. Category A denotes a document cited only to indicate background material. Documents which were published only between the priority and filing dates are additionally categorised by the letter P, indicating relevance under s.2(3) only to a novelty objection; or by the letter E for a reference which may also be effective, although only if the claimed priority date is not effective in respect of subject-matter indicated by the cited document.

As set out below, where there is lack of unity, then claims relating wholly to second or further inventions will not be included in the "claims searched" section of the search report. In addition, independent claims should not be searched if they relate to wholly unpatentable subject-matter. However, claims which are unpatentable as worded but could form the basis of a patentable claim—for example, method of treatment claims which could be converted to a valid second medical use claim—are likely to be searched if they fall within the scope of the first invention.

Further, the MOPP outlines that claims which are completely unsupported and of indeterminate scope should not be searched; in particular, applications containing totally indeterminate claims such as to "any novel matter disclosed". The MOPP indicates that such claims are to be disregarded at the search stage. No reference need be made to them in the search report.

If the examiner determines that the claims comprise plural inventions and the first claimed invention appears to be wholly unpatentable, but one or more subsequent inventions are patentable, then the MOPP indicates that the search should be directed to the first patentable invention.

Additionally, current UK-IPO practice is that, where it is considered that the or each claimed invention is excluded from patentability but that a patentable invention supported by the description can be identified, a search should be directed to the latter and the applicant should be informed of the examiner's views.

The MOPP indicates that, if the examiner's opinion is that the application has no patentable content, a letter suggesting action before search (ABS) (or, if appropriate, action before combined search and examination (ABCSE) may be issued, see §17.06.

Alternatively, the applicant may have an opportunity to provide amendments and/or arguments to address the issues raised in the ABS/ABCSE letter.

Supplementary searches

17.09

If the examiner considers that the claims are directed to two or more inventions not so linked as to form a single inventive concept, he is required (under subs.(6)) to restrict the search to the first-claimed invention and (under r.27(3)) to inform the applicant to this effect. Thus, the applicant should choose the subject of claim 1 with such a possibility in mind, see *Hollister's Application* [1983] R.P.C. 10. The search report will identify those claims that the examiner considers are not directed to the first invention and against which he has not conducted a search. The applicant will then be permitted (under r.27(4)) to request a further search against such claims by filing a further PF 9A and paying the additional search fee therewith.

Although the applicant has up to the beginning of the third month before expiry of the r.30 period in which to do this, the earlier the request is made the more time will be left in which to file a divisional application if the further search is favourable, the filing of a divisional application being excluded once this three-month period has commenced, see r.19(3)(b) and §15.16. If it is established during the substantive examination under s.18(2) that the examiner's decision that the claims are not directed to a single invention or inventive concept is wrong, the additional search fee paid on the further search may be refunded by way of rectification of an irregularity in procedure under r.107, see §123.65.

A further search under subs.(6) may be requested only where the examiner has reported that some claims define a further invention. A further search under subs.(6) should not be requested in respect of new or amended claims nor in respect of original claims on which the examiner has not so reported. A separate PF 9A is required in respect of each such further invention for which a search is required. Requests on PF 9A for further searches under subs.(6) should not be filed until the initial search report under subs.(5) has been issued, and then only if the examiner has reported under subs.(1) or s.18(3) that the application relates to a plurality of inventions.

The MOPP specifically indicates the current UK-IPO practice that the search examiner should not respond to a request for a further search under s.17(6) by issuing an ABS letter (see §17.06 and §17.08, above) requesting amendment or other action before search.

If the first search report of the examiner indicates that the search has not been completed, but it is unclear from it whether a non-unity objection arises or not, it is suggested that the examiner be asked to clarify whether objection is being raised under subs.(6) because, if it is, the time for requesting further searches under r.27(4) may expire without it being appreciated that r.27(3) has been applied by the examiner.

Subsection (8) comes into play only when the applicant amends or corrects the specification in a manner that renders the original search ineffective or defective. If that happens, an official letter will be issued notifying the applicant of the need for a supplementary search. Unless the Comptroller should direct otherwise, the supplementary search under this provision requires a fee to be and a further PF 9A to be filed, see r.27(6). It should be possible to contest the need for the supplementary search, and if such a contest is successful after the fee has been paid it should be possible to obtain a refund of the fee under r.107 because of an irregularity in procedure, see §123.65.

Subsection (7) is applied to both subss.(5) and (6) and requires a search report to be issued following any supplementary search. PF 9A requires that, where an additional search is requested, the area for that search should be fully identified on that form by reference to the claims to be searched. If this is not done, the further search will be carried out on the second invention in the previous search report, as Notes (c) and (d) on PF 9A make clear. For a discussion on the search report issued on a divisional application, see §15.32.

If a divisional application is filed for an invention on which a search report has already been drawn up upon the parent application, the search fee paid on the divisional application may be refunded on request (r.106(2)(b)), see §123.65. However, it is always necessary to pay the search fee on the divisional application in the first instance to enable the preliminary examination to take place, see §15.32.

Amendment after the search

17.10   Once the applicant has received the search report, he may voluntarily amend his application. Voluntary amendment is discussed in §19.04.

Amendments made to the description before the publication under s.16 are not included in the printed "A-specification", but any amendments to the claims and/or any additional claims, filed before the preparations for publication are complete, will be printed together with the claims as originally filed. Such amended claims should be filed in a communication marked "URGENT—SECTION 16 PUBLICATION IMMINENT".

Whilst there is no obligation on the applicant to offer any amendment upon receipt of the search report, it is relevant to early amendment of the claims that the rights arising under ss.55 and 69 on publication of the application refer to the claims as they were immediately before completion of the preparations for publication of the application under s.16, that is, the form in which they were originally published, or deemed to be published, under that section.

SECTION 18

Substantive examination and grant or refusal of patent

18.01   **18.**—(1) Where the conditions imposed by section 17(1) above for the comptroller to refer an application to an examiner for a search are satisfied and at the time of the request under that subsection or within the prescribed period—

> (a) a request is made by the applicant to the Patent Office in the prescribed form for a substantive examination; and
>
> (b) the prescribed fee is paid for the examination;

the comptroller shall refer the application to an examiner for a substantive examination; and if no such request is made or the prescribed fee is not paid within that period, the application shall be treated as having been withdrawn at the end of that period.

(1A) If the examiner forms the view that a supplementary search under section 17 above is required for which a fee is payable, he shall inform the comptroller, who may decide that the substantive examination should not proceed until the fee is paid; and if he so decides, then unless within such period as he may allow—

(a) the fee is paid, or

(b) the application is so amended so as to render the supplementary search unnecessary,

he may refuse the application.

(2) On a substantive examination of an application the examiner shall investigate, to such extent as he considers necessary in view of any examination **carried out under section 15A** above and search carried out under section 17 above, whether the application complies with the requirements of this Act and the rules and shall determine that question and report his determination to the comptroller.

(3) If the examiner reports that any of those requirements are not complied with, the comptroller shall give the applicant an opportunity within a specified period to make observations on the report and to amend the application so as to comply with those requirements (subject, however, to section 76 below), and if the applicant fails to satisfy the comptroller that those requirements are complied with, or to amend the application so as to comply with them, the comptroller may refuse the application.

(4) If the examiner reports that the application, whether as originally filed or as amended in pursuance of section **15A** [*17*] above, this section or section 19 below, complies with those requirements at any time before the end of the prescribed period, the comptroller shall notify the applicant of that fact and, subject to subsection (5) and sections 19 and 22 below and on payment within the prescribed period of any fee prescribed for the grant, grant him a patent.

(5) Where two or more applications for a patent for the same invention having the same priority date are filed by the same applicant or his successor in title, the comptroller may on that ground refuse to grant a patent in pursuance of more than one of the applications.

Note. Subsection (1A) was added by Sch.5 para.4 to the CDPA 1988, with effect from January 7, 1991 (SI 1990/2168). The modification of subs.(4) was introduced by the Regulatory Reform (Patents) Order 2004 (SI 2004/2357) with effect from January 1, 2005.

RELEVANT RULES—RULES 28–30

Rule 28—Request for substantive examination under section 18

28.—(1) A request under section 18 for a substantive examination of an application must be made on Patents Form 10.   **18.02**

(2) Subject to paragraphs (3) and (4) and rules 60 and 68(4), the period prescribed for the purposes of section 18(1) is six months beginning [with] immediately after the date the application was published.

(3) Where the comptroller has given directions under section 22(1) or (2) in relation to information contained in the application, the period prescribed for the purposes of section 18(1) is the relevant period.

(4) Paragraphs (2) and (3) do not apply to a new application.

(5) In relation to a new application, the period prescribed for the purposes of section 18(1) is—

(a) two months beginning [with] immediately after its initiation date; or

(b) if it expires later, the relevant period,

and the reference in paragraph (7) to the date of filing of the application is a reference to the date of filing of the earlier application.

(6) But where the new application is filed less than six months before the compliance date, the period prescribed for the purposes of section 18(1) is the period ending with its initiation date.

(7) For the purposes of this rule the relevant period is two years beginning [with] immediately after—

(a) where there is no declared priority date, the date of filing of the application; or

(b) where there is a declared priority date, that date.

Note. Rule 28(5)(a) was amended as from October 1, 2011 by The Patents (Amendment) Rules 2011 (SI 2011/2052).

Rule 29—Substantive examination reports

18.03
29.—(1) Whenever the examiner reports to the comptroller under either section 18(3) or (4) on whether the application complies with the requirements of the Act and these Rules, the comptroller must send a copy of that report to the applicant.

(2) The comptroller may, if he thinks fit, send to the applicant a copy of any document (or any part of it) referred to in the examiner's report.

(3) For the purposes of rules 30 and 31—

(a) "first substantive examination report" means the first report sent to the applicant under paragraph (1); and

(b) "first observations report" means a report sent to the applicant under paragraph (1) which meets the condition in paragraph (4).

(4) The condition is that—

(a) a person has made observations to the comptroller under section 21(1) on the question whether the invention is a patentable invention;

(b) the examiner has reported to the comptroller, as a consequence of those observations, that the invention does not comply with the requirements of the Act or these Rules; and

(c) the comptroller has not previously sent to the applicant a report, relating to those observations, under paragraph (1).

Rule 30—Period for putting application in order

18.04
30.—(1) The period prescribed for the purposes of sections 18(4) and 20(1) (failure of application) is the compliance period.

(2) For the purposes of paragraph (1), subject to paragraphs (3) and (4), the compliance period is—

(a) four years and six months beginning [with] immediately after—

    (i) where there is no declared priority date, the date of filing of the application, or

    (ii) where there is a declared priority date, that date; or

(b) if it expires later, the period of twelve months beginning [with] immediately after the date on which the first substantive examination report is sent to the applicant.

(3) Subject to paragraph (4), where a new application is filed the compliance period is—

(a) where it is filed under section 8(3), 12(6) or 37(4)—

    (i) the period specified in paragraph (2) in relation to the earlier application, or

    (ii) if it expires later, the period of eighteen months beginning [with] immediately after the initiation date; and

(b) where it is filed as mentioned in section 15(9), the period specified in paragraph (2) in relation to the earlier application.

(4) Where the first observations report is sent to the applicant during the last three months of the period specified in paragraphs (2) or (3), the compliance period is three months beginning [with] immediately after the date on which that report is sent.

Note. Rule 30 was amended as from October 1, 2011 by The Patents (Amendment) Rules 2011 (SI 2011/2052).

COMMENTARY ON SECTION 18

Scope of the section

The first two stages of the examination procedure are the preliminary examination **18.05** under s.15A and the search required by s.17, both as discussed above in the commentaries on them. The third stage is the substantive examination prescribed by subss.(1) and (2). Subsection (1A) deals with the possible suspension of the substantive examination when a fee is required for a supplementary search under s.17 until appropriate action is taken, for which see §§17.05 and 17.09. Subsections (3)–(5) deal with refusal, amendment and grant of the application as the result of the examination.

There are corresponding provisions in arts 94, 96 and 97 of the EPC and rr.51 and 52 of the EPC, but s.18 is not one of the sections specified in s.130(7) as being intended to have the same effect as the corresponding provisions of the EPC. The international preliminary examination under Ch.II of the PCT is a substantive examination but results only in an international preliminary examination report, which a national office can regard as advisory rather than determinative of patentability.

The section is in conformity with art.62(2) and (4) of the TRIPS Agreement which read:

"TRIPS Article 62—Acquisition and maintenance of intellectual property rights and related inter-partes procedures

2. Where the acquisition of an intellectual property right is subject to the right being granted or registered, Members shall ensure that the procedures for grant and registration, subject to compliance with the substantive conditions for acquisition of the right, permit the granting or registration of the right within a reasonable period of time so as to avoid unwarranted curtailment of the period of protection.

4. Procedures concerning the acquisition or maintenance of intellectual property rights and, where a member's law provides for such procedures, administrative revocation and *inter partes* proceedings such as opposition, revocation and cancellation shall be governed by the general

principles set out in paragraphs 2 and 3 of Article 41." (Reprinted at §61.03.)

Rule 28 governs the method and time for filing the request for substantive examination; r.29 governs the nature and content of the reports that result from an examination under r.28; and r.30 governs the period within which the substantive examination under the Act is to be completed, see §§18.02–18.04.

The amendments to s.18(4) (set out in §18.01) are a consequence of the changes made at the end of 2004 to separate the stages of preliminary examination and search into new s.15A and amended s.17.

Request for substantive examination (subs.(1))

18.06   By subs.(1) and r.28(1), a request for substantive examination is made by filing PF 10 and paying the prescribed fee (referred to in this commentary as the "examination fee").

In the case of a normal application, such request must be made and the examination fee paid within six months immediately after the date of publication of the first printing of the application under s.16, see r.28(2) above. When a European application is converted into a national UK application under s.81, this period is two years from the declared priority date, if any, or otherwise from the date of filings (r.60); and where an international application for a patent UK enters the UK national phase, this period is 33 months from the declared priority date, if any, or otherwise from the date of filing, although here with a minimum of two months beginning immediately after the date of entry into the UK national phase (r.68(4)), each as respectively discussed in §81.10 and §89A.29.

These date requirements are to be compared to the analogous provision for requesting substantive examination under the EPC or PCT. Thus, under EPC art.94(2) and EPC r.70, a six-month period is allowed for requesting examination of a European patent application reckoned from the date of mention of the publication of the search report in the EPB; and under PCT arts 39 and 40 a demand made to the competent International Preliminary Examination Authority for an international preliminary examination of an international patent application is to be made within 22 months from the priority date (or within three months of issue of the Written Opinion of the International Searching Authority, whichever is the later).

In the case of a "new application", i.e. either a divisional application filed under s.15(9), or a replacement application filed under ss.8(3), 12(6) or 37(4) following entitlement proceedings, the prescribed period for filing PF 10 and paying the examination fee is only two months beginning with its initiation date or, if later, a period of two years starting on the date of filing of the earlier application from its declared priority date, or from the filing date if there is no declared priority date, but where the application is filed less than six months before the compliance date, PF 10 and its fee is required to be paid by its initiation date, i.e. PF 10 must be filed when lodging the new application if such two-year period has already expired, see also §15.21.

Under r.28(3), the period for paying the examination fee on an application of which publication under s.16 is prohibited by a direction under s.22(2) is two years from the declared priority date or, if there is no declared priority date, from the filing date.

By subs.(1), failure to request examination and pay the examination fee within the prescribed period, or the two-month extension period obtainable as of right under r.108(2) by filing PF 52, will result in the application being deemed to have been withdrawn at the end of this period, unless that period can be further or alternatively extended at the Comptroller's discretion under r.108(3) (discussed in §123.72 and §123.74). However, as rr.28, 30, 60 and 68 are each listed in Pt 3 of Sch.4 to the Rules, any such extension(s) may only be of two months each and cannot be sought more than two months after the expiry of the last extended period, as explained in §15.17 and more generally in §123.72.

Subsection (1A) was added in 1990 to deal with a situation where an examiner, in preparing the examination report, considers that a further prior art search is necessary to complete the report. He can then inform the Comptroller of this who may then decide that a supplementary search should be required under subs.(1A) should be carried out under the terms of s.17(8)(b), for which s.17(6) provides, see §17.05. This requires the filing of a further PF 9A and the payment of a further search fee. Then, if this fee is not paid within the period prescribed by r.27, i.e. not later than three months before the compliance date, or by then the application has been amended so as to make the supplementary search unnecessary, the application may be refused.

If refusal or deemed withdrawal does occur, it may be possible to reinstate the application under s.20A, but only if the Comptroller is satisfied that the failure of the applicant to comply with the Act or rules was "unintentional", see the commentary on s.20A. Also, the situation may be correctable (although with considerable difficulty) under r.107 if it could be shown that non-compliance arose from an irregularity attributable, at least in part, to a default, omission or error by the Comptroller, an examiner or the UK-IPO, as discussed in §§123.61 and 123.62.

Refund of the examination fee

If an application is irrevocably withdrawn after the examination fee has been paid, but before the first examination report has issued, the examination fee may be refunded, and usually is, but this is discretionary only (*Spectra-Tech's Application* [1999] R.P.C. 187). **18.07**

Substantive examination (subss.(2) and (3))

The purpose of the substantive examination under subs.(2) is to determine whether the application complies with the requirements of the Act and the Rules, other than the formal requirements which are dealt with in the preliminary examination under s.15A. **18.08**

The principal object of the substantive examination is to determine whether the Comptroller is satisfied that the invention as claimed is patentable. The Comptroller has power to call for a supplementary search and a fee for it (ss.17(7) and (8) and 18(1A), as discussed in §18.09). This examination will concentrate on assessing whether the proposed claims have the required elements of novelty and inventive step (as required by ss.2 and 3), particularly in the light of the prior art revealed by the s.17 search. However, the examination is also required to be directed to whether: (a) the claims extend to subject-matter deemed unpatentable by ss.1(2) and 4A; (b) the claimed subject-matter has industrial utility (as required by s.4); (c) the description of the invention contained in the application is sufficient to enable the skilled person to practise it and the claims are supported by the description (as required respectively by s.14(3) and s.14(5); and (d) whether amendments have been made which offend against s.76(2). All these matters are discussed in depth in the commentaries on each of the indicated sections, it only being necessary here to indicate the broad scope of the substantive patentability examination possible under s.18. However, the examiner can only judge these matters of the basis of the facts available to him as assessed on the balance of probabilities as he sees them, see the MOPP (para.18.09.2).

In the event that the examiner takes a view that the application that he has examined fails to comply with the Act and Rules and so reports to the Comptroller, the Comptroller is required by subs.(3) to provide the applicant with a copy of the examination report (which r.29(3)(a) defines as "the first substantive examination report") and give him an opportunity to make observations and amendments within a specified period, but new matter must not be added, see s.76(2) and the commentary on s.76. With this first examination report there are provided (under r.29(2)) copies of the documents cited, unless the examiner does not think this appropriate in a particular circumstance, e.g. where to do so would be inconvenient in view of the size of the document, as mentioned in §17.04.

The practice which follows receipt of the first substantive examination report is discussed in more detail in §§18.15–18.20, but it may consist of arguments provided in writing in which the applicant seeks to convince the examiner that objections to patentability are not sound or have been met by amendments put forward in the response. This process may follow through a series of examination "section 18(3)" reports and responses to it, perhaps with (further) amendments being put forward, at least on a proposed basis, until the examiner is satisfied that the application is in condition for acceptance for the grant of a patent. Provided that the compliance period prescribed by r.30 (reprinted above) has not expired, the examiner then issues a report under subs.(4)—a "section 18(4) report"—stating that the application will now proceed to the grant process, for which see §18.10.

Amending the application during the substantive examination is governed by s.19 and r.31 (reprinted at §19.02), as discussed in the commentary on that section. The object here will be to convince the examiner to issue a s.18(4) report and an informal telephone discussion or a personal discussion (both will be internally minuted) may assist an attorney in securing at least tentative approval of amendments which he proposes to make.

The period set for response to each s.18(3) report is specified by the Comptroller in it and this period may be extended by exercise of his discretion. Response periods for first examination reports are set out in items 4 to 6 of the UK-IPO practice note dated December 6, 2010. Where the first examination report on an application is issued under s.18(3) three and a half years or more after the earliest priority date (or, where there is no priority claim, the filing date) of the application, the standard period for response is two months from issue of the examination report. This period may be extended as of right by two months by providing a written request under r.108.

In the case where the first examination report is issued less than three and a half years after the earliest priority date (or, where there is no priority claim, the filing date) of the application, the standard period for response will be four months from issue of the examination report or, for combined search and examination cases, two years from the earliest date. This period may also be extended as of right by two months.

However, the examiner has discretion to set different time periods in certain cases. For example, first examination reports on divisional applications received close to the compliance date of the parent application may have a shorter response period in view of the period for putting the application in order.

Because the s.18(3) response period is not specified in the Act or prescribed by the Rules, it can be extended at the Comptroller's discretion under r.108(1), and without limit of time, but the amendment request must be in writing and state why the extension is being requested so that it can easily be seen whether the necessary discretion should be exercised without further investigation, as to which see §18.16. Requests for extension of the compliance period set out in r.30 are also possible, but because r.30 is listed in Pt 3 of Sch.4 to the Rules each extension of the r.30 period is limited under r.108(5) and (7) to no more than two months and application therefor must be made within two months of the expiry of the last extension granted, as explained in §15.17 and more generally in §§123.69–123.76.

Section 21 provides for a person other than an applicant to make observations in writing to the Comptroller on the question whether the invention described in a published application is patentable invention, stating reasons for such observations. The procedure under s.21, and its attendant r.33 (reprinted at §21.02) is discussed in the commentary on s.21, but for present purposes it is important to note that the Comptroller (under r.33(1), reprinted at §21.02) is normally required to send to the applicant a copy of such s.21 observations and any documents referred to. The applicant is entitled to submit observations in reply, but is not obliged to do so. The examiner is also required to consider such observations and if he then thinks that such observations have previously not been part of a s.18(3) report and, as a consequence of these observations, he has reported to the Comptroller that, in his opinion, and in the light of the received observations, the application does not comply with the Act and Rules, then such observations are termed "the first observations report", see r.29(2)(b). The applicant is then put on notice to deal with these observations as if made by the examiner under s.18(3) and to the satisfaction of the Comptroller within the compliance period, if thought appropriate by an amendment under r.31. However, if the s.21 observations are only sent to the applicant within the last three months of the otherwise stipulated "compliance period", that period is extended to three months from the date when this report was sent to him (r.30(4)).

Throughout the examination process, it is important that applicants, and particularly their appointed representatives, act in an appropriate and constructive manner. A code of practice for patent applicants and agents, available on the website *http://www.ipo.gov.uk*, has been drawn up and the UK-IPO hopes that it will be routinely followed throughout the substantive examination process in order to lead with expedition to an amicable and satisfactory settlement of disagreement between an applicant and the examiner carrying out the substantive patentability examination. It must be remembered that the task of the UK-IPO is to grant, not refuse to grant, patents. However, the examiners have an overriding obligation to see, to the best of their knowledge and ability, that a granted patent should comply with the statutory requirements.

If the examiner cannot be persuaded to accept the arguments put forward on behalf of the applicant, then before the Comptroller's discretion is exercised adversely under s.18(3) (for which see §18.15 and §18.16), or r.31(4) or r.108(1), a hearing before a senior examiner (acting for the Comptroller as "hearing officer") can be requested under s.101, for which see the commentary on it. Such hearing request must be granted, see §101.04. This is not an appeal as such, but a re-examination at a higher level of the views put forward by the examiner. This hearing will lead to the issue of a formal decision that will be made public. If the decision is adverse to the applicant, s.97(1) provides for appeal to the Patents Court with further appeal (both on facts and the law), with leave, to the Court of Appeal or even to the Supreme Court, see s.97 and the commentary on it. Although s.97(5) provides for further appeals in Scotland, r.88 (reprinted at §98.05) does not provide for hearings of the Comptroller under s.18 to be held in Scotland because these do not involve any person other than the applicant.

During substantive examination, the examiner may raise any objection arising under the Act or Rules, including formal requirements. Indeed, an application may be rejected under subs.(3) at any time (even before PF 10 is filed for substantive examination) if the Comptroller holds—if necessary after a hearing, if requested—that the specification is such that it cannot be brought into compliance with the Act and Rules, for example because it describes a device which can only function in a manner contrary to established natural laws (*Paez's Application* BL O/176/83; *Simon's Application* BL O/139/86 and C/6/87; and *Rohde and Schwarz's Application* [1980] R.P.C. 155). In the light of these decisions, the Comptroller has refused, prior to carrying out any prior art examination, applications as not describing a patentable invention in view of s.1(2)(c), see *Asher and Moultrie's Application* BL O/21/93 and *Toshiba's Application* BL O/22/93. In *Microsonics' Application* [1984] R.P.C. 29, it was doubted whether, despite the use of the word "may" in the final words of s.18(3), the Comptroller has any real discretion not to refuse an application once he had held that an objection to grant existed. See for example, *Blacklight Power Inc v Comptroller General of Patents* [2009] R.P.C. 6.

Where the search under s.17 has revealed major issues that will have to be addressed at substantive examination, such as where the scope of the independent claim is so wide that numerous anticipating documents exist, the examiner may provide early warning of such issues in an "examination opinion" to encourage early amendment before examination. If the applicant does not amend, the first substantive examination report under s.18 will be similar in content to the examination opinion and specify a two-month period for response.

As explained in the MOPP, an examiner should now identify equivalent cases and in particular WO cases, EP cases (to be inspected using the *EPOline* register), US cases (to be inspected using USPTO PAIR) and also corresponding Japanese and Korean applications. The status of such applications will now normally be checked before forwarding an application to grant (see MOPP).

An abbreviated examination report may be issued where an examination opinion identifying major defects has been identified at the search stage, or where an International Search report or International Preliminary Report on Patentability has indicated that major amendments are required.

Supplementary searches (subs.(1A))

Under subs.(1A), if the examiner decides that a correction or amendment has resulted in **18.09** the need for a supplementary search, a fee will normally become payable (see s.17(8) and §17.09). Under subs.(1A), it is possible to suspend the substantive examination until the fee has been paid (and also presumably until the supplementary search has been carried out) or until the application is amended to remove the need for the supplementary search. If examination is suspended and then the supplementary search fee is not paid, and the specification is not amended to remove the need for the supplementary search, the application may be refused. However, it would appear that the Comptroller could exercise his discretion on this and, therefore, the applicant ought to be provided with an opportunity of contending (if desired, at a hearing held under s.101, with the possibility of appeal under s.97(1)) that no supplementary search is necessary even without amendment, see further §17.05 and §17.09.

Grant of the patent (subs.(4))

18.10   After the examiner has issued a s.18(4) report, i.e. that the application complies with the Act and Rules, then (save for subs.(5), for which see §18.12; and s.22, for which see §22.06), the application will proceed to the grant of a patent and the applicant is notified accordingly. If the first report of the examiner, is issued under s.18(4), rather than under s.18(3), a period of two months is set for (a) the possible filing of a divisional application under r.19(3)(a) (reprinted in §15.04) and/or (b) voluntary amendment under r.31(4)(a) (reprinted in §19.02). Grant for the purposes of ss.1 to s.23, (i.e. "administrative grant") takes place after this two-month period has elapsed. If expedited grant is required, these opportunities can be waived. If objection under s.18(3) has previously been taken, the notification is simply a statement that administrative grant took place on the date of the notification. From that date, the filing of a divisional application is precluded by r.24(2)(c), and pre-grant amendment is no longer possible, see §19.09. The notification of administrative grant also states that notice of the grant will be published in the *Patents Journal* on a specified date, several weeks later. The grant under subs.(4) terminates the possibility of any further proceedings under ss.1–23. The grant, though made when the aforesaid notification of grant is given to the applicant, does not actually take effect until the notice of the grant has been published in the *Patents Journal* under s.24(1), see §24.11, but (since February 1997) the notification of grant has been recorded in the *Patents Journal* because of the importance of this date in preventing the filing thereafter of observations under s.21.

A similar situation arises on the grant of a European patent. The decision to grant a European patent under EPC art.97 terminates the application procedure, though the European patent does not take effect until the grant is mentioned in the *European Patents Bulletin* (EPC art.97(3)). A difference between the United Kingdom and European procedures is that a European application (or a country designation) may be withdrawn right up to the date of publication of the mention of the grant. This is important if it is preferred to have a national, rather than a European, patent for any particular country. If a European patent (UK) is granted, a corresponding patent which has already been granted under the Act is open to revocation for "double patenting" by the Comptroller acting on his own initiative, see §73.06. Another important difference is that a divisional application can be filed on a European patent right up until the publication of the mention of grant of the parent. Further, advance warning of grant is provided in the European procedure, in the form of a Communication under EPC r.71(3).

Once a notice under s.18(4) has been issued, the Comptroller has held that he has no power to withdraw it (under s.14(9)), or allow the filing of a divisional application (under s.15(9)), or consider an amendment, the request for which cannot then be filed until s.27 is effective after notice of the grant has been published in the *Patents Journal* (*ITT's Application* [1984] R.P.C. 23). In *Nokia's Application* [1996] R.P.C. 733; BL O/148/95, the examiner discovered new prior art after having issued a notice (under subs.(4)) that the application was in order for allowance. The Comptroller held that this notice could be withdrawn and the examination re-opened but, on appeal, the Patents Court held that the notice had been final and that the Comptroller could not invoke r.100 (now r.107) to withdraw that notice. Once the conditions for grant exist, the act of grant is mandatory and thus no hearing is appropriate in an attempt to secure its rescission (*Luk Lamellan's Application* [1997] R.P.C. 104), the Patents Court in any event seeing no jurisdiction permitting rescission of grant once made.

No form or fee for securing grant has been prescribed under subs.(4). For the certificate of grant and for its effect, see §24.06.

There is no provision in the Act for pre-grant opposition, as there was under previous patent statutes. Accordingly, grant is now mandatory once the examiner has reported under subs.(4) that the application complies with the requirements of the Act and the Rules. However, an application for revocation under s.72 may be made to the Comptroller at any time after grant.

If the examiner becomes aware, after the administrative act of grant has occurred, of a prior-dated application citable under s.2(3), such may be cited after grant under s.73(1), see §73.06.

Time for complying with Act and Rules

The period prescribed under ss.18(4) and 20(1) for meeting the requirements of the Act and Rules is determined by r.30 (reprinted at §18.04 above). Under the present form of this rule, the period within which an application must be placed in compliance with the Act and Rules, if a patent is to be granted thereon, is defined as "the compliance period" (r.30(1) and normally is four years and six months from the earliest declared priority date, or from the filing date if no priority is claimed (see r.30(2)(a)), but this period is automatically extended to provide a minimum of 12 months from the date when the first substantive examination report under s.18 is sent to the applicant (see r.30(2)(b)). The later date is increasingly more common, particularly in the case of ex-PCT applications. However, for a "replacement application" (i.e. one filed under s.8(3), 12(6) or 37(4) following entitlement proceedings), the aforesaid compliance period of four years, six months is calculated from the priority or filing date of the original earlier application, but with a minimum of 18 months from its initiation date (see r.30(3)(a)); and, for a "divisional application" (i.e. one filed under s.15(9)), the period is that applying under r.30(2) (see §15.25 and §15.34), but applied to the priority or filing date of the earlier application and not from the initiation date for the filing of the divisional application (r.30(3)(b)).

18.11

A further general provision for extension of the normal compliance period for acceptance (applicable to all types of applications) is provided by r.30(4): when third party observations are made under s.21 and lead to a new objection of patentability, sent to the applicant (as a first observations report, as defined in r.29(3)(b)) within the last three months of the normal compliance period, this period is extended to the end of three months after the s.21 observations are sent to the applicant.

The compliance date is not altered if a priority date is lost or withdrawn after preparations for publication under s.16 are completed (see r.2(1), reprinted in §123.04, as to "declared priority date" and r.30(2)(a)(ii) as to the start of the compliance period) and the compliance period is also not affected by a secrecy order under s.22(1).

However, if priority is dropped after the preparations for the publication of the application have been completed, for example because, while the required priority document was filed (without which publication under s.16 will not occur, see §16.04), the required translation was not filed in the (extended) time permitted (although this is generally no longer required), the declared priority date still remains valid for the purpose of calculating time limits (see r.2(1), reprinted in §123.04), particularly the period for complying with requirements under r.30. It is of note that the time limit for filing of divisional applications under r.19 is also dependent upon the r.30 period (the time limit being three months from the end of the compliance period).

Should a response be awaited from the examiner close to the end of the compliance period on an application where no notification of grant has been received, the examiner should be telephoned to determine the status of the case.

For possible extension of the compliance period, see §15.14 and more generally §§123.69–123.76.

If at the end of the r.30 period there is an outstanding, but unanswered, official letter of objection, the Comptroller must decide whether in fact there were then any outstanding valid objections (*Helmy's Application* BL O/150/93).

If an appeal to the Patents Court is pending, the time for placing the application in order may be extended by the court, or (if the period for lodging an appeal has not expired, but an appeal has not been lodged) the time for placing the application in order extends to the end of such appeal period or any extension thereof (s.20(2)). Furthermore, when secrecy directions under s.22(1) are revoked, the Comptroller may extend the time for doing anything, including placing the application in order for grant (s.22(5)(e)).

Corresponding identical patents (subs.(5))

18.12   Under subs.(5) two patents may not be granted to the same person in respect of the same invention. This is a statutory statement of a long-held principle preventing so-called double patenting and it will be followed by the Comptroller in amendment proceedings after grant, although an objection on this ground is not one which can be raised as such in an opposition under s.27 (*Securistyle's Patent* BL O/61/94). Objection can lie under subs.(5) if there is a common applicant (or a successor in title of him) for the two applications, even if there is another applicant not common to the two applications. If the priority dates of the two applications are not the same, then one application will be citable as prior art against the other. The applications must be ones made under the Act, including international applications (UK) that are treated as so made once the national UK phase has been entered. While the subsection does not apply to European patent applications (UK), if a proprietor of a United Kingdom patent obtains the grant of a European patent (UK) for the same invention and having the same priority date, the Comptroller will, probably, revoke the United Kingdom patent on his own initiative under s.73(2), though only after giving an opportunity for observations and amendments, see §73.03. For the meaning of "the same invention" in the context of this provision, see §73.06 in relation to the interpretation given to s.73(2).

In *International Business Machines' (Barclay and Bigar's) Application* [1983] R.P.C. 283, a second application was refused under subs.(5) despite the argument that in it the subject-matter was defined more precisely than in the first application which had employed a functional definition. The hearing officer held that refusal was mandatory unless the situation giving rise to the objection was overcome and that this would not occur by surrender of the patent on the first application because that would not amount to revocation of its grant, see §29.06. Cases decided under the analogous provisions of s.73(2) are also relevant, for which see §73.06.

In *Sun Microsystems' Application* BL O/252/06, two applications had the same description but different claims. It was held that double patenting here did exist, but the applicant was given time to decide whether to overcome this by abandoning the first application (which was then ready for grant) rather than have the second application rejected under s.18(5).

EPO decisions concerning double patenting are at present conflicting. The prohibition on double patenting was affirmed in T 307/03 *ARCO/Double patenting* [2009] E.P.O.R. 28 where the later claim had been more broadly formulated. In particular, where the subject-matter which would be double-patented is the preferred way of carrying out the invention both of the granted patent and of the pending application under consideration, the extent of double patenting cannot be ignored as de minimis, see T 587/98 *KOMAG/Divisional claim not followed* [2001] E.P.O.R. 19.

However, in T 1423/07 *BOEHRINGER INGELHEIM/Cyclic amine derivative* the Board of Appeal noted that only UK and Ireland excluded double patenting by statute, and that there was a prohibition on double patenting in Germany on the ground that there was no legitimate interest in the grant of several patents to the same applicant with identical content and priority dates. It concluded that there was no general principle of law recognised in the contracting states of the EPC for refusal on the ground of double patenting, and there was no basis for refusal under EPC art.125. Nor should T 307/03 *ARCO/Double patenting* be followed as to EPC art.60, and there was no prohibition on double patenting irrespective of whether or not the applicant had a legitimate interest, the fact that the EPC contains no specific provisions relating to double patenting being decisive. Furthermore, where the relevant applications have different filing dates, there is no conflict with decisions G 1/05 *XXX/Exclusion and objection* [2007] E.P.O.R. 17 and G 1/06 *SEIKO/Sequences of divisionals* [2007] E.P.O.R. 47.

PRACTICE UNDER SECTION 18

Request for substantive examination

18.13   In normal circumstances, if the application is to be further prosecuted, the request for examination must be made by filing PF 10 and the fee for it paid, both within six months after the publication of the application under s.16 (r.28) (see §16.08). Under r.31 (reprinted in §19.02), amendments may be made to the application between the time when the search report is received (under s.17(5)) and the time that the first substantive examination report is sent to the applicant. A convenient time for making such amendments is when PF 10 is filed. The period for filing PF 10 is extensible by right for two months by filing PF 52 and is further or alternatively extensible at the Comptroller's discretion but with restrictions because r.28 is listed in Pt 3 of Sch.4 to the Rules, as explained in §15.17. If PF 10 has not been filed on an extant application, it is thought that the UK-IPO will send a reminder to the address for service two weeks before expiry of the period under r.28, see the MOPP.

The applicant will usually have at least six months in which to come to a decision as to whether to pay the examination fee, since he should receive a copy of the search report issued under s.17(5)(b) before the date of publication under s.16 which starts the six-month period for filing PF 10. He will also have received any written observations already made to the Comptroller under s.21(1). The applicant can allow the application to lapse merely by failing to pay the examination fee; the search fee will not then be refundable. If the applicant desires that the application should not be published, the application must be formally withdrawn before preparations for publication are complete, see §16.10.

It is possible to request examination by filing PF 10 at the same time as making the request on PF 9A for the search. Such combined search and examination occurs automatically when PF 9A and PF 10 are filed at the same time, see §17.04. However, combined search and examination is not possible for an international application entering the United Kingdom national phase if the international search report has already been communicated to the UK-IPO. With a combined search and examination, it remains the aim of the UK-IPO to complete the search within 12 weeks, and the UK-IPO has promised that any response to a report under s.18(3) resulting from such a combined procedure will be considered without delay, see the *Patents Journal* March 22, 1995.

The Comptroller is prepared to accept a request for accelerated substantive examination but, if such request is made before publication of the application, it should be made clear whether accelerated publication (for which see §16.03) is also requested, see e.g. the *Patents Journal* August 2, 2000. A request for accelerated examination will be accepted only if the Comptroller is satisfied that the applicant is suffering substantial hardship, for example if infringement is taking place, or where an investor requires a granted patent before committing funds, or where the invention relates to "green" technology, see *http:// www.ipo.gov.uk/p-fastgrantguide.pdf*. However, as explained in the MOPP, no report under s.18(4) can issue until at least three months after publication in order to allow third party observations under s.21 (although this rule may be waived for divisional applications).

Such a request will normally not be considered as one to which confidentiality restrictions will be applied, and it will thus become publicly available on inspection of the file, for which see §118.14. Once examination has been concluded, the administrative procedure for publication of the B-specification has to take its normal course, see §18.10. Nevertheless, if a request for early publication is made, and combined search and examination is requested, it may be possible for an application to proceed to grant about 12 months from its filing date, see the *Patents Journal* March 22, 1995. However, the normal rule is that three months should be allowed for third party observations under s.21 so that very good reasons are needed to expedite grant when this period has not elapsed: in any event, the grant cycle cannot be reduced to less than three weeks, see [2000] *CIPA* 107 and §24.05.

When PF 10 has been filed, the application is referred to an examiner for investigation under s.18(2). As before the EPO, the UK-IPO endeavours to arrange that the search and substantive examiners are one and the same person. However, the substantive examiner is not bound to consider only the documents cited in the search report and, in particular, should consider documents noted by the search examiner but not included in the search report. Where a relevant document is in a foreign language, the examiner should, if possible, cite an English-language equivalent.

Unless such combined search and examination has been requested, the UK-IPO takes up cases for examination within each classification heading in order of priority (or filing date if there is no declared priority date). The date of filing of PF 10 does not appear to affect this order. This means that no substantive examination takes place until at least six months have elapsed from publication under s.16. The fee paid on PF 10 can be refunded, under exercise of the Comptroller's discretion, if the application is withdrawn before the examiner has commenced work on the substantive examination. It is possible to pay the examination fee before publication, but there appears to be no advantage in so doing apart from avoiding the need to monitor the only period which does not run from the priority date or, if none, the date of filing of the application.

The examiner has the option provided by s.18(1A) of requesting a fee for a supplementary search under s.17(8), in which case r.27(6) (reprinted in §17.02) applies and a further PF 9A is required to be filed.

It is important to preserve the filing receipt after filing PF 10. Should it subsequently be asserted that the form was not filed in due time, so that the application is treated as withdrawn, the onus of proof that discretion for a further extension under r.108(2) or (3) should be exercised, or that there has been a default on the part of the UK-IPO, thereby permitting r.107 to be invoked, will lie on the applicant and this filing receipt could be crucial evidence, see *SRM Hydromechanik's Application* BL O/14/83; as also may entries on the fee sheet lodged at the UK-IPO (*Aoki's Application* [1987] R.P.C. 133). In *Sanyo's Application* BL O/31/88, the records kept by the Patent Office of fee sheets filed and of receipts issued were explained.

Plurality of invention

18.14   If the search examiner considers that the claims are directed to more than one invention and has so indicated in his search report under s.17(6), and no voluntary amendment is made in response, (but see below) a "plurality of invention" objection under s.14(5)(d) can be expected in the first report on the substantive examination under subs.(3). The MOPP explains that the examiner can proceed in one of three ways depending upon his perception of what the applicant is most likely to do in the particular circumstances. One possibility is the suspension of the s.18 examination until the position has been made clear as to requests for supplementary searches, amendment and/or the filing of divisional applications. Often, however, the examiner will call for the claims to be limited to a single invention before he will commence his full examination and will set a period for initial response of between two and four months (see §18.06). In exceptional circumstances, the Comptroller may grant an extension to the specified term for response to his first report (see §18.16). If, however, a further PF 9A has been filed following a plurality objection and this objection is later not pursued or is rescinded, the search fee will usually be refunded by an exercise of discretion, except where the objection was removed by amendment.

The temptation to amend the claims voluntarily before the first substantive examination report has been issued, for the purpose of forestalling a "plurality of invention" objection, should be avoided, unless a divisional application is filed at the same time. If the first substantive examination report should be a favourable one under subs.(4), there would then only be a two-month period (under r.19(3)(a)) for filing any divisional applications.

The filing of divisional applications under s.15(9) is extensively discussed in §§15.16–15.26 and, in relation to "Practice", in §§15.32–15.35.

Substantive examination

—Filing of response

18.15   Where objections are raised during substantive examination that is that the report is an adverse one for patentability under s.18(3), the examiner will, where the report does not arise from the combined search and examination procedure, normally set a period for response of two to four months in the case of a first report.

Where the first examination report on an application is issued under s.18(3) three and a half years or more after the earliest date priority date (or, where no priority is claimed, the filing date) of the application, the standard period for response is two months from issue of the examination report. In the case where the first examination report is issued less than three and a half years after the earliest priority date (or, where no priority is claimed, the filing date) of the application, the standard period for response will be four months from issue of the examination report or, for combined search and examination cases, two years from the earliest priority date (or filing date if no priority is claimed).

With a second and subsequent reports, the set period will normally be two months. However, these periods may be varied in special circumstances, for example where a substantive objection is raised for the first time other than in the first examination report. Nevertheless, in all cases, less time for response may be set if the overall time for putting the application in order has already been severely eroded. If at the end of the r.30 period (for which see §18.11) there is an outstanding, but unanswered official letter of objection, the Comptroller must decide whether in fact there were then any outstanding valid objections (*Helmy's Application* BL O/150/93).

If the examination report is to be one of no objections under s.18(4), then the examination report will not issue until three months after publication under s.16 in order to allow time for third party observations to be lodged under s.21. If such observations are received, then a three-month period for response is set, except possibly in the case of a divisional application the claims of which appeared also in the parent application.

For further information on the UK-IPO practice in setting response times, see the "Period specified for response" section of the MOPP.

In replying to an examination report, the applicant may amend the description and claims to meet the objections raised and/or he may present a reasoned argument in defence of his application. In particular, if the examiner has objected that the invention claimed in any claim is obvious, it is necessary, if this claim is maintained, to overcome the examiner's objection by argument and perhaps also with evidence. If, as is not uncommon, the first examination report simply alleges that the invention claimed is not novel and/or does not involve an inventive step, it may be sufficient to argue that the examiner has not constructed an argument to which proper response can be made, but it will generally be prudent to go somewhat further than this. Point 6 of the Code of Practice (also reproduced in the MOPP) indicates what elements the response to the examination report should contain.

If an applicant thinks that his case against rejection, for example on an objection of obviousness, would be strengthened by the introduction of evidence, it is up to him to seek to introduce evidence. If he does not do so, the Patents Court has stated (*Wistar Institute's Application* [1983] R.P.C. 255; and *Toyama's Application* [1990] R.P.C. 555) that it is unlikely that such evidence will be allowed to be introduced on appeal, unless it should be evidence of the character which is normally admitted on appeal, for which see §97.16. However, such evidence was admitted on appeal in *PCUK's Application* [1984] R.P.C. 482, though here the UK-IPO hearing had taken place near the end of the s.18(4) period.

Care should be taken to file a response to all points in the examination report under s.18(3), even if only to argue that the objection is one that is not soundly based. If a response is considered not to be, or to be less than, a genuine attempt to meet the objections raised, or at least advance the prosecution of the application, the application may be refused, as it was in *General Electric's Application* BL O/94/89, noted I.P.D. 12103. Refusal will also occur if no response is filed within the time set (*Incom's Application* BL O/39/83, noted I.P.D. 6015), though in both cases subject to the applicant being given an opportunity to be heard, see §101.04.

Although they are not binding upon the Comptroller, decisions of the EPO, and especially those of its Appeal Boards, and the EPO Guidelines (all reprinted in the *European Patents Handbook* ("EPH") London: Sweet & Maxwell), are taken note of by examiners, and may be persuasive. It is often worth citing these in a response to a substantive examination report if they are relevant to a point being made. Consideration should also be given to citing the relevant portions of the MOPP, in the EPO: the EPO Guidelines, and for a corresponding US application: the *Manual of Patent Examining Procedure*, because these Manuals contain the instructions on which the examiners base their daily work.

An applicant, or his agent, may request an interview with the examiner to try and overcome the objections by personal argument. However, the substance of the interview will be recorded and placed on the public file and the applicant/agent may be asked to sign a minute of the interview. By prior arrangement, that interview may be in the Welsh language, see §101.05.

—Extension of time for response

18.16   Section 117B deals with extensions of time of periods which have been specified by the Comptroller, rather than specified in the Act or Rules, and hence concerns time extensions of the period set for response to a substantive examination report. As explained in §117B.04, an initial extension of two months is available upon written request for it, but such an extension is terminated at the end of the period for placing the application in order under s.20. Under s.117B(4), a further extension of an initial extension may be possible, but it may be granted subject to such conditions as the Comptroller may think fit.

As stated in §18.08, further extensions of the response times set in a s.18(3) report are a matter of discretion under r.108(1). The general UK-IPO practice on such extensions is explained in the "Extension of the period" section of the MOPP. The MOPP also provides an Annex B setting out the extension of time procedure. This is repeated below.

"An extension further to the as-of-right extension may be requested but:

— is only available if the as-of-right extension was requested.

— the request must be made before the expiry of the period as extended by right.

— is discretionary, but one single extension of up to one month on a given period is generally allowable.

— does not usually need to be requested in writing.

— must give an adequate reason; if no reason is given, one should be asked for.

— may be requested at the same time as the as-of-right extension.

— must take into account how much time is left of the compliance period.

Requests for additional further extensions:

— must be made before expiry of the period as already extended.

— require a strong reason to be allowed.

— should be for the minimum required (normally < 1 month) to fix the problem.

Where a late reply is received and no extension is available because the period for requesting an extension has expired, the reply should be referred to the examiner:

— If no reason is given for the late reply, the examiner should ask for one; if no reason is forthcoming, the application will be refused.

— If a reason is given, the examiner should consider it and decide whether to exercise the discretion provided under section 18(3) to accept the late reply (despite it falling outside the specified period)."

Discretion still exists to grant an extension even if the period set for reply has passed, as the application continues to exist (unless withdrawn) until it is refused. However, in *Nauchno Proizvodstvennoe's Application* BL O/65/82, noted I.P.D. 5038, it was pointed out that the grant of extension should not be presumed, and requests for extensions should be made while time still remains for dealing with the objections. In this case the absence of an inventor on a business trip of uncertain length and the patent agent's absence from his office were each held to be inadequate reasons.

In *Fibre Optic's Application* BL O/156/85, the Comptroller stated that the reason why the applicant did not, or could not, respond within the unextended period should be considered in the exercise of discretion, and in particular the extent to which the burden placed on the applicant exceeded the norm. The applicant "must be seen to have acted reasonably vis-à-vis the public". An extension was refused as it appeared that the need arose mainly because the applicant had decided to abandon the application and then had changed his mind. In *McDonald's Application* BL O/71/96, the agent sought reinstatement on the grounds that he said that he had little experience of prosecution before the United Kingdom Office, and that he had been awaiting the results of searches from other countries: moreover, the applicant had been travelling and the agent had been absent from work because of family health problems. None of these reasons was held sufficient to avoid refusal of the application, the hearing officer commenting that:

"to delay over three months before responding to a letter [the warning letter that no timely response had been filed to the section 18(3) report], seems lacking in diligence and optimistic in anticipating a sympathetic response [from the UK-IPO]".

In *Ezeh's Application* BL O/293/99, it was stated that the grant of an extension requires "exceptional or extenuating circumstances". Here the time for response had been ignored; a later request for extension because the applicant had been "tied down with doing and writing a doctoral thesis" was deemed inadequate; and the applicant had moved without making arrangements for mail to be forwarded.

Other examples where extensions have been refused include: *Goodhart's Application* BL O/242/97, where reversal of the previous decision of abandonment arose from an unexpected availability of funds; *Lintott's Application* BL O/66/82, noted I.P.D. 5077, where the applicant stated he would withdraw the United Kingdom application if an adverse report was received on the corresponding application in the USA; and *Decker's Application* BL O/10/96, where extensions had been previously granted, but the final request was based on the vacations of both the applicant and of the agent.

It is understood that these principles continue to apply. However, they now only apply to further extensions beyond the two months extension automatically allowed.

However, the MOPP indicates that an extension will normally be granted, provided that sufficient time remains of the "rule 30 period", where the applicant desires to ascertain whether any opposition is lodged against a corresponding European patent, or where a German company would itself withdraw the application, but is required by law to consult the inventor and allow him to take over the application should he so wish.

A refusal to grant an extension cannot be circumvented by an attempt to file a divisional application outside the time permitted by r.19, for which see §15.16.

Where r.100 (now r.107) was successfully invoked because an official letter had not been received by the applicant, due to use of an incorrect address, the s.18(4) period was extended to allow time for response (*Opatowski's Application* BL O/74/88), but with the hint that the application would be refused if that response did not put it entirely in order for grant.

In *Lionweld Kennedy's Application* BL O/258/00, a request for response time extension, based on changes in the management organisation of the applicant company that had made it difficult to obtain material and meaningful instructions, was not regarded as the required "exceptional circumstances". A subsidiary factor in refusing extension was that an extension request had not been made earlier. The situation was similar in *Lucent Technologies' Application* BL O/237/04 and in *Abekeh Mensah's Application* BL O/36/06, in each of which the Comptroller was not satisfied that the applicant had had a settled intention to proceed.

In *Smart Card Solutions' Application* [2004] R.P.C. 12 at 273 an extension was requested to the time set under s.18(3) for responding to the substantive examination report to give the agent time to study the International Search Report before responding. Although the agent indicated that this had been his common practice and that similar requests had been granted previously, the application for extension was refused. As stated above, there must be a reason for exercising the discretion to extend and in *MacDonald's Application* BL O/71/96, awaiting results of searches from other countries was not accepted as an excuse for an extension.

A request for an extension of time may now be emailed to the dedicated pateot@ipo.gov.uk email address. All requests sent to the 'pateot' email address will receive an automated acknowledgment confirming receipt: requests for an automatic extension will receive no further response because the act of validly requesting the extension is all that is necessary for it to be obtained. (For a full list of directions under s.124A specifying a particular Office e-mail address, see *http://www.ipo.gov.uk/p-direction-emailaddress.htm.*)

When a request for a discretionary extension is received, this will be sent to the substantive examiner for consideration. Email requests will be noted and imported into the dossier by an Examination Support Officer. They will also check to see if the request has been made on time and that it appears to come from the applicant or appointed agent.

—Examination procedure and refusal

18.17   If no response is filed within the prescribed period, the application becomes dormant. The MOPP indicates that a reminder will then be sent to the address for service some months before the end of the prescribed period for placing the application in compliance with the Act and Rules. However, if the applicant then seeks to file a response, this will be considered only after it has been decided whether (in the Comptroller's discretion) an extension of the time specified for response can be granted, and to obtain this a reasonable explanation must be provided. Nevertheless, if an extension is refused, the Comptroller must then decide whether in fact the application as it then stands is in order for acceptance despite objections made in an unanswered examination report, see *Helmy's Application* BL O/150/93.

The application is thus only treated as refused at the expiry of the period prescribed by s.20(1) as determined by r.30 (discussed in §18.11). There thus remains the possibility of filing a belated response simultaneously with a request for extension of the period for reply to the report under subs.(3) in the inherent discretion of the Comptroller under it. If the r.30 period has already expired, or is about to expire, a simultaneous request under r.108(3) for extension of that period should also be made by filing PF 52.

The MOPP suggests that it is in an applicant's own interest that when letters and faxes are filed close to the end of the compliance period these should be marked prominently "URGENT—compliance period expires on (date)". Such wording can helpfully appear in red.

—Procedure during substantive examination

18.18   Usually an informal interview or telephone discussion can be held with the examiner. This will normally lead to the preparation of an official minute, a copy of which will be sent to the applicant. The minute becomes part of the official file. If the applicant disagrees with any part of the minute, he may register his disapproval in a letter that is also placed in the open part of the file. The applicant or his agent attending a personal interview may be asked to sign the minute.

Although subs.(5) does not apply to concurrent applications under the Act and under the EPC for the same invention (but see s.73(2)), the examiner will often mention the existence of any conflicting application for a European patent (UK) of which he is aware. If the application under the Act is desired to give rise to a patent, it may be appropriate to abandon at least the United Kingdom designation for any such corresponding application for a European patent (UK) before the notice of its grant is published in the EPB (*European*

Patent Bulletin): otherwise the patent under the Act becomes subject to the revocation procedure of s.73(2), for which see §73.06.

Where the applicant is an individual acting without professional assistance, the UK-IPO (gratuitously) tries to assist by making suggestions which might lead to grant rather than total refusal. *Keyes' Application* BL O/103/06 is a good example of this.

If an examiner is minded to refuse an application, the applicant will be informed by an official letter setting a one-month period within which the applicant can request a hearing (see the MOPP). If the offer is accepted the examiner should issue a final communication defining all the issues to be considered at the hearing and setting out the arguments on each issue.

—*Amendments*

Any amendments made to the description and claims should normally be effected by **18.19** filing substitute pages. The need for clean pages arises because the specification of the granted patent is produced by reproduction from any documents filed by the applicant. In practice, examiners will sometimes make very minor amendments by hand on request. In a few exceptional cases, when the amendment to the drawings is very minor, the examiner may, at his discretion, make the amendments himself, since there is no rule forbidding manuscript amendments to the drawings. If an examiner is requested to make an amendment to the drawings, it is prudent to file further copies of the drawings "as filed" together with a copy showing the desired amendment in red, and an offer to furnish substitute formal sheets of drawings, if required. It should be remembered that manuscript amendments will appear exactly as they subsist in the eventually granted B-specification; this may be undesirable for the purist.

In normal written prosecution, the examiner can be assisted in checking retyped pages by the concurrent submission of copies of the previous pages showing by manuscript annotation the changes made in those retyped pages. The UK-IPO welcomes such a practice. Indeed, current para.18.61 of the MOPP states:

"Normally the applicant or agent responds to a report under s.18(3) by filing amendments, and/or observations. Amendments may be filed in electronic form if they are submitted via the Office's website, or using the secure online filing system provided by EPO Online Services if the filer has completed the enrolment procedure for that service. Office policy is that amended pages should not be accepted by email. While it is possible under section 124A(3) to exercise discretion to accept documents submitted by email, this should only be allowed in exceptional circumstances and should not be encouraged. The amendments should normally be in the form of new pages or sheets of drawings to be incorporated into the specification. It is helpful if a further copy of the amended pages is provided indicating the changes made either in manuscript on the original pages or using standard word-processing features since this aids identification by the examiner of the changes and where support is provided for them in the description. However minor amendments may be submitted in manuscript on photocopy pages or may be requested in a letter and be effected by the substantive examiner, provided they can be regarded as de minimis (see 14.37-38). Minor amendments to drawings, eg the insertion of a reference numeral, which can be regarded as de minimis may also be effected by the substantive examiner if requested in a letter and in accordance with 14.28 and 14.40-45. Amendments may also be submitted informally, with a view to filing retyped pages when the allowability of the amendments has been confirmed; this practice should not normally be continued in subsequent actions. When no other matters are outstanding and the substantive examiner asks for new pages to be filed, one month should be specified for reply (unexpired compliance period permitting)."

However, the application cannot proceed to grant until the description and drawings are in a state complying with r.14 (reprinted at §14.04), and therefore also with Pts 1–3 of

Sch.2 to the Rules (reprinted in §14.05) as discussed in §§14.44–14.50. However, at the examiner's discretion, compliance with r.14 can be deferred until the substantive objections have been met, but normally a s.18(3) report will indicate that such compliance remains outstanding (see the MOPP).

The UK-IPO now recommends the use of electronic filing when submitting amended pages or arguments in response to the examiner's objections, whether the original application was filed electronically or not. See the *Code of Practice for Applicants and Agents*, Point 6. Electronic filing procedures are detailed under s.124A, and the relevant direction is reproduced in full at §14.06.

—Miscellaneous

18.20   There is no limit on the number of official reports which may be issued within the compliance period set by r.30 for placing the application in compliance with the Act and Rules.

Where a communication is filed by an applicant after the issue of the examiner's s.18(4) report that the application complies with the requirements of the Act and the Rules, the examiner will need to give such communication urgent attention and any such communication should be marked "URGENT" in a bold and prominent manner.

It is worth noting that reference to the right of the applicant to file a divisional application in a response to a report under s.18(4) can often lead to a brief response from the examiner noting that an application is in order for grant and that a divisional application should be filed as soon as possible. Therefore, it is possible to provide for a measure of forewarning of the notification of grant, although this is not guaranteed.

Grant

18.21   The date of grant for the purposes of the provisions of ss.1 to 24(1) is the date of the letter sent to the applicant notifying him that a patent has been granted see §18.10. The specification of the patent is then republished under the same serial number as the application as published, but followed by the letter B. This "B-specification" is published on the date of publication of the notice of grant in the *Patents Journal*, this being the relevant date of grant for the purposes of s.25 onwards, see §24.11. In *Ogawa Chemical's Applications* [1986] R.P.C. 63, the Comptroller explained the practice of the Office with regard to the issuing of the notice of grant under s.24(1). If the examiner reports the application to be in order when he makes his first substantive examination, the applicant is so notified and informed that he may file voluntary amendments (under r.31(4)(a)) and divisional applications under s.15(9) (under r.19(3)(a)), each within a two-month period from the date of the s.18(4) report. The notice of grant is then issued at the end of that period. However, when the application is found to be in order for grant after an acceptable response to an objection under s.18(3), the administrative act of grant under s.24(1) occurs automatically, see §18.10. Once the administrative act of grant has taken place, further amendment under s.19, and the filing of divisional applications under s.15(9), are each precluded.

Examination may be re-opened to a very limited extent under s.73 after publication of the notice of grant, see §73.06.

SECTION 19

General power to amend application before grant

19.01   **19.**—(1) At any time before a patent is granted in pursuance of an application the applicant may, in accordance with the prescribed conditions and subject to section 76 below, amend the application of his own volition.

(2) The comptroller may, without an application being made to him for the purpose, amend the specification and abstract contained in an application for a patent so as to acknowledge a registered trade mark [*or registered service mark*].

Note. Subsection (2) was initially amended by the Patents, Designs and Trade Marks Act 1986 (c.39) s.2 and then re-amended by the Trade Marks Act 1994 (c.26) Sch.4 para.1(2) and Sch.5.

RELEVANT RULE—RULE 31

Rule 31—Amendment of application before grant

31.—(1) A request to amend an application for a patent under section 19(1)   **19.02**
must be made in writing.

(2) The conditions prescribed under section 19(1) are as follows.

(3) The applicant may amend his application only within the period beginning with the date on which the applicant is informed of the examiner's report under section 17(5) and ending with the date on which the comptroller sends him the first substantive examination report.

(4) But after the end of this period, the applicant may—

   (a) where the first substantive examination report states that his application complies with the requirements of the Act and these Rules, amend his application once before the end of the period of two months beginning [with] immediately following the date on which that report was sent; or

   (b) where the first substantive examination report states that his application does not comply with the requirements of the Act and these Rules—

      (i) amend his application once at the same time as he makes his first observations on, or amendments to, his application under section 18(3), and

      (ii) if the first substantive examination report is sent before preparations for the application's publication have been completed by the Patent Office, amend his application prior to any further amendment he may make under sub-paragraph (b)(i).

(5) However, the conditions in paragraphs (3) and (4) do not apply—

   (a) where the comptroller consents to the amendment; or

   (b) to an amendment of a request for the grant of a patent.

(6) Where the comptroller's consent is required, or the applicant wishes to amend the request for the grant of a patent, the applicant must include the reasons for the amendment.

Note. Rule 31 was amended as from October 1, 2011 by The Patents (Amendment) Rules 2011 (SI 2011/2052).

COMMENTARY ON SECTION 19

Scope of the section

Section 19 concerns amendment of an application at the volition of the applicant   **19.03**
(subs.(1), as governed by r.31, above); and by the Comptroller to acknowledge in the specification or abstract a registered trade mark (subs.(2)). Amendment of a European patent application (necessarily in the EPO) is covered by art.123 of the EPC and r.137 of the EPC, and of an international application (before the International Bureau) by arts 19 and 34(2)(b) of the PCT and rr.46 and 66 of the PCT. Amendment after grant is dealt with under ss.27 and 75 and, at the initiative of the Comptroller, under s.73. For amendment prior to publication of the application under s.16(2), see §16.03.

Amendment is to be contrasted with correction, for which see the commentary on s.117 and s.19 of the MOPP. In the case of an allowed correction, the document is deemed always to have been in the corrected form, see *Braun's Patent* BL O/138/94 so that s.76 has no effect. However, where an application is amended before grant under s.19, the amendment takes effect only from the date when the amendment is allowed, whereas for amendments made after grant (under s.27 or s.75), the amendment is in effect back-dated to the date of grant, i.e. the granted patent is deemed always to have been so amended. However, in all cases of amendment (as compared with correction), s.76(2) may have effect because the question of added matter relates back to the description, as it existed at the date of filing of the application.

Any request to amend any part of an application, i.e. of the description, drawings, claims or abstract, made at the proprietor's volition prior to substantive examination, must be made in writing (r.31(1)), but no form is generally required for such a request, even for making a minor amendment to PF 1. However, the filing of PF 20 (no fee), under r.49 (reprinted at §32.09) needed for amendments which require also a change in the register entry which is created when the application is published under s.16. These matters are discussed in the MOPP at s.19 "Amendments and corrections".

Amendments to the specification

19.04   Although subs.(1) states that the applicant may, of his own volition, amend the application at any time before grant, this generality is restricted by the presence of the words "in accordance with the prescribed conditions", and r.31 provides that an applicant may only amend the application within a defined period which commences when the applicant is informed of the search report under s.17(5) and terminates when the first substantive examination report is sent to him (r.31(3)). No form (or fee) is required for amendment at this stage. However, this time restriction does not apply where the Comptroller consents to the amendment or where the amendment request is directed to of the request for grant, i.e. of PF 1 (r.31.5).

Amendments to the claims which are received by the UK-IPO before the preparations for publication under s.16 are complete (i.e. before this defined period has commenced) should appear in the "A–specification", together with the claims as originally filed, but in practice there is little time available within which to achieve this, see §16.04. As explained in §16.04, the letter forwarding the search report under s.17(5) now states the date when the preparations for publication of the application under s.16 will be completed. This should be not earlier than 15 months after the declared priority date (or the filing date, if no priority date is claimed) and not less than four weeks after the date of the letter. This is intended to provide a short time within which amendments occasioned by the contents of the search report may be submitted to be included within the application as published. However, publication of these amendments in the "A–specification" cannot be guaranteed, though they will appear in the file, which becomes available for public inspection (under s.118) from the date of the publication under s.16. When an applicant files an amendment to the specification before the search report issues, the UK-IPO holds the amendment and treats it as effectively filed upon the issuance of the search report. This is because of r.31(3). Nevertheless, the examiner may take the proposed amendments into consideration on an informal basis, see the MOPP.

Once substantive examination has commenced with the issue of a report under s.18(3), the above-defined period expires, but the applicant has a right under r.31(4)(b)(i) to amend the description, claims and drawings, but only once, at his own volition in response to the examiner's report on the substantive examination with the object of meeting the requirements of the Act, see §18.08. However, this voluntary amendment must be filed at the same time as the applicant replies to the s.18(3) report in the sense of submitting a fully considered response to the substantive examination objections. However, where combined search and examination has been requested, for which see §18.13, it is possible that the examination report is issued prior to publication under s.16; the right of voluntary amendment prior to the response to the examination report under s.18(3) or (4) is then preserved with a right to amend further at a later date in response to the examination report whether this is one under s.18(3) or (4) (by r.31(4)(b)(ii)). If the examiner's first report is made under s.18(4), that is that the requirements for grant have been met, then a single voluntary amendment request can be filed within two months of the report (r.31(4)(a)).

After a considered response to the first official report on the substantive examination has been lodged, the opportunity for voluntary amendment under r.31(4) has been exercised or lost, but r.31(5)(a) provides that voluntary amendments may be made provided that the Comptroller gives consent thereto, as discussed in the MOPP. Such amendment request is to be made in writing and consent therefor should be sought in an accompanying letter. Note that, if an amendment voluntarily put forward under r.31(4)(a) following a favourable report under s.18(4) is not found acceptable, and a further amendment is then put forward, the Comptroller's consent to this will need to be sought under r.31(5)(a), as only one voluntary amendment may be made under r.31(4)(a). The MOPP para.19.20 indicates that, if amendments requested under r.31(6) are considered allowable, the necessary consent required by that rule will normally be given.

The right to amend under s.19 is lost with effect from the date of a letter sent to the applicant notifying him that administrative grant under s.18(4) has occurred, for which see §24.11. But, as explained, amendment under s.27 is not possible until notice of the grant has been published in the *Patents Journal* under s.24(1), that is until after the grant has taken effect under s.25(1). The right to amend is also lost once the application is deemed to have been withdrawn for failure to meet a set time limit, unless the application can be revived under either r.107 or by an extension granted under r.108. This is because the amendment provisions of the section cannot be used to circumvent a specific requirement of the Act, see *Payne's Application* [1985] R.P.C. 193 and §117.07.

Any amendments sought under any part of r.31 must be clearly identified in some way, but there is no longer a need to show the amendments in red ink on a copy of the specification, unless the Comptroller so requires, see §19.10.

Limitations on allowable amendments

The allowability of amendment under s.19 is fettered by the provisions of s.76(2) (as amended) according to which no amendment to the specification is to be allowed if this "results in the application disclosing matter extending beyond that disclosed in the application as filed", see §76.05. This, and similar, wording has been interpreted as a severe restriction on possible amendments, see §§76.06–76.20. Breach of the terms of s.76(2) provides a ground of revocation of the patent under s.72(1)(d), see §72.15.

19.05

A voluntary amendment under s.19, which is made within the periods prescribed in r.31(3) and (4), does not entail exercise of the Comptroller's discretion. In particular, any amendment to the claims filed before preparations for publication under s.16 have been completed for the purpose of inclusion in the "A–specification" is not examined for allowability prior to the substantive examination under s.18. It is not clear whether any amended or new claim which contains additional matter and therefore contravenes s.76(2) may be taken into account for the purposes of ss.55(5)(b) and 69(2)(b).

Neither r.31 nor s.76(2) applies to corrections under s.117 and therefore these can be treated differently, see §117.06, but a "correction" (unlike an amendment) requires an unchanged intent of the draftsman.

Amendment of documents other than the specification

—General

Section 19 concerns amendment to an application, for which r.31 provides certain time limits for seeking voluntary amendment, particularly of the description, claims and drawings, as discussed in §19.04 and §19.05. However, an application to amend the request (usually made by seeking to amend PF 1) is not fettered by any prescribed conditions and may be lodged at any time before issue of the letter notifying administrative grant of the patent under s.18(4), but the amendment must be sought in writing (r.31(1)).

19.06

Nevertheless, s.19 cannot be used to add a declaration of priority or convert an independent application into a divisional one, since that would result in a specific provision of the statute being overridden, see *P's Application* [1983] R.P.C. 269. Amendment of the abstract at any time also seems possible, but any such amendment, once publication of the "A–specification" has occurred under s.16, has little point as the abstract is not re-published in the granted patent (the "B–specification").

—Change of applicant

19.07   An applicant may be added or deleted by submitting, in writing a request to amend PF 1. The reasons for the amendment must be given (under r.31(6)) either on PF 1 or separately. When PF 7 is subsequently filed, the statement of the right to the grant thereon must be consistent with the reasons supplied for the amendment of PF 1. Also, PF 21 may be filed to record a change of ownership, but there must then be compliance with the requirements of r.47, as explained in §32.19. To change the applicant once PF 7 has been filed and the application has been published under s.16, PF 20 (no fee) must be filed because the details entered on that PF 7 will have been recorded in the register of patents (under r.44, reprinted at §32.04) upon that publication.

Alteration of an address, or address for service, under r.44, no longer requires a form: notification in writing is all that is required (r.49(3)), see §§32.25 and 32.24 respectively. Note that correction under s.117, and not amendment under the present section, is involved if the name or address of the applicant was incorrectly stated on PF 1 when originally filed.

For further information following a change in the applicant entity, or merely a change of name, and whether such change is regarded as an amendment under s.19 or a correction under s.117, see the MOPP ("Amendment of the Request for Grant" section).

—Change in designated inventorship

19.08   If the statutory period for filing the statement of inventorship on PF 7 has not expired, a new PF 7 can be simply substituted for that originally filed, see §13.13. Otherwise, PF 7 may be corrected under s.117 and r.105, see §117.12. For the correction of an error of translation or transcription, clerical error or mistake as the case may be, see §117.05.

Acknowledgment of registered trade mark (subs.(2))

19.09   Subsection (2) gives the Comptroller power himself to insert into the specification and abstract an acknowledgment that a trade mark is a registered trade mark. This power can be exercised by examiners and senior examiners, see §130.04. There is no corresponding rule, and the subsection does not, apparently, require the Comptroller to give notice to the applicant that the reference is being made. A similar power (under s.27(4)) exists as regards amendment of the specification of a granted patent. While these provisions are each expressed in discretionary terms, under which an applicant or patentee would have a right under s.101 to be heard before a decision is made, with appeal possible under s.97(1), the Comptroller has held, under the somewhat similar wording of s.73(2), that in fact he has no discretion once the wording of the provision is found to have been met, see §73.06.

Although the Comptroller may insert an acknowledgement of a registered trade mark before publication of the application under s.16, the usual practice is for the applicant to be invited to insert such an acknowledgement during substantive examination, but see the MOPP.

The subsection refers merely to a registered trade mark and not to a mark registered in or for the United Kingdom. There is no definition of "trade mark" in s.130(1), so that it would appear that the Comptroller has power unilaterally to make a reference to registration, even where the applicant uses a trade mark to identify a product obtained abroad under that trade mark and there is no evidence that the material obtainable under the registered trade mark (i.e. in the United Kingdom) is the same product.

PRACTICE UNDER SECTION 19

Amendment of description, claims or drawings

19.10 Any request to amend the description, claims or drawings of an application must be accompanied by replacement documents prepared in accordance with r.14 and Sch.2 to the Rules (reprinted respectively at §14.04 and §14.05). In order to comply with these requirements, it is usually necessary to file replacement sheets whenever amendment is made, but very minor amendments can be inserted in manuscript without contravening this rule. Because publication under s.16 takes place by reproduction of the specification in the form supplied by the applicant, pages of new or amended claims should be self-explanatory and should preferably be headed "Amendments to the claims".

It is also understood that, when a request for amendment is filed after issuance of a favourable examination report under s.18(4), and within the two-month period permitted for it by r.1(4)(a), it is the practice of the UK-IPO both to acknowledge receipt of the request and indicate whether or not the requested amendments have been found acceptable. When such amendments are filed, the accompanying letter should be prominently marked "URGENT" in order to alert the UK-IPO to the need to deal with the requested amendments prior to the administrative act of grant; and similarly upon filing amendments when less than six months remains of the period under r.30 for placing the application in order for acceptance, especially where the application is: a divisional application filed under s.15(9); a converted European application (UK) filed under s.81; or an international application (UK) entering the national phase under s.89, as in such cases the compliance period will be shorter, see §18.11.

When the Comptroller's discretion is sought to make a further amendment under r.31(6), the application must not only be in writing but the amendment sought must be clearly identified (either on PF 1 or in a separate document) and the reasons for seeking the amendment must be stated.

The UK-IPO now recommends the use of electronic filing when submitting amended pages, whether the original application was filed electronically or not. See the Code of Practice for Applicants and Agents, Point 6. Electronic filing procedures are detailed under s.124A, and these directions are reproduced in §14.06 above.

Amendment of the request (PF 1)

19.11 To record a change of applicant before publication under s.16 has taken place, leave to amend should be sought in writing. No particular form needs to be used but a copy of the request (PF 1) can usefully be supplied on which the amendments are shown in red ink. However, what is important is that the proposed amendments are clearly identified, perhaps in a separate document if this can be done without ambiguity. Reasons for the requested amendment must be stated, either on PF 1 or in a separate document. For a change of name, proof of the change should be supplied, and the initial entry in the register, which is made only after publication under s.16 (r.44(1)), will then record the new name. If this is done before preparations for publication of the application have been completed, the "A–specification" will show the new name. The UK-IPO prefers that an application to record an alteration in the proprietor's name is not made after preparations for publication have been completed and before publication (for which see §16.04), whereafter such application should be made on PF 20 to amend the register entry which is created (under r.44, upon such publication), see §32.16 and §32.25. The procedure for correction of, or updating, an applicant's address is similar provided that the proposed amendments are otherwise clearly identified without ambiguity, either in a separate document or on a copy of the PF 1 already on file.

The distinction between a request for amendment and one for correction has been noted in §19.03 and §19.05, on which see also the MOPP.

SECTION 20

Failure of application

20.01 **20.**—(1) If it is not determined that an application for a patent complies before the end of the prescribed period with all the requirements of this Act and the rules, the application shall be treated as having been refused by the comptroller at the end of that period, and section 97 below shall apply accordingly.

(2) If at the end of that period an appeal to the court is pending in respect of the application or the time within which such an appeal could be brought has not expired, that period—

(a) where such an appeal is pending, or is brought within the said time or before the expiration of any extension of that time granted (in the case of a first extension) on an application made within that time or (in the case of a subsequent extension) on an application made before the expiration of the last previous extension, shall be extended until such date as the court may determine;

(b) where no such appeal is pending or is so brought, shall continue until the end of the said time or, if any extension of that time is so granted, until the expiration of the extension or last extension so granted.

COMMENTARY ON SECTION 20

Scope of the section

20.02   Section 20 provides for the refusal of an application which is not brought into a condition in compliance with the Act and Rules within the period prescribed by r.30 (reprinted at §18.04) and extends that period when an appeal is lodged. It is not a section specified in s.130(7) as having the same effect as a corresponding provision of the EPC; but the EPC prescribes no period for placing a European application in order.

Subsection (1) complements s.18(3). Section 18(3) does not mention the prescribed period for compliance with the Act and Rules, but empowers the Comptroller to issue a decision of refusal at any time. Subsection 20(1) provides for an application to be treated as refused (no decision of refusal need be issued) if it does not comply with the Act and Rules within the prescribed "compliance period", i.e. that specified in r.30.

Period for acceptance

20.03   Because ss.18(4) and 20(1) do not specify the period in which the application is to be brought into compliance, the period for compliance can be altered when circumstances warrant without a change in the Act. Both the period for complying with the Act and Rules and the possibility of extending it under r.108 are discussed in §18.10 and §18.11, see also §15.18 in relation to "new applications".

Appeal from refusal

20.04   Under subs.(1), an application is to be treated as having been refused by the Comptroller if it does not comply with the requirements within the due period. The refusal is therefore a decision taken by the Comptroller and as such is subject to appeal under s.97(1). Further appeal from an initial decision of the Patents Court under s.20 (whether on fact or law) can be taken, with leave, to the Court of Appeal under s.97(3).

—Time for appeal

20.05   An appeal against refusal of an application must be brought (under CPR 63.15; 52.6(1) and 52.6(2)) within 28 days from the date of the Comptroller's decision. Neither the parties by agreement, nor the Comptroller, can grant any extension of this period; though the Patents Court could, but would be unlikely to, do so. Thus, if a decision of refusal is issued under s.18(3), the period for bringing the appeal is four weeks from the date of the decision and meanwhile the compliance period may expire. If s.20(1) applies, because by the end of the r.30 period there has been no determination on compliance with the Act and Rules, the application is treated as having been refused "at the end of that period", which suggests that there is a notional decision of refusal at the end of the r.30 period. However, the r.30 period is automatically extended by subs.(2) to the end of the appeal period, but this extension applies only to the r.30 period and is not a cumulative extension with the appeal period, see the MOPP paras 20.09 and 20.10. Thus, the appeal period runs from the date of the decision and not from the end of the r.30 period, so that any extension obtained by discretion under r.108(2) or (3), and presumably also under either r.107 or 108(4), runs concurrently with the extension of the r.30 period provided by subs.(2), see *P's Application* [1983] R.P.C. 269.

Since an extension to the r.30 period may be applied for under r.108(3) up to two months after the end of the period, it would be possible to obtain an effective post-dating of the date of the deemed decision under s.20(1) by means of such an extension, and thus post-date the deadline for filing an appeal. In such a case, the Comptroller might refuse discretion under r.108(3), but under s.97 that refusal would itself be subject to appeal.

Under CPR 63.16, the procedure in appeals from the Comptroller is now governed by the general rules for appeals set out in CPR Pt 52. For the appeal procedure, see §97.12.

In *Degussa-Hüls' Application* BL O/180/04, it was noted that, under s.20(2) the r.30 period for placing the application in order for acceptance is automatically extended to the end of the appeal period of 28 days; and it was pointed out that this extension runs concurrently with any extension under r.108(3) and not consecutively, reference being made to the MOPP para.20.10.

—Effect of appeal

If an appeal is duly lodged, the period for acceptance may be extended to a date specified by the court (subs.(2)). It is customary for the Patents Court to grant an extension of time sufficient in the circumstances to permit the application to be placed in compliance with the Act and Rules in accordance with the decision of the court, but a request for such an extension should be made immediately after the decision is given. **20.06**

Effect of failing to comply with Act and Rules within prescribed period

The words in subs.(1) "at the end of that period" mean that, if the requirements of the Act and Rules have not been complied with, the application is treated as having been refused at the end of the period specified by r.30 (as extended under r.108, if appropriate). Thus, in *P's Application* [1983] R.P.C. 269, decided before r.108(3) was introduced, it was held that, if what is now PF 52 was not filed within two months of the end of the acceptance period, the application is treated as having been refused when the filing of that form first became due. **20.07**

Since extension of any length of time may be obtained retroactively under r.108(3), it should always be possible to revive an application which has passed the normal acceptance period, provided that the Comptroller is prepared to exercise his discretion, and not more than two months has elapsed since the end of the previous extended period because r.30 is listed in Pt 3 of Sch.4 to the Rules.

The decision in *Farmitalia's Application* BL O/88/87 suggests that the s.20(1) period for complying with the Act and Rules may be extended in appropriate circumstances.

When an application is deemed to be withdrawn because the examiner regards the statutory requirements as not being met in due time, the possibility exists of arguing that the examiner's objections were not justified so that in fact those requirements had been met. Such an argument succeeded in *Akebono Brake's Application* BL O/2/85 and similarly in *Coal Industry's Application* [1986] R.P.C. 57. In each case, r.100 (now r.107) was then invoked to rectify the register, see §123.24.

In *Duncan and Harcombe's Applications* BL O/426/01 a series of errors had been made by private applicants who now sought an extension of time for putting an application in order despite the expiry of the r.30 period. The Comptroller remarked that:

389

"Confusion and ignorance of patent law are not grounds for exercising discretion for time extensions. An applicant must demonstrate a continuing underlying intention to pursue the Application". (See §18.16.)

PRACTICE UNDER SECTION 20

Correspondence towards end of rule 30 period

20.08   While the UK-IPO gives precedence to dealing with applications nearing the end of the permitted acceptance period, it does so by reference to the application numbers. This method of operation does not work for divisional applications, for international applications which have entered the UK phase (s.89A), or for European applications which have been converted to United Kingdom applications (s.81), the application numbers of which do not relate to priority dates in any predetermined way. The Office, therefore, requests that correspondence on all such applications or the like be endorsed prominently at the head of the text with words, such as "DIVISIONAL; URGENT", preferably in red. When less than six months of the period prescribed by s.20 (the "rule 30" or "compliance period" discussed in §18.11) remains, it is also urged that correspondence should be marked "URGENT" in a bold and prominent manner. This is particularly important for the three types of applications mentioned, because for these the date of expiry of the r.30 period is less apparent.

Because of problems which arise when applications are recorded in the register as having been withdrawn and it is later found that an official letter under s.18(3) or a response to it had gone astray, with the result that the register is rectified under what is now r.107 (for which see §123.24), the Office issues shortly before the end of the period provided under s.20 and r.30 a letter forewarning of the intention to treat as having been refused an application on which a report under s.18(3) has been issued and a response to it is overdue, An example of such a letter is reproduced in the judgment in *Anning's Application* [2007] EWHC 2770 Pat Ct; BL O/374/06.

When such response is overdue, other than as the result of some default or omission by the Patent Office, the applicant will still need to seek discretion for an extension of time under s.18(3) in order that a response be permitted to be filed outside the time set therefor in the report, see §18.16. Any such request should likewise be prominently marked "URGENT" in view of the short time that will then remain under r.30.

If a hearing in respect of outstanding objections is requested then, unless this takes place within the r.30 period, all that can then be decided is whether the application was in fact in compliance with the Act and Rules at the end of that period. Thus, an applicant should be prepared to waive the normal 14 days notice of a hearing date, for which see §101.05.

Where a hearing is held towards the end of the r.30 period and leads to a decision of refusal, an extension under r.108(3) may need to be obtained retrospectively to enable an appeal against refusal to be brought (*Shopalotto.com's Application* [2006] R.P.C. 7 at 293; [2006] I.P. & T. 396). In *Touch Clarity's Application* BL O/198/06, a hearing against refusal had been held, but the decision thereon was only given the day after the r.30 period had expired, as also had the time requested by a previous application, so that r.108 no longer permitted the grant of any further extension. However, the examiner had, erroneously, informed the applicant that the r.30 period is effectively suspended once a hearing had taken place pending a decision thereon. This was an irregularity of procedure and, in these circumstances, what was then r.100 (now r.107) was invoked to permit the grant of a two-month extension under s.117B(2), but it was pointed out that s.117B(5) precluded any extension of this two-month period, for which see §§117B.01–117B.03.

Appeals against refusal

20.09   The lodging of an appeal against a decision refusing the application, or because it has not been brought into compliance with the Act and Rules before the end of the r.30 period, is governed by s.97(1) and CPR 63.16, see §97.12. The Comptroller will normally be represented by counsel on the hearing of the appeal and will ask for his costs if the appeal is unsuccessful, see §97.24. If the appeal decision results in patentable subject-matter being found, or conceded, to exist in the application, it will often be necessary to seek an extension of time under subs.(2) from the court, and a specific request for it should be made to the court immediately following the handing down of its decision

As explained in §97.12, an appeal against the Comptroller's refusal of an application can be brought within 28 days from the date of that decision. However, at the date of bringing the appeal, the application must still be in existence. It may therefore be necessary for an extension of the r.104 period to be obtained, on which note the decisions cited in §20.08.

SECTION 20A [ADDED]

Reinstatement of applications

20A.—(1) Subsection (2) below applies where an application for a patent is refused, or is treated as having been refused or withdrawn, as a direct consequence of a failure by the applicant to comply with a requirement of this Act or rules within a period which is—   20A.01

  (a) set out in this Act or rules, or

  (b) specified by the comptroller.

(2) Subject to subsection (3) below, the comptroller shall reinstate the application if, and only if—

  (a) the applicant requests him to do so;

  (b) the request complies with the relevant requirements of rules; and

  (c) he is satisfied that the failure to comply referred to in subsection (1) above was unintentional.

(3) The comptroller shall not reinstate the application if—

  (a) an extension remains available under this Act or rules for the period referred to in subsection (1) above; or

  (b) the period referred to in subsection (1) above is set out or specified—

      (i) in relation to any proceedings before the comptroller;

      (ii) for the purposes of section 5(2A)(b) above; or

      (iii) for the purposes of a request under this section or section 117B below.

(4) Where the application was made by two or more persons jointly, a request under subsection (2) above may, with the leave of the comptroller, be made by one or more of those persons without joining the others.

(5) If the application has been published under section 16 above, then the comptroller shall publish notice of a request under subsection (2) above in the prescribed manner.

(6) The reinstatement of an application under this section shall be by order.

(7) If an application is reinstated under this section the applicant shall comply with the requirement referred to in subsection (1) above within the further period specified by the comptroller in the order reinstating the application.

(8) The further period specified under subsection (7) above shall not be less than two months.

(9) If the applicant fails to comply with subsection (7) above the application shall be treated as having been withdrawn on the expiry of the period specified under that subsection.

Note. Section 20A was added by the Regulatory Reform (Patents) Order 2004 (SI 2004/2357) ("RRO"), with effect from January 1, 2005.

RELEVANT RULE—RULE 32

Rule 32—Reinstatement of applications under section 20A

20A.02   **32.**—(1) A request under section 20A for the reinstatement of an application must be made before the end of the relevant period.

(2) For this purpose the relevant period is—

    (a) two months beginning [with] immediately after the date on which the removal of the cause of non-compliance occurred; or

    (b) if it expires earlier, the period of twelve months beginning [with] immediately after the date on which the application was terminated.

(3) The request must be made on Patents Form 14.

(4) Where the comptroller is required to publish a notice under section 20A(5), it must be published in the journal.

(5) The applicant must file evidence in support of that request.

(6) Where that evidence does not accompany the request, the comptroller must specify a period within which the evidence must be filed.

(7) Where, on consideration of that evidence, the comptroller is not satisfied that a case for an order under section 20A has been made out, he must notify the applicant accordingly.

(8) The applicant may, before the end of the period of one month beginning [with] immediately after the date of that notification, request to be heard by the comptroller.

(9) Where the applicant requests a hearing, the comptroller must give him an opportunity to be heard, after which the comptroller shall determine whether the request under section 20A shall be allowed or refused.

(10) Where the comptroller reinstates the application after a notice was published under paragraph (4), he must advertise in the journal the fact that he has reinstated the application.

(11) In determining the date on which the removal of the cause of non-compliance occurred, the comptroller shall have regard to any relevant principles applicable under the European Patent Convention.

Note. Rule 32 was amended as from October 1, 2011 by The Patents (Amendment) Rules 2011 (2011/2052).

COMMENTARY ON SECTION 20A

Scope of the section

20A.03   Section 20A, to be read in conjunction with r.32, provides for reinstatement of an application which has been refused, or treated as refused or withdrawn as a direct consequence of the applicant failing to comply with a requirements of the Act or any rules within a period which is set out in the Act or Rules, or is one as specified by the Comptroller (subs.(1)). However, reinstatement may only be allowed when the applicant so requests in compliance with the relevant requirements of the Rules (as discussed in §20A.04); and only when he satisfies the Comptroller that this failure to comply was "*unintentional*" (subs.(2)), as to which see §20A.05 below.

Nevertheless (under subs.(3)), the Comptroller may *not* order a reinstatement if: (a) an extension of time remains available for the period for which there was non-compliance; or (b) if the period (i) is one set out or specified in relation to any proceedings before the Comptroller; or (ii) is one for the purpose a declaration of priority under s.5(2)(a); or (iii) is one for the purpose of making a request for reinstatement under the section or is one for an extension (or further extension) of a time limit specified by the Comptroller under s.117B (for which see §117B.02).

Where there are joint applicants, one or some of the applicants may make a reinstatement request without joining the others, provided that the Comptroller so permits (subs.(4)).

Where the application has already been published under s.16, notice of a reinstatement request is to be published in the Journal (subs.(5) and r.32(4)); and, if reinstatement is to be permitted, this must also be advertised in the *Patents Journal* (r.32(10)).

Section 20A has parallels with s.5(2C), under which the late filing of a priority declaration can be allowed if, likewise, the Comptroller can be satisfied that the timely failure to make the declaration had been unintentional; and also to the restoration (under s.28) of a patent where the failure to pay the required renewal fee was "unintentional". Thus, decisions under these other provisions may be applicable to decisions under s.20A and these are discussed in §20A.05 below.

If the Comptroller is not satisfied that the request should be accepted, the applicant is notified; then the applicant can within one month of the date of notification request a hearing. The Comptroller must then provide an opportunity for the applicant to be heard, after which he is to determine whether the request should be allowed or refused (r.32(6)–(8)). There appears to be no provision for the filing of an opposition to a reinstatement request, neither s.20A nor r.32 being mentioned in Pt 7 and Sch.3 to the Rules, as "proceedings heard before the comptroller".

In his determination of the request, the Comptroller is required to "have regard to any relevant principles applicable under the European Patent Convention" (r.32(11)). This presumably means that the Comptroller should take judicial notice of the EPC Implementing Regulations and of decisions of the EPO Boards of Appeal and endeavour to reach an analogous conclusion in relation to the reinstatement of a European application that has been terminated for non-compliance with a specified time limit.

When an order is made under the section for reinstatement of a terminated application under the Act and Rules, it will specify the period (of not less than two months) within which compliance is to take place; and, if this is not done, the application is to be treated as having been withdrawn on the expiry of the period referred to in subs.(1), i.e. that which caused the original termination (subss.(7)–(9)).

The effect of reinstatement is as set out in s.20B, for which see §20B.01 and §20B.02.

Time period for making reinstatement request

A request for reinstatement under the section must be made before the expiry of either (a) two months from "the date on which the removal of the cause of non compliance occurred"; or (b) twelve months from the date when the application was terminated; *whichever is the earlier* (r.32(2)). This period is inextensible (Rules, Sch.4 Pt 1, reprinted at §123.26). The request is to be made on PF 14 with its attendant fee and evidence must be filed sufficient to support the request, in particular to establish to the satisfaction of the Comptroller that the non-compliance was "unintentional" (as required by s.20A(2)(c)). If the evidence is not filed with the request, the Comptroller will specify a period within which this must be done, but this period is extensible with discretion exercised under r.108(1).

20A.04

As regards the shorter two-month period specified in r.32(2)(a), there is some doubt as to the precise meaning to be attached to the words quoted above, see *Anning's Application* [2007] EWHC 2770 Pat Ct; BL O/374/06. Here the point was not decided in the factual circumstances of that case, the longer 12-month period being accepted, perhaps because the application was then held to fail the "unintentional" requirement, as discussed in §20A.05. However, it should always be assumed that the shorter two-month period will normally apply and therefore every possible effort should be made to remove the cause of non-compliance, using any available extensions of time, and file the s.20A request, each as quickly as possible. The alternative 12-month period should therefore be seen as a last resort, as it was in *Anning's Application* (above).

The meaning of "unintentional"

20A.05   As explained in §20A.03, there are three provisions in the Act which use the word "unintentional" This word was used deliberately when the Act was amended to accord with the provisions of the PLT, particularly to provide for the possibility of a late filing of a priority declaration (under the provisions of s.5(2A)–(2C), as discussed in §5.18. It now seems clear that the word is used in a stricter sense than that which applies merely to the exercise by the Comptroller of his general discretion, but nevertheless where it can be shown that the applicant had changed his mind, as in *Heatex's Application* [1995] R.P.C. 546), it seems that it is unlikely that the conduct can be considered as unintentional. Also, in *Al Bahdaini's Application* BL O/356/04, a request for a discretionary extension of time for responding to a s.18(3) report was not allowed because the Comptroller was not satisfied that the applicant had had a continuing underlying intention to proceed with his application.

However, the early decisions given on the meaning of "unintentional" focus on the specific act which caused the application to be refused or withdrawn and judge whether the failure to perform that particular act was unintentional or whether the applicant had simply failed to take adequate care to fulfil the obligations imposed upon him by the Act and Rules. On this general point it should first be noted that each of these decisions denied reinstatement, thereby indicating that the burden of proof under s.20A is a heavy one.

The first two decisions were *Sirna Therapeutics' Application* [2006] R.P.C. 12; BL O/240/05 and *Abaco Machines (Australasia)'s Application* BL O/309/06 where in each case a PCT application had been filed not designating the UK and there was an attempt to make a late claim for priority for a UK national application. However, the PCT application was non-existent for the UK and the later national UK application had been filed intentionally outside the required priority period.

A specific reinstatement request was made under s.20A in *Anning's Application* [2007] EWHC 2770 Pat Ct; BL O/374/06. Here, the applicant (as in the *Al Bahdaini* case, above), had apparently deliberately not responded to a s.18(3) report and, although warned specifically by the UK-IPO and by his agent of the fairly imminent expiry of the compliance period (in a letter reproduced in the appeal judgment) he took no action. Because of this, Pumfrey J. stated:

> "The letter [informing the applicant that no reply to the examination report has been received and warning that the application will be treated as refused at the end of compliance period] does not itself either require any act to be done or extend the period of time for doing that act, and is for this reason not within s. 20A: and the prescribed period under s.20(1) is merely the period during which the requirements of the Act and Rules must be complied with. It imposes no additional requirement on the applicant. It therefore follows that an application may not be reinstated if the only failure by the applicant has been a failure to comply with s.20(1)".

This shows the importance of responding to a s.18(3) report, if necessary on the basis of first obtaining a discretionary extension of time. Then, for example, a failure to meet all the formal presentational requirements within the compliance period may perhaps be seen as unintentional because the applicant had reasonably assumed that his appointed agent would timely meet these.

In *Matsushita Electric's Patent* [2008] R.P.C. 35; [2008] EWHC 2071 Pat Ct, the patentee had merely made a bald assertion that the failure to pay the required renewal fee was unintentional but no evidence by way of explanation or support was filed. In dismissing the application for restoration under s.28(3), Mann J. said:

"the Act requires a judgment to be formed by the Comptroller so that he can be satisfied of the relevant matters. A judgment usually has to be made on the basis of evidence...The evidence required in any particular case where satisfaction is required depends on the nature of the enquiry and the nature and purpose of the decision to be made...[but]...the Act does not require a statement that the failure to pay fees was unintentional. It requires the Comptroller to be satisfied of that fact".

In *Ibrahim Ghulam Murad Ali et al's Application* O/264/10 applicants failed to respond to an examination report and the application was treated as refused on the compliance date. Subsequently, they successfully applied for reinstatement, and a new period was set for responding to the outstanding examination report. However, the applicants were warned that they could now only submit arguments that the application as it stood at the end of the compliance period was in order for grant and that it was too late to submit amendments, see *Anning's Application* above.

However, the hearing officer concluded that the requirement which the applicant must be given a chance to meet following reinstatement was the requirement in s.18(3) to make observations or amendments which bring the application into compliance. Section 20A(7) provided power to specify a period for that requirement to be met, and to do that properly it was necessary to specify both a new period for replying to the examination report and a new period for overall compliance. The court in *Anning* had not dealt with the question whether the compliance period could be extended when reinstatement has been allowed because in that case the request for reinstatement had been refused, so that was the end of the matter.

In the light of *Ali's Application*, the UK-IPO has issued a practice note (March 15, 2011) noting that, where an application is refused, or treated as having been refused or withdrawn, due to a failure by the applicant to comply with a requirement of the Act or rules, the application may be reinstated provided that the requirements of s.20A and r.32 are met. It remains the case that reinstatement of the application will not generally have the effect of extending the compliance period.

However, where an application has been treated as refused at the end of the compliance period due to failure to respond to a substantive examination report, and is subsequently reinstated, both a new period for responding to the examination report and a new period for overall compliance will be specified. This will allow the applicant to respond to the examination report with amendments which bring the application into compliance, if necessary.

The current section of the MOPP relating to s.20A(8) now reflects the change of practice in light of the *Ali* decision. However, at the time of going to press, s.10 of the *Formalities Manual* has yet to be updated.

In *Griffith's Application* O/394/09 a private individual applicant had not prosecuted his patent application as carefully as he should have because of a range of external factors in his life. The time for filing his abstract came and went without any awareness on his part as to this requirement, such that the failure to file was not the result of a conscious decision on his part and could be regarded as unintentional. Thus reinstatement would be allowed.

SECTION 20B [ADDED]

Effect of reinstatement under section 20A

20B.—(1) The effect of reinstatement under section 20A of an application for a patent is as follows. 20B.01

(2) Anything done under or in relation to the application during the period between termination and reinstatement shall be treated as valid.

(3) If the application has been published under section 16 above before its termination anything done during that period which would have constituted an infringement of the rights conferred by publication of the application if the termination had not occurred shall be treated as an infringement of those rights—

    (a) if done at a time when it was possible for the period referred to in section 20A(1) above to be extended, or

    (b) if it was a continuation or repetition of an earlier act infringing those rights.

(4) If the application has been published under section 16 above before its termination and, after the termination and before publication of notice of the request for its reinstatement, a person—

    (a) began in good faith to do an act which would have constituted an infringement of the rights conferred by publication of the application if the termination had not taken place, or

    (b) made in good faith effective and serious preparations to do such an act, he has the right to continue to do the act or, as the case may be, to do the act, notwithstanding the reinstatement of the application and the grant of the patent; but this right does not extend to granting a licence to another person to do the act.

(5) If the act was done, or the preparations were made, in the course of a business, the person entitled to the right conferred by subsection (4) above may—

    (a) authorise the doing of that act by any partners of his for the time being in that business, and

    (b) assign that right, or transmit it on death (or in the case of a body corporate on its dissolution), to any person who acquires that part of the business in the course of which the act was done or the preparations were made.

(6) Where a product is disposed of to another in exercise of a right conferred by subsection (4) or (5) above, that other and any person claiming through him may deal with the product in the same way as if it had been disposed of by the applicant.

(6A) The above provisions apply in relation to the use of a patented invention for the services of the Crown as they apply in relation to infringement of the rights conferred by publication of the application for a patent (or, as the case may be, infringement of the patent). "Patented invention" has the same meaning as in section 55 below.

(7) In this section "termination", in relation to an application, means—

    (a) the refusal of the application, or

    (b) the application being treated as having been refused or withdrawn.

Note. Section 20B was added to the Act by the Regulatory Reform (Patents) Order 2004 (SI 2004/2357) ("RRO") into which subs.(6A) was incorporated by the Patents Act 2004 (c.16) Sch.2(7), all having effect from January 1, 2005.

COMMENTARY ON SECTION 20B

Scope of the section

Section 20(B) specifies the provisions which apply when reinstatement is allowed under **20B.02** s.20A (as discussed in §20A.03) of an application which has been terminated as the result of refusal of the application or where an application has been refused or withdrawn (subs.(7)), the word "termination" as used in the Rules being defined by subs.20B(7), and more generally by an addition to r.2 (definitions), for which see §123.04.

These provisions, which are often called "third party rights" generally follow those which apply (i) when a lapsed patent is restored under s.28 and, therefore, are generally analogous to the provisions set out in s.28A; (ii) to the third party rights which arise under s.117A when an application is resuscitated for having been withdrawn in error or by mistake; and (iii) to such rights which arise under s.64 in a situation of prior secret use, for all of which see the commentaries on these sections, particularly the commentary on s.28A.

Under s.20B, anything done during the period between termination and reinstatement (conveniently termed the "interim period") is treated as valid (subs.(2)); and, where the application had been published under s.16 before the termination occurred, acts which would have constituted an infringement of the rights arising from the existence of the application (under s.69) are to be treated as an infringement of those rights, but only if these acts were done at a time when it was possible for the period specified in s.20A(1) to be extended or the act was a "continuation" or "repetition" of an earlier act infringing those rights (subs.(3)).

However, where the application was published under s.16 before its termination and after the termination and before publication of the request for reinstatement, then third party rights will exist to allow a person who had during such period "begun in good faith" to do what would otherwise have been an infringing act or had made "in good faith effective and serious preparations to do" such an act, that person will have the right to continue to do the act notwithstanding the subsequent reinstatement of the application and the grant of a patent on it, but without a right to grant a licence to another to do the same act (subs.(4). Where such a third party right has been acquired as part of a business, such rights can be exercised by others in the same business and it can be assigned (or transmitted on death or dissolution of a company) to a person acquiring the relevant part of that business (subs.(5)). Where a product is disposed of in exercise of a right acquired under either of subss.(4) or (5), any person receiving that product may deal with it in the same way as if it had been disposed of by the applicant (subs.(6)).

SECTION 21

Observations by third party on patentability

21.—(1) Where an application for a patent has been published but a patent has **21.01** not been granted to the applicant, any other person may make observations in writing to the comptroller on the question whether the invention is a patentable invention, stating reasons for the observations, and the comptroller shall consider the observations in accordance with rules.

(2) It is hereby declared that a person does not become a party to any proceedings under this Act before the comptroller by reason only that he makes observations under this section.

RELEVANT RULE—RULE 33

Rule 33—Observations by third parties on patentability

33.—(1) The comptroller must send to the applicant a copy of any observa- **21.02** tions on patentability he receives under section 21.

(2) But paragraph (1) does not apply to any observation which, in the opinion of the comptroller, would—

(a) disparage any person in a way likely to damage such person; or

(b) be generally expected to encourage offensive, immoral or anti-social behaviour.

(3) The comptroller may, if he thinks fit, send to the applicant a copy of any document referred to in the observations.

(4) The comptroller must send to an examiner any observations on patentability.

(5) But paragraph (4) does not apply where the observations are received after the examiner has reported under section 18(4) that an application complies with the requirements of the Act and these Rules.

Relevant Direction under Section 124A

Submitting third party (section 21) observations by electronic means

21.03   (as updated to May, 2011)

Note. This Direction is reprinted from the website: *http://www.ipo.gov.uk*. Before use, this website should be checked against the update date given above and, if different, the website version should be used instead of that given below. The update date is that given as the "Review date" at the bottom of the left hand panel of this website.

Introduction

1. The comptroller has made the following Directions under section 124A of the Patents Act 1977 ("the Act") to direct the form and manner in which observations made by a third party, under section 21 of the Act, on the question of whether the invention is a patentable invention may be made in electronic form or using electronic communications.

2. These Directions come into force on 25 May 2005.

Interpretation

3. In these Directions:

"digital media" means—

- a compact read-only optical disk that can contain electronic data and conforms to ISO 9660: 1988; or:
- a 3.5'' floppy disk that can contain electronic data; and

"observations" means observations made under section 21 of the Act;

Delivery of observations

4. Observations may be sent by e-mail or delivered on digital media.

5. Observations sent by e-mail shall be sent to the following e-mail address *section21@patent.gov.uk* or *section21@ipo.gov.uk*.

6. No document, other than an e-mail containing observations, shall be sent to that email address.

Content and format of observations

7. Where observations are sent by e-mail, the e-mail shall contain—

- the observations; and

- sufficient information to enable the comptroller to identify the patent application to which the observations relate.

8. Observations delivered on digital media shall be accompanied by a paper document containing—

- a statement that the digital media carries observations;

- sufficient information to enable the comptroller to identify the patent application to which the observations relate.

9. No observations sent by email or delivered on digital media shall be encrypted.

Illegible or incomplete observations and infected observations

10. Where part or all of the observations delivered under these Directions are illegible or incomplete, the whole of the observations shall be treated as not complying with these Directions.

11. Where the observations delivered under these Directions—

- are reported as having a virus (or other malicious software) by the Patent Office's virus checking software; or

- appear to contain a computer program (other than a document), they shall be treated as not complying with these Directions.

12. Where the observations are treated as not complying with these Directions under paragraph 10 or 11, provided that the person making the observations can be identified, he shall be notified of this fact by the comptroller.

Acknowledgement

13. Where the observations have been sent in accordance with these Directions, they shall be treated as delivered only after they have been acknowledged by the comptroller.

14. The time of delivery accorded to an email containing observations shall be that generated by the Patent Office's internal electronic communications network (within the meaning of section 32 of the Communications Act 2003).

RON MARCHANT

Comptroller-General of Patents, Designs and Trade Marks

17 May 2005

Guidance and notes on the Direction

The Directions contain some guidance and explanatory notes, which (as at May 2011) were as reprinted from the website: *http://www.ipo.gov.uk*.

Before use, this website should be checked against the update date given above and, if different, the website version should be used instead of that given below. The update date is that given as the "Review date" at the bottom of the left hand panel of this website beneath the words "IP Policy".

These notes are not part of the Directions. They are intended to provide background and additional information.

The Interpretation Act 1978 applies to these Directions. Therefore, all the definitions set out in that Act apply to these Directions. Further, among other things, generally any words importing the masculine gender include the feminine and words in the singular include the plural and words in the plural include the singular.

Where observations are submitted which do not comply with the Directions, the comptroller may treat the observations as not having been delivered (see section 124A(3) of the Act).

Observations may be submitted as an attachment to an email. The comptroller will try to read attachments in any format, but Microsoft® Word, WordPerfect®, Portable Document Format (PDF) or plain text (RFC822 compliant) are preferred.

Observations sent by email will receive an automatic acknowledgement when they are received by the comptroller.

Computer programs should not be submitted as part of any observations. They will be considered illegible under paragraph 11 of the Directions and consequently the whole of the observations may be treated as not having been delivered.

Any queries about these Directions should be addressed to: Room 3Y26, The Intellectual Property Office, Concept House, Cardiff Road, Newport, South Wales NP10 8QQ; Tel.+44 (0)1633 813572.

The reference in the above Directions to the ipo.gov.uk domain name was introduced by a Direction effective from April 2, 2007.

COMMENTARY ON SECTION 21

Scope of the section

21.04 Section 21 provides the procedure by which any person may make observations formally bringing to the notice of the Comptroller material affecting the patentability of an invention, at any time after publication and before grant. The section is governed by r.33 (reprinted above) and corresponds to art.15 of the EPC; there is no equivalent PCT provision. Subsection (2) provides that the informant does not become a party to the proceedings. He is, therefore, not informed about the outcome of these, but he can obtain this information by inspection of the public file. Supplementary observations may be filed if time permits.

In *Porter Lancastrian's Application* BL O/200/04 the applicant, despite repeated requests from the Patent Office, made no response to observations which had been made under s.21, supported by filed witness statements, and which alleged prior use of the invention. It was held that the applicant had failed to satisfy the Comptroller that the requirements of the Act had been made and, as no application to amend had been filed, the application was refused.

Nature of permitted observations

21.05 The observations to be submitted are those which concern the patentability of the invention. The Comptroller is not required to consider observations which relate to other matters, such as the right to be granted a patent under s.7 or matters which may be raised in revocation proceedings under s.72, e.g. the adequacy of the disclosure under s.14(3) or the wording and content of the claims under s.14(5). The Comptroller is obliged to consider the observations under s.21 so far as they relate to patentability, i.e. to the definition of patentable invention in s.1(1). Also, in view of the decision in *Genentech's Patent* [1989] R.P.C. 147 CA, it is submitted that the examiner ought to take into account observations submitted alleging non-compliance of the claims with s.14(5)(a), (b) or (c), because otherwise such non-compliance cannot, according to that decision, be raised as such post-grant (except possibly on a question of amendment), though over-broad claims may well fail on other grounds, as was held in the *Genentech* case, see §§1.10, 3.25 and 14.25.

Time for making observations

21.06 Observations under subs.(1) may be filed at any time before grant. For this purpose, the date of grant is the administrative date of grant under s.18(4), as explained in §24.06. Thus, before submitting observations under the section, a check should be made whether this is still possible or whether the administrative date of grant under s.18(4) has already taken place. Such check is possible because this date is now recorded in the register, see §18.10. Note that, if combined search and examination has been requested, it is possible for the administrative act of grant to follow three months after publication of the application under s.16 (see §18.15). Therefore, if preliminary observations are contemplated, a register search should be carried out (for which see §32.34) to ascertain if examination has been commenced; and, if so, the filing of these observations should be made without delay.

An acknowledgement of receipt of the observations is issued, but by subs.(2) the person making the observations is expressed not to be a party to any proceedings. Therefore, no estoppel can arise against him in relation to the observations. Likewise, there is no bar to any person who files observations under s.21 from making the same observations in subsequent revocation proceedings under s.72 because no estoppel is created. There is also no restriction on a person making repeated observations under s.21.

Under r.33, there is no obligation on the Comptroller to consider third party observations after the applicant has been informed under s.18(4) that the application may proceed to grant or if the r.30 period for compliance with the Act and Rules (including any extension of time under r.107or r.108) has expired. Otherwise, the observations have to be referred to an examiner who may "consider and comment upon them as he thinks fit" in a (further) report made to the applicant under s.18 (r.33(4)). In any case, the observations must be reported to the applicant (r.33(1)) and copies of documents provided with the observations will also usually be supplied, although this is only if the Comptroller "thinks fit" (r.33(3)) as will be likely if these are considered not suitable for photocopying. In any case, the papers will be placed on the file of the applications where they can be inspected under s.118, unless the Comptroller invokes r.53, as discussed in §21.07.

If an observation under s.21 is received by the examiner before the s.18(4) notification has been dispatched, he is obliged to consider it and raise any apparent objection to patentability with the applicant. The applicant will then be required to deal with the objection within whatever time remains of the s.20 compliance period: see *Secretary of State for Defence's Application* BL O/177/83. However, the hardship of a late report of unpatentability following third party observations made near to the end of the r.30 period for placing an application in compliance with the Act and Rules is now somewhat alleviated by r.30(4), read in conjunction with r.29(4). This allows a minimum three-month period from the date when a first observations report is sent to the applicant during the last three months of the compliance period. In that situation the compliance period is extended to three months from that date of sending, a period which seems to be extensible under r.108(3).

PRACTICE UNDER SECTION 21

By r.33(1), but subject to r.33(2), a copy of any observations filed under s.21 has to be sent to the applicant, whether or not a request for substantive examination under s.18(1) has yet been filed. The applicant will also be supplied with copies of any documents referred to in the observations, unless the Comptroller considers any such document will already be available to the applicant or if the document is not, for some reason, suitable for photocopying (see r.33(3)) and MOPP para.21.04. Where observations are received before the application is published under s.16, a copy will nevertheless be sent to the applicant but the observer will be informed that these will not be considered by an examiner before publication, as only afterwards is the file open to public inspection, see the MOPP para.21.02.1.

Observations under s.21 may now conveniently be filed by electronic means under directions made under s.124A (as reprinted at §21.03). The Directions require observations to be sent by email to *section21@ipo.gov.uk* or to be delivered on digital media. Observations sent electronically to any other address may be treated as not filed, but should not generally be treated in this way if they comply with the other conditions in these Directions and are successfully received at an email address within the Office.

21.07

Observations received at the dedicated email address will be acknowledged by an automatic email reply. This email mentions that if the observations can be treated as made under s.21, they will be forwarded to the examiner for consideration, placed on the open part of the file, and a copy sent to the applicant, see the MOPP para.21.02.1.

Although there is no express right to comment on observations made under the section, it may be assumed that the applicant may do so during that examination. The examiner may himself comment on the observations in his initial report under s.18(3), or in a later additional report also having the effect of a further report under s.18(3), see the MOPP para.21.06. The applicant in his own interest ought to reply to such a report, as otherwise the application may be refused (s.18(3)). If the examiner considers that there is no substance in the observations, he need make no reference to them. If observations are received at a time when the application is in order for grant, the MOPP para.21.07 indicates that the applicant should be informed of the observations and that the application will not be sent for grant for two months (in order to enable him to file voluntary amendments) unless he requests that the application may be so sent earlier. No action on s.21 observations can be taken once the s.18(4) report has issued indicating that the application is to proceed to grant, but it is possible that this report could be rescinded, see the MOPP paras 21.14 to 21.16.

The standard to be met for third party observations to have effect is that of the balance of probabilities (*Colley's Application* BL O/191/98): here, sworn evidence of prior use by two independent witnesses was presented and was found sufficiently compelling in the absence of any counter-evidence. An argument that such matters should not be considered pre-grant, but left to full inter partes proceedings post-grant was rejected. Previously, in *Zannetos' Application* BL O/119/96, amendment had been made to distinguish the claims from an earlier patent to T whose patent attorneys then provided evidence of prior use which led to refusal of the application.

All observations submitted under s.21 should be placed on the public file 14 days after submission, see §118.10 and §118.14, and the MOPP para.21.05 indicates that an application by the informant for confidentiality under r.53 will normally be refused because an examiner's report on the observations should be based only on documents open to public inspection. *Central Research Laboratories' Application* BL O/419/00 is an example of a confidentiality order being made on observations containing commercially sensitive information.

Obvious problems arise where observations are made which may be defamatory of the applicant. However, knowingly to make observations of this character could amount to professional misconduct by a Chartered Patent Attorney. Anyway, r.51(2)(d) (reprinted in §118.02 and commented upon in §118.08) gives the Comptroller power to exclude any document from public inspection which contains disparaging, offensive, immoral or anti-social matter. It is not clear whether, in such circumstances, a report under s.21 may be made by an examiner but without him placing the offending document on the public file of the application, but the Comptroller seems to have no power to refuse to communicate defamatory statements to the applicant, though the applicant could presumably request, under r.53(1), that such statements should not appear on the public file, see further §118.19. The MOPP indicates that the documents may be modified by partial obliteration of offending matter so that the remainder of the document may be made available in the public file.

Since official letters and replies thereto are in the public file of an application after s.16 publication, it is possible for the observer, or any interested third party, to monitor the progress of an application by repeated file inspection and such a person may file observation, or further observations under s.21 whenever and as often as desired., but such person(s) are not entitled to be informed of the action which has been taken on any submitted observations.

Apparently, the UK-IPO will accept s.21 observations that are submitted anonymously see the MOPP, para.21.02.1. In this way an applicant could submit observations on his own application.

Security and safety [Sections 22–23]

SECTION 22

Information prejudicial to national security [defence of realm] or safety of public

22.—(1) Where an application for a patent is filed in the Patent Office (whether **22.01** under this Act or any treaty or international convention to which the United Kingdom is a party and whether before or after the appointed day) and it appears to the comptroller that the application contains information of a description notified to him by the Secretary of State as being information the publication of which might be prejudicial to **national security** [*the defence of realm*], the comptroller may give directions prohibiting or restricting the publication of that information or its communication to any specified person or description of persons.

(2) If it appears to the comptroller that any application so filed contains information the publication of which might be prejudicial to the safety of the public, he may give directions prohibiting or restricting the publication of that information or its communication to any specified person or description of persons until the end of a period not exceeding three months from the end of the period prescribed for the purposes of section 16 above.

(3) While directions are in force under this section with respect to an application—

(a) if the application is made under this Act, it may proceed to the stage where it is in order for the grant of a patent, but it shall not be published and that information shall not be so communicated and no patent shall be granted in pursuance of the application;

(b) if it is an application for a European patent, it shall not be sent to the European Patent Office; and

(c) if it is an international application for a patent, a copy of it shall not be sent to the International Bureau or any international searching authority appointed under the Patent Co-operation Treaty.

(4) Subsection (3)(b) above shall not prevent the comptroller from sending the European Patent Office any information which it is his duty to send that office under the European Patent Convention.

(5) Where the comptroller gives directions under this section with respect to any application, he shall give notice of the application and of the directions to the Secretary of State, and the following provisions shall then have effect—

(a) the Secretary of State shall, on receipt of the notice, consider whether the publication of the application or the publication or communication of the information in question would be prejudicial to **national security** [*the defence of realm*] or the safety of the public;

(b) if the Secretary of State determines under paragraph (a) above that the publication of the application or the publication or communication of that information would be prejudicial to the safety of the public, he shall notify the comptroller who shall continue his directions under subsection (2) above until they are revoked under paragraph (e) below;

(c) if the Secretary of State determines under paragraph (a) above that the publication of the application or the publication or communication of that information would be prejudicial to **national security** [*the defence of realm*] or the safety of the public, he shall (unless a notice under paragraph (d) below has previously been given by the Secretary of State to the comptroller) reconsider that question during the period of nine months from the date of filing the application and at least once in every subsequent period of twelve months;

(d) if on consideration of an application at any time it appears to the Secretary of State that the publication of the application or the publication or communication of the information contained in it would not, or would no longer, be prejudicial to **national security** [*the defence of realm*] or the safety of the public, he shall give notice to the comptroller to that effect; and

(e) on receipt of such a notice the comptroller shall revoke the directions and may, subject to such conditions (if any) as he thinks fit, extend the time for doing anything required or authorised to be done by or under this Act in connection with the application, whether or not that time has previously expired.

(6) The Secretary of State may do the following for the purpose of enabling him to decide the question referred to in subsection (5)(c) above—

(a) where the application contains information relating to the production or use of atomic energy or research into matters connected with such production or use, he may at any time do one or both of the following, that is to say,

(i) **inspect the application and any documents sent to the comptroller in connection with it;**

(ii) **authorise a government body with responsibility for the production of atomic energy or for research into matters connected with its production or use, or a person appointed by such a government body, to inspect the application and any documents sent to the comptroller in connection with it; and**

(b) in any other case, he may at any time after (or, with the applicant's consent, before) the end of the period prescribed for the purposes of section 16 above inspect the application and any such documents;

and where a government body or a person appointed by a government body carries out an inspection which the body or person is authorised to carry out under paragraph (a) above, the body or (as the case may be) the person shall report on inspection to the Secretary of State as soon as practicable.

(7) Where directions have been given under this section in respect of an application for a patent for an invention and, before the directions are revoked, that prescribed period expires and the application is brought in order for the grant of a patent, then—

(a) if while the directions are in force the invention is worked by (or with the written authorisation of or to the order of) a government department, the provisions of sections 55 to 59 below shall apply as if—

(i) the working were use made by section 55;

      (ii) the application had been published at the end of that period; and

      (iii) a patent had been granted for the invention at the time the application is brought in order for the grant of a patent (taking the terms of the patent to be those of the application as it stood at the time it was so brought in order); and

  (b) if it appears to the Secretary of State that the applicant for the patent has suffered hardship by reason of the continuance in force of the directions, the Secretary of State may, with the consent of the Treasury, make such payment (if any) by way of compensation to the applicant as appears to the Secretary of State and the Treasury to be reasonable having regard to the inventive merit and utility of the invention, the purpose for which it is designed and any other relevant circumstances.

(8) Where a patent is granted in pursuance of an application in respect of which directions have been given under this section, no renewal fees shall be payable in respect of any period during which those directions were in force.

(9) A person who fails to comply with any direction under this section shall be liable—

  (a) on summary conviction, to a fine not exceeding **the prescribed sum** [*£1000*]; or

  (b) on conviction on indictment, to imprisonment for a term not exceeding two years or a fine, or both.

Notes

1. The section heading and subss.(1), (5) and (6) were amended as a result of the Patents Act 2004 s.16(1), Sch.2 paras 1, 8.

2. Subsection (9)(a) was amended as a result of the Magistrates' Courts Act 1980 (c.43) s.32(2).

3. The reference to "indictment" in subs.(9)(b) is treated as a reference to "information" for the Isle of Man (SI 2003/1249).

COMMENTARY ON SECTION 22

Scope of the section

Section 22, which should be read in conjunction with s.23, takes account of the EPC and PCT, in neither of which is there any corresponding provision. It relates to patent applications which contain subject-matter relating not only to national security (subs.(1)), but also to subject-matter which may be prejudicial to safety of the public (subs.(2)). Because of this section, every application filed at the UK-IPO, which (by virtue of s.23) must include any initial filing by a United Kingdom resident of a filing under the EPC or PCT, is initially scrutinised by the Security Section of the UK-IPO. This scrutiny may result in "directions" being given under either of subss.(1) and (2), as discussed in §22.03. The remainder of s.22 deals with the restrictions which result from the giving of such directions and the procedure which follows, or may follow, after such directions have been given. Subsection (9) prescribes the maximum penalties which may be imposed for non-compliance with those directions.

    The amendments made by the Patents Act 2004 to s.22 do not change its scope as such, but its terminology is updated by changing the reference to "defence of the realm" to "national security". The amended wording also addresses an anomaly caused by removal of duties from the United Kingdom Atomic Energy Authority (UKAEA), see §22.05. While it could be argued that amendment of the phrase "prejudicial to the defence of the

22.02

realm" to "prejudicial to national security" represents a broadening of the scope of the section, it is understood that this is not intended. Certainly, the phrase "national security" is vague and can be given such meaning as one wants. However, it is understood that the Comptroller's view as to the meaning of the words is likely to be guided by the rules which regulate the export of goods and information as found in the Export of Goods, Transfer of Technology and Provision of Technical Assistance (Control) Order 2003 (SI 2003/2764) (together with its subsequent amendments), particularly the goods falling within the definitions of Schs 1 and 2 thereof, and that there is likely to be little or no change in practice under the section. Guidance as to whether particular subject matters are likely to be found to fall within the terms of s.22(1) can be obtained by enquiry to the Security Section of the UK-IPO, see also §22.14.

Power to give prohibition directions (subss.(1) and (2))

22.03   By subss.(1) and (2) the Comptroller is empowered to give directions (often called "secrecy" or "prohibition" orders) if the application contains information of a description having relevance for national security (subs.(1)) or for the safety of the public (subs.(2)). The directions given will prohibit or restrict publication of information concerning the application and the information contained in it, though consent may be sought for disclosure to specified persons. The directions will also restrict the filing of corresponding applications in other countries, see s.23(1)(b). The description by which the defence relevance is decided by the Comptroller is as notified to him by the Secretary of State. However, where prohibition is imposed on grounds of public safety, under subs.(2) and at the discretion of the Comptroller, the directions given cannot endure longer than three months after the end of the normal period prescribed for publication of the application, i.e. not longer than 21 months after the declared priority date (subs.(2)) unless the prohibition is explicitly extended under subs.(5)(b) and (e). Because of the provisions of the Landmines Act 1998 (c.33), the Comptroller has announced his intention to act under subs.(2) in relation to applications concerning landmines, see §1.21.

By the Interpretation Act 1978 (c.30) Sch.1, the term "Secretary of State" as used in any statute, means "one of Her Majesty's Principal Secretaries of State". Throughout s.22 he is (generally speaking) the Secretary of State for Defence, whereas elsewhere in the Act he is the Secretary of State for Business Innovation and Skills, see §130.04.

No claim against the Secretary of State in respect of the exercise of powers under s.22 would seem to be possible by virtue of the Crown Proceedings Act 1947 (c.44) s.3(2)(b), as amended and reprinted in §129.02, and possibly also by virtue of s.116(b). Nor is it possible to appeal from any decision of the Comptroller under subs.(1) and (2) (s.97(1)(c)).

UK-IPO examination procedure while directions are in force (subss.(3) and (4))

22.04   By subss.(3) and (4), while directions under subs.(1) or (2) are in force, the normal examination procedure is to be followed. However, if the application is for a European patent, it must not be sent to the EPO (EPC art.77 so permitting); and, if it is an international application, it must not be forwarded to WIPO or the international searching authority (PCT r.22.1(a) so permitting). By s.118(3)(a), information concerning an application for a European patent may be sent to the EPO by the Comptroller, but only if it is his duty so to do. Article 77 of the EPC would seem to remove this duty once directions have been given under s.22(1), but this is not necessarily so when the directions are given under subs.(2) as such may perhaps not be regarded as given "in the interests of the State".

If the imposition of directions prevents an application for a European patent from being received by the EPO within 14 months from the declared priority date (as required by EPC art.77(5)), conversion of the European application into national applications is possible under EPC art.135(1)(b) provided that consent to the filing of foreign applications can be obtained. For conversion into a United Kingdom application under the Act, see s.81 and the commentary on it. There is no corresponding provision for conversion of an international application when directions under s.22 prevent this from being received in due time by the International Bureau so that such is then deemed to be withdrawn (PCT art.12(3) and PCT r.22.3). However, such an application may upon request be treated as an application under the Act (see the MOPP). Further information on conversion of European and international applications is given in §23.09.

Notice of directions to Secretary of State (subss.(5) and (6))

22.05

The Comptroller is required to give notice of his action under subss.(1) or (2) to the Secretary of State who must then consider whether the directions should be maintained (subs.(5)(a)). If so, they are continued (subs.(5)(b)) until revoked under subs.(5)(e). At the time the original directions are given, the Secretary of State has no right to examine the documents of the application. He may do so only after the end of the period normally allowed for publication, unless the consent of the applicant to earlier inspection is obtained. The amendments made by the Patents Act 2004 to subs.(6) is to reflect the change that the UKAEA is no longer responsible for inspection of applications relating to atomic energy or research into such matters. However, if the application concerns atomic energy or research into such matters there is a right for the Secretary of State itself to inspect it at any time under subs.(6)(a)(i) or provision for inspection by an authorised appropriate government body or a person appointed by an appropriate government body under subs.(6)(a)(ii) to make an inspection on which a report in the latter case is to be made to the Secretary of State (subs.(6)(b)). Provision for this inspection is made in s.118(3) by way of exception to the general rule that the contents of applications shall not be accessible to third parties before publication.

Where the subject-matter of the application relates to atomic energy or research into such matters, the UK-IPO also has obligations to communicate information to the Euratom Commission under the Euratom Treaty (Cmnd.4865), see §22.09.

If the directions are to be maintained, a notification from the Secretary of State to the Comptroller is necessary where the relevance is for the safety of the public because of the time limit in subs.(2). While directions continue to be maintained the matter must be reconsidered by the Secretary of State during a period of nine months following the date of application and at least once in every subsequent period of 12 months (subs.(5)(c)). On a prohibition order being lifted by the Secretary of State under subs.(5)(d), the Comptroller is empowered to grant any necessary extension of time (subs.(5)(e)).

Effect of application during continuance of directions (subs.(7))

22.06

So long as directions are in force the patent will not be granted, but, if the application has been brought into order for grant and if the invention is used for the services of the Crown, that use is to be treated as though the patent had been granted at the date it was so brought into order, and the provisions of ss.55–59 apply from that date (subs.(7)(a)). Where the prohibition direction is considered by the Secretary of State to have caused hardship, a payment by way of compensation can be made to the applicant: this payment is to be one considered "reasonable" by the Secretary of State and the Treasury having regard to the "inventive merit" of the invention, as well as its "utility" and "the purpose for which it is designed and any other relevant circumstances" (subs.(7)(b)).

Where a patent has not been granted for an invention of an employee-inventor because of the subsistence of directions under s.22, it would seem that the employee cannot make an application for compensation under s.40, even though the employer may well have derived benefit from the patent application brought into order for grant, e.g. by virtue of subs.(7), because each of subss.(1) and (2) of s.40 is predicated on the patent being "granted". On the other hand, s.39(3) mentions copyright, so perhaps it may be argued that "granted" should not be taken entirely literally.

Renewal fees during continuance of directions (subs.(8))

22.07

Renewal fees are not required to be paid in respect of a patent granted on an application which has been the subject of directions for the period during which directions were in force (subs.(8)). If a prohibition order is lifted, any renewal fee falling due between the date of rescission and grant of the patent must be paid within three months of the grant, see §22.11. Otherwise, the normal provisions of r.36 of the Patents Rules 2007 apply.

Penalties (subs.(9))

22.08

The offence under subs.(9) is one indictable either way, i.e. by summary conviction in a magistrates' court or on indictment before the Crown Court. The maximum penalty in the former case, the "prescribed sum", is now equated with the fine of the "statutory maximum" (Criminal Justice Act 1982 (c.48) s.74). This was increased to £5,000 by the Criminal Justice Act 1991 (c.53) s.17. There is no maximum fine on indictment, except that the penalty imposed must not be excessive in the circumstances, see §109.02. For offences by companies, see s.113 and §113.02.

PRACTICE UNDER SECTION 22

Procedure on imposition, and effect, of prohibition order

22.09   Correspondence concerning applications subject to a prohibition order, and any other matters involving s.22 or s.23, should be addressed or delivered by hand to "The UK-IPO, Room GR70, Concept House, Newport, South Wales NP10 8QQ", where the Security Section of the UK-IPO is located, the documents being enclosed in an envelope clearly marked "For the attention of Room GR70". Enquiries about practice or procedure in relation to prohibition orders should also be directed to that Room (tel. 01633 813 558). Applications and documents to which s.22 applies, or may apply, may also be delivered by hand to the London Office of the UK-IPO during the opening hours of that office (for the address and times of which, see §123.53), likewise in envelopes marked "For the attention of Room GR70". Persons delivering such documents should indicate to the receptionist that a Room GR70 filing is required. Fees for applications subject to a prohibition order should be paid separately from those on normal applications, and such applications (and those upon which an agent thinks it likely that a prohibition order will be imposed) should *not* be filed by fax. For so long as the prohibition order may remain in force, the application will be dealt with solely by an examiner within the Security Section.

When a prohibition order is imposed before or within six weeks after filing an application, no details of that application appear either in the *Patents Journal* or in the register of patent applications. However, if the prohibition order is lifted during the five-year period an entry is made in the register of patent applications, but no entry is made in the Journal.

When drafting applications it is desirable not to include a cross-reference to another application which has attracted, or is likely to attract, a prohibition order, because the existence of that cross-reference will then require both applications to be treated likewise. Even if the imposition of a prohibition order is anticipated, it is undesirable that the specification and drawings included in the application should bear markings to indicate the classified nature of the subject-matter. Such markings become an embarrassment if and when the prohibition order is lifted. Also, when registering assignments, separate documentation should be used for any applications subject to a prohibition order as:

> "it is a basic security requirement that there should be no reference in potentially open documents to the application numbers, titles or contents of cases subject to section 22 direction" (1985–86) 15 *CIPA* 215.

When a prohibition order is imposed, the UK-IPO invites the applicant to agree to early inspection of the application. Agreement is advisable since the prohibition order is unlikely to be lifted until an inspection has been made. It is acceptable to the UK-IPO that agreement is given over the signature of the appointed agent.

Where the subject-matter of the invention relates to the production or use of atomic energy, or research into matters connected with such production or use, the Security Section will refer the application to the Secretary of State where it will itself inspect or authorise a government body or a person authorised by such a government body for inspection of the application under subs.(6)(a)(ii). Also, where the subject-matter of the application relates specifically to nuclear matters, the applicant is invited to give his consent to inspection of the application by the Euratom Commission under the terms of art.16(1) of the Euratom Treaty (for which see §22.05). If this consent is not given within two months, the existence of the application is notified to this Commission. If the Commission seeks to inspect the application, the applicant's consent is sought again; but, even if this is not given, the Treaty requires the UK-IPO to forward a copy of the application to the Euratom Commission within 18 months of the filing date, unless the application has been withdrawn. Where, however, the application relates only to other atomic matters directly connected with and essential to the development of nuclear energy within the European Community, then art.16(2) of the Euratom Treaty requires the UK-IPO merely to notify the Euratom Commission of the existence of the application, and this is done without reference to the applicant automatically 17 months after the filing date, see the MOPP.

Although a prohibition order imposes a blanket prohibition against disclosure of the information in the application, permission for disclosure to specified persons may be given by the Comptroller in appropriate cases subject to conditions regarding transmittal of documents and procedures to prevent unauthorised disclosure.

Subsection (5)(c) requires reconsideration of the prohibition order after the first nine months and thereafter at least annually, but the UK-IPO does not notify the applicant that such reconsideration has taken place. Nevertheless, an applicant may at any time enquire whether there are now circumstances in which the prohibition order could be revoked and presumably make representations that publication of the subject-matter would no longer be prejudicial to the national security or the safety of the public.

Persons handling applications on which a prohibition order is in force should inform the Security Section of the UK-IPO if any document relating to the application is destroyed, see the *Patents Journal*, August 12, 1998.

Avoidance of prohibition orders on subsequent applications

When a prohibition order is revoked on an application which may later serve as a priority document, it is often the practice of the UK-IPO to inform the applicant that a prohibition order may reasonably be expected on any subsequent application claiming priority from it, but that this may be avoided if a letter is written to the Security Section at the UK-IPO stating whether changes have been made compared with the earlier application and, where this is so, supplying a copy of the later application together with any drawings showing where these changes occur, see the MOPP. These documents are retained in the Security Section and therefore do not at any time become open to public inspection. Likewise, correspondence with the Security Section on other matters, e.g. seeking permission to file corresponding applications in certain foreign countries, is not placed on that part of the file which becomes open to public inspection, see the MOPP. Rule 51 of the Patents Rules 2007 now appears to provide the basis for this.

22.10

Procedure upon revocation of prohibition order

When a prohibition order is revoked after 18 months from the earliest declared priority date (or, if none, from the date of filing), arrangements are immediately made to publish the application under s.16. The publication will contain the claims in their form at the date of such revocation; and if this takes place after the application has been put in order, the published claims will be those in their final form. If the revocation occurs before a search has been carried out, the application then proceeds in the normal way. If the search report has already been issued, the application is transferred to the appropriate examining group for the substantive examination, and the examiner may carry out a further search additional to that performed by the examiner in the Security Section. If revocation occurs after the substantive examination has been commenced, the examination may be continued by the Security Section examiner or transferred to the normal examining group, whichever is more expedient. In such a case, it is possible to extend the period under r.30 of the Patents Rules 2007 for putting the application in order for grant under the provision of subs.(5)(e). Of course, there must have been timely filing throughout of Patents Forms 7, 9A and 10. If at the date of revocation the application has already been put in order, then (after arrangements are made for publication under s.16) the application proceeds to grant.

22.11

As noted in §22.07, no renewal fees are due for any period during which the prohibition order was in force (subs.(8)). Also, when a prohibition order is revoked, no renewal fee is payable for the remainder of the year in which the prohibition order was revoked. The basis is that, under r.37 of the Patents Rules 2007, a renewal fee is prescribed to be paid prior to the year in which it is to be effective. When a prohibition order is revoked prior to grant, but after a date three months before the expiration of the fourth year of the patent, the renewal fee is due within three months from the date on which the patent is granted (r.37(3)). Since this rule is made under s.25(3), which is a "following provision" as referred to in s.25(1), this date of grant will be the date on which the notice of grant is published in the *Patents Journal* under s.25(1) and not the administrative date of grant referred to in s.24(1), for which see §24.11. Should a prohibition order be lifted in any year after the fourth, and the anniversary of the filing date falls between the date of rescission of the prohibition order and the date of grant, the renewal fee for the year starting with that anniversary is likewise payable within three months of publication of the notice of grant (r.37(3)).

Withdrawal of prohibited application

22.12   Under ss.16(1) and 22(3)(a), it is possible to withdraw an application while still under a prohibition order (and even perhaps a little later) and thereby avoid publication even though the period prescribed by s.16(1) has expired.

Effect of other statutes

—Official Secrets Act

22.13   If any invention is in fact of a military nature, then the transmission of information about it is governed, not only by s.22, but also by the Official Secrets Acts 1911 to 1989. In particular, s.1A thereof (inserted by s.9 of the 1920 Act) reads:

> "If any person having in his possession or control any sketch, plan, model, article, note, document or information which relates to munitions of war, communicates it directly or indirectly to any foreign power, or in any other manner prejudicial to the safety or interests of the State, that person shall be guilty of a misdemeanour".

Section 9 also inserted the following definition in s.12 of the 1911 Act:

> "The expression 'munitions of war' includes the whole or any part of any ship, submarine, aircraft, tank or similar engine, arms and ammunition, torpedo or mine, intended or adapted for use in war, and any other article, material, or device, whether actual or proposed, intended for such use".

—Export of Goods (Control) Order

22.14   Under the Export of Goods (Control) Act 2002 (c.28) orders can be made specifying specific categories of goods or technology which it is unlawful to export to certain countries. The Export of Goods, Transfer of Technology and provision of Technical Assistance (Control) Order 2003 (SI 2003/2764), as amended, and especially the forms of Schs 1 and 2 of it as may be applicable at the time, set out the goods and technology concerned. Enquires as to the extent of export restriction can be made to the Export Control Organisation, 3rd Floor, 1 Victoria Street, London SW1H 0ET (Tel: 020 7215 2423 Fax: 020 7215 0531).

The Export Control Order includes a provision exempting from its provisions applications for patents (as well as other forms of protection for innovations, including registered designs), and documents necessary to enable such applications to be made or pursued.. The reason for this exception is the existence of s.23 and the corresponding provisions of the Registered Designs Act 1949.

SECTION 23

Restrictions on applications abroad by United Kingdom residents

23.01   **23.**—(1) Subject to the following provisions of this section, no person resident in the United Kingdom shall, without written authority granted by the comptroller, file or cause to be filed outside the United Kingdom an application for a patent for an invention **if subsection (1A) below applies to that application,** unless—

(a) **an application for a patent for the same invention has been filed in the Patent Office (whether before, on or after the appointed day) not less than six weeks before the application outside the United Kingdom; and**

(b) **either no directions have been given under section 22 above in relation to the application in the United Kingdom or all such directions have been revoked.**

(1A) **This subsection applies to an application if—**

(a) **the application contains information which relates to military technology or for any other reasons publication of the information might prejudicial to national security; or**

(b) **the application contains information the publication of which might be prejudicial to the safety of the public.**

(2) Subsection (1) above does not apply to an application for a patent for an invention for which an application for a patent has first been filed (whether before or after the appointed day) in a country outside the United Kingdom by a person resident outside the United Kingdom.

(3) A person who files or causes to be filed an application for the grant of a patent in contravention of this section shall be liable—

(a) on summary conviction, to a fine not exceeding the prescribed sum; or

(b) on conviction on indictment, to imprisonment for a term not exceeding two years or a fine, or both.

(3A) **A person is liable under subsection (3) above only if—**

(a) **he knows that filing the application, or causing it to be filed, would contravene this section; or**

(b) **he is reckless as to whether filing the application, or causing it to be filed, would contravene this section.**

(4) In this section—

(a) any reference to an application for a patent includes a reference to an application for other protection for an invention;

(b) any reference to either kind of application is a reference to an application under this Act, under the law of any country other than the United Kingdom or under any treaty or international convention to which the United Kingdom is a party.

Notes

1. Subsection (1): Additional wording was inserted by the Patents Act 2004 s.7(1). Subsections (1A) and (3A) were inserted by the Patents Act 2004 s.7(2), (3).

2. An amendment to subs.(3)(a) was effected by the Magistrates' Courts Act 1980 (c.43) s.32(2).

3. The reference to "indictment" in subs.(3)(b) is treated as a reference to "information" for the Isle of Man (SI 2003/1249).

COMMENTARY ON SECTION 23

Scope and general purpose of the section

23.02   Section 23(1) of the Patents Act 1977 (as amended by the Patents Act 2004) requires that no person resident in the United Kingdom shall, except as provided by s.23(1)(a) and (b), without the written authority of the Comptroller file or cause to be filed outside the United Kingdom an application for a patent for an invention if subs.(1A) of s.23 applies to that application. The amendments to this section indicated in §23.01 above greatly ease the burden imposed by the original section, although with some uncertainty of an applicant and his agents. Subsection (1A) covers applications containing "information relating to military technology" or, if for some reason open publication might prejudice national security (e.g. it relates to eavesdropping technology, anti-counterfeiting measures, explosives detection equipment, etc.) or publication "might be prejudicial to the safety of the public".

The references to "military technology" and to "information which might be prejudicial to national security or the safety of public" are potentially far-reaching in their effect, if only because of the vagueness of these terms and their subjective nature. This is particularly so in the case of public safety. However, it is understood that the term "public safety" is not intended to cover inventions which merely could be dangerous if misused and, while no specific examples are appropriate, it is understood that the term is likely only to be applied to an invention, or information presented in a patent application, which the general public would understand as constituting a threat to their safety and security. Where an applicant or agent is in any doubt as to whether permission under s.23 is needed, he is advised not to file abroad without first seeking advice from the Security Section of the UK-IPO.

The EPC and PCT contain no corresponding provisions to s.23, though arts 75 and 77 of the EPC refer to national security requirements, as does r.22.1(a) of the PCT. One effect of s.23 is that, unless the conditions of subs.(1) are met, European and PCT applications containing material to which s.23 refers must be filed with the International Unit of the UK-IPO. Once these are filed the process described in §22.09 will be followed.

Under new subs.(3), breach of the provisions of subs.(1) against unauthorised filing now only makes a person criminally liable in circumstances of deliberate or reckless conduct, see §23.07.

The meaning of the term "resident"

23.03   It is irrelevant that a United Kingdom resident is employed by a foreign company, and this is so even if the invention is made by that resident while temporarily out of the United Kingdom so long as he maintains a residential address within the United Kingdom. It should also be noted that the important criterion is residency and not citizenship or nationality.

The restrictions imposed by s.23 also apply, of course, in the case of joint inventorship with a non-United Kingdom resident or where a United Kingdom resident seeks to be a co-applicant for a foreign patent application. In the case of a joint application with foreign companies or inventors, compliance with s.23 may bring about a conflict between United Kingdom law and equivalent provisions in foreign law, especially those of the United States (see §23.06). In such a situation the Security Section of the UK-IPO may usefully be contacted.

"United Kingdom" here includes the Isle of Man (s.132(2)) and the territorial waters of the United Kingdom (s.132(3)), but does not include the Channel Islands.

Definitions applicable to section 23 (subs.(4))

23.04   An application for a patent is defined by subs.(4)(a) to include an application for any "other protection of an invention"; and, by subs.(4)(b), either kind of application is to be taken as comprising applications abroad or under any treaty or convention to which the United Kingdom is a party. The generality is wide and would seem to extend to applications for design or utility model protection if such an application can be said to be one for "protection of an invention". The section certainly applies to the filing of applications under the European Patent Convention or Patent Cooperation Treaty, unless these are filed at the UK-IPO as receiving office or prior written approval has been received from the Comptroller.

Exceptions to applicability of subsection (1) (subs.(2))

By subs.(2), the restrictions on filing abroad do not apply in respect of an invention for which an application for protection has first been filed abroad by a person resident abroad. In the common case, therefore, in which a United Kingdom company has rights abroad in respect of an invention made by an associated company overseas, and receives a copy of a patent application made by the associated company, there is no need to obtain permission or to wait six weeks before any corresponding application is made in a territory in which the United Kingdom company has such rights. Also, where an application is first filed abroad by a non-resident, it can be assigned to a resident of the United Kingdom or further applications filed by such a person without committing an offence under the section.

23.05

Similar laws in other countries

The laws of several foreign countries contain similar provisions to those of s.23. This can cause complications when inventions are made jointly by a United Kingdom resident and a resident of some other country which imposes a similar restriction against foreign patent filing without prior clearance through home filing and delay or the grant of a clearance certificate. For example, in the United States there is a six-month prohibition on foreign filing without a clearance certificate. It should be noted that breach of a similar restriction against prior communication of inventions outside the United States without first filing a United States patent application, or obtaining a foreign filing licence from the United States Patent and Trademark Office, leads to invalidity of the corresponding United States patent. Thus, where an invention is made by an employee of a United States subsidiary of a British company, and it is desired to file the application first in the United Kingdom, or even have a British patent attorney prepare or review the application prior to filing, the precaution should be taken of obtaining an export licence from that Office.

23.06

Before exporting information, particularly military information, from another country, the laws of that country should be carefully checked. Heavy fines or imprisonment can result from breaches of these laws, particularly as regards the export of military technologies in any form from the United States of America. At present China is considering amendment of its law to require applications to be subject to security scrutiny with the sanction that a patent will not be granted for an invention that has been filed abroad without such scrutiny and with the further risk of a criminal penalty.Those engaged in collaborative research with Chinese individuals or institutions will need to exercise care that any such future requirements are complied with.

Penalties (subs.(3))

The penalties specified in subs.(3) correspond to those in s.22(9), for which see §22.08. Section 113 explains where the liability shall be placed in the case of offences committed by bodies corporate, see §113.02.

23.07

While subs.(2) does not absolve a person from liability for breach of subs.(1) as indicated in §23.05, the effect of the introduction of new subs.(3A) (as indicated in §23.01) seems to have the effect that amended s.23 is only likely to lead to a criminal penalty if an applicant (or his agent), either of whom is "resident" in the United Kingdom, files an application abroad either initially or without waiting until the six-week period has expired without seeking consent from the UK-IPO for foreign filing of an application *when he knows, or ought to have known*, that the application contains information relating to military technology which "might" be prejudicial to national security or the safety of the public. Thus, an honestly held and considered view that filing abroad would not contravene subs.(1), as modified by subss.(1A) and (2), absolves a person from criminal penalty even if that view turns out to have been erroneous. However, obviously, there can be no absolution in the case of an application arising from research and development work carried out under a defence contract, or one obviously relating to technology of military significance. This is especially so where (as often will be the case) the contract contains a provision requiring any patent application to be made under a secure filing procedure on the assumption that a prohibition order under s.22 will be made upon filing.

Practice under Section 23

Obtaining leave to file application abroad

23.08   Clearance under subs.(1) may be sought, and is usually obtainable quite quickly, by application to the Security Section at one of the addresses of the UK-IPO indicated in §22.09. A certificate will normally be despatched from Newport the same day; and, if this is not sufficient, enquiry should be made by telephone (tel: 01633 813 558): *Patents Journal*, April 8, 1992. Clearance in the case of an application for which priority is claimed from an earlier application is facilitated if further subject-matter included in the new application is identified in an accompanying letter or by marking on a duplicate of the specification, see §22.10. These matters were discussed by Fiona Dickson and E. Nodder, *Patent World*, May 1994, 41.

Where application for security clearance for permitted foreign filing is made by post, it is desirable to mark the envelope "For the URGENT attention of Security Section, Room GR70": otherwise, delays have been known to occur.

As mentioned in §22.10, it is often the practice of the UK-IPO, when revoking a prohibition order on an application not claiming priority, to advise the applicant to seek security clearance before filing foreign applications, preferably with marked documents as indicated above for showing any additional matter. As also noted in §22.10, such marked documents are retained by the Security Section and therefore do not at any time become open to public inspection.

Filing application abroad while prohibition order is in force

23.09   While a prohibition order under s.22 is in force on a United Kingdom application, the filing abroad of corresponding patent applications is not impossible. Arrangements exist between the United Kingdom and certain other countries, notably those in the North Atlantic Treaty Organization, for the mutual safeguarding of patent applications subject to prohibition orders. For filing in these countries, the permission of the UK-IPO should be sought. Under the NATO arrangements (see Cmnd.1595: "Agreement for the Mutual Safeguarding of Inventions relating to Defence and for which Applications for Patents have been made". Cmnd.2167 provides implementing procedures), it appears to be a precondition for the permission to be granted that an application covering the invention shall have been filed in the United Kingdom. Similar arrangements also exist with a few non-NATO countries.

It is recommended that, if advantage is being taken of the reciprocal filing arrangements, discussed above, in order to secure protection abroad for an invention in respect of which a prohibition order under s.22 is in force, an approach should be made to the Security Section at the UK-IPO for a permit under s.23 as soon as the proposed filing programme is known. A minimum period of 14 weeks before the desired filing date is suggested. Documents for foreign filing of an application subject to a prohibition order should be transmitted solely through officially recognised, adequately secure communication channels. They should be received by the Ministry of Defence at the address given on the UK-IPO permit at least 10 weeks before the desired filing date for Germany, Italy and France, and six weeks for elsewhere.

If it is desired to seek to file applications for patents in EPC countries for an invention covered by a prohibition order, and the procedure stipulated above leaves insufficient time for the filing of national applications, an applicant may wish to consider filing an application for a European patent with the Security Section at the UK-IPO, designating the EPC Member States for which a permit has been given, and requesting that the prospective European application should be made subject to a prohibition order under s.22. Such an application will not be forwarded to the EPO and, eventually, a notice of withdrawal will be issued by the EPO under EPC art.77(5). The application may then be converted to national applications under EPC art.135 by a request made (for the United Kingdom under s.81) within three months of the date of notice of withdrawal, for which see §§81.05 and 81.08.

No formal, equivalent conversion procedure exists for international applications filed under the PCT but, in the United States, it is theoretically possible to enter the national phase based on a classified international application by filing a continuation application, provided that the international application had a filing number and date and had designated the United States. If the international application were deemed abandoned, the revival process available in the United States appears useable. Other than in the United States, and the United Kingdom (for which see §22.04), no formal procedure has been identified for allowing an international application on which a prohibition order is imposed to be converted to a national filing (but see §23.10 below for alternative approaches which might be adopted in practice).

Where possible conversion of a European application under EPC art.77(5) is pursued to enable national applications to proceed in other EPC countries, all the normal documentation should be submitted, including the application, designation of inventor, designation of countries, PF 23 for certified copies of the priority application and fees for these certified copies. Documents must be received by the patent office of the designated EPC Member State directly from the UK-IPO within 20 months of its declared priority date. European filing and designation fees are not required, unless it is possible that the prohibition order will be rescinded within the period specified in art.77(5) of the EPC. The UK-IPO will prepare the certified copy of the priority document and associate this with the other papers (without returning these to the applicant). If formal permission has not already been sought for filing in the designated countries, it should be sought at the time. The UK-IPO must be given the names and addresses of the nominated foreign agents, security cleared to receive documents, which the applicant proposes to engage in the designated European countries. The relevant EPC patent offices will, on receipt of documents from the United Kingdom, then contact the designated agents to seek supporting documents, e.g. translations, power of attorney, etc. Copies of permits will, however, have been sent directly from the UK-IPO to the patent office of the designated EPC Member State.

To avoid delay in the lifting of any prohibition order, the agent should ensure that the Ministry of Defence is aware of the application numbers of any patent applications outside the United Kingdom for the filing of which authorisation was obtained.

Prohibition conditions for foreign-originating applications

It is understood that a prohibition order under s.22 will be imposed on an application **23.10** from abroad only if the country of origin is one with which the United Kingdom has a reciprocal arrangement, for which see §23.09, and the authorities of that country have imposed a prohibition order on the equivalent case filed in that country. An applicant wishing to file such an application in the United Kingdom should seek approval from his domestic authorities who will give instructions and make arrangements for the transmission of documents for filing through secure channels to the British agent nominated to receive them and act for the foreign applicant in the filing and prosecution of an application under the Act. If the nominated agent is not cleared to receive the documents, applicants will be asked to nominate an alternative agent.

For cases filed in this way, the Ministry of Defence issues guidance to agents on handling of such cases in the United Kingdom and continuing correspondence with the foreign applicant or his associates. So far as dealings with the UK-IPO are concerned, these will be as for similar domestic cases, except that a copy of the application is automatically made available to the appropriate United Kingdom authority for information purposes.

Although no formal conversion procedure exists for international applications filed under the PCT, it appears possible to achieve the same effect for some countries, including the United Kingdom. Under PCT r.22, in the case of a classified international application, the applicant can expect to receive a notification from the receiving office, between the 13th and shortly after the expiry of the 16th month from priority, that the international application is no longer to be treated as such. Before that notice is received, and subject to securing the necessary permits, it appears possible to enter the national phase in those countries designated with whom the United Kingdom has reciprocal security arrangements. Certainly, ss.89, 89A and 89B allow for this in the UK.

Provisions as to patents after grant [Sections 24–29]

SECTION 24

Publication and certificate of grant

24.01   **24.**—(1) As soon as practicable after a patent has been granted under this Act the comptroller shall publish in the journal a notice that it has been granted.

(2) The comptroller shall, as soon as practicable after he publishes a notice under subsection (1) above, send the proprietor of the patent a certificate in the prescribed form that the patent has been granted to the proprietor.

(3) The comptroller shall, at the same time as he publishes a notice under subsection (1) above in relation to a patent publish the specification of the patent, the names of the proprietor and (if different) the inventor and any other matters constituting or relating to the patent which in the comptroller's opinion it is desirable to publish.

(4) **Subsection (3) above shall not require the comptroller to identify as inventor a person who has waived his right to be mentioned as inventor in any patent granted for the invention.**

Note. Subsection (4) inserted by Patents Act 2004 (c.16) s.16 and Sch.2 para.9 with effect from October 1, 2005, SI 2005/2471.

RELEVANT RULE—RULE 34

Rule 34—Certificate of grant

24.02   **34.** The certificate of grant of a patent must be in a form which includes—

(a) the name of the proprietor;

(b) the date of filing of the application; and

(c) the number of the patent.

FORM OF CERTIFICATE OF GRANT OF PATENT

24.03

The wording on the certificate of grant is as set out below:

Certificate of Grant of Patent

Patent Number: *(Patent number appears here)*
Proprietor(s):   *(Proprietor(s) name(s) appears here)*
Inventor(s):   *(Inventor(s) name(s) appears here)*

This is to Certify that, in accordance with the Patents Act 1977,
a Patent has been granted to the proprietor(s) for an invention entitled
"(*Title of invention appears here*)"
disclosed in an application filed (*Filing date appears here*)

Dated (*Date of Certificate appears here*)

(*Comptroller General's signature and name appear here*)

The following notes appear on the rear face of the form:

IMPORTANT NOTES FOR PROPRIETORS OF UNITED KINGDOM PATENTS
1. DURATION OF PATENT AND PAYMENT OF RENEWAL FEES

(i) Your patent took full effect on the date of the certificate, as shown overleaf.

(ii) By paying annual renewal fees, you can keep your patent in force for 20 years from the date of filing of the patent application, which is shown overleaf.

(iii) The date on which the first annual renewal fee is due may be determined as follows: calculate the fourth anniversary of the date of filing, and the last day of the month in which this anniversary falls is the date on which the first renewal fee is due. Subsequent renewal fees will be due for payment, each year, on the same due date. The fee can be paid up to three months before each due date and should be accompanied by Patents Form 12. If the Form with the fee is not received by the UK Intellectual Property Office by the due date, the fee can still be paid at any time during the following six months. However, you may have to pay a late payment fee. The patents will cease if the renewal fee (and any late payment fee) is not paid before the end of the six month period. When renewing the patent it is advisable to check the current fee rates.

(iv) It is important that you should set up and maintain effective renewal arrangements to ensure that renewals fees are paid on time. You should not wait for any reminder from the UK Intellectual Property Office before paying the renewal fee. The UK Intellectual Propety Office will send a reminder to the last recorded address for service, or to the address requested when the previous renewal payment was made, within six weeks after the renewal fee due date, but this reminder is only intended to alert you to the possible failure of your renewal arrangements.

2. PROCEDURE FOR PAYMENT OF RENEWAL FEES

Patents Form 12, together with the fee(s) and fee sheet (FS2) should be addressed to "The Cashier, Concept House, Cardiff Road, Newport, South Wales NP10 8QQ" and may be posted or delivered by hand to this address. Alternatively, they may be delivered by hand to The UK Intellectual Property Office at Harmsworth House, 13–15 Bouverie Street, London, EC4.

Blank Patent Forms 12 and fee sheets (FS2) can be requested by post from The Central Enquiry Unit, Concept House, Cardiff Road, Newport, South Wales NP10 8QQ, by telephone on 08459–500505 (Minicom 08459–222250), by fax on 01633–817777 or by e-mail (enquiries@ipo.gov.uk). The Forms and fee sheets can also be downloaded from the office website (www.ipo.gov.uk).

3. REGISTRATION OF OWNERSHIP AS EVIDENCE OF ENTITLEMENT

Any person who becomes entitled to a patent or to a share or interest in a patent should apply to the UK Intellectual Property Office to register their entitlement, share or interest. The person granting the entitlement, share or interest will have to confirm that they have done so.

(*Address For Service appears here*)

For further information or assistance you can contact the Central Enquiry Unit as indicated above.

COMMENTARY ON SECTION 24

Scope of the section

24.04   Section 24 concerns the notification and publication of grant of patents under the Act. The term of the patent is defined by s.25 and discussed in §25.09.

Unlike the position under former statutes, patents are no longer granted under seal and the Royal prerogative. This makes it inappropriate to refer to patents granted under the present Act as "Letters Patent", and the Act carefully avoids the use of the term "patentee", replacing this with "proprietor". Nevertheless, the term "patentee" is still frequently used in practice.

Notification of grant (subs.(1))

24.05   Subsection (1) requires the Comptroller, as soon as practicable after the patent has been granted, to publish in the *Patents Journal* a notice to that effect. While s.20 requires an application to be brought in order for grant within a prescribed period, the Act is silent on exactly when the patent shall be granted. Prima facie it should be when the requirements of s.18(4) have been met. The applicant is informed when this administrative date of grant has occurred (for which see §24.06) and as to when the notice of grant will be published in the *Patents Journal* several weeks later. This latter date is the date from which the grant produces its monopoly right, but see §24.06. For the meaning of the term "date of the patent", see also §24.06. For the date of grant of European patents (UK), see §24.09.

The Comptroller will give sympathetic consideration to granting patents "out of turn" where the applicant can show he is suffering "real and substantial hardship", for example, where actual infringement is taking place, especially if by importation, see e.g. *Patents Journal*, January 11, 1995. However, the mere fear of possible infringement or the desire to expedite licensing negotiations would probably not be sufficient reason (1980–81) 10 *CIPA* 492. Where expedition is refused, it might still be possible to seek judicial review under CPR 54 [not reprinted herein] to require the Comptroller to perform his statutory duty, though it is not clear that the Comptroller has any duty to carry out examination unusually expeditiously. However, whilst substantive examination can, perhaps, be accelerated when the applicant is suffering hardship, this is not administratively possible for the process of granting the patent after completion of the examination. This grant cycle lasts five weeks, see [2000] *CIPA* 107.

Date of grant

24.06   There are actually two dates of grant of a patent, see the *Patents Journal* September 2, 1982. For the purposes of those sections of the Act preceding s.25(1), i.e. for administrative and pre-grant purposes, the date of grant is that of the date of issue of the letter notifying the applicant that a patent has been granted and informing him of the date (several weeks ahead) when notification will appear in the *Patents Journal*. After that date no withdrawal of the application under s.14(9), no divisional application under s.15(4) and no further amendment under s.19 is admitted, see *ITT's Application* [1984] R.P.C. 23 and *Ogawa Chemical's Application* [1986] R.P.C. 63. To prevent publication of a granted patent, notice of withdrawal must be received before issue of the letter notifying the date of grant. See §16.06 above as to the manner in which withdrawal should now be effected.

However, for the purposes of the "following" sections of the Act, the date of grant is that of the *Patents Journal* in which notice of grant is published (s.25(1)), and it is this date which is entered in the register under r.44(4)(a) as the date of grant. Only after that may amendment be sought under ss.27 and 75. Thus, there is a short time between the date of the letter and the publication in the *Patents Journal* during which amendment of a patent cannot be requested. Also, any assignment executed after the date when notice of grant is given to the applicant and before the publication of the notice of grant in the *Patents Journal* is treated as an assignment of an application, rather than of a patent, as ss.30 and 31 are provisions which "follow" s.24, see e.g. *Patents Journal* April 5, 1989.

Similarly, as set out in the MOPP, if a question of entitlement is referred to the Comptroller between the date on which the grant letter is issued and the date of publication of the notice of grant, then no immediate action can take place under either of ss.8 or 37. Instead, the question is treated as having been referred under s.37.

The two dates of grant could cause confusion in determining the period within which a granted patent may be registered in those countries where patent protection is secured by registration of the United Kingdom patent within a specified time, as some of the Patent Ordinances provide for computing the time from the date of "grant" of the patent (see (1981–82) 11 *CIPA* 414 and (1982–83) 12 *CIPA* 25). It is understood that some territories (e.g. Antigua, Belize, Jersey and Hong Kong) have amended their Ordinances specifically to define the date of grant as the date of the *Patents Journal* publication. The prudent practitioner will compute the time from the earlier of the two dates although it can be argued that, as "patent" is defined in s.130(1) (which is a "following" provision of the Act), the latter date is controlling. For information on the registration of United Kingdom patents in other countries to obtain patent protection there, see §132.06 and the notes to art.168 of the EPC in the *European Patents Handbook* ("EPH") (London: Sweet & Maxwell).

Issue of certificate of grant (subs. (2))

Subsection (2) requires the Comptroller to send a Certificate of Grant to the proprietor as soon as practicable after notification of grant in the *Patents Journal*. For the form of this Certificate, see §24.02 and §24.03. **24.07**

The certificate of grant is dated with its own date of issue and does not mention the actual date of grant. It carries on its reverse side a reminder of the requirement to pay renewal fees (for which see §25.15) if the patent is to be maintained in force from year to year up to the end of its permitted term, for which see §§25.08 and 25.09.

The certificate has no legal force under United Kingdom law, as legal ownership is determined by the entry on the register (by virtue of ss.32(9) and 33, see §32.14). According to the MOPP, the UK-IPO may provide replacement certificates of grant either to correct an error on an original certificate or to replace one that has been lost. Return of the original certificate is not required. Replacement of old-style certificates will be with certificates in the current style. If the certificate or a certified copy is required to support registration of the patent in another country, the UK-IPO will provide an explanatory letter, but this may not be sufficient evidence to obtain registration of the patent abroad. The EPO will not apparently issue a certified copy of a European patent (UK), but will issue a "duplicate patent certificate" to the proprietor or his authorised agent, see (1984–85) 14 *CIPA* 111.

Publication of patent specification (subs. (3))

At the time of publishing the notification of grant in the *Patents Journal* under subs.(1), the Comptroller is required by subs.(3) to publish the specification of the granted patent, the name(s) of the proprietor(s) and inventor(s) and any other matters concerning the patent which he considers desirable. This publication is made under the same number as that given to the application when published under s.16, but with the suffix "B" instead of the former suffix "A", see further §24.12. Unlike the position now with granted European patents (for which see §77.04), the "B-specification" does not indicate whether any divisional applications were filed which could mature into individual patents. **24.08**

The authentic version of the specification of the granted patent is the text as on file in the UK-IPO. It can be inspected, and copies obtained, as from the date when the notice of grant is published in the *Patents Journal*, see §118.10.

Subsection (4) removes the requirement of the Comptroller to identify an inventor, provided that he has waived his right to be mentioned as such in the granted patent. The way in which that waiver can be made is specified in r.11, see §13.12 above.

European patents (UK)

24.09   Under s.77, a European patent (UK) is, as from notice of grant appearing in the EPB, to be treated as though it were published in the *Patents Journal* on that date for the purposes of Pts I and III of the Act. The corresponding provisions of EPC are: EPC art.97, relating to grant and publication; and EPC art.98, relating to publication procedure.

Despite the wording of subs.(3), European patents (UK) are not published as such by the United Kingdom UK-IPO, see §77.04 for a discussion of the propriety of this and the problem which arises on amendment of such a patent.

PRACTICE UNDER SECTION 24

Entries in the register

24.10   When an application proceeds to grant, further entries are made in the register already established when the application was published under s.16. At that time, the entries set out in r.44(1) (reprinted in §32.04) would have been entered, see §16.05. By r.44(4) (reprinted in §32.04), the further entries are the date when the patent is granted (for which see §24.06) and (if different from the previous entries) the name and address of the person(s) to whom the patent is granted, and the address for service. For the requirements as regards furnishing an address for service, see §32.15 and for European patents (UK) §77.12.

Entries in the Patents Journal

24.11   The *Patents Journal* containing notice of grant of a patent also includes its subject-matter classification according to the current United Kingdom classification key (which may be different from that for the specification as published under s.16). The *Patents Journal* lists: (a) in numerical order the patents, the notification of grant of which is being published, together with bibliographic data; (b) a "subject matter index" listing classification codes; (c) a name index of proprietor(s) and inventor(s) with cross-references between them, each list being headed with an explanatory note illustrating typical wording of such an entry; and (d) inventorship details. The cumulated indexes of patent specifications published by the UK-IPO are compiled from the applications published under s.16 and do not include details of granted patents. Full information can be obtained by inspection of the register, for which see §32.34 or from the online register at *http://www.ipo.gov.uk*.

European patents (UK) granted under EPC art.97 are listed in the *Patents Journal* some weeks after notice of their grant has appeared in the EPB, but with only the patent number, publication number and name of proprietor. For information on the status of European patents (UK) and applications for them, see §32.35.

Specification of granted patent

24.12   It is the practice of the UK-IPO to attach to the certificate of grant a copy of the specification of the granted patent, but this does not include the abstract as this does not form part of the patent (s.125(1)). The specification bears the same number as that of the application published under s.16, preceded by the letters "GB" and followed by the letter "B". The "other matters" published are presently presented on a front page which states the date of its publication (the official "date of grant") and reiterates the bibliographic data published under s.16, replaced or supplemented as appropriate, together with a list of the documents cited in the search report or during the substantive examination and revised classification data. This bibliographic data is annotated according to the INID codes referred to in §123.84. It appears that the Comptroller has a wide discretion in respect of the publication of indexes, classified file lists and other information-retrieval tools, see §123.85.

Electronic copies of the patents granted after January 1, 2007 are available on the UK-IPO website. For patents granted earlier than this date, it is difficult to obtain an electronic copy. Some websites, including ESP@CENET, provide the A-specification instead of the B-specification but may also make the B–specification available. Users should check which version they are downloading. Earlier B-specifications can be ordered from the UK-IPO using PF 23 or online from the website.

According to the MOPP, if the B-specification contains a printer's error, whether in the specification, the list of citations, or in the bibliographic or classification data, it may be corrected by the issue of an erratum.

In this context, "printer's error" is interpreted broadly to embrace any error originating within the UK-IPO or during the publication process. However, it does not extend to errors made elsewhere, such as by the applicant. An erratum should not be issued to correct an error in the specification which is detected by the UK-IPO unless the error is significant, in the sense that it misleads or introduces doubt. An erratum should be issued for an error in the specification which is notified by the applicant or by a member of the public or for any error in the bibliographic or classification data

SECTION 25

Term of Patent

25.01

25.—(1) A patent granted under this Act shall be treated for the purposes of the following provisions of this Act as having been granted, and shall take effect, on the date on which notice of its grant is published in the journal and, subject to subsection (3) below, shall continue in force until the end of the period of 20 years beginning with the date of filing the application for the patent or with such other date as may be prescribed.

(2) A rule prescribing any such other date under this section shall not be made unless a draft of the rule has been laid before, and approved by resolution of, each House of Parliament.

(3) Where any renewal fee in respect of a patent is not paid by the end of the period prescribed for payment (the "prescribed period") the patent shall cease to have effect at the end of such day, in the final month of that period, as may be prescribed. [*A patent shall cease to have effect at the end of the period prescribed for the payment of any renewal fee if it is not paid within that period.*]

(4) If during the period **ending with the sixth month after the month in which the prescribed period ends** [*of six months immediately following the end of the prescribed period*] the renewal fee and any prescribed additional fee are paid, the patent shall be treated for the purposes of this Act as if it had never expired, and accordingly—

  (a) anything done under or in relation to it during that further period shall be valid;

  (b) an act which would constitute an infringement of it if it had not expired shall constitute such an infringement; and

  (c) an act which would constitute the use of the patented invention for the services of the Crown if the patent had not expired shall constitute that use.

(5) Rules shall include provision requiring the comptroller to notify the registered proprietor of a patent that a renewal fee has not been received from him in the Intellectual Property Office before the end of the prescribed period and before the framing of the notification.

Notes

1. Subsection 3 substituted subject to transitional provisions specified in SI 2005/2471

art.3 by Patents Act 2004 (c.16) s.8(1) (October 1, 2005: substitution has effect subject to transitional provisions specified in SI 2005/2471 art.3).

2. Words in subs.4 substituted by Patents Act 2004 (c.16) s.8(2) (October 1, 2005).

RELEVANT RULES—RULES 36–39 AND 41

Rule 36—Renewal of patents: general

25.02   **36.**—(1) In this rule and in rules 37 to 41—

"renewal date" has the meaning given in rules 37(2) to (4) and 38(3);
"renewal fee" means the fee prescribed in respect of a renewal date;
"renewal period" means the period prescribed by rule 37 or 38 for the payment of a renewal fee.

(2) If the renewal fee is not paid before the end of the renewal period, the patent shall cease to have effect at the end of the renewal date.

(3) Patents Form 12 must be filed before the end of the renewal period.

(4) But where payment is made under section 25(4) or section 28(3), Patents Form 12 must accompany the renewal fee and the prescribed additional fee.

(5) On receipt of the renewal fee the comptroller must issue a certificate of payment.

Rule 37—Renewal of patents: first renewal

25.03   **37.**—(1) This rule prescribes the period for the payment of a renewal fee in respect of the first renewal date.

(2) Subject to paragraphs (3) and (4)—

(a) the first renewal date is the fourth anniversary of the date of filing; and

(b) the renewal period is three months ending with the last day of the month in which that renewal date falls.

(3) Where a patent is granted under the Act during the period of three months ending with the fourth anniversary of the date of filing, or at any time after that anniversary—

(a) the first renewal date is the last day of the period of three months beginning [with] immediately after the date on which the patent was granted; and

(b) the renewal period begins with the date on which the patent was granted and ends with the last day of the month in which that renewal date falls.

(4) Where the grant of a patent is mentioned in the European Patent Bulletin during the period of three months ending with the fourth anniversary of the date of filing, or at any time after that anniversary—

(a) the first renewal date is the later of—

(i) the last day of the period of three months beginning [with] immediately after the date on which the grant of the patent was mentioned in the European Patent Bulletin (case A), or

(ii) the next anniversary of the date of filing to fall after the date on which the grant of the patent was so mentioned (case B); and

(b) the renewal period is—

    (i) in case A, the period beginning [with] immediately after the date on which the grant of the patent was mentioned in the European Patent Bulletin and ending with the last day of the month in which the first renewal date falls, or

    (ii) in case B, three months ending with the last day of the month in which the first renewal date falls.

Rule 38—Renewal of patents: subsequent renewals

38.—(1) This rule prescribes the period for the payment of a renewal fee in re- **25.04** spect of renewal dates subsequent to the first renewal date.

(2) The renewal period is three months ending with the last day of the month in which the renewal date falls.

(3) For those purposes—

(a) the second renewal date is the next anniversary of the date of filing to fall after the first renewal date; and

(b) each subsequent renewal date is the anniversary of the previous renewal date.

Rule 39—Renewal notice

39.—(1) This rule applies where the renewal fee has not been received by the **25.05** end of the renewal period.

(2) The comptroller must, before the end of the period of six weeks beginning immediately after the end of the renewal period, and if the fee remains unpaid, send a renewal notice to the proprietor of the patent.

(3) The comptroller must send the renewal notice to—

(a) the address specified by the proprietor on payment of the last renewal fee (or to another address that has since been notified to him for that purpose by the proprietor); or

(b) where such an address has not been so specified or notified, the address for service entered in the register.

(4) The renewal notice must remind the proprietor of the patent—

(a) that payment is overdue; and

(b) of the consequences of non-payment.

Rule 41—Notification of lapsed patent

41.—(1) This rule applies where— **25.06**

(a) a patent has ceased to have effect because a renewal fee has not been paid by the end of the renewal period; and

(b) the renewal fee and the prescribed additional fee have not been paid by the end of the period specified in section 25(4) ("the extended period").

(2) The comptroller must, before the end of the period of six weeks beginning immediately after the end of the extended period, send a notice to the proprietor of the patent—

(a) stating that the extended period has expired; and

(b) referring him to the provisions of section 28.

(3) The comptroller must send the notice to the address specified by rule 39(3).

Note. Rule 37 was amended as from October 1, 211 by The Patents (Amendment) Rules (2011/2052).

Commentary on Section 25

Scope of the section

25.07
Section 25 deals, in subss.(1) and (2), with the term of patents granted under the Act (also of European Patents (UK)); and, in subss.(3)–(5), with the payment of renewal fees. The section is in conformity with art.33 of the TRIPS Agreement which specifies that:

> "The term of protection available shall not end before the expiration of a period of twenty years counted from the filing date".

Grant and term of patent (subss.(1) and (2))

25.08
Subsection (1) provides that, for the purposes of the "following provisions" of the Act, a patent granted under the Act is to be regarded as having been granted and as taking effect on the date on which notice of grant is published in the *Patents Journal*, see §24.06, but subject to the payment of renewal fees (for which see §25.15). The term of the patent is 20 years from and including its date of filing. This date is defined in s.130(1) as that specified in s.15 in the case of an application made under the Act, i.e. the date when the minimum requirements have been met, or are treated as having been met, e.g. in the case of a divisional application, see §15.09. In the case of any other application, i.e. one filed under the EPC or PCT, it is the date treated as the date of filing of that application in accordance with the relevant convention or treaty, whatever the outcome of that application in relation to other countries. Consequent on these provisions, the UK-IPO regards a patent as expiring at the end of the day preceding the 20th anniversary of its filing date, see *Patents Journal* July 29, 1992. However, the wording of r.36 (for which see §25.02 and §25.15) allows a renewal fee to be paid on the anniversary of the filing date without attracting the fee for late payment.

Subsection (1) further provides for the possibility of the term of a patent granted under the Act running from some other date to be prescribed by rule, but subject to affirmative resolution by both Houses of Parliament pursuant to subs.(2). These provisions were intended, if activated, to make it possible for the term of a patent to run not from the date of filing but from the declared priority date should this be required by any revised convention to which the United Kingdom may become a party. However, to shorten the patent term in this way would now appear to be contrary to the art.33 of the TRIPS Agreement, see §25.08, but such a rule could perhaps be used to extend the term of patents generally to meet special circumstances, e.g. war, although only by altering the starting date for the prescribed 20-year term. It should be noted that there is no provision for extension of the stipulated patent term as there was in earlier legislation.

Article 63(1) of the EPC similarly provides for a 20-year term for European patents running from the date of application. Section 77(1) incorporates these provisions into the terms of s.25, so that the date of grant of a European patent (UK) is that on which notice of the grant is published in the EPB, irrespective of any opposition filed during the ensuing nine months in the EPO under EPC art.99.

Article 63(2) of the EPC provides a contracting state with: (a) the right to extend European patents on the same terms as national patents in the case of war or similar emergency conditions; or (b) where the patent involves a product which has to undergo an administrative authorisation procedure required by law before it can be put on the market. However, these provisions have not, as yet, been introduced into United Kingdom law, but see §25.10.

Supplementary protection certificates and extension of term

As from January 1993 and February 1997 respectively, EC Regulations Nos 1768/92 **25.09** and 1610/96 have created supplementary protection certificates ("SPCs") for medicinal products and for plant protection products, respectively. These SPCs are intended to compensate a proprietor for the loss of effective protection provided by a patent arising out of the time taken to obtain regulatory approval to market such a product, as a medicinal or plant protection product, to the extent that this was protected by that patent. These Regulations are instruments of law of the European Communities and thus lie outside the ambit of the terms of the EPC.

These regulations are now incorporated into the Act at s.128B and Sch.4A, see §§128B.03–128B.09). In summary, an SPC does not extend the term of the patent itself, but it takes effect at the end of the lawful term of a basic patent protecting a product as such, a process to obtain a product or an application of a product. It extends the protection conferred by that patent, but only in respect of the product covered by the authorisation to place the corresponding medicinal product on the market, and any use of the product as a medicinal product that has been authorised before expiry of the SPC. In the United Kingdom, the marketing authorisation for a medicinal product takes the form of a product licence under the Medicines Act 1968 (c.67, as amended) granted by the Medicines Control Agency of the Department of Health for a pharmaceutical product or the Veterinary Medicines Directorate of the Department for the Environment, Food and Rural Affairs (DEFRA) for a veterinary product; and, for a plant protection product, takes the form of a product approval or authorisation issued by the Pesticides Safety Directorate of the Ministry of Agriculture, Fisheries and Food.

The SPC Rules prescribe, inter alia, the procedure for payment of fees to bring the SPC into effect. Accordingly, s.25(3) and r.36 concerning the payment of renewal fees have no effect in the case of SPCs.

Renewal fees (subs.(3))

Subsection (3) provides that a patent shall lapse if a renewal fee is not paid within the **25.10** prescribed period. Under r.37(2)(a) and (b) (reprinted above), the first renewal date is the fourth anniversary of the date of filing and the renewal period is the three months ending with the last day of the month in which the renewal date falls. Under r.38(2) and (3) (reprinted above), the second and each subsequent renewal date is the anniversary of the date of filing and the renewal period is three months ending with the last day of the month in which the renewal date falls. The certificate of patent grant contains a reminder of these provisions on its reverse side, see §24.07 and §25.15. The three-month limit on pre-payment is inextensible (r.108(1)): it is therefore not possible to pay more than one year's fee at a time in order to avoid paying increased fees.

It is understood that a renewal fee which is sent to the UK-IPO before the date of grant of the patent is known will be refunded; and that a renewal fee sent to the UK-IPO more than one month before the period prescribed in s.25(3) will also be refunded, but a renewal fee received by the UK-IPO up to one month earlier than the start of the s.25(3) period will be retained and accepted as having been filed on the first day of that period, though if a statutory increase in the fee has occurred in the meantime the UK-IPO will seek the balance. For late payment under subs.(4), see §25.11.

Under r.37(3), when grant has not taken place by a date three months before expiration of the fourth year, the appropriate fee (which includes any fee(s) which should have been paid for preceding years had the patent then been granted, as confirmed by *Goddin's Patent* BL O/117/96, noted I.P.D. 19101; and BL C/115/96, noted I.P.D. 20023, discussed at [1997] *CIPA* 120, are to be paid within three months of the date of grant: again this period is not extensible (r.108(1)). The six months' period for late payment of the renewal fee, with fine, then runs from the date when the renewal fee fell due, and not (in this instance) from the anniversary of the filing date.

In the case of a European patent (UK), r.37(4)(a) sets out that, where the grant of a patent is mentioned in the EPB in the period of three months ending with the fourth anniversary of the date of filing, or at any time after that anniversary, the first renewal date is the later of the last day of the period of three months beginning with the date on which the grant of the patent was mentioned in the EPB (case A) or the next anniversary of the date of filing to fall after the date on which the grant of the patent was mentioned (case B). Rule 37(4)(b) sets out that the renewal period for case A is the period beginning with the date on which the grant of the patent was mentioned in the EPB and ending with the last date of the month in which that renewal date falls and for case B it is the period of three months ending with the last day of the month in which the renewal date falls. Each of these periods is also inextensible (r.110(2)). A periodic note in the *Patents Journal* explains these provisions.

Late payment of renewal fees (subs.(4))

25.11   Under subs.(4), a renewal fee can be paid during the six months following the end of the normal period for payment, i.e. the end of the month in which the renewal date falls, provided that an additional fee is paid for each month after the first month of this extension period. As this six months' extension period is specified by statute, it is itself inextensible. This six months' period appears in the Act itself because subs.(4) enacts the requirement under art.5*bis* of the Paris Convention. Where r.37(2) and (4) reset the normal period for renewal fee payment to a date three months after the anniversary date, the six months' period allowed for late payment runs from this later date.

Although subs.(3) states that a patent ceases to have effect if a renewal fee is not paid within the prescribed period, subs.(4) also makes it clear that, if the fee and the additional fee are paid within six months, the patent will be treated as if it had not lapsed. Thus, if the fee is not then paid, the patent is deemed to have lapsed at the end of the normal period for payment, but the register is only then updated with a record "Patent Ceased". This cessation is, however, subject to possible restoration under s.28. It appears to follow that, where fees are increased during this extension period, the old renewal fee scale applies to the renewal fee itself, but the new scale will apply to the additional fee paid after the date of change of the fee scales. When a renewal fee has been paid within the additional period, relief in respect of Crown use or infringement during that period may be refused (ss.58(5) and 62(2)).

Accordingly, it is not safe to treat a patent as having lapsed until six months after the due date for payment of a renewal fee, and even then an application for restoration is possible during the permitted period or it under s.28, see the commentary on that section below. Though a third party may acquire rights under s.28A in respect of acts by him commenced during that period, see §§28A.05–28A.06.

Reminders (subs.(5))

25.12   Pursuant to subs.(5) and r.39(2) (reprinted above), the Comptroller is required to send the proprietor a reminder not later than six weeks after the end of the renewal period for payment pointing out the consequences of non-payment.

The reminder is sent to the address specified by the proprietor when last paying a renewal fee or nominated for the purpose subsequently or otherwise to the address for service entered in the register, neither of which need now be in the United Kingdom (r. 39(3), see above). The present form of r.103 (reprinted at §32.02) provides that every applicant for a patent under the Act must have an address for service within the United Kingdom, another EEA State or the Channel Islands and that, upon grant, that address shall be entered in the register as the address for service under the patent until such time as this may be altered or withdrawn. In the case of a European patent (UK), while the nomination of a United Kingdom address for service is encouraged, this is no longer obligatory, and an overseas address for service will be accepted under the current form of r.103 (as discussed in §32.15). In default of the nomination of any address for service (or upon the withdrawal of a previously nominated address without replacement), the address of the proprietor will be deemed to be the nominated address. However, the nomination of a United Kingdom, EEA or Channel Islands address is obligatory when a party becomes "concerned" in any proceedings under the Act. While the mere payment of a renewal fee (and with additional fee for late payment) is not regarded as "proceedings", an application for restoration is certainly is.

Similarly, under r.41 (reprinted at §25.06), when the renewal fee has not been paid within the additional period provided by subs.(4), a notification of cessation is sent not later than six weeks after the expiry of the additional period drawing attention to the provisions of s.28 (restoration). This notice is also sent to the address specified by r.39(3).

PRACTICE UNDER SECTION 25

Payment of renewal fees

25.13 Renewal fees are paid on PF 12, the fees being those specified in the Schedule to the relevant Patents (Fees) Rules. On PF 12, there must be stated: the patent number; the date on which the renewal fee is due; the number of the year for which it is paid; the amount of the fee being paid; and the name and address of the person paying the fee. For the modes of payment of fees, see §123.64. As there described, these modes include payment by deduction from a deposit account, by credit or debit card, by cheque or bank transfer. Thus, the fee paid need not be recorded on PF 12 and r.36(2) and (3) refers to the filing of PF 12 and payment of the prescribed fee without requiring these two actions to be carried out on the one form or even simultaneously. Details of the renewal fees and PF 12 can be found respectively at *http://www.ipo.gov.uk*.

The UK-IPO must issue a "certificate of payment" (r.36(5)) and this is sent to the address given on PF 12 as that of the person who has paid the fee. Certificates of payment sent to an address outside the United Kingdom are sent by air-mail. PF 12 may be filed by any person, whose address need not be in the United Kingdom, and there is no need to show any relationship to, or authorisation by, the proprietor.

Where a patent is subject to "licences of right", only one-half of the specified renewal fee is payable (s.46(3)(d)).

The additional fee for late payment within the six-month period provided by subs.(4) is also made on PF 12, this fee again being as specified in the Schedule to the Patents (Fees) Rules. This fee for late payment is reduced if the patent is subject to "licences of right".

Section 6 of PF 12 also invites that an address be specified to which any reminder (under r.39(3)) of non-payment of the next renewal fee due should be sent if this is not to be sent to the address for service entered in the register. This address need not be in the United Kingdom. There is also a reminder that, if it is desired to change the address for service entered in the register, a separate letter should be sent, for which see §32.23.

Now that the register is computerised, the date of payment of the last renewal fee is recorded thereon and this can be ascertained, free of charge, via the UK-IPO web site, *http://www.ipo.gov.uk*. Information as to the date of payment of a renewal fee can also be requested by filing PF 23, see r.46.

Patents which have ceased through non-payment of renewal fees, and also patents which have expired through the passing of time, are listed in the *Patents Journal*.

If a patent has lapsed by failure to pay a fee and the next year's fee is tendered, this fee is refunded.

Reminders

—By general notice

25.14 The notice of grant issued by the UK-IPO specifically draws attention to the responsibility of the proprietor to arrange for payment of renewal fees, and advises him to check if any renewal fee is due at the time of grant or in the near future, and to set up a suitable reminder system. A Note on the back of the Certificate of grant reads:

"It is important that you should set up and maintain effective renewal arrangements to ensure that renewals fees are paid on time. You should not await any communication from the UK-IPO before paying the renewal fee. The UK-IPO will send a reminder to the last recorded address for service, or to the address requested when the previous renewal payment was made, six weeks after the renewal fee due date, but this reminder is only intended to alert you to the possible failure of your renewal arrangements."

European patent applications require the payment of renewal fees to the EPO two years after filing and then annually until the year of notice of grant appearing in the EPB. For guidance on the payment of renewal fees on European patent applications, see Ch.11 of the European Patents Handbook ("EPH") (London: Sweet & Maxwell).

—By statutory notice

25.15 The requirement to issue a reminder of non-payment of a renewal fee (r.39(2)), and a notice of lapsing of the patent (r.41) have been discussed in §25.13. The r.39(2) reminder is issued within six weeks after the due payment date, and the r.41 notice of lapsing is issued within six weeks after the expiry of the six months' grace period. Although these notices are not intended to be a back-up to a renewal reminder system operated by the proprietor or his agent, see the discussion in §28.11, the Patents Court has accepted the argument that a proprietor (albeit an individual) is entitled to set up a system for payment of renewal fees which relies on the official r.39(2) reminder telling him of the need to pay renewal fees, see *Ling's Patent and Wilson and Pearce's Patent* [1981] R.P.C. 85 discussed in §28.11.

Legal obligations of agents in respect of statutory notices

25.16 Particular care needs to be taken by a joint proprietor or a licensee who does not have the responsibility for paying renewal fees to check that the fee has been paid, e.g. by filing PF 23 at the date the fee is due. It is dangerous to rely on the caveat system.

SECTION 26

Patent not to be impugned for lack of unity

26.01 **26.** No person may in any proceeding object to a patent or to an amendment of a specification of a patent on the ground that the claims contained in the specification of the patent, as they stand or, as the case may be, as proposed to be amended, relate—

(a) to more than one invention, or

(b) to a group of inventions which are not so linked as to form a single inventive concept.

COMMENTARY ON SECTION 26

26.02 Section 26 concerns unity of invention. While s.14(5)(d) requires that the claims of an application must relate (a) to one invention or (b) to a group of inventions which are so linked as to form a single inventive concept, s.26 provides that no person can in any proceedings object to a patent on the ground that the claims do not comply with that requirement.

This provision makes it clear that objection to a proposed amendment under s.27 or s.75 similarly cannot be based on the ground that the amendment would result in lack of unity. Presumably the same would apply to a correction under s.117. In any event a patent granted under the Act can be revoked only on the specific grounds listed in s.72(1), see *Genentech's Patent* [1989] R.P.C. 147 CA. The MOPP indicates that, if a post-grant amendment would leave the amended claims lacking this requirement of unity, it is not the practice of the UK-IPO to take objection to the amendment on this ground. If it were otherwise, a proprietor might have to relinquish part of the protection to which he is legitimately entitled merely because there is a need to excise some central part of the scope of the claims as granted.

Section 26(b), like s.14(5)(d), makes it clear that the claims can relate to "group of inventions which are so linked as to form a single inventive concept". Also, s.125(2) (discussed in §125.27) states that a priority date is assigned to an "invention" and not to a "claim". This also shows that the claims of a patent can relate to a group of inter-linked inventions, and thus the objection which, in practice, is taken pre-grant is that the claims are not confined to a group of this type. The question of pre-grant objections to lack of unity of invention is dealt with in §14.40.

There is no corresponding provision in the EPC, but art.82 of the EPC corresponds to s.14(5)(d), while the comprehensive grounds of opposition specified in art.100 of the EPC (to which s.72(1) corresponds) do not include lack of unity. Indeed, the EPO has held that lack of unity can have no significance once division is no longer possible: thus, an objection of lack of unity cannot be raised post-grant (G 1/91 *SIEMENS/Unity* OJ EPO 1992, 253; [1992] E.P.O.R. 356).

Although an objection of lack of unity per se cannot be made post-grant, the question may have significance in another context. In *Chiron v Organon Teknika (No.3)* [1994] F.S.R. 202, and on appeal sub nom. *Chiron v Murex* [1996] R.P.C. 535 CA, it was argued that, if a claim covers more than one invention, then the specification should sufficiently describe how each of these related inventions could be practised. However, the courts here held that the claims in issue extended to a single inventive concept and, hence, could not successfully be attacked for insufficiency on the basis that not all embodiments of the invention could be reproduced by the skilled person when it was admitted that at least one of them could be reproduced from the information given.

SECTION 27

General power to amend specification after grant

27.—(1) Subject to the following provisions of this section and to section 76 below, the comptroller may, on an application made by the proprietor of a patent, allow the specification of the patent to be amended subject to such conditions, if any, as he thinks fit. **27.01**

(2) No such amendment shall be allowed under this section where there are pending before the court or the comptroller proceedings in which the validity of the patent may be put in issue.

(3) An amendment of a specification of a patent under this section shall have effect and be deemed always to have had effect from the grant of the patent.

(4) The comptroller may, without an application being made to him for the purpose, amend the specification of a patent so as to acknowledge a registered trademark.

(5) A person may give notice to the comptroller of his opposition to an application under this section by the proprietor of a patent, and if he does so the comptroller shall notify the proprietor and consider the opposition in deciding whether to grant the application.

(6) In considering whether or not to allow an application under this section, the comptroller shall have regard to any relevant principles under the European Patent Convention.

Note. Subsection (6) was added by the Patents Act 2004 (c.16) s.2 with effect from December 13, 2007 when the EPC 2000 revisions came into force.

Rule 35—Amendment of specification after grant

27.02   **35.**—(1) An application by the proprietor of a patent for the specification of the patent to be amended must—

    (a) be made in writing;

    (b) identify the proposed amendment; and

    (c) state the reason for making the amendment.

(2) The application must, if it is reasonably possible, be delivered to the comptroller in electronic form or using electronic communications.

(3) The comptroller may, if he thinks fit, direct the proprietor to file a copy of the specification with the amendment applied for marked on it.

(4) Where the specification of a European patent (UK) was published in a language other than English, the proprietor must file a translation into English of the part of the specification which he is applying to amend and a translation of the amendment.

(5) The comptroller may give such directions as he may think fit with regard to the subsequent procedure.

(6) Where the court or the comptroller allows the proprietor of a patent to amend the specification of the patent, the comptroller may direct him to file an amended specification which complies with the requirements of Schedule 2.

Commentary on Section 27

Scope of the section

27.03   Section 27 provides a route for voluntary amendment of patents post-grant, as opposed to pre-grant for which see s.19, or where the validity of the patent is in issue, for which see s.75. The word "may" in para.1 implies discretion, but that discretion is now subject to the provisions of para.6. In consequence, and in accordance with EPO practice the conduct of the patentee is now no longer relevant, see *Zipher Ltd v Markem Systems Ltd & Anor* [2008] EWHC 1379 (Pat) and MOPP at 27.08 and 27.32.1 where the necessity of the amendments and procedural fairness were held now to be the main, if not the only, factors relevant to the exercise of discretion. The extensive jurisprudence on patentee conduct explained in earlier editions of this work is therefore now of historical interest only. Amendment during revocation proceedings initiated by the Comptroller under s.73 (for which see §§73.03 et seq.) is not governed by the rules relating to amendment under s.27, though there must be compliance with s.76. "Amendment" should not be confused with "correction" under s.117, see §117.06.

No application to amend under s.27 may be made before the date when notice of grant has been published in the *Patents Journal* (s.25(1)), but an application to amend under s.19 is precluded once grant has administratively taken place by issue of the administrative notice of grant under s.18(4). Thus, there is a short period in which an application for amendment cannot be filed at all, as discussed in §24.06.

The Comptroller can permit amendment of the specification of a European patent (UK) after its grant (see s.77(1), as discussed in §75.03). In *Reed's Patent* BL C/74/96, noted I.P.D. 19094, no reason was seen why a lapsed European patent should not be amended in order to remove overlap with a patent granted under the Act, in order to avoid the revocation of that patent under s.73(2). However, a European patent (UK) may also be amended during opposition proceedings in the EPO under art.99 EPC and, following the revisions of EPC 2000, in limitation proceedings under art.105 EPC. Accordingly, s.130(5A) (discussed in §130.07) now states that references in the Act to amendment (whether under the Act or by the EPO) include limitation of the claims. Any amendment made by the EPO has automatic effect, see s.77(4) discussed in §77.06, and therefore if an amendment has been made to a European patent (UK) under the Act, that amendment may be nullified by an amendment or limitation by the EPO.

The types of amendment which may be allowed and those which should be prohibited are largely governed by the terms of s.76. The MOPP indicates at para.27.11 that objection is not raised against proposed amendments on the ground that the claims as amended would lack unity of invention.

Introduction of s.27(6) has removed much incentive for avoiding "covetous claiming" or delaying amendment of a granted patent after a ground of invalidity has come to the patentee's attention. However it is inevitable that a court will view a patent that is resistant to challenge in the form in which that patent is first brought to its attention more favourably than a patent that is only partially valid and requires amendment during the proceedings. Where the relevant defects were or should have been apparent to the patentee at the time when proceedings were launched and no amendment was applied for before proceedings were launched, it appears arguable that there should be a costs sanction reflecting the inconvenience to which a defendant was put by attempted assertion of a patent in a form in which it was or should have been known to be invalid.

Inapplicability of section 27 subs.(2)

As previously explained, by subs.(2), no amendment is to be allowed by the Comptroller under s.27 where there are pending before the court or Comptroller any proceedings in which the validity of the patent may be (not "is") put in issue, such proceedings being called "validity proceedings". Any application in such a case must be made under s.75, see §75.04. **27.04**

Section 74 sets out what are the "validity proceedings" that by operation of s.27(2) exclude amendment under s.27, namely proceedings under: s.61 (infringement of patent); s.69 (notional infringement of application); s.70 (threats); s.71 (declaration of non-infringement); s.72 (revocation); and s.58 (Crown user compensation), irrespective of whether such proceedings take place before the court or before the Comptroller. No other proceedings are relevant here, see s.74(2).

If the application to amend under s.27 is presented to the Comptroller before the commencement of any such "validity proceedings", but the proceedings are commenced subsequently, it appears that the Comptroller must stay the proceedings under s.27. As regards termination of the "validity proceedings", s.27(2) would seem not to apply after expiration of the time for lodging appeal against a final order of the court and disposal of any appeal timely brought, see *Lever Bros' Patent* (1955) 72 R.P.C. 198 CA decided under s.30 of the 1949 Act which applied to the existence of a "proceeding". When proceedings are concluded by consent, the proceedings remain pending until the court has approved the proposed consent order: *Critchley v Engelmann* [1971] R.P.C. 346.

In *Wilkinson Sword v Warner-Lambert* BL C/124/87, proceedings under s.27 were already in being when application was made to the court for a declaration of non-infringement under s.71 and for revocation under s.72. In these circumstances subs.(2) would seem to have required a stay of the amendment application before the Comptroller. The proprietor sought a stay of the court proceedings pending resolution by the Comptroller of the amendment application, but the court refused a stay, indicating that the amendment proceedings should be recommenced before the court under s.75. Subsequently the court allowed the amendment and found the amended patent valid but not infringed, see BL C/36/88.

In *Luk Lamellan's Patent* BL O/379/02 it was made clear that where amendments had been advertised under s.27 and an application for revocation under s.72 was subsequently filed, the amendment application under s.27 would still be stayed since the amendments had not at that point been "allowed". See also §72.19.

PRACTICE UNDER SECTION 27

Applying to amend

Since a licence granted under a patent may contain a covenant prohibiting the proprietor **27.05** from amending the specification without the consent of the licensee, care should be taken to check whether any such licence term exists before applying to amend.

A form is no longer required. Rule 35(1) requires the application (a) to be in writing, (b) to identify the proposed amendments, and (c) state the reasons for making the amendment. The applicant may be required to file a copy of the specification with the amendment applied for marked on it (r.35(3)), although this would seem to be the simplest way to present the amendment anyway. Rule 35(2) requires the applicant "if it is reasonably possible" to deliver the amendment, and the reasons for making it, to the Comptroller electronically. Directions have been made under s.124A and are reproduced in the "Relevant Official Notices and Directions" section of the MOPP. The amendment details should be sent using email entitled "Proposal to amend under s.27" and addressed to litigationamend@patent.gov.uk and presented as a "plain text" message (RFC822-compliant). MS-TNEF/RTF and HTML formats, and encrypted or digitally signed documents are not acceptable. The details may be presented in an attachment. Alternatively, the amendment details may be presented on a data carrier (e.g. on a disk or CD-ROM) delivered to the Patent Office accompanied by a letter. The attached text, or that presented on a data carrier, may be presented in Microsoft Word®, WordPerfect® or PDF formats. A notice on the UK-IPO website states that applicants are encouraged to use conventional word processing features such as mark-up, coloured text and strikeout/strikethrough to set out the amendments on the original version of the text in a way that makes it easy for the reader to appreciate the changes.

Once made, an application to amend may not be withdrawn without the Comptroller's consent, which may not be forthcoming if reasons are seen why discretion to permit amendment should not be exercised, even if the patentee indicates that he intends to allow the patent to lapse (*Wittenborg's Patent* BL O/126/93). Also, the MOPP indicates (by reference to *Emulsol's Application* (1940) 57 R.P.C. 256) that the amendment takes effect from the date when the Comptroller sets out that the requested amendments have been allowed (but not yet advertised for opposition purposes). Thus, thereafter, those amendments cannot be withdrawn or changed, although an application can be filed to make further amendments of a non-broadening nature.

Amendment of European patent (UK)

27.06   Under r.35(4), where a European patent (UK) is sought to be amended and the specification is not in English (i.e. is in French or German), the applicant must also supply a translation of that part of the specification which is proposed to be amended and a translation of the proposed amendment. Copies of the amendment and the translation are available from the UK-IPO. In many cases a total translation of the patent as granted, as formerly required by s.77(6)(a), will already have been filed. Verified translations are not required but, under r.115 (reprinted in §123.32), the Comptroller can take action where he has reasonable doubts about the accuracy of any translation filed. The amendment proceedings will be conducted in English; if the amendment as accepted differs from that originally sought, it must be re-presented in the documents of both languages. Where the European patent is published in the English language, translation of the French and German versions of the claims is not required.

If the patent is under opposition at the EPO or the opposition period has not expired, the applicant is given the option of either: (a) staying the amendment request until the opposition period has expired or the opposition proceedings settled; or (b) proceeding with the amendment application but on the understanding that the amendments may be negated by amendments allowed by the EPO. Thus, if further or different amendments to those made in the EPO after grant are desired, a fresh application under s.27 (or s.75 in court proceedings) may be required.

Statement of reasons for amendment

27.07   Amendment still appears to involve the exercise of an element of discretion, s.27(6) notwithstanding. The reasons for amendment therefore need to be given fully and completely. The prior art sought to be distinguished from has to be identified, see *Clevite*

Corp's Patent [1966] R.P.C. 199 and *Warnant's Application* [1956] R.P.C. 205. In *Waddington's Application* [1986] R.P.C. 158, the Comptroller decided that it is not sufficient to state that amendment "is by way of voluntary amendment as a result of prior art which has come to the applicant's attention". The Comptroller requires that such prior art should be identified, basing this requirement on the provisions of r.82(1)(a) (or its predecessor) under which the Comptroller has power to call for documents to be produced to him, see §72.23. In *Pownall's Patent* BL O/1/04, the reason "to distinguish the invention from new prior art which has recently come to light" was deemed insufficient since it did not identify the prior art and thereby did not enable the Comptroller to determine whether the proposed amendments did or did not cure the defects they were intended to cure. The patentee responded by filing further documents (which were treated as confidential under r.94) but which were deemed to overcome the inadequacy of the reason given for amendment. In *PSC Freyssinet's Patent* BL O/117/91, the patentee was criticised for not referring in the amendment request to a pertinent patent cited in an EPO search report. The amendment request referred only to a German *Gebrauchsmuster*, also cited in that report. However, the amendment was allowed as the opponent had raised the point only at the hearing and the patent, as to which the notice of opposition had been silent, was held not to affect patentability in the absence of evidence from skilled persons. The further fact that the patentee had supplied only the published extract of the *Gebrauchsmuster*, and not the full text, was held in the circumstances not to be sufficient to stand against allowance of the requested amendment.

Advertisement of the application for amendment

Existence of an application to amend is advertised by a preliminary notice in the *Patents Journal* prior to its examination, but without specifying the proposed amendments themselves. The fact that an amendment application has been filed is also recorded in the register. Details of the amendment application can then be inspected at the UK-IPO. **27.08**

Examination of the proposed amendments

The Comptroller will examine the amendments for compliance with s.76(2) and s.76(3). **27.09**
If an amendment is made under either of s.27 or 75 which contravenes s.76(3) by disclosing additional matter or extending the protection conferred by the patent, a basis for revocation will arise under s.72(1)(d) or (e), see §72.15. An application for revocation may be made on these grounds whether or not the applicant for revocation opposed the application to amend.

The Comptroller will also consider whether the reasons given for making the amendments are sufficient and that the amendments remedy the defects that they are intended to rectify. Thus where prior art is cited, the Comptroller will consider whether the subject-matter claimed in the specification as amended is novel and inventive over that prior art. It has been stated, obiter in *Horne Engineering v Reliance Water Controls* [2000] F.S.R. 90, that a court should exercise its discretion against an amendment which would leave a claim non-compliant with s.14(5), i.e. as to its clarity and, presumably, also as regards the requirements for the claims to be supported by the description and not to be unduly prolix, and such objections are routinely considered by the EPO where amendments are submitted during opposition proceedings.

Publication for opposition purposes

When it has been found that proposed amendments appear to be allowable, a notice is **27.10**
published in the *Patents Journal* declaring that the amendments are open to opposition and setting a 4-week term within which opposition may be filed.

An exception to the above procedure arises if the applicant for amendment and the Comptroller have not reached agreement on the permissibility of the amendments and the applicant has asked for a hearing; the Comptroller then publishes the notice that amendment has been sought to ascertain if there is any opposition before he proceeds with the hearing. The notice indicates that the amendments requested have not yet been approved. If there is no opposition, the application will then proceed to a hearing without notice to other parties.

Opposition to application to amend a patent (subs.(5))

27.11   Subsection (5) provides for opposition to amendment. Such proceedings are governed by Pt 7 of the Patents Rules 2007 "Proceedings Heard before the Comptroller" (rr.73 to 91), mostly reprinted at §§123.06–123.21, and the procedure to be followed is discussed in §27.17 below.

An opponent does not have to show an interest in the patent before he is entitled to oppose (*Braun AG's Application* [1981] R.P.C. 355), it being in the public interest that anyone who has evidence which might cast doubt on the bona fides of the applicant's application to amend should be so entitled. Accordingly, in *Sanders Associates' Patent* BL O/89/81, noted I.P.D. 4128, the Comptroller permitted a patent agent to oppose an application to amend as nominee for an undisclosed principal. Although this ruling was challenged on the ground that opposition to the application to amend had to be accompanied by a statement setting out fully the facts on which the opponent relies, the hearing officer declined (following *Dirks' Application* [1960] R.P.C. 1) to decide such a point. This is broadly consistent with the EPO's position on oppositions by nominee opponents, since Enlarged Board Decisions G 3/97 and G 4/97 decided (overruling previous case law) that such oppositions are legitimately filed unless they amount to an abuse of process, for example by allowing self-opposition by the patentee through a nominee, or by allowing a nominee to fulfil the role of a professional representative without being one.

There is power (under r.82(1)(f)) for the Comptroller to stay amendment proceedings on a European patent (UK) where there is a pending opposition against that patent at the EPO. This is because any amendments made in these proceedings, leading to the maintenance of the European patent (UK) in a form different from that in which it was granted, will automatically override (at least initially) any amendment of that patent made separately under the provisions of the Act (i.e. under any of ss.27, 73 or 75), see s.77(4) discussed in §77.06. However, where the patent is subject to infringement proceedings in which validity is challenged, separate application to amend under s.75 is required, see *Petrolite v Dyno* [1998] F.S.R. 190 and §75.04.

Grounds of opposition

27.12   The grounds of opposition to amendment before the Comptroller are not set out in the Act, but usually comprise the following:

(1) that the amendment does not meet the requirements of s.76 for allowability (for which see the commentary thereon);

(2) that favourable exercise of the discretion to allow the amendments ought to be refused, subject now to s.27(6); and

(3) that the proposed amendments would leave the patent still invalid.

It seems clear that an opponent may not raise a general attack on validity. He is normally limited to arguments which can be based on the documents otherwise before the Comptroller and where the invalidity can be established without real controversy, for example as to arguments of ambiguity and insufficiency under s.14(3).

In *Genentech's Patent* [1989] R.P.C. 147 CA, Dillon L.J. observed that an application to amend a granted claim could let in the objection that the claim did not comply with s.14(5) owing to lack of support in the original disclosure. This view may mean that an amendment application could in effect result in re-opening the substantive examination for patentability. It is supported by T 301/87 *BIOGEN/Alpha-Interferons* OJ EPO 1990, 335; [1990] E.P.O.R. 190; discussed at (1988–89) 18 *CIPA* 396, albeit that the latter decision was given under a specific provision (EPC art.102(3)) which has no precise counterpart in the Act. Thus, in *Deepwater Oil Services' Patent* BL O/13/92, noted I.P.D. 15137, amendment was refused because the proposed amended claim was not supported by the original disclosure. However, for an objection under s.14(5) to be raised on amendment the requested amendment must have a sufficient nexus with arguably over-broad claims: *Chiron v Organon Teknika (No.5)* [1994] F.S.R. 258.

In *Bucher-Buyer's Patent* BL O/167/86, an opponent was not permitted to contend that the proposed amendment would add only an obvious feature to the claim, or leave it clearly anticipated by some further prior art, but was permitted to contend that the amendment did not cure the defect which the proprietor had indicated it was his intention that the requested amendment should cure. In *Smith Kline & French (Bavin's) Patent* [1988] R.P.C. 224, a clear distinction was drawn between an opponent raising a new ground of invalidity (not generally permissible) and of contending that the amendments offered will not cure the invalidity which the proprietor has himself indicated in his statement of case may exist. The latter can be raised because the Comptroller is entitled to refuse favourable exercise of discretion to amend if he considers, on the basis of documents put before him by the proprietor, that the proposed claims are clearly invalid; it is therefore considered proper to allow an opponent to assist the Comptroller with evidence and argument directed to this point. In *Minister of Agriculture's Patent* [1990] R.P.C. 61, the opposition statement was allowed to be amended to raise this type of plea, but the opponent was not permitted to base its arguments of invalidity on additional documents. Here the Patents Court pointed out that the patentee was seeking an indulgence and that an opponent should not be denied an opportunity of raising matters, unless injustice would be caused thereby. In *Borden's Patent* BL O/160/86, noted I.P.D. 9116, it was indicated that the amended claim ought, at least prima facie, to be distinguished from the prior art as regards novelty and obviousness, but in that case the unamended claims were held already to be distinguished from the prior art. Amendment was refused in *Contra-vision's Patent* BL O/79/00, noted I.P.D. 23048 because the requested amendment did not cure the defect of lack of novelty and some of the proposed new claims extended to additional subject-matter. Even if allowed, the amendment would have been refused for prolixity of claiming, see §14.27. Amendments were refused on discretion on account of their being considered not to cure the stated defects in *Robinson Willey's Patent* BL O/238/04 and in *Archibald Kenrick v Laird Security Hardware* BL O/67/06; in each case the claim amendments were held not to distinguish from the relevant prior art.

In *Kaiser's Patent (No.2)* BL O/377/99, there was an attempt to re-visit a previous finding in proceedings in which the opponent had not been involved. The Comptroller doubted whether this is permissible, but anyway the substantive contentions against the amendments were here no different from those previously considered: the opposition was therefore rejected.

With regard to surrender of a patent by its proprietor when amendment is opposed, see §29.06.

Procedure on opposition

After the advertisement in the *Patents Journal*, notice of opposition to the amendment **27.13** may be lodged. Opposition proceedings are governed by Pt 7 of the Patents Rules 2007 "Proceedings Heard Before The Comptroller" (rr.73 to 91) (reprinted under s.123) and require the filing of the relevant form (r.76(1)(a)) which is PF 15 (see r.76(3)(c) and the reference to s.27 (5) in Pt 2 of Sch.3 to the Rules) and a statement of grounds (r.76(1)(b)). The opposition period is four weeks (r.76(2)(b)) running from the date of advertisement in the *Patents Journal* of the proposed amendment. This opposition period is inextensible (Pt 1 of Sch.4 to the 2007 Rules), except where validity proceedings are pending before the court or the Comptroller.

Security for costs under s.107(4) may be required from an opponent if the conditions prescribed in r.85 for the purposes of s.107(4) are satisfied. In default of the required security being given the Comptroller may treat the opposition as being abandoned (see s.107(4)).

In *Minister of Agriculture's Patent* [1990] R.P.C. 61 it was said that the Comptroller may allow an opposition statement to be amended in order that this should fully set out the facts relied upon.

The applicant/patentee should respond with a counterstatement in duplicate within a period specified under r.77(5) and believed usually to be six weeks. This period may be extended under r.81(1), even if it has already expired. The subsequent procedure is determined by Pt 7 of the 2007 Rules, of which r.80 relates to evidence rounds and the appointment of a hearing.

Where the patentee fails to file a counterstatement, he is taken under r.77(9) to support the opponent's case and the request for amendment is likely to be considered to have been withdrawn. This is in line with the decision under previous rules in *Norsk Hydro AS's Patent* [1997] R.P.C. 89, although in *Rita Rusk Innovations Ltd's Patent* BL O/109/08, it was held (also under previous rules) that opposition to amendment should continue and be heard, whereupon the amendments were refused for failing to cure the identified defect. Where an opponent files a statement of opposition, but then takes no further part in the proceedings, the Comptroller will consider the case on the papers and issue a formal decision whether amendment can be permitted, see *Minister of Agriculture's Patent* BL O/11/92 and *Le Maitre Fireworks' Patent* BL O/109/93.

Oppositions to amend filed under subs.(5), and the outcome, whether successful or unsuccessful, are published in the *Patents Journal*. Appropriate entries are, of course, also made in the register.

In *Intel's Patent* BL O/87/03 the opponent was unsuccessful in opposing the amendment, which was therefore allowed. Nevertheless the opponent argued that it should have its costs because the applicant for an amendment had been seeking an indulgence in applying to amend its patent. The Comptroller rejected this position as suggesting that anyone might raise spurious objections to amendment with impunity. The opponent was ordered to pay costs on the normal scale.

A supplementary statement by the opponent was admitted in *Archibald Kenrick v Laird Security* BL O/156/05, despite it being recognised that the patentee had been put to inconvenience and delay by the request to have the statement admitted. Costs were, however, awarded in favour of the patentee, although only on the standard scale.

Procedure when amendment is allowed

27.14   If leave to amend is given, a notice appears in the *Patents Journal*. The proprietor is likely to be required to file, within a specified time, a copy of the amended specification prepared in accordance with the formal requirements of Sch.2 to the 2007 Rules (see r.35(6)). The amended specification may then be reprinted or, if the amendments are short, an amendment slip is printed for attachment to printed copies of the specification thereafter distributed. The amended specification carries a "C" (rather than "B") designation. If further amendments are made, the amended specification is given a "C2", "C3", etc. designation. If the amendments are not extensive, they are incorporated into a schedule on the reverse of the front page. If the amendments are more extensive and an amended specification has been filed under r.35(6), the specification is republished with a cover page having a "C" designation. In the case of an amended EP (UK) patent, the cover page has an EP/UK country designation.

After amendment, copies of the specification before amendment can still be obtained from the Office Sales Branch, but only on special application on which it is advisable to state very firmly that the amended specification is not required. If desired, an electronic PF 23 available on the UK-IPO website can be employed. B-specifications published since January 3, 2007 are also available directly on the UK-IPO publication server accessible from the UK-IPO website. C-specifications are now also available.

Effect of amendment (subs.(3))

27.15   By subs.(3) an amendment once allowed is considered to have had effect from the grant of the patent. This suggests that if an invalid patent is infringed, and the invalid patent as subsequently amended into valid form is still infringed, infringement can be considered to have taken place during the time when the claim was in invalid form; and conversely, if a patent is not infringed after amendment, there will have been no infringement at any time. However, amendment may have an effect on an award of monetary relief for infringement prior to amendment. Thus s.62(3) (discussed in §62.05) states that where a patent has been amended, the court or tribunal shall, when considering damages or an account of profits for pre-amendment infringements, take into account inter alia whether the specification as published was framed in good faith and with reasonable skill and knowledge. Section 58(6) applies similar restrictions to Crown user compensation.

Amendments are specifically subject to challenge under s.72(1)(d) and (e), for which see §72.25 and §72.26. In the event of a challenge to an amendment under s.72(1)(d) or (e), the amended and unamended specifications will be compared, see *Bonzel v Intervention (No.3)* [1991] R.P.C. 553 discussed on this point in §76.06.

Amendment subject to conditions

Subsection (1) appears to give the Comptroller unfettered power to attach such conditions as he thinks fit when he permits amendment. The power is seldom exercised, and usually for protecting third parties, in certain circumstances, from subsequent action for infringement of an amended patent, see §75.07.   **27.16**

Although now probably only of historical interest following introduction of s.27(6), an attempt to impose conditions using a different approach occurred in *Autoliv Development AB's Patent* [1988] R.P.C. 425, where the Comptroller found that the granted claims were covetous and that there had been undue delay in seeking amendment, but, as the invention was meritorious, it ought not to be made available to the public royalty-free; he therefore permitted amendment subject to the condition that a "licence of right" entry were first entered in the register. However, on appeal, this approach was condemned and the amendments were disallowed, on the basis that the Comptroller must consider only whether the amendments as such are allowable and may not pay any regard to the merits of the invention.

Acknowledgements of registered trade marks (subs.(4))

Subsection (4) enables the Comptroller to amend a patent of his own volition to make reference to a registered trade mark in the same way as he is able to amend a patent application under s.19(2). The matter is discussed in §19.10, as also is the question of a reference in a specification to a foreign trade mark. There would seem to be no good reason to exclude the provisions of s.101 from operation under ss.19(2) or 27(4). Thus, the Comptroller should give notice to the proprietor of his intention to amend to insert a reference to a registered trade mark and to give him a chance to be heard before he takes a definite decision on the matter, see §19.09 and §101.04. The section applies so long as the trade mark is registered [in, or for, the United Kingdom], the validity of the registration being irrelevant. Presumably, if a registered trade mark has been acknowledged and the registration is subsequently revoked, an amendment to remove that acknowledgment should be allowed.   **27.17**

SECTION 28

Restoration of lapsed patents

28.—(1) Where a patent has ceased to have effect by reason of a failure to pay any renewal fee [*within the prescribed period***], an application for the restoration of the patent may be made to the comptroller within the prescribed period [***under this section within one year from the date on which the patent ceased to have effect***].**   **28.01**

(1A) Rules prescribing that period may contain such transitional provisions and savings as appear to the Secretary of State to be necessary or expedient.

(2) An application under this section may be made by the person who was the proprietor of the patent or by any other person who would have been entitled to the patent if it had not ceased to have effect; and where the patent was held by two or more persons jointly, the application may, with the leave of the comptroller, be made by one or more of them without joining the others.

(2A) Notice of the application shall be published by the comptroller in the prescribed manner.

(3) If the comptroller is satisfied that [—

(a) *the proprietor of the patent took reasonable care to see that any renewal fee was paid within the prescribed period or that that fee and any prescribed additional fee were paid within the six months immediately following the end of that period, and*

(b) *those fees were not so paid because of circumstances beyond his control]*, **the failure of the proprietor of the patent —**

(a) to pay the renewal fee within the prescribed period; or

(b) to pay that fee and any prescribed additional fee within the period ending with the sixth month after the month in which the prescribed period ended,

was unintentional, the comptroller shall by order restore the patent on payment of any unpaid renewal fee and any prescribed additional fee.

(4) An order under this section may be made subject to such conditions as the comptroller thinks fit (including a condition requiring compliance with any provisions of the rules relating to registration which have not been complied with), and if the proprietor of the patent does not comply with any condition of such an order the comptroller may revoke the order and give such directions consequential on the revocation as he thinks fit.

Notes

1. The noted amendment to subs.(1), a first amendment to subs.(3) and the introduction of subss.(1A) and (2A) were made by the Sch.5 para.6 to the Copyright, Designs and Patents Act 1988 ("CDPA 1988"), with effect from January 7, 1991 (SI 1990/2168). The first amendment to subs.(3) omitted the requirement that the failure to pay the fees was because of circumstances beyond the proprietor's control. At the same time, former subss.(5)–(9) (not reprinted) were replaced by new s.28A, for which see §28A.01.

2. Subsection (3) was further amended by the combined effect of art.9 of the Regulatory Reform (Patents) Order 2004 ("RRO") and s.8 of the 2004 Act, with effect from October 1, 2005 (SI 2005/2471), but without application to patents which, before this date, had ceased to have effect (art.23 of the 2004 RRO).

RELEVANT RULE—RULE 40

Rule 40—Restoration of lapsed patents under section 28

28.02   **40.**—(1) An application under section 28 for restoration of a patent may be made at any time before the end of the period ending with the thirteenth month after the month in which the period specified in section 25(4) ends.

(2) The application must be made on Patents Form 16.

(3) The notice of the application must be published in the journal.

(4) The applicant must file evidence in support of the application.

(5) If that evidence does not accompany the application, the comptroller must specify a period within which the evidence shall be filed.

(6) If, on consideration of that evidence, the comptroller is not satisfied that a

case for an order under section 28 has been made out, he must notify the applicant accordingly.

(7) The applicant may, before the end of the period of one month beginning with the date of that notification, request to be heard by the comptroller.

(8) If the applicant requests a hearing, the comptroller must give the applicant an opportunity to be heard before he determines whether to grant or refuse the application under section 28.

(9) Where the comptroller grants the application he must advertise the fact in the journal.

COMMENTARY ON SECTION 28

Scope of the section

Section 28 is concerned with the restoration of patents which have lapsed by failure to pay a renewal fee. The restoration of patents is permitted by the Paris Convention (Stockholm revision), which recognises that the countries of the Union shall have the right to provide for the restoration of patents which have lapsed by reason of non-payment of fees (art.5*bis*). Certain substantive and procedural aspects of the law relating to restoration are laid down by the Patent Law Treaty ("PLT") (art.12 and r.13), which has been ratified by the United Kingdom.

A notice of the need to pay renewal fees is included on the reverse of the certificate of grant for patents. The section does not require the Comptroller to exercise any discretion: he must restore the patent if the conditions of subs.(3) have been fulfilled (*Textron's Patent* [1988] R.P.C. 177). Originally subss.(5)–(9) provided for third party rights upon a patent being restored under the section, but the subject-matter of these provisions has been transferred to s.28A (see Note to §28.01) and these provisions are therefore now dealt with in the commentary thereon.

An application for restoration of a patent may be made by the person who was the proprietor of the patent or by any other person who would have been entitled to the patent had it not ceased to have effect (subs.(2)). The application must be made to the Comptroller within the prescribed period (subs.(1)), which is specified by r.40 as the period ending with the 13th month after the month in which the period specified in s.25(4) ends.

For a patent which lapsed on or after October 1, 2005, if restoration of the patent is to be allowed, the Comptroller must be satisfied that the failure of the proprietor to pay the renewal fee within the prescribed period or to pay the fee and any prescribed additional fee within the period ending with the sixth month after the month in which the prescribed period ended was "unintentional" (subs.(3)). For a patent which lapsed prior to this date, the Comptroller must instead be satisfied that the proprietor had taken:

"reasonable care to see that any renewal fee was paid during the prescribed period or that that fee and any prescribed additional fee were paid within the six months immediately following the end of that period".

In the EPC, restoration after failure to pay a renewal fee in due time is dealt with under the general provision of art.122 of the EPC for re-establishment of rights, for which see the *European Patents Handbook* ("EPH") (London: Sweet & Maxwell). Section 28 is not listed in s.130(7) as a provision framed to have, as nearly as practicable, the same effects as the corresponding provisions of the EPC. The Comptroller has therefore refused to follow EPO decisions under art.122 of the EPC: *Ament's Patent* [1994] R.P.C. 647. For patents which have lapsed since October 1, 2005, the relevant provisions of the Act and the EPC are in any case fundamentally different.

History of the section

The section as originally implemented represented a major change as compared with

28.03

28.04

the restoration provisions in the 1949 Act. Previously, it had been necessary to show that failure to pay the fee was unintentional and that there had been no undue delay. A period of three years from the date on which the patent ceased to have effect was allowed within which to apply for restoration. Under the new section, it initially became necessary to show that reasonable care had been taken and that the failure to pay the renewal fee was beyond the control of the proprietor. The period for filing the restoration application was also initially reduced to 12 months from the date on which the patent ceased to have effect.

There was considerable concern that in many instances the inadvertent lapse of a patent was not discovered within this 12-month period. Commonly, the lapse was discovered only when the next renewal fee was paid, and so a restoration application could be filed only if the rejection of the fee was notified before the end of the 12-month period. There was also concern among patent practitioners as to whether, in considering whether the failure to pay the fee was beyond the proprietor's control, the normal rule that a principal stands in the shoes of his agent applied.

On January 7, 1991, the section was amended. The period within which restoration of a lapsed patent could be sought was changed from 12 months to a period prescribed by rule. At the same time, the second requirement for restoration to be permitted, namely that the fee had not been paid due to circumstances beyond the proprietor's control, was deleted.

On October 1, 2005, the significant further amendments were made to the section. At this time, the remaining requirement for restoration that reasonable care had been taken was replaced with a requirement that the failure to pay the fee was unintentional. This, in fact, restored one of the two criteria for restoration which had existed under the 1949 Act.

Application for restoration (subs.(1))

28.05 An application for restoration must be made to the Comptroller on PF 16. The applicant must file evidence in support of the application, and this evidence may either be filed with the application or within a period specified by the Comptroller after the application has been received.

A notice of the application for restoration is published in the *Patents Journal* and the application is noted in the Register. The publication of the notice in the *Patents Journal* is important because it concludes the period referred to in s.28A(4) in which rights can be accorded to third parties, for which see §28A.06.

Term for filing the application for restoration

28.06 The application for restoration of a patent must be filed within the prescribed period, which is specified by r.40 as the period ending with the 13th month after the month in which the period specified in s.25(4) ends. The period specified in s.25(4) is the grace period for late payment of a renewal fee and is defined as the period ending with the sixth month the after month in which the period prescribed for payment of the renewal fee (the "renewal period") ends.

The renewal period referred to in s.25(4) is specified in rr.37–38. According to r.37, the first renewal date is the fourth anniversary of the date of filing, and the corresponding renewal period is the three months ending with the last day of the month in which that renewal date falls. However, if a patent is granted during the three months ending with the fourth anniversary of the date of filing, or at any time thereafter, then the first renewal date is the last day of the period of three months beginning with the date of grant, and the renewal period then begins with the date of grant and ends with the last day in the month in which that renewal date falls. If the grant of a patent is mentioned in the *European Patent Bulletin* during the three months ending with the fourth anniversary of the date of filing, or at any time thereafter, then the first renewal date is the later of the last day of the period of three months beginning with the date on which grant of the patent was so mentioned or the next anniversary of the date of filing to fall after the date on which grant of the patent was mentioned, and the renewal period then either begins with the date on which grant of the patent was mentioned and ends with the last day in the month in which that renewal date falls or is the three months ending with the last day of the month in which that renewal date falls, respectively.

According to r.38, the second renewal date is the next anniversary of the date of filing to fall after the first renewal date, and each subsequent renewal date is the anniversary of the previous renewal date. The renewal period for each of the second and subsequent renewal dates is the three months ending with the last day of the month in which the renewal date falls.

In all cases, however, the latest day on which an application for restoration can be filed is the last day of the 19th month following the month in which the renewal date falls. The usual *dies non* rule applies, for which see §120.03.

Notably, there is no additional requirement that the application for restoration must be filed within any period relating to the removal of the cause of the failure of the proprietor to attend to the renewal requirements. This contrasts with the corresponding provisions of the EPC and the laws of other European countries, such as Germany, according to which such an application must be filed within two months of the removal of the cause of the failure.

The period for filing an application for restoration cannot normally be extended (r.108 and sch.4, Pt 1). However, if the UK-IPO has failed to issue the reminder required by r.39 or the lapsing notice required by r.41, or either has been issued to the wrong address, or if there has been some other procedural irregularity, then an attempt could be made to invoke r.107 after the period has expired, for which see §§123.26 and 123.27. The Comptroller is required to send these statutory communications to the address specified for this purpose on payment of the previous renewal fee (or another address that has since been notified for the purpose) or, if no such address has been provided, to the address for service entered in the register (r.39(3)). For a European patent (UK), the address of the proprietor is treated as the address for service if the Comptroller has not been notified otherwise.

In *Daido Kogyo KK's Patent* [1984] R.P.C. 97, discretion was exercised under r.100 of the Patent Rules 1978, for correction of irregularities, to allow an application for restoration to be filed out of time because the statutory reminder had not been issued at the proper time. In *Somner's Application* BL O/139/03, discretion was also exercised under r.100 of the Patent Rules 1995 after the UK-IPO failed to make any attempt to contact the proprietor when the reminder notice was returned. It has, however, been held that there is no failure by the Comptroller to carry out his statutory duty where a failure to issue the statutory reminders arises from the fact that no address for service had been provided by the proprietor: *Deforeit's Patent* [1986] R.P.C. 142. An attempt to invoke r.100 of the Patent Rules 1995 also failed in *Chemex Pharmaceutical's Patent* BL O/75/99, where instructions to file a restoration application had been received by the proprietor's agent more than one year before the final date for this, but a diary entry was interpreted as a "target date" and consequently that date was missed by a few days.

Under the previous period for filing the application of 12 months from the date on which the patent ceased to have effect, several unsuccessful attempts were made to convert a renewal fee payment, filed in ignorance that the patent had already lapsed, into an application for restoration: *Dynamics Research and Manufacturing Inc's Patent* [1980] R.P.C. 179 and *Electricité de France (EDF)'s Patents* [1992] R.P.C. 205.

In *Pro Challenge Limited's Application* BL O/090/09, the hearing officer considered whether the provisions of s.117 for correction of errors in patents and applications could be applied to an application for restoration after the prescribed period had expired. An application for the restoration of four patents had been filed within the prescribed period and the applicant had requested that the original application be corrected to include a fifth patent. It was held that s.117 did not allow the fifth patent to be entered into the proceedings because the applicant's error was a procedural omission.

An application filed after expiry of the period prescribed in r.40(1) was successful in *GlycoBioSciences Inc.'s Application* BL O/132/10. The previous year's renewal fee had been paid by the original proprietor of the patent via an official fee sheet and the correct remittance using a personal credit card. The UK-IPO issued a receipt and certificate of payment after first completing a PF 12 and making an email enquiry as to where to send them. The renewal fee for the following year was not paid in the renewal period and the reminder notice under r.39 and the lapsing notice under r.41 were sent to the agent of record, who had been instructed to take no further action. The hearing officer found that the UK-IPO had erred by not gaining all the information required by the PF 12, particularly the box relating to the next renewal reminder. As such, r.107 should be invoked because the proprietor had been deprived of the option of changing the address to which the renewal reminder should be sent.

In *Smith's Application* BL O/166/09, the hearing officer accepted that the UK-IPO had misinformed the applicant on two occasions of the date by which the restoration application had to be filed. However, r.107 was not invoked because, on each occasion, the prescribed period had already expired and so the misinformation had had no bearing on the case.

Persons entitled to make the application for restoration (subs.(2))

28.07   The application for restoration must be made by the person who was the proprietor of the patent or by any other person who would have been entitled to the patent had it not ceased to have effect (subs.(2)).

The proprietor of the patent is the person whose name is at the relevant time entered in the register, or someone who is owner of the rights in respect of the patent at that time. The reference to "any other person who would have been entitled to the patent had it not ceased to have effect" includes a person who has acquired the patent after it has lapsed, for example by assignment: *Border's Patent* BL O/157/79. This reference does not, however, include a potential proprietor to whom the patent would later be assigned if it were to be successfully restored: *Vause's European Patent* BL O/278/00.

Where a patent is held by two or more persons jointly, the Comptroller may permit one of them to apply without joining the others (subs.(2)).

Failure to pay the renewal fee was "unintentional" (subs.(3))

28.08   For a patent which lapsed prior to October 1, 2005, restoration of the patent was only possible if the Comptroller was satisfied that the proprietor has taken "reasonable care" to attend to the renewal requirements, for which see previous editions.

For a patent which lapsed on or after October 1, 2005, restoration of the patent is instead only possible if the Comptroller is satisfied that the failure of the proprietor to attend to the renewal requirements was "unintentional". Since April 30, 2007, it has only been possible to file applications for restoration under this regime. Although the UK-IPO has indicated that a large number of these applications have been successful, formal decisions are not generally issued on successful cases. Decided cases therefore tend to reflect only those cases which failed before the Comptroller, although perhaps they may have succeeded on appeal.

The requirement for the proprietor to show that his failure to attend to the renewal requirements was unintentional is generally a far less stringent test than the "reasonable care" test which applied under the previous regime, but it involves a negative proposition which can never be proved with logical certainty. Thus, circumstantial evidence will need to be produced to enable the Comptroller to decide that the failure by the proprietor was unintentional.

Where restoration of a patent has been allowed under the former test of "reasonable care", the circumstances were probably, although not necessarily, such that they also showed that the failure was "unintentional". However, the converse is not likely to be true, so that refusals to allow restoration in circumstances arising in former decisions concerning restoration are mostly of little value in applying the revised wording.

In *Matsushita Electric Industrial Company Ltd's Patent* [2008] R.P.C. 35; BL O/029/08, the applicant had filed a witness statement asserting that the failure by the proprietor had been unintentional. This, the applicant argued, must satisfy the Comptroller since it was a clear, unequivocal statement of the requirement of the law filed in the evidential format prescribed by the rules. The hearing officer emphasised the meaning of subs.(3) when read in totality which, it was said, not only tacitly charges the proprietor with satisfying the Comptroller that his failure was unintentional, but also requires something of the Comptroller. The hearing officer decided that the approach put forward by the applicant would in effect take away the decision-making role which subs.(3) places upon the Comptroller, since it would substitute the applicant's subjective assertion of compliance for what should be a statement of facts and circumstances which would enable the Comptroller himself to arrive at a reasoned, objective determination. On this basis, it was held that the witness statement filed by the applicant was insufficient to establish the facts needed to satisfy the Comptroller that the failure by the proprietor had been unintentional and the application for restoration was therefore refused. Matsushita's appeal to the Patents Court was dismissed, Mann J. describing the restoration of a patent as a serious, significant act with proprietary effect, not a casual administrative step.

The concept of allowing a defect in procedure to be overcome where it arose unintentionally has been applied by the Comptroller in recent years to the exercise of discretion for the grant of an extension, or further extension, of a time limit under r.108, for which see §123.36. For that rule, the firm attitude of the Comptroller has been that such an extension of time should not be permitted if there is evidence that there has been a change of mind: *Heatex Group's Application* [1995] R.P.C. 546. Although this "continuing underlying intention" test has been referred to in a number of cases relating to other provisions where "unintentional" considerations apply (s.5(2C) for late declarations of priority and s.20A for reinstatement of application), more recent cases have highlighted the dangers of going beyond the clear meaning of the statute and have instead focused on the normal English meaning of the term: *Sirna Therapeutic Inc's Application* BL O/240/05 and *Anning's Application* BL O/374/06. Case law under r.108 may, however, be of relevance if detailed examination of the evidence is required, for example if the intentions of the proprietor are not clear: *Sirna Therapeutic Inc's Application*, above.

For a patent to be restored, it is the failure to attend to the renewal requirements that must be unintentional, not merely the consequences which follow from that failure. Thus, an intention by the proprietor to ultimately maintain the patent does not necessarily mean that a failure by the proprietor to attend to the renewal requirements was unintentional, for example if this was based on a mistaken belief that the failure to attend to the renewal requirements would not be fatal. Similar circumstance applied in *Anning's Application*, above, decided under s.20A, in which, despite a clear intention to maintain the application, it did not follow that a failure by the applicant to respond to a report under s.18 was unintentional, because the applicant had mistakenly understood that the application could be put "on hold". Evidence of the proprietor's intention to maintain the patent may, however, assist in meeting the requirements of subs.(3).

It is also to be noted that the failure to attend to the renewal requirements must be unintentional on the part of the proprietor of the patent at the time the renewal fee could have been paid. Thus, for example, where a person has acquired a patent after it has lapsed, and that person is unable to obtain any statement from the proprietor of the patent at the time the renewal fee could have been paid, it will be difficult to satisfy the Comptroller that the necessary condition for restoration exists: *Alderson's Application* BL O/245/04.

In *Orkli (UK) Ltd's Application* BL O/302/09, the evidence showed that the applicant's agent had never intended to pay the renewal fee because they believed that the GB designation of the European application from which the patent derived had been withdrawn to avoid a conflict with an earlier application. Nevertheless, the hearing officer found that the applicant, who was unaware of the (unsuccessful) withdrawal of the GB designation, had intended to pay the renewal fee. The application was allowed on the basis that it is the proprietor's intentions, and not those of his agent, that should count in determining the outcome of an application for restoration.

In *Porter's Application* BL O/144/09, the hearing officer considered evidence relating to the proprietor's financial position. It was noted that, in circumstances where the funds were not available, it was difficult to see how a failure to pay a renewal fee could have been unintentional.

—The test of "unintentional" applied to restoration under former statutes

Because the present form of subs.(3) restores the requirement which existed under pre- **28.09**

1977 statutes that restoration will only be possible if the lapsing of the patent was "unintentional", cases under the former statutes may be relevant. For example, restoration was allowed when a deceased inventor's widow meant to pay, but forgot, *Spheric Structures' Patent* [1958] R.P.C. 283, and also when a patentee relied on receiving a reminder from the UK-IPO which was not, apparently, received, *Salopian Engineers' Application* [1957] R.P.C. 351. This decision also held that negligence in the keeping of records may not be relevant to the question of intention, nor may the adequacy or otherwise of the system adopted to submit the question of payment to a responsible person or to implement an intention to pay.

In an early decision, *Land's Patent* (1910) 27 R.P.C. 481, it was held that a failure to pay the fee arising from an ignorance of the law did not constitute an unintentional failure. However, in *KSM's Patents* [1974] R.P.C. 229 the hearing officer pointed out that restoration applications often arise out of defective business organisation and, therefore, a broad view should be taken of the evidence, due allowance being made for inconsistencies and imperfections: restoration was here allowed because of administrative chaos in the relevant department of the proprietor.

Before the "directing mind" concept (see §28.10 below) came to be appreciated, and under the pre-1977 statute, restoration was refused in *Whitton Engineering's Patent* [1959] R.P.C. 53 and *General Electric's Patent* [1973] R.P.C. 707, each because a company official had instructed non-renewal, despite being misled by defective internal records which caused him to fail to consider existing licences. In *Hawker Siddeley's Patent* [1975] R.P.C. 302, restoration was refused because a deliberate election not to pay a renewal fee had been made, even though the company official involved had based this election on an erroneous supposition. In the present climate, it might be possible to obtain restoration in the circumstances of these cases if it could be convincingly shown that the official concerned should not, in the circumstances, have been regarded as the "directing mind" of the corporation, as discussed in §28.10.

—The "directing mind" of the proprietor

28.10   In *Textron's Patent* [1989] R.P.C. 441, the House of Lords laid stress on deciding who was the "directing mind" of a corporate entity before considering whether "reasonable care" had been taken to pay the renewal fee. Here, there had been an isolated mistake by a junior employee. In absolving that mistake, some reliance was placed on the criminal responsibility of a corporate entity for actions of its employees, as discussed in *Tesco v Nattrass* [1972] A.C. 153 and [1971] 2 All E.R. 127 HL. In *Textron's Patent* (above), Lord Oliver decided that responsibility of a corporate proprietor as regards patent renewal resides in its "directing mind" and that, in deciding corporate responsibility, a distinction may have to be drawn:

> "between default on the part of a person who is the directing mind of the company and default on the part of a mere employee directed to carry out the task by the directing mind, so that it becomes necessary to determine whether such a person is to be regarded as the company or merely as the company's servant or agent".

These remarks seem entirely apposite under the present restoration regime in assessing whether there had been a valid decision not to renew the patent, in which case the failure to renew could not have been "unintentional". In a corporate organisation, it is commonplace for patent renewal decisions to be delegated to a person or committee. In such instances that person or committee has to be regarded as the corporate "directing mind". Nevertheless, it is important to appreciate that the reason for deciding not to renew a patent is entirely irrelevant to the question whether the decision was taken by the responsible person on the knowledge available to him. An erroneous decision is still a decision.

Even before the *Textron's Patent* case, and under the pre-1977 regime, the Comptroller judged the intention of a company to renew by the action of a person who was acting on its behalf (*Processed Surfaces' Patent* [1958] R.P.C. 480). That must still be the position today, but how should one distinguish between an agent (obviously not the proprietor itself) and a servant (at least part of the proprietor)? In such a situation, full evidence would seem to be necessary to establish what power, if any, for ordering renewal was, or was not, delegated to such a person, not only explicitly, but also by inference. Thus, it will usually be difficult to establish that a person was unauthorised to take the renewal decision, particularly where the alleged invalid decision had been taken in other instances, but the position is likely to be considered more favourably when the decision was an isolated one.

In *Adventec's Patents* BL O/196/97, the chief executive had been only part of the "directing mind", but this was sufficient for a finding of lack of "reasonable care" overall when he left the company. Likewise, where it cannot be established which of two individuals should be regarded as the "directing mind", as in *Lermer's Patent* BL O/14/96, it would seem that it will now be necessary to show that each had an intention to have the patent renewed.

In *Marbourn's Patent* BL O/376/99, the "directing mind" of a company had set up a system for reminders to be sent to him, but following a change in ownership and relocation of offices, the established system was amended by another director who was unaware of it. This could be considered as an example of the decision of non-renewal being taken by a non-authorised person and therefore not a controlling one.

In contrast, in *Sumitomo Rubber's Patent* BL O/351/03, an error in information about the patent made by an employee of 13 years' standing, who was regarded as reliable and well trained, had contributed to a decision to allow the patent to lapse. This was later seen to have been a mistake and restoration was allowed (under the "reasonable care" concept) because the error was seen to be an isolated and unpredictable event. However, it seems doubtful whether restoration would have been allowed under the present "unintentional" regime because here the decision not to pay the fee was deliberate and made by a responsible person, albeit based on information which was later found to have been incorrect.

Cases where "reasonable care" was found to exist because of mistakes which can be seen as ones made by persons other than by the proprietor or by its actual "directing mind", include: *Filtermedia's Patent* BL O/22/04; *Stammitz's Patent* BL O/231/04; *Medisup's Patent* BL O/211/05; *Onder and Ozbay's Patent* BL O/332/05; *Trimtec's Patent* BL O/65/06; and *Best and Lewis's Patent* BL O/84/06.

In *Orkli (UK) Limited's Application*, above, the hearing officer drew a distinction between the intentions of the proprietor and his agent and decided the case on the basis of the former.

Conditions for restoration (subs.(4))

Under subs.(4) the Comptroller has power to impose upon the order restoring the patent **28.11** such conditions as he sees fit, including compliance with any requirement of the rules relating to registration which have not been complied with. These conditions are ones additional to the mandatory conditions, as now set out in s.28A, which are imposed upon restoration. If the proprietor does not comply with any imposed conditions, the Comptroller may revoke the restoration order and give any consequential directions as he sees fit.

In *Daido Kogyo's Patent* [1984] R.P.C. 97 CA, a special condition was imposed on restoration by making the patent subject to the provisions of the then subs.(6), now s.28A(3), up to the date when notice of the application for restoration was actually entered on the register because of the delay which had occurred in giving notice to the public of the possibility of restoration.

The Comptroller has also adopted a policy of imposing similar conditions to those now specified in s.28A when a time limit is extended with discretion exercised under r.107 (for which see §123.24) or r.108 (for which see §123.25).

PRACTICE UNDER SECTION 28

The filing and prosecution of an application for restoration are regulated by r.40. Rule **28.12** 40 also applies to applications for restoration which were filed before the Patent Rules 2007 came into force (Sch.5 para.3 to the Patent Rules 2007).

An application for restoration must be made on PF 16. Applications can be made by fax (for which see §119.05), but not yet by electronic means.

Note (c) on PF 16 is a reminder of the need for evidence in support of an application for restoration. In line with general practice in proceedings before the Comptroller, the evidence should be exclusively concerned with the proving of relevant facts. It is often helpful, however, to include with the application for restoration a statement explaining the reasons for the making of the application and the context and relevancy of the evidence, that is to say subjective arguments in support of the application. This statement can be made in a letter accompanying the PF 16.

An application for restoration can be made without evidence, and the Comptroller will then issue an official letter specifying a period within which the evidence must be filed. The period specified by the Comptroller for filing the evidence is usually 14 days from the date of the letter, although in practice a discretionary extension can generally be obtained under s.117B(2) if there are problems. In such cases, a telephone call to the Restorations Section of the UK-IPO is recommended. If evidence is not provided within the initial period or an extended period set by the Comptroller, then ultimately the application may be deemed never to have been filed.

There is no requirement for an application for restoration to be filed within any period relating to the removal of the cause of the failure of the proprietor to attend to the renewal requirements. There is, however, an incentive to file the application as soon as possible in that the advertisement of the application in the *Patents Journal* concludes the period referred to in s.28A(4) in which rights can be accorded to third parties. It may be necessary to monitor the *Patents Journal* for this advertisement since its date is not directly notified to the applicant and delays have been known to occur.

At the risk of stating the obvious, it is strongly recommended that prior to making a restoration application a check is made that the patent has actually lapsed; and, secondly, who the registered proprietor is in accordance with the register. Checks should also be made to ensure that the person making the application for restoration is either the proprietor of the patent or a person who would have been entitled to the patent if it had not ceased to have effect.

Where an application is made by a person who is not named in the register, the circumstances should be explained in full and supporting evidence provided. The Comptroller may in practice defer consideration of such applications until after the appropriate transaction has been registered (for which see §32.26), and an official letter setting a term for complying with such a requirement may be issued.

The position in relation to an applicant who is an equitable assignee of the patent, for which see §30.04, is somewhat unclear. In *Vause's European Patent* BL O/278/00, the hearing officer took the word "entitled" in subs.(2) to mean "having title to something". On this basis, it would be prudent to ensure that the legal title to the patent has been transferred to the applicant for restoration before the application is filed.

In preparing the application, it will be necessary to provide evidence to satisfy the Comptroller that the failure by the proprietor to attend to the renewal requirements in the year in question was unintentional. In practice, this evidence will usually include circumstantial evidence showing that the proprietor had intended to pay the renewal fee. The quantity of such evidence can be important: if possible, the evidence should establish the proprietor's intention to pay the renewal fee on several different occasions. In such circumstances, the failure to pay the renewal fee will always be attributable to some form of mistake or problem, and it will be important to provide evidence of this mistake or problem, or at least explain how it came about. It is often helpful in this respect to find out exactly how the renewals cycle operated in previous years and to collect all relevant documents relating to the year in which the fee was not paid. Although it is no longer necessary to show that the proprietor took reasonable care to see that the renewal fee was paid, it can be helpful to at least explain how the statutory communications issued by the UK-IPO were handled.

For a patent which lapsed prior to October 1, 2005, the Comptroller continues to apply the former test of whether the proprietor has taken "reasonable care" to attend to the renewal requirements, for which see previous editions.

The Comptroller considers the evidence and any statement filed in support of the application for restoration. If the Comptroller is not satisfied that a case for restoration has been made out, the applicant is usually informed of reasons for it and a one-month term is set for further submissions (see the MOPP at para.28.06). It is important to provide additional evidence if it is called for at this stage, since it may be difficult to file further evidence later in the proceedings or on appeal to the Patents Court: *Ament's Patent* [1994] R.P.C. 647; *Winventive's Patent* BL C/55/83. If the further submissions fail to alter the Comptroller's position, or none is filed within the term, then the applicant is notified accordingly and the application is formally refused unless the application is withdrawn in writing or a hearing is requested within one month (subs.(7)).

Evidence filed in support of the application for restoration should, as far as possible, be intrinsically consistent. However, where later investigations reveal errors in evidence that has been filed, new evidence may be filed and the Comptroller will consider which evidence most accurately represents the true circumstances surrounding the failure to pay the renewal fees. In *Farrow Holding Group Inc.'s Patent* BL O/017/11, the hearing officer was prepared to disregard earlier evidence which contradicted later evidence on the basis that the later evidence set out a more plausible scenario as to the relevant circumstances.

Upon allowance of an application for restoration, a term for filing PF 12 and paying the outstanding renewal fees will be set by the Comptroller (s.28(3)). This term is generally two months from the date of the letter allowing the restoration application, although in practice a discretionary extension can generally be obtained under s.117B(2) if there are problems. Each unpaid renewal fee must be accompanied by an individual PF 12, and the fees are payable at the rate at which they were due originally. The amounts required are indicated in the letter of allowance. An order restoring the patent is issued when conditions, including payment of the fees due, have been made.

Applications for restoration, applications withdrawn and applications allowed are advertised in the *Patents Journal*, and notice of it is also entered in the register.

There is no provision in s.28 (as there was in s.27 of the 1949 Act) for a restoration application to be contested in a formal opposition. However, it is possible that a third party may have evidence that the failure to attend to the renewal requirements was not in fact "unintentional" because of knowledge that a decision not to renew had in fact been made. In such a situation, it is suggested that evidence of this fact be submitted to the UK-IPO before a decision on restoration has been made.

If an appeal is filed against a decision of the Comptroller under s.28 on a particular point, consideration should be given to expressly reserving the position of the applicant. In *Matsushita Electric Industrial Company Ltd v Comptroller* [2009] EWCA Civ 134, the CA refused permission to appeal a decision of the Pat Ct, [2008] R.P.C. 35 not to remit the application for restoration back to the UK-IPO for further consideration on the basis that it was wrong that a party, having taken a view that what they had done was sufficient, should, without reserving their position expressly, argue a point, lose it, and then seek to reargue it on a different basis.

SECTION 28A [ADDED]

Effect of order for restoration of patent

28A.—(1) The effect of an order for the restoration of a patent is as follows.   **28A.01**

(2) Anything done under or in relation to the patent during the period between expiry and restoration shall be treated as valid.

(3) Anything done during that period which would have constituted an infringement if the patent had not expired shall be treated as an infringement—

> **(a) if done at a time when it was possible for the patent to be renewed under section 25(4), or**

   (b) if it was a continuation or repetition of an earlier infringing act.

   (4) If after it was no longer possible for the patent to be so renewed, and before publication of notice of the application for restoration, a person—

   (a) began in good faith to do an act which would have constituted an infringement of the patent if it had not expired, or

   (b) made in good faith effective and serious preparations to do such an act,

he has the right to continue to do the act or, as the case may be, to do the act, notwithstanding the restoration of the patent; but this right does not extend to granting a licence to another person to do the act.

   (5) If the act was done, or the preparations were made, in the course of a business, the person entitled to the right conferred by subsection (4) may—

   (a) authorise the doing of that act by any partners of his for the time being in that business, and

   (b) assign that right, or transmit it on death (or in the case of a body corporate on its dissolution), to any person who acquires that part of the business in the course of which the act was done or the preparations were made.

   (6) Where a product is disposed of to another in exercise of the rights conferred by subsection (4) or (5), that other and any person claiming through him may deal with the product in the same way as if it had been disposed of by the registered proprietor of the patent.

   (7) The above provisions apply in relation to the use of a patent for the services of the Crown as they apply in relation to infringement of the patent.

   Note. Section 28A was added by Sch.5 para.7 of the Copyright, Designs and Patents Act 1988 ("CDPA 1988"), with effect from January 7, 1991 (SI 1990/2168), to replace former s.28(5)–(9), see Note to §28.01.

COMMENTARY ON SECTION 28A

Scope of the section

28A.02   A patent "expires" at the end of the renewal date if the renewal fee for the following year has not been paid before the end of the renewal period (s.25(3)). However, if that renewal fee (together with an additional fee for late payment) is paid within the period ending with the sixth month after the month in which the renewal period ends, the patent is deemed not to have expired at the earlier anniversary date (s.25(4)), see §25.12.

Section 28A provides validity to anything done under or in relation to the patent, such as an assignment, during the period between expiry and restoration (subs.(2)). The section also provides for automatic rights to be accorded to a third party if that party has reasonably relied upon the patent having ceased to have effect, should the patent be later restored under s.28 upon the Comptroller being satisfied that the failure to pay the renewal fee within those periods was unintentional (subs.(4)). These third party rights are in addition to any order which may be made under s.28(4) imposing special conditions upon restoration, for which see §28.11.

Thus, s.28A is concerned with acts carried out between the expiry date for the patent, that is to say, the day after a renewal date in respect of which the renewal requirements have not been met, and the date on which the patent is restored. In this commentary this period is called the "restoration period". It has three parts: (1) the period from the expiry date of the patent to the end of the grace period, i.e. the period allowed for late payment of the renewal fee, under s.25(4), during which a potential third-party user should have appreciated that the patent could have been renewed; (2) the period which follows the grace period and extends up to the date when the notice of an application for restoration is published in the *Patents Journal* under s.28(2A), during which a potential third-party user could reasonably take the view that the patent had lapsed; and (3) the period following that date of publication of the restoration application up to the date when the order for restoration is made, during which a potential third-party user should have appreciated that he was at risk of the patent being re-established.

The effect of the section is similar to the third party rights obtained, under s.64, by a person who used within the United Kingdom the invention of the patent prior to its priority date or made serious and effective preparations to do so. The commentary under s.64 is therefore likely also to be relevant to the construction which should be placed on the present section. Other provisions in which similar third party rights apply include s.20B for re-instatement of an application and s.117A for resuscitation of a withdrawn application.

Similar third party rights may also be imposed as a condition when a time limit is extended with discretion exercised under r.107 (for which see §123.08) or r.108 (for which see §123.09).

Where a European application or patent lapses and is subsequently reinstated under the general provision of art.122 of the EPC for re-establishment of rights, third party rights may also be enjoyed under EPC art.122(5), except when the re-establishment of rights occurs before publication of the application (J 5/79 *Siemens/Continuation of use after adverse decision* OJ EPO 1980, 73). Any such rights are given effect in the United Kingdom by s.77(5) (for which see §77.08) and s.78(6) (for which see §78.04).

Origin of the section

Section 28A was inserted into the statute by the CDPA 1988 (see Note to §28A.01) to replace now-repealed s.28(5)–(9) as originally enacted. Section 28A provides a simplified version of the rights that are accorded to third parties upon patent restoration, but there seems little significant change from the original provisions previously contained in s.28. No transitional provision was contained in the CDPA 1988, as subs.(1) refers to the "effect of an order for the restoration of a patent".   **28A.03**

Imposition of third party rights (subs.(4))

An order for restoration (made under s.28) has automatic effect to validate actions and impose the third party rights set out in s.28A. In *Charalambous's Patent* BL O/408/10, the hearing officer considered whether it was fair and necessary for third party rights to be imposed in circumstances where the failure to pay the renewal fee was due, in part, to a procedural error by the UK-IPO, the statutory renewal reminder having been sent to the wrong address. It was concluded that there was a clear intention by the legislator that third parties acting in good faith should not be adversely impacted once a patent had ceased. The patent was reinstated under r.107 subject to conditions similar to those set out in s.28A(4). By comparison, in *Eveready Battery Co. Inc.'s Patent* [2000] R.P.C. 852, the renewal fee had been validly paid by the proprietor but the payment had not been recorded. It was held, in these circumstances, that the patent had in fact never ceased, that there was no power to exercise then r.100 (the predecessor to current r.107), and that there was accordingly no power to impose conditions in relation to third party rights.   **28A.04**

The period for giving effect to section 28A (subss.(2)–(4))

Firstly, "anything" done during the restoration period under or in relation to the patent is treated as valid (subs.(2)). This provision therefore provides validity to assignments and licences executed during this period which may, for example, have been executed in ignorance that the patent had lapsed.   **28A.05**

Then, anything done which would have constituted an infringement if the patent had then been extant remains treated as an infringement if done either (a) in the grace period under s.25(4), or (b) as a continuation or repetition of some infringing act first carried out before that period (subs.(3)). Thus, acts carried out during the restoration period can be regarded as infringing acts, if these acts "commenced" before the end of the s.25(4) grace period. Subsection (3)(a) does not refer to the period between the expiry date of the patent and the end of the s.25(3) renewal period, but the position in this short period is no doubt the same.

Otherwise, third party rights are provided, but only in respect of acts begun, or effective and serious preparations made to do so, during the second part of the restoration period (subs.(4)). However, no relief is granted in respect of acts begun during the first or the third part of the restoration period, because, in each of these periods, the user had constructive notice either that the patent might be renewed or that an application for restoration of the patent was under consideration by the Comptroller. For the meaning of "begun", see *Minnesota Mining v Bondina* [1973] R.P.C. 491 at 510, which confirmed (under s.27 of the 1949 Act) that the provision gave no relief to a person who was initially an infringer. The present section extends that position to persons who (had they made investigations) should have appreciated that the proprietor was entitled to have the patent renewed merely by paying an increased fee or that he was seeking restoration under s.28.

The acts which give rise to third party rights under the section must be acts carried out "in good faith", so that for example acts carried out in knowledge that the proprietor is considering making a restoration application would appear to be excluded. The act must be an actual one which would, if the patent had been alive, have been an infringing one or must constitute "effective and serious preparations" to do such an act. However, rights are accorded only in respect of acts not previously done, or seriously and effectively considered, during the period prior to expiry of the first part of the restoration period. It is not clear whether the word "began" (in subs.(4)) should apply equally to both "continuations" and "repetitions" of an act (as these words are used in subs.(3)(b)).

The acts which give rise to third party rights under the section must also be acts that would have infringed the patent. Thus, acts carried out outside the United Kingdom (or the Isle of Man), acts of Crown use and acts exempted from infringement by s.60(5) are not covered by s.28A. For further discussion of these points, see §64.05 in relation to the analogous provision in s.64.

Nature of third party rights

28A.06   The person (which can of course be a corporate entity) who carried out the required act (for which see §28A.04) then acquires the right to "continue" to do an act begun during the second part of the restoration period, or to do the act for which effective and serious preparations had then been made, notwithstanding the subsequent restoration of the patent. The right operates as a defence to an action for infringement, and therefore the onus is upon the defendant to prove the existence of this, see *Minnesota Mining v Bondina* [1973] R.P.C. 491.

The right is a personal one to the doer and therefore he may not pass on that right by granting a licence (subs.(4)). Nevertheless, if the act was done, or preparations made, "in the course of a business", the person acquiring the right under subs.(4) may authorise partners in a firm with him to do that act (subs.(5)(a)), or assign that right (or transmit it on death, or dissolution in the case of a body corporate), provided that this is done as part of the acquisition of "that part of the business" in the course of which the necessary act, or the preparations for it, were done (subs.(5)(b)). Also, the rights conferred by subss.(4)–(5) extend to any subsequent dealing by another with a product disposed of according to those rights (subs.(6)); and the provisions of these subss.(4)–(6) apply mutatis mutandis to acts of Crown use (subs.(7)), for which see §55.11. These provisions are analogous to those in respect of third party rights under s.64, discussed in §64.06.

Scope of third party rights

28A.07   The scope of the third party rights accorded by the section remains unclear and awaits judicial evaluation. In particular, it is unclear whether the right to "continue to do the act" permits any change in the nature, or extent, of that act and whether the continuity must be without interruption. It seems likely that this phrase would be construed purposively and not so literally as to preclude any change in that act whatsoever or not to permit resumption of an act which had begun but was then discontinued temporarily, although in

Biegevorrichtung [2002] G.R.U.R. 231, the German Supreme Court held, under the German law equivalent to that provided by s.64, that a prior user cannot use further developments going beyond the prior use.

Thus, "continue" in subs.(4) should probably not be limited to a "continuation", as that word is used in subs.(3)(b), but should embrace acts of repetition also. For a discussion on the meaning of "continue", see *Rotocrop v Genbourne* [1982] F.S.R. 241 and *Astra v Pharmaceutical* [1957] R.P.C. 16.

The same difficulties arise with the right to continue a prior secret use under s.64, as is discussed in §64.07 with particular reference to the differing judicial views which have been expressed, each obiter, on the effect of that section. Thus, doubts surround the questions of whether the level, as well as the character, of the "infringing" acts is restricted by the section, for example as to use of an infringing component in a particular machine or activity; and exactly what is meant by "effective and serious preparations".

A person who has relied on the lapsing of the patent, but who has not taken such steps as bring subs.(4) into play, is in a vulnerable position. This was considered (under the former provisions) in *Dynamics Research's Patent* [1980] R.P.C. 179, where it was indicated that, if appropriate, steps could be taken to safeguard interests which ought to be safeguarded. Presumably, the Patents Court had in mind that restoration could be made subject to a special condition under s.28(4) which would provide third party rights additional to those provided automatically by what is now s.28A(4). This was done in *Daido Kogyo's Patent* [1984] R.P.C. 97 where the third part of the restoration period was added to the second because the making of the restoration application had not been advertised under the then-prevailing provisions (now altered by the addition of s.28(2A)). In circumstances where s.28A(4) cannot be relied on to accord fully the required rights, the person requiring those rights should bring the facts before the Comptroller promptly. After the order for restoration is made, imposition of a special condition under s.28(4) would not seem possible. However, no provision is now made for formal opposition to an application for restoration, as was the position under s.27 of the 1949 Act.

SECTION 29

Surrender of patents

29.—(1) The proprietor of a patent may at any time by notice given to the comptroller offer to surrender his patent.   **29.01**

(2) A person may give notice to the comptroller of his opposition to the surrender of a patent under this section, and if he does so the comptroller shall notify the proprietor of the patent and determine the question.

(3) If the comptroller is satisfied that the patent may properly be surrendered, he may accept the offer and, as from the date when notice of his acceptance is published in the journal, the patent shall cease to have effect, but no action for infringement shall lie in respect of any act done before that date and no right to compensation shall accrue for any use of the patented invention before that date for the services of the Crown.

RELEVANT RULE—RULE 42

Rule 42—Surrender

42.— The notice of an offer by a proprietor to surrender a patent must be in writing and include—   **29.02**

   (a) a declaration that no action is pending before the court for infringement or revocation of the patent; or

(b) where such an action is pending, the particulars of the action.

Note. This rule was introduced by SI 2007/3291 with effect from December 17, 2007.

COMMENTARY ON SECTION 29

Scope of the section

29.03   Section 29 provides for the surrender of a patent. There is no directly corresponding provision in the EPC, but s.29 applies equally to European patents (UK) by virtue of s.77(1).

Offer to surrender (subs.(1))

29.04   Under subs.(1) a proprietor may at any time give notice to the Comptroller of an offer to surrender his patent. By r.75, the offer is advertised in the *Patents Journal.*

Opposition to surrender (subs.(2))

29.05   Subsection (2) affords any person the opportunity to oppose surrender within a four-week period from the date of advertisement in the *Patents Journal.* This period is inextensible by virtue of being listed in Pt 2 of Sch.4 to r.108(1). Under r.76(2)(b) opposition must be lodged. The use of similar wording in s.72 (revocation) suggests that no locus standi is required to oppose, see also *Braun AG's Application* [1981] R.P.C. 355 and §27.11. The most likely opponent would be a licensee. Subsection (2) requires the Comptroller to notify the proprietor of any opposition.

Acceptance of offer to surrender (subs.(3))

29.06   Subsection (3) provides that, if the Comptroller is satisfied that the patent may properly be surrendered, he can accept the offer; the patent then ceases to have effect from the date the acceptance is advertised in the *Patents Journal.*

No action for infringement and no claim in respect of Crown use lies in respect of any act done before the date of the advertisement of the acceptance of the offer to surrender. However, for any other purpose, the patent continues to have effect up to that date, e.g. licence royalties paid cannot be reclaimed.

An offer to surrender does not automatically terminate revocation proceedings and, if the surrender offer is made during revocation proceedings before the Comptroller, the Comptroller's practice is first to reach a decision on the revocation before considering the offer to surrender, see: *Murray's Patents* BL O/73/86, noted I.P.D. 9096; *Don Valley's Patent* BL O/166/86; *Kelsey-Hayes' Patent* BL O/14/87; *Fenton's Patent* BL O/89/98; and *Trichromatic Carpet's Patent* BL O/1/99. In such proceedings, the Comptroller examines the statement of case and any evidence already filed by the applicant for revocation and then, treating each assertion of fact as conceded except insofar as it may be contradicted by any other document before the UK-IPO, will order revocation instead of allowing surrender if prima facie grounds for revocation exist, as was done in *Wellworthy's Patent* BL O/119/81 and *Trichromatic Carpet's Patent* (above).

In *Connaught Laboratories' Patent* [1999] F.S.R. 284, an offer to surrender was communicated to the petitioner for revocation the day before the substantive hearing was due to have been heard because the United Kingdom market was seen not to be sufficiently significant, despite the fact that relief under the European patent (UK) had also been sought from a court in The Netherlands. The court treated the petition as undefended and, having already read the evidence, revoked the patent and imposed an order including some costs on an indemnity basis.

Thus, a proprietor cannot evade a finding of invalidity by offering to surrender his patent (as he could under the 1949 Act).

In *Dyson's Patent* [2003] R.P.C. 24, the patentee had applied to the court to stay the revocation proceedings until the patent was revoked by the Comptroller under s.73(2), there being a corresponding European application still undergoing prosecution. However, the court had declined to order the stay. The patentee then offered to surrender the UK patent.

The UK-IPO initially declined to accept the offer of surrender on the basis that it was not appropriate to accept the offer without the view of the court as to how this would affect the revocation proceedings. Upon the matter being further argued (see [2003] R.P.C. 48), the offer of surrender was accepted, the patentee's reasons being accepted as "satisfactory", no-one, including the applicants for revocation, having opposed the surrender, and the court having expressed no view in the matter, although having been made aware of the surrender application. The hearing officer commented that the surrender would not adversely affect the continuance of the revocation action (should the applicant for revocation wish to proceed with it), but it was not the practice of the UK-IPO to initiate proceedings under s.73(2) if, at the relevant date, the UK patent is no longer in force or if an offer to surrender it has been made (reference being made to para.73.09 of the MOPP). The UK-IPO would therefore take no further action under s.73(2).

It appears that an offer to surrender the patent will not terminate entitlement proceedings under s.37 (*Weston Hydraulics' Patent* BL O/153/90, noted I.P.D. 14117), though here the patent was revoked for anticipation.

The operation of s.73 cannot be avoided by surrender of the United Kingdom part of a European patent (*International Business Machines' (Barclay and Bigar's) Patent* [1983] R.P.C. 283), unless such surrender occurs before the patent under the Act is granted, see s.73(4) and §73.07. If the European patent was granted other than in the English language, a failure to file the required English translation will mean that the European patent (UK) will be deemed always to have been void (s.77(7)), but such does not necessarily avoid revocation under s.73, see §73.07. A European patent will also be revoked for all its designated countries if, during opposition proceedings in the EPO under EPC art.99, the proprietor disapproves the text of the patent: T 186/84 *BASF/Revocation at proprietor's request* OJ EPO 1986, 79; [1986] E.P.O.R. 165.

PRACTICE UNDER SECTION 29

Making an offer of surrender

An offer to surrender is to be made in writing (r.42(a)), but there is no particular requirement as to form. It may be desirable, but is not necessary, to make the offer by way of PF 2. This requires no fee but must contain a declaration that there is no pending action for infringement or revocation before the court (though not before the Comptroller). If there is any such pending action the declaration must be deleted and full particulars of such action provided in writing to the Comptroller. It would be sensible for these particulars to contain consents to the surrender by all parties to that action and for the consent to indicate how the matter of costs in the court proceedings is to be dealt with.

29.07

Opposing surrender

Any notice of opposition is made on PF 15 and must be lodged in duplicate within an inextensible period of four weeks from the advertisement of the offer in the *Patents Journal* (r.76(2)(b) and r.108(1)). The notice of opposition must be accompanied by a statement of the grounds relied on by the opponent (r.76(1)), also filed in duplicate. The statement of grounds must include a concise statement of the facts, details of the remedy sought, and must be verified by a statement of truth (r.76(4)).

29.08

Copies of the PF 15 and statement are sent by the Comptroller to the proprietor and any other party whom the Comptroller deems to have an interest in the proceedings (r.77(1)–(3)) who, if he wishes to contest the opposition, should respond with a counter-statement in duplicate within the period set out by the Comptroller in his notification (r.77(5)), although this period may be extended under r.108(1). However, the Comptroller may shorten this period if he thinks fit (r.81(1)). The subsequent procedure follows that, generally applicable to contentious proceedings before the Comptroller. Appeal lies to the Patents Court (s.97(1)).

Oppositions filed under subs.(2), and this eventual outcome thereof will be published in the *Patents Journal* and appropriate entries will be made in the register.

Property in patents and applications, and registration [Sections 30–38]

SECTION 30

Nature of, and transactions in, patents and applications for patents

30.01 30.—(1) Any patent or application for a patent is personal property (without being a thing in action), and any patent or any such application and rights in or under it may be transferred, created or granted in accordance with subsections (2) to (7) below.

(2) Subject to section 36(3) below, any patent or any such application, or any right in it, may be assigned or mortgaged.

(3) Any patent or any such application or right shall vest by operation of law in the same way as any other personal property and may be vested by an assent of personal representatives.

(4) Subject to section 36(3) below, a licence may be granted under any patent or any such application for working the invention which is the subject of the patent or the application; and—

    (a) to the extent that the licence so provides, a sub-licence may be granted under any such licence and any such licence or sub-licence may be assigned or mortgaged; and

    (b) any such licence or sub-licence shall vest by operation of law in the same way as any other personal property and may be vested by an assent of personal representatives.

(5) Subsections (2) to (4) above shall have effect subject to the following provisions of this Act.

(6) Any of the following transactions, that is to say—

    (a) any assignment or mortgage of a patent or any such application, or any right in a patent or any such application;

    (b) any assent relating to any patent or any such application or right;

shall be void unless it is in writing and is signed by or on behalf of **the assignor or mortgagor** [*the parties to the transaction*] (or, in the case of an assent or other transaction by a personal representative, by or on behalf of the personal representative) [*or in the case of a body corporate is so signed or is under the seal of that body*].

(6A) If a transaction mentioned in subsection (6) above is by a body corporate, references in that subsection to such a transaction being signed by or on behalf of the assignor or mortgagor shall be taken to include references to its being under the seal of the body corporate.

(7) An assignment of a patent or any such application or a share in it, and an exclusive licence granted under any patent or any such application, may confer on the assignee or licensee the right of the assignor or licensor to bring proceedings by virtue of section 61 or 69 below for a previous infringement or to bring proceedings under section 58 below for a previous act.

Note. The Regulatory Reform (Patents) Order 2004 (SI 2004/2357) ("RRO") (art.10) amended subs.(6) and introduced new subs.(6A), as indicated above. These amendments took effect on January 1, 2005, the commencement date of the RRO.

COMMENTARY ON SECTION 30

Scope of the section

Section 30 provides that patents and patent applications are "personal property" and **30.02** prescribes how such property rights may be transferred or licensed. It applies also to European patents (UK) and applications (ss.77(1), 78(2)), but does not extend to transactions concerning the disposition of patent rights under Scots law, to which the provisions of s.31 apply (s.31(1)). The provisions of the section satisfy the requirement of art.28(2) of the TRIPS Agreement which specifies that "Patent owners shall also have the right to assign, or transfer by succession, the patent and to conclude licensing contracts".

A "right" in a patent or application includes an interest in it, and reference to a right in a patent includes reference to a share in it (s.130(1)). The registration of transactions, instruments or events affecting rights in or under patents and applications is dealt with by s.32, see §32.19; for the procedure of registration see §§32.26–32.32. Subsections (2) to (4) are subject to subsequent provisions in the Act. In particular, the non-registration of transfers and licences of patent rights has adverse effects arising under s.33, regarding priority of registration, see §33.03; and under s.68, regarding recovery of legal costs and expenses incurred during infringement proceedings. Changes to s.68 alter the consequences of failing to register a transaction (see the commentaries on ss.33 and 68 below for more details). Where a patent is recorded as jointly owned, any assignment or mortgage, or any licence under the patent must be executed by each of the proprietors (or the consent of each otherwise obtained), see s.36(3).

There is no definition in the Act of the "proprietor" of a patent (the term "patentee" used in former statutes is not strictly appropriate to a patent under the 1977 Act which is not granted under seal, but the term remains commonly used.) The wording of s.68 indicates that a person becomes the proprietor by virtue of a transaction, instrument or event and not by virtue of its registration. Thus, the term ''proprietor'' in relation to a patent means the beneficial owner of the primary right to bring infringement proceedings and is not to be equated with the term "registered proprietor", see *Jensen v Emtech* BL C/45/96 where it was held that the defendant had acquired ownership of a patent consequent to an earlier assignment from the claimant. The fact that the assignment was undated was held irrelevant as s.30 only refers to the need for signatures. Also, in decisions under s.28 (*Border's Patent* BL O/157/79 and *Whiteside's Patent* BL O/44/84), the proprietor has been held to be the owner of the rights in respect of the patent at the time and not necessarily the person whose name is registered as such under s.32. Therefore, the entry of ownership in the register is only prima facie, and not conclusive, evidence of beneficial ownership, see s.32(9), although a proprietor who does not register his right within the time limits set may suffer adverse effects under ss.33 and 68, as already noted.

As mentioned above, under the 1977 Act patents are "personal property", that is they can be considered as moveable incorporeal (intangible) property, the most common variety of which are debts, whereas the most common form of personal property is a (corporeal) chattel, ownership of which can pass by its physical delivery from one owner to another. Subsection (1) changed the position at common law under which Letters Patent were regarded as choses (or things) in action. For that reason, the formerly granted "Letters Patent" could not be seized in execution of a writ of fieri facias (*British Mutoscope v Homer* (1901) 18 R.P.C. 177), but this may now be possible.

Vesting by operation of law

A patent or application, or any right in or under it, vests by operation of law in the same **30.03** way as any other personal property (subs.(3)) on the death or bankruptcy of the proprietor, as also does a licence (subs.(4)(b)). A personal representative must sign a written assent (subs.(6)(b)). Where a personal proprietor has died, but his estate has not yet been distributed, the personal representatives of the deceased should, apparently, sue for infringement in the name of the estate, rather than as successors in title, see *Chauvier v Universal Pool Products* [South Africa], noted [1992] E.I.P.R. D-50.

The Patents Court has held that the vesting of title in a company through a series of mergers and demergers governed by Finnish Law constitutes a vesting "by operation of law" under subs.(3) (*Tamglass Ltd OY v Louyang North Glass Technology Co Ltd* [2006] EWHC 65 Ch; [2006] F.S.R. 32, see commentary at §33.05).

When a United Kingdom corporate applicant or patentee has been dissolved or otherwise removed from the register of companies, the patent is granted, or becomes vested, in the Crown under the doctrine of bona vacantia. The patent does not then disappear by merger and, if the proprietor held the patent as trustee for some other person, the court may make an appropriate vesting order (*Dutton's Patent* (1923) 40 R.P.C. 84). Thus, a lawful claimant may acquire ownership of the patent through an assignment from the Attorney-General, for an instance of which see *Latchworth's Patent* BL O/112/96.

Transfer of rights

30.04   Where joint proprietors are recorded in the register, s.36(3) requires all of them to consent to any assignment or mortgage of a patent or the grant of a licence under it, see §36.05. For questions of disputed entitlement to patent rights, see ss.8, 12, 37 and 82 and the commentaries on those sections. Upon the death of a proprietor or applicant, the deceased's patent rights form part of his estate and may then be vested by assent given by his personal representatives in their distribution according to the will or the rules of intestacy. Where the proprietor is of foreign nationality, a personal representative for the United Kingdom estate (including any patents, etc.) must be appointed before a change of ownership can be recorded, for which see §§32.26–32.28. For the desirability of registration of a change of ownership, or the grant of a licence under the patent, see ss.33 and 68. For the procedure for such registration, see §§32.26–32.32.

A "mortgage" includes a charge for securing money or money's worth (s.130(1)). A covenant by the proprietor of a patent to pay certain profits or royalties may take the form of a charge and bind a legal assignee of the patent having notice of the covenant (*Dansk Rekylriffel Syndicat v Snell* (1908) 25 R.P.C. 421). A mortgagee would appear not to have the powers of a proprietor (*Van Gelder, Apsimon v Sowerby Bridge Flour* (1890) 7 R.P.C. 208 CA).

A licence generally passes no proprietary interest and only makes lawful what would otherwise have been unlawful (*Allen & Hanbury v Generics* [1986] R.P.C. 203 HL *per* Lord Diplock). However, an exclusive licensee has an interest sufficient to prevent an assignee of the patent from granting further licences under the order of a foreign court (*British Nylon Spinners v ICI* (1954) 71 R.P.C. 327) and by s.67 may sue for infringement in his own name, see §67.04.

A licence may be void, or unenforceable, in whole or in part if, e.g.: it contains a provision contrary to arts 101 or 102 of the TFEU, as discussed in Appendix D; or it contains a provision prohibited under either of Pts I or II of the Competition Act 1998 (c.41); or it is one void under the terms of the Unfair Contracts Act 1977 (c.50) as discussed in the Notes on repealed s.44; or it is contained as a term in a contract of employment contrary to s.42(2), see §42.03.

The terms of the instrument determine whether an assignee or exclusive licensee can bring proceedings for previous acts of infringement or Crown use (subs.(7)), and whether a licence can be assigned or mortgaged or whether a sub-licence can be granted (subs.4(a)). Thus, a licence confers no right to grant a sub-licence unless this is so stated or can be inferred from the other terms of the licence. A licensee having no right to sub-license may exercise his powers through an agent, but not by an independent contractor (*Dixon v London Small Arms* (1876) 1 App. Cas. 632 HL; *Allen & Hanbury's (Salbutamol) Patent* [1987] R.P.C. 327 CA).

An equitable assignee of a patent, i.e. a person to whom the proprietor has agreed, or is considered to have agreed, to assign it, e.g. an assignee whose assignment has not been registered under s.32(2)(b), may sue for infringement and obtain an interim injunction, but before either damages or a perpetual injunction can be obtained, the legal proprietor must be added as a co-claimant or the equitable assignment must be converted into a registered legal assignment (*Bowden's Patents Syndicate v Smith* (1904) 21 R.P.C. 438; *Performing Right Society v London Theatre of Varieties* [1924] A.C. 1 HL; *Pfizer v Jiwa* [Hong Kong]

[1988] R.P.C. 15; *Stock v Brisbane City Council* [Australia] (1996) 35 I.P.R. 296; and *Baxter International v Nederlands Produktielaboratorium* [1998] R.P.C. 250). Also, the Comptroller may decide questions of entitlement based on an equitable assignment if satisfied, on the balance of probabilities, that such had taken place, even if only orally or by conduct, see *Polar Bay's Patent* BL O/233/99.

Unlike the position under former statutes, it would not appear that patents and applications under the 1977 Act can be assigned for a part only of the United Kingdom. Also, so far as European patent applications are concerned, the difference in wording in arts 71 and 73 of the EPC with regard to transfer on the one hand and licensing on the other indicates that assignment for part of a contracting state is not possible.

Execution of documents (subs.(6))

An assignment or mortgage is void unless it is signed by or on behalf of the assignor or mortgagor. In the case of an assent or other transaction by a personal representative, the document must be signed by or on behalf of the personal representative. In the case of a body corporate the signature may be replaced by the company seal. This amendment, introduced by the RRO, replaces the previous requirement that an assignment, mortgage or assent be signed by or on behalf of both parties. The amendment removes an anomaly which previously existed between the signature formalities required to make a transfer of a patent in Scotland and elsewhere in the UK, and also mirrors the formality requirements which apply to the transfer of other types of intellectual property.

30.05

It is not necessary for a company registered in England or Wales to have a seal; and (whether or not it does have a seal) a document signed by a director and the secretary of a company (or by two directors, or by one director in the presence of a witness who attests the signature), which is expressed in some way to be executed by the company, has the same effect as if that document had been executed under seal; and such document has the effect of a deed if it is indicated as intended to have that effect (see Companies Act 2006 (c.46) s.44).

The Overseas Companies (Execution of Documents and Registration of Charges) Regulations 2009 came into force on October 1, 2009 and extend to all overseas companies, regardless of whether or not they have established a presence in the UK. The Overseas Companies Regulations 2009 modify the effect of ss.43, 44 and 46 of the 2006 Act. Before this Regulation came into force, there was some doubt as to how overseas companies could validly execute a document. This was especially disconcerting considering the case of *European Environmental Recycling's International Application* BL O/316/99 where an assignment was held to have no legal effect because, after the document had been executed under seal, it had been signed by a purported director and secretary of a company who had not been properly appointed or otherwise authorised in accordance with its Articles of Association.

The Overseas Companies (Execution of Documents and Registration of Charges) Regulations 2009 have now clarified any uncertainty in this area. A document may be executed by an overseas company in one of two ways: (a) by affixing its common seal, or (b) by executing the document in any manner permitted by the laws of the jurisdictions in which the company was incorporated. Additionally, a document that is signed by a person acting under the authority of the company (to be determined in accordance with the laws in which the company was incorporated) will have the effect as if the document had been signed by a company registered in England or Wales under common seal. In relation to the execution of deeds, The Overseas Companies (Execution of Documents and Registration of Charges) Regulations 2009 states that an overseas company must comply with s.1(2)(b) of the Law of Property (Miscellaneous Provisions) Act 1989 for the deed to be validly executed; viz. duly executed by the company (as detailed above), and delivered as a deed.

In *Triten Corp's Patent* BL O/65/88 an assignment instrument, which had validly been created retrospectively under a foreign law, was disregarded (for the purpose of permitting the assignee to rely upon it in restoration proceedings under s.28) because the document failed to comply with s.30(6). From a decision under EPC art.71 it appears that the instrument may consist of two documents each signed by one of the parties, execution under seal not being required, followed by exchange of these separate documents between the parties (J 18/84 *Register of European Patents—Entries in* OJ EPO 87, 215; [1987] E.P.O.R. 321).

A personal seal is not required for an individual. Under English law, a document is executed as a deed if it is signed personally in the presence of a witness who attests the signature and the document indicates that it is to have effect as a deed: Law of Property (Miscellaneous Provisions) Act 1989 (c.34) s.1.

Failure to sign or seal an assignment, mortgage or assent as required by subs.(6) will result in it being at most merely equitable in nature and subject to adverse registration under s.33, as discussed in §33.03. However, a transaction of this nature may still have effect as between the parties, and it is registrable under r.47 (reprinted in §32.07) although the register does not necessarily indicate the equitable nature of the transaction. If the register does not so indicate, a problem arises because an entry in the register is prima facie, or sufficient, evidence of the fact recorded (see s.32(9), discussed in §32.22).

An equitable owner of rights can initiate a claim to enforce those rights, but title to sue has to be regularised by the time of the trial, see: §30.04; *Kakkar v Szelke* [1989] F.S.R. 225; [1989] E.P.O.R. 184 CA; J 19/87 *BURR-BROWN/Assignment* [1988] E.P.O.R. 350; and also §§32.26–32.32.

Note that where the transmission of rights occurs by operation of law (as for example by a statute or court order), the subsection has no application, see *Precast Micro Injection's Patent* BL O/234/98 and J 10/93 *COLLAPSIBLE BOTTLE OF AMERICA/Transfer* OJ EPO 1997, 91. In addition, a licence, even an exclusive one, is a right "under", but not a right "in", a patent and so is another type of transaction not governed by subs.(6) (*Insituform v Inliner* [1992] R.P.C. 83; *Leisure Pleasure Products v Raymond Robert Britner* BL O/360/06).

A licensor may grant a licence under hand or by word of mouth (*Crossley v Dixon* (1863) 10 H.L.C. 293 HL) or by conduct or implication, see *Morton-Norwich v Intercen and United Chemicals* [1981] F.S.R. 337. Also, a person may be estopped, by acquiescence or by some inconsistent act (e.g. sale of means for putting the invention into effect), from denying that a licence has been granted. Furthermore, under the law of estoppel, a licensee may be required to pay royalties where the recitals of the licence agreement refer to patent rights which are later discovered to have always been non-existent (*IMH Investments v Trinidad Home Developments* [Trinidad] [1994] F.S.R. 616).

An agreement to assign, mortgage or license a patent in the future also need not be in writing; and, in the case of a contract of employment, it may be subject to s.42(2) (for which see §42.03). An agreement to perform a future act may be enforced by an order for specific performance.

PRACTICE UNDER SECTION 30

Documentation

30.06   The amendment made to subs.(6), and the introduction of new subs.(6A), removed the former requirement for dual signature of an assignment or mortgage of a patent or application for a patent by both the assignor/mortgagor and assignee/mortgagee. It is now sufficient for such a document to be executed solely by the assignor or mortgagor (subs.(6)). Moreover, where such a person is a body corporate, then application of the seal of that body to an assignment or mortgage of a patent or application satisfies the requirement for "signature by or on behalf of" that body (subs.(6A)).

For registration under s.32 of an instrument recording a transaction, there is no longer any need to file a copy of that transaction instrument or, if the transaction instrument contains information, e.g. financial terms, which the parties wish to keep off the public record, extracts from it. As explained in §§32.26–32.32, it is sufficient to file PF 21 signed by, or on behalf of, all parties to the transaction in the case of an assignment or by (or on behalf of) the grantor alone in the case of a mortgage, licence, sub-licence or security. However, the option remains of filing a copy of the transaction instrument or such extracts. Indeed, the Comptroller has the power to require evidence to be submitted to him, which would become part of the record available to the public.

Any number of patents and applications may be assigned by the same instrument, but an application subject to a secrecy order under s.22 should be dealt with separately so that no reference to it is made in a document open to public inspection, see §22.09.

Where an instrument relates also to patents in other countries or to other intellectual property (e.g. trade marks and/or designs) requiring registration, separate documents should be prepared for each type of registrable right in each country so that a single document exists for each register in which it is to be recorded. Although such a document can be a confirmation of an assignment already executed in some more comprehensive document, this can cause problems: in some countries the comprehensive document may have to be produced and perhaps translated.

An assignment of an application should prudently refer to the assignment of "all right, title and interest" in that application and in any patent granted on the application, so as to avoid difficulty or ambiguity when registering the instrument subsequently. Note that an assignment executed after issue of the notice of grant to the applicant, but before such notice has been published in the *Patents Journal*, is treated as an assignment of an application, see §24.06.

An assignment or exclusive licence may take advantage of subs.(7) by including a provision conferring rights to bring proceedings for previous acts of infringement under either s.61 or s.69 or Crown use under s.58.

For further information on the practicalities of taking security over patents, see "Taking Security over Intellectual Property: A Practical Guide" by V. Bromfield and J. Runckles, [2006] E.I.P.R. 344.

Liability of assignor

When a patent is assigned, the assignment carries with it no implied covenant that the patent is valid (*Hall v Conder* (1857) 26 L.J.C.P. 138 Ex.Ch.). However, under the Law of Property (Miscellaneous Provisions) Act 1994 (c.36), where the disposition instrument is expressed to be made with "full title guarantee", there is implied into the disposition instrument covenants: (1) that the person making the disposition has the right to dispose of the property as he purports to and will take all reasonable steps to effect the same at his own expense; and (2) that such person is disposing of the property free from all charges and encumbrances (except those which the disposer does not and could not reasonably be expected to know about, or which at the time are only potential liabilities and rights in respect of the property). If the transfer is instead expressed to be made with "limited title guarantee", this second implied covenant is changed to one that, since the last disposition of the property for value, the disposer has not charged or encumbered the property or granted any third party rights and is not aware that anyone else has done so since the last disposition for value. All this is subject to any contrary statement in the transfer or licence instrument and to matters which are within the actual knowledge of the transferee or licensee or are a necessary consequence of facts then within his actual knowledge. These implied covenants were discussed by M. Anderson at: [1995] E.I.P.R. 236 and D-138; and in his book *Technology: The Law of Exploitation and Transfer* (London: Butterworths, 1996) at pp.241–248. In the last of these references, it is considered unlikely that these covenants also extend to foreign patents even if the instrument is one governed by English law.

Care is especially needed in the wording of an assignment or licence document where a licence already exists or where there is a possibility of infringement of some other patent by use of the invention. Liability may be excluded contractually in the transfer of a right or interest in a patent, etc. by way of exception to the provisions of the Unfair Contract Terms Act 1977 (c.50) s.1(2); Sch.1 para.1(c), see also §274.09.

Transfer of rights by companies

On the dissolution of a corporate proprietor its patents (and other intellectual property rights) vest in the Crown as bona vacantia (Companies Act 1985 (c.6) s.654 or, after October 1, 2009, Companies Act 2006 (c.46) s.1012). A purchaser from the liquidator should, therefore, take care to obtain an actual legal assignment before the company is

30.07

30.08

dissolved. If this is not done, a subsequent assignment from the Attorney-General is possible, see §30.03.

A charge over a patent, or over a licence under a patent (or indeed over any intellectual property right), which belongs to a limited company is void against creditors and the liquidator (or administrator) unless it is registered at the Companies Registration Office at which the company is registered (Companies Act 1985 (c.6) ss.395, 396(1)(j), and 396(3A), as amended by the Insolvency Act 1985 (c.65) Sch.6 para.10, and by Sch.7 para.31 of the CDPA 1988 or, after October 1, 2009, Companies Act 2006 (c.46) ss.860(7)(i), 861(4) and 874). For companies registered in Scotland, see s.410 of the Companies Act 1985 or, after October 1 2006, ss.878(7)(b)(ii) and 889 of the Companies Act 2006 and §31.04. For companies registered in Northern Ireland, see art.403 of the Companies (Northern Ireland) Order (SI 1986/1032 (NI 6)) or, after October 1, 2009, Companies Act 2006 (c.46) ss.860(7)(i), 861(4) and 874). For the purpose of registration of such a charge, Companies Form M395 (or, after October 1, 2009, such form as will be specified), together with the instrument itself, must be received for registration by the Companies Registration Office within 21 days of the date of the charge, and the Registrar of Companies has no discretion to accept papers that are late or incomplete. It is often prudent also to enter notice of such a charge in the register of patents as a mortgage, see §§32.19 and 32.30.

Maintenance and prosecution

30.09　An assignee of a patent or application ought to ensure that any required procedure for maintaining the patent or prosecuting the application has been, and is being, carried out in due time. It is usually prudent to call for official receipts for documents purportedly filed, or to make independent inquiry of the UK-IPO, rather than rely merely on assurances from the assignor or his patent attorney, see *Thermo Technic's Application* [1985] R.P.C. 109.

Stamp duty

30.10　Where a document which is required to be stamped under the Stamp Act 1891 (c.39, as much amended), but is not so stamped, that document is not receivable in evidence by a court, see *Coflexip Stena's Patent* [1997] R.P.C. 179 and *Parinv v Inland Revenue Commissioners* [1998] S.T.C. 305, noted *The Times* January 13, 1998. In the past this has caused much trouble and the Comptroller has been required to be satisfied that any necessary stamp duty was paid before he should register an assignment of, for example, patent rights. However, this position has been greatly alleviated by the abolition of the imposition of stamp duty on the sale, transfer or other disposition of intellectual property taking place on or after March 28, 2000 (Finance Act 2000 (c.17) s.129(1)). Consequently, for transactions entered into on or after this date, the Comptroller no longer requires any declaration that "any necessary stamp duty has been paid" in respect of an assignment sought to be registered, e.g. in the register of patents.

In this Act, "intellectual property" is defined as:

"(a) any patent, trade mark, registered design, copyright or design right,

(b) any plant breeders' rights and rights under section 7 of the Plant Varieties Act 1997 (c. 66),

(c) any licence or other right in respect of anything within paragraph (a) or (b), and

(d) any rights under the law of a country or territory outside the United Kingdom that correspond or are similar to those within paragraph (a), (b) or (c)".

It is understood that the Comptroller will construe broadly the above-quoted definition of "intellectual property" so that it will include, e.g. supplementary protections certificates, utility models, etc. see the comprehensive article by Patricia B. Harris [2000] *CIPA* 172. Note that "know-how" has never been considered as "property" as regards liability for stamp duty payment.

The definition of "intellectual property" above does not extend to "goodwill". However, the Finance Act 2002 (c.23) s.116, abolished stamp duty on the "sale, transfer or other disposition of goodwill" as regards instruments executed after April 23, 2002, so there is no need for an apportionment of value in assignments executed after that date. For agreements executed prior to that date, there will need to be an apportionment of the consideration "on such basis as is just and reasonable" (Finance Act 2000 (c.17) Sch.34 paras 2 and 3).

For a summary of the position since the abolition of Stamp Duty in relation to the transfer of intellectual property rights, see the article on that subject by R. Williams [2002] *CIPA* 16. For the position for transactions concluded before March 28, 2000, see another article by Patricia B. Harris [1999] *CIPA* 880.

In any global assignment of intellectual property rights, it is also important to consider corresponding or similar fiscal duties payable on such assignment (and on any confirmatory or other assignments executed pursuant to it) according to the laws of other countries. Local advice should therefore be taken—if at all possible before the proposed assignment instrument, and even the global assignment, is executed—if the transaction involves a large overall consideration. Indeed, the best practice in the case of a "global" assignment is for the global document to be couched in terms of an agreement to assign at a future date, specifying separate considerations for each item of intellectual property to be transferred, with a "further assurance" clause to provide for enforcement of this provision should this be necessary. Separate formal assignment documents can then be drawn up for each country, according to local laws and signatory and fiscal requirements, with these documents being prepared in the local language in order to save translation costs.

Value added tax

Value added tax (VAT) is normally payable on royalties for the use or sale of patent **30.11** rights if the proprietor of intellectual property rights is registered for VAT purposes in the UK. The proprietor should therefore see that licences and other agreements provide for any VAT payable to be paid to him in addition to the agreed consideration, and he should supply a VAT invoice or receipt. It should also be noted that payments made in settlement of litigation will often be regarded as made in respect of a supply of services within the scope of VAT, with the consequence that VAT is payable on the settlement sum (*Cooper Chasney v Comm. of Customs and Excise* [1992] F.S.R. 298, discussed in [1993] E.I.P.R. 31).

If the proprietor of intellectual property rights receives royalties from a person established outside the UK, this is outside the scope of UK VAT and therefore no UK VAT will be payable if that person is based in another EU Member State and uses the intellectual property rights for business purposes (in which case the proprietor should ensure he obtains that person's VAT number in the country in which he is established and quotes this number on the invoice) or is otherwise established outside the EU.

The effect of VAT law on intellectual property is considered in more detail in Gallafent, Eastaway and Dauppe, *Intellectual Property: Law and Taxation* 7th edn (London: Sweet & Maxwell, 2008).

Income and corporation tax

The taxation in the United Kingdom of payments made and received in respect of patent **30.12** licences and assignments is now primarily governed by Pt 8 of the Corporation Tax Act 2009, the Income Tax (Trading and Other Income) Act 2005 and the Capital Allowances Act 2001. Broadly, Pt 8 aims to tax and relieve profits and losses in respect of intangibles of a company as income, generally in accordance with the way these items are recognised in the accounts of the company. Part 8 applies only to corporations; the tax issues that arise in relation to IP held by individuals are treated differently. The two fundamental issues that need to be considered regarding the income tax treatment of patent rights are (a) determination of deductions and allowances which may be claimed with respect to monies expended on patent rights, and (b) determination of the taxation treatment of the monies received in respect of such rights. The answers to these questions depend on the particular facts at hand including, for example, when the patent was created or acquired, who owns the asset, and where the asset is located. Expenses incurred in devising an invention and patenting it are normally incurred wholly for the purposes of trade and so are deductible (Income Tax (Trading and Other Income) Act 2005 (c.5) ss.25, 87–88: expenses of research and development), and capital expenditure on the acquisition of patent rights may be written-down each year at the rate of 25 per cent of the outstanding amount of the expenditure (Capital Allowances Act 2001 (c.2) ss.472–475). It is worth noting that even where, under accounting rules, a cost is treated as capitalised, for UK purposes, the amount may be deductible under the research and development relief. Losses and profits under Pt 8 give rise to debits and credits respectively. Debits and credits in respect of assets held for a trade are treated as expenses/receipts of that trade and taxed accordingly.

SECTION 31

Nature of, and transactions in, patents and applications for patents in Scotland

31.01   **31.**—(1) Section 30 above shall not extend to Scotland, but instead the following provisions of this section shall apply there.

(2) Any patent or application for a patent, and any right in or under any patent or any such application, is incorporeal moveable property, and the provisions of the following sub-sections and of section 36(3) below shall apply to any grant of licences, assignations and securities in relation to such property.

(3) Any patent or any such application, or any right in it, may be assigned and security may be granted over a patent or any such application or right.

(4) A licence may be granted, under any patent or any application for a patent, for working the invention which is the subject of the patent or the application.

(5) To the extent that any licence granted under subsection (4) above so provides, a sub-licence may be granted under any such licence and any such licence or sub licence may be assigned and security may be granted over it.

(6) Any assignation or grant of security under this section may be carried out only by writing **subscribed in accordance with the Requirements of Writing (Scotland) Act 1995 [c. 7]** [*probative or holograph of the parties to the transaction*],

(7) An assignation of a patent or application for a patent or a share in it, and an exclusive licence granted under any patent or any such application, may confer on the assignee or licensee the right of the assignor or licensor to bring proceedings by virtue of section 61 or 69 below for a previous infringement or to bring proceedings under section 58 below for a previous act.

Note. Subsection (6) was amended by the Requirements in Writing (Scotland) Act 1995 (c.7) Sch.4(49).

COMMENTARY ON SECTION 31

Scope of the section

31.02   Section 31 provides for Scotland similar provisions on the nature of, and transactions in, patents and applications as apply elsewhere under s.30, but modified so as to conform with Scots legal practice and terminology. Like s.30, s.31 applies also to European patents (UK) (s.77(1)); and European applications (UK) (s.78(2)).

Nature of patents and patent rights under Scots law (subss.(2)–(5))

31.03   Under Scots law "any patent, application for a patent, and any grant in or under any patent or any such application" (herein called "a patent right") is "incorporeal moveable property" (subs.(2)). Both s.30 (applicable to England) and s.31, therefore, seem to accept that the *situs* of a patent right is not where the register which records its existence is kept but rather is the part of the UK where the transaction affected is taking place. However, in contrast to this, it should be noted that, for the taxation of capital gains, "patents...are situated where they are registered" (Taxation of Chargeable Gains Act 1992, c.12 s.275(1)(h)).

Although the only United Kingdom patent register is kept at the UK-IPO (in Wales), the general rule of jurisdiction—that proceedings which have as their object the validity of entries in public registers may only be brought in the courts for the place where that register is kept—does not apply to proceedings in Scotland concerning the validity of entries in registers of patents, designs or other similar rights required to be deposited or registered (Civil Jurisdiction and Judgments Act 1982, c.27, Sch.8, as amended by the Civil Jurisdiction and Judgments Order SI 2001/3929). This means that proceedings relating to the validity of patents registered at the UK-IPO may thus be brought in the Court of Session under Sch.8(2)(n) of this Act, subject to the rules of jurisdiction (see §98.05).

The differences between ss.30 and 31 are generally linguistic rather than substantive, with the important exceptions of: (1) the method of granting security over a patent, which is discussed in §31.05; and (2) the required manner of execution of instruments of transfer under Scots law, discussed in §31.06.

Thus, subss.(3)–(5) correspond generally to subss.30(2)–(4) in relation to: "assignations" (corresponding to "assignments" under English law); the grant of licences and (if permitted by the terms of the head licence) also of sub-licences; and the "grant of security" (corresponding to "mortgages", but not "charges", under English law). These subsections provide the necessary power for such transfers and grants to be valid if they took place under Scots law. Also such transfers and grants are, as under s.30, subject to the terms of s.36 in the case of patent rights that are held in joint names, see s.36(3) and §36.05.

The commentaries under s.30 and ss.32–36 therefore generally apply to transactions, instruments and events occurring under Scots law, and therefore under s.31.

Applicability of section 31

The factor which determines whether s.30 or 31 applies to a particular transaction, instrument or event is whether it is the law of Scotland or England which applies. Since 1991, this has been governed by the Contracts (Applicable Law) Act 1990 (c.36) ("the 1990 Act") which was enacted to give effect to the Rome Convention of 1980 ("the Convention"). The Convention was intended to harmonise the position among the new EU States as to the law to be applied when considering the validity and effect of contractual obligations. Although the explanatory report by Professors M. Giuliano and P. Lagarde accompanying the Convention indicated that it does not apply to contracts concerning intellectual property, neither the Convention nor the 1990 Act make any exception for such contracts, and the better view seems to be that it is the 1990 Act which governs the contractual aspects of an agreement concerning the disposition or licence of an intellectual property right, but not necessarily the property aspects of it. **31.04**

Under this 1990 Act, a contract will generally be governed by the law chosen by the parties. However, if the parties have not made a choice of law, the applicable law for that contract shall be "the law of the country with which [the contract] is most closely connected". The general presumption is that this country is where the party who has to effect the characteristic performance of the contract has, at the time of conclusion of the contract, his habitual residence or (in the case of a corporate body) its central administration.

But, if the contract is entered into in the course of that party's trade or profession, the applicable law will be that of the country in which the principal place of business is situated, or, where under the terms of the contract the performance is to be effected through a place of business other than the principal place of business, the country in which that other place of business is situated.

This suggests that unless the contract states otherwise, s.31 rather than s.30 will govern any transfer or licence of a patent right which takes place under Scots law, for example in the case of the distribution of the estate of a person who died domiciled in Scotland, or when the principal party (i.e. the assignor or licensor) is habitually resident in Scotland, or is a company incorporated there. Nevertheless, whenever it is intended that s.31 should apply, it is advisable for the instrument of transfer or grant to expressly state that it is governed by Scots law.

Grant of security under Scots law

31.05   The provisions of s.31 differ from s.30 in relation to the method of the grant of security under Scots law. A grant of security under Scots law can only be effected by an absolute assignation *ex facie*, with a "back letter" for re-transfer on redemption, or by an assignation-in-security; that is an assignation expressed in its text to be "in security", see the articles by: J. McLean, "Security over intellectual property: A Scottish perspective" [1988] E.I.P.R. 155; T. Guthrie and A. Orr, "Fixed security rights over intellectual property in Scotland" [1996] E.I.P.R. 597; and D.P. Sellar, "Rights in security over Scottish patents" (1996) S.L.P.Q. 1(2), 137–144. The assignation must be in writing and delivered by the grantor to the assignee.

It is important to note that the whole area of assignations and security over incorporeal moveable property including intellectual property (and therefore patents) is currently the subject of a review being conducted by the Scottish Law Commission, as part of its 8th Programme of Law Reform (SCOT LAW COM No. 220 paras 2.4-2.6). A Discussion Paper is due to be published in the second half of 2011.

An assignation amounts to a transfer of ownership which, of course, has important implications. For example, it means that the assignee is the owner of the patent and any use by the assignor or cedent will infringe the assignee's rights. This is illustrated by *Buchanan v Alba Diagnostics* [2000] R.P.C. 367, where it was held that the pursuer was not entitled to the patent because of a previous assignment of security of another patent, together with "improvements" on the invention therein claimed, the patent-in-suit being regarded as an improvement on the first invention because the changes from it were not so radical as to render the second invention "quite distinct" from the first. This decision was upheld in appeal to both the Inner House of the Court of Session (see [2001] R.P.C. 43) and subsequently in the House of Lords (see [2004] R.P.C. 34; [2004] S.L.T. 255). The Court of Session's appeal decision provides a useful synopsis of precedent decisions on the meaning of improvement inventions, although each case must be decided on its own facts. This House of Lords decision makes it clear that an improvement is not a term of art but is a question of fact and degree in each case and according to the context (see Amanda Michaels "An Improvement to the Law of Improvements" [2005] E.I.P.R. 158). Here, as the later patent fell within the claim of the first patent with an additional feature, designed to solve a defect with the first patent it was clearly an improvement. Lord Hoffmann in his House of Lords judgment emphasised that the context here, being to protect the commercial value of a patent which was the security for a loan, was important and meant that the patent had to be given a broad and commercial rather than a narrow and technical meaning. The decision is also helpful in making it clear that an assignation of further improvements is not per se an unreasonable restraint of trade.

As explained in the above article by Guthrie and Orr, there are also important differences between an *ex facie* ("on the face of it") absolute assignation and an assignation in security. There is further some doubt whether an assignee can perfect its title to a patent application until the patent is actually granted. Section 31(3) seems to allow security to be taken over an application prior to grant. Whilst it does this and such a charge is valid against a company, notwithstanding that it has not been registered under the Companies Act, it is not clear what happens when the status alters from application to grant.

As under English law, such a grant of security requires registration, without which the security will be ineffective under Scots law. The procedure for effecting this required registration is the same as that under English law, save for differences in nomenclature and the nature of the security instrument, and is discussed in §30.08, though as regards registration of a grant of security made by a company with its registered office in Scotland, ss.878 and 860 of the Companies Act 2006 (c.46) applies.

Manner of execution of assignations and grants of security under Scots law (subs.(6))

Section 31(6) (as amended) requires that execution of the assignation (transfer instru-   **31.06** ment), or grant of security (mortgage), must be by an assignation (see §31.05), carried out by writing subscribed in accordance with the Requirements of Writing (Scotland) Act 1995 (c.7) ["ROWA"]. This means that a document which comes within the terms of s.31 and is governed by Scots law need only be executed by the grantor of the document. A transmission under such a document will be registered under r.44(6) and will have full legal effect.

ROWA should be referred to in detail for its terms. However, the general principles as they apply to assignations and grants of security under s.31(6) are as follows. Under the terms of the ROWA, a Scottish document is validly executed by an individual if it is subscribed by its grantor (s.2(1)). No further formalities are required, but it is thought generally advisable to have signing take place in the presence of a single witness, who should sign and add his/her address. Such an act confers "self-proving" status upon the document (s.3(1)). Valid execution by a partnership requires the document to be signed on behalf of the partnership by a partner (using either his/her own name or the name of the firm), or by a person authorised to sign the document on the partnership's behalf (Sch.2(2)(1)). Again, the witnessing of the signature to make it "self-proving" is thought to be advisable, though not essential.

A document is validly executed under Scots law by a company if it is signed on its behalf by a director, or by the secretary of the company, or by a person authorised to sign on its behalf (Sch.2(3)(1)). This provision has been applied more generally to all registered companies, see §30.05. Once again, under Scots law, it is thought desirable to have the signature made "self-proving" by arranging to have the signing party's signature witnessed by a single witness (see Sch.2(3)(5), in relation to companies).

"Self-proving" status is also accorded to documents executed by companies in terms of the ROWA (s.3(1A)).The effect is that a document is "self-proving" if it is signed on behalf of the company by two directors of the company, or by one director and the company secretary, or by two persons bearing to have been authorised to sign the document on behalf of the company.

It should be noted that, in contrast with English law (as noted in §30.05), there is no presumption under Scots law that a person signing as a director or the company secretary has such a position, or that a purported authorised signatory was in fact so authorised: thus, it may be appropriate to request proof of capacity upon delivery of the executed instrument.

Under the ROWA (s.3(1C)), there is no presumption that such a subscriber is in fact a director, company secretary or authorised person. If there is any challenge to their authority to sign, this would need to be proved, but see §30.05

In terms of s.48 of the Companies Act 2006 (c.46), a company registered in Scotland need not have a company seal. Provided the document is validly executed in terms of ROWA that will suffice.

ROWA contains specific provisions relating to signature by limited liability partnerships (Schedule 2(3A)), local authorities (Schedule 2(4)), Ministers of the Crown and office-holders (Schedule 2(6)) and other bodies corporate (Schedule 2(5)).

Transfer of rights of action (subs.(7))

Subsection (7) corresponds to s.30(7) and permits an assignation of patent rights, or the   **31.07** grant of an exclusive licence, to pass therewith rights of action in relation to pre-assignation or pre-licence events, whether these rights be under ss.69 or 70 for infringement or under s.58 for compensation for Crown use, see §30.04.

SECTION 32 [SUBSTITUTED]

Register of patents etc.

32.01   **32.**—(1) The comptroller shall maintain the register of patents, which shall comply with rules made by virtue of this section and shall be kept in accordance with such rules.

(2) Without prejudice to any other provision of this Act or rules, rules may make provision with respect to the following matters, including provision imposing requirements as to any of those matters—

    (a) the registration of patents and of published applications for patents;

    (b) the registration of transactions, instruments or events affecting rights in or under patents and applications;

(ba) the entering on the register of notices concerning opinions issued, or to be issued, under section 74A below;

    (c) the furnishing to the comptroller of any prescribed documents or description of documents in connection with any matter which is required to be registered;

    (d) the correction of errors in the register and in any documents filed at the Patent Office in connection with registration; and

    (e) the publication and advertisement of anything done under this Act or rules in relation to the register.

(3) Notwithstanding anything in subsection (2)(b) above, no notice of any trust, whether express, implied or constructive, shall be entered in the register and the comptroller shall not be affected by any such notice.

(4) The register need not be kept in documentary form.

(5) Subject to rules, the public shall have a right to inspect the register at the Patent Office at all convenient times.

(6) Any person who applies for a certified copy of an entry in the register or a certified extract from the register shall be entitled to obtain such a copy or extract on payment of a fee prescribed in relation to certified copies and extracts; and rules may provide that any person who applies for an uncertified copy or extract shall be entitled to such a copy or extract on payment of a fee prescribed in relation to uncertified copies and extracts.

(7) Applications under subsection (6) above or rules made by virtue of that subsection shall be made in such manner as may be prescribed.

(8) In relation to any portion of the register kept otherwise than in documentary form—

    (a) the right of inspection conferred by subsection (5) above is a right to inspect the material on the register; and

    (b) the right to a copy or extract conferred by subsection (6) above or rules is a right to a copy or extract in a form in which it can be taken away and in which it is visible and legible.

(9) [*Subject to section 12 below,*]The register shall be prima facie evidence of anything required or authorised by this Act or rules to be registered and in Scotland shall be sufficient evidence of any such thing.

(10) A certificate purporting to be signed by the comptroller and certifying

that any entry which he is authorised by this Act or rules to make has or has not been made, or that any other thing which he is so authorised to do has or has not been done, shall be prima facie evidence, and in Scotland shall be sufficient evidence, of the matters so certified.

(11) Each of the following, that is to say—

(a) a copy of an entry in the register or an extract from the register which is supplied under subsection (6) above;

(b) a copy of any document kept in the Patent Office or an extract from any such document, any specification of a patent or any application for a patent which has been published,

which purports to be a certified copy or a certified extract shall[, *subject to section 12 below,*] be admitted in evidence without further proof and without production of any original; and in Scotland such evidence shall be sufficient evidence.

[(12) *In the application of this section to England and Wales nothing in it shall be taken as detracting from section 69 or 70 of the Police and Criminal Evidence Act 1984 [c.60] or any provision made by virtue of either of them.*]

(13) In this section "certified copy" and "certified extract" mean a copy and extract certified by the comptroller and sealed with the seal of the Patent Office.

(14) In this Act, except so far as the context otherwise requires—

"register", as a noun, means the register of patents;

"register", as a verb, means, in relation to any thing, to register or register particulars, or enter notice, of that thing in the register and, in relation to a person, means to enter his name in the register;

and cognate expressions shall be construed accordingly.

Notes

1. The present s.32 was substituted for its original version by the Patents, Designs and Marks Act 1986 (c.39) s.1 and Sch.1 para.4 with s.35 then being repealed, each with effect from January 1, 1989 (SI 1988/1824), though only from April 1, 1989 for the Isle of Man (SI 1989/493). The original version of the section appears now to have no relevance and is therefore not reprinted.

2. Subsection 32(2) was amended by the Patents Act 2004 (c.16) s.13(3), with effect from October 1, 2005 (SI 2005/2471), by the addition, after sub-para.(b), of sub-para.(ba).

3. Subsection 12 was repealed by the Youth Justice and Criminal Evidence Act 1999 (c.21) Sch.6 and, as a consequence, in subs.(9) the words "Subject to subsection 12 below" and in subs.(11) the words, "subject to subsection (12) below", were each subsequently deleted by the Criminal Justice Act 2003 (c.44) Sch.37(6).

RELEVANT RULES—RULES 103 AND 104 AND 44–50

Rule 103—Address for service

103.—(1) For the purposes of any proceeding under the Act or these Rules, an address for service must be furnished by—

(a) an applicant for the grant of a patent;

(b) a person who makes any other application, reference or request or gives any notice of opposition under the Act; and

32.02

(c) any person opposing such an application, reference, request or notice.

(2) The proprietor of a patent, or any person who has registered any right in or under a patent or application, may furnish an address for service by notifying the comptroller.

(3) Where a person has furnished an address for service under paragraph (1) or (2), he may substitute a new address for service by notifying the comptroller.

(4) An address for service furnished under paragraph (1)(a) or (2) must be an address in the United Kingdom, another EEA State or the Channel Islands.

(5) An address for service furnished under paragraph (1)(b) or (c) must be an address in the United Kingdom, unless in a particular case the comptroller otherwise directs.

Rule 104—Failure to furnish an address for service

32.03   **104.**—(1) Where—

> (a) a person has failed to furnish an address for service under rule 103(1); and
>
> (b) the comptroller has sufficient information enabling him to contact that person,

the comptroller shall direct that person to furnish an address for service.

(2) Where a direction has been given under paragraph (1), the person directed shall, before the end of the period of two months beginning [with] immediately after the date of the direction, furnish an address for service.

(3) Paragraph (4) applies where—

> (a) a direction was given under paragraph (1) and the period prescribed by paragraph (2) has expired; or
>
> (b) the comptroller had insufficient information to give a direction under paragraph (1), and the person has failed to furnish an address for service.

(4) Where this paragraph applies—

> (a) in the case of an applicant for the grant of a patent, the application shall be treated as withdrawn;
>
> (b) in the case of a person mentioned in rule 103(1)(b), his application, reference, request or notice of opposition shall be treated as withdrawn; and
>
> (c) in the case of a person mentioned in rule 103(1)(c), he shall be deemed to have withdrawn from the proceedings.

(5) In this rule an "address for service" means an address which complies with the requirements of rule 103(4) or (5).

Note. Amended by the Patents (Amendment) Rules 2011 (SI 2011/2052).

Rule 44—Entries in the register

32.04   **44.**—(1) When an application for a patent is published, the comptroller must enter each of the following matters in the register—

> (a) the name of the applicant;
>
> (b) the name and address of the person identified as the inventor;
>
> (c) the address of the applicant and his address for service;

(d) the title of the invention;

(e) the date of filing of the application for a patent;

(f) the application number;

(g) where a declaration has been made for the purposes of section 5(2)—

    (i) the date of filing of each earlier relevant application specified in the declaration,

    (ii) its application number, and

    (iii) the country it was filed in or in respect of; and

(h) the date of the application's publication.

(2) But where a person's application under rule 11(1)(a) or (b) has been accepted by the comptroller, the comptroller may omit from the register his name and address (or, as the case may be, his address) as that of the person believed to be the inventor.

(3) Where an application for a patent has been published, the comptroller must enter each of the following matters in the register as soon as practicable after the event to which they relate—

(a) the date on which a request is made by an applicant for the substantive examination of his application;

(b) the date on which an application is terminated or withdrawn.

(4) When the patent is granted, the comptroller must enter each of the following matters in the register—

(a) the date on which the comptroller granted the patent;

(b) the name of the proprietor of the patent;

(c) where the address of the proprietor or his address for service was not entered in the register under paragraph (1), that address or address for service.

(5) In relation to a request for an opinion under section 74A, the comptroller must enter each of the following matters in the register as soon as practicable after the event to which they relate—

(a) a notice that a request under section 74A(1)(a) or (b) has been received;

(b) a notice that such a request has been refused or withdrawn;

(c) a notice that an opinion has been issued.

(6) A notice of any transaction, instrument or event mentioned in section 32(2)(b) or 33(3) must be entered in the register as soon as practicable after it occurs (or, if later, when the application is published).

(7) The comptroller may, at any time, enter in the register such other particulars as he thinks fit.

Rule 45—Advertisement in relation to register

45. The comptroller may publish or advertise such things done under the Act or these Rules in relation to the register as he thinks fit.   **32.05**

Rule 46—Copies of entries in, or extracts from, the register and certified facts

46.—(1) An application under section 32(6) for a certified copy of an entry in   **32.06**

the register, or a certified extract from the register, must be made on Patents Form 23.

(2) A person may apply on Patents Form 23 for an uncertified copy of an entry in the register or an uncertified extract from the register and, on payment of the prescribed fee, he shall be entitled to such a copy or extract.

(3) A person may apply on Patents Form 23 for a certificate which certifies that—

(a) an entry has or has not been made in the register; or

(b) something which the comptroller is authorised to do has or has not been done.

Rule 47—Registrations of transactions, instruments and events

32.07   **47.**—(1) An application to register (or in the case of an application for a patent which has not been published, to give notice of) any transaction, instrument or event mentioned in section 32(2)(b) or 33(3) must—

(a) be made on Patents Form 21; and

(b) include evidence establishing the transaction, instrument or event.

(2) The comptroller may direct that such evidence as he may require in connection with the application shall be sent to him within such period as he may specify.

Rule 48—Copies of documents

32.08   **48.**—(1) A person may apply to the comptroller for a certified copy of any relevant document and, on payment of the prescribed fee, he shall be entitled to such a copy.

(2) A person may apply to the comptroller for an uncertified copy of any relevant document and, on payment of the prescribed fee, he shall be entitled to such a copy.

(3) But a person is not entitled to a copy of a relevant document where—

(a) it is not available for inspection under section 118; or

(b) making or providing such a copy would infringe copyright.

(4) For the purposes of this rule a relevant document is any of the following—

(a) an application for a patent which has been published;

(b) a specification of a patent;

(c) any other document, or extract from any such document, kept at the Patent Office.

(5) An application under paragraph (1) or (2) must be made on Patents Form 23.

Rule 49—Correction of name, address and address for service

32.09   **49.**—(1) Any person may request that a correction be entered in the register or made to any application or other document filed at the Patent Office in respect of any of the following—

(a) his name;

(b) his address;

(c) his address for service.

(2) A request under paragraph (1)(a) to correct a name must be made on Patents Form 20.

(3) Any other request under paragraph (1) must be made in writing.

(4) If the comptroller has reasonable doubts about whether he should make the correction—

(a) he must inform the person making the request of the reason for his doubts; and

(b) he may require that person to file evidence in support of the request.

(5) If the comptroller has no doubts (or no longer has doubts) about whether he should make the correction, he must enter the correction in the register or make it to the application or document.

(6) For the purposes of this rule a request for a correction includes a correction made for the purposes of section 117.

Rule 50—Request for correction of error

50.—(1) Subject to rule 49, any person may request the correction of an error **32.10** in the register or in any document filed at the Patent Office in connection with registration.

(2) The request must be—

(a) made in writing; and

(b) accompanied by sufficient information to identify the nature of the error and the correction requested.

(3) If the comptroller has reasonable doubts about whether there is an error—

(a) he shall inform the person making the request of the reason for his doubts; and

(b) he may require that person to furnish a written explanation of the nature of the error or evidence in support of the request.

(4) If the comptroller has no doubts (or no longer has doubts) about whether an error has been made he shall make such correction as he may agree with the proprietor of the patent (or, as the case may be, the applicant).

PATENTS (COMPANIES RE-REGISTRATION) RULES 1982

(SI 1982/ 297)

1. These Rules may be cited as the Patents (Companies Re-registration) Rules 1982 and **32.11** shall come into operation on April 5, 1982.

2. Where a body corporate has re-registered under the Companies Act 1980 [c.22] with the same name as that with which it was registered immediately before the re-registration save for the substitution as, or the inclusion as, the last part of the name (in either upper or lower case of letters and with or without punctuation marks) of—

(a) the words "public limited company" or their equivalent in Welsh; or

(b) the abbreviation "p.l.c." or its equivalent in Welsh,

then references to the name of the body corporate in any application to the comptroller, in the register and in any other record kept at, or any document issued by, the Patent Office and relating to patents shall be treated on and after the date of such re-registration as references to the name with which the body corporate is so re-registered.

32.12   Note. These rules are now of historical interest only as the necessary changes of name were effect many years ago, see §32.19.

COMMENTARY ON SECTION 32

Scope of the section

32.13   Section 32 continues the register of patents kept under previous statutes, the word "register" now being defined in subs.(14). The section applies to applications as well as patents, and to European patents (UK) and applications (ss.77(1), 78(2)). However, entries relating to European applications are dealt with directly in the register of European patents at the EPO (see *European Patents Handbook* ("EPH") (London: Sweet & Maxwell) Ch.17) because no separate register of applications for European patents (UK) is kept, see §32.19.

Subsection (2) gives power to make rules relating to the recording of certain matters in the register of patents, but notice of a trust may not be entered in the register (subs.(3)). This rule-making power is additional to the general rule-making power provided by s.123(1), and rr.44–50, are to be regarded as made under it. Rule 45 empowers the Comptroller to publish and advertise such things done under the Act or Rules in relation to the register "as he may think fit". Such publication normally takes place in the *Patents Journal* and matters which are normally the subject of such advertisement are mentioned here, as appropriate, in relation to practice under the relevant sections.

No entry is made in the register before publication of an application (r.44(1); *Hartington Conway's Patent Applications* [2004] R.P.C. 6 at 137, [16]) though notice may be given to the Comptroller, for example for the purpose of s.33(1)(b), and this will afterwards be registered under r.44(6), see §33.03. An entry regarding licences of right may be made under s.46(1), see §46.05, or s.48(1)(b), see §48.03, or under s.51, see §51.05.

Subsections (4)–(13), which effectively replaced the now repealed s.35 (see the Note to §32.01), deal with the evidential status of entries in the register, falsification of which is a criminal offence under s.109, see §109.02.

The register as evidence

32.14   Subsection (9) provides that an entry in the register of patents is prima facie evidence (or, in Scotland, sufficient evidence) of the thing registered. This was confirmed in *Fraser v Oystertec* [2004] F.S.R. 22 at 427. However, subs.9 strongly implies that the prima facie position is rebuttable. Moreover, the Act itself contemplates actions by proprietors who are not registered; s.68 restricts the right to claim damages for infringements occurring prior to registration. Subsection (4) allows for the register to be kept in a non-documentary, e.g. computerised, form and it need no longer be kept at the UK-IPO. Indeed, for all patents granted and applications filed under the 1977 Act, the register is completely computerised. Subsection (5) provides a right of inspection of the register, and subs.(6) provides for obtaining extracts in accordance with rules made under subs.(7). Subsection (8) provides for inspection of a computerised entry and obtaining an extract thereof. This is discussed in §§118.14 and 118.19. The register may conveniently be inspected free of charge on the UK-IPO website: *http://www.ipo.gov.uk*, see §32.34.

Subsections (9)–(13) provide for copies of entries from the register, certified by the Comptroller under seal (subs.(13)), to be received in legal proceedings as "prima facie" (in Scotland, "sufficient") evidence of the extracted entry, though with a saving for the evidential requirements for computer records in criminal proceedings. These matters are discussed further in §§32.37 and 32.38.

Address for service (r.103)

32.15   The previous rule (r.30), now repealed, required each applicant for a patent or any other person (whether applicant, patentee or otherwise) taking part in any proceedings before the Comptroller to provide an address for service within the United Kingdom (or the Isle of Man by virtue of s.132(2)). However, this requirement was deemed contrary to art.49 of the EC Treaty, which prohibits discrimination against other European Union Members States (see Regulatory Impact Assessment to SI 2006/760). An equivalent provision is also contained in art.36 of the Agreement creating the European Economic Area (the "EEA").

The new rule now set out in r.103 has therefore been liberalised so that, for the purposes of any proceedings under the Act or Rules, any applicant for the grant of a patent may file an address for service in the UK (or the Isle of Man), another EEA state or the Channel Islands (r.103(1)(a)). Note that this does not include Switzerland, which is not in the European Union nor the EEA.

The requirement to provide an address for service in the UK (or Isle of Man) remains unchanged in contested cases and in relation to any other applications unless the Comptroller directs otherwise (r.103(1)(b)).However, this is currently under review following a complaint from the European Commission and the Editors expect a further change soon to bring inter partes cases into line with the ex parte situation.

Also, where an application relates to "military technology", it is likely that the Comptroller will require that prosecution can only proceed by using an address for service which is within the UK (or the Isle of Man) because of the provisions of s.22.

The proprietor or any person who has already registered any right in or under a patent may file an address for service anywhere in the UK, Channel Islands, Isle of Man or EEA: r.103(2). However, any other person who wishes to register a new interest in a patent will need to submit a United Kingdom (or Isle of Man) address for service as this will be done by means of an "other application" under r.103(1)(b).

No form or fee is prescribed for recording such an address.

The term "proceeding", as now used in r.103, is not defined and thus, whether or not this term excludes the mere act of filing a translation of a European patent granted in the French or German language or the mere act of paying a renewal fee, or the mere act of filing a priority document, is not specified. However, the UK-IPO has taken the view under the former rules that these acts were not "proceedings" and accepted them without an address for service being furnished and, in the case of payment of a renewal fee, sent the renewal fee receipt to a foreign address where this was specified on PF 12, and this practice will presumably continue, see further §25.13 and [1994] *CIPA* 305. The UK-IPO will take the EPO representative's address as the address for service for a European Patent (UK) on grant unless it has been told of another address it should use.

While a recorded address for service is clearly the address to which the Comptroller can send communications to meet his obligations under the Act and Rules, this address may now also be used for proceedings before the Patents Court or the Patents County Court. Thus, the provisions of CPR 63.14 provide that notice of any proceedings relating to a patent (including proceedings for revocation, declaration as to non-infringement or groundless threats of infringement proceedings or any other proceedings of a kind mentioned in CPR 63 (which includes proceedings relating to a supplementary protection certificate, see CPR 63.1(2)(e))) may alternatively be served at the address for service recorded in the register. However, CPR 63.14(2)(a) allows service on an address for service recorded at the UK-IPO only if this is "within the jurisdiction" (i.e. within England and Wales and not anywhere else in the EEA). If the address for service provided under r.103 is outside of the UK, the claim form might be served on this address without the court's permission in the circumstances set out in CPR 6.20, which requires the defendant to be domiciled within the EEA. If, however, it is not possible to serve under CPR 6.20, service will need to be effected under the other provisions of CPR 6 (e.g. on a place of business of the foreign corporation within England and Wales) or the court's permission will be needed to either serve out of the jurisdiction under CPR 3 or by an alternative method under CPR 6.8. There may also be problems with serving on the address on the register if the courts take the view that there is no formal address for service under r.103 after grant, as to which see §32.16 below. These problems have been highlighted by A.W. White [2006] *CIPA* 633.

Service on the address recorded in the register is deemed to have been effected on the date on which the document was served at that address, but any time limit running from the date of service receives an automatic extension of seven days. For such proceedings before the Patents Court, this address for service ceases to be effective as soon as the receiving party has provided an address for service to the court.

An address for service can be altered or corrected merely by notifying the Comptroller of the same in writing (r.49(1)(c)) and some of the Patents Forms provide an opportunity to record a change in the registered address for service by completing a specific part of the form provided for this purpose: otherwise, the address for service entered on the form will have effect only for the purpose of the proceedings connected with the filing of that form.

Failure to provide an Address for Service

32.16 Rule 104 allows the Comptroller to direct a person to file an address for service where one has not been provided under r.103. Any application, opposition or reference will be treated as withdrawn if an address for service is not filed within two months of the Comptroller direction. (However, there is no sanction where, following an assignment, a new proprietor refuses to provide a new address for service.)

The provisions of the former r.30(2) and (3) have now been removed: these had provided that, upon grant of a patent, the initial address for service entered in the register was that previously provided to the UK-IPO in respect of the application or, in the case of a European patent (UK), the address of the proprietor as recorded in the EPO (each unless an alternative address was furnished). Former r.30(4) has also been removed: this allowed the withdrawal of a recorded address for service without the provision of an alternative address after the date of publication of the patent because the address of the applicant or proprietor previously provided continued to be treated as an address for service under the Patent Rules. The removal of r.30(4) means it may no longer be possible for an agent to relieve himself of any obligations, e.g. under the Supply of Goods and Services Act 1982 (c.29) by withdrawing his address as the address for service.

The UK-IPO considered these old rules to be superfluous in the light of its continuing practices of: (i) treating the address for service on the register as continuing after grant, unless and until a new address for service is substituted; and (ii) sending reminders of non-payment of renewal fees to the address for service entered on the register unless an alternative address was specified on payment of the previous renewal or otherwise notified by the proprietor (see r.39(3), which does not limit the notification address to the UK).

Whilst the UK-IPO may, in practice, treat the address for service as the same before and after grant, it is not clear that the courts will take the same view in the absence of an express provision to this effect. Therefore it is possible that, following grant, there may be no formal address for service (to which all correspondence can be sent relating to matters under the Patent Rules) because one is only required (and can only be directed under r.104) for patent applications or patents upon which "proceedings" have been or are being instituted.

Rule 103(3) only allows a proprietor to "substitute" a new address for service, implying that a new address must always be provided when the old one is withdrawn. The UK-IPO has indicated that, in practice, if an agent indicates that he no longer wishes to act as an address for service, it will require the proprietor to file a new address for service at the start of any "proceedings" (under r.104), but will continue to treat the "old" address as the address for service for proceedings under the Act until a new address is provided.

Entries made automatically (r.44)

32.17 When an application is published under s.16, or when an international application for a patent (UK) satisfies the conditions of s.89A(3) (for which see §§89A.11–89A.16), all the items listed in r.44(1) are then entered in the register, including the country, date of filing and file number of any application from which priority is claimed under s.5(2), but the address(es) of inventor(s) can be kept off the register upon application by the applicant(s), see the proviso in r.44(2). This can be important for the reasons given in §13.12, where it is also explained that, even if application is made to keep such addresses off the register, this will be only partially effective unless steps are taken to avoid giving the home address(es) of the inventor(s) on PF 7 and it is there indicated how this could perhaps be achieved.

Subsequently, entry is made of the further items listed in r.44(3) and 44(4)(b), including the date of requesting substantive examination under s.18(1) and the date on which the application is granted (the publication of notice of grant in the *Patents Journal* under s.24(1)) or the date on which it is refused, withdrawn or deemed to be withdrawn. Entry is made under r.51 of any reference to the Comptroller of a question about entitlement under s.8, 12, or 37, see §37.12. For recording alterations in the name or address of a proprietor, see §32.26.

Under r.44(7) the Comptroller is given a general discretion to enter in the register other particulars. Entries are customarily made in respect of such "events" as: cessation due to non-payment of a renewal fee, although only after expiration of the grace period allowed under s.25(4); and the institution before the Comptroller of such proceedings as (this list does not purport to be comprehensive; always check with the UK-IPO): disputes between joint applicants (s.10 or s.12(4)); disputes concerning licences (s.11(5) or s.38(5)); inventorship disputes (s.13); amendment (under s.27 or s.75); restoration (s.28); surrender (s.29); licence of right proceedings (under s.46 or s.47); compulsory licence proceedings (s.48 or s.51); infringement proceedings (s.61(3); declaration of non-infringement (s.71); revocation (s.72); and correction (s.117), as well as details of any application for, or grant of, a supplementary protection certificate, for which see Appendix B. The grant by the court of a certificate of contested validity under s.65 is also entered provided that notice of it is given to the Comptroller.

Entries are normally made when such events have actually occurred, but sometimes this is only on conclusion of the proceedings, rather than on their institution. However, entries are now made in respect of all applications for restoration, even if submitted out of time or if apparently unarguable (*Daido Kogyo's Patent* [1984] R.P.C. 97). Also, applications to register a transaction, instrument or event under the present s.32 are often noted; and the computerised register contains, under an entry for a published parent application, details of any divisional application filed under s.15(4), see §§15.32 et seq. Where proceedings before the Comptroller are continued by way of appeal to the Patents Court, Court of Appeal or Supreme Court, such information is also entered in the register where known to the Comptroller.

There is now mechanism whereby the UK-IPO is notified of revocation proceedings instituted by a court. By CPR r.63.14 (reprinted in §F63.14) a copy of the Grounds of Invalidity needs to be sent to the Comptroller at the same time as service on the patentee. The rule also requires requiring service on the Comptroller of a claim form and accompanying documentation regarding rectification of a patent. However, there does not appear to be any sanction for non-compliance with this rule. When this happens, the papers are placed on the file of the patent and it appears that an entry is also then made in the register to notify the public of the existence of the revocation application.

No entry has been made since June 14, 1982 of the nationality of any person, but the names and addresses of applicants, and of persons named as inventors, are recorded (r.44(1)). Also, since that date, payment of a renewal fee under r.39 has not been recorded in the register, but information is available by filing PF 23, see §118.16, or from the UK-IPO website, see §32.35.

Register of European patents

The UK-IPO no longer maintains any register of European applications (UK). Reliance **32.18** for the status of such applications is therefore now totally placed on the register maintained by the EPO itself, an entry in which is created upon the publication (under EPC art.93) of an application for a European patent. Thus, the Comptroller will not record an assignment of an application for a European patent (UK), requiring this to be registered in the EPO, see §78.06.

A separate register of European patents (UK) is, however, created on the publication by the EPO of its notice of grant, although files of them are only created as and when needed.

Copies of any entries made in the European register after grant of a European patent (UK), for example of an assignment sent to the EPO for recording before the date of grant, are not entered automatically in the United Kingdom register, but only if requested. Any such request should be accompanied by a copy of the notice of change in the EPO register issued by the EPO (EPO Form 2544 or 1132) as evidence that the assignment was one which was registered as of a date before grant occurred. The German Federal Patent Court has held (*Decision/4W (pat) 110/84* [Germany] OJ EPO 1987, 438) that an assignment of the European patent during the opposition period is effective only for proceedings in the EPO. Rule 20 of the EPC now makes this a firm rule. Thus, the UK-IPO will not accept an entry made in the EPO register which was requested after the date of grant and will require registration of such an assignment in the normal way. The EPO has also held that, once the opposition period has expired or opposition proceedings have been concluded, the request for grant ceases to have any legal basis and jurisdiction passes to the national patent offices (J 17/91 *COHEN/Registering of licence* OJ EPO 1994, 225; [1994] E.P.O.R. 317).

For a paper on the transfer of rights and their registration in the European patent register, see Lise Dybdahl (1998) 29 I.I.C. 387.

Transactions, instruments and events (rr.49 and 76)

32.19   Alterations to names and/or addresses of proprietors and applicants, as distinct from changes in ownership, are made under r.49 (see reprint, above), see §32.25. However, where the names of United Kingdom public limited companies were required by statute to be altered, the Patents (Companies Re-registration) Rules 1982 (SI 1982/297 reprinted above), deemed the former name to be treated as the new name without formal application for alteration. A notice to this effect is entered upon any certified copy of a register entry where the proprietor is a United Kingdom limited company. However, these Re-registration Rules have no effect in relation to foreign patents or on entries on the register of European patents maintained at the EPO.

Subsection (4)(b) and r.47 (reprinted above) provide for registration of any transaction, instrument or event of the kind listed in s.33(3). Entries can be registered after expiry or lapse of the patent (*Darchem's Patent* BL O/111/86, noted I.P.D. 9073), as the patent may still be involved in proceedings for infringement under s.61, or compensation for Crown use under s.58, or an inventor may make an application for compensation under s.40. However, the MOPP indicates that for such patents the proprietor will first be asked to confirm that such registration is actually intended. The procedure for effecting registration is discussed at §§32.27–32.33. Assignments and other changes in proprietorship, mortgages and licences fall into this category and are discussed generally under s.30. The effect of registration is considered under s.33. Notification may be made before publication under s.16, and the name of the new proprietor is then entered in the register under r.44(6) when the register entry for the application is created upon this publication.

While transactions, instruments and events can be registered in the EPO in respect of a pending application for a European patent and have effect as from publication, in the case of an international application there is no similar facility in the International Bureau for registration of a licence, as distinct from an assignment. For an international application (UK), no licence can be recorded until the international application enters the United Kingdom national phase even though there may have been publication by the International Bureau (s.89B(2)). This could entail a loss of rights under s.69.

Damages or an account of profits are not awarded to an assignee or exclusive licensee for the period between the date of the instrument and the date of registration unless the entry is made within six months from the date of the instrument or can be shown to have been made as soon as practicable (s.68, discussed at §68.03).

Although subs.(3) prohibits entry of notice of a simple trust, an equitable interest can be registered if it is of such a nature that specific performance could be enforced to affect the proprietorship of the patent, whether by creating a trust or otherwise: *Stewart v Casey* (1892) 9 R.P.C. 9 CA, applied in *Kakkar v Szelke* [1989] F.S.R. 225 [1989] E.P.O.R. 184 CA; see also J 19/87 *BURR-BROWN/Assignment* [1988] E.P.O.R. 350. On this basis, an agreement to assign can be registered, see *Coflexip Stena's Patent* [1997] R.P.C. 179, but it will be registered only as a transaction affecting title and not one transferring it. A letter to the Comptroller relating to an equitable right or claim is available on the public file under r.48(1) (reprinted above), even if the letter itself gives no legal or equitable right and could not be registered (as in *Fletcher's Patent* (1893) 10 R.P.C. 252).

It is not clear whether the presence of information concerning an equitable interest (such as a trust) in the file open to public inspection, but not entered in the register, gives constructive notice of that equitable interest sufficient to defeat a claim under the general rule of equity by a subsequent purchaser that he was a bona fide purchaser without notice of the equitable interest and therefore took what he purchased free of that interest, see §33.03. In *Coflexip Stena's Patent* (above), it was indicated that, while an agreement to assign conveys an equitable interest, it does not actually result in the intended assignee acquiring ownership; thus, such an agreement falls outside the terms of s.33, and hence also of s.68. However, the acquisition of rights against third parties would seem to be dependent on the giving of notice of the equitable assignment; notifying the UK-IPO of its existence should assist in this regard.

Rules 47 and 49 limit the obligation on applicants to provide evidence to those situations where the Comptroller has doubts about the relevant issue.

Legal proceedings

For documents to be served on the Comptroller where proceedings have been launched in the Patents Court or Patents County Court see CPR r.63.14 (reproduced in Appendix F). **32.20**

CPR 63 PD 14.1 (reprinted in §F63PD.14) requires a party in whose favour an order is made affecting the validity of an entry in the register too serve a copy of that order on the Comptroller within 14 days. Such documents as served upon the Comptroller under the Practice Directions become available to the public on the file of the patent-in-suit. There is no sanction for a failure to comply with this rule so a court order for revocation could remain unrecorded and consequently not generally known to the public. However, if there is no implementation of an order permitting amendment, the patent would appear to be unenforceable against anyone who becomes aware of such order. When an action is settled and proceedings are stayed or discontinued without formal order, no entry will occur in the register.

Where a court order permits amendment of the patent, the Comptroller can require the submission to him (within a time specified) of an amended specification prepared in accordance with Sch.2 to the Rules, see r.35(6) (see reprint, above).

Correction of errors

Correction of errors in the register, or in any document filed in connection with registration, is provided for by subs.(2)(d) and r.50 (see reprint, above), see §32.33. Where an error has occurred in the register attributable wholly or in part to an error, default or omission on the part of the UK-IPO, correction can be made under r.107, as was done, e.g. in *Coal Industry's Application* [1986] R.P.C. 57. **32.21**

The register may be rectified by the court under s.34, see commentary on it.

Rule 50 limits the obligation on applicants to provide evidence to those situations where the Comptroller has doubts about the relevant issue.

Register entries as prima facie evidence (subss.(9)–(13))

The terms "prima facie evidence", and in Scotland "sufficient evidence", in subss.(9) and (10) mean evidence which, if not balanced or outweighed by other evidence, is sufficient to establish a particular contention. Subsections (11) and (13), as supplemented by s.7 of the Civil Evidence Act 1995 (c.38) in relation to the presentation of evidence of a "hearsay" nature (as discussed in §123.50), allow certified copies impressed with the seal of the UK-IPO to be admitted in evidence without the need to produce the original, and irrespective of the computerised nature of the register. However, an entry in the register is not conclusive evidence and, if its erroneous nature can be established by evidence, the register should be rectified accordingly, as in *Eveready Battery's Patent* [2000] R.P.C. 852 discussed in §123.27. **32.22**

Subsection (12) has been repealed such that it is no longer necessary to obtain a certificate from the UK-IPO for evidence of the state of the register in criminal proceedings. Instead the Criminal Justice Act 1988 (c.88) contains general provisions as regards to the admissibility of hearsay evidence in criminal proceedings, including evidence from computerised records.

Unrepealed s.64 of the Patents and Designs Act 1907 (reprinted in §A20) provides generally that impressions of the seal of the Patent Office shall be judicially noted and admitted in evidence.

For inspection of the register and of documents filed at the UK-IPO and caveats for entries or prospective entries in the register, see §§32.34–32.36 and s.118 generally.

PRACTICE UNDER SECTION 32

Furnishing address for service

32.23   Rule 103 liberalises the previous requirement to furnish an address for service within the United Kingdom (or the Isle of Man) in certain circumstances, as discussed in §32.15 above. The rule now requires, for the purposes of any "proceedings" under the Act or Rules:

(a) any applicant for the grant of a patent (which should include further prosecution of an international application for a patent (UK) entering the United Kingdom phase under the PCT) to file an address for service in the UK (including the Isle of Man under s.132) or any EEA state or the Channel Islands;

(b) any person making an application, reference or notice of opposition under the Act or opposing any such application notice or reference to file an address for service within the UK.

In relation to European (UK) patents, the initial address for service is that of the proprietor and a United Kingdom address for service need only be furnished once the proprietor becomes involved in any contested proceeding under the Act or Rules.

Under r.104 the UK-IPO can direct a person to file an address for service where one has not been provided under r.103. Any application, opposition or reference will be treated as withdrawn if an address for service is not filed within two months of this direction.

Unlike in previous versions of the Rules, there is now no express provision that, upon grant of a patent, the address for service already recorded for the applicant becomes the address for service for the granted patent. Nevertheless, the UK-IPO practice is to treat an address for service on the register as continuing after grant, and to send to that address all correspondence relating to matters under the Patent Rules, (by airmail for addresses outside of the UK), unless and until the proprietor substitutes a new address for service. Although payment of a renewal fee does not appear to involve "proceedings" under the Act or the Rules, reminders of non-payment of renewal fees continue to be sent to the address for service entered on the register unless a different address was specified on payment of the previous renewal or otherwise notified by the proprietor.

Rule 103(3) does not expressly allow the simple withdrawal of an address for service, it merely refers to the "substitution" of a new address. This should prevent the existence of a period when there is no address for service on the register following the withdrawal of a previous address. In practice, if an agent indicates that he no longer wishes to act as an address for service, the UK-IPO will require the proprietor to file a new address for service at the start of any "proceedings" and will continue to treat the former address as the address for service for proceedings under the Act until a new address is provided.

Any proprietor or person who has already registered any right in or under a patent may file an address for service anywhere in the UK, Channel Islands, Isle of Man or EEA (although there does not appear to be any sanction for not doing so). On the other hand, any other person who makes an application to register a new interest in a patent is required to submit an address for service within the United Kingdom or Isle of Man.

"Proceedings" includes any further prosecution and, therefore, r.103 requires a United Kingdom address for service to be furnished when an international application for a patent (UK) enters the UK phase under the PCT (as discussed in §§89A.08 et seq.).

In an application made under the Act, the initial address for service is that contained in the request for grant filed under r.12(1) (see §14.10). For an international application it may conveniently be furnished on PF NP.1 when the national fee is paid (for which see §89A.22). Alternatively, PF 51 can be used, though this is not a prescribed use of this form, see (1984–85) 14 *CIPA* 155 and *Patents Journal* December 2, 1987. For a European patent (UK), the professional representative responsible for the application in the EPO has no standing, see *Deforeit's Patent* [1986] R.P.C. 142. The initial address for service is that of the proprietor, but an address for service must be furnished in compliance with r.103 once the proprietor becomes "concerned" in any proceedings under the Rules. The ways in which the address for service for a European Patent (UK) can be conveniently supplied are discussed in §77.12. No fee is required on furnishing an address for service. A simple letter will suffice. For alteration of an address for service, see §32.24.

An application to record in the register a change of proprietor or his address is likely to be regarded as "proceedings under the Rules"; thus it would require the submission of an EEA or Channel Island address.

Alteration of address for service

Written notification is all that is required to alter an address for service recorded in the register (see r.49)(1) and (3), above). The alteration can also be made at no extra cost on any PF 20 or PF 21 that is filed. However, where PF 21 is filed to record a change of proprietor, the specific question is asked whether there should be a change in the address for service in the register, and if so, this change can be made by completing Pt 4B of that form. The register is altered accordingly. If the Comptroller has any doubts about whether he should make the correction, he must inform the person making the request of the reason for his doubts.

32.24

Appointment of a new agent, as discussed in §274.06, alters the address for service only for the proceedings specified on PF 51. Where an "address for service" stated on any other patents form differs from the address for service entered on the register, the register is likewise not altered, and the address on the form is treated as an address for service only for those proceedings, see e.g. *Patents Journal* July 19, 1989.

Alteration of name or address of proprietor

A request under r.49 (see reprint, above) by the proprietor or applicant to record a change of his name (and if desired his address and/or his address for service) on the register is made by filing PF 20 for which there is at present no fee. However, the use of PF 20 is optional where the alteration is only of an address (either of the proprietor or of his address for service): notification of such in writing is all that is then required: r.49(1) and (3). No proof of change of address is normally required. Where the change is effected by amendment to the application form (PF 1), the register is updated automatically, no separate notification of change of name or address of the applicant then being required.

32.25

To record a change of name, there is required (in addition to PF 20) satisfactory evidence of the error in the name already recorded or of the change of name. Such evidence can be, for example:

for a United Kingdom company: a certificate from the Registrar of Companies;

for a United States company: a certificate from the Secretary of State of the state of incorporation;

for a German company: an appropriately certified extract from the commercial register (the Handels register);

for a French company: an original print or a certified copy of the formal announcement of change of name in, for example, "Les Petites Affiches".

In general, an official announcement in a government gazette of the change of name is sufficient for the purpose. A verified English translation must accompany any document in a foreign language (r.113(1), reprinted at §123.30). There is no need to request correction of the register where a body corporate has become a "public limited company" or "plc" (or the Welsh equivalent) with its name otherwise unchanged. Under the Patents (Companies Re-registration) Rules 1982 (see reprint, above), references to the name in the register (and in any application to the Comptroller and in any other record kept at, or any document issued by, the Office and relating to patents) are treated from the date of the change as references to the new name. If a request to amend the applicant's name on PF 1 is allowed, the register is amended in the same respect.

Patents Form 20 may be filed by an agent in his own name although the Comptroller may require him to establish his authority to do so. A single PF 20 may be used to effect the same change for a number of patents and applications listed in an annexed schedule.

Registration of transactions, instruments and events

—General

32.26 An application under r.47 (see reprint, above) to register or notify a transaction, instrument or event is made on PF 21. It is not essential for PF 21 to be accompanied by any further evidence of the transaction, instrument or event provided that this form is signed at Pt 7 by, or on behalf of, *all* parties in the case of an assignment, or by (or on behalf of) the grantor alone in the case of a mortgage, licence, sub-licence or security. The abolition of stamp duty on intellectual property assignments, for which see §30.10, has also simplified the registration of transfers of patent rights. Thus, there is now no requirement to file any supporting documents as may "suffice to establish the transaction" as was required under old r.46(2), this requirement being deemed to be met by the required signatures on PF 21. If, nevertheless, any such documents are also filed, they are normally simply placed on the file as part of the record made available to the public.

The words "on behalf of" used on PF 21 enable persons representing a party (for example a patent attorney) to sign this form, but it is advisable for such a person first to obtain written authorisation to effect that signature from the party or parties to the transaction who are required by r.47(2) to be the, or one of the, signatories for this form. The obligations and potential liabilities of an agent signing this form on behalf of one or both of the parties to the transaction, etc. to be registered was discussed in relation to an analogous requirement when registering a trade mark assignment by M. Hiddleston (*Trademark World*, November 1995, 31).

Nevertheless, the Comptroller retains the power to call for evidence to be provided (r.47(2)). Where such documentation is required to be filed under this provision, for example because the Comptroller is not satisfied with the signatures on PF 21, filing of the original document is not required; a copy certified by someone who has verified it against the original or an earlier certified copy suffices, and relevant certified extracts may be provided where disclosure of the entire document is not desired. The certification may be in the form "I certify that this is a true copy of [an extract of]...". A verified English translation must be supplied of any document in a foreign language (r.113(1)) and, if the translator works from the original, he may provide a combined certification and translation, see §§123.81 and 123.82.

If there has been a chain of successive assignments, fees can be saved by seeking to register only the final transaction in the chain. However, signatures for all the parties, or copies of each of the assignments, will need to be produced in order to satisfy the Comptroller of the entitlement of the ultimate assignee to be registered as proprietor. However, if that is done, the intermediate "links" in the chain will not be recorded in the register.

Where there has been a global assignment of patents in a variety of countries, and the patent agent has been asked to register the assignment of the United Kingdom patent, a "short form" assignment referring only to the United Kingdom was, in the past, frequently executed for the purposes of registration under s.32. However, it was confirmed in *Coflexip*

Stena's Patent [1997] R.P.C. 179 that where in such a case the rights had actually been assigned by a first assignment (as distinct from a mere agreement for future assignment), the second assignment is in principle a nullity as the rights intended to be assigned thereby had already been assigned. In this *Coflexip Stena* case, the position was saved for the patentee principally because the first assignment had not been stamped and was therefore not receivable in evidence. Thus, it could not there be proved that the second assignment was in law a nullity, see: A. Pickford [1996] *CIPA* 264; I. Karet [1996] E.I.P.R. 404; and §30.10. Note that, if the second assignment can be proved to be a nullity, the fact that it was registered should not prevent s.68 from curtailing the assignee's rights to claim monetary relief.

Where the transfer of ownership arises from the death of the registered proprietor, the Comptroller requires a certified copy of the grant of probate or of the letters of administration, followed by completion of an assignment by the executor(s), but where the executor is also the beneficiary, a signed copy of the will or a signed statement from the executor suffices (see also §§30.04 and 32.29). As there noted, where the deceased proprietor is domiciled abroad, a personal representative of the United Kingdom estate must be appointed to arrange the change of ownership.

It is possible to record a change of ownership even after the patent/application has lapsed, if only because proceedings (or compensation proceedings under s.69) may still be possible for past acts of infringement, though not if the patent has been revoked since then it is deemed never to have existed.

It is understood that an application to register an assignment of a lapsed patent, which is subject to a restoration application under s.28 can now proceed without a stay, pending the registration decision; and likewise for assignment of a patent which is the subject of proceedings before the Comptroller, whether inter partes or ex parte, although for inter partes proceedings a subsequent application will be required for substitution or addition of a party. However, where an application or patent is the subject of entitlement proceedings, an assignment will only be registered before the completion of these proceedings if consent to it is given by all parties to the dispute, or where there are special circumstances. Where entitlement proceedings are known to be pending before the court, there will normally be a stay unless all parties to the dispute consent to the registration or if evidence is provided that the court is content for the substitution of the parties (CPR 63 PD 16(3), reprinted in F63.16). In all cases, a notice will be published in the *Patents Journal* of the application to register the assignment.

—Inter-company transfers

Where company A assigns rights to company B and is then dissolved, and B subsequently changes its name to A, the latter is a different legal entity and the name of the old A should not be allowed to remain as the registered proprietor. Both the assignment and the subsequent change of name should be recorded under rr.47 and 49, using PF 21 and PF 20 respectively. **32.27**

Where a right-holding company A merges into company B, and A does not survive (whether or not there is a change of name) the merger is treated as an "event". A certificate (original or certified copy) from the state of incorporation of either company (e.g. from the Secretary of State for that State in the case of a US corporation) is required as evidence of this, together with PF 21. On the other hand, if company B merges into company A (with company A surviving) a PF 20 will suffice for recording any consequential change of name.

If a German company is converted without liquidation, but is dissolved by the conversion, a notarially certified copy of the resolution for conversion and officially certified copies of entries in the commercial registers of both previous and subsequent owners are required, together (under r.113(1)) with certified translations of these.

For further information concerning disposition of rights following a company demerger situation, see §30.03.

—Transmission on death or insolvency

32.28   On death of an individual, the original or an office copy of the grant of probate or letters of administration is required. For a foreign patentee, this will require the appointment of a personal representative resident in the United Kingdom. Where the grant is in respect of a will containing a gift of the patent or application, and the personal representative has not been registered as the proprietor, the UK-IPO will register the beneficiary under the will (if supplied with a certified copy) without requiring an assent. Until the grant is extracted from the Probate Registry, the UK-IPO regards no person as authorised to act in respect of a pending application; extensions of time are granted under r.110(1) (discussed at §123.36), but even in the absence of formal authority it may be important to file any necessary documents under the rules specified in r.110(2) where extensions or further extensions are not available.

The UK-IPO (Assignments Branch) should be consulted for its requirements in cases such as insolvency, receivership or the appointment of an administrator, or in any unusual or complex matter.

—Execution of documents

32.29   The requirements for execution of assignments, etc. by the parties are discussed at §30.05 and (under Scots law) at §31.06. Where several copies of a document were produced simultaneously on "no carbon required" paper, one of the lower copies bearing the signature in blue print was accepted for registration by the EPO as the "original" under EPC art.72 and EPC r.20(1) (J 18/84 *Register of European Patents-Entries in* OJ EPO 1987, 215; [1987] E.P.O.R. 321).

—Filing request for registration

32.30   The application for registration under r.47, see §32.07, may be made by, or on behalf of, any of the parties, but is normally filed by the beneficiary (assignee, licensee, mortgagee, etc.) to protect his interest.

The fact that PF 21 has been filed is normally entered immediately in the register and, though the requested entry may not be made for some time, it is effectively backdated under s.33(4) for the purposes of s.33(1)(a), though not necessarily for the purposes of s.68 (see *Minnesota Mining v Rennicks* [1992] R.P.C. 331 at 367). If the instrument to be recorded is a mortgage given by a United Kingdom registered company, to be effective it must also be registered as a charge at the Companies Registration Office, see §30.08.

Where the devolution of title or rights arises in the same manner for more than one patent and/or application, a single PF 21 may be filed with an annexed schedule listing them. However, if several transactions (e.g. successive assignments) are each to be entered on the register, the devolution of title is not the same; the UK-IPO then prefers the filing of a separate PF 21 for each devolution.

Where the event is an order or direction by the court (s.33(3)(e)), a copy of the order must be served on the Comptroller within 14 days (CPR 63 PD 15.1, reprinted in §F63PD.15.)

—Comptroller's requirements

32.31   The Comptroller's requirement that he be satisfied that the rights stated in the application to have been acquired is discussed in §32.27. For the possible liability to pay stamp duty, see §30.10.

Where there are joint proprietors, the Comptroller also requires to be satisfied that there has been compliance with s.36(3), see §36.05. Otherwise, if the documentation for registration appears to be in order, the circumstances under which the transaction was entered into are not considered. Challenge to its validity must then be by legal proceedings, presumably by an application for rectification of the register under s.34. The court may, where appropriate, grant an injunction restraining any disposal or licensing of specified patents pending resolution of disputed ownership (*Landi den Hartog v Sea Bird* [1975] F.S.R. 502).

—Documents placed on public file

Any document supplied for registration is placed on the patent file and becomes a matter of public record and a copy may be requested under s.118 and anyone may request a copy once the relevant patent application has been published, see r.48(1) (reprinted above). If the original (or an additional copy) is furnished, the UK-IPO endorses it as having been registered and returns it. In order to prevent terms in an instrument becoming open to public inspection, either PF 21 signed by all parties should be (without a copy of the instrument) filed, without a copy of the instrument, or extracts only of the relevant parts of the instrument should be filed with the PF 21, as described in §32.27.

32.32

Correction of errors in register or documents

An address for service, or the address of a proprietor, may be corrected under r.49(10), for which see §§32.25 and 32.26. A request for any other correction is made under r.50 on PF 11. The nature of the correction sought must be clearly identified, either on PF 11 or on a document annexed to it. However, the correction need not be presented in coloured ink, unless the Comptroller should so require to clarify the correction sought. If the error is not self-evident, or the person filing PF 11 is not obviously entitled to request correction, the Comptroller is likely to call for supporting evidence under r.82(1)(a). If the error is one which arose in the UK-IPO, correction can be requested under r.107 (discussed in §§123.25–123.27).

32.33

Requests for correction of the register are now advertised in the *Patents Journal*.

Inspection of register and documents

The easiest way of obtaining information as to whether a renewal fee has been paid (for which see §25.11), is to access relevant information on the UK-IPO website (*http://www.ipo.gov.uk*) by entering either the publication or application number (prefaced by GB) and viewing the details. This requires no fee. In this way, it can also be ascertained whether search and examination fees have been paid. The register (or entries or reproductions of entries in it) is available by the public at the Office in Newport or London between the hours of 9am and 5pm on weekdays, other than Saturdays and days which are specified as excluded days for the purposes of s.120. In the case of a non-documentary part of the register, the right of inspection is a right to inspect the material on the register.

32.34

For other ways of inspecting the register; and for obtaining copies of entries in the register, and/or copies of documents on the public file, and/or for information as to payment of renewal fees, see §118.19. For the certification of such copies, see §32.38. For information on the status of supplementary protection certificates, see §§118.18 and B20. However, r.48(3) expressly restricts the copying of documents which are not open to public inspection.

On occasion the register has erroneously indicated that a patent has lapsed, and in an important case it is prudent to ask for the Comptroller's certificate that the patent has lapsed rather than rely on inspection of the register. However, it is not clear whether the Comptroller would be liable for loss arising if he issued such a certificate in error of the true position, on which see §123.27. The UK-IPO has requested, through the Chartered Institute, that it be notified if any inconsistencies or irregularities in register entries should be discovered: (1991–92) 21 *CIPA* 157.

For further information on documents open to public inspection, see §§118.07–118.15.

There is maintained at the Science, Technology and Business Section in Science 1 South of the British Library at 96 Euston Road, London NW1 2DB (tel. 020 7412 7919/7920) an index known as the Assignment Index. This is arranged yearly in alphabetical order of assignees, etc. It includes entries relating to recorded changes of proprietorship arising from assignments, mergers, or changes of name, as well as licences and mortgages in respect of granted patents; and, since 1992, of applications (whether published or unpublished). This Index is available for inspection without fee. It provides a useful supplement to the published name indexes of applicants (for which see §123.50) to cover those cases where assignment of the application has resulted in a change in proprietorship.

Inspection of Register of European Patents

32.35   The European register maintained by the EPO in the form of the EPIDOS database may be accessed directly by computer link (as described in §118.08) or (without charge) by telephone inquiry during normal office hours to the EPO information desk at Munich (00 49 89 2399 4538) or The Hague (00 31 70 90 67 89) (see OJ EPO 1987, 197). The EP publication number should be quoted if possible, though the application number may be used.

The Register of European Patents (UK) is incorporated into the register of patents maintained by the UK-IPO and can be accessed in the same way, including internet access as described in §32.35. Indeed, it has been noticed that the information provided here about European patents (UK) can contain information generated pre-grant which is additional to that provided by an EPIDOS printout of the European register obtained from the EPO. However, the United Kingdom register contains no details of applications for a European patent (UK) other than their number, with no differential indication whether such an application has failed or is still pending. For information on these, the European register should thus be directly accessed.

A request for information concerning an application for a European patent (UK) will be met by supply of a current extract of the European register in the form of a computer printout. Facilities also exist at the British Library (Science, Technology and Business Section) for obtaining information from the register of European patents; for the location of which see §32.35.

Caveats

32.36   A request for certain kinds of information, known as a "caveat", may be filed under s.118(1) and r.54, as discussed more fully in §§118.16–118.18. Application is made on PF 49 for information to be given when an entry is made in the register or an application is made for the making of an entry. If such a caveat is filed in respect of an application to register an assignment or licence, registration is suspended for a short time to give the caveator (enquirer) an opportunity to prevent registration, e.g. by seeking an injunction from the court. In a proper case registration may be stayed to await the outcome of legal proceedings, see §32.31.

Certificate from Comptroller

32.37   Rules 46 and 48(2) (reprinted above) require PF 23 to be filed to obtain any certificate of the Comptroller. The person filing the form must be duly authorised if it is filed in respect of a document not yet open to public inspection. This constitutes evidence in accordance with subss.(11) and (12). Thus, if an application has not yet been published under s.16, PF 23 will only be accepted if filed by the applicant or his previously authorised agent, see §118.19. However, anyone may obtain a certified copy of the register or of any document open to public inspection under r.48(1) (reprinted above). The wording on PF 23 suggests that the address for dispatch of the certificate need not be in the United Kingdom.

The person making the request on PF 23 must state whether he has any special requirements, such as the need for patent register extracts or details of renewal payments made, and the number and type of certificates required divided as between those authenticated by a rubber stamp impression and those for which the certificates are to be signed and sealed. A separate fee is charged for each certificate required. There is a higher fee for a certificate sealed with the seal of the UK-IPO (whether or not attached to documents). There is now no separate copying charge.

A request can be made for a certified copy of a specification indicating that a correction or amendment has been made and the date when it was requested and/or allowed. This may be important in registering a granted United Kingdom patent abroad. Where certification of a printed specification is required, if requested, the UK-IPO supplies the printed copy without charge.

Section 118(4) states that an entity may make a request to inspect and obtain copies of the register when it is notified that: (i) an application has been made but not yet published; and (ii) the applicant will, if the patent is granted, bring proceedings against the recipient in the event of his doing an act specified in the notice after the application is published. In such circumstances, the Comptroller should supply copies as well as or allowing inspection without charge (*Burralls of Wisbech Ltd's Application* [2004] R.P.C. 14). Nevertheless r.48(3) expressly imports the restrictions prescribed under s.118(2), which prevent the Comptroller from communicating information about unpublished applications to third parties. Accordingly, if an application has not yet been published under s.16, PF 23 will only be accepted if filed by the applicant or his previously authorised agent or the circumstances of s.118(4) apply.

Certification of priority documents

Certified copies of United Kingdom applications for use as priority documents under the Paris Convention must be ordered on PF 23 so they can be "signed and sealed" (Notice in the *Patents Journal* of December 17, 2003). A separate charge is no longer made to cover the cost of copying. If a certified copy is required urgently, this should be stated prominently on PF 23, preferably in red ink. **32.38**

Where a withdrawn application under the Act serves as a priority document for a later application under r.6(3)(b), a single request on PF 23 suffices for a certified copy of both applications. If an earlier United Kingdom application was withdrawn without being open to public inspection and leaving no rights outstanding, the Comptroller will certify accordingly in the terms of art.4C(4) of the Paris Convention: *Patents Journal* September 19, 1962.

Certified copies of priority documents are now created within the formalities units of the UK-IPO. Enquiries concerning expedited or delayed certification should be addressed to the appropriate unit, followed up if necessary by a general inquiry to 0044 (0)1633 814611: (1990–91) 20 *CIPA* 415. Certified copies of applications not yet open to public inspection are, however, only supplied to the applicant personally or to his agent of record, see §118.19.

The countries for which the copies are required can be specified, and the UK-IPO can then provide certification appropriate for each. For example, a copy of PF 7 is automatically included in a certified copy for the United States; and, where legalisation is necessary, the certificate bears the manuscript signature of the Comptroller which can be authenticated by the Foreign and Commonwealth Office before this is legalised by the appropriate consulate. However, if it is not desired to identify to persons later inspecting the file all the countries for which priority documents have been requested, it is recommended that PF 23 itself should simply state the number of certificates required, with only the countries listed for which specially worded certificates are required.

When an application is abandoned, withdrawn, taken to be withdrawn or refused before publication under s.16, the UK-IPO file is now normally destroyed at the end of the seventh year from its date of filing, but there are exceptions (for which see §118.19 and *Patents Journal* March 18, 1998). Certified copies, as may still be required for foreign applications, will then not be available and should therefore have been obtained in advance of destruction. However, the date of destruction can be obtained from the UK-IPO who are also prepared to re-certify a copy of a previously certified document obtained from some other UK-IPO, see (1990–91) 20 *CIPA* 415.

SECTION 33

Effect of registration, etc., on rights in patents

33.—(1) Any person who claims to have acquired the property in a patent or **33.01**

application for a patent by virtue of any transaction, instrument or event to which this section applies shall be entitled as against any other person who claims to have acquired that property by virtue of an earlier transaction, instrument or event to which this section applies if, at the time of the later transaction, instrument or event—

(a) the earlier transaction, instrument or event was not registered, or

(b) in the case of any application which has not been published, notice of the earlier transaction, instrument or event had not been given to the comptroller, and

(c) in any case, the person claiming under the later transaction, instrument or event, did not know of the earlier transaction, instrument or event.

(2) Subsection (1) above shall apply equally to the case where any person claims to have acquired any right in or under a patent or application for a patent, by virtue of a transaction, instrument or event to which this section applies, and that right is incompatible with any such right acquired by virtue of an earlier transaction, instrument or event to which this section applies.

(3) This section applies to the following transactions, instruments and events—

(a) the assignment or assignation of a patent or application for a patent, or a right in it;

(b) the mortgage of a patent or application or the granting of security over it;

(c) the grant, assignment or assignation of a licence or sub-licence, or mortgage of a licence or sub-licence, under a patent or application;

(d) the death of the proprietor or one of the proprietors of any such patent or application or any person having a right in or under a patent or application and the vesting by an assent of personal representatives of a patent, application or any such right; and

(e) any order or directions of a court or other competent authority—

(i) transferring a patent or application or any right in or under it to any person; or

(ii) that an application should proceed in the name of any person;

and in either case the event by virtue of which the court or authority had power to make any such order or give any such directions.

(4) Where an application for the registration of a transaction, instrument or event has been made, but the transaction, instrument or event has not been registered, then, for the purposes of subsection (1)(a) above, registration of the application shall be treated as registration of the transaction, instrument or event.

COMMENTARY ON SECTION 33

Scope of the section

33.02 Section 33 deals with the effect of entries in the register of patents concerning rights in patents. It applies to applications as well as patents and also to European patents (UK) and applications (ss.77(1), 78(2)). It applies to the transactions, instruments and events listed in subs.(3): these affect title to a patent or application and are considered generally under s.30.

The Intellectual Property (Enforcement, etc.) Regulations 2006 (SI 2006/1028, reg.2(2) and Sch.2(4)) amended the effect of a failure to register a transaction, instrument or event to which s.33 applies. For discussion of these changes, and the consequences of non-registration on the recovery of costs and expenses in litigation, see the commentary on s.68, and in particular §§68.02 and 68.04.

Article 33 of Council Regulation (EC) No 44/2001 of 22 December 2000 on Jurisdiction and the Recognition and Enforcement of Judgments in Civil and Commercial Matters requires EU Member States to recognise judgments given in other Member States without further proceedings. This applies unless the judgment is irreconcilable with an earlier judgement between the same parties in the UK or an earlier judgment in another Member State able to be given recognition. Denmark is not covered by this Regulation, but is party to the Brussels Regulation 44/2001 (previously Convention), and Iceland, Switzerland and Norway are signatories of the Lugano Convention on Jurisdiction and Enforcement of Judgments in Civil and Commercial Matters, which makes very similar provisions. Therefore an application to enter a court order on the register transferring a patent or application, or stating that the application is to proceed in the name of another person, made by a court in the European Economic Area, should be accepted unless it cannot be reconciled with an earlier court order.

Priority by registration or notice (subss. (1) and (2))

Subsections (1) and (2) provide that a person who acquires the property in, or a right in **33.03** or under, a patent or application is not affected by an earlier transaction, instrument or event if he did not know of it at the time of his own acquisition and if at that time it had not been registered or (if the application had not yet been published under s.16) notified to the Comptroller under s.32, see §32.19. Thus, a bona fide purchaser without notice of some unregistered defect in the title which he has acquired is likely to retain ownership despite that defect. The degree of "knowledge" which is required to override this provision is discussed in §33.04 and the importance of the section was discussed by A.K. Lewis [1979] E.I.P.R. 217. Subsection (4) provides that, for the purpose of the section, registration is backdated to the date of application for the entry to be made in the register: but, for the purposes of s.68 (loss of monetary relief prior to registration), it is the date of registration which is critical, see §68.03. The later transaction, instrument or event need not itself be registered, but will only take effect as against subsequent transactions when notice of it has been given to the public by an application to register it. In *Mölnycke AB v Proctor & Gamble Ltd* [1994] R.P.C. 49 at 138 the Court of Appeal rejected the argument that entry in the register of a notice that a s.32 application had been filed was equivalent to registration. The purpose of subs.(4) is to secure priority for a person who claims an interest in a patent and seeks registration. It is not to substitute for the requirement of registration of the particular transaction or instrument a lesser requirement that an application has been made for registration of an unspecified transaction or instrument.

Knowledge

Besides prior registration, knowledge of the earlier transaction, instrument or event **33.04** deprives a person of the benefit of subss.(1) and (2) even if that knowledge is not definite or complete. In *Transfer Systems v International Consultants* BL O/1/05, the hearing officer held that the beneficiaries of an earlier assignment of a patent were entitled to be registered as proprietors, despite the fact that they had failed to register their assignment, as the subsequent assignee (who had registered his assignment) had knowledge of the earlier assignment.

It is not clear whether subs.(1)(c) requires actual knowledge, or whether constructive or imputed knowledge would suffice, see §32.19.

In *Morey's Patent* (1858) 25 Beav. 581; 53 E.R. 759), where a patentee had assigned half the patent to A and afterwards assigned the whole to B by a deed reciting that he had already granted a "licence" to A, and B's assignment was registered first, the court held that B had constructive notice of A's rights and ordered an entry to be made in the register that the "licence" referred to in B's assignment was the subsequently registered assignment to A. More generally, proof of knowledge on the part of a person may be based on evidence that he:

"had deliberately shut his eyes to the obvious or refrained from inquiry because he suspected the truth but did not wish to have his suspicion confirmed" (*Westminster City Council v Croyalgrange* [1986] 2 All E.R. 353; [1986] 1 W.L.R. 674 HL *per* Lord Bridge).

Whether this imposes an obligation to inspect the file of the patent as well as its register entry remains to be decided, see §32.19.

Decided cases

33.05   In *Tamglass Ltd OY v Luoyang North Glass Technology Co Ltd* [2006] EWHC 65 Ch; [2006] F.S.R. 33, the High Court considered issues of whether a transfer of title to a patent, which had been effected by a series of corporate mergers and demergers under Finnish law, fell within one of the categories of transfer set out at s.33(3). Mann J. held that the transfer could not be an assignment under s.33(3)(a), since an assignment should be construed as being affected by an inter partes consensual document. He also held that the transfer was not an "order or directions of a court or competent authority" despite the fact that the Finnish mergers authority had approved the mergers/de-mergers, since this approval did not amount to an order effecting the transfer. As a result, the transfer of title in issue fell outside of s.33(3), and hence fell outside of s.68, with the result that the claimant was able to recover damages for the period in which the correct title holder had not been registered as such. The judge did not come to his decision lightly, and expressed some discomfort about the conclusion he had reached. In the later case of *Siemens Schweiz AG v Thorn Security Ltd* [2007] EWHC 2242 Ch., the same judge reluctantly held that a transfer of a patent by operation of Swiss merger law, via the Swiss doctrine of universal succession (which process resulted in the transferral of assets, including the patent in suit, by operation of law, without the need for what Mann J. called any "special acts of assignment") similarly fell outside the scope of s.33(3). However, on appeal and reported sub nom. *Thorn Security Ltd v Siemens Schweiz AG* [2009] R.P.C. 3, the Court of Appeal held that "…'assignment' is inherently capable of more than one meaning" and warned against a narrow literal approach, continuing that in s.33(3) the expression "transactions, instruments or events" was "wide and open-textured". Thus "there is no reason why an assignment, if given a wide meaning, should not be an instrument in some circumstances and an event in other circumstances" or a combination of them. Hence the transfer was ordered to be recorded, and *Tamglass* as well as Mann J.'s decision expressly overruled. Thus the relevant provisions apply to an assignment by operation of law where there is no assignment document, see also §68.02.

In *Finecard International Ltd v Urquhart-Dykes & Lord* [2005] EWHC 2481, the High Court held that an exclusive licence which replaced and extended the scope of a registered exclusive licence must itself be registered.

PRACTICE UNDER SECTION 33

General

33.06   Registration of any transaction, instrument or event to which s.33 applies is governed by r.47 and is dealt with under s.32.

Desirability of registration and inspection of register and file

33.07   Registration is obviously desirable to prevent the proprietor or former proprietor purporting to grant incompatible rights in the future. In the absence of registration, rights to monetary relief for infringement may be lost, see s.68. Where there is doubt as to registerability of a claim to have an interest in or under a patent or application, the application on PF 21 should be accompanied by a letter to the Comptroller setting out the claim, see §32.19. A third party who inspects the file, or who deliberately refrains from such inquiry, may then be fixed with knowledge of the claim and may be unable to rely on subss.(2) and (3), even if no entry is made in the register, see §§32.19 and 33.04.

Conversely, a person seeking to rely on the protection of subs.(2) or (3) should inspect the public file under r.51 at the same time as the register. A single request on PF 23 suffices for both.

SECTION 34

Rectification of register

34.—(1) The court may, on the application of any person aggrieved, order the register to be rectified by the making, or the variation or deletion, of any entry in it. **34.01**

(2) In proceedings under this section the court may determine any question which it may be necessary or expedient to decide in connection with the rectification of the register.

(3) Rules of court may provide for the notification of any application under this section to the comptroller and for his appearance on the application and for giving effect to any order of the court on the application.

Commentary on Section 34

Scope of the section

Section 34 provides for rectification of the register by the court. It is applicable also to European patents (UK), but not to applications for European Patents (UK), because no separate register is created for these, see §§32.18 and 78.06. The section provides a remedy for wrongful refusal by the Comptroller to register a transaction, instrument or event under s.32, as discussed in §32.19; and also a remedy in respect of an entry in the register which should not have been made. As indicated in §32.33, errors in the register can be corrected by direct application to the Comptroller under r.49(3), r.50 or r.107. **34.02**

It is uncertain whether a patent granted by the Comptroller ultra vires, e.g. because a time limit was not met which the Comptroller had no power to excuse (see *E's Applications* [1983] R.P.C. 231 HL), is a nullity and thus subject to rectification of the register; if the grant is merely voidable and not void, s.72(1) specifies the only grounds upon which it could be revoked, see §72.09.

The Comptroller should be served with a claim form for rectification and any accompanying documentation (CPR 63.14) at the same time as other parties. Any order affecting the validity of an entry on the register must be served on the Comptroller by the court and the party in whose favour the order is made within 14 days (CPR 63 PD 14.1).

Forum for rectification

Application for rectification of the register under s.34 must be made to the court. The "court" is defined in s.130. The courts of Scotland, Northern Ireland and the Isle of Man appear also to have jurisdiction in addition to the Patents Court and Patents County Court, see §96.24. The Civil Jurisdiction and Judgments Act 1982 (c.27) by s.17, Sch.5 para.2 and Sch.8 para.4(2), appears specifically to exclude provision for exclusive jurisdiction of any one court of the United Kingdom (excluding for this purpose the Isle of Man). **34.03**

Applicant for rectification

An applicant for rectification under s.34 must be a "person aggrieved" (subs.(1)). This may be a person who has some proprietary interest in the patent in question, as in *Manning's Patent* (1903) 20 R.P.C. 74 where the purchaser of a share of a patent was held to be a person aggrieved by the entry of an assignment of a share purporting to have been made by someone who in fact was a bankrupt. However, the proprietor himself is not a "person aggrieved"; thus under analogous provisions in Ireland a patentee failed to rectify the register to delete a priority date claimed for his patent (*Beecham Group's Irish Application* [Ireland] [1983] F.S.R. 355). **34.04**

Where an applicant seeking to rectify the register to annul the recording of a purported assignment is being sued by the currently registered proprietor, that applicant is "a person aggrieved" within the meaning of s.34, as s.68 may protect him from damages for infringement until such time as the currently registered proprietor may become properly registered, see *Coflexip Stena's Patent* [1997] R.P.C. 179 discussed in §§30.10 and 32.26.

Effect of rectification

34.05   A court order for rectification is given effect by serving a copy upon the Comptroller at the same time as other parties under CPR 63.14. CPR Pt 63 is reprinted in Appendix F. Rectification will not be ordered if the entry in the register, although incorrect when proceedings began, is no longer incorrect at the date of the hearing (*Manning's Patent* (1903) 20 R.P.C. 74, see also *Coflexip Stena's Patent* [1997] R.P.C. 179).

PRACTICE UNDER SECTION 34

Procedure for rectification before the Patents Court

34.06   Any application for rectification of the register made to the Patents Court requires a copy of the claim form to be served on the other party or parties and on the Comptroller (CPR 63.14). The Comptroller is entitled to take part in the proceedings once the documents have been served on him (CPR 63.15). Accordingly, once the Comptroller has received the documents, he then usually indicates (via the Treasury Solicitor) whether he wishes to appear and be heard. This generally depends on whether there is any other respondent to the application. If the Comptroller does appear, his costs become an issue in the proceedings as with any other party. Proceedings in relation to a foreign patentee (who ought to be a respondent to them) can be served upon the address for service recorded in the register of patents provided the address is within the jurisdiction (CPR 63.14(2)(a)), as discussed in §32.15.

The proceedings need not come before the judge for directions as to the conduct of the proceedings where the parties have agreed the pre-trial directions which should be given, see *Patents Court Guide*, para.4.2 (reprinted in Appendix G). As there stated, the agreed order can then be obtained by supplying a draft of it, together with the written consent of all the parties' respective solicitors or counsel, to the Clerk in charge of the Patents List. Often such directions will include provision for evidence to be given by written witness statements with liberty to cross-examine the witnesses. The directions may include liberty to apply to the master if any further directions are required.

Effecting rectification of the register

34.07   Rectication will follow automatically from a decision of the court when an office copy of the court order is transmitted to the UK-IPO within 14 days, see §32.30. An order for revocation of the patent should also be served on the Comptroller within 14 days as discussed above.

SECTION 35 [REPEALED]

Evidence of register, documents, etc.

35.01   **35.** [...]

Note. Section 35 was repealed by the Patents, Designs and Marks Act 1986 (c.39) s.3 and Sch.3, as from January 1, 1989 (SI 1988/1824), with no continuing effect, because the provisions of the section were at the same time re-enacted in modified form in substituted s.32(4)–(13), see §32.01. These provisions are discussed in §§32.14, 32.22 and 32.37.

SECTION 36

Co-ownership of patents and applications for patents

36.01   **36.**—(1) Where a patent is granted to two or more persons, each of them shall, subject to any agreement to the contrary, be entitled to an equal undivided share in the patent.

(2) Where two or more persons are proprietors of a patent, then, subject to the provisions of this section and subject to any agreement to the contrary—

    (a) each of them shall be entitled, by himself or his agents, to do in respect of the invention concerned, for his own benefit and without the consent of or the need to account to the other or others, any act which would apart from this subsection and section 55 below, amount to an infringement of the patent concerned; and

    (b) any such act shall not amount to an infringement of the patent concerned.

(3) Subject to the provisions of sections 8 and 12 above and section 37 below and to any agreement for the time being in force, where two or more persons are proprietors of a patent one of them shall not without the consent of the other or others—

    (a) amend the specification of the patent or apply for such an amendment to be allowed or for the patent to be revoked, or

    (b) grant a licence under the patent or assign or mortgage a share in the patent or in Scotland cause or permit security to be granted over it.

(4) Subject to the provisions of those sections, where two or more persons are proprietors of a patent, anyone else may supply one of those persons with the means, relating to an essential element of the invention, for putting the invention into effect, and the supply of those means by virtue of this subsection shall not amount to an infringement of the patent.

(5) Where a patented product is disposed of by any of two or more proprietors to any person, that person and any other person claiming through him shall be entitled to deal with the product in the same way as if it had been disposed of by a sole registered proprietor.

(6) Nothing in subsection (1) or (2) above shall affect the mutual rights or obligations of trustees or of the personal representatives of a deceased person, or their rights or obligations as such.

(7) The foregoing provisions of this section shall have effect in relation to an application for a patent which is filed as they have effect in relation to a patent and—

    (a) references to a patent and a patent being granted shall accordingly include references respectively to any such application and to the application being filed; and

    (b) the reference in subsection (5) above to a patented product shall be construed accordingly.

Note. Subsection (3) was amended by the Patents Act 2004 (c.16) s.9, with effect from October 1, 2005 (SI 2005/2471).

COMMENTARY ON SECTION 36

Scope of the section

Section 36, in the absence of agreement to the contrary, defines the respective rights and **36.02** obligations of co-owners of patents (except those who have become co-owners as trustees or personal representatives, see subs.(6)), and it also protects those who purchase patented articles from a co-owner or supply a co-owner with means for putting the patented invention into effect. Section 36 applies also to applications (subs.(7)) and to European patents (UK) and applications (ss.77(1), 78(2)).

In *Henry Bros v Ministry of Defence* [1999] R.P.C. 442, the Court of Appeal was critical of the drafting of this and other sections of the Act relevant to co-ownership and recommended that, in any revision of Act and the EPC, the relative rights of co-owners should be specifically considered. For example, there are problems in interpreting s.36, for which see §36.04. Also, at that time it was not clear whether a co-owner could himself apply to amend the patent—a point which the courts avoided in the *Henry* case—or whether a co-owner could seek revocation of the patent in order to promote competition against the other co-owner. However, with effect from October 1, 2005, the 2004 Act clarified both of these points by adding in subs.(3)(a), which makes it clear that amendment of the patent, or an application for revocation requires the consent of the co-owner. For a review of joint ownership of intellectual property, see J. Marchese [1999] E.I.P.R. 364, although this predates this amendment.

Disputes between co-owners can be resolved by proceedings under s.37. Where the application is still pending, then any dispute as to how the application should proceed can be referred to the Comptroller under s.10 (see commentary above under that section).

Prima facie entitlement of co-owners to equal undivided shares in patent

36.03   Co-ownership of property generally may be as joint tenants, where the survivor acquires ownership of the whole automatically, or as tenants in common, where ownership of a deceased owner's share devolves on his personal representatives; and the share of a company which is dissolved becomes vested in the Crown as bona vacantia. The wording of subs.(1) provides that, unless otherwise agreed, two or more persons to whom a patent is granted hold it as tenants in common in equal shares. An allegation by a co-owner that he had a greater share was rejected on the evidence in *Florey's Patent* [1962] R.P.C. 186—but this was under the 1949 Act.

Trustees *inter se* hold property as joint tenants, and subs.(6) preserves their position in this respect. The existence of a possible constructive trust of ownership was in issue in *Kakkar v Szelke* [1989] F.S.R. 255; [1989] E.P.O.R. 184 CA. For the registrability of equitable interests of this type, see §32.19.

Where joint proprietors acquire their interest after grant, the instrument by which they do so normally indicates whether they hold the property as tenants in common (and, if so, in what shares), or as joint tenants. The former is usual, and is implied in a business relationship or where the co-owners contribute unequally to the cost. For the terms which are implied into an instrument for the disposition of property rights by the laws of property, see §30.07.

In *Magill's Application* BL O/256/00, a payment default provision in an agreement providing a condition for assignment of "30% of the patent application" was held to be void for uncertainty, such phrase having no clear meaning, particularly in view of the wording of s.36.

M. Anderson has discussed (*Patent World*, October 1990, 24) the application of real property laws to intellectual property, with particular reference to s.34 of the Law of Property Act 1925 (c.20); and, following the amendment of other sections of that Act by the Law of Property (Miscellaneous Provisions) Act 1994 (c.36), again at pp.241–255, and in particular at pp.254–255, of his book *Technology: The Law of Exploitation and Transfer* (Butterworths, 1996).

Rights and freedom of each co-owner (subss.(2), (4) and (5))

36.04   Subsection (2) provides that, unless they have agreed otherwise (and subject to the position of trustees or personal representatives under subs.(6)), any of the co-owners may for his own benefit do any act which would otherwise be an infringement of the patent. There is no obligation for the co-owner to account to the other co-owners for such acts.

Minnesota Mining's International Application [2003] R.P.C. 28 at 541 considered the rights of co-owners and whether there should be an order for cross-royalties to be paid between two co-owners. Although it was held that such an order would be possible under s.36, it was considered inappropriate in this case. The decision also considered the division of patenting costs, and marking requirements.

There is, however, an exclusion to the rule of one co-owner not accounting to the other when it comes to acts of Crown use, so that compensation under ss.55(4) and 57A (discussed at §55.19, §57A.02–57A.07 and §58.05) is due to all the co-owners if one of them is authorised to use the invention for the services of the Crown (*Patchett's Patent* [1963] R.P.C. 90—but this was under the 1949 Act). This right extends to a co-owner's agents (which term here does not seem to have its normal legal meaning, and has been held to protect "home use" so that a co-owner may have the patented product made for him) (see *Henry Bros v Ministry of Defence* [1997] R.P.C. 693; and [1999] R.P.C. 442 CA). Here, "home use", at least by the Crown, was held by the Court of Appeal to have a very wide scope and includes use of the patent by the Crown's agents for the Crown's own benefit. How far this right of home use does, however, extend is unclear; the Court of Appeal went little further than stating that it does not extend to the large-scale corporation through the grant of licences, see also *Howard & Bullough v Tweedales & Smalley* (1895) 12 R.P.C. 519 for a discussion of infringements by "agents" under the common law formerly applicable.

Subsections (4) and (5) save a supplier to one co-owner from being an indirect infringer under s.60(2) (discussed at §60.08) and also protect persons acquiring a patented product from one co-owner only. The protection extends to acts done before grant of the patent, see subs.(7)(b). "Patented product" is defined in s.130(1) (discussed in §60.03). It includes a product to which a patented process has been applied, as well as the "products" referred to in s.60(1)(a) and (c).

Rights not exercisable by co-owners individually without consent (subs.(3))

The amendment of s.36(3) places an additional restraint on a co-owner in that, without consent of all other co-owners, or by virtue of a prior agreement, no application may be made to amend or revoke the patent, nor may the patent be amended. For example, if A and B are the original proprietors, but in entitlement proceedings C, rather than B, is found to be a rightful co-owner, C is not entitled to have the patent revoked. Instead, C (under s.37) should apply to be added as a co-owner and for B to be removed. If A and B were found both to be wrongly entitled, with C and D found to be the rightful co-owners, the patent could be revoked and leave granted to the filing of a replacement application by C and D, provided that both agree to do this.

36.05

Except where so directed by an order made in proceedings under s.37 (see ss.37(1)(c) and 37(2)(c), discussed at §37.10), one co-owner cannot license the patent, or assign or mortgage his share in it, without the consent of all the others (subs.(3)). This prohibition is expressly reserved in ss.30(2) and (4) and 31(2). The consent given by other co-owners for the purpose of overriding subs.(3) need not be in writing, but written evidence of it is required if the licence, assignment or mortgage is to be registered under s.32, see §32.30.

A co-owner can apply to the Comptroller for an order that he be able to grant a licence, whether or not there is an entitlement dispute. In *Hughes v Paxman* [2007] R.P.C. 2; [2006] EWCA Civ 818 (appealing BL O/143/05; and [2005] EWHC 2240 Pat Ct, noted [2005] *CIPA* 398, and 735), the Court of Appeal held that the Comptroller did have discretion to grant a licence, but the co-owner seeking to have the licence granted had to set out the terms he wanted, as the court doubted that the Comptroller had the power to grant one co-owner an untrammelled right to license the patent generally. Section 36(3) was subject to the provisions of ss.8, 12, and 37 and there was no need for there to be an entitlement dispute before the Comptroller had the power to grant a licence, but he had to act rationally, fairly and proportionately. However, the Comptroller only has "a power to produce a fair commercial solution when co-owners cannot agree". The Comptroller has subsequently interpreted this (*Hughes v Paxman* BL O/217/08) as requiring the parties first to show that they are deadlocked and then whether the terms sought represent a fair and commercial solution. In *Hughes v Paxman*, he found that he did not need to intervene as the parties had reached agreement previously and a licence had been granted to a third party with the royalties being split equally between the co-owners.

Rights against infringers

36.06   Each co-owner has the rights of the proprietor as regards infringement of the patent (s.66(1)), and one co-owner may sue for infringement, or claim compensation for Crown use, without joining the others as claimants, as in *Turner v Bowman* (1925) 42 R.P.C. 29 where the co-owner had exceeded his authority to act. In such circumstances another co-owner may himself be sued for infringement. In any case, other co-owners must be made parties to the proceedings, if only as nominal defendants, so that at least they have notice of it, see s.66(2) and s.58(13) discussed respectively in §66.02 and §58.07.

PRACTICE UNDER SECTION 36

36.07   Section 36 provides only a basic framework of the rights and obligations of co-owners: this is often unsatisfactory in practice, see §36.02 and §36.04. Co-ownership should, therefore, only be entered into on the basis of an agreement between the co-owners which clearly defines the rights and obligations of each. The provisions of subss.(2) and (3) can be overridden by agreement (*Young v Wilson* (1955) 72 R.P.C. 351—in relation to the 1949 Act), and this may be particularly important where one co-owner has facilities to work the invention himself but another can only do so by licensing a third party. An agreement between co-owners should indicate whether co-ownership is as tenants in common (and, if so, in what shares—although note *Magill's Application* BL O/256/00 where the wording chosen was uncertain and rendered the agreement void) or joint tenants, see §36.03, and it should define the responsibility for paying renewal fees, suing infringers and resisting revocation or compulsory licensing. The agreement should also state how any money which may be received from the patent by way of assignment, licensing, damages or compensation for Crown use is to be shared. It should also provide for what would happen if the parties cannot agree over revocation or amendment.

The possible dangers of failing to comply with obligations in a co-ownership agreement are illustrated by *BICC v Burndy* [1985] R.P.C. 273 CA, where one party had failed to reimburse the other for renewal fees and was saved from having to relinquish its share in the patents only by the court exercising its discretion in equity against forfeiture.

SECTION 37

Determination of right to patent after grant

37.01   **37.**—(1) After a patent has been granted for an invention any person having or claiming a proprietary interest in or under the patent may refer to the comptroller the question—

(a) who is or are the true proprietor or proprietors of the patent,

(b) whether the patent should have been granted to the person or persons to whom it was granted, or

(c) whether any right in or under the patent should be transferred or granted to any other person or persons;

and the comptroller shall determine the question and make such order as he thinks fit to give effect to the determination.

(2) Without prejudice to the generality of subsection (1) above, an order under that subsection may contain provision—

(a) directing that the person by whom the reference is made under that subsection shall be included (whether or not to the exclusion of any other person) among the persons registered as proprietors of the patent;

(b) directing the registration of a transaction, instrument or event by virtue of which that person has acquired any right in or under the patent;

(c) granting any licence or other right in or under the patent;

(d) directing the proprietor of the patent or any person having any right in or under the patent to do anything specified in the order as necessary to carry out the other provisions of the order.

(3) If any person to whom directions have been given under subsection (2)(d) above fails to do anything necessary for carrying out any such directions within 14 days after the date of the order containing the directions, the comptroller may, on application made to him by any person in whose favour or on whose reference the order containing the directions was made, authorise him to do that thing on behalf of the person to whom the directions were given.

(4) Where the comptroller finds on a reference under this section that the patent was granted to a person not entitled to be granted that patent (whether alone or with other persons) and on application made under section 72 below makes an order on that ground for the conditional or unconditional revocation of the patent, the comptroller may order that the person by whom the application was made or his successor in title may, subject to section 76 below, make a new application for a patent—

(a) in the case of unconditional revocation, for the whole of the matter comprised in the specification of that patent; and

(b) in the case of conditional revocation, for the matter which in the opinion of the comptroller should be excluded from that specification by amendment under section 75 below;

and where such new application is made, it shall be treated as having been filed on the date of filing the application for the patent to which the reference relates.

(5) On any such reference no order shall be made under this section transferring the patent to which the reference relates on the ground that the patent was granted to a person not so entitled, and no order shall be made under subsection (4) above on that ground, if the reference was made after the end of the period of two years beginning with the date of the grant, unless it is shown that any person registered as a proprietor of the patent knew at the time of the grant or, as the case may be, of the transfer of the patent to him that he was not entitled to the patent.

(6) An order under this section shall not be so made as to affect the mutual rights or obligations of trustees or of the personal representatives of a deceased person, or their rights or obligations as such.

(7) Where a question is referred to the comptroller under this section an order shall not be made by virtue of subsection (2) or under subsection (4) above on the reference unless notice of the reference is given to all persons registered as proprietor of the patent or as having a right in or under the patent, except those who are parties to the reference.

(8) If it appears to the comptroller on a reference under this section that the question referred to him would more properly be determined by the court, he may decline to deal with it and, without prejudice to the court's jurisdiction to determine any such question and make a declaration, or any declaratory jurisdiction of the court in Scotland, the court shall have jurisdiction to do so.

(9) The court shall not in the exercise of any such declaratory jurisdiction determine a question whether a patent was granted to a person not entitled to be granted the patent if the proceedings in which the jurisdiction is invoked were commenced after the end of the period of two years beginning with the date of

the grant of the patent, unless it is shown that any person registered as a proprietor of the patent knew at the time of the grant or, as the case may be, of the transfer of the patent to him that he was not entitled to the patent.

Notes

1. Section 130(7) requires subs.(5) to be construed in conformity with the corresponding provisions of the EPC, CPC and PCT. The relevant provision here is art.23(1)–(3) of the CPC (reprinted below). This appears to have been given effect by s.37(5) even though the CPC has never come into effect.

2. Subsections (1), (4), (7) and (8) were amended by the CDPA 1988 (c.48) Sch.5(9) with effect from January 1, 1991 (SI 1990/2168), but the previous form of the section (as explained at the end of §37.04) now has only historical significance.

RELEVANT CONVENTION PROVISION

CPC Article 23—Claiming the right to the Community Patent

37.02   **23.**—(1) If a Community patent has been granted to a person who is not entitled to it under article 60(1) of the European Patent Convention, the person entitled to it under that provision may, without prejudice to any other remedy which may be open to him, claim to have the patent transferred to him.

(2) Where a person is entitled to only part of the Community patent, that person may, in accordance with paragraph 1, claim to be made a joint proprietor.

(3) Legal proceedings in respect of the rights specified in paragraphs 1 and 2 may be instituted only within a period of not more than two years after the date on which the European Patent Bulletin mentions the grant of the European patent. This provision shall not apply if the proprietor of the patent knew, at the time when the patent was granted or transferred to him, that he was not entitled to the patent.

RELEVANT RULES—RULES 20, 73–88

37.03   The rules reprinted at §§123.06–123.21 are those of Pt 7 of the Patents Rules 2007 and are general in nature to govern procedure in all proceedings to be heard before the Comptroller. These specifically include proceedings under s.37(1). These rules are discussed under the heading "Practice under Section 123", but are also mentioned, as appropriate, in the commentary and practice sections below. Rule 20 (reprinted in §8.02 above) is also relevant to the filing of a new application under s.37(4).

Note. For "replacement" applications filed under s.37(4), rr.21, 28(4)–(7) and 30(3) and (4) (reprinted respectively at §§15.06, 18.02 and 18.04) are also relevant.

COMMENTARY ON SECTION 37

Scope of the section

37.04   Section 37 is part of a series of sections dealing with ownership and entitlement. Section 7 deals with the right to apply for and obtain a patent. Sections 8–12 and 37 deal with disputes regarding the entitlement or progress of UK and overseas patents and applications, with s.36 regulating the rights of co-owners. Section 13 deals with the right to be mentioned as inventor. Section 39 deals with the issue of entitlement as between an employer and an employee.

Subsections (1)–(7) provide for the determination by the Comptroller of questions of entitlement to granted patents which have been referred to him under s.37. The nature of the claim will be based on the provisions of s.7(2) (see *Yeda v Rhône-Poulenc Rorer* [2008] R.P.C. 1; [2007] UKHL 43—where it was held that s.7(2) provides a complete code for entitlement—as discussed at §7.06). Because s.9 provides that entitlement proceedings initiated under s.8, but not determined before the application has proceeded to grant, are then to be continued under s.37, this section tends in practice to govern the determination of most entitlement disputes and the relief available. Accordingly, with the exception of matters specific and unique to s.8, the commentary on s.37 is equally applicable to s.8. As discussed at §§8.04 and 9.02, an entitlement application made between the issue of a letter of intention to grant and the publication of the grant will not be processed until after the grant has occurred.

Section 37 applies also to granted European patents (UK).

Under s.37(1)(c), questions over licences can also be referred to the Comptroller, see *Leisure Pleasure Products Ltd v Raymond Robert Britner* BL O/360/06.

The Comptroller has no power to decide entitlement questions concerning foreign patents under s.37. However, by reference to s.12 (see *Vet Health's Patent* BL O/49/90, noted I.P.D. 13165), he can adjudicate on entitlement to foreign applications (including European and international applications, as limited by s.82 in the case of European applications) but only if the entitlement reference under s.12 is made to the Comptroller before grant of the foreign patent, as the wording of s.12(1) excludes a post-grant application under that sub-section (see *Magill's Application* cited at §12.03). Issues relevant to the entitlement of UK patents are often also applicable to ownership of foreign applications. Accordingly, with the exception of matters specific and unique to s.12, much of the commentary on s.37 is equally applicable to s.12.

Indeed, the courts tend to treat these sections as interchangeable and a decision under s.8 or s.12 will have cause of action estoppel against later proceedings under s.37 (*Cinpres v Melea* [2008] R.P.C. 17; [2008] EWCA Civ 9).

Where the claim to entitlement involves an allegation of incorrect naming of inventors, then the provisions of s.13 apply. Whilst under the 1995 Rules it was necessary to have separate proceedings under each section, which would then be consolidated, see *Brockhouse's Patent* [1985] R.P.C. 332, it is now no longer necessary to do this and all grounds should be raised in the same application.

By subs.(8), the Comptroller can decline to deal with an application under the section, requiring instead that the matter be referred for determination to a court (as defined in s.130(1)). Such a court also has an inherent power to give a declaratory judgment as to a patent entitlement issue, but is bound by the same restraints as the Comptroller, see subs.(9). Thus, as discussed in §37.08, the Patents County Court in England and Wales (but not a Sheriff Court in Scotland), has jurisdiction in such matters. Also, proceedings under the section before the Comptroller can be heard in Scotland (r.88, reprinted at §98.05 and discussed in §98.23). For Patents County Court jurisdiction and procedure, see §287.05 and §§61.40 et seq.

A decision in proceedings under the section that a patent has been granted to a person not entitled under the Act to be granted the patent, or a share of it, cannot in itself lead to its revocation under s.72(1)(b). However, although validity issues used to be irrelevant to proceedings on either inventorship or entitlement, see *Norris's Patent* [1988] R.P.C. 159 and *Viziball's Application* [1988] R.P.C. 213, even when the evidence presented indicated prior use of the invention (*Monk Construction's Patent* BL O/119/98), this is no longer good law and in *Markem v Zipher* [2005] R.P.C. 31; [2005] EWCA Civ 267, the Court of Appeal held that the Comptroller ought to take clear-cut validity issues into account and it was in the public interest to remove invalid monopolies at the earliest opportunity. This is discussed at §7.08. Further, proceedings under the section can be coupled with an application for revocation under s.72; or a claimant can seek a declaration of entitlement and then seek revocation under s.72(1)(b) based on that declaration (*Kokta's Patents* BL O/88/91, noted I.P.D. 15018). In fact, by virtue of s.72(2), a finding of non-entitlement under s.37, or a declaration from the court, is a prerequisite to revocation under s.72(1)(b), but it is sufficient if a declaration is made before an order for revocation is itself made, see *Henry Bros v Ministry of Defence* [1997] R.P.C. 693 overruling the decision on this point in

Dolphin Showers v Farmiloe [1989] 1 F.S.R. 1. Thus, as discussed in §72.13 and §74.05, entitlement and subsequent revocation could (under the 1995 Rules) be decided in concurrent proceedings, see §72.13, and can now be decided in the same proceedings. However, note the restriction on a co-owner seeking revocation in §36.05.

Entitlement issues can also be relevant to a defence to infringement proceedings, as the patent cannot be infringed by its proprietor (*Buchanan v Alba Diagnostics* [2000] R.P.C. 367 at 387). Also, a third party may also be able to rely on the lack of title of the registered proprietor to challenge that person's ability to bring a claim (*Cinpres v Melea* [2008] R.P.C. 17; [2008] EWCA Civ 9 at [116] and [117]), even if, by virtue of s.72(2), he cannot rely on it to invalidate the patent under s.72(1)(b).

Also, where the patent is revoked on other grounds, there is nothing left to decide under pending entitlement (or inventorship) proceedings and references under the relevant sections abate (see *Simon Bibby & Bernard Ward* BL O/195/07).

Any decision of the Comptroller under ss.8 and 37 is appealable to the Patents Court (s.97(1)), or (if heard in Scotland) to the Court of Session (s.97(4)), and thereafter, with leave, to the Court of Appeal (or, in Scotland, to the Inner House of the Court of Session), whether or not a question of law is involved (s.97(3) and (5)).

Section 37 was amended by the CDPA 1988 at the same time as amendment was made to s.72(1)(b) which had failed to provide adequately for a situation involving joint inventors and/or proprietors, where only some of those so named properly gave rise to entitlement to grant. It is surprising that ss.8(1) and 12(1) were not amended similarly to subs.(1), in view of their original similar wording, but one explanation could be that these two sections concern entitlement disputes determined pre-grant, rather than post-grant. However, the present form of the section continues to cause problems in relation to co-inventor situations, and the application of the section can be opaque in some situations, as illustrated by S. Thorley [1995] *CIPA* 104 and the call for clarification of the wording of s.72(1)(b) and (2) expressed in the appeal decision in *Henry Bros v Ministry of Defence* above; and [1999] R.P.C. 442 CA.

Types of entitlement questions which can arise under sections 8, 12 or 37

37.05   Section 37 complements ss.8 and 12 which relate to entitlement proceedings before grant. Proceedings under these sections, whether commenced by an employer or by his employee, afford means for resolving any dispute there may be as to ownership of an invention under s.39; that is in respect of inventions made by persons mainly employed in the United Kingdom or having a United Kingdom employer (s.43(2)).

Under the current form of subs.(1), any person "having or claiming a property right in or under the patent" (the "claimant" (r.73)) may seek determination by the Comptroller as to: (a) who is or are the true proprietor(s) of the patent; (b) whether the patent should have been granted to the person(s) to whom it was granted; or (c) whether any right in or under the patent should be transferred or granted to any other person(s)). The Comptroller's primary duty is, therefore, to determine these questions and to declare accordingly. He may "make such order as he thinks fit" to give effect to that determination. As subs.(1) refers to "any right in or under" the patent, consideration of entitlement is not limited to the contents of the application as originally filed, but can consider the claims currently present (*Egerton's Patent* BL O/219/98, noted I.P.D. 22022). For the same reason, the Comptroller can reach a decision on entitlement based on an equitable assignment if satisfied that the existence of this has been established on the balance of probabilities, see *Polar Bay's Patent* BL O/233/99. However, as noted in §37.04, the Comptroller does not have the power to revoke a patent if only entitlement proceedings are in being before him. However, following the introduction of the 2007 Rules, he might well allow a late amendment of the statements of case under r.82(1)(e) (reprinted in §123.15) to add such a request (applying the overriding objective), rather than insisting on the issue of fresh proceedings, with further delay and increased costs, if the issue of validity was to be decided anyway.

Although a claimant may show that he is an inventor of (part of) the subject-matter claimed, so that the person(s) granted the patent may not have (full) entitlement to it, the claimant's own rights may be subjugated to another by virtue of an agreement, either explicit or implied, or to his employer by virtue of s.39, as discussed in §§39.07–39.14.

Entitlement is no longer to be decided on a claim by claim basis. Following the Court of Appeal in *Markem v Zipher* [2005] R.P.C. 31; [2005] EWCA Civ 267, the issue for the court will be to see what is "the heart of the invention" and, even though there may be more than "one heart", that may not mean that each claim is "a heart". This is discussed at §7.08.

If the entitlement asserted is based on some contractual obligation, the principles of contract law must be shown to have been satisfied, i.e. there must have been an "offer", subsequently "accepted"; there must have been "consideration"; there must have been an intention for the parties to the agreement to create a legal relationship inter se; and the terms of the agreement made must be tolerably clear and free from ambiguity. Such a contract can be one made orally, but the existence and terms of such will be more difficult to prove. These criteria were held not to have been met in *James Industries' Patent* [1987] R.P.C. 235. If the patent was granted to an assignee and it is shown that the assignor had no entitlement to the patent rights, that assignment can have no effect (*Kitelane's Application* BL O/15/94). If there has been an agreement to assign which has not been implemented, no entitlement can arise from that agreement without an order for its specific performance having first been obtained (*Westend Investments' Applications* BL O/36/94). However, where the assignment appears valid, but the claimant alleges that not all of the consideration has been paid, then the assignment may still be upheld and the claimant may instead have to seek damages (*Denne v Electro Magnetic Rams* BL O/160/07).

In *Magill's Application* BL O/256/00, entitlement was claimed (under s.12) under a payment default provision in an agreement between two companies (CRL and IC, a company apparently owned by the applicant, M) specifying that, if IC defaulted on the agreed payments (as was held to have happened) "CRL will be assigned 30% of the patent application". This phrase was found to have no clear meaning (s.36 requiring a 50 per cent ownership for co-proprietors) and so was held void for uncertainty, leaving the patent rights seemingly with M. However, the agreement was seen as evidence that IC was the true owner of the rights. The Comptroller therefore made an order for assignment of the rights to IC forthwith: BL O/362/00. However, no order could be made under s.12 in respect of the United States application which had already proceeded to grant.

In *Technology Fund's Patent* BL O/96/04, noted [2004] *CIPA* 294, the claimant asserted that the assignment of the patent from the claimant to the defendant was invalid and that the patent should be put back into the name of the claimant. The defendant obtained a judgment from the Singapore court that the assignment was valid and thereafter the claimant did not appeal or file any evidence or argument to support its case. The application was dismissed.

In *Transfer Systems v International Consultants* BL O/1/06, noted [2006] *CIPA* 123, the applicants successfully claimed ownership due to an earlier unregistered assignment, the current registered proprietor having been aware of that before executing a later assignment to them which they had registered.

In *Ogden and McKenzie's Patent* BL O/142/06, noted [2006] *CIPA* 485, McKenzie had agreed to fund the application for Ogden's invention. So they were co-owners on the basis of an oral agreement, but another applicant had no rights and should not have been a co-applicant. The same declaration as to ownership (and exploitation) was subsequently made (see BL O/158/07) in respect of all the overseas applications McKenzie had filed.

In *Ritchie v Envireneer Marine Cranes* BL O/220/06, the inventor claimed ownership by virtue of a "Product Royalties Agreement" which contained a "reversion" clause. However, the employer was found to be the true owner of the invention and this agreement did not have the effect of transferring rights to Ritchie. Further, it had not been registered and was not known to the new owner at the date when it took an assignment from the liquidator of Ritchie's employer.

As examples of alleged subjugation by reason of a prior agreement, see: *Rig Technology's Application* BL O/83/95, where the original applicant was held entitled to be the proprietor on the basis of an informal agreement; and *Temple v Protophot* BL C/77/95, noted I.P.D. 19002, where the claimant-inventor was held to have agreed to assign the patent rights to the defendant and, moreover, had acted in conformity with it so that he was therefore estopped from subsequently claiming entitlement.

Issues of potential estoppel were also discussed in *Yeda v Rhône-Poulenc Rorer* [2008] R.P.C. 1; [2007] UKHL 43, where the proposition was put to the court that if the inventor had stood by and allowed someone else to apply for the patent and expend money on "the risky and expensive development work to bring [the product] to market", then that could give rise to complete or partial defence to the entitlement proceedings by the application of the equitable rules of proprietary estoppel.

In relation to equitable transfers of rights to inventions and the subsequent filing of patent applications, see the discussion at §7.06, above.

In *Shape and Potemkin's Applications* BL O/140/92 and C/68/94, noted I.P.D. 18033, although P proved inventorship, his position as a consultant to S at the time he made the invention was held sufficient to entitle S to the patent rights because it was held to be an implied term of P's consultancy contract that his inventions should belong to S. However, this may not always be so; and, unless ownership has been specifically dealt with in the consultancy contract, there may be uncertainty as to ownership of inventions made by an independent consultant working in conjunction with company employees, see comment by A. Shindler *MIP*, July/August 1998, 39.

It is important to appreciate that, if a claimant was, at the time of making the invention, an employee within the scope of s.39(1), that is, making the invention was within the scope of his normal or specially assigned duties (as discussed in §§39.07–39.14), it is impossible for him to succeed on an entitlement application because either he will fail to prove inventorship or the invention will be found to properly belong to his employer, see *Blagden Industries' Application* BL O/42/93. Also, in *Peerless Nursery Products' Application* BL O/44/96, it was held that, as the inventor had made the invention prior to him being dismissed as an employee, his application to file a replacement application in his own name was refused; but in *Novacare Products' Application* BL O/112/95 it was held that the inventor had made the invention before becoming an employee of the applicant and hence was entitled to become the applicant in substitution. In *JGB Steelcraft's Patent* BL O/22/94, it was held that the patentee had been working on a prototype before the referrer had been engaged as a consultant to the patentee: the reference therefore failed.

Shortly before the hearing in *Expotech's Patent* BL O/95/04, noted [2004] *CIPA* 294 it became apparent that there were two inventions in the patent and not one. The hearing officer found that an employee of the patent applicant was responsible for one of these and an employee of the claimant was responsible for the other. The parties had collaborated and it was conceded that the employers were entitled to the inventions of their employees. Joint ownership was awarded.

In *Environ's Application* BL O/3/94, although C was held to have made the invention before becoming an employee of the applicant, it was only fully developed after that. As C had consented to the filing, he was held not to have discharged the onus of proving complete entitlement, but the applicant E was likewise not fully entitled to ownership under s.39. Thus, in equity, neither should have exclusive rights and joint ownership was not appropriate. The most pragmatic solution was seen to be to allow the application to proceed in the name of the applicant, but with C having an irrevocable, royalty-free, non-exclusive licence with power to sub-license (but see *Hughes v Paxman* [2007] R.P.C. 2; [2006] EWCA Civ 818 discussed at §37.10). However, no amicable settlement was reached and, as E was seen to have lost interest in the patent, it was later ordered that the application should proceed in the name of C with such a licence granted to E: BL O/137/94.

Thus, the date when the invention was made may be significant. For example, in *Imperial Chemical Industries' Application* BL O/159/98, one inventor claimed joint ownership on the basis that at the time the invention was made he had been an independent consultant, this date being asserted to be when the experiments which verified the invention were complete. However, these experiments were held to be only corroborative so that the invention had been made by a date when W had been an employee of a company whose successor in title had relinquished all rights to the applicant who had thus acquired full rights to the invention.

The claim in *Lawson and McGarry's Application* BL O/56/04, noted [2004] *CIPA* 165, arose out of the fact that Lawson was an employee and director of the claimant. The claim under s.39(1)(a) was not pursued but the claim under s.39(1)(b) would have been made out were it not for the fact that there was sufficient evidence of the invention having been conceived before the company was incorporated. See further at §39.06 and §39.11.

In *Enston's Applications* BL O/206/04, noted [2004] *CIPA* 484 two brothers were in dispute as to which of them first came up with the invention and whether it should belong to the company of which both had been directors. Claim 1 was found to be overbroad, and, although the hearing officer ignored possible validity questions, he still found the invention to be something narrower. The claimant, P, failed show that he had communicated the invention to his brother prior to the priority date. Indeed, once the narrower view of the invention was taken, the hearing officer was unable to find that P had thought of that at all. It was acknowledged that all the embodiments had been devised by the patent applicant, E, who would be at least a joint inventor and a claim to that was pursued under s.37. In a subsidiary point, Counsel sought to argue that the invention belonged to the company by way of constructive trust as the patent applicant and alleged inventor had been a director of the company when the invention was made. However, as this argument in relation to "fiduciary duty" only appeared in the skeleton and had not been foreshadowed in the pleadings which had relied on a purported contract of employment, the hearing officer did not allow what was, in effect, a very late amendment to the pleadings.

The provisions of s.36 (co-ownership of patents) and s.39(2) (no joint ownership between employer and employee) need further to be borne in mind, see §§36.03–36.06 and §39.07 and §39.17 respectively. Thus, a referrer who claims to be the true inventor should be careful to make it clear whether he contends that he is the sole inventor or whether only a joint inventor. See *Shop-A-Long Bingo's Application* BL O/115/93 and BL O/4/94 where W and S were held to have been joint inventors with S having been employed by the applicant, and it was thought appropriate that the application should proceed in the joint names of the two inventors, any dispute as to the prosecution of the application then being resolvable under s.10.

Where joint ownership arises, either from joint inventorship or from an assignment, difficult questions arise both under s.37(1)(a) and s.74(4), see *La Baigue Magiglo v Multiglow Fires* BL C/56/93 from which it appears that if, in s.37 proceedings, it is held that a person (B) should have been a joint grantee, then the other grantee (A) cannot allege infringement by B either because of s.36(2)(a) or on general equitable principles. See also §74.05.

Du Pont's (Rebouillat's) Applications [1996] R.P.C. 740 further illustrates the complexity which can arise in entitlement disputes. Here the referrers initially claimed a breach of a confidentiality agreement providing for no publication of data generated under a joint development programme. Accordingly, the referrers claimed that patent applications filed disclosing that data should be held on constructive trust for them. When the patentee claimed that the agreement only provided for secrecy in respect of data provided in writing and identified as "confidential", the referrers sought to add a plea of breach of a non-contractual obligation of confidence, and were allowed to amend their statement of case because it was held that this plea raised no truly new issue, though the patentee was given time to file further evidence in answer.

In *Minnesota Mining's International Application* [2003] R.P.C. 28 at 541, a third party had made a non-confidential disclosure which was communicated to an inventor employed by the applicant and which then found its way into the application in suit. The applicant contended that since the disclosure had not been subject to confidentiality restrictions they were entitled to treat it as though it were in the public domain. It was, however, held that the disclosure had contributed to the inventive concept of some of the claims, and the third party was thus entitled to be a joint applicant in respect of them. However, some of the claims derived only from the work of the applicant's employee and some only from the work of the third party so that further time was allowed for the parties to make submissions as to the appropriate order in the circumstances (see §36.04).

In *GE Healthcare v PerkinElmer* [2006] EWHC 214 Pat Ct; noted [2006] *CIPA* 2000, PerkinElmer ("PE") claimed ownership in the event that the patent was valid, on the basis of confidential discussions between the parties' predecessors over a number of years. However, in the light of the evidence, the court found that the inventive concept was made by the patent applicant's employee before these discussions and had not been derived from PE.

Allergan v Merz Pharma BL O/271/06, noted [2006] *CIPA* 679, was an unusual case in that the proprietor sought a declaration that it was entitled to the patent. Although s.37 allows anyone "having or claiming an interest" to apply and this included the proprietor, a claim of right had to have been asserted first (see *Re Clay* [1919] 1 Ch. 66, as approved in *Unilever v Proctor & Gamble* [2000] F.S.R. 344). Also, the hearing officer doubted whether such proceedings could be effective, as the patentee would have to put forward the case for the other party. In this case, the proceedings were struck out.

Although the same thing happened in *Auckland (Paul) and Enderby Construction Ltd* BL O/343/06, with the proprietor bringing the claim, his employer, Enderby, had then also asked the Comptroller for a declaration that it owned the rights. The question was which had the burden of proof, and this was held to be with the party seeking to change the ownership and hence overturn the presumption in s.7(4).

Raising questions of entitlement

37.06   The onus of proof in all types of entitlement proceedings is on the claimant (*Viziball's Application* [1988] R.P.C. 213), with this proof to be established on the test of the "balance of probabilities", as is usual in civil litigation, but see the comment on *Peart's Patents* BL O/209/87 in §39.11. If there is a conflict of evidence which cannot be resolved, the claimant must fail (*Alsop's Application* BL O/120/84 and *Brockhouse's Patent (No.2)* BL O/100/85); and, likewise, where neither party files evidence and there is a conflict in the pleaded facts (*Steel's Patent* BL O/139/94). Thus, where the referrer and applicant (now "claimant" and "defendant" (r.73)) each claimed to have made the same invention independently, the referrer failed to establish entitlement as he had not disproved the applicant's entitlement (*Sofitech's Patent* BL O/442/99). See also *A.C. Egerton's Patent* BL O/170/00, noted I.P.D. 23075 where the referrer alleged that the patentee had obtained the invention from it, but failed to identify any inventor(s) within its own organisation of three features in the patent claim, nor that the patentee had received any confidential information from it, thus suggesting that any similarity between the devices produced by each party was due to independent, contemporaneous derivation, although even then not by the referrer. See also *Mackie's Patent* BL O/299/05, noted [2005] *CIPA* 799 where neither side provided adequate evidence as to who contributed to the inventive concept.

Where a considerable period of time has elapsed between the making of the invention and the entitlement claim, the evidence to prove the claimant's case may not be available. As was noted by Jacob L.J. in *Yeda Research v Rhône-Poulenc Rorer* ([2007] R.P.C. 9 at paras 4 and 5), "entitlement disputes often involve conflicting evidence as to who exactly contributed what and who said what to whom". So to decide cases many years after the event is deeply unsatisfactory. In *Farr v Orbis* BL O/214/11, the defendant has been unable to supply documents or witnesses due to the relevant R&D being more than 10 years old and all the relevant employees having left the business. The business had also been transferred from one entity to another. This left the claimant at a considerable disadvantage, especially when the defendant chooses not to appear at the hearing. The onus was still on the claimant to show that the relevant features which he claimed to have contributed had not been derived from the defendant's employees. It is not clear why the Comptroller declined to compel witnesses in this case given the Comptroller's powers concerning evidence discussed at §123.55. There is further discussion of procedure in entitlement disputes at this topic at §37.12.

Although the onus of proof in all types of entitlement proceedings is on the claimant, note the reversal which occurred in *Statoil v University of Southampton* BL O/268/05, noted [2005] *CIPA* 735, see §12.04), where the onus was put on the University on the question as to whether the law differed in other countries, and hence whether the University could retain the overseas applications, following loss of the UK patent.

Conflicts should be tested by disclosure of documents (for which see §§61.67–61.73) and cross-examination (for which see §97.18 and *Norris's Patent* [1988] R.P.C. 159). In *Amateur Athletic Association's Applications* [1989] R.P.C. 717, the referrer largely proved his case because of the more complete circuit diagram filed in his own application the following day, whereas the application-in-suit contained only outline details of this essential feature of the invention (see also *Brueton's Patent* BL O/104/90, noted I.P.D. 14012).

Where one party wishes to impugn the character of the other parties' witnesses, then the witnesses must first be challenged on the facts and counsel should not just leave it to the judge to draw adverse findings. See the Court of Appeal in *Markem v Zipher* [2005] R.P.C. 31; [2005] EWCA Civ 267, relying on the House of Lords in *Browne v Dunn* (1894) 6 R. 67 and the Australian case of *Allied Pastoral Holdings v Federal Commissioner of Taxation* (1983) 44 A.L.R. 607.

Although the traditional position was that validity should not be taken into consideration when deciding questions of entitlement (*Norris's Patent*, above), this did not mean that there was no need to look for any contribution from the referrer to the very feature which distinguishes the claims of the contested application/patent from the prior art (*Derbyshire Maid's Patent* BL O/40/97). Now, following *Markem v Zipher*, the issue can be explored, even without a request for revocation, and where there is a clear and unarguable attack, then there is no point in the Comptroller passing such claims from the defendant to the claimant: see the discussion at §7.08.

Notice of any reference in an entitlement proceeding must be given to any person who it appears may be entitled to a share in the invention or any right in or under the patent (s.8(6); s.37(7)). To ensure this, a caveat can be lodged by a potential claimant by filing PF 49, see §118.19. The fact that a reference has been made is usually entered in the register but r.44(4) of the 1995 Rules, which provided for this, has been omitted.

Where the Comptroller makes a finding which does not entirely accord with the contentions advanced by either party, findings will be made and the matter adjourned for further argument as to the form of the eventual order, examples of which are given in §37.10.

Under ss.8(7), 12(2) and 37(8), the Comptroller may refuse to deal with a question of entitlement if he considers this should more properly be determined by the court. It is then necessary for application to be made to a court (as defined in s.130(1)), for which see §37.08. However, a party has no power to require the Comptroller to transfer the matter to the court for decision. This is to be decided by the Comptroller of his own motion (*Brockhouse's Patent* [1985] R.P.C. 332), as also discussed in §37.08.

—*Types of relief available under sections 8 and 37*

Without prejudice to the generality of subs.(1), subs.(2) of each of ss.8 and 37 gives the following specific remedies in relation to a subsisting application (s.8) or to a granted patent (s.37): **37.07**

  (i) refusal of the application (s.8(2)(c));

  (ii) amendment to exclude the matter in dispute (s.8(2)(c));

  (iii) transfer of the application or patent to the person or persons making the reference (ss.8(2)(a), (b) and 37(2)(a));

  (iv) inclusion of the person making the reference alongside other applicants or proprietors, with or without the exclusion of any specified applicant or proprietor (ss.8(2)(a) and 37(2)(a));

  (v) directions to grant a licence or other right in or under the application or patent or to transfer a licence or other right in or under the application (ss.8(2)(d) and 37(2)(c));

  (vi) order to register any transaction, instrument or event by which the referrer has acquired any right in or under the patent (s.37(2)(b)); and

(vii) directions to the proprietor or any other person having some right in or under the patent to implement an order providing a remedy (s.37(2)(d)).

This last-mentioned power is supported by s.37(3) which permits the Comptroller to authorise the beneficiary of the order to perform the required act on behalf of a person who has been directed to perform it, but has failed to do so. The procedure is discussed in §37.12. There is equivalent wording in s.8(2)(d) to give directions, but it is unclear whether this was intended to refer to the provisions of s.8(2)(d) only or to any order under s.8(2).

The claimant may also be permitted to file a new (back-dated) application for the whole or part of the invention, see s.8(3) and s.37(4) (discussed in §37.09); and the Comptroller may order a transfer or assignment of any right in the application or patent to any other person (s.8(4); s.37(2)(b)).

If the Comptroller decides that there should be a variation in entitlement, he may need to consider whether the rights of the apparently entitled parties are subordinated to one or more employers under the provisions of s.39(1), as discussed in §37.05. This may lead to adjournment of the case for further argument and evidence, particularly in the light of possible subjugation to the superior interest of the employer of an employed inventor, as illustrated in §37.10. Also, where the Comptroller decides that co-ownership is appropriate, he will often delay a final decision to permit the parties to make submissions as to whether such co-ownership should be on the basis of s.36(3) or on some more appropriate basis having regard to the underlying prospects for commercialisation of the invention from the commercial standing of each party involved, see e.g. *Minnesota Mining's Patent* BL O/237/00. At times, the Comptroller has felt that he could not make an appropriate order. For example, following the initial decision of joint entitlement in *Minnesota Mining's Patent* BL O/237/00, the parties failed to reach agreement and the Comptroller could then do no more than order (see BL 0/452/00) joint ownership under the terms of s.36 despite the fact that the customers of the new co-owner (E) would be required to obtain a licence from the original owner (M), but it was pointed out to M:

"that it is incumbent on them to recognise how E carry out their business as suppliers of adhesives in order that E might gain some advantage from the patents".

However, subsequently in *Hughes v Paxman* [2007] R.P.C. 2; [2006] EWCA Civ 818, appealing BL O/143/05; and [2005] EWHC 2240 Pat Ct, the Court of Appeal held that the Comptroller did have discretion to allow the co-owner to grant a licence under the UK patent, see also §36.05 and §37.10.

If an order under any of heads (iii)–(v) above is to be made, notice of the reference must be given to any person not party to the reference who is alleged to be entitled to the patent or to have any right in or under it (s.8(6) or 37(7)), unless such notice had been given earlier in the proceedings. However, no directions are to be given under ss.8(8) and 37(6) which would affect the mutual rights or obligations, or the rights and obligations as such, either of trustees or of personal representatives of deceased persons. Thus, it seems that probate disputes should not be resolved under ss.8 and 37.

In addition to the remedies provided by ss.8, 12, 37 and 82 in questions of entitlement, it would also appear possible to seek a declaration from the Comptroller that the referrer has an equitable interest in the application or patent as a result of a constructive trust having arisen, see *Kakkar v Szelke* [1989] 1 F.S.R. 225 CA.

If a patent application made by a person held to have been a wrongful applicant has been allowed to lapse, no order can be made under s.8(2), but a new application may be filed under s.8(3), see *Jessamine Holdings' Application* BL O/138/85 and §37.09; or a declaration can be made under s.37(1), see *Szucs' Application* BL O/4/86 and *Cryogenic Consultants' Application* BL O/1/94: for subsequent proceedings in the *Szucs'* case, see §37.10.

When (under s.8 or 12) an application is ordered to proceed with any new applicant under s.8(4), s.11 applies, see §§11.05–11.07.

When an order is made under s.8(2)(d) or (4) or s.37(2)(c) for a licence to be granted or an assignment made, subs.(5) applies: for which see §37.11. If there is non-compliance with such an order, any person in whose favour the order was made may apply, within the existing proceedings to the Comptroller, for authority to take the requisite action on behalf of the person ordered, see further also at §37.11. Where an order is made for the transfer of proprietorship of the patent, s.38 comes into play with respect to licences already granted under the patent and to persons who, in good faith, had made "effective and serious" preparations to work the invention in the United Kingdom, see the commentary on s.38.

Section 8 contains no time limit on the powers of the Comptroller, nor is there a time bar imposed on the court. By contrast, s.37(5) and (9) impose a definite time bar on the powers of the Comptroller and the court, respectively, to entertain entitlement proceedings, and this has the effect of severely limiting the relief which can be granted in cases of improper grant due to a wrongful claim to entitlement, as discussed in §37.11.

The power of the Comptroller under ss.8 and 37 does not include the provision of a priority date which was not claimed at the date of filing the application. Thus, in a case where it was alleged that an earlier application had been filed in contravention of rights and an application to revoke the resulting patent was pending, the Comptroller refused to allow the later application to proceed because it had been anticipated by the publication of a foreign specification corresponding to the allegedly improper application, and held that there was no power to overcome this by effective back-dating of the application (*Georgia Pacific's Application* [1984] R.P.C. 467). However, where the referrer was held entitled to file a replacement application for an application which had been abandoned, but which had served as a priority document for a second application, the referrer was also allowed to file a second replacement application claiming priority from the first (*Amateur Athletic Association's Applications* [1989] R.P.C. 717; and *Coin Control's Application* BL O/95/89, noted I.P.D. 13034).

In *Quantum Glass v Spowart* [Scotland], [2000] ScotCS 76, noted [2001] *CIPA* 99, the Court of Session thought it appropriate to impose interim interdicts upon a patent applicant and inventor preventing them from further prosecuting an international application pending full trial of the issues of entitlement to this application and of alleged breach of confidence in its disclosure, even though the outcome of these interdicts seemed likely to be that the application could not proceed within the required time limits. However, generally the Comptroller does not suspend prosecution of an application under the 1977 Act or prevent the applicant from allowing the application to lapse pending resolution of an entitlement dispute and probably would not have the jurisdiction to make any such order in relation to an international application—see §§8.04, 8.07 and §12.03.

In *Yeda Research v Rhône-Poulenc Rorer* BL O/277/05; [2006] R.P.C. 24 the hearing officer thought that the Comptroller could make any order that he thought fit, which included ordering sole or joint ownership without requiring amendment of the pleading. Although this was overturned on the appeal, the Court of Appeal (see [2007] R.P.C. 9) holding that a claim to joint ownership does not encompass a claim to sole ownership, even if a claim to sole ownership does encompass a claim to joint ownership, the House of Lords (see [2008] R.P.C. 1; [2007] UKHL 43) reversed that finding and upheld the hearing officer. It was the reference of the question as to who was entitled that had to be made in time and not the particulars of that reference. The proposed amendment to include a claim to sole ownership was not time barred (see §37.11).

In *Ogden v McKenzie and Projectile* BL O/219/05, noted [2005] *CIPA* 608, the hearing officer allowed the proceedings under s.37 to be extended to cover the PCT application under s.12 as the wording of the two documents was identical.

Powers of the Comptroller and court to determine entitlement disputes

Sections 8, 12 and 37 do not exclude an application to the court for a declaration or other relief concerning ownership of a patent or application for which it has relevant jurisdiction; and the Comptroller may decline (under ss.8(7), 12(2) or 37(8)) to deal with a question referred to him under any of these sections (although note the different focus in the wording between s.37(8) and those in ss.8(7) and 12(2)). Where there is jurisdiction to

37.08

decide entitlement of a European patent application under s.82, then the court and the Comptroller are given concurrent jurisdiction (see §82.06). Any party then wishing to have the dispute resolved must himself initiate proceedings before a court, see *Stringer and Colby's Patent* BL O/55/92. The "court" for such purposes is one defined in s.130(1) and is not necessarily the Patents Court: other courts, including the Patents County Court (as to which see §287.05 and §§64.40 et seq.), and courts in Scotland, Northern Ireland and the Isle of Man have a concurrent jurisdiction (for which see §96.06). Normally, where the Comptroller declines to deal with an entitlement matter, the dispute will be referred to the Patents Court under the procedure described in §37.14. However, another of the defined courts may be chosen although the jurisdiction of the courts of Scotland, Northern Ireland and the Isle of Man requires an appropriate connection of at least one of the parties with such jurisdiction, as determined under the terms of the Civil Jurisdiction and Judgments Act 1982 (c.27), as discussed in §96.09.

The mere fact that questions of entitlement to the United Kingdom patent are raised is not conclusive as to whether the matter ought to be decided by the Comptroller. In *GAF Corp v Amchem* [1975] 1 Lloyd's Rep. 601, the Court of Appeal refused to allow an entitlement dispute which involved patent applications in several countries (including the United Kingdom) to be litigated in the English court, holding that the question was one which would not be appropriate for the English court to decide having regard to the foreign residence of each of the parties. This is particularly so where the parties are domiciled within the EEA or in Switzerland because here the matter is regulated by the Jurisdiction (or: Brussels) Regulation (Council Regulation (EC) No.44/2001 of 22 December 2000) or, where that does not apply (e.g. to Denmark (which is not bound by this Regulation) and non-EU states), the Brussels and Lugano Conventions (as enacted into United Kingdom law by the said 1982 Act). Under the Jurisdiction Regulation and these Conventions, subject to certain conditions, a defendant has to be sued in a court of his domicile (in the sense of habitual residence). One such exception provides exclusive jurisdiction to a national court in proceedings concerned with the validity or registration of patents (art.16(4) of the Brussels Convention and art.22(4) of the Jurisdiction Regulation), but this provision has no applicability to questions of patent entitlement (*Duijnstee v Göderbauer* (288/82) [1983] E.C.R. 363; [1985] 1 C.M.L.R. 220; [1985] F.S.R. 221 ECJ).

In *Ross's Application* BL O/188/04, noted [2004] *CIPA* 482, the Comptroller was also asked to adjudicate on the related and overlapping family of patents and applications filed by the claimant, Crabtree. Ross had not filed the PF 2 then required to initiate proceedings in respect of those patents and applications. At that time, this was not a mere irregularity which the Comptroller could overlook, nor would it be sensible completely to ignore the other family as any finding in the current case on inventorship would affect that family too. (Under the 2007 Rules, there is no need to commence separate proceedings where the matters are sufficiently linked and the Comptroller might instead agree to amend the statements of case if this was in line with the "overriding objective".) So the hearing proceeded on the basis that the Comptroller would rule on the inventorship issues for the patents in dispute but not those that were not before him and then allow the parties to make submissions as to the order to be made. The Comptroller also noted that he had no jurisdiction to decide anything under s.12 in relation to granted foreign Crabtree patents and that he could only decide "so far as he is able to" which required evidence as to the appropriate foreign law.

The Comptroller's practice in exercising his discretion to decline jurisdiction in favour of the court has been completely re-written following the decision by Warren J. in *Luxim v Ceravision* [2007] R.P.C. 33; [2007] EWHC 1624 overturning the decision of the hearing officer not to decline jurisdiction: BL O/143/06. This was the culmination of an interesting "misunderstanding" by the Patent Office, of judicial comment by the Court of Appeal in *IDA v Southampton* [2006] R.P.C. 21; [2006] EWCA Civ 145 and *Yeda Research v Rhône-Poulenc Rorer* [2007] R.P.C. 9; [2006] EWCA Civ 1094, and the Comptroller's continuation of his practice to be "cautious" or "sparing" over declining to hear matters to which Parliament had given the Comptroller primary jurisdiction. The new practice is set out in the *Hearings Manual*, at Ch.2, paras 2.77–2.83 and was applied in *Northern Light Music v*

Conversor Products BL O/296/07. This is a question for the Comptroller to determine of his own motion, regardless of whether one or more parties have made such a request. Indeed, there is no provision for a party to compel transfer, but appeal from the Comptroller's decision on this issue lies to the Patents Court under CPR Pt 52.

When considering whether or not the matter or question would "more properly be determined by the court" and whether he should decline jurisdiction, the Comptroller will now approach this in the same way, regardless of whether he is dealing with a case under, e.g. s.8, where the UK-IPO has primary jurisdiction, or under, e.g. s.40 where the UK-IPO and the court have concurrent jurisdiction. However, there are differences in wording between the sections which may call for closer consideration. Under ss.8(7) and 12(2), the Comptroller has to consider whether the reference of a question under that section "involves matters" which would more properly be determined by the court. Whereas, under s.37(8), it is whether "the question referred" would more properly be determined by the court.

In declining jurisdiction, the UK-IPO is not abdicating responsibility for matters given to it by Parliament. That is not the right approach. There is a hierarchy between tribunals and courts and, even if the UK-IPO could perfectly well deal with a matter and do justice between the parties, it must nonetheless form a view as to whether, in any particular case, it or the court is the more appropriate forum.

Warren J. was careful not to lay down any test on complexity. So it is not a question of the UK-IPO retaining jurisdiction only in "straightforward" cases or only referring "highly complex" cases. The standard of what is "complex" will move, depending on what is the normal run of cases and the experience of the hearing officers. The UK-IPO does have experience of dealing with complex matters, including examining facts through cross-examination and expert evidence on foreign law issues. Now the UK-IPO must look at both the complexity of the individual issues, and also at the complexity that comes from the number and the interaction of such issues.

In *Northern Lights* (above), the hearing officer took up the four sorts of issues set out in *Luxim*: (a) technical issues; (b) factual issues unrelated to the technical issues; (c) patent law issues; and (d) non-patent law issues. Hearing officers are usually well able to deal with technical issues and patent law issues, whether English or foreign patent law. However, where the case includes making findings of fraud or breach of fiduciary duty, or of understanding and applying foreign insolvency law, then this may well begin to tilt the balance in favour of the court. The position on costs, with cost recovery in the UK-IPO being generally limited to scale fees, is also to be taken into consideration, but will not be decisive. This might be cancelled out if the party seeking to rely on that is also indicating that it will use all the tiers of appeal (at which point, removing one of them by not also running the case in the UK-IPO may become a relevant factor—see *Luxim*).

In *Mastermailer v Data Security & Stephen Black* (BL O/433/10), the main factor which caused the Comptroller to decline jurisdiction was the issue of Mr Black's fiduciary duty to the claimant's subsidiary. That fiduciary relationship was already in issue in High Court proceedings, although the precise breach was different. So although there was no risk of conflicting decisions, the Comptroller still felt that this was a matter better determined by the Court.

In *Azam v Livesey* (BL O/438/10), the main factors which caused the Comptroller to decline jurisdiction were that one party had accused the other of fabricating evidence and there was a question of interpretation of a contract.

Following *Luxim* and *Northern Lights*, the prior decisions must now be treated with care, including the UK-IPO's practice of declining jurisdiction simply because both parties agree (for example *Pico's Patent* BL O/303/00, where the Comptroller declined jurisdiction solely because this was the unopposed wish of the proprietor, although otherwise no sufficient ground had been put forward as to why jurisdiction should be declined under subs.(8)). Where there are, or are going to be, parallel proceedings in the court for breach of contract or breach of confidence, etc. (for which matters the Comptroller does not have jurisdiction—see §8.04), then this may continue to be a good reason for the Comptroller to decline jurisdiction, but even then, there may be circumstances where the Comptroller should retain that case. The following are examples of cases under the previous test and should be applied with caution, although the outcome may have been the same if the new test had been applied:

The absence of financial support to some, but not all, of the parties was a relevant factor in *Baldwin's Patent* [1998] R.P.C. 415. On the substantive hearing (*Baldwin's Patent (No.3)* BL O/167/99), the referrer failed because the acute conflict of evidence meant that she had not discharged the necessary onus of proof. However, it was indicated that the position could have been different if certain witnesses had been called for cross-examination and/or if the referrer had claimed joint, rather than sole, entitlement.

The Comptroller has declined to deal with entitlement questions when these related to the contractual relationship between the parties: *Downs (J) (Jersey)'s Application* BL O/66/90, noted I.P.D. 13146, although here the relationship was an alleged oral contract probably arising under Scots law. Also, where the referrer himself sought transfer to the Patents Court because one of the patents was already the subject of infringement proceedings brought against him with a counterclaim for its revocation for non-entitlement, the Comptroller acceded to the request in order that all the patents could be dealt with in one set of proceedings (*Instance's Patents* BL O/128/96). In *Stringer and Colby's Patent* (above), the Comptroller also declined to deal further with the reference because the referrer had already commenced court proceedings and the Comptroller held that the parallel disputes ought to be heard by the same court, and likewise in *Oilphase Sampling's Application* BL O/85/94, *Ecoprogress's PCT Application* BL O/36/95 and *West Pharmaceuticals International Application* BL O/58/2. In *Cinpres Gas Injection v Melea* BL O/348/03, the Comptroller held that it would be manifestly undesirable not to decline jurisdiction in the face of both parties' wishes, not least because the referrer was seeking to re-open previous litigation which had already been heard on appeal before both the Patents Court and the Court of Appeal, on the grounds that the inventor had fraudulently given false evidence in the first case.

By contrast, the Comptroller has on occasions refused to decline jurisdiction over an entitlement question. Thus, in *La Baigue's Patent* BL O/124/89, the Comptroller refused to refer an entitlement question to the court under s.37(8) even though infringement proceedings were then pending. He considered that the proceedings before the Comptroller would be conducted more cheaply and, if resolved one way, would terminate the infringement proceedings. Subsequently, the parties asked the Comptroller to dismiss these proceedings without making any finding: this was done, but the Comptroller pointed out that, until any such finding, the register would reflect the status quo: BL O/9/90, noted I.P.D. 13042. Reference to the court was also refused in *Vet Health's Patent* BL O/49/90, noted I.P.D. 13165 because, although infringement proceedings were there pending, these did not involve the person claiming entitlement so that revocation under s.72(1)(b) would not be possible in those proceedings, see §72.13 and §74.05. In the *Brockhouse* case (above), it was decided that there should be no transfer because non-transferable inventorship proceedings under s.13 were also involved.

In *Actineon's Applications* BL O/309/05, noted [2005] *CIPA* 799, the hearing officer declined to transfer the case to the court, despite the Californian company indicating that there were complex contractual issues, as it was not uncommon for such issues to be raised in UK-IPO proceedings. In that case, the means of the individual applicant were an important consideration, as were the fact that there were no co-pending High Court proceedings. However, one reason for the decision was that the hearing officer felt that declining to hear this would be an abdication of the responsibilities given to the Comptroller by parliament but that is no longer the right test to apply.

In *Gerkros Boilers v Alley Enterprises* BL O/82/06, noted [2006] *CIPA* 273 (not an entitlement case), the hearing officer declined to transfer the case, notwithstanding the issues of perjury and fabrication of evidence to be resolved. In distinguishing *IDA v Southampton*, the hearing officer found that the facts of this case were not complex enough to fall into the category of cases which he had understood the Court of Appeal as indicating should be transferred—again, this is no longer the correct test.

While the court has an inherent jurisdiction to grant relief by way of a declaration of rights, the powers of the court otherwise to deal with wrongly claimed entitlement are not clear. On general principles, it is thought that the court could grant any relief of the types specifically available to the Comptroller under s.8(2) or s.37(2), but presumably the court would not have power to permit filing of a replacement application under subs.(4). In particular, there would seem to be no reason in principle why the court should not hold that a patent is held on some form of trust for the benefit of one or more others, see *Kakkar v Szelke* [1989] F.S.R. 225 CA. However, where the court exercises its jurisdiction under the Act, then s.99 gives it all the powers of the Comptroller.

Section 37(9) imposes a statutory limitation on the jurisdiction of a court under the section. As with proceedings before the Comptroller, where subs.(5) applies, a time bar is imposed for exercising its declaratory jurisdiction, as discussed in §37.11.

Filing of replacement application under section 37(4) after order for revocation

37.09

Under subs.(4), if the Comptroller finds that the patent was granted to a person not entitled to it (or to all of it), then the person or persons found by the Comptroller to be entitled to the patent can make an application under s.72(1)(b) to revoke the patent (or part of it), though revocation is only possible after the decision on entitlement has been made by the Comptroller or the court (s.72(2)(a)). If the Comptroller then makes an order for conditional or unconditional revocation of the patent, he may permit the person or persons making the revocation application to make a new application for a patent, which will be treated as having been made on the same date as the original patent application (subs.(4)).

It is not clear whether such a "replacement application" can be permitted by the Comptroller if he has declined to deal with the entitlement issue under subs.(8) and has left the court to decide this, or if the entitlement issue has been initiated solely before the court leading to a declaratory judgment of non-entitlement. A separate (further) application to the Comptroller under subs.(1) may then be a necessary prerequisite to obtaining permission for a replacement application to be filed under subs.(4).

Section 72(1)(b) is discussed in §7.12 as well as in §72.13. As s.72(2)(a) states that an application for revocation on the ground specified in s.72(1)(b), which is the ground relevant to s.37, can be made only by a person who "has been found" by the Comptroller to be entitled to the patent or a part of it on a reference to him of a matter under s.37, it would appear that the procedure first requires the reference to be made to the Comptroller under s.8 or s.37, or to the court under its inherent jurisdiction, for the question of entitlement to be determined, with a separate request for revocation under s.72(1)(b). In *Henry Bros v Ministry of Defence* [1997] R.P.C. 693, it was held that the decision in *Dolphin Showers v Farmiloe* [1989] F.S.R. 1 was incorrect in that it held that revocation proceedings under s.72(1)(b) could not be started until a declaration of non-entitlement had been obtained. In *Henry Bros*, it was held sufficient that such a declaration has been made before an order for revocation could itself be made. Thus, entitlement and subsequent revocation could then occur in concurrent proceedings, see §7.12 and §72.13. However, under the 2007 Rules, only one set of proceedings in the UK-IPO are required and issues under both sections can be brought in the same proceedings—see the further discussion in the commentary on s.123.

Where concurrent revocation proceedings are not in being, but the Comptroller determines that the patent was granted to a person not entitled, it is not clear whether the Comptroller will merely issue the order which he is required to make (under s.37(1)) to give effect to his determination of the matter, or whether he will indicate to the person or persons referring the matter to him that, subject to the outcome of an application under s.72(1)(b), he will issue an appropriate order giving effect to the proceedings under both sections. However, if all the relevant persons have been parties to the s.37 proceedings, or their equivalent before the court, the revocation proceedings under s.72(1)(b) can only be a formality because the doctrine of res judicata would prevent the entitlement question from being re-litigated in the revocation proceedings and, accordingly, the proprietor would appear not to be competent to oppose the application for revocation.

Any replacement application filed under s.37(4) (in the same way as those filed under s.8(3) or s.12) cannot proceed if it contains any additional matter over that contained in the original, improperly filed, application, see s.76(1) discussed in §76.02 and §76.03. However, none of s.8, s.12 or s.37 is listed in s.76(3) and hence there is no direct prohibition against the claims of the replacement application extending the protection conferred by the (improperly granted) patent, although this seems unlikely as indicated in §8.08 and §76.07. Indeed, the Comptroller has indicated that relief under ss.8(3), 12(2) and 37(4), which permit the filing of "replacement applications" should only be considered if no other satisfactory order can be found (*Szucs' Application* BL O/4/86 and O/27/88, noted I.P.D. 11014, where relief of this nature was not considered appropriate). However, replacement applications under s.37(4) were permitted (in proceedings commenced under s.8) in *Jessamine Holdings' Patent* BL O/138/85; *Viziball's Application* [1988] R.P.C. 213; and *Miller and Law's Application* BL O/46/86.

For a discussion on the time limits applicable to any such application see §§8.08, 8.11, 12.05, 12.06 and 37.13.

Relief granted under sections 8, 12 and 37

37.10 To establish entitlement to relief under s.8 and s.37, the onus of proof, as in proceedings under s.12, lies firmly with the claimant (or prior to the 2007 Rules, the "referrer"). Several cases have failed because, on a conflict of evidence, the claimant/referrer was then held to have failed to establish case for relief, as discussed in §37.06. However, the Comptroller is generally prepared to grant relief when the parties consent, as in *Bowling & Smith's Patent* BL O/35/90 where it was agreed the patent should be transferred to the referrer. In *Precast Micro Injection's Patent* BL O/234/98, a Malaysian court had granted, by consent, an Order for assignment of the patent to another company. The Comptroller held that this Order constituted sufficient evidence upon which he would make a transfer of ownership under s.37(1)(c). In *Cinpres v Melea* [2008] R.P.C. 17; [2008] EWCA Civ 9, the Court of Appeal said that the judge at first instance had had the:

> "unenviable task of deciding, as between two liars and perjurers, what the truth was (or at least what was most likely) about the making and ownership of the invention."

The lack of written documents may not be fatal to a claimant. In *Solenzaro's Patents* BL O/156/01 it was held not fatal to an argument that rights in the relevant patent had been transferred that no written documents had been signed because the Comptroller was entitled to take account of the position in equity, and the actions of the parties were consistent with transfer having taken place.

Where there is a written document, the onus will be on the claimant to prove his assertion that the agreement (pursuant to which the parties were co-proprietors) was void. So, in *Meider v Whitfield* (BL O/171/10), even though the relationship between them had broken down completely and joint ownership was not a "thrilling prospect" to either co-owner, the patent was to continue in the name of both parties. However, the Comptroller urged them to mediate the dispute.

The Comptroller may order, under s.8 or s.12, that a patent application be deemed as having always been filed in the name of the claimant (ex tunc), as opposed to an order that it be in the name of the claimant from the date of the order (ex nunc) (see *Lancaster University Business Enterprises Ltd and the University of Lancaster* BL O/040/09). Such an order may be a useful way of correcting matters where a priority application has been assigned, together with the right to claim priority, but the application has been mistakenly filed in the name of the party who originally filed the priority application.

In *Statoil v University of Southampton* BL O/204/05, noted [2005] *CIPA* 538, the hearing officer found that it was Statoil's employees, rather than the University's, who were the inventors and transferred the patents to Statoil. The position regarding the overseas applications was delayed to the second hearing and they were then also transferred to Statoil, the University having been given the opportunity but failed to show that different considerations applied. The order was stayed pending the outcome of the appeal, with provisions to ensure that the pending applications were prosecuted without detriment to Statoil.

In both *Kokta's Patents* BL O/88/91, noted I.P.D. 15018 and *Staeng's Patent* [1996] R.P.C. 183, the referrer was found to be a co-inventor on one of the referred patents, but his rights as co-owner had been subjugated to the patentee via the referrer's employer.

In *Robert Bion's Patent* BL O/66/86, noted I.P.D. 9068, two features of the main claim were held (on the balance of probabilities) to have been respectively invented by employees of different companies then collaborating with each other. The non-applicant company was ordered to become a co-proprietor under subs.(2)(a). Had the collaborative development been that of a sub-claim, it would appear that a licence to the referrer would have been ordered under subs.(2)(c).

In *Szucs' Application* BL O/4/86 a declaration was made (under s.8(1)) that certain defined subject-matter had been invented during the course of the applicant's former employment and that, accordingly, that subject-matter belonged to his former employer. The s.8 proceedings were then continued under s.37 with the request that the employer should become sole proprietor under subs.(2)(a), or become a licensee under subs.(2)(c). Sole proprietorship was rejected and co-proprietorship was held to be unattractive, (the decision not at this point having considered the effect of s.39(2)) and it was decided that the patent should remain in the sole ownership of the inventor, but that the former employer should be granted a free licence under the patent. The filing (under s.37(4)) of a replacement application for the non-entitled part of the patent was not considered appropriate, see §37.09.

In *Stanelco Fibre Optics v Bioprogress [Consequential Orders]* [2004] EWHC 2627 at 2630; C. Floyd QC November 2, 2004; noted [2004] *CIPA* 709, B was entitled to sole ownership of all but claims 6 and 7, to which S had contributed. Joint ownership was recorded in respect of a first patent, but in view of S only contributing to claims 6 and 7, the Order was to contain a proviso that S could not practice the inventions of any of the other claims. It was not felt necessary to give B the right to claim priority from the priority application filed by S, as this was seen to depend upon the wording of the priority document, rather than its ownership.

In *James Industries' Patent* [1987] R.P.C. 235 and *Hook's Patent* BL O/70/87, applications under s.37 were combined with applications under s.72 so that, if the referrer failed to establish entitlement, the patent might nevertheless not be an obstacle to his commercial activities. In *James*, both applications failed, the entitlement proceedings failing because the referrer did not establish an unconditional acceptance of an oral offer of an agreement between the parties for sharing of patent rights; but, in *Hook*, the plea for the revocation succeeded after a finding under s.37 that the proprietor was entitled only to part-ownership because his employer had provided other persons to assist him in developing his personal invention. Under the 2007 Rules, there is no need to begin separate proceedings under each section and these can all form part of the same application.

Also, in *Norris's Patent* [1988] R.P.C. 159, although the referrer failed to establish that he was entitled to the patent in substitution of the original applicant/proprietor, he was held to have contributed to a significant aspect of the claimed invention and was therefore entitled to become a co-proprietor of the patent which had by then been granted. Subsequently, the referrer claimed that the original applicant's share should be assigned to their then common employer (see BL O/179/88), and it was held that there was no issue estoppel which would exclude such a claim, as the original proceedings had only concerned the referrer's own entitlement. In yet further proceedings (see BL O/130/91, noted I.P.D. 15085), it was held that the invention had been made in the applicant's own time and that the rights had never belonged to his then employer; and, moreover, that a subsequent "arrangement" between him and a company set up to exploit the invention had never been sufficiently definite to be an agreement to transfer ownership of the patent.

In *Du Pont's (Rebouillat's) Applications* [1996] R.P.C. 740, the applicant accepted that the contested applications should be held on a constructive trust with the referrer having an equal undivided share in the patent rights. However, the Comptroller held that the referrer should not be required to contribute to the prosecution costs up to the date of agreement but should bear 50 per cent of such costs thereafter. Where the inventors had agreed to assign their rights to a company on the promise of allocations of shares, it was held that the inventors could not rescind that agreement merely because the promised shares had not been issued (*Edenlist's Patent* BL O/121/97).

In *Walter's Applications* BL O/272/05 and O/2/06, noted [2006] *CIPA* 122, the UK patent was awarded to Shannon Biotechnologies Limited, as entitlement was found under s.39 (see §39.06 and §39.11), but there was additional matter in the PCT which had been added by Dr Walters after terminating his relationship with Shannon, and so co-ownership of the PCT was awarded.

In *Leighton v Vickerys Holdings* BL C/59/91, noted I.P.D. 14158, the claimant (an employee) threatened to sue the agent who had filed an application on behalf of the defendant (his employer) if the agent took any action on it other than on claimant's instructions. The agent interpleaded in the entitlement proceedings brought before the court and successfully claimed his costs to be borne equally by the claimant and defendant, pending determination of the main proceedings.

From the similarity of the wording of s.36(1) and s.54(1) of the 1949 Act, it would appear that the decision in *Florey's Patent* [1962] R.P.C. 186 would still be relevant. In that case the Comptroller ordered that one of the proprietors should join in the sale of the patent desired by the others and it was held that the order could not be inconsistent with s.54 of the 1949 Act, and that each proprietor should share equally in the proceeds of the sale.

Where it appears to the Comptroller that there is no obviously satisfactory remedy to apply to a particular factual situation as found by him, the hearing has been adjourned for the parties to submit proposals or to seek to resolve the situation by voluntary action in line with the findings of fact made. Thus, in *Inrad's Application* BL O/164/88, where the parties to an entitlement dispute under s.8 were agreed that one of the four named inventors was not such, the Comptroller ordered PF 7 to be endorsed with his decision; a correction slip to be issued for the specification; and publication of the order in the *Patents Journal*. The proceedings were then adjourned for the remaining inventors to put forward proposals on proprietorship. Meanwhile, the application could not be amended or abandoned. Also, in *Hopkins' Application* BL O/83/88, a referrer was held to be entitled to be named as a co-inventor, but whether the resulting co-proprietorship should be with the referrer or to his employer was left to be decided after further submissions. In *BNOS Electronics' Patent* BL O/270/98 and O/239/99, the Comptroller held that the referrer (one of the named inventors) was not entitled to be named as an inventor, even though this had not been challenged by the proprietor.

In *Hughes v Paxman* [2007] R.P.C. 2; [2006] EWCA Civ 818, appealing BL O/143/05; and [2005] EWHC 2240 Pat Ct, the Court of Appeal held that the co-owner could be allowed to grant a licence under the UK patent, even though there was no entitlement dispute. However, the pleading was defective as it did not set out the terms of the licence sought. Without deciding the point, the Court of Appeal thought that the Comptroller could not grant to one co-owner an uncontrolled right to sublicense. The Comptroller had the power to grant a licence, but he had to act rationally, fairly and proportionately. Before the Comptroller and Kitchin J. the question of whether the Comptroller could also grant licences for overseas patents had been raised. It had been accepted below that this was not possible and the issue was not raised again in the Court of Appeal. However, as the Court of Appeal held that ss.8, 12 and 37 were interchangeable, it is possible that the Comptroller could make such orders in respect of pending foreign applications, if not in respect of the granted overseas patents.

Therefore, while not specifically overturning the prior practice on the grant of licences, the Court of Appeal has thrown doubt on it. However, even after *Hughes v Paxman*, the Comptroller has continued his practice of allowing joint applicants unfettered rights to exploit the patent independently of each other on the basis that: (1) he needs to be fair to both parties and; (2) it is in the public interest for the invention to be worked (see *Ogden and McKenzie's Patent* BL O/158/07). If the parties are already at loggerheads, then a requirement for consent will only give rise to further disputes. When *Hughes v Paxman* came back to the Office (see BL O/217/08), the Comptroller was able to avoid making any orders for licensing on the basis that the parties were not deadlocked as there had been co-operation since the breakdown in the relationship to license a third party. His criteria for exercising this power were to see whether there was a deadlock and then to see what represented a fair and commercial solution. He does not seem to have paid any attention to the Court of Appeal's doubt on the extent of that jurisdiction. So set out below are cases where the Comptroller granted rights to a co-proprietor to license the patent, and which he is still treating as good law.

In *Goddin and Rennie's Application* [1996] R.P.C. 141, G and R had jointly filed the application as co-inventors, but subsequently G (together with a company W which he partly owned) sought relief contending that R either had no entitlement or had filed the application in breach of confidence. Initially, these submissions failed with a finding by the Comptroller (in proceedings held in Scotland under what was then r.108 (but is now r.88)) that R had made an independent contribution to certain features of the invention, but (on appeal to the Scottish Court of Session) the decision of the Comptroller was criticised and varied as regards features of the patented design which, it was held, had been devised by R under an implied contractual arrangement that the rights should belong to the company making that arrangement, W. Thus, the patent should be granted to G alone, but as R had devised two features prior to entering that arrangement, the patent should be granted subject to the grant of an irrevocable exclusive licence to R with power to sub-license under two of the sub-claims.

Somewhat similarly, in *Andrews' Application* BL O/21/98, decided under s.8, joint inventorship was found, with each inventor having contributed different features and neither having sole entitlement to ownership. An order for joint ownership was seen to lead to difficulties and to be impracticable for both parties. The Comptroller thought this could best be resolved by the referrer accepting the previously refused offer of the applicant to sell his rights under the application in return for the costs incurred in filing the applications. However, if no agreement could be reached, the Comptroller was minded to make an order: either (under s.8(2)(a)) that the application should proceed in the name of the referrer, but (under s.8(2)(d)) with an irrevocable exclusive licence granted to the applicant with power to grant sub-licences in respect of articles incorporating the feature the applicant had devised; or an order that the application should proceed in the name of the applicant with a like licence to the referrer in respect of articles having the described features contributed by him but not the feature contributed by the applicant. The matter was then adjourned for consideration of these possible solutions. As no agreement was reached, an order was made that the referrer should have an irrevocable, exclusive, royalty-free licence with power to sub-license in respect of articles having incorporated one or both of the features contributed by him, provided that these did not have the feature contributed by the applicant. A similar case is *McGriskin's Patent* BL O/36/99 and O/135/00 where the Comptroller held that an order under s.37 following a finding of joint inventorship should result in equal treatment between the inventors and that such an order could override the statutory provisions on co-ownership set out in s.36; consequently, it was ordered that the referrer (W) should be joined as a co-owner with the original proprietor (M), with each co-owner having the right to license out without agreement or interference by the other; and with each responsible for paying half of each renewal fee, and not allowing the patent to lapse without the agreement of the other; and, if a renewal fee should not be timely paid by either party, the other was given the right to return the matter to the UK-IPO for further relief. In fact, the parties came back (see BL O/410/00) as M failed to pay her half share of a renewal fee "in a timely manner" as required. An order was therefore made for W to become the sole proprietor, but with M having an irrevocable, royalty-free, non-exclusive licence with power to grant sub-licences, but any party granted a sub-licence must be required to provide to W a bi-annual report of the amount of product produced and sold by it. W was also required to pay the other half-renewal fee which was accepted out of time.

In *Expotech's Patent* BL O/95/04; *(No.2)* BL O/189/04, noted [2004] *CIPA* 416; and *(No.3)* BL O/129/05, noted [2005] *CIPA* 397, it had been decided that E (the current applicant) had sole entitlement to claim 1, but that the claimant (BSB) had sole entitlement to some of the other claims. There should be a declared addition of the BSB inventor and joint ownership of the patent with mutual cross-licences. When the parties could not agree royalty rates, the hearing officer set them at zero. E had taken the "comparables approach",

BSB had taken the "profits available approach", but BSB was based in the UK and would have had to account on each act of manufacture, no matter where the machine was sold and E would only be exploiting by licensing and so only needed to account where the occasional sale was in the UK. So the zero rate minimised unfairness, but there should be no repayment of royalties already paid. The parties had leave to apply to amend the licence in the event that claim 1 was struck out in subsequent proceedings as its validity had already been impugned, and the loss of claim 1 would mean that the rights in the patent would now be predominantly with BSB. Provisions were also made regarding allowing either party to amend and in relation to infringement proceedings.

In *Ross's Application* BL O/188/04, noted [2004] *CIPA* 482 and *Crabtree and Ross's Applications/Patents* BL O/185/05 and O/267/05, noted [2005] *CIPA* 537, 668, the hearing officer followed the *Expotech* case and awarded cross-licences between the co-owners at nil rate royalty, there being no evidence to show any other suitable basis. The Comptroller also used the wide discretion of s.37 to allow sub-licensing by one co-owner without the consent of the other and without accounting to the other.

In *Advanced Extrusion's Patent* BL O/76/98, the referrers failed to establish that the applicant had not been the sole inventor. However, the inventor had broken a contractual arrangement with the referrers that the rights should not be assigned without their consent so that an assignment made was invalid. Subsequently (see BL O/57/99 and O/137/99), it was held that the application should now stand in the name of the sole inventor; the prior arrangement should be terminated; but the business operated by the referrers should have a royalty free, non-exclusive licence.

In *Crilly v New Age Radiators Ltd and Ray Fisher Construction Ltd* BL O/239/09, the Comptroller declined to make a costs award despite the lack of a counter-statement being taken as the defendants supporting the claimant's application, including the application for costs. The first scale fee is for both preparing the statement and consideration of the counter-statement, so this situation was not contemplated. A token award, below the bottom of the scale, was unlikely to serve a useful purpose, as it would cost more to collect than had been awarded.

Costs will be awarded against a claimant under s.8 who withdraws an application after evidence has been filed, even where the claimant is also challenging validity through the submission of third party observations. In *Ford v Threeway Pressings Ltd* O/060/09, the Comptroller found that the defendant had been put to expense in dealing with the s.8 application which could have been avoided if the claimant had sought advice earlier. The question of validity was not considered, as this would be left for the examiner in the event that substantive examination was requested.

Time bar for orders under section 37 (subss.(5) and (9))

37.11   A claim for entitlement may be brought at any time. However, there are restrictions as to what remedies may be obtained if the claim is brought too late. Subsection (5) imposes a time limit of two years from grant on a reference to the Comptroller under s.37 for an order transferring the patent in suit on the ground that it was granted to a person not entitled. The MOPP now clarifies that this period runs from the mention of grant in the *Journal*. Thus the period for launching the application expires the day **before** the second anniversary. Although subs.(5) is supposed to correspond to art.23 of the CPC and (by s.130(7)) is to be construed in conformity with it, notwithstanding that the CPC never came into force (see, e.g. Jacob L.J. para.27 *Yeda v Rhône-Poulenc Rorer* [2007] R.P.C. 9), the wording of the time limit for this type of application is not the same and that difference in wording was not in issue in *Yeda*. The CPC time limit is "not more than two years after the date on which the European Patent Bulletin mentions the grant" and this does expire **on** the second anniversary. These provisions were considered in *Rigcool v Optima Solutions* BL O/149/11, as the application had been filed on the second anniversary. Following the issue of Tribunal Practice Notice 4/2010, which had restated the time limits for lodging trade mark oppositions, the IPO had realised that it had been applying the wrong time limits under subs.(5). In view of its earlier practice and guidance, the Comptroller corrected the irregularity under r.107 in these proceedings, thus deciding that *Rigcool's* *application* (BL O/182/11) had been filed in time. However, this will not be available to later claimants. These decisions applied both to Rigcool's application for entitlement under s.37 and for its application for revocation under s.72(1)(b).

To avoid this time limit from biting, the claimant will have to show "knowledge" of the patentee or assignee at the relevant date—see further below.

As noted above, the two-year time limit does not apply to other forms of relief under s.37 (see *Lockheed Martin v Hybrid Air Vehicles* BL O/235/08—where the Comptroller allowed amendment to the statement of claim to include an earlier granted patent, even though the claimant had not made out a case on knowledge to overcome the two year bar for an ownership claim. Also see *Farr v Orbis* BL O/214/11, where the application had been filed late, and the claimant was not able to establish actual knowledge—see further below). This aspect of entitlement claims may not have been drawn to the attention of the courts in *Yeda Research v Rhône-Poulenc Rorer* [2008] R.P.C. 1; [2007] UKHL 43 (see §37.07) where the Court of Appeal seems to suggest that the two-year window was expected to be a "back-stop" for entitlement claim (see [2007] R.P.C. 9 at paras 4 and 5 and §37.06). But s.37 encompasses a greater range of disputes than can be brought under art.23 CPC and all other subsections of s.37 are omitted from s.130(7).

Subsection (9) is not cited in s.130(7) and could therefore be construed differently from art.23 of the CPC. This subsection was presumably intended to impose the same time limit on the court's exercise of its "declaratory jurisdiction" which refers back to subs.(8) where that phrase is used with reference only to proceedings referred by the Comptroller to the court in Scotland. However, the better view is surely that this phrase is used in subs.(9) in its general sense of referring to the inherent jurisdiction to grant declaratory relief of any "court" within the meaning defined by s.130(1), for which see §96.06 and §37.06. However, the wording in subs.(9) is different from that in subs.(5). In subs (9), the wording prevents the court from exercising its declaratory jurisdiction to decide whether a patent was granted to a person not entitled to it. In subs.(5), the wording is less restrictive. It does not prevent the Comptroller from, e.g. ruling on entitlement or granting licences, but it does prevent him from making certain types of order that would otherwise be open to him under s.37—namely transferring the patent or allowing a new application to be filed under s.37(4). The time limit set out in subs.(9) is expressed in the same language as subs.(5) and so presumably also expires the day **before** the second anniversary.

The time bars imposed by subss.(5) and (9) are mirrored in ss.72(2)(b) and 74(4)(b) which provide respectively that revocation and challenge to validity, each under s.72(1)(b), is only to be entertained if entitlement proceedings (under s.37 or before the court under its inherent jurisdiction) have been brought within two years from the date of grant of the patent, unless it is shown that any registered proprietor "knew" at the date of grant, or on the date of transfer of the patent to him, that he was not entitled to the patent, although in the case of a transfer of ownership knowledge acquired after the end of the two-year period is presumably irrelevant. In *Rigcool v Optima* the Comptroller found that, contrary to his earlier practice, the two-year period began on the day of grant and therefore expired on the day before the second anniversary and not on the anniversary itself (see above). Although the wording of s.74(4)(b), is not discussed in *Rigcool*, considering that it is the same as the wording in ss.37(5) and 72.(2)(b), the period should be calculated in exactly the same way.

Note also the comments on s.74(5) at §74.05.

Previous editions of this Work have speculated as to what is meant by "knew" in the context of subss.(5) and (9) (and, by analogy, ss.72(2)(b) and 74(4)(b)). Is the test subjective or objective? Did the test encompass "ought to have known" (cf. s.60(1)(b) and s.60(2) which contain the phrase "knows or it is obvious to a reasonable person in the circumstances"), even though no phrase about wider knowledge was is set out in these subsections?

In *Lockheed Martin v Hybrid Air Vehicles* BL O/235/08, the hearing officer held that the test of knowledge is subjective, not objective, and disagreed with the discussion in the previous editions of this Work. Although that was an interim decision as to whether the claimant could amend its statement of claim to add a claim for transfer to it of an earlier patent outside the period of two years from grant of that patent (the defendant having objected that the claimant had not given sufficient particulars of knowledge), the IPO has looked at the issue again in *Farr v Orbis* (above): first, in a contested application to strike out Farr's claim (BL O/161/11), and then in an uncontested substantive hearing (BL O/214/11).

The barrier set by subs.(5) is intended to be a high one so that legal certainty can be achieved. "Must have known" was not enough. It is for the claimant to establish that the patentee (or assignee) had knowledge that the patent should not have been granted to him. The IPO was not persuaded that even if the inventors had known that a relevant feature had derived from the claimant that that would have fixed their employer with knowledge. Nor would it have been enough if claimant's letter to the patentee indicating that he would challenge validity had carried with it a clear statement that validity was being challenged on the basis of entitlement (which it had not): the Hearing Officer stated that just because the claimant believed that it was entitled to the patent, it did not necessarily follow that the defendant knew that it was not entitled.

The words "not so entitled" in subs.(5) have been held to refer to the entitlement to the patent, and not to the grant of the patent but, where there was a dispute as to whether the applicant had agreed to assign the patent to a company, the two-year period was immaterial because either the applicant had not so agreed or, if he had, then he "knew" that he was not entitled to the patent, as not being the "true proprietor" under subs.(1)(a) (*Cartwright's Patent* BL O/74/93).

In *Peart's Patent* BL O/209/87, an application under s.37 to transfer ownership of the patent was refused on other grounds, but the Comptroller stated that anyway he would have refused it as being made more than two years after its grant. He said that knowledge by the proprietor that the referrer was disputing proprietorship was not sufficient to excuse the lapse of more than two years, and that that did not establish that the proprietor knew that he was not entitled to the grant.

In *Parr's Patents* BL O/46/94, noted I.P.D. 17130, the patentee (P) was a director of a company which the referrer alleged should have been the proprietor, but the referrer did not prove that P was at the time an employee and, as the company had not challenged P's ownership for several years, it was not proved that P "knew" that he was not entitled to the patent. An unsupported assertion that an experienced director would or ought to have had the requisite knowledge was not sufficient.

In cases such as *Farr v Orbis*, (see comments at §37.06 re lack of available evidence in relation to who devised the invention) and *Parr's Patents*, there would appear to be a lack of evidence from which the claimant could shift any aspect of the burden of proof to the defendant. It may be that in another case there would be stronger evidence as to who knew what and whether the defendant had turned a deliberate blind eye which would not be forgiven: for example, where the proprietorship has resulted from an assignment of the patent in circumstances where the defendant really ought to have had knowledge that entitlement to the grant of a patent was unlikely to exist.

In *Norris's Patent* BL O/130/91, noted I.P.D. 15085 the original order for the referrer to become a joint proprietor had been discharged on appeal pending further determination of possible employer ownership, see [1988] R.P.C. 159. However, when this had been done, it was then held too late to make a further order to this effect because of the time bar under subs.(5). Thus, it is important that a referrer seeks an order within the two-year time limit of this subsection.

The time limit in s.37(5), for bringing claims under this section against granted patents, does not prevent a claim for joint ownership from being amended after the expiry of the time limit to add a claim to sole ownership *Yeda Research v Rhône-Poulenc Rorer* [2008] R.P.C. 1; [2007] UKHL 43, see §37.07.

For additional discussion on the effect of the two-year limit on proceedings under s.37 and the meaning of "knew" in ss.37(5) and (9), 72(2)(b) and 74(4)(b), see the article by M. G. Harman (1986–87) 16 *CIPA* 274 and §72.13 and §74.05. Also, the ingenious, but doubtful, suggestion has been made (see (1980–81) 10 *CIPA* 254) that it may be possible to circumvent this time bar by application under s.34 to rectify the register rather than seek relief for wrongful entitlement under ss.37, 72 and/or 74. Reference is made in *Northern Light Music v Conversor* BL O/296/07 to an attempt to bring such an application in the High Court while entitlement proceedings were before the Comptroller. That application was reportedly dismissed as "procedurally misconceived and brought at the wrong time to the wrong court". However, the Comptroller, although not deciding the point, did not suggest that such an application was impossible, but the two-year time period was not in issue in that case.

Perhaps a better way round the time bar, in appropriate circumstances, would be to contend that the patent is held by its legal owner on a constructive trust for the referrer-beneficiary, who may then apply to the court: (a) to terminate the trust; (b) to order the trustee to assign the patent to the equitable owner, the beneficiary; and (c) to order the trustee to account to the beneficiary for the profits that have accrued from the trust. If viable, this procedure would seem to have a considerable added advantage over filing a new application under s.37(4). Thus, it would avoid the problem involved in suing the grantee-trustee for infringement: since the original patent would (under s.72(1)(b)) be revoked, and revoked ab initio, the owner of the new patent would seem to be disabled from suing the original patentee for infringement in respect of acts committed before its grant, and (under s.69) for damages in respect of acts committed after publication of the new application. However, by parity of reasoning with *Kakkar v Szelke* [1989] F.S.R. 225 CA, it may be that a claim for the holding of a trust is held to be a mere ruse and is really tantamount to a claim of entitlement outside the time bar.

Neither s.37 nor the rules set any time limit for filing the application for revocation consequent on a finding under s.37, but under r.82 (reprinted in §123.15) the Comptroller has a general discretion with regard to the procedure subsequent to formal filing of evidence in the matter referred to him, and therefore he has power to impose a time limit for making a revocation application.

PRACTICE UNDER SECTION 37

Proceedings under section 37 before the Comptroller

The powers and duties of the Comptroller under s.37 to determine questions of entitle-**37.12**
ment to a patent, and to issue an order to give effect to his decision, are closely parallel to his powers and duties under s.8 in connection with a United Kingdom application and under s.12 in connection with an application in a foreign country. A reference to the Comptroller under any of these sections is made on PF 2 and the procedure is now governed by Pt 7 of the 2007 Rules. One set of proceedings may cover references under different sections. The "claimant" (defined in r.73(3)) files the PF 2 in duplicate, together with two copies of the statements of grounds (r.76(1)). The statement of grounds must set out the grounds and the facts relied upon and the other matters referred tor.76(4). A copy is sent to the patent applicant and may be sent to others who appear to the Comptroller to be interested and they will be set a term to serve any counter-statements (r.77). The Comptroller does not need to notify anyone who has already provided written consent to the claimant's case and any party not responding to the Comptroller's notice is deemed to support the claimant's case. See *Farmer v Yardley* BL O/52/08, for a request for an extension of time for filing a counter-statement. The counter-statement must be filed in duplicate and is then sent to the claimant. For further discussion of the procedure, including directions, evidence and hearings see the commentary on s.123.

An applicant not residing within the European Community may be required to give security for costs (under s.107(4), see §107.05 and r.85, reprinted at §123.18).

Under the 1995 Rules, in *Advanced Extrusion's Patent* BL O/24/97, the patentee's counter-statement was filed late due to a misunderstanding as to the state of settlement negotiations. It was held that the 1995 Rules permitted a discretionary extension of the period set for this and that this extension could be granted retrospectively. It was also held that the patentee had not behaved so negligently that it should be made to suffer the consequence of the entitlement reference being unopposed. Under the 2007 Rules, r.82 (reprinted at §123.15) gives the Comptroller specific power to extend or shorten any period he sets under Pt 7 and to do this even after the period has expired. So such a case could still be decided in the same way.

Where the parties are and the witnesses are based in Scotland, then the Comptroller may hear the case there, under r.88(2) (see *James Campbell v University of Aberdeen* BL O/274/08 and §12.04).

Where a co-proprietor had died and all attempts to elicit some response on behalf of his estate, an application for his removal as co-proprietor was treated as uncontested (*Atha and Griffiths' Patent* BL O/68/97).

The Comptroller has refused to make an interim order that the patent (under which a reference under s.37 has been made) should be kept in force pending his decision: it was pointed out that the referrer could be given an opportunity to file a replacement application under subs.(4) if he is eventually successful (*Vet Health's Patent* BL O/49/90, noted I.P.D. 13165). Here it was also pointed out that no relief in respect of any foreign patent or application is possible under s.37, though there may be a possibility of parallel proceedings under s.12 in respect of any foreign applications not yet granted.

In *Fritsch's Patent* BL O/115/91, noted I.P.D. 15016, the Comptroller ordered a stay of proceedings under ss.37 and 72(1)(b), and under art.22 of the Brussels Convention (now Jurisdiction Regulation 44/2001, for which see §61.04), because proceedings already pending before the Irish court were sufficiently related to the matters referred to the Comptroller, and discretion to grant a stay should be exercised because the Irish Court was the *forum conveniens* for resolution of the dispute. However, the issues before the two tribunals were not identical and thus no automatic stay under art.21 of that Convention was required. Articles 21 and 22 of the Brussels Convention are equivalent to arts 27 and 28 respectively of the Jurisdiction Regulation. A stay was ordered in *Keith Dixon Roche*; *Oil & Gas Installations Ltd*; *Pipeflex Ltd v N V Bakaert SA*; *Luc Bourgois*; *Ludo Adriaensen*; and *Daniel Mauer* BL O/366/06, pending the outcome of entitlement proceedings in Belgium. As all parties agreed to the stay and there were no public interest issues, the hearing officer declined to go into any issues under the Jurisdiction.

In *Yeda Research v Rhône-Poulenc* BL O/163/05, the application for a stay pending the outcome of the EPO opposition, and the US and German entitlement proceedings, was refused. The EPO opposition was already stayed pending the outcome of the entitlement proceedings. The German court had indicated that it was unlikely to stay its entitlement proceedings. The US proceedings were due on for trial at around the same time as the UK proceedings, but might well be appealed. Other factors such as relative costs, the large sizes of the parties, the likely contribution to a settlement and the age of one alleged inventor was also taken into account. The risk of inconsistent judgments was seen as irrelevant, due to lack of harmonisation of the two national laws. So issue estoppel was remote. The issue in conducting the balancing exercise was essentially one of discretion to be exercised under the general principles of the *Comptroller's Tribunal Practice Note No.1/2000* [2000] R.P.C. 587—that brought the overriding objective into consideration, but it is now set out in r.74.

In *Thibierge & Connor's Application* BL O/345/01, an application for a stay of entitlement proceedings before the Comptroller when parallel proceedings had been commenced in France was refused. It was held that the applicant for the stay had the onus of showing that it was appropriate. A relevant consideration was the relative speed of proceedings before the English and French courts (the English proceedings being likely to be quicker) but not the availability of cross-examination and disclosure of documents because it would be improper to decide that one national procedure would be superior to another. The Comptroller's decision was upheld when this case came before the Patents Court in *Thibierge & Comar v Rexam* [2002] R.P.C. 18 at 379; see also §97.09.

In *JKN Polymers' Patent* BL O/119/97, the Comptroller granted a stay of entitlement proceedings for about a year because revocation proceedings had been commenced before the court and it was appropriate to see how these progressed, as to which the parties were to keep him informed. However, a stay was refused in *Egerton's Patent* BL O/219/98, noted I.P.D. 22022 pending a decision in an appeal to be lodged by the referrer against maintenance of the patent in an amended form in EPO opposition proceedings as these might "continue for a very long time", it being unrealistic to suppose that the proprietor would seek to maintain the European patent for other countries if the entitlement proceedings under s.37 succeeded. Likewise, stays were refused in *Polar Bay's European Application* BL O/263/98 and *Oxford Brookes University's Patents* BL O/37/00 where it was observed that the EPO would not be able to deal with the issue of entitlement during the pending opposition proceedings.

Where the parties took no steps in the proceedings for some two years because of an agreed but uncompleted settlement, the Comptroller ordered termination of the proceedings in the public interest (*Parker and Parker's Patent* BL O/57/92); and, likewise, in *Carruthers' and M&P's Patent* BL O/68/98, where the proceedings had been pending for over six years with various stays requested and granted, the Comptroller (after giving due warning) deemed the proceedings to be withdrawn.

In *Toland & Coates Smith* BL O/79/08 (proceedings begun before the applications were published), there was not enough in common between the "ideas" that the claimant said he had invented and the inventions set out in the applications. Further, the applications had ceased, leaving "no bone" and there was a want of prosecution. So the proceedings were struck out.

Where a referrer withdraws his application for entitlement before the hearing on the ground that evidence has been given showing that the patent is invalid, costs will normally be awarded against him unless he takes steps convincingly to demonstrate that the patent is invalid, e.g. by bring a successful application for revocation, see *Brisco Engineering's Patent* BL O/251/99. In *Compaction Technology's Patent* BL O/313/99, the Comptroller expressed his disapproval of a referrer withdrawing his application and immediately re-filing it in order to obtain further time for presenting his case, but declined to make an exceptional award of costs in the withdrawn proceedings. As the 2007 Rules now require that cases be decided in accordance with "overriding objective" (r.74), such a case may no longer be useful precedent.

If a person to whom directions have been given fails to carry them out within 14 days of the order, the Comptroller can be requested in writing to authorise the person in whose favour the order was made to do anything necessary himself (s.8(5); s.37(3)). Schedule 3 does not mention applications under either s.8(5) or 37(3), so it is not necessary to apply on form PF 2. These will be applications in the existing proceedings and so it is not necessary to begin new proceedings. See para.37.13 of the MOPP which states that applications under s.37(3) should nonetheless set out fully the facts upon which the applicant relies and the nature of the authorisation sought.

Filing of replacement application under subsection (4)

Where a replacement application is permitted to be filed under subs.(4), for which see **37.13** §37.09, r.20 (reprinted at §8.02) requires this to be filed within three months from the date on the order under s.37 is made (if it is not appealed), or (if appeal is brought) three months from the date when that appeal is finally disposed of. However, the Comptroller has power to shorten these periods if he thinks fit, upon giving notice of this to the parties and "subject to such conditions as [he] may direct" (r.20(4)) or he may extend the term on application under r.108, discussed in §§123.69–123.75). Under s.20(1), and r.30(3) as amended by the 2011 Rules, (reprinted in §18.04), any such application has to be placed in compliance with the Act and Rules within 18 months from its actual date of filing, unless the normal period of four years and six months from the declared priority date (or, if none, the deemed date of filing) should expire later. This provision is subject to r.30(4), that is, a possibility of extension of the "acceptance period" in the case of a late receipt of the first substantive examination report to three months after the report is sent. The periods under r.30 can be extended as of right by two months under r.108(2) by filing PF 52, and further on application under r.108(3), on filing PF 52 with supporting evidence, in the discretion of the Comptroller (also see above under §8.11 and §12.06). Nevertheless, if an appeal to the court has been brought before the end of this acceptance period, such period can be extended at the court's discretion under s.20(2)(a).

In any case, it is necessary to file with any such application the requests for search (on PF 9) and examination (on PF 10) as well as ensuring that an abstract and the claims have been filed. Copies of the inventorship statement (on PF 7), the priority document(s) and any necessary verified translations thereof must, in practice, also be filed with the application, see §15.23 or within such extended times as the Rules may permit, for which see §§15.18–15.25.

In a situation where, during entitlement proceedings, papers are filed which disclose information which ought to have been included in the patent specification to render it sufficient, it is important to seek confidentiality restrictions. In *David Singer Design's Patent* BL O/13/96, this was not done: the patent in suit was insufficient and could not be rendered sufficient by amendment, as this would result in subject-matter being added to it, contrary to s.76, and a completely new application could not be filed because of the public disclosure in the papers of the entitlement proceedings.

Procedure before the court in entitlement proceedings

37.14   If the Comptroller declines, under any of ss.8(7), 12(2) or 37(8), to deal with a matter, requiring this to be referred to a court for determination, then a person entitled to do so, i.e. a party to the proceedings before the Comptroller, is required (assuming a reference to the English Court is chosen) by CPR 63.11 (see Appendix F) to initiate a claim before the Patents Court or Patents County Court within 14 days of the Comptroller's decision. Presumably, the other parties to the previous proceedings should be named as "defendants" to that claim. Similar provisions can be expected to be applied in the other courts available, that is before the Court of Session in Scotland, the High Court in Northern Ireland or the High Court of the Isle of Man, as discussed in §96.06. However, presumably, a claim for declaratory relief may be commenced before such a court at any time under its inherent jurisdiction, although the relief available may then be curtailed, see §37.08.

Any application for the rectification of the register under s.34 (as a possible alternative method of proceeding, as suggested in §37.11) should be brought before the Patents Court or Patents County Court by a claim under CPR 63 PD, although there appears to be no express provision except where the comptroller has declined to deal, see CPR r.63.11 reproduced in Appendix F.

If a party wishes to bring allegations of breach of confidence, etc. then these should be brought at the same time as the entitlement proceedings. This may mean bringing the proceedings in the court, as the Comptroller does not have jurisdiction to adjudicate breach of confidence claims, although he does have jurisdiction to consider breach of confidence issues and other questions of general law such as breach of contract in the course of entitlement proceedings. In the *Markem* entitlement dispute, it had not been asserted that the employees had done anything wrong or unlawful. In response to points raised in the entitlement proceedings, the employees had started declaratory proceedings to clear their names of wrong doing. These had been stayed following *Markem's* application but post-trial, *Markem* sought to bring a new breach of confidence action, based on the same facts. This was struck out by the Court of Appeal (see [2005] R.P.C. 31; [2005] EWCA Civ 267) as an abuse of process, relying on *Henderson v Henderson* (1843) 3 Hare 100 as reiterated by the House of Lords in *Johnson v Gore Wood* [2002] 2 A.C. 1:

"the parties [should]…bring their whole case before the court so that all aspects of it may be finally decided…once and for all…".

For comment as to whether proceedings should be brought in the UK-IPO or the court see §37.08.

SECTION 38

Effect of transfer of patent under section 37

38.01   **38.**—(1) Where an order is made under section 37 above that a patent shall be transferred from any person or persons (the old proprietor or proprietors) to one or more persons (whether or not including an old proprietor), then, except in a case falling within subsection (2) below, any licences or other rights granted or created by the old proprietor or proprietors shall, subject to section 33 above and to the provisions of the order, continue in force and be treated as granted by the person or persons to whom the patent is ordered to be transferred (the new proprietor or proprietors).

(2) Where an order is so made that a patent shall be transferred from the old proprietor or proprietors to one or more persons none of whom was an old proprietor (on the ground that the patent was granted to a person not entitled to be granted the patent), any licences or other rights in or under the patent shall, subject to the provisions of the order and subsection (3) below, lapse on the registration of that person or those persons as the new proprietor or proprietors of the patent.

(3) Where an order is so made that a patent shall be transferred as mentioned in subsection (2) above or that a person other than an old proprietor may make a new application for a patent and before the reference of the question under that section resulting in the making of any such order is registered, the old proprietor or proprietors or a licensee of the patent, acting in good faith, worked the invention in question in the United Kingdom or made effective and serious preparations to do so, the old proprietor or proprietors or the licensee shall, on making a request to the new proprietor or proprietors **or, as the case may be, the new applicant** within the prescribed period, be entitled to be granted a licence (but not an exclusive licence) to continue working or, as the case may be, to work the invention, so far as it is the subject of the new application.

(4) Any such licence shall be granted for a reasonable period and on reasonable terms.

(5) The new proprietor or proprietors of the patent **or, as the case may be, the new applicant** or any person claiming that he is entitled to be granted any such licence may refer to the comptroller the question whether that person is so entitled and whether any such period is or terms are reasonable, and the comptroller shall determine the question and may, if he considers it appropriate, order the grant of such a licence.

Note. Subsections (3) and (5) were amended by the Patents Act 2004 (c.16) Sch.2(10) with effect from January 1, 2005 (SI 2004/3205).

RELEVANT RULES—RULES 73–88 AND 90

The rules reprinted at §§123.06–123.21 are those of Pt 7 of the Patents Rules 2007 and are general in nature to govern procedure in all proceedings to be heard before the Comptroller. These specifically include proceedings under s.38(5). These rules are discussed in the commentary under s.123, but are also mentioned, as appropriate, in the commentary and practice sections below. Rule 90 (reprinted in §11.02 above) is also relevant to licences following entitlement proceedings under s.37. **38.02**

COMMENTARY ON SECTION 38

Scope of the section

Section 38 is the counterpart of s.11 which deals with licences and other rights where the Comptroller has made an order changing the proprietorship of an application, with **38.03** s.38 dealing correspondingly with such matters where an order has been made under s.37 changing the proprietorship of a patent. Where an order has been made under s.37 affecting proprietorship, the position with respect to any licences or other rights (e.g. mortgages) depends upon whether or not the new proprietor(s) include the old proprietor(s) or any of them. The provisions of s.38 also apply to a patent resulting from a new application filed under s.37(4).

Effect of transfer of a patent under section 37

38.04   Subsection (1) deals with the first case where the new proprietor(s) include(s) the, or at least one of the, old proprietor(s). Here, any existing licences or other rights will continue in force, and will be treated as having been granted by the new proprietor(s).

Subsection (2) deals with the case where the new proprietors do not include the old proprietors or any of them. Here, any licences or rights cease as from the date of registration of the new proprietors, unless the order for transfer of the patent provides otherwise. However, in these circumstances, under subs.(3) (as under s.11(3), (3A) and (4)), an old proprietor or his licensee who, acting in good faith, had worked the invention in the United Kingdom or made effective and serious preparations to do so before the entitlement proceedings commenced is entitled, on request to the new proprietors, to be granted a non-exclusive licence to continue to work or to work the invention for a reasonable period and on reasonable terms (s.38(3), (4)).

The amendments made to subss.(3) and (5) by the Patents Act 2004 clarify that these provisions apply both when the successful party has opted to continue with the existing patent and when a choice has been made to file a replacement application. Similar provisions in relation to the right to seek the licence under a replacement application were introduced to s.11 by the Patents Act 2004. However, the transitional provisions which apply to s.11 do not apply to s.38, as s.38 already included a right to seek the licence under the replacement application, notwithstanding the clarifying amendments.

The terms "good faith" and "effective and serious preparations" also arise in s.28A(4) and s.64(1) and are discussed particularly in §28A.06 and §64.06. For the possibility of this provision being contrary to Community law, see §64.03. The term "non-exclusive licence" is defined in s.130(1) by reference to "exclusive licence". It would seem appropriate to construe "reasonable", both in relation to the duration and the terms of the ordered licence, as connoting an objective test as between willing, but arm's length, parties in the light of usage in the relevant industrial sector.

Under subs.(5), the new proprietor or the person making the request can refer to the Comptroller the question of whether or not the request is justified, and the Comptroller can then decide the matter, including the terms of the licence, and may order the grant of a licence. No time limit is specified for the making of a reference under s.38(5). If such a licence is ordered, it takes effect as a deed executed by all necessary parties, see s.108 and §108.02.

If, as a result of a reference under s.8, 12 or 37, an employer-owned patent resulting from an employee's invention were transferred to a third party who is not a person connected with the employer, the employee's rights to compensation under s.40 would be confined thereafter to the benefit derived by the employer from the transfer, see §41.04, and, since an order to transfer ownership would not be retroactive, such an employee could also rely on any right to compensation which had accrued up to the date of the transfer.

Result of making an order falling within subsection (2)

38.05   Under the 1995 Rules, the Comptroller was obliged to notify all original proprietors and their licensees of whom he was aware that he had made an order falling within subs.(2). There is no longer a rule to this effect. The term for making such a request to the new proprietor under subs.(3) is two months from the date of the order itself (see r.90—reprinted at §11.02). (Existing licensees had longer under the 1995 Rules—but now there is only one period for all potential new licensees.) However, presumably all interested parties will already be aware of the entitlement proceedings either because the Comptroller must notify the proprietor of the proceedings under s.37 (or s.8, if they began before grant) when they start (r.77(1)) or because when the proceedings start he may notify any person who appears to him to be likely to have an interest in the case (r.77(2)). Although this does not impose a duty on the Comptroller to notify a licensee or mortgagee, the MOPP states at para.123.05.5 that:

"Generally the Comptroller will notify any person named in the register of patents or in the statement of grounds and any other person who appears likely ona case-by-case basis to have an interest".

Further, at para.38.05, the MOPP states: "the Office notifies all existing proprietors and their licensees of whom it is aware of the making of the order".

The periods under r.90 are extensible at the Comptroller's discretion under r.108(1).

PRACTICE UNDER SECTION 38

Since a request under subs.(3) is to be made directly to the new proprietor, no form is specified for the request. Nor is it required that the Comptroller be notified of the request though it may be prudent to do so; the request would then become of public record on the file of the patent. **38.06**

Any reference to the Comptroller, either by the new proprietor or the person seeking a licence, is to be made on PF 2 under Pt 7 (reprinted at §§123.06–123.21). For more detail see the commentary on these provisions as they apply to an application under s.11(5) in §11.07 (which will also apply here mutatis mutandis) and the commentary on s.123.

Employees' inventions [Sections 39–43]

SECTION 39

Right to employees' inventions

39.—(1) Notwithstanding anything in any rule of law, an invention made by an employee shall, as between him and his employer, be taken to belong to his employer for the purposes of this Act and all other purposes if— **39.01**

    (a) it was made in the course of the normal duties of the employee or in the course of duties falling outside his normal duties, but specifically assigned to him, and the circumstances in either case were such that an invention might reasonably be expected to result from the carrying out of his duties; or

    (b) the invention was made in the course of the duties of the employee and, at the time of making the invention, because of the nature of his duties and the particular responsibilities arising from the nature of his duties he had a special obligation to further the interests of the employer's undertaking.

(2) Any other invention made by an employee shall, as between him and his employer, be taken for those purposes to belong to the employee.

(3) Where by virtue of this section an invention belongs, as between him and his employer, to an employee, nothing done—

    (a) by or on behalf of the employee or any person claiming under him for the purposes of pursuing an application for a patent, or

    (b) by any person for the purpose of performing or working the invention,

shall be taken to infringe any copyright or design right to which, as between him and his employer, his employer is entitled in any model or document relating to the invention.

Note. Subsection (3) was inserted by the CDPA 1988 (c.48) Sch.5(11), with effect from January 7, 1991 (SI 1990/2168).

COMMENTARY ON SECTION 39

General scope of provisions for "employees' inventions" (ss.39–43)

39.02   Section 39 is the first of a group of sections (ss.39–43) headed "Employees' Inventions". This group defines a self-contained code for determining ownership of an invention (s.39); regulates circumstances in which it would be "just" for an employer of such an employee to be obliged to make payments by way of "compensation" to that employee for the benefit which the employer has derived from a patent which has been granted for an invention or (where the patent application is filed on or after January 1, 2005) the invention, made by the employee (s.40); lays down guidelines for determining the quantum of such compensation (s.41); renders unenforceable certain clauses in contracts of employment widely used before 1978 (s.42); and limits the applicability of this group of sections to inventions made on or after June 1, 1978 and by persons "mainly employed" in the United Kingdom (including the Isle of Man). Some of the words used in the preceding sentence are defined in s.43 (which is, in effect, a mini-interpretation section for ss.39–42) and in s.130(1). These all receive discussion below and in the commentaries on the following ss.40–43. In particular, "patent" as used in these sections means under s.43(4) a patent or other protection and to its being granted whether under the law of the United Kingdom or the law in force in any other country or under any treaty or international convention; see further §43.05.

In relation to employee inventions, the provisions of ss.39–43 set out the law as from the commencement of the Act (June 1, 1978) and are not a consolidation of the previous case law. Thus the case law prior to June 1, 1978 has no application for determining ownership of inventions, save to the limited extent that it can give any guidance in relation to the assessment of an employee's duties (see *LIFFE v Pinkava* [2007] R.P.C. 30; [2007] EWCA Civ 217 the Chancellor at paras 42, 44 and 57 and Jacob L.J. at paras 91–92).

There is a general discussion of this subject in the book by Chandler and Holland, *Information: Protection, Ownership and Rights* (Blackstone Press, 1992), and the provisions of ss.39–43 were summarised, from the point of view of industrial relations, in a paper by Susan Cox (1991) 3(1) I.P.B. 2.

The provisions of s.10 of the Patents Act 2004 made a significant change to the operation of the provisions for compensation claims under s.40 and s.41. For inventions where the patent application is filed on or after January 1, 2005, the benefit derived from the invention will also be taken into consideration, as well as the benefit derived from the patent. We await the impact of that change. Applications filed on or after 2005 have now been granted. However, it is usually necessary to wait a few years before being able to assess whether an invention or patent or combination of the two has proved to be of outstanding benefit. So what case law there is relates to the old provisions, but these will continue to have effect in relation to patents filed before January 1, 2005 until these expire.

For a discussion on the comparative rights of ownership of employee inventions within the context of the comparative rights of employees to compensation across a number of European countries, see Senna Wolk, "Remuneration for employee inventors—is there a common European ground?" ([2011] June *CIPA* 352–358 for Part 1 and [2011] July *CIPA* 440–445 for Part 2.)

Scope of section 39

39.03   Section 39 is a provision of substantive, rather than procedural, law. It has effect in relation to the settlement of entitlement disputes under s.8, 12, 37 or 82; and to the question of "compensation" under s.40. It relates to rights in inventions made after June 1, 1978 (s.43(1)) by persons normally resident in the United Kingdom (s.43(2)), and has effect in relation to "patents and other protection" generally irrespective of where or how granted, see s.43(4) and §43.05. For the meaning of the term "invention" in this context, see §39.04.

Put simply, the section specifies (in subs.(1)) the circumstances in which an invention made by such an employee will automatically, by operation of law, vest in the employer but, if none of the circumstances set out in subs.(1) exist, then under subs.(2) ownership of the invention belongs entirely to the employee in his own right, overriding any enactment made before June 1, 1978 and any agreement between the employer and employee of different effect (s.42(2)). These provisions, however, only apply to situations where the invention was made by a person "mainly employed" in the United Kingdom, or by a person not employed anywhere, or employed at an indeterminate location, where his employer had a place of business in the United Kingdom to which the employee was attached, whether or not also attached elsewhere, see s.43(2), as discussed in §43.03. The section has to be applied to the employment situation as it existed at the time the invention was made (*Harris's Patent* [1985] R.P.C. 19 and *French v Mason* [1999] F.S.R. 597), a point discussed in §37.05.

In deciding which of these subsections governs a particular factual situation, it must first be decided who is the "inventor" (for which see the discussion at §7.10), whether he is an employee and what is the "invention", for which see the discussion at §7.08.

The section applies to European, international and foreign applications, but there are no provisions in the EPC, CPC or PCT relating to ownership of patent rights in inventions made by employees, except that disputes on entitlement (and hence disputes arising from a dispute as to the applicability of subs.(1) to a particular situation) may have to be settled in another country if an agreement exists between the employee and employer so stating, and assuming that such an agreement is not void under s.42(2), discussed in §42.02 and §42.03 (Protocol on Recognition, to which effect is given by s.82(9), see §82.02 and §83.02 and the commentary on ss.82 and 83). Otherwise, ownership of an employee's invention falls to be determined by individual national laws, generally applicable only to persons normally employed in the country in question.

Section 39 has no applicability to inventions made solely by non-employees. The disposition of patent rights arising from inventions made by such persons, however, remains subject to possible contractual obligations, for example in the case of research work commissioned from a non-employee. A contract between an employer and a third party concerning the disposition of patent rights of employee inventions can have no effect on patent rights which belong to an employee under subs.(1). That contract may then become incapable of fulfilment, the consequences of which will depend upon the default provisions therein and the doctrine of frustration in the law of contract. The section also has no effect upon the ownership of inventions made before June 1, 1978 (s.43(1)).

Meaning of "invention" in sections 39–43

"Invention" (as used in s.39) is a term clearly wider than "patentable (or patented) invention", but is not defined in the Act: ss.1, 125 and 130, inter alia, deal only with inventions for which a patent under the Act has been applied for or granted. See also the discussion at §7.08, where "invention" is likewise not confined to an invention patentable under the Act. In *Viziball's Application* [1988] R.P.C. 213, it was held that "invention", as used in s.8, encompasses unpatentable subject-matter, whether because already known or because expressly excluded from the ambit of the Act (e.g. by s.1(2), 1(3) or 4(2)). In *LIFFE v Pinkava* [2007] R.P.C. 30; [2007] EWCA Civ 217, the "invention" related to software and the only patent applications were in the US. For the purposes of s.39, it is immaterial whether a patent application has been filed or not, but the nature of the alleged invention needs to be assessed in relation to the duties of the employee, as discussed in §§39.07–39.11. The phrase in the introductory part of subs.(1) "for…all other purposes"; and the reference in s.43(4) to "other protection", needs to be noted, particularly as this provision had been amended specifically to relate also to s.39, see §39.16 and §43.05. Also, it is inferable (from introduced subs.(3)) that the provisions of subss.(1) and (2) are capable of affecting things that may be called "inventions", but which are (also) protected

39.04

(at least in relation to certain aspects) by copyright or design right and, at least by implication, registered designs.

This wide meaning of "invention", including (per s.43(3)) activities by one of a number of co-inventors (but not including the mere contribution of advice or other assistance to the work of a co-employee), may well encompass many "suggestions" submitted by employees under company suggestion schemes. Care should, therefore, be taken to ensure that any rules of such schemes purporting to regulate the ownership of the submitted suggestions remain in harmony with the provisions of s.39. The effect of s.42(2) (unenforceable terms) may also need to be considered, see §42.03, as may s.42(3) (confidentiality), see §42.04.

Although not a s.39 case, the nature and effect of the law of confidence in relation to suggestion schemes was examined in *Prout v British Gas* [1992] F.S.R. 478.

Meaning of "employee" for sections 39–43

39.05 "Employee" is defined for the purposes of the Act in s.130(1) by reference to a "contract of employment", a definition closely similar to that for "employee" now contained in s.230(1) of the Employment Rights Act 1996 (c.18), but the definition used initially in the 1977 Act was extended by the Armed Forces Act 1981 (c.55), by amendment of s.42(4) and s.130(1) to add the words "or a person who serves (or served) in the naval, military or air forces of the Crown" (see §42.01 and §130.01), thereby equating members of the armed forces to employees [of the Crown] for the purposes of ss.39–43. However, as noted at §42.05, the definition of Crown employee in s.42(4) includes those working for any officer or body exercising on behalf of the Crown functions conferred by any enactment, as well as those working for government departments or in the armed forces, whereas the definition of employee at s.130(7) does not.

The Act does not contain a definition of "contract of employment". However, the Employment Rights Act 1996 defines "contract of employment" at s.230(2) as a "contract of service or of apprenticeship" and the CDPA 1988 defines "employee", for the purposes of copyright and design law respectively, as employment "under a contract of service or of apprenticeship" (CDPA 1988 ss.178 and 263(1)). This definition of a "contract of employment" is also to be found in s.295 of the Trade Union and Labour Relations (Consolidation) Act 1992 (c.52). Thus inventions made by apprentices are likely to follow the same rules as those which relate to other employees.

Attention is also drawn to the definition of "worker" in s.230(3) of the Employment Rights Act 1996. Employees are a sub-group of "workers" and not all "workers" are "employees". "Limb (b) workers" (those working not under a contract of employment, but under any other contract whereby the individual undertakes to do or perform personally any work or services for another who is not a client or customer of a profession or business carried on by the individual) are not employees, but have some statutory rights, although not all of the statutory rights enjoyed by "employees". The distinction is discussed by the Court of Appeal and by the Supreme Court, respectively in *Autoclenz Ltd v Belcher* [2009] EWCA Civ 1046 and [2011] UKSC 41. Employers will not have the same rights to intellectual creations of "limb (b) workers", as they have to those of employees.

The status of the inventor as employee

39.06 In most cases, the status of the inventor as employee is not in doubt, but difficult problems can arise with regard to: directors (*Parsons v Parsons* [1979] F.S.R. 254), who are not necessarily employees (*Parr's Patents* BL O/46/94, noted I.P.D. 17130); consultants, see *Shape and Potemkin's Applications* BL O/140/92 and C/68/94, noted I.P.D. 18033 discussed in §37.05; education and university staff; hospital staff; and "home workers". In such cases one must first determine if there is a contract at all, and then, if so, whether the contract is one "of service" (i.e. "employment") or "for services" (i.e. provided on a "self-employed" basis). The question is one of law, and also the facts of the case in question (*Davies v Presbyterian Church of Wales* [1986] 1 W.L.R. 323; [1986] I.R.L.R. 194 HL). An equity-holding partner in a firm is an employer of its staff and cannot therefore be said to be employed by it himself, but the ownership of shares in a company, even by a majority shareholder, is irrelevant as the company is an entity quite separate from its members (*Salomon v Salomon & Co Ltd* [1897] A.C. 22 HL).

Given the crucial difference in treatment of employees for tax and national insurance purposes, as well as for entitlement to social security benefits and employment protection rights (e.g. as regards redundancy, unfair dismissal, health and safety provisions, protection of pay when the employer becomes insolvent, etc.) a huge body of case law on the point has built up in employment law. To do more than provide the briefest of outlines here is beyond the scope of this commentary.

For a contract to be capable of being one of service (i.e. an employment contract) there are three elements which must be present: mutuality of obligation, personal service and control. The precise meaning of mutuality of obligation is frequently before the courts, but at its basis is the irreducible minimum of an obligation on the employee to perform work for the employer and an obligation on the employer to provide work (see *Carmichael v National Power Plc* [2000] I.R.L.R. 43). The personal service requirement was originally set out in *Ready-Mixed Concrete (South East) v Minister of Pensions and National Insurance* [1968] 2 Q.B. 497 and requires an obligation on the employee to provide his or her own work and skill. Included in this element of the test is the right to provide a substitute. Generally, an employee must not be able to provide a substitute to do his or her work (see *Express and Echo Publications Ltd v Tanton* [1999] I.R.L.R. 367) although, as with all the elements, this is not a conclusive test and will be only one of a number of facts considered. Historically, the test for employment status was simply about control: the existence of a contract of service turned on the presence or absence of a right for the "master" to give orders and a corresponding duty on the "servant" to obey. However, with the increased regulation of the employment relationship, there has been a move away from a reliance solely on control. Now whilst the existence of a right for the employer to control how work is performed will not automatically lead to a finding that there exists a contract of service, the absence of control will preclude such a finding (*Ready-Mixed Concrete (South East) v Minister of Pensions and National Insurance* [1968] 2 Q.B. 497, approved in *Autoclenz*, above). If all the three elements exist, whether or not the contract is one of service and therefore the individual an employee, will depend on the circumstances of each particular case: the contract must be looked at as a whole, weighing up all the relevant terms of the contract. In many employment cases, the contracts appear to show that the individuals are not employees of the company—thereby not enjoying employment rights and getting different tax treatment. In contrast, in IP cases, there is often a desire to show that the individual was an employee and hence that the company owns the IP in question.

The Court of Appeal further considered the question of whether or not agreements between companies and those who worked for them represented the true nature of the relationship or were a sham, see *Protectacoat Firthglow Ltd v Szilagyi* [2009] EWCA Civ 98 and *Autoclenz Ltd v Belcher et al*, above. In both cases, the agreements stated that the individuals were independent contractors. In *Protectacoat*, the individuals had first signed a partnership agreement between them (which Protectacoat had provided for them) and the partnership had then contracted with Protectacoat. However, in each case the court looked at the true obligations of the parties.

The court considered the position of whether or not a person was an employee in *Ultraframe v Fielding* [2004] R.P.C. 24; [2003] EWCA Civ 1805. This was a case regarding the ownership of design rights. There the Court of Appeal approved (and the Supreme Court has also approved in *Autoclenz*) the conditions in *Ready Mixed Concrete v Minister of Pensions and National Insurance* [1968] 2 Q.B. 497 at 515:

"(i) The servant agrees that, in consideration of a wage or other remuneration he will provide his own work and skill in the performance of some service for his master.

(ii) He agrees, expressly or impliedly that in the performance of that service he will be subject to the other's control in a sufficient degree to make that other master.

(iii) The other conditions of the contract are consistent with its being a contract of service.

Freedom to do a job either by one's own hands or by another's is inconsistent with a contract of service, though a limited or occasional power of delegation may not be."

The Supreme Court went on to say that there were three further propositions:

(i) "There must ... be an irreducible minimum of obligation on each side to create a contract of service"*Nethermere (St Neots) v Gardiner* [1984] I.C.R. 612.

(ii) If a genuine right of substitution exists, this negates an obligation to perform work personally and is inconsistent with employee status: *Express & Echo Publications Ltd v Tanton* (" *Tanton*") [1999] ICR 693, at p.699G.

(iii) If a contractual right, as for example a right to substitute, exists, it does not matter that it is not used. It does not follow from the fact that a term is not enforced that such a term is not part of the agreement: see e.g. *Tanton* at p.697G.

Cases in which it was held that that a creator was not an employee at the relevant time are: *Coffey's Registered Designs* [1982] F.S.R. 227, where the designer was at the time only a partner in an informal partnership under no trust obligation to it or to a company incorporated only subsequently; *Gleave's Patent* BL O/22/88, where a referrer in s.37 proceedings failed to prove that the patent proprietor was an employee at the relevant time and where it appeared that the alleged employer company had not then been incorporated (see also *Lawson and McGarry's Application* BL O/56/04, noted [2004] *CIPA* 165— where again the company had not been incorporated at the date of the invention); and *Westco's Application* BL O/133/97, where no contract of employment was found for a short period prior to formal employee engagement, the invention being held to have been made during this period for which no salary had been paid.

The question as to whether either or both of two brothers were employees of the business was raised in *Enston's Applications* BL O/206/04, noted [2004] *CIPA* 484. One brother, P, said that at most he was a consultant, but that the other brother was an employee as well as being the managing director. E said that he had been trying to resign as director, although he did not file the relevant forms until later, but he had not been remunerated by the company during Autumn 1999 and the payments made to him in the summer had more of a flavour of expenses and profit sharing than a regular wage. Accordingly, P had not made out his case that E was employed nor what the terms of that employment were, and if E had been an employee, then this could not have survived into the period when he was not paid.

On the other hand, in *Stablocel's Applications* BL O/3/91, noted I.P.D. 14101, the referrer in entitlement proceedings failed to prove that he had made the invention during a short period when he was unemployed following redundancy from, and liquidation of, his former employer and his re-engagement by its successor. In *Walter's Applications* BL O/272/05, noted in [2006] *CIPA* 122, where there were regular payments to the inventor and he held himself out to third parties as representing the company or even as the commercial director or the CEO of the company, the Comptroller held that this pointed to his being an employee rather than a consultant.

Where an employee is seconded by the employer to a third party then, in the absence of a contrary agreement, his/her inventions will in the circumstances described in subs.(1) belong to the employer and not to the third party, although of course the employer is free to assign all rights in the invention to that third party (*Defence Technology's Application* BL O/77/93, noted I.P.D. 16124).

Ownership of employee inventions by an employer

—The basic rule

39.07   The introductory phrase of subs.(1) simply sweeps away any rule evolved under the common law before June 1, 1978 (*Harris's Patent* [1985] R.P.C. 19; and *LIFFE v Pinkava* [2007] R.P.C. 30; [2007] EWCA Civ 217). This renders precedents decided under the common law of no assistance for subs.(1)(a) cases and of only limited help in subs.(1)(b) cases, but see the comment in §39.10. Note, however, Jacob L.J.'s comment in *LIFFE* that the common law may re-appear to a limited extent by the "back door" where the employee's ownership rights clash with his or her duties of confidentiality, see below on the commentary on s.42(3) at §42.04.

The general structure of s.39 suggests that an invention made by an employee will belong wholly to the employee (subs.(2)) unless it is one which fits the tests laid down in subs.(1) for it to belong wholly to the employer. Hence, the scheme of the section completely excludes joint ownership between the employee and the employer for a particular invention. However, the subject-matter of a patent application may go beyond any such single invention and so could belong to both the employer and the employee. This structure is then glossed by subs.(3) under which the exploitation by an employee of an employee-owned invention, which invention is protected (additionally) by other intellectual property rights which are owned by the employer by virtue of the provisions of ownership under legislation for the protection of such other intellectual property rights, receives immunity from infringement of those other rights, e.g. ss.11 and 215 of the CDPA 1988.

The subsection recognises that an "invention" not necessarily covered by a patent may exist as a copyright work, e.g. circuitry diagrams (*Ibcos Computers Ltd v Barclays Mercantile Highland Finance Ltd* [1994] F.S.R. 275), or as an unregistered design, that is to say, protected by IP rights which are neither "granted" nor are true monopolies, cf. *Kelly and Chiu v GE Healthcare*, [2009] R.P.C. 12, [2009] EWHC 181 Pat Ct and the discussion of "other protection" in s.43(4) at §43.05, below.

In *French v Mason* [1999] F.S.R. 597 the phrase "taken to belong to his employer for the purposes of this Act and all other purposes" was considered in a context where the employee sought to establish a constructive trust to retain beneficial ownership of an invention as against the employer. The court concluded that this phrase talks of ownership:

> "in a sense which is not technical and which does not distinguish between legal and equitable ownership. It is talking of ownership which permits the owner to deal with the patent and to work under it".

Although the question of onus of proof under s.39 is not free from doubt, it is submitted that, on the above analysis of the structure of the section, an employee will own his invention by virtue of subs.(2) unless his employer can prove that the situation under either part of subs.(1)(a) or under subs.(1)(b) exists in fact. However, in entitlement proceedings under s.8, 12, 37 or 82, the Comptroller holds the view that the claimant (previously called the referrer) has the onus of proving its contentions. This view, based on s.7(4), for which see §7.11, i.e. when a patent application has already been filed, is open to the criticism that it overlooks the effect of s.39(2). It is submitted that the better view, supported by *Harris's Patent* (above), is that, when s.39 is under consideration, the onus should be on the employer to show that the facts correspond to one of the situations in s.39(1) irrespective of whether it was the employer or the employee who was the applicant of the disputed application.

The factual situation can be proved under subs.(1)(a) either by reference to the employee's "normal duties" or to other duties "specifically assigned to him", whereas subs.(1)(b) provides a third gateway through which an employer can claim rights, by reference to the employee's duties giving rise to "particular responsibilities" and an ensuing "special obligation", though still provided that the invention was made within the scope of the duties of that employee.

For each of the three gateways of subs.(1) a two-stage inquiry is required, the first stage being broadly common to each of these, viz. the establishment of the actual duties of the employee. The second stage is then: (in both parts of subs.(1)(a)) consideration whether the performance of those duties might result in the making of inventions and, if so, the type of invention; and (in subs.(1)(b)) consideration of whether those duties carried responsibilities and obligations for the employee. As *Harris* (above) shows, the Comptroller or court will not be satisfied with job titles but will "lift the veil" to establish the detailed facts.

These facts will often show that a person, though an employee, engages in a number of activities at different times. Not all those activities may be "duties" of employment at all. For example, the position of university lecturers is particularly obscure in relation to their research activities if they are engaged primarily to teach, with spare time allowed for research, but no obligation to carry it out. The position of such persons was discussed by W.R. Cornish in "Rights in university innovations: The Herchel Smith lecture for 1991" [1992] E.I.P.R. 13. See also the decision of the Federal Court of Australia in *University of Western Australia v Gray (No.20)* [2008] F.C.A. 498, dated April 17, 2008, subsequently upheld by the Full Court of the Federal Court of Australia, [2009] FCAFC 116 (September 3, 2009) (link: *http://www.austlii.edu.au/au/cases/cth/FCAFC/2009/116.html*). Although Australia does not have a provision equivalent to s.39 and accordingly makes its decisions under the common law, the judge was not prepared to accept that, as a general proposition, there should be a presumption at law that all inventions made by research staff should automatically belong to the University—it would all depend on the circumstances of the case, including the provisions of the relevant employment contract.

In *LIFFE v Pinkava* [2007] R.P.C. 30; [2006] EWHC 595 Pat Ct, noted [2006] *CIPA* 270 the court took an extensive look at LIFFE's business and the role of Pinkava ("P") within it. It looked at what were the normal and assigned duties and whether an invention of the relevant type was expected to result. The case started in the High Court with LIFFE alleging breach of contract and misuse of confidential information in the filing of four US software and business method patents. P applied under s.12 for a declaration that these belonged to him, but this was transferred to the High Court: BL O/317/05. When the case reached the Court of Appeal, that court's detailed review of the facts led it to conclude that the inventor's duties had evolved over time, with duties which had originally been "assigned duties" becoming "normal duties": [2007] R.P.C. 30; [2007] EWCA Civ 217.

Subsections (1) and (2) are mutually exclusive as between employer and employee, where the invention in question arose at a particular point in time. It is submitted that this overrides the Comptroller's discretionary powers under ss.8 and 37 to grant a patent to joint proprietors where these would be employer and employee and confirms the position under the 1949 Act, as decided in *Patchett v Sterling* (1955) 72 R.P.C. 50 HL. However, where there are a sequence of events with multiple inventions in the same patent application, then it is possible that the employee may own some and (where his duties had changed or he became an employee after some initial work, such that s.39(1) is then satisfied) the employer may own others. In *Szucs' Application* BL O/27/88, noted I.P.D. 11014 (decided under s.37), ownership was awarded to the employee even though part of the subject-matter of the application had been made during employment, but with a free licence under the patent to the employer. The Comptroller stated that joint proprietorship was unattractive, and had ruled out sole proprietorship.

In *Peart's Patent* BL O/209/87 the Comptroller did not accept an argument that conception of an invention outside working hours (where the employee had been charged with finding the outcome of a particular problem) fell outside the scope of an employee's duties. While accepting that the invention was not made in the course of the referrer's normal or specifically assigned duties for the purposes of subs.(1)(a), it was held that the employee's position required him to further the interests of the employer and so the invention belonged to the employer. The decision can be criticised because, for the purposes of subs.(1)(b), it must first be shown that the invention was made in the course of the duties of the employee, before proceeding to focus on the "special obligations", i.e. more is required than the general duty of fidelity.

The Comptroller has been prepared to hold (in an uncontested case) that all rights in an invention belong to the employer when the inventor had apparently been employed to carry out duties relating to the invention (*Travenol Laboratories' Application* BL O/45/90, noted I.P.D. 13141); but in *Hamill's Application* BL O/149/92, he was careful to find that the invention had been made in the course of the normal duties of the employee and was the type of invention which could be expected to result from the carrying out of those duties. In *Defence Technology's Application* BL O/77/93, noted I.P.D. 16124, the referrer failed to prove his invention was not made in those circumstances. In an interim application in a copyright case, it was held not to be unarguable that "moonlighting" falls within the phrase "in the course of employment" (*Missing Link Software v Magee* [1989] F.S.R. 361).

The inventor in *Szewczyk's Application,* BL O/301/04, noted [2004] *CIPA* 655, fell fully within s.39(1)(a)—he had made the inventions during his employment, his normal duties included product development, the inventions in question related to a project that was on-going at the time—and so the patent was transferred to the employer.

—The employee's normal duties

In *Harris's Patent* [1985] R.P.C. 19, the "normal duties" of an employee were defined **39.08** as the actual duties which he was employed to do. Thus, an employee's "normal duties" will be those defined by his contract of employment, including additional terms which may be implied, e.g. the duty of good faith, and terms which are incorporated from collective agreements between employers and trade unions, from custom and practice, and from ancillary documents such as pre-employment correspondence, engagement letters, handbooks, works rules, notices on notice boards, etc. In *Harris* (above), it was held never to have been part of the duties of the employee to apply his mind to solving technical problems.

In *LIFFE v Pinkava* [2007] R.P.C. 30; [2007] EWCA Civ 217, the Court of Appeal found that the employee's duty is primarily contractual, although some terms will be implied by law. An overstatement of the duties was likely to be struck down by s.42(2) (see s.42(2) and (3)). However, these could be expected to be expanded or contracted over time by "a continuous process of subtle variation". Also the performance reviews resulted in further documents which recorded responsibilities on promotion and contained both statements from the employee as to how he saw his role and objectives set by the employer for the next period.

Harris (above) also settled the controversy over the scope of the implied term of an employee's duty of good faith, sometimes referred to as the duty of fidelity: it is co-extensive with, and does not go beyond, contractual duties. In this, *Harris* followed *United Sterling v Felton and Mannion* [1974] R.P.C. 162 in which it was stated that the duty of fidelity expires at the moment the contract of employment terminates, though there is a continuing obligation not to disclose the employer's confidential information (*Faccenda Chicken v Fowler* [1986] F.S.R. 291 CA), and see s.42(3) discussed in §42.04. It should also be noted that contractual duties beyond that of fidelity may be implied in certain, usually non-industrial circumstances: *Attorney-General v Guardian Newspapers (No.2)* [1989] 2 F.S.R. 181; [1988] 3 All E.R. 545, the "Spycatcher" case.

In *Secretary of State for Defence's Application* BL O/135/89, noted I.P.D. 13063, the Comptroller saw no distinction between "official" and "normal" duties, and, where research workers had investigated whether a particular topic should become an approved research product, this was regarded as part of their normal duties. In *British Gas's Application* BL O/176/92, the employed inventor was unsuccessful in his claim to ownership. Some years after he had left his employer's service division and while working on his own initiative, though with the knowledge of the employer and using the employer's materials, the invention was made. The inventor reported this and suggested the filing of a patent application. In these circumstances the invention was held to have been made during the course of the inventor's normal duties.

In *Greater Glasgow Health Board's Application* BL O/136/94 and [1996] R.P.C. 207, the inventor was employed as a clinical hospital registrar and research facilities were made available to him. The Comptroller held that his normal duties included trying to improve patient treatment and that this included considering the modification of an existing ophthalmic instrument, but on appeal the decision was reversed, it being held that the employee's normal duties (as a hospital junior consultant) were limited to clinical responsibilities and that it was unrealistic to hold that these duties extended to all aspects of patient care: in effect that would emasculate s.39(1)(a). For case comment thereon, see P.A. Chandler [1997] E.I.P.R. 262. Following *Greater Glasgow Health Board's Application*, it was held that the job description for a hospital surgeon had merely provided a hope, rather than an obligation, that research would be done under the employment contract. Hence, the surgeon should have entitlement to an invention made by him in his own time and not during either his normal, or specially assigned, duties (*Bradford Hospital's Application* BL O/37/01). However, in *Marchbanks' Applications* BL O/12/96, the normal duties of a person employed by an Institute were held to include research when he admitted that he spent about 20 per cent of his time on that activity. (Although see also *University of Western Australia v Gray* for the duties of academics, discussed at §39.07).

—Duties specifically assigned to employee

39.09   In *Secretary of State for Defence's Application* BL O/135/89, noted I.P.D. 13063, specifically assigned duties were stated to be duties which are not the standard or everyday duties for which a person is normally employed. Given that it is an implied term of a contract of employment that an employee must obey lawful orders, and that an order to carry out duties outside the contract is a breach of that contract and is thus unlawful (unless an employee agrees and there is some consideration to support the consensual variation), an employee who carries out specifically assigned duties under protest and reserving his position may not be caught by subs.(1)(b); and see §39.12.

For a discussion of an employee's duties falling outside of his normal duties, but specifically assigned to him, see the article by B. Bercusson [1980] E.I.P.R. 257.

At first instance in *LIFFE v Pinkava* (above), it was held that the inventions in question fell within duties which had been assigned. However, on appeal, it was found that his duties had evolved over time and what might once have been "assigned" had, by the relevant date, become "normal".

—Performance of normal or specifically assigned duties

39.10   The second stage of inquiry under subs.(1)(a) is concerned with whether the performance of the duties, as established in the first stage, is expected to result in an invention. Although, in *Harris*, "an invention" was found to mean such an invention as that made and that the second stage of the enquiry ("expected to result") is met if it is "an invention which achieves…the aim…to which the employee's efforts in carrying out his duties were directed" (*Harris's Patent* [1985] R.P.C. 19 at 29), in *LIFFE v Pinkava* (above), this was confined to the facts of that case. The words "an invention" have a narrower meaning than "any invention", and are wider in scope than "the invention the subject of the dispute", but it is not acceptable to substitute a judicial test for that set out in the Act. There may be uncertainty as to whose expectations are decisive, the employer's or the employee's, and whether the time of the expectation is the date of commencement of the duties in question or (it is submitted the better view) the date when the invention is made and it may be relevant to consider, in a dispute, what other inventions the employee has made since the commencement of the particular duties. A first invention made several years into the particular job may be an indication that there was no expectation that the performance of the duties in question would result in the making of an invention. However, as Jacob L.J. suggested in *LIFFE v Pinkava*, a research chemist whose first invention comes after ten years of seeking a cancer cure is unlikely to succeed in claiming ownership to himself.

At first instance in *LIFFE v Pinkava*, a number of factors were considered important in dealing with reasonable expectation: the employer had an interest in maintaining its competitive position through innovation, even if it had no history of filing patent applications; the employee was obliged to develop new products as part of his normal duties and was known as "an ideas man"; the task in question did not have an obvious solution and so any result was likely to be innovative; but a "quantum leap" level of invention was not going to take it outside the scope of s.39(1). On appeal, the majority held that although the test is objective, the ability of the employee in question could not be ignored. One could not decide the issue of "expectation" by reference to the substitution of a hypothetical less brilliant employee. The expectation had to arise due to the fact that the duties were carried out by an intelligent person, not just from the fact that an intelligent person carried out those duties.

Whilst this test helps where an employee is arguing that his invention is so radical that there could be no expectation of any such result, the dissenting judge (Jacob L.J.) could not see why a "thick" employee should have a better chance than a "brilliant" one of retaining ownership of an invention, merely because no-one would have expected the "thick" one to invent anything.

Even where some inventions might be expected to result, it will be necessary to consider whether this invention arose in the course of normal duties, assigned duties or outside the course of either. Thus, at first instance in *LIFFE v Pinkava*, P's normal duties did include innovating, but the invention in question was found to arise out of his assigned duties rather than the normal ones, although this point was overturned on appeal. Although P's invention had wider application than just the market in which LIFFE operated, hence the fact that there were four applications, the court found that these all stemmed from the same inventive concept and LIFFE was entitled to all of them.

In determining whether or not there is an "expectation", see also *West Glamorgan's Application* BL O/235/01 and *Paul Auckland v Enderby Construction Ltd* BL O343/06.

In *West Glamorgan's Application*, it was held that, in contrast to the situation in *Harris's Patent* [1985] R.P.C. 19 the inventor had not been asked to apply himself to any technical problem so that although the invention had been made in the course of his normal duties, these were not such that the invention might reasonably have been expected to result, so the inventor was entitled to the invention. The Comptroller also held in this case that "specially assigned duties" under s.39(1)(a) must be outside "normal duties".

In *Paul Auckland v Enderby Construction Ltd*, the invention was found to fall within the employee's normal duties, but those were not such that an invention might be expected to result and so the patent belonged to the employee.

It is arguable that subs.(1)(a) achieves the same result as had been reached by 1977 under the common law, albeit by a different route. Thus, in *Electrolux v Hudson* [1977] F.S.R. 312, a clause in a contract of employment under which the employer claimed ownership of an employee's invention was declared void as being wider than required to protect the employer's legitimate interest and therefore against public policy and in restraint of trade, in effect for not being confined to inventions flowing naturally from the performance of the employee's duties. On this basis former precedents (as discussed in §39.14) may still be of interest, but since *LIFFE v Pinkava* (above), they are unlikely to have much persuasive value.

—Employees with special obligations

39.11 Subsection (1)(b) provides the third gateway whereby an employer can establish ownership of an invention made by an employee. The invention must still be one made "in the course of the duties of the employee". Then, in addition, the employee must be one who, at the relevant time, had a special obligation to the employer, arising from the nature of his duties and responsibilities, to further the interest of the employer's undertaking. The omission of "normal" in the reference to "duties" was no doubt deliberate and in contrast to subs.(1)(a). Subsection (1)(b) clearly covers employees in senior management whose duties are not so closely definable as to make "normal" meaningful in relation thereto. Thus, in *Peart's Patent* BL O/209/87, a works manager was held not to have discharged the onus on him to show that he did not have an obligation which extended to an invention he made at a time when he had been instructed not to involve himself in research and development matters. However, just how far down in the hierarchy of a given organisation one can go before an employee will cease to be covered by subs.(1)(b), irrespective of his inventions being covered by subs.(1)(a), will always be a difficult mixed question of fact and law.

In *Defence Technology's Application* BL O/77/93, noted I.P.D. 16124, a high-grade employee was seconded to a key position in the organisation of a third party and made an invention, the ownership of which he disputed. There were no written provisions as to ownership of inventions by the employer, the employee or the third party. It was held that the duties of the employee were such that he owed a special obligation to further his employer's interests and thus the latter owned the invention. In the actual case, on the balance of probabilities, the employer would have assigned the rights under the invention to the third party. The fact that, shortly after making the invention, the employee became employed by the third party without any real change in his job duties but under a contract which did deal with ownership of inventions, supported the finding that the invention made during the secondment should also belong to the third party.

In *Unitec Systems' Application* BL O/143/94, the applicants had been joint managing directors of a company. Although the normal duties of each of them did not include the making of inventions, their executive position was such that their invention rights were owned by that company. In *SCS Consultancy Services' Application* BL O/174/00, the referrer was a major shareholder and former managing director of a company. Due to ill-health he had handed over managing duties, remaining a non-executive director and working part-time on technical matters. He asserted that the invention (of which he was found to be a co-inventor) had been made outside that part-time working. This was doubted, but anyway, the referrer was held to have had a special obligation to further the interest of the company which he had still regarded as "his company". A less clear case of an inventor having a special obligation to further the interests of his employer because of his seniority and executive responsibilities is *Staeng's Patent* [1996] R.P.C. 183, a decision criticised by P.A. Chandler [1997] E.I.P.R. 262.

In *West Glamorgan's Application* BL O/235/01, the Comptroller also held that the "special obligation" referred to in s.39(1)(b) must be something special over and above the obligations which any employee has to his employer.

In *Lawson and McGarry's Application*, BL O/56/04, noted [2004] *CIPA* 165, Lawson was a director and an employee. There was no real dispute that s.39(1)(b) would apply, but Lawson still argued that his duties did not involve invention and that the invention in question had been made before the company was incorporated. He succeeded on the latter point, but lost on the former. The hearing officer found that the invention did fall within the spectrum of the company's activities and so could have belonged to the company under s.39(1)(b), if it had not been made before the company was incorporated.

A person holding themselves out as commercial director or CEO may have a special obligation to further the interests of the company, even if that person has not been formally appointed with forms returned to the relevant authority (*Walter's Applications*, BL O/272/05 noted in [2006] *CIPA* 122).

In *Enston's Applications*, BL O/206/04, noted [2004] *CIPA* 484, the inventor, E, probably made the invention while he was still a director of the company, but was not employee at that time, so the application under s.39(1)(b) failed. The claim to ownership by reason of the fiduciary duty of the director (i.e. outside the scope of s.39), was brought up for the first time in the skeleton argument and the hearing officer refused, in his discretion, to allow so late an amendment to the pleading.

—Employer holding invention on constructive trust for employee

39.12   Where it is established that the employee is entitled to the benefit of an invention held on trust for him by the employer, the common law of constructive trusts will come into force, as discussed in the book by J. Phillips and M. J. Hoolahan, *Employees' Inventions in the United Kingdom* (ESC Publishing Ltd, 1982). In such a trust the employee not only takes the benefit, but also the liabilities, of the resulting trusts (*Triplex v Scorah* (1938) 55 R.P.C. 21). The employee is then entitled to compensation for any expenditure he may have incurred in developing and protecting the invention, as was required in *Hindmarch and Horner's Application* BL O/158/80, noted I.P.D. 3147. In the case where an employer solicits the aid and services of an employee beyond the scope of his normal duties without any "consideration" or promise of remuneration subsequent to his performance of the requested services, the employee may have a quasi-contractual remedy of quantum meruit to recover the value of those services from the employer.

However, in a situation where employer ownership arises under subs.(1), a claim that the patent is held by the employer on a constructive trust for the employee must fail (*French v Mason* [1999] F.S.R. 597). Here it was held that no constructive trust would arise from breach of a personal relationship between two persons who were shareholders and directors of the employing company because a company owes no fiduciary duty to its directors, and the directors owe no such duty to its shareholders; and there was no nexus between the alleged breach and the remedy sought of a constructive trust of a patent in the name of the company. It was also held that the question of ownership of an invention has to be considered as of the date on which it was made (on which point see §7.06). If there was any trust governing ownership of the invention in favour of the employee, it must have arisen at that date. Moreover, for a constructive trust to be imposed, one must consider the circumstances in which the disputed invention came into the alleged trustee's hands and there must have been some improper behaviour by the alleged trustee, e.g. unconscionable dealing, a breach of trust or a breach of a fiduciary obligation.

Cf. the position in design and copyright law as exemplified in *Ultraframe v Fielding* [2004] R.P.C. 24; [2003] EWCA Civ 1805 where the director was not an employee, but, by virtue of his fiduciary duties to the company, held the design right on trust for the company.

Application of section 39 to particular cases

The application of the principles set out in s.39(1) to particular facts usually arises in proceedings under s.8, 12, 37 or 82 (determination of entitlement to patent ownership). Decisions on these are therefore discussed mainly in the commentary on s.37, and see also §8.07. The applicability of s.39 to members of the academic staff of a university has been discussed by W.R. Cornish, see §39.07, along with the rather different rule for ownership of copyrights created by an employee and see also *University of Western Australia v Gray* also discussed at §39.07.

39.13

Before applying the principles of s.39, it may be necessary to determine an inventorship dispute, which can arise under s.13 (mention of inventor) or under s.8, 12, 37 or 82 (determination of entitlement to patent ownership). The procedure for resolving such disputes, and the relevant time limits for bringing a claim, are discussed in the commentaries on these sections and in the commentary under on s.123.

Decisions under the common law

Precedents decided under common law principles should be treated with considerable caution, see §39.07. This is partly due to the inconsistency of pre-1978 cases such as *British Syphon v Homewood* [1956] R.P.C. 225 and *Selz's Application* (1953) 71 R.P.C. 158; and partly because these cases were generally concerned to determine, as a first step, whether the invention was made "in the course of employment", for example as in *Hindmarch and Horner's Application* BL O/158/80, noted I.P.D. 3147, decided under the 1949 Act s.56. It is submitted that the phrase "duties of an employee" in s.39(1) has a narrower meaning. Whether an act was "in the course of employment" has been the subject of numerous labour law cases involving, e.g. employers' vicarious liability for their employees' acts, and is closely bound up with the concept of authorisation, express or implied, for a given act.

39.14

Further in *LIFFE v Pinkava* [2007] R.P.C. 30; [2007] EWCA Civ 217, the Court of Appeal has held that ss.39 to 43 provide a new code and are not a codification of the common law. To the extent that the prior cases are of assistance, it will only be in relation to the determination of the employees' duties, especially his duty of confidentiality.

Settlement of disputes by employers

Employers will naturally seek to settle inventorship disputes with, or between, their employees by informal and internal procedures. If this is to be done, it is important that the

39.15

procedures used by the employer should be fair, not too lengthy, and generally comply with rules of natural justice. One aspect of fairness is (where the application has yet to be filed) the strict preservation of confidentiality of the invention by both parties to the dispute, pending determination of the question of ownership so as not to pre-empt the rightful owner's freedom to apply for patent protection.

There is an overriding implied term in a contract of employment that employers will not, without reasonable and proper cause, conduct themselves in a manner calculated or likely to destroy or seriously damage the implied (or express) obligation of trust and confidence between employer and employee, see *Malik v BCCI* [1997] 3 W.L.R. 95; [1997] 3 All E.R. 1; [1997] I.R.L.R. 462. The application of this implied term can prohibit actions which would on the face of the contract be legitimate for the employer (such as, e.g. forbidding inclusion of an "enabling disclosure" of the disputed invention in the patent application to render its description sufficient under s.14(3)), and insofar as an express contractual term gives an employer a discretion, it should be exercised reasonably and not in a capricious way, see *White v Reflecting Roadstuds Ltd* [1991] I.R.L.R. 331 EAT.

In an interim decision (*Newns v British Airways* [1992] I.R.L.R. 575), the Court of Appeal stated that there was an implied contractual duty of "good faith" on the employer, requiring fair dealing with employees, and a breach of this duty could be restrained by an injunction. It may therefore be argued that the implied term enunciated in *Malik* (above), and possibly the implied duty found in *Newns*, is a fundamental term in the contract of employment a breach of which entitles an employee (with a qualifying period of service, currently of one year) to resign and claim compensation for unfair constructive dismissal under the current s.95(1)(c) of the Employment Rights Act 1996 (c.18), see in general *Western Excavating v Sharp* [1978] Q.B. 761; [1978] 1 All E.R. 713 CA which still stands as the basis for this area of law.

Consideration should also be given to s.42(2), as any contractual term which diminishes the employee's rights in the invention will be void (see s.42(2) and (3)).

Contrast with employer ownership of copyrights and design rights created during employment

39.16   Sections 11(2) and 215(3) of the CDPA 1988 have effect respectively to pass first ownership of copyrights and design rights created by an employee "in the course of his employment" automatically to the employer, subject in the latter case only to the prior right of one who commissioned the making of the design. A topography right is treated in the same way as a design right, except that here the statutory provision may be varied by a written agreement (Design Right (Semiconductor Topographies) Regulations 1989, SI 1989/1100, rr.2, 5), as amended by SI 1993/2497. First ownership of registered designs, as between employer and employee, is also now governed as for a design right (Registered Designs Act 1949 (c.88) s.2(1B) as inserted by s.267 of the CDPA 1988. This provision has not been changed by subsequent amendments to the Registered Designs Act. If, as seems to be clearly the case, the phrase "in the course of his employment" is wider in scope than the combined effect of the three gateways of s.39(1), then decisions in relation to these other types of intellectual property rights will have no direct effect on the interpretation of s.39. (This wording can be contrasted with that in Council Regulation 6/2002, which provides for the employer to own Community designs:

"developed by an employee in the execution of his duties or following the instructions given by his employer...unless otherwise agreed or specified under national law".

Conversely, having regard to the lack of definition of "invention" in s.39 and the presence in the introductory passage of subs.(1) of the phrase "for the purposes of this Act *and all other purposes*" (emphasis added), it might be argued that s.39 had the unexpected effect of modifying the ownership regimes in the above-mentioned Acts and Regulations if the design or copyright work can be said to be an "invention". See the discussion at §43.05.

Aside from the argument whether a design or copyright work is nevertheless also an "invention", a dichotomy between employees' rights in different species of intellectual property will often arise from the same, or closely associated, acts leading to a position where, even though an employee may own patent rights because the employer is unable to establish any of the criteria of subs.(1), the employer may own associated copyrights, design rights, registered designs, etc. because these have been created by the same employee "in the course of his employment", but see §39.17.

Employees' immunity under associated copyrights and design rights (subs.(3))

To alleviate the position set out in §39.16, subs.(3) was added, and an amendment made to s.43(4), by the CDPA 1988 Sch.5 para.11. Under this subsection, where by virtue of subs.(2) an invention belongs to an employee rather than to the employer, then nothing done by or on behalf of the employee, or his successor in title, for the purpose of prosecuting an application for a patent, or by any person for the purpose of performing or working the invention, "shall be taken to infringe any copyright or design right" in "any model or document" to which the employer is entitled, rather than the employee. It seems slightly odd that subs.(3) does not include a reference to registered designs, but a possible explanation is that the legislator could not conceive of a registrable design as an "invention", given the exclusions from registrability in s.1 of the Registered Designs Act 1949, as amended by the CDPA 1988, or it may have been that as these are also registered rights, they were deliberately excluded from the ambit of this immunity, the employee being required to find a different form for its embodiment. Also, see the discussion at §40.04, in the event that such documents are confidential to the employer. **39.17**

Thus, employers will not be able to use these other intellectual property rights to prevent employees from obtaining patents on their own inventions. Also, subs.(3)(b) provides an immunity from any action for infringement of any copyright or design right arising from a model or document to which the employer is entitled. However, this provision may not be as wide as it seems at first sight. It is clearly intended to apply to copyrights of which the employee in question is the author (designer) but, as regards documents or models created by the employee's colleagues, the resulting copyright or design right may not perhaps be a right "between him [the employee] and the employer".

What is perhaps curious is that subs.(3)(b) is not restricted to persons performing or working the invention with the consent of the employee, but instead apply to any person, whether they are infringing the patent owned by the employee or not.

This section could also have some interesting ramifications where an employee licenses his invention to the employer and then works on the implementation of that invention as part of his employment. Despite the employer paying the employee to work up the implementation and owning the resulting IP rights in those drawings and models, the employer will then not be able to enforce those IP rights. In such circumstances, the employer might be well advised to use a different employee, so that the effects of this section will not bite.

The amendment to s.43(4) has the effect that any reference to "patent" in s.39 extends to a "patent or other protection" granted, whether under the law of the United Kingdom or otherwise. This provision is discussed further in §43.05. However, in its application to s.39(3) (the word "patent" not appearing otherwise in s.39), it is difficult to see how United Kingdom law can effectively provide a defence to an action brought in another country for infringement of an intellectual property right in that country unless perhaps a United Kingdom court would grant an injunction against the employer entity to prevent it from seeking to assert its foreign "protection" contrary to s.39(3)(b), as extended by s.43(4) discussed in §43.05.

PRACTICE UNDER SECTION 39

Keeping of records

Whether s.39(1) applies to an invention made by an employee depends on the circumstances in which an invention was made. In the interest of both employer and employee, it is most desirable to set out in writing the employee's normal duties, whether the employee has any special duties or obligations, to record any change in the employee's normal **39.18** duties and when any other duties are specifically assigned to the employee with the employee's consent, as well as the relevant consideration. It is worth bearing in mind that performance appraisals may have an effect on this and these too should be kept in the employee's file.

It must be a question of fact whether an employee might reasonably be expected to make inventions in carrying out his/her normal, or assigned and accepted, duties. An attempt can be made to deal with this point in the contract of service, but in cases of doubt past experience of the employer as to whether a particular class of employee (e.g. a sales engineer) has made, or been expected to make, inventions as a result of carrying out the employee's normal duties might be relevant in determining ownership of the invention—although, since *LIFFE v Pinkava* [2007] R.P.C. 30; [2007] EWCA Civ 217, this may be of less relevance where the employees are of different levels of intelligence.

In the interests of certainty it may be desirable, before a patent application is filed, that an employee-inventor be asked to sign a declaration as to the ownership of the invention. In any event, personnel records of inventors should be maintained for at least one year after the patent has ceased to have effect, see r.91 reprinted at §40.02, although the fact that this can term can be retrospectively extended under r.108 (reprinted at §123.25), may mean that these should be kept for an even longer period. An attempt may be made to claim inventorship many years after the application was filed, see §13.14, particularly if an unacknowledged inventor perceives a lucrative chance to claim for compensation under s.40.

Papers by K. Hodkinson in *The Company Lawyer* (1986) Vol.2, 146 and 183 contain useful hints on the keeping of records of employee inventions, the handling of ownership claims, and the management of employee inventions. Specimen documentation is provided at the end of his second paper.

SECTION 40

Compensation of employees for certain inventions

40.01 40.—(1) Where it appears to the court or the comptroller on an application made by an employee within the prescribed period that—

(a) **the employee has made an invention belonging to the employer for which a patent has been granted,**

(b) **having regard among other things to the size and nature of the employer's undertaking, the invention or the patent for it (or the combination of both) is of outstanding benefit to the employer, and**

(c) **by reason of those facts it is just that the employee should be awarded compensation to be paid by the employer,**

[*the employee has made an invention belonging to the employer for which a patent has been granted, that the patent is (having regard among other things to the size and nature of the employer's undertaking) of outstanding benefit to the employer and that by reason of those facts it is just that the employee should be awarded compensation to be paid by the employer,*] the court or the comptroller may award him such compensation of an amount determined under section 41 below.

(2) Where it appears to the court or the comptroller on an application made by an employee within the prescribed period that—

(a) a patent has been granted for an invention made by and belonging to the employee;

(b) his rights in the invention, or in any patent or application for a patent for

538

the invention, have since the appointed day been assigned to the employer or an exclusive licence under the patent or application has since the appointed day been granted to the employer;

(c) the benefit derived by the employee from the contract of assignment, assignation or grant or any ancillary contract ("the relevant contract") is inadequate in relation to the benefit derived by the employer from the [*patent*] **invention or the patent for it (or both)**; and

(d) by reason of those facts it is just that the employee should be awarded compensation to be paid by the employer in addition to the benefit derived from the relevant contract;

the court or the comptroller may award him such compensation of an amount determined under section 41 below.

(3) Subsections (1) and (2) above shall not apply to the invention of an employee where a relevant collective agreement provides for the payment of compensation in respect of inventions of the same description as that invention to employees of the same description as that employee.

(4) Subsection (2) above shall have effect notwithstanding anything in the relevant contract or any agreement applicable to the invention (other than any such collective agreement).

(5) If it appears to the comptroller on an application under this section that the application involves matters which would more properly be determined by the court, he may decline to deal with it.

(6) In this section—

"the prescribed period", in relation to proceedings before the court, means the period prescribed by rules of court, and

"relevant collective agreement" means a collective agreement within the meaning of the Trade Union and Labour Relations [*Act 1974 [c. 52]*] **(Consolidation) Act 1992 [c. 52]**, made by or on behalf of a trade union to which the employee belongs, and by the employer or an employers' association to which the employer belongs which is in force at the time of the making of the invention.

(7) References in this section to an invention belonging to an employer or employee are references to it belonging as between the employer and the employee.

Notes

1. Subsections (1) and subs.(2) were amended by the Patents Act 2004 (c.16) s.10, with effect from January 1, 2005 (SI 2004/3205). However (under s.10(8) of the 2004 Act), these amendments only apply in relation to an invention where a patent application is filed on or after that date, the term "patent" having the meaning given by s.43(4).

2. Subsection (6) was amended by the Trade Union and Labour Relations (Consolidation) Act 1992 (c.52) Sch.2.

RELEVANT RULE—RULE 91

Rule 91—Period prescribed for applications by employee for compensation

91.—(1) The period prescribed for the purposes of section 40(1) and (2) shall   **40.02**

be the period beginning with the date of grant of the patent and ending one year after the patent ceased to have effect.

(2) But if an application for restoration is made under section 28 and—

    (a) the application is granted, the period prescribed under paragraph (1) shall continue as if the patent had remained continuously in effect; or

    (b) the application is refused, the period prescribed for the purposes of section 40(1) and (2) shall be—

        (i) the period prescribed under paragraph (1); or

        (ii) if it expires later, the period of six months beginning [with] immediately after the date on which the application was refused.

Note. Amended by the Patents (Amendment) Rules 2011 (SI 2011/2052).

Other Relevant Rules—Rules 73–88

40.03   The rules in Pt 7 of the Patents Rules 2007 (as amended by the 2011 Rules) govern procedure in all proceedings to be heard before the Comptroller. These specifically include proceedings under s.40(1) and (2). These rules are discussed and reprinted in §§123.06–123.21, but are also mentioned, as appropriate, in the commentary and practice sections below. Also r.51(3)(a) (reprinted in §118.02 and discussed and reprinted in §118.10) applies with respect to documents filed in the UK-IPO.

Commentary on Section 40

Scope of the section

40.04   Section 40 is the second of the group of ss.39–43 relating to inventions made by employees. There is no corresponding provision in the EPC, CPC or PCT.

This section is concerned with an employee-inventor making a claim for "compensation" from his employer. It has two limbs relating respectively to employer-owned patented inventions (subs.(1)), and patented inventions originally owned by the employee but assigned or exclusively licensed to the employer (subs.(2)). Under either limb an award of compensation is based on a number of prerequisites. First, the invention must be one for which a "patent" (as defined in an extended sense in s.43(4), see §43.05) has been granted, which precludes the case where the patent has not been granted due to a secrecy order (though see §40.09). Second, the ownership of the invention must already have been determined in accordance with s.39. But in order to get home, the employee will have to jump two hurdles: he must show that the patent and/or (for applications filed after January 1, 2005) the invention, is "of outstanding benefit to the employer" is "of outstanding benefit to the employer" and it must be "just" to make an award in favour of the employee (*Shanks v Unilever* [2011] R.P.C. 12, [2010] EWCA Civ 1283). For discussion regarding "outstanding benefit", see §40.12 and for discussion of "just", see §40.07.

Compensation is to be assessed under either head in relation to the benefit which the employer (including persons "connected with him", see s.41(1) and (2)) derived from the "patent" and/or (where the patent application is filed on or after January 1, 2005) the "invention". For cases where the employer or the employee dies before an award under s.40 is made, see s.43(5) and (6) discussed in §43.07and §43.08 respectively.

For a discussion on the comparative rights of employees to compensation across a number of European countries, see Senna Wolk, "Remuneration for employee inventors—is there a common European ground?" ([2011] June *CIPA* 352–358 for Part 1 and [2011] July *CIPA* 440–445 for Part 2.)

Who may claim?

40.05   The person claiming for compensation under ss.40 and 41 must be an "actual deviser" of the invention and not one who "merely contributes" to the invention, even though it may be "unjust to compensate inventors, whilst leaving others who contribute to the invention uncompensated", see *Kelly & Chiu v GE Healthcare* [2009] R.P.C. 12, [2009] EWHC 181 Pat Ct, at [11]. For further discussion of the case law on this point, see the commentary on s.7.

Note that in subs.(1)(a), there is a need to show that the employee made an invention belonging to the employer. Section 40 does not contain an express requirement for the employee claiming under this section to have first been identified as an inventor. However, r.10(1) does require that all inventors are identified either initially or in an addendum or erratum. So if the employee is not already named as inventor, an application under r.10(2) seems to be required, although as multiple claims can now be made using a single PF2, this can probably be brought at the same time as the compensation claim. This is also discussed further at §13.14 and in the *Litigation Manual* at Ch.10, para.10.02.

However, making both applications together has other difficulties. As noted at §40.09, compensation claims can be brought too early. On the other hand, leaving claims for determination of inventorship too late is likely to be detrimental as there may be a lack of relevant evidence which will make it difficult for the claimant to prove his case. See §37.06—the points about the practical difficulties of disputing entitlement late, also apply to disputing inventorship.

Determination of the employer

A claim under the section must be made against the entity that was the employee's **40.06** employer at the time the invention was made. References in the Act to ability to take into account benefits to be derived, when the employer dies, by the personal representatives or the person in whom the benefit of the invention (where the patent application is filed on or after January 1, 2005) or patent then vested with their assent (s.43(5) and see §43.06) or benefits to be derived where an assignment or licence is to a connected person (s.41(2) and see §41.04), will extend the scope of the enquiry but not add further defendants.

Where there is a company reorganisation, particularly if that includes the sale and subsequent renaming of the company which was the employer, and/or this happens after an employee has left, identifying the company that was the employer can become a forensic exercise (see *Fellerman's Application* BL O/11/96 where there was extensive correspondence between the parties in order to try to identify the company which had been the "employer"). However, as was made clear in *Fellerman's Application*, the claim does not lie against the patent owner, even if ownership of the patent was retained within the group of the original employer, but should instead be directed to the employer company, even when that company was transferred to another group of companies.

Nor can the people who were the directors of the employer be joined in the action, even if they have caused the company to assign the patent to them at an undervalue (*Price v Elf Print Media* [2001] EWCA Civ 622).

Where the Transfer of Undertakings (Protection of Employment) Regulations 2006 ("TUPE") (SI 2006/246) applies, the claim may have to be brought against the new employer rather than the old one. TUPE provides that all the transferor's rights, powers, duties and liabilities under, or in connection with, a contract of employment of a person who immediately before the transfer was employed by the transferor are transferred with the undertaking. So it is possible that the new employer assumes the responsibilities of the former employer under s.40; the new employer may not be a mere assignee, but rather may be regarded as a "continuing" employer. In line with the court's general efforts to protect employees where possible, the Regulations have been held to apply to a wide variety of situations, including departments being outsourced. The case law on TUPE is extensive and the exact extent of the Regulations is a topic in its own right: suffice it to say that, where a business or part of it is being transferred, the implication of the Regulations should be considered.

Co-ownership of the patent by the employer with a third party is apparently irrelevant to an application against the employer, see subs.(7).

When a compensation award may not be "just"

It is not easy to envisage situations where the patent or (where the patent application is **40.07** filed on or after January 1, 2005) the invention is of outstanding benefit and yet it would not be "just" for the employee to receive compensation, particularly because the circumstances in which it may not be "just" for the employee to receive compensation must be "by reason of those facts", namely the facts of a patent having been granted for the invention, and that the patent or (where the patent application is filed on or after January 1, 2005) the invention is of outstanding benefit to the employer. These words were held in *Kelly and Chiu v GE Healthcare* [2009] R.P.C. 12, [2009] EWHC 181 Pat Ct to be there to ensure that the court should not proceed mechanically to assess the compensation, once the required facts had been established, and that it was neither desirable or sensible to categorise the situations where an award would be unjust—the court would recognise it where it arose. The judge also remarked that the fact that the inventors waited several years after leaving the defendants' employment did not make an award unjust: this they were fully entitled to do under the Act.

Nevertheless, it has been stated that, where the nature of an invention is such that it was the expected and reasonable result of the inventor's duties and responsibilities for which he was paid, the benefits arising from the existence of the patent should be exceptional for it to be "just" that the inventor should be further compensated (*Memco-Med's Patent* [1992] R.P.C. 403). Given the change in the law for patent applications filed after January 1, 2005, it can only be presumed that the court will take a similar view with respect to the benefit derived from the invention.

In any case, since both subss.(1) and (2) use the word "may", the making of an award is discretionary and the maxim that he who comes to Equity must come with clean hands applies. Thus, it is possible that circumstances in which it would not be just for the employee to receive compensation could arise in highly unlikely situations in which the employee has engaged in inequitable conduct in relation to "those facts", e.g. actively hindering or sabotaging the patent granting procedure, or actively hindering the commercialisation of the invention (for those patent applications filed on or after January 1, 2005), or the defence or enforcement of the patent against third parties etc. Despite the restriction to "those facts" it may be that a tribunal would use this rubric to apply general equitable considerations to punish, e.g. misuse of confidential information or other acts inconsistent with the employee's general duty of fidelity and honesty. For the position of fiduciaries, see *Boardman v Phipps* [1967] 2 A.C. 46 HL; and generally *Bell v Lever Bros* [1932] A.C. 161 HL.

Determination of amount of compensation

40.08   The amount of compensation payable under s.40 is to be determined according to the principles set out in s.41. See *Kelly and Chiu v GE Healthcare* [2009] R.P.C. 12, [2009] EWHC 181 Pat Ct, discussed in more detail at §40.12. Section 40 does not apply to patents granted on inventions made before June 1, 1978 (s.43(1)), nor where the inventor was not mainly employed, or attached to employment, in the United Kingdom (s.43(2)). However, s.40 does extend to joint inventors (s.43(3)) and to foreign patents and "other protection" (s.43(4)), see further §43.05 where how far, if at all, s.40 is applicable to copyrights, design rights and designs is discussed, and see also §39.16. For the time when an invention is made, see §7.06.

Section 43(7) requires that "benefit" (as referred to in ss.40 and 41) means benefit in "money or money's worth", see §43.09, thus excluding mere fame or kudos. Also, the effect of s.41(1) and (2) has to be borne in mind with regard to benefit obtained by an employer from persons "connected" with him, see §41.04. Where the employer has died see s.43(5) and §43.06. For the definition of "employee", see §39.05.

In s.130(1), it is stated that "'employer', in relation to an employee, means ''the person by whom the employee is or was employed". This excludes from consideration any benefit derived from the patent or (where the patent application is filed on or after January 1, 2005) the invention by an assignee or licensee, unless such is a "connected person", see §41.04. If that current proprietor is not a "connected person" with the original employer, the value placed on the patent or (where the patent application is filed on or after January 1, 2005) the invention at the time of its transfer would seem to limit the amount of benefit received from it by the original employer.

In *Fellerman's Application* BL O/11/96, the applicant tried to show that the group of companies to which his employer company had belonged had retained considerable benefit to itself by conducting a re-organisation of assets between connected companies before parting with the employer company in an asset sale. However, the hearing officer held that this was not benefit to the employer or connected companies (the claim, in any event, having been misdirected against the previous employer's group at the date of employment and not against the previous employer (see §40.06).

In *Shanks v Unilever* [2011] R.P.C. 12, [2010] EWCA Civ 1283, the court doubted that the employee could argue that the benefit (both for meeting the threshold of "outstanding benefit" and for computing the benefit of which the claimant sought a "fair share" (although the claimant dropped the latter point before the Court of Appeal)) would include a "putative benefit" which would take the amount beyond the actual benefits (money or money's worth) realised by the employer's group of companies. This argument was based on a reading of s.41(2) which is discussed at §41.04.

Time for making application for compensation

An application under s.40 can be made either to the Comptroller or to the court and must be made within a prescribed period. This is the period from grant of the patent to one year after it has ceased to have effect, or six months after any application for restoration under s.28 has been refused (subs.(6); r.91 and CPR r.63.12 and CPR 63 PD.12 (reprinted at §§F63.12 and F63PD.13)). **40.09**

The Comptroller now has discretion to extend the period of time set out in r.91 (as amended, see §40.02) following an application under r.108(1) reprinted at §123.25, even if the application is made after that period has expired r.108(6). The Comptroller will give notice to the parties of the application to extend the period and may impose conditions r.108(5). The court may also have latitude to accept an application made out of time.

CPR 63 PD.12 provides for the court to give directions as to how evidence is to be given and the time limits for filing witness statements or affidavits, and for inspection of and taking extracts from books of account.

An employee will not necessarily know when an employer decides not to renew a patent and so may be unaware when the prescribed final period starts to run. Thus, he would be well advised to file the appropriate request to be notified of a relevant event (caveat) for this purpose under r.54(1) and (6) on PF 49 at the UK-IPO, and to take similar precautions (if available) in respect of corresponding foreign patents. Equally, he might wish to file a further PF 49 to be informed of any assignments or licences recorded at the UK-IPO in the register of patents. The filing of caveats is explained in §§118.16–118.18.

In *British Steel's Patent* [1992] R.P.C. 117, the application was made only a few months after the patent grant. In those circumstances the case for compensation at that stage (being limited at that time to relying only on the benefit derived from the patent) would have had to have been "an exceptional one". Even though the amount of compensation that can be awarded can include an element for the future (s.41(1)), this is not taken into account when determining whether there "is outstanding benefit" (s.40(2)) in order to give rise to a right of compensation (see §40.12). So an application can be brought too early.

Where a patent has not been granted for an invention of an employee-inventor because of the subsistence of "secrecy" directions under s.22, prima facie that employee cannot make an application for compensation under s.40, even though his or her employer may well have derived benefit from the patent application having been brought into order for grant, e.g. by virtue of s.22(7), because both subs.(1) and (2) or s.40 are predicated on the patent being "granted". (Arguably, the inclusion of IP rights in s.39(3) which are not "granted" may assist in pressing for a liberal interpretation.) It may be doubted whether this exclusion of employees who have made "secret" inventions reflects what Parliament intended (or would have intended had it addressed its mind to it); and it may be possible for the employee to argue that a patent application subject to a secrecy order is "other protection" granted under the law of the United Kingdom (see s.43(4)).

Forum for seeking an award of compensation

Applications under s.40(1) or (2) (or under s.41(8), for which see §41.10) may be **40.10** brought before the Comptroller or a "court" (as defined in s.130(1), for which see §96.06). Thus, proceedings under these provisions arising in England or Wales may be brought either before the Patents Court or before the Patents County Court. Proceedings are also possible before certain defined courts of Scotland, Northern Ireland or the Isle of Man, see §40.17.

The choice of forum could be influenced if some form of legal aid could be available, which is not the case for UK-IPO proceedings (Access to Justice Act 1999 (c.22)) s.6; Sch.2 para.2(1), providing a Community Legal Service to replace legal aid under the Legal Aid Act 1988 (c.34) s.14; Sch.2 Pt I. However, few litigants are likely to qualify for aid under whichever of these statutes may apply. Also, the provisions of s.106 may have a bearing on the choice of forum as, under that section, the court shall have regard to the financial position of the parties in determining an award of costs (or, in Scotland, expenses), see §106.02.

Invention belonging to the employer (subs.(1))

—Basis of compensation

40.11   By subs.(1), an employee/inventor is entitled to be compensated in respect of an invention which, as between the employer and employee (see subs.(7)), belongs to the employer under s.39(1), and for which a patent has been granted, but only if the patent or (where the patent application is filed on or after January 1, 2005) the invention has provided a benefit to the employer which is "outstanding" having regard (among other things) to the size and nature of the employer's undertaking, and it is "just" to do so. Such compensation is to be determined according to the guidelines set out in s.41(1) and (4), see §41.05.

Compensation is not to be construed in the restrictive sense of "remedying some loss" or to "compensation for . . . damage" to the employee. Nor will it place the employee in the same position as an external patentee or licensor. Once the invention is shown to be of outstanding benefit, then the amount of compensation "is to be determined in the light of all the available evidence in accordance with s.41 so as to secure a just and fair reward to the employee", see *Kelly & Chiu v GE Healthcare* [2009] R.P.C. 12, [2009] EWHC 181 at [60(xiii)]. "What is being compensated...is the disparity between the benefit[s]" received by each of the employer and the employee. Remuneration already received by the employee for his/her efforts in making the invention are factors to be taken into consideration when determining the fair share and not when looking at the threshold as to whether any award should be made: *Kelly and Chiu v GE Healthcare*, above.

—Meaning of "outstanding benefit"

40.12   Until January 1, 2005, subs.(1) required that a successful application could only be made where "the patent is of outstanding benefit to the employer". And in that respect it is the patent, and not the invention, from which the outstanding benefit to the employer has to derive. These provisions continue to apply to all patents filed before January 1, 2005.

When effective, the changes to subss.(1) and (2) (noted at §40.01) are significant. Under the new terms, compensation may be awarded to an employee, not only where the patent has been of outstanding benefit to the employer, but also where the invention (or a combination of the patent and the invention) has provided such benefit. So for those inventions to which the new law applies, the decisions in *Memco-Med's Patent* [1992] R.P.C. 403 and *Kelly and Chiu v GE Healthcare* [2009] R.P.C. 12, [2009] EWHC 181 Pat Ct have therefore no application to the extent that only benefit arising directly from "the patent" can be taken into account when assessing compensation under s.40. Benefits arising from the invention as such can also now be taken into account.

This is one of the hurdles which the employee must jump before he can obtain compensation, in addition to showing that it is "just" that compensation should be awarded. *Shanks v Unilever* [2011] R.P.C. 12, [2010] EWCA Civ 1283.

However, the case law discussed below arises under the "old regime" which will continue to apply to patents applied for prior to January 1, 2005, and therefore the following text will continue to refer to the "patent" being of outstanding benefit, with passing comments to the invention being of outstanding benefit, where it seems appropriate to do so, in the absence of any case lawon the new provisions. In any event, the "old regime" will still apply until at least 2025, i.e. one year (plus any granted extensions) after the last patent filed before the end of 2004 has expired.

In *Memco-Med's Patent* [1992] R.P.C. 403, the Patents Court (disapproving the Comptroller's earlier decision in *GEC Avionics' Patent* [1992] R.P.C. 107), held that, on normal principles, the onus lies on the applicant for compensation to prove the assertion that the patent is of outstanding benefit. (The change to the section by the 2004 Act will not affect the onus of proof.) While, in *British Steel's Patent* [1992] R.P.C. 117, where the claim was dismissed, the words "outstanding benefit" were referred to as connoting a superlative, subsequently (in the *Memco-Med* case) the Patents Court stated that it is not useful to try to paraphrase "outstanding": it denotes something out of the ordinary, more than merely substantial or good, and courts will not have appreciable difficulties in recognising an outstanding benefit when they see one. These decisions were the subject of comment by P.A. Chandler [1992] J.B.L. 600. In *Kelly & Chiu* above, at [60(iv)], the court held "'Outstanding' means 'something special' or 'out of the ordinary' and more than 'substantial', 'significant' or 'good'. The benefit must be something more than one would normally expect to arise from the duties for which the employee is paid".

Nevertheless, a degree of caution is necessary as it is worthy of observation that there is an increasing tendency, in both the civil and criminal courts, to resist construing ordinary words in too technical a manner (insofar as they have not become terms of art). Rather, they are to be construed according to their natural meaning, in the way a jury would construe them. Lord Diplock's famous phrase "purposive construction" in *Catnic v Hill and Smith* [1982] R.P.C. 183 HL is an aspect of that tendency. Thus, in accordance with the underlying philosophy of s.40, it is submitted that the courts should look on "outstanding" as a normative word and take a fairly broad and robust view of its meaning, as indeed was envisaged in *Memco-Med*, above.

The patent will usually confer benefit by protecting sales of a product or by way of licence or assignment income. For patents filed before January 1, 2005, there must be a causal connection between the patent and the outstanding benefit, but a "but for" test is not the right approach. There may be multiple causes of the benefit. Where other factors are important, they will fall into the difficult question of apportionment of benefit. One test of "benefit" propounded by the court in the *Memco-Med* case, was to examine what the employer's position would have been if the patent had never been granted, in comparison with the actual position. It was also held here that the factors leading to good sales have to be teased apart to isolate those attributable to the existence of the patent; and that a patent which is not exploited, but which blocks competitors, may also be of benefit, even though the quantum of this will be difficult to assess. In *Kelly & Chiu* above, the court also considered the benefit obtained from the period of data exclusivity in relation to the marketing authorisation which made it more difficult for a generic product to be placed on the market in competition with the patented product. At [30] and [60(viii)], the court said "Where outstanding benefit is shown, the presence of other causes may have a significant impact on the share of the benefit which the employee may claim". So care must be taken not to elide the hurdle of "outstanding benefit" in s.40(1) with the subsequent calculation under s.41 as to the compensation to be paid, although it may be that the "benefit" to be considered is the same for both sections—see the *Unilever* case at para.27: "in this sense s.41 reaches through to s.40".

It is submitted that an indicator of more-than-ordinary benefit might be where the patented product is sold at a higher profit margin, free of undercutting by competitors, than the employer's other products; or where there is no substitute available for the patented product. For inventions protected by patents filed after January 1, 2005, the test may made considerably easier, for example it might simply be based on significant sales of a product embodying the patented invention, without the need to show that there was a margin achieved which could be attributed to the presence of a monopoly right.

Proof of future benefit is of no avail, see *Memco-Med's Patent* (above) where the word "is" was emphasised by the court. This means that the patent must, at the time of the decision, have been of benefit to the employer, with such being measured in money or money's worth (s.43(7)), see §43.09. The UK-IPO decision in the latter case was sceptical about, but did not exclude the possibility of, including in the "benefit calculations" the benefit that accrued in the post-publication but pre-grant period. However, in an application for summary judgment in *Entertainment UK's Patent* [2002] R.P.C. 11 at 291, the Comptroller was not prepared to make a ruling that, although s.40 used the words "is of outstanding benefit", no future benefit (as referred to in s.41(1)) could be taken into account. Although the UK patent had only been granted recently, there were foreign patents and utility models which had been granted earlier and the question of benefit derived while the patent application was pending was also left open for future argument. Note that whilst, in order to bring the claim, the employee must show outstanding benefit in the present, that does not preclude the making of a compensation order which includes what may accrue the employer in the future.

The validity of the patent appears to be immaterial. Thus, a patent which had attracted licence fees during much of its term before being held invalid would no doubt be considered to have given benefit. Equally, a patent might not qualify for an award even though it was for an invention of merit and originality in a field where the employer had a dominant position for other reasons (e.g. by virtue of some earlier dominating patent), so that the patent of itself contributed little to the benefit of the employer. The reference to the patent, and the limitation of the period in which an application for compensation can be made, substantially confines consideration to benefits obtained from the patent during its subsistence.

In the *Memco-Med* case (above), the claimant failed because it was shown that the customer for the patented product had a long-established history of dealing with the employer and always came to the employer for a new product, irrespective of whether it was patented.

Milner's Inventorship Application (No.2) BL O/164/98, noted I.P.D. 21128 also did not succeed, it being held that the inventor had failed to prove that the patent had been of outstanding benefit to the employer, or that such benefit as there was had resulted from the patent. In *Garrison's Patent* BL O/44/97, there was failure to obtain compensation because the employer's benefit from the patent was not seen as "outstanding", this apparently only being from 2–3 per cent of the total turnover of a small company manufacturing snooker cues.

Likewise, an application was rejected in *Electrolux's Patents* BL O/75/98 where there were 17 patents in issue, some of which involved other inventors. The position was further complicated because of changes (and exchanges) of the names of the companies which had been involved in the exploitation and ownership of the patents, this requiring these companies to be identified by their registration numbers, and had resulted in an earlier application being rejected as not made against the actual employer, see *Fellerman's Application* BL O/11/96 noted in §40.06 and §40.08. Moreover, the companies had been sold, but ownership of the patents had been retained and assigned for a nominal value of £1. It was held that the applicant had failed to establish any credible figure for the benefit which the employer had obtained from the patents in issue, reliance on statements made in the Annual Reports of the company being insufficient for this purpose.

Notwithstanding the recent judgment in *Kelly and Chiu v GE Healthcare* (above), there will still no doubt be an incentive to resolve such disputes by the employer and employee reaching a settlement of the dispute as it is in each of their interests to do so: the employer so as not to create a further precedent vis-à-vis other employees and so as not to risk divulging commercially sensitive information as to sales and profit margins even if that information is kept confidential to the parties (e.g. see r.51(3) reprinted §118.02 and discussed at §118.10); and the employee because a settlement may be more tax-efficient than an award, see §40.18. *Kelly and Chiu v GE Healthcare* will, however, give a boost to employees seeking compensation.

The recommendation of the Government Green Paper (Intellectual Property Rights and Innovation, Cmnd.9117, December 1983), that employee-inventors should be given the right to take title in their inventions which are not being exploited by their employer, has not been adopted. However, if the invention is being inadequately exploited, there is the possibility for the employee-inventor to obtain a compulsory licence under s.48.

—*Meaning of employer's undertaking*

To assist in interpreting "outstanding" in subs.(1), the only guideline provided recog-   **40.13**
nises that a given size of benefit will signify more to a small employer than to a giant multi-national corporation. In *GEC Avionics' Patent* [1992] R.P.C. 107, it was considered relevant to examine whether the invention belonged to the main field of the employer's operations. While there was evidence of substantial benefit arising to a medium-sized company at least in part from the patent, there was also evidence of comparable benefit from the sale of a similar, but unpatented product, and accordingly the employee-applicant was held not to have proved that the benefit from the patent was "outstanding", the burden of which was upon him. The outcome of this case might be different where the new regime applies, as the employee might have been able to show that the invention was "outstanding", even if the patent itself did not give rise to the benefit.

In *British Steel's Patent* [1992] R.P.C. 117, the term "employer's undertaking" was taken, somewhat reluctantly by the Comptroller and on the case as pleaded, as the entire business of the proprietor. The invention had found use in only one of the British Steel locations and, though this had led to significant economic savings in absolute terms, the savings represented only a very small proportion of the total turnover and profit of the employer: it was held not germane that the employer could have made greater efforts to exploit the invention. Then, in *Memco-Med's Patent* [1992] R.P.C. 403, in a laconic comment, the Patents Court implied that, if proper and persuasive evidence is put forward, the employer's undertaking may be taken to be a division of the employer's business rather than its whole, and the benefit may then be ascertained in relation to the size and nature of that division "and all the surrounding circumstances", see also *Milner's Inventorship Application (No.2)* BL O/164/98, noted I.P.D. 21128.

In *Electrolux's Patents* BL O/75/98, 17 patents were in issue, some of which involved other inventors with a complex situation as to ownership because of changes (and exchanges) of the names of the companies which had been involved in the exploitation and ownership of the patents, but it appears that all the companies were "connected companies" and, once an appropriate company had been selected as the target of the application, the term "employer's undertaking" seems to have been applied collectively to the group of companies; see §40.11. If the aim is to argue that the benefit is derived from "connected companies", then it is hard to see how they can then be left out of the determination of the size of the "employer's undertaking".

In *Shanks v Unilever* [2011] R.P.C. 12, [2010] EWCA Civ 1283, Jacob L.J. doubted that Parliament would have intended that employees of big companies had to show a larger benefit to their employer than employees of smaller companies. As the patent had been assigned within the employer's group, the claimant sought to rely on a "putative benefit" (see §40.08) to meet the test for "outstanding benefit" in relation to the size of the employer's group. The court felt that, in this respect s.41 reached through to s.40, and the benefit to be considered was not just the actual benefit obtained by the employer, but also that realised by the connected company (see also §41.04).

—*Post-invention employer-employee agreements (subs.(4))*

There is a question as to the extent to which an employer may enter into an agreement   **40.14**
with an employee after the making of an invention, which restricts the ability of the employee to seek compensation under this section. Section 42(2) (discussed in §42.02 and §42.03) renders contracts which diminish the "employee's rights [as distinct from benefits] in inventions" unenforceable. However, there is then a separate provision in subs.(4) which preserves the employee's position under subs.(2) regardless of any contract to the

contrary. Given that subs.(4) only refers back to subs.(2), does that then imply that it is possible to enter into contracts with an employee-inventor after he has made an invention which belongs to the employer under s.39(1) and which includes conditions excluding the employee making a claim under s.40(1)?

On the one hand, it would seem that such agreement would be binding so as to exclude the operation of s.40(1), even if "outstanding benefit" to the employer results, despite the fact that in this way the object of the statute might be frustrated, but see s.42 discussed in §42.02 and §42.03. Alternatively, the court might declare such an agreement void as being contrary to public policy, but such agreement could be beneficial to the inventor as giving him additional reward even though the patent turned out not to be of outstanding benefit to the employer. As noted above, subs.(4) prevents a contract of this type from being enforceable in the case of an invention belonging to the employee under s.39(2)—the compensation provisions of subs.(2) cannot be excluded. It is not easy to discern the policy considerations between this differential treatment of situations under subss.(1) and (2).

Invention or patent assigned to the employer (subs.(2))

40.15   Subsection (2) relates to the situation where: (i) an employee has made an invention which, as between the employee and his employer (subs.(7)), belongs to the employee under s.39(2) and which the employee has "patented" (in the extended sense of s.43(4)); (ii) the employee has made over to the employer all rights in the invention or under the patent, by way of assignment or exclusive licence; and (iii) it appears subsequently that the benefit obtained by the employee from the contract was inadequate having regard to the benefit to the employer from the patent, see §40.04.

For subs.(2) to be operative, the employee must have made over to the employer (presumably to whomsoever was the employer at the time of making the invention) "his rights" under the patent. Such handing over can be by assignment or exclusive licence. Where there has been such a valid assignment or exclusive licence, the employee may seek compensation under the subsection. Any such application is to be determined according to the principles set out in s.41, particularly s.41(1) and (5), see §41.05 and §41.06. The application must be made within the same (prescribed) period as applies under subs.(1), see §40.09.

The term "exclusive licence" is defined in s.130(1) and means a licence from the proprietor conferring on the licensee, or on him and persons authorised by him, to the exclusion of all other persons (including the proprietor), any right in respect of the invention to which the patent relates. This term is discussed more fully in §67.03. Although an "exclusive licence" as such can be in respect of "any right" under the patent, for the purpose of s.40(2) it might be argued that an exclusive licence must pass all "his rights" under the patent so that an exclusive licence which is limited territorially, or to part of the invention, or to some kind of act only, may be insufficient to permit compensation to be claimed under s.40(2).

Thus, the existence of a sole or non-exclusive licence granted by an employee to his employer does not permit compensation to be claimed under subs.(2). This is because, with such an arrangement, the employee-patentee has retained the right to obtain benefit from the patent by his own efforts or by licensing a third party.

An employee's negotiating position with respect to his own employer may be considerably more difficult than with an arm's length third party. However, if the right granted to an employer is non-exclusive and for low value, then that may still make it impossible, as a matter of practicality, for the employee to exploit it himself or through another licensee.

To have effect under the subsection, the assignment or exclusive licence must be one made after the making of the invention. This is because agreements made before an invention is made, (e.g. an agreement to assign future inventions to the employer), are not enforceable if they diminish the employee-inventor's rights in or under inventions (s.42(2)).

Collective trade union agreements (subs.(3))

40.16   Under subs.(3) an employee is, apparently, precluded from making a claim under subss.(1) or (2) if, at the time of making the invention, he belonged to a trade union which has negotiated a "relevant collective agreement" (as defined in subs.(6), now by reference to the Trade Union and Labour Relations (Consolidation) Act 1992 (c.52), referred to in this paragraph as "the 1992 Act"), which provides for payment of compensation in respect of inventions of the same description to employees of the same description as the employee. An employee who does not belong to the relevant trade union is free to make a claim under subs.(1) or (2). The agreement has to be in force and the employee has to have been a member of the trade union concerned at the time of making the invention; an employee who subsequently leaves such a union would, presumably, still be bound by the collective agreement and not able to make a claim for compensation.

"Collective agreement" is now defined in s.178(1) of the 1992 Act as any agreement or arrangement made by or on behalf of one or more trade unions and one or more employers or employers' associations and relating to one or more of the matters included in s.178(2) of that Act. These matters do not refer to inventions as such, but reward for the making of inventions could be included under the head of "terms and conditions of employment" under s.178 of the 1992 Act. Few such collective agreements are believed to exist, but the articles by K. Hodkinson, noted in §39.18, include two examples.

It is noteworthy that collective agreements are not normally legally enforceable. Thus, under s.179 of the 1992 Act, collective agreements are not intended to have legal effect unless the parties expressly so provide: yet they may override statutory provisions.

Procedure, hearing, costs and appeals

Applications under s.40 may be made either to the Comptroller (under Pt 7 of the Rules discussed and mainly reprinted in §§123.06–123.21) or to the court. The court must be one as defined in s.130(1), for which see §96.06. In England and Wales, the court will be the Patents Court or the Patents County Court, but the definition of "court" in s.130(1) enables applications to be made to the appropriate courts in Scotland, Northern Ireland or the Isle of Man. If the proprietor is domiciled in these parts of the United Kingdom, any application to the court under s.40 may have to be made to the court of that part of the United Kingdom, having regard to the Civil Jurisdiction and Judgments Act 1982 (c.27).

40.17

No document filed in connection with an application under s.40 will be available for inspection, unless the Comptroller decides otherwise. (see r.51(3) reprinted §118.02 and discussed at §118.10).

Under subs.(5), the Comptroller may decline to deal with an application made to him if it involves matters more properly dealt with by the court. If this happens, the applicant must, at least in England and Wales, then make his application to the court within 14 days. For the principles upon which the Comptroller exercises his discretion whether to decline to deal with an application made to him for proceedings under ss.40(1), 40(2) or 41(8), see §§37.08.

It can be expected that application will normally be made to the Comptroller because of the reduced expense. The Comptroller now has power retrospectively to extend the period for making the application (see §40.09). The Comptroller can appoint advisers to assist him in assessing compensation; see the commentary on s.123(2)(g) at §123.68. The Comptroller can hear proceedings in Scotland (but not apparently in Northern Ireland); see the commentary on s.123(2)(f) at §123.67.

During the debates on the Patents Bill, concern was expressed at the prospect of an inventor having to face heavy legal costs in contesting proceedings before the court, particularly on appeal. Consequently, s.106 provides the court with broad powers (whether in initial proceedings or on appeal from the Comptroller) to make special awards of costs in s.40 proceedings, taking into account the relevant circumstances, particularly the financial position of the parties, see §106.02. However, in *Memco-Med's Patent* [1992] R.P.C. 403, costs of £700 were awarded by the Comptroller against the unsuccessful applicant and this sum would appear to have been on the normal scale for costs in proceedings before the Comptroller applicable at that time, for which see §107.03 and §107.04. The question of the availability of financial assistance for s.40 proceedings is also discussed in §40.10 and §106.02. In addition, lawyers may accept instructions from an employee under a Conditional Fee Agreement, a topic that will not be further discussed here.

In making an application, care should be taken that all foreign patents from which benefit is alleged to have resulted are included in the application (*British Steel's Patent* [1992] R.P.C. 117); otherwise late amendment may be refused. Likewise, applications for disclosure should be made in good time (*Memco-Med's Patent*, above), with documents relating to profit accruing from sales of patented products only being disclosable if the patent has played a major part in securing these.

From the decision in *British Steel* (above), it would appear that the several headings of benefit (under s.41(4)) are a useful checklist of matters to which evidence should be directed. The Comptroller also there indicated that the amount of any compensation should be settled at the substantive hearing, and not left to a subsequent enquiry, with the procedure being similar to that in settling the terms of a licence of right under s.46(3).

Any decision of the Comptroller under s.40 is subject to appeal to the Patents Court (s.97(1)) and thereafter, with leave, to the Court of Appeal whether or not a question of law is involved (s.97(3)). CPR 63.16 (reprinted at §F63.16) is relevant to such appeals. If proceedings take place in Scotland, any appeal would be to the Court of Session (s.97(4) and (5)).

Taxation of compensation

40.18   Compensation under s.40 may be a lump sum, periodical payments or both (s.41(6)) and the employee should seek to have compensation paid to him in a manner which minimises his liability to tax on the sum received. This subject has been briefly considered by N. Eastaway, (1981) N.L.J. April, p.375, and is more fully dealt with in the books directed to taxation of intellectual property, for which see §30.11. HM Revenue & Customs take the view that compensation arising under s.40(1) or s.40(2) should be caught by the PAYE system, although arguments could be raised that payments under either subsection should not be regarded as being by reason of employment and hence not subject to PAYE deductions. This point has not been tested in court. It is expected that ex gratia payments made by an employer in lieu of compensation under s.40 are taxable in the same way as payments under s.40.

PRACTICE UNDER SECTION 40

Application to the Comptroller

40.19   The procedure for making an application to the Comptroller under the section is governed by Pt 7 of the Rules (discussed and mainly reprinted in §§123.06–123.21). It may well be sensible to see whether there can be a resolution of the case without resorting even to Patent Office proceedings. If an application is filed without notice and subsequently withdrawn, then adverse cost orders can be made (see *Entertainment UK's Patent* O/447/01).

Under r.76, the application is made on PF 2, filed in duplicate with a statement of grounds (also in duplicate) setting out fully the facts and grounds relied upon (r.76(4)). If foreign patents are contended to have contributed to, or be the cause of, the outstanding benefit claimed to have been derived by the employer (as is permissible under s.43(4)), these patents should be identified by number in the statement of case (*GEC Avionics' Patent* [1992] R.P.C. 107; and *British Steel's Patent* [1992] R.P.C. 117). Application can be made at any time after grant of the patent, but not later than one year after the patent has ceased to have effect, or six months after refusal of any application for restoration whichever is the later (r.91). This period can now be extended under r.108(1), even after the period for filing the application has expired: r.108(6); see §123.72.

The Comptroller notifies the proprietor of the patent that the application has begun and sends a copy of the PF 2 and statement of grounds inviting, if the application is to be contested, the filing of a counter-statement within a period which he specifies (r.77). The Comptroller will also notify any other person who appears to him to be likely to have an interest in the case. This will include an employer who is not the patentee. Provisions relating to the content of the counterstatement are set out in r.78. The Comptroller then sends a copy of the counter-statement to the employee inviting the submission of evidence within a period specified by the Comptroller (r.80, reprinted in §123.13). Thereafter the Comptroller will make such case management rules as are required, including provision for the employer to file evidence and the employee to file evidence in reply. Further evidence can be filed, with leave or direction of the Comptroller at any time (r.80(2)). A hearing must be offered (s.80(3)). See §§123.06–123.21 for more details on the procedure generally.

In proceedings before the Comptroller under ss.40(1), 40(2) or 41(8), no document filed at the Patent Office becomes open to public inspection unless the Comptroller otherwise directs (r.51(3) reprinted §118.02 and discussed at §118.10. M. J. Hoolahan has pointed out in (1985–86) 15 *CIPA* 121 that it is, apparently, not the practice of the Comptroller to direct that any such inspection of documents filed in these proceedings should take place and that this rule creates a difficulty in following the progress of applications already made under s.40 to the Comptroller. However, this rule does not prevent the publication of decisions given under the section after a hearing held in public (*Ibstock Building Products' Patent* BL O/64/88).

In the *Ibstock* case, requests for extensive disclosure of documents and financial data from the patent proprietor had been requested and conceded, see BL O/1/89. As a result, as the preliminary hearing noted above indicates, the proceedings may take several years to resolve: indeed, it is understood that the Ibstock case was settled before a substantive hearing was held. On the other hand, without extensive disclosure and the submission of financial data, it will usually be very difficult for the employee to discharge the burden of proving that the benefit of the patent has been "outstanding", as happened in *GEC Avionics' Patent* (above). In *Communication & Control's Patent* BL O/77/93, noted I.P.D. 16136 disclosure was refused as having been requested too late in the proceedings. Also, the requested documents were not seen to be "necessary" to support the applicant's case.

The difficulties which an inventor has to overcome in order to establish any sort of case under s.40 against an employer, especially one which operates through a group of subsidiary companies which have been the subject of a series of corporate re-arrangements, involving transfer of assets and businesses, is well illustrated by the facts in *Electrolux's Patents* BL O/75/98, discussed in §40.12 and §40.13. Here the employer did not seek an award of costs when the application failed, an action which the hearing officer regarded as "generous". A subsequent application for extension of time for appeal in order that legal aid could be sought was readily granted (*Electrolux's Patents* BL O/135/98).

In *Milner's Inventorship Applications* BL O/209/97, the applicant sought compensation under s.40 and also subsequently sought an order that he be declared the only inventor for the patent in contention. The patentee argued that the inventor had not been employed by the parent company (D) but by a subsidiary (S) and the application was then amended to make a claim against S. D sought an award of costs, but this was held to be premature as the Comptroller was not entirely satisfied that D's involvement had unambiguously ended. The applicant sought disclosure and consolidation of the two proceedings. The respondent objected and it was held that the issue of whether the respondent had received "outstanding benefit" from the patent should be tried as a preliminary point, as this might resolve the main dispute and hence save costs. Disclosure was also contested, but unsuccessfully, as the Comptroller held that the request had been carefully framed for production of a restricted class of documents of possible relevance and the applicant had agreed to confidentiality restrictions on the information disclosed.

The Comptroller refused to order summary judgment for the patentee in *Entertainment UK's Patent* [2002] R.P.C. 11 at 291, holding that the power to do so did exist, but should only be exercised in a clear case in accordance with what is now CPR 63.12, reprinted in Appendix F. Although unlikely to be able to show "outstanding benefit" on the facts, the applicant's case was not hopeless. However, it was too poorly pleaded to go forward as it stood and the question then arose as to whether a revised statement should be prepared next or whether the employer's group should give disclosure. Without a clear statement of case it was going to be hard to scope the disclosure and in the end the applicant agreed to file a revised statement of case (the transcript is at O/319/01). However, the application was subsequently withdrawn without prejudice to bringing another and the proprietor sought its costs. £500 was awarded for the costs of reviewing the statement and preparing the counterclaim on the basis that the application had been launched with no prior warning, an action which the hearing officer deplored (see O/447/01).

Application to the court

40.20

An application to the Patents Court or to the Patents County Court is made by issuing a claim form within the same period as under r.91. The time limit is set out in CPR 63.12. The initial hearing is one for the giving of directions as to future procedure, including directions as to the manner of presentation of "accounts of expenditure and receipts relating to the claim" and for providing "reasonable facilities for inspecting and taking extracts from the books of account by which the defendant proposes to verify such accounts" (CPR 63 PD.12). In the usual case it can be expected that the giving of evidence by affidavit will be ordered, but in proceedings before the court cross-examination of witnesses cannot be avoided if requested. If extensive cross-examination is likely to be required, then the Patents County Court may no longer be a suitable jurisdiction, as cases should only last for up to two days. As regards costs in s.40 proceedings, see §106.02.

If the proceedings are taken to the court by way of appeal from a decision of the Comptroller, such appeal must be brought to the Patents Court (unless the hearing took place in Scotland). The procedure for appeal to the Patents Court is governed by CPR 63.16 and the appeal will be by way of re-hearing on the evidence before the Comptroller, see §§97.08–97.19.

SECTION 41

Amount of compensation

41.01

41.—(1) An award of compensation to an employee under section 40(1) or (2) above shall be such as will secure for the employee a fair share (having regard to all the circumstances) of the benefit which the employer has derived, or may reasonably be expected to derive, from any of the following—

(a) the invention in question;

(b) the patent for the invention;

(c) the assignment, assignation or grant of—

(i) the property or any right in the invention, or

(ii) the property in, or any right in or under, an application for the patent,

to a person connected with the employer.

[*An award of compensation to an employee under section 40(1) or (2) above in relation to a patent for an invention shall be such as will secure for the employee a fair share (having regard to all the circumstances) of the benefit which the employer has derived, or may reasonably be expected to derive, from the patent or from the assignment, assignation or grant to a person connected with the employer of the property or any right in the invention or the property in, or any right in or under, an application for that patent.*]

(2) For the purposes of subsection (1) above the amount of any benefit derived or expected to be derived by an employer from the assignment, assignation or grant of—

(a) the property in, or any right in or under, a patent for the invention or application for such a patent; or

(b) the property or any right in the invention;

to a person connected with him shall be taken to be the amount which could reasonably be expected to be so derived by the employer if that person had not been connected with him.

(3) Where the Crown or a Research Council in its capacity as employer assigns or grants the property in, or any right in or under, an invention, patent or application for a patent to a body having among its functions that of developing or exploiting inventions resulting from public research and does so for no consideration or only a nominal consideration, any benefit derived from the invention, patent or application by that body shall be treated for the purposes of the foregoing provisions of this section as so derived by the Crown or, as the case may be, Research Council.

In this subsection "Research Council" means a body which is a Research Council for the purposes of the Science and Technology Act 1965 [c. 4] **or the Arts and Humanities Research Council (as defined by section 1 of the Higher Education Act 2004)**.

(4) In determining the fair share of the benefit to be secured for an employee in respect of [*a patent for*] an invention which has always belonged to an employer, the court or the comptroller shall, among other things, take the following matters into account, that is to say—

(a) the nature of the employee's duties, his remuneration and the other advantages he derives or has derived from his employment or has derived in relation to the invention under this Act;

(b) the effort and skill which the employee has devoted to making the invention;

(c) the effort and skill which any other person has devoted to making the invention jointly with the employee concerned, and the advice and other assistance contributed by any other employee who is not a joint inventor of the invention; and

(d) the contribution made by the employer to the making, developing and working of the invention by the provision of advice, facilities and other assistance, by the provision of opportunities and by his managerial and commercial skill and activities.

(5) In determining the fair share of the benefit to be secured for an employee in respect of [*a patent for*] an invention which originally belonged to him, the court or the comptroller shall, among other things, take the following matters into account, that is to say—

(a) any conditions in a licence or licences granted under this Act or otherwise in respect of the invention or the patent **for it**;

(b) the extent to which the invention was made jointly by the employee with any other person; and

(c) the contribution made by the employer to the making, developing and working of the invention as mentioned in subsection (4)(d) above.

(6) Any order for the payment of compensation under section 40 above may be an order for the payment of a lump sum or for periodical payment, or both.

(7) Without prejudice to section **12 and 14** [*32*] of the Interpretation Act **1978**

[c. 30] [*1889*] (which provides that a statutory power may in general be exercised from time to time), the refusal of the court or the comptroller to make any such order on an application made by an employee under section 40 above shall not prevent a further application being made under that section by him or any successor in title of his.

(8) Where the court or the comptroller has made any such order, the court or he may on the application of either the employer or the employee vary or discharge it or suspend any provision of the order and revive any provision so suspended, and section 40(5) above shall apply to the application as it applies to an application under that section.

(9) In England and Wales any sums awarded by the comptroller under section 40 above shall, if a county court so orders, be recoverable **under section 85 of the County Courts Act 1984 [c. 28]** [*by execution issued from the county court*] or otherwise as if they were payable under an order of that court.

(10) In Scotland an order made under section 40 above by the comptroller for the payment of any sums may be enforced in like manner as **an extract registered decree arbitral bearing a warrant for execution issued by the sheriff court of any sheriffdom in Scotland.** [*as a recorded decree arbitral*]

(11) In Northern Ireland an order made under section 40 above by the comptroller for the payment of any sums may be enforced as if it were a money judgment.

(12) In the Isle of Man an order made under section 40 above by the comptroller for the payment of any sums may be enforced in like manner as an execution issued out of the court.

Notes

1. Subsections (1), (4), (5) and (10) were amended by the Patents Act 2004 (c.16) s.10(1) and Schs 2(11) and (3) all with effect from January 1, 2005 (SI 2004/3205). However, under s.10(8) of this 2004 Act, these amendments only apply in relation to an invention the patent for which has been applied for on or after that date, the term "patent" here having the meaning given by s.43(4). The amendment of subs.(10) brings its wording into conformity with the wording already existing in ss.93(b) and 107(3) and also as now added by new s.61(7).

2. Subsection (9) was prospectively amended by the Tribunals, Courts and Enforcement Act 2007 (c.15) s.62(3) and Sch.13.

3. The amendment to subs.(7) was effected by the Interpretation Act 1978 (c.30) s.25(2).

4. Subsection 12 was added by SI 1978/621 and SI 2003/1249.

RELEVANT RULE—RULES 73–88

41.02   The rules in Pt 7 of the Patents Rules 2007 govern procedure in all proceedings to be heard before the Comptroller. These specifically include proceedings under s.41(8) (see Sch.3 Pt 1). These rules are mainly reprinted in §§123.06–123.21, but are also mentioned, as appropriate, in the commentary and practice sections below. Also r.51(3)(a) (reprinted in §118.02 and discussed in §118.10) applies with respect to documents filed in the UK-IPO.

COMMENTARY ON SECTION 41

Scope of the section

Section 41 is the third of the group of ss.39–43 which relates to employee inventors. It **41.03** deals with the basis on which compensation under either s.40(1) or (2) is to be computed. There is no counterpart in the EPC, CPC or PCT.

For inventions where the patent application is filed on or after January 1, 2005, the benefit may be derived from the invention itself or the patent, as well as assignments of either to a connected person. This is discussed further at §40.12.

The phrase in subs.(1) "may reasonably be expected to derive" makes it clear that, at the time when a determination of the amount of compensation is made, not only the employer's past benefit, but also his future benefit, will be taken into account. This is in contrast to the requirement, enunciated in *Memco-Méd's Patent* [1992] R.P.C. 403 and *British Steel's Patent* [1992] R.P.C. 117, and based on the word "is" in s.40(1) and (2)(c), that the patent (or, presumably for patents filed after January 1, 2005, the invention) must be of actual, not potential, benefit for the purposes of s.40. The test of future benefit seems to be an objective one and not the employer's subjective evaluation. It appears to be irrelevant in the assessment of the benefit that this could have been greater had the employer exploited the patent or (presumably for patents filed after January 1, 2005 the invention) more effectively (*British Steel's Patent*, above).

The assessment of compensation under s.41, must be made in the light of the available evidence as to the benefit actually achieved. It is incorrect to approach this on the basis of a hypothetical valuation: see *Kelly and Chiu v GE Healthcare* [2009] R.P.C. 12, [2009] EWHC 181 Pat Ct for a detailed analysis of how this applies to patents filed before January 1, 2005.

Connected persons

The phrase "person connected with" the employer occurs in both subss.(1) and (2). By **41.04** subs.(2), where an employer entity assigns or licences the invention or the patent to a person connected with it, the benefit obtained is that benefit which would have been obtained by a transaction at arm's length. From this it would appear that, if the employer assigns the patent to an unconnected person by an arm's length transaction, the benefits to be attributed to the employer from the patent or (where the patent application is filed on or after January 1, 2005) the invention will be frozen at that point in time as the benefits accruing before assignment together with the consideration obtained therefor. Equally, where an employer licenses the patent to a third party at arm's length for a royalty, and the licensee derives a large benefit from the patent under the agreement, the employee will not be able to claim any share of that benefit and his claim will be limited to any upfront payments made to and the royalty receipts of his employer. Where the payments of royalties are expressed to be for use of the patent, there is unlikely to be a separate benefit for use of the invention (where the patent application is filed on or after January 1, 2005). However, where there is a mixed patent and know-how licence, then it may be possible to identify payments for know-how transfer and use of that know-how, which might be viewed as benefit derived from the invention, as opposed to the patent itself.

The definition of "connected person" contained in s.839 of the Income and Corporation Taxes Act 1988 ("ICTA") (c.1), as amended, which is to be applied (s.43(8), as putatively amended, s.533 of the Income and Corporation Taxes Act 1970 having been replaced), refers to persons related by marriage or civil partnership or ascent or lineal descent, to trustees and beneficiaries, and to partnerships (and relatives of partners). It also defines companies as being connected if the same person (or group of persons) has control of each company, or if one company controls the other company; and persons acting together to secure or exercise control of a company are treated in relation to that company as being connected with one another. The word "control" is itself defined in s.416 of the same Act. By this, a person has control of a company if he/she is able or entitled to exercise or acquire direct or indirect control over the company's affairs, particularly if he/she possesses or is entitled to acquire the greater part of the issued share capital or voting power of the company or be entitled on a distribution or winding up of the company to the greater part of its income or assets. In *Steele (Inspector of Taxes) v EVC International* [1995] S.T.C. 31; and [1996] S.T.C. 785 CA, it was held that control of the affairs of a company meant control at the level of general meetings of shareholders as being the forum where ultimate decisions as to the business of a company are made.

For further discussion of what constitutes a "connected person", see *Fellerman's Application* BL O/11/96, discussed in §40.06 and §40.08. This case makes it clear that a transfer of the employer's business outside of the group of companies of which it formed a part at the time the invention was made, while patent ownership is retained within that group, means that the patent ownership is no longer with a "connected person" according to the terms of the definition in s.43(8). In *Garrison's Patent* BL O/44/97, the employer had gone into voluntary liquidation, but the patent had been assigned by the liquidator to a company having the same directors, shareholders and address. As the application under s.40(1) failed (see §40.08 and §40.12), no decision was required as to whether or not the new patentee was a "connected person" within the terms of s.41(1).

However, note the comments in *Shanks v Unilever* [2011] R.P.C. 12, [2010] EWCA Civ 1283, that the definition of "connected person" in ICTA, does not apply to the Crown, hence the provisions in s.41(3) discussed at §41.07.

In *Kelly and Chiu v GE Healthcare* (above), it was held that hypothetical valuation is not the way to approach the assessment of compensation, but s.41(2) requires that the benefit when the employer has disposed of or licensed the patent to a connected company "shall be taken to be the amount which could reasonably be expected to be derived by the employer if that person had not been connected with him". In *Shanks v Unilever* BL O/138/09, [2009] EWHC 3164 (Ch); [2010] R.P.C. 11 and on appeal, as above, the difficulties with the drafting of s.41(2) were first considered by the Hearing Officer, by Mann J. in the High Court and then by Jacob L.J. in the Court of Appeal, who considered that the section was "so ill-drafted that one has to be guided by its evident purpose". The court should therefore follow an approach to construction called by the late Thomas Blanco White QC "sewing the fly buttons on the statute" (see para.32). There should not be "a notional auction of the invention at the time of the assignment". By ruling out any such "notional auction", cases of this sort "should be able to proceed to determination without a mass of evidence about hypothetical considerations about a hypothetical transaction which would have taken place years ago" (see para 33(ii)).

The "paradigm case" is where the employer exploits the invention itself. One had to take the employer as it was and there was no "best endeavours to exploit" requirement. Section 41(2) does not permit the claimant to substitute the actual assignee with a hypothetical party who would pay a "market value" for the patent and so cause the "benefit" to be in excess of what the employer's group of companies had actually obtained (the "putative benefit" see also §40.08). Nor did it allow the employer to argue that, given the uncertainties at the date of the assignment and when the invention had not been exploited, that it would only have realised a modest sum. It was therefore held that "that person" in s.41(2) means an actual assignee with its actual attributes and was to be read consistently with s.41(1) to embrace that actually obtained within the employer's group of companies at the time of the compensation application.

Further, the Court of Appeal suggested that s.41 "reached through" to s.40, suggesting that in dealing with the hurdle in s.40(1), that the employee must show that the patent (or invention) was of "outstanding benefit" to his employer, the benefit is not confined to that actually obtained by the employer itself, but can include the benefit to other companies in the group, notwithstanding that there is no mention in s.40 of persons connected to the employer. (See also §40.08 and §40.13.)

For discussion as to what happens when the employer dies and the patent passes to a personal representative or another in whom it vests see §43.06.

Fair awards (subss. (1), (4) and (5))

41.05   Subsection (1) sets out the worthy principle that the award (whether under s.40(1) or (2)) is to be "fair" having regard to all the circumstances. However, it includes no definition of the word "fair" and its wording affords little assistance in this regard. The concept of a "fair" award, having regard to the contributions made by other employees to the development of the invention, was inconclusively discussed, obiter, in *British Steel's Patent* [1992] R.P.C. 117 and in *Kelly and Chiu v GE Healthcare* [2009] R.P.C. 12, [2009] EWHC 181 Pat Ct, the court was unable to single out anyone other than the joint inventors for a significant contribution. However, as the "benefit" now under consideration is that derived from both the patent and (where the patent application is filed on or after January 1, 2005) the invention, factors which cause one product to sell better than another, e.g. design, branding or advertising, which may all have been contributions by other employees, and these may or may not count as "joint inventors" by virtue of s.43(3) (see §43.04) and there may be "other forms of protection" granted in respect of their inventions (see s.43(4) and §43.05) which might entitle them to compensation as well.

Subsections (4) and (5) set out the factors which have to be taken into account when arriving at a decision as to what is a fair award. Subsection (4) applies to a claim under s.40(1), in respect of an invention owned by the employer, when account is to be taken of: the employee's duties; his remuneration and other advantages he derived from his employment or the invention; his skill and the contributory skill of others; and the contribution to the invention by the employer. Subsection (5) applies to a claim under s.40(2), in respect of an invention owned by the employee, when account is to be taken of: the conditions of any licences granted under the invention or patent; the contribution by any other joint inventor; and the contribution made by the employer. But despite these general directions there still remains considerable scope for deciding what is "fair" in any particular case.

Factors set out in subss.(1) and (4) were considered in *Kelly and Chiu v GE Healthcare* above. However, it is not clear how each of these subsequently contributed to the "fair share" which was then awarded to the two inventors who made the claim. Although Floyd J. had found the invention to be of outstanding benefit, in being "fair" to the employer, he then took—in his own words—a very conservative view as to the benefit to be attributed to the patent and held that that value was in the order of £50 million, with one inventor receiving £1 million and the other £1/2 million, the inventors' shares having been assessed as 2 per cent and 1 per cent of that figure respectively, and the total representing about 0.1 per cent of turnover. (See also §40.12.) It may be noted that the wording in the statute is about securing a "fair share" for the employee. It may be debated as to whether this is the same as being "fair" to the employer. For a discussion on whether or not the amount awarded was "fair to the inventor" see Salmon, "A fair share: a judgment of Solomon: *Kelly & Chiu v GE Healthcare*" [2009] June *CIPA* 606–610.

It may take many years before the amended provisions have to be considered in relation to an application filed after January 1, 2005. So one can only speculate as to whether the sums could have been considerably higher had the court been asked to consider the benefit of the invention, as opposed to the benefit of the patent. The sales in this case had exceeded £1.3 billion by the end of 2007, although the profits in relation to that were not disclosed.

A. N. Devereux, in an article on employee-inventor compensation in (1985–86) 15 *CIPA* 47, suggested that the Crown Awards Scheme, under which Crown employees have in the past been rewarded for their inventive contributions, may provide, by analogy, a method of assessing compensation for employee inventors under s.40.

The words "among other things" which appear in both subss.(4) and (5) indicate that the factors listed are not to be taken as exhaustive. It is interesting to contrast the criteria in s.41 with those applying to an owner of a secret, not granted, patent application who is compensated for hardship under the provisions of s.22(7): in the latter, among all other relevant circumstances, the inventive merit and utility of the invention and the purpose for which it is designed are singled out for specific mention. The first two of these criteria would no doubt be present in virtually all cases of patents of "outstanding benefit" under s.40, but perhaps not necessarily so with regard to the third criterion.

"Developing" occurs both in subss.(4)(d) and (5)(c). Whilst this word must include developing the first germ of an idea to the stage where it is a feasible, or at least a patentable, proposition (since otherwise there will be no granted patent upon which to base the claim), it seems possible that it means more: developing the invention to the stage of production and marketability because of the way the word is sandwiched between "making" and "working", implying a chronological sequence. Although for inventions made before January 1, 2005, it might be right to say that, if *Memco-Med* [1992] R.P.C. 403 is correct and one is confined to the benefit derived from the "patent", then "developing" too ought to be confined to the stage where there is an "enabling disclosure" in an application for a patent, i.e. that its description is "sufficient" (under s.14(3)). Now, where the patent application is filed on or after January 1, 2005, both the benefit derived from the invention and the benefit derived from the patent are taken into account, so the argument for confining "developing" to material required for the patent application and excluding other work done in relation to the invention, e.g. to a commercial product or process, loses its force.

Payment of compensation (subs.(6))

41.06   By subs.(6), payment can be a lump sum or a periodical payment or both. Any order made may subsequently be varied, discharged, suspended or revived (subs.(8)) by application made by either employee or employer to the Comptroller or to the court under s.40. Any award made under s.40 may be enforced in the same way as for an order for payment made by a court, as set out in subss.(9)–(11) for the various constituent parts of the United Kingdom, and in subs.(12) for the Isle of Man. Given that in reaching the award, the court or Comptroller will be looking also at the benefit which may be derived in the future, this ability to make periodic payments, coupled with the provisions of subs.(8) for either party to apply to vary, suspend or discharge such periodic payments, gives considerable flexibility the court and the Comptroller as to what sort of award to make.

In *Kelly and Chiu v GE Healthcare* [2009] R.P.C. 12, [2009] EWHC 181 Pat Ct, the court was invited to make "a once and for all award" and did so, the application for compensation having been made towards the end of the life of the various patents concerned.

Documents filed in connection with an application under s.41(8) are not open for inspection unless the Comptroller decides otherwise. (See r.51(3) reprinted at §118.02 and discussed at §118.10).

Crown and Research Councils (subs.(3))

41.07   Subsection (3) refers to the circumstances where the employer is the Crown or a Research Council (as defined under s.1 (as amended) of the Science and Technology Act 1965 (c.4)) and the patent or any right under it is assigned to a body devoted to exploitation. Benefit to such a body is to be treated as benefit obtained by the Crown or the Research Council (see §41.04 regarding extent of "connected persons").

Under secondary legislation made under the Science and Technology Act 1965 (c.4), the following are designated as "research councils" under that Act: the Biotechnology and Biological Sciences Research Council; the Economic and Social Research Council; the Engineering and Physical Sciences Research Council; the Medical Research Council; the National Environment Research Council; and the Science and Technology Facilities Council. The Arts and Humanities Research Council was established by the Higher Education Act 2004, and subs.(3) amended by the Sch.6 of that Act and brought into force by the Higher Education Act 2004 (Commencement No.2) Order 2004 (SI 2004/3255).

Unsuccessful applications (subs.(7))

41.08   By subs.(7), where an application under s.40 has been unsuccessful, the employee (or successors in title after death) may make a further application under that section. It is not clear whether "a further" application means one further or includes more than one: it is likely to be the latter in view of the Interpretation Act 1978 (c.30) s.6. Also the provisions of subs.(8), allow either party, where the application was successful, to come back to the court or the Comptroller to suspend or revive provisions of an award, as the circumstances change. So it would be consistent with that provision not to restrict an unsuccessful party to a single further application. The provisions of the Limitation Act 1980 (c.58) do not appear to affect the position since the exploitation of a patent or (where the patent application is filed on or after January 1, 2005) the invention, is a continuing event and r.91 (as amended, reprinted in §40.02) sets a wide period within which applications for compensation may be made. However, as with an infringement action, it might be possible to argue that the Limitation Act 1980 should restrict the period of time over which the compensation is assessed, although this point does not appear to have been considered in *Kelly and Chiu v GE Healthcare* above. There is also the question whether the Limitation Act would override the effect of s.42(2). Although the patentee complained that the employee-inventors' delay affected the "justness" of any award, the court did not accept this point, as mentioned in §40.07, above.

Procedure

A foreseeable difficulty in applying s.41 to proceedings under s.40 is the fact that in the **41.09** majority of cases the applicant for an award of compensation will not be in possession of the information on which the application needs to be based so that, if the application is to be justly considered, it will be necessary for the employer to produce, voluntarily or by order for disclosure, the details of benefit derived from the patent or (where the patent application is filed on or after January 1, 2005) the invention. However, applications for disclosure in proceedings under s.40 have been refused, or limited in several instances, see §40.19. CPR 63.12 and CPR 63 PD 12.1(2) make provision for disclosure and verification of financial information and books of account of the employer and the Comptroller can make similar directions under r.82(1)(a), for which see §123.15. Where no such information is available, or is incompletely available (and the relevant period may extend over most of the term of the patent) the court or Comptroller may need to resort to educated estimation, but nevertheless the onus lies on an applicant to prove his case, see *Memco-Med's Patent* [1992] R.P.C. 403. However, although companies are obliged to retain financial records for tax reasons, those records would not necessarily be retained for 21 years and so if the claim is left too long, the relevant information may no longer be available.

PRACTICE UNDER SECTION 41

An application to vary, discharge, suspend or revive an award of compensation to an **41.10** employee under s.40 may be made under subs.(8). As with an application under s.40, the application may be made to the Comptroller or to the court and the Comptroller may decline to deal with such an application made to him (s.40(5)), as discussed in §40.17 in relation to the similar proceedings under s.40(1) or (2). Application to the Comptroller is made under Pt 7 of the Rules (rr.73–91, mainly reprinted at §§123.06–123.21) by filing PF 2 in duplicate and a statement of grounds (also in duplicate) setting out fully the facts relied upon and the relief sought (r.76(1) and (4)). Oppositions/counterstatements can be filed in duplicate under r.77(6) within the period specified (r.77(5)). For further details see r.77 onwards and §§123.44 et seq. and see also the practice under s.40 at §40.19 and §40.20.

Documents filed in connection with an application under s.41(8) are not open for inspection unless the Comptroller decides otherwise. (See r.51(3) reprinted at §118.02 and discussed at §118.10.)

For the procedure in any application to the Patents Court or Patents County Court, see CPR 63 as discussed above. Any appeal from a decision of the Comptroller is now governed by CPR 63.16, for which see the commentary on s.97 generally.

SECTION 42

Enforceability of contracts relating to employees' inventions

42.—(1) This section applies to any contract (whenever made) relating to **42.01** inventions made by an employee, being a contract entered into by him

(a) with the employer (alone or with another); or

(b) with some other person at the request of the employer or in pursuance of the employee's contract of employment.

(2) Any term in a contract to which this section applies which diminishes the employee's rights in inventions of any description made by him after the appointed day and the date of the contract, or in or under patents for those inventions or applications for such patents, shall be unenforceable against him to the extent that it diminishes his rights in an invention of that description so made, or in or under a patent for such an invention or an application for any such patent.

(3) Subsection (2) above shall not be construed as derogating from any duty of confidentiality owed to his employer by an employee by virtue of any rule of law or otherwise.

(4) This section applies to any arrangements made with a Crown employee by or on behalf of the Crown as his employer as it applies to any contract made between an employee and an employer other than the Crown, and for the purposes of this section "Crown employee" means a person employed under or for the purposes of a government department or any officer or body exercising on behalf of the Crown functions conferred by any enactment **or a person serving in the naval, military or air forces of the Crown.**

Note. Section 42(4) was amended by the Armed Forces Act 1981 (c.55, s.22).

COMMENTARY ON SECTION 42

Scope of the section

42.02   Section 42 is the fourth of the group of ss.39–43 which relates to employee inventors. It deals with the enforceability of certain contracts between employees and employers. There is no counterpart in the EPC, CPC or PCT.

Section 42 relates to contracts between an employer and an employee (including Crown employees, subs.(4)), whether made before or after the Act came into force, and provides that no contract is enforceable to the extent that it diminishes the "rights" of an employee in any invention made by the employee after the appointed day, June 1, 1978, and after the date of the contract. The section applies also to any contract between an employee and a third party made at the request of the employer, or in pursuance of the employee's contract of employment (subs.(1)). Under subs.(2), a contract which diminishes the employee's "rights" is unenforceable to the extent that it does so, see §42.03, but with no derogation from a duty of confidentiality owed by an employee to his/her employer (subs.(3)). "Rights", in relation to any patent or application, are defined in s.130(1) as including an "interest" therein. "Right", in relation to an invention, is not mentioned in s.130(1), but would presumably include an "interest" in the invention.

The difficulty is that neither "right" nor "interest" is capable of precise definition. Jurisprudentially, many different classifications exist, e.g. legal rights and moral rights; rights and duties (obligations); rights in personam and rights in rem; personal rights and proprietary rights; legal rights and equitable rights, etc. A basis of right is interest, but not every interest is protected by a legal right. In relation to property, both "interest" and "right" appear to converge into a connection a person has with a thing entitling him to make a claim in respect of it. Elsewhere in the Act, there are references, inter alia, to: the right to apply for and obtain a patent (s.7); any right in or under a patent or application (ss.8, 10, 12, 37, 38, 82 and 86); a right to be mentioned as inventor (s.13); "continuing rights" under restored patents and applications (ss.28A, 77(5) and 78(6)); personal property rights (ss.30, 31, 33); rights of third parties in respect of Crown use (s.57); the right to receive payment for Crown use (s.58, referring to s.55(4) which itself does not use the term "right"); the right to bring proceedings for infringement (ss.67, 69); rights of appeal; the right to continued use (s.64); and right of audience (s.102). In many instances the Act uses "entitlement" in preference to "right".

From this survey one may conclude that "right", for the purposes of s.42(2), is capable of bearing a meaning wider than rights of mere ownership as, for example, arising under s.39. Further discussion awaits judicial construction of subs.(2) in relation to particular factual situations.

Section 40 does not use the term "right" in respect of an employee's ability to bring proceedings for compensation where the invention or patent is of outstanding benefit. Hence the question raised in §40.14, as to whether this is a "benefit" and not a "right" and consequently the circumstances in which that could be restricted. If this is a "right" to make a claim, then a clause which diminished an employee's rights to make an application under s.40 would be void. However, where the employee received compensation in exchange for agreeing not to make a claim under s.40(1) then interesting questions might arise as to whether or not the employee had received proper compensation or whether his "rights" to compensation had been "diminished". See the discussions at §40.14 and §42.03.

In *LIFFE v Pinkava* [2007] R.P.C. 30 at [93]; [2007] EWCA Civ 217, Jacob L.J. suggests that the provisions of subs.(2) apply even to the term of the employment contract that mirrors s.39. In his view s.39 provides the complete code to the issue of ownership. These provisions will also strike down contractual terms which overstate the employee's duties.

Unenforceability of contracts with employees (subs.(2))

The section applies only to contracts entered into by an "employee" acting as such, and **42.03** thus does not have effect in the case of a contract entered into between a company and one of its shareholders acting as such, even if that shareholder is also an employee (*Buchanan v Alba Diagnostics [Scotland]* [2000] R.P.C. 367).

Under subs.(2) a contract is unenforceable only to the extent that it diminishes the employee's rights: the remainder of the contract will therefore remain enforceable provided the unenforceable provisions are severable from the remainder of the contract.

As to severability, the reader is referred to standard textbooks on contract law (e.g. *Chitty on Contracts* 30th edn (London: Sweet & Maxwell, 2010) for the general principles governing the doctrine of severance and the leading case of *United City Merchants v Royal Bank of Canada* [1982] Q.B. 208 CA; [1983] A.C. 168 HL. In the field of employment contracts containing covenants imposed on an employee in restraint of trade, it was said in *Mason v Provident Clothing* [1913] A.C. 724 HL that the courts should be "reluctant" to sever such contracts or parts of them. However, in *Stenhouse Australia v Phillips* [1974] A.C. 391 HL, it was held that there should be no special rule for covenants in employment contracts and that where (but only where) the parts of a contract in reality amount to separate and independent covenants they may be severed from one another. An important consideration is whether the provision in the clause goes to substantially the whole, or only to part, of the consideration. If it is merely subsidiary to the main purpose of the contract, severance may be possible; e.g. a clause in a service contract purporting to oust the jurisdiction of the courts.

It appears irrelevant that severance of void parts of a contract results in a total transformation of the economic balance of interest between the parties, see *Chemidus Wavin v Soc. pour la Transformation* [1977] F.S.R. 19; [1977] F.S.R. 181 where certain clauses were excised as contrary to what is now art.101 TFEU.

Under subs.(2), not only are clauses purporting to regulate ownership of the employee's future inventions void, but so also are the frequently encountered clauses requiring employees to give their employers a first refusal or option on their inventions. In *Quadrant Holdings v Quadrant Research* BL C/86/98, noted I.P.D. 22025, a clause in an employee's service agreement which stated that all inventions made by him should be the direct property of an associated company was held invalid under the terms of the section, even though that clause was stated to be "subject to the provisions of the Patents Act 1977".

An area of controversy concerns the frequently occurring clause in contracts of employment requiring an employee to disclose his/her inventions to the employer. If under s.39 the invention belongs to the employee, does this clause diminish the employee's "rights in inventions ... made by him"? Given the possibility of wide interpretation of "rights" (see §42.02), it probably does; but how can an employer claim rights in an invention if he is unaware of its existence? One practical solution may be based on the implied term of the employee's duty of fidelity, which in this context may mean a requirement to disclose for the initially limited purpose of determination of ownership; and also the need to give the contract of employment business efficacy. Anyway, as long as the clause is not central to the contract it will probably be severable. Including a "severability" clause in the contract may also assist. In any event, employers requiring such disclosure should bear in mind the need to maintain the confidentiality of the employee's submission pending determination of its ownership, see *Prout v British Gas* [1992] F.S.R. 478 from the neighbouring field of suggestion schemes where an employee's submission was held to give rise to a contractually enforceable obligation of confidence or alternatively an equitable obligation arising from the fiduciary relationship between the employee and the employer. Reference should also be made to §39.15 concerning the possibility of a claim for unfair constructive dismissal by failure to treat an employee reasonably.

The commentary on s.40 at §40.14 suggests that it may be possible for an employer to make a binding agreement with an employee which could override the provisions of s.40(1), though not those of s.40(2). Note from the comment of J. Phillips [1980] E.I.P.R. 347 that if the "rights" referred to in s.42(2) that cannot be "diminished" do not also include the right to compensation under s.40(1), much of the latter and/or s.42 could be rendered ineffective.

The impact of subs.(2) on company suggestion schemes needs to be considered carefully in the light of the comments in §39.04 and the *Prout* case (above).

Duty of confidentiality (subs.(3))

42.04   Subsection (3) provides that subs.(2) is not to derogate from any duty of confidentiality which an employee may have to his employer. It is advisable to spell out this duty of confidentiality in conditions of employment. If an invention belongs to an employee he/she has the right to apply for a patent for it, but care must be taken not to disclose in the specification matter which is confidential to the employer. Very probably, an employer could obtain an injunction against an employee disclosing such confidential information, for example in a patent application made by the employee under s.39(2). Although see also the obiter comments of Jacob L.J. in *LIFFE v Pinkava* [2007] R.P.C. 30, at 100; [2007] EWCA Civ 217, where he considers that, if the employee is obliged to keep the invention confidential, then it would probably belong to the employer as "Parliament cannot have intended such a stalemate". However, this misses the point that inventions (particularly improvements) do not sit in isolation and, in order to explain it or even to work it might require the use of the employer's confidential information.

It is also interesting to contrast this section with s.39(3), which allows the employee effectively to ignore an employer's copyright and design rights in models and documents relating to the invention which he makes in the course of his employment. However, s.39(3) makes no reference to any obligations of confidence which relate to such models or documents and, presumably, if these had remained confidential, then the employer could prevent the employee from using them in a way which breached the obligation of confidence. See also §39.17.

The Court of Appeal, in *Faccenda Chicken v Fowler* [1986] F.S.R. 291, and again in *Lancashire Fires v SA Lyons* [1996] F.S.R. 629, reviewed the general principles governing the law of confidence and stated that in every case the starting point is the contract of employment. If the contract contains no express terms protecting confidential information, the implied term of the duty of confidence, itself a facet of the implied duty of good faith, must be considered. The scope of the duty after termination of employment is more restricted than during it, but a limited duty will survive if the degree of confidentiality is high enough. The distinction between confidential information and information which forms part of an employee's stock in trade formulated in *Printers & Finishers v Holloway* [1965] R.P.C. 239 was affirmed, and see the comments in *Ocular Science* (below). The following factors were held to assist in the determination whether a particular item of information falls within the implied duty of confidence: (i) the nature of the employment and status of the employee; (ii) the nature of the information; (iii) whether the employer expressly indicated to the employee that the information was confidential; and (iv) the severability of the confidential information from non-confidential information. The court also said that an express restrictive covenant to protect information is valid only if that information is properly "confidential". In *Faccenda*, the employee's contract of employment contained no restrictive covenant and the employer relied on the implied term in every contract of employment of good faith and fidelity. Nevertheless, even where a contract did contain in wide terms an express obligation of confidentiality to restrain misuse of confidential information, the employer's action for an injunction failed because the court found no evidence of specific, identifiable trade secrets: see *Mainmet Holdings v Austin* [1991] F.S.R. 538.

However, in *Ocular Sciences v Aspect Vision Care* [1997] R.P.C. 289, it was suggested that in *Faccenda Chicken* the Court of Appeal may have muddled confidentiality on the one hand and the employee's skills and expertise on the other. While an employee works for an employer he/she is bound by an implied obligation of good faith and must therefore deploy his/her skill and expertise for the benefit of the employer and no-one else, whether or not the skill and expertise contain confidential information. It is therefore doubtful if the *Faccenda* proposition that the employee is free to disclose to anyone information which belongs to the employer if it is trivial while the employment relationship subsists, is correct. After termination of that relationship, for public policy reasons an employee must be left free to put at the disposal of a new employer all his/her skill and experience. The borderline is very difficult to determine, as was acknowledged both in *Lancashire Fires* and in *Ocular Sciences* (both above). The borderline was also considered in *Vestergaard Frandsen et al v Bestnet Europe et al* [2009] EWHC 657 (Ch), with the court finding that the relevant information (contained in a database) was a trade secret rather than part of the employee's skill and knowledge.

Where an employer is in repudiatory breach of contract (e.g. where an employee is dismissed in contravention of the termination provisions in the contract of employment) any outstanding contractual obligations of the employee are extinguished upon the ending of the contract, and thus any clause of restraint of trade becomes unenforceable: see *General Bill Posting Co v Atkinson* [1909] A.C. 118. It is an open question whether, in relation to trade secrets, the employer's breach discharges the employee's express or implied obligations of confidentiality. Moreover, following a Law Commission Report (1999), it seems that new legislation may impose criminal sanctions against the mis-use of confidential information.

As discussed above, clearly, an employee-owned invention making use of employer-owned confidential information has the potential to lead to an impasse under s.42(3). It is interesting to speculate whether the employer could obtain an injunction against the UK-IPO to prevent publication under s.16 of an application filed by the employee for such an invention, but see *Rex Co v Muirhead and Comptroller-General* (1927) 44 R.P.C. 38.

Crown and Government employees (subs.(4))

At first sight it is hard to see the purpose of this subsection, as the definition of "employee" in s.130(1) already covers those in the employment of a government department or serving in the armed forces. However, the crucial word may be "arrangement", in that Crown employees and those serving may not have a "contract of employment". **42.05**

Section 22 of the Armed Forces Act 1981 (c.55) states that:

"The Patents Act 1977 shall have effect, and be deemed always to have had effect, with the following amendments (being amendments to secure that members of the Armed Forces are 'employees' for the purposes of that Act)"

and then adds the words shown in bold type at the end of subs.(4). This amendment appears to have been made to remove any possible doubt that members of the armed forces are "Crown employees" for the purposes of the Act. A similar amendment has been made in the definition of "employee" in s.130(1), see §39.05.

The definition of "Crown employee" in subs.(4) differs from the definition of "employee" in s.130(1) in that subs.(4) includes "or any officer or body exercising on behalf of the Crown functions conferred by any enactment". Also subs.(4) is expressed only in the present, whereas the definition in s.130(1) refers to those who have been employed or have served. However, it is unlikely that anything would turn on this as if a clause of a contract or arrangement had been unenforceable while the person concerned was employed or serving, it is hard to see why the court would find that it became enforceable after that relationship had terminated and could thereafter be enforced.

SECTION 43

Supplementary

43.01

43.—(1) Sections 39 to 42 above shall not apply to an invention made before the appointed day.

(2) Sections 39 to 42 above shall not apply to an invention made by an employee unless at the time he made the invention one of the following conditions was satisfied in his case, that is to say—

(a) he was mainly employed in the United Kingdom; or

(b) he was not mainly employed anywhere or his place of employment could not be determined, but his employer had a place of business in the United Kingdom to which the employee was attached, whether or not he was also attached elsewhere.

(3) In sections 39 to 42 above and this section, except so far as the context otherwise requires, references to the making of an invention by an employee are references to his making it alone or jointly with any other person, but do not include references to his merely contributing advice or other assistance in the making of an invention by another employee.

(4) Any references in sections **39** [*40*] to 42 above to a patent and to a patent being granted are respectively references to a patent or other protection and to its being granted whether under the law of the United Kingdom or the law in force in any other country or under any treaty or international convention.

(5) For the purposes of sections 40 and 41 above the benefit derived or expected to be derived by an employer from **an invention or** [*a*] patent shall, where he dies before any award is made under section 40 above in respect of **it** [*the patent*], include any benefit derived or expected to be derived from **it** [*the patent*] by his personal representatives or by any person in whom it was vested by their assent.

(5A) For the purposes of sections 40 and 41 above the benefit derived or expected to be derived by an employer from an invention shall not include any benefit derived or expected to be derived from the invention after the patent for it has expired or has been surrendered or revoked.

(6) Where an employee dies before an award is made under section 40 above in respect of a patented invention made by him, his personal representatives or their successors in title may exercise his right to make or proceed with an application for compensation under subsection (1) or (2) of that section.

(7) In sections 40 and 41 above and this section "benefit" means benefit in money or money's worth.

(8) Section **839** [*533*] of the Income and Corporation Taxes Act **1988** [c.1] [*1970*] (definition of connected persons) shall apply for determining for the

purposes of section 41(2) above whether one person is connected with another as it applies for determining that question for the purposes of the Tax Acts.

Notes

1. Subsection (4) was amended by the CDPA 1988 (c.48) Sch.5(11)(2), effective from January 7, 1991 (SI 1990/2168).

2. By s.10 of the Patents Act 2004 (c.16), subs.(5) was amended, and subs.(5A) added, each with effect from January 1, 2005 (SI 2004/3205), but **only** in relation to an invention the patent (as defined in subs.(4)) for which was applied for on or after that date. These amendments are consequential upon the amendments made to s.40(1) and (2) as discussed in the commentary on s.40.

3. Subsection (8) was effectively amended by the Income and Corporation Taxes Act 1988 (c.1) Sch.30(21)(3).

COMMENTARY ON SECTION 43

Scope of the section

Section 43 is the last of the group of ss.39–43 relating to the rights of employees in inventions which they make and sets out a number of supplementary provisions which affect the operation of the other sections of this group, mainly by providing definitions of the terms used. These sections have no counterpart in the EPC, CPC or PCT. **43.02**

Subsection (1) provides that ss.39–42 apply only to inventions made on or after June 1, 1978. For the time of making an invention, see §7.06.

Employee's place of employment (subs.(2))

Subsection (2) limits the operation of ss.39–42 to an invention made by an employee who at the time was mainly employed in the United Kingdom, or by an employee whose main place of employment is indeterminate, but the employer has a place of business in the United Kingdom to which the employee was attached. This wording is similar to the original s.196 of the Employment Rights Act 1996 under which certain employment rights did not apply to employees who worked "wholly or mainly outside Great Britain" unless he/she "ordinarily worked" in Great Britain. This provision was however repealed in October 1999, and instead the position was then left to international principles and case law. Whilst employment case lawcannot be definitive as to how the provisions of subs.(2) will be interpreted, a review of judicial discussion of the issues may be useful. A series of conflicting decisions, in particular in relation to the right to claim unfair dismissal in Great Britain, left the employment law position regarding an employee's place of employment unclear. The latest decision from the House of Lords on this point did not provide the clarity hoped for. In *Lawson v Serco Ltd, Botham v Ministry of Defence and Veta Ltd v Crofts* [2006] UKHL 3, their Lordships chose not to follow any of the tests suggested by prior judgments and instead reverted to general principles. They expressed their support for the "employed in Great Britain" test, although they noted that this was a general principle rather than a firm rule. In the case of a "peripatetic employee" who does not perform services in one particular territory, their base should be treated as the place of their employment. Finally, their Lordships ruled that the position regarding expatriate employees was less clear and the "employed in Great Britain" test might not be adequate. No definitive test was laid down but an employee posted abroad to work for a business carried on in Britain or working abroad in a British enclave will need to show a strong connection with Great Britain and UK employment law for there to be jurisdiction. **43.03**

The Employment Protection (Offshore Employment) Order 1976 (SI 1976/766, as amended) has now been supplemented by the Employment Relations (Offshore Employment Order 2000 (SI 2000/1828). These take effect under s.201 of the Employment Rights Act 1996 (c.18) and extend employment protection to offshore employment in UK territorial waters and to designated waters of the continental shelf so as to cover employees on offshore oil and gas exploration and production installations. The present Act extends to acts occurring at these locations, see s.132(3) and (4), discussed in §132.08.

The Isle of Man is also part of the United Kingdom for the purposes of the Patents Act, see s.132(2) and implementing regulations discussed in §132.07.

Joint inventions (subs.(3))

43.04   Subsection (3) provides that ss.39–42 relate to joint inventions and joint inventors as they relate to a sole invention and inventor, but excludes from joint inventorship any person whose contribution is merely by way of advice or assistance. No doubt, subs.(3) is intended to minimise disputes as to inventorship which often arise where inventions are made in large research organisations or by a research team, but in the absence of definitions of "advice" and "assistance" the operation of the subsection, or the assistance it gives in resolving questions of joint inventorship, is difficult to foresee. Some guidance may be available from *BNOS Electronics' Patent* BL O/270/98 where only one out of four named co-inventors was found to have made the invention, and, more importantly, from the discussion on the definition of "inventor" in §7.10, especially in the light of cases such as *IDA v University of Southampton* [2006] R.P.C. 21; [2006] EWCA Civ 145 CA; *University of Southampton's Patent Applications* [2006] R.P.C. 21, where a distinction was drawn between inventive and non-inventive contributions. See also the discussion in *Kelly and Chiu v GE Healthcare* [2009] R.P.C. 12, [2009] EWHC 181 Pat Ct, where it was found to be inherent in ss.40 and 41 that those who were not joint inventors could not receive an award, however invidious this may be to the running of a business.

Extension to other forms of protection (subs.(4))

43.05   Subsection (4) extends the scope of ss.39–42 to include other forms of protection and to protection in other countries. Under this provision, benefit under a United States patent was in issue in *GEC Avionics' Patent* [1992] R.P.C. 107. There is no indication of whether "other protection" is intended to cover only closely similar forms of protection, such as petty patents, which exist for the protection of patentable or near-patentable inventions, or whether a broader view is to be taken so that these sections apply also to, for example, registered designs, which may or may not involve "inventions" in the broad sense of s.39 and which are "granted"; and copyright, design and topography rights, each of which again may or may not embody an "invention", but which in United Kingdom law are not "granted" and which, moreover, are not necessarily new and do not necessarily involve an inventive step. In any event, copyright can be "granted" in certain foreign jurisdictions, e.g. in the United States. A registrable trade mark may include an invented word, but whether for the purpose of s.43 a registered trade mark thereby can be considered to be an invention in respect of which protection is "granted", as distinct from registered, is doubted. It may or may not be relevant that some invented trade marks have proved to be of great commercial value, no less than that of many patents. That the broader view should be preferred is supported by the contrast with s.12(7)(a) where the word "other" before "protection" is omitted, see §12.03: see also the discussion in the context of "for all other purposes" in s.39(1) in §39.16 and the discussion of s.39(3) in §39.17.

It may be argued that the essential test is whether an "invention" receives "protection" under the law and that protection confers such benefit on the employer that the employee should receive "a fair share (having regard to all the circumstances)", see s.41(1) discussed in §41.05. If that is correct, then it might be argued that confidential information should also be covered by the words "other protection". One reason in support of this proposition is to argue that otherwise the anomalous situation could arise that an employee-inventor is unable to claim compensation in respect of inventions belonging to, or acquired by, an employer who decides to keep the invention secret and to whom the protection of the law of confidentiality may well afford considerable benefit. It may also be noted in this connection that s.64 confers potentially very valuable rights which, moreover, are (within certain limits) assignable for valuable consideration. However, it is hard to see a court finding merit in such a broad interpretation, especially in the light of the amendments to ss.40 and

41 made by the Patents Act 2004, as compensation may now be obtained where there is benefit derived from the invention (for those patent applications filed on or after January 1, 2005) or the assignment of "any right in the invention", and not just the patent, s.41(1)(a) and (c)(i) but where it is a prerequisite to the compensation claim that a patent has been granted s.40(1) and s.40(2)(a) and the period of time for assessing that benefit is only while the patent subsists (s.43(5A). Protection conferred by obligations of confidentiality would probably not meet this hurdle, both because there is no act of "grant" specific for a property right and because there is no publication. Also, since the insertion of subs.5A, it can be argued that the concepts of "expiry", "surrender" and "revocation" would also need to apply to such "other forms of protection" and such language does not sit easily with the nature of confidential information.

Although decided in relation to the pre-January 1, 2005 amendment of the Act, in *Kelly and Chiu v GE Healthcare* above, Floyd J. looked at whether the phrase "or other protection" extended to regulatory data exclusivity regimes for pharmaceutical products. Without deciding on the outer limits of the phrase, he concluded that data exclusivity did not fall within the phrase and distinguished between:

"a form of protection which grants a monopoly in respect of manufacture and sale of a product or use of a process (such as a patent or utility model); and a form of 'protection' which merely makes it more difficult for a competitor to enter the market (as in the case of a product where the generic competitor has to generate his own safety and efficacy data)".

It is therefore interesting to speculate whether the grant of a Supplementary Protection Certificate (SPC), would count as "other protection". As the section of the MOPP on SPCs makes clear at para.SP0.03: "A certificate takes effect at the end of the lawful term of the basic patent but does not extend the term of the patent itself. It extends the protection conferred by the patent in respect of the product covered by the authorization ......". This period can be very important to the patentee, and "is intended to compensate a patentee for the loss of effective protection arising out of the time taken to obtain regulatory approval to place [the product] on the market" (MOPP SP0.01). It therefore would seem right that the inventor should also be entitled to a fair share in the benefits derived at this time.

The words "grants a monopoly" may need to be reconsidered one day in the light of the provisions of s.39(3), see §39.17.

With regard to protection outside of the United Kingdom, in *GEC Avionics' Patent* above, it was said that the application under s.40 should explicitly identify the foreign patent(s) in respect of which it is made, and that it is insufficient to rely on the implication that, e.g. foreign equivalents of a specified United Kingdom patent are automatically included in the claim by virtue of s.43(4), see also *British Steel's Patent* [1992] R.P.C. 117.

The amendment of subs.(4) extending its scope to refer also to s.39 follows the introduction of s.39(3) by the CDPA 1988, and is discussed in §39.17. However, this amendment may also cast doubt on an overly broad interpretation of "other protection", since s.39(3) carries the implication that different rights may end up in different ownership, notwithstanding that they relate to the same invention. If the implication of "other protection" in subs.(4) is so wide as to cause s.39(1) to be interpreted as affecting the ownership of IP rights such as copyright and unregistered design rights, it would be overriding the operation of the ownership provisions in the CDPA 1988; moreover, given that the ownership of the other rights would then also belong to the employee and s.39(3) would appear to be otiose.

But on the other hand again, no judicial interpretation has yet been given to the words in s.39(1) "for the purposes of this Act *and all other purposes*" (emphasis added) and it has been argued that despite its later date such a wording could cover matters dealt with under the CDPA 1988, the Registered Designs Act 1949 et al.

Deceased employer (subs.(5))

Subsection (5) provides that, where an employer has died, account shall be taken for the   **43.06** purposes of ss.40 and 41 of any benefit derived from the patent or (for patents filed after January 1, 2005) the invention by his personal representatives or any person in whom it has been vested with the assent of the personal representatives. Section 40 requires claims to be made to the "employer" who is the person by whom the employee is or was employed (s.130). Thus, when the patent becomes vested in another, the employee still looks for compensation to whoever was the employer at the time of making the invention, see also s.41(2) and §40.06, but subject to what is said in §40.06 in situations where the Transfer of Undertakings (Protection of Employment) Regulations 2006 (SI 2006/246) apply.

However, when the employer dies, subs.(5) provides for benefit enjoyed by the personal representatives, or by a person in whom the patent becomes vested with their assent, to be included in the benefit of the "employer" as such, just as if these were all "connected persons", see subs.(8) and §41.04. Nevertheless, it would seem that a claim may have to be made against the deceased employer's personal representatives and such persons may need to make provision for possible compensation claims before completing their distribution of the employer's estate. Should the employer be an incorporated business, rather than an individual, and go into liquidation or be wound up, the employee's claim will probably have to be made without delay since at a later date there may be no assets left against which to enforce a claim for compensation under s.40(1) and no entity against which to make the claim (but subject to any potential application of TUPE: see §40.06).

Benefit only during the existence of the patent (subs.(5A))

43.07 This section was added at the same time as the extensions of ss.40 and 41, to allow the employee to be compensated for the benefit derived from more than just the patent itself, where that patent application is filed on or after January 1, 2005. This makes it clear that the period of time over which the benefit is assessed is only that during which the patent subsists.

Deceased employee (subs.(6))

43.08 Subsection (6) provides that, where an employee has died, the personal representatives of the employee or their successors may make a claim under s.40(1) or (2) on behalf of the deceased's estate.

Meaning of "benefit" (subs.(7))

43.09 Subsection (7) defines "benefit" as benefit in "money or money's worth". "Money's worth" probably means any benefit which is capable of being assessed in monetary terms and when this term has been used in other statutes it has been given a broad meaning. For example, it includes a purchase at more than the full value of a property (*Attorney-General v Lethbridge* [1970] A.C. 19 HL), and also a purchase for a nominal consideration (*Midland Bank Trust v Green* [1981] 1 All E.R. 153; [1981] 2 W.L.R. 28 HL), and also the protection of business against generic competition which would otherwise occur on the expiry of a regulatory data exclusivity period and the ability to achieve corporate deals and transform the business: *Kelly and Chiu v GE Healthcare* [2009] R.P.C. 12, [2009] EWHC 181 Pat Ct, but does not include a consideration represented by a mere rearrangement of assets already held (*Attorney-General v Smith-Marriott* [1899] 2 Q.B. 595). Thus, it perhaps excludes the type of benefit which is incapable of having a value assigned to it, such as an increase in the goodwill of the employer's business or, for instance, an award such as the Queen's Award. Also, promotion of an employee in recognition that he made a meritorious invention may be irrelevant to "benefit", except insofar as this results in a direct or indirect increase of income.

If relevant, an award might include an element to have regard to the changed value of money over a period of inflation, but it seems unlikely that an award can include a separate element for interest.

In the context of intellectual property, the phrase "money or money's worth" also appears in s.263(1) of the CDPA 1988 in the definition of a "commission" which can create first ownership of a design right according to s.215(3) of the CDPA 1988; and, likewise, in relation to the first ownership of a commissioned registered design in s.2(1A) of the

Registered Designs Act 1949 (c.88), as inserted by s.267 of the CDPA 1988. Any cases decided under these provisions may therefore be of particular assistance in the interpretation of the present subs.(7).

Connected persons (subs.(8))

Subsection (8) now has the effect that connections between companies, for the purposes **43.10** of s.41(2), are as defined in s.839 of the Income and Corporations Taxes Act 1988 (c.1), as amended. This definition is discussed in §41.04, including the fact that it does not apply to the Crown. In fact, the MOPP points out that when s.533 of the Income and Corporation Taxes Act 1970 was repealed, s.43(8) was not amended to reflect this. However, s.839 of the Income and Corporation Taxes Act 1988 is the section which replaced s.533.

Contracts as to patented products, etc. [Sections 44–45]

SECTION 44 [REPEALED]

Avoidance of certain restrictive conditions

[**44.**—(1) *Subject to the provisions of this section, any condition or term of a* **44.01** *contract for the supply of a patented product or of a licence to work a patented invention, or of a contract relating to any such supply or licence, shall be void in so far it purports—*

(a) *In the case of a contract for supply, to require the person supplied to acquire from the supplier, or his nominee, or prohibit him from acquiring from any specified person, or from acquiring except from the supplier or his nominee, anything other than the patented product;*

(b) *in the case of a licence to work a patented invention, to require the licensee to acquire from the licensor or his nominee, or prohibit him from acquiring from any specified person, or from acquiring except from the licensor or his nominee, anything other than the product which is the patented invention or (if it is a process) other than any product obtained directly by means of the process or to which the process has been applied;*

(c) *in either case, to prohibit the person supplied or licensee from using articles (whether patented products or not) which are not supplied by, or any patented process which does not belong to, the supplier or licensor, or his nominee, or to restrict the right of the person supplied or licensee to use any such articles or process.*

(2) *Subsection (1) above applies to contracts and licences whether made or granted before or after the appointed day, but not to those made or granted before 1st January 1950.*

(3) *In proceedings against any person for infringement of a patent it shall be a defence to prove that at the time of the infringement there was in force a contract relating to the patent made by or with the consent of the plaintiff or pursuer or a licence under the patent granted by him or with his consent and containing in either case a condition or term void by virtue of this section.*

(4) *A condition or term of a contract or licence shall not be void by virtue of this section if—*

(a) *at the time of the making of the contract or granting of the licence the supplier or licensor was willing to supply the product, or grant a licence to work the invention, as the case may be, to the person supplied or licensee, on reasonable terms specified in the contract or licence and without any such condition or term as is mentioned in subsection (1) above; and*

(b) *the person supplied or licensee is entitled under the contract or licence to relieve himself of his liability to observe the condition or term on giving to the other party three months' notice in writing and subject to payment to that other party of such compensation (being, in the case of a contract to supply, a lump sum or rent for the residue of the term of the contract and, in the case of a licence, a royalty for the residue of the term of the licence) as may be determined by an arbitrator or arbiter appointed by the Secretary of State.*

(5) *If in any proceeding it is alleged that any condition or term of a contract or licence is void by virtue of this section it shall lie on the supplier or licensor to prove the matters set out in paragraph (a) of subsection (4) above.*

(6) *A condition orterm of a contract or licence shall not be void by virtue of this section by reason only that it prohibits any person from selling goods other than those supplied by a specific person or, in the case of a contract for the hiring of or licence to use a patented product, that it reserves to the bailor (or, in Scotland, hirer) or licensor, or his nominee, the right to supply such new parts of the patented product as may be required to put or keep it in repair.]*

Note. Section 44 was repealed by the Competition Act 1998 (c.41) s.70; Sch.14(1), with effect from March 1, 2000, but with continuing effect only in respect of any agreement made before that date under the Competition Act 1998 (Transitional, Consequential and Supplemental Provisions) Order 2000 SI 2000/311, art.3). However, the conduct formerly prohibited by this section continues to be affected by the Competition Act 1998, irrespective of its repeal or saving provisions, see the following commentary.

Commentary on Repealed Section 44

Purpose of the repealed section and its replacement

44.02   Although there are no corresponding provisions in the EPC, PCT and CPC, s.44 provided a sanction against the inclusion in a patent licence or assignment of a "tying-in" clause preventing or requiring the supply or use of unpatented goods, or of any patented process, as a condition of being granted rights under the patent. The section had its origin in the Patents and Designs Act 1907 (c.29) s.38 at a time when competition law did not exist, as such. Consequently, with the advent of a more comprehensive code of competition law now provided by the Competition Act 1998 (c.41), the section became redundant, with the mischief dealt with by the section being subsumed within the more general area of activity deemed by the Competition Act to be unlawful.

Also to be considered are the provisions of arts 101 and 102 of the TFEU (formerly arts 85 and 86 of the EC Treaty),, reprinted in Appendix D at §§D06 and D07 respectively. These provisions apply to restrictive conditions imposed in an agreement, arrangement or concerted practice, or to an abuse of a dominant position, if thereby trade between Member States of the European Community is affected, or is likely to be affected thereby. Appendix D discusses the operation of art.101 TFEU, particularly by reference to the Technology Transfer Regulation (No.772/2004) under which certain types of technology transfer agreement receive automatic exemption under art.101(3). Thus, as discussed more fully in §§44.04–44.08 below, the circumstances under which the former provisions of s.44 had effect are now likely to fall instead within the scope of the Competition Act 1998 s.2 of which corresponds to art.101 of the TFEUwhile s.18 corresponds to art.102. Indeed, an abuse of a dominant position can particularly arise in "making the conclusion of contracts" subject to acceptance by the other parties of supplementary obligations which, by their nature or according to commercial usage, have no connection with the subject of such contracts, see art.102(d) TFEU.

However, whereas s.44 provided the unique remedy by making a patent, to which an agreement containing "tying-in" provisions applied, unenforceable and against anyone so long as those provisions continued to apply, the remedies under the Competition Act and under the TFEU are that the provision is void and therefore unenforceable. Infringing contractual/procedural conduct can also give rise to the imposition of civil fines by the Office of Fair Trading or European Commission as the case may be.

Section 45, which provided certain powers to enable a licensee to determine a continuing patent licence agreement upon the expiry of relevant licensed patents, has similarly been repealed in view of the provisions of the Competition Act with regard to such conduct, as discussed in the commentary on that repealed section.

Contracts for the sale of goods

The Competition Act 1998 (c.41), effective from March 1, 2000, repealed the Restrictive Trade Practices Act 1976 (c.34) and the Resale Prices Act 1976 (c.53) and made several changes to the Fair Trading Act 1973 (c.41) and to the Competition Act 1980 (c.21). The 1998 Act provides a comprehensive code of law against anti-competitive trade practices having an effect solely in the United Kingdom and hence outside the scope of EC competition law, but in terms consistent with, and in fact parallel to, the prohibitions contained in arts 101 and 102 TFEU. (For completeness, it should be noted that the Enterprise Act 2002 (c.40), effective from June 2003, amended UK competition legislation in a number of ways including by making changes to the Fair Trading Act and the Competition Act. The Enterprise Act also introduced a new and separate criminal cartel offence).

44.03

Chapter I (ss.1–16) of the 1998 Act (in terms parallel to art.101 in relation to trade across national boundaries within the EU) prohibits (unless exempted by other provisions under this Act) "agreements between undertakings, decisions by associations or undertakings or concerted practices which: (a) may affect trade within the United Kingdom; and (b) have as their object or effect the prevention, restriction of distortion of competition within the United Kingdom" (s.2(1)).

Similarly, Ch.II (ss.17–24) of the 1998 Act mirrors art.102 TFEU in prohibiting "any conduct on the part of one or more undertakings which amounts to an abuse of a dominant position in a market if it may affect trade within the United Kingdom" (s.18(1)). Thus, whereas the provisions of the TFEU (as extended by the EEA Agreement) are directed at practices within the "common market" of the Member States of the European Economic Area, the Competition Act 1998 similarly prohibits the same types of conduct insofar as these may, or are intended to, affect trade within the United Kingdom. The consequences of any conduct prohibited under the provisions of Chs I and II of the Competition Act 1998 are analogous to those under the TFEU, namely that the agreement is void and of no effect (unless a void term can be severed from the remainder of the agreement, for which see §44.08) and the parties to an agreement which is unlawful under the provisions of the Act may have fines imposed upon them by the OFT, subject to appeal to the Competition Appeal Tribunal.

Detailed discussion of the provisions of the 1998 Act is beyond the scope of this Work, but attention is drawn to the book *Competition Law* by Richard Whish, 6th edn (Oxford, 2008) and to the parallel provisions in the TFEU which are set out and discussed in Appendix D. That Appendix describes and discusses European competition law in general terms and particularly describes and discusses the provisions for block exemption from the provisions of art.101 TFEU for certain types of "technology transfer agreements". As in the case of art.101(3) TFEU, the Competition Act 1998 makes provision for exemption from the Ch.I prohibition. Undertakings must conduct a self-assessment of whether an agreement that infringes the Ch.I prohibition and, if so, whether the agreement satisfies the criteria contained in s.9 of the Competition Act, which mirror art.101(3). When considering the s.9 criteria, the OFT has said that it will have regard to the European Commission's Guidelines on the application of art.81(3) of the Treaty OJ [2004] C 101/97. Note also that s.10 of the Competition Act provides for so-called "parallel exemption" where an agreement would benefit from one of the EC block exemptions if it were to affect trade between Member States.

—Patent licensing and competition law

44.04   Given that a patentee holds an exclusive right to produce and sell the patented goods, it might be argued that competition law should not apply to any restrictions included in patent licences at all. After all, without the licence (albeit restrictive) there may be less competition in the relevant market. In addition, it might be argued that it is only competition in relation to the patented technology itself (so-called "intra-technology" competition) which is being restricted and that competition from other sources including other patentees (inter-technology competition) remains unaffected.

In fact, this was largely the view taken by the European Commission in the 1960s as reflected in its 1962 Notice on Patent Licensing Agreements.

However, the Commission's approach began to become more interventionist in the late 1960s. Indeed, in the 1966 case of *Consten v Grundig* (C 56 and 58/64) [1966] E.C.R. 299) the European Court of Justice held that it was the assignment of an IP right (in that case a trade mark) to a distributor which enabled it to prevent imports from other countries, thus infringing the competition rules.

Consistent with this approach, the EC competition rules have been applied to restrictions in patent licences which restrict intra-technology competition where the EU single market may be undermined. For example, in 2005, the Commission fined AstraZeneca €60 million for preventing parallel imports from other EU Member States (Commission Press Release IP/05/737) and for abusing a position of dominance by delaying market access for generic versions of one of its products.

Restrictions may also fall foul of competition law where they affect inter-technology competition, e.g. tie-in clauses where a patentee with market power requires a licensee to use certain other products/services when using the patented technology. A position of market dominance is not in itself objectionable under EC/UK competition law. However, the law intervenes, for example, when attempts are made to leverage that market power into other markets, foreclosing competition from other, potentially more efficient, suppliers. Attempts by the patentee to extend its power beyond the protection granted to it by statute may also infringe the competition rules.

In summary, it cannot be assumed that the exclusive nature of a patent legitimises the imposition of restrictions in a licence. A useful analysis of the pro and negative effects of IP licensing under EC competition law is set out in paras 141–145 of the Technology Transfer Guidelines.

—Separate application to "tying-in" provisions in licences

44.05   As mentioned above, tying-in provisions in licensing arrangements may fall within the scope of s.18 of the Competition Act—i.e. the rules prohibiting the abuse of a dominant position which draw heavily on the text of art.102—see D07.

In the 2004 *Microsoft* decision (Case COMP/C-3/37.71 2) the Commission found that Microsoft had abused its dominant position in the PC operating market by licensing its operating system only in a bundle with its media player.

A further example of the European Commission investigating tie-ins in the context of IP licences is the European Commission's ongoing investigation into Alcan. On February 22, 2008, the European Commission confirmed that it had sent a Statement of Objections to Alcan outlining its preliminary view that Alcan had infringed the rules on abuse of dominance by tying its dominant aluminium smelting technology with handling equipment sold by its subsidiaries (Commission MEMO/08/11).

Although s.2 of the Competition Act 1998 (applying to agreements between companies) also refers to the conclusion of contracts subject to the acceptance by other parties of supplementary obligations as being capable of falling within the Ch.I prohibition, it is, in practice, unlikely that a tying-in provision would infringe competition law in the absence of market power.

Settlement of litigation

44.06 It is important to mention here that EC and UK competition law must not be overlooked when negotiating and finalising a settlement of litigation. Helpful guidance is contained in the European Commission's Technology Transfer Guidelines (Commission Notice—Guidelines on the application of art.81 to Technology Transfer Agreements OJ [2004] C100/2) which rehearse the issues arising when licensing is used as a means for settling disputes. The Guidelines explain that where the parties to a dispute agree, as part of a settlement, to license, or to cross-license, competition issues may arise—although the terms of the license may be covered by the Technology Transfer Block Exemption in the usual way. The Commission explains that cross-licences which impose restrictions on the parties' use of their technologies may infringe the rules—especially where the parties have market power or when the license imposes restrictions which are not indispensable i.e. which go beyond what is actually required in order to give access to the disputed technologies. The Commission will also check that the settlement agreement does not preclude the ability of the parties to compete in the future—for example through innovation. A straightforward example of where a settlement may infringe the competition rules is when the settlement involves an element of market sharing. Representative cases in this category are: *Toltecs and Dorcet Trade Marks* [1983] 1 C.M.L.R. 412; [1983] F.S.R. 327; on appeal *BAT v EC Commission (35/83)* [1985] E.C.R. 363; [1985] 2 C.M.L.R. 470; [1985] F.S.R. 533 ECJ, where the true purpose of the agreement was held to be market sharing; and *Oy Airam v Osram* [1982] 3 C.M.L.R. 614; [1983] F.S.R. 108, another case relating to trade mark use.

The Unfair Contract Terms Act 1977

44.07 It is also convenient here to mention the Unfair Contract Terms Act 1977 (c.50). This generally renders void conditions in contracts which are deemed to be unfair, often because of a perceived inequality in bargaining power between the contract parties, for example as will often be the case with contracts entered into by a domestic consumer. However, this Act does not void clauses in a patent licence agreement which have the effect of excluding the proprietor (or head licensee in the case of a sub-licence) from liability resulting from his negligence or breach of contract or from any indemnity in respect thereof. This is because Sch.1 of this Act excludes the operation of ss.2–4 of it to "any contract so far as it relates to the creation or transfer of a right or interest in any patent...or other intellectual property, or relates to the termination of any such right or interest". However, this phrase will apparently be construed narrowly and therefore not be applied to terms which are concerned with other aspects of the contract, such as a warranty of performance (*Salvage Association v CAP Financial Services* [1995] F.S.R. 654).

—Severability of void conditions from patent licence agreements

44.08 Contractual provisions which infringe EC/UK competition law (and which do not qualify for exemption) are void. However, a court is not required to sever a void condition from a contract leaving the remainder to be enforced, unless there is a specific clause in the contract for severance of conditions which may be held to be void, or unless the governing statute which causes the condition to be a void one indicates that the agreement should be construed by omission of the void clause, as for example in s.42(2) which only requires a "term" of the contract to be unenforceable. In any case, the void clause must be capable of being severed from the remainder of the agreement, for example by mere excision (as in the "blue pencil" test). For a case where severance was not possible, see *Hansen v Magnavox* [1977] R.P.C. 301 CA. However, if the void condition is capable of severance, then it appears that the court will strive to do so rather than deprive the agreement of any validity whatever, and this is so even if the severance of the void parts transforms the economic balance of interest of the parties, see *Chemidus Wavin v Soc. pour la Transformation* [1977] F.S.R. 19 and 181 CA, where a minimum royalty clause was maintained irrespective of the possible invalidity of other clauses. However, in that case the Court of Appeal indicated that the position could be different if, after the excisions (which now would be required by art.101) had been made, the contract remaining would fail for lack of consideration or because of a fundamental change in its character.

SECTION 45 [REPEALED]

Determination of parts of certain contracts

45.01 [**45.**—(1) *Any contract for the supply of a patented product or licence to work a patented invention, or contract relating to any such supply or licence, may at any time after the patent or all the patents by which the product or invention was protected at the time of the making of the contract or granting of the licence has or have ceased to be in force, and notwithstanding anything to the contrary in the contract or licence or in any other contract, be determined, to the extent (and only to the extent) that the contract or licence relates to the product or invention, by either party on giving three months' notice in writing to the other party.*

(2) *In subsection (1) above "patented product" and "patented invention" include respectively a product and an invention which is the subject of an application for a patent, and that subsection shall apply in relation to a patent by which any such product or invention was protected and which was granted after the time of the making of the contract or granting of the licence in question, on an application which had been filed before that time, as it applies to a patent in force at that time.*

(3) *If, on an application under this subsection made by either party to a contract or licence falling within subsection (1) above, the court is satisfied that, in consequence of the patent or patents concerned ceasing to be in force, it would be unjust to require the applicant to continue to comply with all the terms and conditions of the contract or licence, it may make such order varying those terms or conditions as, having regard to all the circumstances of the case, it thinks just as between the parties.*

(4) *Without prejudice to any other right of recovery, nothing in subsection (1) above shall be taken to entitle any person to recover property bailed under a hire-purchase agreement (within the meaning of the Consumer Credit Act 1974) [c. 39].*

(5) *The foregoing provisions of this section apply to contracts and licences whether made before or after the appointed day.*

(6) *The provisions of this section shall be without prejudice to any rule of law relating to the frustration of contracts and any right of determining a contract or licence exercisable apart from this section.*]

Note. Section 45 was repealed by the Competition Act 1998 (c.41) s.70; Sch.14(1), with effect from March 1, 2000, but with continuing effect in respect of any application made, or notice given, under the section before this date under the Competition Act 1998 (Transitional, Consequential and Supplemental Provisions) Order 2000 (SI 2000/311, art.3). However, the CDPA 1988 must now be taken into account in considering the type of situation previously covered by this former section, see the commentary below.

COMMENTARY ON REPEALED SECTION 45

Purpose and continuing effect of the repealed section

Section 45 provided for the termination, on three-months' notice in writing by either **45.02** party, of patent licences or of contracts to supply patented products following the cessation, from any cause, of relevant patents. However, the Competition Act 1998 (c.41) made the section redundant.

The subject-matter of the repealed section and its replacement

In the repealed s.45, subs.(1) provided for a licensee (or licensor) to abrogate (on three **45.03** months' notice) the terms of a patent licence granted for the supply of a patented product or licence to work a patented invention once the licensed patent had ceased to be in force, but only insofar as the licence related to that patented product or invention. Thus, other provisions of the contract or licence were seemingly not affected. The terms "patented product" and "patented invention" were specially defined in subs.(2) for the purposes of s.45 so that patent applications pending at the date of the contract or licence were treated as patents. For the severability of contract terms, see §44.08. Under subss.(1) and (2), only a patent "by which the product or invention was protected" could be relevant; and, if any particular product or invention was no longer protected, there was a right to terminate the licence only to the extent that such product or invention was concerned. Under subs.(3), on application to the court by either party, the court could order variation of unjust terms or conditions after cessation of the relevant patent or patents, but there appears to have been no decision on this provision. By subs.(4), there was provision to prevent subs.(1) being used to recover property subject to a hire-purchase agreement as defined in the Consumer Credit Act 1974 (c.39), but this statute would not prevent a hirer from determining such an agreement.

By subs.(6) other legal rights concerning the frustration of contracts or any right of determination of a contract or licence were not affected by an action taken under s.45 so that the provisions of the section were wholly additional to any other remedies existing under the law of contract. Accordingly, the powers provided by the now repealed s.45 were limited in scope.

Relevant Community jurisprudence

Under Community jurisprudence, at one time, an attempt to collect royalties for use of **45.04** an expired patent, at least when calculated on sales taking place after termination, was likely to be held to be contrary to what is now art.101 TFEU, unless such royalties were paid in respect of know-how that remained secret (*Cartoux v Terrapin* [1981] 1 C.M.L.R. 182), or the licensee had the ability to terminate the licence as in *Ottung v Klee (320/87)* [1989] E.C.R. 1177; [1991] F.S.R. 657; [1990] 4 C.M.L.R. 915 ECJ discussed in §D23.

However, the approach of the Commission to such royalty obligations appears to have softened. Indeed, para.159 of the current Technology Transfer Guidelines explains that although the Technology Transfer block exemption will only apply as long as the underlying technology is valid and in force, the parties can normally agree to extend royalty obligations beyond the period of validity of the licensed intellectual property rights without falling foul of what is now art.101(1) TFEU.

The explanation for this is that once these rights expire, third parties can legally exploit the technology in question and compete with the parties to the agreement. Such actual and potential competition will normally suffice to ensure that the obligation in question does not have an appreciable anti-competitive effect.

However, the Guidelines do not deal with the potential application of art.102 TFEU (or the Ch.II prohibition of the Competition Act in the UK) and it cannot be excluded that the imposition of royalty obligations after the validity of a patent could amount to an abuse of a dominant position. Of course, a counter-argument may well be that payments need to be structured over a longer term to make payments more affordable to the licensee. However, an analysis of excessive pricing and other exploitative conduct which may amount to an abuse of dominance is beyond the scope of this Work.

Licences of right and compulsory licences [Sections 46–54]

SECTION 46

Patentee's application for entry in register that licences are available as of right

46.01 46.—(1) At any time after the grant of a patent its proprietor may apply to the comptroller for an entry to be made in the register to the effect that licences under the patent are to be available as of right.

(2) Where such an application is made, the comptroller shall give notice of the application to any person registered as having a right in or under the patent and, if satisfied that the proprietor of the patent is not precluded by contract from granting licences under the patent, shall make that entry.

(3) Where such an entry is made in respect of a patent—

(a) any person shall, at any time after the entry is made, be entitled as of right to a licence under the patent on such terms as may be settled by agreement or, in default of agreement, by the comptroller on the application of the proprietor of the patent or the person requiring the licence;

(b) the comptroller may, on the application of the holder of any licence granted under the patent before the entry was made, order the licence to be exchanged for a licence of right on terms so settled;

(c) if in proceedings for infringement of the patent (otherwise than by the importation of any article **from a country which is not a member State of the European Economic Area *[Community]***) the defendant or defender undertakes to take a licence on such terms, no injunction or interdict shall be granted against him and the amount (if any) recoverable against him by way of damages shall not exceed double the amount which would have been payable by him as licensee if such a licence on those terms had been granted before the earliest infringement;

(d) if the expiry date in relation to a renewal fee falls after the date of the entry, that fee shall be half the fee which would be payable had the entry not been made.

(3A) An undertaking under subsection (3)(c) above may be given at any time before final order in the proceedings, without any admission of liability.

(3B) For the purposes of subsection (3)(d) above the expiry date in relation to a renewal fee is the day at the end of which, by virtue of section 25(3) above, the patent in question ceases to have effect if that fee is not paid.

(4) The licensee under a licence of right may (unless, in the case of a licence the terms of which are settled by agreement, the licence otherwise expressly provides) request the proprietor of the patent to take proceedings to prevent any infringement of the patent; and if the proprietor refuses or neglects to do so within two months after being so requested, the licensee may institute proceedings for the infringement in his own name as if he were proprietor, making the proprietor a defendant or defender.

(5) A proprietor so added as defendant or defender shall not be liable for any costs or expenses unless he enters an appearance and takes part in the proceedings.

Note. Subsection (3)(c) was amended, and subs.(3A) added, by Sch.5 para.12 to the CDPA 1988, and the word "Community" then added in subs.(3)(c) was subsequently effectively amended to "Area" by the European Economic Area Act 1993 (c.51) s.2(1). Subsection (3)(d) was amended, and subs.(3B) added by the Patents Act 2004 (c.16) s.8(4)(b), with effect from December 13, 2007 (SI 1907/3396).

RELEVANT RULES—RULES 43 AND 89

Rule 43—Application for, and cancellation of, an entry that licences are available as of right

43.—(1) An application under section 46(1) must be made on Patents Form 28.   **46.02**

(2) Where an entry is made in the register to the effect that licences under a patent are to be available as of right, the comptroller must advertise the entry in the journal.

(3) An application under section 47(1) for the cancellation of an entry made under section 46 must be made on Patents Form 30.

(4) The period prescribed for the purposes of section 47(3) is two months beginning [with] immediately after the date on which the entry was made under section 46.

Note. Amended by the Patents (Amendment) Rules 2011 (SI 2011/2052).

Rule 89—Proceedings started under section 46(3) by a person other than the proprietor

89.—(1) An application by a person other than the proprietor to the comptroller under section 46(3)(a) or (b) must be—   **46.03**

(a) made on Patents Form 2; and

(b) accompanied by two copies of the draft of the licence he proposes should be granted.

(2) The comptroller must notify the proprietor of the patent that an application has been made.

(3) The comptroller must send a copy of the draft licence with the notification.

(4) In the notification, the comptroller must specify a period within which the proprietor may file a statement of grounds.

(5) The proprietor must file a statement of grounds in accordance with rule 76(4); otherwise he shall be treated as supporting the applicant's case.

(6) Proceedings shall continue under this Part as if they had been started under rule 76(1) and for those purposes the proprietor shall be "the claimant" and the applicant shall be "the defendant".

Note. These rules (and Pt 7 of the same rules referred to in this section) were introduced by SI 2007/3291 with effect from December 17, 2007.

COMMENTARY ON SECTION 46

Scope of the section

Section 46 provides a procedure under which a proprietor may have an entry made in   **46.04**
the register that licences under the patent are "available as of right" (subs.(1)). An applica-

tion for such an entry is notified by the Comptroller to any licensee or other person, for example a mortgagee, shown in the register as having an interest in or under the patent (subs.(2)). The consequences of such an entry are set out in subs.(3), viz.: (a) an entitlement to a licence on terms to be settled by the Comptroller if not otherwise agreed; (b) an order by the Comptroller for an existing licence under the patent to be exchanged for a new one on terms settled by the Comptroller in the absence of agreement; (c) a potential limit on the grant of an injunction or award of damages in infringement proceedings; and (d) a reduction by half in the renewal fees payable on the patent. A licensee under a licence of right can institute infringement proceedings under the patent if the proprietor will not do so (subss.(4), (5)).

An appeal lies from any decision of the Comptroller (s.97(1)), with further appeal to the Court of Appeal, but only on a point of law and with leave (s.97(3)). There is no provision for a party domiciled in Scotland to require proceedings to be held in Scotland, see s.123(2)(f) and §98.07.

For "new existing patents", that is those granted under the Patent Act 1949 which had more than five years of term remaining on June 1, 1978, licences of right were deemed to be available under the section during the extended life of these patents, that is from the end of their 16th year (when, under the Patent Act 1949, they would have expired) to a maximum of 20 years (as under the present Act). Consequently, there were on these patents numerous cases of settlement of licence terms, often decided in fiercely contested proceedings, particularly in the pharmaceutical field. However, this activity diminished greatly with the addition (by s.293 of the CDPA 1988) of paras 4A and 4B to Sch.1 to the Act which enabled a declaration to be filed which had the effect of cancelling the deemed endorsement in respect of "medical" or "pesticidal" products. This activity ceased altogether with the expiry of the last of these "existing patents" on May 31, 1998.

However, the decisions given during this period serve as precedents still applicable for the settlement of terms sought by application under subs.(3) upon a patent for which a "licences of right" entry has been entered in the register voluntarily by the patentee under subs.(1). Nevertheless, such cases will be rare, because the usual reason for having such an entry made in the register is to economise on the amount of renewal fees payable and, if a potential licensee declares his interest in a licence, negotiations will normally ensue with licence terms then settled by agreement, these terms often being prefaced by arrangement with the putative licensee that an application should first be made by the patentee to re-scind the entry on the register. This can be done by application under s.47 (as discussed in §47.02 et seq.).

The practice which developed, and the decisions given, under s.46(3), before it lost its importance as indicated, may also be of guidance as to appropriate terms in patent licence agreements and they can be of some importance in other fields of intellectual property, particularly because the concept of "licences of right" applies to a design right during the last five years of its term (CDPA 1988 s.237). But the decisions given on "licences of right" under this intellectual property right have been held to have a different basis because, under s.46, regard has to be had to the general principles for the grant of compulsory licences set out in s.50, as discussed in §50.02.

For all these reasons, the decisions previously given under s.46(3) now seem to have a greatly reduced relevance and, consequently, are dealt with quite briefly in this commentary on the section.

Application for entry in register (subss.(1) and (2))

46.05   Under subs.(1), the proprietor of the patent can apply for the entry to be made at any time after grant. Application is under r.43 (reprinted above and discussed in §46.18). The application is not advertised, but subs.(2) requires the Comptroller to give notice to any person registered as having a right in or under the patent. If the Comptroller is satisfied that the proprietor is not precluded by contract from granting licences, he must make the entry. After it has been made, a notice is published in the *Patents Journal*.

Settling terms of licence of right (subs.(3)(a) and (b))

—The basic procedure

Subsection (3)(a) states that, after the register entry has been made, any person is **46.06** "entitled as of right to a licence under the patent". This means that the procedure can be invoked by any person intending to take a licence, even if only as an insurance against infringement (*Du Pont's (Blades') Patent* [1988] R.P.C. 479). The proceedings are essentially different from those under s.48, where there is an issue whether a licence should be ordered at all (see *Halcon's Patent* [1989] R.P.C. 1), because only the terms of the licence, and not its grant, are in issue. Section 108 does not apply to an order for the grant of a licence under this section..

Subsection (3)(b) provides for an existing licensee to have his licence exchanged for one settled under subs.(3)(a). The procedure is the same as for the settlement of terms of a new licence.

A licence of right cannot take effect until its terms have been settled by agreement or, in default of agreement, by the Comptroller on application by either the proprietor or the prospective licensee (*Allen & Hanburys v Generics* [1986] R.P.C. 203 HL). An applicant for a licence cannot be frustrated by an application to cancel the endorsement made under s.47; but, after this licence has been granted, the endorsement can be cancelled with the consent of the licensee, see *Cassou's Patent* [1971] R.P.C. 91. The Comptroller can adjudicate only between the proprietor and prospective licensee; and, in *Kaken Pharmaceutical's Patent* [1990] R.P.C. 72, the Comptroller decided that the current exclusive licensee had shown neither a right nor a need to be joined as party to the proceedings under s.46(3). However, the eventual licence can be granted as a sub-licence from the existing exclusive licensee (*Research Corp's (Carboplatin) Patent* [1990] R.P.C. 663). In *Cabot Safety's Patent* [1992] R.P.C. 39, the corporate partners of a foreign unincorporated partnership (a German "*Kommanditgesellschaft*") were required to be named as joint licensees because of the possible difficulty of recovering debts from such an entity under English law.

The procedure for settlement of the terms of a licence of right is governed by r.89 (reprinted above and discussed in §46.19).

—Limitations on power of Comptroller

The Comptroller is required to settle the terms of a licence only in default of agreement **46.07** between the proprietor and the prospective licensee. Thus, if during proceedings under subs.(3)(a) or (b) the terms are no longer contested, there is nothing left for the Comptroller to settle. Default of agreement between the parties, however, is not a pre-condition for making an application to the Comptroller to settle terms. This is because the application will contain a draft licence and, if the other party objects to the terms suggested by the applicant, there is then the necessary default of agreement, see *Roussel-Uclaf (Clemence and Le Martret's) Patent* [1987] R.P.C. 109.

Subsection (3) does not give the Comptroller power to review an existing licence (*Diamond Shamrock's Patent* [1987] R.P.C. 91 at 105), although the licensee can apply for an additional licence (as was done in that case) or seek to exchange the licence for a new one under subs.(3)(b). In proceedings under s.46(3), the Comptroller cannot grant a licence under any intellectual property right other than the patent in issue, but presumably an application under s.46 could be combined with an application for a "licence of right" under a design right or design copyright. In *Eurofix and Bauco v Hilti* [1988] OJ EC L65/19, abridged [1988] F.S.R. 473, the proprietor gave an undertaking (under pressure from the European Commission) not to enforce its copyrights against those who had obtained licences of rights under its patents.

—The basic principles for settlement of terms

No guidance is given in s.46 itself as to the criteria on which terms should be settled, **46.08** but the terms to be settled in a licence of right are those which, notionally, would be agreed between a willing licensor and willing licensee (*Allen & Hanburys v Generics*

[1986] R.P.C. 203 HL), even if the proprietor would not of his own free will have been prepared to grant any licence to that prospective licensee; and, as there stated, some guidance can be found in the criteria set out in s.50 (as it then was) because s.53(4) requires a "licences of right" entry imposed by s.48 or s.51 to have the same effect as an entry made under s.46. Thus, the principle of s.50(1)(b), that the proprietor should receive "reasonable remuneration having regard to the nature of the invention", assumes importance. In *Smith Kline & French's (Cimetidine) Patents* [1990] R.P.C. 203 CA, assistance was also found in various provisions contained in ss.48 and 50 as each then stood, though it was stated that payment is only for use of the invention and is not to be assessed as compensation to the patentee for the loss suffered by the grant of the licence.

While, in order to comply with arts 30 and 31 of the TRIPS Agreement (for which see §§48A.02–48A.03), s.50(1)(b) now only applies where the patent proprietor is a "WTO proprietor" (for which see §48.04), it is not thought that this principle has been altered as a "licence of right" under s.46 is not a "compulsory licence", but is more akin to a voluntary act because the patentee himself applied for the "licence of right" entry in the register and also has the option of seeking to remove this entry by application under s.47.

The *Allen & Hanburys* case also decided that the licence terms should not compensate the proprietor for any loss of manufacturing profit; and that the Comptroller has discretion to impose any terms appropriate to restrict acts of the licensee which (in the absence of a licence) would infringe the patent. However, positive obligations cannot be imposed on the proprietor.

For limitations on the Comptroller's powers, see §46.07; and, because the licence is one to be granted as "of right", the suitability of the prospective licensee to hold a licence is irrelevant. Also, validity of the patent is not relevant when considering its commercial value (*Cabot Safety's Patent* [1992] R.P.C. 39): a prospective licensee acts on the assumption that the patent is valid.

If there are multiple applications for licences under the same patent, each licence has to be settled on the basis of the evidence presented. Where royalty rates have been separately calculated in different applications under the same patent, the conclusion has generally been the same in each case, see *Smith Kline & French's (Cimetidine) Patents* (above). Terms imposed to deal with a particular corporate structure of one applicant, e.g. to permit sub-licensing to an associated company, will not necessarily be included in another licence under the same patent (*Hilti's Patent* [1988] R.P.C. 51).

Assessment of royalty terms

—The different approaches

46.09   The basic criterion is that the royalty rate should be that which would be agreed between a willing licensor and a willing licensee, see §46.09. To achieve this (albeit in cases where the licensor was certainly not a "willing" person), three distinct approaches have been used: (a) a comparison with licences granted by the proprietor or accepted by the licensee where the circumstances can be seen to be comparable and/or a comparison with royalty terms decided in licences of right or compulsory licences concerning inventions of similar nature; (b) an accounting assessment of the value of the patent to the proprietor as such (disregarding manufacturing profits earned by the proprietor); and (c) a profit-sharing approach between the proprietor and the licensee or a consideration of what the licensee can afford to pay. These approaches are separately considered at §§46.10–46.12.

—By considering "comparables"

46.10   Of the three approaches to the assessment of the appropriate royalty rate for a licence of right outlined in §46.09, the "comparables" approach is the most reliable guide to what would be agreed between a willing licensor and willing licensee (*Smith Kline & French's (Cimetidine) Patents* [1990] R.P.C. 203 CA), particularly where the patented invention, or one of a similar commercial nature, has been licensed on such a basis at a proved royalty rate. This approach is best seen in relation to inventions which the proprietor exploits only by licensing, when the licence of right will be settled on terms providing him with an equivalent royalty and rates of royalty voluntarily accepted under the patent in suit by others have been held to be a firm guide as to the appropriate royalty, see for example *Syntex's Patent* [1986] R.P.C. 585. In *American Cyanamid's (Fenbufen) Patent* [1990] R.P.C. 309 and [1991] R.P.C. 409 CA, the "comparables" approach was applied in respect of royalties previously settled under s.46(3) for similar drugs, themselves also the subject of voluntary licences though these were supply contracts which justified a slightly lower royalty than would otherwise be agreed for a voluntary licence. In *Cabot Safety's Patent* [1992] R.P.C. 39, a licence granted under a corresponding United States patent was held not strictly comparable because it arose in the settlement of litigation and was the subject of a lump sum payment.

In cases where there is little or no evidence of comparable licences, the Comptroller has regarded 5 to 7 per cent as a normal royalty, at least for mechanical engineering inventions, see: *Cassou's Patent* [1971] R.P.C. 91 and *Patchett's Patent* [1967] R.P.C. 237. To obtain a higher royalty than 5 per cent for a mechanical invention, it appears that a proprietor must seek to justify this based on some special factor, e.g. as in *Shiley's Patent* [1988] R.P.C. 97, relating to a heart valve prosthesis. However, patents for pharmaceutical products have generally justified much higher royalties, and, for surgical devices or the like, the norm was generally about 15 per cent, as in *Shiley's Patent* (above), and see *Cabot Safety's Patent* (above).

Licence agreements concluded under the patent at an early stage in the development of the patented product may not be truly "comparable" because of the development expenditure borne by the licensee, see *Research Corp's (Carboplatin) Patent* [1990] R.PC. 663.

Each party to proceedings under s.46(3)(a) can expect to have to disclose licence agreements already entered into under arguably comparable circumstances. Such disclosure will be either by normal application for it or upon requirement by the Comptroller under r.82(1)(a) (as in *Smith Kline & French's (Cimetidine) Patents* [1988] R.P.C. 148), for which see §123.47. All such disclosures are normally treated as confidential documents under r.53, and sometimes with special provisions limiting disclosure to legal advisers of the receiving party, for which see §§46.20 and 123.48.

—The section 41 [1949] calculations

Under s.41 of the 1949 Act, compulsory licences were available under patents relating **46.11** to food, medicine or a surgical or curative device on terms which made these items available to the public at the lowest prices consistent with the patentees' deriving a reasonable advantage from their patent rights. Although the principles of the accounting exercises used in assessing royalty rates under that section were applied in many of the early cases under s.46(3)(a), s.50(1)(b) requires the proprietor to receive reasonable remuneration having regard to the nature of the invention rather than a reasonable advantage from the patent. The s.41 of the 1949 Act approach could, therefore, be no more than a guideline to what is reasonable remuneration for the proprietor (*American Cyanamid's (Fenbufen) Patent* [1991] R.P.C. 409 CA) and, consequently this approach became discredited. Nevertheless, it may be of some help generally in cases where the "comparables" approach does not give a clear indication, but it must be borne in mind that this approach was conceived for use with patents in the pharmaceutical field.

The accounting exercise under s.41 of the 1949 Act involved separate calculations of three elements: the proprietor's research and development costs; promotional expenditure in creating and maintaining a market for the patented product; and an appropriate profit margin. For detailed examples, see *Geigy's Patent* [1964] R.P.C. 391 and *Smith Kline & French's (Cimetidine) Patents* [1990] R.P.C. 203 CA.

—By considering the profits available

46.12   While it is not a relevant consideration whether the licensee can trade profitably at the royalty rate settled (*Research Corp's (Carboplatin) Patent* [1990] R.P.C. 663), one method that has been urged for the assessment of an appropriate royalty is to consider the profits likely to be earned by the licensee and then to consider sharing these in some proportion with the proprietor, but it was said that the "profit sharing" approach should be used only as a last resort, see *Smith Kline & French's (Cimetidine) Patents* [1990] R.P.C. 203 CA.

However, this approach has found greater favour in the settlement of "licence of right" terms under design rights and design copyrights, see *Pioneer Tools' Licence of Right (Copyright) Application* [1997] R.P.C. 573 and *E-UK Controls' Licence of Right (Copyright) Application* [1998] R.P.C. 833. In each of these cases, the "profits available" approach was stated to be essentially a realistic commercial approach, with the arguments against its use in patent cases being perhaps less relevant in the case of design right or design copyright because of the absence therefor of any link with criteria such as set out in s.50(1). In the *E-UK* case, the profits split was 2:1, it being stated that a 1:1 split would probably never be accepted by a willing licensor.

—Basis on which royalty rate is to be paid

46.13   The royalty rate is usually expressed initially as a percentage of the proprietor's selling price. If there is a legitimate expectation that the licensee will then sell at a significantly lower price than the patentee—which has usually been the case for a pharmaceutical product—the royalty rate so calculated has then normally been converted into a fixed sum per unit quantity sold, see *Smith Kline & French's (Cimetidine) Patents* [1990] R.P.C. 203 CA and *Research Corp's (Carboplatin) Patent* [1990] R.P.C. 663. This effectively imposes a floor beneath which the licensee cannot cut prices. The parties may expressly agree on some other basis, as in *Diamond Shamrock's Patent* [1987] R.P.C. 91, where the patent was for a coated electrode and the royalty was based on the area of that coating. Occasionally the terms settled have included provision for indexation of the fixed sum in accordance with some published price index, see *Shiley's Patent* [1988] R.P.C. 97 and *Hilti's Patent* [1988] R.P.C. 51.

—Miscellaneous points on royalty terms

46.14   Where an applicant requires terms to be settled under two patents of the same proprietor, there can be a single licence, but the proprietor must provide evidence for any split of royalty between the patents (*Smith Kline & French (Cimetidine) Patents* [1988] R.P.C. 148). In *Research Corp's (Carboplatin) Patent* [1990] R.P.C. 663, the licence of right was granted as a sub-licence to an existing licence so as to share the royalty with the existing licensee who had undertaken the cost of development and of securing regulatory approval. Attempts by applicants to have clauses of the "most favoured nation" type included in the licence have invariably been rejected, as in *Diamond Shamrock's Patent* [1987] R.P.C. 91. Delay, even culpable delay, in settling the applicable royalty rate is no good ground for reducing it (*Cabot Safety's Patent* [1992] R.P.C. 39).

Where the applicant was resident abroad, security for royalty was ordered, and royalty was required to be paid on stocks of the patented product held in the United Kingdom at the expiry of the licence (*Shiley's Patent* [1988] R.P.C. 97). Quarterly accounting periods for royalty payments are generally specified, with provision for verification of books of account by an independent auditor.

Import and Export prohibitions

46.15   In the past, it was held that settled licence terms could, on request, include a prohibition on importation of the patented product from outside the EEA, but prohibition on importation was imposed only if the proprietor worked the invention within the EEA. A prohibition against importation from elsewhere within the EEA was, however, not permissible (*Allen & Hanbury v Generics* (C-434/85) [1988] 1 C.M.L.R. 701; [1988] F.S.R. 312 ECJ); and see *Generics v Smith Kline & French* (C-191/90) [1993] R.P.C. 333; [1993] 1

C.M.L.R. 89 ECJ where it was held to be contrary to what are now the arts 28–30 of the EC Treaty for a prohibition on importation to depend on whether the proprietor manufactured the patented product in one EEA State rather than another.

In *American Cyanamid's (Fenbufen) Patent* [1990] R.P.C. 309, the Patents Court refused to draw a distinction between a drug, not patented per se, and a broadly claimed composition containing it, because supplying the drug would be an act of indirect infringement under s.60(2): importation from outside the EEA was therefore prohibited both of the raw drug and of compositions containing it. Whether increased demand might result if there were price cutting by a licensed competitor is irrelevant to the imposition of an importation ban, see *Research Corp's (Carboplatin) Patent* [1990] R.P.C. 663.

Since export of a patented product involves an act of infringement by disposal of that product within s.60(1)(a), acts of export can be prohibited by the settled terms of a licence of right. This is likely to be in respect only of countries where parallel patents exist, to give the proprietor a cause of action in the United Kingdom if the licensee infringes a foreign patent, see *Smith Kline & French's (Cimetidine) Patents* [1990] R.P.C. 203 CA and *American Cyanamid's (Fenbufen) Patent* (above). In *Diamond Shamrock's Patent* [1987] R.P.C. 91, a licence to export was explicitly granted at the same rate of royalty as for use of the invention within the United Kingdom.

Each of these decisions probably still stands under s.46, but may be influenced by the terms of arts 30 and 31 of the TRIPS Agreement (reprinted and discussed in §48A.02). However, these articles relate to licences granted under compulsion, whereas a licence of right can be said to be a voluntary act as indicated in §46.08.

Miscellaneous licence terms

A licence of right is personal to the licensee. Provisions against assignment, or for **46.16** termination in the event of a take-over situation, can therefore be included (*Syntex's Patent* [1986] R.P.C. 585).

Although sub-licensing may be permitted, this has often been refused, see e.g. *Hilti's Patent* [1988] R.P.C. 51. However, the question of permitting sub-licensing can be avoided by making the prospective sub-licensee a co-applicant. In *Allen & Hanbury's (Salbutamol) Patent* [1987] R.P.C. 327 CA, sub-contracting was not permitted because the patent had claims to compositions containing the patented product which would have been infringed by the manufacturing operation intended to be sub-contracted: a sub-licence was therefore required rather than an agency agreement. In *Shiley's Patent* [1988] R.P.C. 97, the Comptroller held that the licensee (a foreign entity) should be free to work with the distributor of its choice and not only by setting up a wholly-owned subsidiary company in the United Kingdom to act as its distributor. In an application for a compulsory licence under s.48 to sell an unpatented solvent with the right to pass to customers the right to use it in manufacturing a patented product, the licence was refused for the reason that s.49(1) provides for licences to be granted to the customers and these would need to be named in the application or be party to it. The applicant then sought a licence for a named customer, which was refused, see *Monsanto's CCP Patent* [1990] F.S.R. 93 and §49.02.

Licences of right settled by the Comptroller have included the normal provisions for termination on the insolvency of the licensee or the appointment of a receiver or administrator of its assets, see *Syntex's Patent* (above); or on breach of its terms by the licensee, e.g. by non-payment of royalties due, with an appropriate period of notice for the licensee to rectify the breach: in *Hilti's Patent* (above), 30 days was prescribed for this purpose; and, in *Shiley's Patent* (above), the Comptroller refused to reduce to 14 days the initially proposed period of 28 days.

The Comptroller may also include a term that the licence terminates if the licensee challenges the validity of the patent (*Du Pont's (Blades') Patent* [1988] R.P.C. 479), but see §46.17 where the defendant in infringement proceedings obtains a licence of right.

In *Smith Kline & French v Harris* [1992] F.S.R. 110, the licence of right could be terminated if the licensee became an affiliate of another "operating in the field of the licence". Interpreted literally, the quoted words were held to make the provision void for restraint of trade, and when construed narrowly there was no breach because the acquirer of the licence did not already trade in the patented product, but a further licence was later settled to which the acquirer would be party if the original licence were terminated.

A contractual restriction against "passing off" the licensee's product as that of the proprietor has been rejected (*Syntex's Patent*, above), the proprietor being left to his remedy in passing off. In *Cabot Safety's Patent* [1992] R.P.C. 39, no good reason was seen for the licence to require the licensee to mark the product by reference to the licence of right; and, in *Hilti's Patent* (above), a clause was rejected preventing the licensees from asserting that their products were licensed or approved by the patentee.

Quality control provisions are not usually imposed, because the market place is thought to be the most effective control as to quality, but, in *Hilti's Patent* (above), such a term was ordered to take account of the public interest in avoiding faulty magazines for dangerous nail guns. However, provisions allowing the licensor to carry out a product quality audit have been refused, see the MOPP.

The settled licence will not require the proprietor to bring infringement proceedings against others: s.46(4) empowers the licensee to see that this is done. Likewise, licence terms of the "most favoured nation" type will not be included, because if circumstances change the licensee could make a fresh application for a replacement licence on comparable terms. An arbitration clause is not considered appropriate in a licence "settled" by the Comptroller, even if the parties are prepared to accept it.

Effect of "licences of right" register entry (subss.(3)(c) and (d), (3A), (3B), (4) and (5))

46.17   Except in case of importation from outside the European Community (for which see §46.15), subs.(3)(c) allows a defendant in infringement proceedings under a patent where licences are available as of right to undertake to take a licence and thereby avoid an injunction and limit the damages to twice the amount that would be payable under the licence. The defendant must actually give an undertaking to the court (*Du Pont v Enka (No.2)* [1988] R.P.C. 497); and the terms of the licence of right do not apply until the date when it is granted.

Subsection (3)(c) does not affect an account of profits instead of damages, see *Codex v Racal-Milgo (No.3)* [1984] F.S.R. 87. It appears also not to affect the grant of an injunction in respect of infringement of some other intellectual property right.

Where damages are to be calculated on the basis of a reasonable royalty (for which see §61.24), it is difficult to see why these should not equate to the royalty rate which comes to be settled under s.46(3)(a). This is because a licence of right should be granted at a rate of royalty which would be agreed between a willing licensor and a willing licensee (see §46.08), and that would seem to be the same as the "reasonable royalty", if that should be the basis on which damages for infringement are required to be assessed.

Subsection (3A) allows the defendant to take advantage of subs.(3)(c) while continuing to contend that no licence is needed because of non-infringement or invalidity of the patent in suit. Unlike an application for a compulsory licence under s.48, only the terms of the licence of right are in issue and not the question of whether or not a licence should be granted. The existence of subs.(3A) can be a legitimate reason for seeking a licence of right shortly before patent expiry in order to place a limit on any eventual award of infringement damages. Also, where a defendant does not seek a licence of right immediately, but states that he will do so if he loses at trial, it is not a general rule that an injunction should not be then granted effective until the licence is actually granted; and, anyway, a defendant could only avoid an immediate injunction if he satisfies the court that he would be able to discharge his obligations under any licence granted, see the design right case of *Dyrlund Smith v Turberville Smith* [1998] F.S.R. 774 CA where an interim injunction was imposed on an appeal, but with this suspended for a short time to enable the defendant to seek an immediate licence of right coupled with discharge of the injunction.

Under subs.(3)(d), only half renewal fees are to be paid in respect of such fees whose expiry dates fall after the date when the register entry is made. Subsection (3B) clarifies that the expiry date means the end of that day in the period prescribed for payment, within the meaning of s.25(3), after which the patent shall cease to have effect.

Subsection (4) empowers a licensee of right to call for the proprietor to take proceedings for infringement of the patent. If the proprietor refuses or neglects to do so, the licensee can become the claimant and join the proprietor as a nominal defendant. The licensee takes these proceedings "as if he were proprietor", but it is not clear whether any remedy other than an injunction is available in view of the terms of ss.61 and 67. The proprietor will not be liable for costs unless he enters an appearance in the proceedings (subs.(5)).

An existing licensee under the patent before licences became available as of right cannot proceed under subs.(4), unless and until the licence is exchanged for a licence of right under subs.(3)(b).

PRACTICE UNDER SECTION 46

Making of entry in register

The procedure for making a voluntary "licences of right" entry in the register (under **46.18** subs.(1)) is governed by r.43 (reprinted above). The proprietor makes the application on PF 28 in which he must declare that he is not precluded by contract from granting licences. It seems that the declaration need concern only those contracts which are themselves registered. Where it is recorded in the register that a person has an interest in the patent, notice to that person is given (as required by subs.(2)), and the MOPP indicates that the making of the requested entry in the register is then delayed until a stated period for possible objection (normally 14 days) has elapsed.

If a renewal fee is to be accepted at the half rate, it is not enough simply to file the application before the date on which the fee is due. Although the changes to s.25 (noted in §25.01 above) provide an extended period for the payment of a renewal fee (for which see §25.06 above), the changes made to s.46 (as noted in §46.01 above) ensure that, in order to obtain the advantage of a half fee renewal payment, the application under s.46 must be filed BEFORE the anniversary date, i.e. before the commencement of the next renewal period. At least 10 working days before the renewal date, and longer where there is an interest recorded in the register, should be allowed for the register entry to be made: otherwise the full renewal fee is payable, see the MOPP. Thus, where there is such a recorded interest, and the renewal falls due shortly, it is prudent to supply with the request a signed consent to the entry from the person having that interest. PF 28 contains a tear-off slip to be stamped by the UK-IPO and returned to the address given thereon when the entry has been made in the register.

Rule 43(2) requires the register entry to be published in the *Patents Journal*. This is to bring the entry to the notice of manufacturers. Interested parties then have two months in which to apply for cancellation of the register entry under s.47(3), for which see r.43(3) (reprinted above and discussed in §47.08).

Application for settlement of licence terms

The procedure on application for settlement of the terms of a licence of right under **46.19** subs.(3)(a) or (b) is set out in r.89 (reprinted above). The application is made on PF 2, and must be accompanied by two copies of a draft of the licence proposed, or sought, by the applicant. The application can be made by the proprietor but, more usually, is made by a person seeking a licence. If the applicant is the proprietor, the application must also be accompanied by two copies of a statement of grounds setting out the facts on which he relies (r.76(4)). (The proprietor may prefer to propose the terms of a licence of right by making the application to the Comptroller to settle them, rather than leave the prospective licensee to do so. The necessary "default of agreement" under subs.(3)(a) would arise if the prospective licensee objected to them.) The Comptroller sends these documents to the other party (r.77(1)), and may specify a time limit within which the other party may file a counter-statement setting out fully any grounds of objection (r.77(6)). In an application by a prospective licensee, as governed by r.89, the Comptroller will notify the proprietor that an application has been made (r.89(2)) and will set out a period within which the proprietor may file a statement of grounds (r.89(4)). If a statement of grounds is not filed by the proprietor within the period specified, he shall be treated as supporting the applicant's case (r.89(5)). In filing the statement of grounds, the proprietor may optionally provide the form of licence which he would not contest further. The Comptroller has the power to extend or shorten any time period specified during the course of such applications (r.81(1)), although it is permissible to apply for extensions of time (r.81(2)).

Under Pt 7 of the Rules (rr.73–91, mainly reprinted at §§123.06–123.21), the Comptroller has wide-ranging powers to direct how the procedure then unfolds, for example the power to give leave to either party to file evidence upon such terms as he thinks fit (r.80(2)). The general powers of the Comptroller are set out at r.82, but the procedure is likely to provide for successive periods for filing evidence by the applicant and respondent and by the applicant in reply, followed by a hearing. The periods for filing evidence are at the Comptroller's discretion, but will usually be six weeks with the Comptroller being reluctant to grant extensions unless the other party consents. The date for the hearing may be fixed when the evidence timetable directions are given. It is customary for the form of licence settled by the Comptroller to be appended to his decision and for this to state that the licence takes effect from the date of that decision.

The principles for sufficiency of the statement of case are: (1) to take the place of negotiations between a willing licensor and willing licensee; (2) to set out the facts within the party's knowledge which the Comptroller will reasonably need to settle the terms; and (3) to identify the facts and alleged facts in dispute. It is understood that the licensee need not disclose the source of intended supply of the patented product or the proposed selling price if the royalty rate can be fixed by comparison with other licences.

The Comptroller has power to strike out any part of a statement or counter-statement of case if he is satisfied that such is an abuse of process or is otherwise likely to obstruct the just disposal of the proceedings (r.83(2)), as the court may do under CPR 3.4 (see *Roussel-Uclaf's (Clemence & Le Martret's) Patent* [1989] R.P.C. 405 and *Rhône-Poulenc's (Keto-profen) Patent* [1989] R.P.C. 570), although this power is unlikely to be exercised except in a case seen as exceptional.

It is not customary for any award of costs to be made in proceedings before the Comptroller under s.46(3), but this is not an invariable rule.

—Confidential disclosure during proceedings under subsection (3)(a)

46.20   The evidence filed in an application to settle the terms of a licence of right often includes financial and commercial information, disclosure of which would be valuable to competitors as well as to the other party in the proceedings. An order under r.53(1) may be issued that documents containing such information are treated as confidential (as discussed in §118.20), but departure from the norm of making the documents available to the public must be justified (*Diamond Shamrock's Patent* [1987] R.P.C. 91). A notice on the Comptroller's practice was published:*Patents Journal* May 28, 1987. The parties are expected to provide duplicate documents for the public file of the patent in which the confidential passages have been masked, so that as much of the document as possible may be open to public inspection. Commercial information provided in confidence during the settlement proceedings remains confidential thereafter.

As noted in §46.10, the parties may be ordered to produce licence agreements voluntarily entered into, since these may be relevant to fixing a royalty on the "comparables" approach, and a confidentiality order would then normally be made.

Although the statements and evidence may refer to the fact that "without prejudice" discussions had previously taken place between the parties, the terms offered should not be disclosed in the absence of agreement; and, if this is done, the details may be ordered to be removed.

The order for confidentiality may and often does go beyond the terms of r.53(1), which concerns only documents which would otherwise be open to inspection in the patent file under s.118. Distribution of documents containing particularly sensitive information is often restricted, see §123.48. Where confidential information has been filed in evidence or where a witness is cross-examined about it, the Comptroller has often been prepared to sit in private. The court is much less likely to do so on appeal, but counsel and the judge usually take care that the sensitive information is not disclosed orally during the proceedings and decisions and judgments are worded accordingly. Confidential financial data may be presented in an appendix which is not open to public inspection, following *Geigy's Patent* [1964] R.P.C. 391.

SECTION 47

Cancellation of entry made under section 46

47.—(1) At any time after an entry has been made under section 46 above in respect of a patent, the proprietor of the patent may apply to the comptroller for cancellation of the entry.

47.01

(2) Where such an application is made and the balance paid of all renewal fees which would have been payable if the entry had not been made, the comptroller may cancel the entry, if satisfied that there is no existing licence under the patent or that all licensees under the patent consent to the application.

(3) Within the prescribed period after an entry has been made under section 46 above in respect of a patent, any person who claims that the proprietor of the patent is, and was at the time of the entry, precluded by a contract in which the claimant is interested from granting licences under the patent may apply to the comptroller for cancellation of the entry.

(4) Where the comptroller is satisfied, on an application under subsection (3) above, that the proprietor of the patent is and was so precluded, he shall cancel the entry; and the proprietor shall then be liable to pay, within a period specified by the comptroller, a sum equal to the balance of all renewal fees which would have been payable if the entry had not been made, and the patent shall cease to have effect at the expiration of that period if that sum is not so paid.

(5) Where an entry is cancelled under this section, the rights and liabilities of the proprietor of the patent shall afterwards be the same as if the entry had not been made.

(6) Where an application has been made under this section, then—

   (a) in the case of an application under subsection (1) above, any person, and

   (b) in the case of an application under subsection (3) above, the proprietor of the patent,

may within the prescribed period give notice to the comptroller of opposition to the cancellation; and the comptroller shall, in considering the application, determine whether the opposition is justified.

COMMENTARY ON SECTION 47

Scope of the section

Section 47 concerns the cancellation of entries which have been made in the register under s.46. The relevant provisions in the Rules are those of paras (3) and (4) of r.43 (reprinted in §46.02).

47.02

Application for cancellation (subss.(1)–(5))

The proprietor may apply at any time for the entry to be cancelled (subs.(1)). If the unpaid half fees are paid and the Comptroller is satisfied that there are no licences under

47.03

the patent or that all licensees consent, the entry will be cancelled (subs.(2)). Rule 43 (reprinted at §46.02) applies, as discussed in §47.05.

A person claiming to have an interest in a contract which prevents the proprietor granting licences under the patent has the right to apply for cancellation of an entry made under s.46 (subs.(3)). Part 7 of the Rules (discussed in §47.07) governs the procedure and there is a time limit of two months from the date of the register entry for filing the application (r.43(4)). This period cannot be extended (r.108(1)). If the application under subs.(3) succeeds and the entry is cancelled, then by subs.(4) the proprietor must pay the unpaid half renewal fees, failing which the patent will lapse (see §47.08).

When an entry has been cancelled, the rights and liabilities of the proprietor are the same as if the entry had not been made (subs.(5)).

Opposition to cancellation (subs.(6))

47.04   Where the application for cancellation is made under subs.(1), any person can oppose and does not have to show an interest, but where the application is made under subs.(3) only the proprietor can oppose (subs.(6)). If an opposition succeeds, the "licences of right" entry is cancelled and a period is specified within which the patentee must pay the renewal fees that ought to have been paid if the entry had not been made: otherwise the patent lapses, see §47.08.

Proceedings for the cancellation of a "licences of right" endorsement should not, apparently, put in issue the validity of the patent, see *Glaverbel's Patent* [1987] R.P.C. 73 CA. Also, when an application has been made for settlement of terms of a licence of right under s.46(3)(c), a request to cancel a "licences of right" entry (voluntarily entered under s.46(3)(a)) will not be entertained until the terms of the licence of right have been settled, see *Cassou's Patent* [1971] R.P.C. 91 and §46.06.

In *Serenyi's Patent* (1938) 55 R.P.C. 228, it was held that an opposition to cancellation of a "licences of right" endorsement should not be treated as if it were an application for a compulsory licence: cancellation was allowed in that case as being in the best interests of the public.

Practice under Section 47

Application under subsection (1) by proprietor for cancellation of entry under section 46

47.05   An application by the proprietor under s.47(1) for cancellation of the entry "licences of right" in the register is made on PF 30 under r.43(3) (reprinted at §46.02). This form includes a declaration that all licensees consent to the application.

The application must be accompanied by PF 12 and the unpaid half renewal fees. PF 30 contains a confirmation slip which the Comptroller uses to inform the applicant that the entry has been cancelled. The return address need not be the address for service recorded in the register.

Application under subsection (3) by interested party for cancellation of entry under section 46

47.06   An application under subs.(3) by an interested party for cancellation of a "licence of right" entry under s.46 is made on PF 2 under r.76(3)(b) within two months from the date of the entry (r.43(4)), supported by a statement of grounds setting out, inter alia, the facts on which the applicant relies, all in duplicate. The Comptroller then sends a copy of the application and statement of grounds to the proprietor (r.77(4)), and the application is now advertised in the *Patents Journal* (r.75).

The two month period in r.43(4) (which cannot be extended under r.108(1)) runs from the date of entry under s.46 and not necessarily from the date of the *Patents Journal* advertising that entry. Rule 43(2) does not require the Comptroller to correlate those dates.

Opposition to cancellation of "licences of right" entry

47.07   Part 7 of the Rules (rr.73–88,as amended in 2011, mainly reprinted at §§123.06–

123.21), governs opposition to a cancellation application whether made under subs.(1) or (3). By r.75, all such applications are advertised in the *Patents Journal* and opposition may then be filed within four weeks (extensible under r.81(1)) of the date of the advertisement.

If the application to cancel the "licences of right" entry is made by the proprietor, the mechanism under r.76(2)(b) is triggered. The opposition must be filed on PF 15 (under r.76(3)(c)) and supported by a statement of grounds, each in duplicate, within four weeks of the date of the advertisement of the proprietor's application in the *Patents Journal*. The Comptroller sends copies of the PF 15 and statement of grounds to the proprietor who is then permitted to file a counter-statement in duplicate, within such period as may be specified by the Comptroller (r.77(5)). Any such period can be extended by discretion under r.81(1). The Comptroller sends a copy of the counter-statement to the opponent.

If the application to cancel the "licences of right" entry is made by a person other than the proprietor, the Comptroller will notify the proprietor pursuant to r.77(1). The proprietor is then permitted to file a counter-statement in duplicate, compliant with r.78, before the end of the period of four weeks beginning with the date of the advertisement in the *Patents Journal* of the application to cancel the "licences of right" entry.

Thereafter the procedure is at the discretion of the Comptroller but is likely to follow that generally adopted for contentious matters before the Comptroller, as discussed in §§123.06 et seq. Appeal lies to the Patents Court (s.97(1)) and thereafter, but only on a point of law and with leave, to the Court of Appeal (s.97(3)).

Effecting the cancellation of "licences of right" entry

If, on an application made under subs.(3), the Comptroller cancels the entry, he informs **47.08** the proprietor and sets a period within which the proprietor must pay any unpaid half renewal fees, failing which the patent lapses at the end of that period.

SECTION 48 [SUBSTITUTED]

Compulsory licences: general

48.—(1) At any time after the expiration of three years, or of such other **48.01** **period as may be prescribed, from the date of the grant of a patent, any person may apply to the comptroller on one or more of the relevant grounds—**

(a) **for a licence under the patent,**

(b) **for an entry to be made in the register to the effect that licences under the patent are to be available as of right, or**

(c) **where the applicant is a government department, for the grant to any person specified in the application of a licence under the patent.**

(2) Subject to sections 48A and 48B below, if he is satisfied that any of those grounds are established, the comptroller may—

(a) **where the application is under subsection (1)(a) above, order the grant of a licence to the applicant on such terms as the comptroller thinks fit;**

(b) **where the application is under subsection (1)(b) above, make such an entry as is there mentioned;**

(c) **where the application is under subsection (1)(c) above, order the grant of a licence to the person specified in the application on such terms as the comptroller thinks fit.**

(3) An application may be made under this section in respect of a patent

even though the applicant is already the holder of a licence under the patent; and no person shall be estopped or barred from alleging any of the matters specified in the relevant grounds by reason of any admission made by him, whether in such a licence or otherwise, or by reason of his having accepted such a licence.

(4) In this section "the relevant grounds" means—

    (a) in the case of an application made in respect of a patent whose proprietor is a WTO proprietor, the grounds set out in section 48A(1) below;

    (b) in any other case, the grounds set out in section 48B(1) below.

(5) A proprietor is a WTO proprietor for the purposes of this section and sections 48A, 48B, 50 and 52 below if—

    (a) he is a national of or is domiciled in a country which is a member of the World Trade Organisation, or

    (b) he has a real and effective industrial or commercial establishment in such a country.

(6) A rule prescribing any such other period under subsection (1) above shall not be made unless a draft of the rule has been laid before, and approved by resolution of, each House of Parliament.

Note. For the reasons set out in §48.05, the Patents and Trade Marks (World Trade Organisation) Regulations 1999 (SI 1999/1899) replaced (as from July 29, 1999) s.48 with new wording, introduced new ss.48A and 48B (reprinted and discussed respectively in §§48A.01 and 48B.01) and substituted a new form of s.52 (for which see §52.01). This substituted section has been applied to the Isle of Man by SI 2003/1249.

COMMENTARY ON SECTION 48

The provisions for the grant of compulsory licences

48.02   Section 48 is the first of a group of sections (ss.48–54) which concern the grant of compulsory licences where there has been abuse of the monopoly rights. In 1999, this section was substituted by new wording and further ss.48A and 48B were then introduced. Of the other sections in this group: s.49 provides for the grant of licences to customers of the applicant for a compulsory licence under s.48; s.50 (as amended) in s.50(2) sets out the principles and criteria for the grant of a compulsory licence under s.48 upon the grounds now set out in either of s.48A or s.48B, according to which is applicable having regard to the nature of the patent proprietor, with s.50(1) setting out additional principles and criteria when s.48B applies; s.51 provides for relief following a report from the Competition Commission of a practice contrary to the public interest; s.52 (also substituted by new wording in 1999) provides for oppositions, appeals and possible arbitration in respect of applications for compulsory licences; and ss.53 and 54 contain various supplementary provisions particularly relating to international aspects of possible abuse of monopoly rights.

    The amendments to ss.48–54 were effected by the Patents and Trade Marks (World Trade Organisation) Regulations 1999 (SI 1999/1899), purportedly made under powers provided by the European Communities Act 1972 (c.68, as amended by s.1 of the European Economic Area Act 1993, c.51). However, irrespective of whether these powers extend to implementation of the TRIPS Agreement, as to the doubt about which see §D10, the changes can probably be seen as an amplification of the pre-existing provision of s.53(5) (reprinted in §53.01) which prevents ss.48 to 51 being operated in a way which is "at variance with any treaty or international convention to which the United Kingdom is a party", see §53.05.

There is a regime for cross-licences between patents and plant breeders' rights under The Patents and Plant Variety Rights (Compulsory Licensing) Regulations (SI 2002/247), see further §48.07. Note that the procedure under s.48(1) is taken to apply to proceedings under the Regulations, but the provisions of ss.48, 48A, 48B, 49, 50 and 52 do not otherwise apply to compulsory patent licences and cross-licences obtained under these Regulations.

Scope of the section

The replacement of s.48 (as noted in §48.01) was brought about by the need to comply **48.03** with arts 30 and 31 of the TRIPS Agreement (reprinted in §48A.02). As a consequence, the grounds upon which a compulsory licence may be granted are now significantly more restricted when (as normally will be the case) the proprietor of the patent is a "WTO proprietor" (for the meaning of which see §48.04), in which case new s.48A applies (subs.(4)(a)). The restricted availability of licences under s.48A may mean that anti-competitive conduct will now more easily be combated by recourse to s.51 following a finding by the Competition Commission as some of the strictures of these TRIPS articles do not then apply (see TRIPS art.31(k)) as discussed in the commentary on s.51. However, otherwise, the available grounds remain as previously specified in the section, but are now set out in new s.48B (subs.(4)(c)).

Although compulsory licence provisions have existed in the patent statutes for about a century, little use has been made of them, particularly since World War II, and it is unlikely that this will change under the more restricted provisions of the present ss.48–48B. The reason for this is that more effective provisions for controlling an abuse of monopoly are now to be found in provisions of competition law, as discussed by Sir Robin Jacob in the Burrell Competition Lecture (reprinted in *CIPA*, March 2008, pp.144–149), and see the powers now possessed by the Competition Commission as discussed in the following commentaries on ss.50A and 51. Thus, a threat made privately of possible complaint under competition law may be more effective in bringing about an amicable inter partes dispute settlement than would a threat of a making an application under s.48.

In addition to the powers for compulsory licences under the Act, art.12 of the European Biotechnology Directive (reprinted at §C12) requires that compulsory cross-licensing should be available when the exploitation of a plant variety right is impeded by a patent and vice versa. The implementation of this article is discussed in §48.07.

The former form of s.48 is not reprinted herein as the substituted section (with new ss.48A and 48B) had immediate effect, including effect as to existing licences, and applications therefor, made under the previous form of the section, see the transitional provisions reprinted in §48A.03.

The amendments to ss.48–54 also have the consequence of bringing the statute into compliance with European law by removing the previous provisions which could have the effect of limiting trade between the United Kingdom and other members of the EEA, as was held to be improper in *EC Commission v United Kingdom (C-30/90)* [1993] R.P.C. 283; [1992] 1 E.C.R. 829; [1992] 2 C.M.L.R. 709 ECJ. The earlier decision in *Allen & Hanbury v Generics (C–434/85)* [1988] F.S.R. 312; [1988] 1 C.M.L.R. 701 ECJ is also relevant on this point.

Once a ground for the grant of a licence under the section has been established, under s.48A or 48B as the case may be, the Comptroller has no discretion: he then has a duty to settle the terms of a licence taking into account the criteria set out in s.50, but these criteria do not create any additional hurdle for the applicant to overcome before he is entitled to a licence, see *Therma-Tru's Patent* [1997] R.P.C. 777. However, in this decision, the Patents Court disagreed with the Comptroller and held that it is wrong in principle to grant a licence to an applicant who does not intend to work the invention itself but only through a sub-licensee, albeit a subsidiary company. The application was dismissed for this reason alone, even though grounds for the grant of a licence under the former law had been made out.

The date of a licence granted under the section is that when its terms were before the Comptroller and settled by him (*Geigy's Patent* [1966] R.P.C. 250).

It is to be noted that the ECJ has decided that the "exhaustion of rights" doctrine, under which parallel imports of a patented article may not be prevented when that article has first been put on the market within the EEC by the proprietor or with his consent (as discussed in §D15), does not apply where the first marketing within the European Community (probably now within the EEA) took place under a compulsory licence, because this was not with the "consent" of the proprietor (*Pharmon v Hoechst (19/84)* [1985] E.C.R. 2281; [1985] 3 C.M.L.R. 775; [1986] F.S.R. 108, for case comment on which see D. Guy, [1986] E.I.P.R. 252). However, whether a "licence of right" granted on an existing patent compulsorily endorsed is subject to the exhaustion of rights doctrine is not clear.

Besides the provisions in the Act (and under European Community law and the TRIPS Agreement), there are occasions when an industry itself sets up (or tries to set up) a voluntary system for making licences available on demand. This is particularly desirable when the subject of a patented invention becomes an industry standard when it would be obviously undesirable if a patentee is in a position to enforce a monopoly right to exclude all others from complying with that standard, or charging extortionate royalties for the privilege of having access to it. However, no clear solution to this problem has emerged, for which see "European standards for mobile communications: The tense relationship between standard and intellectual property rights" by R. Bekkers and Isabelle Liotard [1999] E.I.P.R. 110.

The term "WTO Proprietor" (subs.(5))

48.04 The grounds upon which a compulsory licence may be granted are limited to those set out in s.48A when the patentee is a "WTO proprietor", a term which is defined in s.48(5) as a person or entity who or which: (a) is "a national of, or is domiciled in a country which is a member of the World Trade Organisation" ("WTO"); or (b) has a real and effective industrial or commercial establishment in such a country. The member countries of the WTO are indicated in §90.03 and include most of the economically important countries of the world. However, at least at the time of writing, some of the former constituent parts of the USSR are not WTO Members, holding only an Observer status. Also, for the purposes of ss.48 and 48A, the United Kingdom is a WTO country, whereas it is not for the purposes of priority under s.5, see s.5(6) set out in §5.01. Consequently, most applications for compulsory licences will be governed by the more restrictive requirements and conditions now set out in s.48A.

When the patentee is *not* a WTO proprietor, the applicable grounds are those set out in s.48B, but this section will have rare effect because few applications will fall within its scope because the patentee is much more likely to be a "WTO proprietor".

Where a State becomes a WTO Member, a patent proprietor can be regarded as a "WTO proprietor" only from the date of accession of that State to the WTO Treaty. Note that, if a licence is granted under s.48B and the patent proprietor then becomes a "WTO proprietor", application can be made under s.52 for that licence to be modified so that it complies with the provisions of s.48A and, if this is not possible, for that licence to be cancelled, see §48A.03.

When application can be made, by whom and for what (subss.(1)–(3) and (6))

48.05 By subs.(1), an application can be made by any person to the Comptroller at any time after the expiration of three years from grant of the patent, that is from the date of publication of the grant in the *Patents Journal*, see §24.11. Unlike an application for a licence of right, which can be filed in advance of the first date from which it can be granted (see §46.06), subs.(1) does not permit an application to be made before the end of this three-year period so that there will be an inevitable delay thereafter before relief under the section can be obtained. The period of three years may be modified by rule, but only by affirmative resolution passed by each House of Parliament (subs.(6)).

Under the section, an application can be made:

(a) for a licence (subs.(1)(a)), which (if the application is successful) can lead to an order that the applicant be granted a licence under the patent "on such terms as the comptroller thinks fit" (subs.(2)(a)); or

(b) for an entry in the register that licences are to be available as of right (subs.(1)(b)), which (if successful) can lead to such an entry in the register, whereupon a licence can be sought and settled under s.46(3)(a), as discussed in §§46.06–46.20; or

(c) if the applicant is a government department, for the grant of a licence to any person specified in the application (subs.(1)(c)), which, again if successful can lead to an order for the grant of a licence as under (a) above.

Subsection (3) provides that an application under s.48 can be made by a licensee under the patent, who is not to be estopped by any terms in his licence or otherwise from raising any of the grounds specified in the section. Subsection (3) is to be read in conjunction with s.49(2), discussed in §49.01. Thus, an application for a compulsory licence can proceed even if the applicant does not admit, or indeed is contesting, that the actions for which he seeks a licence would infringe the patent, such being an alternative type of plea in case infringement proceedings should succeed against him, or in case the applicant has not yet decided whether to work the patent, see subs.(3) and *Halcon's Patents* [1989] R.P.C. 1 where the patent was later held not to be infringed (*Halcon v BP Chemicals* BL/100/87, noted I.P.D. 10072).

Where an order is made for the grant of a licence, s.108 provides that the order itself shall have the effect as if it were a deed, executed by the proprietor and other necessary parties, granting a licence in accordance with that order, for which see §108.02. Also (under s.49(4), discussed in §49.01) a licensee under any licence granted pursuant to ss.48–48B has a right to call upon the patentee to institute infringement proceedings, failing which the licensee can do this himself, making the patentee a nominal defendant, as under s.46(4) and (5), discussed in §46.17. Where an entry "licences of right" is ordered to be made in the register, the provisions of ss.46–47 thereafter have effect with regard to that entry (s.53(4)).

Hearing and appeal

A hearing must be held if requested before a decision is given by the Comptroller **48.06** (s.101). Appeal from the Comptroller's decision lies to the Patents Court (s.97(1)) with further appeal to the Court of Appeal only on a point of law and with leave (s.97(3)). There is no provision for proceedings to be held in Scotland, see §98.08.

Other relevant provisions in other sections

Section 50 sets out the general objects and principles which the Comptroller has to **48.07** consider in exercising his powers under s.48.

Opposition to the grant of a compulsory licence can be filed under s.52(1) by the proprietor of the patent concerned and special provisions then apply as regards possible reference of the matter to arbitration and for appearance on the hearing of any appeal, see §§52.06 and 52.05 respectively. If the proprietor does not lodge opposition under s.52(1), he is precluded from being heard on the settlement of the terms of the licence if the Comptroller decides that one should be granted, see *Ultimatte Corp's Patents* BL O/1/84, noted I.P.D. 6141 and §52.03.

There are further provisions with regard to the granting of licences of right in ss.53 and 54. Section 53 concerns (with the numbering referring to the pertinent subsections: (2) reports of the Competition Commission; (3) entries in the register irrespective of any contract, with such entry having the same effect as an entry under s.46; and (4) any entry under ss.48–51 having to be consistent with international agreements. Section 54 provides for certain cases where an invention is being worked abroad. For further discussion on these points, see the commentaries on ss.53 and 54.

The 1977 Act did not include any provision for revocation of a patent where an order for compulsory licence fails to cure the abuse of monopoly, as existed under repealed s.42 of the 1949 Act, on which there were no cases; or for compulsory licences automatically to be available under patents for certain types of invention, as existed under s.41 of the 1949 Act for inventions relating to "food or medicine", on which there were many cases particularly during the 1960 decade.

Article 12 of the Biotechnology Directive (reprinted in §C12) provides for possible compulsory cross-licensing between patents and plant breeders' rights. This article is given effect by a statutory instrument entitled "The Patents and Plant Variety Rights (Compulsory Licensing) Regulations" (SI 2002/247) which took effect on March 1, 2002. These Regulations provide for compulsory cross-licences between patents and plant breeders' rights which are not in common ownership and where the exploitation of a patent is impeded by a plant variety right, or the exploitation of a new plant variety is impeded by a patent, and in either case where the impeded act would constitute significant technical progress of considerable economic interest compared with the earlier right. These stringent provisions will probably cause these Regulations to have little effect in practice.

The Regulations require that, before an application for a licence can be made, the applicant must have unsuccessfully requested a voluntary licence and demonstrate that the acquisition or exploitation of a plant variety right would otherwise infringe upon the patent concerned (reg.3). The applicant will also have to show that the proposed exploitation will constitute significant technical progress of considerable economic interest.

An application for a patent licence will have to be made to the Comptroller (when the practice under s.48 is to be followed) and an application for a licence under a plant breeders' right will have to be made to the Controller of Plant Variety Rights. Any such licence that is granted cannot be exclusive, and must entitle the patent proprietor to an appropriate royalty and to a cross-licence to the new plant variety on reasonable terms (reg.7). The process for applying for a compulsory licence under these Regulations lies parallel and in addition to the s.48 process the provisions of ss.48, 48A, 48B, 49, 50 and 52 do not apply to any licences grantedunder them (reg.26(2)).

Practice under Section 48

48.08   The procedure for an application for a compulsory licence under s.48 follows the general procedure for proceedings before the Comptroller as set out in Pt 7 of the Rules (rr.73–81, as amended mainly reprinted at §§123.06–123.21, and discussed in §§123.42 et seq). An application for a licence under s.48(1) must be made on PF 2, and be accompanied by a statement of grounds (in duplicate) comprising, inter alia, the facts on which the applicant relies and the terms of the licence which the applicant believes to be reasonable (r.76). The application will be published in the *Patents Journal* (r.75) and the Comptroller will notify the proprietor of the patent and any other party likely to have an interest (r.77).

The former rules required that the applicant must establish, by his initial evidence, a prima facie case that it would be appropriate to grant a licence to him, but this does not form part of the procedure under the new rules. Upon receiving notification from the Comptroller of the application for a compulsory licence, the proprietor has a period of four weeks from the date of the advertisement of the application in the *Patents Journal* (r.77(8)) within which to file a counter-statement setting out his case. Failure to file a counter-statement is deemed to be an acceptance of the applicant's request (r.77(9)).

When the application can proceed, the application is advertised in the *Patents Journal* and copies of the documents are sent to the proprietor and any other person shown on the register as having an interest in the patent.

The Pt 7 procedure also applies to an application for the cancellation of a compulsory licence (under s.52(2)), as discussed in §52.02, or the making of a "licence or right" entry in the register (under s.51), as discussed in §51.06.

Once proceedings under s.48 have commenced, the Comptroller has ruled that they should continue unless there is good reason to postpone them, but it is not open to the applicant merely to request adjournment, especially if the opponent (here an exclusive licensee) has objected to this (*Montgomerie Reid's Application* BL O/198/82, noted I.P.D. 5112). However, where (in *Halcon's Patents* [1989] R.P.C. 1) there were concurrent infringement proceedings, the compulsory licence application proceedings were stayed because these would be costly and lengthy while the infringement proceedings were then well advanced.

Because most applications for a compulsory licence under s.48 are opposed by the patentee under s.52, further matters of procedure are considered in relation to practice under that section, see §§52.06–52.08.

SECTION 48A [ADDED]

Compulsory licences: WTO proprietors

48A.—(1) In the case of an application made under section 48 above in respect of a patent whose proprietor is a WTO proprietor, the relevant grounds are—   **48A.01**

(a) where the patented invention is a product, that a demand for the product in the United Kingdom is not being met on reasonable terms;

(b) that by reason of the refusal of the proprietor of the patent concerned to grant a licence or licences on reasonable terms—

    (i) the exploitation in the United Kingdom of any other patented invention which involves an important technical advance of considerable economic significance in relation to the invention for which the patent concerned was granted is prevented or hindered, or

    (ii) the establishment or development of commercial or industrial activities in the United Kingdom is unfairly prejudiced;

(c) that by reason of conditions imposed by the proprietor of the patent on the grant of licences under the patent, or on the disposal or use of the patented product or on the use of the patented process, the manufacture, use or disposal of materials not protected by the patent, or the establishment or development of commercial or industrial activities in the United Kingdom, is unfairly prejudiced.

(2) No order or entry shall be made under section 48 above in respect of a patent whose proprietor is a WTO proprietor unless—

(a) the applicant has made efforts to obtain a licence from the proprietor on reasonable commercial terms and conditions; and

(b) his efforts have not been successful within a reasonable period.

(3) No order or entry shall be so made if the patented invention is in the field of semi-conductor technology.

(4) No order or entry shall be made under section 48 above in respect of a patent on the ground mentioned in subsection (1)(b)(i) unless the comptroller is satisfied that the proprietor of the patent for the other invention is able and willing to grant to the proprietor of the patent concerned and his licensees a licence under the patent for the other invention on reasonable terms.

(5) A licence granted in pursuance of an order or entry so made shall not be assigned except to a person to whom the patent for the other invention is also assigned.

(6) A licence granted in pursuance of an order or entry made under section 48 above in respect of a patent whose proprietor is a WTO proprietor—

(a) shall not be exclusive;

(b) shall not be assigned except to a person to whom there is also assigned the part of the enterprise that enjoys the use of the patented invention, or the part of the goodwill that belongs to that part;

(c) shall be predominantly for the supply of the market in the United Kingdom;

(d) shall include conditions entitling the proprietor of the patent concerned to remuneration adequate in the circumstances of the case, taking into account the economic value of the licence; and

(e) shall be limited in scope and in duration to the purpose for which the licence was granted.

Note. Section 48A was inserted by the Patents and Trade Marks (World Trade Organisation) Regulations 1999 (SI 1999/1899). This added section has been applied to the Isle of Man by SI 2003/1249.

Relevant Provisions of the TRIPS Agreement

TRIPS Article 30—Exceptions to rights conferred

48A.02   **30.** Members may provide limited exceptions to the exclusive rights conferred by a patent, provided that such exceptions do not unreasonably prejudice the legitimate interests of the patent owner, taking account of the legitimate interests of third parties.

TRIPS Article 31—Other use without authorization of the right holder

31. Where the law of a Member allows for other use [that is, use other than that allowed under Article 30] of the subject matter of a patent without the authorization of the right holder, including use by the government or third parties authorized by the government, the following provisions shall be respected:

(a) authorization of such use shall be considered on its individual merits;

(b) such use may only be permitted if, prior to such use, the proposed user has made efforts to obtain authorization from the right holder on reasonable commercial terms and conditions and that such efforts have not been successful within a reasonable period of time. This requirement may be waived by a Member in the case of a national emergency or other circumstances of extreme urgency or in cases of public non-commercial use. In situations of national emergency or other circumstances of extreme urgency, the right holder shall, nevertheless, be notified as soon as reasonably practicable. In the case of public non-commercial use, where the government or contractor, without making a patent search, knows or has demonstrable grounds to know that a valid patent is or will be used by or for the government, the right holder shall be informed promptly;

(c) the scope and duration of such use shall be limited to the purpose for which it was authorized, and in the case of semi-conductor technology shall only be for public non-commercial use or to remedy a practice determined after judicial or administrative process to be anti-competitive;

(d) such use shall be non-exclusive;

(e) such use shall be non-assignable, except with that part of the enterprise or goodwill which enjoys such use;

(f) any such use shall be authorized predominantly for the supply of the domestic market of the Member authorizing such use;

(g) authorization for such use shall be liable, subject to adequate protection of the legitimate interests of the persons so authorized, to be terminated if and when the circumstances which led to it cease to exist and are unlikely to recur. The competent authority shall have the authority to review, upon motivated request, the continued existence of these circumstances;

(h) the right holder shall be paid adequate remuneration in the circumstances of each case, taking into account the economic value of the authorization;

(i) the legal validity of any decision relating to the authorization of such use shall be subject to judicial review or other independent review by a distinct higher authority in that Member;

(j) any decision relating to the remuneration provided in respect of such use shall be subject to judicial review or other independent review by a distinct higher authority in that Member;

(k) Members are not obliged to apply the conditions set forth in subparagraphs (b) and (f) where such use is permitted to remedy a practice determined after judicial or administrative process to be anti-competitive. The need to correct anti-competitive practices may be taken into account in determining the amount of remuneration in such cases. Competent authorities shall have the authority to refuse termination of authorization if and when the conditions which led to such authorization are likely to recur;

(l) where such use is authorized to permit the exploitation of a patent ("the second patent") which cannot be exploited without infringing another patent ("the first patent"), the following additional conditions shall apply:

   (i) the invention claimed in the second patent shall involve an important technical advance of considerable economic significance in relation to the invention claimed in the first patent;

   (ii) the owner of the first patent shall be entitled to a cross-licence on reasonable terms to use the invention claimed in the second patent; and

   (iii) the use authorized in respect of the first patent shall be non-assignable except with the assignment of the second patent.

TRANSITIONAL PROVISIONS

In order to give s.48A retrospective effect, the Patents and Trade Marks (World Trade Organisation) Regulations 1999 (SI 1999/1899) provided, in regulation 8 thereof, the following transitional provisions: **48A.03**

8.—(1) A WTO proprietor of a patent in respect of which an order or entry has been made under section 48 of the 1977 Act before the relevant date may apply to the comptroller—

   (a) to have the order revoked or the entry cancelled on the grounds that the grounds on which the order or entry was made are not set out in subsection (1) of section 48A of that Act; or

   (b) to have the conditions subject to which any licence was granted before that date in pursuance of the order or entry modified on the grounds that the licence does not satisfy the requirements set out in subsection (6) of that section.

(2) If it appears to the comptroller on an application under paragraph (1)(a) that the grounds on which the order or entry was made are not set out in section 48A(1) of the 1977 Act, he may—

(a) revoke the order or cancel the entry; or

(b) terminate any licence granted to a person in pursuance of the order or entry subject to such terms and conditions as he thinks necessary for the protection of the legitimate interests of that person.

(3) If it appears to the comptroller on an application under paragraph (1)(b) that the conditions of the licence should be modified, he may modify the conditions accordingly; but in doing so he shall have regard to the need to protect the legitimate interests of the holder of the licence.

(4) Subsections (1), (4) and (5) of section 52 of the 1977 Act shall apply to an application under paragraph (1) as they apply to an application under sections 48 to 51 of that Act, but as if the reference in subsection (1) to the proprietor of the patentor any other person were a reference to any person.

(5) Section 48A(5) of the 1977 Act shall apply to a licence granted on or after the relevant date in pursuance of an entry made before that date in relation to a patent whose proprietor is a WTO proprietor, if the entry was made—

(a) before the commencement date and on the ground mentioned in section 48(3)(d)(ii) of that Act [*i.e.* that by reason of the refusal of the proprietor of the patent to grant a licence or licences on reasonable terms, the working or efficient working in the United Kingdom of any other patented invention which makes a substantial contribution to the art is prevented or hindered]; or

(b) on or after that date and on the ground mentioned in section 48B(i)(d)(ii) of that Act [which provision corresponds to that set out under (a) above].

(6) Section 48A(6) of the 1977 Act shall apply to a licence granted on or after the relevant date in pursuance of an entry made before that date in relation to a patent whose proprietor is a WTO proprietor.

(7) A proprietor is a WTO proprietor for the purposes of this regulation if—

(a) he is a national of, or is domiciled in, a country which is a member of the World Trade Organisation; or

(b) he has a real and effective industrial or commercial establishment in such a country.

(8) In this regulation—

"the commencement date" means the date of the coming into force of these Regulations [*i.e.* July 29, 1999];

"the relevant date" means the commencement date or, if later, the date on which the proprietor of the patent became a WTO proprietor.

COMMENTARY ON SECTION 48A

Scope of the section

48A.04   Section 48A applies to an application for a compulsory licence where the owner of the patent in issue is (or subsequently becomes) a "WTO proprietor", which term includes a proprietor resident or incorporated within a Member of the World Trade Organisation, including the United Kingdom, each as discussed in §48.04.

The section must be construed in conformity with arts 30 and 31 of the TRIPS Agreement, as reprinted above. Note that this art.30 only permits limited exceptions to the exclusive rights conferred by a patent, such as the grant of a compulsory licence, provided that the legitimate interests of the patent owner are not unreasonably prejudiced, but with account taken of the legitimate interests of third parties. The general principles of art.30 are particularised in art.31 with the consequence that the grounds upon which a compulsory licence may be granted under s.48A are quite limited—much more so than under the former law, which is therefore now largely inapplicable.

The grounds upon which a compulsory licence may be granted to a patent when s.48A applies are set out in subs.(1) and are:

1. where demand for a patented product in the United Kingdom is not being met on reasonable terms (subs.(1)(a), as discussed in §48A.07); or

2. where the proprietor has refused to grant a licence on reasonable terms and either exploitation of another patented invention, which "involves an important technical advance of considerable economic significance" in relation to the patented invention "is prevented or hindered" (subs.(1)(b)(i)), but subject to the specific limitation of subs.(4), each as discussed in §48A.08); or

3. where the establishment or development of commercial or industrial activities in the United Kingdom "is unfairly prejudiced" (subs.(1)(b)(ii), as discussed in §48A.09); or

4. where, by reasons of conditions imposed by the proprietor, unpatented activities are unfairly prejudiced (subs.(1)(c), as discussed in §48A.10).

Paragraph (1)(a) corresponds to former subs.48(3)(b)(i); the two sub-paragraphs of para.(b) correspond respectively to former sub-paras 48(3)(d)(ii) and (iii); and para.(c) corresponds to former subs.48(3)(e)).

It is possible that more than one of these grounds can be established for the grant of a licence under the section. This could be important because, if at a later date the conditions upon which the licence was granted cease to exist, the patentee may seek cancellation or modification of the licence under substituted s.52, as discussed in §48A.11.

However, in accordance with TRIPS art.31(b) and in part (c), each of these grounds is further restricted by subss.(2) and (3). Thus: to obtain a compulsory licence under s.48A, the applicant must previously have, without success within a reasonable period, "made efforts to obtain a licence from the proprietor on reasonable terms and conditions" (subs.(2)); and the patent must not be one "in the field of semi-conductor technology" (subs.(3), as discussed respectively in §§48A.05 and 48A.06). Further conditions also apply when the application is made under subs.(1)(b)(i) (as discussed in §48A.06).

Even when any of the grounds specified in subs.(1) is established outside these exemptions, a compulsory licence may only be granted in limited terms, see subs.(6) (in conformity with TRIPS art.31(d)–(h)), as discussed in §48A.11.

Article 31(a) of TRIPS also requires any application for compulsory licence to be considered on its individual merits and judicial review must be available both as to decisions granting a licence and as to its compensatory terms (TRIPS art.31(i) and (j)). These conditions are met by the provisions of ss.48 and 49 as regards procedure for adjudicating on an application for a compulsory licence and the terms of such a licence, while s.52 provides for administrative review of such an application via its opposition procedure, from which appeals may be taken at least to the Patents Court.

Note that the former ground for a compulsory licence where the United Kingdom demand for a patented product is met to a substantial extent by importation is now only available in the unlikely case that the patentee is not a WTO proprietor, a situation discussed in §48B.02.

In *EC Commission v United Kingdom* (C-30/90) [1993] R.P.C. 283; [1992] 1 E.C.R. 829; [1992] 2 C.M.L.R. 709, the ECJ ruled that a law is contrary to what is now art.34 TFEU (for which see §§D03 and D13) if it permits the grant of a compulsory licence on the ground of insufficiency of exploitation of the patent within only part of the European Community, when the demand for the patented product is satisfied by importation from other Member States. The main reason for this view is, apparently, that a reference to working (or lack of it) merely within the United Kingdom, as distinct from the Community as a whole, acts as a disguised restriction on trade between Member States. Thus, s.48A(1) has to be interpreted to meet this criterion, as extended to apply to all EEA States. However, it appears that care has been taken over the wording of the section to see that this requirement has been achieved, particularly as all the EEA Member States are WTO members.

Meijer's Plant Variety Right (noted [2002] E.I.P.R. N–38) was the first application to the Controller of Plant Varieties for a compulsory licence under the Plant Varieties Act 1997 (c.66), and was unsuccessful. It was held that nothing in the Act required the rights holder to grant a licence so the Controller had a wide discretion. A compulsory licence should only be granted when to do so was clearly in the public interest, and then only if at least one of the prescribed grounds was seen to be met. The same principles could be held to apply to an application for a patent compulsory licence, when made by a WTO proprietor under this section.

The requirement for a prior application for a voluntary licence (subs.(2))

48A.05   Under subs.(2) (in conformity with TRIPS art.31(a)), it is a pre-condition for an application under the grounds of s.48A(1) that the applicant must have already sought a licence from the patentee "on reasonable commercial terms and conditions" and that such a licence had not been "successful within a reasonable period".

To satisfy these pre-conditions, the applicant will need to provide evidence of his efforts to secure a voluntary licence, specify the terms which he proposed and of the refusal of the patentee to grant him a licence, on such terms or at all, and demonstrate that a "reasonable period" has elapsed since the first approach to the patentee. It is probably also necessary for the applicant to adduce evidence why the terms he proposed should be considered reasonable in all the prevailing circumstances, and that the applicant is able and willing to pay the royalty terms included within these proposals. For an example of application of similar provisions, see *Delta's Patent [South Africa]* (noted [1996] E.I.P.R. D–359). However, it does not appear essential that the refusal to grant a licence was made to the applicant for the compulsory licence.

Under a similar provision contained in s.37(2)(d) [1949], it appeared that, before an application could succeed on that ground, there had to have been a concrete refusal by the patentee to grant a reasonable licence (*Loewe Radio's Application* (1929) 46 R.P.C. 479). Moreover, an insistence by the patentee that the licence must be a bulk licence including other patents did not then constitute such a refusal (*Brownie Wireless' Application* (1929) 46 R.P.C. 457); nor, in *Monsanto's CCP Patent* [1990] F.S.R. 93, was an offer of a worldwide licence for a lump sum payment of $1m regarded as unreasonable. Since s.37(2)(d) [1949] referred only to the patentee, it did not apply where an exclusive licensee refused to grant a licence (*Colbourne Engineering's Application* (1955) 72 R.P.C. 169). That still appears to be the case under the present wording.

However, this relevant TRIPS provision (art.31(b)) allows exceptions to the provisions spelled out in subs.(2) for cases of "a national emergency or other circumstances of extreme urgency or in cases of non-commercial use". Such exceptions can be applied (without recourse to s.48A) under the Crown user provisions of ss.55–59 of the Act, expanded by at least the provisions of s.56(2) and possibly by other statutes. TRIPS also provides for an exception "to remedy a practice determined after judicial or administrative process to be anti-competitive" (TRIPS art.31(k)) and this is available under s.51 when the Competition Commission has issued a report finding anti-competitive conduct to exist.

No licence in field of semi-conductor technology (subs.(3))

48A.06   Subsection (3) (in conformity with TRIPS art.31(c)) provides that no licence under s.48A can be granted where the patented invention is "in the field of semi-conductor technology". There is no definition of "the field of semi-conductor technology" and this phrase would seem to be of broader scope than the "semiconductor topography right" which, in any event, is an aspect of the law protecting a "mask work" or computer chip as an unregistered design right, rather than by a patent. However, while the wording is seemingly broad, the principle should apply that, as an exclusionary provision, it should be interpreted narrowly.

There is also an exception to the exclusion imposed by subs.(3) which is in similar, although not identical, terms to the exception to the pre-condition of subs.(2)), that is, an exception in the case of a licence "for public non-commercial use or to remedy a practice determined after judicial or administrative process to be anti-competitive" (see TRIPS art.31(c)). Thus, for a patent in this field, any application for a licence would have to result from a complaint to the Competition Commission, followed by action under s.51, or by the application of Crown user provisions under ss.55–59 or under some other statute providing authority for use of a patent for a "public non-commercial use", for which see the discussion in §48A.05). Thus, where grounds for a compulsory licence might exist under s.48A, but the subject-matter of the patent appears to involve "semi-conductor technology", it would seem prudent also to try and have the Competition Commission investigate the circumstances so that relief could, alternatively, be obtained under s.51.

Failure to meet demand for patented product (subs.(1)(a))

The ground of subs.(1)(a) is that the patented invention is a product and the demand for **48A.07** it is not being adequately met on reasonable terms. It corresponds to former s.48(3)(b)(i), but the additional ground (in former s.48(3)(b)(ii)) that demand in the United Kingdom is "being met to a substantial extent by importation" is not now available under s.48A, but see s.48B(1)(b)(ii) (discussed in §48B.04) if the patent should not be owned by a WTO proprietor and the importation in question comes from a non-WTO country.

The corresponding ground in s.37(2)(b) [1949] referred to the "patented article". It is not clear whether this change was for the purpose only of consistency, or whether any change of meaning was intended. There are numerous references in the Act to a product or patented product (e.g. in ss.2, 4, 36, 44, 45, 60, 61, 62 and 64), and in these sections a product would appear to be anything which has been made, without reference to the manner in which it has been made: that is, an article. However, "article" is used in some sections (e.g. in ss.46, 110, 111 and 122) where the use of "product" might have been equally appropriate. In any case, use of the phrase "where the invention is a product" would seem to have been chosen deliberately to draw a distinction with the term "patented product" used elsewhere in the Act and defined in s.130(1) as:

"a product which is a patented invention or, in relation to a patented process, a product obtained directly by means of the process or to which the process has been applied".

Thus, the phrase here may exclude products resulting from carrying out a patented method or use. The "product" to be considered is, in any event, one described in the patent and not some product which happens to embody, inter alia, the claimed invention, see *Quantel's Patents* BL O/128/90, noted I.P.D. 14010 discussed in §48A.10. The definition of "patented product", which still leaves doubt as to the meaning of "product", is discussed further in §§55.15 and 60.05.

The significance of the reference to "a demand" in s.37(2)(b) [1949] was said to be obscure: under the 1907–46 Acts the expression was "the demand" and it was then established that the demand referred to was the public demand and not that of an individual person or company (*Robin Electric Lamp's Petition* (1915) 32 R.P.C. 202). Whether the present wording has changed this position is unclear. However, it was evident that, though the demand in one particular field might be fully satisfied, an application could be made under the 1949 Act in respect of an unsatisfied demand in another field, and presumably this remains the law, see *Quantel's Patents* (above). Also, it does not seem that the meeting of the demand has to result from the activities of the patentee or his licensees; meeting a demand by an infringing product would also seem to avoid application of the provision.

The demand "on reasonable terms" is that which exists under the prevailing conditions, so that it is irrelevant that price cutting by a licensee might increase the existing demand (*Research Corp's (Carboplatin) Patent* [1990] R.P.C. 663), or that a previous demand has been satisfied (*Cathro's Patent* (1934) 51 R.P.C. 475). A potential future demand is also not relevant (*Cathro's Patent*, above).

An example of a compulsory licence case in which the question of a failure to supply was considered (application failed on the facts) is *Swansea Imports v Carver Technology* BL O/170/04.

Exploitation of another patent prevented or hindered (subss.(1)(b)(i), (4) and (5))

48A.08   The ground under subs.(1)(b)(i) is that the "exploitation" of another patented invention is being "prevented or hindered" by the patent under which the application is made for a compulsory licence, but this prevention or hindrance must be "by reason of" the refusal of the patentee to grant a licence or licences to the applicant "on reasonable terms". This reference to "exploitation" may be a little less restrictive than under the former law (maintained for non-WTO cases by s.48B(1)(d)(ii)) which referred instead to the "working or efficient working" of the invention of the later patent. Otherwise, the current provision is similar. Nevertheless, the required prevention or hindrance must be a direct consequence of the refusal of the patentee to grant a voluntary licence on reasonable terms. Consequently, when application is made on this ground (and/or one made under subs.(1)(b)(ii), as discussed in §48A.09), it must not only be proved that there has been a refusal to grant a voluntary licence, but also that such refusal is the cause of the alleged prevention or hindrance of the exploitation. This would seem to require that it is quite clear that the projected exploitation would constitute an infringement of the first patent. However, if the "other patent" is capable of being exploited in a non-infringing manner, this should not preclude the grant of a licence under subs.(1)(b)(i) because this refers to exploitation of another "patented invention" and not to exploitation merely of "another patent".

Subsection (1)(b)(i), by referring to the exploitation of a patented invention "in the United Kingdom" is not contrary to European law (e.g. as laid down in *EC Commission v United Kingdom* (C-30/90) [1993] R.P.C. 283; [1992] 1 E.C.R. 829) because the purpose of European law is to abolish barriers to trade within the single market of the EEA and the grant of a compulsory licence assists in achieving this overall aim.

However, the grant of a licence under the provision is subject (in conformity with TRIPS art.31(l)) to three conditions which are set out respectively in subss.(1)(b)(i), (4) and (5).

First, subs.(1)(b), in accordance with TRIPS art.31(l)(l)(i)), requires that the applicant must prove, to the satisfaction of the Comptroller, that the other patented invention "involves an important technical advance of considerable economic significance in relation to the invention for which the patent concerned was granted", that is, the patent under which a compulsory licence is being sought. The use of such words as "important" and "considerable" suggest that, in practice, it will be quite difficult to establish this ground for the grant of a compulsory licence. Under the former form of this provision (now still applicable to applications made against a patent not owned by a WTO proprietor and set out in s.48B(1)(d)(ii)), it was only necessary to show that the patent under which a licence was sought made "a substantial contribution to the art", as discussed in §48B.06, and the wording now having effect under s.48A is clearly significantly more restrictive than this.

Secondly (under subs.(4), in conformity with TRIPS art.31(l)(ii)), the Comptroller must be satisfied that the proprietor of this other patent "is able and willing to grant a licence" to the proprietor of the patent under which a compulsory licence is sought, as well as to that proprietor's licensees, with such licences being "on reasonable terms". Section 48B(5) repeats this unchanged requirement in the case of applications where the patent is not owned by a WTO proprietor. Thus, the grant of a compulsory licence under subs.(1)(b)(i) (as well as under s.48B(1)(d)(ii)) requires the grant of a cross-licence under the other patent which meets the above-mentioned criteria, the existence of which prevents or hinders the exploitation, in the United Kingdom, of the invention of the "other patent". However, so long as this reciprocity of licences can be guaranteed if a compulsory licence is granted, it does not appear to be necessary that the applicant is the proprietor of the "other patent": the applicant could be a licensee.

The third condition (imposed by subs.(5), in conformity with TRIPS art.31(l)(iii)) is that any licence granted under the provision to the proprietor of "the other patent" is unassignable except with the assignment of that patent.

Commercial or industrial activities prevented or hindered (subs.(1)(b)(ii))

The ground of subs.(1)(b)(ii) is applicable where it can be shown to the Comptroller's satisfaction that "the establishment or development of commercial or industrial activities in the United Kingdom is unfairly prejudiced". However, the required prejudice must (as with the ground under subs.(1)(b)(i)) be "by reason of" the refusal of the patentee to grant a licence "on reasonable terms", a phrase which is discussed in §48A.08. As the aim of European law is to establish as single market within the EEA, this provision is also not contrary to that law for the same reason as discussed in §48A.08 in relation to the ground of subs.(1)(b)(i). **48A.09**

The phase "development of commercial or industrial activities" in s.37(2)(d)(iii) [1949] was held to include an increase in the size of a business (*Kamborian's Patent* [1961] R.P.C. 403).

Prejudice due to imposed licence conditions (subs.(1)(c))

The ground set out in subs.(1)(c) is applicable irrespective of whether the patentee is, or is not, a WTO proprietor, subs.48B(1)(e) having equivalent wording. **48A.10**

This ground is that, by reason of conditions imposed by the proprietor on the grant of licences under the patent, or on the disposal or use of the patented product or process, the manufacture or use or disposal of materials not protected by the patent or the establishment or development of commercial or industrial activities in the United Kingdom is unfairly prejudiced. As these provisions again refer only to a state of affairs within the United Kingdom, and such state would be exacerbated (rather than restricted) by activities elsewhere in the European Economic Area, this provision meets the rationale of the ECJ decision in *EC Commission v United Kingdom* (C-30/90) [1993] R.P.C. 283; [1992] 1 E.C.R. 829; [1992] 2 C.M.L.R. 709. The wording of the ground resembles that used in s.37(2)(e) [1949] but reference is now made to "disposal" of the product or materials, instead of "sale" thereof. This change is consistent with the definition of infringement enacted in s.60.

The applicant for the compulsory licence has the onus of proving the necessary "unfair prejudice". This must be more than showing a mere wish to exploit the patent, or relying on a statement of advantage contained in the patent (*Monsanto's CCP Patent* [1990] F.S.R. 93). Also, a mere refusal to grant a licence under the patent is not, in itself, an act of unfair prejudice under this provision, see *Quantel's Patents* BL O/128/90, noted I.P.D. 14010. In *Kamborian's Patent* [1961] R.P.C. 403, the phase "development of commercial or industrial activities" (in s.37(2)(d)(iii) [1949]) was held to include an increase in the size of a business, and that would seem to apply under the present provisions of subs.(1)(c) and of s.48B(1)(d)(iii). The terms "patented product" and "patented process" have been discussed in §48A.07.

Where this ground is established, licences may also be granted by the Comptroller to "such customers of the applicant as he thinks fit" (s.49(1)), see §49.02.

Restrictions on terms of licences ordered under the section (subs.(6))

Subsection (6) places five further conditions on the grant of a licence under the section. **48A.11**

Firstly, the licence shall not be exclusive (subs.(6)(a), in conformity with TRIPS art.31(d) which states that the permitted use under the patent "shall be non-exclusive"). This presumably means that the patentee must not find himself fettered by a compulsory licence from exploiting the patent personally or through any licence which may have already been granted or which he may in future wish to grant. However, there is no prohibition as such against a compulsory licence including a power to grant sub-licences, but any such power is likely to be a restricted one, for example to pass licences to use a patented product made by the licensee under the compulsory licence granted. Any such sub-licence is subject to possible termination, as explained under "Fifthly" below.

Secondly, the licence can only be assigned with that part of the applicant's "enterprise" that enjoys the permitted use of the patented invention or the part of the goodwill which comes to belong to that part (subs.(6)(b), in conformity with TRIPS art.31(e) which states that "such use shall be non-assignable, except with that part of the enterprise or goodwill which enjoys such use"). Although differently worded, this provision presumably has similar effect to the provision of s.64(2)(b) in relation to the assignability of a prior user right, for which see §64.07.

Thirdly, the licence is to be "predominantly for the supply of the market in the United Kingdom" (subs.(6)(c), in conformity with TRIPS art.31(f) which states that "any such use shall be authorized predominantly for the supply of the domestic market of the Member authorizing such use". However, it is arguable that the words "domestic market" in the TRIPS provision should have been construed as referring to the "single market" of the EEA in accordance with the prior ECJ decisions in *Allen & Hanbury v Generics (C–434/85)* [1988] F.S.R. 312; [1988] 1 C.M.L.R. 701 and *EC Commission v United Kingdom (C-30/90)* [1993] R.P.C. 283; [1992] 1 E.C.R. 829; [1992] 2 C.M.L.R. 709.

Fourthly, the compulsory licence is to include conditions entitling the patentee "to remuneration adequate to the circumstances of the case, taking into account the economic value of the licence" (subs.(6)(d), in conformity with TRIPS art.31(h)). This provision overrides the provision of s.50(1), which now only applies to cases considered under s.48B, although the other conditions of s.50(1)(b) do apply, for which see §50.02. It remains to be seen how this provision will come to be interpreted, but probably the extensive case lawestablished for the grant of a "licence of right" under s.46 when that section had more relevance than it now does (see §46.04) will be taken into account in assessing the royalty terms for a compulsory licence under s.48A, for which see §§46.11–46.16.

Fifthly, any licence granted has to be "limited in scope and duration to the purpose for which the licence was granted" (subs.(6)(e), in conformity with TRIPS art.31(c)). This means that a licensee under s.48A (and any permitted sub-licensee) is forever at risk that his licence may be terminated, or modified, in the light of changed circumstances, for example if the patentee can satisfy the Comptroller that, if the application were now to be made, it would not succeed, at least on the terms on which the licence was previously granted. The proprietor can (under s.52, as discussed in §52.03), at any time seek a review of the terms of the licence, or its termination.

Indeed, an application can now be made under s.52 for the review of a licence granted under the former form of s.48 on the ground that such a licence would not at the time of such an application be granted under s.48A, see the transitional provisions set out in §48A.03.

Thus, any licence granted under s.48A (or one previously granted under the original form of s.48) has but a temporary character. This again may indicate (as previously noted in §48.03) that at least a concurrent complaint for the Competition Commission to review alleged anti-competitive conduct may be appropriate as this could lead to an order under s.51. As noted in §§48A.05 and 48A.06, such an order could override some of the provisions of s.48A, for example by leading to a "licence of right" entry in the register, thereby permitting settlement of the terms of such a licence under s.46(3)(a). Such terms might not have to comply with the terms of s.48A (and the provisions of TRIPS art.31) because such a licence would technically be with the authorisation of the right holder, thereby excluding it from the terms of this TRIPS article, see its preamble.

SECTION 48B [ADDED]

Compulsory licences: other cases

48B.01   **48B.—(1) In the case of an application made under section 48 above in respect of a patent whose proprietor is not a WTO proprietor, the relevant grounds are—**

   (a) where the patented invention is capable of being commercially

worked in the United Kingdom, that it is not being so worked or is not being so worked to the fullest extent that is reasonably practicable;

    (b) where the patented invention is a product, that a demand for the product in the United Kingdom—

        (i) is not being met on reasonable terms, or

        (ii) is being met to a substantial extent by importation from a country which is not a member State;

    (c) where the patented invention is capable of being commercially worked in the United Kingdom, that it is being prevented or hindered from being so worked—

        (i) where the invention is a product, by the importation of the product from a country which is not a member State,

        (ii) where the invention is a process, by the importation from such a country of a product obtained directly by means of the process or to which the process has been applied;

    (d) that by reason of the refusal of the proprietor of the patent to grant a licence or licences on reasonable terms—

        (i) a market for the export of any patented product made in the United Kingdom is not being supplied, or

        (ii) the working or efficient working in the United Kingdom of any other patented invention which makes a substantial contribution to the art is prevented or hindered, or

        (iii) the establishment or development of commercial or industrial activities in the United Kingdom is unfairly prejudiced;

    (e) that by reason of conditions imposed by the proprietor of the patent on the grant of licences under the patent, or on the disposal or use of the patented product or on the use of the patented process, the manufacture, use or disposal of materials not protected by the patent, or the establishment or development of commercial or industrial activities in the United Kingdom, is unfairly prejudiced.

(2) Where—

    (a) an application is made on the ground that the patented invention is not being commercially worked in the United Kingdom or is not being so worked to the fullest extent that is reasonably practicable; and

    (b) it appears to the comptroller that the time which has elapsed since the publication in the journal of a notice of the grant of the patent has for any reason been insufficient to enable the invention to be so worked,

he may by order adjourn the application for such period as will in his opinion give sufficient time for the invention to be so worked.

(3) No order or entry shall be made under section 48 above in respect of a patent on the ground mentioned in subsection (1)(a) above if

    (a) the patented invention is being commercially worked in a country which is a member State; and

    (b) demand in the United Kingdom is being met by importation from that country.

(4) No entry shall be made in the register under section 48 above on the ground mentioned in subsection (1)(d)(i) above, and any licence granted under section 48 above on that ground shall contain such provisions as appear to the comptroller to be expedient for restricting the countries in which any product concerned may be disposed of or used by the licensee.

(5) No order or entry shall be made under section 48 above in respect of a patent on the ground mentioned in subsection (1)(d)(ii) above unless the comptroller is satisfied that the proprietor of the patent for the other invention is able and willing to grant to the proprietor of the patent concerned and his licensees a licence under the patent for the other invention on reasonable terms.

Note. Section 48B was inserted by the Patents and Trade Marks (World Trade Organisation) Regulations 1999 (SI 1999/1899). This added section has been applied to the Isle of Man by SI 2003/1249.

Commentary on Section 48B

Scope of the section

48B.02   New s.48B, nominally effective from July 29, 1999, applies to an application for a compulsory licence where the owner of the patent in issue is not a "WTO proprietor", as defined in new s.48(5) (reprinted in §48.01) and discussed in §48.04. As the restricted conditions upon which a compulsory licence may be granted when the patent proprietor is within the definition need not apply in other situations, s.48B was introduced largely to retain the former law in situations when the provisions of the arts 30 and 31 of the TRIPS Agreement (reprinted in §48A.02) do not apply.

When the section is applicable, a compulsory licence may be granted if one or more of the individual grounds specified in subs.(1) can be established to the satisfaction of the Comptroller. The grounds available to the applicant in support of the application are limited to those set out in subs.(1)(a)–(e). They are, in principle, that there has been what used to be called an "abuse of monopoly rights". However, these words are not used in the section, and the emphasis is rather that there should be the fullest practical use of a patented invention and that patent rights should be exercised without prejudice to the development of industry. These grounds are individually discussed in §§48B.03–48B.08.

Because these grounds are, in may cases, similar to those which existed under the 1907 and 1949 Acts (as well as under the original form of s.48 until its wording was replaced in 1999 by that now set out in §48.01), decisions under the former statutory provisions may continue to be applicable. The historical evolution of s.37 [1949], and the early cases, were discussed by W. V. Higgs (Trans. Chart. Inst., LXXIII (1954–55), C65).

Section 37 [1949] had as its object the encouragement of manufacture rather than mere selling (*Co-operative Union's Applications* (1933) 50 R.P.C. 161), and presumably this still applies. It may be noted that there is no positive requirement in the Act that a patentee should work his invention or exercise his patent rights in any particular way, but if he (not being a WTO proprietor) embarks on any action or inaction as specified in subs.(1) he opens himself to an application under the section.

However, in conformity with the ECJ decisions in *EC Commission v United Kingdom* (C-30/90) [1993] R.P.C. 283; [1992] 1 E.C.R. 829; [1992] 2 C.M.L.R. 709 ECJ and *Allen & Hanbury v Generics* (C–434/85) [1988] F.S.R. 312; [1988] 1 C.M.L.R. 701, the grounds now specified in subss.(1)(b)(ii) and (1)(c)(i) include limitations in order to avoid the creation of some barrier to trade with another "member State". Although the term "member State" as used in these provisions is not defined as such, their underlying purpose (in accordance with these ECJ decisions) is to refer to any Member State of the European Economic Area, that is to give this term the same meaning as one specifically set out in s.46(3)(c), as amended, and as effectively further amended (see the Note to §46.01).

The grounds for application under the section (subs.(1))

—Insufficient domestic working (subss.(1)(a), (2) and (3))

Ground (a) is that the patent is not being adequately worked (that is not being commercially worked, or not being so worked "to the fullest extent that is reasonably
practicable") in the United Kingdom while being capable of being so worked. Under
subs.(2), the Comptroller has power to adjourn consideration of an application on the
ground of subs.(1)(a) where the time which has elapsed since the publication of the patent
grant "has for any reason been insufficient to enable the invention to be so worked", for
such period as he considers appropriate in order to give sufficient time for the invention to
be so worked. Also, no order (or entry in the register) is to be made under this provision
where the patented invention is being commercially worked in another EEA State when
demand in the United Kingdom is being met by importation from that State (subs.(3)).

48B.03

In *Therma-Tru's Patent* [1997] R.P.C. 777, this ground (under the former s.48) was
seen to cover at least three cases, viz. that the demand for the invention was not being met
at all; that there is a demand which is unsatisfied; and that an existing demand is satisfied
but not to the fullest extent reasonably practicable. The court stated that "once it is shown
that manufacture in the United Kingdom is possible and that demand is being met by
importation", ground (a) is established (although now provided that subs.(3) does not apply); and, if the patentee can show that future United Kingdom manufacture (now
manufacture within the EEA) is in principle likely, the correct procedure should be to adjourn the application under what is now s.48B(2), not to dismiss the application on this
ground as the Comptroller had done.

Apart from the new exclusory provision of subs.(3), ground (a) is the same as that
under s.37(2) [1949]. Thus, the observations on what is meant by the "fullest extent" of
working found in *Kamborian's Patent* [1961] R.P.C. 403 presumably still apply. "Commercially worked" has been given a plain meaning and held to be satisfied by "straightforward manufacture of goods for the purposes of trade" (*Enviro-Spray's Patents* [1986]
R.P.C. 147). Here the proprietor's argument that the invention had been imperfectly
developed for commercial working was rejected, partly because the invention was being
worked abroad and so was "capable of being commercially worked in the United
Kingdom". However, neither a mere statement of potential interest, nor the maintenance
of the patent, is sufficient to prove a capability of commercial working (*Monsanto's CCP
Patent* [1990] F.S.R. 93). A compulsory licence was granted under the equivalent of this
provision in *Gebhart's Patent* [1992] R.P.C. 1 because a United Kingdom licensee had
ceased trading and no other licence had been granted: working in Germany was not then
considered, although this would now be necessary under subs.(3). Here, the patentee was
not allowed time for re-establishment of United Kingdom working following the demise
of the first licensee, it being held that what is now subs.(2) is primarily concerned with allowing time from grant to establish working, and here 11 years had passed.

—Demand not being met or met by importation (subs.(1)(b))

Ground (b) requires it to be established that, in respect of a patented product, either (i) a
demand for that product in the United Kingdom is not being met on reasonable terms; or
(ii) is being met to a substantial extent by importation from a country outside the EEA.
The first (but not the second) of these grounds applies (under s.48A(1)(a)) also when the
patentee is a "WTO proprietor", and has been discussed in §48A.07.

48B.04

As regards ground (ii), only importation from outside the EEA can be considered for
the reason indicated in §48B.02. There appears to be no decision which has explored the
meaning of the phrase "met to a substantial extent by importation", but obviously this
ground can only be applied when an application under subs.(1)(b)(i) would fail because
demand for the patented product is being sufficiently met.

—Commercial working hindered by importation (subs.(1)(c))

48B.05   Grounds (c)(i) and (c)(ii) refers to "working" of an invention, respectively where the invention is a product and where it is a product of an invented process. Whereas ground (a) (as discussed in §48B.03) refers to inadequate working of an invention within the United Kingdom, and ground (b)(ii) (discussed in §48B.04) refers to a "demand" for a patented product being met by importation (other than from an EEA State), ground (c) refers to prevention or hindrance of "working" within the United Kingdom because of the importation (also from outside the EEA) of (i) an invented product, or (ii) the direct product of an invented process or a product to which an invented process has been applied. The words "or to which the process has been applied" were not present in the previous parallel provision of s.37(2)(c) [1949], and would seem to extend the phrase "product obtained directly by means of the process", a phrase which appears in s.60(1)(c), as discussed in §60.07.

Thus, while ground (c) overlaps to some extent with grounds (a) and (b), it predominantly applies when grounds (a) and (b)(i) fail because local manufacture is being "prevented or hindered" because of importation from outside the EEA. However, as with ground (a), it is necessary to establish that the patented invention "is capable of being commercially worked in the United Kingdom" and the powers available under subss.(2) and (3) under ground (a), as discussed in §48B.03, do not apply to ground (c), presumably because the availability of imported material itself indicates that the invention is capable of being worked, at least outside the EEA. *Fette's Patent* [1961] R.P.C. 396 may be relevant on this point.

—Refusal to grant licence on reasonable terms (subs.(1)(d))

48B.06   Ground (d) is that, "by reason of the refusal of the proprietor to grant a licence on reasonable terms", either:

(i) an export market is not being supplied, or

(ii) the working of another substantial invention is prevented or hindered, or

(iii) the establishment of commercial or industrial activities in the United Kingdom is unfairly prejudiced.

It is to be noted that each of these three grounds specifies only to a state of affairs existing in the United Kingdom, as distinct from conduct within the EEA. However, when analysed, this would seem to be correct because none of these grounds provides a barrier to inter-State trade within the EEA which needs to be remedied under the section, bearing in mind that each of the EEA Member States is a WTO member so that s.48B cannot apply where the patentee is domiciled or established within the EEA. However, the Comptroller has power to limit any licence granted under this provision to restrict the countries in which the licensed product can be disposed of or used, as he may consider expedient, see subs.(4).

Ground (d)(i) refers to non-availability of an export market for goods made in the United Kingdom as a result of the patentee's conduct in refusing to grant a licence for such on reasonable terms. However, the ground would seem to require a total non-supply of a product, the subject of a United Kingdom patent, so that a minimal supply of that product may defeat an application under this provision.

In *Penn Engineering's Patent* [1973] R.P.C. 233, in which there had been no manufacture in the United Kingdom and accordingly s.37(2)(a) [1949] (corresponding to s.48B(1)(a)) was satisfied, a licence including power to export was granted. A contention by the patentee that such a licence should not be granted unless a case was made out that there was an unsupplied export market was dismissed, the Patents Appeal Tribunal holding that a provision corresponding to present s.48B(1)(d)(i) applied only to cases in which an export market for goods made in the United Kingdom was not being satisfied, thus partly overruling *Brownie Wireless' Application* (1929) 46 R.P.C. 457.

Ground (d)(ii) refers to "the working or efficient working of any other patented invention which makes a substantial contribution to the art" being "prevented or hindered". Although this provision is more liberal than that which applies to the grant of a licence under a dominating patent to permit operation of a later patent ("the other patent", the commentary on s.48A(1)(b)(i) (in §48A.08) has some relevance under s.48B(1)(d)(ii). However, "the other patent" need only make a "substantial contribution to the art". This has, of course, to be assessed on the evidence, but the provision protects the patentee against claims for compulsory licences by third parties merely with minor advances to their credit. There appear to be no decisions on the meaning of "substantial contribution to the art". Moreover, the restriction on the grant of a licence under s.48B(1)(d)(ii) is limited to requiring it established that the patentee for "the other patent" is "able and willing" to grant to the proprietor of the patent, under which a compulsory licence is sought, a cross-licence "on reasonable terms", see subs.(5).

Ground (d)(iii) refers to "the establishment or development of commercial or industrial activities in the United Kingdom being prevented or hindered". This ground is also available under s.48A (see s.48A(1)(b)(ii)) and the contents of §48A.09 therefore also apply under s.48B.

—Prejudice due to imposed licence conditions (subs. (1)(e))

Ground (e) extends ground (d)(iii) to a situation where "the manufacture, use or **48B.07** development of commercial or industrial activities within the United Kingdom" is "unfairly prejudiced" "by reason of conditions" imposed by the patentee on the grant of licences under the patent, or on the disposal or use of the patented process or use of the patented process. This ground also applies under s.48A, and therefore the contents of §48A.10 apply likewise under s.48B.

Cases decided under the 1977 Act

Relatively few applications were made under the former form of s.48 and the decisions **48B.08** have to be treated with caution because of the differences in the more restricted grounds available under whichever of ss.48A or 48B apply.

An early case was *Extrude Hone's Patent* [1982] R.P.C. 361 and [1984] R.P.C. 105 with the full terms of the licence granted being set out in the latter report.

In *Penn Engineering's Patent* [1973] R.P.C. 233, a licence to export was ordered despite the existence of an exclusive licence which precluded the patentee himself from granting such a licence.

In *Monsanto's CCP Patent* [1990] F.S.R. 93, the application failed because the applicant failed to discharge the onus upon him, partly because the licence was needed to allow the applicant's customers to work the invention and there was insufficient evidence that this would be done, there being no evidence from the prospective customer on whose behalf a licence was also sought under s.49, see §49.02.

In *Montgomerie Reid's Application* BL O/145/83, noted I.P.D. 5112 the only real dispute concerned the rate of royalty. The invention was a particular mechanism for a forklift truck and the expert evidence on the two sides led to widely disparate views on the appropriate royalty. It was held that the royalty must be one which the applicant was capable of bearing, even if the patentee was entitled to reasonable remuneration (s.50(1)(b)), and that this should be determined as that which would be negotiated between a willing licensor and a willing licensee. The conclusion was that the royalty should be based on five per cent of the value of the mechanism which was seen "as close to the lower end of the general range for invention in the mechanical field". However, as this mechanism was not sold separately, it was then estimated that the mechanism contributed 20 per cent. to the price of the truck and, accordingly, the royalty was fixed at "1 per cent. of the full ex-works selling price of each truck falling within the claims of the patent".

A further case under the Act is *Enviro-Spray's Patents* [1986] R.P.C. 147 mentioned in §48B.03.

SECTION 49

Provisions about licences under section 48

49.01 **49.**—(1) Where the comptroller is satisfied, on an application made under section 48 above in respect of a patent, that the manufacture, use or disposal of materials not protected by the patent is unfairly prejudiced by reason of conditions imposed by the proprietor of the patent on the grant of licences under the patent, or on the disposal or use of the patented product or the use of the patented process, he may (subject to the provisions of that section) order the grant of licences under the patent to such customers of the applicant as he thinks fit as well as to the applicant.

(2) Where an application under section 48 above is made in respect of a patent by a person who holds a licence under the patent, the comptroller—

(a) may, if he orders the grant of a licence to the applicant, order the existing licence to be cancelled, or

(b) may, instead of ordering the grant of a licence to the applicant, order the existing licence to be amended.

[(3) *Where, on an application under section 48 above in respect of a patent, the comptroller orders the grant of a licence, he may direct that the licence shall operate—*

(a) *to deprive the proprietor of the patent of any right he has to work the invention concerned or grant licences under the patent;*

(b) *to revoke all existing licences granted under the patent.*]

(4) Section 46(4) and (5) above shall apply to a licence granted in pursuance of an order under section 48 above and to a licence granted by virtue of an entry under that section as it applies to a licence granted by virtue of an entry under section 46 above.

Note. Subsection (3) was repealed by Sch.5 para.13 CDPA 1988 and Sch.8 CDPA 1988, with effect from August 1, 1989 (SI 1989/816).

COMMENTARY ON SECTION 49

Scope of the section

49.02 Subsection (1) gives the Comptroller power to grant licences to customers of an applicant under s.48 (in addition to the applicant himself) where the applicant successfully establishes the ground that the use or disposal of materials not covered by the patent is unfairly prejudiced by the action of the proprietor of the patent in regard to the granting of licences, that is where an application succeeds under either of ss.48A(1)(c) or 48B(1)(e). Such a licence will be in such terms as the Comptroller sees fit, subject to the other provisions of ss.48–48B, and the provisions of s.50 presumably apply also.

However, in *Monsanto's Patent* BL O/45/88, it was held that the applicant should not be granted a licence permitting it to sell unpatented solvent with the right to pass therewith a licence to customers to use this in manufacturing the patented product. It was stated that the customers would need to be named in the compulsory licence application or be a party to it. The fact that the supply of the solvent would be an act of infringement of the patent under s.60(2) or s.60(3) did not mean that this is part of the protection conferred by the patent (as referred to in s.125(1)). The applicant then sought a licence for a named potential customer, but the application was refused (under s.50(2)(b)) because the Comptroller was not satisfied that this customer would work the invention if the licence were granted (*Monsanto's CCP Patent* [1990] F.S.R. 93). However, for the grant to customers of a "licence of right" under s.46, see *Suspa-Federungstechnik's Patent* BL O/113/85, noted I.P.D. 8084.

Subsection (2) refers to the case where an application is made under s.48 and where the applicant is already a licensee under the patent. It empowers the Comptroller either (a) to cancel the existing licence when ordering a new licence, or (b) to amend the existing licence.

Subsection (3) was deleted by the Copyright, Designs and Patents Act 1988 ("CDPA 1988"). It had provided for the possibility of the Comptroller ordering a compulsory licence to be exclusive, even of the patentee. However, operation of the provision appears never to have been seriously considered and its existence was an embarrassment to the Government in resisting the implementation of similar provisions by some developing nations.

Subsection (4) provides that s.46(4) and (5), giving a licensee who has obtained a "licence of right" the power to sue for infringement, shall apply to a licensee under a compulsory licence granted under s.48. For further discussion on this provision, see §46.17.

An appeal lies under s.49 as it does under s.48 and likewise an order for a licence under s.49 operates as a deed (s.108), see §§48.06 and 48.05 respectively.

Effect of treaty obligations

Section 49 is governed by the further provisions of s.53 and therefore, by virtue of **49.03** s.53(5), as discussed in §53.05, no compulsory licence can be granted which would offend the provisions of art.101 of the TFEU or of the EPC. It would appear that this provision also requires compliance with the TRIPS Agreement so that any defect in the wording of ss.48 and 48A (but not s.48B) in relation to the wording of this Agreement would have to be ignored, see *Allen & Hanbury v Controller of Patents* [Ireland] [1997] F.S.R. 1.

SECTION 50

Exercise of powers on applications under section 48

50.—(1) The powers of the comptroller on an application under section 48 **50.01** above in respect of a patent **whose proprietor is not a WTO proprietor** shall be exercised with a view to securing the following general purposes—

    (a) that inventions which can be worked on a commercial scale in the United Kingdom and which should in the public interest be so worked shall be worked there without undue delay and to the fullest extent that is reasonably practicable;

    (b) that the inventor or other person beneficially entitled to a patent shall receive reasonable remuneration having regard to the nature of the invention;

    (c) that the interests of any person for the time being working or developing an invention in the United Kingdom under the protection of a patent shall not be unfairly prejudiced.

(2) Subject to subsection (1) above, the comptroller shall, in determining whether to make an order or entry in pursuance of **any application under section 48 above** [*such an application*], take account of the following matters, that is to say—

    (a) the nature of the invention, the time which has elapsed since the publication in the journal of a notice of the grant of the patent and the measures already taken by the proprietor of the patent or any licensee to make full use of the invention;

(b) the ability of any person to whom a licence would be granted under the order concerned to work the invention to the public advantage; and

(c) the risks to be undertaken by that person in providing capital and working the invention if the application for an order is granted,

but shall not be required to take account of matters subsequent to the making of the application.

Note. Subsections (1) and (2) were each amended as indicated by the Patents and Trade Marks (World Trade Organisation) Regulations 1999 (SI 1999/1899). The amendments noted for subss.(1) and (2) were each applied to the Isle of Man by SI 2003/1249.

COMMENTARY ON SECTION 50

Scope of the section

50.02   Section 50 sets out the objects and principles which are to be considered by the Comptroller when settling the terms of a licence granted under s.48. While the considerations set out in subs.(2), (as discussed in §50.03) apply to applications made on any patent, the considerations to be taken into account under subs.(1), as discussed in §50.03, now only apply to applications proceeding under s.48B, that is where the patentee is not a "WTO proprietor" (on which see §48.04). This is because the objects specified in subs.(1)(a) and (c) are directed to activities in the United Kingdom and thus are contrary to the principle of the TRIPS Agreement requiring equal treatment for persons domiciled in all WTO States. However, the principle set out in subs.(1)(b), of reasonable remuneration for the patentee when a compulsory licence is to be granted, has its counterpart in s.48A(6)(d) (discussed in §48A.11) when the patent is owned by a "WTO proprietor".

Whether or not the proprietor is a "WTO proprietor", the objects and principles set out in either of the subsections must be exercised in conformity with the overriding principle of Community law (enshrined in arts 34–36, 101 and 102 of the TFEU, reprinted in §§D03–D07 and discussed in §§D13–D16) that there should be free trade between the Member States of the European Economic Area. However, the wording of ss.48A and 48B does seem to be in compliance with this principle as indicated in the commentaries on these sections, but should there be doubt on any point this principle must prevail under the wide powers given to the Comptroller, particularly that of s.53(5), discussed in §53.05. This provides that no order may be made under s.48 or s.50 which is at variance with any treaty or international convention. This, of course, includes the TFEU. Thus, the principle of free trade between the EEA States can be expected to be incorporated into the terms of any compulsory licence, whether granted under s.48A or s.48B.

As the terms of s.50 have been held relevant to the terms upon which a "licence of right" should be settled by the Comptroller under s.46 (*Allen & Hanbury's v Generics* [1986] R.P.C. 203 HL), the decisions given under s.46 on such "settlement" applications may have relevance to the application of s.50 to the grant of compulsory licences under s.48. These decisions are discussed in §§46.06–46.20.

Grant of compulsory licences (subs.(1))

50.03   Subsection (1) sets out the general purposes of, or objects which underlie, the grant of a compulsory licence (under s.48B) in the rare case that the patent is not owned by a "WTO proprietor". These are that: (a) inventions which can be worked in the United Kingdom should be worked promptly and fully, where such working is in the public interest; (b) the inventor or beneficial owner shall be reasonably remunerated; and (c) the interests of anyone working or developing an invention in the United Kingdom under the protection of a patent shall not be unfairly prejudiced.

Although the words "United Kingdom" have been retained in subs.(1)(a) and subs.(1)(a), it is probable that, in practice, these words should be notionally replaced by "the European Economic Area" for the reason explained in §50.02. This is because a clear preference for United Kingdom manufacture over foreign manufacture is likely to be taken as contrary to the terms of the Community and EEA Treaties unless by "foreign manufacture" is meant manufacture which has taken place outside the EEA.

In *Therma-Tru's Patent* [1997] R.P.C. 777, the Comptroller was not satisfied that the applicant had demonstrated that it was in the public interest that local working under a compulsory licence should be permitted, although so far working had been solely by importation. However, on appeal, the Patents Court stated that there was no overlying discretion and that, once the Comptroller is satisfied that a ground for a licence had been made out, no further hurdle under s.50(1) had to be overcome, but the balancing operation required by s.50(2) must be carried out and, if this shows that the general purposes set out in subs.(1) were best achieved by the grant of a licence on particular terms, the Comptroller should grant a licence.

In *Montgomerie Reid's Application* BL O/145/83, it was held that the royalty for a compulsory licence under s.48 should be one that would be negotiated between a willing licensor and a willing licensee. Subsequently, this principle was held also to be that to be applied in settling the terms of a "licence of right" under s.46(3), see *Allen & Hanbury's v Generics* [1986] R.P.C. 203 HL. Thus, the criteria employed for settling the terms of a licence of right under s.46(3) (as discussed in §§46.06–46.20) may be expected to have general applicability to the application of s.50 under either s.48A or s.48B, subject of course to the specific provisions thereof.

However, in the *Montgomerie Reid* case (above), it was held that the royalty to be paid for the licence should be such that the applicant would be able to bear it, but s.50(1)(b) requires a non-WTO proprietor to receive "reasonable remuneration", while s.48A(6)(d) requires a WTO proprietor to receive "remuneration adequate in the circumstances of the case, taking into account the economic value of the licence". Also, as it was subsequently held (*Research Corp's (Carboplatin) Patent* [1990] R.P.C. 663) that it is not a relevant consideration that the licensee (under a "licence of right") can trade profitably at the royalty rate settled, it is submitted that this principle should also be applied to a compulsory licence under either s.48A or s.48B.

Principles for grant of compulsory licences (subs.(2))

Subsection (2) sets out the matters, or principles, upon which the Comptroller is to exercise his power to grant compulsory licences and fix the terms thereof, whether or not the patent is owned by a "WTO proprietor". The subsection requires the Comptroller, in coming to a decision, to take account of: (a) the nature of the invention, the time which has elapsed since grant, and the action of the proprietor or licensee in developing full use of the invention; (b) the ability of the intending licensee to work the invention to the public advantage; and (c) the risks to be taken by that person in providing capital and working the invention. However, account need not be taken of matters subsequent to the filing of the application.

50.04

In subs.(2)(a), the reference to the time which has elapsed since publication of the notice of grant indicates, in the light of the fact that an application can be made under s.48 at any time after three years from grant, that the Comptroller is empowered to give the proprietor further time. The former corresponding provision (s.39(2)(a) of the 1949 Act) was considered in *Hamson's Application* [1958] R.P.C. 88.

In *Enviro-Spray's Patents* [1986] R.P.C. 147, a licence was refused because the applicant had not demonstrated to the Comptroller's satisfaction (as required by subs.(2)(b)) that he was capable of working satisfactorily a licence found to be justified under what is now s.48B(1)(a). It was pointed out that an applicant for a compulsory licence had an obligation to explain as far as possible what he expected to do and put the Comptroller in a position where he can form some estimate of the licensee's likelihood of achieving that aim; and terms, which would effectively defer a decision on whether or not to grant a licence, could not form part of a licence granted under ss.48 and 48. Also, in *Monsanto's CCP Patent* [1990] F.S.R. 93, a licence was refused partly because the Comptroller was not satisfied that the proposed licensee would work the patent; see §49.02 further on this case. This principle of the licensee having to satisfy the Comptroller that, if granted, the licence would be worked would seem applicable to any ground upon which a compulsory licence can now be granted, particularly in the case of a WTO proprietor having regard to the terms of s.48A(6), discussed in §48A.11.

In *Halcon's Patents* [1989] R.P.C. 1, the applicant was permitted to attack the validity of the patent as the extent to which the claimed process represented a major advance would be a factor in settling an appropriate royalty.

The final words of subs.(2) are to the effect that the Comptroller need not take into account any action by the proprietor subsequent to the application under s.48. This means that a proprietor who remedies his errors after such an application may not thereby be protected. These words were noted in *Halcon's Patent* (above) with regard to a refusal to order discovery of a licence agreement offered to the applicant after the making of the application. However, the wording of the subsection is permissive, and merely relieves the Comptroller of being "required" to take this into account. In such an event subs.(1)(c) might nevertheless be relevant.

SECTION 50A [ADDED]

Powers exercisable following merger and market investigations

50A.01 **50A.**—(1) Subsection (2) below applies where—

(a) section 41(2), 55(2), 66(6), 75(2), 83(2), 138(2), 147(2) or 160(2) of, or paragraph 5(2) or 10(2) of Schedule 7 to, the Enterprise Act 2002 (powers to take remedial action following merger or market investigations) applies;

(b) the Competition Commission or (as the case may be) the Secretary of State considers that it would be appropriate to make an application under this section for the purpose of remedying, mitigating or preventing a matter which cannot be dealt with under the enactment concerned; and

(c) the matter concerned involves

(i) conditions in licences granted under a patent by its proprietor restricting the use of the invention by the licences; or

(ii) a refusal by the proprietor of a patent to grant licences on reasonable terms.

(2) The Competition Commission or (as the case may be) the Secretary of State may apply to the comptroller to take action under this section.

(3) Before making an application the Competition Commission or (as the case may be) the Secretary of State shall publish, in such manner as it or he thinks appropriate, a notice describing the nature of the proposed application and shall consider any representations which may be made within 30 days of such publication by persons whose interests appear to it or him to be affected.

(4) The comptroller may, if it appears to him on an application under this section that the application is made in accordance with this section, by order cancel or modify any condition concerned of the kind mentioned in subsection (1)(c)(i) above or may, instead or in addition, make an entry in the register to the effect that licences under the patent are to be available as of right.

(5) References in this section to the Competition Commission shall, in cases where section 75(2) of the Enterprise Act 2002 applies, be read as references to the Office of Fair Trading.

(6) References in section 35, 36, 47, 63, 134 or 141 of the Enterprise Act

2002 (questions to be decided by the Competition Commission in its reports) to taking action under section 41(2), 55, 66, 138 or 147 shall include references to taking action under subsection (2) above.

(7) Action taken by virtue of subsection (4) above in consequence of an application under subsection (2) above where an enactment mentioned in subsection (1)(a) above applies shall be treated, for the purposes of sections 91(3), 92(1)(a), 162(1) and 166(3) of the Enterprise Act 2002 (duties to register and keep under review enforcement orders etc.), as if it were the making of an enforcement order (within the meaning of the Part concerned) under the relevant power in Part 3 or (as the case may be) 4 of that Act.

Note. Section 50A was added by the Enterprise Act 2002 (c.40) Sch.25 para 8. Under the Enterprise Act 2002 (Protection of Legitimate Interests) Order 2003 (SI 2003/1592), s.50A(1)(a) has effect as if it included references to art.12(7) of, and para.5(2) and 10(2) of Sch.2 thereof; and in subs.(6), the references to ss.63 and 66 of the Enterprise Act 2002 (c.40) have effect as if they included (respectively) references to arts 6 and 12 of this Order; and, in subs.(7), the reference to Pt 3 of the Enterprise Act 2002 also has effect as if it included a reference to that Order.

COMMENTARYON SECTION 50A

Scope of the section

Added s.50A, which took effect on June 20, 2003, expands the scope of s.51 (and also relocates some of the provisions of s.51) by providing that, in certain circumstances, the Competition Commission, or the Secretary of State (as the case may be), can apply to the Comptroller for him to vary the terms of a licence under a patent or to make an entry in the register of patents that licences under the patent are to available as of right. The circumstances under which s.50A applies is where a decision has been made, or a report issued by the Competition Commission or the Secretary of State (as the case may be) each acting under the terms of the Enterprise Act 2002 (c.40) that a merger situation, or marketing activities, may have an adverse effect on the public and, accordingly, that some remedial action is desirable in relation to the exercise of patent rights or for the variation of conditions in an existing patent licence. These powers are wider in effect than those under the form of s.51 which existed prior to its amendment as a consequence of the addition of s.50A (for which see §51.01). This is because the terms of the Enterprise Act 2002 (c.40) are considerably more extensive, particularly as regards mergers and marketing activities, than those which were previously applied under the terms of the Competition Act 1980 (c.21). Section 53(2) has been consequentially amended to provide that reports made under Pts 3 or 4 of the Enterprise Act 2002 shall also be prima facie (or sufficient) evidence of the matters stated. Section 52 governs the procedure for opposition, arbitration and appeal under this section. **50A.02**

PRACTICE UNDER SECTION 50A

Applications under subs.2

An application must be preceded by a 30-day notice period of the intention to file an application, during which notice period the Competition Commission or Secretary of State must consider representations made by interested parties (subs.(3)). An application by the Competition Commission or (as the case may be) the Secretary of State pursuant to subs.(2) must follow the procedure set out in Pt 7 of the Rules for hearings before the Comptroller. The application must be made on PF 2 (r.76(3)(b)) and be accompanied, inter alia, by a statement of grounds upon which the applicant replies, both in duplicate (r.76(1)). The Comptroller will then notify the proprietor of the patent (and, if deemed appropriate, any interested party) that proceedings have been started (r.77(1)). The proprietor will be sent a copy of the application (r.77(4)), and will have a period of four weeks **50A.03** from the date of the advertisement of the application in the *Patents Journal* to file any counter-statement (r.77(8)). For more detail on the opposition procedure, see the discussion at §§52.06 et seq.

SECTION 51 [SUBSTITUTED]

Powers exercisable in consequence of report of Competition [Monopolies and Mergers] Commission

51.01   **51.—(1) Where a report of the Competition [*Monopolies and Mergers*] Commission has been laid before Parliament containing conclusions to the effect—**

[(a) *on a monopoly reference, that a monopoly situation exists and facts found by the Commission operate or may be expected to operate against the public interest,*

(b) *on a merger reference, that a merger situation qualifying for investigation has been created and the creation of the situation, or particular elements in or consequences of it specified in the report, operate or may be expected to operate against the public interest,*]

(c) **on a competition reference, that a person was engaged in an anti-competitive practice which operated or may be expected to operate against the public interest, or**

(d) **on a reference under section 11 of the Competition Act 1980 [c. 21] (reference of public bodies and certain other persons), that a person is pursuing a course of conduct which operates against the public interest,**

the appropriate Minister or Ministers may apply to the comptroller to take action under this section.

(2) Before making an application the appropriate Minister or Ministers shall publish, in such manner as he or they think appropriate, a notice describing the nature of the proposed application and shall consider any representations which may be made within 30 days of such publication by persons whose interests appear to him or them to be affected.

(2A) Where—

(a) **on a reference under section 5 of the Competition Act 1980, a report of the Commission, as laid before Parliament, contains conclusions to the effect that—**

(i) **any person was engaged in an anti-competitive practice in relation to a description of goods which consist of or include patented products or in relation to a description of services in which a patented product or process is used, and**

(ii) **that practice operated or might be expected to operate against the public interest; or**

(b) **on a reference under section 11 of that Act, such a report contains conclusions to the effect that—**

(i) **any person is pursuing a course of conduct in relation to such a description of goods or services, and**

(ii) **that course of conduct operates against the public interest,** the appropriate Minister or Ministers may, subject to subsection (3) below, apply to the comptroller for relief under subsection (5A) below in respect of the patent.

(3) If on an application under this section it appears to the comptroller that the matters specified in the Commission's report as being those which in the Commission's opinion operate, or operated or may be expected to operate, against the public interest include—

(a) conditions in licences granted under a patent by its proprietor restricting the use of the invention by the licensee or the right of the proprietor to grant other licences, or

(b) a refusal by the proprietor of a patent to grant licences on reasonable terms

he may by order cancel or modify any such condition or may, instead or in addition, make an entry in the register to the effect that licences under the patent are to be available as of right.

(4) In this section "the appropriate Minister or Ministers" means the Minister or Ministers to whom the report of the Commission was made.

Notes

1. This form of the section was substituted for its former wording by Sch.5 para.14 to the CDPA 1988, with effect from August 1, 1989 (SI 1989/816) with the words "Monopolies and Mergers Commission" being changed to "Competition Commission" by SI 1999/506, as from April 1, 1999. Previously, the original wording of the section had been amended by the Competition Act 1980 (c.21) s.14, but this original wording had no continuing effect.

2. The wording of s.11 of the Competition Act 1980 (c.21), referred to in subs.(1)(d) has been amended in several respects by subsequent Acts.

3. Section 51(1)(a) and (b) have now ceased to have effect (Enterprise Act 2002 (c.40) Sch.15 para.8(3)), but the powers provided by these provisions are now to be found, in expanded form, in the added s.50A (reprinted in §50A.01) as briefly discussed in §50A.02.

4. The amendments noted for the title and subs.(1) were each applied to the Isle of Man by SI 2003/1249.

COMMENTARY ON SECTION 51

Scope of the section

Section 51 concerns the right of a Government Minister to apply for a licence under a **51.02** patent, or seek an entry in the register that licences are obtainable as of right, in each case when a report of the Competition Commission has been laid before Parliament under the responsibility of that Minister.

The wording of the section was totally revised (though not amended in substance) by the CDPA 1988 in order to consolidate the previous wording which had been augmented over its original wording by amendments made by the Competition Act 1980 (c.21) s.14, see note to §51.01, although many of the provisions of this Act (although not the substance of its s.11) have been replaced by provisions in the Competition Act 1998 (c.41), in force from March 1, 2000, see §44.03.

In addition to the powers given to a Minister under the section, a government department is enabled to make an application for a compulsory licence to be granted to a specified person under s.48(1)(c), or more generally under s.48(1)(a) for a licence under the patent or s.48(1)(b), for a "licence of right" entry to be made in the register, each as discussed in §48.05. However, any application under s.48 can only result in a licence, or entry in the register, where one or more grounds is established under s.48A(1) or s.48B(1) as the case may be according to whether the patent proprietor is or is not a "WTO proprietor", on which see §48.04.

While under s.90 of the Fair Trading Act 1973 (c.41) a Minister has a general power to declare things unlawful if found contrary to the public interest and to prohibit the carrying out of existing agreements, he is not permitted thereby to cancel or modify conditions in licences granted by the proprietor of a patent or registered design, or to require licences to be available as of right (s.90(5) of that Act). These effects can now be achieved by action taken under the current form of s.51 as substituted by the CDPA 1988. At the same time the CDPA 1988 also created powers analogous to those now provided by the substituted s.51 in respect of other forms of intellectual property, viz. for registered designs (by s.270 of the CDPA 1988, inserting a new s.11A in the Registered Designs Act 1949 (c.88), see Sch.4 para.11A to the CDPA 1988); for design rights (by s.238 of the CDPA 1988); and for copyrights (by s.144 of the CDPA 1988). These increased powers were presumably provided because it was thought that there was a need which was not met by the terms of the Fair Trading Act (s.90), for which see the Reports on the Ford Motor Company (Cmnd.9437) (noted *Re Ford's Replacement Parts* [1986] F.S.R. 147) and that on the policy of the British Broadcasting Corporation as regards listings of television programmes (Cmnd.9614). The form of the section at the time did not permit the application of s.51 to the situation (which in each of these cases involved copyrights, rather than patents) and so far it appears that no use has been made of the section, in whatever form.

Relevant conclusions of the Competition Commission (subs.(1))

51.03   Subsection (1) now operates when a report of the Competition Commission (set up under the Competition Act 1998, c.41) has been laid before Parliament containing conclusions which arise from a reference to that Commission of one of the following types:

(a) a "competition reference," that is one now made by way of appeal to the Competition Commission from a decision of the Director General of Fair Trading under either Ch.I or II of Pt 1 of the Competition Act 1998 (c.41); or

(b) a reference under s.11 of the Competition Act 1980 (c.21), as this section stands amended by various subsequent statutory provisions.

The offending conclusions which arise from any such reference are that a situation, practice or course of conduct exists which "operates against the public interest"; or, in the case of a reference under (c), which "may be expected to operate against the public interest".

Such a report from the Competition Commission will be addressed to a particular government Minister or Ministers, and it is only such a person (or persons) who can then take advantage of the provisions of the section by making an application to the Comptroller (subs.(4)).

The now-repealed provisions relating to "monopoly" and "merger" references are now the subject of a separate s.50A, for details of which see §51.01, above.

Procedure under section 51

51.04   When a Competition Commission report, which contains a conclusion as indicated in §51.03, has been laid before Parliament, the relevant "Minister or Ministers" (i.e. the Minister or Ministers to whom the report is made (subs.(4)) may propose taking action under the section, but before so doing an appropriate notice of intention has to be published, in such manner as the Minister(s) think appropriate, and 30 days allowed for representations to be made by any person "whose interests appear to be affected" (subs.(2)), e.g. by the patentee or a licensee under the patent. The Minister(s) must consider any representations so made. Thereafter, the Minister(s) may make application to the

Comptroller for him to take action under the section. An application can also be made to the Comptroller for exercise by him of similar powers in respect of other forms of intellectual property; see §51.02. The procedure for such an application is described in §51.06 and, despite already having had the opportunity to make representations to the Minister, the patentee, and/or other interested parties (e.g. licensees) can lodge formal opposition to the s.51 application, as noted in §§51.05 and 51.06.

Powers of the Comptroller (subs.(3))

On application duly made to him by a Minister under subss.(1) and (2), the practice for **51.05** which is discussed in §51.06, the Comptroller may order the cancellation or modification of any conditions in licences granted under the patent (and/or other forms of intellectual property) which either restrict the use of the invention by the licensee or the right of the proprietor to grant other licences (subs.(3)(a)), if such condition has been found by the Competition Commission to operate against the public interest. Surprisingly, the provisions of s.108 (Order to take effect as licence under deed) do not appear to extend to a licence granted or modified by order under s.51.

Alternatively, the Comptroller may order a "licence of right" entry to be made in the register in respect of the patent(s) in issue (subs.(3)(b)). In this case, any person may then seek a licence under the patent which the Comptroller will settle, if necessary, under s.46(3)(a), for which see §§46.06–46.20, which the patentee and/or licensees will be able to oppose even if they had previously made representations to the Minister(s) under subs.(2).

However, by virtue of s.53(5) (discussed in §53.05), the Comptroller may not make any order under s.51 which would not conform with the provisions of the TRIPS Agreement. Thus, where the patent in issue is owned by a "WTO proprietor" the provisions of art.31 of the TRIPS Agreement (reprinted in §48A.02) would have to be respected. Nevertheless, the exceptions stated in art.31(b), (c) and (k), especially those specified in art.31(k), may allow some types of order to be made under s.51 which would not be permissible in an application made under s.48 with grounds required to be established under s.48A(1).

Analogous powers to those of s.51 for patents now exist for registered designs, design rights and copyrights, as noted in §51.02.

PRACTICE UNDER SECTION 51

The procedure is as set out in Pt 7 of the Rules. An application under s.51 is to be made **51.06** on PF 2 and is to be accompanied by a statement of grounds (both in duplicate) containing, inter alia, the facts on which the applicant relies. The procedure is thereafter as set out from r.77 onwards and is the same as with an application under s.48, for which see §48.08, with statements contained in a report of the Competition Commission being taken to be prima facie evidence of it; see s.53(2) and §53.03.

By s.52, opposition to the application can be filed, the procedure for which see §§52.06–52.08.

SECTION 52 [SUBSTITUTED]

Opposition, appeal and arbitration

52.—(1) The proprietor of the patent concerned or any other person wish- 52.01 ing to oppose an application under sections 48 to 51 above may, in accordance with rules, give to the comptroller notice of opposition; and the comptroller shall consider the opposition in deciding whether to grant the application.

(2) Where an order or entry has been made under section 48 above in respect of a patent whose proprietor is a WTO proprietor—

(a) the proprietor or any other person may, in accordance with rules,

apply to the comptroller to have the order revoked or the entry cancelled on the grounds that the circumstances which led to the making of the order or entry have ceased to exist and are unlikely to recur,

(b) any person wishing to oppose an application under paragraph (a) above may, in accordance with rules, give to the comptroller notice of opposition; and

(c) the comptroller shall consider any opposition in deciding whether to grant the application.

(3) If it appears to the comptroller on an application under subsection (2)(a) above that the circumstances which led to the making of the order or entry have ceased to exist and are unlikely to recur, he may—

(a) revoke the order or cancel the entry; and

(b) terminate any licence granted to a person in pursuance of the order or entry subject to such terms and conditions as he thinks necessary for the protection of the legitimate interests of that person.

(4) Where an appeal is brought—

(a) from an order made by the comptroller in pursuance of an application under sections 48 to 51 above;

(b) from a decision of his to make an entry in the register in pursuance of such an application;

(c) from a revocation or cancellation made by him under subsection (3) above; or

(d) from a refusal of his to make such an order, entry, revocation or cancellation,

the Attorney General, the appropriate Law Officer within the meaning of section 4A of the Crown Suits (Scotland) Act 1857 [c. 44] or the Attorney General for Northern Ireland, or such other counsel as any of them may appoint, shall be entitled to appear and be heard.

(5) Where an application under sections 48 to 51 above or subsection (2) above is opposed, and either—

(a) the parties consent, or

(b) the proceedings require a prolonged examination of documents or any scientific or local investigation which cannot in the opinion of the comptroller conveniently be made before him,

the comptroller may at any time order the whole proceedings, or any question or issue of fact arising in them, to be referred to an arbitrator or arbiter agreed on by the parties or, in default of agreement, appointed by the comptroller.

(6) Where the whole proceedings are so referred, unless the parties otherwise agree before the award of the arbitrator or arbiter is made, an appeal shall lie from the award to the court.

(7) Where a question or issue of fact is so referred, the arbitrator or arbiter shall report his findings to the comptroller.

Note. The section was substituted for the original form (as amended by SI 1978/621) to apply to the Isle of Man, and by the Arbitration Act 1996 (c.21) by the Patents and Trade

Marks (World Trade Organisation) Regulations 1999 (SI 1999/1899) consequent with the substitution of original s.48 by new ss.48, s.48A and s.48B. This substituted section was applied to the Isle of Man by SI 2003/1249 with changes to subs.(4) deleting "or" after "1857 [c. 44]" and adding after "Northern Ireland" the words "or the Attorney General for the Isle of Man".

COMMENTARY ON SECTION 52

Scope of the section

Section 52 permits opposition by a proprietor or any other person wishing to oppose an application under any of ss.48–51. Such other person could be an existing licensee under the patent. The new form of the section (in compliance with TRIPS arts 30 and 31) extends the previous provisions so that the section now not only deals with an opposition to the making of an order for a compulsory licence or the entry in the register that the patent is subject to "licences of right" (covered by subs.(1)), but also extends (but only where the patentee is a "WTO proprietor", for which see §48.04) to an application for revocation of such an order or cancellation of any such entry in the register: **52.02**

"on the grounds that the circumstances which led to the making of the order or entry have ceased to exist and are unlikely to recur" (see subs.(2)).

Under subs.(3), a successful application under s.52(2)(a) can lead to such revocation or cancellation, as well as the termination of any licence already granted, but subject to such terms and conditions as the Comptroller thinks necessary for the protection of the legitimate interests of the licensee (see subs.(3)). Subsection (2)(b) provides for opposition to an application for such revocation or cancellation, which the Comptroller must consider (subs.(2)(c)).

The Patents and Trade Marks (World Trade Organisation) Regulations 1999 (SI 1999/1899) also contain (in reg.8, reprinted in §48A.03) transitional provisions effectively back dating the provisions of s.48A to orders already made, or sought, under s.48 before the commencement of these Regulations on July 29, 1999. Thus, a WTO proprietor who, before this date had already had an order made for a compulsory licence or for a "licences of right" entry in the register, may apply to the Comptroller to have the order revoked or the entry cancelled on the grounds that the grounds on which the order or entry was made are not set out in s.48A(1), or to have the conditions subject to which any licence granted before that date modified on the grounds that the licence does not satisfy the requirements now set out in s.48A(6), and powers are granted to the Comptroller to make such orders. These transitional provisions also take effect when a patentee becomes a "WTO proprietor" after an order has been made, or sought, when at that time the proprietor did not have this status.

Opposition to compulsory licence application (subs.(1))

Subsection (1) gives the patent proprietor or "any other person" the right to oppose any application under ss.48–51 and requires the Comptroller to consider the opposition in deciding whether to grant that application. An opponent who resides outside the European Community and the Member States of the Lugano Convention may be required to give security for costs, see s.107(4), r.85, and §107.05. **52.03**

It is imperative that the proprietor lodge opposition under subs.(1) if he wishes to be heard on the terms of any licence which the Comptroller may decide should be granted on an application under s.48, which otherwise will be decided in ex parte proceedings (*Ultimatte Corp's Patents* BL O/1/84, noted I.P.D. 6141). However, by agreement in that case, and because the Comptroller is entitled to consider any material information obtained from whatever source, the proprietor was permitted to make submissions in writing on the terms of the licence to be granted, but with consideration of these restricted to proceedings held in his absence, see also *Zanetti-Streccia's Patent* [1973] R.P.C. 227 discussed in §52.08.

Appeals under ss.48–51 (subs.(2))

52.04   Subsection (2) refers to appeals, and gives to the Attorney-General (or his equivalent in other parts of the United Kingdom) the right to appear, or to be represented by counsel, and be heard, in any appeal on an application under ss.48–51, irrespective of whether the application was opposed. It seems that there is no such right of audience in the initial proceedings before the Comptroller. Where the Attorney-General does so appear on such an appeal, there is precedent for him being permitted to call evidence should he so wish, see *Hoffmann-La Roche v Bamford* [New Zealand] [1976] R.P.C. 346 decided under the corresponding enactment in New Zealand.

Any appeal lies to the Patents Court under s.97(1) and further to the Court of Appeal, but only if a point of law is involved and with leave (s.97(3)). There is no provision for the proceedings to take place in Scotland, see s.123(2)(f).

Arbitration (subss.(5)–(7))

52.05   By subs.(5), if the parties agree, or the proceedings become protracted, the Comptroller can refer the matter to an agreed or appointed arbitrator, or in Scotland an appointed arbiter. The reference to "arbiter" suggests the possibility of arbitration proceedings in Scotland despite s.123(2)(f), see §52.05.

Subsection (6) states that (unless there is prior agreement) the decision of the arbitrator/arbiter is subject to appeal to the court. However, this is now the normal rule in an arbitration, see the Arbitration Act 1996 (c.23). By subs.(7) the arbitrator/arbiter reports his finding to the Comptroller. Presumably, where the Comptroller does not refer the whole proceedings to an arbitrator/arbiter, the proceedings will eventually return to the Comptroller for decision taking into account the questions decided, or facts found, in the arbitration. No use of these provisions has become apparent.

Practice under Section 52

Procedure on opposition

52.06   The procedure on opposition is governed by Pt 7 of the Rules, establishing procedure for hearings before the Comptroller. The Rules distinguish between (i) oppositions made under s.52(1) to oppose an application for a compulsory licence (or under ss.50A or 51), oppositions made under s.52(2)(b) to oppose an application to cancel a compulsory licence; and (ii) an application to cancel a compulsory licence pursuant to s.52(2)(a). In the former instance, proceedings are deemed to have already started, whereas in the latter instance it is the application itself which commences proceedings.

In the case of oppositions under case (i) in the previous paragraph, the Comptroller will notify any interested parties that the application has been made (r.77(1) and r.77(2)). The period within which the counter-statement for opposition must be filed is four weeks from the date of the advertisement in the *Patents Journal* of the application which is being opposed (r.77(8)). The opposition need not be filed in any particular form, but it may be advantageous to file it by way of a PF 15, in duplicate. Failure to file a counter-statement within the allotted time after notification is deemed to be an indication of support for the application (r.77(9)).

In the case of opposition under case (ii) above, proceedings are started when the applicant files a PF 15 and a statement of grounds in duplicate (r.76(1)). The statement of grounds must contain, inter alia, a concise statement of the facts on which the application is based (r.76(4)). The Comptroller will then notify the proprietor of the patent and any other interested parties (which is likely to include any party taking a compulsory licence) that the application to cancel the licence has been made (r.77(1)), unless the applicant is one of those parties, in which case no such notification will be made (r.77(2)). The notified parties are then at liberty to oppose the application following the process noted in the preceding paragraph.

The subsequent procedure is flexible at the Comptroller's discretion (r.82), but will follow that used in proceedings before the Comptroller as set out in Pt 7 of the Rules, for which see mainly §§123.06–123.21. In *Halcon's Patent* [1989] R.P.C. 1, the proceedings were stayed until pending infringement proceedings (and subsequently on appeal) were completed so that it could first be determined whether the applicant's activities did infringe the patent and whether this was valid.

Disclosure during opposition proceedings under section 52

The practice of the Comptroller concerning disclosure in contentious proceedings before him is discussed in §123.47, with §123.48 discussing the restrictions which have been imposed in particular cases, not only to protect the confidentiality of commercially sensitive information put forward in the proceedings by means of orders under r.53 (for which see §118.20), but also orders made for limiting disclosure of specified documents to legal advisers of the other party, and sometimes other specified persons on conditions designed to secure the secrecy, and provide protection against potential misuse, of the information contained in those documents. **52.07**

Such orders have often been made in proceedings for the settlement of terms of a "licence of right" under s.46(3)(a) (for which see §46.20), or in oppositions under the present section. On the latter ground, the cases include: *Heathway Machine's Compulsory Licence Application* BL O/111/80, which was a preliminary to *Extrude Hone's Patent* [1982] R.P.C. 361 and [1984] F.S.R. 105, discussed in §48B.08, concerning discovery (as disclosure was then called) of a licence agreement between the patentee and the applicant; *Geigy's Patent* [1964] R.P.C. 391, and *Smith, Kline & French's Patent* [1965] F.S.R. 98, each of which concerned accountancy evidence filed on behalf of the patentee in proceedings under s.41 of the 1949 Act; and *Halcon's Patents* BL O/118/86, noted I.P.D. 9081, which concerned an assessment of costs and profitability which was presumed had been made by the applicant for a compulsory licence, but other requests for discovery (now disclosure) were here left for determination after the pending infringement proceedings had been completed, for which see [1989] R.P.C. 1.

Appeals

In *Zanetti-Streccia's Patent* [1973] R.P.C. 227, the patentee failed, as the result of a muddle, to enter opposition under the corresponding s.43(3) of the 1949 Act to the grant of a compulsory licence, and when the licence was granted he appealed under the corresponding s.44 of the 1949 Act. Since s.44 of the 1949 Act did not speak of an appeal from an opposition but an appeal from an order of the Comptroller, it was held that the patentee had locus to enter appeal if he could make a complaint about anything appearing on the face of the order made by the Comptroller. Subsection (2) also refers to an appeal brought from an order of the Comptroller and the general provisions for appeal in s.97 would not appear to alter the law, in this respect at least, from that prevailing under the 1949 Act. The main ground of the appeal in the *Zanetti* case was that negotiations for the grant of a voluntary licence to another company, which had begun after the application for the compulsory licence, were known to the Comptroller and should have prevented him from ordering a compulsory licence. The Patents Appeal Tribunal, noting that s.39 of the 1949 Act concluded by observing that the Comptroller should not be required to take account of matters subsequent to the making of the application, declined to interfere with the Comptroller's discretion and dismissed the appeal. The same provision is now to be found in subs.(2). **52.08**

SECTION 53

Compulsory licences; supplementary provisions

53.—[(1) *Without prejudice to section 86 below (by virtue of which the Community Patent Convention has effect in the United Kingdom), sections 48 to 51 above shall have effect subject to any provision of that convention relating to the grant of compulsory licences for lack or insufficiency of exploitation as that provision applies by virtue of that section.*] **53.01**

(2) In any proceedings on an application **made under section 48 above in respect of a patent** [*in relation to a patent under sections 48 to 51 above*], any statement with respect to any activity in relation to the patented invention, or with respect to the grant or refusal of licences under the patent, contained in a report of the **Competition Commission** [*Monopolies and Mergers Commission*] laid before Parliament under Part VII of the Fair Trading Act 1973 [c. 41, ss. 81–83] or section 17 of the Competition Act 1980 [c. 21] **or published under Part 3 or 4 of the Enterprise Act 2002 [c. 40]** shall be prima facie evidence of the matters stated, and in Scotland shall be sufficient evidence of those matters.

(3) The comptroller may make an entry in the register under sections 48 to 51 above notwithstanding any contract which would have precluded the entry on the application of the proprietor of the patent under section 46 above.

(4) An entry made in the register under sections 48 to 51 above shall for all purposes have the same effect as an entry made under section 46 above

(5) No order or entry shall be made in pursuance of an application under sections 48 to 51 above which would be at variance with any treaty or international convention to which the United Kingdom is a party.

Notes

1. Subsection (1) (which had never been brought into force) was deleted by the Patents Act 2004 (c.16) Schs 2 para.12 and 3 on January 1, 2005 (SI 2004/3205, art.2(f)(g)(k)) as part of the removal from the Act of all references to the CPC which never came into force.

2. Subsection (2) was amended by Sch.5 para.15 to the CDPA 1988; and also in consequence of the replacement of the "Monopolies and Mergers Commission" by the "Competition Commission" (SI 1999/506), as from April 1, 1999. Moreover, ss.81 and 83 of the Fair Trading Act 1973 have been amended by the Competition Act 1998 (c.41) Sch.12 para.4. It was further amended by the Enterprise Act 2002 (Sch.25(8)(4)) by adding after the words "Competition Act 1980 [c. 21] the words: or published under Part 3 or 4 of the Enterprise Act 2002 [c. 40]".

COMMENTARY ON SECTION 53

Scope of the section

53.02   Section 53 contains certain supplementary provisions relating to compulsory licences arising from ss.48–51, but, as the CPC did not come into force, subs.(1) was never itself brought into force and was ultimately deleted. Any new version of the CPC would be subject to arts 30 and 31 of the TRIPS Agreement (reprinted in §48A.02) as all Member States of the European Union are WTO Members.

Reports of Competition Commission (subs.(2))

53.03   Subsection (2) has the same effect as s.43(6) of the 1949 Act and states that, in respect of proceedings under ss.48–51, a statement of facts concerning a patent in a report of the Competition Commission (which has replaced the former Monopolies and Mergers Commission) is to be taken as prima facie evidence of those facts. This means that these facts are to be presumed to be true unless a challenger is able to disprove them, the onus being upon him to do so. The subsection is most likely to be of relevance in proceedings under s.51.

Entries in the register (subss.(3) and (4))

53.04   Subsection (3) gives the Comptroller power to make an entry in the register under ss.48–51, notwithstanding any contract which would have precluded the entry on an application by the proprietor under s.46(1). Such an entry would be one stating that "licences of right" are available under the patent. Subsection (4) states that an entry under ss.48–51 is to have the same effect as an entry under s.46. Thus, if the Comptroller makes a "licence of right" entry as the result of an application for a compulsory licence under s.48 (or in proceedings instituted by a Minister under s.51), thereafter any person can take advantage of that entry and obtain a licence with its terms settled, in default of agreement between the parties, by the Comptroller under s.46(3)(a). The proceedings for such settlement are discussed in §§46.06–46.20.

Conformity with treaties and international conventions (subs.(5))

Subsection (5) is the same as s.45(3) of the 1949 Act and prohibits the making of any order or entry which would be at variance with any international agreement to which the United Kingdom is a party. Such agreement could be the Paris Convention, EPC, CPC, PCT, the TFEU or the TRIPS Agreement (under the GATT Treaty) Thus, subs.(5) makes these conventions self-executing in relation to the grant of compulsory licences, even as to conventions, treaties and the like entered into subsequently to the coming into force of the subsection, as the Irish High Court (under a statutory provision similar in wording to s.53(5)) so held, see *Allen & Hanbury's v Controller of Patents* [Ireland] [1997] F.S.R. 1. Thus, the terms of the TRIPS Agreement were, from the entry into force of that Agreement, apparently automatically part of United Kingdom law without recourse to further legislation. However, the revisions of ss.48, 50 and 52, with the concomitant introduction of s.48A, made in 1999 were intended to bring the compulsory licence provisions in the Act into conformity with arts 30 and 31 of the TRIPS Agreement (reprinted in §48A.02) with retroactive transitional provisions (for which see §48A.03).   **53.05**

However, even though the subsection appears to have this automatic effect, ECJ, nowCJEU did not consider its terms to be sufficient to avoid a finding that certain of the provisions of the original forms of ss.48 and 50 were contrary to Community law (*EC Commission v United Kingdom* (C-30/90) [1993] R.P.C. 283; [1992] 1 E.C.R. 829; [1992] 2 C.M.L.R. 709 ECJ), see §48.03.

SECTION 54

Special provisions where patented invention is being worked abroad

54.—(1) Her Majesty may by Order in Council provide that the comptroller may not (otherwise than for purposes of the public interest) make an order or entry in respect of a patent in pursuance of an application under sections 48–51 above if the invention concerned is being commercially worked in any relevant country specified in the Order and demand in the United Kingdom for any patented product resulting from that working is being met by importation from that country.   **54.01**

(2) In subsection (1) above "relevant country" means a country other than a member state **or a member of the World Trade Organisation** whose law in the opinion of Her Majesty in Council incorporates or will incorporate provisions treating the working of an invention in, and importation from, the United Kingdom in a similar way to that in which the Order in Council would (if made) treat the working of an invention in, and importation from, that country.

Note. Subsection 2 was amended by the Patents and Trade Marks (World Trade Organisation) Regulations 1999 (SI 1999/1899). The amendment was applied to the Isle of Man by SI 2003/1249.

COMMENTARY ON SECTION 54

Subsection (1) provides that, by Order in Council to that effect, the Comptroller may not   **54.02** grant a compulsory licence under ss.48–51 if the invention in question is being worked in a foreign country named in the Order, and the demand in the United Kingdom is being met by importation from that country. Section 54 originally contemplated reciprocal arrangements between the United Kingdom and non-EEC countries regarding the working of patents, but (by the amendment to subs.(2) made in 1999) was restricted to apply only to such arrangements between the United Kingdom and any country which is not a member of the World Trade Organization, the members of which are indicated in §90.03. The section therefore would now only apply to those rare compulsory licence applications which fall to be judged under s.48B (or under s.51, if the exceptions in art.31 of the TRIPS Agreement should apply, for which see §51.05), and then only if an order has been made under subs.(1). However, no such order has yet been made so that the section has no current effect.

Use of patented inventions for services of the Crown [Sections 55–59]

SECTION 55

Use of patented inventions for services of the Crown

55.01

55.—(1) Notwithstanding anything in this Act, any government department and any person authorised in writing by a government department may, for the services of the Crown and in accordance with this section, do any of the following acts in the United Kingdom in relation to a patented invention without the consent of the proprietor of the patent, that is to say—

(a) where the invention is a product, may—

    (i) make, use, import or keep the product, or sell or offer to sell it where to do so would be incidental or ancillary to making, using, importing or keeping it; or

    (ii) in any event, sell or offer to sell it for foreign defence purposes or for the production or supply of specified drugs and medicines, or dispose or offer to dispose of it (otherwise than by selling it) for any purpose whatever;

(b) where the invention is a process, may use it or do in relation to any product obtained directly by means of the process anything mentioned in paragraph (a) above;

(c) without prejudice to the foregoing, where the invention or any product obtained directly by means of the invention is a specified drug or medicine, may sell or offer to sell the drug or medicine;

(d) may supply or offer to supply to any person any of the means, relating to an essential element of the invention, for putting the invention into effect;

(e) may dispose or offer to dispose of anything which was made, used, imported or kept in the exercise of the powers conferred by this section and which is no longer required for the purpose for which it was made, used, imported or kept (as the case may be),

and anything done by virtue of this subsection shall not amount to an infringement of the patent concerned.

(2) Any act done in relation to an invention by virtue of this section is in the following provisions of this section referred to as use of the invention; and "use", in relation to an invention, in sections 56 to 58 below shall be construed accordingly.

(3) So far as the invention has before its priority date been duly recorded by or tried by or on behalf of a government department or the United Kingdom Atomic Energy Authority otherwise than in consequence of a relevant communication made in confidence, any use of the invention by virtue of this section may be made free of any royalty or other payment to the proprietor.

(4) So far as the invention has not been so recorded or tried, any use of it made by virtue of this section at any time either—

    (a) after the publication of the application for the patent for the invention; or

    (b) without prejudice to paragraph (a) above, in consequence of a relevant communication made after the priority date of the invention otherwise than in confidence;

shall be made on such terms as may be agreed either before or after the use by the government department and the proprietor of the patent with the approval of the Treasury or as may in default of agreement be determined by the court on a reference under section 58 below.

(5) Where an invention is used by virtue of this section at any time after publication of an application for a patent for the invention but before such a patent is granted, and the terms for its use agreed or determined as mentioned in subsection (4) above include terms as to payment for the use, then (notwithstanding anything in those terms) any such payment shall be recoverable only—

    (a) after such a patent is granted; and

    (b) if (apart from this section) the use would, if the patent had been granted on the date of the publication of the application, have infringed not only the patent but also the claims (as interpreted by the description and any drawings referred to in the description or claims) in the form in which they were contained in the application immediately before the preparations for its publication were completed by the Patent Office.

(6) The authority of a government department in respect of an invention may be given under this section either before or after the patent is granted and either before or after the use in respect of which the authority is given is made, and may be given to any person whether or not he is authorised directly or indirectly by the proprietor of the patent to do anything in relation to the invention.

(7) Where any use of an invention is made by or with the authority of a government department under this section, then, unless it appears to the department that it would be contrary to the public interest to do so, the department shall notify the proprietor of the patent as soon as practicable after the second of the following events, that is to say, the use is begun and the patent is granted, and furnish him with such information as to the extent of the use as he may from time to time require.

(8) A person acquiring anything disposed of in the exercise of powers conferred by this section, and any person claiming through him, may deal with it in the same manner as if the patent were held on behalf of the Crown.

(9) In this section "relevant communication", in relation to an invention, means a communication of the invention directly or indirectly by the proprietor of the patent or any person from whom he derives title.

(10) Subsection (4) above is without prejudice to any rule of law relating to the confidentiality of information.

(11) In the application of this section to Northern Ireland, the reference in subsection (4) above to the Treasury shall, where the government department referred to in that subsection is a department of the Government of Northern Ireland, be construed as a reference to the Department of Finance for Northern Ireland.

Other Relevant Statutes and Secondary Legislation

Defence Contracts Act 1958 (c.38)—Section 2

Provision for use of other technical information by Crown contractors for production and supply of defence materials

55.02 **2.**—(1) For the purposes of any contract or order for the production of defence materials, any person authorised in that behalf by a competent authority may make use of any technical information to which this section applies of which he is in possession, and supply articles produced by means of the use of any such information, discharged—

  (a) from any restriction imposed by any agreement to which he is party (whether made before or after the commencement of this Act); and

  (b) from any obligation to make payments to any other person in pursuance of any such agreement in respect of the use or supply.

(2) Any authorisation given for the purposes of subsection (1) of this section shall be given in writing, and shall—

  (a) describe the defence materials in connection with which the authorisation is given; and

  (b) identify the restrictions or obligations from which the person to whom the authorisation is given is thereby discharged;

and so much of any agreement (whether made before or after the commencement of this Act) as restricts the disclosure of terms of that or any other agreement shall be of no effect in relation to the disclosure to a competent authority of information required by that authority for the purpose of compliance with paragraph (b) of this subsection.

(3) Any authorisation given for the purposes of subsection (1) of this section may apply to things done before as well as after the date on which it is given.

(4) Where any person is discharged by virtue of an authorisation under this section from the obligation to make payments in respect of the use of any technical information or the supply of any articles, so much of any agreement (whether made before or after the commencement of this Act) as provides for the making by any other person of payments in respect of the use of the information or the supply of articles of that description shall be of no effect in relation to any use or supply in respect of which the first-mentioned person is so discharged.

(5) Nothing in this section shall affect any restriction or obligation imposed by an agreement to which any Government department are party.

(6) Nothing in this section or in any authorisation given thereunder shall be construed as authorising the disclosure to a competent authority or any other person of any technical information to which this section applies in contravention of any agreement.

(7) The technical information to which this section applies is any specification or design for articles, and any process or technique used in the production of articles (not being in any case a patented invention or registered design), and any drawing, model, plan, document or other information relating to the application or operation of any such specification, design, process or technique; and references in this Act to the use of technical information include references—

    (a) to the production of articles to any such specification or design, or by means of any such process or technique, as aforesaid; and

    (b) to the reproduction of any such drawing, model, plan or document as aforesaid.

Defence Contracts Act 1958 (c.38)—Section 3

Procedure in connection with authorisations under section 2

3.—(1) Subject to subsection (3) of this section, a competent authority shall, before giving to any person an authorisation under section two of this Act in respect of any restriction or obligation, serve on that person a notice in writing requesting him to treat with the party entitled to enforce that restriction or obligation for such waiver or modification as will enable the technical information to be used or the articles supplied upon terms approved by the competent authority; and the authorisation shall not be given unless either—   **55.03**

    (a) at the expiration of such period, not being less than three months beginning with the date of the service of the notice, as may be specified therein, no agreement for such waiver or modification as aforesaid has been concluded to the satisfaction of the competent authority; or

    (b) before the expiration of the said period, the person on whom the notice was served has given notice in writing to the competent authority that no such agreement is likely to be concluded within that period.

(2) Where an authorisation is given under the said section two in respect of any restriction or obligation, the competent authority shall, subject to subsection (3) of this section, give notice to that effect to the person who, apart from the authorisation, would be entitled to enforce that restriction or obligation, and to such other persons (if any) as appear to the authority, after making such enquiries as are reasonably practicable in the circumstances, to be persons whose interests are affected by the authorisation.

(3) An authorisation under the said section two may be given by a competent authority without compliance with subsection (1) of this section in any case where it appears to the authority, and is certified in the authorisation, that the disclosure of the production or supply of the defence materials concerned would be prejudicial to the safety of the State; and in any such case—

    (a) the competent authority shall not be required to give notice of the authorisation in pursuance of subsection (2) of this section unless and until they are satisfied that the disclosure would no longer be prejudicial as aforesaid; and

    (b) unless and until the competent authority, being satisfied as aforesaid, otherwise direct, the person to whom the authorisation is given shall be discharged thereby from any obligation to which he would otherwise be subject by virtue of any agreement to give information to any other person in respect of the use of the information or the supply of articles to which the authorisation relates.

Defence Contracts Act 1958 (c.38)—Section 4

Payments for use and determination of disputes

55.04   **4.**—(1) A competent authority by whom an authorisation is given under section two of this Act shall pay to the person entitled to the benefit of any restriction or obligation in respect of which the authorisation is given, or of any such provision of an agreement as is mentioned in subsection (4) of that section (whether or not he would himself be entitled, apart from the authorisation, to enforce the restriction, obligation or provision by legal proceedings) such sum (if any) as may be agreed upon between him and the competent authority with the approval of the Treasury or as may, in default of such agreement, be determined by the court under this section to be just having regard—

(a) to the extent of the use made in pursuance of the authorisation;

(b) to the value of any services performed by that person in connection with the conception, development, improvement or adaptation of any specification, design, process or technique used in pursuance of the authorisation;

(c) to any benefit or compensation which that person or any person from whom he derives title may have received, or may be entitled to receive, directly or indirectly from any Government department in respect of any technical information so used; and

(d) to any other relevant circumstances.

(2) Any dispute between a competent authority and any other person as to the exercise of powers conferred by section two of this Act, as to the making of a payment under this section, or as the amount of any such payment, shall be determined by the court upon a reference made by either party to the dispute in such manner as may be prescribed by rules of court.

(3) Without prejudice to any rule of law enabling a court to sit in camera, the court may make such orders for the exclusion of the public from proceedings under this section, and for prohibiting the publication of any technical information to which section two of this Act applies so far as disclosed or recorded in such proceedings, as appear to the court to be necessary or expedient in the public interest or in the interests of any parties to the proceedings.

(4) In this section "the court" has the same meaning as in the **Patents Act 1977**.

Notes

1. The amendment to subs.(4) was effected by Sch.5 para.4 to the 1977 Act.

2. In its application to Northern Ireland, s.4 has effect with omission from subs.(2) of the words "in such manner as may be prescribed by rules of court" (Northern Ireland Act 1962 (c.30) Sch.1).

Defence Contracts Act 1958 (c.38)—Section 5

Expenses

5. There shall be defrayed out of moneys provided by Parliament ... any sums required by a competent authority for making payments under section four of this Act.   **55.05**

Note. The omitted words relate to spent provisions.

Defence Contracts Act 1958 (c.38)—Section 6

Interpretation, etc.

6.—(1) In this Act the following expressions have the meaning hereby respectively assigned to them, that is to say: **55.06**

    "agreement" includes any substance or material, and any plant, machinery or apparatus, whether affixed to land or not;

    "article" includes any substance or material, and any plant, machinery or apparatus, whether affixed to land or not;

    "competent authority" means a Secretary of State.

    "defence materials" means—

        (a) articles required for the armed forces of the Crown or for any such supply to the governments of countries outside the United Kingdom, or to the United Nations, as is authorised by the enactments amended by section one of this Act, being articles designed or adapted for the use of armed forced or components of articles so designed or adapted;

        (b) articles required for purposes of civil defence within the meaning of the Civil Defence Act, 1948 [c. 5], being articles designed or adapted for use for those purposes or components of articles so designed or adapted;

        (c) articles required by the Secretary of State for Defence for the production of any such articles as aforesaid;

    "production" includes repair, maintenance, testing and development..

(2) This Act shall apply in relation to restrictions subsisting by reason of the existence of copyright in any work as it applies in relation to restrictions imposed by an agreement.

Note. The definition of "competent authority" and subs.(c) of the definition of "defence materials", each in subs.(1), were amended by the Ministry of Aviation Supply (Dissolution) Order 1971 (SI 1971/719) Sch. para.4(2).

Defence Contracts Act 1958 (c.38)—Section 8

Citation, construction, commencement and extent

8.—(1) This may be cited as the Defence Contracts Act 1958   **55.07**

(2) ...

(3) This Act shall come into operation at the expiration of the period of one month beginning with the date on which it is passed.

(4) This Act shall extend to the Isle of Man; and it is hereby declared that this Act extends to Northern Ireland.

Note. Subsection (2) refers to certain amendments originally made to the 1949 Act by s.1 of the 1958 Act, but, now relates only to the Registered Designs Act 1949 (c.88).

VISITING FORCES AND INTERNATIONAL HEADQUARTERS (APPLICATION OF LAW) ORDER 1999—ARTICLE 6 AND SCHEDULE 4

(SI 1999 /1736)

Article 6—Use of intellectual property rights

55.08
6. Schedule 4 shall have effect with respect to the use for the purposes of a visiting force or headquarters of intellectual property rights.

SCHEDULE 4

Use of patented inventions

2.—(1) Subject to sub-paragraph (2), the power conferred by section 55(1) of the Patents Act 1977 (c. 37) on a government department, or person authorised in writing by a government department, in relation to the use of patented inventions for the services of the Crown shall be exercisable for the purposes of a visiting force or headquarters to the extent that it would be exercisable if the visiting force or headquarters were part of any of the home forces.
(2) Sub-paragraph (1) shall not have effect to authorise—
    (a) the doing of any act falling within section 55(1)(a)(ii) or (c) of the Patents Act 1977, or
    (b) the doing of anything which is for a purpose relating to the production or use of atomic energy or research into matters connected therewith.
(3) In relation to the exercise of the powers conferred by sub-paragraph (1), sections 55 to s.58 of the Patents Act 1977 (apart from section 56(2) to (4)) shall have effect with any reference in those provisions to the use of a patented invention for the services of the Crown being construed as a reference to the use of such an invention for the purposes of a visiting force or headquarters.
Note. Paragraphs 4(1) and (3) of Sch.4 to the SI 1999/1736 provide respectively corresponding provisions for the use of registered designs and design rights.

COMMENTARY ON SECTION 55

Scope of the section
55.09
Section 55 is the first of a group of sections, ss.55 to 59, which concern the use by the Crown of patented inventions, including those of European patents (UK). If Community patents should ever be granted, it is thought that art.45 of the Community Patent Convention (1989) ("CPC 1989") should be broad enough to cover Crown use of Community patents. Section 55 is supplemented by the provisions of ss.122 (Crown's right to sell forfeited articles) and 129 (Application of Act to Crown), for which see the commentary on those sections.

Subsections (1) and 55(2) define the extent of permitted Crown use under the section, and subs.(4) provides (except in a case covered by subs.(3) where there has been a prior recording of the invention) for the payment of compensation to the proprietor for such use, with the consent of the Treasury (or Department of Finance for Northern Ireland—subs.(11)), and as limited by the provisions of subs.(5), and without prejudice to the law for protecting confidential information (subs.10)). Subsection (6) provides for the Crown to give authority for use of the invention by a third party on behalf of the Crown, and any disposal of a product made under a s.55 authorisation is treated as if this were a disposal of that product by a patentee (subs.(8)). Subsection (7) provides for notification to the patent proprietor of any authorisation under the section, unless this would be contrary to the public interest.

The powers conferred by s.55 have been extended by the Visiting Forces and International Headquarters (Application of Law) Order 1999 (SI 1999/1736) art.6 and

Sch.4(2). This allows certain specified rights of use for the services of the Crown to be exercisable for the purposes of a visiting force or headquarters to the extent that they would be exercisable if the visiting force or headquarters were part of the home forces.

Section 56 modifies the provisions of s.55 in certain defined circumstances. Sections 57 and 57A provide that compensation payable under subs.(4) may be required to be shared with, or passed to, a third party who has suffered direct loss, or has lost profits, arising from Crown use of a patented invention. If questions of the amount of compensation to be paid for Crown use under ss.55–57A cannot be resolved by negotiation, the matter may be taken to the court for resolution under the provisions of s.58. Section 59 provides the Crown with additional powers of use of patented inventions, but these powers may be exercised only during a period of a declared "emergency". For discussion of these other provisions, see the commentaries on these sections.

Sections 55–59 provide in effect for compulsory licences for Crown use of a patented invention, though they are not "licences" in law because Crown use of a patented invention is deemed (by the final phrase of subs.55(1)) not to be an act of patent infringement. It is therefore a moot question whether arts 30 and 31 of the TRIPS Agreement (reprinted in §48A.02) have effect in relation to these Crown user provisions.

Crown use of other forms of intellectual property

Other legislation covering Crown use of intellectual property is to be found as follows: **55.10**

(a) for all forms of intellectual property, in:

    (i) the Defence Contracts Act 1958 (c.38), (reprinted, so far as relevant, above); and

    (ii) the Deregulation and Contracting Out Act 1994 (c.40) s.75 and Sch.15 which gives Government Departments and Local Authorities powers to set aside legal, contractual or other obstructions preventing use of confidential information for the purpose of contracting out functions of the Department or Authority;

(b) for registered designs, in s.12 of, and Sch.1 to, the Registered Designs Act 1949 (c.88), as amended by the CDPA 1988, and re-presented in Sch.4 to the CDPA 1988; and

(c) for unregistered design rights (which includes rights in a "semiconductor topography", Design Right (Semiconductor Topographies) Regulations 1989 (SI 1989/1100), as amended by SI 1993/2497), in ss.240–244 to the CDPA 1988; and

(d) for European registered and unregistered designs under para.5 and the Schedule to the Community Design Regulations 2005 (SI 2005/2339).

In contrast to the position for patents and registered designs, and unless s.57 applies, Crown use of the unregistered design right under s.240 of the CDPA 1988 is limited to use for certain health purposes and for home and foreign defence purposes and Crown use of Community registered and unregistered designs under SI 2005/2339 is limited to essential defence and security needs. The Defence Contracts Act is restricted to "defence" and relates to technical information in the possession of a contractor or proposed contractor, which is subject to a restrictive agreement with a third party or the use of which for the contract purpose is subject to copyright. The Defence Contracts Act could, therefore, presumably be used to authorise use of software for defence purposes. For a short commentary on the Defence Contracts Act, see §55.12. Crown use authorisations given to third parties in respect of patents and registered designs (including Community registered designs) may be given by appropriate civil servants. Government Departments themselves can use without additional authorisation, see for example the wording of s.55(1), but Ministers must give any authorisation under the Defence Contracts Act. A similar assurance was given in respect of authorisations for Crown use under the unregistered design right during the passage of the CDPA 1988 and industry (the Defence Manufactures

Association) has been informed by the Ministry of Defence's Director of Intellectual Property Rights that this practice will also apply to authorisations in respect of unregistered Community designs.

Principles of Crown use

55.11   Sections 55–59 maintain the principle of previous patent statutes in that the Crown, and in particular its agents (i.e. government departments, and persons authorised in writing by a government department), have the right to use patented inventions without the consent (or indeed even prior knowledge) of the patent proprietor, provided that such use is "for the services of the Crown" in the United Kingdom (including the Isle of Man and territorial waters of the United Kingdom, see s.132) and is of a kind specified in subs.(1). The word "agents" is used here not in a legal sense, but as a convenient word to embrace the bodies specified. The armed forces are direct servants of the Crown, and it has been put beyond doubt that the term "Crown employees" includes members of the armed forces by the amendment of the definition of employee in s.130(1), see §130.01.

However, it should be noted that the term "government department" is not defined in the Act, and it can sometimes be a matter of some difficulty to discover the status of a public body. The point was discussed in *Pfizer v Minister of Health* (1965) R.P.C. 261 HL. In general, a nationalised industry is not a government department, and it has become customary to include in legislation setting up new public bodies under statute a definition disclaiming Crown status for that body. Therefore, in the case of public corporations set up under statute, that statute (as possibly amended) should be checked for any provision defining the status of that corporation vis-à-vis the Crown. Health Care Trusts, although not Government Departments, exercise functions of the Secretary of State, as devolved through the provisions of the legislation establishing the National Health Service, and any use of an invention thereby is accordingly Crown use (*Dory v Sheffield Health Authority* [1991] F.S.R. 221).

While the Crown cannot infringe a patent in its private capacity (see s.129), the Crown can be liable under s.3 of the Crown Proceedings Act 1947 (c.44, as amended, reprinted at §129.02) for other types of infringement outside the scope of the exceptions specified in s.55(1), see §129.03.

Thus, the right to sue the Crown for patent infringement under s.60 is subject to the exclusion of Crown use to the substantial extent permitted by s.55. It is otherwise possible to bring action against the Crown for infringement by Crown servants or agents, including government departments, for example in respect of any sales not provided for by s.55(1).

Since Crown use of inventions within the terms of s.55 is not regarded as an act of infringement, there are certain consequences. For example, the definition of infringement included in s.60 does not apply, and the extent to which a patent is used by the Crown is to be judged by s.55 only. Thus, the acts specified in s.60(5) as excluded from infringement (e.g. private, experimental use, and use on ships and aircraft) will not be excluded from Crown use if they are with Crown authority, but will be excluded from infringement if they are not with Crown authority. By s.60(6)(a) the right under s.60(2) to supply means relating to an essential element of the invention to a person entitled to use is extended to a person entitled by virtue of s.55, see also §55.09. Also, no rights arise under s.64 (right to continue use begun before priority date) where the prior use is one falling within the terms of either ss.55(1) or 59(1), since the s.64 right arises only in respect of acts which would be ones of "infringement" if carried out after the date of patent grant, see §64.05. It is, however, difficult to envisage a Government Department paying compensation for acts equivalent to those which are exempted from infringement under s.60(5) and s.64.

Various of the provisions relating to infringement in s.60 are made applicable to Crown use by specific recital in s.58, but otherwise the reliefs available to a proprietor of a patent in a case of infringement, such as injunction and recovery of damages, or an account of profits, are not available as against the Crown in respect of the use of the invention by the Crown. However, s.55(4) provides for compensation to be paid for use of the patented invention by the Crown and, in some circumstances, compensation for loss of manufacturing profit can now also be awarded under s.57A, see §§55.13 and 57A.02–57A.07.

The Defence Contracts Act 1958

This Act (the "DCA"), the relevant parts of which are reprinted above, provides (in s.2) **55.12** powers for a Secretary of State (herein called a "competent authority") to authorise persons (conveniently called "suppliers") to make use of technical information for the purpose of any contract or order for the production of "defence materials" without restriction under any agreement which the supplier may have with another (a "licensor"), or restriction arising under copyrights, and free from any obligation to make payment to such licensor or copyright owner (DCA s.2(1)). Accordingly, the DCA should be read alongside the Crown user provisions of s.55, and those for Community designs and for registered designs and design rights in the CDPA 1988.

"Technical information" is defined in s.2(7) of the DCA to include any specification or design and any drawing, model, plan, document or information, and the power given includes power to "reproduce" the same. Also the "restrictions" which can be overridden by the Act specifically include any arising from the existence of copyrights (DCA s.6(2), reprinted above). The authorisation must be in writing, define the "defence materials" in question and identify the restrictions and obligations to be discharged by the authorisation (DCA s.2(2)). The authority may be given retroactively (DCA s.2(3)), but the authorisation does not override any obligation which the supplier has to respect regarding confidentiality in the technical information received from his licensor (DCA s.2(6)). Before any authorisation should be given under s.2, the Secretary of State is required to serve a notice upon the supplier requiring him to treat with his licensor for the purpose of obtaining his agreement to the supply of the defence materials, and to wait for three months (unless the supplier indicates sooner that agreement is unlikely) (DCA s.3(1) and (2)). However, this requirement can be waived if the Secretary of State certifies that disclosure of the production or supply of the defence materials concerned would (presumably in his opinion) be prejudicial to the safety of the State (DCA s.3(3)).

Section 4 of the DCA provides for compensation to be paid to the licensor with regard to the use by the supplier of the technical information, the subject of the authorisation. Such compensation is to be settled by the court in default of agreement. "Court" here has the same meaning as in s.130(1) of the 1977 Act which therefore means the Patents Court, a Patents County Court and the corresponding courts having appropriate juridsiction in Scotland, Northern Ireland and the Isle of Man. Proceedings in England and Wales can be expected to be heard by the Patents Court under CPR 63.3(2) (reprinted at §F63.02).

Section 1 of the DCA (not reprinted here) also applies to the Crown use of registered designs.

Acts for services of the Crown (subss.(1) and (2))

Subsection (1) lists the acts which are permitted to be done "for the services of the **55.13** Crown". These are individually discussed in the following §§55.15–55.19. All such acts are "Crown use" for the purposes of subss.(4)–(11) and for ss.56–58. The definitions in s.130(1) of "services of the Crown" and "use for the services of the Crown" refer to the meanings given in s.56(2), for which see §56.04.

In addition, in relation to the use of biological material, the Crown has the right to obtain, without the undertaking otherwise required by Sch.1, para.5(1) to the Rules (reprinted in §125A.07), a sample of biological material deposited with a depositary institution for the purpose of Crown use of a patent, the specification of which refers to such a deposited material; and this is so even if the patentee has required that such a sample shall be made available only to an "expert", see Sch.1, para.6(6) to the Rules (reprinted in §125A.08).

—Where the invention is a product (subs.(1)(a))

In subs.(1), para.(a)(i) provides that, where the invention is a product, the Crown may **55.14** make, use, import or keep the product or, incidentally thereto, sell or offer the product for sale; and para.(a)(ii) comprehends the right to sell such a product for foreign defence purposes or for the production or supply of specified drugs or medicines, or to dispose of the product otherwise than by selling. Use of the invention for "foreign defence purposes" is defined in s.56(3) and is discussed in §56.05. The extension of s.55 rights under the SI 1999/1736 to visiting forces or headquarters excludes such extension of s.55(1)(a)(iii) or s.55(1)(c) and also excludes such extension to cover the doing of anything relating to production or use of atomic energy or associated research.

Although the term "patented product" is defined in s.130(1), the term "product" alone covers more than the product of a patented process and appears to mean any article or substance which can be made by, or which results from, a process. Indeed, it has been held that the word "product" is a perfectly general one apt to describe any article (*Therm-a-stor v Weatherseal* [1981] F.S.R. 579 CA), see also §60.05. It therefore seems clear that all patented inventions are to be classed as either a product or a process. In *Pfizer* (see above, §55.11), it was held that the right to authorise importation must include the right of sale to the government department concerned.

—Where the invention is a process or a specified drug or medicine (subs.(1)(b) and (c))

55.15   By subs.(1), para.(b), if the invention is a process, the Crown has similar rights in relation to the process, or the product obtained directly by means of it; and, by para.(c), the Crown specifically has the right to sell or offer to sell the invention where it, or the product directly obtained from it, is a specified drug or medicine; "specified drugs and medicines" are defined in s.56(4), as discussed in §56.06. Paragraphs (a), (b) and (c) thus give to the Crown wide powers in relation to drugs and medicines for Crown use, including use for the National Health Service, and for other services where the Secretary of State has specified that the use of such drugs or medicines is required in accordance with s.56(4). It would appear, however, that the Crown has the right to sell surgical or curative devices (not being drugs or medicines as such) only where such selling is incidental or ancillary to the making, using, importing or keeping of such things for the services of the Crown.

—Supply of contributory means (subs.(1)(d))

55.16   By para.(d) of subs.(1), the rights of Crown user extend to the supply of, or an offer to supply, the means relating to an essential element of the invention for putting the invention into effect. This paragraph reflects the provisions for indirect infringement in s.60(2) and (3), but it is not in the same terms as s.60(2) because, in order that the powers of the Crown should have appropriate breadth, there is no need for the same measure of qualification.

—Disposals by the Crown (subs.(1)(e))

55.17   By subs.(1), para.(e), the Crown can dispose of, or offer to dispose of, anything which has been made or obtained by virtue of the section, provided that this is no longer required for its intended purpose. However, no claim can be made for Crown use of a patented invention unless that use falls within the definition of s.55. Thus, it seems that, where an act is done by the Crown with the consent of the proprietor, a claim for Crown user compensation under subs.(4) should not arise.

Outside the terms of s.55, the Crown also has the right to dispose of, or use, articles forfeited under the laws relating to Customs and Excise, see s.122.

Prior recording of invention (subs.(3))

55.18   Under subs.(3), the Crown is given the right to use, free of royalty or payment, any invention which has been duly recorded or tried by or for a government department or the United Kingdom Atomic Energy Authority (UKAEA), provided that the recording or trial took place before the priority date of the invention and otherwise than as the result of a "relevant communication" made in confidence, this term being defined (in subs.(9)) as being a communication directly or indirectly from the proprietor.

Research and development work of a purely commercial nature carried out by the UKAEA, funded independently, e.g. by industry, will not constitute a prior record for the purposes of subs.(3). The position is probably the same with any other privately funded research activity carried out by a government department. Thus, it may be that subs.(3) does not apply unless the recording or trial takes place within the function of a government department acting in its capacity as such.

Some ambiguities are encountered in practice and it is not clear how wide an interpretation should be put on the words "so far as ... duly recorded", that is whether this last expression gives to the Crown the right to use only that which has been "duly recorded" or whether it gives to the Crown the right to use anything which falls within a claim which covers that which has been "duly recorded". It is understood that government departments, perhaps not unnaturally, adopt the latter view, though this would not seem to be supported by a literal meaning of the provision. In *Henry Bros v Ministry of Defence* (1997) R.P.C. 693, there was no prior recording of the invention when a Crown employee sought a tender from an unrelated contractor and that contractor suggested a construction within the scope of a subsequent patent applied for by another.

Compensation (subs.(4))

Subsection 4 provides that, where an invention has not been so duly recorded, the proprietor of the patent can make a claim in respect of its use after publication of the application or at any time after the priority date as a result of a communication otherwise than in confidence. Use is on terms as agreed, or as settled by the court where agreement cannot be reached (s.58). A co-proprietor may claim compensation, but any payment is, apparently, to be paid to all the co-proprietors jointly, see *Patchett's Patent* (1963) R.P.C. 90 and §36.04. **55.19**

Where a patent has been restored after lapse, rights of continuing use are provided by s.28A to provide an exception to acts which would otherwise be acts of infringement. This exception also applies to exclude compensation for Crown use in the same circumstances (s.28A(7)); and, likewise, where a European patent (UK) is revoked under the EPC and subsequently restored (s.77(5)) upon re-establishment of rights under a European application (UK) (s.78(6)). Similar exceptions apply to continuing rights arising from corrected translations of a European patent (UK), see s.80(4) and §80.07.

The compensatory terms will normally be on a willing licensor/willing licensee basis, not taking into account loss of manufacturing profit, as determined in *Patchett's Patent (No.2)* [1967] R.P.C. 237 CA. However, if the proprietor, or an exclusive licensee, was in a position to supply the product, or use the process concerned, loss of manufacturing profit can now be compensated under s.57A. The terms are to be agreed by the Treasury; or by the Department of Finance for Northern Ireland if appropriate (subs.(11)). Subsection (10) provides that subs.(4) is subject to the rule of law concerning confidentiality and appears to preserve any right which may exist to proceed on the basis of breach of confidence.

A limitation is imposed by s.5 of the Atomic Energy Authority (Weapons Group) Act 1973 (c.4) (as amended by Sch.5 para.6) to the effect that, in respect of patents owned by the United Kingdom Atomic Energy Authority, any remuneration for Crown use is to be determined by the Secretary of State for Defenceand not by the court. Compensation for Crown use is also provided for under s.22(7) when directions have been imposed under s.22 and a patent application has been put in order for grant, but not yet granted under s.22(3) (see the commentary on s.22).

The taxation of sums received by way of compensation for Crown use is equated with the taxation of sums in respect of patent licences under provisions now re-enacted in ss.520–533 of the Income and Corporation Taxes Act 1988 (c.1), see particularly its s.533(4) (as amended to include reference to the 1977 Act by the Finance Act 1988 (c.39) s.146, Sch.13, Pt I, paras 1 and 5.

Use before grant (subs.(5))

In respect of Crown use of an invention after publication but before grant, subs.(5) places the Crown in a position equivalent to an infringer under s.69(2). Section 78(7) **55.20** provides likewise in respect of use between publication of an application for a European patent (UK) and grant. There is in s.58(10) an equivalent of s.69(3) affecting an award of compensation in circumstances set out in s.62(2) (late payment of renewal fee); or s.62(3) (relief after patent amendment), for which see §62.05.

Retrospective authorisation (subs.(6))

55.21   Retrospective authorisation of use for the Crown is permitted by subs.(6). A slight doubt persists as to whether one joint proprietor alone may be authorised, but the reference to "any person" appears to cover the point, see *Patchett's Patent* (1963) R.P.C. 90 and [1967] R.P.C. 77; [1967] R.P.C. 237 CA.

In *Dory v Sheffield Health Authority* [1991] F.S.R. 221, the Secretary of State, acting for the Crown, gave retrospective authorisation for use of a patented medical apparatus in the National Health Service after proceedings for infringement had been commenced. The court then held that the proceedings should be struck out as involving no cause of action, the claimant having to pay the costs of the aborted proceedings.

Notification to proprietor (subs.(7))

55.22   Under subs.(7), information on the extent of Crown use has to be given to the proprietor, though only after the patent has been granted, and even then not if it appears to the government department that it would be contrary to the "public interest" to do so. This term is presumably wider than merely "national security".

Rights on acquisition (subs.(8))

55.23   Subsection (8) gives to a person who acquires anything disposed of in accordance with the section a continuing right to use. This position may obtain anyway under the Community "exhaustion of rights" doctrine, for which see §D15.

Position in Northern Ireland and the Isle of Man

55.24   In the applicability of the section to Northern Ireland, the term "government department" includes "a Department of the Government of Northern Ireland" (s.131(b)) and reference to "the Crown" includes "the Crown in right of Her Majesty's Government in Northern Ireland" (s.131(c)).

There is no special provision defining a "government department" as regards the Isle of Man. The application of s.55 to the Isle of Man therefore may raise a constitutional question.

PRACTICE UNDER SECTION 55

55.25   Many contracts issued by government departments contain standard conditions which require a contractor to notify the relevant authority if he is aware of relevant intellectual property rights thought to be necessary for performing the contract, and to refer any claim which arised from it.

Where a contact name and address is not given in a contract, compensation claims for Crown use, and enquiries in relation thereto, can be addressed to the Defence Intellectual Property Rights, MOD Abbey Wood, Bristol BS34 8JH.

SECTION 56

Interpretation, etc., of provisions about Crown use

56.01   **56.**—(1) Any reference in section 55 above to a patented invention, in relation to any time, is a reference to an invention for which a patent has before that time been, or is subsequently, granted.

(2) In this Act, except so far as the context otherwise requires, "the services of the Crown" includes—

(a) the supply of anything for foreign defence purposes;

(b) the production or supply of specified drugs and medicines; and

(c) such purposes relating to the production or use of atomic energy or research into matters connected therewith as the Secretary of State thinks necessary or expedient;

and "use for the services of the Crown" shall be construed accordingly.

(3) In section 55(1)(a) above and subsection (2)(a) above, references to a sale or supply of anything for foreign defence purposes are references to a sale or supply of the thing—

(a) to the government of any country outside the United Kingdom, in pursuance of an agreement or arrangement between Her Majesty's Government in the United Kingdom and the government of that country, where the thing is required for the defence of that country or of any other country whose government is party to any agreement or arrangement with Her Majesty's Government in respect of defence matters; or

(b) to the United Nations, or to the government of any country belonging to that organisation, in pursuance of an agreement or arrangement between Her Majesty's Government and that organisation or government, where the thing is required for any armed forces operating in pursuance of a resolution of that organisation or any organ of that organisation.

(4) For the purposes of section 55(1)(a) and (c) above and subsection (2)(b) above, specified drugs and medicines are drugs and medicines which are both—

(a) required for the provision of—

(ai) primary medical services under the National Health Service Act 2006, the National Health Service (Wales) Act 2006, part I of the National Health Service (Scotland) Act 1978 or any corresponding provisions of the law in force in Northern Ireland or the Isle of Man or primary dental services under the National Health Service Act 2006, the National Health Service (Wales) Act 2006, or any corresponding provisions of the law in force in Northern Ireland or the Isle of Man, or

(i) pharmaceutical services, general medical services or general dental services under Chapter 1 of Part 7 of the National Health Service Act 2006 or Chapter 1 of Part 7 of the National Health Service (Wales) Act 2006 (in the case of pharmaceutical services), Part II of the National Health Service (Scotland) Act 1978 (in the case of [pharmaceutical services or] general dental services), or the corresponding provisions of the law in force in Northern Ireland or the Isle of Man, or

(ii) personal medical services or personal dental services provided in accordance with arrangements made under Section 17C of the 1978 Act (in the case of personal dental services), or the corresponding provisions of the law in force in Northern Ireland or the Isle of Man, or

(iii) local pharmaceutical services provided under a pilot scheme established under section 134 of the National Health Service Act 2006, or section 92 of the National Health Service (Wales) Act 2006, or an LPS scheme established under Schedule 12 to the National Health Service Act 2006, or Schedule 7 to the

National Health Service (Wales) Act 2006, or under any corresponding provision of the law in force in the Isle of Man,

[(iiia) pharmaceutical care services under Part 1 of the National Health Service (Scotland) Act 1978 [c. 29]] and

(b) specified for the purposes of this subsection in regulations made by the Secretary of State.

Note. Subsection (4)(a) has been amended into the form reprinted above. The previous forms of this subsection and the many amendments made to it are too complex to indicate and are probably unimportant, but for the record, the amending legislation was:

1. The National Health Service (Scotland) Act 1978 (c.29) Sch.16(48);

2. The National Health Service (Primary Care) Act 1997 (c.46) Sch.2(2);

3. The Health and Social Care Act 2001 (c.15) Sch.5(4);

4. SI 2002/1475 (W.147) (The Health and Social Care Act 2001 (Commencement No.2) (Wales) Order 2002), for Wales;

5. SI 2003/53 (The Health and Social Care Act 2001 (Commencement No.11) Order 2002), for England;

6. The Health and Social Care (Community Health and Standards) Act 2003 (c.43) Schs 11(6) and 14(4);

7. SI 2004/288 (The Health and Social Care (Community Health and Standards) Act 2003 Commencement (No.2) Order 2004), for England;

8. SI 2004/480 (W.49) (The Health and Social Care (Community Health and Standards) Act 2003) (Commencement No.1) (Wales) Order 2004), for Wales;

9. SI 2004/957 (S.2) (The Primary Medical Services (Scotland) Act 2004 (Consequential Modifications) Order 2004), for Scotland;

10. SI 2005/2925 (The Health and Social Care (Community Health and Standards) Act 2003 (Commencement No.8) Order 2005), for England;

11. SI 2006/345 (W.42) (The Health and Social Care (Community Health and Standards) Act 2003 (Commencement (Wales) No.4) Order 2006), for Wales;

12. SI 2006/1056 (The Smoking, Health and Social Care (Scotland) Act 2005 (Consequential Modifications) (England, Wales and Northern Ireland) Order 2006), but the deletion of the bracketed words in subpara.(i) and the addition of subpara.(iiia) is dependent on the coming into force of s.20 of the Smoking, Health and Social Care (Scotland) Act 2005 (asp.13); and

13. National Health Service (Consequential Provisions) Act 2006 (c.43) Sch.1(58).

COMMENTARY ON SECTION 56

Scope of the section

56.02   The section provides various definitions, or modifications of definitions, for the purposes of s.55 (Use of patented inventions for the services of the Crown). In particular, the section defines for these purposes the terms: "patented invention" (subs.(1)); "the services of the Crown" (subs.(2)); "foreign defence purposes" (subs.(3)); and "specified drugs and medicines" (subs.(4)). The section also needs to be read in conjunction with the Defence Contracts Act 1958 (c.38) (the relevant sections of which are reprinted at §§55.02–55.07) and the Visiting Forces and International Headquarters (Application of Law) Order 1999 (SI 1999/1736) which is reprinted at §55.08. Any dispute under that Act which is referred to the High Court in England and Wales will be heard by the Patents Court (CPR 63.2, reprinted at §F63.02).

Definition of "patented invention" (subs.(1))

By subs.(1), a reference to a "patented invention" in s.55 includes reference both to an invention that is already patented at the relevant date, and also to one which subsequently becomes patented. In this respect the definition is different from that which applies elsewhere in the Act, see s.130(1), and also §125.04.

56.03

Definition of "services of the Crown" (subs.(2))

The definition of the term "services of the Crown" contained in subs.(2) is not exhaustive. The subsection merely states that the term "includes" the three following matters (a), (b) and (c), and then "except so far as the context otherwise requires". To this extent, the definition differs from that which applied at the time of the decision in *Pfizer v Minister of Health* (1965) R.P.C. 261 HL, and thus the precise meaning of the term remains somewhat unclear. However, it clearly also covers the position of undoubted Crown servants acting in the course of their normal duties, as has been discussed in §55.10 above.

56.04

During a period of a declared emergency, the term "services of the Crown" has a special meaning, see s.59 and §59.03.

By subs.(2)(a) the "services of the Crown" includes the supply of anything for foreign defence purposes, these being defined in subs.(3), see §56.05. Similarly, the production or supply of specified drugs and medicines included by virtue of subs.(2)(b) is defined in subs.(4), see §56.06.

Subsection (2)(c) further defines the term to include such purposes relating to the production or use of atomic energy or research into matters connected therewith as the Secretary of State may consider necessary or expedient. It is possible that the Secretary of State will not now apply this provision to research and development work of a purely commercial nature carried out by the United Kingdom Atomic Energy Authority or other governmental establishments and funded by industry. Thus, those seeking to place research contracts with such establishments may wish to check the position before entering into such a contract. Presumably, for the purpose of subs.(2)(c), the Secretary of State will be the Secretary of State for Defence; and, for the purpose of subs.(4), it will be the Secretary of State for Health.

Foreign defence purposes (subs.(3))

By subs.(3)(a) use for foreign defence purposes includes sale or supply to a foreign government, in pursuance of an agreement or arrangement with that country, of anything for the defence of that country or any other country party to a defence agreement or arrangement with the Government. "Arrangement" covers Memoranda of Understanding and like documents which are often used as vehicles for putting into effect collaboration between governments.

56.05

Subsection (3)(b), relating to use in connection with United Nations resolutions, falls under the head of use for foreign defence purposes, but distinction is made between things required for defence in para.(a) and things required for "any armed forces" in para.(a).

"Specified drugs and medicines" (subs.(4))

The "specified drugs and medicines" referred to in s.56(2)(b) are defined in subs.(4) as drugs and medicines required for the services set up as part of the National Health Service in the various parts of the United Kingdom and Isle of Man. Subsection (4) has been the subject of a number of amendments since the commencement of the Act in line with the enactment of numerous changes in Health Service arrangements. It is to be noted in particular that personal medical and dental services are covered in s.56(4)(a)(ii) as these are defined in the legislation governing the operation of the National Health Service. However, drugs and medicines for the National Health Service, e.g. for use in the hospital services, are not required to be "specified" as this supply falls under s.55(1)(a). The supply of surgi-

56.06

cal or curative devices, and ameliorating devices such as hearing aids, by implication appears to be confined within the limits of s.55(1)(a).

While no regulations have been issued under subs.(4)(b), these would only be necessary if the services referred to in subs.(4)(a) were held not already to be "services of the Crown", and the amendment of this subsection at least removes the doubt left by *Pfizer v Ministry of Health* (above and at §55.11) as to whether the supply of drugs and medicines through channels other than hospital services, such as on prescription issued by a general medical practitioner, falls within the meaning of "services of the Crown".

SECTION 57

Rights of third parties in respect of Crown use

57.01   **57.**—(1) In relation to—

(a) any use made for the services of the Crown of an invention by a government department, or a person authorised by a government department, by virtue of section 55 above, or

(b) anything done for the services of the Crown to the order of a government department by the proprietor of a patent in respect of a patented invention or by the proprietor of an application in respect of an invention for which an application for a patent has been filed and is still pending,

the provisions of any licence, assignment, assignation or agreement to which this subsection applies shall be of no effect so far as those provisions restrict or regulate the working of the invention, or the use of any model, document or information relating to it, or provide for the making of payments in respect of, or calculated by reference to, such working or use; and the reproduction or publication of any model or document in connection with the said working or use shall not be deemed to be an infringement of any copyright or design right subsisting in the model or document **or of any topography right**.

(2) Subsection (1) above applies to a licence, assignment, assignation or agreement which is made, whether before or after the appointed day, between (on the one hand) any person who is a proprietor of or an applicant for the patent, or anyone who derives title from any such person or from whom such person derives title, and (on the other hand) any person whatever other than a government department.

(3) Where an exclusive licence granted otherwise than for royalties or other benefits determined by reference to the working of the invention is in force under the patent or application concerned, then—

(a) in relation to anything done in respect of the invention which, but for the provisions of this section and section 55 above, would constitute an infringement of the rights of the licensee, subsection (4) of that section shall have effect as if for the reference to the proprietor of the patent there were substituted a reference to the licensee; and

(b) in relation to anything done in respect of the invention by virtue of an authority given under that section, that section shall have effect as if the said subsection (4) were omitted.

(4) Subject to the provisions of subsection (3) above, where the patent, or the right to the grant of the patent, has been assigned to the proprietor of the patent or application in consideration of royalties or other benefits determined by reference to the working of the invention, then—

(a) in relation to any use of the invention by virtue of section 55 above, subsection (4) of that section shall have effect as if the reference to the proprietor of the patent included a reference to the assignor, and any sum payable by virtue of that subsection shall be divided between the proprietor of the patent or application and the assignor in such proportion as may be agreed on by them or as may in default of agreement be determined by the court on a reference under section 58 below; and

(b) in relation to any act done in respect of the invention for the services of the Crown by the proprietor of the patent or application to the order of a government department, section 55(4) above shall have effect as if that act were use made by virtue of an authority given under that section.

(5) Where section 55(4) above applies to any use of an invention and a person holds an exclusive licence under the patent or application concerned (other than such a licence as is mentioned in subsection (3) above) authorising him to work the invention, then subsections (7) and (8) below shall apply.

(6) In those subsections "the section 55(4)" payment means such payment (if any) as the proprietor of the patent or application and the department agree under section 55 above, or the court determines under section 58 below, should be made by the department to the proprietor in respect of the use of the invention.

(7) The licensee shall be entitled to recover from the proprietor of the patent or application such part (if any) of the section 55(4) payment as may be agreed on by them or as may in default of agreement be determined by the court under section 58 below to be just having regard to any expenditure incurred by the licensee—

(a) in developing the invention, or

(b) in making payments to the proprietor in consideration of the licence, other than royalties or other payments determined by reference to the use of the invention.

(8) Any agreement by the proprietor of the patent or application and the department under section 55(4) above as to the amount of the section 55(4) payment shall be of no effect unless the licensee consents to the agreement; and any determination by the court under section 55(4) above as to the amount of that payment shall be of no effect unless the licensee has been informed of the reference to the court and is given an opportunity to be heard.

(9) Where any models, documents or information relating to an invention are used in connection with any use of the invention which falls within subsection (1)(a) above, or with anything done in respect of the invention which falls within subsection (1)(b) above, subsection (4) of section 55 above shall (whether or not it applies to any such use of the invention) apply to the use of the models, documents or information as if for the reference in it to the proprietor of the patent there were substituted a reference to the person entitled to the benefit of any provision of an agreement which is rendered inoperative by this section in relation to that use; and in section 58 below the references to terms for the use of an invention shall be construed accordingly.

(10) Nothing in this section shall be construed as authorising the disclosure to a government department or any other person of any model, document or information to the use of which this section applies in contravention of any such licence, assignment, assignation or agreement as is mentioned in this section.

Note. Subsection (1) was amended by Sch.7 para.20 to the CDPA 1988, effective from August 1, 1989 (SI 1989/816): the definition of "design right" thereby inserted includes rights in a "semiconductor topography" (Design Right (Semiconductor Topographies) Regulations 1989, SI 1989/1100, as amended by SI 1993/2497).

COMMENTARY ON SECTION 57

Scope of the section

57.02   Section 57 concerns the rights of third parties in respect of Crown use under ss.55 and 56. The language of the section is involved and its interpretation not free from difficulty. The provisions extend not only to Crown use of granted patents, but also to the use by the Crown of an invention which is the subject of a pending published application.

Under the section, Crown use of an invention (including any model, document or information relating to it) is not inhibited by the existence of any licence, assignment (assignation in Scotland) or agreement, made between the proprietor of the invention or a successor in title and a third party other than a government department, and making use of any such model or document does not amount to any infringement of any relevant copyright or design right (subss.(1) and (2)). Subsections (9) and (10) provide some consequential provisions in relation to the use of models, documents or information as permitted by subs.(1).

Subsections (3)–(8) provide for various situations where the patent has been assigned (subs.(4)) or where an exclusive licence has been granted under the patent (subss.(3) and (5)). These subsections specify the person entitled in these circumstances to compensation under s.55(4), this depending upon the particular nature of the exclusive licence and the possibility of the patent proprietor being authorised to work the patent himself despite having assigned his rights under the patent. Subsections (6)–(8) concern the possible sharing of compensation under s.55(4) between the proprietor and his exclusive licensee (subs.(7)); and the position of a licensee when the proprietor has recourse to the court to settle an amount of compensation under s.55(4) (subs.(8)).

Position under licences or assignments (subss.(1) and (2))

57.03   Any Crown use is not to be subject under subs.(1) to any restraint by virtue of an existing licence or agreement between the proprietor and any third party. Typically, a licensee of the proprietor may by authorisation under s.55 be discharged from certain obligations under the licence for the purposes of the Crown use.

Subsection (1) refers to items, such as models and documents, which might have been passed by a patentee to, typically, a licensee or assignee in connection with a patent agreement. The provision enables the Crown, in placing a contract with such a person, to set aside an agreement which, through its terms or by the existence of copyright or unregistered design right (including rights in a "semiconductor topography", see Note to §57.01), could inhibit that party from fulfilling a contract which the Crown may wish to place with that party, the copyright and design right thereby being overridden. In addition, subs.(1) enables the Crown to set aside any royalty or other payment otherwise required by such an agreement. When payments under a licence are set aside, settlement with the proprietor of the patent concerned is made by way of compensation under s.55(4); and, if the licensee is an exclusive licensee, that person can now claim, under s.57A, for loss of his manufacturing profit.

The agreement in question can be between the proprietor or any person who derives title from him and "any person whatever" other than a government department. This comprehensive wording would apparently include a joint proprietor, whose position under the Registered Designs Act 1949 was considered in *Patchett's Patent* [1963] R.P.C 90 and [1967] R.P.C 77 and 237 CA.

The position of a non-royalty-paying exclusive licensee (subs.(3))

57.04   Subsection (3) puts in the same position as the proprietor an exclusive licensee who has acquired his right for a lump sum or for some other consideration not based on use. The term "exclusive licensee" is defined in s.130(1) and discussed in §67.03.

Assignments for royalty (subs.(4))

Where the patent has been assigned for a consideration based on use, subs.(4) provides **57.05** that the assignor shall be treated in some respects as if he were a joint proprietor. Sums payable in respect of Crown use are to be divided between the assignor and the proprietor. However, if the latter himself is a contractor, it would appear equitable that payments under s.55(4) should be paid to the assignor, as the latter could now presumably have made a claim under s.57A if he had not been awarded the contract in question. Section 57(1)(b) makes clear that such a proprietor may be required to supply articles for Crown use, but it seems unlikely that he would then be entitled to compensation under s.55(4). However, any "dispute" between a proprietor-contractor and the Crown can be referred to the court under s.58.

Entitlement of certain exclusive licensees (subss.(5)–(8))

Subsection (5), in conjunction with subss.(7) and (8) to which it refers, provides for a **57.06** royalty-paying exclusive licensee to have a right to an agreed or settled portion of the payment by the Crown for the use of the invention, defined in subs.(6) as "the section 55(4)" payment; and for the consent of such an exclusive licensee to be necessary for any agreement between the Crown and the proprietor as to payment for the use of the invention. In the event of the court being requested to settle the payment under s.58, the exclusive licensee must be informed, and he then has the right to be heard (subs.(8)).

Use of documents, models and information (subss.(9) and (10))

Subsection (9) concerns the position of parties to an agreement rendered inoperative by **57.07** virtue of s.57. The subsection provides that there is a right of claim in respect of use of models, documents and information where an agreement is ineffective by virtue of s.57, and subs.(10) precludes disclosure of matter in breach of an agreement with which the section is concerned.

The Defence Contracts Act (the relevant provisions of which are reprinted at §§55.02–55.07 and discussed in §55.12) covers use for "defence" purposes of technical information in the possession of contractors, or potential contractors, who are subject to restrictions imposed by agreements or copyrights. Access to other relevant intellectual property rights has now been provided by the CDPA 1988, see §55.10.

SECTION 57A [ADDED]

Compensation for loss of profit

57A.—(1) Where use is made of an invention for the services of the Crown, **57A.01** the government department concerned shall pay—

    (a) to the proprietor of the patent, or

    (b) if there is an exclusive licence in force in respect of the patent, to the exclusive licensee,

compensation for any loss resulting from his not being awarded a contract to supply the patented product or, as the case may be, to perform the patented process or supply a thing made by means of the patented process.

(2) Compensation is payable only to the extent that such a contract could have been fulfilled from his existing manufacturing or other capacity; but is payable notwithstanding the existence of circumstances rendering him ineligible for the award of such a contract.

(3) In determining the loss, regard shall be had to the profit which would have been made on such a contract and to the extent to which any manufacturing or other capacity was under-used.

(4) No compensation is payable in respect of any failure to secure contracts to supply the patented product or, as the case may be, to perform the patented process or supply a thing made by means of the patented process, otherwise than for the services of the Crown.

(5) The amount payable shall, if not agreed between the proprietor or licensee and the government department concerned with the approval of the Treasury, be determined by the court on a reference under section 58, and is in addition to any amount payable under section 55 or 57.

(6) In this section "the government department concerned", in relation to any use of an invention for the services of the Crown, means the government department by whom or on whose authority the use was made.

(7) In the application of this section to Northern Ireland, the reference in subsection (5) above to the Treasury shall, where the government department concerned is a department of the Government of Northern Ireland, be construed as a reference to the Department of Finance and Personnel.

Notes

1. Section 57A was inserted by Sch.5 para.16(1) to the Copyright, Designs and Patents Act 1988 ("CDPA 1988").

2. The operation of s.57A has become subject to the provisions of the Visiting Forces and International Headquarters (Application of Law) Order 1999 (SI 1999/1736) for which see §55.08.

Commentary on Section 57A

Scope of the section

57A.02   Section 57A was introduced by the CDPA 1988 and provides for compensation in respect of loss that a manufacturing patentee or licensee incurs as a result of not being awarded a contract which, but for the exercise of powers under s.55, he might reasonably have expected to have received. Compensation under this head is additional to compensation payable to a patentee under s.55(4) or to a third party under s.57(4) (subs.(5)). In some cases this additional compensation could increase very markedly the compensation payable for Crown use of a patented invention, and the section has the effect of overruling in part the decision in *Patchett's Patent* (1967) R.P.C. 237 CA. In the absence of agreement, a claimant or the relevant government department may, by subs.(5), refer the question of compensation, or its quantum, under the section to the court under amended s.58, for which see the commentary on that section.

The CDPA 1988 has made similar provision in the case of registered designs (by adding para.2A to Sch.1 to the Registered Designs Act 1949, c.88, re-presented in Sch.4 to the CDPA 1988; and, in the case of unregistered design rights, by s.243 of the CDPA 1988.

Entitlement to compensation under section 57A (subs.(1))

57A.03   By subs.(1), compensation is payable either to the patentee or, if there is an exclusive licensee under the patent, to the exclusive licensee. Compensation is not payable to a non-exclusive licensee under either s.55 or s.57A.

"Use" in subs.(1) is defined in s.55(2).

Extent of compensation (subs.(2))

57A.04   Under subs.(2), compensation is payable to a person only to the extent that the contract for the Crown use could have been fulfilled by him from his existing manufacturing capacity. The first part of subs.(2) suggests that only circumstances outside the direct control of the claimant are intended to make the section applicable. Thus, for example, inadequate quality control systems may exclude an otherwise valid claim under the section, at least to the extent that the circumstances extended over a particular period of time; and, in the case of repeat orders, the circumstances will apparently need to be judged in relation to each contract. However, under the second part of the subsection, compensation is payable if circumstances outside the control of the claimant (such as security or public policy) render him ineligible for the contract.

It is clear, therefore, that in determining eligibility, consideration will have to be given to the ability of the claimant to have met the requirements of the contract in terms of specification, delivery time and quality. It appears that any refusal to pay compensation under s.57A can be referred to the court under s.58, though subs.(5) is silent on the point. It is by no means clear how eligibility for compensation could be established in the face of a decision from a government department that the potential contractor could not have met the order in question.

Quantum of compensation (subs.(3))

Under subs.(3), regard is to be had to the profit which would have been made on such a contract and to the extent to which manufacturing or other capacity was under-used. Presumably, a government department will take the view that "profit" should be determined by the conventional rules applied by government departments for determining profit under government contracts. Whether the court would take the same view is more problematical. If a claimant is due to make payments to a third party under a licence or other agreement relating to the patent, "profit" should be determined after deduction of such payments. Compensation to that other party, if he is entitled, will then be determined under ss.55 and 57A and will take the place of royalty. **57A.05**

Exclusions (subs.(4))

Subsection (4) makes clear that the section applies only to failure to secure contracts for "the services of the Crown", as that term has been construed in relation to s.55, for which see §§55.13 and 56.04. Loss sustained through failure to secure other contracts continues to be dealt with, if at all, as infringement under s.60. **57A.06**

Compensation under s.57A will not be payable if the Crown can establish that the patent in question is not valid, or (by analogy with s.62) that any valid claims do not cover the matter in issue. This stems from the fact that compensation is payable only in respect of a "patented product" or "patented process". However, there might still be a claim under the equivalent design right provision contained in s.243 of the CDPA 1988 if a design right can be shown to be involved in the contract.

Miscellaneous points (subss.(5)–(7))

The arrangements in subs.(5) for approval by the Treasury, and settlement of disputes by the court under a reference under s.58, are similar to those provided for in s.55(4) for compensation under s.55, but subs.(5) makes it clear that compensation under s.57A is additional to any other compensation payable to the proprietor under s.55 or to a third party under s.57. **57A.07**

Subsection (6) provides a special definition of a "government department" for the purposes of the section, viz. that which gave the authority for Crown use under s.55.

Subsection (7) mirrors s.55(11) and the position in Northern Ireland, and the Isle of Man, is therefore the same as that under s.55, for which see §55.24.

PRACTICE UNDER SECTION 57A

Section 57A is unlike any previous provision relating to Crown use. However, cases decided under s.50 may be relevant. For example, in *Enviro-Spray's Patents* (1986) R.P.C. 147, an applicant for a compulsory licence was not able to demonstrate satisfactorily that he was capable of working the invention. Subsection (2) makes it clear that an applicant for compensation under s.57A cannot be successful unless he had the ability and capacity **57A.08** to have fulfilled the order in question, though it is not clear whether the onus lies to establish an eligibility or an ineligibility. The words "only to the extent that" suggest the latter, see §57A.04.

Applications for compensation should be addressed in writing to the Department concerned, but in the case of the Ministry of Defence it is appropriate to write to the Head of Defence Intellectual Property Rights at the address given in §55.25 who can also be contacted on any query arising under the section.

As Government Departments follow the process of arts 30 and 31 of the TRIPS Agreement (see §48.02), the circumstances in which a successful claim under the section could be made are likely to be very rare indeed.

SECTION 58

References of disputes as to Crown use

58.01   **58.—(1) Any dispute as to—**

(a) **the exercise by a government department, or a person authorised by a government department, of the powers conferred by section 55 above,**

(b) **terms for the use of an invention for the services of the Crown under that section,**

(c) **the right of any person to receive any part of a payment made in pursuance of subsection (4) of that section, or**

(d) **the right of any person to receive a payment under section 57A,**

may be referred to the court by either party to the dispute after a patent has been granted for the invention.

[(1) *Any dispute as to the exercise by a government department or a person authorized by a government department of the powers conferred by section 55 above, or as to the terms for the use of an invention for the services of the crown thereunder, or as to the right of any person to receive any part of a payment made or agreed to be made in pursuance of subsection (4) of that section or determined by the court in pursuance of that subsection and this section may be referred to the court by either party to the dispute after a patent has been granted for the invention.*]

(2) If in such proceedings any question arises whether an invention has been recorded or tried as mentioned in section 55 above, and the disclosure of any document recording the invention, or of any evidence of the trial thereof, would in the opinion of the department be prejudicial to the public interest, the disclosure may be made confidentially to counsel for the other party or to an independent expert mutually agreed upon.

(3) In determining under this section any dispute between a government department and any person as to the terms for the use of an invention for the services of the Crown, the court shall have regard—

(a) to any benefit or compensation which that person or any person from whom he derives title may have received or may be entitled to receive directly or indirectly from any government department in respect of the invention in question;

(b) to whether that person or any person from whom he derives title has in the court's opinion without reasonable cause failed to comply with a request of the department to use the invention for the services of the Crown on reasonable terms.

(4) In determining whether or not to grant any relief **under subsection (1)(a), (b) or (c) above** [*under this section*] and the nature and extent of the relief granted the court shall, subject to the following provisions of this section, apply the principles applied by the court immediately before the appointed day to the granting of relief under section 48 of the 1949 Act.

(5) On a reference under this section the court may refuse to grant relief by way of compensation in respect of the use of an invention for the services of the Crown during any further period specified under section 25(4) above, but before the payment of the renewal fee and any additional fee prescribed for the purposes of that section.

(6) Where an amendment of the specification of a patent has been allowed under any of the provisions of this Act, the court shall not grant relief by way of compensation under this section in respect of any such use before the decision to allow the amendment unless the court is satisfied that—

(a) the specification of the patent as published was framed in good faith and with reasonable skill and knowledge, **and**

(b) the relief is sought in good faith.

(7) If the validity of a patent is put in issue in proceedings under this section and it is found that the patent is only partially valid, the court may, subject to subsection (8) below, grant relief to the proprietor of the patent in respect of that part of the patent which is found to be valid and to have been used for the services of the Crown.

(8) Where in any such proceedings it is found that a patent is only partially valid, the court shall not grant relief by way of compensation, costs or expenses except where the proprietor of the patent proves that—

(a) the specification of the patent was framed in good faith and with reasonable skill and knowledge, **and**

(b) the relief is sought in good faith,

and in that event the court may grant relief in respect of the part of the patent which is valid and has been so used, subject to the discretion of the court as to costs and expenses and as to the date from which compensation should be awarded.

(9) As a condition of any such relief the court may direct that the specification of the patent shall be amended to its satisfaction upon an application made for that purpose under section 75 below, and an application may be so made accordingly, whether or not all other issues in the proceedings have been determined.

(9A) The court may also grant such relief in the case of a European patent (UK) on condition that the claims of the patent are limited to its satisfaction by the European Patent Office at the request of the proprietor.

(10) In considering the amount of any compensation for the use of an invention for the services of the Crown after publication of an application for a patent for the invention and before such a patent is granted, the court shall consider whether or not it would have been reasonable to expect, from a consideration of the application as published under section 16 above, that a patent would be

granted conferring on the proprietor of the patent protection for an act of the same description as that found to constitute that use, and if the court finds that it would not have been reasonable, it shall reduce the compensation to such amount as it thinks just.

(11) Where by virtue of a transaction, instrument or event to which section 33 above applies a person becomes the proprietor or one of the proprietors or an exclusive licensee of a patent (the new proprietor or licensee) and a government department or a person authorised by a government department subsequently makes use under section 55 above of the patented invention, the new proprietor or licensee shall not be entitled to any compensation under section 55(4) above (as it stands or as modified by section 57(3) above), **or to any compensation under section 57A above**, in respect of a subsequent use of the invention before the transaction, instrument or event is registered unless—

(a) the transaction, instrument or event is registered within the period of six months beginning with its date; or

(b) the court is satisfied that it was not practicable to register the transaction, instrument or event before the end of that period and that it was registered as soon as practicable thereafter.

(12) In any proceedings under this section the court may at any time order the whole proceedings or any question or issue of fact arising in them to be referred, on such terms as the court may direct, to a Circuit judge discharging the functions of an official referee or an arbitrator in England and Wales, **the Isle of Man** or Northern Ireland, or to an arbiter in Scotland; and references to the court in the foregoing provisions of this section shall be construed accordingly.

(13) One of two or more joint proprietors of a patent or application for a patent may without the concurrence of the others refer a dispute to the court under this section, but shall not do so unless the others are made parties to the proceedings; but any of the others made a defendant or defender shall not be liable for any costs or expenses unless he enters an appearance and takes part in the proceedings.

Notes

1. Subsection (1) was replaced, and subss.(4) and (11) amended, by CDPA 1988 (c.48) s.295 and Sch.5 para.16(2) and (3) with effect from August 1, 1989, SI 1989/816.

2. Subsection (12) was amended by SI 1978/621.

3. Subsections (6) and (8) were amended and subs.(9A) added by the Patents Act 2004 with effect from December 13, 2007, SI 2007/3396.

4. The operation of s.58 has become subject to the provisions of the Visiting Forces and International Headquarters (Application of Law) Order 1999 (SI 1999/1736) for which see §55.08.

5. The inclusion of the reference to the Isle of Man in subs.(12) is as a consequence of SI 2003/1249.

Commentary on Section 58

Scope of the section

58.02   Section 58 specifies the procedure to be followed if a dispute arises concerning the use, or the terms of use, by the Crown of a patented invention, or the entitlement to payment under ss.55(4), 57(3) or 57A. Any award under s.57A is in addition to any award under s.55 or s.57 (s.57A(5)). Several of the detailed provisions of the section mirror those applicable to actions for infringement and are needed because acts of Crown use do not rank as acts of infringement, see §55.11. The Crown cannot prevent a dispute being referred to a court under s.58, even apparently in matters concerning use by a proprietor-contractor. *Patchett's Patent* (1963) R.P.C. 90; and (1967) R.P.C. 77; (1967) R.P.C. 237 CA is relevant to the position of co-proprietors.

The provision formerly present in s.48(2) of the 1949 Act that, in the event of a dispute being brought before the court, the Crown can put the validity of the patent in issue, is now to be found in s.74(1)(e). Thus, as formerly, a proprietor wishing to have a dispute resolved by the court must face the possibility of the expense of full validity proceedings. If validity is put in issue then s.75(1) operates, and the court may allow the specification to be amended.

A referral under s.58 may be made to any court as defined in s.130(1) (as amended), for discussion of which see §96.06. However, it is to be expected that proceedings under the section will normally be commenced in the High Court, when they will come before the Patents Court, see CPR 63.3(2) (reprinted in §F63.02). The Patents Court is also required to hear any dispute arising under the Defence Contracts Act 1958 (c.38) (the relevant sections of which are reprinted in §§55.02–55.07, and discussed in §55.12). On the possible jurisdiction of patents county courts in relation to s.58, see §58.06.

Reference of disputes (subs.(1))

Subsection (1) was amended by the CDPA 1988 to provide for disputes under s.57A, **58.03** but no longer providing for settlement of disputes as to payments agreed, or determined, but not paid. If a dispute arises as to the exercise by a government department of its rights under s.55, or the terms of use of an invention, or as to a division of payments, or as to compensation under s.57A, either party may refer the matter to the court provided that a patent has been granted.

In theory, it may not be easy to determine at what stage of negotiations a dispute can be said to have arisen, but the difficulty can be circumvented if one party desires to put the matter before the court.

Disclosure of prior record of invention (subs.(2))

In the case of a dispute whether a prior record had been made of an invention with reference to s.55(3), subs.(2) provides for counsel or an agreed expert to examine, in **58.04** confidence, records of the prior record or trial if, in the opinion of the government department, disclosure of the documents or evidence of the prior activities would be prejudicial to the public interest.

Determination of relief (subss.(3)–(11))

Under subs.(3)(a) the court must have regard to any benefit or compensation the claimant may have received from a government department in respect of the invention when **58.05** settling payment.

Subsection (3)(b) provides that the court is to have regard also to whether the claimant has failed to comply with a request to use the patent for the services of Crown on reasonable terms, but the provision gives no indication of the way in which the court is to relate the failure to offer reasonable terms to the payment made.

Subsection (4) provides that in determining whether or not to grant relief, the court is to adopt the same principles as those adopted before the appointed day in granting relief under s.48 of the 1949 Act. The wording is similar to that adopted in s.61(6), concerning relief in respect of infringement. The direct effect of the provision is not clear. Few cases reached the court under s.48 of the 1949 Act and principles can scarcely be said to have developed, except possibly the "willing licensor and willing licensee" of *Patchett's Patent* (1967) R.P.C. 237 at 252, but the effect of this case has been considerably changed by the introduction of s.57A.

The later subsections of s.58 make Crown use of patented inventions subject to certain provisions which apply in the case of infringement of a patent, such as those referred to in s.62 of the Act, but which would not otherwise apply to Crown use since, by s.55, Crown use is not infringement. Thus, subs.(5) gives to Crown use the same dispensation as arises with an infringement committed in the six months allowed for belated renewal of a patent as is provided in s.62(2), but s.25(4)(c) provides that use in the further period allowed is to be taken as Crown use for the purpose of s.55(4).

Similarly, subs.(6) concerns the case where the patent in question has been amended; the proprietor must show that the specification as published was framed in good faith and with reasonable skill and knowledge. The subsection parallels s.62(3) concerning infringement. Subsections (7) and (8) deal with a similar situation with regard to a partially valid patent. Section 63 provides that where a partially valid patent is infringed, relief may be granted if the specification was framed in good faith and with reasonable skill and knowledge, and subss.(7) and (8) similarly provide for relief in respect of Crown use in such circumstances. Likewise, in subs.(9), the court can call for amendment of the specification of a partially valid patent, as under s.63(3) with an infringement action. A similar provision is applied in the case of a partially valid European patent (UK), see s.77(3).

The amendments made to subss.(6) and (8) by the 2004 Act parallel those made to ss.62(3) and 63(2) and have effect to provide that, in the case of a patent found to be only partially valid or which has been amended, relief for Crown use is predicated on the patentee satisfying the court that, not only was the patent framed in good faith and with reasonable skill and knowledge, but also that the proceedings for relief were "brought in good faith". Thus, Crown use compensation may be denied where the patentee knew, or ought to have known, that during a period in respect of which a claim for compensation is made, or was threatened, the patent was not wholly valid. In relation to a claim for compensation for Crown use of a European patent (UK), subs.(9A) has similar effect to that of new s.63(4), as discussed in §63.04.

Subsection (10) applies to Crown use of a patent before grant, a condition similar to that which applies to infringement under s.69(3): it must be reasonable to expect that a patent would be granted on the basis of the application as published covering the use, and if not the court has power to vary the compensation.

Subsection (11) provides that, where a patent is the subject of an event warranting registration under s.33, the right to claim compensation for Crown use is diminished in the same way as are the rights to relief for infringement diminished by s.68: the event must be registered within six months, or as soon as may be, or the right for compensation for use thereafter until registration is forfeited.

The commentaries on the above provisions are therefore also relevant to the consideration of points arising under s.58.

Reference to a circuit judge (subs.(12))

58.06   Subsection (12) permits the court to refer part or whole of the dispute to a circuit judge acting as an arbitrator or the equivalent in parts of the United Kingdom other than England and Wales. It is possible that similar powers could also provide for a referral of proceedings, or certain questions arising in them, to a patents county court, the jurisdiction of which is discussed in §287.05, but this does not appear so at present.

Joint proprietors (subs.(13))

58.07   Subsection (13) requires that, as in infringement proceedings under s.66(2), where there are joint proprietors of a patent concerned in a dispute all must be joined as parties to the matter, but if joined as a defendant any joint proprietor will not be liable for costs if he does not appear.

PRACTICE UNDER SECTION 58

58.08   If proceedings under s.58 are brought in the Patents Court, CPR 63.3 (reprinted in Appendix F at §F63.03) applies along with the practice directions under it. The procedure will then generally follow that described in the commentary on practice under s.61, below.

SECTION 59

Special provisions as to Crown use during emergency

59.—(1) During any period of emergency within the meaning of this section **59.01** the powers exercisable in relation to an invention by a government department or a person authorised by a government department under section 55 above shall include power to use the invention for any purpose which appears to the department necessary or expedient—

(a) for the efficient prosecution of any war in which Her Majesty may be engaged;

(b) for the maintenance of supplies and services essential to the life of the community;

(c) for securing a sufficiency of supplies and services essential to the well-being of the community;

(d) for promoting the productivity of industry, commerce and agriculture;

(e) for fostering and directing exports and reducing imports, or imports of any classes, from all or any countries and for redressing the balance of trade;

(f) generally for ensuring that the whole resources of the community are available for use, and are used, in a manner best calculated to serve the interests of the community; or

(g) for assisting the relief of suffering and the restoration and distribution of essential supplies and services in any country or territory outside the United Kingdom which is in grave distress as the result of war;

and any reference in this Act to the services of the Crown shall, as respects any period of emergency, include a reference to those purposes.

(2) In this section the use of an invention includes, in addition to any act constituting such use by virtue of section 55 above, any act which would, apart from that section and this section, amount to an infringement of the patent concerned or, as the case may be, give rise to a right under section 69 below to bring proceedings in respect of the application concerned, and any reference in this Act to "use for the services of the Crown" shall, as respects any period of emergency, be construed accordingly.

(3) In this section "period of emergency" means any period beginning with such date as may be declared by Order in Council to be the commencement, and ending with such date as may be so declared to be the termination, of a period of emergency for the purposes of this section.

(4) A draft of an Order under this section shall not be submitted to Her Majesty unless it has been laid before, and approved by resolution of, each House of Parliament.

COMMENTARY ON SECTION 59

Scope of the section

Section 59 has effect only during a period for which a "declaration of emergency" has **59.02** been made. Subsection (3) provides that a period of emergency is one declared so to be by an Order in Council; by subs.(4) the draft of such an order must be approved by both

Houses of Parliament. Since the 1977 Act came into force no such declaration has been made: the South Atlantic conflict in 1982 did not lead to the declaration of an emergency for the purposes of this section.

Extension of powers

59.03   Section 59 provides wider powers during a declared emergency for use by the Crown of inventions. Subsection (1) refers alone to "use" which, in subs.(2), is defined as including that which constitutes Crown use as defined by s.55 and also anything which, but for s.55, would be an infringement of the patent and anything which would fall within s.69.

However, the power provided by the section may be curtailed in its application as a consequence of European law, having regard to the decision in *EC Commission v United Kingdom* (C-30/90) [1993] R.P.C. 283; [1992] 1 E.C.R. 829 ECJ, (discussed in §48A.04), and/or of accession to the TRIPS Agreement, having regard to arts 30 and 31 (reprinted at §48A.02), even though s.59 has not been amended to meet the requirements of either of these. On these points, it is to be noted that s.53(5) (discussed in §53.05) does not apply to s.59. While art.31 of the TRIPS Agreement does allow for a compulsory licence to be granted without prior application to the patentee "in situations of national emergency or other circumstances of extreme urgency" (see TRIPS art.31(b), discussed in §48A.05), it would otherwise appear to be a breach of the United Kingdom's obligations under this Agreement to exercise the power provided by s.59, but any such breach would be a matter solely for the World Trade Organisation to rule upon, such breach not providing any remedy to an individual affected by it, see *Lenzing's European Patent* (1997) R.P.C. 245 discussed in §77.06.

Also, the provisions of s.59 are limited to patents, but similar rights exist for registered designs and unregistered design rights respectively under the Registered Designs Act 1949 (c.88) (Sch.1 para.4, as amended by the CDPA 1988 Sch.3 para.37(4) and (5)), and re-presented in Sch.4 to the CDPA 1988 (para.4 of it), and CDPA 1988 s.244. "Topography rights" are also now included within the concept of "design rights", see §55.10. Whilst there appear to be no corresponding emergency provisions, apart from those of s.57(1), in relation to copyrights, it is possible that the Defence Contracts Act 1958 (c.38), the relevant sections of which are reprinted in §§55.02–55.07, could be used in appropriate circumstances.

The definition in s.130(1) of "services of the Crown" and of "use for the services of the Crown" for the purposes of s.59 are those in s.59 itself, see s.130(1).

War-time legislation

59.04   On the outbreak of any war, it is likely that further legislation would be enacted for confiscation of enemy-owned intellectual property rights, e.g. as was done under the Trading with the Enemy Act 1939 (c.89); and also for the taking of even wider powers in relation to the ordering of compulsory licences. However, the Patents, Designs, Copyright and Trade Marks (Emergency) Act 1939 (c.107) remains in force. This Act was amended by the CDPA 1988 (Sch.7 para.3) to refer to "design rights" (including rights in a "semiconductor topography", Design Right (Semiconductor Topographies) Regulations 1989 (SI 1989/1100, as amended by SI 1993/2497); and by the Trade Marks Act 1994 (c.26) Sch.4 para.3 in relation to trade marks. It provides powers which could be exercised in a time of war for the compulsory licensing of any patent, registered design, trade mark, design right or copyright in which an "enemy or enemy subject" has an interest, as these terms are defined in the Trading with the Enemy Act 1939 (c.89) see s.2). This "Emergency" Act has effect only during a declared "state of war", and so has no present effect. The address of a proprietor entered in the appropriate register on patents, designs and trade marks as being in an "enemy" country is prima facie evidence of enemy status under the Patents, Designs, Copyright and Trade Marks (Emergency) Act (s.7).

This "Emergency" Act also makes provision for the continued validity of grants, assignments and licences of intellectual property rights arising from "enemy subjects", notwithstanding the terms of the Trading with the Enemy Act 1939, and the Comptroller is given power to revoke or vary such an existing licence upon application to him (s.1). The

Comptroller is also empowered to grant licences (which can be exclusive) under intellectual property rights of "enemy subjects", and any such licensee is given power to bring infringement proceedings (s.2).

Despite a "state of war", the grant of intellectual property rights to "enemy" persons can continue (s.4); and the status of an enemy country as a "convention country" (for the purposes of s.159 of the CDPA 1988) or a country enjoying reciprocal copyright or design right protection is not affected (s.5). Section 6 provides a general power to the Comptroller to extend time limits having regard to circumstances arising out of a person being on active service or otherwise due to a state of war.

Although this 1939 Act has not been updated to replace references to the Patents and Designs Act 1907 by references to either the 1949 or 1977 Act, s.10(3) appears to be an automatic updating provision. There is power to make Rules and levy fees (s.9), but no such Rules presently exist.

Infringement [Sections 60–71]

SECTION 60

Meaning of infringement

60.—(1) Subject to the provisions of this section, a person infringes a patent for an invention if, but only if, while the patent is in force, he does any of the following things in the United Kingdom in relation to the invention without the consent of the proprietor of the patent, that is to say— **60.01**

    (a) where the invention is a product, he makes, disposes of, offers to dispose of, uses or imports the product or keeps it whether for disposal or otherwise;

    (b) where the invention is a process, he uses the process or he offers it for use in the United Kingdom when he knows, or it is obvious to a reasonable person in the circumstances, that its use there without the consent of the proprietor would be an infringement of the patent;

    (c) where the invention is a process, he disposes of, offers to dispose of, uses or imports any product obtained directly by means of that process or keeps any such product whether for disposal or otherwise.

(2) Subject to the following provisions of this section, a person (other than the proprietor of the patent) also infringes a patent for an invention if, while the patent is in force and without the consent of the proprietor, he supplies or offers to supply in the United Kingdom a person other than a licensee or other person entitled to work the invention with any of the means, relating to an essential element of the invention, for putting the invention into effect when he knows, or it is obvious to a reasonable person in the circumstances, that those means are suitable for putting, and are intended to put, the invention into effect in the United Kingdom.

(3) Subsection (2) above shall not apply to the supply or offer of a staple commercial product unless the supply or the offer is made for the purpose of inducing the person supplied or, as the case may be, the person to whom the offer is made to do an act which constitutes an infringement of the patent by virtue of subsection (1) above.

(4) *[Without prejudice to section 86 below, subsections (1) and (2) above shall not apply to any act which, under any provision of the Community Patent*

*Convention relating to the exhaustion of the rights of the proprietor of a patent,
as that provision applies by virtue of that section, cannot be prevented by the
proprietor of the patent.*]

(5) An act which, apart from this subsection, would constitute an infringement
of a patent for an invention shall not do so if—

(a) it is done privately and for purposes which are not commercial;

(b) it is done for experimental purposes relating to the subject-matter of the
invention;

(c) it consists of the extemporaneous preparation in a pharmacy of a
medicine for an individual in accordance with a prescription given by a
registered medical or dental practitioner or consists of dealing with a
medicine so prepared;

(d) it consists of the use, exclusively for the needs of a relevant ship, of a
product or process in the body of such a ship or in its machinery, tackle,
apparatus or other accessories, in a case where the ship has temporarily
or accidentally entered the internal or territorial waters of the United
Kingdom;

(e) it consists of the use of a product or process in the body or operation of a
relevant aircraft, hovercraft or vehicle which has temporarily or accidentally entered or is crossing the United Kingdom (including the air
space above it and its territorial waters) or the use of accessories for such
a relevant aircraft, hovercraft or vehicle;

(f) it consists of the use of an exempted aircraft which has lawfully entered
or is lawfully crossing the United Kingdom as aforesaid or of the
importation into the United Kingdom, or the use or storage there, of any
part or accessory for such an aircraft;

**(g) it consists of the use by a farmer of the product of his harvest for
propagation or multiplication by him on his own holding, where
there has been a sale of plant propagating material to the farmer by
the proprietor of the patent or with his consent for agricultural use;**

**(h) it consists of the use of an animal or animal reproductive material
by a farmer for an agricultural purpose following a sale to the
farmer, by the proprietor of the patent or with his consent, of breeding stock or other animal reproductive material which constitutes or
contains the patented invention;**

(i) it consists of—

**(i) an act done in conducting a study, test or trial which is neces-
sary for and is conducted with a view to the application of
paragraphs 1 to 5 of article 13 of Directive 2001/82/EC or
paragraphs 1 to 4 of article 10 of Directive 2001/83/EC, or**

**(ii) any other act which is required for the purpose of the ap-
plication of those paragraphs.**

(6) For the purposes of subsection (2) above a person who does an act in relation to an invention which is prevented only by virtue of paragraph (a), (b) or (c)
of subsection (5) above from constituting an infringement of a patent for the
invention shall not be treated as a person entitled to work the invention, but—

(a) the reference in that subsection to a person entitled to work an invention includes a reference to a person so entitled by virtue of section 55 above, and

(b) a person who by virtue of **section 20B(4) or (5)** above or **section 28A(4) or (5)***[28(6)]* above or section 64 below **or section 117A(4) or (5) below** is entitled to do an act in relation to the invention without it constituting such an infringement shall, so far as concerns that act, be treated as a person entitled to work the invention.

(6A) Schedule A1 contains—

(a) provisions restricting the circumstances in which subsection (5)(g) applies; and

(b) provisions which apply where an act would constitute an infringement of a patent but for subsection (5)(g).

(6B) For the purposes of subsection (5)(h), use for an agricultural purpose—

(a) includes making an animal or animal reproductive material available for the purposes of pursuing the farmer's agricultural activity; but

(b) does not include sale within the framework, or for the purposes, of a commercial reproduction activity.

(6C) In paragraphs (g) and (h) of subsection (5) "sale" includes any other form of commercialisation.

(7) In this section—

"relevant ship" and "relevant aircraft, hovercraft or vehicle" mean respectively a ship and an aircraft, hovercraft or vehicle registered in, or belonging to, any country, other than the United Kingdom, which is a party to the Convention for the Protection of Industrial Property signed at Paris on 20th March 1883 **or which is a member of the World Trade Organisation**; and

"exempted aircraft" means an aircraft to which **section 89 of the Civil Aviation Act 1982** (aircraft exempted from seizure in respect of patent claims) applies.

" **Directive 2001/82/EC" means Directive 2001/82/EC of the European Parliament and of the Council on the Community code relating to veterinary medicinal products as amended by Directive 2004/28 of the European Parliament and of the Council;**

" **Directive 2001/83/EC" means Directive 2001/83/EC of the European Parliament and of the Council on the Community code relating to medicinal products for human use, as amended by Directive 2002/98/EC of the European Parliament and of the Council, by Commission Directive 2003/63/EC and by Directives 2004/24/EC and 2004/27/EC of the European Parliament and of the Council.**

Notes

1. Subsection (4) was repealed by Patents Act 2004 (c.16) Sch.3 para.1 (SI 2004/3205) with effect from January 1, 2005.

2. Subsections (5)(g) and (h) were added by the Patents Regulations 2000 (SI 2000/2037) reg.4(a) with effect from July 28, 2000.

3. Subsection (5)(i) was added by the Medicines (Marketing Authorisations Etc.) Amendment Regulations 2005 (SI 2005/2759) reg.3(a) with effect from October 30, 2005.

4. The words "section 20B(4) or (5) above or" and "or section 117A(4) or (5) below" were added to subs.6(a) by the Regulatory Reform (Patents) Order 2004 (SI 2004/2357) ("RRO") art.11(a) and art.11(b) respectively with effect from January 1, 2005. The words "section 28A(4) or (5)" were substituted by the CDPA 1988 (c.48) s.295, Sch.5 para.8(a).

5. Subsections (6A), (6B) and (6C) were added by the Patents Regulations 2000 (SI 2000/2037) reg.4(b) with effect from July 28, 2000.

6. In subs.(7), the words "or which is a member of the World Trade Organisation" were added to the definition of "relevant ship" by the Patents and Trade Marks (World Trade Organisation) Regulations SI 1999/1899 Pt II reg.7(5) with effect from July 29, 1999. The words "section 89 of the Civil Aviation Act 1982" were substituted in the definition of "exempted aircraft" by the Civil Aviation Act 1982 (c.16) s.109, Sch.15 para.19. Definitions to Directives 2001/82/EC, 2001/83/EC, and 2002/98/EC were inserted by the Medicines (Marketing Authorisations Etc.) Amendment Regulations SI 2005/2759 reg.3(b) (October 30, 2005).

7. The definitions of Directives 2001/82/EC, 2001/83/EC, and 2002/98/EC were inserted by the Medicines (Marketing Authorisations Etc.) Amendment Regulations (SI 2005/2759) reg.3(b) with effect from October 30, 2005.

Section 60(5)(g)

SCHEDULE A1

Derogation From Patent Protection in Respect of Biotechnological Inventions

Interpretation

60.02

1. In this Schedule–

"Council Regulation" means Council Regulation (EC) No.2100/94 of 27th July 1994 on Community plant variety rights;

"farmer's own holding" means any land which a farmer actually exploits for plant growing, whether as his property or otherwise managed under his own responsibility and on his own account;

"the gazette" means the gazette published under section 34 of the Plant Variety and Seeds Act 1964;

"protected material" means plant propagating material which incorporates material subject to a patent;

"relevant activity" means the use by a farmer of the product of his harvest for propagation or multiplication by him on his own holding, where the product of the harvest constitutes or contains protected material;

"relevant rights holder" means the proprietor of a patent to which protected material is subject;

"seed" includes seed potatoes;

"seed year" means the period from 1st July in one year to 30th June in the following year, both dates inclusive.

Specified species

2. Section 60(5)(g) applies only to varieties of the following plant species and groups:

Name	Common Name
Fodder plants	
Cicer arietinum L.	Chickpea milk vetch
Lupinus luteus L.	Yellow lupin
Medicago sativa L.	Lucerne
Pisum sativum L.(partim)	Field pea
Trifolium alexandrinum L.	Berseem/Egyptian clover
Trifolium resupinatum L.	Persian clover
Vicia faba	Field bean
Vicia sativa L.	Common vetch
Cereals	
Avena sativa	Oats
Hordeum vulgare L.	Barley
Oryza sativa L.	Rice
Phalaris canariensis L.	Canary grass
Secale cereale L.	Rye
X Triticosecale Wittm.	Triticale
Triticum aestivum L. emend. Fiori et Paol.	Wheat
Triticum durum Desf.	Durum wheat
Triticum spelta L.	Spelt wheat
Potatoes	
Solanum tuberosum	Potatoes
Oil and fibre plants	
Brassica napus L. (partim)	Swede rape
Brassica rapa L. (partim)	Turnip rape
Linum usitatissimum	Linseed with the exclusion of flax

Liability to pay equitable remuneration

3.—(1) If a farmer's use of protected material is authorised by section 60(5)(g), he shall, at the time of the use, become liable to pay the relevant rights holder equitable remuneration.

(2) That remuneration must be sensibly lower than the amount charged for the production of protected material of the same variety in the same area with the holder's authority.

(3) Remuneration is to be taken to be sensibly lower if it would be taken to be sensibly lower within the meaning of Article 14(3) fourth indent of the Council Regulation.

Exemption for small farmers

4.—(1) Paragraph 3 does not apply to a farmer who is considered to be a small farmer for the purposes of Article 14(3) third indent of the Regulation.

(2) It is for a farmer who claims to be a small farmer to prove that he is such a farmer.

Information to be supplied by farmer

5.—(1) At the request of a relevant rights holder ("H"), a farmer must tell H–
   (a) his name and address;
   (b) whether he has performed a relevant activity; and
   (c) if he has performed such an activity, the address of the holding on which he performed it.

(2) If the farmer has performed such an activity, he must tell H whether he is–

(a) liable to pay remuneration as a result of paragraph 3; or

(b) not liable because he is a small farmer.

(3) If the farmer has told H that he is liable to pay remuneration as a result of paragraph 3, he must tell H–

(a) the amount of the protected material used;

(b) whether the protected material has been processed for planting; and

(c) if it has, the name and address of the person who processed it.

(4) The farmer must comply with sub-paragraph (2) and (3) when complying with sub-paragraph (1).

(5) If the farmer has told H that he is liable to pay remuneration as a result of paragraph 3, he must (if H asks him to do so) tell H–

(a) whether he used any protected material with the authority of H within the same seed year; and

(b) if he did, the amount used and the name and address of the person who supplied it.

Information to be supplied by seed processor

6.—(1) On the request of a relevant rights holder, a seed processor shall supply the following information–

(a) the name and address of the seed processor;

(b) the address of the seed processor's principal place of business; and

(c) whether the seed processor has processed seed of a species specified in paragraph 2 above.

(2) If the seed processor has processed seed of a species specified in paragraph 2 above he shall also supply the following information with the information referred to in sub-paragraph (1)–

(a) the name and address of the person for whom the processing was carried out;

(b) the amount of seed resulting from the processing;

(c) the date processing commenced;

(d) the date processing was completed;

(e) the place where processing was carried out.

Information to be supplied by relevant rights holder

7. On the request of a farmer or a seed processor a relevant rights holder shall supply the following information–

(a) his name and address; and

(b) the amount of royalty charged for certified seed of the lowest certification category for seed containing that protected material.

Period in respect of which inquiry may be made

8. A request may be made under paragraphs 5, 6 and 7 in respect of the current seed year and the three preceding seed years.

Restriction on movement for processing from the holding

9. No person shall remove or cause to be removed from a holding protected material in order to process it unless–

(a) he has the permission of the relevant rights holder in respect of that protected material;

(b) he has taken measures to ensure that the same protected material is returned from processing as is sent for processing and the processor has undertaken to him that the processor has taken measures to ensure that the same protected material is returned from processing as is sent for processing; or

(c) he has the protected material processed by a seed processor on the list of processors referred to in the gazette as being permitted to process seed away from a holding.

Confidentiality

10.—(1) A person who obtains information pursuant to this Schedule shall owe an obligation of confidence in respect of the information to the person who supplied it.

(2) Sub-paragraph (1) shall not have effect to restrict disclosure of information–

    (a) for the purposes of, or in connection with, establishing the amount to be paid to the holder of rights pursuant to paragraph 3 and obtaining payment of that amount,

    (b) for the purposes of, or in connection with, establishing whether a patent has been infringed, or

    (c) for the purposes of, or in connection with, any proceedings for the infringement of a patent.

Formalities

11.—(1) A request for information under this Schedule, and any information given in response to such a request, must be in writing.

    (2) Information requested under this Schedule must be given–

    (a) within 28 days; or

    (b) if the request specifies a longer period, within the specified period.

Remedies

12.—(1) If, in response to a request under this Schedule, a person–

    (a) knowingly fails to provide information which he is required by this Schedule to give, or

    (b) refuses to provide any such information,

the court may order him to provide it.

    (2) Sub-paragraph (1) does not effect any of the court's other powers to make orders.

    (3) A person who knowingly provides false information in response to a request under this Schedule is liable in damages to the person who made the request.

    (4) In any action for damages under sub-paragraph (3) the court must have regard, in particular to–

    (a) how flagrant the defendant was in providing the false information, and

    (b) any benefit which accrued to him as a result of his providing false information,

and shall award such additional damages as the justice of the case may require.

Commentary on Section 60

Origin and scope of the section

Prior to the 1977 Act, there was no statutory definition of acts of infringement. These **60.03** were governed by the common law as applied to the prohibitions expressed in the wording of the Letters Patent grant. This system was replaced by s.60 creating a statutory tort of patent infringement. The origin for this was the "Declaration on the Adjustment of National Patent Law" which was annexed to the 1975 version of the CPC and effective upon its signature, i.e. independent of ratification. This Declaration obliged the Community Member States to bring their laws into conformity, as far as practicable, with corresponding provisions of the EPC, CPC and PCT. Section 60 is, accordingly, specified in s.130(7) as a section which has been so framed as to have, as nearly as practicable, the same effects in the United Kingdom as the corresponding provisions of (in this case) the CPC in the territories to which that Convention was intended to apply.

The relevant provisions of the CPC (as revised in 1989) are CPC arts 25–28. These are reprinted as part of the commentaries on the particular parts of s.60 to which they relate.

In considering the effect of s.60, attention should also be paid to provisions in the TRIPS Agreement because, presumably, s.60 has to be construed as being in conformity with TRIPS. The relevant TRIPS provisions are reprinted below in the paragraphs in which they are discussed.

Within s.60, subs.(1) defines the tort of substantive (or direct) infringement of a patent (including a European patent (UK)), while subss.(2) and (3) brought contributory (or indirect) infringement into the scope of infringing acts by defining a further aspect of the tort of patent infringement. Subsection (4) was never brought into force and has now been repealed because it dealt with exhaustion of rights under a Community patent.

Section 60 is also applicable to actions taken under s.69 for infringement of rights conferred by publication of a pending application (including a European application (UK)), see the commentary on s.69.

Section 60 can be invoked by the registered proprietor of the patent. It can also be invoked by an assignee or by the holder of a licence which is exclusive at least as to some aspect of the exercise of the patent rights, see s.68 and the commentary on that section. For the position concerning a joint proprietor, see s.66 and its commentary. Where an assignment or transmission of rights (valid under s.30 or s.31) has been entered into, or an exclusive licence has been granted, the subsequent proprietor or an exclusive licensee may be entitled to initiate a claim, but can then only obtain monetary relief under the conditions of s.68 which prevents the grant of such relief for acts of infringement prior to the registration of title in the register of patents unless the transaction, instrument or event was so registered within six months of it taking effect, see the commentary on s.68. Of course, there will be a valid defence to a claim for infringement if the defendant can show that the claimant is no longer the proprietor of the patent by virtue of some assignment (as in *Buchanan v Alba Diagnostics* [Scotland] [2000] R.P.C. 367; upheld on appeal [2001] R.P.C. 43 at 851 CA and [2004] R.P.C. 34 at 681 HL; see §31.05); and, likewise, if it is shown that a claimant claiming as an exclusive licensee is not so entitled having regard to the definition of an "exclusive licence", as discussed in the commentary on s.67.

The "extent of invention" protected by a patent is defined in s.125. Questions of infringement which depend on the scope of the patent, in the sense of the technical extent of the protection which it confers, are therefore dealt with in the commentary on that section. Accordingly, the present commentary deals only with liability under the law of torts for infringement of a patent, now made a statutory tort. Here, it must be remembered that Crown use (for which see ss.55–59 and the commentaries on those sections) is permitted use and is therefore not infringement under s.60.

The following ss.61–71 contain further provisions relating to infringement. Thus: ss.61–63 and 65 relate to procedure and remedies (including restrictions); s.64 provides a right of continuing use to persons who worked, or planned to work, the patented invention before its priority date; ss.66–68 specify the persons who can bring actions for infringement under s.60; s.69 applies s.60 to the rights arising from published pending applications; s.70 makes certain threats of infringement actionable as a separate, but related, tort; and s.71 relates to declarations of non-infringement. These matters are discussed in the respective commentaries on these sections.

Section 60 applies to infringement of patents granted under the Act (s.130(1)), and to European patents (UK) (s.77(1)). The section has displaced any residual element of common law in relation to infringement (*Genentech's Patent* [1989] R.P.C. 147 CA), though the former common law test of infringement may still apply when considering infringement of a United Kingdom patent registered in a (former) colony, see *Blackburn v Boon Engineering* [Brunei] [1991] F.S.R. 391. Since infringement is now a statutory tort, it is not permissible to plead a parallel alleged unlawful interference in the conduct of the patentee's business, such being a duplication of a right and remedy provided by this section (*Powerbreaker v Volex* BL CC/39/95).

Direct (or substantive) infringement (subs.(1))

—Scope of subsection (1)

60.04 Subsection (1) corresponds to art.25 of the CPC and by s.130(7) has to be interpreted (so far as possible) in conformity with it. Article 25 of the CPC reads:

"**CPC ARTICLE 25—Prohibition of direct use of invention**

A Community patent shall confer on its proprietor the right to prevent all third parties not having his consent:

(a) from making, offering, putting on the market or using a product which is the subject-matter of the patent, or importing or stocking the product for these purposes;

(b) from using a process which is the subject-matter of the patent or, when the third party knows, or it is obvious in the circumstances, that the use of the process is prohibited without the consent of the proprietor of the patent, from offering the process for use within the territories of the Contracting States;

(c) from offering, putting on the market, using, or importing or stocking for these purposes the product obtained directly by a process which is the subject-matter of the patent."

Subsection (1) should also be construed in conformity with art.28(1) of the TRIPS Agreement, which reads:

"TRIPS ARTICLE 28—Rights conferred

1. A patent shall confer on its owner the following exclusive rights:

   (a) where the subject matter of a patent is a product, to prevent third parties not having the owner's consent from the acts of: making, using, offering for sale, selling or importing for these purposes that product [but subject to any issue of the exhaustion of intellectual property rights];

   (b) where the subject matter of a patent is a process, to prevent third parties not having the owner's consent from the act of using the process, and from the acts of: using, offering for sale, selling or importing for these purposes at least the product obtained directly by that process."

Thus, the subsection classifies infringing acts according to whether the invention is: (a) a product; (b) a process; or (c) the product of a process.

In *Monsanto v Merck* [2000] R.P.C. 709 there was held to be no infringement where the presence of the alleged infringing product would not have been greater than an amount of 10^{-9} of the total product. Although the decision as to non-infringement was reversed on other grounds in *Pharmacia v Merck* [2002] R.P.C. 41 at 775 this aspect of the judgment was not discussed. However, in *Monsanto v Cargill (No.2)* [2008] F.S.R. 16; [2007] EWHC 3113 it was observed that:

"there is, generally, no authority in favour of trace quantities of infringing material being held not to infringe, and some authority against it"

although this latter authority was not identified.

The terms "product" and "process" are not defined as such in the Act, but "patented product" is defined in s.130(1) as:

"a product which is a patented invention or, in relation to a patented process, a product obtained directly by means of the process or to which the process has been applied".

Thus, the definition of "patented product" extends beyond that of a product which is the subject of a per se claim to certain products of a patented process. First, a product obtained directly by means of a patented process is deemed to be a patented product and this seems to be in accordance with s.100; and, secondly, a product to which a patented process "has been applied" is also deemed to be a patented product.

Thus, where a substance or article is treated according to a patented process, the substance or article after such treatment is also deemed to be a patented product even if, *qua* product, it has not been altered by the treatment. For example, if the patented process is one for moving an article from one location to another, the article after having been so moved could, in theory, be regarded for the purposes of the Act as a "patented product", but it seems unlikely that a court would hold that the use of a patented truck or conveyor to transport a staple article, say a tin of baked beans, would convert the tin into a "patented product". Thus, the courts can be expected to construe the product of a patented process as a matter of substance, rather than according to the literal form of the claim, see the remarks (in a different context) in *Wilderman v Berk* (1925) 42 R.P.C. 79 concerning the use of a patented steam hammer to make a battleship; and the reference in *Celanese International v BP Chemicals* [1999] R.P.C. 203 (discussed in §61.28) to a "patented tin whistle" and a claim to a ship with the whistle affixed.

Under s.100, where a patent is granted for a process for making a *new* product, the onus is placed on the defendant to prove that such product has not been made by the patented process, the legal presumption being that it has been so made, see the commentary on s.100. However, the section probably has little effect because, if another process for making the specified product is not apparent, a court is likely to conclude that the defendant's product has been prepared by the patented process in the absence of evidence to the contrary.

The onus of proving infringement always rests upon the patentee and it is not necessary for a defendant to prove non-infringement, see *Imperial Chemical Industries v Montedison* [1995] R.P.C. 449 and also *Bayer v Octapharma* BL C/9/99, noted I.P.D. 22033 where experiments intended to demonstrate infringement were held inconclusive, even after an attempt at statistical analysis of the results.

Relief for infringement (such as an injunction) is not excused when the infringing act occurred over a short time when precautions to avoid infringement had failed, see *Hadley Industries v Metal Sections* BL C/68/98; or when the defendant had relied upon a (fraudulent) statement that the product he had imported had been made by a different process to that claimed, see *Nutrinova v Scanchem* [2001] F.S.R. 42 at 797. It is sufficient for a finding of infringement if the court is satisfied that a machine has been operated in an infringing manner on at least some occasions (*Charlesworth v Relay Roads* BL C/8/99, noted I.P.D. 22052).

The development during the life of a patent of an infringing product, including the making of a prototype, has been seen as involving infringement for which post-expiry relief may be appropriate, see *Dyson v Hoover (No.2)* [2001] R.P.C. 27 at 544 discussed in §61.21.

—Infringement of product invention (subs.(1)(a))

60.05   Subsection (1)(a) deals with infringement of a product invention and, differing in some respects from art.25 of the CPC, it specifies that, when the invention is a product, infringement occurs in the acts of making, disposing of, offering to dispose of, using or importing the product or keeping it whether for disposal or otherwise. In art.25 of the CPC, importing and stocking of the product are prohibited only for the purposes of making, offering, putting on the market or using the product. In *Smith, Kline & French v Harbottle* [1980] R.P.C. 363, "keeping" was construed in conformity with art.25 of the CPC (then CPC art.29) so that the mere activities of a warehouseman did not infringe the patent, see article by M. Howe [1979] E.I.P.R. 287. However, maintaining a stock of the patented material for use as and when the stockholder may find it beneficial is not an act of mere "keeping" (*McDonald v Graham* [1994] R.P.C. 407).

While "dispose of" is broader than "vend" (as under the former common law test of infringement), e.g. as covering a gift which may not be an "exercise" of the invention, it should be remembered that the mere inclusion of an article in a price list, or its exposure in a shop window, is not necessarily an offer to dispose of it: it may be merely an "invitation to treat", that is, a willingness to consider sale if a suitable offer is made, see the copyright case of *Norgren v Technomarketing* (*The Times*, March 3, 1983). However, a quia timet injunction should be obtainable in such circumstances to restrain a threat to infringe. The words "offer to dispose of" have been construed purposively, rather than literally, and therefore it is legitimate to make an offer to supply a patented product, provided that it is made clear that the supply would only take place after expiry of the patent, see *Gerber Garment v Lectra Systems* [1995] R.P.C. 383 where such clarity had not been expressed.

Applying to a regulatory authority in the United Kingdom for a Marketing Authorisation to sell a patented medicinal product is not itself an act of infringement (*Upjohn v Thomas Kerfoot* [1988] F.S.R. 1). However, the supply of a patented product to such an authority, or to a Government department, to obtain permission under regulatory control to sell that product is likely to be an infringing act (*Smith, Kline & French v Douglas Pharmaceuticals* [New Zealand] [1991] F.S.R. 522), for case comment on which see B. Brown [1992] E.I.P.R. 20. A similar view is taken by courts elsewhere in Europe, in certain of which countries the supply of a sample of the product in question may be part of the regulatory process for medicinal products, which is not the case in the United Kingdom, as further discussed in §60.15.

In respect of a patent granted under the 1949 Act (and therefore governed by the common law approach as regards infringement, it was held that any possession of infringing goods for the purposes of trade, and from which a profit to the alleged infringer had resulted, was to be regarded as an infringement of the patentee's rights (*Hoffmann-La Roche v Harris Pharmaceuticals* [1977] F.S.R. 200). Importation with subsequent re-export was also held to infringe in relation to a patent under the 1949 Act (*Smith-Kline v DDSA* [1978] F.S.R. 109) on the basis that this was a trading transaction carried out in the United Kingdom from which the defendants had derived profit, it being immaterial that the patentee had not suffered any loss. It is submitted that these general principles should still be valid under the 1977 Act definition of infringement.

In *SABAF v MFI and Meneghetti* [2005] R.P.C. 10 at 209; [2004] UKHL 45 the arrangements for importation into the United Kingdom were made by the Italian manufacturer. On appeal (see [2003] R.P.C. 14 at 264) the finding of infringement at first instance was reversed on the basis that a seller who had no title to goods but made the contract of carriage did not import the goods for the purposes of s.60(1)(a). The House of Lords agreed with the finding of non-infringement—see also §§60.20 and 60.27 below, and the case comment by E. Cheyrey in *Patent World*, February 2003 (No.149), p.18.

Despite the unfettered reference in subs.(1)(a) to "importation", not all acts of importation of a patented product will amount to infringement because of the doctrine of exhaustion of rights applicable under Community law by virtue of art.101 TFEU (formerly Treaty of Rome art.30). This subject is discussed more fully in Appendix D. For present purposes it can be noted that (under art.101 TFEU) a United Kingdom patent (including a European patent (UK)), may not be invoked to prevent the free movement of goods within the European Community, now extended to EEA countries, as explained in Appendix D. Thus, once the patented product has been placed on the market within the EEA, by the patent proprietor or with his voluntary consent (express or implied), parallel patents in other such countries may not be invoked against such already marketed product when that product is moved elsewhere within the EEA, see in particular *Allen & Hanbury's (Salbutamol) Patent* [1987] R.P.C. 327 and *Merck v Primecrown* [1996] I E.C.R. 6285; [1997] F.S.R. 237; [1997] 1 C.M.L.R. 83 where action was not possible against import of the patentee's own products from elsewhere within the European Community into the United Kingdom.

It was observed the Court of Appeal in *Virgin Atlantic Airways v Delta Airways* [2011] R.P.C. 18, [2011] EWCA Civ 162, reversing a summary judgment determination of non-infringement, that the issue of whether the manufacture in the UK of a complete kit of parts for assembling a patented device could infringe a patent was highly fact-sensitive and was not suitable for determination on a summary judgment application.

—Infringement of process invention (subs.(1)(b))

Subsection (1)(b) deals with infringement of a process invention and specifies as an infringement use of the process or offering such process for use. In the case of an offer for use it must be obvious to a reasonable person that the use will infringe. The provision is intended to conform to art.25(b) of the CPC (reprinted at §60.04 above), but this does not refer to a "reasonable person" and instead uses the phrase "obvious in the circumstances".

60.06

Where the claim required certain concentrations of catalyst to "be maintained within the reaction medium during the course of the reaction", infringement could occur at any time (other than on de minimis occasions) in the course of a continuous process in which the required concentrations varied from time to time. There was no obligation on a defendant to keep records of non-infringement, although any destruction of records would be held against a defendant (*Hoechst Celanese v BP Chemicals [Carbonylation]* [1998] F.S.R. 586).

In *Furr v Truline* [1985] F.S.R. 553, where the defendant was directing purchasers to use certain articles in a way which was not the way of the method claim of the patent (even on the claimant's construction of that claim, which the court did not accept), it was held that the defendant could not be said to have offered a process for use as required by subs.(1)(b) as it clearly did not intend that the articles should be used in the claimed way. See also the comment in §60.26 on *CBS Songs v Amstrad* [1988] R.P.C. 567 HL.

Where a method claim is alleged to be infringed by importation of the product of that method, a positive case of infringement must be shown, at least if an interim injunction is to be granted (*Jakob Schlaepfer v Frankle* BL C/9/88).

In *MMI Research v Cellxion* [2009] EWHC 418 Pat Ct it was held that in order to infringe under s.(1)(b) it is only necessary to offer a method, the use of which will obviously infringe, even if a device that is sold will infringe only some of the time. Moreover, infringement on this basis was not avoided by selling a device with a user-settable parameter, only some of the settings of which infringed, as the vendor was offering a range of processes made up of each of the possible settings of that parameter.

—Infringement by direct product of patented process (subs.(1)(c))

60.07　　Subsection (1)(c) clarifies the law on the protection afforded to the product of a process invention. This provision corresponds to art.25(c) of the CPC and art.64(2) of the EPC which reads:

> **"EPC Article 64—Rights conferred by a European patent**
>
> (2) If the subject-matter of the European patent is a process, the protection conferred by the patent shall extend to the products directly obtained by such process."

These provisions will be of use mainly in situations where: (a) there is no claim to the product as such; and (b) where the process is carried out abroad and a product from that process is imported into the jurisdiction of the court. As noted in §60.04, s.100 provides for reversal of the burden of proof when the product is "new". It is not apparent that infringement extends under subs.(1)(c) to an article when made by a patented apparatus but this may be arguable, see R. F. Haslam (1982–83) 12 *CIPA* 319.

For infringement under subs.(1)(c), the product must have been obtained *directly* by means of the patented process. As the extent of protection is to be determined primarily by the wording of the claims (s.125(1)), prima facie the direct product of a patented process will be that specified in the process claim itself. Often this will be worded as "A process for the production of X". Prima facie, X should then be considered as the direct product of that process. However, a court might think otherwise where the specified process steps lead to a different product which is subsequently converted into X, see the comments in §60.04 on *Wilderman v Berk* (1925) 42 R.P.C. 79 and *Celanese International v BP Chemicals* [1999] R.P.C. 203.

The meaning of "directly" was first considered in *Pioneer Electronics v Warner Music* [1995] R.P.C. 487; [1997] R.P.C. 757 CA where the claims were directed to apparatus for making a master optical disc and it was only discs made from this master which had been imported into the United Kingdom. The Patents Court construed the word "directly" as meaning "without intermediary", and on this basis struck out the action. In doing so, the court relied upon the German and French texts of art.64(2) of the EPC and the way in which corresponding provisions have been construed under German and Dutch law. In particular, reliance was placed on a paper (in German) by K. Bruchhausen [1979] G.R.U.R. 743. The conclusion reached in that paper is that, for a product to be regarded as within the scope of a process claim, the imported product must retain either the essential identity or the essential properties of the product which immediately results from carrying out the process claimed. On that basis, where that immediate product can no longer be identified in the imported product, and that product has qualities different from that of the immediate product, the imported product should not be considered an infringement of a process claim directed to manufacture of a chemical intermediate for the imported product. The Court of Appeal agreed that the test of whether an imported product is the "direct product of the patented process" depends on whether the product with which the patented process ended had lost its identity or not. For case comment on this appeal, see Heidi Hurdle [1997] E.I.P.R. 322. The meaning of "directly" was further considered in *Halliburton v Smith International* [2006] R.P.C. 2 at [26], where it was held that a drill bit manufactured in accordance with parameters that were themselves the result of the claimed method of designing a drill bit was nonetheless the direct product of such claimed process as it was "not ... sensible to view manufacture and design as in some way resulting in separate products". In coming to this conclusion, the court had regard, in addition to the decision in *Pioneer Electronics*, which seemed to exclude further processing, to the decision in *"Halbleiter-bauelement"* in the *Landgericht Düsseldorf* (May 6, 1997), which suggested that further use or processing may take place provided that its effect is not to obscure the qualities of the product directly obtained. In *Monsanto v Cargill (No.2)* [2008] F.S.R. 16; [2007] EWHC 3113, it was held that meal produced from the progeny of parent soya bean plants had not been "directly obtained" from such parent plants which were the product of the claimed process.

For claims of the so-called "Swiss form", it is thought (based on the fundamental concept that a claim must be construed in the same way when considering infringement as when considering its validity) that there will only be infringement under subs.(1) when the claimed product is supplied in a manner which is in some way associated with a statement that the product should be used for the specified purpose; and, likewise, only when the claimed "use" is carried out within the jurisdiction with an intention to effect that purpose, although not necessarily within the jurisdiction.

Nutrinova v Scanchem [2001] F.S.R. 42 at 797 involved infringement by importation of the product specified in a process claim, where the defendants had been assured by the foreign manufacturer that a prior art process had been used, but the evidence produced (including a report obtained as a result of an order for disclosure made by a United States court) satisfied the court that the defendant had been misled and that the patented process had been used, with the manufacturer having produced forged evidence. See also the article by S. Chen and N. Stoate [2000] B.S.L.R. 246.

Where infringement is alleged under s.60(1)(c), it may be important to join the foreign manufacturer as a co-defendant in order to have the benefit of disclosure against that company in order to provide evidence as to the process used by it. However, this will only be possible if the circumstances are such that the court accepts that the supplier and importer may be joint tortfeasors as having acted in a common design, for which see §60.26.

In *Medimmune v Novartis Pharmaceuticals* [2011] EWHC 1669 Pat Ct, the case law as to what constituted the direct product of a patented process was extensively reviewed. The Court rejected an argument on the part of the Defendant to the effect that it should not be held to infringe because the invention, if any, lay in a particular upstream aspect of the claimed process and that it was only as a result of incorporating, downstream, a conventional manufacturing step as part of the claims that the patentee could allege infringement. Although the Court accepted that this was an attractive argument, it rejected it because the case law was expressed in terms of how the claims were drafted rather than what was the inventive concept. It also rejected a further argument, based on art.8(2) of the Biotechnology Directive, because the processes claimed by the claims in issue were not processes that enabled a "biological material", as defined in the Biotechnology Directive, to be produced.

In *Ranbaxy (UK) v AstraZeneca* [2011] EWHC 1831 Pat Ct, the Court observed that the skilled person would generally understand a "Swiss form" claim to mean that the subject medicament must contain the active ingredient for which the new and inventive use has been found, and although such a construction was not mandatory in every case it should be applied in this one; thus here a "Swiss form" claim to use of a medicament of a certain purity was not infringed by a product manufactured abroad by a process that started with a product of such purity but which had been "spiked" with impurity so that the imported product was not of the claimed purity.

Indirect (or contributory) infringement under subs.(2)

—Historical derivation

60.08   The term "contributory infringement" arose as a doubtful concept under the common law and is thus hallowed by traditional usage. However, the term "indirect infringement" may be more apposite to the statutory tort defined in subs.(2) in contrast to the tort of direct infringement under the terms of subs.(1).

The difference is well-illustrated by the facts which arose in *Innes v Short* (1898) 15 R.P.C. 449. Here, an injunction was granted to restrain the sale of packets of powdered zinc bearing instructions for its use in the patented method (of preventing corrosion in water boilers). The correctness of this decision as a finding of patent infringement was doubted, although it could nowadays be justified as arising from an act of joint tortfeasorship (for which see §60.26). However, this situation would now be an act of (indirect) infringement under subs.(2).

—Scope of subs.(2)

60.09   Subsection (2) corresponds to art.26(1) of the CPC and (by s.130(7)) has to be interpreted (so far as possible) in conformity with it. Article 26(1) of the CPC reads:

> **"CPC Article 26—Prohibition of indirect use of the invention**
>
> 1. A Community patent shall also confer on its proprietor the right to prevent all third parties not having his consent from supplying or offering to supply within the territories of the Contracting States a person, other than a party entitled to exploit the patented invention, with means, relating to an essential element of that invention, for putting it into effect therein, when the third party knows, or it is obvious in the circumstances, that these means are suitable and intended for putting that invention into effect."

Thus the subsection permits action to be brought for an indirect act of patent infringement against any person who supplies or offers to supply any of the means, relating to an essential element of the invention, for putting the invention into effect, except where that essential element is a staple commercial product which is not supplied or offered for the purpose of inducing infringement under subs.(1) (as to which see subs.(3) and §60.10). It has always proved difficult to define the scope of indirect acts of this nature and establish a distinction between the rights of the inventor and those of the public. Subsections (2) and (3) reflect this difficulty which remains to be resolved by case law. In this respect, United States cases may be of assistance because the wording of art.26 of the CPC reflects some of the definition of infringement in the patent law of the USA, (contained in 35 U.S.C. 271), as noted by I. C. Baillie (1980–91) 10 *CIPA* 56. Various aspects of the law of contributory (indirect) infringement have also been discussed in articles by: M. Vitoria [1979] E.I.P.R. 91; M. G. Harman (1981–82) 11 *CIPA* 1; R. J. Hart (1981–82) 11 *CIPA* 131; and J. Turner [1983] E.I.P.R. 131.

A major difficulty lies in the scope of the phrase "means relating to an essential element …". It would be reasonable to suppose that "means" was intended to imply a tangible and physical means for implementing a function, and not, for example, an intellectual means, such as an instructional manual or a magazine article or even mere know-how, or the grant of a licence as has been contended. An argument that directions in an instruction manual to use a machine in a particular allegedly infringing way could constitute "means" for the purposes of subs.(2) was rejected in *Agilent v Waters Corp* [2004] EWHC 2992 Ch.; [2005] EWCA Civ 987 CA. "Essential" is also difficult to define in this context; it could have the meaning of necessary, or it could mean necessary to the exclusion of any alternative, or it could mean that it relates to an element of the invention as claimed without which the invention would be incomplete.

Also, subs.(2) provides that, for liability under it, the person who supplies or offers to supply within the United Kingdom the alleged "essential means" must know, or be taken to know (in the sense that "it is obvious to a reasonable person in the circumstances"), that such "means" are suitable for the infringing purpose and that person must also have intended that there should be infringement in the United Kingdom. This double territorial requirement should be noted. However, proof of substantive infringement under subs.(1) does not seem necessary for a finding of infringement under subs.(2).

It is to be noted, however, that art.26(1) of the CPC does not refer to a "reasonable person" and is otherwise also worded slightly differently. Nevertheless, it is submitted that the phrase "obvious to a reasonable person in the circumstances" is probably synonymous with the phrase "has reason to believe" found in s.22 of the CDPA 1988 in relation to secondary infringement of copyright. This latter phrase has been held to be satisfied if a person knew facts from which a reasonable person would have arrived at that belief, but is not satisfied by a mere suspicion that such facts may exist (*L.A. Gear v Hi-Tech Sports* [1992] F.S.R. 121). But the degree of knowledge required by the subsection does not include knowledge of the existence of the patent, but only some awareness of some inventive concept as emphasised by the reference to "an essential element of the invention", see *Ward Building Systems v Hodgson Steels* BL C/47/97 where infringement would also have been found had the patent been valid. A German court has held that a supplier of a part of a patented combination infringes under the equivalent provision when he knows, or ought to have known, that the customer would use the part supplied in that combination, actual knowledge not being required, and this even when the part supplied has other uses (*D.I. BV v H.S.* [Germany] [2000] E.N.P.R. 194). A finding of infringement under subs.(2) was made in *Helitune v Stewart Hughes* [1991] R.P.C. 78; [1991] F.S.R. 171 where the defendant was held to have had the requisite knowledge of the use to which his customer would put the product sold to him.

For another case where contributory infringement was held to have occurred, see *Rhône-Poulenc v Dikloride Herbicides* [Malaysia] [1988] F.S.R. 282 where the claimant proved, on the balance of probabilities, that the defendant's composition was designed to be used in the same manner as the claimant's product was used, i.e. according to the patented method. Other cases where infringement has been found on the basis of subs.(2) are *Precision Metal Forming v McConnell Roofing* BL CC/41/95 and *Renaissance Design v Greenscreen* BL CC/46/96.

In *Furr v Truline* [1985] F.S.R. 553, it was held, in refusing an interim injunction, that the defendant had not intended its articles to be used in the claimed manner and that it would not have been obvious to a reasonable person that the articles were intended to be used in that manner, as required by subs.(2).

For claims of the so-called "Swiss form", the same problems arise under subs.(2) as in relation to the direct product of a patented process under subs.(1)(c), for which see §60.07. It may, therefore, be surmised that infringement of these types of claim would only be held under subs.(2) where the defendant had made the essential means available within the United Kingdom specifically for the stated purpose.

The supply of an essential part knowing that it is for repair of an infringing apparatus will be an infringement under subs.(2), unless there is an implied licence (for example, under the conditions of sale under which the apparatus was originally sold) that the apparatus can be kept in good repair, for which see §60.22. For example, it is explicit in subs.(2) that, if the person who is supplied (or to whom the offer of supply is made) is a licensee, or other person entitled to work the invention, no action for contributory infringement will lie. However, as noted in §60.22, there may be no such defence available to a manufacturer of spare parts for a machine, where either such part is the subject of a patent claim or that part is an essential element of the patented machine, nor to a person who supplies or offers to supply such parts on the open market.

The wording of subss.(1) and (2) seems not to cover all acts which may perhaps be regarded as contributing to infringement, mainly because of the double territoriality requirement discussed above. Thus, while the supply of a patented apparatus in a dismantled form for use in the United Kingdom is clearly an infringement under subs.(2), where the dismantled apparatus is for export there would appear to be no infringement. Likewise, it seems that export of less than a complete apparatus does not fall within either subs.(1) or (2), but against this must be considered the interpretation to be given to the extent of the claim in accordance with s.125; see the commentary on that section. However, in *Menashe v William Hill* [2002] R.P.C. 47 at 950; [2003] R.P.C. 31 at 575 CA the patent related to a gaming system. The claims called for a host computer, terminal computer(s), a communication means between them and a program means for operating the terminals. The host computer in the defendants' system was placed abroad, in the Netherlands Antilles. The court was asked to determine as a preliminary point of law the question:

> "Is it a defence to the claim under section 60(2) of the Patents Act 1977, if otherwise good, that the host computer claimed in the patent in suit is not present in the UK, but is connected to the rest of the apparatus claimed in the patent".

In answering "no" to the question, the judge said that the patentee's invention was in substance *the combination* of elements. The invention was the system and the words of the subsection therefore looked to where the effect of the system was felt. The Court of Appeal agreed. The location of the host computer was irrelevant to a user supplied with software by the defendant. That person used the invention on his own terminal and it was "not a misuse of language to say that that he used the host computer in the United Kingdom". Thus the supply of software on CD by the defendant was intended to put the invention into effect in the UK. See the case comment by D. Knight in *Patent World*, February 2003 (No.149), p.20.

These principles were applied in *Research In Motion v Motorola* [2010] EWHC 118 Pat Ct, where it was held that there was no infringement under subs.(2), because the messaging gateway system in issue was operated outside the UK.

In *Norsk Hydro's Patent* BL O/85/05, the Patent Office rejected an argument that a declaration of non-infringement ought not to be granted as the product in issue could be deployed or modified in such a way as contributorily to infringe one of the process claims, observing that such an argument "could be applied in the circumstances of almost every declaration of non-infringement applied for, at least to the Comptroller".

In *Cranway v Playtech* [2010] F.S.R. 8 (CA: [2010] F.S.R. 18); [2009] EWHC 1588 Pat Ct it was held that whereas the question of whether means are suitable for putting an invention into effect was purely objective, that of whether they are intended to put an invention into effect has an element of subjective intention (although the court's view as to whose knowledge and intention was relevant as to this was disapproved of by the Court of Appeal in *Grimme v Scott*—see below). The court also held that the essential means supplied need not necessarily be the same thing as is used to work the invention.

In *Grimme v Scott* [2009] EWHC 2691 Pat Ct, [2010] EWCA Civ 1110 it was held, by the Court of Appeal, after an extensive review of the background to and the commentary on the subsection, that the "means" need not be incomplete for the provision to apply, and (thus disapproving the observations to the contrary in *Cranway v Playtech* referred to above) that the knowledge and intention requirements of the provision were satisfied if, at the time of supply or offer of supply, the supplier knows, or it is obvious in the circumstances, that ultimate users will intend to put the invention into effect. The Court went on to observe that these requirements were to be proved on the usual standard of balance of probabilities, and that although it was not enough merely that the means were suitable for putting the intention into effect (for that is a separate requirement), it was likely to be the case where the supplier proposes or recommends or even indicates the possibility of such use in his promotional material. For these reasons infringement under subs.(2) was found in the case of the sale of potato separating machines which did not themselves fall within the claims of the patent in suit but in which the rollers could be readily replaced with ones which would render them infringing, this being a feature on which basis the machines were marketed.

In *KCI v Smith & Nephew* [2010] F.S.R. 8, [2009] EWHC 2691, [2010] F.S.R. 31, [2010] EWCA Civ 1260 the Court of Appeal, reversing a finding of non-infringement under subs.(2) at first instance, observed that there was no requirement that the ultimate users must have decided to use the means to put the invention into effect at the time they first take possession of the means, and that the relevant intention may be formed at a later time. Nevertheless, the supplier must know (or it must be obvious to him in all the circumstances) that some ultimate users will indeed form that intention.

As mentioned in §60.05, it was observed by the Court of Appeal in *Virgin Atlantic Airways v Delta Airways* [2011] R.P.C. 18, [2011] EWCA Civ 162, reversing a summary judgment determination of non-infringement, that the issue of whether the manufacture in, and export from, the UK of an incomplete kit of parts for assembling abroad a device which falls within a patent claim infringed under subs (2) was highly fact sensitive and was not suitable for determination on a summary judgment application.

Involving supply of a staple product (subs.(3))

Subsection (3) corresponds to art.26(2) of the CPC and (by s.130(7)) has to be **60.10** interpreted (so far as possible) in conformity with it. Article 26(2) of the CPC reads:

> **"CPC ARTICLE 26—Prohibition of indirect use of the invention**
>
> (2) Paragraph 1 shall not apply when the means are staple commercial products, except when the third party induces the person supplied to commit acts prohibited by Article 25."

As noted in *Cranway v Playtech* [2010] F.S.R. 3, [2009] EWHC 1588 Pat Ct it was observed in *Menashe v William Hill* [2003] 1 W.L.R. 1462 that CPC art.26(2) made it clear that what is contemplated by use of the word "infringement" in subs.(3) is a direct act of infringement, namely one falling within subs.(1).

Thus, the subsection provides that the doctrine of indirect infringement defined in subs.(2) shall not apply to the supply or offer of a staple commercial product unless the supply or offer is made for the purpose of inducing a direct infringement under subs.(1).

The expression "staple commercial product" is not defined but, in *Pavel v Sony* BL CC/14/93, noted I.P.D. 16070, the Patents County Court construed the term as the corresponding CPC provision had apparently been interpreted under German law, namely as a product of the kind needed every day and generally obtainable. It was also there noted that the product should be one generally available when the specification was published, it otherwise being presumed that it had only been put into circulation as a result of the invention.

However, the origin of this subsection is actually a corresponding provision in United States patent law, as explained by I. C. Baillie in his article cited in §60.09. This, and other usages, suggests a definition of a generally available raw product or commodity of commerce suitable for uses of which at least some are non-infringing. Thus, in the United States, a toothpaste containing potassium nitrate has been held not to be a staple article of commerce merely because toothpaste and potassium nitrate, individually, were such (*Milton Hodosh v Block Drug* [USA] (1987) 4 U.S.P.Q. (2d) 1935). Other cases under United States law were summarised by F. Calvetti and C. Hughes [1993] *CIPA* 108.

From these cases, it would appear that, in order to be liable for the supply of a staple commercial substance or article, a defendant has, in effect, to be a joint tortfeasor, i.e. engaged in a common design with a direct infringer, see §60.26. As to the requirement of inducement, this must be an act of procurement: mere facilitation of the act of infringement by another is not sufficient. For a case where the direct infringer was not proved to have used the essential means for performing the invention in issue at the instigation of another defendant, so that the other defendant was held not to be an infringer under the equivalent of subs.(3), see *Decision of 26 September 1986, [Tribunal de Grande Instance, Paris]* OJ EPO 1991, 544.

Obtaining evidence of infringement from third parties

While it is a well-established principle of English law that proceedings cannot be **60.11** brought against a mere witness to compel him to disclose the evidence which he would be able to give in proceedings, even if that evidence is essential to establish the identity of the prospective defendant (for example, to identify a hit-and-run driver in a motor accident, or a person seen to be importing infringing goods), it may be possible to bring proceedings against a party who has so involved himself, i.e. has intermeddled, in the infringing activity, that it would not be proper to allow him to avoid responsibility even though he may have acted under, for example, a statutory duty and may himself not be an infringer. This was established in *Norwich Pharmacal v Commissioners of Customs and Excise* [1974] R.P.C. 101 HL. However, in such a case, the proprietor will have to bear the costs of the action, but he can recoup these as a head of damage in a subsequent infringement action against a person identified as a result of the first action, see §61.27.

It appears from the explanatory note to reg.4 of the Intellectual Property (Enforcement, etc.) Regulations 2006 (SI 2006/1028), (as reprinted at §98.03) implementing art.8 of the Enforcement Directive as to Scotland to provide for a new type of court order, for disclosure of information about infringing goods and services, that the *Norwich Pharmacal* type of order was considered not to be available in Scotland (see §§98.12 et seq). The explanatory note also observes that, by reason of the availability of such order already in England & Wales, no provision is needed to implement that article there.

The principle of the *Norwich Pharmacal* case has been extended to require a defendant in interim proceedings to disclose the identity of the foreign source from whom the patented product had been imported (*Smith, Kline & French v Global Pharmaceutics* [1986] R.P.C. 394). For forced disclosure of documents identifying a foreign supplier of infringing goods, see also *Société Romanaise v British Shoe Corp* [1991] F.S.R. 1. It is also common practice for a Search (formerly *Anton Piller*) Order (for which see §61.49) to require a defendant to disclose the identity of those to whom he has disposed of the alleged infringing goods.

Also, as J. Watts and B. Cordery have pointed out (*Patent World*, No.115, September 20, 1999), under CPR 31.17 it is now possible to obtain an order for disclosure of documents by a third party to the litigation, or projected litigation, see §61.67.

Exhaustion of rights (subs.(4))

60.12   Subsection (4), which was never brought into force, has now been repealed (see §60.01, above). However it had always been redundant, not only because the CPC never came into effect, but also because of the primacy of the doctrine of exhaustion of rights (as developed under arts 81 and 82 EC), as discussed further in Appendix D.

Acts exempted from infringement (subs.(5))

60.13   Paragraphs (a)–(f) of subsection (5) correspond to art.27 of the CPC and by s.130(7) have to be interpreted (so far as possible) in conformity with it. Article 27 of the CPC reads:

"CPC Article 27—Limitations of the effects of the Community patent
    The rights conferred by a Community patent shall not extend to:
    (a) acts done privately and for non-commercial purposes;
    (b) acts done for experimental purposes relating to the subject-matter of the patented invention;
    (c) the extemporaneous preparation for individual cases in a pharmacy of a medicine in accordance with a medical prescription nor acts concerning the medicine so prepared;
    (d) the use on board vessels of the countries of the Union of Paris for the Protection of Industrial Property, other than the Contracting States, of the patented invention, in the body of the vessel, in the machinery, tackle, gear and other accessories, when such vessels temporarily or accidentally enter the waters of Contracting States, provided that the invention is used exclusively for the needs of the vessel;
    (e) the use of the patented invention in the construction or operation of aircraft or land vehicles of countries of the Union of Paris for the protection of Industrial Property, other than the Contracting States, or of accessories to such aircraft or land vehicles, when these temporarily or accidentally enter the territory of the Contracting States;
    (f) the acts specified in Article 27 of the Convention on International Civil Aviation of 7 December 1944 [Cmd. 8742], where these acts concern the aircraft of a State, other than the Contracting States, benefiting from the provisions, of that Article."

Paragraphs (g) and (h) to subsection (5) were added to implement art.11 of the Biotechnology Directive (reprinted in §C11). Paragraph (i) to subs.(5) was added to implement certain provisions of Directives 2001/82/EC and 2001/83/EC, see §60.18.

Sub-paragraph (g) concerns plant propagating material and provides an exception from infringement when a farmer uses the product of his harvest of patent-protected plant or seeds, i.e. his own plant crop, for further propagation or multiplication by him on his own farm, but this exception only applies in respect of the particular species listed in para.2 of Sch.A1 (above), see subs.(6A), and then only when the holder of the patent has sold, or (under subs.(6C) has otherwise supplied) commercially, the plant propagating material, e.g. seeds, to the farmer, or that this has been done with the holder's consent *and* for agricultural use. That sale and initial use of material purchased with the holder's consent is itself outside the scope of the patent by virtue of the so-called "farmer's privilege" introduced by art.10 of the Biotechnology Directive, incorporated into the Act in Sch.A2 para.10 (reprinted under s.76A) and (except in respect of the specific plant species listed in Sch.A1 para.2), the re-sale or re-planting of protected plant propagating material (the plant crop) constitutes an act of patent infringement, as also does the use of such material in the hands of a subsequent purchaser (under arts 8 and 9, incorporated into the Act in Sch.A2 paras 7–9 and also discussed in §125.25).

Where the exception under subs.(5)(g) does apply (i.e in respect of the species listed in Sch.A1 para.2), the terms of that exception are circumscribed by the other provisions of Sch.A1. In particular, those farmers making use of this exception of permission to re-plant seeds, etc. of such species are required to pay to the patent proprietor "equitable remuneration", although at a lower rate than would be otherwise charged for purchase of seeds from the proprietor or his licensee.

New para.(h) in subs.(5) provides a similar privilege to that of para.(g), but in respect of an animal or animal reproductive material, rather than plant propagating material. The principle behind para.(h) is the same as that behind para.(g), i.e. of limiting the "privilege" to farmers producing animals, or animal material, derived from a sale, or other commercialisation, in respect of a patent with subject-matter involving breeding stock or other animal reproductive material continuing to make use of the invention covered by that patent, the privilege likewise being limited to the farmer's own agricultural activity without the power to sell or otherwise commercialise the breeding stock or animal reproductive material derived from the animal or animal material originally sold, or commercially supplied, to him. However, there is no counterpart to Sch.A1 which is applicable only to the exception in relation to plant propagating material provided by para.(g), and then only in respect of the species listed in Sch.A1 para.2.

Another difference between the provisions of paras (g) and (h) is that the former may be affected by the existence of concurrent plant breeders' rights, whereas there are no specific rights in respect of animal breeds, other than may be obtainable under the patent system.

These subsections should also be construed in conformity with art.30 of the TRIPS Agreement, which reads:

"TRIPS ARTICLE 30—Exceptions to Rights Conferred

Members may provide limited exceptions to the exclusive rights conferred by a patent, provided that such exceptions do not unreasonably conflict with a normal exploitation of the patent and do not unreasonably prejudice the legitimate interests of the patent owner, taking account of the legitimate interests of third parties."

Although at first glance the types of exempted acts specified in subsection (5) and art.27 of the CPC are of a disparate nature, it is submitted that they have the underlying unifying philosophy that there are some types of act which the general public interest should not be regarded as capable of monopolisation. This was recognised under the common law when Jessel M.R. stated in *Frearson v Loe* (1878) 9 Ch. D. 48:

"Patent rights were never granted to prevent persons of ingenuity exercising their talents in a fair way. But if there be neither using or vending of the invention for profit, the mere making for the purposes of experiment, and not for a fraudulent purpose, ought not to be considered within the meaning of the prohibition, and if it were, it is certainly not the subject of an injunction."

The exemptions set out in paras (d)–(f) of the subsection also owe their origin to overriding notions of public interest. It is therefore submitted that, in considering the ambit of each of the exemptions of the subsection, including the new paras (g), (h) and (i), the general public interest should be taken into account, particularly bearing in mind that the raison d'être of the patent system is the encouragement of innovation.

Nevertheless, the general philosophy of statutory construction requires that a stated exception be narrowly construed, as is recognised by art.30 of the TRIPS Agreement. Here, it is to be noted that subs.(6) (discussed in §60.19) prevents the exemption from infringement under (a), (b) or (c) of subs.(5) from being relied upon to avoid indirect infringement under subs.(2). Also, decisions under the common law concerning phrases such as "reasonable trial or experiment" are no longer of assistance in construing the now statutory exemptions (*Monsanto v Stauffer* [1985] R.P.C. 515 CA).

—Private and non-commercial acts (subs.(5)(a))

60.14 Under subs.(5)(a), which appears to be in conformity with art.27(a) of the CPC, acts which are both private (that is to say acts not carried out in public and for the person's own use and benefit), and not having a commercial purpose, are exempt from being considered as acts of patent infringement. However (as discussed in §60.19), a person who supplies or offers to supply a private, non-commercial user may nevertheless be liable for direct infringement under subs.(1) and for indirect infringement under subs.(2).

It is submitted that the words "purposes which are not commercial" mean that there must be no immediate commercial purpose, an ultimate commercial purpose being irrelevant since almost any act can be said to be carried out in the hope that it may ultimately prove to have commercial value, as discussed further in §60.15. If the acts have a dual purpose, one non-commercial (e.g. for the purpose of testing the validity of some other patent) and the other leading to valuable commercial information, the exemption may not apply (*Smith, Kline & French v Evans Medical* [1989] 1 F.S.R. 513); but, if the acts relate *solely* to an attack on the validity of the patent, the exemption appears to be available. However, acts carried out with the aim of invalidating a patent which interferes with commercial plans of a business and allows that business to carry on a commercial activity which otherwise it could not do, are less likely to fall within this particular exemption; and keeping a patented product for possible future commercial use has been held not to be a private and non-commercial act within this exception (*McDonald v Graham* [1994] R.P.C. 407).

An interesting question arises in relation to patents with claims directed to "research tools" or their use. These tools will normally be used in private and such use, if done as part of "pure" research, would not seem to have at least an immediate commercial purpose. Also, as noted in §60.13, the purpose of the patent system is to encourage innovation so that to inhibit the use of a research tool by treating that use as an act of patent infringement would be contrary to the ethos of the patent system. Of course, the supply of a research tool would not give rise to an exemption under subs.(5)(a) since the exemption is confined to private acts.

—Acts done for experimental purposes (subs.(5)(b))

60.15 Subsection (5)(b), in conformity with art.27(b) of the CPC (see above), exempts acts done for experimental purposes provided that these relate to the subject-matter of the invention. For detailed discussion of the metes and bounds of the experimental exemption to patent infringement under various legal systems, see the book *Experimental Use and Patents* by D. Gilat, IIC Studies, Vol.16 (Max Planck Institute, 1995); and *A European Perspective as to the Extent to Which Experimental Use, and Certain Other, Defences to Patent Infringement, apply to Differing Types of Research* by T.M. Cook (Intellectual Property Institute, July 2006).

Unlike the exemption of subs.(5)(a), discussed in §60.14, there is no reference here to the experimental work not having a commercial purpose. Thus, an act exempt under this provision may have in view an ultimate commercial purpose (*Monsanto v Stauffer* [1985] R.P.C. 515 CA). In this case, it was held that:

"I would regard the sort of experimental activity which was considered by the Supreme Court of Canada in *Microchemicals Ltd v Smith Kline and French* (1971 2 CPR (2d) 193, 25 DLR (3d) 79, [1972] SCR 506), viz, a limited experiment to establish whether the experimenter could manufacture a quality product in accordance with the specification of a patent, as being covered by the words 'for experimental purpose relating to the subject matter of the invention.'"

It was also held that:

"trials carried out in order to discover something unknown, or to test an hypothesis, or even in order to find out whether something which is known to work in specific conditions, e.g. of soil or weather, will work in different conditions can fairly ... be regarded as experiments. But trials carried out in order to demonstrate to a third party that a product works or, in order to amass information to satisfy a third party, whether a customer or a [regulatory] body such as the PSPS or ACAS, that the product works as its maker claims are not to be regarded as acts done for 'experimental purposes'".

Also, keeping a patented product for possible future commercial use is not an experimental use within this exception (*McDonald v Graham* [1994] R.P.C. 407).

Since then, the German Supreme Court has held that this exemption permits the carrying out of clinical trials on a patented drug to ascertain its effect in medical indications not indicated in the patent (*Klinische Versuche (Clinical Trials)–I* [Germany] [1997] R.P.C. 623). In a subsequent decision (*Klinische Versuche (Clinical Trials)–II* [Germany] [1998] R.P.C. 423), tests carried out to ascertain whether another substance falling within the ambit of the patent claim worked as well as (or better than) the patentee's own commercial product were also held exempt. In these two decisions the *Bundesgerichtshof* emphasised that the only question of relevance is whether the acts complained of were in the nature of an experiment which related to the subject-matter of the patent, it being irrelevant whether or not those acts had a commercial purpose: see the comment by Corinna Vossius [1997] B.S.L.R. 106.

Although there is no definition of "experimental", it is submitted that the above-quoted statement from the *Monsanto* decision can be rationalised as saying that an act is an "experiment" if it seeks to generate genuinely new information and the act is not an experiment if it seeks to do no more than verify existing knowledge. That view seems to be endorsed by these two decisions of the German Supreme Court. For further reviews of the experimental exemption to infringement, see W. R. Cornish (1998) 29 I.I.C. 735. However, there is another rationale for extending the experimental exception to infringement, as was indicated by the Japan Supreme Court in *Clinical Trials III* [Japan], noted [1999] E.I.P.R. N–140; (1999) 30 I.I.C. 448, namely that:

"extending patent protection to cover also clinical trials conducted by generic drug makers carried out for the purpose of obtaining government approval would effectively prolong the life span of a patent, a benefit that cannot be said to be intended by the Patent Act".

The supply of a sample of the patented product to a regulatory authority as part of the process for obtaining a marketing authorisation can scarcely be an experimental act, as has been decided in the Netherlands (*Pharbita v ICI* [Netherlands], noted OJ EPO 1994, 220), but the supply of a sample of the product for which marketing authorisation is sought is not, in the United Kingdom, a requirement of the regulatory process for medicinal products. In the area of biocidal products, where such sample submission would appear to be necessary, making a composition purely for the purpose of getting an official marketing approval, and "not to discover something unknown or to test a hypothesis" was held not to be a defence under subs.(5)(b) (*Auchincloss v Agricultural & Veterinary Supplies* [1997] R.P.C. 649; [1999] R.P.C. 397 CA). Although in the Netherlands clinical trials have been held ineligible for the research exemption because of their overall purpose, unless aimed at researching a further medical indication of the patented product (*Applied Research Systems v Organon* [Netherlands] Decision of Netherlands Supreme Court No. 15,706 of June 23, 1995), the exemption there has the extra requirement that the act be done *exclusively* for experimental purposes.

In *McDonald v Graham* (above), it was also stated that experiments could be carried out for the purposes of litigation on the basis of an order made under what is now CPR 63PD.7 (reprinted in Appendix F at §F63PD.07); but, in *Smith, Kline & French v Evans Medical* [1989] 1 F.S.R. 513, it was held that experiments for the purposes of litigation are only exempted under this provision if they relate to the subject-matter of the invention found in the claims of the patent alleged to be infringed, in the sense of having a real and direct connection with it. Thus, experiments performed for the purpose of invalidating some other patent are not covered by subs.(5)(b); but see §60.14 for an exemption under subs.(5)(a) when the experiments do not have a secondary commercial purpose.

The purchaser of an infringing product which is used for experimental purposes appears (under subs.(5)(b)) to escape infringement, but not necessarily the supplier. It also does not seem that a supplier of a product, which happens then to be used experimentally, is excused by the provisions: such supply is not itself an act done for experimental purposes. The difficulties which arise under these provisions when the supplier is outside of the United Kingdom were the subject of comment by M. J. Butler (1982–83) 12 *CIPA* 317, but see also the discussion in Cook (Intellectual Property Institute, July 2006, above) as to this.

The application of the exemption of subs.(5)(b) to early stage research has become of increasing interest. In *Inhale Therapeutics v Quadrant* [2002] R.P.C. 21 at 419, the defendant raised a defence of experimental use, but this failed on the facts because the defendant was trying to exploit and sell its technology to third parties, which is not experimental use. For a discussion of the extent to which the defence to patent infringement under subs.(5)(b) covers biomedical and biotechnical research tools, see *Exemptions to Patent Infringement Applied to Biotechnology Research Tools* by Fiona Bor at [2006] E.I.P.R. 28(1), 5–14, and the discussion in Cook (Intellectual Property Institute, July 2006, above).

It is to be expected that for generic medicinal products many situations which would previously have been addressed under subs.(5)(b) will now be addressed under new subs.(5)(i), as to which see §60.18.

The principles established in *Klinische Versuche (Clinical Trials) I (X ZR 99/92), Re* [1997] R.P.C. 623 BGH were applied in *CoreValve v Edwards Lifesciences* [2009] F.S.R. 8, [2009] EWHC 6 Pat Ct, where it was noted that there must be outward limits to such principles, one of which should involve consideration of whether the immediate purpose of the transaction in question is to generate revenue. Thus the clinical trials of the medical device here in issue, which had been revenue raising, were held unable to benefit from the defence. A similar point had in fact been made in *Klinische Versuche (Clinical Trials) II (X ZR 68/94)* [1998] R.P.C. 423, BGH, which was, however, not mentioned in *CoreValve*.

—Extemporaneous pharmaceutical preparations (subs.(5)(c))

60.16   Subsection (5)(c), which appears to be in conformity with art.27(c) of the CPC, excludes the extemporaneous preparation in a pharmacy of medicine for an individual to a prescription by a registered medical practitioner or dentist. "Extemporaneous" is not defined, but may be taken as meaning as and when required, so that medicines prepared for stock in advance of a specific need arising are probably not exempt; and, in any case, the preparation must be "for an individual". It would appear that a veterinary preparation is not exempted by the provision as such a preparation would not be provided for an individual, this presumably meaning a human being. Anyway, it is rare nowadays for a pharmacy itself to prepare a medicine since medicinal products are normally supplied to the pharmacy in a pre-packed condition. Thus, the acts exempted under the provision are probably of little consequence in modern practice.

—Acts done on transiently visiting ships, aircraft, etc. (subs.(5)(d)–(f))

Subsection (5)(d), (e) and (f) refers to use of inventions on ships, aircraft, etc. Section 60(5)(d) gives effect to art.5 *ter* of the Paris Convention as inserted by The Hague revision conference of 1925. However, its true origin is the Patent Law Amendment Act 1852 (c.83) s.26 which was enacted to overturn the decision in *Caldwell v Vanvlissengen* (1851) 9 Hare 415; 68 E.R. 571, as explained in *Brown v Duchesne* [USA] (1856) 60 US (19 How.) 183. Article 5*ter* also provides exceptions to infringement for aerial and terrestrial vehicles, but in somewhat different terms. Hence, these exceptions are the subject of s.60(5)(e), but these overlap with the exceptions of s.60(5)(f) which arise from the Convention on International Civil Aviation, signed on 7th December 1944, known as the Chicago Convention. Hovercraft are specifically mentioned in para.(e) and "ship" and "vehicle" are used rather than "vessel" and "land vehicle" in art.27 of the CPC and in the Stockholm revision of art.5 *ter* of the Paris Convention.

60.17

Subsection (5)(d) and (e) relates to "relevant" ships, aircraft, hovercraft and vehicles, these being ones "registered in, or belonging to, any country, other than the United Kingdom", which is a member of the Paris Union established by the Paris Convention of 1883, or (following the amendment to subs.(7)) to any member of the World Trade Organization, again other than the United Kingdom. For a list of countries falling into either category, see §90.03. Note that the definition of "convention country" applied by ss.5 and 90 for the purpose of according a priority date for an invention is not applicable here; and that, while subs.(7) provides automatic designation of member countries of the Paris Union for the purposes of these exemptions from acts of infringement, such countries are only "convention countries" for the purposes of priority under s.5 if designated under s.90 or unless they are members of the WTO, see §90.02.

Subsection (5)(f) relates to "exempted" aircraft. These are defined in subs.(7) (as amended) by reference to the Civil Aviation Act 1982 (c.16). Under s.89 of that Act, foreign aircraft coming temporarily into the United Kingdom (and spare parts and equipment for such aircraft) are exempted from claims of patent infringement. This provision gives effect to the Chicago Convention, but Sch.12 to the Aviation Act 1982 also extends s.89 of that Act to patent claims against aircraft not protected under that Convention. The precise definition of exempted aircraft is in fact based upon Orders in Council designating specified countries. The Order presently effective for this purpose is The Aircraft (Exemption from Seizure on Patent Claims) Order 1977 (SI 1977/829), originally made under s.53 of the Civil Aviation Act 1949 (c.6) which was repealed by s.89 of the 1982 Act, but with previous Orders made under the 1949 Act given continuing effect. This 1977 Order does not appear to have been updated to reflect current membership of the Chicago Convention.

For a discussion about problems arising under these provisions, particularly with regard to extra-territorial activities, see the paper by D. Stauder [1995] *CIPA* 520. Also, the exclusion, in the definitions of a "relevant" ship, aircraft, hovercraft or vehicle set out in subs.(7), of such means of transport being "registered in, or belonging to, any country, *other than the United Kingdom*" would seem to be contrary to European Community law, for similar reasons to those explained in §64.03 in relation to the operation of s.64. Probably, therefore, the above-italicised words need to be read as "other than a Member State of the European Union", or even perhaps as "other than a Member State of the EEA".

A German court has held that, where a defendant loses control of a vehicle within the jurisdiction, that vehicle has not entered the country temporarily (*"Carrying carts for plants" ("Pflanzen-Transportwagen")* [Germany] noted (1990) 21 I.I.C. 99). In *Stena v Irish Ferries* [2002] R.P.C. 50 at 990 and [2003] R.P.C. 36 at 668 CA the defendants' vessel was held to fall within valid claims of the patent. However, infringement was avoided because the vessel (a ferry operating between its home port of Dublin and Holyhead) was deemed only ever to be "temporarily" in UK waters and therefore to be exempted under s.60(1)(d). The judge agreed with a decision of the German District Court of Hamburg (*Rolltraller* (1973) G.R.U.R. Int. 703) that the underlying purpose of the subsection and that of subs.(e) was to promote international trade. An argument that the exemption only applied to products and processes used on ships and not to the ship itself was rejected on a purposive construction of the subsection. A case comment on the *Stena* case by R. Sharma and H. Forrest was published at [2003] E.I.P.R. 430.

Exemptions for clinical or veterinary trials of medicinal products

60.18   (Note: subs.60(5)(g) and (h) are discussed in §60.13).

New subs.60(5)(i) relates to the exemption for clinical or veterinary trials of medicinal products introduced by SI 2005/2759 (reg.3). It implements art.10(6) of Directive 2001/83/EC [2001] OJ EC L311/67 on the Community code for medicinal products for human use, substituted by art.1(8) of Directive 2004/27/EC of the European Parliament and of the Council [2004] OJ EC L136/34, and art.13(6) of Directive 2001/82/EC of the European Parliament and of the Council on the Community code relating to veterinary medicinal products [2001] OJ EC L311/1, substituted by art.1(6) of Directive 2004/28/EC [2004] OJ EC L136/58. These articles provide that the conduct of tests and trials for the purposes of art.10(1) to (4) of Directive 2001/83/EC and corresponding art.13(1) to (5) of Directive 2001/82/EC, and the consequential practical requirements, shall not be regarded as contrary to patent rights for medicinal products.

This para.60(5)(i) therefore introduces a limited form of regulatory review or clinical trial defence into UK patent law (the so-called *Bolar*-type exemption, from the name given to the US version of the defence), which supplements but does not supplant the experimental use defence of para.(b). Paragraph (i) contains two sub-paragraphs, numbered (i) and (ii), which leads to some awkwardness in its citation. Paragraph (i)(i) ("eye-one") operates to introduce the exemption for "an act done in conducting a study, test or trial which is necessary for and is conducted with a view to, the application of" the relevant paragraphs of the appropriate Directive, and para.(i)(ii) ("eye-two") also exempts "any other act which is required for the purpose of the application of those paragraphs". The wording which this implements, however, is somewhat different, in that for example art.10.6 of Directive 2001/83/EC, as amended, provides that:

> "conducting the necessary studies and trials with a view to the application of [the relevant paragraphs] and the consequential practical requirements shall not be regarded as contrary to patent rights or to supplementary protection certificates for medicinal products".

The para.(i)(ii) wording therefore appears to implement this "consequential practical requirements" provision, which is believed to cover manufacturing, importing and processing the active material for the necessary studies.

The particular paragraphs of the two Directives to which para.(i)(i) refers are however all concerned with abridged applications for the authorisation of generic medicinal products, and so the studies and trials that this provision covers will typically be the bioequivalence and stability studies conducted by those wishing to secure a marketing authorisation for a generic version of an already authorised medicinal product. Thus, and in contrast to the US version of the *Bolar*-type exemption, the UK provision has no application to Phase I, Phase II and Phase III clinical trials on a medicinal product containing a new active substance that has not yet received an authorisation in any medicinal product. However, the *Clinical Trials* cases (see §60.15), which concerned Phase III trials, provide authority for such trials, as well as those in Phase I and II, to be regarded as covered by the defence for "use for experimental purposes in relation to the subject matter of the invention". It may be noted however that many other jurisdictions in Europe, when implementing the amendments of the 2001 Directive introduced by the 2004 one in their national laws, have gone further than mandated and further than the UK has done, and have covered all clinical trials in relation to medicinal products. In France and Germany this has been done with a broad provision that is expressed to be distinct from the experimental use defence, whereas in Italy and Spain it has been done by including a broad provision in relation to clinical trials within the scope of the experimental use defence. These national implementations, and the background to this provision, are discussed in *A European Perspective as to the Extent to Which Experimental Use, and Certain Other, Defences to Patent Infringement, apply to Differing Types of Research* by T.M. Cook (Intellectual Property Institute, July 2006).

Entitlement of persons to work the invention (subs.(6))

60.19 Subsection (6) corresponds to art.26(3) of the CPC and (by s.130(7)) has to be interpreted (so far as possible) in conformity with it. Article 26(3) of the CPC reads:

"CPC ARTICLE 26—Prohibition of indirect use of the invention

3. Persons performing the acts referred to in Article 27(a) to (c) shall not be considered to be parties entitled to exploit the invention within the meaning of paragraph 1."

The amendments made to subs.6(b) expand the immunity from infringement proceedings also to situations where a patent has been restored under s.28, with effect under s.28A and to the new situations where a lapsed application has been reinstated under new s.20A, with effect under new s.20B or resuscitated under new s.117A.

Although subss.(5)(a)–(c) exempt certain acts from being considered as patent infringement, associated contributory acts of the type covered by subs.(2) (rather than by subs.(1)) are apparently, by subs.(6), not exempted. Thus, in *Monsanto v Stauffer* [1985] R.P.C. 515 CA, the Patents Court accepted the claimant's argument that the supply of the patented product would have been an infringement under subs.(2), notwithstanding that the activities of the person supplied were exempted under subs.(5)(b). The Court of Appeal declined to express an opinion on the point, but it indicated there was force in the argument.

Besides persons entitled to work a patented invention under the provisions of subs.(5), others so entitled include those carrying out acts authorised by the Crown under s.55. Also entitled to work the invention are persons who have acquired rights under s.28A(4) or (5). Also entitled is a person whose activities before the priority date give him the right to work the invention by virtue of s.64 (for which see §§64.06–64.07), but in all cases only so far as concerns the permitted infringing act.

The Crown also has the right to dispose of, or use, articles forfeited under the laws relating to customs and excise, see s.122, but otherwise proceedings for patent infringement against the Crown can lie, see §129.03.

Territorial scope of infringement

60.20 Section 60 is only primarily applicable if an act of infringement takes place in the United Kingdom. For the purposes of the Act, the "United Kingdom" includes the Isle of Man (s.132(2), for which see §132.07), and also the territorial waters of the United Kingdom (s.132(3), for which see §132.08). As discussed also in §132.08, s.132(4) (as amended) extends the operation of the Act to acts done:

"in an area designated by Order under s.1(7) of the Continental Shelf Act 1964 [c.29] or specified under s.22(5) of the Oil and Gas (Enterprise) Act 1982 [c. 23]".

The present paragraph is limited to a discussion of the territorial effect on issues of infringement (noting that here "territorial" means within the jurisdiction of the court hearing the case, for which see §61.04). However, a person who has acted in the matters in issue solely outside the jurisdiction of the court can nevertheless be held liable as a "joint tortfeasor" for having carried out the separate tort of having taken part in a "common design" with someone who himself has committed the primary tortious act of infringement under s.60 within the court's jurisdiction, as discussed in §§60.27 and 60.28. However, it may be noted that in recent years there has been an increasing tendency to name a foreign entity as a defendant in order to obtain disclosure of documents against that entity. Otherwise, the desired disclosure might not become available to the claimant from a defendant resident within the jurisdiction of the court, see §60.27 (from which it will be seen that the court has not found such practice objectionable as a matter of law).

In *Kalman v PCL Packaging* [1982] F.S.R. 406 the word "disposal" was construed as requiring a disposal of property within the jurisdiction so that, where property in goods passed abroad under an f.o.b. [free-on-board] contract, there was no infringement by the vendor. However, there may be liability if the vendor retains any lien on the goods while in transit to the United Kingdom, this being another reason for the defendant being found liable in *Morton-Norwich v Intercen* [1978] R.P.C. 501. In the *Kalman* case, it was also held that an "offer to dispose of goods" requires both the offer and the subsequent disposal to take place within the United Kingdom for such to constitute infringement under s.60, but it is possible that the restrictive effect of this decision could be overcome by giving the word "supply" a broader construction, see (1983–84) 13 *CIPA* 105. In *SABAF v MFI and Meneghetti* [2003] R.P.C. 14 at 264 HC, [2004] UKHL 45 and [2005] R.P.C. 10 at 209 HL, in which the Italian manufacturer entrusted its products to an independent haulier for transport to the English retailer for sale in England, the Court of Appeal (reversing a finding of infringement at first instance) held that it is artificial to regard someone as importer who has no legal or beneficial interest in the goods, so the Italian company was held not liable for importation for the purposes of s.60(1)(a). The House of Lords agreed with the finding of non-infringement. See also §60.28 below in which the facts were not found sufficient to establish a common design between the manufacturer and the customer.

Also excused will be acts of a foreign state which enjoy immunity under the State Immunity Act 1978 (c.33). However, a UK court has jurisdiction, and indeed the duty, to enforce a patent relating to printing of bank notes within the United Kingdom for the benefit of a foreign bank, the keeping for disposal of foreign bank notes not being a sovereign act but one of dealing in a commodity within the purview of the English courts, see *A Ltd v B Bank* [1997] F.S.R. 165.

Authorised use of invention

60.21   Infringement only occurs if the act in question has taken place without the consent of the proprietor of the patent (subss.(1) and (2)). Obviously, the proprietor's consent may be given indirectly by a licensee. "Proprietor" is not directly defined in the Act but its meaning is evident from ss.30 and 31. The proprietor is prima facie the person entered (or entitled to be entered) as such in the register. From s.30(6) it appears that consent, as distinct from assent, need not be in writing, see §30.05. Consequently, the consent of the proprietor to the alleged act may be express (as in the case of a formal written or provable oral licence) or implied from the acts or conduct of the proprietor or a licensee, whose licence may itself be implied.

A defendant putting forward a defence of licence has the onus of proof and this may involve complicated issues of contract law which may have to be resolved under foreign law if the alleged licence agreement has to be construed other than under the law normally applied by the adjudicating court. For an example of the failure of such a defence see *Oxford Gene Technology v Affymetrix and Beckman* [2000] F.S.R. 741, where the defendant unsuccessfully argued that it was entitled to a licence under the terms of a licence granted to another and, alternatively, that he had purchased the assets of that other company which included its licence, although this decision was partially overturned on appeal (see [2001] F.S.R. 12 at 136 CA), it being held that there had been a purchase of a "business", giving that word a broad meaning.

Under domestic UK law, it is the concept of implied licence, rather than that of "exhaustion of rights", as set out in *United Wire v Screen Repair Services* [Scotland] [2001] R.P.C. 24 at 439 HL that explains why, notwithstanding the apparent breadth of the patentee's rights, a person who has acquired the product with the consent of the patentee may use or dispose of it in any way he pleases. It is well established that an implied licence to use or re-sell a patented product arises in the case of an ordinary sale of the product by the patentee (*Betts v Willmott* (1871) LR 6 Ch. App. 239) and presumably such implied licence can also arise in the case of the supply of means for putting the invention into effect under subs.(2). If there is to be any restriction on future use or resale of a patented article, notice must be given at the time of its sale (*Smith, Kline & French v Salim* [Malaysia] [1989] 1 F.S.R. 407). In principle, such a notice limiting permission to use the invention in specified ways can be given and will be effective if the notice is sufficiently prominent, see *National Phonograph v Menck* (1911) 28 R.P.C. 229; [1911] A.C. 336 Pat Ct; *Sterling Drug v Beck* [1972] F.S.R. 529 and *Dunlop v Longlife Battery* [1958] R.P.C. 473. However, such a notice (or any other contractual restraint) will be ineffective if it seeks to impose an unlawful prohibition such as resale price control (see §44.03) or affect trade between Community Member States, such as preventing export to another such State (as discussed in Appendix D).

The doctrine of notice was in issue in *Christian Salvesen v Odfjell Drilling* [Scotland] [1985] R.P.C. 569, see §68.03. Also, in *Roussel Uclaf v Hockley International* [1996] R.P.C. 441, the claimant asserted that, though the alleged infringing product had been made by it, it had been sold for use in China only. However, the evidence did not establish that any such limitation on future use had been "brought home" to purchasers, and certainly not to the subsequent purchasers who had imported the product into the United Kingdom. The necessary notice that the product had been supplied only under a limited licence for re-sale had not been established and an application for summary judgment was therefore dismissed with costs to be taxed and paid forthwith. For case comment, see D. Wilkinson [1997] E.I.P.R. 319. In *Sandvik v Pfiffner* BL C/91/97, noted I.P.D. 21015, a Chinese company was allowed to intervene and become a party to infringement proceedings in which the defendant alleged that its sales had been licensed by that Chinese company, who had asserted that one of the claimants had granted it worldwide distribution rights for the products in question. If this defence were not substantiated, the court saw the possibility of a substantial claim being made by the defendant against the Chinese company which therefore had a direct interest in becoming a party to the proceedings.

However, where the reseller has purchased a product manufactured by the licensee of a non-UK patent, the concept of implied licence does not apply where the patentee has parallel rights in the UK. Accordingly, any import of such a product into the UK would constitute an act of infringement (*Minnesota Mining & Manufacturing Company v Geerpres Europe Ltd* [1974] R.P.C. 35, applying *SA des Manufactures de Glaces v Tilghman* (1883) 25 Ch. D.1 followed in *The Wellcome Foundation v Discpharm* [1993] F.S.R. 433). In *Discovision v Pioneer Electronics* BL C/55/98, noted I.P.D. 21103, there had been no exhaustion of rights by the patentees when equipment had been sold on to the defendants. The vendor had had a licence to use (and sell products from that use) but with no power to grant sub-licences. The patentees had not consented to the sale of the equipment to the defendants, or to their use by them, and "consent is the cornerstone of the exhaustion doctrine".

The historical development of the separate doctrines of restriction of a licence by notice, express or implied, and of the exhaustion of rights upon first sale of a patented product (for which see §60.12 and Appendix D), and the consequent absence of an overriding rule of general applicability to control the course of patented articles placed in the stream of commerce, are the subject of the paper by D. Gladwell [1986] E.I.P.R. 366.

For infringement of a patent where there are joint proprietors, see §§36.06 and 66.02.

Implied licence to repair

Now that infringement is defined in s.60, the question whether an act of alleged repair **60.22** of a patented article is an act of infringement depends on whether that act is one which falls within the terms of s.60, i.e. has the defendant "made" a product within the claim, taking into account the nature of the invention claimed and what had been done by the defendant, see *United Wire v Screen Repair Services* [2000] F.S.R. 204 CA; [2001] R.P.C. 439 HL where the issue was whether the reconditioning by the defendant of vibratory screens for use in the recycling of oil drilling mud should be regarded as repairs. Although the defendant had re-used the original frames made by the claimant, it had added the mesh members and tensioned these as required. No licence could be implied (as under an exhaustion of rights principle) as this would have amounted to a licence to manufacture, rather than an exercise of a right to quiet enjoyment of a screen made by the claimant, and the acts of the defendant had been one of "making" the patented article contrary to s.60(1)(a), see also *Hazel Grove v Euro-League Leisure* [1995] R.P.C. 529.

Under the former common law test it was held that an implied authorised use of an invention arises from the licence which is implied to a purchaser of a patented article that he may repair and maintain that article, but that such a licence to repair does not extend to renewing a patented article under the guise of repair (*Sirdar Rubber v Wallington Weston* (1907) 24 R.P.C. 539 HL), as approved in *United Wire* (above). For a successful plea of implied licence to repair, both under patent and copyrights, see *Solar Thomson v Barton* [1977] R.P.C. 537, a case which can be seen as not involving "making" the patented article.

The cases on implied right to repair were reviewed in *Dellareed v Delkim* [1988] F.S.R. 329, where it was held that an implied licence to modify a purchased product is no wider than the implied licence to repair it. The defendant had therefore broken a previous undertaking not to modify the patented apparatus because it had, in effect, changed that apparatus into a new article. The English and United States authorities on the repair of patented articles were also reviewed in *Dana Corp v Rhobrake* [South Africa], noted [1993] E.I.P.R. D–111 with the question being whether the defendant was manufacturing new patented clutches or merely repairing those previously manufactured by the patentee. For case comment, see *Patent World* 53, June 1993, p.10.

In any event, it is somewhat uncertain whether the implied licence to permit repair of a patented article extends to open offers for sale of spare parts in relation to patented articles, as was held to apply under the law of copyright, see *British Leyland v Armstrong* [1986] R.P.C. 279 HL. Here, a distinction was apparently drawn between the implied licence to repair arising under true monopoly rights, such as patents (and presumably also registered designs), and those arising from copyright; and it was only with copyrights that the House of Lords held that intellectual property rights may not be invoked to prevent a purchaser of an article from keeping it in good repair by procuring the spare part from another because otherwise there would be a derogation from the grant implied upon sale of the article. However, this doubtful distinction between patent rights and copyrights was not pursued in the subsequent decision of the Privy Council in *Canon v Green Cartridge Company* [Hong Kong] [1997] F.S.R. 817, but this held that the exception to copyright infringement created by the *British Leyland* judgment has to be applied with caution, and in particular only in cases where there is a strong analogy with repair. Accordingly, it was there held that the exception should not apply to the supply of patented replacement cartridges of toner for laser printers where replacement would normally be required at a stage when nothing whatever in the photocopier required repair. Likewise, re-calibration of apparatus cannot be classified as a "repair" (*Mars UK v Teknowledge* [2000] F.S.R. 138).

In *Schütz v Werit* [2011] EWCA Civ 303, [2010] EWHC 660 Pat Ct, where the claims were to an assembly of an outer protective cage and a removable plastic inner bottle, it was held by the Court of Appeal, reversing the Patents Court, that retrofitting plastic bottles to the patentee's assemblies without the licence of the patentee (which the defendants characterised as "re-manufacturing") did constitute the "making" of a product that was within the claims to such assemblies, even though the inventive concept was wholly embodied in the cage and not the inner container.

Laches, acquiescence and estoppel

60.23   If a proprietor either delays unduly in bringing an action, or makes a representation that he does not propose to do so and the defendant acts upon that representation, the proprietor may be held to be estopped from bringing an action at all, and in the second case perhaps even if the limitation period (for which see §60.30) has not expired. One basis for this is that the proprietor has impliedly consented to (i.e. has acquiesced in) the defendant's acts; another is that it would be unconscionable in equity to allow the claimant to enforce his rights (either because of the delay, laches, or because of an implied estoppel), see the statement of principle in the passing-off case of *Habib Bank Ltd v Habib Bank AG* [1982] R.P.C. 1 CA. For further examples see the copyright cases of *Hoover v Hulme* [1982] F.S.R. 565 and *Redwood Music v Chappell* [1982] R.P.C. 109.

To establish a defence of acquiescence on the basis of unconscionable conduct, the defendant must prove more than that he was merely innocent of the existence of the patent, so that, in *Hadley Industries v Metal Sections* BL C/68/98, a plea of acquiescence failed as the patentee was held to have made no representation of acceptance of the defendant's product. Also, mere delay in commencing proceedings does not provide a defence (*Lux Traffic v Pike Signals* [1993] R.P.C. 107). In *Monsanto v Cargill* [2006] EWHC 1679 Pat Ct, the court, holding that the general factual matrix needed to be explained, refused to strike out a plea in an action concerning genetically-modified soybeans that the claimant's action was estopped on the ground that it had acquiesced in the growing of soybeans in Argentina in the knowledge that the product would be exported to other countries. However, on full trial in *Monsanto v Cargill (No.2)* [2008] F.S.R. 16; [2007] EWHC 3113 the defence was rejected as no representation was found to have been made by Monsanto or relied on by Cargill to its detriment. In cases of mere delay, it should be remembered that the Limitation Act 1980 (c.58) s.2 provides a normal period of six years within which proceedings in respect of an alleged tort can be brought, see §60.30, and that in many cases infringement is a continuing act.

An example of a promissory estoppel which entitled the defendant to succeed in having no order made against him for an activity which was held to have been an infringement is *Hazel Grove v Euro-League Leisure* [1995] R.P.C. 529. However, the promise here not to sue could be terminated upon reasonable notice and this notice period was held to be deemed to have expired upon the judgment finding infringement, but a new action would be necessary before the claimant could obtain interim relief.

However, in *Dellareed v Delkim* [1988] F.S.R. 329, a plea of acquiescence was not upheld, though the claimant had delayed for a year after its initial complaint before sending a "letter before action", it being held that the defendant should have realised that the claimant intended to proceed. Failure to take action in respect of one act of infringement does not preclude proceedings in respect of later infringing acts (*Raychem v Thermon* [1989] R.P.C. 423). Also, in *Mars v Azkoyen* BL C/57/89, noted I.P.D. 12079 and [1989] E.I.P.R. D–219, a failure to sue under a corresponding Spanish patent did not preclude later action in the United Kingdom.

No estoppel is created by a judgment in other proceedings unless the two proceedings involve identity of parties and identity of subject-matter and there has been a final judgment in the first proceedings (*Carl-Zeiss-Stiftung v Rayner and Keeler* [1967] R.P.C. 497 HL). Thus, where proceedings have been brought against one tortfeasor and have failed, further proceedings can be brought against others involved in the same alleged acts of infringement provided that there was no privity of interest between the different defendants (*Gleeson v Wippell* [1977] F.S.R. 301). However, in *Harrison v Project & Design [Damages]* [1987] R.P.C. 151 CA, the defendant was held, in an enquiry into damages, to be estopped from putting forward arguments of non-infringement which could have been raised at the trial of the issue of liability.

In *Building Products v Sandtoft Roof Tiles* [2004] F.S.R. 41 at 834, the court had excluded from the damages inquiry in an earlier action certain products which had not been specifically pleaded in that case, because these had to be considered different types of infringement. Upon the claimants launching a new action in respect of these products, the action was struck out on the basis of issue estoppel because infringement by these products could have been included in the earlier case. In accordance with CPR 63 PD 4.1(1)(b), it is important that each type of infringement be specifically pleaded.

For circumstances in which there may be an estoppel to a challenge to validity, see §74.04.

Infringement of an amended patent

Where the patent in suit has been amended, s.75(3) provides that the amended specification is deemed to have had effect from the grant of the patent, so that, if an infringement has taken place and the patent is then amended so that infringement no longer occurs, the infringement before amendment will be deemed not to have taken place. However, if in these circumstances damages (or an account of profits) have already been paid, it is possible that the defendant may not be able to recover those payments because of the principle that money paid under a mistaken view of the law is generally not recoverable.

60.24

To recover damages on an patent held to be only "partially valid", see §63.02. In such a situation, the patentee must be able to satisfy the court that the specification was framed in good faith and with reasonable skill and knowledge (s.63(2), discussed in §63.03, and see also s.62(3) discussed in §62.05 regarding amendment). However, where these conditions do not apply, it may still be possible to amend an invalid patent in order to avoid revocation, but this should be without effect on the defendant (at least for acts prior to the amendment) as there can no infringement of an invalid patent (*Pittevil v Brackelsberg* (1932) 49 R.P.C. 23), and the patent would have been invalid prior to the date of amendment.

Terms of full licence to work the invention

60.25   Under the previous common law, the acts reserved to the patentee by the wording of the Letters Patent grant were those of "making, using, exercising and vending" the invention. It was therefore customary to draft licence agreements in those terms, or some of them if the licence was to be restricted. Having regard to the extension of the concept of infringement by subss.(2) and (3), the specific exemptions from infringement of subss.(5)–(7) and the exclusion of rights exhausted under Community law and of Crown use by s.55, it has become more difficult to define the terms of a full licence. If a licensee wishes to ensure that his licence under the patent is total, he should perhaps ask that the grant clause of the licence gives him the right "to do any act which would otherwise be an infringement of the patent". Even then, such terms (without additional wording) may not provide a right to grant a sub-licence under the patent, other than that of selling or reselling on goods manufactured or sold under the licence which will (in the absence of express words to the contrary) be implied from the grant of a licence for such manufacture and/or sale.

Joint tortfeasance in relation to patent infringement

—The tort of "procuring" infringement

60.26   A proprietor is concerned, if he can, to preserve the monopoly in the invention afforded by the patent by stopping unlicensed use of the invention and/or obtaining compensation for such use. Prospective unlicensed users must also be discouraged or prevented. The relative importance of each of these aims will depend on the commercial situation, but proceedings for infringement under s.60(1) and/or (2) will usually be the principal course of action leading to the types of relief set out in s.61. However, action may also be taken against a defendant for inducing or procuring infringement of an intellectual property right. This is because it has been held (*CBS Songs v Amstrad* [1988] R.P.C. 567 HL) that a defendant who procures a breach of a right (in that case copyright) is liable jointly and severally with the actual infringer for the damages suffered by the claimant as a result of the acts of infringement. In such circumstances the procurer, or inducer, is a joint infringer (tortfeasor) on the basis that he intends and procures and shares a common design that infringement shall take place. This principle applies to patent rights.

However, in *CBS Songs v Amstrad* (above), the House of Lords held, contrary to the previous suggestion in *Belegging v Witten* [1979] F.S.R. 59 CA, that there is no separate tort of inducing, inciting, or persuading someone to commit an act of infringement of an intellectual property right, and that:

"generally speaking, inducement, incitement, or persuasion to infringe must be by a defendant to an individual infringer and must identifiably procure a particular infringement in order to make defendant liable as a joint infringer".

In this case, Amstrad sold twin-tape copiers. It was recognised that the machines could be used to infringe a third party's copyright, but they could also be used without infringement. Amstrad made no suggestion that the machines should be used to infringe copyright, and indeed they were sold with a specific warning about copyright infringement and its consequences. Once they had been sold, Amstrad had no control over, or interest in, their use and therefore had no control over any copying which a purchaser might carry out in infringement of a claimant's copyright, and it was held that Amstrad had not done anything to procure a particular infringement. For case comment on this case, see I. Purvis [1988] E.I.P.R. 345.

A clear distinction is therefore to be drawn between: "facilitating" infringement, which is not unlawful; and "inducing" infringement, which is a tortious act. For example, *Kalman v PCL Packaging* [1982] F.S.R. 406 involved only "facilitating" patent infringement, as also in *PLG Research v Ardon* [1993] F.S.R. 197; and though, in *Dow Chemical v Spence Bryson* [1984] R.P.C. 397 and 598 and [1984] R.P.C. 359, "procuring" was held to have occurred, for liability here such procuring must have occurred within the United Kingdom.

Joint tortfeasance by acting in a "common design"

Acts other than "procuring" infringement (as discussed in §60.26) can also be tortious acts, the common denominator being whether a person has acted in a "common design" with an actual infringer. For example, in *Rotocrop v Genbourne* [1982] F.S.R. 241, a defendant manufacturer who made and sold (under the 1949 Act) compost bins which, when assembled, would infringe a patent, together with assembly instructions, was held liable with its customers, though under the present Act such a manufacturer would appear to be directly liable for infringement under subs.(2). In that case, as in *Innes v Short* (1898) 15 R.P.C. 449, discussed in §60.08, where the defendant sold powdered zinc with specific instructions to the purchaser to infringe a process patent, the vendor and the purchaser had a common design to carry out an infringing act and both decisions can now be seen as ones of joint tortfeasorship. In *Lacroix Duarib v Kwikform* [1998] F.S.R. 493, it was held not unarguable that the supply of a kit of parts for assembly abroad into the claimed product could be regarded as an act of joint tortfeasorship.

In such cases of common design to commit an infringing act, relief can be claimed against either or both of the joint tortfeasors, even as regards a defendant out of the jurisdiction who trades with, but not in, the United Kingdom, as was established in *Morton-Norwich v Intercen* [1978] R.P.C. 501 and *Beecham Group v Norton* [1997] F.S.R. 81), in each of which supplier and importer were considered as joint tortfeasors.

A number of allegations of joint tortfeasorship have, however, been used, not so much as to claim relief against a foreign-based defendant, but to secure from him disclosure of documents thought likely to be useful in assisting the claimant to prove his case against a defendant based in the United Kingdom. This practice was seen by the courts as a legitimate litigation tactic and, provided that the claimant is able to establish that he had a "serious case to be tried" against such a defendant, the court would grant (and sustain) leave to serve an alleged joint tortfeasor outside the jurisdiction of the court, provided that the foreign defendant can be seen to have committed some act within the court's jurisdiction. This was not the case in *Dow Chemical v Spence Bryson* [1982] F.S.R. 397; [1982] F.S.R. 598; [1984] R.P.C. 359 and *Def Lepp Music v Stuart-Brown* [1986] R.P.C. 273. However, there should be less need for use of such a practice to secure disclosure these days, given the terms of CPR Pt 31.17 and the scope for third party disclosure that it confers, and as ordered, for example, in *American Home Products Corp v Novartis* [2001] EWCA Civ 165.

In *Electric Furnace Co v Selas* [1987] R.P.C. 23 CA, leave was given to serve proceedings out of the jurisdiction against a foreign defendant who had designed and supplied the second defendant in the United Kingdom with a furnace, the use of which was alleged to infringe a method claim, it being sufficient that the remedy in damages might be more advantageous against the foreign defendant either in scope or in enforceability, and in any event an account of profits (for which see §61.28) could be claimed against both defendants if they were joint tortfeasors. Subsequent cases have been:

- *Unilever v Gillette* [1989] R.P.C. 583 CA; where the claimant was held to have a good arguable case that a United States parent company and its United Kingdom subsidiary had acted in concert pursuant to a common design resulting in infringement;

60.27

- *Puschner v Tom Palmer* [1989] R.P.C. 430, where the existence of a joint marketing agreement between a foreign supplier and his domestic customer (under which the foreign supplier supplied sales and promotional literature and helped to train the sales staff of his customer) was held sufficient to establish the necessary "common design" for the supplier to be sued as a joint tortfeasor;

- *Mars v Azkoyen* BL C/57/89 and [1989] E.I.P.R. D–219, where the fact that the claimed apparatus required a setting-up operation which was carried out by the parent company in Spain was considered sufficient for an interlocutory injunction to be imposed if adequate security for damages was not forthcoming from the defendants;

- *Intel v General Instrument (No.2)* [1991] R.P.C. 235, where the foreign parent company had given the address of its subsidiary as its United Kingdom sales office and the subsidiary distributed the sales literature of the foreign parent company;

- *Mölnlycke v Procter & Gamble (No.4)* [1992] R.P.C. 21 CA, where a high degree of coordination was shown between German and British subsidiaries of a United States company as to what was marketed in the United Kingdom (the products for this being manufactured by the German company, even though the British company ultimately decided which of the products would be marketed in the United Kingdom; and

- *Lubrizol v Esso* [1992] R.P.C. 281 HC; [1992] R.P.C. 467 CA where joinder of a foreign parent company was permitted on a showing that it appeared to place its worldwide business in the hands of local subsidiaries with research being done in one country for the benefit of others, this indicating a sufficient "common design".

In this last case, it was stated that a claimant should be allowed to sue whom he wished provided the reason for it is not merely vexatious and harassing. In *Allied Colloids v American Cyanamid* BL C/24/93, noted I.P.D. 16073, an affidavit by a patent agent of belief of an act of infringement was held sufficient.

However, the basis for joinder must be an arguable case of joint tortfeasance and not merely a desire to obtain disclosure, shareholder control being insufficient (*Unilever v Chefaro* [1994] F.S.R. 135 CA). Here, the claimant failed to establish the necessary good arguable case against a parent company because the research and development in respect of which disclosure was desired had been carried out by an unidentified subsidiary. Hoffmann L.J. commented upon an apparent lacuna in the rules of disclosure as against subsidiary entities of a multi-national corporation for which outsiders may have difficulty in ascertaining its precise operating structure. This decision was followed in *Sepracor v Hoechst* BL C/5/99, noted I.P.D. 22034; [1999] F.S.R. 746 where it was made clear that joint tortfeasorship does not arise unless there is some act "in furtherance of a common design" and that it is not sufficient for a defendant knowingly to have facilitated or assisted an act of infringement. In particular, a parent–subsidiary relationship, of itself, does not make the foreign parent company a joint tortfeasor, see: *Mead Corp v Riverwood* [1997] F.S.R. 484; *Coin Controls v Suzo* [1997] F.S.R. 660 and *Napp v Asta Medica* [1999] F.S.R. 370, although in *Warheit v Olympia Tools* BL CC/45/01; [2003] R.P.C. 6 at 95 an exception was made on the basis that the foreign company had given the subsidiary's customers a lifetime warranty and had provided financial support to the subsidiary.

Likewise, there is no act of joint tortfeasorship in a normal relationship of seller and buyer, see *Allergan v Sauflon Pharmaceuticals* BL C/81/00, noted I.P.D. 23030. In *SABAF v MFI and Meneghetti* [2003] R.P.C. 14 at 264, HC the Italian manufacturer supplied its products to the English retailer for sale in England and supplied instruction manuals in the English language to facilitate their sale here, but this was not held sufficient to establish that it had a common design to market the products in England. The goods were its standard products and the retailer "could have decided to store or destroy the stock or send them to a market where there were no SABAF patents". This aspect of the case was upheld on appeal. The Italian company was merely acting as a supplier of goods to its English customer (MFI) and did not thereby "make MFI's infringing acts its own". The

House of Lords (see [2005] R.P.C. 10 at 209; [2004] UKHL 45) agreed with the finding of non-infringement. The question of common design was not argued before the House. In *Generics UK v Lundbeck* [2006] EWHC 804 Ch; [2007] R.P.C. 32 amendment of the particulars of claim to join an Indian manufacturer as a defendant, on the basis of an allegation that it had supplied to the UK Regulatory Authority a document purporting to set out the process used in India to make the product in issue, was refused, as the allegation alone if proved was insufficient to render the manufacturer a joint tortfeasor with the proposed UK importer.

In *MMI Research v Cellxion* [2009] EWHC 418 Pat Ct, a consultant to the corporate defendants was found to be jointly liable with such defendants as he shared a common design with them to market the device in issue. He intended and procured the sales which were the subject of the allegation of infringement, and actively participated in the sales effort. Above all others he knew exactly how the device operated, and that, at least some of the time, it would operate in an infringing manner.

In *Fabio Perini v LPC* [2009] EWHC 1929 Pat Ct; [2010] EWCA Civ 525 a foreign supplier of infringing machines was held to be jointly liable with its UK customer. It did not merely sell the machines into the United Kingdom, knowing that they would be used in a way which would infringe, but the supplier's employees were specifically engaged to (a) supervise the assembly of the machines at the customer's UK premises, (b) supervise the starting up of the machines (not merely for a day or so), and (c) supervise the training of the customer's staff in the use of the machines (again for a number of days). All such services, performed in the customer's premises in the United Kingdom, were undertaken to enable, assist and join in with the customer's use of the machines in infringement of the patent in suit.

Liability of directors

The principle that participation in a common design renders each participant a joint tort- **60.28** feasor separately liable for any unlawful activity involved in that design, as discussed in §§60.26 and 60.27, is applicable to the liability of a director for patent infringement committed by his company. Thus, in Australia, it has been held that, where a director has authorised and been personally involved in his company's infringement, he is also personally liable to pay infringement damages (*Martin Engineering v Nicaro* [Australia] (1991) 20 I.P.R. 241). This case was not discussed in the extensive review of the status (under Australian law) of directors as joint tortfeasors in *Inverness Medical Switzerland v MDS Diagnostics [Australia]* [2010] F.C.A. 108, which also cited only Australian and Canadian case law.

Previously, in *Evans v Spritebrand* [1985] F.S.R. 267, the Court of Appeal had indicated (in a copyright case) that a director should be in no more favourable position than an employee who would be liable for tortious acts which he carries out personally. Accordingly, it would appear that a director will be personally liable for acts of patent infringement carried out by his company if he has personally participated in the carrying out of the infringing act, though in the *Evans* case, the Court of Appeal indicated that:

"where there is no knowing, deliberate wilful quality in the participation the court may naturally be more reluctant to hold the director personally liable".

See also *Besson v Fulleon* [1986] F.S.R. 319.

It would therefore appear sufficient to join a director of a defendant as a further defendant to patent infringement proceedings if the pleadings show that there is a good arguable case that the director could have acted in a common design with another defendant (*PLG Research v Ardon* [1992] F.S.R. 59), though at the trial (see [1993] F.S.R. 197) the director was here held to have facilitated, but not procured (on which see §60.26), the acts held to be ones of infringement and so was not personally liable.

In *Charlesworth v Relay Roads* BL C/8/99, noted I.P.D. 22052, three individuals were each held to have operated a machine in an infringing manner on at least some occasions, but it was held that it had not been proved that any of these individuals should be held liable for the totality of the infringement carried out by corporate defendants.

In *Boegli-Gravures v Darsail-ASP* [2009] EWHC 2690 Pat Ct, a director of the infringing defendant company was held to have gone beyond merely performing his constitutional role in the company and thus to be joint tortfeasor with the company where he personally dealt with a prospective customer throughout the negotiations and together with his two co-directors made the decision to supply the infringing products to the customer.

Liability under the Sale of Goods Act

60.29   Liability can also arise under the Sale of Goods Act 1979 (c.54) ss.12(1), (2)(b) and 14(2), as amended by the Sale and Supply of Goods Act 1994 (c.35) ("the SGA") where a purchaser of goods finds himself unable to use these goods because of the existence of a third-party patent, see *Niblett v Confectioners' Materials* [1921] 3 K.B. 387 CA. This can be so even apparently where the patent only issues some time after the sale has taken place, see *Microbeads v Vinhurst* [1976] R.P.C. 19 CA, liability then arising from breaches of a seller's implied warranties of his right to sell the goods imposed by the SGA s.12(1) and/or of the buyer's right of quiet enjoyment of the goods imposed by the SGA, s.12(2)(b) and/or of the seller's implied warranty that the goods are of merchantable quality imposed by the SGA, s.14(2), unless these warranties have validly been excluded or avoided by the terms of the contract, as to which see s.6 of the Unfair Contract Terms Act 1977 (c.50), as discussed further in §44.07.

The effect of the Limitation Acts

60.30   Actions for infringement may be brought before the English court within six years of the act complained of (Limitation Act 1980, c.58, s.2). After that period, an action becomes statute-barred so that damages (or an account of profits) are not claimable for acts done more than six years before the date of the claim. In *Sorota v Gardex* [1984] R.P.C. 317 CA, the pleadings were not permitted to be amended also to allege infringement in respect of unmodified articles sold more than six years prior to the application for amendment, when the action had originally been brought alleging infringement solely by a later-modified article.

However, the limitation period will not run if there has been concealed fraud, see *Morton-Norwich v Intercen and United Chemicals* [1981] F.S.R. 337, referred to in §61.27.

In Scotland, limitation would appear to arise if only five years elapse without proceedings being commenced or an acknowledgement of liability being given by the defender (Prescriptions and Limitations (Scotland) Act 1973, c.52, s.6), but various ancillary provisions of this Act may alter the limitation period in Scotland in particular cases.

Possible continuing liability after expiry of the patent

60.31   Upon expiry of the patent, there can be no further liability for acts committed after that date, and any injunction then in force will automatically lapse, each as regards acts which otherwise would have constituted patent infringement. However, it is possible that an injunction could be specifically couched in post-expiry terms, as in *Dyson v Hoover (No.2)* [2001] R.P.C. 27 at 544 see §61.21.

Nevertheless, despite the expiry of the patent, a proprietor may continue to have some residual rights. For example, if he has built up a reputation for producing the patented article in a distinctive get-up, he may be able to restrain imitation of that get-up, see *Hoffmann-La Roche v DDSA* [1969] F.S.R. 410 and *Industrie Diensten v Beele (6/81)* [1982] E.C.R. 707; [1982] 3 C.M.L.R. 102, abridged [1983] F.S.R. 119 ECJ, though a registered trade mark for the patented product may become invalid if there is no reasonable alternative name for the product (Trade Marks Act 1994, c.26, s.46(1)(c)). It should also be remembered that trade marks may now be registered in the UK and the EU for the shape of goods or their packaging, but not where the shape is "necessary to obtain a technical result" (Trade Marks Act 1994 s.3(2)(b)).

It should also not be assumed that copyright or design rightin the drawings present in a patent specification has necessarily lapsed with the patent. Although Whitford J. so held at first instance in *Catnic v Hill & Smith* [1982] R.P.C. 183, that decision was based on a concession by counsel which was withdrawn on appeal citing the registered design case of *Werner Motors v Gamage* (1904) 21 R.P.C. 621. Also, the *Catnic* decision on this point was specifically disapproved in *Merrell Dow v Norton* [1994] R.P.C. 1, particularly in view of several subsequent decisions in other common law countries which had firmly indicated a contrary view. In any event, the drawings in a patent specification will rarely indicate dimensions (although they did by implication in the *Catnic* case) and design right protection is, therefore, likely to exist in more detailed drawings which were not included in the patent specification.

SECTION 61

Proceedings for infringement of patent

61.—(1) Subject to the following provisions of this Part of this Act, civil **61.01**
proceedings may be brought in the court by the proprietor of a patent in respect of any act alleged to infringe the patent and (without prejudice to any other jurisdiction of the court) in those proceedings a claim may be made—

    (a) for an injunction or interdict restraining the defendant or defender from any apprehended act of infringement;

    (b) for an order for him to deliver up or destroy any patented product in relation to which the patent is infringed or any article in which that product is inextricably comprised;

    (c) for damages in respect of the infringement;

    (d) for an account of the profits derived by him from the infringement;

    (e) for a declaration or declarator that the patent is valid and has been infringed by him.

(2) The court shall not, in respect of the same infringement, both award the proprietor of a patent damages and order that he shall be given an account of the profits.

(3) The proprietor of a patent and any other person may by agreement with each other refer to the comptroller the question whether that other person has infringed the patent and on the reference the proprietor of the patent may make any claim mentioned in subsection (1)(c) or (e) above.

(4) Except so far as the context requires, in the following provisions of this Act—

    (a) any reference to proceedings for infringement and the bringing of such proceedings includes a reference to a reference under subsection (3) above and the making of such a reference;

    (b) any reference to a **claimant** or pursuer includes a reference to the proprietor of the patent; and

    (c) any reference to a defendant or defender includes a reference to any other party to the reference.

(5) If it appears to the comptroller on a reference under subsection (3) above that the question referred to him would more properly be determined by the court, he may decline to deal with it and the court shall have jurisdiction to determine the question as if the reference were proceedings brought in the court.

(6) Subject to the following provisions of this Part of this Act, in determining whether or not to grant any kind of relief claimed under this section and the

extent of the relief granted the court or the comptroller shall apply the principles applied by the court in relation to that kindof relief immediately before the appointed day.

(7) If the comptroller awards any sum by way of damages on a reference under subsection (3) above, then—

(a) in England and Wales, the sum shall be recoverable, if a county court so orders, by execution issued from the county court or otherwise as if it were payable under an order of that court.

(b) in Scotland, payment of the sum may be enforced in like manner as an extract 49 registered decree arbitral bearing a warrant for execution issued by the sheriff court of any sheriffdom in Scotland;

(c) in Northern Ireland, payment of the sum may be enforced as if it were a money judgment.

Note. The Patents Act 2004 (c.16) Sch.2 para.14 formally changed the term "plaintiff" in subs.(4) to "claimant" in conformity with the current practice under the CPR, and (by s.11) also inserted new s.61(7), both changes being effective from January 1, 2005 (SI 2004/3205 art.2(d)(f)(k)).

Relevant Statutory Instrument

INTELLECTUAL PROPERTY (ENFORCEMENT, ETC.) REGULATIONS 2006

(SI 2006/ 1028)

61.02   These Regulations, effective from April 29, 2006 with no transitional provision, implement European Directive No. 2004/48/EC OJ EC L157, 30.4.2004, p.45, with corrigendum OJ EC L195, 2.6.2004, p16 [the "Enforcement Directive"] requiring harmonisation of the relief generally to be available for infringement (within the EEA Area) of intellectual property rights (whether registered or unregistered). Regulation 3 of this Statutory Instrument applies generally to the assessment of damages for infringement of such rights when this has occurred in the circumstances specified thereby. This Regulation has the potential therefore to modify the scope of section 61(1)(c) and, for patent infringement, can be regarded as a potential amendment to it. It reads:

3.—(1) Where in an action for infringement of an intellectual property right the defendant knew, or had reasonable grounds to know, that he engaged in infringing activity, the damages awarded to the claimant shall be appropriate to the actual prejudice he suffered as a result of the infringement.

(2) When awarding such damages—

(a) all appropriate aspects shall be taken into account, including in particular—

(i) the negative economic consequences, including any lost profits, which the claimant has suffered, and any unfair profits made by the defendant; and

(ii) elements other than economic factors, including the moral prejudice caused to the claimant by the infringement; or

(b) where appropriate, they may be awarded on the basis of the royalties or fees which would have been due had the defendant obtained a licence.

(3) This regulation does not affect the operation of any enactment or rule of law relating to remedies for the infringement of intellectual property rights except to the extent that it is inconsistent with the provisions of this regulation.

(4) In the application of this regulation to—

(a) Scotland, "claimant" includes pursuer; "defendant" includes defender; and "enactment" includes an enactment comprised in, or an instrument made under, an Act of the Scottish Parliament; and

(b) Northern Ireland, "claimant" includes plaintiff.

COMMENTARY ON SECTION 61

Scope of the section

Section 61 defines the relief obtainable as the result of a finding of infringement under **61.03** s.60 (or, in the case of infringement pre-grant, under s.69).Unless otherwise stated in the Act, relief is to be available according to the principles applied by the court under former statutes (subs.(6)), with a continued prohibition against an award of both damages and account of profits in respect of the same infringement (subs.(2)).

Section 61 provides for infringement proceedings to be brought before "the court" (subs.(1)) as that term is defined, for which see §61.04. Also, by agreement between the proprietor and the alleged infringer, proceedings may be brought before the Comptroller (subs.(3)), although little use has been made of this facility, see further §61.38. In such proceedings the Comptroller can refer the case to the court for decision (subs.(5)).

As s.61 lays down the types of relief which can be awarded for acts of patent infringement (for which see ss.60 and 125 and the commentaries on those sections), it is convenient here to provide a commentary on the procedure for infringement proceedings before the Patents Court and the Patents County Court ("PCC"). This is discussed in "Practice under Section 61" at §§61.40–61.87 and also see the commentary on s.291 of the CDPA 1988 as regards the PCC. Practice in proceedings before the Comptroller is discussed in the commentary on s.123.

The CPR, which almost entirely replaced the Rules of the Supreme Court ("RSC") in April 1999, introduced several important changes of nomenclature, the most important of which were to replace: "plaintiff" by "claimant"; "writ" by "claim form"; "pleadings" by "statement of case"; "discovery" by "disclosure"; "interlocutory relief" by "interim relief"; and "inter partes" and "ex parte" proceedings by "hearing with/without notice" respectively.

It is thought that s.61 (together with other provisions in the Act and the terms of the CPR) meet the obligations under Pt III of the TRIPS Agreement, the relevant articles of which are reprinted where relevant in the paragraphs which follow.

"TRIPS Article 41—General obligations

1. Members shall ensure that enforcement procedures as specified in this Part are available under their law so as to permit effective action against any act of infringement of intellectual property rights covered by this Agreement, including expeditious remedies to prevent infringements and remedies which constitute a deterrent to further infringements. These procedures shall be applied in such a manner as to avoid the creation of barriers to legitimate trade and to provide for safeguards against their abuse.

2. Procedures concerning the enforcement of intellectual property rights shall be fair and equitable. They shall not be unnecessarily complicated or costly, or entail unreasonable time-limits or unwarranted delays.

3. Decisions on the merits of a case shall preferably be in writing and reasoned. They shall be made available at least to the parties to the proceeding without undue delay. Decisions on the merits of a case shall be based only on evidence in respect of which parties were offered the opportunity to be heard.

4. Parties to a proceeding shall have an opportunity for review by a judicial authority of final administrative decisions and, subject to jurisdictional provisions in a Member's law concerning the importance of a case, of at least the legal aspects of initial judicial decisions on the merits of a case. However, there shall be no obligation to provide an opportunity for review of acquittals in criminal cases.

5. It is understood that this Part does not create any obligation to put in place a judicial system for the enforcement of intellectual property rights distinct from that for the enforcement of law in general, nor does it affect the capacity of Members to enforce their law in general. Nothing in this Part creates any obligation with respect to the distribution of resources as between enforcement of intellectual property rights and the enforcement of law in general."

"TRIPS Article 42—Fair and Equitable procedures

Members shall make available to right holders' civil judicial procedures concerning the enforcement of any intellectual property right covered by this Agreement. Defendants shall have the right to written notice which is timely and contains sufficient detail, including the basis of the claims. Parties shall be allowed to be represented by independent legal counsel, and procedures shall not impose overly burdensome requirements concerning mandatory personal appearances. All parties to such procedures shall be duly entitled to substantiate their claims and to present all relevant evidence. The procedure shall provide a means to identify and protect confidential information, unless this would be contrary to existing constitutional requirements."

Proceedings cannot be commenced under s.61 (or under s.69) until notice of the patent grant has been officially published, see §24.05, and for European patents (UK) see §77.05. The proprietor of the patent may sue (subs.(1)), as may one or more joint proprietors (s.66). Non-exclusive licensees have no power to claim relief for infringement of the patent under which they are licensed, and proceedings by an exclusive licensee are subject to s.68 with consequences for failing to register timely an exclusive interest in the patent, for which see §§68.02–68.04. In *Xtralite (Rooflights) v Hartington Conway* [2004] R.P.C. 7 at 161, it was held that the word "proprietor" did not necessarily mean "registered proprietor" and the statutory right of action was conferred on the person who could trace his title as set out in s.7 of the Act. Section 30(6) requires the specified transactions to be written, but an estoppel at common law could operate to bind the true owner notwithstanding the lack of writing. For the meaning of "proprietor", see also §60.21.

The forum for infringement proceedings

61.04   "Court", for the purposes of the Act, is defined in s.130(1). In England and Wales this means either "the High Court" or a "patents county court" as designated under s.287 of the CDPA 1988, for which see §287.01 and §287.02. In Scotland, Northern Ireland and the Isle of Man, "court" means the local equivalent of the High Court in England and Wales, as defined in s.130(1) (as amended), see §96.06. Infringement proceedings in England and Wales are, by CPR 63.1 (see Appendix F), assigned to the Patents Court constituted as part of the Chancery Division of the High Court, see §96.06. For the position in Scotland, Northern Ireland and the Isle of Man, see §§96.10, 131.03 and 132.07, respectively.

The traditional view has been that no court in the United Kingdom has any jurisdiction to entertain proceedings concerning a foreign patent, but this position was changed by the Civil Jurisdiction and Judgments Act 1982 (c.27) as amended, as regards EU Member States except Denmark by virtue of the Brussels Convention (now replaced by the Brussels I Regulation) and also as regards the other EEA Member States (Iceland, Liechtenstein and Norway) as well as Denmark and Switzerland by virtue of the Lugano Convention. Thus, in the copyright case *Pearce v Ove Arup* [1997] F.S.R. 641 and [1999] F.S.R. 525, it was held that, where the defendant is domiciled within the United Kingdom and is sued in a court of its domicile (as primarily stipulated in art.2 of the Brussels Convention and of the Brussels I Regulation) for a tort committed abroad in a Member State of the Brussels I Regulation or Lugano Convention, the United Kingdom court has no discretion but must accept jurisdiction irrespective of the doctrine of *forum conveniens* and despite the court's reluctance to deal with infringement of a foreign intellectual property right, as discussed in §96.11. For further discussion of the implications of the decision in *Pearce v Ove Arup*, and the issues as to choice of law as to jurisdiction, justiciability and actionability of acts of intellectual property infringement committed out of the jurisdiction of the court, see R. Arnold [1999] I.P.Q. 389.

However, under art.22(4) of the Brussels I Regulation (replacing art.16(4) of the Brussels Convention and a corresponding provision in the Lugano Convention), a challenge to patent validity may only be heard in a national court for which the patent was granted and art.25 of the Brussels I Regulation (replacing art.22 of the Brussels Convention) requires a court to decline jurisdiction when an issue under art.22 of the Brussels I Regulation (replacing art.16 of the Convention) arises for determination in another court. Accordingly, in *Coin Controls v Suzo* [1997] F.S.R. 660, the Patents Court struck out claims for alleged infringement of a European patent for Germany and Spain because the defendant indicated that it would be challenging validity and because there can be no infringement of an invalid patent. In doing so, the court noted that:

"national patents which start out as identical may end up being different in different countries. So obliging infringement and validity to be run together may have significant advantages. The alternative of leaving infringement to be determined in one country and validity in another has nothing to commend it and is only likely to result in an unhelpful proliferation of proceedings"

However, where the Patents Court was asked to impose an anti-suit injunction against a Dutch claimant from seeking relief for an interim injunction covering the United Kingdom in circumstances where it seemed improbable that an English court would grant interim relief because the product had been marketed without previous challenge in this country for five years, and where the Patents Court was informed that the Dutch courts did not, apparently, accept the rationale of the *Coin Controls* decision (for which see *Palmaz v Boston Scientific* [Netherlands] [1998] F.S.R. 199), the Patents Court nevertheless declined to grant anti-suit relief (*Fort Dodge v Akzo Nobel* [1998] F.S.R. 222). The court stated that to do so would be usurping the jurisdiction of the Dutch court, and it saw the application for relief as one amounting to an assertion that the *Coin Controls* decision was undoubtedly right and that the Dutch courts could not be trusted to follow it.

This conflict over the true effect of arts 22(4) and 25 of the Brussels I Regulation (replacing arts 16(4) and 19 of the Brussels Convention) has to a significant extent been resolved in favour of the *Coin Controls* approach by the ECJ in *GAT v LuK* (C-4/03) [2006] F.S.R. 45 at 967; [2006] OJ EC C224/1, which ruled that:

"Article 16(4) of the [Brussels] Convention is to be interpreted as meaning that the rule of exclusive jurisdiction laid down therein concerns all proceedings relating to the registration or validity of a patent, irrespective of whether the issue is raised by way of an action or a plea in objection."

However, where validity is not disputed, there remains power for courts in other countries of the EU (and the other members of the parallel Lugano Convention) to determine disputes concerning infringement of intellectual property rights by acts carried out, or threatened to be carried out, in the United Kingdom. This is because art.5(3) of the Brussels Convention (and the Brussels I Regulation) which is enacted into UK law by Sch.1 art.5(3) of the 1982 Act provides that, in matters relating to tort, a person domiciled in a Contracting State may be sued either in his country of domicile or in the courts of the place where the harmful event occurred. Indeed, apparently, where parallel actions are brought in another contracting state, a United Kingdom court may be required to cede jurisdiction to a foreign court and may choose to do so where related actions are involved. Nevertheless, by virtue of art.22(4) of the Brussels I Regulation, the validity of a patent granted by or for the United Kingdom should only be justiciable within the United Kingdom. Thus, foreign courts may well hold themselves to have jurisdiction to decide questions of infringement (but not validity) of United Kingdom patents and courts in both the Netherlands and Germany have imposed extra-territorial injunctions in respect of patent infringement anywhere within the EU, see §96.10.

The basis for such pan-European infringement jurisdiction has often been founded on art.6(1) of the Brussels Convention and the Brussels I Regulation, by which jurisdiction may also be seized over "closely connected" claims against multiple defendants, some national courts taking the view that in some cases claims in relation to different national designations of a European patent are "closely connected". In *Roche Nederland v Primus and Goldenberg* (C-539/03) [2007] F.S.R. 5, [2006] OJ EC C224/1, a decision given on the same day as that in *GAT v LuK*, the ECJ considered the scope of art.6. The reference, from the Netherlands Supreme Court, concerned the "spider in the web" theory of the Netherlands courts which, in their view, enabled proceedings to be brought in the Netherlands for acts of patent infringement carried out elsewhere in the EU where there were parallel European patents and the various defendants were members of the same group of companies. Here the patentees had sued Roche Nederland in the Netherlands together with eight other companies of the Roche Group established in other EU States alleging infringement of a European patent designating the Netherlands and the other EU

States in question. They alleged that the Dutch courts should hear all these actions together under art.6(1) of the Brussels Convention which allows multiple defendants to be sued in a single court, and the consequence of which under art.22 of the Convention is to require the courts of other Member States to cede jurisdiction to the EU court first seized of related actions in order to avoid a multiplicity of similar actions being tried in different EU Member States. The patentees argued that, as the defendants were related companies, the patents in different EU Member States were identically worded, the acts of infringement were the same and the substantive law was the same, art.6 should be applied to allow a consolidated action against all the defendants initiated before a single court of an EU Member State for which a relevant patent had been granted. The Roche defendants took the opposite view.

The ECJ ruled that art.6 could only be used where there was no scope for differing decisions to be given in patent infringement proceedings brought in different EU States in respect of acts committed in one or more of those States. However, as under the EPC infringement was a matter for national law, the alleged acts of infringement could not be assumed to be the same because the defendants were different, the patents were individual ones under the EPC, and the alleged infringements, being committed in different EU States, were not necessarily the same. Note was also taken of the *GAT v LuK* decision, noted above, as an additional ground for holding art.6(1) not to apply because validity of each of the patents was being challenged and only national courts could decide upon the validity of European patents granted for various EPC States because of art.16 of the Brussels Convention (discussed above). The ECJ therefore held that:

> "Article 6(1) of the [Brussels] Convention must be interpreted as meaning that it does not apply in European patent infringement proceedings involving a number of companies established in various Contracting States in respect of acts committed in one or more of those States even where those companies, which belong to the same group, may have acted in an identical or similar manner in accordance with a common policy elaborated by one of them."

The effect of these two decisions, taken together, is severely to curtail the scope for securing pan-European relief for patent infringement, especially where validity is in issue, once the court first seized of an action has applied these principles, which may however take time. One area not, however, addressed by these decisions is that of interim relief under art.31 of the Brussels Regulation (replacing art.24 of the Brussels Convention). However the ECJ, in *St Paul Dairy Industries NV v Unibel Exser BVBA* (C-104/03) [2005] E.C.R. I-3481 observed that, as an exception to the system of jurisdiction set up by the Convention, this article must be interpreted strictly, and held in that case that an order in the Netherlands for the provisional hearing of a witness, in relation to a dispute in relation to which the Belgian courts would have jurisdiction, but before any proceedings were issued, was not within the scope of the exception conferred by the article for "provisional, including protective, measures".

Appeals

61.05　　The normal procedure for appeals applies to patent infringement proceedings, but since January 1, 1999, leave to appeal *any* decision of the High Court or a county court to the Court of Appeal has been required, save in an exceptional case involving a loss of personal liberty, see §97.19. Leave to appeal should not, apparently, be given if the appeal would have "no realistic prospect of success" (*Plumb v Ayres*, noted *The Times*, May 11, 1999). A further appeal is possible to the Supreme Court, but again only with leave. All such leave can be given either by the court which gave the decision or by the court before which it is sought to being an appeal. Apart from the question of whether or not a decision can be appealed as of right or requires leave, the position in other parts of the United Kingdom is similar. In Northern Ireland an appeal from the High Court in Northern Ireland is made to the Court of Appeal in Northern Ireland. In Scotland, appeal lies from the Outer House of the Court of Session to the Inner House thereof; and in the Isle of Man, the final appeal would be to the Judicial Committee of the Privy Council.

An appeal from a decision of the Comptroller under subs.(3) lies as of right to the Patents Court, but then to the Court of Appeal only with leave (s.97(3)(a)), see §97.06, and for appeals if the Comptroller hears proceedings in Scotland, see §97.07.

The scope to seek leave to appeal was held in *Pozzoli v BDMO* [2007] EWCA Civ 588; [2007] F.S.R. 37 to comply with the obligation under art.32 of the TRIPS Agreement that "an opportunity for judicial review of any decision to revoke or to forfeit a patent shall be available." As to whether or not the trial judge should grant leave, the Court of Appeal observed at para.10, as to patent cases:

"Unless the case is very clear and can be understood sufficiently readily in an hour or so, the better course is normally for permission to be granted by the trial judge. For, unlike the trial judge, the Court of Appeal judge(s) who have to decide whether permission should be granted (where the trial judge has refused it) will not be immersed in the technology and evidence in the same way as the trial judge. Faced with but an incomplete understanding and a plausible skeleton argument seeking permission, the Court of Appeal will generally be likely to grant permission, even if later it discerns that the case is indeed clear."

In *Les Laboratoires Servier v Apotex* [2009] F.S.R. 3 at 220; [2008] EWCA Civ 445; noted [2008] *CIPA* 276, the Court of Appeal observed that the case had not satisfied the test in *Pozzoli* (above) as there was no realistic prospect of upsetting the critical finding of fact on which the patent had been found bad for lack of novelty and obviousness and so leave to appeal ought not have been given by the trial judge. It should also be noted that in relation to appeals about obviousness, Lord Hoffmann in *Biogen v Medeva* [1997] R.P.C. 1 at 45 stated:

"Where the application of a legal standard such as negligence or obviousness involves no question of principle but is simply a matter of degree, an appellate court should be very cautious in differing from the judge's evaluation."

When reversing a judge on his assessment of inventive step in *Wake Forest v Smith & Nephew* [2009] F.S.R. 11, [2009] EWCA Civ 848 it was observed by the Court of Appeal that the observations in *Biogen* had been directed not at the facts as found by a judge but to his evaluation of them in the context of the ultimate question of obviousness. If a judge has adopted the wrong approach to obviousness—for instance taking a mistaken view as what is disclosed by the prior art or what the difference between the prior art and the claim under attack is—then the Court of Appeal has to form its own evaluation on the basis of the facts as found by the judge or which appear clearly from the documents or other evidence without having been expressly mentioned in the judgment.

In *Leo Pharma v Sandoz* [2009] EWCA Civ 1188 the unsuccessful appeal had involved attacking the Judge's findings of fact, evaluations of the evidence and value-judgment conclusions, which as observed by the Court of Appeal amounted to an attack of "perversity" in that to have succeeded on appeal the Judge's conclusions would have to have been such that no judge could reasonably have reached them on the evidence.

Defence of invalidity

While the validity of the patent in suit may always be put in issue as a defence to proceedings under s.60 (s.74(1)(a)), the right to counterclaim for revocation of the patent sued upon, previously specified under s.61 of the 1949 Act, was not re-enacted. Consequently, and strictly speaking, to secure revocation, as distinct from merely pleading invalidity (since an invalid patent cannot be infringed, see *Pittevil v Brackelsberg* (1932) 49 R.P.C. 23, a cross-petition or application under s.72 would appear to be necessary when the patent in suit is one granted under the Act, but in such cases the former practice of seeking revocation in a counterclaim (under the CPR terms a "Part 20 claim") seems not to have been questioned by the Patents Court.

A defence of invalidity is available where the patentee brings action only under a subclaim in the patent and the defendant pleads that the main claim is invalid, because the in-

61.06

validity of any claim makes it revocable unless amendment is permitted. Thus, in *Petrolite v Dyno* [1998] F.S.R. 190, discussed by M. Molyneaux [1998] E.I.P.R. 225, the claimant sought to delay amendment of the patent until this could be done in parallel EPO opposition proceedings, but meanwhile had commenced infringement proceedings without seeking amendment under s.75. It was held that, unless amendments were proposed and communicated to the Comptroller for advertisement within 14 days, the defendant would be entitled to summary judgment because of a prior use against which the patentee would not be defending; and, also, as an abuse of process because the patentee had been drawing the patent to the attention of others without indicating an intention to amend. However, when amendment had been requested, the patentee was permitted to amend its pleadings to add a plea of infringement of a further claim (*Petrolite v Dyno* [1998] F.S.R. 646).

The defence of invalidity is not available when the action is for breach of a contractual undertaking not to infringe (*Van der Lely v Maulden Engineering* [1984] F.S.R. 157), see also s.74(1). In *Biogen v Medeva* [1993] R.P.C. 475, the defendant claimed a declaration in respect of allegations of infringement made by a third party and sought to join that party as a further defendant to its counter-claim for revocation of the patent in order to obtain disclosure from it. This pleading was struck out as an abuse of the process of court, there being no real interest in the relief claimed and no real interest in deciding the pleaded issues as between itself and the third party.

Relief (subs.(1))

61.07   The claimant may claim the reliefs set out in subs.(1), paras (a)–(e). These are discussed separately in §§61.21–61.31, but include: (a) granting an injunction (interdict in Scotland) against the defendant (defender in Scotland); (b) an order for delivery-up or destruction of infringing articles or products; (c) damages; (d) an account of profits; and (e) a certificate of contested validity. Subsection (2) makes damages and an account of profits alternative remedies, but in proceedings before the Comptroller (under subs.(3)) relief is limited to (c) and (e) above. By subs.(6), in determining relief, the court or Comptroller is to apply the same principles as before June 1, 1978 so that there was then no change in the law. In addition the successful party will normally be entitled to an award of costs, for which see §§61.34–61.37.

It is believed that these types of relief are fully in accord with arts 44–47 of the TRIPS Agreement, which read as follows:

"TRIPS Article 44—Injunctions

1. The judicial authorities shall have the authority to order a party to desist from an infringement, *inter alia* to prevent the entry into the channels of commerce in their jurisdiction of imported goods that involve the infringement of an intellectual property right, immediately after customs clearance of such goods. Members are not obliged to accord such authority in respect of protected subject matter acquired or ordered by a person prior to knowing or having reasonable grounds to know that dealing in such subject matter would entail the infringement of an intellectual property right.

2. Notwithstanding the other provisions of this Part and provided that the provisions of Part II specifically addressing use by governments, or by third parties authorized by a government, without the authorization of the right holder are complied with, Members may limit the remedies available against such use to payment of remuneration in accordance with subparagraph (h) of Article 31. In other cases, the remedies under this Part shall apply or, where these remedies are inconsistent with a Member's law, declaratory judgments and adequate compensation shall be available."

"TRIPS Article 45—Damages

1. The judicial authorities shall have the authority to order the infringer to pay the right holder damages adequate to compensate for the injury the right holder has suffered because of an infringement of that person's intellectual property right by an infringer who knowingly, or with reasonable grounds to know, engaged in infringing activity.

2. The judicial authorities shall also have the authority to order the infringer to pay the right holder expenses, which may include appropriate attorney's fees. In appropriate cases, Members

may authorize the judicial authorities to order recovery of profits and/or payment of pre-established damages even where the infringer did not knowingly, or with reasonable grounds to know, engage in infringing activity."

"TRIPS ARTICLE 46—Other remedies

1. In order to create an effective deterrent to infringement, the judicial authorities shall have the authority to order that goods that they have found to be infringing be, without compensation of any sort, disposed of outside the channels of commerce in such a manner as to avoid any harm caused to the right holder, or, unless this would be contrary to existing constitutional requirements, destroyed. The judicial authorities shall also have the authority to order that materials and implements the predominant use of which has been in the creation of the infringing goods be, without compensation of any sort, disposed of outside the channels of commerce in such a manner as to minimize the risks of further infringements. In considering such requests, the need for proportionality between the seriousness of the infringement and the remedies ordered as well as the interests of third parties shall be taken into account."

"TRIPS ARTICLE 47—Right of Information

1. Members may provide that the judicial authorities shall have the authority, unless this would be out of proportion to the seriousness of the infringement, to order the infringer to inform the right holder of the identity of third persons involved in the production and distribution of the infringing goods or services and of their channels of distribution."

"TRIPS ARTICLE 48—Indemnification of the Defendant

1. The judicial authorities shall have the authority to order a party at whose request measures were taken and who has abused enforcement procedures to provide to a party wrongfully enjoined or restrained adequate compensation for the injury suffered because of such abuse. The judicial authorities shall also have the authority to order the applicant to pay the defendant expenses, which may include appropriate attorney's fees.

2. In respect of the administration of any law pertaining to the protection or enforcement of intellectual property rights, Members shall only exempt both public authorities and officials from liability to appropriate remedial measures where actions are taken or intended in good faith in the course of the administration of that law."

It used to be the position that a successful claimant was required to make the election required by subs.(2), that is, between having an inquiry into damages or the taking of an account of profits, immediately upon judgment being given that the patent is valid and infringed. However, following the copyright case of *Island Records v Tring International* [1995] F.S.R. 560, it is now possible to delay making an election between an award of damages or taking an account of profits until after some basic, though not detailed, disclosure has been given by the infringer-defendant so that the successful claimant can make that election on an informed basis, see: *Honeywell v Appliance Components* BL C/62/96; *Celanese International v BP Chemicals* [1999] R.P.C. 203; and *Minnesota Mining v Jeffries* [Australia] [1993] F.S.R. 189.

If a claimant seeks to withdraw his allegation of infringement prior to trial, he will normally be required to give an undertaking to the defendant that he will not hereafter commence fresh proceedings, or threaten new proceedings, against the defendant in respect of the same alleged acts, see *Albright & Wilson v SB Chemicals* [1994] R.P.C. 608; and an undertaking may be required to go further than this, see *Biogen v Medeva* BL C/59/93, noted I.P.D. 16143.

In *Union Carbide v BP Chemicals* [1998] F.S.R. 1, an amendment to claim additional relief for "unjust enrichment" was refused as relating to acts occurring outside the United Kingdom and for processes not covered by the patent, but the court indicated that, in some circumstances, relief might be possible outside the terms of s.61 in furtherance of the policy of the Act in respect of acts which were not themselves ones of infringement, for example the possibility of relief in respect of acts occurring after the expiry of the patent arising from infringing acts committed during the patent term, as to which see in *Dyson v Hoover (No.2)* [2001] R.P.C. 27 at 544 and §61.23. See also *Kirin-Amgen v Transkaryotic Therapies (No.2)* [2002] R.P.C. 3 at 203.

Practice Direction 29.2 (reprinted in §F63PD.29), made in partial implementation of the Enforcement Directive (see §61.02 above), adds scope for the court, where it finds that an intellectual property right has been infringed and where the claimant so requests it, to order appropriate measures for the dissemination and publication of the judgment, at the defendant's expense.

Interim injunctions

—The principles upon which pre-trial relief is granted

61.08   Article 50 of the TRIPS Agreement reads:

"TRIPS ARTICLE 50—Provisional Measures

1. The judicial authorities shall have the authority to order prompt and effective provisional measures:

    (a) to prevent an infringement of any intellectual property right from occurring, and in particular to prevent the entry into the channels of commerce in their jurisdiction of goods, including imported goods immediately after customs clearance;

    (b) to preserve relevant evidence in regard to the alleged infringement.

2. The judicial authorities shall have the authority to adopt provisional measures *inaudita altera parte* where appropriate, in particular where any delay is likely to cause irreparable harm to the right holder, or where there is a demonstrable risk of evidence being destroyed.

3. The judicial authorities shall have the authority to require the applicant to provide any reasonably available evidence in order to satisfy themselves with a sufficient degree of certainty that the applicant is the right holder and that the applicant's right is being infringed or that such infringement is imminent, and to order the applicant to provide a security or equivalent assurance sufficient to protect the defendant and to prevent abuse.

4. Where provisional measures have been adopted *inaudita altera parte*, the parties affected shall be given notice, without delay after the execution of the measures at the latest. A review, including a right to be heard, shall take place upon request of the defendant with a view to deciding, within a reasonable period after the notification of the measures, whether these measures shall be modified, revoked or confirmed.

5. The applicant may be required to supply other information necessary for the identification of the goods concerned by the authority that will execute the provisional measures.

6. Without prejudice to paragraph 4, provisional measures taken on the basis of paragraphs 1 and 2 shall, upon request by the defendant, be revoked or otherwise cease to have effect, if proceedings leading to a decision on the merits of the case are not initiated within a reasonable period, to be determined by the judicial authority ordering the measures where a Member's law so permits or, in the absence of such a determination, not to exceed 20 working days or 31 calendar days, whichever is the longer.

7. Where the provisional measures are revoked or where they lapse due to any act or omission by the applicant, or where it is subsequently found that there has been no infringement or threat of infringement of an intellectual property right, the judicial authorities shall have the authority to order the applicant, upon request of the defendant, to provide the defendant appropriate compensation for any injury caused by these measures.

8. To the extent that any provisional measure can be ordered as a result of administrative procedures, such procedures shall conform to principles equivalent in substance to those set forth in this Section."

It is thought that these requirements are met by the procedure for the grant of interim relief, as described below.

The grant of interim (formerly "interlocutory") remedies by the Patents Court or the Patents County Court is now governed by CPR 25. Practice Direction C under it relates to the grant of interim injunctions, see particularly its para.3. Such an injunction is one granted by the court as an interim measure to hold the ring pending full trial, while avoiding pre-judging the issues then to be contested and becoming involved in factual issues of considerable complexity at the pre-trial stage when cross-examination of witnesses is rare and matters are necessarily dealt with in some haste.

In England and Wales, whether or not to grant such an injunction was for over 20 years decided on the principles established in the patent infringement case of *American Cyanamid v Ethicon* [1975] R.P.C. 513 HL, and then applied generally to cases of all kinds, including those outside the field of intellectual property. These principles require, first, that the claimant show that there is "a serious issue to be tried". Then, the court considers where lies the "balance of convenience", later called the "balance of injustice"; and, if there is no such imbalance, then preservation of the status quo becomes the deciding factor.

However, in *Series 5 Software v Clarke* [1996] F.S.R. 273, it was stated that the determination of the "balance of convenience" should only be a subsidiary factor in a decision to grant or withhold interim relief, at least in relation to infringement of intellectual property rights, and that it is appropriate, in considering whether to grant interim relief, to take into account the relative strengths of the parties' cases and for the court to state a view of the merits. Indeed, it was suggested that the main criterion for the grant of an interim injunction should be the demonstration of a "strong prima facie case", as was the position before *American Cyanamid*. However, the view taken in *Series 5 Software* has not been generally adopted. For comment on the *Series 5 Software* decision, see M. Edenborough and G. Tritton [1996] E.I.P.R. 234. Anyway, the difference between the *American Cyanamid* and *Series 5 Software* decisions have become somewhat academic because, in an appropriate case, the Patents Court now tends towards fixing an early trial thereby circumventing any need to consider the "balance of convenience". Accordingly, a claimant seeking an interim injunction from the Patents Court is advised to make inquiries and investigations as to the estimated length of trial and possible trial dates, see the *Patents Court Guide* (reprinted in Appendix G). Thus, the former tactic of seeking an interim injunction to put pressure on a defendant to cease its activities or enter into a settlement, without any real intention to take the claimant's case to full trial, is now likely to backfire with the court imposing an early trial date which will put the claimant under undesired pressure to have his case ready for trial in time, even if he does wish to proceed to this.

In the following paragraphs, the various factors which have influence the court in the granting or denial of interim injunctions for patent infringement under the *American Cyanamid* principles are discussed on the basis that these principles are still followed.

In Scotland, the grant of interim relief (by way of an interim interdict) is decided on somewhat different principles and the *American Cyanamid* approach is not followed, see §98.18.

—Delay in seeking interim relief

Because interim relief is an equitable remedy for cases of some urgency, undue delay in seeking it will cause this relief to be denied. Even if delay is not itself fatal, it can be a factor in the "balance of injustice". However, delay is not undue when the claimant is under some restraint from commencing proceedings, as for example in *Quantel v Electronic Graphics* [1990] R.P.C. 272 where the patentee had had to give an undertaking to the court in other proceedings that further proceedings would not be commenced until its application to amend the patent had been considered. **61.09**

An interim injunction was refused (but a speedy trial ordered) in *KCI Licensing Inc v Smith & Nephew* [2009] EWHC 2143, where the product in issue had been on the market for four months. The court observed that had the patentee succeeded in establishing, as it had argued, that the defendants had successfully concealed this fact from the patentee the result might have been different. An interim injunction was also refused in *Mölynlycke Healthcare v BSN Medical* [2009] EWHC 3370 primarily on account of the patentee's delay of several months in bringing the application.

—The claimant's cross-undertaking

If granted an interim injunction, the claimant must give a "cross-undertaking" to the court to pay the defendant (or a third party potentially damaged by the injunction but who **61.10** is a made a party to the order) damages if he is unsuccessful at full trial. For cases where an interim injunction has been granted to a claimant who has later failed at full trial, damages for breach of this cross-undertaking are to be assessed as for a breach of contract (*Helitune v Stewart Hughes* [1994] F.S.R. 422).

If third parties, such as the defendant's licensees (not protected by the cross-undertaking), would be prejudiced, this is a reason for not granting an interim injunction (*Standard Telephones v Plessey* BL C/171/82).

In *SmithKline Beecham v Apotex [Damages for unjustified injunction]* [2003] EWHC 3185 Pat Ct, noted I.P.D. 27029, the court refused to stay an enquiry on a cross-undertaking pending appeal and gave directions as to the future conduct of such enquiry. The nature and history of cross-undertakings were fully reviewed in an appeal in subsequent proceedings in the same dispute, *SmithKline Beecham v Apotex [Damages on cross-undertaking]* [2006] EWCA 658; [2007] F.S.R. 16, on appeal from *SmithKline Beecham v Apotex* [2005] F.S.R. 44 at 930; [2006] 2 All E.R. 53; [2006] I.P. & T. 307 and in which an application by third parties which alleged they had suffered loss from the grant of the interim injunction and which sought to benefit from the cross-undertaking, despite their not having been parties to the action or the order setting out the cross-undertaking, was rejected.

The court discussed the principles to be applied in assessing liability under a cross-undertaking in damages in *Les Laboratoires Servier v Apotex* [2008] EWHC 2347 and applied these to make an award against the patentee of £17.5 million in relation to an interim injunction that had lasted for eleven months, as discussed in M. Royle et al "A price worth paying for patentees?" [2008] *CIPA* 628. The annual value of market that the patentee had sought to protect was worth about £80 million, although there was unchallenged evidence that the patentee had paid other potential generic market entrants £40 million in total not to enter the market. However shortly before judgment the patentees applied to amend to argue that the successful alleged infringer could not claim damages for being prevented from selling a product whose manufacture abroad, in a jurisdiction where there was a subsisting patent that was found valid and infringed by that product, would thus have been unlawful. In *Les Laboratoires Servier v Apotex* [2011] R.P.C. 20, [2011] EWHC 730, the patentee's claim abroad having succeeded, it was held that the alleged infringer's claim was indeed so barred.

The cross-undertaking on the interim injunction that was granted in *Wake Forest v Smith & Nephew* [2009] F.S.R. 11, [2009] EWHC 45 was ordered to be framed in such a way as to allow customers of the patentees who had paid for the patentees' products and/or services covered by the injunction to claim the benefit of the cross-undertaking in the event that it came to be enforced, so that it was clear that a customer of the patentee may claim retrospectively loss suffered from the date of the grant of the injunction until the eventual discharge of the injunction, if it is ever discharged.

—The requirement for the claimant to show a "serious issue to be tried"

61.11   Under the principles laid down in *American Cyanamid v Ethicon* [1975] R.P.C. 513 HL, a claimant seeking an interim injunction must first demonstrate to the satisfaction of the court that there is a "serious issue to be tried". It was sometimes said that the claimant must merely have "an arguable case", but sometimes it has been said that a "real and substantial prospect of success at trial" must be shown, see *Mothercare v Robson Books* [1979] F.S.R. 466. Anyway, a claimant should adduce precise evidence on the merits of his case and should not expect the court to invent hypotheses of fact on which he could succeed, see *Re Lord Cable* [1977] 1 W.L.R. 7.

In patent actions it is not usually hard to show a mere "arguable case". First, the fact that the patent-in-suit has been granted is likely to outweigh an allegation of invalidity unless a strong attack can be based on points not previously considered; this is so even when the patent-in-suit is a European patent (UK) which is under opposition in the EPO (*Improver Corp v Innovations* BL C/16/88, noted I.P.D. 11002). Secondly, as to infringement, the Protocol to EPC art.69 can be applied to show an arguable case of infringement, as in *Improver Corp v Remington* [1989] R.P.C. 69 CA, but not so in *Jakob Schlaepfer v Frankle* BL C/9/88. However, a patentee does not have an arguable case if proceedings to amend the patent are pending: the status of the patent is then in limbo, and while this is so the court could not adjudicate on a contempt motion for breach of the injunction (*Mölnlycke v Procter & Gamble (No.2)* [1990] R.P.C. 487). The ease of demonstrating there to be "arguable case" was emphasised by *Abbott Laboratories v Ranbaxy* [2004] EWHC 2723 Pat Ct, noted I.P.D. 27111 where, had it not been for a determination on summary judgment that the claim in issue lacked novelty, an interim injunction would have been granted in the light of the inadequacy of damages as a remedy, despite what the court characterised as a strong argument of obviousness.

—The balance of injustice

The principles laid down in *American Cyanamid v Ethicon* [1975] R.P.C. 513 HL **61.12** require the court to consider the "balance of convenience". This involves assessment of whether the risk of injustice will be less according to whether the claimant is granted an injunction after full trial but is denied that relief until this has been held; or whether an immediate injunction is imposed upon the defendant but at full trial this is found to have been unjustified because the defendant succeeds on his defence. In other words, the court has to consider whether the claimant will be adequately compensated in damages if successful at full trial but denied an injunction meanwhile; and, likewise, whether the defendant will be adequately compensated under the cross-undertaking if a pre-trial injunction is imposed and it is successful at full trial; and in each case whether the party prospectively liable to pay the damages will be able to pay them. Thus, the "balance of convenience" has also been stated to be a "balance of the risk of doing an injustice," see *Fleming Fabrications v Albion Cylinders* [1989] R.P.C. 47 CA, applying *Allen v Jambo* [1980] 1 W.L.R. 1253 and *Cayne v Global Natural Resources* [1984] 1 All E.R. 225 CA. This balance of injustice scarcely has to be considered if the defendant is not seen to have an arguable defence, see *Quantel v Electronic Graphics* [1990] R.P.C. 272 where the patent bore a certificate of validity granted in *Quantel v Spaceward Microsystems* [1990] R.P.C. 83. However, where another defendant was prepared to challenge the same patent, it was held that it had an arguable case and, upon that defendant giving a bank guarantee of £2 million, an interim injunction was refused as causing the lesser degree of injustice where the defendant's damages, though not the claimant's, would not be readily quantifiable (*Quantel v Shima Seiki* [1990] R.P.C. 436).

In *SmithKline Beecham v Generics UK* BL C/50/01, noted I.P.D. 25005, the court said that it was impossible to judge the merit of the defendant's proposed defences based on non-infringement and invalidity of the patent at the stage of an interim injunction request and so proceeded to an analysis of the *American Cyanamid* questions. The claimants had entered into an agreement with another generics manufacturer to assist in marketing the relevant product after patent expiry and the court held that although both parties were likely to suffer unquantifiable and irreparable damage, that likely to be suffered by the claimant would be the greater. The judge also noted that, if the indicated defences had been strong, the defendant could have brought revocation proceedings or sought a declaration of non-infringement, but had not done so. Therefore an injunction was imposed, limited to acts of sale or offers for sale but not so as to prohibit importation or any experiments for the purposes of possible challenges to validity. Another such case (and under the same patent) is *SmithKline Beecham v Apotex* [2003] F.S.R. 30 at 524 in which the entry of the defendant into the market would have given rise to substantial but not adequately quantifiable damage and the judge again commented that the defendant could have cleared its way by proceedings for revocation or a declaration of non-infringement, but had chosen not to do so. This view was upheld by the Court of Appeal (see [2003] F.S.R. 31 at 544), which found that the judge had been entitled to take into account that, by failing to seek revocation, the defendant had "walked into the situation they find themselves in with their eyes open to the risk they were taking" but if they turned out to be right "the court would have to do the best it can to compensate them under the cross-undertaking". See the case comment by E. Nettleton and B. Cordery, *Patent World*, March 2003 (No.150), p.14. Since this decision it has become the norm in cases concerning the introduction of generic pharmaceuticals, where irreparable damage could be done to the patentee in terms of massive and immediate price depression, for prospective generic entrants who might be at risk of an action for patent infringement to seek to "clear the path" before product introduction by seeking a declaration of non-infringement and/or revocation of the patent. Absent that, they are at significant risk of an interim injunction pending trial. Examples of such cases where interim injunctions have been granted against the market entry of generic pharmaceuticals are provided by *Wyeth v Alpharma* [2003] EWHC 3196 Pat Ct; *Les Laboratoires Servier v Apotex* [2009] F.S.R. 3 at [220]; [2006] EWHC 2137 Pat Ct; and *Les Laboratoires Servier v KRKA Polska* [2006] EWHC 2453 Pat Ct (see a case comment on this case by Dr. M. Royale, K. Fox-Murphy and S. Cohen in [2008] *CIPA* 628); *Novartis AG v Dexcel-Pharma Ltd* [2008] EWHC 1266 Pat Ct; and *Leo Pharma A/S v Sandoz* [2008] EWHC 541 Pat Ct; upheld [2008] EWCA Civ 850.

An interim injunction was granted in *Wake Forest v Smith & Nephew* [2009] F.S.R. 11, [2009] EWHC 45, where one important factor in the balance of convenience was the relatively short period between the application and a date that could be fixed for full trial given the limited nature of the likely attacks on validity and in the light of the progress of, and date fixed for trial of, an application by a third party that was already under way to revoke the patent in suit.

Although the primary reason for refusing an interim injunction in *Mölynlycke Healthcare v BSN Medical* [2009] EWHC 3370 was the patentee's delay in bringing the application, in assessing the balance of convenience the court expressed scepticism, in the light of the evidence, as to the degree of downward pressure on pricing in the medical device market in issue here, as opposed to the pharmaceuticals market.

—Maintaining the status quo

61.13   If the court finds the balance of justice evenly divided, it is directed by *American Cyanamid v Ethicon* [1975] R.P.C. 513 HL to maintain the *status quo ante bellum*, i.e. to maintain the commercial situation which existed immediately prior to the commencement of the proceedings. Discussion of the meaning of this status quo is found in *Garden Cottage Foods v Milk Marketing Board* [1984] A.C. 130; [1983] C.M.L.R. 13, noted [1984] F.S.R. 23 HL. In *Beecham Group v Norton* BL C/36/96 and *New Holland v Massey Ferguson* BL C/43/96 interim injunctions were imposed under the basic *American Cyanamid* principle of, in the last resort, maintaining the status quo: though, in the *Beecham* case, the injunction was limited to a three-month period in order to encourage an early trial.

This status quo is to be determined at the date of service, rather than the date of issue, of the claim (*Graham v Delderfield* [1992] F.S.R. 313). In this case interim relief was denied because of the delay in seeking it, on which see also *PLG Research v Ardon* BL C/17/91, noted I.P.D. 14100 where the status quo was determined at the date of the application for the interim injunction.

—The relative merits of the parties

61.14   According to the principles set down in *American Cyanamid* [1975] R.P.C. 513 HL, it is only if the court is unable to decide between the parties after it has assessed the balance of injustice that it is permitted to consider the relative merits of the case. Indeed, these principles were formulated because an application for an interim injunction is normally decided only on written evidence and in a situation where "hearsay" evidence is more readily accepted by the court; where it is unusual to have had any disclosure from the defendant; and where the court is unlikely to have been assisted by cross-examination of those who have presented witness statements or affidavits. In these circumstances, it is not practicable for a court to reach more than a tentative conclusion on the merits of the case.

Thus, it was only in rare cases that the perceived relative strengths of the claimant's and defendant's cases can be seen to have been an overt determining factor, as in *Entec v Abacus Mouldings* [1992] F.S.R. 332 CA. Nevertheless, an interim injunction was refused when the defendant is seen to have much the stronger case (*Merrell Dow v Norton* [1994] R.P.C. 1). A judge would be less than human if his judgment on the balance of justice were not (perhaps subconsciously) influenced by his perception of those merits, and accordingly the merits were inevitably canvassed to some extent in the evidence for and against the grant of an interim injunction; and an injunction was likely to be refused, for one reason or another, if the court thought that the claimant would be likely to lose at full trial, for example as in *Newsweek v BBC* [1979] R.P.C. 441. Conversely, an interim injunction was more likely to be granted if the court doubted whether the defendant had a genuine intention of defending the main action, for example because he is reluctant to reveal his defence (*Smith (T.J.) & Nephew v 3M United Kingdom* [1983] R.P.C. 92). Also, if the interim proceedings were likely to determine the whole proceedings because neither party would have an interest in full trial, it was held appropriate to consider the merits, see: *Associated Newspapers v News Group Newspapers* [1986] R.P.C. 515; *Reckitt & Colman v Borden* [1987] F.S.R. 228 CA; and the article by P. Prescott [1989] E.I.P.R. 259. As noted in §61.08, the decision in *Series 5 Software v Clarke* [1996] F.S.R. 273 saw the relative merits of the parties as much more potent issue than it was hitherto, but see the further comments in that paragraph.

In *Cephalon v Orchid Europe* [2010] EWHC 2945 Pat Ct the Court, in refusing an interim injunction on traditional balance of convenience grounds but ordering a speedy trial, discussed the case law as to the circumstances in which it might be appropriate to review the respective strengths of the parties' cases on an application for an interim injunction, but did not consider this to be such a case.

—The adequacy of damages as a remedy

Under the *American Cyanamid* principles, each party will seek to satisfy the court that **61.15** the balance of injustice is in its favour because without, or with, an injunction that party is likely to suffer damage which is unquantifiable. This is because, if damages are an adequate remedy and the defendant has the ability to pay them, under the *American Cyanamid* principles, no injunction is normally granted (*Garden Cottage Foods v Milk Marketing Board* [1984] A.C. 130; [1983] C.M.L.R. 13, noted [1984] F.S.R. 23 HL; *Polaroid v Kodak* [1977] R.P.C. 379); and *Zaidener v Barrisdale* [1968] R.P.C. 488). An interim injunction was refused in *Hilbar Plastics v Panda Plastics* [1990] E.I.P.R. D–75; BL C/18/90 because damages were an adequate remedy for the claimant and the defendant could afford to pay these; and, likewise, in *Neotronics v B.N.O.S. Meditech* BL C/11/82, noted I.P.D. 15129. In *Peaudouce v Kimberly-Clark* [1996] F.S.R. 680, damages were likely to be relatively low because the claimant had only a relatively small share of a large market, and the defendant was well able to pay those damages, an interim injunction was refused, even though the patent-in-suit had been successfully litigated against others and possessed a certificate of contested validity.

Thus, if the claimant has granted a licence on a royalty basis, damages for infringement are likely to be seen as calculable on a like basis and, hence, the grant of an interim injunction should be precluded if the defendant has the ability to pay such sums; and, likewise, it will be asserted that damages can more readily be calculated on a royalty basis where the patentee has exploited his invention only by importation (*Mölnlycke v Procter & Gamble (No.2)* [1990] R.P.C. 487). However, the decisions in *Gerber Garment v Lectra Systems* [1995] R.P.C. 383; and [1997] R.P.C. 443 CA provide basis for contending that the claimant is entitled to unquantifiable additional damages over mere loss of sales of a patented product, see §61.24.

Arguments which have successfully been used to show that the claimant's pre-trial loss will be unquantifiable are:

— where the defendant may establish a bridgehead or springboard position in the market, as in *American Cyanamid v Ethicon* [1975] R.P.C. 513 HL; *Corruplast v Harrison*

[1978] R.P.C. 761; *Netlon v Bridport-Gundry* [1979] F.S.R. 530; and *Monsanto v Stauffer* [1984] F.S.R. 574, particularly where such might cause price erosion (*Smith, Kline & French v Global Pharmaceutics* BL C/167/83, noted I.P.D. 6125, there being no appeal on this point, see [1986] R.P.C. 394);

— where there will be an adverse effect on the claimant's research programme (as also in the *Netlon* case, above);

— where the claimant is in the process of establishing a market for the patented article, see the *Netlon* case also, and *E.A.R. Corp v Protector Safety Products* [1980] F.S.R. 574; and

— where there is a difficulty of estimating lost sales, particularly where continued infringement would lead to a snowball effect with other infringers appearing.

Although the "snowball" or "rapid and irremediable price depression" argument did not succeed in *Conder International v Hibbing* [1984] F.S.R. 312, it later had some success in *Hallen v Brabantia* [1988] E.I.P.R. D–17; BL C/70/87, noted I.P.D. 10069; *Improver Corp v Innovations* BL C/16/88, noted I.P.D. 11002; *Imperial Chemical v Montedison* BL C/75/88, noted I.P.D. 11047; *Fleming Fabrications v Albion Cylinders* [1989] R.P.C. 47; *Helitune v Stewart Hughes* BL C/94/88, noted I.P.D. 13015; *Neotronics v Anglo-Nordic* BL C/96/88, noted I.P.D. 11046; and *Improver Corp v Remington* [1989] R.P.C. 69 CA. A further factor in the *Neotronics* case was that the product was predicted to have only a short market life. However, these cases all date back to a time when it took much longer to get actions to full trial than it does now, when even without a specific order for an early trial date actions in the Patents Court can come on for trial typically within a year. Nowadays, the "rapid and irremediable price depression" argument only really has practical application in the English courts in relation to the launch of generic pharmaceuticals, see §61.12.

—The relative financial standings of the parties

61.16   Where there is a doubt whether a defendant has the financial resources to pay damages after full trial, an interim injunction has been avoided by the defendant paying a proportion of its sales revenue from the alleged infringing activities into a trust account, e.g. one held jointly by the respective solicitors, see *Vernon v Universal Pulp* [1980] F.S.R. 179 and *Brupat v Sandford Marine* [1983] R.P.C. 61 CA or provide security for damages in some other way (*Mars v Azkoyen* [1989] E.I.P.R. D-219; and BL C/57/89, noted I.P.D. 12079). Also, where an early trial can be arranged and the defendant is prepared to pay a sizeable proportion of his asserted profit into a blocked bank account, any balance of justice in favour of the claimant is minimised, see *Beecham Group v Sanderson Ltd* BL C/46/93 where an interim injunction was denied on these considerations.

Analogously, an impecunious claimant, or one from outside the European Community, may be required to provide security to back his cross-undertaking in damages, see *Pellew v Hunters Leathercraft* BL C/24/81, noted I.P.D. 4034 and *Pall Corp v Owens* BL C/29/86, noted I.P.D. 9035; and particularly *Improver Corp v Remington* BL C/78/88, noted I.P.D. 11048 and C/19/89, where a bank guarantee for £5.5 million was eventually required. However, a probability that the claimant would not be able to meet a liability under his cross-undertaking is not the end of the road, particularly where its financial position owes much to persons connected with the defendant, see *Fleming Fabrications v Albion Cylinders* [1989] R.P.C. 47.

—Interim injunctions granted without notice

61.17   In urgent cases an application for an interim injunction can be requested, even before the formal start of proceedings, on an application made to the court without notice to the (putative) defendant, formerly called an ex parte application. The procedure is now governed by CPR 25.3. However, a case of alleged patent infringement would have to be exceptional for relief of this nature. Any relief on an application made without notice is granted for a short term only, until a hearing can be arranged with notice to be attended by the defendant, formerly known as an inter partes hearing, and this must be done without delay (*Hong Kong Toy Co v Tomy* [1994] F.S.R. 593). In such cases, the *Cyanamid* principles have been applied solely to the period until the application for an interim injunction can be re-argued on full evidence with the defendant present (*Chiron v Organon Teknika* BL C/16/92, noted I.P.D. 15104).

An application for an interim injunction made without prior notice and on incomplete evidence failed in *Mayne Pharma v Teva* [2004] EWHC 2934 Ch, noted I.P.D. 28011, as an early effective date for an inter partes interim injunction hearing was available and the court was not satisfied that there was the real urgency for an injunction coupled with a threat of immediate damage requiring intervention by the court. However in *Les Laboratoires Servier v Apotex* [2009] F.S.R. 3 at [220]; [2006] EWHC 2137 Pat Ct; BL C/84/06), the court was prepared to grant an emergency interim injunction sought without full notice over to an inter partes interim injunction hearing.

In *Cinpres v Melea* [2006] F.S.R. 36 at 647, an interim injunction secured without any notice and preventing contact with a witness, whom it was alleged had received an abusive telephone call from a party to the proceedings, was discharged, and the failure even to try to alert the other side's solicitors as to the application for it was criticised, as was the failure to record fully at the time what took place on the hearing of the application. However, the injunction was replaced by another of similar effect.

—The discretionary nature of interim relief

The grant of any interim injunction is a discretionary remedy. In *Roussel-Uclaf v Searle* **61.18** [1977] F.S.R. 125, it was indicated, obiter, that the court might refuse an injunction when this would have the effect of preventing a life-saving drug, different from that marketed by the patentee, from being made available to the public. However, in *Chiron v Organon Teknika* [1992] F.S.R. 512, an alleged public interest in having the defendants' products available for reasons of public health was held to be only one of the factors to be weighed in the balance as to whether an interlocutory injunction should be granted (though not here determinative because Crown user provisions could be exercised to achieve this end if thought appropriate). Also, in *Biogen v Medeva* [1993] R.P.C. 475, it was indicated that, because also of the existence in the Patents Act of provisions for compulsory licences, and although the court had a discretion in the matter, it would be rare to deprive a successful patentee of the usual remedy of an injunction after full trial. Indeed, although an argument to this effect was subsequently presented in *Chiron v Organon Teknika (No.10)* [1995] F.S.R. 325, it was withdrawn during the hearing and replaced by an application for a stay of the injunction pending appeal, for which see §61.21. However, an exception to the injunction for a particular diagnostic device, for which the claimants had no corresponding device, was there allowed.

—Form of interim injunction

If an interim injunction is granted, this will normally be in specific terms, since an **61.19** injunction in terms of a prohibition on infringing the patent would require a full trial to determine whether such had been breached, see *Staver v Digitext* [1985] F.S.R. 512 and *Video Arts v Paget Industries* [1988] F.S.R. 501. A more robust view was taken in *Spectravest v Aperknit* [1988] F.S.R. 161, but the grant of an injunction in specific, rather than general, terms has now been advocated, even after full trial, see §61.21.

—Other forms of interim relief

There are also special forms of interim relief of an injunctive nature. These are: the now **61.20** so-called "Search Order", formerly called an *"Anton Piller* Order"; the now so-called "Freezing Injunction", formerly called a *"Mareva* Injunction", for freezing the assets of a defendant; and the *ne exeat regno* order, to restrain a defendant from leaving the jurisdiction of the court.

The "Search Order" is discussed in more detail in §61.49, but the "Freezing" and *"ne exeat regno"* Orders are not often required in patent litigation and are therefore considered outside the scope of this Work. However, the Freezing Order (as well as the Search Order) are fully discussed in the books: R. N. Ough *The Mareva injunction and Anton Piller order* 2nd edn (Butterworths, 1993); M. S. W. Hoyle *The Mareva injunction and related orders* 3rd edn (London: Lloyd's of London, 1997); S. Gee *Mareva injunctions and Anton Piller Relief* 4th edn (London: Sweet & Maxwell, 1998). A specimen form of a "Freezing Injunction Order" is set out in an Annex to CPR PD 25A (not reprinted in this Work).

In *Eli Lilly & Company Ltd v Neopharma Ltd* [2008] EWHC 415, where undertakings through to trial had already been given in place of an interim injunction but it was later, and before trial, discovered that before the undertakings were given supplies of the allegedly infringing product had been made to large wholesalers, the court granted an order that the defendant disclose the names of such customers, so that patentee could prevent sales of the product by such wholesalers.

For the grant by the Patents County Court of a freezing (then *Anton Piller*) Order, and associated (*Mareva*) injunction, see *McDonald v Graham* [1994] R.P.C. 407.

Relief by post-trial injunction (subs.(1)(a))

61.21   An injunction is always a discretionary remedy of the court and may therefore be refused in an appropriate case, though this will generally be unlikely, see §61.18. No injunction can be granted once the patent has expired (*Monsanto v Stauffer* [South Africa] [1988] F.S.R. 57), and any injunction then in force automatically lapses. In *Proctor & Gamble v Unilever* [Canada] (1996) 33 I.P.R. 627 an injunction was denied after full trial because the patent would shortly expire.

However, in the Netherlands, where the defendant had supplied a sample of the patented product to the medicines regulatory authority in order to have approval for marketing after patent expiry, that supply was held to be an infringing act and a post-expiry injunction was granted for 14 months, this being the average time taken for marketing approval to be granted and justified on the basis that the defendant should not profit from his infringing act. The ECJ upheld this as a proper exercise of the powers of the court and held it to be non-discriminatory and acceptable within the terms of what is now art.28 EC (*Generics v Smith Kline & French* (C-316/95) [1997] R.P.C. 801; [1997] E.C.R. I-3929). In *Dyson v Hoover (No.2)* [2001] R.P.C. 27 at 544 the English court granted a post-patent expiry injunction, noting that s.61(1) does not preclude other relief for infringement and that under the Senior Courts Act 1981 (c.54) s.37 an injunction can be granted where it appears "just and convenient" to do so. Springboard damages for post-expiry acts had been found allowable in *Gerber Garment v Lectra Systems* [1995] R.P.C. 383; and [1997] R.P.C. 443 CA, but such damages were seen as notoriously difficult to assess and a post-expiry injunction could be granted to ameliorate that difficulty. However (as held in *Gerber Garment*), an award of damages has to be limited to damages which were "foreseeable, caused by the wrong and not excluded by public policy". As Hoover had taken about 12 months to develop the infringing device (such development itself being an infringing act), an injunction was ordered to run for the same period from the patent expiry date, but this would be limited in scope to the device upon which the trial had taken place. A request for an injunction against use of the trade mark used to promote marketing of the infringing device was rejected as not being a foreseeable consequence of the patent infringement; any goodwill generated by that use having conveyed the message of a new Hoover product regardless of how it had been made. In *Tamglass v Luong North Glass and Novoglaze [Post Trial Order]* [2006] EWHC 444 Ch, noted I.P.D. 29031-2, a post-expiry injunction of one month duration was imposed. However, there is still some uncertainty about the jurisdiction. Thus, in *Mayne Pharma v Pharmacia Italia* [2005] EWCA Civ 294, noted I.P.D. 28034, the Court of Appeal, when making an agreed order that the patentees be at liberty to apply for a post-expiry injunction, observed that whether there was jurisdiction in the court to grant such an order was a matter that one day would "have to be considered very carefully" and identified the copyright case of *Chappell v Columbia Graphophone* [1914] 2 Ch. 745 as an authority which ought to be considered in such connection.

Also, where a defendant had undertaken to take a licence of right under an existing patent, an injunction was nevertheless granted to restrain importation of the patented product from outside the EEA (*Knuttson v Roulette Wheel Co* BL CC/49/96).

In *Coflexip v Stolt Comex* [1999] F.S.R. 473, following a finding of infringement on a purposive construction of the claim wording (see BL C/1/99, noted I.P.D. 22035), as discussed in the commentary on s.125, the Patents Court declined to impose a generalised injunction against future "infringement", but limited the injunction to "that act" upon which the case had been fought because it was not thought appropriate to expose the defendants to an action for contempt in respect of a modification which they might honestly consider clearly to fall outside the ambit of protection on the construction given to the claims by the court, as had happened in *Multiform v Whitmarley* [1956] R.P.C. 143 CA; and [1957] R.P.C. 260 HL. However, on appeal (see [2001] R.P.C. 9 at 182 CA) that order was seen as defective as not having been limited to the life of the patent; injuncting acts (such as private or experimental acts) not falling within the statutory definition of "infringement"; and raising problems of construction. It thus needed change and, anyway, no case had been made out in this instance why an injunction in the traditional general form (prohibiting further acts of "infringement") was not appropriate: the injunction order was therefore amended accordingly. Previously, in *Nutrinova v Scanchem (No.2)* [2001] F.S.R. 43 at 831 where the defendant had acted in good faith but had been misled by his supplier (for which see §60.04), an injunction was imposed limited to prohibition of further purchases from that supplier.

It is possible for an injunction to have extra-territorial effect by restraining acts carried out abroad which are likely to lead to infringing acts within the United Kingdom, see the passing-off case of *Dunhill (Alfred) v Sunoptic* [1979] F.S.R. 337 and also *North Western Trailer v Itel* BL HC/PC/41/79, noted *The Times*, December 19, 1979. Another case where the court granted an injunction having extra-territorial effect, and against a foreign company, was the copyright case of *Hospital for Sick Children v Walt Disney* [1967] 1 All E.R. 1005 CA, where the defendant had no assets within the jurisdiction of the court against which the injunction could be enforced, but there was the possibility of future assets within the jurisdiction. However in *Kirin-Amgen v Transkaryotic Therapies (No.2)* [2002] R.P.C. 3 at 203, a patent case, the claimant sought an injunction extending to activities outside the United Kingdom. The court refused the relief holding that it was highly questionable as going beyond the ambit of the patent which relates only to activities in the United Kingdom in the absence of any special facts. The claimant was permitted to amend its pleadings to claim "springboard" relief (as approved in *Dyson v Hoover (No.2)*, above) in respect of any losses arising after expiry as a result of pre-expiry infringing activities. In a further hearing relating to the same patent (*Kirin-Amgen's Patent* [2002] R.P.C. 43 at 851; [2002] I.P. & T. 331) an injunction pending the hearing of the appeal was imposed with certain caveats. The substantive appeal subsequently succeeded (*Kirin-Amgen v Transkaryotic Therapies* [2003] R.P.C. 31), and the patentee eventually lost in the House of Lords: see [2005] R.P.C. 9 at 169.

At the end of the substantive trial the court has a discretion whether to stay an injunction pending appeal. In deciding whether to order a stay or not, the court must balance the injustices which may occur one way or the other (*Unilever v Chefaro* [1994] R.P.C. 567). Thus, if a stay is granted, safeguards against eventual non-payment are likely to be required; and, if a stay is refused, a cross-undertaking to pay damages if the appeal is successful is likely (as where an interim injunction is imposed, for which see §61.10). Thus, there is no general rule and the court has to consider all circumstances. For the separate question as to whether there should be a stay, pending appeal, on the assessment of monetary relief for infringement, see §61.30. For example, in *American Cyanamid v Ethicon* [1979] R.P.C. 215, the interim injunction granted in 1975 was ordered to be continued during the prosecution of an appeal by the defendant against findings of infringement and validity on the ground that thereby the claimant's cross-undertaking in damages would be continued. However, in *Rotocrop v Genbourne* [1982] F.S.R. 241, the court, following *Bugges v Herbon* [1972] R.P.C. 197 at 214, stayed an injunction upon undertakings to keep an account of sales and to pay 10 per cent of the sale price into a special account and to serve promptly a notice of appeal. In *Quantel v Spaceward Microsystems (No.2)* [1990] R.P.C. 147, an injunction was stayed pending appeal, but only upon guarantees being given as to costs and damages and with payment of 20 per cent of sales receipts into a blocked bank account; and, likewise, in *Mentor v Hollister* BL C/65/91, noted I.P.D. 15027 where the defendant also had to undertake to seek an expedited hearing of its appeal and to procure that a new company recently formed to take over the infringing activities should be liable for damages if the appeal failed and should give disclosure on the inquiry into damages. In *Minnesota Mining v Rennicks* [1992] R.P.C. 331 a stay was refused because of the likely inability of the only defendant within the jurisdiction to pay either damages or costs and because the patent would, before an appeal would be heard, have become endorsed "licences of right". In *Unilever v Chefaro* (above), a general injunction was ordered but qualified to allow the defendants to continue selling a modified device on which there was a pending action for a declaration of non-infringement, see §71.04. A stay pending the hearing of an appeal against the finding of validity was also refused in *Chiron v Organon Teknika (No.10)* [1995] F.S.R. 325, though with an exception for a particular device for which the claimants then had no corresponding product. In *SmithKline Beecham v Apotex [Interim Injunction Continued]* [2003] EWHC 3383 Ch, noted I.P.D. 27052, the court continued the already existing interim injunction against the defendant for a short period after delivering judgment in its favour pending a hearing as to whether leave to appeal should be granted.

In *Grimme v Scott* [2010] F.S.R. 11, [2009] EWHC 2691 Pat Ct, [2010] EWCA Civ 1110 the Court of Appeal expressed the preliminary view that an injunction to restrain contributory infringement, where what the defendant sold did not itself infringe and has a non-infringing use, should be expressed in general terms in the same manner as one to restrain direct infringement.

Relief by delivery up or destruction (subs.(1)(b))

61.22   Relief by an order for delivery up or destruction of infringing goods still in the possession of the defendant is ancillary to relief by injunction and is, therefore likewise, a discretionary remedy. Practice Direction 29.1 (reprinted in §F63PD.29), introduced in partial implementation of the Enforcement Directive (see §61.02 above), makes it clear that when the court makes an order for delivery up or destruction of infringing goods, or articles designed or adapted to make such goods, the defendant will pay the costs of complying with that order unless the court orders otherwise. In *Smith Kline & French v Harbottle* [1980] R.P.C. 363, D was ordered to deliver up for destruction supplies of a patented drug consigned at the request of H for delivery by air to H (but which at the time were in the hands of British Airways as warehouseman, the warehousing being a non-infringing act), see §60.05 and an article by M. Howe [1979] E.I.P.R. 287. In *Codex v Racal-Milgo (No.3)* [1984] F.S.R. 87, it was held not sufficient for compliance with an order for delivery up or destruction of infringing apparatus merely to dismantle it without either handing the parts removed to the claimant or destroying the same upon oath, but it was sufficient to deliver up or destroy the elements in the apparatus which caused the act of infringement. The court commented that requests for an order of this nature should perhaps be more specific than had been the custom. However, in *Spectravest v Aperknit* [1988] F.S.R. 161, the order was too specific as covering only articles in the possession of the defendant at the date of the order and not articles coming into its possession subsequently. In *Rockwater v Technip (formerly Coflexip)* [2004] EWCA Civ 522, an order for delivery up was refused, as there was no vessel within the jurisdiction of the court and it was not appropriate to make an order for delivery up, in effect, of future goods. In *Mayne Pharma v Pharmacia Italia* [2005] EWCA Civ 294, noted I.P.D. 28034, an order for delivery up was refused of material which had been imported into the jurisdiction and then re-exported but was still within the control of the defendants. There was no case for delivery up of material which might have had a temporary presence in the jurisdiction. The Court of Appeal observed that the jurisdiction to grant an order for delivery up was nothing more than a way of making sure that the injunction was obeyed and quoted with approval *Roussel Uclaf v Pan Laboratories* [Australia] [1994] 51 F.C.R. 316, in the Federal Court of Australia, dealing with a similar case in which it had been observed that "delivery up is not for punishment of the infringer or compensation to the patentee." The Court of Appeal went on to observe that since the order for delivery up was ancillary to the injunction, "one always has to ask whether it is necessary to be made" and gave the example of a particular machine which has been found to infringe but which could be modified, in which case the court would make the alternative order of modification upon oath. Such was indeed the situation in *Tamglass v Luong North Glass and Novoglaze [Post Trial Order]* [2006] EWHC 444 Ch, noted I.P.D. 29031-2, where the claimants sought an order, which was granted to inspect the modified machine, by whoever they considered best qualified, to ensure that the modification remained in place.

Under the terms of Council Regulation (EC) No.1383/2003 [2003] OJ EC L916/07 it is also possible to take steps to have alleged infringing goods retained by the Customs and Excise authorities against free circulation upon importation into the United Kingdom Notification of the patent (or SPC) right must first be given to the authorities together with such information as may be available as to the likely importation of infringing goods, and their description. The Customs and Excise authorities will then provide notice on receipt of goods suspected of falling within the terms of the notice and detain the goods for up to 10 days. However, the goods will then be released for free circulation (including re-export) unless infringement proceedings have been commenced before a relevant court (including proper service under the rules of that court) within 10 business days from the date when notification has been received. There is provision for permitting inspection of the goods so detained. The relevant provisions are to be found in the Goods Infringing Intellectual Property Rights (Customs) Regulations 2004 (SI 2004/1473). If the infringement proceedings succeed, the goods will be forfeit or condemned under the under the general terms of the Customs and Excise Management Act 1979 (c.2).

Relief by damages (subs.(1)(c))

—Time when damages are assessed

In proceedings for patent infringement, it is customary first to seek a decision on liability to be followed by a continuation of the proceedings through the holding of an inquiry in which the quantum of damages suffered is assessed. Such an inquiry is available as of right to a successful claimant if he has an arguable case of loss suffered (*McDonald's Hamburgers v Burgerking* [1987] F.S.R. 112). If the claimant seeks to proceed with an inquiry into damages despite there being an appeal pending against the substantive decision on liability, he is generally entitled to do so and a stay of the inquiry will only be ordered if there are special reasons for so doing, taking into account all the circumstances (*Strix v Otter (No.3)* [1995] R.P.C. 675). However, in *Hoechst Celanese v BP Chemicals [Carbonylation]* BL C/30/98, it was held that, in a case which involved a single process operated continuously, albeit, with varying reaction conditions, the quantum of any infringement should be decided at the main trial and not left to an inquiry into damages, especially as the appropriate records were before the court; and, in *Smith Kline & French v Doncaster Pharmaceuticals* BL C/119/87, liquidated damages were claimed without an inquiry in a case involving importation without licence from Spain of a patented product produced there by the proprietor's associated company. In *Kirin-Amgen v Transkaryotic Therapies (No.2)* [2002] R.P.C. 3 at 203 the claimant was permitted to amend its pleadings to claim "springboard" relief (as approved in *Dyson v Hoover (No.2)*, see §61.21) in respect of any losses arising after expiry as a result of pre-expiry infringing activities.

The Order made at the end of the trial on liability should give directions for the conduct of the inquiry into damages. If this is not done, the matter must come again before the Patents Court for such directions to be given (*Strix v Otter (No.2)* [1995] R.P.C. 655).

61.23

Where proceedings are continued into a separate stage for the assessment of damages, there will usually be further disclosure of documents, particularly relating to the scale of infringing activities and the financial data associated therewith, see *Catnic v Hill & Smith (No.2)* [1983] F.S.R. 512.

Damages for patent infringement can be expected to be assessed for all acts of infringement occurring in respect of each type of infringement pleaded up-to-date when the inquiry into damages takes place, subject to any expiry of the patent, see *Banks v CBS Songs* [1992] F.S.R. 278.

CPR 25.7 (not reprinted in this Work) provides that a court may order an interim payment in respect of damages in advance of their full assessment. This was done in *Chiron v Murex (No.13)* [1996] F.S.R. 578 where the court thought that a preliminary calculation of damages on the basis of a notional, reasonable royalty (disregarding the claimants' claims under other heads, including additional damages for the depressive effects on the claimants' selling prices), would amount to £6.3 million and ordered an interim payment of £6 million. However, the defendants then assigned some of their assets and went into voluntary liquidation under a new name. A stay of a few months for the inquiry into damages was then obtained (*Chiron v Speciality Diagnostics* BL C/28/96, noted I.P.D. 19080) in order to allow time for the defendants' petition for leave to appeal to the House of Lords to be decided and because it was not seen that the claimants' position would deteriorate further during such a stay, the allowance of which was essentially at the discretion of the court, see *Strix v Otter (No.3)* (above). An interim award of damages was made after a successful appeal on liability in *Ultraframe v Eurocell [Interim damages]* [2005] EWHC 2111 Ch, noted I.P.D. 28074), in which the *Chiron v Murex* decision was cited with approval. There was an urgent need to pay dividends to the claimant's parent company, which had however itself to guarantee repayment in the event of a successful further appeal. An interim award of £800,000 was made, being a reasonable proportion of the lost sales element of the likely final award, which the defendants estimated at £1 million, being 60 per cent of their total sales.

—Basis for assessment

61.24 It is unclear to what extent, if any, reg.3 of the Intellectual Property (Enforcement, Etc.) Regulations 2006 (SI 2006/1028), set out at §61.02 above, will affect the basis of which damages for patent infringement are assessed, as is implicitly recognised by reg.3(3). By recognising royalties and lost profits as bases for such assessments, reg.3 is consistent with the pre-existing practice of the English courts as discussed below. However, insofar as the Regulation makes a distinction between defendants who knew, or had reasonable grounds to know, that they were infringing and those that did not, it may provide some basis for arguing for a more broadly based defence for innocent infringement than that provided by s.62(1), as to which see §62.03.

For many years, there was little authority on the assessment of damages for patent infringement, other that damages should be compensatory and not punitive, see *Catnic v Hill & Smith (No.2)* [1983] F.S.R. 512. In this case, it was held that damages must result from the infringing acts and not merely be caused by them so that so-called "parasitic damages" should not be allowed. However, in *Gerber Garment v Lectra Systems* [1995] R.P.C. 383; and [1997] R.P.C. 443 CA (discussed, as to the decision at first instance, by: P. de Sloan [1995] *CIPA* 195; R. Boulton and M. Bezant, *MIP*, June 1995, 32; and P. Brownlow, *Patent World*, 73, June/July 1995, p.49), it was held that such compensatory damages should be based on any loss which was foreseeable as likely to arise from the infringing acts, including damages for "secondary loss", a term which the court found preferable to "parasitic damages". Thus, in assessing appropriate compensation to the claimant, the court is required to estimate what were the chances that particular events would have occurred if there had been no infringement and reflect those chances in the amount of damages awarded, this necessarily being an imperfect exercise which could reasonably only be based on the general impression received from the evidence as a whole, particularly in a case such as this where the patentee had not granted any licences under the infringed patents. The *Gerber Garment* case concerned automated cloth-cutting machines sold at the best price which the supplier could obtain and damages were claimed on the basis that, but for the infringements, the patentee would have sold the machines which the defendants had done. This was only partially accepted but, for those machines, the court allowed recovery of secondary loss suffered by the patentee in lost sales of associated equipment and of maintenance contracts which it was assessed the patentee could reasonably have expected had it (rather than the defendants) sold the infringing machines; and also any loss which could be established from the infringer having established a commercial "bridgehead" before the expiry of the patent. The court also awarded damages in respect of offers for sale of machines made before the patent expiry though only because the defendants had not limited those offers to supply post-expiry. Otherwise, the court ruled that the words "offer to dispose of" in s.60(1) should be interpreted purposively and not literally so that it is legitimate to make offers to supply a patented product if it is made clear that the supply is only to take place after the patent has expired. In the *Gerber Garment* case, damages in respect of those machines, which the court judged would not necessarily have been purchased from the claimant had the defendant not made the infringing sale, were assessed (as in the *Catnic* case) at a reasonable royalty rate. However, the court rejected the analogy with the "licence of right" cases and, after making an allowance for small sales made by others, assessed the royalty on a split of the profits made by the defendant, though without taking into account the patentee's position as a manufacturer. In *Gerber Garment* at first instance, the defendants also argued that, during a period of infringing sales when the patents had been subject to "licences of right", the damages should be no more than double the reasonable royalty rate which would have been assessed for such a licence. This argument was rejected, the court pointing out that no such licence had in fact been sought and, therefore, the defendants had been liable to be injuncted. On the appeal in the *Gerber Garment* case (discussed by G. Moss and D. Rogers [1977] E.I.P.R. 425 and by A. Cooke [1998] *CIPA* 196), the Court of Appeal stressed that a successful claimant can only obtain damages where it has suffered loss which was foreseeable, caused by the tort, and not excluded from recovery by public or social policy. Moreover, that such a loss has been suffered must be proved, it not being appropriate for the court to assume this. Here, more than half of the damages assessed at first instance were losses suffered by subsidiary companies of the claimant and the Patents Court had assumed that every dollar lost by a wholly-owned subsidiary can be regarded as a corresponding loss by the parent company. However, by a majority, the Court of Appeal held that *Gerber Garment* had not adequately proved that losses by its subsidiaries (who, being non-exclusive licensees, could not themselves claim for patent infringement) would have resulted in losses to itself and, thus, the appeal was successful in reducing the quantum of assessed damages. The appeal was also successful in overturning the large award of interest on future losses, but it is to be noted that the Court of Appeal upheld the principle that damages can be awarded for loss of sales of unpatented articles (and associated service contracts) which resulted as a foreseeable consequence of the infringing acts. This would seem to open up the possibility that, where the defendant changes the alleged infringing product to one which is non-infringing, he may nevertheless be required to pay damages in respect of sales of that substituted product if the court accepts that sales thereof resulted from the initial sales of infringing products, as happened in *Rite-Hite v Kelley* [United States] [1996] F.S.R. 469. In *Ultraframe v Eurocell* [2006] EWHC 1344 Pat Ct, the *Gerber* principles were applied and damages were awarded on a lost profits basis on those infringing sales that it was held that the claimants would have made and on a royalty basis (8 per cent) as to the rest, along with damages for price depression, damages for losses post-infringement caused by price depression and disruption of the market and interest. However, the claimants failed to recover damages for alleged loss of sales of other products or the costs of developing a new product to try to mitigate the damage suffered from the infringing activities. In *Chiron v Murex (No.13)* [1996] F.S.R. 578, claims for damages were made under several heads besides those based on a reasonable royalty, including additional damages for the depressive effects of the infringements on the claimants' selling prices. In an important US case, damages were assessed even on lost sales of non-infringing goods, it being held that these lost sales flowed foreseeably from the infringing acts; damages were also awarded on the basis of a reasonable royalty, assessed at a level corresponding to 50 per cent of the profits of the patentee on the basis that the patentee would not have granted a licence on more favourable terms than this (*Rite-Hite v Kelley*, above).

In *Coflexip v Stolt Comex* [2002] EWHC 1686 Ch, noted I.P.D. 25070 the claimant was ordered to amend its pleadings to specify how and why the use of the invention was causative of the loss of prospect of "infringing contracts" (being contracts entered into between the defendant and its customers), which contracts it was alleged might have been awarded to the claimant. On referral to the Court of Appeal (see [2003] F.S.R. 41 at 728) that court declined to express a view until the facts relating to the contracts had been established, but agreed that detailed re-pleading was required before legal argument could proceed. The claimant would, however, be permitted to plead its view of causation even though that appeared to differ from that of the judge. In a case where the proprietor has shown willingness to license others to use his invention, the royalty then being applied is likely to provide the measure of damages for all the infringing acts (*General Tire v Firestone* [1975] R.P.C. 203 CA; and [1976] R.P.C. 197 HL). In *Harrison v Project & Design* BL C/53/85, damages were assessed on a royalty basis, at 3 per cent of the invoiced price, largely because serious negotiations at such a figure had taken place. (The appeal in that case (see [1987] R.P.C. 151 CA) concerned only the question of whether the previous finding of infringement (see [1978] F.S.R. 81) could be reopened on the inquiry into damages; it was held that the previous findings were res judicata.) In *Morton-Norwich v Intercen and United Chemicals* [1981] F.S.R. 337, the court held that exclusive licensees under the patent were entitled to compensatory damages in the usual way and indicated that, if calculated on a royalty basis, in the circumstances these might be of the order of 20 per cent. In *Smith Kline & French v Doncaster Pharmaceuticals* BL C/119/87, where the infringing product was that marketed in Spain by an associate of the claimant (as noted in §61.23), it was contended that the measure of damages was the difference in price between the Spanish and United Kingdom prices for the proprietor's product, but this argument was rejected in favour of the difference between the Spanish and French (or Belgian) prices of the proprietor, presumably on the basis that importation from those Community countries would not be an infringing act in view of the Community doctrine of "exhaustion of rights" (for which see §D15), not at the time applicable to products sold initially in Spain. Where a patented article is resold, the resale is a separate act of infringement and damages (or an account of profits) can, in theory, be claimed from the second vendor even when damages have already been obtained from the initial vendor (*Catnic v Evans* [1983] F.S.R. 401). However, as damages are intended to compensate the claimant for its financial loss resulting from the infringing acts, the claimant is not entitled to more than that total loss by claiming from separate defendants. The position is different when the claimant elects to take relief for infringement by way of an account of the profits which have resulted from the infringing acts because then it may claim the profits individually made by each infringing defendant, see §61.28. Also, where there is more than one possible defendant in respect of the same act of infringement, then any defendant who pays damages can bring an action for a contribution from the other joint tortfeasors under the Civil Liability (Contribution) Act 1978 (c.47). For a comparative law study in relation to computation of damages based on extensions outside the scope of the patent protection has been published: see G. Karnell [1997] I.P.Q. 92.

A person who incurs costs in defending a patent infringement action, particularly if he is required to pay damages or an account of profits therein, may be able to recover his loss if his act of infringement resulted from his innocent purchase of infringing goods. By s.12(2) of the Sale of Goods Act 1979 (c.54), as amended by the Sale and Supply of Goods Act 1994 (c.35), there is in any sale of goods an implied warranty that the buyer will enjoy quiet possession of those goods except as to any charge or incumbrance on the goods disclosed or known to the buyer. That warranty may not be excluded by the terms of a contract governed by English law (Unfair Contract Terms Act 1977 (c.50) s.6(1) as amended by Sale of Goods Act 1979 (c.54) Sch.2 para.19(a)). Authority for this proposition is to be found in *Microbeads v Vinhurst* [1976] R.P.C. 19 CA, although that case was decided under former statutory provisions, see also *Niblett v Confectioners' Materials* [1921] 3 K.B. 387 CA and §60.29.

—Interest on damages

Interest on damages (on a simple interest basis) is usually awarded (though strictly this **61.25** is at the discretion of the court) in respect of the whole or part of the period between each act of infringement and the date of judgment on the assessment, but a claim therefor must be made (Senior Courts Act 1981 (c.54) s.35A as inserted by s.15 of, and Sch.1 to, the Administration of Justice Act 1982 (c.53) s.15 and Sch.1), see *Hunt v Douglas* [1990] 1 A.C. 398; [1988] 3 All E.R. 823 HL. In proceedings before the Patents County Court, interest upon damages should be claimed under the County Courts Act 1984 (c.28) s.69. After assessment in either the High Court or the county court, interest is also payable (as a judgment debt at a rate fixed under the CPR) on a daily basis for the period between the date of the order on assessment and the date of payment. For interest payable on an award of costs, see §61.34.

For examples of the award of interest on damages, see: *Catnic v Hill and Smith (No.2)* [1983] F.S.R. 512; *General Tire v Firestone* [1975] R.P.C. 203 CA; and *Fablaine v Leygill (No.2)* [1982] F.S.R. 427, the latter two cases arising under the previous enactment relating to interest on an award of damages. *Harrison v Project & Design* BL C/53/85 also contains some observations on the calculation of interest on damages calculated on a royalty basis.

In *Catnic v Hill and Smith (No.2)*, interest was not allowed as a head of damage suffered for the bank financing which was required in the absence of profits from exploitation of the patent by the patentee, although more recently, a defendant's financing costs have been allowed as a deduction from its profits in assessing an account thereof, see *Celanese International v BP Chemicals* [1999] R.P.C. 203 and §61.28.

—Exemplary damages

Exemplary damages will apparently never be awarded for patent infringement even **61.26** when the infringer has cynically made profits greater than the loss suffered by the patent proprietor (*Catnic v Hill and Smith (No.2)* [1983] F.S.R. 512), but an account of profits (for which see §61.28) may be appropriate.

—Effect of Limitation Act

The effect of the Limitation Act 1980 (c.58) on infringement is discussed in §60.30, **61.27** where it is pointed out that, in general, damages are claimable for acts of infringement committed only within the six-year period (five years in Scotland) prior to the date of the claim. Thus, where a further defendant is joined to an infringement action, its liability will normally extend back only to acts committed within the six years prior to the date when that defendant became joined to the action (*Lubrizol v Esso* [1992] R.P.C. 467 CA).

In *Morton-Norwich v Intercen and United Chemicals* [1981] F.S.R. 337, damages were awarded for acts of infringement committed more than six years before the issue of the claim because there had been "concealed fraud" which extended the normal six-year period for claiming relief under the Limitation Acts (see now Limitation Act above, s.2). Damages were here also held to include the cost of proceedings previously brought (*Norwich Pharmacal v Commissioners for Customs and Excise* [1974] R.P.C. 101) in order to discover the identity of the infringers (for which see §60.11), such costs being a foreseeable consequence of the tort committed by the defendants.

Relief by account of profits (subs.(1)(d))

The remedy of an account of profits is one which was not available for patent infringe- **61.28** ment between 1919 and 1950. Being an equitable remedy, its grant is (as with interim relief) strictly speaking a matter for the discretion of the court and in *Beloit Canada v Valmet* [Canada], noted [1997] E.I.P.R. D–236, where the patentee had been aware of the infringement for many years but had not taken action, thereby allowing the defendant to make profits, an account of profits was refused.

The theory behind this type of relief is that, by claiming (as a matter of Equity) the profits made by the infringer, the patentee is prepared to condone these acts as ones of infringement and, hence, he cannot also claim damages resulting from those acts. Thus, when an account of profits is taken, only acts of infringement up to the point where the profit was made are condoned thereby, and subsequent acts of infringement involving the patented product are not apparently franked by the account taken (*Codex v Racal-Milgo (No.3)* [1984] F.S.R. 87). Where there are multiple defendants, the claimant can apparently make a different election as between damages and an account for each defendant (*Electric Furnace Co v Selas* [1987] R.P.C. 23), but there should be no double accounting on the issue of damages, see §61.24. An order for an account of profits (like that of an injunction) is an equitable remedy available, strictly speaking, in the discretion of the court.

In *Bayer Cropscience v Charles River Laboratories* [2010] CSOH 158 a submission that an account of profits could not be awarded in respect of a "springboard" claim relating to post patent expiry sales was rejected.

It has been rare (at least in patent infringement cases before the English courts) for an account of profits to be requested in preference to an award of damages under subs.(1)(c), both not being possible (subs.(2)). This was apparently because of the difficulties in computation, see *Siddell v Vickers* (1892) 9 R.P.C. 152 and the possibility that the computation would show that the defendant suffered a financial loss on its activities, see the copyright case of *Redwood Music v Chappell* [1982] R.P.C. 109 and the passing-off case of *My Kinda Town v Soll* [1983] R.P.C. 15 and 407 CA. In *My Kinda Town*, it was stated that an order for taking an account of profits must be carefully formulated, since otherwise the account ordered may be one that is "virtually impossible to take".

Nevertheless, an account of profits was taken in *Celanese International v BP Chemicals* [1999] R.P.C. 203 and this decision has to be regarded as definitive on the interpretation of subs.(1)(d). It involved the assessment of profits made by BP in using a patented purification method in the final step of its production of acetic acid, for which see *Hoechst Celanese v BP Chemicals [Iodide Removal]* [1997] F.S.R. 547 and [1999] F.S.R. 319 CA. The court held that, first, profits can only be awarded to the extent that the "invention" has been used. This has to be judged as a matter of substance, not form (as in *Lubrizol v Imperial Oil* [Canada] [1996] 71 C.P.R. (3d) 26), so that, although the patent claim was here directed to a method of purification of acetic acid and therefore covered the product of that method as specified, there had to be an apportionment of the total profit made as there is only one profits "pot" and other patents might also have been infringed. In this case, the apportionment allowed was based on the capital expenditure for the purification step as a proportion of the total for the whole plant. In calculating the total profit, a number of matters were here considered, particularly that it is permissible to deduct R&D expenditure according to normal accountancy practice, although allowance should be made for licensing receipts, and also to deduct the cost of funding the plant construction. One of the two plants in issue made both acetic acid and acetic anhydride, and only the acid was subjected to the patented method. There therefore had to be an apportionment of profit from that plant to assess the profit obtained on the acid alone. However, as the anhydride commanded a higher price, BP proved that the acid from this plant had been produced at a loss. Thus, only the profit from the other plant could give rise to an award and, from the base allocated profit arising from these apportionments, the amount of corporation tax that had been paid by BP should be deducted. However, if BP were successful in reclaiming this, the reclaimed tax would also have to be paid over. The conclusion from this decision—for case comment on which, see: N. T. Jenkins and N. Perkins [1999] *CIPA*, 61; T. Moody-Stuart [1999] E.I.P.R. 147; C. Thornton and S. Cohen *Patent World*, 109, February 1999, 30; and [1998/1999] B.S.L.R. 186; and *MIP*, December 1998/January 1999, 6—is that the claimant might have received greater reward if it had sought damages in the conventional manner, for example on the basis of a reasonable royalty, but each case has its own particular facts. These should be carefully assessed before an election is made to have an account of profits taken instead of seeking an award of damages, especially where as here the defendant may be able to prove that at least some of the infringing acts resulted in a financial loss to him.

Prior to the *Celanese* decision, the taking of an account seems to have been more popular in other common law jurisdictions, see below, and, anyway, it will probably be more attractive when the infringing activities have not caused the proprietor any financial loss. The distinction between damages (the loss suffered by the claimant) and an account of profits (the profits made by the infringer) is illustrated by the trade mark case of *Colbeam Palmer v Stock* [Australia] [1972] R.P.C. 303.

Thus, in Canada, there seems to have been a much more restrictive attitude to allowable deductions from gross profits, and consequently a much more generous attitude to the assessment of profits enjoyed by the defendant from an act of patent infringement, than previously seemed possible. This trend seems to have started with *Teledyne v Lido Industrial* [Canada] (1982) 68 C.P.R. (2d) 204, noted [1983] E.I.P.R. D–116. Also, in *Reading & Bates v Baker Energy* [Canada], noted [1992] E.I.P.R. D–259, it was held that the basis for calculating profits must be the entire operation covered by the method claims and should be measured as the difference between the profit made from using the infringing method and that from the alternative method that would most likely have otherwise been used, see further *Beloit Canada v Valmet Oy*, noted [1993] E.I.P.R. D–31. The computation of an account of profits in Canada has been discussed by Coleen L. Kirby [1991] E.I.P.R. 367 and (in relation to infringement of copyright) by L. Bently [1991] E.I.P.R. 5.

In Australia, the computation of an account of profits for patent infringement was comprehensively reviewed in a decision of the High Court of Australia (*Dart Industries v Decor* [Australia] [1994] F.S.R. 567; (1993) 26 I.P.R. 193), discussed by C. Oddie (*Patent World*, 58, December 1993/January 1994, 30). This decision held that overhead expenses could be deducted if these could be shown to have assisted in the production of the profits which resulted from the infringing acts, though "opportunity costs" may not be deducted: approximation rather than precision may be necessary to achieve the aim of arriving as closely as possible at a true profit made from the infringing activity. The reasoning in the Canadian *Teledyne case* (above) was held to be flawed. It was also held that, as the defendants should account for all profits arising from the infringing act, profits made on sales of containers to which the patented seal was applied should be regarded as profits arising from the infringement. In the decision below (*Decor v Dart Industries* [Australia] (1992) 23 I.P.R. 1), the Federal Court of Australia stated that the object of an account of profits is not to punish the defendant, but to ensure that he disgorges, and the claimant receives, an amount which truly represents the profit obtained by the infringement. This view was approved on the above-mentioned appeal.

In *Codex v Racal-Milgo* BL C/135/81, noted I.P.D. 4100, the argument appears to have been accepted that, if the proprietor seeks an account of profits rather than damages, he need not lead evidence that the specification of the patent as published was framed in good faith and with reasonable skill and knowledge, see §§62.05 and 63.03.

In *Spring Form v Toy Brokers* [2002] F.S.R. 17 at 276 the Patents Court determined that while a co-claimant exclusive licensee can claim this relief, there is only one "profits pot" to be shared between him and the patentee. All co-claimants must make the same election between damages and an account. Accounts against multiple defendants needed to be taken together and no payment should be made in respect of any infringing article until the claimant undertakes not to make a claim in respect of the same article against any other defendant, otherwise the taking of an account would become hopelessly complicated.

It is possible to delay making an election between an award of damages or taking an account of profits until after some basic, though not detailed, disclosure has been given by the infringer-defendant so that the successful claimant can make that election on an informed basis, see the copyright case of *Island Records v Tring International* [1995] F.S.R. 560 and §61.07. In *Rockwater v Technip (formerly Coflexip)* [2004] EWCA 1448 Pat Ct the court ordered disclosure of certain financial and commercial information, although less than the claimants had sought, to enable the claimants to make an informed election between claiming damages and seeking an account of profits. For a form of the order made for the purposes of taking an account of profits, see *Glaverbel v British Coal* [1994] R.P.C. 443 at 518.

Accountancy assistance in computation of damages and accounts of profits

61.29 As will be appreciated from the comments in §§61.24, 61.25 and 61.28, the computation of damages and accounts of profits, and the question of which measure should be chosen, is a difficult matter. Accountancy evidence in support of any claim will frequently be desirable. A number of firms of accountants have established litigation support groups which specialise in assessments of damages and accounts of profits.

Stay of inquiry or taking of account pending appeal

61.30 In *Lucas v Gaedor* [1978] R.P.C. 297, the Court of Appeal stated that a stay pending appeal of relief (in that case the taking of an account of profits) should, unless agreed between the parties, be granted only if there are special circumstances, which were then found. In *Minnesota Mining v Rennicks* [1992] R.P.C. 331, no such circumstances were found; and likewise in *Mölnlycke v Procter & Gamble (No.5)* [1994] R.P.C. 49 where no special reasons were seen in the complexity of the inquiry into damages the significant further disclosure required or the need for evidence from experts on the inquiry. Indeed, the courts here indicated that the inquiry should commence before the scent grew cold.

However, in both cases (as well as in *Optical Coating v Pilkington* [1993] F.S.R. 310), undertakings were given which would safeguard the defendants if they were successful on appeal and, in the *Mölnlycke* case, infringing articles were required to be delivered up to the claimants' solicitors for safe-keeping pending the outcome of the appeal. In *Chiron v Organon Teknika* BL C/43/94, noted I.P.D. 17080 a stay of the damages inquiry was refused although the defendants' appeal against a finding of patent validity in an earlier separate action remained to be heard.

For the separate question whether there should be a stay of an injunction pending appeal, see §61.21.

Declaration of validity and infringement (subs.(1)(e))

61.31 When action under s.60 is successful, a declaration (declarator in Scotland) that the patent has been found valid and infringed is given as a matter of course, but such a declaration has only formal effect. It is usual to request that the declaration contain a certificate of contested validity under s.65(1), for the effect of which see §65.03, and such declaration will be granted as a matter of course unless the defendant merely contested infringement and accepted that the patent was valid for the purpose of the proceedings against him. A declaration under subs.(1)(e) is also available in proceedings before the Comptroller under subs.(3).

Relief against a foreign joint tortfeasor

61.32 Where a foreign defendant is found to be a joint tortfeasor, enforcement of an order for monetary relief will depend upon the availability of means for the reciprocal enforcement of foreign judgments. This varies according to the country of domicile of the defendant, but where the defendant is domiciled in a Member State of the Brussels Regulation or Lugano Convention (for which see §61.04 and §96.09) there should be no difficulty because these require courts of their Member States to enforce a judgment given in another Member State, generally automatically without examination of it. However, otherwise, there may be difficulty in enforcing a judgment against a foreign defendant, i.e. against a defendant resident in a State where there is no arrangement for reciprocal enforcement of judgments or where the relief imposed is of an interim nature.

The problem over injunctory relief arises because an English court is generally reluctant to grant relief by an order which it is unable to enforce. Thus, on that basis, the grant of an injunction against continued acts of joint tortfeasance by a foreign entity is problematical, though *North Western Trailer v Itel* (noted, *The Times*, December 19, 1979; BL HC/PC/41/79, and in §61.21) appears to be an example of such. Here, an interim injunction was granted against a German manufacturer who sold goods (collapsible shipping containers) to a United States corporation knowing that goods would then be sold or leased to persons who would inevitably bring them into the United Kingdom where they would infringe a patent, it being held that there was sufficient common design to make the German manufacturer, the United States buyer and the lessee shipping line each a joint tortfeasor as soon as an infringement actually occurred. The balance of justice was held to be in favour of granting an injunction unless the parties could agree on a method of preventing importation pending trial; and such importation would not be exempted under s.60(5)(d) or (e). The decision in this case is an unusually (and perhaps unreasonably) wide extension of the effect of a United Kingdom patent.

Euro-defences

Where the conduct of the claimant has involved breach of the TFEU, particularly arts **61.33** 101 or 102 (reprinted at §§D06 and D07), there is the possibility that he may become disentitled to relief (*Aero-Zipp v Y.K.K.* [1974] R.P.C. 624; and *Application des Gaz v Falks Veritas* [1975] R.P.C. 421). No such defence appears yet to have succeeded before an English court in a case involving intellectual property, but where there is a Pt 20 claim (formerly a "counterclaim") alleging a breach of arts 101 or 102 TFEU, a defendant may be able to secure an injunction against the claimant (*Garden Cottage Foods v Milk Marketing Board* [1984] A.C. 130; [1983] 2 C.M.L.R. 13; noted [1984] F.S.R. 23 HL).

However, generally, the English court has been robust, at least in patent cases, in striking out Euro-defences which seem unlikely to succeed, or where insufficient nexus is seen between the issues for trial and the alleged breach of Community law, see: *Minnesota Mining v Geerpres* [1974] R.P.C. 35 and *Quantel v Electronic Graphics* [1990] R.P.C. 272 in each of which alleged Euro-defences did not prevent an interim injunction; *Ransburg-Gema v Electrostatic Plant Systems* [1990] F.S.R. 287; *Chiron v Organon Teknika (No.2)* [1993] F.S.R. 324 and 567; *Chiron v Murex (No.2)* [1994] F.S.R. 187 CA; and *International Business Machines v Phoenix* [1994] R.P.C. 251. In the first of these *Chiron* decisions, the court accepted that unfair and abusive pricing could be abusive conduct, but on the facts such pricing was not seen to affect trade between Community Member States.

Occasionally, pleadings of Euro-defences have been permitted to remain in order to provide for possible eventual referral to the ECJ in Luxembourg under art.267 TFEU (reprinted at §D08 and discussed in §D12), see: *British Leyland v TI Silencers* [1981] F.S.R. 213; *Dymond v Britton* [1976] F.S.R. 330; *Hagen v Moretti* [1980] F.S.R. 517; [1980] 3 C.M.L.R. 253; and *Lansing Bagnall v Buccaneer* [1984] F.S.R. 241. In the *British Leyland* case, the pleaded Euro-defence was the alleged existence of licensing arrangements contrary to art.101 TFEU, whereas the *Aero Zipp*, *Application des Gaz* and *Lansing Bagnall* cases concerned alleged abuse of a dominant position contrary to art.102 TFEU, discussed further in §D26.

For the possible nature of a "Euro-defence", it is noted that the European Commission has condemned, as being contrary to art.102: contractual provisions for restricting resale of purchased goods; refusal to supply goods to certain persons; and the charging of dissimilar, or unfair, prices for equivalent transactions (*United Brands v EC Commission (27/ 76)* [1978] E.C.R. 207; [1978] 1 C.M.L.R. 429 ECJ); and, indeed, any unfair commercial practice on the part of a dominant enterprise intended to eliminate, discipline or deter small companies is potentially an abuse of marketing power and contrary to art.102 (*Engineering and Chemical Supplies v AKZO* [1986] 3 C.M.L.R. 273), for case comment on which see [1987] E.I.P.R. 86.

However, it is not a breach of the TFEU merely to enforce an intellectual property right which the law provides, see *Keurkoop v Nancy Keen (14/81)* [1982] E.C.R. 2853; [1983] 2 C.M.L.R. 47; [1983] F.S.R. 381 ECJ; *Thetford v Fiamma (35/87)* [1988] 3 C.M.L.R. 549; [1989] F.S.R. 57 ECJ; and §D27. Thus, in *Pitney Bowes v Francotyp-Postalia* [1991] F.S.R. 72, it was stated:

"There is a strong public interest in allowing anyone to assert what he considers to be his legal rights, provided only that he does so in good faith".

Consequently, it is not per se an abuse of a dominant position [contrary to art.102] for a patentee: to enforce his rights; to threaten to do so—even if such enforcement might strengthen a dominant position and might even make it a monopoly; or to refuse to grant a licence on reasonable terms.

Nevertheless, it remains that an intellectual property right must not be used in an abusive manner, and if it is the primacy of art.102 may override the intellectual property right as it did in the copyright case of *Independent Television Publications Ltd v EC Commission* (T-76/89) [1991] 4 C.M.L.R. 745 CFI, upheld on appeal by the ECJ in *RTE v EC Commission and Magill* (C-241/91P and C-242-P) [1995] E.C.R. I-743; [1995] 4 C.M.L.R. 718; [1995] F.S.R. 530, as further discussed in §D27. The principles established in *Magill*, and in which it was said that "the exercise of an exclusive right by the proprietor may, in exceptional circumstances, involve abusive conduct" have been elaborated in a further reference to the ECJ in a copyright case, *IMS Health GmbH & Co OHG v NDC Health GmbH & Co* (C-418/01) [2004] E.C.R. I-5039. The compulsory licensing of IP rights under EC competition law from *Magill* to *Microsoft* was reviewed by D. Curley and Davina Garrod in [2005] *CIPA* 319.

However, the degree to which the *Magill* principles can in practice be applied to patent cases, where there is for example scope for compulsory licensing where a right is not being exploited, which is in general absent with copyright, is unclear. Thus in *Philips Electronics v Ingman* [1999] F.S.R. 112, the *Magill* judgment was explained as arising from an abuse of controlling access to information and not an abuse of exercising intellectual property rights, in this case copyrights, and (following the cases cited above) a Euro-defence based on an alleged abuse under art.102 involving a refusal to license patents on differential terms was held to be unarguable. Also held to be unarguable here was the allegation of void conditions under art.101 because licensees under a standard licence were required to grant back licences under their own future inventions in the field to the licensors, and to other licensees, on "reasonable non-discriminatory conditions"; and also because the standard licence required the payment of uniform royalties irrespective of the number of patents exercised by the licensee. Nevertheless, with reluctance, the allegation that the standard licence conditions were oppressive was allowed to remain in the pleadings, but this issue was ordered to be tried separately from the issue of patent validity and to be stayed pending the outcome of the defendants' complaints to the EC Commission. *Sandvik v Pfiffner* [2000] F.S.R. 17 is a later decision of similar effect where, again, the *Magill* case was seen as exceptional. However, pleadings which alleged an overall anti-competitive conduct by the patentee under art.101 or 102 were here allowed to remain as possibly providing a defence to infringement of a patent which had not been included in a general know-how licence, but see §§D26 and D27.

In *Intel v Via Technologies* [2003] F.S.R. 12 at 175, summary judgment for the claimant was ordered in relation to a series of defences based on arts 101(1) and 102 TFEU. However, on appeal (see [2003] F.S.R. 33 at 574), it was held that, following *Magill* the judge had been wrong to deny a full trial of the issue whether Intel's conduct should be regarded as "exceptional circumstances". The appeal was therefore allowed with an order that the parties should return to the High Court for directions for trial of the "Euro-defences", but the action was subsequently settled. See the case comment on this decision in *Patent World*, October 2002 (No.146), p.12.

Costs

—The principles for award and assessment of costs

61.34   Under the English legal system, the successful party in civil litigation is generally entitled to recover costs from the other party, and an order to this effect will normally be included in the post-trial order of the court, and may be included in any interim order (as to the costs of interim proceedings see §61.36). The terms of such orders are, however, entirely in the discretion of the court, see CPR 44.3 (CPR 44 is not reproduced in this Work) and regard must be had to all the circumstances, including: the conduct of the parties, the extent to which a party has been successful and any payment into court or admissible offer to settle which is drawn to the court's attention, see CPR 44.3(4). Consequently, appeals from a costs order are either impossible or likely to fail. CPR 44.3(4)(b) allows for an issues-based costs order in appropriate cases and "in patent cases, an issues based approach to costs is now the norm" as was stated in *Research in Motion UK Ltd v Visto Corporation* [2008] EWHC 819; [2008] F.S.R. 20. Further cases in which the issues based approach to costs discussed are: *Actavis v Novartis* [2009] EWHC 502 Pat Ct; *Edwards Life Sciences v Cook Biotech* [2009] EWHC 1443; and *Novartis v Johnson & Johnson* [2009] EWHC 2029 Pat Ct.

In *Actavis v Eli Lilly* [2010] EWCA Civ 43 the Court of Appeal refused to vary an order made by the trial Judge for two separate applicants for revocation to share the full costs of the patentee's successful defence of its patent, despite the second applicant to initiate proceedings having also discontinued these before trial, which proceeded with the first applicant alone. The court rejected a submission from the second applicant that it should only pay the patentee's costs in so far as they had been increased by its involvement.

In *Mobiqa v Trinity Mobile* [2010] EWHC 253, where the patentee had discontinued its case but argued that it would have done so much earlier had the applicant for revocation explained its case more fully at an earlier stage the court declined to depart from the provisions of CPR r.38.6 by which a claimant who discontinues is liable for the costs of the other party incurred on or before the date of service of the notice of discontinuance.

It is unclear as yet to what extent the amendments made to s.106 (for which see §106.01) may affect awards of costs in patent litigation. As discussed in §106.02, the new provisions extend the powers under s.106 to proceedings before the court, not only to those under s.40, but also in respect of acts of infringement and/or actions under s.70 and/or s.71, and so require the court in assessing awards of costs in such proceedings to "consider all the relevant circumstances, including the financial position of the parties", as to which see §106.02. These provisions are additional to (or perhaps merely explanatory of) CPR 44.3 which requires the court, when making a costs order, "to have regard to all the circumstances".

The parties have an obligation to inform other parties as to their potential liability in costs and the court can order any party to provide to it, and to all parties, an estimate of costs, such to be done in the form of a standard "Statement of Costs", see CPR 43 PD 43–48 at 4.1. In default of agreement, and upon an order for a detailed costs assessment, the amount of the costs to be paid requires an examination of the files of the solicitor of the successful party, with particular reference being paid to attendance notes and other documents evidencing the work done at each stage of the litigation. In the absence of such supporting documents, costs will either be disallowed or allowed only on a minimal basis. This assessment is carried out in the High Court by a "costs judge" and in a county court by an assigned district judge, called a "costs officer". For the assessment of costs in a county court, with particular reference to the Patents County Court, see [1993] *CIPA* 196. On the assumption that litigation in the Patents County Court follows that of the Patents Court in normally being assigned to the CPR "multi-track" (on which see §G02), the practice of costs in proceedings before either of these courts is covered by CPR Pts 43, 44, 47 and 48.

The normal rule is that a detailed assessment of costs should only be ordered at the conclusion of proceedings (CPR 47.1). For this purpose, the usual split procedure in patent litigation of first deciding liability (infringement and validity), followed by assessment of the quantum of monetary relief is regarded as two separate proceedings, see *Mölnlycke v Procter & Gamble* BL C/78/92. It is, however, nowadays rare in High Court patent litigation to proceed to the considerable trouble and expense of a detailed costs assessment after full trial, either because relatively little remains in issue between the parties after the usual award of an "interim payment" on account of costs has been awarded after trial or, as in *Monsanto v Cargill (No.2)* [2007] EWHC 3113; [2008] F.S.R. 16, the parties have agreed after trial that the trial judge should make an order in absolute terms based on costs schedules put before him. However, in *Research in Motion UK Ltd v Visto Corp*, above, the trial judge declined to make an interim award of costs because the parties were so far apart in their levels of costs (those of the winning party were four times those of the other) that an interim payment would not facilitate agreement. Costs are awarded on either the "standard" or "indemnity" basis as defined by CPR 44.4. Normally the standard basis is applied. This requires the court to consider all the circumstances of the case, and particularly whether the costs claimed were "proportionally and reasonably incurred, or were proportionally and reasonable in amount" and to consider: the parties' conduct; the importance of the matter and its complexity or novelty of the questions raised; the skill, effort, specialist knowledge and responsibility involved; the time spent on the case; and the place where, and the circumstances in which, work for the litigation was carried out, see CPR 44.5 and 44 PD 11. Moreover, the court is required only to allow costs which are "proportionate to the matters in issue", and to "resolve any doubt whether costs were reasonably incurred or reasonable and proportionate in amount in favour of the paying party", see CPR 44.4(2), see also CPR 44 PD 13 made under it. The result is that costs are generally assessed at a level some way below that at which the solicitor was likely to have charged a successful party so that only a proportion of actual costs would be recovered, of the order in practice of two-thirds or three-quarters of the total costs of a party that succeeds on all issues. However, given the degree to which most patent actions involve several separate and not always interconnected issues, and for example an alleged infringer may be able to prevail by succeeding on only one of these the situation is typically considerably more complicated in practice under the "issues-based" approach to costs.

The development of the "issues-based" approach to costs of patent actions under the CPR can be traced back to *McGhan Medical v Nagor* [2002] F.S.R. 9 at 162 where the defendant had succeeded in its arguments that the patent was not infringed but failed in its attack on the validity of the patent. The court considered the appropriate award of costs under CPR 44.3 and concluded that in normal circumstances the overall winner of a patent infringement suit with a counterclaim should get its entire costs, subject only to the possibility of a discretionary discount for any unreasonable conduct on the defendant's part (whether by commission, omission, exaggeration or "over-zealous application"). However, the judge was urged to take into account the observations of Lord Woolf in *AEI Rediffusion Music Ltd v Phonographic Performance Ltd* [1999] R.P.C. 599; [1999] 1 W.L.R. 1507 in which he said that "too robust an application of the 'follow the event principle' ... discourages litigants from being selective as to the points they take ..." and may encourage them to "leave no stone unturned" in their efforts to do so. In the light of that the judge applied a "modest" discount in relation to one aspect of the case (an allegation of prior use) which he held had initially been pleaded as a "makeweight". In the decision on costs in the Court of Appeal in *Pharmacia v Merck* [2002] R.P.C. 41 at 775 (but unreported on this aspect) the defendants had succeeded overall but were unsuccessful on one aspect (infringement), where the appeal was successful in overturning the decision below. The court was not inclined to order assessment of both parties' costs on this aspect but instead applied a discount to the total costs of the overall winner, which in this case was quantified at 10 per cent; see the commentary on this case by Sara Ashby "Costs in United Kingdom Patent Actions: Patent Valid but Not Infringed" [2001] E.I.P.R. 380. The matter was further considered in *Apotex v SmithKline Beecham* [2004] EWHC 964 Ch; and [2004] EWHC 2051 Ch in which the court stated the general principle as follows:

"A party successful on the issue of invalidity will not generally recover its costs of the objections to validity that failed unless they are so tied in with successful objections that it would not be fair to treat them differently. It may, but not must, have to pay the unsuccessful patentee's costs of the issues upon which it fails if those issues were unreasonably raised or persisted in. Where a defendant is successful on the issue of infringement, an order for it to recover its assessed costs of that issue will normally be made unless it is possible at the stage when the order for costs is made to identify discrete 'infringement issues' which failed unreasonably in respect of which it is possible without detailed assessment fairly to make an estimate and so reduce the recovery to that extent. Equally, if in an otherwise successful defence to the allegation of infringement it is clear that the Defendant is responsible for raising issues that failed and in respect of which it is fair that the unsuccessful patent should receive its costs then a further adjustment can be made".

Here the defendant had prevailed at first instance as to both infringement and validity of one of the patents in issue in the proceedings (but the only one the subject of the judgment) and the court went onto observe that:

"it is necessary in a case such as the present to understand that a number of assumptions are being made when a percentage order for costs is made. The first, and perhaps most important, is that there are no general (i.e. unallocatable) costs of the action. All costs are notionally allocated to the issues of either infringement or validity. The successful party is assumed to recover all its reasonable costs of the action, and the percentage deduction is made from that overall sum."

Applying those principles, the court made a reduction of 14 per cent in respect of non infringement arguments that had failed and 10 per cent in respect of invalidity arguments that had failed, thus awarding the defendant 76 per cent of its assessed costs, such assessed costs however to exclude certain identified costs that remained to be dealt with in the context of proceedings on the other patent which had not been the subject of the judgment. The first instance judgment finding the patent invalid having been reversed on appeal, it was accepted in *SmithKline Beecham v Apotex (No.2)* [2005] F.S.R. 24 at 559 that the costs award should be varied to reflect the judgment of the Court of Appeal. The Court of Appeal did not comment on the approach adopted by the first instance judge on costs, and observed that "an issue-by-issue approach is ... one that should be applied so far as it reasonably can" but noted that "such an approach was not the be-all and end-all," given that CPR 44.3(5)(b) makes it a relevant factor whether or not "it was reasonable for a party to raise, pursue or contest a particular allegation." Thus the Court of Appeal did not disturb the 14 per cent reduction at first instance in respect of non-infringement arguments that had failed, but reduced the total award to the defendant by 60 per cent to 16 per cent to take account of the costs attributable to validity, as to some of which the claimant was entitled to costs on an indemnity basis, both under s.65 and in the general exercise of discretion, in relation to an attack on validity that had previously been mounted in other proceedings but had also failed in those.

The principles set out in the first instance *Apotex* judgment were helpfully summarised in *Secretary of State v Frontline Technology [Costs]* [2004] EWHC 1563 Ch, BL C/87/04 and applied in apportioning costs, which was done on an issue-by-issue basis, relating such issues to the percentage of time taken at trial, although in approaching the question of where such costs lay, the court had regard to the principle set out in *Johnson Estates (1990) Ltd v Secretary of State for the Environment* [2001] EWCA Civ 6535 that, in an exceptional case, costs may be awarded in favour of an unsuccessful party without it being necessary to decide whether the allegation on which the successful party had lost had been made improperly or unreasonably. Since then the issues based approach has been applied and discussed in *Actavis v Merck* [2007] EWHC 1625 Pat Ct; *Generics v Lundbeck* [2007] R.P.C. 32 Pat Ct; [2007] EWHC 1606; *Monsanto Technology v Cargill International* [2007] EWHC 3113 Pat Ct; and *Research in Motion UK Ltd v Visto Corp* [2008] EWHC 819; [2008] F.S.R. 20. In the last of these it was observed:

"Where the court decides to disallow the costs of a successful party in relation to a particular issue, it can sometimes go further and order the successful party to pay the unsuccessful party's costs of that issue. It is not necessary to find unreasonable conduct on the part of the successful party in order to make such an order. In *Monsanto v Cargill* Pumfrey LJ (in a case where he was the trial judge) approved of a submission in the form of three questions asked by counsel in *Actavis v Merck* as demonstrating the correct approach:

'Have you won, have you lost a suitably circumscribed issue, so you should be deprived of your costs [of that issue], and is this an exceptional case such as to lead to an adverse costs order on an issue in favour of the overall loser?'"

Indeed, applying these principles the trial judge in *Monsanto* ordered that the successful defendant make a substantial payment made to the patentee because it had won on validity even though it had lost on infringement and thus overall. In *Stena v Irish Ferries (No.2)* [2003] R.P.C. 37 at 681 the Court of Appeal upheld the decision at first instance to award costs on an "issue" basis, where the defendant had been successful on a narrow ground (see §60.17 above) but its substantial attack on validity had failed. Accordingly the claimant was ordered to pay 20 per cent of the defendant's costs, and the defendant 80 per cent of the claimant's. Issues based costs order may not always be appropriate and in *Rambus v Hynix Semiconductor* [2005] F.S.R. 19 at 417, when dismissing actions which been stayed pending EPO oppositions which succeeded, the court declined to make an issues based costs order excluding the costs of an art.82 and another discrete non infringement defence which were never tested.

The costs that can be awarded by the court include "fees, charges, disbursements, expenses, and remuneration", see CPR 43.2(1)(a), and a patent attorney litigator is treated as a solicitor for this purpose, see CPR 43PD 1, but no allowance is made for the executive time incurred by a litigating party. Furthermore, costs may only be recovered in respect of actual or threatened litigation; and, where experiments are carried out by a corporate litigant itself, only a reasonable sum for the actual and direct costs of the work undertaken are likely to be awarded (*Nossen's Patent* [1969] 1 All E.R. 775). *Admiral Management Services v Para Protect Europe* [2002] F.S.R. 59 at 914 applied the principles of *Nossen's Patent* to the costs of an employee of a party acting as an expert witness. *Nossen's Patent* was also applied in *Sisu Capital Fund v Tucker* [2006] F.S.R. 21 at 409 to limit the costs recoverable by the claimant's accountants in relation to the time they had themselves spent on the litigation to the time spent on matters calling for special expertise, such as financial modelling. In *Agassi v Robinson* [2005] EWCA Civ 1507; [2006] 1 All E.R. 900, although the costs of a tax advisor who was not an authorised litigator and had instructed a barrister through the Bar's Licensed Access Scheme could not be recovered as he was treated as a litigant in person, the possibility was left open of recovering costs in relation to ancillary items which might properly be allowed as disbursements under CPR 48.6(3)(a)(ii). In *Inline Logistics v UCL Logistics [Costs: Recovery of Insurance Premium]* [2002] EWHC 519; [2002] I.P. & T. 444 a party was allowed to claim as part of its costs an insurance premium which it had paid shortly before trial to guard against its costs in case it had been unsuccessful in its defence. A party who threatens proceedings but withdraws before they are issued may be liable for the costs of the other party in preparing itself to defend the proceedings, see *Associated Newspaper v Impac* [2002] F.S.R. 18 at 293. In *Lubrizol v Esso* BL C/100/96, but not noted in the reported judgment [1997] R.P.C. 195, the court allowed costs for three counsels on the basis that employment of counsel in a complex case may be more economical than using an extra solicitor, but no justification was seen for the use of three counsels on the appeal (*Lubrizol v Esso* BL C/49/98, noted I.P.D. 21104, CA). In *Connaught Laboratories' Patent* (above), costs for three counsels were also permitted because of the technical complexity of the case.

In *Lenzing's European Patent* [1997] R.P.C. 245, where the European patent (UK) in suit was revoked during the infringement proceedings by an EPO Appeal Board, the defendant obtained its costs on the validity issue as well as that of infringement. The court held that the defendant had acted reasonably in petitioning for revocation upon the patent being upheld by the EPO at first instance and stated that a party should not be discouraged from petitioning for invalidity to defend itself against an infringement action. Where a claim for infringement was sought to be amended to introduce a new allegation while withdrawing that initially pleaded, the court ordered the pleaded claim to be dismissed with costs, leaving the claimant to make a fresh claim for the new allegation (*Texas Electronics v Hyundai Electronics* [2000] F.S.R. 86). In *Nutrinova v Scanchem (No.2)* [2001] F.S.R. 43 at 831, the unsuccessful defendant was awarded its costs of defending an allegation of infringement on one basis which had been replaced before trial by an amended plea on a different basis, although the claimant would obtain its costs (to the extent that the costs officer may regard these as reasonable in the circumstances) on its success on this alternative basis; and, as the patent was held only partially valid, the patentee's costs on the issue of validity were reduced to reflect its only partial success on this point. In *Niche Generics v Lundbeck* [2004] F.S.R. 20 at 392 costs of the attendance of the claimant's experts at an inspection of its process in India were awarded even though the patentee conceded, as a result of the inspection, that the requested declaration of non-infringement should be granted, because the claimants were justified in protecting their interests when the outcome of the inspection was in doubt. In *Merial v Sankyo* [2004] EWHC 3077 Pat Ct, costs were awarded against a defendant patentee that after service of a defence had decided not to contest revocation proceedings but where there had been no letter before action as the court, although observing that such a letter was desirable, did not consider it to be a necessary prerequisite, and held that in any case on the evidence it was unlikely that such a letter would have avoided litigation.

Costs unnecessarily incurred will be disallowed, e.g. as in: *Improver Corp v Remington* BL C/19/89 where all costs of accountants' reports providing evidence on the appropriate security to be given in respect of a cross-undertaking in return for an interim injunction were disallowed; and *Pall Corp v Commercial Hydraulics* [1990] F.S.R. 329 at 358, where the costs of experiments were disallowed as these had been of no value to the court. In *Rediffusion Simulation v Link-Miles* [1993] F.S.R. 369, the court stated:

"In patent actions the costs order should, in appropriate cases, reflect the extent to which significant sums of money have been thrown away by reason of one party, albeit successful overall, raising and pursuing unsuccessful points".

In *Bayer v Octapharma* [1999] F.S.R. 926, (before the issues-based approach became the norm) it was observed that a sensible way to cost the result of a patent infringement action when the validity of the patent had been put in issue was to award the principally successful party a percentage of its costs, but here the costs awarded to the defendant were reduced from two-thirds to one-half because of several omissions or actions on behalf of the defendant that had wasted time unnecessarily. In *Palmaz's European Patents* BL C/42/98, but not included in [1999] R.P.C. 47, the successful party was penalised in costs for an attack against the priority date of the patent-in-suit which was abandoned only shortly before trial. The court may also disallow costs incurred by a party as a result of any improper, unreasonable or negligent act or omission by a legal or other representative, or order these to be paid personally by such representative where the court considers that in the light of such act or omission it is unreasonable for the party itself to pay. Such a representative is defined as any person exercising a right of audience, or right to conduct litigation, on behalf of a party, see CPR 44.14. In exercising these powers as to "wasted costs", the guidelines set out in *Ridehalgh v Horsfield* [1994] 3 W.L.R. 462 CA can be expected to be followed. Under this provision, the Patents County Court has ordered a litigating patent agent to pay the claimant's costs incurred during a period when he acted without the authority of the defendant (*Bell Fruit Manufacturing v Twinfalcon* [1995] F.S.R. 144).

Criticisms by courts of the level of costs or of practices that the courts perceive as wasteful are not uncommon. As mentioned in §61.75 below the judge in *Merck v Generics [Alendronate product]* [2004] R.P.C. 31 at 607 was critical of costs incurred, particularly as a result of experiments. He commented that:

"while the parties must continue to have a major say in the way the litigation is run, this is subject to the court's management responsibilities under the CPR".

In *Mayne Pharma v Pharmacia Italia* [2005] EWCA Civ 137; [2005] I.P. & T. 774, the Court of Appeal criticised the volume of papers copied for the appeal, considering them not to be "relevant to proceedings in the Court of Appeal" within the meaning of CPR 52 PD15.1(1) and suggested that this be taken into account on assessment of costs. The judge in *Research in Motion UK Ltd v Visto Corp*, above, characterised the costs of the party that successfully attacked the validity of the patent as "disproportionately high" and declined to make an interim award of costs. In continuing litigation between these parties, Arnold J. ordered the parties to give an advance estimation of their costs: [2008] EWHC

3025 Pat Ct, noted in [2009] *CIPA* 44. In *Generics v Daiichi* [2008] EWHC 2958 Pat Ct, Kitchin J. observed, by way of guidance to the costs judge, that where £3.4 million had been claimed, "he had been left with the clear impression" that a proportionate gross (i.e. pre-assessment) figure for costs would not be in excess of £2 million, although he declined formally to make a costs-capping order.

Warheit v Olympia Tools (referred to in §60.27 above in relation to a preliminary point) was eventually heard in the Patents County Court. The Court of Appeal reversed the finding of the deputy judge on infringement by one of the defendants' products, but declined to interfere with the finding on validity. The Court of Appeal (reported on the issue of costs only at [2003] F.S.R. 6 at 95) ordered the defendants to pay the claimants' costs in both courts but expressed concern that the amounts claimed were £250,000 for the two-day trial and a further £112,000 for the appeal. It expressed the view that such costs could not have been envisaged by the Lord Chancellor when setting up the Patents County Court as a forum to encourage cheaper litigation. Also, the sums were not such as would normally be recovered in other complex cases in a County Court. Such remarks seem, however, to disregard the lack of any threshold either of financial value or of complexity determining whether cases should be brought in the Patents County Court or in the High Court. Although the technology involved in the case in point was relatively simple, the costs would be broadly in line with what would be expected in a Patents Court hearing, and there is no reason why the costs before the Patents County Court should be significantly different, other things (e.g. the representatives chosen) being equal.

In *CIPLA v Glaxo* [2004] EWHC 819 Ch, noted I.P.D. 27062, an order was made directing the costs judge to consider the costs of four separate and successful revocation actions that had been heard together as if they had been consolidated from the date when it had been ordered that evidence in the fourth action should stand as evidence in the other three and that all four claimants should file a consolidated statement of grounds of invalidity, the court recognising that despite the four applicants only having agreed to be represented by the same counsel at a late stage their commercial position was not entirely the same.

In *Tamglass v Luong North Glass and Novoglaze [Post Trial Order]* [2006] EWHC 443 Ch; BL C/24-25/06, noted I.P.D. 29031-2, a co-defendant who had played no active part in the proceedings and had done no more than not admit validity was made jointly liable with the active defendant for the costs relating to validity, with the exception of the costs of an abortive allegation of prior use. In *Quadrant Holdings v Quadrant Research* [1999] F.S.R. 918, a personal defendant claimed that he should only pay costs in respect of the claims made against him, but it was held that he had been at the centre of the proceedings and his actions were the core of all the issues in dispute and so he should be jointly liable with the other defendants for the costs order made against them jointly.

When the award of costs is to include a punitive element, e.g. when the claimant holds a certificate of contested validity on the patent-in-suit, costs may be awarded on the "indemnity" basis as defined in CPR 44.4(3) and 44.5(1)(b), as discussed in §65.04. In other situations, a court is likely to order that costs be paid on an "indemnity basis" only if satisfied that the paying party has conducted itself unreasonably in the litigation, see *Strix v Otter* [1991] F.S.R. 163 where indemnity costs were refused although the action had been struck out as disclosing no arguable case. In *Connaught Laboratories' Patent* [1999] F.S.R. 284, the case had proceeded to the day before trial when the patentee indicated a wish to surrender the patent (for which see §29.06); the court revoked the patent and ordered the payment of the costs of the petitioner for revocation on an indemnity basis from a date one week after the timetable for trial had been set by the court, thereby indicating that a punitive order for costs may be made when a party is seen to have used its patent as a commercial weapon unjustifiably.

Costs on an indemnity basis were awarded in respect of certain experiments in *Laboratorios Almirall v Boehringer Ingelheim* [2009] EWHC 439 Pat Ct.

When the court makes an order against a party who is not present when the order is made, the solicitor (or patent attorney litigator) has an obligation to notify the client (i.e. any person for whom he is acting or who has instructed him) in writing of that costs order within seven days of its receipt (CPR 44.2, and CPR 44 PD 7), made under CPR 44.2, requires that a solicitor (or patent attorney litigator) must "explain why the order came to be made", and the court may require to be satisfied that the solicitor (or patent attorney litigator) has taken reasonable steps to comply with this rule. Costs ordered must be paid within 14 days of the date of a summary assessment, or within that period from the date of a certificate of award following a detailed assessment (CPR 44.8). Interest on a fixed scale is payable on costs from the date when the trial order is made (*Hunt v Douglas* [1990] 1 A.C. 398; [1988] 3 All E.R. 823 HL).

An order for assessment of costs is not normally to be stayed pending appeal (CPR 47.2), but occasionally this was permitted under the former RSC, see *Minnesota Mining v Rennicks* [1992] R.P.C. 331 where security was ordered for repayment in the event of a successful appeal. Also, in *Lubrizol v Esso* [1997] F.S.R. 844, a stay of assessment of costs pending appeal was granted because of the complexity of the assessment, but only on condition that an interim payment of £1.7 million was made and that the paying party should timely serve its points of objection and any request for further and better particulars of the bill of costs be submitted, this having been for a total of £7.2 million on the standard basis. In *Nutrinova v Scanchem* (above) staged payments by way of an interim award were assessed on the basis of what it was seen the defendant could afford while continuing its other business. In *Canady v Erbe Elektromedizin [Costs]* [2006] EWHC 287 Pat Ct, an interim award of costs was made after trial against the unsuccessful claimant, but payment of this was staged in view of the claimant's evidence as to the award seriously affecting its ability to proceed with its appeal.

On appeal, the appeal court makes its own order as to costs, but it can reverse the costs order made by the court below (see CPR 44.13(2)), e.g. by an order that the successful party on appeal have its costs "here and below". However, no appeal is possible solely on an issue of costs (Senior Courts Act 1981 (c.54) s.18(1)(f), see *Prout v British Gas* [1994] F.S.R. 160).

As noted at §61.39 in proceedings in the Patents County Court there has, since October 1, 2010, by virtue of the Civil Procedure (Amendment No.2) Rules 2010 (SI 2010/1953) (see §G38), been a limit on the costs which a party can be ordered to pay to the other for each stage of a claim, and on the total costs payable to the other on the final determination of a claim relating to liability and on an inquiry as to damages or an account of profits. This does not apply to cases started in the Patents County Court before that date; *Technical Fibre Products v Bell (D.R)* [2010] EWPCC 011.

—The "Earth Closet" or "See v Scott-Paine" order

For over 50 years, it used to be customary that, where a defendant to an infringement **61.35** action sought to amend his defence to allege a new ground of invalidity, the claimant was given a period of time within which he could elect to discontinue the action. If he did so, the normal order as to costs (sometimes called an *Earth Closet* order, from the case in which it was originally devised) is that the defendant had its costs up to the date of serving the original defence, but the claimant had his costs thereafter up to the date of discontinuing the action (*See v Scott-Paine* (1933) 50 R.P.C. 56, approved in *Williamson v Moldline* [1986] R.P.C. 556 CA, and followed in *Vestar v Liposome Technology* [1995] F.S.R. 391). The availability of this order therefore required the defendant to put forward complete particulars of objection at a reasonably early date in the proceedings and it was said that the usual order would be departed from only where the new defence could not, by reasonable diligence, have been discovered earlier, even where there is a late allegation of prior use (*Gill v Chipman* [1987] R.P.C. 209). However, increasingly, when a *See v Scott-Paine* order was sought, the court came to consider the merits in each case and then decided, as a matter of discretion, whether such order should be made and, if so, from what date it should take effect, see *Behr-Thomson v Western Thomson* [1990] R.P.C. 569.

However, since then, the availability and wording of this type of order was increasingly restricted in various decisions, culminating in *GEC Alsthom's Patent* [1996] F.S.R. 415 where it was held that the question of a *See v Scott-Paine* order is essentially one of discretion, to be decided in the light of such factors as the lateness of the application to amend the pleadings, the extent to which that lateness could be explained and the extent to which the patentee would be taken by surprise and particularly whether the attacking party had been reasonably diligent. It was noted that an order of this type is a blunt instrument which could cause injustice and cause a party attacking validity to withhold more pertinent prior art than that already cited because it could not run the risk of the patentee consenting to revocation, yet claiming virtually all of its costs under such an order, which was against the public interest in relation to the validity of the patent. In the circumstances of this case, such an order was refused as amendment was sought shortly before the fixed trial date. In this *GEC* case, although the attacking party had known for some time of the document it now wished to cite, enquiries had had to be made as to its availability to the public, but the patentee had known of the document and so was not taken by surprise. For case comments, see [1997] E.I.P.R. 90 and *Patent World* (107, December 1998/January 1999, 41). Then, in *Hewitt v McCann* [1998] F.S.R. 688, a *See v Scott-Paine* order was held to be inappropriate in circumstances where the defendant was no more guilty than was either party in allowing proceedings to have drifted aimlessly for some time. In *CIL International v Vitrashop* [2002] F.S.R. 4 at 67 the court declined to make such an order, observing that the amendment to the pleadings would have come as no surprise to the claimant, and an allegation that the defendant had not been diligent in making the amendment was dismissed, the application having been made within a month of the facts coming to the defendant's attention. In *Monitoring Technologies v Bell Group* [2003] EWHC 3136 Pat Ct, noted I.P.D. 27015, the court declined in the circumstances to make a *See v Scott-Paine* order, referring to its decision in *GEC Alsthom's Patent* and observing that:

"there is no precision in a decision whether or not to make a *See v Scott-Paine* order ..., it is possible in some cases that a *See v Scott-Paine* order could work an injustice to the defendant by allowing a patentee who already knows it has an extremely fragile case to get out at the last minute with the burden of costs being imposed upon the defendant. So it can present a windfall to a patentee with a very weak patent. On the other hand, it can also act as a useful, and indeed vital, stimulus to defendants to plead properly and early."

It seemed until recently that such orders could still be made on occasion. In *Baxter Healthcare v Abbott Laboratories* [2006] EWHC 2693 Pat Ct the revocation claimant sought to add further allegations of invalidity by the patentee's own prior use arising from disclosure in documents produced by it. Amendment was allowed, but this was followed by a discussion of whether a See v Scott Paine Order would be available to the patentee if it chose to accept invalidity of the patent. Because neither party had initially appreciated the significance of these disclosures, it was held that such an order was available, but only as to costs from the date of the last amendment of the grounds of objection to validity. However, in *Fresenius v Carefusion* [2011] EWCA Civ 1288 the Court of Appeal held that the practice of making such orders was open to challenge and should now be discontinued. Lewison L.J. explained:

"There was some debate about how usual such orders are,although it is right to note that Terrell on Patents (17th edition para.18–122) says that that is the practice that is 'almost invariably followed'. In our judgment the sooner the practice stops the better. The specimen form of order in the Patents Court Guide (and reproduced in the White Book) should be amended to remove the paragraph containing such an order. The Earth Closet order should be consigned to the place that bears its name."

It therefore appears that the provisions included in The Standard Form of the Order for Directions in patent litigation at §G21 para.3 are no longer appropriate and that they will in due course be removed.

—Costs of interim proceedings

As noted in §61.34, the court has power to award interim costs and indeed is encour- **61.36**
aged (by CPR 44 PD 13), to make an immediate order by way of "summary assessment"
at the end of any pre-trial hearing at which one party has been completely successful,
particularly one that has lasted less than one day.

For this purpose, each party who may wish to seek an order for immediate payment of
costs is required to supply every other party with a brief summary of the costs of the application that he would seek to recover if such an order is made, stating the amount and
nature of disbursements, including counsel's fees and the amount of the solicitor's profit
costs (which, if assessed on an hourly rate, specifying the number of hours, the rate per
hour and the grade of the fee earner), together with any VAT to be claimed on it: if this is
not done, the court has to take account of the failure in deciding on the terms of the order
to be made (CPR 44 PD 13.5). Otherwise, the court may make a variety of orders having
effect for postponing the assessment or disallowing costs for particular issues, see for
example the summary of wording used in costs order set out in CPR 44 PD 8.4. In *Goldschmidt v EOC Belgium* BL C/42/99, noted I.P.D. 22083, the defendants who had sought
leave to amend their pleadings seven weeks before the scheduled trial date were given the
option of election (within seven days) either to continue with the trial without amendment
or have leave to amend the pleadings but with: (1) payment to the claimant of all costs occasioned by the amendment on an indemnity basis; all other costs to date to be the
claimant's costs in the case so that if the claimant succeeded the claimant would not have
to pay any costs of the defendant up to the date of this hearing; and (2) a new date for the
trial should be fixed at the earliest date convenient to the claimant, its solicitors and
counsel, although this order should only apply to the one of the three patents in issue for
which the alternative construction was sought to be claimed.

If the court, at the end of a pre-trial hearing, does not undertake a summary assessment
of costs for immediate payment, then, unless there is a specific order that costs "should be
taxed and paid forthwith", any order then made for detailed assessment of costs remains
ineffective until the conclusion of the action. Of course, this will necessarily be so where
the order is one of "costs in the case" or "costs reserved".

Where an application for an interim injunction is not pursued but stood over to the trial,
it has been customary for the costs to be "costs in the case" but, in *Scotnet v Trunature* BL
C/91/96, this practice was seen sometimes to have been too rigidly applied; and, in the
case of a defendant being a small company "fighting for its life", the defendant's costs of
the abandoned interim proceedings were ordered to be taxed and paid forthwith. *Per
contra*, where the claimant has made out a very strong case, the court may be prepared to
award a lump sum of costs for the proceedings for interim relief to be paid within a short
period, as in the trade mark case of *Direct Line Group v Direct Line Estate Agency* [1997]
F.S.R. 374.

In *Novartis v Natco* [2004] EWHC 817 Ch the claimant sought its costs of an application for an interim injunction that it withdrew when the defendant gave suitable undertakings over to trial. Recognising that the claim might fail the court ordered "claimants costs
in cause" (which it assessed at £8,000), which the claimant would accordingly only receive
were it to succeed at trial.

—Effect on costs of offers of settlement

In order to limit liability for costs in proceedings, it is possible to make a payment into **61.37**
court, or to make an offer of settlement, each under the terms of the CPR Pt 36 (not
reprinted in this Work). Where the claimant does not accept this offer within 21 days, then,
if the amount of the payment-in, or offer, is equal to, or greater than, the amount which the
successful party recovers at the end of the proceedings (including any interest element of
the final award), the effect of such a payment or offer is normally to extinguish the paying
party's liability for costs incurred after the time when the other party (normally the claimant) should have accepted the payment and to award the paying party its costs thereafter.
This rule applies because the other party could have taken the payment-in, or accepted the
offer, and obtained all that he was ultimately awarded, and he should have done so and not

wasted the court's time and the parties' money. Thus, a payment into court, or more usually a written offer of a settlement payment, can be a powerful tool in putting pressure upon a claimant to settle proceedings since, if he does not accept the offer in the letter and subsequently fails to recover more at the trial, he will be exposed to a substantial liability in costs, including all the costs of the trial which is normally by far the most expensive part of the action.

However, in patent infringement proceedings, the claimant is normally seeking an injunction and delivery up, in addition to damages or an account of profits. Consequently, accepting the payment-in will not give the claimant everything that he would have been awarded at the trial and, if he is successful and obtains his injunction and delivery up, he will have recovered at the trial more than the payment-in and so be entitled to his costs of the trial and of the subsequent enquiry as to damages. However, under CPR Pt 36, a payment-in, or offer, can be tied to a particular issue or issues; and a payment into court, or settlement offer, may be effective when the patent has expired or the defendant has ceased the alleged infringing acts. An offer of settlement can also be made with specific regard to an interim or preliminary issue and, thus, be effective as regards any summary assessment of costs following resolution of that issue.

An offer to settle the action, as an alternative to making a payment into court, must be made in writing, must state its terms explicitly, and be open for 21 days, see CPR 36.3. Where there has been a "Part 36"payment-in, or settlement offer, the judge must not be informed, or made aware, of this prior to post-trial argument as to a costs order, but is then required to take its terms into account before making a costs order, see CPR 36.13 and 36.14 (not reprinted in this Work). In *Smith, Kline & French v Harbottle* [1980] R.P.C. 363, there was an interesting discussion on the award of costs when the action for infringement succeeded against two defendants, one of whom had made payment into court before trial.

Complex issues as to payment of costs following Pt 36 offers and payments in were addressed in further proceedings in *Dyson v Hoover (No.2) [Costs]* [2003] F.S.R. 21 at 394. In *Kavanagh Balloons v Cameron Balloons* [2004] R.P.C. 5; [2004] F.S.R. 698 at [33]; I.P.D. 27035, the Court of Appeal, having observed that:

"it cannot be right that the practice in relation to costs should be any different as between patent cases in the County Court and those in the High Court",

held that the judge in the Patents County Court had made errors of principle both in not making a costs order based on assessing costs incurred before the making of a Pt 36 offer on an issue by issue basis, and in not awarding the costs after the making of the Pt 36 offer to the defendants making the offer, when this offer had "uncannily predicted most of the conclusions at which the judge had arrived" and when the offer, if accepted, would have disposed of this matter before trial. In *Ultraframe v Eurocell [Costs]* [2006] EWHC 1679 Pat Ct the court refused to award indemnity costs in a damages enquiry against a defendant that had not accepted an offer made by the claimant to settle at the outset of the liability proceedings and another at the outset of the enquiry, as it was not unreasonable for it not to have accepted them.

Proceedings before the Comptroller (subs.(3))

61.38   Infringement proceedings can be held before the Comptroller under subs.(3), and all references in the Act to "infringement proceedings" include proceedings under this subsection (subs.(4)(a)). However, such proceedings can take place only with the consent of the parties, and relief is limited to damages and a declaration under subs.(1)(c) and (e) respectively (for which see §61.23 and §61.31 respectively). A declaration of non-infringement can be sought unilaterally under s.71, see *Hawker-Siddeley v Real Time* [1983] R.P.C. 395, though the reversal of the burden of proof may then be a serious obstacle to use of s.71, see §71.04. In view of the limited relief which the Comptroller can grant, there is some doubt whether subs.(3) is entirely compliant with art.49 of the TRIPS Agreement, which reads:

"TRIPS ARTICLE 49—Administrative procedures

To the extent that any civil remedy can be ordered as a result of administrative procedures on the merits of a case, such procedures shall conform to principles equivalent in substance to those set forth in this Section."

In this Article, the words "this Section" refer to arts 42–48 of the TRIPS Agreement, for which see §§61.03 and 61.07.

Proceedings before the Comptroller cannot be started if there are already any proceedings before the court involving the patent in question, unless the court gives leave, see s.74(7) discussed in §74.06. While an injunction cannot be granted by the Comptroller, a decision on infringement by the Comptroller will probably create an issue estoppel. As a consequence, court proceedings against continuing infringement by the same party could lead to an injunction under summary procedure. However, a defendant could still challenge validity as for this no estoppel is created by the Comptroller's decision in view of s.72(5), see §72.17, but he could then be faced with a certificate of contested validity under s.65, see §65.04.

The apparent advantages of cheapness and expedition of proceedings under subs.(3) have not led to any cases under the present Act. There were only two cases under the analogous s.67 of the 1949 Act, one of which was reported (*Central Electricity v Chamberlain* [1958] R.P.C. 217). Some economies are possible, including representation by the patent attorney alone and the presentation of evidence more succinctly to a technically qualified tribunal, but these are offset because the Comptroller can only grant damages and cannot grant an injunction, nor order delivery up, nor order an account of profits. Under subs.(4)(a) and s.62(1), ignorance of the existence of the patent can be pleaded as affecting the relief granted by the Comptroller.

Now that the Patents County Court is in operation, where the parties do not have to use counsel and can be represented by a single professional, who can be a patent attorney, solicitor or counsel, (for which see §§292.02 and 292.03), it seems likely that subs.(3) will remain unused, in particular because of the wider relief available before the Patents County Court. However, in *Multiform v Whitmarley* [1956] R.P.C. 143 CA; and [1957] R.P.C. 260 HL the Court of Appeal regretted that the parties had not availed themselves of the procedure under s.67 of the 1949 Act to determine whether the defendants were in contempt of an injunction previously imposed when they had introduced a modified device.

The procedure under subs.(3) is set out in Pt 7 of the 2007 Rules (most of which are reprinted in §§123.06–123.21). Proceedings are started when a person files PF 2 in duplicate together with a statement of grounds. The Comptroller will send the relevant form and the statement of grounds to the defendant and specify a period within which the defendant may file a counter-statement which must be filed in duplicate within the period specified by the Comptroller. The Comptroller sends the counter-statement to the claimant and specifies the periods within which evidence may be filed by the claimant and the defendant. The Comptroller must then give the parties an opportunity to be heard and send to the parties notice of a date for the hearing, after which the Comptroller notifies all the parties of his decision, including his reasons for making it. Time periods may be extended under r.81(1), and the general powers of the Comptroller to regulate proceedings before him are set out in rr.82–84.

The Comptroller may decline to deal with the matter and require the matter to be referred to the court (subs.(5)), and the court shall then determine the matter, see CPR 63.11 (reprinted at §F63.11).

If the Comptroller finds the patent invalid, the defendant can then apparently apply under s.72(1) for revocation. Presumably an application for revocation under s.72 could run concurrently with the s.61 proceedings before the Comptroller, just as the two issues of infringement and validity are usually dealt with together in proceedings before the court. The same rules referred to above are stated to apply to proceedings for revocation under s.72 as well as infringement proceedings before the Comptroller under s.61(3). Likewise, there could be concurrent proceedings for amendment under s.27, which are governed by r.35 (see §27.02). A determination by the Comptroller, or on appeal from the Comptroller, that the defendant's act is or is not an infringement will apparently bind the parties in subsequent proceedings based upon similar facts.

The application of the Arbitration Act 1996 (c.23) to subs.(3) proceedings is specifically excluded by s.130(8), see §130.12. Under s.97, the decision of the Comptroller is subject to appeal to the Patents Court and from there, with leave, to the Court of Appeal. If the proceedings before the Comptroller are held in Scotland, the corresponding appellate courts are the Outer House and the Inner House of the Court of Session (s.97(4) and (5)).

New subs.(7) provides a mechanism for enforcement of an award of damages made by the Comptroller under subs.(3). This mechanism is the same as that for enforcement of an award of damages by a county court in England and the corresponding mechanisms in Scotland and Northern Ireland, the wording for Scotland being brought into conformity with that already present in ss.93(b) and 107(3). There is therefore now a uniform mechanism for the recovery of compensation or costs arising from a decision of the Comptroller under any of ss.41, 61, 93 and 107.

Costs in proceedings before the Comptroller are considered in §§107.03 and 107.04.

Infringement proceedings in a Patents County Court

61.39   The CDPA 1988 provided skeleton primary legislation for the creation of one or more patents county courts to operate in England and Wales, under the County Courts Act 1984 (c.28). These provisions are discussed in the commentaries on these sections. To date, only a single such court had been set up, see §287.02. Although this court is constituted under the county court system, unlike the normal county court there are no limits on the amounts which can be claimed in patent infringement proceedings by way of damages, see §288.02.

As in proceedings before the Patents Court, proceedings in the Patents County Court are now governed by the CPR.

Since October 1, 2010, by virtue of the Civil Procedure (Amendment No.2) Rules 2010 (SI 2010/1953) (see §G38) been a limit on the total costs which a party can be ordered to pay to the other for each stage of a claim and on the total costs on the final determination of a claim on certain types of proceeding. The limit on total costs stands at £50,000 on the final determination of a claim relating to liability, and £25,000 on an inquiry as to damages or an account of profits. The limit on the costs that can be ordered in relation to each stage of the claim are set out in a Costs Practice Direction (see §F45PD.01), but the actual costs awarded in respect of each such stage will depend on the nature and complexity of the claim. This does not apply to cases started in the Patents County Court before that date; *Technical Fibre Products v Bell (D.R)* [2010] EWPCC 011. The first judgment applying the new rules to the costs of a full action through to trial, and discussing in detail the approach to be applied in so doing, was *Westwood v Knight (Costs)* [2011] EWPCC 11, which action had concerned largely successful allegations of trade mark and copyright infringement and passing off and which had been transferred to the Patents County Court at an early stage.

PRACTICE UNDER SECTION 61

Scope

61.40   This work is not a textbook on court procedure. Therefore only a very brief introduction to the more general rules is given here. For details of court procedure, more specialised works should be consulted, particularly *Civil Procedure* (the "*White Book*"), (London: Sweet & Maxwell).

The Courts' Jurisdiction to Hear Cases Brought Under Section 61

61.41   Under the provisions of the Senior Courts Act 1981 ss.6 and 62, patent cases are heard by either the Patents Court (a part of the Chancery Division of the High Court) or, under the "special jurisdiction" given to the Patents County Court by virtue of CPDA 1988 s.287.

Practice in both courts is governed by the Civil Procedure Rules (CPR). In addition procedure in patents cases is modified by CPR 63 (Intellectual Property Claims); reprinted in

Appendix F and its accompanying practice direction. Further authoritative guidance on the conduct of patent cases is found in the Chancery Guide, the Patents Court Guide and the Patents County Court Guide (all issued under the authority of the Chancellor of the High Court). For the scope of the jurisdiction of the Patents County Court, and the extent to which it differs from that of a normal County Court, see para 1.2 of the Patents County Court Guide.

Practice before the Comptroller is dealt with in the commentary on s.123. This includes any action for infringement brought before the Comptroller under subs.(3).

For brief remarks on court practice in Scotland, see the commentary on s.98 and, for Northern Ireland or the Isle of Man, see respectively the commentary on ss.131 and 132.

The Differing Roles of the Patents Court and the Patents County Court

A potential litigant must decide in which court to commence its case. Generally, **61.42** complex high value litigation belongs in the Patents Court. In contrast, the Patents County Court is intended for smaller, less complex matters and an important part of its function is to make litigation cheaper and more accessible, particularly for individuals and small- and medium-sized companies (see the report of the Intellectual Property Court Users' Committee entitled "Working Group's Final Report on Proposals for Reform of the Patents County Court", published on July 31, 2009).

Section 1.3 of the most recent edition of the Patents County Court Guide (May 2011) describes the purpose of the Patents County Court as follows:

"In deciding the court in which to commence a claim, users should bear in mind that the Patents County Court was established to handle the smaller, shorter, less complex, less important, lower value actions and the procedures applicable in the court are designed particularly for cases of that kind. The court aims to provide cheaper, speedier and more informal procedures to ensure that small and medium sized enterprises, and private individuals, are not deterred from innovation by the potential cost of litigation to safeguard their rights. Longer, heavier, more complex, more important and more valuable actions belong in the High Court. Parties may agree with each other to maintain a case in the Patents County Court if they wish to make use of the procedures available in it. The court will endeavour to accommodate parties in that respect. The court will however maintain its list in such a way as to ensure that it maintains access to justice for small and medium sized enterprises".

Since the last edition of this Work there has been a profound change in the procedure and practice of the Patents County Court. In particular, costs and damages caps now apply to its proceedings. Furthermore, the rules of procedure are tailored to limit the scope of proceedings and to provide shorter (maximum two-day) cheaper trials. In consequence it is now more important than ever to consider in which court a case should be brought. Save where stated otherwise, the procedure discussed below applies to both the Patents Court and the Patents County Court. The new procedure specific to the Patents County Court is discussed in more detail in §§61.81–87 below.

Both the Patents Court and the Patents County court may be prepared to sit out of London on any intellectual property matter (see Patents Court Guide, para.5, Patents County Court Guide, para.1.5).

Representation

Solicitors and patent attorney litigators may conduct actions in the Patents Court and **61.43** Patents County Court. Advocacy in respect of Patent matters in the Patents Court is generally performed by either barristers or by solicitor advocates with appropriate higher court qualifications. In addition, in the Patents County Court any patent attorney may both conduct and appear in relation to cases falling into the Patents County Court's "special jurisdiction". For other cases in the Patents County Court a patent attorney litigator has a right of audience. Finally a patent attorney may conduct litigation, and has a right of audience, in the Patents Court in relation to matters on appeal from the UK-IPO.

In both the Patents Court and Patents County Court a litigant may appear in person and an appropriately authorised officer of a company may represent that company (see Chancery Guide, Ch.15, paras 15.1–15.11, Patents County Court Guide para.1.7). With permission of the court, an employee of a company may represent the company: see CPR 39.6.

At any hearing it is necessary to supply the court with the name and address of each advocate, his/her qualification or entitlement to act as advocate and the party for which he/she acts (CPR 39A PD 5.1).

Transfer Between Patents Court and Patents County Court and Referral to the Court of Justice (CJEU)

61.44   The CPR provides that the Patents Court may, either on application by a party or by its own motion, transfer a case over which the Patents County Court has jurisdiction to that court, and vice versa (see CPR Part 63.18, 63.25(4) & (5) and CPR 63 PD 30). Note that the Patents Court has no power to transfer a case already in the Patents County Court out of that court, if the case is one which lies within the latter's special jurisdiction (see CPDA s.289(1)).

If an application to transfer to the High Court is made in the Patents County Court, that application must, other than in exceptional circumstances, be made before the Case Management Conference (see Patents County Court Guide ss.1.3 and 2.6). The court has discretion whether or not to transfer. The principles on which the discretion to transfer are exercised are discussed in *ALK-Abello v Meridian* [2010] EWPCC 014 (see also ss.1.3 and 2.6 of the Patents County Court Guide) and *Caljan Rite v Sovex* [2011] EWHC 669 (Ch).

If a case is transferred from the Patents Court to the Patents County Court (even if the case commenced before the new Patents County Court rules) the new rules will apply on transfer (see *Caljan Rite v Sovex* [2011] EWHC 669 (Ch)).

When a "Euro-defence" is put forward (for which see §61.33) it may be necessary to re-mit questions of Community law to the Court of Justice of the European Union ("CJEU") in Luxembourg.

Conduct of an Action

61.45   The general conduct of any action is governed pursuant to the "overriding objective" of the CPR: namely to provide speedy and judicious resolution of disputes (CPR 1.1). The court has extensive case management powers to further this objective (particularly in CPR 3.1). Failure to comply with general case management principles may result in adverse costs awards (including in certain cases against the litigators themselves).

In addition there are various matters of conduct and case management particular to patent cases. The Patents Court Guide draws attention to a number of patent-specific matters such as the need for and scope of admissions, oral testimony, experts, experiments and process/product descriptions, as well as issues of costs and desirability of alternative dispute resolution and/or mediation. Also of note is the requirement to identify those claims of a patent which are alleged to have independent validity.

In technically complex cases the court may order the production of a document setting out basic undisputed technology (a "Primer") (see CPR PD 63 para.5.10, *Hoechst Celanese v BP Chemicals* [1998] F.S.R. 586, *Qualcomm Inc v Nokia Corp* [2008] EWHC 329 Pat Ct).

The Patents County Court has additional and significant differences in matters of case management. These are in the Patents County Court Guide and are discussed below in §61.85.

There are a number of distinct phases in most patent cases, namely pre-action correspondence, pleadings, admissions/further information, disclosure, evidence and trial preparation (including bundling). All such phases are also possible in the Patents County Court. However, as discussed below, some phases, in particular disclosure, are more likely to be excluded as a matter of case management. The directions to be followed to trial are generally ordered at a Case Management Conference after pleadings have closed.

Both the Patents Court (in the Patents Court Guide) and the Patents County Court (in the Patents County Court Guide) provide specimen orders setting out typical directions that will be required for the conduct of a patent action (although, of course, these are liable to be varied on a case by case basis).

In addition, parties may apply for interim remedies to assist in the conduct of the action.

Listing of Cases and Applications

All patent matters are automatically assigned to the multitrack and parties do not need **61.46** to file an allocation questionnaire (CPR 63.8(1))—note however that the possibility of small track and/or fast tracks in the Patents County Court is under consideration, see the Patents County Court Guide, para.5.3. The listing of all hearings in patent matters is made through the Chancery Listing Office (Patents Court Guide s.12). The Patents Court and the Patents County Court form specialist lists for the purposes of CPR 30.5. The procedures for issuing proceedings and applications and for listing in the Patents County Court are set out in s.3 of the current Patents County Court Guide (May 12, 2011).

Applications (Other Than for Case Management Conferences)

If, prior to trial, a party needs the court to determine the course of a step in the action or **61.47** to apply for an interim remedy (for which see below), that party may apply pursuant to CPR 23 for an order to that effect.

Generally, all applications are made on at least three days' notice to the other parties, using an Application Notice (CPR 23.3 and 23.4). The rules also provide that in certain circumstances applications may be made without notice to the other party (i.e. ex parte). Examples of the latter are very urgent interim injunctions and search orders (see below). Applications in the Patents Court are generally, but not inevitably, dealt with by way of a hearing (unless agreed). Applications in the Patents County Court are dealt with without a hearing unless the court considers a hearing necessary (CPR Part 63.25(3)).

Applications in relation to patent matters are applications in specialist proceedings (in accordance with CPR 23.2) and therefore also governed by the Patents Practice Direction, the Patents Court Guide or the Patents County Court Guide. The jurisdiction of Chancery Masters in patent cases is limited (CPR 63 PD 5.2). In consequence the majority of inter-locutory hearings (as well as the trial) are heard by a Patents Judge and therefore must be listed accordingly. The reader is referred to the *White Book* for a more detailed exposition of CPR 23.

Up-to-date copies of the Patents Court Guide, the Patents County Court Guide and the Patents Practice Direction should be consulted to confirm detailed matters of procedure, as these are subject to change. The following are some current matters of note.

For all hearings, except the most urgent ex parte hearings, papers (including skeleton arguments), should be lodged with the judge's clerk usually by noon at least two days before the date fixed for hearing (or 10.30am the previous working day in the Patents County Court, see para.3.4(a) Patents County Court Guide). The texts of important documents, such as the patent-in-suit, the witness statements and expert reports, should also be supplied on a computer disk. All documents should generally be bundled as set out in the Chancery Guide. Short matters not involving a matter of public interest can be dealt with by a telephone conference with the judge and a party may be refused its costs where it ought to have applied for such a conference (see CPR PD 23A para.6.2, CPR PD 63 para.30.1, Patents County Court Guide s.3.5), *Hewitt v McCann* [1998] F.S.R. 688). Since an application will be heard in chambers, attendance on such an application (whether in person or by telephone) may be by a solicitor (or a patent attorney litigator) even though in many cases that application will be heard by an assigned judge of the Patents Court rather than by a Chancery Master.

Where the parties are agreed as to an order they wish the court to make, the order may be made without attendance. A draft of the agreed order, preferably accompanied by a disk recording the agreed terms for the order, should be supplied together with the written consent of all the respective parties' solicitors or counsel, and unless the judge considers a hearing is needed, he will make the order in the agreed terms which will then be drawn up and sent to the parties.

Interim Remedies

61.48   The court has wide powers under CPR 25 to order interim remedies to assist the conduct of an action (including at the pre-action stage). A discussion of the majority of such remedies lies outside the ambit of this book. However, attention is drawn to the availability of interim injunctions, (see §§61.17 et seq) and, as discussed below, search (*"Anton Piller"*) orders, orders for interim payments, and orders for detention and/or inspection of property.

All remedies available in the Patents Court, including the said interim remedies, are available in the Patents County Court. However, it seems likely that the extent to which the Patents County Court is liable to grant such remedies may be curtailed as a matter of case management (for which see §61.85 below).

Interim Remedies: the Search (Formerly Anton Piller) Order

61.49   Where the court can be persuaded that there is a grave danger that vital evidence may be destroyed if the party concerned is forewarned, the court may order pursuant to CPR 25.1(1)(h) that solicitors be authorised to enter the party's premises and remove or take copies of documents in specified categories in order that evidence may be preserved (*Swedac v Magnet & Southern* [1989] F.S.R. 243). This order, formerly known as an *Anton Piller* order, following its approval in *Anton Piller v Manufacturing Processes* [1976] R.P.C. 719 CA, was put on a statutory basis by the Civil Procedure Act 1997 (c.12) s.7. Note, however, that like other forms of relief, search orders are now subject to the EU Enforcement Directive 2004/48/EC as implemented by SI 2006/1028. In the case of search orders this is, however, unlikely to make a significant difference to current practice.

Because of the draconian nature of the relief, a search order is only made when very strict requirements have been satisfied, and there are also very strict requirements as to how any search is executed. As with other forms of interim relief, the claimant seeking such an order must give a cross-undertaking in damages and a foreign claimant may be required to provide security for that undertaking. Because an order of this kind is inevitably made without notice to the (prospective) defendant, there is an obligation upon the claimant to disclose to the court all material facts, even those adverse to the claimant (*Thermax v Schott* [1981] F.S.R. 289). The reader is referred to the *White Book* for a detailed discussion of the requirements and mechanics of obtaining a search order.

Note that failure to comply with a search order is a contempt of court, even if the order is subsequently discharged (*Wardle Fabrics v Myristis* [1984] F.S.R. 263). In *Taylor Made Golf Co v Rata & Rata* [1996] F.S.R. 528, it was held that there had been a cynical and deliberate failure by a partnership to comply with an *Anton Piller* order. While a custodial sentence was not imposed, the court imposed a fine of £75,000.

Interim Remedies: Inspection of Property

61.50   Besides the inspection of documents produced on disclosure under CPR 31 (discussed below), it is possible to obtain an order of interim relief under CPR 25.1(1)(c):

"for the detention, custody or preservation of relevant property; for the inspection of relevant property; for the taking of a sample of relevant property; or for the carrying out of an experiment on or with relevant property",

"relevant property" being property "which is the subject of a claim or as to which any question may arise on a claim". (CPR 25.1(2). See also CPR 63 PD 4.5, reprinted in Appendix F, which provide that the court may order inspection of machine or apparatus where a party alleges such machinery or apparatus was used before the priority date of the claim.)

An order for inspection of third party property may be obtained under CPR 25.5. Such an order is likely to be refused if it is seen as a "fishing" exercise, so that mere suspicion that infringement may be taking place is not sufficient: a prima facie case must first be established (see *British Xylonite v Fibrenyle* [1959] R.P.C. 252; *Wahl v Buhler-Miag* [1979] F.S.R. 183; and *Unilever Plc v Pearce* [1985] F.S.R. 475). Likewise, the scope of the inspection may be limited and/or subject to conditions of confidentiality (*British*

Celanese Ltd v Courtaulds Ltd (1933) 52 R.P.C. 63; and *British Thomson-Houston Co Ltd v Duram Ltd (No.2)* (1920) R.P.C. 475). Nevertheless, in a suitable case, inspection of an alleged infringing process can be carried out even before service of an adequate statement of claim (*Unilever v Pearce*, above). Here the inspection was in confidence, and the claimant's representatives were required to supply to the defendant a report of its inspection; a patent attorney employed by the claimant was permitted to attend this in his professional capacity. Note that leave for employees to attend an inspection was refused as being excessive in *Niche Generics v Lundbeck* [2004] F.S.R. 20.

Additionally, the court also has power to direct a party with access to information not reasonably available to the other party to prepare and file a document recording the information and serve a copy on the other party (CPR 35.9 and CPR 35 PD 4).

Interim Remedies: Security for costs

Under CPR 25.12–25.15, a court may, in its discretion, order that a claimant provide security for some or all of the costs of litigation (including on appeal), provided at least one of four conditions is also satisfied. The conditions are that: (i) the claimant is resident out of the jurisdiction but not resident in a Brussels Contracting State, a Lugano Contracting State or a Regulation State; (ii) the claimant is a company or other body and there is reason to believe that it will be unable to pay the defendant's costs if ordered to do so; (iii) the claimant has changed his address since the claim was commenced with a view to evading the consequences of the litigation; (iv) the claimant failed to give his address in the claim form, or gave an incorrect address in that form; (v) the claimant is acting as a nominal claimant (other than a representative claimant), and there is reason to believe he will be unable to pay the defendant's costs; (vi) the claimant has taken steps in relation to his assets that would make it difficult to enforce an order for costs against him.

61.51

A defendant can also seek security against someone other than the claimant if he can satisfy the court that it would be just to order security to be given having regard to all the circumstances, for example where an assignment of the claim has been made to avoid the possibility of a costs order or where the other party has agreed to contribute to the claimant's costs in return for a share of any financial recovery: note that this could include a lawyer acting on a contingency basis. Security for costs of an appeal can be ordered likewise.

A defendant, however, is entitled to defend proceedings brought against him without being required to give any security for the costs of the action. This applies also to a defendant in patent infringement proceedings who counterclaims for revocation as part of his defence, because a counterclaim is not strictly necessary and does not affect the relief he can enjoy, see *Norprint v S.P.J. Labels* [1979] F.S.R. 126.

If the court is satisfied that a security order is appropriate, it has complete discretion as to the amount of security and the manner in which it shall be given, but in patent litigation it is customary to require a guarantee for costs to be provided by a clearing bank situated in England or Wales or by an indemnity given by a local company with adequate assets to meet a likely award of costs: *GSK v Apotex* [2003] F.S.R. 20.

If the security ordered is not produced within the time set, the action can be dismissed: *Speed Up Holdings v Gough* [1986] F.S.R. 330.

The issue of security is discussed in much greater detail in the *White Book*.

Before Commencing an Action

Unlike many other areas of litigation, the CPR provides no specific pre-action protocol for patent cases. However, this does not relieve a party from the general requirement to conduct pre-action correspondence in accordance with the CPR and in particular the overriding objective and also with the Practice Direction—Pre-Action Conduct (see *http://www.justice.gov.uk/guidance/courts-and-tribunals/courts/procedure-rules/civil/menus/protocol.htm*). An attempt to comply with the Practice Direction may well require entering into comparatively detailed correspondence with the potential defendant identifying matters such as (i) the patent(s) relied upon; (ii) the alleged instances of infringement; (iii) relevant legal analysis (in brief); (iv) a request for undertakings and/or other appropriate

61.52

relief; and (v) the potential claimant's intention in the event that such undertakings are not forthcoming. Failure to conduct adequate pre-action discussion may affect any award of costs. Note however, the possibility that such correspondence may lead to proceedings under the "threats" provisions of s.70 of the Patents Act. Exactly what should, in all the circumstances, be said (and therefore the extent to which the "threats provisions" are engaged), will be a matter of judgment in every case. It follows that care should be taken in respect of drafting such a letter and particular care attention is drawn in particular to the exceptions in s.70(4) and (5) discussed in §§70.07–70.08.

Note that in the Patents County Court, failure to comply with the Practice Direction—Pre-Action Conduct affects the timetable of proceedings (see CPR Part 63.22 and Patents County Court Guide, para.2.4).

Beginning a Claim

61.53 An action, in either the Patents Court or the Patents County Court, is commenced by the issue of a Claim Form in the Royal Courts of Justice (Chancery Registry).

The content of a Claim Form is governed by CPR Part 16 and in the Patents Court and Patents County Court Guide. The Claim Form must set out, amongst other things, a concise statement of the nature of the claim and the nature of the remedy sought (CPR 16.2) and must be verified by a statement of truth (see CPR 22 and in respect of the Patents County Court CPR Part 63.21). The Claim Form must either be marked in the top right-hand corner "Chancery Division Patents Court" or "Patents County Court", below the title of the court in which it is issued, and must state the number of any patent to which the claim relates (CPR 63 PD 3.1).

A Claim Form must be served on the defendant, either within four months of issue or, if service is made outside the jurisdiction within six months. Service is regulated by CPR 6 and see also CPR 7.5.

Depending on the country in question, service outside the jurisdiction may or may not require permission. In either case the court's jurisdiction to hear the claim may be disputed. The rules for service outside the jurisdiction lie outside the scope of this book. The reader is therefore referred to a textbook on procedure (and in particular, the *White Book*). Note, however, that the claimant may be required to demonstrate that he has a "good arguable case", before the court will accept jurisdiction of the claim (*Mölnlycke v Proctor & Gamble (No.4)* [1992] R.P.C. 21 CA). This requires more than a mere assertion from a patent attorney that there is infringement. Consequently, in *Raychem v Thermon* [1989] R.P.C. 423 service was set aside because there was insufficient detail for the court and the defendant to understand the basis upon which the allegations were made. Also, in *Richco Plastic's Patent* [1989] R.P.C. 722, the Comptroller held that a case wholly unsupported by evidence is no case at all and should therefore be dismissed and not proceed to disclosure which might enable a case to be founded.

Once the Claim Form has been served, permission pursuant to CPR 19 is required to add, remove, or substitute a party to the action.

Particulars of Claim

61.54 Generally, Particulars of Claim are set out in a separate document either served with the Claim Form or served within 14 days of service of the Claim Form (CPR 7.4(1) and see CPR 7.5). The content of the Particulars of Claim is governed by CPR 16.4 and by the Patents Court and Patents County Court Guides. It should be noted that the rules concerning the content of the Particulars of Claim is materially different in the Patents Court and the Patents County Court. The following section applies to both. Matters relating specifically to the Patents County Court are discussed below (see §61.81 et seq).

If the Particulars of Claim allege infringement they must identify which of the claims in the specification of the patent are alleged to be infringed and give at least one example of each type of infringement (CPR 63 PD 4.1(1)). Conventionally, such information is set out in "Particulars of Infringement". In this context "type" means the particular kind of infringing act, e.g. manufacture, sale, etc. and the rule is satisfied if reference is made to a particular named product alleged to have been the subject of that type of act: an allegation specifying a particular batch of product is not required (*Lubrizol v Esso (No.3)* [1993] F.S.R. 59). An example of each type of article alleged to infringe must also be included if relief for articles of that sort is to be obtained (*Sorota v Gardex* [1984] R.P.C. 317 CA).

In general in the Patents Court the claimant is not required to plead the construction he puts upon the patent in the Particulars of Infringement. Likewise in the Patents County Court lengthy exposition of patent claims is not required, however parties are expected to identify the claims in issue and identify the relevant features of those claims (see Patents County Court Guide, para.2.4).

It is also long-established practice that a claimant alleging patent infringement is not required positively to aver that the patent is valid; its existence on the register (i.e. the fact that it is in force) is sufficient. (See *Halsey v Brotherhood* (1880) 15 Ch. D. 514.)

Split Trial

Patent infringement actions are almost invariably into two separate trials. The first trial is of liability. The second, assuming infringement is proved, is of quantum of damages. This second trial consists, at the claimant's election, of either an account of profits made by reason of the infringement or an enquiry as to damages made by the infringement. The claimant is entitled to adequate information (often but not always provided by way of disclosure) from the defendant to allow the election to be made (*Island Records v Tring* [1995] F.S.R. 560; and *Brugger v Medic-Aid* [1996] F.S.R. 362). As Patent trials are almost invariably split in this way it is generally not necessary to plead specifically the amounts sought to be recovered until after a successful trial on liability.

61.55

Acknowledgement of Service and Defence

In the Patents Court the normal course for a defendant is to serve a defence within the time limits specified by CPR Rule 15.4 as modified by CPR Rule 63.7. The time limits for serving a defence in the Patents County Court are governed by CPR 63.22 and depend on whether or not the Practice Direction on Pre-Action Conduct has been complied with (see CPR Part 63.22). If the practice direction has been complied with the time limit is 42 days. If it has not, the time limit is 70 days. Note that the rules in CPR Part 63.22 do not allow for extension of these time limits without the prior consent of the judge (see Patents County Court Guide, para.4.1).

61.56

If the defendant is unable to serve a defence in time or wishes to dispute the court's jurisdiction to hear the claim at all, an acknowledgement of service pursuant to CPR Rule 10 should be filed. The time limits for filing an acknowledgement of service are given in CPR Rule 10.3.

If the defendant fails to serve a defence or acknowledge service in accordance with the rules, the claimant may apply for judgment in default pursuant to CPR Rule 12.

The rules require that a defence must address each allegation made in the Particulars of Claim and state whether or not the allegation is admitted, not admitted (i.e. the claimant is put to proof) or denied (CPR 16.5(1)).

The defence may include a counterclaim under CPR 20. A counterclaim will frequently be appropriate when the defence to patent infringement involves a plea of invalidity and therefore the counterclaim is for revocation of the patent. Where the validity of the patent is challenged, Grounds of Invalidity compliant with CPR 63 PD 4.2–4.6 must be served. A copy of the "Grounds of Validity" document must be sent to the Comptroller and, likewise, when any amendment to this document is effected, a copy must also be sent to the Comptroller (CPR 63.14(3)): such document should then appear on the patent file available for inspection in the UK-IPO. Service upon the patentee can be made at the address for service recorded in the Register, see CPR 63.16(2).

In addition to the defences to infringement arising from the Patents Act, attention is drawn to the possibility of defences arising as a result of the Limitation Act 1980, laches, acquiescence, estoppel and "Euro" defences (e.g. exhaustion of rights or acts contrary to the Competition Act 1998). However, it should be noted that failure to oppose the grant of a patent in the EPO does not prevent a party from bringing an action or counterclaim in England or Wales for revocation in relation to the European Patent (UK), see *Buehler AG v Chronos Richardson* [1998] R.P.C. 609 CA.

Further Statements of Case, Amendments to Statements, Further Information

61.57   The claimant may file a reply to the defence. A claimant who does not file a reply, or in a reply fails to deal with a matter raised in the defence, is not taken to admit the matters raised in the defence (CPR 16.7). The time limits are set out in CPR 63.7 (Patents Court) and CPR 63.22 (Patents County Court).

If validity is challenged a claimant should file a defence to counterclaim (CPR 20). This may be served in the same document as the reply (hence a "Reply and Defence to Counterclaim").

Note that where commercial success is raised as a defence in reply to an allegation of obviousness, this must be pleaded out (CPR 63 PD 4.6) in the Defence to Counterclaim. However, a plea of long felt want not including commercial success need not be pleaded (*Schlumberger Holdings Ltd v Electromagnetic Geoservices AS* [2008] EWHC 56 Pat Ct).

If the contents of a statement of case are insufficiently clear, a party may apply for further information pursuant to CPR 18. Requests for further information should be made as soon as is conveniently possible. Note, however, requests for further information which require pleading a particular construction of the patent will not ordinarily be ordered. (*Lux Traffic Controls v Staffordshire Public Works Co* [1991] R.P.C. 73.)

Statements of case may be amended with permission of the court (CPR 17). Amendments are generally allowed only if they will not cause undue prejudice to other parties (e.g. because there is insufficient time to deal with the new pleadings properly). Amendments should therefore be brought forward at the earliest opportunity. Permission to amend is more likely to be refused if there has been delay in seeking permission and if the amendment would cause loss of a fixed trial date. It has been held that it is possible to seek to amend a statement of case to add a new ground of objection to validity even after the trial has taken place, provided that no final order has been signed (*Charlesworth v Relay Roads* [2000] R.P.C. 300). However, this is only likely to be permitted where new evidence has come to light which it would not have been reasonable to locate before the trial.

Where permission is given to amend the Grounds of Invalidity, the order granting permission will generally be in a form which allows the claimant the option of either discontinuing or proceeding with the action. If the action is proceeded with, the defendant pays the costs of the application to amend. If the action is discontinued, the claimant pays the costs up to and including the original particulars of objections and the defendant pays the subsequent costs, all payments being subject to taxation. (See *Edison Telephone Co v India Rubber Co* (1881) L.R. 17 Ch. D. 137; *Williamson v Moldline* [1986] R.P.C. 556; and *CIL International Ltd v Vitrashop Ltd* [2002] F.S.R. 4.) The normal consequence of such a discontinuance will also be the revocation of the patent.

In some circumstances, the court will order the production of a Statement of Case directed to a particular issue. The level of detail in such a document may be much greater than that required in the Particulars of Claim or Particulars of Infringement and, potentially, may bite on matters of construction. For example in *Nokia Corp v Interdigital Technology Corp.* [2007] EWHC 3077 Pat Ct; [2007] F.S.R. 23, the court ordered that detailed statements of case be produced in relation to the question of whether or not certain patents were "essential" to the ETSI telephone standards.

The position in the Patents County Court is modified as discussed below (see §§61.81 et seq).

Availability of Statements of Case to Non-Parties

61.58   CPR 5.4(C)(1)(a) provides that, subject to the requirements of CPR 5.4C(3), the general rule is that:

> "a person who is not a party to proceedings may obtain from the court records a copy of a statement of case, but not any documents filed with or attached to the statement of case, or intended by the party whose statement it is to be served with it".

Likewise, CPR 5.4(C)(2) provides that if the court gives permission a non-party may obtain from the records of the court "a copy of any other document filed by a party, or communication between the court and a party or another person".

Thank you for purchasing CIPA Guide to the Patents Acts, 7th Edition

 ## Don't miss important updates

So that you have all the latest information, **CIPA Guide to the Patents Acts, 7th Edition** is supplemented annually. Sign up today for a Standing Order to ensure you receive the updating supplements as soon as they publish. Setting up a Standing Order with Sweet & Maxwell is hassle-free, simply tick, complete and return this FREEPOST card and we'll do the rest.

You may cancel your Standing Order at any time by writing to us at Sweet & Maxwell, PO Box 2000, Andover, SP10 9AH stating the Standing Order you wish to cancel.

Alternatively, if you have purchased your copy of **CIPA Guide to the Patents Acts, 7th Edition** from a bookshop or other trade supplier, please ask your supplier to ensure that you are registered to receive the new supplements.

All goods are subject to our 30 day Satisfaction Guarantee (applicable to EU customers only)

Yes, please send me new supplements of **CIPA Guide to the Patents Acts, 7th Edition** to be invoiced on publication, until I cancel the standing order in writing.

☐ [All new supplements to the 7th edition]

Title .... Name ....

Organisation ....

Job title ....

Address ....

....

Postcode ....

Telephone ....

Email ....

S&M account number (if known) ....

PO number ....

All orders are accepted subject to the terms of this order form and our Terms of Trading. (see www.sweetandmaxwell.co.uk). By submitting this order form I confirm that I accept these terms and I am authorised to sign on behalf of the customer.

Signed .... Job Title ....

Print Name .... Date ....

UK VAT Number: GB 900 5487 43. Irish VAT Number: IE 9513874E. For customers in an EU member state (except UK & Ireland) please supply your VAT Number. VAT No [   ]

(BC007) V8.1 (11.2011) NB / DA

Delivery charges are not made for titles supplied to mainland UK. Non-mainland UK please add £4/€5 per delivery. Europe - please add £10/€13 for first item, £3/€4 for each additional item. Rest of World - please add £25/€32 for first item, £7/€9 for each additional item.

Goods will normally be dispatched within 3-5 working days of availability. The price charged to customers, irrespective of any prices quoted, will be the price specified in our price list current at the time of dispatch of the goods, as published on our website, unless the order is subject to a specific offer or discount in which case special terms may apply.

UK VAT is charged on all applicable sales at the prevailing rate except in the case of sales to Ireland where Irish VAT will be charged at the prevailing rate. Customers outside the EU will not be charged UK VAT.

Thomson Reuters (Professional) UK Limited – Legal Business (Company No. 1679046). 100 Avenue Road, Swiss Cottage, London NW3 3PF. Registered in England and Wales. Registered office: Aldgate House, 33 Aldgate High Street, London EC3N 1DL. Trades using various trading names, a list of which is posted on its website at sweetandmaxwell.co.uk

"Thomson Reuters" and the Thomson Reuters logo are trademarks of Thomson Reuters and its affiliated companies.

SWEET & MAXWELL

 **THOMSON REUTERS™**

SWEET & MAXWELL

FREEPOST

PO BOX 2000

ANDOVER

SP10 9AH

UNITED KINGDOM

However, the court may on application of a party (or any person identified in a State-ment of Case) prevent or restrict the provision of statements of case/documents to third parties (CPR 5.4(C)(4)).

Note that CPR 5.4(C)(1)(a) came into force on October 2, 2006 and is not retrospective.

Case Management: The Case Management Conference

A key stage in the action is the Case Management Conference ("CMC"). The general **61.59** rules in relation to Case Management Conferences are set out in CPR Part 29.2 and CPR PD 29 paras 5.1–5.9. In the Patents Court additional rules relating to the CMC are found at CPR 63.8 and CPR 63 PD 5.1–5.12. There are additional/different rules in relation to the Patents County Court and these are discussed below in §§61.81 et seq.

Generally the claimant must apply for a CMC within 14 days of the date when all the defendants have served a defence. However, in certain circumstances a CMC can also be called by either the court or one or more of the parties. The CMC is almost always heard before a Patents Judge, although the court may direct a CMC be heard by a Master (CPR 63 PD 5.2).

The court has very wide powers of cases management under CPR 3, and it is usual that the CMC be used to give directions to trial. A specimen minute of order for directions is annexed to the Patents Court Guide. The scope of the CMC is not limited to setting direc-tions to trial. Other applications, such as to strike out pleadings, may also be heard at the CMC.

Each party is required to file and serve an application notice four days prior to the date of the CMC setting out the order which that party intends to seek (CPR 63 PD 5.8). Gener-ally, the claimant will produce a bundle of relevant documents for the CMC in accordance with CPR 63 PD 5.9.

In addition to the directions for trial discussed above, the Patents Practice Direction specifically states that the following matters may be dealt with at the CMC (although this does not preclude the making of other applications): the appointment of a scientific advi-sor, the order for production of a "primer", and the setting of a trial date. Where a trial date has not been fixed by the court, a party may apply for a trial date by filing a certificate which must:

(1) state the estimated length of the trial, agreed if possible by all parties;

(2) detail the time required by the judge to consider the documents;

(3) identify the area of technology; and

(4) assess the complexity of the technical issues involved by indicating the complexity on a scale of one to five (with one being the least and five the most complex).

Case Management: Streamlined Trial

In addition to the normal form of directions to trial, discussed below, a "streamlined **61.60** procedure" exists for the Patents Court. This provides for a simplified form of trial, normally of one day in duration, with limited oral evidence, no experiments and limited or no disclosure. The court will order a streamlined trial by agreement between the parties or where application of the overriding objective indicates that it is appropriate (for example by reason of the simplicity and/or low value of a given case: (*Merck v Generics* [2004] R.P.C. 31 at 607). It has, however, been stated that use of the streamlined procedure depends on all the circumstances of the case, and the speed of a streamlined trial should not be gained at the expense of fairness (*Inpro Licensing Sarl's Patent* [2006] R.P.C. 20; and *Research In Motion v Inpro* [2007] EWCA Civ 51). See also *Generics (UK) Ltd v Synaptech Inc* [2009] EWHC 659 (Ch) and *Synthon BV v Merz Pharma* [2009] EWHC 656 Pat Ct. As the Patents County Court in effect provides a "streamlined" procedure of its own, the number of cases in which the streamlined approach in the Patents Court are ap-propriate may now be more limited.

Case Management: Determination of a Case or Issue without a Trial

61.61   Either court may, on the application of a party or on its own initiative, strike-out the whole or a part of a Statement of Case (whether this is a claim, defence, counterclaim or other Statement of Case) under CPR 3.4 or under the court's inherent jurisdiction (see CPR 3.4(5)). Under CPR 3.4 there are three bases for strike-out: (1) the Statement of Case discloses no reasonable grounds for bringing or defending the claim (CPR 3.4(2)(a)); (2) the Statement of Case is an abuse of the court's process or is otherwise likely to obstruct the just disposal of the proceedings (CPR 3.4(2)(b)); or (3) there has been a failure to comply with a rule, practice direction or order (CPR 3.4(2)(c)).

The court may also, pursuant to CPR 24, give summary judgment against a claimant or a defendant on the whole of a claim or on a particular issue. It will do so if it considers that there is no real prospect of the claimant/defendant succeeding on the claim/issue and there is no other compelling reason why the case or issue should be disposed of at trial.

Case Management: Summary Judgment Pursuant to CPR 12/Strike-Out
  Pursuant to CPR 3.4(2)(a)

61.62   The tests under CPR 3.4(2)(a) and CPR 12 are distinct. However, some common principles apply. In particular, the court will only determine claims for patent infringement without a trial in very clear cases which do not require oral evidence to be heard.

The rules for summary judgment were summarised by the Vice-Chancellor in *Celador Productions v Melville* [2004] EWHC 2362 Ch, as follows:

> "(a) it is for the applicant for summary judgment to demonstrate that the respondent has no real prospect of success in his claim or defence as the case may be;
>
> (b) a 'real' prospect of success is one which is more than fanciful or merely arguable;
>
> (c) if it is clear beyond question that the respondent will not be able at trial to establish the facts on which he relies, then his prospects of success are not real; but
>
> (d) the court is not entitled on an application for summary judgment to conduct a trial on documents without disclosure or cross-examination."

For examples where summary judgment succeeded in a patent action, see *Virgin Atlantic Airways Ltd v Delta Airways Ltd* [2010] EWHC 3094 (Pat), *Abbott Laboratories v Approved Prescription Services* [2004] EWHC 2723 Pat Ct. Note also *Schering v CIPLA* [2005] F.S.R. 25, where an action for infringement was struck out because without being able to rely on a "without prejudice" letter there was no evidence of infringement.

However, see also *Monsanto v Merck* [2000] R.P.C. 77 where a contention that had been struck out by the Patents Court was restored by the Court of Appeal (*Monsanto v Merck* [2000] R.P.C. 709). Also *Tercica v Avecia* [2005] EWHC 984 Ch; *Strix Ltd v Otter Controls Ltd* [1991] F.S.R. 354; *Unilever v Schöller Lebensmittel* [1988] F.S.R. 596; *Southco v Dzus* [1989] R.P.C. 82; *Improver Corp. v Remington* [1990] F.S.R. 181; *Improver Corp. v Raymond Industrial [Hong Kong]* [1990] F.S.R. 422; [1991] F.S.R. 233; and *Upjohn v Thomas Kerfoot* [1988] F.S.R. 1. Furthermore, in *Storage Computer v Hitachi* [2003] EWCA Civ 1155 the court refused to strike out the proceedings even though the case for non-infringement was seen to be "very strong indeed" because it was "not inconceivable" that infringement could be found under the Protocol to art.69 of the EPC.

Where a claimant has sought a novel or unusual form of relief, for example a declaration of non-essentiality to an industry standard, challenges to the court's jurisdiction to grant such relief have been made under CPR Pt 11: see *Nokia Corp. v InterDigital Technology Corp.* at first instance [2006] EWHC 802 Pat Ct; and on appeal [2006] EWCA Civ 1618; [2007] F.S.R. 23.

Where the Patents Court held that a case of infringement should go to trial, but that there was no defence to the counterclaim for invalidity as regards some of the patent claims, the court granted a declaration that these claims were invalid and ordered that a copy of the order be served upon the Comptroller, although an order that the patentee should seek amendment of the patent was refused (*Autopia Terakat v Gwent Auto Fabrications* [1991] F.S.R. 517).

Case Management: Strike-Out Pursuant to CPR 3.4(2)(b): Abuse of Process

CPR 3.4(2)(b) provides the court with the power to strike out a claim as being an abuse **61.63**
of the court's process. However, if the claim or defence is otherwise valid, the Patents
Court has shown a reluctance to strike out proceedings if the abuse can be satisfactorily
addressed in another manner (*Reckitt Benckiser (UK) Ltd v Home Pairfum Ltd* [2004]
EWHC 302 Pat Ct). The reader is referred to textbooks on procedure (e.g. the *White Book*)
for a more detailed discussion of what may constitute an abuse of the court's process.

Case Management: Strike-Out Pursuant to CPR 3.4(2)(c): Failure to Comply with a Rule or Order

Striking out the pleadings (or part thereof) in an action is also the sanction when the **61.64**
court is satisfied that "there has been a failure to comply with a rule, practice direction or
court order". Again the court has been reluctant to strike out a claim on this basis where
other sanctions (such as an award of costs, or payment of money into court) may satisfy
the justice of the case (*Biguzzi v Rank Leisure Plc* [1999] 1 W.L.R. 1926 CA). The reader
is referred to the *White Book* for a more detailed discussion of CPR Pt 3.4(2)(c).

Case Management: Hearing of a preliminary point

The court has the power to order the hearing of a preliminary point. Generally such an **61.65**
order will only be made where the decision on the preliminary point may be decisive of
the whole, or a significant part, of the case and hearing of the preliminary point will not
lead to increased delay and costs. For the interrelationship of a strike-out application and a
hearing of a preliminary point, see *Sandvik v Pfiffner* [2000] F.S.R. 17.

Recent orders for such hearing of a preliminary point were made in *Ranbaxy v Astra-Zeneca* [2011] EWHC 1831 Pat, and *InterDigital Technology Corp v Nokia Corp* [2007]
EWHC 3353 Pat Ct (although in the event that case was settled before the preliminary
point was heard). Also see *Merrell Dow v Norton* [1994] R.P.C. 1; [1995] R.P.C. 233 CA;
and [1996] R.P.C. 76, HL; *American Home Products v Novartis* [2000] R.P.C. 547; and
Cleveland Graphite Bronze v Glacier Metal (1951) 68 R.P.C. 181.

Case Management: Application to stay proceedings

The court has a general, inherent, power to stay proceedings and an express power to **61.66**
stay proceedings pursuant to CPR 26.4 for the purposes of assisting a possible settlement.
The court is generally reluctant to stay proceedings (*Chemithon's Patent* [1966] R.P.C.
365).

The court may, but does not have to, stay infringement proceedings commenced before
an opposition to a European patent was lodged in the EPO. In *Glaxo Group Ltd v Genentech Inc* [2008] EWCA Civ 23; [2008] F.S.R. 18, the Court of Appeal reviewed the case
law and considered the general question in what circumstances the Patents Court should
exercise its inherent power to stay revocation proceedings pending the final outcome of an
opposition in the EPO. The Court of Appeal found that there was no presumption that a
stay should be granted merely because the existence of a UK action would duplicate matters already in suit in the EPO. The Court also identified eight points of guidance as to the
exercise of the discretion (at paras 80–88). In effect a detailed examination of the prejudice
of a stay to each party is required (see also *GlaxoSmithKline Biologicals SA v Novartis AG*
[2009] EWHC 931 Pat).

Note that recently the court has refused to stay UK proceedings in favour of parallel
German proceedings and expressed doubts about using general case management powers
for the purpose of staying proceedings to await the outcome of other parallel proceedings
having no direct legal impact in the UK, unlike proceedings in the EPO which do have
such an impact (*Affymetrix Inv v Multilyte* [2004] EWHC 291 Pat Ct; [2005] F.S.R. 1; and
Baxter Healthcare v Bayer [2006] EWHC 1890 Pat Ct).

The Patents Court also has jurisdiction to stay its proceedings in favour of allowing the determination of an application for a declaration of non-infringement or for revocation in the UK-IPO. It is, however, unlikely that such a stay would be granted save in exceptional circumstances (see *Ferro Corp v Escol* [1990] R.P.C. 651).

Disclosure: General Rules

61.67 Save with the permission of the court, a party may not rely upon any document which it fails to disclose or in respect of which it fails to permit inspection (CPR 31.21).

Disclosure and inspection of documents is governed in general by CPR 31 and its accompanying Practice Direction. A direction relating to disclosure is generally made at the CMC. Unless disclosure is dispensed with by the court, the parties will in the first instance usually be directed to give "standard" disclosure. The scope of such disclosure is defined in CPR Pt 31, and is provided by list using Court Form N265. The list specifies documents available for inspection, documents in respect of which a party claims a right or duty to withhold inspection (primarily documents which are the subject of legal privilege) and documents unavailable for inspection because they are no longer within a party's control. A party is also required to set out the extent of the search for documents it has made (a reasonable search is required).

Legal professional privilege may exist in relation to (amongst other things) communications between solicitors, counsel, patent attorneys and trade mark attorneys. The reader is referred to the *White Book* for a more detailed discussion of the extent of the privilege.

Documents in a party's "control" are defined to be documents which are, or were, in that party's possession, documents that the party has, or has had, the right to possess, and documents that the party has had a right to inspect or take copies of. As a result it has been held that a parent company cannot compel a subsidiary to provide disclosure where to do so would require the subsidiary to alter its articles of association (*Lonrho v Shell* [1980] 1 W.L.R. 627). Likewise, it has been held that disclosure could not be given where a defendant had no power under a licence with his foreign supplier to obtain documents from that supplier (*Unilever v Gillette* [1988] R.P.C. 416). However, note that in some circumstances where a party has previously enjoyed the help of a third party and has in so doing had the cooperation and consent of that third party to inspect, take copies and lists the third party's documents, the documents may be inferred to be within the control of the party with a duty to disclose (*Schlumberger Holdings Ltd v Electromagnetic Geoservices AS* [2008] EWHC 56 Pat Ct).

A party is only required to disclose documents which relate to pleaded issues (*Intel v General Instrument* [1989] F.S.R. 640). Furthermore, under CPR 31.5(2), the court has a general power to restrict disclosure; and, under CPR 31.7(2), a party can seek to restrict its search for relevant documents on the basis of the number of documents involved; the nature and complexity of the proceedings; the ease and expense of retrieval of any particular document; and the significance of any document which is likely to be located during the search.

Note that the disclosure obligation extends to electronic material including emails, databases and word-processed documents (CPR 31.4). Failure to deliver up computers or deliberate deletion of files may amount to a contempt of court (*Marlton v Tectronix UK Holdings* [2003] EWHC 383 Ch).

The fact that a party asserts that a particular document contains confidential information is not a legitimate reason for withholding disclosure and/or inspection. However, the court will frequently restrict the inspection of such documents to a limited number of people, generally those who are signatories to a confidentiality agreement (*Warner Lambert Co v Glaxo Laboratories Ltd* [1975] R.P.C. 354; *Roussel-Uclaf v ICI* [1990] R.P.C. 45 CA; *Centri-Spray v Cera* [1979] F.S.R. 175; and *Format Communications v ITT* [1983] F.S.R. 473 CA). If a document is highly commercially sensitive, such an approach may prevent it being inspected by directors or employees of a party, in particular where the relevance of the document could be assessed via the party's independent expert (*Helitune v Stewart Hughes* [1994] F.S.R. 422). Note that objections to employees who are also patent attorneys receiving confidential information have not been accepted, provided that the patent attorney has first signed a specific undertaking to receive the information only in his/her professional capacity (*Unilever v Pearce* [1985] F.S.R. 475; *Schering's Patent* [1986] R.P.C. 30).

The duty to provide disclosure continues until proceedings are concluded (CPR 31.11). Furthermore, documents which are disclosable in litigation must be preserved. In *Rockwell v Barrus* [1968] 2 All E.R. 98, it was pointed out that solicitors must take positive steps to ensure that their clients appreciate at an early stage of the litigation, promptly after a claim is issued, not only the duty of disclosure and its width but also the importance of not destroying documents which might possibly have to be disclosed. This burden extends to taking steps to ensure that in any corporate organisation knowledge of this burden is passed on to any who may be affected by it. In an inquiry into damages in a copyright action (*Infabrics v Jaytex [Damages]* [1985] F.S.R. 75), the court referred to the *Rockwell* case and admonished the defendant for having destroyed, after the start of the action, invoices and similar documents which ought to have been disclosed during the damages inquiry. In the absence of the defendant's documents, the court may give a claimant the benefit of any doubt on questions of quantum of damages.

In addition to standard disclosure, a party may apply for specific disclosure or specific inspection (CPR 31.12). Disclosure may also be sought against a non-party (CPR 31.17; and see *American Home Products v Novartis* [2001] F.S.R. 41; and *SmithKline Beecham Biologicals v Connaught* [2000] F.S.R. 1), or before an action has commenced (CPR 31.16). Attention is also drawn to the possibility of obtaining disclosure under US domestic law (28 USC 1782) in furtherance of proceedings in the United Kingdom (*Nokia Corp v InterDigital* [2004] EWHC 2920 Pat Ct).

Note that the availability and extent of disclosure in the Patents County Court is, as a matter of that court's case management, liable to be (far) more restricted than in the Patents Court (see §§61.81 et seq below).

Disclosure: Removal of privilege against self-incrimination

Normally a party can claim privilege against any disclosure which might incriminate it **61.68** of committing a criminal offence. However, in proceedings related to intellectual property, s.72 of the Senior Courts Act 1981 (c.54) provides that the privilege against self-incrimination cannot be invoked in such proceedings.

The effect of s.72 is that that privilege against self-incrimination is removed in relation to proceedings brought to prevent an apprehended infringement of intellectual property rights or any apprehended passing off, see *Universal Studios v Hubbard* [1984] R.P.C. 43 CA, even if criminal proceedings are already in being, and in contempt proceedings (*Crest Homes v Marks* [1988] R.P.C. 21; [1987] 1 A.C. 829; [1987] 2 All E.R. 1074 HL). The question is, however, one of discretion, and an order for disclosure should be made unless it would result in injustice (as distinct from disadvantage). Disclosure of the names of potential witnesses is disadvantage, not injustice (*Charles of the Ritz v Jory* [1986] F.S.R. 14). Section 72 of the Senior Courts Act 1981 (c.54) was discussed and applied in *Cobra Golf v Rata (No.2)* [1997] F.S.R. 317, in relation to contempt proceedings based on an undertaking given in previous trade mark infringement proceedings, because the alleged contempts would expose the defendants to a "penalty". See also *Coca-Cola Company and Schweppes Ltd v Gilbey* [1996] F.S.R. 23.

Use of Disclosure Documents

The general rule is unless and until a document is deployed in open court it may only be **61.69** used for the purpose of the action in which it is disclosed (CPR 31.22). Use of such documents for a different purpose may be a contempt of court (*Home Office v Harman* [1983] 1 A.C. 280; *Crest Homes v Marks* [1988] R.P.C. 21; [1987] 1 A.C. 829). However, once a document has been referred to in open court, unless a specific order is made by the court pursuant to CPR 31.22 the protection no longer applies; see *Lilly ICOS v Pfizer* [2002] F.S.R. 54 for a discussion of the considerations relevant to making an order under CPR 31.22. Note that a document has been found to be referred to in open court where it has been read by the judge only out of court but was referred to extensively in the eventual open judgment (*SmithKline Beecham Biologicals SA v Connaught Laboratories* [1999] 4 All E.R. 498 CA).

Where inspection of a document has been allowed inadvertently, use of that document or its contents by the inspecting party requires the permission of the court under CPR 31.20.

Note that in complex and commercially sensitive patent litigation, it is now the frequent practice of the Patents Court to grant a CPR 31.22 order *pro tem* during oral proceedings and to postpone ultimate judgment in relation to whether or not a document should be covered by CPR 31.22 until after judgment.

For consideration of the circumstances in which documents will be kept confidential after deployment, see *Lilly ICOS v Pfizer* [2002] F.S.R. 54 at 809, and *Dyson v Hoover (No.3)* [2002] R.P.C. 42 at 841.

The court may in exceptional circumstances grant permission to use a disclosure document for purposes other than those relating to the action (*SmithKline Beecham v Generics* [2004] F.S.R. 8). Note, however, that permission has been refused for use of documents in an EPO opposition, even when the parties and subject matter of the opposition were the same (*Bonzel v Intervention (No.2)* [1991] R.P.C. 43). Disclosed documents may not be used in proceedings on corresponding patents in other countries where similar disclosure could not be obtained under the law of that country (*Halcon v Shell (Discovery)* [1979] R.P.C. 97), but see also *Bayer v Winter (No.2)* [1986] F.S.R. 357 for a possible contrary case). In *SmithKline Beecham v Apotex* [2004] F.S.R. 133 permission was given to use, in foreign litigation, test results produced in the course of English litigation but not deployed in court.

Breadth of disclosure in patent litigation

61.70   Standard disclosure in patent actions is further limited by CPR 63 PD 6.1, see Appendix F. This provides that standard disclosure does not require the disclosure of documents which relate to:

   (a) the infringement of a patent by a product or process, if before or at the same time as serving a list of documents, the defendant has served on the claimant and any other party full particulars of the product or process alleged to infringe and drawings or other illustrations if necessary (a Product or Process Description);

   (b) any ground on which the validity of a patent is put in issue, except documents which came into existence with the period beginning two years before the earliest claimed priority date and ending two years after the date;

   (c) commercial success.

Disclosure: Product and Process Descriptions

67.71   Full details of the alleged infringing product or process must be given. This requires "particulars sufficient to enable all issues of infringement to be resolved". (*Consafe v Emtunga* [1999] R.P.C. 154. See also *Baxter v Abbott (No.2)* [2006] EWHC 919.)

Unless the content of the description is admitted by the defendant, its content should be proved by a witness (*Technip France SA's Patent* [2004] R.P.C. 46).

Disclosure: Obviousness and Secondary Evidence

61.72   Generally obviousness is considered objectively through the construct of the skilled person having regard to the state of the art (see *Mölnlycke v Proctor & Gamble* [1994] R.P.C. 49 at 113). However, in certain circumstances it may be appropriate to consider what happened in fact (e.g. what was actually done by people in the field or the commercial success of an invention). Such evidence is generally referred to as Secondary Evidence.

The potential importance of secondary evidence was recently explained by Jacob L.J. in *Schlumberger Holdings v EMGS* [2010] R.P.C. 33, [2010] EWCA Civ 819, who stated at para.77 that:

"[Secondary evidence] only comes into play when one is considering the question "if it was obvious, why was it not done before?" That question itself can have many answers showing it was nothing to do with the invention, for instance that the prior art said to make the invention obvious was only published shortly before the date of the patent, or that the practical implementation of the patent required other technical developments. But once all other reasons have been discounted and the problem is shown to have been long-standing and solved by the invention, secondary evidence can and often does, play an important role. If a useful development was, in hindsight, seemingly obvious for years and the apparently straightforward technical step from the prior art simply was not taken, then there is likely to have been an invention".

It follows that a party may have to give disclosure in relation to material relating to the making of the invention (i.e. the inventor's notebooks). For example, in *Halcon v Shell (Discovery No.2)* [1979] R.P.C. 459 disclosure of documents was ordered concerning: (a) research and development in the course of which the invention was made, because this would assist the court in deciding whether an inventive step, or little more than routine work, was involved; (b) experimental work which might show that the patentee had failed in trying to use a certain type of catalyst falling within the scope of protection which, if so, would not be without relevance to the issue of insufficiency; and (c) papers relating to the filing and prosecution of the patent, including the files of the patent attorneys, because the specification and claims differed from those of the basic United States patent. Also, in *SKM v Wagner Spraytech* [1982] R.P.C. 497 CA, it was held that the inventor's notes would be of help either offensively or defensively to the defendant's case in several aspects and, therefore, these should be disclosed, even though such would lead to delay, expense and a substantial addition to the documentation of the case.

Disclosure: Commercial Success

61.73   CPR 63 PD 6.3 replaces the requirement to give disclosure of documents relating to the issue of commercial success with a requirement to serve a schedule: (i) identifying the article, product or process in question; (ii) summarising by convenient periods sales or revenues derived from such articles, products or processes; (iii) summarising for equivalent periods sales or revenues derived from any equivalent prior art article, product or process; and (iv) summarising by convenient periods any expenditure supporting the marketing or use of the articles, products and processes specified under (ii) and (iii).

Admissions

61.74   A party can request another party to admit specified facts, by serving a "notice to admit" no later than 21 days before the trial (CPR 32.18). The court can permit such admissions to be amended or withdrawn. Failure to admit facts, where this ought to be done, can have consequences in costs irrespective of the outcome of the action as a whole. Section 9 of the Patents Court Guide (see Appendix G) highlights the necessity of making admissions at an early stage in the litigation "with a view to early elimination of non-issues". Section 9.2 of the Patents Court Guide notes that a notice to admit facts in patent litigation may include a request to identify points not in dispute with a view to narrowing the ambit of disclosure and of the contents of witness statements and expert reports.

Experiments

61.75   Permission from the Court is required to rely upon experiments conducted for the purpose of patent litigation. Such permission is usually sought at the Case Management Conference. As discussed below (see §§61.81 et seq), experiments are (far) less likely to be permitted in the Patents County Court.

If a party wishes to establish a fact by experimental proof based on experiments conducted for the purpose of patent litigation, it is required first to serve on the other party a notice stating the facts which those experiments are intended to establish and giving full particulars of the experiments proposed to establish them. Note that running a computer program can constitute the performance of an experiment (*Consafe v Emtunga* [1999] R.P.C. 154). There is, however, no obligation on a party to serve a notice of experiments in respect of an experiment conducted in the normal course of research (Practice Direction (Pat Ct; Practice Explanation) [1997] R.P.C. 166).

Experiments that are directed to the issue of construction are not permitted (see *Merck v Generics* [2003] EWHC 2842 Pat).

The procedure for serving particulars of an experiment is given in CPR 63 PD 7. Although an order for experiments requires details of the facts which the party claims to be able to establish by the experiment to be given, that party need only give a reasonable account of such facts and, if it later comes to his attention, without prejudice or detriment to the other party, that the experiments he has done do establish some other facts, then he may apply to amend the notice of experiments, see *Van der Lely v Watveare* [1982] F.S.R. 122. However, as a matter of case management the Court may refuse to admit late experiments (*Monsanto Technology LLC v Cargill International SA* [2008] F.S.R. 7).

Experiments, the results of which are to be given in evidence, will normally be required to be repeated in the presence of representatives of the other party if requested. Conditions may be imposed on such repetitions. For example, in *Roussel-Uclaf v ICI* [1989] R.P.C. 59 CA, experiments which involved the repetition by the claimant's expert of the defendant's secret process disclosed to him (and to the claimant's legal advisers) under a strict order of confidentiality were ordered to be conducted within the jurisdiction of the court in order that the court could impose sanctions if any breach of the confidentiality order occurred.

There is no obligation on a party to disclose experiments on which it does not wish to rely (*Electrolux v Black & Decker* [1996] F.S.R. 595). This led to the Patents Court stating that an expert's report should include the statement: "I know of no experiment which is inconsistent with my evidence"; and practitioners were reminded that it would be contrary to their duty to the court to allow any expert evidence to be given inconsistent with an experiment of which they, but not the expert, had knowledge, see *Practice Explanation (Patents Court)* [1997] R.P.C. 166 and the subsequent Patents Court: *Consolidated Practice Explanation* [1998] R.P.C. 18 at paras 23 and 24, where it was also stated that the reference in the then rule of court to "establishing any fact by experimental proof" includes experiments done in other jurisdictions and any other experiments not done as part of normal research. However, the requirement to include such a statement in an expert's report has not been included as such in the CPR, but a failure to do so will be a legitimate subject for cross-examination of the expert having regard to CPR 35 which regulates evidence given by experts. Furthermore, the duty of the expert is unlikely to allow an expert report contrary to other experiments within his/her knowledge to be advanced.

If experiments are performed which do not assist the court, the performing party may be unable to recover costs in respect of them: *Pall Corp. v Commercial Hydraulics* [1990] R.P.C. 329 at 358. Other cases where the court has been critical of the value of experiments performed include *Merck v Generics [Alendronate process]* [2004] R.P.C. 31 at 607 and *Unilin Beheer v Berry Floor* [2004] F.S.R. 14 at 238.

Evidence

61.76 The general rules under the CPR for the presentation of factual evidence are set out in CPR 32, 33 and 34; and, as regards opinion evidence by an expert in CPR 35. The reader is referred to the *White Book* for a more detailed commentary on these rules.

No evidence relating to an issue of infringement or validity can be given unless that issue has been raised in the particulars of infringement or the particulars of objections, or the court gives permission. In relation to the question of validity, prior use and commercial success must, in general, be proved with factual evidence.

Evidence-in-chief is almost invariably provided by way of a witness statement. The order for directions to trial (see specimen attached to the Patents Court Guide Appendix G) therefore makes provision or exchange of witness statements and expert reports by a set pre-trial date. These witness statements effectively take the place of the examination-in-chief of the witness. As discussed below (see §§61.81 et seq), in the Patents County Court evidence, including relevant evidence, may well be excluded as a matter of case management.

If a party serves a witness statement, and wishes to rely on it at trial, he must call the witness to give oral evidence unless the court orders otherwise or he puts the statement in as hearsay evidence pursuant to CPR 33.2 (see also CPR 32.5). Where a party cannot obtain a witness statement, he can serve a "witness summary" being a summary of evidence which, if known, would have been included in a witness statement; or, if not known, being matters about which the proposed witness would be questioned if he can be called at trial, e.g. in response to a "witness summons" under CPR 34.2.

If service of these witness statements does not take place, the party in default can adduce evidence on the issue in question only with the permission of the court. Where a witness statement is served and the witness gives oral evidence at trial, members of the public can obtain a copy of that statement (CPR 32.13). However, where a witness statement is served but is not tendered in evidence at the trial (or put in evidence by the other party pursuant to CPR 32.5(5)), the general rule is that no other party may make use of the witness statement subsequently (CPR 32.12).

No privilege as such attaches to the contents of a witness statement and therefore such may found the basis of an application for further disclosure (*Black & Decker v Flymo* [1991] F.S.R. 93).

Note that it is now common practice, where a witness is overseas, to arrange for the giving of oral evidence by video link. It should be noted that in order to obtain the use of the High Court's video suite facilities, a direction of the court is required. It has been stated authoritatively that:

"Giving evidence by video link was an entirely satisfactory method of giving evidence if there was a sufficient reason for departing from the normal rule that witness gave evidence in person before court": *Polansk v Condé Nast* [2005] 1 W.L.R. 637 HL.

It should however be borne in mind that the normal practice remains that where a witness will be subject to more than a few questions, or where the witnesses' credibility is seriously challenged, it is normally expected that a witness will attend court.

Expert Evidence

Expert evidence is primarily provided in one or more written reports (CPR 35.5) and **61.77** subject to cross-examination at trial.

The primary function of the expert in patent litigation is to educate the court in the technology in question (*Technip France SA's Patent* [2004] R.P.C. 46 at [12]). Such evidence is admissible in relation to validity, sufficiency, the meaning of technical terms ("terms of art"), and the state of the common general knowledge. What is of primary importance is not the expert's view, but the reasons for that view. (See *SmithKline Beecham v Apotex* [2005] F.S.R. 23 at [51]–[52]; *AB Hässle's Patents* [2002] F.S.R. 564; and *Pfizer's Patent* [2001] F.S.R. 16.)

The specimen order for directions attached to the Patents Court Guide specifies the number of experts which each party may present and requires the parties to provide to each other on a stated date the names of their experts and witnesses. Whilst the aim of the CPR is to reduce the number of experts to a minimum, use of a single joint expert is not normally appropriate in cases in the Patents Court.

The overriding duty of an expert is to assist the court, and this duty overrides any obligation to the party from whom he has received instructions or by whom he is paid (CPR 35.3). In *The Ikarian Reefer* [1993] F.S.R. 563, the duties and responsibilities of expert witnesses were summarised in the following statements:

"1. Expert evidence presented to the court should be, and should be seen to be, the independent product of the expert uninfluenced as to form or content by the exigencies of litigation.

2. An expert witness should provide independent assistance to the court by way of objective, unbiased opinion in relation to matters within his expertise. An expert witness should never assume the role of an advocate.

3. An expert witness should state the facts or assumptions upon which his opinion is based: he should not omit to consider material facts which could detract from his concluded opinion.

4. An expert witness should make it clear when a particular question or issue falls outside his expertise.

5. If an expert's opinion is not properly researched because he considers that insufficient data is available, then this must be stated with an indication that the opinion is no more than a provisional one. In cases where an expert witness, who has prepared a report, could not assert that the report contained the truth, the whole truth and nothing but the truth without some qualification, that qualification should be stated in the report.

6. If, after exchange of reports, an expert witness changes his views on a material matter having read the other side's expert report or for any other reason, such change of view should be communicated (through legal representatives) to the other side without delay and when appropriate to the court.

7. Where expert evidence refers to photographs, plans, calculations, analyses, measurements, survey reports or other similar documents, these must be provided to the other party at the same time as the exchange of reports."

The principle that an expert witness should not adopt a partisan approach to his evidence is illustrated by judicial comments in *Cala Homes v Alfred McAlpine* [1995] F.S.R. 818 that:

"An expert should not consider that it is his job to stand shoulder to shoulder through thick and thin with the side which is paying the bill".

Also, in *Raychem's Patents* [1998] R.P.C. 31, where the court stated:

"The impression I received while watching and listening to [the patentee's expert] in the witness box was that he considered it his primary task to support his employer's case. Balanced and fair answers to technical questions came second. It was apparent on a number of occasions that he was reluctant to answer questions the response to which might benefit the petitioners. This has reduced the reliance I have felt able to put on his evidence";

and in *Cantor Fitzgerald v Tradition* [2000] R.P.C. 95 at 128, where the court observed:

"Where the subject matter of the action lies in a highly technical area it is of particular importance that the expert is scrupulous in putting forward all relevant considerations which occur to him or her as being relevant to the issue to be decided. The court has no points of reference other than those provided by the expert. It is reprehensible for the expert to hold back relevant information. The danger is manifest. If both experts lack objectivity the court is deprived of any proper basis to arrive at a decision".

Likewise, "any pressure, and any act which may have the effect of placing pressure, on a witness may be a contempt of court": *Glaxo Group's Patent* [2004] R.P.C. 43. A recent, and detailed, description of the duties of an expert and also the duties of those legal advisors assisting an expert with his/her report is given by Arnold J. in *Medimmune v Novartis* [2011] EWHC 1669 Pat Ct, the whole of which should be consulted by anyone involved in instructing an expert in a patent case, but the gist of which can be summed up in the following paragraph:

"... lawyers who instruct expert witnesses bear a heavy responsibility for ensuring that an expert witness is not put in a position where he can be made to appear to have failed in his duty to the court even though he conscientiously believes that he has complied with that duty. It is also important that courts should be cautious about criticising an expert witness purely on the basis of omissions from his report unless it is clear that the fault lies with the expert rather than those instructing him, bearing in mind that the court will not usually be privy to the expert's full instructions ...".

CPR 35 and CPR 35.10 require that an expert's report must conclude with a statement that he understands his duty to the court and has complied therewith. The report must also state "the substance of all material instructions, whether written or oral, on the basis of which the report was written". Such instructions are not privileged against disclosure although the court should not normally order disclosure of any specific document or permit any questioning in court other than by the party who instructed the expert unless satisfied that there are reasonable grounds to consider the statement of instructions to be inaccurate or incomplete, see CPR 35.10(4) and also CPR 35 PD 3. For other required details of an expert's report, see CPR 35 PD 1. These requirements include: that the report must be addressed to the court; give details of the expert's qualifications and of the material relied upon in preparing his or her report; contain a summary of the conclusions reached; and be verified by a "statement of truth". For the form of a "statement of truth", see CPR 22 PD 1–4, and for the consequence of this being false to any material degree, see CPR 22 PD.5 and CPR 32.14. For inspection of documents mentioned in an expert's report, see CPR 31 PD.7.

Where the report of more than one expert may cover the same ground, it should be noted that in *Hoechst Celanese v BP Chemicals [Carbonylation]* [1998] F.S.R. 586, statements in the report of an expert witness which duplicated evidence already given by another such witness were ordered to be expunged before the second expert was called to give his testimony.

It is generally inadmissible to present evidence to a court on the interpretation which a patentee puts on his claims, particularly as regards corresponding foreign patents, because construction is a matter for the court relying only on evidence on the meaning of technical terms and the background knowledge of the skilled addressee, and this construction is incapable of being altered by evidence of how such persons subsequently acted upon or interpreted it. See *Glaverbel v British Coal* [1993] R.P.C. 90; [1994] R.P.C. 443; and [1995] R.P.C. 255 CA following *British Celanese v Courtaulds* (1935) 32 R.P.C. 171 at 196 HL.

Scientific Advisers or Assessors

The Patents Court and the Patents County Court may, regardless of whether or not the **61.78** parties themselves proffer expert evidence, appoint a scientific assessor or a scientific assessor to assist the court (see the Senior CourtsAct 1981 s.70(3); CDPA 1988 s.291(1) and (3); CPR PD63 para.5.10 and CPR 35.15). The costs of scientific assessors generally form part of the costs of the action whilst the cost of scientific advisers is paid for by the State. Such assistance is generally only required for the most technologically complex cases (see *Kirin Amgen Inc v Hoechst Marion Roussel Ltd* [2004] UKHL 46, *Schlumberger Holdings Ltd v Electromagnetic Geoservices AS* [2010] R.P.C. 33, [2010] EWCA Civ 819). The Practice Direction specifically provides that the court may order the appointment of a scientific advisor at the Case Management Conference, although there would appear to be no reason in principle why such an adviser may not be appointed at a later date if the technical complexity of the matter only becomes apparent at that date.

The Court of Appeal has said that where a scientific adviser is appointed, a record of the part he or she has played will normally be provided to the parties together with an opportunity to comment on it (*Halliburton Energy Services v Smith International Ltd (No.2)* [2007] R.P.C. 17; [2006] EWCA Civ 1715).

Trial

Mandatory procedural steps to be taken in the run-up to trial are set out in the Patents **61.79** Court Guide (see Appendix G). These steps include the preparation and delivery of the court papers, service of skeleton arguments and provision of a pre-reading guide for the judge. The reader is also referred to CPR Pt 39, and the Chancery Guide (printed in the *White Book*, Vol.2) which give further relevant directions in relation to the conduct of a hearing in general. Differences exist in procedure at trial in the Patents County Court (in particular possibility of no oral hearing, the limitation of any hearing to two days and the degree to which cross-examination may be curtailed or dispensed with). These differences are addressed out in the Patents County Court Guide.

Usually, the party bearing the burden of proof opens the case and calls its witnesses first. Accordingly, in a claim for infringement the patentee will usually go first.

At the trial all oral evidence will be recorded, as also will any judgment, but in patent litigation of any complexity it is usual for the parties to agree that a full transcript of the proceedings be taken with the costs shared between the parties.

The trial will normally be held in public, but may be held in whole or in part "in private" (formerly "*in camera*") if there are special circumstances (CPR 39.2). Consequently, parts of the transcript and/or final judgment may be confidential, as occurred for example in *SmithKline Beecham v Apotex* [2004] F.S.R. 26.

At the trial, any exhibits handed in or produced should be recorded on an exhibit sheet and kept in the custody of the court until the conclusion of the trial. It is then the parties' responsibility to see to their return and to preserve them for the period in which any appeal may take place (CPR 39A PD 7).

In all but the simplest cases, judgment after the substantive trial will be reserved with a written decision handed down at a later date. The written decision will normally be a draft judgment available only to the legal advisers of the parties (and potentially certain key staff of the client) and made available to the public in a final form only after making corrections. When a draft judgment is made available in advance, before the hearing following judgment the parties should exchange drafts of the consequential order which is then to be sought so that no party is taken by surprise at that hearing. When a hearing has taken place in public, anyone can obtain a copy of the transcript of the judgment or of any order made, subject to payment of the appropriate fee (CPR 39A PD 1.11). The Patents Court and the Patents County Court make most of their judgments available online on *http://www.bailii.org*.

Generally, once a judgment has been handed down, a party who disagrees with the result can only dispute it by recourse to an appeal. There are, however, exceptions. First, CPR 40.12 provides that accidental errors and omissions in judgments and orders can be corrected (the so-called "slip rule"). Secondly, the court has jurisdiction to correct its judgment where the judgment does not dispose of all the issues at trial between the parties. Finally, the court may exercise the so-called "Barrell" jurisdiction: where the court has given judgment but no order has been drawn up and entered giving effect to that judgment, the court retains jurisdiction to reconsider its decision and to receive further arguments and even new evidence. The jurisdiction is, however, only exercised in very exceptional circumstances (*Re Barrell Enterprises Ltd* [1973] 1 W.L.R. 19; *Pittalis v Sherefettin* [1986] Q.B. 868; *Stewart v Engle* [2000] 1 W.L.R. 2268; and *Townsend and Robinson v Fernsby* [2003] EWCA Civ 1820). For recent application of the slip rule in a Patent Action (in relation to the interest ordered post judgment) see *Leo Pharma v Sandoz* [2010] EWHC 1911 Pat Ct. A detailed discussion of the *Barrell* jurisdiction lies outside the remit of this book and the reader is referred to a more detailed textbook on procedure, such as the *White Book*.

Appeal

61.80   Appeals are governed by CPR 52 and its Practice Direction (note that CPR 52 also addresses Appeals from the Comptroller, which are addressed at §97.12 et seq.

Permission is required to appeal, or to cross-appeal. As CPR 52 provides, permission to appeal may be sought from the lower court at the hearing at which the decision to be appealed is made or from the appeal court by way of an appeal notice (or both). Unless the court orders otherwise, permission to appeal (and any appellant's notice) must be filed within 21 days after the date of judgment (CPR 52.4(2)(b)). CPR 52.3(6) provides that permission to appeal may only be given where the court considers that the appeal would have a real prospect of success or there is some other compelling reason why the appeal should be heard. The standard to be applied when considering permission in Patent cases was set out by Jacob L.J. *Pozzoli SPA v BDMO* [2007] EWCA Civ 588 as follows:

"I would add this about permission to appeal in patent cases generally. Unless the case is very clear and can be understood sufficiently readily in an hour or so, the better course is normally for permission to be granted by the trial judge. For, unlike the trial judge, the Court of Appeal judge(s) who have to decide whether permission should be granted (where the trial judge has refused it) will not be immersed in the technology and evidence in the same way as the trial judge. Faced with but an incomplete understanding and a plausible skeleton argument seeking permission, the Court of Appeal will generally be likely to grant permission, even if it later discerns that the case is indeed clear".

Note also, that when permission is given the court may limit the issues to be heard on appeal and/or otherwise impose conditions on the appeal (see CPR 52.3).

An appeal is by way of review rather than rehearing. It follows that in general the Court of Appeal will not reconsider findings of fact made at first instance. As the issue of obviousness is primarily a jury (i.e. factual) question, the Court of Appeal will thus rarely overturn a finding of obviousness by the Patents Court (*Biogen Inc v Medeva Plc* [1997] R.P.C. 1 at 45). Likewise, whilst the Court of Appeal has jurisdiction to admit new evidence, it will not do so unless strict criteria are satisfied; namely, that the evidence could not have been obtained with reasonable diligence for use at trial; the evidence would probably have an important influence on the outcome of the case; and the evidence must be credible (*Ladd v Marshall* [1954] 1 W.L.R. 1489 CA; and also *Coflexip SA v Stolt Comex Seaway MS Ltd* [2001] R.P.C. 9).

As at first instance, CPR 63.14 and 63.15 provide that the Comptroller may take part in appeals which concern a remedy relating to the registration of a patent.

A detailed description of the appeal procedure lies outside the scope of this book and the reader is referred to the CPR Pt 52 (and its practice direction), particularly to the time limits stated, and to the commentary in the *White Book*.

Additional Rules of Procedure in the Patents County Court

Since October 1, 2010 the procedure in the Patents County Court has been materially **61.81** different from that in the Patents Court. The position is set out in detail in the Patents County Court Guide, (see Appendix G). It is strongly recommended that an up-to-date copy of the Patents County Court Guide is consulted.

In addition to the rules which apply to the Patents Court, the Patents County Court is governed by CPR Part 63 Section V (general rules), CPR PD 30 paras 9.1 and 9.2 (transfer), CPR Part 45 (costs) and the Patents County Court (Financial Limits) Order 2011.

The new rules of procedure apply as a package and apply only to cases commenced, or transferred, to the Patents County Court on or after October 1, 2010. (see *Technical Fibre Products v Bell* [2010] EWPCC 011 and *Westwood v Knight* [2011] EWPCC 16, para.13).

Patents County Court: Damages Cap

Section 2 of the Patents County Court (Financial Limits) Order 2011 provides that in re- **61.82** lation to all proceedings within the special jurisdiction of the Patents County Court, there is a cap (not including interest or costs) of £500,000 in respect of any claim for damages/ account of profits.

The Order came into force on June 14, 2011. Section 3 of the Order provides transitional provisions in respect of claims made before the Order came into force such that, it appears, no cap applies to such claims.

Patents County Court: Content of Statements of Case

In addition to the general requirements set out above, Statements of Case in the Patents **61.83**

County Court must comply with CPR Part 63.20(1) and must set out concisely all facts and arguments relied upon. The Patents County Court Guide states that "A key purposes of this requirement is to facilitate the conduct of the case management conference which will be conducted on an issue by issue basis. Therefore the Court and the parties need to know what the issues are going to be in sufficient detail for that process to take place. However attention is drawn to the requirement for matters to be set out concisely". Further guidance is set out in s.2.4 of the Patents County Court Guide.

It is important to note that time limits in Patents County Court cases are (a) different from the Patents Court and (b) only extendable with permission of the Court and for good reason (see CPR Part 63.22 and Patents County Practice Direction, para.2.4).

Patents County Court: Statement of Truth

61.84   CPR Part 63.21 modifies the general requirements of a statement of truth as set out in CPR Part 22. The statement of truth must be made by a person (or if necessary persons) who have knowledge of the facts alleged (see Patents County Court Guide para.2.4).

Patents County Court: Case Management

61.85   Case management hearings in the Patents County Court are made in accordance with CPR Part 63.23 and are discussed in detail in para.2.5 of the Patents County Court Guide. They are conducted by the judge and will normally be heard orally (although they may where all the parties consent be determined on paper, see CPR 63.23(3)).

It is to be expected that the court will take a robust attitude to case management. Standard form patent action directions cannot be assumed. On the contrary at the CMC the Patents County Court will consider which issues should be heard at trial and only make appropriate orders in relation to such specific and identified issues as pass a cost benefit test (see CPR PD 63 paras 29.1 and 29.2). Orders in relation to additional material will have to satisfy a significant hurdle (see CPR Part 63.23(2)). The position was set out by HHJ Birss QC in *Westwood v Knight* [2011] EWPCC 16 as follows:

> "36.   [new provisions under CPR Part 63 and its practice direction] present a radical departure from previous English civil procedure, at least as it is practiced in the courts handling intellectual property claims. The provisions are a key element of the new procedure and its purpose in making intellectual property cases less expensive and quicker to resolve. The parties do not have a free rein to call any evidence they want on any topic. The court will control the procedure. Further material will only be permitted on identified points and only if it satisfies the cost benefit test in paragraph 29.2(2). If material has not been permitted in this way, CPR Pt 63.23(2) sets a significant hurdle in the way of its introduction into the case. It seems to me that one important consequence of the provisions is that, subject to proper safeguards, some relevant evidence will be excluded from trials. Merely because some evidence is relevant will not necessarily justify permission being given to adduce it. On the other hand the parties need to know that the court will give permission for evidence to be filed in a proper case since otherwise there will be a temptation to overload the statements of case with unnecessary material.
>
> 37.   Of course powers along these lines were introduced with the CPR itself (see e.g. CPR Pt 1.1 (2) (proportionality) and Pt 1.4 (1) (active case management), (2) (h) (considering whether the likely benefits of taking a step justify the cost of taking it)) but the new procedures create a specific framework in which they can be applied in order to improve the resolution of disputes about intellectual property rights.

The position specifically in relation to amendment a statement of case was also addressed by HHJ Birss QC in *Temple Island v New England Teas* [2011] EWPCC 19, paras 23–33, where it was stated:

> "23.   The power to amend pleadings is in CPR Part 17 rule 17.3. Before me the claimant submitted the usual principles applicable to amendments of pleadings in the High Court applied in the Patents County Court. The classic statement is the passage from the judgment of Peter Gibson LJ in *Cobbold v Greenwich LBC* unreported 9th August 1999 that:

The overriding objective (of the CPR) is that the court should deal with cases justly. That includes, so far as is practicable, ensuring that each case is dealt with not only expeditiously but also fairly. Amendments in general ought to be allowed so that the real dispute between the parties can be adjudicated upon provided that any prejudice to the other party caused by the amendment can be compensated for in costs, and the public interest in the administration of justice is not significantly harmed.
....

33. Every application to amend statements of case involves a balance between allowing the amendment and a consideration of the prejudice the amendment may cause. That is what Peter Gibson LJ is referring to in the passage I have quoted above. When considering an application to amend the statements of case in the Patents County Court in a regime with capped costs, that balancing exercise will include an assessment of whether the likely benefit of the amendment appears likely to justify the cost of taking and dealing with it".

As set out in para.2.5 of the Patents County Court Guide, prior to a CMC hearing the parties will need to consider fully what (if anything) each believes is required by way of evidence/experiments/disclosure/cross-examination etc., and be in a position to justify, on a cost-benefit basis, its position.

At the CMC the Patents County Court will consider whether the trial requires an oral hearing (which will be no more than two days) or whether it can be disposed of on paper. The Patents County Court Guide, (see Appendix G), includes a specimen CMC order. It is the usual practice of the Patents County Court to set a trial date at the CMC (see *Temple Island v New English Teas Ltd* [2011] EWPCC 19, para.14).

Patents County Court: Applications

With the exception of Case Management Conferences, applications will be dealt with **61.86** without a hearing unless the court considers it necessary to hold a hearing (CPR 63.25(3)). A respondent to an application must file a response within five days of the service of the application notice (see Patents County Court Guide, para.2.7). Adverse costs orders may be made if a party has behaved unreasonably (CPR Part 63.26(2).

Patents County Court: Costs

The general rules on costs apply under CPR Part 43.1, 2 and 4 apply to the Patents **61.87** County Court (see *Westwood v Knight* [2011] EWPC, para.8). However, there are important additional rules that apply to the Patents County Court, as set out in Section VII of CPR Part 45. With certain exceptions (relating to (a) abuse of process and (b) cases in which there is a certificate of contested validity) Section VII applies to all Patents County Court proceedings. However, the new costs rules do not automatically apply to costs incurred in the High Court prior to transfer (see *Westwood* para.13). All costs in the Patents County Court are subject to summary assessment (see CPR 45.41(3) and *Westwood* para.14).

CPR Part 45.42 limits costs in the Patents County Court in two ways. First,there is an overall cap after any set off, currently £50,000 in relation to liability and £25,000 in relation to quantum (CPR 45.42(2)). Secondly there are caps as to the sums that can be recovered for the various stages of any proceedings (CPR 45.42(3)). It is important to note that the scale costs are still assessed. Thus, if the assessment produces more than the applicable cap, the cap is ordered. However, if the assessment is less, then a sum less than the cap will be ordered. CPR PD 45 Section 25C, tables A and B of s.25C set out the current scale of costs.

The process of assessment of costs in the Patents County Court is set out in detail in *Westwood* (see also *Indigo Furniture Ltd v Future Look Ltd* [2011] EWPCC 13 and *Temple Island v New English Teas* [2011] EWPCC 19). In addition to the general issues of assessment, attention is drawn to the manner in which the court has dealt with (a) VAT and (b) interest (see *Westwood* paras 44 and 45).

In relation to cases transferred to the Patents County Court, costs before transfer are dealt with on a case by case basis (see Patents County Court Guide, para.2.9 and *Westwood* para.38).

SECTION 62

Restrictions on recovery of damages for infringement

62.01   **62.**—(1) In proceedings for infringement of a patent damages shall not be awarded, and no order shall be made for an account of profits, against a defendant or defender who proves that at the date of the infringement he was not aware, and had no reasonable grounds for supposing, that the patent existed; and a person shall not be taken to have been so aware or to have had reasonable grounds for so supposing by reason only of the application to a product of the word "patent" or "patented", or any word or words expressing or implying that a patent has been obtained for the product, unless the number of the patent accompanied the word or words in question.

(2) In proceedings for infringement of a patent the court or the comptroller may, if it or he thinks fit, refuse to award any damages or make any such order in respect of an infringement committed during **the further period specified in** [*any further period specified under*] section 25(4) above, but before the payment of the renewal fee and any additional fee prescribed for the purposes of that subsection.

(3) Where an amendment of the specification of a patent has been allowed under any of the provisions of this Act, **the court or the comptroller shall, when awarding damages or making an order for an account of profits in proceedings for an infringement of the patent committed before the decision to allow the amendment, take into account the following—**

  (a) whether at the date of infringement the defendant or defender knew, or had reasonable grounds to know, that he was infringing the patent;

  (b) whether the specification of the patent as published was framed in good faith and with reasonable skill and knowledge;

  (c) whether the proceedings are brought in good faith.]

[*no damages shall be awarded in proceedings for an infringement of the patent committed before the decision to allow the amendment unless the court or the comptroller is satisfied that the specification of the patent as published was framed in good faith and with reasonable skill and knowledge.*]

Notes

1. Subsection (2) was amended by the Patents Act 2004 (c.16) Sch.2(15) with effect from October 1, 2005 (SI 2005/2471).

2. An amendment to subs.(3) was prospectively made by the same Act (s.2(3)), but this amendment was not brought into effect and it was repealed by SI 2006/1028 (reg.2(4) and Sch.4) with effect from April 29, 2006. However, by the same SI (reg.2(2) and Sch.2(2)), and with the same date of effect, the subsection was again amended to insert the wording shown above in bold type. This was done to bring the section into compliance with art.13(1) of the European "Enforcement Directive" (No. 2004/48/EC, OJ EC L157, April 30, 2004, p.45, with corrigendum OJ EC L195, June 2, 2004, p.16).

COMMENTARY ON SECTION 62

Scope of the section

62.02   Section 62 provides a patent infringer with the possibility of some relief from the consequences of infringement in certain circumstances, viz. for infringements committed during periods: when he was not aware of the existence of the patent (subs.(1)); when a renewal fee on the patent ought to have been, but had not been, paid (subs.(2)); or where the patent was subsequently amended (subs.(3)). However, each of these provisions is either discretionary or subject to qualifications as explained in §§62.03–62.05 respectively.

The section applies (by virtue of s.61(3)) to infringement proceedings brought before the Comptroller. By virtue of s.69(3), subss.(2) and (3) do not apply to proceedings for infringement of rights in the period between publication of an application and the grant of a patent, but s.69(3) provides for an alternative form of relief in such circumstances, see the commentary on s.69.

The exculpatory provisions of the section do not provide for any relief for infringements committed outside the specified periods; and, apparently, do not prevent the imposition of an injunction against future acts of infringement. While the predecessor s.59(4) of the 1949 Act stipulated that its provisions did not prevent the court from granting an injunction, the present section is silent on the point. Thus, the failure to re-enact this provision might provide a basis for contending, in an appropriate case, that an injunction should not be imposed because of circumstances giving rise to relief under s.62, for example, where heavy expenditure had been incurred by the defendant in erecting a plant, which or the operation of which is covered by the patent, when at the time there was ignorance of the existence of the patent or where the patent was at that time clearly invalid, but subsequently validated by amendment. In any event, the grant of an injunction is always a matter of discretion within the equitable jurisdiction of the court.

Innocent infringement (subs.(1))

By subs.(1), no award of damages, or an account of profits, is to be made against an infringer in respect of infringements committed during a period for which he proves he was unaware of the existence of the patent and had no reasonable grounds for supposing that the patent existed. Marking a product or device with the word "patent" or "patented" is insufficient notice of the existence of the patent unless the patent number is included in that marking. For false marking, see s.110 and the commentary on that section. The onus on establishing this defence rests on the infringer but, if this onus is discharged, relief under the subsection would appear to be mandatory.

62.03

However, no relief is available under the provision against infringements committed after the defendant had been made aware of the existence of the patent, for example by receiving a warning letter or upon the commencement of infringement proceedings. Also, the subsection has no application where an infringer, having actual or constructive knowledge of the existence of the patent, is unaware that his actions amount to an infringement: the subsection concerns only ignorance of the existence of the patent (or application in the case of proceedings under s.69). Ignorance of the former kind can be quite common when use is made of a proprietary product, the composition of which is unknown to the user and perhaps incapable of being revealed by analysis.

The onus of proof for relief under the subsection appears to be a heavy one, see *Benmax v Austin* (1953) 70 R.P.C. 143 and 284 and *Lancer v Henley Forklift* [1975] R.P.C. 307. Also, in *Ward Building Supplies v Hodgson Steels* BL C/47/97, the defendant had been put on notice that a patent existed. A search revealed only a European patent not extending to the United Kingdom. This constituted further notice and a defence under the subsection was held not established. Thus, a company with a research and development department, or its own in-house patent department, would seem rarely to be able to take advantage of the provision because of the presumption that such departments ought to take steps to become aware of patents in their field of interest.

However, the defence is of value to small and medium-sized enterprises and was successful in *Lux Traffic v Pike Signals* [1993] R.P.C. 107, where the claimant conceded that he should obtain no monetary relief for infringements committed up to a date six months after it had sent a warning letter to the defendant. From this, it would appear that the court may be prepared to extend the relief beyond the period of actual innocence up to a date when it was reasonable for the defendant to have investigated the situation and as a consequence brought the infringing activity to an end. Also, in *Texas Iron Works' Patent* [2000] R.P.C. 207 CA, it was accepted that, until receiving a patent agent's letter, the defendant was unaware of the existence of the patent, and had no reason to suppose that it existed. The claimant's product was not marked to indicate the existence of a patent in the United Kingdom (although a US patent number was given), nor had the defendant's article been copied from the claimants' article.

Lost rights after restoration or late renewal (subs.(2))

62.04   Subsection (2) provides a discretionary power to refuse to award damages, or an account of profits, in respect of infringements committed between the end of the period prescribed under s.25(3) for payment of a renewal fee (i.e. the anniversary of the filing date of the patent) and the actual payment of that fee during the following six months, as permitted by s.25(4). The amendment to subs.(2), noted in §62.01 above, conforms the reference to the period which is specified in s.25(4), as amended (for which see §25.01 above). There appear to be no decisions under this provision. In addition to this subsection, s.28A provides for loss of rights during a period between the date when a patent formally lapsed for non-payment of renewal fee (i.e. the anniversary of the filing date of the patent) and the date when it is restored under the provisions of s.28. Such loss of rights is discussed in the commentary on s.28A.

Damages after amendment (subs. (3))

62.05   Subsection (3) is applicable to a situation when the patent has previously been amended, or amended in the course of proceedings. The comparable situation, when a patent is found infringed but only partially valid, is dealt with in s.63, see the commentary on that section. Subsection (3) as now amended has the effect of providing that, where damages or an account is claimed for a period before (validating) amendments are made to the patent, the court or Comptroller has a wide discretion in determining whether award such damages. However, this provision does not apply in respect of acts of infringement occurring after the date of the amendment. The discretion conferred by this subsection is to be exercised having regard to the three factors there set out, namely the state of the defendant's knowledge, whether the patent as published was framed in good faith and with reasonable skill and knowledge, and whether the proceedings were brought in good faith. There is as yet no guidance as to how the courts will exercise such discretion.

Of the three factors taken account of in exercising this discretion the one set out in subs.(3)(a), as to the state of the defendant's knowledge, involves the same type of enquiry as that set out in s.62(1), see §62.03.

Subsection (3)(b), namely "whether the specification of the patent as published was framed in good faith and with reasonable skill and knowledge" is the only one of these three factors which has been the subject of guidance in the case law in this particular context, because it used to be the case under this subsection before it was amended that unless the "specification for the patent as published was framed in good faith and with reasonable skill and knowledge", no damages could be awarded for an infringement committed before the amendment was allowed. There is no reason to assume that guidance under old case law as to what is meant by this expression should not continue to apply. Case law as to the same expression in s.63(2), which has been similarly amended, is also relevant (see §63.03). Thus relief (under the corresponding s.59 of the 1949 Act) was denied in *Rediffusion Simulation v Link-Miles* [1993] F.S.R. 369 because amendment had been carried out carelessly so that the specification "as published" (albeit after amendment) had not been "framed with reasonable skill". Also, in *Mabuchi Motor's Patents* [1996] R.P.C. 387, amendment was allowed on the basis that the Japanese attorney responsible, while knowing of the relevant prior art, accepted the view of the United Kingdom patent agent (who was unaware of that art) that broader claims than requested appeared to be allowable. However, this meant that the original claims had not been drafted with reasonable skill and knowledge, and therefore subs.(3) precluded the award of damages for infringement of the amended claim prior to the date of amendment. The amendment of subs.(3) (as noted in §62.01 above), has the effect of providing that, where damages are claimed for a

period before (validating) amendments are made to the patent, the court is entitled to refuse to award such damages unless it is satisfied, not only that the patent as published was
framed in good faith and with reasonable skill and knowledge, but also that the infringement claim was "brought in good faith". Thus, it could be argued that an award of damages or an account of profits may be denied where the patentee knew, or ought to have
known, that during the period in respect of which the claim is made the patent was not
wholly valid. However, this further provision does not apply in respect of acts of infringement occurring after the date of the amendment.

Relief was not denied in *Mölnlycke v Procter & Gamble (No.5)* [1994] R.P.C. 49 where
the patent had been amended in unsuccessful revocation proceedings before the Comptroller and it was accepted, upon the evidence of the patent draftsman, that the specification
had been drafted with due skill and knowledge, it being irrelevant that, in hindsight, the
patent might have been more clearly drafted. The reference to the "specification of the patent as published" suggests that this criterion of skilful and knowledgeable drafting applies
to the "B-specification"; and, in view of the *Rediffusion* decision, above, the phrase would
also seem to apply to the publication of an amended specification. However, when the
subsection is applied under s.69(1), obviously the reference must be to the publication of
the application under s.16 (the "A-specification"), but see then the special provision of
s.69(3) (discussed in §69.07). Also, s.62(3) applies only where the patent has been
amended post-grant, but this would seem to include amendment of a European patent
(UK) effected during opposition proceedings in the EPO.

Further important cases on s.62(3) are *Nutrinova v Scanchem (No.2)* [2001] F.S.R. 43;
Kirin-Amgen v Transkaryotic Therapies [2003] R.P.C. 3 CA; and *Unilin Beheer v Berry
Floor (No.2)* [2006] F.S.R. 26 at 495, the last two in particular emphasising that any
mistake or negligence by a draftsman must be assessed against the context and the entirety
of the specification. These cases are further discussed in §63.03 below.

SECTION 63

Relief for infringement of partially valid patent

63.—(1) If the validity of a patent is put in issue in proceedings for infringe-   **63.01**
ment of the patent and it is found that the patent is only partially valid, the court
or the comptroller may, subject to subsection (2) below, grant relief in respect of
that part of the patent which is found to be valid and infringed.

(2) Where in any such proceedings it is found that a patent is only partially
valid, the court or the comptroller, **when awarding damages, costs or expenses
or making an order for an account of profits, take into account the following—**

(a) **whether at the date of the infringement the defendant or defender
knew, or had reasonable grounds to know, that he was infringing
the patent;**

(b) **whether the specification of the patent was framed in good faith and
with reasonable skill and knowledge;**

(c) **whether the proceedings are brought in good faith;**

**and any relief granted shall be subject to the discretion of the court or the
comptroller as to costs or expenses and as to the date from which damages
or an account should be reckoned.**

*[shall not grant relief by way of damages, costs or expenses, except where the
plaintiff or pursuer proves that the specification for the patent was framed in
good faith and with reasonable skill and knowledge, and in that event the court
or the comptroller may grant relief in respect of that part of the patent which is*

valid and infringed, subject to the discretion of the court or the comptroller as to costs or expenses and as to the date from which damages should be reckoned.]

(3) As a condition of relief under this section the court or the comptroller may direct that the specification of the patent shall be amended to its or his satisfaction upon an application made for that purpose under section 75 below, and an application may be so made accordingly, whether or not all other issues in the proceedings have been determined.

(4) The court or the comptroller may also grant relief under this section in the case of a European patent (UK) on condition that the claims of the patent are limited to its or his satisfaction by the European Patent Office at the request of the proprietor.

Notes

1. An amendment to subs.(2) was prospectively made by the Patents Act 2004 (c.16) s.2(3), but this amendment was not brought into effect and it was repealed by SI 2006/1028 (reg.2(4) and Sch.4) with effect from April 29, 2006. However, by the same SI (reg.2(2) and Sch.2 para.3), and with the same date of effect, the subsection was again amended to insert the wording shown above in bold type. This was done to bring the section into compliance with art.13(1) of the European "Enforcement Directive" (No.2004/48/EC, OJ EC L157, April 30, 2004, p.45, with corrigendum OJ EC L195, June 2, 2004, p.16).

2. Subsection (4) was prospectively added by the Patents Act 2004 and came into effect on December 17, 2007, when EPC 2000 was brought into force.

COMMENTARY ON SECTION 63

Scope of the section

63.02   Section 63 deals with relief for infringement of a patent which, in the same proceedings, is found to be partially valid (or invalid only partially). It is a precondition for operation of the section that the court has "found" the patent to be partially valid and thus in *SmithKline Beecham v Apotex [Costs]* [2005] F.S.R. 24 at 599, the Court of Appeal held that the words "it is found" at the beginning of s.63(2) mean that the section does not apply insofar as the patentee concedes invalidity of certain claims at the start of trial, because in such a case the court makes no finding as to their validity. It is also a precondition for operation of the section that there has been a finding by the court that the patent could be regarded as "partially valid" (*Lubrizol v Esso* [1998] R.P.C. 727 CA). Here, the judgment had been that the "patent is invalid" and the court had not been asked to make any ruling as to partial validity or invalidity in the light of the evidence presented to the court. Following *Windsurfing v Tabur Marine* [1985] R.P.C. 59, it is important to avoid re-opening the evidence in relation to the allowability of amendment or relief under s.63 and it was noted that, in *Hallen v Brabantia* [1990] F.S.R. 134, the case had been argued on the basis of independent validity of certain claims. Consequently, this *Lubrizol* decision makes it imperative for counsel to seek a finding that, in the event of certain grounds of invalidity being upheld, there should be a concomitant finding that parts of the patent unaffected thereby would be valid if the patent were amended. However, in this decision, it was indicated that putting forward a string of auxiliary requests (as in the EPO) should not be countenanced by the Patents Court. Of course, if it is intended to seek relief under the section or seek amendment effective against other infringers, a stay should be requested of the operation of an order for complete revocation. The Patents County Court ordered such a stay in *Marrero v Elmdene* BL CC/50/96. In *Texas Iron Works' Patent* [2000] R.P.C. 207 CA, it was argued that, where a patent is held invalid for added subject-matter contrary to s.72(1)(d), no finding of "partial validity" is possible, but the point was not decided as the decision below of invalidity for added subject-matter was reversed.

The section does not apply to infringement of rights arising under s.69 under a pending application, see s.69(1)).

Section 63 provides that, although the court or Comptroller may grant relief in respect of that part of a patent which is found valid and infringed, notwithstanding the invalidity of other parts of the patent (subs.(1)), any award of monetary relief and costs (expenses in Scotland) is subject to a discretion which is to be exercised having regard to the three factors set out in subs.(2), and it may be made a condition of the grant of relief under the section that the patent be satisfactorily amended (subs.(3)) or for a European patent (UK) centrally limited (subs.(4)). Where the patent has been amended prior to the infringement proceedings, s.62(3) applies in a similar way to subs.(2), see §62.05. The provisions of s.63(2) and (3) are discussed in §63.03 and §63.04 respectively.

While subs.(1) is silent as to the type of "relief" which may be granted in respect of a partially valid patent, and subs.(2) provides limitations only on monetary relief (by way of damages or an account of profits) and costs (expenses in Scotland), the other types of relief available for patent infringement, i.e. an injunction and an order for delivery up or destruction of infringing articles, are equitable in nature and, consequently, are within the discretion of the court, see the commentary on practice under s.61, even though it is the normal practice for such types of relief to be granted. Consequently, s.63 may mean that all relief for infringement of a partially valid patent is at the discretion of the court (or Comptroller in the case of proceedings under s.63(1)). Nevertheless, an injunction will, apparently, normally be granted, see *Codex v Racal-Milgo* [1983] R.P.C. 369, but the position could be different when there has been a lack of good faith on the basis of the maxim that "he who seeks Equity must have clean hands", though even this was doubted in *Van der Lely v Bamfords* [1964] R.P.C. 54 CA. In the *Codex* decision, as discussed in the previous edition of this Work, the Court of Appeal criticised the distinction then inherent in the original version of s.63(2) (as printed in §63.01 above) as between damages and an account of profits, and whether it was "sensible to let a defendant off damages or an account unless he has actually relied upon something done by the patentee". It was thus questioned whether s.63(2) was consistent with the Enforcement Directive. It is evident that account was taken of these observations in implementing the Directive so as to amend s.63(2) as set out in §63.01, thereby giving the court a broad discretion as to the relief to be ordered in such circumstances. The Court of Appeal in *Unilin Beheer v Berry Floor* [2006] F.S.R. 26 at 495 concluded that from a policy perspective the provision should apply against the patentee only where he had done something which might mislead—see §63.03, and this may therefore give guidance as to how the discretion will be exercised generally.

In *SmithKline Beecham v Apotex* [2003] F.S.R. 30 at 524; and [2003] F.S.R. 31 at 544, no reason was seen why an interim injunction could not be based on a partially valid patent. Also (subject to the limitation period, for which see §60.30), damages or an account of profits will normally run from the date of first infringement unless the partial invalidity has had an effect upon the defendant (*Gerber Garment v Lectra Systems* [1994] F.S.R. 471; and [1995] F.S.R. 492 CA).

While the analogous s.62 of the 1949 Act referred to any claim being found valid despite other claims being found invalid, the present section refers to a "partially valid patent". This seems to suggest that relief is possible under a claim which is itself only invalid to a limited extent. However, it also suggests that it may no longer be sufficient in seeking an interim injunction to sue only on some claims of the patent and argue that the validity of claims not sued upon is irrelevant, as was done in *Hoffmann-La Roche v DDSA* [1965] R.P.C. 503. Indeed, in *Petrolite v Dyno* [1998] F.S.R. 190, where the patentee sued on some claims only, while admitting that other claims were invalid and were to be abandoned in co-pending EPO opposition proceedings, summary judgment of revocation was ordered unless amendment was sought under s.75 within a limited period.

Requirement for good faith, skill and knowledge in patent draftsmanship (subs.(2))

As indicated in §63.02, any award of monetary relief (including costs or expenses and   **63.03** now including both damages and an account of profits after amendment of s.63(2)) on a partially valid patent is subject to a discretion which is to be exercised having regard to the three factors set out in subs.(2). The discretion conferred by this subsection is to be exercised having regard to the three factors there set out, namely the state of the defendant's knowledge, whether the patent as published was framed in good faith and with reasonable skill and knowledge, and whether the proceedings were brought in good faith.

Of the three factors taken account of in exercising this discretion the one set out in subs.(2)(a), as to the state of the defendant's knowledge, involves the same type of enquiry as that set out in s.62(1) (see §62.03).

The language used in subs.(2)(b), namely "whether the specification of the patent was framed in good faith and with reasonable skill and knowledge" was essentially the same in the subsection before it was amended and was the subject of guidance in the case law as to what is meant by this expression which should continue to apply under the amended subsection. Case law as to the same expression in s.62(3), which has been similarly amended is also relevant (see §62.05).

In showing that "the specification for the patent was framed in good faith and with reasonable skill and knowledge" it was usual to offer as a witness the agent(s) who drafted the specification, see: *Page v Brent Toy Products* (1950) 67 R.P.C. 4; *Hallen v Brabantia* [1990] F.S.R. 134; and *Quantel v Spaceward Microsystems* BL C/78/89. However, this is not essential, see *Lucas v Gaedor* [1978] R.P.C. 297.

The requirements for a showing of good faith and reasonable skill and knowledge should normally be considered at the same hearing as an application to amend the patent (for which see §63.03), see *Kahn (David) v Conway Stewart* [1974] R.P.C. 279; and *Hallen v Brabantia* [1990] R.P.C. 307, where the hearing was adjourned for the responsible patent agent to be present to give the necessary evidence, and likewise in *Chiron v Organon Teknika (No.7)* [1994] F.S.R. 458. Unless the defendant admits the point, the witness presented to discharge this onus can be expected to be cross-examined at least as to the instructions given to him by the inventors or the proprietor and his state of knowledge of the relevant prior art at the relevant time. The task of "framing the patent" would seem also to include the framing of any amendment thereto, either before or after grant. As an exercise of discretion is required, it is probable that, if pressed by the defendant, the claimant will be required to make full disclosure of documents, subject to a claim to privilege, as when discretion used to be requested to allow a patent to be amended, for which see §§27.05–27.07.

Cases where the criteria of subs.(2) were not satisfied include: *Ronson v Lewis* [1963] R.P.C. 103, where relief was denied because the patent agent had departed in a material (and erroneous) respect from the instructions which he had been given; *Rediffusion Stimulation v Link-Miles* [1993] F.S.R. 369, where there had been careless amendment of the specification, see §62.05; and *Mabuchi Motors' Patents* [1996] R.P.C. 387 where the United Kingdom patent attorney had not followed the instructions given to him to file narrower claims because he was of the honest opinion that broader claims could be obtained, but he had not been made aware of the relevant art by his instructing Japanese client who did know of the relevant prior art, but accepted the view of the United Kingdom patent agent. In contrast, in *Hallen v Brabantia* (above), the required criterion of reasonable skill and knowledge was held to be satisfied because the patent draftsman had been someone with reasonable skill in drafting patent specifications and a knowledge of patent law and practice, and he had framed the specification with a view to obtaining a monopoly to which he honestly believed, on the information available to him, the applicant was entitled. Discretionary relief was then allowed, particularly because the defendant had received legal advice that he was at risk, and there were no special circumstances, see also *Page v Brent Toy Products* (above). Relief was also allowed in the *Kahn* case (above) and in *Quantel v Spaceward Microsystems* (above). In the latter case, a patentee was not held to be blameworthy when he was aware of the existence of a prior art document, but did not know of its consequences in relation to validity. Indeed, in *Nutrinova v Scanchem (No.2)* [2001] F.S.R. 43 at 831, it was indicated that it is the duty of a patent agent to draft the widest claims which he thought possible and the mere fact that the claims were held invalid for lack of inventive step was no indication of drafting in bad faith, as would probably be the case where claims were maintained in the knowledge of clear lack of novelty. In *Chiron v Organon Teknika* (above), the Patents Court stated that there is "no duty upon a patentee to inform the Patent Office of matters that could affect prosecution of a patent application." However:

"in most cases, it would be wise for a patentee to keep the Patent Office informed, as failure to do so could be relevant to the court's exercise of discretion on amendment and could also amount to lack of good faith."

Also, in *Hoechst Celanese v BP Chemicals [Iodide Removal]* [1997] F.S.R. 547, no lack of good faith was found despite the anticipatory document having been listed in the European search report. This listing was only as a document of background interest and was not relied upon in the subsequent examination report. Evidence was given by both the English and US patent attorneys responsible that it was not their practice to study documents cited only as background interest and the court accepted this, see R. Price and I. de Minvielle-Devaux [1997] *CIPA* 292. Relief was granted in *Kirin-Amgen's Patent* [2002] R.P.C. 43 at 851, the court holding that the fact that:

"a patent may have been drafted so as to include invalid claims should not, in the absence of special factors, prevent the patentee being entitled to the full range of relief against an infringer of one or more of the valid claims, provided it is a case where section 63(2) does not apply".

The court found that errors in a minor proportion of the description had not influenced the decision on the invalidity of the claims sought to be deleted and had not led to the EPO or readers of the specification being particularly adversely affected. The claims were held valid in the Court of Appeal (*Kirin-Amgen v Transkaryotic Therapies* [2003] R.P.C. 3 at 31), but then found invalid by the House of Lords ([2005] R.P.C. 9 at 169). The Court of Appeal reviewed the history of the phrase "reasonable skill and knowledge" in s.63(2) in *Unilin Beheer v Berry Floor* [2006] F.S.R. 26 at 495 and concluded that, from a policy perspective:

"the provision should be construed so as to deprive the patentee of damages only where he had done something which might mislead."

By virtue of subs.(2)(c), involving an enquiry as to whether the proceedings were "brought in good faith", it could be argued that an award of damages or an account of profits may be denied where the patentee knew, or ought to have known, that during the period in respect of which the claim is made the patent was not wholly valid.

Amendment or limitation required as condition of relief on partially valid patent (subss.(3), (4))

As a condition of allowing relief under subs.(2), the court (or the Comptroller in **63.04** proceedings under s.61(3)) may, by s.63(3), direct that the patent be amended to remove its partial invalidity. Alternatively, for a European patent (UK), by s.63(4) the court or the Comptroller may direct that the patentee deal with matters by a patent limitation procedure at the EPO. Similar conditions can be imposed under s.72(4) or (4A) when, in an application for revocation, the applicant's case succeeds only partially. In these circumstances, relief under the partially valid patent is discretionary and, it would appear that, if amendment or limitation cannot be achieved in a timely fashion, it may then be difficult to obtain relief under s.63 as it would be strange if a patentee could obtain damages, etc. while maintaining before the public claims which have been held to be invalid and where therefore prima facie the patent should be revoked unless amended or limited, see *Petrolite v Dyno* [1998] F.S.R. 190, cited in §63.02.

A claim dependent on an invalid claim is not itself invalid prior to amendment or limitation, so that relief thereon can be granted without amendment or limitation first being required (*Hallen v Brabantia* [1989] R.P.C. 307). When amendment in that case was allowed ([1990] F.S.R. 134) the order for amendment was suspended pending the deposition of the patentee's appeal against the decision of partial invalidity.

Where the patent had expired and no one was affected by the absence of amendment, the court did not require this as a condition of granting relief (*Gerber Garment v Lectra Systems* [1994] F.S.R. 471).

SECTION 64 [SUBSTITUTED]

Right to continue use begun before priority date

64.01 **64.**—(1) Where a patent is granted for an invention, a person who in the United Kingdom before the priority date of the invention—

    (a) does in good faith an act which would constitute an infringement of the patent if it were in force, or

    (b) makes in good faith effective and serious preparations to do such an act,

has the right to continue to do the act or, as the case may be, to do the act, notwithstanding the grant of the patent; but this right does not extend to granting a licence to another person to do the act.

(2) If the act was done, or the preparations were made, in the course of a business, the person entitled to the right conferred by subsection (1) may—

    (a) authorise the doing of that act by any partners of his for the time being in that business, and

    (b) assign that right, or transmit it on death (or in the case of a body corporate on its dissolution), to any person who acquires that part of the business in the course of which the act was done or the preparations were made.

(3) Where a product is disposed of to another in exercise of the rights conferred by subsection (1) or (2), that other and any person claiming through him may deal with the product in the same way as if it had been disposed of by the registered proprietor of the patent.

Note. The present s.64 was substituted for its original version by Sch.5 para.17 [CDPA 1988] with effect from January 7, 1991 (SI 1990/2168). The original form of the section has no present applicability and therefore is not reprinted.

Commentary on Section 64

Scope of the section

64.02 In general, the patent laws of continental European countries have not provided for patent invalidity in a case where there has been a prior secret use of the claimed invention, but instead have provided the prior secret user with a right to continue his prior acts unaffected by the grant of the patent. Section 64 is therefore intended to adopt the same principle of providing a third party right, rather than invalidating the patent for prior secret use, as was the case under s.32(1)(l) of the 1949 Act. However, in the light of *EC Commission v United Kingdom* (C-30/90) [1993] R.P.C. 283; [1992] 1 E.C.R. 829, there must be some doubt whether the provisions of the section are ultra vires, as discussed in §64.03. Section 64 provides a person with a right to continue to carry out acts, which would otherwise be an infringement of a patent, if those acts were first done before the priority date of an invention protected by the patent, or where effective and serious preparations were made to carry out such acts, provided always that these prior acts were done, or the preparations made to do them were done, in good faith (subs.(1)). For the concept of "priority date", see the commentary on s.5 and note that this may not be uniform for all the subject-matter covered by the patent, even within a single claim, see §125.27. The right provided by the section is a personal defence to an allegation of infringement and it does not extend to granting a licence to another to do such acts (subs.(1)), except in defined circumstances where the prior act was done in the course of a business (subs.(2)), and where products are disposed of in exercise of rights provided by either subs.(1) or (2) (subs.(3)). This limitation of the right and the exceptions to it are discussed in §64.07. The right is available only in respect of acts which would otherwise by an infringement of the patent and this aspect is discussed further in §64.04. The onus of establishing a right under the section lies with the person who would otherwise be an infringer. The provisions of the section were usefully discussed by Isobel Davies and S. Cohen [1994] E.I.P.R. 239. The present wording of the section is clearer than that of the original provision. The substitution of the section arose from the revision of s.28 and the insertion of s.28A which likewise deals with third party rights, but in relation to intervening acts between the date of a patent lapsing and its restoration under s.28

The requirement for the rights to arise from an "infringing act"

No rights are granted under s.64 except in respect of acts which would otherwise be regarded as acts infringing the patent. Consequently, the onus of establishing the right lies on a person who would otherwise be an infringer. Also, where the alleged prior use has been carried out in public but fails (or is not pleaded) as an anticipation, there seems no prospect of establishing a defence under s.64, see *Hadley Industries v Metal Sections* BL C/68/98. Prior acts only provide rights if they rank as acts of "infringement". Falling outside this category are prior acts of Crown user (for which see the commentary on s.55) and the acts excepted as being infringing acts by the terms of s.60(5): for example, acts done privately and for purposes which are not commercial; or acts done for experimental purposes relating to the invention; or acts carried out on vessels or aircraft coming only temporarily into the United Kingdom; or acts of permitted own farm use (for all of which see §§60.12–60.17). Also excluded from the protection provided by s.64 are prior acts committed outside the United Kingdom; and the Isle of Man by virtue of s.132(2). This is a serious limitation on the effect of the section, particularly because acts of prior use (wherever carried out) are not novelty-destroying unless they make the invention "available to the public" which appears to exclude many prior acts carried out in public from invalidating a patent of later date, see §2.23. Thus, prior user acts carried out abroad, which do not amount to an "enabling disclosure of the invention" and thus do not make the invention "available to the public" do not invalidate the patent, nor do they give rise to any right under s.64 to continue the act of prior use. Consequently, a foreign prior user, whose prior use falls short of the enabling requirement, can, apparently, be prevented from continuing that use in the United Kingdom after the grant of a patent covering the same use, see *PLG Research v Ardon* [1993] F.S.R. 197. However, the territorial limitation imposed by the terms of s.64 may be regarded as a disguised restriction of trade between Community Member States in that prior United Kingdom users have a right not given to prior users in other Member States. In line with the decisions of the ECJ in *Allen & Hanbury v Generics* (C–434/85) [1988] 1 C.M.L.R. 701; [1988] F.S.R. 312, discussed in §46.16; and, in *EC Commission v United Kingdom* (C–30/90) [1993] R.P.C. 283; [1992] 2 C.M.L.R. 709, discussed in §48.03, the terms of s.64 may thus be ultra vires of art.28 EC and not saved by art.30 EC. If this is so, then either the section is of no effect or it has to be interpreted (if such be possible) as providing a prior right in the case of prior acts committed anywhere within the European Community. Indeed, an Opinion from the EU Economic and Social Committee has recommended that consideration should be given to harmonisation of the right of prior use within the EU (see OJ EPO 1998, 328).

J. C. Boff (1989–90) 19 *CIPA* 377 discussed further apparent deficiencies in the wording of the section if the rationale of G 2/88 *MOBIL/Friction reducing additive-III* OJ EPO 1990, 93 and 469; [1990] E.P.O.R. 73, which imports into a claim a stated element of technical purpose, were adopted into the British law of patent infringement. In *Merrell Dow v Norton* [1996] R.P.C. 76, the House of Lords stated that G 2/88 *MOBIL/Friction reducing additive-III* makes it difficult to apply "the traditional United Kingdom doctrine

64.03

of infringement" under which infringement is independent of knowledge or intention, but the *Merrell Dow* case did not require further discussion of this aspect, such that these issues were not resolved. The impact of the *Mobil* decision on s.64, if any, therefore also remains to be seen. Recently Floyd J., in *Actavis UK Ltd v Janssen Pharmaceutica NV* [2008] EWHC 1422; [2008] F.S.R. 35 Pat Ct observed that: "there are signs that the courts in the EPO and in this country are taking quite a limited view of what *Mobil* decided".

Prior acts to be carried out in "good faith"

64.04 The term "good faith" is not defined in the Act but is a term of wide legal application. The requirement for a relevant prior act to have been carried out in "good faith" obviously excludes acts arising from information obtained from the inventor or proprietor and carried out without the proprietor's consent, for example acts which have been carried out in breach of confidence from the inventor or his assigns. The provision probably also excludes acts arising from knowledge of the invention which has been illicitly obtained: but *quaere* the case where the prior user has obtained information which has, unknown to him, been obtained illicitly and in circumstances where he had no reason to suspect this. There is not, as yet, any decision on the point, but the situation seems analogous to confidential information improperly obtained, being passed into a number of hands, some of which were not aware of the confidentiality. Cases relating to such improper use of confidential information may therefore be of some help in construing this particular provision.

Rights arising from "effective and serious preparations"

64.05 The protection provided by the section extends to an act not actually done within the United Kingdom before the priority date of the invention, but for which there had been "effective and serious preparations" to do such an act (i.e. an act within the United Kingdom). This quoted term is also used in s.28A(4)(b) dealing with personal rights which arise after restoration of a patent, but it is not defined in the Act.

The word "effective" causes particular difficulties. It seems to limit the protection to acts which were about to be commenced by the priority date (in a manner which would, post-grant, be an act of infringement), but which had not by then actually been commenced. Thus, the section seems to require, in the absence of an act actually carried out, a settled and firm intention to carry out an act, which later would become an infringing act. In *Helitune v Stewart Hughes* [1991] R.P.C. 78; [1991] F.S.R. 171, it was held that the prior act there in issue was not one which involved doing an act covered by the claims of the patent, nor an act which could be regarded as being an "effective and serious" preparation to do such an act. In *Lubrizol v Esso* [1998] R.P.C. 727 CA, while importation of one batch of a product constituted an invalidating prior use (for which see §2.21), it was held that the preparations taken by the priority date to manufacture that product in the United Kingdom had not been "effective".

The nature and extent of the right provided by section 64

64.06 The right provided by subs.(1) is the right "to continue to do the act" (in the case of a prior act), or the right "to do the act" (in the case of prior effective and serious preparations). Considerable problems arise in deciding what is meant by "the act" in this context. It would clearly be an absurdity to limit the right of continuance to that which is in all respects identical with the prior act that was done, or effectively and seriously planned. Thus, some variation in the prior act ought to fall within the scope of the right provided by the section, but the degree of variation is indefinite. This point was discussed by Helen Jones (1985–86) 15 *CIPA* 342 and by J.U. Neukom [1990] E.I.P.R. 165; and [1991] E.I.P.R. 139. The question has also been discussed in three cases, but in each the judicial remarks were obiter. Firstly, in *Helitune v Stewart Hughes* [1991] R.P.C. 78; [1991] F.S.R. 171, the words "the act" were construed as meaning an act of the same type (i.e. an act of a type as enumerated in s.60(1) or (2), such as an act of manufacture, use or sale). However, presumably a right of manufacture would provide also (either by virtue of subs.(3) or otherwise to make sense of the section) an implied right to sell the goods so manufactured. Secondly, in an interim judgment in *Lubrizol v Esso* [1992] R.P.C. 281, a deputy judge opined that this view was wrong and that the right provided by the section must be much more limited as regards the scope of the technical operations carried out under that right. Here it was pointed out that, if the patent were amended to exclude the prior (contemplated) act, the prior act would no longer fall within the scope of the patent claims. It would thus not now be an act of "infringement" and thus could not enjoy the protection of the section. Thirdly, in the substantive trial in *Lubrizol v Esso* [1997] R.P.C. 195; and [1998] R.P.C. 727 CA, the defence under the section failed on the facts, but the Patents Court indicated that the "existing commercial activity" which could be continued under this section is an activity "which is substantially the same as the prior act or act for which substantial and effective preparations were made", as to which both technical and commercial matters should be taken into account in order to:

> "provide protection to enable a man to continue doing what in substance he was doing before, though the nature of the protected act should not depend on the claims of the patent".

On the appeal, this statement was endorsed, Aldous L.J. stating that the words he had used in the *Helitune* decision had "been read in a way not intended". However, the preparations at issue in this *Lubrizol* case, even if "serious", had not been "effective", see §64.05. In *"Biegevorrichtung"* [2002] G.R.U.R. 231, the German Supreme Court held that the prior user right in German law equivalent to that provided by s.64 does not go beyond what is actually used so that a prior user cannot use further developments going beyond the prior use. This case is noted in *Patent World*, August 2002 (No.144), p.5. Problems arise over the meaning to be ascribed to the word "continue" in subs.(1), in particular whether the right extends to permitting repetitions of the act after a period of time during which it was not carried out. Again, it would be absurd in practical terms to construe the word "continue" literally and thus extinguish the s.64 right if there has been any cessation of the act, but there is no guide as to whether it was the intention of the legislature to treat such cases liberally or not. Nevertheless, to obtain relief under the section, a chain of causation must be established between the alleged prior use and the act of infringement in issue (*Hadley Industries v Metal Sections* BL C/68/98). The question whether an act is a "continuing act" was considered in *Rotocrop v Genbourne* [1982] F.S.R. 241 in another context, namely as regards a continuing act of infringement under the transitional provisions of Sch.4 para.3.

It was conceded in *H. Lundbeck A/S v Norpharma SpA* [2010] R.P.C. 23, [2011] EWHC 907 Pat Ct that the right applied to certain processes conducted in the UK, and to the imports of the direct product of certain processes conducted abroad, but it was also held that it did not apply to the import of the direct product of certain other processes conducted abroad. A submission that the act of importation of a product before the priority date gave the right to import the same product after the priority date even if made by a different process was rejected, although the court observed that the language of s.64 does not sit entirely happily with the case of infringing importation of the direct product of a process.

Limitations on the right

The right of continued use provided by s.64 is a personal one and cannot be licensed **64.07** (subs.(1)), except where the prior act was done in the course of a business when the person entitled to the right may authorise "the doing of that act by any partners of his for the time being in that business" (subs.(2)(a)), and the person entitled to the right may assign that right (or transmit it on death or dissolution) to any person acquiring that part of the business in the course of which the act was done or the preparations were made (subs.(2)(b)). Provided that a genuine transfer of "the business" is proved, it is probably not necessary for transfer of a prior user right existing in that business to be specifically identified in the transfer documentation, see *DV GmbH v AAG B* [Germany] [2000] E.N.P.R. 120). In addition, where a product is disposed of to another in the course of exercising the right granted by s.64, an implied licence is automatically conferred on that other person, and to others who may later deal with that product, as if the disposal had been by the registered proprietor of the patent (subs.(3)). However, this continuing right is limited to dealing with the product "in the same way", whatever these words may mean—on which there is as yet no case law. Presumably, under the principles discussed in §D13, any such right would extend also to subsequent dealings in the product falling under parallel patents in other EEA countries. These provisions are identical to those of s.28A(5) and (6), which are applicable in the case of third party rights granted under s.28A(4) to those who commence acts, or make serious and effective preparations to do so, during a period after the patent had formally lapsed but before the date when there was published a notice of an application to restore the patent, for which see §28A.05. The two provisions would, presumably, be construed in a similar way.

In *Qual-Chem v Corus* [2008] EWPCC 1 a defence based on this section failed on the fact that it was not the party C that sought to rely on it that carried out the "infringing" act, but the other party Q, albeit (on the facts, by necessity) on C's premises. Although the case went to the Court of Appeal, this aspect of HHJ Fysh's finding in the PCC was not appealed.

SECTION 65

Certificate of contested validity of patent

65.01   **65.**—(1) If in any proceedings before the court or the comptroller the validity of a patent to any extent is contested and that patent is found by the court or the comptroller to be wholly or partially valid, the court or the comptroller may certify the finding and the fact that the validity of the patent was so contested.

(2) Where a certificate is granted under this section, then, if in any subsequent proceedings before the court or the comptroller for infringement of the patent concerned or for revocation of the patent a final order or judgment or interlocutor is made or given in favour of the party relying on the validity of the patent as found in the earlier proceedings, that party shall, unless the court or the comptroller otherwise directs, be entitled to his costs or expenses as between solicitor and own client (other than the costs or expenses of any appeal in the subsequent proceedings).

COMMENTARY ON SECTION 65

Scope of the section

65.02   Section 65 provides for the grant of a certificate of contested validity following proceedings in which validity has been unsuccessfully challenged (subs.(1), discussed in §65.03). The effect of such a certificate is to enable a successful patentee in subsequent proceedings to recover his costs substantially on an indemnity basis (subs.(2), discussed in §65.04).

Grant of certificate of contested validity (subs.(1))

65.03   The grant of a certificate of contested validity is in the discretion of the court or Comptroller and may be granted in any proceedings in which validity of the patent was contested and found wholly or partially valid. The certificate may be qualified by reference to certain grounds, or to particular claims, upon which the validity was contested. The required contest can take place in the context of any of the types of proceedings listed in s.74(1), for discussion of which see §74.03.   However, the mere fact that validity was put in issue is not sufficient, since the certificate is granted in respect of contested validity. Nevertheless, where validity was conceded during the course of a trial, but after full argument and evidence, a Scottish court granted a certificate of contested validity even though no decision on validity was required to be given (*Brupat v Smith* [1985] F.S.R. 156); and the Comptroller has issued a certificate where the applicant for revocation failed to support his case by filing evidence, the patent being upheld upon some evidence filed by the patentee (*Albright & Wilson's Patent* BL O/190/92,noted I.P.D. 16028). An example where a certificate was refused in the exercise of discretion is *Moseley Rubber's Patent* BL C/67/ 86. In the Australian case of *Datadot v Alpha Microtech* (2004) 59 I.P.R. 402, the court declined to issue a certificate of contested validity because no evidence had been led on the claim for revocation and therefore there had been no contest to validity. It seems that the Comptroller will routinely grant a certificate upon the failure of an application for revocation brought before him under s.72, for examples of which see *Mölnlycke's and Boussac Saint Frères' Patents* BL O/15/90, noted I.P.D. 13111, *Glaverbel's Patent* BL O/32/91 and *Zip Heaters' Patent (No.2)* BL O/232/05 (the last case relating to a patent the claims of which were only upheld on amendment.)

Subsection (2) provides that, if a proprietor successfully relies upon the finding of validity made in earlier proceedings in which a certificate of contested validity was granted, he shall (unless it is specifically directed otherwise) be entitled to his costs (expenses in Scotland) "as between solicitor and own client" on final order at first instance in the subsequent proceedings, though not on any appeal from it. The quoted words are generally effective as an order for "costs on the indemnity basis", as compared to the normal "costs on the standard basis" (for which see the commentary on practice under s.61). A certificate of contested validity can therefore be a powerful deterrent to further challenges to the validity of the patent, and its availability in the case of an unsuccessful application for revocation brought before the Comptroller under s.72 should be a factor when considering whether to commence revocation proceedings in that forum, particularly as the Comptroller now frequently grants such certificates, as mentioned above. This is so even though no formal estoppel arises as regards the issues unsuccessfully raised in the proceedings before the Comptroller (see s.72(5), discussed in §72.17). A modern example where a certificate of contested validity had been granted and the previously unsuccessful applicant for revocation before the Comptroller failed to convince the court of invalidity in subsequent infringement proceedings is *Mölnlycke v Procter & Gamble (No.5)* [1994] R.P.C. 49 CA) where indemnity costs were ordered by the Patents Court as from the date of the Comptroller's decision, even as regards infringement proceedings which were then in being.

The existence of s.65 might also encourage a proprietor to bring initial infringement proceedings before an infringer of little financial substance, in the hope that a counterclaim for revocation will be made and fail, leading to the grant of a certificate which can then act as a deterrent against other infringers. Such a certificate should extend only to matters which have been contested so that, if there has been no substantial challenge to validity, no certificate should normally be issued, but see §65.03 for an exception (*Brupat v Smith* [1985] F.S.R. 156). This case also indicates the risk that a certificate could be issued if the first defendant to be sued concedes issues of validity. In those circumstances, other potential infringers may find it attractive to assist the first defendant, or to seek leave that their own petitions for revocation should be heard by the court at the same time.

In *SmithKline Beecham v Apotex [Costs]* [2005] F.S.R. 24 at 559, the Court of Appeal questioned whether s.65 served any useful purpose these days given the more sophisticated principles applied to the award of costs. It also held that, although irrational, the wording at the end of s.65(2) made it clear that it does not apply to the costs of appeals in subsequent proceedings, but the Court of Appeal in this case awarded indemnity costs of an equivalent size in the exercise of its general powers.

Effect of certificate of contested validity (subs.(2))

Subsection (2) provides that, if a proprietor successfully relies upon the finding of validity made in earlier proceedings in which a certificate of contested validity was granted, he shall (unless it is specifically directed otherwise) be entitled to his costs (expenses in Scotland) "as between solicitor and own client" on final order at first instance in the subsequent proceedings, though not on any appeal therefrom. The quoted words are generally effective as an order for "costs on the indemnity basis", as compared to the normal "costs on the standard basis" (for which see the commentary on s.61). Generally, see §65.03 above.

65.04

Practice under Section 65

65.05   There is no specific provision in the Rules for entry of a certificate of contested validity on the register but under r.44(7) the Comptroller may at any time enter in the register "such other particulars as he thinks fit". Therefore when a certificate of contested validity is granted by a court, an office copy of the court order may be filed at the UK-IPO under that rule with a request that the Comptroller enter the details of the certificate on the register. This will be advantageous in drawing it to the attention of third parties and potential infringers; although it would seem that such an entry would be voluntary rather than a requirement. Under the previous rules, the Comptroller's practice was to publish notice of such an entry in the *Patents Journal*.

SECTION 66

Proceedings for infringement by a co-owner

66.01   **66.**—(1) In the application of section 60 above to a patent of which there are two or more joint proprietors the reference to the proprietor shall be construed—

    (a) in relation to any act, as a reference to that proprietor or those proprietors who, by virtue of section 36 above or any agreement referred to in that section, is or are entitled to do that act without its amounting to an infringement; and

    (b) in relation to any consent, as a reference to that proprietor or those proprietors who, by virtue of section 36 above or any such agreement, is or are the proper person or persons to give the requisite consent.

(2)   One of two or more joint proprietors of a patent may without the concurrence of the others bring proceedings in respect of an act alleged to infringe the patent, but shall not do so unless the others are made parties to the proceedings; but any of the others made a defendant or defender shall not be liable for any costs or expenses unless he enters an appearance and takes part in the proceedings.

Commentary on Section 66

66.02   Section 66 defines the position of joint proprietors in relation to infringement proceedings. It applies to the infringement of rights arising from a pending application under s.69(1). The section complements the provisions of s.36 which defines the rights, inter se, of patent co-owners, see the commentary on that section. For infringement proceedings brought by an exclusive licensee, see s.67 and its commentary, and for the effect of non-registration of an assignment to a new proprietor or co-proprietor of a patent, see s.68 and its commentary. By subs.(1), the reference in s.60 to a proprietor in respect of a patent of which there are two or more proprietors is to be taken as meaning, in the absence of agreement to the contrary, the proprietor or proprietors who by s.36 would be entitled to do the appropriate act or give the appropriate consent to the use of the patent. Subsection (2) gives a joint proprietor a statutory right by himself to bring infringement proceedings provided that the other proprietors are made parties to the proceedings, at least as nominal defendants; they are not then liable for costs (expenses in Scotland) if they do not enter an appearance. The object of this provision is to ensure that all co-owners of a patent are given notice of infringement proceedings brought by any one of them. If a co-proprietor has, by agreement, accepted that the other co-proprietor(s) should have exclusive rights to work the patent, then that co-proprietor (if he worked the patent) could, apparently, be sued for infringement under his own patent. Where a defendant to infringement proceedings alleged that he derived rights from someone entitled to have been made a co-proprietor, the court held that a defence of implied licence or waiver could be argued (*La Baigue Magiglo v Multiglow Fires* BL C/56/93). Where a co-owner sues under the section, it is not clear whether he can defend a counterclaim by seeking amendment—on which see *Henry Bros v Ministry of Defence* [1997] R.P.C. 693; [1999] R.P.C. 442 CA; and §75.04; or whether a co-owner defendant could counterclaim for revocation of the patent, for example to be able to compete with the other co-owner on the basis of a joint venture with a third party, on which see §72.11. So long as all co-owners have been given the opportunity to be represented in any such proceedings, there would not seem to be any injustice in allowing either amendment or revocation should the court find such to be appropriate on the evidence presented. *Sepracor v Hoechst* BL C/5/98, noted I.P.D. 22034; [1999] F.S.R. 746 is an example of a co-owner being joined as a nominal defendant under the provisions of the section.

In *MMI Research Ltd v Cellxion Ltd* [2007] EWHC 2611, an order was made against a passive joint proprietor joined as defendant in an infringement action under subs.(2) that was not serving a defence, debarring it from adducing any evidence or calling any witnesses contesting any of the allegations made in the counterclaim and granting an order for disclosure against it.

SECTION 67

Proceedings for infringement by exclusive licensee

67.—(1) Subject to the provisions of this section, the holder of an exclusive licence under a patent shall have the same right as the proprietor of the patent to bring proceedings in respect of any infringement of the patent committed after, the date of the licence; and references to the proprietor of the patent in the provisions of this Act relating to infringement shall be construed accordingly. **67.01**

(2) In awarding damages or granting any other relief in any such proceedings the court or the comptroller shall take into consideration any loss suffered or likely to be suffered by the exclusive licensee as such as a result of the infringement, or, as the case may be, the profits derived from the infringement, so far as it constitutes an infringement of the rights of the exclusive licensee as such.

(3) In proceedings taken by an exclusive licensee by virtue of this section the proprietor of the patent shall be made a party to the proceedings, but if made a defendant or defender shall not be liable for any costs or expenses unless he enters an appearance and takes part in the proceedings.

Commentary on Section 67

Scope of the section

Section 67 gives the holder of an exclusive licence the same power as the proprietor of the patent to sue for infringement occurring after the date of the licence, and the word "proprietor" throughout the Act is to be construed (in relation to infringement) accordingly (subs.(1)). The exclusive licensee may then be awarded damages (or an account of profits) for infringement of his rights as exclusive licensee (subs.(2)). The proprietor is to be made a party to the proceedings, at least as a nominal defendant; he is not, however, liable for costs (expenses in Scotland) if he does not put in an appearance (subs.(3)). The section applies to infringement of rights arising from a pending application; see s.69(1). This power is an important one as the exclusive licensee may have suffered loss not suffered by the proprietor as such who cannot therefore claim for that loss. Thus, in *Gerber Garment v Lectra Systems* [1997] R.P.C. 443 CA, a parent company could not claim damages for losses suffered by its wholly-owned subsidiaries because it had failed to prove that these losses had been suffered by itself. To avoid the need to prove that losses by a subsidiary company are, to that extent, losses by the parent company, consideration should be given to appointing the subsidiary as a formal licensee under the patent having some degree of exclusivity under it (for which see §67.04), e.g. an exclusive manufacturing or **67.02** selling right, with registration of that licence so that, when infringement is found to be occurring, the subsidiary can be joined to the infringement proceedings as a co-claimant and thereby claim damages in respect of its own losses.

Definition of "exclusive licence"

67.03   "Exclusive licence" is defined in s.130(1) and means a licence to the exclusion of all others, including the proprietor of the patent (or the applicant where the licence is granted under a pending application) of "any right" in respect of the invention to which that patent or application relates. The words "any right" appear to be very wide. Presumably, a licence comes within the definition if it confers the sole right to manufacture but not the sole right to use a patented invention, or the sole right to make and sell some but not all of the articles covered by the claims. It seems also that a licence limited territorially, e.g. one conferring all the rights in respect of Scotland, is within the definition. Several exclusive licences may, therefore, be granted under one patent, for example as in *Courtauld's Application* [1956] R.P.C. 208. An exclusive sub-licence granted by the licensee with the patentee's consent which conferred the exclusive licence on the sub-licensee to the exclusion of the licensee was accepted as an exclusive licence giving the sub-licensee the entitlement to sue instead of the licensee in *Dendron v Regents of the University of California* [2004] F.S.R. 43 at 861.

However, a licence is not "exclusive" within the definition unless it excludes the proprietor himself. Thus, the holder of a sole, rather than an exclusive, licence is not entitled to sue for patent infringement. Whether an exclusive right is actually possessed may be a mixed question of fact and law, see *Morton-Norwich v Intercen and United Chemicals* [1981] F.S.R. 337 where the licence was held to be partly written and partly oral.

A licence granted other than by a deed or for valuable consideration can be no more than a "bare licence" which estops the proprietor/licensor from suing the licensee for infringement: such a licence cannot, therefore, be an exclusive licence entitling the licensee to sue for infringement (*Gough v Greens Onion Services* BL C/1/92 Pat Cty Ct). Where a licensee appoints an agent to manufacture for him exclusively, the agent (even if the only party so appointed) does not have the rights of an exclusive licensee as this arrangement is not an exclusive licence which has anything to do with the rights under the patent, the head licensee retaining the right to nominate other agents (*Bondax Carpets v Advance Carpet Tiles* [1993] F.S.R. 162).

Right of exclusive licensee to sue for infringement

67.04   So long as a licensee can establish that his licence is "exclusive", even of the proprietor, in respect of some right under the patent, that is sufficient to entitle him to sue in his own right for patent infringement; and, once a claimant (and subject to registration of the licence), he can probably recover damages for any loss suffered according to the usual remoteness of damage principles (*Morton-Norwich v Intercen and United Chemicals* [1981] F.S.R. 337). Indeed, an exclusive licensee has an independent right to bring action and that right is not affected by the illegality of licences entered into by others on a wholly independent basis, see *Chiron v Murex* [1996] R.P.C. 535 where the proprietor could not himself successfully sue because of the existence of a licence offending against s.44 (for which see §44.02).

For entitlement to bring proceedings under the section, the exclusive licence should exist prior to the issue of the claim (*Procter & Gamble v Peaudouce* [1989] F.S.R. 180 CA). However, in *PCUK v Diamond Shamrock* [1981] F.S.R. 427, a party who could only establish an informal de facto licence, exclusive to him as against all others including the proprietor, was held entitled to commence proceedings. Likewise, under the section, the power of an exclusive licensee to sue is limited to actions in respect of infringement occurring after the date, and during the existence, of the licence and its required exclusivity, but ss.30(7) and 31(7) permit an exclusive licence to confer, as a matter of contract, on the licensee the right which the licensor previously had to bring proceedings under either of ss.61 or 69 for a previous act of infringement, or under s.58 for a previous act of Crown use.

In *Cavity Trays v RMC Panel Products* [1996] R.P.C. 361, infringement proceedings were aborted when it appeared that the claimant had previously transferred its licence to another and thus had no entitlement to have commenced the proceedings. Unjustified threats having been made (for which see §70.07), the defendant was permitted to claim the costs of the aborted action (including the preparation of a defence to an interim injunction application) as damages in the action for unjustified threats, see also §70.06.

An exclusive licensee's entitlement to sue does not depend upon registration of the licence. This was confirmed in *Dendron v Regents of the University of California* [2004] F.S.R. 43 at 861. Lack of registration, or delayed registration, may, however, lead to loss of entitlement to costs or expenses in litigation under s.68; see the commentary on that section.

The fact that an exclusive licensee has successfully sued for infringement does not take away from the proprietor any right he may have to be awarded relief in respect of loss suffered, or likely to be suffered, by himself (*Optical Coating v Pilkington* [1993] F.S.R. 310). However, if a proprietor should himself work the patent within the area of exclusivity granted to a licensee, an action for breach of contract will obviously lie. In such a circumstance, there would appear to be no obstacle to the licensee suing the proprietor for infringement of the patent in order to obtain damages in tort which may be available on a wider basis.

SECTION 68

Effect of non-registration on infringement proceedings

68. Where by virtue of a transaction, instrument or event to which section 33 **68.01** above applies a person becomes the proprietor or one of the proprietors or an exclusive licensee of a patent and the patent is subsequently infringed [*the court or the comptroller shall not award him damages or order that he be given an account of the profits in respect of such a subsequent infringement occurring*] before the transaction, instrument or event is registered, **in proceedings for such an infringement, the court or comptroller shall not award him costs or expenses** unless—

   (a) the transaction, instrument or event is registered within the period of six months beginning with its date; or

   (b) the court or the comptroller is satisfied that it was not practicable to register the transaction, instrument or event before the end of that period and that it was registered as soon as practicable thereafter.

Note. In order to comply with art.13(1) of the European "Enforcement Directive" (No.2004/48/EC, OJ EC L157, April 30, 2004, p.45, with corrigendum OJ EC L195, June 2, 2004, p.16), s.68 was amended as shown above in bold type with effect from April 29, 2006 (SI 2006/1028 reg.2(2) and Sch.2 para.4), the previous wording being shown in italics.

COMMENTARY ON SECTION 68

Scope of the section

Section 68 applies only to infringement proceedings and imposes a penalty for non- **68.02** registration, or for unduly delayed registration, of the acquisition of rights under a patent, either as proprietor or as exclusive licensee, such acquisition being one to which s.33 applies. The penalty is now limited to costs (or expenses in Scotland) in litigation, whereas prior to the amendment of the section (to conform to the Enforcement Directive) it precluded the award of damages or an account of profits in respect of infringements before the date of registration of the transaction. Section 33 itself provides for possible total loss of rights of an assignee or licensee by the lack of timely registration in the event of prior registration of a conflicting transaction, instrument or event. For these matters, see the commentary on s.33. Section 68 applies to the infringement of rights arising from a pending application, for which see s.69(1). However, the limitations imposed by s.68 only apply to a "transaction, instrument or event to which section 33 applies" and, accordingly, would not seem to apply to an agreement to assign or create in the future an exclusive licence because such an agreement is not itself registrable under s.33, although notice of it can be given to the UK-IPO and hence to the public, see §32.19. In *Thorn Security Ltd v Siemens Schweiz AG* [2008] EWCA Civ 1161; [2009] R.P.C. 3 it was held that s.68 applied to an assignment by operation of law, and where there had been no assignment document, thereby reversing the first instance decision as to this and disapproving the decision to the contrary in *Tamglass v Luong North Glass* [2006] EWHC 445 Ch. See also *Discovision v Pioneer Electronics* BL C/55/98, noted I.P.D. 21103 discussed in §7.05.

The section, and the effect of the amendment of the penalty in it, was considered in *Schütz (UK) Ltd v Werit UK Ltd & Anor* [2011] EWCA Civ 927 CA where it was held that its effect was that if and in so far as a claim covers a period for which a relevant transaction was not registered when it should have been then any costs incurred during that period cannot be recovered, but that costs incurred outside such non-registration period were recoverable in the usual way. It was recognised that the provision could accordingly accurately be characterised as "toothless", since an exclusive licensee who had failed to get his licence registered would not lose much by way of cost or indeed anything provided he got his licence registered before he started the action, as all or virtually all the costs would be incurred after registration.

Apart from the consequences of the amendment of the penalty under the section, in other respects old case law under this section remains applicable to it as amended.

Avoidance of the penalty imposed by section 68

68.03   To avoid the penalty imposed by s.68, which appears to be mandatory, the rights of the new proprietor or exclusive licensee have to be registered within six months from the date of the transaction, instrument or event which established those rights, except that, if the court or Comptroller is satisfied that it was not practicable to effect such a registration within this six months' period, the penalty may be avoided if the court or Comptroller, as the case may be, is satisfied that registration was effected as soon as practicable thereafter. For registration under s.33 of a change of ownership or of the grant of rights under the patent, see r.47 (reprinted at §32.07). For the registration of an assignment or licence under an application for a European patent (UK), see §78.06.

As the section requires the transaction, instrument or event to be "registered", the imposition of the penalty is not avoided by making an application for registration within the required six months' period. The registration needs to be effected within that period. Thus, registration should be requested in good time and, if necessary, the UK-IPO be asked to expedite registration so that this is complete within six months from the date of the transaction, instrument or event. However, where registration was delayed within the Office, registration was held to have occurred "as soon as practicable", this meaning that the applicant for registration had himself taken all reasonably practical steps (*Mölnlycke v Procter & Gamble (No.5)* [1994] R.P.C. 49 CA); and, where an application had been timely made and a note in the register had recorded this, an exclusive licensee was permitted to claim damages from the date of entry of that note in the register (*Insituform v Inliner* [1992] R.P.C. 83).

Even when a licence has been registered, care needs to be taken when the exclusivity provided to the licensee is only partial. In *Christian Salvesen v Odfjell Drilling* [Scotland] [1985] R.P.C. 569, a registered exclusive licensee for Scotland was refused an interim interdict because he failed to aver that the alleged infringer had had notice of the restriction on use in Scotland of patented apparatus which he had acquired from the head licensor.

Effect of non-registration of an assignment or exclusive licence

68.04   As regards infringement proceedings, the penalty for non-registration of an assignment or exclusive licence since the amendment of s.68 is that the court (or the Comptroller in proceedings under s.61(3), see s.61(4)) shall not award costs (or in Scotland expenses), in proceedings for infringement subsequent to such transaction unless registration is effected within six months of the date of the transaction, instrument or event which established that title, or unless the exception explained in §68.03 is held to apply. This penalty attaches to the claimant, and not to the patent. In *Minnesota Mining v Rennicks* [1992] R.P.C. 331, a written licence was held not to be a mere confirmation of an earlier, informal and unregistered licence, with the consequence that relief was available from the date of the written licence because this had been registered within six months of its execution, whereas otherwise damages would have been available only from the date of this registration as the earlier licence had not been timely registered. In *Spring Form v Toy Brokers* [2002] F.S.R. 17 at 276 the exclusive licence that had not been registered had an "entire agreement" clause and was expressed to run from the commencement date of an earlier one that had been registered. An argument that s.68 should not apply in such a case because the licensee remained, rather than became, an exclusive licensee failed as the later licence was held to replace the earlier one. An attempt in *Finecard v Urquhart Dyke & Lord* [2006] F.S.R. 27 at 505 to revisit this finding in other proceedings on the basis, not advanced in the earlier case that under the proper law of the later licence it did not retroactively revoke any rights arising under the earlier licence, failed, because to succeed it required one in effect to insert the word "first" after the word "person" in the section. The court summarised s.68 as meaning that "where a party wishes to assert a right the relevant transaction . . . which creates the right for the period in question must be registered."

In *H. Lundbeck A/S v Norpharma SpA* [2011] R.P.C. 23, [2011] EWHC 907 Pat Ct it was held that an assignment, expressed to be of the application which led to the patent in suit, but entered into after that date and notified to the EPO, and where no consequential attempt was made to alter the name of the proprietor on the UK register, did not count as a registration for the purposes of s.68. The new proprietor could not rely on s.68(b) even though it had done all that was practicable by instructing his agents to take the steps necessary to register its interest, because, following *Mölnlycke*, the section required an investigation of what was done by the applicant and his agents, and not just the applicant alone.

SECTION 69

Infringement of rights conferred by publication of application

69.—(1) Where an application for a patent for an invention is published, then, subject to subsections (2) and (3) below, the applicant shall have, as from the publication and until the grant of the patent, the same right as he would have had, if the patent had been granted on the date of the publication of the application, to bring proceedings in the court or before the comptroller for damages in respect of any act which would have infringed the patent; and (subject to subsections (2) and (3) below) references in sections 60 to 62 and 66 to 68 above to a patent and the proprietor of a patent shall be respectively construed as including references to any such application and the applicant, and references to a patent being in force, being granted, being valid or existing shall be construed accordingly.

69.01

(2) The applicant shall be entitled to bring proceedings by virtue of this section in respect of any act only—

(a) after the patent has been granted; and

(b) if the act would, if the patent had been granted on the date of the publication of the application, have infringed not only the patent, but also the claims (as interpreted by the description and any drawings referred to in the description or claims) in the form in which they were contained in the application immediately before the preparations for its publication were completed by the Patent Office.

(3) Section 62(2) and (3) above shall not apply to an infringement of the rights conferred by this section, but in considering the amount of any damages for such an infringement, the court or the comptroller shall consider whether or not it would have been reasonable to expect, from a consideration of the application as published under section 16 above, that a patent would be granted conferring on the proprietor of the patent protection from an act of the same description as that found to infringe those rights, and if the court or the comptroller finds that it would not have been reasonable, it or he shall reduce the damages to such an amount as it or he thinks just.

Note. This section is to be interpreted in conformity with relevant provisions in the CPC, EPC and PCT (s.130(7)). This means that the section has to conform predominantly with art.67 of the EPC (and CPC art.32) in the case of a European application, and with art.29 of the PCT in the case of an international application, so that it is intended to have similar effect to that provided by these Convention and Treaty articles. These articles read as at §69.02 and §69.03, below.

RELEVANT CONVENTION PROVISIONS

EPC Article 67—Rights conferred by a European patent application after publication

69.02   **67.**—(1) A European patent application shall, from the date of its publication under Article 93, provisionally confer upon the applicant such protection as is conferred by Article 64, in the Contracting States designated in the application as published.

(2) Any Contracting State may prescribe that a European patent application shall not confer such protection as is conferred by Article 64. However, the protection attached to the publication of the European patent application may not be less than that which the laws of the State concerned attach to the compulsory publication of unexamined national patent applications. In any event, every State shall ensure at least that, from the date of publication of a European patent application, the applicant can claim compensation reasonable in the circumstances from any person who has used the invention in the said State in circumstances where that person would be liable under national law for infringement of a national patent.

(3) Any Contracting State which does not have as an official language the language of the proceedings may prescribe that provisional protection in accordance with paragraphs 1 and 2 above shall not be effective until such time as a translation of the claims in one of its official languages at the option of the applicant or, where that State has prescribed the use of one specific official language, in that language:

(a) has been made available to the public in the manner prescribed by national law, or

(b) has been communicated to the person using the invention in said State.

(4) The European patent application shall be deemed never to have had the effects set out in paragraphs 1 and 2 above when it has been withdrawn or finally refused. The same shall apply in respect of the effects of the European patent application in a Contracting State the designation of which is withdrawn or deemed to be withdrawn.

Note. The corresponding art.32 of the CPC is not reprinted here as, although this is expressed differently from art.67 of the EPC, its effect seems essentially the same; and, were there to be any difference, the provisions of art.67 of the EPC would presumably take precedence as the CPC has not been brought into effect.

PCT Article 29—Effects of the international publication

29.—(1) As far as the protection of any rights of the applicant in a designated State is concerned, the effects, in that State, of the international publication of an international application shall, subject to the provisions of paragraphs (2) to (4), be the same as those which the national law of the designated State provides for the compulsory national publication of unexamined national applications as such. **69.03**

(2) If the language in which the international publication has been effected is different from the language in which publications under the national law are effected in the designated State, the said national law may provide that the effects provided for in paragraph (1) shall be applicable only from such time as:

   (i) a translation into the latter language has been published as provided by the national law, or

  (ii) a translation into the latter language has been made available to the public, by laying open to public inspection as provided by the national law, or

 (iii) a translation into the latter language has been transmitted by the applicant to the actual or prospective authorized user of the invention claimed in the international application, or

 (iv) both the acts described in (i) and (ii), or both the acts described in (ii) and (iii), have taken place.

(3) The national law of any designated State may provide that, where the international publication has been effected, on the request of the applicant, before the expiration of 18 months from the priority date, the effects provided for in paragraph (1) shall be applicable only from the expiration of 18 months from the priority date.

(4) The national law of any designated State may provide that the effects provided for in paragraph (1) shall be applicable only from the date on which a copy of the international application as published under Article 21 has been received in the national Office of or acting for such State. The said Office shall publish the date of receipt in its gazette as soon as possible.

Scope of the section

Section 69 applies only to "applications" and gives a proprietor a right to recover damages in respect of infringements committed during the period between publication of the pending application and the date of patent grant (subs.(1)). However, such relief is claimable only after the patent has been granted, and then only if the act complained of would not only have infringed the patent when granted but also the claims in the form as originally published in the English language (subs.(2)). These are not necessarily the form of claims which were filed originally as they may have been amended prior to publication of the application. Where the patent is granted with claims of different scope than those published, the amount of damages awarded for infringement of the rights provided by the section may be reduced where it was not reasonable to expect, from the application as **69.04** published, that a patent would be granted covering the act of infringement in issue (subs.(3)).

As mentioned above, the section is listed in s.130(7), so that it is intended to have similar effect to the corresponding Convention and Treaty articles, see §69.01.

Applicability of the section

69.05   In s.69, the term "application" includes: an application for a European patent (UK) (s.78(1)); an international application (UK) (s.89(1)); and an international application for a European patent (UK), i.e. a "Euro-PCT application (UK)" (s.79(1)). However, in each case, the right under s.69 applies only as from the date the application is published in the manner prescribed for each of these types of applicable applications. As a general proposition, this is the date of publication when the application is published in the English language, and this will usually not occur before 18 months after the earliest declared priority date; or, if no priority is claimed, 18 months from the filing date.

More specifically, in the case of an application filed under the Act, the date when the s.69 right becomes effective is the date when the application is published under s.16 (subs.(1)). In the case of an application for a European patent (UK), the date is the date when the European application is published (s.78(3)(d)), except when this publication is not in English in which case the date is that on which a certified translation of the claims of the published application is filed at the Office (s.78(7)), see §78.07. In the case of an international application (UK), the date is likewise the date of publication of this if publication takes place in the English language (s.89B(2)) or otherwise the date when an English translation of the international application is published under s.89A(6) (s.89B(3)), for which see §89B.10; and likewise in the case of a Euro-PCT application (UK) (s.79(3)), for which see §79.04. However, s.69 rights can be exercised also in the case of a European, PCT or Euro-PCT application not officially published in English if an English translation of the claims of the published application is sent by post or delivered to the alleged infringer (ss.78(7); 79(3) applying s.78(7); and s.89B(3)).

The date of grant of a patent on any such application is also important under the operation of s.69. From that date, the rights under the section are replaced with the rights stemming from the grant. Also, it is only after that date that the rights conferred on the proprietor of a pending application can be exercised (subs.(2)(a)). For the purposes of s.69, the date of grant of an application filed under the Act (or of an international application processed under the Act) is the date of publication of the grant in the *Patents Journal* (s.25(1)), and not the date when grant for administrative purposes takes place, see §24.06. In the case of a European patent, it is the date when mentioned of its grant is published in the *European Patent Bulletin* (s.77(1)), provided that any required translation is timely filed, see s.77(6) and (7).

Rights conferred by the section (subs.(1))

69.06   Subsection (1) confers on the proprietor, including a co-proprietor (for which see s.66 and the commentary on that section) or an exclusive licensee (for which see s.67 and the commentary its section), not forgetting the requirement of registration of title (for which see s.68 and its commentary), a right to bring proceedings for damages as if the patent had been granted on the date of publication of the application, but only after the date of grant (subs.(2)(a)) and subject to the other limitations of subss.(2) and (3), as discussed in §69.07. Despite the conspicuous omission of any reference to an account of profits in the subsection, in *Spring Form v Toy Brokers* [2002] F.S.R. 17 at 276 it was held that an account of profits could similarly be claimed in respect of infringing activities before the grant of the patent. As to exclusive licensees, although rights under an international application (UK) can take effect from the date of publication of the application in the international phase, it is not possible to register an exclusive licence under such an application until this has entered the national phase, see §32.19.

Thus, for the purposes of s.69, subs.(1) applies the provisions of ss.60–62 (other than those of s.62(2) and (3)) and ss.66–68 as if the word "patent" read "application". The proceedings for enforcing that right are then tantamount to infringement proceedings for a granted patent and can, therefore, be brought before any "court" (as that term is defined in s.130(1), reprinted in §130.01); or under s.61(3) before the Comptroller (for which see §61.38), but in that case s.74(7) prevents proceedings being started if there are already any proceedings before the court, unless the court gives leave, see §74.06. In the case of a continuing act, proceedings under s.69 will normally be combined with proceedings under s.61 for subsequent acts of infringement committed under s.60.

There is no apparent provision for action to be taken against unjustified threats of proceedings for infringement of a s.69 right, as s.70 does not apply under s.69, see subs.(1). However, such a threat can be considered as one to bring proceedings after grant and on that basis be actionable under s.70, for further discussion of which see §70.03. There is also no provision for seeking a declaration of non-infringement of the claims in a pending application, presumably because the form of claims to be granted is not yet certain. Nor can such a declaration apparently be sought after grant in respect of non-infringement of a s.69 right because subs.(1) does not apply s.71 to s.69. However, a declaration made in respect of acts after grant may have effect also for the purposes of s.69 (for example, by creating an issue estoppel on the issue of infringement if the acts and claims in question have not changed).

Limitation of the section 69 right (subss.(2) and (3))

In addition to the proprietor being unable to exercise his right under s.69 before the patent has been granted (subs.(2)(a)), the exercise of that right requires the proprietor to satisfy a double test under subs.(2)(b). This is that the alleged infringing act (apart from the time when it was carried out) falls not only within the scope of protection of the patent as granted, but also that it falls within the scope of protection provided by the claims of the application at the date when the application has been prepared for publication under s.16 (for which see §16.04), the claims being interpreted by the description and drawings referred to in the description and claims, that is, presumably by the application of the principles of art.69 of the EPC and its Protocol, as required for the granted patent by s.125(1) and (3), for which see the commentary on s.125. Thus, if the claims are broadened during prosecution (for the possibility of which see §76.08), the s.69 right may be enforced only in respect of the scope of claim as it existed at the date when the s.69 right became effective.

69.07

A proprietor can, therefore, succeed in his claim for damages for infringement of his s.69 right if the granted claims are equal or narrower in scope than those originally published. However, under subs.(3), damages may be reduced if it would not have been reasonable to expect, from a consideration of the published application, that a patent would be granted in a form in which it is infringed, i.e. with at least one valid claim which is infringed. Thus, the presence in the published application of an unreasonably broad claim is unlikely to avail a defendant who unreasonably disregards another claim which is valid and infringed. It is, therefore, important to file an application with a set of claims of differing scope in order that the application can be seen to contain at least one claim which survives into the granted patent and there held valid and infringed. It is in these circumstances that the discretionary limitation upon relief arising from subs.(3) can most easily be avoided, though the subsection provides for a wide flexibility in its operation.

A literal construction of subs.(2)(b) would be absurd and therefore the word "claims" in it means "at least one claim" (*Unilever v Chefaro* [1994] R.P.C. 567). Here it was held that the defence available under subs.(3) has to be established by a defendant objectively and, therefore, without dependence on any special knowledge he may have. Thus, to succeed in such a defence, the defendant must show that it would not have been possible to expect that the patent would be granted with a claim covering the defendant's acts, and that this will not be an easy task, except in cases where it was not reasonable to suppose that a broad claim would be allowed as supported by the description in accordance with s.14(5). In this *Unilever* case, the defendant could not succeed because it had itself sought a patent for the same invention.

In *Pall Corp v Commercial Hydraulics* BL C/90/89, an inquiry into damages was ordered to run from the date of publication of the application. Although damages for infringement of the s.69 right are not claimable until after patent grant, it seems that pre-judgment interest on such damages can be awarded from the date of the infringing act. Al-though, in *General Tire v Firestone* [1976] R.P.C. 197, interest on pre-grant damages under the 1949 Act was refused in the court's discretion, under the present Act this should not be so because s.69 specifically provides for damages in respect of pre-grant actions, though subject to the limitation of subs.(3). The judgment in *Sevcon v Lucas* [1986] R.P.C. 609 HL), though decided under the 1949 Act, appears to apply by analogy the provisions of the Limitation Act 1980 (c.58) (for which see §60.30) so that relief under s.69 is proba-bly limited to the period of six years prior to the date of the claim, even though the right to issue a claim form arises only as from the date of grant.

The provisions of s.62(2) (no relief for infringement during period of non-payment of a due renewal fee) and s.62(3) (no relief for infringement after amendment unless the published specification was framed with reasonable skill and knowledge) are expressed not to apply under s.69 (subs.(3)). Thus, it appears that an applicant whose application has at some stage been treated as withdrawn, but which has later been revived under the provi-sions of s.123(3A) and r.108(6) (for which see §123.25), does not lose any right under s.69 thereby. However, while in the case of an amended application the proprietor is not required to prove that the published specification was framed with reasonable skill and knowledge, the court or Comptroller may under subs.(3) reduce an award of damages to such an amount "as seems just" so that all factors can be taken into consideration, though the subsection would not appear to apply unless the defendant first proves that it was not reasonable for him to expect that a valid and infringed claim would be granted. In *Unilin Beheer v Berry Floor* BL C/24/05, noted [2005] *CIPA* 259; March 23, 2005, Pats Cty Ct (D. Young Q.C.), the court held that it could not have been intended that a patentee who had not used reasonable skill and knowledge in obtaining a patent could claim damages and costs for pre-grant infringement but would not be entitled to make the same claim post grant if the patent were held to be only partially valid.

SECTION 70

Remedy for groundless threats of infringement proceedings

70.01   **70.—(1) Where a person (whether or not the proprietor of, or entitled to any right in, a patent) by circulars, advertisements or otherwise threatens another person with proceedings for any infringement of a patent, a person aggrieved by the threats (whether or not he is the person to whom the threats are made) may, subject to subsection (4) below, bring proceedings in the court against the person making the threats, claiming any relief mentioned in subsection (3) below.**

(2) In any such proceedings the claimant [*plaintiff*] or pursuer shall, subject to subsection (2A) below, be entitled to the relief claimed if he proves that the threats were so made and satisfies the court that he is a person ag-grieved by them [*be entitled to the relief claimed unless—*]

> (a) *the defendant or defender proves that the acts in respect of which proceedings were threatened constitute or, if done, would constitute an infringement of a patent; and*

> (b) *the patent alleged to be infringed is not shown by the plaintiff or pursuer to be invalid in a relevant respect].*

(2A) If the defendant or defender proves that the acts in respect of which proceedings were threatened constitute or, if done, would constitute an in-fringement of a patent—

> (a) **the claimant or pursuer shall be entitled to the relief claimed only if he shows that the patent alleged to be infringed is invalid in a rele-vant respect;**

    (b) **even if the claimant or pursuer does show that the patent is invalid in a relevant respect, he shall not be entitled to the relief claimed if the defendant or defender proves that at the time of making the threats he did not know, and had no reason to suspect, that the patent was invalid in that respect.**

(3) The said relief is—

    (a) a declaration or declarator to the effect that the threats are unjustifiable;

    (b) an injunction or interdict against the continuance of the threats; and

    (c) damages in respect of any loss which the plaintiff or pursuer has sustained by the threats.

(4) Proceedings may not be brought under this section for—

    (a) **a threat to bring proceedings for an infringement alleged to consist of making or importing a product for disposal or of using a process, or**

    (b) **a threat, made to a person who has made or imported a product for disposal or used a process, to bring proceedings for an infringement alleged to consist of doing anything else in relation to that product or process.**

(5) For the purposes of this section a person does not threaten another person with proceedings for infringement of a patent if he merely—

    (a) **provides factual information about the patent,**

    (b) **makes enquiries of the other person for the sole purpose of discovering whether, or by whom, the patent has been infringed as mentioned in subsection (4)(a) above, or**

    (c) **makes an assertion about the patent for the purpose of any enquiries so made.**

[*It is hereby declared that a mere notification of the existence of a patent does not constitute a threat of proceedings within the meaning of this section*].

(6) In proceedings under this section for threats by one person (A) to another (B) in respect of an alleged infringement of a patent for an invention, it shall be a defence for A to prove that he used his best endeavours, without success, to discover—

    (a) **where the invention is a product, the identity of the person (if any) who made or (in the case of an imported product) imported it for disposal;**

    (b) **where the invention is a process and the alleged infringement consists of offering it for use, the identity of a person who used the process;**

    (c) **where the invention is a process and the alleged infringement is an act falling within section 60(1)(c) above, the identity of the person who used the process to produce the product in question;**

and that he notified B accordingly, before or at the time of making the threats, identifying the endeavours used.

Note. The Patents Act 2004 (c.16) s.12 and Sch.2(17) amended s.70, with effect from January 1, 2005, although the unamended section continues to apply to any alleged threat communicated before that date (SI 2004/3205 arts 2(d)(f)(k) and 9(3)). These amendments substituted new forms of subss.(2), (4) and (5) and inserted new subss.(2A) and (6), and these amendments extensively revise the circumstances in which this section is applicable. The amendments also replace the references to "plaintiff" in subss.(2) and (3) with references to the replacement term "claimant" substituted by the Civil Procedure Rules. The amended versions are shown in bold type and the original versions in italics.

COMMENTARY ON SECTION 70

Scope of the section

70.02   Section 70 provides for relief in certain circumstances against threats of action for patent infringement. Such threats are actionable by whomsoever made, it not being necessary that the person making the threat be the patent proprietor or a licensee. As noted above, the section has been extensively amended with a view to limiting the grounds for bringing a successful action in respect of threats of infringement and so pre-2005 case law should be considered with this in mind. For articles on the revisions to s.70, see: W. Cook, [2004] *CIPA* 698; Vicki Salmon and N. Minogue [2005] *CIPA* 592; and [2005] E.I.P.R. 294; and P. Roberts [2005] E.I.P.R. 334.

The claimant must be "a person aggrieved" (subs.(1)). Such a person is one who has a genuine grievance even though he may not suffer direct loss from the threats, see *Brain v Ingledew Brown* [1995] F.S.R. 552, where the claimant was the sole shareholder of the company threatened, but the reported decision was reversed on appeal as not being one suitable for summary judgment (see [1996] F.S.R. 341 CA). At the eventual substantive trial (*Brain v Ingledew Brown (No.3)* [1997] F.S.R. 511), it was (unsuccessfully) argued that, unless threats were made directly to the claimant, the claimant must prove that he has suffered actual damage before it can be held that he is "a person aggrieved". It was held sufficient that the claimant shows:

"that his commercial interests are or are likely to be adversely affected in a real as opposed to a fanciful or minimal way".

See also *Speedcranes v Thomson* [Scotland] [1978] R.P.C. 221. In *Dimplex v De'Longhi* [1996] F.S.R. 622, threatening letters had been sent to many major retailers of the claimants' goods. It was unsuccessfully contended that, because the patent had been abandoned, the claimant was not a "person aggrieved".

The threats must be groundless (i.e. unjustifiable). This will be so unless the person making the threat proves that the act complained of is a patent infringement and that the patent alleged to be infringed is not held to be invalid in a relevant respect, or that when the threat was made he did not know and had no reason to know of such invalidity (subs.(2A)). In *Icon Health v Precise Exercise Equipment* BL C/29/01, noted I.P.D. 24050 relief for unjustified threats was ordered, the patent being held not to be infringed and it therefore not being necessary to consider the validity of the patent.

The specified relief is: a declaration (in Scotland: declarator) that the threats are unjustifiable; an injunction (in Scotland: interdict) against continuance of the threats; and damages in respect of any loss suffered by the claimant/threatened person (subs.(3)). However, the section is not effective in respect of threats made against a primary act of infringement, i.e. one made in respect of acts of making or importing a product for disposal or of using a process or to someone undertaking such acts (subs.(4)); or where there has been no more than the provision of factual information about the patent, enquiries made for the sole purpose of identifying the primary infringer or making an assertion about the patent for the purpose of such enquiries (subs.(5)).

The section applies to European patents (UK), see s.77(1)(b). Similar provisions exist in relation to threats of infringement: of a registered design, Registered Designs Act 1949 (c.88) s.26; of a design right, s.253 CDPA 1988; and of a registered trade mark, Trade Marks Act 1994 (c.26) s.21, each again with exceptions in respect of primary acts of infringement, although there are important differences between the specifics of each provision. However, there is no corresponding provision in respect of threats for infringement of other (all unregistered) intellectual property rights, e.g. infringement of a copyright, or in respect of a common law tort, such as an alleged "passing off". The absence of similar provisions in other statutes has been held to be deliberate so that threats of litigation of such other intellectual property rights are not actionable, even if presented as an action for wrongful interference with contractual relations (*Granby v Interlego* [1984] R.P.C. 209). However, threats of litigation in respect of some such other intellectual property right which can be made with impunity may nevertheless become actionable if coupled with notification of the existence of an intellectual property right, such as a patent, where such notification by itself is statutorily exempt from being actionable under provisions similar to the present section, see the design case of *Jaybeam v Abru Aluminium* [1976] R.P.C. 308 discussed in §70.08.

The consequence of an action under the section is usually that the defendant contends that the threat was justified because there is an infringement of the patent, with the defendant counter-claiming for infringement (if the defendant is the proprietor or exclusive licensee under the patent in issue and if the claimant, being the person threatened, is alleged to be an actual infringer); and the claimant then counter-claiming to that counterclaim alleging that, even if he is an infringer, the patent is not valid in relation to the alleged infringing activities. An advantage of bringing a threats action under the section is that an interim injunction may be available despite an allegation of justification, see §70.06. Also, the person threatened can seize the initiative. As claimant, he will enjoy the right to open the oral argument and normally to have the final speech as well. Also, the claimant can, at least initially, choose the forum in which the proceedings should be heard, and this is a potent factor now that proceedings for threats, infringement and validity can all be brought before the Patents County Court as an alternative to the High Court, not forgetting the possibility of proceedings in Scotland or Northern Ireland. Indeed, where threats have only been issued in one part of the United Kingdom, an action on it has to be adjudicated in a court for that part, even though this means that infringement and validity may there be put in issue although these issues have also been raised in parallel proceedings in some other part of the United Kingdom (*Demel v Jefferson* BL C/2/98, noted I.P.D. 21050).

In *Kenburn Waste Management v Bergmann* [2002] F.S.R. 44 at 696 the parties had previously settled a threats action by means of undertakings by the German defendant that it would not utter further threats. On the defendant being alleged to have breached the undertakings, questions arose as to the proper forum for adjudication of this further dispute. The defendant argued that because he was domiciled in Germany and operated his business from there, the proper forum for the dispute was Germany. The court considered the relevant provisions of the Brussels Convention (now Regulation 44/2001) and held that because the object of the contract was to achieve results in the UK (fulfilment of the negative obligation not to make threats), and because the contract was concerned with the purely English right of action under s.70, the contract was strongly connected with the UK and therefore the matter was actionable there. The judgment was upheld on appeal ([2002] F.S.R. 45 at 711).

As noted above, s.70 was substantially amended by the Patents Act 2004. The first analysis of the provisions of the section as amended took place in *FNM Corp Ltd v Drammock International Ltd* [2009] EWHC 1294, where, as observed in §70.05, the patentee was able successfully to rely on the new subs.(2A). For a discussion of the current status of these amended provisions in the light of this case and *Zeno Corp v BSM-Bionic Solutions Management* [2009] EWHC 1829, see D. Barron "Early Enforcement Options" [2010] *CIPA* 150.

What constitutes a threat (subs. (1))

To be actionable under the section (subject to the provisions of subss.(2)–(5), as discussed in §§70.05–70.08), there must be a "threat" to bring proceedings for some infringement of a patent, whether past, present or future, but a threat merely of legal proceedings is insufficient (*Easycare v Bryan Lawrence* [1995] F.S.R. 597). Such a threat can be express or implied, but it must be made against "another person" and be made by "circu-

70.03

lars, advertisements or otherwise". Despite the *ejusdem generis* rule of statutory interpretation, which would limit the meaning of "otherwise" to disclosures having a similar nature to "circulars" and "advertisements", the tendency of the courts has been to construe broadly the word "otherwise" in this phrase, see *Speedcranes v Thomson* [Scotland] [1978] R.P.C. 221, where it was also decided that an actionable threat must be addressed to some person, and not merely be a general warning not addressed to anyone in particular. Likewise, in *Alpi v Wright* [1972] R.P.C. 125, where the advertisement announced that an infringement action had been commenced, it was held that an actionable threat must point a finger against the products of some other specified person, though an actionable threat need not be made directly to the actual infringer. Indeed, in *Bristol-Myers v Manon* [1973] R.P.C. 836, there was an actionable threat when a retailer was informed that a claim would be made against the manufacturer, though not against the retailer, of the alleged infringing goods. However, it appears that a court will be reluctant to grant relief in respect of an actionable threat made in the course of "without prejudice" settlement discussions, because such should not be inhibited by litigation arising from what was said during such discussions, see *Unilever v Procter & Gamble* [1999] F.S.R. 849; and [2000] F.S.R. 344 CA and case comments by R. Ashmead [2000] *CIPA* 62 and by Zoë Butler *Patent World*, No.119, February 2000, p.12. In this way, it seems that the requirements of the CPR, that parties must make efforts to settle disputes before commencing litigation, can be met without fear that the attempts to settle would be regarded as an actionable threat, see Alexandra Brodie [1999] *CIPA* 39, but (as there noted) it is important that pre-action correspondence should not merely be marked "Without prejudice", but the words "save as to costs" should be added. Also, mere marking of a communication "Without Prejudice" will not prevent an action for threats made in that communication if its subject-matter was not directed to a negotiation for settlement of potential litigation or to a cause of action by the person making the threat, see *Kooltrade v XTS* [2001] F.S.R. 158 where X had no patent right to protect.

Although an action under the section may be brought by a person who is not an actual or potential infringer, to secure relief that person must satisfy the court that he is a person "aggrieved" by the threats, i.e. that he has suffered actual or potential loss as a result of the threat, see §70.02. In *Brain v Ingledew Brown (No.3)* [1997] F.S.R. 511), some of the threats complained of were directed to a company owned and operated solely by the claimant, but these were not seen to be directed at the claimant personally and were therefore not actionable by him, the company having been struck off the register. However, another letter written to a third party was seen as likely to be understood by that party as applying to the claimant in a personal capacity and was therefore actionable because this made the claimant "a person aggrieved". Letters have amounted to actionable threats where the language used has been such as would convey to a reasonable man that there was an intention to bring proceedings for patent infringement (*C. & P. Development v Sisabro* (1953) 70 R.P.C. 277). In *Continental Linen v Kenpet* [South Africa] [1986] 4 SA 703(t), noted [1987] E.I.P.R. D–87, it was held that the test whether or not a letter constitutes a threat is an objective one to be decided regardless of how the addressee read it, or what the sender intended. See also the trade mark case of *L'Oréal v Johnson & Johnson* [2000] F.S.R. 686 where a letter, the "work of a master of delphic utterances", was held to be a veiled threat muffled by protestations of a continuing state of uncertainty but sufficient to be an intimation to a reasonable man of an intention to enforce rights, it mattering not that the letter was sent in response to an enquiry from the party threatened. In *Bowden Controls v Acco Cable Controls* [1990] R.P.C. 427, a letter addressed to a supplier to car manufacturers, which referred to a German court decision, stated that the patentee had corresponding patents in most other European countries, and that he intended to enforce his rights, was held to be a threat of infringement proceedings, even though the patentee argued that it would be commercial suicide to sue a potential customer in view of the established practice in the industry of requiring dual sourcing of car components. Also, the threat can be in respect of a projected, rather than existing, act of alleged infringement, see *Therm-a-Stor v Weatherseal* [1981] F.S.R. 579 CA. However, to be actionable under the section, it would seem that the threat should be one made within, or reaching, the United Kingdom: otherwise, the Act would have extra-territorial effect contrary to general jurisprudence, see *Norbert Steinhardt v Meth* [Australia] (1960–61) 105 C.L.R. 440; 1A I.P.R. 78.

The section can, apparently, be avoided by issuing a claim form before issuing the threat, even if this form has not been served at the time of the threat. This is because there can scarcely be a threat of infringement proceedings if they are already in being. However, the courts have been prepared to grant relief in cases where the commencement of legal proceedings can be seen as harassment rather than legitimate, especially if allegations of infringement have been insufficiently particularised (*Landi den Hartog v Sea Bird* [1976] F.S.R. 489); or if separate complaints have been issued against customers of an existing defendant (*Jacey v Norton & Wright* [1977] F.S.R. 475), but see *Revlon v Cripps & Lee* [1980] F.S.R. 85 at 98 for a contrary case. A threat issued in respect of a pending application may be incapable of justification, see §70.05.

In *Quads 4 Kids v Campbell* [2006] EWHC 2482, a case on the corresponding threats provisions for designs, it was held that the use by a rights owner of an internet auction website system for asserting ownership of intellectual property rights in articles traded on the site constituted an actionable threat.

Because remarks may so easily be construed as an implied threat, there is frequently a need to give a warning to lay persons, particularly salespersons, not to refer to patents, and in particular not to refer to pending applications except in terms which have previously been approved by a solicitor or patent attorney. Lay persons also need to be told that advertisements may lead to action being taken for unjustifiable threats under the section, see also the warnings in §70.04 in respect of references to pending litigation and the danger of committing a contempt of court or uttering a malicious falsehood if reports of litigation are not entirely accurate and free from contrary innuendo.

In *FNM Corp Ltd v Drammock International Ltd* [2009] EWHC 1294, an email was sent to a third party customer of the defendant, informing the customer that there was a dispute currently existing between the defendant and the patentee. Although this contained no direct allegation against the customer, it was held nonetheless to amount to an actionable threat when viewed from the point of view of the ordinary reader in the position of the actual recipient, which clearly understood this as a threat. Another case in which the question of what constitutes a threat was broadly construed was *Zeno Corp v BSM-Bionic Solutions Management* [2009] EWHC 1829 where a letter sent to a retailer seeking in effect an explanation of why the device in issue did not infringe was held to amount to an actionable threat. In *Best Buy v Worldwide Sales* [2011] EWCA Civ 618, reversing the judge at first instance on this issue at [2010] EWHC 1666 (Ch), the Court of Appeal held that a letter made an actionable threat of trade mark infringement proceedings even though it included an offer to negotiate a settlement and thus might have been thought to attract the privilege accorded to "without prejudice" communications. However, the offer to settle did not contain any concession or admission. Looking at the letter as a whole, the Court of Appeal held that it was unrealistic to treat the offer as amounting to the sort of settlement proposal which should. On the grounds of public policy, be treated as privileged from use in court.

Malicious falsehood and contempt of court

Even if a statement is not an actionable threat, it may nevertheless be actionable as a **70.04** malicious falsehood, or otherwise be a basis for an action for defamation. Also there will be a contempt of court if comment made about a pending litigation could tend to interfere with the course of justice, regardless of any intent that this should be so (Contempt of Court Act 1981 (c.49) s.1). Nevertheless, it is permissible to make an entirely accurate statement that litigation is in progress, particularly to warn the trade of the existence of that litigation, see *Carl-Zeiss-Stiftung v Rayner and Keeler* [1961] R.P.C. 1 and *Easipower v Gordon Moore* [1963] R.P.C. 8 as examples in intellectual property disputes. Care must be taken that such statements are entirely accurate, both in what they say and what they imply. Thus, in a dispute in which records were produced of processes used by the defendant which the claimant alleged to have been forged, the claimant issued statements implying that the court had ordered investigations into the alleged forgery. An order for disclosure as to the origin of these statements was made, the court making it clear that there had as yet been not even a preliminary finding with regard to the allegations (*Lund-*

beck v Lagap BL C/5/03). Moreover, pending judgment, the comment should not state, explicitly or by inference, that the patent is valid or infringed, because these are questions yet to be determined by the court. For example, in *Mentmore v Fomento* (1955) 72 R.P.C. 157, the patent had been held by the Court of Appeal in other proceedings to be valid and infringed. A representative told a buyer for a large store than an injunction had been granted, but did not say that operation of the order had been suspended pending appeal. This was a malicious falsehood. For cases of contempt, see: *Michigan v Mathew* [1966] R.P.C. 47, where a patentee tried to arouse public indignation against the alleged infringer; and *Daw v Eley* (1868) L.R. 7 Eq. Cas. 49, where the defendant's solicitor wrote a tendentious letter to the press under a pseudonym commenting on the litigation.

Justification (subs.(2) and (2A))

70.05   The heading to the section refers to "groundless" threats, though this word is not used in the section, and subs.(3) refers to the threats being "unjustifiable". These words would seem to apply to the conditions set out in subs.(2). These are that a claimant (pursuer in Scotland) is entitled to relief under the section as set out in subs.(3) if he proves (and the onus is on him to do so): (a) that the alleged threat was made; and (b) that he is a person aggrieved by it, subject to new subs.(2A). This provides a defence for the defendant (defender in Scotland) if he proves (a) that the acts for which proceedings were threatened "constitute or, if done, would constitute" an infringement of a patent; and (b) the claimant (pursuer in Scotland) fails to show that that patent is invalid in a relevant respect. New subs.(2A) introduces the possibility for the defendant, even where the patent is shown to be invalid in a relevant respect, to avoid sanction by showing that he did not know, and had no reason to suspect, that the patent was invalid in that respect.

Thus, in *Demel v Jefferson* [1999] F.S.R. 204, partial justification for admitted threats was proved upon a finding of one of the two patents in suit being found valid and infringed, but the invalidity of the other patent was accepted thereby entitling the claimant to relief in that respect. However, in *Goldschmidt v EOC Belgium* [2000] EWHC Patents 175, where two patents were held invalid with a third found valid and infringed, there was justification because the threat had only been made by reference to the third patent. These conditions do not provide for any justification where the threat is made under a patent application rather than a granted patent as the section does not apply under s.69, see §69.06. Indeed, a threat issued in respect of a pending application may be incapable of justification, see *Continental Linen v Kenpet* [South Africa] [1986] 4 SA 703(t), noted [1987] E.I.P.R. D–87, but it is possible that threats made during the pendency of an application can be seen as a threat to take proceedings post-grant. Thus, in *Brain v Ingledew Brown* [1995] F.S.R. 552, threats made under a pending application included a threat of seeking an injunction and, therefore, could only be seen as a threat to bring proceedings after grant; and, anyway, subs.(2) was loosely construed so as to permit the person making the threat to plead that the intervening acts (actionable under s.69) were justifiable because there would have been infringement if the patent had then been granted, but this decision was reversed on appeal as not being one suitable for summary judgment (see [1996] F.S.R. 341 CA) though it was likewise indicated that threats made in relation to a still pending application should be construed as threats to bring proceedings once grant has occurred. However, on that basis, while such proceedings could be commenced before grant, it would be undesirable for the case to be tried before the terms of the claims became certain, at which point their validity could also be judged in the context of deciding whether the threats could be regarded as justified. In subsequent proceedings on this case, the defence of justification was struck out because grant of the European patent was still not imminent, the court holding that there should be no stay of the proceedings and that the claimant was entitled to know details of the plea of justification, i.e. the form of claim alleged to be valid and infringed (*Brain v Ingledew Brown (No.2)* [1997] F.S.R. 271).

In *FNM Corp Ltd v Drammock International Ltd* [2009] EWHC 1294, a threat was held to be protected by the new s.70(2A)(b) introduced by the Patents Act 2004 as although the patent had been held invalid, it would otherwise have been infringed, and the patentee had no reason to suspect that the patent was invalid at the time the threats were made. It was observed that whilst the burden of proof is on the patentee, in practice it is for the party complaining of the threat to suggest why the patentee should have suspected the patent to be invalid. There had to be a specific reason for suspecting invalidity, rather than a mere general awareness that the patent might be held to be invalid, and none here had been identified.

Relief (subs.(3))

The relief available under the section is: (a) a declaration (declarator in Scotland) to the **70.06** effect that the threats are unjustifiable; (b) an injunction (interdict in Scotland) against the continuance of the threats; and (c) damages in respect of any loss which the claimant (pursuer in Scotland) has sustained by the threats. Although subs.(1) states that the claimant is "entitled" to the stated relief, the imposition of an injunction remains in the inherent jurisdiction of the court (*Benmax v Austin* (1953) 70 R.P.C. 143; (1953) 70 R.P.C. 284; and *Tudor Accessories v Somers* [1960] R.P.C. 215). Thus, where a claimant has not been inconvenienced by the threat, and treats his right of action as a weapon in a contractual dispute between the parties, an injunction may be refused. In further proceedings in *Kooltrade v XTS* [2002] F.S.R. 49 at 764, the claimant sought to enforce the court's judgment by joinder of other parties (including a director of the defendant and the solicitors who had issued the threats), the defendant itself having gone into liquidation. The court held that a new trial would be required to assess the liability of the proposed further defendants and fresh proceedings would need to be commenced to deal with any claim against them.

The remedy of an interim injunction against unjustified threats is a most potent one, and such can be granted even if infringement proceedings have already been started, see *H.V.E. v Cufflin* [1964] R.P.C. 149 and *Cerosa v Poseidon* [1973] R.P.C. 882). In *Bowden Controls v Acco Cable Controls* [1990] R.P.C. 427, the interim injunction order also required the patentee to identify the individuals to whom the offending letters had been directed. Although it is well established that an interim injunction will not be imposed in respect of threatened publication of a defamatory statement, provided that the publisher intends to justify the truth of that statement, this principle is inapplicable to threats of patent infringement proceedings (*Johnson Electric v Mabuchi* [1986] F.S.R. 280).

To obtain an award of damages, the claimant must prove a financial loss arising from the threat. Thus, in *Carflow Products v Linwood Securities* BL C/29/98, the retailer had decided to maintain the product in issue in its catalogue despite the threat, and had only withdrawn that product from its catalogue when a claim was initiated against the retailer. In these circumstances, the loss suffered by the supplier to the retailer was held not to have been caused by the threat, see also *Townend Controls v Gilead* [Australia] (1991) 21 I.P.R. 520. However, relief for unjustified threats can extend to a claim for damages to recover the costs of litigation involving those threats which had been aborted when it appeared that the claimant had had no entitlement to bring the proceedings (*Cavity Trays v RMC Panel Products* [1996] R.P.C. 361). In any event, a successful claimant under the section is entitled to an inquiry into damages, even when the court has deep suspicions that he would then recover very little indeed (*Brain v Ingledew Brown (No.3)* [1977] F.S.R. 511), but here it was suggested that, in future cases of this kind, the claimant should ask the court for the issues of liability and quantum to be tried together. In *Dimplex v De'Longhi* [1996] F.S.R. 622, it was contended that the claimant would not have suffered more than minimal damage, but an injunction was granted against further threats and a costs order was made.

Exclusion of threats made to primary infringers (subs.(4))

Subsection (4), which was new in the present Act (with similar provisions now included **70.07** in the corresponding statutory provisions in respect of registered designs, design rights and trade marks, for which see §70.02), excludes action for a threat where this was: (a) made in respect of an act of primary infringement, that is an act of making or importing a product, or of using a process; or (b) made to a person who has undertaken such act. Whereas the exclusionary provision under (a) (which constituted the subsection as originally enacted) is in terms of the nature of the threat rather than in terms of the person threatened, that under (b) (which is significant in the light of much of the earlier case la-wand was introduced by the 2004 Act) is in terms of the person threatened. Thus whereas subs.4(a) relates to threats to bring proceedings for acts of "primary" infringement, subs.(4)(b) relates to threats to bring proceedings in respect of "secondary" acts of in-fringement, i.e. of selling or stocking the patented product or offering the patented product for use, provided that the person threatened has made or imported that product for disposal (or used that process). The subsection may absolve threats made against a manufacturing agent where the alleged infringing act is the making (or importing) of a product for dis-posal, as well as threats against persons who, as indirect infringers under s.60(2), supplied others with products for use in making the claimed products (*Therm-a-Stor v Weatherseal* [1981] F.S.R. 579 CA). Cases decided before the introduction of subs.(4)(b) by the 2004 Act, and which the subsection as originally enacted was held not to exclude the threat from being actionable, but which are likely no longer to be good law (or to be of limited further relevance) as a result of such amendment include: *Neild v Rockley* [1986] F.S.R. 3, where the threat related to acts of sale; and *Johnson Electric v Mabuchi* [1986] F.S.R. 280, where a threat against use of electric motors was held not to be a threat made in respect of manufacture or of use of a process, *Bowden Cable v Acco Cable Controls* [1990] R.P.C. 427), where the threat was against a manufacturer but who had existing stock for sale, *Cavity Trays v RMC Panel Products* [1996] R.P.C. 361 CA where the threat concerned disposal of articles manufactured by the person threatened, and *Brain v Ingledew Brown (No.3)* [1997] F.S.R. 511 which related to use of a process, but where the person threatened might wish to license others to use that process: and where, anyway, there was no guarantee that the then pending application would not issue with a claim to a product which the entity threatened would purchase from others. Where a threat is not actionable under the section because of this subsection, it may nevertheless be possible to obtain a declaration from the court that the threats were unjustified (*Leco Instruments v Land Py-rometers* [1982] R.P.C. 133).

In *FNM Corp Ltd v Drammock International Ltd* [2009] EWHC 1294, a letter that specifically referred only to manufacture was held not to entitle the patentee to the protec-tion of s.70(4) as it had to be read in conjunction with the associated form of undertakings which referred also to supply. Therefore, although the threat was protected in respect of manufacture by s.70(4)(a), it was not protected in respect of supply by s.70(4)(b), as that only protects a threat to a person "who has made. . . a product" and does not protect a threat to a person who is wrongly alleged to have made a product—which was the case here as the defendant was not the manufacturer.

Notifications etc. which will not constitute a threat (subs.(5))

70.08   Subsection (5) as amended by the 2004 Act expands on the wording of the section as enacted to enlarge the definition of acts which cannot be construed as a threat to bring proceedings, previously confined to a "mere notification" of the existence of a patent. These are now:

(a) providing any factual information about the patent (not just the mere notification of its existence);

(b) making enquiries to find out if there has been a primary infringement and, if so, by whom; and

(c) making assertions about the patent for the purposes of making such enquiries.

It is apparently envisaged that, as a result of these changes, an enquirer will be able to make assertions regarding an alleged primary infringement, as part of his attempt to trace the primary infringer, but that assertions regarding an alleged secondary infringement will not necessarily be excluded from the definition of a "threat". Of course, whether an asser-tion does in fact amount to a threat will have to be decided taking into account all the rele-vant circumstances. Thus under the subsection as originally enacted, declaring that:

"mere notification of the existence of the patent is deemed not to be a threat of proceedings within the meaning of the section",

a notification of the existence of a patent could constitute an actionable threat if this was given in such a context that a threat was seen to be intended and this is presumably still the case. For example, in the design case of *Jaybeam v Abru Aluminium* [1976] R.P.C. 308, the notification of the design registration was contained in a letter which clearly threatened proceedings for copyright infringement and an injunction against repetition was granted because, in the context of the letter, reference to the design registration was not a "mere notification", see also *Speedcranes v Thomson* [Scotland] [1978] R.P.C. 221. In *Reymes-Cole v Elite Hosiery* [1964] R.P.C. 255; and [1965] R.P.C. 102, a letter notifying the existence of patents also stated that a number of firms were infringing and that action was being taken against some of them: this was held to be an actionable threat.

See also the discussion in §70.03 of what may constitute threat, and the broad interpretation this word is given in this section, for example in *FNM Corp Ltd v Drammock International Ltd* [2009] EWHC 1294 and *Zeno Corp v BSM-Bionic Solutions Management* [2009] EWHC 1829 which are there discussed.

Defence for threats made when the identity of the primary infringer cannot be ascertained (subs.(6))

New subs.(6), introduced by the 2004 Act, provides a further defence to a claim under **70.09** the section, even when the threat is made against a secondary infringer, although only in limited circumstances. Under this subsection, it is a defence for the person making the threat to prove that he had used his best endeavours, without success, to discover the identity of a person who has made, or imported for disposal, the patented product, or has used the patented process, or has used that process to produce the product in question, although only where the person making the threat had notified the person threatened before, or at the time of making the threat, and has identified the endeavours used. This provision is intended to enable a proprietor to approach, for example, a retailer or stockist, in order to get the infringement dispute resolved, and in doing so threaten the latter with infringement proceedings. However, the defence is only available when "best" endeavours have been used to obtain the information identifying the primary infringer and, when the person threatened is supplied (no later than the time of making the threat) with information setting out the scope of these unsuccessful endeavours.

PRACTICE UNDER SECTION 70

Actions for unjustified threats under the section may be brought before any "court" (as **70.10** defined in s.130(1)), including the Patents County Court. In proceedings before the Patents Court or the Patents County Court, the procedure is governed by CPR r.63 and its associated Practice Direction, with the Patents Court Guide also relevant. CPR 63.2 specifically requires actions under s.70 to be brought in either the Patents Court or a Patents County Court. By CPR 63.14 proceedings may be served initially at the address for service recorded in the register of patents, see §32.15. Where the threatened person commences the proceedings (as distinct from bringing a counterclaim in pending proceedings for patent infringement), he may institute proceedings by serving a claim form pursuant to CPR r.7.2. The defendant/respondent to such proceedings will usually put forward a defence of justification under subs.(2) (see §70.05), and thus serve a counterclaim (a "Part 20 claim" under CPR r.20). The subsequent procedure will then also be governed by CPR r.63 and the Practice Direction and the Patents Court Guide. A counterclaim to the counterclaim alleging invalidity of the patent, at least in a material respect, will then be possible and this counterclaim can also be one for revocation of the patent. In the Patents County Court, the general procedure for proceedings in that court likewise apply. The advantages which arise from commencing proceedings under s.70 are indicated in §70.02. Where threats have only been issued in one part of the United Kingdom, an action thereon has to be adjudicated in a court for that part, even though this means that infringement and validity may there be put in issue, even when parallel infringement and validity proceedings have already been commenced in another part of the United Kingdom (*Demel v Jefferson* BL

C/2/98, noted I.P.D. 21050). Subsequently, a stay of the English proceedings in favour of those commenced in Northern Ireland for infringement was refused (*Demel v Jefferson* [1999] F.S.R. 204).

SECTION 71

Declaration or declarator as to non-infringement

71.01   **71.**—(1) Without prejudice to the court's jurisdiction to make a declaration or declarator apart from this section, a declaration or declarator that an act does not, or a proposed act would not, constitute an infringement of a patent may be made by the court or the comptroller in proceedings between the person doing or proposing to do the act and the proprietor of the patent, notwithstanding that no assertion to the contrary has been made by the proprietor, if it is shown—

(a) that that person has applied in writing to the proprietor for a written acknowledgment to the effect of the declaration or declarator claimed, and has furnished him with full particulars in writing of the act in question; and

(b) that the proprietor has refused or failed to give any such acknowledgment.

(2) Subject to section 72(5) below, a declaration made by the comptroller under this section shall have the same effect as a declaration or declarator by the court.

RELEVANT RULE—RULE 73

71.02   *Note.* The relevant rule for proceedings before the Comptroller for a declaration of non-infringement is r.73, reprinted at §123.06, such proceedings are generally covered by Pt 7 of the Rules (mainly reprinted in §§123.06–123.21 and discussed in the commentary on s.123).

COMMENTARY ON SECTION 71

Scope of the section

71.03   Section 71 provides for the court or Comptroller to make a declaration (declarator in Scotland) of non-infringement of a patent upon application by a person doing, or proposing to do, an act of which full particulars have been furnished in writing to the proprietor and an acknowledgment requested that such act is not, or would not be, an infringement of a specified patent and this acknowledgment has not been given (subs.(1)). The section is without prejudice to the court's inherent jurisdiction to make declarations (or declarators) apart from the section (subs.(1)). The section is applicable to European patents (UK) (s.77(1)(b)), but the section is inapplicable to pending applications (*Acme Signs v AC Edward* BL C/89/87, noted I.P.D. 10071) and so an application must await the grant of the patent under s.25(1), as discussed in §24.06.

An application for a declaration of non-infringement brought under the inherent jurisdiction of the court, rather than under s.71, cannot include an attack on validity because of the provisions of s.74(2), but it may be possible to include in such a claim an application for revocation to be heard concurrently, see *Organon Teknika v Hoffmann-La Roche* [1996] F.S.R. 383 discussed in §74.03. Nor can a declaration be sought from the court based on information given during "without prejudice" settlement discussions because such discussions are to be encouraged and not inhibited by the possibility of legal proceedings arising as a result, see *Unilever v Procter & Gamble* [1999] F.S.R. 849; and [2000] F.S.R. 344 CA, discussed in §70.03. In *Auchincloss v Agricultural & Veterinary Supplies*

[1997] R.P.C. 649, the defendants sought a declaration of non-infringement on a postulated amount of contaminant in their composition, this being one of the factors for possible infringement. The court held that the contaminant might be present in a larger amount and so could not grant a declaration under the section, but it did so under its inherent jurisdiction on the basis that, howsoever the amounts of ingredients were calculated, the proportions fell outside those specified by the claim. In *Nokia v Interdigital Technology* [2005] EWCA Civ 614; [2006] I.P. & T. 8, the Court of Appeal allowed a claim seeking a declaration of "non-essentiality" under the inherent jurisdiction of the court to stand, holding the issue to be clearly enough defined to be the subject of such jurisdiction. Instead of a claim for non-infringement sought under such jurisdiction, this raised the issue of whether patents that had been declared to a standards organisation as "essential" to the licensed practice of the technology were indeed so. In *Nokia v Interdigital Technology* [2006] EWCA Civ 1618; 2007 F.S.R 23, the court allowed a similar claim to stand, the patentees having sought unsuccessfully to distinguish the earlier decision on the basis that no claim of right had been made in the present case and that the declaration to the standards organisation did not in and of itself constitute such a claim. At trial in *Nokia v Interdigital Technology* [2007] EWHC 3077 Pat Ct, and having heard evidence on the matter, the court observed that "the declarations proposed are genuinely useful" but the action settled before a final order was made.

Under subs.(2), when the Comptroller makes a declaration under the section, this has the same effect as one made by the court, but the declaration does not act as an estoppel as regards future revocation proceedings before the court, for which see §72.17 (subs.(2)).

While decisions of the court may be appealed in the usual way for court proceedings, a decision of the Comptroller under the section can be appealed only to the Patents Court (s.97(1)) with further appeal possible only with leave and on a point of law (s.97(3)).

In *Omnipharm v Merial* [2010] EWHC 3059, an applicant for revocation (for which no standing is required) applied to amend its claim in order also to include a declaration under s.71 that what it intended to do would not in any event infringe. This was opposed on the basis that the applicant could not show that it had the requisite intention to carry out the allegedly non-infringing acts because, inter alia it (i) had no website, (ii) had not filed accounts for more than three years and had insufficient assets, (iii) had a registered office care of a firm of accountants and (iv) had no traceable office. The application to amend was allowed, the judge observing that in order to show that it was a person intending to perform the allegedly non-infringing act, it was sufficient for a party to declare only that it should like to do the intended act if it could, although he left open the question of the applicant's standing as being a matter that remained in issue and could perhaps be addressed as a preliminary issue.

The advantages and disadvantages of using the section

An application under the section may be made to the Comptroller or the court (which includes the Patents County Court (see the definition of "court" in s.130(1)); and, in *Sundstrand v Safe Flight Instrument* [1994] F.S.R. 599, that court gave such a declaration. **71.04**

Validity may be put in issue in the same proceedings, see s.74(1)(c); although, if revocation is sought (as distinct from merely seeking a declaration that there is no infringement, which may include an assertion of invalidity, because there can be no infringement of an invalid patent, see *Pittevil v Brackelsberg* (1932) 49 R.P.C. 23) separate proceedings under s.72 are necessary. A finding of invalidity under s.71 does not itself lead to revocation, merely to a declaration in negative form, see *Ziegler's Patent* BL O/64/87. Costs follow the event in the usual way (whereas under former practice the applicant had to pay these in any event). The ability to put validity in issue enables a "squeeze" situation to be set up whereby the proprietor may seek to put forward a broad interpretation of his claims in order to have a declaration of non-infringement denied, but in doing so exposes the patent to objections of invalidity that would perhaps not otherwise arise.

The section is also useful when an alleged infringer has made changes to the accused product and wishes to ensure that his modified product avoids falling foul of any injunction which has been, or may be, granted on the first device, see *Filhol v Fairfax* [1990]

R.P.C. 293, where an injunction had already been granted; and *Rodi & Wienenberger v Showell* [1966] R.P.C. 441 and *Vax v Hoover* [1990] R.P.C. 656, where in each case the application for a declaration in respect of a modified form of the alleged infringement was heard at the same time as the infringement proceedings. In the *Vax* case, the court accepted that the defendant would be in a difficult position if faced with an injunction in general terms, although strictly speaking the cause of action on the counterclaim for a declaration had not existed at the date of the claim for infringement: the modified Hoover device was subsequently found to be non-infringing (see [1991] F.S.R. 307). In *Unilever v Chefaro* [1994] R.P.C. 567, the defendants sought, and obtained, an exception from an injunction against infringement in respect of a modified article in respect of which they had pending proceedings for a declaration of non-infringement, the court accepting that it would not be appropriate to place them at risk of contempt proceedings pending the determination of the s.71 proceedings, see §61.21.

The section facilitates "clearing the path" to market and thus in *Approved Prescription Services v Merck* [2003] EWHC 150 Pat Ct, noted I.P.D. 26026 the Patents Court ordered an early trial of an issue of non-infringement limited to one day where this had the possibility to determine whether or not the claimant could market its product, even though the patent was also the subject of an invalidity challenge by other parties.

The disadvantage of using the section is that the applicant bears the burden of satisfying the court, or the Comptroller as the case may be that, on the balance of probabilities, his acts (or proposed acts) do not amount to infringement of any claim of the patent-in-suit whereas, if the applicant waits to be sued for infringement, this onus of proof will fall upon the patentee (or exclusive licensee), as further discussed in §71.07. The effect of the onus of proof being on a claimant is well-illustrated by *Rohm & Haas v Collag* [2001] F.S.R. 28 at 426 where a declaration was refused under the section, but where a finding of infringement might well have failed had the patentee been the claimant. This view was upheld on appeal, see [2002] F.S.R. 28 at 445.

Requirements for seeking declaration (subs.(1))

71.05 An application under the section can be in respect of an act already committed or a proposed act, but the application can only be made by the person doing, or proposing to do, the act in respect of which the declaration of non-infringement is sought, though a declaration can be sought in the inherent jurisdiction of the court in a case where the applicant seeks a declaration in respect of non-infringement by others, see *Filhol v Fairfax* [1990] R.P.C. 293. The onus of satisfying the court rests upon the applicant for the declaration, see §71.04.

A declaration under the section is limited to one of non-infringement of a United Kingdom patent and the court (in its inherent jurisdiction) will not make a declaration in favour of a party against whom no claim has been formulated because one cannot sue for a declaration of non-liability (*Plastus Kreativ v Minnesota Mining* [1995] R.P.C. 438, citing *Clay (In re)* [1919] Ch. 66). In the *Plastus* case, the court struck out requests for declarations of non-infringement of a European patent valid in France and Germany (as far as those countries were concerned), see further §96.11. Also, the court will not adjudicate on a hypothetical situation. Consequently, where a declaration is sought under the inherent jurisdiction of the court (as distinct from under s.71), the claimant must be able to identify a patent of the defendant against which a claim of infringement has been made. In *Boston Scientific v Cordis* BL C/69/97, noted I.P.D. 20099, the criterion was held not established as, although proceedings in Europe had been threatened, it was only conjecture that these would involve any specific patent in the United Kingdom, it not being sufficient that litigation had been commenced in other countries.

A declaration of non-infringement may still be given even if the patent has lapsed (as in *Wordsworth Holdings' Patent* BL O/145/97) because infringement proceedings would still be possible for previous acts, subject to the provisions of the Limitation Act 1980 (c.58), for which see §60.30.

In *Norsk Hydro's Patent* BL O/85/05, noted [2005] *CIPA* 260, the Office rejected an argument that a declaration of non-infringement ought not to granted as the product in issue could be deployed or modified in such a way as to infringe one of the process claims on a contributory infringement basis under s.60(2), observing that such an argument "could be applied in the circumstances of almost every declaration of non-infringement applied for, at least to the Comptroller".

To obtain a declaration under the section, the applicant must first write to the proprietor seeking an acknowledgment of non-infringement in respect of the act, or proposed act, and full particulars of this must be furnished in writing (subs.(1)(a)), as discussed in §71.06. If the proprietor refuses or fails to provide such an acknowledgment, proceedings under the section can be commenced (subs.(1)(b)). In practice, these proceedings have sometimes been started at the same time as the acknowledgment is sought, because the proprietor can always decide not to contest the proceedings or give a belated acknowledgment, see *MMD Design's Patent* [1989] R.P.C. 131. In *Denman's Patent* BL O/369/01, this practice was disapproved. The applicant in this case had written to the proprietor for an acknowledgement as required, but then applied for the declaration on the next working day. This was held to be at odds with the Civil Procedure Rules in accordance with which "parties are expected to try and settle their disputes first before resorting to litigation." Because the decision in *MMD Design's Patent* had encouraged practitioners to believe that it was acceptable to proceed in this way (or even to defer seeking an acknowledgement until after the application under s.71(1) had been filed), the hearing officer declined to dismiss the application in the *Denman* case. However, it was made clear that the Comptroller is likely to take a different line in future cases. (See [2001] *CIPA* 504). Where the patentee gave an acknowledgment during the course of proceedings, the Comptroller has refused to grant a declaration (*Brupat's Patent* BL O/89/90, noted I.P.D. 13195). In deciding a question of non-infringement, the same tests are applied as for infringement, that is to apply the Protocol to art.69 of the EPC as required by s.125(3) (for which see the commentary on s.125). However, where the applicant for a declaration succeeds in proving non-infringement on a literal construction of the patent claims, it has been held that the onus passes to the patentee to demonstrate that there is a serious case to be tried of non-literal infringement under the Protocol to art.69 of the EPC (*Track Marshall v Caterpillar* BL CC/35/95). Thus, the *Catnic/Improver* questions (for which see §125.07) are used by the Comptroller in proceedings under s.71. In *Weihermüller & Voigtmann's Patent* BL O/15/93 and *Schmersal's Patent* BL O/72/91, these questions were used and applied so as to grant the requested declaration.

However, in *Impro's Patent* [1998] F.S.R. 299, the court held that, when the claim was construed purposively, the "device had certainly not been shown not to infringe"; and, shortly thereafter, the Federal Court of Australia found (by a majority decision) a positive case of infringement under the corresponding patent in that country (*Nesbit Evans v Impro* [Australia] [1998] F.S.R. 306). In a decision in the same court concerning the same patent but by a different judge, *Arjo and Impro v Liko* BL C/52/01, noted [2001] *CIPA* 575, 628; and I.P.D. 25006, the court held that it could not agree with the construction placed on the patent in the previous case and granted a declaration, holding that certain features previously determined as inessential were in fact essential features (see also §125.19).

If appropriate, there should also be taken into consideration any defence of non-infringement arising from s.60(5)–(7), or under s.28A or s.64.

Proceedings under the section cannot be started before the Comptroller if there are any proceedings involving the patent already in being before a court, unless that court gives leave, see s.74(7) discussed in §74.06. Where proceedings under s.71 had already been commenced before the Comptroller, and infringement proceedings were then commenced before the court against the s.71 applicant, the court was prepared to stay the proceedings before it (*Hawker Siddeley v Real Time* [1983] R.P.C. 395; and, subsequently, BL O/84/84, noted I.P.D. 7096 and BL O/24/87). However, in *Wilkinson Sword v Warner-Lambert* BL C/124/87, amendment proceedings were pending before the Comptroller when proceedings were commenced before the court under s.71 and also for revocation under s.72. The court refused to stay these proceedings, and ordered that the amendment proceedings should be recommenced before the court under s.75. Also, where an application to the Comptroller under s.71 was initially defective and, before that could be rectified, infringement proceedings had been commenced before the court, the Comptroller refused an extension of time for placing the s.71 application in order, it being thought that the appropriate course was to seek from the court a stay of the proceedings before it and permission to institute new s.71 proceedings before the Comptroller (*Barton and Cullis's Patent* BL O/73/98). For further discussion on concurrent proceedings, see §72.19.

Required description of the alleged non-infringement

71.06   It is important, in complying with the requirement of subs.(1)(a), that the applicant gives precise and complete information in respect of the article or process alleged not to infringe the stated patent, because no declaration can be granted if there is any doubt that any article, etc. corresponding to the description provided by the applicant could infringe the patent (*Mallory Metallurgical v Black Sivalls* [1977] R.P.C. 321 CA; and *Plasticisers v Pixdane* [1979] R.P.C. 327; [1978] F.S.R. 595). In *WL Gore & Associates GmbH v Geox SpA* [2008] EWHC 462 Pat Ct, a declaration was refused, the court criticising the description provided and observing (at [90]) that what is needed "is a precise technical description of what is present" rather than "statements in argumentative or conclusory terms based on one side's disputed interpretation of a term used in the claim." However, *Minnesota Mining's (Suspension Aerosol Formulation) Patent* [1999] R.P.C. 135) illustrates a difficulty in providing supporting particulars for a declaration of non-infringement when the claim construction is not clear. Here, it was indicated that it ought to be sufficient in seeking such a declaration for an applicant to say: "I should like to do this if I can". This was seen as involving two questions: (1) whether the description provided by the applicant was adequate as a description in relation to which a declaration could be given at all; and (2) if it is, is it nonetheless not a description of a real product? On the basis of the claim construction decided by the court, the product particulars given were held to be adequate and a declaration would have been granted if the patent had been held valid.

The provision can also be satisfied by providing a sample of the alleged non-infringing article, provided that its inspection by competent persons will make clear all aspects of the device material to the question of infringement (*Acme Signs v AC Edwards* BL C/89/87, noted I.P.D. 10071). Indeed, the provision of a sample for examination may be ordered, see *Sumitomo Special Metal's Patent* BL O/145/94. A description to be read in conjunction with a detailed drawing will also suffice (*MMD Design's Patent* [1989] R.P.C. 131). In *Machinery Developments v St Mervyn Meat* [2005] EWCA Civ 29, noted I.P.D. 27086, concerning a declaration in respect of a proposed modification to a device that had previously been held to infringe, it was held by the Patents County Court that s.71 does not require a prototype of the modified device actually to have been produced, provided that it was made clear what the modification would be if it were made. In *Norsk Hydro's Patent* BL O/85/05, noted [2005] *CIPA* 260, a declaration of non-infringement was granted in respect of a probe that was described by only a photograph and diagram, as these provided a clear and unambiguous description to which a sample would have added nothing of significance to the issue to be decided.

It is not appropriate to consider, at least at the pleading stage, whether a described apparatus might infringe as the result of wear or deliberate adjustment (*Bonas Machine's Patent* BL O/25/89, noted I.P.D. 12039). Also, as in *Sumitomo Special Metal's Patent* (above), proceedings were held not to be properly launched until an adequate description (including perhaps a sample) are provided; and, until then, it is not appropriate to consider whether further proceedings should be stayed because of a pending opposition in the EPO, for which see §71.08.

In *HB Clip-Lok's Patent* BL O/145/95, the supplied description of the alleged non-infringing device was held not to "meet the requirements of proper and exact formulation", nor did it "clearly define the true issues between the parties". However, amendment of this description was permitted in order to avoid the filing of a new application, although a fresh request for an acknowledgment of non-infringement was ordered, but in similar circumstances the latter requirement was waived (*Impro's Patent* BL O/181/96).

In *Portasilo Ltd v Manchester Cabins Ltd* BL O/119/09 the patentees argued that although s.74(1)(c) allows validity also to be put in issue in an action under s.71, to do so where the particulars of the potentially infringing act were deficient would be tantamount to mounting a general attack on validity which is prohibited by s.74(2), and that an assertion of invalidity in an action under s.71 could only be made in relation to a specific potentially infringing act. The Comptroller held that where validity is put in issue in s.71 proceedings, the claimant must nevertheless provide full particulars of the potentially infringing act pertinent to all claims which might be found valid, and that "full particulars" means a full description of the potentially infringing act sufficient for the proprietor, or the court or the Comptroller as the case may be, to determine whether the act does or does not fall within the terms of those claims.

Effect of declaration

A declaration by the Comptroller has the same effect as one made by the court. Thus, **71.07** such a declaration creates an estoppel against the patentee afterwards contending that the acts involving the article, etc. which are set out in the declaration, constitutes an infringement of the patent in issue, although no estoppel is created as regards a future application to the court for revocation (subs.(2), creating a saving for s.72(5), discussed in §72.17.

Accordingly, a declaration of non-infringement should be conclusive if action were later brought alleging infringement under s.60 as regards an act to which the declaration applies. However, dismissal of an application for a declaration is not necessarily to be equated with a positive finding that infringement does exist because an applicant has a different onus of proof from that of a claimant in an infringement action. Thus, in electing to seek a declaration of non-infringement, an applicant assumes a burden of proving a positive case of non-infringement, whereas in an infringement action the onus lies with the claimant who must prove that an act of infringement has taken place, see *Mallory Metallurgical v Black Sivalls* [1977] R.P.C. 321 CA. In each case the burden of proof is on the balance of probabilities with the result that the person who initiates the proceedings is required to make good his allegation. Accordingly, if an application for a declaration fails, the decision ought merely to be a finding that the case for non-infringement has not been proven, see *Hirst's Application* (1954) 71 R.P.C. 251.

In *Inpaco Corp's Patent* BL O/79/95, the Comptroller was only satisfied as to one of the alleged features of non-infringement and a declaration of non-infringement was made in the form that the "machine in so far as it uses [that feature] does not infringe the patent".

PRACTICE UNDER SECTION 71

Procedure before the Comptroller

The procedure on application to the Comptroller is governed by Pt 7 of the Rules **71.08** (reprinted at §§123.06–123.21 and discussed in the commentary on s.123) and therefore follow the general procedure applicable to all contested proceedings before the Comptroller. If the counter-statement in the proceedings not only denies non-infringement but seeks to establish a positive case of infringement, the counter-statement should explain the basis of the allegation, though it need not specify any particular construction of the claims in issue, see *Wollard's Patent* [1989] R.P.C. 141 where the patentee's first attempt at amplification of his counter-statement was unsatisfactory, see BL O/13/89.

An application under the section will often be accompanied by a concurrent application for revocation under s.72, although this is not necessary as validity may be put in issue in the s.71 proceedings themselves, though such will then lead only to a finding of invalidity and not to revocation, see §71.04. When concurrent applications are filed under both ss.71 and 72, the proceedings will effectively be conducted as consolidated joint proceedings. It is a matter for the discretion of the Comptroller (and therefore presumably also of the court) whether proceedings under the section should be stayed until after pending opposition proceedings before the EPO should be concluded. Such a stay was refused in *Unilever's Patent* BL O/144/94, noted I.P.D. 18042 because threats of proceedings had been made, but was granted in *Sumitomo Special Metal's Patent* BL O/145/94 though with liberty for the applicant at any time to apply for resumption. However, proceedings under the section are automatically terminated when the European patent in issue is finally revoked by the EPO (*Unilever's Patent* BL O/184/96). In *Ash & Lacy's Patent No.2240558* [2002] R.P.C. 46 at 939, s.71 proceedings were stayed in favour of s.72 proceedings in order that the declarant applicant would not have to make inconsistent statements as to the extent of protection proved by the claims in relation to an insufficiency allegation. It was here noted that s.107(4) provides no power for the Comptroller to order security for costs in proceedings under s.71.

Procedure before the court

71.09   Proceedings under s.71 may be brought before any of the courts specified in the definition of "court" in s.130(1). The normal rules of procedure applicable to the court chosen will then apply. However, CPR 63 and the Practice Direction (reprinted in Appendix F) contain no specific provisions as to s.71 proceedings brought either before the Patents Court or Patents County Court, and the Patents Court Guide (reprinted in Appendix G) is equally silent on this point.

Before the Patents Court, the procedure should be the same as that for the seeking of any other kind of declaratory judgment from the court. The proceedings will be commenced by a claim form asking the court to make a declaration. A form of order is set out in *Flexheat v Bolser* [1966] R.P.C. 374. Under the Patents Court Guide, the parties to all proceedings before the Patents Court (which therefore include applications under s.71) are encouraged to serve notices to admit facts and make admissions at an early stage in the proceedings.

Under CPR 63.14 (reprinted in Appendix F), service of proceedings for a declaration of non-infringement may be served initially at the address for service recorded in the register of patents.

At the conclusion of s.71 proceedings, the court will normally order that costs should follow the event in the normal way, even when the claimant became entitled to the requested declaration as the result of the patent having been declared invalid in other proceedings (*Mölnlycke v Procter & Gamble* [1990] R.P.C. 267).

In *Affymetrix v Multilyte* [2005] F.S.R. 1 at [1] the court refused to stay proceedings for a declaration of non-infringement pending determination of parallel proceedings for infringement brought in Germany. Each party was entitled as of right to bring proceedings in more than one jurisdiction and it was not for the court to compel them to opt for one jurisdiction or another.

For a discussion of those situations in which it may be appropriate to apply to the Comptroller, and as to the procedure to be followed, see A.D. Poore, "IPO Practice in s.71 Applications" [2010] *CIPA* 150.

Revocation of patents [Sections 72–73]

SECTION 72

Power to revoke patents on application

72.01   **72.**—(1) Subject to the following provisions of this Act, the court or the comptroller [*may on the application of any person*] by order revoke a patent for an invention **on the application of any person (including the proprietor of the patent)** on (but only on) any of the following grounds, that is to say—

(a) the invention is not a patentable invention;

(b) the patent was granted to a person who was not [*the only person*] entitled [*under section 7(2) above*] to be granted that patent [*or to two or more persons who were not the only persons so entitled*];

(c) the specification of the patent does not disclose the invention clearly enough and completely enough for it to be performed by a person skilled in the art;

(d) the matter disclosed in the specification of the patent extends beyond that disclosed in the application for the patent, as filed, or, if the patent was granted on a new application filed under section 8(3), 12 or 37(4) above or as mentioned in **section 15(9)** [*section 15(4)*] above, in the earlier application, as filed;

(e) the protection conferred by the patent has been extended by an amendment which should not have been allowed.

(2) An application for the revocation of a patent on the ground mentioned in subsection (1)(b) above—

(a) may only be made by a person found by the court in an action for a declaration or declarator, or found by the court or the comptroller on a reference under section 37 above, to be entitled to be granted that patent or to be granted a patent for part of the matter comprised in the specification of the patent sought to be revoked; and

(b) may not be made if that action was commenced or that reference was made after the end of the period of two years beginning with the date of the grant of the patent sought to be revoked, unless it is shown that any person registered as a proprietor of the patent knew at the time of the grant or of the transfer of the patent to him that he was not entitled to the patent.

[(3) *Rules under section 14(4) and (8) above shall, with any necessary modifications, apply for the purposes of subsection (1)(c) above as they apply for the purposes of section 14(3) above.*]

(4) An order under this section may be an order for the unconditional revocation of the patent or, where the court or the comptroller determines that one of the grounds mentioned in subsection (1) above has been established, but only so as to invalidate the patent to a limited extent, an order that the patent should be revoked unless within a specified time the specification is amended to the satisfaction of the court or the comptroller, as the case may be.

(4A) **The reference in subsection (4) above to the specification being amended is to its being amended under section 75 below and also, in the case of a European patent (UK), to its being amended under any provision of the European Patent Convention under which the claims of the patent may be limited by amendment at the request of the proprietor.**

(5) A decision of the comptroller or on appeal from the comptroller shall not estop any party to civil proceedings in which infringement of a patent is in issue from alleging invalidity of the patent on any of the grounds referred to in subsection (1) above, whether or not any of the issues involved were decided in the said decision.

(6) Where the comptroller refuses to grant an application made to him by any person under this section, no application (otherwise than by way of appeal or by way of putting validity in issue in proceedings for infringement) may be made to the court by that person under this section in relation to the patent concerned, without the leave of the court.

(7) Where the comptroller has not disposed of an application made to him under this section, the applicant may not apply to the court under this section in respect of the patent concerned unless either—

    (a) the proprietor of the patent agrees that the applicant may so apply, or

    (b) the comptroller certifies in writing that it appears to him that the question whether the patent should be revoked is one which would more properly be determined by the court.

Notes

1. Subsection (1) amended by the Patents Act 2004 (c.16) s.16 and Sch.2 para.18, with effect from October 1, 2005 (SI 2005/2471).

2. Subsection (1)(b) was amended and subs.(3) repealed by CDPA 1988 (c.48) Sch.5 para.18 and Sch.8 to the CDPA 1988 respectively, each effective from January 7, 1991 (SI 1990/2168).

3. Subsection (1)(d) was amended by the Regulatory Reform (Patents) Order 2004 (SI 2004/2357) ("RRO") art.12, with effect from January 1, 2005, subject to transitional provisions contained in arts 20–23 of that Order.

4. Subsection (4) was amended and subs.(4A) inserted by the Patents Act 2004 (c.16) s.4 with effect from December 13, 2007 (SI 2007/3396).

Relevant Convention Provisions

Article 138—Revocation of European patents

72.02   **138.**—(1) Subject to Article 139, a European patent may be revoked with effect for a Contracting State only on the grounds that:

    (a) the subject-matter of the European patent is not patentable under Articles 52 to 57;

    (b) the European patent does not disclose the invention in a manner sufficiently clear and complete for it to be carried out by a person skilled in the art;

    (c) the subject-matter of the European patent extends beyond the content of the application as filed or, if the patent was granted on a divisional application or on a new application filed under Article 61, beyond the content of the earlier application as filed;

    (d) the protection conferred by the European patent has been extended; or

    (e) the proprietor of the European patent is not entitled under Article 60, paragraph 1.

(2) If the grounds for revocation affect the European patent only in part, the patent shall be limited by a corresponding amendment of the claims and revoked in part.

(3) In proceedings before the competent court or authority relating to the validity of the European patent, the proprietor of the patent shall have the right to limit the patent by amending the claims. The patent as thus limited shall form the basis for the proceedings.

Article 139—Prior rights and rights arising on the same date

72.03   **139.**—(1) In any designated Contracting State a European patent application and a European patent shall have with regard to a national patent application and a national patent the same prior right effect as a national patent application and a national patent.

(2) A national patent application and a national patent in a Contracting State shall have with regard to a European patent designating that Contracting State the same prior right effect as if the European patent were a national patent.

(3) Any Contracting State may prescribe whether and on what terms an invention disclosed in both a European patent application or patent and a national application or patent having the same date of filing or, where priority is claimed, the same date of priority, may be protected simultaneously by both applications or patents.

CORRESPONDING PROVISION OF TRIPS

Article 32

32. An opportunity for judicial review of any decision to revoke or forfeit a patent shall be available.　　　　**72.04**

RELEVANT CPR PRACTICE DIRECTIONS

Revocation proceedings in the High Court and the Patents County Court are governed　　**72.05**
by the CPR, and in particular by Pt 63—Patents and Other Intellectual Property Claims,
reproduced as relevant to patents in Appendix F, and by the accompanying Practice Direction of which paras 11.2 to 11.5 and 5.1 to 5.2, which deal specifically with revocation, are
also set out below (the order being selected in accordance with the normal sequence of
events). The full Practice Direction as relevant to patent proceedings is reprinted in Appendix F. The full Practice Direction is printed an Appendix F, §F63PD.01ff.

Claim for infringement and challenge to validity (CPR rule 63.6 and 63 PD.4)

63.6 A statement of case in a claim for infringement or a claim in which the　　**72.06**
validity of a patent or registered design is challenged must contain particulars as
set out in Practice Direction 63.

4.2 Where the validity of a patent or registered design is challenged—

(1) the statement of case must contain particulars of—

(a) the remedy sought; and

(b) the issues except those relating to validity of the patent or registered design;

(2) the statement of case must have a separate document attached to and forming part of it headed 'Grounds of Invalidity' which must—

(a) specify the grounds on which validity of the patent or registered design is challenged; and

(b) include particulars that will clearly define every issue (including any challenge to any claimed priority date) which it is intended to raise; and

(3) a copy of each document referred to in the Grounds of Invalidity, and where necessary a translation of the document, must be served with the Grounds of Invalidity.

4.3 Where in an application in which the validity of a patent or a registered design is challenged, the Grounds of Invalidity include an allegation—

(1) that the invention is not a patentable invention because it is not new or

does not include an inventive step, the particulars must specify details of the matter in the state of the art relied on, as set out in paragraph 4.4;

(2) that the specification of the patent does not disclose the invention clearly enough and completely enough for it to be performed by a person skilled in the art, the particulars must state, if appropriate, which examples of the invention cannot be made to work and in which respects they do not work or do not work as described in the specification; or

(3) that the registered design is not new or lacks individual character, the particulars must specify details of any prior design relied on, as set out in paragraph 4.4.

4.4 The details required under paragraphs 4.3(1) and 4.3(3) are—

(1) in the case of matter or a design made available to the public by written description, the date on which and the means by which it was so made available, unless this is clear from the fact of the matter; and

(2) in the case of matter or a design made available to the public by use—

    (a) the date or dates of such use;

    (b) the name of all persons making such use;

    (c) the place of such use;

    (d) any written material which identifies such use;

    (e) the existence and location of any apparatus employed in such use; and

    (f) all facts and matters relied on to establish that such matter was made available to the public.

4.5 In any proceedings in which the validity of a patent is challenged, where a party alleges that machinery or apparatus was used before the priority date of the claim the court may order inspection of that machinery or apparatus.

4.6 If the validity of a patent is challenged on the ground that the invention did not involve an inventive step, a party who wishes to rely on the commercial success of the patent must state in the statement of case the grounds on which that party so relies.

Disclosure and inspection (CPR rule 63.9 and 63 PD6.1)

72.07 63.9— Part 31 is modified to the extent set out in Practice Direction 63.

6.1 Standard disclosure does not require the disclosure of documents where the documents relate to—

(1) [relates to issues of infringement]

(2) any ground on which the validity of a patent is put in issue, except documents which came into existence within the period—

    (a) beginning two years before the earliest claimed priority date; and

    (b) ending two years after that date; and

(3) the issue of commercial success.

6.2 The particulars served under paragraph 6.1(1)(b) must be accompanied by a signed written statement which must state that the person making the statement—

(1) is personally acquainted with the facts to which the particulars relate;

(2) verifies that the particulars are a true and complete description of the product or process alleged to infringe; and

(3) understands that he or she may be required to attend court in order to be cross-examined on the contents of the particulars.

6.3 Where the issue of commercial success arises, the patentee must, within such time limit as the court may direct, serve a schedule containing—

(1) where the commercial success relates to an article or product—

(a) an identification of the article or product (for example by product code number) which the patentee asserts has been made in accordance with the claims of the patent;

(b) a summary by convenient periods of sales of any such article or product;

(c) a summary for the equivalent periods of sales, if any, of any equivalent prior article or product marketed before the article or product in sub-paragraph (a); and

(d) a summary by convenient periods of any expenditure on advertising and promotion which supported the marketing of the articles or products in sub-paragraphs (a) and (c); or

(2) where the commercial success relates to the use of a process—

(a) an identification of the process which the patentee asserts has been used in accordance with the claims of the patent;

(b) a summary by convenient periods of the revenue received from the use of such process;

(c) a summary for the equivalent periods of the revenues, if any, received from the use of any equivalent prior art process; and

(d) a summary by convenient periods of any expenditure which supported the use of the process in sub-paragraphs (a) and (c).

RELEVANT PATENTS RULES

Revocation proceedings before the UK-IPO are governed by Pt 7 of the Patents Rules 2007 (rr.73–88) which are reprinted at §§123.06–123.21.   **72.08**

COMMENTARY ON SECTION 72

Scope of the section

Power is given to a court or to the Comptroller by s.72 to revoke granted patents, includ-   **72.09**
ing European patents (UK), s.77(1).

Subsections (1) and (2) are referred to in s.130(7) as having been intended to have the same effect as the corresponding provisions of the EPC, PCT and CPC. Under s.130(6) references to the EPC apply to that convention as amended, i.e. to EPC 2000, the corresponding provisions of which are arts 138 and 139 which specify the only grounds upon which a European patent may be revoked under the law of an EPC Contracting State. These articles are set out above.

Section 72 appears to be in conformity with art.32 of the TRIPS Agreement which is also set out above. This is because, under s.97(1), there is a right of appeal to the Patents Court against any decision of the Comptroller to revoke a patent. Section 72 also appears to be in conformity with art.62(4) of the TRIPS Agreement (reprinted in §18.05).

Entitlement to make an application for revocation is governed by subs.(1) which provides that any person including the proprietor of the patent may apply for an order revoking the patent. There is no requirement of commercial interest and it is legitimate to obtain a ruling on validity to use in settlement negotiations in other EPO contracting states: *TNS Group Holdings Ltd v Nielsen Media Research Inc* [2009] EWHC 1160 (Pat); [2009] F.S.R. 23 at [23]–[26]. The application may be made to a court or to the Comptroller at any time after the patent has been granted.

The permissible grounds of revocation are those specified in (a)–(e) of subs.(1), and these are the only grounds on which a patent can be declared invalid (and therefore on which the patent can be revoked) either by the court or by the Comptroller, apart from the special provisions of s.73 and, perhaps, subject to rectification of the register under s.34, see §34.02. Section 74(2) precludes the institution of proceedings seeking only a declaration of the validity or invalidity of a patent, and s.74(3) says that the grounds under s.72(1) are the only grounds on which the validity of a patent may be put in issue in any proceedings. Section 72 is, therefore, a concise and comprehensive statement of the manner and nature of proceedings in which validity can be contested. The grounds for revocation set out in subs.(1) are discussed individually below.

Subsection (2) qualifies subs.(1)(b) as to who may make an application under that provision and when.

The effect of subs.(1)(c) is now extended, in the case of inventions relating to biological material, by s.125A(4) which has replaced repealed subs.(3).

Subsection (4) provides for unconditional revocation unless the specification can be validated by amendment under s.75. Subsection (5) provides that proceedings before the Comptroller result in no estoppel in subsequent infringement proceedings in which validity of the patent may be put in issue, but an unsuccessful applicant for revocation may thereafter bring revocation proceedings before the court on that patent only with the leave of the court (subs.(6)). Subsection (7) restricts application to the court by an applicant who is already proceeding before the Comptroller, unless the proprietor so agrees, or the Comptroller certifies that the question of revocation before him is one that ought more properly to be determined by the court.

An application for revocation made to the Patents Court or Patents County Court (other than as a counterclaim in other proceedings) is made by a claim under CPR r.7.2. The procedure is essentially the same as for infringement proceedings before that court and this is therefore discussed in relation to practice under s.61, for which see §§61.40–61.80. An application to the UK-IPO is made on PF 2 and must be accompanied by a statement of grounds in duplicate. Revocation procedure is then governed by Pt 7 of the Patents Rules 2007, for which see §§123.06–123.21.

An applicant for revocation bears the onus of proof. The application for revocation will therefore be dismissed if the applicant fails, on the balance of probabilities, to discharge that onus, see *Haynes International's Patent* BL O/27/90, noted I.P.D. 13145. If the applicant for revocation withdraws his application, the Comptroller will continue nonetheless to deal with it in the public interest, see *Abbott Laboratories' (Chu's) Patent* [1992] R.P.C. 487 and *Emergi-Lite Safety Systems' Patent* BL O/178/00 where a revocation application was withdrawn following a settlement between the parties but where the patent was then revoked for perceived lack of novelty which the patentee failed to contest. Parties considering adducing or challenging expert evidence should consider Arnold J.'s remarks in *Medimmune Limited v Novartis Pharmaceuticals UK Limited, Medical Research Council* [2011] EWHC 1669 (Pat) at [98]–[114] on the balance between the need for careful instruction of the experts and the maintenance of objectivity.

Section 72 gives to the Comptroller the same powers of the court with regard to revocation, save for the absence of estoppel when an application for revocation fails before him. This is quite different from the position before June 1, 1978 when the powers of the Comptroller as regards revocation were much more limited. As with the position under former patent statutes, it is not necessary for a defendant to infringement proceedings to counterclaim for revocation of the patent: he can merely plead invalidity as a sufficient defence, see s.74(1)(a).

Where a patentee company has entered into administration of its affairs, a claim for revocation cannot be made or proceed without the leave of the court, see *Axis Genetics' Patent* [2000] F.S.R. 448 where the Insolvency Act 1985 (c.45) s.11(3) was held applicable and leave was refused. The Enterprise Act 2002 replaced s.11 and inserted Sch.B1 into the Insolvency Act 1986; the equivalent provision to s.11(3)(d) is now in para.43(6) of this Schedule.

Forum for revocation

By virtue of s.72(1) and the definition of "court" in s.130(1) applications for revocation **72.10**
of a patent may be made to any of the following:

- Patents Court

- Patents County Court

- Court of Session in Scotland (see §98.06)

- High Court in Northern Ireland (see §131.03)

- High Court of Justice in the Isle of Man

- Comptroller, UK-IPO

The wording of the Civil Jurisdiction and Judgments Act 1982 (c.27) (the "CJJA"), as discussed on this point in §96.10, is consistent with the wording of the 1977 Act in giving no single court in the United Kingdom exclusive jurisdiction in the matter of revocation, though this has the apparent effect that each court permitted to revoke a patent may do so for the whole of the United Kingdom (including the Isle of Man).

The choice of forum for revocation proceedings depends on many factors. For instance, proceedings before the Comptroller, in contrast to proceedings before the Patents Court, involve an essentially written procedure, usually without disclosure of documents or cross-examination of witnesses, although such are possible under the general provision of rr.80 to 82 (see §§123.13–123.15); and such proceedings can be conducted entirely by a patent attorney (see the commentary on s.102). Consequently, proceedings before the Comptroller are likely to be less expensive than proceedings before the Patents Court, but are likely to involve a less vigorous approach to invalidity than can be expected from the experienced judges of the Patents Court. However, in *Birtcher Medical Systems' Patent* BL O/70/96, where the patent had 120 pages of text, 23 sheets of drawings and 56 claims, several of which were independent, and after the hearing had extended over eight days, the hearing officer commented that bringing proceedings of this complexity in the Comptroller's court is "undesirable if the purpose of the Comptroller's jurisdiction is primarily to provide a relatively quick and inexpensive means of justice". Where the attack on validity has no prospect of success, the Office may short-circuit procedures and enter summary judgment in favour of the patentee: *N Nazareth and Secretary of State for Defence* O/282/10.

An intermediate possibility in England and Wales is the Patents County Court, whose new procedural rules were adopted in October 2010 and are included in CPR Part 63, section V (reprinted in Appendix F). The new rules and procedures are designed to limit costs and the length of proceedings whilst providing specialist judicial expertise and are explained in the 2011 Patents County Court Guide which may be accessed on the website *http://www.justice.gov.uk* (and see Appendix G).

While, under the CJJA, the courts of the United Kingdom had power to consider questions of infringement of patents of other contracting states to the Brussels Convention on Jurisdiction and the Enforcement of Judgments, that Convention (by Article VD of the Protocol annexed thereto and incorporated into the CJJA by Sch.1, art.16(4)) provided that the courts of each of the contracting states who are members of the EPC are to have exclusive jurisdiction, regardless of domicile, in proceedings concerned with the registration and validity of any European patent granted for that State, as well as the registration and validity of national patents in the state in question. The Brussels Convention was superseded by the 'Brussels Regulation' as of March 1, 2002 for EC Member states other than Denmark and July 1, 2007 for Denmark. Article 22(4) of the Brussels Regulation contains equivalent provisions on exclusive jurisdiction over challenges to validity. The Supreme Court summarises the effect of art.22(4) in *Lucasfilm Ltd v Ainsworth* [2011] UKSC 39; [2011] 3 W.L.R. 487 at [87]–[90] by saying that it applies only to intellectual property rights which are required to be deposited or registered, and does not apply to infringement actions in which there is no issue as to validity. A similar provision also applies to the Member States of the Lugano Convention, for which see §96.09. Considerable divergence in the approach to art.16(4)/art.22(4) between the courts of EU Member States has been reduced by decisions of the European Court of Justice in *Gesellschaft für Antriebstechnik mbH & Co. KG (GAT) v Lamellen und Kupplungsbau KG (LuK)* (C–4/03) [2006] E.C.R. I–6509; [2006] F.S.R. 45, holding that jurisdiction was exclusively reserved to the member state of registration even where validity issues arose incidentally, and *Roche Nederland BV v Primus* (C-539/03) [2006] E.C.R. I–6535; [2007] F.S.R. 5, where it was held that joinder rules were not effective to defeat art.16(4). As discussed by the Court of Appeal in *Research in Motion UK Ltd v Visto Corporation* [2008] EWCA Civ 153; [2008] F.S.R. 20, these decisions have not fully resolved all the difficulties.

Proceedings before the Comptroller take the form of the usual judicial process. Therefore, the provisions of the Arbitration Act 1996 (c.23) are made inapplicable, see §130.12.

In revocation proceedings before the Comptroller, it is possible to hold a hearing in Scotland (r.88, reprinted at §98.05 and discussed in §98.23). There is no corresponding provision for Northern Ireland, see §131.04.

Any court dealing with an application for revocation of a European patent is entitled to seek a technical opinion from the EPO under EPC art.25, the procedure for which is governed by EPO Guideline E–XII, see §99A.05. Also, in any proceeding under the Act, the UK-IPO may in principle be asked to inquire into, and report on, any question of fact or opinion. This may be done by the Patents Court (under s.99A, discussed in §§99A.02–99A.04), or in Scotland by the Court of Session (under s.99B, discussed in §99B.02), or by a patents county court (under CDPA 1988 s.291, reprinted in §291.01) It is not known whether similar powers exist for the relevant courts of Northern Ireland and the Isle of Man. The CPR and its Practice Directions contain no specific provision for exercise of these powers by the Patents Court, and there does not appear to have been, as yet, any attempt by any of these courts to use these powers.

When proceedings are brought in the Patents Court or the Patents County Court, CPR 63.14 requires that claims, statements of case and any accompanying documents (which in the Patents Court include a copy of the separate "Grounds of Invalidity" document, and any amendment must be served on the Comptroller).

The fact that opposition proceedings against a European patent (UK) are still possible, or are in being, is no bar to a concurrent application for revocation brought before the Comptroller (*Coflexip Stena's European Patent* BL O/45/96), or before a permissible court of the United Kingdom, see also §72.19.

Who may apply to revoke, and when

72.11   It is not necessary for the applicant for revocation to show a locus standi; any person including the proprietor of the patent can now apply for revocation, except on the ground of non-entitlement (s.72(1)(b)). However, in the case of co-owners, s.36(3) (for which see §36.05, above) makes clear that one co-owner may not seek revocation against the wishes of the others.

In *Cairnstores v AB Hässle* [2002] F.S.R. 35 the defendant tried to have the action struck out as an abuse of process because the defendant company had only recently been incorporated and appeared to lack assets or trading activities. However, the action was allowed to proceed subject to security for costs being given. The court held that the words "any person" in s.72 of the Act did not require a person applying to revoke a patent to have any interest, commercial or otherwise, in the outcome of the proceedings. There were circumstances in which it could be envisaged that the commencement of revocation proceedings might amount to an abuse of process, which the court defined as the use of the court's procedure for an improper or collateral purpose, but there was no suggestion of that in the case in hand. In *Oystertec's Patent* [2003] R.P.C. 29 at 559 a revocation action was allowed to proceed in the name of a firm of patent attorneys, the decision in *Cairnstores* (above) being seen as a precedent binding on the UK-IPO, despite a further argument that to permit an application for revocation in the name of a "man of straw" was contrary to the Human Rights Act 1998. Potential difficulties as to disclosure, cross-examination and estoppel were not seen as sufficient to change that view although they might have had to be considered at a later stage in the proceedings. However, in *British Numberplate Manufacturers Association v Hills Numberplates Ltd* BL/066/05 the hearing officer held that an unincorporated body could not launch proceedings in its own name.

The situation under s.72 may be compared with that under the EPC where art.99(1) of the EPC makes no reference to the patentee and the EPO Enlarged Board has held that "any person" must on a purposive construction mean "any other person" so that self-opposition should not be permitted (G 9/93 *PEUGEOT and RENAULT/Opposition by patent proprietor* OJ EPO 1994, 891; [1995] E.P.O.R. 260). In G 3/97 *INDUPACK/ Opposition on behalf of a third party* OJ EPO 1999, 245; [2000] E.P.O.R. 81, the EPO Enlarged Board of Appeals ruled that nominee oppositions in the name of a third party are not per se objectionable provided that these do not circumvent the law by abuse of process: for example, because the third party is acting as an agent of the proprietor (so that the opposition is a disguised "self-opposition", not permitted as stated above), or because the opponent is acting in the context as a professional representative while not possessing the required qualification of being a qualified "European patent attorney", but there is no objection to a European patent attorney acting in his own name on behalf of a client. Moreover, the onus of establishing such an abuse of process requires clear and convincing evidence by whoever chooses to challenge the bona fides of an opponent. Previously, the EPO had permitted opposition to be lodged by a professional representative acting on his own behalf, but for the purpose of supplementing his professional training (T 798/93 *ROAD TRAIN/Identification of real opponent* OJ EPO 1997, 363; [1998] E.P.O.R. 1).

Since for revocation under s.72, locus standi is not required, the Comptroller has allowed substitution of a new applicant for revocation in place of an existing one, this being less wasteful of time when the new applicant was prepared to adopt the evidence already submitted by the former applicant (*Moore's Patent* BL O/25/92, noted I.P.D. 16007).

An application under s.72 can be made at any time after notice of grant has been published in the *Patents Journal* under s.25(1), even after the patent has lapsed or expired and, if a European patent (UK), even after it has already been opposed in the EPO. Neither the lapsing nor surrender of a patent is sufficient to terminate revocation proceedings, and these continue (normally undefended) in such circumstances, *Ritzerfeld's Patent* BL O/102/81, and see §29.06. Also, failure to pay a renewal fee does not terminate revocation proceedings, see *Fenwick-Wilson's Patent* BL O/5/94, noted I.P.D. 17121.

Grounds of revocation

—Invention is not a patentable invention (subs.(1)(a))

Ground (a) of subs.(1) is that the invention is "not a patentable invention" and covers **72.12** lack of novelty, lack of inventive step, lack of industrial applicability, and exclusion under s.1(2), (3) or s.4A(1). The effect and extent of this ground of revocation is discussed in the commentaries on ss.1–4 and 4A. Selection patents should be considered on general principles and not as a special category of patent, or requiring a special approach to validity: see *Dr. Reddy's Laboratories (UK) Ltd v Eli Lilly and Co Ltd* [2010] R.P.C. 9 at [104].

—Patent granted to person not entitled (subss.(1)(b) and (2))

Ground (b) of subs.(1) is that the patent was granted to some person who was not **72.13** entitled to it. Subsection (2) places two limitations on revocation under subs.(1)(b), viz. (a) that the application for revocation may only be brought by a person "found" to be entitled to be granted the patent; and (b) that the application for revocation is "made" within a restricted period calculated from the date of grant of the patent. The provisions of subs.(1)(b) and (2) need to be construed in conformity with the EPC (by virtue of s.130(7)), both in the previous form of subs.(1)(b) and its current form, and subs.(1)(b) corresponds to art.138(1)(e) of the EPC (see §72.02 above).

As originally worded, subs.(1)(b) was limited in its application to a person who was not entitled to the patent "under section 7(2)", for which see §7.06. However, this original wording was defective as not dealing adequately with issues involving co-inventors and/or co-proprietors. This deficiency was intended to be corrected by amendment of subs.(1)(b) by the CDPA 1988 (Sch.5 para.18, as noted in §72.01), with s.37(1) being amended at the same time, but not the corresponding ss.8(1) and 12(1). It seems doubtful whether or not the amendment actually achieved this objective because, although the section is to be construed in conformity with the EPC, the relevant provision (EPC art.60(1)) does not consider the position of co-owners, see §36.02.

In *Henry Bros v Ministry of Defence* [1997] R.P.C. 693; and [1999] R.P.C. 442 CA, it was held at first instance that the purpose of s.72(2) is to prevent anyone (other than a person truly entitled to apply) from seeking revocation under these provisions, and that a patent is granted to "a person not entitled to apply" if it is not granted to all those entitled to apply. However, the Court of Appeal (likewise in an obiter statement) did not agree with this latter view but considered that, where the patent had been granted to A, and B had joint entitlement, the rights of B would be sufficiently satisfied if B were joined as a joint proprietor with A under s.37(2)(a), as the MOPP suggests. This leaves open the position where (as in the *Henry* case) B does not wish any patent rights to exist. Perhaps B could himself seek revocation because an application for revocation can be made by "any person", see §72.11. However, s.36(3)(a), as amended from January 1, 2005 by the 2004 Act, now prevents B (as co-owner) from applying to revoke the patent without the consent of A (or other co-owner(s)). B could consider applying under s.37(2)(c) for the ability to grant licences which, in effect, deprive A of the benefit of the patent. See also the comments on *Hughes v Paxman* [2007] R.P.C. 2; [2006] EWCA Civ 818 at §37.10.

By subs.(2), revocation under subs.(1)(b) for non-entitlement is only available to an applicant who has already been found by the court or the Comptroller (in the case of the Comptroller as the result of a reference under s.37, which by virtue of s.9 will include proceedings commenced before grant under s.8) to be entitled to the patent or part of the matter comprised in it. In *Henry Bros v Ministry of Defence* (above), it was also held at first instance (contrary to the holding in *Dolphin Showers v Farmiloe* [1989] 1 F.S.R. 1) that the court has jurisdiction under s.72(1)(b) to consider a case without any prior declaration or finding under s.37, but it must first find and declare that the applicant for revocation was the person entitled to apply for the patent. The finding in *Rigcool Ltd v Optima Solutions UK Ltd* O/149/11 in relation to s.37, that the relevant period expires the day before the second anniversary of grant was said also to apply to s.72(1)(b), however, the period could be extended in exercise of discretion: O/182/11 (period now extended by the Patents (Amendment) Rules 2011 (SI 2011/2052)). In other words, the word "made" in subs.(2) does not mean "started", as had been held in the *Dolphin Showers* decision, see further §74.05. Following the *Henry Bros* case, concurrent proceedings under ss.37 and 72(1)(b) took place in *AC Egerton's Patent* BL O/170/00, noted I.P.D. 23075, but were unsuccessful, see §37.06.

Also, the ground of revocation under subs.(1)(b) is, by subs.(2), not available if the action before the court or Comptroller was commenced more than two years after the patent was granted unless the proprietor "knew" at the time of grant (or on transfer of the patent to him) that he was not entitled to it. For a discussion of what is meant by "knew", see further §37.11. These restrictions reflect those of arts 23(3) and 55(1) of the CPC, and they are reiterated in s.74(4), though with a provision (in s.74(5)) that validity can be put in issue even if entitlement proceedings have not yet been commenced. These points are discussed in §74.05, particularly with reference to the *Dolphin Showers* case (above). In that case, it was suggested that, even if revocation could not be sought because of the limitations imposed by s.72(2), an action for infringement could still be defended on the basis of invalidity of the patent. However, as explained in §74.05, the *Henry Bros* case subsequently decided that, if there is any conflict between ss.72(2) and 74(4), the former should prevail.

The question of entitlement is to be determined as at the date of grant. Thus, a post-grant assignment does not alter the position as regards the original grantee (*Dolphin Show-*

ers v Farmiloe, above). Entitlement is more fully dealt with under s.7. Challenge to entitlement is considered mainly in the commentary on s.37, but see also the commentaries on ss.8, 12 and 82 for entitlement questions arising under those sections.

—Insufficient description (subs.(1)(c))

Ground (c) of subs.(1) is that the specification: **72.14**

"does not disclose the invention clearly enough and completely enough for it to be performed by a person skilled in the art".

It corresponds to art.138(1)(b) of the EPC (reprinted above) and adopts the wording of s.14(3) (reprinted in §14.01), and of art.83 of the EPC (reprinted in §14.09), and also art.5 of the PCT and the Strasbourg Convention 1963 art.8(2).

Section 125A provides for special rules in relation to the sufficient description of inventions relating to the use of biological material. Schedule 1 to the Rules (made under r.13, and reprinted at §§125A.03–125A.10) sets out those rules. By s.125A(4), non-compliance with the requirements of these rules also provides a ground of revocation under subs.(1)(c). However, for patent applications filed before July 27, 2000, see paras 7 and 8 of Sch.5 to the Patents Rules 2007 for details of the provisions which apply. These requirements are dealt with in the commentary on s.125A.

Thus, the special sufficiency requirements for inventions involving biological material have been transferred (by r.13) from subs.(3) (now repealed) to Sch.1 to the Rules.

Because a specification cannot be validly amended after its filing date in a manner which would result in it disclosing additional matter, a specification must be "sufficient", in regard to the subject-matter covered by the scope of its claims as of its filing date, or as of its priority date if priority is to be accorded to the invention in issue, see *Biogen v Medeva* [1997] R.P.C. 1 HL.

The wording of ground (c) clearly covers cases (classical insufficiency) where the claimed subject-matter cannot be carried into effect at all see, e.g. the pleaded objections in *Halliburton Energy Services v Smith International* [2006] R.P.C. 2 at 25, or when carried into effect does not achieve a result which is the whole essence of the invention as in *Pharmacia v Merck* [2002] R.P.C. 41. It also covers cases where some embodiments falling within the claim in issue can be made to work whereas others cannot. It has to disclose the subject-matter which, if performed, would necessarily result in an infringement of the patent, *Synthon BV v SmithKline Beecham Plc (No.2)* [2005] UKHL 59, [2006] 1 All E.R. 685 followed in *H Lundbeck A/S v Norpharma SpA* [2011] EWHC 907 (Pat) (Ch D (Patents Ct)). It also apparently covers a parameter in a claim which is inadequately defined so that a skilled reader cannot determine whether or not there is infringement, see *Kirin-Amgen v Hoechst Marion Roussel* [2005] R.P.C. 9 at 169, for example a functional parameter "effective stabilizing amount" for which it must be possible to design a test otherwise the disclosure is insufficient, see *Mayne Pharma v Debiopharm* [2006] F.S.R. 37. CPR 63 PD 4.3(2) (reprinted above) requires that the "Grounds of Invalidity" document must state:

"which examples of the invention cannot be made to work and in which respects they do not work or do not work as described in the specification".

In *Corevalve Inc v Edwards Lifesciences AG* [2009] EWHC 6 (Pat) [2009] F.S.R. 8 at [89]–[93] where the patent claimed "A valve prosthesis. . . for implantation in the body. . .", it was not fatal to validity that the patent did not teach how to implant the prosthesis clinically; the relevant enquiry was whether a skilled manufacturer could make it. The skilled addressee for sufficiency may be a team with a narrower skill set than that for obviousness: *Schlumberger Holdings Ltd v Electromagnetic Geoservices AS* [2010] EWCA Civ 819; [2010] R.P.C. 33 at [35]–[39] (although this latter point is the subject of an appeal to the Supreme Court).

So-called *"Biogen* insufficiency" accepts that the teaching of the patent is adequate to bring the skilled reader within the claims, but asserts that the claims encompass products or processes which owe nothing to the teaching of the patent and which are not enabled. The *Biogen* decision was clarified in *Generics v Lundbeck* [2008] R.P.C. 19; [2008] EWCA Civ 311 CA, confirmed [2009] UKHL 12; [2009] R.P.C. 13, where it was explained that in *Biogen* the claim covered a molecule made by recombinant technology which was a generic expression covering a wide variety of processes by which that molecule might be made, whereas the specification in suit had enabled only a single such process: this was no different from the conventional requirement that where there is a claim to a class the skilled person must be able to work the invention in respect of all members of the class; see also *Zipher Ltd v Markem Systems Ltd* [2008] EWHC 1379; [2009] F.S.R. 1 at 1 Pat Ct. Nonetheless *Biogen* continues to be applied where the specification does not enable performance of the invention across the entire scope of the claim, e.g. *Nokia GmbH v IPCom GmbH & Co KG* [2009] EWHC 3482 (Pat).

Mere ambiguity or lack of clarity is an objection that cannot be raised post-grant, but may result in a patentee being unable to establish infringement since if the invention claimed cannot be defined, then it cannot be concluded that it is being used, see *Scanvaegt v Pelcombe* [1998] F.S.R. 786 CA; BL C/5/97; and *Kirin-Amgen v Roche Diagnostics* [2002] R.P.C. 1. It should be appreciated that the court will use its best endeavours to ascribe a meaning to the words in question, and that it is only in rare cases that ambiguity or lack of clarity will be established.

—Impermissible amendments (subs.(1)(d) and (e))

72.15   Grounds (d) and (e) of subs.(1) represent grounds of invalidity which were new in the 1977 Act. They correspond respectively to art.138(1)(c) and (d) of the EPC (reprinted above) and arise from the prohibitions against amendments which introduce new subject-matter into the content of the application as originally filed as set out in art.123(2) of the EPC and s.76(3)(a) or amendments which extend the protection conferred by the patent at the time of grant as set out in art.123(3) of the EPC and s.76(3)(b). Divisional applications are now made under new s.15(9), rather than under the former s.15(4). Subsection (1)(d) has been amended accordingly.

Grounds of invalidity should identify each and every amendment the subject of objection, and a reply or counter-statement should indicate how each and every amendment is expressly or implicitly supported in the application as filed.

In *Texas Iron Works' Patent* [2000] R.P.C. 207 CA, it was argued that, where a patent is held invalid for added subject-matter contrary to s.72(1)(d), no finding of "partial validity" is possible under s.63, for which see §63.02, but the point was not decided as the decision below of invalidity for added subject-matter was reversed in appeal.

In *Mölnlycke Health Care AB v Wake Forest University* [2009] EWHC 2204 (Pat) an alteration made in opposition proceedings as a mere correction of a mistake, nonetheless widened the protection conferred by the patent and led to revocation.

Partial revocation (subss.(4) and (4A))

72.16   Subsection (4) provides for an order by the court or the Comptroller for unconditional revocation of the patent. However, if the patent is invalid to a limited extent there may instead be an order for revocation unless the specification is satisfactorily amended under s.75 within the time specified. There is a similar provision in s.63(3) where, in the course of infringement proceedings, the patent is found only partially valid, as discussed in §63.02. By ss.27(6) and 75(5) practice in the UK has been aligned with that of the EPO which does not take the proprietor's behaviour into account when exercising discretion to permit or refuse amendment.

An order of revocation, or partial revocation, of a European patent (UK) made by the EPO as the result of opposition proceedings brought under EPC art.99 is to have automatic effect in the United Kingdom under s.77(4) or (4A), see §77.06.

In the case of a European patent (UK) which the court finds to be partially invalid, it may (under new subs.(4A)), instead of ordering this patent to be validated by amendment under s.75, allow the claims of the European patent as a whole to be limited by proceedings in the EPO under EPC art.105A.

Estoppel (subss.(5) and (6))

The principle of res judicata prevents a litigant from re-litigating a matter already **72.17** decided against him (or his privy) in the same proceedings. Thus, in *Chiron v Organon Teknika (No.6)* [1994] F.S.R. 448, the defendants were not allowed to challenge the validity of the patent-in-suit when this had been the subject of previous proceedings between the same parties in which a particular ground of alleged invalidity had been pleaded and abandoned during the first trial only when some experiments required repetition. It was indicated that a postponement of the trial should then have been requested, but as this had not been done, the issue of invalidity had become res judicata as regards those defendants, see also *Parmenter v Malt House Joinery* [1993] F.S.R. 680 CA.

The principle of res judicata has a related principle in the doctrine of "issue estoppel". Under this, any finding of fact which has been, finally, judicially determined between the same parties (or their privies), creates an estoppel preventing that issue being re-litigated between the parties. This principle even applies to matters which could have been litigated in the previous proceedings, but which for some reason were not then litigated, see *Yat Tung v Dao Heng Bank* [1975] A.C. 581 HL. The doctrine also applies to foreign decisions, though with these it is to be applied sparingly and with caution, see *Carl-Zeiss-Stiftung v Rayner and Keeler* [1967] R.P.C. 497 HL where an estoppel was created (though on a narrow point only) as the result of previous findings in trade mark opposition proceedings in India and Pakistan. It has even been suggested that an estoppel will arise from a collateral point, that is where a party has succeeded on one ground (not applicable in some other litigation) but is then not permitted to re-litigate a collateral point on which he either lost or had no need to contest because of his success on the other point, see *Bristol-Myers v Beecham* [Israel] [1978] F.S.R. 553.

In *Kirin-Amgen v Boehringer Mannheim* [1997] F.S.R. 289 CA, an unsuccessful attempt was made to plead "issue estoppel" arising from litigation in the United States. None of the three requirements: identity of subject-matter; identity of parties; and finality of proceedings, was held to be present; and it was stated that:

"the patents are different to those litigated in the USA: the law is different and the facts needed to reach a decision may well be different".

Nevertheless, the court indicated that an issue estoppel could arise in patent actions in appropriate cases, for example whether a particular scientific effect occurs when the invention or a manufacturing process is carried out or how an infringing product is made or as regards the properties of a product or its composition.

By subs.(5) a party is not estopped from raising in infringement proceedings issues of validity covered by a decision of the Comptroller under this section, but by subs.(6) after refusal by the Comptroller of an application for revocation leave of the court is required to make an application to the court under the section (other than in an appeal or a defence in proceedings for infringement).

Section 74 specifies the types of proceedings in which validity can be challenged, so that the proceedings in which subs.(5) can be invoked are those under ss.58, 61, 69, 70, 71 or 72. A successful defence against a threat of revocation under s.73 would also not create an estoppel as only the proprietor and the Comptroller would have been involved.

Although subs.(5) refers only to decisions of the Comptroller, it was held in *Buehler v Chronos Richardson* [1998] R.P.C. 609 that no "cause of action estoppel" arises from a decision in the EPO because this is only a decision to maintain the patent and, as such, is not a decision on the question of invalidity of the patent in revocation proceedings. It was noted that the German Supreme Court had reached a similar conclusion (see *"Regenbecken" (Rain water reservoir)* OJ EPO 1999, 322; [2000] E.P.O.R. 339); and that also no "issue estoppel" arises because the EPO decision is not to be regarded as a "final judgment". Furthermore, although the UK courts should apply the same principles as the EPO (as confirmed in *Generics (UK) Ltd v H Lundbeck A/S* [2009] UKHL 12; [2009] R.P.C. 13, there may be significant differences in the evidence available to the Court and the EPO: *Eli Lilly & Co v Human Genome Sciences Inc* [2010] EWCA Civ 33; [2010] R.P.C. 14.

As a result of subs.(5), a proprietor may be called upon to defend revocation proceedings under s.72, which may prove to be lengthy and expensive; and, if successful in defending validity, he may still find that, if he subsequently institutes infringement proceedings, he may yet again be called upon to defend an attack on validity on the same grounds as before. As subs.(5) refers to "any person", such proceedings could be possibly against the same person. If the proprietor succeeds in obtaining a certificate of contested validity under s.65 (for which see §65.04), the matter of his costs will then to some extent be alleviated. On the other hand, if the proprietor is unsuccessful in proceedings under s.72, the patent is wholly or partly revoked.

Where an applicant for revocation before the Comptroller sought to withdraw some of his grounds of attack, he was required to elect to continue or withdraw unconditionally and subject to an order that he not be permitted to raise the withdrawn grounds in future proceedings before the Comptroller and not before the court except with the leave thereof *Flude's Patent* [1993] R.P.C. 197.

In *Coflexip v Stolt Comex* [2004] F.S.R. 7 at 118; [2004] F.S.R. 34 at 708 the claimants sought a stay of proceedings in the damages enquiry on the basis that the patent-in-suit had been found invalid in subsequent proceedings (*Rockwater v Coflexip* [2004] R.P.C. 46; [2004] EWCA Civ 381, noted I.P.D. 26039). However, the patentee relied on the decision in *Poulton v Adjustable Cover* (1908) 25 R.P.C. 529, 661, where it was held that the decision of patent validity and liability for damages created a cause of action estoppel preventing the defendant from relying on the decision in later proceedings. On that basis the inquiry into damages was ordered to continue. In appeal proceedings *Technip's Patent* [2004] R.P.C. 46 at 919 the decision in the *Rockwater* case was then overturned and the patent again found to be valid. These cases are further mentioned in §§125.10 and 125.16.

For further discussion of estoppel against challenges to patent validity, see §74.04.

Referral to the court (subs.(7))

72.18　Subsection (7) also precludes an applicant for revocation before the Comptroller from applying for revocation to the court under the same patent while his revocation application remains pending, unless the proprietor of the patent agrees (subs.(7)(a)). Under subs.(7)(b), the Comptroller may at any time during s.72 proceedings before him certify in writing that the question whether the patent should be revoked is one which would, in his opinion, be more properly determined by the court. The proceedings before the Comptroller then effectively terminate and the applicant for revocation, if he wishes to proceed, is required to commence proceedings before the court within 14 days, see CPR 63.11(2).The position is not clear where the applicant refrains from commencing court proceedings as ordered. Presumably, the proceedings before the Comptroller would be terminated, but without creating an estoppel against future proceedings before the court, though only after obtaining (under subs.(6)) the leave of the court for such new proceedings as required.

At least where the parties are in agreement, the Comptroller has traditionally declined jurisdiction under subs.(7) (and likewise under other similar provisions such as ss.8(7), 12(2), 37(8), 40(5) and 61(5)). However, the Comptroller's practice in exercising his discretion to decline jurisdiction in favour of the court has changed following the decision by Warren J. in *Luxim v Ceravision* [2007] R.P.C. 33; [2007] EWHC 1624, for which see the commentary at §37.08. Originally, the reason for declining jurisdiction where there was agreement was because "The Comptroller is always mindful that it would be undesirable and wasteful for the same issue to be litigated both before himself and before the court", see *Synthite's European Application* BL O/26/97 which involved entitlement proceedings under s.12. Also, in *Downhole Products' Patent* BL O/7/97, it was stated that "it would be foolish for the Comptroller to attempt to maintain his jurisdiction against the wishes of both sides". Here the issue of a certificate under s.72(7)(b) was seen as a convenient way of terminating the revocation proceedings before the Comptroller to allow the applicant for revocation to put the validity of the patent in issue in infringement proceedings which had since been commenced against it before the Court of Session in Scotland. Similar remarks were also made in *Advance Safe Sustainable Energy's Application* BL O/48/97.

Concurrent proceedings

Without the leave of the court, revocation proceedings before the Comptroller under **72.19** s.72 cannot be instituted if any proceedings involving the patent are already before the court, see s.74(7). In a case where proceedings under s.72 (as well as for a declaration of non-infringement under s.71) had already been commenced before the Comptroller and the proprietor subsequently started infringement proceedings before the court against the applicant for revocation, the court stayed the court proceedings on a plea by the applicant for revocation that he could not afford to defend the court action and was prepared to abide by the Comptroller's decision *Hawker Siddeley v Real Time* [1983] R.P.C. 395. However, this decision was distinguished in *Gen Set v Mosarc* [1985] F.S.R. 302 because: the court proceedings had been commenced first; both parties could afford High Court costs, which were unlikely greatly to exceed those in the Office; and the court felt that a determination of the dispute by the court was likely to be reached more quickly than by an application for revocation brought before the Comptroller. While, prima facie, a claimant has a right to litigate in the forum of his choice, in *Ferro v Escol* [1990] R.P.C. 651, the court felt that the *Hawker Siddeley* case was a special one. In *Ferro*, the parties could afford court proceedings, would anyway be using solicitors and counsel, and would be likely to appeal the Comptroller's decision to the Patents Court. Therefore, the court did not feel that finality would be reached significantly more quickly and cheaply if a stay were ordered. Also, it should be noted that in *Hawker-Siddeley* it was important that there was also an application to the Comptroller for a declaration of non-infringement.

A concurrent application for revocation before the Comptroller of a European patent (UK) and an opposition thereto in the EPO is possible, as in *Coflexip Stena's European Patent* BL O/45/96. Here, an applicant for revocation sought a stay of the United Kingdom proceedings pending determination of the EPO opposition. As the applicant was Norwegian and the patentee French, either forum was convenient and it was thought that proceedings before the Comptroller could be concluded more speedily. No stay of the proceedings before the Comptroller was ordered.

The Patents Court has also firmly taken the view that, despite the existence of a pending opposition in the EPO to a European patent (UK), its validity is a matter for the national court so that proceedings should not be stayed pending determination of the opposition. See *Amersham International v Corning Ltd* [1987] R.P.C. 53; OJ EPO 1987, 558; see also *Pall Corp v Commercial Hydraulics* [1988] F.S.R. 274; [1989] R.P.C. 703 CA. Nor should the existence of the opposition prevent the imposition of an interim injunction, see *Improver v Innovations* BL C/16/88, noted I.P.D. 11002. Stay of proceedings is further discussed in §61.63.

When two proceedings become co-pending before the Comptroller (for example an application for amendment under s.27 and one for revocation under s.72), it was formerly the case that the Comptroller had power to decide which of the proceedings should be heard first, see *Gibbons' Patent* [1957] R.P.C. 158. In *Luk Lamellan's Patent* BL O/379/02 it was pointed out that *Gibbons' Patent* was in fact a case under the 1949 Act and is no longer applicable in view of the express terms of s.27(2) which provide that the amendment cannot be allowed where there are concurrent proceedings as to validity.

Where infringement proceedings are commenced against a defendant who is already seeking revocation before the Comptroller, a stay will be granted if the parties jointly request. However, where these court proceedings had not reached finality after ten years, and in the absence of representations to the contrary, the Comptroller decided that the proceedings before him should be treated as withdrawn *Regal International's Patent* BL O/93/93.

—Appeals

72.20   Applications made to any of the tribunals entitled to hear applications for revocation are subject to appeal. Any decision of revocation made by the Comptroller is appealable as of right to the Patents Court. However, since January 1, 1999, an appeal may only be brought from a decision of the Patents Court or a patents county court by leave of that court or upon leave granted by the Court of Appeal. Further appeal is possible to the Supreme Court (previously House of Lords) but only with leave of the Court of Appeal or of the Supreme Court. There is the possibility of a leapfrog appeal directly from the Patents Court to the Supreme Court under the Administration of Justice Act 1969 (c.58) ss.12, 13. For this, and for appeals from decisions of the Comptroller generally, see s.97 which governs all appeals from the Comptroller and the commentary on that section.

It is thought that an appeal against an order of revocation made by the Court of Session in Scotland may be brought by right to the Inner House of that Court and, thereafter, to the Supreme Court. In Northern Ireland, initial appeal would be to the Court of Appeal in Northern Ireland with further appeal possible, by leave, to the Supreme Court. In the Isle of Man, the final appeal would be to the Privy Council.

An order for revocation has automatic effect unless steps are taken to seek a suspension of the order pending appeal. A request for such suspension will normally be granted, perhaps on an undertaking to prosecute the appeal expeditiously. However, in *Pavel v Sony* [1995] R.P.C. 500 CA, suspension was not requested and it was held that such a request could not be entertained at a later date with the consequence that a corresponding Singapore patent had ceased to exist. If a stay is requested and no appeal is then lodged, no application to amend can thereafter be entertained *Kyowa's Application* [1969] R.P.C. 259. However, where the Comptroller refused to stay an order for revocation pending appeal, and that appeal was eventually successful, it is understood that the patent was simply restored by the Comptroller rectifying the register under the powers provided by s.34.

PRACTICE UNDER SECTION 72

Scope of this Commentary on practice in revocation proceedings

72.21   Inter partes procedure is now reviewed in the commentary under s.123, and in the *Litigation Manual* and the *Patent Hearings Manual*, both available on the website of the UK-IPO. The present commentary is confined to matters specific to s.72.

General procedure in inter partes applications made to the Comptroller

72.22   The "long standing practice" of determining a revocation application in the public interest even when the revocation application is withdrawn, applies where the applicant takes no further action, and even when the patent has lapsed, as in *Acorto's Patent*, BL O/270/05. When this leads to revocation, this operates ex tunc so that the patent is deemed never to have existed. However, in *Myriad Genetics' Patent* BL O/322/05, a revocation application had proceeded in parallel with an EPO opposition. When this opposition concluded with maintenance of the patent as amended, the revocation applicant took no further action despite repeated requests from the UK-IPO. In the light of this inactivity, and the fact that the revocation grounds put forward did not appear to be relevant to the amended patent, it was held that the proceedings need not be continued in the public interest.

Statement of case

72.23   In all proceedings before the UK-IPO, Tribunal Practice Notice (TPN 1/2000) requires claimants to provide a statement of case with a sufficient degree of particularisation for the other side and the Office to have a clear view of the nature of the dispute and supported by a statement of truth (r.78(1)). In particular, it must indicate all grounds which the applicant intends to pursue and which are to be supported by evidence (if appropriate). A precedent for a Statement of Case in s.72 proceedings is provided in an annex to ch.2 of the *Hearings Manual*. The statement of case and supporting document should be supplied in duplicate.

An indication should be given as to which claims are attacked and on which grounds, see *Benz's Application* [1958] R.P.C. 78. All relevant documents to be relied on should be fully cited and preferably be given a label such as the name of the inventor or author in question, see *Du Pont's (Dahlstrom and Bunting's) Patent* [1976] R.P.C. 177 at 195 CA and (1975–76) 15 *CIPA* 269. Copies of cited documents (other than United Kingdom published patent specifications) should be supplied (r.79), together with a translation of any cited document which is not in English (r.113(1)), otherwise the Comptroller may require a translation to be provided (r.82(1)(b)) and if not provided may disregard the document (r.113(4)). It is advisable not to rely on foreign language documents where equivalent documents in English are available, and to cite foreign language references sparingly.

On the sufficiency of the statement, see further CPR 63 PD 4.1–4.4 (reprinted in §F63PD.11), the principles of which can be expected to be followed if objection to its sufficiency is taken, either by the Comptroller or the other party. Thus, in *Coflexip Stena's European Patent* BL O/45/96, an applicant for revocation was required to file a statement of case setting out fully, clearly and consistently the asserted grounds for revocation, failing which the application would be regarded as withdrawn for not being properly launched; and, in *Powerscreen v Finlay* [1979] F.S.R. 108, the court indicated that, in an appropriate case, it would be proper to require an applicant for revocation to make a statement identifying which features of apparatus disclosed in a publication were to be considered as corresponding to the features of the claim under attack for alleged anticipation or obviousness. Any instance of alleged prior use should be fully particularised, see *Gibbons' Patent* [1957] R.P.C. 155. In *Ash & Lacy's Patent No.2240559* BL O/60/02 the claimant's statement of case as originally filed was described as "lamentable", having failed to plead the stated grounds properly, in particular having given no details of alleged "common general knowledge". The claimant was allowed to amend the statement subject to a costs penalty, because it "is not in the public interest for bad patents to remain on the Register". The hearing officer also took note that the claimant could have re-filed the application for revocation and observed that the:

"interests of speedy justice and minimising the period of uncertainty for the public at large would be better served by admitting the amendments than by requiring everything to start all over again."

Counter-statement

TPN 1/2000 requires a counterstatement to set out the basis of the defence, and the **72.24** *Hearings Manual* states that it should reply in a reasonable manner to each of the grounds in issue by way of admission, denial or an offer to amend. A precedent for a counterstatement in s.72 proceedings is also provided in an annex to ch.2 of the *Hearings Manual*.

Where the fact whether a particular document was ever made available to the addressee of the attacked specification and, if so, at what date, is desired to be disputed, a specific denial should be made, thereby requiring the applicant for revocation to prove the facts of publication as part of his evidence, see *Benz's Application* [1958] R.P.C. 78: availability to the public will otherwise be assumed. If the fact of publication is denied, informal proof (for example, a letter from a librarian) can be supplied and the other party asked to consider making a formal admission.

Where claim construction was the basis for an allegation of insufficiency, the patentee was ordered to expand his counter-statement which had made a mere denial of this allegation (*Ash & Lacy's Patent* No.2240558 [2002] R.P.C. 46 at 939).

—Onus of proof

Where an experienced UK-IPO examiner sees a prima facie case of obviousness, the **72.25** onus of proof has been held to shift to the proprietor to show non-obviousness, e.g. by evidence of some unexpected advantage which could perhaps displace that prima facie view: *Degussa-Hüls Application* [2005] R.P.C. 29; [2004] EWHC 3213 Pat Ct.

Amendment of patent during revocation proceedings

In s.72 proceedings, amendments under s.75 may be submitted to the UK-IPO, or under **72.26** the central limitation procedure of art.105A of the EPC. Any amendments under s.75 in revocation proceedings are subject to the limitations imposed by ss.72(1)(d) and (e), 75 and especially s.76, and should if reasonably possible be delivered to the Comptroller in electronic form (e.g. floppy disc or CD-R) or using electronic communications, r.35(2). Amendments may also be filed in paper form. By r.35(4), where the specification of a European patent (UK) was published in a language other than English, the proprietor must file a translation into English of the part of the specification which he is applying to amend and a translation of the amendment. The *Litigation Manual* encourages the use of conventional word processing features such as markup, coloured text and strikeout/ strikethrough to set out the amendments on the original version of the text in such a way as to facilitate appreciation of the changes.

There appears to be no obligation on the Comptroller to advertise the amendment, because any amendment is not sought under s.27 where advertisement is called for, but the Comptroller has a discretionary power under the applicable s.75 to do so. However, advertisement of the proposed amendments normally takes place, particularly if the applicant for revocation withdraws following an offer of unconditional amendment. If the amendment is not advertised, or if advertised and there is no opponent, the amendment proceedings will normally be consolidated into the revocation proceedings. This is an example of the flexible procedure permitted by r.82(1). An applicant for revocation does not need to file opposition to an application to amend the patent-in-suit made under s.75 because he is already a party to proceedings before the Comptroller: *Eickhoff Maschinenfabrik's Patent* BL O/31/87 and *Harding's Patent* BL O/94/90, noted I.P.D. 13215. The proprietor's request to amend the patent will only be supported if the amendment fulfills the requirement of a valid patent claim in of itself: *Robert Leigh v Eurokrete Holdings Ltd Patent* BL O/277/10.

When any amendment is offered during the course of the proceedings, i.e. before any decision has been given on the merits of the case, the proprietor should indicate whether or not the offer to amend is firm and unconditional. If so, it would seem that the Comptroller's decision should deal both with the allowability of the offered amendments and with the objections to validity on the basis of the specification as notionally amended, see *Nippon Seal's Application* [1973] F.S.R. 276. If thought appropriate, the amendment application could be taken to a preliminary hearing. This was done in *Beecham Group's (Amoxycillin) Application* [1980] R.P.C. 261, where amendments were provisionally allowed subject to the issue of discretion being left for decision at the substantive hearing on the validity issue. However, in *Norsk Hydro's Patent* [1997] R.P.C. 89, the Comptroller declined to decide an issue of amendment in a preliminary hearing during revocation proceedings. It is also possible to offer amendments conditional on an adverse finding being made: *Owens-Corning's Application* [1973] F.S.R. 451, in which case the substantive issues should be considered first on the basis of the unamended claim. When an amendment offered by the patentee causes the applicant for revocation to modify his case, the pleadings should be amended, or a supplementary statement filed, before the evidence is closed: *Horville Engineering's Application* [1969] R.P.C. 266.

An unconditional offer to amend should be formally pleaded: *Clading-Boel's Application* [1975] F.S.R. 119, or at least treated as a counterstatement. Such amendments may only be resiled from in an application to amend the pleadings. Where an unconditional offer is made, the Comptroller will normally indicate his prima facie view on the allowability of the amendments and then leave their consideration to the substantive hearing: *Dust Suppression's Application* [1976] F.S.R. 438, but the Comptroller's attitude may lead to some variation of the amendment proposals and thereby shorten the proceedings as a whole.

In *Osterman's Patent* [1985] R.P.C. 579, the counterstatement contained an offer to amend. It was held not necessary that the proprietor should give reasons for proposing amendments as it was presumed (thus differing from proceedings under s.27) that these were put forward to meet the alleged grounds of revocation. It was also here held that there was no reason to depart from the normal procedure, so that the proprietor should not be required to file evidence until after that filed by the applicant for revocation.

When a finding of prior use affects the question only of novelty, and is not relevant to the question of obviousness because no teaching resulted from the prior use, a simple disclaimer of the prior use has been held (under the 1949 Act) to be effective to validate the patent: *Yates Industries' Application* BL O/83/81; and, in T 0629/91 *ICI/Emulsion polymer* [1995] E.P.O.R. 286, the EPO allowed a claim to be validated by disclaimer in order to avoid a prior use which was held not to be the closest state of the art against which inventive step would be judged by the EPO.

When a claim has been disallowed, the patentee's attempts to save it by amendment will be limited by the exercise of discretion according to the facts of each case. For example, an amendment will be disallowed if it does not meet the grounds of attack established (*Bristol-Myers' (Johnson's) Application* [1979] R.P.C. 450). Also, in *Philips' (Bosgra's) Application* [1974] R.P.C. 241, the former Patents Appeal Tribunal indicated that, where broad original claims are maintained from the outset with no part taken in the proceedings after filing a counterstatement, and the broad claims are found to be wholly lacking in merit, subsidiary claims should be approached with caution and the onus of establishing invention in them has shifted. Accordingly, when no assistance is given on the determination of questions raised on the subsidiary claims, it may well be that there should not be an unfettered opportunity to amend the application. In another case when, after three years, no effective attempt to meet the hearing officer's objections had been made, refusal to consider further amendments was held to be justified: *Scholl's Application* [1974] R.P.C. 383. However, limitation to a specified feature was permitted in similar circumstances in *Firth Cleveland's Application (No.2)* [1974] R.P.C. 377, though the proprietor's conduct was criticised. Nevertheless, the primary and overall onus of establishing obviousness always rests on the applicant for revocation and, in *ICOS's Application* [1976] F.S.R. 551, it was indicated that it is only the onus of establishing the truth of particular matters, to be taken into account when deciding the general issue that might shift from party to party. On this basis the shifting onus in the *Philips'* case (above) arose from the unusual facts of that case where no attempt had been made to defend the amended claims. In order to harmonise practice with the EPO, where the question of discretion to permit amendments does not apparently arise, a liberal attitude under s.75(5) to amendments in revocation proceedings is now appropriate.

Where, before an application for revocation before the Comptroller has been concluded, the European patent has been amended in parallel opposition proceedings, and the Comptroller is satisfied that these amendments overcome that application, the proceedings will be terminated without an order: *Du Pont's Patent* BL O/71/99. Where, after a decision by the Patents Court, a European patent has been amended in opposition proceedings before the EPO, the appeal must be conducted on the patent as it now stands amended: *Palmaz's European Patents* [2000] R.P.C. 631 CA.

In arguing a patentee's case, one should be wary in admitting that, if a main claim is lost, a particular sub-claim cannot be supported. In *Firth Cleveland's Application* [1973] R.P.C. 202, such an admission led to refusal of an amended claim, but the former Patents Appeal Tribunal allowed the admission to be withdrawn as having been made by mistake.

Decisions

Because the Comptroller is guardian of the public interest, he may of his own motion **72.27** take the point that an invention is clearly anticipated by some document or rendered unpatentable by common general knowledge of which he may be aware. However, if such an objection is one of obviousness the Comptroller must give the parties a chance to comment and a full opportunity of filing any necessary evidence. If it appears to a hearing officer, while writing his decision, that a claim is objectionable on grounds not argued before him, he ought to recall the parties for further argument after first drawing their attention to the point and giving them the opportunity of dealing with it first by filing evidence: *BOC International's Application* [1980] R.P.C. 122.

SECTION 73

Comptroller's power to revoke patents on his own initiative

73.—(1) If it appears to the comptroller that an invention for which a patent **73.01** has been granted formed part of the state of the art by virtue only of section 2(3) above, he may on his own initiative by order revoke the patent, but shall not do so without giving the proprietor of the patent an opportunity of making any observations and of amending the specification of the patent so as to exclude any matter which formed part of the state of the art as aforesaid without contravening section 76 below.

(2) If it appears to the comptroller that a patent under this Act and a European patent (UK) have been granted for the same invention having the same priority date, and that the applications for the patents were filed by the same applicant or his successor in title, he shall give the proprietor of the patent under this Act an opportunity of making observations and of amending the specification of the patent, and if the proprietor fails to satisfy the comptroller that there are not two patents in respect of the same invention, or to amend the specification so as to prevent there being two patents in respect of the same invention, the comptroller shall revoke the patent.

(3) The comptroller shall not take action under subsection (2) above before—

> **(a) the end of the period for filing an opposition to the European patent (UK) under the European Patent Convention, or**
>
> **(b) if later, the date on which opposition proceedings are finally disposed of;**

and he shall not then take any action if the decision is not to maintain the European patent or if it is amended so that there are not two patents in respect of the same invention.

(4) The comptroller shall not take action under subsection (2) above if the European patent (UK) has been surrendered under section 29(1) above before the date on which by virtue of section 25(1) above the patent under this Act is to be treated as having been granted or, if proceedings for the surrender of the European patent (UK) have been begun before that date, until those proceedings are finally disposed of; and he shall not then take any action if the decision is to accept the surrender of the European patent.

[*(2) If it appears to the comptroller that a patent under this Act and a European patent (UK) have been granted for the same invention having the same priority date and that the applications for both patents were filed by the same applicant or his successor in title, the comptroller may, on his own initiative but only after the relevant date, consider whether to revoke the patent granted under this Act and may, after giving the proprietor of the patent an opportunity of making any observations and of amending the specification of the patent, revoke the patent.*]

[*(3) In this section "the relevant date" means whichever of the following dates is relevant, that is to say—*

> (a) *the date on which the period for filing an opposition to the patent under the European Patent Convention expires without an opposition being filed;*
>
> (b) *the date when any opposition proceedings under that convention are finally disposed of by a decision to maintain the European patent;*
>
> (c) *if later than either of the foregoing dates, the date when the patent under this Act is granted.*]

Note. Subsections (2)–(4) were substituted for the original subss.(2) and (3) by Sch.5 para.19 to the CDPA 1988, effective from January 7, 1991 (SI 1990/2168).

RELEVANT RULE—RULE 35(6)

Rule 35—Amendment of specification after grant

35.—(6) Where the court, or the comptroller allows the proprietor of a patent **73.02** to amend the specification of the patent, the comptroller may direct him to file an amended specification which complies with the requirements of Schedule 2.

COMMENTARY ON SECTION 73

Scope of the section

Section 73 gives the Comptroller power to revoke a patent on his own initiative, but **73.03** only in one of two specific circumstances. These are: (a) where, as a result of the "whole contents" prior art provision of s.2(3), the invention forms part of the state of the art, thus enabling him to deal with cases where conflict between concurrent applications comes to light after grant of the junior patent (subs.(1)); or (b) in cases of double patenting arising from the same priority where a European patent (UK) has been granted for the same invention (subs.(2)). In the latter situation, somewhat similar provisions would apply should simultaneous protection arise from a Community patent, see s.86 implementing art.75 of the Community Patent Convention ("CPC") providing that "the national patent shall be ineffective to the extent that it covers the same invention as the Community patent". Subsection (3) prevents action under subs.(2) until after the European patent (UK) has been confirmed at the end of the period for opposition thereto under art.99 of the European Patent Convention ("EPC"), or the conclusion of any such opposition if such be filed; and subs.(4) provides for surrender of the corresponding European patent (UK) prior to grant of the patent under the Act in order to avoid revocation under subs.(2).

In either of the revocation situations covered by s.73, the proprietor is afforded an opportunity to submit observations and/or to amend the patent to overcome the objection, and thereby avoid revocation under the section. Practice under the section is, therefore, akin to a re-opening of substantive examination, but conducted post-grant.

When the Comptroller takes action under s.73, this is not regarded as proceedings putting validity in issue (s.74(8)). The proprietor has the right to be heard before any action adverse to him under the section is taken (s.101). Appeal against the Comptroller's finding is possible under s.97(1) and then, with leave, to the Court of Appeal.

Amendment under section 73

If revocation under s.73 is to be avoided by an amendment of the patent, the amendment **73.04** must not be one which results in the amended specification describing additional subject-matter or which would extend the extent of protection conferred by the patent (s.76(3)). No form or fee is required and there is no requirement for advertisement of the amendment sought, nor provision for lodging opposition against the requested amendment. Neither can third party observations (under s.21) be permitted as s.21 applies only pre-grant.

In *Reed's Patent* BL C/74/96, noted I.P.D. 19094 no reason was seen why a lapsed European patent should not be amended in order to remove overlap with a patent granted under the Act, in order to avoid the revocation of that patent under s.73(2).

Revocation of patent for anticipation by prior-dated patent specification (subs.(1))

Section 2(3) (as discussed in §§2.11) provides that the contents of an application of **73.05** earlier priority date, which is an application under the Act, an application for a European patent (UK) or an international application (UK), and which was unpublished at the priority date of an invention claimed in the application or patent-in-suit, shall be regarded as part of the state of the art against that later application or patent, though only effective to destroy the novelty of the later application and having no effect as regards the requirement for this to have an inventive step (see s.3). The test for according priority is set out in s.5 and discussed in the commentary on it; and it is to be noted that, in an objection by the Comptroller under s.73(1), such test may need to be applied both to the patent-in-suit and to the cited prior application or patent in order to determine whether the latter is truly to be regarded as part of the state of the art against the former. If this is so, the proprietor may, nevertheless, be able to contend successfully that the invention claimed in the patent-in-suit is not deprived of novelty by the contents of the prior-dated specification. Otherwise, amendment (as discussed in §73.04) will have to be considered to overcome the objection, failing which the Comptroller will order the revocation of the patent, subject to appeal.

Objection under the subsection arises where the existence of the earlier application or patent comes to light only after grant of a patent under the Act. The subsection mainly finds use against a European patent (UK) against which an objection under s.2(3) arises from a prior-dated application or patent under the Act. This is because objection under the parallel EPC art.54(3) can be taken only on the basis of a prior-dated European application. Consequently, a European patent (UK) can be validly granted, despite a conflict with an earlier-dated United Kingdom application (which may have matured into a patent meanwhile). Where this is seen by the Office, objection can then be raised post-grant under subs.(1).

However, if the designation fee for a European patent application (UK) is not paid, it is possible that the prior art effect of that application under s.2(3) may lapse, as discussed in §78.04.

Revocation for double patenting in corresponding European patent (UK) (subss.(2)–(4))

73.06   Subsection (2) provides for revocation on the initiative of the Comptroller where a European patent (UK) is granted "for the same invention" as that for which a patent has been granted under the Act. The subsection therefore corresponds to s.18(5) where there are two applications, each under the Act, which claim the same invention and which were filed by the same applicant with the same priority date, as discussed in §18.12.

The Comptroller has no discretion but to revoke the patent granted under the Act in such a circumstance (as was held in *Turner & Newall's Patent* [1984] R.P.C. 49), and as now confirmed by the subsequent amendment of the subsection to replace the former phrase "may revoke" by "shall revoke", see §73.01. Care therefore needs to be taken if the proprietor wishes to retain his national patent, for example where he wishes to register this in territories that do not register a European patent (UK), or in Hong Kong where a standard patent based on a European patent is subject to revocation if the European patent is itself revoked in opposition proceedings, for which see §77.11.

Subsections (2) and (3) were also amended, together with provision of a new subs.(4), (as noted in §73.01) in a purported attempt to overcome the rigour of the decision in *Turner & Newall's Patent* (above) by providing the proprietor with more time to choose, but prior to the date of grant of the patent under the Act, which of the two patents, i.e. a patent granted under the Act or a corresponding European patent (UK), should be maintained, the eventual maintenance of both not being possible if they are "for the same invention".

In *Turner & Newall's Patent* (above), an attempt was made to amend the granted United Kingdom national patent in order to retain in it solely its omnibus claims, which are not allowed by the practice of the EPO, but the Comptroller regarded these as claims to "the same invention" as contained in the claims of the existing European patent (UK), even though there was a drawing in the patent under the Act which had been omitted from the European patent. Also, in *Maag Gear's Patent* [1985] R.P.C. 532, it was stated that claims do not have to be directed to an invention which has been defined in the two patents in identical terms and that mere differences in scope, such as limitation to an omnibus claim, do not avoid the application of s.73(2).

In *Marley's Patent* [1994] R.P.C. 231, the Court of Appeal (confirming the practice and prior decision in the case by the Comptroller) held that the correct construction of subs.(2)

is the literal one and therefore that its provisions apply if the claims of the patent and the European patent cover "the same invention", "whatever other linked invention may be covered by the claims of either patent", so that revocation will take place when there is overlap between the protections provided by the two patents, unless this overlap is removed by amendment. In this case the Patents Court had reversed the decision of the Comptroller because the European patent had been granted for a process of making articles and the claims of the British patent were directed to those articles per se (evidence having been admitted in the Patents Court indicating that the articles could be made in other ways). However, the Court of Appeal saw claim 1 of the patent under the Act as having two aspects, one of which corresponded to a claim in the European patent and hence objection properly arose under the subsection, and the decision of the Comptroller was therefore restored, although it was indicated that a sympathetic attitude should be shown if an application should be made to limit the claims of the national patent to exclude from its scope the wider protection provided by the European patent. In subsequent proceedings, attempts to overcome the objection by amendment failed as extending the scope of protection contrary to s.76(3) BL O/110/96, noted I.P.D. 20003: the granted claims referred to apparatus "modified as defined in Claim 1" and these words were held to limit the claims to operation according to the process previously claimed so that an unrestricted apparatus claim was not possible.

In *Assing-Collier's Patent* BL O/108/94, the European patent had been allowed to lapse, but the fact that there had been co-existence of the two patents for a short time was sufficient for the patent granted under the Act to be revoked. This patent obtained under the Act was broader in scope than the lapsed European patent, but the omitted features were held to be essential ones and, anyway, the claims embraced the same invention so that the section applied as in the *Marley* case (above). An amendment would, apparently, also not have been possible in *Turner & Newall* (above), because there the claim sought to be maintained in the national patent fell within the scope of the broader protection for which the European patent (UK) had been granted. However, where the claims of the patent granted under the Act and those of a European patent (UK) having the same origin overlap, but are not co-terminous in the sense that constructions can be envisaged which would be an infringement of one patent and not of the other and also vice versa, the Comptroller has been known to allow the national patent to remain on the register: for an example, see Patent No. 2,169,209 and European Patent (UK) No. 0,203,133.

Cases are known where the Comptroller fails to take action under subs.(2). However, where this occurs through inadvertence and the grounds for revocation exist, there seems little point in maintaining the patent granted under the Act as any attempt to enforce this would presumably lead to a complaint to the Comptroller and consequent revocation, the Comptroller having the power to do this at any time.

Avoiding effect of subsection (2)

Subsection (2) cannot be applied if the United Kingdom designation for the European patent is relinquished before the date of publication of notice of its grant in the *European Patents Bulletin* ("EPB"), and this is so even if the designation withdrawal is received by the EPO too late for inclusion on the front page of the patent, or in the EPB or for the register to be corrected before the EPB publication, this only occurring subsequently. Following entry into force of the London Agreement on May 1, 2008 (on the application of art.65 EPC), it is no longer possible to effectively drop the United Kingdom designation by failure to file a translation of a specification published in French or German, see §77.13.

Under subs.(3), the earliest date when the Comptroller can initiate proceedings under subs.(2) is the later of: (a) the last date for lodging opposition to the European patent (UK), i.e. nine months after the date of publication of the mention of its grant in the EPB (EPC r.150(1)); and (b), if any such opposition is lodged, the date when such opposition proceedings are finally disposed of by a decision to maintain the European patent. Before the date when notice of the grant of the patent under the Act is published in the *Patents Journal*, in accordance with s.25(1), it is possible to avoid revocation under subs.(2) by abandoning the European patent (UK), or by amending the European patent by deletion of

73.07

the United Kingdom designation (subs.(3)). Furthermore, revocation under subs.(2) is now capable of being avoided (this was not possible with the previous wording of s.73) by a surrender of the granted European patent (UK) under s.29, but the application to surrender the European patent (UK) must be made before the date of grant under s.25(1) (subs.(4)). This is because such surrender does not take place with retroactive effect, see §29.06, although subs.(4) now has the effect for the purposes of s.73(2) only of backdating the surrender to the date of application for it. Also, failure to pay a renewal fee does not revoke the patent ab initio (*Albright & Wilson's Patent* BL O/142/94). The present form of subs.(3), in contrast to subs.(4), makes it quite clear that not only successful opposition under EPC art.100, but also amendment in the course of such opposition, is of retroactive effect.

The reference to "decision" in subs.(3) means a decision of the Opposition Division of the EPO: therefore the provision cannot be applied to a case where the proprietor decides to surrender the European patent (UK) in an attempt to avoid revocation of a corresponding patent granted under the Act (*Citizen Watch's Patent* [1993] R.P.C. 1). Thus, if revocation under s.73(2) is to be avoided by surrendering the European patent (UK) under s.29, this must be done before the patent under the Act is granted under s.25(1), or at least the application to surrender must have been made before this date, see subs.(4).

Accordingly, although the Comptroller cannot take action under the current form of subs.(2) before the later of the two dates referred to in the current form of subs.(3), the proprietor must act to suppress the European patent (UK) before the grant of the patent under the Act if he is to be certain of avoiding revocation under subs.(2) of the patent granted under the Act, either by relinquishment of the United Kingdom designation for the European patent before this patent is granted or by commencing proceedings for surrender of the European patent (UK) under subs.(4) before the patent under the Act is granted.

If a patent is granted under the Act before the grant of the corresponding European patent (UK), then to be certain of avoiding revocation under subs.(2), the United Kingdom designation for the European application must be relinquished before the European patent is granted, irrespective of any opposition subsequently lodged, though revocation under subs.(2) is postponed until the opposition proceedings are concluded. Subsection (3) provides that such postponement may be of practical value if the opposition succeeds or in response to it the European patent (UK) is amended so that it is in respect of a different invention.

It may also be possible to avoid the effect of subs.(2) by taking action to amend under s.19 the application under the Act before grant takes place so that two patents for the same invention do not come into effect, but note that any such amendment is precluded once the notice of compliance with the Act and Rules has been issued under s.18(4), see §24.06, unless the first report is issued under s.18(4) when two months are allowed for amendment, see §19.04.

Where revocation is ordered under s.73(2), this must be on the normal *ex tunc* basis (*Thomas's Patent* BL O/129/91, noted I.P.D. 15086): however, as there noted, relief for infringement prior to this revocation remains available (under s.69) under the European patent from the date of publication of its application, though subject to any translation requirement having been met.

In *Kimberly-Clark's Patent* BL O/279/04, duplicate applications had been filed in the UK and the EPO for a product involving two features designated as A and B. During prosecution and subsequent opposition in the EPO, the claims of each were amended with the result that the European claims were limited to products containing both features A and B whereas the UK patent claims had been amended to recite only the presence of feature A. The patentee contended that the two sets of claims were directed to separate inventions. It was considered important that the EPO had maintained the patent with claims to the A-B combination which would have been unlikely if feature B was not important. Therefore, on the balance of probabilities, it was held that claims to A and to A-B could here be considered to be separate inventions so that the UK patent could survive attack under s.73.

PRACTICE UNDER SECTION 73

73.08   If the Comptroller is minded to revoke the patent under either of subs.(1) or (2), the proprietor is required to be notified and a period of time will be specified in which to submit observations and/or amend the specification. If amendment is allowed to remove the objection, the Comptroller can require a new specification to be filed, presented in compliance with Sch.2 to the Rules (r.35(6)). It would seem that the right to amend may be lost if unsuccessful appeal is first taken against the decision of the Comptroller to revoke without amendment. Perhaps the amendment should be requested as an initial alternative and the Comptroller asked to stay consideration of it pending determination of the issue of revocation.

Amendment under s.73 requires no form or fee and is not subject to advertisement or to any opposition procedure, see §73.04. Amendments made under s.73 must comply with s.76. If the patent is revoked under s.73, this is noted in the *Patents Journal*.

Putting validity in issue [Section 74]

SECTION 74

Proceedings in which validity of patent may be put in issue

74.—(1) Subject to the following provisions of this section, the validity of a   **74.01** patent may be put in issue—

(a) by way of defence, in proceedings for infringement of the patent under section 61 above or proceedings under section 69 above for infringement of rights conferred by the publication of an application;

(b) in proceedings under section 70 above;

(c) in proceedings in which a declaration in relation to the patent is sought under section 71 above;

(d) in proceedings before the court or the comptroller under section 72 above for the revocation of the patent;

(e) in proceedings under section 58 above.

(2) The validity of a patent may not be put in issue in any other proceedings and, in particular, no proceedings may be instituted (whether under this Act or otherwise) seeking only a declaration as to the validity or invalidity of a patent.

(3) The only grounds on which the validity of a patent may be put in issue (whether in proceedings for revocation under section 72 above or otherwise) are the grounds on which the patent may be revoked under that section.

(4) No determination shall be made in any proceedings mentioned in subsection (1) above on the validity of a patent which any person puts in issue on the ground mentioned in section 72(1)(b) above unless—

(a) it has been determined in entitlement proceedings commenced by that person or in the proceedings in which the validity of the patent is in issue that the patent should have been granted to him and not some other person; and

(b) except where it has been so determined in entitlement proceedings, the proceedings in which the validity of the patent is in issue are commenced before the end of the period of two years beginning with the date of the grant of the patent or it is shown that any person registered as a proprietor of the patent knew at the time of the grant or of the transfer of the patent to him that he was not entitled to the patent.

(5) Where the validity of a patent is put in issue by way of defence or

counterclaim the court or the comptroller shall, if it or he thinks it just to do so, give the defendant an opportunity to comply with the condition in subsection (4)(a) above.

(6) In subsection (4) above "entitlement proceedings", in relation to a patent, means a reference under section 37(1)[*(a)*] above on the ground that the patent was granted to a person not entitled to it or proceedings for a declaration or declarator that it was so granted.

(7) Where proceedings with respect to a patent are pending in the court under any provision of this Act mentioned in subsection (1) above, no proceedings may be instituted without the leave of the court before the comptroller with respect to that patent under section 61(3), 69, 71 or 72 above.

(8) It is hereby declared that for the purposes of this Act the validity of a patent is not be put in issue merely because—

(a) the comptroller is considering its validity in order to decide whether to revoke it under section 73 above, **or**

(b) its validity is being considered in connection with an opinion under section 74A below or a review of such an opinion.

Note. Subsection (6) was amended by Sch.5 para.10 to the CDPA 1988 consequent on the amendment of s.37 (for which see §37.01), with effect from January 7, 1991 (SI 1990/2168). Subsection (8) was amended by the Patents Act 2004 (c.16) s.13(2), with effect from October 1, 2005 (SI 2005/2471).

COMMENTARY ON SECTION 74

74.02 This is an important section. It sets out in subs.(1) the proceedings in which the validity of a patent may be put in issue, with proceedings under s.73 and 74A being specifically excluded (subs.(8)). By subs.(2), the proceedings listed in subs.(1) are the only ones in which the validity of a patent can be put in issue, and then only on the grounds upon which a patent can be revoked under s.72(1) (subs.(3)). Subsections (4)–(6) provide further specialist provisions for entitlement contests and relate to s.72(1)(b): ss.37 and 72(2) are also relevant in this connection. Subsection (7) prevents the commencement, without leave, of proceedings before the Comptroller for infringement, for a declaration of non-infringement, or for revocation, if any proceedings with respect to the patent are already pending before the court. The section, therefore, provides overall a concise and comprehensive statement of the only circumstances in which validity of a patent can be contested after its grant.

There is no directly corresponding provision in the EPC, but subs.(4) corresponds to CPC arts 23(3) and 55(1), with s.130(7) requiring the subsection to be interpreted, if possible, as having the same effect. These CPC provisions, in conjunction with relevant associated provisions, read:

"CPC ARTICLE 23—Claiming the right to the Community patent

1. If a Community patent has been granted to a person who is not entitled to it under Article 60(1) of the European Patent Convention, the person entitled to it under that provision may, without prejudice to any other remedy which may be open to him, claim to have the patent transferred to him.

2. Where a person is entitled to only part of the Community patent, that person may, in accordance with paragraph 1, claim to be a joint proprietor.

3. Legal proceedings in respect of the rights specified in paragraphs 1 and 2 may be instituted only within a period of not more than two years after the date on which the European Patent Bulletin mentions the grant of the European patent. This provision shall not apply if the proprietor of the patent knew, at the time the patent was granted or transferred to him, that he was not entitled to the patent."

"CPC ARTICLE 55—Applications for revocation

1. Any person may file with the European Patent Office an application for revocation of a

Community patent; however, in the case specified in Article 56(1)(e) [An application for revocation of a Community patent may be filed only on the grounds that:...(e) the proprietor of the patent is not, having regard to a decision which has to be recognised in all the Contracting States, entitled under Article 60(1) of the European Patent Convention (Right to a European patent)] the application may be filed only by a person entitled to be entered in the Register of Community Patents as the sole proprietor of the patent or by all the persons entitled to be entered as joint proprietors of it in accordance with Article 23 acting jointly."

Proceedings in which validity may be put in issue (subss.(1)–(3) and (8))

Subsection (1) lists the proceedings in which the validity of a patent may be challenged **74.03** as: infringement (ss.61 and 69); threats (s.70); declaration of non-infringement (s.71); revocation (s.72); and disputes as to Crown use (s.58). Section 73, where the Comptroller revokes on his own initiative, is specifically excluded (subs.(8)) and the revision of subs.(8) (as noted in §74.01 above) provides that proceedings under s.74A (opinion as to validity or infringement) or a review of such an opinion (under s.74B) are not proceedings which are deemed to put validity in issue.

The prohibition in subs.(2) against challenging validity in any type of proceedings other than those listed in subs.(1) has been held, "with regret", to be absolute: *Organon Teknika v Hoffmann-La Roche* [1996] F.S.R. 383; here validity was not allowed to be challenged in an application to the court for a declaration of non-infringement, not under s.71 but in the inherent jurisdiction of the court. The position was rectified by allowing the statement of claim to be amended to raise also an application for revocation which it was held, since proceedings were already in being, need not be brought by petition. The subsection also prohibits proceedings for a mere declaration of validity or invalidity, thereby making statutory previous decisions of the court to this effect. However, the section does not preclude the filing of an opposition against a European patent (UK) because the jurisdiction of the EPO is preserved by s.77(2), see §77.06 and *Organon Teknika v Hoffmann-La Roche* (above). Nor, in *Arrow Generics Ltd v Merck & Co Inc* [2007] EWHC 1900 (Pat); [2007] F.S.R. 39, did s.74(2) preclude the grant of a declaration that products were obvious at the priority date of divisional patent applications. Such a declaration would, if granted, have provided commercial certainty as to whether the products could be marketed in the UK.

Subsection (3) makes clear that the only grounds on which validation may be put in issue are grounds of revocation specified in s.72, as discussed in §72.09.

Apparently in its inherent jurisdiction (no mention being made of s.74), in *Lever Fabergé v Colgate-Palmolive* [2006] F.S.R. 19 at 333, the court granted a declaration that "the patent is, and at all times, has been invalid on the grounds of invalidity served with the particulars of claim" when, just before the patent was due to lapse, prima facie evidence of invalidity was put before the court, which was not contested and as regards which the Court saw no defence.

Estoppel against challenge to validity

There can be circumstances in which a party to proceedings may be estopped from **74.04** contesting validity. For example, where a party has unsuccessfully challenged validity in previous proceedings (other than in revocation proceedings before the Comptroller, for which see §72.17), the doctrine of res judicata is likely to prevent that party from challenging validity again, both on the grounds previously asserted and also on grounds which could have been raised in the earlier proceedings, but which were not, see *Chiron v Organon Teknika (No.6)* [1994] F.S.R. 448 upheld on appeal *Chiron v Organon Teknika (No.14)* [1996] F.S.R. 701 CA, and the registered design case of *Parmenter v Malt House Joinery* [1993] F.S.R. 680 CA. More recently, see the trade mark case *Special Effects Ltd v L'Oréal SA* [2007] R.P.C. 15, where the court regarded opposition proceedings (not inherently final, since invalidity could be challenged subsequently) as distinguishable from invalidity proceedings. This will particularly be so where, as in the *Chiron* case, an allegation of prior publication had been pleaded and only not proceeded with when supporting experiments were criticised and needed repetition: in those circumstances the validity challenger ought to have sought a postponement of the trial to enable further experiments to be carried out.

The doctrines of laches and acquiescence can also lead, effectively, to a litigant becoming estopped from pleading the case it desires, as discussed in §60.23. Partial estoppels can also occur on a particular issue because a party has previously proved (or failed to prove) a particular fact and, as a consequence, has created an "issue estoppel" against himself, for which see §72.17.

Estoppel can further arise as the result of agreement. For example, in *Heinemann v Dorman & Smith* (1955) 72 R.P.C. 60 and 162 CA, the claimant agreed to discontinue an action for infringement in return for a contractual undertaking by the defendant not to infringe. The claimant subsequently sued the defendant for breach of that contract; it was held that the defendant could not defend that action by counterclaiming for revocation of the patent. A consent judgment may, similarly, lead to an estoppel against further challenge to validity on the normal principles of res judicata. Likewise, there cannot be a challenge to validity in contempt of court proceedings for breach of an injunction, see *Multiform v Whitmarley* [1956] R.P.C. 143; [1956] R.P.C. 338 CA; and [1957] R.P.C. 260 HL.

However, a provision in a patent licence agreement that the licensee may not challenge the validity of the patent is invalid under art 101(1) of the Treaty on the Functioning of the European Union (TFEU, ex art.81(1) EC), see *Windsurfing International v EC Commission* (193/83) [1986] E.C.R. 611; abridged [1988] F.S.R. 139 ECJ. However, in the special case of a royalty-free licence, a "no-challenge" clause has been held valid, see *Bayer v Süllhöffer* (65/86) [1990] 4 C.M.L.R. 182; [1990] F.S.R. 300 ECJ. A provision for immediate termination of a licence if the licensee initiates or otherwise becomes involved in a challenge to validity of the licensed intellectual property right, is permitted under the Technology Transfer Block Exemption. See further Appendix D and in particular §D23 on this issue. Also, there is nothing inconsistent in seeking a compulsory licence under a patent while continuing to challenge its validity, see *Halcon's Patents* [1989] R.P.C. 1.

The validity of the rule of "licensee estoppel" has been questioned and discussed by A. Robertson [1991] E.I.P.R. 37. The EPO regards a no-challenge obligation as incompatible with the centralised EPC opposition procedure and will therefore not decline to proceed with opposition proceedings because of the existence of such an obligation: No-challenge obligation OJ EPO 1992, 747.

Once a court has given a final decision upholding the validity of a patent, a party to those proceedings is bound by that judgment, even if further prior art comes to light or the patent is subsequently revoked in separate procedures, see *Coflexip v Stolt Comex* [2004] F.S.R. 7 at 118; and [2004] F.S.R. 34 at 708.

In *Agilent v Waters Corp* [2004] EWHC 2992 Ch, there had been previous litigation under the patent leading to the Court of Appeal giving a different construction to the claim wording upon which this further action alleged infringement by a different machine of the defendants. Although, in these circumstances, it would appear that the defendants would be estopped from re-contesting invalidity, the court expressed some sympathy with the view that a further challenge to validity ought to be possible based upon the new claim construction, but it was not necessary to decide the point.

Allegations of non-entitlement (subss.(4)–(6))

74.05   Subsections (4)–(6) relate to revocation under s.72(1)(b) for non-entitlement, as discussed further in §72.13. These subsections provide that this ground of invalidity may not be raised by any person unless it has been determined, in entitlement proceedings under any of ss.8, 12 and s.37(1), or in court proceedings for a declaration, that the patent was granted to a person not entitled (subs.(6)); or it is so determined in the proceedings in which validity is in issue. However, except where it has been determined otherwise, the proceedings in which validity is in issue must be commenced within two years of grant of the patent unless the proprietor of the patent knew at the time of grant or on transfer of the patent to him that he was not entitled to the patent. The meaning of "knew" in this context is discussed in §§37.11 and 72.13. The provision is to be interpreted in conformity with arts 23(3) and 55(1) of the CPC (each reprinted above), but no cases are known in other countries which have had to interpret similar provisions.

Subsection (5) gives the court or Comptroller discretion to allow a defendant who has raised allegations of invalidity (in a defence or counterclaim) based on entitlement, to obtain a declaration of entitlement in his favour, before the court or comptroller decides the issue of validity, so he is not debarred from contesting validity merely because he has not yet succeeded in entitlement proceedings under s.37, or indeed yet even commenced such proceedings. The defendant will have to establish that it is just for this discretion to be exercised in his favour and this may well include explaining why no such declaration has yet been obtained and when a result is likely to be forthcoming. However, it is not clear whether subs.(5) is broad enough to permit validity to be challenged after the end of the two-year period, if the defendant is not contending that the patentee "knew" that he was not entitled to the patent.

As to the relative timing of entitlement proceedings under s.37(1) and revocation proceedings under s.71(1)(b) and s.72(2), in *Henry Bros v Ministry of Defence* [1997] R.P.C. 693 it was held sufficient that a declaration of entitlement should have been made before an order for revocation could itself be made: thus entitlement and subsequent revocation could occur in the same action, contrary to the view previously taken in *Dolphin Showers v Farmiloe* [1989] F.S.R. 1. In *Henry Bros*, it was stated that, if there is any conflict between the wording of ss.72(2) and 74(4), s.72(2) should prevail. See further §72.13.

The *Dolphin Showers* case held also that only a person with a claim that the patent should have been granted to him had the necessary locus standi to raise the defence; thus a successor in title by virtue of a post-grant assignment has no locus standi to raise such a plea. However, it is possible to argue that the words "should have been granted to him" in subs.(3)(a) do not require that the patent should have been granted to that person as sole proprietor, and therefore that a person who succeeds in proving that he should have been a joint proprietor may be able to take advantage of this provision (*La Baigue Magiglo v Multiglow Fires* BL C/56/93). Indeed, in *Henry Bros*, it was held that a patent is granted to persons not entitled to apply if it is not granted to all those entitled to apply, but it was recommended that the provisions of the EPC and the Act need clarification in relation to questions of co-ownership, on which see also the paper by S. Thorley [1995] *CIPA* 104.

The limit imposed by subss.(4)–(6) on the bringing of entitlement proceedings within two years from the date of grant does not prevent, after that date, amendment of an existing reference for joint ownership to one for sole ownership (*Yeda Research v Rhône-Poulenc Rorer* [2008] R.P.C. 1; [2007] UKHL 43; [2008] R.P.C. 1, overturning the Court of Appeal [2006] EWCA Civ 1094; sub nom *Rhône-Poulenc Rorer v Yeda Research* [2007] R.P.C. 9), this not being a "new claim", impermissible once the two-year period had expired, but rather matters with the question of "who was entitled" which had been referred to the Comptroller within the relevant time period; see also §37.11.

Concurrency of proceedings before the Comptroller and the court (subs.(7))

Subsection (7) prohibits the institution of proceedings before the Comptroller under: **74.06** s.61(3) (infringement of a patent); s.69 (infringement before grant); s.71 (declaration of non-infringement); and s.72 (revocation) while proceedings under any of the provisions specified in subs.(1), i.e. those under ss.58, s.61, or 69–72, are already pending before the court, unless the court gives leave. This provision applies even if the putative applicant before the Comptroller is not a party to the court proceedings. Presumably, to obtain leave he would first need to apply to the court to intervene in the proceedings already before the court. It appears that the court is likely to exercise discretion in favour of allowing proceedings for revocation (under s.72), or for a declaration of non-infringement (under s.71), to take place in the UK-IPO rather than before the court only if one party is unable to afford the costs of High Court proceedings, as in *Hawker-Siddeley v Real Time* [1983] R.P.C. 395, see *Gen Set v Mosarc* [1985] F.S.R. 302.

This practice does not generally apply in reverse when court proceedings are commenced during the pendency of proceedings before the Comptroller, although the effect of s.27(2) appears to be that any amendment proceedings under s.27 must be stayed on the commencement of any proceedings before the court. Thus, in *Wilkinson Sword v Warner-*

Lambert BL C/124/87, proceedings under s.27 for amendment of the patent were already in being when proceedings for a declaration of non-infringement (under s.71) and for revocation (under s.72) were commenced before the court. The Patents Court refused to stay the proceedings before it pending resolution of the amendment proceedings, and indicated that the amendment proceedings should be recommenced before the court under s.75. Subsequently the court allowed the amendments and found the patent valid, but not infringed.

Stay of proceedings pending determination of opposition at the EPO

74.07   The Patents Court has been reluctant to stay infringement proceedings (or other proceedings relating to patents) merely because opposition proceedings are in being before the European Patent Office, see *Amersham International v Corning Ltd* [1987] R.P.C. 53; OJ EPO 1987, 558 and *Pall Corp v Commercial Hydraulics* [1989] R.P.C. 703. In the *Amersham* case it was considered irrelevant that a multiplicity of infringement actions might be avoided if the opposition in the EPO were successful. Here, the defendants had agreed not to seek revocation nationally if the opposition in the EPO were to fail, but in neither the *Amersham* nor in the *Pall* case did the defendant concede the issue of infringement.

In *Beloit v Valmet* [1997] EWCA Civ 993; [1997] R.P.C. 489 CA, a stay was sought because the form of the patent was uncertain, the EPO having indicated that an auxiliary petition with an amended claim might succeed in pending opposition proceedings. The stay was refused because it was uncertain when the EPO proceedings would reach finality, it being indicated that the position could be different if such finality would occur shortly. However, in *Kirin-Amgen's and Boehringer Mannheim's Patents* BL C/15/98, noted I.P.D.21036, a stay for a limited period had previously been granted where patents in contention had been revoked in EPO opposition proceedings, pending appeal, but at the end of the stay these proceedings had still not been completed, a state of affairs which the judge stated was "quite extraordinary and unacceptable". The stay was, nevertheless, continued for a further limited period.

In *Eli Lilly v Human Genome Sciences* [2010] R.P.C. 14, [2010] EWCA Civ 33 there had been cooperation between the UK Court of Appeal and an EPO Appeal Board which was hearing a parallel opposition, such that the hearing of the EPO appeal was expedited and took place before the hearing in the UK Court of Appeal. Jacob L.J. emphasised the need for such cooperation and suggested that where litigation was pending it should be extended to all stages of the opposition procedure.

In *Virgin Atlantic v Premium Aircraft* [2010] R.PC. 8, [2009] EWCA Civ 1513 the patent in issue had been held valid and infringed in the United Kingdom up to the level of the Court of Appeal, but there was the possibility of a further appeal to the Supreme Court and also an appeal in an EPO Opposition which was still pending. The court held that there was no reason why the patentee could not pursue an enquiry as to damages at his own risk as to costs while the appeal was pending, and as regards the EPO opposition validity and infringement were res judicata unless or until the EPO Board of Appeal decided otherwise, see *Unilin Beheer v Berry Floor* [2007] EWCA Civ 364. The court observed:

> "The rule in *Unilin* effectively stretches back to the *Poulton v Adjustable Cover* [1908] 2 Ch 430. Moreover, if the position were otherwise the Patents Court would be partially emasculated. No truly final order could be made until the very often long drawn-out EPO opposition procedure was over. Business could not know in a reasonable time where it stood. Things would be provisional for far too long. Wary or perhaps well-advised inventors might indeed eschew the European Patent Office altogether and apply for a national patent instead—there is no opposition procedure here—for fear that an EPO opposition would make their patents only incompletely or contingently enforceable for the whole period of the opposition."

An application for a stay of revocation proceedings of a European Patent (UK) where there was a parallel EPO opposition and pending proceedings in Belgium was refused in *GlaxoSmithKline Biologicals v Novartis* [2009] EWHC 931 Pat Ct, inter alia because the claimant had waited for over 30 months before bringing proceedings in the United Kingdom.

For further discussion of the grant of a stay until EPO opposition proceedings have been concluded, see §61.63.

Similar issues have arisen in the national courts of other EPC Member States, as to which see the *European Patents Handbook* ("EPH") (London: Sweet & Maxwell) (s.30.6) and some such cases were reported in OJ EPO 1988, 357–363, where a stay of national proceedings was ordered in some, but not all, of these cases. Also, in Germany, it is apparently not permitted to commence national nullity proceedings on a European patent (Germany) during the period when opposition could be commenced in the EPO and, if such opposition is filed, until the opposition proceedings have been finally concluded. For the implications of, and complications which arise from, parallel challenges to validity in the EPO and before a United Kingdom court, see §77.06.

Opinions by Patent Office [Sections 74A–74B]

SECTION 74A

Opinions as to validity or infringement

74A.—**(1) The proprietor of a patent or any other person may request the comptroller to issue an opinion—**   **74A.01**

    (a) as to whether a particular act constitutes, or (if done) would constitute, an infringement of the patent;

    (b) as to whether, or to what extent, the invention in question is not patentable because the condition in section l(l)(a) or (b) above is not satisfied.

(2) Subsection (1) above applies even if the patent has expired or has been surrendered.

(3) The comptroller shall issue an opinion if requested to do so under subsection (1) above, but shall not do so—

    (a) in such circumstances as may be prescribed, or

    (b) if for any reason he considers it inappropriate in all the circumstances to do so.

(4) An opinion under this section shall not be binding for any purposes.

(5) An opinion under this section shall be prepared by an examiner.

(6) In relation to a decision of the comptroller whether to issue an opinion under this section—

    (a) for the purposes of section 101 below, only the person making the request under subsection (1) above shall be regarded as a party to a proceeding before the comptroller; and

    (b) no appeal shall lie at the instance of any other person.

Note. New s.74A was added to the Act by the Patents Act 2004 (c.16) s.13(1) with effect from October 1, 2005 (SI 2005/2471).

RELEVANT RULES—RULES 92–97

PART 8—OPINIONS

Rule 92—Interpretation

92. In this Part—   **74A.02**

"request" means, unless the context otherwise requires, a request for an opinion under section 74A(a);

"requester" means the person who makes that request;

"patent in suit" means the patent to which that request relates;

"patent holder" means the proprietor of that patent and any exclusive licensee of the patent; and

"relevant proceedings" means proceedings (whether pending or concluded) before the comptroller, the court or the European Patent Office.

Note. The reference to "section 74A(a)" in the definition of "request" appears to be erroneous since there is no s.74A(a). This appears to be a typographical error; the definition should refer to "section 74A(1)".

Rule 93—Request for an opinion under section 74A

74A.03

93.—(1) A request must be made on Patents Form 17 and must be accompanied by a copy and a statement setting out fully—

(a) the question upon which an opinion is sought;

(b) the requester's submissions on that question; and

(c) any matters of fact which are requested to be taken into account.

(2) The statement must be accompanied by—

(a) the name and address of any persons, of whom the requester is aware, having an interest in that question; and

(b) particulars of any relevant proceedings of which the requester is aware which relate to the patent in suit and which may be relevant to that question.

(3) However, where the requester is acting as an agent in making the request, the persons referred to in paragraph (2)(a) do not include the person for whom the requester is so acting.

(4) The statement shall be accompanied by a copy of any evidence or other document (except a document which has been published by the comptroller or is kept at the Patent Office) which is referred to in the statement.

(5) Each such statement, evidence or other document must be provided in duplicate.

Rule 94—Refusal or withdrawal of request

74A.04

94.—(1) The comptroller shall not issue an opinion if—

(a) the request appears to him to be frivolous or vexatious; or

(b) the question upon which the opinion is sought appears to him to have been sufficiently considered in any relevant proceedings.

(2) The comptroller shall not issue an opinion if the requester gives him notice in writing that the request is withdrawn.

(3) If the comptroller intends at any time—

(a) to refuse the request because the condition in paragraph (1)(a) or (b) is satisfied; or

(b) to refuse the request because, in accordance with section 74A(3)(b), he considers it inappropriate in all the circumstances to issue an opinion,

he shall notify the requester accordingly.

Rule 95—Notification and advertisement of request

95.—(1) The comptroller must notify each of the following persons of the request (except where the person concerned is the requester)—

    (a) the patent holder;

    (b) any holder of a licence or sub-licence under the patent in suit which has been registered under rule 47;

    (c) any person who has made a request in respect of the patent in suit under rule 54 regarding an opinion being requested under rule 93;

    (d) any person who is specified under rule 93(2)(a).

74A.05

(2) In addition, the comptroller may notify of the request any persons who appear to him to be likely to have an interest in the question upon which the opinion is sought.

(3) The comptroller must send a copy of the form and statement filed under rule 93(1) to each person so notified, together with a copy of such other documents filed under rule 93 as he thinks fit.

(4) The comptroller must advertise a request in such manner as he thinks fit.

(5) However, if the request is refused or withdrawn before a notification has been made under paragraph (1)—

    (a) the patent holder alone must be notified of the request (and of the fact that it has been refused or withdrawn); and

    (b) paragraphs (3) and (4) do not apply.

Rule 96—Submission of observations and observations in reply

96.—(1) If the request has not been refused or withdrawn, any person may, before the end of the relevant period, file observations on any issue raised by the request.

74A.06

(2) Such observations may include reasons why the comptroller should refuse the request.

(3) Any person who files observations under paragraph (1) must ensure that, before the end of the relevant period, a copy of those observations is received—

    (a) where that person is not the patent holder, by the patent holder; and

    (b) by the requester.

(4) A person to whom observations are sent under paragraph (3) may, during the period of two weeks beginning immediately after the end of the relevant period, file observations confined strictly to matters in reply.

(5) Any person who files observations under paragraph (4) must ensure that, within that period of two weeks, a copy of those observations is received—

    (a) where that person is the requester, by the patent holder; and

    (b) where that person is the patent holder, by the requester.

(6) If it is reasonably possible, the observations filed under this rule and the copies of such observations shall be delivered only in electronic form or using electronic communications.

(7) For the purposes of this rule, the relevant period is four weeks beginning [with] immediately after the date of advertisement under rule 95(4).

Note. Directions for submitting observations under r.96 in electronic form or by using electronic communications are set out in the directions reprinted below.

Amended by the Patents (Amendment) Rules 2011 (SI 2011/2052).

Rule 97—Issue of the opinion

74A.07   **97.**—(1) After the end of the procedure under rule 96, the comptroller must refer the request to an examiner for the preparation of the opinion.

(2) The comptroller must issue the opinion that has been prepared by sending a copy to—

    (a) the requester;

    (b) the patent holder; and

    (c) any other person who filed observations under rule 96(1).

DIRECTIONS UNDER SECTION 124A

Note. Rules 92–97 of the Patents Rules 2007 (SI 2007/3291) came into effect on December 17, 2007, replacing rr.77A–77G of the Patents Rules 1995 which had previously governed the new procedures under s.74A.

74A.08   **Submitting opinion observations by electronic means**

(reprinted as updated on December 17, 2007)

Note. These Directions are reprinted from the website: *http://www.ipo.gov.uk.* The original Directions under s.124A were given on September 23, 2005, but were updated on December 17, 2007, bringing them into line with the Patents Rules 2007. Before use, the website should be checked against the update date given above and, if different, the website version should be used. Further information as to the procedure generally is available on the website.

Introduction

1. The Comptroller has made these Directions under section 124A of the Patents Act 1977 ("the Act") to direct the form and manner in which observations on the request for an opinion under section 74A of the Act, filed under rule 96 of the Patents Rules 2007 ("the Rules"), may be delivered in electronic form or using electronic communications.

2. These Directions come into force on 1 October 2005.

Interpretation

3. In these Directions:—

    "digital medium" means—

        • a compact optical disk (CD) containing electronic data conforming to ISO 9660; or

        • a digital versatile disk (DVD) containing electronic data conforming to ISO 9660 or ISO 13346; or

        • a 3.5'' floppy disk;

    "observations" means the observations mentioned in rule 96 of the Rules;

"opinion reference number" means the reference number on the notification sent by the comptroller under rule 95 of the Rules.

Delivery of observations

4. Observations may be sent by email or delivered on digital medium.

5. Observations sent by email shall be sent to: *opinions@ipo.gov.uk*.

Content and format of observations

6. Where observations are sent by email, the email shall contain—

   ● the observations; and

   ● the opinion reference number.

7. Observations delivered on a digital medium shall be accompanied by a paper document containing—

   ● a statement that the digital medium carries observations; and

   ● the opinion reference number.

8. No observations sent by email or delivered on a digital medium shall be encrypted.

Illegible or incomplete observations and infected observations

9. Where part or all of the observations delivered under these Directions are illegible or incomplete, the whole of the observations shall be treated as not complying with these Directions.

10. Where the observations delivered under these Directions are reported as having a virus (or other malicious software) by the Patent Office's virus checking software they shall be treated as not complying with these Directions.

11. Where the observations are treated as not complying with these Directions under paragraph 9 or 10, provided that the person making the observations can be identified, he shall be notified of this fact by the comptroller.

Acknowledgement

12. Where the observations have been received in accordance with these Directions, they shall be acknowledged by the comptroller.

13. The time of delivery accorded to an email containing observations shall be that generated by the Patent Office's internal electronic communications network (within the meaning of section 32 of the Communications Act 2003),

RON MARCHANT

Comptroller-General of Patents, Designs and Trademarks
7 September 2005

Guidance and notes on the Directions

These notes are not part of the Directions. They are intended to provide background and additional information.

The Interpretation Act 1978 applies to these Directions. Therefore, all the definitions set out in that Act apply to these Directions. Further, amongst other things, generally any words importing the masculine gender include the feminine and words in the singular include the plural and words in the plural include the singular.

Where observations are submitted which do not comply with the Directions, the comptroller may treat the observations as not having been delivered (see section 124A(3) of the Act).

Observations in electronic form

Observations may be submitted as an attachment to an email. The comptroller will try to read attachments in any format, but Microsoft® Word, WordPerfect®. Portable Document Format (PDF) or plain text (RFC822 compliant) are preferred.

The acknowledgment referred to in paragraph 12 may not be sent immediately upon receipt of the observations.

Full guidance about opinions and the procedure to be followed is available from this website and you should familiarise yourself with it before submitting observations.

Enquiries concerning these directions should be directed to: Sue Williams, Room 3.Y52, Concept House, Newport, South Wales, NP10 8QQ United Kingdom. Tel: 44(0) 1633 814736; Fax: 44(0) 1633 814491.

COMMENTARY ON SECTION 74A

Scope of the section

74A.09   Section 74A came into effect on October 1, 2005; the associated Rules are now provided by rr.92–97 of the Patents Rules 2007, which came into force on December 17, 2007. Section 74A created a new procedure which enables UK-IPO examiners to issue, on request, non-binding Opinions on questions of validity, although only on issues of novelty and inventive step, as well as on questions of alleged infringement. Once an Opinion has been issued, it is possible to seek a review of it under s.74B and rr.98–100 as discussed further below under s.74B, below.

The Explanatory Notes issued on the Bill which led to the Patents Act 2004 indicate the Government's belief that the ability to request such Opinions from a neutral body, although not leading to the final determination of these issues, should be helpful to parties who wish to settle disputes without launching full proceedings. For example, a person might want an Opinion about whether a certain activity would infringe a patent before investing resources in that activity; and a patent proprietor might want an Opinion about whether "prior art" of which he has just become aware is relevant to the patented invention before he decides whether to seek amendment of the patent. J. Phillips, at [2005] E.I.P.R. 226, elaborated on the reasons which he saw for making use of the new procedure.

Subsections (1) and (2) define the scope of procedure under s.74A. This starts with a "request" made by a "requester" in relation to a specified "patent" owned by a "patent holder" (the actual proprietor and any exclusive licensee under the patent), see r.92, reprinted at §74A.02, above.

An Opinion may be requested as to whether any act constitutes or would constitute an infringement of a patent, and as to whether (or to what extent) the patent is invalid. However, Opinions on validity are limited to the question whether or not the invention is patentable, either because it is not new or because it does not involve an inventive step (s.1(1)(a) or (b)), but not whether the patent lacks industrial applicability or is statutorily unpatentable under s.1(1)(c) or (d) (see Opinions 22/06 and 28/06), nor whether it lacks a sufficient description as required by s.14(3) (see Opinions 04/06 and 05/06), nor whether an amendment has been impermissibly made (see Opinion 02/06).

Under sub.(4) an Opinion is not binding for any purposes. In particular the views expressed by an examiner appointed to give an opinion requested under s.74A(1) have necessarily to be based only upon the permissible matters made the subject of that "request", so that the conclusion which he reaches and issues in response to such matters, and to any response to the request, has to be understood as saying merely that the request, in the Opinion of the appointed examiner, has either "succeeded", or "failed", for the reasons he has set out. The non-binding effect also arises because only an "Opinion", and not a "judgment", is permitted to be given; and also because the Opinion has: (a) necessarily to be given on the facts available to the appointed examiner which he will not have been able to resolve after hearing witnesses and experts testifying on the truth and reliability of the facts and views put forward; and, if thought appropriate, tested by cross-examination on the expressed facts and views, as would happen in proceedings leading to a "judgment"; and also (b) because a court decision to be given in any such future proceedings in relation to the patent might later be re-examined in appeal procedures even up to the highest available level. The effect of the examiner's conclusion, howsoever stated, is to be understood as meaning no more, in effect, than the request made to him was, in his opinion, either justified or unjustified for the reasons he has set out and arrived at in the light of the information that was available to him.

Opinions are limited to the matters set out in the request. Therefore observers must keep observations confined to those matters—Examiners will ignore any other issues raised by an observer. For example, in Opinion 04/07 the patentee requested an Opinion whether an act by a third party infringed his patent. As part of the observations, the third party alleged that the patent lacked novelty. The Examiner declined to deal with that issue since it had not been raised in the request. If an observer wishes to raise the issue of validity of a patent, a request for a separate Opinion should be filed or an application made under s.72 for revocation.

—Standard of Proof

The standard of proof applied by Examiners in the Opinions procedure is that which is used in post-grant work by the UK-IPO, i.e. a balance of probabilities (see para.38 of the *Opinions Manual* which is available online at the UK-IPO website). Where the evidence is not clear it is open to the Examiner to refuse to issue an Opinion under s.74A(3)(b); the likely alternative is that the Examiner will give an opinion that the patent is valid and/or not infringed (see, for example Opinion 20/06 where the Examiner was unable to determine on the evidence if the alleged infringement had the key feature of the claim in question; in the Examiner's view the evidence was "extremely thin" and it was concluded that the claim was not infringed).

74A.10

Unchallenged evidence may be accepted at face value. For example, in Opinion 29/08 an unchallenged witness statement containing drawings and designs of products alleged to have been sold before priority date was accepted as true and accurate. However, the outcome may be different where the evidence is challenged: in Opinion 09/09 part of the evidence submitted by the requester included technical drawings and an invoice. The observer (patentee) challenged whether or not these documents were available to the public. The examiner decided not to consider that part of the evidence because the requester had made no counter-argument and provided no evidence that the documents were available to public.

—Form of Evidence

In Opinion 28/09 the observer (patentee) asserted that non-patent prior art (delivery note, extracts from Argos catalogue, press release and photographs) filed by the requester was not accompanied by a statement of truth and therefore should not be considered. The Examiner noted that r.87(2) relating to the form of evidence in proceedings before the Comptroller is included under Part 7 of the Patent Rules 2007, whereas s.74A is governed by Rules in Part 8. Therefore r.87(2) did not apply to the opinions procedure and there is "no restriction on the form of evidence" admitted for opinions.

—Construction

74A.11 Examiners should apply the usual principles of claim construction (see s.125). In particular, reliance is placed on the judgment of Lord Hoffmann in *Kirin-Amgen v Hoechst Marion Roussel* [2005] R.P.C. 9 at [169] HL, and Examiners ask themselves the now well-known question:

> "what a person skilled in the art would have understood the patentee to have used the language of the claims to mean?"

See further the commentary on s.125.

The Examiner decides on the construction of the claims once all of the rounds of argument and evidence have been completed; that is, after the request, observations (if any) and observations-in-reply (if any). Since arguments in a request may be unopposed, Examiners are tasked with construing the claims having regard to all possible interpretations. However, requesters and observers may put forward their own arguments on construction, although the Examiner will still work through the claim construction process independently (as in Opinion 10/06 where the requester and observer argued for a different construction of the main claim). In Opinion 06/10, rather than submitting arguments on construction, the requester (patentee) submitted an exhibit that it alleged was an embodiment of the invention, but one that was not shown in the patent. The Examiner decided to ignore the exhibit on the grounds that the patent "must stand alone" and that "its disclosure cannot be added to by further documents".

—Wrong finding of invalidity and/or non-infringement

74A.12 Under r.98(5) only the patent holder may apply to the Comptroller for a review of an Opinion and only on the grounds that either the Opinion wrongly concluded that the patent was invalid or partially invalid (r.98(5)(b)), or that by reason of interpretation of the specification the Opinion wrongly concluded that the act in the request is not an infringement of the patent (r.98(5)(b)). Reviews of Opinions 11/06, 14/06, 15/06, 16/06 and 17/06 show instances where the Examiner misconstrued the claims. See the commentary on s.74B.

—Subsection (1)(a)—Infringement

74A.13 Where an Opinion is sought under subs.(1)(a) whether or not a particular act infringes a patent, it is important that evidence is submitted that has sufficient clarity to demonstrate (i) that the product or process falls within the scope of the claims, and (ii) that an act has been (or will be) committed that falls within the scope of s.60. Examiners make a clear distinction between these two aspects in their opinions (see for example Opinion 14/08).

Opinion 12/10 provides an example of where the evidence submitted to support (i) was held insufficient. Here the requester submitted two photographs and a print-out from a website showing products (in this case manhole covers for scaffolding) alleged to fall within the scope of claim 1. Although the Examiner could see that the products had been offered for sale in the UK (it being implied that this evidence was sufficient to be an 'act' within the meaning of s.60), the Examiner was of the view that these photographs simply did not provide sufficient information to determine whether they fell within the scope of claim 1.

Particular difficultly can be encountered when alleging infringement by computer-implemented products and services. For example in Opinion 26/09 an opinion was sought whether or not the well-known SKYPE® voice-over-IP communication system infringed a particular UK patent. The evidence submitted was not clear enough and the Examiner concluded that, whilst it was "possible" that there was infringement, the evidence did "not convincingly show this". A further Opinion was sought (33/09) in which additional evidence was submitted relating to the same infringement. However, this gave rise to issues of possible refusal under r.94(1)(a) (as frivolous or vexatious), for which see §74A.18. Although in that case, the Examiner decided that the additional evidence made a "new or at least extended request", it highlights the importance of gathering as much detailed evidence as possible before asking for an opinion; if the evidence is not clear a further opinion for the same infringement may be refused under r.94(1)(a).

Both acts of primary infringement (s.60(1)) and acts of secondary infringement (s.60(2)) have been considered under this subsection. In Opinion 04/08 the patent related to an apparatus and method for allowing movement of a flat display screen from a viewing position above a fire surround for a fireplace and into a hidden position within the fire surround and vice versa. The independent claims were to "a fireplace apparatus" including a fireplace, fireplace surround and lifting mechanism; and to "a method of operating a fireplace apparatus". The acts specified in the request were sale by a third party of a fire surround and sale of the lifting mechanism respectively. The Examiner was persuaded on the evidence that sale of the fireplace surround was an infringement of the patent under s.60(1), but that "in view of the lack of argument and evidence" in relation to s.60(2) and (3), on the balance of probabilities, there was no contributory infringement relating to the sale of the lifting mechanism per se. This Opinion hints at the importance of the evidence in the Opinions procedure in deciding whether or not an act can be considered to fall under s.60(2). In that particular case evidence would be needed to show firstly whether or not the lifting apparatus was in fact an essential element of the invention, and secondly whether or not it could be considered a "staple commercial product".

In Opinion 08/09 an opinion was sought whether or not the well-known MICROSOFT® OFFICE 2007 suite of software infringed a UK patent under s.60(1) or s.60(2). The Examiner was of the view that there was no literal infringement of claim 1 since it required a "system" which, since the claim required "a processing apparatus", was construed as a computing apparatus programmed in a particular way. On the evidence, the 'wizard' functionality provided by the software to associate MICROSOFT® OUTLOOK and MICROSOFT® ACCESS did not meet this requirement of the claim. However, the Examiner was of the view that supply of MICROSOFT® OFFICE 2007 in the UK would amount to contributory infringement under s.60(2) because it is "sold knowing that its only purpose is for installation on a computer" and that, when installed on a computer, "would result in a system with the processing apparatus elements required by claim 1". Furthermore, despite MICROSOFT® OFFICE 2007 being "ubiquitous", it was not seen as a 'staple commercial product' for the purposes of s.60(3) since "the term is in law taken to relate to a basic everyday product such as a generally available raw product or commodity" (see §60.10 for more detailed commentary on the meaning of 'staple commercial product').

—Subsection (1)(b)—Patentability

Examiners should follow the normal routines of assessing novelty and inventive step. See the commentaries on ss.2 and 3, above, and the UK-IPO's MOPP available online, at *http://www.ipo.gov.uk*.   **74A.14**

For documents and events where the date of disclosure is not immediately apparent, the standard of proof in the Opinions procedure is one of balance of probabilities. Reference in particular is made to §§2.04–2.10, above, for the factors and evidence required to show, on the balance of probabilities, the date and nature of alleged prior disclosure. For example in Opinion 05/06 an allegation of prior use was found not proved because it had not been sufficiently established that the alleged prior use had taken place under non-confidential circumstances.

For the purposes of assessing novelty and inventive step it is open to Examiners to investigate the priority date of the claims of the patent in question. For example in Opinion 10/10 a patent reference submitted by the requester was only relevant under s.2(3) if the claims of the patent were not entitled to their priority date. The Examiner was of the view that, since the MOPP did not require the pre-grant Examiner to assess an application's claim to a particular priority date in detail as a matter of course, this was a question that could be legitimately considered in the Opinions procedure. See Opinion 13/10 for another example of the assessment of priority date.

—Translations of foreign-language references

74A.15   In Opinion 27/09 an unverified translation of a Japanese patent publication was submitted by the requester. The observer questioned the clarity of the translation. In the observations in reply the requester filed a verified translation of the Japanese publication. The observer objected that the two translations differed. The Examiner reviewed both versions and concluded that some of the differences were non-trivial and that it should be the first, unverified translation that is used to form the Opinion.

—Subsection (2)

74A.16   Under subs.(2) an Opinion may be requested in relation to any patent under the 1977 Act, except one which has been revoked. Accordingly, an Opinion on infringement can be given even in relation to an act that has not taken place (see for example Opinions 22/07 and 08/08), and an Opinion on infringement or validity can be given even in relation to a patent which has ceased or expired (see for example Opinions 16/10 and 17/10). Thus an Opinion can be requested which will help someone decide whether it is safe to engage in a particular activity, or which concerns activity that might have taken place before a patent has expired. An Opinion on validity may also be requested where the patent has been surrendered (for instance, if a licensee wishes to argue that licence fees should be repaid).

—Refusal of Request

74A.17   Subsection (3) requires a request for an Opinion to be accepted, except: (a) in prescribed circumstances; or (b) when for any reason, the Comptroller considers that it would be inappropriate to do so. Rule 94 (reprinted at §74A.04, above) specifies the prescribed circumstances as: (a)(i) that the request is seen to be frivolous or vexatious; (a)(ii) the question is seen to have been sufficiently answered in other proceedings; or (b) where the requester has given notice that the request is withdrawn. In any of these circumstances, or when the Comptroller considers it inappropriate to answer the request, the requester is to be informed. Such a decision cannot be the subject of a review under s.74B, see r.98(5) reprinted at §74B.02.

If a request merely seeks to cover old ground rather than raise something new, it is likely to be refused under this subsection (see BL O/289/07). At the time of writing, a number of requests have relied on prior art documents that have been considered earlier, most often those cited during search and/or substantive examination of the patent. The Opinions issued on these requests have made it clear that, to be admissible, such requests must raise a "new argument" in order that they are not refused under this subsection (see Opinions: 26/06—new argument sufficient for request to be admissible; 09/07—acceptability of request raising new inventive step arguments on previously cited prior art; 21/07 and 26/07—request admitted that used "A" category documents which had not previously been used for formal novelty/inventive step objections; 27/07— admissibility of request using seven "old" documents, but which were placed in a new light by one previously unknown citation). However, where a request relies on "X" or "Y" category documents already cited against the patent at any time during the pre-grant phase, it is unlikely, other than in exceptional circumstances, to clear the hurdle of raising a new question or argument (see BL O/370/07). Documents used in earlier Opinions cannot be used to attack the same patent again (see Opinion 06/08).

In determining whether or not to refuse a request that relies on previously cited prior art, it was held in BL O/370/07 that "relevant proceedings" in r.94(1)(b) does not include the normal pre-grant examination process (both before UK-IPO and EPO) and therefore the question of refusal falls under subs.(3)(b) instead. The finding in O/370/07 that "relevant proceedings" in r.94(1)(b) does not include the normal pre-grant examination process was confirmed in BL O/242/09 in which the request related solely to a question considered pre-grant. The approach was followed in Opinion 12/09 in which part of a request was refused under subs.3(b) as some of the documents had already been considered by the EPO pre-grant. In contrast, Opinion 10/09 had a different outcome on the facts: the requester had submitted documents to the UK-IPO which had been filed as third party observations at EPO just before oral proceedings on the patent in question, but which were not mentioned in EPO's decision following those proceedings; furthermore there was no indication in the EPO file that the EPO had considered the third party observations. On balance the Examiner felt that the documents had not been considered pre-grant and would consider them for the purposes of the Opinion. In Opinion 17/09 the Examiner "had no doubt" that "relevant proceedings" in r.94(1)(b) covers the substantive examination process, although this appears to contradict what was held in BL O/370/07 and BL O/242/09 above.

In Opinion 02/05 it was alleged that an estoppel defence to infringement existed and that therefore the Comptroller should refuse to issue an Opinion under subs.(3)(b). The Examiner concluded that there was not normally any need to take account of estoppel since whether or not the act was an infringement was purely a matter of fact; estoppel only becomes an issue once proceedings are launched.

In Opinion 15/07, the patentee (as observer) argued that the Opinions timetable is biased in favour of the requester and therefore that this was in breach of the art.6 of the Convention on Human Rights; although there was no argument that the request should be refused under subs.(3)(b) on this ground. The Examiner commented that the timetable for observations and observations-in-reply had been adopted by Parliament following a full and open consultation; furthermore, the review process under s.74B provides an additional safeguard for patentees in the event that the patent is found invalid or not infringed.

—Refusal under rule 94(1)

In Opinion 21/08 the observer (patentee) argued that the request should be refused, either as vexatious or as having been sufficiently answered in other proceedings. The European patent itself had been the subject of an earlier Opinion (Opinion 08/06), an EPO opposition and a cancellation action before the German courts. However, it was the earlier Opinion and the cancellation action that were the basis of two separate allegations of vexatiousness: first, via the cancellation action the requester was well aware of the documents on which it now relied, and that these documents should have been raised in the earlier Opinion; and secondly that one of the new documents simply showed "conventional prior art", the latter already having been discussed by the observer in its submissions in the earlier Opinion. It was held that the request was not vexatious since the observer had not backed the first allegation with any evidence (or even a reason) why the requester should have been aware of the two documents at the time the earlier Opinion was requested. Perhaps if there were sufficient evidence available the Examiner might have gone on to consider whether the request was vexatious. Regarding the second allegation, the Examiner held that since there were material differences between the observers discussion of the "conventional prior art" and what was shown in the new document, the case for vexatiousness did not succeed. The submission of the observer that the request should be refused as having been considered in the earlier German cancellation proceedings did not succeed either since r.94(1)(b), when read in light of r.92, made it clear that "relevant proceedings" are limited to proceedings before the comptroller, the court or the European Patent Office.

74A.18

In Opinion 20/08 the requester sought an Opinion that the patent was both not novel and not inventive. The observer (patentee) argued that the request should be refused as vexatious since Opinions on validity are limited to the question of whether or not the invention is not patentable, either because it is not new or because it does not involve an inventive step. Accordingly, reliance on multiple grounds of invalidity is not in accordance with "the spirit and intention of the Opinions procedure", and the request should be refused as vexatious. The Examiner disagreed since he could not find any evidence in the Act, Rules or MOPP that it was the intention that only one ground could be submitted per request.

In Opinion 33/09 the requester essentially sought an opinion on the same infringement question that was decided in Opinion 26/09 (see also §74A.13); in the latter case the evidence for infringement was not convincing. In the later opinion the Examiner considered whether or not the request should be refused under r.94(1)(a) as frivolous or vexatious, as an opinion had already been given on the same infringement question. However, the requester had provided some new evidence which "supported and clarified the case for infringement". Therefore the request was admissible as "a new or at least an extended request".

Where there are other relevant proceedings to be considered under r.94(1)(b) the Examiner will not necessarily refuse the whole request; instead it is likely that the Examiner will refuse to consider those parts of the request that overlap with the other proceedings. For example, in Opinion 05/06 there were concurrent revocation proceedings. All of the documents common to both the request and the revocation proceedings would not be considered for the purposes of the Opinion. Furthermore, all of those documents in the request that had been considered pre-grant would not be considered, although one document that had been considered pre-grant in relation to the product claims would be considered in the Opinion in relation to the method claims.

In Opinion 17/07 proceedings had been launched in the Patents County Court by the observer (patentee) one day after the requester had sought an opinion as to infringement and validity of the same patent. The patentee argued that the request should be refused under r.94(1)(a) or (b) either as frivolous or vexatious, or as having been considered in other relevant proceedings. As to the latter, the proceedings had not yet been fully heard by the judge in the PCC, although there had been a preliminary hearing for an extension of time; the patentee alleged that the judge had commented that "the IPO would not issue an opinion in this matter, given concurrent proceedings currently being heard in the PCC". However, the judge had made no order that an opinion should or should not be given. The Examiner was of the view that, in light of this, nothing that the court had ordered impelled refusal of the request under r.94(1)(a). As to refusal under r.94(1)(b), the patentee argued that the court proceedings covered the same issues as the request, that it was inconceivable that the requester would not counterclaim for invalidity based on the same prior art, and therefore that the request should be refused. The Examiner was of the view that if the issues were about to be heard "imminently" by the court, serious consideration would need to be given whether it would be inappropriate in all the circumstances to issue an opinion. However, the full hearing in the PCC was some months off and the Examiner believed an opinion could be helpful. Accordingly the Examiner proceeded to give on opinion on the matters raised in the request.

In Opinion 15/10 the requester had referred inter alia to a US Appeals decision in which the equivalent US patent had been held invalid, and believed that this earlier decision was highly relevant to the opinion. As the requester had not offered any meaningful analysis of why the outcome of the US Appeal might justifiably be applied to the patent in question, the Examiner declined to consider the US proceedings further.

Whilst there is a stay of concurrent court proceedings or proceedings before the Comptroller it appears possible to obtain an Opinion under s.74A (see Opinion 06/07, although in that case neither party objected to the giving of an Opinion) and a review under s.74B. For example, in BL O/345/06 an impecunious applicant for revocation was faced with a request for security for costs by the patentee. The hearing officer believed that the Opinions procedure would be of value in assisting the parties and the Comptroller to assess the strength of the claimant's case for revocation since the dates of publication of some of the alleged prior art was unclear and would need to be established by evidence. In the circumstances the hearing officer stayed the revocation proceedings to give each party an opportunity to consider whether or not to request an Opinion. An Opinion was indeed requested (see Opinion 01/07) which was then the subject of a review (see BL O/053/08). The revocation proceedings were the subject of a further stay (see BL O/137/07) until the outcome of the review under s.74B.

—Non-binding effect & timescale

74A.19 Subsection (4) ensures that an Opinion under the section does not have binding legal effect for any purpose. According to the Explanatory Notes, it is intended that the procedure for delivering Opinions will be as simple and quick as possible. Paragraph 8 of the *Opinions Manual* indicates that an Opinion should be issued no more than three months after a request is made. This is intended to increase the likelihood of an Opinion being helpful in assisting the early settlement of disputes; but an Opinion based on such an abbreviated procedure will not be permitted to make a final binding determination of the issues concerned. However, it is considered that this bar on finality will not prevent the fact that an Opinion had been given from being referred to in subsequent proceedings (see BL O/137/07, for example).

Although an Opinion given under s.74A is to be "non-binding", it would appear possible that this feature could be overridden by an agreement made between the parties. Care should therefore be taken in reaching any agreement as to the conduct of proceedings under s.74A to stress the continuing non-binding nature of the result, if such be intended, in case some inference to the contrary would be possible, particularly where the agreement is an informal one reached in oral discussion.

—Officer of UK-IPO responsible for drawing up Opinion

74A.20 Subsection (5) requires an Opinion to be prepared by an officer of the Intellectual Property Office holding the position of Examiner. These are the officers who carry out the search and examination under ss.17 and 18.

—Right to Hearing

74A.21 Under subs.(6), when read with s.101, the requester of an Opinion has the right to be heard before a request under the section is refused; but no other person (including even the patentee as observer) is to be regarded as a party to the proceedings and such person has no right to be heard on the issues before the Examiner, or to lodge an appeal (as the requester may do) against the refusal. This was confirmed in BL O/370/07 where the observer (patentee) was permitted to attend a Hearing about the refusal of the request, but whilst the written observations filed by the patentee in response to the initial request would be considered, the patentee would not be able to make any submissions during the Hearing. The Explanatory Notes indicate that this is intended to prevent unnecessary delays in a procedure which is designed to be simple and rapid. However, new s.74B provides for a review of an Opinion issued under s.74A, although only by the patentee or an exclusive licensee.

Section 74(8) has been amended to make it clear that proceedings for an Opinion under s.74A are not, as such, to be regarded as proceedings in which the validity of a patent is put in issue. Accordingly, questions of validity may be considered in the context of such proceedings, notwithstanding the exclusive list of proceedings in which the validity of a patent may be put in issue which is laid down by s.74(1) and (2).

—Amendment of Request for Opinion

74A.22 Errors in the documents making up the request for an Opinion would appear to be correctable under s.117 and r.105. However, the *Opinions Manual* contrasts the situation where there is an obvious error on the PF 17, for example, with the situation where there is a mistake in the accompanying statement. The former case is relatively simple, whereas to correct mistakes in the latter case "may be more difficult". For example in Opinions 01/05 and 05/07 the requester was permitted to correct obvious errors in the written statement. In Opinion 05/07 it was obvious that the wrong claims had been referenced in the statement. In other cases, amendment has been refused. In Opinion 08/07, for example, a request to change "infringes" to "meets the terms of" was refused (a case where the patentee sought an Opinion on whether his own product "infringed" the claims of his patent).

Furthermore, any observers must have an opportunity to comment on any amendment or clarification of the statement and/or request. Therefore requests for amendment are unlikely to be permitted once the period for observations is under way. However, in Opinion 05/07 the mention of wrong claims in the request was so fundamental that the observations period was re-started.

—Raising other issues and/or making arguments subsequently

74A.23   In Opinion 23/08 both the observer (patentee) and requester raised other issues in observations and observations in reply. The Examiner refused to deal with these other issues and confined the opinion to matters raised in the original request. This was confirmed in Opinion 28/09 where the observer (patentee) filed further observations after the requester had submitted observations in reply. The Examiner observed that the effect of r.97 is that the observation process is completed after the rounds permitted by r.96. However the Examiner commented that there may be occasional circumstances in which further information may be needed from the parties, but that such further information should not be submitted without being requested by the Examiner. Contrast this with Opinion 27/09 where further correspondence, received after completion of the observation process, was considered despite there being no indication in the opinion that these further submissions were sought by the Examiner.

—Withdrawal

74A.24   Under r.94(2) a request may be withdrawn by the requester at any time. The withdrawal must be in writing. Provided an Opinion has not been issued, the withdrawal permits the same issues to be raised against the patent in a subsequent request.

—Stay

74A.25   It appears possible, by mutual agreement between requester and observer, to obtain a stay in the Opinion proceedings. Such was the case in Opinion 02/05 where a stay of one month was granted pending negotiations between requester and observer. Once an impasse in those negotiations was reached, the Opinions procedure was resumed.

In Opinion 05/06, the Examiner agreed to consider prior art additional to that which was in consideration in a pending EPO opposition brought by another, but not that already in issue in those proceedings. However, the Examiner refused to stay the proceedings pending resolution of the opposition because proceedings under s.74A are intended to be dealt with expeditiously.

—Costs

74A.26   The Opinions procedure is not proceedings before the Comptroller within the meaning of s.107(1) and therefore Examiners have no power to award costs to either the requester or any observer(s). This is in contrast with the reviews procedure, for which see §74B.16.

—Notification to Third Parties (rule 95(2))

In Opinion 16/09 a request was filed asking for an opinion whether or not a marketed product infringed the patent of the requester; no interested parties were identified on the PF 17. Supporting evidence for infringement included photographs of the marketed product which clearly showed two trade marks. Under r.95(2) the UK-IPO exercised their discretion to contact the owners of the trade marks and to give them an opportunity to file observations.

—Effect of the section

The Opinions service has been used by private applicants, companies and patent attorneys. Other than through the number of requests filed, it is impossible to know how useful the Opinions service is as a business tool. In particular, it is not possible to know how useful patent proprietors and third parties find the Opinions service in helping to resolve disputes and/or narrowing the range of issues in a dispute. Having said that, the Opinions service is of undoubted use to private applicants who are able to seek, relatively inexpensively, an impartial Opinion on infringement of their patent. However, this can backfire where a patentee refuses to accept that their patent is not infringed: once the review and appeal processes are used, the patentee risks an award of costs against him (see review O/183/07 where the hearing officer awarded £1,500 against the patentee, and the subsequent appeal *Frank Cunningham v Nokia Corp* [2008] EWHC 1174 Ch, where costs of £20,000 were ordered against the patentee).

74A.27

PRACTICE UNDER SECTION 74A

Making a request for an opinion under section 74A (rr.92–97)

A request under s.74A may be made by anyone, and is quite often made by a patent attorney acting for a principal whose name and address need not be identified (r.93(3)). The requester makes his request on PF 17 on which a fee is required. Rule 93 (reprinted at §74A.03, above) requires PF 17 to be filed in duplicate and accompanied by a statement which sets out fully the question on which an Opinion is requested, together with the requester's submissions and any matters of fact which are asked to be taken into account. In the absence of any specific mention of sub-claims, the request will be taken as not applying to them, see Opinion 03/06.

74A.28

Furthermore, care must be taken that each argument alleging the lack of novelty or inventive step of a dependent claim is sufficient to pass the hurdle presented by r.93(1). For example, in Opinion 15/08 the Requester relied on three prior art documents to allege lack of novelty of claim 1, and also stated that it "seems likely that any two of the documents combined render all of the claims of the present patent obvious". The Examiner held that whilst the statement questioning the novelty of claim 1 met the requirements of r.93, the same was not true of the statement relating to inventive step. Therefore dependent claims 2–17 were not considered in the Opinion either on the ground of novelty or on the ground of inventive step.

This statement is to be accompanied by details (name and address) of any person of whom the requester is aware as having an interest in the submitted question; and also of details of any proceedings of which the requester is aware that have relevance to the patent and to the question. Such proceedings include proceedings in the EPO, whether pending or concluded (r.92). With the statement there should also be filed copies of any documents referred to, with the exception of published specifications of UK patents and applications (r.93(4)) and the PF 17, the statement and any documents or evidence supplied with it must be filed in duplicate (r.93(5))

If the Comptroller refuses to entertain the request, the fee paid may be remitted upon written application to the Comptroller (amended r.106(4), as noted in §123.23).

Under rr.95(4) and 44(5)(a) the making of a request is then advertised on the UK-IPO website: *http://www.ipo.gov.uk*.

The request is also notified to: the patent holder; any registered licensee or sub-licensee; anyone who has filed a "caveat" to be informed under r.54(6)(a) (see §118.05); and any person named in the statement as having an interest in the question. In addition, the

Comptroller is at liberty to notify the request to any other person who appears likely to him to have an interest in the question upon which the Opinion is sought (r.95(2), reprinted at §74A.05, above). Unless the request has been refused or withdrawn before such notification has been made, all such persons who are so notified are sent a copy of the form and statement filed under r.93(1), and, if the Comptroller sees fit, copies of some or all of the other documents submitted; and the request is advertised "as the Comptroller may think fit" (r.95(4)). In practice, such advertisement is not made in the *Patents Journal*, but this contains a reference to the website, in which details of the existence of the request, and its outcome, are included.

All such documents filed with a request are immediately open to public inspection on the patent file under r.53(2)(b), and so are not subject to the normal 14-day period for claiming confidentiality to prevent such inspection (see Opinion 03/05). This should be borne in mind when submitting a request or observations in relation to issues of infringement or prior use.

Responding to notification of a request for an opinion under section 74A (r.96)

—Who may file observations

74A.29   Whether or not officially notified that the request has been made, any person may (provided that the request has not been refused or withdrawn) file "observations" on the request, and ensure that a copy is received by the patent holder when that person is not the patentee, and by the requester (r.96(3)).

—Time limit for filing observations

74A.30   Rule 96(7) requires that these actions should be carried out within four weeks of the date of the advertisement of the request, a period which would appear to be extensible with discretion exercised under r.108. However, see "Extensions of Time" below. Note, however, that this advertisement may not appear in the *Patents Journal*, see §74A.26, above, but only on the UK-IPO website. The filing of any such observations does not require payment of any fee. There is no provision for the filing of evidence outside of this period because the procedure is intended to be a quick one, see Opinion 03/05.

—Observations-in-reply

74A.31   Any person to whom the observations are sent may then file reply observations which are "strictly in reply" to the observations already filed (r.96(4) and (5)). In Opinion 25/08 the requester filed new documents with their observations in reply. The Examiner did not consider them for the purposes of the opinion since they were "new evidence" which the observer (patentee) not had an opportunity to comment on.

—Time limit for filing observations-in-reply

74A.32   This must be done within two weeks of the end of the four-week period specified for the filing of the observations (in chief), a period which, likewise, appears extensible under r.108.

—Extensions of time

74A.33   The procedure under s.74A is intended to be carried out expeditiously and thus good cause may have to be demonstrated to obtain any extension of these four- or two-week periods: indeed the UK-IPO website says that "you can ask us for an extension of time" but:

"will need to have very good reasons why you need this. Any extension is unlikely to be for more than a few days".

According to the *Opinions Manual* an extension of three weeks was granted for the filing of observations on Opinion 08/06 when the only speaker of a relevant foreign language in the agent's office was on holiday for three weeks—the volume of the foreign language documents to be considered being some 130 pages. A request for an extension of two months to the period for filing observations was refused in Opinion 22/06; it was decided that the papers to be considered were not unduly voluminous (25 pages of statement, two witness statements and five other documents).

Rule 96(6) requires that, if it is reasonably possible, all observations (whether "in chief" or in reply) should be submitted only in electronic form or using electronic communications. This is to simplify, and expedite, the proceedings. This use of electronic submission applies both to communications to the Comptroller and to other parties to the proceedings. The procedure for such communications is set out in a direction from the Comptroller, the latest available version of which is reprinted above. The observations should be submitted on a digital medium or sent by email to *opinions@ipo.gov.uk*.

Issue of opinion (r.97)

Rule 97 requires that, when the period for submitting observations has ended, the request **74A.34** is submitted to an examiner for preparation of an Opinion on the questions raised. When the Opinion has been prepared, the Comptroller sends a copy to the requester, the patent holder and any person who filed observations under r.96(1). The issuing of the Opinion is entered in the register, as also is any refusal or withdrawal of the request before an Opinion is issued (r.44(5)(b) and (c)). These matters are also advertised on the website. Other particulars concerning Opinions or requests may also be entered in the register if the Comptroller so thinks fit (r.44(7)).

It is the aim of the UK-IPO to issue an Opinion within three months of the making of the request.

Within three months of the issue of the Opinion the patent holder (but no other person) may seek a review of the opinion under s.74B, as discussed in the commentary below.

Section 74A does not prohibit a requester from seeking a further Opinion on the same patent, although any such further request may be rejected if it does not introduce any new facts, arguments or evidence (see §74A.16). Accordingly, where a request is refused or where an Examiner cannot reach a conclusion on the evidence provided, there is no estoppel preventing the requester making a new request with better evidence.

Availability of Opinion and papers filed in connection with it

Notice that an Opinion has been issued is given on the UK-IPO website and this contains **74A.35** a link to the Opinion itself. This is issued under an Opinion Number in the form "xx/yy" where xx is the consecutive number for the last two digits of calendar year 20yy. The number of the patent involved is stated in this website entry and copies of all papers filed at the UK-IPO, or electronic communications sent, in relation to the request can be examined by an inspection of the file of that patent under s.118(1), as discussed in §118.19.

SECTION 74B

Reviews of opinions under section 74A

74B.—(1) Rules may make provision for a review before the comptroller, **74B.01**
on an application by the proprietor or an exclusive licensee of the patent in question, of an opinion under section 74A above.

(2) The rules may, in particular—

(a) prescribe the circumstances in which, and the period within which, an application may be made;

(b) provide that, in prescribed circumstances, proceedings for a review may not be brought or continued where other proceedings have been brought;

(c) make provision under which, in prescribed circumstances, proceedings on a review are to be treated for prescribed purposes as if they were proceedings under section 61(1)(c) or (e), 71(1) or 72(l)(a) above;

(d) provide for there to be a right of appeal against a decision made on a review only in prescribed cases.

Note. New s.74B was added to the Act by the Patents Act 2004 (c.16) s.13(1) with effect from October 1, 2005 (SI 2005/2471).

RELEVANT RULES—RULES 98–100

Rule 98—Review of opinion

74B.02   **98.**—(1) The patent holder may, before the end of the period of three months beginning [with] immediately after the date on which the opinion is issued, apply to the comptroller for a review of the opinion.

(2) However, such proceedings for a review may not be brought (or if brought may not be continued) if the issue raised by the review has been decided in other relevant proceedings.

(3) The application must be made on Patents Form 2, and shall be accompanied by a copy and a statement in duplicate setting out fully the grounds on which the review is sought.

(4) The statement must contain particulars of any proceedings of which the applicant is aware which may be relevant to the question whether the proceedings for a review may be brought or continued.

(5) The application may be made on the following grounds only—

(a) that the opinion wrongly concluded that the patent was invalid, or was invalid to a limited extent; or

(b) that, by reason of its interpretation of the specification of the patent in suit, the opinion wrongly concluded that a particular act did not or would not constitute an infringement of the patent.

Note. Amended by the Patents (Amendment) Rules 2011 (SI 2011/2052).

Rule 99—Procedure on review

74B.03   **99.**—(1) Upon receipt of the application, the comptroller must send a copy of the form and statement filed under rule 98 to—

(a) to the requester (if different from the applicant); and

(b) to all persons who filed observations under rule 96.

(2) The comptroller must advertise the application in such manner as he thinks fit.

(3) Before the end of the relevant period, any person may file a statement in support of the application or a counter-statement contesting it (which in either case must be in duplicate), and on so doing shall become a party to the proceedings for a review.

(4) or the purposes of paragraph (3) the relevant period is—

  (a) four weeks beginning [with] immediately after the date on which the application is advertised under paragraph (2);

  (b) if it expires later, the period of two months beginning [with] immediately after the date on which the opinion is issued under rule 97(2).

(5) The comptroller shall send to the other parties a copy of each statement or counter-statement filed under paragraph (3).

(6) The rules listed in Parts 4 and 5 of Schedule 3 shall apply to the proceedings for a review and for the purposes of rule 83(3)—

  (a) a reference to "the claimant" is a reference to the applicant for a review; and

  (b) a reference to "the defendant" is a reference to any other party.

Note. Amended by the Patents (Amendment) Rules 2011 (SI 2011/2052).

Rule 100—Outcome of review

100.—(1) On completion of the proceedings under rule 99 the comptroller shall either— **74B.04**

  (a) set aside the opinion in whole or in part; or

  (b) decide that no reason has been shown for the opinion to be set aside.

(2) A decision under paragraph (1)(a) or (b) shall not estop any party to proceedings from raising any issue regarding the validity or the infringement of the patent.

(3) No appeal under section 97 shall lie from a decision to set aside the opinion under paragraph (1)(a), except where the appeal relates to a part of the opinion that is not set aside.

COMMENTARY ON SECTION 74B

Scope of the section

Section 74B enables rules to be made for the filing and resolution of a review against an **74B.05** Opinion issued under s.74A. These rules are now rr.98–100. The section became effective on October 1, 2005 and the rules on December, 17 2007.

The review process is intended to enable patent proprietors or any exclusive licensee to challenge the Opinion given by an Examiner under s.74A. However, the scope of the review is only whether or not it was "wrongly concluded" that the patent was wholly or partially invalid, and/or that the Opinion "wrongly concluded" that a particular act does not constitute an infringement of the patent.

The word "concluded" as used in r.98(5) means that the requested opinion has to be treated as one which "concludes" that the request upon which it issued was either legitimately "justified" or not "justified", i.e. that, in effect, the request made had led to the result that it should be treated as having either "succeeded" or "failed", see §74A.09.

At the conclusion of the review, the Comptroller can either decide to set aside the Opinion, in whole or in part, or decide that no reason has been shown for the Opinion to be set aside (r.100(1)), but any such decision to set aside the Opinion does not create any estoppel from raising the matters in issue in other proceedings (r.100(2)). There is no right of appeal under s.97 from a decision to set aside the Opinion, except where the appeal relates to a part of the Opinion that was not set aside (r.100(3)).

—Applicant

74B.06 According to subs.(1) and r.98(1) only the proprietor or an exclusive licensee of the patent in question may apply for a review of an Opinion.

—Time Limit for Making Application

74B.07 Under r.99(4) an application for review must be made within three months beginning on the date on which the Opinion was issued. In principle this time would appear to be extendible under r.108(1) with the Comptroller's discretion.

—Advertisement of Application

74B.08 Under r.99(2) the Comptroller must advertise the application for review and this is done on the UK-IPO website.

—Circumstances in which Application may be made

74B.09 Rule 98(5) gives effect to subs.(2)(a) and states that an application for review may be made on two grounds only: (i) that the Opinion wrongly concluded that the patent in suit was partially or wholly invalid (r.98(5)(a)); or (ii) that, by reason of its interpretation of the specification of the patent in suit, the Opinion wrongly concluded that a particular act did not or would not constitute an infringement of the patent (r.98(5)(b)).

At the time of writing the leading authority on the scope of the review process and appeals from it is *Re DLP Ltd* [2008] R.P.C. 11; [2007] EWHC 2669 Pat Ct. It was decided in that case that in review proceedings:

> "a Hearing Officer should only decide an opinion was wrong if the examiner has made an error of principle or a reached a conclusion that is clearly wrong."

Plus, furthermore that:

> "it is not the function of the Hearing Officer to express an opinion on the question the subject of the original request."

It was suggested that these two principles also apply to any appeal from a part of the original Opinion that is not set aside by the hearing officer at the end of the review.

It is to be remembered that "conclusions" under s.74A are not binding for any purpose, thereby limiting the basis on which any review under s.74B could be said to succeed. Nevertheless a number of patentees have used the review procedure following unfavourable conclusions under s.74A, see §74B.19.

—Limitation on Availability of Review

74B.10 Rules 98(2) and 98(5) give effect to subs.(2)(b). Rule 98(2) specifies that a review may not be brought (and if brought not continued) if the issue raised by the review has been decided in other relevant proceedings (i.e. before the Comptroller, court or EPO). Furthermore under r.98(4) the applicant must advise the UK-IPO of any relevant proceedings which may be relevant to bringing or continuation of the review proceedings. However, in contrast to the Opinion procedure (see r.94(1)(a) reprinted at §74A.04, above and the commentary in §74A.18) there appears to be no provision for the refusal of an application for review unless the issue raised by the review "has been decided" in other relevant proceedings. Therefore it would seem that, in principle at least, the patentee may seek a review of an Opinion even when proceedings have been commenced and are still pending at the time the application is made and during the review proceedings.

—Review to be Treated as Proceedings under sections 61(1)(c) or (e), 71(1) or 72(1)(a)

Under subs.(2)(c) provision may be made in the rules, in prescribed circumstances, for **74B.11** a review to be treated for prescribed purposes as if they were proceedings under these provisions of the Act, i.e. for the patentee to claim for damages in respect of the infringement (s.61(1)(c)); for a declaration that the patent is valid and infringed (s.61(e)); for the Comptroller to give a declaration of non-infringement (s.71(1)); and to revoke the patent on the ground that it is not a patentable invention (s.72(1)(a)).

However, neither the Patent Rules 1995 (as amended) nor the Patent Rules 2007 have made any provision under this subsection. At para.40 of the consultation paper "The Patents Act 2004: Patent Office Opinions and other changes to the Patent Rules", it is explained that the view of the UK-IPO is that review proceedings should be restricted to setting aside an Opinion or leaving it to stand; and furthermore, that it would not be appropriate for a review of this kind to go on to revoke the patent or make an award of damages for infringement. Since the review proceedings are wholly concerned with whether or not a non-binding opinion should be set aside, it is important that no party is estopped from arguing the points considered in the review proceedings during later proceedings for revocation, infringement or non-infringement.

Section 74(8) has been amended to make it clear that proceedings for a review under s.74B of an opinion given under s.74A are not, as such, to be regarded as proceedings in which the validity of a patent is put in issue. Accordingly, questions of validity may be considered in the context of such review, notwithstanding the exclusive list of proceedings in which the validity of a patent may be put in issue which is laid down by s.74(1) and (2). However, that would not prevent the validity of the patent from being regarded as put in issue where (by virtue of any rules made under s.74B(2)(c)) proceedings on a review might come to be treated as proceedings under ss.61(1)(c) or (e), 71(1) or 72(1)(a)).

—Right of Appeal

Subsection (2)(d) provides for there to be a right of appeal against a decision made on **74B.12** review, but only in prescribed cases. Under r.100(3) that case is where the appeal relates to a part of the Opinion that is not set aside by the hearing officer at the end of the proceedings on review.

While there is normally an automatic right of appeal from a decision of the Comptroller, s.97(4) removes the right in specific instances. Rule 100 effectively adds to these instances by prohibiting any appeal against a decision under s.74B which sets aside an opinion under r.100(1)(a); however, an appeal is possible in respect of a portion of the Opinion which was not set aside by the review proceedings. Appeals are brought before the Patents Court in the same way as any appeal from a decision made by the Comptroller is brought under s.97.

The issue of right of appeal was considered in *Re DLP Ltd* [2008] R.P.C. 11; [2007] EWHC 2669 Pat Ct, and in particular whether an appeal against a decision on review is of the type with which the court should refuse to deal because it can only result in the production of a non-binding opinion (see the commentary under §74A.09 and §74A.18). It was decided that the court should entertain appeals from a decision on review, firstly because the Act and Rules expressly provide for an appeal as of right against an unfavourable decision on review, and secondly because the decision involves a "living issue" namely whether the Opinion reached the wrong conclusion.

—Procedure

The procedure in review proceedings is governed by r.99. The initial procedure **74B.13** provided by r.99(1) and r.99(4) is broadly similar to the Opinions procedure: once the application is received, the UK-IPO send a copy of the application to the requester (if the requester is not the patentee) and any person who filed observations under r.96. After that, any person may file a statement in support of the application or a counter-statement contesting it. Any statement or counter-statement must be filed within four weeks of the date of advertisement of the application or two months from the date of issue of the Opinion, whichever is later. On filing a statement or counterstatement that person becomes a party to the proceedings (with a risk of an award of costs against them, discussed below).

After that, the UK-IPO must give the parties an opportunity to be heard (r.80(4) implemented in review proceedings by r.99(6)). However, the *Opinions Manual* makes it clear that, after the initial rounds provided under r.99, the Comptroller has "wide discretion" to direct subsequent procedure as he sees fit. At this stage it is possible, both in inter partes matters and ex parte matters, for a decision to be made on the papers. Indeed, according to the *Opinions Manual*, most parties have been content for a decision to be made on the basis of the application and any counterstatement.

The wide discretion available to the Comptroller to direct subsequent procedure is provided by r.99(6), which states that Pts 4 and 5 of Sch.3 apply to the proceedings for a review. These parts specify that the following rules apply to the review procedure:

- rule 74 (overriding objective)

- rule 79 (copies of documents)

- rule 80(2) to (6) (evidence and the hearing)

- rule 81 (alteration of time limits)

- rule 82 (general powers of the Comptroller in relation to proceedings before him)

- rule 83 (striking out a statement of case and summary judgment)

- rule 84 (hearings in public)

- rule 85 (security for costs or expenses)

- rule 86 (powers of Comptroller to compel attendance of witness and production of documents)

- rule 87 (evidence in proceedings before the Comptroller)

- rule 88 (proceedings in Scotland)

At the end of the review proceedings the Comptroller either sets aside the Opinion in whole or in part, or decides that no reason has been shown for the Opinion to be set aside.

—Evidence in Review Proceedings

74B.14 Under r.80(2) the Comptroller has the power to admit new evidence at any time from any party to the proceedings.

However, according to the decision in *Re DLP Ltd* [2008] R.P.C. 11; [2007] EWHC 2669 Pat Ct the purpose of a review is not to provide a re-hearing or a second opinion. In BL O/053/08 the hearing officer, applying the ratio decidendi of DLP, refused to consider additional witness statements since "such evidence has no part in a review" of this type. Therefore despite the hearing officer's powers under r.80(2), it would appear that the only kind of evidence that will be considered in review proceedings is that which supports the position that the Examiner made an error of principle or was clearly wrong in the Opinion.

—Withdrawal of Request for Review

74B.15 The applicant may withdraw a request for a review at any time. In BL O/007/07 the applicant withdrew the request before a substantive hearing to address the issue of admissibility of new evidence to the review proceedings, but after the observer had incurred expenses in the pre-Hearing submissions. The hearing officer therefore awarded the observer costs on the standard scale.

—Costs

Rule 98 refers to "proceedings" for review and according to *Frank Cunningham v Nokia Corp* BL O/183/07 (review of Opinion 11/06) hearing officers will treat the review process as proceedings before the Comptroller. Therefore hearing officers will follow the standard procedure when considering the issue of costs. However, the costs to be considered are those relating to the review proceedings only and do not include costs incurred during the Opinion process under s.74A. Accordingly, the behaviour of the parties up to the start of the review process is not relevant to the issue of costs.

74B.16

Costs are usually awarded on the standard published scale (see Ch.5 of the *Hearings Manual*). However, the *Hearings Manual* also makes it clear that hearing officers have the power to award costs off the standard scale where the circumstances warrant it, and the hearing officer reminded the parties about this in BL O/115/07.

—Decisions under section 74B

In BL O/183/07 (a review of Opinion 11/06) the hearing officer decided that claim 1 had been interpreted slightly too broadly. In any event, this did not affect the conclusion that claim 1 was not infringed. The hearing officer's decision was subsequently upheld by the Patents Court in *Frank Cunningham v Nokia Corp* [2008] EWHC 1174 Ch.

74B.17

In BL O/115/07 (a review of Opinion 14/06) the hearing officer found that two particular features of claim 1 had been interpreted too narrowly, but that another feature had been interpreted correctly. Nevertheless, this change in interpretation did not alter the conclusion that there was no infringement under s.60(2). This decision was upheld on appeal (*Re DLP Ltd*; [2008] R.P.C. 11; [2007] EWHC 2669 Pat Ct).

In BL O/200/07 (a review of Opinions 15/06, 16/06 and 17/06) the hearing officer decided that the Examiner had interpreted claim 1 too broadly in the three Opinions, and therefore wrongly concluded that it was invalid in light of a particular piece of prior art.

—Appeal to Patents Court

Rule 100(3) provides that there is no right of appeal under s.97 against a decision on review, except where the appeal relates to a part of the decision that is not set aside.

74B.18

At the time of writing, only two decisions under s.74B have been appealed to the Patents Court: *Re DLP Ltd* [2008] R.P.C. 11; [2007] EWHC 2669 Pat Ct; BL O/115/07; and *Frank Cunningham v Nokia Corp* [2008] EWHC 1174 Ch; BL O/183/07. As discussed above, *DLP* has set the scope of review proceedings and any appeal. The court explained that in any particular request under s.74A two Examiners are quite likely to give two different opinions, but that fact does not make one of them wrong. Similarly, in review proceedings a hearing officer may give an opinion with which the court might not agree. But this simply represents the range of different views within which reasonable people can differ. Accordingly, for an applicant for review or an appellant before the Patents Court to be successful, it is not sufficient merely to show that there is a better alternative opinion falling within the range of opinions of the reasonable person. The applicant/appellant must show that the Examiner or the hearing officer has made an error of principle or has reached a conclusion that is clearly wrong. This appears to be quite a significant hurdle in view of the well-established principles of assessing claim construction, validity and infringement (see §74B.19, below).

Effect of the section

At the time of going to press, 20 applications for review have been filed; of these, two had been withdrawn. Of the remaining 18 issued, two went to appeal, as mentioned at §74B.18, above. There were two decisions outstanding, and of the remainder, two made decisions to set aside part of the Opinion and nine upheld the respective Opinion in full. However, only one of the decisions on review has been made since the judgment in *DLP* (above).

74B.19

The test set down in *DLP* sets what appears to be a difficult hurdle for patentees to overcome in order to have set aside an unfavourable Opinion or a decision on review.

Since the Examiners who review requests under s.74A are experienced senior Examiners it may be unlikely that there will be many cases where an Opinion is given that "makes an error of principle" or is "clearly wrong".

PRACTICE UNDER SECTION 74B

Seeking review of opinion under section 74A (rr.98–100)

74B.20   The procedure for seeking review of an Opinion given under s.74A is closely similar to the procedure for seeking such an Opinion, as discussed in §74A.26, above. The application is made on PF 2 which requires payment of a fee. The application must be made within three months from the date the Opinion is issued, a period which is extensible with discretion exercised under r.108(1), but which will probably be granted only in "wholly exceptional circumstances", see §74A.33. A review may only be requested for the reasons discussed in §74B.05, above.

PF 2 must be accompanied by a statement, in duplicate, setting out fully the grounds on which a review is sought (r.98(3)). It must include particulars of any proceedings of which the applicant is aware which may be relevant to the question whether the review proceedings may be brought or continued (r.98(4)).

Upon receipt of an application for review, the Comptroller sends a copy of the form and statement to the requester (if different from the review applicant) and to all persons who filed observations (under r.99) in the procedure under s.74A. The application is also advertised on the UK-IPO website.

Responding to notification of a request for review of an opinion under section 74A (r.99)

74B.21   The application for review may be supported or contested (by a statement or counter statement as the case may be) filed by "any person" (r.99(3)), i.e. presumably even by a person who was not involved in the proceedings under s.74A. Any such statement or counter-statement (as the case may be) must be filed not later than (a) four weeks from the advertisement of the review application or (b) two months beginning with the date of issue of the Opinion, whichever should be the later date (r.99(4)). These periods appear to be extensible under the same powers as indicated in r.98(1) for the making of the review application (as discussed in §74B.20), but again "wholly exceptional" reasons may have to be shown to obtain such an extension. The Comptroller then sends to the other parties a copy of such statement or counter-statement, after which the procedure is governed by such directions as the Comptroller thinks fit (r.99(5) and (6)).

Although not specifically stated in s.74B, or rr.98–100, the outcome of the review appears on the UK-IPO website and is entered in the register.

General provisions as to amendment of patents and applications [Sections 75–76A]

SECTION 75

Amendment of patent in infringement or revocation proceedings

75.01   **75.**—(1) In any proceedings before the court or the comptroller in which the validity of a patent **may be** [*is*] put in issue the court or, as the case may be, the comptroller may, subject to section 76 below, allow the proprietor of the patent to amend the specification of the patent in such manner, and subject to such terms as to advertising the proposed amendment and as to costs, expenses or otherwise, as the court or comptroller thinks fit.

(2) A person may give notice to the court or the comptroller of his opposition to an amendment proposed by the proprietor of the patent under this section, and

if he does so the court or the comptroller shall notify the proprietor and consider the opposition in deciding whether the amendment or any amendment should be allowed.

(3) An amendment of a specification of a patent under this section shall have effect and be deemed always to have had effect from the grant of the patent.

(4) Where an application for an order under this section is made to the court, the applicant shall notify the comptroller, who shall be entitled to appear and be heard and shall appear if so directed by the court.

(5) In considering whether or not to allow an amendment proposed under this section, the court or the comptroller shall have regard to any relevant principles applicable under the European Patent Convention.

Note. Subsection (1) was amended by the Patents Act 2004 (c.16) Sch.2 para.19, with effect from January 1, 2005, except in relation to proceedings brought before that date (SI 2004/3205, arts 2(f)(k) and 9(4)). Subsection (5) was added by the Patents Act 2004 (c.16) s.2(5) with effect from December 13, 2007.

RELEVANT RULE—RULE 35

Rule 35—Amendment of specification after grant

75.02

Note. Rule 35 is reprinted at §27.02.

COMMENTARY ON SECTION 75

Scope of the section

Section 75 is the third of the three sections relating to the amendment of specifications: s.19 relates to amendment before grant; and ss.27 and 75 to amendment after grant, including amendment of specifications of European patents (UK) (s.77(1)). Section 75 provides for amendment during proceedings before the court or the Comptroller in which validity of a patent "may be put in issue". The words "may be" were introduced by the Patents Act 2004 in substitution for the word "is". This addressed a possible lacuna that may have prevented amendment of a patent by the court or the Comptroller during proceedings in which validity could be, but had not been, put in issue, s.27 being available only in the absence of invalidity proceedings before the court or Comptroller.

75.03

By s.74(1), validity may be put in issue in proceedings under any of ss.58, 61, or ss.69–72, see further §27.04. Otherwise, when no such proceedings are in being, as discussed in §75.04, amendment may be made following application to the Comptroller under s.27 without notice to others. In addition to amendment under ss.19, 27 or 75, amendment may also be allowed in proceedings before the Comptroller under s.73 (for which see §73.05), as well as in opposition and limitation proceedings before the EPO, see §27.03. "Amendment" should not be confused with "correction" under s.117, see the commentary on that section.

The "court" may be the Patents Court, a Patents County Court, the Court of Session in Scotland, the High Court of Northern Ireland or the High Court of Justice in the Isle of Man: see s.130 and §96.06, but the amendment must be sought during proceedings which are in being before that court.

A European patent may be amended in opposition (EPC arts 99–101) or limitation (EPC art 105A–105C) proceedings before the EPO, see §27.03 and 27.06. Section 130(5A) (discussed in §130.07) now states that references in the Act to amendment (whether under the Act or by the EPO) include limitation of the claims. Any amendment made to a European patent during opposition or limitation proceedings has automatic effect on the European patent (UK) (s.77(4)) and thus could have the effect of overriding any amendments made meanwhile to such a patent under any of ss.27, 73 or 75, thereby perhaps necessitating a further amendment application under one of these sections following the establishment of the amendments made in the EPO. However, amendments made during opposition proceedings before the EPO are established only when the opposition proceedings (including any appeals) are finally concluded. These points cause problems, as discussed in §75.04.

Applicability of section 75

75.04   The proceedings in which amendment may be sought under s.75 need not be revocation or infringement proceedings. They can be proceedings of any type as listed in s.74(1) specifying when validity may be put in issue, herein called "validity proceedings". These proceedings may be ones taking place before either the Comptroller or the court and, once such proceedings are pending, no amendment can be allowed under s.27. Section 63(3) further provides for directions as to amendment when validity has been put in issue and the patent has been found only partially valid: see §75.06.

The amendment of subs.(1) allows a proprietor to seek amendment under s.75 during the course of any proceedings in which it is possible to put validity in issue (under s.74(1)) and not merely when validity has actually been put in issue, thus dealing with the "lacuna" in the law identified in *Norling v Eez-Away* [1997] R.P.C. 160 caused by the split of jurisdiction as regards amendment between the courts and Comptroller imposed by ss.27 and 75. That may have prevented amendment of a patent by the court or the Comptroller during proceedings in which validity could have, but had not in fact, been put in issue. This wording appeared to make amendment depend upon validity being actually "in issue", while s.27(2) appears to operate to preclude amendment under s.27 while proceedings are pending in which validity "may be" put in issue, whether or not validity has actually been put in issue in a given case. The amendment to s.75(1) deals with this point and renders discussion of when validity is deemed actually to be in issue in proceedings under s.75 unnecessary.

Section 75 would still seem to be applicable if an application to amend is made during the course of "validity proceedings", but these are concluded without disposing of the application to amend (*Congoleum v Armstrong Cork* [1977] R.P.C. 77).

See §27.11 for further discussions of the circumstances in which the Comptroller will stay amendment proceedings under s.27 when validity proceedings are pending.

The court can order amendment under s.63(3), even if all issues in the proceedings have been determined, but here there must first be a finding of partial invalidity, see §63.02.

It has been stated that, where the parties have in effect settled their dispute, amendment of a patent-in-suit should only be permitted if: (1) the amendments are not substantial in amount or effect; (2) there is no apparent matter of controversy; and (3) no matter of public interest arises: otherwise, application should be made to the Comptroller under s.27 after final order in the court proceedings (*Imperial Chemical v Ram Bathrooms* [1994] F.S.R. 181). Where the court has made an order for revocation but has allowed a stay of this pending appeal or an application to amend, amendment under s.75 would seem to have been contemplated, even if an appeal is lodged and then withdrawn. Anyway, it is understood that the UK-IPO is likely to decline jurisdiction under s.27 in such a circumstance.

In the case of a European patent (UK) which is under opposition in the EPO and the patentee desires to seek amendments in those proceedings, an action for infringement cannot be validly commenced or pursued unless the desired amendments are sought also in parallel under s.75. Thus, in *Petrolite v Dyno* [1998] F.S.R. 190, where the patentee did not intend to contest an invalidating prior user, it was held that summary judgment for the defendant in the infringement proceedings was justified, unless an application to amend was promptly made, see §61.06.

In *Henry Bros. v Ministry of Defence* [1997] R.P.C. 693; and [1999] R.P.C. 442, it was left open whether a co-proprietor may seek amendment without the consent of other co-proprietors, but it would seem unjust to these other persons if this could be done, at least unless the other co-proprietor(s) are parties to the proceedings, on which see also §66.02.

Limitations on amendment

Amendments under s.75 are subject to the severe restrictions of s.76. Thus no amend- **75.05**
ment is to be allowed which (a) results in the specification disclosing additional matter or
(b) which extends the protection conferred by the patent, see the commentary on s.76. If
any amendment is nevertheless made under s.75 which does contravene these restrictions,
a basis then arises for subsequent revocation of the patent under s.72(1)(d) or (e), see
§72.25 and §72.26. An application for revocation on such a ground may be made by
anyone, even if not a party to the proceedings in which the amendment was made.

Discretion

"May allow" in the words of subs.(1) conferring the power to allow amendment, means **75.06**
that this power is discretionary, as were earlier powers to allow amendment under previous United Kingdom patent legislation. However, since the introduction in December
2007 of ss.27(6) and 75(5), the latter of which states that:

"In considering whether or not to allow an amendment proposed under this section, the
court or the comptroller shall have regard to any relevant principles applicable under
the European Patent Convention".

The scope for exercise of discretion has become limited and considerations of delay,
covetous claiming and the patentee's conduct generally are no longer to be considered
relevant. These matters will therefore not be discussed in detail here, although a full commentary on them is contained in the 5th edition of this Work and its 5th Cumulative
Supplement, in the paragraphs relating to s.27 in particular.

The effect of s.75(5) on discretion was considered by Floyd J. in *Zipher Ltd v Markem
Systems Ltd* [2008] EWHC 1379 Pat Ct at [197] to [227]. After discussing the development of the law from *Smith Kline & French v Evans Medical* [1989] 1 F.S.R. 561 and
Kimberley-Clark v Procter & Gamble [2000] R.P.C. 422 and then considering the law and
practice under the EPC, including the effect of arts 105a and 105b, Floyd J. concluded at
para.[219]:

"It follows that if I am to have regard to the principles applicable under the EPC, the
discretion which I have to refuse amendments which comply with the Act has been
limited. Considerations such as those formerly considered relevant to discretion, such
as the conduct of the patentee, are no longer relevant".

Counsel for Markem (opposing the amendment) submitted that this had gone too far,
drawing attention to what the legislature had not done, i.e. changing "may" to "shall" in
the Act, and asking what would happen if the application to amend were an abuse of right.
Floyd J. rejected the first of these points, saying only that it would have been "a much
shorter route to the same objective" if "may" had indeed been changed to "shall". The
second point he answered by saying that the party whose right was abused would be able
to restrain the abuse by enforcement of his right, not by reliance on discretion, and that, if
the application to amend were an abuse of the process of the court, the court would not allow it to be made at all. Indeed, in the later case of *Nokia GmbH v IPCom GmbH* [2010]
EWHC 789 Pat Ct, Floyd J., referring to the Court of Appeal in *Nikken v Pioneer Trading
Co* [2005] EWCA Civ 906, refused a post-trial application for amendment on the basis
that the timing of the application was an abuse of the process of the court.

Subsequent to the judgment in *Zipher v Markem*, the MOPP was amended to include a
new para.75.21.1 which refers to Floyd J.'s following summary of the position under the
EPC:

"(i) in opposition proceedings, appropriateness of the amendments to the proceedings, their necessity and procedural fairness are the main, perhaps only, factors considered relevant to the
discretion to allow amendment;

(ii) in central amendment proceedings, compliance with the procedural requirements gives rise to
a right to have the patent limited in accordance with the request.

(iii) These are therefore the factors which should be taken into account when considering whether or not to allow an amendment [under s75]".

Vector v Glatt [2007] EWCA Civ 805 is a further case in which a post-trial application for amendment was considered and declined. Here Jacob L.J. stated that the *Nikken v Pioneer* "rule" is proper for the conduct of patent disputes and suggested that its having no parallel in the EPO is a reason why delays occur in the EPO.

As for the possible relevance of amendment to the operation of ss.62(3), 63(2), 58(6) and 58(8) with regard to the assessment of damages for infringement and compensation for Crown user, see §27.15 above.

Delay in seeking amendment in court proceedings can arise when the proprietor chooses first to try and support his claims, especially on appeal, and when he fails, then applies to amend. In *Raleigh v Miller* (1948) 65 R.P.C. 141 HL, the grounds on which claims were found invalid had become apparent at an early stage before a lower court, but the patentee had elected to attempt to support them through to a final judgment. A subsequent application to amend was refused: see *Raleigh v Miller* (1950) 67 R.P.C. 226 HL, on the basis that the patentee having failed to enforce his rights, and having persisted too long in the circumstances with his original claims, he should in the court's discretion receive no further chance. In *Windsurfing v Tabur Marine* [1985] R.P.C. 59 CA, leave to amend was refused because the patentee had not sought by his pleadings to support a claim to monopoly on some alternative basis and adduce appropriate evidence for this purpose at the trial. Moreover, the effect of the proposed amendment was to elevate to the status of an essential component the one feature of the allegedly inventive combination previously described in terms which made it entirely clear that it was non-essential, and this was putting forward substantially a different concept. Leave to amend was also refused in *Procter & Gamble v Peaudouce* [1989] 1 F.S.R. 614 because no attempt had been made during the trial and appeal to put forward an alternative plea involving amendment, see also *Lubrizol v Esso* [1998] R.P.C. 727 CA. It is not yet clear whether considerations of this kind will continue to apply in the post-2077 regime.

A distinction has been drawn between an amendment designed to validate an invalid claim (as in the cases cited above) and an amendment designed to assist in the enforcement of a valid claim, especially in cases where the court exercises its power under current s.63(3), as it usually does, to direct amendment under s.75 of a specification held by the court to be only partially valid. Thus, in *Van der Lely v Bamfords* [1964] R.P.C. 54 CA, the patentee was permitted to make amendments by mere excision of invalid claims (with minimum consequential amendment). A similar line was followed in *Bentley Engineering's Patent* [1981] R.P.C. 361, where simple excision of claims 1–3 was allowed, but a recasting amendment was disallowed having regard to the patentees' conduct in asserting the patent in unamended form and their failure to justify their conduct by clear explanation. However, in *Palmaz's European Patents* [1999] R.P.C. 47, discussed by M. Burton and Joanne Green [1999] E.I.P.R. 98, it was questioned whether, under the 1977 Act, a validating amendment by revision of claim wording should be considered as being in a different category from amendment by mere deletion of claims, as cases under previous statutes had done, amendment by simple excision of a claim or claims having been held to be allowable in circumstances where more extensive or textual amendment would probably have been refused.

In *Chiron v Organon Teknika (No.5)* [1994] F.S.R. 258 and on appeal (*Chiron v Organon Teknika (No.11)* [1995] F.S.R. 589 CA), the patentee sought to delete two claims found invalid in proceedings in which the main claim had been upheld despite its alleged undue width (for which see §14.39). The defendants sought in these amendment proceedings to raise the plea of undue width of the claims held valid, but these were struck out, it not being "relevant or right to consider matters which have no nexus with the amendment nor with the cause for the amendment". It was also noted that this view seemed to accord with the view of the EPO as regards amendment in EPC opposition proceedings, though s.75 does not have to be construed in accordance with the EPC as it is not listed in s.130(7).

There is no power to "order" amendment, nor does a patentee "pursue" claims, it can only "defend" them: thus, patentees and opponents to amendment cannot, by agreement, exclude the public interest as to whether an application to amend should, or should not, be allowed: there must always be evidence upon which a decision can be taken whether discretion to permit amendment should be exercised in a particular case, see *Coal Industry's Patent* [1994] R.P.C. 661 where, after these remarks, the amendment application was withdrawn. These comments must however now be read in the light of the changes in practice brought about by the introduction of s.75(5): see §75.06 and §27.05. In *Ancare's Patent [New Zealand]* [2001] R.P.C. 20 at 335 it was held by the Court of Appeal of New Zealand that the possibilityof amendment in revocation proceedings did not permit the validity of the patent to be supported in alternative versions, according to amendments requested before and after trial. That was inconsistent with the requirement for the invention to be clearly defined and the need for competitors to know the scope of the monopoly. The patentee should therefore have submitted all amendments sought before trial.

In *Kirin-Amgen's Patent* [2002] R.P.C. 43 at 851 the court confirmed that "deleting" amendments to claims would normally be permitted, i.e. where there are claims which would be valid in the absence of the invalidity which has been established, but that delay should be taken into account and "any patentee who delays does so at his own risk": conditions might therefore be imposed on the amendment.

In *Merck's [Alendronate] Patents* [2004] F.S.R. 16 at 330, amendments put forward 15 days before an appeal to the Court of Appeal was to be heard were refused by the Court of Appeal on discretion as a result of their timing and also as adding matter (by deletion) unders.76(3)(a).

In *Secretary of State v Frontline Technology* [2005] EWHC 37 Ch, noted I.P.D. 28040, the Patents Court refused, on grounds of discretion and/or abuse of process, to allow amendment to a claim which was intermediate in scope between claims held at trial to be invalid and a claim held to be valid. The court did not, however, consider that the patentee was estopped from putting forward the amendments proposed, whether as a cause of action estoppel or an issue estoppel. However, in *Nikken Kosakusho v Pioneer Trading* [2006] F.S.R. 41 at [4], the Court of Appeal unanimously upheld the judgment of the Patents Court (see [2005] F.S.R. 15 at 259) to exercise its discretion to refuse amendments following a finding of invalidity against all the claims of the patent. The reasons given for refusal were threefold: (1) the application of the principle in *Henderson v Henderson* (1843) 3 Hare 100 that the doctrine of res judicata applies not only to points raised in the earlier litigation but also to points which could have been, but which were not then, put forward only because the party has, from negligence, inadvertence, or even accident, omitted to do so; (2) the fact that the amendments requested would lead, in effect, to a second trial (as had been recognised in the *Windsurfing* and *Lubrizol* cases referred to above); and (3) the CPR was "dead against" such a procedure.

Imposition of conditions

75.07

Subsection (1) appends to the power of the court or the Comptroller to allow amendments the further power to make such conditions "as to advertising", "costs, expenses or otherwise" as are thought fit. It may be that "otherwise" extends no further than permitting a requirement to give notice to the public or ordering provision for costs of opponents or others involved in the proceedings, and that this power to make conditions is more limited than the Comptroller's power, expressed without qualification in s.27, to impose conditions when amendments are made in that jurisdiction, for which see §27.16. Nevertheless, "other" conditions for permitting amendment could possibly be imposed, though occasion may seldom arise, in the exercise of general discretion.

Thus, in a number of amendment cases, most of them arising under earlier statutes, conditions have been considered or imposed to protect in certain circumstances third parties from infringement action under an amended patent. In *Dorr's Application* (1942) 59 R.P.C. 113, the court prohibited the applicant from bringing action in respect of machines begun to be manufactured before the application for leave to amend: the manufacturers in that case had been advised that they did not infringe the unamended claim; prima facie it had been restricted to a drum, and amendment had been allowed on the basis that in the light of the description "drum" was used to include various equivalents. However, conditions were not imposed in *General Tire (Frost's) Patent* [1972] R.P.C. 259; and [1974] R.P.C. 207, nor in *Wilkinson Sword v Gillette* [1975] R.P.C. 101. The *General Tire* case was somewhat analogous to *Dorr's* case, but the Court of Appeal noted that there was no evidence that anyone had infringed the amended claim in reliance on a belief that the original claim was more limited, and that despite allegations of widespread infringement there was only one opponent to the application to amend. In the *Wilkinson* case, the court said that adequate protection would normally be provided under what is now s.62(3).

In *Hallen v Brabantia* [1990] F.S.R. 134, the defendant applied unsuccessfully for the imposition of terms as a condition for allowing amendment of, or relief on, a partially valid patent, and from this case it appears that in order to succeed in obtaining the imposition of such terms, such a defendant must establish that he received reasonable advice (a) that the patent was not infringed or was invalid; (b) that he acted on this advice to his detriment; and (c) that the advice was in some way based on the defect to be cured by the amendment. In *Autoliv Development's Patent* [1988] R.P.C. 425, an attempt to impose conditions using a different approach based on consideration of the perceived merits of the invention was disapproved by the court on appeal (as discussed in §27.16).

For other comments on amendment subject to conditions see §58.05 and §62.05.

Opposition (subs.(2))

75.08   Subsection (2) provides for opposition, with provision for the proprietor to be notified of the opposition and for this to be considered before decision is made on the application to amend, see §§75.11, 75.13 and 75.14. Where the application to amend is made in proceedings before the Comptroller and is advertised, such opposition is governed generally by Pt 7 of the Patents Rules 2007, as discussed in §27.13. The procedure for opposition in proceedings before the court is discussed in §75.11. An opponent does not have to show an interest in the patent and can be an agent for an undisclosed principal, see §27.13.

Effect of amendment (subs.(3))

75.09   By subs.(3), an amendment once allowed is considered to have had effect from the grant of the patent, see the discussion in §27.15 of the similar provision in s.27, and §62.05 for discussion of the effect of allowance of an amendment on the award of damages for infringements committed before amendment. Where a patent claim had been found valid and infringed, but the patentee sought to amend that claim before obtaining relief upon it, it was held that there should be no injunction or damages as there had been no adjudication on either the validity or infringement of the amended claim which now stood (under subs.(3)) as if always present (*PLG Research v Ardon (No.2)* [1993] F.S.R. 698).

Notice of application made to the court (subs.(4))

75.10   Subsection (4) requires that, where application is made to the court under s.75, notice of the application for an order is to be given to the Comptroller, see §75.11. The Comptroller is also given the right to be heard if he wishes, and the court can order him to appear if the court so desires. However, the Comptroller does not normally take an active part in the court proceedings, leaving the parties thereto to raise all appropriate objections, but the UK-IPO will from time to time enquire about progress of the proceedings, and the Comptroller normally requires to be notified of the date of the hearing of the amendment application, though he rarely exercises his right to be represented.

On receipt of a notice to amend, an entry is made in the register.

PRACTICE UNDER SECTION 75

Application to the court

75.11   The procedure for seeking amendment before the Patents Court under s.75 is governed by CPR 63.10 and CPR 63 PD 10 (reprinted in Appendix F at §F63.10 and §F63PD.10).

CPR 63.10(1) requires that the application is by means of an application notice which must give particulars of the proposed amendment and the grounds upon which it is sought and state whether the applicant will contend that the claims prior to amendment are valid. The notice must be served by the applicant on all parties and the Comptroller within seven days of its being filed. The application notice must, if it is reasonably possible, be served on the Comptroller electronically, complying with the requirements which apply in UK-IPO amendment proceedings (CPR 63 PD 63.10.1). Unless the court otherwise orders, the Comptroller will advertise the application to amend in the *Patents Journal*. The advertisement will state that any person may apply to the Comptroller for a copy of the application notice).

Within 14 days of the first appearance of the advertisement, any person who wishes to oppose the application must file and serve on all parties and the Comptroller a notice opposing the application which must include the grounds relied on (CPR 63.10(6)). Within 28 days of the first appearance of the advertisement the applicant must apply to the court for directions (CPR 63.10(7)). Unless the court otherwise orders, the applicant must within seven days serve on the Comptroller any order of the court on the application (CPR 63.10(8)).

By CPR 63 PD 63.10.1, not later than two days before the first hearing date of the application for directions, the applicant, the Comptroller, the parties to the proceedings and any other opponent, must serve a document stating the directions sought.

Generally, the Comptroller has no active involvement in the proceedings and his role does not extend beyond what is stated above and referred to in §75.10, above. In particular, participation by the Comptroller) is now governed by CPR 63.14 and 63.15: CPR 63.14 sets out the documents which must be served on the Comptroller; CPR 63.15 states that the Comptroller (a) may take part in the proceedings and (b) need not serve a defence or other statement of case unless the court orders otherwise.

An amendment is occasionally allowed by the court in the course of contested proceedings. This then becomes the subject of a special order permitting subsequent opposition to be made (for an example, see O.J. July 13, 1988, p.2069). However, where an amendment was sought after a decision of partial invalidity, and where all likely opponents were already before the court, dispensation against advertisement of the proposed amendment was given (*Chiron v Organon Teknika* BL C/63/93).

A common form of the directions order provides for the parties successively to exchange: (1) evidence in support of the amendments, together with disclosure of relevant documents; (2) evidence in support of the opposition, together with disclosure of relevant documents by the opponent; (3) evidence in reply by the applicant; (4) directions that there be liberty to cross-examine witnesses at the hearing on their written evidence; and (5) for that hearing to come before the court either immediately before, or at the same time as, the substantive hearing of the pending proceedings. However, a person who has given evidence in the amendment proceedings, and who is called for cross-examination on that evidence, will not necessarily be exposed to cross-examination on issues related solely to the substantive nature of the remainder of the proceedings in which amendment is being sought (*Du Pont v Enka* [1986] R.P.C. 417).

The procedure is flexible and it will be adapted by the court to fit particular circumstances. Thus, in *Farmhand v Spadework* [1974] F.S.R. 425, the application to amend was made only shortly before the trial of an infringement action; the action was ordered to proceed on the basis of the specification as notionally amended, with the question of amendment being stood over for decision later. On the other hand, where an application was made too late for it to be advertised before the fixed hearing date, the hearing of a revocation petition proceeded with theputative amendment being ignored (*Xyllyx Viewdata's Patent* BL C/10/92). Advertisement may be dispensed with if all likely objectors can be individually notified (*Henry Bros. v Ministry of Defence* [1997] R.P.C. 693).

In *Swintex v Melba Products* [2001] F.S.R. 4 infringement proceedings were settled, subject to an application for amendment which was not contested by the defendant or by any other entity following advertisement. The Comptroller raised no objection to the amendments and, in those circumstances, the court saw no reason for requiring disclosure before exercising discretion to allow the requested amendments which were seen to be allowable.

Where proposed amendments have been advertised, the patentee will probably not be allowed to resile from them, but where the eventual amendments are more extensive than those advertised, re-advertisement will probably not be necessary (*Quantel v Spaceward Microsystems* [1990] R.P.C. 83). Also, pending determination of an amendment application to the court, a patentee will normally have to undertake not to threaten or institute any further proceedings under the patent, see *Quantel v Electronic Graphics* [1990] R.P.C. 272.

In Scotland, the procedure for amendment of a patent in the course of infringement or revocation proceedings is set out in r.55.5 of the Rules of the Court of Session (SI 1994/1443, for which see §98.19). This rule broadly follows the English equivalent procedure, but the time limits specified in it for the various stages of the procedure need to be carefully noted and observed. In *Akzo NV's and Akzo Nobel NV's (Tibolone) Patents* [2006] CSOH 146, the Court of Session held that a contingent application to amend the patent at proof [trial] only if the original claims were invalidated was competent in theory. However, the motion to amend was refused at proof on the grounds that consideration of the proposed amendments would raise a number of issues not covered by the existing dispute and Akzo's opponents could not reasonably be expected to address these issues in the relatively short period between the motion to amend and the proof.

Where amendment had already been sought under s.27 and court proceedings for infringement were subsequently commenced, it was thought prudent in *Demel v Jefferson* [1999] F.S.R. 204 to make a further application and re-advertise the amendments sought under s.75.

Allowance of amendment by the court

75.12   CPR 63.10(8) stipulates that, unless the court otherwise orders, the applicant for amendment must within seven days serve on the Comptroller any order of the court on the amendment application. Rule 35(6) requires that, when so required, by the Comptroller, the proprietor must provide an amended specification conforming to the formal and other requirements of Sch.2 to the Patents Rules 2007. As specifications are published by reproduction of a text supplied by the proprietor, such a request is normally to be expected.

If the court allows amendment of a European patent (UK) with an authentic text in the French or German language, no translation is required following the coming into force of the London Agreement of 2008 and s.77(6)(b) no longer being effective. Notice of an order made by the court under s.75 is inserted at least once in the *Patents Journal*. The amendment is, of course, also recorded in the register.

Applications to the Comptroller

75.13   Applications to the Comptroller are governed by r.35, reprinted in §27.02 above and discussed in §27.05. No form is required. Unlike the position under previous rules, it is now necessary to state the reasons for seeking amendment, just as in ex parte proceedings under s.27. Under the previous rules, it had been assumed that, with contested validity proceedings already in being, the amendments will be put forward to overcome the invalidity objections already raised, see *Osterman's Patent* [1985] R.P.C. 579. The provisions relating to electronic delivery also apply, as discussed in §27.05. Unlike previously, advertisement of the amendments proposed takes place in the *Patents Journal*, as required by r.75 since opposition is possible in accordance with Pt 2 of Sch.3 to the Rules. Opposition may be lodged within an inextensible (see Sch.4 Pt 1) term of two weeks (r.76(2)(a)). If and when amendment is permitted, the Comptroller can make it a precondition of amendment that a new specification be filed, complying with the relevant requirements (r.35(6), reprinted at §27.02). This rule also applies when a European patent (UK) is amended by the Comptroller under s.75.

The MOPP states that any application to amend under the section is recorded in the register and, in due course, the outcome of that application is also so recorded.

In *Clear Focus Imaging v Contra Vision* BL C/54/01, noted I.P.D. 25009, the court held that the issue of re-advertisement was a matter of discretion and did not affect an existing opponent who therefore had no interest in appealing this point. Unless the new amendment was one which would leave the claims significantly wider in scope than those originally proposed, it could not be said that anyone who had not opposed the original amendments could now wish to intervene.

Opposition before the Comptroller

After the advertisement in the *Patents Journal*, notice of opposition to the amendment may be lodged. Opposition proceedings are governed by Pt 7 of the Patents Rules 2007 (as amended in 2011), "Proceedings Heard Before The Comptroller" (rr.73 to 91) and require the filing of the relevant form (r.76(1)(a)) which is PF 15 (see r.76(3)(c) and the reference to s.75(2) in Pt 2 of Sch.3 to the Rules) and a statement of grounds (r.76(1)(b)). The opposition period is two weeks (r.76(2)(a)) running from the date of advertisement in the *Patents Journal* of the proposed amendment, see §27.13 and is inextensible (Sch.4 to the 2007 Rules Pt 1). **75.14**

The patentee should respond with a counterstatement in duplicate within a period specified under r.77(5) and believed usually to be six weeks. This period may be extended under r.81(1), even if it has already expired. The subsequent procedure is determined by Pt 7 of the 2007 Rules, of which r.80 relates to evidence rounds and the appointment of a hearing.

Where the patentee fails to file a counter-statement, he is taken under r.77(9) to support the opponent's case and the request for amendment is likely to be considered to have been withdrawn. Where an opponent files a statement of opposition, but then takes no further part in the proceedings, the Comptroller will consider the case on the papers and issue a formal decision whether amendment can be permitted, see *Minister of Agriculture's Patent* BL O/11/92 and *Le Maitre Fireworks' Patent* BL O/109/93.

Opposition is also permitted even if there has been no advertisement, see subs.(2), and §75.08. There then appears to be no time limit within which such opposition has to be filed because r.78(2) applies only where there has been an advertisement.

If an amendment has already been put forward during revocation proceedings before the Comptroller, the applicant for revocation may oppose the amendment in these proceedings without filing formal opposition on PF 15 (*Eickhoff Maschinenfabrik's Patent* BL O/31/87 and *Harding's Patent* BL O/94/90).

For further discussion of patent amendment during revocation proceedings before the Comptroller, see §72.26.

Costs in an opposition

Where an opponent to an application to amend brought before the court does not present a frivolous case, the practice has been to award him his costs at first instance even if the amendment is allowed (*Mullard v British Belmont* (1938) 55 R.P.C. 197 at 226, and (1939) 56 R.P.C. 1 at 22). This is because the patentee is seeking an indulgence from the court. However, the position can be different, as in *Aumac's Patent* BL C/52/96, noted I.P.D. 20007, where the patentee was entitled to receive costs upon accepting revocation under a *See v Scott Paine* order, for which see §61.35. **75.15**

Before the Comptroller, the normal order of a contribution to costs of the successful party (see §107.03) can be expected. It appears that, unlike previously, certain non-United Kingdom resident opponents can be required to give security for costs (see s.107(4) and r.85).

SECTION 76 [SUBSTITUTED]

Amendments of applications and patents not to include added matter

76.—(1) An application for a patent which— **76.01**

    (a) is made in respect of matter disclosed in an earlier application, or in the specification of a patent which has been granted, and

(b) discloses additional matter, that is, matter extending beyond that disclosed in the earlier application, as filed, or the application for the patent, as filed,

may be filed under section 8(3), 12 or 37(4) above, or as mentioned in section 15(9) above, but shall not be allowed to proceed unless it is amended so as to exclude the additional matter.

(1A) Where, in relation to an application for a patent

(a) a reference to an earlier relevant application has been filed as mentioned in section 15(1)(c)(ii) above; and

(b) the description filed under section 15(10)(b)(i) above discloses additional matter, that is, matter extending beyond that disclosed in the earlier relevant application,

the application shall not be allowed to proceed unless it is amended so as to exclude the additional matter.

(2) No amendment of an application for a patent shall be allowed under section 15A(6), 18(3) or 19(1) if it results in the application disclosing matter extending beyond that disclosed in the application as filed.

(3) No amendment of the specification of a patent shall be allowed under section 27(1), 73 or 75 if it—

(a) results in the specification disclosing additional matter, or

(b) extends the protection conferred by the patent

(4) In subsection (1A) above "relevant application" has the meaning given by section 5(5) above.

COMMENTARY ON SECTION 76

Scope of the section

76.02 Section 76 is concerned: with the permissible content of a new application which is a replacement or divisional application (subs.(1)); with impermissible amendment of applications (subs.(2)); and with impermissible amendment of granted patents (subs.(3)). Thus, although the headnote to the section refers only to amendment, the first subsection deals with the specification content for new filings which are based upon an earlier-filed specification. The present form of subs.(1) (apart from the substitution mentioned below brought about by the Regulatory Reform Order) came into effect from January 7, 1991. The reasons for the changes made then and their consequences are discussed in §76.03. Subsections (1A) and (4) were added by the Regulatory Reform Order (art.13) with effect from January 1, 2005 with the previous version of the section continuing to apply to patents and applications which were then "pending", for the definition of which term see §15.01, Note 1, above. At the same time the references to "section 15(9)" in subs.(1) and "section 15A(6)" in subs.(2) were substituted to reflect other changes brought about by the Regulatory Reform Order.

Subsection (1) limits the allowable content of new applications, i.e. "divisional applications" filed under s.15(9) and "replacement applications" filed under any of ss.8(3), 12(6) and 37(4) by a person granted leave to file such as a result of entitlement proceedings brought under any of ss.8, 12 and 37. If such a new application is filed which discloses additional matter, that is matter extending beyond that disclosed in the earlier case, the application will not be allowed to proceed unless amended to exclude the additional matter, as discussed in §76.03.

Because it is possible to initiate an application by filing a reference to a previous "relevant application" (as defined in s.5(5)), instead of filing a description, subss.(1A) and (4) provide that such an application is not to be allowed to proceed if it contains matter additional to that in the document used to initiate the application until that additional matter has been excluded from the description of the invention initially provided, all as discussed in §15.17, above.

Subsection (2) limits the allowable amendments to patent applications, i.e. amendments made in response to objections during prosecution (under s.15A(6) or s.18(3)), or by way of voluntary amendment under s.19(1). In a similar way to the limitation on the content of new applications as specified under subs.(1), such amendments are not permitted if they result in the application disclosing matter extending beyond that disclosed in the application as filed.

Subsection (3) is concerned with amendment of granted patents under: s.27(1) (amendment after grant); s.73 (amendment pursuant to power of Comptroller to revoke of his own initiative); or s.75 (amendment in the course of pending validity proceedings). This subsection, in subs.(3)(a), is similar to subss.(1) and (2) and forbids the amendment of granted patents which results in the specification disclosing additional subject-matter. Subsection (3)(b) adds for granted patents the further restriction that amendments after grant must not extend the protection conferred by the patent.

In the event that an amendment should be allowed which is contrary to any of subss.(1), (2) and (3)(a), or which is contrary to subs.(3)(b), a ground for revocation ensues under s.72(1)(d) or (e) respectively. Moreover, this may prove fatal to validity, perhaps without the possibility of curing the invalidity by further amendment, see §76.21.

The relationship of the section with the EPC is discussed in §76.04.

It is to be noted that s.76 is concerned with amendment. Correction is dealt with under s.117. The contrast between "correction" and "amendment" is discussed in §117.06.

The previous forms of section 76

76.03

The original version of s.76 was replaced with effect from January 7, 1991 by the version as set out in §76.01 (but without the amendments made by the Regulatory Reform Order). The principal change in 1991 concerned subs.(1) specifying that new applications may not contain additional matter. The original version of s.76 had specified that, if a new application disclosed "matter which extends beyond that disclosed in the earlier application as filed", then that application "shall not be allowed to be filed". This wording meant that, if the new application as filed did contain added matter, the application was forfeit, there being no possibility of saving this, see *Hydroacoustics' Application* [1981] F.S.R. 538. This came to be appreciated as an unduly harsh provision and, consequently, the form of subs.(1) prior to and after the Regulatory Reform Order amendments allows correction of the situation by providing that the new application "shall not be allowed to proceed unless it is amended to exclude the additional matter". Accordingly now, if a new application is filed containing additional matter, the application will be allowed to proceed when that additional matter is cancelled. The EPO much later came to essentially the same conclusion in the Enlarged Board of Appeal cases G 1/05 and G 1/06 [2006] *CIPA* 419.

The other changes in the wording in 1991 were essentially editorial. The 1991 changes were made with no transitional provisions but there was some rearrangement between the subsections which needs to be borne in mind if looking at decisions given under the previous wording, which is set out in the fifth edition of this Work.

Amendment under the EPC

76.04

Section 76 is not referred to in s.130(7) as a section intended to conform with the provisions of the EPC, CPC and PCT. However, if amendment is improperly allowed under s.76, a ground for revocation arises under s.72(1)(d) and/or (e) and these provisions are within s.130(7). Moreover, s.72 is listed in s.130(7) and, consequently, decisions of the EPO under EPC art.123 are relevant under s.76. Quite apart from s.130(7), s.91 requires judicial notice to be taken of the EPC and decisions made under it, as discussed in §91.03. In *B & R Relay's Application* [1985] R.P.C. 1, the Patents Court specifically indicated in relation to s.76 that an attempt should be made to give the same meaning to any provision of the Act as that given to relevant EPC provisions, whichever jurisdiction is being invoked. In *Flexible Directional Indicator's Application* [1994] R.P.C. 207, the Comptroller accepted that s.76 should be construed in conformity with art.123(2) and (3) of the EPC. That this is appropriate was re-iterated by the Patents Court in *Merrell Dow's Patent* BL C/89/96, noted I.P.D. 19111. Similar provisions to those of art.123(2) of the EPC are to be found in arts 28(2) and 41(2) of the PCT, subject in each case to a proviso that the provision can be overridden by national law.

Section 76(2) and (3) respectively correspond to art.123(2) and (3) of the EPC, which, after the amendments of the EPC 2000, read:

> **"EPC ARTICLE 123—Amendments**
>
>   (2) A European patent application or a European patent may not be amended in such a way that it contains subject-matter which extends beyond the content of the application as filed.
>
>   (3) The European patent may not be amended in such a way as to extend the protection conferred."

EPC 2000 amended para.(3) of art.123(3) of the EPC which previously specified that "the claims of" the European patent could not be amended "during opposition proceedings". The first amendment deals with the possibility afforded by the previous wording of allowing a protection-extending amendment brought about by an amendment in the description. This brings art.123(3) of the EPC into line with s.76 which has always referred to amendment "of the specification". The second amendment accommodates the possibility of the European patent being amended in the course of the central limitation procedure of arts 105A–105C of the EPC which was also introduced by EPC 2000.

For European divisional applications, provisions corresponding to s.76(1) can be found in art.76 of the EPC, the relevant part of which, after EPC 2000 (the amendments occasioned by which seem editorial only) reads:

> **"EPC ARTICLE 76—European divisional applications**
>
>   (1) A European divisional application … may be filed only in respect of subject-matter which does not extend beyond the content of the earlier application as filed; in so far as this requirement is complied with, the divisional application shall be deemed to have been filed on the date of filing of the earlier application and shall enjoy any right to priority."

This provision also applies to a new "replacement" European application under EPC art.61(1)(b) and EPC r.17 permitted to be filed by a person becoming entitled (EPC art.61(2)).

In Decisions G 1/05 and G 1/06, referred to in §76.03 above, it was held that the content of a member of a sequence of divisional applications must be disclosed in each of the preceding applications in the sequence as filed, although the claims of a member of a sequence of divisional applications need not be directed to subject-matter within the scope of the claims of the preceding applications in the sequence as filed.

While amendment in the EPO is more fully discussed in the *European Patents Handbook* ("EPH") (London: Sweet & Maxwell), EPO decisions under EPC art.123(2) are discussed in §§76.04, 76.14–76.19, particularly with reference to EPO Guidelines C–VI, 5.2 and 5.3; and EPO decisions under EPC art.123(3) are discussed in §76.22.

As referred to above, the EPC now allows amendment for all designated states in post-grant limitation proceedings under EPC arts 105A–105C. Amendment (but not limitation under arts 105A–105C, see art.105a(2)) is also permitted during EPO opposition proceedings but subject to r.80 which restricts amendments to ones occasioned by a ground for opposition under EPC art.100 but not necessarily one invoked by an opponent.

Meaning of "additional matter" for section 76 (subss.(1), (2) and (3)(a))

76.05   Subsections (1) and (2), on the one hand, and subs.(3)(a), on the other, have slightly different wording in relation to "additional matter". Subsection (1) defines "additional matter" as that matter "extending beyond that disclosed [in the earlier application]"; subs.(2) is in the same terms. However, subs.(3)(a) merely refers to "additional matter". Nevertheless, it is believed that nothing turns on this different wording. Section 76 in its original form likewise used somewhat different wording, but again there would seem to have been little or no difference in effect from that now employed. Therefore, the decisions given under the former wording would seem to be equally applicable under the present form of s.76. Moreover, although these subsections use the word "matter", art.123(2) of the EPC refers to "subject-matter", it would appear that the two terms should be regarded as synonymous, see §76.13.

Decisions involving alleged "additional matter"

—The general principles

From the decisions noted in §§76.06–76.13, it is often difficult to obtain amendments other than claim-narrowing amendments even before grant, although permissible pre-grant amendment can involve broadening of the claims, provided that this does not involve adding subject-matter to the specification. The Comptroller has, however, usually held that claim broadening has involved added matter, see §76.15. In *Bonzel v Intervention (No.3)* [1991] R.P.C. 553, the court ordered revocation on a finding that subject matter had been added to a European application by a revision of the description during the substantive examination. This decision stated (at p.574) that, when examining whether an amendment made during prosecution of a European application had involved adding subject-matter, the following steps of verbal analysis should be carried out:

76.06

"(1) to ascertain through the eyes of the skilled addressee what is disclosed, explicitly and impliedly in the original application;

(2) to do the same in respect of the patent as granted; and

(3) to compare the two disclosures and decide whether any subject-matter related to the invention has been added whether by deletion or addition, this comparison being strict in the sense that subject-matter will be added unless such matter is clearly and unambiguously disclosed in the application either explicitly or implicitly".

In this *Bonzel* case, the Patents Court also stated that it is concerned with "what is disclosed, not with what might have been described", and not with that which the skilled reader might think could be substituted or had been omitted. As this *Bonzel* test has been frequently quoted with approval, as e.g. by the Comptroller in *Flexible Directional Indicators' Application* [1994] R.P.C. 207, it should be regarded as the basic test for compliance with s.76(2).

The test was applied in *Inpro Licensing's Patent* [2006] R.P.C. 20 at 517 to refuse amendments for contravention of s.76(3)(a), in *Ivax v Chugai* [2006] EWHC 756 Pat Ct and, in effect, in *Nikken Kosakusho v Pioneer Trading* [2005] F.S.R. 15 at 259, in each case with the same result.

The *Bonzel* test was also applied in *Cartonneries de Thulin's Patent* BL O/263/04 to refuse an amendment seeking to re-amend claim 1 after it had been held by the Court of Appeal in earlier proceedings to be invalid because of added matter introduced by an amendment made in EPO opposition proceedings.

The test, as elaborated upon to include six features by Kitchin J. in *European Central Bank v Document Security Systems Inc* [2007] EWHC 600 Pat Ct, was applied by the Court of Appeal in *Vector Corp v Glatt Air Technologies Ltd* [2007] EWCA Civ 805; [2008] R.P.C. 10 (see also §76.12). The court confirmed its previously-expressed view that the meaning of s.76(3)(a) is "exactly the same" as art.123(2), despite the difference of wording ("matter"; "subject matter").

Kitchin J. employed the *Bonzel* test when considering and rejecting an amendment designed to address a post-grant extension objection in *Mölnlycke Health Care AB v Wake Forest University and Wake Forest University Health Services* [2009] EWHC 2204. The Court of Appeal also applied the *Bonzel* test in *Napp Pharmaceutical Holdings Ltd v*

Ratiopharm GmbH [2009] R.P.C. 18, [2009] EWCA Civ 252 where Jacob L.J. took the s.76/ art.123 equivalence point further by saying that there was "no point" in referring to the UK provisions as they "mean the same" as those of the EPC. The *Bonzel* test was also applied by Arnold J. in *HTC Corp v Yozmot 33 Ltd* [2010] EWHC 786 Pat Ct. Rejecting an argument that an amendment made during prosecution before the EPO added matter to the application, the judge concluded that the amendment (change of claim 1 from "a method for improving" to "a method for performing") "would make no difference to the skilled reader's understanding of the invention" and "only a lawyer with an excessively detailed attention to minutiae of wording" could suppose otherwise.

The judgment of the Court of Appeal in *Napp v Ratiopharm* was referred to in *Teva UK Ltd v Merck & Co Inc.* [2009] EWHC 2952 Pat Ct as setting out the law on added matter. Arnold J. in *Abbott laboratories Ltd v Medinol Ltd* [2010] EWHC 2865 (Pat) (paras 251 to 264) and in *Datacard Corporation v Eagle Technologies Ltd* [2011] EWHC 244 (Pat) (paras 122 to 127) applied the law as set out by the Court of Appeal in *Vector v Glatt* and *Napp v Ratiopharm*, above. Arnold J.'s "compendious summary" of the law in *Abbott v Medinol* was referred to with approval by Floyd J. in *Gedeon Richter Plc v Bayer Schering Pharma AG* [2011] EWHC 583 (Pat) (paras 71 to 83).

The fact that, apparently, in Germany, the Supreme Court reached the opposite conclusion in the *Bonzel* case to that reached by the Patents Court, see R. Marsh [1998] *CIPA* 981, may mean no more than that court applied the facts to the same type of test in a different way, perhaps in relation to what was seen to be implicit disclosure in the original text as to the nature of the inventive step which had been made. The point here was whether a statement (in the original text) that a tube contiguous with a balloon of about 5 cm in length in an angioplasty catheter of 135 cm in length had a length "about the length of the balloon" was consistent with the statement (in the amended text) that the entrance to that tube should be "near to the balloon".

As subss.(1) and (2) refer to the addition of matter to the original application, i.e. to the whole of the description, any drawings and any claims present at filing, then if the drawings filed initially were informal ones, it is these, not the subsequently filed formal drawings, which must be used for judging the content of the application "as filed". The same principle presumably applies when an application is initiated by reference to another application under s.15(1)(c)(ii), see §15.08 above. In *Armco's Application* BL O/84/85, an attempt was made, which failed on its facts, to find basis for claims of a divisional application in the abstract for its parent. This would seem possible, in theory, because s.76 refers to an "application" as filed and, though an abstract is not part of the "specification" (s.14(2)(b)), it is part of an "application" (s.14). The MOPP (para.76.08) indicates that matter contained in the abstract can be transferred to the description, but that claim broadening based on the wording of the abstract is not normally allowed as this is intended to be only a concise summary of the invention and the absence of a feature from the abstract does not mean that the feature is inessential. However, the EPO has decided that art.85 of the EPC precludes consideration of the abstract as providing support for an amendment, see T 407/86 *FUJITSU/Memory circuit* [1988] E.P.O.R. 254 and T 246/86 *BULL/Identification system* OJ EPO 1989, 199; [1989] E.P.O.R. 344 and T 606/06 *LUDWIG/Heating and Incineration device*.

In *Unilin Beheer v Berry Floor* [2004] F.S.R. 14 at 238 Pat Cty Ct, the fact that certain embodiments fell outside claim 1 of the patent both before and after amendment was not considered to be a valid objection to the amendment.

A priority document does not form part of an "application" (see s.14(2)), as confirmed by *Mitsui Engineering's Application* [1984] R.P.C. 471 and *VEB Kombinat Walzlager's Application* [1987] R.P.C. 405. The EPO has held likewise and also that, while a priority document has evidentiary effect, it cannot be taken into account in establishing the content of the application as filed, even if filed at the same time as the European application (T 260/85 *AMP/Coaxial connector* OJ EPO 1989, 105; [1989] E.P.O.R. 403), see also EPO Guideline C–VI, 5.3.1.

Before a technical analysis of the original disclosure can be made, it is necessary that the claims sought comply with art.84 of the EPC, in particular as to clarity (T 749/94 (unreported)).

—Amendments allowed without contravention of section 76

Most applications for amendment occur during the prosecution stage and, if they should **76.07** then succeed, no reasoned decision is issued. Consequently, the number of formal decisions where an amendment is allowed is much smaller than the total number of cases where amendment has been permitted. This can lead to the published decisions giving an overall impression which belies the true position. Reported decisions, where amendment has been permitted, will generally only arise from: successful appeals or contested inter partes proceedings before the courts or the Comptroller or the EPO Boards of Appeal; or from unsuccessful applications for revocation under s.72(1)(d) or (e). Some instances where, as a point of principle, amendments have been permitted are discussed in §§76.08–76.15.

For example, in *Smith's Patent* BL O/16/86, the Comptroller had permitted amendment and the court subsequently held that this was unobjectionable. In *Philips Electronic's Patent* [1987] R.P.C. 244, the Comptroller permitted amendment to remove reference numerals in the granted claims of a European patent (UK); and to add an omnibus claim of specific wording, neither amendment in the circumstances adding new matter or broadening the claims. Deletion of the French and German translations of the granted claims was also permitted as these served no useful purpose because the authentic text of the specification was in English.

In *Strix v Otter* [1995] R.P.C. 607, amendment was allowed although there was no explicit reference in the description to the feature added to the claim, because this feature was apparent when the description was read in conjunction with the drawings; and, in *Norling v Eez-Away* BL C/37/97, amendments to correct imperfect translations were permitted because "where the meaning of the text is not altered by the amendment, then it adds nothing". In this case, new sub-claims were also permitted to be added in the exercise of discretion, see §27.05. In *Beloit v Valmet* [1995] R.P.C. 705, the alleged broadening concept introduced by an amendment was held to have been disclosed as part of the original statement of the "object of the invention" so that no subject-matter had been added by the prosecution amendments. This holding was not challenged on the appeal, see [1997] R.P.C. 489. In *Demel v Jefferson* [1999] F.S.R. 204, it was contended that, as granted, the claims were ambiguous and that removal of the ambiguity would lead to addition of new matter, but it was held that, when the description was given a commonsense interpretation, rather than an over-literal one, there was no ambiguity and the proposed amendment was therefore only a (permissible) clarification.

In *Southco v Dzus* [1990] R.P.C. 587; [1992] R.P.C. 299 CA, the main claim of the granted patent was worded differently from the application as filed, but both the Patents Court and the Court of Appeal held that the different wording, while (unobjectionably) possibly broadening the claim, did not add "fresh subject-matter" to the application, the claim (even as amended) not extending to cover the alleged infringement. This decision, like some of the others discussed above, illustrates the "squeeze" argument between validity and non-infringement, with the claims being found non-infringed, if given a narrow construction; but infringed, though invalid for added subject-matter, if given a broader construction. *Bonzel v Intervention (No.3)* [1991] R.P.C. 553, discussed in §76.06, might have been in this category. In *A. C. Edwards v Acme Signs* [1990] R.P.C. 621; [1992] R.P.C. 131 CA, the Court of Appeal stressed that the essential question was whether the granted claim disclosed the alleged new subject-matter, it being immaterial that the granted claim covered this, the text of the granted specification (as in the *Southco* case) being substantially unchanged from that of the application as filed. Anyway, the original application and the granted patent must each be (purposively) construed as a whole. In this case, the text of the claims in the original specification was important as providing a disclosure independent of the remainder of the specification, as required by s.130(3). However, subsequently, the effect of that subsection was narrowed by the decision in *Asahi's Application* [1991] R.P.C. 485 HL in regard to a claim providing basis for a priority claim, for which see §§5.23 and 130.07. Also, in *Abbott's Application* BL O/222/98, the Comptroller pointed out that the *A.C. Edwards* decision did not involve claim broadening, but rather a restriction to an intermediate generalisation not explicitly disclosed in the original application, for which see §76.12.

In *Mölnlycke v Procter & Gamble (No.5)* [1994] R.P.C. 49 CA, it was contended, unsuccessfully, that a restricting amendment made during prosecution had changed the emphasis of the specification and hence had added new matter. However, in *Monsanto v Merck* [2000] R.P.C. 709, it was held that subject-matter had been added when, during prosecution, one optional substituent was singled out as a characterising feature of the invention thereby creating a different invention from that originally presented, but a further restricting amendment requested at trial would (had the patent not been held invalid for insufficiency and obviousness) have been allowed as being a straight forward limitation of the disclosure of the original application. The court pointed out that caution should be exercised in a case such as this because otherwise "amendment to disclaim would always amount to a new disclosure, and that is neither desirable nor the law", see also §72.26 and §76.12. The decision was upheld on this point on appeal (reported sub nom. *Pharmacia v Merck* [2002] R.P.C. 41 at 775), the court holding that an amendment to restrict the claim to a substituent already described as optional would not add matter but be a disclaimer which the patentee is entitled to make, see §72.26 above.

In *Haberman v Jackel International* [1999] F.S.R. 683, an allegation of added matter was rejected. Although the claims were directed to devices working solely by suction, three of the drawings illustrated drinking cups which required both suction and lip pressure. The court dismissed the allegation that this feature was also present in the other drawings and so there had been no added matter in referring in the claims to operation (solely) by suction. The said three drawings were allowed to be deleted.

In T 386/90 *PROCTER/Hydrogel* [1997] E.P.O.R. 401, erroneous experimental results were permitted to be deleted from the examples because repetition thereof would show them to be wrong: thus, their retention would mislead the reader and no subject-matter was added by this deletion.

In *Baker Hughes' Patents* BL O/332/02 certain words which described (it was submitted, incorrectly) features mentioned in the patent as belonging to the prior art were allowed to be removed on the exercise of the Comptroller's discretion, on the basis that the amendments would not add new subject-matter or extend the protection conferred by the claims, see also §117.06. On appeal (see [2002] EWHC 2524 Ch; BL C/49/02, noted I.P.D. 26003) the court agreed, seeing no reason why the amendments should not be allowed, but observed that the matter could be revisited in revocation proceedings under s.72(1)(d) as the present decision to allow the amendments would not create an estoppel.

—Expansion of the previously-stated inventive concept

76.08   In *Southco v Dzus* [1990] R.P.C. 587; [1992] R.P.C. 299 CA, discussed in §76.07, it was stated that:

> "section 76 prevents a patentee describing, either by deletion or addition, any inventive concept which was not described before, but not to prevent a patentee claiming the same invention in a different way".

An addition of a further inventive concept was also found in denying divisional status in *Mercury Diagnostics' Application* BL O/104/99 where the parent application had been directed to a combination of an analytical device and a disposable strip having a body fluid sample for insertion and analysis therein and divisional status was sought for claims directed to the described strips per se. The Comptroller quoted his previous comment in *Glatt's Application* [1983] R.P.C. 122 that:

> "Third parties who, potentially, may be affected should not, it seems to me, have to face monopolies which were neither clearly sought nor founded by the inventor at the time of filing, but which were conceived later and claimed post hoc".

Similarly, in *L.B. (Plastics)' Application* BL O/90/86, a per se claim in a divisional application to a component specified in the parent application as part of a combination was held to contravene the prohibition against addition of matter, because there was no suggestion in the parent application that the component was, or could be, of independent applicability.

In *Century Industries' Application* BL O/146/97, the proposed amended claims introduced a feature not mentioned in the specification as originally filed, but which could be deduced from the drawings. The Comptroller considered that the proposed amendments introduced a new inventive concept, because the features to be introduced into the claim "were not present in a form which would alert a reader to them constituting an invention" and consequently should not be allowed. The new concept was indicated in the application abstract, but it was felt that the discrepancy between the original application and its abstract would have indicated to the reader an error in the latter. *Seiko Epson's Application* BL O/83/97 is another instance of added matter arising by deletion (in the claims of a divisional application) of a feature previously indicated (by the claims of the parent application) to be essential.

This concept was put in a slightly different way in *B & R Relay's Application* [1985] R.P.C. 1, where the Patents Court noted that s.14(5)(c) requires claims to be supported by the description and that there was nothing in the original description which could conceivably support a claim omitting those features, so that the proposed divisional application would include additional matter. Likewise, in *Raychem's Applications* [1986] R.P.C. 547, it was held that an amended claim not supported by the original description must offend against s.76. Thus, decisions under s.14(5)(c) (for which see §14.38 and particularly *Glatt's Application*, above) are also relevant to considerations of addition of subject-matter, as discussed more fully in §76.21. However, as there noted, this is not a concept which the EPO appears to accept, perhaps because objections under EPC art.84 (to which s.14(5)(c) is equivalent) may not be raised post-grant, see §76.20.

In *Plantronics' Application* BL O/153/84, it was held that a drawing had to be construed in conformity with the passage entitled "Summary of the invention"; and, in *RCA Corp's Application* BL O/33/87, there was no disclosure in the parent application of the subject-matter of the proposed divisional application, having regard to the previously stated "object of the invention". In *Liversidge's Application* BL O/99/88, "method" claims would have been allowed in an application divided from an application with claims only to a tool if (as was not the case) the method claims had included all the features which the parent specification had indicated the tool should achieve; and see *Université René Descartes' Application* BL O/147/88 noted in §76.12.

—Introduction of subject-matter not specifically described

The permissibility of explicit inclusion of matter previously inherently present only by implication is specifically contemplated by the test from *Bonzel v Intervention (No.3)* [1991] R.P.C. 553, set out in §76.06, although here addition of subject-matter was found as a consequence of revision of the description rather than the claims. However, as indicated in that judgment, the test of implied matter is a strict one. Thus, while the Comptroller has accepted that, in considering objections of added subject-matter under s.76, the "implicit disclosure" of the original specification should be taken into account, this contention has then often been found to fail on the facts of the case, as in e.g. *Saamaan's Application* BL O/181/92 and *Lowndes' Application* BL O/19/93, in each of which it was held that the added matter went beyond what had been impliedly disclosed originally.

76.09

Earlier, the Comptroller had stated, in rejecting divisional status, that:

"the fundamental principle in determining additional subject matter is to decide whether any document presents the informed reader with information relevant to the invention which the other document does not".

See *Van der Lely's Application* [1987] R.P.C. 61 which involved a divisional application specifying "at least one swingable conveyor", when the parent application claimed a baling machine with "three swingable conveyors". Further, in *B & R Relay's Application* [1985] R.P.C. 1, the Patents Court stated that the question to be asked is whether the skilled person would find in the original description an indication that it was important to have the feature now sought to be deleted.

Other statements of principle are to be found: in *Ward's Applications* [1986] R.P.C. 50, where the Comptroller stated:

"matter must not be disclosed which extends, in the sense of enlarging upon, the original disclosure, i.e. which increases the specificity or particularisation of that disclosure";

and in *Flexible Direction Indicators' Application* [1994] R.P.C. 207, where it was stated that the section:

"is concerned with what is disclosed, not with that which the skilled reader might think could be substituted or what has been omitted".

A further statement of principle is to be found in *Texas Iron Works' Patent* [2000] R.P.C. 207 CA that claim broadening before grant is entirely permissible provided that this did not introduce a new inventive concept, and likewise with a restricting amendment.

In a number of EPO decisions, it has been permitted to import into the claims features depicted in the drawings, although not explicitly mentioned in the description, but the imported feature must be one:

"clearly, unmistakably and fully derivable from the drawings by the person skilled in the art and so be relatable by him to the content of the description as a whole as to be manifestly part of the invention".

See T 169/83 *VEREINIGTE METALLWERKE/Wall element* OJ EPO 1985, 193; see also T 75/82 *IBM/Transducer head* [1986] E.P.O.R. 103. The EPO has also stated that, in deciding whether a proposed claim limitation finds basis in the original application, its description should be read in the light of the common general knowledge of the skilled addressee so that an explicit statement of that limitation need not have been present originally (T 343/90 *DSM RESINS/Polyester* [1996] E.P.O.R. 216). The EPO has also permitted a cross-reference to a document to be supplemented by its publication number (T 737/90 (unreported)).

An amendment to introduce an allegedly implicit element will be refused if that element has truly been disclosed only in combination with some other element which it is not proposed to incorporate in the amended claim (T 17/86 *SATAM BRANDT/Refrigeration plant* OJ EPO 1989, 297; [1989] E.P.O.R. 347; see also T 174/86 *BLACK & DECKER/ Brush assembly* [1989] E.P.O.R. 277; and T 284/94 *NEOPOST/Thermal printing* OJ EPO 1999, 464; [2000] E.P.O.R. 24. T 17/86 *SATAM BRANDT/Refrigeration plant* was specifically followed in T 284/94 *ELECTRONIC POSTAGE METER/Thermal printing mechanism* where no unambiguous disclosure was seen that one feature incorporated into the claim was intended to be used in isolation from a second feature not mentioned in the amended claim. Likewise, it is not permissible to replace a specific feature by a functional expression, because the latter will cover equivalents of that feature, which the original disclosure did not (T 416/86 *BOEHRINGER/Reflection photometer* OJ EPO 1989, 308; [1989] E.P.O.R. 327).

In an early EPO decision, but only reported much later, it was held that the content of a divisional application or an amended patent can be taken from the "reservoir" of information provided by the parent or original application (T 190/83 *OTTO BOCK/Artificial knee-joint* [1998] E.P.O.R. 272). Nevertheless, the information content of an original claim (as distinct from the description of the application) may be seen as having little effect in trying to identify the "reservoir" provided by the original application, see T 770/90 *PHILIPS/*

Image enhancement circuit [1992] E.P.O.R. 438. However, this concept of a "reservoir" of disclosure is a dangerous concept because it may include subject-matter which the skilled addressee would immediately perceive as a variation of the subject-matter actually disclosed, either explicitly or implicitly, a point discussed in §76.11.

It is normally not permitted to introduce features disclosed not in the description of the invention as originally filed, but in a document referred to by cross-reference, though this is possible if such introduction would leave the skilled reader in no doubt that the description of the invention as originally filed had made it clear that protection of such a feature was, or may be, sought and that it contributes to achieving the technical aim of the invention and is comprised in the solution of the technical problem underlying the invention the subject of the application, see T 689/90 *RAYCHEM/Event detector* OJ EPO 1993, 616; [1994] E.P.O.R. 157. Other examples of permissible amendment on this basis would appear to be: T 6/84 *MOBIL/Amendment of claims* OJ EPO1985, 238, where a warning was given that the imported feature must not single out a particular feature from a set of features which the referenced document indicated belonged to each other; and T 288/84 *STAMICARBON/Activated support* OJ EPO 1986, 128; [1986] E.P.O.R. 217.

However, amendment by introducing a feature from a referenced document must not involve an act of selection which had not been made in the specification as filed. It is therefore not permissible to derive specific information from drawings stated to be "diagrammatic" or "perspective" (T 17/84 *ICI/Manufacture of fusecord* [1986] E.P.O.R. 274).

Rather more generously than has been the position taken under the Act, the EPO has further stated that a proffered amendment should be judged against the "total information content" of the application as filed, taking into account both its implicit and explicit disclosure (T 514/88 *ALZA/Infusor* OJ EPO 1992, 570; [1990] E.P.O.R. 157), see also (in relation to consideration of novelty) T 666/89 *UNILEVER/Washing composition* OJ EPO 1993, 495; [1992] E.P.O.R. 501. Thus, under this principle, it would appear that words can be introduced into the specification, although not used in the original specification, provided that the skilled person would see that no additional subject-matter was introduced thereby, for example as was held in T 596/88 *COATS/Synthetic yarn* [1994] E.P.O.R. 37.

Where a technical feature has been clearly described in the application, but the effect arising therefrom has not been so mentioned, or not mentioned fully, and yet that effect is readily deducible by the skilled person from the specification, the addition of wording elaborating that effect has been held by the EPO to be mere clarification rather than the addition of new matter, see T 37/82 *SIEMENS/Low-tension switch* OJ EPO 1984, 71. A further case of a permitted clarificatory amendment is T 271/84 *AIR PRODUCTS/Removal of hydrogen sulphide* OJ EPO 1987, 405; [1987] E.P.O.R. 23. However, if the true construction of a claim effectively removes an alleged ambiguity, then there appears no need to amend it, see T 127/85 *IRECO/Blasting composition* OJ EPO 1989, 271; [1989] E.P.O.R. 358.

While "correction" is to be considered quite separately (under s.117) from amendment, see §117.06, if an error can be perceived and rectified by the skilled person from his common general knowledge, amendment to correct the error has been indicated (by the EPO) not to involve adding new subject-matter to the specification, see T 171/84 *AIR PRODUCTS/Redox catalyst* OJ EPO 1986, 95; [1986] E.P.O.R. 210.

Somewhat following this theme, in both T 161/86 *ELI LILLY/Antibiotic* [1987] E.P.O.R. 366) and T 552/91 *MERCK/Chroman Derivatives* OJ EPO 1995, 100; [1995] E.P.O.R. 455 a structural formula in the claim, found after filing to be incorrect, was allowed to be deleted and the claim converted to claim a product "obtainable" by a stated process and possessing certain specified characteristics, each of which had been mentioned in the original specification. This is similar to the amendment allowed, though under the 1949 Act, in *Egyt's Patent* [1981] R.P.C. 99.

An amendment being a combination of disclosed numerical ranges was allowed in T 674/02 (unreported).

An example of an allegation of added subject-matter being dismissed because the added matter consisted of technical matter which the skilled person would have known and taken for granted is *DSM's Patent* [2001] R.P.C. 35 at 675.

Addition of an explanation of the meaning of a trade mark as at the priority date contravenes art.123(2) of the EPC (T 480/98 *CIUFFO GATTO/Trade mark* [2000] E.P.O.R. 494).

The EPO Enlarged Board of Appeal in G 1/03 *PPG/Disclaimer* OJ EPO 2004, 413; [2004] E.P.O.R. 33 at 331 and G 2/03 *AstraZeneca/Priorities from India* considered the question of permitting disclaimers having no support in the application as filed, particularly in overcoming prior art under EPC art.54(3), where only novelty, and not inventive step, can be in issue. The resulting decisions were in identical terms so that only G 1/03 *PPG/ Disclaimer* need be consulted. These decisions largely discredited an earlier decision in T 323/97 *Unilever/Disclaimer* [2002] E.P.O.R. 427 and set out the criteria for allowing a claim to have a disclaiming feature in the following headnote terms:

"1. An amendment to a claim by the introduction of a disclaimer may not be refused under Article 123(2) EPC for the sole reason that neither the disclaimer nor the subject-matter excluded by it from the scope of the claim have a basis in the application as filed.

2. The following criteria are to be applied for assessing the allowability of a disclaimer which is not disclosed in the application as filed:

　　—restore novelty by delimiting a claim against state of the art under Article 54(3) and (4) EPC;

　　—restore novelty by delimiting a claim against an accidental anticipation under Article 54(2) EPC; an anticipation is accidental if it is so unrelated to and remote from the claimed invention that the person skilled in the art would never have taken it into consideration when making the invention; and

　　—disclaim subject-matter which, under Articles 52 to 57 EPC, is excluded from patentability for non-technical reasons.

While these cases were pending, T 525/99 *LUBRIZOL/Flourohydrocarbons* [2004] E.P.O.R. 9 at 85 stated that there is no addition of subject-matter where a disclaimer is inserted into a claim with wording taken solely and directly from a document which is prior art only under EPC art.54(3). This now seems to be the general position under G 1/03 *PPG/Disclaimer*.

The breadth of a disclaimer allowable under G 1/03 *PPG/Disclaimer* [2004] E.P.O.R. 33 was considered in T 8/07 *IDEMITSU KOSAN/Disclaimer* (unreported) where the disclaimer was held to be broader then necessary to restore novelty. In T 788/05 *TERUMO/ Vascular catheter* a disclaimer was replaced in opposition proceedings by a positive, more restrictive, fairly supported and compatible feature without violating art.123(3). In T1120/05 *DELAVAL/Separation an undisclosed negative feature* was held not to constitute an allowable disclaimer in accordance with G 1/03 *PPG/Disclaimer* as the anticipatory document was not considered accidental. In T 1220/07 *CIS BIO/Technetium labelled peptide* an amendment was not allowed because it did not satisfy the "without providing a technical contribution" requirement of G 1/03 *PPG/Disclaimer*.

In T 1076/01 (unreported), the EPO refused an amendment which consisted of a disclaimer directed specifically to octadecanol which was sought to be introduced because experimental tests had shown that the invention lacked reproducibility when that particular monoalcohol was used. The disclaimer was not originally disclosed in the specification. G 1/03 *PPG/Disclaimer* (above) was held not to apply because a disclaimer of the kind sought was not in line with the principles of that decision.

The question "Does a disclaimer infringe Article 123(2) EPC if its subject-matter was disclosed as an embodiment in an application as filed?" was referred to the Enlarged Board of Appeal in T 1068/07 *DNA/Scripps* [2010] E.P.O.R. 40 and was answered as follows in G 2/10:

1a. An amendment to a claim by the introduction of a disclaimer disclaiming from it subject-matter disclosed in an application as filed infringes Article 123(2) EPC if the subject-matter remaining in the claim after the introduction of the disclaimer is not, be it explicitly or implicitly, directly and unambiguously disclosed to the skilled person using common general knowledge, in the application as filed.

1b. Determining whether or not that is the case requires a technical assessment of the overall technical circumstances of the individual case under consideration, taking into account the nature and extent of the disclosure in the application as filed, the nature and extent of the disclaimed subject-matter and its relationship with the subject matter remaining in the claim after amendment.

The application of these answers to the case T 1068/07 is awaited.

—Addition of subject-matter by excision or alteration of text

76.10

EPO Guideline C–VI, 5.3.9 warns that "Alteration or excision of text, as well as the addition of further text, may introduce fresh subject-matter". As has been shown in §76.09, this is a principle which has resulted in disallowance of an amendment (or the filing of a divisional application) in a number of cases decided under the Act. Thus, it should be realised that it is possible to add new matter by implication when an excision to the text or disclaimer to the claims is made. In *Protoned's Application* [1983] F.S.R. 110, amendment to change "mechanical compression spring" to "mechanical spring" was refused, inter alia, for adding new matter, or at least by implication from the mere fact of deleting the word "compression"; and, in *Palmaz's European Patents* [1999] R.P.C. 47, the Patents Court held that subject-matter was added when features only disclosed in a particular context, and not disclosed as having any inventive significance, were introduced into the inventive concept shorn of their original context. However, the EPO subsequently reached the opposite conclusion and, on appeal, the Court of Appeal (see [2000] R.P.C. 631 CA) declined to consider this question as invalidity on other grounds made it academic. A similar case is *Monsanto v Merck* (reported sub nom. *Pharmacia v Merck* [2002] R.P.C. 41 at 775) discussed in §76.12.

Further decisions of this ilk are: *Schering's Patent* BL O/116/84, where it was stated that an applicant or patentee may not later seek to draw from an originally generalised disclosure in such a manner as to create post hoc a teaching, or a specific disclosure, or a specific combination, which could not have been plainly derived from the specification at its filing date; *Air Products' Application* BL O/189/83, where the relevant test for whether a generalisation of a previous claim was allowable is whether or not the proposed claim includes within its scope workable subject-matter not previously described, reference being made to the *Protoned* case; and the attempt to file a divisional application for the use of "a hydrazone" from a parent specification which referred to hydrazones of a specified general formula, the Comptroller being unable to find a positive indication that any hydrazone other than those covered by that formula was contemplated when the original specification was drafted (*Canon KK's Application* BL O/14/85, noted I.P.D. 9095). Further similar cases are: *RTL Contractor's Application* BL C/152/83; *L.B. (Plastics)' Application* BL O/90/86; *Picker International's Application* BL O/3/84; and *Hepworth Electrical's Application* BL O/40/86, noted I.P.D. 9028). Thus, to delete the main drawing, stated to illustrate the principle of the invention, is likely to result in implicit addition of new matter, see *Rockwool International's Patent* BL O/63/90, noted I.P.D. 13164, although this case was decided under the possibly different criteria of s.31(2) of the 1949 Act.

In *Fieldturf's Divisional Application* BL O/192/02 the divisional was not accorded the filing date of its parent because the divisional claimed a two-layer structure instead of the three-layer structure of the parent application, omitting mention of a "base layer" which appeared from the parent to be essential.

Moreover, deletion of a feature from an independent claim will violate art.123(2) of the EPC if that feature was originally presented as an essential feature of the invention (T 260/85 *AMP/Coaxial* connector). However, this was not so in *Texas Iron Works' Patent* [2000] R.P.C. 207 CA where, at first instance, there was a finding that subject-matter had been added by deletion of an alleged essential feature; but, on appeal, the addition was seen as no more than an allowable redefinition of the invention as originally disclosed even though the claim was permissibly broadened thereby, see §76.15. Also, in *Demel v Jefferson* [1999] F.S.R. 204, insertion of reference to subject-matter previously present by implication was held to be unobjectionable.

Also, the silence of a claim as to the presence of a particular feature does not necessarily mean that this must be absent: thus to specify such absence could amount to addition of new matter, see T 170/87 *SULZER/Hot gas cooler* OJ EPO 1989, 441; [1990] E.P.O.R. 14; but a feature can be incorporated into the main claim when this has been disclosed as part of a later, though broader, claim (T 270/89 *OVARD/Splash bar* [1991] E.P.O.R. 540). Indeed, in *Keith's Application* BL O/455/99, the Comptroller took the view that subject-matter is only implicitly disclosed in the original text if it was "inevitable" (to the skilled reader) that such matter was included in the total disclosure; the fact that the alleged added matter could be "derived" from the original wording, or that this matter was one of the possibilities, is not sufficient.

In T 615/95 *CIBA-CORNING/Acridinium Testers* [1999] E.P.O.R. 546, deletion was permitted of one member from each of three lists of substituents in a generic chemical formula as this did not result in singling out any hitherto not specifically mentioned individual compound or groups of compounds, but maintained the remaining subject-matter as a generic group of compounds differing from the original group only by its smaller size.

To change a method claim into one directed to "apparatus for carrying out that method" is a broadening amendment because "for" here simply means "suitable for" and therefore there is an implied addition of subject-matter to apparatus also suitable for carrying out other methods. Nevertheless, claims to apparatus "when suitably programmed for carrying out the claimed method" have been allowed (T 784/89 *GENERAL ELECTRIC/Disclosure of computer-related apparatus* [1992] E.P.O.R. 446). For other cases involving a change of claim category, see §76.21.

An amendment to delete three paragraphs from the specification was refused by the Court of Appeal in *Merck's Patents* [2004] F.S.R. 16 at 330 as this would add matter by deletion.

—Prohibition of addition of obvious subject-matter

76.11   While the common general knowledge in the art has to be taken into account in assessing the implicit disclosure of the original application, the question of subject-matter which is obvious over it is another matter which has to be strictly separated, as obvious subject-matter cannot be added to the original disclosure, as indicated in §76.09 with particular reference to the observation in *Flexible Direction Indicators' Application* [1994] R.P.C. 207, that s.76 "is concerned with what is disclosed, not with that which the skilled reader might think could be substituted or what has been omitted", a sentiment endorsed in T 823/96 *PPG/Coating* [1999] E.P.O.R. 417. Thus, whereas subject-matter present in the original text by implication i.e. subject-matter inherently present can (albeit with difficulty) be explicitly inserted by a permissible amendment, a distinction must be drawn between information inherently present and information which is only obvious to the skilled reader from the explicit text, even when this is read in the light of his common general knowledge. The difference is whether the information sought to be incorporated by the amendment into the specification is "additional", rather than only by way of clarification of subject-matter already inherently present. For a discussion of the difference between implicit disclosure and matter obvious over either explicit or implicit disclosure of the application as originally filed, the first being subject-matter which can probably be permissibly added by amendment and the other not so, see the paper by A.W. White, *MIP*, April 1993, 36.

This distinction between inherent and obvious subject-matter is illustrated by *Chinoin's Application* [1986] R.P.C. 39 where the Comptroller observed:

"the fact that information sought to be added is obvious, as distinct from being already known, does not in my view justify its admission without objection arising under section 76";

and, in *Mayflower Products' Application* BL O/129/86, noted I.P.D. 10002, the Comptroller had recourse to EPO Guidelines C–VI, 5.4 and 5.8 (as they then were—now see C–VI, 5.3.1). and asked the question whether a proposed divisional application would present the skilled reader with information which the earlier application did not, even if that information were obvious to the skilled reader, see also *Gruhn USA's Application* BL O/61/92, noted I.P.D. 16043 where there was a refusal to allow a divisional application to proceed because this did not contain a specific limitation perceived to be a feature of the parent application. In *Rhône-Poulenc Agrochimie's Patent* BL O/20/94, the Comptroller stated that, though the now specified location of temperature-monitoring means might have been regarded as an obvious option to the skilled man, there was no disclosure of it, explicit or implicit, in the specification as filed so that its inclusion in the granted patent constituted added subject-matter.

EPO Guideline C–VI, 5.3.2 (2nd paragraph) apparently indicates that, under the EPC, subject-matter can be added by amendment if that matter, in the context of the invention, is implicit to the person skilled in the art. Thus, in T 32/84 *COMMISSARIAT/Redefining an invention.* OJ EPO 1986, 9; [1986] E.P.O.R. 94, it was held that questions under EPC art.123(2) do not arise in defining an invention in terms of features which have not been shown explicitly in the specification, provided that the invention can be put into practice without need for additional explicit description.

Also, applicants have been permitted to amend claims to cover embodiments which, apparently, would have been obvious to the skilled person from reading the original description (T 192/89 *GEC ALSTHOM/Homogenising immiscible fluids* [1990] E.P.O.R. 287). Whilst the EPO requirement for this type of amendment to be an "obvious clarification" would appear to be the key here, it should not be sufficient merely to show that the additional matter was well-known to the skilled person, but that it was part of his inherent knowledge so that he would read the additional matter as already being present, by inference, in the original specification.

In T 685/90 *FUJITSU/Printer* [1993] E.P.O.R. 183, it was stated that, because the application as originally filed constitutes part of the state of the art as regards later applications, it must be construed as it would be under the law of novelty, that is taking into account its whole disclosure, express or implied, "but not considering subject-matter *obvious over this*" (emphasis added).

Because of the effect of the Protocol to EPC art.69 on the extent of protection provided by a claim (as discussed in §125.05), although an amendment of this type may be regarded as not broadening the scope of the claim, nevertheless it may amount to addition of information which was not "clearly, unmistakably and fully derivable" from the original text, as indicated to be required, see T 169/83 *VEREINIGTE METALLWERKE/Wall element*, discussed in §76.09.

—Restriction to an intermediate generalisation

Limitation to an undisclosed intermediate generalisation is possible only if the proposed words of limitation can be found as at least an inherent feature of the original specification, the fact that the amendment is in the nature of a disclaimer being irrelevant (*Noxell's Application* BL O/137/92, noted I.P.D.16042), and see *A. C. Edwards v Acme Signs* [1990] R.P.C. 621; and [1992] R.P.C. 131 CA), which has been explained as involving an intermediate generalisation permissible on this basis, see *Abbott's Application* BL O/222/98. A good example of this principle is to be found in *Monsanto v Merck* [2000] R.P.C. 709 where claims to a class of chemical compounds had been limited during prosecution to specify the obligatory nature of one substituent, mentioned only as an optional feature in the application as filed. As the application contained no disclosure of the importance, or

76.12

necessity, of this group in combination with the other substituents embraced within the original general formula, the amendment was not seen by the Patents Court as a pure disclaimer or of describing the same invention in a different way, but as an impermissible addition of subject-matter leading to revocation. The court was upheld on this point on appeal (reported sub nom. *Pharmacia v Merck* [2002] R.P.C. 41 at 775) the Court of Appeal finding that the amendment in question amounted to making a new selection of compounds. See §72.10. A similar case is *Palmaz's European Patents* [1999] R.P.C. 47; and [2000] R.P.C. 631 CA, discussed in §72.26). However, in the EPO, amendments of a disclaiming nature were allowed where, on the facts, a skilled person could not derive any information from the amended claim which was not already present in the application as filed; thus that claim did not represent a so-called "new selection" (T 684/96 *BRITISH BIOTECH/ Heterocyclic compounds* [2000] E.P.O.R. 190).

In *Université René Descartes' Application* BL O/147/88, the Comptroller indicated that, in principle, it would be possible to derive a numerical value, not expressly stated in the specification, by calculation or interpolation from the contents of the specification, but such value had to be unequivocally derivable from it and this was not so in this case: to insert the requested value into the claim would also make this objectionable because, under s.14(5)(c), the claim would not then be supported by the description. However, this would only be so if "description" here means only the explicit text which ought not to be the position because (for sufficiency) this is addressed to the person skilled in the art who need not be reminded of subject-matter within his common general knowledge.

In *Discovision v Pioneer Electronics* BL C/55/98, noted I.P.D. 21103, an amendment had been made during prosecution to limit the claims to an intermediate generalisation not indicated as such in the original application. The court noted that this placed the patentees in a dilemma:

"To make good the deficiencies of the disclosure of the application, they must appeal to the common general knowledge, but in so doing they must show that the feature in question is common general knowledge. Since this feature is the only feature of the claim which can give subject matter, the claim must then be obvious. On the whole I prefer the view that this is added matter ".

In the EPO, it has been held not possible to extract numerical figures from the examples of the description and then use these as support for a range embraced by those values, since a series of punctate values does not teach working within that range (*T 526/92 EXXON/Lubricating oil additive* [1995] E.P.O.R. 306). However, it is apparently possible to introduce a parameter from a prior art document if this acts as a disclaimer to distinguish the invention over that prior art, see Enlarged Board of Appeal cases G 1/03 and G 2/03 referred to in §76.09.

In T 201/83 *SHELL/Lead alloys* OJ EPO 1984, 481, amendment was allowed to restrict the lower end of a numerical range to a figure illustrated in one of the examples. In contrast, in T 54/82 *MOBIL/Disclosure* OJ EPO 1983, 446, a disclosure of a range of compounds with "10–50 carbon atoms" did not impliedly disclose, and therefore did not provide a basis for amendment to, a range of "18–24 carbon atoms" in the absence of explicit reference to such a range.

In T 812/00 *SEARLE/Cyclooxygenase 2 inhibitors* [2002] E.P.O.R. 42 at 443 (relating to the same European patent under opposition at the EPO), the Board of Appeal held that for an intermediate generalisation to be acceptable under the EPC, its limits "must themselves be directly and unambiguously derivable from the application as filed in the same was as any other amendment" and that the Boards:

"take a strict view here because to do otherwise would lead to applications being filed with broad speculative claims, the identification of the really significant features only being introduced by later amendments".

In *Tickner v Honda* BL C/68/01, noted I.P.D. 25020 the proposed amendment was rejected as an intermediate generalisation adding matter by disclosing and claiming a new combination which the patentee had never contemplated. Likewise, in T 422/00 *MODINE/ Heat exchanger* [2004] E.P.O.R. 30 at 303, the EPO held that if the inclusion of an intermediate generalisation makes a technical contribution to the subject-matter to be claimed, the amendment is not one "clearly and unambiguously derivable from the original disclosure" as required by G 1/93 *ADVANCED SEMICONDUCTOR PRODUCTS/ Limiting feature*, on which see §76.21 below.

An amendment which consisted of introduction into claim 1 of only one of two features originally disclosed in a dependent claim was allowed in T 755/05 (Unreported) in the circumstances of that particular case. It was unsuccessfully argued that the fact that the two features were present in a single claim at origin resulted in a functional or structural relationship between the features making them inseparable.

In T 126/01 (unreported), an amended claim based on a disclosed embodiment was held to be allowable, despite some aspects of the embodiment being generalised.

In *Vector Corp. v Glatt Air Technologies Ltd* [2008] R.P.C. 10, [2007] EWCA Civ 805, the Court of Appeal overturned Lewison J. at first instance in deciding that a requested amendment constituted an impermissible intermediate generalisation and added an additional requirement resulting in a combination not disclosed expressly or by implication in the specification as filed and which was a true unallowable intermediate generalisation. The added feature could be the subject of significant further debate and could require a fresh trial involving an attack on sufficiency. Accordingly, and in accordance with the rule in *Nikken v Pioneer* [2006] F.S.R. 4, [2005] EWCA Civ 906, amendment should be refused.

—Acknowledgement of prior art

As art.123(2) and (3) of the EPC refer, not to "matter", but to "subject-matter", and as the term "subject-matter" appears to be information pertaining to the invention to be claimed, the EPO does not find objectionable the addition of further reference to the prior art since such is not matter describing the subject of the invention. Thus, EPO Guideline C–VI, 5.3 makes it clear that addition of further reference to the prior art can only serve to define the invention in relation to the prior art and that such added reference cannot be regarded as added "subject-matter", as confirmed by: T 11/82 *LANSING BAGNALL/ Control circuit* OJ EPO 1983, 479; and T 450/97 *PROCTER & GAMBLE/Shampoo composition* OJ EPO 1999, 67; [1999] E.P.O.R. 324.

76.13

In *Merrell Dow's Patent* BL C/89/96, noted I.P.D. 19111, following the definition of "added matter" set out in *Bonzel v Intervention (No.3)* [1991] R.P.C. 553 at 574, as discussed in §76.06, it was stated that "matter" in s.76 means "subject-matter", a term which means that "it is matter which relates to the invention which may not be added" without contravention of these provisions. Here, additional information (unpublished at the priority date) that terfenadine is metabolised to the claimed acid metabolite was not seen as relevant to the invention as now sought to be claimed so that the amendment was allowable to revive the patent held invalid in *Merrell Dow v Norton* [1996] R.P.C. 76 HL by addition of a statement to the prior art reference to terfenadine that ingestion of this forms a specified compound by metabolism of terfenadine in vivo and then adding to the end of the Claim 1 the words, "other than formed by metabolism of terfenadine in vivo". However, a warning was given that:

"the Patent Office should always be careful when an acknowledgment of prior art is being made that the patentee is not subtly adding subject matter in that sort of way".

Subsequently, in *Palmaz's European Patents* [1999] R.P.C. 47, the insertion of reference to prior art was held to be too well-established in the EPO for it to be contrarily challenged by the Patents Court; and, in *Cartonneries de Thulin v CTP White Knight* BL C/85/ 99, noted I.P.D. 22013, it was stated that a court will normally be reluctant to hold that the addition of a reference to prior art in a patent constitutes inadmissible added matter.

However, it was here recognised that matter could (impermissibly) be sought to be added by an acknowledgment of prior art in a way which would result in a different construction of a particular claim from that which the court would otherwise have adopted. In the Court of Appeal ([2001] R.P.C. 107 at [6]) the claims were construed differently in that is was held that the claim wording should not be impliedly limited by reference to the drawing and, on that different view, it was held that subject-matter had been added to the original disclosure, see §125.17.

A reason for making an amendment under s.76 acknowledging prior art would be by way of explanation of a latent ambiguity in the claim wording to clarify that it is not intended that the claims cover the acknowledged prior art, as in *Merrell Dow's Patent* (above); or to overcome prior art amounting to an "accidental anticipation" (such as in *Molins v Industrial Machinery* (1937) 54 R.P.C. 94; and (1938) 55 R.P.C. 31). In each of these cases no valid obviousness argument seems to have been available over that prior art. The EPO is likewise apparently prepared to permit claim amendment by a disclaimer of matter which is an accidental novelty-destroying disclosure, but only if the disclaimer is precisely defined and limited to the prior art disclosure and provided that the disclosure has no relevance to the assessment of inventive step, see Enlarged Board of Appeal Decision G 1/03 *PPG/Disclaimer* and G 2/03 *AstraZeneca/Priorities from India* referred to in §76.09 above and EPO Guideline C–VI, 5.3.11. Where there was an incorrect acknowledgment of prior art—because such was private knowledge of the applicant—its deletion was permitted, particularly to avoid making a misrepresentation as to the state of the art (T 1039/93 (Unreported)). In T 22/83 *FUJITSU/Surface wave acoustic device* [1988] E.P.O.R. 234, the EPO also allowed correction of an erroneous acknowledgement of prior art.

The EPO has also allowed correction of an alleged insufficiency concerning preparation of starting materials for a claimed chemical process, itself adequately described, by insertion of a cross-reference to the prior art document considered to constitute part of the relevant state of the art and describing the preparation of the starting materials, see T 51/87 *MERCK/Starting compounds* OJ EPO 1991, 177; [1991] E.P.O.R. 329, but it can be questioned whether this was addition of "obvious", rather then "inherent" information, as discussed in §76.11.

For comments on EPO practice regarding introducing disclaimers to deal with acknowledged prior art, see §76.09 above.

—Support for divisional application in parent application (subs.(1))

76.14   It is clear from the wording of s.76(1)(a) that, in the case of an application or patent which is derived from an earlier application, such as a divisional application, its contents must not include any matter additional to that contained in that earlier application, and also that contained in the application from which that earlier application is derived, each as originally filed: see Enlarged Board of Appeal Decision G 1/06 discussed at §76.04. For this reason, the EPO regards the case law developed under EPC art.123(2) as applicable to the permissible relationship of a divisional application to its parent, see T 527/88 *WAVIN/ Interconnected bags* [1991] E.P.O.R. 184 and T 873/94 *TOSHIBA/Amended divisional application* OJ EPO 1997, 456; [1998] E.P.O.R. 71. Thus the decisions discussed in §§76.06–76.12 apply under s.76(1), as they do under s.76(2), several of these decisions in fact being decided under subs.(1) rather than subs.(2).

Nevertheless, in relation to finding support for a divisional application in a parent application, a more lenient attitude—at least in the EPO—can be discerned than for permitted amendment of an application or patent, although it is not seen why this should be so since both support for a divisional application and for an amendment have to be found in the parent document because otherwise the proposed divisional or amendment would introduce new subject-matter. For example, in T 176/90 *ICI/Triazoles* [1994] E.P.O.R. 401, all that was required for a divisional application was that the parent application disclosed the invention of the divisional application "in a manner sufficiently clear and complete for it to be carried out by the skilled person". That, however, seems to stray over into the area of subject-matter obvious over, rather than inherent in, the parent application, as discussed (in relation to novelty under s.2(3)) in 2.25 and as shown to be impermissible under EPC art.123(2) and s.76(2), see §76.11.

The possibility of claim broadening before grant

The prohibition of "extending the protection conferred by the patent" applies only post- **76.15** grant (see subs.(3), corresponding to art.123(3) of the EPC compared with subs.(1) and (2)). Thus it is possible to broaden claim scope before patent grant, particularly during prosecution, as was confirmed in *Bonzel v Intervention (No.3)* [1991] R.P.C. 553. However, any such claim broadening is subject to the prohibition against including "additional matter" by amendment, or in a divisional or replacement application, as discussed in detail in §§76.06–76.12. If such a broadening is allowed, it may be challenged after grant in any plea for revocation of the patent under s.72(1)(d).

In *Southco v Dzus* [1990] R.P.C. 587; and [1992] R.P.C. 299 CA, it was considered immaterial whether a pre-grant amendment has the effect of widening (or narrowing) the monopoly claimed, provided that the invention in the amended claims is disclosed in the original application (including its claims by virtue of s.130(3)), when this is read as a whole; and see *A. C. Edwards v Acme Signs* [1990] R.P.C. 621; and [1992] R.P.C. 131 CA, where a distinction was drawn between the disclosure in a claim and the cover which a claim provides. However, as regards the effect of s.130(3), see §76.07.

Also, while s.76(1) requires that a divisional application shall not contain additional matter to that contained in that application as filed, or in its parent application as filed, this does not preclude the broadening before grant of the claims originally filed in the divisional application provided that the claims are based on subject-matter originally contained in each of these applications, see T 441/92 *MOTOROLA/Divisional application* [1998] E.P.O.R. 218; and T 66/85 *AMP/Connector* OJ EPO 1989, 167; [1989] E.P.O.R. 283, where claim broadening was accepted because the skilled person would have seen that, otherwise, some of the illustrated embodiments would have been outside the scope of the claims.

However, the Comptroller has pointed out that the allowability of claim broadening without addition of subject-matter is likely to be rare, see *Abbott's Application* BL O/222/98 where a paragraph in a parent application was held not to provide a basis for broader claims in a divisional application because this paragraph immediately followed the statement of invention and would thus have been read in conformity with it. Here, the Comptroller pointed out that the *A. C. Edwards* decision (above) was not a case of claim broadening, but rather involved limitation to an intermediate generalisation to which different considerations could apply, see §76.12. Nevertheless, subsequently, the Court of Appeal made it clear that claim broadening before grant is entirely permissible provided that this did not introduce a new inventive concept, and likewise with a restricting amendment (*Texas Iron Works' Patent* [2000] R.P.C. 207 CA, see also *Spring Form v Playhut* [2000] F.S.R. 327 holding that a mere difference between wording of claims in the application as filed and the granted patent does not amount to added subject-matter.

An amendment made during prosecution of the application for the patent was held in *HTC Corp.v Yozmat 33 Ltd* [2010] EWHC 786 Pat Ct not to add matter. A further, disclaiming amendment of the granted patent was allowed. However, in *Teva v Merck* [2009] EWHC 2952 Pat Ct amendment to claim 1 was allowed despite an objection that the patent as proposed to be amended disclosed that the relevant feature had technical significance whereas there was no disclosure of the technical significance of that feature in the application as filed so that its selection amounted to an impermissible intermediate generalisation. The court held that once the feature had been disclosed and stated to be preferred its technical significance would at once have been appreciated by a skilled person. It was therefore not necessary to express a view as to whether matter could ever be regarded as added for the purposes of this objection if all that was alleged is that technical significance was being attached to a feature which had been disclosed in the application as filed. Although it was correct that matter could be added by intermediate generalisation, taking a feature which was disclosed only in one context and combining it with other features disclosed in another context, nothing of that nature was effected by the amendment. However, amendment to claim 18 was not allowed on the basis that matter had been added by amendment during prosecution; a further amendment requested after grant was also considered to add matter.

From T 331/87 *HOUDAILLE/Removal of feature* OJ EPO 1991, 22; [1991] E.P.O.R. 194, it would appear that the EPO regards removal of a claim feature as one not violating art.123(2) of the EPC, provided that the skilled person would directly and unambiguously recognise that: (1) the feature was not explained as essential to the disclosure; (2) it is not, as such, indispensable for the function of the invention in the light of the technical problem it seeks to solve; and (3) the removal requires no real modification of the feature to compensate for the change.

This three-part test appears to have been applied in a number of decisions, see: T 467/90 *THOMSON-CSF/Spooling process* [1991] E.P.O.R. 115; T 212/87 *LMG/Sterilising pouch* [1991] E.P.O.R. 144; T 371/88 *FUJI/Transmission apparatus* OJ EPO 1992, 157; [1992] E.P.O.R. 341; and T 691/90 *CRITIKON/Infusion apparatus* [1994] E.P.O.R. 51, in each of which a feature was allowed to be deleted from a claim because the skilled person would have perceived this as an essential limitation. However, a disclosure of a vague and general character will not satisfy this test (T 527/88 *WAVIN/Interconnected bags*), this being a case where a divisional application was not permitted as not being in conformity with its parent.

In T 802/92 *COLORADO/Photovoltaic cell* OJ EPO 1995, 379; [1995] E.P.O.R. 568, a feature was allowed to be removed from a claim when this was held not to provide a technical contribution to the subject-matter of the claimed invention so that there was no change in the technical content of the application; and, in T 187/91 *LELAND/Light source* OJ EPO 1994, 572; [1995] E.P.O.R. 199, restriction to a specific example within a generic disclosure was permitted when it was held that the skilled reader would seriously contemplate such as a possible practical embodiment of the described invention having regard to the context of the remainder of the specification, provided that such reader would not understand to the contrary. Removal of dependency from a claim has also been permitted where it could be seen that there was no close functional or structural relationship between the other dependent features (T 288/89 *NISSAN/Internal combustion engine* [1996] E.P.O.R. 57.

Also, in T 247/96 *ALLEN/Flow restrictor* [1997] E.P.O.R. 519, a broadening amendment was allowed, not only to base the claim on a feature illustrated in the drawing but to the underlying concept thereof, this being what "would be immediately understood by the skilled person". Furthermore, on other occasions, the EPO has permitted removal of a feature from claim wording in a pre-grant amendment, thereby resulting in a broadening of the extent of protection. Thus, in T 190/83 *OTTO BOCK/Artificial knee-joint*, it was permitted to omit two features from the original claim on the basis that the totality of the original disclosure constitutes a "reservoir" from which the applicant can draw when amending the specification. This view was approved in T 133/85 *XEROX/Amendments* [1989] E.P.O.R. 116; abridged OJ EPO 1988, 441, where it was pointed out that such reservoir is that of the original application and that it cannot be expanded after the date of filing. Then, in T 151/84 *Thomson-CSF's Application* [1988] E.P.O.R. 29, a feature was permitted to be deleted from the characterising portion of the main claim because the specification as a whole made it clear that this was an advantageous, but not indispensable, characteristic of the invention. In T 311/99 *FUJITSU/Removal of organic resist* [2000] E.P.O.R. 488, it was permitted to remove the word "used" from the claim phrase "for removing a used organic resist" as the description indicted that working on a "used resist" was only an advantageous, but not an essential, feature of the invention.

Where claim 3 had been granted appendant to claim 2, and it was then sought to incorporate its wording into claim 1, this was allowed because there was no close functional or structural relationship between the features of claims 2 and 3 (T 235/90 *BENDIX/Actuator for brakes* [1996] E.P.O.R. 157). Also, where an application can be seen to contain two independent technical teachings, a divisional application can be filed for the second teaching and having claims which omit features essential to the first teaching (T 211/95 (unreported)).

However, a decision seemingly inconsistent with these decisions is T 147/85 *PHILIPS/Interchangeable disks* [1988] E.P.O.R. 111, where it was stated that it did not assist the applicant that the skilled person would immediately appreciate that a particular feature was unnecessary, see also T 24/85 *DISCOVISION/Lens assembly* [1988] E.P.O.R. 247, though this can perhaps be explained by drawing a distinction between matter implicitly disclosed in the original application and matter deemed obvious over the total information content of that application.

A feature cannot be deleted from a claim if it has previously been presented, expressly or by implication, as an essential feature of the invention (T 685/90 *FUJITSU/Printer*), or if its removal requires modification of other features (T 514/88 *ALZA/Infusor*), and T 248/88 *SGS/Unacceptable generalisation* [1990] E.P.O.R. 274).

Amendment resulting in disunity

The Enlarged Board of Appeal has held in G 1/91 *SIEMENS/Unity* OJ EPO 1992, 253; **76.16**
[1992] E.P.O.R. 183 that it is irrelevant to opposition proceedings that the patent as granted or as amended does not meet the requirements of unity. Section 26 should provide the same effect under the Act, see §26.02.

The concept of "additional matter" present in other provisions

The concept of "additional matter" within art.123 of the EPC (and hence within s.76) **76.17**
has similarities with other concepts arising out of the EPC (and hence also arising under the Act), namely with the concepts of: novelty; according priority; and the presence of supporting description for a claim, as discussed respectively in the following §§76.07–76.09. The extent of the unity relationship between these concepts was discussed by A.W. White, *MIP*, April 1993, 36.

—Relationship of "additional matter" to concept of novelty

First, the concept of "matter contained [in an earlier application]" when considering **76.18**
lack of novelty under EPC art.54(3) (to which s.2(3) corresponds), under which novelty, but not an inventive step, is required (as discussed in §2.25) appears to be an analogous concept to that of "additional matter" arising under EPC art.123 and s.76. Indeed EPO Guideline C–VI, 5.4 (concerned with added matter) specifies that here the test for novelty is applicable, and EPO Guideline C–IV, 7.2 (primarily relevant to the test of novelty) likewise states that the test for novelty is analogous to the test of added subject-matter prohibited under EPC art.123(2). Decisions under ss.2(3) may, therefore, assist in resolving questions arising under s.76.

EPO Guideline C–VI, 5.3.1 suggests that added matter is present if an amendment results in an overall change in the content of the application, whether by way of addition, alteration or excision, which results in the skilled person being presented with information which differs from that previously presented, citing T 201/83 *SHELL/Lead alloys*. This view has alternatively been expressed by saying that the principle under EPC art.123(2) is basically similar to that for lack of novelty (T 133/85 *XEROX/Amendment*), i.e. no new subject-matter must be generated by the amendment (T 17/86, *SATAM BRANDT/Refrigeration plant*. Also, in T 449/90 *CEDARS-SINAI/Treatment of plasma* [1993] E.P.O.R. 54), it was stated that the question of added subject-matter has to be judged "in the same strict and narrow way" as is done in the established case law on the question of novelty.

Although EPO Guideline C–IV, 9.2 states that a novelty destroying document is a document which:

"takes away the novelty of any claimed subject-matter derivable directly and unambiguously from that document including any features implicit to a person skilled in the art in what is expressly mentioned in the document", a warning that care is necessary in applying the lack of novelty test to permissible amendment was given in T 133/85 *XEROX/Amendment* (above), see also T 187/91 *LELAND/Light source*; and the EPO has subsequently, stated that the test for additional subject-matter corresponds to the test for novelty only insofar as both require assessment of whether information is directly and unambiguously derivable from that previously presented, in the originally filed application or in a prior document respectively. See T 194/84 *GENERAL MOTORS/Cellulosic fibres* OJ EPO 1990, 59; [1989] E.P.O.R. 351 and T 339/89 *VMX/Electronic audio communication system* [1991] E.P.O.R. 545.

It then seemed that the "lack of novelty test"should be applied to the change in content of the amended claim and not to the amended claim per se, in that the subject-matter generated by the amendment must not be novel over the specification as filed (T 265/88 *LUNDIA/Diffusion device* [1990] E.P.O.R. 399). Indeed, in T 748/89 *STAUFFER/ Cyclohexanediones* [1999] E.P.O.R. 45, the novelty test for added matter was stressed as applying to the difference between the amended specification and that originally filed so that, when the original subject-matter is notionally disclaimed, residual subject-matter indicates the amendment to be inadmissible, see also T 194/84 *GENERAL MOTORS/ Cellulosic fibres* (above). That appears to be a similar test to that propounded in the Patents Court in *Bonzel v Intervention (No.3)* [1991] R.P.C. 553, discussed in §76.15. For example, an attempt to import a negative feature (the absence of internal fittings) from the drawing has been rejected because such absence did not make it "unequivocally inferable that such feature is to be excluded" (T 170/87 *SULZER/Hot-gas cooler*), but a feature can be imported from the drawings if its presence is clear from them (T 255/88 *WAGNER/Fixing device* [1992] E.P.O.R. 87).

However, more recently, it has been stressed that the applicability of the "novelty test" in relation to art.123(2) of the EPC always depends upon the circumstances, the underlying principle being that a proprietor should not be allowed to improve his position by adding subject-matter which could be damaging to the legal security of third parties (T 873/94 *TOSHIBA/Amended divisional application*, discussed by B. Grennberg, *epi-Information* 1998, 109. In T 824/94 *INSTITUT PASTEUR/Lympdenopathy-associate virus* [2000] E.P.O.R. 436, however, it was reiterated that the test for allowability of amendment under EPC art.123(2) is the same as the test for novelty.

For a discussion on the applicability of various novelty tests to questions of added subject-matter, see D.C. Musker [1995] E.I.P.R. 594.

Care must be taken in construing words, such as "and", used somewhat ambiguously in the original text (T 171/89 *BAYER/Vaccine* [1990] E.P.O.R. 126; and see T 194/84 *GENERAL MOTORS/Cellulosic fibres* (above)).

—Relationship of "additional matter" to according a priority date

76.19   It is stated, in EPO Guideline C–V, 2.2, that the test for according priority from an earlier application "is the same as the test of whether an amendment to an application satisfies the requirement of Art. 123(2)" followed by a reference to EPO Guideline C–VI, 5.3.

The EPO Guidelines reflect the option of the Enlarged Board of Appeal in G 2/98 *X/Same invention* OJ EPO 1998, 509; [2002] E.P.O.R. 17 at 167 in which it was held that priority is to be acknowledged:

"only if the skilled person can derive the subject matter of the claim directly and unambiguously using common general knowledge from the previous application as a whole".

Decision G 2/98 *X/Same invention* resolved a previous uncertainty as to whether or not the test for priority uses the same criteria as the test for added subject-matter, the uncertainty arising from an earlier Technical Board of Appeal decision T 73/88 *HOWARD/ snackfood* OJ EPO 1992 557; [1990] E.P.O.R. 112, and cases which had followed that decision. For a full discussion of G 2/98 *X/Same invention*, see §5.26 above.

—Relationship of "additional matter" to description support for claim

The test of support for claims which is required by s.14(5)(c) may also be relevant. **76.20** Thus, as noted in §76.06, the Comptroller has indicated that the test for claim support may be relevant to that of added matter, but the EPO does not generally regard the test under EPC art.123(2) as the same as that of support for breadth of claim required by art.84 of the EPC, as indicated in T 133/85 *XEROX/Amendments*, discussed in §76.15. This is, apparently, because it is possible to support something which is broad from a narrower base, but an amendment to provide support under EPC art.84 must contravene EPC art.123(2) by adding matter to the disclosure as filed. Thus, use of the word "supported" is inappropriate in relation to art.123(2) of the EPC and T 133/85 *XEROX/Amendments* therefore expressly disapproved T 52/82 *RIETER/Winding apparatus* OJ EPO 1983, 416, where a term in the claim preamble was permitted to be replaced by a more generic term held to be more apt to define a feature present. However, it is possible to overcome an objection of alleged added subject-matter by construing the claim wording in a restrictive way (T 164/90 *LIGHT SIGNATURES/Authenticator device* [1991] E.P.O.R. 289).

In T 7/80 *LICHT DRUCK/Copying process* OJ EPO 1982, 95, an amended claim was rejected because the characterising clause was held not to find sufficient support in the specification as originally filed. Other cases where a lack of support for the amendment in the original specification was found, the amendment not being derivable from the explicit, or implicit, disclosure of that specification, include: T 188/83 *FERNHOLZ/Vinyl acetate* OJ EPO 1984, 555; and T 32/85 *GIST-BROCADES/Biomass preparation* [1986] E.P.O.R. 267.

—Amendment extending the protection conferred (EPC art.123(3) and subs.(3)(b))

Subsection (3)(b), in accordance with art.123(3) of the EPC, prohibits a granted patent **76.21** being amended (under the provisions of ss.27(1), 73 or 75) in such a way as to extend the protection conferred by the patent. This is in contrast to the position pre-grant when this limitation does not apply, see §76.15. The MOPP para.76.26 states that the question to be asked is, is it possible to conceive of any act or apparatus which would infringe the amended claim but would not have infringed any claim of the patent as granted? If the answer is negative, then no objection arises under s.76(3)(b).

It has been suggested in (1980–81) 10 *CIPA* 316 and 403 that the words "extends the protection conferred by the patent" can only apply to a valid claim, as an invalid claim would confer no protection, with the result that allowable amendment would be limited to combining an invalid claim with the whole of one or more sub-claims. If true, this would preclude the curing of invalidity by incorporating into the claims a feature of any specific sub-claim. It would also preclude amendment to a generalisation intermediate between the scope of the invalid claims and that of the valid ones. This argument was run in *Tickner v Honda* BL C/68/01, noted I.P.D. 25020, it being contended that if claim 1 of the patent were invalid, the introduction of a claim narrower than the original claim 1 but broader than any of the sub-claims would result in the protection conferred by the patent being extended (the original claim 1, being invalid, conferring no protection). That argument was rejected, the court saying that "like patents themselves, the EPC and the Act must be construed purposively", but the proposed amendment was nevertheless found objectionable: see §76.12, above. Thus it should probably be assumed that the reference to ''the protection conferred'' relates to the terms of the specification and claims as these stand immediately before amendment, irrespective of the validity of the unamended claims.

In *Siegfried Demel v C&H Jefferson* [1999] F.S.R. 204 it was held that an amendment was permissible which broadened the scope of a dependent claim on the grounds that any case covered by that claim as amended would already have been covered by the earlier broader independent claim. Decisions of the Comptroller under subs.(3)(b) include: *Shoketsu's Patent (No.3)* BL O/60/91, noted I.P.D. 14142, where a patent was amended to leave only an omnibus claim and it was successfully contended that deletion of any of the descriptive matter must necessarily have the effect of broadening the scope of the claim; *Marley's Patent* BL O/110/96, noted I.P.D. 20003, discussed in §73.06; and *Someya's Patent* BL O/199/97, where it was held that changing the claim from "[a] method of purifying water for drinking purposes comprising" to "[a] method of treating water for drinking purposes to render it bacteriostatic comprising" would broaden the claim, as "treating" is a broader term than "purifying", purification requiring a biocidal effect as well as a bacteriostatic one. Similarly, in T 412/04 (unreported) the EPO held that replacement in a granted claim of the feature "to retain the characteristics of fresh meat" by "to extend the shelf life of the fresh meat" extended the protection conferred and therefore offended art.123(3). Other proposed amendments offended art.123(2) or 123(3).

An important decision is G 1/93 *ADVANCED SEMICONDUCTOR PRODUCTS/ Limiting feature* OJ EPO 1994, 541; [1995] E.P.O.R. 97, which disapproved the earlier T 231/89 *BRUYNZEEL/Flat torsion spring* OJ EPO 1991, 13; [1993] E.P.O.R. 418. In G 1/93 *ADVANCED SEMICONDUCTOR PRODUCTS/Limiting feature*, the patent claims had, during prosecution, been restricted to a technical feature which it was held in opposition proceedings found no basis in the specification as originally filed. Deletion of this feature in order to overcome the objection under EPC art.123(2) could not, however, then be permitted because such would have the effect of broadening the extent of protection of the patent as granted, contrary to art.123(3) of the EPC. It was stated that such a patent could only be maintained if there could be found a basis in the application as filed for replacing the added subject-matter without violating art.123(3) of the EPC. The Enlarged Board went on to say that a feature which has not been disclosed in the application as filed but which has been added to the application during examination and which, without providing a technical contribution to the claimed invention, merely limits the protection conferred, is not to be considered as subject-matter extending beyond the content of the application as filed.

Thus, where an inadmissible amendment has been made before grant, it may not be possible to remedy the situation after grant because deletion of that amendment is likely to offend against art.123(3) of the EPC.

The sequel to G 1/93 *ADVANCED SEMICONDUCTOR PRODUCTS/Limiting feature* was that the Board of Appeal which had made the referral to the Enlarged Board stated that deletion of an added feature because it has no technical significance and represents only a restriction in the extent of protection would only appear possible if the skilled reader of the original application would so understand it and if it does not interact with the remaining features of the claim so as to influence the solution to the technical problem as seen from the original application T 384/91 *Conflict between art.123(2) and (3)/II* OJ EPO 1995, 745; [1995] E.P.O.R. 568; [1996] E.P.O.R. 125 sub nom. *ADVANCED SEMICONDUCTOR PRODUCTS/Optical membrane*. The feature was therefore held not to be one which merely limited the protection conferred without providing a technical contribution. The amendment was therefore not allowed.

The draconian effect of art.123(3) of the EPC, involving the inescapable conflict between EPC art.123(2) and 123(3) noted in Decision G 1/93 *ADVANCED SEMICONDUCTOR PRODUCTS/Limiting feature* (above) was the subject of a number of papers at a symposium of European patent judges, as reprinted at (1997) 28 I.I.C. 822–844. Various proposals have been put forward for overcoming it by an amendment of the EPC, possibly by adopting the German "footnote" solution which would allow the amendment previously made to stand but with a note that "no rights or benefit shall be derived from [such wrongly made amendment]", but none of these proposals has found general approval.

Examples where amendment has been refused under EPC art.123(3) are: T 20/84 *WÄRMESTELLE/Annular shaft kiln* [1986] E.P.O.R. 197, where the deletion of several lines from a claim was held to be an impermissible broadening amendment; and T 89/85 *SAB/Vehicle brakes* [1988] E.P.O.R. 105, where an amendment to change a feature from being "stabilized in a substantially vertical position" to being "stabilized in a position parallel to the tread of a wheel" was likewise not permitted. T 136/88 *VAN DER LELY/ Soil cultivating implement* [1996] E.P.O.R. 67 and T 986/93 *EATON CORPORATION/ Central tire inflation system* OJ EPO 1996, 215 are each further examples of revocation following claim broadening by deletion of a feature originally presented as essential to the invention. In T 82/93 *TELECTRONICS/Cardiac pacing* OJ EPO 1996, 274; [1996] E.P.O.R. 409, a patent had been granted with claims subsequently held unallowable as directed to a method of treatment of the human body: an attempt then to direct the claims to apparatus for use in such treatment was rejected as extending the extent of protection conferred by the patent grant because thereby the claims would cover the apparatus whether or not in use.

The EPO held in T 777/02 (unreported) that an amendment without basis introduced during examination did not offend art.123(2) of the EPC because the feature introduced was not critical to the claimed process. Decision G 1/93 *ADVANCED SEMICONDUCTOR PRODUCTS/Limiting feature* was therefore applied to allow the amendment. However, in Decision T 580/03 (unreported), the EPO held that an added feature ("a wireless traffic monitor") could not be regarded as not providing any technical contribution since it performed an essential function so that Decision G 1/93 *ADVANCED SEMICONDUCTOR PRODUCTS/Limiting feature* did not apply and the amendment was refused. In Decision T 23/02 (unreported), an amendment to change to a different method by which the diameter of particles specified in claim 1 was measured was refused under EPC art.123(3). Moreover, removal of the feature (introduced erroneously during prosecution) was refused by application of the principles of Decision G 1/93 *ADVANCED SEMICONDUCTOR PRODUCTS/Limiting feature*. Alternative amendments were also refused.

In T 0567/08 (unreported) a claim to a roll-on cosmetics applicator had been amended during examination to include the undisclosed expression "base footprint" instead of "base" or "first end". The patent was opposed successfully on the ground of art.100(c) (contravention of art.123). On appeal, inclusion of the term was held (on one of its two possible meanings—it was also considered by the Board of Appeal to be ambiguous) to be a "limiting extension" in the terms of G 1/93 which could not be removed without infringing art.123(3). The appeal was therefore dismissed and revocation upheld.

In deciding the scope of protection conferred at grant, it is legitimate to construe the claims by reference to the description and drawings in accordance with art.69 of the EPC and its Protocol, but this must be the description and drawings upon which the patent was granted. Thus, it is not permissible to re-instate wording which had been present in the initial application but which had been deleted before grant, when that wording would cause the claims to be given a broader interpretation, see T 1149/97 *SOLARTRON/Fluid transducer* OJ EPO 2000, 259; [2001] E.P.O.R. 3 at [33]. In any case, using art.69 of the EPC and its Protocol to construe the claims may have the effect of giving a wider meaning to a claim feature than a literal reading would suggest, with the consequence that a clarifying amendment can be made without breach of EPC art.123(3) (T 371/88 *FUJI/Transmission apparatus*). Likewise, where the granted claims, on a literal interpretation, could not (in the light of the description and drawings) be that for which protection was sought, so that the intended meaning must have been that of the amended claims, then on a fair interpretation of the amended claims in the light of the Protocol the protection conferred thereby was seen as not in fact extended: T 108/91 *SEARS/Lockable closure* OJ EPO 1994, 228; [1993] E.P.O.R. 407. Similarly, in T 172/82 *CONTRAVES/Particle analyzer* OJ EPO 1983, 493, it was permitted to delete a feature from a claim on the basis that its removal clarified and/or resolved an inconsistency in the original claim and did not therefore, in the factual circumstances, result in the scope of the protection being extended. For other claim-broadening cases, see §76.15. T 647/91 *TEIJIN/Water-repellant textile fabric* [1998] E.P.O.R. 288) is a further case where the claims were given a non-literal construction in order to avoid an adverse finding under EPC art.123(3).

The effect on the protection conferred by deletion of a statement in the description was considered in T 744/03 (unreported) where it was held that the deletion led to a narrowing of the claim since the claim, when read alone, provided a narrower definition of the invention than when read with the statement in the description. The amendment therefore did not offend art.123(3) of the EPC. In T 1193/05 (unreported), the Board allowed an amended claim 1 which omitted a disclaimer contained in granted claim 1. It was held that the removal of the disclaimer did not extend the protection conferred, on account of the other amendments made.

The EPO has held that art.123(3) of the EPC permits a change in claim category after grant only in exceptional circumstances because of the Protocol to EPC art.69 (T 378/86 *MOOG/Change of category* OJ EPO 1988, 386; [1989] E.P.O.R. 85). In this decision it was stated that art.123(3) of the EPC is contravened when it is obvious that an act can be considered as an infringement of the amended claim, but could not have been so considered in respect of the claims before amendment. However, change of a process claim to an apparatus claim was then permitted because the means of carrying out the process had been described in such detail that the skilled person could readily deduce from the disclosure the apparatus which the amendment sought to claim.

As discussed in §§2.08 and 2.23, in G 2/88 *MOBIL/Friction reducing additive III* OJ EPO 1990, 93 and 469; [1990] E.P.O.R. 73, the EPO Enlarged Board of Appeal confirmed the allowability of changing claim category post-grant by stating that a post-grant change of category of claims can be allowed if the extent of protection (when considered in the light of the Protocol to EPC art.69) is not extended, but in this regard national laws relating to the question of infringement should not be considered. Likewise, claims could be changed from being directed to "a compound" to "a composition including such compound", or to "the use of that compound in a composition for a particular purpose", without offending EPC art.123(2). In T 402/89 *FUJI/Heat developable colour* [1993] E.P.O.R. 81, this decision was explained as not being applicable where a product claim is sought to be converted into a process claim because some contracting states would consider the protection of a process claim to extend only to some of a chain of specified steps, the Board seeing a distinction between the "protection conferred" (as referred to in EPC art.123(2)) and the "rights conferred" (as referred to in EPC art.64), see also T 958/90 *DOW/Sequestering agent* [1994] E.P.O.R. 1.

In T 426/89 *SIEMENS/Pacemaker* OJ EPO 1992, 172; [1992] E.P.O.R. 149, a claim to a method of operating a cardiac pacemaker was allowed to be replaced in opposition proceedings by a claim to the pacemaker per se on the basis that the features of the method referred only to the way in which the pacemaker acted so that, by clarification of the method claim as a product claim, there was no (inadmissible) category change.

EPO Enlarged Board of Appeal decision G 1/99 *3M/Reformatio in peius* OJ EPO 2001, 381; [2001] E.P.O.R. 50 at 391 addressed the issue of an inadmissible amendment made during opposition proceedings. The Enlarged Board (on a reference by a Technical Board of Appeal in T 315/97) decided that, in principle, an amended claim which would put the opponent (who was the sole appellant against the opposition division's decision to maintain the patent in amended form) in a worse situation than if it had not appealed, must be rejected. An exception to this principle was, however, seen to apply in circumstances where the patent would have to be revoked as a direct consequence of the inadmissible amendment. Three possibilities were therefore set out under which remedial action may be possible. One such instance occurred in T 496/04 (unreported), where the inadmissible amendment was allowed to be deleted under the principles set out in G 1/99.

—Amendment in contravention of section 76

76.22   In the event that an amendment should be allowed which has the effect of adding matter, contrary to any of subss.(1), (2) and (3)(a), and/or post-grant which extends the protection afforded contrary to subs.(3)(b), a ground for revocation ensues under s.72(1)(d) and/or (e); see §§72.15. Since such an amendment will have been made only as a deliberate act, it may be difficult (but for the introduction in December 2007 of ss.27(6) and 75(5)) to persuade a tribunal subsequently that its discretion should be exercised in favour of allowing the impermissible amendment to be removed or varied in order to overcome a finding of invalidity under either of these provisions. For discussion of the exercise of discretion in permitting amendment and the effect of statutory amendments made in December 2007, see §§27.04–27.05.

Also (as shown by Decision G 1/93 *ADVANCED SEMICONDUCTOR PRODUCTS/ Limiting feature*, in relation to the corresponding provisions of art.123(2) and (3) of the EPC), where, during prosecution of an application and even though approved by the examiner, a limitation has been inserted in a claim as the result of an impermissible addition of subject-matter contrary to s.76(2)(a), e.g. by a limitation to a feature not part of the disclosure of the application as originally filed, under the current state of the law, it may not be possible after grant to correct this by deletion of the added feature without contravention of s.76(3)(b). This is because removal of that limitation will result in claim broadening, see §76.21.

However, as there explained, there may be a faint possibility of maintaining the patent if the added matter is "without technical contribution" (e.g. where the limitation is by way of citation from the prior art, since such is not "subject-matter", see §76.13), or if there is basis in the original application for replacing the offending limitation without broadening the scope of protection (e.g. by further limitation of the added unsupported feature to a species thereof which was disclosed in the original disclosure). Consequently, great care needs to be taken to see that any limiting amendment put forward is one adequately supported by the original disclosure.

Accordingly, while support can be provided by incorporation of a feature which is implied by, or inherent in, the original disclosure, support cannot be provided by a feature which is obvious over that disclosure, see §76.11; and opinions are likely to differ whether the alleged support is in fact inherent in, or obvious, over, the original disclosure.

Effect of amendment on damages

Under s.62(3)(b), the making of any amendment to the specification of the patent after grant will have the effect of requiring the court or Comptroller when awarding damages or making an account of profit in proceedings for infringement of the patent before amendment, to take into account, inter alia, whether specification of the patent as published was framed in good faith and with reasonable skill and knowledge. However, it is rare for it to be found that such criteria were not met in the drafting of the specification, but see §62.05 for the effect of the section and the method and onus of proof required, see also the commentary on s.63 (relief for infringement of partially valid patent). **76.23**

SECTION 76A [ADDED]

Biotechnological inventions

76A.—(1) Any provision of, or made under, this Act is to have effect in relation to a patent or an application for a patent which concerns a biotechnological invention subject to the provisions of Schedule A2. **76A.01**

(2) Nothing in this section or Schedule A2 is to be read as affecting the application of any provision in relation to any other kind of patent or application for a patent.

Note. This section was added to the Act by the Patents Regulations 2000 (SI 2000/2037) with effect from July 28, 2000. The section was applied to the Isle of Man by SI 2003/1249.

Section 76A
SCHEDULE A2

Biotechnological Inventions

1. An invention shall not be considered unpatentable solely on the ground that it concerns– **76A.01A**
    (a) a product consisting of or containing biological material; or
    (b) a process by which biological material is produced, processed or used.

2. Biological material which is isolated from its natural environment or produced by means of a technical process may be the subject of an invention even if it previously occurred in nature.

3. The following are not patentable inventions–
    (a) the human body, at the various stages of its formation and development, and the simple discovery of one of its elements, including the sequence or partial sequence of a gene;

(b) processes for cloning human beings;

(c) processes for modifying the germ line genetic identity of human beings;

(d) uses of human embryos for industrial or commercial purposes;

(e) processes for modifying the genetic identity of animals which are likely to cause them suffering without any substantial medical benefit to man or animal, and also animals resulting from such processes;

(f) any variety of animal or plant or any essentially biological process for the production of animals or plants, not being a micro-biological or other technical process or the product of such a process.

4. Inventions which concern plants or animals may be patentable if the technical feasibility of the invention is not confined to a particular plant or animal variety.

5. An element isolated from the human body or otherwise produced by means of a technical process, including the sequence or partial sequence of a gene, may constitute a patentable invention, even if the structure of that element is identical to that of a natural element.

6. The industrial application of a sequence or partial sequence of a gene must be disclosed in the patent application as filed.

7. The protection conferred by a patent on a biological material possessing specific characteristics as a result of the invention shall extend to any biological material derived from that biological material through propagation or multiplication in an identical or divergent form and possessing those same characteristics.

8. The protection conferred by a patent on a process that enables a biological material to be produced possessing specific characteristics as a result of the invention shall extend to biological material directly obtained through that process and to any other biological material derived from the directly obtained biological material through propagation or multiplication in an identical or divergent form and possessing those same characteristics.

9. The protection conferred by a patent on a product containing or consisting of genetic information shall extend to all material, save as provided for in paragraph 3(a) above, in which the product is incorporated and in which the genetic information is contained and performs its function.

10. The protection referred to in paragraphs 7, 8 and 9 above shall not extend to biological material obtained from the propagation or multiplication of biological material placed on the market by the proprietor of the patent or with his consent, where the multiplication or propagation necessarily results from the application for which the biological material was marketed, provided that the material obtained is not subsequently used for other propagation or multiplication.

11. In this Schedule:

"essentially biological process" means a process for the production of animals and plants which consists entirely of natural phenomena such as crossing and selection;

"microbiological process" means any process involving or performed upon or resulting in microbiological material;

"plant variety" means a plant grouping within a single botanical taxon of the lowest known rank, which grouping can be:

(a) defined by the expression of the characteristics that results from a given genotype or combination of genotypes; and

(b) distinguished from any other plant grouping by the expression of at least one of the said characteristics; and

(c) considered as a unit with regard to its suitability for being propagated unchanged.

COMMENTARY ON SECTION 76A

The European Biotechnology Directive 98/44/EC

76A.02   Section 76A introduced Sch.A2 (reprinted above) to give effect to the European Biotechnology Directive 98/44/EC [1998] OJ EC L213/13, reprinted in Appendix C. The section applies the provisions of this Schedule to patents and applications which concern "a biotechnological invention". This term is defined by an addition to s.130(1), (for which see §130.01) as an invention which concerns a product consisting of or containing biological material or a process by means of which biological material is produced, processed or used, and where "biological material" is in turn defined as any material containing genetic information and capable of reproducing itself or being reproduced in a biological system. However, this Schedule has no effect on patents and applications which concern subject-matter which is not a "biotechnological invention" as so defined. Under reg.9 of the Patents

Regulations 2000 which introduced these amendments s.76A and Sch.A2 have effect only as regards applications (and patents granted on such applications) dated on or after the "commencement date" of July 28, 2000 for the introduction of these provisions into the statute, but the terms of Sch.A2 are probably largely declaratory of the then existing law, as established by case law.

In the EPO, the date from which the new rules (EPC rr.26–29, formerly rr.23B–23E, corresponding to Sch.A2) was settled, at least for r.28(c) of the EPC, formerly r.23d(c), by the Enlarged Board in G 2/06 *WARF/Stem cells*, which held that the rule applies to all pending applications, including those filed before the entry into force of the rule. This confirms the decision in T 315/03 *HARVARD/Transgenic animals* OJ EPO 2006, 15; [2005] E.P.O.R. 31 at 271 which held that these EPC rules apply to cases which were pending on the date when those rules took effect. See §76A.03 for further details of G 2/06 *WARF/Stem cells*.

The Directive, as such, does not affect countries outside the European Union and thus does not directly affect the EPC, which is not an instrument of the European Community. Nevertheless, the European Patent Organisation decided to implement the provisions of the Directive by the insertion of new rules into the EPC Implementing Regulations, as from September 1, 1999, for which see OJ EPO 1999, 573 Theses rules are now rr.26 to 29 of EPC 2000.

Much of the Act and the Patents Rules as current in July 2000 could be regarded as already in conformity with the requirements of the Directive, at least when these were construed purposively. However, under the powers of the European Communities Act 1972 (c.41) s.2, as amended, the Act was amended by the Patents Regulations 2000 (SI 2000/2037) having effect from July 28, 2000 to give explicit effect to the terms of arts 1–11 by revisions to ss.1, 60, and 130 (for which see §§1.01, 60.01 and 130.01) together with the introduction of new s.76A and Schs A1 and A2, reprinted under ss.60 and 76A respectively. New s.76A requires that, where a patent or application "concerns a biotechnological invention" (as now defined in s.130(1)), the provisions of the entire Act "shall be subject to, and applied or interpreted in accordance with, the provisions of Schedule A2" and it is this Schedule which implements many of the substantive provisions of the Directive. However, these amendments do not formally affect applications (and patents granted on such applications) having a filing date earlier than July 28, 2000, except to the extent that the changes in wording reflected the existing law or practice.

The Directive has an extensive set of recitals and these need to be taken into account in construing the effect of the Directive's Articles which are divided into five Chapters. These concern respectively:

1. patentability (Ch.I, arts 1–7);

2. scope of protection (Ch.II, arts 8–11);

3. compulsory cross-licensing (Ch.III, art.12);

4. deposit, access and re-deposit of a biological material (Ch. IV, arts 13 and 14, discussed under s.125A; and

5. final provisions (Ch.V, arts 15–18).

For a commentary on the substance and context of the Directive, and in particular a comparison between its provisions and the then existing law under the EPC, see Kamstra et al., *Patents on Biotechnological Inventions: The European Directive Special Report* (London: Sweet & Maxwell, 2001).

The most important features of the Directive would seem to be: (1) the provisions denying patentability to the human body at the various stages of its formation and development and, while the simple discovery of one of its elements, including the sequence of partial sequence of a gene, is also unpatentable (under art.5(1) of the Directive, incorporated in the Act by Sch.A2 para.3(a)), an element isolated from the human body or otherwise produced by means of a technical process may be patentable (on which see §4.02), but the specification (as filed) must disclose the industrial application of a sequence or partial sequence of a gene under art.5(2) and (3) of the Directive, incorporated into the Act under Sch.A2 paras 5 and 6 and into the EPC by rr.23D and 23E of the EPC (now EPC rr.26 to 29); (2) the provisions that: "The protection conferred by a patent on a product containing or consisting of genetic information shall extend to all material, save as provided in art.5(1), in which the product is incorporated and in which the genetic information is incorporated and performs its function" (art.9 and Sch.A2 para. 9), as discussed in §125.25; and (3) that: "Inventions which concern plants or animals shall be patentable if the technical feasibility of the invention is not confined to a particular plant or animal variety" (art.4(2), as supported by Recital 31: on which see Sch.A2 para. 3(f).

The UK-IPO has updated the Examination Guidelines for Patent Applications relating to Biotechnological Inventions in the UK Intellectual Property Office ("*The UK Biotech Guidlelines*"). The most recent edition was published in April 2009 and is available online at: *http://www.ipo.gov.uk/biotech.pdf.*

Scope of the exclusions from patentability and types of claim

76A.03   Since the current legislative regime began in 1978, a wide variety of types of claims for products obtained by biotechnological methods, particularly by recombinant DNA technology have been granted both in the United Kingdom and under the EPC. These include claims directed to micro-organisms per se, particularly newly discovered micro-organisms whether or not naturally occurring, provided in the latter case that the claims are distinguished in some way from the naturally occurring product, e.g. by reference to an "isolated" or "purified" product; cell lines per se including those producing monoclonal antibodies; natural products which have undergone alteration through the intervention of man, such as bacterial mutants and attenuated viruses and protozoa; natural products, such as proteins, which have been isolated from animals or micro-organisms; the products of recombinant DNA technology, such as DNA and polypeptides produced therefrom, and materials useful in recombinant DNA technology such as vectors, plasmids, promoters and transformable micro-organisms.

For a detailed review of the types of claim permitted and rejected by the EPO on biotechnology inventions see *From Clones to Claims* by Jaenichen, McDonell, Haley Jr. and Hosoda (Heymans, 2006, ISBN 3-452-24738-4).

Some of the early arguments about patentability of elements isolated from the human body (EPC art.53(a)) and transgenic plants (EPC art.53(b)) have now been disposed of in the wake of the Directive and Enlarged Board case law. For example, the second decision in T 272/95 *HOWARD FLOREY INSTITUTE/Joint opposition* [2000] E.P.O.R. 235, dated October 23, 2002, held that a claim to a DNA fragment encoding a human protein was not excluded from patentability by being contrary to morality. Novelty and inventive step were also acknowledged.

Plants and animals

The meaning of the exclusion from patentability in art.53(b) of the EPC and hence in s.1(3)(b)) led to much debate culminating in G 1/98 *NOVARTIS II/Transgenic plant* OJ EPO 2000, 111; [2000] E.P.O.R. 303. Here, it was explained that the prohibition of art.53(b) of the EPC had been included in the EPC (as in the precedent Strasbourg Convention of 1963) so as not to permit dual protection under both a patent and a plant breeder's right under the UPOV Convention (as this then stood); and, accordingly, was limited to claims directed to a "plant variety" as such. Thus, the claims here in issue were patentable because "in the absence of the identification of specific varieties in the product claims, the subject-matter of the claimed invention was neither limited nor even directed to a variety or varieties"; and, as such, could not anyway be protected by the grant of plant breeder's rights. However, it was stated that "a new plant variety bred as a result of genetically modifying a particular plant variety is still excluded from patent protection, even if the genetic modification is the result of a biotechnological process". In order that the method claims of the *Novartis* application should not cover essentially biological processes, these would be limited to "identifiable method steps".

In early EPO case law, claims were allowed to "Propagating material for cultivated plants treated with X" on the basis that the specified treatment was essentially a chemical one whereas the patentability exclusion corresponding to s.1(3)(b) relates to material produced by an essentially biological process (T 49/83 *CIBA-GEIGY/Propagating material* OJ EPO 1984, 112); and for a process for rapidly developing hybrids and producing hybrid seeds, such a process not being "essentially biological" because the usual order of the cloning and crossing steps had been reversed and a high yield of seed resulted, this being an important technical characteristic of the process, but such hybrid seed lacked stability and could therefore not be classified as a plant variety (T 320/87 *LUBRIZOL/Hybrid plants* OJ EPO 1990, 71; [1990] E.P.O.R. 173).

In T 19/90 *HARVARD/Onco-mouse* OJ EPO 1990, 476; [1990] E.P.O.R. 501, the invention concerned a transgenic non-human mammalian animal whose cells contain an oncogene sequence. It was there held that art.53(b) of the EPC did not preclude protection for living matter, e.g. for animals as such, and it was emphasised that EPC art.53(b) was an exception to the general rule that patents should be granted for all inventions that met the requirements of the EPC; also that there should be a proper balance between the interests of inventors in this field and society's interest in excluding certain categories of animals from patent protection, bearing in mind that there is no alternative industrial property right for the protection of animals. The case was remitted to the Examining Division, who held (*HARVARD/Onco-mouse* OJ EPO 1992, 588; [1991] E.P.O.R. 525) that mammals and rodents constitute higher taxonomic classification units than species, with animal varieties ranking even lower than that, with the consequence that claims to oncogenic non-human mammals are not excluded by EPC art.53(b). However, the resulting patent was opposed and maintained in amended form. On appeal, the Board in T 315/03 *HARVARD/Onco-mouse* [2006] 1 OJ EPO 15; [2005] E.P.O.R. 31 allowed claims for transgenic mice but refused claims encompassing rodents and noted that the relevant date for assessing morality is the priority date of the patent in question. The Board also confirmed that the possible detrimental effects and risks must be weighed and balances against the merits and advantages. In particular, the basic interest of mankind to remedy disease had to be set against environmental protection from uncontrolled dissemination of unwanted genes and the avoidance of suffering to animals, including the possibility of using non-animal alternatives.

T 315/03 *HARVARD/Onco-mouse* also confirmed that, in an assessment under EPC art.53(b), the principle enunciated in G 1/98 *NOVARTIS II/Transgenic plant* concerning plants and "plant varieties" should be followed in the case of animals: a patent should not be granted for a single animal variety (or species or race, depending on which language text of the EPC is used) but can be granted if varieties may fall within the scope of its claims. The patenting of living matter under the terms of the Biotechnology Directive has been upheld by the ECJ in *Kingdom of the Netherlands v European Parliament (C-377/98)* [2002] F.S.R. 574; OJ EPO 2002, 231; [2002] I.P.&T. 121.

It is generally accepted that G 1/98 *NOVARTIS II/Transgenic plant* is in accord with arts.4(2) and (3) of the Directive and of the Act, as now amended as well as EPC rr.26 and 27.

Human stem cells

The question of the patentability of human embryonic stem cells has been resolved, at least in part, in G 2/06 *WARF/Use of embryos*, in which, in addition to deciding that EPC r.28(c) applies to all pending applications, including those filed before the entry into force of the rule (see §76A.02 above), EPC r.28(c) forbids the patenting of claims directed to products which—as described in the application—at the filing date could be prepared exclusively by a method which necessarily involved the destruction of the human embryos from which the products are derived, even if the method is not part of the claims.

It is not of relevance that after the filing date the same products could be obtained without having to recur to a method necessarily involving the destruction of human embryos.

The fact that the wording of the claims in question related to embryonic stem cells per se and not to a method for using (or preparing) them did not help the appellant. The Enlarged Board stated at para.22 that what needed to be looked at was "the technical teaching of the application as a whole as to how the invention is to be performed", and on this approach it was the fact that at the filing date the only way of making the claimed cells involved the destruction of a human embryo that appears to have been decisive for the Enlarged Board. This seems still to leave the door open, therefore, for the patentability of stem cells which at the filing date can be produced without destroying human embryos. Time will tell, but with continuing advances in the field it may be that the decision in G 2/06 in this respect will be seen to be primarily of historical interest.

In addition to answering the referred questions, the Enlarged Board rejected as inadmissible a request for a preliminary ruling on them by the Court of Justice.

G 2/06 *WARF/Stem cells* was analysed by S. Mitchell and G. Schlich in [2008] *CIPA* 708 and [2009] 1 *epi-Information* 11. See also the recent judgment of the CJEU in *Brüstle v Greenpeace eV* (Case C-34/10) discussed below.

The UK-IPO reviewed its practice in light of G 2/06 *WARF/Stem cells*, a notice of which is available at *http://www.ipo.gov.uk/pro-types/pro-patent/p-law/p-pn/p-pn-stemcells-20090203.htm*. The essence of the notice is that (i) patents will not be granted for processes of obtaining stem cells from human embryos; (ii) neither will patents be granted for human totipotent cells which have the potential to develop into an entire human body; and (iii) the UK-IPO will continue in principle to grant patents for inventions involving human embryonic pluripotent stem cells (which arise from further division of totipotent cells, which do not have the potential to develop into an entire human body, and which can be grown in culture and the cell lines stored in cell banks) provided that, at the filing or priority date, the invention could be obtained by means other than the destruction of human embryos.

A recent decision of the UK-IPO on human stem cells is *Cellartis AB's Application* (BL/O/050/11), in which a method for propagating and maintaining isolated xeno-free human blastocyst-derived stem cells (hBS cells) was held not to be patentable by virtue of para.3(d) to Sch.A2 since it was not possible to work the invention without the destruction of a human embryo each time. However, the individual xeno-free hBS cell line SA611 was held not to be excluded from patentability, but as it had not been deposited, it was insufficiently described, not entitled to priority and held to be anticipated by an intervening publication.

In the UK Biotech Guidelines the view is taken in para.105 that the term "embryo" should not be restricted to a live human embryo produced by the fertilisation of a female egg, but should be interpreted to include an embryo produced without such fertilisation, such as one created by cell nuclear replacement (*R (Quintavalle) v Sec of State for Health* [2003] UKHL 13; [2003] 2 All E.R. 113). In addition, those Guidelines adopt the EU Council's reasoning (Official Journal of the EC, C 110/17 at 30, 8.4.98, para.35), saying that all references to a human being should be interpreted as referring to the human being from the embryonic state).

Human embryonic stem cells have also recently come to the attention of the CJEU in *Brüstle v Greenpeace eV* (Case C-34/10). In its judgment of October 18, 2011, the court took a somewhat different approach from that recommended by Advocate-General Bot in his opinion of March 10, 2011 and held:

1 A 'human embryo' within the meaning of art.6(2)(c) of the Biotech Directive is defined broadly to include: any human ovum after fertilisation, any non-fertilised human ovum into which the cell nucleus from a mature human cell has been transplanted, and any non-fertilised human ovum whose division and further development have been stimulated by partheno¬genesis. In the light of this, it is for the referring court to ascertain, in the light of scientific developments, whether a stem cell obtained from a human embryo at the blastocyst stage constitutes a 'human embryo'.

2. The exclusion from patentability concerning the use of human embryos for industrial

or commercial purposes set out in art.6(2)(c) also covers the use of human embryos for purposes of scientific research. Following Recital 42, uses of a human embryo for therapeutic or diagnostic purposes applied to the human embryo are patentable only if they are useful to the embryo.

3. Art.6(2)(c) excludes an invention from patentability where the technical teaching which is the subject-matter of the patent application requires the prior destruction of human embryos or their use as base material, whatever the stage at which that takes place and even if the description of the invention does not refer to the use of human embryos. This exclusion is expressly meant not to be capable of being circumvented 'by skilful drafting of the claim'.

See §§1.21 and 1.22 for further comments on the public policy and plant and animal variety exclusions.

Reach-through claims

In T 1063/06 *BAYER SCHERING PHARMA AG/Reach-through claims* [2010] E.P.O.R. 17, Board 3.3.10 squarely addressed the patentability of so-called reach-though claims, which hitherto had only been dealt with obliquely in such cases as T 609/02 *SALK INSTITUTE/AP-1 complex*. A reach-through claim, historically in the Swiss-style format "Use of a compound [having some in vitro activity in relation to biological molecule X] in the manufacture of a medicament for treating [disease Y]" seeks to define the active ingredient in a medical use claim not in terms of its structure but rather in terms of its function in relation to a biologically active molecule, such as an enzyme or cytokine. Proponents of such claims—typically applicants who have cloned a gene encoding protein found to be useful in a screen of some sort—see them as a vehicle for getting fair reward for their "research tool" invention, by seeking to monopolise the subsequent medical use of a compound identified as being medically useful by means of the screen. The Board did not agree, characterising such claims as being "directed to future inventions based on the one now being disclosed". In the case in point, the claims fell foul of EPC art.83 on the grounds of undue burden, but this conclusion was preceded by a lengthy critique of the formulation of the claim which owes more to general principles than any particular legislative basis.

See also the (pre-T 1063/06) discussion of reach-through claims in the UK-IPO Biotech Guidelines at paras 80–81.

In *MedImmune Ltd v Novartis Pharmaceuticals UK Ltd and Anor* [2011] EWHC 1669 (Pat), it was argued, relying on T 1063/06, that the claims directed to methods for producing a binding molecule (such as an antibody fragment) specific for a particular target epitope or antigen by phage display technology were "reach-through claims by stealth". The judge disagreed, holding at [491] that the invention was a principle of general application that did not depend on the precise identity of the binding molecule. T 1063/06 was distinguished.

Particular forms of claim applicable to biotechnology

Previous editions of this work have devoted considerable space to the particular forms **76A.04** of claim applicable to biotechnology that have been accepted by the UK-IPO and the EPO. Now that this discipline has reached some maturity it is felt no longer necessary to carry such a survey. Accordingly, the treatment that follows highlights certain forms of claim of particular interest, but does not attempt to be comprehensive. For a fuller treatment, please consult the Sixth Edition of the work.

—Cell lines

For a discussion of the patentability of human stem cells, see §76A.03 above. See in **76A.05** particular the discussion of the claimed cell line SA611 in *Cellartis AB's Application* (BL/ O/050/11).

—Recombinant DNA

76A.06   The Court of Appeal's decision is reviewed by Gareth Morgan in "When the TBA just isn't enough" [2010] 4 *CIPA* 227. See also the article by Robert Fitt and Edward Nodder in "Setting the threshold for industrial application: the UK diverges from Europe" (2010) 5(8) *Journal of Intellectual Property Law & Practice* 560–565 and the article by Andrew Sharples "Industrial applicability for genetics patents—divergences between the EPO and the UK" EIPR 2011, 33(2), 72.

The decision of the Supreme Court in *Eli Lilly v Human Genome Sciences* [2011] UKSC 51 is discussed at §4.03.

The *UK Biotech Guidelines* indicate, at para.46, that in the light of the first instance judgment it is permissible for the UK-IPO to use a "problem/solution" approach to inventive step in the United Kingdom, as a departure from the *Windsurfer/Pozzoli* test, in biotech applications where there is an inherent lack of industrial application. Kitchin J.'s "nine principles" relating to industrial application have been incorporated in the *UK Biotech Guidelines* at para.55.

—Plants and animals

76A.07   Article 4 of the Biotechnology Directive, reprinted at §C04 and incorporated into the Act by Sch.A2 paras 3(f) and 4, provides that inventions which concern plants or animals shall be patentable if the technical feasibility of the invention is not confined to a particular plant or variety. Transgenic, or genetically modified (GM), plants and animals are therefore, in principle, patentable. Insofar as national law does not necessarily operate retrospectively in relation to those provisions, the case law is relevant to patents granted before the Patents (Amendment) Rules 2000 took effect on July 28, 2000.

Schedule A2, para.3(f) replaced former subs.(3)(b) as regards applications (and patents granted on such applications) dated on or after the above date. These provisions exclude from patentability "any variety of animal or plant or any essentially biological process for [their production], not being a microbiological process or the product of such a process". The corresponding EPC art.53(b) (explained in EPO Guidelines C–IV, 4.6–4.7) is more direct in its wording, and states that the exclusion does not apply to micro-biological processes or the products thereof. These provisions appear to be in conformity with art.27.3 of the TRIPS Agreement, although only because plant varieties are protectable under other legislation, as discussed further below in relation to the effect of the possible overlapping protection between patents and plant breeders' rights.

The exclusion of plant varieties from patent protection arises from the existence in many EPC Member States of plant breeders' rights as a result of their adherence to the 1964 International Convention for the Protection of New Varieties of Plants ("the UPOV Convention") as revised in 1972 and 1978 (Cmnd.9152). The prohibition on dual patent and plant variety protection in these forms of the UPOV Convention came to be seen as illogical, and it was removed in the further 1991 revision of the Convention, now ratified by the United Kingdom.

Plant breeders' rights originally arose under the Plant Varieties and Seeds Act 1964 (c.14), as amended, principally by the Plant Varieties Act 1983 (c.17), but are now governed by the Plant Varieties Act 1997 (c.66), the provisions of which are summarised in a Guide to the Plant Varieties Act 1997 published by the Food and Environment Research Agency (FERA), an executive agency of the Department for Environment Food and Rural Affairs (DEFRA) and available at *http://www.fera.defra.gov.uk/plants/plantVarieties/*. Although the 1991 version of the UPOV Convention has abolished the former prohibition against the dual protection of plant varieties by both plant breeders' rights and by patent rights, the 1997 Act continues this prohibition for the United Kingdom. For a discussion on the 1991 Convention, see the book "Commentary on the Substantive law of the 1991 UPOV Convention for the Protection of Plant Varieties" by Noel Byrne (Queen Mary and Westfield College, 1994).

Regulation No. 2100/94 Community Plant Variety Rights [1994] OJ EC L227/1; [1995] F.S.R. 396, effective from April 27, 1995, provides Community-wide industrial property rights for plant varieties. If such a right is obtained, then any patent for the protected variety becomes ineffective, at least for that variety (Regulation, art.92).

As well as the Guide to the Plant Varieties Act 1997, other resources are available from FERA's website at *http://www.fera.defra.gov.uk.*

The Patents and Plant Variety Rights (Compulsory Licensing) Regulations (SI 2002/247) came into force on March 1, 2002 (to complete the implementation of art.12 of the Biotechnology Directive), and provide that, where a person cannot acquire or exploit plant breeders' rights without infringing a prior patent, he may apply to the Comptroller for a licence under the patent, subject to payment of an appropriate royalty and an agreement to cross-licence the plant variety right to the owner of that patent. A licence is only available where the new plant variety constitutes significant technical progress of considerable economic interest in relation to the invention. Further, where a proprietor of a patent for a biotechnological invention cannot exploit the invention without infringing prior plant breeders' rights, he may apply to the Controller of Plant Variety Rights for a licence under such rights, but only where the biotechnological invention protected by the patent constitutes significant technical progress of considerable economic interest in relation to the plant variety. It is thought that the Regulations may for this reason find application only in rare circumstances and they are not reproduced in this Work; see also the commentaries on ss.48 and 48A.

—Methods of culture of plants and of breeding animals

Article 2 of the Biotechnology Directive (incorporated into the Act by Sch.A2 para.11), **76A.08** reprinted in §76A.01A, defines a process for the production of plants or animals as essentially biological if it consists entirely of natural phenomena such as crossing or selection. The definition leaves open the issue of whether a process, which merely includes such a step and also includes a step requiring human intervention, is patentable. The issue was referred in G 2/07 and G 1/08 to the Enlarged Board to determine the extent to which the presence of additional steps in an otherwise "essentially biological process" could take the process out of the exclusion from patentability in art.53(b) EPC. The proceedings were consolidated and in the decision of the consolidated proceedings, handed down on December 9, 2010, the Enlarged Board held:

1. A non-microbiological process for the production of plants which contains or consists of the steps of sexually crossing the whole genomes of plants and of subsequently selecting plants is in principle excluded from patentability as being "essentially biological" within the meaning of art.53(b) EPC.

2. Such a process does not escape the exclusion of art.53(b) EPC merely because it contains, as a further step or as part of any of the steps of crossing and selection, a step of a technical nature which serves to enable or assist the performance of the steps of sexually crossing the whole genomes of plants or of subsequently selecting plants.

3. If, however, such a process contains within the steps of sexually crossing and selecting an additional step of a technical nature, which step by itself introduces a trait into the genome or modifies a trait in the genome of the plant produced, so that the introduction or modification of that trait is not the result of the mixing of the genes of the plants chosen for sexual crossing, then the process is not excluded from patentability under art.53(b) EPC.

4. In the context of examining whether such a process is excluded from patentability as being "essentially biological" within the meaning of art.53(b) EPC, it is not relevant whether a step of a technical nature is a new or known measure, whether it is trivial or a fundamental alteration of a known process, whether it does or could occur in nature or whether the essence of the invention lies in it.

The questions referred to the Enlarged Board in in G 2/07 and G 1/08 were framed soley in terms of the production of plants, not animals, and were therefore answered in such terms. Some of the Enlarged Board's reasoning, however, could be taken also to apply to the production of animals.

Prior art issues applicable to biotechnology

76A.09   There is no law or practice which differentiates the approach to issues of lack of novelty or of inventive step in biotechnological cases from those in other fields. However, certain aspects have featured particularly prominently in biotechnological cases, namely:

(a) whether the prior art is part of the common general knowledge or is an enabling disclosure (more generally discussed in the commentary on s.2);

(b) whether the claim is to a desideratum (merely stating the problem to be solved) or whether the route to the subject-matter claimed was obvious to try with a reasonable expectation of success (more generally discussed in the commentary on s.3);

(c) whether particular operations were within the competence of the average skilled person, i.e. whether the specification is sufficient (more generally discussed in commentary on s.14); and

(d) entitlement to priority (more generally discussed in the commentary on s.5).

These topics are discussed, in their application to biotechnology, in the following paragraphs, see particularly §76A.15 which carries a warning of the forced self-anticipation of patent claims which may result from the need for compliance with governmental regulations in relation to experiments involving genetic modification, unless some waiver can be negotiated.

Common General Knowledge

76A.10   In T 890/02 *BAYER/Chimeric gene* [2006] E.P.O.R. 10 at 102, it was held that certain databases, whilst not being *stricto sensu* encyclopaedias or handbooks, can represent the common general knowledge of the skilled person. The conditions are: (a) adequacy—the database must be known to the skilled person as an adequate source for obtaining the required information; (b) appropriateness—the information must be retrievable from the database without undue burden; and (c) correctness—the database must provide the information in a straightforward and unambiguous manner without any need for supplementary searches. In this case, the ENZYME and the EMBL databases were held to be part of the common general knowledge.

—Enabling disclosure

76A.11   While the leading case on this issue is in a non-biotechnological field, namely T 206/83 *ICI/Pyridine herbicides* OJ EPO 1987, 5; [1986] E.P.O.R. 232, biotechnological cases in which it has been affirmed that the prior art must have been enabling to be an effective disclosure include: *Genentech's (Human Growth Hormone) Patent* [1989] R.P.C. 613 at 633; T 261/89 *MERCK/Human hepatitis A virus* (Unreported) and T 923/92 *GENENTECH/Human t-PA*.

A reference in a published scientific paper to a certain plasmid does not make it available to the public in an enabling manner, a presumed scientific custom of free exchange of such material not being sufficient to overcome a presumption of non-availability free of contractual obligations (T 576/91 *NORTH CAROLINA STATE UNIVERSITY/Plasmid pTR2030* [1998] E.P.O.R. 382). In T 128/92 *AJINOMOTO/IL-2* the Board stated at para.13 that for a complex biochemical to be made available to the public, the minimum that would seem to be required for publication was a notice to those in the field that samples of the biochemical could be obtained on request, and clear evidence of exactly what the biochemical was.

—Claims to a desideratum or to matters "obvious to try"

Early gene cloning cases often revolved around the issue of whether a known protein, **76A.12** prepared by a recombinant DNA process of a kind known per se, could be validly claimed. This issue was not resolved by the invalidation of broad product claims in *Genentech's Patent* [1989] R.P.C. 147 CA, the first biotechnology case to come before the Court of Appeal, on the grounds that the starting materials were available, the cloning procedures known per se and the protein encoded (tissue plasminogen activator, "t-PA") being obviously desirable. The UK-IPO's view of Genentech's Patent is that it "has limited value because although all three judges decided the patent was invalid, they did so for different reasons" (*UK-IPO Biotech Guidelines* para.(30)). In the corresponding European patent, oppositions were rejected by the EPO, who upheld a claim directed to a process of preparing (inter alia) t-PA of a defined amino acid sequence, by expression in a recombinant host organism or transforming DNA encoding the protein (T 923/92 *GENENTECH/Human t-PA*). This decision followed T 60/89 *HARVARD/Fusion proteins* OJ EPO 1992, 268; [1992] E.P.O.R. 320 which stated that the notion "obvious to try" must be qualified by the notion of "reasonable expectation of success". On the evidence, particularly concerned with the low abundance and length of the mRNA starting material, they found the claims unobvious.

Following this theme, the Patents Court, in *Chiron v Organon Teknika (No.3)* [1994] F.S.R. 202, upheld claims to a polypeptide comprising an amino acid sequence encoded by the genome of hepatitis C virus (HCV) on a finding that it was by no means obvious which route could be used to achieve such a material, which anyway had not at the time been sufficiently identified by others. These decisions were not challenged on appeal (*Chiron v Murex* [1996] R.P.C. 535 CA).

In *Biogen v Medeva* [1995] R.P.C. 25, the main claim was directed to DNA capable of expressing hepatitis B virus (HBV) antigens. The Patents Court held the inventive concept to be "the idea or decision" to express a polypeptide displaying HBV antigen specificity in a suitable host. The claim was held unobvious, because the factual situation as disclosed in the cited references was more consistent with the evidence for the plaintiff than with the evidence for the defendant, and because there was no evidence to suggest that anyone other than the plaintiff contemplated expression of HBV antigens, despite the incentive to do so. On appeal, the Court of Appeal saw the attempt at the apparently impossible task as a business decision which, once taken, made the actual step of doing the experiment an obvious step to take. The House of Lords (see [1997] R.P.C. 1) did not agree with this approach, but found the claims invalid for reasons concerned with lack of sufficient description. Lord Hoffmann, giving the leading judgment, found that the claims were not supported by the earliest priority application, because of the lack of sufficiency of description in the priority document across the breadth of the claim. Upon denial of this priority date, the claims were then held obvious in view of an intermediate publication (see §3.25). Additionally, the claims were bad for insufficiency for lack of a sufficiently supporting description, Lord Hoffmann stating that: "care must be taken not to stifle further research and healthy competition by allowing the first person who has found a way of achieving an obviously desirable goal to monopolise every other way of doing so", see further the commentary on s.14. This decision was reached despite the claims having been upheld by the EPO in opposition proceedings, see T 296/93 *BIOGEN/Hepatitis B*. More generally, the EPO has historically not had the same aversion to claims to desiderata as the UK courts, with T 595/90 *KAWASAKI/Grain oriented silicon sheet* holding that a product which can be envisaged as such with all the characteristics determining its identity, including its properties in use—i.e. an otherwise obvious entity—may become non-obvious and claimable as such, if there is no known way or applicable (analogy) method in the art to make it and the claimed methods for its preparation are the first to achieve this and do so in an inventive manner. This approach was followed in a number of early gene cloning cases, although the EPO's insistence that the sequence (at least of the encoded protein) be present in the claim meant that the claims did not look like—and to that extent strictly were not—desiderata.

Claims to isolated genes have nowadays become increasingly difficult to obtain with increased knowledge of different genomes (and corresponding proteomes) as well as the vastly increased sophistication of bioinformatics as an analytical and predictive tool. The UK-IPO's position now is that :

"Following the sequencing of various genomes, there is unlikely to be an inventive step in identifying from within a sequenced genome any new gene, even those without known homologues. It is obvious to trawl the genome for previously unidentified genes, and any skilled worker would have some expectation of success." [*UK-IPO Biotech Manual* para.33]

That is not to say that the door is completely shut. In T 1165/06 SCHERING/IL-17 related polypeptide the Board held that, because there was low overall homology between the various gene family members and the available screening methods would not be straightforward, a claim to DNA encoding a new family member—IL-174—was inventive.

In relation to antibodies, in T 499/88 *UNILEVER/Immunoglobulins* [1996] E.P.O.R. 235, it was held that the replacement of monospecific polyclonal antibodies by monoclonal antibodies in an immunopurification process lacked inventive step. T 906/91 *DUPONT/Hybridoma* [1999] E.P.O.R. 423 similarly held it obvious to make a monoclonal antibody when polyclonal antibodies of similar, but less effective, activity were already known.

Although T 60/89 *HARVARD/Fusion protein* stated that "obviousness to try" must be qualified by a reasonable expectation of success, a principle followed in many biotechnology cases, not all relevant EPO cases articulate the necessity for the latter qualification. T 416/01 *THERMO TRILOGY/Controlling fungi* (unreported) and T 73/03 *EXXONMOBIL/Diesel fuel lubricity* (unreported) were cases in point, although it may be argued that a reasonable expectation of success was apparent in the circumstances. However, T 43/02 *MITSUBISHI PHARMA/Remedy for asthma* held that a reasonable expectation of success was still part of the test since the skilled person may easily conceive of inventions, yet realising them may cause problems in view of difficulties known in advance or experienced when practically embarking on a project. It may be, therefore, that the appropriateness of the "reasonable expectation of success" limb is at least in the EPO dependent on the prevailing technical difficulties facing the skilled person at the relevant date (see for example T 694/92 *MYCOGEN/Modifying plant cells*). Note that T 296/93 *BIOGEN/Recombinant DNA* distinguished between a reasonable expectation of success on the one hand with the understandable "hope to succeed" on the other.

In *DSM's Patent* [2001] R.P.C. 35 at 675, claims to a gene sequence of a known enzyme were not seen as either a mere *desideratum* or as something obvious as such a try, but the claims were otherwise held invalid for lack of inventive step and for insufficiency.

In *Hoffmann-La Roche's Application* BL O/192/04, the hearing officer adopted a three-part "obvious to try" test in applying the fourth *Windsurfing* step: (a) would it have been obvious to the addressee to try and obtain an alternative human intestinal sodium phosphate co-transporter? (b) Would a route to this goal have required any degree of invention on the part of the addressee? And (c) assuming there was an obvious route, would the addressee have obtained a polypeptide comprising SEQ ID NO: 01 as the inevitable consequence of following this route?

More recently, and most authoritatively, the House of Lords considered the obviousness to try/reasonable expectation of success issue in *Conor Medsystems Inc (Respondents) v Angiotech Pharmaceuticals Inc (Appellants)* [2008] R.P.C. 28; [2008] UKHL 49. Giving the lead opinion, Lord Hoffmann criticised the judge at first instance for not using the "reasonable expectation of success" limb, and suggested that the reason he had felt the need to avoid it was because he had asked the wrong question in relation to obviousness:

"28. The question was whether that [*i.e.* a taxol-coated stent for preventing or treating restenosis] *was* obvious and not whether it was obvious that taxol (among many other products) *might* have this effect. It is hard to see how the notion that something is worth trying or might have some effect can be described as an invention in respect of which anyone would be entitled to a monopoly. It is therefore perhaps not surprising that the test for obviousness which Pumfrey J devised for such an 'invention' was whether it was obvious to try it without any expectation of success. This oxymoronic concept has, so far as I know, no precedent in the law of patents."

He went on to indicate what he considered to be the correct approach, namely that there must be a fair (or, presumably, reasonable) expectation of success, but how much of an expectation was needed would vary according to the facts of each case:

"42. In the Court of Appeal, Jacob LJ dealt comprehensively with the question of when an invention could be considered obvious on the ground that it was obvious to try. He correctly summarised the authorities, starting with the judgment of Diplock LJ in *Johns-Manville Corporation's Patent* [1967] R.P.C. 479, by saying that the notion of something being obvious to try was useful only in a case in which there was a fair expectation of success. How much of an expectation would be needed depended upon the particular facts of the case. As Kitchin J said in *Generics (UK) Ltd v H Lundbeck A/S* [2007] R.P.C.32, para 72:

'The question of obviousness must be considered on the facts of each case. The court must consider the weight to be attached to any particular factor in the light of all the relevant circumstances. These may include such matters as the motive to find a solution to the problem the patent addresses, the number and extent of the possible avenues of research, the effort involved in pursuing them and the expectation of success.'"

MedImmune Ltd v Novartis Pharmaceuticals UK Limited and Anor [2011] EWHC 1669 (Pat) is a recent example in a biotechnology case of the application of the *Conor* formulation of obviousness to try coupled with a fair expectation of success (at [377]).

—The person skilled in the art

In *Genentech's Patent* [1987] R.P.C. 553; and [1989] R.P.C. 147 CA, the "person   **76A.13**
skilled in the art" in a biotechnological case involving genetic engineering was seen as necessarily involving a team of persons of interacting disciplines. Likewise, in T 60/89 *HARVARD/Fusion proteins*, where it was held that the skilled person was not to be defined as a Nobel Laureate, even if a number were working in the field, but a graduate scientist or team working in laboratories which developed genetic engineering techniques. The patent in suit had a 1978 priority date, but the decision was applied in T 500/91 *BIOGEN/Alpha interferon II*, where the skilled person was held to be "oriented to practicalities and not expected to solve the problems by scientific research in new areas"; see also T 249/88 *MONSANTO/Milk production*. In *Chiron v Organon Teknika (No.3)* [1994] F.S.R. 202, the court stated that it was difficult to draw any inference as to what would be the attitude of the notional skilled addressee of the specification from the opinion of a Nobel prize winner, and in particular from such a person who was not working in the field at the time. In T 412/93 *KIRIN-AMGEN/Erythropoietin*, which related to the cloning of the erythropoietin gene, the parties agreed that in this particular case the skilled person should be treated as a team of three, composed of one PhD researcher with several years' experience in the aspect of gene technology or biochemistry under consideration, assisted by two laboratory technicians fully acquainted with the known techniques relevant to that aspect; the composition of the team might vary depending on the knowledge and skills required by the particular aspect dealt with. In T 455/91 *GENENTECH/Expression in yeast* OJ EPO 1995, 684; [1996] E.P.O.R. 85 it was held at §5.1.3.3:

"In the Board's view, the skilled person in this field is well aware of the fact that even a small structural change in a product (eg a vector, a protein, a DNA sequence) or in a procedure (eg a purification process) can produce dramatic functional changes. Therefore, the said expert would constantly be conditioned by the prior art and, before taking action, would carefully ponder any possible modification, change or adjustment against the background of the existing knowledge. Under these circumstances, in the board's view, the skilled person would adopt a conservative attitude. However, this must not be seen in the sense of being reluctant or opposed to modify or adjust a known product or process, but rather in the sense of being cautious. For example, the skilled person in question would neither go against an established prejudice nor try to enter into "sacrosanct" or unpredictable areas nor take incalculable risks. However, within the normal design procedures, the said expert would readily seek appropriate, manifest changes, modifications or adjustments which involve little trouble or work and no risks or only calculable risks, especially for the sake of obtaining a more handy or convenient product or of simplifying a procedure. In particular, the skilled person working in one field (eg expression in yeast) would regard a means conveniently adopted in a neighbouring field (eg the bacterial art) as being readily usable also in that field, if this transfer of technical knowledge involves nothing out of the ordinary."

In *MedImmune Ltd v Novartis Pharmaceuticals UK Ltd and Anor* [2011] EWHC 1669 (Pat), it was held at [93], following *Schlumberger Holdings Ltd v Electromagnetic Geoservices AS* [2010] EWCA Civ 819, [2010] R.P.C. 33 at [30]-[70], that the skilled person was a team of scientists with differing backgrounds in areas such as immunology (in particular antibody structural biology), molecular biology and protein chemistry, but with a common interest in antibody engineering, to which the case related. The judge held at [97] that the approach of the EPO Boards of Appeal was consistent with the long-standing approach of the courts of the UK of treating the skilled person as being "an unimaginative man with no inventive capacity" (per Lord Reid in *Technograph Printed Circuits Ltd v Mills & Rockley (Electronics) Ltd* [1972] R.P.C. 346 at 355).

Entitlement to priority

76A.14   In *Biogen v Medeva* [1995] R.P.C. 25, the Patents Court held that claim 1 was "akin to an invention for a principle", namely the application of expression techniques to produce hepatitis B virus antigens using a suitable host and conditions. Since the core and surface HBV antigens could be produced from *E. coli*, and since the specification suggested other suitable hosts, the claim was entitled to priority. However, on appeal, the core and surface antigens were seen as separate inventions with only the preparation of the core antigen being sufficiently described in the priority document for priority to be accorded to this "invention". This had the consequence that that part of claim 1 directed to the more important surface antigen was admitted to lack invention in view of the publication (during the priority period) of the sequence of this protein. The Court of Appeal also disagreed that the surface antigen had in fact been made before the claimed priority date. The House of Lords (see [1997] R.P.C. 1) took a somewhat different view in that it saw the success of the inventor as not having established any new principle which his successors had to follow if they were to achieve the same results and, accordingly, priority was denied for this reason, see §5.23. In the corresponding case in the EPO, priority was accorded on the basis of the core and surface antigens being regarded as "the same invention" (T 296/93 *BIOGEN/Hepatitis B*).

Other biotechnological cases on entitlement to priority and include T 301/87 *BIOGEN/Alpha-interferons* although the approach in that case to a document published in the priority interval must no longer be regarded as correct in the light of G 3/93 *Priority Interval* OJ EPO 1995, 018; [1994] E.P.O.R. 521 and T 81/87 *COLLABORATIVE/Preprorennin* OJ EPO 1990, 250; [1990] E.P.O.R. 361 and its parallel cases *Collaborative Research's Patent* BL O/86/94, noted I.P.D. 18004 which reached a similar result. The requirement for claiming priority of "the same invention" referred to in art.87(1) of the EPC, has been explained by the Enlarged Board in G 2/98 *Requirement for claiming priority of the "same invention"* OJ EPO 2001, 413; [2002] E.P.O.R. 17 as meaning that priority of a previous application in respect of a claim in a European patent application in accordance with art.88 of the EPC is to be acknowledged only if the skilled person can derive the subject-matter of the claim *directly and unambiguously*, using common general knowledge, from the previous application as a whole. Identical wording is not required, see T 81/87 *COLLABORATIVE/Preprorennin* (above), but the Boards of Appeal have taken G 2/98 *X/Same invention* as requiring a strict concordance between a sequence in a priority document and that recited in a claim. In T 923/92 *GENENTECH/Human t-PA*, the priority right was not upheld for claims reciting an amino acid sequence which differed three amino acids out of 527 from that recited in the priority document. The same approach was also taken in T 70/05 *GENENTECH/Apoptosis receptors*, where it was explicitly stated that no priority right could be claimed from an earlier application disclosing an amino acid or nucleotide sequence which differs from the sequence in a later application only by unintended sequencing or typing errors, and in T 1213/05 *UNIVERSITY OF UTAH/Breast and ovarian cancer* (the BRCA1 case). The patentee in T 250/06 *UNIVERSITY OF CALIFORNIA/Opioid receptor genes* obtained a more favourable result, but the difference in outcomes may be a result of the different claim wording used (nucleic acids that hybridise to a reference sequence under low stringency conditions in T 250/06 *UNIVERSITY OF CALIFORNIA/Opioid receptor genes*, as opposed to nucleic acids encoding a reference amino acid sequence or encoding an amino acid sequence with at least 95 per cent identity to the reference sequence in T 1213/05 *UNIVERSITY OF UTAH/Breast and ovarian cancer*). H.-R. Jaenichen and O. Malek argue in *epi Information*, 3/2008, 91 for a more lenient approach generally.

In T 903/05 *GEMVAX/Telomerase peptides*, the Board held that the "plausibility" test applied in T 1329/04 (discussed in §76A.16 below) was not relevant for the issue of entitlement to priority. See further the commentary on section 5 in relation to priority issues generally.

In T 666/05 *UNIVERSITY OF UTAH/Mutation*, another case relating to BRCA1, Board 3.3.04 distinguished its earlier decision T 1213/05 (the BRCA1 case) on the facts: T 666/05 related to diagnosing a predisposition for breast cancer by determining whether there was a particular germline mutation in a tissue sample; although there were sequencing discrepancies between the patent and the priority document, they were not fatal to priority since the sequence in question was not here a technical feature of the claimed invention.

In *MedImmune Ltd v Novartis Pharmaceuticals UK Ltd and Anor* [2011] EWHC 1669 (Pat) at [303], Arnold J. adopted his own summary of the law in *Intervet UK Ltd v Merial* [2010] EWHC 294 (Pat) at [180]–[183]. He also held at [304] that the burden of proof in a priority dispute lies on the patentee to establish that the claims in issue are entitled to priority from the priority document in question. On the facts, it was held at [326] that entitlement to the relevant priority date had not been established, with fatal consequences for validity.

Warning against prior publication of a biotechnological invention

Under the Genetically Modified Organisms (Contained Use) Regulations 2000 (SI 2000/2831) as amended by SI 2002/61, SI 2005/2466, it may often be required to seek prior permission to carry out genetic manipulation experiments, or to release genetically modified organisms (GMOs) onto the market or into the environment. Also, prior notification of research experiments with genetically modified pathogenic organisms is required to be given to the Health and Safety Executive. These Regulations affect chiefly inventions in the field of recombinant DNA, cell fusion and transgenics originating from research done in the UK.

76A.15

The forms, which are required to be completed (available at *http://www.hse.gov.uk/forms/genetic/index.htm*), call for a description of the GMO and of the purpose of the experiments. In the case of consents, there is also a public register. These documents may well contain information prejudicial to a later-filed patent application, but they will become available to the public under s.122 of the Environmental Protection Act 1990, at least to the extent that exemption cannot be granted under the limited provisions of its s.123. One such reason for exemption arises when the Executive is requested to exclude certain of the information provided and is satisfied, on the basis of evidence supplied, that this exclusion is necessary to protect information that is commercially confidential (s.123(3)). These issues were the subject of articles by R. K. Percy [1993] *CIPA* 76; and [1994] *CIPA* 395 which indicated to patent practitioners the steps to be taken in connection with experiments with genetically modified organisms in order to safeguard, as far as possible, patent rights arising therefrom.

Since those articles were written, the legislative environment has changed somewhat in that the Environmental Information Regulations 2004 (SI 2004/3391) now also require public bodies, including the Health and Safety Executive, to make available to the public, on request, environmental information. This includes information about genetically modified organisms (reg.2(1)(a)). Regulation 12(5)(c) allows the public body to refuse to make the information available where doing so would adversely affect intellectual property rights. Of course, persons confronted with a patent which describes such an experiment will have an incentive to investigate whether an invalidating disclosure may have occurred as a result of prior notification of the intention to perform an experiment.

—Insufficiency issues in relation to biotechnology

76A.16   The following discussion deals with the need for a sufficient description of a method of performing the invention. For matters relating to deposits of biological material, see the commentary on s.125A.

Where a claim is directed to a sequence or partial sequence of a gene, it is now required by Sch.A2 para.6, that the "industrial application" of the gene shall be disclosed in the patent application "as filed". Failure to do this will render the patent revocable either under s.72(1)(a) for failure to comply with s.(1)(1)(c), as in *Eli Lilly and Company v Human Genome Sciences, Inc* [2008] R.P.C. 29; [2008] EWHC 1903 Pat Ct (July 31, 2008), discussed above in §76A.06or under s.72(1)(c) for failure to comply with s.14(3).

At one time it was said, more frequently than it should have been, that the law of the EPO Boards of Appeal was that only one detailed method of carrying out the invention need be disclosed to satisfy art.83 of the EPC. The original authority generally cited for this dubious proposition was T 292/85 *GENENTECH/Polypeptide expression-I* OJ EPO 1989, 275; [1989] E.P.O.R. 1. However, this view of the law seems to have stemmed from an over-enthusiastically abridged headnote in T 292/85 *GENENTECH/Polypeptide expression-I*, as in the reasons for the decision (para.3.1.5) the Board was careful to note that some knowledge or disclosure of variants on the specific description is required when it said: "any non-availability of some particular variants of a functionally defined component feature of the invention is immaterial to sufficiency *as long as there are suitable variants known to the skilled person through the disclosure or common general knowledge*, which provide the same effect for the invention" [emphasis added]. Later decisions clarified that the "only one method" rule was not the law, if it ever was. Thus, in T 409/91 *EXXON/Fuel oils* the patent claimed a fuel oil which at temperatures at which it solidifies produces wax crystals of less than a defined size. Here it was held that an additive, of which only one specific example was given, was needed to achieve the low crystal size. This single example was insufficient in relation to the width of the claim. This philosophy was subsequently followed in another chemical case (T 435/91 *UNILEVER/Detergents*) and in the biological (and well respected) case of T 694/92 *MYCOGEN/Modifying plant cells* OJ EPO 1997, 408; [1998] E.P.O.R. 114, discussed by L. Kempton ([1997] B.S.L.R. 152). In T 694/92 *MYCOGEN/Modifying plant cells*, the specification described inserting a gene for the plant protein phaseolin, together with its promoter, by a defined method, into a dicotyledenous plant. The main claim was directed to this method as applied to all genes, all promoters and all plants. It was held to relate to an invention insufficiently described, but a claim limited to the method using phaseolin, its promoter and dicot plants was allowed.

At first instance in *Biogen v Medeva* [1995] R.P.C. 25, decided before T 409/91 *EXXON/Fuel oils*, the Patents Court held that it was first necessary to decide whether more than one invention is specified in the claim, but that mere width of claim cannot per se be an indication that it relates to more than one invention. In that case, the main claim covered DNA capable of expressing hepatitis B virus (HBV) surface or core antigen. The court held the claim to relate to only one invention, there being but a single solution to the problem facing the inventors, namely to produce an HBV antigen. However, on appeal (see the same report) the Court of Appeal disagreed with this approach to claim construction, pointing out that, just because the invention was claimed in a single claim, this meant that only a single invention was present, is logic which leads to a conclusion lacking any reality or merit. Thus, the misperceived view of what was held by T 292/85 *GENENTECH/ Polypeptide expression-I* was here distinguished, the Court of Appeal holding that a claim to recombinant antigens to the hepatitis B virus was, in reality, not a claim to a single invention so that it was necessary for sufficiency (and priority) for the preparation of each of the claimed antigens to be adequately described, which was only the case (in the necessary priority application) for the preparation of one of the antigens produced in a single bacterial medium. On further appeal (*Biogen v Medeva* [1997] R.P.C. 1 HL), the position as to the degree of exemplification required to avoid insufficiency was explained as whether the underlying inventive concept could be seen to be one based on the discovery of a new principle or whether the claims cover other ways in which the goods might be delivered, "ways which owe nothing to the teaching of the patent or any principle which it disclosed". On this basis, the *Biogen* claims were not seen to involve any such principle and the decision of the Court of Appeal on that point was disapproved. In the corresponding T 296/93 *BIOGEN/Hepatitis B*, priority was accorded as in the earlier decision of the Patents Court.

In *Chinoin's Application* [1986] R.P.C. 39, a new micro-organism had been isolated from a soil sample. From this a new strain had been derived by breeding and a sample of this strain had been deposited in a culture collection. Other strains had been mutated or modified from the isolated micro-organism, but not deposited. The applicant attempted to claim all such strains as a new species, *Micromonospora rosea*. A claim to the deposited strain was allowed, together with a claim to strains of *Micromonospora rosea* derived therefrom, but a broader claim to all strains of this species was disallowed. The invention of the broader claim was held insufficiently disclosed in the specification under s.14(3) and old r.17(1), whereas that of the narrower claims was held sufficiently disclosed. However, it was held that r.17 (now r.13) did not require the deposit of every strain of a new species to support a claim directed to that species, nor does it require the deposit of the best strain known to the applicant for the intended purpose of the invention.

In *Chiron v Organon Teknika (No.3)* [1994] F.S.R. 202, decided after the *Biogen* case (above) was decided at first instance and before T 409/91 *EXXON/Fuel oils*, the Patents Court stated that it is not a requirement of the law that the specification should provide sufficient instructions to make everything falling within a claimed single invention. The court also pointed out that objections of alleged insufficiency cannot be used as a substitute for an objection that claims of the width of those in suit are not properly supported by the description, a plea which "unfortunately is not available under section 72". Nevertheless, in the *Chiron* case, claims directed to vaccines and to production of the claimed virus *in vitro* were each invalidated for insufficiency of description because the skilled worker would have had to spend an inordinate amount of time before he would have been able to achieve these, the patentee himself only having succeeded several years after filing the patent. An appeal, decided after the availability of T 409/91 *EXXON/Fuel oils* and the Court of Appeal decision in *Biogen* but before the House of Lords decision in that case, was dismissed as regards these points. See the consolidated report (*Chiron v Murex* [1996] R.P.C. 1). The *Chiron* litigation then settled so that whether its decisions would have been influenced by the House of Lords decision in *Biogen* remains a moot point.

A similar approach to *Chiron* was taken in relation to the composition claims in *Eli Lilly and Company v Human Genome Sciences, Inc*, discussed above in §76A.06. Claims to antibodies specifically binding to Neutrokine-α (the subject of the patent) were held to be sufficient, but claims to pharmaceutical or diagnostic compositions containing them were not. Although the judge stated, citing T 226/85 *UNILEVER/Stable bleaches* [1989] E.P.O.R. 18, abridged OJ EPO 1988, 336, that his approach was consistent with that of the EPO, it is not immediately clear that this is so. The EPO's practice is usually that claims to a straightforward pharmaceutical composition are sufficient if the active ingredient is sufficiently described. (A stricter line is taken for second medical use claims (as in, e.g.

T 609/02 *SALK INSTITUTE/AP-1 complex* (unreported) below), but that was not the issue here.) In T 226/85 *UNILEVER/Stable bleaches*, the facts were somewhat dissimilar to those in *Eli Lilly*, as the claimed composition contained two functional limitations which the evidence showed could not be achieved together with a statistically acceptable frequency.

In *Kirin-Amgen Inc v Hoechst Marion Roussel* [2005] R.P.C. 5 at 169 HL a claim to a recombinantly produced erythropoietin having "higher molecular weight by SDS-PAGE from erythropoietin isolated from urinary sources" was held insufficient because the molecular weight of urinary erythropoietin varied according to source and method of preparation. The trial judge and the House of Lords (but not the Court of Appeal) held that the resulting lack of clarity lead to a fatal insufficiency.

It is well-settled law of the EPO Boards of Appeal that the examples of a patent specification need not be precisely repeatable, so long as they are sufficiently nearly repeatable for the benefits of the invention to be obtained. This has been applied in the biotechnological field in, e.g.: T 281/86 *UNILEVER/Preprothaumatin* OJ EPO 1989, 202; [1989] E.P.O.R. 313; T 347/87 *GENENTECH/Cloning vehicle* (Unreported); and T 181/87 *UNIVERSITY OF CALIFORNIA/Hepatitis B.*

In T 315/03 *HARVARD/Transgenic animal*, the Board found that the invention (as ultimately claimed) was sufficiently described, and confirmed the principle articulated in the first ex parte appeal on the onco-mouse technology, see T 19/90 *HARVARD/Oncomouse* OJ EPO 1992, 588; [1991] E.P.O.R. 525 that an objection of insufficiency presupposes that there are serious doubts, substantiated by verifiable facts, that the claimed subject-matter could be reproduced.

In T 1329/04 *JOHNS HOPKINS/Factor-9*, it was held that it must be at least made plausible by the disclosure in an application that its teaching indeed solves the problem it purports to solve. Therefore, even if supplementary, post-published, evidence may in the proper circumstances also be taken into consideration, it may not serve as the sole basis to establish that the application does in fact solve the problem it purports to solve. This decision was taken under EPC art.56 (inventive step) and not EPC art.83 (insufficiency), but it raises an issue which is essentially one of sufficiency of disclosure. This decision was criticised by F. Stolzenburg et al. *epi-Information*, 1/2006, 15–27, but the approach has already been followed (by a slightly differently constituted panel of the same Board) in T 1306/04 *ONO/Cell death peptide* (Unreported) and also in several more recent cases, including T 710/05 *THE CHILDREN'S MEDICAL CENTER/NMDA oxidizing agents* and T 1396/06 *EPIMMUNE/HLA Binding Peptides.*

A requirement for evidence to be present in the application as filed has been found under EPC art.83 in T 609/02 *SALK INSTITUTE/AP-1 complex*. Here it was held that, where the description provides no more than a vague indication of a possible medical use for a chemical compound yet to be identified, later more detailed evidence cannot be used to remedy the fundamental insufficiency of disclosure of such subject-matter. This decision is not dissimilar to the UK decisions in *Hoerrmann's Application* [1996] R.P.C. 341; *McManus' Application* [1994] F.S.R. 558; *Prendergast's Applications* [2000] R.P.C. 446; and *Consultants Supplies' Application* [1996] R.P.C. 348, as discussed in §14.38 above.

The question of whether evidence is required in the application as filed to support medical use claims is still live, with some cases not finding it necessary: T 394/06 *GSK BIOLOGICALS/CASB7439 polypeptide* is a recent example from Board 3.3.04, following (but not citing) T 994/95 MOLECULAR BIOSYSTEMS/Oligonucleotide therapeutic agent, a decision of the same Board. In T 1437/07 ALLERGAN/Botulinum toxin for treating smooth muscle spasm, the same Board cited T 609/02 *SALK INSTITUTE/AP-1 complex* in the context of whether a prior art document had an enabling disclosure of a medical use: it was emphasised that it should be credible that the effect at issue—here relief of pain—has been achieved.

In T 1466/05 *SEREX/Pyridinoline* it was held that the availability of a hybridoma producing one specific antibody together with a general description of the epitope recognised by this antibody did not necessarily put the skilled person in the position to obtain further antibodies with the same specificity, given that no specific antigen had been disclosed. A claim not limited to antibodies sharing the same complementarity determining regions (CDRs) therefore gave rise to an undue burden and a finding of insufficiency.

For a further discussion of sufficiency in relation to biotechnology inventions, see "Enabling Biotechnological Inventions in Europe and the United States" by Sven Bostyn, *EPOscript* Vol.4 (European Patent Office, 2001).

See the discussion of reach through claims, which includes a discussion of T 1063/06 and *MedImmune Ltd v Novartis Pharmaceuticals UK Ltd and Anor* [2011] EWHC 1669 (Pat), which distinguished T 1063/06, in §76A.03 above.

Sequence listing

It is a requirement of the EPO (under EPC r.30), and under the PCT where the EPO is a **76A.17** receiving office, that any nucleotide or amino acid sequences disclosed in a European patent application must be listed in writing in a standardised form, and must also be submitted to the EPO by online filing or on a prescribed data carrier (normally a disk), together with a statement of identity of this with the written sequence listing; and, if a the written sequence listing and electronic version on the data carrier are not identical the application may be refused. The applicant has a non-extendible period of two months to remedy any such deficiency and pay a late furnishing fee. Where a sequence listing is filed or corrected after the filing date, a statement is required that this does not include matter going beyond the disclosure in the application as filed and any sequence listing filed after the date of filing does not form part of the specification, for all of which see "Decision of the President of the EPO and the EPO Notice" Special edition No.3 OJ EPO 2007, C1 and C2 (July 12, 2007).

The standardised form in which the sequence listing is required to be presented is that of WIPO Standard ST.25, also published as an Annex in Supplement No.2 to Issue 11/98 of the OJ EPO and further as Annex C to the Administrative Instructions under the PCT. BiSSAP (Biological Sequence Submission Application for Patents) is a new sequence submission tool. Version 1.0 is freely available from the EPO at *http://www.epo.org/ applying/online-services/online-filing/auxiliary/bissap.html* and can be used to prepare and verify sequences, generate the sequence listing files for submission, import existing sequence listings in WIPO ST.25 and convert between sequence listing formats (WIPO ST.25 and the proposed XML-based standard). It also contains a batch verification module allowing users to verify collections of sequence listings. The old PatentIn software is also still acceptable, and version 3.5.1 is available from the USPTO at *http://www.uspto.gov/ patents/resources/tools/checker/patentinrel.jsp*.

While the use of the standardised mode of listing nucleotide and amino acid sequences in biotechnology applications is not obligatory under the Act and Rules, it has been recommended (see *Patents Journal* November 18, 1998) that the aforesaid "statement of identity", which is required to accompany the supply of a copy of the sequence on a data carrier (normally a disk) should be in the form:

"It is hereby stated that the information recorded on the data carrier is identical to the written sequence listing."

The United States and Japanese Patent Offices have adopted the same WIPO standard ST.25.

The Sequence Listing has become a separate item from the rest of the description, with its own page numbering (Standard 25, art.4).

The Sequence Listing is intended mostly to be a stand-alone document not requiring translation. This has been enabled by the use of standard numbers as identifiers, e.g. <400 = Sequence. An identifier <233 is provided for free text, but any such free text must be repeated in the main part of the description, preferably in a section headed "Sequence Listing Free Text" (Standard 25, art.36).

Under the current wording of r.70(5), noted in §89A.06, the translation of the international application may exclude a sequence listing provided that this has been supplied to the International Bureau in accordance with Annex C to the PCT Administrative Instructions (for which see above).

Breadth of claim issues in relation to biotechnology

76A.18   The United Kingdom and European Patent Offices have each normally allowed claims which include functional expressions. Leading EPO cases in the biotechnological field on permissible breadth of claim are, still: T 292/85 *GENENTECH/Polypeptide expression-I*; T 320/87 *LUBRIZOL/Hybrid plants* OJ EPO 1990, 71; [1990] E.P.O.R. 173; T 347/87 *GENENTECH/Cloning vehicle*; and T 923/92 *GENENTECH/Human t-PA*. Two important principles from the EPO case law are that: (1) mere breadth of claim does not automatically give rise to a lack of clarity under EPC art.84 (T 238/88 *KODAK/Crown ether* OJ EPO 1992, 709; [1993] E.P.O.R. 100; and T 688/91 *SIEMENS/Vorrichtung zur Steuerung von Informationsverarbeitungsabläufen*); and (2) the disclosure the invention must be sufficient to enable a person skilled in the art to carry out the invention in the whole claimed range, so that the scope of the claim is commensurate with the contribution made by the invention to the art (T 409/91 *EXXON/Fuel oils*; T 435/91 *UNILEVER/Detergents*; T 694/92 *MYCOGEN/Modifying plant cells*; and T 939/92 *AGREVO/Triazoles* OJ EPO 1996,309; [1996] E.P.O.R. 171).

In *Kirin-Amgen Inc v Hoechst Marion Roussel* [2005] R.P.C. 9 HL, the House of Lords considered obiter the question whether claims relating to recombinant DNA encoding erythropoietin would be insufficient if they covered the defendant's process, which involved the activation of an endogenous erythropoietin gene, in the light of the description which disclosed only how to make erythropoietin by introducing exogenous DNA coding for EPO into a host cell. As the defendant's process was held not to infringe, no settled conclusion was needed or expressed. However, Lord Hoffmann said at [2005] R.P.C. 9 at [117], "unlike the Court of Appeal, I think that the breadth of claim objection may well have been a good one".

Also in *Kirin-Amgen*, it was restated at [2005] R.P.C. 9 at [102] that the requirement for sufficiency is as set out in *Biogen v Medeva* [1997] R.P.C. 1 at 48, namely that the disclosure must enable the invention to be performed to the full extent of the monopoly claimed. In *American Home Products Corp v Novartis Pharmaceuticals UK Ltd* [2001] R.P.C. 8 at 159, the patentee claimed that the known drug rapamycin and any of its derivatives could be put to a new use. But the claim for such use of all derivatives was not enabled because only some derivatives could be so used and the specification did not enable the skilled person to identify which they were. As explained in *Kirin-Amgen* [2005] R.P.C. 9 at [112], if there is a "principle of general application", i.e. an element of the claim which is stated in general terms, one must reasonably expect the invention to work with anything which falls within the general term for the claim to be sufficiently enabled.

In the EPO, useful guidance on the issue of inoperative embodiments can be had from *G 2/03 Disclaimers* OJ EPO 2004, 448, which noted at para.2.5.2 of the reasons that if a claim comprises non-working embodiments, this may have different consequences, depending on the circumstances.

Either there is a large number of conceivable alternatives and the specification contains sufficient information on the relevant criteria for finding appropriate alternatives over the claimed range with reasonable effort. If this is the case, the inclusion of non-working embodiments is of no harm (T 238/88 *KODAK/Crown ether*, OJ EPO 1992, 709; [1993] E.P.O.R. 100; T 292/85 *GENENTECH/Polypeptide expression I*, OJ EPO 1989, 275; T 301/87 *Biogen/Alpha-interferons*, OJ EPO 1990, 335).

In *DSM's Patent* [2001] R.P.C. 35 at 675, two claims were seen as of undue breadth and were held invalid for insufficiency (see §14.24 above). If the claim, which referred to hybridised material, was of broad scope (as was held), it was admitted to be unworkable and to extend to material unrelated to the inventive concept; and, if a narrower functional imitation were to be impliedly read into the claim wording (as the patentee contended), then the patent provided no teaching as to the appropriate conditions which should be used to achieve the production of only related DNA material. However, if the claims had been valid, they would not have been seen as limited to the precise sequences discovered and it was recognised that a patent draftsman has a problem in identifying the "relation" between the natural product in issue: "so as to be clear and sufficient on the one hand, while, on the other hand, putting forward a formula which has commercial efficacy".

In T 617/07 *LAY LINE/Monoclonal NGF-antagonist antibodies*, claimed monoclonal antibodies partly by their structure (the sequence of the CDRs) and partly by their function (especially, "which prevents the functional activation of TrkA by NGF"). The Board acknowledged that the structural definition included antibodies that did not have the desired function; nonetheless, because of what was known from the art about the structure-function relationship of an antibody, they considered that the skilled person would be able in a straightforward (even though possibly time-consuming) manner to provide antibody variants having the functional requirements indicated in the claim. EPC art.83 was satisfied.

Trade secrecy in relation to biotechnology

76A.19 The alternative to patenting, i.e. keeping a new invention secret, has its advocates for those inventions: (a) which cannot sufficiently be described without a deposit of biological material; and/or (b) can be commercially exploited without being reproducible by others. This typically arises where the invention involves the product of a living cell formed by some chance event, such as random mutagenesis or the random fusion of different cell types, and may be more attractive if only narrow patent protection at best is available. However, a strategy of trade secrecy is somewhat at the mercy of third party rights, in spite of the protections afforded in the UK by s.64 (see the commentary on that section), and it is easy to underestimate the advances in technology over the next twenty years which may facilitate the reverse engineering of the means of production from the product. It is consequently a matter for careful consideration.

Biodiversity and traditional knowledge

76A.20 The debates about biodiversity, traditional knowledge and their relationships to intellectual property laws still continue without, at least as yet, producing any legislative result that directly affects the United Kingdom.

Established by the WIPO General Assembly in October 2000 (document WO/GA/26/6), the WIPO Intergovernmental Committee on Intellectual Property and Genetic Resources, Traditional Knowledge and Folklore (IGC) is undertaking text-based negotiations with the objective of reaching agreement on a text of an international legal instrument (or instruments) which will ensure the effective protection of traditional knowledge (TK), traditional cultural expressions (TCEs)/folklore and genetic resources. The IGC has been requested to submit such a text to the 2011 WIPO General Assembly, which will decide on convening a Diplomatic Conference.

Scope of protection in relation to biotechnology

76A.21 In *Monsanto Technology LLC v Cefetra BV* (C-428/08) [2011] F.S.R. 6, the District Court of The Hague had referred to the ECJ (as it then was) several questions relating to residual patented DNA molecules present in transgenic soy meal imported into The Netherlands. In response to the Patentee's infringement argument, the importers argued that art.9 of the Biotechnology Directive provides that the scope of protection of the patent does not extend to situations where the DNA molecules, if present at all, are residually present and are incapable of performing the function for which the patent was granted, in this case endowing the plant with glyphosate tolerance. Essentially, the questions referred are: (1) whether art.9 of the Biotechnology Directive is referring to the DNA performing its function *at the time of the alleged infringement*; (2) whether art.9 stands in the way of national law which defines patent protection absolutely (i.e. without any reference to the DNA performing its function); (3) whether the answer to question (2) depends on the date of grant of the patent (before or after the Biotechnology Directive was adopted); and (4) whether the TRIPS Agreement, especially arts 27 and 30, should be taken into account.

On July 6 2010, the Court of the Justice of the EC handed down their judgment. The court ruled that the scope of protection of a patent relating to genetic sequences is limited to situations where the genetic information is currently performing the function described in the patent. Specifically, the court held:

1. Article 9 of the Biotech Directive (Directive 98/44/EC on the legal protection of

biotechnological inventions) is to be interpreted as not conferring patent right protection in circumstances such as those of the case in the main proceedings, in which the patented product is contained in the soy meal, where it does not perform the function for which it is patented, but did perform that function previously in the soy plant, of which the meal is a processed product, or would possibly again be able to perform that function after it had been extracted from the soy meal opinion The opinion, and its background and inserted into the cell of a living organism.

2. Article 9 of the Directive effects an exhaustive harmonisation of the protection it confers, with the result that it precludes the national patent legislation from offering absolute protection to the patented product as such, regardless of whether it performs its function in the material containing it.

3. Article 9 of the Directive precludes the holder of a patent issued prior to the adoption of that directive from relying on the absolute protection for the patented product accorded to it under the national legislation then applicable.

4. Articles 27 and 30 of the Agreement on Trade-Related Aspects of Intellectual Property Rights, constituting Annex 1C to the Agreement establishing the World Trade Organisation (WTO), signed at Marrakesh on 15 April 1994 and approved by Council Decision 94/800/EC of 22 December 1994 concerning the conclusion on behalf of the European Community, as regards matters within its competence, of the agreements reached in the Uruguay Round multilateral negotiations (1986–1994) do not affect the interpretation given of art.9 of the Directive.

See the article by Michael Kock: "Court of Justice of the European Union Limits Patents on DNA Sequences: Much Ado About Nothing or the Beginning of Erosion for Biotech Patents?" BSLR 11(1) 3-12, in which it is suggested that a claim to a process for the production of soy meal would have helped solve the problem, as possibly would, at least in theory, plant variety protection. Interestingly, a claim to soy meal per se may not have been the answer, at least in the EPO, because a claim to the 'dead' soy meal would probably not have involved an inventive step shared with the claimed genetic material (at least in this case, given that it related to glyphosate tolerance).

In *MedImmune Ltd v Novartis Pharmaceuticals UK Ltd and Anor* [2011] EWHC 1669 (Pat), Arnold J. considered the scope of art.8(2) of the Directive. The relevant claims were for methods of producing "a binding molecule specific for a particular target epitope or antigen" and "a molecule with binding specificity for a particular target". Novartis had argued that these claims meant that the patent was "on a process that enables a biological material to be produced" and therefore within the scope of art.8(2), with the consequence that their protection was restricted by its wording, by analogy with the CJEU's treatment of art.9 in *Monsanto*, to the production of (reproducible) biological material—i.e. so as not to cover proteins. The judge rejected this submission, holding that: (1) the correct approach is to consider the protection conferred by the relevant claim [567 and 573]; (2) neither the "binding molecule" nor the "molecule with binding specificity" in the claims was "biological material" within the sense of art 2(1)(a) of the Directive, which defined "biological material" as "capable of reproducing itself or of being reproduced in a biological system" [573]; (3) the surprising consequence of Novartis' argument if correct would be that such method claims could never, or only with difficulty, cover the production of proteins [575]; and (4) following Advocate-General Jacobs' analysis in Case C-377/98 (*Kingdom of the Netherlands v European Parliament and Council of the European Union* [2001] E.C.R. I–7079), the purpose of art.8(2) is not to limit the protection conferred by process claims in patents for biotechnological inventions, but, if anything, to extend it [576].

PROVISIONS ABOUT INTERNATIONAL CONVENTIONS

European patents and patent applications [Sections 77–85]

SECTION 77

Effect of European patent (UK)

77.—(1) Subject to the provisions of this Act, a European patent (UK) shall, as **77.01** from the publication of the mention of its grant in the European Patent Bulletin, be treated for the purposes of Parts I and III of this Act as if it were a patent under this Act granted in pursuance of an application made under this Act and as if notice of the grant of the patent had, on the date of that publication, been published under section 24 above in the journal; and—

> (a) the proprietor of a European patent (UK) shall accordingly as respects the United Kingdom have the same rights and remedies, subject to the same conditions, as the proprietor of a patent under this Act;
>
> (b) references in Parts I and III of this Act to a patent shall be construed accordingly; and
>
> (c) any statement made and any certificate filed for the purposes of the provision of the convention corresponding to section 2(4)(c) above shall be respectively treated as a statement made and written evidence filed for the purposes of the said paragraph (c).

(2) Subsection (1) above shall not affect the operation in relation to a European patent (UK) of any provisions of the European Patent Convention relating to the amendment or revocation of such a patent in proceedings before the European Patent Office.

(3) Where in the case of a European patent (UK)—

> **(a) proceedings for infringement, or proceedings under section 58 above, have been commenced before the court or the comptroller and have not been finally disposed of, and**
>
> **(b) it is established in proceedings before the European Patent Office that the patent is only partially valid,**

the provisions of section 63 or, as the case may be, of subsections (7) to (9) of section 58 apply as they apply to proceedings in which the validity of patent is put in issue and in which it is found that the patent is only partially valid.

[(3) *Sections 58(7) to (9) and 63 above shall apply to the case where, after proceedings for the infringement of a European patent have been commenced before the court or the comptroller but have not been finally disposed of, it is established in proceedings before the European Patent Office that the patent is only partially valid as those provisions apply to proceedings in which the validity of a patent is put in issue and in which it is found that the patent is only partially valid.*]

(4) Where a European patent (UK) is amended in accordance with the European Patent Convention, the amendment shall have effect for the

purposes of Parts I and III of this Act as if the specification of the patent has been amended under this Act; but subject to subsection (6)(b) below.

[(4) *Subject to subsection (6) below, where a European patent (UK) is amended or revoked in accordance with the European Patent Convention, the amendment shall be treated for the purposes of Parts I and III of this Act as if it had been made, or as the case may be the patent shall be treated for those purposes as having been revoked, under this Act.*]

(4A) Where a European patent (UK) is revoked in accordance with the European Patent Convention, the patent shall be treated for the purposes of Parts I and III of this Act as having been revoked under this Act.

(5) Where—

    (a) under the European Patent Convention a European patent (UK) is revoked for failure to observe a time limit and is subsequently restored **or is revoked by the Board of Appeal and is subsequently restored by the Enlarged Board of Appeal**; and

    (b) between the revocation and publication of the fact that it has been restored a person begins in good faith to do an act which would, apart from section 55 above, constitute an infringement of the patent or makes in good faith effective and serious preparations to do such an act;

he shall have the rights conferred by section **28A(4) and (5) above, and subsections (6) and (7)** [*28(6) above, and subsection (8) and (9)*] of that section shall apply accordingly.

(6) While this subsection is in force—

    (a) subsection (1) above shall not apply to a European patent (UK) the specification of which was published in French or German, unless a translation of the specification into English is filed at the Patent Office and the prescribed fee is paid before the end of the prescribed period;

    (b) subsection (4) above shall not apply to an amendment made in French or German unless a translation **into English of the specification as amended** [*of the amendment into English*] is filed at the Patent Office and the prescribed fee is paid before the end of the prescribed period.

(7) Where **such a translation is not filed** [*a translation of a specification or amendment into English is not filed in accordance with subsection (6)(a) or (b)*], the patent shall be treated as always having been void.

(8) The comptroller shall publish any translation filed at the Patent Office under subsection (6) above.

(9) Subsection (6) above shall come into force on a day appointed for the purpose by rules and shall cease to have effect on a day so appointed, without prejudice, however, to the power to bring it into force again.

Notes

1. Subsection (6) was brought into force from September 1, 1987 by an order made under subs.(9) (Patents (Amendment) Rules 1987 (SI 1987/288) r.4), but with no effect on European patents (UK) whose grant had been published in the *European Patent Bulletin* before that date. This rule remains in force.

2. Subsections (3)–(7) were each amended, and subs.(4A) added, by Sch.5 paras 8 and 21 to the CDPA 1988, each with effect from January 7, 1991 (SI 1990/2168).

3. Subsection (5)(a) was amended by Patents Act 2004 (c.16) Sch.1 para.2 with effect from December 13, 2007.

4. For the purposes of subs.(9), and (under SI 2005/687 r.33) subs.(6) ceased to have effect on May 1, 2008 when the London Agreement came into force.

RELEVANT RULE—RULE 56

Rule 56—Translations of European patents (UK)

56.—(1) A translation into English of either—   77.02
   (a) the specification of the European patent (UK), which is filed under section 77(6); or
   (b) the claims of the specification of the application for a European patent (UK), which is filed under section 78(7),
must be accompanied by Patents Form 54.

(2) The translation must comply with the requirements set out in Parts 1 to 3 of Schedule 2.

(3) The translation and Patents Form 54 must be filed in duplicate.

(4) But paragraph (2) does not apply where a translation is delivered in electronic form or using electronic communications.

(5) Where the specification includes any drawings all annotations in French or German must be replaced with annotations in English.

(6) The period prescribed for the purposes of section 77(6)(a) is three months beginning with the date on which the grant of the patent was mentioned in the European Patent Bulletin.

(7) The period prescribed for the purposes of section 77(6)(b) is three months beginning with the date of publication, by the European Patent Office, of the specification as amended.

(8) No translation may be filed under section 77(6)(a) or (b) before the beginning of the period prescribed for the purposes of that provision.

(9) On a day appointed under section 77(9), section 77(6) and paragraphs (1)(a) and (5) to (8) of this rule shall cease to have effect.

(10) The day appointed for the purpose of paragraph (9) shall be the day of the coming into force of the Agreement on the application of Article 65 of the Convention on the Grant of European Patents made in London on 17th October 2000.

Note. Parts 1 to 3 of Sch.2 are reprinted in §14.05. The London Agreement noted in r.56(10) came into force on May 1, 2008.

COMMENTARY ON SECTION 77

Scope of the section

Sections 77 to 95 constitute Pt II of the Act and relate to international conventions. Section 77 is the first of a group of ss.77–89B, which are concerned with patents and applications under the EPC and PCT, to give effect to them under domestic patent law of the United Kingdom and to provide for related matters. Articles 63–70 of the EPC are gener-   77.03

ally relevant, and s.77 arises from art.64 of the EPC, with the following ss.78–83 dealing with other aspects of the assimilation of European patents (UK) and applications for them into the British patent system. Of these ss.77–83, only ss.82 and 83 (entitlement to European patents) are stated by s.130(7) to have been drafted so as to have the same effect as provisions of the EPC, for which see §§130.09–130.11.

The terms "European Patent Convention", "European patent", "European Patent (UK)", "European Patent Bulletin" and "European Patent Office" are each defined in s.130(1) and (6) (see §130.08), though these definitions are largely self-evident. Definitions for PCT applications filed with the EPO (often known colloquially, as "Euro-PCT applications", see §79.02) have been inserted into s.130 as subss.(4A), and (5A), for which see §130.08.

The purpose of s.77 is to give the proprietor of a European patent (UK) the same rights as he would have had if he had applied for the patent under the Act and to give the court and the Comptroller jurisdiction over a European patent (UK). Section 78 deals likewise with an application for a European patent (UK). Neither s.77 nor s.78 gives the court or the Comptroller any jurisdiction over the prosecution of the application for, and the grant of, the European patent, although jurisdiction over entitlement is provided under s.12, subject to s.82.

Effect of European patent (UK) (subs.(1))

77.04   Subsection (1) provides that a European patent (UK) has the same effect as a patent granted under the Act, as from publication of the grant in the *European Patent Bulletin* ("the EPB"), as if such publication had taken place under s.24. Thus, Pts I and III of the Act (viz.: ss.1–76 and 96–132) apply mutatis mutandis to such patents. Accordingly, the European patent (UK) has a life of 20 years from the (deemed) date of application (see s.25, discussed in §25.08) and may give rise to a supplementary protection certificate (for which see Appendix B). Also, the proprietor of a European patent (UK) has the same rights and remedies as a proprietor of a patent under the Act; and, where there has been a prior disclosure at an international exhibition, any certificate filed under EPC art.55(2) is deemed to comply with s.2(4)(c). Indeed, the MOPP indicates that, where before the EPO there has been validly claimed an exemption from the prior art effect of display of the invention at an international exhibition, the requirements of s.2(4) and r.5 are deemed to have been met if they were met before the EPO; and, likewise, as regards disclosure of deposited biological material, if the requirements of the EPC Regulations were duly met before the EPO (for which see §125A.20). The Patents Rules have effect to govern European patents (UK) from their date of grant, even when these rules have effect by virtue of Pt I of the Act (*Deforeit's Patent* [1986] R.P.C. 142).

The authentic text of a European patent (UK) is the text on file in the EPO on which the grant was made. Therefore, misprints in a published version have no effect and the EPO can correct these, the printed text having no binding character (*EPO Legal Advice* 17/90 OJ EPO 1990, 260).

It has been pointed out in (1984–85) 14 *CIPA* 14 that, apparently, the Comptroller is required to publish the specification of a European patent (UK) because the provisions of s.24(3) seem to apply to it in view of the wording of s.77(1). However, this is not the practice, and the *Patents Journal* merely lists the numbers of European patents (UK) that have been granted, together with the corresponding EPO application number and the name of the proprietor. Nevertheless, when a European patent (UK) is amended in proceedings under either of ss.27 and 75, the European patent (UK) is republished by the UK-IPO either as a "C-specification", or as an addendum slip to be attached to the existing "B-specification", but in each case stating that the amendment applies to the United Kingdom only. If the European patent is one in the French or German language, this reprint is also in that language. The same procedure is adopted when correction of a European patent (UK) is allowed under s.117 and r.91(1).

The printed version of a European patent now indicates any applications which were divided out of it and which may therefore mature into individual patents.

Registration of European patents (UK) in other countries

77.05   It is by no means certain that the effect of a European patent (UK) is the same as one granted under Pt I of the Act as regards the obtaining of patents in some of those countries which provide for patent rights to be obtained in them by registration of granted United Kingdom patents. In addition, it appears that any revocation of a European patent during opposition proceedings in the EPO will cause a Hong Kong standard patent based on it likewise to be revoked, whereas revocation in the United Kingdom of a national patent or a European patent (UK) does not affect the status of that patent in Hong Kong.

Although there may be some doubt as to the exact date of grant of patents granted under Pt I of the Act when computing the period permitted for such foreign registrations of the patent (see §24.11), no such doubt arises with regard to European patents (UK) because s.77(1) makes it clear that the date of grant of such patents for all purposes is the date of publication of grant in the EPB.

Effect of revocation or amendment of a European patent by the EPO (subss.(2), (4) and (4A))

Subsections (2), (4) and (4A) assimilate the effects of any revocation or amendment of a European patent (UK) made under EPC arts 102, 111, 112 or 123 as if such had occurred under Pts I and III of the Act. Any decision by the EPO of amendment or revocation of such a patent is deemed to be a decision taken under the Act (subss.(4) and (4A)).   **77.06**

However, it is only possible to revoke or amend a European patent by proceedings in the EPO, by way of opposition lodged under EPC art.99 initiated within nine months of the publication in the EPB of the notice of grant of the European patent, or by way of third party intervention (under EPC art.105) in existing opposition proceedings because infringement proceedings under the European patent have been commenced against the intervener. At one time, amendment of the European patent as a whole could be secured by self-opposition filed during the nine-month opposition period, but this is no longer possible (G 9/93 *PEUGEOT and RENAULT/Opposition by patent proprietor* OJ EPO 1994, 891; [1995] E.P.O.R. 260), see §72.11. It should also be noted that a designation of the United Kingdom for the European patent can be withdrawn only before the date of its grant (EPC art.79(3)) and therefore not during any such opposition proceedings.

Thus, during the nine-month opposition period, and while any opposition (and any appeal) remain unresolved, there is the possibility of challenges to validity being adjudicated in parallel in the EPO and in a British court, or before the Comptroller, with potentially conflicting results. However, if the eventual EPO decision is one of revocation or amendment, then the effect of subss.(4) and (4A) is that the EPO decision has automatic and binding effect on the European patent (UK), though probably without effect on awards of damages already ordered. No appeal against such a decision is possible, other than one to an EPO Board of Appeal from the initial decision of its Opposition Division. This was confirmed by *Lenzing's European Patent (UK)* [1997] R.P.C. 245, discussed by W. Cook [1997] E.I.P.R. 367 and I. Karet [1997] I.P.Q. 244. Here, an unsuccessful attempt was made to remove from the United Kingdom register notice of revocation by an EPO Board of Appeal, but it was held that decisions of the EPO Boards of Appeal must be accepted without question. It was also held that the Boards of Appeal do constitute a means of judicial review of a decision so that there is no breach of art.32 of the TRIPS Agreement which requires the possibility of such review, even if that Agreement gives rights to individuals (which were also held not to be so). Also, where attempts were being made to have an EPO Board of Appeal decision of revocation reviewed in the EPO, no basis was seen (because of the *Lenzing* judgment) for any revival of the European patent (UK) even if this review succeeded, as the revocation had removed the patent from the United Kingdom register with no provision for its restoration (*Kirin-Amgen and Boehringer Mannheim's Patents* BL C/15/98, noted I.P.D. 21036). The Bavarian Administrative Court has also held that a decision given by a Board of Appeal of the EPO revoking a patent is final and cannot be re-visited before a German court, see *National review of EPO decisions II* [Germany] OJ EPO 2000, 205.

A final decision of an EPO Board of Appeal revoking a patent is conclusive and must be taken (at least within the EPO) as res judicata (G 1/97 *ETA/Request with review to revision* OJ EPO 2000, 322; [2001] E.P.O.R. 1 at [1]).

In *Virgin Atlantic v Premium Aircraft* [2010] R.P.C. 8, [2009] EWCA Civ 1513 the question was raised of whether it is reasonable to arguable, if the EPO United Kingdom designation is a nullity, that the act of the UK-IPO in registering the patent based on a nullity is also a nullity. Jacob L.J. questioned whether the rule is that the national court cannot go behind a purported act of the EPO, and said that the question would turn on the true interpretation of s.77. The question is whether the publication of the mention of the grant of a patent in the *European Patent Bulletin* is conclusive for the purposes of s.77 even if that act of publication is ultra vires the EPO. The question was not answered, however, as in this case the question of validity was res judicata as far as United Kingdom law is concerned as the case was not concerned with issue estoppel but cause of action estoppel.

In *ITP v Coflexip* [Scotland] [2004] S.L.T. 1285, BL C/150/04, noted *The Times*, November 29, 2004 and I.P.D. 28002, there had been a finding of infringement at first instance, but then the patent in suit was revoked by a decision of an EPO Board of Appeal. The patentee made an application to the European Court of Human Rights for review of the decision in the light of alleged defects and sought a stay of the Scots proceedings pending that decision. The court held that it was clear that under s.77(4A) of the Act the court had to accept the EPO decision as final notwithstanding any further challenge, and therefore the original decision on infringement must be overturned.

Because an amendment to a European patent approved during opposition proceedings in the EPO does not take effect until the conclusion of these proceedings, any court or the Comptroller hearing parallel proceedings on the European patent (UK) must treat the patent as unamended until a final EPO decision is given and the appeal period has expired without an appeal being filed, or if such an appeal is filed, until the issue of the formal decision terminating those proceedings. Also, an EPO decision of amendment may be subject to the filing of an English translation of the amendment when the European patent is in French or German, see §77.09. If this is required but is not done, the European patent (UK) is treated as always having been void (subs.(7)). Thus, although a European patent may eventually be maintained in modified form at the conclusion of opposition proceedings in the EPO, an order for revocation of the European patent (UK) will not be stayed to await the outcome of those proceedings (*Beloit v Valmet* [1997] R.P.C. 489 CA).

Of course, amendment of the European patent (UK) can be separately sought in concurrent proceedings before the court under s.75, or (if no court proceedings are pending) by proceedings before the Comptroller under s.27. While there is, apparently, no obligation to seek separate amendment, failure to do so is likely to jeopardise the maintenance of the patent in the national enforcement proceedings. Indeed, in *Petrolite v Dyno* [1998] F.S.R. 190, where the patentee did not contest a prior use but stated he would be seeking amendment in pending parallel EPO opposition proceedings, infringement proceedings were ordered to be struck out unless amendments were submitted to the Comptroller for advertisement within 14 days, see §61.06. Accordingly, separate amendment of the European patent (UK) should be requested if a decision on revocation is likely to be given in the United Kingdom before the opposition proceedings are concluded.

The binding effect of amendments eventually made in EPO proceedings may result in amendments already made to the European patent (UK) under any of ss.27, 73 or 75 being overridden, see §75.03. This could cause a problem when amendment is made in the EPO proceedings after a court has given a ruling in the infringement proceedings, but when an appeal against this has yet to be heard. This is because the amendments are deemed always to have had effect, see ss.27(3), 75(3) and 77(4) and this may affect the decision at first instance as to infringement. Probably, in such a circumstance, the Court of Appeal would feel that it had little alternative but to remit the case back to the court at first instance for a further ruling based on the amended patent. It is, therefore, suggested that, if amendments are put forward in the EPO opposition proceedings, it would be prudent to seek the same amendments before the UK court hearing the infringement proceedings. Otherwise, the claimant could find himself penalised in costs for proceeding with an infringement action on a patent for which amendments were being sought in another forum with such eventually being overriding if allowed.

It remains to be decided what the position is when amendments to a European patent (UK) are made in proceedings under ss.27 or 75 and different, or additional, amendments are subsequently made in parallel EPO opposition proceedings. It is submitted that, in such a situation, if the effect of the amendments made in the EPO is to extend the protection conferred by the (already amended) European patent (UK), that patent will be invalid under s.72(1)(e), unless and until likewise amended. However, where the EPO proceedings were finalised subsequent to a decision of the Patents Court but before an appeal against that decision was heard, the Court of Appeal was adamant that the appeal had to be conducted on the basis of the amended patent (*Palmaz's European Patents* [2000] R.P.C. 631 CA). At first instance the amended claims had been held to embrace additional subject-matter, but the EPO had taken a contrary view. As the patent was held invalid on other grounds, the Court of Appeal did not opine on these conflicting decisions, see §76.12.

If the EPO maintains the patent, its decision has no legal effect on a British court or on the Comptroller, each of whom is entitled to find the European patent (UK) wholly or partially invalid, the EPO decision creating no estoppel, see *Buehler v Chronos Richardson* [1998] R.P.C. 609 CA. The position is, of course, likewise as to a finding by the EPO that the patent can be maintained by it in a restricted form, although the amendment itself is a binding determination of the maximum scope of protection of the European patent as maintained in the EPO proceedings.

Since January 1984, an entry has been made in the European register if no opposition is timely filed in the EPO; and an analogous entry is also now made when errors in the specification are allowed by the EPO to be rectified (see OJ EPO 1983, 458). Also, when a European patent (UK) is revoked by the EPO as a result of opposition proceedings timely brought before it, a notice to that effect is published in the *Patents Journal*, in addition to an entry being made in the register. The European register also contains much information on the progress of European patent applications and of the prior art coming to light after the European search report has been established, and this information is accessible via the website *http://www.epoline.org*, for which see §118.08. Details of the progress of opposition proceedings can be ascertained only from an inspection of the EPO file, see §118.14 and P.A. Smith [1993] *CIPA* 139 and 245. Access to the European register is also discussed in §32.35.

Effect of finding by EPO of partial invalidity of European patent (UK) (subs.(3))

Subsection (3) assimilates for the purposes of s.58(7)–(9) (patent found partially valid in Crown use proceedings) and s.63 (relief for infringement of a partially valid patent) an EPO decision resulting in partial invalidity. The amendment made to subs.(3) by the 1988 Act clarifies the way in which the provisions in the Act for relief in infringement proceedings and compensation for Crown use under s.58 respectively operate in the case of a European patent (UK) which is amended as a result of opposition proceedings before the EPO, for which see the commentaries on ss.63 and 58 respectively. The revised wording of subs.(3) also makes it clear that it relates only to a European patent (UK). **77.07**

Intervening rights on restoration of European patent (UK) or application for it (subs.(5))

Subsection (5) provides for the application of intervening rights to a European patent (UK) which has been revoked for failure to observe a time limit, and has subsequently been restored. These intervening rights arise on the same basis as in s.28A(4)–(7), that is the right to continue intervening acts or acts that would otherwise infringe or fall under s.55 (Crown use) between expiry and an application to restore a lapsed patent, as discussed in §§28A.05 and 28A.06. Such is most likely to arise following restitution of a pending European patent application under EPC art.122. **77.08**

Subsection (5) has been amended to ensure that intervening rights are available to third parties when a European patent has been revoked and is later restored by the new procedure for a review of a decision of an EPO Board of Appeal under EPC art.112A.

Translation of European patents (UK) (subss.(6)–(9))

Subsections (6)–(8) are concerned with translations where the European patent (UK) is **77.09** in French or German (see EPC art.65), but the London Agreement has the effect that translations of European patents are no longer required where the specification of the patent was published after May 1, 2008 when that Agreement came into force because s.77(9) has the effect of disapplying subss.(6)–(8) to such specifications, and was brought into effect by the Patents (Translations) Rules 2005 (SI 2005/687) as of that date. Thus, these subsections now apply only to European patents (UK), the mention of the grant of which was published on or after September 1, 1987, and before May 1, 2008 and then irrespective of any amendment of a European patent (UK) granted before that date which is made in opposition proceedings at the EPO and thereafter published by the EPO, see note 1 to §77.01. The present rules under these subsections are those made under r.56 (reprinted at above). It should also be noted that subs.(9) permits the making of rules which would allow the provisions of subss.(6)–(8) to be subsequently reimposed.

Paragraphs (1)(a) and (5) to (8) of r.56 also ceased to have effect as from May 1, 2008. Article 9 of the London Agreement makes transitional provision to the effect that the Agreement applies to European patents in respect of which the mention of grant is published in the *European Patent Bulletin* on or after the date the agreement comes into force. However, there are no similar transitional arrangements for r.56 which has the effect that patent proprietors may take advantage of the three-month period prescribed for filing a translation. European patents granted from February 1, 2008 therefore do not require a translation to be filed in order to enter into force in the UK.

Rule 56 prescribes the requirements for providing translations of European patents (UK) having their text in the French or German language. Rule 56(6) prescribes that any translations required by subs.(6)(a) are to be filed, and the prescribed fee paid, within three months of the date of mention of the grant of the European patent (UK) in the EPB; and r.56(7), if applicable, likewise, requires a translation of any amendment of such a patent to be filed within three months from the date of publication by the EPO of the amended specification. The period for filing the translation is extensible by two months as of right by filing PF 52 under r.108(2); and for a longer period if discretion can be exercised under r.108(3). If a required translation is not filed within the prescribed (extended) period, the European patent (UK) would be treated "as always having been void" (subs.(7)). When this happens, the MOPP indicates that any renewal fees paid are not refunded.

Thus, the result of subs.(6) is that, for patents granted before February 1, 2008, until the translation has been filed as required, the European patent (UK) has no effect in the United Kingdom. All formal requisites for the filing of the translation may, therefore, need to be met before the proprietor is able to take advantage of his patent rights. The effect of failing to file a translation therefore appears to be the same as withdrawing the United Kingdom designation for the European patent, although that can be done, as such, only before grant of the European patent.

In the case of amendment of a European patent (UK), for example in opposition proceedings before the EPO, r.56(7) requires a translation to be provided of "the specification as amended", rather than merely of a "translation of the amendment".

The filing of the translation under subs.(6), if required, is recorded in the register and advertised in the *Patents Journal*. The translations are published, in accordance with subs.(8), by printing them in the same manner as the B-specifications of patents granted under Pt I of the Act and are distributed to the same libraries in the United Kingdom as those B-specifications. For this reason the translation must be filed in conformity with the presentation requirements of Pts 1 to 3 of Sch.2 to the Rules. The original translation can be inspected, and copies provided, under r.51 (reprinted at §118.02) in the usual way for inspection of documents filed at the UK-IPO, for which see §§118.10 and 118.19.

Care should always be taken in preparing a translation of a patent because a less than completely accurate translation can cause problems in subsequent litigation. For example, in *Coflexip v Stolt Comex* BL C/1/99, noted I.P.D. 22035, the French phrase "conduite flexible" was translated as "flexible conduit". This led to an attack against validity which was saved by the court purposively construing the phrase as "flexible pipe" in accordance with customary terminology in the art, see §125.15.

The European Court of Justice has ruled that it is not incompatible with art.28 of the PCT that a European patent in a particular country should become void ab initio if no required translation is filed within the permitted period (*BASF v President of the German Patent Office* (C-44/98) [1999] E.C.R. I-6269).

Irrespective of whether a translation is not required, translation problems can arise when construing technical features specified in a foreign language text, as happened in *Siemens Schweiz v Thorn Security* [2008] R.P.C. 4; [2007] EWHC 2242 Ch, noted [2007] *CIPA* 554 when the meaning of certain technical language in a claim was much discussed. Here, the court adopted a literal translation of the German text as being more in conformity with the tenor of the specification when read as a whole.

Legal effect of translation filed under subsection (6)

77.10 The legal effect of a translation filed under subs.(6) is obscure. The authentic text of a European patent (UK) for the purposes of any proceedings in the United Kingdom remains that of the specification of the European patent in the language of the proceedings before the EPO (s.80(1)), but see the discussion in §80.04. Only if the translation filed under s.77(6) is narrower than the protection conferred by the authentic text is the translation to be substituted for that authentic text until this is corrected, and even then not in proceedings for the revocation of the patent (s.80(2), discussed in §80.05). If and when so corrected, the new translation replaces the original translation of the authentic text (s.80(3), discussed in §80.06), but subject to interim loss of rights, see s.80(3) and (4), discussed in §§80.06 and 80.07. Therefore, if the translation is of the same, or wider, scope than the authentic text, it is the authentic text which has effect. Thus, the translation under s.77(6) mainly has effect for information purposes and may be relied upon in legal proceedings only if it is admitted that this is of the same or narrower scope than the authentic text.

In proceedings before the Comptroller, no further translation needs to be filed under r.114(2) (reprinted in §123.31). Thus, a translation filed under s.77(6) is prima facie accepted by the Comptroller, but its existence is evidential and, as with any evidence, is subject to challenge, even though the translation has been verified to the satisfaction of the Comptroller. Otherwise, and especially in proceedings before the court, a translation will need to be provided and supported by evidence, unless it has been made the subject of a formal admission or agreement between the parties.

General obligations on proprietor of European patent (UK)

77.11 A note on EPO Form 2005 (communication under EPC r.71) reminds proprietors of the desirability of supplying an address for service for every European patent (UK) (in compliance with r.103 (reprinted at §32.02). It has been suggested that the address for service should be notified as soon as it becomes apparent that an application for a European patent (UK) is going to mature into a patent, e.g. on the issue of the letter under EPC r.71. This can have the advantage that any reminders concerning the filing of a translation, or the payment of a renewal fee, are sent to the United Kingdom agent. Should an English translation be required, but not supplied within the prescribed three-month period, as extended by two months (r.108(2)), the UK-IPO sends a letter to the address for service, notifying that the European patent (UK) is deemed void. This gives an early opportunity to apply for a further extension under r.108(3) should the voiding have been unintentional.

There is no need to provide any form of authorisation of agent: provision of an address suffices for this purpose, see §274.04. However, if opposition proceedings are commenced against the European patent in the EPO within the permitted nine-month period from the notification of grant in the EPB under EPC art.99, the representative who is to act before the EPO will need to be authorised in accordance with normal EPO practice see, e.g. *Patents Journal* July 19, 1989.

PRACTICE UNDER SECTION 77

Providing the address for service

77.12 There is currently no necessity for a proprietor of a European patent (UK) to appoint an address for service in the United Kingdom (or the Isle of Man) until such time as the proprietor may become concerned in some proceedings before the Comptroller under the Patents Rules, see r.103. Neither the mere filing of a translation of the patent, nor the payment of renewal fees thereon, is regarded as being a relevant proceeding under the Rules. It is good practice for a United Kingdom address for service to be recorded in the register, since otherwise official reminders (e.g. of the non-payment of a renewal fee) may take time to arrive at the proprietor's address and may then be ignored because the proprietor may think that his affairs have been entrusted to an agent, whereas that agent will not now receive the reminder and, anyway, not being the address for service, may consider that the proprietor has made other arrangements for effecting renewal. The UK-IPO will accept notification of an address for service as from the date when the EPO issues a communication under EPC r.71 of its intention to grant the patent in a particular form.

No form or fee has been prescribed for entering an address for service in the United Kingdom register for a European patent (UK): a simple letter suffices. However, it is recommended to use PF 51 (in duplicate), even though this is not a prescribed use of this form (*Patents Journal* December 2, 1987). If such letter or form is filed in duplicate, receipt will be acknowledged by returning the copy. The publication number of the European patent should be quoted in preference to its application number. The letter or form can be signed by an agent.

Filing and form of translations

77.13   European patents (UK) granted in the French or German language on or after September 1, 1987 and before February 1, 2008 (taking into account the r.108(2) grace period) are deemed always to have been void if no English translation thereof is filed within three months of the mention of grant in the EPB (subs.(7) and r.56(6)). This period is extensible by two months under r.108(2), and further by discretion exercised under r.108(3).

Use of translation in legal proceedings

77.14   The need to provide an English translation of a European patent (UK), or of an application therefor, in any legal proceedings in the United Kingdom involving it, and to support this by evidence, is governed by the general provisions of the CPR. In proceedings before the Comptroller, any translation filed under s.77(6) satisfies the requirements of r.114(1) (reprinted in §123.31) which would otherwise require a translation to be filed, but the accuracy of that translation may be challenged. If the challenge leads the Comptroller to have reasonable doubts as to the accuracy of the translation, he may require the person who furnished that translation to provide evidence that the translation is accurate (r.115).

In court proceedings, it would be sensible for the parties to try to agree a translation before the trial, for example by a request for an admission under CPR 6 3PD 4 and para.2.3 of the Patents Court Guide (see, respectively, Appendices F and G). *Terson v Primeline* BL C/183/82, noted I.P.D. 7005 was a case involving a European patent (UK) in the French language. Here the court observed that no translation had been agreed between the parties and indicated that the question of translation was therefore a matter to be proved in evidence. *Salford Electrical v BSH Industries* [1995] R.P.C. 183 was a case where a dispute concerning translation was resolved on the oral evidence of a translator.

Amendment

77.15   When a European patent (UK) with an authentic text in the French or German language (other than one granted before September 1, 1987 or after February 1, 2008) is amended in the EPO after grant (i.e. as the result of opposition proceedings before the EPO), a translation of the amended specification must likewise be filed within three months from the date of publication by the EPO of the amended specification (s.77(6)(b) and r.56(7)). For this purpose PF 54 is likewise to be used. That translation must also comply with the requirements of Pts 1 to 3, Sch.2 to the Rules. The filing of an amended translation is advertised in the *Patents Journal* see, e.g. *Patents Journal* January 31, 1990.

For the procedure for amending a European patent (UK) which is not in the English language, see §27.06.

Renewal fees

77.16   If four or more years have elapsed following the filing date of an application for a

European patent (UK), annual renewal fees are payable to the UK-IPO but not in respect of any period before publication of the mention of grant of the European patent (UK) in the EPB (r.37(4)). If the anniversary for payment falls less than three months after the date of publication of the grant, the renewal fee may still be paid within this three-month period. These matters are discussed in §25.10 and are the subject of periodic notices in the *Patents Journal.*

If any required translation is not filed with the consequence that the patent is treated as always having been void under subs.(7). Any renewal fees paid are not refunded.

SECTION 78

Effect of filing an application for a European patent (UK)

78.—(1) Subject to the provisions of this Act, an application for a European **78.01** patent (UK) having a date of filing under the European Patent Convention shall be treated for the purposes of the provisions of this Act to which this section applies as an application for a patent under this Act having that date as its date of filing and having the other incidents listed in subsection (3) below, but subject to the modifications mentioned in the following provisions of this section.

(2) This section applies to the following provisions of this Act:—

section 2(3) and so much of section 14(7) as relates to section 2(3);

section 5;

section 6;

so much of section 13(3) as relates to an application for and issue of a certificate under that subsection;

sections 30 to 33;

section 36;

sections 55 to 69;

section 74, so far as relevant to any of the provisions mentioned above;

section 111; and

section 125.

(3) The incidents referred to in subsection (1) above in relation to an application for a European patent (UK) are as follows:—

(a) any declaration of priority made in connection with the application under the European Patent Convention shall be treated for the purposes of this Act as a declaration made under section 5(2) above;

(b) where a period of time relevant to priority is extended under that convention, the period of twelve months **allowed under section 5(2A)(a)** [*specified in section 5(2)*] above shall be so treated as altered correspondingly;

(c) where the date of filing an application is re-dated under that convention to a later date, that date shall be so treated as the date of filing the application;

(d) the application, if published in accordance with that convention, shall, subject to subsection (7)* and section 79 below, be so treated as published under section 16 above;

(e) any designation of the inventor under that convention or any statement under it indicating the origin of the right to a European patent shall be treated for the purposes of section 13(3) above as a statement filed under section 13(2) above;

(f) registration of the application in the register of European patents shall be treated as registration under this Act.

(4) Rules under section 32 above may not impose any requirements as to the registration of applications for European patents (UK) but may provide for the registration of copies of entries relating to such applications in the European register of patents.

(5) Subsections (1) to (3) above shall cease to apply to an application for a European patent (UK), except as mentioned in subsection (5A) below, if—

(a) the application is refused or withdrawn or deemed to be withdrawn, or

(b) the designation of the United Kingdom in the application is withdrawn or deemed to be withdrawn,

but shall apply again if the rights of the applicant are re-established under the European Patent Convention, as from their re-establishment.

(5A) The occurrence of any of the events mentioned in subsection (5)(a) or (b) shall not affect the continued operation of section 2(3) above in relation to matter contained in an application for a European patent (UK) which by virtue of that provision has become part of the state of the art as regards other inventions; and the occurrence of any event mentioned in subsection (5)(b) shall not prevent matter contained in an application for a European patent (UK) becoming part of the state of the art by virtue of section 2(3) above as regards other inventions where the event occurs before the publication of that application.

[*(5) Subsections (1) to (3) above shall cease to apply to an application for a European patent (UK) when the application is refused or withdrawn or deemed to be withdrawn, or the designation of the United Kingdom in the application is withdrawn or deemed to be withdrawn, but if the rights of the applicant are re-established under the European Patent Convention, subsections (1) to (3) above shall as from the re-establishment of those rights again apply to the application.*]

(6) Where, between [*those*] subsections **(1) to (3) above** ceasing to apply to **an application for a European patent (UK)** [*any such application*] and the re establishment of the rights of the applicant, a person—

(a) begins in good faith to do an act which would [*, apart from section 55 above*] constitute an infringement of the **rights conferred by publication of the application** if those subsections then applied, or

(b) makes in good faith effective and serious preparations to do such an act,

he shall have the **right to continue to do the act or, as the case may be, to do the act, notwithstanding subsections (1) to (3) applying again and notwithstanding the grant of the patent** [*rights conferred by section 28A(4) and (5) above, and subsections (6) and (7) of that section shall apply... accordingly*].

(6A) Subsections (5) and (6) of section 20B above have effect for the purposes of subsection (6) above as they have effect for the purposes of that section and as if the references to subsection (4) of that section were references to subsection (6) above.

(6B) Subject to subsection (6A) above, the right conferred by subsection (6) above does not extend to granting a licence to another person to do the act in question.

(6C) Subsections (6) to (6B) above apply in relation to the use of a patented invention for the services of the Crown as they apply in relation to an infringement of the rights conferred by publication of the application (or, as the case may be, infringement of the patent).

"Patented invention" has the same meaning as in section 55 above.

[(6) *Where between those subsections ceasing to apply to any such application and the re-establishment of the rights of the applicant a person begins in good faith to do an act which would, apart from section 55 above, constitute an infringement of the application if those subsections then applied, or makes in good faith effective and serious preparations to do such an act, he shall have the rights conferred by section 28A(4) and (5) above, and subsections (6) and (7) of that section shall apply [28(6) above, and section 28(8) and (9) above shall apply to the exercise of any such right] accordingly.*]

(7) While this subsection is in force, an application for a European patent (UK) published by the European Patent Office under the European Patent Convention in French or German shall be treated for the purposes of sections 55 and 69 above as published under section 16 above when a translation into English of the claims of the specification of the application has been filed at and published by the Patent Office and the prescribed fee has been paid, but an applicant—

    (a) may recover a payment by virtue of section 55(5) above in respect of the use of the invention in question before publication of that translation; or

    (b) may bring proceedings by virtue of section 69 above in respect of an act mentioned in that section which is done before publication of that translation;

if before that use or the doing of that act he has sent by post or delivered to the government department who made use or authorised the use of the invention, or, as the case may be, to the person alleged to have done the act, a translation into English of those claims.

(8) Subsection (7) above shall come into force on a day appointed for the purpose by rules and shall cease to have effect on a day so appointed, without prejudice, however, to the power to bring it into force again.

Notes

* In error, the first printing of the Act referred here to "subsection (6)".

1. Subsection (7) was brought into force from September 1, 1987 by an order made under subs.(8) (Patents (Amendment) Rules 1987 (SI 1987/288) r.5), but with no effect on applications for a European patent (UK) which had not been published by the European Patent Office before that date. This rule remains in force.

2. Subsection (5) was replaced by new subss.(5)and (5A), and subs.(6) amended, by Sch.5 paras 8 and 22 to the CDPA 1988, with effect from January 7, 1991 (SI 1990/2168), but the provision of new subs.(5A) (by virtue of SI 2007/3396, r.3) does not apply to a European application (UK) filed before May 1, 2008.

3. The RRO (art.14) amended subs.78(3)(b) by replacing the words "specified in section 5(2)" by "allowed under section 5(2A)(a)". This amendment took effect from January 1, 2005, the Commencement Date of the RRO, but the previous version of the section continues to apply to applications then "pending", i.e. with a filing date on or before December 31, 2004.

4. The Patents Act 2004 (c.16) Sch.1(3) amended s.78(5A), substituted a new form of subs.(6) and inserted new subss.(6A)–(6C) each as set out, or indicated, above. These amendments were brought into effect when the EPC revisions agreed in 2000 came into effect on December 13, 2007.

COMMENTARY ON SECTION 78

Scope of the section

78.02   Section 78 concerns an application for a European patent which has been accorded a date of filing in the EPO and which then designates the United Kingdom as a country for which protection would be sought. Such application is termed by the Act an "application for a European patent (UK)", see its definition and of "designate" in s.130(1). While such applications may be filed at the EPO in Munich, or at its branches in The Hague or Berlin, an originating application (i.e. not a divisional application) may be filed at a national patent office of an EPC Member State. However, persons normally resident in the United Kingdom must not file such non-divisional applications other than at the UK-IPO unless security clearance has first been obtained, see §23.08. If a secrecy order is imposed on a European application filed at the UK-IPO, the application is not forwarded to the EPO and is deemed to be withdrawn, but application may then be made for its conversion (under s.81, as discussed in §81.07) to an application filed under the Act, see §22.04, with the possibility of other national filings in some EPC countries being permitted, see §23.09.

Following the entry into force of the EPC 2000 on December 13, 2007, an application for a European patent is (under revised EPC art.79) automatically deemed to be an application for a European patent in each of the then contracting states. The definition of "designate" in s.130(1) has been amended accordingly, see §130.01.

Section 78 makes an application for a European patent (UK) equivalent to an application under the Act for certain purposes, particularly in respect of the so-called provisional protection conferred on publication under s.69 and possible conflict between concurrent United Kingdom and European applications under s.2(3). The section implements art.67 of the EPC, but is not required by s.130(7) necessarily to have the same effect as EPC art.67.

Section 79 contains some further provisions in respect of international applications which have designated the United Kingdom for patent protection via a European patent (UK). Such applications are herein called "Euro-PCT applications". Section 80 provides for the authentic text for a European application or European patent and for filing and correcting translations thereof. Section 81 makes provision, in certain limited circumstances, for conversion of a European patent (UK) into an application under the Act. Sections 82 and 83 stipulate the circumstances in which tribunals in the United Kingdom can determine disputes as to entitlement to proprietorship of European applications, whether or not designating the United Kingdom.

Effect of application for European patent (UK) (subss.(1)–(4))

78.03   Subject to the other relevant provisions, subs.(1) provides that an application for a European patent (UK) has the same effect as an application for a patent under the Act as to its filing date and for the purposes of the sections listed in subs.(2). Certain incidents in such applications are to be treated in the same manner as corresponding incidents under the Act: these are listed in subs.(3).

The sections listed in subs.(2) are:

section 2(3): Contents of co-pending application (which exclude, for prior art purposes, the abstract);

section 5: Priority date;

section 6: Disclosure between earlier and later applications;

section 13(3): Mention of inventor;

section 14(7): Abstract;

sections 30–33: Property in patents, register, registration;

section 36: Co-ownership of patents and applications;

sections 55–69: Crown use, infringement and right of prior use;

section 74: Proceedings in which validity can be put in issue;

section 111: Unauthorised claim that a patent has been applied for; and

section 125: Extent of invention to be protected.

The incidents listed in subs.(3) are:

(a) declaration of priority, to be treated as if made under s.5(2);

(b) extended priority period, the 12-month period of s.5(2) is to be altered correspondingly;

(c) re-dated application, to be treated as re-dated accordingly;

(d) publication under the EPC, to be treated as publication under s.16 (subject to any intervening rights, and also subject to the eventual filing of any required translations, for which see: §77.13 (for a granted European patent); §78.07 (for a pending European application); and §79.04 (for a pending Euro-PCT application));

(e) designation of inventor and statement of entitlement, to be treated as a statement under s.13(2) for the purposes of s.13(3) (rectification of inventorship); and

(f) registration, to be treated as registration under the Act.

The reference in subs.(3)(b) to "specified in section 5(2) " has been changed to "allowed under section 5(2A)(a) " in order to accommodate the possible allowed late filing of a priority declaration (by the EPO under a provision analogous to that now provided for an application under the Act, as described in §5.03 above).

Subsection (4) prohibits imposition of formal requirements for the separate entry into the register of details of applications for European patents (UK) by rules made under s.32, but it does allow rules providing for the registration of copies of entries relating to such applications which have been entered in the European register of patents maintained under EPC art.127.

When a divisional application is filed under an application for a European patent, it may be important to pay the United Kingdom designation fee on the patent application as, otherwise, such a designation fee paid on the divisional application may not be effective, see R. Camp [1997] *CIPA* 509.

Effect of refusal, etc. and reinstatement (subss.(5), (5A) and (6))

Subsection (5) nullifies the enabling provisions of subss.(1)–(3) when the application, or designation of the United Kingdom in it, ceases to exist but restores these provisions if the rights of the applicant are re-established under the EPC, though in that case subject to subs.(6) (intervening rights as under s.28A(4)–(7)), for which see §§28A.05 and 28A.06. The operation of subs.(5) (revised from January 7, 1991 when subs.(5A) was introduced and as amended as of December 13, 2007) could raise problems. However, as its terms do not appear to be retrospective, it is probably of practical significance only in relation to the third-party rights arising under subs.(6) if the European application is restored under EPC art.122.

Subsection (5A), inserted as from January 7, 1991, specifically maintains the prior art effect of an application for a European patent (UK), arising on its publication, irrespective of the ultimate fate of that application. This reverses the previous position under the for-

78.04

mer wording of subs.(5), which was that the prior art effect of a European application was lost if that application was withdrawn or deemed to have been withdrawn (see *L'Oréal's Application* [1986] R.P.C. 19). The new subs.(5A) does not have retroactive effect, so that the *L'Oréal* decision would still seem to have effect in respect to European applications which were withdrawn or deemed to have been withdrawn before January 7, 1991, unless a court could be persuaded to overrule that decision having regard to *Pepper v Hart* [1992] 3 W.L.R. 1032; [1993] 1 All E.R. 42 (which now admits the possibility of using *Hansard* as an aid to statutory construction) and the parliamentary debate which led to the wording of the former form of subs.(5) where a Government spokesman said that that wording already had the meaning which is now definitively provided by subs.(5A), see H.L. Deb., Vol. 380, Ser. 42, col. 1544 (March 15, 1977).

However, subs.(5A) has more recently come into conflict with the analogous situation as dealt with under the EPC. This has arisen as a consequence of the amendment, as from July 1, 1997, of art.79(2) of the EPC to permit designation fees to be paid on a European application up to six months after notification of the publication of the search report is published in the EPB. This date will usually be after the application has itself been published. At the same time r.23A of the EPC (under the EPC 1973) was made, stipulating that:

"A European patent application shall be considered as comprised in the state of the art under Article 54, paragraphs 3 and 4, only if the designation fees under article 79, paragraph 2, have been validly paid."

Thus, unless former r.23A of the EPC was ultra vires the EPC 1973, it seemed that (under the EPC 1973) a European application did not enter the state of the art under EPC art.54(3)(4) for the United Kingdom unless and until the designation fee for it was paid. However, s.78(3)(c) stipulates that a European application (UK) enters the state of the art (under s.2(3)) upon its publication, and s.78(5A) has the same effect if the failure to pay the designation fee for the United Kingdom after publication of the European application with a tentative designation for it is regarded as withdrawal of that original designation. These provisions under the Act seem to specify that, once a European application has been published with a United Kingdom designation, it irrevocably enters the state of the art as regards its prior art effect in relation to other inventions, and so such an application may have a prior art effect in the United Kingdom different from that in other countries for which no designation fee is subsequently paid despite publication with the designation therefor indicated.

This conflict has been resolved as a result of the amendments made to art.79 of the EPC in EPC 2000 and to subs.(5A), the latter taking effect as of December 13, 2007. The changes ensure that an application for a European patent (UK) shall have prior art effect under s.2(3) upon publication, regardless of whether the UK remains designated at the time of its publication. This is a consequence of the fact that, under EPC 2000 every European patent application will, upon filing, be deemed to be an application for protection in all the then contracting states (see revised EPC art.79).

The amendments to subs.(6) and the new subss.(6A)–(6C) clarify and expand the previous provisions for intervening rights arising when a European patent application is terminated or refused, and subsequently reinstated, including where the reinstatement arises from a review of a decision of an EPO Board of Appeal under new EPC art.112A, and conform to corresponding new provisions in respect of applications under the Act arising under new ss.20B and 117A.

Subsection (6C) applies these provisions also to a claim for compensation for Crown use of an invention covered by such a revived application.

Translations (subss.(7) and (8))

78.05   Subsection (7) is concerned with translations of claims of a published application for a European patent (UK) when these are published in the French or German language (see EPC art.67(3)). The subsection provides that, when a translation of the claims into English of such an application has been filed at the UK-IPO and a fee paid, the application is given the effect of publication for the purposes of ss.55 (Crown use) and 69 (infringement of application). If the applicant exercises his option of filing such a translation, which is merely permissive but not mandatory, he may recover compensation for Crown use under s.55(5) and/or may bring proceedings under s.69 in respect of acts done even before publication of the application, for which see §§55.20 and 69.02 et seq. Alternatively, the same effect can be achieved against a particular entity from the date when a translation of the claims has been delivered, or sent by post, to that entity, i.e. to the Government department or to the infringer as the case may be. The procedure is governed by r.56. Note that whether the translation is to be filed at the UK-IPO or supplied to an alleged Crown user or infringer, only the claims of the application are required to be translated. Subsection (7) is not applicable to European applications published before September 1, 1987.

Subsection (8) permits the making of rules which would allow the provisions of subs.(7) to be removed, and subsequently re-imposed, on an appointed day. However, no such rule has been made although, following the coming into force of the London Agreement, no translation of a European patent granted in the French or German language and published on or after May 1, 2008 has been required, see §77.09. Thus, the effect of subs.(7) remains an option which could be useful to support an application (after grant of the patent) for damages under s.69, even though a translation of the granted patent is no longer required.

PRACTICE UNDER SECTION 78

Register

The UK-IPO no longer maintains any register of European applications (UK). Reliance **78.06** for the status of such applications is therefore now totally placed on the register maintained by the EPO itself, an entry in which is created upon the publication (under EPC art.93) of an application for a European patent, as discussed in §32.18. Consequently, a change of proprietor (or a change of name thereof) for a European application (UK) can only be effected prior to grant of the European patent by an entry made in the register maintained by the EPO even if the change relates only to the United Kingdom designation.

The procedure and documents required for registering in the EPO an assignment of an application for a European patent were the subject of an official notice from the EPO (see OJ EPO 1980, 305). The then r.72 of the EPC required that such assignment be in writing and signed by "the parties to the contract". This condition was held to be not satisfied when counterparts of an assignment were each signed by the separate parties, but not exchanged between them, though both counterparts were supplied to the EPO (J 18/84 *N.N./Register of European patents—Entries in* OJ EPO 1987, 215; [1987] E.P.O.R. 321). This case also pointed out that it is sufficient if a certified copy of a relevant extract of the instrument of transfer is supplied to the EPO, see r.22 of the EPC, and in this case this had been done by a jointly signed declaration as part of the application's "Request for grant", even though the signatures on this had been only carbon copies.

Thus, under the current form of r.22 of the EPC, it is sufficient, in order to register in the EPO a transfer of interest in a European patent application, simply to supply some document which satisfies the EPO that the transfer has taken place, production of an instrument of transfer being no longer required in the EPO, see the EPO Guideline E–XIII. Under the Act a similar position now obtains, see §32.22. Nevertheless, signature of a document by or on behalf of each party to the transaction remains obligatory, failing which a recorded assignment is regarded as having effect only as transfer of an equitable, but not the beneficial, interest in the patent/application, see §30.05.

The register of European patents can be inspected in the UK-IPO in respect of a European patent (UK) or a published application therefore in the normal way for inspecting documents in the UK-IPO file, for which see §118.19. Information can also be obtained by direct contact with the EPO, see §32.36, or more conveniently by online access via the EPO website *http://www.epoline.org*.

Filing of translation of claims

If advantage is to be taken of s.78(7), for the reason explained in §78.05, the English **78.07** translation of the claims of the application for a European patent (UK), or of the Euro-PCT application for a European patent (UK), must be filed with a PF 54, both in duplicate under r.56(3).

Any translation filed under subs.(7) must comply with the requirements of Pts 1 to 3 of Sch.2 to the Rules (reprinted in §§14.05), for which see §77.16, but no translation of the specification (apart from its claims) is required. Any attempt to file a complete translation may, therefore, be rejected. The filing of the translation is advertised in the *Patents Journal* (*Patents Journal* March 1, 1989) and entered in the register. Copies of translations filed under s.78(7) can be obtained in the normal way for obtaining copies of documents from the UK-IPO file, for which see §118.18.

If an application is made under s.78(7) prior to publication of the application for the European patent (UK), the UK-IPO requests that the expected date of publication be provided. This is because the Office has no ready means of ascertaining that date since at the time there will be no entry in the EPO register (*Patents Journal* September 23, 1987). The filed translation can then be made available as from the date of publication of the European (or Euro-PCT) application. The requirements of Pts 1 to 3 of Sch.2 to the Rules need not be complied with where the translation of the claims is delivered in electronic form or using electronic communications (r.56(4)) for which see the commentary on s.124A.

SECTION 79

Operation of section 78 in relation to certain European patent applications

79.01   **79.**—(1) Subject to the following provisions of this section, section 78 above, in its operation in relation to an international application for a patent (UK) which istreated by virtue of the European Patent Convention as an application for a European patent (UK), shall have effect as if any reference in that section to anything done in relation to the application under the European Patent Convention included a reference to the corresponding thing done under the Patent Co-operation Treaty.

(2) Any such international application which is published under that treaty shall be treated for the purposes of section 2(3) above as published only when a copy of the application has been supplied to the European Patent Office in English, French or German and the relevant fee has been paid under that convention.

(3) Any such international application which is published under that treaty in a language other than English, French or German shall, subject to section 78(7) above, be treated for the purposes of sections 55 and 69 above as published only when it is re-published in English, French or German by the European Patent Office under that convention.

COMMENTARY ON SECTION 79

Scope of the section
79.02   The purpose of s.79 is to render an application made under the PCT which designates a European patent (UK) (a "Euro-PCT" application) equivalent to an application for a European patent filed in the EPO, but subject to certain language requirements and other conditions being met and subject to the provisions of new s.130(4A) and (5A) (for which see §130.08). The general provision contained in subs.(1) provides that, for a Euro-PCT application, any requirement of s.78 arising under the EPC is to be met if a corresponding thing is done under the PCT. The European phase of a "Euro-PCT" application is discussed in detail in the *European Patents Handbook* ("EPH") (London: Sweet & Maxwell) Ch.17.

Prior art effect of Euro-PCT application (subs.(2))
79.03   Under subss.(2), (3) (prior art effect of unpublished application of earlier date) applies

only to Euro-PCT applications when: the relevant fee has been paid to the EPO; and either the international application has been published under PCT art.21 in English, French or German or a translation into one of those languages has been filed at the EPO if the international application was published in another language. Thus, if a Euro-PCT application is withdrawn, or is deemed to be withdrawn, during the international phase, it never forms part of the state of the art for the purposes of s.2(3).

The modifications introduced by the EPC 2000 remove any complications as to the prior art effect of Euro-PCT applications which previously existed under the 1973 text as a consequence of the importance of the payment of the "relevant fee". Although art.79(2) of the EPC provides that designation of a Contracting State may be subject to payment of a fee, EPC art.153(5) and EPC r.157 do not stipulate such payment as a requirement for the application to comprise the state of the art for the purposes of art.54(3) of the EPC. All that is required for the application to form part of the state of the art is the international publication of the application in one of the official langues of the EPC (which will be mentioned in the EPB), or publication by the EPO of a translation of the application in one of the said official languages.

Note that, if the application is not published in the international phase (e.g. because the international application was deemed withdrawn and subsequently converted into a European application under PCT art.25), its prior art effect under s.2(3), if any, will arise by virtue of s.78(2) on publication of the application by the EPO. Also, any amendments made during the international phase are irrelevant to the prior art effect of a Euro-PCT application.

Provisional protection arising from Euro-PCT application (subs.(3))

If the Euro-PCT application is published under PCT art.21 in English, the application **79.04** enjoys so-called "provisional protection", i.e. it is treated as published for the purposes of s.55 (Crown use) or s.69 (infringement of application) as of the international publication date. If it is published in French or German, then, to secure this provisional protection, it is necessary first to file PF 54 and an English translation of the claims at the UK-IPO or to supply such translation to the alleged Crown user or infringer (s.78(7)). For this purpose r.56 provides for the filing of a translation of the claims of a Euro-PCT application designating the United Kingdom, as discussed in §78.03. If such translation is filed at the UK-IPO, it must be supplied in duplicate in the same way as for the translation of the claims of a normal European application, for which see §78.07.

If the Euro-PCT application has not entered the European phase when the translation of the claims is filed (although not if it has so entered) the international publication ("WO") number must be inserted on PF 54. Obviously, the application must be one for which the United Kingdom has been designated. Whilst the filing of the translation is advertised in the *Patents Journal*, there can be no entry in the register since the United Kingdom register entry for a Euro-PCT application is not established until after the application has matured into a granted European Patent (UK).

Since an international application, in which a European patent is requested with a designation of the United Kingdom, is regarded ab initio as a European patent application (EPC art.153(2)), it is unnecessary for any fees to be paid to the EPO before such provisional protection can commence. On the other hand, if the international application is published in a language other than English, French or German, provisional protection cannot be secured until a translation has been filed at, and republished by, the EPO. Furthermore, if the international application is republished by the EPO in French or German, compliance with the s.78 procedure is also necessary to secure provisional protection (EPC art.67(3)).

EPO Procedure

After not less than 18 months from the earliest declared priority date, international ap- **79.05** plications filed in Arabic, Chinese, English, French, German, Japanese, Russian or Spanish are published in that language by the International Bureau or, if filed in any other language, and not translated into one of those languages by the applicant, are translated by and published by the International Bureau in English (PCT r.48.3). The conditions for commencement of processing by the EPO must normally be met by 31 months from the priority date (EPC r.149). If not published in English there may, therefore, be a considerable delay following publication of the international application before it has the above-mentioned effects under ss.2(3), 55 and 69. This delay can be reduced, if needed, by meeting the above-mentioned conditions early and requesting early processing of the international application before the EPO under PCT arts.23(2) or 40(2).

When an initial international application is filed at the EPO, it can be sent to the UK-IPO for onward transmission, provided that at least one person (whether inventor, applicant or agent) is ordinarily resident in the United Kingdom. Indeed, it would appear that this procedure should be adopted in any such instance in order that there should be no breach of the requirements of s.23(1), see further at §23.02. However, fees for such an application must be paid directly to the EPO, for example by an accompanying request for deduction of these from an EPO deposit account, see *Patents Journal* September 8, 1999.

Alternatively, the provisional protection under ss.55 and/or 69 can be achieved by delivering or sending by post a translation to the relevant Government department or to the alleged infringer of the provisional protection under the second half of s.78(7), as discussed in §78.05 and §78.07.

International applications for patents (UK) which are not designated as applications for a European patent (UK) do not involve the EPO. Such applications are governed by ss.89, 89A and 89B: see the commentaries thereon.

SECTION 80

Authentic text of European patents and patent applications

80.01

80.—(1) Subject to subsection (2) below, the text of a European patent or application for such a patent in the language of the proceedings, that is to say, the language in which proceedings relating to the patent or the application are to be conducted before the European Patent Office, shall be the authentic text for the purposes of any domestic proceedings, that is to say, any proceedings relating to the patent or application before the comptroller or the court.

(2) Where the language of the proceedings is French or German, a translation into English of the specification of the patent under section 77 above or of the claims of the application under section 78 above shall be treated as the authentic text for the purpose of any domestic proceedings, other than proceedings for the revocation of the patent, if the patent or application as translated into English confers protection which is narrower than that conferred by it in French or German.

(3) If any such translation results in a European patent or application conferring the narrower protection, the proprietor of or applicant for the patent may file a corrected translation with the Patent Office and, if he pays the prescribed fee within the prescribed period, the Patent Office shall publish it, but—

(a) any payment for any use of the invention which (apart from section 55 above) would have infringed the patent as correctly translated, but not as originally translated, or in the case of an application would have infringed it as aforesaid if the patent had been granted, shall not be recoverable under that section,

(b) the proprietor or applicant shall not be entitled to bring proceedings in respect of an act which infringed the patent as correctly translated, but not as originally translated, or in the case of an application would have infringed it as aforesaid if the patent had been granted, unless before that use or the doing of the act the corrected translation has been published by the Patent Office or the proprietor or applicant has sent the corrected translation by post or delivered it to the government department who made use or authorised the use of the invention or, as the case may be, to the person alleged to have done that act.

(4) Where a correction of a translation is published under subsection (3) above and before it is so published a person—

  (a) begins in good faith to do an act which would not constitute an infringement of the patent [or application] as originally translated, **or of the rights conferred by publication of the application as originally translated**, but would [*(apart from section 55 above) constitute an infringement of it*] **do so** under the amended translation, or

  (b) makes in good faith effective and serious preparations to do such an act,

he shall have the **right to continue to do the act or, as the case may be, to do the act, notwithstanding the publication of the corrected translation and notwithstanding the grant of the patent** [*the rights conferred by section 28A(4) and (5) above, and subsections (6) and (7) of that section shall apply... accordingly*].

(5) Subsections (5) and (6) of section 28A above have effect for the purposes of subsection (4) above as they have effect for the purposes of that section and as if—

  (a) the references to subsection (4) of that section were references to subsection (4) above;

  (b) the reference to the registered proprietor of the patent included a reference to the applicant.

(6) Subject to subsection (5) above, the right conferred by subsection (4) above does not extend to granting a licence to another person to do the act in question.

(7) Subsections (4) to (6) above apply in relation to the use of a patented invention for the services of the Crown as they apply in relation to an infringement of the patent or of the rights conferred by the publication of the application.

"Patented invention" has the same meaning as in section 55 above.

Note. The Patents Act 2004 (c. 16, Sch.1(4)) substituted a new form of subs.80(4) and inserted new subss.(5)–(7). These amendments were brought into effect when the EPC revisions agreed in 2000 came into force on 13 December 2007 (SI 2007/3396).

RELEVANT RULES—RULE 57

Rule 57—Corrected translations

57.—(1) A corrected translation filed under section 80(3) must be accompanied   **80.02**
by Patents Form 54.

(2) The corrected translation must comply with the requirements set out in Parts 1 to 3 of Schedule 2.

(3) Where the corrected translation includes any drawings all annotations in French or German must be replaced with annotations in English.

(4) The corrected translation and Patents Form 54 must be filed in duplicate.

(5) But paragraph (2) does not apply where a translation is delivered in electronic form or using electronic communications.

(6) The period prescribed for the purposes of section 80(3) for payment of the prescribed fee is 14 days beginning [with] immediately after the day the corrected translation is filed.

Notes. Rule 115 (verification of translation), reprinted at §123.32 is also relevant.

Amended by the Patents (Amendment) Rules 2011 (SI 2011/2052).

COMMENTARY ON SECTION 80

Scope of the section

80.03   Section 80 stipulates the authentic text of European patents (UK) and applications therefor and is intended to realise the provisions of art.70 of the EPC. Where European patents (UK) and applications for them are not in the English language, s.80 also provides for the treatment of differences between their authentic text and a purported translation of them which is filed under s.77(6), or of the claims of an application for a European patent (UK) filed under s.78(7), and for correction of such translations.

Authentic text of European patents and applications therefor (subs.(1))

80.04   According to subs.(1), pursuant to art.70(1) of the EPC, the authentic text for proceedings before the Comptroller or the court is the text in the language of the proceedings before the EPO. This, under EPC art.14(3), is the official language (English, French or German) in which the European patent application was filed, or into which it was translated if it was filed under EPC art.14(2), or as an international application in a non-official language.

As pointed out by C. Jones (1987–88) 17 *CIPA* 130, the language of subs.(1) does not clearly take into account the possibility, provided by r.3(1) of the EPC, of continuing written proceedings in any one of the three official languages. As explained in EPO Guideline A-VIII, 1.3, the application nevertheless remains in the initial official language of the proceedings and is published in that language. Accordingly, the definition in subs.(1) of the term "the language of the proceedings" in relation to the language in which the proceedings are to be conducted before the EPO is unfortunate and inconsistent with art.70(1) of the EPC where "language of the proceedings" must mean that determined by art.14(3) of the EPC, i.e. the initial official language of the proceedings when the language of the proceedings before the EPO is changed. Also, in the event of initial filing of the European application in a non-official language, EPC art.70(2) provides that, in proceedings before the EPO, the text in the language of filing is to be taken as the basis for determining whether the subject-matter of the application or patent extends beyond the content of the application as filed, but it is not clear how this provision applies in proceedings before the Comptroller or court where the translation into English, French or German broadens the extent of the invention over the text in the initial non-official language because neither s.76 (amendments of applications and patent not to include added matter) nor the present s.80, is required by s.130(7) to be interpreted in conformity with the EPC.

The translations of the claims filed pursuant to art.14(7) of the EPC, and appearing after the specification of the European patent published under EPC art.98, are for information only and are not part of the authentic text, see §77.04. Where the authentic text is in English, the French and German translations of the claims may be deleted by amendment under s.27 (*Philips Electronic's Patent* [1987] R.P.C. 244). In *Siemens Schweiz AG v Thorn Security Ltd* [2008] R.P.C. 4; [2007] EWHC 2242 Ch, it was held that in infringement proceedings where there was a perceived difference between the meaning and effect of words used in two competing languages of the patent, it might be necessary to consider and interpret both the original and the translation as if they were independent documents. Having interpreted each, it would be necessary to consider whether the English translation gave "narrower" protection. If it did, the English text would be treated as authentic and worked from. If not, the foreign text would be treated as the authentic one. Furthermore, the claims were to be interpreted in context and purposively, the purpose to be gathered from the whole of the patent.

Narrower translation (subs.(2))

For European patents (UK) on which a translation has been filed under s.77, or applica- **80.05** tions for European patents (UK) on which a translation of the claims has been filed or supplied to an alleged infringer under s.78, the translation is regarded as the authentic text for all purposes, other than revocation proceedings, but only if the protection afforded by the translation is narrower than that afforded by the text in the language of the proceedings (subs.(2): this closely follows EPC art.70(3)). By "narrower" is meant the possibility of a product, process or article infringing the claims of the text in the language of the proceedings but not infringing the claims in the translation, see §80.06. Revocation proceedings within the meaning of subs.(2) would include proceedings under s.72 (power to revoke patents on application) or s.73 (Comptroller's power to revoke patents on his own initiative), but it is not clear that they would include proceedings in which validity is put in issue (see s.74) unless revocation is sought.

The effect of subs.(2) therefore is that, in legal proceedings in the United Kingdom, the proprietor will normally wish to rely upon the authentic, foreign language, text since he would not wish to admit that a translation provided narrower, not merely the same, protection. There will then be the need, as there is in all revocation proceedings, to produce a translation of the authentic text into English as part of the evidence, see §77.14.

Correction of translation (subs.(3))

Subsection (3), which has been included in the Act pursuant to art.70(4)(a) of the EPC **80.06** allows translations which afford narrower protection than the authentic text (see the discussion in §80.05) to be corrected by broadening to bring the translation into conformity with the text in the language of the proceedings. This amounts to a specific derogation to the provisions of s.76(2) and (3) which, it is to be noted, do not apply to s.80. However, the patent (or the provisional protection provided by the application) may not be invoked in respect of acts falling within the scope of the corrected translation, but not that of the original translation, which were committed before the corrected translation was published unless the proprietor or applicant has sent the corrected translation by post, or delivered it, to the Government department (in the case of proceedings under s.55) or the alleged infringer of the rights (in the case of proceedings under s.69) as the case may be.

In *Rhône-Poulenc Santé's Patent* [1996] R.P.C. 125, the English translation filed cited a water content of 35–50 per cent, whereas the authentic French text stated "35–80 per cent". Correction was sought under s.117, but it was held that the translation had been published (under the then r.93(4)(a)) 14 days after its submission to the UK-IPO and consequently then took effect so that, while the translation could be corrected, third party rights under subs.(3) would arise. As this would not be so with correction under s.117, to decide otherwise would result in circumvention of the specific provision of s.80(3), contrary to *E's Applications* [1983] R.P.C. 231 HL.

A request for publication of a corrected translation is made on PF 54 under r.56 (see reprint, above). The practice is discussed in §80.10. Presumably, the corrected translation will be laid open to public inspection on the date of receipt of the prescribed fee, or 14 days after receipt of the corrected translation if the fee is not paid (r.56(6)). However, unless the corrected translation is published pursuant to the filing of PF 54 and the prescribed fee paid, it is of no effect, see §80.10.

In contrast to procedure under s.117 (correction of errors in patents and applications) there is no provision for opposition to the filing and publication of a corrected translation filed under subs.(3). Also, it seems that the proprietor may file a corrected translation together with PF 54 requesting its publication as of right and the Comptroller has no power of refusal, unless he considers the corrected translation to be inaccurate whereupon he may notify the person submitting the translation of his doubts (r.115).

Intervening rights (subs.(4))

80.07   Subsection (4) follows the provisions of art.70(4)(b) of the EPC and enables any third party, who has in good faith commenced to do an act which infringes the European patent (UK) in the language of publication, but not the published translation, or has made serious preparations so to do before a corrected translation has been published under subs.(3) (discussed in §80.06), to continue doing or commence to do that act. The position is much the same as that, under s.28A(4)–(7) of a third party who has commenced to work the invention of a lapsed patent which is subsequently restored under s.28. These rights are assignable under s.28A(5), but may not be licensed. For further information, see §§28A.05–28A.06. The replacement of previous subs.(4) and the addition of new subss.(5)–(7) are designed to make the provisions of s.80 consistent with the new subss.78(6)–(6C), as explained in §78.04 above.

Older European patents (UK) and applications for them

80.08   In the case of European patents (UK) published as granted patents under EPC art.98 before September 1, 1987, or applications for European patents (UK) published under EPC art.93 before that date, the provisions of subss.(2)–(4) discussed in §§80.05–80.07 do not apply (Patents (Amendment) Rules 1987 SI 1987/288, rr.4(2) and 5(2) respectively). These two rules remain in force. Thus, any proceedings before the Comptroller in relation to a European patent granted before that date, or the application for which was published before that date in French or German, will be conducted on the basis of any translation required to be filed under r.113(4), see §77.09.

Other corrections to the translation

80.09   The provisions of subss.(2)–(4) involving the filing of a corrected translation are concerned only with the event of the original translation affording a narrower scope of protection than the authentic text. Consequently, the filing of PF 54 with a corrected translation which does not broaden the scope of protection as compared with the uncorrected translation is not appropriate. Instead, such corrections should be requested under s.117 by filing PF 11 and paying the prescribed fee. It is thought that no additional evidence to support the correction should be required. For further details, see §§117.07 and 117.12.

PRACTICE UNDER SECTION 80

Filing of corrected translation (Rule 57)

80.10   Rule 57 (see §80.02, above) requires that a corrected translation under s.80 and a PF 54 be filed in duplicate and comply with the formal requirements of Pts 1 to 3 of Sch.2 to the Rules (reprinted in §77.03). Whilst there is no requirement that the translation supplied to be that of the entirety of the specification and drawings, the MOPP states that the form should be accompanied by a corrected version, in duplicate, of the whole of the incorrect translation of the specification or claims (as appropriate). The requirements of Pts 1 to 3 of Sch.2 to the Rules are discussed in §77.16. It should be noted that following r.56(5), these requirements do not need to be complied with is the translation is delivered in electronic form or using electronic communications, see the commentary on s.124A. The Comptroller is likely to publish the corrected translation when filed, provided that the prescribed fee is paid within 14 days of filing the corrected translation. This period would appear to be extensible by discretion under r.108(2), for which see §123.25.

     If the corrected translation is accepted and the fee paid, the fact is recorded in the register and advertised in the *Patents Journal*. Copies of the corrected translation may then be obtained from the UK-IPO file in the usual way, for which see §118.10.

Use of translation of European patent (UK) in proceedings before the
     Comptroller

80.11   In the case of proceedings before the Comptroller under a European patent (UK) published before September 1, 1987 in French or German, the proceedings will be conducted on the basis of the translation then required to be provided under the then r.113(4) (see §77.14). In any proceedings there is the possibility of challenge to the accuracy of the translation in which case the Comptroller could perhaps reject any translation which in his current opinion is inaccurate and, upon failure to furnish evidence that the translation is accurate, take no further action in respect of the document, (r.115) despite his previous acceptance of it.

If leave is given to amend a European patent (UK) the authentic text of which is in French or German, a translation of the amendment into English from the French or German text is required to be furnished under r.114(3). This will then be substituted for the previous translation filed.

Use of translation of European patent (UK) in proceedings before the court

CPR 63 and the Practice Directions under it (reprinted in Appendix F), in particular **80.12** CPR 63 PD 4.2(3), require that a copy of each document referred to in the "Grounds of Invalidity" document, and where necessary a translation of the document, must be served with that document. On general principles, the party relying on the patent should put forward as part of his evidence a translation into English; if this does not become a document agreed between the parties (for which see §77.14), there will be a need to introduce it by the testimony of the translator. The accuracy of the translation into English could then be tested by cross-examination, with the opposing party putting forward its own translation in similar fashion. For an apparent example, see *Salford Electrical v BSH Industries* [1995] R.P.C. 183. For discussion on the effect of a translation filed under s.77(6) in court proceedings, see §77.14.

SECTION 81

Conversion of European patent applications

81.—(1) The comptroller may direct that on compliance with the relevant **81.01** conditions mentioned in subsection (2) below an application for a European patent (UK) shall be treated as an application for a patent under this Act **where the application is deemed to be withdrawn under the provisions of the European Patent Convention relating to the time for forwarding applications to the European Patent Office.** [*in the following cases: (a)... (b)... European Patent Office*]

(2) The relevant conditions referred to above are [*that*]—

[(a) . . .*relating to the application*];

(b) **that** [*in the case... subsection (4)(b) above*]—

    (i) the applicant requests the comptroller within the relevant prescribed period (where the application was filed with the Patent Office) to give a direction under this section, or

    (ii) the central industrial property office of a country which is party to the convention, other than the United Kingdom, with which the application was filed transmits within the relevant prescribed period a request that the application should be converted into an application under this Act, together with a copy of the application; and

(c) **that** [*in either case*] the applicant within the prescribed period pays the **application** [*filing*] fee and if the application is in a language other than English, files a translation into English of the application and of any amendments previously made in accordance with the convention.

(3) Where an application for a European patent falls to be treated as an application for a patent under this Act by virtue of a direction under this section—

    (a) the date which is the date of filing the application under the European Patent Convention shall be treated as its date of filing for the purposes of this Act, but if that date is re-dated under the convention to a later date, that later date shall be treated for those purposes as the date of filing the application;

    (b) if the application satisfies a requirement of the convention corresponding to any of the requirements of this Act or rules designated as formal requirements, it shall be treated as satisfying that formal requirement;

    (c) any document filed with the European Patent Office under any provision of the convention corresponding to any of the following provisions of this Act, that is to say, sections 2(4)(c), 5, 13(2) and 14, or any rule made for the purposes of any of those provisions, shall be treated as filed with the Patent Office under that provision or rule; and

    (d) the comptroller shall refer the application for only so much of the examination and search required by sections 17 and 18 above as he considers appropriate in view of any examination and search carried out under the convention, and those sections shall apply with any necessary modifications accordingly.

Notes

1. The RRO (art.15) amended subs.(2)(c) by replacing the words "filing fee" by "application fee"; and amended subs.(3)(d) by inserting "15A," after the words "required by sections". These amendments took effect from January 1, 2005, but the previous version of the section continues to apply to applications then "pending", a term defined in Note 1 to §15.01 above, and ss.14(1A) and 15A have no effect thereon (RRO art.22).

2. Further amendments to s.81(1) and (2) were also made by the Patents Act 2004 (c.16, Schs.1(5) and 3). These further amendments (which include the removal of the now redundant subss.(1)(a) and (2)(a)) were brought into effect when the EPC revisions agreed in 2000 came into force on December 13, 2007.

Relevant Rules—Rules 58–60

Rule 58—Procedure for making a conversion request under section 81(2)(b)(i)

81.02   **58.**—(1) A request under section 81(2)(b)(i) must be—

    (a) made in writing; and

    (b) accompanied by a copy of the notification by the European Patent Office that the application has been deemed to be withdrawn.

(2) When making such a request, a person may also request the comptroller to send—

    (a) a copy of his application for a European patent (UK); and

    (b) a copy of the request,

to the central industrial property office of any contracting state designated in the application.

(3) The period prescribed for the purposes of section 81(2)(b)(i) is three months beginning [with] immediately after the date of the notification mentioned in paragraph (1)(b).

(4) Where a request has been made under section 81(2)(b)(i), the period prescribed for the purposes of sections 13(2), 15(10)(d) and 81(2)(c) is two months beginning [with] immediately after the date on which the comptroller received that request.

(5) In paragraph (2) "contracting state" means a country which is a party to the European Patent Convention.

Note. Amended by the Patents (Amendment) Rules 2011 (SI 2011/2052).

Rule 59—Procedure for making a conversion request under section 81(2)(b)(ii)

59.—(1) The period prescribed for the purposes of section 81(2)(b)(ii) is **81.03** twenty months beginning [with] immediately after—

(a) where there is no declared priority date, the date of filing of the application; or

(b) where there is a declared priority date, that date.

(2) Where a request, transmitted under section 81(2)(b)(ii), has been received by the comptroller, he must notify the applicant accordingly.

(3) Where a request has been transmitted under section 81(2)(b)(ii), the period prescribed for the purposes of sections 13(2), 15(10)(d) and 81(2)(c) is four months beginning [with] immediately after the date of that notification.

Note. Amended by the Patents (Amendment) Rules 2011 (SI 2011/2052).

Rule 60—Request for substantive examination following a direction under section 81

60. Where an application for a European patent (UK) falls to be treated as an **81.04** application for a patent under the Act by virtue of a direction under section 81, the period prescribed for the purposes of section 18(1) is two years beginning [with] immediately after—

(a) where there is no declared priority date, the date of filing of the application; or

(b) where there is a declared priority date, that date.

Note. Amended by the Patents (Amendment) Rules 2011 (SI 2011/2052).

COMMENTARY ON SECTION 81

Scope of the section

Section 81 concerns the conversion of European patent applications into applications **81.05** under the Act and implements arts.135 and 137 of the EPC. This subject is more comprehensively discussed in the *European Patents Handbook* ("EPH") (London: Sweet & Maxwell) Ch.15, in relation to "Withdrawal, Abandonment and Conversion to National Application".

Subsection (1) permits conversion only in the circumstances of art.135(1)(a) of the EPC, that is where the European application is deemed to have been withdrawn because the application was not received by the EPO within 14 months after the earliest priority date, when priority has been claimed, or otherwise within 14 months after filing at a national patent office (EPC art.77(3)). Subsection (2) specifies the procedure to be used where conversion is still possible and is the basis for rr.58 and 59 (see reprints, above). Subsection (3) then specifies how a converted European application is to be treated under the 1977 Act.

In the United Kingdom the need for conversion is most likely to arise because the UK-IPO has placed a secrecy order under s.22 upon a European application filed with it as a national filing office in the interests of national security or otherwise, and has therefore declined to pass the application to the EPO, for an example of which see EPO Decision J 3/80 [1980] R.P.C. 381; OJ EPO 1980, 92. A need for conversion could also arise due to some accident or delay in the transmission of a European application from a national filing office to the EPO. It is understood, however, that administrative arrangements are now in place which should avoid the repetition of the delay which gave rise to this EPO Decision.

Procedure for conversion (subs.(2))

81.06   The amendments made to subss.(1) and (2) clarify the point that, where a European application is deemed to be withdrawn under the revised EPC 2000, because the application has not been forwarded to the EPO within the required time, it may be converted to a national UK application under the Act, provided that the conditions of revised subs.(2) are met. The term "filing fee" has been changed to "application fee" to accommodate the change discussed in §14.09. Where the application was not received by the EPO within the required time, the request for conversion may be filed at the national patent office at which the European patent application was filed, and that Office then sends the request and application papers to the patent offices of the other designated countries. This must be effected within 20 months of the earliest priority date (or the filing date where priority is not claimed) if the equivalence of the European patent application to national filings in the designated countries under EPC art.66 is not to be lost. Subsection (2)(b)(ii) and r.59 (see §81.03, above) enable this route to be implemented, for which see §81.08.

Alternatively, where the European patent application was filed at the UK-IPO, the applicant may proceed under subs.(2)(b)(i) and r.58 (see §81.02, above) by requesting the Comptroller to give a direction under this section. In either case, and assuming that the United Kingdom was designated, to maintain in the United Kingdom the effect of the European patent application the applicant must pay a conversion fee, provide details of inventorship, request preliminary examination and search and file any necessary translations into English. A request for substantive examination must also be timely filed. For these procedural matters, see §§81.08–81.10.

Subject to the provisions of ss.22 and 23, the receipt and forwarding of an application for a European patent under EPC art.75(1)(b) is an administrative procedure as between the UK-IPO and the EPO. The Act does not prescribe any procedures, but a request can be made to the UK-IPO to transmit copies of the application to the patent offices of the EPC Member States specified by the applicant on the form, see r.58(2). These States must have been designated in the European application. It seems that, if the applicant does not wish to pursue the application in the United Kingdom, he should simply so specify in his letter of request for transmission of papers to other national patent offices.

Treatment of converted application (subs.(3))

81.07   Subsection (3) provides that for a converted application: (a) the date of filing of the application (provided that it meets the minimum requirements prescribed under EPC art.80) is treated as the date of filing under the Act; and (b) the application is deemed to satisfy the formal requirements under the Act and Rules if it satisfies the corresponding EPC requirements. If the minimum requirements to establish a date of filing under EPC art.80 were not initially met, MOPP indicates that the application is re-dated to the date when the application is brought into compliance with these minimum requirements. The German

Federal Supreme Court has held that, under the comparable provision of German law, the filing date of the national application and any priority claimed are to be determined solely from the provisions of the EPC (*Roll and Wippbrett (Roller and seesaw board)* [Germany] OJ EPO 1982, 66).

Thus, compliance with the formal requirements for presentation of the specification and drawings is not required, provided that the specification and drawings meet the requirement of the EPC Implementing Regulations. However, any amendments made to the specification after conversion will need to be in compliance with these regulations.

Subsection (3)(c) also has the effect that any statement of prior display of the invention at an international exhibition made in connection with the European application has effect for the converted application as if filed under r.5 (for which see §2.02); and, likewise, information concerning a micro-organism deposit provided with the European application in compliance with r.31 of the EPC will satisfy the requirements of Sch.1 paras 2 and 3 to the Rules. Also, a statement of inventorship made with the European application and in compliance with EPC art.81 and EPC r.19 should satisfy the requirement of s.13(2). Thus, if this has been done for the European application, the subsequent filing of PF 7 should not be required.

Reference to s.15A has been added to subs.(3)(d) to accommodate the relocation of the topic of "preliminary examination" into new s.15A, leaving s.17 dealing only with the topic of "search", see §§15A.03 and 17.07 above.

PRACTICE UNDER SECTION 81

Procedure for conversion

—Initiation of conversion

In the circumstances of subs.(2)(b)(i), i.e. where the application was not received by the EPO in time and was first filed at the UK-IPO, the applicant must make his request for conversion within three months of notification by the EPO that his application is deemed withdrawn (r.58(3) as amended). This request must be made in writing and should be accompanied by a copy of the relevant EPO notification (r.58(1)). This three-month period is inextensible (r.108(1)). Within two months of making the conversion request the applicant must file any translations of the European application and of any priority document if any of these are not in English (r.58(4) and for which see §81.09). **81.08**

In the circumstances of subs.(2)(b)(ii), i.e. where the application was not received by the EPO in time and was first filed at a national patent office outside the United Kingdom which transmits the applicant's request for conversion and a copy of the application to the UK-IPO within 20 months of the declared priority date or filing date, the Comptroller (under r.59(2)) notifies the applicant of receipt of the request. It is to be noted that the applicant has no means of ensuring that the 20-month period prescribed under r.59(1) (as amended) is observed, since it is up to the national office at which the European application was filed to transmit the conversion request and a copy of the application to the UK-IPO. Also, this 20-month period is inextensible (r.108(1)). The applicant is, therefore, advised to lodge his request for conversion in that national office as soon as possible and not to wait until close to expiry of the three-month term prescribed by art.135(2) of the EPC.

On receipt of the Comptroller's notification under r.59(2), the applicant must then (as with a request under r.58 discussed above) file any necessary translations and priority documents, see §81.09. The time for meeting these requirements is, however, four months from the date of the Comptroller's notification (r.59(3)).

The periods of two months (under r.58 (4)) and of four months (under r.59(3)) may each be extended by two months as of right under r.108(2) and further at the discretion of the Comptroller under r.108(3). Such a request can apply to any or all of the matters to be dealt with within the periods prescribed by rr.58 or 59 as the case may be. As noted above, neither of the periods for making the conversion request under r.58(3), or for a conversion request made to another national patent office to be transmitted to the UK-IPO under r.59(1) is extensible, because these periods are pursuant to art.135(2) of the EPC. It would appear doubtful whether failure to meet either of these periods could form the subject of an application for *restitutio in integrum* under EPC art.122. However, even if such application were to succeed, the Comptroller apparently has no power under rr.107 or 108 to implement it in the United Kingdom, and discretionary extension under r.108(3) is also not possible.

The term "declared priority date" in rr.81 and 82 is defined in r.3 (reprinted at §5.06A).

An address for service within the United Kingdom should preferably be supplied, see r.103 (reprinted at §32.02and discussed in §32.15).

—Requirements for priority documents and translations for converted application

81.09   If the European application to be converted is not in the English language, r.113 (reprinted at §123.30) requires that a translation may be required to be filed. In the case of a converted application under s.81(2)(b)(i) this must be done within the two-month period stipulated, for which see §81.08. If this translation is not filed, r.113(1) makes it clear that the application will not be further processed unless the Comptroller otherwise directs (r.113(4)). There is an exemption to the requirement to provide a translation into English for specifications transmitted from foreign industrial property office under s.81(2)(b)(ii) (r.113(2)(e)).

If priority is claimed, a copy of the priority application (translated into English) will also be required (r.9(4)).

Request for substantive examination on converted application

81.10   Under r.60 (as amended) the request for substantive examination must be made within two years from the declared priority date, if any, or otherwise within two years from the date of filing the application for the European patent (UK). This two-year period is extensible by two months under r.108(2) without fee and further at the Comptroller's absolute discretion.

During the last six months of this period, it is prudent to mark correspondence to the examiner prominently with the word "URGENT" as the filing number of the application will not itself alert the examiner to the imminence of expiry of the period, see §20.08.

Result of conversion

81.11   A United Kingdom filing number is allocated to the converted application and the usual particulars of filing are then published in the *Patents Journal*. In due course, the UK-IPO will make an entry in the register under s.32 and will also publish the application or translation in English. The United Kingdom file is not laid open to inspection until such publication by the UK-IPO (i.e. publication as an "A-specification" under s.16) has taken place (EPC r.156).

SECTION 82

Jurisdiction to determine questions as to right to a patent

82.01   **82.**—(1) The court shall not have jurisdiction to determine a question to which this section applies except in accordance with the following provisions of this section.

(2) Section 12 above shall not confer jurisdiction on the comptroller to determine a question to which this section applies except in accordance with the following provisions of this section.

(3) This section applies to a question arising before the grant of a European patent whether a person has a right to be granted a European patent, or a share in any such patent, and in this section "employer-employee question" means any such question between an employer and an employee, or their successors in title, arising out of an application for a European patent for an invention made by the employee.

(4) The court and the comptroller shall have jurisdiction to determine any question to which this section applies, other than an employer-employee question, if either of the following conditions is satisfied, that is to say—

    (a) the applicant has his residence or principal place of business in the United Kingdom; or

    (b) the other party claims that the patent should be granted to him and he has his residence or principal place of business in the United Kingdom and the applicant does not have his residence or principal place of business in any of the relevant contracting states;

and also if in either of those cases there is no written evidence that the parties have agreed to submit to the jurisdiction of the competent authority of a relevant contracting state other than the United Kingdom.

(5) The court and the comptroller shall have jurisdiction to determine an employer–employee question if either of the following conditions is satisfied, that is to say—

    (a) the employee is mainly employed in the United Kingdom; or

    (b) the employee is not mainly employed anywhere or his place of main employment cannot be determined, but the employer has a place of business in the United Kingdom to which the employee is attached (whether or not he is also attached elsewhere);

and also if in either of those cases there is no written evidence that the parties have agreed to submit to the jurisdiction of the competent authority of a relevant contracting state other than the United Kingdom or, where there is such evidence of such an agreement, if the **law applicable to** [*proper law of*] the contract of employment does not recognise the validity of the agreement.

(6) Without prejudice to subsections (2) to (5) above, the court and the comptroller shall have jurisdiction to determine any question to which this section applies if there is written evidence that the parties have agreed to submit to the jurisdiction of the court or the comptroller, as the case may be, and, in the case of an employer–employee question, the **law applicable to** [*proper law of*] the contract of employment recognises the validity of the agreement.

(7) If, after proceedings to determine a question to which this section applies have been brought before the competent authority of a relevant contracting state other than the United Kingdom, proceedings are begun before the court or a reference is made to the comptroller under section 12 above to determine that question, the court or the comptroller, as the case may be, shall stay or sist the proceedings before the court or the comptroller unless or until the competent authority of that other state either—

    (a) determines to decline jurisdiction and no appeal lies from the determination or the time for appealing expires, or

(b) makes a determination which the court or the comptroller refuses to recognize under section 83 below.

(8) References in this section to the determination of a question include respectively references to—

(a) the making of a declaration or the grant of a declarator with respect to that question (in the case of the court); and

(b) the making of an order under section 12 above in relation to that question (in the case of the court or the comptroller).

(9) In this section and section 83 below "relevant contracting state" means a country which is a party to the European Patent Convention and has not exercised its right under the convention to exclude the application of the protocol to the convention known as the Protocol on Recognition.

Notes

1. Section 130(7) requires s.82 to be construed in conformity with the EPC, CPC and PCT. The relevant provisions are in s.1 (arts 1–8) of the Protocol on Recognition attached to the EPC which is reprinted below. Article 60 of the EPC (reprinted at §7.02) is also relevant.

2. Subsections 82(5) and (6) were amended by the Contracts (Applicable Law) Act 1990 (c.36) Sch.4(3).

RELEVANT CONVENTION PROVISIONS

82.02   The EPC Protocol on Recognition: Section I—Jurisdiction

Article 1

1.—(1) The courts of the Contracting States shall, in accordance with articles 2 to 6, have jurisdiction to decide claims, against the applicant, to the right to the grant of a European patent in respect of one or more of the Contracting States designated in the European patent application.

(2) For the purposes of this Protocol, the term 'courts' shall include authorities which, under the national law of a Contracting State, have jurisdiction to decide the claims referred to in paragraph 1. Any Contracting State shall notify the European Patent Office of the identity of any authority on which such a jurisdiction is conferred, and the European Patent Office shall inform the other Contracting States accordingly.

(3) For the purposes of this Protocol, the term 'Contracting State' refers to a Contracting State which has not excluded application of this Protocol pursuant to article 167 of the Convention.

Article 2

2. Subject to articles 4 and 5, if an applicant for a European patent has his residence or principal place of business within one of the Contracting States, proceedings shall be brought against him in the courts of that Contracting State.

Article 3

3. Subject to articles 4 and 5, if an applicant for a European patent has his residence or principal place of business outside the Contracting States, and if the party claiming the right to the grant of the European patent has his residence or principal place of business within one of the Contracting States, the courts of the latter State shall have exclusive jurisdiction.

Article 4

4. Subject to article 5, if the subject matter of a European patent application is the invention of an employee, the courts of the Contracting State, if any, whose law determines the right to the European patent pursuant to article 60, paragraph 1, second sentence, of the Convention, shall have exclusive jurisdiction over proceedings between the employee and the employer.

Article 5

5.—(1) If the parties to a dispute concerning the right to the grant of a European patent have concluded an agreement, either in writing or verbally with written confirmation, to the effect that a court or the courts of a particular Contracting State shall decide on such a dispute, the court or courts of that State shall have exclusive jurisdiction.

(2) However, if the parties are an employee and his employer, paragraph 1 shall only apply in so far as the national law governing the contract of employment allows the agreement in question.

Article 6

6. In cases where neither articles 2 to 4 nor article 5, paragraph 1, apply, the courts of the Federal Republic of Germany shall have exclusive jurisdiction.

Article 7

7. The courts of Contracting States before which claims referred to in article 1 are brought shall of their own motion decide whether or not they have jurisdiction pursuant to articles 2 to 6.

Article 8

8.—(1) In the event of proceedings based on the same claim and between the same parties being brought before courts of different Contracting States, the court to which a later application is made shall of its own motion decline jurisdiction in favour of the court to which an earlier application was made.

(2) In the event of the jurisdiction of the court to which an earlier application is made being challenged, the court to which a later application is made shall stay the proceedings until the other court takes a final decision.

COMMENTARY ON SECTION 82

The EPC Protocol on Recognition

The EPC Protocol on Recognition (which is reproduced in §82.02 above and the full **82.03** name of which is Protocol on Jurisdiction and the Recognition of Decisions in respect of the Right to the Grant of a European Patent) provides, as between the relevant countries, that the judicial authorities of one of the countries shall have exclusive jurisdiction over questions of entitlement to a European patent arising before grant and that the final decision given in that country shall be recognised in all the others. Section 82(9) defines "relevant countries" as those EPC countries bound by the Protocol. It used to be possible for Member States to opt out of the Protocol by reserving their rights under art.167(2)(d) of the EPC. However, that article has now been deleted from the EPC and so it currently appears to be the case that all present EPC countries are bound. This Protocol was discussed by G. Le Tallec (1985) 16 I.I.C. 318 and 356. A more detailed treatment on the subject of jurisdiction is given in Ch.14 of *Intellectual Property in Europe* by Guy Tritton, 3rd edn (London: Sweet & Maxwell, 2007).

Scope of the section

82.04   Section I (Jurisdiction, arts 1–8) of the Protocol cited in §82.02 gives rise to s.82 which serves to determine, by reference to this Protocol, whether there is jurisdiction within the United Kingdom to determine a question of entitlement to a European patent application, and thus e.g. whether an application to the Comptroller under s.12(1), or an application to the court under s.12(2), may lawfully proceed. Accordingly, in any such application involving an application for a European patent, it must first be considered whether the Comptroller or court, as the case may be, has jurisdiction under the terms of s.82: see, for example, preliminary decisions by the Comptroller in *Travenol Laboratories' Application* BL O/45/90, noted I.P.D. 13141 and *Oxford Instruments' Application* BL O/68/93.

It should be noted that the jurisdiction under s.82 is different from that under ss.8, 12 and 37, in that both the court and the Comptroller have concurrent jurisdiction to hear the entitlement dispute. This was commented on in *Luxim v Ceravision* [2007] R.P.C. 33; [2007] EWHC 1624, but without stating whether s.82(8)(b) conferred the Comptroller's order-making powers on the court without a referral. This was contrasted with the jurisdiction to deal with entitlement matters under ss.8, 12 and 37. Although the court will have its inherent jurisdiction to grant declaratory relief, entitlement disputes brought under ss.8, 12 and 37 have to begin in the UK-IPO and the statutory powers of the Comptroller to grant wide ranging relief are only conferred upon the court when the Comptroller declines jurisdiction under ss.8(7), 12(2) and 37(8). See §37.08.

Section 82 is required by s.130(7) to be interpreted not only in accordance with this Protocol, but also to provide as nearly as possible the same effects as corresponding provisions of the EPC, CPC and PCT. The relevant provisions of these conventions appear to be art.60(1) of the EPC and arts 67(b) and 69 of the CPC. These read:

"EPC Article 60—Right to a European patent

1. The right to a European patent shall belong to the inventor or his successor in title. If the inventor is an employee the right to the European patent shall be determined in accordance with the law of the State in which the employee is mainly employed: if the State in which the employee is mainly employed cannot be determined, the law to be applied shall be that of the State in which the employer has his place of business to which the employee is attached."

"CPC Article 67—Jurisdiction of national courts concerning actions relating to Community patents

The following courts shall have exclusive jurisdiction:
(b) in actions relating to the right to a patent in which an employer and an employee are in dispute, the courts of the Contracting State under whose law the right to a European patent is determined in accordance with Article 60(1), second sentence, of the European Patent Convention. Any agreement conferring jurisdiction shall be valid only insofar as the national law governing the contract of employment allows the agreement in question".

"CPC Article 69—Supplementary provisions on recognition and enforcement

1. Article 27(3) and (4) of the Convention on Jurisdiction and Enforcement ["the Brussels Convention"] shall not apply to decisions relating to the right to a Community patent.
2. In the case of irreconcilable decisions relating to the right to a Community patent given in proceedings between the same parties, only the decision of the court first seised of the matter shall be recognized. Neither party may invoke any other decision even in the Contracting State in which it was given."

By subs.(3), s.82 applies only: (a) to "a question arising before the grant of a European patent"; and (b) "whether a person has a right to be granted a European patent, or a share in any such patent". Such a question can be one which involves the grant of a declaration or the making of an order under s.12 (subs.(8)). It is uncertain whether the term "share in the patent" in subs.(3) is broad enough to embrace the question of an application to be named as an inventor in the patent, despite the fact that questions of possible employee-inventor compensation could arise at some future date. However, this term definitely includes a beneficial (equitable) interest under a trust, as distinct from a legal one, as was decided in *Kakkar v Szelke* [1989] F.S.R. 225; [1989] E.P.O.R. 184 CA where it was held the section should be applied to all questions the substance of which is "who is the true owner [or co-owner] of the invention?"

Section 82(3) defines "an employer-employee question" as meaning:

"any such question between an employer and an employee, or their successors in title, arising out of an application for a European patent for an invention made by the employee",

the word "such" referring back to a right to be granted to the whole or a share of a European patent. By subs.(5), but subject to subs.(6) (see §82.05), the powers of the court or Comptroller to determine an "employer–employee question" are restricted to cases where the employee is mainly employed in the United Kingdom or (in the case of a peripatetic or seconded-out employee) the employer has a place of business in the United Kingdom or the parties have agreed, unless the parties have validly agreed otherwise.

The reciprocal situation, i.e. the effect in the United Kingdom of decisions on patent entitlement disputes made in other EPC Member States, is dealt with in s.83.

Jurisdiction under section 82 when there is an agreement between the parties

If there is written evidence that the parties in dispute have agreed that the United **82.05** Kingdom court or the Comptroller shall decide the question, then the court or the Comptroller has jurisdiction (subs.(6)). If the question is an employer–employee question (which is defined in subs.(3)), this is subject to the parties' agreement, or at least the relevant clause, being valid under the law applicable to the contract of employment (subs.(5)). Conversely, there is no jurisdiction in the United Kingdom to decide a question of entitlement if there is written evidence of a valid agreement between the parties to have it decided in another relevant country.

It has, however, been decided by the ECJ (*Duijnstee v Göderbauer (288/82)* [1983] E.C.R. 3663; [1985] 1 C.M.L.R. 220; [1985] F.S.R. 221) that questions of entitlement, to national patents at least, are to be dealt with under national law and within the European Community by that court which has jurisdiction under the Brussels Regulation, (formerly Convention) 44/2001 of 22 December 2000, which in the United Kingdom is made law by the Civil Jurisdiction and Judgments Act 1982 (c.27) (as amended from time to time by Statutory Instrument), that is, usually by the court within whose jurisdiction the defendant is domiciled in the sense of being habitually resident there. This case also decided that art.16(4) of that Convention, now art.22(4) of the Regulation, (reproduced as Sch.1, art.16(4) of that Act), which deals with exclusive jurisdiction in proceedings concerned with the registration and validity of patents, has no applicability to issues of entitlement to the grant of a patent.

Regulation (EC) 44/2001 replaced the Brussels Convention for all EU Member States other than Denmark. Relations with Denmark are still governed by the Brussels Convention and the Lugano Convention applies to the remaining EFTA States.

Jurisdiction under section 82 when there is no prior agreement between the parties

In the absence of any agreement between the parties, the general position under s.82 is **82.06** that jurisdiction lies in the United Kingdom for an employer-employee question only if the employee is mainly employed in the United Kingdom (subs.(5)(a)); and, for other questions, only if the applicant for the European patent has his residence or principal place of business in the United Kingdom (subs.(4)(a)). Thus, in *Kakkar v Szelke* [1989] F.S.R. 225; [1989] E.P.O.R. 184 CA, where the European patent application had been assigned to a Swedish company, it was conceded that subs.(3) (presumably when read with subs.(4)) precludes an entitlement dispute (being one which did not involve an employer-employee dispute, for which see below), from being determined by the Patents Court, though it was questioned whether the concession was appropriate because the applicability of s.82 had arisen by a post-application assignment, the spectre of oscillatory assignments being envisaged. It was then held, by a majority of the Court of Appeal, that equitable, as well as legal, instruments fall under subs.(3) so that s.82 precluded the English courts from considering the case further, a claim based on seeking a declaration of a constructive trust of holding a patent application being held to be essentially tantamount to a claim to entitlement to a share in the patent.

In contrast to *Kakkar v Szelke*, the UK-IPO did have jurisdiction over a Californian-based company where the applicant was resident in the UK: see *Actineon's Applications*, BL O/309/05, noted [2005] *CIPA* 799. There was both an EPC and a PCT application and so s.82 was considered as well as s.12.

In an employer-employee question, jurisdiction also lies in the United Kingdom if the employee has no main place of employment or such place cannot be determined, provided that the employer has a place of business in the United Kingdom to which the employee is attached (subs.(5)(b)).

In the case of questions of other types, jurisdiction lies in the United Kingdom if the applicant does not reside or have his main place of business in any of the relevant countries, provided that the party claiming to be entitled to the patent has his residence or main place of business in the United Kingdom (subs.(4)(b)). If neither party resides or has a main place of business in a relevant country, jurisdiction lies in the German Federal Republic (EPC Protocol on Recognition art.6, see §82.02).

Although the Comptroller or the court is required to be satisfied (even in an uncontested case concerning a European application) that there is jurisdiction under s.82 (as explained in §82.04), if so satisfied, it is not necessary to decide which of these subsections applies (*Travenol Laboratories' Application* BL O/45/90, noted I.P.D. 13141).

Stay of proceedings (subs. (7))

82.07   If entitlement proceedings are first brought in another relevant country and afterwards in the United Kingdom, subs.(7) requires a stay ("sist" in Scotland) of the United Kingdom proceedings unless or until jurisdiction is declined in the other country or a decision is given for which recognition is refused under s.83, for which see §83.05. However, subs.(7) does not apply when the United Kingdom proceedings were commenced first, nor when the court or the Comptroller is asked to decide a different question from that in another EPC Member State because subs.(7) is limited to proceedings brought "to determine that question", i.e. the question brought before the competent authority of a relevant contracting state.

If proceedings are commenced and it is later held that jurisdiction does not exist (by virtue of subs.(3)) to determine any question in issue, then the proceedings are struck out, rather than merely stayed, see *Kakkar v Szelke* [1989] F.S.R. 225; [1989] E.P.O.R. 184 CA.

PRACTICE UNDER SECTION 82

82.08   Rule 61 (reprinted at §83.03) requires that, where s.82 applies, any person seeking recognition of a relevant decision, etc. from another EPC country under the terms of s.83 must file a certified copy of that decision, see further §83.06.

SECTION 83

Effect of patent decisions of competent authorities of other states

83.—(1) A determination of a question to which section 82 above applies by   **83.01**
the competent authority of a relevant contracting state other than the United
Kingdom shall, if no appeal lies from the determination or the time for appealing
has expired, be recognised in the United Kingdom as if it had been made by the
court or the comptroller unless the court or he refuses to recognise it under subsection (2) below.

(2) The court or the comptroller may refuse to recognise any such determination that the applicant for a European patent had no right to be granted the patent,
or any share in it, if either—

(a) the applicant did not contest the proceedings in question because he was
   not notified of them at all or in the proper manner or was not notified of
   them in time for him to contest the proceedings; or

(b) the determination in the proceedings in question conflicts with the determination of the competent authority of any relevant contracting state in
   proceedings instituted earlier between the same parties as in the proceedings in question.

Note. Section 130(7) requires s.83 to be construed in conformity with the EPC, CPC
and PCT. The relevant provisions are contained in s.II (arts 9–11) of the Protocol on Recognition attached to the EPC which is reprinted below.

RELEVANT CONVENTION PROVISIONS

Section II—Recognition

Article 9

9—(1) Subject to the provisions of article 11, paragraph 2, final decisions   **83.02**
given in any Contracting State on the right to the grant of a European patent in respect of one or more of the Contracting States designated in the European patent
application shall be recognized without requiring a special procedure in the other
Contracting States.

(2) The jurisdiction of the court whose decision is to be recognized and the
validity of such decision may not be reviewed.

Article 10

10 Article 9, paragraph 1, shall not be applicable where:

(a) an applicant for a European patent who has not contested a claim proves
   that the document initiating the proceedings was not notified to him
   regularly and sufficiently early for him to defend himself; or

(b) an applicant proves that the decision is incompatible with another decision given in a Contracting State in proceedings between the same parties which were started before those in which the decision to be
   recognized was given.

Article 11

11—(1) In relations between any Contracting States the provisions of this

Protocol shall prevail over any conflicting provisions of other agreements on jurisdiction or the recognition of judgments.

(2) This Protocol shall not affect the implementation of any agreement between a Contracting State and a State which is not bound by the Protocol.

RELEVANT RULE—RULE 61

Rule 61—Recognition of patent decision of competent authorities of other states

83.03

61.—(1) Where in proceedings before the comptroller a person seeks recognition of a relevant determination, he must furnish to the comptroller a copy of the determination duly certified by the relevant official of the competent authority.

(2) In paragraph (1) "relevant determination" means the determination of a question to which section 82 applies by the competent authority of a relevant contracting state other than the United Kingdom.

COMMENTARY ON SECTION 83

Scope of the section

83.04

Under s.83, a question of entitlement to the grant of a pending application for a European patent, if determined by the competent authority of another EPC country bound by the Protocol (see §82.03 above for discussion of the term "relevant country"), is recognised as if it had been made in the United Kingdom, provided that that decision is final in the sense that no appeal lies from it or the time for appealing has expired (subs.(1)), unless the applicant for the European patent did not contest the proceedings because either he was not timely notified of the foreign entitlement proceedings (subs.(2)(a)), or because the foreign decision is in conflict with the determination of the question in earlier proceedings between the same parties in a relevant country (subs.(2)(b)). However, there is no provision for the court or Comptroller to consider whether the authority in another relevant country should have declined jurisdiction but refused to do so.

Section 130(7) provides that the section is to be interpreted in conformity with any relevant provisions of the EPC, or of the CPC or PCT. The provisions of these conventions, which are reprinted in §82.04, would appear to be relevant to the interpretation of s.83, as well as to the interpretation of s.82. In addition, s.83 gives effect to s.II (Recognition) (arts 9–11) of the EPC Protocol on Recognition (reprinted at §83.02 above).

Possible non-recognition of a foreign judgment on entitlement (subs.(2))

83.05

The considerations which may be applied under subs.(2)(a) to deny recognition to a foreign judgment on entitlement to any right arising from an application for a European patent are set out in subs.(2) and are quite limited in scope. Indeed, this scope appears to be more limited than even those which apply under arts 27 and 28 of the Brussels Convention on the mutual recognition of civil judgments within the European Community or under the parallel provisions, arts 34 and 35, of the Council Regulation (EC) 44/2001 of December 22, 2000 on jurisdiction and the recognition and enforcement of judgments in civil and commercial matters ("Jurisdiction Regulation"), which has replaced the Brussels Convention for all EU Member States other than Denmark. Relations with Denmark are still governed by the Brussels Convention and the Lugano Convention applies to the remaining EFTA states.

Between s.83, the EPC Protocol on Recognition (see §83.02, above), the Civil Jurisdiction and Judgments Act 1982 (c.27) (which enacted the Brussels Convention into the law of the United Kingdom) and the Brussels Regulation, (which is implemented under the European Communities Act 1972), an issue may arise over which law takes precedence.

Speculation in relation to this is beyond the scope of this Work and may, in any event, be academic, as neither the Brussels Convention, nor the Brussels Regulation is specifically framed to deal with arguments over ownership of patents and so these could be treated as a special jurisdiction under art.5/art.71. For any further information, see Ch.14 of *Intellectual Property in Europe* by Guy Tritton, 3rd edn (London: Sweet & Maxwell, 2007).

In *Duijnstee v Göderbauer* (C–288/82) [1983] E.C.R. 3633; [1985] 1 C.M.L.R. 220; [1985] F.S.R. 231, the ECJ decided that, in matters relating to patent entitlement, a defendant should be sued only in his place of domicile (in the sense of the place where he is habitually resident), even though only the courts of States within, or for, which patents are actually registered have jurisdiction over the validity of such patents, see the Civil Jurisdiction and Judgments Act 1982 (c.27) Sch.1 art.16(4), reproducing that article of the Brussels Convention. This decision would therefore seem to play a part in the question whether a foreign judgment on entitlement should be recognised under s.83, notwithstanding that for most EU Member States, the Brussels Convention has been replaced by the Jurisdiction Regulation. Note, however, that ss.82 and 83 only concern applications for European patents. This is because once a European patent application is granted it becomes a bundle of equivalent national patents and, so for a European patent (UK), the employer-employee question, as defined in s.82(3), falls to be determined under s.37 or s.72(1)(b), as the case may be.

PRACTICE UNDER SECTION 83

To obtain recognition in the United Kingdom during proceedings under s.82 of a judgment of a competent authority within another EPC Member State with regard to entitlement to the grant of a European patent, a copy of the foreign judgment certified by that Authority must be obtained and produced to the court or Comptroller as the case may be (r.61, reprinted at §83.03 above, applies in relation to proceedings before the Comptroller). If the judgment is not in English, a translation will be required under r.113 (reprinted at §123.30 and discussed in §123.81) in proceedings before the Comptroller. Although it is no longer necessary to verify all translations filed with the UK-IPO, if the Comptroller has reasons to doubt the accuracy of the translation, then under r.115 (reprinted at §123.32 and discussed in §123.82), he may call for further proof and that may involve the filing of verification that the translation is accurate. Failure to file the verification may result in the Comptroller taking no further action in relation to that document. In proceedings before the court, a translation should be agreed between the parties, if possible, but otherwise will need to be the subject of formal evidence.

83.06

SECTION 84 [REPEALED]

Patent agents and other representatives

84. [...]

84.01

Note. Section 84 is not reprinted as it was repealed by Sch.8 to the CDPA 1988, with effect from August 13, 1990 (SI 1990/1440) and with no continuing effect. Its provisions are now to be found mainly in s.277 of the CDPA 1988 (reprinted at §277.01), but see also s.102(4) (reprinted in §102.01); and s.274(2) and s.276(7) of the CDPA 1988 (reprinted respectively in §§274.01 and 276.01), as read in conjunction with CDPA 1988 s.286 (reprinted at §286.01). The new provisions are discussed in the commentary on CDPA 1988 s.277,with the "European list" being discussed in §286.03.

SECTION 85 [REPEALED]

European patent attorneys

85. [...]

85.01

Note. Section 85 is not reprinted as it was repealed by Sch.8 to the CDPA 1988, with effect from August 13, 1990 (SI 1990/1440) and with no continuing effect. Its provisions have been re-enacted in: (i) s.102(4) (reprinted in §102.01); and (ii) s.277 and s.278(2) of the CDPA 1988 (reprinted respectively at and in §§277.01 and 278.01), each read in conjunction with CDPA 1988 s.286 (reprinted at §286.01). The new provisions are discussed in the commentary on CDPA 1988 s.277.

SECTION 86 [REPEALED]

Community patents [Sections 86–88]

Implementation of Community Patent Convention

86.01 **86. [...]**

Notes

1. This section, which had never been brought into force, was repealed by the Patents Act 2004 (c.16) Schs 1(6) and 3, with effect from January 1, 2005 (SI 2004/3205 art.2(g)(i)) as part of the removal from the Act of all references to the CPC which never came into force. The repealed section is therefore only of historical interest and is not here reprinted.

2. The Community Patent Convention ("the CPC") was formulated at a diplomatic conference in Luxembourg in 1975, but was revised in 1985 and 1989 when an "Agreement relating to Community Patents" was concluded to which was annexed a revised form of the 1975 Convention in which many of the original articles, though themselves unchanged, became re-numbered. A "Protocol on Settlement of Litigation concerning the Infringement and Validity of Community Patents" (the "Litigation Protocol") was also agreed. These documents were published: [1989] OJ EC L401, and Cm 1452. The object of the CPC was to establish a "Community Patent" to be granted as a European patent and to have uniform, and indivisible, effect throughout the Member States of the CPC. The setting-up of a Common Appeal Court ("COPAC"), envisaged by the 1989 revision was intended to bring about a uniform approach among the European Community States to questions of interpretation of the CPC, and therefore of patents granted under it.

3. Despite this activity, the revised Convention and this Protocol were not ratified by a sufficient number of signatory states to bring either of them into force and, as political agreement on their acceptability to Member States of the European Community was not forthcoming, the project appears to have been abandoned, as evidenced by the repeal of ss.86–88.

4. Because of this impasse on the implementation of the CPC, in July 1997 the European Commission published a Green Paper (COM (97) 314 Final) as a consultative document to ascertain current opinion on the introduction of a unitary Community patent, either by implementation of the Community Patent Convention or by a European Union Regulation. This Green Paper acknowledged that the cost of translations was a major problem in introducing an indivisible Community patent, but it indicated that such was needed in order to comply with the "single market" philosophy of the European Union, although the continuing existence of the EPC and of national patent systems was recognised. The Chartered Institute responded in full to this Green Paper, see [1997] *CIPA* 816.

5. The EC Commission then held a hearing on the proposals in the Green Paper and concluded this with a list of preliminary conclusions, see [1997] *CIPA* 916. These preliminary conclusions were followed by an Opinion from the EU Economic and Social Committee (reprinted OJ EPO 1998, 328) recommending the adoption of a Regulation for a Community patent system to co-exist with the national and European patent systems, and with the problem of translation met by the EPO preparing a technical summary to be published in English, French and German

when the application is published, with subsequent translation into all the national languages arranged and published by the Commission and with the proprietor only having to provide on grant translations of the claims into the EU national languages, although a full translation would be required before litigation could be instituted. This Opinion also recommended that, in litigation, a national court should only be able to declare invalidity with effect against the litigating party, with revocation for all reserved either to an EPO Revocation Division, or to a new court to be set up, with appeal to a specialised chamber of the European Court of First Instance.

6. However, unless a cheap and acceptable solution to the problem of translations is found, a Community-wide single, and indivisible, patent may not be attractive to users, particularly as Community-wide protection will often be unnecessary to provide adequate protection and, where this is so, protection will usually also be required in Switzerland. This, therefore, suggests that the route to a Community patent, if established, is likely to be via an application for a European patent with designation of all EPC contracting states, followed by conversion when grant is imminent to a Community patent for EU countries. But, it seems likely that such conversion would only be undertaken if there were an adequate incentive, so that any insistence on translation into a national language for each EU Member State would be financially unattractive unless there were a genuine need for patent protection throughout the EU or a real fear that failure to obtain uniform protection throughout the EU would lead to an "exhaustion of rights" situation under which patented articles initially put on the market in part of the EU, where the opportunity for patent protection was not taken, could be held entitled to free circulation throughout the EU irrespective of the patent protection granted for other EU Member States.

SECTION 87

Decisions on Community Patent Convention

87. [...]   **87.01**

Notes

1. Like s.86, s.87 was never been brought into force and was repealed in the same way and for the same reason as with s.86, see §86.01 above. The repealed section is therefore only of historical interest and is not reprinted here.

2. The object of the section was to ensure that all questions of interpretation and effect of the provisions of, or under, the CPC would be treated as matters of law in accordance with decisions made by other courts. The revised form of the CPC was agreed in 1989. It included a Protocol on Litigation and envisaged a Common Patents Appeal Court (COPAC) to be set up on a Community basis. C. Wadlow comprehensively described these proposals: [1986] E.L.R. 295. It is also worth noting that, in drafting s.87, it was the Government's intention that not all EPO decisions should be binding and that, e.g. practice directions issued by the Comptroller in relation to the CPC, should not be subject to s.87, see H.L. Deb., 380, ser. 42, cols. 1568–1569 (March 15, 1977) and Vol.83, ser. 62, col. 77 (May 9, 1977).

SECTION 88 [REPEALED]

Jurisdiction in legal proceedings in connection with Community Patent Convention

88. [...]   **88.01**

Notes

1. The section was never brought into force and was repealed by the CDPA 1988 (Sch.5 para.23 and Sch.8), effective from January 7, 1991 (SI 1990/2168).

2. The section related to jurisdiction in legal proceedings in connection with the CPC but became redundant when effect was given to the 1968 Brussels "Convention on Jurisdiction and Enforcement of Judgments in Civil and Commercial Matters" and subsequently by the substantially corresponding Regulation (EC) 44/2001, as discussed in §61.04 above and Ch.30 of the *European Patents Handbook* ("EPH") (London, Sweet & Maxwell).

International applications for patents [Sections 89–89B]

SECTION 89 [SUBSTITUTED]

Effect of international application for patent

89.01   **89.—(1) An international application for a patent (UK) for which a date of filing has been accorded under the Patent Co-operation Treaty shall, subject to—**

> **section 89A (international and national phases of application), and**
> **section 89B (adaptation of provisions in relation to international application),**

be treated for the purposes of Parts I and III of this Act as an application for a patent under this Act.

(2) If the application, or the designation of the United Kingdom in it, is withdrawn or (except as mentioned in subsection (3)) deemed to be withdrawn under the Treaty, it shall be treated as withdrawn under this Act.

(3) An application shall not be treated as withdrawn under this Act if it, or the designation of the United Kingdom in it, is deemed to be withdrawn under the Treaty—

> **(a) because of an error or omission in an institution having functions under the Treaty, or**
>
> **(b) because, owing to circumstances outside the applicant's control, a copy of the application was not received by the International Bureau before the end of the time limited for that purpose under the Treaty,**

or in such other circumstances as may be prescribed.

(4) *[repealed]*

(5) If an international application for a patent which designates the United Kingdom is refused a filing date under the Treaty and the comptroller determines that the refusal was caused by an error or omission in an institution having functions under the Treaty, he may direct that the application shall be treated as an application under this Act, having such date of filing as he may direct.

Notes

1. The wording of the original section was completely substituted by the CDPA 1988 (c.48) Sch.5(25), when new ss.89A and 89B were added. The original section now has only historic significance.

2. Subsection (4) of the substituted section was repealed by the Patents Act 2004 (c.16) Sch.1(7) and 3 with effect from January 1, 2005 (SI 2004/3205, art.2(g)(i)).

This was because new s.130(4A) (reprinted in §130.01 and discussed in §130.07) made its provisions redundant.

RELEVANT RULES—RULES 64, 65, 71 AND 72

Rules 64, 65, 71 and 72—International applications for patents: sections 89 and 89A

89.02

Rule 64—Interpretation relating to international applications

64.—(1) In this Part the following have the same meaning as they have in the   **89.03**
Patent Co-operation Treaty—
    "competent receiving Office";
    "International Preliminary Examination Report";
    "International Preliminary Report on Patentability";
    "International Search Report";
    "International Searching Authority";
    "receiving Office".

Rule 65—Filing of international applications at the Patent Office

65.—(1) An international application for a patent filed at the Patent Office as a   **89.04**
competent receiving Office under the Patent Co-operation Treaty must be filed—
    (a) in English or Welsh; and
    (b) in triplicate.
(2) Where fewer than three copies of the application are filed, the comptroller may direct the applicant to pay any copying costs.
(3) Where the Patent Office was acting on behalf of the International Bureau as the receiving Office, the comptroller shall only transmit an international application for a patent filed at the Patent Office to the International Bureau and the International Searching Authority after the appropriate fee has been paid.
(4) A request under the Treaty for a certified copy of an international application for a patent (including any corrections to that application) filed at the Patent Office as the competent receiving Office must be filed on Patents Form 23.

Rule 71—Directions under section 89(3) and (5)

71.—(1) The applicant may, before the end of the relevant period, make a writ-   **89.05**
ten request to the comptroller to give a direction under section 89(5).
(2) The applicant may notify the comptroller that the circumstances mentioned in section 89(3) or rule 72 apply to his application.
(3) The request under paragraph (1) must be accompanied by—
    (a) a statement of the reasons for the request; and
    (b) the fee prescribed for the purposes of section 89A(3).
(4) The relevant period is two months beginning [with] immediately after the date on which—

(a) the International Bureau; or

(b) the receiving Office,

notifies the applicant that his international application for a patent (UK) is refused a filing date under the Patent Co-operation Treaty.

(5) Where the applicant has made a request to the comptroller under paragraph (1), the comptroller may direct the applicant to furnish him with any document, information or evidence within such period as the comptroller may specify.

(6) Where the applicant fails, before the end of the period specified, to comply with a direction given under paragraph (5), the comptroller may treat him as having withdrawn his request.

(7) Where section 89(3) applies or a direction has been given under section 89(5) the comptroller may—

(a) alter any period of time (whether it has already expired or not) specified in the Act or listed in Parts 1 to 3 of Schedule 4; and

(b) amend any document kept at the Patent Office in relation to the application,

subject to such conditions as the comptroller may direct.

Note. Amended by the Patents (Amendment) Rules 2011 (SI 2011/2052).

Rule 72—Circumstance prescribed for the purposes of section 89(3)

89.06   72. The other circumstance prescribed for the purposes of section 89(3) is where the comptroller determines that, in comparable circumstances in relation to an application under the Act (other than an international application for a patent (UK)), he would have exercised his powers under rule 107 or 108 to prevent the application being treated as withdrawn.

Note. The "litigation rules" set out in Part 7 of the Rules (rr.73–87) are not stated to apply to any matters under ss.89, 89A or 89B. This is no doubt because inter partes proceedings are not envisaged under these proceedings.

OTHER RELEVANT RULES

89.07   The following rules are also relevant to international applications:

rule 107   (correction of irregularities), reprinted at §123.24;

rule 108   (extension of time limits), reprinted at §123.25;

rule 110   (interrupted days), reprinted at §123.28;

rule 111   (delays in communication services), reprinted at §123.29;

rule 113   (translations), reprinted at §123.30; and

rule 115   (establishing the accuracy of translations) reprinted at §123.32.

COMMENTARY ON SECTION 89

Scope of the section

89.08   Sections 89, 89A and 89B concern the application of the Act to international applications filed under the provisions of the PCT. These three sections were each introduced by the CDPA 1988 and together replace entirely the former repealed s.89. The following general remarks apply to all three sections.

The terms: "international application for a patent (UK)" (more simply called an "international application (UK)"); "international application for a patent" (abbreviated to "international application"); "International Bureau"; "designate"; and "Patent Co-operation Treaty" are each defined in s.130(1), see §130.08, as regards the PCT. The term "receiving office" is defined in r.64 (see reprint, above) as having the same meaning as in the PCT. The PCT definition is at PCT art.2(xv), according to which "receiving office" means the national office or intergovernmental organisation with which the international application has been filed. The competence of the receiving office is determined by PCT r.19 made under PCT art.10, see §89.11. In practice, the expression "receiving office" is also used generally to denote any office which may receive international applications, as well the office at which a particular international application has been filed; see, for example, PCT art.16(2) which obviously does not mean that an international application must have been filed before the competent international searching authority for that application can be specified. Thus, PCT art.16(2) ought to have referred to "each national office which acts as a receiving office", rather than just "each receiving Office"; see, for example, PCT r.19.4(a) which uses such an expression. Note that the term "international application for a patent (UK)" sometimes means a purported, rather than actual, such application, see §89.09.

"Declared priority date" in relation to an international application (UK) is defined at r.2(1) (reprinted in §123.04). This definition is not very satisfactory since, strictly speaking, a priority claim can be neither lost nor abandoned under the provisions of the PCT. Under the PCT, a declaration of priority can be deemed not to have been made but only for the purposes of the PCT (PCT r.26 *bis*.2(b)) or it can be withdrawn (PCT r.90 *bis*.3). In the PCT, "priority date" is defined differently from "declared priority date" (see PCT art.2(xi)). In the language of the PCT, "priority date" includes the international filing date except when repugnant to the context. The term "priority date" is used here,in relation to the international phase, in the same sense.

The objects of subss.89(1)–(3) and (5), and ss.89A and 89B(1)–(3) and (5) are: (i) to provide for the recognition of international applications (UK) as being applications under the Act; (ii) to enable the transfer of the international application from the international phase to the national or UK phase; and (iii) to provide for the recognition of the processing of the application in the international phase. Although the PCT does not anywhere use the expressions "international phase" and "national phase", they have been adopted widely for the purposes of quickly identifying the two distinct stages of processing of the international application. The terms "international phase" and "national phase" are used in ss.89A and 89B. They are defined for this purpose in s.89A(2) and (3), see §§89A.04 et seq. However, the term "UK phase" is used here in preference to "national phase" where the latter might give rise to ambiguity. It is also convenient to speak of "valid entry into the UK phase" to denote the transfer of the international application (UK) from the international phase to the UK phase.

A detailed discussion on the filing of an international application under the PCT and its processing in the international phase are outside the scope of this book. These matters are the subject of a separate book: the *Patent Cooperation Treaty Handbook* ("PCTH") edited and written mainly by Colin Jones for the Chartered Institute of Patent Attorneys, published by Sweet & Maxwell. This contains an extensive discussion of the PCT with emphasis on the international phase and the effect of an international application. Chapter 16 of the *European Patents Handbook* ("EPH") considers the role of the EPO as an international authority, i.e. as: (i) a receiving office; (ii) an international searching authority; and (iii) an international preliminary examining authority. The *PCT Applicant's Guide* is also extremely helpful. Volume I of this covers the international phase, and Vol.II (National Phase) contains basic information on the national phases before the designated offices. The *PCT Applicant's Guide* is published by WIPO in separate English and French editions.

The *PCT Applicant's Guide* is now available only as a web-based publication, available free of charge, and updated weekly on the *PatentScope* website (WIPO's PCT and patent portal) at (for English text): *http://www.wipo.int*. Users may subscribe to an email update service at the above address (*PCT Newsletter* 03/2006, pp.4–5). It is also useful to consult the *PCT Newsletter*, which is a monthly periodical published online at *http://www.wipo.int* in English by WIPO which contains up-to-date news about the PCT, including the latest amounts of fees payable on filing an international application. Also, §§89.17–89.25 discuss aspects of practice before the UK-IPO, in its role as a receiving office under the PCT, and comment on r.65 which relate to those matters which, under the PCT, are left to national authorities to prescribe.

While the UK-IPO will commonly be the receiving office for an applicant for an international application normally resident in the United Kingdom, the international searching authority for such applications is the EPO and not the UK-IPO. Also, the EPO is the international preliminary examining authority for such applications, see §89.17.

Synopsis of section 89

89.09 The provisions of substituted s.89 are first summarised for convenience. Subsection (1) enables an international application (UK) to be regarded as generally equivalent to an application filed under the Act. The term "international application for a patent" (as defined in s.130(1)), must include a purported international application: otherwise, s.89(5) and r.71(1) would have no effect. Subsection (2) is to ensure that a withdrawal or deemed withdrawal of the international application or of the designation of the United Kingdom in the international phase is fully equivalent to a withdrawal under the Act.

Subsection (3) provides for a review of an allegedly wrongful decision made by an international authority whereby the international application or a designation of the United Kingdom was declared to be deemed withdrawn in the international phase. Subsection (4) has been repealed in favour of new s.130(4A) ("Interpretation") which defines an international application for a European patent (UK) as one not to be interpreted also as an international application for a patent (UK), so that ss.89, 89A and 89B do not apply to an international application for a *European* patent (UK). This generally retains the position as under the former subs.(4) (see §89.29), but removal of the limitation "For the purposes of the above provisions" as was present under that subsection arguably makes the position more general and removes a possible lacuna relating to subs.(5) which enables a purported international application designating the United Kingdom to be saved when the application has wrongfully been refused an international filing date.

Advantages of the PCT

89.10 Advantages of the PCT include the relatively low initial cost and the delay in the commencement of the national processing and the expense thereof. If the international search report or commercial considerations arising after filing make further prosecution not worthwhile, the application can be abandoned without incurring any of the costs and expenses involved with national filings abroad. For other expositions of the advantages put forward in favour of filing international applications under the PCT, see the PCTH (noted in §89.08), particularly Ch.3, and the *PCT Applicant's Guide*, at Vol.I, (Introduction to the International Phase), paras 4.001 to 4.026.

Successive amendments to the Regulations under the PCT, with consequential and other amendments to national legislation, have removed many of the earlier pitfalls and patent attorneys are now more aware of those remaining. As a consequence, they are much more willing to recommend the use of the PCT system. Indeed, at the time of writing, a majority of European applications are filed as Euro-PCT applications, see §§79.02 et seq.

With the exception of the period under r.66(3) for making a request for permission to make a late declaration of priority, all prescribed periods relevant to valid entry into the UK phase are now extensible by two months under r.108(2) provided the extension is requested within two months of the normal date, and may also be extended or further extended (at the Comptroller's discretion) under r.108(3), see §123.25. Accordingly, cases on missed time limits, based on the rules before the 1987 amendments thereto came into force, no longer provide useful precedents, so far as practice under ss.89, 89A and 89B is concerned.

The international phase

—International filing

An international application may be filed only with a receiving office which is competent **89.11** having regard to the nationality or country of residence of the applicant or of any of the applicants, if there are more than one; but (subject to any national security issues; see commentary on s.23 at §23.02 et seq) may alternatively be filed with the International Bureau (PCT art.10; PCT r.19.1(a); PCT r.19.2). An applicant is considered to be resident in a country if he has a real and effective industrial or commercial establishment in that country (PCT r.18.1(b)(i)). It is not essential that that country shall have been indicated in the application at the time of its filing as the applicant's country of residence. Particulars of the competent receiving offices are published in the *PCT Gazette* and are reproduced in the *PCT Applicant's Guide*, Vol.I (International Phase), Annexes B1, B2 and C. For the competence of the UK-IPO as a receiving office and for the receiving offices available to residents and/or nationals of the United Kingdom, see §89.17.

If an international application is filed at a receiving office which is not competent, having regard to the residency and nationality of the applicant, it may be transferred to the International Bureau and the non-competent receiving office is deemed to be acting for the International Bureau (PCT r.19.4(a)(i)). Assuming that the applicant is a resident or national of some PCT country, an international filing date may be accorded, which is the date of receipt by the non-competent receiving office (PCT r.19.4(b)). An international application may also be transferred to the International Bureau when the language in which it is filed is not one accepted by the receiving office to which the applicant has submitted his international application (PCT r.19(4)(a)(ii)). The International Bureau will accept any language (*PCT Applicant's Guide*, Vol.I (International Phase), Annex C (IB)). An international application may be transferred to the International Bureau for any other reason, if the receiving office concerned and the International Bureau both agree and the applicant authorises the transfer (PCT r.19.4(a)(iii)).

If the language in which the international application is filed is not one accepted by the international searching authority, the applicant must file, at the receiving office, a translation into a language that is accepted by the searching authority. The competent international searching authorities are indicated in the *PCT Applicant's Guide*, Vol.I (International Phase) in Annex C and details of the competence of the international searching authorities and the language or languages that they will accept are given in the *PCT Applicant's Guide*, Vol.I (International Phase) in Annex D.

The necessary bibliographical and other data must be included in the PCT Request Form (Form PCT/RO/101). The countries for which patents are required must be designated on filing. (The PCT, like the EPC, uses the word "State", rather than "country").

The filing of a PCT request is now deemed to constitute the designation of all contracting states bound by the PCT on the international filing date, for the grant of every kind of protection available and for the grant of both regional and national patents (PCT r.4.9(a)). Also, under EPC art.79 (as revised in EPC 2000) all European patent applications are, likewise, to be deemed to designate all EPC contracting states that are bound by the EPC at the date of filing. These changes are reflected in the revision of the definition of "designate" in s.130(1) (see §130.01) and the insertion of a new s.130(4A) replacing s.89(4), as explained in §89.29.

This regime is generally considered beneficial for applicants, as it largely removes a previous risk of inadvertent omission of designations. However, in certain specific cases, applicants may wish deliberately to omit a particular designation, for example, to avoid "self-collision". The extent that such deliberate omission is possible is discussed further in the PCTH at Ch.18 and in the *PCT Applicant's Guide* Vol.I (International Phase), para.5.016 and Annex B.

There are certain things the applicant can do at the time of filing an international application or, at latest, before completion of technical preparations for international publication to comply with requirements under national laws of designated offices. Such things include: the furnishing of particulars of the deposit of biological material (PCT r.13 *bis*); the furnishing of a statement that a sample of the deposited biological material may be made available only to an expert; and the furnishing of particulars of a non-prejudicial disclosure. The extent that such matters are pertinent to the UK-IPO, as designated office, is discussed briefly in §§89A.33 and 89A.34.

Further, PCT r.4.18 provides that where an international application claims the priority of an earlier application, the applicant may include in the request a "statement of incorporation by reference" such that certain parts or elements of the earlier (priority) application may be incorporated by reference in the international application. Such a statement is pre-printed on the official Request form PCT/RO/101 so should be automatically made when this form is used. The statement is subject to confirmation under PCT r.20.6 within two months of the international filing date (PCT r.20.6 and PCT r.20.7). In certain circumstances, successful use of this provision might "save" priority for omitted parts or elements which were included in a priority (earlier) filing and might even "save" a particular filing date for the international application as a whole. However, although such a "statement of incorporation by reference" will be valuable as a precaution (and should normally be included on filing for that reason), the provision should not be relied on, since individual designated states may apply reservations (PCT r.20.8) so that such incorporation by reference, even if allowed by the relevant receiving office, may not be effective in such designated states (for further details see the PCTH para.13(6)).

Where an international application has an international filing date which is later than the date on which the 12-month priority period expired but within the period of two months from that date, the receiving office may, if requested by the applicant, restore the relevant right of priority if that office finds that a criterion applied by it (a "criterion for restoration") is satisfied (PCT r.26 *bis*.3(a)).

The provisions for restoration of the right of priority are intended to reflect the corresponding provisions of the PLT at art.13(2) to (6) and at r.14(4) to (7).

The "criteria for restoration" are that the failure to file the international application within the priority period either (i) occurred in spite of due care required by the circumstances having been taken; or (ii) was unintentional (PCT r.26 *bis*.3(a)). Subject always to any reservations under national law (for which see below) each receiving office must apply at least one of these criteria and may apply both of them (PCT r.26 *bis*.3(a)).

Each receiving office informs the International Bureau as to which, if any, of the criteria for restoration it applies and of any subsequent changes. The International Bureau publishes such information in the *PCT Gazette* (see also the information in the *PCT Applicant's Guide*, Vol.I (International Phase), Annex C). The UK-IPO has indicated that it will apply the "unintentionality" criterion in considering requests for restoration of the right of priority under PCT r.26 *bis*.3 (*Official Notices PCT Gazette* March 29, 2007, p.56). The meaning and interpretation of the term "unintentional" is discussed generally in the *Manual of Patent Practice* ("MOPP"), para.20A.13 and see also the discussion in §20A.05.

However, the PCT Assembly has adopted the understanding that a receiving office may, if it wishes, apply both criteria for restoration and leave the choice to the applicant as to which criterion is sought to be applied in a specific case. This is presumably because it may be advantageous for the applicant to obtain a positive finding by the receiving office on the more stringent criterion of "due care" as this may be effective in more designated/ elected States than a finding on the less stringent "unintentionality" criterion (WIPO document PCT/A/43/2 Rev). Furthermore, a receiving office is free to apply conditionally, upon request of the applicant, first the "due care" criterion and then, if the receiving office finds that that criterion is not complied with, the "unintentionality" criterion. In the case of the UK-IPO, it might be expected that the UK-IPO may apply the same test for "unintentionality" as for reinstatement of UK applications generally, as discussed in the MOPP, para.20A.13.

A request for restoration of the right of priority under PCT r.26 *bis*.3(a) must be filed with the receiving office within the period of two months from the date on which the priority period expired (i.e. within 14 months from the filing date of the earliest application from which priority is sought to be claimed), provided that it must also be filed before the technical preparations for international publication have been completed if there is a request by the applicant for early publication under PCT art.21(2)(b) (PCT r.26 *bis*.3(e)). The request for restoration must state the reasons for the failure to file the international application within the priority period (PCT r.26 *bis*.3(b)). For further details of the procedures involved and exceptions and reservations see the PCTH, paras 19.5B to 19.5E.

In *Gordon's Application* BL O/374/07 the applicant filed a PCT application claiming priority from an application which had a filing date 14 months earlier. The applicant also made a request to the UK-IPO acting as receiving office under the PCT to restore the right of priority under PCT r.26 *bis*.3. The hearing officer found that due to the circumstances the applicant found himself in at the time the normal 12-month priority period expired, the failure to file the PCT application within the twelve month period was unintentional, the criterion specified in PCT r.26 *bis*.3(a)(ii), and therefore allowed restoration of the right of priority on that ground.

However, in *Crilly's Application* BL O/182/10 it was held that a failure to file a PCT application within the normal 12-month priority period was not unintentional as it was a consequence of the applicant's decision to delay taking any action until entitlement proceedings were resolved. The applicant's request to restore the right of priority was therefore refused in this case. Similarly, in *Jones' Application* BL O/022/09 it was found that the applicant had been acting intentionally in filing a PCT application when he did, albeit that he was acting on the basis of a misunderstanding of the PCT system which meant that he was unaware of the 12-month priority deadline. The hearing officer accepted that the applicant might have acted differently if he had been aware of the deadline, but found that such speculation was not relevant, and the request for restoration of the right of priority was refused.

For a more detailed discussion of the filing of an international application, see the PCTH, in particular Chapters 13 et seq. and the *PCT Applicant's Guide* Vol. I (Introduction to the International Phase) Chapters 5 to 10.

—*International search and amendments to the claims and optional supplementary international search*

After the filing of the international application, it is referred to the appropriate **89.12** international searching authority (PCT art.16), resulting in the establishment of the international search report (PCT art.18) and written opinion (and subsequent International Preliminary Report on Patentability; IPRP). Thereafter, it is possible to file amended claims (but no amendments to the description or drawings) and a statement explaining the amendments (PCT art.19(1)). An advantage of securing a favourable PCT written opinion and/or international preliminary report on patentability is that it may be possible to take advantage of the PCT Patent Prosecution Highway (PCT-PPH) in the national phase in those designated/elected states which are participants in this program. In addition, whilst not part of the PCT-PPH program the UK-IPO has an accelerated examination system in the UK national phase for PCT applications which have a completely positive international preliminary report on patentability ("PCT(UK) Fast Track"; see §89A.40).

For a more detailed discussion of the international search and amendment, see the PCTH, in particular Chapters 29, 29A and 30 and the *PCT Applicant's Guide* Vol. I (Introduction to the International Phase) Chapters 7 to 9.

It is also now possible to request optional Supplementary International Searches from International Searching Authorities which provide such searches. The supplementary international search (SIS) is an entirely optional service that allows additional (complementary) searches to be performed during the international phase (PCT r.45*bis*), in addition to the mandatory international search performed by the applicant's "regular" international searching authority (as discussed above).

In establishing a system for supplementary international search, WIPO has suggested that no single office is always capable of searching even the whole of the PCT minimum documentation in its original language, still less the large volume of other patent and non-patent literature containing original disclosures. The supplementary international search service is thus intended to allow applicants an opportunity to reduce the risk of being faced with new citations during the national phase. It is not expected that supplementary international search will be requested routinely, but rather as a strategic decision by the applicant, taken after consideration of the results of the main international search, the commercial importance of the particular application and the amount of prior art in the particular technical field which is known to be published in a language in which the main ISA is not skilled (*PCT Newsletter* 12/2008, pp.1–4 under the heading "*New PCT Service: Supplementary International Search*").

The supplementary international search is carried out on the application as filed (PCT arts 19 and/or 34 are not considered) and may cover only one invention or group of inventions having unity of invention—there is no expressed option for paying additional fees for the searching of multiple inventions. However, if the main international searching authority has identified a lack of unity before supplementary international search is requested, the latter can be requested to concentrate on an invention which is not necessarily the first one claimed (Rule 45*bis*.1(d) PCT and see *PCT Newsletter* 12/2008, pp.1–4). The request must be filed within 19 months from the priority date (PCT r.45*bis*.1) directly with the International Bureau (NB not the international searching authority itself). Form PCT/IB/375 (Supplementary Search Request) should be used.

A further explanation of the supplementary international search system is provided in the *PCT Newsletter* 12/2008, pp.14–15, under the heading "Practical Advice", which discusses, in particular, the applicability of the system and how to request supplementary international search. For further information, see also the PCTH (paras 29.21 to 29.28) and the *PCT Applicant's Guide* Vol.I (Introduction to the International Phase) Chapter 8. For detailed information about authorities which are competent to conduct supplementary international searches see the *PCT Applicant's Guide* Vol. I (International Phase) Annex SISA.

—International publication

89.13   The international application, including the regular international search report, is published by the International Bureau promptly after the expiry of the period of 18 months from the priority date (PCT art.21).

In accordance with PCT r.48 and s.406(b) of the PCT Administrative Instructions, after April 1, 2006, international publication of international applications and any republications of previously published international applications has taken place wholly in electronic form (*PCT Newsletter* 03/2006, p.3). Thus, since April 1, 2006, the legal publication of international applications has been the electronic publication only. This is available in several different electronic formats on the day of publication on the "*PatentScope*" Portal of the WIPO website: *http://www.wipo.int*. The International Bureau is reported to continue its practice of publishing once a week, usually on Thursdays. As previously, a time limit of 15 calendar days normally applies for completion of technical preparations for international publication (*PCT Newsletter* 03/2006, p.3). Publication takes place under a number "WO yyyy/zzzzz (PCT Administrative Instructions s.404) where yyyy represents the year of publication and zzzzz represents the publication serial number for that year (previously, only the last two digits of the year had normally been used).

After July 1, 2006, the International Bureau ceased to transmit a paper copy of the published international application to the applicant. Instead, that amended Form PCT/IB/311 is sent to the applicant on the date of publication, notifying the applicant that international publication has taken place, of the international publication number, and a reference to the *PatentScope* website portal where the published international application can be searched, viewed and downloaded. However, on request, the International Bureau will send a paper copy of the published international application, free of charge, to the applicant (*PCT Newsletter*, 03/2006, p.3).

This change to electronic publication is stated not to affect the means of communication of published international applications to national Offices and to interested third parties, which may be in either electronic or physical (paper) form, depending on the requirements of the various authorities and offices, as previously.

Normally, any amendments made to the claims are published with the application, but occasionally the preparations for publication are completed before expiry of the applicable time limit under PCT r.46.1 for filing amended claims. In the latter event, the amended claims are published later (PCT r.48.2(h)).

Following the amendment of PCT r.48.2(a)(x), with effect from April 1, 2006, any declaration(s) filed under PCT r.4.17 are now published with the published international application. The front page of the international publication of the international application continues to refer to declarations which have been filed within the time limit under PCT r.26 ter.1 (*PCT Newsletter*, 03/2006, p.3).

When the international application is filed in one of the languages of publication (at the time of writing the languages of publication are Arabic, Chinese, English, French, German, Japanese, Korean, Portuguese, Russian and Spanish), it is published in the language in which it is filed (PCT r.48.3(a)). When the international application is filed in a language other than a language of publication, but a translation into such a language is filed by the applicant at the receiving office for the purpose of the international search (the language in which the international application is filed being one not accepted by the competent international searching authority), the international application is published in the language of that translation (PCT r.48.3(b)). Where the application is not filed in a language of publication and no translation into such a language is filed by the applicant at the receiving office for the purpose of the international search, the applicant should furnish to the receiving office a translation into any language of publication which the receiving office accepts for this purpose (PCT r.14.4(a)). When the international application is published in a language other than English, the search report as published, declaration, title, abstract and any text relating to any figures accompanying the abstract is published both in that language and in English, the translation being prepared under the responsibility of the International Bureau (PCT r.48.3(c)). Certain documents (such as sequence listings, indications relating to biological material filed separately from the description, and various requests, declarations and information) which form part of the publication of the international application are now presented as separate documents. These are made available, where applicable, in the "PatentScope" portal of the WIPO website on the "Documents" tab of the international application concerned (*PCT Newsletter* 01/2008, pp.1–2).

The front sheet of the published PCT application contains all the usual bibliographical data, including a list of the designated states or regions and any priority claim (other than any withdrawn priority claim and any priority claim deemed not to have been made): PCT r.48.2(b) and Administrative Instructions. The data included on the front sheet is also published separately in the *PCT Gazette* (PCT r.86.1).

Copies of published applications and of priority documents appertaining to them can be obtained by directing a request for them to WIPO, Marketing and Distribution Section, PO Box 18, CH-1211 Geneva 20, Switzerland. In the case of international applications filed on or after July 1, 1998, a copy of any document in the file held by the International Bureau (other than any document relating to international preliminary examination) may be obtained from the International Bureau after international publication (PCT r.94.1). For international applications filed before that date, the previous version of PCT r.94 continues to apply, wherein there is no provision for the International Bureau to furnish copies of documents to third parties, except with the authorisation of the applicant. This notwithstanding, the International Bureau will give access to documents which were already expressly available under the PCT and the previous version of the Regulations under it. Such documents include the priority document as well as the published international application (PCT rr.17.2(c) and 48.1(a)).

The *PCT Gazette* (under PCT r.61.4) list the international applications in respect of which a demand has been filed (see §89.16), though this has less significance now that filing of a demand is not in most cases required to delay start of the national phases. Since

2006, the *PCT Gazette* has been published only in electronic form in English and French. The electronic form includes the abstract and possibly a drawing and is available on the internet (at *http://www.wipo.int*). From April 1998 to April 2006 the *PCT Gazette* was published in bilingual (English and French) paper form (which omitted the abstract and any drawing) and in electronic form in English and French. Before April 2, 1998, the PCT Gazette was published in separate English and French editions in paper form only.

For a more detailed discussion of international publication, see the PCTH, in particular Ch.31 and the *PCT Applicant's Guide* Vol.I (Introduction to the International Phase) Ch.9.

—Communication under PCT Art.20

89.14   The international application is communicated to designated offices as soon as possible after the international publication (PCT art.20, PCT r.47.1(a), (b)). This communication consists of a copy of the international application as published or of a copy of the international application as filed if the application is published in a language different from that in which it was filed, or both, depending upon the requirements of the designated offices (PCT r.47.3). The applicant is notified (on Form PCT/IB/308) that such communication has taken place (*PCT Applicant's Guide* at Vol.II (National Phase), para.4.027). All designated countries are obliged to accept such notification as conclusive proof that the communication under art.20 of the PCT has taken place or that furnishing of a copy by the applicant under art.22 of the PCT is not required (PCT r.47.1(c- *bis*)). Most designated offices have waived the right to receive the communication under art.20 of the PCT automatically: they request the International Bureau to supply this communication when the applicant has performed the acts necessary for entry into the national phase (see §89.15). The notification to the applicant on Form PCT/IB/308 indicates which of the designated offices have made such a waiver.

A copy of the priority document (if filed in the international phase) is also furnished to the designated offices (normally with the communication under art.20 of the PCT) unless the designated office does not require one (PCT r.17.2(a)).

—Commencement of national phase

89.15   To enter the national phase, the applicant must pay the national fee required by the national patent office, acting as a designated office, and must also file a translation of the international application if the designated office so prescribes. In the United Kingdom and most other EPC States, there is now a uniform normal period of 31 months from the earliest claimed priority date (or if no priority is claimed, from the international filing date) for entry into the national UK phase, irrespective of whether international preliminary examination has been requested (see r.66 set out in §89A.02).

However, in a few countries, a shorter 20–month time limit may apply, i.e. where a designated country has notified the International Bureau of incompatibility with the national law applied by that country. Information received by the International Bureau concerning such incompatibility is published in the *PCT Gazette*, *PCT Applicant's Guide* and on the WIPO website at: *http://www.wipo.int*.

In relation to any such designated country which has maintained notice of such incompatibility and in which an election has been made within 19 months from the priority date for the purposes of international preliminary examination under Ch.II of the PCT (see §89.16), the national phase normally commences 30 months from the priority date (PCT art.39(1)).

To enter the national phase, the applicant must pay the national fee required by the national patent office, acting as a designated office, and must also file a translation of the international application if the designated office so prescribes: for the United Kingdom, see r.69 (reprinted in §89A.05).

Except in the somewhat rare situation described above, where a demand may still need to be filed within 19 months from the priority date, the time limit for filing a demand simply for international preliminary examination purposes is now the later of (i) three months from the date of transmittal to the applicant of the international search report and the written opinion established under r.43 *bis*.1 of the PCT, or of any declaration under art.17(2)(a) of the PCT, or (ii) 22 months from the priority date.

—International preliminary examination

International preliminary examination, if demanded under Ch.II of the PCT, is **89.16** conducted by the appropriate international preliminary examining authority (PCT art.32) and results in the issuance of an international preliminary examination report (PCT art.35) which is communicated by the International Bureau to the elected offices (PCT art.36). Submissions may be made and amendments may be made to the description, claims and drawings during international preliminary examination, and such amendments, other than superseded amendments, are annexed to the international preliminary examination report (PCT art.34(2)(b), PCT rr.66.1(b) and 70.16). The international preliminary examination report is not binding on the elected office (PCT art.33(1)).

The demand should be submitted directly to the competent international preliminary examining authority or to the chosen examining authority when the applicant has a choice. The competent examining authorities are indicated in the *PCT Applicant's Guide*, Vol.I (International Phase) in Annex C and their details, including the language or languages that they will accept are given in Annex E.

The International Bureau and the international preliminary examining authority are obliged to keep the international examination file confidential at all times, except that the elected offices may be allowed access to the examination file once the international preliminary examination report has been established (PCT art.38). However, the PCT does not require the elected offices themselves to keep the examination file confidential. It has been usual for a copy of the international examination report (but not any arguments presented by the applicant, for example to overcome citations) to be included in the part of the national file relating to an international application open to public inspection at elected offices. For international applications filed on or after July 1, 1998, the examining authorities must, upon reimbursement of costs, supply a copy of the examination file to any elected office that requests it (PCT r.94.2). Provided that the international application has been published, the examining authorities may (not must) allow third parties to have access to the international preliminary examination file but only to the extent that access is afforded to the files of national applications under national law (PCT r.94.3). The EPO has decided to allow access to international preliminary examination files but only for those international applications for which the EPO was the international preliminary examining authority (see OJ EPO 1999, 329). The EPO does not intend to obtain copies of examination files from any other examining authority, unless required by the EPO for its own use. Rule 51(3)(d) (see §118.02) does not require the UK-IPO to allow inspection of the contents of international preliminary examination files where the International Bureau would not be permitted to allow access under the PCT, which means in practice that only the international preliminary examination report or international preliminary report on patentability is available.

For a more detailed discussion of international preliminary examination, see the PCTH, in particular Ch.34 and the *PCT Applicant's Guide* Vol.I (Introduction to the International Phase), Ch.10.

United Kingdom Intellectual Property Office as an international authority

—General

The Act does not contain any provisions prescribing the conduct of proceedings before **89.17** the UK-IPO in its capacity as an international authority, specifically in its capacity of receiving office under art.10 of the PCT and r.19.1(a)(i) and (ii) of the PCT. The filing and processing of international applications in the international phase are governed entirely by the PCT, the Regulations and the PCT Administrative Instructions. Receiving offices are also expected to follow the PCT Receiving Office Guidelines. Details of the Administrative Instructions and the Receiving Office Guidelines are published in the *PCT Gazette* and *PCT Newsletter* from time to time. Consolidated texts of the current Administrative Instructions and Receiving Office Guidelines are available online from the WIPO *Patent-Scope* portal at: *http://www.wipo.int*, (see also the PCTH at Appendices III and V, and the EPH).

The UK-IPO is neither an international searching authority nor an international preliminary examining authority. Pursuant to the Protocol on Centralisation annexed to the s.IV(1)(e) of the European Patent Convention, the UK-IPO relinquished its status as an examining authority from June 1, 1993 (see *Patents Journal* January 6, 1993). The EPO is the competent international searching and preliminary examining authority for international applications filed at the UK-IPO, as receiving office and for international applications filed by residents or nationals of the United Kingdom at the International Bureau, as alternative receiving office (*PCT Applicant's Guide*, Vol.I (International Phase), Annex C (GB); Annex C (IB)). The demand for international preliminary examination should be submitted directly to the EPO, as examining authority and not to the receiving office (PCT art.31(6)(a)).

In view of the Landmines Act 1998 (c.33), the Comptroller has indicated that the UK-IPO, in its capacity of receiving office, would refuse to process any international application relating to the production or use of landmines, see §1.21. Possibly, permission for this stance can be found in art.27(8) of the PCT, which enables a PCT country to apply measures deemed necessary for the protection of economic interests of that country.

Rule 65 (see reprint, above) has been made under the authority of s.123 for the purpose of regulating the business of the United Kingdom Patent Office (UK-IPO) in relation to international applications. This rule prescribes the requirements which pertain to the filing of an international application as required by the PCT and the Regulations to be determined by the receiving office, but does not give the UK-IPO any jurisdiction under the Act in relation to international applications. Indeed the other rules have no applicability to the international phase of an international application (UK): *Kenrick's (Archibald) International Application* [1994] R.P.C. 635. Jurisdiction is *delegated* to the UK-IPO by the PCT itself and the Regulations (PCT art.10; PCT r.19.1(a); and see the definition of "national office" at PCT art.2(xii)). See also *Abaco Machines (Australasia) Pty Ltd's Application* [2007] EWHC 347 which confirmed that the PCT is a complete code and that a PCT application cannot be an application under the 1977 Act except to the extent that that Act says it is. The circumstances in which a PCT application can be treated as an application for a patent under the 1977 Act are dealt with in ss.89, 89A and 89B of the Act.

The UK-IPO, in its capacity of a receiving office, has refused to correct an international application where the international request form was initially omitted so that, within the priority period, no designation of states had been made (*Intelligence Quotient's International Application* [1996] R.P.C. 245). The Comptroller refused to follow J 25/88 *NEW FLEX/Date of filing* OJ EPO 1989, 486; [1990] E.P.O.R. 59, pointing out that the EPC differed from the PCT in its law on precautionary designations and holding that, in any case, he must have exclusive regard to the provisions of the PCT following *Kenrick's (Archibald) International Application* (above).

The UK-IPO is a competent receiving office for nationals or residents of the United Kingdom and the Isle of Man (*PCT Applicant's Guide*, at Vol.I (International Phase), Annex C(GB)). If there are several applicants, it is sufficient for one to be a resident or national of one of these countries. The UK-IPO is not competent to receive an international application to be filed by an applicant who is neither a national of, nor resident in, the United Kingdom or the Isle of Man. With the extension of the PCT to the Isle of Man, it is the practice of the UK-IPO, as receiving office, to treat residents and citizens of the Isle of Man (as it was also for those of Hong Kong until June 30, 1997) as being residents and nationals of the United Kingdom. The international request form should be completed accordingly. Citizens of certain British Dependent Territories are British nationals under the British Nationalities Act 1981 (c.61) and are thereby qualified to file an international application even though the PCT has not been extended to those territories. The UK-IPO is the competent receiving office for such individuals (see *PCT Applicant's Guide*, Vol.I (International Phase), Annex C (GB)). Any such citizen, believing that he/she is qualified by nationality (GB) to file an international application, should check with the International Unit at the UK-IPO (see §89.31) for confirmation before filing.

In the event that the UK-IPO receives an international application and finds that the applicant is qualified by residency or nationality to file an international application, but the Office is not competent to receive that application or if it finds that the international application is not in the English (or Welsh) language, it transfers the application to the International Bureau provided that a fee is paid for this service (r.65(3)). Any other fees received by the Office are refunded to the applicant (*PCT Applicant's Guide*, Vol.I, (Introduction to the International Phase), paras 6.034 and 6.035. The International Bureau may then act as the competent receiving office (PCT r.19.4). However, it may become necessary for the applicant to represent himself or to appoint a representative who is entitled to practise before the national office of the country of which he is a resident or national and/or to file a translation of the international application into a language that is accepted by the international searching authority.

United Kingdom nationals or residents have the option of choosing the EPO as receiving office, but the provisions of ss.22 and 23 then apply (see the discussion of those sections), as they do if the International Bureau is chosen as the receiving office (PCT art.27(8)). An international application lodged at the UK-IPO for onward transmission to the EPO as receiving office (EPC art.152(1), EPC r.104(3)) is accorded, as its filing date, the date of receipt by the former office. There is a parallel with r.19.4 of the PCT, according to which a national office, which acts as a receiving office and from which an international application is transmitted to the International Bureau, is considered to be acting on behalf of the International Bureau. There is also a parallel with art.75(1)(b) of the EPC.

Whether the EPO would consider itself competent to receive international applications from residents of the Isle of Man or from an individual resident in a dependent territory of the United Kingdom, but having United Kingdom citizenship, is not certain. Provided that the international request is completed to show the applicant's residence and/or nationality to be that of the United Kingdom, in accordance with the practice of the UK-IPO described above, the EPO would not be presented with any reason for holding that it is not competent.

—Number of copies (r.65)

Pursuant to r.11.1(b) of the PCT, r.65(1) (see §89.04, above) prescribes that international applications filed at the UK-IPO as receiving office shall be filed in triplicate in English or Welsh. This applies to the request (Form PCT/RO/101) as well as to the description, claims and abstract, and drawings, if any. Rule 65(2) enables the UK-IPO to demand a fee for making any necessary copies if the applicant does not provide sufficient copies to comply with r.65(1).   **89.18**

—Transmittal, international filing and search fees (r.65(3))

Pursuant to rr.14.1, 16 *bis*.2 and 19.4(b) of the PCT, r.65(3) (see reprint, above) makes provision for the payment of certain fees which the PCT leaves to national authorities, acting as receiving offices under this Treaty, to impose should they so wish.   **89.19**

By r.65(3), a transmittal fee (which is for the benefit of the UK-IPO) is required. PCT r.14(1)(c) specifies that any transmittal fee shall be paid within one month of the date of receipt of the international application (not the international filing date—for the significance of this see the PCTH, para.36.4). The PCT international filing and search fees must likewise be paid within one month of the filing date (PCT rr.15.4(a) and 16.1(a)). For each of these fees, if the full fee has not been paid within the relevant time limit, the receiving office must invite the applicant to remedy the deficiency within one month from the date of the invitation and may levy a fee for late payment of this fee (PCT r.16 *bis*.1(a)). Any payment received before the UK-IPO issues an invitation to pay a missing fee or make up a fee shortfall, is deemed to have been received in time (PCT r.16 *bis*.1(d)). Any payment received in response to such an invitation before the UK-IPO declares that the international application (or a designation) is considered withdrawn is deemed to have been received in time (PCT r.16 *bis*.1(e)). Under r.16 *bis*.2 of the PCT, the amount of the fee for such late payment shall be 50 per cent of the amount of the unpaid fees, but not less than the transmittal fee and not more than 50 per cent of the international filing fee (disregarding, for this purpose, any sheets of the international application in excess of 30 in number).

Rule 65(3) prescribes the payment of a fee when an international application is received by the UK-IPO acting on behalf of the International Bureau which is itself to be regarded as the receiving office under r.19.4(a) of the PCT. PCT r.19.4(b) prescribes that such fee shall be equal to the transmittal fee prescribed under PCT r.14.1, mentioned above.

There is no rule requiring the UK-IPO, when acting as receiving office, to impose a late furnishing fee under PCT r.12.3(d) and (e). This is because the possibility for filing translations at the UK-IPO does not normally arise, the main language that the UK-IPO accepts for the filing of international applications being English, which is one of the languages accepted by the EPO for the international search. If the application is filed in Welsh as now permitted by r.65(1)(a), a translation into an official language of the EPC will presumably need to be filed with the EPO for the purposes of the international search.

The amount of the transmittal fee is prescribed in the current Patents (Fees) Rules. The amounts of the international filing fee and the search fee are determined respectively by the Assembly of the PCT Union (PCT art.58; PCT r.96) and by the EPO (PCT r.16.1(a)), see §89.21.

The amount of any of the fees which is required is the fee which was in force at the date of receipt of the international application (not the international filing date) (PCT rr.14.1(c), 15.4 and 16.1(f)).

—Supply of certified copies (r.65(4))

89.20   The preparation of a certified copy of a priority document has been deemed to have been requested by indicating in Box VI on the PCT Request Form that priority from an application filed under the Act is claimed for the international application (*Patents Journal* November 17, 2004). Accordingly, when this indication has been given, accompanied by the prescribed fee, the requisite certified copy will be prepared and transmitted to the International Bureau by the UK-IPO without the need to file PF 23. This is presumed to be still possible, despite the wording of r.65(4) (see reprint, above), because r.4(2) permits the use of a form which is acceptable to the Comptroller and the aforesaid indication on the PCT Request Form has been deemed to be such a form. In some cases it may also now be possible for certified copies to be supplied electronically; see §89.31.

—Fees to be paid in sterling

89.21   Pursuant to rr.15.2(b) and 16.1(b) of the PCT, all fees payable to the UK-IPO as receiving office shall be paid in sterling. The amounts, in sterling, of the international filing fee and the international search fee are determined by agreement with the International Bureau and the EPO (as international searching authority) and are published from time to time in the *PCT Gazette*, in the *PCT Applicant's Guide* and in the *Patents Journal*. Since these fee amounts may change at very short notice, unless a constant watch on the *PCT Gazette* or, preferably, on the *PCT Newsletter* has been kept, it is prudent to check the amounts required with the International Unit at the UK-IPO (tel. 01633 814 586). The amounts of PCT fees are also published regularly in the *Patents Journal* and on the UK-IPO website *http://www.ipo.gov.uk*.

The handling and examination fees for international preliminary examination are payable directly to the EPO as international preliminary examining authority. The amounts of these fees are given in the *PCT Applicant's Guide*, Vol.I (International Phase) at Annex E (EP). For payment of fees to the EPO, refer to the EPH Ch.5.

—Delay or loss in mail (PCT r.82.1)

The provisions of former r.97 of the Patents Rules 1995 no longer apply. **89.22**

By virtue of r.82.1 of the PCT, made pursuant to PCT art.48(1), items addressed to the UK-IPO as "receiving office", and sent by registered post (using airmail where available when sent from abroad) at least five days before the end of a prescribed period, will be deemed to have been filed in time. Note that European mail requires an airmail label. PCT r.82.1 also prescribes that delivery by private courier may be equated to delivery by registered post, provided that the international authority receiving the delivery has notified the International Bureau. So far, it is not clear that the UK-IPO has made express notification. However, it is stated in the *PCT Applicant's Guide* (Annex B1 (GB)) that the UK-IPO would consider evidence of mailing a document, in case of loss or delay, where a delivery service other than the postal authorities is used, with reference to PCT r.82.1. In this connection, the Postal Services Act 2000 (c.26) Sch.8 provides that the use of the terms "post", "registered post", "recorded delivery", and "first class post" in legislation cannot be limited only to services provided by what it calls "the Post Office company". As a result, the UK-IPO now recognises as "post" any items delivered to it by any commercial service which undertakes to deliver mail in exchange for a fee (see §119.03).

—Interruption in the mail service (PCT r.82.2)

Rule 110 (Interrupted Days) and r.111 (Delays in communication services) reprinted at **89.23** §§123.28 and 123.29, do not apply to international applications while they are in the international phase. Instead, r.82.2 of the PCT, also made pursuant to PCT art.48(1), prescribes that, in the event of an interruption of postal services in the locality of the applicant or his agent, a delay in receipt by an international authority of any letter or document or payment by post from such applicant or agent may be excused, provided that the applicant or agent, as the case may be, proves that such interruption commenced within the ten days preceding the due date for that letter or document or payment and that he posted it within the next five days following resumption of mail services. Use of registered mail would assist in providing the necessary proof, although this is not an express requirement.

—No requirement for representation; address for service; right of representation (PCT arts 27(7) and 49)

The UK-IPO, as receiving office, cannot require that any applicant be represented by an **89.24** agent under PCT art.27(7) in the international phase because the UK-IPO does not make any such requirement in connection with national applications. Also, it appears that the UK-IPO, as receiving office, cannot apply r.103 to require the applicant to furnish an address for service in the United Kingdom (or EU/EEA) because this is not embraced by art.27(7) of the PCT. The reference there to "an address in a designated State" is only relevant to an international application that has entered the national phase. Otherwise, the *PCT Applicant's Guide*, Vol.I (International Phase), at Annex C would indicate the requirements of individual receiving offices as to the furnishing an address for service (cf. *PCT Applicant's Guide*, Vol.II (National Phase), at National Chapters, Summaries). Nevertheless, it is in the applicant's interest to have an address for correspondence in the United Kingdom, in order that receipt of communications from the Office will not be delayed.

PCT art.27(7) enables the receiving office to refuse to recognise an agent who does not have the right to represent applicants under national law. Conversely, r.90.1 of the PCT confirms that any agent having a right of representation before that office in connection with national applications may represent the applicant in connection with international applications filed there. To ascertain who is entitled to represent applicants before the UK-IPO in its role as receiving office, it is necessary to refer to ss.102 and 102A and to s.274 of the CDPA. These provisions permit representation by any person, other than one subject to specific prohibition under s.281 CDPA (see §§281.03 et seq.).

An agent, entitled to represent applicants before the UK-IPO and appointed to represent the applicant for an international application filed there, also has the right to represent the applicant before the EPO, as international searching and preliminary examining authority, and before the International Bureau, in connection with that international application in the international phase (PCT art.49). This is irrespective of the offices designated and, so far as the EPO as international searching and international preliminary examining authority is concerned, is not dependent on the agent being on the "European list", see §286.03.

PCT art.49 and PCT r.90 are restricted to the international phase whereas art.27(7) of the PCT is not so restricted, so that an agent appointed to represent the applicant before the receiving office and/or before the international searching and preliminary examining authorities does not automatically enjoy the right to represent the applicant in the national phase before those authorities (offices) as designated or elected offices. A fresh appointment is necessary in the national phase, unless any power of attorney filed in the international phase is so worded as to extend into the national phase. In any event, such agent must be entitled to practise before the designated or elected office or offices concerned in connection with national applications filed there. For representation before the UK-IPO and the furnishing of an address for service in the UK phase, see §89A.16. The UK-IPO, in its capacity as a receiving office, has waived the general requirement under PCT r.90.4(b) and/or r.90.5(a)(ii) to submit a separate power of attorney and/or a copy of a general power of attorney (*PCT Gazette* 16/2004 of April 15, 2004 updating *PCT Gazette* S-01/2004 (E), Annex C (GB), p.276). However, the UK-IPO has indicated that there will be particular instances in which a separate power of attorney or a copy of a general power of attorney will still be required. These include where an agent or common representative, who is not indicated on the Request form at the time of filing, performs an action after filing or where it is unclear that an agent or common representative has power to act on behalf of the applicant. Powers of attorney will also continue to be required for any withdrawal requests, in accordance with rr.90.4(e) and 90.5(d) of the PCT.

—No appeal

89.25   Unfavourable actions by the UK-IPO, in its capacity of a receiving office under the PCT, are not appealable because the PCT deliberately does not provide for such an appeal. An unfavourable action might be: a refusal to accord the application with an international filing date (a "negative determination") (PCT art.11(2)(a); PCT r.20.7); a declaration that the international application or a country designation is considered withdrawn (PCT art.14; PCT rr.12.3(d) and 26); the according of an international filing date that is not correct (PCT art.11(1); PCT rr.20.1–20.5); a declaration that a priority claim is considered not to have been made (PCT r.26 *bis*.2(b)); or a decision not to authorise the correction of an obvious error in the request (PCT r.91.1(e)(i)). Note that the International Bureau (when not acting in its capacity of receiving office) cannot itself invite the applicant to correct certain defects in the international application or declare that an international application or a designation is deemed withdrawn because the application does not comply with the provisions of the PCT and the Regulations, although the International Bureau may make a finding that the international application is considered withdrawn on the ground that it did not receive the record copy (PCT art.12(3); PCT r.22.3). If the International Bureau is of the opinion that the international application contains a correctable defect or that a declaration ought to be made that the international application or a designation is considered withdrawn, it draws the relevant facts to the attention of the receiving office for the latter to issue an invitation to correct or make the appropriate declaration, unless the receiving office disagrees with the opinion of the International Bureau (PCT rr.28 and 29(3)).

Notwithstanding the absence of any express provision in or under the PCT (but see PCT r.29.4) and notwithstanding that s.101 is not applicable to proceedings before the UK-IPO, as receiving office under PCT art.10 and PCT r.19.1(a)(i) and (ii), it is the practice of the UK-IPO, as receiving office, to afford a hearing before or even after making any un-favourable notification, declaration or decision. At such a hearing, the hearing officer is acting on behalf of the receiving office and not on behalf of the Comptroller (this legal nicety is not always observed). Also, it is the practice for any decision taken by the hear-ing officer at or after such a hearing to be subject to judicial review. As a result of a review, either by the receiving officer or his superior or at the directions of the hearing officer or of the judge upon a judicial review, the receiving officer can change his opinion and as a result, can refrain from making an unfavourable notification or declaration or can withdraw that notification or declaration (see, e.g. PCT r.20.8).

By way of illustration, it was pointed out by the hearing officer in *Celltech Ltd's International Application*, as reported in *R. v Comptroller-General Ex p. Celltech Ltd* [1991] R.P.C. 475 that there is no specific provision for hearings under the PCT but it is customary for the UK-IPO to offer informal hearings on matters concerning its receiving office functions. In *Hemosol's Application* BL O/51/87, noted I.P.D. 10111, the hearing officer expressed the view that there is no right of appeal to the Patents Court from a deci-sion by a hearing officer, acting for the receiving office, but it was noted that the possibility existed of a request to the High Court for judicial review of an unfavourable decision under CPR 54. Subsequently, in each of *R. v Comptroller-General Ex p. Celltech Ltd* (above) and *Drazil's Application* [1992] R.P.C. 479, the applicant (unsuccessfully) sought a judicial review of decisions by the UK-IPO, acting in its capacity of receiving office, not to authorise corrections to country designations. In the latter case, the request for leave to pursue a judicial review was heard urgently, since less than a week remained for any ac-tion (unspecified) under the PCT to be taken.

The proper way to seek redress when the international application has been refused an international filing date or when the international application or a designation is deemed withdrawn is to request each of the designated offices to conduct a review under PCT art.25 within the time limit of two months from the date of the notification sent to the ap-plicant (PCT r.51.1 and 51.3). A separate review, with its consequent expense, before each designated office is necessary, as noted in *Fletcher's International Application* BL O/235/98. For the UK-IPO acting as a designated office for the purpose of such a review, see §§89.28 and 89.30. Decisions after a review by the UK-IPO are appealable in the usual way, since invoking the provisions of subs.(3) or (5) brings the international application within the provisions of the Act, but only so far as the designation of the United Kingdom is concerned. In *Intelligence Quotient's International Application* [1996] R.P.C. 245, the UK-IPO, as receiving office, refused to authorise correction of an international application under PCT r.91 to overcome a problem that no State had been designated because the international request form was accidentally omitted from the initially filed papers, whereby no international filing date could be accorded earlier than the belated date of filing of the request form. It was confirmed that art.27(4) of the PCT is not applicable to the international phase so that the rule at that time equivalent to current r.107 could not be invoked. In *Fletcher's International Application* (above), the UK-IPO, as receiving office, held a hearing following a referral from the International Bureau (which was of the opinion that the international application ought to be deemed withdrawn because it did not contain any claims), despite the fact that, before the hearing took place, the UK-IPO, as receiving office, had already made the declaration that the international application was deemed withdrawn. See also now *Penife International's International Application* BL O/382/03 and [2004] R.P.C. 37 at 737.

The *PCT Applicant's Guide*, Vol.I (Introduction to the International Phase), at para.6.054 warns that, if an appeal is entertained by a higher national authority from a finding by the receiving office, designated offices may not necessarily accept the outcome of such an appeal. In any event, the applicant should only contemplate such a step if no other avenue is available. Quite apart from this, time limits in the international phase are very tight and the two-month time limit prescribed at r.51.1 and 51.3 of the PCT for seeking reviews by designated offices under PCT art.25 will run from the date of the notification that an international filing date is refused or the date of the declaration or notification that an international application is deemed withdrawn. Also, it is necessary to observe the time limit prescribed in or under PCT art.22 or 39(1) for filing the translation at the designated offices, if prescribed; and paying the national fee (for the United Kingdom 31 months from the first declared priority date or, if none, the filing date, see §89A.09 and 89A.10§), even if the outcome of an informal appeal or review in the international phase is not known at that time.

Whether or not the international application has been deemed withdrawn, the applicant can request each of the designated offices (when requesting a review under PCT art.25 or when entering the national phase) to correct the international filing date accorded by the receiving office or re-instate a priority claim that the receiving office or the International Bureau has declared to be deemed not to have been made (PCT rr.82 *ter*, 85(1)) or to review a decision not to authorise correction of an obvious error. For the procedure before the UK-IPO, as designated office, see §89B.12.

Effect of an international application (UK) (subs.(1))

89.26   The effect of subs.(1), pursuant to art.11(3) of the PCT, is that an international application (UK) has the effect of a United Kingdom application immediately when filed at a competent receiving office and accorded an international filing date. This is subject to the savings of ss.89A and 89B, particularly s.89A(1) (procedure in the international phase), see §89A.05, and s.89B(3) (provisional protection arising on publication), see §89B.10. Section 89B(1) specifically concerns the filing date, declaration of priority and statement of inventorship, see respectively §§89B.04, 89B.05 and 89B.07.

If a purported international application designating the United Kingdom is not accorded an international filing date, whereby it is not treated as an international application (PCT r.20.7(i)), then it does not come within the provisions of subs.(1) and cannot be treated as an application under the Act by virtue of these provisions. However, it does fall for review under the provisions of subs.(5), see §89.30.

An important consequence of subs.(1) is that an international application (UK) is treated as personal property under s.30(1) or, in Scotland, as incorporeal moveable property (s.31(2)) as soon as an international filing date has been accorded. Thus, the rights enjoyed in the United Kingdom under an international application (UK) may be assigned or licensed or otherwise dealt with in the international phase. Whilst a change of applicant may be recorded at the International Bureau under PCT r.92*bis*, there is no facility for recording licences or any other transactions, such as mortgages, before the application enters the UK phase. Also, the right to an international application may be disputed under s.12 in the international phase (s.89B(4), see §89B.11). Similarly, it may be possible to initiate proceedings (under s.13(1) and/or (3), mention of inventor) in the international phase, as suggested in §89B.07.

For the possible prior art effect of an international application (UK), see §89B.09, and for the provisional protection possibly afforded by a published international application (UK), see §89B.10.

Withdrawal in the international phase (subs.(2))

89.27   Subsection (2) expressly provides that an international application (UK), which is withdrawn or considered withdrawn under the PCT, i.e. in the international phase, shall be regarded as withdrawn under the Act. The same applies to the withdrawal, or deemed withdrawal, of a designation of the United Kingdom. Having regard to s.14(9) (withdrawal), see §14.43, which is in Pt I of the Act, and subs.(1) (see §89.26), the reference to withdrawal in s.89(2) appears superfluous. However, subs.(2) is necessary insofar as it covers withdrawal of the United Kingdom designation and deemed withdrawal in the international phase under circumstances to which there is no equivalent in the Act. Nevertheless, subs.(2) does not apply in the case of wrongful finding of deemed withdrawal (see subs.(3) and §89.28)

UK-IPO review of deemed withdrawal (subs.(3))

89.28   As mentioned at §89.25, the PCT does not provide for any appeal in the international phase. Instead, art.25 of the PCT enables the applicant to have a declaration or finding that the international application or a country designation is deemed withdrawn or a refusal to accord the application with an international filing date reviewed separately by each of the designated offices. Subsections 89(3) and (5) are provided pursuant to art.25 of the PCT. Section 89(3) relates to a review when an international application, in which the United Kingdom is designated without a request for a European patent (UK), has been accorded an international filing date and has subsequently been declared to be deemed withdrawn or the designation of the United Kingdom (not accompanied by a request for a European patent (UK)) has subsequently been declared withdrawn. Subsection (5) provides for a review when the receiving office has refused to accord an international filing date to the application and is discussed at §89.30.

Specifically, s.89(3)(a) provides for a review of a declaration by the receiving office (which could be the UK-IPO) that the international application, or the designation of the United Kingdom, is considered withdrawn when the applicant asserts that such declaration results from an error or omission made by the receiving office.

Section 89(3)(a) also enables the effect of an international application, in which the UK-IPO is a designated office, to be maintained in the United Kingdom if the International Bureau has found the international application to be deemed withdrawn because the record copy had not reached the International Bureau by the expiry of the time limit prescribed at r.22.3 of the PCT, as a result of an error or omission on the part of the receiving office or the International Bureau. That time limit is three months from the date of a notification sent by the International Bureau to the applicant that it has not received the record copy.

The expression "an institution having functions under the Treaty", as used in subs.89(3)(a) appears to embrace all the designated and elected offices as well as all the receiving offices, the International Bureau, all the international searching authorities and all the international preliminary examining authorities. Of these, only the receiving office at which the international application was filed and the International Bureau are in a position to do, or omit to do, anything in error which results in the international application or the designation of the United Kingdom being deemed withdrawn under the Treaty.

Section 89(3)(b) provides for a review in the event that the international application was deemed to be withdrawn because the record copy did not reach the International Bureau before expiry of the three-month time limit of r.22.3 of the PCT owing to circumstances outside the control of the applicant. This overlaps para.(a) but embraces the possibility of the failure of the record copy to reach the International Bureau being the result of an error or omission by someone other than the applicant or by an institution other than one having functions under the Treaty. It may be assumed that the word "limited" appearing in this para.(b) is a mistake for "limit prescribed".

The intention of the provision at the end of s.89(3) to the effect that an application shall not be treated as withdrawn "in such other circumstances as may be prescribed" is to enable rules to be made whereby the applicant can apply to proceed with the UK phase if the application has been deemed withdrawn when an application filed under the Act would not have been deemed withdrawn in comparable circumstances. Specifically, rules can be made to implement the provisions of: PCT art.26, relating to the application of national laws to permit correction; PCT art.27(4), enabling more favourable national provisions as to content and form to be applied; and PCT art.48(2) and PCT r.82 bis, relating to the application of national provisions on time limits and extensions of time. The provision at the end of s.89(3) only enables rules to be made for the case wherein the international application is deemed withdrawn and application for review is made, although the PCT provisions just mentioned are not so limited.

Rule 72 permits a specified time limit (which was missed in the international phase and thereby resulted in the international application being declared to be deemed withdrawn) to be extended; or its non-observance to be excused to avoid the application being deemed withdrawn, when an extension or excusal would be granted in comparable circumstances for an application filed under the Act. Thus, by the application of r.107 (see §123.24), the effect of an international application in the United Kingdom can be maintained at the Comptroller's discretion if the application has been declared to be deemed withdrawn because of a failure to respond to an invitation from the receiving office within the specified period. In general, reinstatement may also be possible where the Comptroller determines that powers would have been exercised under r.107 or r.108 to prevent a non-PCT application from being treated as withdrawn in comparable circumstances (MOPP para.89.07).

Section 89(3) does not expressly include the circumstances envisaged by art.25(2)(b) of the PCT which provides for a review when the record copy did reach the International Bureau but only after expiry of the three-month time limit and when the delay was the fault of the applicant but could be excused for reasons admitted under national law. These last provisions are probably embraced by r.72 under the "other circumstances" mentioned at the end of subs.(3).

An example of the possible application of s.89(3), under the generally corresponding provisions of the Patents Rules 1995, is indicated in *Fletcher's International Application* BL O/235/98. Here, an individual inventor had filed an international application which contained no claims defining the matter for which protection was sought, the inventor thinking that the requirement for "claims" was directed to the description indicating "the benefits" realised by the invention. The UK-IPO, acting as the receiving office, failed to notice this and accorded an international filing date. After receipt of the record copy of the international application, the International Bureau notified the UK-IPO of the relevant facts which should have precluded the according of an international filing date and expressed the opinion that the international application should be considered withdrawn (PCT art.14(4)) for failure to include any claim. The Office agreed and duly declared the international application to be considered withdrawn. The hearing officer confirmed the correctness of this decision, noting later that the applicant had, at least to some extent, been misinformed by the UK-IPO and he would therefore have exercised the equivalent of what is now r.107 had the application been one under the Act. Priority had been claimed from an application under the Act for which no claims had been filed and the invention had been exhibited during the priority year. The hearing officer, although making a decision on behalf of the receiving office and not on behalf of the Comptroller, went on to consider what redress was still available to the applicant, at least so far as the United Kingdom was concerned. He indicated that s.89(3) might be invoked to enable the application to be treated as a United Kingdom application having, as its filing date, the international filing date, thereby enabling the priority claim to be preserved. The late filing of claims could be excused under the rule in effect at that time and, at that time, no filing fee was payable to the UK-IPO. Accordingly, the applicant was recommended to seek a review under subs.(3).

The general discretion under r.101 of the Patents Rules 1995 no longer applies.

Rule 72 (see §89.06) enables rr.110 and 111, reprinted at §§123.28 and 123.29, to be applied if, in any particular circumstances, they are more favourable to the applicant than r.82 of the PCT, but only when the international application, or the designation of the United Kingdom, has been considered withdrawn as a result of a postal delay. Note that, whereas r.82 of the PCT applies to a postal delay or interruption anywhere, rr.110 and 111 apply only to such a delay or interruption within the United Kingdom, even though these rules are not limited to the case where the delayed or lost letter or document is posted within the United Kingdom.

A finding that the international application (or the designation of the United Kingdom) is deemed withdrawn is reviewed upon written request, accompanied by a supporting statement, and the payment of any fee prescribed. The prescribed fee, if any, is quite distinct from the (national) fee payable under s.89A(3) when entering the UK phase in the normal way (r.71) and its amount, as prescribed in the Patents (Fees) Rules is currently zero. According to PCT art.25(1) and (2) and PCT r.51.1 and 51.3, the applicant must request the International Bureau to forward a copy of the international application to the Patent Office and must file any prescribed translation at, and pay the national fee (if any) to, the Patent Office all within two months of the notification that the application is considered withdrawn. However, as pointed out in *Fletcher's International Application* BL O/235/98, neither s.89(3) nor the equivalent rule at that time called for observance of these time limits or even prescribed a time limit for making a request for review. Indeed, neither reflects any of the above PCT provisions, with the exception that r.71 does mention the payment of the prescribed fee, if any, but without a time limit. Also, r.71, in requiring the applicant to state reasons for the request, appears to be at variance with art.25 of the PCT which obliges designated offices to make a decision when the applicant has fulfilled the conditions of art.25 of the PCT, whether or not the applicant has made an express request for a review. On the other hand, it is unlikely that the Comptroller could come to a decision favourable to the applicant without the applicant presenting him with the relevant facts.

Because the request to the International Bureau under PCT art.25(1)(a) or (b) to transmit a copy of the international application to the UK-IPO must be made by the applicant or his agent in the international phase (e.g. in Japan or Australia) and the procedures under the Act must be performed by the representative before the Office in the United Kingdom, good and speedy liaison is essential. Presumably, the International Bureau would refuse to effect the transmittal if the request is received belatedly, there being no provision for any extension of time. It would then become necessary to find some other way for the Office to be provided with a copy of the international application. In the *Fletcher* case (above) this was not a problem, since the UK-IPO, as a designated office, was also the receiving office and was therefore already in possession of a copy (the "home copy"). All that had to be done was for the applicant to request the Office to make a copy of the home copy for use in its national file (PCT art.30(2)(a) and (3)); see the *Fletcher* decision (above). When the UK-IPO was not the receiving office, it would become necessary to find some other way for the UK-IPO to be supplied with an acceptably authenticated copy of the international application and for failure to meet the two-month time limit of PCT r.51.1 to be excused.

According to the MOPP para.89.06, if any document of the international application is not in English or Welsh, a translation is required under r.113(1) and (2) (reprinted in §123.30). It may be implied that, if the translation is not filed within the two-month time limit prescribed in r.51.3 of the PCT, the Comptroller may extend this time limit upon any such terms as he may direct (r.71(7)). Clearly, the UK-IPO cannot examine the application if it is not in English or Welsh and a translation is not supplied, and may not even be able to review the finding that the application or the designation of the United Kingdom is deemed withdrawn. The applicant would be well advised to furnish any translation that may be needed along with the request under subs.(3) for the international application (or the designation of the United Kingdom) to be treated as not withdrawn, rather than speculate as to what provisions in the Act or the Rules enable the Comptroller to require a translation and as to when it should be filed and what extension, if any, is obtainable. In any case, any necessary translation must be furnished to enable the UK phase to begin (s.89A(3)(a)). The need for a translation, where required, is also mentioned in the *PCT Applicant's Guide*, Vol.II, (National Phase), para.6.019 (see the reference thereto in *PCT Applicant's Guide*, National Chapter (GB), para.GB.17). Rule 71 makes no mention of filing PF 9A (or PF 9) and PF 10. This implies that the UK-IPO may come to a decision on the request before PF 9A is filed. Rule 71(5) enables the Comptroller to call for the filing of any document he may specify which presumably may include PF 9A and PF 10.

Rule 71(7) enables the Comptroller to shorten time limits as well as extend them. In particular, he may require PF 9A to be filed well in advance of the normal period of two months from the date on which the national phase begins as prescribed by r.68(3) (see §89B.16) in order that publication under s.16 will not be delayed unduly (see §89B.14). Furthermore, r.71(7)(b) confirms the Comptroller's entitlement to amend documents to implement his decision in the review.

No time limit is prescribed for filing the priority document in support of a priority claim. As noted in §89A.15, the Comptroller must invite the applicant to file the priority document within a reasonable time limit before disregarding a priority claim (PCT r.17.1(c)).

An application to which subs.(1) continues to apply, by virtue of subs.(3), becomes subject to the provisions of ss.89A and 89B, except that those of s.89A(3) may already have been met. The application will effectively be in the same position as one for which early national processing has been expressly requested under PCT art.23(3), and the comments at §§89A.16 and 89B.14–89B.20 thus become applicable.

The decision in *Vapocure Technologies' Application* [1990] R.P.C. 1 CA was not strictly on a review under PCT art.25, because it did not concern the international application, or the designation of the United Kingdom, being deemed withdrawn, nor a refusal to accord an international filing date. What it did relate to was an attempt to enter the UK phase when a rectification, authorised by the receiving office, to add the designations of the United Kingdom and Switzerland was refused by the International Bureau because the authorisation of the rectification did not reach the International Bureau before preparations for publication had been completed (PCT r.91.1(g- *bis*.)). The absence of the designation of the United Kingdom meant that there was no application in existence which could be corrected by the UK-IPO, although the Swiss Patent Office was apparently able to recognise that the designation of Switzerland had been included by the rectification. The correction in the UK phase of errors made in the international phase is discussed further at §89B.12.

For a general discussion on the issues involved in a request for review before designated offices under PCT art.25, see the PCTH at Ch.28.

International application designating the EPO (subs.(4))

89.29   In the case of a Euro-PCT application, i.e. an international application in which a European patent is requested in respect of the designation of the United Kingdom, s.130(4A) ensures that ss.89, 89A and 89B do not operate in respect of such designation. The designation is then governed by the provisions of s.79; see §§79.02 et seq.

Section 130(4A) (see §130.07), which replaced previous s.89(4), now repealed, defines an international application for a European patent (UK) as one not to be interpreted also as an international application for a patent (UK). All new international applications are now deemed to designate all PCT contracting states bound by the Treaty at the international filing date and under EPC 2000 an international application (EP) automatically designates all contracting states, see revised art.79 of the EPC.

For a review under PCT art.25 by the EPO as a designated office, see the EPH at s.17.6.

UK-IPO review of refusal to accord international filing date (subs.(5))

89.30   Whereas subs.(3) covers a wrongful finding in the international phase that an international application (UK) is considered withdrawn, subs.(5) provides for a review of a decision by the receiving office (which could be the UK-IPO) to refuse to accord an international filing date so that, in the absence of a successful review, the international application would fail to come into existence. Thus, the term "international application for a patent" (as used in s.89(5), and in r.71 has to be interpreted as meaning a purported international application, rather than an actual such application as the definition of this term in s.130(1) indicates.

The procedure for review is prescribed at r.71. It is essentially the same as that under subs.(3) (see §89.28) and, likewise, involves: the filing of a written request, together with a supporting statement and payment of the prescribed fee, if any. The Comptroller may call for further documents, information or evidence (r.71(5)). However, there is one important difference in that a copy of the notification by the receiving office refusing a filing date under the PCT must be attached to the request to the International Bureau to forward copies of the international application to the designated offices (PCT r.51.2).

The prescribed fee, if any, replaces the filing fee (currently zero) and is not the same as the (national) fee payable under s.89A(3). The amount of the fee is prescribed in the Patents (Fees) Rules and is currently also zero.

Neither s.89(5) nor r.71 prescribes a time limit for applying for a review under subs.(5) and neither mentions any need for fulfilment of the conditions of art.25(1)(a) and (2)(a) of the PCT, other than the payment of a national fee, if any. These conditions are: requesting the International Bureau to transmit a copy of the purported international application and documents from the file to the Office; the filing of a translation, if required; and compliance with a two-month time limit (PCT r.51.1). What is said in §89.28 on these matters in connection with subs.(3) applies equally to subs.(5), except that s.89A(3)(a) is inapplicable, the application being not treated as an international application.

For a review under PCT art.25 generally, see the PCTH at Ch.28 and for a review by the EPO as designated office, see the EPH, s.17.6.

An example of an application for review under subs.(5) is *Unique Products' Purported International Application* BL O/147/95, noted I.P.D. 18115. Here the United States Patent and Trademark Office, as receiving office, had refused to accord an international filing date to a purported international application because none of the applicants was a resident or national of a PCT Member State. The Comptroller held the refusal to have been correct under the PCT and, accordingly, he could not allow the purported international application to be treated as an application under the Act. The decision might have been different if it had been argued that the applicants (as nationals of Taiwan, not a contracting state) should have been treated by the receiving office as citizens of China (which is such a State), pointing out that the United States Patent and Trademark Office does not operate the procedure prescribed at PCT Administrative Instructions, Section 329 and PCT Receiving Office Guidelines, para.49 for correction of the applicant's state of residence and/or nationality (PCT Receiving Office Guidelines, footnote to para.49; *PCT Applicant's Guide*, Vol.I (Introduction to the International Phase), para.6.036). Also, in *Intelligent Quotient's Application* [1996] R.P.C. 258, an international application was initially filed without the international request form, this being belatedly filed outside the convention priority period. As an international filing date had been accorded, be it one that resulted in a loss of convention priority, the Comptroller held that s.89(5) was inapplicable.

An application which has been refused an international filing date, but allowed to proceed as a United Kingdom application under subs.(5), is thereafter not to be regarded as an international application for the purposes of subss.(1)–(4) and ss.89A and 89B, since subs.(1) requires the international application to be accorded a filing date for that subsection to apply. Therefore, an application refused an international filing date, but allowed to proceed under subs.(5), becomes treated ab initio as an application under ss.14 et seq. and all time limits will be those prescribed under Pt I of the Act and described in the commentaries on the relevant sections. However, r.72 seems to give the Comptroller wide discretion to amend such time limits (by extending them or shortening them) and to amend documents.

An interesting situation might arise if an international application is refused an international filing date because claims have not been filed. The Act has a more favourable requirement than the PCT inasmuch as a filing date can be accorded under the Act without claims being filed (s.15(1)), as discussed in §15.10. Therefore, the way is open for the applicant to invoke art.27(4) of the PCT, when seeking a review under subs.(5), to secure a filing date for the United Kingdom in the absence of claims, although there is no rule, other than possibly r.107, to help the applicant. Now that the United Kingdom filing fee payable on PF 1 is zero, it would not currently matter whether the international and other fees had been paid on the purported international application at the time of filing. A comparable situation arose in the case of *Fletcher's International Application* BL O/235/98, discussed in §89.28. The international application was deemed withdrawn because, after an international filing date had been accorded, it was found that the application did not contain any claim and therefore did not fulfil the minimum requirements for an international filing date to be accorded. The hearing officer, although acting on behalf of the receiving office and not the Comptroller, indicated that it might be possible to treat the application as a United Kingdom application under subs.(3) because the late filing of claims could be excused and because no filing fee was payable to the UK-IPO. Since it is the filing fee and not the national fee that is relevant here and the filing fee is still zero, this observation remains true.

In *Penife International's International Application* BL O/382/03 it was confirmed that the international application could not be accorded a filing date because the application did not contain "a part which on the face of it appears to be a claim or claims" as required by art.11(1)(e) of the PCT. This was upheld on judicial review (see [2004] R.P.C. 37 at 737) on the basis that a distinct claim, identified as such, had to be included in the application, and it was not sufficient that the description contained a "consistory clause" describing the invention. This decision was generally followed in *Knight's International Application* both at first instance BL O/114/06 and on appeal [2007] EWHC 2264.

In the future in this situation, if any priority document contains claims, and the applicant has included a statement of "incorporation by reference" from that priority document (as discussed in §89.11 above) it might now be possible to incorporate the necessary claims by reference argue that this should and thereby secure a filing date. However, particularly since not all designated/elected states may recognise this as effective in the national phase (by reservations notified under PCT r.20(8)), this should be viewed only as a last resort and should not be relied on. It remains safest always to file claims in the normal way to secure an international filing date.

Note that an international application accorded an international filing date, and later considered to be withdrawn under PCT art.14 because the receiving office later found that the international application did not fulfil the minimum requirement of art.11(1) of the PCT, will be entitled to a review under subs.(3) and not under subs.(5). This is illustrated by *Fletcher's International Application* (above).

PRACTICE UNDER SECTION 89

International phase

89.31   Readers wishing to file an international application are strongly recommended to refer to the PCTH, and/or to Vol.I (Introduction to the International Phase) of the *PCT Applicant's Guide*, for guidance on all essential procedures relating to the filing of an international application and its processing in the international phase. As noted above, this is now available only online from the WIPO website, *http://www.wipo.int*. Blank forms, such as the international request form (PCT/RO/101) and the demand for international preliminary examination form (PCT/IPEA/401) are available from the UK-IPO and from the EPO. They are also included in the *PCT Applicant's Guide* as Annexes X and Y in Vol.I (International Phase) and may be copied from there. These Forms are further available on the WIPO website noted above and are accompanied by respective annexes which comprise fee calculation sheets. The forms are also accompanied by respective notes. If meticulous attention is paid to these notes, the applicant should be able to avoid any serious mistakes in preparing and filing an international application. The International Unit at the UK-IPO (tel. 01633 814 586) is also very helpful and may be consulted in any event to check on the current amounts of the fees payable, see §89.21. An e-mail address is also provided in the MOPP para.89.04 (Code of Practice for Applicants and Agents) to which queries and requests for guidance may be directed.

Users of the PCT are also strongly recommended to consult the *PatentScope* portal of the WIPO website. In particular, the section "PCT Resources" (at *http://www.wipo.int*) provides a great many very useful documents and resources, including, for example: current PCT Forms; information on current fees; the full online *PCT Applicant's Guide* (updated regularly); copies of the *PCT Newsletter* (since 2000); current copies of the Patent Cooperation Treaty, Regulations and Administrative Instructions; Guidelines for Authorities and Offices; details of IP Offices' closing dates; information on electronic filing (PCT-SAFE software); details of reservations and incompatibilities; details of time limits for entering national/regional phases; details of power of attorney waivers; a current list of PCT contracting states; ISA and IPEA agreements; a history of the PCT Regulations; Washington Diplomatic Conference on the PCT; and information on PCT seminars, meetings and documents, PCT presentations and forthcoming PCT Reform. Copies of the *PCT Gazette* (from 1998) are available from the website: *http://www.wipo.int*.

All documents, other than the fee calculation sheet, should be filed in triplicate (r.65(1)). The Office also requires the usual fee sheet in addition to the fee calculation sheet. The UK-IPO, in its capacity as a receiving office, has waived the general requirement under PCT rr.90.4(b) and/or 90.5(a)(ii) to submit a separate power of attorney and/or a copy of a general power of attorney (*PCT Gazette* 16/2004 of April 15, 2004 updating *PCT Gazette* S-01/2004 (E), Annex C (GB), p.276). However, the UK-IPO has indicated that there will be particular instances in which a separate power of attorney or a copy of a general power of attorney will still be required. These include where an agent or common representative, who is not indicated on the Request form at the time of filing, performs an action after filing or where it is unclear that an agent or common representative has power to act on behalf of the applicant. Powers of attorney will also continue to be required for any withdrawal requests in accordance with rr.90.4(e) and 90.5(d) of the PCT. Such power of attorney is recognised by all the competent international authorities, see §89.24, as regards rights of representation, but no special form is prescribed for appointment of agent under the PCT. Suitable forms of specific and general powers of attorney can be found in the *PCT Applicant's Guide*, Vol.I (International Phase) at Annex Z.

If priority is claimed from an earlier application (be it a UK national application or an international application) filed at the UK-IPO, a request for the Office to make a certified copy to be transmitted to the International Bureau should be made by checking "Box No. VI" on Form PCT/RO/101 with the prescribed fee for a certificate sealed and attached to documents (see also §89.20). Potentially, under PCT r.17.1(*b-bis*), priority documents may also be made available through the "WIPO Digital Access Service for Priority Documents" (DAS; see the discussion in the *PCT Newsletter* 01/2010, pp.3–4). This is subject to participation of the relevant Offices in the DAS scheme. The UK-IPO is a participant in the Priority Document Access Scheme, as described in the Notice in the *Patents Journal*, January 20, 2010 (Journal 6296, p.6). In particular, the UK-IPO is prepared to make certain priority documents available via DAS or alternatively applicants may request that the International Bureau retrieve a copy of an earlier application from DAS for use as a priority document (see also *PCT Applicant's Guide* Vol. I (International Phase), Annex C (GB) and the Notes entitled "Priority Document Access Service (PDAS)" on the UK-IPO website). However, applicants or their agents wishing to use this service are warned that it is very important to complete all of the various required steps within 16 months from the priority date (*PCT Newsletter*, 03/2010, pp.1–2).

It is recommended that the transmittal fee, the basic fee, the designation fees and the search fee payable in respect of an international application should all be paid when the application is filed in order that none of these is overlooked.

It is possible to file an international application at the UK-IPO by fax. The fax number is 01633 814 444. Details of the provisions for use of fax filing facilities are published regularly in the *Patents Journal*, e.g. *Patents Journal* December 7, 2005, and can also be obtained from the UK-IPO at the following address "Fax Filing, Concept House, Cardiff Road, Newport, South Wales NP10 8QQ" (tel. 01633 814 570), see also [1999] *CIPA* 766. It is also possible to pay fees due on an international application, for which the UK-IPO is the receiving office, by a fax debit order from a deposit account established and held at the Patent Office for fee payments. Use of fax filing is described further at §119.05.

Although the email addresses of the UK-IPO and other international authorities are well publicised and are included in the *PCT Applicant's Guide*, Vol.I (International Phase), Annex B1 (GB), it is not possible, at present, to file international applications by simple email. Also, email should not be used for correspondence in connection with the processing of international applications, particularly when time limits are important, as there is no guarantee as to how email will be handled by the recipient (cf. the Notice dated June 2, 1999 concerning correspondence with the EPO via email; OJ EPO 1999, 509). Fax transmission should be used for urgent correspondence. It should be noted that as far as the International Bureau is concerned, only informal enquiries which are not related to specific international applications may be sent by email by the applicants or their agents. Email cannot be validly used by an applicant or agent to perform any procedural act before the International Bureau (*PCT Newsletter*, 04/2009, p.10).

The PCT request form (PCT/RO/101) includes a field which allows applicants or their agents to include an email address (only one such address can be provided on the form) with their international applications. If provided without marking one of the associated check-boxes, such an address will normally be used only for communications for which telephones or fax would otherwise have been used (*PCT Newsletter* 05/2008, pp.9–10). There are also check-boxes which, if marked, will authorise any PCT Authority to send advance copies of certain notifications by email (*PCT Newsletter* 05/2008, pp.9–10). If the first such box (request for "advance copies followed by paper notifications") is marked, such advance email communications will not replace paper communications and the latter will remain the legal copy. Applicants are warned that if they wish to receive such email notification(s) from the International Bureau, their email system should be set up in such a way as to ensure that any emails originating from WIPO are not treated as "spam" and that the WIPO email address is recognised as a "safe" address so that it is not blocked by any "spam" filter (*PCT Newsletter* 06/2008, p.5). There is also an alternative check-box which allows applicants to specify that such notifications will be sent exclusively by email so that the email notification will be the legal notification and no paper copy will be sent (*PCT Newsletter* 01/2010, pp.6–7). However, it is not clear that it will normally be in an applicant's or agent's interest to mark this latter box, in case for any reason a relevant email is not received. Rather, it would seem to be advisable in most cases not to check this box and instead to check the box for "advance copies followed by paper notifications" so as to continue to receive paper copies of such notifications, at least as a back-up.

It should also be noted that it is not possible to reply by email to the International Bureau and any such email would not be accepted (*PCT Newsletter* 05/2008, pp.9–10).

A PCT Online Document Upload Facility has been established which allows applicants and/or their agents to submit certain electronic documents (currently in PDF form) to the International Bureau via a web interface (*PCT Newsletter*, 01/2010, pp.2–3). It should be noted that this service is not to be used for the initial filing of international applications and is limited to the submission of later-filed documents that are normally addressed to WIPO in its capacity as International Bureau only (and not in its capacity as receiving Office).

The UK-IPO, in its capacity as a receiving office, has now notified the International Bureau under PCT r.89bis.1(d) that it is prepared to receive and process international applications in electronic form (*PCT Gazette* 32/2004, p.18092) using epoline® or PCT-SAFE software. Applications may be filed either online (PCT Administrative Instructions Annex F. Online filing attracts a reduction in the international filing fee and a further reduction if the application is in character coded format. So-called "mixed-mode" filings of nucleotide and/or amino acid sequence listings are no longer allowed, so that international applications including sequence listings must be filed either entirely electronically (in which case there will normally be a cost saving in page fees) or in paper form (in which latter case full page fees will be payable and a data carrier will also need to be provided).

The UK-IPO no longer accepts PCT applications filed using the PCT-EASY mode of the PCT-SAFE software and any application filed in this way will now be treated as a paper filing (*PCT Newsletter* 02/2009, p.4).

For the filing of international applications directly at the International Bureau in electronic form (subject to national security provisions), see the PCT-SAFE page of WIPO's *PatentScope* website: *http://www.wipo.int*. The PCT-SAFE software package is available for downloading from the website or, upon request, the PCT-SAFE Help Desk will send a CD-ROM installation by mail, free of charge. Digital certificates, required for signing and transmitting applications online, can be obtained through the Certificates section of the website in a simple online transaction. Electronic filing presents various potentially complex issues and applicants wishing to file international applications electronically will need to review the technical requirements carefully. Those without previous experience may find it helpful to use the PCT-SAFE software, in "Demo" mode, to send test filings to the "demo" server of the RO/IB (and other receiving offices, provided that the receiving office selected has such an option available), before attempting to file a "real" international application in electronic form. Possible advantages, apart from the modest reductions in fees, include the possibility for immediate confirmation of receipt by the International Bureau in the case of international applications filed online.

In the case of an international application in paper form which discloses one or more nucleotide and/or amino acid sequences, the application may be accompanied by a data carrier containing a sequence listing in accordance with WIPO Standard ST.25 (which is identical to the PCT sequence listing standard at Annex C to the PCT Administrative Instructions) in anticipation of the EPO, as international searching authority, requiring as it does such data carrier (see Supplement No.2 to OJ EPO 11/1998). The UK-IPO forwards the data carrier to the EPO with the search copy of the international application. Any later filed data carrier should be filed directly with the EPO which will in any event invite the applicant to file this within a period to be set by it if such a data carrier is not presented on filing. Compliance with WIPO Standard ST.25 is mandatory before the EPO can conduct the international search or international preliminary examination in respect of subject-matter relating to the sequence as is the filing of a data carrier recording the sequence in the form prescribed, see the *PCT Applicant's Guide*, Vol.1, Annex L and Supplement No.2 to OJ EPO 11/98.

A filing certificate on Form PCT/RO/105 is not issued by the receiving office until the latter has checked that the application fulfils the minimum requirements for an international filing date to be accorded. This may take several weeks. If an applicant, or agent, wishes to receive confirmation that his communication to the UK-IPO has been received, he may file a duplicate of his covering letter and request that this be returned to him as confirmation of receipt (*Patents Journal* February 7, 1990 and (1989–90) 19 *CIPA* 130), but this procedure is no confirmation that the papers filed fulfil the minimum requirements for an international filing date to be accorded. Any invitation to bring the papers into fulfilment may be received too late for a priority claim to be saved, see (1991–92) 21 *CIPA* 194. The UK-IPO does not make use of Form PCT/RO/125 which WIPO makes available for the purpose of confirmation of receipt.

Any amendments to the claims under PCT art.19.1, i.e. after receipt of the international search report, and any explanatory statement, should be filed in single copy but must be filed directly at the International Bureau.

When the UK-IPO is the receiving office for an international application, a demand for international preliminary examination must be filed at the EPO: in Munich, The Hague or Berlin. A single copy suffices. The demand may be filed by fax. The EPO addresses and fax numbers are given in the *PCT Applicant's Guide* at Annex B2(EP). The handling and international preliminary examination fees must also be paid directly to the EPO and may be paid in any of the currencies of the EPC countries, subject to compliance with the EPO Fees Rules. It is convenient that a cheque or deposit account debit order accompany the demand. If the demand is filed by fax, the cheque or deposit account debit order can be sent with a confirmation copy of the fax as the fees can be paid up to one month after the date of an invitation from the examining authority to pay these fees. If any amendments (which should be filed in triplicate) are to accompany the demand, they may likewise be sent with a confirmation of a demand made by fax. Nevertheless, the EPO does not invite written confirmation of a demand itself sent by fax unless the reproduction is inferior; if confirmation is invited, it must be filed within one month of such invitation.

The above deals with points which are, to a certain extent, peculiar to the UK-IPO when the latter is acting as an international authority. A fuller description of practice under the PCT is beyond the scope of this Work and reference should be made to the PCTH and the *PCT Applicant's Guide*.

Request for review (subss.(3) and (5))

A request to the Comptroller for a review under subs.(3) or (5) following a declaration **89.32** by the receiving office or a finding by the International Bureau that the international application or the designation of the United Kingdom is deemed withdrawn or a refusal by the receiving office to accord an international filing date is made by letter which includes a supporting statement, setting out the facts on which the applicant relies, and is accompanied by the prescribed fee, if any (r.71(3). The unofficial PF NP.1 (available on the UK-IPO website *http://www.ipo.gov.uk*) should not be used when making a request for review (see note c) to PF NP.1). Although r.71 does not mention the filing of a translation, the requirement to file a translation is included in art.25(2)(a) of the PCT. The statement should give details of the alleged error or omission or the international authority by which the application, or the designation of the United Kingdom, was declared withdrawn or by which no international filing date was accorded; or, alternatively, of the circumstances by which the international application was not timely received by the International Bureau; or, alternatively, of the other circumstances by which an irregularity or a time limit missed in the international phase and resulting in the international application being found to be deemed withdrawn should be rectified under r.107 or extended under r.108.

A copy of the international application is supplied to the UK-IPO by the International Bureau on a request from the applicant to the International Bureau pursuant to PCT art.25(1) or (2) and PCT r.51. Such a request can at the same time ask the International Bureau to transmit copies to other designated offices. When the request is under subs.(5), it must be accompanied by a copy of the negative determination from the receiving office (PCT r.51.2).

The period for requesting the International Bureau to transmit a copy of the international application is two months from the date of the letter notifying the applicant of the declaration or finding (PCT r.51.1) and is inextensible. Although r.51.3 of the PCT prescribes the same two month time limit for paying the national fee, if any (the fee actually prescribed under subss.(3) and (5) is zero), and filing a translation of the international application, if required, no time limit is prescribed in the Act or the Rules. For a discussion of the effects of this omission, see §89.28. For an explanation of the translation requirements, see §89A.19.

For particulars of other forms and documents which may be required after a request under subs.(3), e.g. PF 7, PF 9A, PF 10, priority document(s) and translation(s) thereof, see §§89A.24–89A.31. After a successful request under subs.(5), the application is to be treated as one under the Act, the documentary requirements for which are listed in §14.36. Under subs.(5), the date of filing for such an application is to be as the Comptroller may direct, and this date will determine the time limits within which other forms and documents must be filed, subject to any alterations to time limits made by the Comptroller under r.71 and such extensions as may be possible under r.108.

PF 9A attracts the full search fee, since an international search report will not have been drawn up.

SECTION 89A [ADDED]

International and national phases of application

89A.01 **89A.**—(1) The provisions of the Patent Co-operation Treaty relating to publication, search, examination and amendment, and not those of this Act, apply to an international application for a patent (UK) during the international phase of the application.

(2) The international phase of the application means the period from the filing of the application in accordance with the Treaty until the national phase of the application begins.

(3) The national phase of the application begins

(a) when the prescribed period expires, provided any necessary translation of the application into English has been filed at the Patent Office and the prescribed fee has been paid by the applicant; or

(b) on the applicant expressly requesting the comptroller to proceed earlier with the national phase of the application, filing at the Patent Office—

(i) a copy of the application, if none has yet been sent to the Patent Office in accordance with the Treaty, and

(ii) any necessary translation of the application into English, and paying the prescribed fee.

For this purpose a "copy of the application" includes a copy published in accordance with the Treaty in a language other than that in which it was originally filed.

(4) If the prescribed period expires without the conditions mentioned in subsection (3)(a) being satisfied, the application shall be taken to be withdrawn.

(5) Where during the international phase the application is amended in accordance with the Treaty, the amendment shall be treated as made under this Act if—

(a) when the prescribed period expires, any necessary translation of the amendment into English has been filed at the Patent Office, or

(b) where the applicant expressly requests the comptroller to proceed earlier with the national phase of the application, there is then filed at the Patent Office—

(i) a copy of the amendment, if none has yet been sent to the Patent Office in accordance with the Treaty, and

(ii) any necessary translation of the amendment into English;

otherwise the amendment shall be disregarded.

(6) The comptroller shall on payment of the prescribed fee publish any translation filed at the Patent Office under subsection (3) or (5) above.

Note. Section 89A was added by the CDPA 1988 (c.48) Sch.5(25), operative from January 7, 1991 (SI 1990/2168).

RELEVANT RULES—RULES 66–70

Rule 66—Beginning of national phase

66.—(1) The prescribed period for the purposes of section 89A(3)(a) and (5)(a) is thirty one months beginning with— **89A.02**

(a) where there is no declared priority date, the date of filing of the application;

(b) where there is a declared priority date, that date.

(2) But where the applicant has been notified under rule 69(5), the period prescribed for the purposes of section 89A(3)(a) and (5)(a) is three months beginning with the date of the notification.

(3) Where an international application for a patent (UK) has begun the national phase, a request for permission to make a late declaration may be made under section 5(2B) before the end of the period of one month beginning with the date the national phase of the application begins.

Rule 67—International exhibitions

67.—(1) Paragraph (2) applies where an applicant, on filing an international application for a patent (UK), states in writing to the receiving office that the invention has been displayed at an international exhibition. **89A.03**

(2) The prescribed period for the purposes of section 2(4)(c) is two months beginning with the date on which the national phase begins.

Rule 68—Altered prescribed periods

68.—(1) This rule applies to an international application for a patent (UK) which has begun the national phase of the application. **89A.04**

(2) The period prescribed for the purposes of section 13(2) is—

  (a) the period prescribed by rule 10(3); or

  (b) if it expires later, the period of two months beginning with the date on which the national phase begins.

(3) The period prescribed for the purposes of sections 15(10)(c) and (d) and 17(1) is—

  (a) the period prescribed by rule 22(2) and (7); or

  (b) if it expires later, the period of two months beginning with the date on which the national phase begins.

(4) The period prescribed for the purposes of section 18(1) is—

  (a) thirty three months beginning with—

    (i) where there is no declared priority date, the date of filing of the application; or

    (ii) where there is a declared priority date, that date; or

  (b) if it expires later, the period of two months beginning with the date on which the national phase begins.

Rule 69—Necessary translations under section 89A(3) and (5)

89A.05   **69.**—(1) A translation is necessary for the purposes of section 89A(3) where any of the following are not in English—

  (a) the international application for a patent (UK) as published in accordance with the Patent Co-operation Treaty;

  (b) where the information mentioned in paragraph 3(2)(a) and (b) of Schedule 1 (biological material) has been provided, that information.

(2) Where the applicant expressly requests the comptroller to proceed with the national phase before the end of the period prescribed by rule 66(1), the translation must include the request and abstract.

(3) But paragraph (2) does not apply where a copy of the application, as published in accordance with the Patent Co-operation Treaty, is available to the comptroller.

(4) A translation of an amendment is necessary for the purposes of section 89A(5) where any amendment made to the application is not in English and has either been—

  (a) published under the Patent Co-operation Treaty; or

  (b) annexed to the International Preliminary Examination Report.

(5) At the end of the period prescribed by rule 66(1), the comptroller must notify the applicant that a necessary translation is missing if—

  (a) a translation of the application has been filed, but a translation of the amendment has not been filed; or

  (b) the information mentioned in paragraph 3(2)(a) and (b) of Schedule 1 (biological material) has been provided, but a translation of that information has not been filed,

and the prescribed fee has been paid.

Rule 70—Requirements of necessary translations

70.—(1) This rule applies to translations which are necessary for the purposes   **89A.06**
of section 89A(3) and (5).

(2) Such a translation is necessary for only that part of the application which
is in a language other than English.

(3) Where the application includes a drawing which is annotated, the translation shall include either—

(a) a copy of the original drawing where the original annotations have been
replaced by annotations in English; or

(b) a new drawing with the annotations in English.

(4) Where a title has been established for the application by the International
Searching Authority, the translation must include that title (and not any title
which was included in the application as it was originally filed).

(5) Where—

(a) the description of the invention includes a sequence listing; and

(b) the listing complies with the relevant requirements of the Patent Co-
operation Treaty,

the translation of the application may exclude a translation of the sequence listing.

(6) This rule applies to translations of amendments as it applies to translations
of applications and accordingly references to "application" shall be construed as
references to "amendment".

OTHER RELEVANT RULES

The following rules are also relevant to international applications entering the UK   **89A.07**
national phase:

rule 2	(Interpretation), reprinted in §123.04;
rule 6	(declaration of priority), reprinted in §5.07;
rule 10	(procedure where applicant is not inventor or sole inventor), reprinted in §13.04;
rule 103	(address for service), reprinted at §32.02;
rule 25	(formal requirements), reprinted in §15A.04;
rule 44	(entries in the register), reprinted at §32.04;
rule 101	(agents);
rule 105	(correction of errors in patents and applications), reprinted at §117.02;
rule 107	(correction of irregularities), reprinted at §123.24;
rule 108	(extension of time limits), reprinted at §123.25;
rule 110	(interrupted days), reprinted at §123.28;
rule 111	(delays in communication services), reprinted at §123.29;
rule 113	(translations), reprinted at §123.30;
rule 115	(establishing the accuracy of translations) reprinted at §123.32; and
Schedule 1	(biological material) reprinted at §125A.03.

COMMENTARY ON SECTION 89A

Scope of the section

89A.08   This is the second of the three sections which concern international applications (UK), and the general remarks at §89.08 are relevant to this section and to s.89B. Section 89A(1) ensures that the provisions of the PCT relating to the processing of the application in the international phase override the corresponding provisions under the Act, notwithstanding s.89(1) (see §89.26). Section 89A(2) defines the international phase, and s.89A(3) defines the national phase and outlines the procedures to secure valid entry into the United Kingdom phase. Section 89A(4) ensures that an international application does not enter the United Kingdom phase if the procedures prescribed in and under s.89A(3) are not completed. Section 89A(5) concerns the effect of amendments made in the international phase. Section 89A(6) concerns publication of a translation of the application and of any amendment made in the international phase and is relevant to so-called provisional protection arising on publication, see §89B.10.

Effect of proceedings in the international phase (subs.(1))

89A.09   Whilst in principle an international application (UK) is treated ab initio as an application under the Act (s.89(1) and see §89.26), s.89A(1) prescribes that the PCT provisions for publication, search, examination and amendment take precedence in the international phase. The PCT provisions are contained mainly in PCT arts 15–19, 21, 31–35, 38 and 41. International search, international publication and international preliminary examination are briefly described at §§89.12, 89.13 and 89.16 respectively. Amendment is discussed in each of these paragraphs. It has been held, in relation to the corresponding provisions of the former (now repealed) s.89(3), (not reprinted herein), that "the provisions of the PCT relating to publication, search, examination and amendment" are to be construed narrowly so as to exclude the provisions of the PCT relating to all other matters, such as corrections of errors and irregularities in procedure (*Prangley's Application* [1988] R.P.C. 187 CA, see §89B.12).

The effect of publication in the international phase is specified in s.89B(2) (see §89B.08). The effects of search and examination in the international phase are taken into account in s.89B(5) (see §§89B.15 and 89B.16). The effect of amendment in the international phase is subject to s.89A(5) and (6) (see §89A.18). The provisions in the Act relating to publication, search, examination and amendment appear principally in ss.16–19, see the commentaries on those sections.

Supply of copy of international application and of the international preliminary examination report to the UK-IPO

89A.10   Article 20 of the PCT prescribes that the International Bureau shall communicate the international application to each designated office except to any designated office that has waived its right, in whole or in part, to receive this communication. In practice, many designated offices, including the UK-IPO, have waived their right in part and only receive this communication at their specific request to the International Bureau and have notified the International Bureau that the applicant is not required to file a copy of the international application, even if the communication under PCT art.20 has not taken place. A specific request for the PCT art.20 communication is made by the UK-IPO when the applicant has indicated that he wishes to enter the UK phase of an international application (*PCT Newsletter*, 04/1997, p.5, under the heading "Practical Advice"). Thus, it is not normally necessary for the applicant to file a copy of the international application when entering the UK phase. An exception arises when the applicant makes an express request for an early start to national processing before the Office, as discussed in §89A.16. The communication under PCT art.20 comprises a copy of the published PCT application (see §89.14) when the application is both filed and published in the same language. It comprises both a copy of the application as filed and a copy of the published PCT application when the application is published as a translation (subs.(3)). The UK-IPO, as the government authority of a PCT Contracting State entrusted with the granting of patents, does receive copies of all published international applications under PCT r.87.

For international applications that have undergone international preliminary examination under PCT Chapter II (§89.16), it is prescribed in PCT art.36(3)(a) that the International Bureau shall communicate the international preliminary examination report, together with its annex, to each elected office. The UK-IPO, as elected office, has not expressly waived its right to receive such communication. However, the international examination report cannot be communicated earlier than 30 months from the priority date (PCT r.73.2). Accordingly, the UK-IPO, as elected office, receives a copy of any international examination report that has been established if and when it receives the communication under PCT r.20 upon a specific request for the latter. If the international examination report is not in the English language, an English translation of the report itself (but not of any annexed amendments to the international application) is made by the International Bureau (PCT r.72.2) and is included in the communication. Similar provisions apply in respect of the written opinion of the International Searching Authority (PCT r.72.2 *bis*).

The applicant in the UK phase

The applicant in the international phase becomes the applicant for the commencement of the United Kingdom phase. This is because an international application (UK) is treated as an application under Pt I of the Act (s.89(1)). It is not possible simply to add or substitute some other person as applicant for the purpose of commencing proceedings in the United Kingdom. If there are several applicants, they are treated as joint applicants in the international phase. If the international application designates different applicants for different designated countries (PCT art.9(3), PCT r.4.5(d) and the *PCT Applicant's Guide*, at Vol.I (Introduction to the International Phase), para.5.039), only the applicant(s) who was/were designated for the United Kingdom are treated as applicant(s) at the commencement of the UK phase. If the international application, or at least the United Kingdom part thereof, is assigned, or the applicant changes his name, and application to record the assignment or name change reaches the International Bureau while the application is still within the period of 30 months from the priority date, the recordal is effective for the international application (UK) (PCT r.92 *bis*). The UK-IPO is entitled to call for evidence of such assignment or name change, but only after the application has entered the UK phase (PCT r.51 *bis*.1(a)(ii) and the *PCT Applicant's Guide*, at Vol.I (Introduction to the International Phase), para.11.018).

89A.11

Valid entry into the UK phase (subss.(2) and (3)(a))

—General

The time limit for entry into the national UK phase irrespective of whether international preliminary examination has been requested, is now a uniform period of 31 months, see §89A.15. The transfer of the international application (UK) from the international phase into the national or UK phase at the end of the prescribed 31-month period is predicated on payment of the fee, if any, prescribed under PCT arts 22 and 39(1), herein called the "national fee", and the filing of an English translation of the international application if this was neither filed nor published in English (subs.(3)(a)), but an early start to processing may be requested under subs.(3)(b). Only if such early start is desired, is it necessary expressly to request national processing. The payment of the national fee, the filing of the translation and the prescribed 31-month period are discussed respectively in §§89A.13, 89A.14 and 89A.15. When entering the UK phase, it is strongly recommended (MOPP para.89A.04) to use PF NP1 (available from the website *www.patent.gov.uk*), but there is no obligation to use any special form (PCT r.49.4).

89A.12

It may be possible, if desired, to complete and "file" PF NP1 online (currently using an Adobe "pdf" document format prepared online). To do this, among other things, the filer must have a valid email address to which the filing receipt can be sent and payments must be made by use of a valid credit/debit card or through a deposit account held with the UK-IPO; see notes to PF NP1.

Subsection (3)(a) contains no reference to a copy of the international application itself. This ensures that valid entry into the UK phase can be secured at the end of the prescribed 31 month period without the applicant filing a copy of the international application (or any amendments thereto), even though the Office will not have received the communication under PCT art.20, see §89A.10. It also ensures, pursuant to PCT arts.23(1), and 40(1) that the UK phase does not commence until expiry of the prescribed 31-month period, even if the national fee, if any, is paid (§89A.13) and the translation, if required (§89A.14) is filed sooner, save that earlier entry into the UK phase can be obtained at the express request of the applicant (subs.(3)(b)), see §89A.16).

By virtue of s.20A(1), reinstatement may be available for international applications which are taken to be withdrawn as a result of an unintentional failure to satisfy the requirements for entry to the UK national phase. The period within which reinstatement must be requested is the first to expire of twelve months from the date on which the application was terminated or two months from the date on which the removal of the cause of non-compliance occurred (r.32). Under s.20A(3) reinstatement is not available if an extension of the relevant period is available under the Act or Rules, but in that case the appropriate remedy would presumably be under those provisions (in particular the two month extension available under r.108).

In *Research In Motion Ltd's Application* BL O/016/08 an international application was filed with all states designated, but due to a clerical error the European regional phase (EP) was not designated. Unaware of this, the applicant pursued a European regional application and did not take steps to enter the UK national phase at the normal time. When the European Patent Office noticed that the European regional phase had not been designated, the European regional application was deemed void. The applicant therefore applied to reinstate the international application for a patent (UK), which had been taken to be withdrawn for failure to enter the UK national phase. The applicant argued that there had been no intention either to pursue or not pursue the application in the UK national phase. The hearing officer found that the applicant had in fact made a decision to pursue the EP regional route and not the UK national route, and had therefore intentionally failed to comply with the UK national phase requirements. The failure to comply was not considered "unintentional", and so reinstatement was not available. The meaning and interpretation of the term "unintentional" is discussed in the MOPP, para.20A.13 and see also the discussion in §20A.05.

—Payment of the national fee

89A.13   It is left to the designated offices to prescribe what is the "national fee" within the meaning of PCT art.22. The "national fee", although so-called in PCT arts 22 and 39(1), is not identified as such in the Act or in the Rules but is so identified in the *PCT Applicant's Guide*, at Vol.II (National Phase) National Chapter (GB), Summary. For the UK-IPO, as a designated office, the national fee is the fee payable under s.89A(3), and prescribed in the Patents (Fees) Rules since this fee is the one (and the only one) to be paid to enable fulfilment of the conditions of subs.(3) and thereby of PCT arts 22 or 39(1). The national fee is a substitute for the application fee. The filing of PF 9A and payment of the United Kingdom search fee are not necessary for the purpose of securing valid entry into the UK phase. The filing of PF 9A and PF 10 and the fees payable are discussed at §§89A.28 and 89A.29. No form is required for paying the national fee, but it is recommended to use PF NP1 (see §89A.12).

The United Kingdom national fee was reduced to zero with effect from October 1, 1998, but (for the reasons explained in §89A.12) was reinstated for international applications (UK) from May 4, 1999. This is now significant only so far as it affects the prior art status of such applications under s.2(3) (MOPP para.89A.06.1).

Neither of the fees mentioned at r.71 (reprinted at §89.05) and payable pursuant to a request for review under s.89(3) or (5) (see §§89.28 and 89.30) is called the "national fee", despite the fact that PCT art.25(2)(a) refers to the "national fee". Such fees are prescribed in the Patents (Fees) Rules quite separately from the national fee under s.89A(3) and are currently each zero.

—Filing of translation of the international application

When the international application (UK) has been initially filed in a language other than **89A.14** English, it becomes necessary to file an English translation at the UK-IPO to secure valid entry into the UK phase, unless the international application has already been published in English translation (subs.(3)). However, in the case, for example, of an international application which was filed and searched (and therefore published) in the Spanish language, but for which an English translation was furnished by the applicant to the competent international preliminary examining authority for the purpose of the international preliminary examination, that translation is not communicated to elected offices. This means that the applicant must submit the English translation to the UK-IPO as elected office in order to secure valid entry into the UK national phase.

Verification of a translation is now only required upon request by the Comptroller (r.115), see §89A.23. If the international application is published in English translation (see §89.13), such translation becomes a part of the international application to be communicated under PCT art.20; so that no verification and no separate translation of the international application need be filed at the UK-IPO by the applicant. If a translation of the wrong document is filed, it cannot be replaced by a translation of the correct document by way of correction of an error under s.117 (*Masuda's Application* [1987] R.P.C. 37).

If the international application has been amended in the international phase and the amendments were filed in a language other than English, an English translation of the amendments should be furnished with the translation of the international application (as filed), as described more fully at §89A.14. Failure to furnish a translation of the amendments does not prejudice valid entry into the UK phase, nor does belated furnishing of a translation of the application (as filed) provided that a translation of the application (as amended) was duly furnished.

Similarly, valid entry into the UK phase is not immediately prejudiced if information concerning the deposit of biological material, such as a micro-organism, has been added to the international application after the international filing date but a translation of such added information has been omitted (PCT r.49.5(h)). Again, the applicant must be given an opportunity to file the missing translation (r.69(5)(b)). Further discussion on international applications containing information ("indications") concerning deposited biological material is to be found in §89A.33.

If the drawings contain any textual matter, the translation should include a copy of the drawings (which may be informal) containing an English translation of that textual matter (r.70(3)). Formal drawings complying with PCT r.11 (PCT r.49.5(j)) can be filed later within a time limit specified in an invitation to file them (PCT r.49.5(e); see §15A.05). The requirements of r.14 and Parts 1–4 of Sch.2 are generally the same as those of PCT r.11 (as for which see §§14.04 and 14.05).

Although any listing of a nucleotide or amino acid sequence filed with the international application forms part of the application, when the sequence listing is in accordance with the PCT sequence listing standard prescribed in Annex C to the PCT Administrative Instructions (reprinted in the PCTH at Appendix III and in the EPH in s.81.1), the "Sequence Listing" part of the description does not require translation so long as it complies with the relevant requirements (described in WIPO Standard ST.25) of the PCT and any free text in the sequence listing also appears in the main part of the description in accordance with PCT r.5.2(b) (r.70(5) and PCT r.49.5(a -*bis*)). Any later filed sequence listing does not form part of the international application (PCT r.13 *ter*.1(e)) and does not need to be translated (unless it is in the form of an amendment annexed to the international preliminary examination report). WIPO Standard ST.25 (Standard for the Presentation of Nucleotide and Amino Acid Sequence Listings in Patent Applications) is a reproduction of the PCT sequence listing standard.

Notwithstanding PCT r.49.5(a), the translation of the international application need not include a translation of the abstract or of the international request form (Form PCT/RO/101), unless an express request is being made to the UK-IPO for an early start to national processing, as described at §89A.16, and the application is not available by virtue of publication in accordance with the PCT (r.69(2)). When such a request is made, the Office will not have received the communication of the international application under PCT art.20, since it does not receive this communication automatically (see §89A.10). The bibliographic data in the request form can always be identified in the frontsheet of the published application and in the *PCT Gazette* by virtue of use of the INID code (for which a summary is usually published quarterly in the *Patents Journal*, see §123.84, and regularly in the *PCT Gazette*). If a translation of the request form is required, a blank English version of this form may be obtained from the Office free of charge and completed for this purpose (PCT r.49.5(b)).

Pursuant to PCT r.49.5(b), r.70(4) prescribes that, when the title established by the International Searching Authority differs from that originally included in the international application, a translation of the original title is not required.

Any amendments that have been superseded or reversed (and therefore are not annexed to the international preliminary examination report) do not need to be translated (*PCT Applicant's Guide*, Vol.II (National Phase), paras 4.019 and 4.020), except for any amendments to the claims under PCT art.19(1) which are to form the basis of provisional protection arising on publication.

—Time limit for entry into the UK phase

89A.15   There is now a uniform period of 31 months from the declared priority date for entry into the national UK phase irrespective of whether international preliminary examination has been requested, see r.66 set out in §89A.02. For a brief discussion of the definition of "declared priority date" at r.2(1) in the case of an international application (UK), see §89.08. For the supply of the priority document and, if necessary, its translation, see §89A.19. The time limits for filing PF 9A, PF 10 and other documents, if needed, are discussed at §§89A.28–89A.35.

An extension of two months under r.108 can be obtained to the 31-month period for paying the national fee and for filing the translation, if required, provided this is requested within 2 months of expiry of the normal due date. PF 52 should be filed and the appropriate fee should be paid. In many cases it is now possible for PF 52 (and associated documentation) to be filed online via a web filing service (see the Guidance Notes in the "Online Patent Services" section of the UK-IPO website). When the description, the claims or the drawings of the international application have been amended in the international phase and the applicant has filed a translation of the application (as filed), but not of the amendment, within the period prescribed by r.66(1) the Comptroller must notify the applicant (r.69(5)). Extension is possible under r.108. Notice is given to the applicant that a necessary translation is missing and requiring the necessary translation to be filed within three months of the date of such notice, in accordance with r.66(2). (MOPP para.89A.09.01 and para.89A.25) For further discussion on the submission of translations of amendments, see §89A.18.

When the period of 31 months for entering the national phase under r.66(1) is extended under r.107 or 108, this may also extend the time limits under rr.67 and 68 for filing PF 9A, etc. and complying with other requirements, as described in §89A.20.

If information concerning a deposit of biological material was added to the international application under PCT r.13 *bis*.4, and this had not been published in English, the Comptroller must notify the applicant that the translation is missing (r.69(5)(b))and should be filed within three months of the date the notification is sent (MOPP para.89A.10). The information in question is the name of the depositary institution and the accession number of the deposit, and (where the biological material has been deposited by a person other than the applicant) the name and address of the depositor and the statement referred to in para.3(2)(b)(ii) of Sch.1 to the Patents Rules 2007 (MOPP para.89A.10). However, the applicant may find it necessary to file PF 7, PF 9A and any other documents mentioned in §89A.20 before filing the translation of the later-filed information concerning the deposit of biological material.

It appears that PCT r.82 (irregularities in the mail service) cannot be invoked because the 31-month time limit is not a time limit fixed in the PCT or the Regulations under it, as required by PCT art.48(1).

Early entry into the UK phase (subs.(3)(b))

Notwithstanding the 31-month prescribed period for valid entry into the UK phase, the **89A.16** applicant has the right expressly to request the start of national processing before the UK-IPO as soon as he wishes after international filing (PCT arts 23(2) and 40(2)). When expressly requesting an early start to national processing, the applicant must himself file a copy of the international application at the UK-IPO (the Office does not receive the communication under PCT art.20 automatically (see §89A.10). Such is necessary even if the international application was initially filed at the UK-IPO as receiving office, because subs.3(b)(1) so provides, the Office (as receiving office) being bound by the confidentiality requirements of PCT art.30(3). The applicant must also pay the national fee and file the translation, if required, as described at §§89A.13 and 89A.14. The periods within which PF 7, PF 9A and PF 10 must be filed are then altered, as respectively described in §§89A.32, 89A.28 and 89A.29.

Although an indication may be given in PF NP1 that the applicant wishes the Comptroller to proceed earlier with the UK phase, if the applicant is not confident that a wish will be construed as an express request, within the meaning of PCT arts 23(2) and 40(2) and subs.(3)(b), an express request can be made in a separate letter. A separate letter is necessary, in any event, if the applicant desires early publication and/or accelerated substantive examination by the Office, for which see §§16.03 and 18.13. An express request to start the national phase early is not, of itself, a request for accelerated prosecution in the national phase, since the express request does no more than relieve the designated office of the restriction under PCT arts 23(1) and 40(1) not to process or examine the international application early. Conversely, however, a specific request for accelerated examination may be considered to be a request for early entry into the national phase (see MOPP, para.89A.21).

Reasons why the applicant might want an early start to national processing include: a desire for early grant to enable infringement proceedings to commence; a desire to have early publication in English to secure provisional protection (see §89B.10); and a wish to have an adverse decision by an international authority (such as a refusal to authorise the correction of an obvious mistake under PCT r.91) reconsidered promptly, especially before publication. This last point is discussed further at §89B.12.

For the possibility of requesting accelerated examination under the PCT(UK) Fast Track system, see §89A.40.

Failure to pay the national fee and file a translation (subs.(4))

Failure to pay the national fee (as discussed at §89A.13) or to file a translation if required **89A.17** (as discussed at §89A.14), within the prescribed period (as described at §89A.15), results in the international application being deemed to be withdrawn (subs.(4), pursuant to PCT arts.24(1) and 39(2)) without the application entering the UK phase because the conditions of subs.(1)(a) will not have been satisfied. Failure to file a translation of the application (as filed) in response to an notification under r.69(5)(a), or failure to file a translation of later-filed information relating to biological material in response to a notification under r.69(5)(b), also potentially results in the international application being deemed withdrawn without having effectively entered the UK phase. Further, if the international application has been published under PCT art.21, such publication is not regarded as published under the Act (s.89B(2), see §89B.08) and has no prior art effect under s.2(3) as against other United Kingdom patents and applications (see §89B.09).

Copy and translation of amendments made in the international phase (subss.(5) and (6))

Amendments made to the claims under PCT art.19(1), and any explanatory statement, **89A.18** are normally included in the communication under PCT art.20 (see §89A.10), and the applicant does not need to file such amendments or statement at the UK-IPO. In the event that the applicant expressly requests an early start to national processing under PCT art.23(2) (see §89A.16), any the amendment or explanatory statement will not have been communicated to the UK-IPO under PCT art.20 and the applicant should supply a copy of such amendment and statement to the UK-IPO when requesting an early start.

If the amended claims are not in English, a translation must be filed within the prescribed 31-month period (r.69(4)). If an amendment to the claims under PCT art.19(1) was accompanied by an explanatory statement, a translation of the latter should be included, since it is considered to be part of the international application (PCT r.49.3).

If a translation of amended claims is not included with a translation of the international application, the applicant is notified (r.69(5)(a)). Failure to meet the specified time limit or any permissible or allowed extension thereto described at §89A.15 results in the amended claims being disregarded (subs.(5)). Note that, if amended claims published with the international application are so disregarded, the provisional protection afforded by ss.55 and 69 (see §89B.10) is then based on the scope of the unamended claims. This should be considered before making any decision as to whether to refrain deliberately from filing a translation of amended claims.

Amendments made to the description, claims and drawings during international preliminary examination under PCT Chapter II are annexed to the international preliminary examination report and are communicated to the UK-IPO that report (see §89A.10). However, if the applicant expressly requests an early start to national processing under PCT art.40(2) and subs.(3)(b) (see §89A.16), it is unlikely that the international preliminary examination report will have been established and the applicant can simply submit any amendments already filed at the international preliminary examining authority as amendments under s.19(1) and r.31 (see §89B.17). If the international preliminary examination report is not in English, the report itself is translated into English by the International Bureau (PCT art.36(2)(b) and PCT r.72.1), and the English translation is included in the above-mentioned communication. However, the applicant is responsible for filing an English translation of the annexed amendments at the UK-IPO before the expiry of the prescribed 31-month period. As with amendments to the claims under PCT art.19(1), if a translation of amendments annexed to the international examination report does not accompany the translation of the application itself, the applicant is notified (r.69(5)(a)). For more on the time limit for submitting a translation of amendments and possible extensions of it, see §89A.15. There is no need to furnish translations of superseded amendments, other than, possibly, superseded amendments to the claims under PCT art.19(1), as mentioned above.

Translations of claims amended under PCT art.19(1) and translations of amendments annexed to the international preliminary examination report need not be verified (r.115), unless verification is requested by the Comptroller.

Any amendments which are made in the international phase, but which are disregarded so far as the UK phase is concerned, can still be requested under s.19(1) in the UK phase (see §89B.17). If conflicting amendments are on file, the latest to be filed are the ones considered unless these are to be disregarded (MOPP paras 89B.15 and 89A.25).

Rule 66(2) actually goes further than is required by PCT r.49.5(*c-bis*), as the latter refers only to claims (as filed) and claims (as amended under PCT art.19(1)). PCT r.76.5(iv) does not contain any reference to the description or to the drawings nor, indeed, any reference to amended claims which are annexed to the international preliminary examination report but were not filed under PCT art.19(1).

Copy and translation of priority document

89A.19   A copy of the priority document is normally forwarded to the UK-IPO by the International Bureau (see §89.14). The UK-IPO cannot require the applicant to file a priority document when one was filed in the international phase in time to reach the International Bureau before publication of the international application (PCT r.17.2). If the priority document was not so furnished in the international phase, the UK-IPO must give the applicant an opportunity to file the priority document within a time limit which shall be reasonable under the circumstances (s.89B(1)(b); r.8(4); PCT r.17.1(c)). Because there is no prescribed time limit, the Office must invite the applicant to file the priority document within a time limit specified in the invitation. There is no express provision for an extension to the time limit so specified. It is thought that, if a time limit so specified proves not to be reasonable in the circumstances, the Comptroller must specify a new time limit.

It would seem that the International Bureau is not under any obligation to transmit a copy of the priority document to designated offices if the document is received after publication of the international application.

The above also applies in the case of a request for an early start to national processing or examination under s.89A(3)(b) (see §89A.12), and in the case of a request for a review under s.89(3) (see §89.28). In the case of a review under s.89(5) (see §89.30), the time limit for filing the priority document is 16 months from the declared priority date (r.8(2)], reprinted in §5.09), since the application in such a case is not treated as an international application, whereby r.8(4) is not applicable. This 16–month time limit is subject to alteration by the Comptroller (r.71, see §89.05).

When the priority document is not in English or Welsh, a translation must be filed under r.9 at the request of the Comptroller or, in any event, before the grant of a patent (r.67). The procedure is described in §5.32. Note that a translation of the international application filed for the purpose of international publication or for the purpose of entry into the UK phase is not the application in suit within the meaning of r.9 so that a declaration in lieu of a translation of the priority document is not appropriate in the case of an international application not filed in English. Such a declaration may be considered by the Comptroller to be appropriate when the international application was filed in English as a complete translation of the priority application.

The priority claim is discussed more fully at §§89B.05 and 89B.06.

Further formalities after entry into the UK phase

Automatic extensions of the periods of time specified by rr.61(1), 66(2) and 68 are available under r.108 see §123.25. However, such extensions are subject to r.108(5) and (7) and may be extended (or further extended) by two months only. In particular, conditions may be applied, and further, no extension may be granted in respect of the periods prescribed by these rules after the end of the period of two months beginning immediately after the period of time as prescribed (or previously extended) has expired (r.108(7)).

89A.20

There is a uniform normal period of 31 months for entry into the national UK phase irrespective of whether international preliminary examination has been requested, see r.66 reprinted above. In addition to paying the national fee and filing the translation, if required (as described at §§89A.13 and 89A.14), the applicant must also file PF 9A and PF 10 and pay the prescribed search and examination fees. PF 9A can be filed within up to 2 months beginning with the date on which the national phase begins (r.68), but it is advisable to file it when paying the national fee in order that the formalities officer can commence his preliminary examination under s.17(2) and (3) and so enable any noted deficiencies in the national fee to be made up or defects in the translation (if required) to be corrected within the two-month extension available under r.108(2) or the discretionary extension available under r.108(3). However, the Office is not obliged to commence its preliminary examination within the first month (*Masuda's Application* [1987] R.P.C. 37). The period for filing PF 10 expires 33 months from the priority date or, if later, 2 months beginning with the date on which the national phase begins (r.68(4)). It is recommended to file PF 10 along with PF 9A, because there will be no publication under s.16 to trigger a reminder. If the inventor is not named in the international application, PF 7 must be filed, the time limit for which is the same as that mentioned above for filing PF 9A (r.68).

When an express request for an early start to national processing by the UK-IPO has been made, the time limit for filing PF 9A is brought forward, as described in §89A.28. If the United Kingdom has not been elected, the time limit for filing PF 10 becomes 6 months from the date of publication under s.16, as described in §89A.29. Upon such an express request for an early start to national processing, the time limit for filing PF 7 is brought forward to 16 months from the priority date or two months from the date of making that request, whichever is later, as described in §89A.32.

When a request for a review by the UK-IPO has been made under s.89(3) or (5), the time limit for filing PF 9A is likely to be altered, again as described in §89A.28, and the time limit for filing PF 10 may also be altered, as described in §89A.29. Also, the time limit for filing PF 7 may be altered, as described in §89A.32.

An address for service must be furnished, but this can be done after entry into the UK phase (r.103; PCT art.27(7)). The address for service may now be an address in the United Kingdom, another EU/EEA state or the Channel Islands (r.103(4)), see §32.23. So far as right of representation before the UK-IPO, as designated office is concerned, any person, other than one subject to specific prohibition, may represent the applicant and what is said at §§281.03 et seq. applies. The name of the appointed agent and the address for service can be included in PF NP1, when it is appropriate to use this form, see §89A.21.

If a statement was included in the international application, specifically in the supplemental box of the request (Form PCT/RO/101), that the invention was disclosed at an international exhibition in the six months preceding the international filing date and if it is desired that such disclosure shall be excluded from the state of the art, so far as the United Kingdom is concerned, a certificate of exhibition must be filed at the UK-IPO within 33 months from the priority date, as the case may be (see §89A.34). Such period is extensible at the Comptroller's discretion under r.108, see §89A.39.

Verification of a translation is now only required upon request by the Comptroller, see §89A.23. Disregarding the translation of the international application results in the application being deemed withdrawn without entering the UK phase (subss.(3)(a) and (4)). Taking no further action in connection with a translation of any amendments results in the amendments being disregarded (subs.(5)).

For the filing of the priority document and any required translation thereof, see §§89A.30 and 89A.31.

For the possibility of requesting accelerated examination under the PCT(UK) Fast Track system, see §89A.40.

Practice under Section 89A

Valid entry into the UK phase

89A.21 When entering the UK phase, it is recommended, but not compulsory, to use unofficial PF NP1, available from the website *http://www.patent.gov.uk* (PCT rr.49.4 and 76.5). This form contains a checklist of the documents to be furnished which serves as a reminder of the procedural steps to be taken. PF NP1 also contains spaces for insertion of an address for service (r.103, discussed at §32.15) and the nationality of the applicant. As regards the latter, when the applicant is an Australian or United States body corporate, the Office requires to know the State of incorporation before it can complete preparations for re-publication, for which see §89B.14.

PF NP1 should not be used when making a request for a review under s.89(3) or (5), see §89.32, but its use is recommended when making an express request under s.89A(3)(b) for an early start to national processing by the Office.

National fee

89A.22 The fee ("national fee") prescribed under s.89A(3), is due to be paid within the prescribed 31-month period, described in §89A.13. It is convenient to use PF NP1 (see §89A.21) when paying this fee, which may be able to be filed online.

The respective fees, if any, payable upon requests for review under s.89(3) and (5) are prescribed in the Patents (Fees) Rules separately from the fee payable under s.89A(3). Unlike the fee payable under s.89A(3), both are zero. For further information on making such a request for review, see §89.32.

Translation of the international application

89A.23 When the international application is neither filed nor published in English, it is necessary to file an English translation (in duplicate) (see §89A.14) within the prescribed 31-

months' period described in §89A.15. This period is extensible under r.108, see §89A.39. It is no longer necessary to verify a filed translation. Instead r.115 (reprinted in §123.32) provides for the Comptroller to make a request for evidence where he has reasonable doubts about the accuracy of any translation filed at the UK-IPO, see §123.82.

If amendments have been made to the claims and/or the description in the international phase, the translation is to include both the text, as filed, and the amendments. Nevertheless, if a translation of the amendments is omitted in the first instance or if only a translation of the text, as amended, is filed initially, the missing translation may be furnished, without any penalty, up to three months after issuance of an invitation to file it. For the translation of amendments, see §89A.24.

If the drawings contain textual matter not in English, the translation must include a copy of the drawings in which the textual matter is translated into English (r.70(3)). Informal drawings will suffice at the time of entry into the UK phase although formal drawings will eventually be required (PCT r.49.5(e)).

If information concerning the deposit of biological material was filed with the international application, the translation of the application must include that information. If such information was filed later, its translation may be furnished up to three months after an invitation to provide it, see §89A.33.

In the case of an international application disclosing a nucleotide or amino acid sequence, any "Sequence Listing" part of the description complying with the PCT sequence listing standard (WIPO Standard ST.25) does not need to be translated (see §89A.14).

The translation need not include the abstract or the request form (Form PCT/RO/101) (again see §89A.14), unless an express request for an early start to national processing is made, as described at §89A.16. When an amended title is established by the international searching authority, only the amended title need be translated (r.70(4), again see §89A.14).

Translation of amendments and explanatory statement
89A.24
When the claims, the description or the drawings of the application have been amended in the international phase and the amendments were not filed in English, an English translation (in duplicate) of those amendments should be filed within the prescribed 31-months' period described in §89A.15 or an English translation of those amendments should be included in the English translation of the international application filed within that prescribed 31-month period. Such amendments are those made to the claims under PCT art.19(1) (see §89.12) or those made to the description, claims or drawings during international preliminary examination under PCT Chapter II and annexed to the international preliminary examination report (see §89.16). Amendments to the drawings are only relevant in this context if the drawings include textual matter. Any amendment which is disregarded through failure to file a translation of that amendment may be resubmitted as an amendment under s.19 (see §89B.17). For the importance of filing a translation of claims amended under PCT art.19(1) for the purpose of provisional protection, see §89B.10.

If amendments to the claims under PCT art.19(1) were accompanied by an explanatory statement not in English, an English translation of such statement should also be filed within the prescribed 31-month period. For further information on the translation of amendments and of any explanatory statement, see §89A.18. For the possible later requirement for verification of the translation, see §89A.25.

Verification of translation of application
89A.25
The current form of r.69, noted in §89A.05, no longer requires any translation filed at the UK-IPO to be automatically verified Instead r.115 provides for the Comptroller to make a request for evidence where he has reasonable doubts about the accuracy of any translation filed at the UK-IPO, see §123.47 and 89A.23 above.

Publication of translation for provisional protection (subs.(6))
89A.26
When the international application was published in a language other than English, pro-

visional protection under ss.55 and 69 during the United Kingdom phase (see §89B.10) can be secured by filing a written request for publication, together with any fee that may be prescribed. This is conveniently done on PF NP1. The translation is laid open to public inspection immediately when both it and this request have been filed (*Patents Journal* February 20, 1980). There is no time limit for filing this request, but it is recommended to do this when the translation of the international application is filed. The laying-open of the translation to public inspection under s.118(1) and r.51 does not give the applicant any legal rights (see §89B.10).

Early national processing (subs.(3)(b))

89A.27 To enable national processing before the UK-IPO to be started early, i.e. before expiry of the prescribed 31-month period, it is necessary to carry out the steps described at §89A.13 and, if the application is not in English, the steps described at §89A.14 and expressly to request the Comptroller to proceed earlier with the national phase, see §89A.16. It is also necessary to file a copy of the international application itself as the communication under PCT art.20 will not have taken place, see §89A.10. To enable the Comptroller to proceed with the preliminary examination, it is necessary to file PF 9A. If accelerated publication and/or examination by the Office is desired, the applicant must make a specific request for this, giving good reasons, and it is necessary to file PF 10 early.

Early national processing under s.89A(3)(b) is now governed by r.68. This specifies that: (1) PF 7 must be filed within the period specified in r.10(3) (see §13.03), or within two months from the date on which the national phase begins, if later; and (2) the search fee and PF 9A must be filed within the period specified in r.22(2) or (7) (12 months from the priority date or two months from the date on which the national phase begins, if later, see §15.04). However, the maximum period for filing PF 10 is the 33 months stated in r.68(4) (see reprint, above) or 2 months from the date on which the national phase begins, if later.

Request for preliminary examination and search (PF 9A)

89A.28 The normal period for filing PF 9A, as well as paying the search fee, is now 2 months from the date on which the national phase begins. However, a shorter period may apply where early national processing is requested, see §89A.27. This period is extensible under r.108 see §89A.20. However, it is recommended to file this form when paying the national fee. In many cases it is now possible for PF 9A to be filed online via a web filing service (see the Guidance Notes in the "Online Patent Services" section of the UK-IPO website), in which case a fee reduction is also available.

In the case of an express request for an early start to national processing, the time limit for filing PF 9A is 12 months from the priority date (or filing date if no priority is claimed) or 2 months from the date on which the national phase begins, if later (r.68(3)). In the case of a request for review under s.89(3) or (5), there is no express time limit for filing this form, because the Comptroller can alter any time limit specified in the Act or the Rules (r.71(7), reproduced in §89.05). Such time limit is likely to be no more than two months from the date of the request for review. In any of the above cases, it is best to file PF 9A when making the express request for an early start or the request for review. Otherwise, the preliminary examination of the application by the Office is likely to be delayed.

Provided that the application has undergone an international search, the amount of the search fee payable on PF 9A is reduced, as shown in the Patents (Fees) Rules. In the case of an express request for an early start to national processing before the international search report has been established, the full fee is payable on PF 9A. Also, in the case of a request for review under s.89(3) or (5), the full fee is payable on PF 9A, because the application will not have been the subject of an international search.

Request for substantive examination (PF 10)

89A.29 The period for filing PF 10 to request substantive examination is now 33 months from the declared priority date or, if none, the date of filing of the international application for a patent (UK), even where early national processing is expressly requested (see r.68(4), above), or 2 months from the date on which the national phase begins, if later. This 33-month period is extensible under r.108, see §89A.39.

The amount of the examination fee payable on this form is the full amount prescribed in the Patents (Fees) Rules. There is no reduction to take into account establishment of an international preliminary examination report. However, in many cases it is now possible for PF 10 to be filed online via a web filing service (see the Guidance Notes in the "Online Patent Services" section of the UK-IPO website *http://www.ipo.gov.uk*), in which case a fee reduction is also available.

In the case of a request for review under s.89(3) or (5), there is no express period for filing PF 10, since the Comptroller can alter any time limit specified in the Act or the Rules (r.71(7), reprinted in §89.05). Such period is likely to be specified so as to expire no later than 6 months from the date of publication under s.16.

Priority document

It is not normally necessary to file a priority document, since this should have been filed **89A.30** in the international phase within 16 months of the priority date. If the priority document has not been duly submitted in the international phase, the UK-IPO must give the applicant an opportunity to furnish this within a time limit that is reasonable under the circumstances (PCT r.17.1(c)), as is discussed more fully in §89A.19. Thus, belated filing or non-filing of the priority document in the international phase does not prejudice the claim to priority, see §89B.06.

Translation of priority document

When the priority document is not in English, a translation thereof must be filed only if **89A.31** requested by the Comptroller. A declaration under r.9(4)(b) (reprinted at §5.10) *in lieu* of a translation of the priority document is not appropriate in the case of an international application not filed in English; see §5.31 for further details.

When a request for a review by the Office has been made under either s.89(3) or (5), a translation of the priority document is likely to be required to be filed within a period specified for the purpose by the Comptroller, again as described in §89A.19.

Statement of inventorship (PF 7)

If information concerning the inventor was omitted from the request form (Form PCT/ **89A.32** RO/101) pursuant to PCT art.4(i)(v) and PCT r.4.6, a statement of inventorship (including the details of the right to the grant of a patent) on PF 7 must be filed.

The normal period for filing this form is now two months beginning with the date the national phase begins (see r.68(3), above). However, where early national processing is requested, this period is (when there is a declared priority date) the last to expire of the period of 16 months starting on the declared priority date (or if no priority is claimed, the filing date) or the period of two months beginning with the date on which the national phase begins, if later (r.68(3)). In many cases it is now possible for Form 7 (if required) to be filed online via a web filing service (see the Guidance Notes in the "Online Patent Services" section of the UK-IPO website.

In the case of a request for review under s.89(3) or (5), there is no express period for filing PF 7, when required because the Comptroller can alter any time limit specified in the Act or the Rules (r.71(7), reproduced at in §89.05). Such period is likely to be no longer than that prescribed under r.68(3).

Inventions involving biological material

To facilitate compliance with the national laws of designated offices as to patent ap- **89A.33** plications for inventions involving biological material, such as micro-organisms, r.13 *bis* of the PCT contains provisions for international applications containing references to deposited biological material. If the performance of an invention, the subject of an international application (UK), requires the use of biological material not available to the public at the international filing date, then information ("indications") concerning a deposit of that material must have been included in the international application or have been filed within the time limit permitted under PCT r.13 *bis*.4(a) for compliance with s.125A. (For r.13(1) and Sch.1 para.3(3) of the Rules see §125A.05). This time limit is 16 months from the priority date, except that any such information reaching the International Bureau before technical preparations for international publication have been completed is deemed to have been received at the end of this time limit. The provisions of r.13 *bis*.4(b) of the PCT, relating to designated offices where a shorter time limit is prescribed under national law, are not applicable to the United Kingdom, as designated office, under the current version of Sch.1.

The information concerning the deposit of the biological material (i.e. the name of the depositary institution concerned, the date of the deposit and the accession number) forms part of the international application and, if not published in English, must be translated. Any such information included in the international application on filing ought to be translated with the remainder of the application. If it is not or if such information is filed later, then, pursuant to r.49.5(h) of the PCT, the period prescribed for filing a translation of that information (which need not be verified) is three months after a notice has been sent by the Comptroller, calling for such translation (r.69(1)). This period may be extensible under r.108. The late filing of a translation of information relating to the deposit of biological material has the effect of deferring entry into the UK phase but only for the purpose of filing that translation.

In addition, it should be noted that where the biological material was deposited by a person other than the applicant, a statement must be filed which identifies the name and address of the depositor, and a statement must be filed which authorises the applicant to refer to the biological material in his application and irrevocably authorises the making available to the public of the biological material in accordance with Sch.1 (2007 Rules Sch.1 para.3(2)(b)).

In order that the so-called "expert solution", described at §125A.28, can apply to an international application (UK), a statement as to the availability of a sample of the deposited biological material to an expert may be filed at the International Bureau before completion of technical preparations for publication (r.13(1) and Sch.1 para.6 reprinted in §125A.08). However, it is recommended that a statement to this effect be filed at the receiving office with the international application so that corresponding requirements of other designated offices, see the *PCT Applicant's Guide*, Vol.1, Annex L, may be satisfied. Such a statement may be included in Form PCT/RO/134 (*PCT Applicant's Guide*, Vol.1, Annex Z). The Chartered Institute has suggested a form of wording for such a statement. see (1991–92) 21 *CIPA* 607. This suggested form of wording can be modified or supplemented, using the information given in the *PCT Applicant's Guide*, Vol.1, Annex L (*PCT Newsletter* 07/1995, p.4, under the heading "Practical Advice").

International exhibition certificate

89A.34   If it is desired that disclosure of the invention at an international exhibition (see §2.28) in the six months preceding the international filing date shall be excluded from the state of the art, so far as the designation of at least the United Kingdom is concerned, a statement concerning non-prejudicial disclosures must have been included in the supplemental box of the request form (Form PCT/RO/101) as filed with the international application (r.67(1)). Although the note to the Supplemental Box in the Notes to the request form (Form PCT/RO/101) implies that the statement concerning non-prejudicial disclosures may be in the description, it is questionable as to whether a statement included in the description is a statement in writing to the receiving office within the meaning of r.67. After entry into the UK phase, it is necessary to file a certificate from the authority organising the exhibition. Such certificate is due to be filed at the Office within 32 months after the priority date (r.67(2) as amended by the 2011 Rules, pursuant to PCT r.51 *bis*.1(a)(vi) and PCT r.51 *bis*.2(a)). These time limits may be extended under r.108, see §89A.39.

Formal drawings

89A.35   It is not normally necessary to file drawings when entering the United Kingdom phase, since these are included in the communication under PCT art.20. However, when the drawings contain textual matter which must be translated (see §89A.23), it becomes necessary to file drawings complying with the formal requirements of r.14 and Pts 1, 3 and 4 to Sch.2 (reprinted at §14.05). Drawings filed with the translation may be informal (PCT r.49.5(d)). When such drawings filed with the translation do not comply with the formal requirements, the formalities officer must specify a reasonable period for the applicant to file formal drawings (PCT r.49.5(e)).

When an express request for an early start to national processing by the UK-IPO has been made under s.89A(3)(b), as described in §89A.16, or a request for a review by the UK-IPO has been made under s.89(3) or (5), as described in §§89.28 and 89.30, the applicant can be requested to file formal drawings when those already filed at the receiving office do not comply with the PCT requirements.

Prosecution and amendment

A United Kingdom application number is allotted to the international application upon payment of the national fee, and a receipt is issued. A United Kingdom publication number is allotted when preparations for re-publication are about to be completed (see §89B.14). In due course, filing particulars are published in the *Patents Journal*.

89A.36

If an international application, or a designation of the United Kingdom, is withdrawn under the PCT, it is treated as withdrawn under the Act (s.89(2)). If such withdrawal is effected after national processing or examination has already started in the office following an express request for an early start, such a withdrawal under the PCT is ineffective so far as concerns the designation of the United Kingdom (PCT r.90 *bis*.6(a)). This raises the question as to when national processing or examination starts (see PCTH, Ch.33, para.33.3). It does not start when re-publication takes place, because designated offices may re-publish before entry into the national phase (PCT art.64(2)(a)(ii)). It remains to be determined whether it starts at the UK-IPO when the Comptroller refers the international application to an examiner under s.89B(5) or when the examiner actually begins his search and examination.

It is the usual practice for the examiner to conduct any search under s.17 and substantive examination under s.18 simultaneously in respect of an international application (UK) (see MOPP, para.89B.12). However, the procedure for a combined search and substantive examination when PF 9A and PF 10 are filed simultaneously (see §§17.04 and 18.13) does not apply when an international search report has been established (*PCT Applicant's Guide*, Vol.II (National Phase), National Chapter (GB), para.GB.09).

The substantive examiner considers the international search report and will normally re-search the application only if he is reasonably sure that the UK files will yield more pertinent art (MOPP, para.89B.12). Otherwise, his searching will be restricted to a "top-up" search and any supplementary search necessitated by allowable amendment of the claims, as with national applications. No search report is normally issued to the applicant. If additional citations are found, these are brought to the applicant's attention in the examination report (this does not apply to a divisional application for which the preparation and issue of a search report is necessary; see MOPP, para.15.38). Copies of additional documents cited by the UK examiner are issued to the applicant. If amendments have been made during the international or national phase which necessitate a supplementary search, a full supplementary search fee will be payable under ss.17(8), 19(1) and 89A(5).

If any citation in the international search report is not in English, the Comptroller may call for a translation of all or part of the citation to be filed within two months of the direction to furnish such translation (r.113(5), reprinted in §123.30). In practice, in the case of a foreign patent specification, the Patent Office may accept an English language equivalent. Alternatively an Examiner may call for a partial translation, e.g. only of the claims, if that is felt likely to be sufficient (MOPP, para.89B.11).

The conduct of the prosecution in the UK phase is the same as for an application filed under the Act, see §17.08 et seq. and §18.13 et seq. Amendments can be made under s.19, see the commentary thereon. However, prosecution is more compact because there is less time available (see §89A.36), even though the international filing date and the declared priority date are taken into account when deciding what precedence the application should be given in relation to other applications within the responsibility of the relevant examining group.

Refunds and remission of fees

89A.37   As in the case of an application filed under the Act, it is the practice for the UK-IPO to refund the search and examination fees in full if the application is withdrawn unconditionally before the United Kingdom search report or first examination report is issued, respectively (see §17.06 and §18.07). A reduced fee is currently payable on PF 9A when the application has been the subject of an international search.It is not necessary for the full amount of the search fee to be paid in the first instance and to request a refund when benefit is to be obtained from the international search report.

The Office does not make any reduction or refund of the fee on PF 10 on the basis of an international preliminary examination report.

Refunds of fees are discussed further at §123.65.

Placing application in order

89A.38   The period prescribed in r.30 under ss.18 and 20 for bringing an international application (UK) into compliance with the Act and Rules is normally four-and-a-half years from the priority date, as discussed in §18.11. This leaves only two years to complete the examination in most cases where early entry to the national phase is not requested. It is thus necessary to prosecute such applications diligently, and correspondence with the UK-IPO during the last six months of this period should be marked "URGENT" (see e.g. *Patents Journal* April 20, 1988). Nevertheless, the period for bringing the application into compliance is one year from the date of the first substantive examination report, if this expires later, see §18.11. This four-and-a-half-year, or one-year period if expiring later, is extensible under r.108, see §89A.39.

Extensions of time

89A.39   The availability of extensions of time is now governed by r.108 and Pts 1, 2 and 3 to Sch.4 (see §123.25–123.26). With the exception of the period under r.66(3) for making a request for permission to make a late declaration of priority, each of the periods specified in r.66 is extensible under r.108. As to the requirement to file a translation of the priority application under r.9, see §§5.32 and 89A.19. Specific mention has been made in these paragraphs where extension is available under r.108(2) and also where discretionary extension under r.108(3) is possible. Extensions of the periods prescribed by rr.66(1) and (2) (entry to national phase) and 68 (altered prescribed periods) are subject to r.108(5) and (7) and may be extended (or further extended) by two months only. In particular, conditions may be applied, and further, no extension may be granted in respect of the periods prescribed by these rules after the end of the period of two months beginning immediately after the period of time as prescribed (or previously extended) has expired (r.108(7)).

Accelerated examination (PCT(UK) Fast Track)

89A.40   Applicants are now able to request accelerated examination in the UK national phase if their international application has received a positive International Preliminary Report on Patentability (IPRP; see the Practice Notice entitled "*PCT(UK) Fast Track*" in the Patents Law and Practice section of the UK-IPO website). This system is not part of any PCT-PPH (Patent Prosecution Highway) program but it is understood that it allows applicants to request accelerated examination in the UK national phase if their international application has received a positive international preliminary report on patentability either under Chapter I or under Chapter II regardless of which Authority has issued that report (see also MOPP para.89B.17.1). To qualify for this service, all claims present in the application on entry to the national phase must have been examined and found to meet the requirements for novelty, inventive step and industrial applicability in the international phase. Thus, if the IPRP states in Box III that certain claims have not been examined, or if any objections to novelty, inventive step or industrial applicability have been raised in Box V of the

IPRP, then acceleration is not available under this service. Moreover, it should be noted that where these requirements have not been met in the international phase, but outstanding objections are overcome by requesting deletion of the objectionable claims on commencement of the national phase, the "Fast Track" service is NOT available. The UK-IPO states that this is because the service is intended to reward applicants who have made such amendments in the international phase (MOPP para.89B.17.1). However, if the IPRP has not yet been issued, a positive written opinion of the international searching authority is also acceptable, as the written opinion will later be reissued as the IPRP under PCT Chapter I (MOPP para.89B.17.1).

Where appropriate, the applicant should request accelerated examination in writing, indicating that the application has received a suitably positive IPRP or written opinion. The UK-IPO has stated that it will not require further reasons. The UK-IPO has also indicated that it is helpful if any correspondence relating to such accelerated applications is clearly marked as such, for example by boldly indicating "URGENT - ACCELERATED PROCESSING REQUESTED". This helps the UK-IPO to more rapidly identify correspondence relating to accelerated applications and ensure that the examiner receives this correspondence as quickly as possible. In the unlikely event that supply by WIPO of a copy of the IPRP is delayed, the UK-IPO may also ask the applicant to provide a copy in order to expedite the process (see the Practice Notice entitled "*PCT(UK) Fast Track*" in the Patents Law and Practice section of the UK-IPO website).

Any request for accelerated examination will be considered by the examiner, who will then advise whether the request is allowed or refused. Reasons for any refusal will be provided. If the request is allowed, accelerated examination will commence. However, whilst a condition for "Fast Track" status, the examiner is not bound by the positive written opinion or IPRP (MOPP para.89B.17.1). The usual opportunity for voluntary amendment under r. 31(4) will also be available after issue of the first examination report.

At the time of writing the UK-IPO has set a target to issue a substantive examination report within two months of receipt of the request for accelerated examination, on at least 90 per cent of cases (see the Practice Notice entitled "*PCT(UK) Fast Track*" in the Patent Law and Practice section of the UK-IPO website).

SECTION 89B [ADDED]

Adaptation of provisions in relation to international application

89B.—(1) Where an international application for a patent (UK) is accorded a filing date under the Patent Co-operation Treaty— **89B.01**

- (a) that date, or if the application is re-dated under the Treaty to a later date that later date, shall be treated as the date of filing the application under this Act,

- (b) any declaration of priority made under the Treaty shall be treated as made under section 5(2) above, and where in accordance with the Treaty any extra days are allowed, the period of 12 months **allowed under section 5(2A)(a) above** [*specified in section 5(2)*] shall be treated as altered accordingly, and

- (c) any statement of the name of the inventor under the Treaty shall be treated as a statement filed under section 13(2) above.

(2) If the application, not having been published under this Act, is published in accordance with the Treaty it shall be treated, for purposes other than those mentioned in subsection (3), as published under section 16 above when the national phase of the application **begins or, if later, when published in accordance with the Treaty** [*the conditions mentioned in section 89A(3)(a) are complied with*].

(3) For the purposes of section 55 (use of invention for service of the Crown) and section 69 (infringement of rights conferred by publication) the application, not having been published under this Act, shall be treated as published under section 16 above—

    (a) if it is published in accordance with the Treaty in English, on its being so published; and

    (b) if it is so published in a language other than English—

        (i) on the publication of a translation of the application in accordance with section 89A(6) above, or

        (ii) on the service by the applicant of a translation into English of the specification of the application of the government department concerned or, as the case may be, on the person committing the infringing act.

The reference in paragraph (b)(ii) to the service of a translation on a government department or other person is to its being sent by post or delivered to that department or person.

(4) During the international phase of the application, section 8 above does not apply (determination of questions of entitlement in relation to application under this Act) and section 12 above (determination of entitlement in relation to foreign and convention patents) applies notwithstanding the application; but after the end of the international phase, section 8 applies and section 12 does not.

(5) When the national phase begins the comptroller shall refer the application for so much of the examination and search under [*section*] **sections 15A**, 17 and 18 above as he considers appropriate in view of any examination or search carried out under the Treaty.

Notes

    1. Section 89B was added by the CDPA 1988 (c.48) Sch.5(25).

    2. The amendments to subss.(1) and (5) indicated above were made by the Regulatory Reform (Patents) Order 2004 (SI 2004/2357) ("RRO"), effective from January 1, 2005. However, neither these amendments, nor s.15A, has any effect on international applications which, by this date, had already entered the UK national phase, see Note 2 to §15.01.

    3. The indicated amendment to subs.(2) was made by the Patents Act 2004 (c.16) Sch.1(8) with effect from January 1, 2005 (SI 2004/3205).

RELEVANT RULES—RULES 66–70

89B.02   The relevant rules applicable to s.89B are rr.66 to 70 (reprinted in §§89A.02 to 89A.06) and the other rules listed in §89A.07.

COMMENTARY ON SECTION 89B

Scope of the section

89B.03   This is the last of the three sections which deal with international applications (UK). The general remarks at §89.08 also apply to the present section. Section 89B(1) equates: (a) the international filing date with a United Kingdom filing date; (b) a declaration of priority under the PCT with a declaration of priority under the Act; and (c) indications concerning the inventor under the PCT with a declaration of inventorship under the Act. Section 89B(2) provides that publication under the PCT is not equated with publication under the Act unless and until the application enters the UK phase. Nevertheless, s.89B(3) ensures that the provisional protection arising on publication may commence as early as the international publication date. Section 89B(4) deals with the Comptroller's power to consider entitlement to international applications. Section 89B(5) concerns the search and examination in the UK phase.

Additionally, correction (in the UK phase) of errors made in the international phase is discussed at §89B.12, and the application of more favourable provisions in the UK phase forms the subject of §89B.13.

Filing date (subs.(1)(a))

The object of s.89B(1)(a) is to ensure that the filing date for the purposes of the Act is **89B.04** the international filing date (PCT art.11(3)). According to art.11(1), (2)(b) of the PCT, an international filing date is accorded when the minimum requirements set forth in art.11(1) of the PCT are fulfilled. However, r.20.3 of the PCT provides for re-dating of the international application where not all sheets are received on the same day. In the event of such re-dating, the newly accorded date is regarded as the filing date for the purposes of the Act. If the minimum requirements are not fulfilled within two months of the date on which sheets were first received (in the case where no invitation to correct under PCT art.11(2)(a) was sent to the applicant) or within a time limit of two months fixed by the receiving office (PCT r.20.7), the application is not accorded an international filing date and is not treated as an international application (PCT r.20.4). Rule 20.3 of the PCT also allows incorporation of parts or elements by reference from a priority document, see §89.11.

Declaration of priority (subs.(1)(b))

A declaration of priority under the PCT is, by virtue of subs.(1)(b), treated as a declara- **89B.05** tion of priority made under the Act. The reference in the previous version of subs.(l)(b) to "specified under section 5(2)" was changed to "allowed under section 5(2A)(a)" in order to accommodate the possible allowed late filing of a priority declaration, as described in §5.17. Also, by virtue of r.8(3) and (4) (reprinted in §5.09), the requirements of r.8(1) and (2) as to the furnishing of the filing number and the filing of the priority document are treated as fulfilled to the extent that the corresponding requirements of the Regulations under the PCT are fulfilled. These requirements are in rr.4.10, 17 and 26 *bis* of the PCT. By analogy with the introduction of s.5(6) (see §§5.01 and 5.29), r.4.10 of the PCT was amended with effect from January 1, 2000 to enable a declaration of priority in an international application to be based on an application in or for a Member State of the World Trade Organisation, even when that WTO Member is not a party to the Paris Convention. It would seem that a priority claim in an international application (UK) must always be recognised in the United Kingdom by virtue of subs.(1)(b), even when that priority claim is based on an application in or for a Paris Convention country which is neither a WTO Member nor a country declared under s.90 to be a convention country for the purposes of s.5, as indicated in §90.02.

Rule 26 *bis* of the PCT was added to the Regulations with effect from July 1, 1998 to permit a priority claim to be added after the filing of an international application and to simplify the provisions for correcting a priority claim. Rule 17 of the PCT was amended with effect from the same date to ensure that the applicant will always have an opportunity to file the priority document at the designated offices in the national phase.

The time limit, applicable in the international phase, for adding a priority claim or for correcting a priority claim (whether voluntarily or in response to an invitation from the receiving office or from the International Bureau) expires four months from the international filing date or 16 months from the priority date, whichever is later (PCT r.26 *bis*). When the correction or addition of the priority claim results in a change of priority date, the 16-month time limit is computed from the earlier of the original and changed priority dates. When a notice of an addition or correction of a priority claim is received after a request for early publication has been made, that notice is considered not to have been submitted unless the request for early publication is withdrawn before the technical preparations for publication have been completed (PCT r.26 *bis*.1(b)). Rule 66(3) expressly provides that where an international application for a patent (UK) has begun the national phase, a request for permission to make a late declaration may be made under s.5(2B) before the end of the period of one month beginning with the date the national phase of the application begins. This period cannot be extended under r.108 (Rules Sch.4 Pt 1). In *Investigen Inc's Application* (BL O/009/08) the applicant filed a PCT application one day after the end of the 12-month period for claiming priority. The hearing officer held that the PCT application needed to enter the national phase before a request to make a late declaration of priority under s.5(2B) could be made, and also found that since not all the relevant requirements had been satisfied the PCT application did not enter the national phase within the fourteen month period required for making a request under s.5(2B). The request to make a late declaration of priority was therefore refused.

Whilst the date and country or office of filing of the earlier application must be included in the priority claim, the priority claim is not prejudiced in the international phase if the filing number of the earlier application is not furnished or if the priority document is not filed or if there is an uncorrected discrepancy between an indication in the priority claim and the corresponding indication in the priority document. If the applicant fails to correct an error in a priority claim in response to an invitation to make the correction, the receiving office or the International Bureau, as the case may be, declares that the priority claim is considered not to have been made, except when the error is the absence of the filing number of the earlier application or a discrepancy between the priority claim and the priority document. In the event of such a declaration which is disputed by the applicant, he can have the disputed priority claim included in the published application. He can also apply to the UK-IPO, as designated office, to have the disputed priority claim re-instated, so far as concerns the United Kingdom, see §89B.12.

The priority document should be filed in the international phase at the receiving office or at the International Bureau (PCT r.17.1(a)). The time limit for this is 16 months from the priority date but the priority document is considered to have been filed at the end of this 16-month time limit provided that it reaches the International Bureau before the date of international publication. When the earlier application on which the priority claim is based was filed at the national office which is acting as the receiving office, the applicant may, instead of filing the priority document, request the receiving office to forward it to the International Bureau (PCT r.17.1(b)). The time limit for this is 16 months from the priority date. If the priority document was not duly furnished in the international phase, the conditions of r.8(4) are not fulfilled but the applicant must be given an opportunity to file the priority document at the UK-IPO within a time limit that is reasonable in the circumstances before the Office can disregard the priority claim (PCT r.17.1(c)). Whilst the rules under the PCT do not contain a corresponding provision for the case in which the filing number of the earlier application is not furnished in the international phase, it would appear that the UK-IPO, as a designated office, cannot reject the priority claim on the ground that the filing number was not furnished in the international phase because the filing number can presumably be ascertained from the priority document and the priority claim will then comply fully with r.8(4). For similar reasons, the Office should give the applicant an opportunity to remove any outstanding discrepancy between the indications in the priority claim and those in the priority document, either by filing corrected indications or by filing a corrected priority document, depending on which contained an error. Subsection (1)(b) takes into account that the priority term of 12 months may be extended under the PCT. Such extension may, for example, be granted pursuant to r.82.2 of the PCT (interruption in the mail service).

The reference in subs.(1)(b) to "specified under s.5(2)" has been changed to "allowed under section 5(2A)(a)" in order to accommodate the possible allowed late filing of a priority declaration, as described in §5.03 above.

The filing of a translation of the priority document, when required (r.9), is discussed at §89A.19. Rule 49 *ter* of the PCT, makes provision for restoration of rights of priority by designated (or elected) offices under the PCT. This is in addition to the procedures available at the receiving office as discussed under §89.11 above. Thus, if an application before the receiving office under PCT r.26 *bis*.3 is unsuccessful (or even overlooked) it may be possible to seek relief in the national phase under PCT r.49 *ter* on a territory-by-territory basis. Conversely, however, some designated/elected states may not recognise a restoration of the right of priority by a receiving office during the international phase, depending among other things on the criteria for restoration which were applied by that receiving office.

For further details on the relevant procedures reference should be made to the *PCT Applicant's Guide* and to the PCTH paras 19.5D and 33.19B.

The UK-IPO has indicated that it will apply the "unintentionality" criterion in considering requests for restoration of the right of priority under PCT r.49 *ter* (*Official Notices* (*PCT Gazette*) 29 March 2007, p.56). The meaning and interpretation of the term "unintentional" is discussed generally in the MOPP, para.20A.13.

Gordon's Application BL O/374/07 discussed at §89.11, above, provides an example of a restoration of the right of priority under PCT r.26 *bis*.3 by the UK-IPO acting in its capacity as a receiving office (and conversely *Jones' Application* BL O/022/09 and *Crilly's Application* BL O/182/10 provide examples where restoration was refused). Similar approaches might perhaps be expected to be taken by the UK-IPO in its capacity as a designated/elected office under PCT r.49 *ter*.

Effect of non-filing of priority document

As described in §89B.05, the UK-IPO must give the applicant an opportunity to file the **89B.06** priority document there if one was not duly furnished in the international phase. Thus, non-filing of the priority document in the international phase does not immediately result in the priority claim being disregarded and the date from which the 31-month time limit for entry into the UK phase is computed is unaltered. If the applicant fails to furnish the priority document to the UK-IPO in response to an invitation, the priority claim may then be disregarded for non compliance with r.8(4) by virtue of non-compliance with r.17.1(c) of the PCT. If the priority date is changed as a result of a priority claim being disregarded, the expiry of time limits computed from the priority date is likewise changed. Such time limits include the 33-month time limit for filing PF 9A and the 33-month time limit for filing PF 10. It is worth noting that no information is published with the international application as to whether a priority document was duly filed in the international phase. It is possible to obtain a copy of the priority document from the International Bureau after international publication, so long as the declaration of priority has not been withdrawn before such publication, and assuming one was filed (PCT r.17.2(c)), see §89.13.

If a notice of withdrawal of a priority claim is filed at the receiving office or the International Bureau or at the international preliminary examining authority when PCT Ch.II applies, prior to expiry of 30 months from the priority date (PCT r.90 *bis*.3), this can displace the date for computing the 31-month time limit for entering the UK phase as well as time limits applicable in the UK phase.

The designation of the inventor for the United Kingdom (subs.(1)(c))

If the inventor is the applicant, or one of several applicants, for an international applica- **89B.07** tion (UK), then the international request form (PCT/RO/101) may say so (PCT art.4(1)(v) and PCT r.4.6), and no action is then required in the UK phase to name the inventor. If the inventor is not an applicant, but he is named on the international request form (PCT/RO/101), again no action is needed in the UK phase. If the inventor is not named in the international phase, then PF 7 must be filed at the UK-IPO on or shortly after entry into the UK phase (see §89A.32).

Just as disputes as to entitlement may be brought and possibly settled in the international phase (see §89B.11), it would appear that disputes as to inventorship may also be brought in the international phase as well as in the national phase. Specifically, a person may apply at any time under s.13 and r.10 (reprinted at §13.04) for himself or any other person to be mentioned as inventor or for a certificate that another person ought not to have been mentioned as inventor and it would seem that this will apply to an international application before it has entered the UK phase. However, any proceedings under s.13 will be confined to the designation of the United Kingdom (not coupled with a request for a European patent), and any decision by the Comptroller will be of no effect so far as the designation of the EPO or of any country, other than the United Kingdom, is concerned because inventorship is determined under national laws. Also, only the applicant or the receiving office may request the International Bureau to alter the name of the inventor in the international phase (PCT r.92 *bis*). Accordingly, it may be difficult to conclude proceedings under s.13 before the international application (UK) has entered the UK phase. If the proceedings under s.13 are not concluded by the time the international application enters the UK phase and are coupled with entitlement proceedings under s.12, where inventorship is in issue, the s.12 proceedings in respect of the international application (UK) are converted to s.8 proceedings (see §89B.11) and the procedure of rr.20, 90(1) and Pt 7 (described at §8.09 thereafter applies to the inventorship issue under s.13 as well as the United Kingdom entitlement dispute (r.10, reprinted in §13.04).

Effect of international publication (subs.(2))

89B.08   When international publication under PCT art.21 takes place in the international phase, as it normally does, then this replaces publication under s.16 (s.89A(1)). However, if the application enters the UK phase before international publication, as may happen when expressly requesting an early start to national processing (see §89A.16), or in the event of a favourable review under PCT art.25 (see §89.28), then the Office must publish the application under s.16 as described at §89B.14. Subsection (2) ensures that, even when international publication takes place after valid entry into the UK phase, such international publication is equivalent to publication under s.16, notwithstanding s.89A(1), but subject to subs.(3), unless actual publication under s.16 takes place before international publication. These matters are relevant to the prior art effect (see §89B.09) and to the provisional protection arising on publication (see §89B.10). The revision of subs.(2) (noted in §89B.01) made it clear that, provided that an international application has been published under the PCT, then it is treated as published under s.16 even when the application enters the national UK phase early. However, if the application has not yet been published under the PCT then the application is not treated as published under s.16 until publication under the PCT has taken place.

Prior art effect under section 2(3)

89B.09   The prior art effect of an international application (UK), for the purposes of s.2(3), comes into being immediately on entry into the UK phase, assuming that international publication has taken place, and cannot subsequently be lost, even if the application is withdrawn or deemed withdrawn in the UK phase. This is consequential to subs.(2). Note that, under s.89A(3), it is not necessary that any documents, other than any prescribed translation, be filed or that any fee, other than the national fee, be paid to secure valid entry into the UK phase. In particular, it is not necessary for PF 9A to be filed. Conversely, an international application (UK) which is withdrawn or deemed withdrawn in the international phase (s.89(2)), or otherwise does not enter the UK phase (s.89A(4)), can never form part of the state of the art for the purposes of s.2(3). Decision T 623/93 (unreported) illustrates this. The prior art effect under s.2(3) is discussed more fully in §§2.11–2.13.

For international applications which entered the UK phase before the present form of ss.89, 89A and 89B came into force, the question as to whether the prior art effect under s.2(3) was lost if the application was withdrawn or deemed withdrawn after entry into the UK phase depends on whether a withdrawal or deemed withdrawal in the UK phase was under s.14(9) or under the former s.89(8) (not reprinted here). Since at this stage the application would have been proceeding under Pts I and III of the Act, an argument could have been developed that the original s.89(8) could not be operative after entry into the UK phase. In any case, this original provision did not cover refusal of the application. It would have been strange if a different result would have obtained, depending on whether the application was withdrawn or refused.

Provisional protection arising on publication (subs.(3))

89B.10   The provisions of subs.(3) are an exception to the generality of subs.(2), according to which an international application (UK) is not deemed to be published for the purposes of the Act (as discussed at §89B.08) until valid entry into the UK phase has taken place. If the international application is published in the international phase in English, the provisional protection (i.e. the right to recover payment under s.55 (Crown use); and the right to recover damages under s.69 (infringement after publication), is retrospective back to the international publication date (subs.(3)(a)). If the international application is published in the international phase in any other language, the provisional protection can be obtained by meeting the relevant conditions and by requesting publication of a translation by filing this with a written request (subs.(3)(b)). There is a space on PF NP.1 for making this request. An additional fee is payable, see the Patents (Fees) Rules, but no separate fee form is designated. Routine re-publication by the UK-IPO (see §89B.14) is of no consequence, since it is not under s.16 (MOPP, para.89A.14.2; *PCT Applicant's Guide*, at Vol.II (National Phase), National Chapter (GB), para.GB.08). Nevertheless, earlier protection can still be obtained by sending a translation to the relevant government department or to the infringer, as the case may be, and this can be done even before entry into the UK phase.

In view of the references to publication in ss.55(4), 69(1) and 89A(3)(b), it is not possible to recover payment or damages in respect of any Crown use or infringement before the international publication date. If the international application (UK) enters the UK phase, and the application is published under s.16 (see §89B.14) before international publication has taken place, the provisional protection arising on publication by virtue of ss.55 and 69 commences when publication under s.16 takes place. As it is not possible to record an exclusive licence in the international phase (see §32.19), rights under s.69 may be prejudiced until the international application (UK) has entered the UK phase, see §69.04—69.05.

For the provisional protection arising from the international publication of a Euro-PCT application, see §79.04.

Disputes as to entitlement (subs.(4))

Subsection (4) ensures that a dispute as to the right to be granted a patent or patents pursuant to an international application is governed in the international phase by s.12 and not by s.8. However, once the application has entered the UK phase (assuming it does), the dispute is then conducted under s.8. Nevertheless, s.12 will continue to apply in respect of a European phase (even if a United Kingdom designation is included in the Euro-PCT application) and in respect of the continued processing of the international application in other countries.

89B.11

In general, the Comptroller does not have any jurisdiction to put into effect any decision he may make under s.12 as to the entitlement to the grant of patents (other than the grant of a patent (UK) or a European patent) pursuant to an international application. Such matters need to be referred to the relevant authorities in each of the designated countries, which might be possible before entry into the national phase, depending on national laws.

For more on the operation of s.12 in the international phase and s.8 in the national phase, see the commentaries on those sections. For disputes as to inventorship arising in the international phase, see §89B.07.

Correction of mistakes arising in international phase

Here, there is considered only the rectification of obvious mistakes which did not result in the international application, or the designation of the United Kingdom, being considered withdrawn or which did not result in the international application being denied an international filing date. Errors which did have such a result and to which r.71 relate exclusively, are discussed in §§89.28, 89.30 and 89.32.

89B.12

Rectification of obvious mistakes can be authorised by the international authorities (PCT r.91), as described in the *PCT Applicant's Guide*, at Vol.I (International Phase), paras 11.033 to 11.044, and see also the PCTH, Ch.35. The rectification of obvious mistakes does not fall within the expression "publication, search, examination and amendment" as used in s.89A(1), so that the UK-IPO may consider that it has a right to review any rectification authorised in the international phase, just as it has been held that the predecessor to r.107 could be applied to correct a demand for international preliminary examination even though this would have retrospective effect (*Prangley's Application* [1988] R.P.C. 187 CA). Such review is provided for in r.91.3(f) of the PCT. As the conditions for rectification of an obvious error under the PCT are no less stringent than the conditions for correction under s.117 and r.105, the UK-IPO seems unlikely to refuse to recognise a rectification authorised by an international authority, unless the international authority itself was wrong to authorise the rectification.

It is open to the applicant to apply under s.117 during the UK phase for correction of an error made in the international phase, even when an international authority has refused to authorise rectification. The UK-IPO is obliged to afford the applicant the more favourable conditions available under s.117 and r.105, particularly in relation to documents other than the description, claims and drawings (PCT art.26). This is discussed further at §89B.13. Rule 71(7)(b) (reprinted in §89.05) empowers the Comptroller to make certain corrections to documents received from the International Bureau, as further described below, and effectively extends some of the powers which the Comptroller has under r.107 (see §123.24) to a case where an irregularity in procedure occurs within an international authority. If authorisation to rectify an obvious error is refused by an international authority, the fact of refusal may, at the applicant's request, be published with the international application (PCT r.91.3(d). In the absence of any publication of the fact that rectification was applied for, it may be essential or advisable to commence early national processing (see §89A.16) in order to have the request for correction considered as soon as possible by the UK-IPO, as the Office must consider the effect on third parties of a correction material to the information revealed by the application as published by the International Bureau (see §89.13). If the fact of refusal to authorise a rectification appears in the international publication of the application, the need expressly to request an early start to national processing may be less pressing.

Historically, the addition of the designation of the United Kingdom to an international application is a rectification that can be authorised by an international authority (see *Vapocure Technologies' Application* [1990] R.P.C. 1 CA). However, now that international applications automatically designate all available contracting states (see §89.11) including the UK, this is likely to be of little or no relevance in the future. Any authorisation for correction of an obvious error must (except in the case of a rectification authorised by an international preliminary examining authority) reach the International Bureau within 26 months from the priority date (see PCT r.91.2). In *Vapocure*, the authorisation of rectification reached the International Bureau too late so that the United Kingdom was not included among the designated countries listed in the published application. The relevant conditions were complied with at the UK-IPO within the then prescribed 20-month period. It was held that there was no United Kingdom application in existence upon which the Comptroller could exercise any discretion in favour of the applicant and that he had no power to add the United Kingdom to the countries designated in the international application.

The authorisation of rectification of obvious mistakes under PCT r.91 by international authorities, and the general effect or otherwise of such corrections, are outside the scope of this Work and reference should be made, for example, to the PCTH and the *PCT Applicant's Guide*.

In the case of an error of translation, rectification may be authorised in the international phase under PCT r.91 or correction may be made in the UK phase under r.105. However, when the translation error is in the description, in the claims or in textual matter in the drawings, it is simpler, when still possible, to seek correction by way of voluntary amendment in the international phase under PCT art.34(2)(b) and PCT r.66.1(b) (see the PCTH, para.35.10) or in the UK phase under s.19(1) and r.31 (reprinted at §19.02). In either case, it is only necessary to show that the amendment does not introduce new matter, which can be done by reference to the text as originally filed, whatever its language.

It is not normally necessary for the provisions of r.91 of the PCT to be invoked to enable the correction of a priority claim in the international phase, because the applicant has the right to amend or add a priority claim under PCT r.26 *bis*, see §89B.05.

There is now no provision directly corresponding to r.85(11) of the Patents Rules 1995, pursuant to r.82 *ter*.1 of the PCT, enabling the Comptroller to correct the international filing date, so far as the United Kingdom is concerned, and to re-instate a priority claim which was considered not to have been made when the according of an incorrect filing date or the denial of the priority claim was the result of an error on the part of the receiving office or the International Bureau. However, it is thought that the effect of that rule can be achieved by virtue of either s.117 or r.108.

Rule 71(7) which gives the Comptroller discretionary power to correct errors and grant extensions, applies only in the case of errors which have resulted in the international application, or the designation of the United Kingdom, being deemed withdrawn or the application being refused an international filing date, as discussed in §§89.28 and 89.30.

In *Intelligence Quotient's Application* [1996] R.P.C. 258, the applicant attempted, unsuccessfully, to have the international filing date corrected under the rule in force at that time by alleging, inter alia, that there existed more favourable provisions of United Kingdom law which could be applied and/or that the late filing of the international request form could be excused under United Kingdom law.

More favourable law and excusing delay (PCT arts 26, 27 and 48)

Article 26 of the PCT requires that the UK-IPO shall not reject an international application (UK) for non-compliance with the PCT or its Regulations without first giving the applicant time to correct the application to the extent that is permissible under the Act and Rules in comparable circumstances. This provision cannot be used to overcome an objection on the ground of non-compliance with an express provision of the Act or Rules pursuant to the PCT, but it does allow the provisions of Pts I and III of the Act and the Rules under it to be applied to things done or not done in the international phase. In connection with art.27(4), (5) and (6) of the PCT, the provisions of the Act relating to such things as novelty, inventive step, industrial application, exclusion from patentability and unity of invention are essentially the same as those of the PCT. Accordingly, the opportunities to use art.26 of the PCT are not great and are confined mainly to errors made by the international authorities, obvious errors and time limits.

89B.13

In *Intelligence Quotient's Application* [1996] R.P.C. 258, the international request form had been initially omitted on filing a purported international application, so that no designation of States had been made and an international filing date could not be accorded until the request form, which included a designation of PCT States, was received. This was after expiry of the Convention period. The applicant failed to have the international filing date "corrected" (under the rule then in force) to the initial date of receipt of documents by the receiving office, thereby to enable the priority claim to be maintained. It was acknowledged that the rule then corresponding to present r.107 might be invoked before the Office as designated office in relation to an irregularity in procedure in the international phase, but was inapplicable in the circumstances. The corresponding Euro-PCT application was ante-dated by the EPO, following J 25/88 *NEW FLEX/Date of filing* OJ EPO 1989, 486; [1990] E.P.O.R. 59, but the Comptroller held that the Office could not reach the same conclusion because there are no provisions under the Act relating to designation of States and therefore no more favourable national provisions in the United Kingdom. The Comptroller observed (at p.279) that, because the EPO had accorded an earlier filing date, s.2(3) would destroy the novelty of the international application (UK), the United Kingdom also having been designated in the Euro-PCT application.

Clerical errors made in the international phase can be corrected under s.117 after the application has entered the UK phase, because the international application is deemed to be a United Kingdom application for the purposes of Pt III of the Act (s.89(1)), see also §89B.12.

It is unfortunate that there is no express provision to implement r.82 *bis* of the PCT (excuse of delays in meeting time limits), other than in the case of a review under s.89(3), see §89.28. Under PCT r.82 *bis*, PCT art.48(2) is applicable, inter alia, to excusing delays in meeting time limits to be observed in the international phase. Whilst r.107 (reprinted at §123.24) may be applied to correct certain irregularities in procedure in the international phase (*Prangley's Application* [1988] R.P.C. 187 and *Vapocure Technologies Ltd's Application* [1990] R.P.C. 1), it is less clear that it can be applied specifically to excuse the missing of time limits to be observed by the applicant in the international phase.

Even in the absence of any express provisions in the Rules, the Comptroller ought to take note of arts 26 and 48(2)(a) of the PCT and r.82 *bis* of the PCT and grant extensions to time limits which were to have been observed in the international phase when, in comparable circumstances, an extension would be available under the Act or the Rules or by virtue of practice under them. Time limits to be observed in the international phase are those prescribed in the PCT or in the Regulations or specified by any office (including the UK-IPO) acting as an international authority. The time limits coming into consideration here include the time limits specified in invitations to pay fees or correct defects found by the receiving office. Such defects, if uncorrected, will result in the international application being considered withdrawn (PCT art.14(1)(b)). Articles 26 and 48(2) of the PCT can in such circumstances be pleaded before the UK-IPO only in conjunction with a simultaneous request for a review under PCT art.25 and s.89(3), see §89.28.

Rule 111 (reprinted at §123.29) might be applied to an interruption in postal services during the international phase. However, the provisions of r.111 appear on the whole to be less favourable than those of r.82 of the PCT, made under PCT art.48(1), particularly as they are confined respectively to mail posted in the United Kingdom and to an interruption in postal services in the United Kingdom. Rule 82.1 and 82.2 of the PCT are discussed respectively in §§89.22 and 89.23.

For the possibility of restoration of a right of priority see §89.11.

It is to be observed that any decision of the Comptroller after valid entry into the UK phase, and involving the applicability of arts 26 and 48 of the PCT and rr.82, 82 *bis* and 82 *ter* of the PCT, is appealable to the Patents Court.

The article by G. Gall, "Excusal of failure to comply with time limits under the new rule 82 *bis*. PCT and application of means of redress under the EPC" (1986) 17 I.I.C. 618, discussed the interrelationship between PCT arts 25 and 48 and PCT rr.82 *bis* and 82 *ter*.

Publication and re-publication

89B.14   Normally, international publication (see §89.13) takes place before entry into the UK phase; in this event, there is no publication under the provisions of s.16 (see §89B.08). Nevertheless, it is the policy of the UK-IPO then to re-publish the application as soon as convenient after entry into the UK phase (MOPP, para.89A.14.2). When the international application is published in English, such re-publication takes the form of a single sheet containing a reference to the international publication, all the usual bibliographical data (see §16.04) and the abstract, together with one or more accompanying figures of the drawings, if any. When a translation of the international application has to be filed to secure valid entry into the UK phase, the re-publication includes such translation in its entirety.

The re-publication just described is an administrative act and is of no legal significance because it is not prescribed by the Act or the Rules. In particular, re-publication including a translation cannot establish provisional protection under the provisions of ss.55 and 69, see §89B.10.

The international application may enter the UK phase when there is to be no international publication or before international publication takes place, e.g. after review under s.89(3) (see §89.28), or after an express request for an early start to national processing under s.89A(3)(b) (see §89A.16). Because s.89A(1) then ceases to apply, the Comptroller must publish the application in full under s.16 by virtue of s.89(1) (see MOPP, para.89A.20.1). In the case of an express request for an early start to national processing, publication under PCT art.21 will also take place in due course.

Such international publication, or publication under s.16, whichever occurs first, establishes the prior art effect (see §89B.09) and (subject to any language requirement) the provisional protection arising on publication (see §89B.10). The position is different in the case of a Euro-PCT application where the designation for the United Kingdom is withdrawn or not implemented by payment of the designation fee, see §79.03.

After valid entry into the UK phase and even before re-publication, the public file of the international application can be inspected at the UK-IPO, see §118.10 et seq.

Search in the UK phase (subs.(5))

This subsection gives the Comptroller discretion to restrict the search made under s.17, having regard to the extent of the international search. It will always be necessary to search United Kingdom, European and international applications published after the international search commenced, in case any such recently published applications have a priority or filing date earlier than the international filing date, which may make them citable under s.2(2) or (3).

89B.15

It would seem that any "top-up" search, taking into account the international search report, is not normally conducted before PF 10 has been filed (see MOPP, paras 89B.10–89B.12).

Examination in the UK phase (subs.(5))

The search in the UK phase is discussed in §89B.15. Reference to s.15A has been added to subs.(5) to accommodate the relocation of the topic of "preliminary examination" into this new section, leaving s.17 dealing only with the topic of "search", see §§15A.05 and 17.08. Pursuant to the filing of PF 10, the Examiner conducts the substantive examination under s.18(2), or just so much examination as is deemed necessary having regard to any international preliminary examination report established under Ch.II of the PCT (subs.(5)). Evidently, notice can be taken of such report, even if it is not established before or does not reach the UK-IPO before the commencement of the UK phase (see MOPP, para.89B.13).

89B.16

Nevertheless, amendments made during international preliminary examination must be disregarded unless they reach the UK-IPO by commencement of the UK phase either by virtue of the timely communication of the international examination report or by being filed by the applicant (see §89A.18). However, such amendments may still be filed under s.19 (see §89B.17).

If any document cited in the international search report or international preliminary examination report is not in English, the Comptroller is entitled to ask for an English translation of all or a part of such documents (see rr.113 and 115, reprinted respectively in §§123.30 and 123.32), and he may make such as request if the specification of a corresponding patent or application in English is not available (MOPP para.89B.11).

The examination under s.18 must include a check to ensure that any amendments made in the international phase as well as any amendments made in the UK phase do not contravene s.76(2) (see §89B.17).

Amendment in the UK phase

As soon as the application enters the UK phase, amendment becomes subject to s.19 and r.31 (reprinted at §19.02). Thus, voluntary amendments may be lodged at any time up to issuance of the first examination report or when responding thereto. These amendments may comprise or include amendments filed in the international phase but disregarded because they did not reach the International Bureau or the international preliminary examining authority in time or did not reach the UK-IPO before the commencement of the UK phase, or because a translation did not reach the UK-IPO in time (see §89A.18). The UK-IPO is obliged to give the applicant at least one opportunity to amend (PCT art.28(1)). No amendment, whether made in the international or UK phase, may contravene s.76(2) (amendment of applications not to include new subject-matter), see also arts 28(2) and 34(2)(b) of the PCT.

89B.17

Division

The PCT contains no provisions as to the filing of divisional applications, but an international application (UK) can be divided in the UK phase in the same way as any application filed under the Act (see §§15.16–15.25). Indeed, as an international application is

89B.18

deemed (by PCT art.11(3)) to have the effect of a national application in each designated office, the possibility would seem to exist of filing, from an international application, a divisional application in the UK-IPO even before that international application has entered the UK national phase; r.19 (reprinted at §15.04) does not preclude such early filing. Note that the time available for placing a divisional application on an international application (UK) in order for grant (see §89B.20) may be very short.

When the parent international application (UK) was filed at the UK-IPO, as receiving office, a copy of the priority document does not have to be provided for the UK divisional application if this is available from the Office's own files (see r.8(4), reprinted in §5.09).

Withdrawal in the UK phase

89B.19 Withdrawal of the application in the UK phase is effected under s.14(9) (discussed at in §14.51). Withdrawal of the application, or of the designation of the United Kingdom, in the international phase, and a finding in the international phase that the application is considered withdrawn, are governed by s.89(2) (see §89.27); and deemed withdrawal in the international phase through failure to pay the national fee and file any necessary translation of the international application within the prescribed 31-month time limit is governed by s.89A(4) (see §89A.17).

Compliance with the Act and Rules

89B.20 An international application (UK) must be placed in order under ss.18 and 20 within the four-and-a-half-year period from the priority date, or the one-year period from the date of the first examination report prescribed by r.30, whichever is the later (see §§89A.38). Because of the "delay" obtained by use of the PCT, the time available for examination by the Patent Office may be reduced as compared with an application initially filed under the Act.

PRACTICE UNDER SECTION 89B

Prosecution in the UK phase

89B.21 Search, examination and amendment in the UK phase are covered by §§89A.36 et seq. which are closely interrelated with the formalities upon, and after, entry into the UK phase.

Convention countries [Section 90]

SECTION 90

Orders in Council as to convention countries

90.01 **90.**—(1) Her Majesty may with a view to the fulfilment of a treaty or international convention, arrangement or engagement, by Order in Council declare that any country specified in the Order is a convention country for the purposes of section 5 above.

(2) Her Majesty may by Order in Council direct that any of the Channel Islands, any colony [*or any British protectorate or protected state*] shall be taken to be a convention country for those purposes.

(3) For the purposes of subsection (1) above every colony, protectorate, and territory subject to the authority or under the suzerainty of another country, and every territory administered by another country under the trusteeship system of the United Nations shall be taken to be a country in the case of which a declaration may be made under that subsection.

Note. Subsection (2) was amended by the Statute Laws (Repeals) Act 1986 (c.12).

COMMENTARY ON SECTION 90

Scope of the section

Section 90 provides for countries, by Order in Council, to be declared "convention countries" for the purposes of the claiming of priority under s.5. As of writing, the most recent Orders are SI 2007/276, the Patents (Convention Countries) Order 2007, which took effect on April 6, 2007, repealing all previous such orders, and consolidating the list of countries designated as "convention countries", and the Patents (Convention Countries) (Amendment) Order 2009 (SI 2009/2746) which came into force on November 12, 2009 and inserted "Cape Verde" into the list of countries in the Schedule to the 2007 Order.

90.02

The TRIPS Agreement (Cmnd.3046) is part of the general Agreement which set up the World Trade Organization ("WTO"), and art.3 requires nationals of other Member States to be given "treatment no less favourable than that it accords to its own nationals with regard to the protection of intellectual property". For this reason, WTO Member States are now automatically designated as "convention countries" for the purposes of s.5, see s.5(6). No distinction is drawn between States which are "convention countries" by virtue of being members of the Paris Convention or because of their membership of the World Trade Organization. A footnote to this art.3 states that:

> "When 'nationals' are referred to in [the TRIPS] Agreement, they shall be deemed, in the case of a separate customs territory member of the WTO, to mean persons, natural or legal, who are domiciled or who have a real and effective industrial or commercial establishment in that customs territory".

Such a person is herein called "a WTO proprietor".

The list of currently designated "convention countries" as provided by the 2007 Order (as amended) is set out in §90.03, and it is there indicated which of these countries are not members of the Paris Convention or WTO Members. Whether a country is, or is not, a WTO Member has particular importance with regard to applications for compulsory licences under s.48, as the grounds upon which such a licence may be granted now differentiate between patents owned by a WTO proprietor (governed by new s.48A) and patents otherwise owned (governed by new s.48B), the 1999 Order replacing ss.48 and 52 and adding the new ss.48A and 48B, see the commentaries on those sections.

The United Kingdom (GB) is itself not a convention country for the purposes of the Act, see *Agfa-Gevaert's Application* [1982] R.P.C. 441, and this position is maintained by a specific exclusion (in new s.5(6), reprinted in §5.01) from the effect of the 1999 Order of the United Kingdom (which for the purposes of the Act includes the Isle of Man), even though the United Kingdom is a WTO Member.

Subsection (2) permits any of the Channel Islands or any colony to be so designated, but the only order so made under this provision was in respect of Hong Kong and the change of status of that territory has not affected this designation.

The list of convention countries under the Paris Union contains minor differences from the list of countries (under the Chicago Convention relating to international means of transportation) to which exempting powers with regard to infringement exist under s.60(4)–(7) and to which s.90 does not apply. However, the 1999 Order also amended s.60(7) to include automatically WTO Members as designated states for the purpose of those infringement exemptions, see further §60.17, and thus the differences between the Paris Union and Chicago Convention territories have been narrowed still further.

Countries designated as "convention countries"

The "convention countries" under the Act, as provided by the 2007 Order discussed in §90.02, are listed below, to which the WIPO standard two-letter codes have been added in parentheses. This list also indicates by the suffix*, if a country is **not** a WTO Member; and by the suffix *, if a country is **not** a Member of the Paris Union.

90.03

Albania (AL)

Algeria (DZ)^x

Andorra (AD)^x

Angola (AO)

Antigua and Barbuda (AG)

Argentina (AR)

Armenia (AM)

Australia (AU)

Austria (AT)

Azerbaijan (AZ)^x

Bahamas (BS)^x

Bahrain (BH)

Bangladesh (BD)

Barbados (BB)

Belarus (BY)

Belgium (BE)

Belize (BZ)

Benin (BJ)

Bhutan (BT)^x

Bolivia (BO)

Bosnia and Herzegovina (BA)^x

Botswana (BW)

Brazil (BR)

Brunei Darussalam (BN)

Bulgaria (BG)

Burkina Faso (BF)

Burundi (BI)

Cambodia (KH)

Cameroon (CM)

Canada (CA)

Cape Verde (CV)^x

Central African Republic (CF)

Chad (TD)

Chile (CL)

China (CN)

Colombia (CO)

Comoros (KM)^x

Congo (CG)

Congo, Democratic Republic of the (ZR)

Costa Rica (CR)

Côte d'Ivoire (Ivory Coast) (CI)

Croatia (HR)

Cuba (CU)

Cyprus (CY)

Czech Republic (CZ)

Denmark (DK)[1]

Djibouti (DJ)

Dominica (DM)

Dominican Republic (DO)

Ecuador (EC)

Egypt (EG)

El Salvador (SV)*

Equatorial Guinea (GQ)^x

Estonia (EE)

Faeroe Islands (FO)^{xx}

Fiji (FJ)*

Finland (FI)

France (including Overseas Departments and Territories) (FR)

Gabon (GA)

Gambia (GM)

Georgia (GE)

Germany (DE)

Ghana (GH)

Greece (GR)

Grenada (GD)

Guatemala (GT)

Guinea (GN)

Guinea-Bissau (GW)

Guyana (GY)

Haiti (HT)

Holy See (VA)^x

Honduras

Hong Kong (HK)*

Hungary (HU)

Iceland (IS)

India (IN)

Indonesia (ID)

Iran, Islamic Republic of (IR)^x

Iraq (IQ)^x

Ireland (IE)

Israel (IL)

Italy (IT)

Jamaica (JM)

Japan (JP)

Jordan (JO)

Kazakhstan (KZ)^x

Kenya (KE)

Korea, Democratic Republic of (KP)^{xx}

Korea, Republic of (KR)

Kuwait (KW)*

Kyrgyzstan (KG)

Lao, People's Democratic Republic (LA)^x

Latvia (LV)

Lebanon (LB)^x

Lesotho (LS)

Liberia (LR)*

Libyan Arab Jamahiriya (LY)^x

Liechtenstein (LD)

Lithuania (LT)

Luxembourg (LU)

Macau (MO)

Macedonia, Former Yugoslav Republic of (MK)^x

Madagascar (MG)

Malawi (MW)

Malaysia (MY)

Maldives (MV)*

Mali (ML)

Malta (MT)

Mauritania (MR)

Mauritius (MU)

Mexico (MX)

Moldova, Republic of (MD)

Monaco (MC)^x

Mongolia (MN)

Montenegro (MG)^x

Morocco (MA)

Mozambique (MZ)

Myanmar (MM)*

Namibia (NA)

Nepal (NP)

Netherlands (NL)

Netherlands Antilles (and Aruba^x) (AN)

New Zealand (including the Cook Isalnds, Niue and Tokelau) (NZ)

Nicaragua (NL)
Niger (NE)
Nigeria (NG)
Norway (NO)
Oman (OM)
Pakistan (PK)
Panama (PA)
Papua New Guinea (PG)
Paraguay (PY)
Peru (PE)
Philippines (PH)
Poland (PL)
Portugal (PT)
Quatar (QA)
Romania (RO)
Russian Federation (RU)ˣ
Rwanda (RW)
Saint Kitts and Nevis (KN)
Saint Lucia (LC)
Saint Vincent and the Grenadines (VC)
San Marino (SM)ˣ

Sao Tome and Principe (ST)ˣ
Saudi Arabia (SA)
Senegal (SN)
Serbia (RS)ˣ
Seychelles (SC)ˣ
Sierra Leone (SL)
Singapore (SG)
Slovakia (SK)
Slovenia (SI)
Soloman Islands (SB)*
South Africa (ZA)
Spain (ES)
Sri Lanka (LK)
Sudan (SD)ˣ
Suriname (SR)
Swaziland (SZ)
Sweden (SE)
Switzerland (CH)
Syrian Arab Republic (SY)ˣ
Taiwan (TW)ˣ*
Tajikistan (TJ)ˣ

Tanzania, United Republic of (TZ)
Thailand (TH)
Togo (TG)
Tonga (TO)
Trinidad and Tobago (TT)
Tunisia (TN)
Turkey (TR)
Turkmenistan (TM)ˣ
Uganda (UG)
Ukraine (UA)ˣ
United Arab Emirates (AE)
United States of America (including Puerto Rico and all territories and possessions) (US)
Uruguay (UY)
Uzbekistan (UZ)ˣ
Venezuela (VE)
Vietnam (VN)ˣ
Yemen (YE)
Zambia (ZM)
Zimbabwe (ZW)

Effect of incorrect designation of convention country on the UK-IPO

The UK-IPO is not in a position to question whether the wording of an Order in Council **90.04** is ultra vires. Therefore, if it is felt that, because of political changes in the status of a country, such ought not to have been treated as a "convention country" under s.90, so that priority under s.5 was improperly accorded by the Comptroller, relief from the court should be sought by way of judicial review, see *Dirks' Applications* [1960] R.P.C. 1.

Miscellaneous [Sections 91–95]

SECTION 91

Evidence of conventions and instruments under conventions

91.—(1) Judicial notice shall be taken of the following, that is to say— **91.01**

    (a) the European Patent Convention, the Community Patent Convention and the Patent Co-operation Treaty (each of which is hereafter in this section referred to as the relevant convention);

    (b) any bulletin, journal or gazette published under the relevant convention and the register of European **patents kept under the European Patent Convention** [*or Community patents kept under it*]; and

    (c) any decision of, or expression of opinion by, the relevant convention court on any question arising under or in connection with the relevant convention.

  (2) Any document mentioned in subsection (1)(b) above shall be admissible

as evidence of any instrument or other act thereby communicated of any convention institution.

(3) Evidence of any instrument issued under the relevant convention by any such institution, including any judgment or order of the relevant convention court, or of any document in the custody of any such institution or reproducing in legible form any information in such custody otherwise than in legible form, or any entry in or extract from such a document, may be given in any legal proceedings by production of a copy certified as a true copy by an official of that institution; and any document purporting to be such a copy shall be received in evidence without proof of the official position or handwriting of the person signing the certificate.

(4) Evidence of any such instrument may also be given in any legal proceedings—

(a) by production of a copy purporting to be printed by the Queen's Printer;

(b) where the instrument is in the custody of a government department, by production of a copy certified on behalf of the department to be a true copy by an officer of the department generally or specially authorised to do so;

and any document purporting to be such a copy as is mentioned in paragraph (b) above of an instrument in the custody of a department shall be received in evidence without proof of the official position or handwriting of the person signing the certificate, or of his authority to do so, or of the document being in the custody of the department.

(5) In any legal proceedings in Scotland evidence of any matter given in a manner authorised by this section shall be sufficient evidence of it.

(6) In this section—

"convention institution" means an institution established by or having functions under the relevant convention;

"relevant convention court" does not include a court of the United Kingdom or of any other country which is a party to the relevant convention; and

"legal proceedings", in relation to the United Kingdom, includes proceedings before the comptroller.

Note. Subsection (1) was amended by the Patents Act 2004 (c.16) Sch.2para.20.

COMMENTARY ON SECTION 91

Scope of the section

91.02   Section 91 is the first of a group of sections (ss.91–95), the effect of which is to give statutory force to certain provisions relating to the EPC, the CPC (which is now redundant as such) and the PCT, and to provide for various consequential matters and publications. As matters of foreign law and practice are regarded as issues of fact which require to be proved before a United Kingdom court may place reliance upon them, the purpose of s.91 is to provide exceptions to the need to provide such proof in relation to matters connected with the operation or construction of these three conventions/treaties, for example by specifying certain matters as ones of which the court may take "judicial notice", that is to accept copy documents without further proof.

Thus, subs.(1) provides that judicial notice is to be taken of: each of the EPC, CPC and PCT ("the relevant convention") (para.(a)), for further details of which see §130.08; any bulletin or publication under the EPC, CPC or PCT and including the European register (para.(b)); and any decision or opinion by a relevant court (para.(c)). The amendment to subs.(1)(b), is a consequence of the removal from the Act of references to the CPC which never came into force. By subs.(2), any document under subs.(1)(b) is to be admissible as evidence; and, by subs.(3), certified copies of instruments issued by a "convention institution" (as defined in subs.(6)) are to be accepted in evidence. By subs.(4), copies of such instruments printed by the Queen's Printer are to be accepted in evidence, as are certified copies of documents in the custody of a government department, without proof of the signature of the officer certifying the copy. Subsection (5) provides for evidence in proceedings in Scotland.

Subsection (6) defines (although only for the purposes of s.91): "convention institution" as an institution established under the relevant convention. The term "relevant convention court" is primarily defined in s.130(1), and it includes a supra-national tribunal established by such an institution, for example the Appeal Boards of the EPO. However, for the purposes of s.91, the term excludes a national court (subs.(6)). The term "legal proceedings" (as used in s.91) includes proceedings before the Comptroller, but it has been held that a national patent office which is processing an international application under the PCT is not a "convention court" within the meaning of the term (*Sonic Tape's Patent* [1987] R.P.C. 251).

Application of section 91 in practice

Section 91 is primarily directed to evidential matters, so that a judgment under the rele- **91.03**
vant convention does not have to be proved as a matter of foreign law (*Genentech's Patent* [1989] R.P.C. 147 CA). However, s.91(1)(c) does not give the decisions of courts outside the United Kingdom, including those of the EPO Appeal Boards, any greater status than they would otherwise have possessed. These decisions have persuasive, but not binding, effect so that United Kingdom courts are free to reach decisions different from those of a "convention court", even in relation to the same patent as was done in *Biogen v Medeva* [1997] R.P.C. 1 HL and in *Minnesota Mining's Patents* BL C/56/97. As Dr K. Bruchhausen (then President of the Patent Senate of the German Supreme Court) stated:

"The EPO must accept the national court's judgment as to the validity and interpretation of the patents it grants and their assessment of the ambit of protection" (*epi*-Information 2-1988, 148 at 164).

Nevertheless, in *Merrell Dow v Norton* [1996] R.P.C. 76 HL, it was stated that great significance should be attached to decisions of the EPO Boards of Appeal. This must be especially so where the provision in issue is one which is required (by s.130(7), discussed in §§130.09–130.11) to have like effect to a provision of the EPC. Indeed, in *Bristol-Myers Squibb v Baker Norton* [1999] R.P.C. 253, Jacob J. stated that, at least for those sections of the Act referred to in s.130(7), and save in the rare event of a specific contention that a provision of the 1977 Act has a different meaning from a corresponding provision of a Convention, the corresponding provisions of the Convention should be regarded as of direct effect. Thus one should work directly from those provisions and not bother with the provisions of the Act, that is, the wording and numbering of the Convention should be used in preference to the wording and numbering of the Act, see §130.09. In this way, harmonisation of interpretation of the EPC articles throughout EPC Member States would be facilitated.

Examples where EPO decisions have been specifically followed by English courts are: *John Wyeth's and Schering's Applications* [1985] R.P.C. 545, where the Patent Court (sitting *en banc*) decided to follow a decision of the EPO Enlarged Board of Appeal in preference to well-established precedents under British law in order to achieve a harmonious interpretation of the EPC, see §4A.10; *Asahi's Application* [1991] R.P.C. 485 HL, holding that a prior art disclosure must have an enabling character, see §2.09; and *Beloit v Valmet* [1995] R.P.C. 705, where the wording of s.6 was interpreted in a strained manner in order to achieve conformity with a decision of the EPO Enlarged Board of Appeal, see §6.02.

The trend seems to be increasing for the UK courts to follow decisions of the EPO Boards of Appeal, particularly those of the Enlarged Board, see *H. Lundbeck v Generics* [2008] EWCA Civ 311; [2008] R.P.C. 28, discussed in §3.29; and *Conor Medsystems v Angiotech* [2008] UKHL 49; [2008] R.P.C. 28, discussed in §3.11. These decisions seem to indicate that the UK courts should follow an EPO decision unless good reason is seen for disagreeing with it, at least on the facts of the particular case under its consideration. For an example where this was done, see *Eli Lilly v Human Genome Sciences* [2010] EWCA Civ 33 now reversed by the Supreme Court see [2011] UKSC 51 and §4.03, as to the binding nature of the reasoning and outcome in the EPO see §3.36.

Although s.91 does not require United Kingdom courts to take judicial notice of decisions given by other national courts under provisions of the international conventions listed in s.91(1)(a), there is an increasing tendency to look to decisions of national courts in other EPC Member States as providing guidance on the interpretation of EPC provisions in order to promote the intended harmonisation of national patent law where this is required to conform with, or is derived from, the provisions of the EPC, CPC or PCT. For example, German decisions influenced the decisions of the English courts in: *PLG Research v Ardon* [1995] R.P.C. 287 CA, see §125.09; *Pioneer v Warner* [1997] R.P.C. 757, see §60.07; and *Buehler v Chronos Richardson* [1998] R.P.C. 609, see §72.17; and, in *Bristol-Myers Squibb's Patent* (above), the court was pleased that it had come to a similar conclusion to that reached by the District Court in the Netherlands, see §4A.10; and in *Conor Medsystems v Angiotech* (above), the House of Lords, specifically took the same view that a Netherlands court had held when it reversed the lower decisions made by both the Patents Court and the Court of Appeal in the case before it.

However, the Comptroller—pending clarification from the British courts—will primarily follow British decisions (which are binding on him), even if these may conflict with EPO decisions, see: *Sharp K.K.'s Application* BL O/75/91, noted I.P.D. 14171; *Crane Ltd's Application* BL O/41/92, noted I.P.D. 15156; and the MOPP at para.2.14, as discussed generally in the commentary on s.1, the UK courts and the Comptroller, at least at present, seem to take a different view from that taken by the EPO as to the patentability or unpatentability (under EPC art.52(2) and (3) and under s.1(2)(c) and (d)) of subject-matter relating to inventions involving computer programs, business methods and the presentation of information, the EPO choosing to base its decisions on these points by concentrating on inventive step (under EPC art.56, rather than on patentability under EPC art.52 as discussed in §1.05, above.

It should be noted that the EPO Guidelines do not have any binding authority. Even to the EPO they are only persuasive authority (T 42/84 *EXXON/Alumina spinel* [1988] E.P.O.R. 387, abridged OJ EPO 1988, 251).

PRACTICE UNDER SECTION 91

91.04   Where s.91 does not apply, as for example in the citation of a decision of a national court or an extract from a foreign national register, as having evidential value, for example as a persuasive legal authority, a certified copy of the decision or extract should be obtained from the foreign court or patent office and the other party should then be asked to admit that such (together with any necessary translation) is a true and accurate copy of the original. Failing this, formal proof would need to be offered to the court and the translator of the document may have to be called as a supporting witness.

SECTION 92

Obtaining evidence for proceedings under the European Patent Convention

92.01   **92.**—(1) Sections 1 to 3 of the Evidence (Proceedings in Other Jurisdictions) Act 1975 [c.34] (provisions enabling United Kingdom courts to assist in obtaining evidence for foreign courts) shall apply for the purpose of proceedings before a relevant convention court under the European Patent Convention as they apply for the purpose of civil proceedings in a court exercising jurisdiction in a country outside the United Kingdom.

(2) In the application of these sections by virtue of this section any reference to the High Court, the Court of Session or the High Court of Justice in Northern Ireland shall include a reference to the comptroller.

(3) Rules under this Act may include provision—

(a) as to the manner in which an application under section 1 of the said Act of 1975 is to be made to the comptroller for the purpose of proceedings before a relevant convention court under the European Patent Convention; and

(b) subject to the provisions of that Act, as to the circumstances in which an order can be made under section 2 of that Act on any such application.

(4) Rules of court and rules under this Act may provide for an officer of the European Patent Office to attend the hearing of an application under section 1 of that Act before the court or the comptroller, as the case may be, and examine the witnesses or request the court or comptroller to put specified questions to the witnesses.

(5) Section 1(4) of the Perjury Act 1911 [c. 6] and article 3(4) of the Perjury (Northern Ireland) Order 1979 [SI 1979/1714] [*section 1(4) of the Perjury Act (Northern Ireland) 1946*] (statements made for the purposes, among others, of judicial proceedings in a tribunal of a foreign state) shall apply in relation to proceedings before a relevant convention court under the European Patent Convention as they apply to a judicial proceeding in a tribunal of a foreign state.

Note. Subsection (5) was amended by SI 1979/1714.

RELEVANT RULE—RULE 62

Rule 62—Procedure for obtaining evidence for proceedings under the European Patent Convention

62.—(1) An application to the comptroller for an order under the Evidence (Proceedings in Other Jurisdictions) Act 1975 as applied by section 92(1) must be—   **92.02**

(a) made in writing;

(b) supported by written evidence;

(c) accompanied by the request as a result of which the application is made, and where appropriate, a translation of the request into English; and

(d) accompanied by the prescribed fee.

(2) The application must be made without notice.

(3) The comptroller may permit an officer of the European Patent Office to attend the hearing and either—

(a) examine the witnesses; or

(b) request the comptroller to put specified questions to the witnesses.

COMMENTARY ON SECTION 92

Section 92 is the second of the group of sections (ss.91–95) which give statutory force to certain provisions relating to the EPC, the CPC and the PCT.   **92.03**

Sections 1–3 of the Evidence (Proceedings in Other Jurisdictions) Act 1975 (c.34) provide for dealing with "letters of request" ("letters rogatory") by which foreign courts ask a United Kingdom court to assist it in the taking of evidence in matters proceeding before the foreign court. Subsection (1) extends the operation of this 1975 statute to proceedings in a relevant convention court under the EPC. In court proceedings, this operation is now governed by CPR 34.21, and in Scotland by the Act of Sederunt (Ch.66), for which see *http://www.scotscourts.gov.uk/session/rules*. By subs.(2), the provisions of these sections of the 1975 Act apply also to proceedings before the Comptroller. The relevant procedure is set out in r.62 (see §92.02, above) which was made under the authority of subs.(3).

The term "relevant convention court" is defined in s.130(1). It includes departments of the EPO and (unlike the position under s.91) also national courts engaged in proceedings under the EPC or PCT.

Subsection (4) is an independent provision which provides for rules to permit the attendance at a hearing before the court or the Comptroller of an officer of the EPO. Rule 62(3) has been made accordingly. On such attendance the EPO officer may examine witnesses or require the Comptroller to put specified questions to a witness. CPR 34.21 provides the court with a similar power. No instance of the use of this power, either by the EPO or by a United Kingdom court, has yet come to light.

Subsection (5) is a further provision independent of the remainder of the section. It extends the application of the perjury statutes to any evidence given before a relevant convention court under the EPC, thereby permitting proceedings for perjury to be brought in the United Kingdom in respect of evidence given under the EPC abroad, for example in proceedings before the EPO.

PRACTICE UNDER SECTION 92

92.04   An application to the Comptroller under s.92(2) and r.62 is made by written request by the relevant convention court or its representative and must be accompanied by written evidence and any fee prescribed. The application must be accompanied by the request as a result of which the application is made, and where appropriate, a translation of the request into English. The request may, for example, be for the attendance of named witnesses, who may be required to produce specified documents and things and who may be required to submit to cross-examination. CPR 34.21(a) and (b) makes similar provisions for corresponding procedure before the High Court.

The application, whether before the court or the Comptroller, is to be made by or on behalf of the convention court without notice (formerly called "ex parte") and will normally lead to the giving of further directions for the procedure to be followed and the scope of the enquiry permitted. The convention court should take care to formulate its request in sufficiently broad terms, as the tribunal may not permit evidence to be given before it which goes beyond the scope of the request, as established by the accompanying written evidence.

Llewelyn and Small have discussed ([1985] E.I.P.R. 81) the probable absence of privilege against self-incrimination during evidence given in response to a request from a foreign court by letters rogatory.

The normal practice on the taking of evidence will be for a transcript of the proceedings before the tribunal to be signed as a correct record of the proceedings and for this then to be transmitted to the court which made the request for assistance.

SECTION 93

Enforcement of orders for costs

93.01   **93.** If the European Patent Office orders the payment of costs in any proceedings before it—

(a) in England and Wales the costs shall, if a county court so orders, be recoverable **under section 85 of the County Courts Act 1984** (c. 28) [*by execution issued from the county court*] or otherwise as if they were payable under an order of that court;

(b) in Scotland the order may be enforced in like manner as **an extract registered decree arbitral bearing a warrant for execution issued by the sheriff court of any sheriffdom in Scotland** [*a recorded decree arbitral*];

(c) in Northern Ireland the order may be enforced as if it were a money judgment;

(d) **in the Isle of Man the order may be enforced in like manner as an execution issued out of the court.**

Note. Amendment of para.(b) was effected by the Debtors (Scotland) Act 1987 (c.18, Sch.6). The addition of subpara.(d) is a consequence of SI 2003/1249. At the time of writing there is a pending amendment to para.(a), which would replace the words "by execution issued from the county court" with "under section 85 of the County Courts Act 1984". This amendment is proposed by the Tribunals, Courts and Enforcement Act 2007 s.62(3), Sch.13 paras 39, 42, but no appointment date has yet been made.

COMMENTARY ON SECTION 93

Section 93 is the third of the group of sections (ss.91–95) which give statutory effect to certain provisions and operation of the EPC and the PCT. It provides for the enforcement of payment of costs awarded by the EPO; payment can be enforced by a county court order or the equivalent in Scotland and Northern Ireland and perhaps also in the Isle of Man in like manner as for costs awarded by the Comptroller, for which see §107.06.

93.02

SECTION 94

Communication of information to the European Patent Office, etc.

94. It shall not be unlawful by virtue of any enactment to communicate the following information in pursuance of the European Patent Convention to the European Patent Office or the competent authority of any country which is party to the Convention, that is to say—

94.01

(a) information in the files of the court which, in accordance with rules of court, the court authorises to be so communicated;

(b) information in the files of the Patent Office which, in accordance with rules under this Act, the comptroller authorises to be so communicated.

RELEVANT RULE—RULE 63

Rule 63—Communication of information to the European Patent Office

63. The comptroller may authorise any information in the files of the Patent Office to be communicated to the European Patent Office or to a competent authority of any country which is a party to the European Patent Convention, except where that information cannot be communicated under section 118.

94.02

COMMENTARY ON SECTION 94

Scope of the section

Section 94 is the fourth of the group of sections (ss.91–95) which makes statutory provision for miscellaneous matters arising under the EPC, the CPC and the PCT. It provides that it is not to be unlawful to convey, in pursuance of the EPC, to the EPO or to the competent authority of any country party to the EPC, information in the files of a court

94.03

which the court orders to be communicated, or information in the files of the UK-IPO which the Comptroller authorises to be communicated.

The section makes lawful only that which a statutory enactment prevents and is discretionary in nature. It also applies only to documents which are in the files of the court or the UK-IPO. Thus, the section does not extend, for example, to documents merely disclosed to the other party in the course of litigation, see §94.05 below.

Disclosure by the Comptroller

94.04   Rule 63 (see reprint above) authorises the Comptroller to act under s.94. The rule provides that the Comptroller may authorise the communication to any competent authority of any country party to the EPC of information as may be disclosed under s.118. Subection 118(1) allows for prescribed restrictions on the Comptroller's disclosure of documents, and these restrictions may be found at r.51.

Disclosure by the Patents Court

94.05   The operation of s.94 in relation to proceedings before the Patents Court or Patents County Court is provided for by CPR 63PD 13.1 (reprinted in Appendix F). A similar rule applies in Scotland under Ch.55.16 of the Act of Sederunt, for which see *http:// www.scotscourts.gov.uk/session/rules*. While sub-para.13.1 of the PD of CPR 63 seems to permit these courts to disclose any information which they may think fit, the following sub-para.13.2 requires the court to afford any party affected "by the request" an opportunity of making representations on whether the information should be disclosed. Thus, disclosure to the EPO is essentially a matter of the court's discretion. Accordingly, before this discretion may be exercised by the Comptroller or by the court, an opportunity must be given for cause to be shown why the discretion should not be exercised in any particular case and, if requested, a hearing first held on the matter.

The section is limited to the disclosure of information which is "in the files of the court", but the files of the Patents Court (except on an appeal from the Comptroller) contain only copies of the pleadings and affidavits filed in interim proceedings (without the exhibits thereto). In particular, the section is inapplicable to documents which are produced only to the other party as part of the required "disclosure" process (*Bonzel v Intervention* [1991] R.P.C. 43), and even witness statements (used at trial as evidence-in-chief (for which see CPR 32.5) will not necessarily be in the files of the Patents Court, as such statements are required only to be exchanged between the parties and will be brought into court solely for use during the trial of the action. However, the position could be different in proceedings before the Patents County Court.

SECTION 95

Financial provisions

95.01   **95.**—(1) There shall be paid out of moneys provided by Parliament any sums required by any Minister of the Crown or government department to meet any financial obligation of the United Kingdom under the European Patent Convention, [*the Community Patent Convention*] or the Patent Co-operation Treaty.

(2) Any sums received by any Minister of the Crown or government department in pursuance of **that convention** [*either of those conventions*] or that treaty shall be paid into the Consolidated Fund.

Note. The indicated amendments to s.94 were made by the Patents Act 2004 (c.16), Schs 2(21)(b) and 3(1), with effect from January 1, 2005 (SI 2004/3205, art.(f)(g)(k)).

COMMENTARY ON SECTION 95

95.02   Section 95 is the last of the group of sections (ss.91–95) which give statutory provision for miscellaneous matters concerning the operation of the EPC and the PCT. The amendments to s.95, noted in §95.01 are a consequence of the removal from the Act of references to the CPC which never came into force. Subsection (1) enables HM Government and Parliament to provide funds for the meeting of monetary obligations imposed upon the United Kingdom by this Convention and Treaty. Subsection (2) provides for any income from these sources to be paid into the Consolidated Fund. However, that position now seems affected by the Patent Office Trading Fund Order 1991 (SI 1991/1796), under art.2 of which there is established a "trading fund" for "all the operations of the Department of Trade and Industry known as the Patent Office", and these (by Sch.1 to that Order) include operations arising out of anything done in pursuance of any international instrument or convention. Thus, the position is now that any surplus funds at the end of a financial year remain available for use in ensuing years by the Patent Office (which now operates under the title "United Kingdom Intellectual Property Office" or "UK-IPO"), whereas this was not the position prior to the commencement of this Order on October 1, 1991.

It seems that it is subs.(1) which enables the UK-IPO to act under PCT r.19.1 as a receiving office and under EPC art.75(1)(b) as an authority with which European patent applications may be filed.

The section is supplementary to unrepealed ss.62 and 63 of the Patents and Designs Act 1907 (c.29) (for which see §A20 in Appendix A) which authorise the provision of funds for the running of, as amended, an office for the person designated as "the comptroller-general of patents, designs and trade marks" which this s.62(1) then states "shall be called the Patent Office". Thus, so long as these provisions are not amended or repealed, the title "the IPO" is merely a name under which the Patent Office chooses to operate.

PART III [SECTIONS 96–132]

MISCELLANEOUS AND GENERAL

Legal proceedings [Sections 96–108]

SECTION 96 [REPEALED]

The Patents Court

96.01 **96.** […]

Note. Section 96 established the Patents Court as part of the Chancery Division of the High Court of England and Wales. However, the section was repealed by the Senior Courts Act 1981 (c.54) Sch.7 ("SCA"), but its contents were in substance re enacted and supplemented by provisions of that Act. These are reprinted below and discussed in the commentary.

96.02 ### SENIOR COURTS ACT 1981 (C.54)

Section 6—The Patents, Admiralty and Commercial Courts

6.—(1) There shall be—

(a) as part of the Chancery Division, a Patents Court; and

(b) […]

(2) The judges of the Patents Court, of the Admiralty Court and of the Commercial Court shall be such of the puisne judges of the High Court as the Lord Chancellor may from time to time nominate to be judges of the Patents Court, Admiralty Judges and Commercial Judges respectively.

Section 54(9)—Court of Appeal: Court of civil division

96.03 **54.**—(9) Subsections (3) and (4) of section 70 (scientific advisers to assist the Patents Court in proceedings under the Patents Act 1949 (c. 87) and the Patents Act 1977 (c. 37)) shall appeal in relation to the civil division of the Court of Appeal and proceedings on apply from any decision of the Patents Court in proceedings under those Acts as they apply in relation to the Patents Court and proceedings under those Acts.

Section 62(1)—Business of Patents, Admiralty and Commercial Courts

96.04 **62.** The Patents Court shall take such proceedings relating to patents as are within the jurisdiction conferred on it by the Patents Act 1977, and such other proceedings relating to patents or other matters as may be prescribed.

Section 70(3) and (4)—Assessors and scientific advisers

96.05 **70.**—(3) Rules of court shall make provision for the appointment of scientific advisers to assist the Patents Court in proceedings under the Patents Act 1949 (c. 87) and the Patents Act 1977 (c. 37) and for regulating the functions of such advisers.

(4) The remuneration of any such adviser shall be determined by the Lord Chancellor with the concurrence of the **Treasury** [*Minister for the Civil Service*] and shall be defrayed out of money provided by Parliament.

Note. Subsection (3) was amended by SI 1981/1670.

COMMENTARY ON SECTION 96 [REPEALED]

Scope of the section

Section 96 provided for the establishment in 1978 of a "Patents Court", as part of the **96.06** High Court of Justice in England and Wales, to deal with such matters relating to patents and other matters as prescribed by Rules of Court. Previously, and since the 1949 Act, matters brought before the High Court relating to patents have been heard within the Chancery Division by a "patent judge" nominated as such by the Lord Chancellor. Such Rules of Court have, since 1978, provided for appeals from the Comptroller to be brought before the "Patents Court" (other than appeals from proceedings before the Comptroller conducted in Scotland, for which see §98.08), whereas previously such appeals (other than from proceedings in Scotland) had been brought before the "Patents Appeal Tribunal", a body which was not part of the High Court but, in practice, was constituted by one of the nominated "patent judges". This change in jurisdiction and the history of the Patents Appeal Tribunal was discussed by Sir Patrick Graham in his paper "The Patents Court in the United Kingdom" (1980) 11 I.I.C. 585. It may be doubted whether the abolition of the Patents Appeal Tribunal was entirely desirable, since the change led to the unsuccessful appellant having to pay costs on the court scale, as opposed to a mere contribution as previously. The prospect of having to pay heavy costs if an appeal fails naturally favours the financially strong over the financially weak (so far as contentious proceedings in the UK-IPO are concerned), and it is now more onerous for a private inventor, or small company, to challenge a decision of the Comptroller given ex parte.

Although s.96 has been repealed, its provisions have been re-enacted and extended by certain provisions of the Senior CourtsAct 1981 (c.54) ("SCA"), reprinted above: viz. s.6, providing for the continuing existence of the Patents Court with a jurisdiction defined in s.62(1); and s.70, providing continuing provision for the appointment of assessors and scientific advisers to assist the Patents Court, with s.54(9) providing likewise for the Court of Appeal on appeals from the Patents Court. It is therefore convenient to discuss these replacement provisions in the present commentary.

The SCA provides (by Sch.1 para.1, as amended) that all causes and matters relating to "patents, trade marks, registered designs, design rights or copyright" shall be assigned to the Chancery Division. Other Divisions of the High Court therefore have no jurisdiction in respect of such matters; and, consequently, the Patents Court is part of the Chancery Division.

Section 130(1) now defines "court" as having different meanings for the different parts of the United Kingdom, as discussed in §61.04. However, it should be noted that a patents county court has no jurisdiction over appeals from decisions of the Comptroller, see the Patents County Court (Designation and Jurisdiction) Order 1994 (SI 1994/1609) art.4, reprinted in §287.02.

The specialist practice in proceedings brought in England and Wales before the Patents Court is now set out in CPR Pt 63 (reprinted in Appendix F), which has taken the place of the former RSC Order 104. This Practice Direction is augmented by the Patents Court Guide (for which see Appendix G). This specialist practice is particularly discussed in relation to practice under s.61 at §§61.41 et seq. The Patents Court is prepared, in an appropriate case, to sit out of London and it sat in Birmingham in *Hadley Industries v Metal Sections* BL C/68/98, noted I.P.D. 22004.

Section 97 contains provisions relating to appeals from the Comptroller, including further appeals to the Court of Appeal in proceedings which commenced before the Comptroller, see the commentary on that section.

A Patents Court Users' Committee was set up in 1990 as a forum in which users of this court can discuss anything affecting them, including procedure, practice and the facilities available. In 1996, this Committee expanded its remit to a consideration of the problems and concerns of intellectual property generally, and became "the Intellectual Property Court Users' Committee", see para.1.6 of the Patents Court Guide. Anyone having views concerning the improvement of intellectual property litigation is invited to make these views known to this Committee, preferably through a relevant professional representative on the Committee.

Subject-matter jurisdiction of the Patents Court

96.07   Section 62(1) of the SCA provides that the Patents Court shall take such proceedings "as may be prescribed". The jurisdiction so designated is now set out in CPR 63.1 (reprinted in Appendix F in §F01), which shows that this jurisdiction now broadly extends to any claim relating to registered or unregistered rights in intellectual property.

Disputes concerning assignments and licensing of patents are normally heard in the Patents Court in any event, an example being *BICC v Burndy* [1985] R.P.C. 273. Where judicial review is sought under CPR 54 (not reprinted in this book), the application has to be made to the Divisional Court of the Queen's Bench Division, but where such an application has involved an issue relating to patents, a nominated judge of the Patents Court has been assigned to hear it as an additional judge of that Division, see: *Omron Tateisi's Application* [1981] R.P.C. 125; *R v Comptroller-General Ex p. Celltech* [1991] R.P.C. 475; *Drazil's Application* [1992] R.P.C. 479; and *Kenrick's (Archibold) International Application* [1994] R.P.C. 635).

The Patents County Court, to which CPR Pt 63 also now applies, provides an alternative forum for the resolution of disputes within the powers of the Patents Court or within the general powers possessed by any other designated "county court", so that its powers extend beyond those merely "relating to patents or designs, together with any claims or matters ancillary thereto or arising therefrom" as set out in s.287 of the CDPA 1988, see §287.01. This alternative jurisdiction is discussed in the commentaries on ss.287–292 of the CDPA 1988, for which see §§287.03 et seq.

Nominated judges for the Patents Court

96.08   The first "patent judge" so nominated was Lloyd-Jacob J. in 1950. He was the sole patent judge until 1969 when Graham J. was appointed as a second patent judge. The practice of nominating two such judges then continued, with Whitford J. being appointed in 1970 on the death of Lloyd-Jacob J., and Falconer J. on the retirement of Graham J. in 1981. Following the retirement of Whitford J. in 1988, Aldous J. became the second nominated judge of the Patents Court, Falconer J. then becoming the senior patent judge. On the retirement in 1989 of Falconer J., Aldous J. became the senior assigned judge for the Patents Court, with other judges being assigned to sit in the Patents Court as necessary in view of his commitments, these including Hoffmann J. who was shortly elevated to the Court of Appeal, and later to the House of Lords where in both these courts he has given important and authoritative judgments.

Jacob J. was appointed as a further specialist patent judge in 1993. In January 1995, Aldous J. was elevated to the Court of Appeal. Laddie J. became a judge shortly thereafter and became the senior patents judge in 1997 when Jacob J. became a general chancery judge and was later elevated to the Court of Appeal from where he retired in the spring of 2011. Pumfrey J. was appointed as a further specialist patent judge in 1997. Laddie J. retired from the bench in mid-2005 and was replaced by Kitchin J. Pumfrey J. was elevated to the Court of Appeal in 2007, but sadly died later that same year. During 2008, Floyd J. was appointed as a specially assigned patents judge and Arnold J. was appointed later that year.

Thus, the specialist judges of the Patents Court are currently Floyd and Arnold JJ., all having considerable experience at the patent bar prior to their judicial appointment, Mr Justice Kitchin having been promoted to the Court of Appeal in October 2011 (where he will be responsible for listing patent cases). Mr Justice Lewison and Mr Justice Patten, who have heard patent cases, have also been promoted to the Court of Appeal. At the time of writing, other judges appointed to sit, as required, in the Patents Court are Floyd, Arnold, Birss, Mann, Norris, Warren, Morgan, Vos and Roth JJ. Contact details for the judges of the Patents Court are given in the Patents Court Guide (for which see Appendix G, §G1.3).

Other former Patents Judges who have sat in the Court of Appeal are: Mummery and Chadwick LJJ. In the House of Lords: Lords Hoffmann, Nicholls, Neuberger and Walker had each given important patent judgments when sitting at first instance.

It should also be noted that (under s.63 of the SCA) other judges can be nominated by the Lord Chancellor on an ad hoc basis; and leading counsel (i.e. Queen's Counsel) are occasionally appointed as deputy judges of the Patents Court, for example when there is a conflict of interest for a newly-appointed judge, or a need to reduce a backlog of cases awaiting trial. Also HH Judge Birss QC, the Patents County Court judge, also serves from time to time as a Deputy Patents Court judge.

Territorial jurisdiction of the Patents Court

—The Brussels Regulation

As explained in §96.06, the constituent parts of the United Kingdom (here including the **96.09** Isle of Man) have their own courts which are competent to hear disputes relating to patents.

However, the jurisdiction of each of these courts is subject to the provisions of the Brussels and Lugano Conventions, now for the UK embodied in Council Regulation 44/2001 ("the Brussels Regulation"), applied by the Civil Jurisdiction and Judgments Act 1982 (c.27) ("CJJA") (as amended). This provides for extra-territorial jurisdiction in certain circumstances. For patent litigation, it particularly applies to claims for infringement, as more extensively discussed in §61.19.

The general (or "golden") rule under these Conventions is that defendants should normally be sued before court of their domicile, but (as one of the permitted exceptions to this general rule) may alternatively be sued before a court for the place where the harmful event occurred. Furthermore:

"a person domiciled in a Contracting State may also be sued where he is one of a number of defendants, in the courts for the place where any one of them is domiciled".

However, exclusive jurisdiction is granted:

"in proceedings concerned with the registration or validity of patents, trade marks, designs or other similar rights required to be deposited or registered, to the courts of the Contracting State in which the deposit or registration has been applied for, has taken place or is under the terms of an international convention deemed to have taken place".

Moreover:

"where a court of a Contracting State is seized of a claim which is principally concerned with a matter over which the courts of another Contracting State have exclusive jurisdiction by virtue of Article 16, it shall declare of its own motion that it has no jurisdiction"

Thus, there is no extra-territorial jurisdiction on questions of patent validity, again see §61.19.

The effect of the CJJA on the jurisdiction of the Patents Court, as regards the judgment of disputes arising solely within the United Kingdom is discussed in §96.10. Then, §96.11 discusses the extent to which extra-territorial jurisdiction has so far been exercised over patent infringement and validity disputes, both in the United Kingdom and elsewhere.

—Assignment of jurisdiction between courts of different parts of the United Kingdom

As explained in §96.09, the provisions of the CJJA, which was primarily enacted to **96.10** implement the terms of the Brussels Convention, discussed in §96.09, also deal with questions of intra-United Kingdom jurisdiction. This was done by modifying the terms of the Brussels Convention for matters of intra-United Kingdom jurisdiction, this "Modified Convention" constituting Sch.4 to the CJJA.

Of foremost present interest are those provisions of the CJJA which have the effect of retaining the jurisdiction of the courts of Scotland and Northern Ireland (as well as that of the Isle of Man) to consider and, if appropriate, revoke a United Kingdom patent. Thus, while Sch.4 to the CJJA governs questions of jurisdiction within the component parts of the United Kingdom, "proceedings concerned with the registration or validity of patents, trade marks, designs or similar rights required to be deposited or registered" are excluded from the provisions of Sch.4 to the CJJA. (CJJA, Sch.5 para.2). For Scotland, additional provisions were required to lead to the same effect (CJJA, Sch.8 paras 2(14) and 4(2)).

As regards proceedings for patent infringement, Sch.4 to the CJJA provides (in conformity with the principles of the Brussels Convention) for a person to be sued in the courts for that part of the United Kingdom in which he is domiciled irrespective of the location of the act of patent infringement (Sch.4 art.2), or (where a person is domiciled in some part of the United Kingdom) alternatively to be sued in another part of the United Kingdom in matters relating to tort, delict or quasi-delict, in the courts for the place where the harmful event occurred, or, in the case of a threatened wrong, is likely to occur, e.g. where the alleged act of patent infringement occurred or has been threatened to occur (Sch.4 art.5(3)).

A person may be joined as a co-defendant to proceedings properly commenced against another defendant elsewhere in the United Kingdom, or be made a third party to such proceedings or be sued on a counterclaim arising from such proceedings (Sch.4 art.6). Furthermore, an agreement between parties as to jurisdiction within the United Kingdom for the purpose of settling disputes between them has effect (Sch.4 art.17); and, irrespective of jurisdiction over a substantive claim, protective proceedings, e.g. seeking an interim injunction or a search (formerly *Anton Piller*) order, may be brought in any part of the United Kingdom (Sch.4 art.24).

While the Brussels Convention contains provisions for a compulsory stay of parallel, or connected, proceedings once a court of one Member State has been seized of a particular dispute, these provisions are not applied in the case of intra-United Kingdom disputes, see the Sch.4 to the CJJA. Accordingly, the question whether a court in one part of the United Kingdom will stay proceedings before it while a court in another part of the United Kingdom decides the same or a connected case brought before it continues to be decided according to the test of *forum conveniens*, for which see *The Spiliada* [1987] A.C. 460; [1986] 3 All E.R. 843 HL and *MacShannon v Rockware Glass* [1978] A.C. 795; [1978] 1 All E.R. 625 HL, even though this test has no applicability under the Brussels Convention. The *Spiliada* principles have also been applied to the choice of forum for patent infringement/validity issues as between the Patents Court and the Patent Office (*Ferro v Escol* [1990] R.P.C. 651), see §72.19. In *Ivax v Akzo Nobel [Stay of proceedings]* [2006] F.S.R. 43 at 888, an application to stay proceedings before the Patents Court because of other proceedings in Scotland was refused. Neither party had any real connection with Scotland and no significance was seen in which action was commenced first. Also, the factual matters involved were not seen to be the same and there was some evidence that the English case could come to trial at an earlier date.

Where a cause of action arises in one part of the United Kingdom, but not in another, the first court seized must assume jurisdiction even if, in so doing, it has also to decide on an issue already in issue before a court of another part of the United Kingdom. Thus, in *Demel v Jefferson* BL C/2/98 and C/33/98, noted I.P.D. 21050, threats had been made in England (but not Northern Ireland) and infringement proceedings had been instituted in Northern Ireland. The Patents Court held that it, alone, had jurisdiction to adjudicate on the threats proceedings, even though this meant that it had to consider whether the threats were justified as relating to acts of infringement of a valid patent, as it then did.

—Extra-territorial jurisdiction

In traditional mode, various judges have stated that it would not be appropriate for an **96.11** English court to decide issues of infringements of intellectual property rights outside of the United Kingdom, see: *Mölnlycke v Procter & Gamble (No.4)* [1992] R.P.C. 21 at 28; the copyright case, *Tyburn Productions v Conan Doyle* [1990] R.P.C. 185, citing *Potter v Broken Hill* [Australia] [1906] 3 C.L.R. 479, and the case comment thereon by R. Arnold [1990] E.I.P.R. 254, or at least the case is not one which the English court should entertain, see *L.A. Gear v Gerald Whelan & Sons* [1991] F.S.R. 670; and *James Burrough Distillers v Speymalt Whisky* [Scotland] [1991] R.P.C. 130.

Indeed, in *Plastus Kreativ. v Minnesota Mining* [1995] R.P.C. 438, where there was struck out a request for a declaration of non-infringement for other countries for which the European patent in issue had been granted (for which see §71.03), Aldous J. stated, obiter:

> "I believe that, if the local courts are responsible for enforcing and deciding questions of validity and infringement, the conclusions reached are likely to commend the respect of the public. Also, a conclusion that a patent is infringed or not infringed involves in this country a decision on validity as in this country no person can infringe an invalid patent … Thus, I believe it is at least convenient that infringement, like validity, is decided in the state in which it arises … I also believe that it would not normally be right for the courts of this country to decide a dispute on infringement of a foreign patent in respect of acts done outside the country, provided that there is an adequate remedy in the relevant country."

One basis for this reluctance was based on the "double actionability rule", formulated in *Phillips v Eyre* (1870) L.R. 6 Q.B. 1 under which an English court should only have jurisdiction over torts committed abroad where the tort would be an unlawful act both where it was committed and also under English law. Infringement of a foreign patent could not satisfy the second rule. This rule was much criticised, but it no longer exists as it was explicitly repealed by the Private International Law (Miscellaneous Provisions) Act 1995 (c.42, s.10).

However, as explained and discussed at length by C. Wardlow in his book *Enforcement of Intellectual Property in European and International Law* (London: Sweet & Maxwell, 1998), the basis upon which English courts have declined to decide questions of infringement of foreign intellectual property rights is more properly based on the so-called "Moçambique Rule" first formulated in *British South Africa Co v Compania do Moçambique* [1893] A.C. 602 HL that, subject to certain exceptions irrelevant for present purposes:

> "the court has no jurisdiction to entertain an action for (1) the determination of the title to, or the right to the possession of any immovable situate out of England; or (2) the recovery of damages for trespass to such immovable".

See *Hesperides Hotels v Aegean Turkish Holidays* [1979] A.C. 508 HL. Although this rule was abrogated for immovable property by the CJJA 1982 (s.30), that abrogation has been held not to apply to intellectual property which is not regarded as immovable property so-called (*Pearce v Ove Arup* [1997] F.S.R. 641; and *Coin Controls v Suzo* [1997] F.S.R. 660). The Moçambique Rule therefore continues to apply as regards patents held in countries outside of the contracting states of the Brussels and Lugano Conventions; and, for such patents, it is quite clear that the English courts will not entertain an action in which either infringement (trespass) or validity is in issue.

For further discussion of the implications of the decision in *Pearce v Ove Arup*, and the issues as to choice of law as to jurisdiction, justiciability and actionability of acts of intellectual property infringement committed out of the jurisdiction of the court, see the articles by E. Bragiel [1999] I.P.Q. 135 and R. Arnold [1999] I.P.Q. 389 and the full discussion of recent decisions in §61.04.

From the recent decisions it seems that the law has now been clarified in that it is not possible for a national court in one EU/EEA Member State to adjudicate upon infringement of a patent granted by, or for, another such State because: different patents are involved (a European patent being a bunch of national patents); different defendants may be involved, even if these are members of the same corporate group; the evidence presented to a court may be different, or at least may not have the same effect in other Member States; and, where validity is, or can be, in issue, only a court in a State for which that patent has effect has the power to deal with questions of its validity or registration.

Where the issue of jurisdiction involves a party domiciled outside the EU/EEA, the normal rule of *forum non conveniens* applies. In two cases (*Celltech v MedImmune* [2005] F.S.R. 21 and *Harrison v Teton Valley Trading Co Ltd* [2005] F.S.R. 10 at 491), involving different patents, in applications to stay proceedings as to the liability to pay royalties for actions in the United States under a licensing agreement which stipulated that all disputes had to be governed by English law, the courts refused to stay the English proceedings in favour of determination of infringement in the USA. It was held that the English courts could well apply US law to the issue of infringement. However, in the second of these decisions it was held that the issue of validity of the US patents in issue should be decided by a US court. These cases were discussed and analysed by Vicky Clark [2004/2005] 7(3) B.S.L.R. 121.

It should also be noted that it is a long-standing principle of the English courts that they do not impose penalties which they are unable to enforce. That, in itself, suggests that a court would not impose an injunction against a foreign entity in respect of acts committed outside the jurisdiction because it would have no ability to enforce that injunction.

The fact that the CJJA grants exclusive jurisdiction to courts of the United Kingdom to adjudicate on the validity of a patent granted in, or for, the United Kingdom suggests that leave from a United Kingdom court, is not required as a prerequisite to bringing those proceedings where the patent proprietor is resident outside the United Kingdom (or the Isle of Man), see *Napp v Pfizer* [1993] F.S.R. 150, although such service can be effected at the address for service recorded in the register of patents, see CPR 63.14 (reprinted in Appendix F at F63.16) and §32.15.

Appointment of scientific advisers

96.12 Section 70(3) and (4) of the SCA 1981, (see §96.05, above), re-enacted the repealed s.96(4) and (5) of the 1977 Act relating to the possible appointment of scientific advisers to assist the Patents Court and for their remuneration. By s.54(9) of the SCA (see reprint, above), the same provisions are made to apply to the appointment of scientific advisers to assist the Court of Appeal. The general rule relating to the appointment of assessors (including scientific advisers) is CPR 35.15. By this, the Patents Court and Patents County Court are given power, by their own motion if thought appropriate, or otherwise on the application of any party, to appoint such an independent assessor either (a) to sit with the judge at the trial, or (b) to enquire and report on any question of fact or opinion not involving a question of law or construction. The question of appointing a scientific adviser should be raised at a Case Management Conference by any party who thinks such a person would materially assist the court. Insofar as parties normally attempt to agree, so far as possible, on a draft of the order they would like the court to make, they should also seek to agree whether or not they consider it would be desirable to appoint a scientific adviser, and, if so, who this should be. Where the court itself appoints as an assessor, see also CPR 35 PD.10.

One or more scientific advisers have been appointed on a number of occasions to sit with the Patents Court, see: *Western Electric v Racal-Milgo* [1981] R.P.C. 253; *Compagnie Française de Télévision v Thorn* [1981] F.S.R. 306; and BL C/181/83; and *Codex v Racal-Milgo* BL C/135/81, noted I.P.D. 4150; and C/77/83, noted I.P.D. 6025. In *Valensi v British Radio* [1973] R.P.C. 337, the Court of Appeal appointed a scientific adviser for the first time since the corresponding rule was introduced under s.84(2) of the 1949 Act. For the hearing of the appeal in *Codex v Racal-Milgo* (noted above), the Court of Appeal appointed two scientific advisers, of whom one was new to the case and the other had sat with Whitford J. at first instance. Likewise, at the appeal stage, there were two scientific advisers in *Compagnie Française de Télévision v Thorn* BL C/98/85 and also in *Biogen v Medeva* [1995] R.P.C. 25 CA. In *Genentech's Patent* [1989] R.P.C. 147 CA, the scientific adviser prepared that part of one of the judgments which set out the genetic engineering background to the case. Other examples are provided by: *Willemijn Houdstermaatschappij v Madge Networks* [1992] R.P.C. 386 CA, which concerned data transmission systems; *Chiron v Organon Teknika (No.3)* [1994] F.S.R. 202, where the adviser was the same person that had advised the Court of Appeal in the *Genentech* case (above); *Imperial Chemical v Montedison* [1995] R.P.C. 449 CA; and in the appeal in *Chiron v Murex* [1996] R.P.C. 535.

In *Biogen v Medeva* [1997] R.P.C. 1, the House of Lords was assisted by two scientific advisers, this apparently being the first occasion on which the House of Lords was assisted in this way. In *Kirin-Amgen v Hoechst Marion Roussel* in the House of Lords (see [2005] R.P.C. 9 at 169), Professor Yudkin of Oxford University gave a series of seminars to the Law Lords in camera before the appeal was heard which was welcomed by Lords Hope and Hoffmann (and no doubt by the others too). Lord Hope suggested this might be adopted in future in cases "where the technology is complex and undisputed and the parties are willing to consent to it". In *PCME v Goyen Controls* [1999] F.S.R. 801, it appears than an examiner from the UK-IPO sat with the judge during part of the trial, presumably in the role of a scientific adviser.

The appointment of scientific advisers appears to be a wholly desirable trend, albeit that it has tended to be employed only in cases of considerable technical complexity. This is because it represents a convergence towards European (in particular German) practice. It also reduces the ability of one party or the other to throw "scientific dust in the eyes of the court" (*per* Lord Russell in *EMI v Lissen* (1939) 56 R.P.C. 23 at 43).

The remuneration of any adviser appointed to assist the Patents Court is determined by the Lord Chancellor with the concurrence of the Treasury and is defrayed out of money provided by Parliament, see §96.05.

The principles to be followed in appointing a scientific adviser to assist a court on appeal from the Office were extensively considered in *Beecham Group v Bristol-Myers (Amoxycillin)* [New Zealand] [1980] 1 N.Z.L.R. 185, as also was the restricted role which the adviser should play, though this was subsequently expanded by agreement (*Beecham Group v Bristol-Myers (Amoxycillin) (No.2)* [New Zealand] [1980] 1 N.Z.L.R. 192). In that case the same adviser also similarly assisted during the hearing of the appeal to the New Zealand Court of Appeal ([1982] F.S.R. 181). These decisions were further discussed and approved in *Genetic Institute v Kirin-Amgen (No. 2)* [Australia] (1997) 39 I.P.R. 155.

The Rules of Court also empowers the court to order that expert evidence on any particular matter should be given by one expert only to be appointed by the court if the parties cannot agree who this should be, or for the respective experts to have discussions between themselves, see CPR 35.7; 35.12 and 35 PD 9. However, any expert should not be asked questions which can be decided only by the court itself, see *Minnesota Mining v Beiersdorf* [Australia] [1980] F.S.R. 449.

Appointment of a person as "assessor", rather than as "scientific adviser" is also possible under the SCA s.70(1) and CPR 35.15 and this was done in *Mullard v Philco* (1936) 52 R.P.C. 261 CA. However, the modern practice is to appoint an "adviser" who takes no part in the decision-making process of the court.

Attention is also drawn to ss.99A and 99B of the Act (inserted by the CDPA 1988) which respectively provide for rules of court to be made for the Patents Court, and the Court of Session in Scotland, to order the UK-IPO to inquire into and report on any question of fact or opinion. Section 291(3) of the CDPA 1988 (reprinted in §291.01) contains similar provisions in respect of Patents County Courts. However, no such rules have apparently been made, see §99A.03.

Decisions of the Patents Court, etc.

For the availability of decisions of the court on patent matters and the publication of law reports, see §§101.07, 101.12 and 123.87.   **96.13**

Although there is no specific rule on the matter, the court has an inherent jurisdiction to correct an error in the reasons (i.e. in its decision) given as the basis for its judgment (strictly only the resulting court order), see *Hazeltine Corp v International Computers* [1980] F.S.R. 521.

SECTION 97

Appeals from the comptroller

97.01   **97.**—(1) Except as provided by subsection (4) below, an appeal shall lie to the Patents Court from any decision of the comptroller under this Act or rules except any of the following decisions, that is to say—

> (a) a decision falling within section 14(7) above;
>
> (b) a decision under section 16(2) above to omit matter from a specification;
>
> (c) a decision to give directions under subsection (1) or (2) of section 22 above;
>
> (d) a decision under rules which is excepted by rules from the right of appeal conferred by this section.

(2) For the purpose of hearing appeals under this section the Patents Court may consist of one or more judges of that court in accordance with directions given by **the Lord Chief Justice of England and Wales after consulting the Lord Chancellor** [*or on behalf of the Lord Chancellor*] [*; and the Patents Court shall not be treated as a divisional court for the purposes of section 31(1)(f) of the Supreme Court of Judicature (Consolidation) Act 1925 (appeals from divisional courts)*].

(3) An appeal shall not lie to the Court of Appeal from a decision of the Patents Court on appeal from a decision of the comptroller under this Act or rules—

> (a) except where the comptroller's decision was given under section 8, 12, 18, 20, 27, 37, 40, 61, 72, 73 or 75 above; or
>
> (b) except where the ground of appeal is that the decision of the Patents Court is wrong in law;

but an appeal shall only lie to the Court of Appeal under this section if leave to appeal is given by the Patents Court or the Court of Appeal.

(4) An appeal shall lie to the Court of Session from any decision of the comptroller in proceedings which under rules are held in Scotland, except any decision mentioned in paragraphs (a) to (d) of subsection (1) above.

(4) **The Lord Chief Justice may nominate a judicial office holder (as defined in section 109(4) of the Constitutional Reform Act 2005) to exercise his functions under subsection (2).**

(5) An appeal shall not lie to the Inner House of the Court of Session from a decision of an Outer House judge on appeal from a decision of the comptroller under this Act or rules—

> (a) except where the comptroller's decision was given under section 8, 12, 18, 20, 27, 37, 40, 61, 72, 73 or 75 above; or
>
> (b) except where the ground of appeal is that the decision of the Outer House judge is wrong in law.

Notes

1. The deletion of the latter part of subs.(2) (as regards the Patents Court not being

treated as a divisional court) was a result of amendment by the Senior Courts Act 1981 (c.54) Sch.7 and is in force on the Isle of Man, pursuant to SI 2003/1249.

2. There is a possible drafting error in that s.97(4) was purportedly, and prospectively inserted by the Constitutional Reform Act 2005 (c.4) Sch.4(1) para.91(3) with effect from April 3, 2006, but a subs.(4) already exists. An additional subs.97(4) is therefore reprinted above after the existing s.97(4). The same instrument effected the further change to subs.97(2), as regards directions to be given by the Lord Chief Justice, etc.

RELEVANT RULES

Note. Practice under s.97 is governed by CPR 63.16 (reprinted at §F63.16) which subsumes the appeal procedure into that for all appeals as set out in CPR 52 and its Practice Directions.   **97.02**

COMMENTARY ON SECTION 97

Scope of the section

Section 97 relates to appeals from the Comptroller to the Patents Court (subss.(1) and **97.03** (2)) and to further appeals to the Court of Appeal (subs.(3)). Subsections (4) and (5) provide for corresponding appeals from proceedings before the Comptroller held in Scotland.

The Patents County Court has no jurisdiction as regards an appeal from a decision taken in the name of the Comptroller, see SI 1994/1609 art.4 (reprinted in §287.02).

The section is in conformity with art.62(4) of the TRIPS Agreement, which is reprinted at §18.05, and also in conformity with arts 32 and 62(5) of it which read:

"TRIPS ARTICLE 32—Revocation/Forfeiture
An opportunity for judicial review of any decision to revoke or forfeit a patent shall be available."

"TRIPS ARTICLE 62—Acquisition and maintenance of intellectual property rights and related inter-partes procedures
5. Final administrative decisions in any of the procedures referred to under paragraph 4 shall be subject to review by a judicial or quasi-judicial authority. However, there shall be no obligation to provide an opportunity for such review of decisions in cases of unsuccessful opposition or administrative revocation, provided that the grounds for such procedures can be the subject of invalidation proceedings."

Right of appeal from Comptroller (subs.(1))

Subsection (1)(a)–(d) specifies certain types of decisions made by the Comptroller (in **97.04** matters mainly of an administrative nature) from which no appeal lies. These are:

(a) section 14(7)—Amendment of abstract by Comptroller;

(b) section 16(2)—Omission of offensive matter from specification before publication;

(c) section 22(1) and (2)—Prohibition of publication of information prejudicial to defence or public safety; and

(d) any other decisions made unappealable by rule.

At present the rules falling under (d) are:
rule 106—Remission of fees;

rule 88—Proceedings in Scotland; and

rule 100(3)—A decision to set aside a Patent Office option after review.

Otherwise, the Act provides a general right of appeal to the Patents Court against all decisions of the Comptroller, see *Omron Tateisi's Application* [1981] R.P.C. 125. In *R. v Comptroller-General, Ex p. Celltech* [1991] R.P.C. 475; *Drazil's Application* [1992] R.P.C. 479; and *Kenrick's (Archibald) International Application* [1994] R.P.C. 635, judicial review was used (unsuccessfully) in respect of a decision of the Comptroller (in his role as a PCT receiving office) for which there was neither a statutory right of appeal nor a statutory exclusion of the same. While judicial review proceedings are normally commenced by making an application without notice to others for leave, notice of intention to seek such leave ought to be given to the Comptroller so that he can be represented if he thinks his appearance would assist the court, see *R. v Comptroller-General, Ex p. Gist-Brocades* BL C/67/85 and *NETWORK 90 Trade Mark* [1984] R.P.C. 549.

As regards any further appeal, it can be noted that there can be no appeal to the European Court of Human Rights unless and until all possible appeal procedures under national law have been explored (*British-American Tobacco v The Netherlands* (1996) 21 E.H.R.R. 409, noted, *The Times* December 11, 1995): that would, presumably, include the seeking of judicial review under United Kingdom law.

An appeal may only be made from a decision of the Comptroller himself. In *Medeva BV v Comptroller General of Patents* [2010] R.P.C. 20, Kitchin J. held that letters from the examiner indicating an opinion that *Medeva's application* should be refused were not decisions against which appeals could properly be filed under s.97.

Composition of Patents Court on appeal from the Comptroller (subs.(2))

97.05   Subsection (2) relates to the composition and status of the Patents Court when hearing appeals from the Comptroller. Normally the Patents Court consists of a single judge, but (for the purpose of hearing appeals) it may consist of two of the nominated judges (including, by the provisions of the Senior CourtsAct 1981, deputy judges appointed ad hoc) sitting *en banc* if the senior judge or, in his absence, another nominated judge so directs (*Practice Direction* [1978] F.S.R. 449). An example of this practice was *John Wyeth's* and *Schering's Applications* [1985] R.P.C. 545.

For the judges assigned to the Patents Court, see Appendix G, §G03.

Further appeals from the Patents Court after appeal from the Comptroller (subs.(3))

97.06   Subsection (3) concerns further appeals from the Patents Court in relation to appeals from the Comptroller, other than those where the proceedings were held in Scotland (for which see §97.07). The subsection is expressed in terms that no further appeal shall lie from a decision of the Patents Court on appeal from the Comptroller except (a) where the Comptroller's decision was given under certain listed sections of the Act; or (b) where the ground of appeal is that the decision of the Patents Court was wrong in law. However, in all cases, such further appeal lies only if specific leave to appeal is given either by the Patents Court or by the Court of Appeal itself. The Access to Justice Act 1999 (c.22) s.55, together with CPR 52.13, specifically precludes "second appeals" unless the Court of Appeal should rule that there is some compelling point of principle or practice or that there is some other compelling reason for a further appeal to be heard. This led to concern whether such a provision overrides the specific terms of s.97(3) which sanction, in specified circumstances, further appeals from a decision of the Comptroller already appealed to the Patents Court. In *Smith International v Specialised Petroleum Services* [2006] F.S.R. 25 at 487; [2006] I.P. & T. 534, the Court of Appeal held that, in the absence of any specific repeal or amendment of s.97(3), such could not be implied and so a further appeal under s.97(3) was not to be considered as a "second appeal" under the 1999 Act and so is not precluded by that Act and the requirements of CPR 52.13; the difference is that leave should be given if the court considers that the appeal would have a real prospect of success, and not subject to the higher requirement of the existence of a compelling point of principle or practice.

The sections listed in subs.(3)(a), as those under which decisions of fact may (with leave) be further appealed are: ss.8, 12 and 37 (Entitlement); ss.18 and 20 (Refusal of application); ss.27 and 75 (Amendment); s.40 (Employee-inventor compensation); s.61(3) (Infringement, decided by the Comptroller); and ss.72 and 73 (Revocation). Further appeals are also possible (with leave) in relation to a decision of the Comptroller concerning a supplementary protection certificate, see s.128B.

It may be noted that subs.(3) does not provide for appeals on questions of fact arising in such proceedings as those under s.46(3) (settlement of terms of a licence of right); s.48 or s.51 (compulsory licences); or s.71 (declaration of non-infringement), but at least in s.46 proceedings this did not in the past seem to have had any significant inhibitory effect, see *Allen & Hanbury's (Salbutamol) Patent* [1987] R.P.C. 327 and *Smith Kline & French's (Cimetidine) Patents* [1990] R.P.C. 203. However, later in *American Cyanamid's Patent* [1991] R.P.C. 415, the Court of Appeal observed that in such cases the court should be asked to intervene only when there is truly an issue of law of general importance to be decided, and this is probably now the position under the CPR. For possible assistance on the construction of subs.(3) when apparently no provision for further appeal exists, see *Beecham Group's Irish Application* [1983] F.S.R. 355.

In *Ladney's and Hendry's International Application* BL C/103/96, the Patents Court refused leave for an appeal against a decision reversing the decision of the Comptroller, for which see §123.55, because the decision was essentially one of fact, not law, but leave was subsequently granted by the Court of Appeal who restored the decision of the Comptroller: [1998] R.P.C. 319.

A final appeal to the Supreme Court is also possible, though only by leave of the Court of Appeal or, if that court refuses leave, by the Supreme Court itself. The possibility also exists of a direct "leapfrog" appeal from the Patents Court to the Supreme Court under the Administration of Justice Act 1969 (c.58) ss.12 and 13, provided that the parties agree and the court certifies that certain conditions are met. The procedure was first used in *American Cyanamid's (Dann's) Patent* [1971] R.P.C. 425 when some doubt was expressed at the desirability of avoiding consideration of the case by the Court of Appeal. Other intellectual property cases which have involved this "leapfrog" procedure are: *YORK Trade Mark* [1981] F.S.R. 33; and *Ford Motor's Design Applications* [1994] R.P.C. 545 and [1995] R.P.C. 167.

Appeals from Comptroller's proceedings held in Scotland (subss.(4) and (5))

Rule 88 provides for the Comptroller to hear certain proceedings in Scotland. When this has occurred, appeal from the Comptroller lies (subject to the same limitations as in subs.(1)) not to the Patents Court but to the Outer House of the Court of Session in Scotland (subs.(4)), with further appeal possible (in analogous circumstances to those under subs.(3)) to the Inner House of the Court of Session (subs.(5). For court procedure in Scottish cases, see the commentary on s.98.   **97.07**

Principles affecting exercise of appellate jurisdiction

—General

The discussion below is centred upon appeals to the Patents Court from the Comptroller. Much of this is applicable also to subsequent appeals from the Patents Court to the Court of Appeal, but it must be borne in mind that generally (although not always) the judges of the Court of Appeal may lack the scientific and technical background of the Comptroller and the primary judges of the Patents Court, for which see §96.08. An example of a case in which the Court of Appeal disagreed with technical findings of fact by a (non-specialist) judge of the Patents Court and allowed an appeal accordingly is *Thorn Security Ltd v Siemens Schweiz AG* [2008] EWCA Civ 1161.   **97.08**

Under CPR 52.11 every appeal will be limited to a review of the decision of the lower court unless—

(a) a practice direction makes different provision for a particular category of appeal; or

(b) the court considers that in the circumstances of an individual appeal it would be in the interests of justice to hold a re-hearing.

The relevant practice direction is CPR 52 PD 9.1 which states that the hearing of an appeal will be a re-hearing (as opposed to a review of the decision of the lower court) if the appeal is from the decision of a minister, person or other body and the minister, person or other body—

(i) did not hold a hearing to come to that decision; or

(b) held a hearing to come to that decision, but the procedure adopted did not provide for the consideration of evidence

The MOPP confirms that an appeal to the Patents Court is limited to a review of the Comptroller's decision, unless the court considers that in the circumstances of an individual appeal, it would be in the interests of justice to hold a re-hearing. This brings the practice for patent appeals into line with that for other intellectual property appeals (e.g. trade mark appeals) and supersedes the previous case lawunder which appeals from the Comptroller were dealt with as re-hearings. In *REEF Trade Mark* [2003] R.P.C. 5, the Court of Appeal confirmed that findings of primary fact would not be disturbed by a court unless the hearing officer made an error of principle or was plainly wrong on the evidence, and that:

"an appellate court should not treat a judgment or written decision as containing an error of principle simply because it was of the opinion that the judgment or decision could have been better expressed."

Thus, an appellant will normally devote a considerable part of his argument to criticising the decision appealed from, and the burden is on the appellant to satisfy the appellate court that the tribunal of fact had erred, recognising that the appellate court will not have seen or heard the witnesses.

—Weight given to Comptroller's decision

97.09   The degree of weight attached to the Comptroller's decision may vary sharply according to the nature of the dispute. In the *REEF* case referred to above, the Court of Appeal said that in considering how reluctant an appellate court should be to interfere evaluation of, and conclusion on, the primary facts, there is no single standard which is appropriate to every case. The most important variables include the nature of the evaluation required, the standing and experience of the fact-finding judge or tribunal, and the extent to which the judge or tribunal had to assess oral evidence. Where the hearing officer did not hear any oral evidence, the court held that:

"an appellate court should show a real reluctance, but not the very highest degree of reluctance, to interfere in the absence of a distinct and material error of principle."

The guidance from this judgment was taken into account in the appeal to the Patents Court in *Hartington Conway Ltd's Patent Applications* [2004] R.P.C. 7, which was heard after Pt 63 of the CPR came into effect. In finding no error in the approach of the hearing officer either to the assessment of the witnesses or to the evidence before him, Pumfrey J. held that this was a case where the highest degree of reluctance should be felt in revisiting the findings of primary fact. Further, following the Court of Appeal's decision in *Merck & Co Inc's Patents* [2004] F.S.R. 16 a ground of appeal that the hearing officer erred "in principle" should actually identify the principle and not be used simply to mask a complaint about the assessment of evidence by the hearing officer. The power to order a re-hearing is contained expressly in CPR 52.11(b) and could be exercised in rare cases in order to allow justice to be done. In *Dyson Ltd's Trade Mark Application* [2003] R.P.C. 47, Patten J. held that art.6 of the European Convention on Human Rights did not compel the court to conduct a re-hearing in the case of any appeal from an ex parte decision.

Broadly speaking, the least weight will be accorded to any decision depending at root on law, since this is a field in which the disparity between the qualifications of the Comptroller and Patents Court is at its greatest. On questions of fact, the weight on technical issues may be marginally higher than on non-technical ones, since undoubtedly the Comptroller is likely to have superior technical expertise to the Patents Court; the Comptroller has a pool of individually more qualified specialist hearing officers on whom to call. But on certain non-technical issues also, for example licence royalty rates, the Comptroller has a vast experience and he will not lightly be upset—unless, of course, some error in his underlying legal approach can be demonstrated, as in *Shiley's Patent* [1988] R.P.C. 97 and *Smith Kline & French's (Cimetidine) Patents* [1990] R.P.C. 203 CA. On discretion, the Patents Court is reluctant to upset decisions in cases involving what might be termed the procedural mechanics of handling patent applications or patent disputes, see *Kiwi Coder's Application* [1986] R.P.C. 106 and also *Owens-Corning's Patent* [1972] R.P.C. 684, which concerned additional citations at a late stage in revocation proceedings.

Great weight is accorded only where there has been cross-examination before the Comptroller on disputed issues of technical fact, and the Comptroller has relied upon the demeanour and manner of the witnesses in resolving such conflict, see particularly on this point *Ladney and Hendry's International Application* [1998] R.P.C. 319 CA, where the Court of Appeal restored the factual decision of the Comptroller largely for this reason. These cases would still seem to be correct in principle under the new regime.

—By the Court of Appeal

The principles under CPR 52.11 apply equally to appeals to the Court of Appeal from lower courts, including the Patents Court or Patents County Court. In the Court of Appeal, it is difficult to upset concurrent findings of technical fact in both tribunals below. In *Hauni-Werke's Application* [1982] R.P.C. 327, the Court of Appeal confirmed that an experienced judge of the Patents Court was entitled to say that a particular technical fact was within his own knowledge, hence equating him in this respect to the Comptroller.   **97.10**

Article 32 of the TRIPS Agreement, (see §97.03, above) states that an opportunity shall be available for judicial review of any decision to revoke a patent, but does the availability of seeking leave from the Court of Appeal to appeal a decision of the Patents Court satisfy this requirement? In *Mayne Pharma v Debiopharm [Leave to Appeal]* [2006] EWHC 1812 Pat Ct Pumfrey J. granted leave to appeal on other grounds, but said that he would welcome guidance from the Court of Appeal on the effect of this art.32.

—Effect of prior decisions

It is reasonably well established that the Comptroller's own decisions have persuasive, but not compelling, impact upon subsequent cases decided in the UK-IPO involving comparable facts. The strength of the persuasion may depend upon the length of time that the preceding decision has been extant and followed; also upon the status of the hearing officer involved. Some hearing officers, like some judges, are regarded as more equal than others. *R, B and F's Application* [1976] R.P.C. 28 is of general interest on the topic.   **97.11**

The Patents Court (like the former Patents Appeal Tribunal) is fully entitled to overrule an existing precedent of the Comptroller, being the higher forum. But it is uncertain whether the Patents Court regards itself as bound by its own precedents. In the High Court generally, judges are not so bound, although naturally close attention is paid to prior decisions of the court.

The precedential power of previous decisions of the Patents Appeal Tribunal upon the Patents Court is also uncertain, but this is now of lesser significance as it will normally be possible to distinguish decisions of the former Tribunal as having been decided under a statute which no longer represents the present law.

As between the Patents Court, the Court of Appeal and the Supreme Court, the normal rules of precedent apply. The Patents Court is bound by decisions of the Court of Appeal and Supreme Court. The Court of Appeal is normally bound by its own decisions (although there are certain categories of exceptional cases) and in any event by those of the Supreme Court. The Supreme Court does have power to depart from its own previous decisions, and will do so in appropriate cases, although these will in general be rare. Decisions of foreign courts are not binding but may have persuasive effect. Likewise decisions of the Privy Council have persuasive effect, but are not binding. In *Conor v Angiotech* [2008] R.P.C. 28; [2008] UKHL 49 it was said by Lord Hoffmann in the House of Lords (as it was then known) that when the question is one of principle, it is desirable that so far as possible there should be uniformity in the way the national courts and the EPO interpret the European Patent Convention ("EPC"). This may indicate a greater tendency on the part of the UK courts to follow decisions of European courts wherever possible. The position is likewise as regards decisions of the Boards of Appeal in the EPO. Thus, in *John Wyeth's and Schering's Applications* [1985] R.P.C. 545, the Patents Court preferred to follow a decision of the EPO Enlarged Board of Appeal for the sake of harmony under the EPC, and in so doing departed from a long-standing authority of the High Court, in allowing "Swiss Form" claims in the UK: see §4A.10. A similar lurch away from domestic, and towards EPO, precedent occurred in *Asahi's Application* [1991] R.P.C. 485 HL; and, likewise, in both *Merrell Dow v Norton* [1996] R.P.C. 76 HL and *Biogen v Medeva* [1997] R.P.C. 1 HL, it was indicated that decisions by these Boards should be given considerable respect, although the House reached a different conclusion from the EPO in the *Biogen decision.*

Practice under Section 97

Appeals from the Comptroller to the Patents Court

—Lodging and service of notice of appeal

97.12   Under CPR 63.16 (reprinted at §F63.16), the procedure for bringing an appeal from the Comptroller to the Patents Court is now governed by the general procedures for appeals set out in CPR Pt 52. As the appeal is not from a county court or high court decision and it is a "statutory appeal" governed by CPR 52 PD.17, no leave to appeal is required under CPR 52.3. The time for appeal is 28 days from the date of the Comptroller's decision, the Comptroller having no power to vary this period. Also (from CPR 52.6), the Comptroller no longer has power to extend this term as was possible under former CPR 49E PD 16.3, although an application may be made to the court to extend the term. However, anomalously, CPR 52.5(4) does not preclude the granting by the Comptroller of an extension of the period for filing a respondent's notice, but any such extension should be granted by an exercise of discretion in the usual way, see *Specialist Petroleum Services v Smith International* BL O/9/05 where a modest extension was granted as this would not damage the appellant's interests or the conduct of the appeal.

In order to appeal to the Patents Court, it is necessary to bring the proceedings formally into the High Court by means of a "Notice of Appeal". Under CPR 52 PD 5.1, an appellant's notice must be filed and served and Court Form N161 (available together with Guidance Notes (N161A) on the court service website at *http://www.hmcourts-service.gov.uk*) should now be used for this purpose. A summary of the position as regards appeals is set out in Tribunal Practice Notice 1/2003 (revised) ([2003] R.P.C. 46 at 817). The Patents Court Guide has been re-issued and is reprinted in Appendix G in which para.20 refers to appeals from the Comptroller, which can (by agreement) be conducted as "appeals on paper only". In *Clear Focus Imaging v Contra Vision* BL C/54/01, noted I.P.D. 25009 the court noted that the opponent's appeal had been defective in naming "The Patent Office" as the respondent, whereas it should have named the patentee as respondent with a copy being served on the Comptroller of Patents. A request for the appeal to be decided on the papers should have been made at the time of service of the appeal.

The Notice of Appeal, with its attendant fee, must be received in the Chancery Chambers by the due date: receipt in the central post room at these courts is not sufficient. During court vacations, particularly during August, the court offices close early. Care must, therefore, be taken at such times when lodging notice of appeal on the last day of the time within which an appeal should be lodged, since otherwise it may be necessary to seek leave to lodge the appeal out of time. For days when the court office is entirely closed, actions due thereon may be taken on the next day that the office is open for business, see CPR 2.8.

The relevant fees are currently set under the Civil Proceedings Fees Order 2008 (SI 2008/1053) as of May 1, 2008, and should be checked as increases may occur without notice. One of the two required copies of the Notice of Appeal is to be stamped with receipt of the appeal fee. It is recommended that fees sent by post are in the form of a Bankers Draft or a postal order made payable to HM Paymaster General as it is not certain that an ordinary cheque will suffice. If the Notice of Appeal is filed by hand, the fee should first be paid in Room 204. Where the decision appealed from is in respect of proceedings relating to two or more patents or applications, a single notice of appeal may be lodged; however, the prescribed fee must be paid in respect of each patent or application involved. Notice of appeal may be given in respect of the whole or any specific part of the appealed decision and normally the grounds of appeal and the relief sought will be limited according to the terms of the notice of appeal.

An appellant must serve a copy on the Comptroller and any other party to the proceedings as soon as is practicable, and in any event, not later than seven days after the notice was first filed (CPR 63.10(2)(c) and 52.4(3)). Although service may be effected by post, care should be taken to ensure the notice arrives within the specified period. Such service may now initially be effected at the address for service recorded in the register, see §32.15.

It is not sufficient merely to lodge a notice of appeal and serve copies on the other parties to the proceedings and upon the Comptroller, it is also necessary to contact the Clerk or other person in charge of the Patents Court list within 14 days of lodging the appeal with a view to arranging a date for the hearing, see §G20 which also contains a reminder that the provisions for the preparation and service of skeleton arguments set out in the Chancery Guide are to be followed, (as discussed in §97.22). Where an appeal involves a point of commercial or public significance, the Comptroller should arrange for an early hearing of the appeal and, likewise, in any later application to the Court of Appeal for leave to appeal, the Comptroller should indicate that importance (*Draco's SPC Application* [1996] R.P.C. 417).

Under CPR 52.6(1), the appellate court can grant an extension of time for lodging appeal provided that the normal period has not already expired. The grounds upon which an extension is likely to be granted are discussed in §72.20; and, in *Edenlist's Patent* BL O/141/97 and in *Electrolux's Patents* BL O/135/98, extensions of time for lodging appeal were granted each to enable an application for legal aid to be made. In the *Edenlist* case, the extension was granted until four weeks after the decision of the Legal Aid Board was made known, but conditions were imposed to cater for various eventualities during such application so that the putative respondent would know the position as soon as this became clear.

When an extension of time is required from the Patents Court in an appeal from a decision of the Comptroller, this must be sought by a formal "application notice" under CPR Pt 23. However (under the former practice), if a consent was filed, and the request was a reasonable one, the Patents Judge would make the order without formal attendance before him: although, if consent had not been given, the matter would have to come before the judge in court: (1991–92) 21 *CIPA* 276. It is possible that this practice survives under the CPR.

—Respondent's notice and cross-appeal

97.13   CPR 63.16 (for which see §F63.16), and the Patents Court Guide (reprinted in Appendix G), are also relevant to the filing of either a respondent's notice or a cross-appeal. A respondent's notice with the required fee (SI 2008/1053) has to be filed wherever the non-appealing party desires to contend that the decision should be varied either in any event or in the event of the appeal being allowed in whole or in part; such a notice should specify the grounds of the contention and the relief sought. A cross-appeal should likewise be filed where it is intended to contend that the Comptroller's decision should be affirmed on alternative grounds (CPR 52.5).

Any such notice, whether a respondent's notice or a notice of cross-appeal, must be served on the Comptroller, on the appellant, and on any other respondent as soon as practicable and in any event within seven days of being filed (CPR 52.5(6)) and lodged in duplicate with the Clerk or other person in charge of the Patents Court list (for which see §G02) within five days after such service. If a party wishes to vary a decision in a direction different from that sought by the other party, a separate appeal should be filed, and the hearing will deal with the two appeals as separate matters.

Once an appeal has been lodged, the Comptroller is required to lodge with the Clerk or other person in charge of the Patents Court list "all papers relating to the matter subject of the appeal". Thereafter, the Comptroller can take no action on the file, e.g. he cannot then consider an application to amend the patent, see §72.20.

—Hearings and representation

97.14   Apart from solicitors, practising barristers and "patent agent litigators" (for which see §292.04) a patent attorney (or a non-practising barrister) has a right to sign, or be served with, any notice of appeal from a decision of the Comptroller, assuming that such person has been registered as the address for service before the UK-IPO (see CPR 63.14(2), Appendix F), and such persons also have a right of audience before the Patents Court when (but only when) it is hearing an appeal from the Comptroller, see §102A.01. Normally, the Comptroller appears on any such appeal by counsel (instructed by the Treasury Solicitor) to support his decision when this has been given in an ex parte proceeding, but does not (unless requested by the Patents Court) appear on an appeal from a decision given inter partes.

Chancery practice also requires that each person who is to appear on the hearing of an appeal shall provide to the Clerk in charge of the Patents Court list (for which see §G03) an estimate for the length of the hearing. A skeleton argument is also to be provided in advance of the hearing for which see the Chancery Guide. For the form of a skeleton argument, see §97.22.

Notice must be given to the Clerk if the appeal is withdrawn and such notice should also be served on the Comptroller and upon any other party to the appeal. Any respondent will then be asked if he consents to the formal dismissal of the appeal.

—Decisions and resulting orders

97.15   The formal order of the court is drawn up automatically, supplied to the parties and entered in the court records. The order will then appear in the public file at the UK-IPO. The decision itself does not, however, appear on the patent file. Indeed, it should be noted that copies of the decision (as distinct from the formal order) are not supplied to the parties automatically, unless the decision is reserved and handed down in writing. Copies of an oral judgment must be ordered from the official shorthand writers.

—Admission of new evidence on appeal

97.16   Procedure on appeals from the Comptroller to the Patents Court is now governed by CPR Pt 52. Under CPR 52.11(b), unless it orders otherwise, the appeal court will not receive oral evidence or evidence which was not before the lower court. Thus any admission of further evidence for the appeal will require the leave of the appeal court (here the Patents Court). Such leave is likely to be granted only for good cause, applying the criteria generally applied for admission of new evidence in the Court of Appeal on appeal from the High Court, as set down in *Ladd v Marshall* [1954] 1 W.L.R. 1489; [1954] 3 All E.R. 745. The *Ladd v Marshall* criteria are that it should be shown that: (1) the evidence could not have been obtained with reasonable diligence for use at the original hearing; (2) if given, the evidence would probably have had an important influence on the result of the case, though it need not be decisive; and (3) the evidence is such as presumably to be believed, i.e. it must be apparently credible, although it need not be incontrovertible. These rules were applied to refuse the admission of further evidence in: *Gebhart's Patent* [1992] R.P.C. 1 (fresh evidence on appeal in a compulsory licence application) showing that it is not sufficient for the new evidence to be important if it could have been presented previously.

As the *Ladd v Marshall* rules were formulated against the background of the full complement of oral evidence (evidence-in-chief, cross-examination and re-examination) normal in a high court case, it may be somewhat easier to adduce fresh evidence (or evidence in the first place) in appeals based on ex parte prosecution matters where the rules, though not excluding the presentation of evidence to the Comptroller, do not make formal provision for an evidence stage, than in inter partes proceedings where there has been such evidence. There may also be prayed in aid the public interest factor present in proceedings before the Comptroller, see *Oxon Italia's Trade Mark Application* [1981] F.S.R. 408. Also, the courts can be expected to "allow fresh evidence when to refuse it would affront common sense, or a sense of justice" (*Mulholland v Mitchell* [1971] A.C. 666 HL) and under the CPR the admission of further evidence will be exercised in accordance with the overriding objective of the CPR, particularly the concept of proportionality, see *Club Europe Trade Mark* [2000] R.P.C. 329. For this reason, a request (made during an appeal) to add a further document to the plea of obviousness was refused in *Coflexip v Stolt Comex* [2001] R.P.C. 9 at 182: this would necessitate a new trial which would not be proportionate for the allocation of the court's resources.

Fresh evidence was refused admission in relation to an obviousness rejection in *Wistar's Application* [1983] R.P.C. 255, and in relation to restoration in *Winventive's Patent* BL O/55/83, noted I.P.D. 6034. However, further evidence was admitted on a late hearing of an obviousness rejection in *PCUK's Application* [1984] R.P.C. 482; and, in *Therma-Tru's Patent* [1997] R.P.C. 777, it was held appropriate for updated financial statements to be considered in relation to an application for a compulsory licence, for which see §50.03. Also, in *Wellcome Foundation's Application* BL C/72/83, noted I.P.D. 6066, an applicant was allowed to submit a primer of background facts by way of explanation, rather than as evidence. A request to cross-examine a witness on the hearing of the appeal is generally considered as an application to admit new evidence (*Sainsbury's Application* [1981] F.S.R. 406).

In *Clear Focus Imaging v Contra Vision* BL C/54/01, noted I.P.D. 25009 a request to file new evidence was supported by a statement which was regarded as inadequate in stating that the opponent had only become aware of the existence of the person giving the statement a short time beforehand. This lack of awareness might have been due to a lack of diligence by the opponents. The hearing officer had exercised his discretion properly to exclude the new evidence.

—Intervention by third party

It may be possible for a person, who was not a party to the original proceedings, to intervene in any appeal under the provisions of CPR 19.2(2), but only when the question in issue is one which actually affects the proposed intervener, a mere point of law not being sufficient for this purpose (*Spelling Goldberg v BPC Publishing* [1981] R.P.C. 283). **97.17**

—Other relevant rules of court

Attention is drawn to some of the practices of the court which are not included within **97.18**

CPR 63 and the relevant Practice Directions and yet can have considerable relevance to appeals from the Comptroller. Such rules relate to:

- *Hearings in private:* The general principle is that a hearing should be held in public, but a hearing (or part of a hearing) may be held in private where a public hearing would defeat the ends of justice, see CPR 39.2(3). The court has complete discretion in the matter, and an application should be made to the court in any appropriate case, e.g. where confidential financial information in a licensing situation, or a trade secret, is being discussed.

- *Cross-examination:* CPR 32.7 empowers the court to order cross-examination of a witness who has previously given his evidence in writing. An application must be made to the court, and if such an order is made and the witness does not attend, his evidence may not be used without permission of the court. However, the use of the power may be restricted by the rules against the admission of new evidence on appeal, see §97.16.

- *Scientific advisers:* CPR 35.15 is apt to cover the appointment of a scientific adviser on an appeal to the Patents Court, for which see §96.12.

Added ss.99A and 99B also respectively provide power whereby the Patents Court or the Court of Session in Scotland (even on appeal from the Comptroller) can order the UK—IPO to inquire into and report on any question of fact or opinion, see §99A.03.

Further appeals from the Patents Court to the Court of Appeal

—General

97.19 The practice is also governed by CPR Pt 52.

Leave to appeal is now required from all decisions made in the Patents Court and not only where s.97(3) applies (see CPR 52.3), although when subs.(3) applies (appeals to the Court of Appeal from a decision of the patents court on appeal from the Comptroller), such leave must be obtained from the Court of Appeal under, see CPR 52.13. According to *Smith International v Specialised Petroleum Services* [2006] F.S.R. 25 at 487; [2006] I.P. & T. 534 referred to in §97.06, a further appeal under s.97(3) is not to be considered as a "second appeal" under the Access to Justice Act 1999 (c.22) s.55 and so the granting of leave should not be subject to the higher requirement of the existence of a compelling point of principle or practice, but leave should be given on the normal principles of CPR 52.3 that permission to appeal may be given only where the court considers that the appeal would have a real prospect of success or there is some other compelling reason why the appeal should be heard.

In *Designers Guild v Russell Williams* [2001] F.S.R. 11, 113 at 122 the House of Lords (as it was then known) said that an appeal court should only reverse a decision based on the facts and evidence if satisfied that an error of principle had been made, see also *Biogen v Medeva* [1997] R.P.C. 1 HL. This approach is being adopted for appeals generally and has been followed by the Court of Appeal in several cases, see, e.g. *Instance v Denny Bros.* [2002] R.P.C. 14 at 321, in which it was noted that it is only the initial tribunal which has the benefit of assessing the witnesses first hand, whereas the appeal tribunal must normally proceed only on the basis of transcripts of the evidence. The Court of Appeal emphasised and followed this principle also in *Pharmacia v Merck* [2002] R.P.C. 41 at 775, and in *Merck's Patents [Alendronate product]* [2004] F.S.R. 16 at 330 took the matter further by saying that:

"in future when it is sought to challenge the trial judge's conclusions on anticipation or obviousness, the Grounds of Appeal should, in respect of each complaint, contain a succinct statement of the principle that the judge is said to have infringed, and . . . unless the matter is self-evident, what is the authority for that principle".

Increased emphasis is now placed on CPR 52.11(3) which says that the appeal court will only allow an appeal where the decision of the lower court was (a) wrong, or (b) unjust because of a serious procedural or other irregularity in the proceedings in the lower court, and under CPR 52 PD.3 the grounds of appeal should set out clearly the reasons why CPR 52.11(3)(a) or (b) is said to apply, and specify, in respect of each ground, whether the ground raises an appeal on a point of law or is an appeal against a finding of fact. As the construction of documents (whether of the patent-in-suit or of a prior art document) is a question of law, and may be a mixed matter of law and fact in a case on obviousness, leave to appeal in such cases may more easily be obtained (as in *Ferag v Muller Martini* [2006] EWHC 378 Pat Ct; BL C/23/06) than when the appeal is based on an allegation that the judge erred in principle in assessing matters of fact.

In *AB Hässle's Patents* [2003] F.S.R. 23; [2003] I.P.&T 266 the Court of Appeal was presented with an unusual situation in which the patentee, instead of appealing the first instance judgment, sought a new trial on the ground that the trial judge's interventions during cross-examination of its expert showed apparent bias. The Court of Appeal decided that the amount of questioning by the judge was not unfair or oppressive and the judge's conduct of the trial was not, and would not be seen, to be such as to render the trial unfair. The application for a new trial therefore failed, and the decision below was upheld.

Where a case has settled before an appeal against revocation has been heard, it has in the past been possible to obtain a decision to reinstate the patent on the papers without a hearing, e.g. where an EPO opposition has resulted in amendment which has cleared the basis for the revocation order. However, as the result of *Halliburton v Smith International* [2006] R.P.C. 2 at 25, the Court of Appeal will now hear the appeal as a matter of substance, rather than of formality, with the Comptroller being permitted to intervene if he should so wish because of the absence of any submissions from the other parties, see particularly *Conor Medsystems v Angiotech* [2008] R.P.C. 28; [2008] UKHL 49 where the patentee needed to appeal the judgments below of invalidity but the original defendant had withdrawn from the proceedings. The Comptroller was asked to present the case for invalidity, but with the patentee being required to bear the Comptroller's costs of so doing.

If the Patents Court refuses leave, leave can then be sought by an application to the Court of Appeal made without notice to others. The matter will then initially be dealt with a single Lord Justice. By requesting leave to appeal, there is no commitment to proceed with this if leave is given. This is because it is much more convenient to request leave when all the parties are already in court. However, an application to the Patents Court for leave to appeal further may be made by a later application made without notice to others, but the hearing of such an application may be adjourned to be heard with notice to other parties. Where this happens an unsuccessful applicant can expect to be required to pay the other side's costs (*International Paint's Application* [1982] R.P.C. 247).

Where leave to appeal is granted by the Patents Court, the notice of appeal must be filed at the court within 21 days after the date of the decision of the Patents Court that the appellant wishes to appeal (CPR 52.4(2)(b)), unless the Patents Court has specified some different period (CPR 52.4(2)(a)). When a notice of appeal is filed, copies must be served on each respondent as soon as practicable and in any event not later than seven days after the notice has been filed (CPR 52.4(3)).

Where the order appealed from is one relating to the revocation of a patent, or is an appeal involving a judgment of the Comptroller at first instance, CPR 52 PD 21.3 requires service of the notice of appeal and any respondent's notice on the Comptroller. Probably, the Comptroller then has a right to appear on the hearing of the appeal. The Notices will then appear on the file of the patent.

The Court of Appeal may appoint a scientific adviser in the same manner as the Patents Court, see §96.12.

A patent attorney has no right of audience before the Court of Appeal, and an appropriate advocate (counsel or a solicitor-advocate) must be instructed by a solicitor for the purposes of this further appeal or when leave to appeal is sought (often at short notice) from the Court of Appeal. Such a person, likewise, has to be in charge of the day-to-day handling of the appeal while awaiting hearing, including such matters as the setting down of the appeal for hearing, lodgment of bundles of documents for the court, and the like.

Remaining issues of practice before the Court of Appeal under the practice direction CPR 52 PD are beyond the scope of this Work although some comments on matters of particular interest to practitioners are made below.

—Scientific advisers

97.20   The question of scientific advisers is discussed in §96.12. It may be particularly acute in the Court of Appeal, especially in a case of substantial scientific complexity, on account of at least some of the selected members of that court lacking sufficient technical comprehension of the art involved, as they have been known at times openly to admit.

—Evidence

97.21   The *Ladd v Marshall* rules, discussed in §97.16, will normally be applied on any application to admit fresh evidence on appeal to the Court of Appeal. However, the presentation of an agreed statement of facts, or a scientific primer, for the instruction of the Court of Appeal on a further appeal from the Comptroller—as was done in *Johns-Manville's Patent* [1967] R.P.C. 479—has to be distinguished from fresh evidence as such.

—Skeleton arguments

97.22   Each party to an appeal before the Court of Appeal is required with the appellant's (or respondent's) notice, or within 14 days thereafter, to submit a "skeleton argument", see CPR 52 PD 5.9. There is active case management of each appeal by a "supervising lord justice", this currently being Jacob L.J. for patent appeals who gives directions concerning the progress and future conduct of an appeal. If a directions hearing is necessary, that is normally before that supervising Lord Justice and is normally in chambers where solicitors also have a right of audience.

The main purpose of the skeleton argument is to identify in advance the principal points likely to be taken by the party at the oral hearing. Points of law should be accompanied by cross-references to the relevant authorities; and points of fact by cross-reference to relevant passages in the written or oral (transcript) evidence. A chronology of relevant dates has also to be provided as a separate document. However, there is no overall set form for the presentation of skeleton arguments, although it should comply with the requirements of CPR 52 PD 5.10. The skeleton argument is usually prepared by the advocate who has the responsibility of providing the actual oral argument at the hearing, with patent attorneys and solicitors to providing assistance in its preparation and in checking its factual accuracy, and in particular the cross-references to the evidence.

—Costs on appeal

97.23   The normal rule is that the successful party should have its costs as assessed unless otherwise agreed. However, unless there is (unusually in patent litigation) an order for fixed costs, the court is now required to consider whether to make a summary assessment of the amount of the costs to be awarded (see CPR 43–48 PD 13.1). Even before the CPR, the Patents Court had indicated its intention to adopt a vigorous approach to costs and that it would consider an application for immediate judicial assessment on the basis of the actual detailed bills sent to clients with an award of a lump sum, thereby avoiding a detailed assessment of costs, see *Patents Court (Consolidated Practice Direction)* [1998] R.P.C. 653. Indeed, it has been indicated that a summary assessment of costs should be the norm at the conclusion of an appeal from a decision of the Comptroller, at least where the hearing takes no more than a single day, see also CPR 43–48 PD 13.2. For an immediate assessment of costs to be paid in a lump sum, estimates should be supplied in advance of the hearing to all other parties to the appeal proceedings, for the details of which see §61.49. A lump sum award can also be made by consent of the parties; as well as in proceedings under s.40 for employee-inventor compensation, see §106.02.

Otherwise, the normal rule for most proceedings in the High Court is that the successful party is entitled to his costs on the "standard basis". On this basis the court is to have regard to all the circumstances in deciding whether costs were: (i) proportionately and reasonably incurred; or (ii) were proportionate and reasonable in amount (CPR 44.5(1)), but with regard to a list of matters set out in CPR 44.5(3).

In the absence of agreement or order for payment of a lump sum, the successful party's bill should be lodged with the Costs Office of the court for assessment by a costs judge. Where the costs relate to an appeal from the Comptroller to the Patents Court and the appeal has been conducted by a patent attorney, it would be prudent for that person to have the bill drawn up by an experienced costs clerk. For the payment of interest on an award of costs, see §61.34.

In appeals from the Comptroller, whether in ex parte or inter partes proceedings, the successful party is awarded costs to be assessed according to the normal practice in the High Court. The Court of Appeal likewise awards costs against the unsuccessful party, see *Associated British Combustion's Application* [1978] R.P.C. 581. It follows that the Comptroller gives, and receives, costs when he appears on an appeal, see: *Associated British Combustion's Application* (above); *Omron Tateisi's Application* [1981] R.P.C. 125; and *ICI's (Richardson's) Application* [1981] F.S.R. 609. If an appeal from the Comptroller on an ex parte matter is lodged and then not proceeded with, the Treasury Solicitor makes a claim for costs incurred up to withdrawal of the appeal. However, the Comptroller does not always enforce the order when obtained, see *McManus' Application* [1994] F.S.R. 558.

Nevertheless, any award of costs remains within the ultimate discretion of the court, and the Patents Court stated in the *Omron* case (above) that:

"There may well be instances when the court will make variations from the normal rules, for example where the court has itself invited the Comptroller to come and assist".

Thus, where an ex parte appeal has been taken to clarify a point of law, the Comptroller may be prepared to settle costs by the award of a realistic sum in lieu of assessment: (1981–82) 11 *CIPA* 351.

On assessment of the costs of an appeal to the Court of Appeal there will normally be no allowance for a patent attorney's assistance or attendance. However, where a patent attorney's has assisted the court, for example by the provision of a background technical explanation, the Court of Appeal can be requested to signify that such assistance has been given so that the costs judge may give the question special consideration, see *Toppan Printing's Application* BL C/116/83.

In TPN 2/2000 at [19] the Comptroller has indicated that she would be willing not to seek costs in cases where a party would be likely to suffer some form of hardship or where a significant point of general legal interest is involved.

Legal Aid

97.24

Legal aid is not available in proceedings before the Comptroller, see §107.02, but is in principle available on appeal. However, with the replacement of the former legal aid scheme by a Community Legal Service by the Access to Justice Act 1999 (c.22) ss.4–11 and Sch.2, it is likely to be even harder than ever to obtain state funding for patent litigation, including appeals from decisions of the Comptroller.

In *Tiefebrun's Application* [1979] F.S.R. 97, the unsuccessful appellant was legally aided but the court indicated that it had no power to order that the costs of attendance of the appellant's instructing patent agent be covered by the legal aid certificate. In *Edenlist's Patent* BL O/141/97 and *Electrolux's Patents* BL O/135/98, extensions of time for lodging appeal were granted by the Comptroller each to enable an application for legal aid to be made, see §97.12.

SECTION 98

Proceedings in Scotland

98.01   **98.**—(1) In Scotland proceedings relating primarily to patents (other than proceedings before the comptroller) shall be competent in the Court of Session only, and any jurisdiction of the sheriff court relating to patents is hereby abolished except in relation to questions which are incidental to the issue in proceedings which are otherwise competent there.

(2) The remuneration of any assessor appointed to assist the court in proceedings under this Act in the Court of Session shall be determined by the Lord President of the Court of Session with the consent of the **Treasury** [*Minister for the Civil Service*] and shall be defrayed out of moneys provided by Parliament].

Note. Subsection (2) was amended by SI 1981/1670.

RELEVANT STATUTORY INSTRUMENT

INTELLECTUAL PROPERTY (ENFORCEMENT, ETC.) REGULATIONS 2006

(SI 2006/ 1028)

98.02   *Notes*

1. The Intellectual Property (Enforcement, etc.) Regulations 2006 (SI 2006/1028), effective from April 29, 2006 with no transitional provision, were made for compliance with Directive 2004/48/EC OJ EC L157/45, 30.4.2004, with *corrigendum* OJ EC L195/16, 2.6.2004 [the "Enforcement Directive"] requiring harmonisation of the relief generally to be available for infringement (within the EEA Area) of intellectual property rights (whether registered or unregistered).

2. Regulation 3 of this Statutory Instrument (reprinted at §61.02, expands the scope of s.61(1)(c) and, for patent infringement, can be regarded as an extension of it, as discussed in the commentary to s.61.

3. Regulations 4 and 5 (effective from April 29, 2006) apply only to proceedings in Scotland and are reprinted below, and are discussed in §98.22 below.

Regulation 4—Order in Scotland for disclosure of information

98.03   **4.**—(1) This regulation applies to proceedings in Scotland concerning an infringement of an intellectual property right.

(2) The pursuer may apply to the court for an order that information regarding the origin and distribution networks of goods or services which infringe an intellectual property right shall be disclosed to him by the relevant person.

(3) The court may only order the information to be disclosed where it considers it just and proportionate having regard to the rights and privileges of the relevant person and others; such an order may be subject to such conditions as the court thinks fit.

(4) The relevant person is—

    (a) the alleged infringer,

    (b) any person who—

        (i) was found in possession of the infringing goods on a commercial scale,

        (ii) was found to be using the infringing services on a commercial scale, or

        (iii) was found to be providing services on a commercial scale, which are used in activities which infringe an intellectual property right, or

(c) any person who has been identified by a person specified in sub-paragraph (b) as being involved in—

    (i) the production, manufacture or distribution of the infringing goods, or

    (ii) the provision of the infringing services.

(5) For the purposes of paragraph (3), the court may order the disclosure of any of the following types of information—

(a) the names and addresses of—

    (i) each producer, manufacturer, distributor or supplier of the infringing goods or services;

    (ii) any person who previously possessed the infringing goods; and

    (iii) the intended wholesaler and retailer of the infringing goods or services; and

(b) information relating to—

    (i) the quantities of infringing goods or the amount of infringing services provided, produced, manufactured, delivered, received or ordered; and

    (ii) the price paid for the infringing goods or infringing services in question.

(6) Nothing in this regulation affects—

(a) any right of the pursuer to receive information under any other enactment (including an enactment comprised in, or an instrument made under, an Act of the Scottish Parliament) or rule of law; and

(b) any other power of the court.

(7) For the purposes of this regulation and regulation 5, "court" means the Court of Session or the sheriff court.

Regulation 5—Order in Scotland for publication of judgments

5. In Scotland, where the court finds that an intellectual property right has been infringed, the court may, at the request of the pursuer, order appropriate measures for the dissemination and publication of the judgment to be taken at the defender's expense.   **98.04**

RELEVANT RULE—RULE 88

Rule 88—Proceedings in Scotland

88.—(1) Where there is more than one party to proceedings, a party to the proceedings may apply to the comptroller to hold proceedings in Scotland.   **98.05**

(2) An application made under paragraph (1) must be granted—

(a) where all the parties consent to the proceedings being held in Scotland; or

(b) where the comptroller considers it appropriate.

(3) A refusal of an application made under paragraph (1) is excepted from the right of appeal conferred by section 97.

Note. The rule is a re-write of the previous r.108 of the 1995 Rules, but is of broader scope, as discussed in §98.23.

COMMENTARY ON SECTION 98

Scope of the section

Proceedings for patent infringement, validity, entitlement and all other types of proceedings under the 1977 Act may be brought before the Court of Session, subject to general rules on jurisdiction (see §98.08). Section 98 specifies that the Court of Session is the   **98.06**

Scottish court with exclusive jurisdiction to hear proceedings relating primarily to patents. Section 130(1) provides that "court", in relation to Scotland, means "the Court of Session". Section 98(1) specifies that the Sheriff Court has no jurisdiction in relation to patent proceedings, except in relation to questions which are incidental to the issue in proceedings which are otherwise competent there. In practice all patent proceedings in Scotland are brought in the Court of Session.

There is no Scottish equivalent to the Patents County Court as exists in England and Wales, see §287.03. The provisions of ss.287–291 of the CDPA 1988 for establishing Patents County Courts apply only to England and Wales (CDPA 1988 s.304(2)(a)).

Patent proceedings in the Court of Session are governed by the Rules of the Court of Session ("RCS"). The RCS derive from the Act of Sederunt (Rules of the Court of Session) Rules 1994 (SI 1994/1443) (as amended). The Court of Session also publishes Practice Notes with further guidance on procedure from time to time. The website *http://www.scotcourts.gov.uk* provides online access to the RCS and recent Practice Notes. Chapter 55 of RCS provides specific rules relevant to intellectual property proceedings, including patent proceedings, as discussed in §98.19.

Section 98(2) corresponds to s.70(2) of the Senior CourtsAct 1981 (c.54) providing for scientific advisers and assessors to assist the Patents Court, see the discussion on this in §96.12.Otherwise, to accommodate other aspects of Scots law; s.31 makes specific provision for the transfer of patent rights under Scots law; and special provision for privilege in patent proceedings in Scotland is provided by s.105, see the respective commentaries on those sections. The statutory limitation period for actions under Scots law is discussed in §60.30; and the "territorial scope of infringement" is discussed in §60.19.

The Scottish Government commissioned Rt. Hon. Lord Gill in February 2007 to review the Scottish Civil Courts procedure. Lord Gill published his report in September 2009 and recommended a number of reforms to improve the various aspects of procedure in the Scottish Civil Courts. The article by G. Grassie, "What's happening in the Scottish world of IP dispute resolution" [2010] *CIPA* 242 provides commentary on the potential implications of Lord Gill's report in the context of intellectual property actions (including patent actions) in Scotland.

The Intellectual Property (Enforcement etc.) Regulations 2006 (SI 2006/1028) extend the options open to IP including patent right holders for the enforcement of their rights by: (1) allowing for enhanced damages where infringement is deliberate; and (2) by providing an explicit statutory equivalent to *Norwich Pharmacal* orders (see §60.11) for the recovery of certain types of information in Scotland. These rights are reprinted above and discussed at §98.22 below.

Provisions parallel to s.98 exist in relation to proceedings in Northern Ireland, see s.131 and the commentary on it; and to proceedings in the Isle of Man, see s.132(2) and §132.07.

Scots' legal terminology

98.07   Cases decided under Scots law use legal terminology with which English solicitors, counsel and patent attorneys may be unaccustomed. The corresponding terms were previously set out in s.103(6) of the 1949 Act as follows, with Scottish terms in parentheses: "injunction" ("interdict"); "chose in action" ("right of action" or "an incorporeal moveable"); "account of profits" ("accounting and payment of profits"); "arbitrator" ("arbiter"); "claimant" ("pursuer"); and "defendant" ("defender"). Other commonly used Scots law terms are set out in parentheses as follows: "assignment" ("assignation"); "tort" ("delict"); "declaration" ("declarator"); "costs" ("expenses"); an order made by the court ("interlocutor"); "disclosure" ("recovery"); procedure used to obtain disclosure ("commission and diligence"); "claim form" ("summons"); "defences" ("answers"); "hearing on legal issues" ("debate"); "case management hearing" ("Procedural Hearing"); "Trial" ("Proof"); and "judgment" ("decree").

Jurisdiction of the Court in Scotland

98.08   Since January 1, 1987, the Civil Jurisdiction and Judgments Act 1982 (c.27) ("CJJA") as subsequently amended has regulated, inter alia, jurisdiction between the component parts of the United Kingdom, as discussed in §96.09. Schedule 4 (subject to Sch.8) to the CJJA regulates the cases where persons must, or may, be sued in the courts of a particular component part of the United Kingdom.

The primary rule is that persons "domiciled" in one particular component part shall be sued in the courts of that part (CJJA Sch.4 para.1), but a court of a component part also has jurisdiction in cases of tort, delict or quasi-delict where the harmful event occurred or may occur in that component part (CJJA Sch.4 para.3(c)).

—Definition of Domicile

"Domiciled" for this purpose is defined in ss.41–46 of the CJJA. In the case of an indi- **98.09** vidual, a person is domiciled in a particular part of the United Kingdom:

> "if and only if (a) he is resident in that part; and (b) the nature and circumstances of his residence indicates that he has a substantial connection with that part"

(s.41(3)), though (b) is not required for someone domiciled in the United Kingdom if its provisions are not satisfied in relation to any particular part of the United Kingdom (s.41(5)).

The "seat" of a corporation or association is treated as its domicile. There are two tests to determine whether a corporation or association has its "seat" in the United Kingdom. These are: (a) whether it was incorporated under the law of a part of the UK and has its registered office or some other official address in the UK; or (b) whether its central management and control are exercised in the UK. If either condition is met, the corporation has a seat in the UK (s.41(3)). A corporation or association has its seat in a particular part of the UK or place if its seat is in the UK and it meets one of the three following conditions: (a) it has its registered office or some other official address in that part; or (b) its central management or control is exercised in that part; or (c) it has a place of business in that part (ss.41(4) and (5)).

—Definition of "place where the harmful event occurred"

The definition of "place where the harmful event occurred" was considered in the pass- **98.10** ing off case of *Modus Vivendi Ltd v British Products Sanmex Co Ltd* [1996] F.S.R. 790 in which the Scottish defendant argued that the English courts did not have jurisdiction. The court held that there were two options for the "place where the harmful event occurred": (a) the place of the event giving rise to the damage; or (b) the place where the damage occurred. The place where the damage was suffered is not of itself the "place where the harmful event occurred". In this passing off case, the claimant argued that the English courts had jurisdiction as the damage was suffered by it in England. However, the court declined jurisdiction because the event which gave rise to the alleged damage (the defendant's allegedly infringing acts) took place in Scotland. Scotland was the place where the harmful event occurred because that was where the alleged tortious conduct (manufacture and export of deceptive goods to Hong Kong) had originated.

—CJJA Schedule 8

The general rules of this modified Brussels Convention, as applied to proceedings in **98.11** Scotland, are subject to the additional provisions of Sch.8 to the CJJA. Besides reiterating the general rules of domicile, with the alternative jurisdiction of the place where the harmful event occurred (Sch.8(1) and (2)(c)), this Schedule provides that proceedings may be taken for an interdict [injunction] before a Scottish court where a wrong is likely to be committed in Scotland (Sch.8(2)(j)), and the Court of Session expressly maintains jurisdiction to adjudicate in proceedings principally concerned with the registration or validity of United Kingdom patents (Sch.8(2)(n) and 5(2)), subject to the doctrine of *forum non conveniens* discussed below. This means that an attack on the validity of a UK or European patent can be mounted in the Court of Session, irrespective of the domicile of either party and any order for revocation would then be effective UK-wide as a matter of course.

—Applicability of forum non conveniens when parallel proceedings commenced elsewhere in the United Kingdom

98.12   Omitted from Sch.4 to the CJJA are provisions corresponding to arts 21–23 of the Brussels Convention (CJJA Sch.1, arts 21–23) which would, otherwise, require or suggest a stay of proceedings in a court when parallel, or connected, proceedings are commenced in different parts of the United Kingdom. Thus, whether any particular litigation should be brought, or continued, in Scotland or England, where similar causes of action occur in both jurisdictions, apparently falls to be decided on considerations based on the doctrine of forum non conveniens, for which the leading case is *The Spiliada* [1987] A.C. 460; [1986] 3 All E.R. 843 HL.

For example, in *Ivax Pharmaceuticals UK Ltd v Akzo Nobel NV* [2005] EWHC 2658 Ch, BL C/103/05 the Patents Court was asked to decline jurisdiction in patent revocation proceedings on the basis that it was *forum non conveniens* and the Scottish Court of Session was the most appropriate forum to determine the dispute, but the Patents Court declined to do so. Here, the claimant, Ivax, was claiming the revocation of a patent of the sole defendant in respect of a certain form of the steroid tibolone. Proceedings were also pending in Scotland relating to two other patents concerning this compound. Ivax applied for a declaration that the Patents Court should decline jurisdiction in favour of the Court of Session. Looking at *The Spiliada* principles, the court noted that the initial question was whether England was not the natural or appropriate forum for the trial, taking into consideration any factors suggesting the action had its most real and substantial connection with another part of the UK. The claimant was registered in England and Wales and carried on business there. The defendant-patentee was a Netherlands company with no real connection with Scotland. The only factor connecting the action to Scotland was the pending Scottish proceedings, but these related to different aspects of the manufacture of tibolone and Ivax itself was not a party to one of the two Scottish actions. Although one of the patents at issue in the Scottish proceedings was to be referred to in the English proceedings it was being considered in England only as part of the prior art and the Patents Court would not have to consider its validity so that there was no significant risk of inconsistent findings of fact. The existence of the Scottish proceedings was therefore no reason to decline jurisdiction in England or to stay the English proceedings. However, the reasoning suggests that, if similar factual issues were to be considered in the Scottish proceedings such that there was a risk of inconsistent findings of fact, a stay of the English proceedings might have been more favourably considered.

The idea of parallel litigation was frowned upon in *Vetco Gray UK Ltd v FMC Technologies Inc* [2007] EWHC 540 Pat Ct. FMC had raised a patent infringement action against Vetco in Scotland and Vetco responded by alleging that FMC's patent was invalid. Two weeks later Vetco applied for revocation of FMC's patent in England and Wales. FMC then applied to stay the English and Welsh proceedings. Mann J. granted the application to stay the proceedings. He found that in this case, Scotland was the more appropriate forum. Both of these sets of proceedings raised the same or substantially similar issues. The alleged infringement by Vetco had taken place in Scotland. Mann J. noted that the costs of the proceedings would be similar in both jurisdictions and that the time advantage of suing in England and Wales was so small it was not material. Mann J. was not going to encourage parallel litigation, especially given that there would be an enormous waste of efforts and money.

The CJJA permits parallel actions to be commenced without leave of the court. Thus, there is the possibility of parallel interim proceedings, see *Union Carbide v BP Chemicals* [1995] F.S.R. 449; [1995] S.L.T. 972, discussed further in §98.21 where the Scottish provision for an order for pre-action recovery of documents (disclosure in English terminology) is described. In this Union Carbide case such an order was granted in order to assist English proceedings, even though it seems doubtful whether the English court would itself have made such an order at the preliminary stage which the proceedings had then reached, see §§61.67.

Scottish procedure generally

Articles on Scottish procedure and jurisdiction includes Grassie, G., "The Scottish **98.13** Courts—the tartan alternative for resolving IP disputes" [2004] *CIPA* 406 and Buchan, R. and Grassie, G. "Intellectual Property Disputes in Scotland" J.I.P.L.P. 2011, 6(2), 120-127.

Interdict effective UK-wide: defender domiciled in Scotland

In relation to an infringer domiciled in Scotland, (which will include a corporate **98.14** infringer with a Scottish registered office address) in order to obtain either a permanent or an interim interdict/injunction which is effective UK-wide and possibly beyond, the infringer must be sued in the Scottish Court of Session. If the infringer is domiciled in Scotland but is sued in England, any injunction (either permanent or interim) would not be enforceable in Scotland without further measures being taken. The precise procedure for enforcing interdicts depends on whether the interdict is permanent or an interim measure. The Scottish court rules relating to the registration and enforcement of foreign judgments (including judgments of the English courts) are set out in Ch. 62 RCS.

Enforcing permanent interdicts granted in one part of the United Kingdom in another part

It is possible to enforce permanent interdicts [injunctions] granted in one part of the **98.15** United Kingdom in another component part thereof under s.18 and Sch.7 to the CJJA. Therefore a Scottish permanent interdict can be enforced in England, Wales and Northern Ireland and vice versa. Rule 62.38 of the RCS (the rules of court relating to patent proceedings in the Court of Session) sets out the procedure for having interdicts as non-monetary provisions of a judgment made elsewhere in the UK registered for enforcement in Scotland.

Rule 62.42 of the RCS sets out the procedure for obtaining a certificate and a certified copy of the judgment to enable the Court of Session's judgment to be registered in another part of the UK. Essentially, any interested party must obtain a certified copy of the judgment from the Court of Session in Edinburgh and then apply to have it registered in the High Court in England, Wales or Northern Ireland.

The effect of registering the judgment is that it has the same force and effect as if it had been granted in the jurisdiction it has been registered in (CJJA Sch.7(6)). The cost of registration is recoverable as if it had been included in the monetary provisions of the original judgment (CJJA Sch.7 para.7).

For an article on enforcing English judgments in Scotland, see Gill Grassie, "Enforcing English Judgments in IP cases in Scotland" [2004] *CIPA* 515.

Seeking interim relief in one part of the United Kingdom when main proceedings in another part

Interim interdicts/injunctions are defined in the CJJA (s.18(5)(d)) as provisional **98.16** measures to which this s.18 does not apply. Interim interdicts cannot therefore be registered under the CJJA (Sch.7). However, it is possible to seek separate interim relief under the CJJA (s.25) in the High Court of England, Wales and Northern Ireland where proceedings have been raised in Scotland. The High Court in England can refuse to entertain an application for interim or protective measures if the fact that this s.25 is the only ground under which it has jurisdiction makes it inexpedient for the Court to grant relief (CJJA s.25(2)). The meaning of "expediency" was considered in the case of *Credit Suisse Fides Trust SA v Cuoghi* [1998] Q.B. 818 where Millett L.J. stated (p.826):

"...the English court should in principle be willing to grant appropriate interim relief in support of substantive proceedings taking place elsewhere, and that it should not be deterred from doing so by the fact that its role is only an ancillary one unless the circumstances of the particular case make the grant of such relief inexpedient."

He went on to state that two material considerations for the court when in personam relief is sought in ancillary proceedings are: (1) the domicile of the person; and (2) the likely reaction of the court seised of the substantive dispute. He stated:

"Where a similar order has been applied for and has been refused by that court, it would generally be wrong for us to interfere. But where the other court lacks jurisdiction to make an effective order against a defendant because he is resident in England, it does not at all follow that it would find our order objectionable. Mr. Cuoghi is resident and domiciled in England. He carries on business here in a substantial way, and he is alleged to have committed acts in England which were part of the fraud. He is believed to have assets in other jurisdictions, but the Swiss court has no power to order him to disclose their whereabouts. Unless we make such an order, C.S.F.T. cannot apply to the courts where the assets are located for appropriate protective measures, and any final judgment obtained in Switzerland may be rendered ineffective. There is no danger of conflicting jurisdictions, and although the Swiss court cannot make an order against Mr. Cuoghi because he is not resident in Switzerland, there is no reason to believe that it would not welcome assistance from the courts of the country where he is resident."

Credit Suisse has been applied in a number of subsequent cases. In the Court of Appeal decision in *Motorola Credit Corporation v Uzan and others (No.2)* [2004] 1 W.L.R. 113, at para.115 Potter L.J. stated that the principles for the court to bear in mind when considering the question of inexpediency are as follows:

"As the authorities show, there are five particular considerations which the court should bear in mind, when considering the question whether it is inexpedient to make an order. First, whether the making of the order will interfere with the management of the case in the primary court e g where the order is inconsistent with an order in the primary court or overlaps with it... Second, whether it is the policy in the primary jurisdiction not itself to make worldwide freezing/disclosure orders. Third, whether there is a danger that the orders made will give rise to disharmony or confusion and/or risk of conflicting inconsistent or overlapping orders in other jurisdictions, in particular the courts of the state where the person enjoined resides or where the assets affected are located. If so, then respect for the territorial jurisdiction of that state should discourage the English court from using its unusually wide powers against a foreign defendant. Fourth, whether at the time the order is sought there is likely to be a potential conflict as to jurisdiction rendering it inappropriate and inexpedient to make a worldwide order. Fifth, whether, in a case where jurisdiction is resisted and disobedience to be expected, the court will be making an order which it cannot enforce."

Thus in cases where it is necessary for the courts in England to grant a parallel interim injunction to an interim interdict granted in Scotland, it is likely that if the defender is domiciled in England, such an injunction will be granted to assist the Scottish courts.

The CJJA, in s.27, provides that the Court of Session in Scotland may grant interim interdict and various other interim remedies where proceedings have been raised elsewhere in the UK. There is no specific option for the Scottish courts to refuse to grant such an order on the ground of inexpediency set out in s.25 (discussed above). However, the wording of the CJJA (s.27) is such that it is in the Court of Session's discretion as to whether to grant the interim relief sought. In cases decided under this section to date, the Court of Session has taken a similar view to that expressed in the *Credit Suisse* case (see above) and has tended to show a willingness to assist the relevant court which is seised of jurisdiction in the main proceedings.

Types of patent proceedings competent in Scotland

98.17   Where infringement, or threatened infringement, occurs in Scotland, proceedings under s.61 can be brought before the Court of Session. Proceedings under s.61 can also be brought against a person domiciled in Scotland, even in respect of infringements occurring, or threatened, in some other part of the United Kingdom. It may also be possible to bring action in Scotland against a person domiciled in Scotland for infringement of a foreign registered patent, but probably not if validity is put in issue in such Scottish proceedings, see §96.11.

Proceedings can also be brought before the Court of Session under any of: s.58 (compensation for Crown use); s.69 (infringement of rights conferred by publication of a patent application); s.70 (remedy for groundless threats of infringement proceedings); and s.71 (declaration of non-infringement). Moreover, where a patent proprietor is domiciled in Scotland, revocation proceedings under s.72 (or register rectification proceedings under s.34) can be brought in the Court of Session. Indeed even when there is no nexus of any of the parties with Scotland, the court is rendered competent for this purpose (CJJA Sch.8(2)(14) and 8(4)(2)) in regard to the validity of UK and EP (UK) patents. There have now been several cases where the court has accepted jurisdiction in such circumstances. However, there are no written decisions so these are not reported. It seems logical that there is such jurisdiction as it is possible that neither party has a connection with any part of the UK at all. In such circumstances both the English High Court and the Scottish Court of Session have concurrent jurisdiction.

The Court of Session can also hear applications for amendment of a patent in the context of proceedings in which validity may be put at issue, in terms of s.75.

The Court of Session can also be expected to hear claims for employee-inventor compensation under s.40, though again probably only when the employee or employer is domiciled in Scotland. If the Comptroller orders employee-inventor compensation under s.40, this can be enforced in Scotland as a recorded decree arbitral (s.41(10)).

An example of an infringement action decided in Scotland is *Conoco Speciality Products v Merpro Montassa* [1994] F.S.R. 99, where the Outer House of the Court of Session held that the approach to claim construction set out in s.125(1) and s.125(3) was the same as that decided under the 1949 Act in *Catnic v Hill and Smith* [1982] R.P.C. 183 HL, see §125.06. In *Trunature Ltd v Scotnet (1974) Ltd* [2006] C.S.O.H. 114 the Court of Session adopted the approach to construction set out in the authoritative judgment of Lord Hoffmann in *Kirin-Amgen v Hoechst Marion Roussel* [2005] R.P.C. 9 HL.

An example of a revocation action before the Scottish courts is *Akzo NV's and Akzo Nobel NV's (Tibolone) Patents* [2006] C.S.O.H. 146, later partially appealed to the Inner House of the Court of Session and reported at [2008] C.S.I.H. 31.

ITP SA v Coflexip Stena Offshore Ltd [2003] S.L.T. 1197 dealt with the effect of concurrent opposition proceedings in the European Patent Office. The Court of Session was not prepared to sist/stay the Scottish proceedings to await the outcome of the EPO and indeed found that a decision of the Opposition Division of the European Patent Office was not a final decision as to validity of a patent within the United Kingdom and had no evidential significance. The court decided that, even if an appeal to the Board of Appeal of the EPO were successful and validity was upheld, the Scottish action should still proceed on the issue of infringement since the UK, and here the Scottish courts, had sole jurisdiction on infringement which could be defended by the alleged infringer on the basis of invalidity of the infringed patent in order to establish the legal position of the patent without delay. This case then went to appeal (*ITP SA v Coflexip Stena Offshore Ltd* [2004] S.L.T. 1285 and the court decided a point relating to the relationship between the European Court of Human Rights and the EPC.

A recent example of a Scottish infringement and revocation action is *Verathon Medical (Canada) ULC v Aircraft Medical Limited* [2011] C.S.O.H. 19. The pursuer also sought to amend its patent in terms of s.75. The case was raised in the Court of Session shortly after the decision of the Opposition Division of the EPO was issued. The EPO Board of Appeal's decision was issued during the course of the Scottish proceedings. [The pursuer had sought various amendments in terms of s.75. Some of the amendments were allowed by the EPO Board of Appeal prior to the final decision of the Scottish Courts. The pursuer also sought various description amendments, which were not objected to by the defender and were allowed by the court. Finally, the pursuer sought to add in two new dependent claims to better distinguish the patent over the prior art. Both new dependent claims mirrored the terms of auxiliary requests which the pursuer had put before the EPO Board of Appeal. The pursuer's main request was upheld by the Board of Appeal and as such, the Board of Appeal was not required to consider the auxiliary requests. The defender objected to the proposed inclusion of these two dependent claims. The court allowed the description amendments but refused to allow the addition of the two new dependent claims, on the grounds that (a) the new dependent claims would extend the scope of protection of the patent in suit contrary to section 76(3)(b); and (b) in any event the court was not persuaded as to the necessity or the appropriateness of the proposed amendments.]

The rules of court applicable to patent proceedings before the Court of Session ("the RCS") are discussed in §98.19.

Principles governing the grant of interim interdict in Scottish proceedings

98.18   The position in respect of the grant of interim injunctive relief is different in Scotland from that in England. The difference was most clearly explained in *NWL v Woods* [1979] 3 All E.R. 614; [1979] 1 W.L.R. 1294 HL, where (at pp.628 and 1309 of the respective reports) Lord Fraser said:

> "The relevant difference between English law on interlocutory [now 'interim'] injunctions and Scots law on the very similar remedy of interim interdict can be appreciated by reference to the decision of this House in *American Cyanamid v. Ethicon* [1975] R.P.C. 513 HL, a decision which does not apply to Scotland. In that case, this House laid down that the court in exercising its discretion as to granting or refusing an interlocutory injunction ought not to weigh up the relative strengths of the parties' cases on the evidence (necessarily incomplete) available at the interlocutory stage. Lord Diplock, with whose speech the other four noble and learned Lords agreed, said:
>
> > 'The Court no doubt must be satisfied that the claim is not frivolous or vexatious; in other words, that there is a serious question to be tried. It is no part of the Court's function at this stage in the litigation to try and resolve conflicts of evidence on affidavit as to facts on which the claims of either party may ultimately depend nor to decide difficult questions of law which call for detailed argument and mature considerations. These are matters to be dealt with at the trial.
> >
> > In Scotland the practice is otherwise, and the Court is in use to have regard to the relative strength of the cases put forward in averment and argument by each party at the interlocutory stage as one of the many factors that may go to make up the balance of convenience.'
>
> That is certainly in accordance with my own experience as Lord Ordinary, and I believe that practice of other judges in the Court of Session was the same. Whether the likelihood of success should be regarded as one of the elements of the balance of convenience or as a separate matter seems to me to be an academic question of no real importance, but my inclination is in favour of the former alternative. It seems to make very good sense; if the pursuer or petitioner appears very likely to succeed at the end of the day, it will tend to be convenient to grant interim interdict and thus prevent the defender or respondent from infringing his rights, but if the defender or respondent appears very likely to succeed at the end of the day it will tend to be convenient to refuse interim interdict because an interim interdict would probably only delay the exercise of the Defender's legal activities."

In the typical action for patent infringement, the pursuer will allege that he is the proprietor of a patent which is being infringed by the defender. The defender is likely to deny infringement and, possibly, claim that the patent should be revoked. When an application for interim interdict is made, the court has to consider the submissions for each side and form a preliminary view firstly whether the pursuer has a "case to argue and a case to answer" (*Reed Stenhouse v Brodie* [1986] S.L.T. 354). If the pursuer has failed to make out such a case, either by averment or by explanation to the court, he will not be granted an interim interdict. If he has made out a case then the court must apply a similar test to what was said by the defender. If the defender's case is weak and the pursuer's case is strong, then the balance of convenience has already tilted substantially in favour of the pursuer. The court must then proceed to consider other factors. These include whether damages will be an adequate remedy for the pursuer, which includes a consideration of whether the defender is likely to be able to pay any damages that may be awarded. Secondly, the court must consider the existing situation in the relevant market place. If one party has been well established in the market place for a considerable time, then the court will normally make an order which does not disturb that party's existing position. Thirdly, the court will consider the likely economic effects on both parties arising from either a grant or refusal of interim interdict. An example of the application of many of these principles is *Conoco Specialty Products v Merpro Montassa* [1991] S.L.T. 222. A common outcome of an application for interim interdict in a patent infringement case is an undertaking by the defender(s) to the court to keep an account of profits made as a result of the alleged infringement.

It should be noted that, in Scotland, applications for interim interdict normally proceed on the basis of the statements in the summons of the pursuer supplemented by statements made orally by counsel at the bar and production of any relevant documents such as the patent, the alleged infringing device or data relating to it and possibly the documents relied upon in support of any claim for revocation. It is possible, though not usual to put the evidence before the court in the form of affidavits, but this is becoming more common in proceedings for an interim interdict.

Although the court has the power to make it a condition of granting interim interdict that security be given for the defender's possible losses arising from that grant, this is very rarely done in Scotland. It is normally only done where the pursuer's financial resources are probably insufficient to pay the defender's claim for wrongful interdict being granted, see *Conoco Specialty Products* [1991] S.L.T. 222. There is thus no direct equivalent to the cross-undertaking for damages which is required upon the grant of an interim injunction under English procedure. However, if at the end of a defended case which goes to trial, in which an interim interdict has been granted at the outset, the pursuer loses his case, the defender will be entitled to claim for damages if he can prove he suffered directly as a result of the interim interdict being in place and preventing him wrongfully from carrying on business. These cases are few and far between. This rule is known as the "*periculo petentis*" rule and essentially amounts to saying the interim interdict is at the pursuer's own risk.

PRACTICE UNDER SECTION 98

Proceedings before the Court

As noted above, the rules of court applicable to proceedings in Scotland under the Act **98.19** are those set out in the Act of Sederunt (Rules of the Court of Session) Rules 1994 (SI 1994/1443) as amended ("RCS"). Specific rules relating to intellectual property actions (including patent proceedings) are set out in Ch.55 RCS.

Under r.55.3(1)(c)(i) of the RCS, provision is made for a procedural hearing (the equivalent to a case management hearing) to be applied for within not longer than five weeks of the close of pleadings. The procedural hearing has taken on considerable significance in recent times in intellectual property actions as an effective form of case management. At that hearing, the Court of Session can consider: whether to remit the case to the Patent Office for a report (see s.99B and the commentary thereon); whether to order parties to exchange any documents; whether to appoint assessors; whether to order that a meeting of experts should be held for the purpose of producing a joint report on the general state of the art; and whether to make orders regulating the making of any experiments, inspections, tests or reports. The court also has discretion to give such further direction as to the conduct of the cause as it thinks fit. Thus, the court has a very wide general discretion as to case management at the procedural hearing.

Most importantly, the court may decide on which type of hearing is appropriate for effective management of the case. Scottish procedure in general offers a choice between a

"Proof" or a "Debate". The former is essentially the equivalent to a trial under English procedure; the latter is a hearing on legal arguments which has no precise equivalent under English procedure. In ordinary actions (i.e. non-intellectual property actions), a Debate can be insisted upon by either party and is often used as a delaying tactic to stall a final resolution. Often a Debate will involve arguments by counsel in relation to a technical pleading point which may not result in any substantive progress of the case. However, under r.55 and the procedural hearing procedure, the IP Judge may take the view that a Debate, if requested by a defender, or indeed by a pursuer, is inappropriate for effectively driving the case forward, and order a Proof instead.

As in English procedure, it is usual for issues of liability and quantum to be dealt with separately, with liability issues being heard first. While any judge of the Court of Session may hear a patent case, the rules provide that one or more judges will be nominated as "Intellectual Property Judges". In addition r.55.2 of the RCS states that all IP cases under Ch.55 shall be brought before one of these IP judges and it is only when one is not available that another judge may deal with the matter. The practice is therefore that most of the patent cases are heard before an Intellectual Property Judge. Currently the Intellectual Property Judges are Lords Emslie, Hodge, Glennie, Malcolm and Lady Smith. With effect from August 8, 2011 they will be Lady Smith, Lord Glennie, Lord Malcolm and Lord Pentland.

Differences between Scottish and English Procedure and Remedies

98.20   Besides the differences in the approach to grant of interim relief, see §98.18, and on the possible approach to and the statutory remedy of aggravated damages (see §98.22), a major difference between patent litigation in Scotland and that in England and Wales is that disclosure of documents is not available as of right in Scotland. Specifically, there is no rule of Scottish analogous to the rules on Standard Disclosure in terms of English CPR 31 as modified by CPR 63 and Practice Direction 63 (see discussion at §61.67–61.70). Rather, disclosure in Scotland is available only upon request to the court, and only in respect of specified classes of documents (utilising the procedure for recovery of documents (commission and diligence procedure or Section 1 procedure discussed at §98.21) set out in Chapter 35 of the RCS). Also, in terms of RCS r.55.3(4)(c)(i), at the Procedural Hearing the judge can order one party to make copies of "any documents" available to the other party, but again in practice this would require a specific application by one of the parties and would be subject to the discretion of the court. In practice, in Scotland disclosure orders in patent actions are relatively rare and are usually confined to issues such as commercial success.

In addition, the pleadings in a Scottish patent infringement action tend to be more detailed than their counterparts in the English High Court. More emphasis is placed on the written pleadings in Scotland and in some respects this may be more akin to the approach in the recently revised Patents County Court Rules. Chapter 55 of the RCS set out various matters which must be addressed in written pleadings relating to patents—see r.55.7 in respect of pleadings relating to infringement and r.55.8 in respect of pleadings relating to validity.

Other differences in approach between the jurisdictions are discussed in the article Buchan, R and Grassie, G. "Intellectual Property Disputes in Scotland" J.I.P.L.P. 2011, 6(2), 120-127.

—Section 1 Procedure: Search and Seize

98.21   There is a type of "search and seize" procedure available in Scotland. Specifically, in terms of the Administration of Justice (Scotland) Act 1972 (c.59) s.1, the Scottish court has the power:

> "to order the inspection, photographing, preservation, custody and detention of documents and other property which appear to the court to be property as to which any question may relevantly arise in any existing civil proceedings before that court or in civil

proceedings which are likely to be brought, and to order the production and recovery of any such property, the taking of samples thereof and the carrying out of any experiment thereon or therewith".

This power is known as the "Section 1 Procedure" and can be a very effective and powerful pre-action weapon in patent cases. The Section 1 Procedure can be used before an action is brought, or during an action. In certain circumstances it is possible to apply for a Section 1 order without notice to the party holding the documents or other property, particularly where there is a concern that the holder might destroy the documents or property if notice is given.

In *Union Carbide v B.P. Chemicals* [1995] F.S.R. 449; [1995] S.L.T. 972, this procedure was successfully invoked even to aid a concurrent action before the Patents Court in England and Wales in a case where, apparently, the claimant considered that there must be infringement of its process patent but was unable to verify this by inspection of the resulting product. The Section 1 Procedure is thus a potent weapon for a claimant (pursuer in Scottish proceedings). It provides a power of pre-trial (or even pre-action) disclosure, which is potentially very wide in scope and has analogies with the saisie procedure available in France. Indeed, by virtue of the Civil Jurisdiction and Judgments Act 1982 (c.27) s.28, it is possible to use this power to obtain evidence for any proceedings which have been brought, or are likely to be brought, in any contracting state of the Brussels or Lugano Conventions, a Brussels I Regulation State or any other part of the UK.

The decision in *Iomega v Myrica* [1998] S.C. 636; noted *The Times* May 28, 1998, has further enhanced the value of the Section 1 Procedure as a weapon for a patentee. This case established that, if on execution of a Section 1 order, evidence is discovered which implicates third parties who might be outside the jurisdiction, the evidence may be used to sue them there—subject to the approval of the Scottish Court being obtained through a simple and inexpensive procedure. This is despite the existence of implied undertakings to limit the use of the materials recovered to the proceedings contemplated at the time of the Section 1 application.

It is also possible, in principle, for Section 1 Procedure to be authorised ex parte in relation to anticipated proceedings to be based on a patent application which has not yet been granted. If it can be demonstrated that court proceedings are likely to be brought and that the patent will or is very likely to be granted, and that there are otherwise circumstances which make a Section 1 Procedure necessary, there is nothing to stop this.

The rules relating to Section 1 applications made before court proceedings have commenced are contained in Chapter 64 of the Rules of the Court of Session ("RCS"). Chapter 64 was amended with effect from October 22, 2000 to ensure the Section 1 Procedure complied with art.8 of the European Convention on Human Rights. The provisions of Chapter 64 detail the requirements of an application (r.64.2) and the necessary accompanying documentation (r.64.3). They also set out the duties of the court-appointed Commissioner (r.64.9) who must be the person to carry out the search order of the court (r.64.8). As one of the duties, the Commissioner must inform the haver (the party who is the subject of the order) of his or her right to seek legal advice (r.64.9(c)). Where the haver chooses to seek legal advice, and the legal advice is to help decide whether to ask the court to vary the order, the Commissioner "shall not commence to search for or to take any other steps to take possession of or preserve the listed items" (r.64.12).

Rule 64.11 sets out certain restrictions on service that directly relate to the issue of human rights and searches. First, the order may only be served Monday to Friday and between the hours of 9am and 5pm, except on cause shown (r.64.11(1)). The order cannot be served at the same time as a search warrant issued in a criminal investigation (r.64.11(2)). There is also a restriction on the people who may accompany the Commissioner, and may include: those the Commissioner considers necessary to execute the order (r.64.11(3)(a)), and the representatives of the petitioner named in the order (r.64.11(3)(b)). If there is an unaccompanied female at the premises, the Commissioner, if not female, must be accompanied by a female (r.64.11(3)(b)), otherwise the Commissioner may not enter the premises (r.64.11(4)).

The rules relating to Section 1 applications made after court proceedings have commenced are set out in Chapter 35 of RCS, which contains the general rules on recovery of evidence in Scottish court proceedings. Essentially, the application is made by motion in the existing proceedings (r.35.2(1)(a)) in accordance with the remainder of the rules set out in that Chapter.

The Intellectual Property (Enforcement etc.) Regulations 2006

98.22   The Intellectual Property (Enforcement etc.) Regulations 2006 (SI 2006/1028) ("the Enforcement Regulations") came into force on April 29, 2006. These Regulations apply to all types of IPR including patents and introduced a new statutory form of disclosure/discovery in Scottish procedure. Under reg.4 (see reprint, above), a pursuer may apply to the Scottish court for an order for disclosure of information about the origin and distribution networks of infringing goods or services. Prior to the bringing into force of the Enforcement Regulations, there were no specific provisions dealing with pre-action disclosure applications of the specific *Norwich Pharmacal* type, or pre-action disclosure applications which are available in England, see §60.11.

In practice, prior to the passing of the Enforcement Regulations the Section 1 Procedure (discussed at §98.21) and the commission and diligence procedure (discussed briefly at §98.20) could be adapted to deal with any gap which might have existed as the orders available under these procedures could be directed against third parties. However, reg.4 puts it beyond doubt that pre-action disclosure may be ordered relating to the origin and distribution networks of goods and services which infringe a patent from either (1) the alleged infringer or (2) any third party who possesses the infringing goods or uses or provides the infringing services on a commercial scale. It may also be ordered in relation to any third party identified by the foregoing parties as being involved in the production of/provision of the infringing goods/services. Regulation 4 outlines the types of information recoverable such as names and addresses of manufacturers, distributors, purchasers and sellers of the infringing goods/services, quantities of infringing goods/services and prices paid for them.

Although reg.4(5) states that an application for such an order can be brought in the Court of Session or the Sheriff Court, in respect of patent proceedings it would be necessary to bring the application before the Court of Session.

Regulation 5 (see §98.04) provides, only for Scotland, that where infringement has been established, the pursuer may request appropriate measures for the dissemination and publication of the judgment at the defender's expense. In any event, all judgments in patent cases are published on the Scottish Courts website at *http://www.scotcourts.gov.uk* and so this provision is likely to relate to further publication and dissemination of such judgments. There have not yet been any reported decisions in respect of this provision.

Regulation 3 provides for enhanced damages for flagrant acts of infringement by providing that where a defender knew or had reasonable grounds to know that he engaged in infringing activity, the damages awarded shall be appropriate to the actual prejudice suffered by the pursuer. All aspects will be taken into account including lost profits suffered by the pursuer, unfair profits made by the defender and account including lost profits suffered by the pursuer, unfair profits made by the defender and elements other than economic factors including moral prejudice to the pursuer. Such damages may be awarded on a royalties basis if appropriate. Regulation 3 is also introduced into English law and procedure and therefore is not actually a difference between the two systems; for the English law on the point, see §60.27. However both systems have different cultures and historical approaches to the issue of "punitive" damages. England has notionally had the concept at common law whereas Scotland did not prior to this Directive and Regulations. Whether this will mean a different approach is adopted in each jurisdiction to how Regulation 3 is implemented remains to be seen as there have not yet been any Scottish decisions citing this Regulation.

The Enforcement Regulations also made some consequential amendments to ss.62, 63, 68 and 130 of the 1977 Act which are mentioned in the reprints thereof.

Proceedings before the Comptroller in Scotland

98.23   Rule 88 (reprinted at §98.05, and made under the authority of s.123(2)(f)) regulates when proceedings before the Comptroller can be held in Scotland. The rule (as amended from that of previous r.108 of the 1995 Rules) is much more simply put than the previous incarnation. It adopts a common set of rules applying to all types of disputes (and not, as previously, merely those under particular sections of the Act). Under r.88, the Comptroller has power to hold a hearing in Scotland in proceedings where there is more than one party, and any party requests that the hearing be held in Scotland. There is no discretion of the Comptroller to refuse the request if all parties consent. The Comptroller's lack of discretion on this point was recently acknowledged by the Comptroller in the decision in *Rigcool Ltd v Optima Solutions UK Ltd* BL O/149/11. Both parties to those proceedings were based in Scotland and had jointly applied to hold the proceedings in Scotland. The Comptroller also has discretion to grant such a request if he considers it appropriate, even if all parties do not agree.

Indeed the hearing can be held in Scotland even if none of the parties reside there if the Comptroller considers this to be "appropriate", presumably if he is satisfied that the balance of convenience is in favour of the hearing being held there.

Under the previous rules, in *Goddin and Rennie's Application* [1996] R.P.C. 141 the Comptroller held the hearing in an entitlement dispute in the building of the Sheriff Court in Kirkwall, because all but one of the witnesses were resident in the Orkney Islands; and, in *Tiefebrun's Application* [1979] F.S.R. 97, the Comptroller sat in Scotland to hear a witness who was unable to travel on medical grounds.

As was the case under the former rule, the decision of the Comptroller, whether or not to hold hearings in any particular proceeding in Scotland, cannot itself be the subject of an appeal (r.88 (3)).

As r.88 is in Pt 7 of the Rules providing for "Proceedings before the Comptroller", the procedure for hearings in Scotland will be governed by the other rules in this Part, particularly by rr.84 (hearings in public) and 86 (powers of Comptroller to compel attendance of witness and production of documents), as discussed in the commentary on s.123.

Appeals in Scottish proceedings

—Appeals from the Comptroller

The procedure for appeal from a decision of the Comptroller given in Scotland under **98.24** r.89 (see §98.05) is set out in rr.55.14 and 55.15 of the RCS.

Appeals under the 1977 Act of a decision of the Comptroller after a hearing in Scotland are heard by the Outer House of the Court of Session (s.97(4) and RCS r.55.14(1)), but there is no right of appeal for decisions falling within the exceptions listed in s.97(1).

An appeal must be lodged within 14 days after the date of the decision appealed against if the issue of the appeal is procedural, or within six weeks if the issue is of any other nature (RCS r.55.14(3)). An appeal can only be lodged outwith these periods with leave of the court or if the Comptroller grants an extension on application within the periods in r.55.14(3) (r.55.14(4)). As well as lodging the appeal with the court, the appeal must be served on every other party to the proceedings the decision in which is being appealed against, and intimation must be given to the Comptroller (RCS r.55.14(6)).

The appeal will be heard before a Lord Ordinary who will be an Intellectual Property judge. The judge will hear the same evidence led before the Comptroller and can only hear further evidence with leave of the court (RCS r.55.14(10)).

—Appeals from the Outer House of the Court of Session

The Inner House of the Court of Session hears appeals or reclaiming motions of deci- **98.25** sions made by the Outer House (such as decisions on validity and infringement). The relevant rules of procedure are set out in Chapter 38 of RCS, which was amended with effect from April 5, 2010. Essentially the new rules are designed to speed up the appeal process and cut down on the judicial time involved in the appeal procedure. Discussion of the changes can be found in Lord Reed, "Streamlining the Inner House" [2010] 55(3) JLSS 17–19.

A reclaiming motion submits for review by the Inner House all the previous interlocutors of the Lord Ordinary awarded in favour of all parties (RCS r.38.6(1)). No leave of the court is required if the interlocutor from the Outer House deals with the whole subject-matter of the cause or the whole merits of the cause (RCS r.38.2(1)). Similarly leave is not needed if the interlocutor relates to one of the matters set out in RCS r.38.2(3) or RCS r.38.2(4)-(5) including interlocutors granting, refusing, recalling or refusing to recall an interim interdict, or allowing, refusing or limiting a proof. For all other interlocutors leave to reclaim must be sought (RCS r.38.2(6)). The rules governing applications for leave to reclaim are set out in RCS r.38.4.

Where leave is not required, a reclaiming motion must be made either 21 or 14 days after the date on which the interlocutor was pronounced, depending on the type of interlocutor being reclaimed. A reclaiming print must be lodged with the motion. This must include the whole pleadings and interlocutors in the cause, and where available, the opinion of the Lord Ordinary (RCS 38.5(2)).

Once the motion has been enrolled and the reclaiming print lodged, the court will issue a timetable for the procedural steps relating to the appeal (including the lodging of grounds of appeal and answers), and will fix a procedural hearing (RCS r.38.13). The procedural hearing is similar to a case management hearing (RCS r.38.16). It may be heard by a single judge of the Inner House, rather than before a full three judge bench as previously required (RCS r.37A.1). At a procedural hearing, the procedural judge may allocate a hearing for the appeal or may make an order to dispense with the appeal. (RCS r.38.16). The procedural judge is to ascertain the state of preparation of the parties and has wide discretion to make orders to ensure the expeditious disposal of the reclaiming motion (the appeal).

A bench of three of the most senior judges of the Court of Session will preside over the substantive hearing relating to the reclaiming motion, although when a case is deemed to be particularly difficult or of particular importance a larger bench can be formed. Often at least one or two of the bench will be a former IP judge or will have experience of patent proceedings.

—Appeals from Inner House to the Supreme Court

98.26   Decisions of the Inner House can be appealed to the Supreme Court. Section 40 of the Court of Session Act 1988 (as amended) determines which decisions may be appealed to the Supreme Court. Section 40(3) provides that it is not possible to appeal to the House of Lords directly from a decision of the Lord Ordinary in the Outer House, unless such a decision has been reviewed by the Inner House.

Unlike the position in England and Wales for appeals from the Court of Appeal, Inner House decisions can be appealed to the Supreme Court without the leave of the Inner House where the judgment is on the whole merits of the cause, or on an interlocutory judgment where there is a difference of opinion or the interlocutory judgment is one sustaining a dilatory defence and dismissing the action (s.40(1)(a)). Most decisions fall into one of these categories. However, although leave of the Court of Session is not required in these circumstances, the notice of appeal must be signed by two counsel, who must certify that the appeal is reasonable (see The Supreme Court of the United Kingdom Practice Direction 1, paragraph 1.2.25). Leave is required to appeal all other interlocutors (s.40(1)(b)). The general view is that it is not appropriate to refer matters of procedure and practice of the Court of Session for decision by the Supreme Court (*Girvan v Inverness Farmers Dairy* 1998 S.C. (HL) 1, 21C–G *per* Lord Hope of Craighead). The procedure for appeals in the Supreme Court is outside the scope of this Work.

An appeal to the Supreme Court will not necessarily delay execution of a decree pronounced by a lower court. This avoids appeals being used as a method of delaying the execution of the decision of the lower court. The Supreme Court therefore has the power to regulate all matters relative to the interim possession, or execution of the decree and discretion for payment of expenses according to the interests of the parties (Court of Session Act 1988 s.41).

SECTION 99

General powers of the court

99. The court may, for the purpose of determining any question in the exercise of its original or appellate jurisdiction under this Act or any treaty or international convention to which the United Kingdom is a party, make any order or exercise any other power which the comptroller could have made or exercised for the purpose of determining that question.

99.01

COMMENTARY ON SECTION 99

Section 99 is a general provision ensuring that the court may exercise original jurisdiction in relation to any matter where such could have been done by the Comptroller. An example of exercise of this power is *Omron Tateisi's Application* [1981] R.P.C. 125, where the court held that, under s.99, it had itself the power to grant a certificate of postal delay which the Comptroller could have granted under what is now r.110, reprinted at §123.28. Presumably, such powers can be exercised by any of the courts designated by s.130(1) as a "court" for the purposes of the Act, for which see §96.06. In *Rhône-Poulenc Rorer International Holdings Inc v Yeda Research and Development Co Ltd* [2006] EWHC 160 (Ch); [2006] R.P.C. 24 at [70], Lewison J. observed that this could result in the court having different powers to those conferred by the Civil Procedure Rules alone. In *Re IGT/ Acres Gaming Inc* [2008] EWHC 568 (Ch) (Ch D (Patents Ct)), Peter Prescott QC (sitting as a Deputy Judge) held it gave discretion in relation to late-stage amendment and re-examination of a patent application where lack of clarity might have led the examiner to miss relevant prior art.

99.02

SECTION 99A [ADDED]

Power of Patents Court to order report

99A.—(1) Rules of court shall make provision empowering the Patents Court in any proceedings before it under this Act, on or without the application of any party, to order the Patent Office to inquire into and report on any question of fact or opinion.

99A.01

(2) Where the court makes such an order on the application of a party, the fee payable to the Patent Office shall be at such rate as may be determined in accordance with rules of court and shall be costs of the proceedings unless otherwise ordered by the court.

(3) Where the court makes such an order of its own motion, the fee payable to the Patent Office shall be at such rate as may be determined by the Lord Chancellor with the approval of the Treasury and shall be paid out of money provided by Parliament.

Note. Section 99A was introduced by Sch.5 para.26 to the CDPA 1988, effective from January 7, 1991 (SI 1990/2168).

COMMENTARY ON SECTION 99A

Scope of the section

Section 99A was inserted into the Act by the CDPA 1988. Subsection (1) requires rules

99A.02

of court to be made whereby the Patents Court becomes empowered to call for an inquiry or report from the Patent Office (now operating as the UK-IPO) on any fact or opinion in a matter before it. Section 99B provides a similar rule-making power for proceedings in the Scottish Court of Session, and s.291(3)–(5) of the CDPA 1988 (reprinted in §291.01 and discussed in §291.02) is analogous for proceedings in the Patents County Court. Subsections (2) and (3) relate to the fees arising upon the exercise of these powers. These powers should be distinguished from the mechanism under s.74A whereby the UK-IPO may give non-binding opinions on validity and infringement at the request of any person.

Request for inquiry and report

99A.03   Under each of the provisions listed in §99A.02, the appropriate court would be able to request the UK-IPO to inquire into, and report on, any question of fact or opinion arising in proceedings before it, and would be able do so on the request of any party to the proceedings or on the initiative of the court itself. However, no such rules have yet been made, from which it may be surmised that none of these courts considers that it is likely to wish to exercise the power provided to it by the section. If any such rules were made, it is envisaged that fees would be payable to the UK-IPO for any such inquiry and report and that these fees would, in due course, become costs allowable on taxation to the successful party (subs.(2)), except when the referral UK-IPO is made on the initiative of the court when the fees would be paid out of central funds (subs.(3)).

Purpose of inquiry and report

99A.04   The purpose of the section would seem to be to provide for modelling patent litigation more on the investigative basis used in Continental systems of law and in the EPO, and therefore to move away from the traditional British adversarial style of litigation. Any such change could have a profound effect on the determination of, for example, questions of obviousness where determination by the courts has tended to be based upon the evidence given at trial by persons skilled in the relevant art at the relevant date, often with special emphasis on the sequence of contemporaneous events at the date of the patent which may rank as indicia of obviousness or non-obviousness, see the commentary on s.3. However, as noted in §99A.03, the courts seem to have no inclination to adopt a practice of seeking assistance from the UK-IPO, at least of their own initiative. Also, no case is known where one of the parties has sought any enquiry or report from the UK-IPO in the context of proceedings before a "court" (as that term is defined in s.130(1), for which see §96.06). Moreover, it is not immediately clear as to how the concept of a report from the UK-IPO could be properly married together with the concept of wholly oral evidence stages, given that the former stage would, logistically, necessarily have to come in advance of the latter.

However, now that evidence-in-chief is normally presented in writing (both in the Patents Court and in the Patents County Court), then it could be that a factual report from the UK-IPO on that evidence (and/or on the case generally) could serve to focus the issues which the court has to decide, in a manner similar to the role of the Advocate-General in proceedings before the Court of Justice of the European Union in Luxembourg. There the Advocate-General prepares for the court a written opinion in which he or she analyses the issues before the court and suggests the decision that should be given. Then, at the oral proceedings, the parties tend to concentrate their arguments by supporting, or criticising, the views of the Advocate-General and, though the eventual decision does not always adopt the view of the Advocate-General, it does so in a majority of cases. Another model is provided by the kind of provisional report issued in opposition proceedings before the EPO under EPC r.71a(1).

Opinion from the European Patent Office

99A.05   Under EPC art.25, a national court trying an infringement action on a European patent can request the EPO to give a technical opinion concerning that patent. The procedure is governed by EPO Guideline E–XII and a fee of EUR3515 is currently stipulated by art.2(1), item 20, of the EPO's Rules Relating to Fees. Note that such an opinion can be given only on "technical" matters. The opinion is given by the Examining Division of the EPO and is not regarded as a decision and so is not subject to any appeal in the EPO. The EPO Guidelines indicate that the EPO will accept submissions from the parties prior to rendering its opinion which, however, must be objective; moreover, care must be taken not to impinge on the decision-making powers of the court which has requested the opinion.

However, no instance is known where there has been any request, from any national court, for an EPO technical opinion under EPC art.25. Indeed, as the term "Patent Office" in ss.99A and 99B does not include the EPO, and in the absence of any reference thereto in CPR 63 or 63 PD, there appears to be no power whereby this EPC provision could be implemented by a court (as defined in s.130(1), for which see §96.06), even if this were desired.

SECTION 99B [ADDED]

Power of Court of Session to order report

99B.—(1) In any proceedings before the Court of Session under this Act the court may, either of its own volition or on the application of any party, order the Patent Office to inquire into and report on any question of fact or opinion.

99B.01

(2) Where the court makes an order under subsection (1) above of its own volition the fee payable to the Patent Office shall be at such rate as may be determined by the Lord President of the Court of Session with the consent of the Treasury and shall be defrayed out of moneys provided by Parliament.

(3) Where the court makes an order under subsection (1) above on the application of a party, the fee payable to the Patent Office shall be at such rate as may be provided for in rules of court and shall be treated as expenses in the cause.

Note. Section 99B was introduced by the CDPA 1988 (c.48) Sch.5(26) with effect from January 7, 1991 (SI 1990/2168).

COMMENTARY ON SECTION 99B

Section 99B is exactly analogous to s.99A in that it provides power for the Court of Session in Scotland to request the UK-IPO to make an inquiry or report on any fact or opinion in proceedings before the Court under the Act.

99B.02

Litigation in Scotland is generally discussed in the commentary on s.98. Rule 55.3(4)(c) of the RCS brings s.99B into effect by providing that at the procedural hearing, the court shall consider whether to remit to the UK-IPO for a report and, if so, what the terms of the report should be.

SECTION 100

Burden of proof in certain cases

100.—(1) If the invention for which a patent is granted is a process for obtaining a new product, the same product produced by a person other than the proprietor of the patent or a licensee of his shall, unless the contrary is proved, be taken in any proceedings to have been obtained by that process.

100.01

(2) In considering whether a party has discharged the burden imposed upon him by this section, the court shall not require him to disclose any manufacturing or commercial secrets if it appears to the court that it would be unreasonable to do so.

COMMENTARY ON SECTION 100

Scope of the section

100.02   Section 100 provides a reversal of the burden of proof in cases of infringement where the patent is for a process for obtaining a new product. If the same product is produced, there is an assumption that that product is made by the patented process, unless the contrary is proved (subs.(1)), so that in such cases it falls upon the defendant to prove non-infringement. There is a provision for protection of the defendant's confidential information (subs.(2)), see §100.04. There were no corresponding provisions in the 1949 Act.

This section is to be interpreted in conformity with relevant provisions in the CPC, EPC and PCT (s.130(7)). This means that the section has to conform with art.35 of the CPC which reads:

> **"CPC ARTICLE 35—Burden of proof**
>
> 1. If the subject matter of a Community patent is a process for obtaining a new product, the same product when produced by any other party shall, in the absence of proof to the contrary, be deemed to have been obtained by the patented process.
>
> 2. In the adduction of proof to the contrary, the legitimate interests of the defendant in protecting his manufacturing and business secrets shall be taken into account."

The section should, probably, also be construed in conformity with art.34 of the TRIPS Agreement which reads:

> **"TRIPS ARTICLE 34—Process Patents: Burden of Proof**
>
> 1. For the purposes of civil proceedings in respect of the infringement of the rights of the owner referred to in paragraph 1(b) of Article 28, if the subject matter of a patent is a process for obtaining a product, the judicial authorities shall have the authority to order the defendant to prove that the process to obtain an identical product is different from the patented process. Therefore, Members shall provide, in at least one of the following circumstances, that any identical product when produced without the consent of the patent owner shall, in the absence of proof to the contrary, be deemed to have been obtained by the patented process:
>
> > (a) if the product obtained by the patented process is new;
> >
> > (b) if there is a substantial likelihood that the identical product was made by the process and the owner of the patent has been unable through reasonable efforts to determine the process actually used.
>
> 2. Any Member shall be free to provide that the burden of proof indicated in paragraph 1 shall be on the alleged infringer only if the condition referred to in subparagraph (a) is fulfilled or only if the condition referred to in subparagraph (b) is fulfilled.
>
> 3. In the adduction of proof to the contrary, the legitimate interests of defendants in protecting their manufacturing and business secrets shall be taken into account."

As shown below, s.100 meets the option of compliance with art.34.1(a) of the TRIPS Agreement, but not art.34.1(b), permissible under art.34.2, with compliance with art.34.3 by virtue of s.100(2).

Section 100 has obvious application to chemical cases, but, because chemical process patents that result in new products which are chemically definable usually have claims to the product per se, the section may have little practical application to such cases. The section therefore applies mainly to a patent that includes no claim to the product per se.

Doubts as to the ambit of subsection (1)

100.03   The section is not clear in several respects. The term "product" is not defined, and there is no guide as to whether it is intended to be given a meaning, appropriate to chemical cases, of a new composition of matter, or whether it is intended to have a broader meaning of anything that is produced; there is no obvious limitation of the section to chemical cases. "New" is also not defined in the context of the section. Section 1 defines an invention as "new" if it does not form part of the state of the art, and this definition could be appropriate to "a new product". But, in that event, a product could be considered new if it is not exactly the same as anything comprised in the state of the art, that is it could be a known product modified or improved in some respect, such as a magnetic material having properties superior to any previously known. It is also not clear what is meant by a process for "obtaining" the new product. This could mean that the process must be directed to synthesising or fabricating the product, but it would seem to be an arbitrary definition of this expression and which would exclude a process of, say, making a melt of materials and heat-treating the melt on cooling in such way as to produce the improved magnetic materials referred to. Whether the section would apply to a patent directed to the method of heat treatment is even more difficult to discern. There is also doubt in chemical cases as to the meaning of "the same product". Thus, difficulty has arisen in those countries where there has been a similar provision. It is beyond the scope of this commentary to examine the law in such countries, but the *Alkylenediamine II* decision of the German Federal Supreme Court (see (1977) 8 I.I.C. 350) gives an indication of the kinds of problems that may arise. In that case the d-isomer used in the defendant's drug was held to be a material of the same composition as the racemic mixture produced by the patented method. The extent to which "the same product" will permit application of the section to a non-identical product, as in this German case, must be a matter for speculation. The term "the same product" is likely also to give rise to difficulty in (at least) non-chemical cases.

Protection of confidential information (subs.(2))

Subsection (2) provides that a defendant under this section may not be forced to disclose manufacturing or commercial secrets if the court thinks this would be unreasonable in all the circumstances. In this context "disclose" presumably means disclose to the claimant. Nevertheless, if the defendant is to discharge the burden of proof imposed upon him by subs.(1), some disclosure must presumably be made. Thus, subs.(2) indicates that such disclosure could be in confidence, for example to legal advisers only, or perhaps also to the claimant under conditions preventing further disclosure, as in: *Warner-Lambert v Glaxo* [1975] R.P.C. 354; *Centri-Spray v Cera* [1979] F.S.R. 175; *Roussel-Uclaf v ICI* [1990] R.P.C. 45; and other cases as noted in §61.67. Without such a safeguard, there would be the possibility of a claimant starting an action mainly to obtain details of a defendant's secret process. **100.04**

The rather different wording of art.35(2) of the CPC (repeated in TRIPS art.34.3), each reprinted in §100.02, is interesting and seems to require disclosure under safeguards to provide protection of manufacturing and business secrets, whereas subs.(2) may provide the court with power to avoid any disclosure of such secrets, even in confidence.

Operation of the section in practice

Although, as yet, there appears to be no instance of s.100 being pleaded in any specific case, *Farmos v Wellcome Foundation* BL C/55/84 CA may be noted as a case where the defendant-patentee was able to prove, without the benefit of the section, infringement of a process claim by importation of a resulting product. This was done by showing the presence of impurities in the imported product, it being held that these indicated (in the absence of a satisfactory explanation from the other party) that the claimed process had been used abroad to make that product. The court refused an application to plead s.100 in an infringement counterclaim in *Generics v Lundbeck* [2006] EWHC 804 Ch; noted I.P.D. 29060. A suggestion by the patentee that in effect the only way in which the presumption of s.100 could be rebutted was by a full trial was rejected, the court observing that whilst that might be so in some cases it might be that, as here, it could be rebutted to the standards for strike out or refusal of permission to serve out of the jurisdiction. The decision was upheld on appeal (see [2006] EWCA Civ 1261; [2008] R.P.C. 19, sub nom *H. Lundbeck A/S v Generics (UK) Ltd*) where it was observed that the presumption of s.100(1) was completely displaced by the material supplied to the regulator and the patentee's experimental evidence did nothing to alter that. **100.05**

SECTION 101

Exercise of comptroller's discretionary powers

101. Without prejudice to any rule of law, the comptroller shall give any party **101.01**

to a proceeding before him an opportunity to be heard before exercising adversely to that party any discretion vested in the comptroller by this Act or rules.

RELEVANT RULES—RULES PART 7 (RULES 73–88)

101.02   In the new 2007 Rules, the UK-IPO adopted a general and more flexible stance on the conduct of proceedings before the Comptroller. These were summarised in TPN 6/2007 (available on the UK-IPO website *http://www.ipo.gov.uk* and now published [2008] R.P.C. 8). On a number of issues, practice under TPN 6/2007 has been superseded by TPN 3/2009.

Part 7 now governs all proceedings before the Comptroller, most of which are reprinted under s.123, but where these are relevant to hearings, as distinct from the proceedings as such, they are discussed below.

Rule 74 (reprinted at §123.07) sets out the overriding objective of these rules in similar vein to those set out in Pt 1 of the CPR governing proceedings before the English courts. Part 4 of Sch.3 to the Rules specifies other rules which particularly apply to hearings, which (besides r.74) are:

> Rule 79 (copies of documents), reprinted at §123.12;
>
> Rule 80(2)–(6) (evidence and the hearing), reprinted at §123.13;
>
> Rule 81 (alteration of time limits), reprinted at §123.14;
>
> Rule 82 (general powers of the comptroller in relation to proceedings before him), reprinted at §123.15;
>
> Rule 84 (hearings in public), reprinted at §123.17; and
>
> Rule 87 (evidence in proceedings before the comptroller), reprinted at §123.20.

101.03   Detailed discussion of the procedural rules for all type of hearings before a "hearing officer", who acts for the Comptroller, is not included in this edition because the *Hearings Manual* ("HM") is now available on the UK-IPO website: *http://www.ipo.gov.uk*.

The HM is updated as appropriate and it contains much useful specific information, particularly concerning unusual situations. It also refers to decisions over the whole range of civil court procedures which illustrate how these decisions are likely to be dealt with by the Comptroller, even if the CPR does not automatically apply to proceedings before the Comptroller. However, reference is made in the commentary below to particular paragraphs of the HM where it is thought they are likely to be of special interest to the reader, see also TPN 6/2007 and TPN 3/2009 noted in §101.02.

COMMENTARY ON SECTION 101

Scope of the section

101.04   Section 101 provides that the Comptroller, before exercising his discretion under the Act adversely to any party to the proceedings, must give that party an opportunity to be heard. The section conforms to the requirements of art.41(3) of the TRIPS Agreement (reprinted in §61.03). The EPO also follows the principle, set out in art.116 of the EPC) of giving adequate opportunity for making submissions, and of being heard, if desired, prior to an adverse decision being given, but here oral proceedings must be requested (unless the EPO considers that a hearing is expedient). The EPO is not required to warn a party that such a request is necessary, see Ch.4.5 of the *European Patents Handbook* ("EPH") (London: Sweet & Maxwell).

The section embodies the general rule of natural justice in administrative law that no one may be penalised by a decision of a tribunal unless he has been given a fair opportunity to know and answer the case against him. This has not been changed by the new practice of providing written Preliminary Evaluations; TPN3/2009 makes clear that these are not binding on a hearing officer, who will reach a decision only once all procedures are complete and representations made. See, also, HM paras 2.01-2. The hearing officer should examine all relevant material before him so that he can come to a fair conclusion on the balance of probabilities. If an objection was raised, the applicant should be given the opportunity of arguing whether or not the objection was sound (*Blacklight Power Inc v*

Comptroller General of Patents Designs and Trade Marks [2008] EWHC 2763 (Pat)). A corollary of this rule is that the person must also be given proper and prior notice of the case he has to meet before the tribunal, e.g. an examiner must have set out adequately his objection to allowing an application to proceed to grant. A further consequence of s.101 is that an application may not be rejected (e.g. under s.18(3)) without the applicant (or his attorney) having been given the chance to be heard (*S's Application* [1977] R.P.C. 367). The procedure follows that used in court proceedings and, under the Tribunals and Inquiries Act 1992 (c.53), the Council of Tribunals has a supervisory role over the conduct of hearings.

In principle, hearings are usually open to members of the public, for which see §101.06 and §123.56. In contrast, proceedings in the EPO before the Receiving Section, Examining Division and the Legal Division cannot be in public (EPC art.116(3)). Rule 84(1) specifies that a hearing before the Comptroller shall normally be held in public, although a party can apply for a hearing to be held in private where there is good reason for it (r.84(2) and (3)). If the hearing relates to an application which has not yet been published, then that hearing must be in private (r.84(4)). Parts of a hearing may be held in private if appropriate (r.84(5)).

Rule 86 (reprinted at §123.19) gives the Comptroller the power of a High Court judge to require the attendance of witnesses and the discovery and production of documents, although he has no power to punish summarily for contempt.

Rule 88 (reprinted at §123.21) allows for hearings before the Comptroller to be held in Scotland, for which see §98.23 and §123.32. Other locations may also be agreed, see TPN 3/2009 para.4.

Reference to the *Hearings Manual* can be useful where further information is desired, and see also the summary in TPN 6/2007 and practice introduced by TPN 3/2009 (cited in §101.02 above).

Procedure for hearings

Hearings may be held in either ex parte proceedings, for example whether an application can proceed to grant under s.18; or in inter partes proceedings, among the commonest of which are those for revocation under s.72. In either type of hearing, the procedure under s.101 is governed by rules presented in Pt 7 of the Rules (as discussed in §101.02). By r.80(5), any party requesting a hearing must be given a date. The date will now be flexible and will be set according to the circumstances (see the HM paras 4.02–4.04), with particular attention being given to the time left before the end of the compliance period under r.30, discussed in §18.11. For practitioners preparing for a hearing or, more generally, involved in any proceedings before the Comptroller, Tribunal Practice Notices TPN 6/2007 and TPN 3/2009, on the Office website and reported at [2008] R.P.C. 8 at [191] and [2009] RPC 000 are essential reading. They deal with statements of case, oppositions, time periods, reviews of opinions, notification of interested parties, case management, including case management conferences, ADR (now applicable in all inter partes cases), expert witness evidence, negotiations during proceedings, and stays.

101.05

Procedure for hearings is now described in detail in the *Hearings Manual*. The Comptroller, and any other party involved, must be given notice of an intention to refer at the hearing to any document, (other than one already mentioned in the proceedings or a report of any decision of a United Kingdom court or of the Comptroller), and he must also supply details of, or a copy of, every such document (r.79). This requirement may be waived, with the consent of the Comptroller and the agreement of other parties, which should only be sought in genuinely unexpected circumstances. It should be noted that the exception to the supply of copies of law reports does not apply to EPO decisions: copies of these should therefore be supplied.

Although there is no need to notify an intention to rely on any precedent decisions of a United Kingdom court or of the Comptroller, it is customary to give notice to the Comptroller and to other parties of any legal precedents to which reference may be made in argument. For further information on procedure at hearings, see the *Hearings Manual* (para.4.112); and for the right of audience at hearings, see substituted s.102, reprinted at

§102.01 and the commentary on that section. The HM also sets out procedural matters, particularly as to the conduct of the hearing and the entitlement of persons authorised to act, in the name of the Comptroller, as "hearing officers".

Inter partes hearings will normally be conducted on the basis of evidence filed at an earlier stage in the proceedings. In ex parte proceedings, the filing of evidence is at the discretion of the party, but if this is not done the party may find himself in an impossible position in the event of a subsequent appeal as the filing of evidence specifically for the appeal is generally not permitted, see *Wistar's Application* [1983] R.P.C. 255 and §97.16. Oral evidence is unusual in proceedings before the Comptroller, but will normally be permitted if requested. Indeed, a party who wishes to challenge the declared or sworn evidence of a witness presented by the other party can seek cross-examination of that witness. It is recognised that the working maximum of two days for hearings may need to be exceeded if cross-examination is required: TPN3/2009 at [3.11]

Although the main UK-IPO is now based in Newport, South Wales, hearings will normally be arranged to be held at the London location (see the HM para.4.07). However, if a hearing or an interview with an examiner is held in Newport, any party attending can insist on speaking in the Welsh language (Welsh Language Act 1993 (c.38) s.22). Nevertheless, prior notice should be given (for which see the HM para.4.47) so that interpretation facilities can be arranged, as required by s.24 of that Act. Hearings may also be held in Scotland and indeed in any other part of the UK if the parties agree and benefits in time and cost can be identified: TPN 3/2009 para.4.

Hearings before the Comptroller and public access to them

101.06   Hearings in the Patent Office are conducted by a "hearing officer" who will normally be a divisional director or, ex parte, a deputy director, see §102.04. However, as such a person acts for and in the name of the Comptroller, decisions given in proceedings conducted in the UK-IPO will be deemed decisions of "the Comptroller", though for many years neither the Comptroller nor an Assistant Comptroller appears to have taken a hearing personally.

Access of the public to hearings in proceedings before the Comptroller is largely governed by r.84. By this rule, where a hearing is in respect of a matter concerning a patent or an application which takes place after publication of the application, the hearing will normally be in public, unless after consultation with the parties concerned at the hearing the Comptroller decides otherwise. However, a decision whether a hearing should be held in private can be given only after representations in that respect of it have themselves been made in public. Cases in which the public has been excluded for at least part of the hearing are those in which sensitive financial information has been disclosed during an application for a compulsory licence or for settlement of the terms of a "licence of right"; and where details of secret manufacturing processes have been given as incidental to an allegation of prior use. An order for proceedings to be held in private may also arise in entitlement or inventorship disputes under any of ss.8, 12, 13, 37 and 82, or in applications for employee-inventor compensation under s.40, each where commercially sensitive information may be disclosed during oral evidence or needs to be discussed during the proceedings. In any event, a member of the Council on Tribunals, or of its Scottish Committee, may attend any hearing in that capacity, see the HM para.8.25.

In an appeal against a decision of the Comptroller in *Macrossan's Application* [2006] EWHC 705 Ch it was alleged that the hearing officer showed bias in her decision because she had been supplied with a document which the UK-IPO refused to disclose as being a private explanatory document to the background to the dispute prepared by an examiner for the benefit of the hearing officer according to the HM (paras 4.15–4.20). However, it was held that proceedings before the Comptroller are not adversarial in nature and the examiner is not a party to the proceedings; and there was no evidence of procedural unfairness. Nevertheless, it is understood that procedures in the UK-IPO were subsequently changed.

Decisions of the Comptroller and their communication

101.07   Once the matter in issue has been decided, after a hearing, or otherwise without a hearing, the parties are informed of the decision. Rule 86 permits the Comptroller not to give a written decision in inter partes proceedings, but he must do so if any party so desires under the provisions of the Tribunals and Inquiries Act 1992 (c.53, ss. 10(1), 14 and Sch.1), although that Act does not make clear whether an invitation for such attendance is required. Thus, if a decision adverse to the applicant is made orally at a hearing then, notwithstanding his stated acceptance of that decision, he may also request a written decision in order that he may consider the possibility of appealing. A decision adverse to the applicant issued subsequent to the hearing is always in the form of a written decision even if a party merely states that he will not attend the hearing, or does not wish to be heard, or that he no longer has any interest in the proceedings. If, in ex parte proceedings, the party withdraws his application, the proceedings become closed, and no decision is necessary.

In addition, if ex parte and the decision is favourable to the party, it is not usual to issue a formal decision, although it would seem that a party could require the Comptroller to give a reasoned decision on any case by virtue of the Tribunals and Inquiries Act 1992. Even if judgment is reserved, an ordinary official letter stating that the objection is withdrawn is all that is required so that action by the Examiner may be resumed or concluded. However, in practice the hearing officer prepares a minute for the file and sends a copy of this to the party or parties unless its substance has already been communicated in a letter. If and when the file becomes open to inspection, this minute will appear in the "open" part of that file and therefore itself becomes available to public inspection. Nevertheless, in such cases—for example where a party is successful in his application for patent restoration—the facts of the case do not become readily available to serve as a precedent for future cases based on similar facts. A consequence of this practice is that written precedents favourable to applicants are available only from successful appeals, and only rarely from UK-IPO decisions. This results in a distorted view of UK-IPO practice being obtained from a study of the Comptroller's decisions which do become available in the British Library's collection of UK-IPO decisions, for which see §101.12 and §123.58.

There are precedents for confidential information to be contained in an appendix to the decision which is made available to the parties and their advisers only, which could prevent a written decision being fully available to the public, see *Geigy's Patent* [1964] R.P.C. 391.

If the hearing officer perceives the possibility of further proceedings, for example the offer of amendments to meet the decision, the decision will be an interim, rather than a final, one and will then state the period within which amendments may be put forward in an attempt to overcome the adverse decision. In *Rhône-Poulenc Rorer International Holdings* [2006] EWHC 160 (Pat), it was held that the hearing officer had erred in assuming that amendments were related to the original reference. Rather, this amendment represented a new claim meaning that the appellant still had their limitation defence for these new claims. Therefore, if the limitation defence was still available, an appeal should have never been allowed by the hearing officer and instead this should have been treated as a new claim. In the case of a pending application, the expiration of the r.30 period will be an important factor, as this period can be extended only in certain circumstances (see §123.69 et seq) or under the provisions of s.20(2) which generally requires the filing of an appeal to the Patents Court.

In ex parte proceedings, there is no award of costs, but in inter partes proceedings the Comptroller normally makes an award in favour of the successful party, for which see the commentary on s.107. Where the hearing is not inter partes, but is taking place as part of a pre-grant procedure, there is a statutory obligation on the comptroller to refuse applications that do not match the requirements of the act. Additionally, the comptroller can act in the public interest to ensure that defective applications do not satisfy the requirements of a grant (*Raytheon Co v Comptroller General of Patents, Designs and Trade Marks* [2007] EWHC 1230 (Pat)). However, an interim decision often, but not necessarily, postpones an award of costs to a successful party until the issue of the final decision in the matter, see §107.03. However, the comptroller did not have jurisdiction to order security for costs when he did not represent a "court" body under s.726 1985 Companies Act (*Abdulhayoglu's Patent Application* [2000] R.P.C. 18).

Appealability of decisions of the Comptroller

101.08   Apart from the matters listed in s.97(1) (for which see §97.04), any decision of the Comptroller given under s.101 is appealable (*Omron Tateisi's Application* [1981] R.P.C. 125), but clear errors in a decision have been corrected by the Comptroller by following CPR 40.12 without the need for appeal (*Eli Lilly's Patent* BL O/180/88). The period within which an appeal can be lodged in the Patents Court against a decision of the Comptroller is now 28 days, see §97.12. This period can only be extended by that court itself.

Once an appeal from a decision of the Comptroller has been brought in the Patents Court under s.97, the UK-IPO file is transferred to the Patents Court and no further action in respect of that file can then take place in the UK-IPO until the appeal proceedings have been concluded, or the Patents Court accepts a submission for the matter to be remitted to the UK-IPO for further treatment prior to the hearing of the appeal.

Practice Under Section 101

Fixing of hearing date

101.09   As explained in the *Hearings Manual* (paras 4.01–4.05), the UK-IPO will normally try to be helpful in fixing a hearing date which is convenient to all the parties and their chosen representatives and to minimise, where possible, gaps between evidence rounds and hearings. The parties will be offered a window of time within which to fix hearings: TPN 3/2009 para.3.9-10. A preliminary notice can be expected following the filing of a counter-statement setting out the timetable for the filing of evidence and indicating the period within which the hearing should be fixed, the objective being that the proceedings should be concluded within 12 months. Following the last round of evidence, an attorney should then promptly inform the hearings clerk as to the manner of intended representation. Then, if counsel is to appear, the hearings clerk will normally liaise directly with counsel's clerk in an attempt to find a date mutually convenient for all concerned. However, without agreement of the parties, hearing dates will not be unduly delayed because of the unavailability of chosen counsel.

Unless the parties agree to a postponement of a hearing date already fixed, the hearing will normally proceed on the appointed date, but a preliminary hearing can be requested and held as to whether the substantive hearing should be postponed. The UK-IPO will normally agree to a postponement if all parties have consented to this but will normally require an alternative date to be put forward. Nevertheless, where the parties indicate that settlement negotiations are in progress, the Comptroller may agree to the abrogation of a hearing date with the question of re-listing itself being postponed.

Location and notice of hearings

101.10   Hearings before the Comptroller will usually take place at the London branch of the UK-IPO at 21 Bloomsbury Street, WC1B 3HF (tel. 020 7438 4700), unless otherwise stated. However, ex parte hearings may be fixed for hearing in the UK-IPO in Newport, Gwent. Procedural and ex parte hearings can also be held by tele-conference link between the UK-IPO in Newport and Bloomsbury Street, or possibly another location if special arrangements are made, see the HM (para.4.08).

Procedure at hearings

101.11   The decision of the hearing officer is made partly in an administrative capacity, because in one sense the hearing is a continuation of the administrative substantive examination, but he must also act judicially. At the hearing, an examiner will normally be in attendance, not as a party but in an administrative capacity to assist the hearing officer. However, in ex parte proceedings, the examiner may express the reasons for the rejection which has led to the request for a formal hearing. Thus, the examiner may not cross-examine the applicant or his representative, although of course the hearing officer may ask such questions as he thinks appropriate to reach a decision on the point in issue. In most contested cases, a tape recording will be made and a shorthand writer will be present. For further information on procedure at hearings, see the HM (paras 4.26–4.43 for inter partes hearings and paras 6.37–6.43 for ex parte hearings).

For representation at hearings, see substituted s.102 (reprinted at §102.01) and the commentary on that section.

The applicant for revocation, who has the general burden of proof of his allegations, will normally be invited to open the oral argument, thus changing the former practice under which the patentee was required to make the first case presentation.

A hearing normally commences at 10.30 a.m., and continues to an adjournment at 4 p.m., unless it seems likely that a conclusion will be reached shortly thereafter. There will normally be a short lunchtime adjournment from 1 p.m. to 2 p.m.

Publication of decisions

The parties are normally given three days' advance notice of an intention to issue a written decision on a stated date. A copy of this notice is also exhibited at Bloomsbury Street and left there for a further 14 days after the date of the decision. The decision is delivered to the parties with the decision simultaneously being made available to the public in the file of patent or application in issue, provided that there has already been a publication of the application under s.16 or the applicant agrees to publication. Notices of final (although not interim) decisions are also published in the *Patents Journal*. **101.12**

When a written decision is given on behalf of the Comptroller on an application which has previously been published, a copy of the decision is also normally passed to the British Library for incorporation in their collection of UK—IPO decisions, though a few days usually elapse before this occurs. The Comptroller's decisions given from 1998 are also now placed on the UK-IPO website.

A case reference of the type BL O/xxx/yy is assigned by the UK-IPO before the decision is passed to the British Library. The British Library's collection of Comptroller's decisions extends back to 1965. The library will prepare photocopies of such decisions on request. This is in contrast to some decisions of the court where some copies of decisions in the BL collection (in which case references are assigned by the Library in the form C/xxx/yy) may be marked "Not to be photocopied until [a date six years after the date of the decision]". Such decisions are then obtainable only on request to the shorthand writers involved.

The Legal Secretariat of the UK-IPO also maintains a separate copy of decisions issued by the Comptroller so that copies of these may continue to be available even after the patent file has been destroyed, for which see §118.19.

SECTION 102 [SUBSTITUTED]

Right of audience, etc., in proceedings before comptroller

102.—(1) A party to proceedings before the comptroller under this Act, or under any treaty or international convention to which the United Kingdom is a party, may appear before the comptroller in person or be represented by any person whom he desires to represent him. **102.01**

(2) No offence is committed under the enactments relating to the preparation of documents by persons not legally qualified by reason only of the preparation by any person of a document, other than a deed, for use in such proceedings.

(3) Subsection (1) has effect subject to rules made under section 281 of the Copyright, Designs and Patents Act 1988 (power of comptroller to refuse to recognise certain agents).

(4) In its application to proceedings in relation to applications for, or otherwise in connection with, European patents, this section has effect

subject to any restrictions imposed by or under the European Patent Convention.

(5) Nothing in this section shall be taken to limit the right to draw or prepare deeds given to a registered patent agent by section 68 of the Courts and Legal Services Act 1990 [c. 41].

Note. Subsections (1)–(4) of the section were substituted for the former version of the section by Sch.5 para.27 to the CDPA 1988, with effect from August 13, 1990 (SI 1990/1400). As the former version has no continuing effect, it is not reprinted here. Subsection (5) was added by the Courts and Legal Services Act 1990 (c.41) Sch.18 para.20(1), effective from January 1, 1991.

COMMENTARY ON SECTION 102

Scope of the section

102.02   Section 102 concerns the right of audience in proceedings before the Comptroller. The section complements s.274 of the CDPA 1988 which governs the right of persons to carry on a business of acting as agent for applicants for patents (whether in the United Kingdom or elsewhere) and in conducting proceedings before the Comptroller in connection with patents. Because of the deregulation of these matters effected by the CDPA 1988 s.102 was substituted to bring it into accordance with s.274, for which see §274.01. A recent court decision which addresses the issue of audience is *Atrium Medical Corp v DSB Invest Holding SA* [2011] EWHC 74 (Pat). In this case the court held that a patent attorney who holds a litigator certificate in accordance with the CIPA Higher Courts Qualification Regulations 2007 has rights of audience under the Legal Services Act 2007 s.18 with regard to royalties under contracts for use of patents.

    The substituted form of s.102, together with s.274, provides for a general freedom for a party to proceedings before the Comptroller (besides being able to appear to conduct the proceedings in person) to be represented by any person whom he desires should act for him.

    The general right of audience before the Comptroller provided by subs.(1) is, however, limited in certain respects by subss.(2)–(4). These limitations are: in relation to the preparation of deeds for use in proceedings before the Comptroller (subs.(2)), except those drawn or prepared by a registered patent agent (subs.(5)); in relation to the Comptroller's general power (under CDPA 1988 s.281) not to recognise certain persons as agents acting for others (subs.(3)), for which see §§281.03 et seq; and subject to restrictions imposed by the EPC (subs.(4)). For the last case, there is a parallel provision in s.274(2) of the CDPA 1988, and these restrictions preserve the position under EPC art.134 according to which (as explained in §274.10) proceedings before the EPO must be conducted either in person, or by a person on the "European List" (for which see §286.03), or by a duly qualified legal practitioner (i.e. a solicitor or barrister in England and Wales), for which also see §286.03. However, proceedings before the Comptroller concerning a European patent (UK) fall outside the scope of art.134 of the EPC, see also §274.10.

    The present commentary is confined to rights of audience before the Comptroller, the more general question of representation by agents being dealt with in the commentary on s.274. Also, the present commentary is particularly directed to appearances before the Comptroller by persons other than those on the Register of Patent Agents. The section applies to proceedings concerning European patents (UK) which come before the Comptroller (s.77(1)).

    Representation in appeals from the Comptroller to the Patents Court is governed by s.102A (reprinted at §102A.01) and discussed in the commentary on that section.

Origin of the section

102.03   Under s.102 as originally enacted in 1977, any person could represent a party in proceedings before the Comptroller, but subject to a rule which permitted the Comptroller to refuse to deal with persons guilty of criminal activity or professional misconduct (as remains the present position, see §281.02) and also entitled the Comptroller to refuse to deal with any person, other than a solicitor (of any part of the United Kingdom), counsel, or a registered patent agent, who in the Comptroller's opinion was:

"engaged wholly or mainly in acting as agent in applying for patents in the United Kingdom or elsewhere in the name of or for the benefit of a person by whom he [was] employed".

Moreover (by now repealed s.114), only a registered patent attorney, formerly agent, could practise, describe himself, or hold himself out as a "patent agent", as that term was defined in s.130(1) (for which see §130.01), a definition which required operations to be carried on "for gain". Thus, in practice, patent proceedings before the Comptroller were largely handled by registered patent agents, with occasional matters handled by solicitors or counsel, by an applicant appearing in person or by a corporate applicant appearing by an "agent" appointed to be the company for the purposes of the proceedings.

However, acceptance by the Government of some of the recommendations contained in ch.6 of the "Review of Restrictions on the Patent Agents' Profession" published by the Office of Fair Trading on September 25, 1986 (noted [1986] E.P.O.R. 348), led to the repeal by the CDPA 1988 of ss.84, 85, 102, 104, 114, 115, 123(2)(k) and the definition of "patent agent" in s.130(1) of the original form of the 1977 Act and the replacement of these provisions by substituted ss.102 and 102A and by certain provisions of Pt V of the CDPA 1988, viz. ss.274–281, 285 and 286 of the CDPA 1988. The result of these changes was the removal of the so-called "monopoly" on representation before the Comptroller "to minimise the anti-competitive effects of the Register".

Hearings before the Comptroller

Although the Act refers to proceedings "before the Comptroller", all hearings to determine matters arising from such proceedings are entrusted to a "hearing officer", who acts in the name of the Comptroller under authority conferred by virtue of s.63 of the Patents & Designs Act 1907 (c.29), for which see Appendix A at §A20. As explained in §130.04, for hearings on an ex parte basis, the hearing officer can be a Deputy Director (formally called a "principal examiner"), but, for cases to be heard inter partes, the hearing officer will be a Divisional Director (formerly called a "superintending examiner") or, in cases of particular principle, a Director (formerly called an "Assistant Comptroller"), see the MOPP (para.130.05). In this Work, the convention has been adopted of describing all decisions made within the UK-IPO as if made by the Comptroller himself, even though the decision will normally have been made under a delegated power, see also §101.06. For the location of hearings, see §101.10.

The Patent Office has issued a *Hearings Manual* ("HM") which explains the procedure and conduct applicable to hearings before the Comptroller. This is available on the UK-IPO website.

102.04

Offences relating to document preparation (subs.(2))

Under s.22 of the Solicitors Act 1974 (c.47), and similar provisions in: the Scotland (Solicitors (Scotland) Act 1980 (c.46) s.32); the Northern Ireland (Solicitors (Northern Ireland) Order 1976, SI 1976/582, art.23); and the Isle of Man (Advocates Act 1976 (Act of Tynwald) s.11), it is an offence for a person not qualified under any of those provisions to draw or prepare for personal benefit (that is for, or in expectation of, any fee, gain or reward) any instrument relating to the transfer or charge of real or personal estate or to any legal proceeding. Subsection (2) provides an exception to this prohibition, except as regards the preparation of a deed, although only in connection with proceedings before the Comptroller, or under any treaty or international convention to which the United Kingdom is a party, e.g. the EPC and the PCT. A corresponding exemption for documents prepared for the purposes of legal proceedings by way of appeal to the Patents Court from a decision of the Comptroller, is limited to "registered patent agents" and non-practising barristers, see §102A.01 and §102A.02.

102.05

However, s.22(2) of the Solicitors Act 1974 has been amended to add to the list of persons there set out as being exempt from the prohibitions of s.22(1) "a registered patent agent drawing or preparing any instrument relating to any invention, design, technical information, trade mark or service mark", although it is not clear whether a similar exception has been granted under the other Acts mentioned above as applying respectively to Scotland, Northern Ireland or the Isle of Man. Sections 102(5) and 102A(6) were added at the same time to give full effect to this amendment of s.22 of the Solicitors Act 1974.

Thus, apart from the exception set out in subs.(2), it is an offence for a person (not being a solicitor or registered patent agent) to prepare for personal benefit an instrument (whether or not a deed) or agreement under seal (or any other deed) for assignment, charge or grant of patent rights, although assignment of patents by deed is not now required, see §30.06. Although there is a general exception to all these provisions for "European lawyers" by the European Communities (Services of Lawyers) Order 1978 (SI 1978/1910), it is questionable whether this covers activities by a "European patent attorney".

SECTION 102A [REPEALED WITH EFFECT JANUARY 1, 2010]

Right of audience, etc., in proceedings on appeal from the comptroller

102A.01
102A.—(1) A solicitor of the Senior Courts or (in relation of this section to Northern Ireland) of the Court of Judicature [*Supreme Court*] may appear and be heard on behalf of any party to an appeal under this Act from the comptroller to the Patents Court.

(2) A registered patent agent or a member of the Bar not in actual practice may do, in or in connection with proceedings on an appeal under this Act from the comptroller to the Patents Court, anything which a solicitor of the Senior Courts or of the Court of Judicature [*Supreme Court*] might do, other than prepare a deed.

(3) The Lord Chancellor, with the concurrence of the Lord Chief Justice of England and Wales, may by regulations—

(a) provide that the right conferred by subsection (2) shall be subject to such conditions and restrictions as appear to the Lord Chancellor to be necessary or expedient, and

(b) apply to persons exercising that right such statutory provisions, rules of court and other rules of law and practice applying to solicitors as may be specified in the regulations;

and different provision may be made for different descriptions of proceedings.

(4) Regulations under this section shall be made by statutory instrument which shall be subject to annulment in pursuance of a resolution of either House of Parliament.

(5) This section is without prejudice to the right of counsel to appear before the High Court.

(6) Nothing in this section shall be taken to limit the right to draw or prepare deeds given to a registered patent agent by section 68 of the Courts and Legal Services Act 1990 [c. 41].

(7) The Lord Chief Justice may nominate a judicial office holder (as defined in section 109(4) of the Constitutional Reform Act 2005 [c. 4]) to exercise his functions under the section.

Notes

1. The section was added (with subss.(1)–(5)) by Sch.5 para.27 to the CDPA 1988, with effect from August 13, 1990 (SI 1990/1400). Subsection (6) was added by the Courts and Legal Services Act 1990 (c.41) Sch.18 para.20(1), effective from January 1, 1991

2. The italicised words (and the noted deletions) in subss.(1) and (2) were added by the Constitutional Reform Act 2005 (c.4) Sch.11 para.23 and the underlined words in subs.(3) and subs.(7) were added by the same Act 2005 (Sch.4 para.92).

3. The repeal of this section was a consequence of the Legal Services Act 2007 (c.29), s.210 and Sch.23 para.1, and was effected by SI 2009/3250 para. 2, sub-para.(i)(iii) with effect from 1 January 2010. However, as explained in §275.09 and further below, the effect of the section will remain unchanged during a "transitional period", which may be lengthy.

COMMENTARY ON SECTION 102A

As noted in note 3 above, Section 102A was repealed with effect January 1, 2010, on which date a "transitional period" commenced, as defined by the Legal Services Act 2007, Sch.5, Part 2, para.3. According to para.15 of Sch.5 of the same Act, "(d)uring the transitional period registered patent attorneys are to continue to have the rights conferred by section 102A(2) of the Patents Act 1977 (c. 37)" and hence although the section is itself repealed the effects of the section still apply during the transitional period. In this respect, the rights of solicitors under subsection (1) are preserved via para.7(1) and (2) of Sch.5 of the Legal Services Act 2007. The aforementioned para.15 in combination with the repealed section 102A therefore export these continuing rights to registered patent attorneys, at least in respect of appeals undertaken in proceedings under the Patents Act 1977, discussed further below.

102A.02

The length of the transitional period is at the time of writing as yet unspecified, and may be of several years duration. It is anticipated that the Intellectual Property Regulation Board (IPReg) will in due course propose a replacement regulation, to replace the provisions of s.102A, as well as those of s.292 of the Copyright, Designs, and Patents Act 1988 (for which see §292.01 et seq. below) and the CIPA Higher Courts Qualifications Regulations 2007, which at present govern the rights of "patent attorney litigators". At the time of writing no formal open consultation had yet been commenced by IPReg, although it is understood that draft rules have been prepared in preparation for such.

The effect is to permit a party to an appeal to the Patents Court from a decision of the Comptroller to be represented by counsel, a solicitor of the Senior Courts (i.e. a solicitor practising in England or Wales), a registered patent agent or a non-practising barrister, but by no other person. This is in contrast to the general power of representation in proceedings before the Comptroller conferred by s.102, for which see §102.02.

Sub-section (2) conferred on registered patent agents the right to do, in or in connection with proceedings on an appeal under this Act from the comptroller to the Patents Court, anything which a solicitor might do, other than prepare a deed (although sub-s.6 ensured that this did not derogate from the rights granted to registered patent agents to prepare deeds in certain circumstances (for which see §102.05) granted by s.68 of the Courts and Legal Services Act 1990). This therefore constituted the basis for patent agent representation on appeal from the comptroller, and permitted a registered patent agent both to instruct counsel or (by virtue of sub-s.(1)) appear directly in the Patents Court. However, it should be noted that the scope of these rights was only in respect of appeal proceedings brought under a section of the Patents Act 1977, and did not apply more generally. Thus, for such persons, there is no right of representation in trade mark appeals taken to the court, or (by virtue of s.251 of the CDPA 1988) on a decision under CDPA 1988 s.246 (subsistence or term of design right or identity of first owner thereof), but appeals relating to registered designs and on licences of right on a design right (under CDPA 1988 s.247 or s.248) come (by virtue of s.249 of the CDPA 1988) before the Registered Designs Appeal Tribunal before which registered patent agents do have a right of representation. Holders of "Litigator Certificates" possess additional rights to those persons who are solely registered patent agents, for which see §280.05.

Note, however, that the right of appearance of the persons specified in s.102A(1) and (2) did not extend to their appearance on the hearing of any subsequent appeal to the Court of Appeal; nor are registered patent agents, as such, permitted to brief counsel directly (as theycan for first instance appearances) on such an appeal to the Court of Appeal, although this was recommended by the Royal Commission of Legal Services (Cmnd.7648), see (1979–80) 9 *CIPA* 155. The right of appearance of the persons specified in s.102A(1) and (2) also did not extend to appearance before the Patents Court in proceedings which are not appeals from the Comptroller. Where registered patent agents have directly instructed counsel on appeals from the comptroller (for example in *Symbian Limited's Application* [2009] R.P.C. 1) this was in the capacity of the holder of a "Litigator's Certificate" under the CIPA Higher Courts Qualifications Regulations 2007.

The right of appearance on an appeal from a decision of the Comptroller to the Patents Court of persons other than practising counsel (whose position continues to be regulated by the practice of the High Court, see subs.(5)) was potentially circumscribed by rules which the Lord Chancellor may make under the power conferred by subss.(3) and (4), although no such rules were made, other than those for "patent agent litigators", for which see §280.05. When a patent attorney (agent) appears before the Patents Court, either in pursuance of the rights granted by the continued effect of the provisions of s.102A during the transitional period, or in the future under whatever rules IPReg propose, he should wear a gown of approved design. The Chartered Institute has a small stock of such gowns which may be hired for this purpose. For patent agent litigators, it is thought that this gown would also meet the requirement of the current *Practice Direction (Court Dress)*.

SECTION 103

Extension of privilege for communications with solicitors relating to patent proceedings

103.01   **103.**—(1) It is hereby declared that the rule of law which confers privilege from disclosure in legal proceedings in respect of communications made with a solicitor or a person acting on his behalf, or in relation to information obtained or supplied for submission to a solicitor or a person acting on his behalf, for the purpose of any pending or contemplated proceedings before a court in the United Kingdom extends to such communications so made for the purpose of any pending or contemplated—

    (a) proceedings before the comptroller under this Act or any of the relevant conventions, or

    (b) proceedings before the relevant convention court under any of those conventions.

(2) In this section—

"legal proceedings" includes proceedings before the comptroller; the references to legal proceedings and pending or contemplated proceedings include references to applications for a patent or a European patent and to international applications for a patent;

and "the relevant conventions" means the European Patent Convention, and the Patent Co-operation Treaty.

(3) This section shall not extend to Scotland.

COMMENTARY ON SECTION 103

103.02   The privilege accorded to disclosure of communications with and between solicitors in connection with any pending or contemplated proceedings before a court in the United Kingdom is a rule of general law and is discussed in §§280.05–280.08. By the Solicitors' Incorporated Practice Order 1991 (SI 1991/2684) art.4 the term "solicitor" as used in this section includes any body corporate recognised by the Council of the Law Society under s.9 of the Administration of Justice Act 1985 (c.61).

Section 103 extends this rule of law to proceedings which can be conveniently termed "patent proceedings", being proceedings more usually conducted by patent attorneys rather than by solicitors. The privilege of patent attorneys, both in such "patent proceedings" and in court proceedings, is the subject of s.280 of the CDPA 1988 (reprinted at §280.01). The present section does not extend to Scotland (subs.(3)), because privilege under Scots law is dealt with by s.105. However, s.280(4) extends "patent agent's privilege" to proceedings in Scotland, and in this respect there appears to be some overlap with s.105, see §105.02.

Subsection (1) provides that solicitors (and persons acting on their behalf) are to have, in respect of "legal proceedings" before the Comptroller under the Act or any of the relevant conventions, or a "relevant convention court" under any of those conventions (although not under the Act), the same privilege from disclosure of documents as they would have in connection with any pending or contemplated proceedings before a court in the United Kingdom, for which see §280.07. Subsection (2) defines the term "legal proceedings", to which subs.(1) refers, as including any proceedings before the Comptroller and provides that these may be proceedings (pending or contemplated) concerning an application for a patent, for a European patent or an international application for a patent. Thus, the protection provided by the section is not intended to be a restricted one. The term "relevant conventions" is defined in subs.(2) as meaning the EPC, the CPC and the PCT, and the term "relevant convention court" (as defined in s.130(1), reprinted in §130.01)as a court or other body having jurisdiction over proceedings under any of these three Conventions. Apart from the reference to "convention courts", the provisions of s.103 were previously to be found in s.15 of the Civil Evidence Act 1968 (c.64), repealed by Sch.6 to the present Act.

For example, s.103 is relevant where an application for employee compensation is made to the Comptroller under s.40, with the applicant being represented by a solicitor, or when a solicitor represents a party in proceedings before the EPO.

For the reasons explained in §275.09 the effect of this section will continue during a "transitional period" set out in the Legal Services Act 2007 (c.29).

SECTION 104 [REPEALED]

Privilege for communications with patent agents relating to patent proceedings

104. [...]   **104.01**

Note. The section was repealed by Sch.8 to the CDPA 1988, with effect from August 13, 1990 (SI 1990/1400). Its subject-matter has been re-enacted in expanded form in s.280 of the CDPA 1988, for which see §§280.01 et seq.

SECTION 105

Extension of privilege in Scotland for communications relating to patent proceedings

105.—(1) It is hereby declared that in Scotland the rules of law which confer   **105.01**
privilege from disclosure in legal proceedings in respect of communications, reports or other documents (by whomsoever made) made for the purpose of any pending or contemplated proceedings in a court in the United Kingdom extend to communications, reports or other documents made for the purpose of patent proceedings [*within the meaning of section 104 above*].

(2) In this section—

"patent proceedings" means proceedings under this Act or any of the relevant conventions, before the court, the comptroller or the relevant convention court, whether contested or uncontested and including an application for a patent; *and*

"the relevant conventions" means the European Patent Convention [*the Community Patent Convention* **] and the Patent Co-operation Treaty.**

Note. Section 105 was amended as indicated: (1) by the CDPA 1988 (c.48) Schs 7(21) and 8, with effect from August 13, 1990 (SI 1990/1400); and (2) by the Patents Act 2004 (c.16) Schs 2(22) and 3, with effect from January 1, 2005 (SI 2004/3205 art.2(k)).

COMMENTARY ON SECTION 105

Privilege under Scots law and scope of the section

105.02   Under Scots law there are two broad categories which confer privilege from disclosure in legal proceedings of communications, reports and other documents.

The first category arises from the confidential nature of the relationship between the parties. Thus, for example, communications between a solicitor and his client are confidential and are protected from disclosure (with certain exceptions) in legal proceedings.

It has not been decided whether communications between a patent attorney and his client fall into this category and thus are similarly protected in terms of Scots common law. However, see the discussion of statutory provisions relating to patent agent privilege at §§280.02 et seq.

The second category relates to documents of any kind which have been brought into existence as part of preparations for litigation. "The general rule is that no party can recover from another material which that other party has made in preparing his case" (*Anderson v St Andrews Ambulance Association* [1942] S.C. 555 at 557). The privilege attaches to materials which are prepared, or come into existence, both after the action has started in court and also to such materials prepared at any time "after it is apparent that there is going to be a litigious contention" (*Admiralty v Aberdeen Steam Trawling* [1909] S.C. 335 at 340). Once litigation is "threatened or mooted", or once the parties "are at arms length or are obviously going to be at arms length", the privilege attaches to all materials prepared after that time which relate to the actual or intended litigation. This protection for materials made *post litem motam* (after the commencement of the suit) is well established in Scotland and applies subject to limited exceptions, not only to communications between a litigant and his legal advisers, but to all materials which came into existence as a result of preparing for the case, whether or not at the date any particular item came into existence the action had started in court.

Section 105 clarifies that privilege arising from the application of the *post litem motam* principle of the second category, attaches to communications, reports or other documents made for the purpose of "patent proceedings". Patent proceedings are defined in s.105(2) as including proceedings before the court, the Comptroller or the relevant convention court (as defined in s.130(1)), whether contested or uncontested, and including an application for a patent. However, as regards legal proceedings in Scotland, "the court" is defined as meaning the Court of Session (s.130(1)). Therefore, so far as concerns litigation before the courts, s.105 applies only to proceedings before the Court of Session. But, insofar as it concerns court proceedings, s.105 is probably superfluous because the common law principles summarised above would already protect all such communications, reports or other documents prepared for the purposes of patent proceedings in court. What s.105 does is to make it clear that the same protection is given when the proceedings are before the Comptroller or a relevant convention court (as defined), and that these proceedings include those involving an application for a patent.

The section applies to such communications, reports or other documents "by whomsoever made" and there is no explicit requirement that the communications, reports or other documents must be made by or to a solicitor. Thus, in *Santa Fé International Corporation v Napier Shipping SA (No.2)* [1986] R.P.C. 72, the provisions of the section were held to apply to prevent disclosure in a patent infringement and validity action of expert advice given by a witness (an employee of the pursuer) to the pursuer's UK patent agent in respect of an application before the comptroller to amend the patent. In this regard s.105 appears to be of wider scope than s.103 (extension of privilege for communications with solicitors relating to patent proceedings), discussed in §103.01, which does not apply to Scotland. The extension of privilege in s.103 applies only to communications made with a solicitor or a person acting on his behalf, or in relation to information obtained or supplied for submission to a solicitor or a person acting on his behalf.

Scottish cases on privilege in connection with intellectual property matters

As with privilege under English law, the mere fact that a document has been provided in **105.03** confidence to a party to proceedings is not in itself sufficient reason for according it privilege, see §280.05. This was specifically confirmed in *Santa Fé (International Corporation v Napier Shipping S.A. (No.1)* [1985] S.L.T 430). Here it was held that, where one party to patent proceedings had entered into contracts with third parties which contained clauses binding that party to hold certain information in strict confidence and not to disclose it to others without the consent of the third party, nevertheless that promise of confidentiality must yield to the public interest that, in the administration of justice, the truth should be established. Therefore, the other party to the litigation was entitled to see those contracts, despite the contractual confidentiality obligations. The judge held that no sufficient ground in law for claiming privilege had been put forward. However, for cases where disclosure of confidential information has been ordered to be disclosed on a restricted basis, e.g. to legal advisers only, see §61.67.

SECTION 106

Costs and expenses in proceedings before the court [under section 40]

106.—(1) In proceedings **to which this section applies** [*before the court under* **106.01** *section 40 above (whether on an application or on appeal to the court),*] the court, in determining whether to award costs or expenses to any party and what costs or expenses to award, shall have regard to all the relevant circumstances, including the financial position of the parties.

(1A) This section applies to proceedings before the court (including proceedings on an appeal to the court) which are—

    (a) proceedings under section 40;

    (b) proceedings for infringement;

    (c) proceedings under section 70; or

    (d) proceedings on an application for a declaration or declarator under section 71.

(2) If in any such proceedings the Patents Court directs that any costs of one party shall be paid by another party, the court may settle the amount of the costs by fixing a lump sum or may direct that the costs shall be taxed on a scale specified by the court, being a scale of costs prescribed by the **rules of court** [*Rules of the Supreme Court or by the County Court Rules*].

Notes

  1. The amendments to the heading of the section, in subs.(1), and the addition of subs.(1A) were made by the Patents Act 2004 (c.16) s.14 with effect from January 1, 2005 (SI 2004/3205, art.2(e)(g)), but (by s.14(4) of that Act) do not apply to proceedings commenced before that date.

2. The amendment in subs.(2) was prospectively made by the Constitutional Reform Act 2005 (c.4) s.59 Sch.11 para.23, the Rules of the Supreme Court and the County Court Rules having both been superseded by the Civil Procedure Rules.

COMMENTARY ON SECTION 106

106.02   Section 106 provides the court with a discretion, when awarding costs, to take into account the financial position of the parties in certain patent proceedings, namely those under s.40 (employee compensation claims), in "proceedings for infringement" (which will usually be brought before the court under s.61(1)), proceedings under s.70 (threats) and/or s.71 (a declaration, or declarator, of non-infringement). Proceedings for revocation, as such, are not included within the ambit of the section, but, where there is a counterclaim for revocation as part of infringement proceedings, it can be argued that the costs of bringing, or defending, invalidity claims should come within its scope. Before its amendment by the Patents Act 2004, the section applied only to proceedings for employee-inventor compensation under s.40 which were brought before the court, either ab initio or on appeal from the Comptroller.

The "court" (which is defined in s.130(1), reprinted in §130.01 and discussed in §96.06; and therefore now which also includes the Patents County Court) is here given broad discretion as regards awarding costs ("expenses" in Scotland) in such proceedings "to any party". Thus, it can be concluded that, in any such proceedings, the presumption is that costs on the normal costs scale ("standard costs" in the High Court) should not be awarded without consideration of the discretion conferred by s.106. This discretion is a wide one, and the court can make such order for costs as it may deem appropriate, particularly after taking into account "the financial position of the parties". Subsection (2) provides, for example, that a costs order by the Patents Court can include the award of a lump sum or may direct assessment according to any scale of costs now prescribed by or under the CPR. No specific rules have been so made, but the scales laid down for cases involving relatively small monetary sums would seem to be applicable. Presumably, for a case coming before a "court", other than the Patents Court or Patents County Court, a similar principle would be followed in the general discretion which such a court has as regards orders for costs or expenses.

The procedure for an application under s.40 to the Patents Court or Patents County Court is governed by CPR 63.12 and CPR 63 PD 12, see Appendix F for their wording. The section had no effect when it related solely to s.40 claims because the adjudicated cases under s.40 have so far arisen from applications made initially to the Comptroller, where the provisions of s.107 solely apply, for which see §§107.02–107.06. As yet there has been no case law on the section under its extended scope. The origin of the section in its original form lay in concerns expressed during the debates leading to the Patents Act 1977 that an (ex-)employee might otherwise face a heavy burden of costs on the normal taxed basis. In view of *Pepper v Hart* [1992] 3 W.L.R. 1032; [1993] 1 All E.R. 42, HL, reference can now be made to these debates to show that Parliament expected that an order for assessment on the normal basis should rarely be made (see H.L. Deb. Vol.386, ser.102, cols.1078–1080, July 27, 1977). Here it was also noted that the provision is one similar to that pertaining to matters brought before the Lands Tribunal. The availability of financial support could influence the choice of tribunal before which s.40 proceedings are commenced, although such support may be difficult to obtain, see §40.10. For example, under previous legislation, legal aid was refused in proceedings aimed to secure a personal benefit from ownership of a patent (*Halpern and Ward's Patent* [1974] F.S.R. 242).

When applied to other types of patent proceedings these amendments provide a specific discretion to the court which is additional to that which at least the Patents Court already has (although the position may be different in Scotland or Northern Ireland) in relation to awards of costs under the CPR Pt 44. The Court of Appeal observed in *Smithkline Beecham Plc v Apotex* [2004] EWCA Civ 1703; [2005] F.S.R. 24 that it created "a special rule as to costs in infringement proceedings which has no counterpart in the Civil Procedure Rules." Its extension to such other types of patent proceedings is intended to redress somewhat the imbalance in the ability to bring, or defend, patent litigation when one party is an individual or an SME (small or medium-sized enterprise), especially where the other party has large financial resources available to it. However, an individual or SME cannot expect to have the discretion given by the section exercised in his/its favour when he/it has behaved in an abusive or irresponsible manner, e.g. having commenced litigation on an unjustified basis. Also, under the section the court has to have regard, not only the financial position of the parties, but also "all the relevant circumstances". It remains to be seen how the Patents Court will treat this amended section. One consequence could be that it will increase the litigation costs for an individual or SME as claims may require justification requiring preparation and presentation of evidence of his/its financial standing.

SECTION 107

Costs and expenses in proceedings before the comptroller

107.—(1) The comptroller may, in proceedings before him under this Act, by order award to any party such costs or, in Scotland, such expenses as he may consider reasonable and direct how and by what parties they are to be paid.   **107.01**

(2) In England and Wales any costs awarded under this section shall, if a county court so orders, be recoverable **under section 85 of the County Courts Act 1984** [c. 28] [*by execution issued from the county court*] or otherwise as if they were payable under an order of that court.

(3) In Scotland any order under this section for the payment of expenses may be enforced in like manner as **an extract registered decree arbitral bearing a warrant for execution issued by the sheriff court of any sheriffdom in Scotland** [*a recorded decree arbitral*].

[(4) *If any of the following persons, that is to say—*

(a) *any person by whom a reference is made to the comptroller under section 8, 12 or 37 above;*

(b) *any person by whom an application is made to the comptroller for the revocation of a patent; any person by whom an application is made to the comptroller for the revocation of a patent;*

(c) *any person by whom notice of opposition is given to the comptroller under section 27(5), 29(2), 47(6) or 52(1) above, or section 117(2) below;*

neither resides nor carries on business in the United Kingdom, the comptroller may require him to give security for the costs or expenses of the proceedings and in default of such security being given may treat the reference, application or notice as abandoned.]

(4) The comptroller may make an order for security for costs or expenses against any party to proceedings before him under this Act if—

(a) the prescribed conditions are met, and

(b) he is satisfied that it is just to make the order, having regard to all the circumstances of the case;

and in default of the required security being given the comptroller may treat the reference, application or notice in question as abandoned.

(5) In Northern Ireland any order under this section for the payment of costs may be enforced as if it were a money judgment.

(6) In the Isle of Man any order under this section for the payment of costs may be enforced in like manner to an execution issued out of the court.

Notes

1. Subsection (2) was prospectively amended by the Tribunals, Courts and Enforcement Act 2007 (c.15) s.62(3) and Sch.13.

2. Subsection (3) was amended by the Debtors (Scotland) Act 1987 (c.18) Sch.6; and subs.(6) was added by SI 1978/621.

3. Subsection (4) was substituted by the Patents Act 2004 (c.16) s.15 with effect from October 1, 2005, SI 2005/2471 but applies only in respect of proceedings commenced on or after October 1, 2005.

COMMENTARY ON SECTION 107

Scope of the section

107.02   Section 107 sets out the powers of the Comptroller and Hearing Officers acting for him (referred to as "the Comptroller") to award costs. It also provides for a mechanism for enforcing awards made, including the power to require security. The section does not erode the parties' freedom to agree costs by mutual consent, for example as part of a settlement agreement.

The s.107 powers are limited to proceedings before the Comptroller only. Costs of an appeal from a decision of the Comptroller to the High Court (or Court of Session in Scotland), or of a further appeal to the Court of Appeal, are awarded according to the normal court practice, for which see CPR 44 and §§61.49–61.52 and §97.24.

As a general rule, an award of costs is made in favour of a successful party in inter partes proceedings. While s.107 does not preclude an award of costs in ex parte proceedings, the practice of the Comptroller is not to award costs in such proceedings; see para.17 of *Tribunal Practice Notice* TPN 2/2000 [2000] R.P.C. 598 (referred to as "TPN 2000"). Moreover, costs are no longer awarded in an undefended opposition, revocation or invalidity action, unless factors exist which suggest otherwise; see para.9 of *Tribunal Practice Notice* TPN 4/2007 [2008] R.P.C. 7 (referred to as "TPN 2007"). Neither are costs awarded when the Comptroller is asked to settle the terms of a licence of right under s.46(3) of this Act; see *Down's Patent* BL O/2/93, noted I.P.D. 16097; also para.15 of TPN 2000.

Regarding the timing of an award of costs, the current practice of the Comptroller is to consider costs when the cause of them arises, rather than leaving the issue for the final hearing as used to be the case; see para.10 of TPN 2007, also paras 12 and 13 of TPN 2000.

Generally, when making submissions on costs, there is no need to send detailed bills in support, although an itemised bill will be required in a claim for costs exceeding the standard scale, as discussed at §107.04; see para.7 of TPN 2007. Costs will not be awarded against any party until it has had an opportunity to make written or oral submissions to the Comptroller, if it wishes. An award of costs is payable no later than seven days after the expiry of the appeal period. If an appeal is lodged, the deadline will be suspended pending the appeal; see para.14 of TPN 2000. A failure to make payment will have implications for the continuation of the case.

In terms of funding, Legal Aid is not available in proceedings before the Comptroller, see the Access to Justice Act 1999 (c.22) s.6; Sch.2 para.2(1), providing a Community Legal Service to replace legal aid under the Legal Aid Act 1988 (c.34) where such aid was equally denied by s.14 and Sch.2 Pt I). However, it seems at least theoretically possible for Legal Aid to be available on appeals from a decision of the Comptroller, on which §97.23. Award of costs when a party to the proceedings before the Comptroller has agreed a conditional fee agreement with their representative is dealt with by para.11 of the *Tribunal Practice Notice* TPN 4/2007 [2008] R.P.C. 7.

The general rule for exercising the Comptroller's powers

107.03   The terms of s.107(1) give the Comptroller a very wide discretion in awarding costs. As a general rule, when awarding costs, the Comptroller relies on the standard scale of costs contained in TPN 4/2007 (for proceedings commenced on or after December 3, 2007) and in TPN 2/2000 (for proceedings commenced on or after May 22, 2000). TPN 4/2007 was supplemented by TPN 6/2008. Both Tribunal Practice Notices are available on the website of the UK-IPO. In order to keep the costs low and predictable, the standard scale costs represent only a contribution towards the full expense. In other words, such costs are not intended to compensate parties for the expense to which they may have been put; see para.6 of TPN 2/2000.

The following scale of costs is applicable in proceedings commenced on or after December 3, 2007:

Preparing a statement and considering the other side's statement	From £200 to £600 depending on the nature of the statements, for example their complexity and relevance.
Preparing evidence and considering and commenting on the other side's evidence	From £500 if the evidence is light to £2,000 if the evidence is substantial. The award could go above this range in exceptionally large cases but will be cut down if the successful party had filed a significant amount of unnecessary evidence.
Preparing for and attending a hearing	Up to £1,500 per day of hearing, capped at £3,000 for the full hearing unless one side has behaved unreasonably. From £300 to £500 for preparation of submissions, depending on their substance, if there is no oral hearing.
Expenses	(a) Official fees arising from the action and paid by the successful party (other than fees for extensions of time). (b) The reasonable travel and accommodation expenses for any witnesses of the successful party required to attend a hearing for cross examination.

While setting a cap on costs, this scale provides for a range of costs as opposed to a fixed sum. This enables the Comptroller to take account of the weight of the evidence, the number of hearing days and so on.

As pointed out by the Hearing Officer acting for the Comptroller in *Loadhog Limited v Polymer Logistics BV*, "as a general rule, it is not intended that any item in the table [above] should apply more than once in any award of costs. If it did, it would defeat one of the fundamental purposes of the published scale—i.e. predictability of costs" (BL O/337/10, September 29, 2010).

As a result, the defendant was not able to recover £7,000 for preparing their evidence and considering that of the claimant (the so-called "evidence element" in the second row of the table above). The sum had been itemised as follows: £2,000 for preparing their own evidence, plus £2,000 for considering the claimant's expert evidence, plus six separate amounts of £500 each for considering six other witness statements filed by the claimant. Noting that "the evidence element of any costs order should be between £500 and £2000 in total", the Hearing Officer awarded the claimant £1,600 only.

The following scale of costs applies to proceedings commenced on or after May 22, 2000 but before December 3, 2007. This scale is less flexible; it aims to give an average award of about £2,000 regardless of the weight of the evidence and the length of the hearing.

1. Application or Notice of Opposition and accompanying statement	£300 plus statutory fee (if any);
2. Considering statement of case in reply	£200 OR
1. Considering Application or Notice of Opposition and accompanying statement	£200;
2. Statement of case in reply	£300;
3. Preparing and filing evidence	Up to £1,500;
4. Considering evidence	One half of item 3;
5. Preparation for and attendance at Hearing	Up to £1,500
6. Where a party appears in person or where attendance of a party's witnesses is required by the opposite party, allowance will be made for general expenses and travelling, but the allowance for general expenses will not normally exceed £250 per person per day, nor an overall maximum per party of £750 per day.	

—Departures from the standard scale of costs

107.04   As an exception rather than the norm, the Comptroller may depart from the standard (contributory) scale of costs considered above (see para.2 of TPN 4/2007 which updates TPN 2/2000). As summarised by TPN 2/2000, para.8, this power is essential for dealing with breaches of rules, delaying tactics or other unreasonable behaviour. As explained by TPN 2/2000, para.9, there is no exhaustive list of circumstances when the Comptroller may make an off-the-scale award partly because of the difficulties of drafting such a list, and partly because an exhaustive list may fetter the Comptroller's discretion. However, the Tribunal Practice Notices give some examples of behaviour that can warrant an off-the-scale award, namely: making an application to amend a statement of case which, if granted, would cause the other side to have to amend its statement or would lead to the filing of further evidence, where such an amendment could have been avoided; filing evidence in respect of grounds which are not pursued at the main or substantive hearing; unreasonably rejecting efforts to settle a dispute; unreasonably declining the opportunity of Alternative Dispute Resolution; and failing to attend a hearing without informing the other side.

Further guidance comes from the case law. In what is still the leading case, *Rizla's Application* [1992] F.S.R. 659, a Deputy Judge of the High Court stated that a compensatory award may be made where the claimant commences or maintains a case without a genuine belief that there is an issue to be tried. Other examples of when the Comptroller may make a compensatory award are deliberate delay and unnecessary adjournment.

An award exceeding the scale was made in the following cases:

Power-Stow v RASN O/305/09, where claimants failed to pursue a reference under s.71 and had given no credible reason why their evidence had not been filed or how they intended to move the case forward. Having applied to have the case struck out, the defendant was awarded an on-scale sum of £400 but full compensatory costs of £1,778 for correspondence with the UK-IPO and the application to strike out;

Stafford Engineering's Licence of Right (Copyright) Application [2000] R.P.C. 797, where the copyright owner did not represent his position honestly while also deliberately abusing the process;

Smartwater's Patent O/32/00, where an applicant for revocation abandoned his case in anticipation of a preliminary hearing set up to deal with deficiencies of his statement, the continuance of the case was seen as an abuse of process and the costs order made included compensation to the patentee for the involvement of counsel;

Haynes International's Patent BL O/105/90, noted I.P.D. 13196, where an unsuccessful applicant for revocation required a witness for cross-examination from the United States; and

Nippon Shinyaku's Application BL O/1/83, where a defendant failed to respond to evidence and did not inform the claimant that he would not attend a hearing until shortly before the hearing, and failed to mention that he had withdrawn his opposition, cf. the case of *Geistlich-Sohne v ND Partners* O/164/09 where the claimants withdrew their application only a day before a preliminary hearing. It was held that costs above the standard scale would not be appropriate because if parties were punished for pulling out at short notice, they might feel obliged to go ahead with the hearing to avoid an award of actual costs, which would not be in the interests of justice. An award exceeding the scale may have been awarded if the claimants deliberately encouraged or allowed the defendant to incur unnecessary expense in preparing for that hearing.

Having dealt with cases where the Comptroller has made an award exceeding the scale, it is worth bearing in mind that in appropriate circumstances he can also make a nominal award of costs lower than the minimum provided by the scale.

Security for costs (s.107(4))

An order for security for costs or expenses is not available in all proceedings. Such an order can be made in entitlement proceedings under ss.8, 12 or 37 and applications for revocation before the Comptroller under s.72. The defendant in an application for amendment under s.27(5); surrender under s.29(2); cancellation of a licence of right endorsement under s.47(6); compulsory licence under s.52(1); and correction of error under s.117(2) may also be able to obtain an order for security for costs or expenses. By contrast, no order for security for costs or expenses can be made in applications for employee-inventor compensation under s.40; for settlement of the terms of a licence of right under s.46(3) or proceedings for a declaration of non-infringement under s.71 (*Ash & Lacy's Patent No. 2240558* [2002] R.P.C. 46 at 939). Regarding infringement proceedings under s.61(3), no order will be made unless the agreement preceding such proceedings requires one of the parties to give security. **107.05**

Because the Comptroller is not a "court" for the purpose of s.1156 of the Companies Act 2006 (c.46), no order for security for costs or expenses may be made against an impecunious corporate referrer in entitlement proceedings (*Abdulhayoglu's Applications* BL O/49/99).

In terms of procedure, the party wishing to obtain security makes an application as the Comptroller no longer awards security on his own initiative. In deciding on the amount of the award, the Comptroller will consider arguments made and evidence provided by the applicant; the old practice of making a standard award in the sum of £900 has been abandoned; see para.16 of TPN 2000.

Monies provided as security may be deposited in an interest bearing account in the joint names of patent attorneys or solicitors authorised to act for the parties. A guarantee given by a UK bank may also suffice.

Enforcement of award of costs (s.107(2), (3), (5) and (6))

By virtue of subss.(2), (3), (5) and (6), while the exact mechanism for enforcing an award of costs varies depending on whether the person ordered to provide security resides in England or Wales, Scotland, Northern Ireland or the Isle of Man, a failure to comply with an order for security is treated in the same way as a debt for a relatively small sum of money. The idea is to keep the costs of enforcement low. **107.06**

SECTION 108

Licences granted by order of comptroller

108. Any order for the grant of a licence under section 11, 38, 48 or 49 above shall, without prejudice to any other method of enforcement, have effect as if it **108.01**

were a deed, executed by the proprietor of the patent and all other necessary parties, granting a licence in accordance with the order.

COMMENTARY ON SECTION 108

108.02   The section removes any doubt as to validity, for want of proper execution, of a licence granted or modified by the Comptroller: where an order is made under the provisions of s.11 or s.38 for the substitution of a new licence for an existing one following an order for change of applicant or proprietor in entitlement proceedings under s.8 or s.37; or where an order is made for the grant of a compulsory licence (under s.48) or for the substitution of an existing licence under s.49. Curiously, the section does not appear to apply to cases where the Comptroller has settled or ordered the terms of a "licence of right" under s.46(3)(a) or (b), or if a modification of an existing licence is ordered under s.51(3), but presumably the terms of these sections are such that the licence ordered takes direct effect rather than as the result of a decision that a licence shall be granted.

Where the powers of s.108 are invoked by making an order under it, the licence would seem to take effect from the date of the Order so that this has effect while any appeal against the making of the Order may remain undecided. These powers could be exercised by the court or the Court of Appeal during appeal proceedings from a decision of the Comptroller under the appointed ss.11, 38, 48 or 49.

Offences [Sections 109–113]

SECTION 109

Falsification of register etc.

109.01   **109.** If a person makes or causes to be made a false entry in any register kept under this Act, or a writing falsely purporting to be a copy or reproduction of an entry in any such register, or produces or tenders or causes to be produced or tendered in evidence any such writing, knowing the entry or writing to be false, he shall be liable—

    (a) **on summary conviction to a fine not exceeding the prescribed sum [*£1,000*],**

    (b) on conviction on indictment, to imprisonment for a term not exceeding two years or a fine, or both.

Note. Subsection (a) was amended by the Magistrates' Courts Act 1980 (c.43) s.32(2). This section isapplied to the Isle of Man by SI 2003/1249 with the substitution of "information" for "indictment" in subs.(b) as applied to the Isle of Man.

COMMENTARY ON SECTION 109

Scope of the section

109.02   The offences under s.109 concern false entries in the register of patents and false copies thereof. Such an offence has existed since 1883, but no case appears to have been brought.

The offence is one triable "either way", i.e. by summary conviction or on indictment. In the summary jurisdiction the maximum fine is the "prescribed sum", a term which has been equated with the term "statutory maximum" which is defined (varyingly for England and Wales, Scotland and Northern Ireland) in the Interpretation Act 1978 (c.30) Sch.1, as amended by the Criminal Justice Act 1988 (c.33) Sch.15 para.58. It presently stands at £5,000 for England and Wales (Criminal Justice Act 1991, c.53 s.17). Although there is no limit specified for a fine on indictment, this must not be excessive (Bill of Rights 1688 (c.2) s.1) and must be within the offender's capacity to pay (*R. v Churchill (No.2)* [1967] 1 Q.B. 190 CCA; and *R. v Garner* [1986] 1 W.L.R. 73; [1986] 1 All E.R. 78 CA). Where a company commits the offence, its officers may be liable under s.113, see §113.01.

Knowing the entry or writing to be false

The offences under s.109 require the offender to have knowledge that the register entry **109.03** or copy is false. A statement which is literally true may be false if an omission creates clearly and intentionally a belief which is wrong (*R. v Bishirgian* [1936] 1 All E.R. 586 CA). Whether the person responsible for the falsehood gains by it is irrelevant (*Barrass v Reeve* [1980] 3 All E.R. 705).

Proof of a person's knowledge can be based on evidence that he:

"deliberately shut his eyes to the obvious or refrained from inquiry because he suspected the truth but did not wish to have his suspicion confirmed".

(*Westminster City Council v Croyalgrange* [1986] 2 All E.R. 353; [1986] 1 W.L.R. 674 HL per Lord Bridge). The knowledge of an employee or agent may be imputed to his employer or principal where control of the work was delegated to the employee or agent (*Vane v Yiannopoullos* [1965] A.C. 486; [1964] 3 All E.R. 820 HL), but, in the absence of control by or delegation to the employee, criminal acts by an employee are not imputed to his employer (*Tesco v Nattrass* [1972] A.C. 153; [1971] 2 All E.R. 127 HL).

SECTION 110

Unauthorised claim of patent rights

110.01

110.—(1) If a person falsely represents that anything disposed of by him for value is a patented product he shall, subject to the following provisions of this section, be liable on summary conviction to a fine not exceeding **level 3 on the standard scale** [*£200*].

(2) For the purposes of subsection (1) above a person who for value disposes of an article having stamped, engraved or impressed on it or otherwise applied to it the word patent or "patented" or anything expressing or implying that the article is a patented product, shall be taken to represent that the article is a patented product.

(3) Subsection (1) above does not apply where the representation is made in respect of a product after the patent for that product or, as the case may be, the process in question has expired or been revoked and before the end of a period which is reasonably sufficient to enable the accused to take steps to ensure that the representation is not made (or does not continue to be made).

(4) In proceedings for an offence under this section it shall be a defence for the accused to prove that he used due diligence to prevent the commission of the offence.

Note. The section was amended by the Criminal Justice Act 1982 (c.48) s.46.

Commentary on Section 110

Scope of the section **110.02**

The offence under s.110 is committed by a false representation that a product, which is disposed of for value, is "patented". The section applies to European patents (UK) (s.77(1)). For the effect of marking on infringement proceedings, see §62.03. However, the section may perhaps not be invoked where the product is marked "patented" and a patent exists in some other EC country, though not in the United Kingdom, see the trade mark case of *Pall Corp v Dahlhausen* (C-238/89) [1990] E.C.R. I-4827, noted *The Times*, February 4, 1991.

The section applies only where a product is "disposed of...for value". Thus, no such offence is committed in the case of a gift, e.g. as with the distribution of free samples. Nor is a mere display of a falsely marked product an offence under the section.

It is here also useful to note that no company or limited liability partnership may be registered under a name which incorporates the word "patent" or "patentee" without the consent of the Secretary of State for Business, Innovation and Skills, see Companies Act 2006 (c.46) s.55 and Company, Limited Liability Partnership and Business Names (Sensitive Words and Expressions) Regulations 2009/2615 s.3 and Pt.1 Sch.1.

Penalties under the section (subs.(1))

110.03   Offences under s.110 are triable only summarily. The maximum fine applicable is now defined by reference to "level 3 on the standard scale". The term "standard scale" is varyingly defined for England and Wales, Scotland and Northern Ireland (under the Interpretation Act 1978 (c.30) Sch.1, as amended by the Criminal Justice Act 1988 (c.33) Sch.15 para.58), and "level 3" currently stands at £1,000 for England and Wales (Criminal Justice Act 1991 (c.53) s.17). Where a company commits an offence under s.110, its officers may be liable under s.113, see §113.01.

Besides giving rise to possible criminal penalties, false marking may also disentitle the marker to discretionary relief from the court, e.g. an injunction against trade mark infringement or passing off (*Cheavin v Walker* (1877) 5 Ch.D. 850 CA and *Cochrane v MacNish* (1896) 13 R.P.C. 100 Pat Ct). False marking is not an offence under the Trade Descriptions Act 1968 (c.29) in view of the definition of "trade description" in s.2(1) of that Act. However, false marking may give rise to an offence under regs 5 and 9 of the Consumer Protection from Unfair Trading Regulations 2008 (SI 2008/1277, which came into force on May 26, 2008): inaccurate marking as to the nature of intellectual property rights associated with an item which causes or is likely to cause the average consumer to take a transactional decision he would not have taken otherwise is deemed to be misleading and is therefore an offence. These Regulations implement the Unfair Commercial Practices Directive (2005/29/EC), so similar protection should be afforded in all European Member States.

Meaning of "patented product"

110.04   An offence under s.110 is committed only by reference to a "patented product", a term defined in s.130(1) and discussed in §60.04. The term includes a product to which a patented process has been applied, as well as the products mentioned in s.60(1)(a) and (c). The fact that the sale of an article could be restrained as a contributory (indirect) act of infringement under s.60(2) (for which see §§60.08–60.10) does not make that article a "patented product".

The patent in question must be subsisting at the time. A fine for unauthorised marking was imposed in *Cassidy v Eisenmann* (1980) F.S.R. 381, where a toy imported from Italy was marked "Brevettato Italia, Espania, Great Britain, France, Deutschland" and only a pending application existed in the United Kingdom. The decision was in line with earlier cases where there had once been a patent which had expired, or where there was at the time only a pending application (*R. v Wallis* (1886) 3 R.P.C. 1; *R. v Crampton* (1886) 3 R.P.C. 367).

Meaning of "falsely represents" (subss.(2) and (3))

110.05   Subsection (2) defines the representation required for an offence to be committed. There is, however, ancient authority that use of the word "patent" is not objectionable where the patent expired long ago and the word has become part of the description of the article (*Sykes v Sykes* (1824) 3 B & C 641; 107 E.R. 834). It is irrelevant that the vendor of an article believes it to be a patented product if this is not so (*Esco v Rolo* (1923) 40 R.P.C. 471). The patent does not have to be represented as his.

Subsection (3) now provides a reasonable period of grace after expiry or revocation of a patent for marking to cease.

The effect of s.110 on trade in second-hand goods is obscure.

Defence of due diligence (subs.(4))

110.06   The burden of proof for the defendant under subs.(4) is a preponderance of probability.

A company may have a defence by proving that the false marking was carried out without its consent (*Tesco v Nattrass* [1972] A.C. 153; [1971] 2 All E.R. 127 HL).

SECTION 111

Unauthorised claim that patent has been applied for

111.—(1) If a person represents that a patent has been applied for in respect of any article disposed of for value by him and— **111.01**

    (a) no such application has been made, or

    (b) any such application has been refused or withdrawn,

he shall, subject to the following provisions of this section, be liable on summary conviction to a fine not exceeding **level 3 on the standard scale** [*£200*].

(2) Subsection (1)(b) above does not apply where the representation is made (or continues to be made) before the expiry of a period which commences with the refusal or withdrawal and which is reasonably sufficient to enable the accused to take steps to ensure that the representation is not made (or does not continue to be made).

(3) For the purposes of subsection (1) above a person who for value disposes of an article having stamped, engraved or impressed on it or otherwise applied to it the words "patent applied for" or "patent pending", or anything expressing or implying that a patent has been applied for in respect of the article, shall be taken to represent that a patent has been applied for in respect of it.

(4) In any proceedings for an offence under this section it shall be a defence for the accused to prove that he used due diligence to prevent the commission of such an offence.

Note. The section was amended by the Criminal Justice Act 1982 (c.48) s.46.

COMMENTARY ON SECTION 111

Scope of the section

The offence under s.111 is committed by a false representation that, in respect of an article disposed of for value, a patent has been applied for, and remains, which will cover that article. It therefore complements s.110 which concerns false representation that a product is "patented". Section 111 applies also to applications for a European patent (UK) (s.78(1) and (2)) and to international applications for a patent (UK) (s.89(1)). However, an earlier application in another country from which priority may be claimed under the Paris Convention is not an "application" for the purpose of s.111, and an offence may therefore be committed by a prospective applicant during the priority interval. **111.02**

Effect and limitations of section 111

An offence under the section is committed if there is no application subsisting when an article, marked for example "patent applied for", is disposed of for value. Disposal by gift, e.g. distribution of free samples, is outside the ambit of the section. Even if an application had once been made, but at the time of disposal of the article had been refused, withdrawn or deemed to be withdrawn, an offence would seem to arise under the section. However, as a defence, it is not necessary that, at the time, the application had been published under s.16 or under the EPC or the PCT. **111.03**

The Act does not define what is meant by a patent applied for "in respect of" an article. The definition of s.69(2)(b) is evidently not intended (cf. "patented product" in s.110, see §110.01). However, for a successful defence, the subsisting application must be one which, at the time, sought to protect the article the subject of the complaint.

For the effect of marking and why it is desirable, see the discussion on s.62, which provision is extended to published applications by s.69(1). For the purpose of s.111 (unlike under s.69(3)), the likelihood of grant of the application is immaterial.

Where a company commits an offence under s.111, its officers may be liable under s.113, see §113.01.

Defences and penalties under section 111

111.04   Subsection (2) gives a period of grace to cease marking after refusal or withdrawal of the application.

The defence under subs.(4) is analogous to that discussed under s.110(4), see §110.06.

An offence under s.111 is triable only summarily. The maximum fine is now defined with reference to "level 3 on the standard scale". The term "standard scale" is varyingly defined for England and Wales, Scotland and Northern Ireland by the Interpretation Act 1978 (c.30) Sch.1, as amended by the Criminal Justice Act 1988 (c.33) Sch.15 para.58, and "level 3" currently stands at £1,000 for England and Wales (Criminal Justice Act 1991 (c.53) s.17).

SECTION 112

Misuse of title "Patent Office"

112.01   **112.** If any person uses on his place of business, or on any document issued by him, or otherwise, the words "Patent Office" or any other words suggesting that his place of business is, or is officially connected with, the Patent Office, he shall be liable on summary conviction to a fine not exceeding **level 4 on the standard scale** [*£500*].

Note. The section was amended by the Criminal Justice Act 1982 (c.48) s.46.

COMMENTARY ON SECTION 112

112.02   An offence is committed under s.112 when the words "Patent Office" are used to suggest, contrary to the fact, some connection with "The Patent Office", a term defined by unrepealed s.62 of the Patents and Designs Act 1907 (reprinted at §A20). Thus, care should be taken not to contravene the section in the wording of advertisements for staff referring to the recruitment for the "patent office" of a particular company or firm.

The offence is triable only summarily, and the maximum fine is now set at "level 4 on the standard scale". The term "standard scale" is varyingly defined for England and Wales, Scotland and Northern Ireland by the Interpretation Act 1978 (c.30) Sch.1, as amended by the Criminal Justice Act 1988 (c.33) Sch.15 para.58. "Level 4" currently stands at £2,500 for England and Wales (Criminal Justice Act 1991 (c.53) s.17). Where a company commits an offence under the section, its officers may be liable under s.113, see §113.01.

If any function of the Comptroller were to be contracted out by an order made under the Deregulation and Contracting Out Act 1994 (c.40) Pt II, for which see §130.04, s.112: "[S]hall not apply in relation to any thing done by a person who is authorised by virtue of the order to exercise any function of the [Comptroller]" (see Sch.16 to that Act).

The Office adopted the operating name "The UK Intellectual Property Office" on April 2, 2007, and in December 2008 adopted a new logo and title "Intellectual Property Office". (This book still uses the abbreviation UK-IPO.) The scope of s.112 would not appear to extend to misuse of this phrase and abbreviation directly, but it might be argued that these amount to ''any other words suggesting that his place of business is, or is officially connected with, the Patent Office''. This would have to be proved ''beyond reasonable doubt'' (the criminal standard of proof) for the offence to be committed.

SECTION 113

Offences by corporations

113.01   **113.**—(1) Where an offence under this Act which has been committed by a body corporate is proved to have been committed with the consent or connivance of, or to be attributable to any neglect on the part of, a director, manager, secretary or other similar officer of the body corporate, or any person who was purporting to act in any such capacity, he, as well as the body corporate, shall be guilty of that offence and shall be liable to be proceeded against and punished accordingly.

(2) Where the affairs of a body corporate are managed by its members, subsection (1) above shall apply in relation to the acts and defaults of a member in connection with his functions of management as if he were a director of the body corporate.

COMMENTARY ON SECTION 113

If a body corporate commits an offence under the Act, an officer or a person managing **113.02** the affairs of such a body is also liable for that offence if it is proved that the offence was committed with the consent or connivance of that person or was attributable to his neglect. Here the term "officer" means a director, manager, company secretary or someone acting in such a role, whatever his formal title. The offences to which the section is applicable are those under: s.22(9) (breach of a secrecy order); s.23(3) (unauthorised filing of foreign patent application); s.109 (falsification of register of patents); s.110 (unauthorised claim of patent rights); s.111 (unauthorised claim of existence of patent application); and s.112 (misuse of title of "Patent Office"). A similar provision exists in s.285(5) of the CDPA 1988 in relation to offences underCDPA 1988 s.276(6) (misuse of terms "patent agent" and "patent attorney").

Section 113 places the onus of proof on the prosecutor, whereas with its predecessor (1949 Act s.93) the accused had the onus of proving his innocence, viz. that the offence was committed without his consent or connivance and that he exercised an appropriate degree of diligence. This shift of onus may be due to the decision in *Tesco v Nattrass* [1972] A.C. 153; [1971] 2 All E.R. 127 HL, under which a company can be convicted for the criminal acts of a director or manager (including those requiring mens rea) only when that person can be identified with the controlling mind and will of the company and was in actual control of its relevant operation. It has also been held, under a statute similarly requiring the consent, connivance or neglect of an officer of a company, that "neglect" does not mean a failure to see that the law was observed: thus, no offence was committed by a director who had no reason to distrust another officer of the company to whom she could properly leave matters, and therefore she had no need to inquire specifically whether there had been compliance with a certain statutory requirement (*Huckerby v Elliott* [1970] 1 All E.R. 189).

Patent agents [Sections 114–115]

SECTION 114 [REPEALED]

Restrictions on practice as patent agent

114. [...] **114.01**

Note. The section was repealed by Sch.8 to the CDPA 1988, with effect from August 13, 1990 (SI 1990/1400). As the section has no continuing effect, it is not reprinted here. It has been replaced by the CDPA 1988 ss.274 and 276, for which see §274.01 and §276.01 respectively.

SECTION 115 [REPEALED]

Power of comptroller to refuse to deal with certain agents

115. [...] **115.01**

Note. The section was repealed by Sch.8 to the CDPA 1988, with effect from August 13, 1990 (SI 1990/1400). As the section has no continuing effect, it is not reprinted here. It was replaced by s.281 of the CDPA 1988, for which see §281.01.

Immunity of department [Section 116]

SECTION 116

Immunity of department as regards official acts

116.01   **116.** Neither the Secretary of State nor any officer of his—

(a) shall be taken to warrant the validity of any patent granted under this Act or any treaty or international convention to which the United Kingdom is a party; or

(b) shall incur any liability by reason of or in connection with any examination or investigation required or authorised by this Act or any such treaty or convention, or any report or other proceedings consequent on any such examination or investigation.

Commentary on Section 116

116.02   Although the 1977 Act makes no statement generally on any presumption of validity of a patent granted under the Act, s.116 protects the Secretary of State and his officers from any implication that the grant of a patent carries with it any warranty of validity. It also excludes all liability arising from any examination or investigation (which would include the search carried out during the preliminary examination of an application) under the Act or any treaty or convention. The section may not, however, absolve the Comptroller from acts of negligence arising in other connections, for example recording that a patent has lapsed when the required renewal fee had been duly paid.

Section 116 provides immunity only as regards acts which can loosely be regarded as "official", i.e. as an act authorised under statute. Thus, the section would not seem to provide any immunity as regards the Search and Advisory Service ("SAS") provided by the UK-IPO, although this operates under the terms of a broad disclaimer of responsibility for the accuracy of its reports. Such a disclaimer, however, is probably only effective if it would be considered "reasonable" under the Unfair Contract Terms Act 1977 (c.50) s.6, see §44.07. However, the SAS was closed as from October 6, 2011.

Under the Interpretation Act 1978 (c.30) Sch.1,"Secretary of State" means any one of Her Majesty's Principal Secretaries of State, see §22.03.

Administrative provisions [Section 117–121]

SECTION 117

Correction of errors in patents and applications

117.01   **117.**—(1) The comptroller may, subject to any provision of rules, correct any error of translation or transcription, clerical error or mistake in any specification of a patent or application for a patent or any document filed in connection with a patent or such an application.

(2) Where the comptroller is requested to correct such an error or mistake, any person may in accordance with rules give the comptroller notice of opposition to the request and the comptroller shall determine the matter.

(3) Where the comptroller is requested to correct an error or mistake in a withdrawal of an application for a patent, and—

(a) the application was published under section 16 above; and

(b) details of the withdrawal were published by the comptroller;

the comptroller shall publish notice of such a request in the prescribed manner.

(4) Where the comptroller publishes a notice under subsection (3) above, the comptroller may only correct an error or mistake under subsection (1) above by order.

Note. New subss.(3) and (4) were added to s.117 by the Regulatory Reform (Patents) Order 2004 (SI 2004/2357) ("RRO") (art.17) with effect from January 1, 2005.

RELEVANT RULE—RULE 105

Rule 105—Correction of errors

105.—(1) A request to the comptroller to correct an error or mistake under section 117 must be made in writing and identify the proposed correction. **117.02**

(2) The comptroller may, if he thinks fit, require the person requesting a correction to produce a copy of the document indicating the correction.

(3) Where the request is to correct a specification of a patent or application, the request shall not be granted unless the correction is obvious (meaning that it is immediately evident that nothing else could have been intended in the original specification).

(4) But paragraph (3) does not apply where the error in the specification of the patent or application is connected to the delivery of the application in electronic form or using electronic communications.

(5) Where the comptroller determines that no person could reasonably object to the correction no advertisement shall be published under rule 75.

(6) Where the comptroller is required to publish a notice under section 117(3), it must be published in the journal.

(7) This rule does not apply to a correction of a name, address or address for service (which may be corrected under rule 49).

COMMENTARY ON SECTION 117

Scope of the section

Subsection (1) gives the Comptroller power to correct errors in various documents filed **117.03** in connection with a patent or application. According to s.14(10), this power is not affected by the provision of s.14(9) that withdrawal of an application may not be revoked. According to s.15(8), the power is not affected, in relation to the filing of missing parts of a specification, by the provisions of s.15(6) and (7). The procedure, which is discussed in §117.12, is that the request for correction is made in writing (a form is no longer required) under r.105(1) and must identify the proposed correction.

However, while subs.(1) refers to the correction of any specification or document filed, r.105 does not apply to changes made under r.49(1) (correction of a name, address or address for service, or under r.57 (correction under s.80(3) of a translation of a European patent (UK); correction of an error in the register is governed by r.50. However, where a correction is made under s.117 of a kind which causes the register then to contain an incorrect entry, that entry is corrected as a consequence of the s.117 correction. For rectification of the register, see s.34 and the commentary on that section.

Section 117 is only concerned with errors in documents. Thus, it has no applicability to the correction of procedural irregularities, for the possibility of correction of which see r.107 (reprinted at §123.24) discussed in §123.61 et seq.

Subsection (2) provides for opposition to any request for correction and requires the Comptroller to determine any opposition, for which see §117.13. For the possible effect on validity of a permitted correction, see §117.06.

Subsections (3) and (4) (added by art.17 of the RRO) provide for the Comptroller to allow, as a result of a request, the correction of a withdrawal of an application which had been made in error or by a mistake. This correction is to be by way of resuscitation of the withdrawn application under s.117A, discussed below. If allowed, the resuscitation will have effect under the provisions of s.117A(2)–(7), as summarised in the commentary on that section.

Subsection (3) requires that, where such a request for resuscitation relates to an application which has already been published under s.16 and details of its withdrawal have also been published, the request is to be published in the *Patents Journal*, in accordance with r.105(6). Where such publication of the request takes place, subs.(4) requires that any correction of an error or mistake in the earlier withdrawal is to be made by order.

It is to be noted that r.105(3), which restricts corrections to specifications, is worded differently from previous r.91(2) in that it requires it to be immediately evident that "nothing else could have been intended in the original specification", rather than that "nothing else could have been intended than what is offered as the correction". The previous wording is closer to that of r.139 of the EPC (formerly r.88) but the difference does not appear to be significant. Indeed, it is understood that the UK-IPO regards the change as not being of significance but rather an updating of language. Rule 91.1(c) of the PCT has wording which is different again but closer to r.139 of the EPC. Section 130(7) does not list s.117 as one of those intended to conform with the provisions of the EPC, the CPC or the PCT. Indeed, in *Alps Electric's Application* BL O/12/90, noted I.P.D. 13083, the Comptroller refused to follow EPO decisions on correction for this reason. Nevertheless, EPO decisions may often having a persuasive effect under the Act. There is also a difference (at least in wording) in the overall scope of r.139 of the EPC compared with that of s.117(1) in that former relates to "linguistic errors, errors of transcription and mistakes", whilst the latter concerns "any error of translation or transcription, clerical error or mistake" For discussion of EPO decisions on correction, see §117.10.

Section 117 applies to the correction of a European patent (UK) as it does to a patent granted under the Act. If this is not in the English language a corrected translation may also be required. However, where it is only the translation which is sought to be corrected, s.80(3) applies, see §80.06. In *Rhône-Poulenc Santé's Patent* [1996] R.P.C. 125, the Comptroller declined to entertain an application for correction under s.117 of a European patent until the period for possible opposition under EPC art.100 had expired because any correction of a European patent (UK) may be overridden by a correction allowed by the EPO during opposition proceedings: the application then failed because the correction involved the translation of the patent and s.80(3) was held to take precedence. In this case, it was argued that the Comptroller had already allowed the correction, subsequently disallowed, but the act in question was one of an administrative officer who is not authorised to act for the Comptroller in such a matter, for which see §130.04. However, as there explained, Examiners and Senior Examiners are authorised to act for the Comptroller under s.117.

In *GMC Tools (UK) Ltd v Makita Corporation* BL O/121/07 the patent was the subject of a revocation action in the Patents County Court. Trial was four weeks away. The patentee (Makita) requested correction of an error under s.117; GMC opposed. The hearing officer decided on balance to stay the correction procedure, principally because there was no time for the opposition procedure to run its course before trial, despite concluding that the chances of unnecessary duplication of effort or inconsistent conclusions were small. The stay was lifted when the revocation action was subsequently discontinued, see BL O/202/07. In the first decision, the hearing officer remarked that the Patents County Court had itself no jurisdiction to decide the correction issue.

Who may apply for correction

117.04 There is apparently no restriction on who may apply for correction under s.117. Thus, it would seem that any person able to give evidence on the occurrence of the error may apply for its correction. For example, a request may apparently be filed in the name of a patent attorney, rather than that of an applicant or proprietor. Indeed, this absence of restriction allows the examiner to make minor corrections of his own initiative during the examination process, but he must do this only where the nature of the error and its correction are beyond reasonable doubt, and where he informs the applicant that he has done this, see the MOPP. Consequently, an applicant, or his patent attorney, may request the examiner to correct minor errors without a formal request under s.117.

Nature of permissible corrections to specifications (r.105(3))

Rule 105(3) is important in that, where the document to be corrected is a specification **117.05**
of an application or patent, the rule explicitly limits the correction thereof to one which is obvious in the sense that it is "immediately evident" that nothing else (but the correction offered) could have been intended "in the original specification". This is a very stringent requirement.

The person to whom the correction has to be immediately evident would seem to be the notional addressee of the specification rather than its draftsman, with the test being objective rather than subjective. Thus, it is submitted that the skilled reader is entitled to read the text in the light of his common general knowledge and, therefore, to take into account not only the express disclosure of the document which is sought to be corrected but also its implicit teaching to the skilled person, as EPO decisions have apparently held, see §117.10.

According to the Comptroller (at least, under previous r.91(2)), it is necessary for grant of the correction request that it is immediately evident from the specification sought to be corrected not only that something has gone wrong but also that what has gone wrong, see: *Antiphon's Application* [1984] R.P.C. 1; *Dukhovskoi's Applications* [1985] R.P.C. 8; and *VEB Kombinat Walzlager's Application* [1987] R.P.C. 405. The position should be no different under r.105(3). For proof of that mistake or error, see §117.09. The Comptroller also requires to be satisfied that what is offered as the correction is that which was originally intended to be expressed in the document sought to be corrected. In *Reeves Wireline's Application* BL O/454/01 the Comptroller held that the then r.91(2) imposed a stringent requirement for an allowable correction, namely (a) is it clear that there is an error?; and (b) if so, is it clear that what is now offered is what was originally intended? Nevertheless, it may be significant that, in each of these three decisions under s.117, the Patents Court specifically refused to endorse the expressed view of the Comptroller as to the requirements for then r.91(2) to be satisfied and decided each case on some other ground.

In the *Antiphon* and *VEB* cases, the Patents Court held that to allow correction to deal with missing drawings would, in the circumstances, circumvent the statutory requirements under s.15(3) of the time. These two decisions, however, now stand overruled by the bringing into effect of s.15(8), referred to in §117.03, which specifically permits correction under s.117 to take place despite any failure to meet the requirements of s.15(6) and (7) as to missing parts of a specification.

While the nature of the mistake must be apparent on the face of the document, the Comptroller allows consideration of all documents filed contemporaneously to establish what was originally intended to be present. These documents include the priority document even if this is filed subsequently, provided that its identity is established on the basis of an identifying number in the file papers, see *Dukhovskoi's Applications* (above). However, the EPO does not permit reference to a priority document to establish the needed correction (G 11/91 *CELTRIX/Glu-Gln* OJ EPO 1993, 125; [1993] E.P.O.R. 245), see §117.10. In any case, a mere discrepancy between the specification and its priority document does not establish an error in the specification, because the discrepancy could have arisen from an error of judgment by its draftsman, see *Tragen's Application* BL O/96/90.

In *Birkett's and Butler's Patent* BL O/401/10 an attempt was made by a third party to use s.117 essentially as a substitute for proceedings under s.13 or s.37. The Hearing Officer reached her decision on the papers and on the assumption that the request was to enter the requester as sole inventor; no evidence was filed. The request was refused. The

Hearing Officer stated that, if her assumption was wrong and the request was to enter the requester also as sole proprietor, the request would also be refused.

The MOPP gives other examples of various types of correction which will, and which will not, be accepted by the Comptroller under s.117.

"Correction" as contrasted with "amendment"

117.06   Section 117 refers to "correction" and not to "amendment". Moreover, s.117 is not mentioned in s.76(2) or (3) as one of the sections to which the limitations contained in s.76 apply. The question nevertheless arises whether addition of matter to a specification, or extension of the scope of protection of a granted patent, each within the meaning of s.76, is allowable by way of correction and whether validity objections could be raised under s.72(1)(d) or (e) that a correction has been made which is in contravention of these provisions.

It is thought that objection under s.72(1)(d) or (e) should be unlikely because correction can be made to a specification only in obvious and evident circumstances. If these criteria are met, the content of the specification and the effective scope of protection as determined by s.125 should not be regarded as having been altered, particularly when the implicit teaching of the specification before correction is taken into account.

In accordance with this view, in G 3/89 *Correction under rule 88* OJ EPO 1993, 117; [1993] E.P.O.R. 376, it was stated that a valid correction cannot possibly add subject-matter because it is simply what a skilled person would automatically read into the specification in any event. Also, while it was stated in G 11/91 *CELTRIX/Glu-Gln* that a correction under EPC r.88 (now r.139) must comply with the requirement of art.123(2) of the EPC in not adding subject-matter to the content of the application as filed, there should be automatic compliance with art.123(2) of the EPC when a correction is allowed under EPC r.139, as the correction will merely set out explicitly what the skilled reader would understand from reading, and notionally correcting in his mind, the erroneous description, as further discussed in §117.10. On this basis, in T 647/91 *TEIJIN/Water-repellant textile fabric* [1998] E.P.O.R. 288, discussed in §117.10, a correction which broadened the literal wording of the claim was allowed, it being stated that objection under art.123(3) did not arise because the true meaning would have been discerned by the skilled worker, this being the test for claim construction under EPC art.69.

In contrast to the position taken by the EPO, in *Braun's Patent* BL O/138/94 the Comptroller stated that corrections allowed under s.117 are not subject to the restrictions of s.76(3)(b) (prohibition against broadening of invention claimed at grant) applicable to permissible amendments, and therefore presumably not either subject to s.76(3)(a) (prohibition against adding subject-matter to the application as originally filed either). However, once it is seen that a correction only clarifies existing subject-matter (as it would be understood by the skilled addressee of the specification), the need for compliance of a correction with either s.76(3) or art.123 of the EPC becomes irrelevant as compliance with the correction provisions leads to automatic compliance with the prohibitions set out in s.76 and in art.123 of the EPC.

However, in *Mönlycke Health Care AB v Wake Forest University and Wake Forest University Health Services* [2009] EWHC 2204 Pat Ct, Kitchin J. found the patent in suit to be invalid and that it should be revoked under s.72(1)(e). The scope of claim 1 had been widened after grant during EPO opposition proceedings as a result of allowance of a request for correction of an error under r.88 (now r.139). The judge held that the correction should not have been allowed as it was not immediately apparent that a mistake had been made. The protection conferred by the patent had therefore been extended in contravention of s.76(3) and, following G 11/91 *CELTRIX/Correction of errors* [1993] E.P.O.R. 245, Kitchin J. decided that it would be wrong in principle that a correction not admissible under r.88/139 (or, presumably s.117) and which resulted in an extension of protection should escape EPC art.123 (or presumably, s.76). The contrast drawn above between the practice of the UK-IPO and of the EPO therefore may no longer be appropriate.

In *Western Electric v Racal-Milgo* [1981] R.P.C. 253 amendment (under the 1949 Act) was not allowed to correct what was agreed to be an obvious mistake on the ground that this has remained undetected for many years and so was not a mistake apparent on the face of the document. The same reasoning might be employed under the 1977 Act and r.105(3), but such a case might now be seen as an appropriate one for the exercise of discretion in favour of making a correction; see further §117.08.

In *Baker Hughes' Patents* BL O/332/02; [2002] EWHC 2524 Ch the amendments were allowed under s.27 but an alternative request to treat them as corrections under s.117 was refused. It was held that for a correction to be made under s.117 it has first to be clear that something is wrong, and that this was not so in the case where the amendment requested was to remove certain words which described features mentioned in the patent as belonging to the prior art.

Corrections to documents other than specifications

Section 117 is general in its application to all documents filed in connection with a pa- **117.07** tent or an application and has been used to correct applications for supplementary protection certificates see, e.g. *Patents Journal* April 6, 1994. However, s.117 relates only to mistakes in documents and not to procedural errors or omissions, such as mistakes in the filing of documents, see: *Klein Schanzlin's Application* [1985] R.P.C. 241; and *Tokan Kogyo's Application* [1985] R.P.C. 244.

Rule 105(3) relates only to corrections in specifications. Accordingly, corrections to documents other than specifications are not required to be obvious in the sense "that it is immediately evident that nothing else would have been intended in the original specification". Rule 139 of the EPC is to like effect and, on this basis, the EPO Boards of Appeal have allowed correction of non-evident mistakes in documents other than specifications, see §117.11.

The extensions of time which are now available under rr.107 and 108 (reprinted and discussed under s.123) and their predecessors have reduced the need to try to apply s.117 to circumstances where the aim in correcting a document was to overcome a deemed failure of an application because of some action not timely taken.

In *Berg's Application* BL O/235/05, the applicant requested that the entire specification of an application which was the UK national phase of an international application be replaced by the specification of the priority document to the international application. This followed the filing of the wrong specification in the international application. The request was refused because the correction was held not to be obvious in the sense of being immediately evident that nothing else could have been intended then for the international application and its priority document to be worded identically. The mistake that had occurred was also held not to be a mistake in a document, but rather that the wrong document had been filed.

Where the number of the priority application has been wrongly stated, this can be corrected without the need to invoke s.117, provided that this is done within the priority year. Likewise, correction of PF 7 (statement of inventorship) is permitted within the period permitted for filing this form. Otherwise, a request under s.117 will be required, together with evidence to establish the error and the proper manner of its correction according to the original intention of the applicant.

Discretion

The allowability of a correction is essentially a matter of the exercise of discretion. For **117.08** this reason, few cases where correction is permitted are recorded in a formal decision, and therefore there are few decisions under the Act which indicate how this discretion is favourably exercised in practice. The impact of the introduction of ss.27(6) and 75(5), discussed in the commentaries on ss.27 and 75 (which require that in cases of amendment regard should be had to the relevant principles applicable under the EPC), remains to be seen, although it can presumably be taken as making discretion less likely to be exercised against correction, even in cases of delay, despite the position taken by the Patents Court in *Western Electric v Racal-Milgo* [1981] R.P.C. 253 (referred to in §117.06).

The other principle appears to be that the exercise of discretion involves drawing a balance between the interest of the applicant (or proprietor) and that of the public who may have acted in reliance on the uncorrected document. Following this principle, in the EPO the correction of a priority date, if not requested early enough for a warning to be included with the publication of the application, requires special circumstances and there has been a refusal to consider correction of an application after its publication when the correction could have had a profound effect on the public, see J 3/81 OJ EPO 1982, 100, and also J 4/82 *YOSHIDA/Priority declaration* OJ EPO 1982, 385 discussed in §117.11. In the *Yoshida* case, it was important that the correction request had been made sufficiently early for it to be included in the publication of the application, though only decided upon thereafter. Otherwise, neither the fact that the missing priority is a later one, nor that the possibility of a mistake is apparent from the documents filed, is seemingly sufficient for correction to be permitted, see J 7/94 *FONTECH/Priority declaration (correction)* OJ EPO 1995, 817.

However, in J 9/91 *Correction/Priority declaration* [1998] E.P.O.R. 352, where a declaration of priority had been omitted from the PCT Request Form and the international application had been published with an indication that correction was being sought and hence the request for correction had been made promptly, correction was allowed, it being indicated that the omission of a priority declaration will, in nearly all cases, be an error capable of correction under EPC r.88 (now r.139).

Also, where the mistake in the particulars of a priority application is apparent on the face of the published application, correction has been allowed by the EPO even though publication has already occurred because the interests of the public should not be adversely affected in view of the apparent discrepancy, see: J 3/91 *UNI-CHARM CORPORATION/ Priority declaration (correction)* OJ EPO 1994, 365; [1994] E.P.O.R. 566; J 6/91 *DU PONT/Priority declaration (correction)* OJ EPO 1994, 349; [1993] E.P.O.R. 318; and J 2/92 *UNITED STATES/Priority declaration (correction)* OJ EPO 1994, 375; [1994] E.P.O.R. 547.

Proof of mistake or error

117.09   Since s.117 concerns only correction of errors and mistakes, the fact that an error or mistake has occurred will need to be proved. Therefore, the requirements of the EPO (noted in §117.10) for submission of strict proof of the error or mistake and appropriate correction should be borne in mind. A similar standard of proof may well be required under s.117, particularly as correction involves the exercise of discretion, and such in turn requires that the applicant for correction must have acted, and be seen to have acted, with the utmost good faith.

In English law there is the maxim that all are presumed to know the law. It would therefore seem doubtful that "error" in s.117(1) can extend to an error of law. This point has been left open by the EPO, see §117.11.

EPO Decisions on correction

—Correction of description, drawings and claims

117.10   As already noted, the terms of the second sentence of r.139 of the EPC are likely to have similar effect to r.105(3). Although s.117 is not listed in s.130(7) as being a provision intended to be in harmony with the EPC, EPO decisions under EPC r.88/139 are illustrative of a parallel way of thought in another jurisdiction, cf. the preamble to the Act. However, no correction under EPC r.88/139 can be effected in the EPO after grant, except during opposition proceedings (J 42/92 (Unreported)).

Also, the EPO Enlarged Board of Appeal has ruled that any correction under EPC r.88/ 139 must not contravene art.123(2) of the EPC, see §117.06. Hence, replacement of the complete documents of an application by the documents which the applicant intended to file cannot be permitted as a correction (G 2/95 *ATOTECH/Replacement of application documents* OJ EPO 1996, 555; [1997] E.P.O.R. 77). This was confirmed in J 5/06 *AGRU-PACION OLCINA, S.L./Correction* under r.88 [2007] E.P.O.R. 21 where a request for a reference to the Enlarged Board of Appeal was refused.

A request for correction under EPC r.88/139 must be accompanied by sufficient evidence for the EPO to be satisfied: (1) that a mistake has been made; (2) what the mistake was; and (3) what the correction should be (J 8/80 OJ EPO 1980, 293, also reported as *Appeal Practice Decision No.4* [1981] R.P.C. 60). This decision also stressed the need to present evidence of the relevant facts fully and frankly, and stated that, where the alleged mistake is not self-evident and where it is not immediately evident that nothing else would have been intended other than that which is offered as the correction, the burden of proving the facts will be a heavy one. This decision also warns that, if the evidence put forward is incomplete, obscure or ambiguous, the request for correction should be rejected.

It follows that, for an error to be correctable, the correction must be one that is unequivocal from the specification as filed, see T 32/85 *GIST-BROCADES/Biomass preparation* [1986] E.P.O.R. 267 and T 581/91 *JOHNSON & JOHNSON/Polylactide* [1994] E.P.O.R. 259 in each of which correction was refused, though in the latter case an alternative amendment was allowed which had the effect of correcting the error. Thus, the proper correction of an error is not immediately evident if more than one possibility for correction can be envisaged and the correction chosen must be the one which the application as a whole clearly implies (T 13/83 *Erroneous technical calculation* OJ EPO 1984, 428).

However, it is not clear that this is the same as the UK test under r.105(3) because r.105(3) seems to require that the requested correction must be in terms of the only possibility as to what was originally intended, so that substitution of wording which is the most obvious correction would not be sufficient. Nonetheless, it has since been held that the requirements of r.88/139 of the EPC are not fulfilled when there are two equally plausible ways in which the apparent error could be corrected, as in T 158/89 *GENERAL ELECTRIC/Ortho-alkylation catalyst* [1996] E.P.O.R. 246. Likewise, in T 955/92 *FINA/Crystalline silicas I* [1997] E.P.O.R. 7 correction was not permitted because the intended meaning of a term could only be ascertained from two possibilities by conducting an experiment which needed more than common general knowledge.

In T 200/89 *BOEING/Obvious error* OJ EPO 1992, 46; [1990] E.P.O.R. 407, the EPO allowed correction because the claims and description were inconsistent and the error was identifiable in the claims: otherwise all of the examples would have been outside their scope. Analogously, in T 726/93 *RIETER/Textile machines* OJ EPO 1995, 478; [1996] E.P.O.R. 72 an application was filed with drawings corresponding to those in the accompanying priority document, but with a description obviously unrelated thereto: substitution of the description of the priority document was allowed, it being immediately evident that this was what had been intended.

The name of a chemical product has also been permitted to be corrected throughout the specification upon acceptance of evidence that careful reading of the specification (and especially the acknowledgement of the prior art therein) would have informed the skilled reader of the name that had been intended (T 990/91 *PFIZER/Correction of chemical name* [1992] E.P.O.R. 32). Also, in T 647/91 *TEIJIN/Water-repellant textile fabric, correction* was allowed on the basis that the skilled worker would appreciate that an error had occurred in a formula and that this had resulted from an erroneous conversion into metric units. Although the correction broadened the literal wording of the claim, objection under art.123(3) did not arise. The EPO has also held that there is no insufficiency of description when an error in the sole illustrative example of the specification could be seen and rectified by the skilled reader using his common general knowledge (T 171/84 *AIR PRODUCTS/Redox catalyst* OJ EPO 1986, 95; [1986] E.P.O.R. 210), although this was indicated to be an exceptional case.

Thus, it can be considered that the EPO allows correction to be made when the error and the manner of its correction are derivable from the "total information content" provided by the document which is sought to be corrected. This appears from G 11/91 *CELTRIX/Glu-Gln* (above). Here, the Enlarged Board of Appeal was asked to consider questions concerning the documents which could be used to show the existence of a self-evident error; and whether correction might be made in a manner which, in the case of an amendment, would offend against the prohibition of adding new subject matter by amendment or broadening the extent of protection after grant. These questions were answered by the Enlarged Board of Appeal as follows:

"1. The parts of a European patent application or of a European patent relating to the disclosure (i.e. the description, the claims and the drawings) may be corrected under rule 88 [now r.139], second sentence, EPC only within the limits of what a skilled person would have derived directly and unambiguously, using common general knowledge, and viewed objectively as at the date of filing, from the totality of those documents as filed. Such a correction is of a strictly declaratory nature and thus does not infringe the prohibition of extension under article 123(2) EPC.

2. Evidence of what was common general knowledge on the date of filing may be furnished in connection with an admissible application for correction in any appropriate form."

Decision G 3/89 *Correction under rule 88* is a decision to similar effect. In other words, a valid correction cannot possibly add subject-matter because it is simply what a skilled person would automatically read into the specification in any event.

In the light of these two decisions of the EPO Enlarged Board of Appeal, a correction may not be established, at least before the EPO, on the basis of statements made in either the abstract or priority document: thus J 4/85 *ETAT FRANÇAIS/Correction of drawings* OJ EPO 1986, 205; [1986] E.P.O.R. 331 has been overruled in this respect. Here, a priority document was considered in determining an applicant's intention, and, on this basis, replacement was allowed of an incorrect drawing initially filed.

In T 487/89 *ASAHI/Polyamide fibre* [1992] E.P.O.R. 32, a calculation error was not permitted to be corrected, though in the circumstances the uncorrected specification was found sufficient.

T 3/88 *HOECHST/Melting point* [1988] E.P.O.R. 377 is a case where a typing error (where two numerals had been transposed) was permitted to be corrected as an error of transcription. Also, an obvious printing error was corrected in T 268/89 *LATZKE/Magnetic plaster* OJ EPO 1994, 50; [1994] E.P.O.R. 469.

In T 200/89 *BOEING/Obvious error* (above), the EPO held that correction is retrospective, whereas amendment is not, but it should be noted that in the United Kingdom, any amendment of a patent after grant has retrospective effect, see ss.27(3) and 75(3) (reprinted in §27.01 and §75.01 respectively), and likewise for a European patent (UK) under s.77(4) (reprinted in §77.01).

In T 1728/07 *SCHERING/Process for preparing intermediate to florfenicol* the allowability under r.88 (now r.139) of a correction made during examination was challenged during opposition appeal proceedings under art.100(c). The error involved an incorrect substituent being shown in a structural formula. The Board of Appeal held that the correction was allowable and did not offend art.100 (c) by extending the subject-matter of the application as filed. In reaching this view, the Board concluded that, by mapping atoms from the starting material to the product, the skilled person would immediately recognise that there was an inconsistency in the substitution pattern of the molecule depicted in the formula. Arguments that it could not be excluded that the incorrect formula was in fact the correct one and that the skilled person would not know how to correct the formula were rejected.

—Correction of other documents

117.11   The limitation in r.139 of the EPC that an allowable correction must be self-evident applies (like that in r.105(3)) to a correction only of a description, drawing or claim. The EPO has shown a fairly benevolent attitude to corrections of other documents where it has been satisfied that the document as filed did not accord with the applicant's intention, and where the correction could be made in time for the public not to be prejudiced by it, or where the need for correction was almost self-evident from the incorrect document, on which point see §117.08.

For example, the EPO has permitted: correction of omissions in the designation of States on the application form (J 8/80, also reported as *Appeal Practice Decision No.4*

[1981] R.P.C. 60); and J 4/80 OJ EPO 1980, 351, reported also as *Appeal Practice Decision No.5* [1981] R.P.C. 65); correction of an erroneous withdrawal of designation of a State (J 10/87 *INLAND STEEL/Retraction of Withdrawal* [1989] E.P.O.R. 437, abridged OJ EPO 1989, 323), see §14.51; and correction of a priority declaration: J 4/82 *YOSHIDA/ Priority Declaration*; J 3/91 *UNI-CHARM CORPORATION/Priority declaration (correction)*; J 6/91 *DU PONT/Priority declaration (correction)*; and J 2/92 *UNITED STATES/ Priority declaration (correction)*, though only because the correction was sought at an early stage in the life of the application, see §117.08, or otherwise would not have deceived the public (J 11/92 *BEECHAM/Priority declaration (correction)* OJ EPO 1995, 25; [1996] E.P.O.R. 141).

Further, in J 7/80 OJ EPO 1981, 137, correction was allowed of the identity of the applicant in a case where the wrong and correct applicants were both companies within the same group: full evidence was required to substantiate the correction. A correction substituting the name of the applicant was also allowed in J 18/93 *CARDIAC/Correction of mistake* OJ EPO 1997, 326; [1998] E.P.O.R. 38, but it was stressed that, although r.88 of the EPC (now r.139) is not applicable to corrections of other documents, to avoid any abuse of its provisions, the burden of proving the necessary facts for correction is a heavy one. However, omission of a priority declaration will normally be seen as not expressing the true intention of the applicant so that, in such a case, special evidence is not normally needed (J 9/91 *Correction/Priority declaration*).

Moreover, J 19/80 OJ EPO 1981, 65, reported also as *Appeal Practice Decision No.6* [1981] R.P.C. 277 allowed correction under EPC r.88 where half a sheet of drawings was missing from the application as filed, but where the nature of the correction was unambiguous from the priority document which contained the full drawing and where the relevant portion of the text was in identical terms to the specification as filed at the EPO: thus it was clear that nothing else would have been intended than what was offered as the correction. However, correction was refused under EPC r.88 in a later case where a sheet of drawings with a complete figure was omitted: post-dating for late filing of the drawings was then the remedy (J 1/82 OJ EPO 1982, 293). The effect of these decisions now needs to be reconsidered in view of s.15(8), referred to in §117.03 above.

The EPO has left open whether an error of law can be recognised as a mistake, see J 3/81 OJ EPO 1982, 100; but, in D 6/82 OJ EPO 1983, 337, it was indicated that a mistake in law does not, as a general rule, constitute a ground for re-establishment of rights under EPC art.122. Also, r.88/139 of the EPC applies only to mistakes in documents and, therefore, a mistake of fact in not paying an opposition fee could not be corrected by seeking to correct a notice of opposition to include a request for the fee to be deducted from a deposit account (T 152/85 *SANDVIK/Unpaid opposition fee* OJ EPO 1987, 191; [1987] E.P.O.R. 258).

In T 713/02 *AVECIA/Phosphoramidites* OJ EPO 2006, 267; [2005] E.P.O.R. 46 at [486], an application to claim an earlier priority date to overcome a prior art objection under EPC art.54(2) was refused. The mistake in not claiming the priority claimed from the original of a US continuation-in-part application was only discovered when the earlier document was cited, but an attempt was then made to overcome this by a disclaiming amendment with the claim for correction only being made some time later. Thus, the public had been misled as to priority for over three years from publication of the application and therefore the correction application had to be refused, even though earlier allowed by a formalities officer.

PRACTICE UNDER SECTION 117

Request for correction

117.12 The procedure for requesting correction is governed by r.105, and by r.105(1), a request for correction has to be made in writing and identify the proposed correction. No form is required. It is not necessary to show the correction on a copy of the document to be corrected unless the Comptroller so requires (r.105(2)). The correction may then have to be shown in red ink on a copy of the document sought to be corrected. The application will need to be accompanied by appropriate evidence to establish the matters required for correction to be permitted, for which see §117.05 and §117.09.

Advertisement of the correction request is not obligatory (see r.105(5)) and is not normally required before grant, but advertisement is usual in any but the most trivial case for correction sought after grant. Advertisement takes place in the *Patents Journal* and sets out the nature of the correction sought. When s.117(3) applies, advertisement of the request is obligatory under r.105(6). Section 117(4) stipulates that, in such circumstances correction may only be by order.

When a correction is allowed before publication, a notice stating that correction under s.117(1) has been allowed is included on the front page of the "A-specification". When correction is allowed after grant, a "C-specification" is published, just as such is published when amendment of a granted patent occurs under either s.27 or s.75. This C-specification is either a fully corrected specification or a reprinted front page listing a schedule of the corrections made to the "B-specification".

The MOPP indicates that consideration of an application for correction may be stayed pending conclusion of co-pending revocation proceedings. Generally, however, it would seem better to stay the revocation proceedings until the form of the specification to be considered has been decided.

Opposition to correction

117.13   Any person may oppose an application for correction (see s.117(2)). The period of opposition is four weeks after advertisement (r.76(2)(b) as amended by the 2011 Rules and Sch.3 Pt 2); this time is inextensible (Sch.4 Pt 1). It is not clear whether opposition can be lodged should the Comptroller decide to dispense with advertisement. Any person may oppose, e.g. a nominee for an undisclosed principal, and he need not demonstrate locus standi, see §27.11, but an opponent resident outside specific territories may be required to give security for costs. The opposition must be limited to the allowability of the correction, and, in particular, validity may not be put in issue in the s.117 proceedings, although it is possible to file a parallel application for revocation under s.72.

Opposition to the request is to be on PF 15 (rr.76(1) and 76(3)(c)) and must be supported by a statement of grounds (r.76 (1)(b)). Both are required to be filed in duplicate r.76(1). The copy of PF 15 and statement are sent by the Comptroller to the applicant for correction who is invited, if he desires to proceed, to file within a specified period (usually six weeks) calculated from the date of dispatch of the statement by the Comptroller, a counter-statement in duplicate (r.77(4)–(6)), of which the Comptroller will send a copy to the opponent (r.80(1)(a)). Both statement and counter-statement must set out fully the facts relied upon. The subsequent procedure is at the discretion of the Comptroller but is likely to be similar to that in other inter partes proceedings before the Comptroller. See the commentary under s.123. The entire procedure is subject to the "overriding objective" set out in r.74.

Appeal

117.14   There is provision for appeal under the general terms of s.97(1), see §97.01.

SECTION 117A [ADDED]

Effect of resuscitating a withdrawn application under section 117

117A.01   117A.—(1) Where—

(a) the comptroller is requested to correct an error or mistake in a withdrawal of an application for a patent; and

(b) an application has been resuscitated in accordance with that request,

the effect of that resuscitation is as follows.

(2) Anything done under or in relation to the application during the period be-

tween the application being withdrawn and its resuscitation shall be treated as valid.

(3) If the comptroller has published notice of the request as mentioned in section 117(3) above, anything done during that period which would have constituted an infringement of the rights conferred by publication of the application if the application had not been withdrawn shall be treated as an infringement of those rights if it was a continuation or repetition of an earlier act infringing those rights.

(4) If the comptroller has published notice of the request as mentioned in section 117(3) above and, after the withdrawal of the application and before publication of the notice, a person—

    (a) began in good faith to do an act which would have constituted an infringement of the rights conferred by publication of the application if the withdrawal had not taken place, or

    (b) made in good faith effective and serious preparations to do such an act,

he has the right to continue to do the act or, as the case may be, to do the act, notwithstanding the resuscitation of the application and the grant of the patent; but this right does not extend to granting a licence to another person to do the act.

(5) If the act was done, or the preparations were made, in the course of a business, the person entitled to the right conferred by subsection (4) above may—

    (a) authorise the doing of that act by any partners of his for the time being in that business, and

    (b) assign that right, or transmit it on death (or in the case of a body corporate on its dissolution), to any person who acquires that part of the business in the course of which the act was done or the preparations were made.

(6) Where a product is disposed of to another in exercise of a right conferred by subsection (4) or (5) above, that other and any person claiming through him may deal with the product in the same way as if it had been disposed of by the applicant.

(7) The above provisions apply in relation to the use of a patented invention for the services of the Crown as they apply in relation to infringement of the rights conferred by publication of the application for a patent (or, as the case may be, infringement of the patent).

"Patented invention" has the same meaning as in section 55 above.

Note. The Regulatory Reform (Patents) Order 2004 (SI 2004/2357) ("RRO") art.18 added new s.117A and subs.(7) was later added by the Patents Act 2004 (c.16) Sch.2 para.23.This section came into effect on January 1, 2005 (the Commencement Date of theRRO) (for subs.(7), by s.17(2) and Patents Act 2004 Sch.2 para.23). This section applies even to applications which, on January 1, 2005 were pending in the sense of Note 1 to §15.01.

COMMENTARY ON SECTION 117A

Scope of the section

Section 117A specifies the provisions which apply when reinstatement of an application **117A.02** is allowed as a correction of a withdrawal of an application. These provisions generally follow those which apply under s.20B when a withdrawn application is reinstated under s.20A, as discussed in §20B.02. However, the availability of "continuing rights" conferred by publication of the application, under s.117A(3), limited by s.117A(4), starts on the date when the request for correction under s.117(3) was published rather than the date of publication of notice of the request for reinstatement as under s.20B. Otherwise, the commentary on s.20B (in §20B.02) applies mutatis mutandis. As also noted in §20B.02, third party rights under s.117A(4) are generally similar to those which are imposed under s.28A when a lapsed patent is restored and under s.64 for prior secret users of an invention of a granted patent. The commentaries on these sections may, therefore, also be applicable to the situation of resuscitation of an application which has lapsed through error or mistake.

SECTION 117B [ADDED]

Extension of time limits specified by comptroller

117B.01   **117B.**—(1) Subsection (2) below applies in relation to a period if it is specified by the comptroller in connection with an application for a patent, or a patent.

(2) Subject to subsections (4) and (5) below, the comptroller shall extend a period to which this subsection applies if—

    (a) the applicant or the proprietor of the patent requests him to do so; and

    (b) the request complies with the relevant requirements of rules.

(3) An extension of a period under subsection (2) above expires—

    (a) at the end of the period prescribed for the purposes of this subsection, or

    (b) if sooner, at the end of the period prescribed for the purposes of section 20 above.

(4) If a period has already been extended under subsection (2) above—

    (a) that subsection does not apply in relation to it again;

    (b) the comptroller may further extend the period subject to such conditions as he thinks fit.

(5) Subsection (2) above does not apply to a period specified in relation to proceedings before the comptroller.

Note. The Regulatory Reform (Patents) Order 2004 (SI 2004/2357) ("RRO") art.18 added new s.117B. This section came into effect on January 1, 2005 (the Commencement Date of the RRO). This section applies even to applications which, on January 1, 2005, were pending in the sense of Note 1 to §15.01.

Relevant Rule—Rule 109

Rule 109—Extension of time limits specified by comptroller

117B.02   **109.**—(1) A request under section 117B(2) must be—

    (a) made in writing; and

    (b) made before the end of the period prescribed by paragraph (2).

(2) The period prescribed for the purposes of section 117B(3) is two months beginning immediately after the expiry of the period to which section 117B(2) applies.

Relevant Direction under Section 124A

Requesting an Extension of Time by Email

117B.03   (as updated to December 12, 2007)

Note. This Direction is reprinted from the website: *http://www.ipo.gov.uk.*
Before use, this website should be checked against the update date given above and, if different, the website version should be used instead of that given below. The update date is that given at the bottom of the left hand panel of this website.

Introduction

1. The comptroller has made the following Directions under section 124A of the Patents Act 1977 ("the Act") to direct the form and manner in which written requests made in accordance with rule 109 of the Patents Rules 2007 to extend a specified period may be made using electronic communications.

2. These Directions come into force on 1 January 2005.

3. In these Directions "email request" means an electronic mail document requesting an extension of a specified period under section 117B of the Act.

Electronic Address

4. An email request using electronic communications shall be sent to one of the following email addresses pateot@ipo.gov.uk

5. No document, other than an email request, shall be sent to those email addresses.

Content of email message

6. An email request shall include sufficient information to enable the comptroller to identify—

the patent application or patent to which the request relates; and

the specified period which is the subject of the request.

7. An email request to extend a specified period under section 117B(4) shall include a statement of the reasons for the request.

Format of email message

8. An email request shall be in plain text (RFC822 compliant) and shall not include any attachments.

Illegible or incomplete email requests and infected emails

9. Where part or all of an email request delivered under these Directions is illegible or incomplete, the whole email request shall be treated as not complying with these Directions.

10. Where an email request delivered under these Directions is reported as having a virus (or other malicious software) by the Patent Office's virus checking software, the email request shall be treated as not complying with these Directions.

11. Where an email request is treated as not complying with these Directions under paragraph 9 or 10, provided the person making the request can be identified, he shall be notified of this fact by the comptroller.

Acknowledgment and time of delivery

12. Where an email request has been sent in accordance with these Directions, it shall be treated as delivered only after it has been acknowledged by the comptroller.

13. The time of delivery accorded to the email request shall be that generated by the Patent Office's internal electronic communications network (within the meaning of section 32 of the Communications Act 2003).

Ron Marchant

Comptroller-General of Patents, Designs and Trade Marks
23 December 2004

Guidance notes to the Directions
(as updated to December 11, 2007)

Note. The Directions contain some guidance and explanatory notes, which are reprinted from the website: *http://www.ipo.gov.uk.*

Before use, this website should be checked against the update date given above and, if different, the website version should be used instead of that given below. The update date is that given at the bottom of the left hand panel of this website.

These notes are not part of the Directions. They are intended to provide background and additional information to readers.

- The Interpretation Act 1978 applies to these Directions. Therefore, all the definitions set out in that Act apply to these Directions. Further, amongst other things, generally any words importing the masculine gender include the feminine and words in the singular include the plural and words in the plural include the singular.

- Where an email request is submitted which does not comply with the Directions, the comptroller may treat the email request as not having been delivered (see section 124A(3) of the Act).

- It should be noted that extensions are not available under section 117B of the Act to periods specified in relation to proceedings before the comptroller.

- The comptroller will not accept an email request that has been encrypted.

- It should be noted that the time accorded to an email request will be when it enters the Patent Office's internal electronic communications network (email system). This will not be the exact time it was sent nor the exact time it was received by the Patent Office's external server. An acknowledgement of receipt will normally be sent automatically.

- The processing of an email request within the Patent Office will be facilitated if the patent or patent application number is entered into the subject line of the email. For requests under section 117B(4) please also add the word "DISCRETIONARY" in capital letters.

- "pateot" found at the start of the email address stands for "patent extensions of time."

Any queries about this Direction should be addressed to Patents Legal Section:
Concept House
Cardiff Road
Newport
South Wales
NP10 8QQ
United Kingdom
Tel: +44 (0)1633 814083

COMMENTARY ON SECTION 117B

Scope of the section

117B.04   Section 117B, which is to be read together with r.109 (see §117B.02, above), applies to time limits in relation to an application or a patent which have been set by the Comptroller rather than by the Act or the Rules, (subs.(1)). The section does not apply to periods set by the Comptroller during proceedings before him (subs.(5)). Thus, periods set by the Comptroller at the end of proceedings, e.g. allowing a period to put forward amendments which might save an application from being refused, cannot be extended as of right under the section, see *Touch Clarity's Application* BL O/198/06 and *Sun Microsystems' Application* BL O/252/06. Similarly, periods set by the Comptroller in pre-hearing correspondence cannot be extended as of right under the section.

The section provides for the extension of such a time limit upon request, provided that the request complies with the relevant requirements of other rules (subs.(2)). The request must be in writing and made within the two months following the expiry of the time limit set by the Comptroller (r.109(1)). This period is inextensible (under 2007 Rules Sch.4 Pt 1 reprinted at §123.26). Any extension so granted cannot extend beyond the end of the compliance period prescribed under s.20 and r.30(1) (subs.(3) and r.109(2)), for which see §18.11.

A further extension of an extended period provided by s.117B is possible, but the Comptroller may make this subject to such conditions as he thinks fit (subs.(4)). A request for a further extension no longer needs be in writing (as was required by r.110A(3) of the 1995 Rules), although this may continue to be required in certain cases. Any request for a further extension should include a statement of reasons for the request. A further extension under subs.(4) is only available if an extension as of right under subs.(2) has been obtained, see *Barry Mellor's Application* BL O/087/08.

PRACTICE UNDER SECTION 117B

Although an application under s.117B must be made in writing (r.109(1)(a)), this includes making the application by electronic communication. For this, directions have been issued under s.124A which are reprinted (together with associated guidance notes) above. The UK-IPO hopes that most applications under the section will be made in this way, but it is important to ensure that an application made by email has actually been received, as will be indicated by a return email receipt, without which an enquiry should immediately be made by telephone. The Office's practice is not to acknowledge a request for an extension under s.117B other than by standard automated acknowledgment by email. Lack of an acknowledgment does not amount to an error default or omission, see *Irwin Industrial Tool Company's Application* BL O/247/09. If some irregularity within the UK-IPO has occurred, r.107 may permit an alternative extension to be obtained, as in *Touch Clarity's Application* BL O/198/06. **117B.05**

SECTION 118

Information about patent applications and patents, and inspection of documents

118.—(1) After publication of an application for a patent in accordance with section 16 above the comptroller shall on a request being made to him in the prescribed manner and on payment of the prescribed fee (if any) give the person making the request such information, and permit him to inspect such documents, relating to the application or to any patent granted in pursuance of the application as may be specified in the request, subject, however, to any prescribed restrictions. **118.01**

(2) Subject to the following provisions of this section, until an application for a patent is so published documents or information constituting or relating to the application shall not, without the consent of the applicant, be published or communicated to any person by the comptroller.

(3) Subsection (2) above shall not prevent the comptroller from—

(a) sending the European Patent Office information which it is his duty to send that office in accordance with any provision of the European Patent Convention; or

(b) publishing or communicating to others any prescribed bibliographic information about an unpublished application for a patent;

nor shall that subsection prevent the Secretary of State from inspecting or authorising the inspection of an application for a patent or any connected documents under section 22(6)[*(a)*] above.

(4) Where a person is notified that an application for a patent has been made, but not published in accordance with section 16 above, and that the applicant will, if the patent is granted, bring proceedings against that person in the event of his doing an act specified in the notification after the application is so published, that person may make a request under subsection (1) above, notwithstanding that the application has not been published, and that subsection shall apply accordingly.

(5) Where an application for a patent is filed, but not published, and a new application is filed in respect of any part of the subject-matter of the earlier application (either in accordance with rules or in pursuance of an order under section 8 above) and is published, any person may make a request under subsection (1) above relating to the earlier application and on payment of the prescribed fee the comptroller shall give him such information and permit him to inspect such documents as could have been given or inspected if the earlier application had been published.

Note. Subsection (3) was amended by Sch.5 para.28 to the CDPA 1988 (c.48), effective from January 7, 1991 (SI 1990/2168).

RELEVANT RULES—RULES 51–55

Rule 51—Restrictions on inspection of documents

118.02   **51.**—(1) For the purposes of section 118(1) the prescribed restrictions are those set out in paragraphs (2) and (3).

(2) No document may be inspected—

(a) where that document was prepared by the comptroller, an examiner or the Patent Office for internal use only;

(b) where the circumstances specified in section 118(4) exist, before the end of the period of 14 days beginning [with] immediately after the date of the notification under rule 52(2);

(c) where that document is a request or application made under section 118 or rule 46(2), 48(2) or 54(1); or

(d) where that document includes matter—

(i) which in the comptroller's opinion disparages any person in a way likely to damage him, or

(ii) the inspection of which would in his opinion be generally expected to encourage offensive, immoral or anti-social behaviour.

(3) Unless in a particular case the comptroller otherwise directs, no document may be inspected—

(a) where that document was filed at the Patent Office in connection with an application under section 40(1) or (2) or 41(8);

1100

(b) where that document is treated as a confidential document under rule 53;

(c) where—

    (i) that document was prepared by the comptroller, an examiner or the Patent Office other than for internal use, and

    (ii) it contains information which the comptroller considers should remain confidential;

(d) where that document relates to an international application for a patent and the International Bureau would not be permitted to allow access to that document under the Patent Co-operation Treaty; or

(e) where—

    (i) the comptroller has accepted a person's application under rule 11(1)(a) or (b), and

    (ii) that person's name and address can be identified from that document as those of the inventor or of the person believed to be the inventor (or, as the case may be, his address can be so identified).

(4) In this rule references to a document include part of a document.

Note. Amended by the Patents (Amendment) Rules 2011 (SI 2011/2052).

Rule 52—Request for information where section 118(4) applies

52.—(1) Where the circumstances specified in section 118(4) exist, a request **118.03** under section 118(1) must be accompanied by evidence verifying their existence.

(2) The comptroller must notify the applicant for the patent of any request.

(3) The notification must be accompanied by a copy of the request and the accompanying evidence.

(4) The applicant may, before the end of the period of 14 days beginning [with] immediately after the date of the notification, inform the comptroller that the circumstances specified in section 118(4) do not exist; otherwise the comptroller may treat him as accepting that those circumstances exist.

Note. Amended by the Patents (Amendment) Rules 2011 (SI 2011/2052).

Rule 53—Confidential documents

53.—(1) Where a person files a document at the Patent Office or sends it to an **118.04** examiner or the comptroller, any person may request that the document be treated as a confidential document.

(2) The comptroller must refuse any request where it relates to—

(a) a Patents Form; or

(b) any document filed in connection with a request under section 74A.

(3) A request to treat a document as confidential must—

(a) be made before the end of the period of 14 days beginning [with] immediately after the date on which the document was—

    (i) filed at the Patent Office, or

    (ii) received by the comptroller, an examiner or the Patent Office; and

(b) include reasons for the request.

(4) Where a request has been made under paragraph (1), the document must be treated as confidential until the comptroller refuses that request or gives a direction under paragraph (5).

(5) If it appears to the comptroller that there is good reason for the document to remain confidential, he may direct that the document shall be treated as a confidential document; otherwise he must refuse the request made under paragraph (1).

(6) But where the comptroller believes there is no longer a good reason for the direction under paragraph (5) to continue in force, he must revoke it.

(7) In this rule references to a document include part of a document.

Note. Amended by the Patents (Amendment) Rules 2011 (SI 2011/2052).

Rule 54—Requests for certain information

118.05 **54.**—(1) Where a person requests to be notified of a relevant event, he must use Patents Form 49.

(2) Where a person has made such a request, the comptroller must notify him that the relevant event has occurred as soon as practicable after the event.

(3) But the comptroller shall not give him information or permit him to inspect a document unless he would be entitled to such information or to inspect such a document under section 118.

(4) A request on Patents Form 49 must be for information regarding a single relevant event only.

(5) For the purposes of paragraph (1), in relation to an application for a patent, each of the following is a relevant event—

(a) an applicant requesting, or failing to request, a substantive examination before the end of the period prescribed for the purposes of section 18(1);

(b) the application being published;

(c) the notice of grant of the patent being published under section 24;

(d) the application being terminated or withdrawn.

(6) For the purposes of paragraph (1), in relation to a patent, each of the following is a relevant event—

(a) a request for an opinion under section 74A;

(b) the patent ceasing to have effect by reason of section 25(3);

(c) the renewal fee and any additional fee being paid during the period specified in section 25(4);

(d) an application being made for the restoration of the patent which has ceased to have effect.

(7) For the purposes of paragraph (1), in relation to a patent or an application for a patent, each of the following is a relevant event—

(a) an entry being made in the register;

(b) a document becoming available for inspection under section 118 (by reason of a prescribed restriction no longer applying to the document);

(c) an application to register a transaction, instrument or event being made under rule 47;

(d) a matter being published in the journal.

Rule 55—Bibliographic information about an unpublished application

55. For the purposes of section 118(3)(b) the following bibliographic informa-   **118.06**
tion is prescribed—

(a) the name of the applicant;

(b) the title of the invention;

(c) the number of the application;

(d) the date of filing of the application;

(e) where a declaration has been made for the purposes of section 5(2)—

   (i) the date of filing of each earlier relevant application specified in the declaration,

   (ii) its application number, and

   (iii) the country it was filed in or in respect of;

(f) where an application has been terminated or withdrawn, that information;
and

(g) where a transaction, instrument or event mentioned in section 32(2)(b) or
33(3) is notified to the comptroller, that information.

Scope of the section

Section 118 concerns the availability to the public of information and documents relat-   **118.07**
ing to patents and applications for patents under the Act, including the effects on such
availability arising from publication of an application under s.16. The applicable rules are
rr.51–55 (see §§118.02–118.06, above). By operation of s.89B(2), s.118 also applies to
international applications which have been published under the PCT and which have
entered the national phase in the United Kingdom by paying the necessary fees to the UK-
IPO and filing any necessary translations. The provisions also apply to such documents relating to European patents (UK) as may exist in the UK-IPO, though the Office creates no
file for an application for a European patent (UK) before the notice of its grant appears in
the *European Patent Bulletin*, and then only when a need for it arises. For information
available on the internet, see §118.10 for applications/patents filed or granted under the
Act and §118.08 for European applications/patents and for published international
applications.

Information about the status of patents and applications is available online from the
UK-IPO website.

The general availability to the public of papers filed at the UK-IPO (which commenced
in November 1968) is in marked contrast to the rules and practice of the High Court. CPR
Pt 5 (available on the websites: *http://www.justice.gov.uk* and *http://www.dca.gov.uk*) sets
out (in CPR 5.4–5.4D) the documents which can be obtained from court files, this availability being different for requests by parties and by non-parties to a particular dispute.
These rules apply also to the Patents County Court. Under these provisions, a party to the
proceedings, or a person identified in a claim form, may apply to the court for an order
restricting persons from obtaining such copies, even a copy of the claim form. Only the
claim form (but not the accompanying statement of case) and judgments and orders in the
proceedings are available, other than to parties to the proceedings or with the leave of the
court (CPR 5.4C, and see also CPR 5 PD 5A). To attempt to obtain unauthorised access to
court files constitutes a contempt of court (*Dobson v Hastings* [1992] Ch. 394; [1992] 2
All E.R. 94).

Copies of documents having a bearing on validity may be supplied from court records relating to a discontinued patent action to a third party commercially active in a technical field to which the patent relates, as this would allow them to make sensible commercial decisions (*Pfizer v Schwarz* [2010] EWHC 3236 (Pat)).

Availability of information on European patents and applications and on international applications

118.08   The EPC and its Implementing Regulations contain similar provisions relating to information obtainable from the files of European patent applications, see arts 127 and 128 of the EPC and r.143 of the EPC. The EPO Bulletin is published weekly on-line and contains the information specified by these provisions. The European Patent Register (*register.epo.org*) provides online file inspection for patent applications handled by the EPO, including detailed information of dates of all examination reports, responses, dates of other communications (e.g. notices of appeal filed), payment of maintenance fees, etc. The information relating to the official part of the database (i.e. that kept in accordance with arts 127 and 128 of the EPC) is updated each week and is more up-to-date than the official *European Patent Bulletin*. The (unofficial) information relating to the progress of a European patent application is updated in a different manner, but is said by the EPO to be up-to-date. At least for more recently filed applications, the full file of the application (and any opposition) can be inspected, and links to cited patent documents in the Espacenet database (see below) are provided.

The European Patent Register can be searched in various ways including by application or publication number, by name of the applicant/patentee, by application or priority date, by representative name, and under the classification codes of the International Patent Classification.

The Register Alert service (formerly WebRegMT) is an online alerting service which allows users to monitor the development of patent applications at the EPO. Again, access is free.

In relation to international applications filed before July 1, 1998, the only information or copies which can be obtained from WIPO are a copy of the priority document(s), the international application as published and the date of filing of any demand for international preliminary examination, each of which can be obtained on request in writing from the International Bureau in Geneva (see §89.13) after the international application has been published. Procedural information, including the date of filing of any demand for international preliminary examination and of states not elected, is available from the *PCT Gazette* which is published fortnightly. Information on international patent applications is also available on the Espacenet database.

In relation to international applications filed on or after July 1, 1998, third parties may additionally obtain a copy of any document in the file of the International Bureau except for documents relating to international preliminary examination, and again only after the international application has been published.

Changes in the PCT Regulations effective from July 1, 1998 have enabled an elected office to request copies from the International Preliminary Examining Authority of any document in its file, provided the application was filed after that date (PCT r.94.2); and the files of an international application held by an elected office are now open to inspection by third parties to the same extent as the files of that office themselves may be available for inspection under the applicable national law (PCT r.94.3). This means that the files of a Euro-PCT application are now open to inspection in the same way as are European applications following their publication.

The UK-IPO has asked the International Bureau (under new r.94.1(c) of the PCT) to supply it with copies of Preliminary Examination Reports for international applications which have been published (see *Patents Journal* December 31, 2003). These should therefore become available on the UK-IPO file as and when the international application enters the UK national phase.

Searches for worldwide published patent documents and information on patents and patent applications can be carried out on the EPO's Esp@cenet database, accessible for free (*worldwide.espacenet.com*). The Esp@cenet® database provides links to patents and applications in which a patent or application has been cited as a prior art document by the EPO. Much information concerning patents in most countries is also available via the IN-PADOC service administered by the EPO. This is based on the same raw data as the Esp@cenet database. However, unlike the "also published as" feature in Esp@cenet, which only shows almost identical documents, an INPADOC family search should retrieve all documents relating in any way to the root document.

Exceptions from copyright protection

No infringement of copyright occurs when copies of documents are made available at **118.09** the request of a third party from the file of a patent or published application by an appropriate person (e.g. by the Comptroller), see ss.47, 48 and 50(1) of the CDPA 1988. The saving provision of s.47 of the CDPA 1988 has been extended to copies produced by the Comptroller of documents open to public inspection in the EPO under the EPC or at WIPO under the PCT (Copyright (Material Open to Public Inspection) (International Organisations) Order 1989 SI 1989/1098). Furthermore, under the CDPA 1988 s.47(3), the Comptroller has authorised the copying of specifications of United Kingdom patents and patent applications laid open to public inspection pursuant to statutory requirements, and also English translations of European patents (UK) filed at the UK-IPO under s.77, "for the purpose of disseminating information about matters of general scientific interest, technical, commercial or economic interest": *Patents Journal* March 6, 1991.

It is understood, however, that the UK-IPO has been advised that providing full online file inspection is prevented by copyright law. In January 2011 the UK-IPO issued a consultation document proposing a new s.118A to provide an exception to copyright infringement for documents made available for inspection under s.118(1), which would permit full online access to the public file. The IPO has since launched an interim service known as Ipsum (*http://www.ipo.gov.uk/p-ipsum.htm*), providing online access to documents on the public file published on or after January 1, 2008, i.e. with a publication number of GB2439518 or greater. At present, this does not include some documents sent to the IPO. For documents unavailable on Ipsum, see *http://www.ipo.gov.uk/p-ipsum/p-ipsum-documents.htm*. For a copy of all available documents forming part of the public file for an application, a request with PF 23 is therefore still required (see §118.19).

Access to register and to documents filed at the UK-IPO (subs.(1))

Subsection (1) gives the right to obtain information and inspect documents of, or relat- **118.10** ing to, a patent or an application for a patent after its publication under s.16. The information which can be requested by a specific enquiry in relation to patents and applications under the Act is set out in r.54(5)–(7) (see §118.05, above). By r.54(1) and (4), a request for information under r.54 is made on PF 49; a separate form is required in respect of each item of information required. A request for such information is often called a caveat.

Rule 51 (see reprint, above) provides that all documents filed or kept at the UK-IPO in relation to a published application, or to a patent granted thereon, can be inspected subject to certain specified restrictions. The restrictions are set out in r.51. As the register for all 1977 Act patents and published applications is now computerised using the UK-IPO OPTICS database, a register extract for 1977 Act patents and published applications is presented in the form of a printout from the OPTICS system and is now available free of charge from the UK-IPO website. Information about the status of a supplementary protection certificate is obtainable by telephone enquiry to the UK-IPO helpline (tel. 08459 500505).

Enquiries about the date of payment of a renewal fee may be made to the UK-IPO (either in London or at Newport). A record of the renewal fees paid on all patents in force is also kept on the OPTICS system, and thus the information is also now in the form of a printout from the OPTICS system and it may conveniently be obtained by an internet enquiry as indicated above. Such an enquiry may be made informally, but, if a certificate of renewal fee payment is required, PF 23 has to be used, see §118.19. Such enquiry is usefully combined with a request for copy documents from a file or for information from the register. This request (unless made informally, e.g. by telephone) now attracts a fee (currently £5) whether or not a written copy is requested on PF 23. The request may be made for this fee to be met from a deposit account, for which see §123.64.

When inspecting the United Kingdom register to ascertain the status of a European patent (UK), it must be remembered that the patent may be the subject of an opposition in the EPO which remains unresolved either by the Opposition Division or on appeal. It is therefore prudent always to inspect the EPO online file via the online European Patent Register, for which see §118.08.

If a document is physically within the UK-IPO (even though initially filed in the Chancery Chambers as additional evidence in appeal proceedings), the Comptroller has, in view of s.32(11)(b), no discretion to refuse inspection, provided that neither of r.51(2) or (3) (for which see §118.02) applies (*Marley's Patent* BL O/91/93, noted I.P.D. 16155). For a similar reason, the Patents Court has upheld the Comptroller's decision that evidence filed during subsequently abandoned proceedings for revocation (under the 1949 Act s.33) should not be removed from the file and returned to the parties as had been requested (*Wisconsin Alumni Research Foundation's Patent* BL C/45/88).

In *Haberman v Comptroller* [2004] R.P.C. 21 at 414 the claimant sought from the Patents Court an order for the Comptroller to receive evidence and determine the date of withdrawal of a UK application. A subsequent European application, claiming priority from a later-filed UK application, had been found not entitled to its claimed priority date (and as a consequence had been revoked), on the ground that at the time of filing the UK priority application the earlier UK application had not been withdrawn as required by art.87(4) of the EPC. There was uncertainty about the date of withdrawal because of possible errors in the attorney's files, and the UK-IPO had been unable to confirm the date of withdrawal because its own files relating to the withdrawn application had been destroyed in accordance with its normal practice. The deputy judge held that he had sympathy with the claimant, seeing no purpose in the requirement for withdrawal of the earlier application prior to filing of the later, but was unable to assist. Given that the question of entitlement to priority would be a matter for the EPO to determine, he said that her recourse was "to trust in the good sense of the Board of Appeal and those other tribunals before whom the question of the priority date may come".

—Documents available concerning pre-1977 Patents Act patents

118.11   The only information that can now be obtained as of right from the file of a pre-1977 Patents Act patent is the result of searches made under ss.7 and 8 of the 1949 Patents Act (1968 Rules r.32 as amended and PF 8). A request for inspection of any other document from the file of an existing patent that has not been destroyed (for which see §118.19) will be considered by the UK-IPO on its individual merits.

Unpublished applications (subss.(2) and (3))

118.12   Subsection (2) provides that documents or information relating to a patent application shall not be available for inspection or otherwise published until after the application has been published under s.16, but this is subject to the exceptions of subss.(3)–(5).

Subsection (3) empowers the Comptroller to provide or otherwise publish information in certain specified circumstances, notwithstanding the restrictions of subs.(2). In particular, the Comptroller may forward information to the European Patent Office as required by any provision of the European Patent Convention and confirms the right of the Secretary of State to inspect or authorise the inspection of an unpublished application for the purposes of security as required under s.22, for which see §22.05.

Furthermore, the Comptroller may publish bibliographic data about unpublished applications to the limited extent prescribed, that is as to the matters set out in r.55 (see §118.06, above). Such data comprises: the application number; the application date; the priority details; the name(s) of the applicant(s); the title of the invention; and an indication if the application has been withdrawn. The first five of these items are generally published in the *Patents Journal* about five weeks after the application has been filed. The *Patents Journal* from April 2008 onwards can now be searched online on the UK-IPO website, and journals dated from August 12, 1998 to March 26, 2008 are available for viewing or downloading. Thus, it is possible in the United Kingdom (unlike in many other countries) to carry out a name search of applicants to obtain some basic details of patent applications which are as yet unpublished. The status of unpublished applications can also be searched online.

Subsection (3) also permits the Secretary of State further to inspect application papers in his annual review of the continuance of a secrecy order pursuant to s.22(5)(c), for which see §22.05.

—Inspection of unpublished applications (subss.(4) and (5))

Subsection (4) provides that, where a person has been warned that proceedings will be **118.13** instituted for infringement of a patent to be granted on an application not published at the date of the warning, the person warned may inspect the UK-IPO file. Subsection (5) relates to a further circumstance in which the documents of an unpublished application can be examined. In the case of a divisional application, or an application filed as a result of an order made under the entitlement provisions of s.8, if that later application but not the earlier application has been published, the earlier application can be inspected as though it had been published.

A request for inspection in the circumstances of subs.(4) or (5) can be made by a written request, although PF 23 can also be used. In the case of an application under subs.(4), a statutory declaration as the evidence required by r.52(1) (see §118.03, above) should be filed at the same time, and compliance with the request is delayed until the applicant has been notified of the request (r.52(2) and (3)), see §118.03. No evidence is required to support a request under subs.(5), but note that r.52 does not apply under this subsection; nor does subs.(5) extend to permit the inspection of the file of an unpublished application from which priority under s.5 has been claimed.

It is not apparent whether the applicant of the relevant application under subs.(4) or (5) may, on receipt of notice of the request and any accompanying documents, contest the request for inspection, e.g. by disputing the statements of the person making the request, since neither the Act nor the Rules makes any specific provision for inter partes proceedings in such circumstances. Thus, in *Buralls of Wisbech Ltd's Applications* [2004] R.P.C. 14, the hearing officer refused a request from the patent applicant to impose confidentiality restrictions on the inspection of documents.

In *Saunders' Application* BL O/144/92, where entitlement proceedings under s.8 or 12 had been commenced in relation to an unpublished application, the Comptroller felt unable to order that, in the absence of consent from the applicant, a referrer should be permitted to inspect the file of an unpublished application against which he had filed an entitlement reference, this not being a circumstance to which subs.(5) applies.

It is not clear what record, if any, will be made of the actual inspection of any documents in accordance with the provisions of subs.(4) or (5), as distinct from authority to inspect having been given, and there may be some ambiguity as to the effect of a nominal publication of this kind in consideration of patent novelty in countries abroad and, in view of r.52, the effective date of such publication.

Documents not available for inspection (r.51(2) and (3))

As already mentioned in §118.10, r.51(2) and (3) (see §118.02, above) place restric- **118.14** tions on what can be inspected in the UK-IPO file. In particular, the following documents are excluded from inspection by an absolute bar: internal UK-IPO papers; and requests for information. In addition, unless in a particular case the Comptroller otherwise directs, the following documents are excluded from inspection:

(a) documents filed in connection with applications under ss.40 and 41 (compensation of inventors), although it is understood that decisions on such applications will be made available;

(b) documents which are treated as confidential by the UK-IPO on request under r.53;

(c) any documents issued by the UK-IPO which the Comptroller considers should be treated as confidential;

(d) documents relating to PCT applications where the International Bureau would not be permitted to allow access to that document under the PCT; or

(e) where the name and/or address of an inventor has been allowed not to be published, documents from which his name and address can be identified.

Paragraph (4) ensures that all references in the rule to a document apply to any part of a document.

Rule 51(3)(c) provides the Comptroller with very wide power and could be used to restrict inspection of published specifications. A similar rule (1968 Rules r.158) was introduced in 1975, when it was discovered that specifications describing the preparation of a banned hallucinogenic drug and a chemical warfare agent had been published.

Rule 51(2)(d) specifically bars public inspection any part of a document which, in the Comptroller's opinion, disparages any person; or which would, if published or exploited, be generally expected to encourage offensive, immoral or anti-social behaviour. The previous rule (1995 Rules r.93(6)) preventing appeal of a decision of the Comptroller under this provision has been removed. Apparently, the reason for the rule against derogatory material was a fear by the Comptroller that he might be held liable under the law of defamation for publishing a derogatory statement, but it is probable that any such publication would be the subject of a proper claim to privilege as arising from a publication made in pursuance of a statutory duty.

Confidentiality

118.15 Rule 53 (see §118.04, above) provides for documents or parts of documents lodged at the UK-IPO to be treated as confidential and therefore not available for public inspection. By r.53(1), where a document (other than a patent form) is filed at or sent to the UK-IPO, and the person filing or sending the document or any party to the proceedings to which the document relates so requests, giving reasons, within 14 days of the filing or sending of the document, the Comptroller may then direct that the document be treated as confidential and not laid open to public inspection while the matter is being determined.

There is no longer a general rule preventing public disclosure of all documents filed at the UK-IPO for 14 days. This is a consequence of the move within the UK-IPO to electronic files. The software used, as developed by the EPO, automatically enters all documents filed into the public access electronic file. Therefore, a request for a document to be treated as a confidential document should be made on filing and should be very prominent. Where such a request is made, the document is not placed on the public file until a ruling has been given on the request. If a request for a document to be treated as a confidential document is made later within the 14-day period, the document will be removed from the public file while the request is considered. However, it is likely that the document would, at least temporarily, have been made available to the public.

It is also clearly prudent to indicate to any party to whom the document is sent that the document is to be treated as "confidential", at least until the Comptroller has given a ruling.

Rule 53(7) makes it clear that the request for confidentiality, or the order for it, may be in terms of part of the document.

Since the public is generally entitled to inspect documents relating to a patent or, after publication of an application, relating to the application, a request for confidentiality is granted only when it is considered justified for the reasons given in the request. The MOPP indicates that observations by an applicant in response to an official objection (e.g. of lack of novelty or inventive step), communications concerning disclosure of matter obtained unlawfully or in breach of confidence and third party observations should not be treated as confidential, but that information concerning individuals' health or personal circumstances is likely to be treated as confidential.

For instance, in inter partes proceedings, evidence filed by one party, such as details of licence agreements, may be treated as confidential if its disclosure risks being harmful (e.g. commercially) to the party to an extent which overrides the requirement for public access. However, mere statements of the kind that the material in question "contains sensitive commercial information" are regarded as too vague to give good grounds for consideration and do not necessarily justify confidentiality; a more precise indication of the reasons should be given (*Diamond Shamrock's Patent* [1987] R.P.C. 91). In this case, the Patents Court allowed information to remain confidential where its disclosure would be against the wish of a third party and would have no relevance to any interest of the public in the case.

It should be noted that r.53 only deals with a request to keep documents off the file for public inspection. Where, in inter partes proceedings, it is desired that the other party should itself have restricted access to documents for which confidentiality under r.53 is being requested, it should be made clear that such is an additional request. Good reasons will have to be given and it is unlikely that the Comptroller would agree that even the legal representatives of the other party should not be permitted to see the document. However, where a confidentiality order is imposed under r.53 beyond non-availability of the document in the publicly available file, disclosure is quite commonly limited to specified categories of persons, independent of the other parties to the proceedings, for which see §61.67 where confidentiality orders imposed by the court are more generally discussed. For some examples of orders for restricted access to documents in inter partes proceedings, see §46.20.

In proceedings to settle a licence of right (*Knutsson and Björk's Patent* [1996] R.P.C. 461), the patentee requested that its main declaration, and all the exhibits thereto, should not only be kept off the public file but also that only the applicant's legal advisers and one named independent expert should be permitted to see these and then only after signing an undertaking not to use the information for any other purpose. The Comptroller noted that the exhibits contained details of other licences of a comparable nature, and that the patentee was seeking to rely upon its own profits. It was considered that the public interest required that information on these points should not be kept from them unless a clear case for non-disclosure were made out, following the principles enunciated in *Diamond Shamrock's Patent* (above). Consequently, only a few sentences of the evidence were held to be confidential, and even these could be used in parallel proceedings in the Patents County Court without further leave.

The Comptroller has refused an order for confidentiality in respect of evidence filed where that evidence had previously been before the Patents Court without any suggestion that it was to be treated as confidential in those proceedings (*Coal Industry's Patent* BL O/11/90, noted I.P.D. 13081). However, in *Dines' Patent* BL O/231/99 some of the evidence given in restoration proceedings, including part of the transcript of the proceedings, was of a sensitive nature and was made subject to confidentiality restrictions.

The importance of requesting confidentiality of documents filed in proceedings before the Comptroller is illustrated by *David Singer Design's Patent* BL O/13/96. Here, in entitlement proceedings, information was disclosed which was missing from the patent-in-suit, thereby making it invalid for insufficiency. Amendment could not be permitted because this would add subject-matter contrary to s.76, nor could a fresh application be made because of the public disclosure in the papers of the entitlement proceedings, for which no confidentiality request had been made.

In *University of Southampton's Applications* BL O/444/02 and O/456/02, confidentiality orders as to issues involving a third party were refused, on the principle that the subject-matter in issue should be in the public domain, but the university was given time to decide whether it wished to withdraw its evidence as an alternative to making the information public.

Under the analogous provisions of art.128(4) and r.144(d) of the EPC, the EPO has excluded medical documents and other information about personal circumstances of the applicant, inventor or representative from inspection, although other, commercial, reasons will almost certainly not be sufficient for the EPO to keep that matter confidential ("Information from the EPO" OJ EPO 1985, 316). The general rule in the EPO is that documents filed as evidence in opposition proceedings must remain on the file during those proceedings and for at least five years afterwards, but there can be an exception when the filing party itself wishes to have the document withdrawn, unconsidered, when its interest prevails over those of the other parties to the opposition and that of the public interest, for example where the documents were filed in breach of a court confidentiality order, did not refer to the state of the art, and the other parties agreed with the request (T 760/89 *BURLINGTON/Return of documents* OJ EPO 1994, 797; (1995) E.P.O.R. 224). Previously, in T 516/89 *SCHERING/Confidential papers* OJ EPO 1992, 136; [1992] E.P.O.R. 476, papers marked confidential were returned to the party concerned without taking any note of their contents.

The period of 14 days allowed under r.53(3)(a) can be extended under r.108(1). If the extension is granted after the expiry of the original 14 days allowed, there is no right to inspect during the extended period or until the matter is determined by the Comptroller (r.53(4)). Any person affected by a request for confidentiality, or revocation of a confidentiality direction under para.(6), is entitled to be heard before a decision adverse to that person is made under r.53, see s.101 and §101.04.

Under r.53(2), no request for confidentiality may be made as regards a Patents Form or any document filed in connection with a request for an opinion under s.74A.

Although it is no longer required by the rules (as under the 1995 Rules r.94(3)), the Comptroller will continue to consult the person who made a request for a document to be treated as confidential (where possible) before revoking any direction.

Very rarely, confidential treatment can be accorded for a limited period only.

Rule 51(2)(b) provides an exclusion period before inspection of documents under s.118(4) (inspection of an unpublished application by a person threatened with infringement proceedings under a patent granted on that application). The exclusion period is 14 days beginning with the date of notification of the applicant under r.52(2).

PRACTICE UNDER SECTION 118

Information given on request

118.16   Information under r.54(5)–(7) is obtained by filing PF 49 (r.54(1)). This is often called a caveat (a formal notice or caution) and is usually filed for information about a possible future event. This form can be used likewise to obtain information in respect of European patents (UK) and patents granted on international applications, and also in respect of applications for supplementary protection certificates and other proceedings involving these (for which see §118.18), but not in respect of applications for European patents.

A separate form and fee are required in respect of each item of information requested.

An answer to a request under r.54(5)(b) as to when a specification of a United Kingdom application has been published will include the case where that specification has been made available as a priority document in the file of a subsequent application upon publication of the later application.

—Wording on caveats

118.17   It is important to note that a caveat request under r.54, made on PF 49 (current fee £25), is exhausted as soon as one answer has resulted, even if an event giving rise to a second answer subsequently occurs. Thus, careful wording of caveats is required to minimise the number necessary to cover eventualities, and it may be necessary to file a further caveat once an initial caveat has elicited a response.

A caveat can also be filed for information whether a request for one or more certified copies of the application has been requested, even if the application has been withdrawn, provided that the application has been published. Such request may assist in ascertaining whether corresponding foreign applications, for example a European or international application, were filed. However, the UK-IPO will probably not indicate for what countries the copies have been requested, but that information may perhaps be available on the file of the application which can be inspected if published, for which see §32.38 and §118.15 and (1980–81) 10 *CIPA* 411.

The UK-IPO has indicated that it is prepared to consider any request for information and to respond to such request if satisfied that it falls within the provisions of r.54. For example, the Office has agreed to accept a caveat in respect of the possibility of a lapsed patent being revived under previous provisions corresponding to r.108(3), and a caveat may be filed for information concerning a supplementary protection certificate, for which see §118.18.

It is important to note that the information given in response to a caveat request is correct only as at the date on which it is given, and that, in particular, leave may subsequently be given under r.108(3) to extend the period for taking any action which has not been timely taken, for which see §§123.69 et seq., so that an application indicated to be treated as withdrawn might subsequently be revived under this rule. Presumably, it is also possible to file a caveat to be informed if a request has been made under r.108(3) to extend retrospectively a time limitation period that has apparently expired.

Information concerning Supplementary Protection Certificates ("SPCs")

Information concerning the status of SPCs is available from the UK-IPO website, via **118.18** the searchable *Patents Journal* or a dedicated SPC search service. Information concerning revocation actions and other legal proceedings on an SPC is included in the status information record of the relevant patent.

Section 128B and Sch.4A deal with Supplementary Protection Certificates and applications for them. Caveats in respect of an application for, or a granted SPC can be filed under r.54 for events which apply to SPCs. Rule 54(7)(d) is particularly relevant to SPCs, since the following events occurring with these are published in the *Patents Journal*, and the Office will thus be able to respond to requests for information concerning them, i.e. information concerning:

— the filing of an application for an SPC;

— the grant of an SPC;

— rejection of an application for an SPC;

— entry into force of an SPC (which is consequent upon payment of the necessary fees);

— lapse of an SPC;

— termination of lapse of an SPC for withdrawal of marketing authorisation; and

— declaration of invalidity of an SPC.

For suitable economical wording for caveats for information in these categories, see J.M. Davies [1994] *CIPA* 11.

If a request for other information concerning a possible SPC is made, it is understood that the UK-IPO would consider the request and comply if possible or otherwise notify the requester that it is not considered possible for the UK-IPO to comply with the request.

Inspection of register and file

All files are stored at the UK-IPO in Newport, Wales, but a public search room exists at **118.19** 21 Bloomsbury Street, London, WC1B 3HF, at which register and file inspections may be made. However, preferably at least 48 hours' notice is required for files to be transported from Newport to London for inspection in London. Prior applications should therefore be made to the search room by telephone (tel. 020 7596 6530). Files and register entries may also be inspected at Newport (tel. 01633 814560 or 814657). Inspection is also possible of ex-PCT applications between valid entry into the national phase and republication of the ex-PCT United Kingdom application: see (1990–91) 20 *CIPA* 414. Photocopying facilities are available in the London search room which can be used to obtain uncertified copies of papers from inspected files after purchase from the search room of a pre-paid photocopy card. Alternatively, the file can be returned to Newport and the requested copies dispatched from there.

Patent files are kept for at least seven years following termination (i.e. abandonment, lapsing, withdrawal, revocation, expiry, etc.) of the application or patent. Where there has been a divisional or replacement application, the file is retained until the demise of that application or patent granted on it; and, likewise, where there is a supplementary protection certificate granted on a patent, the file of that patent is retained for seven years after the demise of the SPC. Also, the UK-IPO maintains files of applications and patents which are seen as having established some legal precedent for at least 25 years from the date of the application. Moreover, where the Comptroller has issued a decision during the life of the patent/application, a copy of this may be available in a separate file maintained by the Legal Secretariat (for which see §101.12) from whom it may be possible to obtain a certified copy of the decision should this be required.

A request to inspect the register or a file, or to obtain information on the payment of a renewal fee now requires no form or fee. Indeed, the register is now most conveniently accessed (free of charge) via the UK-IPO website *http://www.ipo.gov.uk*, as described more fully in §32.34. Details of granted European patents (UK) can be obtained in the same way, see §32.35. The register of supplementary protection certificates is a separate register, but information concerning the existence and status of SPCs is available online, see §118.18.

Requests for copies of documents held on patent files, or uncertified copies of extracts from the register, should be made in writing to Room GY25, The UK-IPO, Cardiff Road, Newport, Gwent NP10 8QQ, or by fax to 01633 817777 (*Patents Journal* May 14, 1997). Such requests must be accompanied by PF 23 and by the required fee (currently £5, which includes the cost of providing the copy document requested, irrespective of its length, see rr.46 and 48). Where certified copies are requested, a separate PF 23 is required for each patent/application, but for uncertified copies a single PF 23 suffices for a plurality of requests. Certified and uncertified copies should not be requested on the same PF 23. Holders of a deposit account at the UK-IPO may make such a request by submitting the PF 23 by fax and requesting deduction of the fee from their deposit account, the number of which must then be quoted. On request, uncertified copies will be sent by fax to the holder of a deposit account at an additional cost, currently £1 per page. For the setting up and use of a deposit account for the payment of UK-IPO fees, see §123.64.

Since June 2002, the papers on the UK-IPO files which are open to public inspection have been recorded in electronic form. A direction under s.124A (available together with notes and guidance on the UK-IPO website) provides for on-line filing of PF 23. This can be done via links from the website. Note that it is not possible to use the UK-IPO's online service to request a paper uncertified copy or to request an electronic uncertified copy by filing a paper Form 23.

Payment (currently £5) can be made on-line from a deposit account or by credit or debit card. Documents are sent by email (on CD if over 10 MB). It is understood that there are currently no plans for full online file inspection at the UK-IPO for copyright reasons.

Requests for a copy of a register extract and/or information of a renewal fee payment may be made, and PF 23 (as well as a caveat request on PF 49, as to which see §118.17) may be filed, each by an agent without disclosing the identity of his principal. None of these requests and forms for file inspection themselves become open to subsequent inspection (r.51(1)(c)).

As the register is now computerised for patents in force and for pending applications, a request for inspection of the register will normally be met by providing a copy of the entry from the UK-IPO "OPTICS" database which for a patent automatically contains the date when the last renewal fee was paid if the patent remains in force. The same information is available from the UK-IPO website *http://www.ipo.gov.uk*.

Whilst a copy of a priority document, for example, may be obtained by a simple written request, certified copies of priority documents can be obtained only by using PF 23, see §32.38.

To obtain the results of a search made under ss.7 and 8 of the 1949 Act, see §118.11.

As a matter of administrative convenience, PF 12 (filed when a renewal fee is paid) is not placed on the patent file, nor are copies of the statutory reminder letters on non-payment of renewal fees issued under rr.39(3) and 41. However, it is understood that these forms can be made available for inspection if a specific request is made for them.

If an application has not yet been published under s.16, PF 23 will be accepted only if filed by the applicant or his previously authorised agent. Where a request for inspection of documents in the special circumstances of s.118(4) is made, the request on PF 23 must be accompanied by evidence of the facts and any supporting material which the Comptroller may require (r.52(1)). The Comptroller then sends a copy of the documents to the applicant in question (r.52(2)), and compliance with the request is delayed for 14 days (r.51(2)(b)).

Requesting confidentiality

Any request for confidentiality under r.53(1) should be made at the same time as the **118.20** document is filed to prevent publication from taking place. A later request for confidentiality (within the 14 day period permitted by r.53(3)(a)) is unlikely to prevent temporary publication from taking place (see §118.15). This is all the more so since the inception of the online publication service Ipsum, see §118.02, above. A request by the person filing the document should be by letter accompanying it, and parties to whom copies of the documents are sent directly should be sent a copy of that letter or otherwise informed of the request. Sometimes it will be such a recipient who will wish to seek an order under r.53, and any such request should be made promptly and, in any event, within 14 days of the date of filing; preferably, any such letter should be marked "URGENT" and supported by a telephone request and notification to the party which filed the document in question.

It is quite common in making requests for confidentiality not only to seek to keep documents off the public file under r.53, but also to seek restricted availability to other parties to the proceedings in which the document has been lodged, for example, by seeking to limit availability to the legal advisors, including patent attorneys, of the parties. As indicated in §118.15, such an order will be made only where there are strong reasons for so doing, such as when information in the document would disclose valuable commercial information to a competitor. For examples, see §61.67.

Where a patent attorney is an employee of a party who is to be restricted as to access, he has been required to give undertakings to receive the documents solely in a personal professional capacity, not to copy then and to return them at the end of the proceedings; and his employer has been required to give an undertaking not to seek disclosure from him, see *Unilever v Pearce* [1985] F.S.R. 475 and *Schering A.G.'s Patent* [1986] R.P.C. 30. Presumably, similar undertakings would be required if an employee solicitor were involved in the proceedings.

Where possible, a request for confidentiality should be sought for only part of a document, and a copy of that document, with the confidential part or parts obliterated, should be supplied so that this "masked" copy document can be placed in the public file, as was ordered in *Marley's Patent* BL O/91/93, noted I.P.D. 16155. Alternatively, the confidential information can sometimes be conveniently presented in an exhibit for which confidentiality can then be requested as a separate document.

The person who made the request will be notified when the request has been allowed.

SECTION 119

Service by post

119. Any notice required or authorised to be given by this Act or rules, and any **119.01** application or other document so authorised or required to be made or filed, may be given, made or filed by post.

COMMENTARY ON SECTION 119

Scope of the section

119.02   Section 119 provides for the sending of notices and documents by post. For the address of the UK-IPO, see §123.88.

Rule 110 (reprinted at §123.28) makes provision for interruptions of the postal services or the normal operation of the UK-IPO, permitting the Comptroller to extend periods allowed for any acts to the day which follows the end of the interruption of services, see §123.78 and §123.79. For the computation of time limits, see §123.77.

The MOPP specifies that s.119 does not preclude other methods of filing documents, e.g. by hand; or by facsimile transmission ("fax"), for which see §119.05. Filing of documents by hand can be done at the special counter at 21 Bloomsbury Street, London, WC1B 3HF, for which see §123.41. Documents can be sent to the UK-IPO by private courier service. The reference to "post" is construed widely to mean any item of mail delivered by any service in exchange for payment (not necessarily by the Post Office).

Rules 110 and 111 are respectively reprinted at §123.28 and §123.29. Rule 110 extends time limits where events or circumstances cause an interruption in the normal operation of the UK-IPO, as well as any general dislocation in the postal services of the United Kingdom. When this occurs the days involved are called "interrupted days", provided that they have been certified as such. There is then an automatic extension to the next day which is not an "interrupted day" or is a day which is an "excluded day" under s.120 (for which see §120.03 and §120.04). Rule 110 does not apply to dislocations in foreign postal services nor to services which are not "by post", although on this see §119.03 below.

Rule 111 further provides for extension of any period of time specified in the Act or the Rules where the Comptroller is satisfied that the failure to do something was "wholly or mainly attributable to a delay in, or failure of, a communication service". Such service means "a service by which documents may be sent or delivered and includes service by post, electronic communication or courier" (r.111(3)) and is thus broadly defined. However, where r.111 is sought to be applied to inter partes proceedings, a time extension under it is only made after giving other parties to the proceedings such notice as the Comptroller thinks appropriate and to such conditions as he may think it appropriate to impose (r.111(2)).

Since January 2, 2001, it has also been possible to file documents at the UK-IPO by sending them to Hays Document Exchange addressed to "DX 722540 CLEPPA PARK 3". Receipt at that address is deemed to be receipt at the UK-IPO, see *Patents Journal* January 3, 2001. Filing in this way is not, however, regarded as a use of the "post".

Delivery in the ordinary course of post

119.03   Section 7 of the Interpretation Act 1978 (c.30) requires that s.119 is applicable only when a letter containing the document(s) in question has been properly addressed and posted with pre-paid postage. Thus, delivery of documents to the UK-IPO made by an employee of a patent attorney does not constitute "service by post" (*Fujisawa's Application* [1978] F.S.R. 187). Handing a letter to a clerk for subsequent posting is not in itself "service by post" (*S and B's Application* BL O/1/85).

Documents are accorded the date of receipt at the UK-IPO. Where a communication sent by post is received on an excluded day it is treated as having been received on the next non-excluded day.

By contrast, under the former r.97 of the 1995 Rules, documents sent to the UK-IPO by post were deemed delivered on the day when they would have arrived "in the ordinary course of post". This applied to any document posted prior to December 17, 2007. The Comptroller regarded first class post as arriving on the first working day after posting provided that the post mark was legible and second class post (including that sent under official paid labels and foreign mail) as arriving four working days (excluding Saturdays, Sundays and Bank Holidays) after posting. It is understood that the Comptroller ante-dated first-class mail automatically to the first working day after posting provided that the post mark was legible, but that there was no corresponding ante-dating of second-class mail. Most Saturdays are working days of the UK-IPO, though only for certain purposes, see directions under s.120 (reprinted at §120.01, and §120.05). For the meaning of "post", see §119.03.

Care should be taken to post bulky documents in stout envelopes, as delays can occur when damage occurs during normal handling.

Postal delays under the EPC and the PCT

The PCT allows documents in relation to international applications sent at least five days before a due date to be deemed to have arrived in time to meet the due date, provided that the documents were sent by registered post, regardless of when (or if) the documents actually arrive (PCT r.82.1(a)). **119.04**

Rules 110 and 111 (discussed in §119.02) have no effect on communications with either the EPO or the International Bureau to which only the EPC or PCT rules have application.

PRACTICE UNDER SECTION 119

Filing by fax

Relevant information is provided on the UK-IPO website. Any document which is required to be filed at the UK-IPO may be transmitted by fax to a special telephone number: 01633 817777. The UK-IPO fax machines are open to receive transmissions on a continuous basis (24 hours a day, 7 days a week) and the time and date of receipt will be recorded automatically. The filing date accorded is the date of receipt if the UK-IPO is open for that class of documents at the time of receipt or, if not, the next working day. Users are requested not to submit confirmation copies of documents other than evidence and PCT applications unless requested to do so. Confirmation copies should be marked as such. **119.05**

When filing by fax, the sender is responsible for ensuring legibility. No checking of legibility of the fax is carried out by the UK-IPO on immediate receipt. Perhaps fax should be used only in cases where there is no other means for obtaining the required date because of the risks involved, especially with the transmission of drawings. Documents which might include information of relevance to national defence or security should not be transmitted by fax.

Where a document transmitted by fax requires a fee to be paid, the fee maybe paid by credit or debit card or from a deposit account. A fee sheet should be included in the fax transmission. Where a deposit account is used, the account must be in credit to the amount of the fee.

A fax-back service is available whereby the UK-IPO will fax back within 30 minutes a copy of the transmission received by the UK-IPO for a fee, though the service is available only on working days between 9 am and 4.30 pm. The fee for this "fax-back service" is currently £25. If this service is required, this should be mentioned on an accompanying fee sheet. Telephone enquiries concerning fax filing at the UK-IPO can be made to 01633 814570.

Advertisement of filing date

If a filing date has been altered as the result of a successful application under the former r.97 of the 1995 Rules, the *Patents Journal* and the BL card index will have nevertheless recorded the original date of filing. Consequently, in an important case, the date of filing recorded in these ways should be checked against the file of the application once this has been published. **119.06**

SECTION 120

Hours of business and excluded days

120.—(1) The Comptroller may give directions specifying [*Rules may* **120.01**

specify] the hour at which the Patent Office shall be taken to be closed on any day for purposes of the transaction by the public of business under this Act or any class of such business, and **the directions** may specify days as excluded days for any such purposes.

(2) Any business done under this Act on any day after the hour so specified in relation to business of that class, or on a day which is an excluded day in relation to business of that class, shall be taken to have been done on the next following day not being an excluded day; and where the time for doing anything under this Act expires on an excluded day that time shall be extended to the next following day not being an excluded day.

(3) Directions under this section shall be published in the prescribed manner.

Note. Section 120(1) was amended and s.120(3) added by the Patents Act 2004 (c.16) Sch.2 para.24. The amendments took effect from September 22, 2004 via the Patents Act 2004 (Commencement No.1 and Consequential and Transitional Provisions) Order 2004 (SI 2004/2177).

RELEVANT DIRECTIONS

Hours of Business and Excluded Days

120.02   (as updated to September 26, 2007)

Note. This Direction is reprinted from the UK-IPO website.

Before use, this website should be checked against the update date given above and, if different, the website version should be used instead of that given below. The update date is that given at the bottom of the left hand panel of this website.

Introduction

1. The comptroller has made the following Directions under section 120(1) of the Patents Act 1977.

2. These Directions come into force on 17 December 2007.

Interpretation

3. In these Directions:

"the Office" means the Patent Office;

"the Act" means the Patents Act 1977;

"business" means business transacted by the public under the Act or any class of such business;

"excluded day" means a day excluded for any such business or class of business;

"applications" means applications for patents filed under the Act;

"forms" means documents containing the information required by the relevant Patents Forms as set out in directions under section 123(2A) of the Act.

Hours of Business

4. The Office shall be deemed to be closed at the following hours for the transaction of business of the classes specified—

a) on weekdays other than Saturdays, at midnight for the filing of applications, forms and other documents, and at 5pm for all other business; and

b) on Saturdays, at 1pm for the filing of applications in respect of which no declaration for the purpose of section 5(2) of the Act is made.

Excluded Days

5. The following shall be excluded days for all purposes under the Act:

a) all Sundays

b) Good Friday and Christmas Day

c) any day specified as or proclaimed to be a bank holiday in England in or under section 1 of the Banking and Financial Dealings Act 1971; and

d) any Saturday immediately preceded by one of the above.

6. Saturdays not falling within paragraph 5 above shall be excluded days for all purposes except the filing of applications in respect of which no declaration for the purposes of section 5(2) is made.

7. Tuesday 4 January 2000 is an excluded day for all purposes under the Act.

Guidance notes to the Directions
(as updated to September 26, 2007)

Note. The UK-IPO Directions contain some guidance and explanatory notes, which are reprinted from the UK-IPO website.

Before use, the website should be checked against the update date given above and, if different, the website version should be used instead of that given below. The update date is that given at the bottom of the left hand panel of this website.

(a) These notes are not part of the Directions. They are intended to provide background and additional information.

(b) The Interpretation Act 1978 applies to these Directions. Therefore, all the definitions set out in that Act apply to these Directions. Further, amongst other things, generally any words importing the masculine gender include the feminine and words in the singular include the plural and words in the plural include the singular.

(c) Section 120(1) of the Patents Act allows the comptroller to give directions specifying the hours during which the Office is closed for the transaction of business under the Patents Act, and the days that are excluded for any such purposes. This power was brought in by the Patents Act 2004, which amended s.120 and came into force in September 2004 via the Patents Act 2004 (Commencement no. 1 and Consequential and Transitional Provisions) Order 2004 (SI 2004/2177). The power to give directions replaced the previous provision which authorised the making of rules to prescribe the days and hours when the Office is closed for business. Under the above Order, rules 98 and 99 of the Patents Rules 1995 were revoked and the comptroller was deemed to have given directions specifying the Office's hours of business and excluded days as being those specified in rules 98 and 99 immediately prior to being revoked.

(d) These Directions replace the directions that were deemed to have been given by virtue of the above Order. The Office's hours of business and excluded days remain unchanged.

(e) Any queries about these Directions should be addressed to Patents Legal Section:

> Concept House
> Cardiff Road
> Newport
> South Wales
> NP10 8QQ
> United Kingdom
> Tel: +44 (0)1633 814083

COMMENTARY ON SECTION 120

Scope of the section

Section 120 provides for the making of rules concerning the working times of the Intel- **120.03** lectual Property Office and concerning days which are to be *dies non*. Directions (see reprint, above) are made under s.120 and detail the hours and days during which documents may and may not be lodged at the UK-IPO. These directions are differential in character, i.e. specifying different hours for the receipt of new applications from those for other types of business. For the two official addresses of the UK-IPO, see §123.41 and §123.88.

Subsection (2) provides that any business done, or due to be done, on an excluded day is considered to have been done, or due to be done, on the next day not being an excluded day. Similar rules apply under the EPC and the PCT, see r.134(1) and (3) of the EPC and r.80.5 of the PCT.

Rule 110 (reprinted at §123.28 and discussed in §123.77 and §123.78) provides a separate power to deal with interruption of postal services and other disruptions of UK-IPO business, for example, as a result of strike action or weather problems. However, "excluded days" under the directions are not days which come under r.110 as involving a "general interruption in the post".

Rule 111 deals with extensions of time limits where there has been a dislocation in the normal operations of the UK-IPO or in the postal services or in some other communication service. These rules are reprinted at §123.28 and §123.29, and are discussed in §119.02. The definition of "excluded day" (see §120.04 below) applies in relation to the extent of a time extension which automatically arises under the new form of r.110.

Subsection (3) requires that these directions are to be "published in the prescribed manner". This is publication in the *Patents Journal* (under r.117(b)), but the directions are also published as a separate item on the UK-IPO website.

The statutory "excluded days"

120.04   The excluded days are defined as being: all Sundays; Good Friday and Christmas Day; the days specified as a "bank holiday" in England and Wales or under s.1 of the Banking and Financial Dealings Act 1971 (c.80); and any Saturday immediately preceded by one of those days; Tuesday, January 4, 2000 was also made an excluded day under the rule. Section 1(1) of this 1971 Act specifies the regular "bank holidays" as: Easter Monday; the last Monday in May; the last Monday in August; December 26, if not a Sunday; and December 27, in a year in which December 25 or 26 is a Sunday, unless a proclamation be issued to the contrary. In addition, there is a power to declare further "bank holidays" by proclamation. Since 1974, it has been customary to declare New Year's Day, and, since 1978, the first Monday in May, to be additional bank holidays.

The effect of the direction is that the UK-IPO is closed for all classes of business on the Saturday following Good Friday and Saturdays on which December 27 and January 2 falls. Thus, over the Christmas and Easter holiday periods, there are many days when it is not possible to secure a priority date by an initial filing at the UK-IPO. Perhaps in these circumstances, an initial filing in some other country could be made to secure priority over a projected disclosure of the invention (with permission then being sought retroactively under s.23(1) if necessary for the foreign filing).

From Monday to Friday, the front desk at the London branch of the UK-IPO is open from 9 am to 5 pm (*Patents Journal* May 6, 1998). The Direction is, apparently, interpreted by the UK-IPO as stipulating only minimum opening hours so that documents received while the UK-IPO is open for receipt of those documents are dated as and when received. In particular, the MOPP makes it clear that documents may be filed before 9 am. The UK-IPO is officially open on Saturdays only until 1 pm and then only for the filing of new applications with no priority claim. On Saturdays, and Mondays to Fridays after the hours of 5 pm (up to midnight) or before 9 am, it is necessary to hand the documents to the custodian at Newport, South Wales or at the London Branch. In the case of bulky packages, it may be possible to persuade the custodian to accept them, see *Patents Journal* August 5, 1992. Documents may also be filed by fax, see §119.05.

Note that applications likely to be subject to secrecy directions under s.22 may be filed in person at the Newport or London offices but only between the hours of 9 am and 5 pm (see also §22.09). Documents may also now be filed electronically, see §124A.03.

PRACTICE UNDER SECTION 120
The procedure for filing documents at the UK-IPO outside the hours of 9 am to 5 pm on **120.05**
Mondays to Fridays is as follows:

(1) All documents must be in sealed packages (inspection of the contents of packages is available on request until 7 pm at the London office)

(2) Packages must be handed to the custodian on duty at the Newport office (it may be necessary to telephone at the gatehouse to gain access) or in London as described above (§120.03).

(3) All packages handed in under the above procedures will be stamped with the date and time of receipt.

In all cases, payment must be enclosed for any fees which are due, see *Patents Journal* December 31, 1980.

SECTION 121

Comptroller's annual report

121. Before 1st **December** [*June*] in every **financial** year the comptroller shall **121.01** cause to be laid before both Houses of Parliament a report with respect to the execution of this Act and the discharge of his functions under the European Patent Convention[, the Community Patent Convention] and the Patent Co-operation Treaty, and every such report shall include an account of all fees, salaries and allowances, and other money received and paid by him under this Act, **that convention** [*those conventions*] and that treaty during the previous **financial year**.

Note. This section was amended as indicated by The Patents Act 2004 (c.16) Sch.2 para.25 and Sch.3 para.1 with effect from January 1, 2005 (SI 2004/3205, art.2(f), (g), (k)).

COMMENTARY ON SECTION 121

Section 121 requires the Comptroller to make an annual report to be placed before **121.02** Parliament. The section is in similar terms to provisions which have appeared in the patent statutes since the office of Comptroller was established in 1883 and now requires the report to include reference to the discharge of the functions of the Comptroller under the EPC and the PCT, and the accounts of fees, etc. must also refer to thisconvention and treaty. The report also covers matters arising under: the Trade Marks Act 1994 (c.26) s.71; and the Registered Designs Act 1949 (c.88) s.42, as amended for the purpose by Sch.5 para.3of the 1977 Act.

As a consequence of the UK-IPO acquiring "Trading Fund" status from October 1, 1991 (for which see §A20), the Comptroller's annual report is now prepared for each financial year ending March 31st and has to be presented to Parliament before November 30th, the 1991 report covering the extended period to March 31, 1992 (SI 1991/1796). The present form of the report contains the accounts of the UK-IPO and is now analogous in form to the annual report of a registered company as required under the Companies Acts.

The Comptroller's annual reports, copies of which may be inspected in the British Library or on the UK-IPO's website, provide a wealth of statistical data concerning the operations of the UK-IPO and, therefore, of the relative levels of activity from time to time occurring in relation to various provisions of the patent statutes, and of the geographical origin of applications filed. Much of this statistical data has been summarised, and commented upon, by N. Davenport in his book, *The United Kingdom patent system: A brief history* (Kenneth Mason, 1979) which also briefly summarised the historical development of the United Kingdom patent system. This book can still be obtained but has not been updated, so is of historical interest only.

The changes made to s.121, noted above, bring the date for the Comptroller's Annual Report into line with the Patent Office Trading Fund Order and are a consequence of the removal from the Act of references to the CPC which never came into force.

Supplemental [Sections 122–132]

SECTION 122

Crown's right to sell forfeited articles

122.01   122. Nothing in this Act affects the right of the Crown or any person deriving title directly or indirectly from the Crown to dispose of or use articles forfeited under the laws relating to customs or excise.

COMMENTARY ON SECTION 122

122.02   Section 122 provides that nothing in the Act affects the right of the Crown to dispose of articles seized by the Customs and Excise; and forfeited under the laws relating to customs and excise. Without this provision, such disposal would be an act of infringement of the patent having regard to the limited powers of the Crown as regards sale of patented products under s.55, see §55.17, nor would such disposal be absolved by s.129 which defines the liability of the Crown for acts of patent infringement, for which see §129.03.

SECTION 123

Rules

123.01   123.—(1) The Secretary of State may make such rules as he thinks expedient for regulating the business of the Patent Office in relation to patents and applications for patents (including European patents, applications for European patents and international applications for patents) and for regulating all matters placed by this Act under the direction or control of the comptroller; and in this Act, except so far as the context otherwise requires, "prescribed" means prescribed by rules and "rules" means rules made under this section.

(2) Without prejudice to the generality of subsection (1) above, rules may make provision—

   (a) prescribing the form and contents of applications for patents and other documents which may be filed at the Patent Office and requiring copies to be furnished of any such documents;

   (b) regulating the procedure to be followed in connection with any proceeding or other matter before the comptroller or the Patent Office and authorising the rectification of irregularities of procedure;

   (c) requiring fees to be paid in connection with any such proceeding or matter or in connection with the provision of any service by the Patent Office and providing for the remission of fees in the prescribed circumstances;

   (d) regulating the mode of giving evidence in any such proceeding and empowering the comptroller to compel the attendance of witnesses and the discovery [now "disclosure"] of and production of documents;

   (e) requiring the comptroller to advertise any proposed amendments of patents and any other prescribed matters, including any prescribed steps in any such proceeding;

(f) requiring the comptroller to hold proceedings in Scotland in such circumstances as may be specified in the rules where there is more than one party to proceedings under section 8, 12, 37, 40(1) or (2), 41(8), 61(3), 71 or 72 above;

(g) providing for the appointment of advisers to assist the comptroller in any proceeding before him;

(h) prescribing time limits for doing anything required to be done in connection with any such proceeding by this Act or the rules and providing for the alteration of any period of time specified in this Act or the rules;

(i) giving effect to an inventor's rights to be mentioned conferred by section 13, and providing for an inventor's waiver of any such right to be subject to acceptance by the comptroller; [*giving effect to the right of an inventor of an invention to be mentioned in an application for a patent for the invention*];

(j) without prejudice to any other provision of this Act, requiring and regulating the translation of documents in connection with an application for a patent or a European patent or an international application for a patent and the filing and authentication of any such translations;

[(k) *requiring the keeping of a register of patent agents and regulating the registration of patent agents and authorising in prescribed cases the erasure from the register of patent agents of the name of any person registered therein or the suspension of the right of any such person to act as a patent agent;*]

(l) providing for the publication and sale of documents in the Patent Office and of information about such documents.

(2A) The comptroller may set out in directions any forms the use of which is required by rules; and any such directions shall be published in the prescribed manner.

(3) Rules may make different provision for different cases.

(3A) It is hereby declared that rules—

(a) authorising the rectification of irregularities of procedure, or

(b) providing for any alteration of any period of time,

may authorise the comptroller to extend or further extend any period notwithstanding that the period has already expired.

[(4) *Rules prescribing fees shall not be made except with the consent of the Treasury.*]

[(5) *The remuneration of any adviser appointed under rules to assist the comptroller in any proceeding shall be determined by the Secretary of State with the consent of the Treasury and shall be defrayed out of moneys provided by Parliament.*]

(6) Rules shall provide for the publication by the comptroller of a journal (in this Act referred to as "the journal") containing particulars of applications for and grants of patents, and of other proceedings under this Act.

(7) Rules shall require or authorise the comptroller to make arrangements for the publication of reports of cases relating to patents, trade marks, [*service marks,*] [*and*] registered designs **or design right** decided by him and of cases relating to

patents (whether under this Act or otherwise), trade marks, [*service marks*,] registered designs, [*and*] copyright **and design right** decided by any court or body (whether in the United Kingdom or elsewhere).

Notes

1. Subsection (2)(k) was repealed by Sch.8 to the CDPA 1988, effective from August 13, 1990 (SI 1990/1400), but has effectively been replaced by CDPA 1988 s.275 reprinted at §275.01 and discussed in §§275.02–275.04.

2. Subsection (3A) was added by Sch.5 para.29 to the CDPA 1988, with the effect from November 15, 1988 (CDPA 1988 s.305(1)).

3. In subs.(7): the references to "service marks" were inserted by the Patents, Design and Trade Marks Act 1986 (c.39) s.2 and then removed by the Trade Marks Act 1994 (c.26) Sch.4 para.1(2) and Sch.5; and the other amendments to this subsection were made by Sch.7 para.22 to the CDPA 1988.

4. The Patents Act 2004 (c.16) Sch.2 para.26(3) and (4) inserted new subs.(2A) and deleted subss.(4) and (5). These provisions were given effect by SI 2004/2177 from September 22, 2004.

5. The same instrument amended subs.(2), with effect from October 1, 2005 (SI 2005/2471) by replacing para.(i) as indicated above.

123.02   *Note.* The rules relevant to particular sections of the Act are reprinted under each such section, and discussed as required in the commentary on that section. See pp.1327 et seq. for a concordance showing where each rule is reprinted. The rules reprinted below are not reprinted under any other sections and are therefore discussed here as required. These relate mainly to administrative matters and interpretation, the conduct of proceedings before the Comptroller, extentions of time limits, and the finishing of translations; see further §123.38.

RELEVANT RULES—RULES 1, 2, 4, 73–88, 102, 106–115, 117–120

Rule 1—Citation and commencement

123.03   **1.** These Rules may be cited as the Patents Rules 2007 and shall come into force on 17th December 2007.

Note. These Rules (SI 2007/3291) replace all of the previous Patents Rules applicable under the 1977 Act, except that rr.4 and 5 of the Patents (Amendment) Rules 1987 (SI 1987/288) continue in force, see notes in §§77.01 and 78.01 respectively.

Rule 2—General Interpretation

123.04   **2.**—(1) In these Rules—

"the Act" means the Patents Act 1977 and "section", unless the contrary intention appears, means a section of the Act;

"application number" includes file number;

"compliance date" means the last day of the compliance period;

"compliance period" means the period prescribed by rule 30;

"declared priority date" has the meaning given to it by rule 3(1);

"initiation date" means the date on which a new application was initiated by documents, mentioned in section 15(1), being filed at the Patent Office;

"new application" means a new application filed under section 8(3), 12(6) or 37(4) or as mentioned in section 15(9);

"no declared priority date" has the meaning given to it by rule 3(2);

"Patents Form" has the meaning given to it by rule 4(1);

"priority application" means an earlier relevant application specified in a declaration for the purposes of section 5(2);

"sequence" and "sequence listing" have the same meaning as they have under the Patent Co-operation Treaty;

"start date" means, in relation to rules 106(6)(a) and 116 on supplementary protection certificates, the first day following the day on which the basic patent expires; and

"termination" has the meaning given by section 20B(7) and "terminated" shall be construed accordingly.

(2) Where a period of time has been altered under rules 20(4), 71(7), 81 or 107 to 111, any reference in these Rules to the period of time shall be construed as a reference to the period as altered.

(3) For the purposes of these Rules a document is available to the comptroller where—

(a) it is in electronic storage (whether in the Patent Office or elsewhere) and he can access it by using electronic communications; or

(b) it is kept at the Patent Office,

and he has been furnished with sufficient information to obtain a copy of the document.

(4) But a document may be treated as unavailable to the comptroller where—

(a) its accuracy cannot be verified to his satisfaction; or

(b) he has to pay to access it.

Rule 4—Forms and documents

4.—(1) The forms of which the use is required by these Rules are those set out in directions under section 123(2A) and are referred to in these Rules as Patents Forms. **123.05**

(2) Such a requirement to use a form is satisfied by the use of a form which is acceptable to the comptroller and contains the information required by the form as so set out.

(3) Such directions must be published in accordance with rule 117(c).

(4) Unless the comptroller otherwise directs, to file any form or other document under the Act or these Rules only one side of each sheet of paper must be used and the other side must remain blank.

(5) But where the information is delivered in electronic form or using electronic communications—

(a) a requirement under these Rules to use a form; and

(b) the requirements in paragraph (4),

do not apply.

(6) Where any form or other document is delivered to the comptroller in electronic form or using electronic communications, any requirement in these Rules for multiple copies of that form or document to be filed does not apply.

PART 7—Proceedings Heard Before The Comptroller

Rule 73—Scope and interpretation; list of proceedings heard before the comptroller (Schedule 3)

123.06   73.—(1) This Part applies to the following proceedings heard before the comptroller—

(a) applications, references and requests under the provisions mentioned in Part 1 of Schedule 3;

(b) oppositions under the provisions mentioned in Part 2 of that Schedule.

(2) The rules listed in Part 4 of that Schedule apply to any proceedings heard before the comptroller under the Act.

(3) In this Part—

"claimant" means a person who starts proceedings or is treated as starting proceedings under rule 76(1);

"defendant" means a person who files a counter-statement under rule 77(6) or (8);

"statement of case" means the statement of grounds or the counter-statement and references to a statement of case include part of the statement of case;

"statement of grounds" means a statement filed by the claimant;

"statement of truth" means a statement that the person making the statement believes that the facts stated in a particular document are true; and

"witness statement" means a written statement signed by a person that contains the evidence which that person would be allowed to give orally.

Rule 73

SCHEDULE 3

Proceedings Heard Before the Comptroller (Rule 73)

PART 1

APPLICATION, REFERENCES AND REQUESTS

Patents Act 1977

section 8(1) (reference regarding entitlement in relation to a patent under the Act)

section 10 (request for directions for handling a joint application)

section 11(5) (reference regarding entitlement to a licence to continue working after transfer of application)

section 12(1) (reference regarding entitlement in relation to a foreign or convention patent)

section 12(4) (reference involving joint applications on entitlement in relation to a foreign or convention patent)

section 13(3) (application to comptroller to remove person mentioned as inventor)

section 37(1) (determination of right to patent after grant)

section 38(5) (reference regarding entitlement to a licence to continue working after transfer of patent)

section 40 (application for compensation by an employee)

section 41(8) (application to vary order for compensation for certain inventions)

section 46(3) (application to settle terms of licence available as of right)

section 47(3) (application to cancel licence available as of right)

section 48(1) (application for a compulsory licence)

section 50A(2) (application following merger and market investigation)

section 51(1) (application by Minister following report of Competition Commission)

section 52(2)(a) (application to cancel compulsory licence)

section 61(3) (reference on question of infringement before the comptroller)
section 71 (declaration of non-infringement)
section 72 (application to revoke patent)

Patents Rules 2007

rule 10(2) (application to be mentioned as inventor)
rule 88(1) (application to hold proceedings in Scotland)
paragraph 7(4) of Schedule 1 (notice of objection to expert)

Compulsory Licensing Regulation

Article 5(c) of the Compulsory Licensing Regulation (application to terminate EU compulsory licence)
Article 6(1) of that Regulation (application for an EU compulsory licence)
Article 10(8) of that Regulation (application to access books and records)
Article 16(1), second paragraph, of that Regulation (application for a review of an EU compulsory licence)
Article 16(4) of that Regulation (application for modification of an EU compulsory licence)

Medicinal Products Regulation and Plant Protection Products Regulation

Article 14(d) of the Medicinal Products Regulation and the Plant Protection Products Regulation (request to review lapse of supplementary protection certificate)
Article 15 of those Regulations (application for declaration of invalidity of supplementary protection certificate)
Article 15a of the Medicinal Products Regulation (application for revocation of an extension of the duration of a supplementary protection certificate)

PART 2

OPPOSITIONS WHICH START PROCEEDINGS

Patents Act 1977

section 27(5) (opposition to amendment of specification after grant)
section 29(2) (opposition to surrender of patent)
section 47(6) (opposition to cancellation of licence available as of right), where the application was made by the proprietor of the patent
section 75(2) (opposition to amendment during infringement or revocation proceedings)
section 117(2) (opposition to correction of error in patents and applications)

PART 3

OPPOSITIONS AFTER PROCEEDINGS HAVE STARTED

Patents Act 1977

section 47(6) (opposition to cancellation of licence available as of right), where the application was made by a person other than the proprietor of the patent
section 52(1) (opposition to an application for compulsory licence or under section 50A or 51)
section 52(2)(b) (opposition to an application to cancel a compulsory licence)

PART 4

RULES WHICH APPLY TO ANY PROCEEDINGS HEARD BEFORE THE COMPTROLLER

Patents Rules 2007

rule 74 (overriding objective)
rule 79 (copies of documents)
rule 80(2) to (6) (evidence and the hearing)
rule 81 (alteration of time limits)
rule 82 (general powers of the comptroller in relation to proceedings before him)
rule 84 (hearings in public)
rule 87 (evidence in proceedings before the comptroller)

Rule 74—Overriding objective

123.07 **74.**—(1) The rules in this Part set out a procedural code with the overriding objective of enabling the comptroller to deal with cases justly.

(2) Dealing with a case justly includes, so far as is practicable—

(a) ensuring that the parties are on an equal footing;

(b) saving expense;

(c) dealing with the case in ways which are proportionate—

(i) to the amount of money involved,

(ii) to the importance of the case,

(iii) to the complexity of the issues, and

(iv) to the financial position of each party;

(d) ensuring that it is dealt with expeditiously and fairly; and

(e) allotting to it an appropriate share of the resources available to the comptroller, while taking into account the need to allot resources to other cases.

(3) The comptroller shall seek to give effect to the overriding objective when he—

(a) exercises any power given to him by this Part; or

(b) interprets any rule in this Part.

(4) The parties are required to help the comptroller to further the overriding objective.

Rule 75—Publication of notices

123.08 **75.** The comptroller must advertise in the journal any event to which it is possible to object under any of the provisions mentioned in Part 2 or 3 of Schedule 3, subject to rule 105(5).

Rule 76—Starting proceedings

123.09 **76.**—(1) Proceedings are started when a person files in duplicate—

(a) the relevant form; and

(b) his statement of grounds.

(2) Any person may give notice of opposition—

(a) in the case of section 75(2), before the end of the period of two weeks beginning [with] immediately after the date of the relevant notice; and

(b) in the case of any of the other provisions mentioned in Part 2 of Schedule 3, before the end of the period of four weeks beginning [with] immediately after the date of the relevant notice.

(3) For the purposes of this rule and rule 77—

"relevant form" means —

(a) in relation to applications or requests under the provisions of the Medicinal Products Regulation or the Plant Protection Products Regulation mentioned in Part 1 of Schedule 3, Patents Form SP3;

(b) in relation to applications, references or requests under any other provision mentioned in Part 1 of that Schedule, Patents Form 2; and

(c) in relation to oppositions under the provisions mentioned in Part 2 of that Schedule, Patents Form 15; and

"relevant notice" means the advertisement in the journal mentioned in rule 75.

(4) A statement of grounds must—

(a) include a concise statement of the facts and grounds on which the claimant relies;

(b) in the case of rule 89(5), include the grounds of objection to the draft licence;

(c) where appropriate, include the period or terms of the licence which he believes are reasonable;

(d) specify the remedy which he seeks;

(e) where it accompanies an application under the Compulsory Licensing Regulation, include any information required by that Regulation;

(f) be verified by a statement of truth; and

(g) comply with the requirements of Part 1 of Schedule 2.

Note. Amended by the Patents (Amendment) Rules 2011 (SI 2011/2052).

Rule 77—Notification of the parties

77.—(1) The comptroller must notify the applicant for, or proprietor of, the patent which is the subject matter of the case that proceedings have started.   **123.10**

(2) In addition, the comptroller may notify any persons who appear to him to be likely to have an interest in the case that proceedings have started.

(3) But where a person mentioned in paragraph (1) or (2)—

(a) is the claimant; or

(b) has indicated in writing to the comptroller that he supports the claimant's case,

the comptroller has no duty to notify him.

(4) The comptroller must send the relevant form and the statement of grounds with the notification under paragraph (1) or (2).

(5) In that notification, the comptroller must specify a period within which the persons notified may file a counter-statement.

(6) Any counter-statement must be filed in duplicate before the end of the period specified under paragraph (5).

(7) But paragraphs (5) and (6) do not apply to an opposition under any of the provisions mentioned in Part 3 of Schedule 3.

(8) In such oppositions, any counter-statement must be filed in duplicate before the end of the period of four weeks beginning [with] immediately after the date of the relevant notice.

(9) Where—

(a) a person was notified under paragraph (1) or (2); and

(b) that person fails to file a counter-statement under paragraph (6) or (8),

the comptroller shall treat him as supporting the claimant's case.

(10) The period prescribed for the purposes of giving notice to the comptroller

under section 47(6) of opposition to cancellation of an entry made under section 46 that licences are available as of right is the period prescribed by paragraph (8).

Note. Amended by the Patents (Amendment) Rules 2011 (SI 2011/2052).

Rule 78—The counter-statement

123.11 **78.**—(1) Any counter-statement filed by the defendant must—
   (a) state which of the allegations in the statement of grounds he denies;
   (b) state which of the allegations he is unable to admit or deny, but which he requires the claimant to prove;
   (c) state which of the allegations he admits;
   (d) be verified by a statement of truth; and
   (e) comply with the requirements of Part 1 of Schedule 2.
   (2) Where the defendant denies an allegation—
   (a) he must state his reasons for doing so; and
   (b) if he intends to put forward a different version of events from that given by the claimant, he must state his own version.
   (3) A defendant who fails to deal with an allegation in a counter-statement shall be taken to admit that allegation.
   (4) But a defendant who—
   (a) fails to deal with an allegation; but
   (b) has set out in his counter-statement the nature of his case in relation to the issue to which the allegation is relevant,
shall be taken to require the allegation to be proved.

Rule 79—Copies of documents

123.12 **79.**—(1) Where a relevant statement refers to any other document, a copy of that document must accompany the relevant statement.
   (2) Where more than one copy of a relevant statement is filed, each copy of the statement must be accompanied by a copy of any document referred to in the statement.
   (3) But paragraphs (1) and (2) do not apply where—
   (a) the relevant statement is sent to the comptroller; and
   (b) the document referred to in the relevant statement was published by the comptroller or is kept at the Patent Office.
   (4) In this rule "relevant statement" means a witness statement, statement of case, affidavit or statutory declaration.

Rule 80—Evidence rounds and the hearing

123.13 **80.**—(1) When the defendant files a counter-statement, the comptroller must as soon as practicable—
   (a) send the counter-statement to the claimant;
   (aa) specify the period in which the claimant must file Patents Form 4; and
   (b) specify the periods within which evidence may be filed by the claimant and the defendant.

(1A) If the claimant wishes to continue the proceedings following receipt of the counter-statement the claimant must file Patents Form 4.

(2) The comptroller may, at any time he thinks fit, give leave to either party to file evidence upon such terms as he thinks fit.

(3) Under this rule, evidence shall only be considered to be filed when—

(a) it has been received by the comptroller; and

(b) it has been sent to all the other parties to the proceedings.

(4) The comptroller must then give the parties an opportunity to be heard.

(5) If any party requests to be heard, the comptroller must send to the parties notice of a date for the hearing.

(6) When the comptroller has decided the matter he must notify all the parties of his decision, including his reasons for making the decision.

Rule 81—Alteration of time limits

81.—(1) The comptroller may extend or shorten (or further extend or shorten) **123.14** any period of time which has been specified under any provision of this Part.

(2) An extension may be granted under paragraph (1) notwithstanding the period of time specified has expired.

Rule 81A—Failure to file Patents Form 4

81A. If a claimant fails to file Patents Form 4 within the period specified by the **123.14A** comptroller the claimant shall be deemed to have filed a request to withdraw from the proceedings.

Rule 82—General powers of the comptroller in relation to proceedings before him

82.—(1) Except where the Act or these Rules otherwise provide, the comptrol- **123.15** ler may give such directions as to the management of the proceedings as he thinks fit, and in particular he may—

(a) require a document, information or evidence to be filed;

(b) require a translation of a specification of a patent or application or any other document which is not in English;

(c) require a party or a party's legal representative to attend a hearing;

(d) hold a hearing and receive evidence by telephone or by using any other method of direct oral communication;

(e) allow a statement of case to be amended;

(f) stay the whole, or any part, of the proceedings either generally or until a specified date or event;

(g) consolidate proceedings;

(h) direct that part of any proceedings be dealt with as separate proceedings; and

(i) direct that the parties attend a case management conference or pre-hearing review.

(2) The comptroller may control the evidence by giving directions as to—

(a) the issues on which he requires evidence;

(b) the nature of the evidence which he requires to decide those issues; and

(c) the way in which the evidence is to be placed before him,

and the comptroller may use his power under this paragraph to exclude evidence which would otherwise be admissible.

(3) When the comptroller gives directions under any provision of this Part, he may—

(a) make them subject to conditions; and

(b) specify the consequence of failure to comply with the directions or a condition.

Rule 83—Striking out a statement of case and summary judgment

123.16   **83.**—(1) A party may apply to the comptroller for him to strike out a statement of case or to give summary judgment.

(2) If it appears to the comptroller that—

(a) the statement of case discloses no reasonable grounds for bringing or defending the claim;

(b) the statement of case is an abuse of process or is otherwise likely to obstruct the just disposal of the proceedings; or

(c) there has been a failure to comply with a section, a rule or a previous direction given by the comptroller,

he may strike out the statement of case.

(3) The comptroller may give summary judgment against a claimant or defendant on the whole of a case or on a particular issue if—

(a) he considers that—

(i) that claimant has no real prospect of succeeding on the case or issue, or

(ii) that defendant has no real prospect of successfully defending the case or issue; and

(b) there is no other compelling reason why the case or issue should be disposed of at a hearing.

Rule 84—Hearings in public

123.17   **84.**—(1) Subject to paragraphs (3) and (4), any hearing before the comptroller in proceedings relating to an application for a patent, or a patent, shall be held in public.

(2) Any party to the proceedings may apply to the comptroller for a hearing to be held in private.

(3) The comptroller may grant an application under paragraph (2) where—

(a) he considers there is good reason for the hearing to be held in private; and

(b) all the parties to the proceedings have had an opportunity to be heard on the matter,

and where the application is granted the hearing must be held in private.

(4) Any hearing—

(a) of an application under paragraph (2); or

(b) relating to an application for a patent which has not been published,

shall be held in private.

(5) For the purposes of this rule a reference to a hearing includes any part of a hearing.

Rule 85—Security for costs or expenses

85.—(1) The conditions prescribed for the purposes of making an order for se- **123.18** curity for costs under section 107(4) are that the party against whom the order is made—

(a) is resident outside the United Kingdom, but not resident in—

    (i) a Brussels Contracting State,

    (ii) a Lugano Contracting State, or

    (iii) a Regulation State,

as defined in section 1(3) of the Civil Jurisdiction and Judgments Act 1982;

(b) is a company or other body (whether incorporated inside or outside the United Kingdom) and there is reason to believe that it will be unable to pay another party's costs if ordered to do so;

(c) has changed his address for service with a view to evading the consequences of the litigation;

(d) has furnished an incorrect address for service; or

(e) has taken steps in relation to his assets that would make it difficult to enforce an order for costs against him.

(2) In relation to proceedings in Scotland, references in this rule to costs are references to expenses.

Rule 86—Powers of comptroller to compel attendance of witnesses and production of documents

86. The comptroller shall have the powers of a judge of the High Court (in **123.19** Scotland, the Court of Session) as regards—

(a) the attendance of witnesses; and

(b) the discovery and production of documents,

but he shall have no power to punish summarily for contempt.

Rule 87—Evidence in proceedings before the comptroller

87.—(1) Subject to paragraphs (2) to (5), evidence filed under this Part may be **123.20** given—

(a) by witness statement, statement of case, affidavit, statutory declaration; or

(b) in any other form which would be admissible as evidence in proceedings before the court.

(2) A witness statement or a statement of case may only be given in evidence if it includes a statement of truth.

(3) Evidence is to be by witness statement unless the comptroller directs or any enactment requires otherwise.

(4) A witness statement, affidavit or statutory declaration must comply with the requirements of Part 1 of Schedule 2, unless the comptroller otherwise directs.

(5) For the purposes of this Part a statement of truth must be dated and signed by—

(a) in the case of a witness statement, the person making the statement; and

(b) in any other case, the party or his legal representative.

Rule 88—Proceedings in Scotland

123.21   **88.**—(1) Where there is more than one party to proceedings, a party to the proceedings may apply to the comptroller to hold proceedings in Scotland.

(2) An application made under paragraph (1) must be granted—

(a) where all the parties consent to the proceedings being held in Scotland; or

(b) where the comptroller considers it appropriate.

(3) A refusal of an application made under paragraph (1) is excepted from the right of appeal conferred by section 97.

PART 9—Miscellaneous

Rule 102—Appointing advisers

123.22   **102.** The comptroller may appoint an adviser to assist him in any proceeding before him and shall settle any question or instructions to be given to the adviser.

Rule 106—Remission of fees

123.23   **106.**—(1) A person may apply to the comptroller for the remission of a fee.

(2) The comptroller may remit the whole or part of a search fee where—

(a) in relation to an international application for a patent (UK), a copy of the International Search Report (as defined in rule 64) for that application is available to the comptroller; or

(b) a new application for a patent is filed as mentioned in section 15(9) and, in connection with the earlier application, the applicant has already paid the search fee for the invention described in the new application.

(3) The comptroller may remit the whole or part of any fee where—

(a) a person has requested the comptroller or an examiner to do something in accordance with the Act or these Rules; and

(b) the request is withdrawn before it is carried out.

(4) The comptroller may remit the whole or part of the fee payable in respect of a request for an opinion under section 74A where he has refused the request.

(5) Where a supplementary protection certificate lapses or is declared invalid, the comptroller must remit any fee which has been paid in respect of the relevant period.

(6) In paragraph (5) "the relevant period" is the period—

(a) beginning with the next anniversary of the start date following the date the certificate lapsed or was declared invalid; and

(b) ending with the date the certificate would have expired but for its lapse or invalidity.

(7) Any decision of the comptroller under this rule is excepted from the right of appeal conferred by section 97.

Rule 107—Correction of irregularities

107.—(1) Subject to paragraph (3), the comptroller may, if he thinks fit, authorise the rectification of any irregularity of procedure connected with any proceeding or other matter before the comptroller, an examiner or the Patent Office. **123.24**

(2) Any rectification made under paragraph (1) shall be made—

(a) after giving the parties such notice; and

(b) subject to such conditions,

as the comptroller may direct.

(3) A period of time specified in the Act or listed in Parts 1 to 3 of Schedule 4 (whether it has already expired or not) may be extended under paragraph (1) if, and only if—

(a) the irregularity or prospective irregularity is attributable, wholly or in part, to a default, omission or other error by the comptroller, an examiner or the Patent Office; and

(b) it appears to the comptroller that the irregularity should be rectified.

Rule 108—Extension of time limits

108.—(1) The comptroller may, if he thinks fit, extend or further extend any period of time prescribed by these Rules except a period prescribed by the provisions listed in Parts 1 and 2 of Schedule 4. **123.25**

(2) The comptroller shall extend, by a period of two months, any period of time prescribed by the provisions listed in Part 2 of Schedule 4 where—

(a) a request is filed on Patents Form 52;

(b) no previous request has been made under this paragraph; and

(c) that request is filed before the end of the period of two months beginning [with] immediately after the date on which the relevant period of time expired.

(3) The comptroller may, if he thinks fit, extend or further extend any period of time prescribed by the rules listed in Part 2 of Schedule 4 where—

(a) a request is filed on Patents Form 52; and

(b) the person making the request has furnished evidence supporting the grounds of the request, except where the comptroller otherwise directs.

(4) Each request under paragraph (2) or (3) for a period of time to be extended must be made on a separate form unless—

(a) each of those requests relate to the same patent or application for a patent; and

(b) the grant of each of those requests would result in the expiry of all the extended periods of time on the same date,

in which case those requests may be combined and made on a single form.

(5) Any extension made under paragraph (1) or (3) shall be made—

(a) after giving the parties such notice; and

(b) subject to such conditions,

as the comptroller may direct, except that a period of time prescribed by the rules listed in Part 3 of Schedule 4 may be extended (or further extended) for a period of two months only.

(6) An extension may be granted under paragraph (1) or (3) notwithstanding the period of time prescribed by the relevant rule has expired.

(7) But no extension may be granted in relation to the periods of time prescribed by the rules listed in Part 3 of Schedule 4 after the end of the period of two months beginning immediately after the period of time as prescribed (or previously extended) has expired.

Note. Amended by the Patents (Amendment) Rules 2011 (SI 2011/2052).

SCHEDULE 4

Extension of time limits

PART 1

PERIODS OF TIME THAT CANNOT BE EXTENDED

123.26

rule 6(2)(b) (declaration of priority for the purposes of section 5(2) made after the date of filing)

rule 7(1) (period for making a request to the comptroller for permission to make a late declaration of priority)

rule 32(1) (application to reinstate a terminated application)

rule 37 and 38 (renewal of patents)

rule 40(1) (application to restore a lapsed patent)

rule 43(4) (application to cancel entry that licence available as of right)

rule 58(3) (request for a direction under section 81)

rule 59(1) (request from a foreign industrial property office for a direction under section 81)

rule 66(3) (period for making a request to the comptroller for permission to make a late declaration of priority in respect of an international application for a patent (UK))

rule 76(2) (notice of opposition), except in relation to an opposition under section 27(5) where there are pending before the court or the comptroller proceedings in which the validity of the patent is put in issue

rule 77(8) and (10) (opposition periods)

rule 104(2) (period for filing an address for service), in relation to an application for a patent

rule 109 (extension of time limits specified by comptroller)

rule 116(2) (fee for supplementary protection certificate)

paragraph 8(5) of Schedule 1 (new deposits of biological material)

PART 2

PERIODS OF TIME THAT MAY BE EXTENDED UNDER RULE 108(2) OR 108(3)

rule 8(1) and (2) (filing of information and priority documents)

rule 10(3) (filing of statement of inventorship and the right to be granted a patent)

rule 18(1) (missing parts)

rule 21 (extensions for new applications)

rule 22(1), (2) and (5) (periods prescribed for the purposes of sections 15(10) and 17(1))

rule 28(2), (3) and (5) (request for substantive examination)

rule 30 (period for putting an application in order)

rule 56(6) and (7) (filing of a translation of European patent (UK) specifications)

rule 58(4) (request under section 81(2)(b)(i))

rule 59(3) (request under section 81(2)(b)(ii))

rule 60 (request for substantive examination following a direction under section 81)

rule 66(1) and (2) (international applications for patents: entry into national phase)
rule 68 (international applications for patents: altered prescribed periods)
paragraph 3(2) of Schedule 1 (filing of information in relation to the deposit of biological matter)

PART 3

PERIODS OF TIME TO WHICH RULE 108(5) AND 108(7) RELATE

rule 10(3) (filing of statement of inventorship and the right to be granted a patent)
rule 12(3) and (9) (filing of name and address and translations)
rule 19 (new applications filed as mentioned in section 15(9))
rule 21(1)(a) and (2)(a) (extensions for new applications)
rule 22 (periods prescribed for the purposes of sections 15(10) and 17(1))
rule 28 (request for substantive examination)
rule 30 (period for putting application in order)
rule 58(4) (request under section 81(2)(b)(i))
rule 59(3) (request under section 81(2)(b)(ii))
rule 60 (request for substantive examination following a direction under section 81)
rule 66(1) and (2) (international applications for patents: entry into national phase)
rule 68 (international applications for patents: altered prescribed periods)

Rule 109—Extension of time limits specified by comptroller

109.—(1) A request under section 117B(2) must be—   **123.27**

(a) made in writing; and

(b) made before the end of the period prescribed by paragraph (2).

(2) The period prescribed for the purposes of section 117B(3) is two months beginning immediately after the expiry of the period to which section 117B(2) applies.

Rule 110—Interrupted days

110.—(1) The comptroller may certify any day as an interrupted day where—   **123.28**

(a) there is an event or circumstance causing an interruption in the normal operation of the Patent Office; or

(b) there is a general interruption or subsequent dislocation in the postal services of the United Kingdom.

(2) Any certificate of the comptroller given under paragraph (1) shall be displayed in the Patent Office and advertised in the journal.

(3) The comptroller shall, where the time for doing anything under the Act expires on an interrupted day, extend that time to the next following day not being an interrupted day (or an excluded day).

(4) In this rule—

"excluded day" means a day specified as an excluded day in directions given under section 120; and

"interrupted day" means a day which has been certified as such under paragraph (1).

Rule 111—Delays in communication services

111.—(1) The comptroller shall extend any period of time specified in the Act   **123.29**
or these Rules where he is satisfied that the failure to do something under the Act or these Rules was wholly or mainly attributable to a delay in, or failure of, a communication service.

(2) Any extension under paragraph (1) shall be made—

(a) after giving the parties such notice; and

(b) subject to such conditions,

as the comptroller may direct.

(3) In this rule "communication service" means a service by which documents may be sent and delivered and includes post, electronic communications, and courier.

Rule 112—Copies available to the comptroller

123.29A   **112.**—(1) This rule applies where an applicant is not required to file a copy of an application at the Patent Office because that application or a copy of that application is available to the comptroller.

(2) Where this rule applies the comptroller shall make a copy (or further copy) of that application and certify it accordingly.

Rule 113—Translations

123.30   **113.**—(1) Where any document filed at the Patent Office, or sent to the comptroller, is in a language other than English or Welsh it must be accompanied by a translation into English of that document.

(2) But paragraph (1) does not apply to the following documents—

(a) where the documents filed to initiate an application for a patent include something which is or appears to be a description of the invention, the document containing that thing;

(b) a priority application;

(c) a copy of an application provided under section 15(10)(b)(ii);

(d) a copy of a specification of a European patent (UK) filed in connection with an application by the proprietor to amend the specification;

(e) a copy of an application for a European patent (UK) provided under section 81(2)(b)(ii);

(f) an international application for a patent (UK), where a translation of the application or an amendment to it is a necessary translation;

(g) a document referred to in paragraph (5).

(3) Where more than one copy of the document mentioned in paragraph (1) is filed or sent, a corresponding number of translations shall accompany it.

(4) Where a document to which paragraph (1) applies is not accompanied by a translation, the comptroller may, if he thinks fit, take no further action in relation to that document.

(5) In relation to an international application for a patent (UK), where any document which is in a language other than English or Welsh is—

(a) referred to in an International Search Report or International Preliminary Report on Patentability; or

(b) cited in an International Preliminary Examination Report,

and the relevant report is filed at the Patent Office, the comptroller may direct that a translation into English of that document be filed.

(6) Where a direction is given under paragraph (5) a translation of that docu-

ment must be filed before the end of the period of two months beginning [with] immediately after the date on which the direction is given; otherwise the comptroller may, if he thinks fit, take no further action in relation to the application.

(7) Subject to rule 82(1)(b), where a patent application or any document related to such application is filed at the Patent Office or sent to the comptroller in Welsh, and is not accompanied by a translation into English, the comptroller must obtain such a translation.

(8) In this rule a reference to a document includes a reference to a part of a document; and in paragraph (5) "International Preliminary Examination Report", "International Preliminary Report on Patentability" and "International Search Report" and have the same meaning as in rule 64.

Note. Amended by the Patents (Amendment) Rules 2011 (SI 2011/2052).

Rule 114—Translations in proceedings in relation to a European Patent (UK)

114.—(1) Where—   **123.31**

(a) proceedings are started before the comptroller in relation to a European patent (UK); and

(b) the specification of that patent was published in French or German,

the person who starts those proceedings shall file at the Patent Office a translation into English of the specification.

(2) But paragraph (1) shall not apply where—

(a) a translation into English of the specification has been filed under section 77(6); or

(b) the comptroller directs that a translation is unnecessary.

(3) Where, in the course of such proceedings, leave is given to amend the specification of the patent, the proprietor shall file at the Patent Office a translation of the amendment into the language in which the specification of the patent was published.

(4) This rule applies to making a request for an opinion under section 74A as it applies to proceedings started before the comptroller.

Rule 115—Establishing the accuracy of translations

115. If the comptroller has reasonable doubts about the accuracy of any transla-   **123.32**
tion of a document that has been filed at the Patent Office by any person in accordance with the Act or these Rules—

(a) he shall notify that person of the reasons for his doubts; and

(b) he may require that person to furnish evidence to establish that the translation is accurate,

and where that person fails to furnish evidence the comptroller may, if he thinks fit, take no further action in relation to that document.

Rule 117—The journal

117. The comptroller must publish a journal containing—   **123.33**

(a) particulars of applications for and grants of patents and of other proceedings under the Act;

(b) any directions given under section 120(1) specifying hours of business or excluded days;

(c) any directions under section 123(2A) setting out forms; and

(d) any other information that the comptroller considers to be generally useful or important.

Rule 118—Reports of cases

123.34   118. The comptroller must make arrangements for the publication of—

(a) reports of cases relating to patents, trade marks, registered designs or design right decided by him; and

(b) reports of cases relating to patents (whether under the Act or otherwise), trade marks, registered designs, copyright and design right decided by any court or body (whether in the United Kingdom or elsewhere).

Rule 119—Publication and sale of documents

123.35   119. The comptroller may arrange for the publication and sale of copies of documents (in particular, specifications of patents and applications for patents) in the Patent Office.

Rule 120—Transitional provisions and revocations

123.36   120.—(1) Schedule 5 (transitional provisions) shall have effect.

(2) The instruments set out in Schedule 6 (revocations) shall be revoked to the extent specified.

RELEVANT STATUTORY INSTRUMENT

PATENT OFFICE TRADING FUND ORDER 1991

(SI 1991/ 1796)

Citation and commencement

123.37   1. This Order may be cited as the Patent Office Trading Fund Order 1991 and shall come into force on 1st October 1991.

Establishment of the fund

2. As from 1st October 1991 for all the operations of the Department of Trade and Industry known as the Patent Office, which operations are more particularly described in Schedule 1 to this Order, there shall be established a trading fund to be known as the Patent Office Trading Fund (hereinafter referred to as "the fund").

Source of loans

3. The Secretary of State is hereby designated as the source of issues to the fund by way of loan.

Assets, liabilities and public dividend capital

4.—(1) The Crown assets and liabilities set out in Schedule 2 to this Order shall be appropriated as assets and liabilities of the fund.

(2) The sum of £8,489,000 shall be treated as public dividend capital.

Limitation of indebtedness

5. The maximum amount that may be issued to the fund by way of loan under section 2B of the 1973 Act shall be £75,000,000.

Annual reports

6. [*Insofar as the provisions of:*

(a) *section 121 of the Patents Act 1977 [c. 37] (Comptroller's annual report);*

(b) *section 42 of the Registered Designs Act 1949 [c. 88] (Annual report of Registrar); and*

(c) *section 71 [45] of the Trade Marks Act 1994 [c. 26] [1938, c. 22] (Annual report of Registrar), require a report to be prepared and laid before both Houses of Parliament before 1st June in every year in respect of the preceding calendar year, that requirement shall be treated as satisfied:*

    (i) *...; and*

    (ii) *thereafter, by the preparation of a report in respect of each financial year and by the laying of the same before both Houses of Parliament on or before 30th November next following the end of the financial year.*]

Note. Article 6 of this Order was revoked by the Patents Act 2004 (c.16) s.16(3), with effect from January 1, 2005 (SI 2004/3205 art.2(h)). This is consequent on the changes made at the same time to s.121, as noted in §121.01.

SCHEDULE 1

Funded operations

The operations to be funded by the fund are all the operations of the Patent Office, relating to or connected with:

(a) copyright;

(b) design rights;

(c) patents;

(d) patent and trade mark agents;

(e) registered designs;

(f) rights in performances;

(g) trade marks and service marks;

including, without prejudice to the generality of the foregoing—

1. operations concerned with the promotion and administration of legislation relating to the foregoing;

2. operations arising out of anything done or being proposed by the European Communities or any of their institutions or any international organisation, or in pursuance of any international instrument or convention, in relation to or in connection with the foregoing;

3. the provision and dissemination of information and the procurement of publicity and advertising relating to or in connection with the foregoing;

4. operations incidental, conducive or ancillary to the operations described above.

SCHEDULE 2

Assets and liabilities

Assets

1. Freehold land and buildings at Concept House, Newport, South Wales.

2. Plant, equipment and computers as at 1st October 1991 used or allocated for use in the funded operations.

3. The accumulated and deferred costs as at 1st October 1991 of the relocation of the Patent Office from premises in London to Concept House, Newport.

4. Sundry debtors.

Liabilities

1. Repayment to the Department of Trade and Industry of the accumulated and deferred costs of relocations as at 1st October 1991.

2. Deposits held for publications customers.

3. Value owed in respect of fees received in advance of services yet to be rendered.

4. Fees held on behalf of the European Patent Office and the World Intellectual Property Organisation from time to time prior to transfer.

5. Sundry creditors and accruals.

Note. This Order was made under the Government Trading Funds Act 1973 (c.63), as amended by the Government Trading Act 1990 (c.30) and the Finance Act 1991 (c.31) s.119.

COMMENTARY ON SECTION 123

Scope of the section

123.38   Section 123 (together with s.124, reprinted at §124.01) largely contains enabling provisions empowering the Secretary of State to make Rules for the purpose of implementing the various provisions of the Act. The Rules so made appear to be consistent with the requirement of art.62(1) of the TRIPS Agreement which reads:

> "**TRIPS Article 62—**
>
>   1. Members may require as a condition of the acquisition or maintenance of the intellectual property rights provided for under Sections 2 through 6 of Part II, compliance with reasonable procedures and formalities. Such procedures and formalities shall be consistent with the provisions of this Agreement."

For a listing of the current Patents Rules 2007, indicating where each is reprinted in this book, see pp.1327 et seq. The UK-IPO itself (still formally called "the Patent Office") is constituted under the powers set out in unrepealed s.62 of the Patents and Designs Act 1907 (c.29), for which see §A20, but its financial and trading status is governed by the Patent Office Trading Fund Order 1991 (SI 1991/1796) (for which see above and §123.89) made under the Government Trading Funds Act 1973 (c.63), as amended.

Subsection (1) refers to the making of rules for regulating the business of the Patent Office in connection with patent matters, and includes reference to European patents. The subsection also defines "prescribed" and "rules" for the purpose of s.130(1). Further, and quite far-reaching, powers have been provided by the terms of the Deregulation and Contracting Out Act 1994 (c.40), and subsequently by the Regulatory Reform Act 2001 (c.6), including powers for amendment of statutes as to minor matters, and the Regulatory Reform (Patents) Order 2004 (SI 2004/2357) ("RRO") was made under these powers.

Subsection (2) lists at length various matters on which rules can be made, without prejudice to the generality of subs.(1), and these rules can make different provision for different cases (subs.(3)).

Subsection (3A), inserted by the CDPA 1988, declares the Comptroller to have power to deal with an application or a patent, even if it had, apparently, ceased to exist, and is discussed in §123.75. Subsections (4) and (7) relate respectively to: fees (for which see

§123.64) and the publication of the *Patents Journal* and the R.P.C. law reports (for which see respectively §§123.86 and 123.87).

Under the Tribunals and Inquiries Act 1992 (c.53) ss.1, 8 and Sch.1, the Secretary of State may not make "procedural rules" for the Comptroller without prior consultation with the Council on Tribunals established under that Act.

Definitions for Patents Rules (rr.2 and 3)

Rule 2, reprinted above, defines various terms used in the Patents Rules 2007. By s.11 of the Interpretation Act 1978 (c.30), the definitions contained in the Patents Act 1977 themselves apply also for the purposes of the Rules made under its provisions. Thus, the term "United Kingdom" in the Patents Rules includes the Isle of Man by virtue of s.132(2). **123.39**

Form and content of documents (subs.(2)(a))

Subsection (2)(a) provides that rules may be made prescribing the form and contents of patent applications, see rr.12–15 reproduced with accompanying schedules at §§14.02–14.05 and 14.07. It also permits rules to be made prescribing the form of other documents which may be filed at the UK-IPO, e.g. rr.76(4)(g) and 78(1)(e) which provide that statements of case and counter-statements must comply with Part 1 of Schedule 2. This requires matt white A4 paper, free from tears, folds or similar damage and avoidance of the use of frames. It further permits the Patents Forms to be specified in the Rules. However, under new s.123(2A) effective from September 22, 2004 (SI 2004/2177) it is no longer required for the Patents Forms to be prescribed formally by the rules, and instead they are now prescribed under directions issued by the Comptroller and published in the *Patents Journal*. The Forms may be freely downloaded from the UK-IPO website. **123.40**

The use of replica or modified forms is permitted, provided that the substitute form contains the information required by the official form and is otherwise also acceptable to the Comptroller (see r.4(2), above), so that agents can reproduce the forms without the explanatory notes. However, since many of the forms have been designed for easy reading by UK-IPO staff, the general layout of a home-made form has to be closely similar to the official form if such is to be found acceptable. If such a form fails to satisfy the Comptroller, presumably time would be permitted (at least under r.110(4)) to rectify the deficiency, but this cannot be guaranteed if necessary information has been omitted from the form. For possible conflict between the official forms and the Rules relating to them, see R. Camp (1991–92) 21 *CIPA* 466.

Where electronic filing of a form is permitted (as discussed in the separate commentaries for such forms), r.4 modifies the requirements for forms and in particular disapplies the need to provide multiple copies. The supply of a single copy of a required form is generally necessary where a fee needs to be paid. It is to be noted that r.4(2) is broad enough to cover the use of any indication which satisfies the Comptroller of the intention of the applicant, see, e.g. §89.20where an indication on the PCT Request Form that priority is being claimed is sufficient to obviate the need to file PF 23 requesting a certified copy of the priority application to be made and transmitted to the International Bureau.

Procedure before the Comptroller (subs.(2)(b))

—Filing of documents at the Patent Office

Documents are most conveniently filed at the UK-IPO in electronic form, as to which see the *Directions under Section 124A of the Patents Act 1977*, reprinted at §14.06. **123.41**

As the UK-IPO is based in Newport, South Wales (for which see §123.88), all filing receipts emanate from there, but documents can be sent, or hand-delivered, to the London address of the UK-IPO at 21 Bloomsbury Street, London WC1B 3HF where they are date-stamped and then forwarded, unopened, to Newport. However, for documents taken by hand to the London office between its opening hours of 9 am and 7 pm on Mondays to Fridays, it is possible for the agent to provide a checklist listing the documents delivered in an unsealed or re-sealable package. However, no check can be made as to whether the cheque contained in the package is sufficient to pay the fees due on the patent forms included in the envelope. A receipt is issued for all documents filed by hand in London. If the documents are filed outside the opening hours of the London Office, the receipt can be collected on the next working day.

When documents are filed by post, or filed sealed or filed open for checking, the outside of the envelope should be marked with the sender's name and address and an identifying number added to assist in tracing envelopes in the case of later queries on the filing date. It is also possible, when sending a package of documents to the UK-IPO by post, to enclose a self-addressed stamped reply card. The UK-IPO will endorse this and return the card as evidence of receipt of the package but will not at that stage check that the contents of the package are complete. Obviously, care needs to be taken to identify the reply card with a particular package: see (1991–92) 21 *CIPA* 353.

It is also possible to file documents at the UK-IPO by fax transmission. The procedure which has to be adopted is discussed in §119.05.

Proceedings heard before the Comptroller (Part 7, rr.73–88)

—Scope of this commentary on practice in revocation and other proceedings

123.42   The Rules concerning proceedings heard before the Comptroller have been rewritten and consolidated and are now contained in rr.73–88 set out above. They should be read with TPN 1/2000, TPN 6/2007 (now partly superseded) and TPN 3/2009, all downloadable from the UK-IPO website, and which have been incorporated into the *Litigation Manual* which can be regarded as a reliable source of information for current practice. Costs are dealt with in TPN 4/2007.

Rule 74 explains that the rules in Pt 7 set out a procedural code with the overriding objective of enabling the Comptroller to deal with cases justly. The objectives in this rule are modelled on the overriding objective in Pt 1 of the CPR. This is amplified in ch.2 of the *Hearings Manual* which explains at para.2.00.2 that the parties should avoid behaving obstructively and that at para.2.00.3 that the Office will aim to complete inter partes proceedings within 12 months of the filing of the counterstatement.

—Starting proceedings

123.43   As set out in r.76, proceedings are stated by filing in duplicate the relevant form (r.76(3)) and a statement of grounds complying with r.76(4). That form is Patents Form 2 which requires identification of the number of the patent or application, the full name of each applicant or proprietor, the name, address and postcode of all those initiating the proceedings and the relevant legal provisions which are listed in the notes to that form.

The accompanying statement of grounds should set out fully the matters in issue, the facts relied on and the relief sought. This means that the pleading must be such that the proprietor is left in no doubt as to the nature and scope of each of the allegations made. It should be verified by a statement of truth so that it can be given in evidence, and should be signed and dated. Suitable language for the statement of truth is: "I/we confirm that the information contained in this statement of grounds is true to the best of my/our knowledge and belief" or "I/we believe the information contained in this statement of grounds to be true". Although a professional representative can sign the statement of truth (r.87(5)(b)), he can do so only on the information provided to him by his client, and his signature could potentially give rise to witness/advocate difficulties if he both signs the statement of truth and subsequently appears as advocate at the subsequent hearing. It is therefore more appropriate for the statement of grounds to be signed by the client or if a corporation by a duly authorised officer of that corporation. Precedents for statements of grounds are annexed to the *Hearings Manual*.

The relationship between Patents Form 2 and the accompanying statement of grounds was explained by Lord Hoffmann in *Yeda Research & Development v Rhone-Poulenc Rorer* [2007] UKHL 43. Once the primary statutory question has been identified by filing the form, the comptroller is seized of that question and must determine it. The accompanying statement is not analogous to a claim form asserting a cause of action in the sense contemplated by the Limitation Act 1980 or the Civil Procedure Rules. In considering amendment (in this case of a reference under s.37) the question was whether the proposed amendment to the statement of facts would have made the reference into a new reference, which in this instance it did not. The former r.100 (now r.107) gave the Comptroller a broad discretion which he had to exercise in accordance with what appears to be fair and just in the particular circumstances of the case.

The Comptroller examines the form and statement of grounds for formal matters, e.g defects in the statement of grounds or missing documents, and when any objections have been resolved (normally within a response term of one month from an official letter notifying any objection(s)) must notify any person with an interest in the proceedings and must set a time for filing a counterstatement, r.77.

A wholly speculative case may be dismissed in limine because "a case wholly unsupported by evidence is in reality no case at all" (*Ricoh Plastic's Patent* [1989] R.P.C. 722), although this dictum is more likely to apply to other proceedings before the Comptroller rather than ones for revocation, the Ricoh case being a speculative application for a compulsory licence.

As explained above, amendment of a statement of grounds, or the filing of a supplementary statement, may be allowed in the exercise of the Comptroller's discretion. The counterstatement may then be amended or a supplementary counter-statement filed.

An allegation which has not been adequately particularised in the statement of grounds (particularly one of improper amendment under s.72(1)(d)) will not be permitted to be raised in argument at the hearing, because the patentee will not have had proper notice of it and no proper opportunity of dealing with it in his evidence: *Mölnlycke's and Boussac Saint Frères' Patents* BL O/15/90, noted I.P.D. 13111. However, late amendment of the statement is more likely to be permitted in the public interest if the new allegation is one of prior use by the patentee: *Moore's Patent* BL O/116/90, noted I.P.D. 14083.

In *Archibald Kenrick v Laird Security* BL O/156/05 which concerned an opposition to an application for amendment under s.27, an opponent to the application to amend was allowed to supplement a wholly unsatisfactory initial statement because each case should be dealt with not only expeditiously but also fairly and any prejudice caused by an amendment of pleading can be compensated in costs if the public interest in the efficient administration of justice is not significantly harmed. It was here held that the patentee would not be materially prejudiced by admission of a further pleading, particularly as there was no case for dismissing or striking out the opposition. However, an immediate interim award of costs was ordered to be paid by the opponent.

—Counter statement

The period for filing the counter-statement is now set by the Comptroller, and a period **123.44** of six weeks is the norm, see TPN 6/2007 para.2.5. The required contents of the counter-statement and the consequences of non-compliance are set out in r.78. As for the statement of grounds, signature can be by the party or his legal representative (r.88(5)(b)).

The counter statement should correspond to a defence to an action before the court and should, therefore, fully set out the grounds upon which the application is contested. Indeed, Patent Office Tribunal Practice Note TPN 1/2000 ([2000] R.P.C. 587, discussed generally in §72.23) requires in paras 23–25 that, in his counter-statement, the defendant must state which of the allegations in the statement of grounds are denied, and why, and if an alternative version of events is to be put forward what that version is; which of the allegations in the statement the defendant is unable to admit or deny, but requires the claimant to prove; and which of the allegations in the statement are admitted. The counter-statement should also contain a statement of truth.

Thus, any positive defence to be relied upon should be properly pleaded (*Du Pont's (Werner's) Patent* [1975] F.S.R. 193), see also *Wollard's Patent* [1989] R.P.C. 141 supporting the proposition that a party making a positive allegation (in this case in contesting an application for a declaration of non-infringement on the ground that there would be infringement) should explain the basis for that allegation. Any allegation in the statement of case not specifically denied is likely to be taken to be admitted. *Concrete Repairs' Patent* BL O/67/97 indicates that where a counter-statement responds to the majority of the allegations made and is not a mere denial, a request for an expanded counter-statement is likely to be refused.

The counter-statement must be filed in duplicate. The period of six weeks for filing the counter-statement is extensible with discretion.

Failure to file a counter-statement will mean that the application for revocation is undefended; see *Fontaine's Patent* [1959] R.P.C. 72 and *Curtis' Patent* [1965] F.S.R. 59 in each of which there was an inability to take action. The Comptroller may then revoke the patent or he may proceed to decide the matter, as he will also do if the patent is allowed to lapse or is offered to be surrendered, see *Ritzerfeld's Patent* BL O/102/81. The position is similar in entitlement proceedings where the applicant/patentee declines to oppose, actively, the referrer's contentions, see *Coventry University's Application* BL O/223/00.

An application for leave to amend a counter-statement was allowed as a matter of discretion in *Robinson Wiley's Patent* BL O/228/02, the amendments being largely by way of clarification and not substantive.

—Continuation of proceedings before the Comptroller

123.44A   In contested proceedings started after April 6, 2010, after the counterstatement has been filed the Comptroller sets a period (normally two weeks) for the claimant to file Patents Form 4 requesting continuation of the proceedings and to pay the appropriate fee. If this is not done, the claimant is deemed to have filed a request for withdrawal from the proceedings. If the proceedings are uncontested, filing of Patents Form 4 and payment of a fee are not required.

On receipt of Patents Form 4, the Office makes a register entry recording that the form has been filed and the proceedings are to continue, and informs both parties that the proceedings will be reviewed and the Office will consider the best way of proceeding with the case.

If Form 4 is not received in due time, the Office sends a standard letter pointing out the deficiency, indicating that the proceedings are proposed to be withdrawn and giving the claimant a period of two weeks within which to submit comments. If no response is then received, a further letter is sent to the claimant confirming that the proceedings are to be treated as withdrawn with no matters outstanding. The defendant is also advised that the proceedings are withdrawn and invited to submit comments.

—Establishing the further procedure to be followed

123.45   After the counterstatement and Patents Form 4 have been received Litigation section will require the parties to set a mutually acceptable date for a hearing within a proposed window of one to two months. The intention is that the hearing date will not be changed once it has been fixed, TPN 3/2009 at 3.9.

The case is referred to a hearing officer who has a range of available actions for which standard letters are set out as Annexes to Chapter 1 of the *Litigation Manual*.

He should consider the appropriate procedure for the filing of evidence, TPN 3/2009 at 3.7–3.8. He could direct the parties to exchange their main evidence simultaneously and then allow a short period for both parties to file their evidence in reply. That option could shorten the overall duration of the procedure and could focus the minds of the parties on key issues, avoiding proliferation of unnecessary evidence. He could alternatively order sequential evidence rounds as has been usual in proceedings before the UK-IPO, with evidence first by the claimant, then by the respondent and finally by the claimant strictly in reply. Sequential exchange may be needed where a defendant cannot file evidence until the evidence against him has been filed, and where simultaneous exchange would cause the defendant to have to cover a wider range of possibilities than is really necessary. He may also consider whether a joint report from expert witnesses is required, see TPN 3/2009 at 3.9 TPM 6/2007 at s.4. The former practice of an administrative check by the UK-IPO on the evidence filed is now discontinued, TPN 3/2009 at 3.14.

Evidence was given by video link in *Interfilta (UK)'s Patent* [2003] R.P.C. 22 at 411 and an application to reopen the hearing on the ground that the witness had been accompanied and assisted by his own attorney such that his evidence was tainted was refused. It was indicated however that the *Hearings Manual* (see para.4.79) had been amended to make it clear that in future such cases the Patent Office would insist on the witness being supervised by an attorney who is independent of the parties.

Once a timetable for the proceedings has been set, extensions of time will now be granted only in exceptional circumstances and will be only as long as is strictly necessary, TPN 3/2009 at 3.13. As explained in the *Hearings Manual* at 1.41 if the comptroller is to exercise discretion to extend time, there must be some material on which he can exercise discretion otherwise a party in breach would have an unqualified right to an extension and the purpose of the rules in providing a timetable for the conduct of the dispute would be defeated. Under CPR r.3.9(1) relevant factors include the interests of the administration of justice, whether an application for relief has been made promptly, whether non-compliance was intentional, whether there is a good explanation for the non-compliance, whether non-compliance was caused by the party or by his legal representative, whether the hearing date can still be met if the requested extension is given, the effects of non-compliance on each party, the effects of granting an extension on each party and the less formal nature of proceedings before the Comptroller.

The hearing officer should consider whether to issue one or more non-binding preliminary evaluations (PEs) and if so whether these should be before or after the evidence rounds or at some other stage in the procedure. TPN 3/2009 records a wish by users to receive PEs similar to those produced by EPO Appeal Boards and accordingly they are now issued in most inter partes cases. Their aim is to focus the minds of the parties on key issues by exposing the strength or weakness of their respective cases, and so lead to more efficient conduct of the proceedings. In some cases questions considered to be important may be highlighted, in other cases a provisional view may be indicated. Where validity is in issue a PE may highlight the need for the patentee to identify claims alleged to have independent validity, and may also identify prior art considered to have no real relevance to the issues to be decided.

PEs have little value if the parties ignore them. Therefore when awarding costs the hearing officer will consider whether a party has acted unreasonably in the light of a PE by, for example, pursuing aspects of a case which have been notified as irrelevant to the final outcome. If in the event it transpires that they were indeed irrelevant, such unreasonable behaviour could attract off-scale costs. For an example of a PE issued in connection with entitlement proceedings, see *Meider v Whitfield* O/171/10 where a copy of the PE is annexed to the decision. It will be apparent that in appropriate cases a PE can be in similar detail to an opinion under s.74A.

He may propose alternative dispute resolution (ADR), which is now encouraged for all proceedings including those where validity is disputed, although if a settlement is reached the hearing officer will in order to protect the public interest and in accordance with current practice come to a view on the validity of the patent on the basis of the submissions before him. Stays for ADR are not given automatically but may be given at the request of the parties. The former position under TPN 1/2000 no longer applies and *Farrow System's Patent* BL O/8/05 and *Yeda Research v Rhône-Poulenc* BL O/163/05 no longer represents current practice.

The hearing officer may call a case management conference to deal with procedural matters, giving the parties an opportunity to raise additional issues and identifying any documents needing to be supplied in advance. For an example of a decision following a case management conference in entitlement proceedings see *Campbell v Aberdeen University* O/269/97 in which the matters were clarification of the statement and counterstatement, a timetable for the remainder of the proceedings and consideration of mediation or other alternative dispute resolution (ADR). In *Northern Lights Music v Conversor Products* O/060/07 issues recorded are a deadline for ordering specific disclosure and security for costs. In *Vibrant Technology v Protex Healthcare* O/261/06 which concerned revocation under s.72 the issues concerned amendment of the statement of case to include a new paragraph relating to prior use and admission of a late filed witness statement.

The powers which are exercisable at such a conference include those provided by r.82(1) and power to strike out a statement of case or give summary judgment (r.83), e.g. as in *Meider v Whitfield* O/171/10. In *Sony's Patent* BL O/56/05, it was held that the Comptroller has the power to strike out an application for revocation if this is seen either to have no hope of success or to be an abuse of process, the latter ground requiring a finding that the proceedings had been launched deliberately as a vehicle for the allegations made. Here, the allegation in support of either entitlement or revocation was that the invention had been stolen from the applicant, but this was not seen to be substantiated. A strike out was ordered because no prospect of success could be seen on the facts which had been put forward.

In *Ash & Lacy's Patent No.2240558* [2002] R.P.C. 46 at 939, a Case Management Conference was held to decide various procedural disputes and an immediate award of costs was made to the party wholly successful at that Conference. In a subsequent decision (see BL O/175/01), although the application for revocation had been withdrawn, the Comptroller in accordance with "long-standing practice" went on to consider whether to accept the notice of withdrawal or whether there were questions which should be considered further in the public interest. Having done so, it was held that the grounds for revocation of the patent had not been made out. The power of the Comptroller to continue the proceedings in this way was upheld in an application for judicial review of that decision before Mr Justice Laddie sitting as a judge of the Queen's Bench Division (Administrative Court) (*R v Comptroller-General ex parte Ash & Lacy Building Products* [2002] R.P.C. 46 at [939]; [2002] I.P. & T. 709). The same patent was then the subject of proceedings in the Patents County Court (*Ash & Lacy v Fixing Point* (PCC July 24, 2002)). The patentee argued for a broader construction of claim than that given by the Patent Office but validity was upheld on the basis of a relatively narrow construction, which then led to a finding that it was not infringed by the defendant's product. So, in effect, the Patent Office's decision was vindicated.

—Onus and standard of proof

123.46   Onus of proof is discussed in the *Hearings Manual* at paras 3.11–3.13. In *Dunlop's Application* [1979] R.P.C. 523, there are useful remarks concerning onus. The legal burden always rests on the party that has to prove the allegations relied on, e.g. on an applicant for revocation, but the evidential burden can shift, sometimes quite readily, to the patentee and then, perhaps, shift back to the applicant for revocation. Where the patentee does not defend an application for revocation, the applicant for revocation must still prove his case, see *McCann's Patent* BL O/125/97.

The standard of proof required is the normal civil standard of the "balance of probabilities" *Lubrizol v Esso* [1998] R.P.C. 727 CA, even in cases of alleged prior use *O'Shei's Application* [1958] R.P.C. 72; *McCann's Patent* (above) and especially *Kavanagh Balloons v Cameron Balloons* [2004] R.P.C. 5 at [97] or whether a disclosure was one not made in confidence *Visx v Nidek* [1999] F.S.R. 405. In contrast, the EPO may require an allegation of prior publication or prior use to be proved "up to the hilt", see T 472/92 *SEKISUI/Shrinkable sheet* OJ EPO 1998, 161; [1997] E.P.O.R. 432 and §§2.05 to 2.08 especially where an opponent's own prior use is relied on.

As regards the provision of evidence of background knowledge of the art in question, a hearing officer can be assumed to have a general, but not a detailed, knowledge of the art in question (*Eickhoff Maschinenfabrik's Patent* BL O/31/87). If an apparent admission of prior use is made in written evidence, the onus lies on the party producing that evidence to establish that the admission was not properly made (*Fernberg's Patent* [1958] R.P.C. 133). Where a witness gives affidavit evidence in relation to anticipation or obviousness, and in doing so makes assertions in relation to his experience and that of his employer, it is possible that the witness or the employer could be issued with a subpoena to produce internal documents of a specified class which relate thereto, see *Lucas v Hewitt* [Australia] [1980] F.S.R. 208.

—Disclosure and power to require production of documents

Rule 86 gives the Comptroller the powers of a judge of the High Court, or in Scotland **123.47** the Court of Session, as regards the production of documents and current practice is as set out in paras 33–37 of TPN 1/2000 and paras 3.40–3.57 of the *Hearings Manual*.

Although there is power to order disclosure at any stage in the proceedings and even before proceedings have started (CPR r.31.16) it would not normally be appropriate to do so before the issues have been defined by statements of case, and it may be preferable to await the evidence of the parties so as to avoid unnecessary disclosure.

Current Office practice has been explained in *I.D.A. Limited v University of Southampton*)/067/02 as follows:

"As stated in TPN 1/2000 at paragraphs 33–37, disclosure is not common in proceedings before the comptroller and that was not expected to change. The tests laid down in *Merrell Dow Pharmaceuticals Inc's (Terfenadine) Patent* [1991] RPC 221, namely whether the documents should relate to the matters in question and whether their disclosure is necessary to dispose fairly of the proceedings or to reduce costs, are still seen as an appropriate way of taking into account the circumstances of a case and the overriding objectives which are stated at paragraph 5 of TPN 1/2000. It is however accepted that the Office should put greater emphasis on the principle of proportionality and on the need to ensure that proceedings are dealt with expeditiously."

It is unlikely that the Comptroller will ever order "standard disclosure" (i.e. all relevant documents in a party's control) because that would negate the advantage of the comptroller as a relatively inexpensive jurisdiction in comparison to the High Court and he is more likely to order "specific disclosure" (usually of specific documents or classes of documents), see *Yeda Research v Rhône-Poulenc Rorer* BL O/277/05. As explained in *Yeda*, before approaching the comptroller for a disclosure order, the party requesting it should have attempted to reach a voluntary agreement with the other party as to what documents should be disclosed, and when applying for specific disclosure should explain its reasons in full and should identify the documents or classes of documents that it seeks as clearly as possible, see also *Secretary of State for Defence v Farrow System* BL O/308/05.

In *Merrell Dow's Patent* [1991] R.P.C. 221, the Patents Court pointed out that documents should be disclosed if they "relate" to issues, not merely if they are "relevant" to them. Subsequently, the Comptroller ruled that it is implicit in this *Merrell Dow* decision that a party seeking documentary disclosure before the Comptroller will need to present a stronger argument than might be the case in the High Court (*Du Pont's Application* BL O/146/94, noted I.P.D. 18090). Also, disclosure cannot be used to establish a case, the onus for which is on the applicant: there must first be indicated the existence of evidence sufficient to meet that onus (*Ricoh Plastic's Patent* [1989] R.P.C. 722).

Examples of cases in which the Comptroller has ordered some disclosure are now given by way of example.

In *Coflexip Stena's Patent* BL O/20/96, in licence of right proceedings, disclosure was ordered of documents from previously decided entitlement proceedings under s.37. In *Baldwin's Patent (No.2)* BL O/79/99, a reasonable request for disclosure was allowed in entitlement proceedings, despite this being submitted at a late stage, because such was in the interests of justice and inventorship records would be of assistance, particularly because of several changes of ownership of the patent in dispute; and, in *Abdulhayoglu's Application (No.2)* (above), disclosure of correspondence was ordered in view of a conflict in the contentions of employment status in an entitlement dispute.

In connection with a prior use allegation in *Alley Enterprises' Patent* BL O/304/05, disclosure was ordered under a number of headings, including certain events which had occurred outside the two year periods before and after the priority date, but limited to specific matters and to "documents that support or adversely affect a party's case". The applicant for revocation was also asked to send a letter to a testing authority (GRE) asking them to waive the confidentiality provision which it had imposed upon them, but it was noted that this would provide no guarantee that GRE would co-operate. The terms on which inspection of domestic boilers in individual homes should be carried out to ensure minimum disruption were also agreed, including limitation of those present to one expert, one legal representative and one patent agent from each side and a engineer from G (other than two named individuals).

Disclosure was not ordered in *Intel's Patent* [2002] R.P.C. 48 at [957], it being stated that disclosure was not always necessary in amendment proceedings and that the obligation on the patentee to give full and frank "disclosure" as required in *Smith Kline & French v Evans Medical* [1989] 1 F.S.R. 561 was met in the first instance by the statement of reasons.

In *University of Southampton's Applications* [2002] R.P.C. 44 at [906] which concerned an inventorship dispute limited disclosure was ordered under former r.106 concerning corresponding applications in other countries and of a draft application relevant to the issue of inventorship. Further disclosure was refused at this stage pending the filing of evidence, but further orders were made when the matter came back before the Comptroller at a later stage, see BL O/456/02. The rule has also been applied, in an application to settle the terms of a licence of right under s.46(3), to require production of previous licence agreements, see *Smith Kline & French's Cimetidine Patents* [1988] R.P.C. 148. Here it was observed that documents produced on an order made under r.106 became available as evidence in the case even if not relied upon by either party to a contested proceeding. If disclosure is ordered, claims to "privilege" can be made which (if successful) result in non-disclosure of the documents held, or conceded, to be privileged. The question of privilege is discussed in the commentary on CDPA 1988 s.280. Where the Comptroller orders production of documents, it would appear that he could order even privileged documents to be produced, see *McIlwraith v Paracel [Australia]* (1991–92) 23 I.P.R. 177. Here a previous partial waiver of privilege assisted the order for production.

—Restrictions on disclosure of discovered documents

123.48   Where disclosure is ordered confidentiality orders may be imposed see, e.g. the *Hearings Manual* at para.3.57, *Halcon International Inc v The Shell Transport Co* [1979] R.P.C. 97; *Bonzel & Schneider (Europe) AG v Intervention Ltd* [1991] R.P.C. 43; and *Apple Corps Ltd v Apple Computer Inc* [1992] F.S.R. 389. Thus, where circumstances so (require because documents disclose commercially sensitive information which would be valuable in the hands of the other parties to the proceedings for reasons unconnected with those proceedings, for example details of sales and revenue in applications to settle the terms of a "licence of right") it has become commonplace for the Comptroller to order that a party should have limited access to the documents produced on disclosure. This follows the steps taken by the court to protect trade secrets necessarily disclosed to meet the obligations of disclosure, for which see §61.67 and §61.69. As regards the file of the application in the Patent Office, confidentiality orders under r.53 (reprinted at §118.04) can be requested, see §118.20.

In *Glaverbel's Patent* BL O/15/96, a "confidentiality club" of persons entitled to inspect documents ordered to be produced on disclosure was established to prevent the use of the information in corresponding litigation in other countries, persons directly involved in this being excluded from that club; and, in *Cooper Roller Bearings' Design Rights* BL O/66/

97, in view of the commercial nature of the documents produced on disclosure, inspection thereof was limited to legal advisers and experts, see also the remarks in *LIFESAVERS/ Trade Mark* [1997] R.P.C. 563.

—Written evidence

As explained in the *Hearings Manual*, the general rule is that all of the facts in issue or **123.49** relevant to the issue in a given case must be proved by evidence. If a party fails to prove an essential fact the other side may well succeed even though the required evidence was in fact available. The claimant should adduce evidence to prove the facts pleaded in his or her statement or to refute the defendant's evidence. Similarly, the defendant should file evidence to support the facts pleaded in his or her counter-statement or to refute the claimant's evidence. However matters which have been admitted, of which judicial notice is taken, or which are presumptions of law need not be proved by evidence.

Rule 87 provides for evidence to be given by witness statement, affidavit, statutory declaration or any other form which would be admissible as evidence in court proceedings, but r.87(2) provides that evidence is to be by witness statement unless the Comptroller otherwise directs. It should be noted that a statement of grounds or a counterstatement which is required to be verified by a statement of truth is also admissible in evidence.

The Practice Direction supplementing CPR Pt 32 defines a witness statement as a written statement signed by a person which contains the evidence which that person would be allowed to give orally. An affidavit or witness statement should so far as possible be in the deponent's or witness's own words, must indicate which of his statements are made from his own knowledge, and which on the basis of his information and belief, and in the latter case the source of any matters of information or belief must be indicated. It may only be given in evidence if it includes a statement of truth, r.87(2).

The format for evidence is set out in the *Litigation Manual* at paras 3.61–3.69. Evidence in a foreign language is permitted and should be accompanied by a translation into English made by a qualified translator, and by an affidavit made by the translator confirming that the translation is true. The three documents and any exhibits must be filed together.

A witness statement, affidavit or statutory declaration should:

(a) if the if the person is giving evidence in his professional, business or other occupational capacity, give the address at which he works, the position he holds and the name of his firm or employer;

(b) state whether the witness is a party to the proceedings or is an employee of a party to the proceedings;

(c) give evidence in the first person (I, me and so on);

(d) have each paragraph numbered, with so far as possible each paragraph confined to a distinct portion of the subject;

(e) have each page numbered and where possible, be bound;

(f) express dates, sums and other numbers in figures not words;

(g) end with a statement of truth or jurat on the same page as the last page of the written evidence.

As set out in CPR Pt 32 PD 18.3 a document referred to in a witness statement should be produced to and verified by the person making that statement and should remain separate from that statement. It should be filed with the evidence and should be exhibited, normally with an appropriately headed fly sheet bearing a title and an identification code.

It should be noted that merely exhibiting a document does not in itself give any evidence about it or about the relevance or truth of its contents. The exhibited document should therefore be discussed by the witness, relevant portions of the document or information in it should be identified and where its contents are true either to the personal knowledge of the witness or on information and belief this should be explicitly stated. Failure of the witness to provide a full discussion of each relevant part of each relevant document may have the consequence that significant information contained in an exhibited document may not be available to be relied on at the subsequent hearing because it has not been put to and discussed by the witness.

Non-documentary evidence should be exhibited and handled in accordance with CPR Pt 32 PD.

In *Wordsworth Holdings' Patent* BL O/145/97 the Comptroller decided the case on documents annexed to the statement of case, but not formally included in a statutory declaration or affidavit, though only because no objection was raised against this and it was pointed out that difficulties would consequently arise on any appeal. A copy of an affidavit used in court proceedings did not satisfy the requirements of former r.103, see *Taylor's Patent* [1970] R.P.C. 108 and would probably not be accepted under r.87.

Particularly in entitlement disputes, the Comptroller increasingly places importance upon written evidence having been personally prepared by the witnesses, rather than by lawyers, and not being at variance with factual evidence and not contradicted during cross examination, see: *Expotech's Patent* BL O/95/04 and *University of Southampton's Applications* BL O/86/04 and [2005] R.P.C. 11 at [220], in each of which some evidence was wholly disregarded as being "unreliable" for these reasons.

—Hearsay

123.50   The Civil Evidence Act 1995 (c.38) abolished with effect from January 31, 1997 the previous general prohibition against the receipt of hearsay evidence in civil litigation subject to a notice procedure which is now set out in CPR 33.1–33.5. The 1995 Act (in s.1(2)) defines "hearsay" as "a statement made otherwise by a person while giving oral evidence in the proceedings which is tendered as evidence of the matters stated", and is not limited to hearsay evidence repeated at first hand. Under s.4 of this Act, the weight (if any) of the hearsay evidence is to be estimated by the court having regard to any circumstances from which any inference can be drawn as to the reliability or otherwise of the evidence. In particular, regard is to be had to:

"(a) whether it would have been reasonable and practicable for the party by whom the evidence was adduced to have produced the maker of the original statement as a witness;

(b) whether the original statement was made contemporaneously with the occurrence or existence of the matters stated;

(c) whether the evidence involves multiple hearsay;

(d) whether any person involved had any motive to conceal or misrepresent matters;

(e) whether the original statement was an edited account, or was made in collaboration with another or for a particular purpose; and

(f) whether the circumstances in which the evidence is adduced as hearsay are such as to suggest an attempt to prevent proper evaluation of its weight."

This 1995 Act applies to proceedings before the Comptroller, but in a Patent Office Practice Notice on Evidence (see [1999] R.P.C. 294), it was stated that, as normally evidence in proceedings before the Comptroller is given by statutory declarations or affidavits filed in advance of the hearing, such filing will be taken as the notice required under this Act.

Although evidence given by affidavit or statutory declaration is itself strictly of a hearsay nature, because it is not given orally, no objection arises merely because evidence before the Comptroller is given in this form, since such is specifically permitted by r.87 made under the powers of s.123(2)(d) (*Peckitt's Application* [1999] R.P.C. 337). However, where such written evidence itself contains statements of a hearsay nature, the Practice Notice referred to above that the evidence "should contain sufficient details to enable the other party or parties to deal with the matters arising out of its containing such evidence". Also, if the provision of further particulars relating to the evidence is reasonable and practical in the circumstances for that purpose, such particulars should be given on request; and, following CPR 33.2, it seems that the hearsay statements and the makers of such statements should each be identified and an indication given why those persons are not themselves giving evidence in the proceedings.

Another party to the proceedings is entitled to call the maker of the hearsay statement for cross-examination (CPR 33.4), but this power may not be effective when such a person cannot be traced or is resident abroad, although an unfulfilled reasonable request to present a witness for cross-examination should reduce (perhaps to zero) the weight to be given to that evidence.

The Comptroller has found unacceptable evidence presented as un-sworn statements exhibited to statutory declarations of others; and has said that, where the authenticity of documents has been questioned, the originals should be produced or an explanation given of their non-availability (*Brooks and Cope's Application* BL O/71/93).

In *Genentech's Patent* BL C/66/87, the Patents Court gave the claimants leave, under the then Civil Evidence Acts, to give in evidence at the trial "all statements contained in the documents disclosed by the defendants".

Note that, since the Civil Evidence Act 1972 (c.30) a witness has been able to give evidence of an opinion nature and (particularly in view of the increased acceptance of evidence of a hearsay nature since the 1995 Act) this would seem to extend to giving an opinion on the very question which the court has before it for decision, see I. Purvis (1998] *CIPA* 588, as was accepted in the copyright case of *Designers Guild v Russell Williams* [1998] F.S.R. 803. Even before the 1995 Act, it had been suggested that the court should be entitled to receive evidence as to whether an expert himself considered the invention to be obvious *Mölnlycke v Procter & Gamble (No.5)* [1994] R.P.C. 49. However, in *Scanvaegt v Pelcombe* [1998] F.S.R. 786 it was stated that "the dicta of Lord Tomlin in *British Celanese v Courtaulds* (1935) 52 R.P.C. 171 at 196 HL that 'an expert witness is not entitled to say, nor is counsel entitled to ask him, what the specification means' remains entirely apt".

A brief discussion of hearsay and "similar fact" evidence appears in the *Hearings Manual* at 3.87–3.91.

—Evidence of expert witnesses

The duties of an expert witness are explained in *The Ikarian Reefer* [1993] 2 Lloyd's Rep. 68 at 81–82 and in *Anglo Group Plc v Winther Brown & Co* March 1, [2000] and are now governed by CPR Pt 35 and the accompanying Practice Direction see in particular the following: **123.51**

"2.1 ... An expert's report should be addressed to the court and not to the party from whom the expert has received his instructions.
2.2 ... An expert's report must:

(1) give details of the expert's qualifications;

(2) give details of any literature or other material which the expert has relied on in making the report;

(3) contain a statement setting out the substance of all facts and instructions given to the expert which are material to the opinions expressed in the report or upon which those opinions are based;

(4) make clear which of the facts stated in the report are within the expert's own knowledge;

(5) say who carried out any examination, measurement, test or experiment which the expert has

used for the report, give the qualifications of that person, and say whether or not the test or experiment has been carried out under the expert's supervision;

(6) where there is a range of opinion on the matters dealt with in the report—

    (a) summarise the range of opinion, and

    (b) give reasons for his own opinion;

(7) contain a summary of the conclusions reached;

(8) if the expert is not able to give his opinion without qualification, state the qualification; and

(9) contain a statement that the expert understands his duty to the court, and has complied and will continue to comply with that duty."

Expert evidence is extensively discussed in the *Hearings Manual* at paras 3.70–3.83 where the above requirements are emphasised. Furthermore, if both parties file expert evidence, the Comptroller will in advance of any hearing require the expert witnesses to provide a statement setting out the issues on which they agree and the issues on which they disagree including a summary of disputed matters, see the model Office letter at Annex 9 to Chapter 1 of the *Litigation Manual*.

The role of a technical expert in patent cases has been considered in *SmithKline Beecham Plc v Apotex Europe Ltd* [2004] EWCA Civ 1568; [2005] F.S.R. 24 and *Alan Nuttall Ltd v Fri-Jado UK Ltd* [2008] EWHC 1311. An expert may survive criticism that he was not actually working in the relevant field at the time if the technology of the case is such that he could read into it and detailed knowledge as not required. However, if in cross-examination he is shown to lack impartiality and not to be prepared to accept what is obvious and basic then it is legitimate for the tribunal to conclude that his opinions are tainted and to disregard his evidence in its entirety, see *Tickner v Honda Motor Co Ltd* [2002] EWHC 8 Pat Ct, see also *Alan Nuttall Ltd* (above).

A non-exhaustive list of issues on which an expert might be asked to give evidence is set out below:

— the technical background to the invention;

— the common general knowledge in the relevant art;

— attributes of individuals working in the relevant art, and where the skilled addressee is a team the likely make-up of that team;

— the meaning of specialised or technical terms, see *Glaverbel SA v British Coal Corp* [1994] R.P.C 443 at 486 but not the construction of a patent specification, see *British Celanese Ltd v Courtaulds Ltd* (1935) 52 R.P.C. 171; and *ICI v Montedison (UK) Ltd* [1995] R.P.C. 449 at 460;

— what a skilled person would see in a drawing or photograph, see *Van der Lely v Bamfords* [1959] R.P.C. 99;

— what a document would disclose to an appropriately skilled reader, or what he would understand from a prior document's teaching, including features that are implicit or obvious to a skilled reader but are not apparent on the face of the document;

— whether a skilled person would regard a prior document as a worthwhile starting point for further development or as having any relevance to the technical problem under consideration, or whether he would put it to one side, see *Eli Lilly and Company v Human Genome Sciences, Inc* [2008] EWHC 1903; [2008] R.P.C. 29 at [733] Pat Ct;

— whether and if so how a skilled person could put the disclosure of a prior document into practice, see *Eli Lilly & Company v Human Genome Sciences* [2008] EWHC 1903; [2008] R.P.C. 29 at [733] Pat Ct;

— what a skilled person would have done next on the basis of a prior disclosure;

— whether there was any reason why a feature alleged to be obvious had not been included in a prior disclosure;

— whether the differences between the claimed subject matter and the prior art were mere workshop modification; and

— if a step beyond a prior disclosure was taken what resulting behaviour or properties were surprising or were predictable.

In *Specialist Petroleum Services' Patent* BL O/352/04, written witness statements presented as expert evidence in revocation proceedings were criticised, the hearing officer saying: "None of these [statements] said [as the CPR requires] what their instructions were or that they understood their duty was to the tribunal rather than their client or employer". Consequently, the credibility of these witnesses was not enhanced. In particular, one witness statement referred to case lawand other legal matters, but there was no indication that the witness was an expert in these matters.

Patent attorneys cannot be regarded as experts on scientific facts and therefore their statements on such matters are likely to be disregarded or given little weight as, e.g. in *Schwibag's Patent* BL O/29/04 and *Cunningham Covers v Airmat Safety Products* BL O/302/04.

—Evidence of experiments

Evidence of the results of experiments can be given, but experiments carried out in proceedings before the Comptroller should always comply with the Rules of Court *Raufoss' Patent* BL C/102/86, for which see CPR 63 PD 7.1 discussed in §61.75. This means that the other party should be given the opportunity of witnessing the carrying out of the experiments, or a repetition of them, failing which the evidence may be given less than full weight (*British Cast Iron's Patent* [1976] R.P.C. 33 at 48), or not admitted at all as in *British Railways' Patent* BL O/41/85. **123.52**

Experimental evidence should normally be presented in evidence-in-chief, see *Union Carbide's (Hostettler's) Application* [1972] R.P.C. 601 and *Scragg's Application* [1972] R.P.C. 679. In *Timbale Corp.'s Patent* BL O/152/90, experimental evidence was allowed to be filed as reply evidence, without opportunity for repetition before the other party's observers, in order not to delay the hearing, but the question of admission of the evidence was reserved to the hearing.

—Attestation of evidence given by statutory declaration or affidavit

A statutory declaration should be in the form: **123.53**

"I, A.B., of ... do solemnly and sincerely declare that ... And I make this solemn declaration conscientiously believing the same to be true, and by virtue of the provisions of the Statutory Declarations Act 1835."

An affidavit is made on oath and the affiant is subject to the penalties specified for making a false oath. It should be in the form:

"I, A.B., of ... make oath [or affirm] and say as follows: ... "

Each of these types of written evidence should be headed with reference to the proceedings for which it is to be made and conclude with the signature of the declarant/affiant followed by a jurat reading:

Declared/Sworn [Affirmed] at ...

this ... day of ... 20..
before me:

and the qualification of the attesting officer should be stated, e.g. as "A solicitor entitled to administer oaths". The affidavit/declaration would appear to be void if the attesting officer is a solicitor to any of the parties or if he has an interest in the proceedings for which it is made (Commissioners for Oaths Act 1889 (c.10) s.1(3)), see also CPR 32 PD 9.

Under the Solicitors Act 1974 (c.47) s.81, an affidavit or declaration can be attested in the United Kingdom, inter alia, by any practising solicitor, who now automatically has the status of a Commissioner for Oaths. Any registered patent agent having the status of an "authorised litigator" (for which see §102A.02) would also be able attest statutory declarations and affidavits within the United Kingdom, in each case subject to that person not having an interest in the proceedings.

Outside the United Kingdom, the most convenient procedure is to arrange attestation by a notary public or authorised consular officer, but within the Commonwealth or the Republic of Ireland, attestation can be by anyone authorised by law to administer an oath in that country for the purpose of any legal proceedings with no further attestation needed. However, under CPR 32.17 this freedom (for use in proceedings before a court, including a county court) is now extended to execution abroad in any country, provided that the affidavit is signed in accordance with the formalities of the place where it is made. There would seem to be no good reason for the Comptroller to object to a foreign attestation in accordance with this rule.

—Timetable for the evidence stages and hearing

123.54   Following dispatch of the counter-statement, the Comptroller sets a timetable for the evidence stages and for the hearing which as explained above is to take place within nine months from the date when the counter-statement is sent to the claimant. The timetable will normally provide that successive periods each of six weeks, each calculated from the date of dispatch of the initiating document, are provided for the submission of evidence. For example in proceedings under s.72 the applicant files his evidence-in-chief first, the proprietor then files his evidence (which should include both his evidence-in-chief and that in reply to the applicant for revocation), and finally the applicant for revocation files further evidence, which must be strictly in reply to that of the proprietor. In each case the filing party should automatically send a copy of the evidence directly to the other party at its address for service. Each of these six week periods is extensible by exercise of discretion, but the Comptroller also has power to shorten any such period (r.81). However, a shortened timetable with simultaneous exchange of evidence may be set, see §123.45.

After these set evidence stages, further evidence can be filed but requires leave of the Comptroller (r.80(2)). If the applicant does not file any evidence, the proprietor's time for filing evidence commences when the time for the applicant's evidence (including any extension sought and granted) expires. As the Comptroller will decide on the allegations in the public interest, the proprietor should not assume that evidence to support patentability is not required merely because the applicant has chosen not to file any evidence himself. For example, an alleged anticipation may not need any evidence to establish it.

In each case, the evidence (in the form of affidavits, witness statements or statutory declarations) is filed at the UK-IPO (together with original exhibits) and the party filing the same supplies a copy directly to the address for service of the other party. In addition, there is the possibility of submitting oral evidence at an ensuing hearing, although only with leave of the Comptroller. Where a solicitor omitted to supply the other party directly with a copy of his party's evidence, the Comptroller termed this a "trivial irregularity" and did not impose any penalty (*Bere's Patent* BL O/84/91), but a less lenient attitude could be shown in other cases. Where exhibits cannot be copied, they can be inspected at the UK-IPO. Each of the six week periods is extensible by discretion exercised under r.81.

The third round of evidence must be "strictly in reply" and therefore supplementary evidence which could (and should) have been included in the evidence-in-chief may be struck out as inadmissible, see *Scragg's Application* [1972] R.P.C. 679. For examples of inadmissible reply evidence, see *Ford Motor's (Nastas') Application* [1968] R.P.C. 220 and *Timbale Corp's Patent* BL O/152/90, in the latter of which some parts of a declaration were ordered to be deleted as not being "evidence strictly in reply". In *AEA Technology's Reference* BL O/166/98, it was held that evidence in answer to "evidence-in-reply" should only be admitted in exceptional circumstances, but here a challenge to that evidence as not being "strictly in reply" failed. However, where purported evidence in reply is largely a repetition of evidence given in chief, it need not be struck out (*Peckitt's Application* [1999] R.P.C. 337).

Late-filed evidence will be admitted if it is "both relevant and decisive" (*Rohm and Haas' Application* [1966] F.S.R. 403), and also when amendments are put forward which change the situation (*Reuter's Patent* [1973] R.P.C. 83).

If an applicant for revocation under s.72 withdraws, the Comptroller will decide the application in the public interest, and this is so even if the patentee indicates his intention to allow the patent to lapse by non-renewal (*N.L. Petroleum's Patent* BL O/112/90, noted I.P.D. 14043). This is because revocation has complete retroactive effect, see *Abbott Laboratories' (Chu's) Patent* [1992] R.P.C. 487 where the procedure in *General Motors' (Turney and Barr's) Application* [1976] R.P.C. 659 under the 1949 Act was followed with approval. For the procedure when the applicant for revocation withdraws and the patentee wishes to amend the patent, see the MOPP (para.72.49).

—Powers of the Comptroller concerning evidence

The powers of the Comptroller to regulate the issues on which he requires evidence and the mode of giving evidence before him are set out in r.82(2). **123.55**

On a conflict of written evidence, an application for revocation should fail *General Electric's (Cox's) Patents* [1977] R.P.C. 421 because the onus of proof (on the balance of probabilities) lies with the applicant for revocation.

However, rr.82(1)(d) and 87(1)(b) provide for oral evidence in addition to, or in lieu of, the normal written form of evidence. In *Sainsbury's Application* [1981] F.S.R. 406, the Court of Appeal was informed that it was (at that time) not the practice of the patent bar to cross-examine deponents in Patent Office proceedings. In refusing leave to cross-examine a witness on appeal to the Patents Court, the Court of Appeal stated:

> "If that be the practice, it is one which is a bad practice, because if there is good reason for wanting to cross-examine a deponent, then the proper time to do this is before the superintending examiner and not on appeal to the Patents Court".

The *Hearings Manual* states that in accordance with *Peckitts Application* [1999] R.P.C. 337 if cross-examination is requested it will normally be allowed unless the Comptroller directs otherwise. A failure to challenge testimony by cross-examination can, therefore, be relevant (*Laguerre's Patent* [1971] R.P.C. 384 CA and *Technic's Application* [1973] R.P.C. 383 at 406 CA).

In the *Patent Office Practice Notice on Evidence* [1999] R.P.C. 294, the Comptroller stated that reasonable notice—normally of at least four weeks—should be given of any request to present a witness for cross-examination, with longer notice if the witness is resident abroad or would otherwise find it difficult to attend at the time when the hearing is likely to be held and that co-operation between the parties is expected so that difficulties can be avoided. As to refusal by a witness to attend a hearing and the possibility of applying to the court for an enforcement order by way of subpoena see the *Hearings Manual* at 4.76.

In *Norris's Patent* [1988] R.P.C. 159, a failure by the parties to request cross-examination (as well as disclosure of documents) was criticised. However, where cross-examination takes place, the witness must not be confronted with documents which have not previously been introduced into the proceedings, see *Staeng's Patent* [1996] R.P.C. 183 at 186.

In *Ladney and Hendry's International PCT Application* BL O/84/96, the hearing officer had been faced with allegations of lying by the respective witnesses, but had felt able to conclude that there was no real conflict of evidence, although he refused to admit into evidence a transcript of cross-examination held previously in the offices of a patent agent, see BL C/103/96, noted I.P.D. 20025. On appeal, the Court held that the hearing officer had failed to give proper weight to certain evidence before him which had not been the subject of challenge and allowed an appeal, but the Court of Appeal restored the decision of the Comptroller (see [1998] R.P.C. 319) because it felt that the hearing officer had properly evaluated the evidence before him. The Court of Appeal stated that the Comptroller's decision on matters of fact should not be reversed except in a clear case.

Under r.86 it appears that the Comptroller has power to issue a witness summons, or alternatively in his aid the High Court or a country court could do so (CPR 34A PD 2.1). However, the Comptroller has no power to punish a witness for non-attendance. Further, there is no power by which a witness summons can be issued against a witness who is resident outside England, Wales and Scotland. The principles which should be considered when cross-examination of a witness is resisted were extensively discussed in the case of *Beecham Group v Bristol-Myers (No.2)* [New Zealand] [1979] 2 N.Z.L.R. 625.

In *Loewy's Application* (1952) 69 R.P.C. 3, it was argued that a declaration by a declarant who, although he had been summoned, failed to attend for cross-examination, should not be received or read, but the Comptroller received it in the exercise of his discretion. However, in *PyMah's Patent* BL O/68/95, the Comptroller entirely discounted the evidence of a witness who was not presented for cross-examination despite a request having been made. In *Plasser Bahnbaumaschinen's Patent* BL O/76/93, the Patentee's expert was asked to attend for cross-examination on his evidence but did not do so. The Comptroller revoked the patent for lack of inventive step after finding the opposing testimony credible. In *Shop-A-Long Bingo's Application* BL O/115/93, the Comptroller considered sworn evidence submitted by the referrer in entitlement proceedings even though he chose not to attend the hearing; this evidence was given due weight and found to be sufficient for a finding in favour of the referrer. In *European Environmental Recycling's International Application* BL O/316/99, evidence from one declarant, who failed to appear for cross examination because he was on holiday, was struck out upon application by the other party.

Evidence given in other proceedings is not necessarily evidence in the proceedings in issue, and an attempt to exhibit such other evidence has been disallowed *Coal Industry's Patent* BL O/11/90, noted I.P.D. 13081. However, where a joint hearing is held on two related patents, oral evidence given at that hearing may be considered in respect of both patents (*Mölnlycke's and Boussac Saint Frères' Patents* BL O/15/90, noted I.P.D. 13111).

Note that r.79(1) requires supply of a copy of any document referred to in any evidence (see also r.82(1)). There is no apparent power to waive strict compliance with this rule. In *Coflexip Stena's Patent* BL O/20/96, where an affidavit had indirectly referred to documents which the other party sought to inspect, it was ordered that either the documents be produced or the parts of affidavits referring to them be withdrawn.

Although the Comptroller has no power to issue an injunction, under r.86 he can restrain a party from using before him any evidence which is shown to be subject to legal privilege, see *Sonic Tape's Patent* [1987] R.P.C. 251; and, in *AEA Technology's Reference* BL O/166/98 a declaration was struck out because it was held to refer to a meeting which had been held on a "without prejudice" basis, and other evidence relating to the admissibility of that declaration should play no further part on the proceedings. In *JAT Extrusions' Patent* BL O/167/95, an applicant for revocation (a former employee and director of the proprietor) sought to rely upon documents addressed to him in his former capacity by a patent agent. The Comptroller held that these documents were the subject of privilege enjoyed by the proprietor so that the applicant for revocation was not free to disclose them to others; it was ordered that they "not be used in the case and kept confidential".

Rule 103(3) and (4) gives the Comptroller no power to punish summarily for contempt of court.

In proceedings under ss.48–51, a statement made in a report of the Competition Commission concerning any activity in relation to a patented invention is to be taken as prima facie evidence and does not require any supporting declaration or affidavit (s.53(2)).

On the possible admission of further evidence on appeal, see §97.16.

After the rounds of evidence provided by the rules, further evidence may be admitted at the discretion of the Comptroller. This discretion will not be exercised for evidence which could have been filed earlier, especially where it would result in delay because of the need to provide an opportunity for response, see *Baker Hughes' Patents* BL O/1/01.

Requests for admission of further evidence and for cross-examination were allowed in *Hartington Conway's Application* BL O/438/02.

In *Intel's Patent* [2002] R.P.C. 48 at [957] it was commented that it was normal practice in amendment proceedings before the Patent Office for the opponent to put in its evidence first, but the practice in the High Court was for the patentee to go first. There was seen to be no good grounds for this difference in practice so the practice in the Patent Office should be changed to align it with the court and therefore the patentee was ordered to file its evidence first.

Hearings

As explained above, a hearing date is normally fixed shortly after the counter-statement is filed.

123.56

Normally, hearings will be held in London, rather than Newport. If a hearing is held in Newport, the Welsh language can be used, but prior notice of this must be given in order that interpretation can be provided. For the addresses of these locations, see §123.88. The provisions for fixing hearings, and the practice in relation to them, are dealt with in §101.09. As regards the right of audience at hearings, see §102.02; and, as regards the procedure at hearings before the Comptroller, see §§101.05 and 101.11. In *AEA Technology's Reference* BL O/166/98, it was suggested at a preliminary hearing that, before the substantive hearing, the parties should try and agree upon textbooks which gave clear and correct definitions of the technical terms in issue and that, if possible, the parties should prepare an agreed technical primer to be used at that hearing. This was done and was stated to have facilitated the subsequent substantive hearing, see BL O/36/99. Under TPN 1/2000 (para.45), it is generally to be expected that parties, especially those represented by professional practitioners, will supply the hearing officer with skeleton arguments, together with authorities, at least two days before the date of a hearing. For the content of skeleton arguments, see §97.22.

It has long been the tradition that, except in cases of entitlement to the invention (formerly called "obtaining"), the patentee should open the proceedings at a hearing in the UK-IPO. However, this practice was changed by para.43 of TPN 1/2000 so that he who has the general burden of proof should be invited at least to open the oral proceedings.

When late-filed evidence is not admitted, and the party putting forward that evidence indicates his intention to appeal that decision, the Comptroller has felt obliged to postpone the substantive hearing, see *Upjohn and Takeda's Patents* BL O/21/87.

For the holding of a hearing in Scotland, see s.98.

Advisers

Under r.102 made under the authority of s.123(2)(g) the Comptroller may appoint one or more advisers to assist him in any particular case. The provision was new in the present Act and does not extend to the appointment of an "assessor", as distinct from an "adviser", the difference between which is explained in §96.12. Section 123(2)(g) may reflect the increased power of the Comptroller to revoke patents for lack of inventive step under the provisions of s.72, and the desirability of affording the Comptroller expert assistance in the same way as the court may have under the re-enactment of s.96. However, the choice of the Comptroller is unfettered and is not limited to scientific advisers as in the case of advisers to the court.

123.57

While r.102 explicitly gives the Comptroller power to settle the question of instructions to be given to the adviser, there is no direction as to the manner in which assistance by an appointed adviser is to be given, for example whether the adviser will appear at any hearing and, if so, whether the parties will have the right to address the adviser. It is not even clear whether the advice given by the adviser will be disclosed to the parties. In the past, where an assessor has assisted the judge or judges in infringement actions, the assessor has remained tacit, but an assessor has a different legal function from an adviser, as explained in §96.12. It is also not clear that the adviser must come from outside the UK-IPO. Thus, the rule may legitimise the practice of an examiner sitting with the hearing officer in hearings before the Comptroller, though otherwise no instance of an appointment of an adviser to assist the Comptroller has been noted.

For a discussion of the role to be played by an adviser, see particularly *Beecham Group v Bristol-Myers [Amoxycillin]* [New Zealand] [1980] 1 N.Z.L.R. 185 and 192.

In the debates on the Bill which led to the 1977 Act, the impression was given that the Comptroller would often wish to appoint lay advisers in proceedings under s.40 for inventor compensation (H.C. Official Report, Standing Committee D, July 5, 1977 (AM), cols. 120–128). However, this has not yet happened in practice.

Decisions

123.58   The mode of giving decisions is dealt with in §101.07 and the publication of decisions in §101.12. The Comptroller may give an interim decision, and it is his practice to do so if he thinks that any amendment could save part of the patent. The question of costs was normally deferred to the final decision; since December 3, 2007 hearing officers are likely to be more willing to award costs following interlocutory or preliminary hearings, see Patent Office Tribunal Practice Note TPN 4/2007. An interim decision is subject to appeal as if it were a final decision, and if appeal is lodged the revocation proceedings are suspended pending its resolution. Thus a proprietor faced with an interim decision of patent invalidity must decide whether he wishes to appeal or apply to amend, but if he chooses the latter, he will forfeit his right to the former, see *Nachf's Application* [1983] R.P.C. 87.

Very rarely a hearing before the Comptroller will result in an extempore decision. In such circumstances the parties can obtain a copy of the decisions only by application to the shorthand writers, see the notice in O.J. May 2, 1973 which also explains that applications for extension of time for lodging appeal will then be entertained while the decision is studied, if this is requested within 14 days of the decision being given. Otherwise, the decision will be issued in writing and a copy will (unless the decision involves an unpublished application) be provided to the British Library and made available on the website of the UK-IPO.

Where the Comptroller orders revocation and the patentee desires to appeal, it is prudent to request a stay of the revocation order pending the determination of the appeal. Where this was not done, and the appeal succeeded, the order of the Court was a declaration that the register should be rectified to restore the patent *Rockwool International's Patent* BL C/34/93.

Appeals from decisions of the Comptroller

123.59   Under CPR 63.16, appeals from the Comptroller to the Patents Court are now governed by the general rules for appeals set out in CPR 52, as discussed in §§97.12–97.18. Permission to appeal is not required.

Costs

123.60   The question of costs (and the giving of security for costs) in proceedings before the Comptroller is governed by s.107. The principles for such awards of costs and the amounts that are normally allowed and of orders for security for such costs to be awarded are discussed in the commentary on that section. In proceedings before the Comptroller the costs awarded are only a contribution to actual costs. However, on appeal, costs (taxed if not agreed) are awarded to the successful party on the normal "standard" basis for proceedings in the High Court, even if that party be the Comptroller, but the Comptroller does not always enforce an order for his costs, even though he routinely asks for these when an ex parte applicant makes an unsuccessful appeal from a decision of the Comptroller, see §97.23.

A party may be awarded costs, even if he does not appear and was not represented, if he expended time and labour on the preparation of his case (*Rhodes (Edgar's) Patent* [1975] F.S.R. 135).

In *Ash & Lacy's Patent No.2240559* BL O/60/02, the hearing officer awarded costs against the claimant for having filed an inadequate statement of case, but in a later decision (see BL O/144/02), when the patentee decided not to defend its patent, costs in an equal amount were awarded against it, so the costs orders cancelled out.

Following *Oystertec's Application* in which a revocation action was allowed to proceed in the name of a firm of patent attorneys, it was contended that the agents' firm should be treated as a litigant in person and therefore not be able to recover costs for work done by them. It was held (see BL O/525/02) that this principle did not apply to proceedings before the Comptroller in which costs awarded "are not intended to compensate parties for their expenses but are merely a lump sum contribution to those expenses" and an appropriate award of costs was therefore made.

Miscellaneous

—Rectification of errors under rules 105 and 107

Subsection (2)(b) specifies the regulation of procedure before the Comptroller and the UK-IPO and the rectification of irregularities of procedure. This, together with s.117(1), is the direct authority for rr.105 and 107. **123.61**

As presently worded, r.105 gives the Comptroller discretion to amend any document filed in proceedings before him and r.107 gives the power to rectify any irregularity of procedure in or before the UK-IPO, but with the important proviso that no time or period specified in the Act, or in the Patents Rules, may be altered unless there had been an irregularity, or prospective irregularity, "which is attributable, wholly or in part, to a default, omission or other error by the Comptroller, an examiner or the Patent Office", see r.107(3). However, this is without prejudice to the grant of extensions of time in the circumstances permitted by rr.108 or 109.

The decisions relating to "default, omission or other error" and the discretionary nature of relief under r.107 is discussed in §123.62. Some occasions on which there may still be an incentive or need to obtain an extension of time under r.107 (rather than under some part of r.108) are indicated in that paragraph.

The wording of r.105 permits amendment to correct an error or mistake under s.117. Section 117(1) provides that the Comptroller may, subject to any rules, correct an error of translation, a clerical error or a mistake in any document filed in connection with a patent or application, see §§117.03 et seq. While r.105 does not specifically limit amendment to that sought by an applicant, comparison with the wording of s.19 suggests that it is not the intention to give the Comptroller power under this rule to make a correction of his own volition. In any dispute under r.105, the proprietor or applicant has a right to be heard, see §101.04. The Comptroller also has limited powers under rr.71 and 72 to rectify irregularities in procedure which occur during the international phase of an international application for a patent (UK), for which see §89B.12.

Applications for amendments under r.105, and the eventual result, are now (but were not for some years) advertised in the *Patents Journal* by virtue of r.105(6). Part 2 of Sch.3 to the 2007 Rules clearly states that an opposition to a correction of an error in a specification is a process which will trigger proceedings before the Comptroller.

—Irregularity in procedure

Operation of r.107 in practice requires an "irregularity" of procedure connected with any matter before the Comptroller, an examiner or the UK-IPO. In *E's Applications* [1983] **123.62**

R.P.C. 231 HL, it was uncompromisingly laid down in relation to the original form of the rule that the rule could not be used to override any limitation imposed by virtue of any statute or other rule, but this principle is now varied to the extent set out in current r.107(2).

The MOPP indicates (by reference to *M's Application* [1985] R.P.C. 249 CA) that, for r.107 to be invoked to extend a time limit: (1) the UK-IPO must be shown to have been guilty of some error, default or omission (with "omission" being of something which the UK-IPO has some sort of obligation to do); (2) that such error, default or omission must have contributed to the failure to meet the time limit; and (3) that such has played an active causative role in the irregularity that has taken place, though it need not be the sole cause of the irregularity.

There has been no irregularity of procedure when there has merely been a change of mind of the applicant (or his agent) (*P's Application* [1983] R.P.C. 269). There is also no irregularity in procedure, at least within the UK-IPO, when the Comptroller fails to draw attention to a mistake by the applicant or his agent in circumstances where the Comptroller is not under a legal duty so to do, for example: replying to routine letters within any particular time (*M's Application*, above); noting that a wrong translation of an international application had been filed (*Masuda's Application* [1987] R.P.C. 37); authorising a renewal fee refund without drawing attention to the lapsing of the patent (*Borg-Warner's Patent* [1986] R.P.C. 137); and giving information directly to the patentee in response to a telephone call from him, with this not being communicated to the agent recorded as the address for service, there being no obligation (and therefore no omission by the Patent Office) to communicate advisory correspondence, as distinct from statutory notices, to the address for service (*Danev's Patent* BL O/142/96).

However, the position is different where the Comptroller has a moral duty to act in a certain way because he has previously indicated he will do so, see *Mills' Application* [1985] R.P.C. 339 CA, or by virtue of custom and expected practice, see *Mitsubishi Jidosha's Application* [1988] R.P.C. 449, *Alphaplan's Application* BL O/127/93, noted I.P.D. 17004 and *Rigcool v Optima Solutions* O/182/11. A further example may be where the UK-IPO gives erroneous advice, as has been accepted by the EPO, see *J 6/79 Rhône-Poulenc* [1980] R.P.C. 515; OJ EPO 1980, 225.

Examples of procedural irregularities which have led (or which would probably have led, but for the proviso of present r.107(2)), to the grant of relief under r.107 are:

- issue of Patent Office receipt causing agent to believe, according to custom and practice, that all necessary papers had been duly filed (*Mitsubishi Jidosha's Application*, above); or that a received cheque had been post-dated (*Alphaplan's Application*, above);

- failure to respond to a request to correct formal defects when the telephone call was unrecorded in the Patent Office (*Davison's Application* BL O/47/95);

- omission of "UK" from the list of designated states for an international application though "United Kingdom (EPO)" had been listed (*Prangley's Application* [1988] R.P.C. 187 CA);

- non-receipt by the agent of a complimentary copy of the patent specification, contrary to expected and advertised practice (*Mills' Application*, above);

- application wrongly recorded as being withdrawn (*Alsthom-Atlantique's Application* BL O/49/84; and *Akebono Brake's Application* BL O/2/85), where the agent had understood the application to have been placed in order; and *Minnesota Mining's Application* BL O/86/86, where the request for substantive examination had been misfiled because it bore an incorrect number);

- letter of further objections never received by the agent (*Coal Industry's Application* [1986] R.P.C. 57; and *Opatowski's Application* BL O/74/88);

- non-receipt of response to substantive examination objections (*Bosch's Application* BL O/175/86) and loss of a letter in the Patent Office (*Kangaroos USA's Application* BL O/136/85);

- wrongly according priority in a published application when the necessary certified priority document had not been filed (*Brossmann's Application* [1983] R.P.C. 109);

- failure by the Patent Office to send out promptly a statutory reminder of failure to pay a renewal fee or of lapsing of the patent (*Daido Kogyo's Patent* [1984] R.P.C. 97);

- wrongly recording a patent as having lapsed (*Costolin's Patent* BL O/7/98);

- receipt of renewal fees for some years though the patent should have been recorded as lapsed because of a failure to pay the renewal fee in some earlier year (*Phillips Petroleum's Patent* BL O/20/84, noted I.P.D. 7069);

- erroneous telephone advice given to a person challenging the view expressed by the Patent Office in correspondence concerning the extent of renewal fees due (*Goddin's Patent* BL O/117/96, noted I.P.D. 19101; and BL C/115/96, noted I.P.D. 20023);

- revoking a patent (under s.73(2)) when amendments had been filed, unbeknown to the hearing officer (*Albright & Wilson's Patent* BL O/46/95); and

- deciding the allowability of amendments without consideration of observations by a proper party (*Harding's Patent* BL O/94/90, noted I.P.D. 13215).

However, r.107 was not invoked: when a late applicant for restoration had been sent the customary "pack of information" (*Mohmand's Patent* BL O/62/97), it being stated that the Patent Office could not be responsible for any failure by an agent to forward correspondence; nor where payment was not made directly to a bank account of the Patent Office (*Migowski's Patent* BL O/134/97, discussed in §123.64). Also, there is also no obligation upon the Comptroller to harmonise the Patents Rules with the Implementing Regulations under the EPC or indeed to amend the Rules at all since such amendments are made by the Secretary of State, see *Chemex Pharmaceuticals' Patent* BL O/75/99 discussed in §28.06. Although there is no obligation upon the Comptroller to issue a warning notice that an application will be treated as deemed to have been refused if no timely response to an examination report and no application for extension of the specified period has been made, the issue of a "warning of refusal letter" has become customary so that a failure in receipt of such could be a ground for application of r.107(2), but the onus of proof of non-receipt of such a letter lies upon the applicant once the UK-IPO has shown that such a letter was, according to its records, dispatched: in *Kaye's Application* BL O/353/99, the applicant failed to establish non-receipt of such a letter.

As to allegations of loss of papers in the UK-IPO after alleged due filing, it should be noted that the Office keeps copies of receipts issued in bound books, and they are able to retrieve the fee sheets which should have accompanied the filing of fee-bearing forms (*Sanyo's Application* BL O/31/88). In *Aisin Seiki's Application* BL O/74/90, noted I.P.D. 13139, the Comptroller refused self-certification by the patent agent that a priority document had been filed when no trace of this, or a receipt, could be found and pointed out that the agent's evidence did not go beyond an intention to file the document, not that it had been filed: reinstatement of the claimed priority was, however, allowed by alternative means.

In *Norsk Hydro's Amendment Application*, noted I.P.D. 18006, the amendments requested were wrongly advertised. Re-advertisement was proposed but the applicants objected to this re-setting of the period for opposition. It was decided that the re-advertisement should take the form of an explanation rather than a rectification (under r.107) of the original notice, with the opposition period not formally being re-set, although with the question to be reconsidered if an attempt at late opposition were to be made.

Relief under rule 107 is discretionary and may be conditional

The application of r.107 is a matter of discretion. Thus, in *Lebelson's Application* [1984] R.P.C. 136, the Patents Court observed that in such circumstances it is important to see

123.63

what had been done by the applicant and his agent to secure compliance with the requirements of the Act and Rules. Also, in *Application des Gaz's Application* [1987] R.P.C. 279, it was pointed out that applicants for the exercise of discretion are under an obligation to make a full disclosure of all relevant matters, and it has to be seen whether the activities and actions of the applicants (and their agents, both in this country and abroad) have been such as to justify the exercise of discretion in their favour. In particular, the blameworthiness of the agent(s) cannot be separated from that of the applicants themselves, but see now *Textron's Patent* [1989] R.P.C. 441 HL discussed in §28.10. Also, because relief under r.107 is discretionary, the delay in seeking this is a factor to be considered (*Jovanovic's Patent* BL O/115/90, noted I.P.D. 14028—an extreme case, where the patent sought to be restored (if r.107 could be invoked), had lapsed 13 years previously).

Since relief under r.107 involves an exercise of discretion, it may be granted subject to conditions, see *Roussel-Uclaf's (Clemence & Le Martret's) Patent* [1987] R.P.C. 109 where the Comptroller held that r.107 provides him with authority to rectify any irregularity in procedure (other than as regards time limits, unless r.100(3) is satisfied) on such terms as he may direct. Thus, where information as to the status of an application or patent has been given to the public which then falls to be corrected under r.107, the Comptroller appears, almost invariably, to make his order subject to conditions to protect third parties similar to those now imposed under s.28A when a patent is restored, for which see §§28A.05 and 28A.06. Indeed, where the UK-IPO erroneously recorded several patents as having lapsed when renewal fees had been paid, the Comptroller regarded the need to protect the public as paramount and insisted that the register could only be corrected if the proprietor accepted such third party conditions, but on appeal it was held that the patent had never lapsed as the fee had been timely paid. Thus, the Comptroller here had no power to impose third party conditions. The register should be rectified and, if the public had been affected by the wrong register entry, their remedy was certainly not against the patentee (*Eveready Battery's Patent* BL O/452/99 and C/22/00, noted I.P.D.23054 and reported as [2000] R.P.C. 852).

In *Howmet's Patent* [2006] R.P.C. 27 at 657, the Comptroller declined to exercise discretion under r.107 to rescind grant of the patent to allow a divisional application to be filed because he held that a conscious decision had been taken to stay action for the time being despite the fact that the Office had failed to warn the applicant of the imminent grant which would preclude such a filing. However, in allowing an appeal, it was stated that:

"Once it has been shown that the applicant would not have failed to take the step in question if the Office had not been guilty of an error, default, etc., there can be few reasons why the Comptroller's discretion should be exercised against him".

Rule 107 was applied in *Touch Clarity's Application* BL O/198/06 to allow a two month extension of the r.30 period (itself inextensible) where an examiner had erroneously advised that the period is effectively suspended once a hearing on patentability had taken place; and, likewise, in *Sun Microsystems' Application* BL O/252/06 where the applicant had been misled as regards maintenance of a further objection.

Other examples where such conditions have been imposed are: *Elf Union's Application* BL O/96/81, noted I.P.D. 5011; *Coal Industry's Application* [1986] R.P.C. 57; *Kangeroos USA's Application* BL O/136/85; *Costolin's Patent* BL O/7/98; and *Tristram's Patent* BL O/133/98. In at least the *Kangaroos'* and *Costolin's* cases, there had been no fault at all by the applicant, the UK-IPO having lost a letter in the first and wrongly recording a patent as having lapsed in the second, but in each instance third party conditions were imposed to protect third parties who might have relied upon the incorrect register entry, albeit only during a defined and limited "window period", but see now *Eveready Battery's Patent* (above).

Where the Comptroller purports to have exercised his discretion to extend a time period, and it can be shown that he had in fact no power to do so under the Act or Rules, it can be argued that the subsequent grant of a patent was made ultra vires and that, consequently, the patent is a nullity, see §34.02.

Fees and remission of fees (subss.(2)(c) and (4))

—Fees

Subsection (2)(c) authorises the current form of the Patents (Fees) Rules. The repeal of **123.64** subs.(4) (for which see §123.01) and the consequent amendment of the "Trading Fund Status" of the Patent Office (for which see §123.89), means that the specific consent of the Treasury is no longer required for rules setting the level of fees charged by the UK-IPO. However, these fees still need to be made by rules signed by the Secretary of State and to be subject to annulment by a resolution of either House of Parliament.

Fees must be paid in money (Public Offices (Patents, Designs and Trade Marks) Order 1964, SI 1964/45) and may be paid by credit or debit card, deposit account, cheque, and bank transfer. All cheques should be crossed "Account Payee Only" and made payable to "The UK Intellectual Property Office". Overseas customers should pay in sterling drawn on a United Kingdom Clearing Bank.

Also, fees can be paid by direct bank transfer to the Account of "The UK Intellectual Property Office" at Barclays Bank Plc, 121 Queen Street, Cardiff CF10 2XU (Account number, Sort code and other details are published on the UK-IPO website), but a reference should be quoted in order that the payment becomes linked with forms sent separately (*Patents Journal* October 9, 1991). Also, when remitting payments by direct bank transfer, care must be taken to direct these directly to this account. This Bank is the agent of the UK-IPO and any delay in the bank transferring the payment to the UK-IPO account can then be excused. However, in *Migowski's Patent* BL O/134/97, the direct bank transfer (from abroad) was made to the Midland Bank who took two days to transfer the sum to the Bank of England (then the UK-IPO's bank) with the consequence that the fee was received too late and r.107 could not be invoked as there had been no default on the part of the UK-IPO or its agent.

It is further possible to pay fees by debit from funds previously deposited in a UK-IPO deposit account. Obviously, it is necessary to ensure that sufficient funds are available in this account for payment of the fees requested. Otherwise, the form will not be accepted, although it is understood that the UK-IPO will try and contact the payer by telephone so that alternative arrangements can be made in time, but this may not always be possible. The same deposit account can also be used for purchase of UK-IPO publications, such as specifications of applications and patents, and for copies of papers from the files which are open to public inspection. Arrangements can be made for the regular provision of statements of the funds held in these accounts and of payments from them; and there are security arrangements designed to prevent the misuse of such funds. For queries on the opening or operation of such a deposit account, details can be found on the UK-IPO website.

The UK-IPO has also instituted a system for cash payment of fees by regular "customers", that is by agents and industrial patent departments who regularly file forms requiring payments and who choose not to ask for debit from a pre-arranged deposit account (as described above). Each such "customer" is allocated a "customer account number", together with a "customised fee sheet" bearing a unique bar code allocated to that customer, as well as a "customised publication sales order form", again containing that account number and its associated bar code. For further details see the UK-IPO website.

When fees are increased, care needs to be taken to ascertain whether the fee revision takes effect from the date when the fee is actually tendered (as is normally the case, e.g. see notice in *Patents Journal* November 6, 1991), or whether (when an extension of time for fee payment is permitted), exceptionally, the previous fee remains applicable if the due date preceded the payment date.

It may be noted that no rule pertaining to fees is mentioned in r.108, and, therefore, if a form (such as PF 52) is timely filed, other than under a specific provision in the Act, and the fee is omitted from that form, the time for paying that fee might be extensible by discretion exercised under r.108(1).

The Department of Trade and Industry (Fees) Order 1988 (SI 1988/93), made under s.102 of the Finance (No.2) Act 1987 (c.51), gave power to the Secretary of State to fix UK-IPO fees at levels which not only cover the direct cost of providing the service in question, but also to cover deficits incurred or to be incurred, as well as to secure a return on an amount of capital, and in respect of depreciation of assets. Under the amendment of this Order by the Department of Trade and Industry (Fees) (Amendment) Order 1990 (SI 1990/1473) the Secretary of State has been further enabled to take into account, in fixing the level of UK-IPO fees, "any other function of the Secretary of State and the Comptroller in relation to patents", including work done on legislative proposals and developments and any European Community institution or international convention.

—Remission of fees (r.106)

123.65   Subsection (2)(c) also authorises r.106. This provides for the remission of the search fee where this has already been paid by the applicant under the PCT (r.106(2)(a)), or in the case of a divisional application where the search fee has already been paid on an earlier application under s.15(9) (r.106(2)(b)). A request for fee remission should be submitted in writing (addressed to the Comptroller); there is no provision in r.106 that any remission should be automatic. The only obligation on the Comptroller to remit a fee is in the case of a supplementary protection certificate which has lapsed or been declared invalid and where fees have been paid in advance (r.106(5)). No appeal on fee remission is permitted (r.102(7)).

On a divisional application filed under s.15(9), the search fee is, in practice, remitted in full upon written application, but no remission of the examination fee is allowed. However, there is no provision for remission of the search fee on a later application when a corresponding search has been made on an earlier United Kingdom application from which the later application claims priority, r.106(2)(b) being limited to the case of divisional applications filed under s.15(9). The EPO has also ruled that remission of fees is not a matter of equity and can take place only where a rule so provides (J 20/87 *UPJOHN/Refund of search fee* OJ EPO 1989, 67; [1989] E.P.O.R. 298).

Although there is power to do so, it is the present practice not to refund any part of the fee for substantive examination when an international preliminary examination report has already been established on an international application before this enters its national phase before the Office, see §89A.37.

Advertisements (subs.(2)(e))

123.66   Subsection (2)(e) requires the Comptroller to advertise any proposed amendments of patents, that is those requested under s.27 or s.75 (and r.35), and any other matters as prescribed. Thus, under r.117 (see reprint, above), the Comptroller is required (by ss.16 and 24) to advertise in the *Patents Journal* the publication of an application and grant of a patent. Details of applications withdrawn are published in the *Patents Journal* under the authority of s.118(3)(b) and r.55(f), as discussed in §118.12. The following rules also require the Comptroller to advertise in the *Patents Journal* certain other proceedings, viz. those under:

- section 28 and r.40 (restoration), for which see §28.02;

- section 46 and r.43 (making "licence of right" entry), for which see §46.02; and

- section 117 and r.105 (correction), for which see §117.02.

Subject to r.105(5), r.75 requires the Comptroller to advertise in the *Patents Journal* any event to which it is possible to object under the provisions of Pts 2 and 3 of Sch.3 to the 2007 Rules, namely those events which are amenable to opposition. These include amendment of specification of grant (s.27(5)), surrender of patent (s.29(2)), cancellation of licence being available as of right (s.47(6)), amendment during infringement or revocation proceedings (s.75(2)), correction of error in specifications (s.117(2)), application for compulsory licence (s.52(1)), and application to cancel a compulsory licence (s.52(2)(b)).

Under r.45, the Comptroller has a general discretionary power to advertise things done under the Act or rules in relation to the register. Under this power, the Comptroller now advertises in the *Patents Journal* details of proceedings, and their outcome, under: ss.8, 10, 12(1) and (4) (entitlement to application); s.13 (inventorship); s.32 (notice of transactions, instruments or events entered in the register); s.37(1) (entitlement to patent); s.40 (employee-inventor compensation); s.46(3) (applications for settlement of licences of right); s.71(applications for declaration of non-infringement); and ss.72 and 73 (revocation). There are published details of applications for revival of applications, and, if these lead to the application or patent being restored, this fact is also advertised in the *Patents Journal*. Each of these matters ought to be picked up by the British Library in the compilation of their unofficial ledgers of states of progress of applications and patents.

However, it appears that details are not published of proceedings under: s.61(3) (infringement proceedings before the Comptroller); s.71 (declaration of non-infringement); or s.82 (entitlement disputes under European patent).

Proceedings in Scotland (subs.(2)(f))

Subsection (2)(f) is the authority for r.88 (reprinted at §98.05 and §123.21 above and discussed in §98.23) in relation to proceedings in Scotland under the Act.   **123.67**

Under the Act, hearings in proceedings before the Comptroller can be conducted in Scotland, where the conditions of r.88 are met, in matters under ss.8, 12 and 37 (entitlement), ss.40 and 41 (rewards to inventors), s.61(3) (action for infringement before Comptroller), s.71 (declaration of non-infringement) and s.72 (revocation), but not apparently in proceedings under any other section. The conditions of r.88 are that all parties consent to the proceedings being held in Scotland, or that the Comptroller considers it appropriate for the proceedings to be so held. For instances of the exercise of this power, see §98.23. A refusal by the Comptroller of an application for the proceedings to be held in Scotland is excepted from the right of appeal conferred by s.97 (r.88(3)).

Advisers (subss.(2)(g) and (5))

Subsection (2)(g) is the authority for the appointment by the Comptroller under r.102 of an adviser or advisers to assist him, see §123.57 above. The remuneration of such an adviser was previously determined by the Secretary of State with the consent of the Treasury under subs.5, but since the repeal of this subsection and the consequent amendment of the "Trading Fund Status" of the UK-IPO), the remuneration to be paid to an adviser no longer needs the consent of the Treasury, although it remains to be determined by the Secretary of State.   **123.68**

Time limits (subs.(2)(h) and r.108)

—*Scope of r.108*

Subsection (2)(h) is the authority for r.108 which deals with the alteration of those time periods which are specified in the Rules, which (if not complied with) will lead to a deemed withdrawal of the application.   **123.69**

In principle, any such period can be extended, unless this is precluded or limited by other provisions set out in r.108 (r.108(1)). Those rules which are inextensible are listed in Pt 1 of Sch.4 to the Rules (reprinted above, and see the discussion in §123.70 below).

Besides the position as to time periods specified in the Act and Rules, s.117B formalises the position that extensions can be granted by the Comptroller of time limits set by him (other than in proceedings before him), see the commentary on s.117B where the conditions applicable to such extensions are explained.

Section 20A permits the reinstatement of an application that has been terminated by failure to meet the time periods required by the rules, and s.117A permits the resuscitation of an application which had been withdrawn by error or mistake, in each case subject to the possible imposition of third party rights, as set out and described respectively in the commentary on those sections.

Automatic extensions (under r.108(2)) by two months of the periods specified in those rules which are listed in Pt 2 of this Sch.4 (see §123.26 and §123.71 below) are possible upon request to the Comptroller and payment of the prescribed fee, but provided that the request is one being made under r.108(2) for the first time and is made within a period of two months of the date when the relevant period expired.

Further extensions of the periods specified in those rules which are listed in Pt 2 of Sch.4 are possible (under r.123(3), as discussed in §123.71 below), if a request is made and supported by evidence following which the Comptroller exercises his discretion and, if he allows the request, a further fee is then paid.

However, in respect of some of the rules which are listed in Pt 3 of Sch.4 (see §123.26 above) the possible extension period is limited to only two months (r.110(5)) and then only if the extension is granted within the two months following the expiry of the period, or extended period, of time prescribed by the relevant rule (r.123(7)).

Where a period of time is one not specified in the lists of any part of Sch.4, a discretionary extension should be available under r.108(1), as discussed in §123.74 below, but any such extension under r.12(3) and (9) (filing of name and address and translations); or r.19 (divisional applications) may not exceed two months (Rules, Sch.4, Pt 3).

An extension can be granted under either of rr.108(1) or (3) notwithstanding that the period prescribed by the rules has already expired (s.123(3A) and r.108(6)).

Under r.108(5), the Comptroller may, if he thinks fit, alter any period of time under any of r.108(1) and (3) upon such notice and upon such terms as he may direct. However, presumably, this is intended to be a general rule-making power, rather than one to be exercised in specific cases, and simply removes the need for a formal SI amending any of these time limits. Thus, it is thought that the power of r.108(5) should not be used to nullify the normal application of r.108(1)–(4) without appropriate notice given well in advance of the intention to alter specified time periods set out in the Rules, subject to appropriate transitional provisions.

Extensions of time are thus obtainable in the following ways which have been discussed, or will be discussed, in the following paragraphs:

(1) by general discretion exercised under r.108(1), which, however, is applicable only in the case of time periods arising under rules (other than those listed in Pts 1 and 2 of Sch.4 to the rules);

(2) by automatic extension of two months (r.108(2)) or re-extension for a discretionary period of time (r.108(3)) for those periods listed in Pt 2 of Sch.4;

(3) by extension of two months as of right upon application under s.117B and r.109;

(4) in cases of "error, default or omission by the Patent Office" under r.107(3); and

(5) in cases of postal or other disruption under rr.110 and 111.

—The inextensible time periods under r.108 (Rules Sch.4. Pt 1)

123.70   The rules which specify time limits that cannot be extended are listed in Pt 1 of Sch.4 to the Rules (see §123.26 above). Where these rules prescribe a period for opposition this (inextensible) period is generally only two months from the date of advertisement in the *Patents Journal*.

—Limited extension as of right (automatic extensions) of certain time periods (r.108(2))

123.71   Rule 108(2) states that the Comptroller *shall* extend the periods of time to which that rule is applicable, so that under the provisions of that rule issues of discretion do not arise. The rules which specify time limits under which automatic extensions of time can be obtained under r.108(2) are listed in Pt 2 of Sch.4 to the Rules (see §123.26 above). The extensions available under r.108(2) are a uniform two months.

An extension request under r.108(3) must be made on PF 52 (r.108(2)(a)) and before the end of the period of two months following the date when the time period expired (r.108(2)(c)), although the Comptroller has power to alter this two month period under r.108(5) upon such notice and terms as he may direct. Only one extension under r.108(2) is possible in respect of each period to be extended (r.108(2)(b)) so that any further extension of the same period must be sought under r.108(3).

However, under r.108(5) and (7), in certain cases only a *single* discretionary extension (or further extension) under r.108(1), (2) or (3) of two months can be granted and then only if the request is made within the two months period immediately following the expiry of the period, or extended period, under the relevant rule. This is the position for those rules listed in Pt 3 of Sch.4 to the Rules (see §123.26 above).

Where multiple parallel extensions are requested on the same application, they may be made on a single PF 52 provided that all the periods sought to be extended would then expire on the same date (r.108(4)).

The two-month extension under r.108(2) is obtainable automatically by filing PF 52 but is subject to payment of a large fee. Under this sub-rule only one extension of each period is permitted and PF 52 must be filed before the end of the extended period. If PF 52 is not filed during the two-month extension period, the application is deemed to have been withdrawn at the end of the normal period (*P's Application* [1983] R.P.C. 269), though with the possibility of further extension under r.108(3). Note that, because extension under r.108(2) is obtainable as of right, there is no question of the imposition of any third party rights as a condition for permitting extension.

An interesting situation arises where PF 52 is timely filed together with the form required by a rule specified in r.110(3), but the fee is paid only on this latter form. The filing of PF 52 would appear itself to provide the extension, and extra time for paying the missing fee on the PF 52 could then be allowed by discretion under r.108(1) on the basis that none of the rules under which fees are now prescribed and which require that a form be accompanied by the specified fee, is listed in either Pts 2 or 3 of Sch.4 to the Rules. A similar position may arise when any form, other than one filed under rule specified in either of Pts 2 or 3 of Sch.4 to the Rules, is filed but the fee omitted.

—Request for discretionary extension of the time periods covered by rule 108(2) and (3)

123.72 The provisions for allowing a further discretionary extension of a period to which an automatic limited extension can be obtained under r.108(2) (as discussed in §123.71 above) are set out in r.108(3).

The allowance of an extension under r.108(3) requires the filing of a further PF 52 together with evidence supporting the request. Such an extension may be granted notwithstanding that the prescribed period of time had already expired at the date of the extension request (r.108(6)), but this is not possible for the rules listed in Pt 3 of Sch.4 (for which see §123.26). For extensions under these listed rules an extension request must be made within the two month period immediately following the expiry date of the period (or extended period) prescribed by the relevant rule (r.108(7)).

As with extensions requested under r.108(2), multiple requests for extensions under different rules can be made on the same form, but only if all the altered time periods would expire on the same date (r.108(4)).

A lack of care (as distinct from inadvertence) in making the decision not to proceed is not a determining factor and an underlying intention to proceed with the application or patent is therefore seen by the Comptroller as a necessary requirement in both cases. Consequently, discretion is unlikely to be exercised under r.108 where there has been a change of mind by whoever had the responsibility for deciding whether the required action should be timely taken (*Heatex Group's Application* [1995] R.P.C. 546; *P's Application* [1983] R.P.C. 269; and *Institut Pasteur's Patent* BL O/198/97, noted I.P.D. 21006).

In the *Institut Pasteur* case, the Comptroller was asked to exercise discretion to permit (under then r.110(4)) the late filing of the required translation of a European patent. The procedure within the proprietor's organisation was for a committee to review all patents annually, but subject to any comment from the inventor. This committee had decided to recommend that the patent in issue should lapse, but the inventor confused the request for comment as one applying to another patent and so took no action. It was argued that the failure had been that of the inventor and not of the patentee and so discretion could be exercised. However the hearing officer saw the matter as one where there had been a change of mind of the review committee precluding exercise of discretion under r.108(3). Anyway, he indicated, it would not be right for the public to be faced with a new monopoly right some three years after the patent had been (erroneously) abandoned by a decision within the patentee's organisation and advertised as being void.

In *Meunier's International Application* (BL O/13/01), an application to grant an extension of time under the corresponding rules of the Patent Rules 1995 to allow late entry of an international application into the UK phase was refused. The applicant was seen to have changed his mind in having instructed his agent to pursue protection only via the EPO, and it was unfortunate that the European designation for the United Kingdom had later been dropped as a result of a mistake by his agent.

A similar case is *Pilat's International Application* [2003] R.P.C. 13 at 253 in which the applicant had intended to pursue protection in the UK via the "Euro–PCT" route but due to an error the PCT request form did not include a European regional designation. By the time this was realised it was too late to correct the request form and so the applicant sought an extension of the period for entering the UK national phase under old r.110(4) (equivalent to r.108(3)). This was refused as it was held that the applicant had no continuing underlying intention to pursue the national phase route for protection in the UK so that to allow the extension would have given him the opportunity effectively to change his mind.

In *MacMullen's Application* BL O/307/03 evidence of the applicant's efforts to raise money to pay the fee for PF 9 was accepted as evidence of a continuing underlying intention to file the request and pay the fee and discretion was exercised in favour of the applicant. Likewise in *Chalmor's Application* BL O/256/05 financial investment in developing the invention was accepted as evidence of a continued intention to proceed with the application. However, in *Al Bahdaini's Application* BL O/356/04, the Comptroller was not satisfied that the applicant had had a continuing underlying intention to proceed with his application and the request for extension was therefore refused.

It appears that most applications made under r.108(3) do succeed, indicating that the Comptroller does not exercise his discretion under the rule in a restrictive manner. Nevertheless, it seems doubtful whether a missed priority date could be retrieved under r.108(3), not only because such action would probably be contrary to the Paris Convention, but also because at the relevant time there would have been no application in existence under the Act to which r.108(3) could be applied. However, the PCT Regulations may enable this to be done in the case of an international application (UK), see §89B.05.

Since the forerunner of r.108(3) was introduced, the UK-IPO sends out warning letters when time periods are about to expire, or have just expired. These include a request that any desired restorative action be taken promptly, e.g. within the two-month period allowed for extension under r.108(2), or within a week or so thereafter. If, thereafter, restorative action is not promptly requested, it will obviously be more difficult to obtain a discretionary extension under r.108(3).

An extension may be granted notwithstanding that the prescribed period of time had already expired at the date of the extension request (r.108(6)), but this is not possible for the rules listed in Pt 3 of Sch.4 (for which see §123.26 above). For extensions under these listed rules, an extension request must be made within the two month period immediately following the expiry date of the period (or extended period) prescribed by the relevant rule (see r.108(7), as discussed in §123.25 above).

As with extensions requested under r.108(2), multiple requests for extensions under different rules can be made on the same form, but only if all the altered time periods would expire on the same date (r.108(4)).

—Grant of discretionary extension of the time periods covered by rule 108(2) and (3)

If the Comptroller allows extension after an application under r.108(3), then the exten-   **123.73**
sion is obtained only upon the filing of PF 52 with which a fee is required.

In contrast to the automatic extension of time available under r.108(2), it can be
expected that any extension ultimately granted under r.108(3) will be made subject to third
party rights, unless the extension is requested for an application as yet unpublished, and
especially if the application or patent has already been advertised as having lapsed, see
MOPP. But, before the Comptroller can impose a notice of such third party rights, the applicant should be given an opportunity to seek an oral hearing, see *Systemsovereign's Application* BL O/100/96 where such rights were nevertheless imposed. In *Chitolie's Application* BL O/078/04, upheld on appeal [2004] EWHC 1549 (Ch), the third party rights
were similar to those employed (under s.28A) upon patent restoration being allowed under
s.28, for which see the commentary on s.28A. Similar conditions are imposed when r.100
is invoked.

Where a patent (or application) is reinstated under r.108(5), after advertised lapsing, a
notice appears in the *Patents Journal*, with notice if the reinstatement is subject to the "attachment of terms to protect third parties". A notice is also published in the *Patents Journal*
when an advertised application for reinstatement is rejected.

—Discretionary extension without fee (r.108(1))

Under r.108(1), any time period which is prescribed by a rule is extensible with the   **123.74**
exercise of discretion by the Comptroller provided that the rule is *not* one of those listed
under the Rules, Sch.4 Pts 1 and 2 (see §123.26 above). Such an extension can be granted
notwithstanding that the prescribed period under the relevant rule has already expired
(s.123(3A) and r.108(6)). However, any such extension of the periods specified in r.12(3)
and (9); or r.19 may not exceed two months.

In *Abbott Laboratories' SPC Application* [2004] R.P.C. 20 at 391 the period for applying for an SPC in the UK was extended under old r.110(1) (equivalent to r.108(1)); see
§128B.70 below.

Discretion to grant an extension is likely to be exercised when to allow some extension
in the circumstances is seen, on balance, to be proportionate and not unduly prejudicial in
the interests of justice and the administration of justice, see *Hills Numberplates' Patent*
BL O/130/06, where an extension was granted although less than that requested, and *Enston's Application* BL O/130/06, where the balance was seen to be such that an extension
should not be granted.

While, in *Bloomberg's Application* BL O/254/06, it was noted that an extension of the
time for filing PF 53 can be granted under old r.110(1) (equivalent to r.108(1)), here it
should be refused because it was not considered reasonable that the applicant should await
the outcome of an appeal against refusal before paying the fee required to activate an
extension granted, with discretion, under old r.110(4) (equivalent to r.108(3)). Here, it was
noted that old r.110(8)(b) and 110(10) (equivalent to r.108(5)(b) and r.108(7))limit the
duration of a permissible extension under old r.110(4) (equivalent to r.108(3)).

A further instance where r.108(1) is applied is where a sole applicant has died.
Discretionary extensions of periods not covered by r.108(2) or (3) are then allowed until
after probate has been granted or letters of administration issued.

A request for time extension under r.108(1) should be made as soon as the need for it is
seen and while time still remains for taking the necessary action. The request should be
supported by full reasons why discretion should be exercised in the applicant's favour, and
it should not be presumed that the extension will be granted. The request is made by letter
and no fee is required. It may be noted that a request for an extension of time for the term
set for response to an official letter issued during substantive examination under s.18(3)
does not fall within r.108(1) as this is not a time limit set by the Act or Rules. It is thought

that the same principles apply to the exercise of discretion under r.108(1) as have been applied under s.18(3), for which see §18.16.

For many types of contested proceedings, the Rules set time limits for the filing of counter-statements and evidence of four weeks, which periods are extensible under r.81(1), but the Comptroller has in most, although not all, of these cases the power to shorten the period if he thinks fit, upon such notice to the parties and upon such terms as he may direct. Where the practice under these rules has been discussed herein, the existence of this power has been noted.

—Extension after lapsing (subs.(3A)) and r.108(6))

123.75   Subsection (3A) was inserted by the CDPA 1988. It formally permits the Comptroller (subject to the Patent Rules) to extend any period of time specified in the Act or Rules, notwithstanding that such period may already have expired and hence the application or patent has apparently become void. Accordingly, r.108(6) now specifically provides for an extension to be granted even though, without the extension, the time period prescribed by the relevant rule has expired. As an example of the application of this rule, Application No. 2,129,502 can be noted: this was revived some years after it had erroneously been abandoned by failure to respond to a substantive examination objection.

However, it is not seen that the operation of new s.123(3A) has any effect in a case where no application for a patent under the Act ever came into existence, as distinct from one deemed to have lapsed. For the possible correction of errors occurring in the international phase of an international application for a patent (UK), see §§89B.12.

The subsection is expressed in declaratory form, but this still leaves open the question whether any extension granted before its commencement (on November 15, 1988) in respect of an already expired period was one granted ultra vires, thereby rendering void any patent granted see §34.02.

—Extension under section 117B (r.109)

123.76   §§117B.01–117B.03 set out in detail the conditions under which an extension can be sought under s.117B. It applies to any period by the Comptroller in connection with an application for a patent, or a patent, and is put into practice by way of r.109. A request under s.117B must be submitted in writing and within a two-month window after the expiry of the period for which extension is sought.

—Calculation of time limits

123.77   The Patents Rules do not contain any rule indicating how time limits are to be computed, other than in the specific circumstances set out in r.110 (discussed in §123.78). Therefore, in cases of doubt the Civil Procedure Rules are likely to be followed. These are set out in CPR 2.8–2.10. Under these rules: a "month" means a calendar month; and a period of time expressed as a number of days means "clear days", that is excluding the days on which the period begins and on which it ends (CPR 2.8(2) and (3)).

However, where the specified period is five days or less, any Saturday, Sunday, Bank Holiday (as defined in the Banking and Financial Dealings Act 1971 (c.80) s.1), Christmas Day or Good Friday does not count (CPR 2.8(4)); and, where the period for doing an act at the court office ends on a day on which that office is closed, that act can be done in time on the next day when the court office is open (CPR 2.8(5)).

For filing notices of appeal from decisions of the Comptroller, note that during a court vacation the court office may close early, see §97.12. For the calculation of time limits under the EPC and the PCT, see respectively r.131 of the EPC and r.80 of the PCT, discussed respectively in the *European Patents Handbook* ("EPH") (London: Sweet & Maxwell) and *Patent Cooperation Treaty Handbook* ("PCTH") (London: Sweet & Maxwell).

When a time limit is to be calculated from a "declared priority date", this date is to be determined according to the definition in r.3 (reprinted in §5.06A).

Extensions arising from interrupted and excluded days (r.110)

Rule 110 makes provision for the Comptroller to certify a day as being an "interrupted **123.78**
day" if there is interruption to the normal operation of the UK-IPO, or if there is a general interruption to the operation of the UK postal system. If such a certification is made, a notification to that effect will be advertised in the *Patents Journal* and displayed at the UK-IPO. While clearly intended to provide for the possibility of industrial action within the UK-IPO, the provision can also be applied when the event or circumstances are external to the UK-IPO, for example dislocation of transport services due to weather conditions.

If a time limit, already extended or otherwise, expires on an interrupted day as so certified (or on an excluded day under rules made under s.120), the Comptroller is obliged to extend that time limit to the next day not being an interrupted or excluded day (r.110(3)). There is however, no provision for extending a time limit if a day within the time limit and not being the day of expiry is certified as being interrupted or excluded.

While an interruption or subsequent dislocation of postal services of the United Kingdom must be certified by the Comptroller, it appears that such a certificate can be issued retroactively and, if the Comptroller refuses so to do, by the court on appeal to it under s.97(1), see *Omron Tateisi's Application* [1981] R.P.C. 125.

Rule 110 cannot be used to give additional time to an individual whose problem is of a purely personal kind. In relation to postal delays, the rule is concerned only with exceptional circumstances where there has been a general interruption or subsequent dislocation in the postal service over and above the provisions for excluded days which might bring about such an interruption, see *Armaturjonsson's Application* [1985] R.P.C. 213. Here, mail was delayed over the Christmas holiday period, but this did not amount to a "dislocation" in the postal service. The Post Office was then misinformed as to the day when the agent's office would re-open after the holiday period with the consequence that delivery was further delayed, but the Comptroller and the court each held that this did not amount to a "subsequent" dislocation in the post enabling the convention priority date to be saved. However, the harshness of this situation is now alleviated by r.111, for which see §123.79.

The EPO has held that the provisions of r.134(2) of the EPC, which are analogous to those of r.110(3), may be invoked whenever a general interruption in the postal service has been certified and that it is not necessary for the applicant to show that his non-observance of the set time limit was due to that disruption (T 192/84 *DAIKIN KOGYO/ Interruption in delivery of mail* OJ EPO 1985, 39). A similar conclusion would seem to be possible under r.110. The EPO has also held that a general interruption in the postal service is a question of fact, and it has accepted letters from the UK-IPO that such interruption had occurred and that such would have been certified if a request had been made (J 11/88 *LELAND STANFORD/Postal strike* OJ EPO 1989, 433; [1990] E.P.O.R. 50). A "general" disruption can be a local, rather than a national one, provided that it is of general effect in that locality (J 3/90 *FISCHER SCIENTIFIC/Postal strike* OJ EPO 1991, 550; [1992] E.P.O.R. 148; and J 4/90 *MARELLO/Postal strike* [1990] E.P.O.R. 576).

—Extensions arising from delays in communication services (r.111)

Rule 111(1) is a rule which experience has shown to be increasingly necessary. It al- **123.79**
lows the Comptroller to extend any period of time specified in the Act or in the Rules where he is satisfied that the failure to meet the time limit was wholly or mainly attributable to the delay or failure of a "communication service", such term being defined in r.111(3) as including (but not being limited to) post, courier, and electronic communications. Previously, r.111 had been held to apply only to postal delays occurring within the United Kingdom (*Koehring's Application* BL O/91/86). Here it was stated that the rule protects an applicant from the effects of delays incurred in the United Kingdom on documents posted outside of the United Kingdom:

"just as rule 97 protects United Kingdom residents from the effects of delays incurred within the United Kingdom in relation to documents posted therein".

The r.97 referred to in that case has been revoked as of the 2007 Rules, and the rule as it now stands makes no restriction on geographic territory of which communication service may invoke the rule, so there would not appear to be any reason why an applicant could not seek an extension of time based on breakdown of a communication service based overseas. This is particularly relevant with the case of electronic submissions to the UK-IPO, whereby communications sent via such means are liable to pass through foreign jurisdictions en route to the UK-IPO's receiving section.

The onus of proof will be on the applicant, and proof of timely submission to the relevant communication service can be expected to be required. If an extension is granted under rule, the Comptroller can require notification of the extension to other parties (presumably including insertion of a notice in the *Patents Journal*). He can also make the extension subject to terms, for example by granting third parties certain rights, such as those that arise under s.28A when a patent is restored, for which see §§28A.05 and 28A.06. Previously, it had been held that r.111 (in its former form) could not be invoked in respect of an isolated instance of failure to deliver a letter, see *Tiszai Vegy's Application* BL O/109/87 where again the end of the Christmas period was involved, but presumably this (and the *Armaturjonsson* case, §123.78 above) would now be differently decided under new r.111.

Naming of inventor (subs.(2)(i))

123.80   Subsection (2)(i) provides for rules to be made to give an inventor the right to be named in an application. Such right is inherent in the procedure of s.13 and r.10 and is discussed in §13.13. The difficulties arising from the meaning of "invention" are discussed in the commentary on s.13. The concomitant difficulty with "inventor" is discussed in §7.10.

The amendment to para.(2)(i) (noted at §123.01 above) has provided the basis for rules to be made setting out the way in which an inventor (subject to acceptance by the Comptroller) can waive his rights to be mentioned as such or for the omission of publication of his address (see §13.12). Rule 11 (replacing r.15A under the 1995 Rules) has been made to deal with the question of waiver and amendments as regards omission of publication of an inventor's name, or at least his address, have been made in rr.26, 44 and 51 (as noted in §§16.02, 32.04 and 118.02).

Translations (subs.(2)(j) and rr.113 and 114)

123.81   Subsection (2)(j) is the authority for r.113 (see reprint, above). Separate rules, however, deal with the provision of translations in particular circumstances, see, for example, r.35 for translation of a proposed amendment to a European patent (UK).

The general rule is that any document sent to the UK-IPO which is not in English or Welsh must be "accompanied" by an English translation, and be supplied in the same number of copies as the document translated (r.113(3)). Verification and the form of the translation are discussed in §123.82. The word "accompanied" in r.113(1) can be regarded as defining an infinitely short period of time which may perhaps be extended under r.108(1) (*Rohde and Schwarz's Application* [1980] R.P.C. 155). While discretion with respect to r.113(1) was not exercised in that case, the decision of the hearing officer does contain the more general statement that "the Comptroller must allow a period of time to put the description into conformity with rule 20(1) [as it now is]". Rule 113(1) does not apply, by virtue of r.113(2), to the following documents:

(a) where the documents filed to initiate an application for a patent include something which is or appears to be a description of the invention, the document containing that thing;

(b) a priority application;

(c) a copy of an application provided under s.15(10)(b)(ii);

(d) a copy of a specification of a European patent (UK) filed in connection with an application by the proprietor to amend the specification;

(e) a copy of an application for a European patent (UK) provided under s.81(2)(b)(ii);

(f) an international application for a patent (UK), where a translation of the application or an amendment to it is a necessary translation; and

(g) in relation to an international application for a patent (UK), where any document which is in a language other than English or Welsh which is referred to in an International Search Report or International Preliminary Report on Patentability; or cited in an International Preliminary Examination Report.

No translation of a priority application is now required to be filed unless and until a direction may be made by the Comptroller requiring this to be filed, and then only if the validity of the priority claim is regarded as relevant to whether of not the claimed invention is novel and involves an inventive step, see r.9. When an initial filing is made involving reference to an earlier application in lieu of a formal description, a certified copy of that earlier application is required to be filed (unless a copy thereof is already on file in the UK-IPO), together with a translation of this if not in the English language, as discussed in §5.23.

Unless a translation of a European patent (UK) has been supplied (as will probably not have been the case for such patents granted before September 1, 1987), r.114(1) requires that a person instituting proceedings before the Comptroller in relation to such a patent must furnish a translation. However, under r.114(2), the Comptroller may direct that such a translation in unnecessary, and furthermore, r.114(1) does not apply if an English translation has already been filed under s.77(6). Note that if such proceedings are commenced by a person other than the patentee (for example by an applicant for revocation of the patent), that person has the duty of supplying the translation under r.114(1), and not the patentee. If such a European patent (UK) is to be amended in the course of those proceedings (which proceedings could be solely for amendment under s.27), a translation of the amendment must then be furnished (r.114(3)). Where drawings with foreign language annotations were submitted in revocation proceedings, the applicant for revocation was permitted to file these without translations of the annotations, though at the risk that the document would be disregarded if the drawing did not "speak for itself" (*JAT Extrusions' Patent* BL O/167/95).

For amendment of a European patent (UK) not in the English language, see §27.14. For the correction of translations initially filed under s.77(6), see s.80(3); as discussed in §§80.06, 80.09 and 80.10. For the legal effect in proceedings before the court of a translation filed under s.77(6) or r.113, see §77.14.

Rule 113(4) gives the Comptroller power to take no further action in respect of a document which ought to have been furnished alongside a translation of its contents, but which translation is absent.

—Verification of translations

Rule 115 takes the place of the previous rule requirements that translations filed at the Patent Office should be "verified to the satisfaction of the comptroller". Instead, r.115 provides that, where the Comptroller has "reasonable doubts about the accuracy of any [such] translation", he shall notify the person who has filed the translation of the reasons for his doubts and he may also require that person to furnish evidence that the translation is accurate. If this is not done, then the Comptroller is empowered, if he thinks fit, to take no further action in relation to that document.

123.82

Publications by the UK-IPO (subs.(2)(1))

Subsection (2)(1) is the authority for r.119 reprinted above, which rule gives power to the Comptroller to publish and sell copies of specifications of patent applications and

123.83

granted patents, as well as indexes to, and abridgements or abstracts of such documents. The historical evolution of this rule was discussed by R.M.C. Arnot (1978–79) 8 *CIPA* 287, where he deplored the removal of the reference to the provision of indexes, previously present in the statute itself (s.94(1)(d) of the Patents Act 1949), into a rule from which it could readily be deleted. In addition, the UK-IPO publishes the Official Journal (Patents) (the *"Patents Journal"*). The Reports of Patent Cases ("R.P.C.") are also published on its behalf, for which see §§123.86 and 123.87 respectively.

The UK-IPO publications are available online from the Patents Publication Enquiry Service which covers all GB applications published and granted after January 3, 2007 and all GB corrected documents published after April 1, 2010. Specifications can also be accessed electronically via the esp@cenet database and through commercial databases. Paper copies of specifications can be purchased from the Sales Branch, The UK-IPO, Concept House, Cardiff Road, Newport, South Wales, NP10 8QQ. An ESPACE-UK CD ROM is available from the Sales Branch by subscription. Details of these publications are available on the UK IP Office website.

The British Library, at 96 Euston Road London NW1 2DR, holds a full range of UK-IPO publications and enquiries in relation to patent publications may be directed to its British Patents Enquiry Desk. See also the British Library website at: *http://www.bl.uk.* The Science Museum Library, Imperial College Road, South Kensington, London SW7 5NH also holds a comprehensive collection of GB patent publications and copies of at least GB patents are also held by the Central Libraries in Aberdeen, Belfast, Birmingham, Bristol, Coventry, Glasgow, Leeds, Liverpool, Manchester, Newcastle upon Tyne, Plymouth, Portsmouth and Sheffield who constitute the "Patent Information Network (PIN)" libraries of the United Kingdom.

—Specifications and abstracts

123.84   Specifications are published in three series: the specification as filed published under s.16 which is given a two million series number with the suffix "A" (the "A-specification"); the specification of the granted patent under the same number with the suffix "B" (the "B-specification" and under the same number with the suffix C denoting a patent specification that has been amended or corrected post grant (the "C-specification"). If an amended patent is further amended, the suffix becomes "C2" and so on. If a European patent (UK) is amended under the Act, its number is preceded by the prefix "EP/UK", see §27.14. Although specifications were initially printed in letterpress, neither form is now typeset but is reproduced directly from the typed specification provided by the applicant: hence the rigid requirements of r.14 (and Pts 1 and 2 of Sch.2) discussed in §14.47.

The front pages of each of these publications carries bibliographic data which uses the international INID code numbers and the two letter country codes of WIPO Standards ST3 and ST9. These are explained in a booklet obtainable from the Patent Office Classification Section and the BL, and details are usually published in the final issues of the *Patents Journal* for January, April, July and October, see also the EPH, Ch.60.1.

The front page of the "A-specification" also carries the abstract with an associated drawing, and these pages are available separately as "Abstracts". The weekly batches of "A-specifications" are arranged according to the divisions of the classification scheme before the seven figure number is allotted.

The Patents Publication Enquiry Service adds newly published A specifications on a weekly basis each Wednesday at or shortly after 13.00 UK time on the day of publication, so avoiding the possibility of earlier publication dates in different time zones.

—Indexes

123.85   Name searches for published applications and granted patents are conveniently carried out using the esp@cenet database. Annual indexes of published specifications and granted patents are available for those conducting historical research.

The Journal (subs.(6))

The Journal is published under the authority of r.117 (for which see §123.33). The **123.86** journal (now known as the *"Patents Journal"*) used to be published as "The Official Journal (Patents)", but (from February 5, 1997) the Journal was renamed under the title "The Patents and Designs Journal". There is no obligation to publish the Journal at any prescribed interval, nor that it should have any particular name. It adopted the present title in March 2008.

The "Journal" is not to be confused with the Official Journal of the European Patent Office (referred to as the "OJ EPO") or with the Official Journal of the European Communities (referred to as the "OJ EC").

The *Patents Journal* normally appears each Wednesday and contains details of proceedings under the 1977 Act. Since August 2, 2000 the *Patents Journal* has been placed on the UK-IPO website. Apart from an alphabetical index of new applications and information on applications published under s.16, which is given fully and with indexes, much of the other information is in the form of lists of patent or application numbers in respect of which some event has occurred. The extent of information provided in the *Patents Journal*, as regards various proceedings before the Comptroller, has expanded and also now contains bibliographic details of granted patents, i.e. of the "B-specifications", in numerical order together with details of inventors, priorities claimed, etc. but the title is restricted to 158 characters, see also §24.12.

The *Patents Journal* further contains numerical lists of European patents (UK) that have been granted; and details of the translations of European patents (UK) and applications filed respectively under ss.77(6) and 78(7) with details of the application number and proprietor. The *Patents Journal* also now contains lists of European applications which have become void. Much of this information is transcribed by the Library staff into informal registers.

The *Patents Journal* further provides details of the classification of patent specifications, advertises the commercial services available from the UK-IPO, provides details of the libraries in the United Kingdom which maintain collections of United Kingdom patent specifications, and generally gives notice of items of interest to patent practitioners, e.g the adherence of further States to various international Conventions and Treaties relating to intellectual property, and of decisions of the Comptroller and of the courts received into the British Library collections.

Patent law reports (subs.(7))

Very many decisions of Patent Offices and courts are available online. Decisions of the **123.87** Comptroller since 1998 are available on the IP Office website *www.ipo.gov.uk* in a database searchable by year of decision, BL number (see below), publication number, parties and keyword. A database of decisions of the EPO Appeal Boards is available on the EPO website: *http://www.epo.org* and gives access to the full text of each decision with links both to cited decisions and also to subsequent citing decisions. For decisions of the UK courts including the Patents Court and the Patents County Court see *http://www.bailli.org*. Transcripts of judgments in Intellectual Property cases can also be obtained via commercial databases such as "Lexis" and "Westlaw" but this will generally require payment whether by subscription or otherwise. To find a decision online it frequently suffices to enter the name of the decision into Google or another search engine.

Subsection (7) is the authority for r.118 (see reprint, above) and provides for the official publication of reports of patent and other cases (the "R.P.C."). Rule 118 is mandatory in terms and particularly refers to the publication of cases which the Comptroller has decided, and which relate to intellectual property rights in courts both in the UK and elsewhere. The selection of cases from the court is made by the editor who is traditionally a practising member of the patent bar.

The R.P.C. is rare among United Kingdom law reports as being sanctioned by and published under statute and published, unlike most other law reports which are organised privately. It commenced publication in 1883 with Vol.1, and its volumes were numbered annually up to Vol.72 (1955). Thereafter, the volumes have been designated solely by their year of publication. The R.P.C. appears irregularly in about 25 issues per year together with an annual digest which, until 1985, contained classified abridgements of the cases reported in the volume for that year. This digest continues to include various lists of cases and statutes cited in those cases. A consolidated Digest of Volumes 1–71 (1883–1955) was issued in three volumes, which has now been independently reprinted. Copies of each individual issue of the R.P.C. are kept in print and are available for purchase as described below.

The UK-IPO maintains responsibility for sales of these law reports for years up to 1997 with individual copies being obtainable from the UK-IPO Sales Branch.

From 1998 until 2007 inclusive Sweet & Maxwell published the R.P.C. and issues for this period can be purchased from Customer Services at Sweet & Maxwell, Cheriton House, PO Box 2000, Andover, SP10 9AH.

The R.P.C. is currently published by Oxford University Press and issues starting from 2008 can be purchased from Journals Customer Service Department, Oxford University Press, Great Clarendon Street, Oxford OX2 6DP.

The Fleet Street Law Reports ("F.S.R.") is a series of law reports which has been privately published since 1963. It presently also is published by Sweet & Maxwell and has the same editor as the R.P.C. It aims to produce its reports more quickly, though with a less authoritative headnote, and to publish in addition cases of lesser or more transient importance than those generally reported in R.P.C. as well as including cases arising under European Community law.

Selected decisions of the EPO and its Appeal Boards are published in the OJ EPO and in a private series of law reports, European Patent Office Reports ("E.P.O.R."), produced by Sweet & Maxwell. These decisions are not now reported in the R.P.C. or the F.S.R.

Decisions of the European Commission and of the Court of Justice of the European Union ("ECJ") in Luxembourg are reported in Common Market Law Reports ("C.M.L.R."), but the authentic reports of cases decided by the ECJ are contained in the European Court Reports ("E.C.R."), which are published somewhat later in parallel volumes in the individual languages of the EU Member States.

Copies of transcripts of decisions of the High Court, the Court of Appeal and the Supreme Court (House of Lords) in proceedings relating to intellectual property are normally received automatically by the British Library ("BL"), see (1983–84) 13 *CIPA* 411 and (1985–86) 15 *CIPA* 155. Here they are numbered, and the names of the parties indexed, in a "C/-/-" series. Copies of decisions in the UK-IPO are also supplied to the BL and filed in a separate "O/-/-" series and indexed accordingly. The transcripts are eventually bound into yearly volumes. Since the former Science Reference and Information Service ("SRIS") of the British Library no longer exists under that name, it has been thought appropriate herein to use the prefix "BL" to denote decisions included in these two collections instead of "SRIS" which was used in earlier editions of this Work, and which has been used in other books and in the Patent Office MOPP.

Photocopies of UK-IPO decisions contained in the BL collection can be obtained from the British Library or from the UK-IPO quoting the BL reference designation. However, for six years after judgment, unless otherwise stated, transcripts of court decisions (and of UK-IPO decisions given orally and recorded by the shorthand writers) may perhaps be obtained only by application to the firm of shorthand writers responsible for providing the transcript. To obtain these, the date of the judgment and the name of the judge should be identified, as well as the names of the parties. The cost of obtaining such copies is quite high as the shorthand writers base their charges on transcription, rather than copying, cost. However, there is an increasing tendency for the judges to produce their own judgments in written form rather than have transcripts prepared by shorthand writers and many of the judgments (including those of the House of Lords) are now supplied to the BL collection, without any restriction placed on them being photocopied. Such decisions are stamped in the BL collection with the rubric "No copyright restriction". However, photocopying restrictions continue to apply to those judgments which are transcribed from a recording of an oral judgment.

Practice Direction (Form of Judgments, Paragraph Marking and Neutral Citation) of January 11, 2001 (see [2001] 1 W.L.R. 194; [2001] 1 All E.R. 193) and Practice Direction (Neutral Citations) of January 14, 2002 (see [2002] 1 W.L.R. 346) provide for numbering of all High Court judgments with a unique number. Decisions of the Patents Court are now designated as, e.g. [201X] EWHC yyyy Pat Ct; general decisions of the Chancery Division as e.g. [201X] EWHC yyyy Ch; decisions of Court of Appeal (Civil Division) as e.g. [201X] EWCA yyyy Civ; decisions of the House of Lords as e.g. [201X] UKHL yyy and decisions of the Supreme Court as [201X] UKSC yyy. These references may be used to access decisions via the BAILII website as given above.

Since decisions are now being issued with numbered paragraphs, a full citation of a particular paragraph would include the paragraph number thus: *Smith v Jones* [2002] EWHC 123 at [59]. Although the Practice Directions indicate that it is intended that this form of citation be used as much as possible, the main series of patent law reports, R.P.C. and F.S.R., still adopt their own citation references which are used in this book. Unreported judgments continue to be referred to by their British Library (BL) reference numbers or references to other sources (e.g. I.P.D. or *The Times*) where available. Neutral citations are now given where available decisions are not formally reported. Where a cited court decision is available on the BAILII website, the reference to the availability of the decision in the British Library collection of court judgments is no longer being included.

Attention is drawn to the existence on the CIPA website *http://www.cipa.org.uk* of a link to indexes of decisions which have been noted in the *CIPA Journal*. These indexes are updated to include information on the subsequent appearance of decisions in the formal law reports.

Since 2001, the R.P.C., F.S.R. and E.P.O.R. reports have allocated to each decision a citation, or case, number. The practice has started of placing this number in square brackets after the page number for the initial page traditionally used for citation of a reported judgment. Unfortunately, judgments sometimes cite earlier judgments using only this citation number and this can cause confusion as being mistaken for its initial page number.

Address of the UK Intellectual Property Office

The Gowers Review of Intellectual Property recommended a change of the name of the Patent Office to the UK Intellectual Property Office (UK-IPO) "to reflect the breadth of functions the office has, and to dispel confusion". The Patent Office adopted a new "UK-IPO" branding from April 2, 2007, but, in November 2008 adopted a new logo and the name "Intellectual Property Office". This book has retained use of the abbreviation UK-IPO as the term Intellectual Property Office or IPO is also used by other institutions around the world. The new name is an "operating name" of the Patent Office which is still its formal name until the necessary changes can be made by statute, see §A16.   **123.88**

There is not now (as there was formerly) an official address for the UK-IPO designated by a statutory instrument. However, the main office is at The UK-IPO, Cardiff Road, Newport, South Wales NP10 8QQ. There are also filing, search and hearing facilities at a London office located at 21 Bloomsbury Street, London WC1B 3HF. However, the London branch office contains no examining staff and all correspondence is dealt with in the Newport office. Correspondence with individuals at the Patent Office may be made by email, but such emails should be restricted to correspondence only and, in particular, should not attach other documents. The general email address for inquiries is "enquiries@ipo.gov.uk". Such enquiries can even be directed to a known individual under the designation "firstname.surname@ipo.gov.uk". A notice in the *Patents Journal* of July 11, 2001 gives general information on communicating with patents staff by email. The UK-IPO website (*http://www.ipo.gov.uk*) offers a wide range of information about intellectual property and the publications and services of the UK-IPO, and contains contact details and telephone numbers for various departments.

To protect against the remote possibility of documents and fees going astray between London and Newport, additional copies of the forms and documents may be sent by fax transmission on the same day as the primary documents and fees are filed, though these will only serve to provide prima facie evidence of original filing. The filing of original documents can also be effected by fax transmission. Of course, care has to be taken that any fee required is also paid, for example by including in the transmission a valid request for the fee to be deducted from a named deposit account, see §119.05. Enquiries concerning this facility for fax filing can be made by telephone, or further details obtained from the website above.

Trading Fund status of the UK Intellectual Property Office

123.89   From October 1, 1991, the UK-IPO became financially independent of the Department of Trade and Industry by being given "trading fund status" under the Government Trading Funds Act 1973 (c.63), as amended by the Government Trading Act 1990 (c.30) and the Finance Act 1991 (c.31), see §123.37 where the Patent Office Trading Fund Order 1991 (SI 1991/1796) is reprinted, and also §A16. This Order led to alteration of the form and date of the Comptroller's Annual Report, as required by s.121, for which see §121.02. A further consequence of this Order was that the UK-IPO is now administered through a board of management of which the Comptroller is the "Chief Executive Officer".

The Order establishes the "Patent Office Trading Fund" ("the Fund"), on the basis of a specified sum to be treated as public dividend capital and the power for loans to be made to the Fund. From this, there is funded all operations of the UK-IPO, including obligations under European Community or other international institutions. The provision and dissemination of information and advertisement of its activities is also borne by the Fund, see Sch.1 to the Order, and the Fund at its creation had the assets and liabilities specified in Sch.2 to the Order. It is not thought that the Order alters the position concerning the level of fees which the Secretary of State can require to be imposed to obtain a specified return on assets, for which see §123.64.

SECTION 124

Rules, regulations and orders; supplementary

124.01   **124.**—(1) Any power conferred on the Secretary of State by this Act to make rules, regulations or orders shall be exercisable by statutory instrument.

(2) Any Order in Council and any statutory instrument containing an order, rules or regulations under this Act, other than an order or rule required to be laid before Parliament in draft or an order under section 132(5) below, shall be subject to annulment in pursuance of a resolution of either House of Parliament.

(3) Any Order in Council or order under any provision of this Act may be varied or revoked by a subsequent order.

Note. The rule-making powers under this section have been extended by SI 1992/3091 and SI 1996/3120 to provide for rules governing Supplementary Protection Certificates, see s.128B.

COMMENTARY ON SECTION 124

Scope of the section and rule-making powers

124.02   Section 124 provides general rule-making powers additional to the specific provisions contained elsewhere in the Act, mainly in s.123. These powers are exercisable by the Secretary of State or by Order in Council. Under the Interpretation Act 1978 (c.30) Sch.1, "Secretary of State" means any one of Her Majesty's Principal Secretaries of State. In relation to the operation of the patent statutes, the powers of the "Secretary of State" were formerly exercised by the Secretary of State for Trade and Industry, but are now exercised by the Secretary of State for Innovation Universities and Skills.

Besides the rule-making powers conferred by s.123 and discussed in the commentary on that section, powers to make specific rules are also contained in s.25(5) (notice of overdue renewal); s.32(1) and (2) (entries in the register); s.92(3) and (4) (evidence for use under the EPC); s.120(1) (hours of business and excluded days); s.125A (availability of samples of deposited biological material); and s.130(2) (statement of international exhibition). The rules made under these powers are discussed in the commentaries on those sections.

Variation of Act by executive order

In addition to these rule-making powers, powers to vary provisions of the Act by execu- **124.03** tive order are given by s.1(5) (non-inventions) and s.25(2) (date of commencement of patent), but each subject to affirmative resolution of each House of Parliament; s.48(2) (period required before compulsory licence application can be filed); s.77(9) (translation of European patent); and s.78(8) (translation of claims of European application).

There are also provisions for Orders in Council, permitting amendment of the application of the Act, in: s.54(1) (foreign working of inventions); and s.59(3) and (4) (declaration of period of emergency: each after affirmative resolution by each House of Parliament); and in s.90 (designation of convention countries); and in s.132(2) (application of the Act to the Isle of Man), as discussed in the commentaries on those sections. Repealed s.86 formerly provided for the making of "regulations" for implementing the CPC.

In addition to these specific powers contained within the Act to vary its provisions, the Act can be amended by a statutory instrument issued under powers contained in the European Communities Act 1972 (c.68), but only in order to bring the statute into conformity with European Union Regulations and Directives and then only after affirmative resolution of each House of Parliament, as was done for amending the Act in order to implement the EU Biotechnology Directive (reprinted in Appendix C) by the Patents Regulations 2000 (SI 2000/2037). However, it is doubtful whether these powers extend to matters arising out of a revision of the EPC which is a Convention existing outside of the laws of the European Union, but the position may be different in respect of amendments to bring the statute into conformity with the TRIPS Agreement as the Commission co-signed this together with each of EU Member States. Also, the European Commission has expressed the view that the EU should accede to the EPC in its own name, but this has not yet happened.

A further possibility of amendment of the Act under secondary legislation is provided by the terms of the Deregulation and Contracting Out Act 1994 (c.40), see §123.38.

Annulment of amendments made by secondary legislation (subs.(2))

Subsection (2) provides that, unless otherwise stated, any Order in Council or statutory **124.04** instrument made under the Act is subject to negative resolution (i.e. a prayer for annulment) by either House of Parliament, but in the absence of any such resolution the Order or instrument comes into force automatically on the date specified.A prayer for annulment of an Order in Council or a statutory instrument can, however, only relate to the Order or instrument as a whole, so that Parliament cannot debate any specific variation of it.

SECTION 124A [ADDED]

Use of electronic communications

124A.—(1) The comptroller may **give** [*make*] directions as to the form and **124A.01** manner in which documents to be delivered to the comptroller—

    (a) in electronic form; or

    (b) using electronic communications,

are to be delivered to him.

(2) A direction under subsection (1) may provide that in order for a document to be delivered in compliance with the direction it shall be accompanied by one or more additional documents specified in the direction.

(3) Subject to subsections (14) and (15), if a document to which a direction under subsection (1) or (2) [*If a document to which a direction under* *subsection (1)*] applies is delivered to the comptroller in a form or manner which does not comply with the direction the comptroller may treat the document as not having been delivered.

(4) Subsection (5) applies in relation to a case where—

(a) a document is delivered using electronic communications, and

(b) there is a requirement for a fee to accompany the document.

(5) The comptroller may **give** [*make*] directions specifying—

(a) how the fee shall be paid; **and**

(b) when the fee shall be deemed to have been paid.

(6) The comptroller may **give** [*make*] directions specifying that a person who delivers a document to the comptroller in electronic form or using electronic communications cannot treat the document as having been delivered unless its delivery has been acknowledged.

(7) The comptroller may **give** [*make*] directions specifying how a time of delivery is to be accorded to a document delivered to him in electronic form or using electronic communications.

(8) A direction under this section may be given—

(a) generally;

(b) in relation to a description of cases specified in the direction;

(c) in relation to a particular person or persons.

[(9) *Repealed*]

[(10) *Repealed*]

(11) A direction under this section may be varied or revoked by a subsequent direction under this section.

[(12) *Repealed*]

(13) The delivery using electronic communications to any person by the comptroller of any document is deemed to be effected, unless the comptroller has otherwise specified, by transmitting an electronic communication containing the document to an address provided or made available to the comptroller by that person as an address of his for the receipt of electronic communications; and unless the contrary is proved such delivery is deemed to be effected immediately upon the transmission of the communication [*Where the comptroller delivers a document using electronic communications then, unless the contrary intention has been specified by the comptroller, the delivery is deemed to be effected by the comptroller properly addressing and transmitting the electronic communication*].

(14) A requirement of this Act that something must be done in the prescribed manner is satisfied in the case of something that is done—

(a) using a document in electronic form, or

(b) using electronic communications,

only if the directions under this section that apply to the manner in which it is done are complied with [*Where the comptroller makes a direction under this section which applies in addition to or in place of rules, to the extent that the direction applies—*

(a) *"prescribed" in this Act includes prescribed by the direction;*

(b) *references in this Act to compliance with rules or requirements of rules include compliance with the direction or requirements of the direction].*

(15) In the case of an application made as mentioned in subsection (14)(a) or (b) above, a reference in this Act to the application not having been made in compliance with rules or requirements of this Act includes a reference to its not having been made in compliance with any particular directions under this section

[In this section—

(a) *references to a document include anything that is or may be embodied in paper form;*

(b) *references to delivery to the comptroller include delivery at, in, with or to the Patent Office;*

(c) *references to delivery by the comptroller include delivery by the Patent Office;*

and cognate expressions must be construed accordingly].

(16) This section applies—

(a) **to delivery at, in, with or to the Patent Office as it applies to delivery to the comptroller; and**

(b) **to delivery by the Patent Office as it applies to delivery by the comptroller.**

Note. Section 124A was added by the Patents Act 1977 (Electronic Communications) Order 2003 (SI 2003/512) with effect from April 1, 2003, and applied to the Isle of Man by SI 2003/1249. The term "electronic communication" was then defined by an addition to s.130(1), see §130.01. Section 124A was amended by SI 2006/1229 (with effect from October 1, 2006).

Directions on Electronic Communications made under Section 124A

Under the powers provided by section 124A, the Comptroller has issued directions on the following matters: **124A.02**

- Filing patent applications by electronic means (reprinted in §14.06).

- Filing documents relating to pending patent applications by electronic means (reprinted in §14.06).

- Requests for electronic uncertified copies from patent files (discussed in §118.19).

- Withdrawal of patent applications by email (discussed in §14.51 and §16.06).

- Requesting an extension of time by email (reprinted in §117B.03).

- Submitting observations concerning the patentability of an invention (reprinted in §21.03).

- Submitting post-grant amendments by email (discussed in §27.13).

- Submitting Opinion observations by email (reprinted in §74A.08).

These directions are all available on the UK-IPO website.

COMMENTARY ON SECTION 124A

Section 124A was introduced into the Act in order to facilitate the use of electronic communications with the Patent Office by providing enabling powers for new Rules or for amended Rules having this objective.   **124A.03**

At the time of writing, the communication options included in the directions were as follows:

— web interface (for filing applications, subsequent documents and PF 23);

— online filing using epoline® smart-card software (for filing applications and subsequent documents);

— email (for withdrawal of applications, requesting extensions of time, filing third party observations, filing post-grant amendments and filing observations in opinion proceedings); and

— digital media (CDs, DVDs and floppy disks) accompanied by covering letter.

Some important points are set out below.

The epoline® smart-card software can be used to prepare documents for online filing or for filing on digital media. Smart-card documents which require a signature can include a facsimile signature, a text string signature (normally in the form/name/) or an electronic signature using a PIN. The smart-card documents can be saved. By contrast, the UK-IPO web interface requires the documents to be prepared and filed in a single session.

Online filing using epoline® smart-card software requires the user to be registered with the UK-IPO, to have an account with the UK-IPO and to be registered for electronic signature. Filing via the web interface simply requires an email address to be given. On-line filing can take place at any time except between 01.00 and 02.30 hours UK time. Fees due with an online filing can be paid from a deposit account or by credit or debit card. A receipt indicating the date and time of delivery and documents received is sent electronically. Where documents are illegible or incomplete, or are reported as containing a virus, they are treated as not complying with the directions and the sender is notified. When a digital medium is used a receipt indicating the date and time of delivery and documents received is sent by post.

No paper confirmation of documents filed online or on digital media is required (but note that covering letters are required for documents filed on digital media).

Rule 35(2) (for which see §27.02) provides that amendments to a granted patent which are sought from the Comptroller should, whenever possible, be delivered in electronic form.

SECTION 125

Extent of invention

125.01 **125.**—(1) For the purposes of this Act an invention for a patent for which an application has been made or for which a patent has been granted shall, unless the context otherwise requires, be taken to be that specified in a claim of the specification of the application or patent, as the case may be, as interpreted by the description and any drawings contained in that specification, and the extent of the protection conferred by a patent or application for a patent shall be determined accordingly.

(2) It is hereby declared for the avoidance of doubt that where more than one invention is specified in any such claim, each invention may have a different priority date under section 5 above.

(3) The Protocol on the Interpretation of Article 69 of the European Patent Convention (which Article contains a provision corresponding to subsection (1) above) shall, as for the time being in force, apply for the purposes of subsection (1) above as it applies for the purposes of that Article.

Note. Subsection (1) is defectively worded. The words "for a patent" in line 1 ought to appear after the word "application" such that the subsection should read:

"For the purposes of this Act an invention for which an application for a patent has been made or for which a patent has been granted...".

RELEVANT PROVISIONS OF THE EUROPEAN PATENT CONVENTION

EPC Article 69(1)—Extent of protection

69.—(1) The extent of the protection conferred by a European patent or a   **125.02**
European patent application shall be determined by the claims. Nevertheless, the description and drawings shall be used to interpret the claims.

Note. Amended by EPC 2000, entering into force 13 December 2007. The previous wording referred to the extent of protection being determined by "the terms of the claims". Most decisions so far have referred back to the old wording in force at the relevant time but the change is not likely to have any material effect on the operation of the article.

PROTOCOL ON THE INTERPRETATION OF ARTICLE 69 OF THE CONVENTION

Article 1—General principles

Article 69 should not be interpreted as meaning that the extent of the protec-   **125.03**
tion conferred by a European patent is to be understood as that defined by the strict, literal meaning of the wording used in the claims, the description and drawings being employed only for the purpose of resolving an ambiguity found in the claims. Nor should it be taken to mean that the claims serve only as a guideline and that the actual protection conferred may extend to what, from a consideration of the description and drawings by a person skilled in the art, the patent proprietor has contemplated. On the contrary, it is to be interpreted as defining a position between these extremes which combines a fair protection for the patent proprietor with a reasonable degree of legal certainty for third parties.

Article 2—Equivalents

For the purpose of determining the extent of protection conferred by a European patent, due account shall be taken of any element which is equivalent to an element specified in the claims.

Note. Amended, and art.2 added, by EPC 2000, entering into force December 13, 2007. The amendments to art.1 are largely editorial, the only change of any possible substance being the word "legal" added before "certainty" in the last line. This is presumably a point of clarification, not likely to have any significant effect on the interpretation of the Protocol.

COMMENTARY ON SECTION 125

Introduction and scope of section

Since the publication of the Sixth Edition of this Work, judges in patent cases have gen-   **125.04**
erally confirmed that the exercise of construction of a patent should be carried out in accordance with the decision of the House of Lords in *Kirin-Amgen Inc v Hoechst Marion Roussel* [2005] R.P.C. 9 at 169 (otherwise cited as *Kirin-Amgen v Transkaryotic Therapies (No.2))* and in particular the speech of Lord Hoffmann in that case which is now recognised as the leading authority in this jurisdiction on the question of interpretation.

The usual approach, typified in a recent case by HH Judge Birss QC sitting as a judge of the High Court in *Convatec v Smith & Nephew* [2011] EWHC 2039 (Pat) and *Mölnlycke v Brightwake* [2011] EWHC 376, is to point out (as stated in the Sixth Edition) that the House of Lords comprehensively reviewed the principles applicable to claim construction under the 1977 Act in *Kirin Amgen*, and thus the process of construction is purposive in nature and the question is always to work out what the person skilled in the art would have understood the patentee to be using the language of the claim to mean. See also Arnold J. in *Abbott v Medinol* [2010] EWHC 2865 and *KCI v Smith & Nephew* [2010] EWHC 1487 in the same vein. Cases often refer to the fact that in *Kirin-Amgen* the judgment of Jacob L.J. in *Technip* [2004] EWCA Civ 381 was approved "subject to one point" (for that see §125.08 below). The same principles have also been acknowledged in Scots law, e.g. *Verathon v Aircraft Medical* [2011] CSOH 19. Perhaps the most succinct statement of these principles is that of Jacob L.J. in *Virgin Atlantic v Delta* [2011] EWCA Civ 162: "This [the patent claim] is to be construed on familiar *Kirin-Amgen* principles: what would the person skilled in the art have understood the patentee to be using the language of the claim to mean?" Indeed in the *Virgin* case on appeal, Jacob L.J. said that "one might have thought there was nothing more to say on this topic after *Kirin-Amgen*".

On the other hand, it is still possible for the Court of Appeal to get through a whole case involving an important point of construction without even referring to *Kirin-Amgen*, nevertheless coming to the same conclusions by the same reasoning: see *Tate & Lyle Technology v Roquette Frères* [2010] EWCA Civ 1049 in which the court referred to Lord Diplock's warnings in *Catnic* against meticulous verbal analysis, it having been argued that the judge had adopted "an over-abstract and linguistic approach which ultimately departed from the whole teaching of the specification". In several cases, reference is made to *Virgin v Premium Aircraft* [2009] EWHC 26 (Pat) in which Lewison J. provided "a helpful summary" of the principles of construction as applied to patents with reference back to Lord Diplock's speech in *Catnic*.

In the above light, this section discussing s.125 could be very short. However, as always, some historical perspective and discussion of cases in general will be valuable to an understanding of the principles involved.

There being no definition as such of "invention" in the Act or the EPC, it is for s.125(1) to establish what the invention "covered by" a patent or application is deemed to be, namely that which is specified in a claim of the specification. Under the Patents Act 1949 and former patent statutes, the scope of protection was left to be determined by the common law based on the wording of the grant of the Letters Patent, and the definition of a patentable invention in the Statute of Monopolies of 1623, as discussed further in Appendix A. The fact that s.125(1) is clumsily worded, as pointed out in the note to §125.01, has not affected its interpretation in practice. Indeed in *Schütz v Werit* [2011] EWCA Civ 303 Lord Justice Jacob, as noted below, implied that the wording of s.125(1) is no longer of real importance, the true source of the law on construction now being art.69 EPC.

Thus, it is the function of the claims to define the invention for the purpose of determining the legal monopoly conferred by the patent, whereas the description and drawings disclose the means of performing the invention. The patent, when granted, will only confer protection on the invention as specified in the claims, but the claims are to be interpreted in the light of the description and drawings. The construction of the claims is thus crucial in determining the extent of protection provided for the invention by the patent under the Act, and is therefore pivotal to any considerations of infringement (ss.60 and 69); validity (ss.2 and 3); priority date (s.5); and amendment (s.76).

Section 125 is one of those declared by s.130(7) to be so framed as to have, as nearly as practicable, the same effects in the UK as the corresponding provisions of the EPC, the CPC and the PCT. Thus, there is an obligation to construe s.125 in a manner which will harmonise as far as possible with those measures and with decisions and opinions of relevant convention courts, judicial notice of which is to be taken in accordance with s.91. In particular, as provided in s.125(3), the Protocol on the Interpretation of art.69 of the EPC applies for the purposes of subs.(1).

In *Schütz v Werit* [2011] EWCA Civ 303 Lord Justice Jacob, giving the decision of the Court of Appeal, pointed out that s.125(1) nevertheless has no direct parallel in the EPC or the CPC. He concluded the effect of s.130(7) must be that so far as the Conventions do provide for the extent of protection of a patent, the same is intended to apply in the UK. That means that art.69 EPC "is what matters, and nothing else".

Given that all EPC Member States should apply art.69(1) of the EPC and the Protocol in the same way, this should lead to uniformity of interpretation of claims. However, because of differences between national court procedures and of differences in the reception and assessment of evidence, such uniformity has not generally been attained in practice.

Section 125 defines what is meant by an invention "except where the context otherwise requires". In *Schütz v Werit* (above) Lord Justice Jacob considered that the use of this expression was effectively meaningless as the phrase forms no part of the EPC provisions and therefore did not assist one way or the other in the interpretation of s.125. In his view this was just an example of less than optimal drafting. In prior editions of this Work, some attempt was made to give some meaning to this phrase by postulating circumstances where the context might require "invention" to be a reference to something other than an invention specified in a claim which would include, for example, when claims have not yet been drawn up (ss.7(3), 15(1), 22(1), 23, 39, 42 and 43). Then it appears that "invention" can have any meaning which suits the context in which the word is used. For example, "a description of the invention" as required by s.14(2)(b) and s.14(3) requires the invention to be disclosed in a manner which is clear enough and complete enough for it to be performed by a person skilled in the art. In *Viziball's Application* [1988] R.P.C. 213 (in entitlement proceedings), "invention" was held to encompass anything devised by the inventor and to include both patentable and non-patentable discoveries. Given that Lord Justice Jacob's comment was made in the context of the case before him, in which these other circumstances were not relevant, it is submitted that this discussion may be of some value in other contexts. It should be noted also that the term "invention" is, therefore, not synonymous with a "patentable invention", as is evident in any case from s.1(1) which says that patents may only be granted for an "invention" which fulfils the criteria there set out, s.1(3) which says that patents cannot be granted for certain inventions and s.72(1)(a) which says that a patent for an invention can be revoked if "the invention is not a patentable invention".

Section 125 makes no reference to validity, and, accordingly, the definition of invention evidently includes an alleged invention. Consequently, the "extent of protection conferred" may be defined by a claim which is invalid. This is relevant to questions of amendment and covered in the commentary on s.76.

The modern approach to claim construction will be discussed in the following paragraphs, from which it will be clear that what is all important is what would the person skilled in the relevant art think that the claim wording meant upon reading it at the date of first publication, not what the patent draftsman thought, or hoped, it would mean. Although it is submitted that *Kirin-Amgen* did not change the existing law, and indeed it emphasised the continued validity in the UK of the "purposive construction" approach famously expounded by Lord Diplock in *Catnic*, the decision synthesises the legal principles of construction as developed in the UK and in other jurisdictions and is almost a text book on the subject in its own right. Lord Hoffmann, who had considerable influence over the development of the law in this area over his extensive career, has now retired, but continues his interest and influence as Honorary Professor of Intellectual Property Law at Queen Mary, University of London.

The modern approach to claim construction in the UK under the principles of article 69(1) and the Protocol

As noted in §125.04, subs.(1) is required by s.130(7) to be interpreted in conformity **125.05** with art.69(1) of the EPC, and is to be read in conjunction with subs.(3) which imports the concept of the Protocol to EPC art.69 in defining the extent of protection conferred by a patent or patent application.

Article 69(1) states that the extent of the protection conferred by a patent application shall be determined by the claims, with the description and drawings being used to interpret the claims. This general principle (that the extent of protection is defined by the claims) is in accordance with the former English approach, for example as set forth by Lord Russell of Killowen in *Electrical and Musical Industries v Lissen* (1939) 56 R.P.C. 23:

> "The function of the claims is to define clearly and with precision the monopoly claimed, so that others may know the exact boundary of the area within which they will be trespassers. Their primary object is to limit and not to extend the monopoly."

In *Nobel v Anderson* (1895) 12 R.P.C. 164 HL, it was stated: "What is not claimed, is disclaimed" and, in *Electrical and Musical Industries v Lissen* (above), it was said that there was:

> "no canon or principle which would justify one in departing from the unambiguous and grammatical meaning of a claim and narrowing or extending its scope by reading into it words which are not in it".

See also *Norton and Gregory v Jacobs* (1937) 54 R.P.C. 58 and 271 CA. The above quotations, and the words of Lord Porter in *Electrical and Musical Industries v Lissen*:

> "If the Claims have a plain meaning in themselves, then advantage cannot be taken of the language used in the body of the Specification to make them mean something different."

epitomise the perception that the English rules of construction would lead to a literal construction of the scope of the claims. Only if the language of the claim was ambiguous could the court could have regard to the context provided by the specification and drawings, and if that was insufficient to resolve the ambiguity, to extrinsic evidence.

This did not conform to the approach adopted in other countries, in particular Germany and Holland. There the practice was more to regard the claims as a starting point in determining the extent of protection, looking towards the essence of the invention or the inventive achievement or concept to be found from reading the specification as a whole, using the claim merely as a guide or signpost to what the patentee intended. The combined effect of art.69(1) and the Protocol is to define an approach to construction which is designed to be adopted as the common standard within Europe, not necessarily corresponding precisely to any of the approaches previously adopted, and therefore requiring a fresh appraisal.

As already discussed in §125.04, *Kirin-Amgen* is now recognised as the leading UK authority on interpretation. In that case Lord Hoffmann gives a thorough exposition of how the rules of construction have evolved over the years since the Patents Act 1977 and the EPC came into force, and how they now compare with what went before, in particular as expounded by his predecessor Lord Diplock in *Catnic v Hill & Smith* [1982] R.P.C. 183, from which he concludes that Lord Diplock's emphasis on "purposive construction" is still valid and in accordance with the principles of the Protocol. In the course of a thorough review of historical and recent cases on construction, including case law from Germany, the Netherlands and the United States, he summarised the philosophy of the Protocol and art.69 as being "so far as is possible in an imperfect world, not to disappoint the reasonable expectations" of the patentee or third parties. To that end, a construction which would give fair protection to the patentee would be one:

> "which would give him the full extent of the monopoly which the person skilled in the art would think he was intending to claim".

Likewise, reasonable certainty for third parties would be achieved by a principle:

> "which would not give the patentee more than the full extent of the monopoly which the person skilled in the art would think that he was intending to claim".

Lord Hoffmann points out in *Kirin-Amgen* that the Protocol relates to the interpretation of art.69, not as such to the interpretation of claims. It sets forth what might be viewed as a compromise designed to reconcile the two approaches to interpretation it describes or at least to define a "middle way" between them. Thus, although the common law principle of using the claims to determine the extent of protection is adopted, it seeks to avoid the possibility that the principles of construction adopted in the UK courts might result in claims being given a narrow and literal construction. Nor should the "essence of the invention" approach be adopted so as to risk giving the claims an over generous interpretation. Thus the Protocol makes it clear that it is not permissible to use art.69 to restrict the extent of protection to the strict, literal meaning of the wording used in the claims, the sole purpose of the description and drawings being to resolve ambiguities, nor to go beyond the claims to what, on the basis of the specification as a whole, it appears that "the patentee has contemplated". The overriding approach, as defined in the final sentence, is to strive to achieve "a fair protection for the patent proprietor with a reasonable degree of legal certainty for third parties". This is as Lord Russell recognised; but not just from the point of view of others who need to know the area "within which they will be trespassers" but also in the interests of the proprietor, who needs to be able to avoid a wide construction which would invalidate the patent by being deemed to cover the prior art.

To the extent that the prior UK rules on construction meant that the court, unless it could find some ambiguity in the language, had to construe the document literally, even to the extent of adopting a construction which a reasonable reader would not have thought the author intended, they could cause injustice. To counteract this, judges were sometimes forced into using some level of "inventiveness" themselves to find the "ambiguity" which would enable them to come to a more appropriate interpretation of the document in its proper context. In the words of Lord Hoffmann again in *Kirin-Amgen*,

> "the attempt to treat the words of the claim as having meanings 'in themselves' and without regard to the context in which or the purpose for which they were used was always a highly artificial exercise".

The Protocol therefore clearly rejects this approach, but in fact it was already outmoded even in English law by the time the Patents Act 1977 came into force. Even before the famous "purposive construction" speech of Lord Diplock in *Catnic* the English courts had begun to recognise that a document ought not to be construed in a way that gives the author's words a meaning different from how they would be understood by the audience to which they were actually addressed. This is true of legal documents generally, not just of patent specifications. Although such documents may generally be written by lawyers or patent attorneys, they are practical documents addressed to, and to be used by, "real" people in relation to practical situations. Thus Lord Diplock's famous warning against "the kind of meticulous verbal analysis in which lawyers [which for this purpose at least includes patent attorneys] are too often tempted by their training to indulge" still resonates.

Whilst it may be tempting to conclude that the last words on construction have been spoken, the extent to which there may still be scope for the courts to create further change in the effect of claim construction, even after *Kirin-Amgen*, is discussed in a paper by D.J. Brennan *The evolution of English Patent Claims as Property Definers* [2005] I.P.Q. (No.4), 361.

Purposive construction

In *Catnic*, which was a case about a patent granted under the 1949 Act, Lord Diplock **125.06** propounded the principle of "purposive construction" in the following passage, which has frequently been quoted in subsequent judgments. As noted above, this approach has been found to be still applicable to the test to be applied under s.125(1) and (3), and thus in conformity with the Protocol to EPC art.69. Therefore it is still appropriate to quote extensively from Lord Diplock's speech:

> "My Lords, a patent specification is a unilateral statement by the patentee, in words of his own choosing, addressed to those likely to have a practical interest in the subject matter of his invention (i.e. 'skilled in the art') by which he informs them what he

claims to be the essential features of the new product process for which the letters patent grant him a monopoly. It is those novel features only that he claims to be essential that constitute the so-called 'pith and marrow' of the claim. A patent specification should be given a purposive construction rather than a purely literal one derived from applying to it the kind of meticulous verbal analysis in which lawyers are too often tempted by their training to indulge. The question in each case is: whether persons with practical knowledge and experience of the kind of work in which the invention was intended to be used, would understand that strict compliance with a particular descriptive word or phrase appearing in a claim was intended by the patentee to be an essential requirement of the invention so that any variant would fall outside the monopoly claimed, even though it could have no material effect upon the way the invention worked. The question, of course, does not arise where the variant would in fact have a material effect upon the way the invention worked. Nor does it arise unless at the date of publication of the specification it would be obvious to the informed reader that this was so. Where it is not obvious, in the light of then-existing knowledge, the reader is entitled to assume that the patentee thought at the time of the specification that he had good reason for limiting his monopoly so strictly and had intended to do so, even though subsequent work by him or others in the field of the invention might show the limitation to have been unnecessary. It is to be answered in the negative only when it would be apparent to any reader skilled in the art that a particular descriptive word or phrase used in a claim cannot have been intended by a patentee, who was also skilled in the art, to exclude minor variants which, to the knowledge of both him and the readers to whom the patent was addressed, could have no material effect upon the way in which the invention worked. The essential features of the invention that is the subject of claim 1 of the patent in suit in the instant appeal are much easier to understand than those of any of the three patents to which I have referred; and this makes the question of its construction simpler. Put in a nutshell the question to be answered is: Would the specification make it obvious to a builder familiar with ordinary building operations that the description of a lintel in the form of a weight-bearing box girder of which the back plate was referred to as 'extending vertically' from one of the two horizontal plates to join the other, could not have been intended to exclude lintels in which the back plate although not positioned at precisely90° to both horizontal plates was close enough to 90° to make no material difference to the way the lintel worked when used in building operations No plausible reason has been advanced why any rational patentee should want to place so narrow a limitation on his invention. On the contrary, it would render his monopoly for all practical purposes worthless, since any imitator could avoid it and take all the benefit of the invention by the simple expedient of positioning the back plate a degree or two from the exact vertical."

Neuberger J. in *Kirin-Amgen v Roche Diagnostics* [2002] R.P.C. 1 (otherwise cited as *Kirin-Amgen v Transkaryotic Therapies (No.1)*) felt that the rules for construction of patents did not differ substantially from those for other legal documents. The fact that a patent was a unilateral document did not seem to him to be a relevant distinction since the approach to the construction of notices (i.e. other unilateral documents) was the same as for the construction of contracts.

The Court of Appeal in *Pharmacia v Merck* [2002] R.P.C. 41 at 775 elaborated on the approach to the construction of patent claims under the Protocol in some detail, comparing it with the approaches to construction of contracts, statutes and wills, and finding both similarities and differences. In that the court had to determine the intentions of the patentee, there was most similarity with the interpretation of wills. However, this was only one step in the process because the court was required by the Protocol to balance the interests of the patentee with that of third parties. Under the Protocol, it might be necessary to fill in a gap or to depart from the precise terms of the patent in suit but only if the court was satisfied that this could be done as a matter of interpretation. The weight to be given to the concepts of reasonableness and fairness under the Protocol has yet to be fully articulated by the courts but may be guided by policy considerations such as that identified by Lord Hoffmann in *Biogen v Medeva* [1997] R.P.C. 1:

"care is needed not to stifle further research and healthy competition by allowing the first person who has found a way of achieving an obviously desirable goal to monopolise every other way of doing so".

However, the court acknowledged that "it would be unfair to the patentee to construe a patent beyond its intended ambit. …To do so may make his patent invalid." See also the article *Purposive Construction of Unambiguous Terms in a Claim* by L. Kempton and A. Cooke [2002] *CIPA* 24.

Thus, what has to be decided in each case is whether persons of relevant practical knowledge and experience would understand that the patentee intended strict compliance with a particular descriptive word or phrase to be an essential requirement of the invention, so that any variant would fall outside the monopoly claimed even though it could have no material effect upon the way the invention worked. On the facts of the *Catnic* case, there seemed no good reason why the word "vertical" should be given a meaning so as to exclude a member not positioned at precisely 90 degrees to the horizontal yet close enough to make no material difference to its function. Accordingly, infringement was found.

In *Nokia v IPCom* [2009] EWHC 3482 Pat Ct, Floyd J. explained the "now well settled" rules of construction under *Kirin Amgen* and *Technip* as clarified in *Halliburton*, and went on to say that where a patentee has used general language in a claim, but has described the invention by reference to a specific embodiment, it is not normally legitimate to write limitations into the claim corresponding to details of the specific embodiment, if the patentee has chosen not to do so. The specific embodiments are merely examples of what is claimed as the invention, and are often expressly, although superfluously, stated not to be "limiting". There is no general principle which requires the court to assume that the patentee intended to claim the most sophisticated embodiment of the invention. The skilled person understands that, in the claim, the patentee is stating the limits of the monopoly which it claims, not seeking to describe every detail of the manifold ways in which the invention may be put into effect.

In this case it had been contended that claim 1 defined an entire scheme, and did not allow steps which are not specified to be interposed between the steps prescribed in the claim. In that connection it was pointed out that, in describing the steps, the claim stated that the stage is "split into" a number of steps, rather than saying that the stage "comprises" those steps, "comprise" being said to be patent attorney's code for saying that the claim allows for other things, whereas "split into" suggests they are part of a whole into which nothing else is admitted. The judge rejected that interpretation, concluding that the claim would not be read as excluding other steps and that the skilled reader would not attach much importance to the patentee's use of "split into" as opposed to "comprise". There was nothing to suggest that other steps could not be used, and it would be "odd, to say the least," if infringement could be avoided by the use of some additional step.

In a further submission the judge was asked to imply into the claim a feature not expressly set out in it but which was said to be necessary for it to work. In the absence of being referred to any authority on the implication of claim features, the judge held, by analogy with the principles applied to the interpretation of contracts, that a term should not be implied into a patent claim unless it is necessary to do so, for example where it is necessary to imply a feature to make technical sense of the claim. In this case it was held that the relevant feature should not be implied as it would result in a significant limitation of the claim, and there was no reason why the draftsman should be presumed to have wanted to build in such a limitation when the claim made technical sense without it.

Further, it was commented that whilst it is unusual for the same term to carry a different meaning at different points in the same claim, it is not impossible for this to occur. In the present case the different stages of the process had a different purpose, and although it was said that "the specification does its best to make this point obscure, and it is tempting to visit the consequences on the patentee", on balance the judge favoured an interpretation derivable from the purpose and context of the relevant term which would be consistent with the skilled person's understanding of what the claim required. The decision was upheld on appeal: [2011] EWCA Civ 6.

In *Ratiopharm v Alza* [2009] EWHC 213 Pat Ct, having referred to the correct approach to construction as set out in *Kirin Amgen*, the judge referred back to the words of Aldous J. in *Rediffusion Simulation v Link-Miles* [1993] F.S.R. 369, that there is seldom a case where a person asked to look at every word of a specification to try to destroy it, cannot make out a case of potential ambiguity. The specification is to be read through the eyes of the skilled person attempting to give it a practical meaning and ascertain the intention of the draftsman rather than take it apart word by word. With that in mind the judge rejected the defendants' submission that the claim was completely unclear and accordingly could not be infringed and was insufficient, in favour of giving it a modified construction contended for by the patentee which took account of the range of humans to whom the drug of the invention might be administered and their inherent variability.

In *Medtronic CoreValve v Edwards* [2010] EWCA Civ 704 the Court of Appeal held that to construe a the word "cylindrical" as capable of including a shape in which the diameter varied along its length was to put far too great a strain on the word.

"Of course in some cases a patentee by the use of a particular geometric term may not have intended mathematical precision (the classic case is 'vertical' in *Catnic*). But it is quite another thing to strike it out altogether".

The "Improver" questions

125.07   In *Improver Corp v Remington* [1990] F.S.R. 181, Hoffmann J. (as he then was) saw that Lord Diplock's speech in *Catnic* involved three questions. He formulated these as follows:

"The proper approach to the interpretation of patents registered under the Patents Act 1949 was explained by Lord Diplock in *Catnic Components Ltd v Hill & Smith Ltd* [1982] R.P.C. 183. The language should be given a 'purposive' and not necessarily a literal construction. If the issue was whether a feature embodied in an alleged infringement which fell outside the primary, literal or acontextual meaning of a descriptive word or phrase in the claim ('a variant') was nevertheless within its language as properly interpreted, the court should ask itself the following three questions:
(1) Does the variant have a material effect upon the way the invention works If yes, the variant is outside the claim. If no—
(2) Would this (i.e. that the variant had no material effect) have been obvious at the date of publication of the patent to a reader skilled in the art. If no, the variant is outside the claim. If yes—
(3) Would the reader skilled in the art nevertheless have understood from the language of the claim that the patentee intended that strict compliance with the primary meaning was an essential requirement of the invention, If yes, the variant is outside the claim.
On the other hand, a negative answer to the last question would lead to the conclusion that the patentee was intending the word or phrase to have not a literal but a figurative meaning (the figure being a form of synecdoche or metonymy) denoting a class of things which included the variant and the literal meaning, the latter being perhaps the most perfect, best-known or striking example of the class. Thus in *Catnic* itself the claim of a patent for a lintel of box construction required that the upper plate be supported upon the lower plate by two rigid supports, one in the front and the other 'extending vertically' from the one plate to the other at the rear. The defendant's lintel had a rear support which was inclined 6° or 8° from the vertical. The House of Lords decided that this variation had no material effect upon the load-bearing capacity of the lintel or the way it worked and that this would have been obvious to the skilled builder at the date of publication of the patent. It also decided that the skilled reader would not have understood from the language of the claim that the patentee was insisting upon precisely 90° as an essential requirement of his invention. The conclusion was that 'extending vertically' meant 'extending with the range of angles which give substantially the maximum load-bearing capacity and of which 90° is the perfect example'. In the end, therefore, the question is always whether the alleged infringement is covered by the

language of the claim. This, I think, is what Lord Diplock meant in *Catnic* when he said that there was no dichotomy between 'textual infringement' and infringement of the 'pith and marrow' of the patent and I respectfully think that Fox L.J. put the question with great precision in *Anchor Building Products Ltd v Redland Roof Tiles Ltd* [1990] R.P.C. 283 CA when he said the question was whether the absence of a feature mentioned in the claim was 'an immaterial variant which a person skilled in the trade would have regarded as being *within the ambit of the language*' (my emphasis). It is worth noticing that Lord Diplock's first two questions, although they cannot sensibly be answered without reference to the patent, do not primarily involve questions of construction: whether the variant would make a material difference to the way the invention worked and whether this would have been obvious to the skilled reader are questions of fact. The answers are used to provide the factual background against which the specification must be construed. It is the third question which raises the question of construction and Lord Diplock's formulation makes it clear that on this question the answers to the first two questions are not conclusive. Even a purposive construction of the language of the patent may lead to the conclusion that although the variant made no material difference and this would have been obvious at the time, the patentee for some reason was confining his claim to the primary meaning and excluding the variant. If this were not the case, there would be no point in asking the third question at all."

The three questions set forth in the judgment quoted above have come to be known as the *Improver* questions, sometimes termed the "Protocol" questions. In the *Improver* case, the court was prepared to accept that a bent slitted rubber rod could be regarded as a variant of the term "helical spring" used in the claim, so that the first two of the questions posed by Hoffmann J., could be answered as "no" and "yes" respectively, thereby proceeding to the third question. However, here the words chosen by the patent draftsman were seen to be such as not to permit the slitted rubber rod to be covered by the term "helical spring" so that infringement was not found. The Court of Appeal in Hong Kong reached a similar conclusion, see *Improver Corp v Raymond Industrial* [Hong Kong] [1991] F.S.R. 233, but the dispute was settled globally before either of these decisions progressed to a further appeal. However, in other countries there were findings of infringement. An explanation for some of these decisions may be found submerged in the facts of the case, although not clear from the judgments. This is that the patent required the "helical spring" to be bent and the drawings showed many possible configurations, all of which bent the spring through at least 180 degrees, and usually much more. Yet it appears to have been admitted that the *Remington* slitted rubber rod could not be rotated axially, as required, if bent to more than 120 degrees. In other words, the defendant's device could not be made in any of the embodiments illustrated in the *Improver* patent.

The importance of the third question was stressed by Hoffmann L.J. (as he had by then become) in *Société Technique de Pulverisation STEP v Emson* [1993] R.P.C. 513 where he said:

"The well known principle that patent claims are to have a purposive construction does not mean that an integer can be treated as struck out if it does not appear to make any difference to the inventive concept. It may have some other purpose buried in the prior art and even if this is not discernible, the patentee may have had some reason of his own for introducing it."

And in *Beloit v Valmet* [1995] R.P.C. 705, Jacob J. said:

"In all this it must be remembered that it is the patentee who has set out the limits of his monopoly. Moreover, those reading his claim are entitled to see that it has a scope that goes thus far and no further and to design around the patent. There is no such thing as the tort of non-infringement."

In *Kirin-Amgen*, Lord Hoffmann (as he was by that time) took the opportunity to review the whole field of claim construction and "equivalents" and to place the *Improver*/Protocol questions (Lord Hoffmann uses the latter term) in their proper context. Lord Hoffmann refers to the questions formulated (by him) in *Improver* as being "only guidelines, more useful in some cases than in others". They ought not to be treated as "legal rules":

"the determination of the extent of protection conferred by a European patent is an examination in which there is only one compulsory question, namely that set by Art. 69 and its Protocol: what would a person skilled in the art have understood the patentee to have used the language of the claim to mean? Everything else ... is only guidance to a judge in trying to answer that question".

Lord Walker of Gestingthorpe, in concurring with the opinion of Lord Hoffmann, went further in noting that neither *Catnic* nor *Improver* were concerned with high technology inventions and saying that:

"in a rapidly developing, high-technology field the *Improver* questions may have no useful function, and may be a distraction from the one compulsory question set by Art. 69 and its Protocol".

It seems likely that the courts will in future see themselves as free to use the *Improver* questions where they feel that they will aid the process of construction but will not feel obliged to follow them slavishly in all cases, particularly in "rapidly developing, high technology" fields, in which at least the first two questions may prove difficult to answer. It is notable that in the cases which have considered the question of construction since the last edition of this Work, there has been very little reference to the *Improver* Questions, the courts, as discussed above, confining themselves to reference to *Kirin-Amgen* and Lord Hoffmann's reformulation of the principles of construction as discussed at length above.

In *Sara Lee v Johnson Wax* [2001] EWCA Civ 1609, noted I.P.D. 25008, the Court of Appeal said that the second "Protocol" (*Improver*) question was designed to ensure a reasonable degree of certainty for third parties:

"To be fair to the patentee a party cannot necessarily avoid infringement by taking the invention in a disguised but equivalent form. However to be fair to the public the equivalence must be clear or obvious to the skilled addressee . . . He should not have to build the device and test it . . . if the variant is not obviously immaterial, it would normally be wrong for the public to be prevented from making that variant. It is the patentee who chooses the words of the claim".

The Court of Appeal in *Pharmacia v Merck* (above) developed this theme further by viewing the *Improver* questions as analogous to the process of filling in gaps in statutes. They are used as a tool of analysis and the disciplined approach offered promotes consistency and transparency. The court applied the *Improver* questions to conclude that the claim in this case ought to be construed to cover the variant (the *keto* tautomer), thus overturning the first instance decision (cited as *Monsanto v Merck* [2000] R.P.C. 709) on this point. Another way in which this is put in the same case is that the *Improver* questions are normally a useful tool to arrive at the middle ground required by the Protocol. But sometimes the questions cannot be used without modification. The court was satisfied that its conclusion on interpretation in this case would not prevent there being a reasonable degree of certainty for third parties, and one of the members of the Court of Appeal sums this up by saying that "the *Improver* questions are no more than guidelines: the final conclusion on interpretation must be found by asking the Protocol questions"—by which is presumably meant the two limbs of fairness for the patentee and reasonable certainty for third parties as formulated in the Protocol itself.

In *Kirin-Amgen v Roche Diagnostics* [2002] R.P.C. 1, infringement by one defendant was found on a literal reading of the claim. The other defendant used different technology but was also found to infringe based on an application of the "Protocol" (*Improver*) questions, the defendant having made use of the "technical contribution" of the patent. In the Court of Appeal (sub. nom. *Kirin-Amgen v Transkaryotic Therapies* [2003] R.P.C. 3 at 31) this decision was overturned as incompatible with art.69 of the EPC and the Protocol. See the case comment by H. Sheraton and A. Sharples [2002] E.I.P.R. 596. In the House of Lords the finding of non-infringement was upheld following Lord Hoffmann's review of the law referred to above.

In the appeal in *City Technology v Alphasense* [2002] EWCA Civ 347; [2002] I.P. & T. 767, noted (2002) 25(6) I.P.D. 25038 referred to in §125.20, the defendant conceded that the variant present in its device had no material effect on the way the invention worked and that this had been obvious, thus answering the first two *Improver* questions in the patentee's favour. It argued however that the patentee had indicated, by the words used in the specification, that it intended strict compliance with the words of the claim, i.e. that the third question should be answered in the defendant's favour. That submission was rejected, the court holding that the specification followed a "familiar pattern" for mechanical inventions, and there was nothing to indicate that fair protection for the patentee should be limited to a literal interpretation. The court said that it did not believe that third parties would be surprised by that conclusion (thus, presumably, implying that the test of certainty for third parties was also fulfilled).

In *Merck v Generics* [2004] R.P.C. 31 at 607, referred to in §125.08, the patent concerned the use of sulphonic acids in a manufacturing process. The claim specified methanesulphonic acid (MSA), but the patentee sought to show by experiments that it was possible to substitute other sulphonic acids without having any material effect on the process, and that this would have been obvious to the skilled reader at the relevant date, in an attempt to see that the first two *Improver* questions would be answered in its favour. The judge referred to the *Improver* questions as "normally useful tools", but said that there was nothing to suggest that they were intended as:

"a rigid checklist with three boxes, each of which needs to be ticked appropriately for there to be infringement. . . . They are not a substitute for the Protocol".

Given that the patentee had clearly limited the acid in the claim to MSA, he was deemed to have made a decision not to seek protection for other sulphonic acids, whether or not he was aware of their existence or whether or not they might work. The third *Improver* question was therefore answered in favour of this construction.

The *Merck* case illustrates that it is the third *Improver* question which comes closest to Lord Hoffmann's formulation of looking at what the person skilled in the art would think the patentee was intending to claim. Literal construction is of course banned by the Protocol, but this does not mean that departure from the plain words of the claim should be permitted on a routine basis. If a precise expression is used, the meaning of which would be clear to the person skilled in the art (such as the name of a specific chemical compound), the patentee will be deemed to have chosen it with due regard for that meaning. Where less precise expressions are used, such as words like "vertically", as in *Catnic*, there may be more scope for arguing about the patentee's intentions. The *Merck* case has been criticised by P.G. Mole in [2004] *CIPA* 50 as a case which should never have been brought, and he is also critical of the drafting of the claims. Patent attorneys should first and foremost be skilled draftsmen, and despite repeated references in the cases to the intentions of the patentee, it is inevitably a patent attorney who chooses the language of the claims. The *Improver* questions are not a substitute for the Protocol, as the judge says, but nor should the Protocol be seen as a substitute for good drafting. The judge's barbed comment in *Merck* should be noted:

"the courts are not a branch of the social services whose job it is to help the infirm or the unwise and the Protocol does not require them to be so".

Principles of construction

For a synopsis of the canons of construction to be applied to the interpretation of patent **125.08** claims, see *Dyson v Hoover* [2001] R.P.C. 26 at 473. For comment on this decision, see A. Inglis and S. Cotrill *Patent World* 128, December 2000/January 2001, 15. It is usual in the United Kingdom for the courts first to construe the claims of the patent in suit and determine the extent of protection provided by them. This is done without reference to the prior art (e.g. as in *Molins v Industrial Machinery* (1938) 55 R.P.C. 31 CA), other than perhaps that acknowledged in the patent specification. Having done this, the court can proceed to consider whether the construction of claim adopted by the court leads to validity, or invalidity, of the patent and to its infringement or non-infringement. An example of these principles is *Glaverbel v British Coal* [1994] R.P.C. 443, where it was said that the specification:

"... must be read as a whole in the light of the surrounding circumstances . . . and without regard to the alleged subsequent infringement or the subsequent conduct of the patentee"

and

"... it is not permissible to construe the claims by reference to the subjective thoughts, intentions, purposes and opinions of the patentee or his witnesses or by reference to his actions before or after the grant of the patent."

On appeal in this case (see [1995] R.P.C. 255 CA), the same principles of construction were adopted, but the claim was given a wider construction as, otherwise, it would have been invalid for ambiguity, see the case comment by S. Conroy [1995] E.I.P.R. 199. In *Nobel v Anderson* (1894) 11 R.P.C. 519 at 524 CA, it was stated that the specification and claims should be construed without reference to the alleged infringement: in fact "as if the defendant had never been born". However, in *Pifco v Philips* BL C/83/98, noted I.P.D. 22026, it was pointed out that this is no longer possible, bearing in mind the need to consider possible variants of the literal wording of the claims and whether the patentee intended that strict compliance with any particular descriptive word or phrase is an essential requirement of the invention, as required by purposive construction. In *Pifco*, it was also remarked that "it would be surprising if the principal claim of the patent failed to cover one of the alternative embodiments" and, on this basis, the court held the main claim to have a broader construction than had been sought by either the patentee or the defendant.

In *Hewlett Packard v Waters*, noted I.P.D. 24071 the court said that it was:

"not in general possible finally to come to a conclusion as to the proper construction of the claim until the nature of the alleged infringement has been considered".

This was stated to be because of "the need [arising from the *Catnic* and *Improver* cases] to identify variants from the literal meaning of the claim which are represented by the alleged infringement." However, on appeal, a different construction was given to the claims and infringement was then found: [2002] EWCA Civ 612; [2002] I.P. & T. 5.

As a matter of principle, according to Neuberger J. in *Kirin-Amgen v Roche Diagnostics* [2002] R.P.C. 1, questions of claim construction and infringement of the claim are separate, and there are "obvious dangers" in determining construction having regard to the infringement. But "some issues of construction only arose because of the nature of the alleged infringement". In the same case the court said that expressing something in non-quantitative terms could lead to uncertainties, difficulties and difference of opinion, but these "fuzzy edges" were inevitable in science and technology and it would be unrealistic to construe a patent in an unnatural way "simply because it would otherwise result in the odd occasion" in which there could be such uncertainties, etc.

In *Merck v Generics* [2004] R.P.C. 31 at 607, the judge examined the meaning of the Protocol in some detail. He explained this in terms of a balance between width of protection and validity, and said that "it is up to the patentee to choose the level of risk he wishes to run". The monopoly sought by the patentee must be discernible from the patent, and it "cannot be right that [the reader] needs to carry out experiments to determine the width of the monopoly".

"The Protocol is directed at allowing protection for the discernible intention of the patentee, to be derived from the words used to express that intention".

The Protocol:

"says expressly that the context may be looked at even when no question of ambiguity of the claim arises. What it does not say ... is that by looking at the claims in the context of the specification the exclusive rights can be extended beyond that which the patentee wanted to cover".

The concept of fair protection for the patentee was also seen in the context of the disadvantages that the patentee might suffer if his claim were construed more broadly than he intended:

"There is no canon of construction which would justify the courts in granting a patentee more protection than that which, objectively assessed, he indicated he wanted. Indeed to do so would not be 'fair' to the patentee. It could expose him to a greater risk of invalidity than he was prepared to shoulder".

On the other hand It is not appropriate to narrow down the proper meaning of claims by importing limitations not to be found in those claims, but only in the description, as such does not provide the required "reasonable certainty for third parties" (*Cadcam Technology v Proel* BL CC/61/00).

The courts will generally try to ensure that the claim construction adopted will be a sensible one. Thus, they will strive to avoid a claim construction which would exclude the stated principal object since that would not be a purposive construction (*Scanvaegt v Pelcombe* [1998] F.S.R. 786) and also one that would cause the illustrated products to fall outside its ambit (*Oneac v Raychem* BL C/32/98, noted I.P.D. 21085), or a construction contrary to the required mode of operation of the claimed machine (*Taylor v Ishida*, noted I.P.D. 22114; [2001] EWCA Civ 1092). Likewise, in *Minnesota Mining v Plastus Kreativ* [1997] R.P.C. 737 CA, the word "opaque" was construed according to the stated purpose and non-infringement was found because the defendant's device failed to meet the inventive criteria indicated by the use of that word. Another example is *Hoechst Celanese v BP Chemicals [Iodide Removal]* [1997] F.S.R. 547 and [1999] F.S.R. 319 CA. At first instance, the words "physical dimension" were given their literal meaning as referring to pore diameter, rather than pore volume, as "volume" is not a true "dimension" and, if volume had been meant, the claim would not have covered the use of a number of known resins which seemed unlikely. On the appeal, the same construction was adopted, but on the different basis of construing the document particularly in the context in which the word "dimension" had been used in the patent rather than according to its strict technical meaning, such being seen as construing the claim "having regard to the purpose of the words used". The Court of Appeal noted that, if this word had been used to mean volume (as the defendants contended), then a significant number of commercially available materials would have been excluded, but the specification gave no indication of this and, accordingly, this construction was not seen to be the intention of the draftsman, nor would it "give fair protection to the patentee". In T 79/96 *APV ANHYDRO/Granulation by spray drying* [2001] E.P.O.R. 40 at 309, the EPO said that when assessing the novelty of claimed subject-matter, an expression in a claim should be given its broadest technically sensible meaning.

The court should not, if it can help it, arrive at a construction of the claim which has the result that the claim will read on to prior art referred to in the patent. That principle has been relied on in a number of cases: see e.g. *Beloit v Valmet* [1995] R.P.C. 705 at 720, lines 30–33, and *Ultraframe v Eurocell* [2005] R.P.C. 36 at [47]; [2005] EWCA Civ 761; on the basis that "it can hardly have been the inventor's purpose to cover that which he expressly recognises was old" but it was said in *Actavis v Janssen* [2008] EWHC 1422 Pat Ct that this is "not a rigid rule", referring to Lewison J.'s discussion of the relevant principles in the *Ultraframe* case at first instance [2004] EWHC 1785 at [72] to [73].

In *Mayne Pharma v Pharmacia Italia* [2005] EWCA Civ 137; [2005] I.P.&T. 774, Jacob L.J. in the Court of Appeal took the opportunity to restate the principles of construction as he had summarised them in *Technip's Patent* [2004] R.P.C. 46 at 919 (also cited as

Rockwater v Technip) which he said had been approved ("save for one minor matter") by the House of Lords in *Kirin-Amgen*. Accordingly, "as a practical working guide" he said it would generally be sufficient to use this summary as approved. In *Mayne Pharma* it was agreed that the "Protocol questions" did not assist in the construction of the claim.

The "minor matter" referred to related to Jacob L.J.'s original para.(e) in the *Technip* formulation in which he had said:

"(e) When ascertaining the inventor's purpose, it must be remembered that he may have several purposes depending on the level of generality of his invention. Typically, for instance, an inventor may have one, generally more than one, specific embodiment as well as a generalised concept. It is the latter which matters when construing the claim, particularly the widest claim. Otherwise one is in danger of being unfair to the inventor".

Of this Lord Hoffmann said that he would question that summary in as far as it says that to be "fair to the patentee" one must use "the widest purpose consistent with his teaching". Lord Hoffmann said that this would be to confuse the purpose of the utterance with what it would be understood to mean. He said that:

"the purpose of a patent specification is no more nor less than to communicate the idea of an invention. An appreciation of that purpose is part of the material which one uses to ascertain the meaning. But purpose and meaning are different. If, when speaking of the widest purpose, Jacob L.J. meant the widest meaning, I would respectfully disagree. There is no presumption about the width of the claims. A patent may, for one reason or another, claim less than it teaches or enables."

With this in mind, Pumfrey J. in *Halliburton v Smith* [2006] R.P.C. 2 at 25 applied the list in *Technip* with para.(e) reformulated in accordance with Lord Hoffmann's analysis.

In *Ferag v Muller Martini* [2006] EWHC 225 the principles of *Technip* as modified in *Halliburton* were applied, as they were also in *Pozzoli v BDMO* [2006] EWHC 1398 Pat Ct, and it is submitted that in this form these can now be taken to be the most authoritative statement of the principles of construction, having the approval of judges at all levels of the English judiciary, and they are therefore set out below, stripped down to "bare essentials", as *per* Jacob L.J. in *Mayne Pharma*, but with para.(e) reformulated as *per* Pumfrey J. in *Halliburton*.

This formulation is in essence just a restatement of the basic principles of construction formulated by Lord Diplock in *Catnic* and approved as in accordance with art.69 and the Protocol by Lord Hoffmann in *Kirin-Amgen*, as discussed above, but is being referred to in many cases. The most comprehensive statement of the law on construction would be as set out for example in *Medimmune v Novartis* [2011] EWHC 1669 (Pat), in which Arnold J. set out the law referring to the previous cases as follows:

"In *Virgin Atlantic Airways Ltd v Premium Aircraft Interiors UK Ltd* [2009] EWCA Civ 1062, [2010] RPC 8 at [5] the Court of Appeal summarised the general principles applicable to the construction of patent claims as follows:

One might have thought there was nothing more to say on this topic after *Kirin-Amgen Inc v Hoechst Marion Roussel Ltd* [2005] RPC 9. The judge accurately set out the position, save that he used the old language of Art.69 EPC rather than that of the EPC 2000, a Convention now in force. The new language omits 'the terms of' from Art.69. No one suggested the amendment changes the meaning. We set out what the judge said, but using the language of the EPC 2000:

The task for the court is to determine what the person skilled in the art would have understood the patentee to have been using the language of the claim to mean. The principles were summarised by Jacob LJ in *Mayne Pharma Pty Ltd v Pharmacia Italia SpA* [2005] EWCA Civ 137 and refined by Pumfrey J in *Halliburton Energy Services Inc v Smith International (North Sea) Ltd* [2005] EWHC 1623 (Pat) following their general approval by the House of Lords in *Kirin-Amgen Inc v Hoechst Marion Roussel Ltd* [2005] RPC 9. An abbreviated version of them is as follows:

"(i) The first overarching principle is that contained in Article 69 of the European Patent Convention.

(ii) Article 69 says that the extent of protection is determined by the claims. It goes on to say that the description and drawings shall be used to interpret the claims. In short the claims are to be construed in context.

(iii) It follows that the claims are to be construed purposively - the inventor's purpose being ascertained from the description and drawings.

(iv) It further follows that the claims must not be construed as if they stood alone - the drawings and description only being used to resolve any ambiguity. Purpose is vital to the construction of claims.

(v) When ascertaining the inventor's purpose, it must be remembered that he may have several purposes depending on the level of generality of his invention. Typically, for instance, an inventor may have one, generally more than one, specific embodiment as well as a generalised concept. But there is no presumption that the patentee necessarily intended the widest possible meaning consistent with his purpose be given to the words that he used: purpose and meaning are different.

(vi) Thus purpose is not the be-all and end-all. One is still at the end of the day concerned with the meaning of the language used. Hence the other extreme of the Protocol - a mere guideline - is also ruled out by Article 69 itself. It is the terms of the claims which delineate the patentee's territory.

(vii) It follows that if the patentee has included what is obviously a deliberate limitation in his claims, it must have a meaning. One cannot disregard obviously intentional elements.

(viii) It also follows that where a patentee has used a word or phrase which, acontextually, might have a particular meaning (narrow or wide) it does not necessarily have that meaning in context.

(ix) It further follows that there is no general 'doctrine of equivalents.'

(x) On the other hand purposive construction can lead to the conclusion that a technically trivial or minor difference between an element of a claim and the corresponding element of the alleged infringement nonetheless falls within the meaning of the element when read purposively. This is not because there is a doctrine of equivalents: it is because that is the fair way to read the claim in context.

(xi) Finally purposive construction leads one to eschew the kind of meticulous verbal analysis which lawyers are too often tempted by their training to indulge."

The Court of Appeal went on at [6]-[22] to hold that the skilled reader is to be taken to know the purpose of (i) including reference numerals in patent claims, (ii) dividing claims into pre-characterising and characterising portions and (iii) filing of divisional applications, and to bring that knowledge to bear when he considers the scope of the claim."

In decisions in the Patent Office in giving opinions under s.74A, the examiners have summarised the approach more succinctly, for example in Opinion Number 10/06 (THREE-D Signs (Proprietory) Ltd) the hearing officer said:

"The parties are agreed that I should use the usual principles of claim construction, set out in *Kirin-Amgen*…. I must put a purposive construction on the claims; interpret them in the light of the description and drawings as instructed by section 125(1) and take account of the Protocol to Article 69 of the EPC. In simpler language I must decide what a person skilled in the art would have understood the patentee to have used the language of the claim to mean."

Note that in *Conor v Angiotech* [2008] UKHL 49 (a major decision on obviousness decided after *Kirin-Amgen* and discussed in the commentary on s.3), Lord Hoffmann said in relation to construction that:

"the invention is the product specified in a claim and the patentee is entitled to have the question of obviousness determined by reference to his claim and not to some vague paraphrase based upon the extent of his disclosure in the description",

which seems to be a warning against using the principles of "purposive construction" under the Protocol to try to bend the wording of the claims too far by reference to the description.

Conformity of interpretation with EPC

125.09   In practice, over the past 30 years since the EPC came into force, there has been substantial divergence of interpretation of the effect of art.69 of the EPC and its accompanying Protocol in the courts of the EPC Member States, even in cases involving the same alleged infringing device and a European patent with identically worded claims for its designated states. The United Kingdom courts have continued are likely to continue to apply the test of "purpose construction" as already discussed. However, the courts in other EPC countries have also continued, to a greater or lesser extent, also to follow their traditional methods of claim interpretation which treated the claim more as a signpost indicating the invention rather than (as in the United Kingdom) as a boundary delimiting the extent of the invention. This has led to apparently conflicting decisions. For example, German and Dutch courts found infringement of the same European patent in the circumstances of the *Improver* case (see *Epilady* [Germany] and *Epilady* [Netherlands], noted (1993) 24 I.I.C. 838 and 852), whereas the opposite conclusion was reached in the United Kingdom (*Improver Corp v Remington* [1990] F.S.R. 181); in Hong Kong (*Improver Corp v Raymond Industrial* [Hong Kong] [1990] F.S.R. 422 and [1991] F.S.R. 233); and in Austria (*Epilady V* [Austria], noted (1992) 23 I.I.C. 391).

Of course, the divergences which have occurred between different European courts considering similar acts of infringement under identical European patents may arise because of differences in the presentation of the case before different courts, in the approaches taken by expert witnesses and in the availability and effect of disclosure of internal documents in some jurisdictions and not in others. Nevertheless, these differences seem largely to be overlooked in criticisms of these seemingly inconsistent decisions. In many Continental jurisdictions it is usual to include obvious equivalents within the extent of protection, see, e.g. *BP BV v W GmbH* [Germany] [2000] E.N.P.R. 1 and *DV GmbH v A AG B* [Germany] [2000] E.N.P.R. 120, whereas art.69(1) requires that the extent of protection be defined by the claims, with some flexibility from the requirement that the claims be interpreted in the light of the description of the patent and any drawings. More recently, the German Supreme Court has begun to emphasise the need for the extent of protection of a patent to be decided after paying particular attention to the requirement of the Protocol that there should be reasonable certainty for third parties, see " *Batteriekastenschnur*" ["*Handle cord for battery case*"] OJ EPO 1993, 463.

Until *PLG Research v Ardon* [1995] R.P.C. 287 CA, there was little attempt by the English courts to consider European jurisprudence on the effect to be given to art.69 of the EPC and the Protocol, but in that case several German judgments (including "*Batteriekastenschnur*") were cited to the Court of Appeal and that court was invited to adopt what was said to be the German approach of deciding non-literal infringement by a test of "functional equivalence" with the third *Improver* question no longer to be considered. However, the Court of Appeal expressly rejected that contention, holding that such would be contrary to s.125(1) and the Protocol. The cited German decisions were reviewed and it was noted that emphasis had there been placed on the need for interpretation of claims in the light of the description and drawings and that these courts had held that, while the extent of protection goes beyond the literal content of the claim to cover functional equivalents, it does not go beyond functional equivalents which are deducible from the words of the claim. It is necessary that the patent be construed so as to afford a fair measure of protection for the patentee, but:

"the determination of the scope of protection requires that the meaning of the content of the patent claims, to be determined by interpretation, constitutes not only a point of departure but the decisive basis for the determination of the scope of protection".

The Court of Appeal then pointed out that, if the "purposive construction" approach of the *Catnic* case is the same as the test required by the Protocol, reference to Lord Diplock's formulation in *Catnic* is unnecessary, while, if they are different, it is dangerous to do so, so that in future, it said, more attention should be paid to the wording of the Protocol in art.69 of the EPC and, hopefully, also to the developing European jurisprudence, rather than on the former approaches (including *Catnic*) devised under the common law. However, in *Kirin-Amgen* Lord Hoffmann agreed with the "masterly judgment" of Aldous J. (as he then was) in *Assidoman Multipack v The Mead Corp* [1995] R.P.C. 321, in which he explains why the *Catnic* approach accords with the Protocol. In that decision the court had to consider two patents, one being an existing patent (granted under the 1949 Act) and therefore subject to the *Catnic* test of "purposive construction" and a later patent governed by s.125. Aldous J. held that the *Catnic* case "fits squarely within the guidelines of the Protocol" and that "purposive construction provides a structured way to determine the ambit of the invention claimed". The remarks of the Court of Appeal in *PLG* were regarded as obiter and it was held that the *Catnic* approach should be followed for both patents in suit, if only (for the later patent) because no better guidance could be seen which would lead to consistent decisions between courts of the United Kingdom and those of other parties to the EPC. Infringement was then found on the basis that a feature specified (in a claim to a package blank) for the top of the package could be regarded as its bottom because, "one man's top is another man's bottom" and also on the basis that broad wording of a claim should not be limited by a statement in the description.

In *Kastner v Rizla* [1995] R.P.C. 585, Aldous L.J. (as he had by then become) approved his decision in the Patents Court in *Assidoman*. Then, in June 1998, the Court of Appeal stated, in *Hoechst Celanese v BP Chemicals* [1999] F.S.R. 319, that (at least in that court) it had been settled by the *Kastner* case that "purposive construction" as propounded by Lord Diplock in *Catnic* and as explained in *Improver* is the correct means:

"of navigating between Scylla, the rock of literal construction, and Charybdis, the whirlpool of guided freedom as required by the Protocol. It enables the court to arrive at a result which gives fair protection to the patentee with a reasonable degree of certainty for third parties".

Thus, the principle of "purposive construction" continues to be employed by the Patents Court and Court of Appeal.

It must also be appreciated that any liberal construction of a claim broadening the extent of the protection which it provides carries with it an increased risk to the patentee that the claim will (on that construction) lack validity, either over the prior art or for insufficiency of description, or perhaps for added subject-matter. Anyway, it is clear from his remarks in *Kirin-Amgen* that this approach is approved by Lord Hoffmann and therefore has the authority of the House of Lords, and is likely to continue to be adopted by the UK Courts as being consistent with and carrying out the principles mandated by art.69(1) and the Protocol.

When considering any difference between Continental and British decisions under the Protocol, it should be appreciated that the Continental decisions may themselves be based on vestigial concepts under former national laws, rather than on a proper approach to the meaning of the Protocol. Where a claim is in the recommended two-part European form with a prior art part and a characterising part, a court (on an unsuccessful striking-out action) said (prior to the *PLG* decision) that it is not unarguable that a court should more readily give a liberal construction to the applicant's description of the prior art than to the part of the claim in which he describes the point of his invention (*Mead Corp v McLaren Packaging* BL C/51/90, noted I.P.D. 14021). In The Netherlands, this has been done to such an extent that the Supreme Court in one case chose to disregard an apparent limitation appearing in the pre-characterising part of the claim (*Meyn v Stork* [Netherlands], noted (1992) 23 I.I.C. 529). However, it is difficult to see how these two cases can be reconciled with the Protocol's exhortation to provide an interpretation of the extent of protection which provides a reasonable degree of legal certainty to third parties as indeed a Dutch court has more recently observed, see *Decision of the Netherlands Supreme Court*

No. 15,390, June 17, 1994, *Applied Research Systems v Organon* described (with a further decision of the same court) at (1995) 26 I.I.C. 596, and noted [1995] E.I.P.R. D–99. The answer, of course, lies in competent drafting of the patent claims so that they are as extensive in their breadth of wording as the prior art will allow. As this breadth cannot be expanded after grant (since then the claim would become invalid under s.72(1)(e)), there can be little justification for allowing this to happen through an over-generous interpretation of the extent of protection. Yet, such often seems to lie at the heart of those Continental decisions which focus on the application of the so-called "doctrine of equivalents". For the view of Lord Hoffmann that there is now little difference between the outcome of claim construction questions in Germany and the UK, although the method of approach is different, see his paper "Patent Construction" reprinted at [2006] *CIPA* 727. In this he recounts interesting instances where the use of an obviously wrong word (as in a malapropism) was automatically corrected by the recipient so that the utterance should be understood in its intended sense.

In *Ranbaxy and Arrow Generics v Warner-Lambert* [2007] R.P.C. 4; [2006] EWCA Civ 876 the court declined to admit evidence of statements made in other jurisdictions as having no effect upon the issue of construction. However in *Braun's Patent* BL O/138/94, the Comptroller stated that, while a decision by the EPO on the construction to be given to a European patent is not binding upon him, this should have considerable persuasive authority in the interests of harmonisation within the EPC countries.

In *Occlutech v AGA Medical* [2009] EWHC 2013 Pat Ct, in deciding that the judge at first instance had been right in his construction of the claim and dismissing the appeal, the Court of Appeal noted that the same issue of construction had met with a divided response from the courts of the contracting states in which the issue of infringement had been considered. In particular the Düsseldorf Higher Regional Court (on appeal from the Civil Division of the Regional Court) had upheld a different construction from the English High Court.

This approach to the construction of the claims by the Düsseldorf Court was expressed in the judgment to be based on the case of *Kunstoffrohrteil* [2002] G.R.U.R. 511, a decision of the *Bundesgerichtshof* which is cited by Lord Hoffmann in *Kirin-Amgen* (at para.[75]) as confirmation that the German courts have adopted an approach similar to that in *Catnic* in relation to the application of EPC art.69 in cases where equivalents are in issue. Counsel for the patentee drew attention to an article in the *Yale Law Journal* ("The Doctrine of Equivalents in Various Patent Regimes—Does Anybody Have It Right?" [2009] 11 Yale J.L. & Tech 261) co-authored by the late Pumfrey L.J. and other distinguished judges, in which the section on German law concludes with the following summary:

"The German approach to the question of equivalents can be summarized as follows: The main basis for the determination of the scope of patent protection is the patent claim and an understanding by a person skilled in the art of the technical teaching embodied in such a claim. For this purpose, a patent claim has to be interpreted in conjunction with both the description of the invention and the drawings. In doing so, the basic principles of function-aimed interpretation of the terms used in the patent claim, as well as a context-based interpretation, are to be followed. A contested embodiment which falls within the meaning of the claim so construed infringes the patent literally.

A patent can also be infringed if the contested embodiment does not fall within the 'literal' scope of the patent claim. This extension in the scope of the patent is to bring about an adequate level of protection of the inventive achievement in a way that also ensures the highest possible level of legal certainty. This optimal balance is achieved by protecting only those variants that the patent claim (and not just the prior art) has made obvious to a person skilled in the art, on the priority date. That is the case, if the following questions 1 to 3 are answered in the affirmative and, in addition, question 4 is answered in the negative:

1. Does the modified embodiment solve the problem underlying the invention by means which have objectively the same technical effect?

2. Was the person skilled in the art enabled by her specialist knowledge on the priority date to find that the modified means would have the same effect?

3. While answering question 2, are the considerations that the person skilled in the art applies drawn from the technical teaching of the patent claim (so that the person skilled in the art took the modified embodiment into account as being an equivalent solution)?

4. Is the modified embodiment anticipated or made obvious by the state of the art?"

The court noted that this summary of the German position does not contain anything similar to the third *Improver* question, i.e.:

"(3) Would the reader skilled in the art nevertheless have understood from the language of the claim that the patentee intended that strict compliance with the primary meaning was an essential requirement of the invention? If yes, the variant is outside the claim."

This on one view is likely to deprive the skilled addressee of one possible explanation of the words used, i.e. that they have been deliberately chosen by the patentee so as to narrow the scope of the claims over the prior art.

See also the article by P. England, "Towards a single pan-European standard—Scope of patent protection and inventive concept" [2010] 32(5) E.I.P.R. 195.

Equivalents

There is a natural reluctance on the part of the courts to apply a construction which **125.10** would permit someone to avoid infringement by making a trivial change to the invention as defined in the claims. In English case law, this led to the idea that a claim might be held infringed by "taking the pith and marrow of the invention" or using a chemical or mechanical "equivalent" of, or even disregarding, some (inessential) integer of the claim, see *Raleigh v Miller* (1948) 65 R.P.C. 141 HL and *Rotocrop v Genbourne* [1982] F.S.R. 241, where it was said that the claims should not be construed as strictly as a conveyancing document. These decisions were, however, seen as exceptions to the usual rule of literal claim construction, see *Van der Lely v Bamfords* [1963] R.P.C. 61 HL; and *Rodi and Wienenberger v Showell* [1969] R.P.C. 367 HL. The pith and marrow doctrine was seen as "necessary to prevent sharp practice" (*per* Lord Reid in *Van Der Lely NV v Bamfords*) but is referred to by Lord Hoffmann in *Kirin-Amgen* as having always been "a bit vague'', and he says that it is unclear whether it operated as a principle of construction or as an extension of protection outside the claims. However, the "pith and marrow" concept in English law came to be replaced by the principle of purposive construction after *Catnic* as has been seen.

In *Technip's Patent* [2004] R.P.C. 46 at 919, in overturning the decision of the Patents Court in *Rockwater v Coflexip* [2003] EWHC 812 Ch, noted I.P.D. 26039 in which the Patents Court had held invalid, over new prior art, the patent previously held valid in *Coflexip v Stolt Comex* [2001] R.P.C. 9 at 182, the Court of Appeal commented on the concept of "doctrine of equivalents" in the context of the Protocol and the principle of purposive construction. In holding that no general "doctrine of equivalents" is created by the Protocol, the court said:

"purposive construction can lead to a conclusion that a technically trivial or minor difference between an element of a claim and the corresponding element of the alleged infringement nonetheless falls within the meaning of the element when read purposively. This is not because there is a doctrine of equivalents: it is because that is the fair way to read the claim in context".

It is not clear that the ambit of purposive construction should be limited only to "technically trivial or minor" variants between the claim and the alleged infringement; the overriding test, as emphasised by Lord Hoffmann in *Kirin-Amgen*, being what a person skilled in the art would have understood the author to mean by the words used.

In the United States on the other hand, the "doctrine of equivalents" does allow the patentee to extend his monopoly beyond the claims. In Lord Hoffmann's opinion in *Kirin Amgen*:

"both the doctrine of equivalents in the United States and the pith and marrow doctrine in the United Kingdom were born of despair. The courts felt unable to escape from interpretations which "unsparing logic" appeared to require and which prevented them from according the patentee the full extent of the monopoly which the person skilled in the art would reasonably have thought he was claiming. The background was the tendency to literalism which then characterised the approach of the courts to the interpretation of documents generally and the fact that patents are likely to attract the skills of lawyers seeking to exploit literalism to find loopholes in the monopoly they create. (Similar skills are devoted to revenue statutes)."

Lord Hoffmann's solution, following Lord Diplock, is to "abandon literalism" and:

"to adopt a principle of construction which actually gave effect to what the person skilled in the art would have understood the patentee to be claiming."

This equates, in his view, to the *Catnic* approach which he finds to be "precisely in accordance with the Protocol".

In the above analysis there has now to be considered the effect of the new art.2 added to the Protocol by EPC 2000. See §125.03 above. Lord Hoffmann considered this issue in *Kirin-Amgen* even though the new article had not at that stage come into force. In his view art.69 prevents consideration of equivalence from extending protection outside the claims, but:

"there is no reason why it cannot be an important part of the background of facts known to the skilled man which would affect what he understood the claims to mean."

Assuming that approach to be followed by the UK courts, the new art.2 should not have any radical effect on the interpretation of claims in the UK, and clearly should not have the effect of introducing a US-style "doctrine of equivalents" extending protection to embodiments not within the scope of the claims. However, it may have wider effects in other European jurisdictions (e.g. Germany) which already incline towards a "doctrine of equivalents" approach and it will be interesting to see how the law develops in the different jurisdictions in this respect.

"File wrapper estoppel"

125.11   In US case law, the operation of the doctrine of equivalents is tempered by the operation of prosecution history or "file wrapper" estoppel, which provides that the doctrine of equivalents cannot be invoked where relevant restrictions have been introduced by amendment during prosecution. In *Festo Corp v Shoketsu Kinzoku*, reported at [2003] F.S.R. 10 at 154, the US Court of Appeals for the Federal Circuit had held that estoppel arose from any amendment that narrowed a claim to comply with the Patent Act and when estoppel applied it stood as a complete bar against any claim of equivalence for the element that was amended. This caused concern that the doctrine of equivalents was effectively abolished for any element of a claim which had undergone amendment during prosecution. The US Supreme Court (see [2004] F.S.R. 186) held that estoppel required an examination of the subject-matter surrendered by the amendment. To establish a rule barring all equivalence was inconsistent with the purpose of applying the estoppel, namely to hold the inventor to the representations made during prosecution and the inferences that might reasonably be drawn from the amendment. By amending, the inventor was deemed to concede that the patent did not extend as far as the original claim. It did not follow, however, that the amended claim became so perfect in its description that no-one could devise an equivalent. Language remained an "imperfect fit" for invention. The narrowing amendment might demonstrate what the claim was not, but it might still fail to capture precisely what the claim was. When the court was unable to determine the purpose underlying a narrowing amendment, the patentee should bear the burden of showing that the amendment did not surrender the particular equivalent in question.

Applying an estoppel approach leads to the result that the true construction and scope of the patent cannot be determined without review of the patent office file. Lord Hoffmann was firmly against this concept in *Kirin-Amgen*, commenting that American litigants "pay dearly for results which are no more just or predictable than could be achieved by simply reading the claims", and that:

"the meaning of the patent should not change according to whether or not the person skilled in the art has access to the file and in any case life is too short for the limited assistance which it can provide."

There have nevertheless been some cases in which the concept of estoppel has been discussed and in which some account has been taken of events in the prosecution history before the UK-IPO or the EPO, and such considerations manifest themselves not infrequently when patents come into focus in the context of litigation, and the attentions of batteries of lawyers come to be turned to the meaning of limitations introduced by the unwitting patent attorney or his assistant when trying to get the application through examination.

In *Furr v Truline* [1985] F.S.R. 553, an interlocutory injunction was refused on the basis that the applicant in prosecuting his application had made an admission against interest which had become available to the public in the UK-IPO file, and the claims should not be widened by construction to include certain members when they had been limited to exclude such members from their ambit in order to meet the objections raised by the examiner.

As already mentioned, the court is not concerned with what the patentee may have thought or what he intended, but only with what he actually said in his claims, see *Reynes-Cole v Elite Hosiery* [1965] R.P.C. 102 at 108 and 116 CA, and the claims must be construed without regard to his subsequent conduct, see *Glaverbel v British Coal* [1994] R.P.C. 443; [1995] R.P.C. 255. Thus, it seems that evidence of statements made during patent prosecution will not be determinative of the construction to be put upon the claims. If a patentee has persuaded an examiner that his claim should be allowed on the basis of an asserted narrow construction of its scope, the court is free to disagree and consequently invalidate the patent or to construe the claim in a different way to find it infringed or non-infringed.

In *Electrolux v Black & Decker* [1996] F.S.R. 595, the court stated that the wording of claims which have been adjudicated upon in other decisions offers little guidance on claim construction; and, in *Norling v Eez-Away* BL C/37/97, evidence was rejected of statements made by the patentee when prosecuting the basic Swedish application because "The meaning of the claims is a matter for the court", with an expert's view as to the meaning of these statements "being of no value". Therefore, to construe a claim according to representations made by the proprietor in other proceedings is an illegitimate approach (*Palmaz's European Patents* [1999] R.P.C. 47). In *Bristol-Myers Squibb v Baker Norton* [1999] R.P.C. 253, it was stated that there is a difference between using the prosecution history to widen a claim and using that history to narrow it, it being unfair on the public if material they would not normally look at could serve as a basis for supporting a wide construction.

In the appeal in *Rohm & Haas v Collag* [2002] F.S.R. 28 at 445 a key issue in the case was the meaning of the word "surfactant". A question was raised whether statements made in a letter to the EPO in the course of prosecution of the patent should be taken into account in construing the claims. The Court of Appeal (in a statement which would appear to be obiter) said that had it been necessary to take account of the letter in order to resolve the issue of construction, the judge would have been entitled to do so. Some commentators (see L. Cohen [2001] *CIPA* 571 and A. Rich [2001] *CIPA* 583) have seen this as a step towards the acceptance of a doctrine of file wrapper estoppel in the United Kingdom along the lines of the United States model, but it is submitted that the decision (apart from being obiter on this point) may go no further than *Furr v Truline* above in which the patentee was not allowed to resile from an "admission against interest" held to have been made in the UK-IPO file.

In *Wesley Jesson v Coopervision* [2003] R.P.C. 20 at 355 the judge of the Patents County Court took account of amendments made during prosecution of the patent application before the EPO in reaching a finding of non-infringement under the Protocol. However, in *Machinery Developments v St Merryn Meat* PAT 03 061; BL C/50/04, he explained that decision as relating to a "key word" in the claims, and in which he had reached his conclusion on infringement without reference to the prosecution file such that this was "a makeweight point". In stating that he did not find the notion of prosecution history estoppel helpful in deciding the issues in the case before him, the judge echoed the cautionary comments of Jacob J. in *Celltech Chiroscience v Medimmune* BL C/36/01, noted I.P.D. 24074, as to the undesirability of introducing such a doctrine into English law, particularly in the context of cases to be decided in accordance with the procedures of the Patents County Court, which "was set up to cater for the needs of litigants . . . of modest means". This seems also to be in accordance with the concerns of Lord Hoffmann as quoted above.

In *Celltech* (above), a judge of the English High Court had to construe the claims of a US patent in order to determine whether payment of royalties was due under a licence (which was under English law, but required royalties to be paid in respect of products falling within the US patent). In this initial decision the determination of this question was stayed pending the decision of the US Supreme Court in *Festo*. In subsequent proceedings (*Celltech (Adair's) US Patent* [2003] F.S.R. 25 at 433), when the scope of the US doctrine of file wrapper estoppel had been clarified by the *Festo* decision, the English court found that the patent was not infringed, the application of the doctrine of equivalents having been precluded by arguments made during prosecution, "argument estoppel". On appeal (see [2004] F.S.R. 3 at 35), the Court of Appeal upheld (by a majority) the judge's finding on "argument estoppel" but also allowed the defendant's cross-appeal that the assertion of infringement was precluded by "amendment estoppel" as well. The case is also of interest in view of remarks made by the judge at first instance about the undesirability of introducing a doctrine of file wrapper estoppel into European law. These views were reinforced by a different judge in the Patents Court in *Russel Finex v Telsonic* [2004] EWHC 474 Pat Ct; I.P.D. 27050, in saying that:

> "Patents and their claims are meant to be statements made by the patentee to the relevant public. Their meaning and effect should be discernible from the face of the document".

In this case, the judge declined to rule on the issue because the meaning of the claim appeared clear to him without resorting to the prosecution history.

The same conclusion (as to non-infringement) was reached when the case again came before the Patents Court (*Celltech R & D v Medimmune* [2005] F.S.R. 21 at 491) for a finding on the same facts but in relation to the corresponding European patent and under the German law relating to infringement. The German law was seen as broadly in line with the *Improver* approach, and in particular the statement by the German Supreme Court in *Custodial II* (G.R.U.R. 2002, 527) that:

> "the German law of infringement does not allow one to correct mistakes made by the patentee. If the patentee has imposed a clear limit on his monopoly which addressees recognise as being unnecessary or based on mistaken science, it is still effective"

which was seen as involving essentially the same test as the third *Improver* question.

In *Occlutech v AGA Medical* [2009] EWHC 2013 Pat Ct; [2010] EWCA Civ 702, reference was made to the corresponding judgment of the Dutch court, in which some reliance had been placed on a letter from the patentee's patent attorney to the examiner which appeared to indicate that a particular feature of claim 1 had been included in order to avoid a novelty objection based on the prior art, and the contents of the prosecution file appeared to be admissible under Dutch law for the purpose of construing what the claims were intended to convey to the skilled addressee. Whilst recognising the issues of principle involved and the reservations of Lord Hoffmann as to the relevance of the file, the court acknowledged that there is no clear English authority as to whether the file should be regarded as material available to the addressee and likely to be looked at by him in deciding how to interpret the claims, cf. *Rohm and Haas Co v Collag Ltd* [2001] EWCA Civ 1589. In the circumstances of this case the Court of Appeal agreed with the judge that it should be assumed that the skilled addressee would not have had the benefit of access to the file.

It is thus likely to continue to be difficult to argue for a concept of "file wrapper estoppel" in UK patent law except perhaps in the case of very clear "admissions against interest", as in *Furr v Truline*.

Other general principles

Although the overriding principles governing construction of the extent of protection conferred by a patent are set out in s.125(1), read together with art.69(1) and the Protocol, leading to a "purposive construction" approach in the UK, some further specific principles can be derived from the case law (including where appropriate cases decided under former statutes) and these principles are discussed in the following paragraphs.   **125.12**

—The need for a uniform construction of the extent of protection

The extent of protection conferred by a patent, and therefore the construction of the claims as regards the invention covered, is relevant in several contexts. For example, the claims need to be construed to determine their validity, in particular in relation to prior art, and to determine whether the patent is infringed. A claim should not be construed narrowly for the purposes of validity, but widely when considering infringement, the claim then being held infringed by something found in the prior art. This raises the issue of whether validity and infringement should be considered by the same tribunal in the same proceedings, as is the usual practice of the UK courts, in contrast to that in Germany, the Netherlands and Sweden, in which infringement and validity are dealt with in separate courts, with the possibility of differences in construction arising. It is also to be noted that when validity is considered in opposition proceedings, the EPO generally has no regard to how the claims might be construed in the context of subsequent infringement proceedings in the courts of an EPC Member State. A Board of Appeal has stated that determination of the extent of protection is not a matter for it (T 175/84 *KABELMETAL/Combination claim* OJ EPO 1989, 71; [1989] E.P.O.R. 181). Where patent claims have been construed in a previous action by the Court of Appeal, the Patents Court will normally regard that construction as binding upon it (*Filhol v Fairfax* [1990] R.P.C. 293).   **125.13**

However, in *Novartis v Dexel-Pharma* [2008] EWHC 1266 Pat Ct the judge held (obiter) that it was seriously arguable that a subsequent court was not bound by a previous court's conclusion as to the correct construction of a patent specification if that conclusion turned on evidence that was either lacking in the prior case or which was materially different in the subsequent case. The court referred to *Apotex Europe v SmithKline Beecham* [2003] EWHC 2939 Pat Ct; [2004] F.S.R. 26 in which it was held that a previous judgment of the Court of Appeal in a different action on the same patent had no bearing on the proceedings before the court, save on questions of construction. So far as questions of fact were concerned, the parties could not be affected by the manner in which the parties to the previous action decided to put their case, and the evidence they decided to call. On the other hand, the construction of the documents themselves was a question of law, and could not change from case to case. But the construction of the documents was not the end of the question. Their disclosure was still a question of fact, upon which evidence would be admissible. In the *Novartis* case, the judge thought that there was a stark difference between the question for consideration in the prior Court of Appeal case and the matters then before the court, and therefore Novartis would not be precluded by the findings in the previous case from contending that specific examples in its patent were covered by the claims.

—Construction is a question of law

125.14   The meaning of the patent is a matter of law for the court itself to decide. Construction is not concerned with what the author himself actually "meant" to say. Generally, the author cannot be consulted on that point, nor would his view be determinative even if that were the case. This was expressly stated by Lord Tomlin in *British Celanese v Courtaulds* (1935) 52 R.P.C. 171 at 196 HL:

> "an expert witness is not entitled to say, nor is counsel entitled to ask him, what the specification means".

A patent specification or any other legal document is fixed in time and cannot be subject to the possibility that the author can "change his mind" about what he meant by it afterwards. That should be left to the authors of political speeches. Construction has to be objective in the sense that it is concerned with what a reasonable person would have understood the author to mean by the words used. This is not simply a matter of rules of grammar and dictionary definition. It is highly sensitive to context and depends not just on the words the author has chosen but also to whom the words are addressed and the attributes of that addressee. In the case of a patent specification, the notional addressee is of course the person skilled in the art, who comes to the specification with the benefit of common general knowledge.

Thus, the court should not receive evidence as such as to what the claim means to its skilled reader. That is a matter to be decided by the court after it has been instructed by experts as to: (a) the meaning of technical terms and (b) the background of the common general knowledge of the presumed addressee. This was reiterated by the statement in *Glaverbel v British Coal* [1995] R.P.C. 255 CA that:

> "Interpretation of a patent is a question of law, not a jury question. The patent is to be construed objectively, through the eyes of a skilled addressee. Evidence of the patentee as to what he intended it to mean should not be admitted, nor indirect evidence said to point to his intention"

and, at first instance in that *Glaverbel* case [1994] R.P.C. 443, it was said:

> "It is for the court, not for any witness, however expert, to decide the question of construction in accordance with the meaning of the language used. Experts can give evidence to enlighten the judge on the meaning which those skilled in the art would give to technical or scientific terms and phrases and on unusual or special meanings given by such persons to words which might otherwise bear their ordinary meaning."

and

> "The specification must be read as a whole in the light of the surrounding circumstances as at the date of its publication and must be construed without the aid of reference to:
> (a) the alleged infringement;
> (b) the subjective thoughts, intentions, purposes and opinions of the patentee or his witnesses;
> (c) the way in which the invention was developed by experiment and research;
> (d) the patentee's actions before or after the grant of the patent;
> (e) documents subsequent to the specification; and
> (f) the prior documents relied on as a ground of invalidity."

In *Glaverbel*, the Court of Appeal also said that "subsequent conduct is not available as an aid to interpretation of the document", citing *L Schuler AG v Wickman Machine Tool Sales Ltd* [1974] A.C. 235 at 251; [1973] 2 All E.R. 39 at 45 HL; and that a claim must not be construed with an eye on prior material, in order to avoid its effect, citing *Molins v*

Industrial Machinery (1938) 55 R.P.C. 31 at 39 CA. Also, reading the document as a whole does not allow the reader to ignore one of the characterising features of the claim, or to lift words out of the specification for the purpose of changing the clear meaning of a claim, see *Norton and Gregory v Jacobs* (1937) 54 R.P.C. 58 and 271 CA and *Norling v Eez-Away* BL C/37/97.

In *Brugger v Medic-Aid (No.2)* [1996] R.P.C. 635, the court also stated that claim construction is a matter for the court unless the claims and specification contain technical expressions which need explanation. On the other hand, in *Sara Lee v Johnson Wax* BL C/60/01, noted I.P.D. 25008 the Court of Appeal deplored that the parties had "inflicted upon the judge" evidence of professors as to the meaning of the terms "liquid-permeable closure" and "porous mass". As these were not technical terms, their construction was entirely a matter for the court, and could not be delegated to scientific witnesses.

Note also the comments in of the court in *Apotex Europe v SmithKline Beecham* [2003] EWHC 2939 Pat Ct; [2004] F.S.R. 26, applied in *Novartis v Dexel-Pharma* [2008] EWHC 1266 Pat Ct in which it was held that although the construction of documents was a question of law, and could not change from case to case, construction was not the end of the question. Their disclosures contained in the documents was still a question of fact: see §125.13 above.

—The patent must be read as a whole

Article 69 of the EPC requires that the description and drawings *shall* be used to **125.15** interpret the claims, not only that they may be used if needed. It was already a settled principle in English law that the patent must be read as a single document, the terms used in the claims being defined by the wording used in the description and as illustrated in the drawings, if any. Thus, it was stated in *Glaverbel v British Coal* [1995] R.P.C. 255 CA, citing *Electrical & Musical Industries v Lissen* (1939) 56 R.P.C. 23 at 39 HL, that:

"The whole document must be read together, the body of the specification with the claims, but if the meaning of a claim is clear it cannot be extended or cut down by reference to the rest of the specification. If there is any uncertainty as to the meaning of the claim then recourse might be had to the body of the specification to resolve that uncertainty"

and, at first instance in that same case (see [1994] R.P.C. 443), it was held that:

"The court must construe the specification as a whole to discern its relevant purpose and determine the scope of the claims, and then decide whether the claims are sufficiently or clearly defined and are fairly based. The court should examine the structure and wording of the claims in the context of the rest of the specification, and must be wary of the danger of losing the true meaning in a literal word-by-word or line-by-line textual dissection of the language. ... The clear language of a claim must not be restricted, expanded or amended by reference to a limitation or gloss used in the earlier part of the specification but not repeated in the claim itself. It is legitimate, however, to refer to the rest of the specification to explain the background to the claims, to ascertain the meaning of the technical terms, and to resolve ambiguities in the construction of the claims".

It is submitted that these statements are still valid except that it is clear that that recourse may, and indeed should, be had to the description and drawings other than just for the purpose of resolving ambiguities or uncertainties. Note that the contents of the abstract may not be used to determine the extent of protection, because this is not part of the description of the patent, see s.14(2)(b) and (1984–85) 14 *CIPA* 93.

Where the claims are clear and mirror the terminology in the remainder of the specification, this may not be significant; however, the drafter should always be aware of how words used elsewhere in the specification compare to those used in the claims and be wary of inadvertently affecting the extent of the protection to be conferred by the patent by the use of such words. For example, where different words have been used, it is generally to be taken that they refer to different things or concepts, see *Sara Lee v Johnson Wax* [2001] F.S.R. 17 at 261 where "permeable" was held not to be synonymous with "porous".

It has been held that claims may be used in the interpretation of other claims: for example in *Glaverbel* (above):

"Guidance on the true construction of a claim might properly be obtained from a subordinate claim of narrower scope appended to it",

so that the earlier claim should be interpreted as having a broader extent than a subordinate claim dependent on it, and two claims should not be construed to have identical scope; for an example of this, see *Adhesive Dry Mounting v Trapp* (1910) 27 R.P.C. 341. It is submitted that this remains valid although not expressly stated in s.125(1) or in art.69 or the Protocol.

In *Red Spider v Omega* [2010] EWHC 59 (Ch) it was held that the process of construction does not require that one hunts through the specification to find an invention. Even if the description contains something which is said to be inventive, it does not follow that that is within the claim. In this case, the question was whether a "cutaway" feature could be an inventive step, even though the claim did not refer to it. The judge found that there was not the slightest hint of any such thing in claim 1, which in his view seemed to point at something different. Even from the description one did not come to the conclusion that the cutaway is what the claim meant. On its proper construction there were other embodiments which might not include that shape or feature, and the cutaway therefore could not be the invention because the invention could be achieved without it.

In *Research In Motion v Motorola* [2010] EWHC 118 Pat Ct, the judge rejected a construction of the word "transmittable" which "robbed the word of its meaning and effect", and also rejected an alternative formulation which did not find any support in the description, preferring a construction which was supported by considering the technical purpose of other integers of the claim.

—The meaning to be given to technical terms

125.16   Under the common law the specification was regarded as its own dictionary, with the claims to be interpreted according to common sense, see *Henriksen v Tallon* [1965] R.P.C. 434 HL and *Ransburg v Aerostyle* [1968] R.P.C. 287 HL. Also, technical terms were required to be construed in the way the skilled addressee of the specification would have read them in the light of his general knowledge of the art, see *British Thomson-Houston v Corona* (1922) 39 R.P.C. 49 HL; and *Cleveland Graphite v Glacier Metal* (1950) 67 R.P.C. 149 HL. It is submitted that this basic approach remains valid and therefore reference is made below to some of the pre-1977 Act law in this context.

A classic case of the construction of technical and functional terms is *British Thomson-Houston v Corona* (1922) 39 R.P.C. 49 HL, where a "filament of large diameter" can now be seen to have been given a purposive construction, i.e. the meaning which it enjoyed in the mind of the skilled addressee of the specification. Technical terms must be construed as the addressee would construe them, since it is to such a person skilled in the relevant art that the patent has to provide instructions as to how the claimed invention can be performed. For example, see *Glaverbel* [1995] R.P.C. 255, citing *Catnic v Hill & Smith* [1982] R.P.C. 183 at 243 HL:

"The court should admit evidence of the meaning of technical terms.. . . The question is what such a person would understand to be the essential features of the invention and, when carrying it out, how he would understand the meaning of the words".

The judgment in *American Cyanamid v Ethicon* [1979] R.P.C. 215 contains an extended discussion of the way in which a court should treat expert evidence on the meaning of technical terms. It was held that the word "polymer" was not necessarily a precise term excluding copolymers and that, on the facts of the case and the construction to be placed on the specification, a claim which referred to a certain polymer was infringed by use of a copolymer with about 10 per cent of a co-monomer. Likewise, in *Minnesota Mining v Beiersdorf* [Australia] [1980] F.S.R. 449, the court construed the word "inextensible" not in absolute terms, but as a practical matter in the light of its context. In *Dow Chemical v Spence Bryson* [1984] R.P.C. 359, the Court of Appeal can be seen to have construed "rapid" in a purposive manner. They also gave "pourable" a pragmatic meaning but defined the term "elevated temperature" as meaning "a temperature above room temperature". On these constructions the claims were found invalid and not infringed.

In *A.C. Edwards v Acme Signs* [1990] R.P.C. 621; and [1992] R.P.C. 131 CA, an extended meaning was given to the word "spring", an attempt at limiting this meaning being dismissed as trying to import a feature that was not there; and, in *Bonzel v Intervention (No.3)* [1991] R.P.C. 553, the word "near" was construed according to the perception of the skilled man in the light of the problem which the invention set out to solve. In *Minnesota Mining v Rennicks* [1992] R.P.C. 331, the word "adhesion" was construed in conformity with the specification, particularly because, if given the wider meaning contended for, no method was indicated or known whereby this parameter could be measured. In *Kimberly-Clark v Procter & Gamble* [2001] F.S.R. 22 at 339, specification of a dual purpose structure could be infringed by the use of two individual layers defining a separable structure, but not (as in the case) where those two layers had entirely separate functions. See also: *Beecham v Bristol* [1978] R.P.C. 153 HL; *Monsanto v Stauffer* [1984] F.S.R. 574; and *Monsanto v Stauffer* [New Zealand] [1984] F.S.R. 559.

In *Imperial Chemical v Montedison* [1995] R.P.C. 449 CA, the word "whereby" in a claim was construed as requiring the stated result to be at least predominantly achieved by the claimed combination, so that this was the *causa sine qua non* of the result, it being insufficient if the result was achieved mainly by the presence of some feature used by the defendant but not mentioned in the patent. In *Coflexip v Stolt Comex* [1999] F.S.R. 473, a reference in the claim to "the pull" involving a flexible conduit and tensioning means was construed as meaning "substantially all the pull", rather than the whole of the pull, provided that the total pull did not result in damage to the system which the invention set out to avoid. On this basis, the claim was infringed. Other wording in the claim was given a narrower purposive construction to find the claim valid. These decisions were upheld on appeal, see [2001] R.P.C. 9 at 182.

In *Auchincloss v Agricultural & Veterinary Supplies* [1997] R.P.C. 649; and [1999] R.P.C. 397 CA, a claim to a composition defined in terms of comprising specified ingredients each specified as present in a range of "parts by weight" was construed by considering only the amounts of the specified ingredients, while ignoring the presence of other incidental ingredients. The term "sodium chloride" in the context of a dry composition was also construed as excluding ingredients which caused both sodium and chlorine ions to be present in a wet solution; and the fact that sodium chloride as such was only present as an unintended contaminant in one of the other ingredients (when supplied from a particular source) was held not to avoid infringement in the instances when the composition was formulated from that source.

In *Evans Medical's Patent* [1998] R.P.C. 517, the word "purified" was construed as not to require any particular level of purification of a biological product, provided that some purification procedure had been carried out on that product. However, the words "substantially free from X" were construed fairly strictly; and other words contained in the claim (apparently inserted at the behest of the EPO) were held to have no limiting effect and therefore to be redundant as regards claim construction.

In the EPO the term "substantially free" has been held to be construed according to the circumstances of the case (T 79/99, *GASCO/Solid lipid microspheres* [2000] E.P.O.R. 419) which here required the phrase to mean "free in so far as is practically and realistically feasible". Also, the term "naizatidine" included not only the pure chemical but also the "real product" sold under that generic name (T 55/99 *ELI LILLY/Naizatidine* [2000] E.P.O.R. 430).

Neuberger J. in *Kirin-Amgen v Roche Diagnostics* [2002] R.P.C. 1 considered that "[q]uestions as to the meaning of words in documents can rarely, if ever, be determined by reference to dictionaries". Dictionary definitions are "shorn of any relevant context" and "represent the view of a particular person who is required to summarise a definition in a few words". Expressions "may have slightly different meanings to different scientists in the field".

In the Court of Appeal decision in *Dyson v Hoover* [2002] R.P.C. 22 at 465 the court did not find the evidence of professors as to the meaning of words and phrases in the claims helpful as "they did not seek to attribute to these the meaning required by the Protocol". See also *Sara Lee v Johnson Wax* [2001] EWCA Civ 1609, noted I.P.D. 25008, in which the Court of Appeal said that scientific witnesses are not experts in the construction of patent specifications and their expertise "which requires precise use of words, is not useful when applying the Protocol".

The broader meaning given to a term in a claim by the Court of Appeal in *Coflexip v Stolt Comex* [2001] R.P.C. 9 at 182 led to the patent subsequently being held invalid over different prior art (*Rockwater v Coflexip* [2003] EWHC 812 Ch, noted I.P.D. 26039)—see the case comment on this case by N. Coulson and D. Brown at *Patent World* No.153 (June 2003). However, on appeal, the decision on invalidity was reversed, and the patent again found valid and infringed (*Technip's Patent* [2004] R.P.C. 46 at 919—see the case comment by Katharine Stephens in [2004] *CIPA* 224).

In T 728/98 *ALBANY/Pure Terfenadine* [2002] E.P.O.R. 1 at [1] the EPO held that claims comprising unclear technical features entailed doubts as to the subject-matter covered by the claim, particularly where the unclear feature was essential for delimiting the claimed subject-matter from the prior art. For example, purity as such is an unreliable characteristic in the pharmaceutical field and is a "rather hazy concept having a variable meaning shifting with time and progress in analytical chemistry". So a term such as "substantially pure" was unclear and did not allow determination of the scope of the claim without ambiguity.

In *Ancon v ACS Stainless Steel Fixings* [2009] EWCA Civ 498 Lord Justice Jacob "diffidently" added three observations of his own to the principles of construction quoted in §125.08:

"The first is merely the trite principle that the addressee of the specification is the person skilled in the art, who approaches the document with the common general knowledge. Secondly, there may be obscurities and difficulties in a claim that cannot be resolved by an appeal to context. It is very rare that some sensible meaning cannot be attributed to the words used in a patent claim, but where a claim permits alternative interpretations it is possible to be left with no alternative but to take the most straightforward. Finally, and most importantly, over-meticulousness is not to be equated to carefulness. Care in working out what the patentee was aiming at when he chose the words he used is absolutely necessary."

The instant case required construction of the term "Elliptical cone shape" which was, as a matter of pure geometry, something of a nonsense—the patentee must be trying to define something which is not exactly or precisely geometrical. But the patent was not directed to a geometer but to a practical designer and manufacturer of fixings for buildings—much the same sort of person as the *Catnic* patent was aimed at. To gain an idea of what such a skilled reader would have understood the patentee to convey by "generally elliptical cone" the judge pointed out that one needs to think like him. He would know about the prior art bolts and channels, but he would never have seen anything like the invention before. And he would be told of the advantages thereby achieved. In that context, what would he understand the phrase to mean? What shape is the patentee trying to convey to him? The patentee here was faced with a familiar problem. He was trying, in the words of Lord Hoffmann in *Kirin-Amgen* "to describe something which, at any rate in his opinion, is new; which has not existed before and of which there may be no generally accepted definition." That is particularly hard when you are trying to describe a complicated shape.

By and large you need to start from some point of reference to a known sort of shape (here ellipse and cone) but it would be wrong to suppose that he was taking a strictly geometrical approach and calling for a mathematical cone shape or a perfect geometrical ellipse.

In *Boegli-Gravures v Darsailand Pyzhov* [2009] EWHC 2690 Pat Ct, the defendant contended that "pyramidal", in relation to the shape of teeth on the surface of a roller should be construed as meaning shaped precisely like a regular geometric pyramid with a square base and four equal triangular sides meeting at an apex (or which would meet at an apex if the top were not flattened). The claimant contends that "pyramidal" should be construed as meaning roughly pyramid-shaped. The judge rejected the argument that "pyramidal" was a term of art in the relevant field (embossing packaging foil), "Pyramidal" is an ordinary English word defined in *The Oxford English Dictionary*, from which it was clear that "pyramidal" and "pyramid" are often used in a figurative sense.

The skilled reader would appreciate that the teeth were unlikely to be required to be perfect pyramids in the defendants' sense because manufacturing methods and tolerances would make it difficult to achieve perfect pyramids to begin with and because the prior art describes the continued use of the teeth when they are worn. The addressee would conclude that the precise geometric shape of the teeth is unimportant, and the word "pyramidal" was being used in its figurative or extended sense to denote something shaped roughly like a pyramid and not merely in the restricted sense of a geometric pyramid with a square base and an apex. He would also conclude that the criterion for what is sufficiently like a pyramid must be a functional one: can the teeth perform the required functions?

Counsel for the defendants sought to draw a contrast between this case and what was said by Jacob L.J. in *Ancon* [2009] EWCA Civ 498, above, in that in the present case the patentee had used a known term to denote a known shape. The judge held that, as in *Ancon*, the patentee had done as Jacob L.J. described, namely use a known shape as a point of reference. Just as in *Ancon*, there was no reason to suppose that it was taking a strict geometric approach.

The defendant sought to argue further on the basis of the application of the *Improver* or "Protocol" questions, but the judge said that it was neither necessary nor particularly helpful to resort to the Protocol questions in the present case. However, in case that was wrong, the judge considered the three questions and concluded in favour of infringement, compliance with the primary, literal or a contextual meaning of "pyramidal" as a precise geometric pyramid with a square base and an apex not being a requirement of the claim.

In *Novartis v Dexcel-Pharma* [2009] EWHC 336 Pat Ct, the patent was concerned with microemulsions. The judge rejected the defendant's construction of the claim because it was based on linguistic analysis rather than consideration of the technical purpose of the elements of the claim. The skilled reader would come to the patent with the relevant common general knowledge about the formation of an emulsion. The specification tells him everything he needs to know about microemulsions and how they are formed. Reading the specification in context and having regard to the inventor's purpose he would understand the requirements for the production of the microemulsion of the invention, and this would even allow him to resolve an apparent "conundrum" in the wording of the claims.

In *Ratiopharm v Napp* [2008] EWHC 3070 Pat Ct; [2009] EWCA Civ 252; [2009] R.P.C. 18, the judge at first instance had concluded that the word "granule" should have a wide interpretation and that "spheroid", meaning a spheroidal granule, should be construed accordingly:

". . . the skilled reader would have no reason to think that the term 'granule' was being used in any particularly limited sense. He would know that a wide range of processes exist for arriving at a spheroidal particle by agglomerating smaller particles. He would have no reason to suppose that the patentee wanted to exclude any of them."

Before the Court of Appeal, it was asserted that the "spheroid" should have a more limited meaning, being spheroids produced by a process of spheronisation using a spheronising agent. This followed, it was suggested, from a submission (accepted by the judge) about the limited meaning of "spheronising agent".

On appeal it was held that the judge had been right about the meaning of "spheroid". There was no purposive reason to limit it as suggested, and every purposive reason to say it meant any spheroidal particle made up of smaller particles. Since all would work, why would the patentee have intended a limited meaning to his claims? However, the judge had been wrong to give a limited meaning to "spheronising agent." Having reached the correct conclusion that "spheroid" was not limited to the process by which the product was made, it was wrong for him to interpret "spheronising agent" narrowly so that it only referred to certain types of non-water soluble materials.

In *Dyson v Samsung* [2009] EWHC 55 Pat Ct; [2009] F.S.R. 15, there was an issue of construction of the term "vacuum cleaner" which on one submission was contended to have a broad meaning and cover any apparatus that sucks up dust and dirt from a surface, but on another contention should be interpreted more narrowly, as being restricted to machines for domestic and light industrial cleaning duties. Neither party had suggested that "vacuum cleaner" was a technical term of art and the judge said that "to [his] surprise", neither party had referred him to any dictionary definition of the term. The judge therefore referred to the definition in the Oxford English Dictionary which is "an electrical appliance for removing dust (from carpets and other floorings, soft furnishings, etc.) by suction". Considering the submissions of the experts, it was held that the inventor's technical purpose in using the term "vacuum cleaner" appeared to have been a fairly broad one, and not one limited to domestic or quasi-domestic machines. Nor could the judge see why the inventor would have wished to restrict the scope of his claims to such machines. Accordingly, he accepted the broader construction as being correct.

The "Gillette" defence and "squeeze" arguments

125.17   In Frost's *Patent Law and Practice* (3rd edn (1906)) it was stated:

"Sometimes in a patent case a conclusion may be arrived at in favour of the defendant by considering the infringement apart from the patent. If it can be shown that the alleged infringement is an act which, having regard to the state of public knowledge prior to the date of the patent is obvious (i.e., passing from what was actually known or done to the act complained of involved no inventive step), the patentee cannot complain. He is in this dilemma, either the patent includes that which was actually done before or that which the public had a right to do—that is, something which involved no invention—in which case the patent is bad for want of novelty; or it does not include it, in which case the defendant is not an infringer" (Vol.1, p.56).

A few years later, the same view was expressed by Lord Moulton in *Gillette v Anglo-American* (1913) 30 R.P.C. 465 at 480 HL, and this has since become known as "the *Gillette* defence". A feature of this approach is that it appears to allow a conclusion to be reached on infringement and/or validity without actually construing the claim itself, because the essence of the defence involves comparing the invention with the prior art.

The same notion can be expressed by the maxim: "What would infringe, if later, anticipates, if sooner", a phrase which apparently has its origin in the patent law of the United States; or, as Laddie J. put it in *PCME v Goyen Controls* [1999] F.S.R. 801,

"One way of looking at [the issue of anticipation] is to consider the question of infringement. Subject to the issue of enablement where, in accordance with recent jurisprudence, it appears anticipation and infringement differ, something which falls within and infringes a claim if it post-dates the patent, will anticipate the claim if published or used before the priority date".

A similar theme was developed by B. C. Reid in his article "The right to work" [1983] E.I.P.R. 6; and its principle has also been adopted by the German Supreme Court, see *Formstein ("Moulded kerbstone")* [Germany] [1991] R.P.C. 597; OJ EPO 1987, 551. However, the *Gillette* defence is not recognised as a formal defence, and there appear to be exceptions to it, particularly in the case of a prior use, see §2.08. Nevertheless, its principle may be regarded as a cornerstone of patent law, and it was applied in *Merrell*

Dow v Norton [1994] R.P.C. 1; [1995] R.P.C. 233 CA; and [1996] R.P.C. 76 HL, but the House of Lords indicated that this defence is now not necessarily available in situations of prior secret or uninformative prior use, see §§2.07 and 2.08.

A variation of the *Gillette* defence is the so-called "squeeze" argument. This particularly arises when there is the possibility of an elastic interpretation of a claim so that a defendant can contend that a claim will be either invalid if construed broadly, or not infringed if construed more narrowly. For example, in *Pifco v Philips* BL C/83/98, noted I.P.D. 22026, it was noted that a broad construction was undesirable for the patentee in view of the state of the art; and, for the defendant, it made a finding of infringement more likely. While a squeeze argument will often be put before the court, the decision will normally be based on a particular construction of the claim with a consequent finding of infringement or non-infringement and/or of validity or invalidity as the case may be. Such a squeeze argument is usually between infringement and lack of novelty or of inventive step. An example is *Reynes-Cole v Elite Hosiery* [1964] R.P.C. 255; and [1965] R.P.C. 102 CA.

Analogously, in *Merrell Dow v Norton* (above), a disclosure of oral administration of a drug, which led to the *in vivo* production of the claimed chemical compound, was held to have destroyed the novelty of the claim, though the same legal result could have been achieved by construing the claim more narrowly to that compound in a purified or isolated state, when the finding would have been of non-infringement, rather than of invalidity. In the parallel cases in Germany and the United States, the courts so held, see §2.08.

A further illustration of the use of the squeeze argument is *Fairfax v Filhol* [1986] R.P.C. 499 CA, though here the argument failed, the court finding a construction of claim which left it neither anticipated nor obvious and yet infringed by a modification of the illustrated embodiment, a decision criticised by D. R. Cowan (1986–87) 16 *CIPA* 179.

In *Novamedix v NDM* BL C/78/97, noted I.P.D. 20108, the patent was directed to a medical appliance producing a particular effect. "On the balance of probabilities", the patentee established infringement by experiments which showed that the defendants' appliance produced the required effect when fitted in a particular way. The description of a prior art device was silent about that effect, its author having no apparent intention to produce it. However, in view of the similarity of that device to that illustrated in the patent, the Court of Appeal held (reversing the judgment at first instance, BL CC/60/95), again on the balance of probabilities, that, if fitted in the same way, the prior art device would have provided the same effect and so the patent claim lacked novelty, see §2.24.

It may also be useful to consider whether the alleged infringement could itself have been patented over the prior art, as the German Supreme Court has held should be done, see the German decision *Formstein ("Moulded kerbstone")* [Germany] (above). A squeeze argument between infringement and insufficiency is possible, see *American Home Products v Novartis* [2000] R.P.C. 547; [2001] R.P.C. 8 CA where (as held by the Court of Appeal, contrary to the decision of the Patents Court) that, if the claim had been infringed (which the Court of Appeal held not to be the case), it would have been invalid for insufficiency.

For an example of the squeeze argument being used between infringement and added subject-matter, see *Bonzel v Intervention (No.3)* [1991] R.P.C. 553. Here, either the claim had a narrow meaning so that there was no infringement (as was in fact held not to be the case), or it had a broader meaning and was then invalid for added subject-matter because of lack of support for this in the description of the original application (as was so held), see §76.06. Likewise, in *Cartonneries de Thulin v CTP White Knight*, noted I.P.D. 22013 and [2001] R.P.C. 6 at 107 CA, the Patents Court construed the claim more narrowly than its literal wording and hence found no infringement. The Court of Appeal reversed that finding using the literal wording of the claim, but then held that this included a feature not to be found in the application as filed, hence finding invalidity for added subject-matter.

Decisions on claim construction

The sections below indicate some of the recent decisions in which the courts (mainly the Patents Court at first instance) have applied the Protocol to specific factual situations as illustrating the judicial attitudes being applied. This is done by first considering those

125.18

decisions where there was a finding of non-infringement, followed by decisions where infringement was found outside what might be regarded as the literal meaning of the words of the claim, decisions which seem to be based on a more restricted construction than might be suggested by their literal wording, and by reference to the construction of claims containing numerical limits, reference numerals, or a statement of purpose or which relate to biological material.

Many of the decisions mentioned in the following paragraphs were decided pre-*Kirin-Amgen* but might well have been decided in the same way under the principles summarised in that case, and therefore it is still thought appropriate to refer to them with the caveat that *Kirin-Amgen* should still be regarded as the leading authority and is likely to be referred to as such in future decisions on construction.

A review of cases on the protocol by H. Dunlop was published in [2003] E.I.P.R. 342 under the title "Court of Appeal gets to grips with the Protocol", and provides a detailed analysis of many decisions given by the English courts during the period 1993–2003, but not the most recent cases including the House of Lords' decision in *Kirin-Amgen*, which were of course published after that article went to press.

Perhaps the decisions discussed below indicate that a court will try to produce a result which appears to it to be "just" in all the circumstances of the case. Accordingly, the value of underlying merit in the invention itself is usually significant, although whether or not a defendant has copied the claimant's product should be irrelevant.

—Decisions finding non-infringement

125.19   In *Wheatley v Drillsafe* [2001] R.P.C. 7 at 133, the Court of Appeal (by a majority) reversed a finding of infringement below, holding that the defendant's device had not been in contemplation by the patentee and that the wording of the description precluded that the claim wording should be given an expanded meaning. Aldous L.J. interpreted the claim in the light of the overall object of the invention and, on this basis, would have found the claim to be infringed in order to provide "fair protection", but the judge at first instance and the other two Lords Justices, adopting a stricter approach to the *Improver* questions, took the contrary view that the wording of the claim should be given a more literal construction, particularly as it was seen that the alleged infringement had never occurred to the patentee and so was not an obvious variant. This approach should also be seen in the context of the remarks of Lord Hoffmann in *Kirin-Amgen* that the *Improver* questions are "only guidelines, more useful in some cases than in others", and ought not to be treated as "legal rules".

In *Beloit v Valmet* [1995] R.P.C. 705, the wording of a subsidiary claim was seen as more likely to be limited to its precise wording, so that here "third" should not be held to mean "third or more". On appeal (see [1997] R.P.C. 489 CA), it was held that the word "third" would be seen by the skilled reader as having been used deliberately and was therefore a limitation, even though he would not have known why such a limitation had been introduced.

In *Palmaz's European Patents* [1999] R.P.C. 47; and [2000] R.P.C. 631 CA, where features of a claim were not present in the alleged infringement, no scope was seen for arguing for the presence of some "variant", particularly "where the specification does not describe the reason for the presence of the features in the claim, which had been added by amendment". Here, no construction of the claim which managed to cover the alleged infringement could be said to satisfy the requirement of a reasonable degree of certainty for third parties.

In *Consafe v Emtunga* [1999] R.P.C. 154, as well as in *Union Carbide v BP Chemicals* [1999] R.P.C. 409, it was noted that, in relation to the *Improver* questions, whether the variant has a material effect upon the way in which the invention works depends upon the degree of generality with which one approaches the question of how the invention works. In *Consafe*, the skilled reader of the patent would see that a deliberate choice had been made by the draftsman and the claim could not be re-worded to omit a specified essential feature, but this was not so in the *Union Carbide* case.

In *Visx v Nidek* [1999] F.S.R. 405, the defendants' devices were each found not to "work in the same way", and to be inventive over the disclosure of the patent: it was therefore not seen as a mere "variant" of the claimed apparatus. Likewise, in *American Home Products v Novartis* [2000] R.P.C. 547; [2001] R.P.C. 8 CA, the Court of Appeal overturned a finding of infringement by the Patents Court of a claim (in the "Swiss form") to the use of rapamycin for making a medicament useful as an immuno-suppressant by the defendant's product which was a derivative of rapamycin, the title of the patent stating that the invention related to rapamycin and its derivatives, with references given to documents describing some such derivatives. The Patents Court had seen that the defendant had made use of the underlying discovery and saw that the protection provided by the claim should extend (despite its wording) to those rapamycin derivatives which provided a similar immuno-suppressive effect. However, obviously, not all such derivatives would produce this effect and the reader of the patent had no way of determining which of such derivatives would do so, and which would not. This was held to preclude any extension of the wording of the claim beyond the use of the single compound rapamycin, the second *Improver* question being answered in the negative, while the third of these questions (if it had been relevant) would also have been answered to deny infringement. Had the position been otherwise, the claim would have to fail for insufficiency of description as regards the selection of those rapamycin derivatives which did have a similar immuno-suppressive property, for which see §14.24.

Where a claim contains a term which is so vague and ambiguous as to be incapable of any reasonable meaning, an argument may succeed that such claim can never be infringed *Milliken Denmark v Walk Off Mats* [1996] F.S.R. 292, though the point did not succeed in that case.

The court found non-infringement in *Tickner v Honda* [2002] EWHC 8 Pat Ct, noted I.P.D. 25020 where the claimant's alleged construction would have given "more than fair protection to the patentee, covering something he never envisaged either specifically or generally". It also would not give third parties reasonable certainty "catching them even though what they do owes nothing to the inventor's conception in its widest form".

In *Canady v Erbe Elektromedizin* [2005] EWHC 2946 Pat Ct, the court had to construe the word "handle" and associated terms and said that it had done so giving them "as wide a meaning as I think they can reasonably bear." Nevertheless there was no infringement, applying the principles of construction in *Mayne Pharma*, see §125.08. It would appear that this is an example of a word of general meaning being used without sufficient consideration for its context, leading to the word being given an unintended restrictive meaning based on that context.

In *Amersham v Amicon*, noted I.P.D. 24011, it was argued that the stated object of the invention could be ignored as not being correct, but the court held that there could be no infringement in such a situation. In the Court of Appeal (see [2001] EWCA Civ 1042, noted I.P.D. 24078) the judgment was upheld on this point and it was commented that the Protocol did not introduce "a doctrine of infringement by equivalent effect by use of a different mechanism. That may be for the future" and:

"third parties should be able to discern, from the terms of the patent, which equivalent mechanisms, if any, are included within the claim".

Infringement (in the context of an application under s.71) had been found in *Impro's Patent* [1998] F.S.R. 299 (see §71.05). In *Arjo and Impro v Liko* BL C/52/01, noted [2001] CIPA 575, 628; I.P.D. 25006 the court disagreed with the construction placed on the patent in the previous case (by a different judge), holding that the "Protocol" (*Improver*) questions could not be used to:

"allow one to ignore limitations in the claim which a skilled reader would understand to have been deliberately included to achieve a particular, stated and wanted, technical effect".

Certain features previously determined as inessential were held to be essential features, being "features which the inventor put forward as central to his alleged technical contribution to the art", even though it appeared that these features were not in fact essential to the working of the invention.

In *Sara Lee v Johnson Wax* [2001] EWCA Civ 1609, noted I.P.D. 25008, infringement was not found where the defendant's device used a feature which could not be held to be a "liquid permeable closure" as required by the words of the claim. Accordingly the words of the claim were not apt to cover the alleged infringement, which operated in a different way. There may have been "equivalence of result, but not of construction".

In *Ranbaxy v AstraZeneca* [2011] EWHC 1831 (Pat) the claim were in Swiss form and concerned magnesium esomeprazole with an optical purity of 99.8 per cent. It was accepted that the end product which was the subject of the declaration of non-infringement did not contain an active ingredient of that optical purity, although that had been used as part of the process of manufacture of the product in India. Considering the various sets of claims contained in the patent the judge considered that the skilled person would understand the claims to be directed to the use of such magnesium esomeprazole to manufacture a medicament which contained that active ingredient. On that construction there was no infringement and the applicants were entitled to the declaration.

—Decisions finding infringement

125.20   In *Kastner v Rizla* [1995] R.P.C. 585 CA, discussed by P. Oliver [1996] E.I.P.R. 28 and by P.G. Cole [1997] E.I.P.R. 617, a finding of non-infringement by the Patents County Court was reversed by the Court of Appeal applying a more purposive interpretation of the claim holding that two variations of the defendant's apparatus (for making packets of interleaved cigarette papers) from that claimed were each inessential features of the claim, fulfilling the same purpose by the same, though more complicated, type of operation and making use of the patentee's inventive effort. It was held that the skilled person would have seen that these variations were each obvious alternatives to the patentee's device and there was nothing in the specification which made the varied features essential ones for the working of the invention. Thus, each of the *Improver* questions was answered in the way which led to a finding of infringement, the Patents County Court being held to have reached a wrong conclusion as to "the essence of the invention".

In *Strix v Otter* [1995] R.P.C. 607, infringement was found on the basis that the phrase "co-operates with" would not be read narrowly by the skilled reader to mean "engages with" and that a leaf spring could be regarded both as the required "actuating member" and "operating member", the skilled person not seeing that these members should be separate parts of an integral construction. In *Beloit v Valmet* [1995] R.P.C. 705, the word "tier" was held not to be limited to a horizontal row resulting in a finding of infringement, a finding upheld on appeal, see [1997] R.P.C. 489 CA.

A variant which has advantages over the articles specifically described in the patent can still fall within the ambit of its protection if the skilled reader would not believe that it was intended to be excluded from the monopoly claim and if he would realise that it would have no material effect on the way the inventive concept of the patent worked, see *Insituform v Inliner* [1992] R.P.C. 83 and *Strix v Otter* (above), in each of which infringement was found.

In *Mabuchi Motor's Patents* [1996] R.P.C. 387, the use of a bent-over flap having a relief hole was held to serve the same purpose as the required "plurality of projections", and to be an obvious and immaterial variant of that feature of the claim, but in the corresponding case in Germany (*Johnson Electric v Mabuchi Motor* [Germany] [1996] R.P.C. 411), infringement was not found on the basis that, by using the word "plurality", the patentee had definitively limited the claim to exclude a single projection. In England, infringement was denied on a different point which did not arise in the German proceedings. In *Honeywell v Appliance Components* BL C/21/96, the claim specified a return means (a spring) "which is capable of returning" the claimed valve motor to a degaussed state, but it was held that this did not require the spring force alone to achieve this objective.

Findings of infringement based on a non-literal construction of the patent claims, but following the *Catnic* approach, occurred in *B & H (Nottingham) v Sicame* BL C/29/95, noted I.P.D. 18096; where it was regarded as immaterial whether screw holes for an electrical connector should be in the "open channel member" (as claimed) or in the associated "cover member"; and in *Spring Form v Playhut* [2000] F.S.R. 327 where, although the claim referred to "third means" and "fourth means" it was held that both means could be provided by the same component. The skilled reader of the patent would see that a deliberate choice had been made by the draftsman and the claim could not be re-worded to omit a specified essential feature.

In *Union Carbide v BP Chemicals* [1999] R.P.C. 409, the court found infringement despite the omission of a specified feature which was seen to be an inessential one. In *Stoves v Baumatic* BL C/27/00, noted I.P.D. 23086, infringement would have been found (had the claim been valid), the variant being seen as obviously having no effect upon the performance of the invention and not excluded by the wording of the claim. A similar decision is *City Technology v Alphasense* BL C/42/00; [2001] I.P. & T. 326; noted I.P.D. 23102 where the word "wick" was interpreted functionally and as not limited to a unitary element. The decision was upheld on appeal, see [2002] EWCA Civ 347; [2002] I.P. & T. 767, noted I.P.D. 25038.

In *American Home Products v Novartis* [2000] R.P.C. 547; [2001] R.P.C. 8 CA, the Patents Court held there to be infringement even though the defendant's product fell outside the literal wording of the claim, but the Court of Appeal reversed that judgment holding that a strict interpretation of the claim wording was required as, otherwise, the claims were invalid for insufficiency.

In the Court of Appeal decision in *Dyson v Hoover* [2002] R.P.C. 22 at 465 the test of the Protocol was applied to the meaning of the term "frustro-conical" which it was held should not be given a precise mathematical definition, but construed purposively to encompass a shape, generally frustro-conical, which achieved the effect desired by the patent.

Infringement was found by the Court of Appeal in *Pharmacia v Merck* [2002] R.P.C. 41 at 775 overturning the first instance decision (cited as *Monsanto v Merck* [2000] R.P.C. 709) on this point.

In *Ranbaxy and Arrow Generics v Warner-Lambert* [2006] F.S.R. 14 at 209, it was held that, at the priority date, the skilled reader would know that, in the case of a chiral product, it was highly likely that only one of the enantiomers would be responsible for any pharmaceutical activity and there was a modern tendency to prefer exploitation as a single entantiomer when resolution of the racemic mixture of enantiomers is practicable. Therefore, although the patent did not explicitly describe making any enantiomer form, the skilled reader would not consider the claims to be limited to the racemic mixtures of the described compounds. In the words of the judge:

"every time the skilled person sees [the formula] he will see it with eyes that tell him that in that racemate, there is a single enantiomer that is the effective compound, and that he can resolve the racemate using conventional techniques to extract that enantiomer. ...In my view, the claim covers the racemate and the individual enantiomers."

Alternatively, it would be a proper approach to construction:

"to ask why the patentee, who has covered a two-element composition for use in a drug, would wish not to cover one element of that composition which any reader would know was the effective element and which could be isolated using routine techniques."

The declaration of non-infringement sought was therefore refused. The decision was upheld in the Court of Appeal (see [2006] EWCA Civ 876; [2007] R.P.C. 65 at [4]) in which the court said:

"Overshadowing everything is the fact that the skilled reader would know that the R,R-enantiomer was the form which had all or by far the preponderance of the pharmaceutical activity. He would expect the patentee to know that too.. . .There simply is no rational basis for supposing that the patentee would want to exclude the pure enantiomer which he would have known was the substance which really mattered." The claim should not be interpreted "in a way that no rational patentee would have intended."

—Limitation of literal wording

125.21   While the "fair position" required by the Protocol to EPC art.69 may often result in claims being interpreted more broadly than their literal construction, there are occasions where the court may limit the literal wording of the claim in the interests of fairness and certainty. Thus a particular term in a claim may be given a technical meaning which is more restricted than its literal meaning would suggest: see the restricted meaning given to "fluid" in *Barking Brassware v Allied Ironfounders* [1962] R.P.C. 210 in order to find the claim valid, with a broad meaning then being given to "concentric" to find the claim infringed; and the restricted meaning given to the word "workbench" in *Hickman v Andrews* [1983] R.P.C. 147 in order to limit the claim and avoid a finding of lack of novelty. This did not happen in *Merrell Dow v Norton* [1994] R.P.C. 1; [1995] R.P.C. 233 CA; and [1996] R.P.C. 76 HL, see §2.08, but in Germany the claims of the corresponding patent were restrictively interpreted to reach a decision of non-infringement rather than one of invalidity, see *Terfenadin* [Germany] [1998] F.S.R. 145.

Thus, "purposive construction" can result in a narrowing of the claim over its literal meaning. Indeed, courts will often use statements in the body of the specification as an aid to claim construction; and, in *Bühler v Satake* [1997] R.P.C. 232, the "crux of the invention" was stated to require the presence of means "independently from the main frame" so the claim could not be construed to cover a case of only partial independence. In *Coflexip v Stolt Comex* [1999] F.S.R. 473, the words "flexible conduit" were purposively construed as "flexible pipe", thereby narrowing the claim and avoiding the prior art. Another feature of the claim was purposively construed more broadly to find the claim infringed. The broader meaning given to the claim by the Court of Appeal led to the patent subsequently being held invalid over different prior art (*Rockwater v Coflexip* [2003] EWHC 812 Ch, noted I.P.D. 26039)—see the case comment on this case by N. Coulson and D. Brown at *Patent World* No.153 (June 2003)). However, on appeal, the decision on invalidity was reversed, and the patent again found valid and infringed (*Technip's Patent* [2004] R.P.C. 46 at 919—see §125.10, and the case comment by Katharine Stephens in [2004] *CIPA* 224).

However, it is incorrect to limit the clear words in a claim by reference to statements made in the included "Examples" of the invention (*Lubrizol v Esso* [1998] R.P.C. 727 CA), see also *Cartonneries de Thulin v CTP White Knight* [2001] R.P.C. 6 at 107 CA, noted I.P.D. 22013 and 23068, CA.

The EPO has also held that, where a specification specifies a feature to be an overriding requirement of the invention, that feature should be read into the claim in the light of the Protocol to EPC art.69 (T 416/87 *JSR/Block copolymer* OJ EPO 1990, 415; [1991] E.P.O.R. 25; and T 860/93 *AQUALON/Protective coating compositions* OJ EPO 1995, 47; [1995] E.P.O.R. 391). Also, interpretation of a claim in accordance with examples in the specification has been applied in preference to its strictly literal interpretation (T 361/88 *DU PONT/Hollow filaments* [1991] E.P.O.R. 1).

It also noted that, in *Du Pont's (Witsiepe's) Application* [1982] F.S.R. 303 HL, two law lords specifically left open the point that, where a patent is in respect of a selection invention, the use of the selected member for the purpose described for the prior art class may perhaps be regarded as outside the extent of the protection conferred by the patent for an invention of selection based on previously unspecified advantages. On this point, see the comments by J. G. Drysdale and J. Woolard (1981–82) 11 *CIPA* 262 and 328 respectively.

—Claims containing numerical limits

In *Auchincloss v Agricultural & Veterinary Supplies* [1997] R.P.C. 649, discussed by I.   **125.22**
Karet and Kerry Watson [1998] E.I.P.R. 192, it was stated that the *Improver* questions
could only be applied to a term which was capable of variation and so had no place where
the patentee had chosen to state a particular numerical range, but in *Lubrizol v Esso* BL
C/100/96 (not included in the abridged report at [1997] R.P.C. 195) and [1998] R.P.C. 727
CA, a minimum parameter of "1.3" was seen as expressed only to two significant figures,
so that this was met by a result of 1.25 or above. This was not a flexible interpretation of
the numerical parameter, but a construction according to how that parameter would be
read by one skilled in the art. Likewise, in *Goldschmidt v EOC Belgium* [2000] EWHC
Patents 175, the claim referred to a "pH value of 5 to 8" and, as it was customary to record
such a value to one decimal point, with an uncertainty of measurement of from 0.2–0.5
units, the court concluded that the skilled person would not have read the claim language
as referring to a range of "5.0–8.0", but would have understood the claim to state the range
to one significant figure only. Thus, infringement was found by a reaction controlled at a
pH value between 4.5 and 5.5.

In *Zeno v BSM-Bionic and Riemser* [2009] EWHC 1829 Pat Ct, the claim referred to
temperature ranges. Following *Auchinloss v Agricultural & Veterinary Supplies* [1997]
R.P.C. 649, it was held that the temperatures given in the claim were to be read as accurate
to two significant figures.

In *FNM Corp v Drammock International* [2009] EWHC 1294 Pat Ct, it was established
that a composition is non-flammable if it contains up to 45 per cent flammable components,
but the precision to which the figure of 45 per cent was expressed in the specification was
to two significant figures (i.e. the figure was not stated to be 45.0 per cent). It was therefore
held that claim 1 covered compositions with a total flammable content of up to 45.4 per
cent.

—Claims containing reference numerals

The Act does not contain any equivalent to rule 29(7) of the EPC which indicates that   **125.23**
reference signs present in claims in parentheses, and relating to features of the drawings,
are not to be construed as limiting the claims, although that effect may, but not necessarily,
arise by virtue of s.130(7) applying EPC principles to s.125, see the satirical article by J.
C. H. Ellis (1982–83) 12 *CIPA* 2 and the article by F. W. B. Leistikow (1982–83) 12 *CIPA*
205.

The effect of reference numerals in claims was analysed in *Philips Electronic's Patent*
[1987] R.P.C. 244. On the basis that such numerals did not limit the scope of protection,
having regard to s.125(1) and the Protocol to art.69 of the EPC, amendment was permitted
to remove the numerals from the claims of a European patent (UK). In T 237/84 *PHILIPS/
Reference signs* OJ EPO 1987, 309; [1987] E.P.O.R. 310, the EPO would not allow deletion of reference numerals from the claims but did allow the insertion into the specification
of a statement that these numerals were not to be regarded as limiting the scope of the
claims, though the view was expressed that the applicant's fears in this regard were probably groundless, at least for the United Kingdom, having regard to the decision in *Philips
Electronic's Patent* (above). They were probably also groundless because, in *Rodi and
Wienenberger v Showell* [1964] R.P.C. 441 CA; and [1965] R.P.C. 367 HL, such numerals
were present and were ignored by the judges, Lord Reid stating (at 378) that "it would be
wrong to use such numbers as in any way limiting the scope of the claim".

In *Russel Finex v Telsonic* [2004] EWHC 474 Pat Ct, I.P.D. 27050, the judge commented that reference numerals in the claim "may, depending on the circumstances, help
to illustrate that the inventor intended a wide or narrow scope for his claim", but "cannot
be used to import into the claim restrictions which are not foreshadowed by the language
of the claim itself".

In *Virgin Atlantic Airways Ltd v Premium Aircraft Interiors UK Ltd* [2009] EWCA Civ
1062, [2010] R.P.C. 8 the Court of Appeal held that the skilled reader is to be taken to
know the purpose of (i) including reference numerals in patent claims, (ii) dividing claims
into pre-characterising and characterising portions and (iii) filing of divisional applications, and to bring that knowledge to bear when he considers the scope of the claim.

Since the Implementing Regulations to the EPC provide that reference signs shall not be construed as limiting the claim, the question is does the skilled reader assume that the patentee knew this rule? Further, must the skilled reader be taken to understand a two-part claim as defined under the Regulations so that he at least expects the pre-characterising portion to describe matter which is part of the prior art?

The court thought that the answers to these questions followed from *Kirin-Amgen* itself, in which Lord Hoffmann said that the skilled reader:

"... reads the specification on the assumption that its purpose is to both describe and demarcate an invention—a practical idea which the patentee has had for a new product or process"

and:

"... it must be recognised that the patentee is trying to describe something which, at any rate in his opinion, is new ..."

and:

"the words will usually have been chosen on skilled advice. The specification is not a document *inter rusticos* for which broad allowances must be made."

So in the view of the court the skilled reader is taken to suppose that the patentee knew some patent law. It would be "unrealistic—indeed perverse" for the law to say that the reader, probably also with the benefit of skilled advice, would not know and take into account the explicit drafting conventions by which the patent and its claims were framed.

The court therefore went on to address how the skilled person would interpret the claim in the light of the two explicit drafting rules above and referred to *Telsonic AG's Patent* [2004] EWHC 474; [2004] R.P.C. 38 in which Laddie J. had said that:

"Reference numerals. . . are designed to be, and can be, useful tools to elucidate the inventor's intention. As such they may, depending on the circumstances, help to illustrate that the inventor intended a wide or narrow scope for his claim. On the other hand they cannot be used to import into the claim restrictions which are not foreshadowed by the language of the claim itself."

The court held that formulation to be "not quite right", in particular it did not think that numerals should influence the construction of the claim at all—they do not illustrate whether the inventor intended a wide or narrow meaning.

"The patentee is told by the rule that if he puts numerals into his claim they will not be used to limit it. If the court subsequently pays attention to the numbers to limit the claim that is simply not fair. And patentees would wisely refrain from inserting numbers in case they were used against them. That is not to say that numbers are pointless. They help a real reader orient himself at the stage when he is trying to get the general notion of what the patent is about. He can see where in the specific embodiment a particular claim element is, but no more. Once one comes to construe the claim, it must be construed as if the numbers were not part of it. To give an analogy, the numbers help you get the map the right way up, they do not help you to read it to find out exactly where you are."

As regards the use of the two-part claim, because the skilled reader knows that the patentee is trying to claim something which he, the patentee, considers to be new, he will in any event be strongly averse to ascribe to the claim a meaning which covers that which the patentee acknowledges is old. So if the patentee acknowledges that a particular piece of prior art is old and then has a pre-characterising clause which is based on it, the skilled reader will be even more strongly inclined to read that clause as intended to describe that old art. This approach was followed in *Boegli-Gravures v Darsailand Pyzhov* [2009] EWHC 2690 Pat Ct.

Further, there was a question whether the skilled reader would know about the practice of divisional applications which might affect his understanding of a claim because he will know that there are, or may be, aspects of what is described in the patent which are actually claimed in some other patent or patents divided out from the original application. When there is a reference to the patent being a divisional application, the court thought it would be "perverse" to work on the basis that the skilled person would not know what that means:

> "A real skilled man reading a patent which, as in the case of the Patent, refers to 'the parent application' would surely say 'what's a parent application?'—and he would go on to ask a man who knows, probably a patent agent."

—Claims containing a statement of purpose

The decision of the EPO Enlarged Board of Appeal (G 2/88 *MOBIL/ Friction reducing* **125.24** *additive* OJ EPO 1990, 93 and 469; [1990] E.P.O.R. 73), discussed in §2.08, has put in doubt the rule of construction hitherto understood in English law that claims which specify a purpose for which the claimed article or process is intended to be used shall have no effect on the scope of the claims. In this decision, it was held that novelty can be conferred on a claim by inclusion of a mere statement of novel purpose for obtaining a technical effect, here a reduction in friction. This EPO decision ought to have the effect of narrowing the scope of a claim when considering both novelty and infringement, and thus overruling the special rule of construction enunciated in *Adhesive Dry Mounting v Trapp* (1910) 27 R.P.C. 341, and previously applied under the present Act in *Furr v Truline* [1985] F.S.R. 553, that a claim for an article "suitable for use" in a specified method is a claim to that article *per se* whatever might be the purpose for which it is used.

In *Folding Attic Stairs v The Loft Stairs* [2009] EWHC 1221 Pat Ct, consideration had to be given to the meaning of the terms "predetermined" and "preset" in patent claims. Despite difficulties in interpreting such terms, they would not be considered meaningless and of no effect. A reader skilled in the art would think the patentee was using such terms in order to try to tell him something, and would read the patent as a whole to find out the meaning of the term. The deputy judge therefore determined that "spaced a preset distance" meant that the separation between the relevant members was chosen by the manufacturer (or one to whom he leaves the decision) with the aim of coping with a variety of spaces in which the invention (a folding loft ladder) might be used, while avoiding excessive bending or cranking of its metal arms. The judge was satisfied that a third party could tell whether he was inside the claim, because he could tell whether he was presetting the distance in order not to bend the metal arms too much, because he was doing it himself and it depended on his own intentions.

Quoting the words of Bowen L.J. in *Edgington v Fitzmaurice* (1885) 29 Ch.D 459:

> "the state of a man's mind is as much a fact as the state of his digestion. It is true that it is very difficult to prove what the state of a man's mind at a particular time is, but if can be ascertained it is as much a fact as anything else".

The judge was happy that, in normal circumstances, although it might be difficult for the patentee to prove the necessary intent, it would be possible to establish this as a question of fact. Commenting that "there is an old prejudice or tradition in patent law that words of intent should not be used in patent claims", the judge pointed out that there had been an abandonment of the concept in many pharmaceutical patents whose claims are in so-called "Swiss" form, and in *Actavis v Merck* [2008] EWCA Civ 444 claims had been allowed based on the intention to treat a condition with a different dosage regimen. Such claims imply a test of purpose or intentionality on the part of the manufacturer. If that is permissible in pharmaceutical cases, the judge did not see why it could not be so in other industries, and commented that if the words "predetermined" or "preset" have long been used by patent draftsmen for the purpose of indicating intentionality, albeit rather covertly, why not admit it openly?

The interpretation of the word "for" as meaning "suitable for" was explored at considerable length by Arnold J. in *FNM Corp v Drammock International* [2009] EWHC 1294 Pat Ct, which should be consulted for a thorough examination of the UK and EPO case law. It was also noted that the EPO Guidelines for Examination state at C-III para.4.13 (April 2009 edition) that:

> "If a claim commences with such words as: 'Apparatus for carrying out the process etc. . . . ' this must be construed as meaning merely apparatus suitable for carrying out the process."

Taking *Actavis v Merck* [2008] EWCA Civ 444; [2008] R.P.C. 26 as the leading UK authority on these issues, it was not possible to find that the Court of Appeal had there said that one should no longer construe the word "for" in a product claim as meaning "suitable for". The Court of Appeal "went out of its way" to emphasise the importance of the English courts following the jurisprudence of the EPO, "and can therefore have hardly intended to put us in direct conflict with that jurisprudence". Accordingly the judge concluded that the relevant integer should be interpreted to mean that the composition in question was suitable for the relevant purpose.

In *Zeno v BSM-Bionic and Riemser* [2009] EWHC 1829 Pat Ct, Lewison J. expressed some doubts whether the word "for" in a patent claim always means "suitable for", tracing the history of this back to *Adhesive Dry Mounting v Trapp* (1910) 27 R.P.C. 341, but in the end concluding that he would accept "the received wisdom" on this point.

In *Virgin v Delta* [2011] EWCA Civ. 162 Lord Justice Jacob noted that in *Zeno* Lewison J. had only been shown *Adhesive Dry Mounting* and *Coflexip*, and that although "for" might sometimes mean "intended for" depending on the specification as a whole, that would not normally make a difference on construction.

In this case (which was about seating systems for aircraft) he thought that the construction of "system for an aircraft" should be approached "with a very strong predilection for understanding it as meaning suitable for", and that only if compelled by the rest of the claim read in the light of the specification as a whole should it be construed as limited to a system when fitted on an aircraft.

There is an exception to this general principle where the claim is to a known substance or composition for use in a surgical, therapeutic or diagnostic method when the specified method is one specifically precluded from patent protection now under s.4A, see *John Wyeth's and Schering's Applications* [1985] R.P.C. 545 discussed in §4A.08. In both these applications, claims directed to methods of making a medicament suitable for use in (novel) therapeutic treatments of the human body (i.e. for protecting a further medical indication of a known medicament) were held to possess novelty even though the medicaments as such were not novel by traditional standards of English patent law.

In *Merrell Dow v Norton* [1996] R.P.C. 76, the House of Lords stated that *MOBIL/ Friction reducing additive* makes it difficult to apply "the traditional U.K. doctrine of infringement" under which infringement is absolute, i.e. independent of knowledge or intention on the part of the infringer. In *Bristol-Myers Squibb v Baker Norton* [1999] R.P.C. 253, a plea was made for G 2/88 *MOBIL/ Friction reducing additive* to be re-visited in an infringement context, although on appeal (see [2001] R.P.C. 1) the EPO decision was distinguished. Meanwhile, the Comptroller has declined to follow this EPO decision in the absence of guidance from the English Courts, see *Crane Ltd's Application* BL O/41/92, noted I.P.D. 15156, and see the reference to G 2/88 *MOBIL/ Friction reducing additive* in the MOPP, in which it is stated that these EPO decisions should not be followed and the existing practice of the Office should continue pending clarification or guidance from the courts.

A Swiss court has stated that indications of statements of purpose, effect or function in a claim do not, generally, have the effect of limiting the scope of protection. However, where the claim is limited to a particular production or use of the product, such limitation is binding: thus, where a claim referred to apparatus for coating non-textile substrates, the claim did not cover machines constructed according to the patent but used for coating textile substrates (*Coating apparatus* [Switzerland], noted (1998) 29 I.I.C. 706).

In *Actavis v Janssen* [2008] EWHC 1422 Pat Ct, which had to consider the effect of a "Swiss-type" of claim, the court construed claim 1 as restricted to the use of the relevant compounds in such a way as actually to achieve the technical effect, in line with the *Mobil* decision.

In *Ranbaxy v AstraZeneca* [2011] EWHC 1591 (Pat) Mr Justice Kitchin considered the history and evolution of claims in the "Swiss" form and concluded that the skilled person would generally understand a Swiss form claim to mean that the medicament must contain the active ingredient for which a new and inventive use has been found. But for the exclusion contained in art.52(4) EPC 1973, the claim would have been directed to the new and non obvious use of that ingredient. However, it did not follow that a claim cast in Swiss form must always be construed in that way. The proper meaning of the claim must be determined having regard to the words of the claim when construed purposively. The skilled person would appreciate that to construe it otherwise than as above would render the claim vulnerable to an attack of insufficiency, referring to *American Home Products v Novartis* [2001] R.P.C. 8 in that context, in which the Court of Appeal construed the claim so as to avoid insufficiency; see §14.38. This case required the judge to consider the position prior to *ABBOTT RESPIRATORY/dosage regime*, G2/08 under which claims may no longer be granted in Swiss form. Issues of construction of this particular form of claim will therefore recede in the future.

—*Claims relating to biological material*

By arts 8–12 of the Biotechnology Directive 98/44/EC [1998] OJ EC L213/13; OJ EPO **125.25** 1999, 101, (reprinted at §§C08–C12) there are special rules of construction for claims directed to certain biological material or to its preparation. These articles have been incorporated into the Act as Sch.A2 paras 7–10) and as s.76A, reprinted in §76A.01. They apply to all patents and applications concerning a "biotechnological invention" (a term defined in an addition to s.130(1), reprinted in §130.01) particularly in relation to "biological material" (also defined in an addition to s.130(1)), although perhaps only as regards patents granted on applications filed on or after July 28, 2000 (on which see §76A.02). These provisions have the effect in some respects of broadening the protection provided by a patent claim beyond its wording (even when this is given a purposive construction). Thus, art.8(1) (Sch.A2 para.7) extends the protection conferred by a patent of a biological material possessing "specific characteristics" as a result of the invention to "any biological material derived from that biological material through propagation or multiplication in an identical or divergent form and possessing those same characteristics", i.e. the protection is extended to progeny of the invented biological material provided that this continues to have specific characteristics which are a feature of the invented material; and art.8(2) (Sch.2 para.8) provides similar protection to progeny of biological material having such characteristics and directly obtained through a patented process. It is thought that these provisions mean that, if the claimed invention is directed to biological material (or the production of biological material) which is characterised by having a particular amino acid protein sequence, or is a material replicated by a particular DNA sequence, then (if that sequence is specified in the patent) the extent of protection provided by such a patent extends to any material which continues to possess that same sequence data. Article 9 (Sch.A2 para.9) further extends these provisions to products "containing or consisting of genetic information" to all material (other than to "the human body, at its various stages of development", which are excluded from patentability by art.5(1) of the Directive, as discussed in §76A.02) in which the patented product is "incorporated and in which the genetic information is contained and performs its function".

However, the provisions of arts 7, 8 and 9 (Sch.A2 paras 7–9), by art.10 (Sch.A2 para.10) do not extend to biological material obtained from the propagation or multiplication of biological material placed on the market by the patent proprietor or with his consent (that is, for example, to the crop obtained from purchased seeds), where such arises from the application for which the biological material was marketed, but this exception does not apply to the obtained material when subsequently used for other propagation or multiplication, that is in a replanting exercise: indeed, when unauthorised re-planting takes place, then the exception provided by this provision for the initial planting appears to be annulled retroactively. Thus, this provision applies (albeit perhaps only temporarily) the doctrine of exhaustion of rights for a purchaser of biological material to use it for propagation or multiplication when that was the purpose of the purchase, that is the biological material may be freely used in the planting process intended by the authorised vendor, but the patentee's right to control re-planting is not exhausted and therefore the extension of protection (by arts 8 and 9; Sch.A2 paras 7–9) to cover progeny of biological material extends to a re-planting exercise of protected material (e.g. a first crop obtained from it), although not to the initial planting, with even that initial planting exception being annulled if the planting takes place in circumstances where material derived from the initial planting is then re-planted, even perhaps if this was not the original intention of the first planter. This is the so-called "farmer's privilege".

There is an exception to the prohibition on re-using plant propagating material, but this applies only to a limited number of species for which personal re-planting is permitted and applies only under stringent conditions requiring the payment of "equitable remuneration", see art.11(1) incorporated into the Act as s.60(5)(g) (discussed in §60.13) and Sch.A1 (reprinted in §60.02). A further, somewhat more general, exception is provided in respect of the commercialisation of breeding stock or other animal reproductive material by a farmer for an agricultural activity, but not for sale within the framework or for the purpose of a commercial reproduction activity (see art.11(2) and (3) incorporated into the Act by s.60(5)(h), also discussed in §60.13).

The provisions of Sch.A2 paras 7–9, in relation to the extension of claims to "biological material" to cover its progeny, is likely to cause evidential difficulties for a defendant. This is because he may have purchased, or otherwise himself produced, genetically-modified material quite unknowing that it has the specific character the subject of a patent, and yet infringement does not require a defendant to have knowledge that his acts amount to patent infringement, even if he knows of the existence of the patent, see §62.03. Certainly, these provisions seem to go beyond the Protocol to EPC art.69 so that the terms of the EPC have been extended, at least for acts carried out within the European Union.

The limitation under art.10 of the extension of protection provided by Article 8 also has the potential to cause considerable evidential problems both for a patentee proving an act of infringement and for a defendant trying to prove that his actions fall within the limited exception of a first, but not a subsequent, propagation or multiplication of purchased material. Thus, how arts 8–12 of the Biotechnology Directive will come to be interpreted by the courts is at present almost impossible to assess, but the evidential problems outlined above may mean that they have little effect in practice.

Technical opinions

125.26   Article 25 of the EPC provides that, on request from a national court trying an infringement or revocation action, the EPO can give a technical opinion concerning a European patent the subject of such action. The procedure is governed by EPO Guideline E–XII and is discussed further at §99A.05. It should be noted, however, that the EPO is empowered only to give a "technical opinion", and it takes the view that this precludes giving any opinion on the extent of protection under EPC art.69 and the Protocol (EPO Guideline E–XII, 2.2).

Sections 99A, 99B and 291(3)(b) of the CDPA 1988 respectively provide power for the Patents Court, the Court of Session in Scotland and a Patents County Court to ask the UK-IPO to inquire into and report on any question of fact or opinion. Presumably, this could include a report on construction of a patent claim in the light of the common general knowledge at the date of publication of the patent as perceived by the UK-IPO. However, as noted in the commentaries on these sections, no rules of court have been made for implementation of these provisions.

Priority dates

Subsection (2) was intended to overrule *Thornhill's Application* [1962] R.P.C. 199 and **125.27** to harmonise with art.88(2) of the EPC following s.5 which accords priority to an "invention", whereas formerly priority was attributed to a claim so that (as was held in *Thornhill*) a claim under the 1949 Act could have only a single priority date. On a literal construction, subs.(2) provides for "claim splitting", but on an automatic and notional basis. Thus, if more than one invention is "specified" as an alternative in a claim, each so specified invention can take its own priority date in the same manner as if the claim had been "split" by amendment. No difficulty arises if the separately specified inventions can be seen as specific linguistic alternatives in the claim (as in American *Markush*-type claims), but difficulty can be expected if the claim is truly generic, for instance if it specifies a range or a continuum of species rather than alternative subgenera. The "alternatives" construction was adopted in *Hallen v Brabantia (No.2)* [1990] F.S.R. 134, where the claims were not truly generic in the same way as a generic chemical formula and, in *Biogen v Medeva* [1997] R.P.C. 1, the House of Lords, differing from the Court of Appeal (see [1995] R.P.C. 25 CA), did not see the claim as a truly generic one, as would have been the case had it been directed to a newly discovered principle, see §§5.23, 14.25 and 14.26.

Cases where the EPO has applied multiple priorities to a single claim are: T 85/87 *CSIRO/Arthropodicidal compounds* [1989] E.P.O.R. 24; and T 310/87 *BIOGEN/Alpha-interferons*OJ EPO 1990, 335; [1990] E.P.O.R. 190.

SECTION 125A

Disclosure of invention by specification: availability of samples of biological material [micro-organisms]

125A.—(1) Provision may be made by rules prescribing the circumstances **125A.01** **in which the specification of an application for a patent, or of a patent, for an invention which <u>involves the use of or concerns biological material</u> [*requires for its performance the use of a micro-organism*] is to be treated as disclosing the invention in a manner which is clear enough and complete enough for the invention to be performed by a person skilled in the art.**

(2) The rules may in particular require the applicant or patentee—

(a) to take such steps as may be prescribed for the purposes of making available to the public samples of the <u>biological material</u> [*micro-organism*], and

(b) not to impose or maintain restrictions on the uses to which such samples may be put, except as may be prescribed.

(3) The rules may provide that, in such cases as may be prescribed, samples need only be made available to such persons or descriptions of persons as may be prescribed; and the rules may identify a description of persons by reference to whether the comptroller has given his certificate as to any matter.

(4) An application for revocation of the patent under section 72(1)(c) above may be made if any of the requirements of the rules cease to be complied with.

Notes

1. The section was added by the Copyright, Designs and Patents Act 1988 (Commencement No.6) Order 1990 (SI 1990/2168) Sch.5 para.30, with effect from January 7, 1991.

2. The section was further amended by the Patents Regulations 2000 (SI 2000/2037) with effect from July 28, 2000, when the words denoted by underlining replaced those presented in italic type.

3. The amendments noted for the title and subss.(1) and (2)(a) were each applied to the Isle of Man by SI 2003/1249.

RELEVANT RULES—RULE 13 AND SCHEDULE 1

Rule 13—Biological material and sequence listings

125A.02   **13.**—(1) The provisions of Schedule 1 prescribe the circumstances in which the specification of an application for a patent, or of a patent, for an invention which involves the use of or concerns biological material is to be treated as disclosing the invention in a manner which is clear enough and complete enough for the invention to be performed by a person skilled in the art.

(2) Where the specification of an application for a patent discloses a sequence, it must include a sequence listing.

(3) Where an applicant has not provided a sequence listing on filing the application, the comptroller may specify a period within which the applicant must provide the sequence listing; and if it is not provided within this period, the comptroller may refuse the application.

(4) Where a sequence listing is provided after the date of filing the application, the listing must be accompanied by a declaration that it does not contain matter extending beyond the sequence disclosed in the application.

(5) The sequence listing must comply with any requirements and standards adopted under the Patent Co-operation Treaty for the presentation of sequence listings in patent applications.

(6) A sequence listing shall, if it is reasonably possible, be delivered to the comptroller in electronic form or using electronic communications, even where the application for the patent is not delivered in electronic form or using electronic communications.

(7) A sequence listing may be set out either in the description or at the end of the application, but if set out at the end of the application rule 12(4) shall not apply.

Notes

1. Rule 13 Patent Rules 2007 has replaced r.17 of the 1995 Rules

2. Para.13(1) has been drafted to closely relate to s.125A compared to the previous provisions in r.17.

3. Paras 13(2) to (7) have been added to provide for sequence listings.

SCHEDULE 1

Biological Material

Paragraph 1—Introductory

1. In this Schedule— **125A.03**

"authorisation certificate" means a certificate issued by the comptroller authorising a depositary institution to make available a sample of biological material;

"Budapest Treaty" means the Treaty on the International Recognition of the Deposit of Micro-organisms for the purposes of Patent Procedure signed at Budapest on 28th April 1977, as amended on 26th September 1980, and includes references to the regulations made under that Treaty;

"depositary institution" means an institution which—

    (a) carries out the functions of receiving, accepting and storing biological material and the furnishing of samples of such biological material (whether generally or of a specific type); and

    (b) conducts its affairs, in so far as they relate to the carrying out of those functions, in an objective and impartial manner;

"expert" means independent expert;

"first requirement" means the first requirement in paragraph 3;

"international depositary authority" means a depositary institution which has acquired the status of international depositary authority as provided in the Budapest Treaty; and

"second requirement" means the second requirement in paragraph 3.

Note. Schedule 1 to the Patent Rules 2007 has replaced Sch.2 of the 1995 Rules. In particular, para.1 replaces para.7 of Sch.2 (amended by SI 2001/1412). Paragraph 1 now includes definitions from para.7(1): the Budapest Treaty and depositary institution. New definitions for authorisation certificate and expert have been included. The other definitions in para.1 replace those in para.7(2) of the 1995 Rules.

Paragraph 2—Specification of an application for a patent, or of a patent, for an invention which involves the use of or concerns biological material

2.—(1) This paragraph applies where the specification of an application for a patent, or of a patent, **125A.04** for an invention which involves the use of or concerns biological material does not disclose the invention in a manner which is clear enough and complete enough for the invention to be performed by a person skilled in the art.

(2) Where this paragraph applies, the specification is to be treated as disclosing the invention in a manner which is clear enough and complete enough for the invention to be performed by a person skilled in the art, if—

    (a) the first requirement and the second requirement are satisfied; and

    (b) the specification of the application as filed contains such relevant information as is available to the applicant on the characteristics of the biological material.

Note. Paragraph 2(1) replaces some of para.1(1) of Sch.2 to the 1995 Rules and more closely reflects the wording of s.125A. Paragraph 2(2) replaces the rest of paras 1(1) and 2(2)(b) includes wording from art.13(1)(b) of the Biotechnology Directive 98/44/EC.

Paragraph 3—The first and second requirements

3.—(1) The first requirement is that— **125A.05**

    (a) on or before the date of filing of the application, the biological material has been deposited in a depositary institution; and

    (b) that institution will be able to furnish subsequently a sample of the biological material.

(2) The second requirement is that before the end of the relevant period—

    (a) the name of the depositary institution and the accession number of the deposit are included in the specification; and

    (b) where the biological material was deposited by a person other than the applicant ("the depositor")—

        (i) a statement is filed which identifies the name and address of the depositor, and

(ii) a statement by the depositor has been filed, which authorises the applicant to refer to the biological material in his application and irrevocably authorises the making available to the public of the biological material in accordance with this Schedule.

(3) The relevant period is the first to expire of—

(a) the period of sixteen months—
  (i) where there is no declared priority date, beginning with the date of filing of the application; or
  (ii) where there is a declared priority date, beginning with that date;

(b) where the applicant has made a request under section 16(1) to publish the application during the period prescribed for the purposes of that section, the period ending with the date of the request; or

(c) where the applicant was notified under rule 52(2), the period of one month beginning with the date of the notification.

(4) Where—

(a) the application is filed with the European Patent Office and documents have been filed under the provisions of the European Patent Convention corresponding to sub-paragraph (2); or

(b) the application in suit is an international application for a patent (UK) and documents have been filed in accordance with the Patent Co-operation Treaty under the provisions of the Treaty corresponding to sub-paragraph (2),

the second requirement shall be treated as having been met.

(5) In this paragraph—

"accession number" means the number given to the deposit by a depositary institution;

"specification" means the specification of an application for a patent.

Notes

1. Paragraph 3 replaces para.1(2) to (4) of Sch.2 to the Patents Rules 1995 (as substituted by SI 2001/1412). The first requirement in para.3(1) is based on para.1(2)(i) of Sch.2 to the 1995 Rules. The second requirement in para.3(2) is based on para.1(2)(ii) of Sch.2 to the 1995 Rules, but the wording now more closely reflects Patent Act 1977 wording instead of art.13(1)(a) of the Biotechnology Directive 98/44/EC. Paragraph 2(b) is based on para.1(2)(ii) of Sch.2 to the 1995 Rules. The definition of "relevant period" in para.3(3) replaces the time provision contained in para.3 of Sch.2 to the 1995 Rules. Paragraph 3(4) replaces para.1(2)(b) of Sch.2 to the 1995 Rules.

2. A new definition has been added in para.3(5) for "accession number".

Paragraph 4—A request by a person for biological material to be made available

125A.06

4.—(1) This paragraph applies when paragraph 7 does not apply.

(2) Where an application for a patent has been published, any person may request the comptroller to issue an authorisation certificate.

(3) Where the application has not been published, a person who has been notified in accordance with section 118(4) may request the comptroller to issue an authorisation certificate.

(4) A request must be made on Patents Form 8.

(5) Where the biological material has been deposited at an international depositary authority, the request must be accompanied by the relevant form required by the Budapest Treaty.

(6) Where the comptroller grants the request, he must send copies of the request and the certificate (and any form required by the Budapest Treaty) to—

(a) the applicant for, or the proprietor of, the patent;
(b) the depositary institution; and
(c) the person making the request.

Note. Paragraph 4 replaces para.2(1) to (3) to Sch.2 to the 1995 Rules (as substituted by SI 2001/1412) and only applies where a sample availability is not to be limited to experts. Paragraph 4(2) and (3) replace para.2(1) of Sch.2 to the 1995 Rules. Paragraph 4(4) and

(5) replaces para.2(2) of Sch.2 to the 1995 Rules. Paragraph 4(6) replaces para.2(3) of Sch.2 to the 1995 Rules.

Paragraph 5—The undertaking

5.—(1) A request made under paragraph 4 or 7 shall include an undertaking by the person making the request— **125A.07**

(a) not to make the biological material, or any material derived from it, available to any other person; and

(b) not to use the biological material, or any material derived from it, except for experimental purposes relating to the subject matter of the invention,

subject to the following sub-paragraphs.

(2) The applicant for, or the proprietor of, a patent may agree to limit the effect of the undertaking in a particular case.

(3) The undertaking shall cease to have effect—

(a) when the application for a patent is terminated or withdrawn (but it will continue to have effect if the application is reinstated or resuscitated); or

(b) when the patent ceases to have effect.

(4) Where a request is made—

(a) by a government department or any person authorised in writing by a government department; and

(b) for the purposes of using the patented invention for the services of the Crown,

no undertaking is required and any undertaking by the government department or the person so authorised shall not have effect.

(5) Where—

(a) a licence under the patent to which the undertaking relates is available as of right; or

(b) a compulsory licence in respect of the patent to which the undertaking relates has been granted, any undertaking made shall have no effect to the extent necessary to give effect to any such licence.

Notes

1. Paragraph 5 replaces para.2(4) to (8) of Sch.2 to the 1995 Rules (as substituted by SI 2001/1412). Paragraph 5(1) replaces para.2(4)(a), (b) of Sch.2 to the 1995 Rules; para.5(2) replaces para.2(6) of Sch.2 to the 1995 Rules; para.5(3) replaces the other parts of para.2(4) of Sch.2 to the 1995 Rules.

2. Paragraph 5(3)(a) and (b) replace para.2(4)(i) and (ii) of Sch.2 to the 1995 Rules so that the undertaking ceases to have effect when the application is withdrawn (unless reinstated or resuscitated under s.20A, s.117 or s.117A of the Patents Act 1977 respectively) or the patent ceases to have effect.

3. Paragraph 5(4) replaces para.2(5) of Sch.2 to the 1995 Rules; para.5(5) replaces para.2(7) of Sch.2 to the 1995 Rules; and provision equivalent to para.2(8) of Sch.2 to the 1995 Rules regarding references to material derived from deposited biological material is not included as it is not mentioned in the Biotechnology Directive 98/44/EC.

Paragraph 6—Restriction of availability of biological material to experts

6.—(1) Where the first or the second condition is met (except in relation to Crown use), paragraph 7 applies until the end of the relevant period. **125A.08**

(2) The first condition is—

(a) the applicant requests on Patents Form 8A that a sample of the biological material should only be made available to an expert; and

(b) that request is made before the preparations for the application's publication have been completed by the Patent Office.

(3) The second condition is that, in relation to an international application for a patent (UK), the applicant made a reference to the deposited biological material in accordance with the Patent Co-operation Treaty.

(4) Where the first condition is met, the comptroller shall, when he publishes the application, include a notice that the provisions of paragraph 7 apply.

(5) In paragraph 6(1) "the relevant period" is—

(a) where the patent is granted, the period ending with the date on which the patent was granted; and

(b) where the application is terminated or withdrawn, twenty years beginning with the date of filing.

(6) Nothing in this or the following paragraph affects the rights under section 55 of any government department or any person authorised in writing by a government department.

Notes

1. Paragraph 6 replaces para.3 of Sch.2 to the 1995 Rules (as substituted by SI 2001/1412).

2. The first and second conditions reflect those in para.3(1) and (3) of Sch.2 to the 1995 Rules respectively. Paragraph 6(4) and (5) replaces para.3(2)(a) and (2)(b) of Sch.2 to the 1995 Rules respectively. Paragraph 6(6) replaces para.4(7) of Sch.1 to the 1995 Rules.

Paragraph 7—Request for a sample to be made available to expert

125A.09

7.—(1) A request for a sample to be made available to an expert must be made on Patents Form 8 and must include details of the expert.

(2) Where the biological material has been deposited at an international depositary authority, the request must be accompanied by any form required by the Budapest Treaty.

(3) The comptroller must send a copy of Patents Form 8 to the applicant for the patent.

(4) Before the end of the period of one month beginning with the date on which a copy of Patents Form 8 is sent by the comptroller, the applicant may give notice of his objection to the particular expert, and where he objects the comptroller shall determine the matter.

(5) Where—

(a) the applicant does not object to the sample being made available; or

(b) following an objection, the comptroller decides that the sample should be made available to the particular expert,

the comptroller must issue a certificate authorising the release of a sample to the expert.

(6) A copy of Patents Form 8 (and any form required by the Budapest Treaty) and any certificate issued under sub-paragraph (5) must be sent to—

(a) the applicant for the patent;

(b) the depository institution where the sample of the biological material is stored;

(c) the expert; and

(d) the person who made the request.

Notes

1. Paragraph 7 replaces para.4 of Sch.2 to the 1995 Rules (as substituted by SI 2001/1412).

2. Paragraph 7(1) and (2) replaces para.4(1)(a) of Sch.2 to the 1995 Rules; para.7(3) replaces para.4(2) of Sch.2 to the 1995 Rules.

3. Paragraph 7(4) states that an applicant may file a notice of objection to the expert within one month of PF 8 being sent by the Comptroller. The Comptroller has discretion to grant an extension of this period under r.108.

4. Paragraph 7(5) and (6) replaces para.4(4) and (3) of Sch.2 to the 1995 Rules respectively.

Paragraph 8—New deposits

125A.10

8.—(1) This paragraph applies where the first, second or third circumstance occurs.

(2) The first circumstance is that the biological material ceases to be available at the depositary institution because it is no longer viable.

(3) The second circumstance is that—

    (a) the depositary institution is, for any other reason, unable to supply the biological material; or

    (b) the place where the biological material is deposited is no longer a depositary institution for that type of material (whether temporarily or permanently).

(4) The third circumstance is that the biological material is transferred to a different depositary institution.

(5) The first requirement and the second requirement shall be treated as having been complied with throughout the relevant period, if and only if—

    (a) where the first or second circumstance occurs—

        (i) a new deposit of biological material is made at the relevant depositary before the end of the relevant period, and

        (ii) that deposit is accompanied by a statement, signed by the person making the deposit, that the biological material deposited is the same as that originally deposited; and

    (b) in all circumstances, the applicant or proprietor, before the end of the relevant period, applies to the comptroller to amend the specification of the application for the patent, or the patent, so that it meets the second requirement.

(6) For the purposes of paragraph (5) "the relevant period" is the period beginning when the first, second or third circumstance occurs and ending—

    (a) three months after the date on which the depositor is notified by the depositary institution that the first, second or third circumstance occurred; or

    (b) where it expires later, three months after the date on which that circumstance is advertised in the journal.

(7) The relevant depositary is—

    (a) where only the first circumstance occurs, the depositary institution where the original deposit was made; or

    (b) in any other case, any depositary institution.

Notes

1. Paragraph 8 replaces para.5 of Sch.2 to the 1995 Rules (as substituted by SI 2001/1412).

2. Paragraph 8(2) relating to the first circumstance replaces para.5(1)(a)(i) of Sch.2 to the 1995 Rules; para.8(3) relating to the second circumstance replaces para.5(1)(a)(ii) and (b) of Sch.2 to the 1995 Rules; and para.8(4) relating to the third circumstance, is based on para.5(1)(b) of Sch.2 to the 1995 Rules.

3. Paragraph 8(5) replaces para.5(2) of Sch.2 to the 1995 Rules and para.8(5)(a)(ii) replaces para.5(5) of Sch.2 to the 1995 Rules.

4. Paragraph 8(6) defines the "relevant period" and if this period expires the patent may be revoked for inadequate disclosure.

5. Paragraph 8(7) replaces para.5(3) of Sch.2 to the 1995 Rules.

SCHEDULE 4

Extension of Time Limits

PART 1

PERIODS OF TIME THAT CANNOT BE EXTENDED

[...]

paragraph 8(5) of Schedule 1 (new deposits of biological material)

125A.11

PART 2

PERIODS OF TIME THAT MAY BE EXTENDED UNDER RULE 108(2) OR 108(3)

[...]

paragraph 3(2) of Schedule 1 (filing of information in relation to the deposit of biological matter)

SCHEDULE 5

Transitional Provisions

Paragraph 7—Patent applications filed before 7th January 1991

125A.12   7.—(1) This paragraph applies to an application for a patent filed before 7th January 1991 and to a patent granted in pursuance of such application.

(2) Schedule 1 has effect with the following modifications.

(3) In paragraph 2, for the words "involves the use of or concerns biological material" substitute the words "requires for its performance the use of a micro-organism".

(4) In paragraph 5(3)(b), insert at the beginning the words "in the case of an undertaking given in accordance with paragraph 1(a)," and insert at the end the word "or" followed by:

"(c) in the case of an undertaking given in accordance with paragraph (1)(b), when the patent is granted.".

(5) Any reference to "biological material"—

(a) in paragraphs 3(1)(a), 4, 5 and 8 is a reference to "culture of the micro-organism"; and

(b) other than in those provisions, is a reference to "micro-organism".

(6) For the purposes of paragraph 3(2) the relevant period is the period of two months beginning with the date of filing of the application for a patent.

(7) The following provisions do not have effect—

paragraph 3(3) (defining relevant period);

paragraph 6 (restriction of availability of biological material to experts)

paragraph 7 (request for sample to be made available to expert).

Paragraph 8—Patent applications filed between 7th January 1991 and 27th July 2000

125A.13   8.—(1) This paragraph applies to an application for a patent filed during the period beginning with 7th January 1991 and ending with 27th July 2000 and to a patent granted in pursuance of such application.

(2) Schedule 1 to these Rules has effect with the following modifications.

(3) In paragraph 2, for the words "involves the use of or concerns biological material" substitute the words "requires for its performance the use of a micro-organism".

(4) In paragraph 5(3)(b), insert at the beginning the words "in the case of an undertaking given in accordance with paragraph 1(a)," and insert at the end the word "or" followed by:

"(c) in the case of an undertaking given in accordance with paragraph (1)(b), when the patent is granted.".

(5) Any reference to "biological material"—

(a) in paragraphs 3(1)(a), 4, 5, 6(3), 7(2) and 8 is a reference to "culture of the micro-organism"; and

(b) other than in those provisions, is a reference to "micro-organism".

(6) Paragraph 2(2)(b) (requirement that application contains relevant information) does not have effect.

(7) In paragraph 6(5)(b), for the words from "the period of 20 years" to the end of that provision substitute "the period ending with the date on which the application was terminated or withdrawn".

(8) The specification of an application for a patent, or of a patent, must mention any international agreement under which the micro-organism is deposited.

COMMENTARY ON SECTION 125A

Scope of the section

125A.14   By the CDPA 1988 s.125A replaced the former s.14(4) and (8) of the 1977 with effect from January 1991. Its provisions relate to inventions which require for their performance the use of micro-organisms, and now particularly for the deposit of samples of other forms of biological material necessary to render the specification sufficient to enable the claimed invention to be practiced by the world at large after the expiry of the patent. Consequently, the commentary on this section discusses only the requirements and procedure for deposit of biological material. For a more general treatment of issues particularly arising in relation to inventions which involve the production or use of biological material, particularly by processes of recombinant DNA technology, see the commentary on s.76A.

The words "biological material" replaced the word "micro-organism" in s.125A with effect from July 28, 2000. It may be that the same amendment would be seen, by implication, as having been made on that date to r.17 and Sch.2 to the 1995 Rules. Anyway, the term "micro-organism" had, as a matter of practice, been interpreted for some years in the broader sense of meaning any "biological material" where, without a deposit of the same, the description of the patent would be insufficient to allow the claimed invention to be practised. For this reason, the term "biological material" is used in the following commentary on s.125A instead of the former term "micro-organism", although this may not strictly be accurate for applications and patents with filing dates prior to whichever of the aforesaid dates is actually controlling.

The term "biological material", as now used in s.125A, is defined by art.2 of the Directive (and also in s.130(1) and r.26 of the EPC) as meaning "any material containing genetic information and capable of reproducing itself or being reproduced in a biological system" and "microbiological process" is defined as meaning "any process involving or performed upon or resulting in microbiological material" (see Appendix C and Sch.A2 reprinted under s.76A and r.26 of the EPC). Consequently, wherever the term micro-organism has appeared in any decision given under the former provisions, this may now be required to be understood in the broader sense of meaning "biological material" as so defined. Whether this is so for patents and applications filed before July 28, 2000, however, remains in some doubt (see above).

In s.125A, subs.(1) authorises, as did former s.14(4), the necessary rules for ensuring that the specification in a case involving biological material complies with s.14(3) as to the adequate disclosure of the way in which the invention is to be performed. Subsection (2) authorises, as did former s.14(8), rules concerning the availability to the general public of samples of the biological material; and subs.(3) (which had no previous counterpart) authorises rules concerning the availability of the samples to nominated experts: the so-called "expert solution". Subsection (4) makes non-compliance with the rules a ground of revocation under s.72(1)(c) (insufficiency).

The detailed rules made under the section are to be found in Sch.1 to the Patents Rules, with r.13 merely serving to introduce the provisions of this Schedule, see above, and references to "Sch.1" in this commentary are references to that Schedule of the 2007 Rules. The transitional provisions in Sch.5 to the Patent Rules deal with applications filed under the former provisions.

Rule 17 (and Sch.2) of the 1995 Rules in any of their forms were, and r.13 and Sch.1 to the Patents Rules 2007 remain, confined to the case where the biological material referred to in the patent specification was not available to the public at the time of filing the application. Thus, not all applications for inventions which require the use of biological material require the making of a deposit of that material. This issue is discussed further in §125A.21, and see also §125A.15.

Articles 13 and 14 of the Biotechnology Directive (reprinted in Appendix C) require that national laws of EU Member States meet minimum standards as to the deposition of biological material which, at the date of filing a patent application, was not available to the public.

—The need for a deposit to establish sufficiency

The following discussion deals with insufficiency issues where a deposit is needed to **125A.15** ensure that the invention can be carried out by a person skilled in the art. For matters relating to sufficiency of description, see §76A.16.

Issues relating to deposition of biological material are dealt with in §§125A.16–125A.22, with the practice involved being discussed in §§125A.23–125A.28. A deposit is not necessary, but still highly advisable, when the biological material, such as a micro-organism, is already available to the public at the date of filing the application. This is discussed more fully in §125A.21.

A deposit of biological material is usually necessary whenever that material is required for performance of the invention. This may be, for example when the invention includes biological material per se; when it is used to obtain a chemical substance from it, or for a microbiological or genetic transformation process; or when biological material is required for use of the invention, e.g. to convert a claimed novel intermediate into a final useful product. In many recombinant DNA inventions, a deposit is unnecessary, since, once the DNA has been prepared and its sequence revealed, it is usually possible to obtain it by a shorter route. The benefit of the invention can then be realised without repeating the steps actually taken by the inventors, and the requirement for "performance" in the invention thereby satisfied. Even in those cases, however, a deposit can in the right circumstances be a useful safeguard against sequencing errors. However, the fact is that cases that require a deposit are becoming increasingly rare, and probably never were as common as was originally envisaged.

Cases in which a patent has been held insufficient because of lack of a deposit are too numerous to mention.

Cases in which the patent or application have been held sufficient without a deposit are too numerous to mention.

Where a deposit is necessary, failure to make one or to comply with the prescribed conditions for deposit constitutes a ground of revocation under s.72(1)(c), and failure to maintain the deposit, at least for the life of the patent and any supplementary protection certificate, is confirmed by s.125A(4) as a ground of revocation. Normally no special action is required by the applicant to maintain the deposit, as this is done by the depositary authority, but in some cases the depositor may be called on to supply a fresh sample (for which see §125A.19) and failure to comply would be a breach of Sch.2 to the 2007 Rules which would also be a ground for revocation by virtue of the same subsection.

In T 816/90 *ALKO/CBH II* [2003] E.P.O.R. 45 at 414, certain sub-claims were held invalid for insufficiency because the required deposits had not been made, even though the main claim (on which the sub-claims were dependent) was allowed as relating to a process which was inventive in itself.

Avoiding an objection of insufficiency is not the only reason why a deposit may be useful. In *Cellartis AB's Application* (BL/O/050/11), a method for propagating and maintaining isolated xeno-free human blastocyst-derived stem cells (hBS cells) was held not to be patentable by virtue of para.3(d) to Sch.A2 since it was not possible to work the invention without the destruction of a human embryo each time. However, the individual xeno-free hBS cell line SA611 was held not to be excluded from patentability, but as it had not been deposited it was insufficiently described, not entitled to priority and held to be anticipated by an intervening publication.

Deposit of biological material (2007 Rules, Sch.1)

125A.16   Section 125A provides that, where practice of an invention requires use of a biological material which is not itself available to the public, sufficiency of the description can be established by the deposit of a sample of that biological material in a recognised depositary institution from which members of the public can obtain a sample, but only at certain times and under certain conditions. This principle is enshrined in the Budapest Treaty (defined in 2007 Rules Sch.1 para.1), and reprinted in Ch.88 of the EPH) is also set out in art.13 of the Biotechnology Directive (reprinted in Appendix C).

Paragraph 2 of Sch.1 to the 2007 Rules lays down the general conditions under which a deposit of biological material may overcome an otherwise deficiency of sufficiency of description to enable the claimed invention to be practised. Thus, compliance with the deposit requirements (as set out in the Budapest Treaty) is only necessary where performance of the invention involves the use, or concerns, biological material not available to the public at the filing date of the application, and which cannot be described in the specification in a manner enabling the invention to be performed by a skilled person. However, when deposit is required then certain conditions must be satisfied.

These conditions are that: (i) on or before the filing date, a sample of the biological material has been deposited with a depositary institution able to furnish a sample; (ii) the name of that institution and the accession number of the deposit are given in the specification; and (iii) where the biological material was deposited by a person other than the applicant, a statement is filed which identifies the name and address of the depositor, and a statement by the depositor has been filed which authorises the applicant to refer to the biological material in his application and irrevocably authorises the making available to the public of the biological material in accordance with Sch.1 (Sch.1 para.3).

Where the relevant application is a European or international application, it is the respective requirements of the EPC or PCT which must be satisfied (Sch.1, para.3(4)). These are the provisions of r.31 of the EPC, or r.13 *bis* of the PCT as the case may be, which are of generally similar effect to those for applications filed under the Act and which are discussed in the *European Patents Handbook* ("EPH") (London, Sweet & Maxwell) and *Patent Cooperation Treaty Handbook* ("PCTH") (London: Sweet & Maxwell) respectively, but for international applications see §89A.33. Although the period for late submission of the data required to be present in the application is not extensible in the EPO, *restitutio in integrum* is, in principle, available, see: G 2/93 *UNITED STATES OF AMERICA II/Hepatitis A virus* OJ EPO 1995, 275; [1995] E.P.O.R. 437; and T 221/97 *LINDAHL/ Micro-organism deposit* unreported, but noted I.P.D. 22007.

Article 13(1)(a) of the Biotechnology Directive requires the biological material to be deposited with a "recognised depositary institution" and specifies that any depositary institution which has acquired this status by virtue of "the Budapest Treaty of 28 April 1977 on the international recognition of the deposit of micro-organisms for the purposes of patent procedure" (the "Budapest Treaty", reprinted with its Implementing Regulations in Ch.88 of the EPH) shall be so recognised, on which see further §125A.25. For further information concerning the Budapest Treaty and operations thereunder, see the *WIPO Guide to the Deposit of Micro-organisms under the Budapest Treaty* (WIPO Publication 661 and available at *http://www.wipo.int*, under Budapest Treaty). However, under the 2007 Rules, no limitation is imposed on the depositary institution which an applicant can use for an application filed under the Act. It is deemed sufficient that the applicant/ proprietor should satisfy himself that the chosen institution is one which will store the biological material, furnish samples thereof, and conduct its affairs relating to patent deposits in an objective and impartial manner, failing which the applicant/proprietor would be at risk of suffering loss of the application or patent if the conditions required of a depositary institution were not met or did not continue to be met throughout the life of the patent.

In contrast, the EPO has always (now by EPC r.31) required deposit with one of the depositary institutions specifically recognised by it for the purpose, a list of which is required (by EPC r.33(6)) to be published in the OJ EPO. For the current form of this list see Ch.89 of the EPH. For details of depositary institutions situated in the United Kingdom and contained in this EPO list, see §125A.25.

For access to the deposited material, see §125A.17 and §125A.18.

If at any time the deposit made ceases to be viable in the sense that it can be used successfully to perform the claimed invention or for any other reason the depositary institution is unable to supply a sample of the deposited biological material, a new deposit (a "re-deposit") must be made as discussed in §125A.19 where it is also noted that further steps should be taken if and when a deposit is voluntarily transferred to another depositary institution (Sch.1 para.8).

Under Sch.1 para.2(2)(b) there is a requirement that:

"the specification of the application as filed contains such relevant information as is available to the applicant on the characteristics of the biological material".

Read literally, this requirement is a very onerous one and could leave any patent to which it applies vulnerable to possible revocation for non-compliance if it comes to light that the proprietor had, at the date of filing, information on the characteristics of the biological material additional to that present in the specification at its filing date. It will be all too easy to overlook the apparent requirement to update the information on these characteristics contained in a priority document by additional information which came to the applicant's attention between the priority and filing dates. However, the missing information must be "relevant", and presumably this applies to the characteristics of the biological material which are necessary for practice of the invention or for the biological material to be identified, for example in an alleged infringement situation.

For some discussion on the meaning of "relevance" in this context, see EPO Guideline C–II, 6.3 (2010 revision) and the wording of the Budapest Treaty and its Implementing Regulations. This EPO Guideline suggests that "relevant information" includes:

"the classification of the biological material and significant differences from known biological material. For this purpose, the applicant must, to the extent available to him, indicate morphological and biochemical characteristics and the proposed taxonomic description".

The EPO Guideline notes that:

"the information on the biological material in question which is generally known to the skilled person on the date of filing is as a rule presumed to be available to the applicant and must therefore be provided by him. If necessary, it has to be provided through experiments in accordance with the relevant standard literature."

Bergey's Manual of Determinative Bacteriology is cited as an example of the standard literature—although of course many forms of biological material other than bacteria may be deposited. The main reason for the applicant having to provide information is to enable it to be successfully cultured and used for the purposes of the claimed invention by a third party requesting and obtaining a sample of the deposited material. So, the EPO Guideline points out that suitable media should be identified, especially where a medium has been modified from a standard preparation, and notes the particular importance of describing conditions for replicating biological material that cannot replicate itself unaided (e.g. viruses, bacteriophages, plasmids, vectors or free DNA or RNA). Note that host cells or helper viruses may themselves need to be deposited and appropriately characterised. Onerous as all this may appear, in many cases it will be information that will have already been provided to the depository institution (and typically prompted for on the deposit form), but care should be taken to incorporate it into the application—which is another good reason for assessing the need for, and if necessary making, a deposit in good time before the planned filing date of an application.

If the "relevant information" is omitted on filing, it would not seem to be possible to add further information on such characteristics to the specification after filing, because to do so would apparently result in the addition of subject-matter contrary to s.76, thereby making a patent granted on the application revocable under s.72(1)(d).

While the conditions of requirement (i) must be satisfied on or before the date of filing, requirements (ii) and (iii) may be met at a somewhat later date before the end of the "relevant period". The relevant period is the first to expire of: (a) sixteen months where there is no declared priority date, beginning with the filing date of the application, or where there is a declared priority date, beginning with that date; (b) where the applicant has made a request under s.16(1) to publish the application, during the period prescribed for the purposes of that section, the period ending with the date of the request; or (c) where the applicant was notified under r.52(2), the period of one month beginning with the date of the notification. This period of time may be extended by request under r.108 (Sch.4 Pt 2): see §125A.11.

It is not clear what happens when the application/patent is assigned. Such may cause the depositor and the applicant to be different persons, even if this is not so originally, and will cause the required consent under point (iii) to be no longer relevant. It is prudent that, with or following any assignment of the application/patent, the new proprietor should furnish to the UK-IPO a document providing his unreserved and irrevocable consent to the deposited material being made available to the public in accordance with point (iii) above.

Obtaining a sample of deposited biological material by a non-expert (2007 Rules, Sch.1 para.4)

125A.17

Access to a sample of biological material which has been deposited under the Act in accordance with the 2007 Rules Sch.1 para.2 or under the EPC or PCT in accordance with the 2007 Rules Sch.1 para.3(4) (for which see §125A.05 and §125A.16), depends upon whether or not the deposit was made under the options now available under the Biotechnology Directive, to activate the so-called "expert solution" which restricts access to the deposited material to a greater extent than when this expert solution has not been chosen. When the expert solution has *not* been chosen, which is rare in practice, then access to the deposited material is governed by the Sch.1 para.4, discussed below. However, where the "expert solution" has been elected, accessibility to the deposited material is governed by paras 6 and 7 of this Schedule, discussed in §125A.18.

The first rule is that, before the application is published (whether under s.16 or under the provisions of the EPC or PCT) access to the deposited material is denied, *except* where a request has been received by the Comptroller under s.118(4) and r.62 and allowed under s.118(1) for early inspection of the unpublished application (on which see §118.13) and accordingly para.3(3) of Sch.1 to the 2007 Rules has been applied, as explained in §125A.16 (2007 Rules Sch.1 para.4(3)). Thereafter, where the "expert solution" has *not* been applied, there is completely unrestricted access to a sample of the deposited material once a patent has been granted on the application, or from the time when the application may be (finally) withdrawn, taken to be withdrawn, refused, or taken to be refused, and notwithstanding any revocation or cancellation of the patent (Sch.1 para.4(2)).

For the release of a sample of the deposited material at a time so permitted, a request must be made to the Comptroller by filing PF 8. The procedure for this is explained in §125A.28. Such a request must include undertakings as set out in Sch.1 para.5, viz. (a) not to make the sample supplied, or any material derived from it, available to any other person; and (b) not to use the sample, or any material derived from it, for other than experimental purposes related to the subject-matter of the invention with these undertakings to lapse when an application is withdrawn of terminated. However, it will continue to have effect if the application is reinstated (s.20A) or resuscitated (s.117; s.117A). The undertaking also ends when the patent ceases to have effect (i.e. if it lapses and is not renewed) (Sch.1 para.5(3)(b)). The relaxation of the deemed undertakings in the case of Crown use of a deposited material is provided for by Sch.1 para.5(4). Schedule 1 para.5(5) provides that the undertakings are not to apply: (a) where the patent has been made subject to "licences of right" under s.46(1); or (b) where a compulsory licence is granted under s.48, though in either case only to the extent for effect to be given to any such licence.

Nothing has been prescribed as to what remedy might be available to the applicant or proprietor for any breach of any undertaking given on PF 8, and no case has yet appeared to deal with the effect of such undertaking. Nonetheless, it is thought that the undertaking would be construed as a contractual (or quasi-contractual) undertaking given by the requester to the applicant as it is evident that the undertakings are for the benefit of the applicant/proprietor (although it would be clearer if the wording of r.33(2) of the EPC, namely "if the requester has undertaken vis-à-vis the applicant for or proprietor of the patent", had been adopted). This ought to have avoided the former rule of English contract law which made a breach of contract actionable only by a party to that contract. However, this rule was repealed by the Contracts (Rights of Third Parties) Act 1999 (c.31), although only for contracts dated on or after May 11, 2000. In any event, a remedy may lie in respect of the tort of breach of a statutory duty.

These undertakings may be varied by way of derogation by an agreement between the applicant or proprietor and the person giving the undertaking (see Sch.1 para.5(2) and §125A.07).

In the case of an international application (UK), a request for a sample must be made to the UK-IPO, not to the receiving office or to the International Bureau in Geneva. If both the applicant and the culture collection are agreeable to the release of a sample, there is no need for the requester to file any form at the UK-IPO (see Budapest Treaty r.11(2)). In such a case, it would be up to the applicant and the person wanting the sample to negotiate what undertakings should be given in relation to use of that sample.

—Obtaining a sample when access has been restricted to an expert (2007 Rules, Sch.1 para.6)

125A.18   The Budapest Treaty provides the possibility for an applicant to limit the availability of access to a deposited sample prior to grant of the patent to an "expert", provided that an application for this "expert solution" is timely made, i.e. (for an application under the Act) before the technical preparations for publication under s.16 have been completed.

Since July 6, 2001, it has been possible (under the revised 1995 Rules Sch.2 para.3(2)(b)(ii), and now under 2007 Rules Sch.1 para.6(5) not only to apply the "expert solution" (i.e. that provision of a sample of deposited material shall be limited to an expert) for the period between publication and grant or failure of the application, in the latter case, but also that such provision shall apply during the period of 20 years from the date of filing the application where the application was withdrawn, taken to be withdrawn, refused or taken to be refused before grant, i.e. when the application fails and does not proceed to grant. Thus, under this second aspect of the "expert solution", an applicant may eventually have the choice between: (1) allowing the application to proceed to grant, whereafter the deposited sample will become available to anyone; or (2) withdrawing the application, or otherwise allowing this to fail, and thereby retain limitation of access to the deposited material to an expert for the remainder of the 20-year period running from the filing date of the application.

To implement this "expert solution" for these effects, it is necessary to file PF 8A before the "technical preparations for publication have been completed" (2007 Rules Sch.1 para.6(2)). Once the preparations for publication of the application under s.16 have been completed, it will be impossible to request the "expert solution" to be applied.

Where the "expert solution" is requested under para.6, a notice of it is published with the application (2007 Rules Sch.1 para.6(4)). In the case of a European application, any application of the "expert solution" is published in the EPB. Note also that the second (20 year) aspect of the restriction to an expert following failure of an application was made available for European applications from an earlier date in 1999.

When the "expert solution" has been applied, the Comptroller may not issue a certificate directed to the depositary institution for release of deposited material except in conformity with the provisions of para.7 of Sch.1 to the 2007 Rules (see reprint, above). The procedure for this is generally the same as when the "expert solution" does not apply (for which see §125A.17).

Thus, the application for a sample of the deposited material to be made available is made on PF 8 and this must nominate the "expert" to whom release is requested and, at the same time, undertakings by that expert are to be supplied (2007 Rules Sch.1 para.5). These undertakings are to be to the same effect as those specified for release to a non-expert.

Following the filing of PF 8, together with the required undertakings from the nominated expert, the Comptroller supplies a copy to the applicant for the patent specifying that the applicant may object to the deposited biological material being made available to the nominated expert within one month of the PF 8 being sent (Sch.1 para.7(4)), but this does not affect the rights of Crown user under s.55 (2007 Rules, Sch.1 para.6).

The applicant then has one month within which he can send to the Comptroller a written objection to a sample of the deposited biological material being sent to the nominated expert and giving his reasons for that objection. In the absence of such objection, the Comptroller must then send a copy of PF 8, together with a certificate authorising release of the sample to the expert to: (a) the applicant; (b) the depositary institution concerned; (c) the expert; and (d) the requester (Sch.1 para.7(6)). If, however, the applicant lodges a written objection (within the period specified under para.7(4)), which period may be extended under r.108 at the Comptroller's discretion, the Comptroller is required to adjudicate upon the suitability of the expert, having regard to his knowledge, experience, independence and technical qualifications (para.7(5)).

Renewal of deposited biological material (2007 Rules, Sch.1 para.8)

The requirements for a renewal of deposited biological material are to be found in Sch.1 para.8 thereof. These provisions apply to deposits where, a sample of deposited material ceases to be available from the institution with which it was deposited because it is either no longer viable, or "for any other reason the depositary institution is unable to supply samples"; the place where the biological material is deposited is no longer a depository institution for that type of material (temporarily or permanently); or the material is transferred to a different depositary institution (Sch.1 para.8(1)). **125A.19**

This para.8 implements art.14 of the Biotechnology Directive which requires that a new deposit of the material (a "redeposit") has to be permitted on the same terms as those laid down in the Budapest Treaty. These include that any such redeposit must be accompanied by a statement signed by the depositor certifying that the newly deposited material "is the same as that originally deposited" (see 2007 Rules Sch.1 para.8(5)), a phrase which presumably means that the material at least has essentially the same biological activity. The term "depositary institution" is defined in para.8(7) of Sch.1.

In accordance with the Budapest Treaty, sub-para.(5) sets out the circumstances in which an interruption of availability is deemed not to have occurred. If the conditions of this sub-paragraph are not met, then the interruption in availability is not condoned and, accordingly, the patentability of the application, or validity of the patent, as the case may be may then be impugned for insufficiency under either of ss.14(3) or 72(1)(c).

If the original depositary institution should notify the depositor that it has already transferred the deposited material to another depositary institution, all the applicant/proprietor need do is to satisfy himself that the new institution can carry out its required storage of the sample in a satisfactory manner, except that it is also necessary for an application to be made to amend the application/patent so as to include information as to the new deposit number and name of the new depositary institution, as to which see below.

If the depositor should be notified the original institution cannot now satisfy a valid request to make a sample of the deposited material available, "for any reason", then a fresh deposit must be made and, where the notification is that the originally deposited sample "is no longer viable", the redeposit must be made with the same institution, but otherwise a new institution may be chosen (Sch.1 para.8(7)). Note the requirement to supply a statement that the redeposited material "is the same as that of the original deposited material", see above.

When the applicant or proprietor is notified by the relevant depositary institution that its ability to supply samples of the deposited material has been interrupted, the redeposit must take place (again with a certificate of identity), and an application must be made to amend the application or patent to provide details of the redeposit, within three months of the date of that notification (Sch.1 para.8(5)). This three-month period is inextendible (see Sch.4 Pt 1 and §125A.11). However, where the original depositary institution (a term which presumably includes a depositary institution which has already been validly substituted, with the application/patent amended to record that fact) ceases to be recognised for the purposes of Sch.1, or has discontinued performance, whether temporarily or permanently, of its functions as regards deposited biological material, and notice of it from the depositary institution is not received within six months of that event occurring, the above-mentioned three month period begins only on the date when that event is announced in the *Patents Journal* (Sch.1 para.8(6)). This period is also inextendible under the Sch.4 Pt 1—see §125A.11.

To avoid a loss of rights arising from a failure to note such an entry in the *Patents Journal*, it would be prudent to file a caveat requesting that notification of any such entry in the *Patents Journal* should be provided, for which see §118.17. The filing of such a caveat will be particularly important where the applicant/proprietor is not (or is no longer) the person recognised by the depositary institution as the depositor because an official notification from that institution may then never reach the applicant/proprietor. The notification may also not reach the applicant/proprietor if that person has changed his address. However, even the filing of a caveat may not be sufficient when this occurs, unless the address for reply thereto is amended upon that change of address.

Paragraph 8(5)(b) of Sch.1 requires that, where a new deposit is made following notification of an interruption in the availability of a deposited sample, a request for amendment of the application or patent (specified to be made under s.19 or s.27, but presumably not precluding application under s.75 when court proceedings are pending) must also be made so as to include the accession number of the new deposit and the name of the new depositary institution (as in 2007 Rules, Sch.1 para.3(2)). Again, this period is inextendible under Sch.4 Pt 1 see §125A.11.

Comparison with EPC and PCT provisions

125A.20   Since 1999, r.28 of the EPC (now EPC r.32) and r.13 *bis* of the PCT have provided (as Sch.1 also does) that, if the applicant has so requested, during the period following publication of the patent application up to grant of a patent, or for 20 years from the filing date if the application is refused or withdrawn, and a request was filed before the technical preparations for publication of the application had been completed, the sample may only be made available to a nominated expert. This option (sometimes called the "expert solution") is supposed to be virtually equivalent to maintaining inaccessibility of the deposit during whichever of those periods should apply, because the expert is independent and must not make the culture available to the requester or any other third party. Whereas, under the Act, a time limit exists for putting the application in order for grant (s.20, r.30), see §18.11), no such time limit is provided under the EPC. Therefore, an applicant wishing to keep his deposit inaccessible for as long as possible might continue to find the EPC or the Euro-PCT route more advantageous than the national or the PCT (UK) route.

While, under the United Kingdom rules, an applicant has an almost unlimited choice of depositary institutions, under the EPC the depositary institution has to be one named in the prescribed list, see §125A.25 above. The Biotechnology Directive requires that this institution shall be a "recognised" one, but this does not necessarily mean that there should be a recognised list, and Sch.1 to the 2007 Rules continues to permit the recognition of any depositary institution chosen by the applicant. However, problems can arise if a non-recognised institution is chosen for the initial deposit and the application under the Act is then abandoned but used as a priority document for a European or Euro-PCT application.

An updated procedural notice from the EPO dated July 7, 2010 concerning inventions which involve the use of or concern biological material was published at OJ EPO 2010 498 and is reproduced at pp.99–114 of the *Ancillary Regulations to the EPC* 2010 edn. This notice supersedes from January 1, 2011 the previous notice dated July 18, 1986.

Biological material already available to the public

125A.21   If the invention involves the use of biological material which is available to the public at the date of filing of the application, a deposit for patent purposes is not necessarily required, and therefore there is no relevant rule. For compliance with s.14(3), the specification as originally filed must still give such relevant information as is available to the applicant at the date of filing, including mention of how a sample of that material can be obtained. It is an interesting question to what extent it is the responsibility of the applicant, and subsequently the proprietor of the patent, to ensure that the biological material required to practise the invention remains available to the public at least until the lapse or expiry of the patent. A strong case can be made that it is the applicant or proprietor's responsibility to do so, as otherwise the specification would not continue to enable a person skilled in the art to perform the invention, and this is clearly the prudent line to take. Nonetheless, it should be recalled that in *Biogen Inc v Medeva Plc* [1997] R.P.C. 1 it was held at para.54 that the relevant date for establishing sufficiency was the filing date, and there is clearly a

TRIPS-based argument that this must apply "without discrimination as to...the field of technology" (TRIPS art 27.1).

As a practical matter, though, applicants should beware of relying upon the continuing availability or viability of biological material deposited by others, sold or available by gift, but should themselves make a (fresh) deposit.

Generally, a deposit under the Budapest Treaty is greatly to be preferred for this purpose: under this, the deposit is kept for at least 30 years or five years after the most recent request for a sample, whichever is the longer (Budapest Treaty r.9.1). Unless such a deposit is made before the patent application is filed, there is the risk of an interruption of availability which would probably be regarded as fatal, at least if occurring after s.16 publication, see §125A.24.

Where the application has already been filed and reliance placed on the availability of the biological material by way of sale or gift, it is suggested that a deposit be made under the Budapest Treaty *and* that this deposit be made freely available to the public without any restriction, thus ensuring that the same public availability pertaining before the application was filed continues for the same period under the Budapest Treaty (r.9.1), explained above.

Inadequate deposits

In Germany, a non-Budapest Treaty deposit of a micro-organism in a collection potentially controlled by the applicant itself was held to be an insufficient deposit (*Methylomonas* [Germany] OJ EPO 1986, 285; [1986] E.P.O.R. 325). The EPO also challenged the status of a deposit made by an applicant's subsidiary, but eventually held that this did satisfy r.28 of the EPC, though only because the parent company had effective control over the deposit (T 118/87 *CPC/Amylolytic enzymes* OJ EPO 1991, 474; [1990] E.P.O.R. 298). In this decision the Appeal Board interpreted r.28 of the EPC as requiring that the depositor of a micro-organism and the applicant must "in principle" be one and the same. However, in 1996, r.28 of the EPC was amended to provide explicitly that the applicant and depositor need not be the same entity, although where this is so the name and address of the depositor must be given in the application and a document must be filed in which the depositor explicitly gives his unreserved and irrevocable consent, before the filing date of the application, to the deposited material being made available to the public in accordance with the remainder of the rule, see r.28(1)(d) of the EPC (now EPC r.31). This requirement is incorporated into Sch.1 para.3, on which see §125A.05. For continued compliance with this requirement that a depositor different from the proprietor provides express consent to making the deposited available, it is advisable that an assignment of the application/patent should expressly include an assignment of the deposit; and that the new proprietor should provide to the UK-IPO a document providing his unreserved and irrevocable consent to the deposited material being made available to the public, on which see also §125A.16.

125A.22

PRACTICE UNDER SECTION 125A

Procedure for deposit of biological material

—General

The term "biological material" (as now defined in s.130(1) in conformity with art.2 of the Biotechnology Directive, includes any self-replicating living matter and any matter capable of being replicated in a biological system. Thus, plant and animal cells, and naked DNA such as phages and plasmids, are to be regarded as "biological material". Likewise the term "culture", which formerly appeared in the Rules under the Act or the EPC, should now, if still used, be read as synonymous with the material deposited or the replication thereof. Naked DNA cannot be cultured as such, and this is a reason for not depositing it in this form but as bacteria containing a vector in which the DNA of interest is present,

125A.23

which can much more easily be handled by the depositary institution and would not require multiple samples to be submitted.

The overriding principle is that the material which is deposited is such that it can be made use of to practise the claimed invention either directly or indirectly, in the latter case the material being first used to produce some other material thereby enabling the claimed invention itself to be practised.

—Time limits for deposit of biological material with a depositary institution

125A.24 If an invention, for which a United Kingdom patent application is about to be filed, requires the use of biological material not available to the public, the provisions of Sch.1 will usually require a sample of some biological material (which is of such a nature that this can be used to practise the invention, either directly or indirectly, see §125A.23) to have been deposited with a depositary institution on or before the United Kingdom application date, see particularly §125A.16. Where a corresponding application has already been filed in another country, the situation should be checked carefully for full compliance with the provisions of this Sch.1. Any deficiency might require urgent action to be taken to deposit before the deadline for filing the application. The deposition process may take at least a week, depending on the material deposited, in order to have the viability checked (essential for a Budapest Treaty deposit) before the application is filed.

It is *not* adequate to rely on a mere mention in the specification of the culture collection, deposit number and filing date. Unless the specification states that the deposit was made for the purposes of a United Kingdom patent application or under the Budapest Treaty, it is not necessarily a valid deposit. Thus, where an applicant had made a deposit in the American Type Culture collection and had paid the lower fee for a deposit valid only for United States patent purposes, a higher fee being required for an EPO or Budapest Treaty deposit, and the specification gave no indication of this limitation of the deposit, it was held in several cases that such a deposit did not fulfil the EPC requirements, see, e.g. T 239/87 *NABISCO/Micro-organisms* [1988] E.P.O.R. 311. In these cases, a short time failure to meet the EPO requirements was excused, exceptionally, because the EPO had not previously clarified the position for applicants. The EPO then warned applicants (see OJ EPO 1986, 269) that an application should indicate clearly at the time of filing the legal status of deposited biological material. A "US-only" deposit should therefore be converted before filing other applications.

—Factors influencing choice of depositary institution

125A.25 Before a patent application is filed abroad, consideration should be given to the earliest date in any foreign country when the deposit can be accessed by application to the foreign patent office.

The responsibility for arranging for deposit will devolve directly on the United Kingdom patent attorney when he or she is entrusted with the first filing of a patent application on the invention. Wherever possible, it is advisable to choose a depositary institution which is an International Depositary Authority (IDA) under the Budapest Treaty. Under the Biotechnology Directive, an IDA is called a "depositary institution". If a deposit is to be made therewith, the institution chosen should be one which meets the requirements of those countries in, or for, which corresponding applications have been, or are to be, filed. The choice of IDA will depend largely on: (1) whether the IDA is authorised to accept biological material of the kind in question; (2) whether it can store, replicate and check for viability the particular material deposited; and (3) the convenience of making the deposit. Use of an IDA situated in the United Kingdom will obviously be more convenient for a United Kingdom resident depositor, especially if the biological material has any tendency to deteriorate in transit or may be subject to carriage or import restrictions.

There are at present six IDAs situated in the United Kingdom and each is authorised under the Budapest Treaty to accept certain defined types of biological material only. The location, telephone number and the broad outline of what they can accept are as follows:

(1) National Collections of Industrial, Food and Marine Bacteria (NCIMB) at NCIMB Ltd., Ferguson Building, Craibstone Estate, Bucksburn, Aberdeen AB21 9YA (tel. 01224 711100; fax 01224 711299; email *enquiries@ncimb.com*; web *http:// www.ncimb.com*), which accepts bacteria, yeasts, bacteriophages and plasmids, including recombinants, provided that their hazard rating and physical containment requirements are no greater than ACDP category 2 or ACGM class 1, and orthodox seeds (i.e. those which can be dried to a low moisture content and stored at –20°C (or lower) without damage; all arable crops and many small seeded tree species produce orthodox seeds).

(2) The European Collection of Cell Cultures ("ECACC") and the National Collection of Type Cultures ("NCTC") are now both part of the Health Protection Agency ("HPA") Culture Collections at Health Protection Agency, Centre for Emergency Preparedness and Response, Porton Down, Salisbury SP4 0JG (tel. 01980 612512; fax: 01980 611315; email: *hpacultures@hpa.org.uk*; web: *http:// www.hpacultures.org.uk*. NCTC accepts bacteria as patent deposits, including those of ACDP Hazard Group 3, that can be preservedwithout significant change to their properties by freeze-drying and which are pathogenic to man and/or animals; they should also be free-living and grow on ordinary laboratory media. ECACC accepts the following types of patent deposits: human and animal cell lines including genetically modified lines up to GMO2, hybridomas, viruses up to and including ACDP Hazard Group 3 pathogens and eukaryotic and viral recombinant DNA either as naked DNA or cloned into a host organism. Viruses are processed on behalf of ECACC by the National Collection of Pathogenic Viruses ("NCPV"). HPA Culture Collections laboratory operations remain at their original parent sites at Porton Down, Colindale and Bristol in order to exploit the particular scientific expertise of each site. However the sales, marketing, financial and quality management has been centralised at Porton Down, based on the original ECACC organisation.

(3) CABI, Genetic Resource Collection at Bakeham Lane, Egham, Surrey TW20 9TY (tel. 01491 829080; fax 01491 829100; email *microbiologicalservices@cabi.org*; web *http://www.cabi.org*), which accepts nematodes, fungal isolates (including yeasts) and bacteria (including actinomycetes), other than known human and animal pathogens that can be preserved without significant change to their properties by methods of preservation in use. Organisms up to and including ACDP* Category 2 deposits are accepted.

(4) National Collection of Yeast Cultures (NCYC) at the Institute of Food Research, Norwich Research Park, Colney, Norwich NR4 7UA (tel. 01603 255274; fax 01603 458414; email *ncyc@ncyc.co.uk*; web *http://www.ncyc.co.uk*), which accepts yeasts, other than known pathogens.

(5) Culture Collection of Algae and Protozoa (CCAP) at SAMS Research Services Ltd, Scottish Marine Institute, Oban, Argyll PA37 1QA (tel. 01631 559000 or 559268 (direct dial); fax 01631 559001; email *ccap@sams.ac.uk*; web *http:// www.ccap.ac.uk*), which accepts freshwater and terrestrial algae and cyanobacteria, non-pathogenic free-living protozoa and marine algae and cyanobacteria, other than large seaweeds.

(6) The UK Stem Cell Bank, hosted by the National Institute for Biological Standards and Control (NIBSC) at Blanche Lane, South Mimms. Potters Bar, Herts., EN6 3QG (tel. 01707 641000; fax 01707 646730; email *enquiries@nibsc.ac.uk* (or use the enquiry form on the web site); web *http://www.ukstemcellbank.org.uk/ patentdepositservice.cfm*. The UK Stem Cell Bank's deposits are not confined to human stem cells. As well as human embryonic and somatic stem cell lines it accepts other human cell lines, animal cell lines and genetically modified animal and human cell lines.

There are no United Kingdom IDAs for animals. In difficult cases, for example pathogenic protozoa and viruses, it is always worth checking thoroughly with United Kingdom IDAs before trying abroad. Before using a foreign IDA, it is essential to check that the carrier is willing to accept the consignment of biological material and that no problems will arise in importing the biological material into the foreign country. Official clearances are particularly likely to be needed where a virus is involved, and obtaining such could be very time consuming.

Where the collection used is not an IDA, it is advisable to check that it complies with the requirements of the relevant foreign laws and practice, at least insofar as they affect priority, especially with regard to permanence of deposit and ensuring that the deposit will be released to the public at the time required by national law, see particularly the United States "Manual of Patent Examining Practise" and the "Notice of the EPO" OJ EPO 2006, 317 reproduced in *Ancilliary Regulations to the EPC 2007* edn (EPO) p.390. (Unfortunately this list has not been reproduced in the 2010 edn.) The same warning applies to biological material which is publicly available or has been deposited by a third party, see §125A.22.

Lists of depositary institutions including non-IDAs, which are believed by the UK-IPO to be willing to meet the obligations prescribed in r.13 and Sch.1 to the 2007 Rules are published from time to time in the OJ Lists of IDAs are published by WIPO in January in "Industrial Property", and similar lists including other depositary institutions appear in a January issue of the *PCT Gazette* and periodically in the OJ EPO. The OJ EPO lists any culture collections abroad which are not IDAs but are recognised by the EPO. For a full list of the depositary institutions recognised by WIPO for international applications, and therefore which must be recognised by the EPO and by the Comptroller, see *http://www.wipo.int/export/sites/www/treaties/en/registration/budapest/pdf/ida.pdf*, although be warned that some of the information may not be up to date.

—Arranging the deposit

125A.26   To arrange the deposit, it is advisable to obtain forms from the depositary institution and "tail" them to make clear that the scientist who sends the material to be deposited does so as the agent of the patent applicant, who should be named as depositor, and not as a depositor on his own behalf (unless, of course, he is the patent applicant). It is sensible also to speak with the depositary institution to tell them of the impending deposit and enquire if there are likely to be any special requirements. If the depositary institution's forms do not make it clear, and if a Budapest Treaty deposit is possible and desired, as will nearly always be the case, the forms should be annotated accordingly.

A United Kingdom depositary has to make a risk assessment under the Genetically Modified Organisms (Contained Use) Regulations 2000 (SI 2000/2831) as amended by SI 2002/61, SI 2005/2466 and SI 2010/2840. The depositary institution is likely to request the depositor to make this assessment.

When deposit is made, the date of the deposit will be that on which the sample is received by the culture collection. However, if the sample turns out to be of the wrong biological material, heavily contaminated or non-viable, the date is likely to be refused. Therefore, it is extremely important to allow enough time for possible re-deposit before filing. An IDA must issue the depositor with a receipt (Budapest Treaty r.7.1) and viability statement (Budapest Treaty r.10.2) which should be carefully checked to ensure that the biological material is correctly identified and that the depositor is correctly stated.

—Fees for deposit

125A.27   Most culture collections, including all the IDAs, require payment of fees. These vary greatly. It should be ascertained whether the fees must be paid at the time of deposit in order for the deposit to be validly made.

Obtaining sample of deposited biological material micro-organism

125A.28   To obtain a culture of deposited biological material to which a United Kingdom patent specification (including an international application designating the United Kingdom) refers and which was not available to the public at the time of filing of the application, PF 8 must first be completed in duplicate, and in accordance with the Notes on the form, and filed at the UK-IPO in order to obtain a certificate authorising the release of the culture. The UK-IPO sends a copy of this form to the applicant or proprietor (2007 Rules, Sch.1 para.7(6)). The certificate must be presented to the depositary institution holding the deposited biological material, together with the request (made on PF 8) for a sample to be supplied as specified on that form.

When the depositary institution is an international depositary authority, PF 8 must be accompanied by Form BP/12. This form, which must be filed in duplicate, is one prescribed under r.11.3(a) of the Budapest Treaty. It is a combined certificate (to be signed by the UK-IPO) and is a request for release of a deposited material.

When PF 8A has been filed for operation of the "expert solution", and the request is made during a period when para.6 of Sch.1 is operative, so that a sample may then only be supplied to an independent expert, the procedure under para.6 of Sch.1 applies instead of that under para.4 thereof.

SECTION 126 [REPEALED]

Stamp duty

126. [...]   126.01

Note. Section 126 concerned matters under the CPC and never had any effect, its object being to relieve from United Kingdom stamp duty instruments relating to dispositions of rights in Community patents. It was repealed by the Finance Act 2000 (c.17) s.156 and Sch.40 Pt III consequent upon the abolition (by s.129 of that Act) of stamp duty on instruments for the sale, transfer or other disposition of intellectual property.

SECTION 127 [SPENT]

Existing patents and applications

127. [...]   127.01

Notes.

1. Section 127 introduced the transitional provisions of Schs 1 to 4 to have effect in relation to applications filed, and patents granted, under the 1949 Act which the 1977 Act replaced. These were defined as "existing patents" and "existing applications", but as 35 years has now passed,, they can now be regarded as spent and these schedules are therefore not reprinted in this work, but for historical reasons, some brief notes on these Schedules are given below.

2. **Schedule 1 (Application of the 1949 Act to existing Patents and Applications):**
   As the term of existing patents under the 1949 Act was only 16 years, provision was made by this Schedule (para.4) for the new term of 20 years to apply to these existing patents having more than five years of life after the appointed day. However, these "new existing patents" were subject to deemed endorsement "licences of right" and this led to many contested disputes as to the terms on which such licences should be granted, as discussed in the commentary on s.46. Eventually, provisions were enacted (by amending para.4(2)(c) and inserting paras 4A and 4B, effected by ss. 293 and 294 of the CDPA 1988) whereby patents relating to medicinal or pesticidal products could be excused from the "licence of right" regime. Extension of term (under ss.23–25 of the 1949 Act) remained possible for the other "existing patents" (i.e. "old existing patents"), but for not more than four years.

3. **Schedule 2 (Application of this Act to Existing Patents and Applications):**

This Schedule applied to "existing" patents and applications, that is those with a filing date for their complete specification prior to June 1, 1978 ("the appointed day"), but subject to the transitional provisions of Sch.4, particularly as applied to Crown user and infringement of "existing patents" (for which see note 5). The provisions of the 1949 Act continued to apply to the validity and amendment of "existing patents".

4. Schedule 3 (repeals of Provisions of 1949 Act
   Subject to the provisions of Sch.4 (for which see note 5 below), this Schedule listed certain sections which were to have no effect under the 1977 Act. Significantly, these repeals included (as from the date of the Royal assent, see §132.09) that of s.41 of the 1949 Act, under which compulsory licences had been available under patents relating to food or medicine.

5. **Schedule 4 (Transitional Provisions):**
   This Schedule set out various transitional provisions effective as regards the continuance of 1949 Act. Para.I of the Schedule reads:
   "1.In so far as any instrument made or other thing done under any provision of the 1949 Act which is repealed by virtue of this Act could have been made or done under a corresponding provision of this Act, it shall not be invalidated by the repeals made by virtue of this Act but shall have effect as if made or done under that corresponding provision."
   In this way, assignments and licences executed before June 1, 1978 continued to have effect.
   Paragraphs 2 and 3 provided that Crown use and infringement of existing patents should be dealt with under the provisions of ss.55–71 of the 1977 Act, except for the continuance of acts commenced before "the appointed day" (June 1, 1978). Proceedings commenced before that day were to continue under the provisions of the 1949 Act (paras 4 and 6–8, 10–13), as well as appeals already instituted from such proceedings; but, otherwise, appeals would take place under the 1977 Act provisions (paras 10–13 and 15).
   Orders in Council designating specified countries to be "convention countries" had their effect continued (para.9), now under s.90 of the 1977 Act, and the power to make rules under s.123) was extended also to "existing patents" (para.24).
   Secrecy orders made on "existing patents" and "existing applications" (either under the 1949 Act or the Atomic Energy Act 1946 (c.80) s.12(1), each repealed by Sch.6 were also continued (para.5). It is possible that some of these survive since such an order can prevent publication of the subject matter of a patent even after its expiry. However, the amendment made to s.13(2) of the 1949 Act (made by Sch.5 para.1 to the CDPA 1988) enabled "existing applications", which were subject to secrecy orders on the appointed day, to be withdrawn without publication.

Appendix A summarises some of the principles of the former patent statutes so that expressions to be found in the earlier reported cases can be understood. This Appendix also deals with some provisions relating to patents which are contained in other pre-1977 statutes and are still effective.

SECTION 128 [SPENT]

Priorities between patents and applications under 1949 Act and this Act

128.01 **128.** [...]

Note. Section 128 is not reprinted here as its provisions are considered to be spent. The section provided a necessary transitional provision for resolving conflicts of priority between patents granted under the 1949 Act and patents (including European patents (UK)) granted under the present Act. However, as all patents granted under the 1949 Act have now expired, as also have patents granted during the early years of operations under the present Act, any such conflicts are likely to be of historical interest only.

SECTION 128A [ADDED]

EU compulsory licences

128A.—(1) In this Act an "EU compulsory licence" means a compulsory licence granted under Regulation (EC) No 816/2006 of the European Parliament and of the Council of 17 May 2006 on compulsory licensing of patents relating to the manufacture of pharmaceutical products for export to countries with public health problems[a] **(referred to in this Act as "the Compulsory Licensing Regulation").**

128A.01

(2) In the application to EU compulsory licences of the provisions of this Act listed in subsection (3)—

(a) references to a licence under a patent,

(b) references to a right under a patent, and

(c) references to a proprietary interest under a patent,

include an EU compulsory licence.

(3) The provisions referred to in subsection (2) are—

sections 32 and 33 (registration of patents etc);

section 37 (determination of right to patent after grant);

section 38 (effect of transfer etc of patent under section 37), apart from subsection (2) and subsections (3) to (5) so far as relating to subsection (2);

section 41 (amount of compensation);

section 46(2) (notice of application for entry that licences are available as of right);

section 57(1) and (2) (rights of third parties in respect of Crown use).

(4) In the following provisions references to this Act include the Compulsory Licensing Regulation—

sections 97 to 99B, 101 to 103, 105 and 107 (legal proceedings);

section 119 (service by post);

section 120 (hours of business and excluded days);

section 121 (comptroller's annual report);

section 123 (rules);

section 124A (use of electronic communications);

section 130(8) (disapplication of Part 1 of Arbitration Act 1996).

(5) In section 108 (licences granted by order of comptroller) the reference to a licence under section 11, 38, 48 or 49 includes an EU compulsory licence.

(6) References in this Act to the Compulsory Licensing Regulation are to that Regulation as amended from time to time.

[a] [2006] OJ L157/1.

Note. This section was inserted by the Patents (Compulsory Licensing and Supplementary Protection Certificates) Regulations 2007 (SI 2007/3293) reg.2, with effect from December 17, 2007.

COMMENTARY ON SECTION 128A

Scope of the section

128A.02 This is the first of two new sections (the other being s.128B) inserted by the Patents (Compulsory Licensing and Supplementary Protection Certificates) Regulations 2007 (SI 2007/3293). Regulation 2 of the instrument amends the Patents Act 1977 to apply certain procedural provisions of the Act in relation to applications and other proceedings under Regulation (EC) No.816/2006 of the European Parliament and the Council, on compulsory licensing of patents relating to the manufacture of pharmaceutical products for export to countries with public health problems. The EC Regulation came into effect on June 29, 2006, implementing a Decision of August 30, 2003 of the General Council of the World Trade Organisation (WTO) on the implementation of para.6 of the Doha Declaration of November 14, 2001 on the Agreement on Trade-Related Aspects of Intellectual Property Rights (TRIPS) and Public Health. As noted at §48A.02, the TRIPS Agreement allows governments to issue licences to companies who wish to manufacture patented products without the permission of the patent holder, under certain conditions. One condition is that holders of compulsory licenses may only produce for the national or domestic market. The Doha Declaration recognised that WTO Members with insufficient or no manufacturing capacity in the pharmaceutical sector could face difficulties in making effective use of compulsory licensing. In order to remedy this situation, the WTO agreed in to a "Decision" which would waive the "national" requirement relating to the manufacture of pharmaceutical products produced under compulsory licensing, allowing developing countries to source cheaper medicines manufactured outside their boundaries. The issuing of compulsory licences under the Regulation is intended to impose clear conditions upon the licensee as regards the acts covered by the licence, the identification of the pharmaceutical products manufactured under the licence and the countries to which the products will be exported. The intention is that products manufactured as a consequence of the grant of a compulsory licence under the Regulation reach only those who need them and that they are not diverted from those for whom they were intended.

Section 128A does not implement those provisions of the Regulation that are directly applicable in relation to UK patents. Nor do the provisions apply in the Isle of Man.

Definition of "EU compulsory licence" and "Compulsory Licensing Regulation"

128A.03 Subsection (1) defines the term "EU compulsory licence" as a compulsory licence granted under Regulation (EC) No.816/2006 and the term "Compulsory Licensing Regulation" is defined accordingly. Subsections (2) and (3) makes it clear that references to a licence, right or proprietary interest under a patent in certain provisions of the Act include an EU compulsory licence and subs.(4) clarifies in which provisions references to the Act include the Compulsory Licensing Regulation. Similarly, subs.(5) makes it clear that in s.108 (licences granted by order of Comptroller) reference to a license includes an EU compulsory licence.

Interpretation

128A.04 In sub.(6), references to the Compulsory Licensing Regulation are to that Regulation "as amended from time to time". Such "ambulatory references" to Community instruments are permitted under para.1A of Sch.2 to the European Communities Act 1972, which was inserted by s.28 of the Legislative and Regulatory Reform Act 2006, where it appears to the person making the legislation (in this case, the Secretary of State) that it is necessary or expedient for the reference to be construed to as a reference to the instrument as amended from time to time. Use of this power avoids the need for the legislation to have to be amended regularly in the future simply to reflect the updating of the Community instrument.

SECTION 128B [ADDED]

Supplementary protection certificates

128B.—**(1) Schedule 4A contains provision about the application of this Act in relation to supplementary protection certificates and other provision about such certificates.** 128B.01

(2) In this Act a "supplementary protection certificate" means a certificate issued under—

    (a) **Council Regulation (EEC) No 1768/92 of 18 June 1992 concerning the creation of a supplementary protection certificate for medicinal products,**[a] **or**

    (b) **Regulation (EC) No 1610/96 of the European Parliament and of the Council of 23 July 1996 concerning the creation of a supplementary protection certificate for plant protection products.**[b]

[a] OJ No L 182, 2.7.92, pl. 128B.02

[b] OJ No L 198, 8.8.96, p30.

Note. This section was inserted by the Patents (Compulsory Licensing and Supplementary Protection Certificates) Regulations (2007/3293) reg.2, with effect from December 17, 2007. Council Regulation (EEC) No 1768/92 was replaced and repealed by Regulation (EC) No 469/2009 of May 6, 2009 with effect from July 6, 2009.

SCHEDULE 4A

Supplementary Protection Certificates

References to patents etc

1.—(1) In the application to supplementary protection certificates of the provisions of this Act listed in sub-paragraph (2)— 128B.03

    (a) references to a patent are to a supplementary protection certificate;

    (b) references to an application or the applicant for a patent are to an application or the applicant—

        (i) for a supplementary protection certificate, or

        (ii) for an extension of the duration of a supplementary protection certificate;

    (c) references to the proprietor of a patent are to the holder of a supplementary protection certificate;

    (d) references to the specification of a patent are to the text of a supplementary protection certificate;

    (e) references to a patented product or an invention (including a patented invention) are to a product for which a supplementary protection certificate has effect;

    (f) references to a patent having expired or having been revoked are to a supplementary protection certificate having lapsed or having been declared invalid;

    (g) references to proceedings for the revocation of a patent are to proceedings—

        (i) for a decision that a supplementary protection certificate has lapsed, or

        (ii) for a declaration that a supplementary protection certificate is invalid;

    (h) references to the issue of the validity of a patent include the issue of whether a supplementary protection certificate has lapsed or is invalid.

    (2) The provisions referred to in sub-paragraph (1) are—

    section 14(1), (9) and (10) (making of application);

    section 19(1) (general power to amend application before grant);

    sections 20A and 20B (reinstatement of applications);

    section 21 (observations by third party on patentability);

    section 27 (general power to amend specification after grant);

section 29 (surrender of patents);

sections 30 to 36, 37(1) to (3) and (5) to (9) and 38 (property in patents and applications, and registration);

sections 39 to 59 (employees' inventions, licences of right and compulsory licences and use of patented inventions for services of the Crown);

sections 60 to 71 (infringement);

section 74(1) and (7) (proceedings in which validity of patent may be put in issue);

section 75 (amendment of patent in infringement or revocation proceedings);

sections 103 and 105 (privilege for communications relating to patent proceedings);

section 108 (licences granted by order of comptroller);

sections 110 and 111 (unauthorised claim of patent rights or that patent has been applied for);

section 116 (immunity of department as regards official acts);

sections 117 to 118 (administrative provisions);

section 123 (rules);

section 130 (interpretation).

128B.04   2.—(1) In the case of the provisions of this Act listed in sub-paragraph (2), paragraph 1 applies in relation to an application for a supplementary protection certificate only if the basic patent expires before the certificate is granted.

(2) The provisions referred to in sub-paragraph (1) are—

section 20B(3) to (6A) (effect of reinstatement under section 20A);

section 55(5) and (7) (use of patented inventions for services of the Crown);

section 58(10) (disputes as to Crown use);

section 69 (infringement of rights conferred by publication of application);

section 117A(3) to (7) (effect of resuscitating a withdrawn application under section 117).

References to this Act etc

128B.05   3.—(1) In the provisions of this Act listed in sub-paragraph (2)—

(a) references to this Act include the Medicinal Products Regulation and the Plant Protection Products Regulation, and

(b) references to a provision of this Act include any equivalent provision of the Medicinal Products Regulation and the Plant Protection Products Regulation.

(2) The provisions referred to in sub-paragraph (1) are—

sections 20A and 20B (reinstatement of applications);

section 21 (observations by third party on patentability);

section 69 (infringement of rights conferred by publication of application);

section 74(1) and (7) (proceedings in which validity of patent may be put in issue);

sections 97 to 99B, 101 to 103, 105 and 107 (legal proceedings);

section 116 (immunity of department as regards official acts);

sections 117 and 118 to 121 (administrative provisions);

section 122 (Crown's right to sell forfeited articles);

section 123 (rules);

section 124A (use of electronic communications);

section 130 (interpretation).

Other references

128B.06   4.—(1) In the application of section 21(1) (observations by third party on patentability) to supplementary protection certificates, the reference to the question whether the invention is a patentable invention is to the question whether the product is one for which a supplementary protection certificate may have effect.

(2) In the application of section 69(2) (conditions for infringement of rights conferred by publication of application) to supplementary protection certificates, the condition in paragraph (b) is that the act would, if the certificate had been granted on the date of the publication of the application, have infringed not only the certificate as granted but also the certificate for which the application was made.

Fees

128B.07   5. A supplementary protection certificate does not take effect unless—

(a) the prescribed fee is paid before the end of the prescribed period, or

(b) the prescribed fee and any prescribed additional fee are paid before the end of the period of six months beginning immediately after the prescribed period.

Interpretation

6.—(1) Expressions used in this Act that are defined in the Medicinal Products Regulation or the Plant Protection Products Regulation have the same meaning as in that Regulation. **128B.08**

(2) References in this Act to, or to a provision of, the Medicinal Products Regulation or the Plant Protection Products Regulation are to that Regulation or that provision as amended from time to time.

7. In this Act— **128B.09**

(a) "the Medicinal Products Regulation" means Council Regulation (EEC) No 1768/92 of 18 June 1992 concerning the creation of a supplementary protection certificate for medicinal products, and

(b) "the Plant Protection Products Regulation" means Regulation (EC) No 1610/96 of the European Parliament and of the Council of 23 July 1996 concerning the creation of a supplementary protection certificate for plant protection products.

Note. Schedule 4A was inserted by the Patents (Compulsory Licensing and Supplementary Protection Certificates) Regulations 2007 (SI 2007/3293) reg.2, with effect from December 17, 2007.

Note. Regulation (EC) No.469/2009 repealed and replaced Council Regulation (EEC) **128B.10** 1768/92, of June 18, 1992, which came into force January 2, 1993. That Regulation had been amended by the Act of Accession of Austria, Sweden and Finland (adapted by Council Decision 95/1/EC, Euratom, ECSC) and by Regulation (EC) No.1901/2006 of the European Parliament and of the Council of December 12, 2006 on Medicinal Products for Paediatric Use and amending Regulation (EEC) No.1768/92, Directive 2001/20/EC, Directive 2001/83/EC and Regulation (EC) 726/2004. The Regulation was also amended by the Act concerning the conditions of accession of the Czech Republic, the Republic of Estonia, the Republic of Cyprus, the Republic of Latvia, the Republic of Lithuania, the Republic of Hungary, the Republic of Malta, the Republic of Poland, the Republic of Slovenia and the Slovak Republic and the adjustments to the Treaties on which the European Union is founded and the Act of accession of Bulgaria and Romania. These amendments, which concern transitional provisions relating to the enlargement of the Community are not relevant in the United Kingdom.

The new regulation is a codification of all amendments made to the earlier regulation which is intended to fully preserve the content of the acts being codified and do no more than bring together the previous legislation with only such formal amendments as are required by the codification exercise itself.

The recitals have been numbered for the first time. However, as the first recital relates to the need for codification, the numbering of the remaining recitals does not correspond to the informal numbering used in judgments and patent office decisions referring to the former regulation. For example, the reference to Recital 9 of Regulation 1768/92 in the Plant Protection Products Regulation, at Recital 17, should now be to Recital 10 of Regulation 469/2009.

Recitals 10, 11 and 12 of the former regulation have been deleted in the codification. These related to transitional provisions whose purpose is now redundant. The definition of "basic patent" at art.1(c) has been amended from "a patent which protects a product as defined in (b) as such" to "a patent which protects a product as such". Given that no changes of substance may be made to the instruments affected by codification, this amendment would appear to be merely editorial. The second sentence of art.3(b), inserted into the former regulation following the Act of Accession of Austria, Sweden and Finland, which required that a marketing authorisation granted in accordance with national legislation of Austria, Finland or Sweden is to be treated as a corresponding community authorisation, has been deleted.

For clarity, art.8(1)(a), (1)(b) and (2) in the former regulation, which relate to aspects of the content of an application for a certificate, have been renumbered as art.8(2), (3) and (4). Former art.15a, which relates to the revocation of a paediatric extension, has been renumbered as art.16, and former arts 16, 17 and 18 renumbered accordingly. Former art.19, which related to transitional provisions, has been deleted. Although of no consequence to UK practice, art.19a, which related to transitional provisions following EU enlargements in 2004 and 2007 is now art.20. Former art.20, which relates to further transitional measures is now art.21. Former art.21 related to now redundant transitional measures, and has been deleted. The provision of former art.22, which related to the effect of patent extensions granted under national law before the coming into force of Regulation 1768/92, has been moved to art.13(4).

The correlation between the numbering of recitals and articles between the former regulation and the new regulation, together with paragraph reference is as follows:

Regulation (EEC) No 1768/92	Regulation (EC) 469/2009
[new]	Recital 1
Recital 1	Recital 2
Recital 2	Recital 3
Recital 3	Recital 4
Recital 4	Recital 5
Recital 5	Recital 6
Recital 6	Recital 7
Recital 7	Recital 8
Recital 8	Recital 9
Recital 9	Recital 10
Recital 10	[deleted]
Recital 11	[deleted]
Recital 12	[deleted]
Recital 13	Recital 11
Article 1	Article 1
Article 2	Article 2
Article 3, introductory wording	Article 3, introductory wording
Article 3, point (a)	Article 3, point (a)
Article 3, point (b), first sentence	Article 3, point (b), first sentence
Article 3, point (b), second sentence	[deleted]
Article 3, points (c) and (d)	Article 3, points (c) and (d)
Article 4 to 7	Article 4 to 7
Article 8(1)	Article 8(1)
Article 8(1)(a)	Article 8(2)
Article 8(1)(b)	Article 8(3)
Article 8(2)	Article 8(4)
Article 9 to 12	Article 9 to 12
Article 13(1), (2) and (3)	Article 13(1), (2) and (3)
Article 14 and 15	Article 14 and 15
Article 15a	Article 16
Article 16, 17 and 18	Article 17, 18 and 19
Article 19	[deleted]

Article 19a, introductory wording	Article 20, introductory wording
Article 19a, point (a) to (l): Non UK transitional provisions	*Article 19a, point (a) to (l): Non UK transitional provisions*
Article 20	Article 21
Article 21	[*deleted*]
Article 22	Article 13(4)
[*new*]	Article 22
Article 23	Article 23

Regulation (EC) No 469/2009 of the European Parliament and of the Council of 6 May 2009 concerning the supplementary protection certificate for medicinal products

(codified version)

THE EUROPEAN PARLIAMENT AND THE COUNCIL OF THE EUROPEAN UNION,

Having regard to the Treaty establishing the European Community, and in particular Article 95 thereof,

Having regard to the proposal from the Commission,

Having regard to the opinion of the European Economic and Social Committee,

Acting in accordance with the procedure laid down in Article 251 of the Treaty,

Whereas:

(1) Council Regulation (EEC) No 1768/92 of 18 June 1992 concerning the creation of a supplementary protection certificate for medicinal products has been substantially amended several times. In the interests of clarity and rationality the said Regulation should be codified.

(2) Pharmaceutical research plays a decisive role in the continuing improvement in public health.

(3) Medicinal products, especially those that are the result of long, costly research will not continue to be developed in the Community and in Europe unless they are covered by favourable rules that provide for sufficient protection to encourage such research.

(4) At the moment, the period that elapses between the filing of an application for a patent for a new medicinal product and authorisation to place the medicinal product on the market makes the period of effective protection under the patent insufficient to cover the investment put into the research.

(5) This situation leads to a lack of protection which penalises pharmaceutical research.

(6) There exists a risk of research centres situated in the Member States relocating to countries that offer greater protection.

(7) A uniform solution at Community level should be provided for, thereby preventing the heterogeneous development of national laws leading to further disparities which would be likely to create obstacles to the free movement of medicinal products within the Community and thus directly affect the functioning of the internal market.

(8) Therefore, the provision of a supplementary protection certificate granted, under the same conditions, by each of the Member States at the request of the holder of a national or European patent relating to a medicinal product for which marketing authorisation has been granted is necessary. A regulation is therefore the most appropriate legal instrument.

(9) The duration of the protection granted by the certificate should be such as to provide adequate effective protection. For this purpose, the holder of both a patent and a certificate should be able to enjoy an overall maximum of 15 years of exclusivity from the time the medicinal product in question first obtains authorisation to be placed on the market in the Community.

(10) All the interests at stake, including those of public health, in a sector as complex and sensitive as the pharmaceutical sector should nevertheless be taken into account. For this purpose, the certificate cannot be granted for a period exceeding five years. The protection granted should furthermore be strictly confined to the product which obtained authorisation to be placed on the market as a medicinal product.

(11) Provision should be made for appropriate limitation of the duration of the certificate in the special case where a patent term has already been extended under a specific national law,

HAVE ADOPTED THIS REGULATION:

Article 1—Definitions

128B.11 For the purposes of this Regulation:

(a) 'medicinal product' means any substance or combination of substances presented for treating or preventing disease in human beings or animals and any substance or combination of substances which may be administered to human beings or animals with a view to making a medical diagnosis or to restoring, correcting or modifying physiological functions in humans or in animals;

(b) 'product' means the active ingredient or combination of active ingredients of a medicinal product;

(c) 'basic patent' means a patent which protects a product as such, a process to obtain a product or an application of a product, and which is designated by its holder for the purpose of the procedure for grant of a certificate;

(d) 'certificate' means the supplementary protection certificate;

(e) 'application for an extension of the duration' means an application for an extension of the duration of the certificate pursuant to Article 13(3) of this Regulation and Article 36 of Regulation (EC) No 1901/2006 of the European Parliament and of the Council of 12 December 2006 on medicinal products for paediatric use.

Article 2—Scope

128B.12 Any product protected by a patent in the territory of a Member State and subject, prior to being placed on the market as a medicinal product, to an administrative authorisation procedure as laid down in Directive 2001/83/EC of the European Parliament and of the Council of 6 November 2001 on the Community code relating to medicinal products for human use or Directive 2001/82/EC of the European Parliament and of the Council of 6 November 2001 on the Community code relating to veterinary medicinal products may, under the terms and conditions provided for in this Regulation, be the subject of a certificate.

Article 3—Conditions for obtaining a certificate

A certificate shall be granted if, in the Member State in which the applica- **128B.13**
tion referred to in Article 7 is submitted and at the date of that application:
(a) the product is protected by a basic patent in force;
(b) a valid authorisation to place the product on the market as a medicinal
product has been granted in accordance with Directive 2001/83/EC or
Directive 2001/82/EC, as appropriate;
(c) the product has not already been the subject of a certificate;
(d) the authorisation referred to in point (b) is the first authorisation to place
the product on the market as a medicinal product.

Note. As far as applications in the United Kingdom are concerned, the term "market" in
paras (b) and (d) means the United Kingdom.

Article 4—Subject matter of protection

Within the limits of the protection conferred by the basic patent, the protec- **128B.14**
tion conferred by a certificate shall extend only to the product covered by the authorisation to place the corresponding medicinal product on the market and for
any use of the product as a medicinal product that has been authorised before the
expiry of the certificate.

Note. As far as applications in the United Kingdom are concerned, the term "market"
means the United Kingdom.

Article 5—Effects of the certificate

Subject to the provisions of Article 4, the certificate shall confer the same **128B.15**
rights as conferred by the basic patent and shall be subject to the same limitations
and the same obligations.

Article 6—Entitlement to the certificate

The certificate shall be granted to the holder of the basic patent or his suc- **128B.16**
cessor in title.

Article 7—Application for a certificate

—1. The application for a certificate shall be lodged within six months of **128B.17**
the date on which the authorisation referred to in Article 3(b) to place the product
on the market as a medicinal product was granted.

2. Notwithstanding paragraph 1, where the authorisation to place the product
on the market is granted before the basic patent is granted, the application for a
certificate shall be lodged within six months of the date on which the patent is
granted.

3. The application for an extension of the duration may be made when lodging
the application for a certificate or when the application for the certificate is pending and the appropriate requirements of Articles 8(1)(d) or 8(2), respectively, are
fulfilled.

4. The application for an extension of the duration of a certificate already granted shall be lodged not later than two years before the expiry of the certificate.

5. Notwithstanding paragraph 4, for five years following the entry into force of Regulation (EC) No 1901/2006, the application for an extension of the duration of a certificate already granted shall be lodged not later than six months before the expiry of the certificate.

Note. As far as applications in the United Kingdom are concerned, the term "market" means the United Kingdom.

Article 8—Content of the application for a certificate

128B.18

—(1) The application for a certificate shall contain:
(a) a request for the grant of a certificate, stating in particular:
    (i) the name and address of the applicant;
    (ii) if he has appointed a representative, the name and address of the representative;
    (iii) the number of the basic patent and the title of the invention;
    (iv) the number and date of the first authorisation to place the product on the market, as referred to in Article 3(b) and, if this authorisation is not the first authorisation for placing the product on the market in the Community, the number and date of that authorisation;
(b) a copy of the authorisation to place the product on the market, as referred to in Article 3(b), in which the product is identified, containing in particular the number and date of the authorisation and the summary of the product characteristics listed in Article 11 of Directive 2001/83/EC or Article 14 of Directive 2001/82/EC;
(c) if the authorisation referred to in point (b) is not the first authorisation for placing the product on the market as a medicinal product in the Community, information regarding the identity of the product thus authorised and the legal provision under which the authorisation procedure took place, together with a copy of the notice publishing the authorisation in the appropriate official publication;
(d) where the application for a certificate includes a request for an extension of the duration:
    (i) a copy of the statement indicating compliance with an agreed completed paediatric investigation plan as referred to in Article 36(1) of Regulation (EC) No 1901/2006;
    (ii) where necessary, in addition to the copy of the authorisation to place the product on the market as referred to in point (b), proof of possession of authorisations to place the product on the market of all other Member States, as referred to in Article 36(3) of Regulation (EC) No 1901/2006.

(2) Where an application for a certificate is pending, an application for an extended duration in accordance with Article 7(3) shall include the particulars referred to in paragraph 1(d) of this Article and a reference to the application for a certificate already filed.

(3) The application for an extension of the duration of a certificate already granted shall contain the particulars referred to in paragraph 1(d) and a copy of the certificate already granted.

(4) Member States may provide that a fee is to be payable upon application for a certificate and upon application for the extension of the duration of a certificate.

Notes.

1. As far as applications in the United Kingdom are concerned, the term "market, as referred to in Article 3(b)" means the United Kingdom.

2. The terms "on the market as a medicinal product in the Community", as used in art.8(1)(c), means (as from July 1, 1994) the then existing Member States of the European Community, together with the then EFTA countries, Austria, Finland, Iceland, Norway and Sweden (Decision No.7/94 of the EEA Joint Committee [1994] OJ EC L160/1), as modified by Council Decision of January 1, 1995, upon the accession to the European Community of Austria, Finland and Sweden [1995] OJ EC L1/1 and (from May 1, 1995) also Liechtenstein (Decision No.1/95 of the EEA Council [1995] OJ EC L86/58). Thus, at least for authorisations issued after May 1, 1995, the "Community" means the EEA. Although Switzerland did not become an EEA Member State, until July 1, 2005, marketing authorisations for Switzerland automatically extended to Liechtenstein with immediate effect and therefore are to be taken into account for SPC applications filed from May 1, 1995 to May 31, 2005. On June 1, 2005, a modification to the bilateral agreement between Switzerland and Liechtenstein relating to the recognition by Liechtenstein of authorisations delivered by Swissmedic, the Swiss regulatory body, came into force, according to which authorisations granted by Swissmedic would no longer be recognised immediately in Liechtenstein, but in principle only after 12 months. The Czech Republic, the Republic of Estonia, the Republic of Cyprus, the Republic of Latvia, the Republic of Lithuania, the Republic of Hungary, the Republic of Malta, the Republic of Poland, the Republic of Slovenia and the Slovak Republic acceded to the EU on May 1, 2004. Bulgaria and Romania acceded to the EU on January 1, 2007.

Article 9—Lodging of an application for a certificate

—1. The application for a certificate shall be lodged with the competent **128B.19** industrial property office of the Member State which granted the basic patent or on whose behalf it was granted and in which the authorisation referred to in Article 3(b) to place the product on the market was obtained, unless the Member State designates another authority for the purpose.

The application for an extension of the duration of a certificate shall be lodged with the competent authority of the Member State concerned.

2. Notification of the application for a certificate shall be published by the authority referred to in paragraph 1. The notification shall contain at least the following information:

   (a) the name and address of the applicant;
   (b) the number of the basic patent;
   (c) the title of the invention;
   (d) the number and date of the authorisation to place the product on the market, referred to in Article 3(b), and the product identified in that authorisation;
   (e) where relevant, the number and date of the first authorisation to place the product on the market in the Community.
   (f) where applicable, an indication that the application includes an application for an extension of the duration.

3. Paragraph 2 shall apply to the notification of the application for an extension of the duration of a certificate already granted or where an application for a certificate is pending. The notification shall additionally contain an indication of the application for an extended duration of the certificate.

Note. For the meaning of the terms "market" and "market in the Community" in this article, see the Notes to § 128B.18.

Article 10—Grant of the certificate or rejection of the application

128B.20
—1. Where the application for a certificate and the product to which it relates meet the conditions laid down in this Regulation, the authority referred to in Article 9(1) shall grant the certificate.

2. The authority referred to in Article 9(1) shall, subject to paragraph 3, reject the application for a certificate if the application or the product to which it relates does not meet the conditions laid down in this Regulation.

3. Where the application for a certificate does not meet the conditions laid down in Article 8, the authority referred to in Article 9(1) shall ask the applicant to rectify the irregularity, or to settle the fee, within a stated time.

4. If the irregularity is not rectified or the fee is not settled under paragraph 3 within the stated time, the authority shall reject the application.

5. Member States may provide that the authority referred to in Article 9(1) is to grant certificates without verifying that the conditions laid down in Article 3(c) and (d) are met.

6. Paragraphs 1 to 4 shall apply *mutatis mutandis* to the application for an extension of the duration.

Article 11—Publication

128B.21
—1. Notification of the fact that a certificate has been granted shall be published by the authority referred to in Article 9(1). The notification shall contain at least the following information:
   (a) the name and address of the holder of the certificate;
   (b) the number of the basic patent;
   (c) the title of the invention;
   (d) the number and date of the authorisation to place the product on the market referred to in Article 3(b) and the product identified in that authorisation;
   (e) where relevant, the number and date of the first authorisation to place the product on the market in the Community;
   (f) the duration of the certificate.

2. Notification of the fact that the application for a certificate has been rejected shall be published by the authority referred to in Article 9(1). The notification shall contain at least the information listed in Article 9(2).

3. Paragraphs 1 and 2 shall apply to the notification of the fact that an extension of the duration of a certificate has been granted or of the fact that the application for an extension has been rejected.

Article 12—Annual fees

Member States may require that the certificate be subject to the payment of annual fees.   128B.22

Article 13—Duration of the certificate

—1. The certificate shall take effect at the end of the lawful term of the basic patent for a period equal to the period which elapsed between the date on which the application for a basic patent was lodged and the date of the first authorisation to place the product on the market in the Community reduced by a period of five years.   128B.23

2. Notwithstanding paragraph 1, the duration of the certificate may not exceed five years from the date on which it takes effect.

3. The periods laid down in paragraphs 1 and 2 shall be extended by six months in the case where Article 36 of Regulation (EC) No 1901/2006 applies. In that case, the duration of the period laid down in paragraph 1 of this Article may be extended only once.

4. Where a certificate is granted for a product protected by a patent which, before 2 January 1993, had its term extended or for which such extension was applied for, under national law, the term of protection to be afforded under this certificate shall be reduced by the number of years by which the term of the patent exceeds 20 years.

Note. For the meaning of the term "market in the Community" in this article, see Note 2 to §128B.18.

Article 14—Expiry of the certificate

The certificate shall lapse: 128B.24
- (a) at the end of the period provided for in Article 13;
- (b) if the certificate-holder surrenders it;
- (c) if the annual fee laid down in accordance with Article 12 is not paid in time;
- (d) if and as long as the product covered by the certificate may no longer be placed on the market following the withdrawal of the appropriate authorisation or authorisations to place on the market in accordance with Directive 2001/83/EC or Directive 2001/82/EC. The authority referred to in Article 9(1) of this Regulation may decide on the lapse of the certificate either of its own motion or at the request of a third party.

Note. As far as applications in the United Kingdom are concerned, the term "market" in this article means the United Kingdom.

Article 15—Invalidity of the certificate

—1. The certificate shall be invalid if: 128B.25
- (a) it was granted contrary to the provisions of Article 3;
- (b) the basic patent has lapsed before its lawful term expires;

(c) the basic patent is revoked or limited to the extent that the product for which the certificate was granted would no longer be protected by the claims of the basic patent or, after the basic patent has expired, grounds for revocation exist which would have justified such revocation or limitation.

2. Any person may submit an application or bring an action for a declaration of invalidity of the certificate before the body responsible under national law for the renovation of the corresponding basic patent.

Article 16—Revocation of an extension of the duration

128B.26
—1. The extension of the duration may be revoked if it was granted contrary to the provisions of Article 36 of Regulation (EC) No 1901/2006.

2. Any person may submit an application for revocation of the extension of the duration to the body responsible under national law for the revocation of the corresponding basic patent.

Article 17—Notification of lapse or invalidity

128B.27
—1. If the certificate lapses in accordance with point (b), (c) or (d) of Article 14, or is invalid in accordance with Article 15, notification thereof shall be published by the authority referred to in Article 9(1).

2. If the extension of the duration is revoked in accordance with Article 16, notification thereof shall be published by the authority referred to in Article 9(1).

Article 18—Appeals

128B.28
The decisions of the authority referred to in Article 9(1) or of the bodies referred to in Articles 15(2) and 16(2) taken under this Regulation shall be open to the same appeals as those provided for in national law against similar decisions taken in respect of national patents.

Article 19—Procedure

128B.29
—1. In the absence of procedural provisions in this Regulation, the procedural provisions applicable under national law to the corresponding basic patent shall apply to the certificate, unless that law lays down special procedural provisions for certificates.

2. Notwithstanding paragraph 1, the procedure for opposition to the granting of a certificate shall be excluded.

Article 20—Additional provisions relating to the enlargement of the Community

128B.30
[This Article is not relevant in the UK.]

Article 21—Transitional provisions

128B.31
—(1) This Regulation shall not apply to certificates granted in accordance with the national legislation of a Member State before 2 January 1993 or to ap-

plications for a certificate filed in accordance with that legislation before 2 July 1992.

With regard to Austria, Finland and Sweden, this Regulation shall not apply to certificates granted in accordance with their national legislation before 1 January 1995.

(2) This Regulation shall apply to supplementary protection certificates granted in accordance with the national legislation of the Czech Republic, Estonia, Cyprus, Latvia, Lithuania, Malta, Poland, Slovenia and Slovakia prior to 1 May 2004 and the national legislation of Romania prior to 1 January 2007.

Article 22—Repeal

Regulation (EEC) No 1768/92, as amended by the acts listed in Annex I, is repealed.   **128B.32**

References to the repealed Regulation shall be construed as references to this Regulation and shall be read in accordance with the correlation table in Annex II.

Note. Annex II is reproduced in the Note to §128B.10.

Article 23—Entry into force

This Regulation shall enter into force on the 20th day following its publication in the *Official Journal of the European Communities*.   **128B.33**

This Regulation shall be binding in its entirety and directly applicable in all Member States.

Regulation (EC) No. 1610/96 of the European Parliament and of the Council of 23 July 1996 concerning the creation of a supplementary protection certificate for plant protection products

THE EUROPEAN PARLIAMENT AND THE COUNCIL OF THE EUROPEAN UNION   **128B.34**

Having regard to the Treaty establishing the European Community, and in particular Article 100a thereof,

Having regard to the proposal from the Commission [[1994] OJ EC, C390/21],

Having regard to the opinion of the Economic and Social Committee [[1995] OJ EC, C155/14],

Acting in accordance with the procedure referred to in Article 189b of the Treaty [Opinion of the European Parliament, [1995] OJ EC C166/89; common position of the Council, [1995] OJ EC C353/36; and decision of the European Parliament, [1996] OJ EC C96/30],

(1) Whereas research into plant protection products contributes to the continuing improvement in the production and procurement of plentiful food of good quality at affordable prices;

(2) Whereas plant protection research contributes to the continuing improvement in crop production;

(3) Whereas plant protection products, especially those that are the result of long, costly research, will continue to be developed in the Community and in Europe if they are covered by favourable rules that provide for sufficient protection to encourage such research;

(4) Whereas the competitiveness of the plant protection sector, by the very nature of that industry, requires a level of protection for innovation which is equivalent to that

granted to medicinal products by Council Regulation (EEC) No 1768/92 of 18 June 1992 concerning the creation of a supplementary protection certificate for medicinal products [[1992] OJ EC L182/1];

(5) Whereas, at the moment, the period that elapses between the filing of an application for a patent for a new plant protection product and authorisation to place the said plant protection product on the market makes the period of effective protection under the patent insufficient to cover the investment put into the research and to generate the resources needed to maintain a high level of research;

(6) Whereas this situation leads to a lack of protection which penalizes plant protection research and the competitiveness of the sector;

(7) Whereas one of the main objectives of the supplementary protection certificate is to place European industry on the same competitive footing as its North American and Japanese counterparts;

(8) Whereas, in its Resolution of 1 February 1993 [[1993] OJ EC C138/1] on a Community programme of policy and action in relation to the environment and sustainable development, the Council adopted the general approach and strategy of the programme presented by the Commission, which stressed the interdependence of economic growth and environmental quality; whereas improved protection of the environment means maintaining the economic competitiveness of industry; whereas, accordingly, the issue of a supplementary protection certificate can be regarded as a positive measure in favour of environmental protection;

(9) Whereas a uniform solution at Community level should be provided for, thereby preventing the heterogeneous development of national laws leading to further disparities which would be likely to hinder the free movement of plant protection products within the Community and thus directly affect the functioning of the internal market; whereas this is in accordance with the principle of subsidiarity as defined by Article 3b of the Treaty;

(10) Whereas, therefore, there is a need to create a supplementary protection certificate granted, under the same conditions, by each of the Member States at the request of the holder of a national or European patent relating to a plant protection product for which marketing authorisation has been granted is necessary; whereas a Regulation is therefore the most appropriate legal instrument;

(11) Whereas the duration of the protection granted by the certificate should be such as to provide adequate, effective protection; whereas, for this purpose, the holder of both a patent and a certificate should be able to enjoy an overall maximum of fifteen years of exclusivity from the time the plant protection product in question first obtains authorisation to be placed on the market in the Community;

(12) Whereas all the interests at stake in a sector as complex and sensitive as plant protection must nevertheless be taken into account; whereas, for this purpose, the certificate cannot be granted for a period exceeding five years;

(13) Whereas the certificate confers the same rights as those conferred by the basic patent; whereas, consequently, where the basic patent covers an active substance and its various derivatives (salts and esters), the certificate confers the same protection;

(14) Whereas the issue of a certificate for a product consisting of an active substance does not prejudice the issue of other certificates for derivatives (salts and esters) of the substance, provided that the derivatives are the subject of patents specifically covering them;

(15) Whereas a fair balance should also be struck with regard to the determination of the transitional arrangements; whereas such arrangements should enable the Community plant protection industry to catch up to some extent with its main competitors, while making sure that the arrangements do not compromise the achievement of other legitimate objectives concerning the agricultural policy and environment protection policy pursued at both national and Community level;

(16) Whereas only action at Community level will enable the objective, which consists in ensuring adequate protection for innovation in the field of plant protection, while

guaranteeing the proper functioning of the internal market for plant protection products, to be attained effectively;

(17) Whereas the detailed rules in recitals 12, 13 and 14 and in Articles 3(2), 4, 8(1)(c) and 17(2) of this Regulation are also valid, *mutatis mutandis*, for the interpretation in particular of recital 9 and Articles 3, 4, 8(1)(c) and 17 of Council Regulation (EEC) No 1768/92.

HAVE ADOPTED THIS REGULATION

Article 1—Definitions

For the purposes of this Regulation, the following definitions shall apply: **128B.35**

1. "plant protection products": active substances and preparations containing one or more active substances, put up in the form in which they are supplied to the user, intended to:

- (a) protect plants or plant products against all harmful organisms or prevent the action of such organisms, in so far as such substances or preparations are not otherwise defined below;
- (b) influence the life processes of plants, other than as a nutrient (*e.g.* plant growth regulators);
- (c) preserve plant products, in so far as such substances or products are not subject to special Council or Commission provisions on preservations;
- (d) destroy undesirable plants; or
- (e) destroy parts of plants, check or prevent undesirable growth of plants;

2. "substances": chemical elements and their compounds, as they occur naturally or by manufacture, including any impurity inevitably resulting from the manufacturing process;

3. "active substances": substances or micro-organisms including viruses, having general or specific action;

- (a) against harmful organisms; or
- (b) on plants, parts of plants or plant products;

4. "preparations": mixtures or solutions composed of two or more substances, of which at least one is an active substance, intended for use as plant protection products;

5. "plants": live plants and live parts of plants, including fresh fruit and seeds;

6. "plant products": products in the unprocessed state or having undergone only simple preparation such as milling, drying or pressing, derived from plants, but excluding plants themselves as defined in point 5;

7. "harmful organisms": pests of plants or plant products belonging to the animal or plant kingdom, and also viruses, bacteria and mycoplasmas and other pathogens;

8. "product": the active substance as defined in point 3 or combination of active substances of a plant protection product;

9. "basic patent": a patent which protects a product as defined in point 8 as such, a preparation as defined in point 4, a process to obtain a product or an application of a product, and which is designated by its holder for the purpose of the procedure for grant of a certificate;

10. "certificate": the supplementary protection certificate.

Article 2—Scope

128B.36   Any product protected by a patent in the territory of a Member State and subject, prior to being placed on the market as a plant protection product, to an administrative authorisation procedure as laid down in Article 4 of Directive 91/ 414/EEC [[1999] OJ EC L230/1, as last amended by Directive 95/36/EC [1995] OJ EC L172/8], or pursuant to an equivalent provision of national law if it is a plant protection product in respect of which the application for authorisation was lodged before Directive 91/414/EEC was implemented by the Member State concerned, may, under the terms and conditions provided for in this Regulation, be the subject of a certificate.

Article 3—Conditions for obtaining a certificate

128B.37   —1. A certificate shall be granted if, in the Member State in which the application referred to in Article 7 is submitted, at the date of that application:

(a) the product is protected by a basic patent in force;

(b) a valid authorisation to place the product on the market as a plant protection product has been granted in accordance with Article 4 of Directive 91/414/EEC or an equivalent provision of national law;

(c) the product has not already been the subject of a certificate;

(d) the authorisation referred to in (b) is the first authorisation to place the product on the market as a plant protection product.

2. The holder of more than one patent for the same product shall not be granted more than one certificate for that product. However, where two or more applications concerning the same product and emanating from two or more holders of different patents are pending, one certificate for this product may be issued to each of these holders.

Article 4—Subject-matter of protection

128B.38   Within the limits of the protection conferred by the basic patent, the protection conferred by a certificate shall extend only to the product covered by the authorisations to place the corresponding plant protection product on the market and for any use of the product as a plant protection product that has been authorised before the expiry of the certificate.

Article 5—Effects of the certificate

128B.39   Subject to Article 4, the certificate shall confer the same rights as conferred by the basic patent and shall be subject to the same limitations and the same obligations.

Article 6—Entitlement to the certificate

128B.40   The certificate shall be granted to the holder of the basic patent or his successor in title.

Article 7—Application for a certificate

128B.41   —1. The application for a certificate shall be lodged within six months of the date on which the authorisation referred to in Article 3(1)(b) to place the product on the market as a plant protection product was granted.

2. Notwithstanding paragraph 1, where the authorisation to place the product on the market is granted before the basic patent is granted, the application for a certificate shall be lodged within six months of the date on which the patent is granted.

Article 8—Content of the application for a certificate

—1. The application for a certificate shall contain: **128B.42**

(a) a request for the grant of a certificate, stating in particular:
- (i) the name and address of the applicant;
- (ii) the name and address of the representative, if any;
- (iii) the number of the basic patent and the title of the invention;
- (iv) the number and date of the first authorisation to place the product on the market, as referred to in Article 3(1)(b) and, if this authorisation is not the first authorisation for placing the product on the market in the Community, the number and date of that authorisation;

(b) a copy of the authorisation to place the product on the market, as referred to in Article 3(1)(b), in which the product is identified, containing in particular the number and date of the authorisation and the summary of the product characteristics listed in Part A.1 (points 1–7) or B.1 (points 1–7) of Annex II toDirective 91/414/EEC or in equivalent national laws of the Member State in which the application was lodged;

(c) if the authorisation referred to in (b) is not the first authorisation to place the product on the market as a plant protection product in the Community, information regarding the identity of the product thus authorised and the legal provision under which the authorisation procedure took place, together with a copy of the notice publishing the authorisation in the appropriate official publication or, failing such a notice, any other document proving that the authorisation has been issued, the date on which it was issued and the identity of the product authorised.

2. Member States may provide that a fee to be payable upon application for a certificate.

Article 9—Lodging of an application for a certificate

—1. The application for a certificate shall be lodged with the competent **128B.43**
industrial property office of the Member State which granted the basic patent or on whose behalf it was granted and in which the authorisation referred to in Article 3(1)(b) to place the product on the market was obtained, unless the Member State designates another authority for the purpose.

2. Notification of the application for a certificate shall be published by the authority referred to in paragraph 1. The notification shall contain at least the following information:

(a) the name and address of the applicant;

(b) the number of the basic patent;

(c) the title of the invention;

(d) the number and date of the authorisation to place the product on the market, referred to in Article 3(1)(b), and the product identified in that authorisation;

(e) where relevant, the number and date of the first authorisation to place the product on the market in the Community.

Article 10—Grant of the certificate or rejection of the application

128B.44   —1. Where the application for a certificate and the product to which it relates meet the conditions laid down in this Regulation, the authority referred to in Article 9(1) shall grant the certificate.

2. The authority referred to in Article 9(1) shall, subject to paragraph 3, reject the application for a certificate if the application or the product to which it relates does not meet the conditions laid down in this Regulation.

3. Where the application for a certificate does not meet the conditions laid down in Article 8, the authority referred to in Article 9(1) shall ask the applicant to rectify the irregularity, or to settle the fee, within a stated time.

4. If the irregularity is not rectified or the fee is not settled under paragraph 3 within the stated time, the authority shall reject the application.

5. Member States may provide that the authority referred to in Article 9(1) is to grant certificates without verifying that the conditions laid down in Article 3(1)(c) and (d) are met.

Article 11—Publication

128B.45   —1. Notification of the fact that a certificate has been granted shall be published by the authority referred to in Article 9(1). The notification shall contain at least the following information:

(a) the name and address of the holder of the certificate;

(b) the number of the basic patent;

(c) the title of the invention;

(d) the number and date of the authorisation to place the product on the market referred to in Article 3(1)(b) and the product identified in that authorisation;

(e) where relevant, the number and date of the first authorisation to place the product on the market in the Community;

(f) the duration of the certificate;

2. Notification of the fact that the application for a certificate has been rejected shall be published by the authority referred to in Article 9(1). The notification shall contain at least the information listed in Article 9(2).

Article 12—Annual fees

128B.46   Member States may require the certificate to be subject to the payment of annual fees.

Article 13—Duration of the certificate

128B.47   —1. The certificate shall take effect at the end of the lawful terms of the basic patent for a period equal to the period which elapsed between the date on which the application for a basic patent was lodged and the date of the first authorisation to place the product on the market in the Community reduced by a period of five years.

2. Notwithstanding paragraph 1, the duration of the certificate may not exceed five years from the date on which it takes effect.

3. For the purposes of calculating the duration of the certificate, account shall be taken of a provisional first marketing authorisation only if it is directly followed by a definitive authorisation concerning the same product.

Article 14—Expiry of the certificate

The certificate shall lapse: **128B.48**
(a) at the end of the period provided for in Article 13;
(b) if the certificate-holder surrenders it;
(c) if the annual fee laid down in accordance with Article 12 is not paid in time;
(d) if and as long as the product covered by the certificate may no longer be placed on the market following the withdrawal of the appropriate authorisation or authorisations to place on the market in accordance with Article 4 of Directive 91/414/EEC or equivalent provisions of national law. The authority referred to in Article 9(1) may decide on the lapse of the certificate either of its own initiative or at the request of a third party.

Article 15—Invalidity of the certificate

—1. The certificate shall be invalid if: **128B.49**
(a) it was granted contrary to the provisions of Article 3;
(b) the basic patent has lapsed before its lawful term expires;
(c) the basic patent is revoked or limited to the extent that the product for which the certificate was granted would no longer be protected by the claims of the basic patent or, after the basic patent has expired, grounds for revocation exist which would have justified such revocation or limitation.

2. Any person may submit an application or bring an action for a declaration of invalidity of the certificate before the body responsible under national law for the revocation of the corresponding basic patent.

Article 16—Notification of lapse or invalidity

If the certificate lapses in accordance with Article 14(b), (c) or (d) or is in-   **128B.50**
valid in accordance with Article 15, notification thereof shall be published by the authority referred to in Article 9(1).

Article 17—Appeals

—1. The decisions of the authority referred to in Article 9(1) of the body   **128B.51**
referred to in Article 15(2) taken under this Regulation shall be open to the same

appeals as those provided for in national law against similar decisions taken in respect of national patents.

2. The decision to grant the certificate shall be open to an appeal aimed at rectifying the duration of the certificate where the date of first authorisation to place the product on the market in the Community, contained in the application for a certificate as provided for in Article 8, is incorrect.

Article 18—Procedure

128B.52
—1. In the absence of procedural provisions in this Regulation, the procedural provisions applicable under national law to the corresponding basic patent and, where appropriate, the procedural provisions applicable to the certificates referred to in Regulation (EEC) No 1768/92, shall apply to the certificate, unless that law lays down special procedural provisions for certificates as referred to in this Regulation.

2. Notwithstanding paragraph 1, the procedure for opposition to the granting of a certificate shall be excluded.

TRANSITIONAL PROVISIONS

128B.53 **Article 19**

—1. Any product which, on the date on which this Regulation enters into force, is protected by a valid basic patent and for which the first authorisation to place it on the market as a plant protection product in the Community was obtained after 1 January 1985 under Article 4 of Directive 91/414/EEC or an equivalent national provision may be granted a certificate.

2. An application made under paragraph 1 for a certificate shall be submitted within six months of the date on which this Regulation enters into force.

Article 20

128B.54
In those Member States whose national law did not, on 1 January 1990, provide for the patentability of plant protection products, this Regulation shall apply from 2 January 1998.

Article 19 shall not apply in those Member States.

FINAL PROVISION

128B.55 **Article 21—Entry into force**

This Regulation shall enter into force six months after its publication in the *Official Journal of the European Communities* [that is, on 8 February 1997].

This Regulation shall be binding in its entirety and directly applicable in all Member States.

RELEVANT RULE—RULE 116

Rule 116—Supplementary protection certificates

128B.56
116.—(1) An application for—

(a) a supplementary protection certificate shall be made on Patents Form SP1; and

(b) an extension of the duration of a supplementary protection certificate under Article 8 of the Medicinal Products Regulation shall be made on Patents Form SP4.

(2) The period prescribed for the purposes of paragraph 5(a) of Schedule 4A to the Act is—

(a) three months ending with the start date; or

(b) where the certificate is granted after the beginning of that period, three months beginning with the date the supplementary protection certificate is granted.

(3) The comptroller must send a notice to the applicant for the certificate—

(a) before the beginning of the period of two months immediately preceding the start date; or

(b) where the certificate is granted as mentioned in paragraph (2)(b), on the date the certificate is granted.

(4) The notice must notify the applicant for the certificate of—

(a) the fact that payment is required for the certificate to take effect;

(b) the prescribed fee due;

(c) the date before which payment must be made; and

(d) the start date.

(5) The prescribed fee must be accompanied by Patents Form SP2; and once the certificate has taken effect no further fee may be paid to extend the term of the certificate unless an application for an extension of the duration of the certificate is made under the Medicinal Products Regulation.

(6) Where the prescribed fee is not paid before the end of the period prescribed for the purposes of paragraph 5(a) of Schedule 4A to the Act, the comptroller shall, before the end of the period of six weeks beginning immediately after the end of that prescribed period, and if the fee remains unpaid, send a notice to the applicant for the certificate.

(7) The notice shall remind the applicant for the certificate—

(a) that payment is overdue; and

(b) of the consequences of non-payment.

(8) The comptroller must send the notices under this rule to—

(a) the applicant's address for service; and

(b) the address to which a renewal notice would be sent to the proprietor of the basic patent under rule 39(3).

Extension to the Isle of Man

The Patents (Compulsory Licensing and Supplementary Protection Certificates) Regulation 2007 (SI 2007/3293) revoked both the Patents (Supplementary Protection Certificates for Medicinal Products) Regulations 1992 (SI 1992/3091) (the "1992 Regulations") and the Patents (Supplementary Protection Certificate for Plant Protection Products) Regulations 1996 (SI 1996/3120) (the "1996 Regulation"). The 1992 SPC Regulations were replicated in the Isle of Man by virtue of the Patents (Medicinal Products) Regulations [Act of Tynwald], Statutory Document No.447/93. Similarly, the 1996 SPC Regulations (SI 1996/3120, relating to plant protection products) were replicated in the Isle of Man by

128B.57

virtue of the Patents (Plant Protection Products Regulations) Statutory Document No.746/99. It seems that this remains the position in Isle of Man and the Patents Act 1977 as applied to them has not yet been amended to reflect the changes made by SI 2007/3293. It appears that it was not possible to extend SI 2007/3293 to the Isle of Man because it was an instrument under the European Communities Act 1972. Therefore, it remains for the Isle of Man to bring forward—if it wishes—an order under s.132(2) of the Patents Act 1977 to modify the version of the Act as it applies to it, so that it includes the changes made by SI 2007/3293. This route was used when the Manx government wanted to apply the changes made in the UK as a result of the EC Biotechnology Patents Directive, and it resulted in the Patents Act 1977 (Isle of Man) Order 2003 (SI 2003/1249).

COMMENTARY ON SECTION 128B AND SUPPLEMENTARY PROTECTION CERTIFICATES GENERALLY

Scope of the section

128B.58   This is the second of two new sections (the other being s.128A) inserted into the Patents Act 1977 by the Patents (Compulsory Licensing and Supplementary Protection Certificates) Regulations 2007 (SI 2007/3293). Together with Sch.4A, which is also inserted into the 1977 Act by the same instrument, this section sets out how certain provisions of the Act apply to supplementary protection certificates ("SPCs") and applications for SPCs. SPCs are available under two Community Regulations, Regulation (EC) No 469/2009 of May 6, 2009 which repealed and replaced Council Regulation (EEC) No.1768/92 of June 18, 1992 which created SPCs for medicinal products (referred to at para.7 of the Schedule as "the Medicinal Product Regulation") and Regulation (EC) No.1610/96 of the European Parliament and of the Council of July 23, 1996 which created SPCs for plant protection products (referred to at para.7 of the Schedule as "the Plant Protection Products Regulation"). Both these Regulations are reprinted above.

Under these two Regulations, it is possible to protect certain medicinal and plant protection products beyond the normal 20-year patent term by means of an SPC. According to art.19 of the Medicinal Product Regulation and art.18 of the Plant Protection Product Regulation, in the absence of procedural provisions in the Regulations, the procedural provisions applicable under UK law to the patent which is the subject of the SPC shall apply to the certificate, unless that law lays down special procedural provisions for SPCs. Until the coming into force of this section, although certain rules had been enacted (notably SI 1992/3091 and SI 1996/3120, see below), the provisions of the Act could only be applied to SPCs in a rather general way, for example in relation to rights conferred by an SPC application pending at the time of expiry of the basic patent.

Further, the Medicinal Product Regulation provides for a six-month extension to the term of the SPC for medicinal products if the product in question has undergone approved testing for paediatric use.

With the coming into force of this section, all proceedings before the Comptroller in relation to SPCs are dealt with under Pt 7 of the Patent Rules 2007, the relevant rules being reprinted in §§123.06–123.21, and reg.4 revokes the 1992 and 1996 SPC rules, SI 1992/3091 and SI 1996/3120 which previously implemented the relevant provisions of the SPC Regulations in the UK.

References to patents, etc.

128B.59   Paragraph 1 of Sch.4A sets out the circumstances in which references to a patent extend to SPCs. These include for example, s.14(1), (9) and (10), (the making of an application) and s.21 (observations by third party on patentability). As far as third party observations are concerned, para.4(1) of the Schedule clarifies that the reference to the question whether the invention is a patentable invention is to the question whether the product is one for which an SPC has effect. Such observations have previously been considered by the Comptroller, see for example *Draco's SPC Application* [1996] R.P.C. 417. Third party observations were considered by the judge in *Astellas Pharma Inc v Comptroller General of Patents* [2009] EWHC 1916 Pat Ct, who commented that this should not be taken as accepting that this was an appropriate method for what amounted to the submission of an amicus curiae.

Other references that are modified in their meaning in relation to SPCs include references to the proprietor, which becomes the holder of a SPC and references to the specification of a patent which becomes the text of an SPC. References to a patent product or an invention (including a patented invention) are to a product for which an SPC has effect, which clarifies how s.60 applies to SPCs.

Paragraph 2 of the Schedule sets out certain provisions which apply only if the basic patent expires before the SPC is granted. These include s.69 (infringement of right conferred by publication of an application). Paragraph 4(2) of the Schedule makes it clear that in the application of s.69(2) to SPCs, the condition is that the act would, if the SPC had been granted on the date of the publication of the application, have infringed not only the certificate as granted but also the certificate for which the application was made.

References to the Patents Act, etc.

Paragraph 3 extends certain provisions of the Act to the two SPC Regulations and provides that references to a provision in the Patents Act include any equivalent provision of the SPC Regulations. These provisions are ss.20A, 20B, 21, 69, 74(1) and (7), 97 to 99B, 101 to 103, 105, 107, 116, 117, 118 to 123, 124A and 130. **128B.60**

Interpretation

In accordance with para.6(2), the references in the Act to the two SPC Regulations are "ambulatory", see the commentary on s.128A at §128A.04. **128B.61**

The legal basis for supplementary protection certificates

The object of creating supplementary protection certificates for certain types of products is to provide some compensatory monopoly protection for products the exploitation of which has suffered delays due to the requirement first to obtain an administrative regulatory marketing permission, as in the case of medical and veterinary medicines (defined as "medicinal products"), later extended also to agrochemical products (defined as "plant protection products"). The SPC scheme is, therefore, not one for the general protection of the fruits of research, but rather to provide some compensation for time lost in the exploitation of patented inventions due to delays in obtaining a marketing authorisation, see *Draco's SPC Application* [1996] R.P.C. 417. **128B.62**

Accordingly, supplementary protection certificates ("SPCs"), have the effect of extending the term of certain aspects of certain patents after their expiry. They have resulted from an original Proposal for a Supplementary Protection Certificate for Medicinal Products dated April 19, 1990 [1990] OJ EC C114/10 which led eventually to two EC Regulations (the "Regulations" or "Regs"), the first in 1992 for medicinal products (Council Regulation (EEC) No.1768/92, the "Medicinal Products Regulation", effective from January 2, 1993 and published [1992] OJ EC L182/1; OJ EPO 12/1992, 812); and the second in 1997 for plant protection products (Regulation (EC) No.1610/96, the "Plant Protection Products Regulation", effective from February 8, 1997 and published [1996] OJ EC L198/30). These Regulations were originally implemented into UK law by the Patents (Supplementary Protection Certificate for Medicinal Products) Regulations 1992 (SI 1992/3091) and the Patents Supplementary Protection Certificates for Plant Protection Products) Regulations 1996 (SI 1996/3120) now revoked by the Patents (Compulsory Licensing and Supplementary Protection Certificates) Regulations 2007 (SI 2007/3293), which introduced s.128B and Sch.4A as discussed above.

Although SPCs are created under Community Regulations, they take effect only under national law. Consequently, the Regulations may have differing effect in different States of the European Community, but only their application to the United Kingdom is considered here, particularly by reference to the above-mentioned Compulsory Licensing and SPCs regulations. Here SPCs are granted on application to the UK-IPO. The MOPP contains an extensive commentary on SPCs.

An SPC may only be granted in respect of a particular product and in relation to a "basic patent". When granted, the SPC only takes effect from the end of the term of that patent and, in effect, regrants that patent for a period not exceeding five years, but only in respect of that "product", the definition of which is discussed in §128B.66. While SPCs are, formally, a sui generis intellectual property right, the applications, and the SPCs when granted, are treated mutatis mutandis with the provisions of the patent statutes and the rules (including rules of court) made in relation to them.

The validity of the Medicinal Product Regulation was challenged by the Kingdom of Spain on the basis of alleged lack of competence to make this form of regulation or that it was adopted on an incorrect legal basis, but that challenge failed (*Kingdom of Spain v EU Council* (C-350/92) [1996] F.S.R. 73; [1996] 1 C.M.L.R. 415 ECJ).

Both Regulations have been amended to take account of the enlargement of the Community from 12 Member States at the time of coming into force of Regulation 1768/92 to the present 27 Member States following the accession of Austria, Finland and Sweden in 1995, the 2004 act of enlargement bringing in 10 new Member States and the addition of Bulgaria and Hungary in 2007. Further, both Regulations are included within the scope of the EEA Agreement, such that they each apply to Iceland and Norway (but not Liechtenstein, where by virtue of a treaty, Swiss SPCs take effect).

The Interpretation of the Regulations—Role of the Recitals

128B.63   The Plant Protection Products Regulation is generally similar to the earlier Medicinal Products Regulation but, besides the different types of products to which they are directed (for which see §128B.66), there are differences in wording and it would seem that these differences were intended to apply also to the interpretation of the earlier Medicinal Products Regulation because Recital (17) of the later Regulation (see reprint, above) states (where the reference to Recital 9 must now be construed as Recital 10 of Regulation 469/2009):

"Whereas the detailed rules in recitals 12, 13 and 14 and in Articles 3(2), 4, 8(1)(c) and 17(2) of this Regulation are also valid, *mutatis mutandis*, for the interpretation in particular of Recital 9 and Articles 3, 4, 8(1)(c) and 17 of Council Regulation (EEC) No 1768/92."

Whether such a provision actually has a modifying effect in law on the earlier regulation remains to be decided. A reference was pending before the ECJ on this point, raising also the point that, if the later Regulation amends the earlier one, from what date that amendment had effect (*Wellcome Foundation v Nycomed Austria* (C-330/98)), but the reference appears to have been abandoned. In *Hässle AB and Ratiopharm GmbH* (C-127/00), in a footnote, A.G. Stix-Hackl stated that the question is left open whether the "principle of precision" ("*Bestimmtheitsgrundsatz*"—one expression of the principle or requirement of legal certainty) is satisfied where the Community legislature provides for the specific legal consequences of a Regulation to be determined by a particular interpretation of that Regulation and where that interpretation is itself provided for in another Regulation, and even then, only in the recitals.

The Recitals to the Regulations have often been used by the European Court to assist in the interpretation of the provisions of the articles. For example, in *Novartis AG v Comptroller-General, Ministre de l'Economie v Millennium Pharmaceuticals Inc* (C-207/03 and C-252/03) [2005] R.P.C. 33, the European Court referred to recital 4 of reg.1610/96, which states that innovation in the plant protection sector requires a level of protection which is equivalent to that granted to medicinal products by reg.1768/92 (now reg.469/2009). This was then used as a basis for interpreting the definition of "product" in art.1(3) of the Medicinal Product Regulation in the light of art.1(8) of Regulation 1610/96, even though different wording is used. In *Pharmacia Italia SpA v Deutsches Patentamt* (C-31/03) [2005] R.P.C. 27; [2004] E.C.R. I–10001, in rejecting an interpretation of the term "first marketing authorisation in the Community" proposed by Pharmacia, the court noted that the proposal would prevent the realisation of the objective of the sixth recital of reg.1768/92 (now the seventh recital of reg.469/2009), which is to provide a uniform solution at Community level to the problem of inadequate patent protection. In *Massachussetts Institute of Technology* (C-431/04), a broader interpretation of the term "active ingredient" favoured by the Advocate General, based on the first, second, fourth and eighth recitals of reg.1768/92 was rejected by the court, also on the basis of the need for uniformity as set out in the sixth recital of reg.1768/92. The court took the view that without legal certainty, there may be disparities between Member States in the certificates granted.

Scope of the Community Regulations under United Kingdom law and practice

The Community SPC Regulations provide (in the United Kingdom) for the grant of a SPC for a "product" which is: (1) either a "medicinal product" or a "plant protection product" (each as respectively defined in the Regulations, see §128B.11 and §128B.35); (2) protected by a patent which is in force in or for the United Kingdom; and (3) which is subject, prior to its being placed on the market in the United Kingdom, to an administrative procedure. **128B.64**

The administrative procedures giving rise to a marketing authorisation permitting the holder to sell a medicinal product or a plant protection product have been harmonised in the Community. Marketing authorisations for medicinal products may be granted either by the United Kingdom's Medicines and Healthcare Products Regulatory Agency (MHRA), in accordance with Directive 2004/24, e.g. using the mutual recognition procedure, or may be granted at the Community level, by the European Medicines Agency (EMEA), in accordance with reg.726/2004 (which replaced reg.2309/93). A Community authorisation allows a medicinal product to be sold throughout the Community (but not the EEA states of Norway, Iceland and Liechtenstein) and the single authorisation may be used to initiate applications for SPCs in each Member State of the EU in which there is a basic patent.

For plant protection products, the procedure is governed by the Control of Pesticides Regulations 1986 (SI 1986/1510, as amended) and the Plant Protection Products Regulations 1995 (SI 1995/887) each made under the Food and Environmental Protection Act 1985 (c.48), but subject to the terms and conditions of the plant protection product Regulation (EEC) No.1610/96 (art.2, §128B.36).

These enactments provide that SPCs (whether for medicinal or plant protection products) are available in the United Kingdom only where the first authorisation to place the product on the market anywhere within the European Community (which, in effect, generally means the EEA and, in certain circumstances, Switzerland, see §128B.73), and in the form of such a product, was obtained after January 1, 1985 (Regs, art.19(1)). It is thought that the Comptroller should interpret this as requiring him to ignore any marketing authorisation granted in a country which, at the date of the grant of the SPC, was not then a Member State of the European Community, even if that state had become one by the date of application for the SPC. However, as explained in §128B.73, from July 1, 1994, the Medicinal Products Regulation was extended to cover all Member States of the EEA with this being extended to Liechtenstein from January 1, 1995 when that country joined the EEA; and, likewise, for the Plant Protection Products Regulation from August 1, 1997 for Liechtenstein and from January 2, 1998 for Iceland and Norway. It would seem, therefore, that the two Regulations require a first marketing authorisation in an EFTA country to be taken into account even if this was granted at a date before the relevant Regulation came into effect for that country, except where this occurred before the entry into force of the EEA Agreement on July 1, 1994, see MOPP paras SP0.08 and SP0.09. For example, the UK SPC for toremifine, granted on a basic patent with a normal expiry of May 2003, therefore expired in December 2003, because the product was first authorised in Finland in December 1988, even though an EC authorisation was not granted until February 1996. For the effect of a first marketing authorisation in Switzerland, see §128B.73.

Conditions for obtaining an SPC

Article 3 in both Regulations sets out the conditions to be fulfilled at the date of making the application for a certificate in the United Kingdom. To obtain a valid certificate at the date of making application, there must be: **128B.65**

(a) a patent in force in the United Kingdom protecting "the product", being eitner a "medicinal product" as defined in art.1 of the Medicinal Products Regulation or a "plant protection product" as defined in art.1 of the Plant Protection Products Regulation;

(b) a valid authorisation for marketing the product in the United Kingdom as a "medicinal product" under Directives 2001/83/EC or 2001/82/EC, or as a "plant protection product" under Community Directive 94/414/EEC or an equivalent national provision;

(c) the product must not already have been the subject of a certificate; and

(d) the United Kingdom authorisation referred to in (b) must be the first authorisation to place the product on the United Kingdom market as a medicinal or plant protection product as the case may be (Regs, art.3, §§128B.05 and 128B.37).

The Comptroller, in interpreting these terms (*BASF's SPC Application* [2000] R.P.C. 1), was guided by the original Proposal for a Supplementary Protection Certificate for Medicinal Products dated April 19, 1990 ([1990] OJ EC C114/10).

At the application date, the basic patent protecting the product must be in force in the United Kingdom, the product must not previously have been the subject of a certificate in the United Kingdom, there must be a valid marketing authorisation to place the product, as a medicinal product or plant protection product, as appropriate, on the market in the Member State and the marketing authorisation must be the first authorisation to place the product on the market as a medicinal/plant protection product in the United Kingdom (although there may have been an earlier authorisation elsewhere in the community). Although the basic patent may expire before the certificate is granted, it is not possible to apply for an SPC after patent expiry.

The ninth recital of the Medicinal Products Regulation and the eighth recital of the Plant Protection Products Regulation each state that the duration of protection granted by the certificate should be such as to provide adequate effective protection. The proprietor of a patent and an SPC subsequently granted in relation to it will enjoy an overall maximum of 15 years of exclusivity from the time the medicinal product in question first obtains authorisation to be placed on the market in the community. Nonetheless, the Regulations do not define what is meant by "protected". As the European Court pointed out in *Farmitalia Carlo Erba S.r.L's SPC* (C-392/97) [2000] R.P.C. 580, the provisions concerning patents have not yet been made the subject of harmonisation at Community level or of an approximation of laws. The extent of protection of the basic patent is therefore a question for national law, which, however, will be interpreted in accordance with the normal canons of claim construction. The MOPP further indicates that, in *Takeda's SPC Application* No. SPC/GB93/017 (unreported oral decision, noted in MOPP para.SPM3.02), a patent claiming a peptide was regarded as protecting an acetate salt of that peptide applying the usual canons of construction for patent claims, it perhaps being significant that the specification referred to this salt although it did not fall within the literal wording of the patent claims.

On one view this might imply that the test for whether or not a product is protected by the basic patent is whether or not the product, if sold by a third party, would infringe that basic patent. But this test has been rejected on a number of occasions, at least in relation to a product which is a combination of active ingredients and where the basic patent concerns only one of the active ingredients of the combination.

In *Takeda Chemical Industries' SPC Applications (No.3)* [2004] R.P.C. 37, requests for SPCs covering combinations of lansoprazole and an antibiotic were refused because the basic patent related to lansoprazole itself and not the combination, which was not protected by a basic patent and therefore did not comply with art.3(a). However, in *Gilead Sciences, Inc's SPC Application* [2008] EWHC 1902 Pat Ct, the correctness of the reasoning in *Takeda (No.3)* was questioned, the judge (Kitchin J.) believing that the issues raised merited further consideration by a higher court and perhaps even the Court of Justice.

Nonetheless, similar rulings in relation to combinations have been made elsewhere in the Community: Sweden, *AB Hässle*, January 2, 2000, Supreme Administrative Court

Case Number 3248-1996; Denmark, *Merck and Co. Inc v The Patent Board of Appeal*, December 12, 2003, Eastern Division of the High Court, B-2667-01; and France, *Abbott Laboratories v M. le Directeur de l'INPI*, January 19, 2005, Cours d'Appel, 04/14435.

In *Gilead*, a claim directed to a composition comprising tenofovir (amongst other compounds) together with a carrier and optionally other active ingredients was held to protect a product comprising the combination of tenofovir and emtracitabine. Objections from the Comptroller that the basic patent did not disclose the particular active ingredients and that the skilled person would have attached no particular significance to the claim, would not have considered it inventive and would not have thought it was the result of any significant research effort were rejected, on the ground that it can be no part of a determination as to whether a product is protected by a basic patent to embark upon an analysis of whether the patent or the claim in issue is obvious or invalid for any other reason. The scheme of the Regulation is to provide a simple and straightforward system for the grant of SPCs based only upon a consideration of the requirements laid down in the Regulation.

In *Astellas Pharma Inc v Comptroller General of Patents* [2009] EWHC 1916 Pat Ct, the basic patent disclosed emodepside, but not prazaquantel or a combination of emodepside and praziquantel, for the treatment of cats with roundworm. A marketing authorisation had been obtained for a veterinary medical product comprising both emodepside and praziquantel. Astellas sought an SPC for the combination, which was refused on the ground that the patent did not protect the combination. Arnold J. referred to *Farmitalia* (C-392/97) [1999] E.C.R. I-5553; *Takeda No.3* [2004] R.P.C. 37, [2003] EWHC 649 Pat Ct; and *Gilead* [2008] EWHC 1902 Pat Ct, but was not convinced that *Takeda* was wrong and so left the question of a reference to the ECJ for any appeal.

In *Medeva's SPC Applications* [2010] EWCA Civ 700, on appeal from the High Court [2010] EWHC 68 Pat Ct, in turn on appeal from BL O/357/09, in both instances the applications having been rejected, the Court of Appeal referred several matters relating to the interpretation of art.3a and art.3b in relation to combination products, in particular multi-disease vaccines, to the CJEU for a preliminary ruling under *Medeva v Comptroller General of Patents* (C-322/10), summarised as follows:

1. What is meant in art.3(a) of the Regulation by "the product is protected by a basic patent in force" and what are the criteria for deciding this?

2. In a case involving a medicinal product comprising more than one active ingredient, are there further or different criteria for determining whether or not "the product is protected by a basic patent" according to art.3(a) of the Regulation and, if so, what are those further or different criteria?

3. In a case involving a multi-disease vaccine, are there further or different criteria for determining whether or not "the product is protected by a basic patent" according to art.3(a) of the Regulation and, if so, what are those further or different criteria?

4. For the purposes of art.3(a), is a multi-disease vaccine comprising multiple antigens "protected by a basic patent" if one antigen of the vaccine is "protected by the basic patent in force"?

5. For the purposes of art.3(a), is a multi-disease vaccine comprising multiple antigens "protected by a basic patent" if all antigens directed against one disease are "protected by the basic patent in force"?

6. Does the SPC Regulation and, in particular, art.3(b), permit the grant of a Supplementary Protection Certificate for a single active ingredient or combination of active ingredients where:
   (a) a basic patent in force protects the single active ingredient or combination of active ingredients within the meaning of art.3(a) of the SPC Regulation; and
   (b) a medicinal product containing the single active ingredient or combination of active ingredients together with one or more other active ingredients is the subject of a valid authorisation granted in accordance with Directive 2001/83/EC or 2001/

82/EC which is the first marketing authorisation that places the single active ingredient or combination of active ingredients on the market?

In *Georgetown University, Loyola University of Chicago, and University of Rochester's SPC applications* BL O/401/09, which involved multi-ingredient vaccines, the hearing officer rejected the SPC applications on the grounds that they did not satisfy the requirements of art.3(b) of the Regulation as the marketing authorisations related to products with multiple active ingredients. The marketing authorisations comprised further active ingredients in addition to the active ingredient listed in the product definition of the SPC application. Thus a valid authorisation to place the product (for which an SPC had been applied) on the market as a medicinal product had not been supplied. On appeal, the Patents Court referred to the CJEU, as C-422/10, a question identical to the sixth question in *Medeva*.

By order of January 12, 2011, *Medeva* and *Georgetown University* were joined for the purposes of the oral procedure and the judgement. The opinion of AG Trstenjak delivered on July 13, 2011 rejects the "infringement" test (which had been supported by the UK government in its submissions), stating that it would not be compatible with the mandatory requirements of art.1c for a national court, relying on national patent law, to invoke the protective effect of the patent for a specific active ingredient in order to declare the patent to be the basic patent for all combinations in which the patented active ingredient was to be used. It would seem that this was because AG Trstenjak took the view that the definition of basic patent laid down in art.1c requires that, in the application of that definition, regard is always to be had to the subject-matter of the patent in question, and not to its protective effects. Having decided that this apparently literal interpretation of art.1c ruled out an SPC being granted for a multi-disease vaccine in which the combination of active ingredients is only "partly patented", but that the aim of the regulation was to extend the term of patent protection for active ingredients, AG Trstenjak concluded, from an analysis that is not easy to follow, that the condition for the classification of an active ingredient or combination of active ingredients of a medicinal product as a product within the meaning of art.3a is that that active ingredient or combination of active ingredients forms the subject-matter of a basic patent within the meaning of art.1c.

Whether an active ingredient or combination of active ingredients of a medicinal product forms the subject-matter of a basic patent within the meaning of art.1c and whether that active ingredient or combination of active ingredients is protected by a basic patent in force in accordance with the requirement of art.3a are determined, in principle, according to the rules governing the basic patent. However, the definition of the basic patent laid down in art.1c of the regulation precludes use of the protective effect of the basic patent from being invoked as a criterion for the purpose of answering the question whether an active ingredient or combination of active ingredients of a medicinal product forms the subject-matter of a basic patent.

As far as the second and third questions are concerned, the AG has taken the view that there are no further or different criteria for determining whether a product within the meaning of art.3a exists and whether that product is protected by a basic patent in force. The proposed answers to the fourth and fifth questions is that they must, principle, be answered according to the rules governing the basic patent. However, the protective effect of the basic patent must not be used as a criterion for the purpose of answering the question whether a product within the meaning of art.3a exists. For the sixth question referred in *Medeva* and the sole question referred in *Georgetown University*, the AG proposes that this should be answered to the effect that a valid authorisation to place the product on the market as a medicinal product within the meaning of art.3b exists for a single active ingredient or combination of active ingredients where that active ingredient or combination of active ingredients is contained together with one or more other active ingredients in a medicinal product which was the subject of a valid marketing authorisation granted in accordance with Directive 2001/83 or Directive 2001/82.

Following an appeal from the hearing officer's decision in *University of Queensland & CSL Limited* BL O/335/10, a case which again involved multi-disease vaccines, in addition to referring the first, second, fourth and sixth questions of *Medeva* to the CJEU (as questions 1, 2, 4 and 7 respectively), the Patents Court referred the following further questions, C-630/10:

3. Is one of these further or different criteria [for deciding whether a product is protected by a basic patent in force] whether the active ingredients are admixed together rather than being delivered in separate formulations but at the same time?

5. In a case like the present one involving a medicinal product comprising more than one active ingredient, is it relevant to the assessment of whether or not 'the product is protected by a basic patent' according to art.3a that the basic patent is one of a family of patents based on the same original patent application and comprising a parent patent and two divisional patents which between them protect all the active ingredients in the medicinal product?

8. Does the answer to Question [6 in *Medeva*] differ depending on whether the authorisation is for the single active ingredient admixed with the one or more other active ingredients rather than being delivered in separate formulations but at the same time?

A further reference relating to combination products, this time arising from a combination of two chemical entities, in which only one was the subject of the patent which was the subject of the SPC application arose on an appeal from the a hearing officer's decision in *Sankyo Company Limited (now Daiichi Sankyo Company)*, BL O/271/10, in which in addition to referring the first and second questions of *Medeva*, two further questions were referred to the CJEU, raising explicitly for the first time in relation to the construction of art.3a the possible impact of art.4:

3. In order for a combination of active ingredients cited in an authorisation for placing a medicinal product on the market to be the subject of an SPC, and having regard to the wording to art.4, is the condition that the product be 'protected by a basic patent' within the meaning of art.1 and 3 satisfied if the product infringes the basic patent under national law?

4. In order for a combination of active ingredients cited in an authorisation for placing a medicinal product on the market to be the subject of an SPC, and having regard to the wording to art.4, does satisfaction of the condition that the product be 'protected by a basic patent' within the meaning of art.1 and 3 depend upon whether the basic patent contains one (or more) claims which specifically mention a combination of (1) a class of compounds which includes one of the active ingredients in the said product and (2) a class of further active ingredients which may be unspecified but which includes the other active ingredient in the said product; or is it sufficient that the basic patent contains one (or more) claims which (1) claim a class of compounds which includes one of the active ingredients in the said product and (2) use specific language which as a matter of national law extends the scope of protection to include the presence of further other unspecified active ingredients including the other active ingredient in the said product?

At the date of application, the United Kingdom marketing authorisation must already have been granted (*Yamanouchi's SPC Application*, BL O/112/93, noted I.P.D. 17136; and BL C/67/94, noted I.P.D. 18007, upheld on appeal to the ECJ: *Yamanouchi Pharmaceuticals Co Ltd v Comptroller-General of Patents, Designs and Trade Marks* (C-110/95) [1997] R.P.C. 844), and discussed by Natalie Young [1997] B.S.L.R. 81). A marketing authorisation for the same product in another Member State, or granted later in the same Member State after patent expiry, will not suffice. An authorisation must, inter alia, include a summary of product characteristics ("SmPC") as required by art.8(1)(b) see §128B.42 above. This appears to rule out the granting of permission by a regulatory authority for a product to be supplied for a clinical trial to be considered as an appropriate marketing authorisation, as the required summary SmPC will not be available.

As regards (b) above, a full "marketing authorisation" is required, a letter granting permission to carry out a clinical trial not being sufficient (*British Technology's SPC Application* [1997] R.P.C. 118). A conditional marketing authorisation, granted in accordance with Regulation 507/2006, which are valid for one year on a renewable basis would appear to constitute a valid authorisation for marketing a product as a medicinal product, as it granted under a procedure falling within the scope of Regulation 726/2004. According to the Plant Protection Products Regulation (see art.13(3), reprinted at §128B.47 above) a provisional marketing authorisation (which is granted under art.8.1 of Directive 91/414) may suffice if it is "directly followed by a definitive authorisation concerning the same product" and this position has been confirmed by the CJEU in *Hogan Lovells International LLP v Bayer CropScience AG* (C-229/09).

The Medicinal Products Regulation does not explicitly extend to medical devices. However, in *Genzyme Biosurgery Corp. v Industrial Property Office*, BIE 70 (2002) 360-362 (Netherlands), the District Court in the Hague was asked to consider whether in respect of a medical device, authorised in accordance with the Medical Device Directive 93/42, which incorporates as an integral part a substance which if used separately can be considered to be a medicinal product within the meaning of Directive 65/65, an SPC could be obtained for that substance. The court was of the opinion that although art.2 of the Regulation does not refer to Directive 93/42, that need not be a bar to the application of the Regulation if the safety, quality and usefulness of the substance for which an SPC was being sought was verified as part of the authorisation procedure, being a procedure analogous to that for a medicinal product. Similar arguments may apply to the other device Directives, namely Directive 90/385 on active implantable medical devices and Directive 98/79 on in vitro diagnostic medical devices, but this interpretation has not yet been considered by the European Court and there is no established practice on this point at the UK-IPO.

Following an appeal from the German Patent Office rejecting an application for an SPC for Yttrium-90 Glass Microspheres, based on an authorisation under Council Directive 90/385, rather than Directive 65/65, the German Patent Court in 14W (pat) 12/07 ruled that authorisations granted under the device Directives 93/42 and 90//385 are to be considered as analogous to those granted under Directive 65/65 (now replaced by Directive 2001/83) and so the applicant was entitled to the grant of an SPC for the product in question. The German court specifically referred to the similar practice of the Dutch court in *Genzyme Biosurgery Corp.*

A literal interpretation of para.3(a) in the Medicinal Product Regulation seems to rule out the grant of a certificate for a product which is already the subject of a certificate in the United Kingdom. The Explanatory Memorandum accompanying the Commission Proposal for the Regulation suggests that the intention of this provision was to prevent a new SPC being granted each time that there was a minor change in the medicinal product, e.g. a new formulation, leading to a new marketing authorisation. This in turn would lead to extension of the duration of the term of the SPC protection for the product. However, in *Takeda's SPC Applications (No.2)* [2004] R.P.C. 20 it was held that under art.3(c) of the SPC Regulation, which states that an SPC can only be granted where "the product has not already been the subject of a certificate", applications for SPCs based on different marketing authorisations for combinations containing the patented active ingredient were refused as the relevant "product" was the same in each case, namely the active ingredient which was the subject of the patent.

In *Chiron and Novo-Nordisk's SPC Application* [2005] R.P.C. 24 two other companies had already obtained SPCs relating to a particular product under different patents, and the present applicants sought a further SPC under their own patent which had been granted subsequently. Article 3(c) was here given a "teleological"(object-based) interpretation as limited to the situation where multiple SPCs would be granted to the same applicant, but not where different applicants were involved. The present application was therefore allowable, and could be distinguished from *Takeda*, above. The practice established by the UK-IPO in *Chiron* has now been confirmed following the ECJ's ruling in *AHP Manufacturing BV v BIE* (C-482/07) [2009] E.C.R. I-7295.

Recital (17) of reg.1610/96 (the Plant Protection Regulation) suggests that art.3 is to be interpreted in accordance with art.3(2) of the new regulation which states:

"2. The holder of more than one patent for the same product shall not be granted more than one certificate for that product. However, where two or more applications concerning the same product and emanating from two or more holders of different patents are pending, one certificate for this product may be issued to each of these holders."

The second sentence of this provision is consistent with the ruling of the European Court in *Biogen Inc v SmithKline Beecham Biologicals* (C-181/95) [1997] R.P.C. 833, which stated that where a medicinal product is covered by a basic patent, the Regulation does not preclude the grant of an SPC to each holder of a basic patent. The European Court has not explicitly considered the situation in which two or more applications for the same product emanate from one patent holder, but the practice of many patent offices is to allow only one SPC from such applications, see for example *Takeda Chemical Industries Ltd's Applications* [2004] R.P.C. 2. The same reasoning was applied in *Knoll AG's application* BL O/138/05, where the applicant filed two co-pending applications relating to the same product based upon common marketing authorisations, but different basic patents. The applicant's argument that under a literal interpretation of art.3(c) of the Medicinal Products Regulation no objection could be made was rejected, as was the argument that art.3(2) of the Plant Protection Regulation No.1610/96 could not be used in the interpretation of art.3 of the Medicinal Products Regulation. In particular, the hearing officer found that it was not inequitable to deny a patent holder more than one certificate for a product whilst allowing other patent holders one certificate for that product. This decision is consistent with that of the same hearing officer in *Takeda No.2* (above).

Note: It appears that relationships between companies will be disregarded in determining whether SPCs should be granted to multiple applicants. Thus the UK-IPO has granted SPCs relating to the same product where the basic patents are in the name of different companies apparently belonging to the same group.

Definition of "product" for which a supplementary protection certificate can be granted

Although the Regulations create SPCs for "medicinal (or plant protection) products", **128B.66** the SPC is actually granted for a "product". The term "product" is defined in art.1 of the respective Regulations.

Under the Medicinal Products Regulation, the term "product" means "the active ingredient or combination of active ingredients of a medicinal product" (art.1(b)), and this latter term means "a substance or combination of substances presented for treating or preventing disease in humans or animals and any substance or combination of substances which may be administered to human beings or animals with a view to making a medical diagnosis or to restoring, correcting or modifying physiological functions in humans and animals".

In the Plant Protection Regulation, the definition of the term "plant protection products" is more complex. As stated in its art.1, this term means "active substances and preparations containing one or more active substances put up in the form in which they are supplied to the user and intended to have certain function or activity (for which see the detailed definition set out in §128B.35). This article then also defines: "substances" as meaning "chemical elements and their compounds, as they occur naturally or by manufacture, including any impurity inevitably resulting from the manufacturing process"; "active substances" as meaning "substances or micro-organisms including viruses, having general or specific action against harmful organisms or on plants, parts of plants or plant products"; and "preparations" as meaning "mixtures or solutions composed of two or more substances, of which at least one is an active substance". The article also defines the terms: "plants"; "plant products"; and "harmful organisms", with "product" also being defined as "the active substance [as defined above] or combination of active substances of a plant protection product".

In the discussion in the EC Council which led to the Medicinal Products Regulation, it was apparently understood that the term "product" may cover salts and esters of the active ingredient, but the possibility was not ruled out of obtaining a new certificate for a salt or ester regarded as a new active ingredient, see the article by Whaite and Jones [1992] E.I.P.R. 324. This position appears to have been clarified by Recitals (13) and (14) of the Plant Protection Products Regulation, and the following Recital (17) may have the effect of importing these Recitals into the earlier Regulation. Thus, this Recital (13) states that "where the basic patent covers an active substance and its various derivatives (salts and esters), the certificate confers the same protection"; and Recital (14) states that: "the issue of a certificate for a product consisting of an active substance does not prejudice the issue of other certificates for derivatives (salts and esters) of the substance, provided that the derivatives are the subject of patents specifically covering them".

In English, "active ingredient" is generally understood to be the actual active substance in the (medicinal) product that has been authorised, e.g. amlodipine besylate as opposed to amlodipine maleate. However, in the French version of the Regulation, product is defined as "principe actif", which in normal usage means either the substance in the (medicinal) product or the active moiety, e.g. "amlodipine". In some national marketing authorisations, the active substance is only described in terms of the active moiety, and not in terms of the actual substance used, which may be a salt, e.g. a hydrochloride salt, and may further be solvated, e.g. as a trihydrate.

In *Massachusetts Institute of Technology* ("MIT") (C-431/04) OJ C165, 9 (July 15, 2006), the ECJ ruled that art.1(b) of the Medicinal Products Regulation No.1768/92 must be interpreted so as not to include in the concept of "combination of active ingredients of a medicinal product" a combination of two substances, only one of which has therapeutic effects of its own for a specific indication, the other rendering possible a pharmaceutical form of the medicinal product which is necessary for the therapeutic efficacy of the first substance for that indication. The case concerned the medicinal product Gliadel Implant, which consists of the drug substance, carmustine and polymeric, biologically degradable excipient, polifeprosan. Whilst the ECJ accepted that the Regulation does not define the concept of "active ingredient", the ECJ noted that it was common ground in the case that the expression "active ingredient" is generally taken in pharmacology not to include substances forming part of a medicinal product which do not have an effect of their own on the human or animal body. The ECJ also argued that this interpretation is consistent with the Plant Protection Regulation, which, according to Recital 4, is intended to give a level of protection which is equivalent to that granted in the Medicinal Products Regulation. Article 1(8) of that Regulation defines "product" as the active substance or combination of active substances of a plant protection product. An active substance is defined as a substance having general or specific action against harmful organisms or on plants. The interpretation sought by *MIT*, and which had been approved by A.G. Léger in his Opinion published on November 25, 2005, extended the concept of combination to include a combination of two substances, only one of which has therapeutic effects of its own for a specific indication, the other rendering possible a pharmaceutical form of the medicinal product which is necessary for the therapeutic efficacy of the first substance for that indication. In rejecting this approach, the ECJ noted that whether a substance without any therapeutic effect of its own is necessary for the therapeutic efficacy of the active ingredient cannot be regarded as a sufficiently precise test. In *Yissum Research and Development Company of the Hebrew University of Jerusalem v Comptroller-General of Patents* (C-202/05), the applicant sought to obtain an SPC for calcitriol for a particular therapeutic indication, when calcitriol had previously been had already been granted authorisation to be placed on the market for other uses. Following an appeal from a decision of the Comptroller (BL O/222/04) and referral from the Patents Court to the ECJ, the Court ruled that art.1(b) of the Regulation is to be interpreted as meaning that in a case where a basic patent protects a second medical use of an active ingredient, that use does not form an integral part of the definition of "product". The court further noted the same interpretation can be inferred from the judgment in *Pharmacia Italia* (C-31/03) [2004] E.C.R. I–10001, in which the court held that "the decisive factor for the grant of the certificate is not the intended use of the medicinal product and . . . the purpose of the protection conferred by the certificate relates to any use of the product as a medicinal product without any distinction between use of the product as a medicinal product for human use and as a veterinary medicinal product".

In *BASF v BIE* (C-258/99) [2002] R.P.C. 9 at 274, the ECJ dismissed an appeal by BASF against refusal of the Netherlands Patent Office (upheld on national appeal) to grant an SPC for a plant protection product with fewer impurities than a corresponding product for which a marketing authorisation had been granted. In 1967, BASF was granted an authorisation for a pesticide containing a substance which consisted of two isomers, one of which was active and the other which was inactive and considered an impurity. BASF was granted a patent for a process for making the substance which allowed a greater proportion of active to inactive isomer to be obtained. Following the grant of a marketing authorisation for a pesticide containing the substance made by this process, BASF applied for an SPC, arguing that a product within the meaning of Regulation 1610/96 includes the active substance and the impurities. There is therefore a different product where the proportion of active substance to impurities is substantially altered. It was argued therefore that the earlier marketing authorisation should not prevent the grant of an SPC based on the later process patent. The ECJ held that the SPC Regulation covers chemical elements and their compounds as they occur naturally or by manufacture, including any impurity inevitably resulting from the manufacturing process, and that two products, which differ only in the proportion of the active chemical compound to the impurity they contain, must be regarded as the same product within the meaning of the Regulation. The fact that a marketing authorisation must be obtained for a product prepared by the new process is not relevant for the purposes of establishing whether or not the products are the same for this purpose. The conditions laid down in art.3(1)(a) and (d) of the Regulation are therefore not satisfied where a product differs from a previously authorised product only in the proportion of impurity it contains.

The UK-IPO view has been that the term "active ingredient" covers any closely related derivative of it for which a marketing authorisation has been obtained and which is protected by the basic patent, unless the derivative in question can be regarded as a new active ingredient, see MOPP para.SP1.03 and *BASF's SPC Application* (above). The MOPP (para.SPM2.04) also indicates that SPCs have been granted for a compound "optionally in derivative form", e.g. "X optionally in the form of a pharmaceutically active salt such as the hydrochloride".

The Recitals of the SPC Regulations indicate that the protection granted should be confined to the product which obtained authorisation. Consequently it was held, in *Draco's SPC Application* [1996] R.P.C. 417, that an SPC should be "strictly limited" to "the active ingredient of that which is presented for treatment". Here, the product for which an SPC was sought differed from that of an earlier product licence only as to physical form and it was held that this was not sufficient to make the later product licence one for a different product. Thus, it was here too late to obtain an SPC because the basic patent for the active ingredient in issue had expired too long ago, and research leading to a new formulation could not itself have led to an SPC.

A related problem is when separate authorisations have been granted by the different authorities for marketing the same active ingredient as a human and a veterinary medicine. However, it has been held that the term "first marketing authorisation" means an authorisation for either type of medicine (*Farmitalia Carlo Erba's SPC Application* [1996] R.P.C. 111).

In *Generics (UK) Ltd v Daiichi Pharmaceutical Co Ltd* [2008] EWHC 2413; [2009] R.P.C. 4, the validity of the SPC for levofloxacin, an antibiotic, was challenged on the basis that it did not comply with art.3(d). Levofloxacin was the (-) entantiomer of ofloxacin, which had received a marketing authorisation in the UK as a racemic mixture some seven years earlier. Generics (UK) claimed that since ofloxacin was a 50:50 mixture of the levofloxacin with its (-) enantiomer, the earlier marketing authorisation was the first to put levofloxacin on the market as a medicinal product. Dismissing this argument, it was found that the earlier authorisation was a permission to place ofloxacin on the market as a medicinal product and the active ingredient was duly named as oflaxacin. Ofloxacin, levofloxacin and the (-) enantiomer each had different properties, with the (-) enantiomer having some antimicrobial activity. Ofloxacin could be considered as a combination of two active ingredients, namely levofloxacin and the (-) enantiomer. The (-) enantiomer was not an inactive impurity (cf. *BASF*, above); nor is it an excipient (cf. *MIT*, above). This conclusion was consistent with the scheme and objects of the SPC Regulation. Invention was required to make levofloxacin. There was a delay of 11 years between the filing of the patent application for that invention and the grant of the first marketing authorisation in the Community for the active ingredient. Without the SPC, Daiichi would only have had nine years of protection from the date of first authorisation, which was precisely the vice at which the SPC Regulation was aimed. Further, the SPC did not result in an undue extension of protection contrary to Recitals (8) and (9), as the SPC did not cover the previously authorised oflaxacin.

The decision in *Generics (UK) Ltd v Daiichi Pharmaceutical Co Ltd* was upheld on appeal in [2009] EWCA Civ 646. Levofloxacin was a new and better product than ofloxacin. It needed a new marketing authorisation and was a new product from all practical points of view. It was unrealistic to regard ofloxacin as no more than Levofloxacin with an impurity. They were not regarded as such by patent law or by the law regarding the marketing of medicines. There was no reason why the law of SPCs which was built on these two branches of law should go off in a different direction. Successive SPCs were not available for mere minor variants of an active substance but here Levofloxacin was not a minor variant of ofloxacin, but was a novel and inventive improvement with its own bioavailability and toxicity.

In *Yeda Research and Development Co Ltd v BIE*, Case No.200809060/1/H3, the Netherlands Council of State rejected an application for an SPC in which the product was identified by the applicant as "human monoclonal antibody against tumor necrosis factor-alpha" whereas the marketing authorisation identified the active ingredient as adalimumab. The applicant argued that a reasonable interpretation of *Farmitalia* implies that therapeutically equivalent variants of the product cited in the market authorisation may be included in the product description of a certificate to the extent that these are protected by the basic patent. Since the basic patent in question also protected other monoclonal antibodies which it may be assumed are therapeutically equivalent to adalimumab, the applicant argued that the certificate should include a broader product description. Rejecting an appeal from the decision of the District Court of the Hague, the Council of State held that this case, involving a biological medicinal product, differed fundamentally from the situation in *Farmitalia* and that it cannot be assumed that the therapeutic value of the monoclonal antibodies against tumour necrosis factor-alpha related to adalimumab is in principle the same. At the UK-IPO it seems to be established practice that for macromolecules such as monoclonal antibodies, the product is defined in terms of the INN (International Non-Proprietary Name).

In *Neurim Pharmaceuticals (1991) Ltd v Comptroller General of Patents* [2010] EWHC 976 Pat Ct, dismissing an appeal from a decision of the hearing officer (BL O/384/09), the court held that an earlier authorisation of a product (melatonin) as a veterinary medicinal product prevented the grant of an SPC based on a later authorisation for the same product as a human medicinal product, under art.3d. Although Arnold J. took the view that the interpretation of art.3d was 'acte claire', on further appeal [2011] EWCA Civ 228, the CA referred the following questions to the CJEU, C-130/11:

1. In interpreting art.3 when a marketing authorisation (A) has been granted for a medicinal product comprising an active ingredient, is art.3d to be construed as precluding the grant of an SPC based on a later marketing authorisation (B) which is for a different medicinal product comprising the same active ingredient where the limits of the protection conferred by the basic patent do not extend to placing the product the subject of the earlier MA on the market within the meaning of art.4?

2. If the grant of the SPC is not precluded, does it follow that in interpreting art.13(1) "the first authorisation to place the product on the market in the Community" needs to be an authorisation to place a medicinal product on the market within the limits of the protection conferred by the basic patent within the meaning of art.4?

3. Are the answers to the above questions different if the earlier marketing authorisation has been granted for a veterinary medicinal product for a particular indication and the later marketing authorisation has been granted for a medicinal product for human use for a different indication?

4. Are the answers to the above questions different if the later marketing authorisation required a full application for marketing approval in accordance with Article 8 (3) of Directive 2001/83/EC?

5. Are the answers to the above questions different if the product covered by authorisation (A) to place the corresponding medicinal product on the market is within the scope of protection of a different patent which belongs to a different registered proprietor from the SPC applicant?

Definition of "basic patent" upon which a supplementary protection certificate can be granted

The SPC is granted under a "basic patent", which term is defined (Regs, art.1, §128B.11 **128B.67** and §128B.35) as a patent designated by its proprietor for the purpose of the SPC. Such patent may be one granted under the 1977 Act or by virtue of s.77(1) of the 1977 Act) a European patent (UK). However, the designated patent must be one which protects, inter alia: the "product" (as defined by the United Kingdom marketing authorisation); or a "preparation" in the case of a plant protection product; a process to obtain such a product; or a patent which protects an application for such product. Thus, *Centocor's SPC Application* [1996] R.P.C. 118 was refused because the product licence had been granted for a single active ingredient and the patent upon which the SPC was sought had claims only to a combination of this with another active ingredient. Also, the UK-IPO questionably takes the view that a patent for a process can only give rise to a SPC if that process leads to a new product, see MOPP para.SPM1.05.

According to art.3(2) of the Plant Protection Regulations (§128B.37), only one SPC can be granted to any one holder for each such "product" (or a preparation of it in the case of a plant protection product), or for the production or any application of any such product, although it is possible for two holders each to have an SPC for the same product, see §B09. However, as a patent can cover more than one authorised product, separate SPCs can be granted for each such product under a single patent. This is because art.3(c) and (1)(c) of the respective Regulations state that "*the product* has not already been the subject of a certificate" (emphasis added) and so the same patent may be used as the basis for multiple certificates for different products. Thus, in *Biogen v SmithKline Biologicals* (C-181/95) [1997] R.P.C. 833; [1997] R.P.C. 23; [1997] 1 E.C.R. 386, where the European Court stated that "under Article 3(c) of the [medicinal product] Regulation, only one certificate may be granted for each basic patent", it is submitted that this statement was made per incuriam.

In *Takeda Chemical Industries Ltd's SPC Applications (No.2)* [2004] R.P.C. 2, the hearing officer considered what the ECJ had meant in its judgment in *Biogen* and concluded that this statement could not be taken at face value. Rather, the Court had intended that if a patent holder has more than one patent for the same product, he should not be able to obtain more than one certificate for that product. He also concluded that when deciding whether the present requests were allowable, he should consider not only the explicit condition of art.3(c) but also the additional, implicit condition which emerges from a consideration of the principles underlying Regulation (EEC) No.1768/92 and which is made explicit by art.3(2) of Regulation 1610/96. These two conditions were:

1. a certificate shall not be granted for a product if at the date of application for the certificate, the product has already been the subject of a certificate; and

2. the holder of more than one patent for the same product shall not be granted more than one certificate for that product.

Applying these conditions to the six requests the hearing officer decided that only one certificate for each of the three different products could have been granted if all six requests had not already been rejected in the earlier decision.

It is to be noted that the patentee need not necessarily designate the earliest of a group of patents which protect the "product" in issue, but can choose to designate, as "the basic patent", that patent which it considers to be the most protective of its market, with an important factor being the relative dates of expiry of the possible patents which could be the subject of the single permitted SPC for any particular product.

Obviously, difficulties will arise in the case of products marketed under licence from the patentee, because only the registered proprietor of the basic patent can be granted an SPC upon it (Regs, art.6, §§128B.16 and 128B.40), but the licensee cannot frustrate an SPC application made by the patentee, see *Biogen v SmithKline Biologicals* (C-181/95) (above).

Yeda Research and Development Co Ltd (formerly Imclone Systems Inc Ltd & Aventis Holdings Inc) v Comptroller General of Patents [2010] EWHC 1733 Pat Ct, was an appeal from a decision of the hearing officer (BL O/066/10) rejecting two SPC applications identifying the same marketing authorisation and basic patent. The patent claimed the combination of a monoclonal antibody (cetuximab) and an anti-neoplastic agent (irinotecan). The marketing authorisation was for cetuximab. Dismissing the appeal in relation to the first SPC application, which identified the product as "cetuximab in combination with irinotecan", the court agreed with the hearing officer that the marketing authorisation was for cetuximab alone and so failed to comply with art.3b. The court held that although cetuximab was authorised for use with irinotecan and the patent claimed the combination when administered separately, the use of a product was not part of the definition of the product itself. The second SPC application identified the product as "cetuximab", the applicant arguing that protection of the product under art.3a arose by virtue of the supply of cetuximab for use in conjunction with irinotecan. This putting the invention into effect was, it was argued, a secondary infringement under s.60(2). Dismissing that appeal, the court found that cetuximab (as opposed to the combination of cetuximab and irinotecan) was not protected by the patent and so failed to comply with art.3a. However, leave to appeal was given in relation to this second SPC application, and the Court of Appeal referred the matter to the ECJ, C-518/10, asking if the criteria for deciding whether a product is "protected by a basic patent in force" under art.3a include or consist of an assessment of whether the supply of the product would infringe the basic patent, does it make any difference to the analysis if infringement is by way of indirect or contributory infringement based on s.60(2)?

Subject-matter of protection

128B.68 An SPC protects only the product covered by the marketing authorisation. Although the third paragraph of the ninth recital to the Regulation states that the protection granted should be "strictly confined" to the product which obtained authorisation to be placed on the market, Recital (13) of Regulation 1610/96, which according to Recital (17) of that Regulation can be used to interpret both the ninth Recital and art.4, states that the certificate confers the same rights as those conferred on the basic patent; consequently, it continues, where the basic patent covers an active substance and also its various derivatives (salts and esters), the certificate confers the same protection. This is consistent with the European Court's comments in *Farmitalia Carlo Erba* (C-392/97) [2000] R.P.C. 580; [1999] E.C.R. I–5553; [2000] 2 C.M.L.R. 253 where an active ingredient in the form of a salt is referred to in the marketing authorisation and the salt is protected by a basic patent in force, the certificate is capable of covering the active ingredient as such and also its various derived forms such as salts and esters, as medicinal products, insofar as they are covered by the protection of the basic patent.

In *Generics v Daiichi* (see above), the claimant accepted that the SPC to the (-) enantiomer did not give protection against the sale of the racemate, even though the racemate could be considered to be a combination of the (-) enantiomer and the (-) enantiomer. This is consistent with the requirement of art.4 that the protection conferred by a certificate extends only to the product covered by the authorisation to place the corresponding product on the market as a medicinal/plant protection product.

As the European Court noted in *Pharmacia Italia v Deutsches Patentamt* (C-31/03) [2005] R.P.C. 27, the protection conferred by the certificate relates to any use of the product as a medicinal product without any distinction between use of the product as a medicinal product for human use and as a veterinary medicinal product. Thus a product first authorised as a veterinary medicinal product could not be granted an SPC following its authorisation as a human medicinal product. On the other hand, medicinal products are frequently authorised for further uses before the expiry of the certificate. For example the SPC for a product first authorised for the treatment of stress incontinence in women, and then later, for the treatment of severe depression, will cover both uses, provided that the relevant basic patent protects both uses.

Infringement actions relating to SPCs have until recently been very rare. However, there have been two rounds of litigation across Europe in relation to SPCs for a monoproduct [A] and whether sale of a medicinal product having [A] in combination with [B] constituted an infringement. A first round of cases resulted in conflicting decisions being given by the Tribunal de Grande Instance de Paris, France ("TGI") and Court of Appeal of Brussels, Belgium in February 2010. The claimant was the holder in France and Belgium of an SPC to the product, losartan, whose duration had been extended six months following the completion of paediatric studies. A further SPC to the product, losartan in combination with hydrochlorothiazide expired two weeks before the losartan SPC. The defendant sought to put a combination product on the market in both France and Belgium after the expiry of the combination SPC but before the expiry of the losartan SPC. The claimant argued that sale of the combination product, which included losartan, was an infringement of its losartan SPC. In interim proceedings, *DuPont de Nemours et al v Mylan, R.K.* 14/2010, the Belgian Commercial Court found that the two products were separate products and the subject of different marketing authorisations, which had given rise to SPCs for losartan alone and losartan in combination with hydrochlorothiazide. A literal interpretation of art.4, read in the light of art.1b); could only conclude that the scope of the losartan SPC did not extend to losartan in combination with hydrochlorothiazide. This decision was upheld on appeal by the Brussels Court of Appeal, 8th Chamber, AR 2010/KR/53. In contrast, in interim proceedings involving the same parties, RG 10/51453, the French TGI de Paris enjoined the defendant from putting the combination product on the market until the SPC for losartan expired.

The second round of cases involved the valsartan SPC and the medicinal product, valsartan in combination with hydrochlorothiazide. In interim proceedings, *Novartis AG v Actavis Deutschland GmbH & Co. KG*, 4b O 280/10, March 8, 2011, the *Landgericht* (District Court) Düsseldorf held that sale of the combination medicinal product was an infringement of the SPC to the monoproduct. The court observed that the function of art.4 is to define the subject-matter of protection and in this context identified three criteria. First, it declared that the absolute limit of protection is defined by the scope of protection of the basic patent. Second, the product is identified in order to delimit the protected active ingredient from other compounds which may be a further subject-matter of protection of the basic patent. Finally, art.4 provides for a purpose bound compound protection by limiting the subject-matter of protection to authorised uses. Article 4 accordingly leads to a hypothetical patent claim which is related to the product and the purpose. Article 5 then requires that subject to these limitations, the SPC confers the same rights as conferred by the basic patent. So sale of the medicinal product containing [A] in combination with [B] is an infringement of the [A] SPC.

In the related case, *Novartis AG v Actavis UK Ltd*, in the Patents Court, Floyd J. referred the following questions to the CJEU, as C-442/11:

> "Where a supplementary protection certificate has been granted for a product as defined by the Regulation for an active ingredient, are the rights conferred by that certificate pursuant to art.5 in respect of the subject matter as defined in art.4:
>
> i. by a medicinal product that contains that active ingredient (in this case valsartan) in combination with one or more other active ingredients (in this case hydrochlorothiazide); or
>
> ii. only by a medicinal product that contains that active ingredient (in this case valsartan) as the sole active ingredient?"

Entitlement to the certificate

128B.69   The holder of the basic patent and the holder of the marketing authorisation that initiates the application procedure for a certificate are frequently not the same. The holder of the marketing authorisation may be, for example, a European subsidiary of the American company which holds the patent. Alternatively, the marketing authorisation holder may be a licensee of the patent holder. In principle, it would seem that anyone may apply for a certificate, although ultimately the certificate shall be granted to the holder of the basic patent or his successor in title. Whilst the applicant may be required by the UK-IPO to justify that the basic patent protects the product, it appears that the UK-IPO does not require that the applicant demonstrates a contractual or any other relationship with holder of the marketing authorisation.

Where the holder of the marketing authorisation is not the patentee and does not wish to collaborate with the patentee in providing a copy of the marketing authorisation which is required to be filed (by the patentee) to support an application for an SPC. This was the background to *Biogen v SmithKline Biologicals* (C-181/95) [1997] R.P.C. 833; [1997] 1 E.C.R. 386; [1997] 1 C.M.L.R. 704 where the product in issue was marketed under patent licences from two separate licensors and the holder of the marketing authorisation contended that it was entitled to choose which, if either, patentee should have the benefit of an SPC and hence the receipt of continuing royalty payments. The ECJ was asked to rule whether the holder of a marketing authorisation is legally obliged to provide a copy of the authorisation to the patentee who has a patent covering the product in order that thereby an SPC can be obtained and the ruling was that the provision of a copy of the marketing authorisation is not a prerequisite to a successful application so long as the patentee can adduce extrinsic evidence of its existence. However, as indicated above, in such circumstances separate SPCs will be granted to both patentees, see also §128B.67.

Deadline for filing the application for a certificate

128B.70   Usually the patent will be granted before grant of the marketing authorisation, in which case the application for the certificate must be filed within six months of the date of grant of the marketing authorisation. However, where the marketing authorisation is granted before the patent, the application for the certificate must be filed within six months of patent grant. Where the basic patent is a European patent validated in the UK which has been opposed, the patent may still be designated under the SPC Regulation, although if the patent is revoked, then any certificate granted to the patent will also be treated as being revoked.

Care needs to be taken with establishing the date of grant of the marketing authorisation, used to calculate the six-month period for lodging an application. For a marketing authorisation for a medicinal product granted under the centralised procedure according to Regulation 726/2004, the date of grant of the marketing authorisation is generally taken to be the date of the Commission decision to approve the medicinal product in accordance with Directive 2001/83 or Directive 2001/82, as appropriate. This date appears on the front page of the Commission decision. The situation may not be so clear with national authorisations, where some national regulatory authorities do not refer to the date of grant of the marketing authorisation, but merely inform the applicant for the authorisation, in a letter, that the medicinal product has been authorised. The usual practice is to take the date of the grant of the authorisation in such circumstances to be the date of the letter. The UK-IPO in *Abbott Laboratories' SPC Application* [2004] R.P.C. 20 at 391 took the view that the relevant date is the actual date of grant of the of the authorisation, but other patent offices, e.g. the Italian, have taken the view that the date is the date of publication in the relevant Official Gazette. In *Health Research Inc* (C-452/07), the German Supreme Court has referred the question of whether the "date on which the authorisation referred to in Article 3(b) to place the product on the market as a medicinal product was granted", referred to in art.7(1) is determined according to Community law or whether it refers to the date on which authorisation takes effect under national law to the ECJ for a preliminary ruling. If the date is determined by Community law, the ECJ has also been asked to rule on which date must be taken into account for that purpose; however, it appears that this reference was withdrawn in September 2008.

There have been occasions when the applicant has missed the six-month deadline for filing the SPC the application. Article 19 of the Medicinal Product Regulation and art.18 of the Plant Protection Regulation each provides that in the absence of procedural provisions in the Regulation, the procedural provisions under national law to the corresponding basic patent shall apply to the certificate, unless that law lays down special procedural provisions for certificates. In *Abbott* the period for applying for an SPC in the UK was extended by six days, the application having been late filed because of genuine misunderstandings (occasioned by a transfer of rights) and prompt action having been taken once the position had been revealed. It was therefore decided that the relevant period (which was held to run from the actual date of grant of the marketing authorisation, and not from the (later) date of publication of the authorisation in the London Gazette) could be extended at the Comptroller's discretion under r.110(1) of the Patents Rules 1995, now r.108(1) of the Patents Rules 2007.

Application for, and grant of, a supplementary protection certificate in the United Kingdom

Application for an SPC in the United Kingdom is made to the UK-IPO (Regs art.9, §§128B.19 and 128B.43). The procedure is governed by r.116. It requires the filing of PF SP1 (see r.116(1)) and a fee (£250 at the time of printing), see SPC Rules Sch.4. The application is given a number in the form "SPC/GB93/001". Notice of the application is published in the *Patents Journal* (2007 Rules r.44(7)). This notice includes: the name and address of the applicant; the number of the basic patent; the title of the invention; the number and date of the UK marketing authorisation upon which the SPC is requested; and, if different, the number and date of the first marketing authorisation for the product within the EEA (Regs art.9(2)). **128B.71**

The application is then subjected to examination in a manner similar to the examination of patent applications, although there is no overall time limit by which that examination must be concluded. Reasonable individual periods for response to each letter outlining an objection to the SPC grant will be set and the Comptroller will not reject an application without having given the applicant an opportunity of being heard, as s.101 of the 1977 Act applies. Any such rejection may be made the subject of an appeal under s.97 of the 1977 Act initially to the Patents Court and thereafter, with leave, to the Court of Appeal and possibly the House of Lords (Medicinal Product Reg art.18, Plant Protection Reg art.17, §§128B.28 and 128B.51). There is also the possibility of reference to the ECJ for an interpretation of the Regulation under what is now art.234 EC and this has happened, see for example, §128B.63. The rejection of an application has to be advertised in the Patents Journal (2007 Rules r.44(7), implementing Regs, art.11(2)). As art.3(c) and (1)(c) of the Regulations stipulate only that an application must be one where "the product has not already been the subject of a certificate", refusal of an SPC application does not preclude a later application (*British Technology's SPC Application* [1997] R.P.C. 118).

If the requirements of the appropriate Regulation appear to be met, the Comptroller must grant the certificate (Regs, art.10(1)). Grant of the SPC is then made and the certificate indicates the date of expiry of its maximum period and that its entry is subject to the payment of the prescribed fees, for which see §128B.78. Under the 1997 SPC Rules, the form of a certificate was set out in Sch.3 to those rules, but no such provisions are included in the 2007 Rules. However, essentially the same format is used as before, which identified the SPC number, the grantee, the product, the basic patent number and its title, as well as the date on which the certificate will take effect (subject to the payment of fees) and the maximum expiry date of the SPC. Notice of the grant is published in the *Patents Journal* (r.44(7), implementing Regs, art.11), and the published information reflects that published for the application (for which see above), together with the duration of the SPC (Regs, arts.11(1)). An entry is also made in the register of patents, but in the case of SPCs granted on "existing patents" that register is maintained manually and for information on this a special application has to be made, see §118.18, There is no publication of an SPC as such, nor of an application for one (see MOPP paras SPM9.02 and SPM11.03). The granted SPC retains the same number as its application, for which see above (and see MOPP para.SPM10.15). Opposition to the grant of an SPC is precluded (Regs, art.18(2)), but third parties may submit observations under s.21, for which see §§21.06 and 128B.03.

The *Patents Journal* also gives notice when an SPC comes into force.

In practice it is not easy for industrial property offices to verify whether or not the authorisation referred to in the application is the first authorisation to place the product on the market as a medicinal product. In Case COMP/A. 37.507/F3 *AstraZeneca*, the European Commission fined AstraZeneca €60 million relating to abuse of art.82 of the EC Treaty (now art.102 TFEU), a key aspect of which was the finding that in applying for SPCs, AstraZeneca made misleading representations to patent offices, including the UK-IPO, about the dates of marketing authorisations which the national industrial property offices concerned were under no obligation to verify. In *AstraZeneca v the Commission* (T–321/05), the General Court confirmed the majority of the findings of the European Commission that AstraZeneca's practices in relation to SPC filings were an abuse of art.82 of the EC Treaty (now art.102 TFEU), but reduced the fine to take account of a different date for the start of the abuse.

The documentary requirements for an application for an extension of the duration of a certificate already granted have been clarified in *El du Pont Nemours & Co v UK Intellectual Property Office* [2009] EWCA Civ 966; [2010] R.P.C. 6, allowing an appeal against a decision of the Patents Court [2009] EWHC 1112 (Ch); [2010] R.P.C. 5, which in turn was an appeal from a decision of the hearing officer in BL O/096/09; [2010] R.P.C. 4. The hearing officer held that any deficiency in the documentary requirements for making the extension application could not be rectified afterwards. However, construing art.10(3) (which requires that the patent office asks the applicant to rectify any irregularity in art.8 broadly), Jacob L.J. held that the Comptroller should take into account all relevant factors, including the reason for the failure to include all the art.8(1) materials in the application, the extent to which the applicant was guilty of unreasonable conduct or delay, and how close to the date of the expiry of the SPC full compliance was expected. Unless the applicant had behaved unreasonably, time should be extended so that it got its reward.

Fees and the time for their payment

128B.72   The Regulations provide for the possibility of both application and annual fees (Regs, arts 8(2) and 12), and the United Kingdom has exercised both these options, (Sch.4A para.5 and r.116(5)), although the "annual fees" must be paid cumulatively in a single payment. Thus, besides a fee payable with the application (Fee Rules [2007], Sch.1), the SPC becomes effective only when the "prescribed fee" have been paid in accordance with r.116(5).

The "prescribed fee" is payable before the start date of the certificate, this being the date when the SPC would take effect at the end of the lawful term of the basic patent, and thus not later than the 20th anniversary of its filing date, but the fees cannot be paid more than three months before that date (r.116(2)(a)). Where the certificate is granted after the expiry of the basic patent, the period for payment expires three months after the grant of the certificate (r.116(2)(b)). If not paid by the due date, the appropriate fees can be paid within the following six months on payment also of an additional fee (Sch.4A para.5).

In BL0/252/11, *Tulane's SPC application*, the proprietor failed to pay the prescribed fee for bringing a SPC into effect within the prescribed period or within the period of six months following the end of the prescribed period and requested restoration under s.28. The proprietor argued s.28 applied to SPCs, as art.12 referred to annual fees for the maintenance of the SPC. Rejecting the request, the hearing officer found the fee was not an annual or renewal fee and so s.28 could not apply, and in any event s.28 was not one of the sections listed in point 1(2) of Sch.4A as applying to SPCs. The decision has been appealed.

The "prescribed fee" is determined by the maximum possible duration of the certificate. At the time of writing, when the certificate expires during the period of one year beginning with the start date, the fee is £600. Thereafter, the "prescribed fee" increase steeply for each additional year, with the prescribed fee for a certificate expiring during the fourth anniversary of the start date being £4,000. Unlike patent renewal fees, which are payable annually, a single payment has to be made which is the cumulative total for the maximum period for the duration of the SPC. There is no express provision for permitting the holder of the certificate to maintain the certificate for some lesser period, however, if a fee for a lesser period than the maximum is paid, the SPC may not subsequently be extended (r.116(5)).

Rule 116(5) provides for the Comptroller to send a reminder, not later than six weeks from the start date, notifying the certificate holder of that date and indicating the fees payable in respect of each of the effective years which make up the maximum period of the certificate, and indicating the latest date by which the fees must be paid for the SPC to take effect. Payment is then made with PF SP2.

The notices under r.116(5) of the 2007 Rules are sent to the UK address for service notified by the SPC applicant and, if different, to the address in the United Kingdom which is the last address specified by the proprietor of the basic patent on payment of the final renewal fee (or any address subsequently replacing this); or, in the absence of any such address, to the address (if any) entered in the register of patents for the basic patent under r.10 of the 2007 Rules (r.116).

If the fees are not paid within even the extended six-month period, the SPC is regarded as having lapsed on the expiry of the basic patent, i.e. the SPC never came into effect, and the certificate holder is notified of this by the UK-IPO (see MOPP para.SPM12.14).

If the SPC is surrendered, or declared invalid (for which see §§128B.27 and 128B.74), after the appropriate fees have been paid, the Comptroller is required to remit the fees paid for any whole effective year following the date when the SPC ceased to have effect (SPC r.6), see MOPP para.SPM14.10. There is no special procedure for requesting such fee remission. However, unless the certificate is surrendered, remission will not be made when the certificate lapses because of withdrawal of the underlying marketing authorisation. This is because that withdrawal may subsequently be rescinded, or a new authorisation granted, whereupon the SPC would automatically again have effect unless surrendered, see §128B.74 and MOPP para.SPM14.11.

Duration of the certificate and meaning of "Community"

128B.73

While an application for an SPC must be filed before patent expiry, it does not take effect until the expiry of the lawful term of "the basic patent". Thus, since the basic patent expires the day before the 20th anniversary of its filing date, the SPC in the United Kingdom will take effect from the 20th anniversary. Thereafter, provided the necessary fee has been paid, the SPC has a duration of a period not exceeding five years which is a period "equal to the period which elapsed between the date on which the application for the basic patent was lodged and the date of the first authorisation to place the product on the market in the Community, reduced by a period of five years" (Regs, art.13, §§128B.23 and 128B.47).

Such an authorisation is deemed to be that provided for any purpose under the product licence regulations. Thus, where there had been a prior authorisation of a veterinary formulation, in a UK application, the hearing officer held that the SPC was to have effect from that date and not from the much later date when the active ingredient was first approved for human use (*Farmitalia Carlo Erba's SPC Application* [1996] R.P.C. 111). This practice of the UK-IPO has subsequently been confirmed by the European Court in *Pharmacia Italia SpA* (C-31/03) [2004] E.C.R. I–10001, where the ECJ ruled that the authorisation of a veterinary product was the first authorisation in the Community for an SPC application for a human medicinal product, therefore precluding the grant of a certificate for the human medicinal product.

Where the term of the basic patent is 20 years, the maximum duration of an SPC will be 15 years from the date of the first marketing authorisation in the Community or five years from the date of normal patent expiry, whichever is the shorter. The patent must have run its full term for the SPC to take effect, so must not have been revoked or lapsed prior to normal patent expiry. The duration of the SPC will be less than the period under art.13 if the holder of the certificate fails to pay all the required annuity fees, either deliberately or inadvertently.

In the context of art.13 of the two Regulations, the word "Community" has been effectively replaced by "the EEA" (for the Medicinal Products Regulation as from July 1, 1994, see Patents Journal November 30, 1994, although for Liechtenstein only from January 1, 1995 when that country joined the EEA; and for the Plant Protection Products Regulation from August 1, 1997 for Liechtenstein, and from January 2, 1998 for Iceland and Norway). Thus, since July 1, 1994 (or January 1, 1995 for Liechtenstein), the first marketing authorisation (for a medicinal product) within the EEA (that is within the European Community as it then was, together with Austria, Finland, Iceland, Norway and Sweden) has been the controlling date for the duration of a medicinal product SPC, see note on PF SP1; and, since August 1, 1997 (or January 2, 1998 as regards Iceland and Norway), the first marketing authorisation for a plant product SPC within the present EEA (that is within the present European Community, together with Iceland, Liechtenstein and Norway) has been that controlling date, as indicated in §128B.64. Since Liechtenstein is a member of the EEA, and since marketing authorisations granted in Switzerland until June 1, 2005 automatically extended to Liechtenstein, Switzerland was also considered to be a country to be taken into account in determining the country for which the "first marketing authorisation" was issued: *Patents Journal* January 3, 1996. The effect of a Swiss marketing authorisation, granted before the June 1, 2005, on the duration of an SPC under the Regulation was addressed by the European Court in *Novartis AG, University College London, Institute of Microbiology and Epidemiology v Comptroller-General of Patents, Designs and Trade Marks for the United Kingdom* and *Ministre de l'Economie v Millennium Pharmaceuticals Inc* (C-207/03 and C-252/03) [2005] E.C.R. I–3209 ECJ, April 21, 2005, where the Court ruled that as Swiss marketing authorisation was automatically recognised by Liechtenstein, it constituted the first authorisation in the Community. In coming to this conclusion, the Court noted that if Swiss marketing authorisations were precluded from constituting a first marketing authorisation for the purposes of art.13, the duration of SPCs would have to be calculated by reference to a marketing authorisation issued subsequently in the EEA. In *Millennium*, the Swiss authorisation for the relevant medicinal product was granted two years before the Community authorisation under the centralised procedure. From June 1, 2005, the Swiss–Liechtenstein union was modified so that Swiss marketing authorisations no longer automatically extend to Liechtenstein, but instead are be subject to a minimum of a year's delay before taking effect, see press release, "*Secretariat d'Etat à l'Economie SECO, Confederation Suisse*", April 21, 2005, *http://www.seco.admin.ch*.

As a consequence of the EEA Agreement, an authorisation to place a product on the market granted in accordance with national legislation of an EFTA State may be treated as an authorisation granted in accordance with EU legislation (e.g Directive 65/65 and its successors). Thus, where the first authorisation in the Community (e.g. in Portugal, Spain or Greece) was not in accordance with Directive 65/65, because at the time of granting the authorisation the Member State in question had not yet implemented the Directive, the marketing authorisation is still treated as the first authorisation in the Community. In the UK, Netherlands, Italy and Sweden, SPCs were granted for aceclofenac, expiring in March 2005, based on a Portuguese marketing authorisation granted in March 1990, even though the first authorisation in the Community in accordance with Directive 65/65 was not granted (in the UK) until April 1995. In Germany, in 14 W (pat) 42/04 *Aceclofenac*, July 18, 2006, the Federal Patent Court took a different view, basing the duration of the SPC on the UK marketing authorisation, relying on the reasoning set out in *Hässle AB and Ratiopharm GmbH* (C-127/00) [2003] E.C.R. I–14781 ECJ. However, in a later nullity action in Belgium, the court of first instance in *NV Merck v Almirall Prodesfarma*, Docket Nr 06/10.756/A, Register Nr. 07/26125, June 15, 2007 found that the duration of the aceclofenac SPC should be determined by the Portuguese marketing authorisation and allowed correction of the SPC to change the date of expiry from March 2009 to March 2005, relying in part in the reasoning set out by the Advocate General in *Novartis*.

The question of whether an earlier marketing authorisation not in accordance with EU legislation can determine the duration of an SPC was referred to the ECJ in two separate and unrelated proceedings, *Synthon v Merz Pharma* [2009] EWHC 656 Pat Ct and *Generics v Synaptech* [2009] EWCA Civ 1119 (on appeal from [2009] EWHC 659 (Ch)), as C-195/09 and C-427/09 respectively. In *Synthon*, the active ingredient memantine was placed on the German market before 1976, under legislation which predated Directive 65/65/EEC (the precursor of Directive 2001/83/EC). In 1983, a marketing authorisation was granted in Luxembourg, but this relied on the German authorisation, and no safety or efficacy studies were carried out. Both these marketing authorisations concerned memantine in the treatment of Parkinson's disease. However, in 2002, following safety and efficacy studies a community authorisation (under Regulation 2309/93) was granted for the use of memantine as a medicinal product in the treatment of Alzheimer's disease, and the earlier authorisations withdrawn. In the UK, an SPC was granted, identifying a basic patent which related to use of memantine in the treatment of Alzheimer's disease and citing the 2002 marketing authorisation as the first authorisation in the community, for the purpose of determining the duration of the SPC under art.3. Four questions were referred to the ECJ following an action to invalidate the SPC or to fix its term at zero:

1. For the purposes of art. 13 and 19 of [Reg. 1768/92], is an authorisation a "first authorisation to place . . . on the market in the Community" if it is granted in pursuance of a national law which is compliant with [Directive 65/65], or is it necessary that it be established in addition that, in granting the authorisation in question, the national authority followed an assessment of data as required by the administrative procedure laid down in that directive?

2. For the purposes of art.13 and 19 of [Regulation No 1768/92], does the expression "first authorisation to place . . . on the market in the Community" include authorisations which had been permitted by national law to co-exist with an authorisation regime which complies with [Directive 65/65]?

3. Is a product which is authorised to be placed on the market for the first time in the EEC without going through the administrative procedure laid down in [Directive 65/65] within the scope of [Reg. 1768/92] as defined by art. 2?

4. If not, is an SPC granted in respect of such a product invalid?'

Dealing with the third question first, the Court took the view that it would be contrary to the objective of offsetting the time taken to obtain a marketing authorisation—which requires long and demanding testing of the safety and efficacy of the medicinal product concerned—if an SPC, which amounts to an extension of exclusivity, could be granted for a product which has already been sold on the Community market as a medicinal product before being subject to an administrative authorisation procedure as laid down in Directive 65/65, including safety and efficacy testing and so ruled that the answer to that question was no. In answering the fourth question, the Court, following the reasoning in *Hässle*, held that because of the connection between art.19 and art.3, the SPC was invalid, irrespective of whether or not art. 15.1 was an exhaustive list of the grounds of validity of an SPC. In view of the answers to the third and the fourth questions, the first and second questions were not answered. In *Generics v Synaptech*, which concerned an active ingredient, galantamine, which had been on sale as a medicinal product in various European countries for over 40 years, the Court came to essentially similar conclusion.

Where the certificate is granted with an incorrect duration because the first marketing authorisation within the Community (EEA or Switzerland) set out in the SPC application was incorrect, an appeal is now possible, see art.17(2) of the Plant Protection Regulation probably applicable also to medicinal product SPCs, see §128B.63 and MOPP para.SPM17.02. In *Novartis*, the European Court was asked whether the authorities of the EEA Member States were obliged to rectify certificates, the duration of which had been erroneously calculated. As a result of finding that the duration had been correctly calculated, the court did not address this question. However, in his opinion in the case,

Advocate General Ruiz-Jarabo Colomer expressed the view that national authorities are obliged to rectify the dates used to determine the duration of the certificate if, when they were set, a mistake had been made. In the absence of Community legislation, he continued, it is for the domestic legal systems of the Member States to make provision about the detailed procedural rules for obtaining rectification. In general, UK practice before the *Novartis* referral was to take account of an earlier Swiss authorisation in determining the duration of an SPC, and whilst the reference was pending before the European Court, all pending UK SPC applications whose duration would have been effected by a change in practice were stayed, so no rectification of the duration of SPCs was necessary.

Until the coming into force the amendment of the Medicinal Product Regulation by the Paediatric Regulation (EC) 1901/2006, which is now incorporated into Reg.469/2009, the maximum combined effective protection of patent and an SPC was 15 years. Accordingly, where the first marketing authorisation in the Community was granted less than five years after the filing date of the basic patent, an SPC would have no duration and was not granted. Following the coming into force of the Paediatric Regulation, which permits the term of an SPC to be extended by six months where an application for a marketing authorisation includes the results of all studies conducted in accordance with an agreed paediatric investigation plan as set out in art.36 of that Regulation, the UK-IPO in *Merck and Co Inc's SPC Application* BL O/108/08 has granted a negative term SPC, which will only take effect if an application for a paediatric authorisation is made and an extension to the SPC is applied for.

Practice has developed unevenly in the Community in relation to the grant of "negative term" SPCs under the Medicinal Products Regulation, with the Netherlands and Bulgaria following the UK practice. However, the German and Estonian patent offices have rejected SPC applications in which the term of the SPC would be negative. Following an appeal to the German Patent Court, 15W (pat) 36/08, the case parallel to that decided in *Merck and Co Inc's SPC Application*, BL O/108/08, has been referred to the ECJ as *Merck and Co Inc v Deutsches Patent- und Markenamt* (C-125/10). The opinion of AG Bot, delivered on June 9, 2011 is that an SPC can be granted if the period between the date on which the application for the basic patent was lodged and the date of the first MA for the product in the Community is less than five years, in which case the six-month term provided for in art.13(3) starts from the date determined by subtracting from the date of the expiry of the patent the difference between five years and the period which has elapsed between the filing of the patent application and the grant of the first MA.

Lapse or invalidity of the supplementary protection certificate

128B.74   While an SPC (which has come into effect by the due payment of the appropriate fees, for which see §128B.72) will normally lapse at the end of the period for which it was granted, it can lapse prematurely if the SPC is surrendered by its holder (using s.29 of the 1977 Act) or if the product has been ordered to be withdrawn from the market (Regs, art.14, §§128B.24 and 128B.48).

Although a third party cannot oppose the grant of an SPC as such (Regs, art.18(2)), any person can seek a declaration, either from the Comptroller or the court (2007 Rules Pt 7), that the certificate is invalid on a ground that:

(a) it was granted contrary to the provisions of art.3 of the Community Regulations (for which see §128B.65);

(b) the basic patent had lapsed before its lawful term expired; or

(c) the basic patent is revoked or limited to the extent that the product for which the SPC was granted is no longer protected by its claims; or, after the basic patent expired, grounds for revocation exist which would have justified such revocation or limitation. (Regs, art.15(1))

Although this is on its face an exhaustive list, in *Hässle AB and Ratiopharm GmbH* (C-127/00) [2003] E.C.R. I-14781 ECJ, the European Court ruled that a certificate that has been delivered contrary to the requirements of the transitional provisions of art.19 is invalid pursuant to art.15 and remarked that this must be so even it is not possible to infer from the wording or origin of art.15(1) that the list of grounds of invalidity of a certificate set out there is not exhaustive.

An application may also be made by any person for a decision that the SPC has lapsed on the grounds that the authorisation referred to in art.14(d) of the Regulations has been withdrawn so that the product may no longer be lawfully marketed. Such an application may be made only to the Comptroller, as the SPC grant authority (2007 Rules Pt 7).

For proceedings to seek from the Comptroller a decision of lapsing or a declaration of invalidity, an application is made on PF SP3. The fee payable with this form is currently £50, and the form must be accompanied by a statement of case in duplicate. For the subsequent procedure, see §128B.79. Any decision of the Comptroller under these provisions must be published in the *Patents Journal* (Regs, art.16, §§128B.27 and 128B.50); and is recorded in the register of patents (MOPP paras SPM15.01 and SPM16.01). The Comptroller's decision is appealable in the normal manner (Regs, art.17, §§128B.28 and 128B.51), see §128B.71. Likewise, any decision of the court should also be appealable in the normal manner for appeals from a decision of the court in question.

A withdrawal of the underlying marketing authorisation only affects the SPC when the product is ordered to be withdrawn from the market. Often, a marketing authorisation is withdrawn and replaced by a modified one, perhaps in favour of a different entity, and such replacement has no effect upon the SPC. Also, an order for the product to be withdrawn from the market may be only a temporary one so that there is the possibility that the lapsing of the SPC under art.14(d) of the Regulations may also only have temporary effect. Provision for this is made by the opening words to this article: "If and as long as the product may no longer be placed on the market". Consequently, unless the SPC holder surrenders his certificate, for example to obtain a remission of fees (for which see §128B.72), grant of a subsequent marketing authorisation, or rescission of the withdrawal thereof, has the automatic effect of the SPC once more being in force. In such a circumstance, the SPC holder should advise the UK-IPO so that appropriate notice of termination of lapse can be published in the *Patents Journal* (MOPP para.SPM14.07). It is also possible for any person to apply to the Comptroller for a declaration that the ground of lapse under art.14(d) no longer exists. This procedure could be useful when the marketing authorisation is granted to a licensee under the basic patent who retains his licence under the SPC. No formal requirements govern such a procedure (MOPP para.SPM14.08).

If and when an SPC lapses, either at the end of the period for which the fees were paid, or because of loss of the UK marketing authorisation referred to in art.14(d) of the Regulations, or if the certificate is declared invalid, then the fact is published in the *Patents Journal* (SPC r.10(d) and (f), implementing Regs, art.16, §§128B.27 and 128B.50), and an entry is also made in the register of patents (MOPP para.SPM14.01).

In *Generics v Daiichi* (see above), the validity of the SPC for levofloxacin was challenged on the basis of art.15(a) and (c) it should not have been granted.

Effect of a supplementary protection certificate

CPR 49E PD 1 has been replaced by CPR 63.1–63.3 (reprinted in Appendix F). **128B.75**

The SPC is not itself a "patent", nor an extension of the basic patent as such. Nevertheless, the certificate has effect to extend (up to its expiry) the protection conferred by the basic patent on its proprietor for the further term of the SPC, though only in respect of the single "product" (or a preparation thereof in the case of a plant protection product, or of the production or application of any such product), for which the SPC was granted and for any use of the product as a medicinal or plant protection product that is authorised before and during the life of the SPC (Regs, arts 4 and 5, §§128B.14 and 128B.38 and 128B.15 and 128B.39), as discussed in §128B.66. Otherwise, the SPC confers the same rights as the basic patent and is subject to the same limitations and obligations, as discussed below.

The grant of an SPC is dependent upon the basic patent being in force at the date of expiry of its lawful term (Regs, art.15(1)(b) and (c)), and the due payment of the prescribed fees, for which see §128B.72. Thus, if the basic patent is revoked with the consequence that it is deemed never to have had existence, the SPC is itself invalid (cf. Regs, art.15(1)(c)). The position is likewise if the basic patent is amended so as to exclude the "product" for which the SPC is granted, because such amendment is deemed to have had effect from the grant of the patent (ss.27(3), 75(3), 76(6) of the 1977 Act). The SPC can also be declared invalid after the expiry of the basic patent where grounds for revocation exist which would have justified such revocation or amendment of the basic patent (cf. Regs, art.15(1)(c)).

However, while the SPC can extend to further authorisations given in respect of the same product after the initial UK marketing authorisation, e.g. to enable the product to be marketed for a further medical indication, there is no provision for updating the information supplied to the UK-IPO. Nevertheless, presumably, an SPC holder can notify the UK-IPO of such further authorisations so that the information is available to interested persons via inspection of the SPC file at the UK-IPO. The SPC will, in any event, be given in respect of "the product", as specified on the certificate, and in practice marketing of that product, as a "medicinal (or plant protection) product" will be possible only where there is a marketing authorisation for the product.

It appears that the monopoly protection granted by an SPC may be enforced by action for infringement as if the SPC were a patent, and that the effect of the SPC Regulations art.5 is that proceedings for infringement may be brought before any forum (before which proceedings for patent infringement may be brought, the term "court" having the same meaning as under the 1977 Act (Regs, art.2, §§128B.04 and 128B.36), and that such proceedings can lead to the same relief as is available against acts of patent infringement, i.e. as available under ss.61–68 of the 1977 Act. There should also be the possibility of action against unjustified threats of SPC infringement under the 1977 Act s.70, and for seeking a declaration of non-infringement under the 1977 Act s.71. However, a certificate of contested validity granted in respect of the "basic patent" may not have automatic effect as regards infringement of an SPC based on it, but an award of costs is always a question of judicial discretion so that it should not be assumed that costs on an indemnity basis will not be awarded in infringement proceedings on an SPC for which the basic patent had such a certificate.

Other consequences of the SPC Regulations art.5 and the effect of Sch.4A (see §128B.75) are, for example: that an SPC may be surrendered under art.14 of the Community Regulations in accordance with the provisions of s.29 of the 1977 Act, see §128B.75; that it may be assigned (under the 1977 Act s.30); that it is subject to employee-inventor compensation (s.40 of the 1977 Act); and that the provisions for Crown use and compensation apply (ss.55–59 of the 1977 Act). However, not only does an SPC confer upon its holder the same rights as it had under the basic patent, but that these rights are subject to the same limitations and obligations (Regs, art.5, §§128B.15 and 128B.39). While there may be a little doubt that this applies to limitations and obligations imposed by statute, the position is not so clear with regard to limitations and obligations which have their origin in inter partes contracts, such as those contained in an agreement which granted a licence under the "basic patent". This is because the term "patent" cannot, on the face of it, be read as including reference to an SPC, unless there is some indication in the contract which gives that effect.

However, it has been held that an SPC is subject to "licences of right" if the patent which is replaced was so subject (*Research Corp's SPC* [1994] R.P.C. 387 and [1994] R.P.C. 667 CA) and, by analogy, a licence agreement which grants a licence under a patent should be construed as extending to an SPC which becomes effective upon expiry of that patent, absent clear words in the contract to the contrary. If this were not so, then the licensee would become an infringer of the SPC upon expiry of the patent, and hence also expiry of his licence. A purposive construction of the terms of the contract would not lead to such an inequitable result. Indeed, on appeal in this case the Patents Court stated "A SPC gives no more nor less rights than those that existed under the basis patent". In the substantive decision settling the terms of the licence of right in this case (*Research Corp's SPC (No.2)* [1996] R.P.C. 320), the Comptroller followed this view by holding that, though the SPC was solely for the previously patented substance, importation of formulated compositions containing that product would fall under the protection of the SPC and should therefore be covered by the licence of right with royalties payable thereon.

Another consequence of the SPC being treated as if it were a patent, and an application for an SPC being treated as if it were an application, is that errors in the documents submitted are correctable under s.117. For an example of this, see *Patents Journal* March 8, 1995.

To give full effect to these provisions, general arrangements have been made to extend the law and practice of Great Britain and Northern Ireland to SPCs as if they were patents, see Sch.4A, §§128B.03–128B.09. Consequently, for proceedings in the UK-IPO involving SPCs or applications for them, the same Patents Forms are to be used, and the same fees (if any) are applicable, as if the proceedings involved a patent or application therefor, except where any of Forms SP1, SP2 or SP3 are required to be used (2007 Rules r.4). Also, CPR 63 (reprinted in Appendix F) embraces proceedings based on an SPC (see r.63.1(2)(e)). Consequently all proceedings in the High Court of England and Wales concerning such certificates must come before the Patents Court, as will appeals from the Comptroller relating to SPCs. Proceedings (other than appeals from the Comptroller) can also be brought before any other defined court, for which see §96.06.

Period within which application for a supplementary protection certificate in the United Kingdom must be filed

For products for which the first marketing authorisation within the Community was obtained after January 1, 1985, but before the entry into force of the Community Regulations on January 2, 1993 (for medicinal products) or February 8, 1997 (for plant protection products), an SPC could still be obtained in the United Kingdom, provided that the basic patent was extant on that date of entry into force of the appropriate Regulation and provided that any such application for a "transitional SPC" was submitted not later than six months thereafter (Regs, art.19(1) and (2)). However, the basic patent must still have been in force at the date of the application for the SPC (Regs, art.3(a) and (1)(a)), and here it must be borne in mind that a patent in the United Kingdom is treated as expiring at midnight on the day preceding the 20th anniversary of its filing date, see §25.08. Thus, these transitional provisions had an extremely limited life. **128B.76**

PRACTICE CONCERNING SUPPLEMENTARY PROTECTION CERTIFICATES

Procedure for obtaining a supplementary protection certificate

Application for an SPC is made on PF SP1 accompanied by the prescribed fee (currently £250, see the 2007 Fee Rules Sch.1). **128B.77**

There must be given: the name and address of the applicant, who need not be the registered proprietor of the basic patent or his successor in title, though the SPC must be granted to such person (Regs, art.6, §§128B.16 and 128B.40); the name of any agent appointed to act for the applicant in the matter; and a United Kingdom address for service for future communications.

Where the patentee is a foreign company, the marketing authority for the United Kingdom will normally have been granted to a licensee (perhaps an unregistered one in the case of a subsidiary of the foreign patentee). This raises no problems when the patentee (who would normally make the application, because the certificate has to be granted to him) and the licensee can readily collaborate. However, even though the licensee may not wish an SPC to be granted to the patentee the patentee may still apply for an SPC, see *Biogen v SmithKline Biologicals* (C-181/95) [1997] R.P.C. 833; [1997] 1 E.C.R. 386; [1997] 1 C.M.L.R. 704 ECJ, discussed in §128B.67.

The same PF SP1 is used for applications for a certificate under Reg.469/2009 (medicinal products) and Reg.1610/96 (plant protection products) and the applicant is required to indicate under which Regulation the application is being made (s.5). A very small number of products have been authorised both as a plant protection product and as a medicinal product.

The applicant is required to identify the protect for which protection is sought (s.6). Although art.8(1)(b) implies that the product should be described in the same manner that it is referred to in the marketing authorisation, e.g. dopexamine hydrochloride, the UK-IPO has long accepted formats such as X opinionally in the form of the hydrochloride or X optionally in the form of a pharmaceutically acceptable salt such as the hydrochloride or X optionally in the form of a pharmaceutically acceptable salt (see MOPP para.SPM2.04). However, this approach is not consistently followed across the EEA, the German patent office (and courts) preferring the format "X in all forms protected by the basic patent". This format also seems to be accepted by the UK-IPO and may be more suitable to ensure a uniform approach across the EEA.

As the active ingredient of a medicinal product is usually identified by its international non-proprietary name (INN), but referred to by its systematic IUPAC name (for a chemical) or a code name (for a biological product, such as a monoclonal antibody), it will often be necessary to set out what is meant by the INN. Proposed and accepted INN are published in "WHO Drug Information", which is a useful source of this information.

The "basic patent" upon which the SPC is to be granted must be specified by number, title and expiry date; and the product for which protection by the SPC is sought must be specified. Also, if necessary, sufficient information must be given to enable the Comptroller to determine that the product is protected in some way by the basic patent, e.g. by specifying a claim of the basic patent which refers to the product or indicating how the product is derived from a general formula in a claim (see MOPP para.SP8.06).

The first authorisation for placing the product on the market within the United Kingdom, as a medicinal product in accordance with either of Directives 2001/83/EC (for human medicines), 2001/82/EC (for veterinary medicines), or as a plant protection product in accordance with Directive 91/414/EEC, must be identified by number and date, and a copy of this authorisation must be supplied. This authorisation must be valid at the date of the application, and the copy must contain a summary of the product characteristics listed in art.11 of Directive 2001/83/EC or art.5A of Directive 81/851/EEC.

In the case of a pharmaceutical product, it is necessary to file a complete copy of the Product Licence granted by the MHRA granted under the Medicines Act 1968 (c.67), together with a Marketing Authorisation issued under the Medicines for Human Use (Marketing Authorisation etc.) Regulations 1994 (SI 1994/3144). Alternatively, the marketing authorisation can be one issued by the central European Medicines Agency (the EMEA) in the form of a Commission decision incorporating a grant document (bearing a number in the form "EU/1/97/001/001") issued under Council Regulation (EC) 726/2004, formerly Regulation (EEC) 2309/93. The copy of the authorisation filed should include the attached Schedule or authenticated copy of the licence application, commonly called the "product characteristics". This requirement can be satisfied by supply of information published on the electronic Medicines Compendium, available at *http:// emc.medicines.org.uk*, replacing information previously available as a data sheet for the compendium of approved pharmaceutical products distributed by the Association of the British Pharmaceutical Industry. In the case of a veterinary product, there should be supplied a copy of the Veterinary Product Licence granted by the Veterinary Medicines Directorate of the Department for the Environment, Food and Rural Affairs, commonly referred to as DEFRA (including the accompanying Schedule) granted under the Medicines Act 1968 (c.67) and a Marketing Authorisation issued under the Veterinary Medicinal Products Regulations 1994 (SI 1994/3142), see MOPP para.SP2.01 and notes on PF SP1.

In the case of a plant protection product, it is necessary to supply a *complete* copy (including any schedules and annexes) of an approval issued by the Pesticides Safety Directorate of DEFRA under the Control of Pesticides Regulations 1986 (SI 1986/1510, as amended), or of an authorisation issued under the Plant Protection Product Regulations 1995 (SI 1995/887, as amended). The Guide indicates approvals and authorisations for plant protection products usually consist of a Notice of Approval and a covering letter, both of which should be filed. The Guide also indicates that approvals issued by the Pesticides Registration Section of the Health and Safety Executive do not generally relate to plant protection products as defined in this Plant Protection Products Regulation.

As the detailed contents of such authorisation documents usually contain valuable information not usually available to competitors, it is prudent to request, at the time of filing, that the document (or at least part of it) should be kept confidential under r.53 of the 2007 Rules, as discussed in §128B.80.

If the basic patent was granted only after the date of the first UK authorisation, the date of the patent grant must also be specified.

Also to be provided are details of the first authorisation to place the product on the market within the European Community (or EEA or Switzerland, if appropriate, for which see §§128B.64 and 128B.71). For this, the State, the number and the date of such authorisation must be given as well as information identifying the product thus authorised and the legal provision under which this authorisation took place. A copy of the notice publishing such authorisation in the appropriate official publication should also be provided. In the case of the first authorisation having been obtained in the United Kingdom, this official publication would appear to be the notice which appears in the London Gazette when a marketing authorisation is granted under the above-mentioned Directives. If no such notice is published in respect of the "first marketing authorisation", it is now permitted to file "any other document proving that the authorisation has been issued, the date on which it was issued and the identity of the product authorised", see the Plant Protection Products Regulation (art.8(1)(c)), probably also applicable to medicinal products, and see Recital (17) of that Regulation, discussed in §128B.63.

PF SP1 must also be signed and dated. The signature of an agent appointed on s.2 of that Form will suffice for this in accordance with r.101 of the 2007 Rules. All documents submitted to the UK-IPO (presumably, other than copies of the regulatory documents required to be provided with the application) must comply with the physical requirements of r.20; and any document not in the English language must be accompanied by a verified translation in accordance with r.113 of the 2007 Rules, for which see §123.30.

The application is then referred for formality and substantive examinations as with patent applications. The substantive examiner has to determine that: (a) the product is protected by the specified basic patent; (b) a valid authorisation exists for marketing the product in the United Kingdom as a medicinal product; and (c) the product has not already been the subject of a United Kingdom SPC, all as required by art.3 of the Regulations (see MOPP para.SP10.04). However, although art.10(5) of the Regulations permits an investigation whether the authorisation specified was the first authorisation for marketing the product in the United Kingdom as a medicinal (or plant protection) product, as it must be according to art.3(d) and (1)(d) of the Regulations, at present the Office does not examine this requirement, but will raise an objection if such seems to arise, e.g. because of information supplied by an applicant, or by a third party informant (acting under the 1977 Act s.21) or information contained in a parallel application as in *Draco's SPC Application* [1996] R.P.C. 417, see MOPP para.SPM10.05.

If the examiner is of the view that there is a formality irregularity and/or that the requirements for the grant of an SPC are not met, an objection is raised in writing, and a time for response and rectification (usually two months) is then set, in accordance with art.10(3) and (4) of the Regulations. Where an application is deficient as regards the supply of required particulars or documents, the applicant is normally given an opportunity to rectify these deficiencies without loss of filing date (see MOPP para.SPM10.08.1). Extensions of the time set for response may also be requested and (as for patent applications) will be allowed at the Comptroller's discretion.

Before any rejection of the application, the applicant has the opportunity of being heard (under the 1977 Act s.101), and any adverse decision is appealable to the Patents Court (under the 1977 Act s.97).

Payment of fees to make a supplementary protection certificate effective
The onus is upon the certificate holder to pay the appropriate fees to make the SPC effective within the required period, which runs from three months before the lawful date of expiry of the basic patent up to the 20th anniversary of the filing of this, but the Office has to send a reminder if the fees are not paid by the due date, see r.116(6) of the 2007 Rules. **128B.78**

If the fees are not paid within this time, they may be paid within the following six months with a 50 per cent surcharge; and, again, the Office must send a reminder if the fees have not been paid by the due date, see also §128B.72. Also explained in §128B.72 is how the fee required is to be calculated, with the possibility of paying for less than the maximum possible duration of the SPC, although without possibility of its extension after that.

These fees are to be paid together with the filing of PF SP2. A form containing the same information can be used, (2007 Rules r.4(2)). This form requires identification of the number of the SPC, the name of its holder(s) and the due date for payment of the so-called "annual fees", together with a statement of the desired effective period for the certificate and the amount of the fees (and any extension fee required for late payment). Also to be identified is the person making the payment and the address to which the certificate of payment of fees should be sent. It is not clear whether or not it is possible to pay the fee electronically, in contrast to this possibility with patents, trade marks and design fees.

For information whether fees have been paid, the caveat system can be used, see §§128B.80 and 118.18.

Procedure for challenge of grant or refusal of a supplementary protection certificate

128B.79   For challenge to the validity of an SPC, or for a decision that such is to be regarded as having lapsed because of the withdrawal of the underlying United Kingdom marketing authorisation for the product, PF SP3, or a replica of it, is required, accompanied by a statement of case in duplicate setting out fully the facts upon which the applicant relies and the relief sought (SPC r.7(3)). The Comptroller sends a copy of the PF SP3 and the Statement of Case to the SPC holder. If the holder wishes to contest the application, he must, within two months, file a counter-statement in duplicate setting out in full the grounds on which the application is contested, and the Comptroller then sends a copy of this to the applicant and gives such directions as he thinks fit for the subsequent procedure. No further statement or counter-statement is possible without leave or direction of the Comptroller (2007 Rules Pt 7; MOPP paras SPM14.03; SPM15.03). The subsequent procedure is then likely to follow that used for an application to the Comptroller for revocation of a patent, for which see §72.21 et seq. Proceedings concerning an SPC should be brought before the Patents Court, or the Patents County Court, in the same way as if the SPC were a patent, see [1993] *CIPA* 284, but proceedings are also possible in the courts of Scotland and Northern Ireland, and perhaps also in the Isle of Man (on which see §128B.57).

In *Generics v Daiichi*, see above, the validity of an SPC was challenged in the High Court on the grounds that the basic patent was invalid and that the SPC should not have been granted.

Inspection of documents filed at the UK-IPO in connection with supplementary protection certificates and applications therefor

128B.80   Information about SPCs is available on the UK-IPO website *http://www.ipo.gov.uk* under both the basic patent (using the patent number in the form EP1234567 or GB2345678, as appropriate) and the SPC number (in the form SPC/GB12/345). In general, the register entry for the basic patent carries the complete history of the SPC, from application to grant, rejection or withdrawal, whereas the SPC register gives only the current status of the SPC or its application. Where an SPC is associated with an EP(UK) patent or a GB patent, the register entry at the top is marked with the hyperlink "View the Supplementary Protection Certificate that exists for this Patent". Where more than one application for a certificate has been made, the link connects to a listing of all the applications.

Data relating to an application for an SPC is usually made available on the UK-IPO website within two weeks for the application being made. Besides publication of details of applications for, and grant and revocation of, SPCs which are published in the *Patents Journal*, and the entries which are made in the register, the documents filed or sent to the UK-IPO become open to public inspection 14 days after it under the 2007 Rules r.51, unless a confidentiality direction is sought and granted under the 2007 Rules r.53. Thus, as regards such documents, the position is the same as that applying to documents filed at, or sent to, the UK-IPO in connection with patents and applications, and copies of such non-confidential documents are obtainable on request under the 2007 Rules r.52. It is normal practice for applicants to request, and be granted, confidentiality in respect of marketing authorisation documents, because the regulatory authorities do not allow these to be inspected, and any schedules to the marketing authorisation may contain details of the manufacturing methods used to prepare the authorised product. Care should therefore be taken to request confidentiality within the 14 days specified in the 2007 Rules r.53. However, since, for medicinal products, the summary of product characteristics (SmPC) is now published shortly after the authorisation of a medicinal product by either the MHRA or the EMA (formerly the EMEA), a request for confidentiality of the SmPC is not appropriate.

Since all information concerning the application for, and the grant and maintenance of, SPCs is required to be published in the *Patents Journal* and as entries are made in the register of patents accordingly, it is possible to use the caveat system for notification of such entries to persons interested. The files of SPCs, together with the files of the basic patents on which the SPCs were based, are maintained for seven years after the demise of the SPC: *Patents Journal* March 18, 1998.

Procedure for obtaining an extension to a supplementary protection certificate

Application for an extension to an SPC, following is made on PF SP4 accompanied by **128B.81** the prescribed fee (currently £200, see the 2007 Fee Rules Sch.1). The request should specify a granted certificate number or certificate application number (s.2). If filing for an extension at the same time as making an application for a certificate, the UK-IPO will fill in this part. If the applicant already has a granted certificate, then its number and its expiry date should be given. Current practice requires that where the certificate is granted, a copy should be supplied. The applicant is required (s.5) to identify the active ingredient(s) or active substance(s), using, if possible, the chemical or generic names. If a certificate has already been granted, the applicant should use the definition of the product on the granted certificate. The number, title and expiry date of the basic patent (GB or EP(UK)) must be given (s.6), the number and date of the authorisation containing the statement of compliance with an agreed completed paediatric investigation plan as referred to in art.36(1) of Regulation (EC) No 1901/2006 (s.7) and an indication whether the product has been authorised in all member states by either a "centralised" authorisation issued by the EM(E)A or by national authorisations granted by each member state (s.8). The applicant is also required to state if a copy of the authorisations required at ss.7 and 8 respectively is filed with the SP4. Following *E I Du Pont Nemours & Co v UK Intellectual Property Office* [2009] EWCA Civ 966, [2010] R.P.C. 6, failure to provide these two documentsat the time of submitting the application for an extension to a certificate is an irregularity which may be remedied after the date of application, during examination under art.10(3).

MOPP at SPM8.12 notes that except where it is immediately apparent, the applicant should also provide whatever information is necessary to enable the Comptroller to confirm that the product in question satisfactorily completed the agreed paediatric investigation plan. This is challenging for a medicinal product that was not authorised through the centralised route, as evidence of authorisations will, in principle at least, be required in each of the 27 member states of the EU (but not the additional member states of the EEA).

SECTION 129

Application of Act to Crown

129. This Act does not affect Her Majesty in her private capacity, but subject **129.01** to that, it binds the Crown.

OTHER RELEVANT STATUTE

Crown Proceedings Act 1947 (c.44)—Section 3

Infringement of intellectual property rights

129.02   3.—(1) Civil proceedings lie against the Crown for an infringement committed by a servant or agent of the Crown, with the authority of the Crown, of—

(a) a patent,

(b) a registered trade mark,

(c) the right in a registered design,

(d) design right, or

(e) copyright;

but save as provided by this subsection no proceedings lie against the Crown by virtue of this Act in respect of an infringement of any of those rights.

(2) Nothing in this section, or any other provision of this Act, shall be construed as affecting—

(a) the rights of a government department or any part of the Scottish Administration under section 55 of the Patents Act 1977, Schedule 1 to the Registered Designs Act 1949 [c.88] or section 240 of the Copyright, Designs and Patents Act 1988 (Crown use of patents and designs) or,

(b) the rights of the Secretary of State under section 22 of the Patents Act 1977 or section 5 of the Registered Designs Act 1949 (security of information prejudicial to defence or public safety).

Note. This section was substituted by the CDPA 1988 Sch.7 para.4(1)(2) and is reprinted here as amended by various other statutes and instruments.

COMMENTARY ON SECTION 129

129.03   The section has to be read in conjunction with s.3 of the Crown Proceedings Act 1947 (c.44) (the "CrPA") reprinted above. The combined effect of the section and the CrPA is that a patent cannot be applied against acts of the Crown carried out in a private capacity; and acts within the permitted scope of Crown user rights of s.55 are also no longer regarded as authorised acts "infringement". The right of action against the Crown for patent infringement which remains is therefore a narrow one, probably confined to public instances of "sale" by the Crown of patented articles, i.e. acts not covered by the Crown user provisions of s.55. Even then, an exception exists as regards sales of articles which have been forfeited under Customs and Excise legislation, see s.122 and §122.02. Also, no injunction can be granted against the Crown (CrPA s.21). The section does not, however confer any immunity on any foreign state, see the State Immunity Act 1978 (c.33) s.7.

The historical derivation of s.129 is that, prior to the CrPA, the Crown was immune from actions in tort on the legal principle that the Crown could do no wrong. The CrPA altered that principle, and the Crown user provisions of the 1949 Act merely provided for compensation for acts of permitted Crown user while leaving these still technically acts of infringement. Moreover, until the 1977 Act, patents were granted under the Royal prerogative and, as one cannot infringe one's own grant, the Crown was inherently immune at least in its private capacity. Thus, the section preserves the former inherent immunity of the Crown in relation to patents even though now granted by statute rather than under the prerogative.

By Sch.7 para.4 to the CDPA 1988, s.3 of the CrPA was extended in its effect apply generally to all forms of intellectual property; and the reference to "design right" includes a topography right (Design Right (Semiconductor Topographies) Regulations, SI 1989/1100, as amended by SI 1993/2497).

SECTION 130

Interpretation

130.—(1) In this Act, except so far as the context otherwise requires—

    "application fee" means the fee prescribed for the purposes of section 14(1A) above;

    "application for a European patent (UK)" and (subject to subsection (4A) below) "international application for a patent (UK)" each mean an application of the relevant description which, on its date of filing, designates the United Kingdom.

    "appointed day", in any provision of this Act, means the day appointed under section 132 below for the coming into operation of that provision;

    "biological material" means any material containing genetic information and capable of reproducing itself or being reproduced in a biological system;

    "biotechnological invention" means an invention which concerns a product consisting of or containing biological material or a process by means of which biological material is produced, processed or used;

    "Community Patent Convention" means the Convention for the European Patent for the Common Market [*and Community patent means a patent granted under that convention*];

    "comptroller" means the Comptroller-General of Patents, Designs and Trade Marks;

    "Convention on International Exhibitions" means the Convention relating to International Exhibitions signed in Paris on 22nd November 1928, as amended or supplemented by any protocol to that convention which is for the time being in force;

    "court" means

        (a) as respects England and Wales, the High Court **or any patents county court having jurisdiction by virtue of an order under section 287 of the Copyright, Designs and Patents Act 1988 [c. 48];**

        (b) as respects Scotland, the Court of Session;

        (c) as respects Northern Ireland, the High Court in Northern Ireland;

        (d) as respects the Isle of Man, Her Majesty's High Court of Justice in the Isle of Man;

    "date of filing" means—

        (a) in relation to an application for a patent made under this Act, the date which is the date of filing that application by virtue of section 15 above; and

        (b) in relation to any other application, the date which, under the law of the country where the application was made or in accordance with the terms of a treaty or convention to which that country is a party, is to be treated as the date of filing that application or is equivalent to the date of filing an application in that country (whatever the outcome of the application);

    "designate" in relation to an application or a patent, means designate the country or countries (in pursuance of the European Patent Convention or the Patent Co-operation Treaty) in which protection is sought for the invention which is the subject of the application or patent **and includes a**

130.01

**reference to a country being treated as designated in pursuance of
the convention or treaty**;

**"electronic communication" has the same meaning as in the Electronic
Communications Act 2000 (c. 7).**

"employee" means a person who works or (where the employment has
ceased) worked under a contract of employment or in employment under
or for the purposes of a government department **or a person who serves
(or served) in the naval, military or air forces of the Crown**;

"employer", in relation to an employee, means the person by whom the employee is or was employed;

"enactment" includes an Act of Tynwald;

"European Patent Convention" means the Convention on the Grant of
European Patents, "European patent" means a patent granted under that
convention, "European patent (UK)" means a European patent designating the United Kingdom, "European Patent Bulletin" means the bulletin
of that name published under that convention, and "European Patent Office" means the office of that name established by that convention;

"exclusive licence" means a licence from the proprietor of or applicant for a
patent conferring on the licensee, or on him and persons authorised by
him, to the exclusion of all other persons (including the proprietor or applicant), any right in respect of the invention to which the patent or application relates, and "exclusive licensee" and "non-exclusive licence"
shall be constructed accordingly;

"formal requirements" means those requirements designated as such by rules
made for the purposes of section 15A above;

"international application for a patent" means an application made under the
Patent Co-operation Treaty;

"International Bureau" means the secretariat of the World Intellectual Property Organization established by a convention signed at Stockholm on
14th July 1967;

"international exhibition" means an official or officially recognised international exhibition falling within the terms of the Convention on International Exhibitions or falling within the terms of any subsequent treaty or
convention replacing that convention;

"inventor" has the meaning assigned to it by section 7 above;

"journal" has the meaning assigned to it by section 123(6) above;

"mortgage", when used as a noun, includes a charge for securing money or
money's worth and, when used as a verb, shall be construed accordingly;

"1949 Act" means the Patents Act 1949 [c. 87];

"patent" means a patent under this Act;

[*"patent agent" means a person carrying on for gain in the United Kingdom
the business of acting as agent for other persons for the purposes of applying for or obtaining patents (other than European patents) in the
United Kingdom or elsewhere or for the purpose of conducting proceedings before the comptroller;*]

"Patent Co-operation Treaty" means the treaty of that name signed at
Washington on 19th June 1970;

"patented invention" means an invention for which a patent is granted and
"patented process" shall be construed accordingly;

"patented product" means a product which is a patented invention or, in relation to a patented process, a product obtained directly by means of the process or to which the process has been applied;

"prescribed" and "rules" have the meanings assigned to them by section 123 above;

"priority date" means the date determined as such under section 5 above;

"published" means made available to the public (whether in the United Kingdom or elsewhere) and a document shall be taken be published under any provision of this Act if it can be inspected as of right at any place in the United Kingdom by members of the public, whether on payment of a fee or not; and "republished" shall be construed accordingly;

"register" and cognate expressions have the meanings assigned to them by section 32 above;

"relevant convention court", in relation to any proceedings under the European Patent Convention, [*the Community Patent Convention*] or the Patent Co-operation Treaty, means that court or other body which under that convention or treaty has jurisdiction over those proceedings, including (where it has such jurisdiction) any department of the European Patent Office;

"right", in relation to any patent or application, includes an interest in the patent or application and, without prejudice to the foregoing, any reference to a right in a patent includes a reference to a share in the patent;

"search fee" means the fee prescribed for the purposes of section 17(1) above;

"services of the Crown" and "use for the services of the Crown" have the meanings assigned to them by section 56(2) above, including, as respects any period of emergency within the meaning of section 59 above, the meanings assigned to them by the said section 59.

(2) Rules may provide for stating in the journal that an exhibition falls within the definition of international exhibition in subsection (1) above and any such statement shall be conclusive evidence that the exhibition falls within that definition.

(3) For the purposes of this Act matter shall be taken to have been disclosed in any relevant application within the meaning of section 5 above or in the specification of a patent if it was either claimed or disclosed (otherwise than by way of disclaimer or acknowledgment of prior art) in that application or specification.

(4) References in this Act to an application for a patent, as filed, are references to such an application in the state it was on the date of filing.

(4A) An international application for a patent is not, by reason of being treated by virtue of the European Patent Convention as an application for a European patent (UK), to be treated also as an international application for a patent (UK).

(5) References in this Act to an application for a patent being published are references to its being published under section 16 above.

(5A) References in this Act to the amendment of a patent or its specification (whether under this Act or by the European Patent Office) include, in particular, limitation of the claims (as interpreted by the description and any drawings referred to in the description or claims).

(6) References in this Act to any of the following conventions, that is to say—

(a) The European Patent Convention;

(b) The Community Patent Convention;

(c) The Patent Co-operation Treaty;

are references to that convention or any other international convention or agreement replacing it, as amended or supplemented by any convention or international agreement (including in either case any protocol or annex), or in accordance with the terms of any such convention or agreement, and include references to any instrument made under any such convention or agreement.

(7) Whereas by a resolution made on the signature of the Community Patent Convention the governments of the member states of the European Economic Community resolved to adjust their laws relating to patents so as (among other things) to bring those laws into conformity with the corresponding provisions of the European Patent Convention, the Community Patent Convention and the Patent Co-operation Treaty, it is hereby declared that the following provisions of this Act, that is to say, sections 1(1) to (4), 2 to 6, 14(3), (5) and (6), 37(5), 54, 60, 69, 72(1) and (2), 74(4), 82, 83, [*88(6) and (7),*] 100 and 125, are so framed as to have, as nearly as practicable, the same effects in the United Kingdom as the corresponding provisions of the European Patent Convention, the Community Patent Convention and the Patent Co-operation Treaty have in the territories to which those Conventions apply.

(8) **Part I of the Arbitration Act 1996 [c. 23]** [*The Arbitration Act 1950 [c. 27]*] shall not apply to any proceeding before the comptroller under this Act.

(9) Except so far as the context otherwise requires, any reference in the Act to any enactment shall be construed as a reference to that enactment amended or extended by or under any other enactment, including this Act.

Notes

1. The definition of "application fee" was inserted into subs.(1) by the Regulatory Reform (Patents) Order 2004 (SI 2004/2357) ("RRO") with effect from January 1, 2005.

2. The definitions of "biological material" and of "biotechnological invention" were inserted into subs.(1), by SI 2000/2037, with effect from July 28, 2000, but as to this effect see §76A.02.

3. The definition of "court" was amended: as to (a) by Sch.7 para.23 to the CDPA 1988; and as to (d) by SI 1978/621, as now applied by SI 2003/1249.

4. The definition of "designate" was amended by the Patent Act 2004 (c.16) Sch.1(9)(2)(b), with effect from January 1, 2005 (SI 2004/3205 art.2(i)(j))

5. The definition of "electronic communication" was inserted by SI 2003/512, with effect from January 1, 2005.

6. The definition of "employee" was amended by the Armed Forces Act 1981 (c.55) s.22.

7. The definition of "enactment" was added by SI 1990/2295.

8. The definition of "patent agent" (printed as amended by the Administration of Justice Act 1985 (c.61) s.60) was repealed by Sch.8 to the CDPA 1988 with effect from August 13, 1990 (SI 1990/1400), then to be replaced by ss.275 and 276 of the CDPA 1988, for which see §275.01 and §276.01 respectively.

9. The definition of "search fee" was amended by Sch.5 para.5 to the CDPA 1988 with effect from January 7, 1991 (SI 1990/2168).

10. Subsection (4A) was inserted by the Patents Act 2004 (c.16) Sch.1(9)(3), with effect from January 1, 2005 (SI 2004/3205).

11. Subsection (5A) was inserted by the Patents Act 2004 (c.16) Sch.1(9)(4), with effect from December 17, 2007.

12. Subsection (7) was amended by Sch.8 to the CDPA 1988, with effect from January 7, 1991 (SI 1990/2168).

13. Subsection (8) was amended by the Arbitration Act 1996 (c.23) Sch.3 para.33 and by The Arbitration (Scotland) Act 2010 (Consequential Amendments) Order 2010 (Scottish SI 2010/220) Sch.5.

14. The definitions of "court", "biotechnological invention", "electronic communication" and "enactment" were each applied to the Isle of Man by SI 2003/1249.

COMMENTARY ON SECTION 130

Scope of the section

Subsection (1) defines many of the various terms used in the Act, and the whole of s.130 **130.02** has an important bearing on the interpretation of many sections of the Act. The definitions are, however, qualified by the proviso in the preamble to subs.(1) "except so far as the context otherwise requires".

Specific definitions

Most of the specific definitions listed in subs.(1) are dealt with in the commentaries of **130.03** the particular section to which they relate.

Note: the term "published" in respect of a patent application under the Act has special meaning, see subs.(5) and §130.07.

Definition of "comptroller"

The office of Comptroller-General of Patents, Designs and Trade Marks referred to in **130.04** this definition is authorised by s.62 of the Patents and Designs Act 1907 (c.29) which remains in force, see Appendix A at §A20. By s.62(3) (as amended), any officer in the Patent Office may be authorised by the Secretary of State to act instead of the Comptroller. It is under this provision that the powers of the Comptroller are delegated to others in the UK-IPO, particularly to take hearings and issue decisions in the name of the Comptroller.

Thus, hearings involving the exercise of the Comptroller's judicial functions are taken normally, not by the Comptroller himself, but by a "hearing officer". Accordingly, while throughout this Work the convention has been adopted of referring to "decisions of the Comptroller", it should be realised that these decisions will normally have been given by a Divisional Director (formerly a "Superintending Examiner"), or occasionally by a Deputy Director (formerly a principal examiner) or by a Director (formerly an Assistant Comptroller), these titles having changed in December 1998, each acting for the Comptroller under such delegated powers, as explained in §102.04. For the appointment of other officers in the UK-IPO, see s.63 of the 1907, reprinted in at §A20.

As set out in the MOPP (para.130.05), the manner of this delegation by the Comptroller is that: the Directors and Divisional Directors are authorised to act for the Comptroller in all proceedings under the 1977 Act and CDPA 1988; Deputy Directors are authorised to act for the Comptroller in ex parte proceedings; Senior Patent Examiners and Patent Examiners may (with certain exceptions) act for the Comptroller in respect of pre-grant matters such as opposed requests, references and applications or the refusal of applications and requests when disputed; administration staff of the rank of SPAN A2 or A3 may act in connection with unopposed requests, references and applications so far as technical content is not involved; and staff of grades SPAN B1 or B2 may act on certain provisions under the Rules, including the alteration of time limits under r.110(1).

However, otherwise, administrative officers are not authorised under s.62(3) of the 1907 Act to act for the Comptroller in any judicial capacity (*Rhône Poulenc Santé's Patent* [1996] R.P.C. 125).

By the Interpretation Act 1978 (c.30) Sch.1 the term "Secretary of State" in any statute means "one of Her Majesty's Principal Secretaries of State". The powers of the Secretary of State under the Act are currently administered (unless otherwise stated) by the Head of the Department of Innovation, Universities and Skills (the "DIUS").

The Deregulation and Contracting Out Act 1994 (c.40) has made provision (in Pt II of that Act, ss.69–79 and Schs 15 and 16) for the services and functions of the Comptroller (as specifically designated in its s.74(4)(c)) to be contracted out by a Minister of the Crown (s.69), though for not more than ten years at a time, s.69(5) and subject to positive resolution of each House of Parliament (s.77(2)). However, this does not apply to any function, the exercise of which would constitute the exercise of any jurisdiction of any tribunal which exercises the judicial power of the State, or any power or duty to make subordinate legislation (s.71(a) and (d)). The effect of any such contractorisation is to provide that anything done, or not done, by a contractee shall have effect as if done, or not done, by the Minister or the office-holder (such as the Comptroller) whose powers and functions have been delegated under the contracting out order (s.74): this includes a variation of the effect of s.112, see §112.02. The power to contract out statutory functions and duties specifically extends to the functions of examiners and other officers of the Office (s.79(5)) and anything done by a person delegated to exercise such functions is to be treated as if done "by or in relation to an examiner or other officer of the Office in his capacity as such" (s.72(2), as modified by s.79(6)). However, at the time of writing, no order under these provisions has been made affecting the Comptroller or the UK-IPO.

Definition of the "1949 Act"

130.05   The term "1949 Act" means the Patents Act 1949 (c.87). The previous substantive patent statute to this was the Patents and Designs Act 1907 (c.29) which had been amended by various Acts in 1908 (c.4); 1914 (c.18); 1919 (c.80); 1928 (c.3); 1932 (c.32); 1938 (c.29); 1939 (c.32 and c.107); 1942 (c.6); 1946 (c.26 and c.44) and 1947 (c.10). This Act was then further amended by the Patents and Designs Act 1949 (c.62), but, before this was brought into force, the Patents Act 1949 (c.87) and the Registered Designs Act 1949 (c.88) were each passed in order to split the two subjects into separate statutes and at the same time consolidate the amended provisions. These two Acts were then brought into force, and the Patents and Designs Act 1949 was itself almost entirely repealed by the Patents Act 1949. As all patents granted under the 1977 Act have now expired, the surviving provisions of the 1949 Act are considered to be "spent" (see Appendix A), and are not further considered except where reference to them may assist in understanding the provisions of the present statute, or as an aid to the understanding of judgments. The surviving provisions of the 1907 Act which remain in force are set out and considered in Appendix A at §A20.

Definition of "patent"

130.06   The term "patent" as used throughout the Act normally means only a patent granted under the 1977 Act, see *Wellcome's Two Patent Applications* [1983] R.P.C. 200. However, a European patent (UK) is to be treated as a patent granted under the Act, though only for the purposes of Pts I and III of the Act, i.e. excluding the provisions of ss.77–95. The Act contains no definition of "patentee" (as did s.101 of the 1949 Act) and indeed does not use this term. The owner of a patent granted under the Act is termed a "proprietor", though this term is also not defined in the Act. It would, therefore, appear to be the better practice to use the term "proprietor" to refer to a beneficial owner and, in respect of a title entered in the patent register, to refer to a "registered" proprietor or other types of rights ownership. Nevertheless, the term "patentee" is still frequently used informally.

Miscellaneous further definitions (subss.(2)–(5))

130.07   Subsection (2) provides for rules defining an international exhibition for the purposes of s.2(4)(c). Rule 5, reprinted in §2.02, was made under this provision. It is discussed in §2.16.

Subsection (3) is of relevance in the determination of priority under s.5, for which see §5.24. The subsection extends the disclosure of a priority or original specification to include the wording of the claims of that specification. However, while the wording of claims in a priority or original application thus constitutes part of that application, such wording is not an independent disclosure (*Asahi's Application* [1991] R.P.C. 485 HL). The claims must, accordingly, be read in context with the specification of which they form a part, and their subject-matter is not to be confused with their breadth (*A.C. Edwards v Acme Signs* [1990] R.P.C. 621; and [1992] R.P.C. 131 CA). The presence of claims in a priority application has also been held to limit its disclosure, so that a divisional application with a broader claim was not permitted to claim priority (*Van der Lely's Application* [1987] R.P.C. 61).

The provisions of the subsection, however, exclude from the "disclosure" of a priority or original specification matter present in that specification which is presented "by way of disclaimer or acknowledgment of prior art". There is no decision whether the disclaimer can be implied, e.g. by inference from an absence of claim but certainly express words of disclaimer in a specification cannot be used as part of the "disclosure" of that specification for the purposes of either of ss.5 or 7. Likewise, an acknowledgment of prior art contained in a specification is not part of its "disclosure", presumably even if the acknowledgment is an inaccurate one.

Subsection (4) provides that an application "as filed" is an application in the state it was on its date of filing. This is of importance in the assessment of whether a divisional or replacement application can be allowed to proceed under s.76(1), for which see §76.14 and whether any amendment made after the original filing is permissible within the terms of s.76(2) and (3)(a), for which see §§76.11–76.15. A priority document is not part of an application, even when filed with it, nor is the abstract. However, the UK-IPO is apparently prepared to allow other papers filed contemporaneously to be regarded as part of the specification as originally filed, see Ch.16 of the MOPP (paras 16.10–16.13). New subs.(4A) makes it clear that an international application which is treated as an application for a European patent (UK) is not also to be treated as an international application for a patent (UK).

Subsection (5) defines "publication of an application" as that which occurred pursuant to s.16, but this definition includes publication of a European application (UK), as this is deemed to be published under s.16 (s.78(3)(d)) and also an international application for a patent (UK) published under PCT art.21 which is also deemed to be published under s.16 provided that it validly enters the United Kingdom national phase (s.89B(2)), though subject for certain purposes to the filing of a translation, see s.89B(3), discussed in §89B.10. Publication of an application is discussed further in §16.03.

New subs.(5A) puts a gloss on the term "amendment" (of a patent, but not of an application) whenever this (and cognate terms) appears in the Act so as to include an amendment which limits the scope of the claims whether under either of ss.27 or 75 or by way of limitation proceedings before the EPO of a European patent as a whole under new art.105A of the EPC.

Definitions of the EPC, the CPC and the PCT (subs.(6))

Subsection (6) defines the terms "European Patent Convention" ("EPC") "Community **130.08** Patent Convention" ("CPC") and "Patent Co-operation Treaty" ("PCT") each for the purpose of references in the Act. The definitions, in each case, extend to future agreements replacing, amending or supplementing any of these conventions, including any annexes or protocols, and also any instrument made under any such convention or agreement. The full titles of these conventions, and their official publications in English, are:

— the EPC: "Convention on the Grant of European Patents", signed in Munich on October 5, 1973, published November 1974 as Cmnd.5657 with revisions signed in 2000 and published as Cm.5615;

— the CPC: "Convention of the European Patent of the Common Market (Community Patent Convention)", signed in Luxembourg on December 15, 1975, published August 1976 as Cmnd.6553, but this was amended and replaced by "Agreement relating to Community Patents" signed in Luxembourg on December 15, 1989, published March 1991 as Cm.1452, and this is the CPC version to which reference is made throughout this Work; and

— the PCT: "Patent Co-operation Treaty", signed in Washington on June 19, 1970, published December 1970 as Cmnd.4530.

The English language texts of the EPC, together with its protocols and regulations (as amended), are set out fully in the European Patents Handbook ("EPH") likewise the updated PCT documents are published in the *Patent Cooperation Treaty Handbook* ("PCTH") each compiled by the Chartered Institute of Patent Attorneys and published by Sweet & Maxwell, London. It must be borne in mind that the CPC has never been ratified and now seems unlikely ever to come into force.

The long title of the Act (reprinted at §0.02) indicates that an object of the Act is to give effect to certain conventions, that is to the EPC, the CPC and the PCT. As a result the title of the Act gives rise to the applicability of the rule of statutory construction laid down by the House of Lords in *The Escherheim* (sub nom. *The Jade*) [1976] 1 All E.R. 920 that, where there is any difference between the language of the statute provision and that of the corresponding provision of the convention which the statutory provision is to enact, the statute language should be construed in the same sense as that of the convention if the words of the statute are reasonably capable of bearing that meaning. However, this decision has no applicability if the wording of the statute (or rule) is "plain", even if this wording leads to breach of an international obligation under a Convention or Treaty. Thus, in *E's Applications* [1983] R.P.C. 231 HL, it was held that the wording of s.89(3) and the then r.110 (each as they then stood) was too "plain" for a reference to the wording of the PCT to be made.

Meaning and effect of subsection (7)

130.09   Subsection (7) is an important provision because it specifies those sections of the Act which, being deemed to have equivalents in the EPC, the CPC or the PCT, are to be taken as having been intended to be framed so as to have, as nearly as practicable, the same effect in the United Kingdom as the corresponding provision of the relevant convention. This adds some specificity to the general object of the Act noted above. At the time of its enactment, the provision of subs.(7) was unique in United Kingdom statute law, but other examples are arising as the strict interpretation of United Kingdom statutes comes to be adapted to the interpretation of Continental civil law which is often expressed in terms of principles rather than means. A particular example of this new legislative technique is the Civil Jurisdiction and Judgments Act 1982 (c.27), outlined in §96.09.

The effect of subs.(7) would seem to be that, in interpreting those sections of the Act listed, due weight should be given not only to the wording of the corresponding provisions in the EPC, the CPC and the PCT, but also to their travaux préparatoires, for example the official minutes of the conferences which led to the adoption of the final wording of these conventions. Subsection (7), in effect, directs the Comptroller and the courts to treat the wording of these conventions, their travaux préparatoires and foreign decisions construing these as persuasive authorities. Indeed, in *Fothergill v Monarch Airlines* [1981] A.C. 251; [1980] 2 All E.R. 696, the House of Lords, reversing previous authorities, held that such preparatory works could be taken into account in interpreting any statute which purported to enact into United Kingdom law the terms of an international convention ratified by the United Kingdom. Another decision of similar effect is *The Escherheim* [1976] 1 All E.R. 920 noted §130.08, see also *Wavin v Hepworth* [Ireland] [1982] F.S.R. 32. Moreover, it is now possible, as an aid to statutory construction, to have reference to Parliamentary documents, such as the Hansard Reports of Parliamentary proceedings, although only where the wording of legislation appears to be ambiguous, obscure or to lead to an apparent absurdity, and where this is clarified by a clear statement by a minister or other promoter of the legislation, see *Pepper v Hart* [1992] 3 W.L.R. 1033; [1993] 1 All E.R. 42.

For these reasons, Jacob J. commented (in *Beloit v Valmet* [1995] R.P.C. 705; and in *Lenzing's European Patent* [1997] R.P.C. 245) that it would have been preferable, here and elsewhere in the Act, if the draftsman had used the same language as that in the EPC, since any attempt to "clarify" the Convention wording by other wording "simply causes extra complications", and therefore legal uncertainty and costs. This theme was taken further by the same judge in *Bristol-Myers Squibb v Baker Norton* [1999] R.P.C. 253 when he indicated that, at least for those sections of the Act referred to in subs.(7), and save in the rare event of a specific contention that a provision of the 1977 Act has a different meaning from a corresponding provision of a Convention, the corresponding provisions of the Convention should be regarded as of direct effect and that one should work directly from those provisions and not bother with the provisions of the Act, that is the wording and numbering of the Convention should be used in preference to the wording and numbering of the Act. In each of *Unilin Beheer v Berry Floor* [2005] F.S.R. 6 at 56; *Yeda Research v Rhône-Poulenc* [2006] R.P.C. 24 at 605; and *Aerotel v Telco* [2006] EWCA Civ 1371; [2007] R.P.C. 117 at [4] cases, Jacob L.J. repeated his previous criticisms that the draftsman of the 1977 Act should not have tried to implement the wording of provisions of a Convention or Treaty in different wording when s.130(7) requires the UK law to have the same effect. In the *Yeda* case, it was argued that there was no need to interpret s.37 in accordance with the CPC as this Convention had never come into force. That argument was seen to be wrong. It would mean a change in the law if and when the CPC did come into force and that could not have been contemplated. In this book each section to which s.130(7) refers is followed by a reprint of the corresponding EPC, PCT or CPC article.

As discussed in the commentary on that section, s.91 requires judicial notice to be taken of the three Conventions as well any decision of, or expression of opinion by, a "relevant convention court" of an organisation set up under the Convention, such as the EPO and its Boards of Appeal. Primarily, this merely means that these decisions may be considered by a court without formal proof of their existence, but in practice the decisions of such "convention courts" are to be taken into account in interpreting the provisions of the EPC, particularly in construing those provisions of the Act listed in s.130(7). Nevertheless, such decisions would appear to be of persuasive, rather than decisive, authority under English law. Likewise, the International Convention of Paris is only a guide to, but not a rule of, interpretation of the Act. The EPO takes a similar view as regards any conflict between this Convention and the EPC, the latter being regarded by the EPO as a self-contained code, see J 15/80 OJ EPO 1981, 213. However, in that decision, and later in T 301/87 *BIOGEN/Alpha-interferons* OJ EPO 1990, 195; [1990] E.P.O.R. 337, it was held that, if possible, the provisions the EPC should be interpreted in conformity with those of the Paris Convention.

Those provisions of Act required to conform with the EPC, the CPC and the PCT under subsection (7)

130.10 The provisions of the Act to which subs.(7) applies the corresponding EPC or CPC provisions (despite the fact that the CPC has not, and now seems unlikely that it ever will, come into force) are the following:

Type of provisions	1977 Act(s.)	Corresponding EPC, PCT or CPC Article
(a) Definition of patentability	1(1)–(4)	EPC art.52
	2–4	EPC arts 52–57
	14(3), (5)	EPC arts 83, 84
(b) Definition of priority	5, 6	EPC arts 87–89

Type of provisions	1977 Act(s.)	Corresponding EPC, PCT or CPC Article
(c) Limitation of period within which allegations of improper ownership of the patent may be raised	37(5), 74(4)	CPC art.23
(d) Treating use abroad as local use when considering abuse of monopoly	54 [*not in force*]	CPC art.46
(e) Definitions of act of infringement of patents and applications	60	CPC arts 25–28, 32
	69	EPC art.67; PCT art.29; CPC art.32
(f) Definition of grounds of revocation	72(1), (2)	EPC arts 138, 139; CPC art.56
(g) Determination of right to a European patent application (UK) and the recognition of foreign judgments thereon	82	EPC art.60; CPC art.67
	83	Protocol on recognition, arts 9–11
(h) Definition of burden of proof in relation to patented processes	100	CPC art.35
(i) Definition of extent of protection of the patent	125	EPC art.69 and Protocol thereto

The most important of these provisions is the application of subs.(7) to s.125 which defines the scope of protection of a patent for the purposes of the Act. This is because s.125(3) applies to the Act the Protocol to EPC art.69, just as the Protocol modifies the meaning of EPC art.69. This makes it clear that the scope of patents granted under the Act (and of European patents (UK) by virtue of s.77(1)) is not to be limited to the strict wording of their claims. The point is more fully dealt with in the commentary on s.125.

Application of subsection (7) in decided cases

130.11   The first application of s.130(7) was in *Smith, Kline & French v Harbottle* [1980] R.P.C. 363, where s.60(1)(a) was construed in conformity with CPC art.29, see §60.05; and, in *Monsanto v Stauffer* [1985] R.P.C. 515 CA, the CPC was used as an interpretive aid to s.60(5)(b), see §60.15. For the application of the Protocol to EPC art.69 in assessing the extent of protection of a patent claim, see the commentary on s.125.

There is some doubt whether sections of the Act not listed in subs.(7) should, nevertheless, be construed in conformity with the EPO or EPO decisions applied mutatis mutandis. In *Daido Kogyo's Patent* [1984] R.P.C. 9, the Patents Court and Court of Appeal each indicated, *obiter*, that s.28 (not listed in subs.(7)) should be construed in conformity with the Long Title to the Act (for which see §0.02), and therefore in accordance with the principles of the EPC. Also, in *Lowndes' Application* BL O/19/93, the Comptroller held that s.76 (although not listed in s.130(7)) should be interpreted uniformly with art.123 of the EPC because s.76 arose under s.72 and EPC art.123 arose under EPC art.138 and s.72 is listed in s.130(7)).

However, in any event, the House of Lords has stressed in *Merrell Dow v Norton* [1996] R.P.C. 76, that great significance should be attached to decisions of the EPO Boards of Appeal with the consequence that, in *Bristol-Myers Squibb v Baker Norton* [1999] R.P.C. 253, the Patents Court declined to consider whether decisions of the EPO Enlarged Board of Appeal had been wrongly decided, that being a matter for higher courts. Accordingly, it is considered that, whether or not a provision of the Act is referred to in s.130(7), interpretations given by the EPO to analogously worded provisions of the EPC or its rules should be taken into consideration in construing provisions intended to have a similar effect. This was done in *John Wyeth's and Schering's Applications* [1985] R.P.C. 545, see §4A.03; and in *B&R Relays Ltd's Application* [1985] R.P.C. 1, see §76.04.

Nevertheless, the Comptroller feels himself bound by decisions of the Patents Court, even if these are not in accord with decisions in the EPO; and likewise the Patents Court will hold itself bound by a decision of the Court of Appeal, whatever the view of the EPO on the same or analogous point, as also will the Court of Appeal faced with a decision of the House of Lords.

Arbitration (subs.(8))

Subsection (8) (as amended) states that Pt I of the Arbitration Act 1996 (c.23) does not apply to proceedings before the Comptroller. **130.12**

For the purposes of the Tribunals and Inquiries Act 1992 (c.53) Sch.1, the Comptroller is defined as a "tribunal". Proceedings before the Comptroller are therefore to be considered as taking place in a tribunal which should follow fully the legal principles of natural justice and the legal principles and practices used in the High Court, unless the Act should imply otherwise. Appeals from the Comptroller are governed entirely by the Act (s.97) and the Civil Procedure Rules, see §§97.03 et seq.

Amendment of, and reference to, other statutes (subs.(9))

Subsection (9) provides that, where the Act refers to another enactment, the relevant provision is to be construed as a reference to any amendment or extension of that enactment by any subsequent enactment. **130.13**

The term "enactment" now includes as Act of Tynwald in respect of the Isle of Man, see §132.02.

Included in the preliminary pages to this book are Tables of Statutes referred to.

SECTION 131

Northern Ireland

131. In the application of this Act to Northern Ireland— **131.01**

    (a) "enactment" includes an enactment of the Parliament of Northern Ireland and a Measure of the Northern Ireland Assembly;

    (b) any reference to a government department includes a reference to a Department of the Government of Northern Ireland;

    (c) any reference to the Crown includes a reference to the Crown in right of Her Majesty's Government in Northern Ireland;

    (d) any reference to the Companies Act **1985** [*1948*] includes a reference to the corresponding enactments in force in Northern Ireland; and [(e) *the Arbitration Act (Northern Ireland) 1937 [c.8 (N.I.)] shall apply in relation to an arbitration in pursuance of this Act as if this Act related to a matter in respect of which the Parliament of Northern Ireland had power to make laws.*]

(f) any reference to a claimant includes a reference to a plaintiff.

Note. Paragraph (d) was amended by the Companies Consolidation (Consequential Provisions) Act 1985 (c.9) s.30 and Sch.2 and para.(e) was repealed by the Arbitration Act 1996 (c.23) Sch.4. Paragraph (f) was added by the Patents Act 2004 (c.16) Sch.2(28) with effect from January 1, 2005 (SI 2004/3202 art.2(f)(k)).

Commentary on Section 131

Scope of the section

131.02   The Act applies to Northern Ireland, see §132.06. Northern Ireland has its own legal and judicial system, though the main differences in its legal system from that of England and Wales are procedural ones. Consequently, there is no need for special substantive provisions of law, such as those of s.31 (transfer of patent rights) and s.105 (privilege in patent proceedings in Scotland), as is required to provide for the differences in Scots law. Thus, s.131 provides only for some variation in nomenclature in the application of the Act to Northern Ireland, in terms which are self-explanatory. The enactment referred to in s.131(d) is now the Companies (Northern Ireland) Order 1986 (SI 1986/1032 (NI 6)). The corresponding provisions for proceedings in Scotland are contained in s.98. The Arbitration Act 1996 (c.23) now governs arbitration in Northern Ireland and, consequently, para.(e) was repealed thereby as redundant. New para.(f) was added to the section because the term "plaintiff" continues to be used in Northern Ireland, whereas the term "plaintiff" has been changed to "claimant" in the other sections such as ss.60, 63 and 70 where the term "plaintiff" formerly appeared.

Jurisdiction of the court in Northern Ireland

131.03   By s.130(1), the word "court" as used throughout the Act means, in relation to Northern Ireland, the High Court in Northern Ireland. That court has jurisdiction in all matters under the Act wherein reference is made to bring matters before "the court". Thus, provided that there is a sufficient nexus with Northern Ireland of the parties or the acts involved, the High Court in Northern Ireland has jurisdiction, inter alia, in relation to infringement (s.61), revocation (s.72) and employee-inventor compensation (s.40). There is, however, no provision for a county court jurisdiction for patents in the province, ss.287–292 of the CDPA 1988 providing a Patents County Court with jurisdiction only in England and Wales.

There is no judge specially assigned to hear patent matters in the High Court in Northern Ireland. Patent litigation there is infrequent, but, when there have been cases, the pleading practice appears to have followed more that used in the Republic of Ireland than under the former RSC Order 104. Nevertheless, it can be expected that the general principles set out in CPR Part 63 and the Patents Court Guide (for which see Appendices F and G, respectively) will at least have persuasive effect in that court.

The question of jurisdiction between the various courts of the United Kingdom is discussed in §96.09 where the effect of the Civil Jurisdiction and Judgments Act 1982 (c.27) ["the CJJA"] is indicated. Schedule 4 of the CJJA regulates the intra-jurisdiction of the courts of the various component parts of the United Kingdom (i.e. England and Wales, Scotland and Northern Ireland, with provision for extension to other territories, such as the Isle of Man), and its provisions are discussed in relation to patent proceedings in Scotland in §98.05. These comments apply, mutatis mutandis, to patent proceedings before the High Court in Northern Ireland, except that no parallel provisions to those for Scotland contained in Sch.8 to the CJJA were needed. The power of the High Court in Northern Ireland to determine revocation proceedings under s.72 appears to have been maintained by the absence from Sch.4 to the CJJA of a provision corresponding to art.16(4) of the

Brussels Convention which would otherwise have restricted such proceedings to the court for that part of the United Kingdom where the register of patents is kept (i.e. in England and Wales) (see CJJA s.16(2); Sch.1 art.16(4); and Sch.4 art.16)).

Under the CJJA, it may no longer be possible for a defendant domiciled in Northern Ireland, and sued for an act of patent infringement committed in that territory, voluntarily to submit to the jurisdiction of the court in England, as happened in *Dow Chemical v Spence Bryson* [1982] F.S.R. 397.

An award of employee-inventor compensation by the Comptroller may be enforced in Northern Ireland as if it were a money judgment (s.41(11)).

Hearings before the Comptroller in Northern Ireland

Unlike Scotland (for which see r.88, reprinted at §98.05), there are no provisions for the Comptroller to sit in Northern Ireland. This seems an unfortunate omission, at least in respect of claims for employee-inventor compensation under s.40.   **131.04**

SECTION 131A

Scotland

131A. In the application of this Act to Scotland—   **131A.01**

(a) "enactment" includes an enactment comprised in, or in an instrument made under, an Act of the Scottish Parliament;

(b) any reference to a government department includes a reference to any part of the Scottish Administration; and

(c) any reference to the Crown includes a reference to the Crown in right of the Scottish Administration.

Note. Section 131A was added by the Scotland Act 1998 (Consequential Modifications) (No.2) Order 1999 (SI 1999/1820 art.4; Sch.2 Pt I para.58), with effect from July 1, 1999.

COMMENTARY ON SECTION 131A

Section 131A sets out some definitions for the application of the 1977 Act to Scotland and provide for exercise in relation to them of the powers now devolved to the Scottish Parliament. These are generally self-explanatory, but if necessary are mentioned in the commentaries on those sections of the 1977 Act which particularly pertain to Scotland, viz. ss.31, 98, 99B and 105.   **131A.02**

SECTION 132

Short title, extent, commencement consequential amendments and repeals

132.—(1) This Act may be cited as the Patents Act 1977.   **132.01**

(2) This Act shall extend to the Isle of Man, subject to any modification contained in an Order made by Her Majesty in Council, and according subject to any such order, references in this Act to the United Kingdom shall be construed as including references to the Isle of Man.

(3) For the purposes of this Act the territorial waters of the United Kingdom shall be treated as part of the United Kingdom.

(4) This Act applies to acts done in an area designated by order under section 1(7) of the Continental Shelf Act 1964 [c. 29], **or specified by order under section 10(8) of the Petroleum Act 1998 [c. 17]** [*section 22(5) of the Oil and Gas (Enterprise) Act 1982 [c. 23]*] in connection with **any activity falling within section 11(2) *[23(2)]* of that Act** [*the exploration of the sea bed or of subsoil or*

exploitation of their natural resources], as it applies to acts done in the United Kingdom.

(5) This Act (except sections 77(6), (7) and (9), 78(7) and (8), this subsection and the repeal of section 41 of the 1949 Act) shall come into operation on such day as may be appointed by the Secretary of State by order, and different days may be appointed under this subsection for different purposes.

(6) The consequential amendments in Schedule 5 shall have effect.

(7) Subject to the provisions of Schedule 4 to this Act, the enactments specified in Schedule 6 to this Act (which include certain enactments which were spent before the passing of this Act) are hereby repealed to the extent specified in column 3 of that Schedule.

Notes.

1. Subsection (2) applies the Act to the Isle of Man with appropriate modifications, as discussed in §132.05 below.

2. Subsection (4) was first amended by the Oil and Gas (Enterprise) Act 1982 (c.23) Sch.3 para.39 and the references to it then updated by the Petroleum Act 1998 (c.17) Sch.4.

RELEVANT STATUTORY INSTRUMENTS

132.02   Under s.132(2): Patents Act 1977 (Isle of Man) (Variation) Order 1990/2295; Patents Act 1977 (Isle of Man) Order 1978/621; Patents Act 1977 (Isle of Man) Order 2003/1249.

Under s.132(5): Patents Act 1977 (Commencement No. 1) Order 1977/2090; Patents Act 1977 (Commencement No. 2) Order 1978/586.

Application of the 1977 Act to the Isle of Man

The Patents Act 1977 (Isle of Man) Order 2003 (SI 2003/1249), effective from June 10, 2003, currently specifies the forms of the modifications of the provisions of the Patents Act 1977 (c.37) which are to be applied in the application of this Act to the Isle of Man. This Order, effective from June 10, 2003, replaced and expanded the previous Order of the same name (SI 1978/621) as later varied by the Patents Act 1977 (Isle of Man Variation) Order 1990 (SI 1990/2295).

Since that Variation Order the basic Order has contained a new art.4:

"**4.** The Patents Act 1977 shall, in its extension to the Isle of Man, be construed—

(a) as if references to the Crown included the Crown in right of the Government of the Isle of Man;

(b) as if references to a Government department included references to a Department of the Government of the Isle of Man, and in relation to such a Department as if references to the Treasury were references to the Treasury of the Isle of Man; and

(c) for the purposes of any arbitration in pursuance thereof and of the application thereto of the Arbitration Act 1976 (an Act of Tynwald), as if it were an Act of Tynwald."

The Schedule to the current 2003 Order made the Act (as already amended) applicable with necessary modifications and omissions also to the Isle of Man as indicated in the reprints of, and commentaries on, ss.1, 5, 22, 23, 41, 44, 45, 48, 48A, 48B, 50, 51, 52, 54, 58, 60, 76A, 93, 96, 97, 107, 109, 124A, 125A, 130 (definitions of "court" and "enactment") and, Schs A1 and A2.

The amendments made to the 1977 Act by the Patents Act 2004 (c.16), and the Regulatory Reform (Patents) Order 2004 (SI 2004/2357) ("RRO"), as set out and discussed above in relation to the sections thereby amended, each apply also in the application of the 1977 Act to the Isle of Man (Patents Act 2004 (c.16) s.18(2) and RRO art.1(3)).

Also, some further changes, as to the effect of the 1977 Act for the Isle of Man, were made by provisions contained in the CDPA 1988 as indicated in the following §132.03.

Application of the CDPA 1988 to the Isle of Man

While ss.293 and 294 of the CDPA 1988 (amendment of licence provisions for certain **132.03** existing patents), and Sch.5 paras 24 and 29 to the CDPA 1988 (amendment of s.89 and power to extend time limits) were given automatic effect in the Isle of Man (CDPA 1988 s.305(1)), the other provisions of the CDPA 1988 have had to be applied to the Isle of Man by further Orders in Council, as indicated below.

The Copyright, Designs and Patents Act 1988 (Isle of Man) (No.2) Order 1989 SI 1989/1292), inter alia, brought into effect (from August 1, 1989) further amendments to ss.46, 49, 51, 53, 57A and 58 of the 1977 Act effected by Sch.5 paras 12–16 to the CDPA 1988 so far as concerns the extension of these sections to the Isle of Man. This Order also contained the provision that:

"Any reference in any of these provisions to an Act of Parliament or to a provision of such an Act shall be construed, unless the contrary intention appears, as a reference to that Act or provision as it has effect in the Isle of Man."

This Order further extended to the Isle of Man the repealing provisions of Sch.7 paras 5, 20, 22 and 23 and Sch.8 to the CDPA 1988.

The Copyright, Designs and Patents Act 1988 (Isle of Man) Order 1990 (SI 1990/1505) extended to the Isle of Man the provisions of the CDPA 1988 relating to patent attorneys, i.e. ss.274–281, 285 and 286 of the CDPA 1988, including the repeals or partial repeals of ss.84, 85, 104, 105, 114, 115, 123(2)(k) and 130(1) of the 1977 Act effected by CDPA 1988 Sch.8, but with some amendment of ss.278, 280, 284 and 285 of the CDPA 1988 in relation to their application to the Isle of Man, as noted in the reprinting of the amended ss.278 and 280.

The remainder of the CDPA 1988 was given effect to in the Isle of Man by the Copyright, Designs and Patents Act 1988 (Isle of Man) (No.2) Order 1990 (SI 1990/2293). This extended to the Isle of Man the amendments to the 1977 Act effected by Sch.5 paras 1–11, 17–23, 25, 26, 28 and 30 to the CDPA 1988, and the repeals in CDPA 1988 Sch.8 of ss.14(4) and (8), 28(3) and (5)–(9), 72(3), 88, 130(7) and Sch.5 paras 2, 7 and 8 of the 1977 Act, with effect from January 7, 1991. These modifications to the 1977 Act were also made subject to the same construction provision as set out in art.4 of SI 2003/1292 quoted in §132.02 above.

COMMENTARY ON SECTION 132

Scope of the section

Section 132 provides the official title to the Act (subs.(1)) and extends operation of the **132.04** Act to the Isle of Man (subs.(2)), to territorial waters (subs.(3)) and to other designated areas (subs.(4)). It also provided for the commencement of the provisions the Act on varying dates (subs.(5)) and for certain consequential amendments to, and repeals of, other statutes by Schs 5 and 6 (subss.(6) and (7)).

Title (subs.(1))

Subsection (1) provides that the official title of the Act is "The Patents Act 1977". The **132.05** Act is Chapter 37 in the 1977 volume of Public General Acts and it can be cited more fully as "The Patents Act 1977 (c.37)". The "long title" of the statute is that given as the preamble to the Act, see §0.02. Of significance is that this commences with the words "An Act to establish a new law of patents . . ." so that it is not to be presumed that the pre-1977 law or decisions, have any continuing effect. Nevertheless, this is by no means an absolute rule, as the commentaries above have indicated.

Extension of the Act beyond the United Kingdom

132.06   The "United Kingdom" consists of the countries of England, Wales, Scotland and Northern Ireland, and, in the absence of any statement to the contrary, the Act applies automatically to them all. Subsections (2)–(4) provide for extension of the Act outside the United Kingdom as such, particularly to the Isle of Man (subs.(2)), as discussed in §132.07 below. However, Act has no direct applicability to other territories for which the United Kingdom has some responsibility, for example, to its remaining colonies, protected territories or even the Channel Islands, although United Kingdom patents are automatically extended to the British Indian Ocean Territory: (1983–84) 13 *CIPA* 459.

Nevertheless, patent protection in such areas is, for many of these territories, obtainable by registration of a granted United Kingdom patent within a specified period from grant, that registration then having effect (with or without the payment of renewal fees) so long as the United Kingdom patent remains in force. Further reference to such registration will be found in the commentary on s.77 at §77.05. Nevertheless, where a United Kingdom patent is registered abroad, this is under local law, and the provisions of the present Act (or its amendments or extensions) may not necessarily apply in the country of registration, see *Blackburn v Boon Engineering* [Brunei] [1991] F.S.R. 391.

It may be noted that United Kingdom patents, but not necessarily European patents (UK), may still have automatic effect in Swaziland.

—Extension of the Act to the Isle of Man (subs.(2))

132.07   By subs.(2), the Act is extended to the Isle of Man with provision for modification of the Act by Order in Council, to adapt its provisions to Manx legislation and terminology, and the term "enactment" used in the Act includes an Act of Tynwald (s.130(1)). The Orders that have been made in this regard are summarised in §132.02 and §132.03 dealing respectively with the application and modification of the 1977 Act and the patent provision of the CDPA 1988 each in relation to the Isle of Man. It is to be noted that these Orders now contain more generalised provisions for application of these Acts to matters arising in, or in relation to, the Isle of Man, as noted in §132.02 and §132.03. The PCT has been extended to the Isle of Man (see OJ EPO 1983, 465).

However, although the Isle of Man is not part of the European Community, by the Act of Accession of the United Kingdom to the European Communities 1972, the Isle of Man is part of the customs union of the EEC as now expanded to the EEA. Consequently, the EEC Regulations for supplementary protection certificates do not apply as such to the Isle of Man, but these can be applied by separate Isle of Man legislation, as it appears at least partially to have been done by Isle of Man Statutory Documents SD 447/93 and 748/99 see the Manual, §SPD,005 and §128B.57.

By amended s.130(1), "court", in relation to the Isle of Man, means "Her Majesty's High Court of Justice in the Isle of Man", and that court is therefore given the same powers under the Act as the other United Kingdom courts designated in s.130(1). Thus, for example, jurisdiction is extended to the Isle of Man for infringement (s.61), revocation (s.72) and employee-inventor compensation (s.40), though there must be sufficient nexus with the Isle of Man of the parties of the acts involved for the Isle of Man Court to assume this jurisdiction given to it. The question of jurisdiction between the various United Kingdom courts is discussed in general terms at §96.09. Here, reference is made to the Civil Jurisdiction and Judgments Act 1982 (c.27), an Act under which there is power to extend its provisions by Order in Council to the Isle of Man. Final appeal from the court in the Isle of Man is to the Judicial Committee of the Privy Council.

Court procedure in the Isle of Man High Court is governed by its own rules of court, SD [Statutory Document] 352/09, available as updated on *www.courts.im/rules of court*. These seem generally to follow the CPR.

Because, at least for some purposes, the Isle of Man is not part of the European Community, the application of the doctrine of "exhaustion of rights" in relation to products first, or subsequently, placed on the market in the Isle of Man could be different from that where that first marketing occurs within the European Community as such. For the extent to which the ECJ considers itself competent to decide matters of the law of the Isle of Man, see the employment law case of *DHSS (Isle of Man) v Barr* (C-355/89) [1991] 3 C.M.L.R. 325 ECJ.

There is no provision for the Comptroller to sit in the Isle of Man, but an order for employee-inventor compensation made by the Comptroller can be enforced in the Isle of Man in like manner as an execution issued out of the court (s.41(11)).

—Extension of the Act to territorial waters and the continental shelf (subss.(3), (4))

Subsection (3) states explicitly that the Act applies to the territorial waters of the United **132.08** Kingdom, while subs.(4) gives a United Kingdom patent effect on the continental shelf of the United Kingdom as defined by Orders made under s.1(7) of the Continental Shelf Act 1964 (c.29). The "United Kingdom Continental Shelf" is the area around the United Kingdom designated as such by the Geneva Convention on the High Seas (1958); a "designated area" is one designated by Order in Council under s.1(7) of the 1964 Act. Various such Orders, known as the Continental Shelf (Jurisdiction) Orders, have designated specified areas of the United Kingdom Continental Shelf as areas to which English, Scottish and Northern Ireland civil law is to apply. Such Orders may govern which court has jurisdiction under the Civil Jurisdiction and Judgments Act 1982 (c.27) over acts of patent infringement committed in one of the designated areas.

The amendment made to subs.(4) has been stated to have the effect (broadly speaking) of extending the application of the Act to specified areas which are in a foreign sector of the continental shelf and which comprise part of geological structure which extends into the foreign sector from an area designated under s.1(7) of the Continental Shelf Act 1964; and also as redefining the off-shore activities to which the Act applies in a way which corresponds to other off-shore legislation: *Patents Journal* August 11, 1982.

Thus, subss.(3) and (4) extend possibly infringing acts to those done in connection with the exploration of specified areas of the sea bed or subsoil or exploitation of their natural resources. Also, in connection with areas specified under the 1982 Act (within the terms of subs.(4)), acts of possible patent infringement include activities carried out from, by means of, or on, or for purposes connected with, installations for carrying out such exploitation, the storage or recovery of gas, the conveyance by a pipe and the provision of accommodation for workers on an off-shore installation, as now set out in the Petroleum Act 1998 (c.17) s.11.

In *Rockwater Ltd v Coflexip SA* [2003] EWHC 812 (Pat) at [1], the counterclaim for infringement alleged use of a patented pipelaying method offshore in the Leadon and East Foinaven fields; jurisdiction under s.132(4) was not disputed. On appeal the patent was held valid and infringed: [2004] EWCA Civ 381; [2004] R.P.C. 46.

The position as regards off-shore territorial areas near to the Isle of Man seems somewhat obscure.

Commencement of the Act (subs.(5))

The Act received the Royal Assent on July 29, 1977, but this brought into operation **132.09** only subs.(5) and the provisions specified in that subsection. Thus, the only immediate effect of the Royal Assent was the repeal of s.41 of the 1949 Act, other than as regards existing licences.

On December 31, 1977 ss.84, 85, 114 and 130 were brought into operation by the Patents Act (Commencement No.1) Order 1977 (SI 1977/2090); and, on June 1, 1978, all the remaining provisions of the Act (except for ss.53(1), 60(4) and 86–88) were brought into operation by the Patents Act (Commencement No.2) Order 1978 (SI 1978/586).

By s.130(1), the term "appointed day" in any provision of the Act means "the day appointed under section 132 for the coming into operation of that provision." Accordingly, June 1, 1978 was "the appointed day" for all provisions of the Act with the exceptions noted above.

While s.77(6) and (7) (requiring the proprietor of a European patent (UK) to file at the Office a translation of the specification from the French or German language into English if this is not already its language, and for the patent to become void if this is not done within the time specified), and s.78(7) (enabling applicants for such patents to file such a translation in order to take advantage of s.69) were "in operation" from June 1, 1978, these provisions had no effect before September 1, 1987 when rules were made under ss.77(9) and 78(8) (Patents (Amendment) Rules 1987, SI 1987/288 r.1(3) and (6)). However, s.77(6) was disapplied as from December 17, 2007 (under r.56(9) and (10)) upon the coming in to effect of the London Agreement, as discussed in §77.09. But the provisions in ss.77(9) and 78(8) remain to be re-activated at a subsequent date, without the need for further primary legislation. Thus the filing of translations of European patents and applications, is now only a voluntary matter, see further the commentaries on ss.77 and 78.

Provisions of the Act not yet in operation

132.10   The provisions of ss.53(1), 60(4), 86 and 87 were never brought into force, but have now each been formally repealed, so that there is now only s.54 which has not been brought into force.

Amendments to, and repeals of, other statutes (subss.(6) and (7))

132.11   Subsection (6) introduced Sch.5 which made amendments to certain statutes in order that references to earlier patent enactments were replaced with references to the corresponding provisions of the present Act.

Subsection (7) introduced Sch.6 which repealed the enactments listed to the extent specified. This list included s.47(1) of the Patents & Designs Act 1907 (c.29) provided for the Patent Museum. This museum was later transferred to, and made part of, the Science Museum (National Heritage Act) 1983 (c.47) ss.12, 13 and Sch.1 para.15).

Thus, with these historical notes, Schs.5 and 6 are considered each to be spent so that their re printing in this Work is considered unnecessary.

Unrepealed former patent statutes

132.12   Large portions of the 1949 Act remain unrepealed but, now that more than 35 years has elapsed since "the appointed day", these provisions can be considered to be spent. Consequently, this Work now has no discussion of the 1949 Act. However, in Appendix A there are some brief notes which describe the principal features of that Act which no longer appear in the current statute in order that terms appearing in reported decisions under this (and earlier) patent statutes can be more readily understood.

In Appendix A are also reprinted, or summarised, some provisions from other earlier statutes which continue, or may continue, to have effect. These provisions are—

— **Patents and Designs Act 1907** (c.29): s.62(1)–(3) and s.63 of this Act continue to provide for the existence and name of the Patent Office and of the Comptroller-General and the staff of the Office as discussed in the commentary on s.130 of the 1977 Act at §130.02 and §A20; and s.64 which provides for recognition of the seal of the Patent Office, although this is no longer used to provide a sealed Letters Patent document, as occurred under previous patent statutes. Sections 88, 91 and 91A of the 1907 Act also remain in force, but each has been amended so that these now relate only to trade marks.

— **Patents, Designs, Copyright and Trade Marks (Emergency) Act 1939** (c.107): the provisions of this Act are inactive until a "state of emergency" should be declared. This Act is not reprinted, but its existence is mentioned in §A21, and see the commentary on s.59.

— **Defence Contracts Act 1958** (c.38 ss.2–4, 6, 7(2) and (3) and 8(1) and (4), printed in §§55.02–55.07, and discussed in §55.11) relate to Crown useof intellectual property, for which see the commentaries on ss.55–58.

Appendix A also reprints (for historical reasons) unrepealed s.6 of the Statute of Monopolies 1623 (c.3), this being the basis for the concept of patentability in United Kingdom patent law until the advent of the present Act and the European Patent Convention, see §A06.

Schedules

SCHEDULES TO THE ACT

The Act (as now amended) contains eight Schedules, as listed below with indication of where these (unless spent) are reprinted and (for those unspent) are discussed in the paragraphs noted below.

SCH.00

Schedule	*Title*
Sch.A1 [Added]	Derogation from Patent Protection in respect of Biotechnological Inventions
Sch.A2 [Added]	Biotechnological Inventions
Sch.1 [Spent]	Application of 1949 Act to Existing Patents and Applications
Sch.2 [Spent]	Application of this Act to Existing Patents and Applications
Sch.3 [Spent]	Repeals of Provisions of 1949 Act [Spent]
Sch.4 [Spent]	Transitional Provisions [Spent]
Sch. 4A [Added]	Supplementary Protection Certificates
Sch.5 [Spent]	Consequential amendments
Sch.6 [Spent]	Enactments repealed

SCHEDULE 1 [SECTION 127]

Application of 1949 Act to Existing Patents and Applications

SCH.01

Note. The provisions of this Schedule can be regarded as spent and are therefore not reprinted. It lists those provisions of the 1949 Act which continued to apply to patents granted on applications filed before June 1, 1978 ("the appointed day"). The Schedule defined these patents as "existing patents". The main such provisions were those pertaining to validity and amendment, but infringement of such patents fell to be decided under the 1977 Act (save for continuing acts commenced before the appointed day).

As the term of existing patents under the 1949 Act was only 16 years (from the date of the complete specification), provision was made by this Schedule (para.4) for the new term of 20 years to apply to these existing patents having more than five years of life after the appointed day. However, these "new existing patents" were subject to deemed endorsement "licences of right" and this led to many contested disputes as to the terms on which such licences should be granted, as discussed in the commentary on s.46. Eventually, provisions were enacted (by amending para.4(2)(c) and inserting paras 4A and 4B, effected by ss.293 and 294 of the CDPA 1988) whereby patents relating to medicinal or pesticidal products could be excused from the "licence of right" regime. Extension of term (under ss.23–25 of the 1949 Act)remained possible for the other "existing patents" (i.e. "old existing patents"), but for not more than four years. All these provisions are now spent, and so need not be discussed further.

SCHEDULE 2 [SECTION 127]

Application of this Act to Existing Patents and Applications

SCH.02

Note. The provisions of this Schedule (introduced by s.127(3)) can be regarded as spent and are therefore not reprinted. It listed those provisions of the 1977 Act which were to be applied to "existing" patents and applications, that is those with a filing date for their complete specification prior to June 1, 1978 ("the appointed day"), but subject to the transitional provisions of Sch.4 (for which see §SCH.04). The provisions of the 1949 Act continued to apply to the validity and amendment of "existing patents". As regards Crown user and infringement of "existing patents", see §SCH.04.

SCHEDULE 3 [SECTION 127]

Repeals of Provisions of 1949 Act

SCH.03

Note. Subject to the provisions of Sch.4 (for which see §SCH.04), this Schedule listed certain sections which were to have no effect under the 1977 Act. These provisions are now of no importance and, hence, the Schedule is not reprinted. However, it is of historical significance that these repeals included (as from the date of the Royal assent, see §132.09) that of s.41 of the 1949 Act, under which compulsory licences had been available under patents relating to food or medicine.

SCHEDULE 4 [SECTION 127]

Transitional Provisions

SCH.04

Note. This Schedule set out various transitional provisions effective as regards the continuance of patents granted under the provisions of the 1949 Act. As all such "existing patents" have now expired, the Schedule is not reprinted, and is considered to be spent.

However, para.1 of the Schedule may have some importance. It reads:

"1. In so far as any instrument made or other thing done under any provision of the 1949 Act which is repealed by virtue of this Act could have been made or done under a corresponding provision of this Act, it shall not be invalidated by the repeals made by virtue of this Act but shall have effect as if made or done under that corresponding provision."

Thus, e.g. any instrument made or other thing done under any provision of the 1949 Act had continuing effect insofar as it could have been made or done under the present Act. In this way, assignments and licences executed before June 1, 1978 continued to have effect.

Paragraphs 2 and 3 deal with Crown use and infringement of existing patents. They provided that these matters should be dealt with under the provisions of ss.55–71 of the 1977 Act, except for the continuance of acts commenced before "the appointed day" (June 1, 1978). Proceedings commenced before that day were to continue under the provisions of the 1949 Act (paras 4 and 6–8, 10–13), as well as appeals already instituted from such proceedings; but, otherwise, appeals would take place under the 1977 Act provisions (paras 10–13 and 15).

Orders in Council designating specified countries to be "convention countries" had their effect continued (para.9), now under s.90 of the 1977 Act, and the power to make rules (under s.123) was extended to apply also to "existing patents" (para.14). There were also certain saving provisions, now of no importance (paras 16–18).

Secrecy orders made on "existing patents" and "existing applications" (either under s.18 of the 1949 Act or the Atomic Energy Act 1946 (c.80) s.12(1)), each repealed by Sch.6, were also continued (para.5). It is possible that some of these survive since such an order can prevent publication of the subject-matter of a patent even after its expiry. However, the amendment made to s.13(2) of the 1949 Act (made by Sch.5 para.1 of the

CDPA 1988) enabled "existing applications", which were subject to secrecy orders on the appointed day, to be withdrawn without publication.

SCHEDULE 4A [ADDED] [SECTION 128B]

[Supplementary Protection Certificates]

SCH.04A

Note. This new Schedule was inserted into the Act by reg.2 of the Patents (Compulsory Licensing and Supplementary Protection Certificates) Regulations 2007 (SI 2007/3293), having effect from December 17, 2007. By this means, the European Regulations for Supplementary Protection Certificates arising from Council Regulation (EEC) No.1768/92 of 18 June 1992 and from Regulation (EC) No.1610/96 of 23 July 1996, and of any amendments made, or subsequently made, to them have been brought specifically within the ambit of the Act. Schedule 4A is reprinted at §§128B.03–128B.09.

SCHEDULE 5 [SECTION 132]

Consequential amendments

SCH.05

Note. Schedule 5 is introduced by s.132(6). It effected some consequential amendments to certain other statutes. These amendments, to the extent that they even in theory still have effect are merely summarised as follows:

"Paragraph 1 amended s.3 of the Crown Proceedings Act 1947 (c.44). This section (as subsequently further amended) is reprinted in §129.02.

Paragraph 6 amended s.5(2) of the Atomic Energy Authority (Weapons Group) Act 1973 (c.4) by inserting, after the first "Patents Act 1949", the words "the Patents Act 1977"; and, after the second "Patents Act 1949", the words "section 55(4) of the Patents Act 1977". This Act may have some relevance to Crown use and is mentioned in §55.19.

Paragraph 7 amended some provisions in the Fair Trading Act 1973 (c.41)in relation to the services of "patent agents" and "European patent attorneys", but the present state of these services is now discussed at §276.02 for "patent agents", and at §277.02 for "European patent attorneys".

SCHEDULE 6 [SECTION 132]

Enactments repealed

SCH.06

Note. This Schedule contained a list of enactments repealed by the 1977 Act, including former patent statutes and other provisions. It is not reprinted here. A repeal does not (unless the contrary intention appears) revive anything not then in force or affect the previous operation of any enactment (Interpretation Act 1978 (c.30) ss.15 and 16).

SCHEDULE A1 [ADDED] [SECTION 60]

[Derogation from Patent Protection in respect of Biotechnological inventions]

SCH.A1

Note. This new Schedule was inserted into s.60 of the Act, together with new subss.(6A), (6B) and (6C), by the Patents Regulations 2000 (SI 2000/2037), with effect from July 28, 2000. Schedule A1 is reprinted at §60.02 and discussed in the commentary on s.60.

SCHEDULE A2 [ADDED] [SECTION 76A]

[Biotechnological Inventions]

SCH.A2

Note. This new Schedule was inserted the Act (as part of new s.76A) by the Patents Regulations 2000 (SI 2000/2037), with effect from July 28, 2000. Schedule A2 is reprinted at §76A.01A and discussed in the commentary on s.76A.

The Patents Rules 2007

(SI 2007/3291)

PART 3
GRANTED PATENTS

Certificate and amendment

Renewal

Surrender and cancelling entry that licences available as of right

PART 4
THE REGISTER AND OTHER INFORMATION

The register

Copies of documents and corrections in relation to the register

Requests for information or documents

PART 7
PROCEEDINGS HEARD BEFORE THE COMPTROLLER

Introductory

Conduct of hearings

Miscellaneous

Forms

The forms for use in business before the UK-IPO were those set out in Sch.1 to the **PR.02** Patents Rules 1995. However, under the authority of new s.123(2A) (for which see §123.05 above), the forms are no longer prescribed by formal rules, but are based upon directions issued by the Comptroller. As these forms may change in the future by simple direction from the Comptroller, and because they are now readily available by download-ing them (in their current form) from the UK-IPO website: *http://www.ipo.gov.uk*, they are no longer reprinted in this Work.

Fees

PR.03   The fees payable under the Patents Rules (including the fees payable to the UK-IPO when filing an International application under the PCT) are governed by separate Patents (Fees) Rules. Because these are likely to change from time to time, the current schedule of fees is not reprinted in this Work. A pamphlet is available from the Office setting out the current level of fees.

Copyright, Designs and Patents Act 1988 (c.48)

["the CDPA 1988 "]

ARRANGEMENT OF RELEVANT SECTIONS

Part V   **274.00**

Patent Agents and Trade Mark Agents

Part VI

PATENTS

Patents county courts

An Act ..., to make provision with respect to patent agents and trade mark agents; to confer patents and designs jurisdiction on certain county courts; to amend the law of patents; ...; and for connected purposes.

[15th November 1988]

PATENT AGENTS AND TRADE MARK AGENTS

Patent Agents [Sections 274–281]

SECTION 274

Persons permitted to carry on business of a patent agent

274.—(1) Any individual, partnership or body corporate may, subject to the **274.01** following provisions of this Part and to the **Legal Services Act 2007** [c.29], carry on the business of acting as agent for others for the purpose of—

(a) applying for or obtaining patents, in the United Kingdom or elsewhere, or

(b) conducting proceedings before the comptroller relating to applications for, or otherwise in connection with, patents.

(2) This does not affect any restriction under the European Patent Convention as to who may act on behalf of another for any purpose relating to European patents.

Notes

1. This section came into force on August 13, 1990 (SI 1990/1400) but was amended by the Legal Services Act 2007 (c.4) s.185 and Sch.21(76) when that Act came into force on January 1, 2010 (SI 2009/3250). See §275.04 for a discussion of the effects of the Act.

RELEVANT RULE—RULE 101

Rule 101—Agents

—(1) Any act required or authorised by the Act or these Rules to be done by **274.02** or to any person in connection with an application for a patent, or any procedure relating to a patent, may be done by or to an agent authorised by that person orally or in writing—

(a) where an agent is appointed when a person starts or joins any proceeding under the Act, once the comptroller has been notified of his appointment in writing; or

(b) where an agent is appointed after a person has started or joined any proceeding under the Act, once Patents Form 51 has been filed in duplicate.

(2) Where an agent has been authorised under paragraph (1), the comptroller may, in any particular case, require the signature or presence of his principal.

COMMENTARY ON SECTION 274

Scope of the section

Section 274 of the CDPA 1988 is complementary to substituted s.102 (reprinted at **274.03** §102.01). While s.102 provides a general freedom of appearance and audience in proceedings before the Comptroller, s.274 provides a like general freedom for persons to carry on the business of a "patent agent", defined as an agent for others for the purpose of applying for and obtaining patents (whether in the United Kingdom or elsewhere) or of conducting proceedings before the Comptroller relating to applications for, or otherwise in connection with, patents; and such agency representation may be by an individual, by a partnership or by a body corporate (subs.(1)). Accordingly, s.274 of the CDPA 1988 provides a freedom for those not on the Register of Patent Attorneys (the title of the register was altered from "Agents" by the Legal Services Act 2007) (and not being a solicitor) to carry on the business of a "patent agent" (as that term was formerly defined in s.130(1), for which see §102.03), with this freedom extended to cover business relating to European patents and patent applications (except in proceedings before the EPO). The origin of this freedom is discussed in §102.03, see also P. R. B. Lawrence (1988–89) 18 *CIPA* 88.

The freedom of practice for persons who are not "registered patent attorneys" (for which see s.275), which is provided by s.274 of the CDPA 1988, and the freedom of audience before the Comptroller provided by s.102, are, however, subject to the restrictions specified in the remainder of Pt V of the CDPA 1988, i.e.: in ss.275–281 of the CDPA 1988, particularly the restriction against use of the terms "patent agent", "patent attorney" and the like (as discussed in the commentaries on ss.276 and 278 of the CDPA 1988); and subject to the restrictions set out in s.102(2)–(4) and discussed in §102.02; and to a limitation on appearance on appeal from a decision of the Comptroller to the Patents Court, not permitted by the terms of s.102A, (which was repealed on the entry into force on January 1, 2010 of Sch.4 of the Legal Services Act 2007, the rights to conduct litigation and the right of audience in the High Court now being limited to "authorised persons" as defined in s.18 and Sch.5 of that Act); and without effect on the provisions of the EPC as discussed in §274.10. Moreover, the Comptroller continues to have power to refuse to recognise certain persons as agents, see s.281 and its commentary. However, the freedom provided by ss.102 and 274 includes exemption in connection with proceedings before the Comptroller from the offence of preparation of documents (other than a deed) by legally unqualified persons, see s.102(2) and §102.05.

Representation by an agent

—Appointment of agent

274.04   Notwithstanding that subs.(1) permits a party to any proceedings before the Comptroller (either under the Act or under any treaty or international convention to which the United Kingdom is a party) to be represented by another (herein called an "agent"), although subject to possible non-recognition by the Comptroller of certain persons under s.281 of the CDPA 1988 and rules made under it, for which see §§281.02 et seq., such a person must be authorised under r.101 reprinted above at §274.02 (which replaced r.90 of the 1995 Rules), and an appointed agent must have an address for service which is in the United Kingdom, another EEA state or the Channel Islands (r.103, reprinted at §32.02, replacing r.30 of the 1995 Rules, as amended in 2006). The appointed agent can be a firm, or body corporate, rather than an individual (subs.(1)). The personal signature of documents is not required, though the Comptroller may enquire whether signature of a particulardocument was properly authorised by its apparent maker, i.e. by a partner in the case of a firm.

While, at least in the period from 1950 to the commencement of the new provisions at the end of 1990, there does not appear to have been any non-recognition by the Comptroller of persons acting as agent contrary to the previous wording of r.101 and its predecessors, nevertheless the provision acted as a deterrent. Although the position has now changed by a shift of emphasis towards representation by "anyone", there so far appears to have been little shift in practice, even though the way has been opened to representation in proceedings before the Comptroller by foreign patent professionals, particularly those situated elsewhere in the European Community. It is not necessary for a formal authorisation of agent to be filed at the UK-IPO when an application is filed or proceedings commenced.

This change (made in 1982) brought proceedings before the Comptroller into line with the position of a solicitor commencing proceedings before the court. However, when the UK-IPO is acting as receiving office under the PCT, an authorisation must be filed under PCT r.90. For the provision of a signed authorisation for proceedings in the EPO, see §274.10.

Nevertheless, attention is drawn to r.82(1)(a) (reprinted at §123.15 and replacing r.106 of the 1995 Rules). This enables the Comptroller to direct that there should be furnished to him, within a period which he specifies, such documents and/or evidence as he may require. Accordingly, under the power of r.82(1)(a), the Comptroller can at any time require that he be satisfied that an agent was duly authorised by his principal to file the application or instigate the proceeding in question. Presumably, if the form naming the agent is directly signed by the principal, that will suffice, as also would the provision of a pre-dated authorisation or a statutory declaration (or other acceptable evidence) from the principal that the agent had been duly authorised: for example by oral instructions or by implication from the nature of the relationship between the agent and principal, or as a result of the requests made by the principal to the agent. There seems to be no reason why the authorisation should not arise by sub-delegation and it may even be possible for the principal to adopt the actions of his agent retroactively. However, a prudent agent may wish to protect himself against a subsequent repudiation of authority from the principal (for example, in a dispute over payment of costs). He may therefore deem it a wise precaution to seek a signed authorisation from the principal and retain this on his file. The signing of an authorisation is also a useful way of an agent ensuring that he has correctly stated the name and address of the principal.

If an authorisation is provided, care should be taken that its terms are broad enough to cover the acts performed, or to be performed, by the agent. For example, a general authorisation for the filing of applications, for obtaining grant and for subsequent proceedings in respect of the patent so obtained may not have broad enough wording (unless modified) to authorise the agent to act in proceedings against third parties, such as in applications for revocation under s.72. If it is desired to have the principal execute an authorisation, a suitable form, which can be adapted as either a specific or general authorisation, was published in the *Patents Journal* March 30, 1978. This is in the form:

Patents Act 1977
Authorisation of Agent

I/We (a)...

have appointed (b)...

to act for me/us in proceedings concerning

(1) my/our application for a patent or a patent identified as follows
(c) ....
....

(d)

(2) all applications for patents and patents in my/our name.

and request that notices, requisition and communications relating thereto be sent to such agent at the above address.

I/We hereby revoke all previous authorisations given by me/us in this connection.

Dated this ....day of ....19.....

(e)...

Notes.

(a) State name and address of applicant(s).

(b) State name and address of agent.

(c) State here the title of the invention if not yet filed or the application or patent number if available.

(d) Delete (1) or (2) whichever is inapplicable.

(e) To be signed by the person(s) appointing the agent.

However, modification of this is necessary if it is intended to provide an authorisation to act in proceedings relating to third party patents.

Where a possible conflict of interest can be seen, the court may grant (at least on an ex parte basis pending further review on an inter partes basis) an injunction against representation by a particular firm or person, see *Chiron v Murex* BL C/17/95 where the defendants desired to change their representation to a firm of solicitors of which a partner had formerly been a partner with the plaintiff's solicitors even though that partner had not been involved in the litigation in question. However, the injunction was not continued after an inter partes hearing (*Re A Firm of Solicitors* [1995] F.S.R. 783), the court then deciding that there was, on the facts, no good and sufficient reason to deprive a litigant of its solicitor of choice, there being no evidence that the new solicitor possessed any relevant confidential information.

Many of the patent forms now provide space for entry of an ADP number for the specified agent. This is an automatic data processing number which has been assigned to agents as part of the computerisation of UK-IPO procedures. If the agent's ADP number is known this should be used, but care is necessary to insert this correctly. Note that different ADP numbers are allocated for patent and trade mark matters.

It is important to note that, in proceedings before the EPO, documents (if not signed personally by the applicant) must be signed personally by a duly authorised representative, see further §274.10. However, personal signature is not, in practice, required by the UK-IPO. It is sufficient that the person appending a requisite signature has authority, express or implied, to sign on behalf of the authorised agent. It is on this basis that a partnership or firm may be authorised to act collectively. Thus, in *General Motors (Longhouse's) Application* [1981] R.P.C. 41, it was held that a signature of an employee on behalf of an authorised agent had been made with at least implied authority, unless it could be shown that the employee had acted "on a frolic of his own".

—Location of agent

274.05 Section 281(5) of the CDPA 1988 (reprinted in §281.01) requires the Comptroller not to recognise as agent a person appointed to represent another in "business under the Patents Act 1949, the Registered Designs Act 1949 (c.88) or the Patents Act 1977" unless such person resides, or has a place of business, in the United Kingdom, the Isle of Man or a Member State of the European Community. This broadened the former position (under the now repealed s.115(2)) which required such location to be "in the United Kingdom". However, r.103 (reprinted at §32.02) now requires an agent to furnish an address for service which (for the filing and prosecution of a patent application) is one within the United Kingdom (or the Isle of Man) or within the EEA or the Channel Islands; and, for other proceedings before the Comptroller, such address must be one in the United Kingdom (or the Isle of Man).

—Change of agency

274.06 Rule 101(1) requires that, where an agent is appointed for the first time, the Comptroller must be notified of his appointment in writing before that agent can act, and where an agent is appointed after the commencement of proceedings, a declaration of authorisation must be filed in duplicate on PF 51 (for which no fee is required). Under r.104(1), where an address for service required under r.103(1) has not been furnished, the Comptroller shall issue a direction that one must be filed within two months. Rule 108 cannot be used to extend this period, as this rule is listed in Pt 1 of Sch.4 to the 2007 Rules as not being extendible. When one agent replaces another, PF 51 is required to be filed in duplicate so that the Comptroller can send one copy to the agent formerly acting to inform him of the new agency, thereby giving him the chance to object if appropriate (r.101(1)(b)).

If the new agent is to act only in a limited manner and the previous agency is not to be revoked (or at least not totally), this should be made clear on PF 51, if necessary with deletion or amendment of the instruction to send all correspondence to the address of the new agent. When PF 51 relates to a published patent application or to a granted patent, it is not treated as a change of the address for service recorded in the register. For this, the filing of PF 20 is required see, e.g. *Patents Journal* July 19, 1989 and §32.24.

It has been suggested that the procedure of being able to nominate oneself as a new agent during the course of proceedings is open to abuse. See A. J. Hewlett (1981–82) 11 *CIPA* 417, and also N. J. Flower (1982–83) 12 *CIPA* 119. However, any such abuse by a registered patent attorney would constitute gross professional misconduct leading to possible penalty for breach of the Code of Conduct for Patent Attorneys, Trade Mark Attorneys and Other Regulated Persons, issued by IPReg (for details of which see §275.04) and possible refusal of recognition under s.281, for which see §281.04. Such actions as envisaged would also be likely to be criminal as being part of a conspiracy to defraud and possibly obtaining a pecuniary advantage by deception. Moreover, the persons concerned would be liable to civil law actions for damages for deceit and breach of warranty of authority.

—Obstacles to practice by unqualified person

While, as stated in §102.03, the representation, for financial gain, of a party to proceed-　**274.07**
ings before the Comptroller is no longer restricted to registered patent attorneys (and solicitors), others (here termed "unqualified persons") suffer disadvantages compared to registered patent attorneys, previously and still known also as "patent agents", (and solicitors) in that unqualified persons do not enjoy any of the privileges of registered patent attorneys (for which see §275.08). In particular, unqualified persons may not use the terms "patent agent" or "patent attorney", or similar terms, (for which see the commentary on s.276 of the CDPA 1988) and the term "European patent attorney" is restricted to those on the European list (s.277 of the CDPA 1988, reprinted at §277.01 and discussed in the following commentary). Also, unqualified persons have no right to conduct or appear in, appeals to the Patents Court from decisions of the Comptroller (s.102A, discussed §102A.02) or instruct counsel directly. Further, unqualified persons do not enjoy the legal privilege of patent attorneys and solicitors in respect of communications relating to inventions, etc., (CDPA 1988 s.280 discussed in the commentary on it), though an unqualified person may enjoy a like privilege under Scots law, see §105.03; and unqualified persons may also have a problem over the availability of professional indemnity insurance, see the paper by W. E. Caro (1986–87) 16 *CIPA* 150 and the Seminar Report (1986–87) 16 *CIPA* 399.

—Advantages of representation by a "Chartered Patent Attorney (formerly Agent)"

Prior to the entry into force on January 1, 2011 of the relevant parts of the Legal Ser-　**274.08**
vices Act 2007 (c.29) and the consequential revision of s.275 of the CPDA, with the addition of a new s.275A (for which see §275.01 et seq.), ultimate responsibility for regulating the patent and trade mark attorney professions lay with the UK-IPO, acting on behalf of the Secretary of State, but regulation of the professions is now the responsibility of an independent regulatory board appointed by and acting in the name of CIPA, with a similar regulatory board appointed by and acting in the name of ITMA for the trade mark attorney profession. In practice, the two regulatory boards act jointly as the IP Regulation Board (IPReg).

Previously, an attorney could be removed from the relevant register by order of the UK-IPO, acting for the Secretary of State, on the grounds of "conduct discreditable to a patent (or trade mark) attorney", but there was no definition of this and there was no code of conduct for patent or trade mark attorneys. The former CIPA Rules of Professional Conduct (which ceased to have effect on that date, being replaced by a Code of Conduct introduced by IPReg as applicable to registered patent attorneys, registered trade mark attorneys and "other regulated persons") were used by the UK-IPO as the yardstick to determine whether the patent attorney had been guilty of discreditable conduct. Breaches of the Code of Conduct and the Special Rules of Professional Conduct applicable to all registered patent attorneys undertaking litigation work are subject to investigation and the imposition of sanctions under IPReg's Rules of Disciplinary Procedure, which can be found on the IPReg website *www.ipreg.org.uk.*

From 2010, with IPReg now responsible for full regulation of the patent and trade mark attorney professions, its Code of Conduct, which is largely based on the previous CIPA Rules, governs the conduct of all registered patent attorneys. However, membership of CIPA, with the use of the title "Chartered Patent Attorney", continues to offer advantages to registered patent attorneys, as they have access to guidance from CIPA and its Committees, for example the Business Practice Committee, and to continuing professional development seminars which enable them to maintain their knowledge up-to-date, this being one of the requirements of the IPReg Code of Conduct.

While a registered patent attorney need not be a member of the Chartered Institute of Patent Attorneys, the vast majority of registered patent attorneys are members of this professional body. Fellowship of CIPA, which gives entitlement to use of the title "Chartered Patent Attorney" and the designatory letters "CPA" is open to all registered patent attorneys.

Those members of the Chartered Institute who are also European patent attorneys (as most of them are) are also bound, at least in respect of their activities before the EPO, by the Code of Professional Conduct of the Institute of Professional Representatives before the EPO ("epi") for which see §286.05, membership of which is compulsory for European patent attorneys. As noted in §277.05, the restrictions there are more "severe" for example, as regards restrictions on offering services by way of advertisements, whereas the IPReg Code of Conduct mentioned above permits more freedom as regards professional advertising.

—Liability of agents for negligence

274.09   Any person providing a service for the benefit of another is liable to that other person (either in contract or in tort) for any negligence in the performance of these duties, or actions in respect thereof, because a general duty of care is assumed to exist in such circumstances: *Hedley Byrne v Heller* [1964] A.C. 465 HL. Also, under s.13 of the Supply of Goods and Services Act 1982 (c.29), there is an implied term in a contract for the supply of a service (where the supplier is acting in the course of a business) that the supplier will carry out the service with reasonable care and skill. However, there has been exempted from this particular provision:

> "the services of an advocate in court or before any tribunal, inquiry or arbitrator and in carrying out preliminary work directly affecting the conduct of the hearing".

(Supply of Services (Exclusion of Implied Terms) Order, SI 1982/1771): this would appear to cover anyone appearing before the Comptroller under s.102(1). The application of these principles to the principles of patent agency work is the subject of a paper by T. Z. Gold (1990–91) 20 *CIPA* 120.

Under s.2(2) of the Unfair Contract Terms Act 1977 (c.50) ["UCTA"], liability for negligence cannot be excluded by a contract term or a notice except (other than for death or personal injury) as such term or notice satisfies a requirement for reasonableness (as defined in s.11 of the UCTA). However, the UCTA does not extend to:

> "any contract so far as it relates to the creation or transfer of a right or interest in any patent, trade mark, copyright or design right (including a 'topography right'), registered design, technical or commercial information or other intellectual property, or relates to the termination of any such right or interest":

(UCTA Sch.1 para.1(c), as amended by: Sch.1 para.1(2)(f) [1986 Act]; CDPA 1988 Sch.7 para.24; and SI 1989/1100 itself amended by SI 1993/2497). Thus, agents acting for others in matters relating to patents could exclude, or limit, liability for their negligence in respect of much of the work carried out by them. However, most "Chartered Patent Attorneys" (i.e. Fellows of the Chartered Institute of Patent Attorneys, for which see §275.09) are unlikely to exclude such liability, regarding it as inimical to their professional character and relying instead on professional indemnity insurance, a subject which has been discussed in above-mentioned articles on professional indemnity insurance. Unqualified persons, to whom such insurance is unlikely to be available (see §274.07), are more likely to adopt such a practice. The IPReg Code of Conduct (r.17) states that any limitation of liability for negligence must be clearly drawn to the attention of a client and be understood and accepted by him.

Andrew Master Hones v Cruikshank and Fairweather [1980] R.P.C. 16 was a case of negligence against a firm of patent agents. A breach of contract between client and patent agent was held to have occurred when the agent did not exercise the degree of knowledge and care to be expected from a notional duly qualified person practising in the profession. The agent in question was negligent in that he had taken a superficial and incorrect view of the prior art which he had failed to apply to all the claims. He had also failed to ascertain from his client the features which distinguished the invention from the prior art and which resulted in its practical success. Moreover, on the evidence, the patent could have been effective against competitors irrespective of its validity. Consequently, the agent should not have assumed, without further inquiry, that the applicant, by his silence, had taken the agent's advice to abandon the application. An inquiry into damages was ordered on the basis that there was good reason to think that valid claims could have been obtained which would not readily have been circumvented by competitors. On appeal (see [1981] R.P.C. 389), it was conceded that there had been some degree of negligence and a breach of contract, but it was held that the degree of negligence was much less than the judgment at first instance indicated. Thus, none of the claims of the specification in the form which existed when the application lapsed was valid, and the claims could easily have been avoided. In these circumstances the Court of Appeal thought that damages, although not purely nominal, were unlikely to be large.

Another case of negligence is *Lee v Walker* (1872) L.R. 7 C.P. 121, where a patent agent was held to have been negligent when he had failed to act in accordance with a legal decision of the previous year of which he ought to have been aware.

Halifax Building Society v Urquhart-Dykes and Lord [1997] R.P.C. 55 was a case of negligence by a trade mark agent and, although in the circumstances of the case, nominal damages only were awarded, the court stated that the duties of a trade mark agent extend to advising in relation to all legal pitfalls reasonably connected with a trade mark application, including: (1) keeping his client informed of any legal problems which might arise and warning the client to consider any commercial problems which might arise as a result of the legal problems which he, as a trade mark agent, might reasonably discern; and (2) informing his client of any matter in relation to which he needed instructions on the facts in order for him to give proper advice. These remarks would seem to apply equally to the duties of a patent agent. However, a patent agent is entitled to rely upon information provided by persons consulted abroad within the scope of their expertise and is not negligent in not obtaining documentation supporting advice received from abroad: *Arbiter Group v Gill Jennings & Every* [2001] R.P.C. 4 at 67; and [1999] R.P.C. 686.

In *Kalsep v X-Flow* BL C/13/01 terms in a patent licence agreement (which failed to provide for termination of the licence or any warranty as to patent validity and where the relevant application had not proceeded to grant) were described as being "grossly improvident" and the court opined that English advisers, if instructed and aware of the facts, would have been negligent in not advising the licensee to terminate the agreement.

Agency under the EPC

But for the presence of subs.(2) (which parallels s.102(4), reprinted in §102.01), s.274 **274.10** of the CDPA 1988 would have been in conflict with art.134 of the EPC. This article restricts representation before the EPO to those on the list of professional representatives maintained by the EPO ("the European list", as defined in s.286 of the CDPA 1988, reprinted at §286.01 and discussed in §286.03), or by a duly qualified legal practitioner, see §102.03. Accordingly, while a person not covered by art.134 of the EPC may be refused recognition by the EPO, he or she is apparently free under the present statutes to carry on in the United Kingdom the business of acting as agent for others for the purpose of applying for European patents (s.102(4)), but the restrictions imposed by the EPC in respect of proceedings before the EPO remain effective (subs.(2)).

It is not clear whether any person not on the European list is free to file in the United Kingdom an international application for a European patent. It would seem that such a person is free, because art.49 of the PCT provides that any:

"person, having the right to practice before the national office with which the international application was filed shall be entitled to practice in respect of that application before: the International Bureau (WIPO); the competent International Searching Authority [e.g. the EPO]; and the competent International Preliminary Examination Authority [e.g. also the EPO]".

It would seem wholly illogical for someone so entitled not to be free to file the application itself and this view must be strengthened by the provision in art.150(2) of the EPC that, in case of conflict, PCT provisions prevail over those of the EPC.

For representation before the EPO, see the *European Patents Handbook* ("EPH") (London: Sweet & Maxwell). It is here noted that if an applicant or other party to proceedings in the EPO uses a representative for those proceedings, an authorisation for a duly qualified representative to act must be filed under EPC r.101(4) if the appointed representative is not on the "European list", i.e. if that person is a general lawyer or an employee of the applicant, patentee or opponent (OJ EPO 1991, 489). It is also to be noted that, when an appointed representative acts before the EPO under the EPC, his communications must be personally signed, as discussed in §277.03. On the other hand, when representation in proceedings before the Comptroller is by a partnership or body corporate, communications from it to the UK-IPO can be signed in the name of such a firm or company.

SECTION 275 [PROSPECTIVELY REPLACED]

The register of patent attorneys

275.01 275.—(1) There is to continue to be a register of persons who act as agent for others for the purpose of applying for or obtaining patents.

(2) In this Part a registered patent attorney means an individual whose name is entered on the register kept under this section.

(3) The register is to be kept by the Chartered Institute of Patent Attorneys.

(4) The Secretary of State may, by order, amend subsection (3) so as to require the register to be kept by the person specified in the order.

(5) Before making an order under subsection (4), the Secretary of State must consult the Legal Services Board.

(6) An order under this section must be made by statutory instrument.

(7) An order under this section may not be made unless a draft of it has been laid before, and approved by a resolution of, each House of Parliament.

Regulation of patent attorneys

275A.—(1) The person who keeps the register under section 275 may make regulations which regulate—

(a) the keeping of the register and the registration of persons;

(b) the carrying on of patent attorney work by registered persons.

(2) Those regulations may, amongst other things, make—

(a) provision as to the educational and training qualifications, and other requirements, which must be satisfied before an individual may be registered or for an individual to remain registered;

(b) provision as to the requirements which must be met by a body (corporate or unincorporate) before it may be registered, or for it to remain registered, including provision as to the management and control of the body;

(c) provision as to the educational, training and other requirements to be met by regulated persons;

(d) provision regulating the practice, conduct and discipline of registered persons or regulated persons;

(e) provision authorising in such cases as may be specified in the regulations the erasure from the register of the name of any person registered in it, or the suspension of a person's registration;

(f) provision requiring the payment of such fees as may be specified in or determined in accordance with the regulations;

(g) provision about the provision to be made by registered persons in respect of complaints made against them;

(h) provision about the keeping by registered persons or regulated persons of records and accounts;

(i) provision for reviews of or appeals against decisions made under the regulations;

(j) provision as to the indemnification of registered persons or regulated persons against losses arising from claims in respect of civil liability incurred by them.

(3) Regulations under this section may make different provision for different purposes.

(4) Regulations under this section which are not regulatory arrangements within the meaning of the Legal Services Act 2007 are to be treated as such arrangements for the purposes of that Act.

(5) Before the appointed day, regulations under this section may be made only with the approval of the Secretary of State.

(6) The powers conferred to make regulations under this section are not to be taken to prejudice—

(a) any other power which the person who keeps the register may have to make rules or regulations (however they may be described and whether they are made under an enactment or otherwise);

(b) any rules or regulations made by that person under any such power.

(7) In this section—

"appointed day" means the day appointed for the coming into force of paragraph 1 of Schedule 4 to the Legal Services Act 2007;

"manager", in relation to a body, has the same meaning as in the Legal Services Act 2007 (see section 207);

"patent attorney work" means work done in the course of carrying on the business of acting as agent for others for the purpose of—

(a) applying for or obtaining patents, in the United Kingdom or elsewhere, or

(b) conducting proceedings before the comptroller relating to applications for, or otherwise in connection with, patents;

"registered person" means —

(a) a registered patent attorney, or

(b) a body (corporate or unincorporate) registered in the register kept under section 275;

"regulated person" means a person who is not a registered person but is a manager or employee of a body which is a registered person."

Note

Sections 275 and 275A entered into force on 1st January 2010, on which day s.185 of the Legal Services Act 2007 (c29) also entered into force. The sections replaced the previous s.275.

COMMENTARY ON SECTION 275

Scope of the section

275.02 Section 275 (as amended by the Legal Services Act 2007) of the CDPA 1988 provides for the continuation of the Register of Patent Attorneys (previously the Register of Patent Agents) and designates CIPA to keep the register. Subsections 4 to 7 set out the procedure for appointing another person or body to keep the register. These subsections, which would apply if CIPA wished to cease to keep the register or if it were found to be failing properly to discharge its duties, involve consultation with the Legal Services Board, which was set up by the Legal Services Act 2007, and require the approval of both Houses of Parliament of a draft statutory instrument.

Section 275A is a new enabling section providing in subsection (1) for regulations to be made concerning the keeping of the Register of Patent Attorneys, and for the carrying out of "patent attorney work" by registered persons, this term being defined in subs.(7). Subsection (2) contains a non-exhaustive list of matters which the regulations ("regulatory arrangements") may cover, while subs.3 ensures that all regulatory arrangements, however they are described, are treated as regulatory arrangements for the purposes of the Legal Services Act 2007. Subsection (5) ensures that the regulatory arrangements were in place on the coming into force of the Legal Services Act and consequently of the new s.275A, while subsection (7) is an interpretation clause.

Thus, the Register (first established by s.1 of the Patents, Designs and Trade Marks Act 1888 (c.50)), the history of which was reviewed by F. W. B. Kittel (1986–87) 16 *CIPA* 195, continues to provide the public with information of those who are specifically qualified by examination (for which see §275.05) to act for others as agents in relation to matters concerning patents (and indeed most other forms of intellectual property as well).

Section 275 of the CDPA 1988 originally replaced subs.123(2)(k) (now repealed) in providing for rules governing the Register of Patent Agents and defining the term "registered patent agent" as a person entered in this Register (subs.(1)). This definition replaced the definition of "patent agent" previously contained in s.130(1) which was in terms of functions performed and activity carried out, though by s.114 (now repealed) the title "patent agent" could not be used except by a person entered in this register. The revised wording of the section now amends the name of the register to the usually-used title of "patent attorney". As noted in the commentary on section 274, anyone may perform the functions and carry out the activity of acting as an agent for others (for which see §102.02 and §274.03), but it remains the position that only a registered patent attorney is entitled to use the term "patent agent" or "patent attorney", see s.276 of the CDPA 1988, discussed in §§276.02 et seq., although s.278 permits a solicitor or a firm of solicitors to use the expression "patent attorney" without contravening section 276.

There is now no nationality requirement for entry in the Register of Patent Attorneys, but the Comptroller is required to refuse to recognise a patent agent who neither resides nor has a place of business in the United Kingdom, the Isle of Man or a Member State of the European Community (CDPA 1988 s.281(5), discussed in §281.05).

THE LEGAL SERVICES ACT 2007 (C.29)
SCHEDULE 5

Authorised Persons

PART 1

CONTINUITY OF RIGHTS

Rights of audience and conduct of litigation

1.—(1) For the purposes of section 18 (authorised persons), in the case of a person who is authorised by a listed body—   **275.03**

    (a) to exercise a right of audience before a court in relation to any proceedings, or

    (b) to conduct litigation in relation to any proceedings,

it is irrelevant whether the person's authorisation was granted before or on or after the appointed day.

  (2) The "listed bodies" are—

    (c) The Chartered Institute of Patent Attorneys.

PART 2

RIGHTS DURING TRANSITIONAL PERIOD

The transitional period

3.—(1) In this Part of this Schedule references to "the transitional period" are to the period which—

    (a) begins with the appointed day (within the meaning given by paragraph 19), and

    (b) ends with the day appointed by the Lord Chancellor by order for the purposes of this paragraph.

  (2) Different days may be appointed under sub-paragraph (1)(b) for different purposes.

Patent attorneys

14.—(1) During the transitional period, every registered patent attorney is deemed to be authorised by the Chartered Institute of Patent Attorneys to carry on reserved instrument activities.

  (2) During that period, every authorised patent attorney is deemed to be authorised by the Chartered Institute of Patent Attorneys to administer oaths.

  (3) During that period, every patent attorney body is deemed to be authorised by the Chartered Institute of Patent Attorneys to carry on the activities in sub-paragraph (4).

  (4) Those activities are any activities which are reserved legal activities within sub-paragraph (5) and which—

    (a) if the body is a partnership, any partner who is a registered patent attorney is authorised to carry on;

    (b) if the body is a body corporate, any director who is a registered patent attorney is authorised to carry on.

  (5) Those activities are—

    (a) the exercise of a right of audience;

    (b) the conduct of litigation;

    (c) reserved instrument activities;

    (d) the administration of oaths.

  (6) The authority conferred by any of sub-paragraphs (1) to (3) is exercisable in accordance with and subject to the regulatory arrangements of the Chartered Institute of Patent Attorneys.

  (7) In this paragraph—

"authorised patent attorney" means a registered patent attorney who is authorised by the Chartered Institute of Patent Attorneys to carry on one or both of the following activities—

(a) the exercise of a right of audience;

(b) the conduct of litigation;

"patent attorney body" means —

(a) a partnership all the partners of which are registered patent attorneys,

(b) a body corporate all the directors of which are registered patent attorneys,

(c) a partnership or body corporate which satisfies the conditions prescribed under section 279 of the Copyright, Designs and Patents Act 1988 (c. 48), or

(d) a body corporate to which section 276(4) of that Act applies;

"registered patent attorney" has the meaning given by section 275(2) of that Act;

and, in the case of a patent attorney body to which section 276(4) of that Act applies, the reference in sub-paragraph (4)(b) to a director includes a reference to the manager (within the meaning of section 276(4) of that Act) of the company.

Patent attorneys

15.—(1) During the transitional period registered patent attorneys are to continue to have the rights conferred by section 102A(2) of the Patents Act 1977 (c. 37) and section 292 of the Copyright, Designs and Patents Act 1988 (c. 48).

(2) In this paragraph "registered patent attorney" has the same meaning as in paragraph 14.

PART 3

INTERPRETATION

19. In this Schedule—

"the appointed day" means the day appointed for the coming into force of section 13 (entitlement to carry on a reserved legal activity);

Note

These sections entered into force of January 1, 2010.

Effects of the Legal Services Act 2007 (c.29)

275.04   The Legal Services Act 2007 (c.29), the relevant parts of which entered into force on January 1, 2010, provides for the establishment of a Legal Services Board to oversee the regulation of persons carrying out certain reserved legal activities. These reserved legal activities include rights to conduct litigation and rights of audience before the courts and all patent attorneys have previously been granted certain litigation rights under s.292 of the CDP Act 1988. Both CIPA and ITMA were subsequently granted the right under ss.27–29 of the Courts & Legal Services Act 1990 (c.41) (now repealed and replaced by the rights afforded by the Legal Services Act 2007) to award to suitably qualified and experienced members certificates entitling them to conduct litigation in the High Court. The Legal Services Act 2007 now recognises the patent attorney and trade mark attorney professions as part of the legal professions and thus falling within the scope of that Act. The Chartered Institute and the Institute of Trade Mark Attorneys are both designated as "Approved Regulators"; s.185 of this Act contains provisions relating to patent attorneys and s.184 contains similar provisions relating to trade mark attorneys. These provisions include a substitution for s.275 of the CDPA 1988 and a new s.275A. Also, there were amendments to ss.276, 280, 281 and 286, and deletion of s.279 (see the relevant commentaries below for details of these changes). Similar amendments were made to the provisions relating to trade mark attorneys in the Trade Marks Act 1994. However, thereafter there is a "transitional period" during which reserved activities permitted for authorised persons under the pre-existing legislation can continue as before, as discussed in §275.10 below.

The titles of the Registers were changed to "The Register of Patent Attorneys" and "The Register of Trade Mark Attorneys". Thus, the designations by which those on either register are known has formally changed to "patent attorney" and "registered trade mark attorney" and it is to be expected that the use of "agent" will very largely cease.

Revised s.275 provides for the continuation of the register and for the Chartered Institute to continue to keep the register. New s.275A provides for the Chartered Institute to make regulations ("regulatory arrangements") relating to the keeping of the register and for the registration both of individuals (as hitherto) and of entities (a new provision). The Act requires the separation of the regulatory decision-making functions of the approved regulators from their representative decision-making functions. The Chartered Institute has set up a Patent Regulation Board ("PRB") and ITMA has set up a similar Trade Mark Regulation Board ("TRB"). Because many patent attorneys are dually-qualified also as trade mark attorneys, and also because patent and trade mark attorneys practise together in mixed partnerships (see the discussion in the commentary of s.279) and these firms will be entered in both registers, in actuality PRB and TRB function as a joint IP Regulation Board, to which is delegated most of the regulatory functions of both of the Institutes. However, the IP Regulation Board formally takes the decisions in the names of the separate Institute Regulation Boards, since it is the Institutes which are separately named as the approved regulators. A few functions have been reserved for decisions to be taken separately by the Institute Regulation Boards, but in practice this separation has not yet proved to be necessary.

The regulatory arrangements prepared in the name of the Chartered Institute and approved by the Legal Services Board have replaced the Register of Patent Agents Rules 1990 (SI 1990/1457),which were revoked when the new ss.275 and 275A were brought into effect on January 1, 2010.

Under the previous s.275 of the CDPA 1988 and the RPA Rules, the power of removal of the name of a registered patent agent from the register lay with the Secretary of State (a function delegated to the UK-IPO) after a hearing. The regulatory arrangements made under the new s.275A [2007] give this power to the Chartered Institute, to be exercised under regulatory and disciplinary procedures to be introduced by the IP Regulation Board. The regulatory arrangements also include a Code of Conduct for Patent and Trade Mark Attorneys and Other Regulated Persons (see Appendix x) and regulations covering the qualification and registration of individual patent and trade mark attorneys and regulations for the registration of firms of patent and/or trade mark attorneys. The CIPA Rules of Professional Conduct which applied to members of the Chartered Institute ceased to have effect on January 1, 2010, when the IPReg Code of Conduct replaced them.

Prior to the coming into force of the new arrangements, the disciplinary procedures of the Chartered Institute did not distinguish between complaints of poor service and those alleging misconduct, both type of complaint being dealt with under a common procedure. However, under the Legal Services Act, a new Office for Legal Complaints (operating as the Legal Ombudsman) has been set up under the Legal Services Board and this Office acts as the gateway for all complaints against legal services providers and itself deals with poor service complaints, referring to the appropriate regulator any misconduct issues which require to be considered.

Patent Attorney and Trade Mark Attorney Qualification and Registration Regulations

These regulations, which were promulgated by IPReg and approved by the Legal Services Board, replaced the former Register of Patent Agents Rules 1994 when those rules were revoked on the entry into force of the Legal Services Act and new s.275A of the CDP Act on January 1, 2010. The regulations make provision for the appointment of Registrars for maintaining the patent attorney and trade mark attorney registers; the procedures for, and the circumstances in which, individuals may be entered into the patent attorney register and/or the trade mark attorney register; the duration and renewal of registrations and the circumstances in which registration will expire or may be revoked; and appeals relating to registration of individuals in the patent attorney and trade mark attorney registers.

275.05

This Register of Patent Attorneys contains the names of each person entitled to be registered under the regulations, together with his business address, date of registration and qualifications for registration (r.3.3). The register is generally open to public inspection (r.3.5), and IPReg is required to publish by April 1 annually an alphabetical list of the entries in the register as at the end of the previous year (r.3.6). This copy of the register is posted on the website of IPReg and the Chartered Institute publishes on its website *www.cipa.org.uk* on behalf of IPReg a searchable database of registered patent attorneys updated on a daily basis. However, the Chartered Institute also publishes on its website a directory of firms of Chartered Patent Attorneys, which is of greater use for members of the public seeking to engage the services of a patent attorney. The Chartered Institute also publishes a "Membership List", again in electronic and printed forms, which contains more information than the current form of the register and is thus of greater use to members of the Chartered Institute.

Entry to the register is on the basis of passing an examination (for which see §275.07), and completing a period of practice in the field of intellectual property, this period being at least two years of supervised practice or at least four years of full-time practice, in each case "including substantial experience in patent agency work", but for unsupervised practice this experience must be gained in the UK, whereas supervised practice does not carry this restriction see r.4.2).

The regulations also make provision for the making of regulations requiring registered attorneys to carry out a prescribed amount of continuing professional development activities each year; also provision is made for regulations relating to disciplinary procedures under which IPReg may direct that a registered patent attorney or a registered trade mark attorney who has been found guilty of misconduct or other material breach of any of its rules and regulations be erased or suspended from the relevant register. Under s.281 and the Rules made under it, the Comptroller may refuse to recognise as agent for any business under the Patents Act 1949, the Patents Act 1977, or the Registered Designs Act 1949, any person whose name has been erased from the Register and not restored to it (see §§281.01 et seq.)

IPReg is empowered by the regulations (r.12), in consultation with CIPA and ITMA and with the approval of the Legal Services Board, to set and levy fees payable in connection with initial and continued registration of individuals

The regulations also provide for the accreditation by IPReg of examination agencies to be responsible to them for the management and control of the qualifying examinations pertaining to admission to one or both of the Registers, for details of which see §275.07 below.

Patent Attorney and Trade Mark Attorney Registered Bodies Regulations (Registration of Entities)

275.06   Section 275A for the first time allows for the making of regulations for the registration of entities (corporate or unincorporate), and for them to remain registered, including provision as to the management and control of the body. IPReg has promulgated these regulations, which can be found on the IPReg website: at *http://www.ipreg.org.uk*.

Under the regulations, which came into force on January 1, 2010, all partnerships and bodies corporate entitled under s.276 of the Copyright Designs and Patents Act 1988 as amended on the day immediately prior to that date to carry on a business under any name or other description which contains the words "patent agent" or "patent attorney" were deemed to be registered as registered bodies in the patent attorney register effective as of the commencement date, subject to payment of an entity registration fee.

New registrations will be approved if the entity provides "patent attorney work" services and confirms that it will abide by the Code of Conduct of IPReg. In addition, for a partnership, at least one partner must be a registered patent attorney, at least 75 per cent of the partners must be lawyers, and all other partners must be approved by IPReg as managers in accordance with the requirements of the regulations. Similar conditions apply to the managers of an LLP or a company.

The letterhead, website and e-mails of firms and sole practitioner registered persons in private practice must show the words "regulated by the Intellectual Property Regulation Board" or "regulated by IPREG".

Entities which are entered in the register are entitled to use the title "Patent Attorneys", in accordance with s.276 (see the commentary on this section at §276.02 et seq.).

Examinations for entry into the Register of Patent Attorneys

Under the previous Register of Patent Agents Rules 1994 (now repealed), the Chartered **275.07** Institute of Patent Attorneys and the Institute of Trade Mark Attorneys had each been given power, in consultation with the other Institute and with the approval of the comptroller, to make provision for the examinations leading to qualification for registration in the relevant Register. The Institutes had delegated their respective responsibilities for the qualifying examinations to a Joint Examination Board ("JEB") consisting of an equal number of registered patent attorneys and registered trade mark attorneys. The constitution of the JEB was reproduced: [1996] *CIPA* 111, but see also [1997] *CIPA* 260. The Institute of Trade Mark Attorneys has recently revised the requirements for the qualifying examinations for registration as a trade mark attorney and these changes are working through, so that after the Final level trade mark examinations to be set in November 2012, the JEB will no longer be involved in setting the qualifying examinations for registration as a trade mark attorney and it is likely that the JEB will be dissolved and be reformed as a Committee of CIPA to provide only qualifying examinations for registration as a patent attorney.

As noted in §275.05 above, the Patent Attorney and Trade Mark Attorney Qualification and Registration Regulations, which entered into force on January 1, 2010 replacing the RPA Rules, provide in reg.5 for the accreditation of one or more Examination Agencies to be responsible to IPReg for the management and control of the qualifying examinations for registration of individuals. Pursuant to this power, IPReg issued the "Rules for the Examination and Admission of Individuals to the Registers of Patent and Trade Mark Attorneys 2011", effective from June 6, 2011, which are available on the IPReg website.

The new Rules continue the existing arrangements of Foundation Level and Final (Advanced in the JEB regulations) Level examinations to be managed and controlled by Examination Agencies, provided that the examinations have been determined by IPReg on an application by the relevant Examination Agency as meeting the requisite overall standard and general content (r.3.1). An Examination Agency may be empowered and accredited to run either or both Foundation and Final level examinations (r.3.2), each Examination Agency being required to publish in advance details of its qualifying examinations (r.3.4).

The JEB and the academic institutions which it recognised as providing courses giving exemptions from various papers of the qualifying examinations set by the JEB have been accredited as Examination Agencies, so that the arrangements for the qualifying examinations remain essentially as they were before the new Rules were promulgated.

The examinations are organised on a modular basis with candidates having to satisfy the examiners in relevant "foundation papers" and then pass certain "advanced papers" according to whether they wish to qualify for entry into the Register of Patent Attorneys (under the present section), or the Register of Trade Mark Attorneys (now under the Trade Marks Act 1994 (c.26) s.83, as amended by the Legal Services Act), or both. Notes have been published on the procedures adopted for these examinations, explaining particularly how the papers are set and marked, syllabuses for the papers and the methods available for making complaints against the marks awarded (*Patents Journal* June 21, 1995).

The principles underlying these examinations is that entry into the register should indicate a competent knowledge of intellectual property law and of patent practice both for the United Kingdom and for overseas countries generally. Copies of the current form of the Examination Regulations can be obtained from the Chartered Institute of Patent Attorneys, 95 Chancery Lane, London, WC2A 1DT, or can be downloaded from the website of the Joint Examination Board at *http://www.jointexaminationboard.org.uk*.

For qualification as a "European patent attorney", see §286.04.

The privileges of a registered patent attorney

The entry of an individual's name in the Register of Patent Attorneys entitles that person **275.08** to use the title "patent attorney" or "patent agent" as a description in the course of business, which use would otherwise be an offence under s.276(1) of the CDPA 1988, see §276.02 and §278.02. Also, a registered patent attorney can be a partner in a partnership, a member of a limited liability partnership, or a director in a body corporate, which describe themselves as a firm or company of patent attorneys or patent agents, provided that the provisions of s.276(2) or (3) of the CDPA 1988 (as amended by the Legal Services Act) are met, for which also see §276.02. The terms "patent agent" and "patent attorney" may not be used otherwise, except that a solicitor and his firm may use the term "patent attorney" or "patent attorneys" (CDPA s.278(1)); but only if appropriate, see §278.02.

Other privileges of registered patent attorneys possessed in common with solicitors, but denied to other persons, are those referred to in §274.07, viz.: rights as regards representation and appearance in, and preparing documents for, appeals from a decision of the Comptroller to the Patents Court (s.102A, discussed in §102A.02); and rights as regards legal privilege (CDPA 1988 s.280, discussed in §§280.02et seq.), perhaps also enjoyed in Scotland by unqualified persons, see §105.03. Also, whereas counsel may normally only receive instructions from solicitors, by tradition registered patent attorneys may instruct counsel directly, see *Reiss Engineering v Harris* [1987] R.P.C. 171.

Furthermore, agreements relating to services provided by "patent attorneys" and "European patent attorneys" as such can be exempted from the effects of Pt I of the Competition Act 1998 (c.41) s.3(1); Sch.4 by an order made by the Secretary of State that such is to be regarded as "a professional rule".

The extent of the lien which a patent attorney may have over the papers of his client who has failed to make proper payment to him has been explained by R. P. Lloyd (1988–89) 18 *CIPA* 30, see also (1988–89) 18 *CIPA* 133 and 135; it is also covered in the Code of Conduct of IPReg.

It appears that, while an individual's name remains in the Register of Patent Attorneys, the Comptroller cannot refuse to recognise that individual as an agent in respect of business under the Patents and Registered Designs Acts, see s.281 of the CDPA 1988 (reprinted at §281.01 and dealt with in §§281.02 et seq.).

For a discussion of the effects of the Legal Services Act 2007 (c.29) in this area, see §275.04.

The Chartered Institute and "Chartered Patent Attorneys"

275.09　　The Chartered Institute of Patent Attorneys is a professional body established in 1882 and incorporated under a Royal Charter granted in 1891. The history of the Chartered Institute was described in a special "Commemorative Issue" of its monthly journal: *CIPA* (1981–82) 11 *CIPA* 470. Since 1891, the term "Chartered Patent Agent" has been a title approved by the Privy Council for use by those Fellows of the Chartered Institute who are also registered patent attorneys (Charter of Incorporation of the Institute, 1891, clause 29). Clause 29 of a Third Supplemental Charter granted to the Chartered Institute on September 13, 1991 added the right to use of the term "Chartered Patent Attorney". On February 11, 2009 CIPA was granted a new, enabling, Charter and revised Bye-laws, in order for it to be able to delegate its regulatory functions to the newly created Intellectual Property Regulation Board (IPReg). In Bye-law 4, it is now stated that:

"Fellows of the Institute who have qualified as patent attorneys may use the designations 'Chartered Patent Agent' and 'Chartered Patent Attorney' (but not together or otherwise so as to imply two separate qualifications) and after their names the initials 'C.P.A.' representing either designation".

It should, however, be noted that the abbreviation "F.C.I.P.A." is not approved by the Privy Council, see (1973–74) 3 *CIPA* 170 and 265. It may also be noted that Fellows of the Chartered Institute who have retired from practice and are no longer "registered patent attorneys" would appear, strictly speaking, to be committing an offence if they continue to describe themselves as a "Chartered Patent Agent" or "Chartered Patent Attorney", though only if this is done "in the course of a business", see s.276(1)(b).

The expressions "Chartered Patent Agents" and "Chartered Patent Attorneys" should only be used by firms (or bodies corporate) which are entered in the Register of Patent Attorneys (see §275.07 above) and in which all principals who are "patent attorneys" are Fellows of the Chartered Institute, and such expression should only appear first or more prominently in the letterhead, etc. of a mixed partnership (or body corporate) only when the majority of its principals are patent agents, see [1995] *CIPA* 550 and [1996] *CIPA* 211.

The designations "CHARTERED PATENT AGENT"; "CHARTERED PATENT AGENTS"; "CHARTERED PATENT ATTORNEY"; "CHARTERED PATENT ATTORNEYS"; "C.P.A."; and "CPA" have each been registered as collective trade marks under the Trade Marks Act 1994. The Regulations governing the use of these marks by Fellows of the Chartered Institute were published [1996] *CIPA* 905–909, with prospective amendment [1997] *CIPA* 164.

Chartered Patent Attorneys were previously bound by the Rules of Professional Conduct adopted from time to time by the Chartered Institute, the Rules being amplified by a set of guidelines concerning the observance of the rules. However, on the entry into force on January 1, 2010 of the Legal Services Act 2007 and the amendment of s.275 with the addition of the new s.275A, the regulation of the patent attorney profession passed to the IP Regulation Board and the Chartered Institute is no longer able to impose its Rules, since these are of a regulatory nature. The CIPA Rules of Professional Conduct have accordingly been superseded by the IPReg Code of Conduct for Patent Attorneys, Trade Mark Attorneys and Other Regulated Persons.

Members of the Chartered Institute, when acting as litigators, either in the Patents County Court or as an "authorised litigator" under the Courts and Legal Services Act 1990 (c.41) ss.27, 28 and 119, for which see §275.10, are subject to additional rules of professional conduct, these being the Special Rules of Professional Conduct (reprinted in Appendix K). Any breach of either of these sets of Rules can lead to the imposition of sanctions under IPReg's Rules of Disciplinary Procedure.

The Chartered Institute's former rules of professional conduct (now superseded by IPReg's Code of Conduct) have been recognised by the Patents Court, who noted that they draw no distinction between those Chartered Patent Agents in private practice and those employed in industry, the Government or public service. Thus, in *Schering's Patent* [1986] R.P.C. 30, it was held that, because all Chartered Patent Agents are bound by the same rules of professional conduct, there was no good reason why an employed patent agent, as regards the receipt of evidence in confidence in proceedings under s.46, should be put in a different position from that of an independent patent agent, though conditions were imposed on his employer to ensure his independence, see also *Unilever v Pearce* [1985] F.S.R. 475 and §280.02—280.09.

Registered patent attorneys as "authorised litigators"

Under the Chartered Institute of Patent Agents Order 1999 (SI 1999/3137), the **275.10** Chartered Institute was designated as "an authorised body for the purposes of ss.27 and 28 of the Courts and Legal Services Act 1990" as from November 25, 1999. Under the powers thereby provided, a Litigator Accrediting Board was established by the Chartered Institute and was able (under conditions) to issue a "Litigator Certificate" to a Chartered Patent Attorney appointing that person as an "authorised litigator" within the terms of this 1990 Act to act within the limits set out in that certificate. Such a person is termed a "patent attorney litigator". The conditions for such an appointment were set out in the CIPA Higher Courts Qualification Regulations 2007, made by the Council of the Chartered Institute, as approved under this 1990 Act. These Regulations include the requirement for a candidate for issue of a Litigator Certificate to have passed certain examinations. However, up to November 25, 2001, the Chartered Institute had the power to waive this requirement for those of its members who were able to demonstrate to the Litigator Accrediting Board that they had had significant experience in being involved with intellectual property litigation.

From January 1, 2010, when the Legal Services Act 2007 entered into force, the IP Regulation Board (for which see §§275.04 and 274.08) took over responsibility for regulating the patent attorney and trade mark attorney professions, including the power to award litigator certificates. IPReg adopted CIPA's Higher Court Regulations and has set up a Litigator Accrediting Board to consider applications for the award of a litigators certificate.

Schedule 5, para.15 of the Legal Services Act maintains the rights of all registered patent agents to conduct litigation in, and appear before a patents county court conferred by s.102A of the Patents Act 1977 and s.292 of the CDPA 1988 during a transitional period (as discussed in §292.02).

The power of a patent attorney litigator to act as an "authorised litigator" is limited to the conduct of litigation in the county courts, the High Court and the Court of Appeal which involves intellectual property, provided that this is of a technical character (i.e. excluding copyright protection of aesthetic subject-matter). However, neither IPReg, nor previously CIPA, has the right to appoint registered patent attorneys as "authorised advocates" so that patent attorney litigators do not have a right of appearance in the High Court (except when it is sitting in Chambers) or in the Court of Appeal. However, in July 2011 IPReg issued a consultation paper on litigation rights for patent and trade mark attorneys and proposes to introduce procedures for granting these rights to patent or trade mark attorneys who undertake suitable further training.

For other rights and privileges enjoyed by "authorised litigators", see §292.04.

All registered patent attorneys, whether or not patent attorney litigators, who undertake litigation work, whether in proceedings in a patents county court or (in the case of a patent attorney litigator) in intellectual property litigation in the High Court or the Court of Appeal), are bound by the Special Rules of Professional Conduct of IPReg (for which see §274.08) and are subject to the Disciplinary Procedure of IPReg referred to in that paragraph.

SECTION 276

Persons entitled to describe themselves as patent agents

276.01 **276.**—(1) An individual who is not a registered patent attorney shall not—

(a) carry on a business (otherwise than in partnership) under any name or other description which contains the words "patent agent" or "patent attorney"; or

(b) in the course of a business otherwise describe himself, or permit himself to be described, as a "patent agent" or "patent attorney".

(2) A partnership or other unincorporated body shall not—

(a) carry on a business under any name or other description which contains the words "patent agent" or "patent attorney"; or

(b) in the course of a business otherwise describe itself, or permit itself to be described as, a firm of "patent agents" or "patent attorneys",

unless the partnership or other body is registered in the Register kept under section 275.

(3) A body corporate shall not—

(a) carry on a business (otherwise than in partnership) under any name or other description which contains the words "patent agent" or "patent attorney"; or

(b) in the course of a business otherwise describe itself, or permit itself to be described as, a "patent agent" or "patent attorney",

unless the body corporate is entered in the register kept under section 275.

(4) Subsection (3) does not apply to a company which began to carry on business as a patent agent before 17th November 1917 if the name of a director or the manager of the company who is a registered patent attorney is mentioned as be-

ing so registered in all professional advertisements, circulars or letters issued by or with the company's consent on which its name appears.

(5) Where this section would be contravened by the use of the words "patent agent" or "patent attorney" in reference to an individual, partnership or body corporate, it is equally contravened by the use of other expressions in reference to that person, or his business or place of business, which are likely to be understood as indicating that he is entitled to be described as a "patent agent" or "patent attorney".

(6) A person who contravenes this section commits an offence and is liable on summary conviction to a fine not exceeding level 5 on the standard scale; and proceedings for such an offence may be begun at any time within a year from the date of the offence.

(7) This section has effect subject to—

- (a) section 277 (persons entitled to describe themselves as European patent attorneys, etc.), and
- (b) section 278(1) (use of term "patent attorney" in reference to solicitors).

Notes

1. This section which originally came into force on August 13, 1990 (SI 1990/1400) was amended by the provisions of Sch.21, para.76 of the Legal Services Act 2007 when that Schedule entered into force on January 1, 2010.

2. The amendments were the replacement of the word "agent" by "attorney" in subss.(1) and (4); the insertion in subs.(2) of "or other unincorporated body" after "partnership" (in the first place); the substitution of "the partnership or other body is registered in the register kept under s.275" for "all the partners" to the end; and the substitution of "the body corporate is registered in the register kept under s.275." for "all the directors" to the end in subs.(3).

COMMENTARY ON SECTION 276

Scope of the section

Section 276 of the CDPA 1988 replaced s.114 (now repealed), but with one notable **276.02** omission consequent upon the Government's acceptance of part of recommendation 6.6c of the Report of the Office of Fair Trading of September 1986 (for which see §102.03), viz. criminal sanctions against the practice of patent agency by unqualified persons. This omission followed naturally from the provisions of substituted s.102 and s.274 of the CDPA 1988, discussed respectively in §§102.02 et seq. and 274.03 et seq. However, the second arm of that recommendation—to remove all protection from the title "patent agent"—was not accepted. Indeed, the Government eventually went further than the protection for this title provided by the former s.114, by also providing protection for the term "patent attorney", and for other expressions indicating activity in the area of patent agency (as discussed and illustrated in §§276.04 and 276.05), and by officially sanctioning the use (by registered patent agents and by appropriate solicitors) of the term "patent attorney", see s.278(2) of the CDPA 1988 and §§278.02 et seq.

The process of securing the use of "patent attorney" was completed with the entry into force of the Legal Services Act 2007 (c.29) on January 1, 2010, this Act recognising "patent attorney" as the main title used, although the use of "patent agent" continues to be reserved to those on the register and unregistered persons (other than solicitors) continue to be prohibited from using that title. The name of the register was also changed to the Register of Patent Attorneys.

Subsection (1) prohibits an individual from practising under, or using in the course of a business, the title "patent agent" or "patent attorney", unless registered in the Register of Patent Attorneys, for which see s.275 of the CDPA 1988 and §§275.03 and 275.04. The prohibition is clear and would presumably apply to foreign patent agents and patent attorneys not on the register, although those persons on the European list (for which see §286.01) may use the title "European patent attorney" or "European patent agent" (CDPA 1988 s.277, see §§277.02 et seq.).

Subsections (2) and (3), as amended by the Legal Services Act 2007 on January 1, 2010, extend the prohibition of subs.(1) respectively to partnerships, other bodies unincorporate and bodies corporate, unless the entity is entered in the Register of Patent Attorneys; see §275.06 for a discussion of the requirements for registration of an entity.

Prior to that date, the requirement for a partnership or a body corporate to be entitled to use the expressions "patent agent" or "patent attorney" was that all of the partners or directors (which term would be deemed to include the chief executive or other senior manager of the company) had to be entered on the register, or the body had to satisfy conditions prescribed with respect to the section. Those conditions were set out in the Patent Agents (Mixed Partnerships and Bodies Corporate) Rules 1994 (SI 1994/362) which were made under s.279. That section was repealed and the Rules were revoked when the amended wording for subss.276(2) and 276(3) came into effect on January 1, 2010. The rules of SI 1994/362 became effective from March 24, 1994. These permitted the use of the expressions "patent agent" and "patent attorney" by mixed partnerships, or bodies corporate with mixed directors, of patent agents/attorneys and registered trade mark agents/attorneys (the latter originally registered under s.282 of the CDPA 1988 latterly registered under the Trade Marks Act 1994 (c.26), s.83), provided that at least one quarter of the partners/directors were "patent agents" (i.e. entered on the Register of Patent Agents, for which see s.275 and its commentary on it); and that, where the names of the partners/directors appeared on business papers, each partner/director so named must be identified as a patent agent or patent attorney. Reciprocal provisions were made in respect of registered trade mark agents by the Registered Trade Mark Agents (Mixed Partnerships and Bodies Corporate) Rules 1994 (SI 1994/363). At the same time, these mixed partnerships were added to the list of partnerships which are exempted from a limit of 20 partners (Partnerships (Unrestricted Size) No.11 Regulations (SI 1994/644).

Subsection (4) retains the previous exemption (previously contained in now repealed s.114(2)(a)) in favour of companies which started business "as a patent agent" before November 17, 1917, but at least one director or the manager of such a company must be a registered patent attorney and the name of at least one of these must be mentioned in all professional advertisements, circulars or letters issued by the company on which its name appears.

Subsection (5) extends the prohibitions of s.276 of the CDPA 1988 to expressions "which are likely to be understood as indicating that [the person or entity in question] is entitled to be described as a "patent agent" or "patent attorney". This provision was especially inserted to close a gap revealed by litigation under former statutes and deal with the problem of unregistered persons using expressions in reference to themselves which, whilst not including the forbidden words, imply that they are registered, or otherwise qualified, as "patent agents" or "patent attorneys", for which see §§276.04 and 276.05.

Patent agents are excused from the limitation on partnerships to a maximum of 20 persons by the Partnerships (Unrestricted Size) No. 1 Regulations 1968 (SI 1968/1222); and the services they provide are exempted by s.15 and Sch.4 to the Fair Trading Act 1973 (c.41) from some of the provisions of that Act.

J.C. Boff [2005] *CIPA* 517 has discussed the complex position as to the various persons who are entitled to use the terms: "patent agent(s)" or "patent attorney(s)"; "European patent attorney" or "European patent attorneys"; "registered trade mark agent(s)"; "trade mark attorney(s)"; and "Chartered Patent Agent(s) or "Chartered Patent Attorneys".

Penalty for offence under the section (subs.(6))

276.03   Subsection (6) prescribes that an offence under the section is triable only summarily and proceedings must be commenced within a year from the date of the offence. However, this latter provision is not clear in respect of an offence of a continuing, rather than an isolated, nature. The maximum penalty is prescribed as a fine "not exceeding level 5 on the standard scale". The term "standard scale" is defined by s.37(2) of the Criminal Justice Act 1982 (c.48). The amount of the fine corresponding to stated levels on the standard scale may be increased by order made under s.143 of the Magistrates' Courts Act 1980 (c.43) or otherwise, and "level 5" presently stands at £5,000 (Criminal Justice Act 1991 (c.53) s.17).

Protection of titles of "patent agent", "patent attorney" and analogous expressions

The propriety of use of the term "patent attorney" (reserved under CDPA 1988 s.276(1)) **276.04** by a registered patent attorney in the course of business is now not in doubt (as it was before the CDPA 1988), because s.278(2)(a) of the CDPA 1988 makes specific provision for use of this term alone by a registered patent attorney, just as use of the title "European patent attorney" by a person on the European list continues to be sanctioned (by CDPA 1988 s.278(2)(b)) as it formerly was under now repealed s.85(1). As is noted in §275.08, following the entry into force of the relevant sections of the Legal Services Act 2007 (c.29), Sch.4(1), the term "patent attorney" has become the designated term for those on the register, which itself has become the Register of Patent Attorneys. However (by CDPA 1988 s.278(1)), the title "patent attorney" may also be used by any solicitor, even if not also a registered patent attorney.

Because s.274 of the CDPA 1988 (without subs.(5) of it), together with ss.276(1)–(3), would have merely changed the law back to the unsatisfactory position which obtained between 1888 and 1919, concern was felt as to titles which might be used by persons acting for others in patent matters, but who are not registered patent agents or solicitors. Past decisions on appeal during the former period suggested that the use of names very similar to "patent agent" would not be held to be prohibited, as it did not then prove possible for the Chartered Institute to stop the use of such titles. Thus, for example, prosecutions by the Chartered Institute failed in the following instances: "Agent for the Applicant" (*Graham v Fanta* (1892) 9 R.P.C. 164); "Patent Office", "Inventors' Medium Limited", "patent expert" and "If you want a patent agent, I am the man for you" (*Graham v Eli, Hughes and Barlow* (1898) 15 R.P.C. 259); "Agent for preparing patent specifications" (*Graham v Tanner* (1912) 29 R.P.C. 683); and "Patent Agency" (*Hans v Graham* [1914] 3 K.B. 400). After 1919, when the statute was amended into a form substantially similar to that of now repealed s.114, further prosecutions failed to prove that the defendant was acting "as a patent agent", in cases involving: "negotiation of all foreign patents" (*Thompson v Bettinger (No.2)* (1929) 46 R.P.C. 189); "acting as agent for a foreign patent attorney" (*Thompson v Joseph Benton* (1932) 49 R.P.C. 33); and "assisting applicant by attending interview with Patent Office examiner" (*Thompson v Arthur Edward Brown* (1933) 50 R.P.C. 389).

While it is not thought that these decisions would necessarily be repeated in modern times, a criminal statute is construed strictly, and therefore it was appropriate for the protection of the title of "patent agent" to be safeguarded against the use of other expressions implying registration when this is not the case. Also, with the increasing interest in other forms of intellectual and industrial property, the public is beginning to recognise the term "intellectual property" as covering patents, trade marks, service marks, designs (both registered and unregistered, and semiconductor topographies) and copyrights. Nevertheless, it remains to be seen whether the term "intellectual property agent" will be held as being understood as indicating that its user is a registered patent attorney. Of even more concern, would be a decision which permitted the use of foreign-language terms corresponding to the prohibited wording, such as "*Patentanwalt*", "*Conseil en brevets*", "*Patentombud*" or "*Octrooigemachtigde*".

The Chartered Institute has also stated that:

"Where a person not on the register of Patent Agents, but qualified as a Patent Agent in a jurisdiction outside the United Kingdom, describes himself (but not his business) by a title containing the words 'Patent Agent' placed in juxtaposition with a clear and unambiguous indication of the jurisdiction in which he is qualified, the Institute will not seek to challenge such use on the basis of section 276(1)(b)" [1995] *CIPA* 313.

It may be noted that, while the term "registered trade mark attorney" is likewise reserved to persons entered in the register of trade mark attorneys, there is no provision corresponding to s.276(5) of the CDPA 1988 making it an offence to use similar expressions indicating that the person is a registered trade mark attorney when such is not the case. Thus, it remains to be seen whether the former cases in relation to "patent agents" will still be applied in modern times in relation to registered trade mark attorneys. However, s.17 of the Legal Services Act 2007 makes it an offence for any person to pretend to be entitled to carry out "reserved legal activities" when not entitled to do so, or to take or use any name, title or description with the intention of implying falsely that the person is so entitled. Advocacy and litigation rights, as granted to and exercised by registered patent attorneys or registered trade mark attorneys are reserved legal activities, although "patent attorney work" and "trade mark attorney work" are not.

Cases brought under the section

276.05   In order to enforce the provisions prohibiting use of the terms "patent agent", "patent attorney" and the like by persons not entitled to use these expressions under the terms of s.276, the Chartered Institute has set up a "Protected Titles Committee" to monitor, and take action in respect of, any improper use of these protected titles (1990–91) 20 *CIPA* 417. The work of this Committee was described by C. Lees [1993] *CIPA* 184. Members of the Chartered Institute have been asked to check published directories and report to this Committee any listing under these headings of a person not entitled to use such a designation: [1996] *CIPA* 824.

As a consequence of these provisions, in 1991 the Chartered Institute took action against a directory entry by a firm of solicitors under the heading "Patent Agents", and also against use by the same firm of the description "patent agency", (1991–92) 21 *CIPA* 149, but these complaints were withdrawn after the solicitors had given undertakings acceptable to the Chartered Institute to change their use of these terms: (1991–92) 21 *CIPA* 277.

In 1992, the DTI brought a successful prosecution in the Magistrates' Court of Kingston-upon-Hull against a person who, his name having been removed from the Register by order of the UK-IPO acting for the Secretary of State, continued to describe himself as a "Chartered Patent Agent" when not on the Register of Patent Agents (as it then was), nor a Fellow of the Chartered Institute: [1993] *CIPA* 43.

SECTION 277

Persons entitled to describe themselves as European patent attorneys, etc.

277.01   **277.**—(1) The term "European patent attorney" or "European patent agent" may be used in the following cases without any contravention of section 276.

(2) An individual who is on the European list may—

(a) carry on business under a name or other description which contains the words "European patent attorney" or "European patent agent", or

(b) otherwise describe himself, or permit himself to be described, as a "European patent attorney" or "European patent agent".

(3) A partnership of which not less than the prescribed number or proportion of partners is on the European list may—

(a) carry on a business under a name or other description which contains the words "European patent attorneys" or "European patent agents", or

(b) otherwise describe itself, or permit itself to be described, as a firm which carries on the business of a "European patent attorney" or "European patent agent".

(4) A body corporate of which not less than the prescribed number or proportion of directors is on the European list may—

    (a) carry on a business under a name or other description which contains the words "European patent attorney" or "European patent agent", or

    (b) otherwise describe itself, or permit itself to be described as, a company which carries on the business of a "European patent attorney" or "European patent agent".

(5) Where the term "European patent attorney" or "European patent agent" may, in accordance with this section, be used in reference to an individual, partnership or body corporate, it is equally permissible to use other expressions in reference to that person, or to his business or place of business, which are likely to be understood as indicating that he is entitled to be described as a "European patent attorney" or "European patent agent."

Note. This section came into force on August 13, 1990 (SI 1990/1400).

COMMENTARY ON SECTION 277

Scope of the section

Section 277 of the CDPA 1988 provides exceptions to the prohibition in s.276 of the use of the titles "patent agent", "patent attorney" or the like by persons other than those on the Register of Patent Attorneys, for which see §§276.02 et seq., by the use of the title "European patent attorney" or "European patent agent". In doing so, the section also provides that these terms may be used only by persons on the "European list", this being defined in s.286 of the CDPA 1988 as "the list of professional representatives maintained by the European Patent Office in pursuance of the European Patent Convention". Were it not for s.277, use of either of these titles by persons on the European list, but who are not registered patent attorneys, would have been a contravention of s.276 of the CDPA 1988; and, but for s.278(2) and (3), there might also have been a contravention of other statutes, see §278.02.

277.02

The recommended title for persons on the European list is "European patent attorney", see §277.06, though the title "European patent agent" is also sanctioned by the section as an equivalent title. The prohibitions against use of these titles by persons not on the European list extend to the use of other references which are likely to be understood as indicating that the person is entitled to be described as a European patent attorney or European patent agent (subs.(5), for which the decisions under the corresponding s.275(5) will be relevant by analogy, see §§276.04 and 276.05).

Subsections (2)–(4) set out in positive terms the use that may be made of these titles by a person on the European list, rather than negatively forbidding certain actions to those not on the European list as with repealed s.84. The unintended effect of this seems to be that a registered patent attorney, who is not on the European list, commits no offence under the 1988 Act by using the title "European patent attorney", but the terms of s.278(2)(b) of the CDPA 1988 seem to be such that an offence as to use of the word "attorney" may then be committed under the enactments specified in s.278(3) of the CDPA 1988, as to which see §278.02, unless exemption could be claimed under s.278(2)(a).

The Partnerships (Unrestricted Size) (No.12) Regulations 1997 (SI 1997/1937) excuse professional representatives before the European Patent Office from forming partnerships of more than 20 persons provided that such representatives constitute the majority of members of that partnership; and the services these persons provide are exempted (by s.15 and Sch.4 to the Fair Trading Act 1973 (c.41)) from some of the provisions of that Act.

J.C. Boff [2005] *CIPA* 517 has discussed the complex position as to the various persons who are entitled to use the terms: "patent agent(s)" or "patent attorney(s)"; "European patent attorney" or "European patent attorneys"; "registered trade mark agent(s)"; "trade mark attorney(s)"; and "Chartered Patent Agent(s) or "Chartered Patent Attorneys".

Use of title "European patent attorney" by partnerships and bodies corporate (subss.(3) and (4))

277.03   Subsection (3) refers specifically to partnerships, and subs.(4) to bodies corporate, in both cases requiring "a prescribed number or proportion" of partners, or directors, to be on the European list, if the partnership, or body corporate, is permitted to use the title "European patent attorney(s) [or agent(s)]". Power to make rules prescribing that number or proportion was provided by s.279, but that section was repealed on January 1, 2010 on the entry into force of the relevant sections of the Legal Services Act 2007 (c.29) and no such rules had been made before that date.

On this point it is to be noted that, under the EPC, persons generally practise before the EPO as individuals, even though they may be members of a partnership or body corporate (EPC r.152). While, under EPC r.152(11), an association (whether a partnership or a body corporate) of representatives is allowed to be authorised to act before the EPO as such, this requires prior confirmation by the EPO. For many years, this was given only to partnerships or companies of which all the partners or directors are on the European list and in private practice (see OJ EPO 1979, 92), but this position was reversed by J 116/96 *NN/ Association of representatives* [1999] E.P.O.R. 202 where an association of professional representatives formed from members of a corporate patent department was permitted to practise as such, that is to be authorised as an "association" rather than singly, but all members of that association must be on the European List. When an "association" of professional representatives is recognised, any change in the composition of that association requires notification to, and approval by, the EPO. Even with that authority, all communications from such an association must be personally signed by a person who has been notified to the EPO as a member of that association. Section 285(5) of the CDPA 1988 is relevant to the liability of officers of a partnership or company for offences committed by such an entity, for which see §285.02.

Penalties arising under section 277

277.04   As s.277 of the CDPA 1988 is permissive and introduces no offence, there are no penalties under the section as there were under repealed s.84. However, an individual, partnership or body corporate using the title "European patent attorney(s)" (or "European patent agent(s)"), and not satisfying any of s.277(2)–(4), would contravene s.276 of the CDPA 1988 and therefore be liable for penalty under s.276(6), for which see §276.03.

Approval of titles under the EPC

277.05   The use of the title "European patent attorney" was eventually approved by EPOAC (see OJEPO 1979, 452) and by the *epi* Council, (1979–1980) 9 *CIPA* 453, 455, though only after considerable controversy, see (1979–80) 9 *CIPA* 100. However, as these notices indicate, use by a person on the European list of a national title, together with the designation "European" (e.g. "European patent agent"), has been disapproved of by both EPOAC and the epi Council, even though (by CDPA 1988 s.277) its use by a person on the European list, is unexceptional under British law.

Because of the more stringent restrictions existing in Continental Europe than exist in the United Kingdom on advertising by professional persons, and particularly because of the stringent rules for professional conduct applying to *epi* members, it was recommended that advertisements should not make explicit reference to a person being a "European patent attorney" or like expression since this could amount to professional misconduct in the eyes of the *epi*, see *epi-Information* 3/1993, 170 and 4/1995, 137. Subsequently, the European Commission held that the *epi* Code of Professional Conduct violated provisions of the EC Treaty. As a result, these rules were revised. For the current form of this Code, see §286.05.

Privileges of a "European patent attorney"

277.06   Legal professional privilege, now accorded (by CDPA 1988 s.280, as amended by the

Legal Services Act 2007)to communications with patent attorneys, which term is defined as "registered patent attorneys" and persons "on the European list", is also accorded to partnerships and bodies corporate of it (CDPA 1988 s.280(3)). However, it is not certain that a person on the European list, who is not also a registered patent agent, benefits from the exceptions to the prohibition on document preparation by legally unqualified persons provided by s.102(2), see §102.05. See also §§280.02 et seq.)

SECTION 278

Use of the term "patent attorney": supplementary provisions

278.—(1) The term "patent attorney" may be used in reference to a solicitor, **278.01** and a firm of solicitors may be described as a firm of "patent attorneys", without any contravention of section 276.

(2) No offence is committed under the enactments restricting the use of certain expressions in reference to persons not qualified to act as solicitors—

> (a) by the use of the term "patent attorney" in reference to a registered patent agent, or
>
> (b) by the use of the term "European patent attorney" in reference to a person on the European list.

(3) The enactments referred to in subsection (2) are section 21 of the Solicitors Act 1974 [c.37], section 31 of the Solicitors (Scotland) Act 1980 [c.46] and Article 22 of the Solicitors (Northern Ireland) Order 1976 [S.I. 1976 No. 582 (N.I. 12)].

Notes

1. This section came into force on August 13, 1990 (SI 1990/1400).

2. In the application of this section to the Isle of Man: in subs.(1), the references to "solicitor" and "solicitors" are substituted by "advocate" and "advocates" respectively; subs.(2) is re-written to read:

> "(2) No offence is committed under section 1 of the Legal Practitioners Registration Act 1986 (an Act of Tynwald) (which restricts the use of certain expressions in reference to persons not qualified to act as advocates)"; and subs.(3) is omitted (SI 1990/1505).

COMMENTARY ON SECTION 278

Section 21 of the Solicitors Act 1974 (c.37), as well as s.31 of the Solicitors (Scotland) **278.02** Act 1980 (c.46) and art.22 of the Solicitors (Northern Ireland) Order 1977 (SI 1976/582 (N.I. 12)), make it an offence for legally-unqualified persons to use a title suggesting that such qualification is possessed. It is uncertain whether the term "attorney" would be embraced by these provisions, at least as regards use in England and Wales, because of its apparent disuse as an expression of legal qualification, see J.C.H. Ellis (1987–88) 17 *CIPA* 289, but subs.(2) puts the matter beyond doubt so far as the terms "patent attorney" and "European patent attorney" are concerned by expressly legalising such use under these three statutes (as listed in subs.(3)). Also, by subs.(1), a solicitor is permitted to use the term "patent attorney" without contravention of s.276 of the CDPA 1988, for which see §§276.01 et seq. However, the Law Society view is that a solicitor should not use such a title unless he holds himself out to be skilled in the work of patent agency.

This section remained unchanged when the Legal Services Act 2007 (c.29) Sch.4(1) entered into force on January 1, 2010, so that the situation discussed above did not alter.

Although the register became the Register of Patent Attorneys, the Act refers to "registered patent attorneys" in relevant places, thus distinguishing those on the register from any use by solicitors of the title "patent attorney".

J.C. Boff [2005] *CIPA* 517 has discussed the complex position as to the various persons who are entitled to use the terms: "patent agent(s)" or "patent attorney(s)"; "European patent attorney" or "European patent attorneys"; "registered trade mark agent(s)"; "trade mark attorney(s)"; and "Chartered Patent Agent(s) or "Chartered Patent Attorneys".

SECTION 279 [REPEALED]

Note.

279.01   This section, which originally came into force on August 13, 1990 (SI 1990/1400) provided power for the Secretary of State to make rules prescribing the conditions to be satisfied for partnership or body corporate to use the title "patent agent", without breaching the provisions of s.276 above. The section was repealed by the Legal Services Act 2007 (c.29), s.185 and Sch.23 and the Rules made under the section were revoked and replaced by regulatory arrangements made by the IP Regulation Board for the Patent Regulation Board, as discussed in §275.04 above.

SECTION 280

Privilege for communications with patent agents

280.01   **280.**—(1) This section applies to—

(a) communications as to any matter relating to the protection of any invention, design, technical information, **or trade mark** [*trade mark or service mark*], or as to any matter involving passing off, and

(b) **documents, materials or information relating to any matter referred to in paragraph (a).**

(2) Where a patent attorney acts for a client in relation to a matter mentioned in subsection (1), any communication, document, material or information to which this section applies is privileged from disclosure in like manner as if the patent attorney had at all material times been acting as the client's solicitor.

[(2) *Any such communication—*

(a) *between a person and his patent agent, or*

(b) *for the purpose of obtaining, or in response to a request for, information which a person is seeking for the purpose of instructing his patent agent,*

is privileged from disclosure in legal proceedings in England, Wales or Northern Ireland in the same way as a communication between a person and his solicitor or, as the case may be, a communication for the purpose of obtaining, or in response to a request for, information which a person seeks for the purpose of instructing his solicitor.]

(3) In subsection (2) "patent **attorney**" means—

(a) a registered patent **attorney** or a person who is on the European list,

(b) a partnership entitled to describe itself as a firm of patent **attorneys** [*agents*] or as a firm carrying on the business of a European patent attorney, [*or*]

(ba) **an unincorporated body (other than a partnership) entitled to describe itself as a patent attorney, or**

(c) a body corporate entitled to describe itself as a patent attorney or as a company carrying on the business of a European patent attorney.

Notes

1. This section came into force on August 13, 1990 (SI 1990/1400).

2. Subsection (1) was first amended by the Trade Marks Act 1994 (c.26) Sch.4, para.8(3).

3. In the application of this section to the Isle of Man: in subs.(2), the words "England, Wales or Northern Ireland" and "solicitor" are respectively substituted by "the Isle of Man" and "advocate"; and subs.(4) is omitted (SI 1990/1505).

4. The other amendments indicated above have been prospectively made by the Legal Services Act 2007 (c.29) s.185 and Schs 21 and 23 and are expected to come into force during 2009.

COMMENTARY ON SECTION 280

Scope of the section

Section 280 of the CDPA 1988 relates to the extent to which "privilege" can be claimed **280.02** to prevent disclosure during the course of litigation of documents, the contents of which it would not be appropriate to disclose to another party to litigation for one reason or another, where such documents are generated or referred to by patent attorneys in the course of their work for clients. Legal professional privilege normally attaches to communications (whether documents or oral advice) to and from a solicitor (or barrister) for the purpose of seeking or giving legal advice, or documents which came into being (at the request of the lawyers) for the purposes of litigation which is in progress or seriously contemplated. The nature of this privilege and the grounds for claiming it are more fully discussed in §§280.05–280.08. Section 280 gives statutory extension of the concept of privilege to patent attorneys.

The principle of extending this privilege, in connection with what may loosely be called solicitor's documents, was first applied to documents created by or for patent agents by the Civil Evidence Act 1968 (c.64) s.15. This provision was replaced by s.104 of the 1977 Act, and this section was itself replaced (as from August 13, 1990) by s.280 of the CDPA 1988, with s.104 then being repealed. Section 280 of the CDPA 1988 is to be further amended by the Legal Services Act 2007, when it is brought into force, as set out above. Each of these provisions has progressively extended the scope of patent attorney's privilege, though it should always be remembered that the privilege is that of the client and therefore that the client (but not the solicitor, barrister or patent attorney, without the client's consent) may waive a claim to privilege which may otherwise be possible, or refuse to waive privilege against the wishes of the solicitor, barrister or patent attorney.

Section 280 of the CDPA 1988 extends to "patent attorneys [agents]" (as that term is defined in subs.(3)) the same rights of privilege as apply to a solicitor in relation to disclosure of communications in legal proceedings in England, Wales and Northern Ireland (subs.(2)), as also discussed in §280.03, although only in respect of the matters set out in subs.(1). The rules of privilege pertaining to legal proceedings in Scotland were previously dealt with in subs.(4), but that subsection is prospectively repealed by the Legal Services Act 2007 and as a result the remainder of the section as amended will apply in Scotland also when that provision comes into effect, as discussed in §280.09. The extent of a solicitor's common law privilege has itself been extended by s.103 with respect to "patent proceedings" (as defined commentaries), and with a further extension under Scots' law by s.105, for which see the on these sections.

Extent of the privilege extended to patent attorneys (subss.(1) and (2))

The extension of patent attorneys' privilege provided by s.280 is restricted in that this is **280.03** limited to "communications as to any matter relating to the protection of any invention, design, technical information or trade mark or as to any matter involving passing off" (subs.(1)); and thus may not extend to any other matter relating to "intellectual property" as that term has been defined, for example in the Senior Courts Act 1981 (c.54) s.72(5), see §280.03. The section does not therefore appear to extend to matters of copyright, unrelated to designs or protection of "inventions".

This does beg the question as to what "invention" means in this context. It seems unlikely that it should be restricted only to inventions which are patentable under the Act, as that would be to deprive advice in relation to inventions which turn out not to be patentable for whatever reason of privilege. Therefore this may be wide enough to cover any protection for an invention, e.g. advice in relation to copyright protection for source code of a computing invention. See also the commentary under s.43 as to the meaning of "invention" and "other forms of protection".

The presence of the word "protection" may also provide scope for argument as to whether it is limited to the act of "protection" (e.g. the obtaining of a patent or the contesting of validity or infringement proceedings) or whether it applies to any question relating to a type of protection for an invention, etc. and so also covers issues relating to ownership and exploitation of that protection. See the Governmental assurances described by Jacqueline Needle (1988–89) 18 *CIPA* 130. It is thought that the word "protection" should be construed purposively to extend, at least, to any proceedings which relate to the existence, or possible existence, or non-existence of, e.g. a patent or patent application, SPC, etc. but the matter remains one of some doubt.

The recent decision in *Atrium Medical Corporation and another v DSB Invest Holding SA* [2011] EWHC 74 (Pat), related to these issues. There had been a technology transfer from the defendant to the claimant companies of various aspects of intellectual property relating to medicine. The agreement provided for a lump sum payment payable in stages and also a royalty in the event that Atrium sold anything incorporating the technical information. The defendant later asserted that the claimants were selling a product that fell within the scope of the agreement. The claimants issued proceedings seeking a declaration that the product did not fall within the scope of the agreement. Since the claimants owned the rights under the agreement, there was no question of infringement by them. The claimants' case was conducted by a patent attorney holding a patent litigator certificate. The defendants questioned whether his certificate entitled him to conduct the litigation, with the issue as to whether he attracted professional privilege being a dependant issue. The defendants argued that there was a difference between cases which relate to the protection of inventions etc, which may be litigated by appropriately qualified patent attorney litigators, and cases which merely related in some way to intellectual property.

Holding that the patent attorney was entitled to conduct the litigation, Lewison J. held that the litigation was 'Intellectual Property Litigation' within the meaning of reg.3 of the CIPA Higher Courts Qualification Regulations 2007. Regulation 3 included inventions, whether they were patented or not, and it also included technical information, which was not further defined. He held that the technology, as defined by the agreement, fell within that part of reg.3 which referred to technical information in purely general terms. He stated that the proprietor of a patent might protect his invention in a number of ways: by manufacturing the thing that is covered by the patent and suing infringers; or by licensing the right to manufacture what is claimed by the patent. The defendant, in effect, protected its intellectual property rights by selling them on terms; and it was the working out of those terms which was the subject-matter of the action. Alternatively, the claim to a royalty for the use of the technical information and for the use of matter falling within the claims of a patent was a "similar right" to a claim to protect the invention or the technical information. The court held that the patent attorney was as a result entitled to conduct the litigation, and additionally to assert legal professional privilege on behalf of his client to the same extent as could be claimed by a solicitor.

The extent of the protection afforded by the section was discussed by A. J. Webb (1990–91) 20 *CIPA* 477; and, outside this field, communications by or to a patent agent do not enjoy legal professional privilege, see *Wilden Pump v Fusfeld [Privilege]* [1985] F.S.R

159 CA), a case which was decided under the former s.104 under which privilege was accorded only to documents created "for the purpose of pending or contemplated patent proceedings" (though including proceedings "whether contested or uncontested and including an application for a patent", see repealed s.104(4)). However, note that the reasoning in *Wilden Pump* was held no longer applicable after the enactment of s.280 of the CDPA 1988 by Aldous J. in *IBM v Phoenix* [1995] 1 All E.R. 413, [1995] F.S.R. 184 in which he commented that:

"At the date when those cases were decided, patent agents were not considered to be lawyers and therefore legal professional privilege could not be claimed. Since then, legislation has recognised the change in professional status of patent agents".

Thus, despite the extension which it provides, s.280 falls short of the full privilege accorded to solicitor's documents. Under that privilege, documents are protected irrespective of the subject-matter to which they relate, provided that they relate to the giving of legal advice or that they came into being for the purposes of actual or contemplated litigation, see §§280.05–280.08. The amendments to be made by the Legal Services Act 2007 expressly extends the privilege from mere "communications" to cover "documents, materials or information" and so is intended unequivocally to cover preparatory documents which are not actually communicated to the client.

In particular, it is to be noted that, though patent attorneys may now conduct litigation before the Patents County Court, in this respect they are not "authorised litigators" or "authorised advocates" as those terms are defined in the Courts and Legal Services Act 1990 (c.41) s.119, for which see §292.04. As a consequence, a patent attorney conducting litigation (unless accredited as a "patent agent litigator", for which see §275.07), or acting as an advocate in the Patents County Court may have a lesser degree of privilege in respect of those proceedings, because the extent of that privilege is determined by the present section, for which see §280.04, whereas the privilege of authorised litigators and authorised advocates is additionally determined by s.63 of the Courts and Legal Services Act 1990. Whilst this indicates that the privilege is equated with that which a solicitor would enjoy when carrying out such a function, where a Chartered Patent Attorney is a "patent agent litigator" because he holds a litigation certificate he will only have the same privilege as if he were a solicitor to the extent that he acts within the terms of that certificate. The certificate is limited in terms of subject-matter and so will not cover all topics upon which a solicitor advises. However, as that certificate also covers "similar rights" and "ancillary matters", the privilege under Courts and Legal Services Act 1990 s.63 is arguably broader than that under CDPA 198 s.280.

The relevant provisions of The Courts and Legal Services Act 1990 are:

"Section 63—Legal Professional Privilege

63.—(1) This section applies to any communication made to or by a person who is not a barrister or solicitor at any time when that person is—

      (a) providing advocacy or litigation services as an authorised advocate or authorised litigator;

      (b) [...]

(2) Any such communication shall in any legal proceedings be privileged from disclosure in like manner as if the person in question had at all material times been acting as his client's solicitor.

    (3) [. . .]"

"Section 119—Interpretation

    "authorised litigator" means any person (including a solicitor) who has a right to conduct litigation granted by an authorised body in accordance with the provisions of this Act".

119.—(1)

Section 280 of the CDPA 1988 contains no geographical limitation, and, therefore, it would appear that legal advice privilege (see §§280.06 and 280.07 for the distinction between "legal advice privilege" and "litigation privilege") may now be accorded, under English law, to documents prepared in connection with foreign patent applications, this not being so (except for proceedings under the EPC or the PCT) under the former s.104, see *Sonic Tape's Patent* [1987] R.P.C. 251. In *Société Francqise Hoechst v Allied Colloids* [1992] F.S.R. 66 it was held that a report prepared in connection with French proceedings was a privileged document under common law principles, and it did not matter that it had been prepared at the instigation of a patent agent who, having regard to the *Wilden Pump* case, was not to be regarded as a legal adviser. The court said that documents which are prepared, whether at the instigation of a patent agent or by anybody for the purpose of legal proceedings are privileged.

Under s.103, litigation privilege will only be extended to the "patent proceedings" defined in that section, i.e. before the Comptroller or relevant convention court and under the Act, under the EPC or under the PCT. "Relevant convention court" is defined in s.130(1) and includes the EPO itself and WIPO itself or potentially a foreign patent office insofar as it relates to the applications under either of those treaties. However, it may not extend to proceedings under the foreign national law.

Privilege as applied to European patent attorneys is discussed at §277.06. However, additional privilege is now conferred under the EPC for authorised representatives, in relation to proceedings before the EPO.

"Rule 153—Attorney evidentiary privilege

(1) Where advice is sought from a professional representative in his capacity as such, all communications between the professional representative and his client or any other person, relating to that purpose and falling under Article 2 of the Regulation on discipline for professional representatives, are permanently privileged from disclosure in proceedings before the European Patent Office, unless such privilege is expressly waived by the client.

(2) Such privilege from disclosure shall apply, in particular, to any communication or document relating to:

      (a) the assessment of the patentability of an invention;

      (b) the preparation or prosecution of a European patent application;

      (c) any opinion relating to the validity, scope of protection or infringement of a European patent or a European patent application."

"Regulation on discipline for professional representatives
Article 2—Professional secrecy
A professional representative shall be bound not to disclose information accepted by him in confidence in the exercise of his duties, unless he is released from this obligation."

UK patent attorneys may also be able to claim privilege for certain communications under other statutes and statutory instruments. For example, a patent attorney who is also a registered trade mark attorney will be able to claim privilege in relation to trade mark and design matters under Trade Marks Act 1994 s.87. Where that person is a European designs attorney, then privilege may be claimed under reg.4 Community Design Regulations 2005 (SI 2005/2339), and where that person is a European trade mark and design attorney, then privilege may be claimed under Community Trade Mark Regulations 2006 reg.11 (SI 2006/1027). However, it is worth noting that none of the UK or Community legislation relating to obtaining trade marks and designs contains an equivalent of s.103 of the 1977

Act: so there is no statutory provision extending the litigation privilege of solicitors to trade mark and designs proceedings before the relevant Office, although legal advice privilege may apply to some communications.

Persons entitled to privilege under the section (subs.(3))

Privilege under the section is accorded only in relation to communications by or to "patent attorneys [agents]", as that term is defined in subs.(3). By this definition, "patent attorneys [agents]" are: either (i) registered patent attorneys [agents], i.e. those on the register of patent attorneys [agents] under s.275 of the CDPA 1988 (for which see §§275.02 et seq.); or (ii) those on the "European list" of persons entitled to practise before the EPO (as defined in CDPA 1988 s.286, and discussed in §286.03), i.e. "European patent attorneys" (a term defined by s.277 of the CDPA 1988, and discussed in §§277.02 et seq. (subs.(3)(a)). However, privilege is also accorded to "partnerships" and "bodies corporate", as defined in s.276(2) and (3) of the CDPA 1988 in relation to "patent attorneys [agents]", for which see §276.02. It would also extend to "partnerships" and "bodies corporate" practising (by subs.(3)(b) and (c)) as "European patent attorneys" as these forms of professional association are permitted, for which see §277.03.

280.04

While, in contrast to the extension of privilege for solicitor's documents conferred by s.103(1), the reference to "patent attorney [agent]" does not explicitly include "a person acting on his behalf" (such as a technical assistant or a secretary). This may be a mere technicality, insofar as it relates to private practice, as such persons are within the partnership or body corporate (bodies corporate not being natural persona must act through their officers and servants) which the client has retained. However, the position may be less clear insofar is it relates to the non-patent attorneys within an in-house patent department.

These principles will be affected by the Legal Services Act 2007 (c.29) s.190 when that comes into force.

The nature of privilege

—General and the grounds of privilege

The question of privilege is closely allied to that of disclosure of documents during the course of litigation. See the commentary on s.61 for further discussion on disclosure. For present purposes, it is sufficient to note that, as part of the pre-trial litigation process in proceedings in the Patents Court or Patents County Court a party is obligated to give "standard disclosure" under CPR 31.6, but limited in relation to the issues of infringement and validity proceedings by CPR 63.9 and CPR 63PD.6, see Appendix F. Other parties to those proceedings may then require inspection of the listed documents under CPR 31.3, unless a successful claim is made to the withholding from inspection of certain documents either because privilege in them is validly claimed or that to allow inspection would be disproportionate to the value in the litigation (CPR 31.3(2)), on which see CPR 63.9 and CPR 63PD.6.

280.05

The question of according privilege to production of particular documents in the course of litigation is a complex one and outside the scope of this Work. Here the position is briefly summarised, particularly to the extent that it is likely to affect patent attorneys claiming privilege under the provisions of s.280 of the CDPA 1988. "Patent agent litigators", that is Fellows of the Chartered Institute holding a litigation certificate from that Institute stand in the same position as solicitors as regards privilege when acting in their capacity as an "authorised litigator" and within the scope of their certificates. It is possible that this is marginally broader than that accorded to patent attorneys under s.280, see §280.03.

The mere fact that a document contains confidential information is not a basis for a claim to privilege and thus, of itself, is no excuse against production of that document: *Crompton (Alfred) v Customs & Excise Commissioners (No.2)* [1974] A.C. 405; [1973] 2 All E.R. 1169 HL. While it is well settled that, where trade secrets are involved, a court may restrict inspection of discovered documents, the discovering party has the onus of seeking a special order in this regard, and of justifying any limitation of the general right of the public to know all the evidence upon which a case is decided: *Roussel-Uclaf v ICI* [1990] R.P.C. 45. If so satisfied, the court may limit inspection of documents to legal or independent advisers. It is permissible to mask out those portions of documents which contain confidential matter which is irrelevant for the purposes of the litigation disclosure, but inferences may then be drawn from the extent of that masking, see the judgment of Buckley L.J. in *Beecham Group's (Amoxycillin) Application* [1980] R.P.C. 261 CA).

Privilege against disclosure of documents can be claimed on any of three broad grounds: legal professional privilege (discussed in §§280.06–280.08); self-incrimination; and public policy. (See below for "without prejudice" communications). In the context of this work, little needs to be said about the latter two: except to note that privilege against self-incrimination (i.e. against disclosing documents which may tend to show the commission of a criminal offence by the party required to give disclosure) has been virtually abolished for proceedings relating to intellectual property, e.g. for England and Wales by s.72 of the Senior CourtsAct 1981 (c.54), see §280.03; and that a claim to public policy privilege usually arises only when a government department (whether or not a party to the proceedings in question) thinks disclosure of a document would be inimical to the public interest, which, for patent proceedings, would be most likely in proceedings for Crown use, compensation under s.58 or relating to inventions having a national defence purpose.

Legal professional privilege itself involves two distinct classes of documents, depending on whether or not litigation was pending or contemplated at the time the document came into existence: these are respectively discussed in §§280.06 and 280.07. Also, for the general nature of "legal professional" and "legal advice" privilege, and the possible limitation of privilege for patent agents, see A. J. Webb (1989–90) 19 *CIPA* 279, with comment by J. C. H. Ellis (1989–90) 19 *CIPA* 380. A more recent discussion of privilege, including changes brought about by EPC 2000, by W. Cook and A. McLean was published in [2007] *CIPA* 616.

In addition, correspondence marked "without prejudice", or obviously communicated on such a basis, may not be disclosed to the court except in special circumstances, see §280.07. However, where that correspondence arises within the context of the litigation in question, then it is already known to the parties to that correspondence, so the "privilege" relates to not showing that correspondence to the court, rather than withholding it from disclosure, although it may be withheld from other parties to the same litigation. For public policy considerations behind the without prejudice privilege see Robert Walker L.J. in *Unilever v Procter & Gamble* [2000] 1 W.L.R. 2436 at 2448H–2449, approved by Lord Mance in *Bradford & Bingley v Rashid* [2006] UKHL 37 at [91]: "Parties cannot speak freely at a without prejudice meeting if they must constantly monitor every sentence, with lawyers or patent agents sitting at their shoulders as minders".

It must, however, be noted that any privilege enjoyed is that of the client, not his lawyer, and such privilege may be waived, although only by the client or with his consent. Such waiver can occur even inadvertently, with an argument available that waiver of privilege for one document has the effect of waiving privilege in further documents, such as those the subject of a cross-reference or for documents within the same class. However, privilege is not waived when inspection of a document submitted to the taxing master on a taxation of costs is permitted to the other party: *Bourns Inc v Raychem* [1999] F.S.R 641 CA.

—Legal professional privilege arising from request for, or giving of, legal advice

280.06 First, irrespective of whether or not proceedings are pending or contemplated, documentary communications which have passed between a party and its legal adviser (which term includes a patent attorney if the document relates to matter as defined in s.280(1) for the purpose of seeking, or the passing of, advice on the party's legal position, are privileged against production even if the documents pass through an intermediate hand, unless it appears to the court that the party may have engaged in fraudulent or dishonest conduct, see *Gamlen v Rochem* [1983] R.P.C. 1.

An important decision on the general scope of "legal advice privilege" is *Three Rivers DC v Bank of England (Disclosure) (No.64)* [2004] UKHL 48, [2005] 1 A.C. 610. Here the House of Lords overturned the Court of Appeal by finding that the privilege attached to advice about the presentation of evidence and what should sensibly do done and not merely advice on legal rights and remedies. See also *Balabel v Air India* [1988] 2 W.L.R. 1036; [1988] 2 All E.R. 246 CA. However, the House of Lords declined to review the Court of Appeal's narrow definition (*Three Rivers District Council v Governor and Company of the Bank of England (No.5)* [2003] Q.B. 1556) as to who the "client" was. Of course, the legal advisor must have been acting as such, which may not have been so where the advisor is an employed solicitor (or patent attorney) acting in an executive capacity and not all communications with a legal adviser are capable of exclusion from disclosure under this head. The effect of the *Three Rivers* case, and the differences between the concepts of "legal advice privilege" and "litigation privilege", were usefully discussed by N. Beckett [2005] *CIPA* 23 and 102, the latter being augmented in a note by T.C. Stancliffe on the following p.103 which extended these remarks to s.103 of the 1977 Act.

—Legal professional privilege arising from actual or contemplated proceedings

Secondly, legal professional privilege also attaches to documents which are communications between a solicitor (or, for proceedings in the relevant fields, a patent attorney) and a non-professional agent or third party, whether communicated directly or through an agent, provided that these documents have come into existence for the purpose of obtaining or giving advice in relation to pending or contemplated proceedings, for obtaining or collecting evidence to be used in such proceedings or for obtaining information which may lead to the obtaining of such evidence (including drafts of affidavits and witness statements). The underlying principle to privilege in this category is whether there is a public interest factor which overrides the factor that, for the proper administration of justice, there should normally be full disclosure of documents which are relevant to the issues to be decided in the litigation: *Re Barings* [1998] 1 All E.R. 673. **280.07**

The proceedings which give rise to the privilege can be foreign proceedings, for example documents created in the course of United States litigation and subject to a protective order prohibiting their use outside those proceedings (*Minnesota Mining v Rennicks* [1991] F.S.R 97), although the document must be one to which privilege properly attaches under United Kingdom law, see *Lubrizol v Esso (No.4)* [1993] F.S.R 64. However, privilege does not extend to evidence given in foreign proceedings, even though not made public because of a protective order, especially where the party claiming privilege has itself relied on that evidence abroad, thereby being deemed to have waived any privilege it might have had: *Visx v Nidek* [1999] F.S.R 91.

For privilege in this category to be accorded, the dominant purpose for which the document was created must be related to legal proceedings: *Waugh v British Railways Board* [1980] A.C. 521; [1979] 2 All E.R. 1169 HL. It is questionable whether, for proceedings to be contemplated, a decision must have already been taken that they should be instituted or defended, see *Crompton (Alfred) v Customs & Excise Commissioners (No.2)* [1974] A.C. 405; [1973] 2 All E.R. 1169 HL. The Patents Court has held that such contemplation must be genuine (*Bishop v Adwest* BL C/20/83); and there must be more than a mere fear of litigation (*Rockwell v Serck* [1987] R.P.C. 89), where it was observed that a contemplated patent application would bring proceedings within the terms of the former s.104). In *USA v Philip Morris and British American Tobacco* [2003] All E.R. (D) 191 (Dec), approved by Court of Appeal, [2004] All E.R. (D) 448 (Mar), the "mere possibility", "general apprehension of future litigation" or even "the distinct possibility that sooner or later someone might make a claim" was insufficient. However, that did not mean that there had to be a greater than 50 per cent chance of litigation.

It should be noted that, under this head of privilege, where communications are between a solicitor and a patent attorney, then the solicitor's rights to privilege will apply to the communication in any event, regardless of whether the patent attorney has an additional privilege. On the other hand, legal professional privilege does not attach to copies of documents where the originals are not privileged documents, unless the copies tend to indicate the legal advice that was either sought or given, see *Lubrizol v Esso (No.4)*, above.

Communications between the parties, conducted on a "without prejudice" basis, are privileged and may be disclosed to the court only in reserved circumstances, for example as to an eventual award of costs as in *Cutts v Head* [1984] Ch. 290; [1984] 1 All E.R. 597 CA or, after settlement, in relation to a dispute as to the terms of that settlement (*Rush & Tompkins v GLC* [1988] 3 W.L.R. 939; 3 All E.R. 737 HL).

—Limitations on privilege

280.08   Privilege can stem only from a party to the proceedings, see *Reeves v Reed (Lewis)* [1971] R.P.C. 355 where a licensee could not claim privilege in proceedings in which the licensor, but not the licensee, was a party. However, once a document has become privileged in one set of proceedings, it remains privileged in future proceedings, unless the party from whom the privilege stems chooses to waive the claim to that privilege.

In *Sonic Tape's Patent* [1987] R.P.C. 251, the personal recipient of letters from a patent agent was an employee of the applicant. After leaving that employment, the recipient sought to make use of copies of the letters in an inventorship dispute under s.13. It was held that he had received those letters both in a personal capacity and as a representative of his employer, and, on this basis, the employer could claim privilege for their contents as against third parties, but not as against that person. Letters received solely by the employer could not be used in the dispute upon privilege being claimed. However, no similar privilege was accorded in respect of communications relating to a United States patent application, even though filed initially under the PCT, but on this point the *Sonic Tape* decision (decided under s.104) may no longer be good law in view of the new wording of s.280 of the CDPA 1988, see §280.03.

The protection to be afforded by s.280 of the CDPA 1988 is broad within the relevant field, but, where the patent attorney is acting for a foreign client, the effect may be reduced by the client being called upon to comply with an order for disclosure/discovery in his native country and against which the United Kingdom legislation is ineffective so far as his client is concerned. Here it may be noted that in the United States the scope of legal professional privilege appears considerably less than in the United Kingdom, though in *Detection Systems v Pittway* [USA] (1984) 220 U.S.P.Q. 716 it was suggested that United States courts should not insist on disclosure of documents prepared by a foreign patent agent/attorney which are privileged according to his own law. Here it may be important that s.280 of the CDPA 1988 now appears to provide privilege in respect of foreign patent applications, which was not formerly the case, as noted in §280.03; and that privilege for a British patent attorney, as a non-lawyer, was denied by a US court in *Chubb v National Bank of Washington* (1985) 224 U.S.P.Q. 1002. It should also be noted that a United States court may deny privilege for communications between a British patent agent and his correspondents in other countries in relation to parallel patent applications, see *Burroughs Wellcome v Barr Laboratories* (1992) 25 U.S.P.Q. (2d), 1274. For a discussion on privilege under US law, see Yoshida, D. "The applicability of the Attorney-Client Privilege to Communications with Foreign Legal Professionals" (1997) *Fordham Law Review* 209. It appears that patent agents (or lawyers acting as such) do not obtain privilege in Canadian litigation, see [1996] *CIPA* 1030. This applies even to UK patent attorneys, see *Lilly Icos v Pfizer Ireland Pharmaceuticals* 2006 FC 1465. Also, in Australia, advice of a UK patent attorney was held not privileged either at common law or under the local statute (as not being a registered Australian patent attorney) in *Eli Lilly v Pfizer Ireland Pharmaceuticals (No.2)* [2004] F.C.A. 850, although amending legislation is being considered. It appears at least possible that the same reasoning might apply in reverse in the UK as regards Australian or other foreign patent attorneys who are not lawyers, UK registered patent attorneys or EPAs. Here it may be noted that at a meeting called by the World Intellectual Property Organization (WIPO) and held in Geneva in May 2008, it was agreed that the issue of privilege should be included in the negotiations in the WIPO Standing Committee on the Law of Patents (SCP) directed at harmonising substantive patent law around the world. A paper on the issue of client-attorney privilege, to be prepared by the WIPO Secretariat will be considered at the SCP meeting expected to be held in the first quarter of 2009.

Under European law arising from the EC Treaty "CT", privilege is not accorded to lawyers unless they are independent, that is not bound to their client by a relationship of employment and unless they are EU registered lawyers (*Australian Mining & Smelting v EC Commission (155/79)* [1982] 2 C.M.L.R. 264, abridged [1982] F.S.R 474 ECJ). The European Court of Justice held that the confidentiality of written communications between lawyers and clients should be protected at Community level. However, the Court stated that protection was subject to two cumulative conditions. First, the exchange with the lawyer had to be connected to 'the client's rights of defence' and, second, that the exchange must emanate from 'independent lawyers', that is to say 'lawyers who are not bound to the client by a relationship of employment'. As to the second condition, the Court observed, that the requirement as to the position and status as an independent lawyer, which had to be fulfilled by the legal adviser from whom the written communications which may be protected emanate, was based on a conception of the lawyer's role as collaborating in the administration of justice and as being required to provide, in full independence and in the overriding interests of that cause, such legal assistance as the client needed. The counterpart to that protection lay in the rules of professional ethics and discipline which are laid down and enforced in the general interest. That court held that it followed, that the requirement of independence meant the absence of any employment relationship between the lawyer and his client, so that legal professional privilege did not cover exchanges within a company or group with in-house lawyers. Similar issues with respect to in-house counsel arose in *Akzo Nobel Chemicals and Akcros Chemicals v Commission* (joined cases T 125/03, T 253/03). The CFI followed the ECJ in *AMS v Commission*, at first instance. By their appeal in *Akzo Nobel Chemicals Ltd v Commission* C 550/07 P, the appellants sought to set aside the judgment of the Court of First Instance of the European Communities in Joined Cases T-125/03 and T-253/03 *Akzo Nobel Chemicals* and *Akcros Chemicals v Commission*, in so far as it rejected the claim of legal professional privilege for correspondence with the appellants' in-house lawyer. Those documents had been examined by the European Commission in the course of investigations in competition law. The ECJ took the view that the concept of the independence of lawyers was determined not only positively, by reference to professional ethical obligations, but also negatively, by the absence of an employment relationship. It held that an in-house lawyer, despite enrolment with a Bar or Law Society with the attendant professional ethical obligations, did not enjoy the same degree of independence from his employer as a lawyer working in an external law firm did in relation to his client. Consequently, an in-house lawyer would be less able to deal effectively with any conflicts between his professional obligations and the aims of his client. Accordingly, following *AM & S Europe v Commission*, the Commission had been entitled to refuse the documents created by the appellant's in-house lawyers professional privilege.

English law does not discriminate between independent and employed lawyers in this way, though an employed lawyer may claim privilege only for communications which have arisen in his capacity as lawyer and not as employee. In any event, all legal advice given on matters which may come to the attention of the European Commission should be clearly headed "Professional Legal Advice: Private and Confidential", and such advice should not be given by employed legal advisers if there may be a future desire to claim privilege in respect of it.

—Privilege under Scots law for communications with or relating to patent agents (subs.(4))

Subsection (4) declared that the rules of law which confer privilege under Scots law extend to the types of communications mentioned in the remainder of the section. These **280.09** rules of law have been explained in §105.02 in connection with the extension of that privilege by s.105 to "patent proceedings" before the court, the Comptroller or a "relevant convention court" (as defined in s.130(1)). The section has now been omitted under s.208 and para.77(e) of sch.21 of the Legal Services Act 2007.

SECTION 281

Power of comptroller to refuse to deal with certain agents

281.01 **281.**—(1) This section applies to business under the Patents Act 1949 [c. 87], the Registered Designs Act 1949 [c. 88] or the Patents Act 1977 [c. 37].

(2) The Secretary of State may make rules authorising the comptroller to refuse to recognise as agent in respect of any business to which this section applies—

(a) aa person who has been convicted of an offence under section 88 of the Patents Act 1949 [c. 87], section 114 of the Patents Act 1977 [c. 37] or section 276 of this Act;

(b) a person whose name has been erased from and not restored to, or who is suspended from, the register of patent attorneys on the ground of misconduct;

(c) a person who is found by the Secretary of State to have been guilty of such conduct as would, in the case of a person registered in the register of patent attorneys, render the person liable to have the person's name erased from the register on the ground of misconduct;

(d) a partnership or body corporate of which one of the partners or directors is a person whom the comptroller could refuse to recognise under paragraph (a), (b) or (c) above.

(3) The rules may contain such incidental and supplementary provisions as appear to the Secretary of State to be appropriate and may, in particular, prescribe circumstances in which a person is or is not to be taken to have been guilty of misconduct.

(4) Rules made under this section shall be made by statutory instrument which shall be subject to annulment in pursuance of a resolution of either House of Parliament.

(5) The comptroller shall refuse to recognise as agent in respect of any business to which this section applies a person who neither resides nor has a place of business in the United Kingdom, the Isle of Man or another member State of the European Economic Community.

Note. This section originally came into force on August 13, 1990 (SI 1990/1400) and subss.(2)(b) and (2)(c) were amended in their references to the name of the register when the Legal Services Act 2007 (c.29) Sch.2(78) entered into force on January 1, 2010. At the same time, references to "individual" in subss.(2)(b) and (2)(c) were amended to "person".

THE PATENT AGENTS (NON-RECOGNITION OF CERTAIN AGENTS BY COMPTROLLER) RULES 1990

(SI 1990/ 1454)

281.02 **1.** These Rules may be cited as the Patent Agents (Non-recognition of Certain Agents by Comptroller) Rules 1990 and shall come into force on 13th August, 1990.

2. In these Rules—

"the Act" means the Copyright, Designs and Patents Act 1988 [c. 48],

"the Comptroller" means the Comptroller-General of Patents, Designs and Trade Marks;

"the register" means the register of patent attorneys required to be kept in accordance with section 275 of the Act.].

3. The Comptroller is hereby authorised to refuse to recognise as agent in respect of any business under the Patents Act 1949 [c. 87], the Registered Designs Act 1949 [c. 88] or the Patents Act 1977 [c. 37]—

(a) a person who has been convicted of an offence under section 88 of the Patents Act 1949, section 114 of the Patents Act 1977 or section 276 of the Act;

(b) a person whose name has been erased from and not restored to the register on the ground of misconduct;

(c) a person who is found by the Secretary of State to have been guilty of such conduct as would, in the case of a person registered in the register, render the person liable to have the person's name erased from the register on the ground of misconduct;

(d) a partnership or body corporate of which one of the partners or directors is a person whom the Comptroller could refuse to recognise under paragraph (a), (b) or (c) above.

Note.

These Rules were amended in the same way as s.281 was amended on the entry into force on January 1, 2010 of the Legal Services Act 2007, with the additional amendments of the change of the name of the register and the amendment of "pursuant to rules made under" to "in accordance with".

COMMENTARY ON SECTION 281

Scope of the section

Section 281 of the CDPA 1988 provides the basis for specifying in what circumstances **281.03** the Comptroller may (or shall) refuse to recognise as an agent a person appointed to act for a party to proceedings before him. The section replaced s.115 of the 1977 Act (now repealed) and has its origin in s.89 of the 1949 Act. However, various changes have been made to suit the new provisions as regards persons acting as agents for others in matters relating to patents, for which now see s.274 of the CDPA 1988 (reprinted at §274.01) and substituted s.102 of the 1977 Act (reprinted at §102.01), each discussed in the commentaries on these sections at §§274.02 et seq. and 102.02 et seq. respectively. Consequent upon the repeal of s.32 of the Registered Designs Act 1949 (c.88) by Sch.8 to the CDPA 1988, the section is applied to business under that Act, as well as covering business under the Patents Act 1949 and 1977 (subs.(1)).

Subsection (2) authorises the making of rules specifying the terms and conditions upon which the Comptroller can refuse to recognise as agent for representing parties to proceedings before him four specified classes of persons. Such rules are applied also in relation to appearances before the Comptroller at hearings, see s.102(3). They may contain such incidental and supplementary provisions as may appear to be appropriate, particularly in prescribing circumstances of deemed misconduct (subs.(3)). Rules made under the section are subject to annulment by resolution in either House of Parliament (subs.(4)). The rules now made under this subsection are the Patent Agents (Non-recognition of Certain Agents by Comptroller) Rules 1990 (SI 1990/1454), see above. These Rules were amended as a consequence of the entry into force of the Legal Services Act 2007 (c.29), the relevant provisions of which entered into force on January 1, 2010. These provisions (s.185) revised s.275 of the CDPA 1988 (see the commentary on s.275 above), particularly by amending the name of the register to the Register of Patent Attorneys and extending its scope to include both individuals and entities. Previously, similar provisions were made as part of the earlier r.90, but its replacement r.101 (reprinted at §274.02) now deals only with the appointment of an agent to represent a party in proceedings before the Comptroller, for a discussion of which see §274.04.

Subsection (5) is mandatory in form and requires the Comptroller to refuse to recognise as agent a person who does not reside within the European Community (or the Isle of Man).

Rules for refusal of recognition of agent (subss.(2) and (3))

281.04
Apart from one small point noted below, the rules made under subs.(2) (the "Non-recognition Rules") are in identical terms with the powers provided by this subsection, and there are no incidental or supplementary provisions (under subs.(3)), other than r.2 which defines the terms used in the substantive r.3. The four classes of persons set out in subs.(2) concern respectively:

(a) those convicted of offence of misusing the terms "patent agent", "patent attorney" or the like (for which see §§276.02 et seq.);

(b) an individual whose name has been erased from the register of patent attorneys on the ground of misconduct under Regulation 9 of the Patent Attorney and Trade Mark Attorney Qualification and Registration Regulations as issued by the IP Regulation Board (see Appendix H), as discussed in §275.05: while subs.(2)(b) allows rules for non-recognition of agents who have been suspended from this register, this provision has not found its way into the Non-recognition Rules;

(c) a person (not on the register of patent attorneys) who has been found to have committed such misconduct (as under (b) above) as would have made him subject to that provision had he been on the register; and

(d) partnerships and bodies corporate where one of the partners or directors is a person whom the Comptroller could refuse to recognise under any of (a)–(c) above.

Apparently, a person remaining on the Register, and not suspended therefrom, must be recognised by the Comptroller in the absence of a conviction under s.276 of the CDPA 1988 (or its predecessors), see subs.(2)(a). Also, apparently, the misconduct referred to in subs.(2)(c) (and perhaps also in subs.(3), which at present is not reflected in the rules), is linked to such conduct as would render a person liable to actual or possible erasure from the register of patent attorneys. Thus, though an unregistered person describing himself as a "patent attorney" or "patent agent" would commit a criminal offence under s.276 of the CDPA 1988, it is not clear that that person would be considered as having committed such misconduct as would entitle the Comptroller to refuse to recognise that person as an agent, unless and until a conviction has been obtained for an offence under s.276 of the CDPA 1988, thereby enabling non-recognition under subs.(2)(a).

The Non-recognition Rules also apply to agents appearing at hearings before the Comptroller, see s.102(3), but it is not clear whether the Comptroller has the power selectively to refuse to recognise an agent as a representative for hearings or for conducting proceedings or any type of proceedings. There is no obligation upon the Comptroller to give notice to the public of any exercise by him of his powers under the Non-recognition Rules. Although no action is believed to have been taken to refuse to recognise a particular agent under the predecessors of the section (1977 Act s.114 and 1949 Act s.88), nor apparently were any cases brought in respect of alleged offences under these sections, action has been taken under the present section. An example of a disciplinary case brought before the Comptroller is that referred to in *Law v Chartered Institute of Patent Agents* (1919) 36 R.P.C. 163, where an accusation of "disgraceful professional conduct" was not upheld.

Residence or place of business of agent (subs.(5))

281.05
An agent representing a party to proceedings before the Comptroller may now have a

residence or place of business outside the United Kingdom or the Isle of Man, provided that this is elsewhere within the European Community (cf. repealed s.115(3) of the 1977 Act). However, the agent may not be located solely in the Channel Islands. The provision applies only to "business" activity and, here at least, the Comptroller is understood to have taken the prima facie view that the payment of renewal fees is not a "business".

Subsection (5) is tied in practice to r.103 (reprinted at §32.02) which, as noted in §274.05 above, now requires that an address for service notified to the Comptroller need not be one within the United Kingdom (including the Isle of Man), provided that such an address is one within the EEA or the Channel Islands and is only used for the filing and prosecution of patent applications, as distinct from proceedings before the Comptroller for which an address for service within the United Kingdom (including the Isle of Man) is still required. Thus, while an agent from another Community Member State may represent a party to proceedings before the Comptroller, the address for service provided to the Patent Office for those proceedings must be within the United Kingdom (or the Isle of Man). There is nothing in subs.(5), or the Non-recognition Rules, which prevents the Comptroller exercising his powers under those Rules to refuse to recognise as agent a person who neither resides nor has a place of business in the United Kingdom, though natural justice would require the Comptroller to ensure that an agent based within the European Union, but not within the United Kingdom, is given adequate notice of charges of misconduct, etc., made against him and an opportunity of making representations and of being heard before an order of non-recognition should be made, but the mandatory nature of this subsection may create a different situation in the case of a person apparently having no residence or place of business within any European Union Member State (or the Isle of Man).

Trade mark agents [Sections 282–284]

282–284. [...]   282.01

Note. These sections have been repealed, replaced and augmented by ss.82–88 of the Trade Marks Act 1994 (c.26). As they relate to trade marks, rather than patents, they are outside the scope of this Work but are discussed in *The Trade Mark Handbook* (Sweet and Maxwell).

Supplementary [sections 285–286]

SECTION 285

Offences committed by partnerships and bodies corporate

285.—(1) Proceedings for an offence under this Part alleged to have been com-   285.01
mitted by a partnership shall be brought in the name of the partnership and not in that of the partners; but without prejudice to any liability of theirs undersubsection (4) below.

(2) The following provisions apply for the purposes of such proceedings as in relation to a body corporate—

    (a) any rules of court relating to the service of documents;

    (b) in England, Wales or Northern Ireland, Schedule 3 to the Magistrates' Courts Act 1980 [c. 43] or Schedule 4 to the Magistrates' Courts (Northern Ireland) Order 1981 [S.I. 1981 No. 1675 (N.I. 26)] (procedure on charge of offence).

(3) A fine imposed on a partnership on its conviction in such proceedings shall be paid out of the partnership assets.

(4) Where a partnership is guilty of an offence under this Part, every partner,

other than a partner who is proved to have been ignorant of or to have attempted to prevent the commission of the offence, is also guilty of the offence and liable to be proceeded against and punished accordingly.

(5) Where an offence under this Part committed by a body corporate is proved to have been committed with the consent or connivance of a director, manager, secretary or other similar officer of the body, or a person purporting to act in any such capacity, he as well as the body corporate is guilty of the offence and liable to be proceeded against and punished accordingly.

Note. This section came into force on August 13, 1990 (SI 1990/1400).

COMMENTARY ON SECTION 285

285.02   Section 285 of the CDPA 1988 concerns the handling of offences committed by partnerships and bodies corporate under Pt V of the CDPA 1988 (i.e. for present purposes under CDPA 1988 s.276). Section 113 covers offences by corporations under the 1977 Act, but does not refer to partnerships.

Subsection (1) simplifies proceedings for such offences by partnerships by requiring these to be brought in the name of the partnership, rather than against each individual partner named as such, but each individual partner is likewise also guilty of the offence unless that partner is able to prove that he was either ignorant of the offence or tried to prevent its commission (subs.(4)).

Subsection (2) enables partnerships to be treated on the same basis as bodies corporate as regards rules of court, as to service of documents upon them and as to procedure by the application thereto of Sch.3 to the Magistrates' Courts Act 1980 (c.43) in England and Wales, and in Northern Ireland of Sch.4 to the Magistrates' Court (Northern Ireland) Order 1981 (SI 1981/1675 (N.I. 26)): Scottish partnerships are, anyway, treated as bodies corporate. Subsection (3), likewise, makes the partnership as such responsible for the payment of any fine imposed upon it, in lieu of or in addition to any fines imposed on the individual partners under subs.(4).

Subsection (5) concerns bodies corporate and repeats (for the purposes of CDPA 1988 s.276) the substance of s.113, for discussion of which see §.113.02 However, proof of guilt of any individual charged under s.285 of the CDPA 1988 requires the connivance or consent of that person, rather than the mere "neglect" required for offence by an individual under s.113. This appears to be the equivalent of the defence of ignorance afforded to individual partners by subs.(4).

SECTION 286

Interpretation

286.01   **286.** In this Part—

"the comptroller" means the Comptroller-General of Patents, Designs and Trade Marks;

"director", in relation to a body corporate whose affairs are managed by its members, means any member of the body corporate;

"the European list" means the list of professional representatives maintained by the European Patent Office in pursuance of the European Patent Convention;

"registered patent attorney" has the meaning given by section 275(1) [*"registered trade mark agent" has the meaning given by* section 280(1)].

Notes

1. This section came into force on August 13, 1990 (SI 1990/1400). The definition of "registered trade mark agent" was repealed by the Trade Marks Act 1994 (c.26) Sch.5 and re-enacted in s.84 of that Act.

2. The section was amended by the Legal Services Act 2007 (c.29) Sch.21(79) when it entered into force on January 1, 2010, the amendments being the change of "agent" to "attorney" and amendment of the reference to s.275(1) to s.275(2).

COMMENTARY ON SECTION 286

Scope of the section

Section 286 of the CDPA 1988 provides certain definitions for use with ss.274–285 of the CDPA 1988. Of these: the definition of "the Comptroller" repeats that in s.130(1), for which see §130.04; the definition of "director" in relation to a body corporate is made sufficiently broad as to cover any member of that body who plays a role in the management of that body; and the definition of "registered patent attorney" is merely a reference to s.275(2) of the CDPA, which itself states its meaning. The remaining definition is that of the European list, for which see §§286.03 et seq.

286.02

Definition of the "European list"

Section 286 of the CDPA 1988 defines "the European list" as the list of professional representatives maintained by the EPO in pursuance of the EPC. The provisions for such a list are to be found in EPC arts 133 and 134, with EPC rr.91(1)(h), 101 and 102 also making reference to "representatives" (i.e. agents who act for others in proceedings before the EPO).

286.03

The European list was established in January 1978 (OJ EPO 1978, 85), together with a "Regulation on the Establishment of an Institute of Professional Representatives before the EPO" (which has officially adopted the acronym "*epi*"), for which see §286.05, and a "Code of Professional Conduct". Following objection to the form of this Code by the EC Commission under what is now art.101 TFEU, it was revised and then approved by the Commission, as discussed in §286.05 and was published in OJ EPO 2003, 523 ff. There is also a "Regulation on Discipline for Professional Representatives", published in OJ EPO 1980, 183. The texts of these Regulations, and the Code of Professional Conduct, are reprinted in the *European Patents Handbook* (2nd edn) Chs 96 and 98. Breaches of the Code of Professional Conduct may be dealt with, at least in the first instance, by the *epi*, for which see §286.05.

While the use of a representative is not obligatory before the EPO, under EPC art.134 any such representation must be by a person on the European list except that EPC art.134(7) also allows representation by "any legal practitioner qualified in a Contracting State and having his place of business in that State, to the extent that he is entitled in that State to act as a professional representative in patent matters". A registered patent attorney, who is not also a person on the European list, is not a "duly authorised legal practitioner" under EPC art.134 (J 19/89 *N.N./Legal practitioner* OJ EPO 1994, 425; [1991] E.P.O.R. 44).

In G 2/94 *HAUTAU/Representation-II* OJ EPO 1996, 401 and G 4/95 *BOGASKY/ Representation* OJ EPO 1996, 412, the Enlarged Board of Appeal held that, in both ex parte and inter partes proceedings, a non-qualified person, at the discretion of the Board of Appeal, present part of a party's case, although only under the continuing responsibility and control of the appointed professional representative, see also T 598/91 *VMI EPE/Tyre* OJ EPO 1994, 912. Advance application should be made for this facility stating the name and qualification of such person and specifying the subject-matter of his/ her proposed oral submissions.

Qualification for entry to the European list

The transitional period under EPC art.163, during which admission to the European list was open to representatives by virtue of national qualifications or practice, ended on October 5, 1981 (except for nationals of newly joining EPC Member States). Since that date, entry to the European list has been solely by the European qualifying examination under EPC art.134, for which a "Regulation on the European Qualifying Examination for

286.04

Professional Representatives before the EPO" was adopted, the latest version of which was published in a Supplement to OJ EPO 2011, 3 and can be found on the EPO website in a special section relating to the EQE and training for it. Before being permitted to enter this examination the candidate must satisfy the EPO that he/she has been engaged for three years in full-time training and active involvement in proceedings before the EPO under the supervision of a professional representative already on the European list; alternatively, this pre-examination training requirement may be satisfied by full-time employment for three years within an EPC Member State involving representation of the employer over a wide range of activities before the EPO, or working for this period under the direct supervision of such a person (art.10(2) of the Regulation). These provisions can present difficulty to persons practising under the provisions of s.274 of the CDPA 1988 and s.102 who have not already satisfied this service requirement, particularly because the supervision is required to include "constantly taking part in activities pertaining to patent application procedures before the EPO of which the supervising representative is in fact in charge" (D 4/86 *European Qualifying Examination* OJ EPO 1988, 26), and because it is not sufficient for the supervisor to be merely a patent attorney registered to practice only before a national patent office (D 14/93 *Training period* OJ EPO 1997, 561).

The European Patents Institute or "epi"

286.05   The "*epi*", an organisation with the full title "Institute of Professional Representatives before the EPO" (see §286.03), has a general secretariat in an office in Munich and has the postal address: PO Box 260112, D–80058 München, Germany and a website at *http://www.patentepi.com*, see the EPH. Membership of *epi* is compulsory for those on the European list. Such persons are subject to certain disciplinary rules, including the requirement to pay annual subscriptions and notify changes of address in due time and adherence to the code of professional conduct referred to in §286.03. A paper by B.I. Cawthra (1983–84) 13 *CIPA* 46 describes the bodies which enforce these disciplinary rules and the fines which have been imposed, for example for late or non-payment of subscriptions.

For many years, the Code of Professional Conduct of *epi* members did not permit them to advertise, but consequent upon a complaint by the European Commission, the Code was revised and then generally approved by the Commission (see "*EPI Code of Conduct*" [1999] OJ EC L106/14, [1999] 5 C.M.L.R. 540, reprinted OJ EPO 1999, 537; *epi-Information* 2/1999, 60. Under the revised Code, advertising is generally permitted. Also, there is the provision (in art.5(c)) that a representative may not discuss with a potential client a specific case which is or was handled by another representative unless the client declares his wish for an independent view or to change his representative. The representative may inform the first representative only if the client agrees. The EU Commission declared this to be illegal, but on appeal, the Court of First Instance of the European Communities annulled that part of the Commission's decision and reinstated art.5(c), see *epi Information* 2/2001, 75. This revised *epi* Code is now more in line with the code of conduct of the IP Regulation Board (for which see §275.04) under which responsible advertising is generally unobjectionable. Under the previous regime, mail shots and other similar means of drawing the attention of the public to the availability of patent agents, made by United Kingdom patent agents who were also European patent attorneys, had to avoid mentioning the latter qualification, see Disciplinary Case CD 4/91 (*epi Information* 1993, 170) and Disciplinary Case CD 1/92 (*epi-Information* 1993, 326). Unsolicited approaches to potential clients were also in breach of the code (Disciplinary Case CD 3/93 epi-Information 1994, 65). These activities should now be unobjectionable under the revised *epi* Code of Conduct.

PATENTS

Patents county courts [Sections 287–292]

SECTION 287

Patents county courts: special jurisdiction

287.—(1) The Lord Chancellor may, with the concurrence of the Lord Chief   **287.01**
Justice, by order made by statutory instrument designate any county court as a
patents county court and confer on it jurisdiction (its "special jurisdiction") to
hear and determine such descriptions of proceedings—

(a) relating to patents or designs, or

(b) ancillary to, or arising out of the same subject matter as, proceedings relating to patents or designs,

as may be specified in the order.

(2) The special jurisdiction of a patents county court is exercisable throughout
England and Wales, but rules of court may provide for a matter pending in one
such court to be heard and determined in another or partly in that and partly in
another.

(3) A patents county court may entertain proceedings within its special jurisdiction notwithstanding that no pecuniary remedy is sought.

(4) An order under this section providing for the discontinuance of any of the
special jurisdiction of a patents county court may make provision as to proceedings pending in the court when the order comes into operation.

(5) Nothing in this section shall be construed as affecting the ordinary jurisdiction of a county court.

(6) The Lord Chief Justice of England and Wales may nominate a judicial office holder (as defined in section 109(4) of the Constitutional Reform Act 2005
[c. 4]) to exercise his functions under this section.

Notes

1. This section came formally into force on August 1, 1989 (SI 1989/816).

2. The amendment of subs.1 and the addition of subs.(7) were prospectively made by
   the Constitutional Reform Act 2005 (c.4) Sch.4 para.200.

PATENTS COUNTY COURT (DESIGNATION AND JURISDICTION) ORDER 1994

(SI 1994/ 1609 AS AMENDED SI 2005/587)

Title and commencement

1. This order may be cited as the Patents County Court (Designation and Juris-   **287.02**
diction) Order 1994 and shall come into force on 11th July 1994.

Designation as Patents County Court

2. The Central London County Court is hereby designated as a patents county
court.

3. As a patents county court, the Central London County Court shall have jurisdiction, subject to article 4 below—

    (a) to hear and determine any action or matter relating to patents or designs over which the High Court would have jurisdiction, together with any claims or matters ancillary to, or arising from, such proceedings; and

    (b) under the following provisions of the Trade Marks Act 1994

        (i) sections 15, 16, 19, 23(5), 25(4)(b), 30, 31, 46, 47,

        (ii) paragraph 12 of Schedule 1; and

        (iii) paragraph 14 of Schedule 2,

to include jurisdiction to hear and determine any claims or matters ancillary to, or arising from proceedings brought under such provisions.

4. The jurisdiction conferred by article 3 above shall not include jurisdiction to hear appeals from the comptroller.

5. ...

Notes

1. The first county court designated under the CDPA 1988 was the Edmonton County Court, designated by SI 1990/1496 as from September 3, 1990, which was therefore the first Patents County Court. The present Order (SI 1994/1609) replaced the original order consequent on the move from the Edmonton County Court to the Central London County Court. Article 3 of the Order was amended by SI 2005/587 into the form shown above in bold with effect from April 1, 2005 to provide the court with jurisdiction for litigation under the Trade Marks Act 1994.

2. The provisions of para.5 of the order relating to the transfer of jurisdiction from the Edmonton County Court to the Central London County Court are now spent.

COMMENTARY ON SECTION 287

Scope of the section

287.03   Section 287 of the CDPA 1988 provided for the institution of the Patents County Court.

The remaining ss.288–292 of Pt VI of the CDPA 1988 contain further enabling provisions. The Patents County Court at the Central London County Court (designated as such with effect from July 11, 1994) is the only court currently designated for this purpose and is therefore referred to as "the Patents County Court" ("the PCC") in the following paragraphs.

In Autumn 2011, the PCC moved to the Rolls Building, 7 Rolls Buildings, London, EC4A 1NL.

Although ss.287–292 of the CDPA 1988 came formally into force on August 1, 1989, the PCC was designated to be operative only from September 3, 1990. Upon the commencement of these sections, the definition of "court" in s.130(1) was also amended to include "patents county courts" within the definition of "court" for the purposes of the 1977 Act; and the definition of "court" for the purposes of the Registered Designs Act 1949 (c.88) s.27 was also likewise extended to cover the PCC (CDPA 1988 Sch.3 para.16). However, by para.4 of this Order, the PCC has no jurisdiction to hear appeals from the Comptroller.

The reader is referred to §§61.40 et seq for a discussion of the practice and procedure before the Patents Court and the PCC and the contrast between the procedure in the two courts. The following paragraphs deal with aspects of the legislation setting up the PCC.

The history of the development of the Patents County Court jurisdiction

287.04   The creation of the patents county court jurisdiction in 1990 represented the first serious attempt by parliament to modernise the system of patent litigation in the United Kingdom. The need for such improvement had been extant for well over a century, see the famous speech by Lord Esher M.R. in *Ungar v Sugg* about the complexity and expense of patent litigation, see (1892) 9 R.P.C. 113 at 116–117.

The origin of the new jurisdiction was an adverse reaction from the legal profession to the proposal in the 1986 White Paper "Intellectual Property Rights and Innovation" (Cmnd.9712) that patent litigation should in the first instance be brought before the Comptroller. As a result, the Lord Chancellor set up an inquiry under Sir Derek Oulton. It was the report of this inquiry ("the Oulton Report") which recommended the creation of the PCC as part of the county court system. Sections 287–293 of the CDPA 1988 then implemented that Report. This background to the institution of the new forum was described in articles by D. Gladwell and S. Wilcox (1989–90) 19 *CIPA* 422 and B. C. Reid [1988] E.I.P.R. 35.

The first phase of the PCC's existence (at Edmonton) saw an attempt to introduce new rules of procedure having the effect of "front loading" some of the costs of litigation with a view to encouraging fuller pleading of cases, and was not generally regarded as a success. This was followed by a phase, coinciding with the appointment of HHJ Michael Fysh QC, SC, in which the rules of procedure in the PCC (and other county courts) were aligned with those of the High Court as a consequence of the Woolf reforms. This was generally seen as removing much of the incentive for the use of the PCC, in particular as an effective forum for SMEs.

The PCC is now in effect in a third phase of its development with the appointment of HHJ Judge Colin Birss QC in October 2010, and the revision of its rules to incorporate limits on costs and recovery of damages as described in more detail in §§61.40 et seq. Early signs are that the PCC under this new regime has taken on a new lease of life and has a much busier case load than formerly, although only a minor proportion of its work actually involves patent matters. Proposals to change the name of the court to describe more accurately its work as an Intellectual Property County Court, which would require legislation, have not moved forward at the time of writing.

Jurisdiction of patents county courts

The jurisdiction of the PCC is limited to England and Wales, the separate legal systems   **287.05** of Scotland, Northern Ireland and the Isle of Man at present having no similar lower court jurisdiction over patent and design matters. In addition to the PCC having all the normal powers of a county court (subs.(5)), subs.(1) provides for the PCC's special jurisdiction, for which see §287.06.

While county courts generally cannot make search (*Anton Piller*) orders, or grant freezing (*Mareva*) injunctions, the PCC can do so (County Courts (Remedies) Regulations 1991, SI 1991/1222 r.3). An example of such a case is *McDonald v Graham* [1994] R.P.C. 407, though here it was noted that the power probably would not extend to matters outside the special jurisdiction of the PCC. Appeals from a decision of the PCC proceed to the Court of Appeal in the normal way under s.77 of the County Courts Act, but there is power (under its s.77(2)) for the Lord Chancellor, by order, to limit appeals on specified matters unless leave is granted either by the county court or the Court of Appeal. The procedure for appeal from the PCC to the Court of Appeal is the same as for an appeal from the High Court, any such appeal now requiring leave, either from the PCC or from the Court of Appeal itself, as discussed in §97.20.

—Subject-matter limits to jurisdiction

The PCC has jurisdiction in normal actions for infringement and challenges to the va-   **287.06** lidity of patents or registered designs, even if only one of these matters is in issue as well as "proceedings" related to patents and designs which would seem to be capable of covering virtually any kind of dispute involving patent rights, e.g. disputes as to entitlement (employer-employee or otherwise), unjustified threats and priority as between licensees. It is also clear that actions involving either a patent or a registered design, together with a companion cause of action, are encompassed. In *Prout v British Gas* [1992] F.S.R. 478, an action for patent infringement was combined with an action for breach of confidence, the claimant failing on the former but succeeding on the latter. It is also clear that the term "designs" covers both registered designs and "design rights", as created by Pt III of the CDPA 1988. In *PSM International v Specialised Fastener Products* [1993] F.S.R. 113, the PCC held that it had jurisdiction in a copyright case involving designs recorded in design documents prior to commencement of the CDPA 1988 for which copyright protection akin to the new design right remained in effect for a transitional period under CDPA 1988 Sch.1 para.19; and, in *McDonald v Graham* [1994] R.P.C. 407 CA, an action for infringement of literary and artistic copyright was held to be "ancillary" within the meaning of the section.

Indeed, the Court of Appeal here stated that the phrase "claims or matters ancillary thereto or arising therefrom" should be construed sensibly and, if convenient, widely drawn, though unrelated matters could not be introduced. However, the term "designs" in Pt VI of the CDPA 1988 might be limited to registered designs and "design rights". Although the original PCC jurisdiction was limited as defined in s.287 of the CDPA 1988 to matters relating to patents and designs, the Courts and Legal Services Act 1990 (c.41) s.1 provided extension of the powers of county courts (of which the PCC is one) the same powers (with a few exceptions) as those of the High Court, see §289.02. Also, in 2005, the PCC was given explicit powers to decide certain types of trade mark disputes, see §287.02.

SECTION 288

Financial limits in relation to proceedings within special jurisdiction of patents county court

288.01

288.—(1) Her Majesty may by Order in Council provide for limits of amount or value in relation to any description of proceedings within the special jurisdiction of a patents county court.

(2) If a limit is imposed on the amount of a claim of any description and the plaintiff has a cause of action for more than that amount, he may abandon the excess; in which case a patents county court shall have jurisdiction to hear and determine the action, but the plaintiff may not recover more than that amount.

(3) Where the court has jurisdiction to hear and determine an action by virtue of subsection (2), the judgment of the court in the action is in full discharge of all demands in respect of the cause of action, and entry of the judgment shall be made accordingly.

(4) If the parties agree, by a memorandum signed by them or by their respective solicitors or other agents, that a patents county court shall have jurisdiction in any proceedings, that court shall have jurisdiction to hear and determine the proceedings notwithstanding any limit imposed under this section.

(5) No recommendation shall be made to Her Majesty to make an order under this section unless a draft of the Order has been laid before and approved by a resolution of each House of Parliament.

Notes

1. This section came formally into force on August 1, 1989 (SI 1989/816).

2. The word "plaintiff" in subs.(2) is now to be interpreted as meaning "claimant" in view of this replacement of the term in the CPR.

THE PATENTS COUNTY COURT (FINANCIAL LIMITS) ORDER 2011

Citation and commencement

1. This Order may be cited as the Patents County Court (Financial Limits) Order 2011 and shall come into force on 14th June 2011.   **288.02**

Financial limits

2.—(1) In relation to all proceedings within the special jurisdiction of a patents county court and in which a claim is made for damages or an account of profits, the amount or value of that claim shall not exceed £500,000.

(2) In determining the amount or value of a claim for the purpose of paragraph (1), a claim for—

(a) interest, other than interest payable under an agreement, or

(b) costs,

shall be disregarded.

Transitional provision

3. A patents county court has jurisdiction to hear and determine a claim for damages or an account of profits for an amount or value exceeding the limit imposed by article 2 where, before the coming into force of this Order—

(a) the claim has been made in a patents county court in proceedings within its special jurisdiction, or

(b) the High Court orders the proceedings in which the claim has been made to be transferred to the special jurisdiction of a patents county court, or

(c) an application has been made to the High Court for transfer of the proceedings in which the claim has been made to a patents county court and, after the coming into force of this Order, the High Court orders the transfer of the proceedings to the special jurisdiction of a patents county court.

COMMENTARY ON SECTION 288

The Patents County Court (Financial Limits) Order 2011 (2011/1402) set out above   **288.03**
provides for a limit of £500,000 in relation to claims for damages or an account of profits for all proceedings within the special jurisdiction of the PCC and contains transitional provisions relating to actions commenced before the coming into force of the Order.

SECTION 289

Transfer of proceedings between High Court and patents county court

289.—(1) No order shall be made under section 41 of the County Courts Act   **289.01**
1984 [c.28] (power of High Court to order proceedings to be transferred from the county court) in respect of proceedings within the special jurisdiction of a patents county court.

(2) In considering in relation to proceedings within the special jurisdiction of a patents county court whether an order should be made under section 40 or 42 of the County Courts Act 1984 (transfer of proceedings from or to the High Court), the court shall have regard to the financial position of the parties and may order

the transfer of the proceedings to a patents county court or, as the case may be, refrain from ordering their transfer to the High Court notwithstanding that the proceedings are likely to raise an important question of fact or law.

Notes

1. This section came formally into force on August 1, 1989 (SI 1989/ 816).

2. Sections 40 and 42 of the County Courts Act 1984 (c.28) have been substituted by new wording, and s.41 amended by the Courts and Legal Services Act 1990 (c.41) s.2.

COMMENTARY ON SECTION 289

Scope of the section

289.02 Subsection (1) prevents the High Court from ordering of its own motion the transfer of proceedings from the PCC to itself under s.41 of the County Courts Act 1984 (c.28). Sections 40 and 42 of that Act provide for transfer of cases from or to a county court, but in making any order under these provisions in relation to its special jurisdiction the court is required to have regard to the financial position of the parties, even when the proceedings are likely to raise an important question of fact or law (subs.(2)).

However, ss.40–42 of the County Courts Act 1984 were amended by the Courts and Legal Services Act 1990 (c.41) s.2 and then empowered the Lord Chancellor to make orders for cases in general to be transferred from the High Court to a county court, and vice versa, when these cases fell within certain categories as specified by order. The principles for transfer between the High Court and a county court, and vice versa, are now set out in the CPR Pt 30 and these augment the criteria for judging whether transfer of patent proceedings should, or should not, be ordered, as discussed in §289.03. For the issue of transfer between the courts, see also §61.44.

Criteria for transfer between the High Court and Patents County Court

289.03 The Patents County Court Guide contains the following guidelines to assist users in determining which of the two courts is suitable:

- Size of the parties. If both sides are small or medium sized enterprises then the case may well be suitable for the Patents County Court. If one party is a small or medium sized enterprise but the other is a larger undertaking then again the case may be suitable for the Patents County Court but other factors ought to be considered such as the value of the claim and its likely complexity.

- The complexity of the claim. The procedure in the Patents County Court is streamlined and trials last no more than 2 days. A trial which would appear to require more time than that even with the streamlined procedure of the Patents County Court is likely to be unsuitable.

- The nature of the evidence. Experiments in a patent case may be admitted in the Patents County Court but a case which will involve substantial complex experimental evidence will be unsuitable for the Patents County Court.

- Conflicting factual evidence. Cross-examination of witnesses will be strictly controlled in the Patents County Court. The court is well able to handle cases involving disputed factual matters such as allegations of prior use in patents and independent design as a defence to copying; but if a large number of witnesses are required the case may be unsuitable for the Patents County Court.

- Value of the claim. Putting a value on a claim is a notoriously difficult exercise, taking into account factors such as possible damages, the value of an injunction and the possible effect on competition in a market if a patent was revoked. The likely damages to be recovered in an infringement claim is a factor which should be considered. [Although no limit on damages in the Patents County Court has been introduced (yet),]* if the damages are likely to be well in excess of £500,000 then the claim may not be appropriate for the Patents County Court. As a general rule of thumb, disputes where the value of sales, in the UK, of products protected by the intellectual property in issue (by the owner, licensees and alleged infringer) exceeds £1 million per year are unlikely to be suitable for the Patent County Court in the absence of agreement.

[*this version of the Guide (the latest available at the time of writing) dates from May 2011, before the coming in to force of The Patents County Court (Financial Limits) Order 2011 (see §288.02 above).]

Transfer from the PCC to the High Court was refused in *Wesley Jessen Corp v Coopervision* BL C/31/01 the court holding that the onus for transfer lay with he who sought it. There is no case for transfer just because the parties are big or that expert and experimental evidence is in prospect. However, transfer to the Patents Court was ordered in *Aerotel v First National Telecom* [2005] EWHC 2539 Pat Ct, noted I.P.D. 29009 because it was uncertain whether the PCC could (a) grant a letter of request to a US court; or (b) enforce an award of costs from the PCC in a foreign court.

In *Halliburton v Smith International* BL C/6/04 actions between the same parties had been started, almost simultaneously, before the PCC and the Patents Court. The PCC considered that it was desirable for all actions to be tried in the same court, but which court was a matter for the Patents Court to decide. A transfer order of the PCC actions was therefore made without prejudice to a re-transfer to the PCC if the Patents Court thought this appropriate.

Factors which influence applications for transfer in practice

Where both parties consent to transfer, then little difficulty arises—apart from attending to the transfer formalities, for which see §289.05. Such transfer by consent is by no means exceptional. In a case where it appears at an interim stage that the potential quantum of damages could hardly justify the use of the Patents Court procedure, there is an obvious incentive to move to a more modest forum. Conversely, there may be a case where it appears at an interim stage that large-scale disclosure or elaborate experiments are desirable. In such instances, there may be a counter-incentive to move from the more modest forum to one which is more powerful from a procedural standpoint, e.g. as in *Mannesmann v Microsystem Design* [1992] R.P.C. 569.

289.04

Where the parties disagree as to transfer, the position is more complex, although a tendency can be discerned for both the High Court and the PCC each to decline to transfer a case first brought before it, at least in the absence of related proceedings having been brought in the other jurisdiction. It appears reasonably clear that the mere wish of one party or the other to transfer from the Patents Court to the PCC, or vice versa, is not in itself decisive: justification for the proposed transfer has to be shown: *GEC-Marconi v Xyllyx Viewdata* [1991] F.S.R. 319. Nor, in the case of conflicting jurisdictions—e.g. where one party commences infringement proceedings in one forum and the other party petitions for revocation in the other—is it decisive which action was commenced first (*Symbol v Opticon* [1993] R.P.C. 211; and *Pharma Plast A/S v Bard* BL CC/19/93), though this is a powerful reason (within the discretion of the judge) for transfer so that both cases can be heard in the same forum (*Mentor v Colorplast* [1994] F.S.R. 175 CA).

The financial position of the parties remains a most important factor (*Memminger v Trip-Lite* [1992] R.P.C. 227 CA). However, in refusing transfer where the parties were each of sufficient size to afford High Court proceedings, the PCC has taken into account that the patented product represented only a small proportion of the claimant's turnover from which it was deduced that high litigation costs could be significant to it in relation to the profitability of that product and therefore held that this factor militated against transfer to a more expensive forum (see *Pharma Plast A/S v Bard*).

A party's desire to save costs by being represented by his patent attorney does, however, provide a strong (although not necessarily a compelling) reason for transfer to the PCC, since the underlying concept of this court was to reduce costs and hence enable those of lesser means to litigate in the patent and design fields (*Memminger v Trip-Lite*). From a practical standpoint, costs in the PCC can undoubtedly be lower—and in many cases considerably lower—than comparable proceedings in the Patents Court, provided a truncated legal team is employed. The following factors assist in that end: the abbreviated interim procedure; the greater degree of preparation by the court itself (leading in turn to a shorter duration of trial); and the more flexible requirements as to representation (in particular, the possibility for the entire action to be conducted by a party's patent agent, for which see s.292(1) and §292.03).

Indeed, the court has in the past assumed that proceedings (taken to full trial) before the PCC will be somewhat quicker and cheaper than if fought in the Patents Court; and that, accordingly, extensive evidence on these points is not necessary on an application for transfer (*Composite Gutters v Pre-formed Components* [1993] F.S.R. 305).

In *Slope Indicator v Monitoring Systems* [1995] F.S.R. 867, transfer from the Patents Court to the PCC was refused; it was contended that the defendant was a start-up company whose business as a whole was threatened by the litigation, but it was conceded that a trial before the PCC would not be any quicker, and that the defendant would wish to use counsel.

The Patents Court has also stated that "the primary aim of the Patents County Court should not be blunted by large companies litigating part of a substantial portfolio of patents", this being "better dealt with by procedures which have evolved and are practised in the High Court" (see *Symbol v Opticon*); and has refused transfer where the defendant wished the case to remain with the Patents Court in order to obtain full disclosure and both parties were companies of significant size, see *Mannesmann v Microsystem Design*.

Also, a party may wish to resist transfer because it sees the need for it to use the services of more than one expert witness, whereas the PCC may seek to limit each party to one expert witness, see *Optical Recording Corp v Hayden Laboratories* BL C/3/93 CA and the comment on the case by P. Langley and S. Jones [1993] E.I.P.R. 136.

Mechanics of transfer of a case from or to the Patents Court

289.05   The procedure when the Patents Court orders transfer to the PCC, or vice versa, is governed generally by CPR 30 PD. Unless objection is taken, the pleadings in the initial court should stand before the second court on transfer.

SECTION 290 [PROSPECTIVELY REPEALED]

Limitation of costs where pecuniary claim could have been brought in patents county court

290.01   [**290.**—(1) *Where an action is commenced in the High Court which could have been commenced in a patents county court and in which a claim for a pecuniary remedy is made, then, subject to the provisions of this section, if the plaintiff [now "claimant"] recovers less than the prescribed amount, he is not entitled to recover any more costs than those to which he would have been entitled if the action had been brought in the county court.*

(2) *For this purpose a plaintiff [claimant] shall be treated as recovering the full amount recoverable in respect of his claim without regard to any deduction made in respect of matters not falling to be taken into account in determining whether the action could have been commenced in a patents county court.*

(3) *This section does not affect any question as to costs if it appears to the High Court that there was reasonable ground for supposing the amount recover-*

able in respect of the plaintiff's [claimant's] claim to be in excess of the prescribed amount.

(4) *The High Court, if satisfied that there was sufficient reason for bringing the action in the High Court, may make an order allowing the costs or any part of the costs on the High Court scale or on such one of the county court scales as it may direct.*

(5) *This section does not apply to proceedings brought by the Crown.*

(6) *In this section "the prescribed amount" means such amount as may be prescribed by Her Majesty for the purposes of this section by Order in Council.*

(7) *No recommendation shall be made to Her Majesty to make an Order under this section unless a draft of the Order has been laid before and approved by a resolution of each House of Parliament.*]

Note. This section came formally into force on August 1, 1989 (SI 1989/816), but was prospectively repealed by the Courts and Legal Services Act 1990 (c.41) Sch.20, although that repeal has not been activated. However, as no order has been made under the section, it presently has no effect.

COMMENTARY ON SECTION 290

Scope of the section

This section contemplated a restriction in costs recovery where the claimant in fact litigated in the Patents Court even though he could have litigated instead in the Patents County Court.   **290.02**

The section was not implemented and has been prospectively repealed by the Courts and Legal Services Act 1990, ss.124(3), 125(7), Sch.20.

Costs in the Patents County Court are now subject to a cap provided by CPR Part 45.42. Subject to certain limited exceptions the court will not order a party to pay total costs of more than £50,000 on the final determination of a claim in relation to liability and no more than £25,000 on an inquiry as to damages or account of profits. See further the Patents County Court Guide and §61.87.

SECTION 291

Proceedings in patents county court

291.—(1) Where a county court is designated a patents county court, Lord   **291.01**
Chief Justice shall, after consulting the Lord Chancellor, nominate a person entitled to sit as a judge of that court as the patents judge.

(2) County court rules shall make provision for securing that, so far as is practicable and appropriate—

    (a) proceedings within the special jurisdiction of a patents county court are dealt with by the patents judge, and

    (b) the judge, rather than a registrar or other officer of the court, deals with interlocutory [now "interim"] matters in the proceedings.

(3) County court rules shall make provision empowering a patents county court in proceedings within its special jurisdiction, on or without the application of any party—

    (a) to appoint scientific advisers or assessors to assist the court, or

    (b) to order the Patent Office to inquire into and report on any question of fact or opinion.

(4) Where the court exercises either of those powers on the application of a party, the remuneration or fees payable to the Patent Office shall be at such rate as may be determined in accordance with county court rules and shall be costs of the proceedings unless otherwise ordered by the judge.

(5) Where the court exercises either of those powers of its own motion, the remuneration or fees payable to the Patent Office shall be at such rate as may be determined by the Lord Chancellor with the approval of the Treasury and shall be paid out of money provided by Parliament.

(6) The Lord Chief Justice may nominate a judicial office holder (as defined in section 109(4) of the Constitutional Reform Act 2005 [c. 4]) to exercise his functions under subsection (1).

Note

1. This section came formally into force on August 1, 1989 (SI 1989/816).

2. The amendment of subs.1 and the addition of subs.(6) were prospectively made by the Constitutional Reform Act 2005 (c.4) Sch.4 para.201.

COMMENTARY ON SECTION 291

Judges of the Patents County Court (subss.(1) and (2))

291.02   Section 291 of the CDPA 1988 is an enabling section providing for the special appointment of a "patents judge" to sit as a judge in the PCC (subs.(1)); and for special county court rules to be made providing for that judge, so far as practicable and appropriate, to hear all matters, including interim matters, in that court (subs.(2)). The section also provides that the county court rules shall make provision for the appointment of scientific advisers or assessors to assist the PCC, and to require the UK-IPO to make inquiry into and report on any question of fact or opinion, with consequent financial provisions (subss.(3)–(5)).

Counsel of the Patent Bar may also sit as deputy judges in the PCC.

The first judge of the PCC was HHJ Peter Ford, a former member of the English Patents Bar and subsequently chairman of a Legal Board of Appeals of the European Patent Office. HHJ Michael Fysh QC, SC was appointed as judge of the PCC in 2001. HHJ Colin Birss QC was appointed in October 2010, see also §287.04.

Procedure in the Patents County Court

291.03   Procedure before the Patents County Court and the contrast between the procedure there and in the High Court (Patents Court) is dealt with in this Work under the heading of Practice under Section 61, in §§61.40 et seq.

SECTION 292 [REPEALED WITH EFFECT JANUARY 1, 2010]

Rights and duties of registered patent agents in relation to proceedings in patents county court

292.01   **292.**—(1) A registered patent agent may do, in or in connection with proceedings in a patents county court which are within the special jurisdiction of that court, anything which a solicitor of the Supreme Court might do, other than prepare a deed.

(2) The Lord Chancellor may by regulations provide that the right conferred by subsection (1) shall be subject to such conditions and restrictions as appear to

the Lord Chancellor to be necessary or expedient; and different provision may be made for different descriptions of proceedings.

(2A) The Lord Chancellor may make regulations under subsection (2) only with the concurrence of the Lord Chief Justice.

(3) A patents county court has the same power to enforce an undertaking given by a registered patent agent acting in pursuance of this section as it has, by virtue of section 142 of the County Courts Act 1984 [c. 28], in relation to a solicitor.

(4) Nothing in section 143 of the County Courts Act 1984 [c. 28], (prohibition on persons other than solicitors receiving remuneration) applies to a registered patent agent acting in pursuance of this section.

(5) The provisions of county court rules prescribing scales of costs to be paid to solicitors apply in relation to registered patent agents acting in pursuance of this section.

(6) Regulations under this section shall be made by statutory instrument which shall be subject to annulment in pursuance of a resolution of either House of Parliament.

(7) The Lord Chief Justice may nominate a judicial office holder (as defined in section 109(4) of the Constitutional Reform Act 2005 [c. 4]) to exercise his functions under this section.

Notes

1. This section came formally into force on August 1, 1989 (SI 1989/816).

2. The addition of subss.(2A) and (7) was made by the Constitutional Reform Act 2005 (c.4) Sch.4, para.202(2) and (3) respectively.

3. The section was repealed by the Legal Services Act 2007 (c.29) Sch.23, on January 1, 2010 (SI 2009/3250, para.2(i)(vi)), but the section continues to have effect during the "transitional period" provided by that Act, see §275.09 above.

COMMENTARY ON SECTION 292

Scope of the section

As noted in note 3 above, Section 292 was repealed with effect 1 January 2010, on **292.02** which date a "transitional period" commenced, as defined by the Legal Services Act 2007, Sch.5, Part 2, para 3. According to para. 15 of Sch.5 of the same Act, "(d)uring the transitional period registered patent attorneys are to continue to have the rights conferred by ... section 292 of the Copyright, Designs and Patents Act 1988", and hence although the section is itself repealed the effects of the section still apply during the transitional period. As explained in § 102A.02 above, the length of the transitional period is at the time of writing as yet unspecified, and may be of several years duration. It is anticipated that the Intellectual Property Regulation Board (IPReg) will in due course propose a replacement regulation, to replace the provisions of s.102A of the Patents Act 1977 (which although repealed remain effective via the same legislative mechanism as the present section), as well as those of Section 292 and the CIPA Higher Courts Qualifications Regulations 2007, which at present govern the rights of "patent attorney litigators". At the time of writing no formal open consultation had yet been commenced by IPReg, although it is understood that draft rules have been prepared in preparation for such.

Whereas only counsel (besides non-corporate litigants in person) normally have a right of audience in the High Court, and are required to be instructed either by a solicitor or, for intellectual property litigation, by a patent attorney litigator (except in relation to proceedings before the Patents Court by way of appeal from the Comptroller, for which see §102A.02), in proceedings before a county court solicitors also have a right of audience. Section 292 of the CDPA 1988 also provided for a "registered patent attorney [agent]" to do anything in proceedings before a patents county court which a solicitor may do (subs.(1)), other than prepare a deed, but subject to such conditions and restrictions as the Lord Chancellor may deem necessary or expedient (subs.(2)), as set out in regulations to be made by statutory instrument subject to negative resolution by either House of Parliament (subs.(6)). The term "registered patent attorney [agent]" is defined in s.275(1) of the CDPA 1988, see s.286 of the CDPA 1988 (reprinted respectively in §§275.01 and 286.01), and is discussed in §275.02.

The position of registered patent attorneys conducting litigation in the PCC was further equated with that of solicitors acting in a similar capacity, as regards the giving of undertakings to the court (subs.(3)) and as to the scale of costs which may be prescribed to be paid to such persons (subs.(5)), while subs.(4) removed (as regards registered patent attorneys acting under the section) the prohibition against persons other than solicitors receiving remuneration for their services in proceedings before a county court. Fellows of the Chartered Institute of Patent Attorneys are also subject to a special code of conduct for patent litigators (reprinted in Appendix K), which is supported by a special disciplinary procedure for which see §J14 in Appendix J. Regarding scale costs in the Patents County Court, regard must now be had to CPR Pts 45.41 and 45.42. as well as the Costs Practice Direction, which sets out in detail the scale costs applicable in PCC proceedings. Further information is also available in *The Patents County Court Guide*, (reprinted in Appendix G) issued by the Lord Chancellor on May 12, 2011.

The apparent prohibition in subs.(1) that prevented a patent attorney from preparing a deed may have been overruled by the Courts and Legal Services Act 1990 (c.41) s.68. This amended s.22 of the Solicitors Act 1974 (c.47) to provide a further exception to the monopoly power of solicitors to draw deeds so as to allow this to be done by "a registered patent agent drawing or preparing any instrument relating to any invention, design, technical information, trade mark or service mark", see §102.05.

For Chartered Patent Attorneys who have received a "Litigation Rights Certificate" as an "authorised litigator" under the Courts and Legal Services Act 1990, the powers of s.292 have been superseded because such "patent agent litigators" can have the conduct of litigation concerning intellectual property of a technical nature whether this takes place in the High Court, a county court or the Court of Appeal, as explained in §275.10. However, although s.292 of the CDPA 1988 provides such a person with the right to act as an advocate before the Patents County Court, the CIPA Higher Court Qualification Regulations were amended in 2007 (following the introduction of trade mark jurisdiction to certain county courts) to give those with Litigation Rights Certificates the additional right of advocacy in county court proceedings in intellectual property litigation, see also §275.10 and §292.04. Therefore, if at the end of the transitional period noted above no replacement for s.292 CDPA has been promulgated, the only registered patent attorneys with either litigation rights or rights of audience in the PCC will be patent agent litigators.

Effect of the section in practice

292.03   At a practical level, the PCC welcomes representation by patent attorneys, and the recent revision to the PCC procedural rules to provide for more of an "EPO-style" approach to litigation (for more details of which see §§61.81 et seq. above) has made the court a more inviting forum for patent attorneys, particularly for lower value disputes. However, patent attorneys should be wary of acting as advocate in a case where they may be required to give factual testimony, for example in patent amendment proceedings, because of the tradition that an advocate stands apart from the evidence, see P. A. Smith [1993] *CIPA* 121.

It is significant that the wording of the side-note to the s.292 of the CDPA 1988 referred to the "rights and duties" of registered patent agents. Clearly, patent attorneys who practise before the PCC, whether as litigators or advocates, ought to be subject to similar disciplinary rules and procedures as apply to solicitors as "officers of the Supreme Court." However, no regulations were made under subs.(2), and, consequently, it is not clear whether in fact patent attorneys are to be regarded as "officers of the court" in the same way as solicitors and, therefore, whether the court has disciplinary powers over patent attorneys as it does over solicitors engaged in litigation before it. Nevertheless, it should not be assumed that such disciplinary power is lacking and, anyway, the Chartered Institute has promulgated its own rules of conduct and disciplinary procedures for those of its members who engage in litigation work whether as litigators or advocates, and whether or not the member is acting within the power of a litigation rights certificate held by him or her, see the Special Rules of Professional Conduct made by the Chartered Institute (reprinted as Appendix K).

In any event, subs.(3) provided that undertakings given by a registered patent agent in the course of proceedings before the PCC are just as enforceable (under the County Courts Act 1984 (c.28) s.142) as those given by a solicitor on behalf of his client. Accordingly, patent attorneys should be wary of giving any undertaking in proceedings before the PCC unless specifically authorised so to do and, even then, only to give an undertaking with which he is satisfied his client will comply.

In consequence of these perceived duties, patent attorneys practising before the PCC ought to have adequate professional indemnity insurance, as is required of solicitors. There is no indemnity fund (as there is with solicitors) to cope with a mishandling of a client's funds entrusted to a patent attorney for the purposes of litigation. Likewise, there is no obligation for a patent attorney to maintain clients' money in a separate bank account, although a Chartered Patent Attorney who may be paid money in advance to cover costs in litigation can be expected to comply with rules of professional conduct imposed by the Chartered Institute (for which see §275.06) and prudently take steps to safeguard his client's interests. Also, Chartered Patent Attorneys are required to have professional indemnity insurance of at least £250,000, see §J17.

"Authorised litigators" and "authorised advocates"

The Courts and Legal Services Act 1990 (c.41) (the "1990 Act") regulates the rights of audience before a court (s.27) and the right to conduct litigation (s.28), although the right of registered patent agents to conduct litigation before a patents county court is not affected by this subsequent statute. This is because persons having rights under the 1990 Act can be, inter alia, those having a right "granted by or under any enactment". Consequently, the rights of registered patent agents to represent litigants before the PCC and to appear before it (as had previously been conferred by the present section) are preserved. However, a registered patent agent is not an "authorised advocate" or an "authorised litigator" (as defined in s.119 of the 1990 Act), because these definitions apply only where the "right" has been granted by an authorised body in accordance with that Act.

292.04

As explained in §275.05, the Chartered Institute has the power to grant a "Litigator Certificate" under which a Fellow of the Institute who is deemed to have met the required qualification criteria (reprinted in Appendix K) becomes an "authorised litigator" within the terms of the 1990 Act. The holder of such a certificate has, effectively, the same powers as a solicitor for the conduct of litigation of the type specified in that certificate. In the case of "patent agent litigators", this is the power granted by the CIPA Higher Courts Qualification Regulations 2007 to conduct litigation before the County Court, High Court and the Court of Appeal and act as an advocate in the County Court (but not to act as advocate in open court in the High Court or Court of Appeal), in addition to the power granted under s.292 of the CDPA 1988 for proceedings in a patents county court.

Differences in rights between registered patent agents who do not hold "litigator certificates" and those who do would appear to be that:

(1) a registered patent agent providing advocacy or litigation services before the Comptroller or the Patents County Court may obtain slightly less legal professional privilege for communications made to or by him in the conduct of litigation: s.63 of the 1990 Act would not apply, though he will enjoy privilege under the terms of

s.280 of the CDPA 1988, and s.103 of the 1977 Act (which extends a solicitor's litigation privilege to proceedings before the Comptroller) see §280.03, or perhaps in relation to proceedings or contemplated proceedings in the Patents County Court by implication under the provisions of the present section itself;

(2) legal aid was not available for representation of a litigant by a patent agent in proceedings before the PCC, see Sch.18 paras 60 and 63(4) to the 1990 Act, though a patent agent could be paid out of the Legal Aid Fund when assisting a solicitor in legally aided litigation;

(3) there is no entitlement to administer oaths and hence use the title "Commissioner for Oaths".

Nevertheless, a registered patent agent, when acting as an advocate, enjoys immunity from actions for negligence or for breach of contract if a barrister would have a like immunity (s.62 of the 1990 Act).

Regarding (1) above, that a non-PAL registered patent attorney has lesser privilege than a PAL was confirmed by the judgment of Lewison J. in *Atrium Medical v DSB* [2011] EWHC 74 (Pat), where it was held that the wording of Regulation 3 of the CIPA Higher Courts Qualification Regulations 2007 (which sets out the scope of patent attorney litigator rights, and which, by virtue of s.190 of the Legal Services Act 2007 is also the basis for the scope of patent attorney litigator privilege) is broader than that of s.280 of the CDPA, in that it refers to "similar rights" to those mentioned in CDPA s.280 as well as "any ancillary matters thereto". In the case in question, which related to the interpretation of the scope of licensed technology in a royalty agreement, Lewison J. found that the dispute in question fell within the scope of "technical information" mentioned in both CDPA s.280 and Regulation 3, but that if he was wrong on this then it fell within the "similar rights" definition of Regulation 3. Whilst the case was brought in the High Court, and hence the point in question was whether the responsible PAL even had rights to conduct the case, if a similar case had instead been in the PCC and brought by a non-PAL patent attorney then although the right to bring the case under the present section would have been clear, following Lewison J.'s reasoning on the difference between patent attorney and PAL privilege, it is possible that privilege would not be granted to the non-PAL patent attorney.

Licences of right in respect of certain patents [Sections 293-294]

SECTION 293 [SPENT]

Restriction of acts authorised by certain licences

293.01   **293.** [...]

Note. This section amended Sch.1 para.4(2)(c) to the 1977 Act and inserted new para.4A within it, but its provisions are now spent.

SECTION 294 [SPENT]

When application may be made for settlement of terms of licence

294.01   **294.** [...]

Note. This section inserted para.4B in Sch.1 to the 1977 Act, but this can be considered to be spent.

Patents: miscellaneous amendments [Section 295]

SECTION 295

Patents: miscellaneous amendments

295.01   **295.** [...]

Note. This section introduced Sch.5 tothe CDPA 1988 by which, inter alia, several amendments were made to the 1977 Act: these amendments have been noted individually in the reprinting of these sections as so amended.

Appendices

APPENDIX A

HISTORY OF UNITED KINGDOM PATENT LAW

The scope of this Appendix

A01   This Work is a Guide to the current patent law of the United Kingdom which has been explained for practitioners and discussed in the above commentaries, but it is important to appreciate how this law has been created and evolved over many centuries under the Common Law of England which governs its judicial system. This Appendix briefly explains this by a trawl through its history.

The early years before 1623

A02   It is thought that a Venetian law of 1474 provided an early reference to the devising and invention of ingenious devices which deserved an exclusive monopoly for a limited period in the following words:

> "There are men in this city, and also there come other persons every day from different places by reason of its greatness and goodness, who have most clever minds, capable of devising and inventing all kinds of ingenious contrivances. And should it be legislated that the works and contrivances invented by them could not be copied and made by others so that they are deprived of their honour, men of such kind would exert their minds, invent and make things that would be of no small utility and benefit to our State.
>
> Therefore, the decision has been made that, by authority of this Council, any person in this city who makes any new and ingenious contrivances not made heretofore in our Dominion, shall, as soon as it is perfected so that it can be used and exercised, give notice of the same to the office of our Provveditori di Comun, having been forbidden up to ten years to any other person in any territory and place of ours to make a contrivance in the form and resemblance of that one without the consent and license of the author.
>
> And if nevertheless someone should make it, the aforesaid author and inventor will have the liberty to cite him before any office of this city, which office will force the aforesaid infringer to pay him the sum of one hundred ducats and immediately destroy the contrivance. But our Government will be free, at its complete discretion, to take and use for its needs any of the said contrivances and instruments, with this condition, however, that no one other than the authors shall operate them."

It is to be noted that this proclamation was directed to new and ingenious contrivances. However, this was not so in England and here towards the end of the sixteenth Century, many such grants of exclusive privilege for trading practices were granted by the Crown in exercise of its prerogative and as a means of raising money for the Crown outside the writ of Parliament. Complaints were made to it but without success as the Crown contended that the Crown's prerogative was absolute. One such patent was one granting a monopoly for the importing, manufacturing and selling of playing cards. This came before the court and was held to be a monopoly illegal at common law, see *Darcy v Allin* (1602) 1 W.P.C. 1 and 5, but the Crown stoutly asserted that, this was an isolated case and the Crown prerogative would remain supreme. This led to several debates in Parliament which eventually resulted in the passing of a statute which became known as the Statute of Monopolies.

—The Statute of Monopolies

A03   The Statute of Monopolies 1623 (21 Jac. 2, c.3, enacted in 1624) declared all grants of privilege void and of no effect with the **exception** (expressed in its s.6) of those for the working or introduction of new inventions within the realm. This section can be regarded as the foundation stone of the British patent system, and indeed of the systems of many other countries, e.g. the USA, Australia, Canada, India and New Zealand.

This s.6 (which remains on the statute books, although no longer explicitly part of the 1977 Act, as it was in its previous statutes) reads:

"Provided also, [and be it declared and enacted], that any Declaration before-mentioned shall not extend to any letters patent and grants of privilege for the term of fourteen years or under, hereafter to be made, of the sole working or making of any manner of new manufactures within this realm, to the true and first inventor and inventors of such manufactures which others at the time of making such letters patent and grants shall not use, so as also they be not contrary to the law, nor mischievous to the state, by raising prices of commodities at home, or hurt of trade, or generally inconvenient: the said fourteen years to be accounted from the date of the first letters patent, or grant of such privilege hereafter to be made, but that the same shall be of such force as they should be, if this Act had never been made, and of none other."

Note. The bracketed words were deleted by the Statute Law Revision Act 1888 (51 Vic. c.3, s.1, Sch. pt.1).

Thus, the British patent system is founded on the philosophy that monopolies as such are odious except as regards those that encourage the introduction of new and ingenious contrivances which were an exception to a prohibition on the grant of monopoly rights because this provides an incentive to technical and commercial progress which is in the general public interest, a principle which still applies as a general proposition.

The importance of this s.6 lies foremost in its definition of a patentable invention, that is one for "any new manner of manufacture within the realm which others at that time did not use and which were not contrary to the law, nor mischievous to the State, by raising prices of commodities at home, or hurt of trade, or generally inconvenient". That definition remained in effect until the commencement of the 1977 Act when it was replaced by definitions of types of innovation which are not to be regarded as patentable inventions for the purposes of the 1977 Act.

It should also be noted that this s.6 defined the quality of novelty as limited to information and use "within the realm". Accordingly, foreign prior art had no effect on patentability under the pre-1977 patent law of the United Kingdom, but the 1977 Act adopted the then widely accepted principle of universal, rather than only local, novelty. This universal principle then applied to all UK patents granted on applications filed on or after June 1, 1977.

Arguments were presented in *The Most Powerful Idea in the World, A Story of Steam, Industry and Innovation* by W. Rosen (Jonathan Cape, 2010 ISBN 24681097531) that the patent system as it existed in the UK in the seventeenth and eighteenth centuries helped create a framework in which the industrial revolution could develop (in contrast to France where patents for inventions were discouraged following the revolution of 1789 for inconsistency with the principle of equality), although as discussed below the practical details of the UK system long remained antiquated and inefficient.

The Middle Ages of patent law

—Patent statutes 1624–1852

Under the post-1624 procedure, no specific description of the nature of the invention was required **A04** at the time of application, but such general information as to express the object and intention of the invention was considered sufficient e.g. by the wording of the title. But, dating from the reign of Queen Anne, within six months from grant a specification had to be enrolled in the High Court of Chancery and was required to be sufficiently clear and explicit that an ordinary workman engaged in the relevant trade could make the patented article or carry out the patented process. The specification had to deal with two matters: the nature of the invention and the manner in which it was to be performed and any deficiency in the disclosure was fatal, see *Rex v Arkwrght* Webs. Pat. Ca. 66 (S.C.). There was no requirement for claims, so that inventors were understandably confused about how to prepare their specifications. James Watt in 1769 invented and patented inter alia a separate condenser for improving the fuel-efficiency of a Newcomen atmospheric engine. On advice he disclosed in his patent the general principles underlying his improved engine, but not any specific embodiment for fear of his protection being limited by inconsequential detail, with the consequence that although the patent was upheld in litigation, the sufficiency of the disclosure became a major issue, see a booklet *James Watt and the Patent System* by A.N. Davenport (British Library, 1989, ISBN 0 7123 0752 4).

A recognisably modern system for examination and grant of patents was established in the US by the Patent Act of 1836 which created a Patent Office attached to the Department of State. Requirements for a description and claims were set out in s.6:

> "But before any inventor shall receive a patent for any such new invention or discovery, he shall deliver a written description of his invention or discovery, and of the manner and process of making, constructing, using, and compounding the same, in such full, clear, and exact terms, avoiding unnecessary prolixity, as to enable any person skilled in the art or science to which it appertains, or with which it is most nearly connected, to make, construct, compound, and use the same; and in case of any machine, he shall fully explain the principle and the several modes in which he has contemplated the application of that principle or character by which it may be distinguished from other inventions; and shall particularly specify and point out the part, improvement, or combination, which he claims as his own invention or discovery. He shall, furthermore, accompany the whole with a drawing, or drawings, and written references, where the nature of the case admits of drawings . . ."

By s.7 provision was made for pre-grant examination as to novelty, utility, "importance", and defects or insufficiency in the description. A patent granted under the 1836 Act that came before the US Supreme Court in *Winans v Denmead* 56 U.S. 15 How. 330 (1853) concerned a truck for coal of enhanced carrying capacity and was in recognizably modern form. It was accepted by the court that the scope of protection was defined by the wording of the claims and one of the main issues was whether the claim language relating to the shape of the truck body "a frustum of a cone" covered a body of octagonal shape.

In contrast, the procedure for obtaining a patent in the UK remained unreformed until the second half of the nineteenth century. It entailed several petitions to various officers of the Crown, each of whom required fees which, in those days, were very significant sums of money. This procedure was summarised by A. N. Davenport in his book *The United Kingdom Patent System: A brief history with Bibliography* (Kenneth Mason 1979, ISBN 085937 1 573) and graphically explained by Charles Dickens in his story *A poor man's tale of a patent* (1850; re-published by J. Phillips, ESC Publishing Ltd, 1984, ISBN 0 906214 30 0. The Protection of Inventions Act, 1851 (15 Vict. c.6) saw the appointment of "Commissioners for Patents and Inventions" to oversee the operation of the patent system and made it possible for patents to be granted for the whole of the United Kingdom and Ireland with the possibility of extension to "Her Majesty's Colonies and Plantations". The effect of establishing a "Commissioners' Office" was to reduce "the proceedings to obtain the grant from a wearisome, and oftentimes dangerous, formality to the dimensions of an ordinary business-like transaction", see John Coryton, *A Treatise on the Law of Letters-Patent*, Sweet, 1855, Preface, vii.

The Protection of Inventions Act 1851 (15 Vict. c.6) which entered into force in 1852 provided for the filing of a provisional specification with a petition for a patent which was examined by a law officer for sufficiency, and that could be followed within six months by a complete specification. In contrast to the reforms in the US, there was no provision for examination as to novelty and no requirement to include claims.

The complexity of the former grant procedure, only partially alleviated by the 1852 Act explains why there grew up, from about 1840, a profession of "patent agents", that is persons who were knowledgeable of the intricacies of this procedure, and subsequently of persons skilled in preparing the specification upon which the patent grant came to be based. This led, in 1882, to the formation of an Association of Patent Agents which, upon receiving a Royal Charter in 1891 became "The Chartered Institute of Patent Agents", a body (now re-named as "The Chartered Institute of Patent Attorneys"). This body continues to represent those who specialise in the grant, maintenance and enforcement, not only of patents but of intellectual property rights in general. However, for recent changes in its powers, see §A24 below.

In 1875 the British legal system was fundamentally reformed and the current structure of the English High Court set up.

—Patent statutes 1853–1883

A05   After 1853, the mechanical age accelerated with increased industrial use of power and the continued growth of travel by steam ships and by the railways and a more modern patent system was required. As stated below in §A14, in 1883 the Paris Union was formed for the reciprocal protection of inventions among Member States so that patents could be granted also to foreigners. This Union also created the "Paris Convention" which instituted a priority period which avoided having to make corresponding patent applications at the same time in all countries for which patent protection was desired lest the filing in one country would act as prior art against the grant of a parallel patent in another country.

As a result of these demands and to provide for the Paris Convention, the first comprehensive statute of intellectual property law was enacted in the Patents, Designs and Trade Marks Act 1883 (c.57). This required, for the first time (but some 47 years behind the US), that the patent should contain "claims" defining the monopoly sought. It also replaced the Commissioners of Patents with a Patent Office headed by "The Comptroller", who had the full title of "The Comptroller-General of Patents, Designs and Trade Marks", a position and title which survives under the present Act, see §A20 below. There was still no provision for examination as to novelty.

This 1883 Act also provided for the publication of a series of law reports, "The Reports of Patent, Design and Trade Mark Cases" ("the RPCs"); and for patent applications to be referred to "Examiners" within the Patent Office, although initially their obligation was merely to report whether the accompanying specification contained a "fair description" of the invention for which a patent was sought. In 1902, this examination was extended to questions of novelty and prior grant of the patent claims.

—Patent statutes 1884–1949

In 1907, the 1883 Act was wholly replaced by the Patents and Designs Act 1907 (c.29), the subject   **A06**
of trade marks having been placed in a separate statute by the Trade Marks Act 1905 (c.15). This 1907 Act followed a report ("the Fry Report") of a government committee set up to review the working of the 1883 Act, as it had since been amended. Some provisions of this 1907 Act still remain in force as they are the authority under which the United Kingdom Patent Office remains constituted, see §A20 below. Some 71 years after their US counterparts, examiners in the UK Patent Office were finally given the power to refuse applications on the ground of lack of novelty.

A further government committee was set up in 1929 and this resulted in the "Sargent Report" of 1931 (Cmd.3829) which in turn led to an amending statute, the Patents and Designs Act 1932 (c.32). Until this Act, the validity of a granted patent could only be challenged on the general ground that it should not have been granted because the invention claimed was not "a manner of **new** manufacture", or had been the subject of prior public use, or because the accompanying specification did not fairly describe the invention claimed or was not useful. The procedure, prior to the changes in legal structure in 1875, was by way of a writ of scire facias, replaced in that year by a petition for revocation on any ground upon which the patent could, before 1875, have been revoked by such a writ (Patents and Designs Act 1907 (c.29) s.25). This 1932 Act by its s.32 substituted a new form of s.25 in the 1907 Act. This particularised the specific grounds upon which a patent could be revoked, although the general ground of *scire facias* remained as a fall-back provision. This 1932 Act specified for the first time that lack of novelty and lack of inventive step should be regarded as separate and distinct grounds for patent revocation.

The Patents Act 1949 ("the 1949 Act")

At the end of the Second World War, a governmental committee was set up under the Chairman-   **A07**
ship of Sir Kenneth Swan QC to consider and report on any changes "desirable in the Patents and Designs Act, and in the practice of the Patent Office, and the Courts in relation to matters arising therefrom". The resulting "Swan Report" (Cmd.7206) was published in September 1947. It led to the Patents and Designs Act 1949 (c.62), which further amended the Patent and Designs Act 1907. However, this Act was immediately repealed upon it coming into force to be replaced by separate consolidated statutes, the Patents Act 1949 (c.87) and the Registered Designs Act 1949 (c.88).

A principal feature of the 1949 Act was that there was provided a continuing power, to be exercised during examination of applications within the Patent Office, to refuse an application if any of its claims lacked novelty (within the United Kingdom), but a lack of inventive step could only lead to rejection of an application published as suitable for grant in third party opposition proceedings commenced within the following three months, or in an application for revocation brought before the Comptroller within 12 months of the date when the patent was "sealed" at the end of the opposition period or following any opposition filed during that period, and then, in each case as regards inventive step, only on the ground that a claim "was obvious and clearly did not involve an inventive step". The grounds for possible revocation by the court were slightly amended and the reserve *scire facias* provision was removed. In addition to this limitation of the power of refusal in opposition proceedings (or in subsequent revocation, commonly called "belated opposition", proceedings) to a "clear" lack of inventive step, only some of the grounds for revocation by the High Court were made available for action by the Comptroller even in such opposition or belated opposition proceedings. Obviously, at that time, it was thought that the Comptroller and his staff ought not to be able to apply the full powers which a court had to decide on patent validity.

The Patents Appeal Tribunal, staffed by a judge of the High Court, was also created to hear appeals from decisions of the Comptroller, and a specialist patents judge was appointed to hear proceedings in the High Court relating to patents and registered designs, although the now existing specialist Patents Court originated only later.

—Infringement of UK patent rights from 1624 to 1950

A08   Under the 1949 Act and its predecessors, the terms of grant of a UK patent gave its owner the "sole working or making" of the new manner of manufacture for which the patent had been granted. However, this phrase came to be elaborated in the wording of the Letters Patent grant by which (in the terms eventually applied by under the 1949 Act (Sch.4, as amended), the Crown gave unto the person(s) named in the grant (and their heirs and successors):

> "our especial licence, full power, sole privilege, and authority, that the patentee or any agent or licensee of the patentee and no others, may subject to the conditions and provisions prescribed by any statute or order for the time being in force at all times hereafter during the term of years herein mentioned, make, use, exercise and vend the said invention within our United Kingdom of Great Britain and Northern Ireland, and the Isle of Man, and that the patentee shall have and enjoy the whole profit and advantage from time to time accruing by reason of the said invention during the term of sixteen years from the date hereunder written of these presents: AND to the end that the patentee may have and enjoy the sole use and exercise and full benefit of the said invention. We do by these presents for Us, our heirs and successors strictly command all our subjects whatsoever within our United Kingdom of Great Britain and Northern Ireland, and the Isle of Man, that they do not at any time during the continuance of the said term either directly or indirectly make use of or put in practice the said invention, nor in anywise imitate the same, without the written consent, licence or agreement of the patentee, on pain of incurring such penalties as may be justly inflicted on such offenders for their contempt of this our Royal command, and of being answerable to the patentee according to the law for damages thereby occasioned:
> PROVIDED ALWAYS that these letters patent shall be revocable on any of the grounds from time to time by law prescribed as grounds for revoking letters patent granted by Us, and the same may be revoked and made void accordingly".

Thus, under the 1949 Act and its predecessors, it was these words (as construed under the Common Law) which governed the tests used by the courts for judging the issue of patent infringement, with the emphasis on the words which declared that, without permission of the patentee, others should not "make, use, exercise and vend the invention".

The present current patent law of the United Kingdom

—The Patents Act 1977

A09   The current patent law statute is the Patents Act 1977 (c.37), as later amended particularly by Pts V and VI of the Copyright, Designs and Patents Act 1988 (c.48, "the CDPA 1988") This Work reprints all these extant statutory provisions in their current forms, while indicating how and when any has been amended, sometimes only prospectively and/or with transitional provisions. The Work's contents include extracts from other legislation (including relevant International Conventions and Treaties) and to Rules for operation of these provisions as well as detailed commentaries on their provisions and practice. It is thus intended that the Work has comprehensive coverage of all aspects of the practice of patent law within all parts of the United Kingdom, including the Isle of Man.

—Origin and purpose of the 1977 Act

A10   The Long Title of the 1977 Act (reprinted in full at the start of §0.02) importantly states that it is "an Act to establish a new law of patents [and] to give effect to certain international conventions on patents". The "old law" on patents was then the Patents Act 1949 (c.87). Not only had this become outmoded in the increasingly international world of commerce, but discussions had been on-going for several years to try to create means for international co-operation over the granting of similar patents for the same invention by multiple applications in a number of countries. This had led to a considerable duplication of effort and consequent delays in the grant of patents in an increasingly technological environment, especially within the European Community which had come into being in 1963, although the United Kingdom did not join this until 1972.

In the light of these factors, the then UK Government set up in 1967 a Committee under Mr (later Sir) Maurice Banks "To examine and report with recommendations upon the British patent system and patent law, in the light of the increasing need for international collaboration in patent matters and, in particular, of the United Kingdom Government's intention to ratify the recent Council of Europe "Convention on Patent Laws". The report of this Committee (known as "the Banks Report") was published in July 1970 (Cmnd.4407). The Convention referred to in its terms of reference was the Strasbourg Convention on the unification of certain parts of substantive law on patents for inventions signed in 1963 (Cmnd.2362), but not then ratified.

However, by the time the Banks Report was published, this Strasbourg Convention had largely been overtaken by concomitant discussions to establish, on a much wider basis, three further Conventions for international and European co-operation whereby the cost and effort of filing substantially similar applications for protection before national patent offices, each to be subjected to duplicated search and examination procedures before patents came to be granted thereon, could be reduced. These Conventions were: (1) the Patent Co-operation Treaty ("the PCT"), signed in Washington in December 1970 (Cmnd.4350); (2) the European Patent Convention ("the EPC"), signed in Munich in 1973 (Cmnd.5656); and (3) the Community Patent Convention ("the CPC"), signed in Luxembourg also in 1973 (Cmnd.6553). The Strasbourg Convention was eventually ratified in 1980 and republished as Cmnd.8002, but the CPC never came into force because of the plurality of languages used within what is now the "European Union" ("the EU") and the fact that few industries want or need protection in each of the EU Member States.

The formulation of the 1977 Act was delayed to take account of these further then envisaged Conventions and the Bill for the 1977 Act was preceded by a Green Paper (ISBN 0 11 511639 7) issued in 1975. The Act received the Royal Assent on July 29, 1977, but was timed to come into force on June 1, 1978 ("the appointed day") as this was the date upon which both the PCT and the EPC also came into force. Accordingly, the Act set out to replace the then existing patent law of the United Kingdom—largely based on the Common Law (as discussed in §A16 below) with an entirely new administrative law based upon the principles of substantive patent law set out in this Strasbourg Convention and in the EPC and to make provision for the operation of the EPC and PCT within the United Kingdom.

The EPC and the Implementing Regulations of the PCT were each significantly revised in 2000 and the two systems are now widely used, although individuals and small and medium enterprises perhaps having little commercial interest outside the UK often continue to use the traditional method of, at least initially, filing only for protection in the UK. However, to a large extent the PCT and EPC have become the prime methods whereby patents for the United Kingdom are now obtained, so that these conventions have great significance to the modes of procedure whereby patent protection for innovative inventions within the UK is now obtainable. The basic provisions of the EPC and its operation were well described in *Unilin Beheer v Berry Floor* ([2007] EWCA Civ 364; [2007] F.S.R. 25).

Thus, there are three distinct methods by which patent protection with effect for the UK can be obtained. However, it is important to note that these are methods for obtaining the grant of a patent, the effect of which is governed solely by the laws of the United Kingdom save that several (but not all) of the specific provisions of this 1977 Act are required (by s.130(7)) to be interpreted as being in accordance with corresponding provisions of the EPC.

—The traditional UK national application procedure

Under this system which, in principle, has been in operation since 1907, an application for the grant of a patent is filed at the United Kingdom Patent Office (now trading under the name "UK Intellectual Property Office ("the UK-IPO")) where, after formality checking, it is sent to an examiner employed by that Office for him to decide whether it meets the criteria as to its suitability for grant. Objections raised may (since 1977) arise under any ground on which a court may (after a trial) declare it invalid, but any objection may be contested by evidence, argument and, if necessary, appeal. If found suitable, the (perhaps amended) application will proceed to grant of a patent which then has a life of 20 years from the application's filing date provided that required renewal fees are timely paid and the patent is not finally declared by a judicial tribunal to have been invalidly granted when it is revoked and then held never to have existed. **A11**

—The "PCT route"

The PCT (which now has a wide membership among the World's nations) provides for the filing, with the "International Bureau" of the World Intellectual Property Organisation ("WIPO"), or with a recognised national patent office of a single application bearing designations for all (or only some) of **A12** the individual PCT Member States in (or for) which patent protection is intended eventually to be sought. This "international application" is then the subject of a central search, and optionally a subsequent central advisory patentability examination, each under the aegis of WIPO, but carried out for WIPO by designated "international searching authorities" and "international preliminary examining authorities".

After receipt of the "international search report" from the international searching authority, or optionally after requesting and obtaining a "preliminary examination report" from the "international preliminary examining authority", the applicant may then (within a defined time limit) seek to enter the national phase in such of the originally designated PCT Member States for which he continues to desire to obtain patent protection. This is done on the basis of the original application (which could have become more limited by this time as a result of the applicant putting forward more restricted claims) accompanied by the "international search report" and, perhaps also, by an advisory "international preliminary examination report".

Further examination is then carried out by the individual national patent offices to which the international application is submitted for further processing in separate national phases and thus leading to a bundle of national patents of possibly differing scope following these national processing stages. An international application designating the United Kingdom is called "an international application (UK)" but, if and when granted, it leads (now under the provisions of ss.89, 89A and 89B of the 1977 Act) to a patent granted under this Act, just as if this had been obtained via the traditional national route.

The main advantage of the PCT system is the avoidance of preparing translations of parallel applications into the various national languages until after at least a prior art search has been carried out and perhaps also an advisory substantive examination so that the applicant is in a better position to judge whether a patent is likely to be obtained and, of course, at a time when he is better able to decide whether the commercial outlook for exploitation of the invention will justify the cost of obtaining a patent in any particular country.

The PCT is the subject of a comprehensive book, the *PCT Handbook* written, like the present work, by members of the Chartered Institute of Patent Attorneys and published by Sweet & Maxwell, with frequent updating of its loose-leaf pages.

—The "European and Euro-PCT routes"

A13   While the PCT provides for a single application leading to a bundle of individual national applications in designated PCT Member States, the EPC in contrast provides for a single application (for designated EPC Member States) to be examined and granted as a "European patent" which is, in effect, a bundle of national patents usually of identical content. Under the EPC, an application for a European patent may be filed in one of the three official EPC languages, English, French and German. This application is then subjected to a novelty search, followed by examination at the European Patent Office ("the EPO") in Munich; and, if and when granted, this application for a European patent results in a bundle of "European patents" in those EPC Member States for which a designation fee has been paid and, where necessary, a translation of the patent into a national language of that State has been filed.

For the United Kingdom, such a patent is called a "European patent (UK)" and an application which designated the United Kingdom for the eventual grant of a European patent is called an "Application for a European patent (UK)". The Member States of the EPC are not limited to those of the European Union although all EU Member States are now EPC Members and European patents can also be granted for a number of non-EU countries, particularly for Iceland, Norway, Switzerland and Turkey.

For a period of nine months after its date of grant, the European patent (that is the bundle of individual European patents for the designated Member States) may be opposed centrally within the EPO. If this opposition is wholly successful, there is central revocation of all patents in that bundle; and, likewise, if the European patent is maintained in an amended form by the EPO, all patents in that bundle are deemed always to have been in that form. However, this central opposition procedure does not supersede individual revocation or amendment procedures conducted in a national forum against one or more of the existing individual European patents in that "bundle", even if the granted European patent is then subject to ongoing opposition proceedings. Thus, apart from a special circumstances arising from prior-dated conflicting applications effective in some but not all of the designated States, each patent in the bundle of national patents which constitutes that European patent will initially have uniform wording, but which may come to be amended or revoked to a different extent in the various designated EPC States. Under the provisions of ss.77–83 of the 1977 Act, such European applications and patents are treated, from their date of grant as a "European patent (UK)" (that is as patents obtained via the "European route"), on the same terms as a UK patent obtained via either the national or PCT routes. After grant, each of such patents is subject to the timely payment of renewal fees under the individual laws of the country for which the European patent was granted.

It is also possible to combine the PCT and European routes to obtaining patent protection for the United Kingdom by the international application designating the grant of a patent for the United Kingdom as a European patent (UK). Such an application is colloquially called a "Euro PCT application", with special provisions therefor in s.79 of the 1977 Act, but apart from its origin via the PCT route, the resulting patent (obtained by this "Euro-PCT route") is simply a bundle of individual European patents for the countries designated when the international application was originally filed and for which the appropriate designation fees have subsequently been paid.

An agreement (the "London Agreement" of October 17, 2000), effective from May 1, 2008, now allows those States which have acceded to it (which includes the UK) to accept European patents granted in French or German under their law without translation, into an official language of that State, although translation may still be required if that patent becomes the subject of litigation.

However, in 2009 proposals were put forward for a new Treaty providing for a voluntary system for a single indivisible patent covering the full territory of the European Union, but in March 2011, the Court of Justice of the European Communities ("the EUECJ") ruled this not to be possible under the Lisbon European Treaty ("the TFEU") unless disputes arising from it are justiciable by the central European Courts of Justice. Thus, for the now foreseeable future, the European patent system (as outlined above will remain for the grant of a plurality of individual, though parallel, patents effective in individual European countries with disputes adjudicated by national courts using their individual legal systems, as discussed in §A16 below.

The EPC is the subject of a comprehensive book, the *European Patents Handbook* ["the *EPH*"] written, like the present work, by members of the Chartered Institute of Patent Attorneys and published by Sweet & Maxwell, with frequent updating of its loose-leaf pages.

The Paris International Convention

The PCT and EPC each rely and build upon the first international convention providing for **A14** international co-operation in the field of intellectual property (then called "industrial property" as it did not cover copyright protection). This was the International Convention of Paris signed in 1883, its current text being that agreed in Stockholm in 1967. The United Kingdom was one of the founder members of this Convention and, today, almost all nations are Member States of it.

The main provisions of the Paris Convention are: (1) that its Member States agree to operate their patent, design and trade mark laws on the basis of reciprocity, so that foreign persons and entities shall enjoy intellectual property rights in a Member State to the same extent as do nationals of that Member State; and (2) that an applicant for a registration of a patent, design or trade mark shall enjoy a priority period during which corresponding applications for obtaining corresponding registrations in other Member States can be filed, effectively as if filed initially in that form in that other Member State on the date of the initial filing.

For patents, this priority period is the inextensible period of 12 months from the date of the first filing for protection of the invention in any Member State of the Paris Union. Effect is given to this priority right by s.5 of the 1977 Act. This priority right has now been extended on the same terms to all Member States of the World Trade Organisation ("the WTO"), see s.5(6) as discussed in §90.02. A complete list of these Member States in either or both categories is set out in §90.03.

—The changes to United Kingdom patent law initiated by the 1977 Act

Besides the provisions in the 1977 Act for giving effect to the provisions of the PCT and EPC, this **A15** Act also particularly harmonised the substantive law for patents with the provisions of the EPC; and the Comptroller was given equal power with the courts to revoke patents and to refuse applications on any ground upon which the patent could, after grant, be revoked (see s.72). These grounds include the requirement to judge novelty and inventive step against the world-wide "state of the art", and not only against prior knowledge and use existing in the United Kingdom as with the former statutes and under the Common Law. Also of major significance, was: (1) the codification of the acts pertaining to patent infringement, so that the former common law tests ceased to be applicable, this codification following provisions in the proposed CPC; and (2) the harmonisation of the effect of patent claims, in conformity with the requirements of the EPC (art.69, and its accompanying Protocol), see §§125.01 and 125.02.

The Patents Court was also created as part of the Chancery Division of the High Court of England and Wales, to deal with all proceedings in the High Court relating to patents and registered designs, and also to hear appeals from decisions of the Comptroller, with continuation of the system whereby patent cases before the High Court would be heard by an "assigned judge" usually having scientific and/or patent law experience. The right of patent agents to appear before the former Patents Appeal Tribunal was continued as a right to appear before the new Patents Court, although only on appeals from the Comptroller, but now also to appear before the Patents County Court, see §§A18 and A24 below.

The previous system of being able to file a "provisional specification" as a priority document, to be followed within one year with a "complete specification" was abolished, but the same effect was achieved by providing that an application could claim priority from a earlier application filed within the inextensible period of the previous 12 months. Such claiming of an "internal priority" was not possible under previous statutes, although an "external priority" could be claimed when a "convention application" was filed. Such an application could claim (under the Paris Convention), as a priority date, the date of filing of a corresponding application in a "convention country" (the United Kingdom not being designated as such under the statutes) within the inextensible period of 12 months from the "first foreign filing" for the invention, see further on this point §A14.

The term of patents was also extended to 20 years, this term having been increased from 14 to 16 years in 1938.

—The differing systems of law and judicial background

A16   Of fundamental importance in relation to UK patents, obtained through one of the national UK, EPC or PCT routes, is the fact that the law of England is based upon what is called the system of Common Law which has evolved over centuries and has also been adopted in many English-speaking countries, notably the United States of America. This system is based on law arising from statutes and secondary legislation enacted by or with the consent of the legislature. For the elucidation of the meaning of the statutory wording in its application to a state of facts, a court must rely upon historical precedent under which courts should, generally, follow previous judicial decisions (especially those from a superior court) based on the same (or very similar) facts. In olden times, such facts would be determined by a jury of common people who would collectively judge the evidence placed before them and were required to ignore their own knowledge. Although juries are not now used in non-criminal UK litigation (but may still be used in the USA), the judge must act according to the principles of jury trial, i.e. by basing his judgment on the facts presented to him by witnesses who testify on their own actual knowledge and, where there is conflicting testimony, deciding which of the witnesses should be seen as having greater credibility. Oral examination of witnesses (and their cross-examination by opposing lawyers) is considered very important in this exercise.

This is a different system to that used in other parts of the world which have a "Civil" system of law, largely based on the ancient principles of Roman Law. Under this, the written law is all-controlling and a judge applies its application to the factual situation as he himself assesses the position. Consequently, evidence given by witnesses to the facts actually experienced by them is often thought to be irrelevant to judges under the civil system of law as they merely have to interpret the meaning of the written law. Consequently, the court procedure is largely a written one and oral advocacy carries much less weight than it does under the Common Law system.

A further difference in the United Kingdom is that the judges, particularly those in charge of patent litigation, are recruited solely from the ranks of litigation lawyers ("counsel") who have many years experience of practising before the courts and have learned the manner in which a lawyer can present the facts of any particular dispute in a way best suited to the wishes of the party which has chosen him to press the case in the client's favour. Thus, UK judges are well experienced in assessing the quality of the oral submissions made to them, and are able to assess which is the more credible evidence put before them and then apply this to the written law. Moreover, most counsel who practise in patent litigation, and therefore the best of whom are elevated to be patent judges, have a background of having themselves been science graduates in their past, so that they can more easily see if an argument presented to them is, in reality, based on a scientific fallacy.

Thus, European patents (UK) are subject to the procedure of the English Common Law, particularly as regards enforcement (infringement) of a patent right, determination of its validity (though in accordance with the EPC wording) and as regards ownership of the patent right. However, Scotland has a somewhat different legal procedure, see the commentary on s.98 of the 1977 Act.

Also, it must be recognised that grant of a patent by the EPO does not guarantee its validity under UK law and there have been some cases where an English court has invalidated a European Patent (even if previously upheld by an EPO Board of Appeal) because it has considered that such patent should not have been granted in the light of the factual evidence which has been put before the UK court. These procedural differences were explained by Jacob L.J. in *Eli Lilly v Human Genome Sciences* ([2010] EWCA Civ 33, [14]–[37]), see also the decision of the Supreme Court [2011] UKSC 51 where the issue is reviewed and the distinction is emphasised between the approach which should be followed and the reasoning and/or outcome which need not.

As this "new law" became largely harmonised with the provisions of the EPC, and as increasingly the European route to UK patents (for which see §A13) is being followed, decisions given by the Boards of Appeal of the EPO can be used as persuasive precedents in proceedings before the Comptroller and the UK patent courts. Consequently, such decisions are cited where it is thought they may have some precedential value. Nevertheless, these precedents do not have a binding authority on any UK court, but UK superior courts have advised that UK courts of lower status should have good reason if they wish to take a different view from the effect of the EPC, particularly as set out by decisions of the EPO Enlarged Board of Appeals.

However, a decision by the EPO to maintain a patent creates no estoppel in proceedings before a United Kingdom court, see *Buehler v Chronos Richardson* ([1998] R.P.C. 609); but a decision of the EPO to revoke a European patent is final as no patent then exists for it to be brought for review before a United Kingdom court, see *Lenzing's European Patent (UK)* ([1997] R.P.C. 245).

For those involved with patents granted in the USA, it should be noted that s.282 of the US patent statute (35 USC 282) states that a granted US patent has a presumption of validity: this means that a US court can only declare a US patent to be invalid over prior art if it is proved (beyond reasonable doubt) that the USPTO made a mistake in granting the patent on the material which was then before it.

The transitional provisions of the 1977 Act provided that patents granted under the 1949 Act, together with patents for which applications had been filed before the "appointed day" of June 1, 1978, should be styled as "existing patents" and should have their validity, and any amendment, determined according to the criteria required by the 1949 Act, but with acts of infringement which commenced after the appointed day to be judged under the 1977 Act. As all "existing patents" are now non-existent, the provisions of the 1949 Act are herein regarded as "spent" and references in this Guide to the provisions of the 1949 Act are confined to those of historical significance.

The Act is supplemented by Rules which are re-issued periodically. The current rules are set out in the Patents Rules 2007 (SI 2007/3291, effective from December 17, 2007), and subsequently amended in fairly minor respects. These rules (as amended) are reprinted in this Work near to the location of the section of the Act to which they mainly apply or under s.123 for those rules of general application, particularly as regards the conduct of proceedings before a hearing officer appointed by the Comptroller. For the specific locations for such presentations, see the List in §PR.01.

Major changes made subsequent to the 1977 Act

—Representation in proceedings within the UK-IPO

In December 1983 there issued, without prior notice, a Green Paper, *Intellectual Property Rights and Innovation* written by the Chief Scientific Adviser to the Cabinet Office (Cmnd.9117). This "Nicholson Report" made a number of suggestions for streamlining the patent system and recommended that "the policy on intellectual property rights should aim to reduce the need for mandatory reliance on professional advice" and that "the case for the monopoly right of representation [in proceedings before the Patent Office then] held by patent agents should be reviewed". This last point led to an enquiry by the Office of Fair Trading into the profession of patent agency and its Report *Review of Restrictions on the Patent Agents' Profession*, recommended that there should be a complete freedom on representation in proceedings before the Office and that the criminal sanctions on use of the title "patent agent" should be deleted from the 1977 Act. **A17**

The Government accepted only the first of these recommendations and consequently Part V of the subsequent Copyright, Designs and Patents Act 1988 (c.48) ("the CDPA" or "the 1988 Act"), not only retained the Register of Patent Agents, but also protected the term "patent attorney" as an alternative to the traditional title of "patent agent". This has led to an increasing use of the term "patent attorney" by those on this Register and the renaming of the professional body as "The Chartered Institute of Patent Attorneys".

However, the Legal Services Act 2007 (c.29) has more recently stipulated that professional bodies should be entirely representational in their activities and that all decisions as to who can be regarded as an "authorised lawyer" (a term which includes registered patent attorneys) should be decided by independent organisations. Consequently an "IP Registration Body" ("the IPReg.") has been formed for the governance of the registration and conduct of patent attorneys and trade mark attorneys, and this is discussed in the commentaries on ss.274–281 of the CDPA.

—The creation of a Patents County Court

In April 1986, a White Paper *Intellectual Property and Innovation* (Cmnd.9712) was published, **A18** the main purpose of which was to pave the way for reform of the law of copyright and of that for the protection of industrial designs. However, this paper also recommended that patent litigation should be removed from the purview of the courts and be adjudicated exclusively by the Comptroller who should be given power to grant injunctions. This proposal met much criticism and the controversy led to the establishment of an inter-professional working party under Sir Derek Oulton of the Lord Chancellor's Office. In turn, this led to the "Oulton Report" which advocated the creation of a Patents County Court as an alternative, rather than a substitute, forum for patent litigation. This proposal was accepted by the Government and enabling legislation was then enacted in Pt VI of the 1988 Act, for which see the commentaries on ss.287–295 of that Act in this Work.

The first Patents County Court ("the PCC") was instituted on September 3, 1990 with a jurisdiction parallel to that of the High Court of England and Wales, although then limited to matters relating to patents and registered designs, together with any claims or matters ancillary thereto or arising therefrom, it later being held that the PCC (as a stipulated "county court") could also be used for litigation based on other forms of intellectual property rights, particularly trade marks, copyrights etc.

Parties to litigation before this court need not be represented in court by a barrister, nor need the litigation be conducted by a solicitor, patent attorneys having been given power to conduct litigation in that court. They (and solicitors) have also been provided with a statutory right of audience before this court, for which see above the commentary on s.287of the CDPA 1988.

In 2010, the Civil Procedure Rules were significantly amended to provide for a simplified trial procedure before the PCC with severe limits on the time allowed for trial, the costs to be borne by the parties, and on the amount on an award of damages. This quite recent development is discussed in the commentary on s.291 of the CDPA 1988 and obviously will develop considerably over time to enable IP litigation to be conducted at lower cost by smaller and medium sized enterprises. However, such developments are largely a matter for the future and must await further editions of this Work.

—The creation of "Supplementary Protection Certificates"

A19   By 1992, the pharmaceutical industry had satisfied the European Commission that some further protection should be provided for their inventions as the 20-year term for pharmaceutical patents was unduly short given the delays in the marketing of medicinal products which resulted from the need first to obtain a marketing approval certificate which is only granted after a governmental authority is satisfied as to the efficacy and safety of a new pharmaceutical product. Consequently, the effective term of a patent protecting such a product was curtailed by external considerations which made the pharmaceutical industry a special case.

This resulted in an EC Regulation (Regulation No. 1768/92) making provision for the grant of a "supplementary protection certificate" having the effect, from the date of expiry of the patent protecting a specified medicinal product, of providing equivalent rights limited to that product for a period (not exceeding five years) deemed to compensate for the delays necessarily incurred in obtaining the marketing authority required in order to supply that product. This period is measured from the date of the first marketing authorisation within the EEA so that the effective extension of patent rights granted in this way have a uniform duration throughout at least this territorial area. In 1996, a similar Regulation (Regulation (EC) No. 1610/96) was issued to grant supplementary protection certificates likewise for "plant protection products".

At the end of 2007, these Regulations were incorporated into the 1977 Act by new s.128B and Sch.4A, and their application and effect are discussed above in the commentary thereon.

Former Patent Statutes having continuing effect

—Unrepealed provisions of the Patents and Designs Act 1907 (c.29)

A20   Sections 62–64 of the 1907 Act remain in force and are the basis for the current operations of the Patent Office and the powers of the Comptroller (for which see also §A12). These sections are set out above.

Thus, s.62 of the 1907 Act continues to provide the statutory basis for the existence of the Patent Office and the requirement that the Treasury provide "all requisite buildings and conveniences" for the office of the comptroller which "shall be called the Patent Office". This explains that the currently applied terminology of referring to the Patent Office as "the United Kingdom Intellectual Property Office (abbreviated to IPO or UK-IPO in this Work) may be no more than an operational or trading name, and seemingly one of dubious validity pending amendment of this s.62.

This section also provides for the post of "Comptroller" to act at the behest of the Secretary of State, who himself may act in place of the Comptroller. For the definition of the term "Comptroller", see §130.04.

By the Interpretation Act 1978 (c.30, Sch.1) the term "Secretary of State" in any statute covers "any of Her Majesty's Principal Secretaries of State". The powers of the Secretary of State under the patent statutes (except for some matters relating to national security or defence applications) are carried out by a designated Secretary of State. Also associated with the Office is an Intellectual Property Policy Directorate which has responsibility for formulating governmental policy in relation to matters of intellectual property law and practice.

Since October 1, 1991, all operations of the Office have been carried out under a trading fund established under the Government Trading Act 1990 (c30), (Patent Office Trading Fund) Order 1991 (SI 1991/1796), for which see §95.02 and §123.37). This Office is governed by a Steering Board and the Comptroller-General acts as its Chief Executive Officer. Under this Act and Treasury Minutes, the Office, in addition to its statutory duty to balance its income and expenditure, is expected (taking one year with another) to achieve an operating surplus expressed as a percentage of average net assets employed at then current values.

Section 63 of the 1907 Act provides for the appointment of the Comptroller, "examiners, other officers and clerks", all by the Secretary of State. While the Comptroller and examiners in the Office may be appointed in this manner, their duties are nevertheless often defined in the statutes. It would appear that these persons may not be given instructions to ignore or act in non-compliance with their statutory duties; at least it has been so decided in the Republic of Ireland under a similar statutory provision (*Rajan v Ministry for Industry and Commerce [Ireland]* [1988] F.S.R. 9). In §130.04, it is explained that the functions, duties and certain powers of the officers of the Patent Office, and of its examiners, are now subject to possible delegation by contract under the powers of the Deregulation and Contracting Out Act 1994 (c.40).

Before the 1977 Act, patents were granted under seal as "Letters Patent". Until 1883, the Great Seal of the Realm was used for this purpose, but from 1883 the seal of the Office replaced this. This seal is still used when request is made on PF23 for a "signed and sealed" certificate of the Comptroller, see §32.37.

—Emergency legislation for use in time of war

The Patents, Designs, Copyrights and Trade Marks (Emergency) Act 1939 (c.107) remains in force, but would only have effect during a declared "state of war". Accordingly, this statute is not reprinted here, but its provisions are discussed in §59.04.

A21

—The Defence Contracts Act 1958

The Defence Contracts Act 1958 (c.38) exists to govern the powers of the Crown in relation to contracts for the use of intellectual property which may override the rights of patent proprietors. The relevant provisions of this Act are reprinted at §§55.02–55.07 and are discussed at §55.12.

A22

—The TRIPS Agreement

Part of the Agreement establishing the World Trade Organisation ("the WTO") is an Agreement on Trade-Related Aspects of Intellectual Property Rights (the "TRIPS Agreement", Cm.3046) signed in Marrakech April 15, 1994 and in force from January 1, 1995. This Agreement sets minimum standards to be provided by the national laws of WTO Member States for the creation, maintenance and enforcement of intellectual property rights. The articles governing the "standards concerning the availability, scope and use of intellectual property rights" are set out in arts 27–34 (in Pt II, s.5) of the TRIPS Agreement; and Pt III (governing the "enforcement of intellectual property rights") sets out: the general obligations for such enforcement required of WTO Member States (s.1, art.41); the minimum requirements for civil and administrative procedures and remedies (s.2, arts 42–49); and the required availability of provisional measures (s.3, art.50). There are also minimum standards set for the "acquisition and maintenance of intellectual property rights and related inter partes proceedings" (Pt IV, art.62) and for "dispute prevention and settlement" (Pt V, arts 63 and 64).

An EC Directive 2004/48/EC ("the Enforcement Directive") was issued to meet the requirements of arts 27–34 of the TRIPS Agreement, for which see §61.02.

Although, where appropriate, articles of the TRIPS Agreement have been reprinted in this Work, the provisions of the TRIPS Agreement relate only to the conduct of Member States and do not create any private rights, see *Lenzing's European Patent (UK)* ([1997] R.P.C. 245). Consequently, any al-

A23

leged non-compliance of national law with the provisions of the TRIPS Agreement is a matter for complaint by another Member State requesting that a WTO dispute resolution panel be set up to investigate and rule on the validity of that complaint, which, if upheld, may then lead to sanctions against that State being imposed.

However, it is possible for a statute to provide for automatic compliance with an international treaty, convention or agreement, and often secondary legislation will be made to achieve this. However, in other cases, the provisions of the TRIPS Agreement will probably have persuasive effect upon the courts since a judge is unlikely to wish to interpret the statute as not being in compliance with the TRIPS Agreement if this can be avoided by a different interpretation of existing primary and secondary legislation.

For books which explain further the TRIPS Agreement and its derivation and its later developments, see the website *http://www.tripsagreement.net*.

The future for patent law in and for the United Kingdom

A24   This Appendix has discussed how the current law of patents in and for the UK has developed over the past 600 years. It has stood the test of time. The fundamental Statute of Monopolies 1623 drew a vital distinction between arbitrary grants of privilege as a form of taxation and subservience to the Crown and specific grant of limited monopoly rights designed to foster innovation, the growth of trade and development of technological advance.

The USA followed the Statute of Monopolies by a provision in its original constitution of 1789 (art.1, s.8, Clause 8) that:

"The Congress shall have power "to promote the progress of Science and useful Arts, by securing for limited Time to Authors and Inventors the exclusive Right to their Writings and Discoveries".

This led almost immediately to the first US patent statute in 1790 for which its drafters were much influenced by the Statute of Monopolies although, in view of their recent Declaration of Independence and the absence of any more specific UK statute at that time, they wrote up the doctrine in their own terms. However, their formulation of the desired statute of patent law was so imperfect as to the patent application and grant procedure, that the 1790 Statute was replaced shortly after by one of 1793; and it was only in 1952 that the current US patent statute was enacted with more advanced and specific wording.

During the nineteenth century, a few countries, particularly The Netherlands, cancelled their patent laws, but this cancellation existed for a very few years as it was found that there was an increasing amount of patenting throughout the developing world which could not be ignored and that the creation and fostering of technological advance was to be encouraged, not inhibited.

Not only is a patent law a "good thing", no other system has emerged which better meets its essential criteria of advancing the concept of innovation.

Patent Office

62.—(1) The Treasury may continue to provide for the purposes of the Patents Act 1977 . . . an office with all requisite buildings and conveniences, **which shall be called, and is in this Act referred to as, the Patent Office.** (emphasis added).

(2) The Patent Office shall be under the immediate control of the comptroller, who shall act under the superintendence and direction of the Secretary of State.

(3) Any act or thing directed to be done by or to the comptroller may be done by or to any officer authorised by the Secretary of State.

Officers and clerks

63.—(1) There shall continue to be a comptroller-general of patents, designs and trade marks, and the Secretary of State may, subject to the approval of the Treasury, appoint the comptroller, and so many examiners and other officers and clerks, with such designation and duties as the Secretary of State thinks fit, and may remove any of those officers and clerks.

(2) The salaries of those officers and clerks shall be appointed by the Secretary of State.

Seal of the Patent Office

64. Impressions of the seal of the Patent Office shall be judicially noticed and admitted in evidence.

APPENDIX B

SUPPLEMENTARY PROTECTION CERTIFICATES

Note. The application of the 1977 Act in relation to Supplementary Protection Certificates (SPCs) is now governed by the new s.128B inserted into the 1977 Act by the Patents (Compulsory Licensing and Supplementary Protection Certificates) Regulations 2007 (SI 2007/3293), with effect from December 17, 2007. This instrument inserts a new Sch.4A into the Act containing provisions about the application of the Act to SPCs. The commentary on SPCs is therefore now set out under s.128B, where the relevant rules and European Regulations on this topic are also reprinted.

APPENDIX C

THE BIOTECHNOLOGY DIRECTIVE

Directive 98/44/EC of THE EUROPEAN PARLIAMENT AND THE COUNCIL of 6 July 1998 on the legal protection of biotechnological inventions

[1998] OJL175/1

Recitals

THE EUROPEAN PARLIAMENT AND THE COUNCIL OF THE EUROPEAN UNION,

Having regard to the Treaty establishing the European Community, and in particular Article 100a thereof,

Having regard to the proposal from the Commission [[1996] OJEC C296/4 and [1997] OJEC C311/12],

Having regard to the opinion of the Economic and Social Committee [[1996] OJEC C295/11],

Acting in accordance with the procedure laid down in Article 189b of the Treaty [Opinion of the European Parliament] [1997] OJEC C286/87; Council Common Position, [1998] OJEC C110/17; Decision of the European Parliament [1998] OJEC C167; and Council Decision of June 16, 1998],

(1) Whereas biotechnology and genetic engineering are playing an increasingly important role in a broad range of industries and the protection of biotechnological inventions will certainly be of fundamental importance for the Community's industrial development;

(2) Whereas, in particular in the field of genetic engineering, research and development require a considerable amount of high-risk investment and therefore only adequate legal protection can make them profitable;

(3) Whereas effective and harmonised protection throughout the Member States is essential in order to maintain and encourage investment in the field of biotechnology;

(4) Whereas following the European Parliament's rejection of the joint text, approved by the Conciliation Committee, for a European Parliament and Council Directive on the legal protection of biotechnological inventions [[1995] OJEC C68/26], the European Parliament and the Council have determined that the legal protection of biotechnological inventions requires clarification;

(5) Whereas differences exist in the legal protection of biotechnological inventions offered by the laws and practices of the different Member States; whereas such differences could create barriers to trade and hence impede the proper functioning of the internal market;

(6) Whereas such differences could well become greater as Member States adopt new and different legislation and administrative practices, or whereas national case-law interpreting such legislation develops differently;

(7) Whereas uncoordinated development of national laws on the legal protection of biotechnological inventions in the Community could lead to further disincentives to trade, to the detriment of the industrial development of such inventions and of the smooth operation of the internal market;

(8) Whereas legal protection of biotechnological inventions does not necessitate the creation of a separate body of law in place of the rules of national patent law; whereas the rules of national patent law remain the essential basis for the legal protection of biotechnological inventions given that they must be adapted or added to in certain specific respects in order to take adequate account

of technological developments involving biological material which also fulfil the requirements for patentability;

(9) Whereas in certain cases, such as the exclusion from patentability of plant and animal varieties and of essentially biological processes for the production of plants and animals, certain concepts in national laws based upon international patent and plant variety conventions have created uncertainty regarding the protection of biotechnological and certain microbiological inventions; whereas harmonisation is necessary to clarify the said uncertainty;

(10) Whereas regard should be had to the potential of the development of biotechnology for the environment and in particular the utility of this technology for the development of methods of cultivation which are less polluting and more economical in their use of ground; whereas the patent system should be used to encourage research into, and the application of, such processes;

(11) Whereas the development of biotechnology is important to developing countries, both in the field of health and combating major epidemics and endemic diseases and in that of combating hunger in the world; whereas the patent system should likewise be used to encourage research in these fields; whereas international procedures for the dissemination of such technology in the Third World and to the benefit of the population groups concerned should be promoted;

(12) Whereas the Agreement on Trade-Related Aspects of Intellectual Property Rights (TRIPS) [[1994] OJEC L336/213] signed by the European Community and the Member States, has entered into force and provides that patent protection must be guaranteed for products and processes in all areas of technology;

(13) Whereas the Community's legal framework for the protection of biotechnological inventions can be limited to laying down certain principles as they apply to the patentability of biological material as such, such principles being intended in particular to determine the difference between inventions and discoveries with regard to the patentability of certain elements of human origin, to the scope of protection conferred by a patent on a biotechnological invention, to the right to use a deposit mechanism in addition to written descriptions and lastly to the option of obtaining non-exclusive compulsory licences in respect of interdependence between plant varieties and inventions, and conversely;

(14) Whereas a patent for invention does not authorise the holder to implement that invention, but merely entitles him to prohibit third parties from exploiting it for industrial and commercial purposes; whereas, consequently, substantive patent law cannot serve to replace or render superfluous national, European or international law which may impose restrictions or prohibitions or which concerns the monitoring of research and of the use or commercialisation of its results, notably from the point of view of the requirements of public health, safety, environmental protection, animal welfare, the preservation of genetic diversity and compliance with certain ethical standards;

(15) Whereas no prohibition or exclusion exists in national or European patent law (Munich Convention) which precludes *a priori* the patentability of biological matter;

(16) Whereas patent law must be applied so as to respect the fundamental principles safeguarding the dignity and integrity of the person; whereas it is important to assert the principle that the human body, at any stage in its formation or development, including germ cells, and the simple discovery of one of its elements or one of its products, including the sequence or partial sequence of a human gene, cannot be patented; whereas these principles are in line with the criteria of patentability proper to patent law, whereby a mere discovery cannot be patented;

(17) Whereas significant progress in the treatment of diseases has already been made thanks to the existence of medicinal products derived from elements isolated from the human body and/or otherwise produced, such medicinal products resulting from technical processes aimed at obtaining elements similar in structure to those existing naturally in the human body and whereas, consequently, research aimed at obtaining and isolating such elements valuable to medicinal production should be encouraged by means of the patent system;

(18) Whereas, since the patent system provides insufficient incentive for encouraging research into and production of biotechnological medicines which are needed to combat rare or "orphan" diseases, the Community and the Member States have a duty to respond adequately to this problem;

(19) Whereas account has been taken of Opinion No. 8 of the Group of Advisers on the Ethical Implications of Biotechnology to the European Commission;

(20) Whereas, therefore, it should be made clear that an invention based on an element isolated from the human body or otherwise produced by means of a technical process, which is susceptible of industrial application, is not excluded from patentability, even where the structure of that element is identical to that of a natural element, given that the rights conferred by the patent do not extend to the human body and its elements in their natural environment;

(21) Whereas such an element isolated from the human body or otherwise produced is not excluded

from patentability since it is, for example, the result of technical processes used to identify, purify and classify it and to reproduce it outside the human body, techniques which human beings alone are capable of putting into practice and which nature is incapable of accomplishing by itself;

(22) Whereas the discussion on the patentability of sequences or partial sequences of genes is controversial; whereas, according to this Directive, the granting of a patent for inventions which concern such sequences or partial sequences should be subject to the same criteria of patentability as in all other areas of technology: novelty, inventive step and industrial application; whereas the industrial application of a sequence or partial sequence must be disclosed in the patent application as filed;

(23) Whereas a mere DNA sequence without indication of a function does not contain any technical information and is therefore not a patentable invention;

(24) Whereas, in order to comply with the industrial application criterion it is necessary in cases where a sequence or partial sequence of a gene is used to produce a protein or part of a protein, to specify which protein or part of a protein is produced or what function it performs;

(25) Whereas, for the purposes of interpreting rights conferred by a patent, when sequences overlap only in parts which are not essential to the invention, each sequence will be considered as an independent sequence in patent law terms;

(26) Whereas if an invention is based on biological material of human origin or if it uses such material, where a patent application is filed, the person from whose body the material is taken must have had an opportunity of expressing free and informed consent thereto, in accordance with national law;

(27) Whereas if an invention is based on biological material of plant or animal origin or if it uses such material, the patent application should, where appropriate, include information on the geographical origin of such material, if known; whereas this is without prejudice to the processing of patent applications or the validity of rights arising from granted patents;

(28) Whereas this Directive does not in any way affect the basis of current patent law, according to which a patent may be granted for any new application of a patented product;

(29) Whereas this Directive is without prejudice to the exclusion of plant and animal varieties from patentability; whereas on the other hand inventions which concern plants or animals are patentable provided that the application of the invention is not technically confined to a single plant or animal variety;

(30) Whereas the concept "plant variety" is defined by the legislation protecting new varieties, pursuant to which a variety is defined by its whole genome and therefore possesses individuality and is clearly distinguishable from other varieties;

(31) Whereas a plant grouping which is characterised by a particular gene (and not its whole genome) is not covered by the protection of new varieties and is therefore not excluded from patentability even if it comprises new varieties of plants;

(32) Whereas, however, if an invention consists only in genetically modifying a particular plant variety, and if a new plant variety is bred, it will still be excluded from patentability even if the genetic modification is the result not of an essentially biological process but of a biotechnological process;

(33) Whereas it is necessary to define for the purposes of this Directive when a process for the breeding of plants and animals is essentially biological;

(34) Whereas this Directive shall be without prejudice to concepts of invention and discovery, as developed by national, European or international patent law;

(35) Whereas this Directive shall be without prejudice to the provisions of national patent law whereby processes for treatment of the human or animal body by surgery or therapy and diagnostic methods practised on the human or animal body are excluded from patentability;

(36) Whereas the TRIPS Agreement provides for the possibility that members of the World Trade Organisation may exclude from patentability inventions, the prevention within their territory of the commercial exploitation of which is necessary to protect *ordre public* or morality, including to protect human, animal or plant life or health or to avoid serious prejudice to the environment, provided that such exclusion is not made merely because the exploitation is prohibited by their law;

(37) Whereas the principle whereby inventions must be excluded from patentability where their commercial exploitation offends against *ordre public* or morality must also be stressed in this Directive;

(38) Whereas the operative part of this Directive should also include an illustrative list of inventions excluded from patentability so as to provide national courts and patent offices with a general guide to interpreting the reference to *ordre public* and morality; whereas this list obviously cannot presume to be exhaustive; whereas processes, the use of which offend against human dignity, such

as processes to produce chimeras from germ cells or totipotent cells of humans and animals, are obviously also excluded from patentability;

(39) Whereas *ordre public* and morality correspond in particular to ethical or moral principles recognised in a Member State, respect for which is particularly important in the field of biotechnology in view of the potential scope of inventions in this field and their inherent relationship to living matter; whereas such ethical or moral principles supplement the standard legal examinations under patent law regardless of the technical field of the invention;

(40) Whereas there is a consensus within the Community that interventions in the human germ line and the cloning of human beings offends against *ordre public* and morality; whereas it is therefore important to exclude unequivocally from patentability processes for modifying the germ line genetic identity of human beings and processes for cloning human beings;

(41) Whereas a process for cloning human beings may be defined as any process, including techniques of embryo splitting, designed to create a human being with the same nuclear genetic information as another living or deceased human being;

(42) Whereas, moreover, uses of human embryos for industrial or commercial purposes must also be excluded from patentability; whereas in any case such exclusion does not affect inventions for therapeutic or diagnostic purposes which are applied to the human embryo and are useful to it;

(43) Whereas pursuant to Article F(2) of the Treaty on European Union, the Union is to respect fundamental rights, as guaranteed by the European Convention for the Protection of Human Rights and Fundamental Freedomssigned in Rome on 4 November 1950 and as they result from the constitutional traditions common to the Member States, as general principles of Community law;

(44) Whereas the Commission's European Group on Ethics in Science and New Technologies evaluates all ethical aspects of biotechnology; whereas it should be pointed out in this connection that that Group may be consulted only where biotechnology is to be evaluated at the level of basic ethical principles, including where it is consulted on patent law;

(45) Whereas processes for modifying the genetic identity of animals which are likely to cause them suffering without any substantial medical benefit in terms of research, prevention, diagnosis or therapy to man or animal, and also animals resulting from such processes, must be excluded from patentability;

(46) Whereas, in view of the fact that the function of a patent is to reward the inventor for his creative efforts by granting an exclusive but time-bound right, and thereby encourage inventive activities, the holder of the patent should be entitled to prohibit the use of patented self-reproducing material in situations analogous to those where it would be permitted to prohibit the use of patented, non-self-reproducing products, that is to say the production of the patented product itself;

(47) Whereas it is necessary to provide for a first derogation from the rights of the holder of the patent when the propagating material incorporating the protected invention is sold to a farmer for farming purposes by the holder of the patent or with his consent; whereas that initial derogation must authorise the farmer to use the product of his harvest for further multiplication or propagation on his own farm; whereas the extent and the conditions of that derogation must be limited in accordance with the extent and conditions set out in Council Regulation (E.C.) No. 2100/94 of 27 July 1994 on Community plant variety rights [[1994] OJEC L227/1, as amended by Regulation 2506/95/EC [1995] OJEC L258/3];

(48) Whereas only the fee envisaged under Community law relating to plant variety rights as a condition for applying the derogation from Community plant variety rights can be required of the farmer;

(49) Whereas, however, the holder of the patent may defend his rights against a farmer abusing the derogation or against a breeder who has developed a plant variety incorporating the protected invention if the latter fails to adhere to his commitments;

(50) Whereas a second derogation from the rights of the holder of the patent must authorise the farmer to use protected livestock for agricultural purposes;

(51) Whereas the extent and the conditions of that second derogation must be determined by national laws, regulations and practices, since there is no Community legislation on animal variety rights;

(52) Whereas, in the field of exploitation of new plant characteristics resulting from genetic engineering, guaranteed access must, on payment of a fee, be granted in the form of a compulsory licence where, in relation to the genus or species concerned, the plant variety represents significant technical progress of considerable economic interest compared to the invention claimed in the patent;

(53) Whereas, in the field of the use of new plant characteristics resulting from new plant varieties in genetic engineering, guaranteed access must, on payment of a fee, be granted in the form of a

compulsory licence where the invention represents significant technical progress of considerable economic interest;

(54) Whereas Article 34 of the TRIPS Agreementcontains detailed provisions on the burden of proof which is binding on all Member States; whereas, therefore, a provision in this Directive is not necessary;

(55) Whereas following Decision 93/626/EEC [[1993] OJEC L309/1] the Community is party to the Convention on Biological Diversity of 5 June 1992; whereas, in this regard, Member States must give particular weight to Article 3 and Article 8(j), the second sentence of Article 16(2) and Article 16(5) of the Convention when bringing into force the laws, regulations and administrative provisions necessary to comply with this Directive;

(56) Whereas the Third Conference of the Parties to the Biodiversity Convention, which took place in November 1996, noted in Decision III/17that "further work is required to help develop a common appreciation of the relationship between intellectual property rights and the relevant provisions of the TRIPS Agreement and the Convention on Biological Diversity, in particular on issues relating to technology transfer and conservation and sustainable use of biological diversity and the fair and equitable sharing of benefits arising out of the use of genetic resources, including the protection of knowledge, innovations and practices of indigenous and local communities embodying traditional lifestyles relevant for the conservation and sustainable use of biological diversity", HAVE ADOPTED THIS DIRECTIVE:

CHAPTER I–Patentability

ARTICLE 1

C01   1. Member States shall protect biotechnological inventions under national patent law. They shall, if necessary, adjust their national patent law to take account of the provisions of this Directive.

2. This Directive shall be without prejudice to the obligations of the Member States pursuant to international agreements, and in particular the TRIPS Agreement and the Convention on Biological Diversity.

ARTICLE 2

C02   1. For the purposes of this Directive,
    (a) "biological material" means any material containing genetic information and capable of reproducing itself or being reproduced in a biological system;
    (b) "microbiological process" means any process involving or performed upon or resulting in microbiological material.

2. A process for the production of plants or animals is essentially biological if it consists entirely of natural phenomena such as crossing or selection.

3. The concept of "plant variety" is defined by Article 5 of Regulation (E.C.) No. 2100/94.

ARTICLE 3

C03   1. For the purposes of this Directive, inventions which are new, which involve an inventive step and which are susceptible of industrial application shall be patentable even if they concern a product consisting of or containing biological material or a process by means of which biological material is produced, processed or used.

2. Biological material which is isolated from its natural environment or produced by means of a technical process may be the subject of an invention even if it previously occurred in nature.

ARTICLE 4

C04   1. The following shall not be patentable:

(a) plant and animal varieties;

(b) essentially biological processes for the production of plants or animals.

2. Inventions which concern plants or animals shall be patentable if the technical feasibility of the invention is not confined to a particular plant or animal variety.

3. Paragraph 1(b) shall be without prejudice to the patentability of inventions which concern a microbiological or other technical process or a product obtained by means of such a process.

ARTICLE 5

1. The human body, at the various stages of its formation and development, and the simple discovery of one of its elements, including the sequence or partial sequence of a gene, cannot constitute patentable inventions. **C05**

2. An element isolated from the human body or otherwise produced by means of a technical process, including the sequence or partial sequence of a gene, may constitute a patentable invention, even if the structure of that element is identical to that of a natural element.

3. The industrial application of a sequence or a partial sequence of a gene must be disclosed in the patent application.

ARTICLE 6

1. Inventions shall be considered unpatentable where their commercial exploitation would be contrary to *ordre public* or morality; however, exploitation shall not be deemed to be so contrary merely because it is prohibited by law or regulation. **C06**

2. On the basis of paragraph 1, the following, in particular, shall be considered unpatentable:

(a) processes for cloning human beings;

(b) processes for modifying the germ line genetic identity of human beings;

(c) uses of human embryos for industrial or commercial purposes;

(d) processes for modifying the genetic identity of animals which are likely to cause them suffering without any substantial medical benefit to man or animal, and also animals resulting from such processes.

ARTICLE 7

The Commission's European Group on Ethics in Science and New Technologies evaluates all ethical aspects of biotechnology. **C07**

CHAPTER II–Scope of protection

ARTICLE 8

1. The protection conferred by a patent on a biological material possessing specific characteristics as a result of the invention shall extend to any biological material derived from that biological material through propagation or multiplication in an identical or divergent form and possessing those same characteristics. **C08**

2. The protection conferred by a patent on a process that enables a biological material to be produced possessing specific characteristics as a result of the invention shall extend to biological material directly obtained through that process and to any other biological material derived from the directly obtained biological material through propagation or multiplication in an identical or divergent form and possessing those same characteristics.

ARTICLE 9

C09   The protection conferred by a patent on a product containing or consisting of genetic information shall extend to all material, save as provided in Article 5(1), in which the product is incorporated and in which the genetic information is contained and performs its function.

ARTICLE 10

C10   The protection referred to in Articles 8 and 9 shall not extend to biological material obtained from the propagation or multiplication of biological material placed on the market in the territory of a Member State by the holder of the patent or with his consent, where the multiplication or propagation necessarily results from the application for which the biological material was marketed, provided that the material obtained is not subsequently used for other propagation or multiplication.

ARTICLE 11

C11   1. By way of derogation from Articles 8 and 9, the sale or other form of commercialisation of plant propagating material to a farmer by the holder of the patent or with his consent for agricultural use implies authorisation for the farmer to use the product of his harvest for propagation or multiplication by him on his own farm, the extent and conditions of this derogation corresponding to those under Article 14 of Regulation (E.C.) No. 2100/94.

2. By way of derogation from Articles 8 and 9, the sale or any other form of commercialisation of breeding stock or other animal reproductive material to a farmer by the holder of the patent or with his consent implies authorisation for the farmer to use the protected livestock for an agricultural purpose. This includes making the animal or other animal reproductive material available for the purposes of pursuing his agricultural activity but not sale within the framework or for the purpose of a commercial reproduction activity.

3. The extent and the conditions of the derogation provided for in paragraph 2 shall be determined by national laws, regulations and practices.

CHAPTER III–Compulsory cross-licensing

ARTICLE 12

C12   1. Where a breeder cannot acquire or exploit a plant variety right without infringing a prior patent, he may apply for a compulsory licence for non-exclusive use of the invention protected by the patent inasmuch as the licence is necessary for the exploitation of the plant variety to be protected, subject to payment of an appropriate royalty. Member States shall provide that, where such a licence is granted, the holder of the patent will be entitled to a cross-licence on reasonable terms to use the protected variety.

2. Where the holder of a patent concerning a biotechnological invention cannot exploit it without infringing a prior plant variety right, he may apply for a compulsory licence for non-exclusive use of the plant variety protected by that right, subject to payment of an appropriate royalty. Member States shall provide that, where such a licence is granted, the holder of the variety right will be entitled to a cross-licence on reasonable terms to use the protected invention.

3. Applicants for the licences referred to in paragraphs 1 and 2 must demonstrate that:

(a) they have applied unsuccessfully to the holder of the patent or of the plant variety right to obtain a contractual licence;

(b) the plant variety or the invention constitutes significant technical progress of considerable economic interest compared with the invention claimed in the patent or the protected plant variety.

4. Each Member State shall designate the authority or authorities responsible for granting the licence. Where a licence for a plant variety can be granted only by the Community Plant Variety Office, Article 29 of Regulation (E.C.) No. 2100/94 shall apply.

CHAPTER IV–Deposit, access and re-deposit of a biological material

ARTICLE 13

1. Where an invention involves the use of or concerns biological material which is **C13**
not available to the public and which cannot be described in a patent application in such a manner as to enable the invention to be reproduced by a person skilled in the art, the description shall be considered inadequate for the purposes of patent law unless:

    (a) the biological material has been deposited no later than the date on which the patent application was filed with a recognised depositary institution. At least the international depositary authorities which acquired this status by virtue of Article 7 of the Budapest Treaty of 28 April 1977 on the international recognition of the deposit of micro-organisms for the purposes of patent procedure, hereinafter referred to as the "Budapest Treaty", shall be recognised;

    (b) the application as filed contains such relevant information as is available to the applicant on the characteristics of the biological material deposited;

    (c) the patent application states the name of the depository institution and the accession number.

2. Access to the deposited biological material shall be provided through the supply of a sample:

    (a) up to the first publication of the patent application, only to those persons who are authorised under national patent law;

    (b) between the first publication of the application and the granting of the patent, to anyone requesting it or, if the applicant so requests, only to an independent expert;

    (c) after the patent has been granted, and notwithstanding revocation or cancellation of the patent, to anyone requesting it.

3. The sample shall be supplied only if the person requesting it undertakes, for the term during which the patent is in force:

    (a) not to make it or any material derived from it available to third parties; and

    (b) not to use it or any material derived from it except for experimental purposes, unless the applicant for or proprietor of the patent, as applicable, expressly waives such an undertaking.

4. At the applicant's request, where an application is refused or withdrawn, access to the deposited material shall be limited to an independent expert for 20 years from the date on which the patent application was filed. In that case, paragraph 3 shall apply.

5. The applicant's requests referred to in point (b) of paragraph 2 and in paragraph 4 may only be made up to the date on which the technical preparations for publishing the patent application are deemed to have been completed.

ARTICLE 14

1. If the biological material deposited in accordance with Article 13 ceases to be **C14**
available from the recognised depositary institution, a new deposit of the material shall be permitted on the same terms as those laid down in the Budapest Treaty.

2. Any new deposit shall be accompanied by a statement signed by the depositor certifying that the newly deposited biological material is the same as that originally

deposited.

CHAPTER V–Final provisions

ARTICLE 15

C15   1. Member States shall bring into force the laws, regulations and administrative provisions necessary to comply with this Directive not later than 30th July 2000. They shall forthwith inform the Commission thereof.

When Member States adopt these measures, they shall contain a reference to this Directive or shall be accompanied by such reference on the occasion of their official publication. The methods of making such reference shall be laid down by Member States.

2. Member States shall communicate to the Commission the text of the provisions of national law which they adopt in the field covered by this Directive.

ARTICLE 16

C16   The Commission shall send the European Parliament and the Council:

(a) every five years as from the date specified in Article 15(1) a report on any problems encountered with regard to the relationship between this Directive and international agreements on the protection of human rights to which the Member States have acceded;

(b) within two years of entry into force of this Directive, a report assessing the implications for basic genetic engineering research of failure to publish, or late publication of, papers on subjects which could be patentable;

(c) annually as from the date specified in Article 15(1), a report on the development and implications of patent law in the field of biotechnology and genetic engineering

ARTICLE 17

C17   This Directive shall enter into force on the day of its publication in the *Official Journal of the European Communities* [July 30, 1998].

ARTICLE 18

C18   This Directive is addressed to the Member States.

Done at Brussels, 6 July 1998.

For the European Parliament   *For the Council*
The President   *The President*
J. M. GIL-ROBLES   R. EDLINGER

25 July 1999

APPENDIX D

THE TREATY ON THE FUNCTIONING OF THE EUROPEAN UNION (TFEU)

Scope of this Appendix

The articles of the EC Treaty, usually called "The Community Treaty" have been incorporated into the Lisbon Treaty, which came into force on December 1, 2009 and is now officially called the "Treaty on the Functioning of the European Union" (TFEU), which may also be referred to as the 'EU Treaty'.　**D01**

It was published OJEC 2008, 115/1 and its text may be inspected by use of the website *http://eur lex.europa.eu*.　**D02**

RELEVANT ARTICLES OF THE TFEU

ARTICLE 34 TFEU (EX ART.28 EC)

Quantitative restrictions on imports and all measures having equivalent effect shall, without prejudice to the following provisions, be prohibited between Member States.　**D03**

ARTICLE 35 TFEU (EX ART.29 EC)

Quantitative restrictions on exports, and all measures having equivalent effect, shall be prohibited between Member States.　**D04**

ARTICLE 36 TFEU (EX ART.30 EC)

The provisions of Articles 34 and [formerly arts 28 and 29 EC] shall not preclude prohibitions or restrictions on imports, exports or goods in transit justified on grounds of public morality, public policy or public security; the protection of health and life of humans, animals or plant; the protection of national treasures possessing artistic, historic or archaeological value; or the protection of industrial and commercial property. Such prohibitions or restrictions shall not, however, constitute a means of arbitrary discrimination or a disguised restriction on trade between Member States.　**D05**

ARTICLE 101 TFEU (EX ART.81 EC)

1. The following shall be prohibited as incompatible with the common market: all agreements between undertakings, decisions by association of undertakings and concerted practices which may affect trade between Member States and which have as their object or effect the prevention, restriction or distortion of competition within the common market, and in particular those which:　**D06**
    (a) directly or indirectly fix purchase or selling prices or any other trading conditions;
    (b) limit or control production, markets, technical development, or investment;
    (c) share markets or sources of supply;
    (d) apply dissimilar conditions to equivalent transactions with other trading parties, thereby placing them at a competitive disadvantage;

  (e) make the conclusion of contracts subject to acceptance by the other parties of supplementary obligations which, by their nature or according to commercial usage, have no connection with the subject of such contracts.

  2. Any agreement or decisions prohibited pursuant to this Article shall be automatically void.

  3. The provisions of paragraph 1 may, however, be declared inapplicable in the case of:

   — any agreement or category of agreements between undertakings;

   — any decision or category of decisions by associations of undertakings;

   — any concerted practice or category of concerted practices;

which contributes to improving the production or distribution of goods or to promoting technical or economic progress, while allowing consumers a fair share of the resulting benefit, and which does not:

  (a) impose on the undertakings concerned restrictions which are not indispensable to the attainment of these objectives;

  (b) afford such undertakings the possibility of eliminating competition in respect of a substantial part of the products in question.

ARTICLE 102 TFEU (EX ART.82 EC)

D07 Any abuse by one or more undertakings of a dominant position within the common market or in a substantial part of it shall be prohibited as incompatible with the common market in so far as it may affect trade between Member States.

  Such abuse may, in particular, consist in:

  (a) directly or indirectly imposing unfair purchase or selling prices or other unfair trading conditions;

  (b) limiting production, markets or technical development to the prejudice of consumers;

  (c) applying dissimilar conditions to equivalent transactions with other trading parties, thereby placing them at a competitive disadvantage;

  (d) making the conclusion of contracts subject to acceptance by the other parties of supplementary obligations which, by their nature or according to commercial usage, have no connection with the subject of such contracts.

ARTICLE 267 TFEU (EX ART.234 EC)

D08 The Court of Justice shall have jurisdiction to give preliminary rulings concerning:

  (a) the interpretation of this Treaty;

  (b) the validity and interpretation of acts of the institutions, bodies, offices or agencies of the Union;

  Where such a question is raised before any court or tribunal of a Member State, that court or tribunal may, if it considers that a decision on the question is necessary to enable it to give judgment, request the Court of Justice to give a ruling thereon.

  Where any such question is raised in a case pending before a court or tribunal of a Member State, against whose decisions there is no judicial remedy under national law, that court or tribunal shall bring the matter before the Court.

ARTICLE 345 TFEU (EX ART.295 EC)

D09 This Treaty shall in no way prejudice the rules in Member States governing the system of property ownership.

COMMENTARY ON THE EC (NOW EU) TREATY

Incorporation of the Treaty into United Kingdom law

D10 On January 1, 1973, the United Kingdom joined the then European Economic Community and effect was given to this by the European Communities Act 1972 (c.68). This provides in s.2(1) that:

  "All such rights, powers, obligations and restrictions from time to time created or arising by or under the Treaties, and all such remedies and procedures from time to time provided by for or under the Treaties, as in accordance with the Treaties are without further enactment to be given legal effect or used in the United Kingdom shall be recognised and available in law, and be enforced, allowed and followed accordingly: and the expression 'enforceable Community right' and similar expressions shall be read as referring to one to which this subsection applies".

Then, provision was made (by s.2(2)) for future amendment of the laws of the United Kingdom by subordinate legislation in order to bring them into conformity with the provisions of any "European Directive", which the European Commission (now in conjunction with the European Parliament) decrees are to be enacted in some way or other into the national legislation of EU Member States, or to give formal effect to a European Regulation (as agreed by the Commission and accepted by the European Parliament) which has to have direct effect under the law of the Community from a speci-fied date. However, it is to be noted that this provision only permits legislation by secondary legisla-tion to bring United Kingdom law into conformity with the law of the European Community and thus, probably, cannot be used to bring patent law into conformity with more general international agree-ments, such as the TRIPS Agreement, although perhaps this is possible in this instance because the European Union is itself a party to this Agreement, although only having joint competence with the Member States to conclude this Agreement, save for exclusive competence as regards cross-border trade in counterfeit goods, see *ECJ Opinion 1/94 on the WTO Agreement* [1994] E.C.R. I–5267.

The EEC, EC and EU Treaties

The "EC Treaty" was originally the European Economic Treaty (EEC), also styled the "Treaty of **D11** Rome". As the then three "European Communities" progressed into a single European Community within the "European Union", that Treaty was revised and augmented, first by the Maastricht Treaty and then by the Amsterdam/Nice Treaties into what became known as the EC Treaty ("EC"). There are currently 27 Member States. A "Reform Treaty" was signed in Lisbon in December 2007 and formally renamed the European Community as the European Union when it came into force on December 1, 2009. The, current, consolidated treaty is the TFEU.

EU competition law is contained in Chapter 1 of Part VII of the TFEU which consists of arts 101–106. Note that in 1991, the European Community and the Member States of the European Free Trade Association signed an agreement to establish the European Economic Area (the "EEA"). It consists of the Member States of the European Community, Norway, Iceland and Lichtenstein. The EEA agree-ment entered into force in 1994 and includes rules on competition which mirror those contained in the EU Treaty.

The Member States of the European Union and the EEA now have a system of competition law modelled to a greater or lesser extent upon arts 101 and 102 of the TFEU. For example, the Competi-tion Act 1998 of the UK contains two prohibitions—the Chapter I prohibition and the Chapter II pro-hibition—which are modelled on TFEU arts 101 and 102 respectively.

Interpretation of the Treaty by the European Court of Justice

The "European Court of Justice" in Luxembourg was formally named "the Court of Justice", but **D12** now officially bears the name of the "Court of Justice of the European Union" and so the abbreviation "CJEU" should now be used rather than the shortened abbreviation "ECJ" which does continue to be colloquially used. However "the Court of First Instance" has become an integral part of the CJEU and has been renamed as "the General Court" for which the abbreviation "EUGC" can be used instead of the term "CFI". The judgments of the Court of Justice bear the prefix "C-" whereas cases originating in the General Court have the prefix "T-". However, significant judgments from both courts (as well as opinions provided by the Advocates-General) can often easily be accessed through the BAILII website, see *http://www.bailii.org/eu/cases/EUECJ/*. The official European Court Reports (ECRs) are not always available for very recent cases.

Under the TFEU, the Court of Justice of the European Union ("CJEU") is the final arbiter of its interpretation. The CJEU often follows the principles which it sees as enshrined in the TFEU, even if they are not expressed there as such. Its rulings are therefore conditioned on the creation and preser-vation of a true "single market" within which there are no barriers to trade between Member States. However, it is important to note that the CJEU does not follow a strict doctrine of precedent, as exists under the English common law. Because of this, the CJEU is able to change its attitude more easily and thus depart from the rationale of its earlier decisions. As such, CJEU decisions made many years ago may have no more than doubtful precedent effect.

It is against this background that the inherent conflict between the freedom of a single market and the barrier to trade which a nationally based intellectual property right (legitimately) creates comes sharply into focus. The CJEU has had a varying bias towards one or other of these principles, (see in particular the former insistence of the difference between the "existence" and the "exercise" of intellectual property rights discussed in §D14). However, in recent years, there are signs that the CJEU is prepared to recognise, to a greater extent than previously, that role of intellectual property in promoting commercial endeavour.

The great majority of cases relevant to intellectual property reach the CJEU in Luxembourg because of requests for preliminary rulings concerning the interpretation of the Treaty under art.267 TFEU. Under this article, any court of a Member State may request the CJEU to give a ruling when it considers this to be "necessary" so that the national court itself can give judgement on the case before it. A court of final jurisdiction in the Member State must make such request if a question of interpretation regarding any of the Community Treaties arises. However, it is not clear which is the court of final jurisdiction in the United Kingdom when leave to appeal to the Supreme Court is refused and that Court itself declines to hear an appeal, see *Chiron v Murex (No.8)* [1995] F.S.R. 309. It is by this procedure that litigants can, if successful in such an application, effectively transfer a case from a national court to the CJEU. For example, a party to a lawsuit in the UK may argue that the interpretation of the EU Treaty to a particular fact situation is not clear and that the UK court should therefore seek a preliminary ruling on the point from the CJEU.

The first cases in which art.267 TFEU was considered by the English Court of Appeal were *Löwenbräu München v Grünhalle Lager* [1974] R.P.C. 492; [1974] 1 C.M.L.R. 1; and *Bulmer v Bollinger*[1975] R.P.C. 321; [1974] 2 C.M.L.R. 91. In the latter case, the view expressed was that the point of Community law in issue must be decisive of the proceedings (but it is doubtful if that is correct). The reference can take place before full trial. This was done in the patent cases of *Hagen v Moretti* [1980] F.S.R. 517; [1980] 3 C.M.L.R. 253 CA; and *Thetford v Fiamma* [1987] F.S.R. 244; [1989] E.C.R. 3585; CA; and in relation to the Community Regulation for supplementary protection certificates (*Yamanouchi's SPC Application* (C–110/95) [1997] R.P.C. 844). In *R. v Pharmaceutical Society, Ex p. Association of Pharmaceutical Importers* [1987] 3 C.M.L.R. 951 CA, the court made a reference under what is now art.267 TFEU, even without a full hearing having been held. The CJEU has since given guidance to national courts on when it is appropriate for a case to be referred to the CJEU for an opinion (ECJ "Guidance Note" [1997] 1 C.M.L.R. 78). This Guidance Note stressed that the factual and legal content of the questions to be put to the CJEU should first have been fully determined by the national court, and that both parties should have been heard prior to a reference being made.

A court, other than a court of final jurisdiction, is not required to refer a question if it considers that the law in issue is "*acte claire*". Thus, in *Azrak-Hamway's Licence of Right* [1997] R.P.C. 134, although the Comptroller held that he has the power to refer a question to the CJEU under this article, he refused to do so in the case (see the comment by Julia McCormick [1997] E.I.P.R. 205). There was also a refusal to refer the case to the CJEU in *Research Corp's SPC* [1994] R.P.C. 387; and [1994] R.P.C. 667 CA, but the Court of Appeal took a different view, see Appendix B. In *British Horseracing Board v William Hill* [2001] EWCA Civ 1268 noted I.P.D. 24059, a referral was made to the CJEU largely because a Swedish court had reached an opposite conclusion to that of the judge at first instance, see [2001] R.P.C. 31. Accordingly the Court of Appeal felt that the issue could not be "*acte claire*".

Some judgments of the CJEU (also made following referral under what is now art.234 TFEU) have led to revision of the Patents Act 1977 so the national law would conform to the law as laid down by the Court.

The principle of free trade between EEA Member States (arts 34–36 TFEU)

—Free movement of goods within the EEA

D13   Articles 34 and 36 of the TFEU state that quantitative restrictions on imports and exports between Member States are not permitted, but this is subject to an express derogation now stated in art.36 of the TFEU. Article 36 TFEU provides that prohibitions or restrictions on imports, exports, etc. can be justified on the ground of protection of industrial and commercial property, provided that such does not "constitute a means of arbitrary discrimination or a disguised restriction on trade between Member States". Thus, art.36 of the TFEU allows a compromise between the rights of an intellectual property holder and the rights of, and the desire for, free movement of goods within the common market. The latter has to prevail, unless it is the specific subject-matter of the right that is in question. The guiding principle is that what is lawful or unlawful in any one Member State with regard to the supply of goods or services must not depend on the origin of those goods or services, provided that this is within the EEA.

Accordingly, the CJEU decisions in *Allen & Hanbury v Generics (C-434/85)* [1988] 1 C.M.L.R. 701; [1988] F.S.R. 312; and in *Generics v SmithKline and French (C-191/90)* [1993] R.P.C. 333;

[1993] 1 C.M.L.R. 89 resulted in amendment of s.46 (of the Patent Act 1977) so that, in the case of a patent bearing a "licence of right" entry, those who infringe by importation from another EU Member State are treated in the same way as a domestic manufacturer infringer.

A further consequence of requiring intra-Community trade to be treated on the same basis as domestic trade is that those provisions in ss.48 and 50 of the 1977 Act, which provide a distinction between working an invention within the United Kingdom and elsewhere in the Community with regards to the possible grant of compulsory licences, have been held to be contrary to European law (*EC Commission v United Kingdom* (C-30/90) [1993] R.P.C. 283; [1992] E.C.R. I–829). This topic was reviewed by N. Macfarlane, Clare Wardle and J. Wilkinson [1994] E.I.P.R. 525 in a paper, which discussed generally the tension between national intellectual property rights and Community law. However, the matter was probably dealt with in the amendments made to ss.48 and 50 under the Patents and Trade Marks (World Trade Organisation) Regulations (SI 1999/1899) promulgated to bring ss.48–54 into conformity with the TRIPS Agreement (for which see the commentaries on these sections).

For further discussion, see C. Stothers, *Parallel Trade in Europe: Intellectual Property, Competition and Regulatory Law* (2007, Hart).

—The "existence" and "exercise" of intellectual property rights

The CJEU first considered intellectual property rights in *Parke, Davis v Probel* (C-24/67) [1968] **D14** E.C.R. 55; [1968] F.S.R. 393. Here, the court observed that the national character of the protection of industrial property was capable of creating obstacles both to the free movement of patented products and to competition within the Community. However, it was held that the holder of a patent or trade mark right protected under the law of Member State X could properly oppose the importation of an article manufactured by a third party in Member State Y where he could not obtain a patent. In Germany, the same principle has been held to apply where a patent in Member State Y could have been, but was not, obtained (*Pfizer v Denkavit, "Carbadox"* [Germany] (1983) 14 I.I.C. 107). In other words, the holder of intellectual property rights in two Member States can choose in which State to sue an infringer of those rights. It should be noted that in these cases the defendant had not obtained his product from the patentee, or with the patentee's consent, otherwise it would likely have been an "exhaustion of rights" as discussed in §§D15 and D16.

The *Parke, Davis* case was decided in 1968. There are subsequent cases in which the CJEU considered more deeply the problem presented by the apparent conflict between art.345 (which states that the Treaty shall in no way prejudice the rules in Member States governing the system of property ownership) and art.36 TFEU (where the derogation from the general provisions of the Treaty is much more circumscribed) (see in §D13). In narrowly construing art.345 TFEU, the CJEU has drawn a distinction between the "existence" and "exercise" of property right. This was first done in *Deutsche Grammophon v Metro* (C-78/80) [1971] E.C.R. 487; [1971] C.M.L.R. 631. This case concerned records manufactured by the claimant in Germany and sold to its subsidiary in France. The defendant, Metro, obtained the records in France and attempted to resell them in Germany. The CJEU said that the exercise of the industrial property right (copyright) did not fall within art.101 TFEU, but its compatibility with the Treaty had to be considered with respect to art.102 TFEU and with the principle of the free movement of goods. Consequently, the re-importation could not be prevented, the "existence" of the right not being called into question.

Nevertheless, in *Generics v SmithKline & French (C-316/95)* [1997] R.P.C. 801; [1997] E.C.R. I–3929, the CJEU held that a post-expiry injunction to compensate for an act of patent infringement committed pre-expiry is justifiable under art.36 TFEU in order to avoid effective encroachment by the infringer upon the patentee's monopoly.

—"Exhaustion of rights" in intra-Community trade

In order to fulfil the aims of the EU "single market", the CJEU has adopted what has come to be **D15** called the "exhaustion of rights" doctrine applied under what are now arts 34 and 36 TFEU. Under this doctrine, the first marketing within the EEA of a product protected anywhere within the EU by an industrial property right "exhausts" that industrial property right, not only in the country of first sale, but also in any other country within the EEA, provided that such first marketing was carried out by the holder of that right or with his express or implied consent. This subject is dealt with more thoroughly in the European Patents Handbook (EPH).

In relation to patent rights, this doctrine was first set out in *Centrafarm v Sterling Drug* (C-15/74) [1974] E.C.R. 1147; [1975] F.S.R. 161 ECJ and was elaborated upon in *Merck v Stephar* (C-187/80) [1981] E.C.R. 2063; [1981] 3 C.M.L.R. 463, abridged [1982] F.S.R. 57 ECJ) and was elaborated upon in *Merck v Stephar* (C-187/80) [1981] E.C.R. 2063; [1981] 3 C.M.L.R. 463, abridged [1982] F.S.R. 57 ECJ). In the latter case, the patentee could not at the time have obtained a patent in the country (Italy) where the patented drug was first put on the market. It was held that a Dutch patent could not be enforced against an importer of the Merck product from Italy because that product had been marketed there with the express consent of the patentee, and it was immaterial that no patent existed there because the patentee had had the choice whether to market in that country or not. In the latter case, the patentee could not at the time have obtained a patent in the country (Italy) where the patented drug was first put on the market, but it was held that a Dutch patent could not be enforced against an importer of the Merck product from Italy because that product had been marketed there with the express consent of the patentee, and it was immaterial that no patent existed there because the patentee had had the choice whether to market in that country or not. That decision was seen as having an anti-patent character because the patentee was suffering from an inequality in patent law within the Community. Consequently, more recently, in *Merck v Primecrown* (C-267/95) [1997] F.S.R. 237; [1996] E.C.R. I–6285), a determined effort was made to reverse the *Merck v Stephar* decision, but the CJEU declined to vary it significantly, despite the advice of its Advocate General that it would be appropriate to do so.

Thus, the position remains that arts 34 and 36 of the TFEU preclude the enforcement of national patents against the importation of the patented product from an EEA Member State in which that product has been placed on the market by the patentee or with his consent, even though at the time the patentee was not able to obtain a patent for that product in the country of that first marketing, unless (as stated in *Merck v Primecrown*, above), exceptionally, the patentee can show that the circumstances were then such that it had a legal (as distinct from ethical) obligation to market the product in that State despite the absence of patent protection for it.

Also, the CJEU has held that, because of the existence of this "exhaustion of rights" doctrine, a prohibition in a national patent law against importation of a patented product from another Member State is discriminatory and not justified under what is now art.36 TFEU when domestic manufacturers would be able to market the product (*Allen & Hanbury v Generics (C-434/85)* [1988] 1 C.M.L.R. 701; [1988] F.S.R. 312 ECJ), a decision which led to the amendment of s.46 of the 1977 Act (settlement of terms of a "licence of right"), as noted in §D13, where it is pointed out that ss.48 and 50 of the Patents Act 1977 (grant of compulsory licences) have also had to be amended for a similar reason.

However, the "exhaustion of rights" doctrine relies heavily upon the first sale having been made either by the rights holder or with his consent, expressly or impliedly. Thus, in *Pharmon v Hoechst (C-19/84)* [1985] E.C.R. 2281; [1986] F.S.R. 108 ECJ, where the first sale arose under a United Kingdom compulsory licence, the product was held not to have been put on the market with the patentee's consent, an infringement action could therefore be brought under a parallel patent. Likewise, where patents exist in some, but not all, EU States and the patentee has deliberately not granted licences under those patents, although a general know-how licence may have been granted, there is no exhaustion of right when goods manufactured under the know-how licence are imported into a State where no patent licence was granted. Similarly, this is because consent cannot exist where a licence had not been given.

While, in *Allen & Hanbury v Generics* (C-434/85) (above), the "licence of right" provisions of s.46 of the 1977 Act were considered equivalent to the grant of compulsory licence, as the "licence of right" endorsement in this case had been made involuntarily. The position could be different if the patentee elects so to endorse his patent.

Because connected companies are deemed not to be separate entities under Community law, an inter-group transfer of goods does not lead to any exhaustion of intellectual property rights (*Musik-Vertrieb v GEMA* [Germany] [1982] 1 C.M.L.R. 630, noted [1982] F.S.R. 355).

At one time, a further facet of the "exhaustion of rights" doctrine was whether the parallel intellectual property rights had previously been in common ownership. However, this no longer appears to be a relevant consideration, see §D17.

—"Exhaustion of rights" in international trade

D16   Under English law, the sale of a right protected product normally carries with it an implied licence under that right for the purchaser to use or re-sell the product without fetter, as was established in *Betts v Willmott* (1871) L.R. 6 Ch. App. 239. There was no distinction drawn as to whether that first sale occurred inside or outside the United Kingdom. The position is, however, different where the first sale was made with an express prohibition against specified future conduct, such as resale or an export prohibition. This is because no licensee can grant rights in excess of those which have been granted to him so that re-sale or export in breach of the condition imposed on the occasion of the first sale makes the subsequent purchaser an infringer of the right, see *National Phonograph Company v*

Menck (1911) 28 R.P.C. 229 Pat Ct; *Incandescent Gas Light v Brogden* (1899) 16 R.P.C. 179; and *Dunlop v Longlife Battery* [1958] R.P.C. 473.

However, assuming that the imposition of that condition is not itself void under competition law principles (as discussed in §§44.04 and 44.07 and exemplified by *Soc. de Vente de Ciments v Kerpen* [1985] 1 C.M.L.R. 511, noted [1985] F.S.R. 281), the restrictive condition will only be effective against a subsequent purchaser of the goods if notice of that condition has been "brought home" to him by some express or constructive notice, see *SmithKline & French v Salim* [Malaysia] [1989] F.S.R. 407. The *Zino Davidoff* decision (noted below) shows that to do this in practice may be quite difficult, save by an express, and irremovable, marking on the product itself.

Thus, under the laws of the United Kingdom, this doctrine of "implied licence" accompanying sale of a product can be seen to be similar to the CJEU doctrine of the "exhaustion of rights". However, the doctrine has been applied under English law not only to "domestic exhaustion" (i.e. sale and re-sale within the United Kingdom) but also to "international exhaustion" (i.e. sale outside the United Kingdom and re-sale within the United Kingdom). However, this has not been the law in many European countries, thereby leaving open whether the application of the doctrine to intra-Community sales also applies to situations where the first sale occurs outside the EEA and when the product is then re-sold within the EU, a situation which has become known as "international exhaustion".

It was first established in the copyright case of *EMI v CBS (C-51/75)* [1976] E.C.R. 811; [1976] F.S.R. 457 where the CJEU held that, because the "exhaustion of rights" doctrine is based on the requirement to establish a true "single market" for the EU, the doctrine does not apply where a protected product is first marketed by the rights-holder or his licensee outside the Community and then imported without the consent of the rights-holder. This was also held to be so where a licensee under a patent outside the Community lawfully first imported the patented product into a Member State where no parallel patent existed and that product was then imported into another Member State where a parallel patent did exist but for which no right to sell had been granted: *SmithKline & French v Global Pharmaceutics* BL C/167/83, noted I.P.D. 6125; and [1986] R.P.C. 394; and *"Patented Bandagaging Material"* [Germany] [1988] 2 C.M.L.R. 359; [1988] F.S.R. 505.

This theme was pursued in *Silhoutte v Hartlauer (C-355/96)* [1998] F.S.R. 729; [1998] 2 C.M.L.R. 953, where the CJEU held that, in order to eliminate disparity between the variations in the extent of the exhaustion of rights doctrine in different EU States, no doctrine of "international exhaustion of rights" should be recognised where trade-marked products had been sold by the rights-holder outside the EEA on the apparent express condition that these goods should not re-enter the EEA. Thus, action for trade mark infringement was appropriate when the goods were re-sold in an EEA country.

Moreover, it appears from the subsequent trade mark case (*Zino Davidoff v A & G Imports* [1999] R.P.C. 631) that (under English law) consent to subsequent marketing of the goods will always exist to provide an exhaustion of the trade mark right unless a specific prohibition against import into the EU has been brought home to the importer of the goods into the United Kingdom, but it was also indicated that the function of a trade mark is a guarantee of origin of the goods. However, in the further judgment in *Sebago v GB-Unic SA* [2000] R.P.C. 63, the CJEU stated that any consent to marketing "must relate to each individual item of the product in respect of which exhaustion was pleaded", seemingly suggesting that consent should normally be presumed to be absent unless specifically granted.

Nevertheless, it should be noted that the reasoning in each of the *Silhoutte*, *Davidoff* and *Sebago* decisions was based on a specific provision in trade mark Directive 89/104/EEC, albeit codifying earlier case lawas with Regulation 40/94 on the Community trade mark. Thus the position could be different with patented products for which no similar provision (yet) exists. The TRIPS Agreement, quite deliberately, took no view as to whether international exhaustion should, or should not, be a permitted aspect of international trade, see art.6 of the TRIPS Agreement, which reads:

"ARTICLE 6—Exhaustion

For the purposes of dispute settlement under this Agreement, subject to the provisions of Articles 3 and 4 above [National treatment and Most-favoured-nation treatment] nothing in this Agreement shall be used to address the issue of the exhaustion of intellectual property rights."

However, a ruling of no international exhaustion was made in relation to copyright protected goods in *Laserdisken v Kulturministeriet* (C-479/04) [2006] E.C.R. I–8089, which suggests that a similar.

Following the ruling of *L'Oreal Norge AS v Per Aarskog AS* [2008] E.T.M.R. 60, the doctrine of no international exhaustion extends to European Free Trade Association (EFTA) countries. It was also established in *Class International BV v Colgate-Palmolive Co* (C-405/03) [2005] E.C.R. I–873. and applied in *Eli Lilly and Co v 8PM Chemists Ltd* [2008] F.S.R. 12 that, if consignments in transit were physically present in an EU country but destined for a third country, as long as they were not "released for circulation", they should not be regarded as undermining the rights owners right of first sale in the EU.

For further discussion of these issues and the continued applicability of *EMI v CBS* (above), see papers by Helen Norman and Jessica Jones [2000] E.I.P.R. 159 and 171; Maria Mercedes Frabboni [2007] Ent LR 70.

Principle of "common origin"

D17   The CJEU at one time relied on a principle of common origin, rather than the principle of "exhaustion", when considering the free movement of goods from one Member State to another where those goods bear the same trade mark. That principle has been applied to prevent the owner of a trade mark in one Member State from exerting that right against goods bearing the same mark applied by a now-unconnected entity when originally the two marks had been in common ownership. However, in *IHT v Ideal Standard* (C-9/93) [1994] 3 C.M.L.R. 857; [1995] F.S.R. 59 ECJ, it was held that, where a trade mark had in the past been voluntarily assigned to an unconnected undertaking, the assignor could assert a parallel trade mark in another country which it had retained, on the basis that the national intellectual property rights were independent of each other and, where retained, should continue to be upheld under the Community law. It would therefore appear that there is no separate, or related, doctrine of "common origin" and that the issue of "exhaustion of rights" should be decided on the principles set out in §D15, see the discussion on this case by G. Tritton [1994] E.I.P.R. 422. This would mean that parties relying on the principle of "common origin" as a defence are likely to have the case to be struck out or summarily dismissed at an early stage of the proceedings. In recent years, there has been a shift of attitude in the English courts. In *Doncaster Pharmaceuticals Group Ltd v The Bolton Pharmaceutical Company 100 Ltd* [2006] EWCA Civ. 66, the Court of Appeal found that a summary judgement would not be sufficient to assess the legitimacy of such a defence. The circumstances in which the assignments were made require detailed examination at trial to determine whether they were intended as a market-partitioning mechanism to give the owners control over the use of the trademarks.

Anti-trust provisions of the TFEU (arts 101 and 102 TFEU)

D18   Articles 101 and 102 TFEU are the basis of EU competition, or anti-trust, policy. Article 101 TFEU is concerned with co-operative market behaviour which may have an effect upon trade between Member States, as may be expressed in the form of agreements between undertakings or decisions of associations of undertakings; or of concerted practices; and art.102 of the TFEU is concerned with instances of an abuse of a dominant position within the EU.

The basic legal position is that any provision of a licence agreement which falls within art.101(1) of the TFEU is void unless the agreement is qualifies for exemption under TFEU art.101(3).

In broad terms, art.101(3) of the TFEU exemption is available if the restrictive effects of the agreement in question are outweighed by its benefits and that the restrictions go no further than is necessary in order to generate those benefits.

Recognising that a complex assessment is required in order to verify whether art.101(3) of the TFEU can be relied upon, the Commission has issued a number of Block Exemption Regulations for different types of agreements, of which the most important for present purposes is the Technology Transfer Regulation (TTR) discussed in §§D20–D23.

Neither art.101 nor art.102 of the TFEU is applicable unless the behaviour in question is one which affects trade between Member States, but the Commission and the CJEU have each readily been prepared to find that this factor is present if other conditions for the applicability of these articles exist, see *Vaessen v Morris* [1979] 1 C.M.L.R. 511; [1979] F.S.R. 259 and *Remia v Nutricia* [1987] 1 C.M.L.R. 1; [1987] F.S.R. 190.

Cases generally dealing with what is meant by agreements between undertakings, decisions of association of undertakings and concerted practices are not cited here, but the TFEU assumes that an undertaking acting unilaterally cannot threaten competition unless it occupies a dominant position within the meaning of art.82 EC, and companies in common ownership, such as parent and subsidiary, are not regarded as separate entities in this regard (*Centraform v Sterling Drug (C-15/74)* [1974] E.C.R. 1147; [1974] 2 C.M.L.R. 480, but see *Konica's Agreements* [1988] OJ EC L78/34 for an exception when subsidiaries did not receive parental instructions for day-to-day running of their businesses and *Viho Europe BV v Commission* C-73/95 P [1996] E.C.R. I–05457.

Since May 1, 2004, the Commission shares the competence to apply arts 101 and 102 of the TFEU with national competition authorities ("NCAs") and national courts in the EU. In the UK, the OFT and sectoral regulators are designated NCAs. Under the Modernisation Regulation (Regulation 1/2003) NCAs are obliged to apply TFEU arts 101 and 102 insofar as the agreements under consideration have an effect on trade between Member States.

Also, the Competition Act 1998 (c.41), in force from March 1, 2000, makes domestic behaviour carried on within the United Kingdom likewise objectionable if it is of the type which would have been contrary to either of arts 101 or 102 TFEU if carried on across national borders within the EEA, see the commentary on repealed s.44. Any agreement, etc. exempted under an EU Block Exemption Regulation is automatically exempted under the Competition Act 1998 s.10.

—Exemption under TFEU article 101(3)

No exemption is provided for under TFEU art.102, but an agreement which is objectionable under TFEU art.101(1) may nonetheless be exempt (without any prior decision to that effect being required) where it satisfies the four conditions contained in art.101(3) of the TFEU. **D19**

However, in the interest of legal certainty, the Commission has developed a number of "block exemptions". If an agreement is drafted in such a way to fall within the scope of a block exemption, the parties can be satisfied that the agreement will not be exposed to sanctions (e.g. unenforceability and fines). The most relevant block exemption for patents is the Technology Transfer Block Exemption which is considered in §D20 below.

The Commission's Notice on Agreements of Minor Importance is also relevant, for the latest version of which see *Patents Journal* [2001] C368/07. This Notice reflects the Commission's view that agreements between undertakings which affect trade between Member States do not appreciably restrict competition within the meaning of art.101(1) of the TFEU if the aggregate market share held by the parties to the agreement does not exceed 10 per cent of the relevant markets affected by the agreement where the agreement is made between undertakings which are actual or potential competitors or 15 per cent if the undertakings are not actual or potential competitors in any of these markets. In cases where it is difficult to classify the agreement as either an agreement between competitors or non-competitors the 10 per cent threshold is applicable. Thus the Notice draws a distinction between horizontal and vertical agreements, and, in conjunction with Commission Recommendation 96/280/EC of April 3, 1996 concerning the definition of small and medium-sized enterprises (as subsequently revised) also provides a further ground for exemption where the agreements involve companies with fewer than 250 employees and either a turnover of less than €50 million or an annual balance-sheet total not exceeding €43 million. This Notice and the TTR (discussed in the following paragraphs) are dealt with further in the EPH and attention can also usefully be paid to any of the books listed in §D02. For guidance on market definition, see *Commission notice on the definition of relevant market for the purposes of Community competition law* [1997] OJ C 372/00.

The Technology Transfer Regulation

The TTR (Commission Regulation (EC) No 772/2004) came into force on May 1, 2004, replacing the 1996 Technology Transfer Regulation. **D20**

In some respects the new TTR is wider in scope than the 1996 Regulation

In particular, it is structured so that the exemption applies to all restrictions, subject to a list of hardcore restrictions (art.4) which, if included, would take the entire agreement outside the exemption, and a list of excluded restrictions (art.5), which are not covered by the exemption and are subject to an individual assessment under TFEU art.101(3) but (subject to applicable laws of contract) are severable from the rest of the agreement.

The previous exemption had a more complicated structure containing a list of restrictions which had to be present in order for the exemption to apply; a "white list" of restrictions do not generally restrict competition; a "black list" of restrictions whose inclusion would remove the benefit of the block exemption and a procedure for a "fast track" individual exemption for restrictions were neither expressly permitted under the exemption nor black listed.

The structure of, and key concepts in the TTR, are considered below, followed by an assessment of how common provisions in patent licenses may be treated under EC competition law.

The Guidelines which accompany the TTR (see OJ [2004] C101/02) provide further guidance on its application. They also discuss the provisions which the Commission considers are not caught by art.101 of the TFEU at all, the circumstances where an agreement falls outside the terms of the TTR but where restrictions may satisfy the conditions of art.101(3) of the TFEU, and situations where the principles of the TTR may provide assistance in analysing licences of IPRs which are not covered by it.

Structure of the TTR

● Article 2—exemption **D21**

Article 2 contains the terms of the exemption. The exemption covers "technology transfer agreements entered into between two undertakings permitting the production of contract products".

- Article 3—market share thresholds, which relate both to the market for contract products and the market for licences, or 'technology market'.
  Article 3 sets out the condition that the exemption will only apply provided that certain market share thresholds are not exceeded:

  — 20 per cent combined market share in the case of agreements between competitors;

  — 30 per cent (for each party) in the case of agreements between non-competitors.

- Article 4—hardcore restrictions
  Article 4 lists those restrictions whose inclusion removes the benefit of the exemption. There are two lists of restrictions, one for agreements between competitors and one for agreements between non-competitors.

- Article 5—excluded restrictions
  Article 5 lists those restrictions which are not covered by the exemption. Such restrictions are severable—their inclusion will not take the entire agreement outside the scope of the TTR.

- Article 6—withdrawal in individual cases
  Article 6 sets out the circumstances in which the Commission, or the competition authority of a Member State, may withdraw the benefit of the exemption, in particular where the cumulative effect of parallel networks of similar restrictive agreements is to foreclose access to markets.

- Article 7—non-application of the regulation
  Article 7 describes the circumstances where the Commission may declare that the TTR is not to apply

- Article 8—application of the market share thresholds
  Article 8 sets out how the market share should be calculated for the purposes of applying the thresholds and provides that the TTR will continue to apply for a period of two calendar years if the parties' market share(s) were originally below the thresholds, at the commencement of the agreement, but subsequently rise above it.

- Article 9—repeal
  Article 9 repeals the 1996 Technology Transfer Regulation.

Key concepts in the TTR

—Scope

D22   The Article 2 exemption applies to "technology transfer agreements" between two undertakings. This includes "licensing" agreements and also assignments "where part of the risk associated with exploitation of the technology remains with the assignor".

The exemption only applies to agreements "permitting the production of contract products"—art.2. For these purposes "products" includes goods and services. It does not apply to the purchase of goods and services. Provisions relating to the purchase and sale of products may however be covered provided that the purchase and sale is not the primary object of the agreement and they are directly related to the application of the licensed technology.

The TTR covers the licensing of patents, know-how, software copyright and mixed licences of the same (art.1(1)(b)). "Patents" is widely-defined and includes "patents, patent applications, utility models, applications for registration of utility models, designs, topographies of semiconductor products, supplementary protection certificates for medicinal products or other products for which such supplementary protection certificates may be obtained and plant breeder's certificates" (art.1(1)(h)).

—Market share

The market share thresholds apply to both technology and product markets. On the technology market, a licensor's market share is calculated based on the value of all products incorporating the licensed technology produced by the licensor and its licensees, as a percentage of the relevant product market—see art.3(3) and Guidelines, paragraph 70.

A party's market share on the product market is the value of the products it produces, whether or not using the licensed technology, as a percentage of total market value.

If the market share thresholds are exceeded on either market, the exemption does not provide an automatic 'safe harbour' for the agreement.

—Concept of competitors

The TTR, recognising that agreements between competitors are likely to give rise to greater competition law concerns than agreements between non-competitors, makes a distinction between agreements between "competitors" and "non-competitors" for the purposes of permitted/hardcore restraints. "Competing Undertakings" are parties who are either:

(a) actual competitors on a relevant technology market; or

(b) actual or potential competitors (a company is a potential competitor if it would realistically "make the investments to enter the market in response to a small, permanent increase in price within one to two years")—art.1(1)(j) and Guidelines, paragraphs 26–33.

Application of the TTR to particular provisions

—Sales Restrictions—territorial and customer group protection

The most common restrictions in technology licences are those that relate to restrictions on the territory into which, and the customers to whom, the licensee(s) and licensor may sell. The restriction may be one of three kinds:

D23

- protection for the licensor's territory or selected customers from competition from the licensee;

- protection for the licensee's allocated territory or customers from competition from the licensor;

- protection for other licensees' allocated territories or customers from competition from the licensee.

Between competitors, all territorial or customer restrictions are considered hardcore unless one of the listed exceptions applies—art.4(1)(c). This reflects the Commission's concern that restrictions on the licensee's or licensor's ability to sell in certain territories or to certain customers will lead to the allocation of markets and customers between competitors.

In licences between competitors, an obligation on the licensor not to sell (both actively and/or passively) in the licensee's territory or customer group is permitted only in non-reciprocal agreements between competitors and, provided that the territory or customer group is exclusive to the licensee—art.4(1)(c)(iv). An exclusive customer group is a group of customers to which only one undertaking is allowed to sell the contract products—art.1(1)(m). An obligation on the licensee not to sell (both actively and/or passively) into the licensor's territory or customer group is permitted under the same conditions.

The licensor may also restrict active sales by a licensee into the exclusive territory or customer group of another licensee, provided that such exclusive licensee was not a competitor at the time of its appointment—art.4(1)(c)(v).

Between non-competitors, the TTR is more permissive. A licensor can always prevent a licensee making active sales of the products outside its allocated territory or customer group, except in the context of selective distribution.

—Licensee's downstream distribution

It is common for a licensor to require that its licensees impose restrictions on their distributors/resellers, in order to protect the integrity of the system that the licensor has set up at the licensee level. Such a requirement is covered by the TTR, provided that the restrictions themselves comply with EC competition law—Guidelines, paragraph 39.

—Pricing

In agreements between competitors and non-competitors, the licensor may not set a fixed or minimum price for the products incorporating the technology—art.4(1)(a) and art.4(2)(a).

This includes indirect measures such as fixing the maximum level of any discount, limiting the sales price to the sales price of competitors or threats to terminate. It can also include penalties structured such that if a product price is reduced below a certain level, royalty rates change. However, an obligation on a licensee to pay a certain minimum royalty is not considered to be price fixing.

Maximum and recommended prices are permitted in agreements between competitors but are hardcore restrictions in agreements between competitors—Guidelines, paragraphs 79 and 97.

—Output restrictions

Limitations on the quantity that the licensee can produce (including, for example, a limit on the licence to a particular site with a specified capacity) are permitted in non-reciprocal agreements between competitors. In reciprocal agreements between competitors, limitations may be placed on one licensee—art.4(1)(b) and Guidelines, paragraphs 82–83 and 175–178. Output restrictions are exempted in agreements between non-competitors.

—Captive use restrictions

In both agreements between competitors and non-competitors, the licensor may restrict the licensee to using the products incorporating the technology only for its own use. However, the licensee must be free to make active and passive sales of the products as spare parts for its own products, including selling to third parties who perform after sales services in respect of its products—art.4(1)(c)(vi), art.4(2)(b)(iii) and Guidelines, paragraph 92.

—Field of use restrictions

Field of use restrictions (i.e. restrictions limiting the right to produce with the technology only within one or more technical fields of use or one or more product markets) on licensees are permitted in agreements between competitors (art.4(1)(c)(i)). However, in a reciprocal agreement between competitors, a field of use limitation on the licensor is a hardcore restraint—Guidelines, paragraph 183.

—Limits on right to exploit own technology and carry out R&D

In agreements between non-competitors, any restriction on the licensee's ability to exploit its own technology or to carry out its own research and development is not covered by the TTR, unless the restriction on research and development is indispensable to prevent the disclosure of the licensed know-how to third parties (art.5(2)). Such a restriction requires individual assessment—Guidelines, paragraphs 114–116.

In agreements between competitors such a restriction is hardcore (art.4(1)(d)), as it is likely to limit competition between the parties.

—Improvements

The TTR permits an obligation on the licensee to grant an exclusive licence or an assignment of improvements in, or new applications of, the licensed technology (i.e. these are not hardcore restraints) provided that the improvements are not severable from the licensed technology. However, if the improvement is severable, that is, capable of being exploited without infringing the intellectual property rights in the original technology (art.1(1)(n)), then an exclusive licence or assignment in favour of the licensor is not covered by the TTR (art.5(1)(a) and (b)), although not hardcore.

—No challenge clauses

Obligations on the licensee not to challenge the validity of the licensor's intellectual property fall outside the TTR and are subject to individual assessment (art.5(1)(c)). A right to terminate the license agreement in the event of a validity challenge by the licensee is covered by the TTR (art.5(1)(c)).

In *Bayer v Sullhofer (C-65/86)* [1988] E.C.R. 5249; [1990] F.S.R. 300 though, the CJEU held that art.101 TFEU did not necessarily catch restrictions on challenge and, in *Moosehead* OJ [1990] 100/32 the Commission held that a restriction on challenging the validity of a trade mark did not fall within art.101 TFEU where the trade mark was comparatively new to the territory and, consequently, would not constitute an appreciable barrier to entry.

—Royalties

Certain royalty structures (e.g. an increase in the royalty rate due in the event that products are sold below a certain price) may amount to price fixing, in which case they are hardcore restrictions and are prohibited. (They are also likely to attract fines). Minimum royalties are permitted.

In *Ottung v Klee* C-320/87; [1090] ECR 1177; [1990] 4 C.M.L.R. 915, the CJEU held that a provision requiring the licensee to pay royalties following termination would not infringe art.101 TFEU if the licensee could terminate the licence on giving a reasonable period of notice. In its Guidelines, the Commission states that, generally, parties can extend the payment of royalties beyond the life of the IPRs. The fact that, at that stage, third parties are free to exploit the technology in question, means that such a provision is unlikely to have an appreciable anti-competitive effect—Guidelines, paragraph 159.

—Other terms

The Guidelines also make clear that the following terms, which are frequently found in licence agreements, generally do not restrict competition and fall outside art.101(1) TFEU:

(i) confidentiality obligations;

(ii) obligations on licensees not to sub-license;

(iii) obligations not to use the licensed technology after the expiry of the agreement (provided that the IPR remains valid);

(iv) obligations to assist the licensor in enforcing its IPRs

(v) obligations to pay minimum royalties or to produce minimum quantities; and

(vi) obligations to use the licensor's trademark or to indicate the name of the licensor on the product—Guidelines, paragraph 155.

Agreements for collaborative research and development

Agreements for joint ventures are generally outside the scope of this Work, but, as noted in the **D24** EPH, there are other Block Exemption Regulations of possible relevance to the subject-matter of this Work. These include: (1) Reg1217/2010 for research and development agreements; (2) Reg1218/2010 for "specialisation" agreements; and (3) Reg 330/2010 for agreements of a "vertical" nature, usually concerned with arrangements for product sales made via intermediaries.

Decisions of relevance to the application of Article 101 TFEU

Decisions of the Commission given before the advent of the TTR are generally now of little **D25** relevance to the application of art.101, but some such decisions are worthy of note because they illustrate the then thinking of the Commission, or the thinking of the CJEU, and it is possible that such decisions may be relied upon in a situation where it is being argued that an agreement has, or has not, terms forbidden by art.101(1) and not exemptible under TFEU art.101(3), this (and not the terms of the TTR) being the ultimate test. However, it must be remembered that the tests under TFEU art.101(1) and (3) are essentially economic, rather than legal, and thus their application may varyas economic circumstances change. Decisions on the application of art.101(1) and (3) of the TFEU can, therefore, be no more than a general guide, and older decisions probably have little or no value. Consequently, only selective decisions are discussed below.

Windsurfing International v EC Commission (C-193/83) [1986] E.C.R. 611; [1986] 3 C.M.L.R. 489, abridged [1988] F.S.R. 139 ECJ was the first case considered by the CJEU with respect to the detailed clauses commonly found in a licence agreement. In the EU, Windsurfing were the owners of patents only in the United Kingdom (subsequently found invalid, see *Windsurfing v Tabur Marine* [1985] R.P.C. 59 and Germany (where a court had found as a fact that the scope of the patent was restricted to a rig for a sailboard). At first instance, the Commission found (ignoring the British patent position, then *sub judice*) that the following licensing practices of Windsurfing were objectionable.

(1) limitation of the licence to manufacture to a country where a patent existed, with the effect that royalties were to be paid even on products sold in parts of the Union where no patent protection existed;

(2) the presence of provisions for terminating the licence if the licensee changed its manufacturing location;

(3) requirements for a licensee's design to be approved, other than for objective reasons of quality control or safety factors based on the specific subject-matter of the patent;

(4) provisions requiring marketing to be accompanied by a notice of the licence, even when no patent or other right requiring a licence existed in the country of sale;

(5) limitation of a licensee's power to supply the rig and the board separately;

(6) the requirement that the licensee should acknowledge the validity of the licensed trade mark;

(7) the placing of a notice that the product was marketed under licence on a part of the combination which was not the subject of the patent; and

(8) charging a royalty based on the unpatented combination of the board and rig.

On appeal, the CJEU generally upheld the initial decision of the Commission with the exception that the court felt it was reasonable, for convenience, to base the royalty on the complete sailboard, rather than on the rig only, provided that it could be shown that the royalty based on the value of the rig alone was not excessive. For discussion of the basis of the fines imposed in this case, see §D28.

In *Jus-Rol and Rich Products' Agreement* [1988] 4 C.M.L.R. 527; abridged [1988] F.S.R. 528 the Commission granted negative clearance (i.e. they found that the agreement did not fall within what is now art.81(1)) to an agreement relating to the licensing by Rich Products of its technology for the manufacture of frozen yeast dough products. The licensee was allowed to use the secret know-how, which was indicated to be substantial when the licensee agreed to pay for its use and which was apparently here identified as a body of written confidential non-patented information, for a period of ten years, but there was a right of termination by either party after five years. At the conclusion of the agreement, the licensee was not permitted to use the know-how for a period of ten years. It was clearly stated by the Commission that such a clause was not within what is now art.101(1) of the TFEU and that, if it were not possible for a licensor to require that a licensee should stop using the non-patented technical know-how, it would ultimately be harmful to the general transfer of technical knowledge. For comment see [1989] E.I.P.R. 291.

In *DDD and Delta Chemie's Agreement* [1989] 4 C.M.L.R. 535, abridged [1989] F.S.R. 52 and 497, an exclusive know-how licence was granted exemption under what is now art.101(3), with a prohibition on use of the licensor's know-how after the end of the agreement, but the licensee was permitted then to use the improvements to it developed by itself provided that such would not involved use of the licensor's know-how. Also, while the licensee was required to collaborate in the prosecution of infringers, this provision is not to be taken as preventing the licensee from challenging the validity of the licensed right. Individual exemption was also granted in *Brown Boveri and NGK Insulators' Agreement* [1988] OJ EC L301/68, where, in a research and development agreement, one party undertook not to export into the Union for ten years, the high risk of the project justifying the exemption.

In *Konica's Agreement* [1988] OJ EC L78/34, the Commission found objectionable (under what is now TFEU art.101) the conduct of Konica of Japan, and of some of its wholly-owned subsidiaries in Europe, on the basis that these subsidiaries did not receive instructions from Japan on the day-to-day running of their business. In other words, it is no longer safe to assume that any licensing practice as between a parent and its subsidiaries cannot be objected to under TFEU art.101.

In *Bayer v Sullhofer (C-65/86)* [1988] E.C.R. 5249; [1990] F.S.R. 300 ECJ, the CJEU held:

(1) A "no challenge" clause included in a patent licence agreement may, in the light of the legal and economic context, restrict competition within the meaning of what is now art.101 TFEU, but a national court must determine whether such a clause involves a restriction on the licensee's freedom of action which restricts competition to an appreciable extent bearing in mind the relative positions held by the licensor and licensee in the market for the products concerned.

(2) A "no challenge" clause in a royalty-free licence does not restrict competition; and, similarly, there is no restriction in competition if the licence relates to a technically-outdated process which the licensee does not use, even when royalties are called for by such a clause.

This case arose because of the possibility under German law that, if the "no challenge" clause was invalid, the whole agreement might be void.

Abuse of a dominant position (TFEU art.102)

Article 102 of the TFEU deals with "abuse of a dominant position". This phrase is not defined as such in the Treaty, but its sub-paragraphs provide some illustrative examples. Thus, art.102(d) TFEU states that an abuse may exist by making the conclusion of a contract subject to acceptance by the other party of supplementary obligations, which have no connection with the subject of such a contract. This provision leads fairly directly on to a situation where, for example, a purchaser is forced to buy unpatented goods from a patentee when taking a licence. Accordingly, care has to be taken to avoid infringement of art.102 TFEU in circumstances where it can be argued that a patent licensor has a "dominant position", which could be the case merely from the existence of his patent (although this is not necessarily the case). **D26**

In *Hugin v EC Commission (C-22/78)* [1979] E.C.R. 1869; [1979] 3 C.M.L.R. 345 ECJ, the court found that Hugin did not have a dominant position within the Community with respect to the sale of cash registers, as its share of the market for this product was only about 12 per cent. However, the spare parts for its registers were mostly not interchangeable with spare parts for other registers, and there therefore existed a dominant position with respect to the reconditioning and repair of Hugin registers.

In *Eurofix and Bauco v Hilti* [1988] OJ EC L65/19, abridged [1988] F.S.R. 473, the defendant was heavily fined by the Commission for abuse of a dominant position because, inter alia, it had attempted to control the supply of unpatented nails for use with its patented fastening guns. Arguments that Hilti was restricting supplies only on safety grounds, and/or that the complainant was selling inferior nails, were rejected. A fine was also levied for operating selective and discriminatory practices directed against the business of both competitors and competitors' customers, including "frustrating and delaying legitimately-available licences of right" in proceedings for the settlement of terms thereof under s.46(3). Besides the fine, Hilti agreed not to assert its copyrights in respect of present and future operations under "licences of right" applying to the patents in question. In dismissing the appeal (*Hilti AG v EC Commission (T-30/89)* [1992] F.S.R. 210 CFI), the General Court held that Hilti had abused its dominant position in the specific market for consumable items (nails) for use with products (nail guns) by seeking in licence of right proceedings (under s.46(3)) a royalty about six times higher than that ultimately awarded by the Comptroller. Here, the court made it clear that it was more concerned to see that the rules of competition within the Community are effective and were thus prepared to disregard submissions that product liability by a manufacturer could be a good ground for refusing to permit competition. A further appeal was dismissed (*Hilti AG v EC Commission (C-53/92P)* [1994] 4 C.M.L.R. 614 ECJ), as discussed by S. Topping [1994] E.I.P.R. 543.

In *Elopak v Tetra-Pak (No.2)* [1992] OJ EC L72/1; [1992] 4 C.M.L.R. 551, abridged [1992] F.S.R. 542, the Commission, in imposing a record fine on Tetra-Pak (a Swedish company) for numerous breaches of what are now arts 101 and 102 TFEU, criticised, inter alia:

(1) that customers or licensee were obliged to inform Tetra-Pak of any technical improvement and to grant Tetra-Pak ownership of intellectual property rights for such improvements or modifications—a practice which is obviously contrary to the principles of free competition; and

(2) that Tetra-Pak had a practice of patenting all its basic technology and all modifications, however minor, giving rise to a monopolistic abuse at a time when the basic technology developed in the 1960s was still in use and yet some two hundred patents still existed covering

alleged patentable modifications, though this second ground was not in fact taken into account in computing the record fine.

This second criticism gives rise to some concern, because it is difficult to decide whether any particular improvement at the time it is made may eventually turn out to be significant; and yet it seems that a company can be regarded as guilty of abusive conduct in seeking patent protection for each and every improvement which it devises to its basic technology. Appeals in each case were dismissed: *Tetra-Pak v EC Commission (T-83/91)* [1994] E.C.R. II–755; [1997] 4 C.M.L.R. 726 CFI; and *Tetra-Pak v EC Commission (C-333/94)* [1996] E.C.R. I–595; [1997] 4 C.M.L.R. 602 ECJ.

In 2005, the Commission fined AstraZeneca €60 million for abusing its dominant position in the market for proton pump inhibitors by misusing its patent. The Commission concluded that AstraZeneca abused its position of dominance by blocking or delaying market access for generic versions of its products and by preventing parallel imports (see Commission Press Release IP/05/737). The case was appealed to the CJEU and judgment was given in July 2010, *AstraZeneca v Commission (Competition)* (T-321/05) [2010] CJEU. The conduct of *AstraZeneca* was held to have included a serious abuse of a dominant position as regards its applications for SPCs and the heavy fine previously imposed was only slightly reduced. This decision must be seen as a warning to IP practitioners and this was discussed in two papers by D. Curley, "A duty of transparency: the General Court rules in the AstraZeneca competition case" [2010] *CIPA* 412 and B. Batchelor [2010] *CIPA* 478.

In 2009, the Commission imposed a large fine of €1.06 billion against Intel Corporation for violating EU Competition law on the abuse of a dominant market position. The Commission found that Intel Corporation had engaged in illegal practices to exclude competitors from the market for computer chips called x86 central processing units (CPUs). First, Intel gave wholly or partially hidden rebates to computer manufacturers on condition that they bought all, or almost all, their x86 CPUs from Intel. It was believed that such rebates and payments would have prevented consumers from choosing alternative products. Second, Intel made direct payments to computer manufcturers to halt or delay the launch of specific products containing competitors' x86 CPUs and to limit the sales channels available to these product (see Commission Press Release IP/09/745).

—Mere exercise of rights

D27   It is not apparently per se an abuse of a dominant position for a patentee to seek, in good faith, to enforce a legal right which he thinks he has, or to threaten to do so (*Pitney Bowes v Francotyp-Postalia* [1991] F.S.R. 72). Thus, it is not an abuse of a dominant position merely to exercise an intellectual property right, even though a similar right does not exist in the Member State of first sale, provided that the "exhaustion of rights" doctrine, as expounded in §D15, is not breached. Thus, by *Parke, Davis v Probel* (C–24/67) [1968] E.C.R. 55; [1968] F.S.R. 393 ECJ, discussed in §D14, a patentee is not obliged to enforce his right in the country where the infringer's first sale occurs. Also, if a rights-holder possesses more than one type of right, he may enforce those remaining when others have expired. For example, in *Industrie Diensten v Beele (C-6/81)* [1982] E.C.R. 707; [1983] F.S.R. 119 ECJ, action was permitted to be taken under a law against unfair competition to prevent slavish copying of the device of an expired patent.

A difference between a national intellectual property law and parallel laws in other Member States is also not to be taken into account in the absence of a harmonisation requirement. Thus, in *Keurkoop v Nancy Kean (C-144/81)* [1982] E.C.R. 2853; [1983] F.S.R. 381 ECJ, a Benelux-registered design was enforced against an importation from Taiwan, even though the design registered had itself been imported from Taiwan, apparently without the knowledge of the actual designer, this being permitted under the Benelux Designs law. Another case of a similar kind is *Thetford v Fiamma (C-35/87)* [1988] 3 C.M.L.R. 549; [1989] 1 F.S.R. 57 ECJ, where a patent was held enforceable even if it would have been anticipated but for the "50-year rule" then exempting certain prior art from consideration (under 1949 Act s.50(1)).

Nevertheless, if an intellectual property right conferring market power is exercised in a way which restricts competition, this may amount to an infringement of art.102 of the TFEU. Thus, in *RTE v EC Commission and Magill (C-241/91P and C-242P)* [1995] F.S.R. 530; [1995] E.C.R. I–743 ECJ, where television companies had enjoyed a monopoly in the information underlying an intellectual property right (their copyrights in the listings of the programmes which they transmit), it was held that they had abused this monopoly by denying others the ability to market a unique product (weekly, as distinct from daily, programme listings making use of that copyright) for which a public demand was seen.

However, the *RTE* case has been explained as not inhibiting the mere exercise of patent rights (*Philips Electronics v Ingman* [1999] F.S.R. 112), as discussed by N. Jones [1988] E.I.P.R. 352;

[1998] B.S.L.R. 68; and, in *Sandvik v Pfiffner* [2000] F.S.R. 17, the *RTE* case was described as an exceptional case. Nevertheless (as in this *Sandvik* case), doubtless it will be argued that the rationale of the *RTE* case should be applied against any patentee who refuses a licence under his patent for the making available of a product which he himself chooses not to supply, or allow his voluntary licensees to supply.

Imposition of fines by European Commission

Under Regulation 1/2003, the Commission can impose fines of up to 10 per cent of an undertaking's worldwide turnover. The Commission will have regard to the duration and gravity of the infringement. In 2005, the Commission fined AstraZeneca €60 million for a TFEU art.102 infringement.   **D28**

In *Windsurfing International v EC Commission (C-193/83)* [1986] E.C.R. 611; [1986] 3 C.M.L.R. 489, abridged [1988] F.S.R. 139 ECJ, the facts of which are discussed in §D25, a fine was imposed, inter alia, because of the existence of "no challenge" clauses both as to patent and trade mark rights. The CJEU stated that "it is in the public interest to eliminate any obstacle to economic activity which may arise where a patent was granted in error". Other reasons for imposing a fine in this case were:

(a) the existence of effective export restrictions to other parts of the Community;

(b) the requirement to pay royalties on sales of unpatented components alone, and limitation of a licensee's power to supply components separately;

(c) the limitation of licensed manufacture to a country where a patent existed, with the effect that royalties were paid even on products manufactured and sold in Member States where no patent protection existed;

(d) the presence of provisions for terminating the licence if the licensee changed his manufacturing location;

(e) the requirement for a licensee's designs to be approved, other than for objective reasons for quality control or safety factors based on the specific subject of the patent; and

(f) provisions requiring marketing to be accompanied by a notice of the licence even when no patent or other right requiring a licence existed in the country of sale and no know-how had been supplied by the licensor.

For comment on this case, see G. I. F. Leigh [1986] E.I.P.R. 27; P. A. Stone [1986] E.I.P.R. 242; and J. S. Venit (1987) 18 IIC 1, see also §D26.

APPENDIX E

THE CIVIL PROCEDURE RULES

Form and purpose of the Civil Procedure Rules

The Civil Procedure Rules (the "CPR") were initiated in 1999 and have now emerged as a new and unified set of rules for litigation in England and Wales both in the High Court and a county court. The CPR have now replaced the former Rules of the Supreme Court ("RSC") and the former County Court Rules ("CCR"). The CPR are set out in 79 Parts which individually comprise a set of sub-rules, the numbers of which commence with the number corresponding to the number of that Part and often amplified by specific Practice Directions. However, with the exceptions of: (a) Part 1, which sets out the "Overriding Objective" of the CPR and is reprinted at §§E01–E04; and (b) Part 63, which is directed to "Patents and other intellectual property claims" and, together with its associated Practice Directions, is reprinted (as regards litigations involving patents) in Appendix F, the other Parts of the CPR are not reprinted in this book. Nevertheless, a reference to a particular CPR is included where it is thought important to acquaint the reader with the number of the appropriate CPR and perhaps a Practice Direction made under it.

Regular litigation practitioners will usually have ready access to *The White Book*, published by Sweet & Maxwell which not only reprints each CPR but also has commentary on the use of that rule. The full text of the CPR and of its associated Practice Directions ("PD") may also be freely accessed via the official website of the Ministry of Justice which is updated with details of any amendment made here. This website has the address: *http://www.justice.gov.uk*.

The CPR introduced new terminology, so that all litigation in either the High Court or a county court is now commenced with a "claim form", replacing the former ways of commencing proceedings by way of a "writ", "petition", "originating notice of motion", etc. Accordingly, the CPR replaced the terms "plaintiff", "petitioner" and "applicant" by the single term "claimant", although the term "defendant" remains. The former "pleadings" have been replaced by the comprehensive term "statement of case", within which the "particulars of claim", "defence" and any "reply" each become incorporated as these documents are served. A counterclaim is now included within the term "additional claim" sometimes referred to as a "Part 20 claim". The former procedure of "discovery" of documents has been replaced by the concept of "disclosure" which is of more restricted scope than the former discovery procedure. According to their complexity, and the amount of money at stake, cases are categorised as "small claims" or allocated to the "fast track" or to the "multi-track". Patent litigation will normally fall into the multi-track category.

Evidence is now given mainly in written form by "witness statements", accompanied by a signed "statement of truth". Thus, a sworn affidavit should now rarely be required in litigation before either the High Court or a county court. The requirement for a signed "statement of truth" has also been extended as being a required element of various other litigation documents, including the contents of: a claim form; a defence; a reply: particulars of claim; and an additional claim including a counterclaim and, likewise, in proceedings before the Comptroller. An expert's report must also contain such a statement. Also, as part of the new process of "disclosure", the "list" of relevant documents must be accompanied by a signed statement indicating the steps taken to produce that list and the basis for the required expressed belief that complete disclosure has been made.

The CPR have the "overriding objective" of ensuring that parties to litigation settle their differences expeditiously, fairly and without undue expenditure, see CPR Pt 1 reprinted below. The same objective is now applied to proceedings before the Comptroller concerning patent and applications, see r.74 of the Patents Rules 2007 (reprinted at §123.07 above).

As one theme of the CPR is to use the courts only as a last resort in the settlement of civil disputes, parties are encouraged at all times to consider mutual settlement, perhaps as the result of some type of mediation or arbitration ("alternative dispute resolution"). To assist in this there has been appended to the CPR a general "Pre-action Protocol" as a prelude to a series of detailed pre-action protocols for various forms of litigation (see also the Patents and Patents County Court Guide in Appendix G below).

Another of the overriding objectives of the CPR is that the judges should adopt a pro-active approach to litigation before them and seek ways of bringing cases to trial at the earliest practical date; and that the length of the trial should be curtailed by limiting the issues to those which can be seen to involve a genuine dispute. To this end, there are various provisions for "case management", including a case management conference or a pre-trial review and these must be attended by persons who have authority to take decisions on the spot on the issues which the judge should permit to proceed to full trial, on which see §G08 in the Patents and Patents County Court Guide.

PART 1—Overriding Objective

The overriding objective

1.1—(1) These Rules are a new procedural code with the overriding objective of en-   **E01**
abling the court to deal with cases justly.

(2) Dealing with a case justly includes, so far as is practicable—

  (a) ensuring that the parties are on an equal footing;

  (b) saving expense;

  (c) dealing with the case in ways which are proportionate—

     (i) to the amount of money involved;

     (ii) to the importance of the case;

     (iii) to the complexity of the issues; and

     (iv) to the financial position of each party;

  (d) ensuring that it is dealt with expeditiously and fairly; and

  (e) allotting to it an appropriate share of the court's resources, while taking into account the need to allot resources to other cases.

Application by the court of the overriding objective

1.2 The court must seek to give effect to the overriding objective when it—   **E02**

(a) exercises any power given to it by the Rules; or

(b) interprets any rule subject to rule 76.2.

[Rule 76.2 says that the overriding objective and rules must be read and given effect to in a way which is compatible with the duty of the court to ensure that information is not disclosed contrary to the public interest as defined further under Pt 76 which relates to Proceedings under the Prevention of Terrorism Act 2005.]

Duty of the parties

1.3 The parties are required to help the court to further the overriding objective.   **E03**

Court's duty to manage cases

1.4—(1) The court must further the overriding objective by actively managing cases.   **E04**

(2) Active case management includes—

  (a) encouraging the parties to cooperate with each other in the conduct of the proceedings;

  (b) identifying the issues at an early stage;

  (c) deciding promptly which issues need full investigation and trial and accordingly disposing summarily of the others;

   (d) deciding the order in which issues are to be resolved;

   (e) encouraging the parties to use an alternative dispute resolution procedure if the court considers that appropriate and facilitating the use of such procedure;

   (f) helping the parties to settle the whole or part of the case;

   (g) fixing timetables or otherwise controlling the progress of the case;

   (h) considering whether the likely benefits of taking a particular step justify the cost of taking it;

   (i) dealing with as many aspects of the case as it can on the same occasion;

   (j) dealing with the case without the parties having to attend at court;

   (k) making use of technology; and

   (l) giving directions to ensure that the trial of a case proceeds quickly and efficiently.

APPENDIX F

PART 63 OF THE CIVIL PROCEDURE RULES

PATENTS AND OTHER INTELLECTUAL PROPERTY CLAIMS

(As updated to October 2010 and available on *http://www.justice.gov.uk*)

Notes:

1. Part 63 (as reprinted in the Main Work) was completely replaced, as from October 1, 2009, by the Civil Procedure (Amendment No.2) Rules, SI 2009/2092 (r.12; Sch.1).

2. To enact these changes, Pts 45 and 63 of the Civil Procedure Rules have been further amended by the Civil Procedure (Amendment No.2 Rules) 2010, SI 2010/1953 (rr.5, 8; Schs 1, 2), which come into force on October 1, 2010.

3. Part 63, in its amended form is set out below, followed by the relevant changes to Pt 45 and its practice direction. The Practice Directions issued in relation to Pt 63 are printed in this Appendix after the reprinting of the Rules of Pt 63 and are identified by the numbering 63PD.XX. The Costs Practice Direction is identified at the end of this Appendix by the numeral 45PD.XX.

RULE 1— SCOPE OF THIS PART AND INTERPRETATION

Scope of this Part and interpretation

63.1—(1) This Part applies to all intellectual property claims including–   **F63.01**
   (a) registered intellectual property rights such as–
      (i) patents;
      (ii) registered designs; and
      (iii) registered trade marks; and
   (b) unregistered intellectual property rights such as –
      (i) copyright;
      (ii) design right;
      (iii) the right to prevent passing off; and
      (iv) the other rights set out in **Practice Direction 63.**
(2) In this Part –
   (a) 'the 1977 Act' means the Patents Act 1977;
   (b) 'the 1988 Act' means the Copyright, Designs and Patents Act 1988;
   (c) 'the 1994 Act' means the Trade Marks Act 1994;
   (d) 'the Comptroller' means the Comptroller General of Patents, Designs and Trade Marks;
   (e) 'patent' means a patent under the 1977 Act or a supplementary protection certif-

icate granted by the Patent Office under Article 10(1) of Council Regulation (EEC) No. 1768/92 or of Regulation (EC) No. 1610/96 of the European Parliament and the Council and includes any application for a patent or supplementary protection certificate;

(f) 'Patents Court' means the Patents Court of the High Court constituted as part of the Chancery Division by section 6(1) of the Senior CourtsAct 1981;

(g) 'Patents County Court' means a county court designated as a Patents County Court under section 287(1) of the 1988 Act;

(h) 'patents judge' means a person nominated under section 291(1) of the 1988 Act as the patents judge of a patents county court;

(i) *omitted*

(j) 'the register' means whichever of the following registers is appropriate –

(i) patents maintained by the Comptroller under section 32 of the 1977 Act;

(ii) designs maintained by the registrar under section 17 of the Registered Designs Act 1949;

(iii) trade marks maintained by the registrar under section 63 of the 1994 Act;

(iv) Community trade marks maintained by the Office for Harmonisation in the Internal Market under Article 83 of Council Regulation (EC) 40/94; and

(v) Community designs maintained by the Office for Harmonisation in the Internal Market under Article 72 of Council Regulation (EC) 6/2002; and

(vi) plant varieties maintained by the Controller under regulation 12 of the Plant Breeders' Rights Regulations 1998; and

(k) 'the registrar' means –

(i) the registrar of trade marks; or

(ii) the registrar of registered designs,whichever is appropriate.

(3) Claims to which this Part applies are allocated to the multi-track.

I Patents and Registered Designs

RULE 2—SCOPE OF SECTION I AND ALLOCATION

Scope of Section I and Allocation

F63.02   **63.2**—(1) This Section applies to–

(a) any claim under–

(i) the 1977 Act;

(ii) the Registered Designs Act 1949;

(iii) the Defence Contracts Act 1958; and

(b) any claim relating to–

(i) Community registered designs;

(ii) semiconductor topography rights; or

(iii) plant varieties.

(2) claims to which this Section applies must be started in–

(a) the Patents Court; or

(b) a patents county court.

RULE 3—SPECIALIST LIST

Specialist list

F63.03   **63.3** Claims in the Patents Court and a patents county court form specialist lists for the purpose of rule 30.5.

RULE 4—OMITTED

Patents judge

63.4 *Omitted*   **F63.04**

Note: Rule 4 has been omitted by SI 2010/1953 r.8.

RULE 5—STARTING THE CLAIM

Starting the claim

63.5 Claims to which this Section of this Part applies must be started –   **F63.05**
(a) by issuing a Part 7 claim form; or
(b) in existing proceedings under Part 20.

RULE 6—CLAIM FOR INFRINGEMENT OR CHALLENGE TO VALIDITY OF A PATENT OR REGISTERED DESIGN

Claim for infringement or challenge to validity of a patent or registered design

63.6 A statement of case in a claim for infringement or a claim in which the validity of   **F63.06**
a patent or registered design is challenged must contain particulars as set out in Practice
Direction 63.

RULE 7—DEFENCE AND REPLY

Defence and reply

63.7 Part 15 applies with the modification –   **F63.07**
(a) to rule 15.4(1)(b) that in a claim for infringement under rule 63.6, the period for filing a defence where the defendant files an acknowledgment of service under Part 10 is 42
days after service of the particulars of claim;
(b) that where rule 15.4(2) provides for a longer period to file a defence than in rule
63.7(a), then the period of time in rule 15.4(2) will apply; and
(b) to rule 15.8 that the claimant must –
(i) file any reply to a defence; and
(ii) serve it on all other parties,
within 21 days of service of the defence.

RULE 8—CASE MANAGEMENT

Case management

63.8—(1) Parties do not need to file an allocation questionnaire   **F63.08**
(3) The following provisions only of Part 29 apply –
(a) rule 29.3(2) (legal representatives to attend case management conferences);
(b) rule 29.4 (the court's approval of agreed proposals for the management of
proceedings); and
(c) rule 29.5 (variation of case management timetable) with the exception of
paragraph (1)(b) and (c).
(4) As soon as practicable the court will hold a case management conference which
must be fixed in accordance with Practice Direction 63.

RULE 9—DISCLOSURE AND INSPECTION

Disclosure and inspection

F63.09   **63.9** Part 31 is modified to the extent set out in Practice Direction 63.

RULE 10—APPLICATION TO AMEND A PATENT SPECIFICATION IN EXISTING PROCEEDINGS

Application to amend a patent specification in existing proceedings

F63.10   **63.10**—(1) An application under section 75 of the 1977 Act for permission to amend the specification of a patent by the proprietor of the patent must be made by application notice.

(2) The application notice must –

    (a) give particulars of –

        (i) the proposed amendment sought; and

        (ii) the grounds upon which the amendment is sought;

    (b) state whether the applicant will contend that the claims prior to amendment are valid; and

    (c) be served by the applicant on all parties and the Comptroller within 7 days of its issue.

(3) The application notice must, if it is reasonably possible, be served on the Comptroller electronically.

(4) Unless the court otherwise orders, the Comptroller will forthwith advertise the application to amend in the journal.

(5) The advertisement will state that any person may apply to the Comptroller for a copy of the application notice.

(6) Within 14 days of the first appearance of the advertisement any person who wishes to oppose the application must file and serve on all parties and the Comptroller a notice opposing the application which must include the grounds relied on.

(7) Within 28 days of the first appearance of the advertisement the applicant must apply to the court for directions.

(8) Unless the court otherwise orders, the applicant must within 7 days serve on the Comptroller any order of the court on the application.

(9) In this rule, 'the journal' means the journal published pursuant to rules made under section 123(6) of the 1977 Act.

RULE 11—COURT'S DETERMINATION OF QUESTION OR APPLICATION

Court's determination of question or application

F63.11   **63.11**—(1) This rule applies where the Comptroller–

    (a) declines to deal with a question under section 8(7), 12(2), 37(8) or 61(5) of the 1977 Act;

    (b) declines to deal with an application under section 40(5) of the 1977 Act; or

    (c) certifies under section 72(7)(b) of the 1977 Act that the court should determine the question whether a patent should be revoked.

(2) Any person seeking the court's determination of that question or application must start a claim for that purpose within 14 days of receiving notification of the Comptroller's decision.

(b) A person who fails to start a claim within the time prescribed by rule 63.11(2) will be deemed to have abandoned the reference or application.

(c) A party may apply to the Comptroller or the court to extend the period for starting a claim prescribed by rule 63.11(2) even where the application is made after expiration of that period.

Rule 12—Application by employee for compensation

Application by employee for compensation

63.12—(1) An application by an employee for compensation under section 40(1) or (2) of the 1977 Act must be made –   **F63.12**

(a) in a claim form; and

(b) within the period prescribed by paragraphs (2), (3) and (4).

(2) The prescribed period begins on the date of the grant of the patent and ends 1 year after the patent has ceased to have effect.

(3) Where the patent has ceased to have effect as a result of failure to pay renewal fees, the prescribed period continues as if the patent has remained continuously in effect provided that –

(a) the renewal fee and any additional fee are paid in accordance with section 25(4) of the 1977 Act; or

(b) restoration is ordered by the Comptroller following an application under section 28 of the 1977 Act.

(4) Where restoration is refused by the Comptroller following an application under section 28 of the 1977 Act, the prescribed period will end 1 year after the patent has ceased to have effect or 6 months after the date of refusal, whichever is the later.

II Registered trade marks and other intellectual property rights

Rule 13—Allocation

Allocation

63.13 Claims relating to matters arising out of the 1994 Act and other intellectual property rights set out in Practice Direction 63 must be started in –   **F63.13**

(a) the Chancery Division;

(b) a patents county court; or

(c) save as set out in Practice Direction 63, a county court where there is also a Chancery District Registry.

III Service of documents and participation by the Comptroller

Rule 14—Service of documents

Service of documents

63.14—(1) Subject to paragraph (2), Part 6 applies to service of a claim form and any document in any proceedings under this Part.   **F63.14**

(2) A claim form relating to a registered right may be served –

(a) on a party who has registered the right at the address for service given for that right in the United Kingdom Patent Office register, provided the address is within the United Kingdom; or

(b) in accordance with rule 6.32(1), 6.33(1) or 6.33(2) on a party who has registered the right at the address for service given for that right in the appropriate register at –

        (i) the United Kingdom Patent Office; or

        (ii) the Office for Harmonisation in the Internal Market.

(3) Where a party seeks any remedy (whether by claim form, counterclaim or application notice), which would if granted affect an entry in any United Kingdom Patent Office register, that party must serve on the Comptroller or registrar –

    (a) the claim form, counterclaim or application notice;

    (b) any other statement of case where relevant (including any amended statement of case); and

    (c) any accompanying documents.

Rule 15—Participation by the Comptroller

Participation by the Comptroller

F63.15   **63.15** Where the documents set out in rule 63.14(3) are served, the Comptroller or registrar –

    (a) may take part in proceedings; and

    (b) need not serve a defence or other statement of case unless the court orders otherwise.

IV Appeals

Rule 16—Appeals from decisions of the Comptroller or the registrar

Appeals from decisions of the Comptroller or the registrar

F63.16   **63.16**—(1) Part 52 applies to appeals from decisions of the Comptroller and the registrar.

(2) Appeals about patents must be made to the Patents Court, and other appeals to the Chancery Division.

(3) Where Part 52 requires a document to be served, it must also be served on the Comptroller or registrar, as appropriate.

V Patents Country Court (as inserted by SI 2010/1953)

Rule 17—Scope of this Section

Scope of this Section

F63.17   **63.17** This Part, as modified by this Section, applies to claims started in or transferred to a patents county court.

Rule 18—Transfer of proceedings

Transfer of proceedings

F63.18   **63.18** When considering whether to transfer proceedings to or from a patents county court, the court will have regard to the provisions of Practice Direction 30.

Rule 19—Patents judge

Patents judge

F63.19   **63.19**—(1) Subject to paragraph (2), proceedings in a patents county court will be dealt with by the patents judge of that court.

(2) When a matter needs to be dealt with urgently and it is not practicable or appropriate for the patents judge to deal with it, the matter may be dealt with by another judge with appropriate specialist experience nominated by the Chancellor of the High Court.

Rule 20—Statements of case

Statements of case

63.20—(1) Part 16 applies with the modification that a statement of case must set out concisely all the facts and arguments upon which the party serving it relies. **F63.20**

(2) The particulars of claim must state whether the claimant has complied with paragraph 7.1(1) and Annex A (paragraph 2) of the Practice Direction (Pre-Action Conduct).

Rule 21—Statement of truth

Statement of truth

63.21 Part 22 applies with the modification that the statement of truth verifying a statement of case must be signed by a person with knowledge of the facts alleged, or if no one person has knowledge of all the facts, by persons who between them have knowledge of all the facts alleged. **F63.21**

Rule 22—Defence and reply

Defence and reply

63.22—(1) Rule 63.7 does not apply and Part 15 applies with the following modifications. **F63.22**

(2) Where the particulars of claim contain a confirmation in accordance with rule 63.20(2), the period for filing a defence is 42 days after service of the particulars of claim unless rule 15.4(2) provides for a longer period to do so.

(3) Where the particulars of claim do not contain a confirmation in accordance with rule 63.20(2), the period for filing a defence is 70 days after service of the particulars of claim.

(4) Where the claimant files a reply to a defence it must be filed and served on all other parties within 28 days of service of the defence.

(5) Where the defendant files a reply to a defence to a counterclaim it must be filed and served on all other parties within 14 days of service of the defence to the counterclaim.

(6) The periods in this rule may only be extended by order of the court and for good reason.

Rule 23—Case management

Case management

63.23—(1) At the first case management conference after those defendants who intend to file and serve a defence have done so, the court will identify the issues and decide whether to make an order in accordance with paragraph 29.1 of Practice Direction 63. **F63.23**

(2) Save in exceptional circumstances the court will not consider an application by a party to submit material in addition to that ordered under paragraph (1).

(3) The court may determine the claim on the papers where all parties consent.

Rule 24—Disclosure and inspection

Disclosure and inspection

63.24—(1) Rule 63.9 does not apply. **F63.24**

(2) Part 31 applies save that the provisions on standard disclosure do not apply.

RULE 25—APPLICATIONS

Applications

F63.25 63.25—(1) Part 23 applies with the modifications set out in this rule.

(2) Except at the case management conference provided for in rule 63.23(1), a respondent to an application must file and serve on all relevant parties a response within 5 days of the service of the application notice.

(3) The court will deal with an application without a hearing unless the court considers it necessary to hold a hearing.

(4) An application to transfer the claim to the High Court or to stay proceedings must be made before or at the case management conference provided for in rule 63.23(1).

(5) The court will consider an application to transfer the claim later in the proceedings only where there are exceptional circumstances.

RULE 26—COSTS

Costs

F63.26 63.26—(1) Subject to paragraph (2), the court will reserve the costs of an application to the conclusion of the trial when they will be subject to summary assessment.

(2) Where a party has behaved unreasonably the court will make an order for costs at the conclusion of the hearing.

(3) Where the court makes a summary assessment of costs, it will do so in accordance with Section VII of Part 45.

PRACTICE DIRECTION—PATENTS AND OTHER INTELLECTUAL PROPERTY CLAIMS

1.1 CONTENTS OF THIS PRACTICE DIRECTION

F63PD.01 This practice direction is divided into five sections –

- Section I – Provisions about patents and those other rights within the scope of Section I of Part 63
- Section II – Provisions about registered trade marks and other intellectual property rights
- Section III – Provisions about appeals
- Section IV – Provisions about final orders
- Section V – Provisions about proceedings in a patents county court

SECTION 1—PROVISIONS ABOUT PATENTS AND THOSE OTHER RIGHTS WITHIN THE SCOPE OF SECTION I OF PART 63

Practice Direction 63.2—Scope of Section I

Scope of Section I

F63PD.02 2.1 This Section applies to claims within the scope of Section 1 of Part 63.

Practice Direction 63.3—Starting the claim (rule 63.5)

Starting the claim (rule 63.5)

F63PD.03 3.1 A claim form to which this Section applies must –

(a) be marked 'Chancery Division Patents Court' or 'Patents County Court' as the case may be, in the top right hand corner below the title of the court, and

(b) state the number of any patent or registered design to which the claim relates.

Practice Direction 63.4—Claim for infringement or challenge to validity (rule 63.6)

Claim for infringement or challenge to validity (rule 63.6)

4.1 In a claim for infringement of a patent –   **F63PD.04**

(1) the statement of case must –

(a) show which of the claims in the specification of the patent are alleged to be infringed; and

(b) give at least one example of each type of infringement alleged; and

(2) a copy of each document referred to in the statement of case, and where necessary a translation of the document, must be served with the statement of case.

4.2 Where the validity of a patent or registered design is challenged –

(1) the statement of case must contain particulars of –

(a) the remedy sought; and

(b) the issues except those relating to validity of the patent or registered design;

(2) the statement of case must have a separate document attached to and forming part of it headed 'Grounds of Invalidity' which must –

(a) specify the grounds on which validity of the patent or registered design is challenged; and

(b) include particulars that will clearly define every issue (including any challenge to any claimed priority date) which it is intended to raise; and

(3) a copy of each document referred to in the Grounds of Invalidity, and where necessary a translation of the document, must be served with the Grounds of Invalidity.

4.3 Where in an application in which the validity of a patent or a registered design is challenged, the Grounds of Invalidity include an allegation –

(1) that the invention is not a patentable invention because it is not new or does not include an inventive step, the particulars must specify details of the matter in the state of the art relied on, as set out in paragraph 4.4;

(2) that the specification of the patent does not disclose the invention clearly enough and completely enough for it to be performed by a person skilled in the art, the particulars must state, if appropriate, which examples of the invention cannot be made to work and in which respects they do not work or do not work as described in the specification; or

(3) that the registered design is not new or lacks individual character, the particulars must specify details of any prior design relied on, as set out in paragraph 4.4.

4.4 The details required under paragraphs 4.3(1) and 4.3(3) are–

(1) in the case of matter or a design made available to the public by written description, the date on which and the means by which it was so made available, unless this is clear from the fact of the matter; and

(2) in the case of matter or a design made available to the public by use –

(a) the date or dates of such use;

(b) the name of all persons making such use;

(c) the place of such use;

(d) any written material which identifies such use;

(e) the existence and location of any apparatus employed in such use; and

(f) all facts and matters relied on to establish that such matter was made available to the public.

4.5 In any proceedings in which the validity of a patent is challenged, where a party alleges that machinery or apparatus was used before the priority date of the claim the court may order inspection of that machinery or apparatus.

4.6 If the validity of a patent is challenged on the ground that the invention did not involve an inventive step, a party who wishes to rely on the commercial success of the patent must state in the statement of case the grounds on which that party so relies.

Practice Direction 63.5—Case management (rule 63.8)

Case management (rule 63.8)

F63PD.05 5.1 The following parts only of the practice direction supplementing Part 29 apply –
(1) paragraph 5 (case management conferences) –
(a) excluding paragraph 5.9; and
(b) modified so far as is made necessary by other specific provisions of this practice direction; and
(2) paragraph 7 (failure to comply with case management directions).
5.2 Case management shall be dealt with by –
(1) a judge of the Patents Court, a patents judge or a Master, but
(2) a Master may only deal with the following matters –
(a) orders by way of settlement, except settlement of procedural disputes;
(b) applications for extension of time;
(c) applications for permission to serve out of the jurisdiction;
(d) applications for security for costs;
(e) other matters as directed by a judge of the court; and
(f) enforcement of money judgments.
5.3 The claimant must apply for a case management conference within 14 days of the date when all defendants who intend to file and serve a defence have done so.
5.4 Where the claim has been transferred, the claimant must apply for a case management conference within 14 days of the date of the order transferring the claim, unless the court held or gave directions for a case management conference when it made the order transferring the claim.
5.5 Any party may, at a time earlier than that provided in paragraphs 5.3 and 5.4, apply in writing to the court to fix a case management conference.
5.6 If the claimant does not make an application in accordance with paragraphs 5.3 and 5.4, any other party may apply for a case management conference.
5.7 The court may fix a case management conference at any time on its own initiative.
5.8 Not less than 4 days before a case management conference, each party must file and serve an application notice for any order which that party intends to seek at the case management conference.
5.9 Unless the court orders otherwise, the claimant, or the party who makes an application under paragraph 5.6, in consultation with the other parties, must prepare a case management bundle containing –
(1) the claim form;
(2) all other statements of case (excluding schedules), except that, if a summary of a statement of case has been filed, the bundle must contain the summary, and not the full statement of case;
(3) a pre-trial timetable, if one has been agreed or ordered;
(4) the principal orders of the court; and
(5) any agreement in writing made by the parties as to disclosure, and provide copies of the case management bundle for the court and the other parties at least 4 days before the first case management conference or any earlier hearing at which the court may give case management directions.
5.10 At the case management conference the court may direct that –
(1) a scientific adviser under section 70(3) of the Senior Courts Act 1981 or under section 63(1) of the County Courts Act 1984 be appointed; and
(2) a document setting out basic undisputed technology should be prepared.
(Rule 35.15 applies to scientific advisers)

5.11 Where a trial date has not been fixed by the court, a party may apply for a trial date by filing a certificate which must –

(1) state the estimated length of the trial, agreed if possible by all parties;

(2) detail the time required for the judge to consider the documents;

(3) identify the area of technology; and

(4) assess the complexity of the technical issues involved by indicating the complexity on a scale of 1 to 5 (with 1 being the least and 5 the most complex).

5.12 The claimant, in consultation with the other parties, must revise and update the documents, referred to in paragraph 5.9 appropriately as the case proceeds. This must include making all necessary revisions and additions at least 7 days before any subsequent hearing at which the court may give case management directions.

Practice Direction 63.6—Disclosure and inspection (rule 63.9)

Disclosure and inspection (rule 63.9)

6.1 Standard disclosure does not require the disclosure of documents that relate to –   **F63PD.06**

(1) the infringement of a patent by a product or process where –

(a) not less than 21 days before the date for service of a list of documents the defendant notifies the claimant and any other party of the defendant's intention to serve –

(i) full particulars of the product or process alleged to infringe; and

(ii) any necessary drawings or other illustrations; and

(b) on or before the date for service the defendant serves on the claimant and any other party the documents referred to in paragraph 6.1(1)(a);

(2) any ground on which the validity of a patent is put in issue, except documents which came into existence within the period –

(a) beginning two years before the earliest claimed priority date; and

(b) ending two years after that date; and

(3) the issue of commercial success.

6.2 The particulars served under paragraph 6.1(1)(b) must be accompanied by a signed written statement which must state that the person making the statement –

(1) is personally acquainted with the facts to which the particulars relate;

(2) verifies that the particulars are a true and complete description of the product or process alleged to infringe; and

(3) understands that he or she may be required to attend court in order to be cross-examined on the contents of the particulars.

6.3 Where the issue of commercial success arises, the patentee must, within such time limit as the court may direct, serve a schedule containing –

(1) where the commercial success relates to an article or product –

(a) an identification of the article or product (for example by product code number) which the patentee asserts has been made in accordance with the claims of the patent;

(b) a summary by convenient periods of sales of any such article or product;

(c) a summary for the equivalent periods of sales, if any, of any equivalent prior article or product marketed before the article or product in sub-paragraph (a); and

(d) a summary by convenient periods of any expenditure on advertising and promotion which supported the marketing of the articles or products in sub-paragraphs (a) and (c); or

(2) where the commercial success relates to the use of a process –

(a) an identification of the process which the patentee asserts has been used in accordance with the claims of the patent;

(b) a summary by convenient periods of the revenue received from the use of such process;

(c) a summary for the equivalent periods of the revenues, if any, received from the use of any equivalent prior art process; and

(d) a summary by convenient periods of any expenditure which supported the use of the process in sub-paragraphs (a) and (c).

Practice Direction 63.7—Experiments

Experiments

F63PD.07   7.1 A party seeking to establish any fact by experimental proof conducted for the purpose of litigation must, at least 21 days before service of the application notice for directions under paragraph 7.3, or within such other time as the court may direct, serve on all parties a notice –

(1) stating the facts which the party seeks to establish; and

(2) giving full particulars of the experiments proposed to establish them.

7.2 A party served with a notice under paragraph 7.1 –

(1) must within 21 days after such service, serve on the other party a notice stating whether or not each fact is admitted; and

(2) may request the opportunity to inspect a repetition of all or a number of the experiments identified in the notice served under paragraph 7.1.

7.3 Where any fact which a party seeks to establish by experimental proof is not admitted, that party must apply to the court for permission and directions by application notice.

Practice Direction 63.8—Use of models or apparatus

Use of models or apparatus

F63PD.08   8.1 A party that intends to rely on any model or apparatus must apply to the court for directions at the first case management conference.

Practice Direction 63.9—Time estimates for trial, trial bundle, reading guide and detailed trial timetable

Time estimates for trial, trial bundle, reading guide and detailed trial timetable

F63PD.09   9.1 Not less than one week before the beginning of the trial, each party must inform the court in writing of the estimated length of its –

(1) oral submissions;

(2) examination in chief, if any, of its own witnesses; and

(3) cross-examination of witnesses of any other party.

9.2 At least four days before the date fixed for the trial, the claimant must file –

(1) the trial bundle; and

(2) a reading guide for the judge; and

(3) a detailed trial timetable which should be agreed, if possible.

9.3 The reading guide filed under paragraph 9.2 must –

(1) be short and, if possible, agreed;

(2) set out the issues, the parts of the documents that need to be read on each issue and the most convenient order in which they should be read;

(3) identify the relevant passages in text books and cases, if appropriate; and

(4) not contain argument.

Practice Direction 63.10—Application to amend a patent specification in existing proceedings (rule 63.10)

Application to amend a patent specification in existing proceedings (rule 63.10)

F63PD.10   10.1 Where the application notice is served on the Comptroller electronically under rule

63.10(3), the applicant must comply with any requirements for the sending of electronic communications to the Comptroller.

10.2 Not later than two days before the first hearing date the applicant, the Comptroller if wishing to be heard, the parties to the proceedings and any other opponent, must file and serve a document stating the directions sought.

Practice Direction 63.11—Request to limit a European patent (UK) under the European Patent Convention

Request to limit a European patent (UK) under the European Patent Convention

11.1 Paragraphs 11.2 to 11.4 apply where there are proceedings before the court in which the validity of a European patent (UK) may be put in issue. **F63PD.11**

11.2 Where the proprietor of the European patent (UK) intends to file a request under Article 105a of the European Patent Convention to limit the European patent (UK) by amendment of the claims, the proprietor must serve on all the parties to the proceedings a copy of the intended request (including a copy of the intended complete version of the amended claims and, as the case may be, of the amended description and drawings) at least 28 days prior to filing the request with the European Patent Office.

11.3 Where a copy of an intended request is served on the party in accordance with paragraph 11.2, any party may apply to the court for such directions or other order as may be appropriate.

11.4 Reference to 'European Patent Convention' means the Convention on the Grant of European Patents of 5th October 1973 as amended from time to time.

Practice Direction 63.12—Application by employee for compensation (rule 63.12)

Application by employee for compensation (rule 63.12)

12.1 Where an employee applies for compensation under section 40(1) or (2) of the 1977 Act, the court will at the case management conference give directions as to – **F63PD.12**

(1) the manner in which the evidence, including any accounts of expenditure and receipts relating to the claim, is to be given at the hearing of the claim and if written evidence is to be given, specify the period within which witness statements must be filed; and

(2) the provision to the claimant by the defendant or a person deputed by the defendant, of reasonable facilities for inspecting and taking extracts from the accounts by which the defendant proposes to verify the accounts in sub-paragraph (1) or from which those accounts have been derived.

Practice Direction 63.13—Communication of information to the European Patent Office

Communication of information to the European Patent Office

13.1 The court may authorise the communication of any such information in the court files as the court thinks fit to – **F63PD.13**

(1) the European Patent Office; or

(2) the competent authority of any country which is a party to the European Patent Convention.

13.2 Before authorising the communication of information under paragraph 13.1, the court will permit any party who may be affected by the disclosure to make representations, in writing or otherwise, on the question of whether the information should be disclosed.

Practice Direction 63.14—Order affecting entry in the register of patents or designs

Order affecting entry in the register of patents or designs

14.1 Where any order of the court affects the validity of an entry in the register, the **F63PD.14** party in whose favour the order is made, must serve a copy of such order on the Comptroller within 14 days.

14.2 Where the order is in favour of more than one party, a copy of the order must be served by such party as the court directs.

Practice Direction 63.15—European Community designs

European Community designs

F63PD.15

15.1 The Patents Court and the patents county court at the Central London County Court are the designated Community design courts under Article 80(5) of Council Regulation (EC) 6/2002..

15.2 Where a counterclaim is filed at the Community design court, for a declaration of invalidity of a registered Community design, the Community design court will inform the Office for Harmonisation in the Internal Market of the date on which the counterclaim was filed, in accordance with Article 86(2) of Council Regulation (EC) 6/2002.

15.3 On filing a counterclaim under paragraph 15.2, the party filing it must inform the Community design court in writing that it is a counterclaim to which paragraph 15.2 applies and that the Office for Harmonisation in the Internal Market needs to be informed of the date on which the counterclaim was filed.

15.4 Where a Community design court has given a judgment which has become final on a counterclaim for a declaration of invalidity of a registered Community design, the Community design court will send a copy of the judgment to the Office for Harmonisation in the Internal Market, in accordance with Article 86(4) of Council Regulation (EC) 6/2002.

15.5 The party in whose favour judgment is given under paragraph 15.4 must inform the Community design court at the time of judgment that paragraph 15.4 applies and that the Office for Harmonisation in the Internal Market needs to be sent a copy of the judgment.

SECTION II—PROVISIONS ABOUT REGISTERED TRADE MARKS AND OTHER
INTELLECTUAL PROPERTY RIGHTS

Practice Direction 63.16—Allocation (rule 63.13)

Allocation (rule 63.13)

F63PD.16

16.1 The other intellectual property rights referred to in rule 63.13 are –

(1) copyright;

(2) rights in performances;

(3) rights conferred under Part VII of the 1988 Act;

(4) design right;

(5) Community design right;

(6) association rights;

(7) moral rights;

(8) database rights;

(9) unauthorised decryption rights;

(10) hallmarks;

(11) technical trade secrets litigation;

(12) passing off;

(13) protected designations of origin, protected geographical indications and traditional speciality guarantees;

(14) registered trade marks; and

(15) Community trade marks.

16.2 There are Chancery district registries at Birmingham, Bristol, Caernarfon, Cardiff, Leeds, Liverpool, Manchester, Mold, Newcastle upon Tyne and Preston.

16.3 The county courts at Caernarfon, Mold and Preston do not have jurisdiction in relation to registered trade marks and Community trade marks.

Note. Rules 17.1–24.1 are outside the scope of this work and are not here reproduced.

SECTION III—PROVISIONS ABOUT APPEALS

Practice Direction 63.25—Reference to the court by an appointed person

Reference to the court by an appointed person

25.1 This paragraph applies where a person appointed by the Lord Chancellor to hear and decide appeals under section 77 of the 1994 Act, refers an appeal to the Chancery Division under section 76(3) of the 1994 Act.

F63PD.25

25.2 The appellant must file a claim form seeking the court's determination of the appeal within 14 days of receiving notification of the decision to refer.

25.3 The appeal will be deemed to have been abandoned if the appellant does not file a claim form within the period prescribed by paragraph 25.2.

25.4 The period prescribed under paragraph 25.2 may be extended by –

(1) the person appointed by the Lord Chancellor; or

(2) the court

where the appellant so applies, even if such application is not made until after the expiration of that period.

SECTION IV—PROVISIONS ABOUT FINAL ORDERS

Practice Direction 63.26—Costs

Costs

26.1 Where the court makes an order for delivery up or destruction of infringing goods, or articles designed or adapted to make such goods, the person against whom the order is made must pay the costs of complying with that order unless the court orders otherwise.

F63PD.26

26.2 Where the court finds that an intellectual property right has been infringed, the court may, at the request of the applicant, order appropriate measures for the dissemination and publication of the judgment to be taken at the expense of the infringer.

SECTION V—PROVISIONS ABOUT PROCEEDINGS IN A PATENTS COUNTY COURT

Practice Direction 63.27—Scope of Section V

Scope of Section V

27.1 Except as provided for in paragraph 27.2 this Practice Direction, as modified by this Section, applies to claims in a patents county court.

F63PD.27

27.2 Paragraphs 5.10 to 9.1 and paragraph 9.2(3) do not apply to a claim in a patents county court.

Practice Direction 63.28—Claims for infringement or challenge to validity

Claims for infringement or challenge to validity

28.1 Paragraph 4.2(2) is modified so that the grounds for invalidity must be included in the statement of case and not in a separate document.

F63PD.28

Practice Direction 63.29—Case management (rule 63.23)

Case management (rule 63.23)

F63PD.29 29.1 At the case management conference referred to in rule 63.23 the court may order any of the following—

(1) specific disclosure;

(2) a product or process description (or a supplementary product or process description where one has already been provided);

(3) experiments;

(4) witness statements;

(5) experts' reports;

(6) cross examination at trial;

(7) written submissions or skeleton arguments.

29.2 The court will make an order under paragraph 29.1 only —

(1) in relation to specific and identified issues; and

(2) if the court is satisfied that the benefit of the further material in terms of its value in resolving those issues appears likely to justify the cost of producing and dealing with it.

Practice Direction 63.30—Applications (rule 63.25)

Applications (rule 63.25)

F63PD.30 30.1 Where the court considers that a hearing is necessary under rule 63.25(3) the court will conduct a hearing by telephone or video conference in accordance with paragraphs 6.2 to 7 of Practice Direction 23A unless it considers that a hearing in person would be more cost effective for the parties or is otherwise necessary in the interests of justice.

Practice Direction 63.31—Determination of the claim

Determination of the claim

F63PD.31 31.1 Where possible, the court will determine the claim solely on the basis of the parties' statements of case and oral submissions.

31.2 The court will set the timetable for the trial and will, so far as appropriate, allocate equal time to the parties. Cross-examination will be strictly controlled by the court. The court will endeavour to ensure that the trial lasts no more than 2 days.

PART 45 OF THE CIVIL PROCEDURE RULES

45.01.F45.40 *Note*: Rules 45.01–45.40 are outside the scope of this work and are not here reproduced.

VII Scale costs for claims in a Patents County Court

RULE 41 — SCOPE AND INTERPRETATION

Scope and interpretation

F45.41 **45.41**—(1) Subject to paragraph (2) this Section applies to proceedings in a patents county court.

(2) This Section does not apply where—

(a) the court considers that a party has behaved in a manner which amounts to an abuse of the court's process; or

    (b) the claim concerns the infringement or revocation of a patent or registered design the validity of which has been certified by a court in earlier proceedings.

    (3) The court will make a summary assessment of the costs of the party in whose favour any order for costs is made. Rules 44.3(8), 44.3A(2)(b) and (c), 44.7(b) and Part 47 do not apply to this Section.

    (4) "Scale costs" means costs as defined in rule 43.2(1)(a).

RULE 42—AMOUNT OF SCALE COSTS

Amount of scale costs

45.42—(1) Subject to rule 45.43 the court will not order a party to pay total costs of more than—   **F45.42**

    (a) £50,000 on the final determination of a claim in relation to liability; and

    (b) £25,000 on an inquiry as to damages or account of profits.

    (2) The amounts in paragraph (1) apply after the court has applied the provision on set off in accordance with rule 44.3(9)(a).

    (3) The maximum amount of scale costs that the court will award for each stage of the claim is set out in the Costs Practice Direction.

    (4) The amount of the scale costs awarded by the court in accordance with paragraph (3) will depend on the nature and complexity of the claim.

    (5) Where appropriate, value added tax (VAT) may be recovered in addition to the amount of the scale costs and any reference in this Section to scale costs is a reference to those costs net of any such VAT.

RULE 43—SUMMARY ASSESSMENT OF THE COSTS OF AN APPLICATION WHERE A PARTY HAS BEHAVED UNREASONABLY

Summary assessment of the costs of an application where a party has behaved unreasonably

45.43 Costs awarded to a party under rule 63.26(2) are in addition to the total costs that may be awarded to that party under rule 45.42   **F45.43**

After paragraph 25B.1 of the Practice Directions under CPR Part 45 (not reprinted herein), insert—

PRACTICE DIRECTION—COSTS PRACTICE DIRECTION

Section 25C   **Scale costs for proceedings in a patents county court**

25C.1 Tables A and B set out the maximum amount of scale costs which the court will award for each stage of a claim in a patents county court.   **F45PD.01**

25C.2 Table A sets out the scale costs for each stage of a claim up to determination of liability.

25C.3 Table B sets out the scale costs for each stage of an inquiry as to damages or account of profits.

TABLE A

Stage of a claim	Maximum amount of costs
Particulars of claim	£6,125
Defence and counterclaim	£6,125

Reply and defence to counterclaim	£6,125
Reply to defence to counterclaim	£3,000
Attendance at a case management conference	£2,500
Making or responding to an application	£2,500
Providing or inspecting disclosure or product/process description	£5,000
Performing or inspecting experiments	£2,500
Preparing witness statements	£5,000
Preparing experts' report	£7,500
Preparing for and attending trial and judgment	£15,000
Preparing for determination on the papers	£5,000

TABLE B

Stage of a claim	Maximum amount of costs
Points of claim	£2,500
Points of defence	£2,500
Attendance at a case management conference	£2,500
Making or responding to an application	£2,500
Providing or inspecting disclosure	£2,500
Preparing witness statements	£5,000
Preparing experts' report	£5,000
Preparing for and attending trial and judgment	£7,500
Preparing for determination on the papers	£5,000

THE PATENTS COURT AND PATENTS COUNTY COURT GUIDE

Note. The Patents Court and Patents County Court Guide is reproduced below in the form issued on July 7, 2008 by authority of the Chancellor of the High Court, but subsequently amended most recently on February 24, 2010. A separate guide for the Patents County Court, also reproduced below, was issued on May 12, 2011 and should now be used as the primary reference for matters relating to the Patents County Court.

Some sections of the guides have been omitted here, particularly those which summarise provisions of the Civil Procedure Rules which may be found at Appendix F.

The full guides are available at *http://www.justice.gov.uk/downloads/guidance/courts-and-tribunals/courts/patents-court/patents__court__guide.pdf* and *http://www.justice.gov.uk/downloads/guidance/courts-and-tribunals/courts/patents-court/patents-court-guide.pdf* respectively. The website *http://www.justice.gov.uk* should be checked for any more recent updating of the guides.

The two guides reproduced here refer to the Chancery Guide which may be found at *http://www.justice.gov.uk/guidance/courts-and-tribunals/courts/chancery-division/*.

Since the guides were last issued or amended a number of important changes have occurred:

(i) Both the Patents Court (as part of the Chancery Division) and the Patents County Court have moved to the Rolls Building, 7 Rolls Buildings, London, EC4A 1NL.

(ii) It is understood that the telephone numbers listed in the guides are unchanged following the move.

(iii) From June 14 2011, claims issued in the Patents County Court under the special jurisdiction are subject to a damages cap of £500,000 by virtue of the Patents County Court (Financial Limits) Order 2011 (SI 2011/1402).

(iv) From October 1, 2011, claims issued in the Patents County Court under the ordinary jurisdiction are subject to a damages cap of £500,000 by virtue of the Patents County Court (Financial Limits) (No.2) Order 2011 (SI 2011/2222).

The Patents Court and Patents County Court Guide

Issued July 7, 2008 (Revised 24 February 2010)
By authority of the Chancellor of the High Court

CONTENTS

GENERAL

GENERAL

1. INTRODUCTION

G01   This guide applies to both the Patents Court and the Patents County Court.

The general guidance applicable to matters in the Chancery Division, as set out in the Chancery Guide also applies to patent actions unless specifically mentioned below. "63PD" refers to the Practice Direction—Patents and Other Intellectual Property Claims which supplements CPR Part 63. Thus practitioners should consult this guide together with the Chancery Guide.

2. ALLOCATION

G02   Actions proceeding in the Patents Court and the Patents County Court are allocated to the multi-track (Part 63.1(3)). Attention is drawn to Part 63.7 and 63PD.4 (case management).

3. THE JUDGES OF THE PATENTS COURT

G03   Kitchin J (Clerk: Don Bennett—tel 020 7947 6518, fax 020 7947 6439, (*Donald.Bennett@hmcourts-service.gsi.gov.uk*)—Senior Patents judge

Lewison J (Clerk: Olivia Tanner—tel 020 7947 6039, fax 020 7947 6894, (*Olivia.Tanner@hmcourts-service.gsi.gov.uk*)

Mann J (Clerk: Patricia Swales—tel 020 7947 7964, fax 020 7947 6739, (*Patricia.Swales@hmcourts-service.gsi.gov.uk*)

Warren J (Clerk: Elizabeth Collum—tel 020 7947 7260, fax 020 7947 7740, (*Elizabeth.Collum2@hmcourts-service.gsi.gov.uk*)

Floyd J (Clerk: Alison Hall—tel 020 7073 1740, fax 020 7947 6593, (*Alison.Hall@hmcourts-service.gsi.gov.uk*)

Arnold J (Clerk: Alison Lee—tel 020 7073 1789, fax 020 7947 6719, (*Alison.Lee2@hmcourts-service.gsi.gov.uk*)

Morgan J (Clerk: Heather Watson—tel 020 7947 6419, fax 020 7947 6062, (*Heather.Watson@hmcourts-service.gsi.gov.uk*)

Norris J (Clerk: Peter Bucknole—tel 020 7073 1728, fax 020 7947 6649, (*Peter.Bucknole@hmcourts-service.gsi.gov.uk*)

Trials of cases with a technical difficulty rating of 4 or 5 will normally be heard by Kitchin J, Floyd J or Arnold J.

4. Patents County Court

[*Not reproduced—see the separate Patents County Court Guide below.*] **G04**

5. Judges able and willing to sit out of London

If the parties so desire, for the purpose of saving time or costs, the Patents Court and Patents **G05**
County Court will sit out of London. Before any approach is made to the Chancery Listing Officer,
the parties should discuss between themselves the desirability of such a course. If there is a dispute
as to venue, the court will resolve the matter on an application. Where there is no dispute, the
Chancery Listing Officer should be contacted as soon as possible so that arrangements can be put in
place well before the date of the proposed hearing.

6. Intellectual Property Court Users' Committee

[*Not reproduced.*] **G06**

PROCEDURE IN THE PATENTS COURT AND PATENTS COUNTY COURT

7. Statements of Case

Time Limits

7.1 In general, the time limits set out in Part 15 apply to litigation of patents and **G07**
registered designs. However, rule 63.7 modifies Part 15 in respect of the time limits for filing defences and replies.

Content of statements of case

7.2 In general, statements of case (i.e. the pleadings of all parties) must comply with the
requirements of Part 16. Furthermore, they should comply with rule 63.6 and PD63 paras.
4.1–4.6. Copies of important documents referred to in a statement of case (e.g. an
advertisement referred to in a claim of infringement form or documents cited in Grounds
of Invalidity) should be served with the statement of case. Where any such document
requires translation, a translation should be served at the same time.

Independent validity of claims

7.3 Where one party raises the issue of validity of a patent, the patentee (or other relevant party) should identify which of the claims of the patent are alleged to have independent validity as early as possible.

8. Active case management and streamlined procedure

8.1 The claimants should apply for a case management conference ("CMC") within 14 **G08**
days of the date when all defendants who intend to file and serve a defence have done so
(PD63 para.5.3) [Appendix F]. If the claimants fail to do so, then any other party may apply for a CMC (PD63 para.5.5). Any party may apply in writing for a CMC prior to the
above periods. Where a case has been transferred from another division or from another
court, the claimants must file for a CMC within 14 days of the transfer (PD63 para.5.4).

8.2 Almost invariably CMCs in the Patents Court will be conducted by a judge.
However, in the limited circumstances set out in PD63 para.5.2 (see also para.16 below), a
Master may conduct a CMC. Bundles in accordance with PD63 para.5.9 should be filed
with the court. In the Patents County Court, all CMCs are conducted by the judge of the
Patents County Court and not by a district judge.

8.3 In general, parties should endeavour to agree directions prior to the date fixed for the
CMC. Although the court has the right to amend directions which have been agreed, this
will only happen where there is manifest reason for doing so.

8.4 In accordance with the overriding objective, the court will actively manage the case. In making any order for directions, the court will consider all relevant matters and have regard to the overriding objective with particular emphasis on proportionality, the financial position of the parties, the degree of complexity of the case, the importance of the case and the amount of money at stake.

8.5 The parties are reminded of their continuing obligation to assist the court to further the overriding objective. Moreover, it is the duty of the parties' advisors to remind litigants of the existence of mediation or other forms of alternative dispute resolution as a possible means to resolve disputes. In particular, the parties should consider:

(a) The need for and/or scope of any oral testimony from factual or expert witnesses. The court may confine cross-examination to particular issues and to time limits. The parties should consider whether oral testimony of witnesses should be given by video facility.

(b) The need for, and scope of, any disclosure of documents.

(c) The need for any experiments, process or product descriptions.

(d) The need for an oral hearing or whether a decision can be made on the papers. If an oral hearing is considered to be appropriate, the court may order that the hearing be of a fixed duration.

(e) Whether there is a need for a document setting out the basic undisputed technology ("technical primer"), and if so, its scope and the steps to be taken to achieve agreement of it.

(f) Whether a scientific adviser should be appointed.

(g) Whether a costs-capping order should be made.

(h) Whether there should be a stay of proceedings for mediation or other form of alternative dispute resolution.

Streamlined procedure

8.6 Any party may at any time apply to the court for a streamlined procedure in which:

(a) all factual and expert evidence is in writing;

(b) there is no requirement to give disclosure of documents;

(c) there are no experiments;

(d) cross-examination is only permitted on any topic or topics where it is necessary and is confined to those topics;

or for any variant on the above.

8.7 Prior to applying for a streamlined procedure, the party seeking it should put its proposal to other parties in the proceedings and should endeavour to agree a form of order.

8.8 If the parties agree to a streamlined procedure, the proposed form of order should be put to the judge for approval as a paper application.

9. ADMISSIONS

G09   *[Not reproduced.]*

10. ALTERNATIVE DISPUTE RESOLUTION ("ADR")

G10   *[Not reproduced.]*

11. DISCLOSURE

G11   11.1 Parties are obliged to provide disclosure in accordance with Part 31 as modified by rule 63.9 and PD63 paras 6.1–6.3

Process and Product Descriptions

11.2 Where appropriate, parties are encouraged to provide a Process and/or Product Description ("PPD") instead of standard disclosure relating to processes or products which are alleged to infringe or are otherwise relevant to proceedings.

11.3 PPDs must be adequate to deal with the nature of the allegation that has been advanced by the other party or parties. The parties have joint responsibility at an early stage to determine the nature of the case advanced so that the PPD is adequate to deal with that case.

11.4 Parties should bear in mind when preparing a PPD that it must be verified by a statement in accordance with PD63 para.6.2 and that they may be called on to prove it at trial. Any material omission or inaccuracy could result in a costly adjournment with consequential adverse orders, including as to costs.

Descriptions and drawings of processes or products

11.5 Parties are encouraged to agree descriptions and drawings of processes and/or products which are the subject of infringement proceedings or are alleged to constitute relevant prior art.

Models or apparatus of processes or products

11.6 If a party wishes to adduce a model or apparatus at trial, it should, if practicable, ensure that directions for such are given at the first CMC (PD63 para.8.1). Parties should endeavour to view and agree the accuracy of such models or apparatus where possible well in advance of the date of trial.

GENERAL MATTERS RELATING TO HEARINGS OF APPLICATIONS AND TRIALS

12. ARRANGEMENTS FOR LISTING

12.1 The Chancery Listing Officer is responsible for the listing of all work of the Patents **G12** Court and the Patents County Court.

12.2 The Chancery Listing Officer and his staff are located in Room WG04 in the Royal Courts of Justice. The office is open to the public from 10.00 am to 4.30 pm each day. The telephone numbers are 020 7947 6778/6690 and the fax number is 020 7947 7345.

12.3 Appointments to fix trials and interim applications are dealt with on Tuesdays and Thursdays between 11.00 am and 12.00 noon. The applicant should first obtain an appointment from the Chancery Listing Officer and give 3 clear days' notice to all interested parties of the date and time fixed.

12.4 A party should not seek to list an application or cause the opposing advocate or counsel's clerk to "pencil in" a date for hearing prior to raising with the proposed respondent the subject-matter of the application so that, where possible, agreement may be reached on the subject-matter of the application. Applicants who fail properly to consult with the respondents prior to listing an application may be met with an adverse costs order.

Short applications

12.5 Short applications (i.e. those estimated to last no more than 1 hour) will usually be heard before the normal court day starts at 10.30 am, e.g. 9.30 or 10 am. These can be issued and the hearing date arranged at any time by attendance at the Chancery Listing Office. Attention is drawn to 63PD.6 about the filing of documents and skeleton arguments.

Urgent applications and Without Notice applications

12.6 A party wishing to apply without notice to the respondent(s) should contact the Chancery Listing Office. In cases of emergency in vacation or out of normal court hours, the application should be made to the duty Chancery judge.

September sittings

12.7 The Patents Court and Patents County Court will endeavour, if the parties so desire and the case is urgent, to sit in September.

Interim injunction hearings and expedited trials

12.8 Applicants for interim remedies (in particular, interim injunctions) and respondents are encouraged to consider whether an expedited (speedy) trial would better meet the interests of justice. Applications for expedited trials may be made at any time but should be made as soon as possible and notice given to all parties.

12.9 When an application for an interim injunction is made the applicant should, where practicable, make prior investigations with the Chancery Listing Officer about trial dates on an unexpedited and expedited basis having regard to the estimated length of trial.

13. Time estimates

G13   13.1 In providing appropriate time estimates, parties must appreciate the need to give realistic and accurate time estimates and ensure that the time estimate includes a discrete reading time for the court to read the papers prior to the hearing of the application or trial. In general, the court will wish to read the skeleton arguments, the patent (where relevant), the prior art (where relevant), expert reports and other key documents (e.g. important witness statements). Advisors should bear in mind the technical difficulty of the case when considering the reading time estimate. The court will consider the imposition of guillotines where time estimates are exceeded.

Revised time estimates

13.2 Where parties and their legal advisors consider that a time estimate that has been provided (e.g. at the CMC) is unrealistic, they have a duty to notify the new time estimate to the Chancery Listing Office or, where appropriate, the judge's clerk as soon as possible.

14. Documents and timetable

G14   14.1 Bundling for the hearing of applications and trials is of considerable importance and should be approached intelligently. The general guidance given in Appendix 6 of the Chancery Guide should be followed. Solicitors or patent attorneys who fail to do so may be required to explain why and may be penalised personally in costs.

14.2 If it is known which judge will be taking the hearing, papers for the hearing should be lodged directly with that judge's clerk. If there is insufficient time to lodge hard copies before the deadline, faxed documents of significance (and particularly skeleton arguments) should be supplied, followed up by clean hard copies. Alternatively to faxing documents, by agreement, documents may be sent by e-mail to the clerk of the judge concerned.

14.3 It is the responsibility of both parties to ensure that all relevant documents are lodged with the clerk of the judge who will be taking the hearing by noon two days before the date fixed for hearing unless some longer or shorter period has been ordered by the judge or is prescribed by this guide.

14.4 The judges request that all important documents also be supplied to them on disk or via e-mail in a format convenient for the judge's use (normally the current or a recent version of Microsoft Word 2003 for Windows or as a text searchable pdf). These will usually include skeleton arguments, important patents and drawings, the witness statements and expert reports.

14.5 Prior to trial, parties should ensure that they comply with the requirements of 63PD.7 concerning the provision of a trial timetable, trial bundle and reading guide for the judge. The trial timetable should be detailed and set out the times and dates that witnesses will be required to give evidence.

14.6 Where a technical primer has been produced, the parties should identify those parts which are agreed to form part of the common general knowledge. Usually, this should be done shortly after exchange of experts reports but a reasonable time prior to trial.

14.7 Skeleton arguments should be lodged in time for the judge to read them before an application or trial.

(a) In the case of applications, this should normally be 10:30 am the previous working day (or, in the case of short applications, 3pm)

(b) In the case of trials, this should normally be at least two working days before commencement of the trial. In substantial cases, a longer period (to be discussed with the clerk to the judge concerned) may be needed.

14.8 Following the evidence in a substantial trial, a short adjournment may be granted to enable the parties to summarise their arguments in writing before oral argument.

Transcripts

14.9 In trials where a transcript of evidence is being made and supplied to the judge, the transcript should be supplied by e-mail and in hard copy.

15. TELEPHONE APPLICATIONS

15.1 For short (20 minutes or less) matters, the judges of the Patents Court and Patents **G15** County Court are willing to hear applications by telephone conference in accordance with the Practice Direction under Part 23. The party making the application is responsible for setting up the telephone application and informing the parties, Counsels' clerks and Chancery Listing of the time of the conference call.

15.2 It is possible for the application to be recorded, and if recording by the court rather than by British Telecom (or other service provider) is requested, arrangements should be made with the Chancery Listing Officer. The recording will not be transcribed. The tape will be kept by the clerk to the judge hearing the application for a period of six months. Arrangements for transcription, if needed, must be made by the parties.

15.3 This procedure should be used where it will save costs.

MISCELLANEOUS

16. JURISDICTION OF MASTERS

[Not reproduced.] **G16**

17. CONSENT ORDERS

17.1 The court is normally willing to make consent orders without the need for the at- **G17** tendance of any parties. A draft of the agreed order and the written consent of all the parties' respective solicitors or counsel should be supplied to the Chancery Listing Office. Unless the judge considers a hearing is needed, he will make the order in the agreed terms by initialing it. It will be drawn up accordingly and sent to the parties.

17.2 In the Patents County Court, consent orders should be sent to the judge's clerk or to the Chancery Listing Office.

18. DRAFT JUDGMENTS

[Not reproduced—see CPR PD40E paras 2.1–2.9] **G18**

19. ORDERS FOLLOWING JUDGMENT

19.1 Where a judgment is made available in draft before being given in open court the **G19** parties should, in advance of that occasion, exchange drafts of the desired consequential order. It is highly undesirable that one party should spring a proposal on the other for the first time when judgment is handed down. Where the parties are agreed as to the consequential order and have supplied to the judge a copy of the same signed by all parties or their representatives, attendance at the handing down of the judgment is not necessary.

20. APPEALS FROM THE COMPTROLLER-GENERAL OF PATENTS, DESIGNS AND TRADE MARKS ("THE COMPTROLLER")

Patents

G20   20.1 By virtue of statute, these lie only to the High Court and not the Patents County Court. They are now governed by Part 52 (see rule 63.16). Permission to appeal is not required. Note that the Comptroller must be served with an Appellant's Notice (rule 63.16(3)). The appellant has the conduct of the appeal and he or his representative should, within 2 weeks of lodging the appeal, contact the Chancery Listing Officer with a view to arranging a hearing date. The appellant must ensure that the appeal is set down as soon as is reasonably practicable after service of the notice of appeal. Parties are reminded that the provisions about the service of skeleton arguments apply to appeals from the Comptroller.

Registered Designs

20.2 Appeals in registered designs cases go to the Registered Designs Appeal Tribunal. This consists of one of the patent judges sitting as a tribunal. The CPR and PD do not apply to such appeals. Where such an appeal is desired, contact should be made direct with the Chancery Listing Officer.

Trade Marks

20.3 These are assigned to the Chancery Division as a whole, not the Patents Court (rule 63.16(2)). Permission to appeal is not required.

Appeals on paper only

20.4 The court will hear appeals on paper only if that is what the parties desire. If the appellant is willing for the appeal to be heard on paper only, he should contact the respondent and UKIPO at the earliest opportunity to discover whether such a way of proceeding is agreed. If it is, the Chancery Listing Office should be informed as soon as possible. The parties (and the Chancery Listing Officer if he/she desires) should liaise amongst themselves for early preparation of written submissions and bundles and provide the court with all necessary materials.

SPECIMEN MINUTE OF ORDER FOR DIRECTIONS

G21   A draft order is annexed below covering most normal eventualities. The directions are intended only as a guide and are not "standard directions". Not all paragraphs will be applicable in every case.

FORM OF ORDER FOR DIRECTIONS

[Recitals as necessary including the following, where appropriate]

AND UPON the parties' legal advisors having advised the litigants of the existence of mediation as a possible means of resolving this claim and counterclaim

Transfer

1. [This claim and counterclaim be transferred to the Patents County Court.] (If this order is made, no other order will generally be necessary, though it will generally be desirable for procedural orders to be made at this time to save the costs of a further conference in the Patents County Court.)

Amendments to statements of case

2. The claimants have permission to amend their claim form shown in red on the copy [annexed to the application notice/as signed by the solicitors for the parties/annexed hereto] and [to re-serve the same on or before [date]/and that re-service be dispensed with] and that the defendants have permission to serve a consequentially amended defence within [number] days [thereafter/hereafter] and that the claimants have permission to serve a consequentially amended reply (if so advised) within [number] days thereafter.

3. (a) The defendants have permission to amend their defence and counterclaim [and grounds of invalidity] as shown in red on the copy [annexed to the application notice/as signed by the solicitors for the parties/annexed hereto] and [to re-serve the same within [number] days/on or before[date]] [and that re-service be dispensed with] and that the claimants have permission to serve a consequentially amended reply (if so advised) within [number] days thereafter.

[(b) The claimants do on or before [date] elect whether they will discontinue this claim and withdraw their defence to the amended counterclaim and consent to an order for the revocation of Patent No. .... ("the Patent") AND IF the claimants shall so elect and give notice thereof in the time aforesaid:

    (i) the Patent be revoked;

    (ii) the claimants shall pay the defendant's costs of the claim and counterclaim incurred up to and including [..........] (*date of service of original defence and counterclaim*) which shall include the costs of obtaining and giving effect to the order for revocation; and

    (iii) the defendants shall pay the claimants' costs of the claim and counterclaim incurred thereafter.]

(c) The defendants' [claimants'] costs of and caused by the amendments to the claim form [particulars of claim] [defence and counterclaim] [reply] be the defendants [claimants] in any event.

Further Information and Clarification

5. (a) The [claimants/defendants] do on or before [date] serve on the [defendants/claimants] the further information or clarification of the [specify statement of case] as requested by the [claimants/defendants] by their request served on the [defendants/claimants] on [date] [and/or]

(b) The [claimants/defendants] do on or before [date] serve on the [defendants/claimants] [a response to their request for further information] [do answer the requests in their request for further information] or clarification of the [identify statement of case] served on the [defendants/claimants] on [date].

Admissions

6. The [claimants/defendants] do on or before [date] state in writing whether or not they admit the facts specified in the [defendants'/claimants'] notice to admit facts dated [date].

Security

7. The claimants/defendants do provide security for the defendants'/claimants' costs for its claim/counterclaim in the sum of £[state sum] by [paying such sums into court] [specify manner in which security to be given] and that:

    (i) in the meantime the claim [counterclaim] be stayed [and/or];

    (ii) unless security is given as ordered by the above date, the claim [counterclaim] be struck out without further order with the defendants'/claimants' costs of the claim [counterclaim] to be the subject of detailed assessment if not agreed.

Lists of Documents

8. (a) The claimants and the defendants respectively do on or before [state date] make and serve on the other of them a list in accordance with form N265 of the documents in their possession custody or control which they are required to disclose in accordance with the obligation of standard disclosure in accordance with Part 31 as modified by paragraph 5 of the Practice Direction—Patents etc. supplementing Part 63.

(b) In respect of those issues identified in Schedule [number] hereto disclosure shall be limited to those [documents/categories of documents] listed in Schedule [number].

Inspection

9. If any party wishes to inspect or have copies of such documents as are in another party's control, it shall give notice in writing that it wishes to do so and such inspection shall be allowed at all reasonable times upon reasonable notice and any copies shall be provided within [number] working days of the request upon the undertaking of the party requesting the copies to pay the reasonable copying charges.

Experiments

10. (a) Where a party desires to establish any fact by experimental proof, including an experiment conducted for the purposes of litigation or otherwise not being an experiment conducted in the normal course of research, that party shall on or before [date] serve on all the other parties a notice stating the facts which it desires to establish and giving full particulars of the experiments proposed to establish them.

(b) A party upon whom a notice is served under the preceding sub-paragraph shall within [number] days, serve on the party serving the notice a notice stating in respect of each fact whether or not that party admits it.

(c) Where any fact which a party wishes to establish by experimental proof is not admitted that party shall apply to the court for further directions in respect of such experiments.

[Or where paragraph 9 of the Practice Direction—Patents etc. supplementing CPR Part 63 has been complied with.]

11. (a) The claimants/defendants are to afford to the other parties an opportunity, if so requested, of inspecting a repetition of the experiments identified in paragraphs [specify them] of the notice[s] of experiments served on [date]. Any such inspection must be requested within [number] days of the date of this order and shall take place within [number] days of the date of the request.

(b) If any party shall wish to establish any fact in reply to experimental proof that party shall on or before [date] serve on all the other parties a notice stating the facts which it desires to establish and giving full particulars of the experiments proposed to establish them. (c) A party upon whom a notice is served under the preceding sub-paragraph shall within [number] days serve on the party serving the notice a notice stating in respect of each fact whether or not that party admits it.

(d) Where any fact which a party wishes to establish by experimental proof in reply is not admitted the party may apply to the court for further directions in respect of such experiments.

Notice of Models, etc.

12. (a) If any party wishes to rely at the trial of this claim and counterclaim upon any model or apparatus, that party shall on or before [date] give notice thereof to all the other parties; shall afford the other parties an opportunity within [number] days of the service of such notice of inspecting the same and shall, if so requested, furnish the other party with copies or illustrations of such model or apparatus.

(b) No further or other model or apparatus shall be relied upon in evidence by either party save with consent or by permission of the court.

Product or Process Description

13. (a) The defendants/claimants do provide a written description together with relevant drawings of the following [product(s)] [process(es)] to the claimants/defendants by [......].

   (i) [description of product or process];

   (ii) [description of product or process];

etc.

(b) The description served under paragraph (a) shall be accompanied by a signed written statement which shall:

   (i) state that the person making the statement is personally acquainted with the facts to which the description relates;

   (ii) verify that the description is a true and complete description of the product or process; and

   (iii) contain an acknowledgement by the person making the statement that he may be required to attend court in order to be cross-examined on the contents of the description.

Technical Primer

14. The parties shall use their best endeavours to agree on or before [date] a single technical primer setting out the basic undisputed technology and shall on or before [date] indicate which parts of the technical primer are agreed to form part of the common general knowledge.

Scientific Adviser

15. A.B is appointed a scientific adviser to assist the court in this claim and counterclaim, his/her costs to be met in the first instance in equal shares by the parties and to be costs in the claim and counterclaim, subject to any other order of the trial judge.

Written Evidence

16. (a) Each party shall on or before [date] serve on the other parties [signed] written statements of the oral evidence which the party intends to lead on any issues of fact to be decided at the trial, such statements to stand as the evidence in chief of the witness unless the court otherwise directs;

(b) Each party shall on or before [date] serve on the other parties [signed] written statements of the oral evidence which it intends to lead at trial in answer to facts and matters raised in the witness statements served on it under paragraph (a) and (b) above;

(c) Each party may call up to [number] expert witnesses in this claim and counterclaim provided that the said party:

  (i) supplies the name of such expert to the other parties and to the court on or before [date]; and

  (ii) no later than [date/[number days] before the date set for the hearing of this claim and counterclaim] serve upon the other parties a report of each such expert comprising the evidence which that expert intends to give at trial.

[(d)The claimant shall, with the cooperation of the other parties, arrange for the experts to meet on or before [date] to determine on what issues they agree and on what they disagree and the experts shall before[date] file a report stating where they agree and where they disagree and in the latter case, their reasons for disagreeing].

Admissibility of Evidence

17. A party who objects to any statements of any witness being read by the judge prior to the hearing of the trial, shall serve upon each other party a notice in writing to that effect setting out the grounds of the objection.

Non-Compliance

18. Where either party fails to comply with the directions relating to experiments and written evidence it shall not be entitled to adduce evidence to which such directions relate without the permission of the court.

Trial Bundles

19. Each party shall no later than [28] days before the date fixed for the trial of this claim and counterclaim serve upon the other parties a list of all the documents to be included in the trial bundles. The claimants shall no later than [21] days before the date fixed for trial serve upon the defendants .... sets of the bundles for use at trial.

20. The claimants must file with the court no later than [4] days before the date fixed for the trial:

  (i) the trial bundle; and

  (ii) a reading guide for the judge.

Trial

21. The trial of these proceedings shall be before an assigned judge alone in [London], estimated length [number] days which shall include a pre-trial reading estimate for the judge of [number] days. The technical difficulty rating is [ ].

Liberty to Apply

22. The parties are to be at liberty on two days' notice to apply for further directions and generally.

Costs

23. The costs of this application are to be costs in the claim and counterclaim.

The Patents County Court Guide

G22   Issued 12th May 2011

By authority of the Chancellor of the High Court

CONTENTS

1. GENERAL

INTRODUCTION

1.1 This Guide applies to the Patents County Court (PCC). It is written for all users of **G23** the PCC, whether a litigant in person or a specialist IP litigator.

The Guide aims to help users and potential users of the PCC by explaining how the procedures will operate, providing guidelines where appropriate and dealing with various practical aspects of proceedings before the PCC.

The Guide cannot be wholly comprehensive of all issues which may arise before the PCC. In circumstances which are not covered by this guide, reference may be made to the Patents Court Guide and the Chancery Guide.

History of the PCC.

[Not reproduced]

JURISDICTION

1.2 *[Not reproduced]*   **G24**

Legal basis for jurisdiction of the PCC

[Not reproduced]

Legal remedies

[Not reproduced]

Applicable rules of procedure

[Not reproduced—see Appendix F for relevant provisions of the CPR]

ALLOCATION

1.3 There is no sharp dividing line between cases which should be brought in the Patents **G25** County Court and actions which should be brought in the High Court. It is anticipated that a limit on damages in the Patents County Court will be enacted in 2011 (see paragraph 5.3 Plans for the Future below).

In deciding the court in which to commence a claim, users should bear in mind that the Patents County Court was established to handle the smaller, shorter, less complex, less important, lower value actions and the procedures applicable in the court are designed particularly for cases of that kind. The court aims to provide cheaper, speedier and more informal procedures to ensure that small and medium sized enterprises, and private individuals, are not deterred from innovation by the potential cost of litigation to safeguard their rights. Longer, heavier, more complex, more important and more valuable actions belong in the High Court.

Parties may agree with each other to maintain a case in the Patents County Court if they wish to make use of the procedures available in it. The court will endeavour to accommodate parties in that respect. The court will however maintain its list in such a way as to ensure that it maintains access to justice for small and medium sized enterprises.

If a party to litigation in either the Patents County Court or the High Court believes that the other court is a more appropriate forum for the case, they should apply to transfer it. In the Patents County Court an application to transfer to the High Court must be made at or before the case management conference (CPR rule 63.25(4)). Users are referred to *ALK Abello v Meridian* [2010] EWPCC 014 in which the transfer provisions now applicable were considered.

The following guidelines are provided to assist users in determining which of the two courts is suitable:

- Size of the parties. If both sides are small or medium sized enterprises then the case may well be suitable for the Patents County Court. If one party is a small or medium sized enterprise but the other is a larger undertaking then again the case may be suitable for the Patents County Court but other factors ought to be considered such as the value of the claim and its likely complexity.

- The complexity of the claim. The procedure in the Patents County Court is streamlined and trials last no more than 2 days. A trial which would appear to require more time than that even with the streamlined procedure of the Patents County Court is likely to be unsuitable.

- The nature of the evidence. Experiments in a patent case may be admitted in the Patents County Court but a case which will involve substantial complex experimental evidence will be unsuitable for the Patents County Court.

- Conflicting factual evidence. Cross-examination of witnesses will be strictly controlled in the Patents County Court. The court is well able to handle cases involving disputed factual matters such as allegations of prior use in patents and independent design as a defence to copying; but if a large number of witnesses are required the case may be unsuitable for the Patents County Court.

- Value of the claim. Putting a value on a claim is a notoriously difficult exercise, taking into account factors such as possible damages, the value of an injunction and the possible effect on competition in a market if a patent was revoked. The likely damages to be recovered in an infringement claim is a factor which should be considered. Although no limit on damages in the Patents County Court has been introduced (yet), if the damages are likely to be well in excess of £500,000 then the claim may not be appropriate for the Patents County Court. As a general rule of thumb, disputes where the value of sales, in the UK, of products protected by the intellectual property in issue (by the owner, licensees and alleged infringer) exceeds £1 million per year are unlikely to be suitable for the Patent County Court in the absence of agreement.

In the Patents County Court all claims are allocated to the multi-track. There is currently no small claims track or fast track.

THE JUDGES OF THE PATENTS COUNTY COURT

G26   1.4 The patents judge of the Patents County Court and his clerk are:

His Honour Judge Birss QC

Judge's Clerk: Kav Rekhi—tel 020 7947 7754, fax 020 7947 7483, *Kav.rekhi@hmcts.gsi.gov.uk.*

The judges of the High Court, Patents Court are able to sit as judges of the Patents County Court as necessary.

Certain senior members of the Intellectual Property bar are qualified and able to sit as recorders in the Patents County Court when the need arises.

JUDGES ABLE AND WILLING TO SIT OUT OF LONDON

G27   1.5 If the parties so desire, for the purpose of saving time or costs, the Patents County Court will sit out of London. Before any approach is made to the Judge's Clerk, the parties should discuss between themselves the desirability of such a course. If there is a dispute as to venue, the court will resolve the matter on an application. Where there is no dispute, the Judge's Clerk should be contacted as soon as possible so that arrangements can be put in place well before the date of the proposed hearing.

PATENTS COUNTY COURT USERS' COMMITTEE

G28   1.6 *[Not reproduced]*

1.7 *[Not reproduced]* **G29**

2. PROCEDURE IN THE PATENTS COUNTY COURT

BEFORE ISSUING PROCEEDINGS

2.1 Attention is drawn to the Practice Direction—Pre-Action Conduct (a copy of which **G30** can be found at *www.justice.gov.uk/guidance/courts-and-tribunals/courts/procedurerules/ civil/menus/protocol.htm*).

Compliance with this Practice Direction will affect the timetable, once proceedings are issued (see further below). However, as unjustified threats to bring legal proceedings in respect of many IP rights can themselves be subject to litigation, each claimant will have to make their own decision as to whether it is appropriate to write to a prospective defendant to see if matters can be settled before any proceedings are issued.

ISSUING PROCEEDINGS

2.2 The Patents County Court is currently situated at: St Dunstan's House 133-137 Fet- **G31** ter Lane London EC4 1HD. Apart from the issuing of proceedings, all communications with the Court should be addressed to the Clerk to HH Judge Birss QC at this address.

Until 31st March 2011 the issue of claim forms takes place at the Central London County Court offices. See paragraph 3.10 below for contact details.

From 1st April 2011 the issue of claim forms takes place at the Royal Courts of Justice (Chancery Registry). See paragraph 3.10 below for contact details.

Most proceedings are issued using form N1 (*http://www.hmcourtsservice.gov.uk/ courtfinder/forms/n1_0102.pdf*). A claimant should ensure that there is a copy of the claim form for the court and each defendant, as well a copy for itself.

All proceedings when issued are sent to the Clerk to HH Judge Birss QC. Enquiries relating to an existing case in the Patents County Court after the claim form has been issued (except for enforcement) may be addressed to the Clerk to His Honour Judge Birss QC at the address given above (and repeated at paragraph 3.10 below).

SERVICE OF DOCUMENTS

2.3 *[Not reproduced]* **G32**

STATEMENTS OF CASE

Introduction

The statements of case are the documents where each party sets out its case. As **G33** discussed below, these need to be full, but not unnecessarily lengthy. Statements of case can stand as evidence at trial in the PCC, where relevant individuals have verified them with a statement of truth, as discussed further below.

Time limits

[Not reproduced—see CPR r.63.22]

Content of statements of case

In general, statements of case (i.e. the pleadings of all parties) must comply with the requirements of Part 16. Furthermore, they should comply with rule 63.6 and PD 63 paras. 4.1-4.6. Copies of important documents referred to in a statement of case (e.g. an advertisement referred to in a claim of infringement form or documents cited in Grounds of Invalidity) should be served with the statement of case. Where any such document requires translation, a translation should be served at the same time.

A particular feature of statements of case in the Patents County Court is that they should comply with rule 63.20 (1) and must set out concisely all facts and arguments relied on. A key purpose of this requirement is to facilitate the conduct of the case management conference which will be conducted on an issue by issue basis. Therefore the court and the parties need to know what the issues are going to be in sufficient detail for that process to take place. However attention is drawn to the requirement for the matters to be set out concisely. The parties are invited to raise issues with the court before committing excessive time and resources to the production of unnecessarily lengthy statements of case.

Guidance on the statement of case is as follows:

- In a normal case it is unlikely that legal arguments will need to be set out in any detail in the statement of case, all that is likely to be required is a brief statement of the nature of the argument to be relied on.

- Lengthy expositions of construction of patent claims is unlikely to be necessary or desirable. However the parties will be expected to identify the claims in issue (for infringement and validity) and identify the relevant features of those claims.

- It is likely to be necessary to break down a patent claim into suitable integers in order to explain a case on infringement with reference to specific elements of the alleged infringing product or process. This may be most conveniently done in the form of a table or chart annexed to the statement of case. Points on construction should emerge from this exercise and may need to be identified but lengthy argument on them is not required.

- A case of anticipation of a patent is likely to require a similar approach to infringement (i.e. a claim break down, perhaps in the form of a table, with the claim integers compared with the relevant parts of the prior art disclosure(s) relied upon).

- A case of obviousness of a patent is likely to require a statement addressing the allegedly obvious step(s).

- A specific statement of what facts are said to be relevant common general knowledge is likely to be necessary. A short summary of the relevant technical background may be helpful.

- Similarity between marks may not require elaboration but in an appropriate case some detail will be necessary, particularly in relation to allegations that goods or services are similar. Parties to trade mark cases should identify the nature and characteristics of the relevant consumer (if relevant).

- A defence of independent design in a copyright case (or similar) will need to be addressed in appropriate detail.

Independent validity of patent claims

Where one party raises the issue of validity of a patent, the patentee (or other relevant party) should identify which of the claims of the patent are alleged to have independent validity in his reply (or defence) to the allegation of invalidity.

Statements of truth

[Not reproduced – see CPR r63.21]

CASE MANAGEMENT (R 63.23)

G34   2.5 The case management conference ("CMC") in the Patents County Court will be conducted by a judge. The purpose of the CMC is to manage the conduct of the case in order to bring the proceedings to a trial in a manner proportionate to the nature of the dispute, the financial position of the parties, the degree of complexity of the case, the importance of the case and the amount of money at stake. At the first CMC, the court will identify the issues and decide whether to make orders under paragraph 29.1 of PD 63. These include orders permitting the filing of further material in the case such as witness statements, experts' reports and disclosure and orders permitting cross-examination at trial and skeleton arguments. The trial date will be fixed at the CMC.

The date for the CMC will normally be arranged as follows. The claimant should apply for a CMC within 14 days after all defendants who intend to file and serve a defence have done so. Where a case has been transferred from another court, the claimant should apply for a CMC within 14 days of the transfer. Any party may apply for a CMC at an earlier date than these dates. If the claimant has not applied for a CMC within 14 days then the defendant should do so. In any event the Court can and will fix a date for a CMC if the parties have not done so within a reasonable period. These requirements are mandatory for cases within Section I of Part 63 (essentially patents and registered designs; see PD 63 para 5.3–5.7) but should be followed in all cases in the Patents County Court as a matter of efficient case management. All cases are allocated to the multitrack automatically by operation of Rule 63.1(3) and so the Patents County Court generally dispenses with the need for an allocation questionnaire.

The CMC will be conducted as a hearing in open court. However where all parties consent the court may determine the CMC on paper (rule 63.23(3)).

Bundles should be filed with the court at St Dunstan's House (full address below). Although PD 63 para 5.9 applies to the preparation of those bundles, parties must consider the different procedure in the Patents County Court and, where appropriate, include attachments to the statements of case and copies of the documents referred to in the statements of case.

In general, parties should endeavour to agree directions prior to the date fixed for the CMC. The court will still identify the issues and although the court has the right to amend directions which have been agreed, this will only happen where there is manifest reason for doing so.

The CMC is an important part of the procedure because no material may be filed in the case by way of evidence, disclosure or written submissions unless permission is given for it by the judge and the proper time for that permission to be given is the CMC. Save in exceptional circumstances the court will not consider an application by a party to submit material in a case in addition to that ordered at the CMC (rule 63.23(2)).

The basis on which the court will decide whether to permit material to be filed in a case is by applying the cost-benefit test (PD 63 para 29.2(2)) and by giving permission in relation to specific and identified issues only ((PD 63 para 29.2(1)). PD 63 para 29.1 lists the material which the court may order: disclosure of documents, a product or process description, experiments, witness statements, experts' reports, cross-examination at trial, and written submissions or skeleton arguments. The parties need to attend the CMC in a position to assist the court in making appropriate orders on this basis. In particular, the parties should consider:

(a) The need for and scope of any evidence from factual or expert witnesses. Note the court will consider whether there is sufficient evidence in the statements of case or whether further evidence is required.

(b) The need for and scope of any oral testimony and cross-examination. Note that the court will confine any permitted cross-examination to particular issues and to time limits.

(c) The need for, and scope of, any disclosure of documents.

(d) The need for any experiments, process or product descriptions or supply of any samples.

(e) The need for written submissions or skeleton arguments.

(f) The likely timetable up to trial. This may include dates on which disclosure of documents, product and process description and experiments is to take place as well as a schedule for witness statements and experts reports including provisions for any evidence in reply (if required).

(g) The need for an oral hearing or whether a decision can be made on the papers. If an oral hearing is considered to be appropriate, the court will order that the hearing be of a fixed duration of no more than 2 days.

A specimen CMC order is attached to this Guide at Annex A.

TRANSFERS (RULE 63.18 AND RULES 63.25(4) AND (5))

G35 2.6 Applications to transfer a case to the High Court should be made at the case management conference. The court will have regard to the provisions of PD 30 (Transfer) and in particular paragraph 9.1 thereof which relates to transfers between the High Court and Patents County Court. The considerations set out above in section 1.3 Allocation will be taken into account. In addition, in considering an application to transfer to the High Court the following further matters will be taken into account:

- The holder of an intellectual property right who does not wish to incur High Court costs but apprehends that an alleged infringer may seek to have the matter transferred to the High Court, may consider an undertaking to limit the enforcement of their rights; e.g. by foregoing an injunction or by reference to a certain value of sales.

- A defendant seeking transfer to the High Court when the claimant cannot afford the cost of High Court litigation may offer to allow the claimant to withdraw their claim without prejudice to a right to restart litigation and/or without an adverse costs award.

An application to transfer a case to the High Court after the CMC will only be considered in exceptional circumstances.

The High Court has the power to transfer a case before it from the High Court to the Patents County Court.

An application for such an order must be made to the High Court. The High Court has no power to order proceedings within the special jurisdiction to be transferred from the Patents County Court (s.289(1) 1988 Act).

APPLICATIONS (RULE 63.25)

G36 2.7 *[Not reproduced]*

THE TRIAL (PD 63 PARA 31)

G37 2.8 *[Not reproduced]*

COSTS (RULE 63.23)

G38 2.9 Costs in the Patents County Court are subject to a cap provided by Part 45 rules 45.41–45.43 and see also PD 45 Section 25C. Subject to certain limited exceptions the court will not order a party to pay total costs of more than £50,000 on the final determination of a claim in relation to liability and no more than £25,000 on an inquiry as to damages or account of profits.

Tables A and B of Section 25C of the Costs Practice Direction set out the maximum amount of scale costs which the court will award for each stage of a claim in the Patents County Court.

For cases which have been transferred to the Patents County Court from elsewhere, either another county court or the High Court, the Patents County Court will deal with costs incurred in proceedings before transfer on a case by case basis.

ALTERNATIVE DISPUTE RESOLUTION

2.10 *[Not reproduced]* **G39**

3. GENERAL ARRANGEMENTS

ISSUING PROCEEDINGS AND APPLICATIONS

(a) Issuing proceedings

[Not reproduced–see s.2.2 above] **G40**

(b) Transferring proceedings to the Patents County Court

Until 31st March 2011 cases transferred to the Patents County Court are taken first to the offices of the Central London County Court at 26 Park Crescent, London. From 1st April 2011 cases transferred to the Patents County Court will be taken to the Royal Courts of Justice (Chancery Registry). All transferred proceedings are then passed on to the Judge's Clerk at the Patents County Court, St Dunstan's House.

(c) Issuing interim applications

The issue of all interim process will continue to be dealt with as at present by the Clerk to HHJ Birss QC at St Dunstan's House either by post or personal attendance. The payment of the fee will be made at St Dunstan's House.

Users are reminded that:

a. The first case management conference (rule 63.23) will be conducted at a hearing unless all parties consent to determination on paper.

b. The court will deal with all other applications without a hearing unless it considers one necessary (rule 63.25(3)).

The fee will be determined on the face of the application notice when it is issued and prior to consideration (if any) by the court of whether a hearing is necessary. Accordingly applications marked for determination at a hearing will be charged the fee of £80. Applications marked for determination otherwise than at a hearing will be charged the £45 fee.

Personal attendance to issue process

The Fee and the application notice should be taken to the Clerk to HHJ Birss at St Dunstan's House. The Application will be issued and returned.

Postal application to issue process

Applications should be sent the Clerk to HHJ Birss QC at St Dunstan's House. The Clerk will issue and return the application.

ARRANGEMENTS FOR LISTING

3.2 (a) First case management conference (rule 63.23)

If the application is for the first case management conference (rule 63.23), the date for **G41**
the hearing will be fixed at the same time the application is issued as follows:

a. For applications issued by personal attendance on the Clerk to HHJ Birss QC at St Dunstan's House, the Clerk in the presence of the applicant or their representative, whilst the parties are there, will contact the Chancery Judges Listing Office who will supply the date.

b. For applications issued by post, the Clerk will obtain a hearing date and inform the parties.

(b) Interim Applications when a hearing has been ordered

For applications marked for determination at a hearing, the court will promptly consider whether a hearing is necessary. If the court considers it necessary to hold a hearing, the Clerk will then obtain a hearing date and inform the parties.

(c) Trials

Trial dates will be fixed at the Case Management Conference (CMC) and parties attending the Case Management Conference should have the necessary information in order to fix a trial date.

The trial fee (£1,090) must be paid within 14 days of the trial date being set.

TIME ESTIMATES

G42   3.3 The parties must provide time estimates for all applications in respect of which a hearing is sought. Parties must appreciate the need to give a realistic and accurate time estimate and ensure that it includes a discrete reading time for the court to read the papers prior to the hearing of the application. The court will consider the imposition of guillotines where time estimates are exceeded.

At trial the Court will take an active part in controlling the proceedings and setting limits on the time allocated during a trial. To facilitate this process the parties need to provide realistic and accurate time estimates in advance.

Where parties and their legal advisors consider that a time estimate that has been provided is unrealistic, they have a duty to notify the new time estimate to the Judge's Clerk as soon as possible.

The Court will normally hear trials from 10.30am to 4.15 pm with a break from 1pm to 2pm for lunch. CMCs and other hearings will normally be heard at 10.30am but may be heard at a different time if appropriate.

DOCUMENTS AND TIMETABLE

G43   3.3 The preparation of papers for the hearing of applications and trials is of considerable importance and should be approached intelligently. The general guidance given in Appendix 6 of the Chancery Guide should be followed. Legal representatives and litigants in person who fail to do so may be required to explain why and may be penalised personally in costs.

Papers for the hearing should be lodged directly with the Judge's Clerk. If there is insufficient time to lodge hard copies before the deadline, faxed documents of significance (and particularly skeleton arguments) should be supplied, followed up by clean hard copies. As an alternative to faxing documents they may, by agreement, be sent by e-mail to the Judge's Clerk.

It is the responsibility of both parties to ensure that all relevant documents are lodged with the Judge's Clerk by noon two days before the date fixed for hearing unless some longer or shorter period has been ordered by the judge or is prescribed by this guide.

The judge requests that all important documents also be supplied to him on disk or via e-mail in a format convenient for the judge's use (normally the current or a recent version of Microsoft Word or as a text searchable pdf). For trial, these will usually include skeleton arguments, important patents and drawings, the witness statements and expert reports.

Prior to trial, parties should ensure that they comply with the requirements of PD 63 para 9 concerning the provision of a trial bundle and reading guide for the judge. Insofar as the trial timetable has not already have been discussed at the CMC and set out in the Order for Directions, the parties should provide a detailed time table setting out the times and dates that witnesses will be required to be available for any cross-examination already ordered.

Where a technical primer has been ordered at the CMC, the parties should identify those parts which are agreed to form part of the common general knowledge. The time table for this will have been ordered at the CMC.

If they are used, skeleton arguments should be lodged in time for the judge to read them before an application or trial. Any skeleton argument must also be served on the other parties in the case:

(a) In the case of applications, if a skeleton argument is used, it should normally be filed by 10:30am the previous working day (or, in the case of short applications, 3pm).

(b) In the case of trials, skeletons may only be used where they have been ordered at the CMC and they should normally be lodged at least two working days before commencement of the trial.

Transcripts

In trials where a transcript of evidence is being made and supplied to the judge, the transcript should be supplied by e-mail and in hard copy.

TELEPHONE APPLICATIONS

3.5 The Patents County Court will hear applications by telephone conference in accordance with the Practice Direction under Part 23 and PD 63 para 30.1. The party making the application is responsible for setting up the telephone application and informing the parties, Counsels' clerks (where barristers are instructed) and the Judge's Clerk or the Chancery Listing Office of the time of the conference call. **G44**

It is possible for the application to be recorded, and if recording by the court rather than by British Telecom (or other service provider) is requested, arrangements should be made with the Judge's Clerk. The recording will not be transcribed. The tape will be kept by the Judge's Clerk for a period of six months. Arrangements for transcription, if needed, must be made by the parties.

This procedure should be used where it will save costs.

CONSENT ORDERS

3.6 The court is normally willing to make consent orders without the need for the attendance of any parties. A draft of the agreed order and the written consent of all the parties or their respective legal representatives should be supplied to the Judge's Clerk. Unless the judge assigned to hear the application considers a hearing is needed, he or she will make the order in the agreed terms by initialling it. It will be drawn up accordingly and sent to the parties. **G45**

DRAFT JUDGMENTS

3.7 *[Not reproduced—see CPR PD40E paras 2.1–2.9]* **G46**

ORDERS FOLLOWING JUDGMENT

3.8 *[Not reproduced—see §19 of the Patent Court Guide]* **G47**

ENFORCEMENT

3.9 All enforcement will continue to be carried out at the Enforcement Section at Central London CC. **G48**

G49 3.10 *[Information applicable prior to April 1, 2011 omitted]*

From 1st April 2011, the issue of Claim Forms for the Patents County Court and general enquiries relating to claim fees may be addressed to:

Chancery Registry TM 5.04
Royal Courts of Justice
Strand
London WC2A 2LL
DX 44450 STRAND
Tel 020 7947 7783
Fax 020 7947 7422

Enquiries relating to an existing case in the Patents County Court after the claim form has been issued (except for enforcement) may be addressed to:

The Clerk to HHJ Birss QC
St Dunstan's House
133-137 Fetter Lane
London
EC4A 1HD
DX 44450 STRAND
Tel: 020 7947 7754
Fax: 020 7947 7483

The Chancery Listing Office may be contacted at:

The Chancery Listing Department Room WG04
Royal Courts of Justice
Strand
London WC2A 2LL
DX 44450 STRAND
Tel: 020 7947 7717
Fax: 0870 739 5869

Enquiries relating to enforcement may be addressed to: The Specialist Section, Central London Civil Justice Centre at the address above.

4. CHECKLISTS AND MODEL PLEADINGS

G50 The PCC Users' Committee is preparing checklists and model pleadings to assist users in getting to grips with the requirements of the pleading rules applicable in the Patents County Court.

5. MISCELLANEOUS

Information available on the Internet

G51 5.1 *[Not reproduced]*

Monitoring

G52 5.2 *[Not reproduced]*

Plans for the future

G53 5.3 *[Not reproduced]*

ANNEX A

SPECIMEN CMC ORDER

G54 UPON HEARING the Case Management Conference on [date]

IT IS ORDERED THAT:

Disclosure

1. The parties will make and serve on the other of them a list in accordance with form N265 of the documents in their control which relate to [issue X] by [date]. If any party wishes to inspect or have copies of such documents as are in another party's control it shall give notice in writing that it wishes to do so and such inspection shall be allowed at all reasonable times upon reasonable notice and any copies shall be provided within 14 days of the request, upon the undertaking of the party requesting the copies to pay the reasonable copying charges.

Evidence

2. The statements of case shall stand as evidence in chief in relation to [issue U, and issue V].

3. The parties may serve witness statements dealing with [issue X, and issue Y] on or before 4pm on [date].

4. The parties may serve witness statements in reply on or before 4pm on [date].

5. The parties may each serve an expert's report dealing with [issue Z] on or before 4pm on [date].

6. The parties may serve an expert's report in reply on or before 4pm on [date].

7. The witnesses dealing with [issue X] may be cross-examined at trial. No other witness will be cross-examined.

Trial

8. The time allocated for the trial is 1 day. The parties are allocated $^{1}/_{2}$ day each.

9. Time estimates for the cross-examination and speeches of the parties will be filed by 4pm on [date]. The court will consider the estimates and allocate time taking them into account.

10. The parties have permission to file skeleton arguments, on or before 4pm on [date].

11. The trial of the Claim shall take place on [date].

12. Judgment in the action shall be handed down on [date].

Costs

13. The costs of this case management conference shall be costs in the case.

APPENDIX H

PATENT ATTORNEY AND TRADE MARK ATTORNEY QUALIFICATION AND REGISTRATION REGULATIONS 2009

The above Regulations replace the former Register of Patent Agents Rules made by the Chartered Institute of Patent Attorneys.

It is explained that the Patent Regulation Board of the Chartered Institute of Patent Attorneys and the Trade Mark Regulation Board of the Institute of Trade Mark Attorneys working jointly together as the IP Regulation Board (IPREG) made the above Regulations under s.275A of the Copyright Designs and Patents Act 1988 and under s.83A of the Trade Marks Act 1994, respectively, pursuant to ss.185 and 184 of the Legal Services Act 2007. These Regulations make provision as to:

- the appointment of Registrars for maintaining the patent attorney and trade mark attorney registers;

- the procedures for, and the circumstances in which, individuals may be entered into the patent attorney register and/or the trade mark attorney register, the duration and renewal of registration and the circumstances in which registration will expire or may be revoked; and

- appeals relating to registration of individuals in the patent attorney and trade mark attorney registers.

The Regulations can be downloaded from *www.ipreg.org*.

APPENDIX I

RULES FOR EXAMINATION AND ADMISSION OF INDIVIDUALS
2011

(Available on http://www.ipreg.org.uk/document_file/file/Rules_for_Examination_ and_Admission_of_Individuals_2011.pdf.
These Rules were issued by the IP Regulation Board, which is the regulatory body for the professions of patent and trade mark attorneys. The Rules make provision for the accreditation of bodies as Examination Agencies to set some or all of the qualifying examinations leading to entitlement to be registered as a patent or trade mark attorney.

APPENDIX J

RULES OF CONDUCT FOR PATENT ATTORNEYS, TRADE MARK ATTORNEYS AND OTHER REGULATED PERSONS

J00   *The Patent Regulation Board of the Chartered Institute of Patent Attorneys and the Trade Mark Regulation Board of the Institute of Trade Mark Attorneys working jointly together as the IP Regulation Board (IPREG) now make the following provisions under section 275A of the Copyright Designs and Patents Act 1988 and under section 83A of the Trade Marks Act 1994, respectively, pursuant to Sections 185 and 184 of the Legal Services Act 2007.*

Rule 1—Interpretation

J01   1. In these Rules, unless context otherwise requires:

" patent attorney register" means the register kept under section 275 of the Copyright Designs and Patents Act 1988 as amended;

" trade mark attorney register" means the register kept under section 83 of the Trade Marks Act 1994 as amended;

" registered person" means —

   (a) a registered patent attorney;

   (b) a registered trade mark attorney; or

   (c) a body (corporate or unincorporate) registered in the patent attorney register or the trade mark attorney register;

" regulated person" means a registered person, an employee of a registered person, or a manager of a body which is a registered person;

" manager", in relation to a body, has the same meaning as in the Legal Services Act 2007;

" professional work" means any services provided by a regulated person in the course of business providing legal services;

" corporate work" means professional work undertaken by an employed regulated person acting solely as an agent on behalf of —

   (a) their employer;

   (b) a company or organisation controlled by their employer or in which their employer has a substantial measure of control;

   (c) a company in the same group as their employer;

   (d) a company which controls their employer;

   (e) an employee (including a director or a company secretary) of a company or organisation under (a) – (d) above, where the matter relates or arises out of the work of that company or organisation; or

   (f) another person with whom a person under (a) to (e) above has a common interest;

" in private practice" means undertaking professional work which is not solely corporate work;

" client" means principal on whose behalf a regulated person acts as agent and includes any person for whom the regulated person is address for service for any right regardless of the nature of any current relationship. In the case of foreign originating work, for the purposes of these Rules the "client" remains the principal for whom the work is ultimately being done, although the instructions may come from an intermediary foreign patent or trade mark attorney, to whom the regulated person will also owe a duty of professional care. Where a regulated person is instructed via such an intermediary any obligation to provide information to a client under these rules may be discharged by providing such information to that intermediary.

Rule 2—Scope

2. These Rules set out the standards of professional conduct and practice expected of regulated persons undertaking professional work. Registered persons are responsible under these Rules not only for their own acts and omissions, but also for those sanctioned, expressly or otherwise, by them. **J02**

Not every shortcoming on the part of a regulated person, nor failure to comply with these Rules, will necessarily give rise to disciplinary proceedings. The guidance shown in italics accompanying these rules is not mandatory and does not form part of the Rules. Nevertheless, any alleged breach of the rules will be considered with reference to the guidance.

Guidelines to rules 1 and 2

2.1 Rules 1 and 2 define the scope of the Code of Conduct. Individuals, firms and companies registered in the patent attorney register or trade mark attorney register, their managers and employees are subject to the code if they act in the course of a business which undertakes relevant professional work.

2.2 Rules 12 (Complaints handling) and 17 (Professional Indemnity Insurance) are only applicable to registered persons "in private practice" and attorneys employed within industrial departments are not required to comply with these rules provided that such attorneys limit their professional activities to "corporate work". In general, this means only undertaking work on behalf of their employer and individuals or companies associated with their employer.

2.3 Attorneys undertaking "corporate work" may, however, act on behalf of third parties unrelated to their employer where their employer or an associated individual or company has a "common interest" in such work. Typical examples of permitted actions on behalf of third parties would include: maintaining or enforcing patents on behalf of third parties where the patents are licensed to an employer; prosecuting patent applications owned jointly by an employer and a third party; the appointment of an attorney as a joint representative on behalf of an employer and others in revocation or opposition proceedings; and time limited activities arising due to the transfer of assets to or from an employer such as the on-going maintenance of a portfolio of rights whilst a formal transfer was being finalised.

Rule 3—Service of documents

3. Any notice or other document required by or for the purposes of these Rules to be given or sent to a regulated person may be given to them personally or sent by mail to their last known address with proof of such postage. **J03**

Rule 4—Competence

4. Regulated persons shall carry out their professional work with due skill, care and diligence and with proper regard for the technical standards expected of them. **J04**

A regulated person should only undertake work within his expertise or competence.

Guidance

4.1 A regulated person should always consider whether, having regard to

(a) the circumstances (including in particular the gravity, complexity and likely cost) of the work;

(b) the nature of the regulated person's practice;

(c) the regulated person's ability, experience and seniority; and

(d) the regulated person's relationship with the client,

the interests of the client would be served by the regulated person or some other person providing professional services in fulfilment of the client's instructions.

This should be considered as soon as practicable after receiving instructions and from time-to-time thereafter, particularly when circumstances change. If the regulated person considers that the interests of the client would be served by some other person acting, he must advise his client accordingly.

Rule 5—Integrity

J05   5. Regulated persons shall at all times act with integrity putting their clients' interests foremost subject to the law and any overriding duty to any Court or Tribunal.

Guidance

5.1 A regulated person should in all professional activities

(a) practise competently, promptly, conscientiously, courteously, honestly and objectively, avoiding unnecessary expense to the client;

(b) act so as to promote confidence in the intellectual property system;

(c) subject to the law and the regulated person's duty to any Court or Tribunal, put clients' interests foremost and keep clients' affairs confidential.

5.2 A regulated person should not do anything that might compromise

(a) his independence;

(b) the dignity and good standing of the regulated person, or of the patent or trade mark professions;

(c) the freedom of clients to instruct any person or firm to carry out their work or to change their representation.

Rule 6—Client care and service

J06   6. Regulated persons shall carry out their professional work in a timely manner and with proper regard for standards of professional service and client care.

Guideline to rule 6

6.1 Written terms of business should be given to clients at the outset of a relationship and as often as necessary thereafter. Any variations should be communicated to clients as soon as they apply to the client. Regulated persons should ensure that clients receive as often as necessary an explanation, appropriate to the client's reasonably apparent or expected level of understanding, as to the issues in a matter, the progress of the matter and the likely timescale and an update periodically on expenditure incurred or to be incurred. The level of reporting depends on the client relationship and the experience of the client or the person responsible within the client's organisation. For example lay clients may require more care than in-house counsel.

6.2 When instructions are received orally, it is sensible practice, for the avoidance of future disputes as to the precise instructions given, for a regulated person to provide to the client a written note confirming the instructions received.

6.3 When unwilling or unable to provide services to an existing client, or withdrawing from giving services, a regulated person should make reasonable efforts to enable the client to make other arrangements and bear in mind their obligations to put clients' interests foremost. A regulated person should co-operate with a client and any new representative of the client to ensure the client's interests are protected on any change of responsibility.

6.4 Even where there is no ongoing client relationship, absent a formal termination including clear and reasonable notice to the former client that communications will not be forwarded, regulated persons should take timely steps to draw a former client's attention to correspondence or communications received relating to the former client and their rights. A regulated person may seek a fees undertaking where the client relationship has been terminated for the costs involved in forwarding correspondence.

6.5 Every regulated person should have a written file retention/destruction policy which should be made available to the client on request.

6.6 If a regulated person gives an indication (such as an estimate) of the likely cost of work and that indication is not intended to be fixed, the regulated person is responsible for making it clear that the indication is not fixed, and for ensuring that the client is informed in advance whenever reasonably possible if it appears the indication will be materially exceeded.

6.7 Unless otherwise agreed with the client a regulated person should not require as a condition precedent from a sender of correspondence or a communication intended for or relevant to the client, an undertaking to meet the regulated person's fees for forwarding the sender's correspondence or communication to the client or for giving the client advice on the matter.

6.8 This applies typically to requests for consent, licence and so on. There have been instances where regulated persons have refused even to pass on correspondence without comment until their fees are met. Absent the client's agreement, this is a breach of Rules 5, 6 & 7, since the regulated person is putting his own interest in fees before the interest of the client which is in being informed promptly. This does not prevent the regulated person asking the sender for an agreement to meet reasonable costs, but the forwarding of the communication must not be dependent on it. It is up to the regulated person, having regard to his relationship with the client, to determine how matters of this kind should be drawn to the attention of the client and in the absence of any other arrangement, if the regulated person is unwilling to forward the communication "on risk as to costs" the communication should either be returned to the sender (provided that the client is not prejudiced by the resulting delay) or be forwarded without comment or offering assistance on appropriate terms.

6.9 Note that the sender is not liable for any costs until agreement is reached but that any agreement will impose liability regardless of whether the sender receives the benefit or co-operation sought.

Rule 7—Conflicts

7. A regulated person must not act where his interests conflict with those of a client or **J07** of a former client, or where he knows or has reasonable grounds for suspecting that the interests of any partner or regulated person or staff of his firm, conflict with those of a client or of a former client.

Provided in all the circumstances it is reasonable to do so, a regulated person may act for two or more clients, or for a client as against a former client, in relation to the same or a related matter in a situation of conflict, or possible conflict but only if all of the parties have given their informed consent in writing. Regardless of consent a regulated person must, however, refuse to act on behalf of conflicting or potentially conflicting parties in contentious matters, in circumstances where the regulated person's actions would not be seen to be neutral or where accepting instructions from both parties would risk a breach of Rule 5 or if Rule 8 cannot be observed.

Guidance

7.1 If a regulated person acquires or has acquired relevant knowledge concerning a current or a former client in the course of acting for that client in any capacity, the regulated person should not accept instructions to act against that client or should henceforth cease to act against that client. The term "relevant knowledge" should mean knowledge of the client or the client's affairs that is not widely disseminated to the public and that is, or is likely to become, relevant to the action concerned against the client.

7.2 A regulated person must not allow any person to perform work under his supervision when the regulated person knows or has reasonable grounds for suspecting that such a person has a conflict of interest in respect of the work.

7.3 A conflict may not arise simply because the regulated person acts for two or more parties in the same general field of business or technology although on the facts it may do so. More typically a conflict arises by reference to the specific subject matter of a case. However, acting for two or more parties in the same general field of business or technology may give rise to issues of confidentiality under Rule 8.

7.4 Confidentiality safeguards within firms or between branches may be sufficient to "cure" conflict, provided informed written consent is obtained from all parties and suitable arrangements to ensure the confidentiality of information applying to each client are in place. Safeguards - within firms or between branches - cannot, however, "cure" conflicts to enable the same regulated person to act on behalf of opposing parties in a contentious matter.

7.5 All regulated persons should undertake a "conflict check" before taking on a new client. This may take whatever form is considered appropriate in all of the circumstances. The minimum expected is a check with all other relevant persons that acceptance of a named client is not likely to compromise the interests of a client already on the books.

7.6 Unless otherwise agreed, informed consent requires that the parties whose interests do or may conflict are notified in writing of the name(s) of the other party(ies).

7.7 Where there is conflict between the interests of a regulated person, and those of a client, neither informed consent, nor any other arrangement, will enable him to act for that client.

7.8 Nothing in these rules prevents a regulated person from acting as a mediator between parties to a dispute provided the appropriate codes of practice which deal with conflict when acting as a mediator are observed.

Rule 8—Confidentiality and disclosure

J08

8. Regulated persons must keep the affairs of clients and former clients confidential except where disclosure is required and permitted by law or by the client or former client.

Subject to this duty of client confidentially and any circumstance where disclosure of information is prohibited by law, unless a client expressly agrees that no duty to disclose arises or a different standard of disclosure applies, a regulated person should disclose all relevant information of which he is aware to a client.

Regulated persons must not put any clients' confidential information at risk by acting, or continuing to act for another client where that information may be material, unless both clients provide informed consent and in all of the circumstances it is reasonable to do so.

Guidance

8.1 Confidentiality of clients' information is paramount and central to, though distinct from, the issue of conflict of interests.

8.2 Where a regulated person takes on a client where there is already a client on the books in the same area of business or technology, but where the matters for which they have been engaged are not related, they should still ensure that the confidential information associated with one is not allowed to be made available to the other or to any regulated person acting for the other client.

8.3 Regulated persons have a duty to disclose all relevant information, of which they are aware, to their client in respect of the matter in hand. Information of which they are not aware, but is known to others in the same firm, for example, would be exempted, as would information disclosure of which would breach the duty of confidentiality to another client.

8.4 If information is obtained in relation to a prospective client, a regulated person may still be bound by a duty of confidentiality, even if that prospective client does not subsequently instruct that person or their firm. There may be circumstances, however, where a regulated person receives information where there is no real or genuine interest in instructing that person or their firm and that information is unlikely to be confidential.

Rule 9—Relationships with other professionals

9. Regulated persons should not communicate directly with any other party who to his **J09** knowledge has retained a registered person or other legally qualified person as a professional advisor to act in a matter except:

(a) to request the name and address of the other party's professional advisor;

(b) where it would be reasonable to conclude that the other party's professional advisor has refused or failed for no adequate reason either to pass on messages to their client or to reply to correspondence, and has been warned of your intention to contact their client direct;

(c) with that professional advisor's consent; or

(d) in exceptional circumstances.

A regulated person should co-operate with a client and any new representative of the client to ensure the client's interests are protected on any change of responsibility.

Guidance

9.1 When a regulated person has been given explicit notice that another party has engaged a patent attorney, trade mark attorney or other legally qualified person in relation to a specific matter, the regulated person should normally direct all communications about that matter to the appointed advisor rather than directly to the party. The mere recordal of an address for service in relation to a relevant or potentially relevant right does not necessarily on its own constitute explicit notice that an advisor has been appointed in relation to a matter. Rather, it is only where a regulated person has been informed that a party has appointed a professional advisor, or the registered person receives a response from such an advisor, or it is otherwise objectively clear from the facts or circumstances that the recorded address for service is the appointed advisor in the specific matter in question, that the regulated person should avoid direct, or further direct, communication under this rule.

9.2 General communications and publicity undertaken by regulated persons (i.e. communications not relation to a specific matter where another party has retained a professional advisor in relation to that matter) are governed by Rule 18.

9.3 Nothing in this rule shall be taken to prevent a regulated person from exercising a lien over client papers or other materials to the extent permitted by Rule 13.

Rule 10—Fees

10. Regulated persons' fees must be justifiable. **J10**

Guidance

10.1 Fees charged should be based upon the information provided in any letter of engagement or on the basis of any amendment thereto.

Rule 11—Financial matters

11. Regulated persons shall ensure that their professional finances are managed **J11** appropriately.

Guidance

11.1 In the event that a regulated person receives money from a client, other than by way of payment of fees or disbursements or money on account for fees or disbursements paid up front, they should ensure that such money is held on trust for the client in an account which is entirely separate from the regulated person's or the firm's professional business accounts.

11.2 In the event that money may be held on trust for a client, a registered person's terms of business should deal with the issue of ownership of interest earned on money held on behalf of a client.

11.3 It is the responsibility of regulated persons to ensure that they are aware of legislation pertaining to "money laundering" and "proceeds of crime".

Rule 12—Complaints handling

J12   12. Regulated persons in private practice must have an established procedure for dealing with complaints. Written details of the procedure must be available whenever a client requests them and a client should be informed in writing, when first engaging the registered person, that such a procedure for the resolution of a complaint exists..

Rule 13—Liens

J13   13. Regulated persons may exercise a lien over client papers and other materials belonging to a client only when and to the extent that the lien is available in law or the lien is an express term of business to which the client has agreed.

Guidance

13.1 The issue of lien comes up reasonably frequently in complaints. Regulated persons do not benefit from the statutory lien of solicitors and the extent of any lien – if any – at common law has never been clarified. It is best to ensure this is dealt with in written terms.

13.2 Any charges or contractual liens applicable to a transfer of files should be set out in the regulated person's terms of business or should be otherwise agreed, but the absence of agreement should not unreasonably delay effecting the transfer. Regulated persons should note that if they have not dealt with this issue adequately in their terms of business, they may be in no position contractually to recover costs associated with the transfer if no other agreement can be reached.

13.3 Save in exercise of any lien, it is not acceptable to obstruct or unreasonably delay a transfer of responsibility to a new representative when asked to do so by a client.

Rule 14—Duty to act in the interests of justice

J14   14. Regulated persons exercising any right to appear before a court or tribunal or to conduct litigation must comply with their duties to the court or tribunal and act with independence in the interests of justice. Regulated persons must not knowingly deceive or mislead a court or tribunal. Regulated persons exercising any right to appear before a court or to conduct litigation shall observe the Special Rules of Professional Conduct applicable to Litigation Practitioners.

Guidance

14.1 A regulated person must not submit orally or in any documents or pleadings:

(a) statements of fact or contentions that are not supported by the evidence or instruction of the client;

(b) contentions that he cannot justify as prima facie arguable;

(c) allegations of fraud unless clearly instructed to make such an allegation and it is prima facie supported by credible material; note, however that this does not preclude the making of claims of "bad faith" per se (for example, a lack of intention to use a trade mark), unless that claim is specifically directed to substantive fraud.

Rule 15—Anti-Discrimination

J15   15. Regulated persons must not, in the conduct of their practice, unfairly or unlawfully discriminate against any person on grounds of race, religious belief, gender, sexual orientation, age or disability.

Rule 16—Continuing Professional Development

J16   16. Registered patent attorneys and registered trade mark attorneys shall undertake appropriate continuing professional development and, on request, provide details thereof to the appropriate Regulation Board.

Rule 17—Professional Indemnity Insurance

17. Without prejudice to any obligation contained the Special Rules of Professional **J17** Conduct applicable to Litigation Practitioners, each registered person or his firm in private practice must take out and maintain professional indemnity insurance cover, for each and every claim brought in the United Kingdom or elsewhere in the EU, commensurate with the risks at large arising from the extent and size of their practice, with due regard to Rule 4 (Competence). Any limitation of liability for negligence must be clearly drawn to the attention of a client and be understood and accepted by him.

Guidance

17.1 It would be expected that Professional Indemnity Insurance of at least £1m would be required for all registered persons and their firms, unless demonstrably, their practice does not warrant a sum that high.

Rule 18—Publicity

18. Publicity and promotional activity of any kind by regulated persons is permitted if it **J18** is fair, honest, accurate and is not misleading and is not otherwise in breach of these Rules.

The letterhead, website and e-mails of firms and sole practitioner registered persons in private practice must show the words "regulated by the Intellectual Property Regulation Board" or "regulated by IPREG".

Guidance

18.1 What is acceptable promotional activity will inevitably change over time and will be a matter of subjective assessment in each case. For example, whilst creativity is an essential part of promotion, good taste in content and execution is important.

18.2 Cold calling (by any means) of private individuals or to domestic premises unless a business is being conducted from there would generally be unacceptable, and would certainly be so if directed repeatedly to specific individuals or groups.

18.3 Letterheads must comply with the Business Names Act 1985 concerning lists of partners and an address for service on stationery etc. and the Companies (Trading Disclosures) Regulations 2008 (SI 2008/495) regarding the appearance of the company name and other particulars on stationery, etc. If non-partners are named on a partnership's letterhead, their status should be made clear. A printed line is not sufficient in itself to distinguish partners from nonpartners in a list. A similar standard applies to a company or an LLP's letterhead.

18.4 The website and e-mails of any individual or firm providing services to the public in the EU must comply with the provisions of the E-Commerce Directive 2000/31/EC. This requires that the following information is included in electronic communications including e-mails and websites involved in cross-border e-commerce within the EU:

(a) details of the professional body with which a firm is registered, which in the case of patent attorneys and trade mark attorneys would be IPREG;

(b) the professional title and the member state where it was granted – it is recommended to state that the partners/members/directors of the firm are UK registered patent and/or trade mark attorneys; and

(c) a reference to the professional rules applicable to the firm in the member state where the firm is established and the means to access them. This could be achieved by providing a link to the Code of Conduct on the IPREG website.

Rule 19—Information to Regulation Boards

19. Regulated persons shall submit in a timely manner such information as the Regula- **J19** tion Boards may reasonably require.

Rule 20—Co-operation

J20 20. Regulated persons shall co-operate fully with the appropriate Regulation Boards, and with any persons designated by them in connection with their regulatory responsibilities.

Rule 21—Avoidance of regulatory conflict

J21 21. To avoid regulatory conflict as defined in sections 52 - 54 of the Legal Services Act 2007, the appropriate Regulation Boards may waive in writing the provisions of these Rules in any particular case or cases where the professional activities of a regulated person are fully regulated by another professional regulator.

Rule 22—Commencement Date

J22 22. These Rules shall apply from the date on which sections 184 and 185 of the Legal Services Act 2007 come into force with the exception of Rule 18 second sentence which shall come into force 6 months after that date.

APPENDIX K

SPECIAL RULES OF PROFESSIONAL CONDUCT APPLICABLE TO REGULATED PERSONS CONDUCTING LITIGATION OR EXERCISING A RIGHT OF AUDIENCE BEFORE THE COURTS

The Patent Regulation Board of the Chartered Institute of Patent Attorneys and the Trade Mark **K01** Regulation Board of the Institute of Trade Mark Attorneys working jointly together as the IP Regulation Board (IPREG) now make the following provisions under section 275A of the Copyright Designs and Patents Act 1988 and under section 83A of the Trade Marks Act 1994, respectively, pursuant to Sections 185 and 184 of the Legal Services Act 2007.

Rule 1—Interpretation

In these Rules, unless context otherwise requires:

"CIPA" means the Chartered Institute of Patent Attorneys;

"ITMA" means the Institute of Trade Mark Attorneys;

"IPREG" means the Patent Regulation Board of CIPA and the Trade Mark Regulation Board of ITMA working jointly together as the Intellectual Property Regulation Board;

"patent attorney register" means the register kept under section 275 of the Copyright Designs and Patents Act 1988 as amended;

"trade mark attorney register" means the register kept under section 83 of the Trade Marks Act 1994 as amended;

"registered person" means—

a) a registered patent attorney;

b) a registered trade mark attorney; or

c) a body (corporate or unincorporate) registered in the patent attorney register or the trade mark attorney register;

"regulated person" means a registered person, an employee of a registered person, or a manager of a body which is a registered person;

"manager", in relation to a body, has the same meaning as in the Legal Services Act 2007;

"litigation certificate" means a certificate issued by CIPA or ITMA under their authority as authorised bodies under the Legal Services Act 2007 to grant rights of audience or conduct litigation;

"litigation work" shall mean conducting litigation or exercising a right of audience before the UK or community courts including any work undertaken within the scope of a litigation certificate;

"litigation practitioner" shall mean a regulated person undertaking litigation work;

"employed litigation practitioner" shall mean a litigation practitioner who is employed by an employer who is not regulated by IPREG or another legal services regulator under the Legal Services Act 2007.

Rule 2—Scope of Rules

2.1 Subject to Rule 2.2, these Rules and the Rules of Conduct for Patent Attorneys, Trade Mark Attorneys and other regulated persons shall apply to litigation practitioners and shall prevail over any other rules of conduct to which a litigation practitioner is subject.

2.2 Litigation practitioners undertaking litigation work in their capacity as:

(a) a recognised sole practitioner regulated by the Solicitors Regulation Authority;

(b) a self-employed barrister regulated by the Bar Standards Board; or

(c) a Manager or employee of an entity or person authorised by another approved regulator to carry on an activity which is a reserved legal activity

shall be subject to these Rules only to the extent that these Rules are compatible with the rules of the other legal regulator regulating that work.

2.3 A litigation practitioner shall be responsible for ensuring that all litigation work performed by a person under his or her supervision will be conducted in accordance with these Rules.

Rule 3—Duties of a litigation practitioner

3.1 A litigation practitioner conducting litigation or exercising a right of audience has a statutory duty

(a) to the court to act in the interest of justice; and

(b) to comply with these Rules and the Rules of Conduct for Patent Attorneys, Trade Mark Attorneys and other regulated persons

and those duties override any obligation which the litigation practitioner may have (otherwise than under the criminal law) it if is inconsistent with them.

3.2 A litigation practitioner whilst under a duty to do the best for a client must never deceive or mislead the Court.

3.3 A litigation practitioner must not make or instruct Counsel to make an allegation which is intended only to insult, degrade or annoy the other side, a witness or any other person.

3.4 A litigation practitioner is under a duty to attend or arrange for the attendance of a responsible representative throughout any Court hearing attended by Counsel.

3.5 A litigation practitioner must comply with any order of the Court which the Court can properly make requiring the litigation practitioner and his or her firm to take or refrain from taking some particular course of action.

3.6 A litigation practitioner must comply with the letter and spirit of any undertaking given to the Court or other party whether or not that undertaking is supported by consideration.

Rule 4—Conflicts of Interests arising in the course of litigation work

4.1 A litigation practitioner must not accept instructions to act for two or more clients where there is a conflict or a significant risk of conflict between the interests of the clients.

4.2 A litigation practitioner must not continue to act for two or more clients where a conflict of interest arises between those clients.

4.3 Subject to Rule 5, an employed litigation practitioner may only undertake litigation work for a person other than his or her employer if;

(a) he or she declines to act for that person if any conflict arises between the employer and that person; and

(b) he or she informs that person in writing prior to commencing the or each piece of litigation work that he or she is an employee and that he or she must decline to act further for that person if any conflict arises between the employer and that person.

Rule 5—Employed litigation practitioners

5.1 An employed litigation practitioner shall not act in the course of his employment with his employer as a litigation practitioner except in accordance with the following provisions of Rule 5.

5.2 In the course of his employment, an employed litigation practitioner may act for the employer and the following related bodies

(a) the employer's holding, associated or subsidiary company;

(b) a partnership, syndicate or company by way of joint venture in which the employer and others have an interest;

(c) a trade association of which the employer is a member;

(d) a club, association, pension fund or other scheme operating for the benefit of employees of the employer;

(e) where the employer is a public body, for another public body or statutory officer to which the employer is statutorily empowered to provide legal services; or

(f) a person with whom the employer has a joint interest in the outcome of any proceedings, including in particular any licensee or licensor of the employer, or any joint owner with the employer of any intellectual property rights the subject of the relevant litigation work, providing that such joint interest is bona fide for the employer's benefit and is not formed directly or indirectly for securing assistance in legal proceedings.

5.3 Subject to the following provisions, an employed litigation practitioner may also act for the following persons;

(a) a fellow employee;

(b) a director, company secretary or board member of the Employed litigation practitioner's employer; or

(c) an employee, director, company secretary, board member or trustee of the employer or of a related body of the employer within the meaning of Rule 5.2;

Provided that in each case

(a) the matter related to or arises out of the work of such person for the employer;

(b) the employed litigation practitioner is satisfied that such person does not wish to instruct some other representative; and

(c) no charge is made to such person, in relation to the employed litigation practitioner's costs, unless such costs are recoverable from any other source.

5.4 The employed litigation practitioner shall, before accepting instructions to act for the bodies or persons other than the employer in accordance with these Rules, give written notice to the client that the employer is not able, by way of insurance or otherwise, to indemnify the client adequately in the event of a claim against the employed litigation practitioner for which the employer would be vicariously liable, if that be the case.

5.5 The employed litigation practitioner shall before accepting instructions to act for the bodies or persons other than the employer in accordance with these Rules, give written notice to the client that the employed litigation practitioner is not covered by insurance in relation to professional negligence, if that be the case.

5.6 Where an Employed litigation practitioner is acting for a body or person other than the employer in accordance with these Rules, any information disclosed by the Employed litigation practitioner by the client is confidential and cannot be disclosed to the employer except with the express consent of the client.

5.7 Interpretation

1. "holding" and "subsidiary" Company have the meanings assigned to them by the Company's Act 1985 (as amended from time to time) and two companies are "associated"where they are subsidiaries of the same holding company or companies; and

2. any references to a litigation practitioner's employer include the employer's holding, associated or subsidiary company, and any references to an employee include references to an employee of such holding, association or subsidiary company.

Rule 6— Non-discrimination

A litigation practitioner in any instance in which he is providing advocacy services In the course of litigation work must not withhold those services:

(a) on the ground that the nature of the case is objectionable to him or to any section of the public;

(b) on the ground that the conduct, opinions or beliefs of the prospective client are unacceptable to him or to any section of the public; or

(c) on any ground relating to the source of any financial support which may properly be given to the prospective client for the proceedings in question (for example, on the ground that such support will be available under the Access to Justice Act 1999).

Rule 7— Fees

7.1 A litigation practitioner must not charge unjustifiable fees having regard to fees generally charged by professions in the conduct of litigation of comparable complexity and difficulty to the litigation work in question.

7.2 A litigation practitioner who is retained in connection with litigation work shall not enter into any arrangement to receive a contingency fee in respect of that work except if permitted to do so by the Lord Chancellor in accordance with any statute or statutory instrument or otherwise in accordance with any rule of law.

7.3 In order to reduce misunderstandings concerning the levels of fees charged for litigation work, the client must also be informed in writing of the basis on which the work is to be charged.

Rule 8—Community Legal Service Fund

A litigation practitioner is under a duty to consider and advise the client on the availability of funding for litigation services by the Community Legal Service Fund or any funding available from the wider Community Legal Service to which the client might be entitled under the Access to Justice Act 1999 and any Statutory Instruments thereunder or any succeeding Act.

Rule 9—Professional Indemnity Insurance

9.1 Each litigation practitioner or his or her firm must take out and maintain professional indemnity insurance cover for litigation work. When commencing and renewing such insurance, each litigation practitioner or his firm shall ensure that the insurance provides cover in respect of each and every claim brought in the United Kingdom or elsewhere in the European Union of at least the Minimum Value (as defined in the next sentence) prevailing at the time of commencement or renewal. The Minimum Value shall be determined by IPREG from time to time but shall never be a value less than £1,000,000.

9.2 A litigation practitioner shall not limit liability for professional negligence below the Minimum Value.

9.4 The provisions of this Rule 9 shall not apply to an employed litigation practitioner when he is acting within the meaning of Rule 5.2 or 5.3.

Rule 10—Client's Money

10.1 A litigation practitioner must ensure that any money held on behalf of the client in respect of such litigation work is held on trust for the client in an account which is entirely separate from the litigation practitioner's personal or professional business account.

10.2 Money which would have to be kept in the separate account includes that which is intended or which may be required to be:

(a) paid or received from a third party on settlement or as the Court might direct; or

(b) paid into or received from the Court (including without limitation by way of a Part 36 payment or a payment on account of costs following summary or detailed assessment).

10.3 Money in the separate client's account must be held to the order of the client or the Court and any interest accruing in the account must inure to the client.

10.4 Money which the litigation practitioner is not required to keep in such a separate clients' account includes:

(a) any money receiving on account of expected charges for the litigation practitioner's services;

(b) costs to be incurred on the client's behalf; and

(c) money paid in settlement of a debt owed by the client to the litigation practitioner.

Rule 11—Commencement Date and Repeal

11.1 These Rules shall apply to all litigation work effective from 15th September 2011.

11.2 The ITMA Rules of Professional Conduct for Trade Mark Agents holding and acting within the scope of Litigator Certificates and the CIPA Rules of Professional Conduct for Patent Attorneys holding and acting within the scope of Litigator Certificates shall cease to be effective as of that date.

INDEX

LEGAL TAXONOMY

FROM SWEET & MAXWELL

This index has been prepared using Sweet & Maxwell's Legal Taxonomy. Main index entries conform to keywords provided by the Legal Taxonomy except where references to specific documents or non-standard terms (denoted by quotation marks) have been included. These keywords provide a means of identifying similar concepts in other Sweet & Maxwell publications and online services to which keywords from the Legal Taxonomy have been applied. Readers may find some minor differences between terms used in the text and those which appear in the index. Suggestions to *sweet&maxwell.taxonomy@thomson.com.*

(All references are to paragraph number)

Abstracts
 generally, 14.42
 Patents Rules, and, 14.07
 requirements, 14.05
 sale of documents, and, 123.84
 statutory text, 14.01
Abuse of dominant position
 generally, D26–D27
"Abuse of monopoly rights"
 compulsory licences, and, 48.02
Account of profits
 accountancy assistance, 61.29
 generally, 61.28
 stay pending appeal, 61.30
Acknowledgment of service
 infringement proceedings, and, 61.56
Acquiescence
 infringement, and, 60.23
"Acting in common design"
 infringement, and, 60.27
"Acts for services of the Crown"
 See also **Crown use**
 disposals by Crown, 55.17
 introduction, 55.13
 invention is a process, where, 55.15
 invention is a product, where, 55.14
 invention is a specified drug or
  medicine, where, 55.15
 prior recording of invention, 55.18
 supply of contributory means, 55.16
Added subject matter
 acknowledgment of prior art, 76.13
 addition of subject-matter by excision
  or alteration of text, 76.10

Added subject matter—*cont.*
 amendment allowed without
  contravention of section, 76.07
 amendment in contravention of section,
  76.22
 amendment resulting in disunity, 76.16
 case law, 76.06–76.14
 claim broadening before grant, 76.15
 descriptions, and, 76.20
 expansion of previously-stated
  inventive concept, 76.08
 general principles, 76.06
 introduction of subject-matter not
  specifically described, 76.09
 meaning, 76.05
 novelty, and, 76.18
 priority dates, and, 76.19
 prohibition of addition of obvious
  subject matter, 76.11
 relationship with other concepts,
  76.17–76.21
 restriction to intermediate
  generalisation, 76.12
 support for divisional application in
  parent application, 76.14
Additional matter
 See **Added subject matter**
Addresses for service
 alteration, 32.24
 commentary, 32.15–32.16
 correction, 32.09–32.10
 failure to provide
  generally, 32.16
  Patents Rules, and, 32.03

Comptroller of Patents Designs and Trade Marks—*cont.*